The HOLY BIBLE

Contemporary English Version

The HOLY BIBLE

Contemporary English Version

AMERICAN BIBLE SOCIETY
NEW YORK

The HOLY BIBLE

Contemporary English Version

Quotation Rights for the Contemporary English Version

The American Bible Society is glad to grant authors and publishers the right to use up to five hundred (500) verses from the *Contemporary English Version* text in church, religious and other publications without the need to seek and receive written permission. However, the extent of quotation must not comprise a complete book nor should it amount to more than 25% of the work. The proper copyright notice must appear on the title or copyright page.

When quotations from the *CEV* are used in non-saleable media such as church bulletins, orders of service, posters, transparencies or similar media, a complete copyright notice is not required, but the initials *(CEV)* must appear at the end of each quotation.

Requests for quotations in excess of five hundred (500) verses in any publication must be directed to, and written approval received from, the American Bible Society, 1865 Broadway, New York, NY 10023.

ISBN 1-58516-062-8
Printed in the United States of America
English Bible CEV050-106026
ABS-8/01-3,500-34,083—MW3

Congratulations!

You have in your hands one of the most precious books the world has ever seen. It is a book full of profound wisdom and insight about human nature and the character and purpose of the God who created all things. Throughout the centuries people from many lands have opened this book and read from it in their own languages. Here they have learned about God's love and justice. Great leaders and thinkers have searched its pages and explored its truths, looking for the answers to life's problems and challenges.

You are invited to make that same exploration. The following section of special helps is provided to help you begin this rewarding journey.

- *What's in the Bible* gives you a brief summary of every book in the Bible and a handy chart giving an overview of all the books that make up the Bible.
- *How to Read the Bible* provides simple suggestions on how to read the Bible devotionally and to keep notes on the many lessons you'll learn.
- *Read through the Bible in a Year* is a reading plan that is easy to follow and guides you through the entire Old and New Testaments in exactly one year.
- *Some Readings for Special Days* guides you to passages you may want to read on special days like Christmas, Easter, Mother's Day—and even your own birthday.
- *Famous Passages of the Bible* helps you locate those famous Bible stories you've heard time and again, but may never have read for yourself.
- *Finding Help in the Bible* leads you to those passages that can help you when you're facing a difficult problem or special challenge.
- *What the Bible Says about God's Forgiveness* will lead you to places in the Bible where you can learn how much God loves each one of us and what he had done to put us right with himself.

It really doesn't matter where you begin, but it does matter *that* you begin. Use any one of these special reader's helps to get you started on a daily habit of reading the Bible. Discover for yourself the help and hope it has to offer.

The Bible

The word "Bible" comes from the Greek word *biblia,* which means "books." So the Bible is really a collection or library of many books. These books are divided into two main parts, the Old Testament and the New Testament.

Old Testament

The Old Testament tells the history of the people of Israel. This history is based on their faith in the God of Israel and on their religious life as the people of God. The authors of these books wrote about what God had done for them as a people and how they were to worship and obey God in return. The following chart shows the different groups of books that make up the Old Testament.

The Law

Genesis, Exodus, Leviticus, Numbers, Deuteronomy

History

Joshua, Judges, Ruth, 1 Samuel, 2 Samuel, 1 Kings, 2 Kings, 1 Chronicles, 2 Chronicles, Ezra, Nehemiah, Esther

Poetry and Wisdom

Job, Psalms, Proverbs, Ecclesiastes, Song of Songs

Major Prophets

Isaiah, Jeremiah, Lamentations, Ezekiel, Daniel

Minor Prophets

Hosea, Joel, Amos, Obadiah, Jonah, Micah, Nahum, Habakkuk, Zephaniah, Haggai, Zechariah, Malachi

New Testament

The books of the New Testament were written by the followers of Jesus Christ. These followers wanted others to know the Good News about Jesus Christ and the possibility of a "new" life available to them through his death and resurrection. The following chart shows the different groups of books that make up the New Testament. Although scholarly opinion has varied, Paul has traditionally been identified as the author of the letters indicated below.

The Gospels

Matthew, Mark, Luke, John

Paul's Letters

Romans, 1 Corinthians, 2 Corinthians, Galatians, Ephesians, Philippians, Colossians, 1 Thessalonians, 2 Thessalonians, 1 Timothy, 2 Timothy, Titus, Philemon

History

Acts

General Letters

Hebrews, James, 1 Peter, 2 Peter, 1 John, 2 John, 3 John, Jude

Prophecy

Revelation

What's in the Bible

The following are summary capsules for each book of the Bible. It will be obvious from how brief the descriptions are that they are not complete. They should, however, serve as a quick and handy guide to the content of the whole Bible.

Old Testament

GENESIS: In this book of beginnings the stories are about creation, early relationships between God and people, and God's promise to bless Abraham and his descendants.

EXODUS: The name Exodus means "departure" and this book tells about how God led the Israelites out of a life of hardship and slavery in Egypt. God made a covenant with them and gave them the Law to order their lives.

LEVITICUS: This book is named for the priestly tribe of Levi and is made up of laws concerning rituals and ceremonies.

NUMBERS: The Israelites wandered in the wilderness for 40 years before entering Canaan, the promised land. The name of the book comes from two censuses taken during the journey.

DEUTERONOMY: Moses gave three farewell speeches shortly before he died. In them he reviewed the laws of God for the Israelites. This book gets its name—"second law"—from this review.

JOSHUA: Joshua led the Israelite armies into victory over the Canaanites. The book ends with the division of the land among the tribes of Israel.

JUDGES: The Israelites often fell away from God and into the hands of oppressors. God sent "judges" to lead and deliver them.

RUTH: Love and dedication between Ruth and her mother-in-law, Naomi, are the focus of this story.

1 SAMUEL: Samuel was the leader of Israel between the time of Judges and the time of Saul, the first King of Israel. When Saul's leadership failed, David was anointed by Samuel to be king.

2 SAMUEL: Under David's rule, the new nation was strong and unified. But after David committed adultery and murder, his family and nation suffered.

1 KINGS: This book starts with stories about Solomon's reign over Israel. After the death of Solomon, the kingdom went to war with itself, north against south. The result was two nations, Israel in the north and Judah in the south.

2 KINGS: Israel was conquered by Assyria in 721 B.C. Judah was defeated by Babylon in 586 B.C. These events were seen as judgment upon the people because they did not follow the laws of God.

1 CHRONICLES: This book begins with genealogies from Adam to David and then recounts the incidents of David's reign.

2 CHRONICLES: This book covers the same period as 2 Kings but the emphasis is on Judah, the southern kingdom, and its rulers.

EZRA: God's people returned to Jerusalem after being held captive in Babylon for several decades. One of the leaders was Ezra. This book contains his charge to the people to be true to the law of God.

NEHEMIAH: After the Temple was rebuilt, the protective wall around Jerusalem was restored. Nehemiah brought this effort to completion. He also worked with Ezra to restore religious fervor among the people.

ESTHER: This book tells the story of the Jewish queen of Persia who exposed a plot to destroy her people and thus saved all the Jews in that country from destruction.

JOB: The question, "Why do innocent people suffer?" is address in the story of Job.

PSALMS: These 150 prayers and hymns were used by the Hebrew people to express their relationship with God. They cover the whole range of human emotions from joy to anger, from hope to despair.

PROVERBS: This is a book of wise sayings and ethical and common sense teachings on how to live a godly life.

ECCLESIASTES: In a quest for happiness and the meaning of life, this writer, known as "the Philosopher," asks many questions that are still raised in today's society.

SONG OF SONGS: This poem describes the joy and ecstasy of love. It has been understood both as a picture of God's love for Israel and of Christ's love for the Church.

ISAIAH: The prophet Isaiah brought the message of God's judgment on the nations, pointed to a future king like David, and promised a time of comfort and peace.

JEREMIAH: Before Babylon destroyed Judah, Jeremiah foretold God's judgment. While his message was largely of destruction, he also pointed toward a new covenant with God.

LAMENTATIONS: As Jeremiah had warned, Jerusalem fell to the Babylonians. This book records five "laments" for the fallen city.

EZEKIEL: Ezekiel's message was given to the Jews held captive in Babylon. He used stories and parables to speak about judgement, hope and restoration.

DANIEL: Daniel remained faithful to God while facing many pressures as a captive in Babylon. This book includes Daniel's prophetic visions.

HOSEA: Hosea used his commitment to his wife in the face of her unfaithfulness to illustrate the "adultery" Israel had committed against God, whose faithful love never ceased.

JOEL: After a locust plague in Judah, Joel urged the people to repent.

AMOS: During an era of prosperity, this Judean prophet preached judgment on the rich leaders of Israel. Amos urged them to consider the poor and oppressed rather than their own self-satisfaction.

OBADIAH: Obadiah prophesied judgment on Edom, a neighboring country.

JONAH: Jonah did not want to preach to the Ninevites, an enemy people. When he finally brought God's message to them, they repented.

MICAH: Micah's message to Judah was a prophecy of judgment as well as forgiveness and hope for restoration. Especially notable is his single verse summary of what God requires of us (6.8).

NAHUM: Nahum announced that God would destroy the people of Nineveh because of their cruelty in war.

HABAKKUK: Habakkuk's book features a dialogue between Habakkuk and God about suffering and justice.

ZEPHANIAH: Zephaniah announced the day of the Lord, which would bring judgment on Judah and other surrounding nations. This coming day would be one of doom for many, but a humble and faithful remnant will survive to bless the whole world.

HAGGAI: After the people returned from exile, Haggai reminded them to give God their highest priority and to rebuild the Temple before working on their own homes.

ZECHARIAH: Like Haggai, Zechariah urged the people to rebuild the Temple, assuring them of God's help and blessing. His visions point to a glorious future.

MALACHI: After the exiles returned, they became complacent about their religious life. Malachi tried to stir them up by preaching about the day of the Lord.

New Testament

MATTHEW: This Gospel includes many Old Testament quotations, thus appealing to a Jewish audience and presenting Jesus as the Messiah promised in the Hebrew Scriptures. Matthew told the story of Jesus from birth to resurrection and placed emphasis on his teaching.

MARK: Mark wrote a short, action-packed Gospel. He emphasized Jesus' miracles and his life of suffering. His aim was to deepen the faith and commitment of the believers in the community to which he wrote.

LUKE: In this Gospel, the availability of salvation for all people is emphasized. Luke proclaimed this message by showing Jesus' involvement with people who are poor, needy, and on the fringes of society.

JOHN: The Gospel of John stands apart from the others. John organized his message around seven signs that point to Jesus as the Son of God. His writing style is reflective and filled with striking images.

ACTS: When Jesus left his disciples, the Holy Spirit came to abide with them. Written by Luke as the sequel to his Gospel, Acts records key events in the history of the work of the early Christian Church to spread the Gospel throughout the Mediterranean world.

ROMANS: In this important letter, Paul wrote to the Romans about life in the Spirit, which is given to believers in Christ through faith. The apostle tells them about God's great kindness and declares that because of Jesus Christ, God accepts us and sets us free from our sins.

1 CORINTHIANS: This letter deals with the problems the church in Corinth was experiencing: dissension, immorality, public worship, and confusion about spiritual gifts.

2 CORINTHIANS: In this letter, Paul wrote about his relationship with the church of Corinth and the effects of certain false apostles on his ministry.

GALATIANS: This letter addresses freedom from the law through Christ. Paul declares that it is by faith that all who believe are put right with God.

EPHESIANS: A central theme to this letter is that God's eternal purpose is to bring together from many nations and peoples the universal Church of Jesus Christ.

PHILIPPIANS: This letter emphasizes the joy found in any situation when a person believes in Christ. Paul wrote it while in prison.

COLOSSIANS: In this letter Paul tells the people of Colossae to make Christ the center of their faith and to put aside their superstitions.

1 THESSALONIANS: In this letter Paul gives advice to the people of Thessalonica concerning Christ's return.

2 THESSALONIANS: This letter discusses the same topics as the first. Paul teaches the people a way to be ready for the Lord.

1 TIMOTHY: This letter served as a guide to Timothy, a young leader in the church. It contains advice about worship, ministry, and relationships within the church.

2 TIMOTHY: This is Paul's last letter. In it he offers a final challenge to his co-worker.

TITUS: Titus was ministering in Crete. In this letter, Paul gave him advice on how to help Christians follow Christ.

PHILEMON: In this letter, Philemon is urged to forgive his runaway slave, Onesimus, and accept him as a friend in Christ.

HEBREWS: The letter to the Hebrews challenges new Christians to move beyond their traditional rituals and ceremonies and believe that Christ has fulfilled them all.

JAMES: James advises putting beliefs into practice and offers practical ways for Christians to live out their faith.

1 PETER: This letter was written to comfort early Christians who were being persecuted for their faith.

2 PETER: In this letter Peter warns against false teachers and urges Christians to stay loyal to God.

1 JOHN: This letter explains basic truths about the Christian life, with emphasis on the command to love one another.

2 JOHN: This letter, addressed to "the dear Lady and to her children," warns against false teachers.

3 JOHN: In contrast to 2 John, this letter states the need to welcome people who preach Christ.

JUDE: Jude warns against the influence of evil ones outside the fellowship of believers.

REVELATION: This book was written to encourage persecuted believers and affirm their faith that God will care for them. Using visions and symbols, the writer illustrates the triumph of good over evil and the creation of a new heaven and new earth.

How to Read the Bible

Set aside time each day to read from your Bible. Try to make it the same time each day. Be realistic. Commit yourself only to as much time as you honestly feel that you can stick to on an ongoing basis. Before you begin reading ask for God's guidance and blessing. Some people have found that keeping a daily notebook is helpful. Use the following steps to get the most out of your daily Bible reading:

1. Select a passage (perhaps one from the *Read through the Bible in a Year* section that follows).
2. Examine its context:
   a. What kind of book is it drawn from? A biographical book such as one of the Gospel accounts of Jesus' life; a long historical book, such as *The Second Book of Samuel,* which tells of the reign of King David; a brief letter to a person (*The Letters of Paul to Timothy*) or to a specific church (*The Letters of Paul to the Corinthians*)?
   b. What is the overall purpose/intent of this book? (Do not do lengthy research, but feel free to read the opening and closing paragraphs as well as section headings and introductions if your Bible has them.)
   c. What occurs or is discussed in the passages immediately preceding and following the passage you chose?
3. Read the passage quickly for sense.
4. Identify key words or phrases. Are there words or thoughts that are repeated throughout the passage? Are any cause and effect relationships established? (These are often signaled by words like *if* and *then, therefore, because, since,* and *so.*) Are any comparisons made or similarities pointed out? Are any two people, things or concepts contrasted?
5. Read the passage again and ask yourself what is the intent or purpose of the passage. Try to find out what the author is saying. Be honest; don't just look for what you want to hear. The Bible has many strong messages that can change lives!
6. What do you learn about God from this passage? What do you learn about human nature? Ask yourself how this message applies to you. Is there anything you need to change in your life in order to be a more faithful child of God or more loving to your neighbor? Ask for God's help in making this change.
7. Re-read the passage one more time. Is there one verse you would like to commit to memory? Why not write it on an index card and carry it with you throughout the day as a study aid?
8. Thank God for what he has shown you, and ask for his help as you seek to apply this lesson in your life.
9. Share what you have learned with someone else.

Read through the Bible in a Year

Have you ever read the entire Bible all the way through? By committing just twenty or thirty minutes a day you can use the following daily reading plan to help you do just that in one year. The abbreviations used here are explained in the front of the Bible. For help in finding the passages refer to the *How to look up a Bible reference* box. Begin today and discover the riches of God's Word!

JANUARY

1 ☐ Lk 5.27-39 ☐ Gn 1-2 ☐ Ps 1
2 ☐ Lk 6.1-26 ☐ Gn 3-5 ☐ Ps 2
3 ☐ Lk 6.27-49 ☐ Gn 6-7 ☐ Ps 3
4 ☐ Lk 7.1-17 ☐ Gn 8-10 ☐ Ps 4
5 ☐ Lk 7.18-50 ☐ Gn 11 ☐ Ps 5
6 ☐ Lk 8.1-25 ☐ Gn 12 ☐ Ps 6
7 ☐ Lk 8.26-56 ☐ Gn 13-14 ☐ Ps 7
8 ☐ Lk 9.1-27 ☐ Gn 15 ☐ Ps 8
9 ☐ Lk 9.28-62 ☐ Gn 16 ☐ Ps 9
10 ☐ Lk 10.1-20 ☐ Gn 17 ☐ Ps 10
11 ☐ Lk 10.21-42 ☐ Gn 18 ☐ Ps 11
12 ☐ Lk 11.1-28 ☐ Gn 19 ☐ Ps 12
13 ☐ Lk 11.29-54 ☐ Gn 20 ☐ Ps 13
14 ☐ Lk 12.1-31 ☐ Gn 21 ☐ Ps 14
15 ☐ Lk 12.32-59 ☐ Gn 22 ☐ Ps 15
16 ☐ Lk 13.1-17 ☐ Gn 23 ☐ Ps 16
17 ☐ Lk 13.18-35 ☐ Gn 24 ☐ Ps 17
18 ☐ Lk 14.1-24 ☐ Gn 25 ☐ Ps 18
19 ☐ Lk 14.25-35 ☐ Gn 26 ☐ Ps 19
20 ☐ Lk 15 ☐ Gn 27.1-45 ☐ Ps 20
21 ☐ Lk 16 ☐ Gn 27.46-28.22 ☐ Ps 21
22 ☐ Lk 17 ☐ Gn 29.1-30 ☐ Ps 22
23 ☐ Lk 18.1-17 ☐ Gn 29.31-30.43 ☐ Ps 23
24 ☐ Lk 18.18-43 ☐ Gn 31 ☐ Ps 24
25 ☐ Lk 19.1-27 ☐ Gn 32-33 ☐ Ps 25
26 ☐ Lk 19.28-48 ☐ Gn 34 ☐ Ps 26
27 ☐ Lk 20.1-26 ☐ Gn 35-36 ☐ Ps 27
28 ☐ Lk 20.27-47 ☐ Gn 37 ☐ Ps 28
29 ☐ Lk 21 ☐ Gn 38 ☐ Ps 29
30 ☐ Lk 22.1-38 ☐ Gn 39 ☐ Ps 30
31 ☐ Lk 22.39-71 ☐ Gn 40 ☐ Ps 31

FEBRUARY

1 ☐ Lk 23.1-25 ☐ Gn 41 ☐ Ps 32
2 ☐ Lk 23.26-56 ☐ Gn 42 ☐ Ps 33
3 ☐ Lk 24.1-12 ☐ Gn 43 ☐ Ps 34
4 ☐ Lk 24.13-53 ☐ Gn 44 ☐ Ps 35
5 ☐ He 1 ☐ Gn 45.1-46.27 ☐ Ps 36
6 ☐ He 2 ☐ Gn 46.28-47.31 ☐ Ps 37
7 ☐ He 3.1-4.13 ☐ Gn 48 ☐ Ps 38
8 ☐ He 4.14-6.12 ☐ Gn 49-50 ☐ Ps 39
9 ☐ He 6.13-20 ☐ Ex 1-2 ☐ Ps 40
10 ☐ He 7 ☐ Ex 3-4 ☐ Ps 41
11 ☐ He 8 ☐ Ex 5.1-6.27 ☐ Pr 1
12 ☐ He 9.1-22 ☐ Ex 6.28-8.32 ☐ Pr 2
13 ☐ He 9.23-10.18 ☐ Ex 9-10 ☐ Pr 3
14 ☐ He 10.19-39 ☐ Ex 11-12 ☐ Pr 4
15 ☐ He 11.1-21 ☐ Ex 13-14 ☐ Pr 5
16 ☐ He 11.22-40 ☐ Ex 15 ☐ Pr 6.1-7.5
17 ☐ He 12 ☐ Ex 16-17 ☐ Pr 7.6-27
18 ☐ He 13 ☐ Ex 18-19 ☐ Pr 8
19 ☐ Mt 1 ☐ Ex 20-21 ☐ Pr 9
20 ☐ Mt 2 ☐ Ex 22-23 ☐ Pr 10
21 ☐ Mt 3 ☐ Ex 24 ☐ Pr 11
22 ☐ Mt 4 ☐ Ex 25-27 ☐ Pr 12
23 ☐ Mt 5.1-20 ☐ Ex 28-29 ☐ Pr 13
24 ☐ Mt 5.21-48 ☐ Ex 30-32 ☐ Pr 14
25 ☐ Mt 6.1-18 ☐ Ex 33-34 ☐ Pr 15
26 ☐ Mt 6.19-34 ☐ Ex 35-36 ☐ Pr 16
27 ☐ Mt 7 ☐ Ex 37-38 ☐ Pr 17
28 ☐ Mt 8.1-13 ☐ Ex 39-40 ☐ Pr 18

MARCH

1 ☐ Mt 8.14-34 ☐ Lv 1-2 ☐ Pr 19
2 ☐ Mt 9.1-17 ☐ Lv 3-4 ☐ Pr 20
3 ☐ Mt 9.18-38 ☐ Lv 5-6 ☐ Pr 21
4 ☐ Mt 10.1-25 ☐ Lv 7-8 ☐ Pr 22
5 ☐ Mt 10.26-42 ☐ Lv 9-10 ☐ Pr 23
6 ☐ Mt 11.1-19 ☐ Lv 11-12 ☐ Pr 24
7 ☐ Mt 11.20-30 ☐ Lv 13 ☐ Pr 25
8 ☐ Mt 12.1-21 ☐ Lv 14 ☐ Pr 26
9 ☐ Mt 12.22-50 ☐ Lv 15-16 ☐ Pr 27
10 ☐ Mt 13.1-23 ☐ Lv 17-18 ☐ Pr 28
11 ☐ Mt 13.24-58 ☐ Lv 19 ☐ Pr 29
12 ☐ Mt 14.1-21 ☐ Lv 20-21 ☐ Pr 30

How to look up a Bible reference.

Every verse in this Bible is marked by its own *verse number.* To find any one of the passages listed in these reader's helps, you need to find the book, the chapter in the book, and the verse or verses within that chapter. The chapter number immediately follows the name of the book. This is followed by a period (.) which is followed by the number or range of numbers for the verses you seek. For example: 1 Corinthians 12.1-11 is the First Letter of Paul to the Corinthians, chapter twelve, verses one through eleven.

13 □ Mt 14.22-36 □ Lv 22-23 □ Pr 31
14 □ Mt 15.1-20 □ Lv 24-25 □ Ec 1.1-11
15 □ Mt 15.21-39 □ Lv 26-27 □ Ec 1.12-2.26
16 □ Mt 16 □ Nu 1-2 □ Ec 3.1-15
17 □ Mt 17 □ Nu 3-4 □ Ec 3.16-4.16
18 □ Mt 18.1-17 □ Nu 5-6 □ Ec 5
19 □ Mt 18.18-35 □ Nu 7-8 □ Ec 6
20 □ Mt 19.1-15 □ Nu 9-10 □ Ec 7
21 □ Mt 19.16-30 □ Nu 11-12 □ Ec 8
22 □ Mt 20.1-16 □ Nu 13-14 □ Ec 9.1-12
23 □ Mt 20.17-34 □ Nu 15-16 □ Ec 9.13-10.20
24 □ Mt 21.1-27 □ Nu 17-18 □ Ec 11.1-8
25 □ Mt 21.28-46 □ Nu 19-20 □ Ec 11.9-12.14
26 □ Mt 22.1-22 □ Nu 21 □ Sgs 1.1-2.7
27 □ Mt 22.23-46 □ Nu 22.1-40 □ Sgs 2.8-3.5
28 □ Mt 23.1-12 □ Nu 22.41-23.26 □ Sgs 3.6-5.1
29 □ Mt 23.13-39 □ Nu 23.27-24.25 □ Sgs 5.2-6.3
30 □ Mt 24.1-31 □ Nu 25-27 □ Sgs 6.4-8.4
31 □ Mt 24.32-51 □ Nu 28-29 □ Sgs 8.5-14

APRIL

1 □ Mt 25.1-30 □ Nu 30-31 □ Job 1
2 □ Mt 25.31-46 □ Nu 32-34 □ Job 2
3 □ Mt 26.1-25 □ Nu 35-36 □ Job 3
4 □ Mt 26.26-46 □ Dt 1-2 □ Job 4
5 □ Mt 26.47-75 □ Dt 3-4 □ Job 5
6 □ Mt 27.1-31 □ Dt 5-6 □ Job 6
7 □ Mt 27.32-66 □ Dt 7-8 □ Job 7
8 □ Mt 28 □ Dt 9-10 □ Job 8
9 □ Ac 1 □ Dt 11-12 □ Job 9
10 □ Ac 2.1-13 □ Dt 13-14 □ Job 10
11 □ Ac 2.14-47 □ Dt 15-16 □ Job 11
12 □ Ac 3 □ Dt 17-18 □ Job 12
13 □ Ac 4.1-22 □ Dt 19-20 □ Job 13
14 □ Ac 4.23-37 □ Dt 21-22 □ Job 14
15 □ Ac 5.1-16 □ Dt 23-24 □ Job 15
16 □ Ac 5.17-42 □ Dt 25-27 □ Job 16
17 □ Ac 6 □ Dt 28 □ Job 17
18 □ Ac 7.1-22 □ Dt 29-30 □ Job 18
19 □ Ac 7.23-8.1 □ Dt 31-32 □ Job 19
20 □ Ac 8.1-25 □ Dt 33-34 □ Job 20
21 □ Ac 8.26-40 □ Js 1-2 □ Job 21
22 □ Ac 9.1-25 □ Js 3.1-5.1 □ Job 22
23 □ Ac 9.26-43 □ Js 5.2-6.27 □ Job 23
24 □ Ac 10.1-33 □ Js 7-8 □ Job 24
25 □ Ac 10.34-48 □ Js 9-10 □ Job 25
26 □ Ac 11.1-18 □ Js 11-12 □ Job 26
27 □ Ac 11.19-30 □ Js 13-14 □ Job 27
28 □ Ac 12 □ Js 15-17 □ Job 28
29 □ Ac 13.1-25 □ Js 18-19 □ Job 29
30 □ Ac 13.26-52 □ Js 20-21 □ Job 30

MAY

1 □ Ac 14 □ Js 22 □ Job 31
2 □ Ac 15.1-21 □ Js 23-24 □ Job 32
3 □ Ac 15.22-41 □ Jg 1 □ Job 33
4 □ Ac 16.1-15 □ Jg 2-3 □ Job 34
5 □ Ac 16.16-40 □ Jg 4-5 □ Job 35
6 □ Ac 17.1-15 □ Jg 6 □ Job 36
7 □ Ac 17.16-34 □ Jg 7-8 □ Job 37
8 □ Ac 18 □ Jg 9 □ Job 38
9 □ Ac 19.1-20 □ Jg 10.1-11.33 □ Job 39
10 □ Ac 19.21-41 □ Jg 11.34-12.15 □ Job 40
11 □ Ac 20.1-16 □ Jg 13 □ Job 41
12 □ Ac 20.17-38 □ Jg 14-15 □ Job 42
13 □ Ac 21.1-36 □ Jg 16 □ Ps 42
14 □ Ac 21.37-22.29 □ Jg 17-18 □ Ps 43
15 □ Ac 22.30-23.22 □ Jg 19 □ Ps 44
16 □ Ac 23.23-24.9 □ Jg 20 □ Ps 45
17 □ Ac 24.10-27 □ Jg 21 □ Ps 46
18 □ Ac 25 □ Ru 1-2 □ Ps 47
19 □ Ac 26.1-18 □ Ru 3-4 □ Ps 48
20 □ Ac 26.19-32 □ 1 S 1.1-2.11 □ Ps 49
21 □ Ac 27.1-12 □ 1 S 2.12-36 □ Ps 50
22 □ Ac 27.13-44 □ 1 S 3 □ Ps 51
23 □ Ac 28.1-15 □ 1 S 4-5 □ Ps 52
24 □ Ac 28.16-31 □ 1 S 6-7 □ Ps 53
25 □ Ro 1.1-15 □ 1 S 8 □ Ps 54
26 □ Ro 1.16-32 □ 1 S 9.1-10.16 □ Ps 55
27 □ Ro 2.1-3.8 □ 1 S 10.17-11.15 □ Ps 56
28 □ Ro 3.9-31 □ 1 S 12 □ Ps 57
29 □ Ro 4 □ 1 S 13 □ Ps 58
30 □ Ro 5 □ 1 S 14 □ Ps 59
31 □ Ro 6 □ 1 S 15 □ Ps 60

JUNE

1 □ Ro 7 □ 1 S 16 □ Ps 61
2 □ Ro 8 □ 1 S 17.1-54 □ Ps 62
3 □ Ro 9.1-29 □ 1 S 17.55-18.30 □ Ps 63
4 □ Ro 9.30-10.21 □ 1 S 19 □ Ps 64
5 □ Ro 11.1-24 □ 1 S 20 □ Ps 65
6 □ Ro 11.25-36 □ 1 S 21-22 □ Ps 66
7 □ Ro 12 □ 1 S 23-24 □ Ps 67
8 □ Ro 13 □ 1 S 25 □ Ps 68
9 □ Ro 14 □ 1 S 26 □ Ps 69
10 □ Ro 15.1-13 □ 1 S 27-28 □ Ps 70
11 □ Ro 15.14-33 □ 1 S 29-31 □ Ps 71
12 □ Ro 16 □ 2 S 1 □ Ps 72
13 □ Mk 1.1-20 □ 2 S 2.1-3.1 □ Dn 1
14 □ Mk 1.21-45 □ 2 S 3.2-39 □ Dn 2.1-23
15 □ Mk 2 □ 2 S 4-5 □ Dn 2.24-49
16 □ Mk 3.1-19 □ 2 S 6 □ Dn 3
17 □ Mk 3.20-35 □ 2 S 7-8 □ Dn 4
18 □ Mk 4.1-20 □ 2 S 9-10 □ Dn 5
19 □ Mk 4.21-41 □ 2 S 11-12 □ Dn 6
20 □ Mk 5.1-20 □ 2 S 13 □ Dn 7
21 □ Mk 5.21-43 □ 2 S 14 □ Dn 8
22 □ Mk 6.1-29 □ 2 S 15 □ Dn 9
23 □ Mk 6.30-56 □ 2 S 16 □ Dn 10.1-11.2
24 □ Mk 7.1-13 □ 2 S 17 □ Dn 11.2-20
25 □ Mk 7.14-37 □ 2 S 18 □ Dn 11.21-45
26 □ Mk 8.1-21 □ 2 S 19 □ Dn 12
27 □ Mk 8.22-9.1 □ 2 S 20-21 □ Ho 1.1-2.1
28 □ Mk 9.2-50 □ 2 S 22 □ Ho 2.2-23
29 □ Mk 10.1-31 □ 2 S 23 □ Ho 3
30 □ Mk 10.32-52 □ 2 S 24 □ Ho 4.1-10

JULY

1 ☐ Mk 11.1-14 ☐ 1 K 1 ☐ Ho 4.11-5.3
2 ☐ Mk 11.15-33 ☐ 1 K 2 ☐ Ho 5.4-15
3 ☐ Mk 12.1-27 ☐ 1 K 3 ☐ Ho 6.1-7.2
4 ☐ Mk 12.28-44 ☐ 1 K 4-5 ☐ Ho 7.3-16
5 ☐ Mk 13.1-13 ☐ 1 K 6 ☐ Ho 8
6 ☐ Mk 13.14-37 ☐ 1 K 7 ☐ Ho 9.1-16
7 ☐ Mk 14.1-31 ☐ 1 K 8 ☐ Ho 9.17-10.15
8 ☐ Mk 14.32-72 ☐ 1 K 9 ☐ Ho 11.1-11
9 ☐ Mk 15.1-20 ☐ 1 K 10 ☐ Ho 11.12-12.14
10 ☐ Mk 15.21-47 ☐ 1 K 11 ☐ Ho 13
11 ☐ Mk 16 ☐ 1 K 12.1-31 ☐ Ho 14
12 ☐ 1 Co 1.1-17 ☐ 1 K 12.32-13.34 ☐ Jl 1
13 ☐ 1 Co 1.18-31 ☐ 1 K 14 ☐ Jl 2.1-11
14 ☐ 1 Co 2 ☐ 1 K 15.1-32 ☐ Jl 2.12-23
15 ☐ 1 Co 3 ☐ 1 K 15.33-16.34 ☐ Jl 3
16 ☐ 1 Co 4 ☐ 1 K 17 ☐ Am 1
17 ☐ 1 Co 5 ☐ 1 K 18 ☐ Am 2.1-3.2
18 ☐ 1 Co 6 ☐ 1 K 19 ☐ Am 3.3-4.3
19 ☐ 1 Co 7.1-24 ☐ 1 K 20 ☐ Am 4.4-13
20 ☐ 1 Co 7.25-40 ☐ 1 K 21 ☐ Am 5
21 ☐ 1 Co 8 ☐ 1 K 22 ☐ Am 6
22 ☐ 1 Co 9 ☐ 2 K 1-2 ☐ Am 7
23 ☐ 1 Co 10 ☐ 2 K 3 ☐ Am 8
24 ☐ 1 Co 11.1-16 ☐ 2 K 4 ☐ Am 9
25 ☐ 1 Co 11.17-34 ☐ 2 K 5 ☐ Ob
26 ☐ 1 Co 12 ☐ 2 K 6.1-7.2 ☐ Jon 1
27 ☐ 1 Co 13 ☐ 2 K 7.3-20 ☐ Jon 2
28 ☐ 1 Co 14.1-25 ☐ 2 K 8 ☐ Jon 3
29 ☐ 1 Co 14.26-40 ☐ 2 K 9 ☐ Jon 4
30 ☐ 1 Co 15.1-34 ☐ 2 K 10 ☐ Mic 1
31 ☐ 1 Co 15.35-58 ☐ 1 K 11 ☐ Mic 2

AUGUST

1 ☐ 1 Co 16 ☐ 2 K 12-13 ☐ Mic 3
2 ☐ 2 Co 1.1-2.4 ☐ 2 K 14 ☐ Mic 4.1-5.1
3 ☐ 2 Co 2.5-3.18 ☐ 2 K 15-16 ☐ Mic 5.2-15
4 ☐ 2 Co 4.1-5.10 ☐ 2 K 17 ☐ Mic 6
5 ☐ 2 Co 5.11-6.13 ☐ 2 K 18 ☐ Mic 7
6 ☐ 2 Co 6.14-7.16 ☐ 2 K 19 ☐ Nh 1
7 ☐ 2 Co 8 ☐ 2 K 20-21 ☐ Nh 2
8 ☐ 2 Co 9 ☐ 2 K 22.1-23.34 ☐ Nh 3
9 ☐ 2 Co 10 ☐ 2 K 23.35-24.20 ☐ Hb 1
10 ☐ 2 Co 11 ☐ 2 K 25 ☐ Hb 2
11 ☐ 2 Co 12 ☐ 1 Ch 1-2 ☐ Hb 3
12 ☐ 2 Co 13 ☐ 1 Ch 3-4 ☐ Zep 1
13 ☐ Jn 1.1-18 ☐ 1 Ch 5-6 ☐ Zep 2
14 ☐ Jn 1.19-34 ☐ 1 Ch 7-8 ☐ Zep 3
15 ☐ Jn 1.35-51 ☐ 1 Ch 9 ☐ Hg 1-2
16 ☐ Jn 2 ☐ 1 Ch 10-11 ☐ Zec 1
17 ☐ Jn 3.1-21 ☐ 1 Ch 12 ☐ Zec 2
18 ☐ Jn 3.22-36 ☐ 1 Ch 13-14 ☐ Zec 3
19 ☐ Jn 4.1-26 ☐ 1 Ch 15.1-16.7 ☐ Zec 4
20 ☐ Jn 4.27-42 ☐ 1 Ch 16.8-43 ☐ Zec 5
21 ☐ Jn 4.43-54 ☐ 1 Ch 17 ☐ Zec 6
22 ☐ Jn 5.1-18 ☐ 1 Ch 18-19 ☐ Zec 7
23 ☐ Jn 5.19-47 ☐ 1 Ch 20.1-22.1 ☐ Zec 8
24 ☐ Jn 6.1-24 ☐ 1 Ch 22.2-23.1 ☐ Zec 9
25 ☐ Jn 6.25-59 ☐ 1 Ch 24 ☐ Zec 10
26 ☐ Jn 6.60-71 ☐ 1 Ch 25-26 ☐ Zec 11
27 ☐ Jn 7.1-24 ☐ 1 Ch 27-28 ☐ Zec 12
28 ☐ Jn 7.25-52 ☐ 1 Ch 29 ☐ Zec 13
29 ☐ Jn 8.1-20 ☐ 2 Ch 1.1-2.16 ☐ Zec 14
30 ☐ Jn 8.21-47 ☐ 2 Ch 2.17-5.1 ☐ Ml 1.1-2.9
31 ☐ Jn 8.48-59 ☐ 2 Ch 5.2-14 ☐ Ml 2.10-16

SEPTEMBER

1 ☐ Jn 9.1-23 ☐ 2 Ch 6 ☐ Ml 2.17-3.18
2 ☐ Jn 9.24-41 ☐ 2 Ch 7 ☐ Ml 4
3 ☐ Jn 10.1-21 ☐ 2 Ch 8 ☐ Ps 73
4 ☐ Jn 10.22-42 ☐ 2 Ch 9 ☐ Ps 74
5 ☐ Jn 11.1-27 ☐ 2 Ch 10-11 ☐ Ps 75
6 ☐ Jn 11.28-57 ☐ 2 Ch 12-13 ☐ Ps 76
7 ☐ Jn 12.1-26 ☐ 2 Ch 14-15 ☐ Ps 77
8 ☐ Jn 12.27-50 ☐ 2 Ch 16-17 ☐ Ps 78.1-20
9 ☐ Jn 13.1-20 ☐ 2 Ch 18 ☐ Ps 78.21-37
10 ☐ Jn 13.21-38 ☐ 2 Ch 19 ☐ Ps 78.38-55
11 ☐ Jn 14.1-14 ☐ 2 Ch 20.1-21.1 ☐ Ps 78.56-72
12 ☐ Jn 14.15-31 ☐ 2 Ch 21.2-22.12 ☐ Ps 79
13 ☐ Jn 15.1-16.4 ☐ 2 Ch 23 ☐ Ps 80
14 ☐ Jn 16.4-33 ☐ 2 Ch 24 ☐ Ps 81
15 ☐ Jn 17 ☐ 2 Ch 25 ☐ Ps 82
16 ☐ Jn 18.1-18 ☐ 2 Ch 26 ☐ Ps 83
17 ☐ Jn 18.19-38 ☐ 2 Ch 27-28 ☐ Ps 84
18 ☐ Jn 18.38-19.16 ☐ 2 Ch 29 ☐ Ps 85
19 ☐ Jn 19.16-42 ☐ 2 Ch 30 ☐ Ps 86
20 ☐ Jn 20.1-18 ☐ 2 Ch 31 ☐ Ps 87
21 ☐ Jn 20.19-31 ☐ 2 Ch 32 ☐ Ps 88
22 ☐ Jn 21 ☐ 2 Ch 33 ☐ Ps 89.1-18
23 ☐ 1 Jn 1 ☐ 2 Ch 34 ☐ Ps 89.19-37
24 ☐ 1 Jn 2 ☐ 2 Ch 35 ☐ Ps 89.38-52
25 ☐ 1 Jn 3 ☐ 2 Ch 36 ☐ Ps 90
26 ☐ 1 Jn 4 ☐ Ezra 1-2 ☐ Ps 91
27 ☐ 1 Jn 5 ☐ Ezra 3-4 ☐ Ps 92
28 ☐ 2 Jn ☐ Ezra 5-6 ☐ Ps 93
29 ☐ 3 Jn ☐ Ezra 7-8 ☐ Ps 94
30 ☐ Jd ☐ Ezra 9-10 ☐ Ps 95

OCTOBER

1 ☐ Rev 1 ☐ Ne 1-2 ☐ Ps 96
2 ☐ Rev 2 ☐ Ne 3 ☐ Ps 97
3 ☐ Rev 3 ☐ Ne 4 ☐ Ps 98
4 ☐ Rev 4 ☐ Ne 5.1-7.3 ☐ Ps 99
5 ☐ Rev 5 ☐ Ne 7.4-8.12 ☐ Ps 100
6 ☐ Rev 6 ☐ Ne 8.13-9.37 ☐ Ps 101
7 ☐ Rev 7 ☐ Ne 9.38-10.39 ☐ Ps 102
8 ☐ Rev 8 ☐ Ne 11 ☐ Ps 103
9 ☐ Rev 9 ☐ Ne 12 ☐ Ps 104.1-23
10 ☐ Rev 10 ☐ Ne 13 ☐ Ps 104.24-35
11 ☐ Rev 11 ☐ Es 1 ☐ Ps 105.1-25
12 ☐ Rev 12 ☐ Es 2 ☐ Ps 105.26-45
13 ☐ Rev 13 ☐ Es 3-4 ☐ Ps 106.1-23
14 ☐ Rev 14 ☐ Es 5.1-6.13 ☐ Ps 106.24-48
15 ☐ Rev 15 ☐ Es 6.14-8.17 ☐ Ps 107.1-22
16 ☐ Rev 16 ☐ Es 9-10 ☐ Ps 107.23-43
17 ☐ Rev 17 ☐ Is 1-2 ☐ Ps 108
18 ☐ Rev 18 ☐ Is 3-4 ☐ Ps 109.1-19
19 ☐ Rev 19 ☐ Is 5-6 ☐ Ps 109.20-31
20 ☐ Rev 20 ☐ Is 7-8 ☐ Ps 110
21 ☐ Rev 21-22 ☐ Is 9-10 ☐ Ps 111

22 ☐ 1 Th 1 ☐ Is 11-13 ☐ Ps 112
23 ☐ 1 Th 2.1-16 ☐ Is 14-16 ☐ Ps 113
24 ☐ 1 Th 2.17-3.13 ☐ Is 17-19 ☐ Ps 114
25 ☐ 1 Th 4 ☐ Is 20-22 ☐ Ps 115
26 ☐ 1 Th 5 ☐ Is 23-24 ☐ Ps 116
27 ☐ 2 Th 1 ☐ Is 25-26 ☐ Ps 117
28 ☐ 2 Th 2 ☐ Is 27-28 ☐ Ps 118
29 ☐ 2 Th 3 ☐ Is 29-30 ☐ Ps 119.1-32
30 ☐ 1 Ti 1 ☐ Is 31-33 ☐ Ps 119.33-64
31 ☐ 1 Ti 2 ☐ Is 34-35 ☐ Ps 119.65-96

NOVEMBER

1 ☐ 1 Ti 3 ☐ Is 36-37 ☐ Ps 119.97-120
2 ☐ 1 Ti 4 ☐ Is 38-39 ☐ Ps 119.121-144
3 ☐ 1 Ti 5.1-20 ☐ Jr 1-2 ☐ Ps 119.145-176
4 ☐ 1 Ti 5.21-6.21 ☐ Jr 3-4 ☐ Ps 120
5 ☐ 2 Ti 1 ☐ Jr 5-6 ☐ Ps 121
6 ☐ 2 Ti 2 ☐ Jr 7-8 ☐ Ps 122
7 ☐ 2 Ti 3 ☐ Jr 9-10 ☐ Ps 123
8 ☐ 2 Ti 4 ☐ Jr 11-12 ☐ Ps 124
9 ☐ Titus 1 ☐ Jr 13-14 ☐ Ps 125
10 ☐ Titus 2 ☐ Jr 15-16 ☐ Ps 126
11 ☐ Titus 3 ☐ Jr 17-18 ☐ Ps 127
12 ☐ Phm ☐ Jr 19-20 ☐ Ps 128
13 ☐ Jas 1 ☐ Jr 21-22 ☐ Ps 129
14 ☐ Jas 2 ☐ Jr 23-24 ☐ Ps 130
15 ☐ Jas 3 ☐ Jr 25-26 ☐ Ps 131
16 ☐ Jas 4 ☐ Jr 27-28 ☐ Ps 132
17 ☐ Jas 5 ☐ Jr 29-30 ☐ Ps 133
18 ☐ 1 Pet 1 ☐ Jr 31-32 ☐ Ps 134
19 ☐ 1 Pet 2 ☐ Jr 33-34 ☐ Ps 135
20 ☐ 1 Pet 3 ☐ Jr 35-36 ☐ Ps 136
21 ☐ 1 Pet 4 ☐ Jr 37-38 ☐ Ps 137
22 ☐ 1 Pet 5 ☐ Jr 39-40 ☐ Ps 138
23 ☐ 2 Pet 1 ☐ Jr 41-42 ☐ Ps 139
24 ☐ 2 Pet 2 ☐ Jr 43-44 ☐ Ps 140
25 ☐ 2 Pet 3 ☐ Jr 45-46 ☐ Ps 141
26 ☐ Ga 1 ☐ Jr 47-48 ☐ Ps 142
27 ☐ Ga 2 ☐ Jr 49-50 ☐ Ps 143
28 ☐ Ga 3.1-20 ☐ Jr 51-52 ☐ Ps 144
29 ☐ Ga 3.21-4.20 ☐ Lm 1-2 ☐ Ps 145
30 ☐ Ga 4.21-31 ☐ Lm 3-4 ☐ Ps 146

DECEMBER

1 ☐ Ga 5.1-15 ☐ Lm 5 ☐ Ps 147
2 ☐ Ga 5.16-26 ☐ Ez 1 ☐ Ps 148
3 ☐ Ga 6 ☐ Ez 2-3 ☐ Ps 149
4 ☐ Eph 1 ☐ Ez 4-5 ☐ Ps 150
5 ☐ Eph 2 ☐ Ez 6-7 ☐ Is 40
6 ☐ Eph 3 ☐ Ez 8-9 ☐ Is 41
7 ☐ Eph 4.1-16 ☐ Ez 10-11 ☐ Is 42
8 ☐ Eph 4.17-32 ☐ Ez 12-13 ☐ Is 43
9 ☐ Eph 5.1-20 ☐ Ez 14-15 ☐ Is 44
10 ☐ Eph 5.21-33 ☐ Ez 16 ☐ Is 45
11 ☐ Eph 6 ☐ Ez 17 ☐ Is 46
12 ☐ Phil 1.1-11 ☐ Ez 18 ☐ Is 47
13 ☐ Phil 1.12-30 ☐ Ez 19 ☐ Is 48
14 ☐ Phil 2.1-11 ☐ Ez 20 ☐ Is 49
15 ☐ Phil 2.12-30 ☐ Ez 21-22 ☐ Is 50
16 ☐ Phil 3 ☐ Ez 23 ☐ Is 51
17 ☐ Phil 4 ☐ Ez 24 ☐ Is 52
18 ☐ Col 1.1-23 ☐ Ez 25-26 ☐ Is 53
19 ☐ Col 1.24-2.19 ☐ Ez 27-28 ☐ Is 54
20 ☐ Col 2.20-3.17 ☐ Ez 29-30 ☐ Is 55
21 ☐ Col 3.18-4.18 ☐ Ez 31-32 ☐ Is 56
22 ☐ Lk 1.1-25 ☐ Ez 33 ☐ Is 57
23 ☐ Lk 1.26-56 ☐ Ez 34 ☐ Is 58
24 ☐ Lk 1.57-80 ☐ Ez 35-36 ☐ Is 59
25 ☐ Lk 2.1-20 ☐ Ez 37 ☐ Is 60
26 ☐ Lk 2.21-52 ☐ Ez 38-39 ☐ Is 61
27 ☐ Lk 3.1-20 ☐ Ez 40-41 ☐ Is 62
28 ☐ Lk 3.21-38 ☐ Ez 42-43 ☐ Is 63
29 ☐ Lk 4.1-30 ☐ Ez 44-45 ☐ Is 64
30 ☐ Lk 4.31-44 ☐ Ez 46-47 ☐ Is 65
31 ☐ Lk 5.1-26 ☐ Ez 48 ☐ Is 66

How to look up a Bible reference.

Every verse in this Bible is marked by its own *verse number*. To find any one of the passages listed in these reader's helps, you need to find the book, the chapter in the book, and the verse or verses within that chapter. The chapter number immediately follows the name of the book. This is followed by a period (.) which is followed by the number or range of numbers for the verses you seek. For example: 1 Corinthians 12.1-11 is the First Letter of Paul to the Corinthians, chapter twelve, verses one through eleven.

Some Readings for Special Days

New Year's Day
Colossians 3.5-17
Epiphany
Matthew 2.1-12
Martin Luther King, Jr. Day
Exodus 3.1-22
Christian Unity Sunday
John 17
Valentine's Day
1 Corinthians 13; 1 John 4.7-21
Presidents' Day
Isaiah 32.1-8
Ash Wednesday
Psalm 51; Joel 2.12-19;
Matthew 6.1-6; James 1.12-18
St. Patrick's Day
Isaiah 52.7-12
Palm Sunday
Mark 11.1-11; John 12.12-19;
Philippians 2.5-11
Holy (Maundy) Thursday
John 13.1-35; Psalm 116;
Matthew 26.26-30
Good Friday
John 18.1-19.42; Psalm 22;
Isaiah 52.13-53.12
Easter
Matthew 28; Luke 24; John 20;
Acts 10.34-43; Psalm 33
Passover
Exodus 12
Mother's Day
1 Samuel 1.1-28; Proverbs 23.22-25;
Proverbs 31.10-31; Luke 1.26-56
Memorial Day
Isaiah 26.1-19
Pentecost
Acts 2.1-11
Father's Day
Proverbs 4; Proverbs 20.7; Luke 15.11-32
Independence Day
Psalm 33
Labor Day
Genesis 1.26-2.4
Yom Kippur
Jeremiah 31.31-34
Grandparent's Day
Psalm 128
World Communion Sunday
1 Corinthians 11.23-34
All Saints Day
Hebrews 11
Stewardship Day
Matthew 25.14-29; 2 Corinthians 9.1-15
Election Day
1 Peter 2.13-17
Veterans Day
Isaiah 2.1-5
Bible Sunday
2 Timothy 3.10-17
Thanksgiving
Deuteronomy 8.1-10; Psalms 65; 67
First Sunday in Advent
Isaiah 63.15-64.12; Matthew 24.36-44;
Luke 21.25-36; Psalm 25
Second Sunday in Advent
Malachi 3.1-5; Matthew 3.1-12; Psalm 85
Third Sunday in Advent
Isaiah 12.1-6; Matthew 11.2-19;
Luke 3.7-18; Philippians 4.4-9
Fourth Sunday in Advent
Isaiah 7.10-17; Micah 5.2-5; Luke 1.26-56;
Psalm 89.1-18
Christmas
Luke 2.1-20; Matthew 1.18-25;
John 1.1-18; Titus 3.4-7
Personal Birthday
Psalm 145

Famous Passages of the Bible

Stories from the Old Testament

EARLY BEGINNINGS

Creation and Sin
Genesis 2.4-3.24
The First Murder
Genesis 4.1-15
Noah and the Flood
Genesis 6.1-9.17
The Tower of Babel (Babylon)
Genesis 11.1-9
The Call of Abraham
Genesis 12.1-9
The Destruction of Sodom and Gomorrah
Genesis 19.1-28

Hagar and Ishmael
Genesis 16.1-15; 21.9-21
The Birth of Isaac
Genesis 21.1-8
Abraham's Offering of Isaac
Genesis 22.1-19
The Story of Jacob
Genesis 25.19-35.29
The Story of Joseph
Genesis 37-50
Moses in Egypt
Exodus 1-14
Moses' Wilderness Wanderings
Exodus 15.22-20.26;
Exodus 31.18-34.35;
Numbers 20.1-21.25
The Ten Commandments
Exodus 20.1-17;
Deuteronomy 5.1-21
The King of Moab and Balaam
Numbers 22-24

PEOPLE OF GREAT FAITH IN THE OLD TESTAMENT

Rahab Helps the Israelite Spies
Joshua 2
Joshua, Military Strategist
Joshua 3; 6
Deborah, a Woman of Power and Judgment
Judges 4-5
Gideon, the Conqueror
Judges 6.11-8.32
Samson, a Man of Great Strength
Judges 13-16
Ruth, a Woman of Loyalty and Devotion
Ruth 1-4
Samuel, a Prophet Who Listened to God
1 Samuel 1-3; 7-10; 12; 15; 16
Saul, Israel's First King
1 Samuel 8-11; 13; 15; 28; 31
David, the Shepherd King
1 Samuel 16-27; 29.1-30.25;
2 Samuel 2; 11; 12; 15.1-8; 18;
1 Kings 1.1-31; 2.1-11
Solomon, the Wise King
1 Kings 2.12-11.43
Elijah, a Great Prophet
1 Kings 17-19; 21; 2 Kings 1
Elisha, His Successor
2 Kings 2; 4.1-7.2; 13.14-21
Nehemiah, a Heroic Builder
Nehemiah 1; 2; 4
Esther, a Brave Queen
Esther 1-10
Daniel, a Prophet of Courage
Daniel 1-6
Jonah, the Reluctant Missionary
Jonah 1-4

Stories from the New Testament

THE LIFE OF JESUS

The Birth of Jesus
Matthew 1.18-2.15; Luke 2.1-20

Jesus Is Named and Presented in the Temple
Luke 2.21-40

The Boy Jesus
Luke 2.41-52

The Baptism of Jesus
Matthew 3; Mark 1.1-11; Luke 3.21, 22

The Temptation of Jesus
Matthew 4.1-11; Mark 1.12, 13;
Luke 4.1-13

Jesus Calls His First Disciples
Matthew 4.18-22; Mark 1.16-20;
Luke 5.1-11

Jesus Chooses Twelve Apostles
Matthew 10.1-4; Mark 3.13-19;
Luke 6.12-16

The Transfiguration of Jesus
Matthew 17.1-13; Mark 9.2-13

JESUS' DEATH AND RESURRECTION

Jesus' Entry into Jerusalem
Matthew 21.1-11; Mark 11.1-11;
Luke 19.29-44; John 12.12-19

The Last Supper of Jesus
Matthew 26.17-35; Mark 14.12-26;
Luke 22.1-38

Jesus Prays in Gethsemane
Matthew 26.36-46; Mark 14.32-42;
Luke 22.39-46

Jesus' Trial and Crucifixion
Matthew 26.47-27.66;
Mark 14.43-15.47;
Luke 22.47-23.56; John 18; 19

The Resurrection of Jesus
Matthew 28.1-10; Mark 16;
Luke 24.1-12; John 20

The Great Commission
Matthew 28.16-20

The Ascension of Jesus
Luke 24.50-53; Acts 1.1-12

MIRACLES AND HEALINGS OF JESUS

Jesus Turns Water into Wine
John 2.1-11

Jesus Feeds Many People
Matthew 14.13-21; Mark 6.30-44; Luke 9.10-17; John 6.1-15; Matthew 15.32-39; Mark 8.1-10

Jesus Calms a Storm
Matthew 8.23-27; Mark 4.35-41; Luke 8.22-25

The Great Catch of Fish
Luke 5.1-11

Jesus Walks on Water
Matthew 14.22-33; Mark 6.45-52; John 6.16-21

Jesus Heals People with Leprosy
Matthew 8.1-4; Mark 1.40-45; Luke 5.12-16; Luke 17.11-19

Jesus Casts Out Demons
Matthew 8.28-34; Mark 5.1-20; Luke 8.26-39; Matthew 12.22-37; Mark 3.20-30; Luke 11.14-23; Matthew 17.14-21; Mark 9.14-29; Luke 9.37-43; Mark 1.21-28; Luke 4.31-37

Jesus Heals the Blind
Matthew 9.27-31; Matthew 20.29-34; Mark 10.46-52; Luke 18.35-43

Jesus Heals a Deaf Man
Mark 7.31-37

Jesus Heals the Crippled
Matthew 12.9-14; Mark 3.1-6; Luke 6.6-11; John 5.1-9; Luke 14.1-6; Matthew 9.1-8; Mark 2.1-12; Luke 5.17-26

Jesus Heals Many Women
Matthew 9.18-26; Mark 5.21-43; Luke 8.1-3; Luke 8.40-56; Luke 13.10-17; Matthew 15.21-28; Mark 7.24-30

Jesus Heals an Army Officer's Servant
Matthew 8.5-13; Luke 7.1-10

Jesus Heals Peter's Mother-in-Law
Matthew 8.14, 15; Mark 1.29-31; Luke 4.38, 39

Jesus Heals an Official's Son
John 4.46-54

Jesus Revives an Official's Daughter
Matthew 9.18, 19, 23-26; Mark 5.21-24, 35-42; Luke 8.40-42, 49-56

Jesus Raises the Dead
Luke 7.11-17; John 11.1-44

THE TEACHINGS AND PARABLES OF JESUS

The Sermon on the Mount
Matthew 5-7; Luke 6.20-49

The Beatitudes
Matthew 5.3-11; Luke 6.20-26

The Most Important Commandment
Matthew 22.37-39; Mark 12.29-31; Luke 10.27

The Golden Rule
Matthew 7.12; Luke 6.31

The Grain of Mustard Seed
Matthew 13.31, 32; Mark 4.30-32; Luke 13.18, 19

The Parable of the Sower
Matthew 13.1-23; Mark 4.1-20

The Parable of the Growing Seed
Mark 4.26-29

Some Parables about the Kingdom of Heaven
Matthew 13.24-52

The Parable of the Unforgiving Official
Matthew 18.23-35

The Parable of the Workers in the Vineyard
Matthew 20.1-16

The Parable of the Renters in the Vineyard
Matthew 21.33-46; Mark 12.1-11; Luke 20.9-18

The Parable of the Wedding Banquet
Matthew 22.1-14; Luke 14.15-24

The Parable of the Ten Girls (Virgins)
Matthew 25.1-13

The Parable of the Three Servants and Their Coins
Matthew 25.14-30; Luke 19.11-27

The Parable of the Sheep and the Goats
Matthew 25.31-46

What is a parable?

Parables are stories that use typical every-day situations in order to teach important truths. Jesus used many parables to teach his followers about the Kingdom of God.

The Parable of the Good Samaritan
Luke 10.25-37

The Parable of the Shepherd
John 10.1-21

The Parable of the Rich Fool
Luke 12.16-21

The Parable of the Watchful Servants
Luke 12.35-48

The Parable of the Barren Fig Tree
Luke 13.6-9

The Parable of the Lost Sheep
Matthew 18.12-14; Luke 15.3-7

The Parable of the Lost Coin
Luke 15.8-10

The Parable of the Lost Son
Luke 15.11-32

The Parable of the Dishonest Manager
Luke 16.1-13

The Rich Man and Lazarus
Luke 16.19-31

The Parable of the Widow and the Judge
Luke 18.1-8

The Parable of the Pharisee and the Tax Collector
Luke 18.9-14

OTHER NEW TESTAMENT STORIES

The Birth of John the Baptist
Luke 1.57-66

John the Baptist Is Executed
Matthew 14.1-12; Mark 6.14-29

Peter Receives the Keys to the Kingdom of Heaven
Matthew 16.13-20

The Holy Spirit Comes on Pentecost
Acts 2

Stephen, the First Martyr
Acts 6.5-15; 7.54-60

Philip Baptizes the Ethiopian Official
Acts 8.26-39

The Conversion of Paul
Acts 9.1-31

Peter and Cornelius
Acts 10

Peter in Prison
Acts 12.1-19

The Baptism of Lydia
Acts 16.11-15

Paul in Prison
Acts 16.16-40

The Riot in Ephesus
Acts 19.23-41

Paul's Voyage to Rome
Acts 27; 28

Other Famous Passages

SONGS OF THE BIBLE

Moses' Song of Deliverance
Exodus 15.1-18

Deborah and Barak's Song of Victory
Judges 5.1-31

Hannah's Song of Praise
1 Samuel 2.1-10

David's Song of Lament
2 Samuel 17-27

David's Song of Victory
2 Samuel 22; Psalm 18

Solomon's Love Song
Song of Songs 2.10-15

Mary's Song of Praise
Luke 1.46-55

A Hymn to Christ Jesus
Philippians 2.6-11

PRAYERS OF THE BIBLE

Solomon's Personal Prayer
1 Kings 3.5-10

Solomon's Public Prayer
1 Kings 8.22-61
2 Chronicles 6.12-42

Hezekiah's Temple Prayer
2 Kings 19.15-19; Isaiah 37.14-20

David's Prayer of Thanksgiving
2 Samuel 7.18-29; 1 Chronicles 17.16-27

Job's Prayer
Job 42.1-6

Jeremiah's Prayer
Jeremiah 32.16-25

Daniel's Prayer
Daniel 9.3-19

Jonah's Prayer
Jonah 2.1-9

The Lord's Prayer
Matthew 6.9-13

Jesus' Prayer in Gethsemane
Matthew 26.36-44

Jesus' Prayer for His Disciples
John 17

The Disciples' Prayer
Acts 4.24-31

Paul's Prayer for Believers
Ephesians 3.14-21

SPECIAL BLESSINGS FROM THE BIBLE

Invocations and Openings
Psalm 19.14; 1 Corinthians 1.3;
1 Timothy 1.2; 2 John 3;
Revelation 1.4-6

Dismissals and Closings
Numbers 6.24-26; 1 Kings 8.57,58;
Romans 15.5,6,13; Romans 16.25-27;
2 Corinthians 13.13; Ephesians 6.23,24;
Philippians 4.7; Hebrews 13.20,21;
Jude 24,25

Finding Help in the Bible

HELP IN SPECIAL CIRCUMSTANCES

Being a friend
Proverbs 17.17; Luke 10.25-37; John 15.11-17;
Romans 16.1,2

Being a leader
Isaiah 11.1-9; Isaiah 32.1-8; 1 Timothy 3.1-7;
2 Timothy 2.14-26; Titus 1.5-9

Caring for the aged and widowed
Genesis 47.1-12; Ruth 1; Proverbs 23.22;
1 Timothy 5.3-8

Celebrating the birth/adoption of a child
Psalm 100; Proverbs 22.6;
Luke 18.15-17; John 16.16-22

Celebrating a graduation
Psalm 119.105,106; Proverbs 9.10-12;
Galatians 5.16-26; Philippians 4.4-9

Celebrating a marriage
Genesis 2.18-24; Song of Songs 8.6,7;
Ephesians 5.21-33; Colossians 2.6,7

Celebrating a wedding anniversary
Psalm 100; 1 Corinthians 13

Controlling your temper
Proverbs 14.17, 29; 15.18; 19.11; 29.22;
Ecclesiastes 7.9; Galatians 5.16-26

Controlling your tongue
Psalm 12; Psalm 19.14; Proverbs 11.13;
Proverbs 26.20; 2 Thessalonians 2.16,17;
James 3.1-12

Discovering God's will
Psalm 15; Micah 6.6-8; Matthew 5.14-16;
Luke 9.21-27; Romans 13.8-14;
2 Peter 1.3-9; 1 John 4.7-21

Encountering a cult
Matthew 7.15-20; 2 Peter 2; 1 John 4.1-6; Jude

Encountering peer pressure
Proverbs 1.7-19; Romans 12.1,2;
Galatians 6.1-5; Ephesians 5.1-20

Entering college
Proverbs 2.1-8; Proverbs 3.1-18;
Proverbs 4.1-27; Proverbs 23.12;
Romans 8.1-17; 1 Corinthians 1.18-31

Entering military service
2 Samuel 22.2-51; Psalm 91;
Ephesians 6.10-20; 2 Timothy 2.1-13

Experiencing the death of a loved one
Job 19.25-27; John 11.25-27; John 14.1-7;
Romans 8.31-39; Romans 14.7-9;
1 Thessalonians 4.13-18

Experiencing illness
Psalm 23; Mark 1.29-34; Mark 6.53-56;
James 5.14-16

Experiencing suffering and persecution
Psalm 109; Psalm 119.153-160; Matthew 5.3-12;
John 15.18-16.4; Romans 8.18-30;
2 Corinthians 4.1-15; Hebrews 12.1-11;
1 Peter 4.12-19

Facing a difficult decision
1 Kings 3; Esther 4-7; Psalm 139;
Daniel 2.14-23; Colossians 3.12-17

Facing a divorce
Psalm 25; Matthew 19.1-9; Philippians 3.1-11

Facing homelessness
Psalm 90.1,2; Isaiah 65.17-25;
Lamentations 3.19-24; Luke 9.57-62;
Revelation 21.1-4

Facing imprisonment
Lamentations 3.34-36; Matthew 25.31-46;
Luke 4.16-21

Facing life alone
1 Corinthians 7.25-38; 1 Corinthians 12.1-31

Facing a natural disaster
Genesis 8.1-9.17; Job 36.22-37.13; Psalms 29,
124; Psalm 36.5-9; Jeremiah 31.35-37;
Romans 8.31-39; 1 Peter 1.3-12

Facing a trial or lawsuit
Psalm 26; Isaiah 50.4-11; Matthew 5.25, 26;
Luke 18.1-8

Losing your job
Jeremiah 29.10-14; Luke 16.1-13;
Philippians 4.10-13

Losing your property and possessions
Job 1.13-22; Job 42.7-17; Isaiah 30.19-26;
Isaiah 41.17-20; Romans 8.18-39

Managing your time
Proverbs 12.11; Proverbs 28.19; Mark 13.32-37; Luke 21.34-36; 1 Timothy 4.11-16; Titus 3.8-14

Moving into a new home
Psalm 127.1,2; Proverbs 24.3,4; John 14.1-7; Ephesians 3.14-21; Revelation 3.20,21

Overcoming addiction
Psalm 40.1-5, 11-17; Psalm 116.1-7; Provebs 23.29-35; 2 Corinthians 5.16-21; Ephesians 4.22-24

Overcoming a grudge
Leviticus 19.17,18; Matthew 5.23-26; Luke 6.27-36; Ephesians 4.25-32

Overcoming prejudice
Matthew 7.1-5; Acts 10.34-36; Galatians 3.26-29; Ephesians 2.11-22; Colossians 3.5-11; James 2.1-13

Overcoming pride
Psalm 131; Mark 9.33-37; Luke 14.7-11; Luke 18.9-14; Luke 22.24-27; Romans 12.14-16; 1 Corinthians 1.18-31; 2 Corinthians 12.1-10

Overcoming procrastination
Matthew 22.1-14; Matthew 25.1-13; 2 Corinthians 6.1,2

Raising children
Proverbs 22.6; Ephesians 6.4; Colossians 3.21

Respecting civil authorities
Mark 12.13-17; Romans 13.1-7; Titus 3.1, 2; 1 Peter 2.13-17

Respecting parents
Exodus 20.12; Proverbs 23.22; Ephesians 6.1-3; Colossians 3.20

Retiring from your job
Numbers 6.24-26; Psalm 145; Matthew 25.31-46; Romans 12.1,2; Philippians 3.12-21; 2 Peter 1.2

Seeking forgiveness
Psalm 32.1-5; Psalm 51; Proverbs 28.13; Joel 2.12-17; Matthew 6.14-15; Luke 15; Philemon; Hebrews 4.14-16; 1 John 1.5-10

Seeking God's help
Psalms 5, 57, 86, 121, 130; Psalm 119.169-176; Matthew 7.7-12

Seeking justice
Psalms 10, 17, 75, 94; Isaiah 42.1-7; Isaiah 61.1-9; Amos 5.21-24; Habakkuk 1.1-2.4

Seeking salvation
John 3.1-21; Romans 1.16, 17; Romans 3.21-31; Romans 5.1-11; Romans 10.5-13; Ephesians 1.3-14; Ephesians 2.1-10

Seeking strength
Psalms 46, 138; Isaiah 40.27-31; Isaiah 51.12-16; Ephesians 6.10-20; 2 Thessalonians 2.16,17

Seeking truth
Psalm 119.153-160; John 8.31-47; John 14.6-14; John 16.4b-15; 1 Timothy 2.1-7

Sharing your gifts
Exodus 35.20-29; Malachi 3.6-12; Luke 21.1-4; Acts 2.43-47; Acts 4.32-37; Romans 12.9-13; 1 Corinthians 16.1-4; 2 Corinthians 8.1-15; 2 Corinthians 9.6-15

Starting a new job
Proverbs 11.3; Proverbs 22.29; Romans 12.3-11; 1 Thessalonians 5.12-18; 2 Thessalonians 3.6-13; 1 Peter 4.7-11

Understanding your relationship with God
Deuteronomy 5.1-22; Psalm 139; John 15.1-17; Romans 5.1-11; Romans 8.1-17

Understanding your relationship with others
Deuteronomy 5.16-21; Proverbs 3.27-35; Matthew 18.15-17; Matthew 18.21-35; Romans 14.13-23; Romans 15.1-6; Galatians 6.1-10; Colossians 3.12-17; 1 John 4.7-12

Worrying about the future
Isaiah 35; Isaiah 60; Jeremiah 29.10-14; 1 Peter 1.3-5; Revelation 21.1-8

Worrying about growing old
Psalm 37.23-29; Isaiah 46.3,4

Worrying about money
Proverbs 11.7; Ecclesiastes 5.10-20; Matthew 6.24-34; Luke 12.13-21; 1 Timothy 6.6-10

EXPERIENCING TROUBLESOME FEELINGS

Afraid?
Psalms 27, 91; Isaiah 41.5-13; Mark 4.35-41; Hebrews 13.5,6; 1 John 4.13-18

Afraid of death?
Psalm 23; Psalm 63.1-8; John 6.35-40; Romans 8.18-39; 1 Corinthians 15.35-57; 1 Corinthians 5.1-10; 2 Timothy 1.8-10

Angry?
Proverbs 15.1; Matthew 5.21-24; Romans 12.17-21; Ephesians 4.26-32; James 1.19-21

Anxious? Worried?
Psalm 25; Matthew 6.24-34; Matthew 10.26-31; 1 Peter 1.3-5; 1 Peter 5.7

Depressed?
Psalms 16, 43, 130; Isaiah 61.1-4; Jeremiah 15.10-21; Lamentations 3.55-57; John 3.14-17; Ephesians 3.14-21

Disappointed? Let down?
Psalm 55; Psalm 62.1-8; Jeremiah 20.7-18

Discouraged?
Psalm 34; Isaiah 12.1-6; Romans 15.13; 2 Corinthians 4.16-18; Phillippians 4.10-13; Colossians 1.9-14; Hebrews 6.9-12

Doubting your faith in God?
Psalms 8, 146; Proverbs 30.5; Matthew 7.7-12; Luke 17.5,6; John 20.24-31; Romans 4.13-25; Hebrews 11; 1 John 5.13-15

Frustrated?
Job 21.1-16; Job 24.1-17; Job 36.1-26; Matthew 7.13,14

Impatient?
Psalm 13; Psalm 37.1-7; Psalm 40.1-5; Ecclesiastes 3.1-15; Lamentations 3.25-33; Hebrews 6.13-20; James 5.7-11

Insecure? Lacking confidence?
Deuteronomy 31.1-8; Psalm 73.21-26; Psalm 108; Philippians 4.10-20; 1 John 3.19-24

Jealous?
Psalm 49; Proverbs 23.17; James 3.13-18

Lonely?
Psalms 22, 42; John 14.15-31a

Overwhelmed? Experiencing stress?
Isaiah 55.1-9; Matthew 11.25-30; John 4.1-30; 2 Corinthians 6.3-10; Revelation 22.17

Rejected?
Psalm 38; Isaiah 52.13-53.12; Matthew 9.9-13; Luke 4.16-30; John 15.18-16.4; Ephesians 1.3-14; 1 Peter 2.1-10

Tempted?
Psalm 19.12-14; Psalm 141; Luke 4.1-13; Hebrews 2.11-18; Hebrews 4.14-16; James 1.12-18

Tempted by sex?
2 Samuel 11.1-12.25; 1 Corinthians 6.12-20; Galatians 5.16-26

Tired? Weary?
Psalm 3.5,6; Psalm 4.4-8; Isaiah 35.1-10; Matthew 11.25-30; 2 Thessalonians 3.16; Hebrews 4.1-11

Feeling useless? Inferior?
Isaiah 6.1-8; Jeremiah 1.4-10; Galatians 1.11-24; Ephesians 4.1-16; 1 Peter 2.4-10

Vengeful?
Matthew 5.38-42; Romans 12.17-21

What the Bible Says about God's Forgiveness

Every person is separated from God because of sin.
Isaiah 59.1-15
Romans 3.9-20
Romans 5.12-21
Ecclesiastes 7.20
Romans 7.14-25

God has always sought to form a close relationship with people.
Exodus 19.3b-8
Jeremiah 31.31-34
Isaiah 54.1-10
1 Peter 1.1-10
1 John 3.1-10

God has reached out to people in a personal way by sending Jesus Christ.
Colossians 1.15-23
Romans 5.1-11
1 Peter 2.10-25
John 3.1-21
2 Timothy 1.3-10
Ephesians 2.1-10

God's forgiveness through Jesus Christ is available to every person.
Psalm 51.1-17
1 John 1.5-10
Romans 10.5-13
Psalm 32.1-11
Romans 8.31-39
Romans 3.21-26

New life in Christ calls a person to live in a Christ-like way.
Romans 6.1-14
Matthew 20.20-28
Ephesians 4.17-32
Galatians 5.16-26
1 John 4.7-21
Romans 12.1-21

WELCOME TO THE CONTEMPORARY ENGLISH VERSION

Languages are spoken before they are written. And far more communication is done through the spoken word than through the written word. In fact, more people *hear* the Bible read than read it for themselves. Traditional translations of the Bible count on the *reader's* ability to understand a *written* text. But the *Contemporary English Version* differs from all other English Bibles—past and present—in that it takes into consideration the needs of the *hearer*, as well as those of the reader, who may not be familiar with traditional biblical language.

The *Contemporary English Version* has been described as a "user-friendly" and a "mission-driven" translation that can be *read aloud* without stumbling, *heard* without misunderstanding, and *listened to* with enjoyment and appreciation, because the language is contemporary and the style is lucid and lyrical.

The *Contemporary English Version* invites you to *read*, to *hear*, to *understand* and to *share*

the Word of God now
as never before!

THE CONTEMPORARY ENGLISH VERSION

Translation it is that opens the window, to let in the light; that breaks the shell, that we may eat the kernel; that puts aside the curtain, that we may look into the most holy place; that removes the cover of the well, that we may come by the water ("The Translators to the Reader," King James Version, 1611).

The most important document in the history of the English language is the King James Version of the Bible. To measure its spiritual impact on the English speaking world would be more impossible than counting the grains of sand along the ocean shores. Historically, many Bible translators have attempted in some measure to *retain the form* of the King James Version. But the translators of the Contemporary English Version of the Bible have diligently sought to *capture the spirit* of the King James Version by following certain principles set forth by its translators in the document "The Translators to the Reader," which was printed in the earliest editions.

This is the Word of God, which we translate

Accuracy, beauty, clarity, and dignity—all of these can and must be achieved in the translation of the Bible. After all, as the translators of the King James Version stated, "This is the Word of God, which we translate."

Every attempt has been made to produce a text that is faithful to the *meaning* of the original. In order to assure the *accuracy* of the Contemporary English Version, the Old Testament was translated directly from the Hebrew and Aramaic texts published by the United Bible Societies (*Biblia Hebraica Stuttgartensia*, fourth edition corrected). And the New Testament was translated directly from the Greek text published by the United Bible Societies (third edition corrected and compared with the fourth revised edition).

The drafts in their earliest stages were sent for review and comment to a number of biblical scholars, theologians, and educators representing a wide variety of church traditions. In addition, drafts were sent for review and comment to all English-speaking Bible Societies and to more than forty United Bible Societies translation consultants around the world. Final approval of the text was given by the American Bible Society Board of Trustees on the recommendation of its Translations Subcommittee.

We desire that the Scripture . . . may be understood

That the Scripture may be understood even by ordinary people was a primary goal of the translators of the King James Version. And they raised the question, "What can be more available thereto than to deliver God's book unto God's people in a tongue which they understand?" Martin Luther also did his translation for the common people, and he established the following guidelines:

> We do not have to inquire of the literal Latin, how we are to speak German . . . Rather we must inquire about this of the mother in the home, the children on the street, the common man in the marketplace. *We must be guided by their language, the way they speak, and do our translating accordingly.*

Today more people *hear* the Bible read aloud than read it for themselves! And statistics released by the National Center for Education indicate that "almost half of U.S. adults have very limited reading and writing skills." If this is the case, a contemporary translation must be a text that an inexperienced reader can *read aloud* without stumbling, that someone unfamiliar with traditional biblical terminology can *hear without misunderstanding*, and that everyone can *listen to with enjoyment* because the style is lucid and lyrical.

In order to attain these goals of clarity, beauty, and dignity, the translators of the Contemporary English Version carefully studied every word, phrase, clause, and paragraph of the original. Then, with equal care, they struggled to discover the best way to translate the text, so that it would be suitable both for *private* and *public* reading, and for *memorizing*. The result is an English text that is enjoyable and easily understood by the vast majority of English speakers, regardless of their religious or educational background.

In the *hearing* of a translation, even the inclusion of a simple word like "and" can make a significant difference. Matthew 2.9 of the Contemporary English Version reads as follows: "The wise men listened to what the king said, and then left. *And* the star they had seen in the east went on ahead of them until it stopped over the place where the child was."

"And" at the beginning of the second sentence assists both the person who reads the text aloud and those who must depend upon hearing it read. Like all other punctuation marks, the period after "left" is silent, and so the text without "And" could possibly be *heard* as, "The wise men listened to what the king said and then left the star they had seen in the east." However, as the text now stands, the oral reader must pause briefly for a breath before "And," which will signal the hearer that a new sentence has begun.

As another example, try reading the following two sentences aloud: "You yourselves admit, then, that you agree with what your ancestors did" and "for it was better with me then than now." Both suffer from potential tongue twisters ("admit, then, that" and "then than"). But the first is doubly difficult because it consists of a lengthy series of unaccented syllables that do not allow the reader to take a breath. In the Contemporary English Version every attempt has been made to avoid these and other kinds of constructions that could possibly prove problematic for oral reading.

According to the rules of English grammar, the pronoun *he* must refer back to *God* in the following sentence: "The other, however, rebuked him saying, 'Don't you fear *God*? You received the same sentence *he* did.' " But the reference is actually to Jesus, who is mentioned earlier in the passage. Traditional translations assume that the reader can study the printed text and finally figure out the meaning, but the Contemporary English Version is concerned equally with the reader and the *hearer*. And in many situations, the hearer may have only *one* chance to understand what is read aloud.

In poetry, the *appearance of the text on the page* is important, since in oral reading there is a tendency to stress the last word on a line and to pause momentarily before going to the next line, especially if the second line is indented. Compare the three following examples, where the lines of the same text have been broken improperly (left column) and properly (right column):

He brought me out into a broad
    place.
	He brought me out
	    into a broad place.

With the loyal you show yourself
    loyal.
	With the loyal
	    you show yourself loyal.

The Lord my God lights up
    my darkness.
	The Lord my God
	    lights up my darkness.

No fault is to be found with the translation itself. Yet there is a significant difference in the *appearance* of the text on the page, because the lines on the right have been *measured*, in order to prevent unfortunate runovers. In this form, the text not only looks better on the page, but it is easier to read and memorize, and it avoids such disastrous combinations as "He brought me out into a broad" or "With the loyal you show yourself" or "The Lord my God lights up." Moreover, both formats require exactly the same amount of lines.

The first translation in the history of the English Bible to develop a text with measured poetry lines is the Contemporary English Version, in which the translators have consciously created a text that will not suffer from unfortunate line breaks when published in double columns. *Accuracy* is the main concern of translators, but it must be realized that in the translation of biblical poetry, what the reader *sees* is what will be *said*, and what others will *hear*. This means that lines improperly broken can easily lead to a misunderstanding of the text, especially for those who must depend upon *hearing* the Scriptures read.

Hebrew poetry has its own systems of sound, rhyme, and rhythm, as well as a *form* that involves much repetition. It is impossible in English to retain the sounds, rhymes, and rhythms of the Hebrew text, but traditional translations have attempted to reproduce the frequent repetition, in which a second line will repeat or expand, either negatively or positively, the thoughts of the previous line. However, this repetition is often ineffective for those English speakers, who are unaccustomed to the poetic style of the biblical authors. And so, the translators of the Contemporary English Version have followed the example of Martin Luther in the translation of poetry:

> Whoever would speak German *must not use Hebrew style*. Rather he must see to it—once he understands the Hebrew author—that he concentrates on the *sense* of the text, asking himself, "Pray tell, what do the Germans say in such a situation?" Once he has the German words to serve his purpose, let him drop the Hebrew words and *express the meaning freely* in the best German he knows.

The qualities that many critics value most in modern poetry are effortless *economy* and *exactness* of language. It is hoped that readers will discover similar features in the poetry of the Contemporary English Version, which strives for beauty and dignity, as much as for accuracy and clarity. In this translation, the poetry often requires fewer lines than do traditional translations, but the *integrity*, *intent*, and *impact* of the original are consistently maintained. Note, for example, the rendering of Job 38.14,15:

Early dawn outlines the hills
like stitches on clothing
or sketches on clay.

But its light is too much
for those who are evil,
and their power is broken.

Whenever the contents of two or more verses have been joined together and rearranged in the poetic sections of the *CEV*, this is signaled by an asterisk (*) before the first verse number in the series.

In everyday speech, "gender generic" or "inclusive" language is used, because it sounds most natural to people today. This means that where the biblical languages require masculine nouns or pronouns when both men and women are intended, this intention must be reflected in translation, though the English *form* may be very different from that of the original. The Greek text of Matthew 16.24 is literally, "If anyone wants to follow me, *he* must deny *himself* and take up *his* cross and follow me." The Contemporary English Version shifts to a form which is still accurate, and at the same time more effective in English: "If any of *you* want to be my followers, *you* must forget about *yourself*. *You* must take up *your* cross and follow me."

Variety of translations is profitable

The translators of the King James Version said, ". . . variety of translations is profitable for the finding out of the sense of the Scriptures" and "We affirm and avow that the very meanest translation of the Bible in English, set forth by men of our profession . . . contains the Word of God, nay is the Word of God." They even stated, "No cause therefore why the Word translated should be denied to be the Word, or forbidden to be current, notwithstanding that some imperfections and blemishes may be noted in the setting forth of it."

Each English translation is, in its own right, the Word of God, yet each translation serves to meet the needs of a different audience. In this regard, the Contemporary English Version should be considered a *companion*—the *mission* arm—of traditional translations, because it takes seriously the words of the apostle Paul that "faith comes by *hearing*."

It has pleased God in his divine providence

Translating the Bible may be compared to living the life of faith. God has not given us all the answers for our pilgrim journey, but we have been provided with all that we need to know in order to be saved. As the translators of the King James Version observed:

> . . . it has pleased God in His divine providence here and there to scatter those words and sentences of that difficulty and doubtfulness, not in doctrinal points that concern salvation (for in such it has been vouched that the Scriptures are plain), but in matters of less moment, that fearfulness would better beseem us than confidence . . .
>
> For as it is a fault of incredulity, to doubt of those things that are evident; so to determine of such things that the Spirit of God

has left (even in the mind of the judicious) questionable, can be no less than presumption.

Bible translators do not have the privilege and luxury of working from the original manuscripts of either the Old or New Testament. Indeed, there are numerous difficult passages where decisions must be made concerning what word or words actually belong in the text, and what these words may, in fact, mean. At such places, the best a translator can do is to give what seems to be one possible meaning for the difficult text and to indicate this by a note, which was also what the King James translators did: "... so diversity of signification and sense in the margin, where the text is not clear, must needs be good; yea, is necessary, as we are persuaded." Fortunately, these "words and sentences of that difficulty and doubtfulness" do not in any way leave unclear the central message of the Bible or any of its major doctrines.

Having and using as great helps as were needful

The translators of the Contemporary English Version have not created new or novel interpretations of the text. Rather, it was their goal to express mainstream interpretations of the text in current, everyday English. To do so required *listening* carefully to each word of the biblical text, to the way in which English is spoken today, to the remarks of their reviewers, and especially to the Spirit of God. Once again the comments of the translators of the King James Version are appropriate:

> Neither did we think much to consult the translators or commentators ... but neither did we disdain to revise that which we had done, and to bring to the anvil that which we had hammered; but having and using as great helps as were needful, and fearing no reproach for slowness, nor coveting praise for expedition, we have at the length, through the good hand of the Lord upon us, brought forth the work to that pass that you see.

Accordingly, the translators of the Contemporary English Version are indebted to all translators and biblical scholars who have gone before them and have made it possible to understand something of the languages, cultures, and history of biblical times. And, together with the apostle Paul, they confess: *We don't have the right to claim that we have done anything on our own. God gives us what it takes to do all that we do.* (2 Corinthians 3.5)

Offer praise to God our Savior because of our Lord Jesus Christ! (Jude 24,25)

CONTENTS

OLD TESTAMENT

NEW TESTAMENT

ALPHABETICAL LISTING
WITH ABBREVIATIONS

OLD TESTAMENT

NEW TESTAMENT

OTHER ABBREVIATIONS

Circa (around)	c.
Old Testament	OT
New Testament	NT
Septuagint	LXX

The
HOLY BIBLE

The Old Testament
Contemporary English Version

About the Old Testament

The Old Testament is a collection of 39 books written in Hebrew, with a few chapters written in Aramaic. These books are arranged in five groups in English Bibles:

(1) The Pentateuch. The name means "five books," and this group is made up of Genesis, Exodus, Leviticus, Numbers, and Deuteronomy. The group is sometimes called the "Law of Moses" or the "Torah," a Hebrew word referring to God's "law" or "teachings."

(2) The Historical Books. This group is made up of Joshua, Judges, Ruth, 1 and 2 Samuel, 1 and 2 Kings, 1 and 2 Chronicles, Ezra, Nehemiah, and Esther. Together, the Pentateuch and Historical books tell the history of Israel two times. The books of Genesis through 2 Kings tell the history the first time, while the books of 1 Chronicles through Nehemiah tell it the second time from a somewhat different point of view.

(3) The Poetic Books. This group is sometimes called the "Wisdom Books," and it contains Job, Psalms, Proverbs, Ecclesiastes, and the Song of Songs. Lamentations is also one of the poetic books, but in English Bibles it follows Jeremiah, because Jeremiah has often been thought to be its author.

(4) The Major Prophets are the longer books that contain the messages of the prophets Isaiah, Jeremiah, Ezekiel, and Daniel.

(5) The Minor Prophets are the shorter books that contain the messages of the prophets Hosea, Joel, Amos, Obadiah, Jonah, Micah, Nahum, Habakkuk, Zephaniah, Haggai, Zechariah, and Malachi.

GENESIS

ABOUT THIS BOOK

The name "Genesis" comes from a Greek word meaning "beginning." And this is a book of beginnings, because it talks about the beginning of the universe, the beginning of the human race, and the beginning of the people of Israel.

The first part of Genesis (1–11) tells about creation and the human race up to the time of Abraham. Everything God created was good, but the first two human beings, Adam and Eve, disobeyed him and brought evil into the world. People became so sinful that God decided to send a flood to kill everyone except a man named Noah and his family. They worshiped God, and so God told them to build a large boat to save themselves and a few of each kind of animals and birds. After the flood people again spread out over the earth, and most of them stopped worshiping God.

The rest of the book of Genesis (12–50) contains the story of Abram and his family. God chose them to be the beginning of his own special people. God also changed Abram's name to Abraham, and the name of Abram's wife Sarai to Sarah. Abraham and his wife Sarah had no children, but God promised that they would have a child and that their descendants would someday have their own land and be a blessing for all nations.

Abraham and Sarah moved to Canaan, the land that God had promised to give their descendants. Abraham and Sarah had a son, Isaac, when they were very old. Isaac later had two sons, Jacob and Esau. As the book concludes, Jacob's twelve sons and their families are living in Egypt. One of these brothers, Joseph, had become the governor of Egypt. But Joseph knew that God would someday keep his promise to his people:

> *Before Joseph died, he told his brothers, "I won't live much longer. But God will take care of you and lead you out of Egypt to the land he promised Abraham, Isaac, and Jacob."* *(50.24)*

A QUICK LOOK AT THIS BOOK

The Story of Creation (1.1—2.25)
The First Sin and the First Murder (3.1—4.16)
Descendants of Adam before the Flood (4.17—5.32)
Noah and the Flood (6.1—9.28)
The Descendants of Noah and the Tower of Babel (10.1—11.32)
The Lord Chooses Abram (12.1-20)
Abram and Lot (13.1—14.24)
The Lord's Promises to Abram (15.1-21)
Abram, Hagar, and Ishmael (16.1-16)
God Changes Abram's Name to Abraham and Promises Him a Son (17.1—18.15)
Abraham, Lot, Sodom, and Gomorrah (18.16—19.38)
Abraham, Sarah, and Isaac (20.1—23.20)
Rebekah, a Wife for Isaac (24.1-67)
The Death of Abraham (25.1-18)
Isaac and His Family (25.19—28.9)
Jacob and His Family (28.10—35.29)
Esau and His Family (36.1-43)
Joseph Is Sold by His Brothers as a Slave (37.1-36)
Judah and Tamar (38.1-30)

Joseph in Egypt (39.1—41.57)
Joseph and His Brothers (42.1—45.28)
Jacob and His Family Go to Egypt (46.1—47.31)
Jacob Blesses His Family and Dies (48.1—50.14)
Joseph Dies (50.15-26)

The Story of Creation

1 In the beginning God
created the heavens
and the earth.[a]
2 The earth was barren,
with no form of life;[b]
it was under a roaring ocean
covered with darkness.
But the Spirit of God[c]
was moving over the water.

The First Day

3God said, "I command light to shine!"
And light started shining. 4God looked
at the light and saw that it was good. He
separated light from darkness 5and
named the light "Day" and the darkness
"Night." Evening came and then morning—that was the first day.[d]

The Second Day

6God said, "I command a dome to separate the water above it from the water
below it." 7And that's what happened.
God made the dome 8and named it
"Sky." Evening came and then morning—that was the second day.

The Third Day

9God said, "I command the water under the sky to come together in one
place, so there will be dry ground." And
that's what happened. 10God named the
dry ground "Land," and he named the
water "Ocean." God looked at what he
had done and saw that it was good.
11God said, "I command the earth to
produce all kinds of plants, including
fruit trees and grain." And that's what
happened. 12The earth produced all
kinds of vegetation. God looked at what
he had done, and it was good. 13Evening
came and then morning—that was the
third day.

The Fourth Day

14God said, "I command lights to appear in the sky and to separate day from
night and to show the time for seasons,
special days, and years. 15I command
them to shine on the earth." And that's
what happened. 16God made two powerful lights, the brighter one to rule the
day and the other[e] to rule the night. He
also made the stars. 17Then God put
these lights in the sky to shine on the
earth, 18to rule day and night, and to
separate light from darkness. God
looked at what he had done, and it was
good. 19Evening came and then morning—that was the fourth day.

The Fifth Day

20God said, "I command the ocean to
be full of living creatures, and I command birds to fly above the earth." 21So
God made the giant sea monsters and
all the living creatures that swim in the
ocean. He also made every kind of bird.
God looked at what he had done, and it
was good. 22Then he gave the living
creatures his blessing—he told the
ocean creatures to live everywhere in
the ocean and the birds to live everywhere on earth. 23Evening came and
then morning—that was the fifth day.

The Sixth Day

24God said, "I command the earth to
give life to all kinds of tame animals,
wild animals, and reptiles." And that's
what happened. 25God made every one
of them. Then he looked at what he had
done, and it was good.
26God said, "Now we will make humans, and they will be like us. We will
let them rule the fish, the birds, and all
other living creatures."
27So God created humans to be like
himself; he made men and women.
28God gave them his blessing and said:

Have a lot of children! Fill the
earth with people and bring it under
your control. Rule over the fish in
the ocean, the birds in the sky, and
every animal on the earth.

[a]**1.1** *the heavens and the earth*: "The heavens and the earth" stood for the universe.
[b]**1.1,2** *In . . . life*: Or "When God began to create the heavens and the earth, the earth was barren with no form of life." [c]**1.2** *the Spirit of God*: Or "a mighty wind." [d]**1.5** *the first day*: A day was measured from evening to evening. [e]**1.16** *the brighter . . . the other*: The sun and the moon. But they are not called by their names, because in Old Testament times some people worshiped the sun and the moon as though they were gods.

29I have provided all kinds of fruit
and grain for you to eat. 30And I
have given the green plants as food
for everything else that breathes.
These will be food for animals, both
wild and tame, and for birds.
31God looked at what he had done. All
of it was very good! Evening came and
then morning—that was the sixth day.
2 So the heavens and the earth and
everything else were created.

The Seventh Day

2By the seventh day God had finished
his work, and so he rested. 3God blessed
the seventh day and made it special because on that day he rested from his
work.
4That's how God created the heavens
and the earth.

The Garden of Eden

When the LORD God made the heavens and the earth, 5no grass or plants
were growing anywhere. God had not
yet sent any rain, and there was no one
to work the land. 6But streams[f] came up
from the ground and watered the earth.
7The LORD God took a handful of soil
and made a man.[g] God breathed life into
the man, and the man started breathing. 8The LORD made a garden in a place
called Eden, which was in the east, and
he put the man there.
9The LORD God placed all kinds of
beautiful trees and fruit trees in the garden. Two other trees were in the middle
of the garden. One of the trees gave
life—the other gave the power to know
the difference between right and wrong.
10From Eden a river flowed out to water the garden, then it divided into four
rivers. 11The first one is the Pishon
River that flows through the land of
Havilah, 12where pure gold, rare per-
fumes, and precious stones are found.
13The second is the Gihon River that
winds through Ethiopia.[h] 14The Tigris
River that flows east of Assyria is the
third, and the fourth is the Euphrates
River.
15The LORD God put the man in the
Garden of Eden to take care of it and to
look after it. 16But the LORD told him,
"You may eat fruit from any tree in the
garden, 17except the one that has the
power to let you know the difference between right and wrong. If you eat any
fruit from that tree, you will die before
the day is over!"
18The LORD God said, "It isn't good for
the man to live alone. I need to make a
suitable partner for him." 19-20So the
LORD took some soil and made animals
and birds. He brought them to the man
to see what names he would give each
of them. Then the man named the tame
animals and the birds and the wild animals. That's how they got their names.
None of these was the right kind of
partner for the man. 21So the LORD God
made him fall into a deep sleep, and he
took out one of the man's ribs. Then after closing the man's side, 22the LORD
made a woman out of the rib.
The LORD God brought her to the
man, 23and the man exclaimed,

"Here is someone like me!
She is part of my body,
my own flesh and bones.
She came from me, a man.
So I will name her Woman!"[i]

24That's why a man will leave his own
father and mother. He marries a
woman, and the two of them become
like one person.
25Although the man and his wife were
both naked, they were not ashamed.

The First Sin

3 The snake was sneakier than any of
the other wild animals that the LORD
God had made. One day it came to the
woman and asked, "Did God tell you not
to eat fruit from any tree in the garden?"
2The woman answered, "God said we
could eat fruit from any tree in the garden, 3except the one in the middle. He
told us not to eat fruit from that tree or
even to touch it. If we do, we will die."
4"No, you won't!" the snake replied.
5"God understands what will happen on
the day you eat fruit from that tree. You
will see what you have done, and you
will know the difference between right
and wrong, just as God does."
6The woman stared at the fruit. It
looked beautiful and tasty. She wanted
the wisdom that it would give her, and
she ate some of the fruit. Her husband
was there with her, so she gave some to
him, and he ate it too. 7Right away they
saw what they had done, and they realized they were naked. Then they sewed
fig leaves together to make something
to cover themselves.
8Late in the afternoon a breeze began
to blow, and the man and woman heard
the LORD God walking in the garden.
They were frightened and hid behind
some trees.

The Trouble with Sin

9The LORD called out to the man and
asked, "Where are you?"

[f]**2.6** *streams*: Or "mist." [g]**2.7** *man*: In Hebrew "man" comes from the same word as "soil." [h]**2.13** *Ethiopia*: The Hebrew text has "Cush," which was a region south of Egypt that included parts of the present countries of Ethiopia and Sudan. [i]**2.23** *a man . . . woman*: In Hebrew the words "man" and "woman" are similar.

10 The man answered, "I was naked,
and when I heard you walking through
the garden, I was frightened and hid!"
11 "How did you know you were
naked?" God asked. "Did you eat any
fruit from that tree in the middle of the
garden?"
12 "It was the woman you put here with
me," the man said. "She gave me some
of the fruit, and I ate it."
13 The LORD God then asked the
woman, "What have you done?"
"The snake tricked me," she answered. "And I ate some of that fruit."
14 So the LORD God said to the snake:

"Because of what you have done,
you will be the only animal
to suffer this curse—
For as long as you live,
you will crawl on your stomach
and eat dirt.
15 You and this woman
will hate each other;
your descendants and hers
will always be enemies.
One of hers will strike you
on the head,
and you will strike him
on the heel."

16 Then the LORD said to the woman,

"You will suffer terribly
when you give birth.
But you will still desire
your husband,
and he will rule over you."

17 The LORD said to the man,

"You listened to your wife
and ate fruit from that tree.
And so, the ground
will be under a curse
because of what you did.
As long as you live,
you will have to struggle
to grow enough food.
18 Your food will be plants,
but the ground will produce
thorns and thistles.
19 You will have to sweat
to earn a living;
you were made out of soil,
and you will once again
turn into soil."

20 The man Adam[i] named his wife
Eve[k] because she would become the
mother of all who live.
21 Then the LORD God made clothes
out of animal skins for the man and his
wife.
22 The LORD said, "These people now
know the difference between right and
wrong, just as we do. But they must not
be allowed to eat fruit from the tree that
lets them live forever." 23 So the LORD
God sent them out of the Garden of
Eden, where they would have to work
the ground from which the man had
been made. 24 Then God put winged
creatures at the entrance to the garden
and a flaming, flashing sword to guard
the way to the life-giving tree.

Cain Murders Abel

4 Adam[l] and Eve had a son. Then Eve
said, "I'll name him Cain because I
got[m] him with the help of the LORD."
2 Later she had another son and named
him Abel.
Abel became a sheep farmer, but Cain
farmed the land. 3 One day, Cain gave
part of his harvest to the LORD, 4 and
Abel also gave an offering to the LORD.
He killed the first-born lamb from one
of his sheep and gave the LORD the best
parts of it. The LORD was pleased with
Abel and his offering, 5 but not with
Cain and his offering. This made Cain
so angry that he could not hide his feelings.
6 The LORD said to Cain:
What's wrong with you? Why do
you have such an angry look on
your face? 7 If you had done the right
thing, you would be smiling.[n] But
you did the wrong thing, and now
sin is waiting to attack you like a
lion. Sin wants to destroy you, but
don't let it!
8 Cain said to his brother Abel, "Let's
go for a walk."[o] And when they were
out in a field, Cain killed him.
9 Afterwards the LORD asked Cain,
"Where is Abel?"
"How should I know?" he answered.
"Am I supposed to look after my
brother?"
10 Then the LORD said:
Why have you done this terrible
thing? You killed your own brother,
and his blood flowed onto the
ground. Now his blood is calling out
for me to punish you. 11 And so, I'll
put you under a curse. Because you
killed Abel and made his blood run
out on the ground, you will never be
able to farm the land again. 12 If you
try to farm the land, it won't produce
anything for you. From now on,
you'll be without a home, and you'll
spend the rest of your life wandering
from place to place.
13 "This punishment is too hard!" Cain

[i] **3.20** *The man Adam*: In Hebrew "man" and "Adam" are the same. [k] **3.20** *Eve*: In Hebrew "Eve" sounds like "living." [l] **4.1** *Adam*: See the note at 3.20. [m] **4.1** *Cain . . . got*: In Hebrew "Cain" sounds like "got." [n] **4.7** *you would be smiling*: Or "I would have accepted your offering." [o] **4.8** *Cain said to his brother Abel, "Let's . . . walk*: Most ancient translations; Hebrew "Cain spoke to his brother Abel."

said. 14"You're making me leave my
home and live far from you.[p] I will have
to wander about without a home, and
just anyone could kill me."
15"No!"[q] the LORD answered. "Anyone
who kills you will be punished seven
times worse than I am punishing you."
So the LORD put a mark on Cain to warn
everyone not to kill him. 16But Cain had
to go far from the LORD and live in the
Land of Wandering,[r] which is east of
Eden.

More and More People

17Later, Cain and his wife had a son
named Enoch. At the time Cain was
building a town, and so he named it
Enoch after his son. 18Then Enoch had a
son named Irad, who had a son named
Mehujael, who had a son named Me-
thushael, who had a son named Lamech.
19Lamech married Adah, then Zillah.
20-21Lamech and Adah had two sons, Jabal and Jubal. Their son Jabal was the
first to live in tents and raise sheep and
goats. Jubal was the first to play harps
and flutes.
22Lamech and Zillah had a son named
Tubal Cain who made tools out of
bronze and iron. They also had a daughter, whose name was Naamah.
23One day, Lamech said to his two
wives, "A young man wounded me, and I
killed him. 24Anyone who tries to get
even with me will be punished ten times
more than anyone who tries to get even
with Cain."
25Adam and his wife had another son.
They named him Seth, because they
said, "God has given[s] us a son to take
the place of Abel, who was killed by his
brother Cain." 26Later, Seth had a son
and named him Enosh.
About this time people started worshiping the LORD.[t]

Descendants of Adam

5 1-2God created men and women to
be like himself. He gave them his
blessing and called them human beings.
This is a list of the descendants of
Adam, the first man:
3-4When Adam was one hundred
thirty, he had a son who was just like
him, and he named him Seth. Adam had
more children 5and died at the age of
nine hundred thirty.
6When Seth was one hundred five, he
had a son named Enosh. 7Seth had more
children 8and died at the age of nine
hundred twelve.
9When Enosh was ninety, he had a
son named Kenan. 10Enosh had more
children 11and died at the age of nine
hundred five.
12When Kenan was seventy, he had a
son named Mahalalel. 13Kenan had
more children 14and died at the age of
nine hundred ten.
15When Mahalalel was sixty-five, he
had a son named Jared. 16Mahalalel had
more children 17and died at the age of
eight hundred ninety-five.
18When Jared was one hundred sixty-
two, he had a son named Enoch. 19Jared
had more children 20and died at the age
of nine hundred sixty-two.
21When Enoch was sixty-five, he had
a son named Methuselah, 22and during
the next three hundred years he had
more children. Enoch truly loved God,
23-24and God took him away at the age of
three hundred sixty-five.
25When Methuselah was one hundred
eighty-seven, he had a son named
Lamech. 26Methuselah had more children 27and died at the age of nine hundred sixty-nine.
28When Lamech was one hundred
eighty-two, he had a son. 29Lamech said,
"I'll name him Noah because he will
give us comfort,[u] as we struggle hard to
make a living on this land that the LORD
has put under a curse." 30Lamech had
more children 31and died at the age of
seven hundred seventy-seven.
32After Noah was five hundred years
old, he had three sons and named them
Shem, Ham, and Japheth.

The LORD Will Send a Flood

6 1-2More and more people were born,
until finally they spread all over the
earth. Some of their daughters were so
beautiful that supernatural beings[v]
came down and married the ones they
wanted. 3Then the LORD said, "I won't let
my life-giving breath remain in anyone
forever.[w] No one will live for more than
one hundred twenty years."[x]
4The children of the supernatural beings who had married these women became famous heroes and warriors. They
were called Nephilim and lived on the
earth at that time and even later.
5The LORD saw how bad the people on
earth were and that everything they

[p]**4.14** *live . . . you*: At this time it was believed that the LORD was with his people only in their own land. [q]**4.15** *No*: Three ancient translations; Hebrew "Very well!" [r]**4.16** *Wandering*: The Hebrew text has "Nod," which means "wandering." [s]**4.25** *Seth . . . given*: In Hebrew "Seth" sounds like "given." [t]**4.26** *worshiping the LORD*: Or "worshiping in the name of the LORD." [u]**5.29** *Noah . . . comfort*: In Hebrew "Noah" sounds like "comfort." [v]**6.1,2** *supernatural beings*: Or "angels." [w]**6.3** *I won't . . . forever*: One possible meaning for the difficult Hebrew text. [x]**6.3** *No one . . . years*: Or "In fact, they will all be destroyed in about one hundred years" (that is, at the time of the flood).

thought and planned was evil. [6]He was very sorry that he had made them, [7]and he said, "I'll destroy every living creature on earth! I'll wipe out people, animals, birds, and reptiles. I'm sorry I ever made them."

[8]But the LORD was pleased with Noah, [9]and this is the story about him. Noah was the only person who lived right and obeyed God. [10]He had three sons: Shem, Ham, and Japheth.

[11-12]God knew that everyone was terribly cruel and violent. [13]So he told Noah:

> Cruelty and violence have spread everywhere. Now I'm going to destroy the whole earth and all its people. [14]Get some good lumber and build a boat. Put rooms in it and cover it with tar inside and out. [15]Make it four hundred fifty feet long, seventy-five feet wide, and forty-five feet high. [16]Build a roof[y] on the boat and leave a space of about eighteen inches between the roof and the sides.[z] Make the boat three stories high and put a door on one side.
>
> [17]I'm going to send a flood that will destroy everything that breathes! Nothing will be left alive. [18]But I solemnly promise that you, your wife, your sons, and your daughters-in-law will be kept safe in the boat.[a]
>
> [19-20]Bring into the boat with you a male and a female of every kind of animal and bird, as well as a male and a female of every reptile. I don't want them to be destroyed. [21]Store up enough food both for yourself and for them.

[22]Noah did everything the LORD told him to do.

The Flood

7 The LORD told Noah:

> Take your whole family with you into the boat, because you are the only one on this earth who pleases me. [2]Take seven pairs of every kind of animal that can be used for sacrifice[b] and one pair of all others. [3]Also take seven pairs of every kind of bird with you. Do this so there will always be animals and birds on the earth. [4]Seven days from now I will send rain that will last for forty days and nights, and I will destroy all other living creatures I have made.

[5-7]Noah was six hundred years old when he went into the boat to escape the flood, and he did everything the LORD had told him to do. His wife, his sons, and his daughters-in-law all went inside with him. [8-9]He obeyed God and took a male and a female of each kind of animal and bird into the boat with him. [10]Seven days later a flood began to cover the earth.

[11-12]Noah was six hundred years old when the water under the earth started gushing out everywhere. The sky opened like windows, and rain poured down for forty days and nights. All this began on the seventeenth day of the second month of the year. [13]On that day Noah and his wife went into the boat with their three sons, Shem, Ham, and Japheth, and their wives. [14]They took along every kind of animal, tame and wild, including the birds. [15]Noah took a male and a female of every living creature with him, [16]just as God had told him to do. And when they were all in the boat, God closed the door.

[17-18]For forty days the rain poured down without stopping. And the water became deeper and deeper, until the boat started floating high above the ground. [19-20]Finally, the mighty flood was so deep that even the highest mountain peaks were almost twenty-five feet below the surface of the water. [21]Not a bird, animal, reptile, or human was left alive anywhere on earth. [22-23]The LORD destroyed everything that breathed. Nothing was left alive except Noah and the others in the boat. [24]A hundred fifty days later, the water started going down.

The Water Goes Down

8 God did not forget about Noah and the animals with him in the boat. So God made a wind blow, and the water started going down. [2]God stopped up the places where the water had been gushing out from under the earth. He also closed up the sky, and the rain stopped. [3]For one hundred fifty days the water slowly went down. [4]Then on the seventeenth day of the seventh month of the year, the boat came to rest somewhere in the Ararat mountains. [5]The water kept going down, and the mountain tops could be seen on the first day of the tenth month.

[6-7]Forty days later Noah opened a window to send out a raven, but it kept flying around until the water had dried up. [8]Noah wanted to find out if the water had gone down, and he sent out a dove. [9]Deep water was still everywhere, and the dove could not find a place to land. So it flew back to the boat. Noah held out his hand and helped it back in.

[y]**6.16** *roof*: Or "window." [z]**6.16** *leave . . . sides*: One possible meaning for the difficult Hebrew text. [a]**6.18** *boat*: One possible meaning for the difficult Hebrew text of verse 18.
[b]**7.2** *animal . . . for sacrifice*: Hebrew "clean animals." Animals that could be used for sacrifice were called "clean," and animals that could not be used were called "unclean."

10 Seven days later Noah sent the dove
out again. 11 It returned in the evening,
holding in its beak a green leaf from an
olive tree. Noah knew that the water
was finally going down. 12 He waited
seven more days before sending the
dove out again, and this time it did not
return.
13 Noah was now six hundred one
years old. And by the first day of that
year, almost all the water had gone
away. Noah made an opening in the roof
of the boat[c] and saw that the ground
was getting dry. 14 By the twenty-seventh
day of the second month, the earth was
completely dry.
15 God said to Noah, 16 "You, your wife,
your sons, and your daughters-in-law
may now leave the boat. 17 Let out the
birds, animals, and reptiles, so they can
mate and live all over the earth." 18 After
Noah and his family had gone out of the
boat, 19 the living creatures left in groups
of their own kind.

The LORD's Promise for the Earth

20 Noah built an altar where he could
offer sacrifices to the LORD. Then he offered on the altar one of each kind of
animal and bird that could be used for a
sacrifice.[d] 21 The smell of the burning offering pleased God, and he said:

Never again will I punish the earth
for the sinful things its people do.
All of them have evil thoughts from
the time they are young, but I will
never destroy everything that
breathes, as I did this time.

22 As long as the earth remains,
there will be planting
and harvest,
cold and heat;
winter and summer,
day and night.

God's Promise to Noah

9 God said to Noah and his sons:
I am giving you my blessing.
Have a lot of children and grandchildren, so people will live everywhere
on this earth. 2 All animals, birds,
reptiles, and fish will be afraid of
you. I have placed them under your
control, 3 and I have given them to
you for food. From now on, you may
eat them, as well as the green plants
that you have always eaten. 4 But life
is in the blood, and you must not eat
any meat that still has blood in it. 5-6 I
created humans to be like me, and I
will punish any animal or person
that takes a human life. If an animal
kills someone, that animal must die.
And if a person takes the life of another, that person must be put to
death.
7 I want you and your descendants
to have many children, so people
will live everywhere on earth.
8 Again, God said to Noah and his
sons:
9 I am going to make a solemn
promise to you and to everyone who
will live after you. 10 This includes
the birds and the animals that came
out of the boat. 11 I promise every living creature that the earth and those
living on it will never again be destroyed by a flood.
12-13 The rainbow that I have put in
the sky will be my sign to you and to
every living creature on earth. It will
remind you that I will keep this
promise forever. 14 When I send
clouds over the earth, and a rainbow
appears in the sky, 15 I will remember
my promise to you and to all other
living creatures. Never again will I
let floodwaters destroy all life.
16 When I see the rainbow in the sky,
I will always remember the promise
that I have made to every living
creature. 17 The rainbow will be the
sign of that solemn promise.

Noah and His Family

18 Noah and his sons, Shem, Ham, and
Japheth, came out of the boat. Ham later
had a son named Canaan. 19 All people
on earth are descendants of Noah's
three sons.
20 Noah farmed the land and was the
first to plant a vineyard. 21 One day he
got drunk and was lying naked in his
tent. 22 Ham entered the tent and saw
him naked, then went back outside and
told his brothers. 23 Shem and Japheth
put a robe over their shoulders and
walked backwards into the tent. Without
looking at their father, they placed it
over his body.
24 When Noah woke up and learned
what his youngest son Ham had done,
25 he said,

"I now put a curse on Canaan!
He will be the lowest slave
of his brothers.
26 I ask the LORD my God
to bless Shem
and make Canaan his slave.
27 I pray that the LORD
will give Japheth
more and more[e] land
and let him take over
the territory of Shem.
May Canaan be his slave."

[c] 8.13 *made . . . boat*: One possible meaning for the difficult Hebrew text. [d] 8.20 *animal . . . sacrifice*: See the note at 7.2. [e] 9.27 *more and more*: In Hebrew "Japheth" sounds like "more and more."

28 Noah lived three hundred fifty years
after the flood 29 and died at the age of
nine hundred fifty.

The Descendants of Noah

10 After the flood Shem, Ham, and Japheth had many descendants.

The Descendants of Japheth

2-5 Japheth's descendants had their
own languages, tribes, and land. They
were Gomer, Magog, Madai, Javan,
Tubal, Meshech, and Tiras.

Gomer was the ancestor of Ashkenaz, Riphath, and Togarmah.

Javan was the ancestor of Elishah, Tarshish, Kittim, and Dodanim,[f] who settled along the coast.

The Descendants of Ham

6-20 Ham's descendants had their own
languages, tribes, and land. They were
Ethiopia,[g] Egypt, Put, and Canaan.

Cush[h] was the ancestor of Seba, Havilah, Sabtah, Raamah, and Sabteca.

Raamah was the ancestor of Sheba and Dedan.

Cush was also the ancestor of Nimrod, a mighty warrior whose strength came from the LORD. Nimrod is the reason for the saying, "You hunt like Nimrod with the strength of the LORD!" Nimrod first ruled in Babylon, Erech, and Accad, all of[i] which were in Babylonia.[j] From there Nimrod went to Assyria and built the great city of Nineveh. He also built Rehoboth-Ir and Calah, as well as Resen, which is between Nineveh and Calah.

Egypt was the ancestor of Ludim, Anamim, Lehabim, Naphtuhim, Pathrusim, Casluhim, and Caphtorim, the ancestor of the Philistines.[k]

Canaan's sons were Sidon and Heth. He was also the ancestor of the Jebusites, the Amorites, the Girgashites, the Hivites, the Arkites, the Sinites, the Arvadites, the Zemarites, and the Hamathites.

Later the Canaanites spread from the territory of Sidon and went as far as Gaza in the direction of Gerar. They also went as far as Lasha in the direction of Sodom, Gomorrah, Admah, and Zeboiim.

The Descendants of Shem

21-31 Shem's descendants had their
own languages, tribes, and land. He was
the older brother of Japheth and the ancestor of the tribes of Eber.

Shem was the ancestor of Elam, Asshur, Arpachshad, Lud, and Aram.

Aram was the ancestor of Uz, Hul, Gether, and Mash.

Arpachshad was the father of Shelah and the grandfather of Eber, whose first son was named Peleg,[l] because it was during his time that tribes divided up the earth. Eber's second son was Joktan.

Joktan was the ancestor of Almodad, Sheleph, Hazarmaveth, Jerah, Hadoram, Uzal, Diklah, Obal, Abimael, Sheba, Ophir, Havilah, and Jobab. Their land reached from Mesha in the direction of Sephar, the hill country in the east.

32 This completes the list of Noah's descendants. After the flood their descendants became nations and spread all over
the world.

The Tower of Babel

11 At first everyone spoke the same
language, 2 but after some of them
moved from the east[m] and settled in
Babylonia,[n] 3-4 they said:

> Let's build a city with a tower that reaches to the sky! We'll use hard bricks and tar instead of stone and mortar. We'll become famous, and we won't be scattered all over the world.

5 But when the LORD came down to
look at the city and the tower, 6 he said:

> These people are working together because they all speak the same language. This is just the beginning. Soon they will be able to do
> anything they want. 7 Come on! Let's
> go down and confuse them by making them speak different languages—then they won't be able to understand each other.

8-9 So the people had to stop building
the city, because the LORD confused
their language and scattered them all
over the earth. That's how the city of
Babel[o] got its name.

The Descendants of Shem

10-11 Two years after the flood, when
Shem was one hundred, he had a son
named Arpachshad. He had more children and died at the age of six hundred.
This is a list of his descendants:

12 When Arpachshad was thirty-five,

---

[f] **10.2-5** *Dodanim*: Most Hebrew manuscripts; some Hebrew manuscripts and one ancient translation have "Rodanim." [g] **10.6-20** *Ethiopia*: See the note at 2.13. [h] **10.6-20** *Cush*: See the note at 2.13. [i] **10.6-20** *and Accad, all of*: Or "Accad, and Calneh." [j] **10.6-20** *Babylonia*: The Hebrew text has "Shinar," another name for Babylonia. [k] **10.6-20** *Casluhim, and Caphtorim, the ancestor of the Philistines*: Hebrew "Caphtorim, and Casluhim, the ancestor of the Philistines." The Philistines were from Caphtor (see Jeremiah 47.4; Amos 9.7), better known as Crete. [l] **10.21-31** *Peleg*: In Hebrew "Peleg" means "divided." [m] **11.2** *from the east*: Or "to the east." [n] **11.2** *Babylonia*: See the note at 10.6-20. [o] **11.8,9** *Babel*: In Hebrew "Babel" sounds like "confused."

he had a son named Shelah. 13Ar-
pachshad had more children and died at
the age of four hundred thirty-eight.
14When Shelah was thirty, he had a
son named Eber. 15Shelah had more
children and died at the age of four hundred thirty-three.
16When Eber was thirty-four, he had a
son named Peleg. 17Eber had more children and died at the age of four hundred sixty-four.
18When Peleg was thirty, he had a son
named Reu. 19Peleg had more children
and died at the age of two hundred
thirty-nine.
20When Reu was thirty-two he had a
son named Serug. 21Reu had more children and died at the age of two hundred
thirty-nine.
22When Serug was thirty, he had a son
named Nahor. 23Serug had more children and died at the age of two hundred
thirty.
24When Nahor was twenty-nine, he
had a son named Terah. 25Nahor had
more children and died at the age of one
hundred forty-eight.

The Descendants of Terah

26-28After Terah was seventy years old,
he had three sons: Abram, Nahor, and
Haran, who became the father of Lot.
Terah's sons were born in the city of Ur
in Chaldea,[p] and Haran died there before the death of his father. The following is the story of Terah's descendants.
29-30Abram married Sarai, but she was
not able to have any children. And Nahor married Milcah, who was the
daughter of Haran and the sister of
Iscah.
31Terah decided to move from Ur to
the land of Canaan. He took along
Abram and Sarai and his grandson Lot,
the son of Haran. But when they came
to the city of Haran,[q] they decided to
settle there instead. 32Terah lived to be
two hundred five years old and died in
Haran.

The LORD Chooses Abram

12 The LORD said to Abram:
Leave your country, your family, and your relatives and go to
the land that I will show you. 2I
will bless you and make your descendants into a great nation. You
will become famous and be a
blessing to others. 3I will bless
anyone who blesses you, but I will
put a curse on anyone who puts a
curse on you. Everyone on earth
will be blessed because of you.[r]
4-5Abram was seventy-five years old
when the LORD told him to leave the city
of Haran. He obeyed and left with his
wife Sarai, his nephew Lot, and all the
possessions and slaves they had gotten
while in Haran.
When they came to the land of Canaan, 6Abram went as far as the sacred
tree of Moreh in a place called Shechem. The Canaanites were still living in
the land at that time, 7but the LORD appeared to Abram and promised, "I will
give this land to your family forever."
Abram then built an altar there for the
LORD.
8Abram traveled to the hill country
east of Bethel and camped between
Bethel and Ai, where he built another
altar and worshiped the LORD. 9Later,
Abram started out toward the Southern
Desert.

Abram in Egypt

10-11The crops failed, and there was no
food anywhere in the land. So Abram
and his wife Sarai went to live in Egypt
for a while. But just before they got
there, he said, "Sarai, you are really
beautiful! 12When the Egyptians see
how lovely you are, they will murder me
because I am your husband. But they
won't kill you. 13Please save my life by
saying that you are my sister."
14As soon as Abram and Sarai arrived
in Egypt, the Egyptians noticed how
beautiful she was. 15The king's[s] officials
told him about her, and she was taken to
his house. 16The king was good to
Abram because of Sarai, and Abram
was given sheep, cattle, donkeys, slaves,
and camels.
17Because of Sarai, the LORD struck
the king and everyone in his palace with
terrible diseases. 18Finally, the king sent
for Abram and said to him, "What have
you done to me? Why didn't you tell me
Sarai was your wife? 19Why did you
make me believe she was your sister?
Now I've married her. Take her and go!
She's your wife."
20So the king told his men to let
Abram and Sarai take their possessions
and leave.

Abram and Lot Separate

13 Abram and Sarai took everything
they owned and went to the
Southern Desert. Lot went with them.
2Abram was very rich. He owned

[p] **11.26-28** *Ur in Chaldea*: Chaldea was a region at the head of the Persian Gulf. Ur was on the main trade routes from Mesopotamia to the Mediterranean Sea. [q] **11.31** *Haran*: About 550 miles northwest of Ur. [r] **12.3** *Everyone . . . you*: Or "Everyone on earth will ask me to bless them as I have blessed you." [s] **12.15** *the king's*: The Hebrew text has "Pharaoh's," a Hebrew word sometimes used for the king of Egypt.

many cattle, sheep, and goats, and had a
lot of silver and gold. 3 Abram moved
from place to place in the Southern
Desert. And finally, he went north and
set up his tents between Bethel and Ai,
4 where he had earlier camped and built
an altar. There he worshiped the LORD.
5 Lot, who was traveling with him, also
had sheep, goats, and cattle, as well as
his own family and slaves. 6-7 At this
time the Canaanites and the Perizzites
were living in the same area, and so
there wasn't enough pastureland left for
Abram and Lot with all of their animals.
Besides this, the men who took care of
Abram's animals and the ones who took
care of Lot's animals started quarreling.
8 Abram said to Lot, "We are close relatives. We shouldn't argue, and our men
shouldn't be fighting one another.
9 There is plenty of land for you to
choose from. Let's separate. If you go
north, I'll go south; if you go south, I'll
go north."
10 This happened before the LORD had
destroyed the cities of Sodom and Gomorrah. And when Lot looked around,
he saw there was plenty of water in the
Jordan Valley. All the way to Zoar the
valley was as green as the garden of the
LORD or the land of Egypt. 11 So Lot
chose the whole Jordan Valley for himself, and as he started toward the east,
he and Abram separated. 12 Abram
stayed in the land of Canaan. But Lot
settled near the cities of the valley and
put up his tents not far from Sodom,
13 where the people were evil and sinned
terribly against the LORD.

Abram Moves to Hebron

14 After Abram and Lot had gone their
separate ways, the LORD said to Abram:
Look around to the north, south,
east, and west. 15 I will give you and
your family all the land you can see.
It will be theirs forever! 16 I will give
you more descendants than there
are specks of dust on the earth, and
someday it will be easier to count
the specks of dust than to count
your descendants. 17 Now walk back
and forth across the land, because I
am giving it to you.
18 Abram took down his tents and
went to live near the sacred trees of
Mamre at Hebron, where he built an altar in honor of the LORD.

Abram Rescues Lot

14 About this time, King Amraphel
of Babylonia,[t] King Arioch of Ellasar, King Chedorlaomer of Elam, and
King Tidal of Goiim 2 attacked King Bera
of Sodom, King Birsha of Gomorrah,
King Shinab of Admah, King Shemeber
of Zeboiim, and the king of Bela, also
known as the city of Zoar. 3-4 King Chedorlaomer and his allies had ruled these
last five kings for twelve years, but in
the thirteenth year the kings rebelled
and came together in Siddim Valley,
which is now covered by the southern
part of the Dead Sea.
5 A year later King Chedorlaomer and
his allies attacked and defeated the
Rephaites in Ashteroth-Karnaim, the
Zuzites in Ham, and the Emites in
Shaveh-Kiriathaim. 6 They also defeated
the Horites in the hill country of Edom,[u]
as far as El-Paran, near the desert.
7 They went back to the city of En-
mishpat, better known as Kadesh. Then
they captured all the land that belonged
to the Amalekites, and they defeated the
Amorites who were living in Hazazon-
Tamar.
8-9 At Siddim Valley, the armies of the
kings of Sodom, Gomorrah, Admah, Zeboiim, and Bela fought the armies of
King Chedorlaomer of Elam, King Tidal
of Goiim, King Amraphel of Babylonia,
and King Arioch of Ellasar. The valley
10 was full of tar pits, and when the
troops from Sodom and Gomorrah
started running away, some of them fell
into the pits. Others escaped to the hill
country. 11 Their enemies took everything of value from Sodom and Gomorrah, including their food supplies.
12 They also captured Abram's nephew
Lot, who lived in Sodom. They took him
and his possessions and then left.
13 At this time Abram the Hebrew was
living near the oaks that belonged to
Mamre the Amorite. Mamre and his
brothers Eshcol and Aner were Abram's
friends. Someone who had escaped
from the battle told Abram 14 that his
nephew Lot had been taken away. Three
hundred eighteen of Abram's servants
were fighting men, so he took them and
followed the enemy as far north as the
city of Dan.
15 That night, Abram divided up his
troops, attacked from all sides, and won
a great victory. But some of the enemy
escaped to the town of Hobah north of
Damascus, 16 and Abram went after
them. He brought back his nephew Lot,
together with Lot's possessions and the
women and everyone else who had been
captured.

Abram Is Blessed by Melchizedek

17 Abram returned after he had defeated King Chedorlaomer and the
other kings. Then the king of Sodom
went to meet Abram in Shaveh Valley,
which is also known as King's Valley.

[t] **14.1** *Babylonia*: See the note at 10.6-20.

[u] **14.6** *Edom*: The Hebrew text has "Seir," another name for Edom.

18King Melchizedek of Salem was a priest of God Most High. He brought out some bread and wine 19and said to Abram:

“I bless you in the name
of God Most High,
Creator of heaven and earth.
20 All praise belongs
to God Most High
for helping you defeat
your enemies.”

Then Abram gave Melchizedek a tenth of everything.

21The king of Sodom said to Abram, “All I want are my people. You can keep everything else.”

22Abram answered:

The LORD God Most High made the heavens and the earth. And I have promised him 23that I won’t keep anything of yours, not even a sandal strap or a piece of thread. Then you can never say that you are the one who made me rich. 24Let my share be the food that my men have eaten. But Aner, Eshcol, and Mamre went with me, so give them their share of what we brought back.

The LORD’s Promise to Abram

15 Later the LORD spoke to Abram in a vision, “Abram, don’t be afraid! I will protect you and reward you greatly.”

2But Abram answered, “LORD All-Powerful, you have given me everything I could ask for, except children. And when I die, Eliezer of Damascus will get all I own.[v] 3You have not given me any children, and this servant of mine will inherit everything.”

4The LORD replied, “No, he won’t! You will have a son of your own, and everything you have will be his.” 5Then the LORD took Abram outside and said, “Look at the sky and see if you can count the stars. That’s how many descendants you will have.” 6Abram believed the LORD, and the LORD was pleased with him.

The LORD Makes Another Promise to Abram

7The LORD said to Abram, “I brought you here from Ur in Chaldea, and I gave you this land.”

8Abram asked, “LORD God, how can I know the land will be mine?”

9Then the LORD told him, “Bring me a three-year-old cow, a three-year-old female goat, a three-year-old ram, a dove, and a young pigeon.”

10Abram obeyed the LORD. Then he cut[w] the animals in half and laid the two halves of each animal opposite each other on the ground. But he did not cut the doves and pigeons in half. 11And when birds came down to eat the animals, Abram chased them away.

12As the sun was setting, Abram fell into a deep sleep, and everything became dark and frightening. 13-15Then the LORD said:

Abram, you will live to an old age and die in peace.

But I solemnly promise that your descendants will live as foreigners in a land that doesn’t belong to them. They will be forced into slavery and abused for four hundred years. But I will terribly punish the nation that enslaves them, and they will leave with many possessions.

16Four generations later,[x] your descendants will return here and take this land, because only then will the people who live here[y] be so sinful that they deserve to be punished.

17Sometime after sunset, when it was very dark, a smoking cooking pot[z] and a flaming fire went between the two halves of each animal. 18At that time the LORD made an agreement with Abram and told him:

I will give your descendants the land east of the Shihor River[a] on the border of Egypt as far as the Euphrates River. 19They will possess the land of the Kenites, the Kenizzites, the Kadmonites, 20the Hittites, the Perizzites, the Rephaites, 21the Amorites, the Canaanites, the Girgashites, and the Jebusites.

Hagar and Ishmael

16 Abram’s wife Sarai had not been able to have any children. But she owned a young Egyptian slave woman named Hagar, 2and Sarai said to Abram, “The LORD has not given me any children. Sleep with my slave, and if she has a child, it will be mine.”[b] Abram agreed, 3and Sarai gave him Hagar to be his

[v]**15.2** *And . . . own*: One possible meaning for the difficult Hebrew text. [w]**15.10** *cut*: In Hebrew “cut” sounds something like “agreement.” What follows shows that the LORD is making an agreement with Abram. [x]**15.16** *Four generations later*: This may refer to the “four hundred years” of verses 13-15. [y]**15.16** *people who live here*: The Hebrew text has “Amorites,” a name sometimes used of the people who lived in Palestine before the Israelites. [z]**15.17** *smoking cooking pot*: One possible meaning for the difficult Hebrew text. The smoke and fire represent the presence of the LORD. [a]**15.18** *Shihor River:* See Joshua 13.2-7.
[b]**16.2** *Sleep . . . mine:* It was the custom for a wife who could not have children to let her husband sleep with one of her slave women. The children of the slave would belong to the wife.

wife. This happened after Abram had
lived in the land of Canaan for ten
years. 4 Later, when Hagar knew she was
going to have a baby, she became proud
and was hateful to Sarai.
5 Then Sarai said to Abram, "It's all
your fault![c] I gave you my slave woman,
but she has been hateful to me ever
since she found out she was pregnant.
You have done me wrong, and you will
have to answer to the LORD for this."
6 Abram said, "All right! She's your
slave, and you can do whatever you
want with her." But Sarai began treating
Hagar so harshly that she finally ran
away.
7 Hagar stopped to rest at a spring in
the desert on the road to Shur. While
she was there, the angel of the LORD
came to her 8 and asked, "Hagar, where
have you come from, and where are you
going?"
She answered, "I'm running away
from Sarai, my owner."
9 The angel said, "Go back to Sarai
and be her slave. 10-11 I will give you a
son, who will be called Ishmael,[d] because I have heard your cry for help.
And later I will give you so many descendants that no one will be able to
count them all. 12 But your son will live
far from his relatives; he will be like a
wild donkey, fighting everyone, and
everyone fighting him."
13 Hagar thought, "Have I really seen
God and lived to tell about it?"[e] So from
then on she called him, "The God Who
Sees Me."[f] 14 That's why people call the
well between Kadesh and Bered, "The
Well of the Living One Who Sees Me."[g]
15-16 Abram was eighty-six years old
when Hagar gave birth to their son, and
he named him Ishmael.

God's Promise to Abraham

17 Abram was ninety-nine years old
when the LORD appeared to him
again and said, "I am God All-Powerful.
If you obey me and always do right, 2 I
will keep my solemn promise to you and
give you more descendants than can be
counted." 3 Abram bowed with his face
to the ground, and God said:

4-5 I promise that you will be the
father of many nations. That's why I
now change your name from Abram
to Abraham.[h] 6 I will give you a lot of
descendants, and in the future they
will become great nations. Some of
them will even be kings.
7 I will always keep the promise I
have made to you and your descendants, because I am your God and
their God. 8 I will give you and them
the land in which you are now a foreigner. I will give the whole land of
Canaan to your family forever, and I
will be their God.
9 Abraham, you and all future
members of your family must
promise to obey me. 10-11 As the sign
that you are keeping this promise,
you must circumcise every man and
boy in your family. 12-13 From now on,
your family must circumcise every
baby boy when he is eight days old.
You must even circumcise any man
or boy you have as a slave, both
those born in your homes and those
you buy from foreigners. This will be
a sign that my promise to you will
last forever. 14 Any man who isn't circumcised hasn't kept his promise to
me and cannot be one of my people.
15 Abraham, your wife's name will
now be Sarah instead of Sarai. 16 I
will bless her, and you will have a
son by her. She will become the
mother of nations, and some of her
descendants will even be kings.

17 Abraham bowed with his face to the
ground and thought, "I am almost a
hundred years old. How can I become a
father? And Sarah is ninety. How can
she have a child?" So he started laughing. 18 Then he asked God, "Why not let
Ishmael[i] inherit what you have promised me?"
19 But God answered:

No! You and Sarah will have a son.
His name will be Isaac,[j] and I will
make an everlasting promise to him
and his descendants.
20 I have heard what you asked me
to do for Ishmael, and so I will also
bless him with many descendants.
He will be the father of twelve
princes, and I will make his family a
great nation. 21 But your son Isaac
will be born about this time next
year, and the promise I am making
to you and your family will be for
him and his descendants forever.

22 God finished speaking to Abraham
and then left.
23-27 On that same day Abraham
obeyed God by circumcising Ishmael.
Abraham was also circumcised, and so
were all other men and boys in his
household, including his servants and

[c] **16.5** *It's . . . fault*: Or "I hope you'll be punished for what you did to me!"
[d] **16.10,11** *Ishmael*: In Hebrew "Ishmael" sounds like "God hears." [e] **16.13** *Have . . . it*: One possible meaning for the difficult Hebrew text. [f] **16.13** *The God Who Sees Me*: Or "The God I Have Seen." [g] **16.14** *The Well . . . Me*: Or "Beer-Lahai-Roi" (see 25.11).
[h] **17.4,5** *Abraham*: In Hebrew "Abraham" sounds like "father of many nations."
[i] **17.18** *Ishmael*: Ishmael was the son of Sarah's slave Hagar (see 16.1-16). [j] **17.19** *Isaac*: In Hebrew "Isaac" sounds like "laugh."

slaves. He was ninety-nine years old at
the time, and his son Ishmael was thirteen.

The Lord Promises Abraham a Son

18 One hot summer afternoon Abraham was sitting by the entrance
to his tent near the sacred trees of
Mamre, when the Lord appeared to
him. 2Abraham looked up and saw three
men standing nearby. He quickly ran to
meet them, bowed with his face to the
ground, 3and said, "Please come to my
home where I can serve you. 4I'll have
some water brought, so you can wash
your feet, then you can rest under the
tree. 5Let me get you some food to give
you strength before you leave. I would
be honored to serve you."

"Thank you very much," they answered. "We accept your offer."

6Abraham quickly went to his tent
and said to Sarah, "Hurry! Get a large
sack of flour and make some bread."
7After saying this, he rushed off to his
herd of cattle and picked out one of the
best calves, which his servant quickly
prepared. 8He then served his guests
some yogurt and milk together with the
meat.

While they were eating, he stood near
them under the trees, 9and they asked,
"Where is your wife Sarah?"

"She is right there in the tent," Abraham answered.

10One of the guests was the Lord, and
he said, "I'll come back about this time
next year, and when I do, Sarah will already have a son."

Sarah was behind Abraham, listening
at the entrance to the tent. 11Abraham
and Sarah were very old, and Sarah was
well past the age for having children.
12So she laughed and said to herself,
"Now that I am worn out and my husband is old, will I really know such happiness?"[k]

13The Lord asked Abraham, "Why did
Sarah laugh? Does she doubt that she
can have a child in her old age? 14I am
the Lord! There is nothing too difficult
for me. I'll come back next year at the
time I promised, and Sarah will already
have a son."

15Sarah was so frightened that she
lied and said, "I didn't laugh."

"Yes, you did!" he answered.

Abraham Prays for Sodom

16When the three men got ready to
leave, they looked down toward Sodom,
and Abraham walked part of the way
with them.

17The Lord said to himself, "I should
tell Abraham what I am going to do,
18since his family will become a great
and powerful nation that will be a blessing to all other nations on earth.[l] 19I
have chosen him to teach his family to
obey me forever and to do what is right
and fair. Then I will give Abraham many
descendants, just as I promised."

20The Lord said, "Abraham, I have
heard that the people of Sodom and Gomorrah are doing all kinds of evil
things. 21Now I am going down to see
for myself if those people really are that
bad. If they aren't, I want to know about
it."

22The men turned and started toward
Sodom. But the Lord stayed with Abraham, 23who asked, "Lord, when you
destroy the evil people, are you also
going to destroy those who are good?
24Wouldn't you spare the city if there
are only fifty good people in it? 25You
surely wouldn't let them be killed when
you destroy the evil ones. You are the
judge of all the earth, and you do what
is right."

26The Lord replied, "If I find fifty good
people in Sodom, I will save the city to
keep them from being killed."

27Abraham answered, "I am nothing
more than the dust of the earth. Please
forgive me, Lord, for daring to speak to
you like this. 28But suppose there are
only forty-five good people in Sodom.
Would you still wipe out the whole
city?"

"If I find forty-five good people," the
Lord replied, "I won't destroy the city."

29"Suppose there are just forty good
people?" Abraham asked.

"Even for them," the Lord replied, "I
won't destroy the city."

30Abraham said, "Please don't be angry, Lord, if I ask you what you will do
if there are only thirty good people in
the city."

"If I find thirty," the Lord replied, "I
still won't destroy it."

31Then Abraham said, "I don't have
any right to ask you, Lord, but what
would you do if you find only twenty?"

"Because of them, I won't destroy the
city," was the Lord's answer.

32Finally, Abraham said, "Please don't
get angry, Lord, if I speak just once
more. Suppose you find only ten good
people there."

"For the sake of ten good people," the
Lord told him, "I still won't destroy the
city."

33After speaking with Abraham, the
Lord left, and Abraham went back
home.

[k] **18.12** *know such happiness*: Either the joy of making love or the joy of having children.
[l] **18.18** *that will be . . . on earth*: Or "and all other nations on earth will ask me to bless them as I have blessed his family."

The Evil City of Sodom

19 That evening the two angels[m] arrived in Sodom, while Lot was sitting near the city gate.[n] When Lot saw
them, he got up, bowed down low, 2and
said, "Gentlemen, I am your servant.
Please come to my home. You can wash
your feet, spend the night, and be on
your way in the morning."
They told him, "No, we'll spend the
night in the city square." 3But Lot kept
insisting, until they finally agreed and
went home with him. He baked some
bread,[o] cooked a meal, and they ate.
4Before Lot and his guests could go to
bed, every man in Sodom, young and
old, came and stood outside his house
5and started shouting, "Where are your
visitors? Send them out, so we can have
sex with them!"
6Lot went outside and shut the door
behind him. 7Then he said, "Friends,
please don't do such a terrible thing! 8I
have two daughters who have never
been married. I'll bring them out, and
you can do what you want with them.
But don't harm these men. They are
guests in my home."
9"Don't get in our way," the crowd answered. "You're an outsider. What right
do you have to order us around? We'll
do worse things to you than we're going
to do to them."
The crowd kept arguing with Lot. Finally, they rushed toward the door to
break it down. 10But the two angels in
the house reached out and pulled Lot
safely inside. 11Then they struck everyone in the crowd blind, and none of
them could even find the door.
12-13The two angels said to Lot, "The
LORD has heard many terrible things
about the people of Sodom, and he has
sent us here to destroy the city. Take
your family and leave. Take every relative you have in the city, as well as the
men your daughters are going to
marry."
14Lot went to the men who were engaged to his daughters and said, "Hurry
and get out of here! The LORD is going to
destroy this city." But they thought he
was joking, and they laughed at him.
15Early the next morning the two angels tried to make Lot hurry and leave.
They said, "Take your wife and your two
daughters and get out of here as fast as
you can! If you don't, every one of you
will be killed when the LORD destroys
the city." 16At first, Lot just stood there.
But the LORD wanted to save him. So the
angels took Lot, his wife, and his two
daughters by the hand and led them out
of the city. 17When they were outside,
one of the angels said, "Run for your
lives! Don't even look back. And don't
stop in the valley. Run to the hills, where
you will be safe."
18-19Lot answered, "You have done us
a great favor, sir. You have saved our
lives, but please don't make us go to the
hills. That's too far away. The city will be
destroyed before we can get there, and
we will be killed when it happens.
20There's a town near here. It's only a
small place, but my family and I will be
safe, if you let us go there."
21"All right, go there," he answered. "I
won't destroy that town. 22Hurry! Run! I
can't do anything until you are safely
there."
The town was later called Zoar[p] because Lot had said it was small.

Sodom and Gomorrah Are Destroyed

23The sun was coming up as Lot
reached the town of Zoar, 24and the
LORD sent burning sulfur down like
rain on Sodom and Gomorrah. 25He
destroyed those cities and everyone
who lived in them, as well as their
land and the trees and grass that grew
there.
26On the way, Lot's wife looked back
and was turned into a block of salt.
27That same morning Abraham got up
and went to the place where he had
stood and spoken with the LORD. 28He
looked down toward Sodom and Gomorrah and saw smoke rising from all
over the land—it was like a flaming furnace.
29When God destroyed the cities of
the valley where Lot lived, he remembered his promise to Abraham and
saved Lot from the terrible destruction.

Moab and Ammon

30Lot was afraid to stay on in Zoar. So
he took his two daughters and moved to
a cave in the hill country. 31One day his
older daughter said to her sister, "Our
father is old, and there are no men anywhere for us to marry. 32Let's get our
father drunk! Then we can sleep with
him and have children." 33That night
they got their father drunk, and the
older daughter got in bed with him, but
he was too drunk even to know she was
there.
34The next day the older daughter
said to her sister, "I slept with my father
last night. We'll get him drunk again
tonight, so you can go to bed with him,

[m] **19.1** *two angels*: The two men of 18.22. [n] **19.1** *near the city gate*: In a large area where the people would gather for community business and for meeting with friends.
[o] **19.3** *bread*: The Hebrew text has "bread without yeast," which could be fixed quickly when guests came without warning. [p] **19.22** *Zoar*: In Hebrew "Zoar" sounds like "small."

and we can each have a child." 35That
night they got their father drunk, and
this time the younger sister slept with
him. But once again he was too drunk
even to know she was there.
36That's how Lot's two daughters had
their children. 37The older daughter
named her son Moab,[q] and he is the ancestor of the Moabites. 38The younger
daughter named her son Benammi,[r] and
he is the ancestor of the Ammonites.

Abraham and Sarah at Gerar

20 Abraham moved to the Southern
Desert, where he settled between
Kadesh and Shur. Later he went to
Gerar, and while there 2he told everyone
that his wife Sarah was his sister. So
King Abimelech of Gerar had Sarah
brought to him. 3But God came to Abimelech in a dream and said, "You have
taken a married woman, and for this
you will die!"
4-5Abimelech said to the Lord, "Don't
kill me! I haven't slept with Sarah.
Didn't they say they were brother and
sister? I am completely innocent."
6God spoke to Abimelech in another
dream and said:
I know you are innocent. That's
why I kept you from sleeping with
Sarah and doing anything wrong.
7Her husband is a prophet. Let her
go back to him, and his prayers will
save you from death. But if you don't
return her, you and all your people
will die.
8Early the next morning Abimelech
sent for his officials, and when he told
them what had happened, they were
frightened. 9Abimelech then called in
Abraham and said:
Look what you've done to us!
What have I ever done to you? Why
did you make me and my nation
guilty of such a terrible sin? 10What
were you thinking when you did
this?
11Abraham answered:
I did it because I didn't think any
of you respected God, and I was sure
that someone would kill me to get
my wife. 12Besides, she is my half
sister. We have the same father, but
different mothers. 13When God
made us leave my father's home and
start wandering, I told her, "If you
really love me, you will tell everyone
that I am your brother."
14Abimelech gave Abraham some
sheep, cattle, and slaves. He sent Sarah
back 15and told Abraham that he could
settle anywhere in his country. 16Then
he said to Sarah, "I have given your
brother a thousand pieces of silver as
proof to everyone that you have done
nothing wrong."[s]
17-18Meanwhile, God had kept Abimelech's wife and slaves from having children. But Abraham prayed, and God let
them start having children again.

Sarah Has a Son

21 The LORD was good to Sarah and
kept his promise. 2Although
Abraham was very old, Sarah had a son
exactly at the time God had said. 3Abra-
ham named his son Isaac, 4and when
the boy was eight days old, Abraham
circumcised him, just as the LORD had
commanded.
5Abraham was a hundred years old
when Isaac was born, 6and Sarah said,
"God has made me laugh.[t] Now everyone will laugh with me. 7Who would
have dared to tell Abraham that someday I would have a child? But in his old
age, I have given him a son."
8The time came when Sarah no longer
had to nurse Isaac,[u] and on that day
Abraham gave a big feast.

Hagar and Ishmael Are Sent Away

9-10One day, Sarah noticed Hagar's
son Ishmael[v] playing,[w] and she said to
Abraham, "Get rid of that Egyptian
slave woman and her son! I don't want
him to inherit anything. It should all go
to my son."[x]
11Abraham was worried about Ishmael. 12But God said, "Abraham, don't
worry about your slave woman and the
boy. Just do what Sarah tells you. Isaac
will inherit your family name, 13but the
son of the slave woman is also your son,
and I will make his descendants into a
great nation."
14Early the next morning Abraham
gave Hagar an animal skin full of water
and some bread. Then he put the boy on
her shoulder and sent them away.
They wandered around in the desert
near Beersheba, 15and after they had
run out of water, Hagar put her son

[q]**19.37** *Moab*: In Hebrew "Moab" sounds like "from (my) father." [r]**19.38** *Benammi*: In Hebrew "Benammi" means "son of my relative." [s]**20.16** *as proof . . . wrong*: One possible meaning for the difficult Hebrew text. [t]**21.6** *God has made me laugh*: In Hebrew "Isaac" sounds like "laugh." [u]**21.8** *no longer had to nurse Isaac*: In ancient Israel mothers nursed their children until they were about three years old. Then there was a family celebration.
[v]**21.9,10** *Ishmael*: The son of Abraham and Hagar, who was Sarah's slave woman (see 16.1-16).
[w]**21.9,10** *playing*: Hebrew; one ancient translation "playing with her son Isaac."
[x]**21.9,10** *Get rid . . . son*: When Abraham accepted Ishmael as his son, it gave Ishmael the right to inherit part of what Abraham owned. But slaves who were given their freedom lost the right to inherit such property.

under a bush. 16Then she sat down a
long way off, because she could not bear
to watch him die. And she cried bitterly.
17When God heard the boy crying, the
angel of God called out to Hagar from
heaven and said, "Hagar, why are you
worried? Don't be afraid. I have heard
your son crying. 18Help him up and hold
his hand, because I will make him the
father of a great nation." 19Then God let
her see a well. So she went to the well
and filled the skin with water, then gave
some to her son.
20-21God blessed Ishmael, and as the
boy grew older, he became an expert
with his bow and arrows. He lived in the
Paran Desert, and his mother chose an
Egyptian woman for him to marry.

A Peace Treaty

22About this time Abimelech and his
army commander Phicol said to Abraham, "God blesses everything you do!
23Now I want you to promise in the
name of God that you will always be
loyal to me and my descendants, just as
I have always been loyal to you in this
land where you have lived as a foreigner." 24And so, Abraham promised.
25One day, Abraham told Abimelech,
"Some of your servants have taken over
one of my wells."
26"This is the first I've heard about it,"
Abimelech replied. "Why haven't you
said something before? I don't have any
idea who did it." 27Abraham gave Abimelech some sheep and cattle, and then
the two men made a peace treaty.
28Abraham separated seven female
lambs from his flock of sheep, 29and
Abimelech asked, "Why have you done
this?"
30Abraham told him, "I want you to
accept these seven lambs as proof that I
dug this well." 31So they called the place
Beersheba,[y] because they made a treaty
there.
32When the treaty was completed,
Abimelech and his army commander
Phicol went back to the land of the Philistines. 33Abraham planted a tamarisk
tree[z] in Beersheba and worshiped the
eternal LORD God. 34Then Abraham
lived a long time as a foreigner in the
land of the Philistines.

The LORD Tells Abraham To Offer Isaac as a Sacrifice

22 Some years later God decided to
test Abraham, so he spoke to him.
Abraham answered, "Here I am,
LORD."
2The LORD said, "Go get Isaac, your
only son, the one you dearly love! Take
him to the land of Moriah, and I will
show you a mountain where you must
sacrifice him to me on the fires of an altar." 3So Abraham got up early the next
morning and chopped wood for the fire.
He put a saddle on his donkey and left
with Isaac and two servants for the
place where God had told him to go.
4Three days later Abraham looked off
in the distance and saw the place. 5He
told his servants, "Stay here with the
donkey, while my son and I go over
there to worship. We will come back."
6Abraham put the wood on Isaac's
shoulder, but he carried the hot coals
and the knife. As the two of them
walked along, 7-8Isaac said, "Father, we
have the coals and the wood, but where
is the lamb for the sacrifice?"
"My son," Abraham answered, "God
will provide the lamb."
The two of them walked on, and
9when they reached the place that God
had told him about, Abraham built an
altar and placed the wood on it. Next, he
tied up his son and put him on the
wood. 10He then took the knife and got
ready to kill his son. 11But the LORD's
angel shouted from heaven, "Abraham!
Abraham!"
"Here I am!" he answered.
12"Don't hurt the boy or harm him in
any way!" the angel said. "Now I know
that you truly obey God, because you
were willing to offer him your only son."
13Abraham looked up and saw a ram
caught by its horns in the bushes. So he
took the ram and sacrificed it in place of
his son.
14Abraham named that place "The
LORD Will Provide." And even now people say, "On the mountain of the LORD it
will be provided."[a]
15The LORD's angel called out from
heaven a second time:
16You were willing to offer the
LORD your only son, and so he
makes you this solemn promise, 17"I
will bless you and give you such a
large family, that someday your descendants will be more numerous
than the stars in the sky or the
grains of sand along the beach. They
will defeat their enemies and take
over the cities where their enemies
live. 18You have obeyed me, and so
you and your descendants will be a
blessing to all nations on earth."
19Abraham and Isaac went back to the
servants who had come with him, and

[y]21.31 *Beersheba*: Meaning "Well of Good Fortune" or "Peace Treaty Well." [z]21.33 *tamarisk tree*: A tall shade tree that has deep roots and needs little water. [a]22.14 *The LORD Will Provide . . . it will be provided*: Or "The LORD Will Be Seen . . . the LORD will be seen" or "It (a ram) Will Be Seen . . . it (a ram) will be seen."

they returned to Abraham's home in
Beersheba.

The Children of Nahor

20-23 Abraham's brother Nahor had
married Milcah, and Abraham was later
told that they had eight sons. Uz was
their first-born; Buz was next, and then
there was Kemuel who became the
father of Aram; their other five sons
were: Chesed, Hazo, Pildash, Jidlaph,
and Bethuel, who became the father of
Rebekah. 24 Nahor also had another
wife.[b] Her name was Reumah, and she
had four sons: Tebah, Gaham, Tahash,
and Maacah.

Sarah's Death and Burial

23 1-2 When Sarah was one hundred
twenty-seven years old, she died
in Kiriath-Arba, better known as Hebron, in the land of Canaan. After Abraham had mourned for her, 3 he went to
the Hittites and said, 4 "I live as a foreigner in your land, and I don't own any
property where I can bury my wife.
Please let me buy a piece of land."
5-6 "Sir," they answered, "you are an
important man. Choose the best place to
bury your wife. None of us would refuse
you a resting place for your dead."
7 Abraham bowed down 8 and replied,
"If you are willing to let me bury my
wife here, please ask Zohar's son
Ephron 9 to sell me Machpelah Cave at
the end of his field. I'll pay what it's
worth, and all of you can be witnesses."
10 Ephron was sitting there near the
city gate, when Abraham made this request, and he answered, 11 "Sir, the
whole field, including the cave, is yours.
With my own people as witnesses, I
freely give it to you as a burial place for
your dead."
12 Once again, Abraham bowed down
13 and said to Ephron, "In front of these
witnesses, I offer you the full price, so I
can bury my wife. Please accept my offer."
14-15 "But sir," the man replied, "the
property is worth only four hundred
pieces of silver. Why should we haggle
over such a small amount? Take the
land. It's yours."
16-18 Abraham accepted Ephron's offer
and paid him the four hundred pieces of
silver in front of everyone at the city
gate. That's how Abraham got Ephron's
property east of Hebron,[c] which included the field with all of its trees, as
well as Machpelah Cave at the end of
the field. 19 So Abraham buried his wife
Sarah in Machpelah Cave that was in
the field 20 he had bought from the Hittites.

A Wife for Isaac

24 Abraham was now a very old
man. The LORD had made him
rich, and he was successful in everything he did. 2 One day, Abraham called
in his most trusted servant and said to
him, "Solemnly promise me 3 in the
name of the LORD, who rules heaven
and earth, that you won't choose a wife
for my son Isaac from the people here in
the land of Canaan. 4 Instead, go back to
the land where I was born and find a
wife for him from among my relatives."
5 But the servant asked, "What if the
young woman I choose refuses to leave
home and come here with me? Should I
send Isaac there to look for a wife?"
6 "No!" Abraham answered. "Don't
ever do that, no matter what. 7 The LORD
who rules heaven brought me here from
the land where I was born and promised
that he would give this land to my descendants forever. When you go back
there, the LORD will send his angel
ahead of you to help you find a wife for
my son. 8 If the woman refuses to come
along, you don't have to keep this
promise. But don't ever take my son
back there." 9 So the servant gave Abraham his word that he would do everything he had been told to do.
10 Soon after that, the servant loaded
ten of Abraham's camels with valuable
gifts. Then he set out for the city in
northern Syria,[d] where Abraham's
brother Nahor lived.
11 When he got there, he let the camels
rest near the well outside the city. It was
late afternoon, the time when the
women came out for water. 12 The servant prayed:

You, LORD, are the God my master
Abraham worships. Please keep
your promise to him and let me find
a wife for Isaac today. 13 The young
women of the city will soon come to
this well for water, 14 and I'll ask one
of them for a drink. If she gives me a
drink and then offers to get some
water for my camels, I'll know she is
the one you have chosen and that
you have kept your promise to my
master.

15-16 While he was still praying, a beautiful unmarried young woman came by
with a water jar on her shoulder. She
was Rebekah, the daughter of Bethuel,
the son of Abraham's brother Nahor

[b] **22.24** *another wife*: This translates a Hebrew word for a woman who was legally bound to a man, but without the full privileges of a wife. [c] **23.16-18** *Hebron*: The Hebrew text has "Mamre," a place just north of Hebron. [d] **24.10** *northern Syria*: The Hebrew text has "Aram-Naharaim," probably referring to the land around the city of Haran (see also "Paddan-Aram" in 25.20; 28.2, 6; 31.18, 20; 33.18; 35.23-26; 46.8-15; and "Paddan" in 48.7).

and his wife Milcah. Rebekah walked
past Abraham's servant, then went over
to the well, and filled her water jar.
When she started back, 17Abraham's
servant ran to her and said, "Please let
me have a drink of water."
18"I'll be glad to," she answered. Then
she quickly took the jar from her shoulder and held it while he drank. 19-20After
he had finished, she said, "Now I'll give
your camels all the water they want."
She quickly poured out water for them,
and she kept going back for more, until
his camels had drunk all they wanted.
21Abraham's servant did not say a word,
but he watched everything Rebekah did,
because he wanted to know for certain
if this was the woman the LORD had
chosen.
22The servant had brought along an
expensive gold ring and two large gold
bracelets. When Rebekah had finished
bringing the water, he gave her the ring
for her nose[e] and the bracelets for her
arms. 23Then he said, "Please tell me
who your father is. Does he have room
in his house for me and my men to
spend the night?"
24She answered, "My father is
Bethuel, the son of Nahor and Milcah.
25We have a place where you and your
men can stay, and we also have enough
straw and feed for your camels."
26Then the servant bowed his head
and prayed, 27"I thank you, LORD God of
my master Abraham! You have led me to
his relatives and kept your promise to
him."
28Rebekah ran straight home and told
her family everything. 29-30Her brother
Laban heard her tell what the servant
had said, and he saw the ring and the
bracelets she was wearing. So Laban
ran out to Abraham's servant, who was
standing by his camels at the well.
31Then Laban said, "The LORD has
brought you safely here. Come home
with me. There's no need for you to
keep on standing outside. I have a room
ready for you in our house, and there's
also a place for your camels."
32Abraham's servant went home with
Laban, where Laban's servants un-
loaded his camels and gave them straw
and feed. Then they brought water into
the house, so Abraham's servant and his
men could wash their feet. 33After that,
they brought in food. But the servant
said, "Before I eat, I must tell you why I
have come."
"Go ahead and tell us," Laban answered.
34The servant explained:
I am Abraham's servant. 35The
LORD has been good to my master
and has made him very rich. He has
given him many sheep, goats, cattle,
camels, and donkeys, as well as a lot
of silver and gold, and many slaves.
36Sarah, my master's wife, didn't
have any children until she was very
old. Then she had a son, and my
master has given him everything. 37I
solemnly promised my master that I
would do what he said. And he told
me, "Don't choose a wife for my son
from the women in this land of
Canaan. 38Instead, go back to the
land where I was born and find a
wife for my son from among my relatives."
39I asked my master, "What if the
young woman refuses to come with
me?"
40My master answered, "I have
always obeyed the LORD, and he
will send his angel to help you
find my son a wife from among
my own relatives. 41But if they
refuse to let her come back with
you, then you are freed from your
promise."
42When I came to the well today, I
silently prayed, "You, LORD, are the
God my master Abraham worships,
so please lead me to a wife for his
son 43while I am here at the well.
When a young woman comes out to
get water, I'll ask her to give me a
drink. 44If she gives me a drink and
offers to get some water for my
camels, I'll know she is the one you
have chosen."
45Even before I had finished praying, Rebekah came by with a water
jar on her shoulder. When she had
filled the jar, I asked her for a drink.
46She quickly lowered the jar from
her shoulder and said, "Have a drink.
Then I'll get water for your camels."
So I drank, and after that she got
some water for my camels. 47I asked
her who her father was, and she answered, "My father is Bethuel the
son of Nahor and Milcah." Right
away I put the ring in her nose and
the bracelets on her arms. 48Then I
bowed my head and gave thanks to
the God my master Abraham worships. The LORD had led me straight
to my master's relatives, and I had
found a wife for his son.
49Now please tell me if you are
willing to do the right thing for my
master. Will you treat him fairly, or
do I have to look for another young
woman?
50Laban and Bethuel answered, "The
LORD has done this. We have no choice
in the matter. 51Take Rebekah with you;

[e]24.22 *ring for her nose*: Nose-rings were popular jewelry items, as were earrings.

she can marry your master's son, just as
the LORD has said." [52]Abraham's servant
bowed down and thanked the LORD.
[53]Then he gave clothing, as well as silver and gold jewelry, to Rebekah. He
also gave expensive gifts to her brother
and her mother.
[54]Abraham's servant and the men
with him ate and drank, then spent the
night there. The next morning they got
up, and the servant told Rebekah's
mother and brother, "I would like to go
back to my master now."
[55]"Let Rebekah stay with us for a
week or ten days," they answered. "Then
she may go."
[56]But he said, "Don't make me stay
any longer. The LORD has already helped
me find a wife for my master's son. Now
let us return."
[57]They answered, "Let's ask Rebekah
what she wants to do." [58]They called her
and asked, "Are you willing to leave
with this man right now?"
"Yes," she answered.
[59]So they agreed to let Rebekah and
an old family servant woman[f] leave immediately with Abraham's servant and
his men. [60]They gave Rebekah their
blessing and said, "We pray that God
will give you many children and grandchildren and that he will help them
defeat their enemies." [61]Afterwards,
Rebekah and the young women who
were to travel with her prepared to
leave. Then they got on camels and
left with Abraham's servant and his
men.
[62]At that time Isaac was living in the
southern part of Canaan near a place
called "The Well of the Living One Who
Sees Me."[g] [63-65]One evening he was
walking out in the fields, when suddenly
he saw a group of people approaching
on camels. So he started toward them.
Rebekah saw him coming; she got down
from her camel, and asked, "Who is that
man?"
"He is my master Isaac," the servant
answered. Then Rebekah covered her
face with her veil.[h]
[66]The servant told Isaac everything
that had happened.
[67]Isaac took Rebekah into the tent[i]
where his mother had lived before she
died, and Rebekah became his wife. He
loved her and was comforted over the
loss of his mother.

Abraham Marries Keturah

25 Abraham married Keturah, [2]and
they had six sons: Zimran, Jokshan, Medan, Midian, Ishbak, and
Shuah. [3]Later, Jokshan became the
father of Sheba and Dedan, and when
Dedan grew up, he had three sons:
Asshurim, Letushim, and Leummim.
[4]Midian also had five sons: Ephah,
Epher, Hanoch, Abida, and Eldaah.
[5-6]While Abraham was still alive, he
gave gifts to the sons of Hagar and Keturah. He also sent their sons to live in
the east far from his son Isaac, and
when Abraham died, he left everything
to Isaac.

The Death of Abraham

[7-8]Abraham died at the ripe old age of
one hundred seventy-five. [9-10]His sons
Isaac and Ishmael buried him east of
Hebron[j] in Machpelah Cave that was
part of the field Abraham had bought
from Ephron son of Zohar the Hittite.
Abraham was buried there beside his
wife Sarah. [11]God blessed Isaac after
this, and Isaac moved to a place called
"The Well of the Living One Who Sees
Me."[k]

Ishmael's Descendants

[12]Ishmael was the son of Abraham
and Hagar, the slave woman of Sarah.
[13]Ishmael had twelve sons, in this order:
Nebaioth, Kedar, Adbeel, Mibsam,
[14]Mishma, Dumah, Massa, [15]Hadad,
Tema, Jetur, Naphish, and Kedemah.
[16]Each of Ishmael's sons was a tribal
chief, and a village was named after
each of them.
[17-18]Ishmael had settled in the land
east of his brothers, and his sons[l] settled
everywhere from Havilah to Shur, east
of Egypt on the way to Asshur.[m] Ishmael was one hundred thirty-seven
when he died.

The Birth of Esau and Jacob

[19]Isaac was the son of Abraham, [20]and
he was forty years old when he married
Rebekah, the daughter of Bethuel. She
was also the sister of Laban, the Aramean from northern Syria.[n]
Almost twenty years later, [21]Rebekah
still had no children. So Isaac asked the
LORD to let her have a child, and the
LORD answered his prayer.

[f]**24.59** *old family servant woman*: Probably Deborah, who had taken care of Rebekah from the time she was born (see 35.8). [g]**24.62** *Who Sees Me*: Or "I Have Seen." [h]**24.63-65** *covered . . . veil*: Since the veiling of a bride was part of the wedding ceremony, this probably means that she was willing to become the wife of Isaac. [i]**24.67** *took . . . tent*: This shows that Rebekah is now the wife of Isaac and the successor of Sarah as the leading woman in the tribe. [j]**25.9,10** *Hebron*: See the note at 23.16-18. [k]**25.11** *The Well . . . Sees Me*: Or "Beer-Lahai-Roi." (see 16.14). [l]**25.17,18** *sons*: Or "descendants." [m]**25.17,18** *Havilah to Shur . . . Asshur*: The exact location of these places is not known. [n]**25.20** *northern Syria*: See the note at 24.10.

22Before Rebekah gave birth, she
knew she was going to have twins, because she could feel them inside her,
fighting each other. She thought, "Why
is this happening to me?" Finally, she
asked the LORD why her twins were
fighting, 23and he told her:

"Your two sons will become
two separate nations.[o]
The younger of the two
will be stronger,
and the older son
will be his servant."

24When Rebekah gave birth, 25the first
baby was covered with red hair, so he
was named Esau.[p] 26The second baby
grabbed on to his brother's heel, so they
named him Jacob.[q] Isaac was sixty
years old when they were born.

Esau Sells His Rights as the First-Born Son

27As Jacob and Esau grew older, Esau
liked the outdoors and became a good
hunter, while Jacob settled down and
became a shepherd. 28Esau would take
the meat of wild animals to his father
Isaac, and so Isaac loved him more, but
Jacob was his mother's favorite son.

29One day, Jacob was cooking some
stew, when Esau came home hungry
30and said, "I'm starving to death! Give
me some of that red stew right now!"
That's how Esau got the name "Edom."[r]

31Jacob replied, "Sell me your rights
as the first-born son."[s]

32"I'm about to die," Esau answered.
"What good will those rights do me?"

33But Jacob said, "Promise me your
birthrights, here and now!" And that's
what Esau did. 34Jacob then gave Esau
some bread and some of the bean stew,
and when Esau had finished eating and
drinking, he just got up and left, showing how little he thought of his rights as
the first-born.

Isaac and Abimelech

26 Once during Abraham's lifetime,
the fields had not produced
enough grain, and now the same thing
happened. So Isaac went to King Abimelech of the Philistines in the land of
Gerar, 2because the LORD had appeared
to Isaac and said:

Isaac, stay away from Egypt! I will
show you where I want you to go.
3You will live there as a foreigner,
but I will be with you and bless you.
I will keep my promise to your
father Abraham by giving this land
to you and your descendants.

4I will give you as many descendants as there are stars in the sky,
and I will give your descendants all
of this land. They will be a blessing
to every nation on earth,[t] 5because
Abraham did everything I told him
to do.

6Isaac moved to Gerar 7with his beautiful wife Rebekah. He was afraid that
someone might kill him to get her, and
so he told everyone that Rebekah was
his sister. 8After Isaac had been there a
long time, King Abimelech looked out a
window and saw Isaac hugging and
kissing Rebekah. 9Abimelech called him
in and said, "Rebekah must be your
wife! Why did you say she is your sister?"

"Because I thought someone would
kill me," Isaac answered.

10"Don't you know what you've
done?" Abimelech exclaimed. "If someone had slept with her, you would have
made our whole nation guilty!" 11Then
Abimelech warned his people that anyone who even touched Isaac or Rebekah
would be put to death.

12Isaac planted grain and had a good
harvest that same year. The LORD
blessed him, 13and Isaac was so successful that he became very rich. 14In fact,
the Philistines were jealous of the large
number of sheep, goats, and slaves that
Isaac owned, 15and they stopped up the
wells that Abraham's servants had dug
before his death. 16Finally, Abimelech
said, "Isaac, I want you to leave our
country. You have become too powerful
to stay here."

17Isaac left and settled in Gerar Valley,
18where he cleaned out those wells that
the Philistines had stopped up. Isaac
also gave each of the wells the same
name[u] that Abraham had given to them.
19While his servants were digging in the
valley, they found a spring-fed well.
20But the shepherds of Gerar Valley
quarreled with Isaac's shepherds and
claimed the water belonged to them. So
the well was named "Quarrel," because
they had quarreled with Isaac.

21Isaac's servants dug another well,
and the shepherds also quarreled about
it. So that well was named "Jealous."
22Finally, they dug one more well. There
was no quarreling this time, and the
well was named "Lots of Room," be-

[o]**25.23** *two separate nations*: Or "two nations always in conflict." [p]**25.25** *Esau*: In Hebrew "Esau" sounds like "hairy." [q]**25.26** *Jacob*: In Hebrew "Jacob" sounds like "heel." [r]**25.30** *Edom*: In Hebrew "Edom" sounds like "red." [s]**25.31** *rights . . . son*: The first-born son inherited the largest amount of property, as well as the leadership of the family. [t]**26.4** *They . . . on earth*: Or "All nations on earth will ask me to bless them." [u]**26.18** *gave . . . same name*: By doing this Isaac claimed ownership of the wells.

cause the LORD had given them room
and would make them very successful.
[23]Isaac went on to Beersheba, [24]where
the LORD appeared to him that night and
told him, "Don't be afraid! I am the God
who was worshiped by your father
Abraham, my servant. I will be with you
and bless you, and because of Abraham
I will give you many descendants."
[25]Isaac built an altar there and worshiped the LORD. Then he set up camp,
and his servants started digging a well.
[26]Meanwhile, Abimelech had left
Gerar and was taking his advisor Ahuz-
zath and his army commander Phicol to
see Isaac. [27]When they arrived, Isaac
asked, "Why are you here? Didn't you
send me away because you hated me?"
[28]They answered, "We now know for
certain that the LORD is with you, and
we have decided there needs to be a
peace treaty between you and us. So
let's make a solemn agreement [29]not to
harm each other. Remember, we have
never hurt you, and when we sent you
away, we let you go in peace. The LORD
has truly blessed you."
[30]Isaac gave a big feast for them, and
everyone ate and drank. [31]Early the next
morning Isaac and the others made a
solemn agreement, then he let them go
in peace.
[32]Later that same day Isaac's servants
came and said, "We've struck water!"
[33]So Isaac named the well Shibah,[v] and
the town is still called Beersheba.[w]

Esau's Foreign Wives

[34]When Esau was forty, he married
Judith the daughter of Beeri the Hittite
and Basemath the daughter of Elon the
Hittite. [35]But these two women brought
a lot of grief to his parents Isaac and
Rebekah.

Isaac Blesses Jacob

27 After Isaac had become old and
almost blind, he called in his first-
born son Esau, who asked him, "Father,
what can I do for you?"
[2]Isaac replied, "I am old and might die
at any time. [3]So take your bow and arrows, then go out in the fields, and kill a
wild animal. [4]Cook some of that tasty
food that I love so much and bring it to
me. I want to eat it once more and give
you my blessing before I die."
[5]Rebekah had been listening, and as
soon as Esau left to go hunting, [6]she
said to Jacob, "I heard your father tell
Esau [7]to kill a wild animal and cook
some tasty food for your father before
he dies. Your father said this because he
wants to bless your brother with the
LORD as his witness. [8]Now, my son, listen carefully to what I want you to do.
[9]Go and kill two of your best young
goats and bring them to me. I'll cook the
tasty food that your father loves so
much. [10]Then you can take it to him, so
he can eat it and give you his blessing
before he dies."
[11]"My brother Esau is a hairy man,"
Jacob reminded her. "And I am not. [12]If
my father touches me and realizes I am
trying to trick him, he will put a curse
on me instead of giving me a blessing."
[13]Rebekah insisted, "Let his curse fall
on me! Just do what I say and bring me
the meat." [14]So Jacob brought the meat
to his mother, and she cooked the tasty
food that his father liked. [15]Then she
took Esau's best clothes and put them
on Jacob. [16]She also covered the smooth
part of his hands and neck with
goatskins [17]and gave him some bread
and the tasty food she had cooked.
[18]Jacob went to his father and said,
"Father, here I am."
"Which one of my sons are you?" his
father asked.
[19]Jacob replied, "I am Esau, your first-
born, and I have done what you told me.
Please sit up and eat the meat I have
brought. Then you can give me your
blessing."
[20]Isaac asked, "My son, how did you
find an animal so quickly?"
"The LORD your God was kind to me,"
Jacob answered.
[21]"My son," Isaac said, "come closer,
where I can touch you and find out if
you really are Esau." [22]Jacob went
closer. His father touched him and said,
"You sound like Jacob, but your hands
feel hairy like Esau's." [23]And so Isaac
blessed Jacob, thinking he was Esau.
[24]Isaac asked, "Are you really my son
Esau?"
"Yes, I am," Jacob answered.
[25]So Isaac told him, "Serve me the
wild meat, and I can give you my blessing."
Jacob gave him some meat, and he ate
it. He also gave him some wine, and he
drank it. [26]Then Isaac said, "Son, come
over here and kiss me." [27]While Jacob
was kissing him, Isaac caught the smell
of his clothes and said:

"The smell of my son
is like a field
the LORD has blessed.
28 God will bless you, my son,
with dew from heaven
and with fertile fields,
rich with grain and grapes.
29 Nations will be your servants
and bow down to you.

[v]26.33 *Shibah*: In Hebrew "Shibah" sounds something like "good luck" and "promise."
[w]26.33 *Beersheba*: Meaning "Well of Good Fortune" or "Peace Treaty Well."

You will rule over your brothers,
and they will kneel
at your feet.
Anyone who curses you
will be cursed;
anyone who blesses you
will be blessed."

30 Right after Isaac had given Jacob
his blessing and Jacob had gone, Esau
came back from hunting. 31 He cooked
the tasty food, brought it to his father,
and said, "Father, please sit up and eat
the meat I have brought you, so you can
give me your blessing."
32 "Who are you?" Isaac asked.
"I am Esau, your first-born son."
33 Isaac started trembling and said,
"Then who brought me some wild meat
right before you came in? I ate it and
gave him a blessing that cannot be
taken back."
34 Esau cried loudly and begged,
"Father, give me a blessing too!"
35 Isaac answered, "Your brother
tricked me and stole your blessing."
36 Esau replied, "My brother deserves
the name Jacob,[x] because he has already cheated me twice. The first time
he cheated me out of my rights as the
first-born son, and now he has cheated
me out of my blessing." Then Esau
asked his father, "Don't you still have
any blessing left for me?"
37 "My son," Isaac answered, "I have
made Jacob the ruler over you and your
brothers, and all of you will be his servants. I have also promised him all the
grain and grapes that he needs. There's
nothing left that I can do for you."
38 "Father," Esau asked, "don't you
have more than one blessing? You can
surely give me a blessing too!" Then
Esau started crying again.
39 So his father said:

"Your home will be far
from that fertile land,
where dew comes down
from the heavens.
40 You will live by the power
of your sword
and be your brother's slave.
But when you decide to be free,
you will break loose."

41 Esau hated his brother Jacob because he had stolen the blessing that
was supposed to be his. So he said to
himself, "Just as soon as my father dies,
I'll kill Jacob."
42 When Rebekah found out what Esau
planned to do, she sent for Jacob and
told him, "Son, your brother Esau is just
waiting for the time when he can kill
you. 43 Now listen carefully and do what
I say. Go to the home of my brother Laban in Haran 44 and stay with him for a
while. When Esau stops being angry
45 and forgets what you have done to
him, I'll send for you to come home.
Why should I lose both of my sons on
the same day?"[y]
46 Rebekah later told Isaac, "Those Hittite wives of Esau are making my life
miserable! If Jacob marries a Hittite
woman, I'd be better off dead."

Isaac's Instructions to Jacob

28 Isaac called in Jacob, then gave
him a blessing, and said:
Don't marry any of those Canaanite women. 2 Go at once to your
mother's father Bethuel in northern
Syria[z] and choose a wife from one
of the daughters of Laban, your
mother's brother. 3 I pray that God
All-Powerful will bless you with
many descendants and let you become a great nation. 4 May he bless
you with the land he gave Abraham,
so that you will take over this land
where we now live as foreigners.
5 Isaac then sent Jacob to stay with Rebekah's brother Laban, the son of
Bethuel the Aramean.

Esau Marries the Daughter of Ishmael

6 Esau found out that his father Isaac
had blessed Jacob and had warned him
not to marry any of the Canaanite
women. He also learned that Jacob had
been sent to find a wife in northern
Syria[z] 7 and that he had obeyed his
father and mother. 8 Esau already had
several wives, but he realized at last
how much his father hated the Canaanite women. 9 So he married Ishmael's
daughter Mahalath, who was the sister
of Nebaioth[a] and the granddaughter of
Abraham.

Jacob's Dream at Bethel

10 Jacob left the town of Beersheba
and started out for Haran. 11 At sunset
he stopped for the night and went to
sleep, resting his head on a large rock.
12 In a dream he saw a ladder[b] that
reached from earth to heaven, and
God's angels were going up and down
on it.
13 The LORD was standing beside the
ladder[c] and said:

[x] **27.36** *Jacob*: In Hebrew "Jacob" sounds like "cheat." [y] **27.45** *lose . . . day*: Esau would be hunted down as a murderer if he killed Jacob, and so Rebekah would lose both of her sons. [z] **28.2** *northern Syria*: See the note at 24.10. [z] **28.6** *northern Syria*: See the note at 24.10. [a] **28.9** *Nebaioth*: Ishmael's oldest son (see 25.13). [b] **28.12** *ladder*: Or "stairway." [c] **28.13** *the ladder*: Or "Jacob" or "the stairway" (see the note at 28.12).

I am the LORD God who was worshiped by Abraham and Isaac. I will
give to you and your family the land
on which you are now sleeping.
14Your descendants will spread over
the earth in all directions and will
become as numerous as the specks
of dust. Your family will be a blessing to all people.[d] 15Wherever you
go, I will watch over you, then later I
will bring you back to this land. I
won't leave you—I will do all I have
promised.
16Jacob woke up suddenly and
thought, "The LORD is in this place, and I
didn't even know it." 17Then Jacob became frightened and said, "This is a
fearsome place! It must be the house of
God and the ladder[e] to heaven."
18When Jacob got up early the next
morning, he took the rock that he
had used for a pillow and stood it
up for a place of worship. Then he
poured olive oil on the rock to dedicate
it to God, 19and he named the place
Bethel.[f] Before that it had been named
Luz.
20Jacob solemnly promised God, "If
you go with me and watch over me as I
travel, and if you give me food and
clothes 21and bring me safely home
again, you will be my God. 22This rock
will be your house, and I will give back
to you a tenth of everything you give
me."

Jacob Arrives at Laban's Home

29 As Jacob continued on his way to
the east, 2he looked out in a field
and saw a well where shepherds took
their sheep for water. Three flocks of
sheep were lying around the well, which
was covered with a large rock. 3Shep-
herds would roll the rock away when all
their sheep had gathered there. Then after the sheep had been watered, the
shepherds would roll the rock back over
the mouth of the well.
4Jacob asked the shepherds, "Where
are you from?"
"We're from Haran," they answered.
5Then he asked, "Do you know Nahor's grandson Laban?"
"Yes we do," they replied.
6"How is he?" Jacob asked.
"He's fine," they answered. "And here
comes his daughter Rachel with the
sheep."
7Jacob told them, "Look, the sun is
still high up in the sky, and it's too early
to bring in the rest of the flocks. Water
your sheep and take them back to the
pasture."
8But they replied, "We can't do that
until they all get here, and the rock has
been rolled away from the well."
9While Jacob was still talking with the
men, his cousin Rachel came up with
her father's sheep. 10When Jacob saw
her and his uncle's sheep, he rolled the
rock away and watered the sheep. 11He
then kissed Rachel and started crying
because he was so happy. 12He told her
that he was the son of her aunt Rebekah, and she ran and told her father
about him.
13As soon as Laban heard the news,
he ran out to meet Jacob. He hugged
and kissed him and brought him to his
home, where Jacob told him everything
that had happened. 14Laban said, "You
are my nephew, and you are like one of
my own family."

Jacob Marries Leah and Rachel

After Jacob had been there for a
month, 15Laban said to him, "You
shouldn't have to work without pay, just
because you are a relative of mine. What
do you want me to give you?"
16-17Laban had two daughters. Leah
was older than Rachel, but her eyes
didn't sparkle,[g] while Rachel was beautiful and had a good figure. 18Since Jacob was in love with Rachel, he answered, "If you will let me marry
Rachel, I'll work seven years for you."
19Laban replied, "It's better for me to
let you marry Rachel than for someone
else to have her. So stay and work for
me." 20Jacob worked seven years for Laban, but the time seemed like only a few
days, because he loved Rachel so much.
21Jacob said to Laban, "The time is up,
and I want to marry Rachel now!" 22So
Laban gave a big feast and invited all
their neighbors. 23But that evening he
brought Leah to Jacob, who married her
and spent the night with her. 24Laban
also gave Zilpah to Leah as her servant
woman.
25The next morning Jacob found out
that he had married Leah, and he asked
Laban, "Why did you do this to me?
Didn't I work to get Rachel? Why did
you trick me?"
26Laban replied, "In our country the
older daughter must get married first.
27After you spend this week[h] with Leah,
you may also marry Rachel. But you
will have to work for me another seven
years."
28-30At the end of the week of celebration, Laban let Jacob marry Rachel, and
he gave her his servant woman Bilhah.
Jacob loved Rachel more than he did

[d]**28.14** *Your family . . . people*: Or "All people will ask me to bless them as I have blessed your family." [e]**28.17** *ladder*: See the note at 28.12. [f]**28.19** *Bethel*: In Hebrew "Bethel" means "House of God." [g]**29.16,17** *but her eyes didn't sparkle*: Or "and her eyes sparkled." [h]**29.27** *this week*: The wedding feast lasted for seven days (see Judges 14.12, 17).

Leah, but he had to work another seven
years for Laban.
31 The LORD knew that Jacob loved
Rachel more than he did Leah, and so
he gave children to Leah, but not to
Rachel. 32 Leah gave birth to a son and
named him Reuben,[i] because she said,
"The LORD has taken away my sorrow.
Now my husband will love me more
than he does Rachel." 33 She had a second son and named him Simeon,[j] because she said, "The LORD has heard that
my husband doesn't love me." 34 When
Leah's third son was born, she said,
"Now my husband will hold me close."
So this son was named Levi.[k] 35 She had
one more son and named him Judah,[l]
because she said, "I'll praise the LORD!"

Problems between Rachel and Leah

30 Rachel was very jealous of Leah
for having children, and she said
to Jacob, "I'll die if you don't give me
some children!"
2 But Jacob became upset with Rachel
and answered, "Don't blame me! I'm not
God."
3 "Here, take my servant Bilhah,"
Rachel told him. "Have children by her,
and I'll let them be born on my knees to
show that they are mine."
4 Then Rachel let Jacob marry Bilhah,
5 and they had a son. 6 Rachel named him
Dan,[m] because she said, "God has answered my prayers. He has judged me
and given me a son." 7 When Bilhah and
Jacob had a second son, 8 Rachel said,
"I've struggled hard with my sister, and
I've won!" So she named the boy Naphtali.[n]
9 When Leah realized she could not
have any more children, she let Jacob
marry her servant Zilpah, 10 and they
had a son. 11 "I'm really lucky," Leah
said, and she named the boy Gad.[o]
12 When they had another son, 13 Leah
exclaimed, "I'm happy now, and all the
women will say how happy I am." So
she named him Asher.[p]

Love Flowers

14 During the time of the wheat harvest, Reuben found some love flowers[q]
and took them to his mother Leah.
Rachel asked Leah for some of them,
15 but Leah said, "It's bad enough that
you stole my husband! Now you want
my son's love flowers too."
"All right," Rachel answered. "Let me
have the flowers, and you can sleep with
Jacob tonight."
16 That evening when Jacob came in
from the fields, Leah told him, "You're
sleeping with me tonight. I hired you
with my son's love flowers."
They slept together that night, 17 and
God answered Leah's prayers by giving
her a fifth son. 18 Leah shouted, "God has
rewarded me for letting Jacob marry my
servant," and she named the boy Issachar.[r]
19 When Leah had another son, 20 she
exclaimed, "God has given me a wonderful gift, and my husband will praise
me for giving him six sons." So she
named the boy Zebulun.[s] 21 Later, Leah
had a daughter and named her Dinah.
22-23 Finally, God remembered Rachel—he answered her prayer by giving
her a son. "God has taken away my disgrace," she said. 24 "I'll name the boy
Joseph,[t] and I'll pray that the LORD will
give me another son."

Jacob and Laban

25 After Joseph was born, Jacob said
to Laban, "Release me from our agreement[u] and let me return to my own
country. 26 You know how hard I've
worked for you, so let me take my wives
and children and leave."
27-28 But Laban told him, "If you really
are my friend, stay on, and I'll pay whatever you ask. I'm sure[v] the LORD has
blessed me because of you."
29 Jacob answered:
You've seen how hard I've worked
for you, and you know how your
flocks and herds have grown under
my care. 30 You didn't have much before I came, but the LORD has
blessed everything I have ever done
for you. Now it's time for me to start
looking out for my own family.
31 "How much do you want me to pay
you?" Laban asked.
Then Jacob told him:
I don't want you to pay me anything. Just do one thing, and I'll take
care of your sheep and goats. 32 Let

[i] **29.32** *Reuben*: In Hebrew "Reuben" means, "Look, a son!" [j] **29.33** *Simeon*: In Hebrew "Simeon" sounds like "someone who hears." [k] **29.34** *hold me close . . . Levi*: In Hebrew "Levi" sounds like "hold (someone) close." [l] **29.35** *Judah*: In Hebrew "Judah" sounds like "praise." [m] **30.6** *Dan*: In Hebrew "Dan" means "judge." [n] **30.8** *Naphtali*: In Hebrew "Naphtali" means "struggle" or "contest." [o] **30.11** *Gad*: In Hebrew "Gad" means "lucky." [p] **30.13** *Asher*: In Hebrew "Asher" means "happy." [q] **30.14** *love flowers*: Also called "mandrakes," a flowering plant that was thought to give sexual powers. [r] **30.18** *Issachar*: In Hebrew "Issachar" sounds like "reward." [s] **30.20** *Zebulun*: In Hebrew "Zebulun" sounds like "give" and "praise." [t] **30.24** *Joseph*: In Hebrew "Joseph" sounds like "take away" and "add." [u] **30.25** *Release . . . agreement*: Jacob had agreed to work seven years for each of Laban's two daughters (see 29.18). [v] **30.27,28** *I'm sure*: The Hebrew text means to find out by some kind of magic, such as fortunetelling.

me go through your flocks and herds
and take the sheep and goats that
are either spotted or speckled[w] and
the black lambs. That's all you need
to give me. 33In the future you can
easily find out if I've been honest.
Just look and see if my animals are
either spotted or speckled, or if the
lambs are black. If they aren't,
they've been stolen from you.
34"I agree to that," was Laban's response. 35Before the end of the day, Laban had separated his spotted and
speckled animals and the black lambs
from the others and had put his sons in
charge of them. 36Then Laban made Jacob keep the rest of the sheep and goats
at a distance of three days' journey.
37Jacob cut branches from some
poplar trees and from some almond and
evergreen trees. He peeled off part of
the bark and made the branches look
spotted and speckled. 38Then he put the
branches where the sheep and goats
would see them[x] while they were drinking from the water trough. The goats
mated there 39in front of the branches,
and their young were spotted and
speckled.
40Some of the sheep that Jacob was
keeping for Laban were already spotted.
And when the others were ready to
mate, he made sure that they faced in
the direction of the spotted and black
ones. In this way, Jacob built up a flock
of sheep for himself and did not put
them with the other sheep.
41When the stronger sheep were mating near the drinking place, Jacob made
sure that the spotted branches were
there. 42But he would not put out the
branches when the weaker animals
were mating. So Jacob got all of the
healthy animals, and Laban got what
was left. 43Jacob soon became rich and
successful. He owned many sheep,
goats, camels, and donkeys, as well as a
lot of slaves.

Jacob Runs from Laban

31 Jacob heard that Laban's sons
were complaining, "Jacob is now
a rich man, and he got everything he
owns from our father." 2Jacob also noticed that Laban was not as friendly as
he had been before. 3One day the LORD
said, "Jacob, go back to your relatives in
the land of your ancestors, and I will
bless you."
4Jacob sent for Rachel and Leah to
meet him in the field where he kept his
sheep, 5and he told them:
Your father isn't as friendly with
me as he used to be, but the God my
ancestors worshiped has been on
my side. 6You know that I have
worked hard for your father 7and
that he keeps cheating me by changing my wages time after time. But
God has protected me. 8When your
father said the speckled sheep
would be my wages, all of them
were speckled. And when he said
the spotted ones would be mine, all
of them were spotted. 9That's how
God has taken sheep and goats from
your father and given them to me.
10Once, when the flocks were mating, I dreamed that all the rams were
either spotted or speckled. 11Then
God's angel called me by name. I answered, 12and he said, "Notice that
all the rams are either spotted or
speckled. I know everything Laban
is doing to you, 13and I am the God
you worshiped at Bethel,[y] when you
poured olive oil on a rock and made
a promise to me. Leave here right
away and return to the land where
you were born."
14Rachel and Leah said to Jacob:
There's nothing left for us to inherit from our father. 15He treats us
like foreigners and has even cheated
us out of the bride price[z] that should
have been ours. 16Now do whatever
God tells you to do. Even the property God took from our father and
gave to you really belongs to us and
our children.
17Then Jacob, his wives, and his children got on camels and left 18for the
home of his father Isaac in Canaan. Jacob took all of the flocks, herds, and
other property that he had gotten in
northern Syria.[a]
19Before Rachel left, she stole the
household idols[b] while Laban was out
shearing his sheep.
20Jacob tricked Laban the Aramean[c]
by not saying that he intended to leave.
21When Jacob crossed the Euphrates

[w] **30.32** *spotted or speckled*: In ancient times sheep were usually white, and goats were usually black or dark brown; only a few sheep would have black spots, and only a few goats would have white spots. [x] **30.38** *would see them*: It was believed by some that what sheep and goats saw at the time of breeding would determine the color of their young. [y] **31.13** *you . . . Bethel*: Or "who appeared to you at Bethel." [z] **31.15** *bride price*: Usually the husband-to-be paid a bride price to the father of the bride. But Jacob didn't pay Laban a bride price for either Rachel or Leah. Instead he was tricked into working fourteen years to get the bride he loved. So there was no money for either of Laban's daughters. [a] **31.18** *northern Syria*: See the note at 24.10. [b] **31.19** *household idols*: These were thought to protect the household from danger. It is also possible that the person who had them would inherit the family property. [c] **31.20** *the Aramean*: Meaning someone from northern Syria (see the note at 24.10).

River and headed for the hill country of
Gilead, he took with him everything he
owned.

Laban Catches Up with Jacob

22 Three days later Laban found out
that Jacob had gone. 23 So he took some
of his relatives along and chased after
Jacob for seven days, before catching up
with him in the hill country of Gilead.
24 But God appeared to Laban in a
dream that night and warned, "Don't
say a word to Jacob. Don't make a
threat or a promise."
25 Jacob had set up camp in the hill
country of Gilead, when Laban and his
relatives came and set up camp in another part of the hill country. Laban
went to Jacob 26 and said:
Look what you've done! You've
tricked me and run off with my
daughters like a kidnapper. 27 Why
did you sneak away without telling
me? I would have given you a going-
away party with singing and with
music on tambourines and harps.
28 You didn't even give me a chance
to kiss my own grandchildren and
daughters good-by. That was really
foolish. 29 I could easily hurt you, but
the God your father worshiped has
warned me not to make any threats
or promises.
30 I can understand why you were
eager to return to your father, but
why did you have to steal my idols?
31 Jacob answered, "I left secretly because I was afraid you would take your
daughters from me by force. 32 If you
find that any one of us has taken your
idols, I'll have that person killed. Let
your relatives be witnesses. Show me
what belongs to you, and you can take it
back." Jacob did not realize that Rachel
had stolen the household idols.
33 Laban searched the tents of Jacob,
Leah, and the two servant women,[d] but
did not find the idols. Then he started
for Rachel's tent. 34 She had already hidden them in the cushion she used as a
saddle and was sitting on it. Laban
searched everywhere and did not find
them. 35 Rachel said, "Father, please don't
be angry with me for not getting up; I
am having my period." Laban kept on
searching, but still did not find the idols.
36 Jacob became very angry and said
to Laban:
What have I done wrong? Have I
committed some crime? Is that why
you hunted me down? 37 After
searching through everything I have,
did you find anything of yours? If so,
put it here, where your relatives and
mine can see it. Then we can decide
what to do.
38 In all the twenty years that I've
worked for you, not one of your
sheep or goats has had a miscarriage, and I've never eaten even one
of your rams. 39 If a wild animal
killed one of your sheep or goats, I
paid for it myself. In fact, you demanded the full price, whether the
animal was killed during the day or
at night.[e] 40 I sweated every day, and
I couldn't sleep at night because of
the cold.
41 I had to work fourteen of these
twenty long years to earn your two
daughters and another six years to
buy your sheep and goats. During
that time you kept changing my
wages. 42 If the fearsome God[f] worshiped by Abraham and my father
Isaac had not been on my side, you
would have sent me away without a
thing. But God saw my hard work,
and he knew the trouble I was in, so
he helped me. Then last night he told
you how wrong you were.

Jacob and Laban Make an Agreement

43 Laban said to Jacob, "Leah and
Rachel are my daughters, and their children belong to me. All these sheep you
are taking are really mine too. In fact,
everything you have belongs to me. But
there is nothing I can do to keep my
daughters and their children. 44 So I am
ready to make an agreement with you,
and we will pile up some large rocks
here to remind us of the agreement."
45 After Jacob had set up a large rock,
46 he told his men to get some more
rocks and pile them up next to it. Then
Jacob and Laban ate a meal together
beside the rocks. 47 Laban named the
pile of rocks Jegar Sahadutha.[g] But Jacob named it Galeed.[h] 48 Laban said to
Jacob, "This pile of rocks will remind us
of our agreement." That's why the place
was named Galeed. 49 Laban also said,
"This pile of rocks means that the LORD
will watch us both while we are apart
from each other." So the place was also
named Mizpah.[i]
50 Then Laban said:
If you mistreat my daughters or
marry other women, I may not know

[d] **31.33** *two servant women*: Bilhah and Zilpah (see 30.4, 9). [e] **31.39** *you demanded . . . night*: A shepherd was not responsible for sheep and goats killed by wild animals, if the shepherd could supply proof of how they were killed. [f] **31.42** *fearsome God*: One possible meaning for the difficult Hebrew text. [g] **31.47** *Jegar Sahadutha*: In Aramaic "Jegar Sahadutha" means "a pile of rocks to remind us." [h] **31.47** *Galeed*: In Hebrew "Galeed" means "a pile of rocks to remind us." [i] **31.49** *Mizpah*: In Hebrew "Mizpah" sounds like "a place from which to watch."

about it, but remember, God is
watching us! 51-52Both this pile of
rocks and this large rock have been
set up between us as a reminder. I
must never go beyond them to attack you, and you must never go beyond them to attack me. 53My father
Nahor, your grandfather Abraham,
and their ancestors all worshiped
the same God, and he will make sure
that we each keep the agreement.
Then Jacob made a promise in the
name of the fearsome God[j] his father
Isaac had worshiped. 54Jacob killed an
animal and offered it as a sacrifice there
on the mountain, and he invited his men
to eat with him. After the meal they
spent the night on the mountain. 55Early
the next morning, Laban kissed his
daughters and his grandchildren good-
by, then he left to go back home.

Jacob Gets Ready To Meet Esau

32 As Jacob was on his way back
home, some of God's angels came
and met him. 2When Jacob saw them, he
said, "This is God's camp." So he named
the place Mahanaim.[k]
3Jacob sent messengers on ahead to
Esau, who lived in the land of Seir, also
known as Edom. 4Jacob told them to say
to Esau, "Master, I am your servant! I
have lived with Laban all this time, 5and
now I own cattle, donkeys, and sheep, as
well as many slaves. Master, I am sending these messengers in the hope that
you will be kind to me."
6When the messengers returned, they
told Jacob, "We went to your brother
Esau, and now he is heading this way
with four hundred men."
7Jacob was so frightened that he divided his people, sheep, cattle, and
camels into two groups. 8He thought, "If
Esau attacks one group, perhaps the
other can escape."
9Then Jacob prayed:
You, LORD, are the God who was
worshiped by my grandfather Abraham and by my father Isaac. You told
me to return home to my family, and
you promised to be with me and
make me successful. 10I don't deserve all the good things you have
done for me, your servant. When I
first crossed the Jordan, I had only
my walking stick, but now I have
two large groups of people and animals. 11Please rescue me from my
brother. I am afraid he will come
and attack not only me, but my
wives and children as well. 12But you
have promised that I would be a success and that someday it will be as
hard to count my descendants as it
is to count the stars in the sky.
13After Jacob had spent the night
there, he chose some animals as gifts
for Esau: 14-15two hundred female goats
and twenty males, two hundred female
sheep and twenty males, thirty female
camels with their young, forty cows and
ten bulls, and twenty female donkeys
and ten males.
16Jacob put servants in charge of each
herd and told them, "Go ahead of me
and keep a space between each herd."
17Then he said to the servant in charge
of the first herd, "When Esau meets you,
he will ask whose servant you are. He
will want to know where you are going
and who owns those animals in front of
you. 18So tell him, 'They belong to your
servant Jacob, who is coming this way.
He is sending them as a gift to his master Esau.' "
19Jacob also told the men in charge of
the second and third herds and those
who followed to say the same thing
when they met Esau. 20And Jacob told
them to be sure to say that he was right
behind them. Jacob hoped the gifts
would make Esau friendly, so Esau
would be glad to see him when they
met. 21Jacob's men took the gifts on
ahead of him, but he spent the night in
camp.

Jacob's Name Is Changed to Israel

22-23Jacob got up in the middle of the
night and took his wives, his eleven children, and everything he owned across to
the other side of the Jabbok River for
safety. 24Afterwards, Jacob went back
and spent the rest of the night alone.
A man came and fought with Jacob
until just before daybreak. 25When the
man saw that he could not win, he
struck Jacob on the hip and threw it out
of joint. 26They kept on wrestling until
the man said, "Let go of me! It's almost
daylight."
"You can't go until you bless me," Jacob replied.
27Then the man asked, "What is your
name?"
"Jacob," he answered.
28The man said, "Your name will no
longer be Jacob. You have wrestled with
God and with men, and you have won.
That's why your name will be Israel."[l]
29Jacob said, "Now tell me your name."
"Don't you know who I am?" he
asked. And he blessed Jacob.
30Jacob said, "I have seen God face to
face, and I am still alive." So he named
the place Peniel.[m] 31The sun was coming
up as Jacob was leaving Peniel. He was

[j]**31.53** *fearsome God*: See the note at 31.42. [k]**32.2** *Mahanaim*: In Hebrew "Mahanaim" means "two camps." [l]**32.28** *Israel*: In Hebrew one meaning of "Israel" is "a man who wrestles with God." [m]**32.30** *Peniel*: In Hebrew "Peniel" means "face of God."

limping because he had been struck on
the hip, 32and the muscle on his hip joint
had been injured. That's why even today
the people of Israel don't eat the hip
muscle of any animal.

Jacob Meets Esau

33 Later that day Jacob met Esau
coming with his four hundred
men. So Jacob had his children walk
with their mothers. 2The two servant
women, Zilpah and Bilhah, together
with their children went first, followed
by Leah and her children, then by
Rachel and Joseph. 3Jacob himself
walked in front of them all, bowing to
the ground seven times as he came near
his brother.

4But Esau ran toward Jacob and
hugged and kissed him. Then the two
brothers started crying.

5When Esau noticed the women and
children he asked, "Whose children are
these?"

Jacob answered, "These are the ones
the LORD has been kind enough to give
to me, your servant."

6Then the two servant women and
their children came and bowed down to
Esau. 7Next, Leah and her children
came and bowed down; finally, Joseph
and Rachel also came and bowed down.

8Esau asked Jacob, "What did you
mean by these herds I met along the
road?"

"Master," Jacob answered, "I sent them
so that you would be friendly to me."

9"But, brother, I already have plenty,"
Esau replied. "Keep them for yourself."

10"No!" Jacob said. "Please accept
these gifts as a sign of your friendship
for me. When you welcomed me and I
saw your face, it was like seeing the
face of God. 11Please accept these gifts I
brought to you. God has been good to
me, and I have everything I need." Jacob
kept insisting until Esau accepted the
gifts.

12"Let's get ready to travel," Esau said.
"I'll go along with you."

13But Jacob answered, "Master, you
know traveling is hard on children, and
I have to look after the sheep and goats
that are nursing their young. If my animals travel too much in one day, they
will all die. 14Why don't you go on
ahead and let me travel along slowly
with the children, the herds, and the
flocks. We can meet again in the country
of Edom."

15Esau replied, "Let me leave some of
my men with you."

"You don't have to do that," Jacob answered. "I am happy, simply knowing
that you are friendly to me."

16So Esau left for Edom. 17But Jacob
went to Succoth,[n] where he built a
house for himself and set up shelters for
his animals. That's why the place is
called Succoth.

Jacob Arrives at Shechem

18After leaving northern Syria,[o] Jacob
arrived safely at Shechem in Canaan
and set up camp outside the city. 19The
land where he camped was owned by
the descendants of Hamor, the father of
Shechem. So Jacob paid them one hundred pieces of silver[p] for the property,
20then he set up his tents and built an altar there to honor the God of Israel.

Dinah Is Raped

34 Dinah, the daughter of Jacob and
Leah, went to visit some of the
women who lived there. 2She was seen
by Hamor's son Shechem, the leader of
the Hivites, and he grabbed her and
raped her. 3But Shechem was attracted
to Dinah, so he told her how much he
loved her. 4He even asked his father to
get her for his wife.

5Meanwhile, Jacob heard what had
happened. But his sons were out in the
fields with the cattle, so he did not do
anything at the time. 6Hamor arrived at
Jacob's home 7just as Jacob's sons were
coming in from work. When they
learned that their sister had been raped,
they became furiously angry. Nothing is
more disgraceful than rape, and it
should not be tolerated in Israel.

8Hamor said to Jacob and his sons:

> My son Shechem really loves Di-
> nah. Please let him marry her. 9Why
> don't you start letting your families
> marry into our families and ours
> marry into yours? 10You can share
> this land with us. Move freely about
> until you find the property you want;
> then buy it and settle down here.

11Shechem added, "Do this favor for
me, and I'll give whatever you want.
12Ask anything, no matter how expensive. I'll do anything, just let me marry
Dinah."

13Jacob's sons wanted to get even
with Shechem and his father because of
what had happened to their sister. 14So
they tricked them by saying:

> You're not circumcised![q] It would
> be a disgrace for us to let you marry
> Dinah now. 15But we will let you
> marry her, if you and the other men
> in your tribe get circumcised. 16Then
> your families can marry into ours,

[n] **33.17** *Succoth*: In Hebrew "Succoth" means "shelters." [o] **33.18** *northern Syria*: See the note at 24.10. [p] **33.19** *pieces of silver*: Or "lambs" or "cattle." [q] **34.14** *You're not circumcised*: Israelite boys were circumcised when they were eight days old, and no uncircumcised man could be part of the people of Israel.

and ours can marry into yours, and
we can live together like one nation.
17But if you don't agree to get circumcised, we'll take Dinah and
leave this place.
18Hamor and Shechem liked what was
said. 19Shechem was the most respected
person in his family, and he was so in
love with Dinah that he hurried off to
get everything done. 20The two men met
with the other leaders of their city and
told them:
21These people really are friendly.
Why not let them move freely about
until they find the property they
want? There's enough land here for
them and for us. Then our families
can marry into theirs, and theirs can
marry into ours.
22We have to do only one thing before they will agree to stay here and
become one nation with us. Our men
will have to be circumcised like their
men. 23Just think! We'll get their
property, as well as their flocks and
herds. All we have to do is to agree,
and they will live here with us.
24Every grown man followed this advice and got circumcised.

Dinah's Brothers Take Revenge

25Three days later the men who had
been circumcised were still weak from
pain. So Simeon and Levi,[r] two of Dinah's brothers, attacked with their
swords and killed every man in town,
26including Hamor and Shechem. Then
they took Dinah and left. 27Jacob's other
sons came and took everything they
wanted. All this was done because of the
horrible thing that had happened to
their sister. 28They took sheep, goats,
donkeys, and everything else that was
in the town or the fields. 29After taking
everything of value from the houses,
they dragged away the wives and children of their victims.
30Jacob said to Simeon and Levi,
"Look what you've done! Now I'm in
real trouble with the Canaanites and
Perizzites who live around here. There
aren't many of us, and if they attack,
they'll kill everyone in my household."
31They answered, "Was it right to let
our own sister be treated that way?"

Jacob Returns to Bethel

35 God told Jacob, "Return to Bethel,
where I appeared to you when
you were running from your brother
Esau. Make your home there and build
an altar for me."
2Jacob said to his family and to everyone else who was traveling with him:
Get rid of your foreign gods! Then
make yourselves acceptable to worship God and put on clean clothes.
3Afterwards, we'll go to Bethel. I will
build an altar there for God, who answered my prayers when I was in
trouble and who has always been at
my side.
4So everyone gave Jacob their idols
and their earrings,[s] and he buried them
under the oak tree near Shechem.
5While Jacob and his family were
traveling through Canaan, God terrified
the people in the towns so much that no
one dared bother them. 6Finally, they
reached Bethel, also known as Luz. 7Ja-
cob built an altar there and called it
"God of Bethel," because that was the
place where God had appeared to him
when he was running from Esau. 8While
they were there, Rebekah's personal
servant Deborah[t] died. They buried her
under an oak tree and called it "Weeping Oak."

God Blesses Jacob at Bethel

9-11After Jacob came back to the land
of Canaan, God appeared to him again.
This time he gave Jacob a new name
and blessed him by saying:
I am God All-Powerful, and from
now on your name will be Israel[u] instead of Jacob. You will have many
children. Your descendants will become nations, and some of the men
in your family will even be kings. 12I
will give you the land that I
promised Abraham and Isaac, and it
will belong to your family forever.
13After God had gone, 14Jacob set up a
large rock, so that he would remember
what had happened there. Then he
poured wine and olive oil on the rock to
show that it was dedicated to God, 15and
he named the place Bethel.[v]

Benjamin Is Born

16Jacob and his family had left Bethel
and were still a long way from Ephrath,
when the time came for Rachel's baby
to be born. 17She was having a rough
time, but the woman who was helping
her said, "Don't worry! It's a boy."
18Rachel was at the point of death, and
right before dying, she said, "I'll name
him Benoni."[w] But Jacob called him
Benjamin.[x]
19Rachel was buried beside the road
to Ephrath, which is also called Bethlehem. 20Jacob set up a tombstone over

[r] **34.25** *Simeon and Levi*: Dinah's full brothers. [s] **35.4** *earrings*: These would have had symbols of foreign gods on them. [t] **35.8** *Deborah*: See 24.59 and the note there. [u] **35.9-11** *Israel*: See the note at 32.28. [v] **35.15** *Bethel*: See the note at 28.19. [w] **35.18** *Benoni*: In Hebrew "Benoni" means "Son of my Sorrow." [x] **35.18** *Benjamin*: In Hebrew "Benjamin" can mean "Son at my Right Side" (the place of power).

her grave, and it is still there. 21Jacob, also known as Israel, traveled to the south of Eder Tower, where he set up camp.

22During their time there, Jacob's oldest son Reuben slept with Bilhah, who was one of Jacob's other wives.[y] And Jacob found out about it.

Jacob's Twelve Sons

23-26Jacob had twelve sons while living in northern Syria.[z] His first-born Reuben was the son of Leah, who later gave birth to Simeon, Levi, Judah, Issachar, and Zebulun. Leah's servant Zilpah had two sons: Gad and Asher.

Jacob and his wife Rachel had Joseph and Benjamin. Rachel's servant woman Bilhah had two more sons: Dan and Naphtali.

Isaac Dies

27Jacob went to his father Isaac at Hebron, also called Mamre or Kiriath-Arba, where Isaac's father Abraham had lived as a foreigner. 28-29Isaac died at the ripe old age of one hundred eighty, then his sons Esau and Jacob buried him.

Esau's Family

36 Esau, also known as Edom, had many descendants. 2He married three Canaanite women: The first was Adah, the daughter of Elon the Hittite; the second was Oholibamah, the daughter of Anah and the granddaughter of Zibeon the Hivite; 3the third was Basemath, who was Ishmael's daughter and Nebaioth's sister.

4-5Esau and his three wives had five sons while in Canaan. Adah's son was Eliphaz; Basemath's son was Reuel; Oholibamah's three sons were Jeush, Jalam, and Korah.

6Esau took his children and wives, his relatives and servants, his animals and possessions he had gotten while in Canaan, and moved far from Jacob. 7He did this because the land was too crowded and could not support him and his brother with their flocks and herds. 8That's why Esau made his home in the hill country of Seir.

9-14Esau lived in the hill country of Seir and was the ancestor of the Edomites. Esau had three wives: Adah, Basemath, and Oholibamah. Here is a list of his descendants: Esau and Adah had a son named Eliphaz, whose sons were Teman, Omar, Zepho, Gatam, and Kenaz. Timna was the other wife[a] of Esau's son Eliphaz, and she had a son named Amalek.

Esau and Basemath had a son named Reuel, whose sons were Nahath, Zerah, Shammah, and Mizzah.

Esau and Oholibamah had three sons: Jeush, Jalam, and Korah.

Chiefs and Leaders in Edom

15Esau and Adah's oldest son was Eliphaz, and the clans that descended from him were Teman, Omar, Zepho, Kenaz, 16Korah, Gatam, and Amalek. These and Esau's other descendants lived in the land of Edom.

17The clans that descended from Esau and Basemath's son Reuel were Nahath, Zerah, Shammah, and Mizzah.

18The clans that descended from Esau and Oholibamah the daughter of Anah were Jeush, Jalam, and Korah. 19All of these clans descended from Esau, who was known as Edom.

20Seir was from the Horite tribe that had lived in Edom before the time of Esau. The clans that had descended from him were Lotan, Shobal, Zibeon, Anah, 21Dishon, Ezer, and Dishan.

22Lotan's sons were Hori and Heman; his sister was Timna.

23Shobal's sons were Alvan, Manahath, Ebal, Shepho, and Onam.

24Zibeon's sons were Aiah and Anah—the same Anah who found an oasis[b] in the desert while taking the donkeys of his father out to pasture.

25Anah's children were Dishon and Oholibamah.

26Dishon's sons were Hemdan, Eshban, Ithran, and Cheran.

27Ezer's sons were Bilhan, Zaavan, and Akan.

28Dishan's sons were Uz and Aran.

29The clans of the Horites were Lotan, Shobal, Zibeon, Anah, 30Dishon, Ezer, and Dishan, and they lived in the land of Seir.

31-39Before there were kings in Israel, the following kings ruled Edom one after another:

Bela son of Beor from Dinhabah;
Jobab son of Zerah from Bozrah;
Husham from the land of Teman;
Hadad son of Bedad from Avith
  (Bedad had defeated the Midianites
  in Moab);
Samlah from Masrekah;
Shaul from the city of Rehoboth on
  the Euphrates River;
Baal Hanan son of Achbor;
Hadar from the city of Pau (his wife
  Mehetabel was the daughter of
  Matred and the granddaughter of
  Mezahab).

[y]**35.22** *other wives*: See the note at 22.24. Bilhah had been Rachel's servant woman (see 29.28-30). [z]**35.23-26** *northern Syria*: See the note at 24.10. [a]**36.9-14** *other wife*: See the note at 22.24. [b]**36.24** *an oasis*: One possible meaning for the difficult Hebrew text.

40The clans that descended from Esau
took their names from their families and
the places where they lived. They are
Timna, Alvah, Jetheth, 41Oholibamah,
Elah, Pinon, 42Kenaz, Teman, Mibzar,
43Magdiel, and Iram. These clans descended from Esau, who was known as
Edom, the father of the Edomites. They
took their names from the places where
they settled.

Joseph and His Brothers

37 Jacob lived in the land of Canaan,
where his father Isaac had lived,
2and this is the story of his family.
When Jacob's son Joseph was seventeen years old, he took care of the sheep
with his brothers, the sons of Bilhah and
Zilpah.[c] But he was always telling his
father all sorts of bad things about his
brothers.
3Jacob loved Joseph more than he did
any of his other sons, because Joseph
was born after Jacob was very old. Jacob had given Joseph a fancy coat[d] 4to
show that he was his favorite son, and
so Joseph's brothers hated him and
would not be friendly to him.
5One day, Joseph told his brothers
what he had dreamed, and they hated
him even more. 6Joseph said, "Let me
tell you about my dream. 7We were out
in the field, tying up bundles of wheat.
Suddenly my bundle stood up, and your
bundles gathered around and bowed
down to it."
8His brothers asked, "Do you really
think you are going to be king and rule
over us?" Now they hated Joseph more
than ever because of what he had said
about his dream.
9Joseph later had another dream, and
he told his brothers, "Listen to what else
I dreamed. The sun, the moon, and
eleven stars bowed down to me."
10When he told his father about this
dream, his father became angry and
said, "What's that supposed to mean?
Are your mother and I and your brothers all going to come and bow down in
front of you?" 11Joseph's brothers were
jealous of him, but his father kept wondering about the dream.

Joseph Is Sold and Taken to Egypt

12One day when Joseph's brothers
had taken the sheep to a pasture near
Shechem, 13his father Jacob said to him,
"I want you to go to your brothers. They
are with the sheep near Shechem."
"Yes, sir," Joseph answered.
14His father said, "Go and find out how
your brothers and the sheep are doing.
Then come back and let me know." So
he sent him from Hebron Valley.
Joseph was near Shechem 15and wandering through the fields, when a man
asked, "What are you looking for?"
16Joseph answered, "I'm looking for
my brothers who are watching the
sheep. Can you tell me where they are?"
17"They're not here anymore," the
man replied. "I overheard them say they
were going to Dothan."
Joseph left and found his brothers in
Dothan. 18But before he got there, they
saw him coming and made plans to kill
him. 19They said to one another, "Look,
here comes the hero of those dreams!
20Let's kill him and throw him into a pit
and say that some wild animal ate him.
Then we'll see what happens to those
dreams."
21Reuben heard this and tried to protect Joseph from them. "Let's not kill
him," he said. 22"Don't murder him or
even harm him. Just throw him into a
dry well out here in the desert." Reuben
planned to rescue Joseph later and take
him back to his father.
23When Joseph came to his brothers,
they pulled off his fancy coat[d] 24and
threw him into a dry well.
25As Joseph's brothers sat down to
eat, they looked up and saw a caravan
of Ishmaelites coming from Gilead.
Their camels were loaded with all kinds
of spices that they were taking to Egypt.
26So Judah said, "What will we gain if
we kill our brother and hide his body?
27Let's sell him to the Ishmaelites and
not harm him. After all, he is our
brother." And the others agreed.
28When the Midianite merchants
came by, Joseph's brothers took him out
of the well, and for twenty pieces of silver they sold him to the Ishmaelites[e]
who took him to Egypt.
29When Reuben returned to the well
and did not find Joseph there, he tore
his clothes in sorrow. 30Then he went
back to his brothers and said, "The boy
is gone! What am I going to do?"
31Joseph's brothers killed a goat and
dipped Joseph's fancy coat in its blood.
32After this, they took the coat to their
father and said, "We found this! Look at
it carefully and see if it belongs to your
son."
33Jacob knew it was Joseph's coat and
said, "It's my son's coat! Joseph has

[c]**37.2** *Bilhah and Zilpah*: See 30.1-13. [d]**37.3** *fancy coat*: Or "a coat of many colors" or "a coat with long sleeves." [d]**37.23** *fancy coat*: Or "a coat of many colors" or "a coat with long sleeves." [e]**37.28** *Midianite . . . Ishmaelites*: According to 25.1, 2, 12 both the Midianites and the Ishmaelites were descendants of Abraham, and in Judges 8.22-24 the two names are used of the same people. It is possible that in this passage "Ishmaelite" has the meaning "nomadic traders," while "Midianite" refers to their ethnic origin.

been torn to pieces and eaten by some
wild animal."
34 Jacob mourned for Joseph a long
time, and to show his sorrow he tore his
clothes and wore sackcloth.[f] 35 All of Jacob's children came to comfort him, but
he refused to be comforted. "No," he
said, "I will go to my grave, mourning
for my son." So Jacob kept on grieving.
36 Meanwhile, the Midianites had sold
Joseph in Egypt to a man named
Potiphar, who was the king's[g] official in
charge of the palace guard.

Judah and Tamar

38 About that time Judah left his
brothers in the hill country and
went to live near his friend Hirah in the
town of Adullam. 2 While there he met
the daughter of Shua, a Canaanite man.
Judah married her, 3 and they had three
sons. He named the first one Er; 4 she
named the next one Onan. 5 The third
one was born when Judah was in
Chezib, and she named him Shelah.
6 Later, Judah chose Tamar as a wife
for Er, his oldest son. 7 But Er was very
evil, and the LORD took his life. 8 So Judah told Onan, "It's your duty to marry
Tamar and have a child for your
brother."[h]
9 Onan knew the child would not be
his,[i] and when he had sex with Tamar,
he made sure that she would not get
pregnant. 10 The LORD wasn't pleased
with Onan and took his life too.
11 Judah did not want the same thing
to happen to his son Shelah, and he told
Tamar, "Go home to your father and live
there as a widow until my son Shelah is
grown." So Tamar went to live with her
father.
12 Some years later Judah's wife died,
and he mourned for her. He then went
with his friend Hirah to the town of
Timnah, where his sheep were being sheared. 13 Tamar found out that her
father-in-law Judah was going to Timnah to shear his sheep. 14 She also realized that Shelah was now a grown man,
but she had not been allowed to marry
him. So she decided to dress in something other than her widow's clothes
and to cover her face with a veil. After
this, she sat outside the town of Enaim
on the road to Timnah.
15 When Judah came along, he did not
recognize her because of the veil. He
thought she was a prostitute 16 and
asked her to sleep with him. She asked,
"What will you give me if I do?"
17 "One of my young goats," he answered.
"What will you give me to keep until
you send the goat?" she asked.
18 "What do you want?" he asked in return.
"The ring on that cord around your
neck," was her reply. "I also want the
special walking stick[j] you have with
you." He gave them to her, they slept together, and she became pregnant.
19 After returning home, Tamar took
off the veil and dressed in her widow's
clothes again.
20 Judah had his friend Hirah take a
goat to the woman, so he could get back
the ring and walking stick, but she
wasn't there. 21 Hirah asked the people
of Enaim, "Where is the prostitute who
sat along the road outside your town?"
"There's never been one here," they
answered.
22 Hirah went back and told Judah, "I
couldn't find the woman, and the people
of Enaim said no prostitute had ever
been there."
23 "If you couldn't find her, we'll just let
her keep the things I gave her," Judah
answered. "And we'd better forget about
the goat, or else we'll look like fools."
24 About three months later someone
told Judah, "Your daughter-in-law Tamar
has behaved like a prostitute, and now
she's pregnant!"
"Drag her out of town and burn her to
death!" Judah shouted.
25 As Tamar was being dragged off, she
sent someone to tell her father-in-law,
"The man who gave me this ring, this
cord, and this walking stick is the one
who got me pregnant."
26 "Those are mine!" Judah admitted.
"She's a better person than I am, because I broke my promise to let her
marry my son Shelah." After this, Judah
never slept with her again.
27-28 Tamar later gave birth to twins.
But before either of them was born, one
of them stuck a hand out of her womb.
The woman who was helping tied a red
thread around the baby's hand and explained, "This one came out first."
29 Right away his hand went back in,

[f]**37.34** *sackcloth:* A rough dark-colored cloth made from goat ro camel hair and used to make grain sacks. It was worn in times of trouble or sorrow. [g]**37.36** *the king's*: See the note at 12.15. [h]**38.8** *It's your duty . . . child . . . brother*: If a man died without having children, his brother was to marry the dead man's wife and have a child, who was to be considered the child of the dead brother (see Deuteronomy 25.5,6). [i]**38.9** *the child . . . not be his*: When Judah died, Onan would get his dead brother's share of the inheritance, but if his dead brother had a son, the inheritance would go to him instead. [j]**38.18** *ring . . . walking stick*: The ring was shaped like a cylinder and could be rolled over soft clay as a way of sealing special documents. The walking stick was probably a symbol of power and the sign of leadership in the tribe, though it may have been a shepherd's rod.

and the other child was born first. The
woman then said, "What an opening
you've made for yourself!" So they
named the baby Perez.[k] 30When the
brother with the red thread came out,
they named him Zerah.[l]

Joseph and Potiphar's Wife

39 The Ishmaelites took Joseph to
Egypt and sold him to Potiphar,
the king's[m] official in charge of the
palace guard. 2-3So Joseph lived in the
home of Potiphar, his Egyptian owner.
Soon Potiphar realized that the LORD
was helping Joseph to be successful in
whatever he did. 4Potiphar liked Joseph
and made him his personal assistant,
putting him in charge of his house and
all of his property. 5Because of Joseph,
the LORD began to bless Potiphar's family and fields. 6Potiphar left everything
up to Joseph, and with Joseph there, the
only decision he had to make was what
he wanted to eat.

Joseph was well-built and handsome,
7and Potiphar's wife soon noticed him.
She asked him to make love to her, 8but
he refused and said, "My master isn't
worried about anything in his house, because he has placed me in charge of
everything he owns. 9No one in my master's house is more important than I am.
The only thing he hasn't given me is
you, and that's because you are his wife.
I won't sin against God by doing such a
terrible thing as this." 10She kept begging Joseph day after day, but he refused to do what she wanted or even to
go near her.

11One day, Joseph went to Potiphar's
house to do his work, and none of the
other servants were there. 12Potiphar's
wife grabbed hold of his coat and said,
"Make love to me!" Joseph ran out of
the house, leaving her hanging onto his
coat.

13When this happened, 14she called in
her servants and said, "Look! This Hebrew has come just to make fools of us.
He tried to rape me, but I screamed for
help. 15And when he heard me scream,
he ran out of the house, leaving his coat
with me."

16Potiphar's wife kept Joseph's coat
until her husband came home. 17Then
she said, "That Hebrew slave of yours
tried to rape me! 18But when I screamed
for help, he left his coat and ran out of
the house."

19Potiphar became very angry 20and
threw Joseph in the same prison where
the king's prisoners were kept.

While Joseph was in prison, 21the
LORD helped him and was good to him.
He even made the jailer like Joseph so
much that 22he put him in charge of the
other prisoners and of everything that
was done in the jail. 23The jailer did not
worry about anything, because the LORD
was with Joseph and made him successful in all that he did.

Joseph Tells the Meaning of the Prisoners' Dreams

40 1-3While Joseph was in prison,
both the king's[m] personal servant[n] and his chief cook made the king
angry. So he had them thrown into the
same prison with Joseph. 4They spent a
long time in prison, and Potiphar, the official in charge of the palace guard,
made Joseph their servant.

5One night each of the two men had a
dream, but their dreams had different
meanings. 6The next morning, when
Joseph went to see the men, he could
tell they were upset, 7and he asked,
"Why are you so worried today?"

8"We each had a dream last night,"
they answered, "and there is no one to
tell us what they mean."

Joseph replied, "Doesn't God know
the meaning of dreams? Now tell me
what you dreamed."

9The king's personal servant told
Joseph, "In my dream I saw a vine
10with three branches. As soon as it bud-
ded, it blossomed, and its grapes became ripe. 11I held the king's cup and
squeezed the grapes into it, then I gave
the cup to the king."

12Joseph said:

> This is the meaning of your
> dream. The three branches stand for
> three days, 13and in three days the
> king will pardon you. He will make
> you his personal servant again, and
> you will serve him his wine, just as
> you used to do. 14But when these
> good things happen, please don't
> forget to tell the king about me, so I
> can get out of this place. 15I was kid-
> napped from the land of the He-
> brews, and here in Egypt I haven't
> done anything to deserve being
> thrown in jail.

16When the chief cook saw that
Joseph had given a good meaning to the
dream, he told Joseph, "I also had a
dream. In it I was carrying three bread-
baskets stacked on top of my head.
17The top basket was full of all kinds of
baked things for the king, but birds
were eating them."

[k]**38.29** *Perez*: In Hebrew "Perez" sounds like "opening." [l]**38.30** *Zerah*: In Hebrew "Zerah" means "bright," probably referring to the red thread. [m]**39.1** *the king's*: See the note at 12.15. [m]**40.1-3** *the king's*: See the note at 12.15. [n]**40.1-3** *personal servant*: The Hebrew text has "cup bearer," an important and trusted official in the royal court, who personally served wine to the king.

18 Joseph said:
This is the meaning of your
dream. The three baskets are three
days, 19 and in three days the king
will cut off your head. He will hang
your body on a pole, and birds will
come and peck at it.
20 Three days later, while the king was
celebrating his birthday with a dinner
for his officials, he sent for his personal
servant and the chief cook. 21 He put the
personal servant back in his old job
22 and had the cook put to death.
Everything happened just as Joseph
had said it would, 23 but the king's personal servant completely forgot about
Joseph.

Joseph Interprets the King's Dreams

41 Two years later the king° of Egypt
dreamed he was standing beside
the Nile River. 2 Suddenly, seven fat,
healthy cows came up from the river
and started eating grass along the bank.
3 Then seven ugly, skinny cows came up
out of the river and 4 ate the fat, healthy
cows. When this happened, the king
woke up.
5 The king went back to sleep and had
another dream. This time seven full
heads of grain were growing on a single
stalk. 6 Later, seven other heads of grain
appeared, but they were thin and
scorched by the east wind. 7 The thin
heads of grain swallowed the seven full
heads. Again the king woke up, and it
had only been a dream.
8 The next morning the king was upset. So he called in his magicians and
wise men and told them what he had
dreamed. None of them could tell him
what the dreams meant.
9 The king's personal servant said:
Now I remember what I was supposed to do. 10 When you were angry
with me and your chief cook, you
threw us both in jail in the house of
the captain of the guard. 11 One night
we both had dreams, and each
dream had a different meaning. 12 A
young Hebrew, who was a servant of
the captain of the guard, was there
with us at the time. When we told
him our dreams, he explained what
each of them meant, 13 and everything happened just as he said it
would. I got my job back, and the
cook was put to death.
14 The king sent for Joseph, who was
quickly brought out of jail. He shaved,
changed his clothes, and went to the
king.
15 The king said to him, "I had a dream,
yet no one can explain what it means. I
am told that you can interpret dreams."
16 "Your Majesty," Joseph answered, "I
can't do it myself, but God can give a
good meaning to your dreams."
17 The king told Joseph:
I dreamed I was standing on the
bank of the Nile River. 18 I saw seven
fat, healthy cows come up out of the
river, and they began feeding on the
grass. 19 Next, seven skinny, bony
cows came up out of the river. I have
never seen such terrible looking
cows anywhere in Egypt. 20 The
skinny cows ate the fat ones. 21 But
you couldn't tell it, because these
skinny cows were just as skinny as
they were before. Right away, I woke
up.
22 I also dreamed that I saw seven
heads of grain growing on one stalk.
The heads were full and ripe. 23 Then
seven other heads of grain came up.
They were thin and scorched by a
wind from the desert. 24 These heads
of grain swallowed the full ones. I
told my dreams to the magicians,
but none of them could tell me the
meaning of the dreams.
25 Joseph replied:
Your Majesty, both of your dreams
mean the same thing, and in them
God has shown what he is going to
do. 26 The seven good cows stand for
seven years, and so do the seven
good heads of grain. 27 The seven
skinny, ugly cows that came up later
also stand for seven years, as do the
seven bad heads of grain that were
scorched by the east wind. The
dreams mean there will be seven
years when there won't be enough
grain.
28 It is just as I said—God has
shown what he intends to do. 29 For
seven years Egypt will have more
than enough grain, 30 but that will be
followed by seven years when there
won't be enough. The good years of
plenty will be forgotten, and everywhere in Egypt people will be starving. 31 The famine will be so bad that
no one will remember that once
there had been plenty. 32 God has
given you two dreams to let you
know that he has definitely decided
to do this and that he will do it soon.
33 Your Majesty, you should find
someone who is wise and will know
what to do, so that you can put him
in charge of all Egypt. 34 Then appoint some other officials to collect
one-fifth of every crop harvested in
Egypt during the seven years when
there is plenty. 35 Give them the
power to collect the grain during
those good years and to store it in

°**41.1** ***the king*****: See the note at 12.15.**

your cities. 36It can be stored until it
is needed during the seven years
when there won't be enough grain in
Egypt. This will keep the country
from being destroyed because of the
lack of food.

Joseph Is Made Governor over Egypt

37The king[o] and his officials liked this
plan. 38So the king said to them, "No
one could possibly handle this better
than Joseph, since the Spirit of God is
with him."
39The king told Joseph, "God is the
one who has shown you these things.
No one else is as wise as you are or
knows as much as you do. 40I'm putting
you in charge of my palace, and everybody will have to obey you. No one will
be over you except me. 41You are now
governor of all Egypt!"
42Then the king took off his royal ring
and put it on Joseph's finger. He gave
him fine clothes to wear and placed a
gold chain around his neck. 43He also let
him ride in the chariot next to his own,
and people shouted, "Make way for
Joseph!" So Joseph was governor of
Egypt.
44The king told Joseph, "Although I'm
king, no one in Egypt is to do anything
without your permission." 45He gave
Joseph the Egyptian name Zaphenath
Paneah. And he let him marry Asenath,
the daughter of Potiphera, a priest in the
city of Heliopolis.[p] Joseph traveled all
over Egypt.
46Joseph was thirty when the king
made him governor, and he went everywhere for the king. 47For seven years
there were big harvests of grain.
48Joseph collected and stored up the extra grain in the cities of Egypt near the
fields where it was harvested. 49In fact,
there was so much grain that they
stopped keeping record, because it was
like counting the grains of sand along
the beach.
50Joseph and his wife had two sons
before the famine began. 51Their first
son was named Manasseh, which
means, "God has let me forget all my
troubles and my family back home."
52His second son was named Ephraim,
which means "God has made me a success[q] in the land where I suffered."[r]
53Egypt's seven years of plenty came
to an end, 54and the seven years of
famine began, just as Joseph had said.
There was not enough food in other
countries, but all over Egypt there was
plenty. 55When the famine finally struck
Egypt, the people asked the king for
food, but he said, "Go to Joseph and do
what he tells you to do."
56The famine became bad everywhere
in Egypt, so Joseph opened the storehouses and sold the grain to the Egyptians. 57People from all over the world
came to Egypt, because the famine was
severe in their countries.

Joseph's Brothers Go to Egypt To Buy Grain

42 When Jacob found out there was
grain in Egypt, he said to his
sons, "Why are you just sitting here,
staring at one another? 2I have heard
there is grain in Egypt. Now go down
and buy some, so we won't starve to
death."
3Ten of Joseph's brothers went to
Egypt to buy grain. 4But Jacob did not
send Joseph's younger brother Benjamin with them; he was afraid that
something might happen to him. 5So Jacob's sons joined others from Canaan
who were going to Egypt because of the
terrible famine.
6Since Joseph was governor of Egypt
and in charge of selling grain, his brothers came to him and bowed with their
faces to the ground. 7-8They did not recognize Joseph, but right away he knew
who they were, though he pretended not
to know. Instead, he spoke harshly and
asked, "Where do you come from?"
"From the land of Canaan," they answered. "We've come here to buy grain."
9Joseph remembered what he had
dreamed about them and said, "You're
spies! You've come here to find out
where our country is weak."
10"No sir," they replied. "We're your
servants, and we have only come to buy
grain. 11We're honest men, and we come
from the same family—we're not spies."
12"That isn't so!" Joseph insisted.
"You've come here to find out where our
country is weak."
13But they explained, "Sir, we come
from a family of twelve brothers. The
youngest is still with our father in Canaan, and one of our brothers is dead."
14Joseph replied:

It's just like I said. You're spies,
15and I'm going to find out who you
really are. I swear by the life of the
king that you won't leave this place
until your youngest brother comes
here. 16Choose one of you to go after
your brother, while the rest of you
stay here in jail. That will show
whether you are telling the truth.
But if you are lying, I swear by the
life of the king that you are spies!

[o]41.37 *The king*: See the note at 12.15. [p]41.45 *Heliopolis*: The Hebrew text has "On," which is better known by its Greek name "Heliopolis." [q]41.52 *God has made me a success*: Or "God has given me children." [r]41.52 *Ephraim . . . suffered*: In Hebrew "Ephraim" actually means either "fertile land" or "pastureland."

[17]Joseph kept them all under guard
for three days, [18]before saying to them:
Since I respect God, I'll give you a
chance to save your lives. [19]If you
are honest men, one of you must
stay here in jail, and the rest of you
can take the grain back to your
starving families. [20]But you must
bring your youngest brother to me.
Then I'll know that you are telling
the truth, and you won't be put to
death.
Joseph's brothers agreed [21]and said to
one another, "We're being punished because of Joseph. We saw the trouble he
was in, but we refused to help him when
he begged us. That's why these terrible
things are happening."
[22]Reuben spoke up, "Didn't I tell you
not to harm the boy? But you wouldn't
listen, and now we have to pay the price
for killing him."
[23]They did not know that Joseph
could understand them, since he was
speaking through an interpreter. [24]Jo-
seph turned away from them and cried,
but soon he turned back and spoke to
them again. Then he had Simeon tied up
and taken away while they watched.

Joseph's Brothers Return to Canaan

[25]Joseph gave orders for his brothers'
grain sacks to be filled with grain and
for their money[s] to be put in their sacks.
He also gave orders for them to be given
food for their journey home. After this
was done, [26]they each loaded the grain
on their donkeys and left.
[27]When they stopped for the night,
one of them opened his sack to get some
grain for his donkey, and right away he
saw his moneybag. [28]"Here's my
money!" he told his brothers. "Right
here in my sack."
They were trembling with fear as they
stared at one another and asked themselves, "What has God done to us?"
[29]When they returned to the land of
Canaan, they told their father Jacob
everything that had happened to them:
[30]The governor of Egypt was rude
and treated us like spies. [31]But we
told him, "We're honest men, not
spies. [32]We come from a family of
twelve brothers. The youngest is still
with our father in Canaan, and the
other is dead."
[33]Then the governor of Egypt told
us, "I'll find out if you really are honest. Leave one of your brothers here
with me, while you take the grain to
your starving families. [34]But bring
your youngest brother to me, so I
can be certain that you are honest
men and not spies. After that, I'll let
your other brother go free, and you
can stay here and trade."
[35]When the brothers started emptying
their sacks of grain, they found their
moneybags in them. They were frightened, and so was their father Jacob,
[36]who said, "You have already taken my
sons Joseph and Simeon from me. And
now you want to take away Benjamin!
Everything is against me."
[37]Reuben spoke up, "Father, if I don't
bring Benjamin back, you can kill both
of my sons. Trust me with him, and I
will bring him back."
[38]But Jacob said, "I won't let my son
Benjamin go down to Egypt with the
rest of you. His brother is already dead,
and he is the only son I have left.[t] I am
an old man, and if anything happens to
him on the way, I'll die from sorrow, and
all of you will be to blame."

Joseph's Brothers Return to Egypt with Benjamin

43 The famine in Canaan got worse,
[2]until finally, Jacob's family had
eaten all the grain they had bought in
Egypt. So Jacob said to his sons, "Go
back and buy some more grain."
[3-5]Judah replied, "The governor
strictly warned us that we would not be
allowed to see him unless we brought
our youngest brother with us. If you let
us take Benjamin along, we will go and
buy grain. But we won't go without him!"
[6]Jacob asked, "Why did you cause me
so much trouble by telling the governor
you had another brother?"
[7]They answered, "He asked a lot of
questions about us and our family. He
wanted to know if you were still alive
and if we had any more brothers. All we
could do was answer his questions. How
could we know he would tell us to bring
along our brother?"
[8]Then Judah said to his father, "Let
Benjamin go with me, and we will leave
right away, so that none of us will starve
to death. [9]I promise to bring him back
safely, and if I don't, you can blame me
as long as I live. [10]If we had not wasted
all this time, we could already have
been there and back twice."
[11]Their father said:
If Benjamin must go with you,
take the governor a gift of some of
the best things from our own country, such as perfume, honey, spices,
pistachio nuts, and almonds.[u] [12]Also

[s]**42.25** *money*: Probably in the form of small pieces of silver and/or other precious or semi-precious metals; there were no coins or paper money at this time. [t]**42.38** *only son I have left*: Jacob had only two sons by Rachel, his favorite wife. [u]**43.11** *honey, spices, pistachio nuts, and almonds*: Some of these foods were still available in Canaan, but the main food was bread, and there was no grain to make bread.

take along twice the amount of
money for the grain, because there
must have been some mistake when
the money was put back in your
sacks. [13]Take Benjamin with you
and leave right away.
[14]When you go in to see the governor, I pray that God All-Powerful
will be good to you and that the governor will let your other brother and
Benjamin come back home with
you. If I must lose my children, I
suppose I must.
[15]The brothers took the gifts, twice the
amount of money, and Benjamin. Then
they hurried off to Egypt. When they
stood in front of Joseph, [16]he saw Benjamin and told the servant in charge of
his house, "Take these men to my house.
Slaughter an animal and cook it, so they
can eat with me at noon."
[17]The servant did as he was told and
took the brothers to Joseph's house.
[18]But on the way they got worried and
started thinking, "We are being taken
there because of the money that was put
back in our sacks last time. He will arrest us, make us his slaves, and take our
donkeys."
[19]So when they arrived at Joseph's
house, they said to the servant in
charge, [20]"Sir, we came to Egypt once
before to buy grain. [21]But when we
stopped for the night, we each found in
our grain sacks the exact amount we
had paid. We have brought that money
back, [22]together with enough money to
buy more grain. We don't know who put
the money in our sacks."
[23]"It's all right," the servant replied.
"Don't worry. The God you and your
father worship must have put the money
there, because I received your payment
in full." Then he brought Simeon out to
them.
[24]The servant took them into Joseph's
house and gave them water to wash
their feet. He also tended their donkeys.
[25]The brothers got their gifts ready to
give to Joseph at noon, since they had
heard they were going to eat there.
[26]When Joseph came home, they gave
him the gifts they had brought, and they
bowed down to him. [27]After Joseph had
asked how they were, he said, "What
about your elderly father? Is he still
alive?"
[28]They answered, "Your servant our
father is still alive and well." And again
they bowed down to Joseph.
[29]When Joseph looked around and
saw his brother Benjamin, he said, "This
must be your youngest brother, the one
you told me about. God bless you, my
son."
[30]Right away he rushed off to his
room and cried because of his love for
Benjamin. [31]After washing his face and
returning, he was able to control himself
and said, "Serve the meal!"
[32]Joseph was served at a table by himself, and his brothers were served at another. The Egyptians sat at yet another
table, because Egyptians felt it was disgusting to eat with Hebrews. [33]To the
surprise of Joseph's brothers, they were
seated in front of him according to their
ages, from the oldest to the youngest.
[34]They were served food from Joseph's
table, and Benjamin was given five
times as much as each of the others. So
Joseph's brothers drank with him and
had a good time.

The Missing Cup

44 [1-2]Later, Joseph told the servant
in charge of his house, "Fill the
men's grain sacks with as much as they
can hold and put their money in the
sacks. Also put my silver cup in the sack
of the youngest brother." The servant
did as he was told.
[3]Early the next morning, the men
were sent on their way with their donkeys. [4]But they had not gone far from
the city when Joseph told the servant,
"Go after those men! When you catch
them, say, 'My master has been good to
you. So why have you stolen his silver
cup? [5]Not only does he drink from his
cup, but he also uses it to learn about
the future. You have done a terrible
thing.' "
[6]When the servant caught up with
them, he said exactly what Joseph had
told him to say. [7]But they replied, "Sir,
why do you say such things? We would
never do anything like that! [8]We even
returned the money we found in our
grain sacks when we got back to
Canaan. So why would we want to steal
any silver or gold from your master's
house? [9]If you find that one of us has
the cup, then kill him, and the rest of us
will become your slaves."
[10]"Good!" the man replied, "I'll do
what you have said. But only the one
who has the cup will become my slave.
The rest of you can go free."
[11]Each of the brothers quickly put his
sack on the ground and opened it.
[12]Joseph's servant started searching the
sacks, beginning with the one that belonged to the oldest brother. When he
came to Benjamin's sack, he found the
cup. [13]This upset the brothers so much
that they began tearing their clothes in
sorrow. Then they loaded their donkeys
and returned to the city.
[14]When Judah and his brothers got
there, Joseph was still at home. So they
bowed down to Joseph, [15]who asked
them, "What have you done? Didn't you
know I could find out?"
[16]"Sir, what can we say?" Judah
replied. "How can we prove we are

innocent? God has shown that we are
guilty. And now all of us are your slaves,
especially the one who had the cup."
17Joseph told them, "I would never
punish all of you. Only the one who was
caught with the cup will become my
slave. The rest of you are free to go
home to your father."

Judah Pleads for Benjamin

18Judah went over to Joseph and said:
Sir, you have as much power as
the king[v] himself, and I am only
your slave. Please don't get angry if
I speak. 19You asked us if our father
was still alive and if we had any
more brothers. 20So we told you,
"Our father is a very old man. In
fact, he was already old when Benjamin was born. Benjamin's brother
is dead. Now Benjamin is the only
one of the two brothers who is still
alive, and our father loves him very
much."
21You ordered us to bring him
here, so you could see him for yourself. 22We told you that our father
would die if Benjamin left him. 23But
you warned us that we could never
see you again, unless our youngest
brother came with us. 24So we returned to our father and reported
what you had said.
25Later our father told us to come
back here and buy more grain. 26But
we answered, "We can't go back to
Egypt without our youngest brother.
We will never be let in to see the
governor, unless he is with us."
27Sir, our father then reminded us
that his favorite wife had given birth
to two sons. 28One of them was already missing and had not been
seen for a long time. My father
thinks the boy was torn to pieces by
some wild animal, 29and he said, "I
am an old man. If you take Benjamin from me, and something happens to him, I will die of a broken
heart."
30That's why Benjamin must be
with us when I go back to my father.
He loves him so much 31that he will
die if Benjamin doesn't come back
with me. 32I promised my father that
I would bring him safely home. If I
don't, I told my father he could
blame me the rest of my life.
33Sir, I am your slave. Please let
me stay here in place of Benjamin
and let him return home with his
brothers. 34How can I face my
father if Benjamin isn't with me? I
couldn't bear to see my father in
such sorrow.

Joseph Tells His Brothers Who He Is

45 Since Joseph could no longer
control his feelings in front of his
servants, he sent them out of the room.
When he was alone with his brothers,
he told them, "I am Joseph." 2Then he
cried so loudly that the Egyptians heard
him and told about it in the king's[v]
palace.
3Joseph asked his brothers if his
father was still alive, but they were too
frightened to answer. 4Joseph told them
to come closer to him, and when they
did, he said:
Yes, I am your brother Joseph, the
one you sold into Egypt. 5Don't
worry or blame yourselves for what
you did. God is the one who sent me
ahead of you to save lives.
6There has already been a famine
for two years, and for five more
years no one will plow fields or harvest grain. 7But God sent me on
ahead of you to keep your families
alive and to save you in this wonderful way. 8After all, you weren't really
the ones who sent me here—it was
God. He made me the highest official in the king's court and placed
me over all Egypt.
9Now hurry back and tell my
father that his son Joseph says, "God
has made me ruler of Egypt. Come
here as quickly as you can. 10You
will live near me in the region of
Goshen with your children and
grandchildren, as well as with your
sheep, goats, cattle, and everything
else you own. 11I will take care of
you there during the next five years
of famine. But if you don't come, you
and your family and your animals
will starve to death."
12All of you, including my brother
Benjamin, can tell by what I have
said that I really am Joseph. 13Tell
my father about my great power
here in Egypt and about everything
you have seen. Hurry and bring him
here.
14Joseph and Benjamin hugged each
other and started crying. 15Joseph was
still crying as he kissed each of his
other brothers. After this, they started
talking with Joseph.
16When it was told in the palace that
Joseph's brothers had come, the king
and his officials were happy. 17So the
king said to Joseph:
Tell your brothers to load their
donkeys and return to Canaan.
18Have them bring their father and
their families here. I will give them
the best land in Egypt, and they can
eat and enjoy everything that grows

[v]**44.18** *the king*: See the note at 12.15. [v]**45.2** *the king's*: See the note at 12.15.

on it. 19 Also tell your brothers to
take some wagons from Egypt for
their wives and children to ride in.
And be sure to have them bring their
father. 20 They can leave their possessions behind, because they will be
given the best of everything in
Egypt.
21 Jacob's sons agreed to do what the
king had said. And Joseph gave them
wagons and food for their trip home,
just as the king had ordered. 22 Joseph
gave some new clothes to each of his
brothers, but to Benjamin he gave five
new outfits and three hundred pieces of
silver. 23 To his father he sent ten donkeys loaded with the best things in
Egypt, and ten other donkeys loaded
with grain and bread and other food for
the return trip. 24 Then he sent his brothers off and told them, "Don't argue on
the way home!"
25 Joseph's brothers left Egypt, and
when they arrived in Canaan, 26 they
told their father that Joseph was still
alive and was the ruler of Egypt. But
their father was so surprised that he
could not believe them. 27 Then they told
him everything Joseph had said. When
he saw the wagons Joseph had sent, he
felt much better 28 and said, "Now I can
believe you! My son Joseph must really
be alive, and I will get to see him before
I die."

Jacob and His Family Go to Egypt

46 Jacob packed up everything he
owned and left for Egypt. On the
way he stopped near the town of Beersheba and offered sacrifices to the God
his father Isaac had worshiped. 2 That
night, God spoke to him and said, "Jacob! Jacob!"
"Here I am," Jacob answered.
3 God said, "I am God, the same God
your father worshiped. Don't be afraid
to go to Egypt. I will give you so many
descendants that one day they will become a nation. 4 I will go with you to
Egypt, and later I will bring your descendants back here. Your son Joseph
will be at your side when you die."
5-7 Jacob and his family set out from
Beersheba and headed for Egypt. His
sons put him in the wagon that the
king[v] had sent for him, and they put
their small children and their wives in
the other wagons. Jacob's whole family
went to Egypt, including his sons, his
grandsons, his daughters, and his
granddaughters. They took along their
animals and everything else they
owned.
8-15 When Jacob went to Egypt, his
children who were born in northern
Syria[w] also went along with their families.
Jacob and his wife Leah had a total of
thirty-three children, grandchildren, and
great-grandchildren, but two of their
grandchildren had died in Canaan.
Their oldest son Reuben took his
sons Hanoch, Pallu, Hezron, and
Carmi.
Their son Simeon took his sons
Jemuel, Jamin, Ohad, Jachin, Zohar,
and Shaul, whose mother was a
Canaanite.
Their son Levi took his sons Ger-
shon, Kohath, and Merari.
Their son Judah took his sons
Shelah, Perez, and Zerah. Judah's
sons Er and Onan had died in
Canaan. Judah's son Perez took his
sons Hezron and Hamul.
Their son Issachar took his sons
Tola, Puvah, Jashub,[x] and Shimron.
Their son Zebulun took his sons
Sered, Elon, and Jahleel.
Their daughter Dinah also went.
16-18 Jacob and Zilpah, the servant
woman Laban had given his daughter
Leah, had a total of sixteen children,
grandchildren, and great-grandchildren.
Their son Gad took his sons
Ziphion, Haggi, Shuni, Ezbon, Eri,
Arodi, and Areli.
Their son Asher took his sons Im-
nah, Ishvah, Ishvi, and Beriah, who
took his sons, Heber and Malchiel.
Serah, the daughter of Asher, also
went.
19-22 Jacob and Rachel had fourteen
children and grandchildren.
Their son Joseph was already in
Egypt, where he had married Asenath, daughter of Potiphera, the
priest of Heliopolis.[y] Joseph and Asenath had two sons, Manasseh and
Ephraim.
Jacob and Rachel's son Benjamin
took his sons Bela, Becher, Ashbel,
Gera, Naaman, Ehi, Rosh, Muppim,
Huppim, and Ard.
23-25 Jacob and Bilhah, the servant
woman Laban had given his daughter
Rachel, had seven children and grandchildren.
Their son Dan took his son Hushim.
Their son Naphtali took his sons
Jahzeel, Guni, Jezer, and Shillem.
26 Sixty-six members of Jacob's family
went to Egypt with him, not counting
his daughters-in-law. 27 Jacob's two
grandsons who were born there made it
a total of seventy members of Jacob's
family in Egypt.

[v] **46.5-7** *the king*: See the note at 12.15. [w] **46.8-15** *northern Syria*: See the note at 24.10.
[x] **46.8-15** *Jashub*: The Samaritan Hebrew Text and one ancient translation; the Standard
Hebrew Text "Iob." [y] **46.19-22** *Heliopolis*: See the note at 41.45.

28 Jacob had sent his son Judah ahead
of him to ask Joseph to meet them in
Goshen. 29 So Joseph got in his chariot
and went to meet his father. When they
met, Joseph hugged his father around
the neck and cried for a long time. 30 Jacob said to Joseph, "Now that I have
seen you and know you are still alive, I
am ready to die."

31 Then Joseph said to his brothers and
to everyone who had come with them:

> I must go and tell the king[z] that
> you have arrived from Canaan. 32 I
> will tell him that you are shepherds
> and that you have brought your
> sheep, goats, cattle, and everything
> else you own. 33 The king will call
> you in and ask what you do for a liv-
> ing. 34 When he does, be sure to say,
> "We are shepherds. Our families
> have always raised sheep." If you tell
> him this, he will let you settle in the
> region of Goshen.

Joseph wanted them to say this to the
king, because the Egyptians did not like
to be around anyone who raised sheep.

47 1-2 Joseph took five of his brothers
to the king and told him, "My
father and my brothers have come from
Canaan. They have brought their sheep,
goats, cattle, and everything else they
own to the region of Goshen."

Then he introduced his brothers to the
king, 3 who asked them, "What do you
do for a living?"

"Sir, we are shepherds," was their answer. "Our families have always raised
sheep. 4 But in our country all the pastures are dried up, and our sheep have
no grass to eat. So we, your servants,
have come here. Please let us live in the
region of Goshen."

5 The king said to Joseph, "It's good
that your father and brothers have arrived. 6 I will let them live anywhere they
choose in the land of Egypt, but I suggest that they settle in Goshen, the best
part of our land. I would also like for
your finest shepherds to watch after my
own sheep and goats."

7 Then Joseph brought his father Jacob and introduced him to the king. Jacob gave the king his blessing, 8 and the
king asked him, "How old are you?"

9 Jacob answered, "I have lived only a
hundred thirty years, and I have had to
move from place to place. My parents
and my grandparents also had to move
from place to place. But they lived much
longer, and their life was not as hard as
mine." 10 Then Jacob gave the king his
blessing once again and left. 11 Joseph
obeyed the king's orders and gave his
father and brothers some of the best
land in Egypt near the city of Rameses.
12 Joseph also provided food for their
families.

A Famine in Egypt

13 The famine was bad everywhere in
Egypt and Canaan, and the people were
suffering terribly. 14 So Joseph sold them
the grain that had been stored up, and
he put the money[a] in the king's treasury. 15 But when everyone had run out
of money, the Egyptians came to Joseph
and demanded, "Give us more grain! If
you don't, we'll soon be dead, because
our money's all gone."

16 "If you don't have any money,"
Joseph answered, "give me your animals, and I'll let you have some grain."
17 From then on, they brought him their
horses and donkeys and their sheep and
goats in exchange for grain.

Within a year Joseph had collected
every animal in Egypt. 18 Then the people came to him and said:

> Sir, there's no way we can hide the
> truth from you. We are broke, and
> we don't have any more animals. We
> have nothing left except ourselves
> and our land. 19 Don't let us starve
> and our land be ruined. If you'll give
> us grain to eat and seed to plant,
> we'll sell ourselves and our land to
> the king.[b] We'll become his slaves.

20 The famine became so severe that
Joseph finally bought every piece of
land in Egypt for the king 21 and made
everyone the king's slaves,[c] 22 except
the priests. The king gave the priests a
regular food allowance, so they did not
have to sell their land. 23 Then Joseph
said to the people, "You and your land
now belong to the king. I'm giving you
seed to plant, 24 but one-fifth of your
crops must go to the king. You can keep
the rest as seed or as food for your families."

25 "Sir, you have saved our lives!" they
answered. "We are glad to be slaves of
the king." 26 Then Joseph made a law
that one-fifth of the harvest would always belong to the king. Only the
priests did not lose their land.

Jacob Becomes an Old Man

27 The people of Israel made their
home in the land of Goshen, where they
became prosperous and had large families. 28 Jacob himself lived there for seventeen years, before dying at the age of
one hundred forty-seven. 29 When Jacob
knew he did not have long to live, he
called in Joseph and said, "If you really
love me, you must make a solemn
promise not to bury me in Egypt. 30 In-

[z] **46.31** *the king*: See the note at 12.15. [a] **47.14** *money*: See the note at 42.25. [b] **47.19** *the king*: See the note at 12.15. [c] **47.21** *made . . . slaves*: One ancient translation and the Samaritan Hebrew Text; the Standard Hebrew Text "made everyone move to the cities."

stead, bury me in the place where my
ancestors are buried."
"I will do what you have asked,"
Joseph answered.
31 "Will you give me your word?" Jacob
asked.
"Yes, I will," Joseph promised. After
this, Jacob bowed down and prayed at
the head of his bed.

Jacob Blesses Joseph's Two Sons

48 Joseph was told that his father
Jacob had become very sick. So
Joseph went to see him and took along
his two sons, Manasseh and Ephraim.
2 When Joseph arrived, someone told Jacob, "Your son Joseph has come to see
you." Jacob sat up in bed, but it took almost all his strength.
3 Jacob told Joseph:
God All-Powerful appeared to me
at Luz in the land of Canaan, where
he gave me his blessing 4 and
promised, "I will give you a large
family with many descendants that
will grow into a nation. And I am
giving you this land that will belong
to you and your family forever."
5 Then Jacob went on to say:
Joseph, your two sons Ephraim
and Manasseh were born in Egypt,
but I accept them as my own, just as
Reuben and Simeon are mine. 6 Any
children you have later will be considered yours, but their inheritance
will come from Ephraim and Manasseh. 7 Unfortunately, your mother
Rachel died in Canaan after we had
left northern Syria[d] and before we
reached Bethlehem.[e] And I had to
bury her along the way.
8-10 Jacob was very old and almost
blind. He did not recognize the two
boys, and so he asked Joseph, "Who are
these boys?"
Joseph answered, "They are my sons.
God has given them to me here in
Egypt."
"Bring them to me," Jacob said. "I
want to give them my blessing." Joseph
brought the boys to him, and he hugged
and kissed them.
11 Jacob turned to Joseph and told
him, "For many years I thought you
were dead and that I would never see
you again. But now God has even let me
live to see your children." 12 Then Joseph
made his sons move away from Jacob's
knees,[f] and Joseph bowed down in front
of him with his face to the ground.
13 After Joseph got up, he brought his
two sons over to Jacob again. He led his
younger son Ephraim to the left side of
Jacob and his older son Manasseh to
the right. 14 But before Jacob gave them
his blessing, he crossed his arms,
putting his right hand on the head of
Ephraim and his left hand on the head
of Manasseh. 15 Then he gave Joseph his
blessing and said:
My grandfather Abraham and my
father Isaac worshiped the LORD
God. He has been with me all my
life, 16 and his angel has kept me
safe. Now I pray that he will bless
these boys and that my name and
the names of Abraham and Isaac
will live on because of them. I ask
God to give them many children and
many descendants as well.
17 Joseph did not like it when he saw
his father place his right hand on the
head of the younger son. So he tried to
move his father's right hand from
Ephraim's head and place it on Manasseh. 18 Joseph said, "Father, you have
made a mistake. This is the older boy.
Put your right hand on him."
19 But his father said, "Son, I know
what I am doing. It's true that Manasseh's family will someday become a
great nation. But Ephraim will be even
greater than Manasseh, because his descendants will become many great nations."
20 Jacob told him that in the future the
people of Israel would ask God's blessings on one another by saying, "I pray
for God to bless you as much as he
blessed Ephraim and Manasseh." Jacob
put Ephraim's name first to show that
he would be greater than Manasseh.
21 After that, Jacob said, "Joseph, you
can see that I won't live much longer.
But God will be with you and will lead
you back to the land he promised our
family long ago. 22 Meanwhile, I'm giving you the hillside[g] I captured from the
Amorites."

Jacob Blesses His Sons

49 *1 Jacob called his sons together
and said:

My sons, I am Jacob,
your father Israel.
2 Come, gather around,
as I tell your future.

3 Reuben, you are my oldest,
born at the peak of my powers;
you were an honored leader.
4 Uncontrollable as a flood,
you slept with my wife
and disgraced my bed.
And so you no longer deserve
the place of honor.

[d]48.7 *northern Syria*: See the note at 24.10. [e]48.7 *Bethlehem*: The Hebrew text has "Ephrath, that is, Bethlehem." [f]48.12 *move . . . Jacob's knees*: The two boys were placed either on or between Jacob's knees, as a sign that he had accepted them as his sons.
[g]48.22 *the hillside*: Or "a larger share than your brothers, the land."

5 Simeon and Levi,
you are brothers,
each a gruesome sword.
6 I never want to take part
in your plans or deeds.
You slaughtered people
in your anger,
and you crippled cattle
for no reason.
7 Now I place a curse on you
because of
your fierce anger.
Your descendants
will be scattered
among the tribes of Israel.

8 Judah, you will be praised
by your brothers;
they will bow down to you,
as you defeat your enemies.
9 My son, you are a lion
ready to eat your victim!
You are terribly fierce;
no one will bother you.
10 You will have power and rule
until nations obey you[h]
and come bringing gifts.
11 You will tie your donkey
to a choice grapevine
and wash your clothes
in wine from those grapes.
12 Your eyes are darker than wine,
your teeth whiter than milk.

13 Zebulun, you will settle
along the seashore
and provide safe harbors
as far north as Sidon.

14 Issachar, you are a strong donkey
resting in the meadows.[i]
15 You found them so pleasant
that you worked too hard
and became a slave.

16 Dan,[j] you are the tribe
that will bring justice
to Israel.
17 You are a snake that bites
the heel of a horse,
making its rider fall.

18 Our LORD, I am waiting
for you to save us.

19 Gad,[k] you will be attacked,
then attack your attackers.

20 Asher, you will eat food
fancy enough for a king.

21 Naphtali, you are a wild deer
with lovely fawns.[l]

22 Joseph, you are a fruitful vine
growing near a stream
and climbing a wall.[m]
23 Enemies attacked with arrows,
refusing to show mercy.
24 But you stood your ground,
swiftly shooting back
with the help of Jacob's God,
the All-Powerful One—
his name is the Shepherd,
Israel's mighty rock.[n]
25 Your help came from the God
your father worshiped,
from God All-Powerful.
God will bless you with rain
and streams from the earth;
he will bless you
with many descendants.
26 My son, the blessings I give
are better than the promise
of ancient mountains
or eternal hills.[o]
Joseph, I pray these blessings
will come to you,
because you are the leader
of your brothers.

27 Benjamin, you are a fierce wolf,
destroying your enemies
morning and evening.

28These are the twelve tribes of Israel,
and this is how Jacob gave each of them
their proper blessings.

Jacob's Death

29-31Jacob told his sons:
Soon I will die, and I want you to
bury me in Machpelah Cave. Abraham bought this cave as a burial
place from Ephron the Hittite, and it
is near the town of Mamre in
Canaan. Abraham and Sarah are
buried there, and so are Isaac and
Rebekah. I buried Leah there too.
32Both the cave and the land that
goes with it were bought from the
Hittites.
33When Jacob had finished giving
these instructions to his sons, he lay
50 down on his bed and died. 1Jo-
seph started crying, then leaned
over to hug and kiss his father.

[h]49.10 *until . . . you*: One possible meaning for the difficult Hebrew text. [i]49.14 *resting . . . meadows*: One possible meaning for the difficult Hebrew text. [j]49.16 *Dan*: In Hebrew "Dan" means "justice" or "judgment." [k]49.19 *Gad*: In Hebrew "Gad" sounds like "attack." [l]49.21 *with lovely fawns*: Or "speaking lovely words." [m]49.22 *wall*: One possible meaning for the difficult Hebrew text. [n]49.24 *mighty rock*: The Hebrew text has "rock," which is sometimes used in poetry to compare the LORD to a mountain where his people can run for protection from their enemies. [o]49.26 *eternal hills*: One possible meaning for the difficult Hebrew text.

2Joseph gave orders for Jacob's body
to be embalmed, 3and it took the usual
forty days.
The Egyptians mourned seventy days
for Jacob. 4When the time of mourning
was over, Joseph said to the Egyptian
leaders, "If you consider me your friend,
please speak to the king[p] for me. 5Just
before my father died, he made me
promise to bury him in his burial cave
in Canaan. If the king will give me permission to go, I will come back here."
6The king answered, "Go to Canaan
and keep your promise to your father."
7-9When Joseph left Goshen with his
brothers, his relatives, and his father's
relatives to bury Jacob, many of the
king's highest officials and even his military chariots and cavalry went along.
The Israelites left behind only their children, their cattle, and their sheep and
goats.
10After crossing the Jordan River and
reaching Atad's threshing place, Joseph
had everyone mourn and weep seven
days for his father. 11The Canaanites
saw this and said, "The Egyptians are in
great sorrow." Then they named the
place "Egypt in Sorrow."[q]
12So Jacob's sons did just as their
father had instructed. 13They took him
to Canaan and buried him in Machpelah
Cave, the burial place Abraham had
bought from Ephron the Hittite.
14After the funeral, Joseph, his brothers, and everyone else returned to
Egypt.

Joseph's Promise to His Brothers

15After Jacob died, Joseph's brothers
said to each other, "What if Joseph still
hates us and wants to get even with us
for all the cruel things we did to him?"
16So they sent this message to Joseph:

> Before our father died, 17he told
> us, "You did some cruel and terrible
> things to Joseph, but you must ask
> him to forgive you."
> Now we ask you to please forgive
> the terrible things we did. After all,
> we serve the same God that your
> father worshiped.

When Joseph heard this, he started
crying.
18Right then, Joseph's brothers came
and bowed down to the ground in front
of him and said, "We are your slaves."
19But Joseph told them, "Don't be
afraid! I have no right to change what
God has decided. 20You tried to harm
me, but God made it turn out for the
best, so that he could save all these people, as he is now doing. 21Don't be
afraid! I will take care of you and your
children." After Joseph said this, his
brothers felt much better.

Joseph's Death

22Joseph lived in Egypt with his brothers until he died at the age of one hundred ten. 23Joseph lived long enough
to see Ephraim's children and grandchildren. He also lived to see the children of Manasseh's son Machir, and he
welcomed them into his family. 24Before
Joseph died, he told his brothers, "I
won't live much longer. But God will
take care of you and lead you out
of Egypt to the land he promised
Abraham, Isaac, and Jacob. 25Now
promise me that you will take my body
with you when God leads you to that
land."
26So Joseph died in Egypt at the age
of one hundred ten; his body was embalmed and put in a coffin.

[p]**50.4** *the king*: See the note at 12.15.

[q]**50.11** *Egypt in Sorrow*: Or "Abel-Mizraim."

EXODUS

ABOUT THIS BOOK

The title "Exodus" comes from a Greek word meaning "going out," and this book tells how the Lord set his people Israel free from slavery and brought them out of Egypt.

The book of Exodus teaches that the Lord is the one true God and the ruler of all creation. And when the Lord decides to do something, no one can stop him.

Exodus can be divided into three parts. Most of the events in the first part (1–13) take place in Egypt, where the people of Israel had been made slaves by the king. The Lord heard their cries for help and chose Moses to set them free. Moses was an Israelite who had been adopted by an Egyptian princess.

When Moses demanded that the Israelites be set free, the king refused. And so the Lord told Moses to bring ten disasters on Egypt. These disasters have often been called "the ten plagues." Finally, the king let the Israelites leave Egypt.

The second part of the book (14–18) includes events that happened while the people of Israel were on their way to Mount Sinai, God's holy mountain. The king of Egypt quickly changed his mind about setting them free, and he ordered his army to capture them. But the Lord protected Israel and destroyed the Egyptian army. Then, as the Israelites traveled through the desert, the Lord provided food and water for them.

The final part of Exodus (19–40) takes place at Mount Sinai, where the Lord appeared to Moses. The Lord gave him the Ten Commandments, as well as laws for worship, sacrifice, and everyday life, and instructions on making the sacred tent and its furnishings, the altars, and the priestly clothes. But this part also tells how the people made an idol and disobeyed the first of the Ten Commandments:

I am the LORD *your God, the one who brought you out of Egypt where you were slaves.*
Do not worship any god except me. *(20.2, 3)*

A QUICK LOOK AT THIS BOOK

The People of Israel Become Slaves (1.1-22)
Moses Is Born and Grows Up (2.1-25)
God Sends Moses To Speak to the King of Egypt (3.1—6.30)
The First Nine Disasters (7.1—10.29)
The Last Disaster and the First Passover (11.1—13.22)
The People Cross the Red Sea (14.1—15.21)
Moses Leads the People to Mount Sinai (15.22—18.27)
The Ten Commandments and Other Laws (19.1—24.18)
Instructions for the Sacred Tent, Its Furnishings, and the Sacred Chest (25.1—27.21)
Instructions for the Priests, Sacrifices, and the Sabbath (28.1—31.18)
The People Make an Idol (32.1-35)
The Lord Makes Promises, Renews His Agreement, and Gives More Laws to Israel (33.1—35.3)
Offerings and Gifts for the Sacred Tent and the Priestly Clothes (35.4—36.7)
Skilled Workers Make the Sacred Tent and Its Furnishings (36.8—38.31)
The Priestly Clothes Are Made (39.1-31)
The Sacred Tent Is Set Up (39.32—40.38)

The People of Israel Suffer

1 1-5When Jacob went to Egypt, his
son Joseph was already there. So
Jacob took his eleven other sons and
their families. They were: Reuben,
Simeon, Levi, Judah, Issachar, Zebulun,
Benjamin, Dan, Naphtali, Gad, and
Asher. Altogether, Jacob had seventy
children, grandchildren, and great-
grandchildren[a] who went with him.
6After Joseph, his brothers, and everyone else in that generation had died,
7the people of Israel became so numerous that the whole region of Goshen
was full of them.
8Many years later a new king came to
power. He did not know what Joseph
had done for Egypt, 9and he told the
Egyptians:

> There are too many of those Is-
> raelites in our country, and they are
> becoming more powerful than we
> are. 10If we don't outsmart them,
> their families will keep growing
> larger. And if our country goes to
> war, they could easily fight on the
> side of our enemies and escape from
> Egypt.

11The Egyptians put slave bosses in
charge of the people of Israel and tried
to wear them down with hard work.
Those bosses forced them to build the
cities of Pithom and Rameses,[b] where
the king[c] could store his supplies. 12But
even though the Israelites were mistreated, their families grew larger, and
they took over more land. Because of
this, the Egyptians hated them worse
than before 13and made them work so
hard 14that their lives were miserable.
The Egyptians were cruel to the people
of Israel and forced them to make
bricks and to mix mortar and to work in
the fields.
15Finally, the king called in Shiphrah
and Puah, the two women who helped
the Hebrew[d] mothers when they gave
birth. 16He told them, "If a Hebrew
woman gives birth to a girl, let the child
live. If the baby is a boy, kill him!"
17But the two women were faithful to
God and did not kill the boys, even
though the king had told them to. 18The
king called them in again and asked,
"Why are you letting those baby boys
live?"
19They answered, "Hebrew women
have their babies much quicker than
Egyptian women. By the time we arrive,
their babies are already born." 20-21God
was good to the two women because
they truly respected him, and he blessed
them with children of their own.
The Hebrews kept increasing 22until
finally, the king gave a command to
everyone in the nation, "As soon as a
Hebrew boy is born, throw him into the
Nile River! But you can let the girls
live."

Moses Is Born

2 A man from the Levi tribe married a
woman from the same tribe, 2and
she later had a baby boy. He was a
beautiful child, and she kept him inside
for three months. 3But when she could
no longer keep him hidden, she made a
basket out of reeds and covered it with
tar. She put him in the basket and
placed it in the tall grass along the edge
of the Nile River. 4The baby's older sister[e] stood off at a distance to see what
would happen to him.
5About that time one of the king's[f]
daughters came down to take a bath in
the river, while her servant women
walked along the river bank. She saw
the basket in the tall grass and sent one
of the young women to pull it out of the
water. 6When the king's daughter
opened the basket, she saw the baby
and felt sorry for him because he was
crying. She said, "This must be one of
the Hebrew babies."
7At once the baby's older sister came
up and asked, "Do you want me to get a
Hebrew woman to take care of the baby
for you?"
8"Yes," the king's daughter answered.
So the girl brought the baby's mother,
9and the king's daughter told her, "Take
care of this child, and I will pay you."
The baby's mother carried him home
and took care of him. 10And when he
was old enough, she took him to the
king's daughter, who adopted him. She
named him Moses[g] because she said, "I
pulled him out of the water."

Moses Escapes from Egypt

11After Moses had grown up, he went
out to where his own people were hard
at work, and he saw an Egyptian beating one of them. 12Moses looked around
to see if anyone was watching, then he
killed the Egyptian and hid his body in
the sand.

[a]**1.1-5** *seventy children . . . great-grandchildren*: See Genesis 46.8-27. [b]**1.11** *Pithom and Rameses*: This is the only mention of Pithom in the Bible; its exact location is unknown, though it was probably in the northern Delta of Egypt. Rameses is the famous Delta city that was the home of Rameses II; its exact location is also unknown. [c]**1.11** *the king*: The Hebrew text has "Pharaoh," a Hebrew word sometimes used for the title of the king of Egypt. [d]**1.15** *Hebrew*: An earlier term for "Israelite." [e]**2.4** *older sister*: Miriam, the sister of Moses and Aaron. [f]**2.5** *the king's*: See the note at 1.11. [g]**2.10** *Moses*: In Hebrew "Moses" sounds like "pull out."

13When Moses went out the next day,
he saw two Hebrews fighting. So he
went to the man who had started the
fight and asked, "Why are you beating
up one of your own people?"
14The man answered, "Who put you in
charge of us and made you our judge?
Are you planning to kill me, just as you
killed that Egyptian?"
This frightened Moses because he was
sure that people must have found out
what had happened. 15When the king[h]
heard what Moses had done, the king
wanted to kill him. But Moses escaped
and went to the land of Midian.
One day, Moses was sitting there by a
well, 16when the seven daughters of
Jethro, the priest of Midian,[i] came up to
water their father's sheep and goats.
17Some shepherds tried to chase them
away, but Moses came to their rescue
and watered their animals. 18When
Jethro's daughters returned home, their
father asked, "Why have you come back
so early today?"
19They answered, "An Egyptian rescued us from the shepherds, and he
even watered our sheep and goats."
20"Where is he?" Jethro asked. "Why
did you leave him out there? Invite him
to eat with us."
21Moses agreed to stay on with Jethro,
who later let his daughter Zipporah
marry Moses. 22And when she had a
son, Moses said, "I will name him Gershom,[j] since I am a foreigner in this
country."
23After the death of the king of Egypt,
the Israelites still complained because
they were forced to be slaves. They
cried out for help, 24and God heard their
loud cries. He did not forget the promise
he had made to Abraham, Isaac, and Jacob, 25and because he knew what was
happening to his people, he felt sorry
for them.

God Speaks to Moses

3 One day, Moses was taking care of
the sheep and goats of his father-in-
law Jethro, the priest of Midian, and
Moses decided to lead them across the
desert to Sinai,[k] the holy mountain.
2There an angel of the LORD appeared to
him from a burning bush. Moses saw
that the bush was on fire, but it was not
burning up. 3"This is strange!" he said to
himself. "I'll go over and see why the
bush isn't burning up."
4When the LORD saw Moses coming
near the bush, he called him by name,
and Moses answered, "Here I am."
5God replied, "Don't come any closer.
Take off your sandals—the ground
where you are standing is holy. 6I am
the God who was worshiped by your ancestors Abraham, Isaac, and Jacob."
Moses was afraid to look at God, and
so he hid his face.
7The LORD said:

I have seen how my people are
suffering as slaves in Egypt, and I
have heard them beg for my help because of the way they are being mistreated. I feel sorry for them, 8and I
have come down to rescue them
from the Egyptians.

I will bring my people out of
Egypt into a country where there is
good land, rich with milk and honey.
I will give them the land where the
Canaanites, Hittites, Amorites, Perizzites, Hivites, and Jebusites now
live. 9My people have begged for my
help, and I have seen how cruel the
Egyptians are to them. 10Now go to
the king! I am sending you to lead
my people out of his country.

11But Moses said, "Who am I to go to
the king and lead your people out of
Egypt?"
12God replied, "I will be with you. And
you will know that I am the one who
sent you, when you worship me on this
mountain after you have led my people
out of Egypt."[l]
13Moses answered, "I will tell the people of Israel that the God their ancestors
worshiped has sent me to them. But
what should I say, if they ask me your
name?"
14-15God said to Moses:

I am the eternal God. So tell them
that the LORD,[m] whose name is "I
Am," has sent you. This is my name
forever, and it is the name that people must use from now on.

16Call together the leaders of Israel and tell them that the God who
was worshiped by Abraham, Isaac,
and Jacob has appeared to you. Tell
them I have seen how terribly they
are being treated in Egypt, 17and I
promise to lead them out of their

[h]**2.15** *the king*: See the note at 1.11. [i]**2.16** *Jethro, the priest of Midian*: Hebrew "the priest of Midian." But see 3.1; 4.18; 18.1, 2-4 where his name is given. In the Hebrew of verse 18 he is spoken of as "Reuel," which may have been the name of the tribe to which Jethro belonged. [j]**2.22** *Gershom*: In Hebrew "Gershom" sounds like "foreigner." [k]**3.1** *Sinai*: The Hebrew text has "Horeb," another name for Sinai. [l]**3.12** *I will be with you . . . out of Egypt*: Or "I will be with you. This bush is a sign that I am the one sending you, and it is a promise that you will worship me on this mountain after you have led my people out of Egypt." [m]**3.14,15** *LORD*: The Hebrew text has "Yahweh," which is usually translated "LORD" in the CEV. Since it seems related to the word translated "I am," it may mean "I am the one who is" or "I will be what I will be" or "I am the one who brings into being."

troubles. I will give them a land rich
with milk and honey, where the
Canaanites, Hittites, Amorites, Perizzites, Hivites, and Jebusites now
live.
18The leaders of Israel will listen
to you. Then you must take them to
the king of Egypt and say, "The
LORD God of the Hebrews has appeared to us. Let us walk three days
into the desert, where we can offer a
sacrifice to him." 19But I know that
the king of Egypt won't let you go
unless something forces him to. 20So
I will use my mighty power to perform all kinds of miracles and strike
down the Egyptians. Then the king
will send you away.
21After I punish the Egyptians,
they will be so afraid of you that
they will give you anything you
want. You are my people, and I will
let you take many things with you
when you leave the land of Egypt.
22Every Israelite woman will go to
her Egyptian neighbors or to any
Egyptian woman living in her house.
She will ask them for gold and silver
jewelry and for their finest clothes.
The Egyptians will give them to you,
and you will put these fine things on
your sons and daughters. You will
carry all this away when you leave
Egypt.

The LORD Gives Great Power to Moses

4 Moses asked the LORD, "Suppose
everyone refuses to listen to my
message, and no one believes that you
really appeared to me?"
2The LORD answered, "What's that in
your hand?"
"A walking stick," Moses replied.
3"Throw it down!" the LORD commanded. So Moses threw the stick on
the ground. It immediately turned into a
snake, and Moses jumped back.
4"Pick it up by the tail!" the LORD told
him. And when Moses did this, the
snake turned back into a walking stick.
5"Do this," the LORD said, "and the Israelites will believe that you have seen
me, the God who was worshiped by
their ancestors Abraham, Isaac, and Jacob."
6Next, the LORD commanded Moses,
"Put your hand inside your shirt." Moses
obeyed, and when he took it out, his
hand had turned white as snow—like
someone with leprosy.[n]
7"Put your hand back inside your
shirt," the LORD told him. Moses did so,
and when he took it out again, it was as
healthy as the rest of his body.
8-9Then the LORD said, "If no one believes either of these miracles, take
some water from the Nile River and
pour it on the ground. The water will
immediately turn into blood."
10Moses replied, "I have never been a
good speaker. I wasn't one before you
spoke to me, and I'm not one now. I am
slow at speaking, and I can never think
of what to say."
11But the LORD answered, "Who
makes people able to speak or makes
them deaf or unable to speak? Who
gives them sight or makes them blind?
Don't you know that I am the one who
does these things? 12Now go! When you
speak, I will be with you and give you
the words to say."
13Moses begged, "LORD, please send
someone else to do it."
14The LORD became irritated with
Moses and said:
What about your brother Aaron,
the Levite? I know he is a good
speaker. He is already on his way
here to visit you, and he will be
happy to see you again. 15-16Aaron
will speak to the people for you, and
you will be like me, telling Aaron
what to say. I will be with both of
you as you speak, and I will tell each
of you what to do. 17Now take this
walking stick and use it to perform
miracles.

Moses Returns to Egypt

18Moses went to his father-in-law
Jethro and asked, "Please let me return
to Egypt to see if any of my people are
still alive."
"All right," Jethro replied. "I hope all
goes well."
19But even before this, the LORD had
told Moses, "Leave the land of Midian
and return to Egypt. Everyone who
wanted to kill you is dead." 20So Moses
put his wife and sons on donkeys and
headed for Egypt, holding the walking
stick that had the power of God.
21On the way the LORD said to Moses:
When you get to Egypt, go to the
king and work the miracles I have
shown you. But I will make him so
stubborn that he will refuse to let
my people go. 22Then tell him that I
have said, "Israel is my first-born
son, 23and I commanded you to release him, so he could worship me.
But you refused, and now I will kill
your first-born son."

Zipporah's Son Is Circumcised

24One night while Moses was in camp,
the LORD was about to kill him. 25But
Zipporah[o] circumcised her son with a
flint knife. She touched his[p] legs with

[n]4.6 *leprosy*: The word translated "leprosy" was used for many different kinds of skin diseases.
[o]4.25 *Zipporah*: The wife of Moses (see 2.16-21). [p]4.25 *his*: Either Moses or the boy.

the skin she had cut off and said, "My
dear son, this blood will protect you."[q]
26So the LORD did not harm Moses. Then
Zipporah said, "Yes, my dear, you are
safe because of this circumcision."[r]

Aaron Is Sent To Meet Moses

27The LORD sent Aaron to meet Moses
in the desert. So Aaron met Moses at
Mount Sinai[s] and greeted him with a
kiss. 28Moses told Aaron what God had
sent him to say; he also told him about
the miracles God had given him the
power to perform.
29Later they brought together the
leaders of Israel, 30and Aaron told them
what the LORD had sent Moses to say.
Then Moses worked the miracles for the
people, 31and everyone believed. They
bowed down and worshiped the LORD
because they knew that he had seen
their suffering and was going to help
them.

Moses and Aaron Go to the King of Egypt

5 Moses and Aaron went to the king[t]
of Egypt and told him, "The LORD
God says, 'Let my people go into the
desert, so they can honor me with a celebration there.' "
2"Who is this LORD and why should I
obey him?" the king replied. "I refuse to
let you and your people go!"
3They answered, "The LORD God of
the Hebrews, has appeared to us. Please
let us walk three days into the desert
where we can offer sacrifices to him. If
you don't, he may strike us down with
terrible troubles or with war."
4-5The king said, "Moses and Aaron,
why are you keeping these people from
working? Look how many you are keeping from doing their work. Now everyone get back to work!"
6That same day the king gave orders
to his slave bosses and to the men directly in charge of the Israelite slaves.
He told them:

> 7Don't give the slaves any more
> straw[u] to put in their bricks. Force
> them to find their own straw wher-
> ever they can, 8but they must make
> the same number of bricks as be-
> fore. They are lazy, or else they
> would not beg me to let them go and
> sacrifice to their God. 9Make them
> work so hard that they won't have
> time to listen to these lies.

10The slave bosses and the men in
charge of the slaves went out and told
them, "The king says he will not give
you any more straw. 11Go and find your
own straw wherever you can, but you
must still make as many bricks as before."
12The slaves went all over Egypt, looking for straw. 13But the slave bosses
were hard on them and kept saying,
"Each day you have to make as many
bricks as you did when you were given
straw." 14The bosses beat the men in
charge of the slaves and said, "Why
didn't you force the slaves to make as
many bricks yesterday and today as
they did before?"
15Finally, the men in charge of the
slaves went to the king and said, "Why
are you treating us like this? 16No one
brings us any straw, but we are still ordered to make the same number of
bricks. We are beaten with whips, and
your own people are to blame."
17The king replied, "You are lazy—
nothing but lazy! That's why you keep
asking me to let you go and sacrifice to
your LORD. 18Get back to work! You
won't be given straw, but you must still
make the same number of bricks."
19The men knew they were in deep
trouble when they were ordered to
make the same number of bricks each
day. 20After they left the king, they went
to see Moses and Aaron, who had been
waiting for them. 21Then the men said,
"We hope the LORD will punish both of
you for making the king and his officials hate us. Now they even have an excuse to kill us."

The LORD's Promise to Moses

22Moses left them and prayed, "Our
LORD, why have you brought so much
trouble on your people? Is that why you
sent me here? 23Ever since you told me
to speak to the king,[v] he has caused
nothing but trouble for these people.
And you haven't done a thing to help."

6 The LORD God told Moses:

> Soon you will see what I will do to
> the king. Because of my mighty
> power, he will let my people go, and
> he will even chase them out of his
> country.
> 2My name is the LORD.[w] 3But when
> I appeared to Abraham, Isaac, and
> Jacob, I came as God All-Powerful
> and did not use my name. 4I made
> an agreement and promised them
> the land of Canaan, where they were
> living as foreigners. 5Now I have
> seen how the people of Israel are
> suffering because of the Egyptians,
> and I will keep my promise.

[q]**4.25** *My dear son . . . you*: Or "My dear husband, you are a man of blood" (meaning Moses).
[r]**4.26** *you are . . . circumcision*: Or "you are a man of blood." [s]**4.27** *Mount Sinai*: Hebrew "the mountain of God." [t]**5.1** *the king*: See the note at 1.11. [u]**5.7** *straw*: The straw made the mud bricks stronger and kept them from shrinking, cracking, or losing their shape.
[v]**5.23** *the king*: See the note at 1.11. [w]**6.2** *My name is the LORD*: See the note at 3.14, 15.

6Here is my message for Israel: "I
am the LORD! And with my mighty
power I will punish the Egyptians
and free you from slavery. 7I will accept you as my people, and I will be
your God. Then you will know that I
was the one who rescued you from
the Egyptians. 8I will bring you into
the land that I solemnly promised
Abraham, Isaac, and Jacob, and it
will be yours. I am the LORD!"
9When Moses told this to the Israelites, they were too discouraged and
mistreated to believe him.
10Then the LORD told Moses 11to demand that the king of Egypt let the Israelites leave. 12But Moses replied, "I'm
not a powerful speaker. If the Israelites
won't listen to me, why should the king
of Egypt?" 13But the LORD sent Aaron
and Moses with a message for the Israelites and for the king; he also ordered Aaron and Moses to free the people from Egypt.

Family Record of Aaron and Moses

14The following men were the heads
of their ancestral clans:
The sons of Reuben, Jacob's[x] oldest son, were Hanoch, Pallu, Hezron,
and Carmi.
15The sons of Simeon were Jemuel, Jamin, Ohad, Jachin, Zohar,
and Shaul, the son of a Canaanite
woman.
16Levi lived to be one hundred
thirty-seven; his sons were Gershon,
Kohath, and Merari.
17Gershon's sons were Libni and
Shimei.
18Kohath lived to be one hundred
thirty-three; his sons were Amram,
Izhar, Hebron, and Uzziel.
19Merari's sons were Mahli and
Mushi. All of the above were from
the Levi tribe.
20Amram lived to be one hundred
thirty-seven. He married his father's
sister Jochebed, and they had two
sons, Aaron and Moses.
21Izhar's sons were Korah,
Nepheg, and Zichri.
22Uzziel's sons were Mishael,
Elzaphan, and Sithri.
23Aaron married Elisheba. She
was the daughter of Amminadab
and the sister of Nahshon; they had
four sons, Nadab, Abihu, Eleazar,
and Ithamar.
24Korah's sons were Assir, Elkanah, and Abiasaph.
25Aaron's son Eleazar married one
of Putiel's daughters, and their son
was Phinehas. This ends the list of
those who were the heads of clans in
the Levi tribe.
26The LORD had commanded Aaron
and Moses to lead every family and
tribe of Israel out of Egypt, 27and so
they ordered the king of Egypt to set the
people of Israel free.

The LORD Commands Moses and Aaron To Speak to the King

28When the LORD spoke to Moses in
the land of Egypt, 29he said, "I am the
LORD. Tell the king[y] of Egypt everything
I say to you."
30But Moses answered, "You know I
am a very poor speaker, and the king
will never listen to me."

7 The LORD said:
I am going to let your brother
Aaron speak for you. He will tell
your message to the king, just as a
prophet speaks my message to the
people. 2Tell Aaron everything I say
to you, and he will order the king to
let my people leave his country.
3-4But I will make the king so stubborn that he won't listen to you. He
won't listen even when I do many
terrible things to him and his nation.
Then I will bring a final punishment
on Egypt, and the king will let Israel's families and tribes go. 5When
this happens, the Egyptians will
know that I am the LORD.
6Moses and Aaron obeyed the LORD
7and spoke to the king. At the time,
Moses was eighty years old, and Aaron
was eighty-three.

A Stick Turns into a Snake

8-9The LORD said, "Moses, when the
king[y] asks you and Aaron to perform a
miracle, command Aaron to throw his
walking stick down in front of the king,
and it will turn into a snake."
10Moses and Aaron went to the king
and his officials and did exactly as the
LORD had commanded—Aaron threw
the stick down, and it turned into a
snake. 11Then the king called in the wise
men and the magicians, who used their
secret powers to do the same thing—
12they threw down sticks that turned
into snakes. But Aaron's snake swallowed theirs. 13The king behaved just as
the LORD had said and stubbornly refused to listen.

The Nile River Turns into Blood

14The LORD said to Moses:
The Egyptian king[y] stubbornly refuses to change his mind and let the
people go. 15Tomorrow morning take
the stick that turned into a snake,

[x]6.14 *Jacob*: The Hebrew text has "Israel," Jacob's name after God renamed him. [y]6.29 *the king*: See the note at 1.11. [y]7.8,9 *the king*: See the note at 1.11. [y]7.14 *The Egyptian king*: See the note at 1.11.

then wait beside the Nile River for
the king. 16Tell him, "The LORD God
of the Hebrews sent me to order you
to release his people, so they can
worship him in the desert. But until
now, you have paid no attention.
17"The LORD is going to do something to show you that he really is
the LORD. I will strike the Nile with
this stick, and the water will turn
into blood. 18The fish will die, the
river will stink, and none of you
Egyptians will be able to drink the
water."
19Moses, then command Aaron to
hold his stick over the water. And
when he does, every drop of water in
Egypt will turn into blood, including
rivers, canals, ponds, and even the
water in buckets and jars.
20Moses and Aaron obeyed the LORD.
Aaron held out his stick, then struck the
Nile, as the king and his officials
watched. The river turned into blood,
21the fish died, and the water smelled so
bad that none of the Egyptians could
drink it. Blood was everywhere in
Egypt.
22But the Egyptian magicians used
their secret powers to do the same
thing. The king did just as the LORD had
said—he stubbornly refused to listen.
23Then he went back to his palace and
never gave it a second thought. 24The
Egyptians had to dig holes along the
banks of the Nile for drinking water, because water from the river was unfit to
drink.

Frogs

25Seven days after the LORD had
8 struck the Nile, 1he said to Moses:
Go to the palace and tell the
king[y] of Egypt that I order him to let
my people go, so they can worship
me. 2If he refuses, I will cover his entire country with frogs. 3Warn the
king that the Nile will be full of
frogs, and from there they will
spread into the royal palace, including the king's bedroom and even his
bed. Frogs will enter the homes of
his officials and will find their way
into ovens and into the bowls of
bread dough. 4Frogs will be crawling
on everyone—the king, his officials,
and every citizen of Egypt.
5Moses, now command Aaron to
hold his stick over the water. Then
frogs will come from all rivers,
canals, and ponds in Egypt, and they
will cover the land.
6Aaron obeyed, and suddenly frogs
were everywhere in Egypt. 7But the magicians used their secret powers to do
the same thing.
8The king sent for Moses and Aaron
and told them, "If you ask the LORD to
take these frogs away from me and my
people, I will let your people go and offer sacrifices to him."
9"All right," Moses answered. "You
choose the time when I am to pray for
the frogs to stop bothering you, your officials, and your people, and for them to
leave your houses and be found only in
the river."
10"Do it tomorrow!" the king replied.
"As you wish," Moses agreed. "Then
everyone will discover that there is no
god like the LORD, 11and frogs will no
longer be found anywhere, except in the
Nile."
12After Moses and Aaron left the
palace, Moses begged the LORD to do
something about the frogs he had sent
as punishment for the king. 13The LORD
listened to Moses, and frogs died everywhere—in houses, yards, and fields.
14The dead frogs were placed in piles,
and the whole country began to stink.
15But when the king saw that things
were now better, he again did just as the
LORD had said and stubbornly refused
to listen to Moses and Aaron.

Gnats

16The LORD said to Moses, "Command
Aaron to strike the ground with his
walking stick, and everywhere in Egypt
the dust will turn into gnats." 17They
obeyed, and when Aaron struck the
ground with the stick, gnats started
swarming on people and animals. In
fact, every speck of dust in Egypt turned
into a gnat. 18When the magicians tried
to use their secret powers to do this,[z]
they failed, and gnats stayed on people
and animals.
19The magicians told the king,[a] "God
has done this."
But, as the LORD had said, the king
was too stubborn to listen.

Flies

20The LORD said to Moses:
Early tomorrow morning, while
the king[a] is on his way to the river,
go and say to him, "The LORD commands you to let his people go, so
they can worship him. 21If you don't,
he will send swarms of flies to attack you, your officials, and every
citizen of your country. Houses will
be full of flies, and the ground will
crawl with them.
22-23"The LORD's people in Goshen
won't be bothered by flies, but your
people in the rest of the country will

[y]**8.1** *the king*: See the note at 1.11.
[a]**8.19** *the king*: See the note at 1.11.
[z]**8.18** *to do this*: Or "to get rid of the gnats."
[a]**8.20** *the king*: See the note at 1.11.

be tormented by them. That's how you will know that the LORD is here in Egypt. This miracle will happen tomorrow."

24The LORD kept his promise—the palace and the homes of the royal officials swarmed with flies, and the rest of the country was infested with them as well. 25Then the king sent for Moses and Aaron and told them, "Go sacrifice to your God, but stay here in Egypt."

26"That's impossible!" Moses replied. "Any sacrifices we offer to the LORD our God would disgust the Egyptians, and they would stone us to death. 27No indeed! The LORD has ordered us to walk three days into the desert before offering sacrifices to him, and that's what we have to do."

28Then the king told him, "I'll let you go into the desert to offer sacrifices, if you don't go very far. But in the meantime, pray for me."

29"Your Majesty," Moses replied, "I'll pray for you as soon as I leave, and by tomorrow the flies will stop bothering you, your officials, and the citizens of your country. Only make sure that you're telling the truth this time and that you really intend to let our people offer sacrifices to the LORD."

30After leaving the palace, Moses prayed, 31and the LORD answered his prayer. Not a fly was left to pester the king, his officials, or anyone else in Egypt. 32But the king turned stubborn again and would not let the people go.

Dead Animals

9 The LORD sent Moses with this message for the king[a] of Egypt:

The LORD God of the Hebrews commands you to let his people go, so they can worship him. 2If you keep refusing, 3he will bring a terrible disease on your horses and donkeys, your camels and cattle, and your sheep and goats. 4But the LORD will protect the animals that belong to the people of Israel, and none of theirs will die. 5Tomorrow is the day the LORD has set to do this.

6It happened the next day—all of the animals belonging to the Egyptians died, but the Israelites did not lose even one. 7When the king found out, he was still too stubborn to let the people go.

Sores

8The LORD said to Moses and Aaron:

Take a few handfuls of ashes from a stove and have Moses throw them into the air. Be sure the king is watching. 9The ashes will blow across the land of Egypt, causing sores to break out on people and animals.

10So they took a few handfuls of ashes and went to the king.[a] Moses threw them into the air, and sores immediately broke out on the Egyptians and their animals. 11The magicians were suffering so much from the sores, that they could not even come to Moses. 12Everything happened just as the LORD had told Moses—he made the king too stubborn to listen to Moses and Aaron.

Hailstones

13The LORD told Moses to get up early the next morning and say to the king:[a]

The LORD God of the Hebrews commands you to let his people go, so they can worship him! 14If you don't, he will send his worst plagues to strike you, your officials, and everyone else in your country. Then you will find out that no one can oppose the LORD. 15In fact, he could already have sent a terrible disease and wiped you from the face of the earth. 16But he has kept you alive, just to show you his power and to bring honor to himself everywhere in the world.

17You are still determined not to let the LORD's people go. 18All right. At this time tomorrow, he will bring on Egypt the worst hailstorm in its history. 19You had better give orders for every person and every animal in Egypt to take shelter. If they don't, they will die.

20Some of the king's officials were frightened by what the LORD had said, and they hurried off to make sure their slaves and animals were safe. 21But others paid no attention to his threats and left their slaves and animals out in the open.

22Then the LORD told Moses, "Stretch your arm toward the sky, so that hailstones will fall on people, animals, and crops in the land of Egypt." 23-24Moses pointed his walking stick toward the sky, and hailstones started falling everywhere. Thunder roared, and lightning flashed back and forth, striking the ground. This was the worst storm in the history of Egypt. 25People, animals, and crops were pounded by the hailstones, and bark was stripped from trees. 26Only Goshen, where the Israelites lived, was safe from the storm.

27The king sent for Moses and Aaron and told them, "Now I have really sinned! My people and I are guilty, and the LORD is right. 28We can't stand any more of this thunder and hail. Please ask the LORD to make it stop. Your

[a]9.1 *the king*: See the note at 1.11. [a]9.10 *the king*: See the note at 1.11. [a]9.13 *the king*: See the note at 1.11.

people can go—you don't have to stay in
Egypt any longer."
29Moses answered, "As soon as I leave
the city, I will lift my arms in prayer.
When the thunder and hail stop, you
will know that the earth belongs to the
LORD. 30But I am certain that neither you
nor your officials really fear the LORD
God."
31Meanwhile, the flax and barley
crops had been destroyed by the storm
because they were ready to ripen. 32But
the wheat crops[b] ripen later, and they
were not damaged.
33After Moses left the royal palace
and the city, he lifted his arms in prayer
to the LORD, and the thunder, hail, and
drenching rain stopped. 34When the
king realized that the storm was over,
he disobeyed once more. He and his officials were so stubborn 35that he refused to let the Israelites go. This was
exactly what the LORD had said would
happen.

Locusts

10 The LORD said to Moses:
Go back to the king.[c] I have
made him and his officials stubborn,
so that I could work these miracles.
2I did this because I want you to tell
your children and your grandchildren about my miracles and
about my harsh treatment of the
Egyptians. Then all of you will know
that I am the LORD.
3Moses and Aaron went to the king
and told him that the LORD God of the
Hebrews had said:
How long will you stubbornly
refuse to obey? Release my people
so they can worship me. 4Do this by
tomorrow, or I will cover your country with so many locusts[d] 5that you
won't be able to see the ground.
Most of your crops were ruined by
the hailstones, but these locusts will
destroy what little is left, including
the trees. 6Your palace, the homes of
your officials, and all other houses
in Egypt will overflow with more locusts than have ever been seen in
this country.
After Moses left the palace, 7the
king's officials asked, "Your Majesty,
how much longer is this man going to
be a troublemaker? Why don't you let
the people leave, so they can worship
the LORD their God? Don't you know
that Egypt is a disaster?"
8The king had Moses and Aaron
brought back, and he said, "All right,
you may go and worship the LORD your
God. But first tell me who will be going."
9"Everyone, young and old," Moses
answered. "We will even take our sheep,
goats, and cattle, because we want to
hold a celebration in honor of the
LORD."
10The king replied, "The LORD had better watch over you on the day I let you
leave with your families! You're up to no
good. 11Do you want to worship the
LORD? All right, take only the men and
go." Then Moses and Aaron were
chased out of the palace.
12The LORD told Moses, "Stretch your
arm toward Egypt. Swarms of locusts
will come and eat everything left by the
hail."
13Moses held out his walking stick,
and the LORD sent an east wind that
blew across Egypt the rest of the day
and all that night. By morning, locusts
14were swarming everywhere. Never before had there been so many locusts in
Egypt, and never again will there be so
many. 15The ground was black with locusts, and they ate everything left on the
trees and in the fields. Nothing green remained in Egypt—not a tree or a plant.
16At once the king sent for Moses and
Aaron. He told them, "I have sinned
against the LORD your God and against
you. 17Forgive me one more time and
ask the LORD to stop these insects from
killing every living plant."
18Moses left the palace and prayed.
19Then the LORD sent a strong west
wind[e] that swept the locusts into the
Red Sea.[f] Not one locust was left anywhere in Egypt, 20but the LORD made the
king so stubborn that he still refused to
let the Israelites go.

Darkness

21The LORD said to Moses, "Stretch
your arm toward the sky, and everything will be covered with darkness
thick enough to touch." 22Moses
stretched his arm toward the sky, and
Egypt was covered with darkness for
three days. 23During that time, the Egyptians could not see each other or leave
their homes, but there was light where
the Israelites lived.
24The king[g] sent for Moses and told
him, "Go worship the LORD! And take
your families with you. Just leave your
sheep, goats, and cattle."
25"No!" Moses replied. "You must let
us offer sacrifices to the LORD our God,

[b] **9.32** *wheat crops*: The Hebrew text mentions two kinds of wheat. [c] **10.1** *the king*: See the note at 1.11. [d] **10.4** *locusts*: A type of grasshopper that comes in swarms and causes great damage to crops. [e] **10.19** *west wind*: The Hebrew text has "wind from the sea," referring to the Mediterranean Sea (see verse 13). [f] **10.19** *Red Sea*: Hebrew *yam suph*, here referring to the Gulf of Suez, since the term is extended to include the northwestern arm of the Red Sea (see also the note at 13.18). [g] **10.24** *The king*: See the note at 1.11.

26and we won't know which animals we
will need until we get there. That's why
we can't leave even one of them here."
27This time the LORD made the king so
stubborn 28that he said to Moses, "Get
out and stay out! If you ever come back,
you're dead!"
29"Have it your way," Moses answered.
"You won't see me again."

Moses Warns the Egyptians That the LORD Will Kill Their First-Born Sons

11 The LORD said to Moses:
I am going to punish the king[g]
of Egypt and his people one more
time. Then the king will gladly let
you leave his land, so that I will stop
punishing the Egyptians. He will
even chase you out. 2Now go and tell
my people to ask their Egyptian
neighbors for gold and silver jewelry.
3So the LORD made the Egyptians
greatly respect the Israelites, and everyone, including the king and his officials,
considered Moses an important leader.
4Moses went to the king and said:
I have come to let you know what
the LORD is going to do. About midnight he will go through the land of
Egypt, 5and wherever he goes, the
first-born son in every family will
die. Your own son will die, and so
will the son of the lowest slave
woman. Even the first-born males of
cattle will die. 6Everywhere in Egypt
there will be loud crying. Nothing
like this has ever happened before
or will ever happen again.
7But there won't be any need for
the Israelites to cry. Things will be
so quiet that not even a dog will be
heard barking. Then you Egyptians
will know that the LORD is good to
the Israelites, even while he punishes you. 8Your leaders will come
and bow down, begging me to take
my people and leave your country.
Then we will leave.
Moses was very angry; he turned and
left the king.
9What the LORD had earlier said to
Moses came true. He had said, "The
king of Egypt won't listen. Then I will
perform even more miracles." 10So the
king of Egypt saw Moses and Aaron
work miracles, but the LORD made him
stubbornly refuse to let the Israelites
leave his country.

The Passover

12 Some time later the LORD said to
Moses and Aaron:
2This month[h] is to be the first
month of the year for you. 3Tell the
people of Israel that on the tenth day
of this month the head of each family must choose a lamb or a young
goat for his family to eat. 4-5If any
family is too small to eat the whole
animal, they must share it with their
next-door neighbors. Choose either
a sheep or a goat, but it must be a
one-year-old male that has nothing
wrong with it. And it must be large
enough for everyone to have some of
the meat.
6Each family must take care of its
animal until the evening of the fourteenth day of the month, when the
animals are to be killed. 7Some of
the blood must be put on the two
doorposts and above the door of
each house where the animals are to
be eaten. 8That night the animals are
to be roasted and eaten, together
with bitter herbs and thin bread
made without yeast. 9Don't eat the
meat raw or boiled. The entire animal, including its head, legs, and insides, must be roasted. 10Eat what
you want that night, and the next
morning burn whatever is left.
11When you eat the meal, be dressed
and ready to travel. Have your sandals on, carry your walking stick in
your hand, and eat quickly. This is
the Passover Festival in honor of me,
your LORD.
12That same night I will pass
through Egypt and kill the first-born
son in every family and the first-
born male of all animals. I am the
LORD, and I will punish the gods of
Egypt. 13The blood on the houses
will show me where you live, and
when I see the blood, I will pass over
you. Then you won't be bothered by
the terrible disasters I will bring on
Egypt.
14Remember this day and celebrate it each year as a festival in my
honor. 15For seven days you must eat
bread made without yeast. And on
the first of these seven days, you
must remove all yeast from your
homes. If you eat anything made
with yeast during this festival, you
will no longer be part of Israel.
16Meet together for worship on the
first and seventh days of the festival.
The only work you are allowed to do
on either of these two days is that of
preparing the bread.
17Celebrate this Festival of Thin
Bread as a way of remembering the
day that I brought your families and
tribes out of Egypt. And do this each

year. 18 Begin on the evening of the
fourteenth day of the first month by
eating bread made without yeast.
Then continue this celebration until
the evening of the twenty-first day.
19 During these seven days no yeast
is allowed in anyone's home,
whether they are native Israelites or
not. If you are caught eating anything made with yeast, you will no
longer be part of Israel. 20 Stay away
from yeast, no matter where you
live. No one is allowed to eat anything made with yeast!
21 Moses called the leaders of Israel together and said:
Each family is to pick out a sheep
and kill it for Passover. 22 Make a
brush from a few small branches of
a hyssop plant and dip the brush in
the bowl that has the blood of the
animal in it. Then brush some of the
blood above the door and on the
posts at each side of the door of your
house. After this, everyone is to stay
inside.
23 During that night the LORD will
go through the country of Egypt and
kill the first-born son in every
Egyptian family. He will see where
you have put the blood, and he will
not come into your house. His angel
that brings death will pass over and
not kill your first-born sons.
24-25 After you have entered the
country promised to you by the
LORD, you and your children must
continue to celebrate Passover each
year. 26 Your children will ask you,
"What are we celebrating?" 27 And
you will answer, "The Passover animal is killed to honor the LORD. We
do these things because on that
night long ago the LORD passed over
the homes of our people in Egypt.
He killed the first-born sons of the
Egyptians, but he saved our children
from death."
After Moses finished speaking, the
people of Israel knelt down and worshiped the LORD. 28 Then they left and
did what Moses and Aaron had told
them to do.

Death for the First-Born Sons

29 At midnight the LORD killed the
first-born son of every Egyptian family,
from the son of the king[i] to the son of
every prisoner in jail. He also killed the
first-born male of every animal that belonged to the Egyptians.
30 That night the king, his officials, and
everyone else in Egypt got up and
started crying bitterly. In every Egyptian
home, someone was dead.

The People of Israel Escape from Egypt

31 During the night the king[i] sent for
Moses and Aaron and told them, "Get
your people out of my country and leave
us alone! Go and worship the LORD, as
you have asked. 32 Take your sheep,
goats, and cattle, and get out. But ask
your God to be kind to me."
33 The Egyptians did everything they
could to get the Israelites to leave their
country fast. They said, "Please hurry
and leave. If you don't, we will all be
dead." 34 So the Israelites quickly made
some bread dough and put it in pans.
But they did not mix any yeast in the
dough to make it rise. They wrapped
cloth around the pans and carried them
on their shoulders.
35 The Israelites had already done
what Moses had told them to do. They
had gone to their Egyptian neighbors
and asked for gold and silver and for
clothes. 36 The LORD had made the Egyptians friendly toward the people of Israel, and they gave them whatever they
asked for. In this way they carried away
the wealth of the Egyptians when they
left Egypt.
37 The Israelites walked from the city
of Rameses to the city of Succoth. There
were about six hundred thousand of
them, not counting women and children.
38 Many other people went with them as
well, and there were also a lot of sheep,
goats, and cattle. 39 They left Egypt in
such a hurry that they did not have time
to prepare any food except the bread
dough made without yeast. So they
baked it and made thin bread.
40-41 The LORD's people left Egypt exactly four hundred thirty years after
they had arrived. 42 On that night the
LORD kept watch for them, and on this
same night each year Israel will always
keep watch in honor of the LORD.

Instructions for Passover

43 The LORD gave Moses and Aaron the
following instructions for celebrating
Passover:
No one except Israelites may eat
the Passover meal.
44 Your slaves may eat the meal if
they have been circumcised, 45 but no
foreigners who work for you are allowed to have any.
46 The entire meal must be eaten
inside, and no one may leave the
house during the celebration.
No bones of the Passover lamb
may be broken. 47 And all Israelites
must take part in the meal.
48 If anyone who isn't an Israelite
wants to celebrate Passover with
you, every man and boy in that fam-

[i] **12.29** *the king*: See the note at 1.11.

[i] **12.31** *the king*: See the note at 1.11.

ily must first be circumcised. Then
they may join in the meal, just like
native Israelites. No uncircumcised
man or boy may eat the Passover
meal! 49 This law applies both to native Israelites and to those foreigners who live among you.
50 The Israelites obeyed everything the
LORD had commanded Moses and
Aaron to tell them. 51 And on that same
day the LORD brought Israel's families
and tribes out of Egypt.

Dedication of the First-Born

13 The LORD said to Moses, 2 "Dedicate to me the first-born son of
every family and the first-born males of
your flocks and herds. These belong to
me."

The Festival of Thin Bread

3-4 Moses said to the people:
Remember this day in the month
of Abib.[j] It is the day when the
LORD's mighty power rescued you
from Egypt, where you were slaves.
Do not eat anything made with
yeast. 5 The LORD promised your ancestors that he would bring you into
the land of the Canaanites, Hittites,
Amorites, Hivites, and Jebusites. It is
a land rich with milk and honey.
Each year during the month of
Abib, celebrate these events in the
following way: 6 For seven days you
are to eat bread made without yeast,
and on the seventh day you are to
celebrate a festival in honor of the
LORD. 7 During those seven days, you
must not eat anything made with
yeast or even have yeast anywhere
near your homes. 8 Then on the seventh day you must explain to your
children that you do this because the
LORD brought you out of Egypt.
9 This celebration will be like wearing a sign on your hand or on your
forehead, because then you will pass
on to others the teaching of the
LORD, whose mighty power brought
you out of Egypt. 10 Celebrate this
festival each year at the same time.
11 The LORD will give you the land
of the Canaanites, just as he
promised you and your ancestors.
12 From then on, you must give him
every first-born son from your families and every first-born male from
your animals, because these belong
to him. 13 You can save the life of a
first-born donkey[k] by sacrificing a
lamb; if you don't, you must break
the donkey's neck. You must save
every first-born son.
14 In the future your children will
ask what this ceremony means. Explain it to them by saying, "The
LORD used his mighty power to rescue us from slavery in Egypt. 15 The
king[l] stubbornly refused to set us
free, so the LORD killed the first-born
male of every animal and the first-
born son of every Egyptian family.
This is why we sacrifice to the LORD
every first-born male of every animal and save every first-born son."
16 This ceremony will serve the
same purpose as a sign on your
hand or on your forehead to tell how
the LORD's mighty power rescued us
from Egypt.

The LORD Leads His People

17 After the king[l] had finally let the
people go, the LORD did not lead them
through Philistine territory,[m] though
that was the shortest way. God had said,
"If they are attacked, they may decide to
return to Egypt." 18 So he led them
around through the desert and toward
the Red Sea.[n]
The Israelites left Egypt, prepared for
battle.
19 Moses had them take along the
bones of Joseph, whose dying words
had been, "God will come to your rescue, and when he does, be sure to take
along my bones."
20 The people of Israel left Succoth and
camped at Etham at the border of Egypt
near the desert. 21-22 During the day the
LORD went ahead of his people in a
thick cloud, and during the night he
went ahead of them in a flaming fire.
That way the LORD could lead them at
all times, whether day or night.

The Israelites Cross the Red Sea

14 At Etham the LORD said to Moses:
2 Tell the people of Israel to
turn back and camp across from
Pi-Hahiroth near Baal-Zephon,

[j] 13.3,4 *Abib*: Or Nisan, the first month of the Hebrew calendar, from about mid-March to mid-April. [k] 13.13 *donkey*: This was the only "unclean" animal that had to be saved; the first-born of all "clean" animals (sheep, goats, cattle) had to be sacrificed. Donkeys were important because they were the basic means of transportation. [l] 13.15 *The king*: See the note at 1.11. [l] 13.17 *the king*: See the note at 1.11. [m] 13.17 *Philistine territory*: The shortest land route from the Nile Delta to Canaan; it was the southern section of the major road that led to Megiddo and then on to Mesopotamia by way of Asia Minor. [n] 13.18 *Red Sea*: Hebrew *yam suph* "Sea of Reeds," one of the marshes or fresh water lakes, near the eastern part of the Nile Delta. This identification is based on Exodus 13.17—14.9, which lists the towns on the route of the Israelites before crossing the sea. In the Greek translation of the Scriptures made about 200 B.C., the "Sea of Reeds" was named "Red Sea."

between Migdol and the Red Sea.[o]
3 The king[p] will think they were
afraid to cross the desert and that
they are wandering around, trying to
find another way to leave the country. 4 I will make the king stubborn
again, and he will try to catch you.
Then I will destroy him and his
army. People everywhere will praise
me for my victory, and the Egyptians
will know that I really am the LORD.
The Israelites obeyed the LORD and
camped where he told them.
5 When the king of Egypt heard that
the Israelites had finally left, he and his
officials changed their minds and said,
"Look what we have done! We let them
get away, and they will no longer be our
slaves."
6 The king got his war chariot and
army ready. 7 He commanded his officers in charge of his six hundred best
chariots and all his other chariots to
start after the Israelites. 8 The LORD
made the king so stubborn that he went
after them, even though the Israelites
proudly[q] went on their way. 9 But the
king's horses and chariots and soldiers
caught up with them while they were
camping by the Red Sea near Pi-
Hahiroth and Baal-Zephon.
10 When the Israelites saw the king
coming with his army, they were frightened and begged the LORD for help.
11 They also complained to Moses,
"Wasn't there enough room in Egypt to
bury us? Is that why you brought us out
here to die in the desert? Why did you
bring us out of Egypt anyway? 12 While
we were there, didn't we tell you to
leave us alone? We had rather be slaves
in Egypt than die in this desert!"
13 But Moses answered, "Don't be
afraid! Be brave, and you will see the
LORD save you today. These Egyptians
will never bother you again. 14 The LORD
will fight for you, and you won't have to
do a thing."
15 The LORD said to Moses, "Why do
you keep calling out to me for help? Tell
the Israelites to move forward. 16 Then
hold your walking stick over the sea.
The water will open up and make a road
where they can walk through on dry
ground. 17 I will make the Egyptians so
stubborn that they will go after you.
Then I will be praised because of what
happens to the king and his chariots
and cavalry. 18 The Egyptians will know
for sure that I am the LORD."
19 All this time God's angel had gone
ahead of Israel's army, but now he
moved behind them. A large cloud had
also gone ahead of them, 20 but now it
moved between the Egyptians and the
Israelites. The cloud gave light to the Israelites, but made it dark for the Egyptians, and during the night they could
not come any closer.
21 Moses stretched his arm over the
sea, and the LORD sent a strong east
wind that blew all night until there was
dry land where the water had been. The
sea opened up, 22 and the Israelites
walked through on dry land with a wall
of water on each side.
23 The Egyptian chariots and cavalry
went after them. 24 But before daylight
the LORD looked down at the Egyptian
army from the fiery cloud and made
them panic. 25 Their chariot wheels got
stuck,[r] and it was hard for them to
move. So the Egyptians said to one another, "Let's leave these people alone!
The LORD is on their side and is fighting
against us."
26 The LORD told Moses, "Stretch your
arm toward the sea—the water will
cover the Egyptians and their cavalry
and chariots." 27 Moses stretched out his
arm, and at daybreak the water rushed
toward the Egyptians. They tried to run
away, but the LORD drowned them in the
sea. 28 The water came and covered the
chariots, the cavalry, and the whole
Egyptian army that had followed the Israelites into the sea. Not one of them
was left alive. 29 But the sea had made a
wall of water on each side of the Israelites; so they walked through on dry
land.
30 On that day, when the Israelites saw
the bodies of the Egyptians washed up
on the shore, they knew that the LORD
had saved them. 31 Because of the
mighty power he had used against the
Egyptians, the Israelites worshiped him
and trusted him and his servant Moses.

The Song of Moses

15 Moses and the Israelites sang this
song in praise of the LORD:

I sing praises to the LORD
for his great victory!
He has thrown the horses
and their riders
into the sea.
2 The LORD is my strength,
the reason for my song,
because he has saved me.
I praise and honor the LORD—
he is my God and the God
of my ancestors.
3 The LORD is his name,
and he is a warrior!

[o] **14.2** *Red Sea*: Hebrew *hayyam* "the Sea," understood as *yam suph*, "Sea of Reeds" (see also the note at 13.18). [p] **14.3** *The king*: See the note at 1.11. [q] **14.8** *proudly*: Or "victoriously." [r] **14.25** *stuck*: The Samaritan Hebrew text and two ancient translations; Hebrew "came off."

4 He threw the chariots and army
of Egypt's kings[s]
into the Red Sea,[t]
and he drowned the best
of the king's officers.
5 They sank to the bottom
just like stones.

6 With the tremendous force
of your right arm, our LORD,
you crushed your enemies.
7 What a great victory was yours,
as you defeated everyone
who opposed you.
Your fiery anger wiped them out,
as though they were straw.
8 You were so furious
that the sea piled up
like a wall,
and the ocean depths
curdled like cheese.

9 Your enemies boasted
that they would
pursue and capture us,
divide up our possessions,
treat us as they wished,
then take out their swords
and kill us right there.
10 But when you got furious,
they sank like lead,
swallowed by ocean waves.

11 Our LORD, no other gods
compare with you—
Majestic and holy!
Fearsome and glorious!
Miracle worker!
12 When you signaled
with your right hand,
your enemies were swallowed
deep into the earth.

13 The people you rescued
were led by your powerful love
to your holy place.
14 Nations learned of this
and trembled—
Philistines shook with horror.
15 The leaders of Edom and of Moab
were terrified.
Everyone in Canaan fainted,
16 struck down by fear.
Our LORD, your powerful arm
kept them still as a rock
until the people you rescued
for your very own
had marched by.

17 You will let your people settle
on your chosen mountain,
where you built your home
and your temple.
18 Our LORD, you will rule forever!

The Song of Miriam

19The LORD covered the royal Egyptian cavalry and chariots with the sea,
after the Israelites had walked safely
through on dry ground. 20Miriam the
sister of Aaron was a prophet. So she
took her tambourine and led the other
women out to play their tambourines
and to dance. 21Then she sang to them:

"Sing praises to the LORD
for his great victory!
He has thrown the horses
and their riders into the sea."

Bitter Water at Marah

22After the Israelites left the Red Sea,[t]
Moses led them through the Shur
Desert for three days, before finding
water. 23They did find water at Marah,
but it was bitter, which is how that place
got its name.[u] 24The people complained
and said, "Moses, what are we going to
drink?"
25Moses asked the LORD for help, and
the LORD told him to throw a piece of
wood into the water. Moses did so, and
the water became fit to drink.

At Marah the LORD tested his people
and also gave them some laws and
teachings. 26Then he said, "I am the
LORD your God, and I cure your diseases. If you obey me by doing right and
by following my laws and teachings, I
won't punish you with the diseases I
sent on the Egyptians."
27Later the Israelites came to Elim,
where there were twelve springs and
seventy palm trees. So they camped
there.

The LORD Sends Food from Heaven

16 On the fifteenth day of the second
month after the Israelites had escaped from Egypt, they left Elim and
started through the western edge of the
Sinai Desert[v] in the direction of Mount
Sinai. 2There in the desert they started
complaining to Moses and Aaron, 3"We
wish the LORD had killed us in Egypt.
When we lived there, we could at least
sit down and eat all the bread and meat
we wanted. But you have brought us out
here into this desert, where we are going to starve."
4The LORD said to Moses, "I will send
bread[w] down from heaven like rain.
Each day the people can go out and

[s] **15.4** *Egypt's king*: See the note at 1.11. [t] **15.4** *Red Sea*: See the note at 13.18.
[t] **15.22** *Red Sea*: See the note at 13.18. [u] **15.23** *Marah . . . name*: In Hebrew "Marah" means "bitter." [v] **16.1** *the western edge of the Sinai Desert*: Hebrew "the Sin Desert."
[w] **16.4** *bread*: This was something like a thin wafer, and it was called "manna," which in Hebrew means, "What is it?"

gather only enough for that day. That's how I will see if they obey me. 5But on the sixth day of each week they must gather and cook twice as much."

6Moses and Aaron told the people, "This evening you will know that the LORD was the one who rescued you from Egypt. 7And in the morning you will see his glorious power, because he has heard your complaints against him. Why should you grumble to us? Who are we?"

8Then Moses continued, "You will know it is the LORD when he gives you meat each evening and more than enough bread each morning. He is really the one you are complaining about, not us—we are nobodies—but the LORD has heard your complaints."

9Moses turned to Aaron and said, "Bring the people together, because the LORD has heard their complaints."

10Aaron was speaking to them, when everyone looked out toward the desert and saw the bright glory of the LORD in a cloud. 11The LORD said to Moses, 12"I have heard my people complain. Now tell them that each evening they will have meat and each morning they will have more than enough bread. Then they will know that I am the LORD their God."

13That evening a lot of quails came and landed everywhere in the camp, and the next morning dew covered the ground. 14After the dew had gone, the desert was covered with thin flakes that looked like frost. 15The people had never seen anything like this, and they started asking each other, "What is it?"[x]

Moses answered, "This is the bread that the LORD has given you to eat. 16And he orders you to gather about two quarts for each person in your family—that should be more than enough."

17They did as they were told. Some gathered more and some gathered less, 18according to their needs, and none was left over.

19Moses told them not to keep any overnight. 20Some of them disobeyed, but the next morning what they kept was stinking and full of worms, and Moses was angry.

21Each morning everyone gathered as much as they needed, and in the heat of the day the rest melted. 22However, on the sixth day of the week, everyone gathered enough to have four quarts, instead of two. When the leaders reported this to Moses, 23he told them that the LORD had said, "Tomorrow is the Sabbath, a sacred day of rest in honor of me. So gather all you want to bake or boil, and make sure you save enough for tomorrow."

24The people obeyed, and the next morning the food smelled fine and had no worms. 25"You may eat the food," Moses said. "Today is the Sabbath in honor of the LORD, and there won't be any of this food on the ground today. 26You will find it there for the first six days of the week, but not on the Sabbath."

27A few of the Israelites did go out to look for some, but there was none. 28Then the LORD said, "Moses, how long will you people keep disobeying my laws and teachings? 29Remember that I was the one who gave you the Sabbath. That's why on the sixth day I provide enough bread for two days. Everyone is to stay home and rest on the Sabbath." 30And so they rested on the Sabbath.

31The Israelites called the bread manna.[y] It was white like coriander seed and delicious as wafers made with honey. 32Moses told the people that the LORD had said, "Store up two quarts of this manna, because I want future generations to see the food I gave you during the time you were in the desert after I rescued you from Egypt."

33Then Moses told Aaron, "Put some manna in a jar and store it in the place of worship for future generations to see."

34Aaron followed the LORD's instructions and put the manna in front of the sacred chest for safekeeping. 35-36The Israelites ate manna for forty years, before they came to the border of Canaan that was a settled land.[z]

The LORD Gives Water from a Rock

(Numbers 20.1-13)

17 The Israelites left the desert and moved from one place to another each time the LORD ordered them to. Once they camped at Rephidim,[a] but there was no water for them to drink.

2The people started complaining to Moses, "Give us some water!"

Moses replied, "Why are you complaining to me and trying to put the LORD to the test?"

3But the people were thirsty and kept on complaining, "Moses, did you bring us out of Egypt just to let us and our families and our animals die of thirst?"

4Then Moses prayed to the LORD, "What am I going to do with these people? They are about to stone me to death!"

5The LORD answered, "Take some of

[x]16.15 *What is it*: See the note at 16.4. **[y]16.31** *manna*: See the note at 16.4. **[z]16.35,36** *land*: The Hebrew text adds, "An omer is one tenth of an ephah." In the CEV "omer" is usually translated "two quarts." **[a]17.1** *Rephidim*: The last stopping place for the Israelites between the Red Sea and Mount Sinai; the exact location is not known.

the leaders with you and go ahead of
the rest of the people. Also take along
the walking stick you used to strike the
Nile River, 6and when you get to the
rock at Mount Sinai,[b] I will be there
with you. Strike the rock with the stick,
and water will pour out for the people to
drink." Moses did this while the leaders
watched.
7The people had complained and
tested the LORD by asking, "Is the LORD
really with us?" So Moses named that
place Massah, which means "testing"
and Meribah, which means "complaining."

Israel Defeats the Amalekites

8When the Israelites were at
Rephidim, they were attacked by the
Amalekites. 9So Moses told Joshua,
"Have some men ready to attack the
Amalekites tomorrow. I will stand on a
hilltop, holding this walking stick that
has the power of God."
10Joshua led the attack as Moses had
commanded, while Moses, Aaron, and
Hur stood on the hilltop. 11The Israelites
out-fought the Amalekites as long as
Moses held up his arms, but they started
losing whenever he had to lower them.
12Finally, Moses was so tired that Aaron
and Hur got a rock for him to sit on.
Then they stood beside him and supported his arms in the same position until sunset. 13That's how Joshua defeated
the Amalekites.
14Afterwards, the LORD said to Moses,
"Write an account of this victory and
read it to Joshua. I want the Amalekites
to be forgotten forever."
15Moses built an altar and named it
"The LORD Gives Me Victory." 16Then
Moses explained, "This is because I depended on the LORD.[c] But in future generations, the LORD will have to fight the
Amalekites again."

Jethro Visits Moses

18 Jethro was the priest of Midian
and the father-in-law of Moses.
And he heard what the LORD God had
done for Moses and his people, after
rescuing them from Egypt.
2-4In the meantime, Moses had sent
his wife Zipporah and her two sons to
stay with Jethro, and he had welcomed
them. Moses was still a foreigner in
Midian when his first son was born, and
so Moses said, "I'll name him
Gershom."[d]
When his second son was born, Moses
said, "I'll name him Eliezer,[e] because
the God my father worshiped has saved
me from the king of Egypt."[f]
5-6While Israel was camped in the
desert near Mount Sinai,[g] Jethro sent
Moses this message: "I am coming to
visit you, and I am bringing your wife
and two sons."
7When they arrived, Moses went out
and bowed down in front of Jethro, then
kissed him. After they had greeted each
other, they went into the tent, 8where
Moses told him everything the LORD had
done to protect Israel against the Egyptians and their king. He also told him
how the LORD had helped them in all of
their troubles.
9Jethro was so pleased to hear this
good news about what the LORD had
done, 10that he shouted, "Praise the
LORD! He rescued you and the Israelites
from the Egyptians and their king.
11Now I know that the LORD is the greatest God, because he has rescued Israel
from their arrogant enemies." 12Jethro
offered sacrifices to God. Then Aaron
and Israel's leaders came to eat with
Jethro there at the place of worship.

Judges Are Appointed
(Deuteronomy 1.9-18)

13The next morning Moses sat down
at the place where he decided legal
cases for the people, and everyone
crowded around him until evening.
14Jethro saw how much Moses had to do
for the people, and he asked, "Why are
you the only judge? Why do you let
these people crowd around you from
morning till evening?"
15Moses answered, "Because they
come here to find out what God wants
them to do. 16They bring their complaints to me, and I make decisions on
the basis of God's laws."
17Jethro replied:
That isn't the best way to do it.
18You and the people who come to
you will soon be worn out. The job is
too much for one person; you can't
do it alone. 19God will help you if
you follow my advice. You should be
the one to speak to God for the people, 20and you should teach them
God's laws and show them what
they must do to live right.
21You will need to appoint some
competent leaders who respect God
and are trustworthy and honest.
Then put them over groups of ten,
fifty, a hundred, and a thousand.
22These judges can handle the ordinary cases and bring the more difficult ones to you. Having them to

[b]17.6 *Sinai*: The Hebrew text has "Horeb," another name for Sinai. [c]17.16 *This . . . LORD*: One possible meaning for the difficult Hebrew text. [d]18.2-4 *Gershom*: See the note at 2.22. [e]18.2-4 *Eliezer*: In Hebrew "Eliezer" means "God has helped me." [f]18.2-4 *saved . . . Egypt*: See 2.1-15. [g]18.5,6 *Mount Sinai*: Hebrew "the mountain of God."

share the load will make your work
easier. 23This is the way God wants it
done. You won't be under nearly as
much stress, and everyone else will
return home feeling satisfied.
24Moses followed Jethro's advice. 25He
chose some competent leaders from
every tribe in Israel and put them over
groups of ten, fifty, a hundred, and a
thousand. 26They served as judges, deciding the easy cases themselves, but
bringing the more difficult ones to
Moses.
27After Moses and his father-in-law
Jethro had said good-by to each other,
Jethro returned home.

At Mount Sinai

19 1-2The Israelites left Rephidim.[h]
Then two months after leaving
Egypt, they arrived at the desert near
Mount Sinai, where they set up camp at
the foot of the mountain.
3Moses went up the mountain to meet
with the LORD God, who told him to say
to the people:
4You saw what I did in Egypt, and
you know how I brought you here to
me, just as a mighty eagle carries its
young. 5Now if you will faithfully
obey me, you will be my very own
people. The whole world is mine,
6but you will be my holy nation and
serve me as priests.
Moses, that is what you must tell
the Israelites.
7After Moses went back, he reported
to the leaders what the LORD had said,
8and they promised, "We will do everything the LORD has commanded." So
Moses told the LORD about this.
9The LORD said to Moses, "I will come
to you in a thick cloud and let the people hear me speak to you. Then they will
always trust you." Again Moses reported
to the people what the LORD had told
him.
10Once more the LORD spoke to
Moses:
Go back and tell the people that
today and tomorrow they must get
themselves ready to meet me. They
must wash their clothes 11and be
ready by the day after tomorrow,
when I will come down to Mount
Sinai, where all of them can see me.
12Warn the people that they are
forbidden to touch any part of the
mountain. Anyone who does will be
put to death, 13either with stones or
arrows, and no one must touch the
body of a person killed in this way.
Even an animal that touches this
mountain must be put to death. You
may go up the mountain only after a
signal is given on the trumpet.
14After Moses went down the mountain, he gave orders for the people to
wash their clothes and make themselves
acceptable to worship God. 15He told
them to be ready in three days and not
to have sex in the meantime.

The LORD Comes to Mount Sinai

16On the morning of the third day
there was thunder and lightning. A thick
cloud covered the mountain, a loud
trumpet blast was heard, and everyone
in camp trembled with fear. 17Moses led
them out of the camp to meet God, and
they stood at the foot of the mountain.
18Mount Sinai was covered with
smoke because the LORD had come
down in a flaming fire. Smoke poured
out of the mountain just like a furnace,
and the whole mountain shook. 19The
trumpet blew louder and louder. Moses
spoke, and God answered him with
thunder.
20The LORD came down to the top of
Mount Sinai and told Moses to meet
him there. 21Then he said, "Moses, go
and warn the people not to cross the
boundary that you set at the foot of the
mountain. They must not cross it to
come and look at me, because if they do,
many of them will die. 22Only the priests
may come near me, and they must obey
strict rules before I let them. If they
don't, they will be punished."
23Moses replied, "The people cannot
come up the mountain. You warned us to
stay away because it is holy."
24Then the LORD told Moses, "Go
down and bring Aaron back here with
you. But the priests and people must not
try to push their way through, or I will
rush at them like a flood!"
25After Moses had gone back down,
he told the people what the LORD had
said.

The Ten Commandments
(Deuteronomy 5.1-21)

20 God said to the people of Israel:
2I am the LORD your God, the
one who brought you out of Egypt
where you were slaves.
3Do not worship any god except
me.
4Do not make idols that look like
anything in the sky or on earth or in
the ocean under the earth. 5Don't
bow down and worship idols. I am
the LORD your God, and I demand all
your love. If you reject me, I will
punish your families for three or
four generations. 6But if you love me
and obey my laws, I will be kind to
your families for thousands of generations.

[h] **19.1,2** *Rephidim*: See the note at 17.1.

7Do not misuse my name.[i] I am
the LORD your God, and I will punish
anyone who misuses my name.
8Remember that the Sabbath Day
belongs to me. 9You have six days
when you can do your work, 10but
the seventh day of each week belongs to me, your God. No one is to
work on that day—not you, your
children, your slaves, your animals,
or the foreigners who live in your
towns. 11In six days I made the sky,
the earth, the oceans, and everything
in them, but on the seventh day I
rested. That's why I made the Sabbath a special day that belongs to
me.
12Respect your father and your
mother, and you will live a long time
in the land I am giving you.
13Do not murder.
14Be faithful in marriage.
15Do not steal.
16Do not tell lies about others.
17Do not want anything that belongs to someone else. Don't want
anyone's house, wife or husband,
slaves, oxen, donkeys or anything
else.

The People Are Afraid
(Deuteronomy 5.23-33)

18The people trembled with fear when
they heard the thunder and the trumpet
and saw the lightning and the smoke
coming from the mountain. They stood
a long way off 19and said to Moses, "If
you speak to us, we will listen. But don't
let God speak to us, or we will die!"
20"Don't be afraid!" Moses replied.
"God has come only to test you, so that
by obeying him you won't sin." 21But
when Moses went near the thick cloud
where God was, the people stayed a
long way off.

Idols and Altars

22The LORD told Moses to say to the
people of Israel:
With your own eyes, you saw me
speak to you from heaven. 23So you
must never make idols of silver or
gold to worship in place of me.[j]
24Build an altar out of earth, and
offer on it your sacrifices[k] of sheep,
goats, and cattle. Wherever I choose
to be worshiped, I will come down to
bless you. 25If you ever build an altar
for me out of stones, do not use any
tools to chisel the stones, because
that would make the altar unfit.
26And don't build an altar that requires steps; you might expose yourself when you climb up.

Hebrew Slaves
(Deuteronomy 15.12-18)

21 The LORD gave Moses the following laws for his people:
2If you buy a Hebrew slave, he must
remain your slave for six years. But in
the seventh year you must set him free,
without cost to him. 3If he was single at
the time you bought him, he alone must
be set free. But if he was married at the
time, both he and his wife must be given
their freedom. 4If you give him a wife,
and they have children, only the man
himself must be set free; his wife and
children remain the property of his
owner.
5But suppose the slave loves his wife
and children so much that he won't
leave without them. 6Then he must
stand beside either the door or the door-
post at the place of worship,[l] while his
owner punches a small hole through
one of his ears with a sharp metal rod.
This makes him a slave for life.
7A young woman who was sold by
her father doesn't gain her freedom in
the same way that a man does. 8If she
doesn't please the man who bought her
to be his wife, he must let her be bought
back.[m] He cannot sell her to foreigners;
this would break the contract he made
with her. 9If he selects her as a wife for
his son, he must treat her as his own
daughter.
10If the man later marries another
woman, he must continue to provide
food and clothing for the one he bought
and to treat her as a wife. 11If he fails to
do any of these things, she must be
given her freedom without cost.

Murder and Other Violent Crimes

The LORD said:
12Death is the punishment for murder.
13But if you did not intend to kill someone, and I, the LORD, let it happen anyway, you may run for safety to a place
that I have set aside. 14If you plan in

[i]**20.7** *misuse my name*: Probably includes breaking promises, telling lies after swearing to tell the truth, using the LORD's name as a curse word or a magic formula, and trying to control the LORD by using his name. [j]**20.23** *in place of me*: Or "together with me." [k]**20.24** *sacrifices*: The Hebrew text mentions two types of sacrifices: Sacrifices to please the LORD (traditionally called "whole burnt offerings") and sacrifices to ask the LORD's blessing (traditionally called "peace offerings"). [l]**21.6** *at the place of worship*: The Hebrew text has "in the presence of God," which probably refers to the place where God was worshiped. [m]**21.8** *bought back*: Either by her family or by another Israelite who wanted to marry her.

advance to murder someone, there's no
escape, not even by holding on to my
altar.[n] You will be dragged off and
killed.
15 Death is the punishment for attacking your father or mother.
16 Death is the punishment for kidnapping. If you sell the person you kid-
napped, or if you are caught with that
person, the penalty is death.
17 Death is the punishment for cursing
your father or mother.
18 Suppose two of you are arguing, and
you hit the other with either a rock or
your fist, without causing a fatal injury.
If the victim has to stay in bed, 19 and
later has to use a stick when walking
outside, you must pay for the loss of
time and do what you can to help until
the injury is completely healed. That's
your only responsibility.
20 Death is the punishment for beating
to death any of your slaves. 21 However,
if the slave lives a few days after the
beating, you are not to be punished. After all, you have already lost the services of that slave who was your property.
22 Suppose a pregnant woman suffers
a miscarriage[o] as the result of an injury
caused by someone who is fighting. If
she isn't badly hurt, the one who injured
her must pay whatever fine her husband
demands and the judges approve. 23 But
if she is seriously injured, the payment
will be life for life, 24 eye for eye, tooth
for tooth, hand for hand, foot for foot,
25 burn for burn, cut for cut, and bruise
for bruise.
26 If you hit one of your slaves and
cause the loss of an eye, the slave must
be set free. 27 The same law applies if
you knock out a slave's tooth—the slave
goes free.
28 A bull that kills someone with its
horns must be killed and its meat destroyed, but the owner of the bull isn't
responsible for the death.
29 Suppose you own a bull that has
been in the habit of attacking people,
but you have refused to keep it fenced
in. If that bull kills someone, both you
and the bull must be put to death by
stoning. 30 However, you may save your
own life by paying whatever fine is demanded. 31 This same law applies if the
bull gores someone's son or daughter.
32 If the bull kills a slave, you must pay
the slave owner thirty pieces of silver
for the loss of the slave, and the bull
must be killed by stoning.
33 Suppose someone's ox or donkey is
killed by falling into an open pit that
you dug or left uncovered on your property. 34 You must pay for the dead animal, and it becomes yours.
35 If your bull kills someone else's,
yours must be sold. Then the money
from your bull and the meat from the
dead bull must be divided equally between you and the other owner.
36 If you refuse to fence in a bull that is
known to attack others, you must pay
for any animal it kills, but the dead animal will belong to you.

Property Laws

The LORD said:

22 If you steal an ox and slaughter
or sell it, you must replace it with
five oxen; if you steal a sheep and
slaughter it or sell it, you must replace it
with four sheep. 2-4 But if you cannot afford to replace the animals, you must be
sold as a slave to pay for what you have
stolen. If you steal an ox, donkey, or
sheep, and are caught with it still alive,
you must pay the owner double.
If you happen to kill a burglar who
breaks into your home after dark, you
are not guilty. But if you kill someone
who breaks in during the day, you are
guilty of murder.
5 If you allow any of your animals to
stray from your property and graze[p] in
someone else's field or vineyard, you
must repay the damage from the best
part of your own harvest of grapes and
grain.
6 If you carelessly let a fire spread
from your property to someone else's,
you must pay the owner for any crops
or fields destroyed by the fire.
7 Suppose a neighbor asks you to keep
some silver or other valuables, and they
are stolen from your house. If the thief
is caught, the thief must repay double.
8 But if the thief isn't caught, some
judges[q] will decide if you are the guilty
one.
9 Suppose two people claim to own the
same ox or donkey or sheep or piece of
clothing. Then the judges[r] must decide
the case, and the guilty person will pay
the owner double.
10 Suppose a neighbor who is going to
be away asks you to keep a donkey or
an ox or a sheep or some other animal,
and it dies or gets injured or is stolen
while no one is looking. 11 If you swear
with me as your witness that you did
not harm the animal, you do not have to
replace it. Your word is enough. 12 But if
the animal was stolen while in your
care, you must replace it. 13 If the animal

[n] **21.14** *altar*: As a rule, anyone who ran to the altar was safe from the death penalty, until proven guilty. [o] **21.22** *suffers a miscarriage*: Or "gives birth before her time."
[p] **22.5** *graze*: Or "eat everything." [q] **22.8** *some judges*: Or "I." [r] **22.9** *the judges*: Or "I."

was attacked and killed by a wild animal, and you can show the remains of
the dead animal to its owner, you do not
have to replace it.
14 Suppose you borrow an animal from
a neighbor, and it gets injured or dies
while the neighbor isn't around. Then
you must replace it. 15 But if something
happens to the animal while the owner
is present, you do not have to replace it.
If you had leased the animal, the money
you paid the owner will cover any harm
done to it.

Laws for Everyday Life

The LORD said:
16 Suppose a young woman has never
been married and isn't engaged. If a
man talks her into having sex, he must
pay the bride price[s] and marry her.
17 But if her father refuses to let her
marry the man, the bride price must still
be paid.
18 Death is the punishment for witchcraft.
19 Death is the punishment for having
sex with an animal.
20 Death is the punishment for offering
sacrifices to any god except me.
21 Do not mistreat or abuse foreigners
who live among you. Remember, you
were foreigners in Egypt.
22 Do not mistreat widows or orphans.
23 If you do, they will beg for my help,
and I will come to their rescue. 24 In fact,
I will get so angry that I will kill your
men and make widows of their wives
and orphans of their children.
25 Don't charge interest when you lend
money to any of my people who are in
need. 26 Before sunset you must return
any coat taken as security for a loan,
27 because that is the only cover the poor
have when they sleep at night. I am a
merciful God, and when they call out to
me, I will come to help them.
28 Don't speak evil of me[t] or of the
ruler of your people.
29 Don't fail to give me the offerings of
grain and wine that belong to me.[u]
Dedicate to me your first-born sons
30 and the first-born of your cattle and
sheep. Let the animals stay with their
mothers for seven days, then on the
eighth day give them to me, your God.
31 You are my chosen people, so don't
eat the meat of any of your livestock
that was killed by a wild animal. Instead, feed the meat to dogs.

Equal Justice for All

The LORD said:
23 Don't spread harmful rumors or
help a criminal by giving false evidence.
2 Always tell the truth in court, even if
everyone else is[v] dishonest and stands
in the way of justice. 3 And don't favor
the poor, simply because they are poor.
4 If you find an ox or a donkey that has
wandered off, take it back where it belongs, even if the owner is your enemy.
5 If a donkey is overloaded and falls
down, you must do what you can to
help, even if it belongs to someone who
doesn't like you.[w]
6 Make sure that the poor are given
equal justice in court. 7 Don't bring false
charges against anyone or sentence an
innocent person to death. I won't forgive
you if you do.
8 Don't accept bribes. Judges are
blinded and justice is twisted by bribes.
9 Don't mistreat foreigners. You were
foreigners in Egypt, and you know what
it is like.

Laws for the Sabbath

The LORD said:
10 Plant and harvest your crops for six
years, 11 but let the land rest during the
seventh year. The poor are to eat what
they want from your fields, vineyards,
and olive trees during that year, and
when they have all they want from your
fields, leave the rest for wild animals.
12 Work the first six days of the week,
but rest and relax on the seventh day.
This law is not only for you, but for your
oxen, donkeys, and slaves, as well as for
any foreigners among you.
13 Make certain that you obey everything I have said. Don't pray to other
gods or even mention their names.

Three Annual Festivals

(Exodus 34.18-26; Deuteronomy 16.1-17)

The LORD said:
14 Celebrate three festivals each year
in my honor.
15 Celebrate the Festival of Thin Bread
by eating bread made without yeast, just
as I have commanded.[x] Do this at the
proper time during the month of Abib,[y]
because it is the month when you left
Egypt. And make certain that everyone
brings the proper offerings.
16 Celebrate the Harvest Festival[z] each
spring when you start harvesting your
wheat, and celebrate the Festival of

[s] **22.16** *bride price*: It was the custom for a man to pay his wife's family a bride price before the actual wedding ceremony took place. [t] **22.28** *me*: Or "your judges." [u] **22.29** *Don't fail . . . me*: One possible meaning for the difficult Hebrew text. [v] **23.2** *everyone else is*: Or "the authorities are." [w] **23.5** *you*: One possible meaning for the difficult Hebrew text of verse 5. [x] **23.15** *as I have commanded*: See 12.14-20. [y] **23.15** *Abib*: See the note at 12.2.
[z] **23.16** *Harvest Festival*: Traditionally called the "Festival of Weeks" and known in New Testament times as "Pentecost."

Shelters[a] each autumn when you pick your fruit.

17Your men must come to these three festivals each year to worship me.

18Do not offer bread made with yeast when you sacrifice an animal to me. And make sure that the fat of the animal is burned that same day.

19Each year bring the best part of your first harvest to the place of worship.

Don't boil a young goat in its mother's milk.

A Promise and a Warning

The LORD *said:*

20I am sending an angel to protect you and to lead you into the land I have ready for you. 21Carefully obey everything the angel says, because I am giving him complete authority, and he won't tolerate rebellion. 22If you faithfully obey him, I will be a fierce enemy of your enemies. 23My angel will lead you into the land of the Amorites, Hittites, Perizzites, Canaanites, Hivites, and Jebusites, and I will wipe them out. 24Don't worship their gods or follow their customs. Instead, destroy their idols and shatter their stone images.

25Worship only me, the LORD your God! I will bless you with plenty of food and water and keep you strong. 26Your women will give birth to healthy children, and everyone will live a long life.

27I will terrify those nations and make your enemies so confused that they will run from you. 28I will make the Hivites, Canaanites, and Hittites panic as you approach. 29But I won't do all this in the first year, because the land would become poor, and wild animals would be everywhere. 30Instead, I will force out your enemies little by little and give your nation time to grow strong enough to take over the land.

31I will see that your borders reach from the Red Sea[b] to the Euphrates River and from the Mediterranean Sea to the desert. I will let you defeat the people who live there, and you will force them out of the land. 32But you must not make any agreements with them or with their gods. 33Don't let them stay in your land. They will trap you into sinning against me and worshiping their gods.

The People Agree To Obey God

24 The LORD said to Moses, "Come up to me on this mountain. Bring along Aaron, as well as his two sons Nadab and Abihu, and seventy of Israel's leaders. They must worship me at a distance, 2but you are to come near. Don't let anyone else come up."

3Moses gave the LORD's instructions to the people, and they promised, "We will do everything the LORD has commanded!" 4Then Moses wrote down what the LORD had said.

The next morning Moses got up early. He built an altar at the foot of the mountain and set up a large stone for each of the twelve tribes of Israel. 5He also sent some young men to burn offerings and to sacrifice bulls as special offerings[c] to the LORD. 6Moses put half of the blood from the animals into bowls and sprinkled the rest on the altar. 7Then he read aloud the LORD's commands and promises, and the people shouted, "We will obey the LORD and do everything he has commanded!"

8Moses took the blood from the bowls and sprinkled it on the people. Next, he told them, "With this blood the LORD makes his agreement with you."

9Moses and Aaron, together with Nadab and Abihu and the seventy leaders, went up the mountain 10and saw the God of Israel. Under his feet was something that looked like a pavement made out of sapphire,[d] and it was as bright as the sky.

11Even though these leaders of Israel saw God, he did not punish them. So they ate and drank.

Moses on Mount Sinai

12The LORD said to Moses, "Come up on the mountain and stay here for a while. I will give you the two flat stones on which I have written the laws that my people must obey." 13Moses and Joshua his assistant got ready, then Moses started up the mountain to meet with God.

14Moses had told the leaders, "Wait here until we come back. Aaron and Hur will be with you, and they can settle any arguments while we are away."

15When Moses went up on Mount Sinai, a cloud covered it, 16and the bright glory of the LORD came down and stayed there. The cloud covered the mountain for six days, and on the seventh day the LORD told Moses to come into the cloud. 17-18Moses did so and stayed there forty days and nights. To

[a]**23.16** *Festival of Shelters*: The Hebrew text has "Festival of Ingathering" (so also in 34.22), which was the final harvesting of crops and fruits before the autumn rains began. But the usual name was "Festival of Shelters." [b]**23.31** *Red Sea*: Hebrew *yam suph*, here referring to the Gulf of Aqaba, since the term is extended to include the northeastern arm of the Red Sea (see also the note at 13.18). [c]**24.5** *special offerings*: Often translated "peace offerings," which were to make peace between God and his people, who ate certain parts of the sacrificed animal. [d]**24.10** *sapphire*: A precious stone, blue in color.

the people, the LORD's glory looked like
a blazing fire on top of the mountain.

The Sacred Tent
(Exodus 35.4-9)

25 The LORD said to Moses:
2 Tell everyone in Israel who
wants to give gifts that they must bring
them to you. 3 Here is a list of what you
are to collect: Gold, silver, and bronze;
4 blue, purple, and red wool; fine linen;
goat hair; 5 tanned ram skins; fine
leather; acacia wood; 6 olive oil for the
lamp; sweet-smelling spices to mix with
the oil for dedicating the tent and ordaining the priests; 7 and onyx[e] stones
for the sacred vest and the breastpiece.
8 I also want them to build a special
place where I can live among my people. 9 Make it and its furnishings exactly
like the pattern I will show you.

The Sacred Chest
(Exodus 37.1-9)

The LORD said to Moses:
10 Tell the people to build a chest of
acacia wood forty-five inches long,
twenty-seven inches wide, and twenty-
seven inches high. 11 Cover it inside and
out with pure gold and put a gold edging around the lid. 12 Make four gold
rings and fasten one of them to each of
the four legs of the chest. 13 Make two
poles of acacia wood. Cover them with
gold 14 and put them through the rings,
so the chest can be carried by the poles.
15 Don't ever remove the poles from the
rings. 16 When I give you the Ten Commandments written on two flat stones,
put them inside the chest.
17 Cover the lid of the chest with pure
gold. 18-19 Then hammer out two winged
creatures of pure gold and fasten them
to the lid at the ends of the chest. 20 The
creatures must face each other with
their wings spread over the chest. 21 Inside it place the two flat stones with the
Ten Commandments and put the gold
lid on top of the chest. 22 I will meet you
there[f] between the two creatures and
tell you what my people must do and
what they must not do.

The Table for the Sacred Bread
(Exodus 37.10-16)

The LORD said:
23 Make a table of acacia wood thirty-
six inches long, eighteen inches wide,
and twenty-seven inches high. 24-25 Cover
it with pure gold and put a gold edging
around it with a border three inches
wide.[g] 26 Make four gold rings and attach one to each of the legs 27-28 near the
edging. The poles for carrying the table
are to be placed through these rings and
are to be made of acacia wood covered
with gold. 29-30 The table is to be kept in
the holy place, and the sacred loaves of
bread must always be put on it. All
bowls, plates, jars, and cups for wine offerings are to be made of pure gold and
set on this table.

The Lampstand
(Exodus 37.17-24)

The LORD said:
31 Make a lampstand of pure gold. The
whole lampstand, including its decorative flowers, must be made from a single
piece of hammered gold 32 with three
branches on each of its two sides.
33 There are to be three decorative almond blossoms on each branch 34 and
four on the stem. 35 There must also be a
blossom where each pair of branches
comes out from the stem. 36 The lampstand, including its branches and decorative flowers, must be made from a single piece of hammered pure gold. 37 The
lamp on the top and those at the end of
each of its six branches must be made
so as to shine toward the front of the
lampstand. 38 The tongs and trays for
taking care of the lamps are to be made
of pure gold. 39 The lampstand and its
equipment will require seventy-five
pounds of pure gold, 40 and they must be
made according to the pattern I showed
you on the mountain.

Curtains and Coverings for the Sacred Tent
(Exodus 36.8-19)

The LORD said to Moses:
26 Furnish the sacred tent with curtains made from ten pieces of the
finest linen. They must be woven with
blue, purple, and red wool and embroidered with figures of winged creatures.
2 Make each piece fourteen yards long
and two yards wide 3 and sew them together into two curtains with five sections each. 4-6 Put fifty loops of blue cloth
along one of the wider sides of each curtain, then fasten the two curtains at the
loops with fifty gold hooks.
7-8 As the material for the tent, use
goat hair to weave eleven sections fifteen yards by two yards each. 9 Sew five
of the sections together to make one
panel. Then sew the other six together
to make a second panel, and fold the
sixth section double over the front of
the tent. 10 Put fifty loops along one
of the wider sides of each panel 11 and

[e] **25.7** *onyx*: A precious stone with bands of different colors. [f] **25.22** *I will meet you there*: It was believed that God had his earthly throne on the lid of the sacred chest. [g] **25.24,25** *a gold edging . . . wide*: Or "a gold edging around it three inches wide."

fasten the two panels at the loops with fifty bronze hooks. 12-13The panel of goat hair will be a yard longer than the tent itself, so fold half a yard of the material behind the tent and on each side as a protective covering. 14Make two more coverings—one with ram skins dyed red and the other with fine leather.

The Framework for the Sacred Tent

(Exodus 36.20-34)

The LORD said:

15Build a framework of acacia wood for the walls of the sacred tent. 16Each frame is to be fifteen feet high and twenty-seven inches wide 17with two wooden pegs near the bottom. 18-21Place two silver stands under each frame with sockets for the pegs, so the frames can be joined together. Twenty of these frames are to be used along the south side and twenty more along the north. 22For the back wall along the west side use six frames 23-24with two more at the southwest and northwest corners. Make certain that these corner frames are joined from top to bottom. 25Altogether, this back wall will have eight frames with two silver stands under each one.

26-27Make five crossbars for each of the wooden frames, 28with the center crossbar running the full length of the wall. 29Cover the frames and the crossbars with gold and attach gold rings to the frames to run the crossbars through. 30Then set up the tent in the way I showed you on the mountain.

The Curtain inside the Sacred Tent

(Exodus 36.35-38)

The LORD said:

31-33Make a curtain to separate the holy place from the most holy place. Use fine linen woven with blue, purple, and red wool, and embroidered with figures of winged creatures. Cover four acacia wood posts with gold and set them each on a silver stand. Then fasten gold hooks to the posts and hang the curtain there.

34Inside the most holy place, you must put the sacred chest that has the place of mercy on its lid.[h] 35Outside the curtain put the table for the sacred bread on the right side and the gold lampstand on the left.

36For the entrance to the tent, use a piece of fine linen woven with blue, purple, and red wool and embroidered with fancy needlework. 37Cover five acacia wood posts with gold and set them each on a bronze stand. Then put gold hooks on the posts and hang the curtain there.

The Altar for Offering Sacrifices

(Exodus 38.1-7)

The LORD said to Moses:

27 Use acacia wood to build an altar seven and a half feet square and four and a half feet high, 2and make each of the four top corners stick up like the horn of a bull. Then cover the whole altar with bronze, including the four horns. 3All the equipment for the altar must also be made of bronze—the pans for the hot ashes, the shovels, the sprinkling bowls, the meat forks, and the fire pans. 4-5Midway up the altar build a ledge around it, and cover the bottom half of the altar with a decorative bronze grating. Then attach a bronze ring beneath the ledge at the four corners of the altar. 6-7Cover two acacia wood poles with bronze and put them through the rings for carrying the altar. 8Construct the altar in the shape of an open box, just as you were shown on the mountain.

The Courtyard around the Sacred Tent

(Exodus 38.9-20)

The LORD said:

9-15Surround the sacred tent with a courtyard one hundred fifty feet long on the south and north and seventy-five feet wide on the east and west. Use twenty bronze posts on bronze stands for the south and north and ten for the west. Then hang a curtain of fine linen on the posts along each of these three sides by using silver hooks and rods.

Place three bronze posts on each side of the entrance at the east and hang a curtain seven and a half yards wide on each set of posts. 16Use four more of these posts for the entrance way, then hang on them an embroidered curtain of fine linen ten yards long and woven with blue, purple, and red wool.

17-18The curtains that surround the courtyard must be two and a half yards high and are to be hung from the bronze posts with silver hooks and rods. 19The rest of the equipment for the sacred tent must be made of bronze, including the pegs for the tent and for the curtain surrounding the courtyard.

The Oil for the Lamp in the Holy Place

(Leviticus 24.1-4)

The LORD said to Moses:

20Command the people of Israel to supply you with the purest olive oil. Do this so the lamp will keep burning 21in front of the curtain that separates the holy place from the most holy place, where the sacred chest is kept. Aaron and his sons are responsible for keeping

[h]**26.34** *place of mercy on its lid*: It was believed that God had his earthly throne on the lid of the sacred chest, and from this place he showed mercy to his people.

the lamp burning every night in the sacred tent. The Israelites must always obey this command.

The Clothes for the High Priest

(Exodus 39.1-7)

The LORD said to Moses:

28 Send for your brother Aaron and his sons Nadab, Abihu, Eleazar, and Ithamar. They are the ones I have chosen from Israel to serve as my priests. 2Make Aaron some beautiful clothes that are worthy of a high priest. 3Aaron is to be dedicated as my high priest, and his clothes must be made only by persons who possess skills that I have given them. 4Here are the items that need to be made: a breastpiece, a priestly vest, a robe, an embroidered shirt, a turban, and a sash. These sacred clothes are to be made for your brother Aaron and his sons who will be my priests. 5Only gold and fine linen, woven with blue, purple, and red wool, are to be used for making these clothes.

The Vest for the High Priest

(Exodus 39.2-7)

The LORD said:

6-8The entire priestly vest must be made of fine linen skillfully woven with blue, purple, and red wool, and decorated with gold. It is to have two shoulder straps to support it and a sash that fastens around the waist.

9-12Put two onyx[i] stones in gold settings, then attach one to each of the shoulder straps. On one of these stones engrave the names of Israel's first six sons in the order of their birth. And do the same with his remaining six sons on the other stone. In this way Aaron will always carry the names of the tribes of Israel when he enters the holy place, and I will never forget my people.

13-14Attach two gold settings to the shoulder straps and fasten them with two braided chains of pure gold.

The Breastpiece for the High Priest

(Exodus 39.8-21)

The LORD said:

15From the same costly material make a breastpiece for the high priest to use in learning what I want my people to do. 16It is to be nine inches square and folded double 17with four rows of three precious stones: In the first row put a carnelian, a chrysolite, and an emerald; 18in the second row a turquoise, a sapphire, and a diamond; 19in the third row a jacinth, an agate, and an amethyst; 20and in the fourth row a beryl, an onyx, and a jasper.[j] Mount the stones in delicate gold settings 21and engrave on each of them the name of one of the twelve tribes of Israel.

22-25Attach two gold rings to the upper front corners of the breastpiece and fasten them with two braided gold chains to gold settings on the shoulder straps. 26Attach two other gold rings to the lower inside corners next to the vest 27and two more near the bottom of the shoulder straps right above the sash. 28Then take a blue cord and tie the two lower rings on the breastpiece to those on the vest. This will keep the breastpiece in place.

29In this way Aaron will have the names of the twelve tribes of Israel written on his heart each time he enters the holy place, and I will never forget my people. 30He must also wear on his breastpiece the two small objects[k] that he uses to receive answers from me.

The Other High-Priestly Clothes

(Exodus 39.22-26, 30, 31)

The LORD said:

31Under his vest Aaron must wear a robe of blue wool 32with an opening in the center for his head. Be sure to bind the material around the collar to keep it from raveling. 33-34Along the hem of the robe weave pomegranates[l] of blue, purple, and red wool with a gold bell between each of them. 35If Aaron wears these clothes when he enters the holy place as my high priest, the sound of the bells will be heard, and his life will not be in danger.

36On a narrow strip of pure gold engrave the words: "Dedicated to the LORD." 37Fasten it to the front of Aaron's turban with a blue cord, 38so he can wear it on his forehead. This will show that he will take on himself the guilt for any sins the people of Israel commit in offering their gifts to me, and I will forgive them.

39Make Aaron's robe and turban of fine linen and decorate his sash with fancy needlework.

[i]**28.9-12** *onyx*: See the note at 25.7. [j]**28.20** *jasper*: The stones mentioned in verses 17-20 are of different colors: *carnelian* is deep red or reddish white; *chrysolite* is olive green; *emerald* is green; *turquoise* is blue or blue green; *sapphire* is blue; *diamond* is colorless or white; *jacinth* is reddish orange; *agate* has circles of brown and white; *amethyst* is deep purple; *beryl* is green or bluish green; *onyx* has bands of different colors; and *jasper* is usually green or clear.
[k]**28.30** *two small objects*: The Hebrew text has "urim and thummim," which may have been made of wood, stone, or metal, and were used in some way to receive answers from God.
[l]**28.33,34** *pomegranates*: A bright red fruit that looks like an apple.

The Clothes for the Other Priests
(Exodus 39.27-29)

40 Since Aaron's sons are priests, they
should also look dignified. So make
robes, sashes, and special caps for them.
41 Then dress Aaron and his sons in
these clothes, pour olive oil on their
heads, and ordain them as my priests.
42 Make linen shorts for them that
reach from the waist down to the thigh,
so they won't expose themselves.
43 Whenever they enter the sacred tent
or serve at the altar or enter the holy
place, they must wear these shorts, or
else they will be guilty and die. This
same rule applies to any of their descendants who serve as priests.

Instructions for Ordaining Priests
(Leviticus 8.1-36)

The LORD said to Moses:
29 When you ordain one of Aaron's
sons as my priest, choose a young
bull and two rams that have nothing
wrong with them. 2 Then from your
finest flour make three batches of dough
without yeast. Shape some of it into
larger loaves, some into smaller loaves
mixed with olive oil, and the rest into
thin wafers brushed with oil. 3 Put all of
this bread in a basket and bring it when
you come to sacrifice the three animals
to me.
4 Bring Aaron and his sons to the entrance of the sacred tent and have them
wash themselves. 5 Dress Aaron in the
priestly shirt, the robe that goes under
the sacred vest, the vest itself, the
breastpiece, and the sash. 6 Put on his
turban with its narrow strip of engraved
gold 7 and then ordain him by pouring
olive oil on his head.
8 Next, dress Aaron's sons in their special shirts 9 and caps and their sashes,[m]
then ordain them, because they and
their descendants will always be priests.
10 Lead the bull to the entrance of the
sacred tent, where Aaron and his sons
will lay their hands on its head. 11 Kill
the bull near my altar in front of the
tent. 12 Use a finger to smear some of its
blood on each of the four corners of the
altar and pour out the rest of the blood
on the ground next to the altar. 13 Then
take the fat from the animal's insides, as
well as the lower part of the liver and
the two kidneys with their fat, and send
them up in smoke on the altar. 14 But the
meat, the skin, and the food still in the
bull's stomach must be burned outside
the camp as an offering to ask forgiveness for the sins of the priests.[n]
15 Bring one of the rams to Aaron and
his sons and have them lay their hands
on its head. 16 Kill the ram and splatter
its blood against all four sides of the altar. 17 Cut up the ram, wash its insides
and legs, and lay all of its parts on the
altar, including the head. 18 Then make
sure that the whole animal goes up in
smoke with a smell that pleases me.
19 Bring the other ram to Aaron and
his sons and have them lay their hands
on its head. 20 Kill the ram and place
some of its blood on Aaron's right ear
lobe, his right thumb, and the big toe of
his right foot. Do the same for each of
his sons and splatter the rest of the
blood against the four sides of the altar.
21 Then take some of the blood from the
altar, mix it with the oil used for ordination, and sprinkle it on Aaron and his
clothes, and also on his sons and their
clothes. This will show that they and
their clothes have been dedicated to me.
22 This ram is part of the ordination
service. So remove its right hind leg,[o] its
fat tail, the fat on its insides, as well as
the lower part of the liver and the two
kidneys with their fat. 23 Take one loaf of
each kind of bread[p] from the basket,
24 and put this bread, together with the
meat, into the hands of Aaron and his
sons. Then they will lift it all up[q] to
show that it is dedicated to me. 25 After
this, the meat and bread are to be
placed on the altar and sent up in
smoke with a smell that pleases me.
26 You may eat the choice ribs from
this second ram, but you must first lift
them up[q] to show that this meat is dedicated to me.
27-28 In the future, when anyone from
Israel offers the ribs and a hind leg of a
ram either to ordain a priest or to ask
for my blessing, the meat belongs to me,
but it may be eaten by the priests. This
law will never change.
29-30 After Aaron's death, his priestly
clothes are to be handed down to each
descendant who succeeds him as high
priest, and these clothes must be worn
during the seven-day ceremony of ordination.
31 Boil the meat of the ordination ram
in a sacred place, 32 then have Aaron and
his sons eat it together with the three
kinds of bread[r] at the entrance to the sacred tent. 33 At their ordination, a cere-

[m] **29.9** *their sashes*: One ancient translation; Hebrew "the sashes of Aaron and his sons."
[n] **29.14** *for the sins of the priests*: When a sacrifice for the forgiveness of sins was made for someone other than priests, the part that was not burned on the altar could be eaten by the priests (see Leviticus 5.13; 6.26). [o] **29.22** *right hind leg*: This was usually given to the officiating priest (see Leviticus 7.33). [p] **29.23** *each kind of bread*: See verses 2, 3. [q] **29.24** *lift it all up*: Or "wave it all." [q] **29.26** *lift them up*: Or "wave them." [r] **29.32** *three kinds of bread*: See verses 2, 3.

mony of forgiveness was performed for them with this sacred food, and only they have the right to eat it. [34]If any of the sacred food is left until morning, it must be burned up.

[35]Repeat this ordination ceremony for Aaron and his sons seven days in a row, just as I have instructed you. [36]Each day you must offer a bull as a sacrifice for sin and as a way of purifying the altar. In addition, you must smear the altar with olive oil to make it completely holy. [37]Do this for seven days, and the altar will become so holy that anyone who touches it will become holy.

Daily Sacrifices

(Leviticus 6.8-13; Numbers 28.1-8)

The LORD said:

[38]Each day you must sacrifice two lambs a year old, [39]one in the morning and one in the evening. [40-41]With each lamb offer two pounds of your finest flour mixed with a quart of pure olive oil, and also pour out a quart of wine as an offering. The smell of this sacrifice on the fires of the altar will be pleasing to me. [42-43]You and your descendants must always offer this sacrifice on the altar at the entrance to the sacred tent.

People of Israel, I will meet and speak with you there, and my shining glory will make the place holy. [44]Because of who I am, the tent will become sacred, and Aaron and his sons will become worthy to serve as my priests. [45]I will live among you as your God, [46]and you will know that I am the LORD your God, the one who rescued you from Egypt, so that I could live among you.

The Altar for Burning Incense

(Exodus 37.25-28)

The LORD said to Moses:

30 Build an altar of acacia wood where you can burn incense. [2]Make it eighteen inches square and thirty-six inches high, and make each of its four corners stick up like the horn of a bull. [3]Cover it with pure gold and put a gold edging around it. [4]Then below the edging on opposite sides attach two gold rings through which you can put the poles for carrying the altar. [5]These poles are also to be made of acacia wood covered with gold.

[6]Put the altar in front of the inside curtain of the sacred tent. The chest with the place of mercy[s] is kept behind that curtain, and I will talk with you there. [7-8]From now on, when Aaron tends the lamp each morning and evening, he must burn sweet-smelling incense to me on the altar. [9]Burn only the proper incense on the altar and never use it for grain sacrifices or animal sacrifices or drink offerings. [10]Once a year Aaron must purify the altar by smearing on its four corners[t] the blood of an animal sacrificed for sin, and this practice must always be followed. The altar is sacred because it is dedicated to me.

The Money for the Sacred Tent

[11]The LORD said to Moses:

[12]Find out how many grown men there are in Israel and require each of them to pay me to keep him safe from danger while you are counting them. [13-15]Each man over nineteen, whether rich or poor, must pay me the same amount of money, weighed according to the official standards. [16]This money is to be used for the upkeep of the sacred tent, and because of it, I will never forget my people.

The Large Bronze Bowl

(Exodus 38.8)

[17]The LORD said to Moses:

[18-21]Make a large bronze bowl and a bronze stand for it. Then put them between the altar for sacrifice and the sacred tent, so the priests can wash their hands and feet before entering the tent or offering a sacrifice on the altar. Each priest in every generation must wash himself in this way, or else he will die right there.

The Oil for Dedication and Ordination

(Exodus 37.29)

[22]The LORD said to Moses:

[23-25]Mix a gallon of olive oil with the following costly spices: twelve pounds of myrrh, six pounds of cinnamon, six pounds of cane, and twelve pounds of cassia. Measure these according to the official standards. Then use this sacred mixture [26]for dedicating the tent and chest, [27]the table with its equipment, the lampstand with its equipment, the incense altar with all its utensils, [28]the altar for sacrifices, and the large bowl with its stand. [29]By dedicating them in this way, you will make them so holy that anyone who even touches them will become holy.

[30]When you ordain Aaron and his sons as my priests, sprinkle them with some of this oil, [31]and say to the people of Israel: "This oil must always be used in the ordination service of a priest. It is holy because it is dedicated to the LORD.

[s]**30.6** *place of mercy*: See the note at 26.34. [t]**30.10** *four corners*: See 27.2; 30.2.
[u]**31.2** *Bezalel*: Hebrew "Bezalel, son of Uri and grandson of Hur."

[32]So treat it as holy! Don't ever use it for everyday purposes or mix any for yourselves. [33]If you do, you will no longer belong to the LORD's people."

The Sweet-Smelling Incense

[34-35]Mix equal amounts of the costly spices stacte, onycha, galbanum, and pure frankincense, then add salt to make the mixture pure and holy. [36]Pound some of it into powder and sprinkle it in front of the sacred chest, where I meet with you. Be sure to treat this incense as something very holy. [37]It is truly holy because it is dedicated to me, so don't ever make any for yourselves. [38]If you ever make any of it to use as perfume, you will no longer belong to my people.

The LORD Chooses Bezalel and Oholiab

(Exodus 35.30—36.1)

31 The LORD said to Moses:

[2]I have chosen Bezalel[u] from the Judah tribe to make the sacred tent and its furnishings. [3-5]Not only have I filled him with my Spirit, but I have given him wisdom and made him a skilled craftsman who can create objects of art with gold, silver, bronze, stone, and wood. [6]I have appointed Oholiab[v] from the tribe of Dan to work with him, and I have also given skills to those who will help them make everything exactly as I have commanded you: [7-11]the sacred tent with its furnishings, the sacred chest with its place of mercy, the table with all that is on it, the lamp with its equipment, the incense altar, the altar for sacrifices with its equipment, the bronze bowl with its stand, the beautiful priestly clothes for Aaron and his sons, the oil for dedication and ordination services, and the sweet-smelling incense for the holy place.

Laws for the Sabbath

[12-13]Moses told the Israelites that the LORD had said:

The Sabbath belongs to me. Now I command you and your descendants to always obey the laws of the Sabbath. By doing this, you will know that I have chosen you as my own. [14-15]Keep the Sabbath holy. You have six days to do your work, but the Sabbath is mine, and it must remain a day of rest. If you work on the Sabbath, you will no longer be part of my people, and you will be put to death.

[16]Every generation of Israelites must respect the Sabbath. [17]This day will always serve as a reminder, both to me and to the Israelites, that I made the heavens and the earth in six days, then on the seventh day I rested and relaxed.

[18]When God had finished speaking to Moses on Mount Sinai, he gave him the two flat stones on which he had written all of his laws with his own hand.

The People Make an Idol To Worship

(Deuteronomy 9.6-29)

32 After the people saw that Moses had been on the mountain for a long time, they went to Aaron and said, "Make us an image of a god who will lead and protect us. Moses brought us out of Egypt, but nobody knows what has happened to him."

[2]Aaron told them, "Bring me the gold earrings that your wives and sons and daughters are wearing." [3]Everybody took off their earrings and brought them to Aaron, [4]then he melted them and made an idol in the shape of a young bull.

All the people said to one another, "This is the god who brought us out of Egypt!"

[5]When Aaron saw what was happening, he built an altar in front of the idol and said, "Tomorrow we will celebrate in honor of the LORD." [6]The people got up early the next morning and killed some animals to be used for sacrifices and others to be eaten. Then everyone ate and drank so much that they began to carry on like wild people.

[7]The LORD said to Moses:

Hurry back down! Those people you led out of Egypt are acting like fools. [8]They have already stopped obeying me and have made themselves an idol in the shape of a young bull. They have bowed down to it, offered sacrifices, and said that it is the god who brought them out of Egypt. [9]Moses, I have seen how stubborn these people are, [10]and I'm angry enough to destroy them, so don't try to stop me. But I will make your descendants into a great nation.

[11]Moses tried to get the LORD God to change his mind:

Our LORD, you used your mighty power to bring these people out of Egypt. Now don't become angry and destroy them. [12]If you do, the Egyptians will say that you brought your people out here into the mountains just to get rid of them. Please don't be angry with your people. Don't destroy them!

[13]Remember the solemn promise you made to Abraham, Isaac, and Jacob. You promised that someday

[v]31.6 *Oholiab*: Hebrew "Oholiab son of Ahisamach."

they would have as many descendants as there are stars in the sky
and that you would give them land.
14 So even though the LORD had threatened to destroy the people, he changed
his mind and let them live.
15-16 Moses went back down the mountain with the two flat stones on which
God had written all of his laws with his
own hand, and he had used both sides
of the stones.
17 When Joshua heard the noisy shouts
of the people, he said to Moses, "A battle
must be going on down in the camp."
18 But Moses replied, "It doesn't sound
like they are shouting because they
have won or lost a battle. They are
singing wildly!"
19 As Moses got closer to the camp, he
saw the idol, and he also saw the people
dancing around. This made him so angry that he threw down the stones and
broke them to pieces at the foot of the
mountain. 20 He melted the idol the people had made, and he ground it into
powder. He scattered it in their water
and made them drink it. 21 Moses asked
Aaron, "What did these people do to
harm you? Why did you make them sin
in this terrible way?"
22 Aaron answered:
Don't be angry with me. You know
as well as I do that they are determined to do evil. 23 They even told
me, "That man Moses led us out of
Egypt, but now we don't know what
has happened to him. Make us a god
to lead us." 24 Then I asked them to
bring me their gold earrings. They
took them off and gave them to me. I
threw the gold into a fire, and out
came this bull.
25 Moses knew that the people were
out of control and that it was Aaron's
fault. And now they had made fools of
themselves in front of their enemies.
26 So Moses stood at the gate of the
camp and shouted, "Everyone who is on
the LORD's side come over here!"
Then the men of the Levi tribe gathered around Moses, 27 and he said to
them, "The LORD God of Israel commands you to strap on your swords and
go through the camp, killing your relatives, your friends, and your neighbors."
28 The men of the Levi tribe followed
his orders, and that day they killed
about three thousand men. 29 Moses said
to them, "You obeyed the LORD and did
what was right, and so you will serve as
his priests for the people of Israel. It
was hard for you to kill your own sons
and brothers, but the LORD has blessed
you and made you his priests today."
30 The next day Moses told the people,
"This is a terrible thing you have done.
But I will go back to the LORD to see if I
can do something to keep this sin from
being held against you."
31 Moses returned to the LORD and
said, "The people have committed a terrible sin. They have made a gold idol to
be their god. 32 But I beg you to forgive
them. If you don't, please wipe my name
out of your book."[w]
33 The LORD replied, "I will wipe out of
my book the name of everyone who has
sinned against me. 34 Now take my people to the place I told you about, and my
angel will lead you. But when the time
comes, I will punish them for this sin."
35 So the LORD punished the people of
Israel with a terrible disease for talking
Aaron into making the gold idol.

The LORD Tells Israel To Leave Mount Sinai

33 The LORD said to Moses:
You led the people of Israel
out of Egypt. Now get ready to lead
them to the land I promised their ancestors Abraham, Isaac, and Jacob.
2-3 It is a land rich with milk and
honey, and I will send an angel to
force out those people who live
there—the Canaanites, the Amorites,
the Hittites, the Perizzites, the
Hivites, and the Jebusites. I would
go with my people, but they are so
rebellious that I would destroy them
before they get there.
4-5 Even before the LORD said these
harsh things, he had told Moses, "These
people really are rebellious, and I would
kill them at once, if I went with them.
But tell them to take off their fancy jewelry, then I'll decide what to do with
them." So the people started mourning,
6 and after leaving Mount Sinai,[x] they
stopped wearing fancy jewelry.

The LORD Is with His People

7 Moses used to set up a tent far from
camp. He called it the "meeting tent,"
and whoever needed some message
from the LORD would go there. 8 Each
time Moses went out to the tent, everyone would stand at the entrance to their
own tents and watch him enter. 9-11 Then
they would bow down because a thick
cloud would come down in front of the
tent, and the LORD would speak to
Moses face to face, just like a friend. Afterwards, Moses would return to camp,
but his young assistant Joshua[y] would
stay at the tent.

[w] **32.32** *your book*: The people of Israel believed that the LORD kept a record of the names of his people, and anyone whose name was removed from that book no longer belonged to the LORD.
[x] **33.6** *Mount Sinai*: The Hebrew text has "Mount Horeb," another name for Sinai.
[y] **33.9-11** *Joshua*: Hebrew "Joshua son of Nun."

The LORD Promises To Be with His People

12 Moses said to the LORD, "I know that
you have told me to lead these people to
the land you promised them. But you
have not told me who my assistant will
be. You have said that you are my friend
and that you are pleased with me. 13 If
this is true, let me know what your
plans are, then I can obey and continue
to please you. And don't forget that you
have chosen this nation to be your own."
14 The LORD said, "I will go with you
and give you peace."
15 Then Moses replied, "If you aren't
going with us, please don't make us
leave this place. 16 But if you do go with
us, everyone will know that you are
pleased with your people and with me.
That way, we will be different from the
rest of the people on earth."
17 So the LORD told him, "I will do what
you have asked, because I am your
friend and I am pleased with you."
18 Then Moses said, "I pray that you
will let me see you in all of your glory."
19 The LORD answered:
All right. I am the LORD, and I
show mercy and kindness to anyone
I choose. I will let you see my glory
and hear my holy name, 20 but I
won't let you see my face, because
anyone who sees my face will die.
21 There is a rock not far from me.
Stand beside it, 22 and before I pass
by in all of my shining glory, I will
put you in a large crack in the rock. I
will cover your eyes with my hand
until I have passed by. 23 Then I will
take my hand away, and you will see
my back. You will not see my face.

The Second Set of Commandments

(Deuteronomy 10.1-5)

34 One day the LORD said to Moses,
"Cut two flat stones like the first
ones I made, and I will write on them
the same commandments that were on
the two you broke. 2 Be ready tomorrow
morning to come up Mount Sinai and
meet me at the top. 3 No one is to come
with you or to be on the mountain at all.
Don't even let the sheep and cattle
graze at the foot of the mountain." 4 So
Moses cut two flat stones like the first
ones, and early the next morning he
carried them to the top of Mount Sinai,
just as the LORD had commanded.
5 The LORD God came down in a cloud
and stood beside Moses there on the
mountain. God spoke his holy name,
"the LORD."[z] 6 Then he passed in front of
Moses and called out, "I am the LORD
God. I am merciful and very patient
with my people. I show great love, and I
can be trusted. 7 I keep my promises to
my people forever, but I also punish
anyone who sins. When people sin, I
punish them and their children, and also
their grandchildren and great-grandchildren."
8 Moses quickly bowed down to the
ground and worshiped the LORD. 9 He
prayed, "LORD, if you really are pleased
with me, I pray that you will go with us.
It is true that these people are sinful and
rebellious, but forgive our sin and let us
be your people."

A Promise and Its Demands

(Exodus 23.14-19; Deuteronomy 7.1-5; 16.1-17)

10 The LORD said:
I promise to perform miracles for
you that have never been seen anywhere on earth. Neighboring nations
will stand in fear and know that I
was the one who did these marvelous things. 11 I will force out the
Amorites, the Canaanites, the Hittites, the Perizzites, the Hivites, and
the Jebusites, but you must do what
I command you today. 12 Don't make
treaties with any of those people. If
you do, it will be like falling into a
trap. 13 Instead, you must destroy
their altars and tear down the sacred poles[a] they use in the worship
of the goddess Asherah. 14 I demand
your complete loyalty—you must not
worship any other god! 15 Don't
make treaties with the people there,
or you will soon find yourselves
worshiping their gods and taking
part in their sacrificial meals. 16 Your
men will even marry their women
and be influenced to worship their
gods.
17 Don't make metal images of
gods.
18 Don't fail to observe the Festival
of Thin Bread in the month of Abib.[b]
Obey me and eat bread without
yeast for seven days during Abib,
because that is the month you left
Egypt.
19 The first-born males of your
families and of your flocks and
herds belong to me.
20 You can save the life of a first-
born donkey[c] by sacrificing a lamb;
if you don't, you must break the donkey's neck. You must save every
first-born son.
Bring an offering every time you
come to worship.

---

[z] **34.5** *the LORD*: See the note at 3.14, 15. [a] **34.13** *sacred poles*: Or "trees," used as symbols of Asherah, the goddess of fertility. [b] **34.18** *Abib*: See the note at 12.2. [c] **34.20** *donkey*: See the note at 13.13.

21 Do your work in six days and
rest on the seventh day, even during
the seasons for plowing and harvesting. 22 Celebrate the Harvest
Festival[d] each spring when you start
harvesting your wheat, and celebrate the Festival of Shelters[e] each
autumn when you pick your fruit.
23 Your men must come to worship
me three times a year, because I am
the LORD God of Israel. 24 I will force
the nations out of your land and en-
large your borders. Then no one will
try to take your property when you
come to worship me these three
times each year.
25 When you sacrifice an animal on
the altar, don't offer bread made
with yeast. And don't save any part
of the Passover meal for the next
day.
26 I am the LORD your God, and you
must bring the first part of your harvest to the place of worship.
Don't boil a young goat in its
mother's milk.
27 The LORD told Moses to put these
laws in writing, as part of his agreement
with Israel. 28 Moses stayed on the
mountain with the LORD for forty days
and nights, without eating or drinking.
And he wrote down the Ten Commandments, the most important part of God's
agreement with his people.

Moses Comes Down from Mount Sinai

29 Moses came down from Mount
Sinai, carrying the Ten Commandments.
His face was shining brightly because
the LORD had been speaking to him. But
Moses did not know at first that his face
was shining. 30 When Aaron and the others looked at Moses, they saw that his
face was shining, and they were afraid
to go near him. 31 Moses called out for
Aaron and the leaders to come to him,
and he spoke with them. 32 Then the rest
of the people of Israel gathered around
Moses, and he gave them the laws that
the LORD had given him on Mount Sinai.
33 The face of Moses kept shining, and
after he had spoken with the people, he
covered his face with a veil. 34 Moses
would always remove the veil when he
went into the sacred tent to speak with
the LORD. And when he came out, he
would tell the people everything the
LORD had told him to say. 35 They could
see that his face was still shining. So after he had spoken with them, he would
put the veil back on and leave it on until
the next time he went to speak with the
LORD.

Laws for the Sabbath

35 Moses called together the people
of Israel and told them that the
LORD had said:
2 You have six days in which to do
your work. But the seventh day must
be dedicated to me, your LORD, as a
day of rest. Whoever works on the
Sabbath will be put to death. 3 Don't
even build a cooking fire at home on
the Sabbath.

Offerings for the Sacred Tent

(Exodus 25.1-9; 35.10-19)

4 Moses told the people of Israel that
the LORD had said:
5 I would welcome an offering from
anyone who wants to give something. You may bring gold, silver, or
bronze; 6 blue, purple, or red wool;
fine linen; goat hair; 7 tanned ram
skin or fine leather; acacia wood;
8 olive oil for the lamp; sweet-
smelling spices for the oil of dedication and for the incense; or 9 onyx[f]
stones or other gems for the sacred
vest and breastpiece.
10 If you have any skills, you
should use them to help make what I
have commanded: 11 the sacred tent
with its covering and hooks, its
framework and crossbars, and its
post and stands; 12 the sacred chest
with its carrying poles, its place of
mercy, and the curtain in front of it;
13 the table with all that goes on it,
including the sacred bread; 14 the
lamp with its equipment and oil;
15 the incense altar with its carrying
poles and sweet-smelling incense;
the ordination oil; the curtain for the
entrance to the sacred tent; 16 the altar for sacrifices with its bronze
grating, its carrying poles, and its
equipment; the large bronze bowl
with its stand; 17 the curtains with
the posts and stands that go around
the courtyard; 18 the pegs and ropes
for the tent and the courtyard; 19 and
the finely woven priestly clothes for
Aaron and his sons.

Gifts for the LORD

20 Moses finished speaking, and everyone left. 21 Then those who wanted to
bring gifts to the LORD, brought them to
be used for the sacred tent, the worship
services, and the priestly clothes. 22 Men
and women came willingly and gave all
kinds of gold jewelry such as pins, earrings, rings, and necklaces. 23 Everyone
brought their blue, purple, and red wool,
their fine linen, and their cloth made of

[d] **34.22** *Harvest Festival*: See the note at 23.16.
[e] **34.22** *Festival of Shelters*: See the note at 23.16.
[f] **35.9** *onyx*: See the note at 25.7.

goat hair, as well as their ram skins
dyed red and their fine leather. 24 Anyone who had silver or bronze or acacia
wood brought it as a gift to the LORD.
25 The women who were good at weav-
ing cloth brought the blue, purple, and
red wool and the fine linen they had
made. 26 And the women who knew how
to make cloth from goat hair were glad
to do so.
27 The leaders brought different kinds
of jewels to be sewn on the special
clothes and the breastpiece for the high
priest. 28 They also brought sweet-
smelling spices to be mixed with the incense and olive oil that were for the
lamps and for ordaining the priests.
29 Moses had told the people what the
LORD wanted them to do, and many of
them decided to bring their gifts.

Bezalel and Oholiab
(Exodus 31.1-11)

30 Moses said to the people of Israel:
The LORD has chosen Bezalel[g] of
the Judah tribe. 31-33 Not only has the
LORD filled him with his Spirit, but
he has given him wisdom and made
him a skilled craftsman who can
create objects of art with gold, silver,
bronze, stone, and wood. 34 The LORD
is urging him and Oholiab[h] from the
tribe of Dan to teach others. 35 And
he has given them all kinds of artis-
tic skills, including the ability to design and embroider with blue, purple, and red wool and to weave fine
linen.

36 The LORD has given to Bezalel,
Oholiab, and others the skills
needed for building a place of worship,
and they will follow the LORD's instructions.
2 Then Moses brought together these
workers who were eager to work, 3 and
he gave them the money that the people
of Israel had donated for building the
place of worship. In fact, so much
money was being given each morning,
4 that finally everyone stopped working
5 and said, "Moses, there is already more
money than we need for what the LORD
has assigned us to do." 6 So Moses sent
word for the people to stop giving, and
they did. 7 But there was already more
than enough to do what needed to be
done.

The Curtains and Coverings for the Sacred Tent
(Exodus 26.1-14)

8-9 The skilled workers got together to
make the sacred tent and its linen curtains woven with blue, purple, and red
wool and embroidered with figures of
winged creatures. Each of the ten panels
was fourteen yards long and two yards
wide, 10 and they were sewn together to
make two curtains with five panels
each. 11-13 Then fifty loops of blue cloth
were put along one of the wider sides of
each curtain, and the two curtains were
fastened together at the loops with fifty
gold hooks.
14-15 As the material for the tent, goat
hair was used to weave eleven sections
fifteen yards by two yards each. 16 These
eleven sections were joined to make two
panels, one with five and the other with
six sections. 17 Fifty loops were put along
one of the wider sides of each panel,
18 and the two panels were fastened at
the loops with fifty bronze hooks. 19 Two
other coverings were made—one with
fine leather and the other with ram
skins dyed red.

The Framework for the Sacred Tent
(Exodus 26.15-30)

20 Acacia wood was used to build the
framework for the walls of the sacred
tent. 21 Each frame was fifteen feet high
and twenty-seven inches wide 22-26 with
two wooden pegs near the bottom. Then
two silver stands were placed under
each frame with sockets for the pegs, so
they could be joined together. Twenty of
these frames were used along the south
side and twenty more along the north.
27 Six frames were used for the back
wall along the west side 28-29 with two
more at the southwest and northwest
corners. These corner frames were
joined from top to bottom. 30 Altogether,
along the back wall there were eight
frames with two silver stands under
each of them.
31-33 Five crossbars were made for each
of the wooden frames, with the center
crossbar running the full length of the
wall. 34 The frames and crossbars were
covered with gold, and gold rings were
attached to the frames to run the crossbars through.

The Inside Curtain for the Sacred Tent
(Exodus 26.31-37)

35 They made the inside curtain[i] of fine
linen woven with blue, purple, and red
wool, and embroidered with figures of
winged creatures. 36 They also made four
acacia wood posts and covered them
with gold. Then gold rings were fastened to the posts, which were set on silver stands.

[g] **35.30** *Bezalel*: See the note at 31.2. [h] **35.34** *Oholiab*: Hebrew "Oholiab son of Ahisamach."
[i] **36.35** *inside curtain*: Separating the holy place from the most holy place.

37 For the entrance to the tent, they
used a curtain of fine linen woven with
blue, purple, and red wool and embroidered with fancy needlework. 38 They
made five posts, covered them completely with gold, and set them each on
a gold-covered bronze stand. Finally,
they attached hooks for the curtain.

The Sacred Chest
(Exodus 25.10-22)

37 Bezalel built a chest of acacia
wood forty-five inches long,
twenty-seven inches wide, and twenty-
seven inches high. 2 He covered it inside
and out with pure gold and put a gold
edging around the top. 3 He made four
gold rings and fastened one of them to
each of the four legs of the chest. 4 Then
he made two poles of acacia wood, covered them with gold, 5 and put them
through the rings, so the chest could be
carried by the poles.
6 The entire lid of the chest, which was
also covered with pure gold, was the
place of mercy.[j] 7-9 On each of the two
ends of the chest he made a winged
creature of hammered gold. They faced
each other, and their wings covered the
place of mercy.

The Table for the Sacred Bread
(Exodus 25.23-30)

10 Bezalel built a table of acacia wood
thirty-six inches long, eighteen inches
wide, and twenty-seven inches high.
11-12 He covered it with pure gold and put
a gold edging around it with a border
three inches wide.[k] 13 He made four gold
rings and attached one to each of the
legs 14 near the edging. The poles for
carrying the table were placed through
these rings 15 and were made of acacia
wood covered with gold. 16 Everything
that was to be set on the table was made
of pure gold—the bowls, plates, jars, and
cups for wine offerings.

The Lampstand
(Exodus 25.31-40)

17 Bezalel made a lampstand of pure
gold. The whole lampstand, including its
decorative flowers, was made from a
single piece of hammered gold, 18 with
three branches on each of its two sides.
19 There were three decorative almond
blossoms on each branch 20 and four on
the stem. 21 There was also a blossom
where each pair of branches came out
from the stem. 22 The lampstand, including its branches and decorative flowers,
was made from a single piece of hammered pure gold. 23-24 The lamp and its
equipment, including the tongs and
trays, were made of about seventy-five
pounds of pure gold.

The Altar for Burning Incense
(Exodus 30.1-5)

25 For burning incense, Bezalel made
an altar of acacia wood. It was eighteen
inches square and thirty-six inches high
with each of its four corners sticking up
like the horn of a bull. 26 He covered it
with pure gold and put a gold edging
around it. 27 Then below the edging on
opposite sides he attached two gold
rings through which he put the poles for
carrying the altar. 28 These poles were
also made of acacia wood and covered
with gold.

The Oil for Dedication and the Incense
(Exodus 30.22-38)

29 Bezalel mixed the oil for dedication
and the sweet-smelling spices for the incense.

The Altar for Offering Sacrifices
(Exodus 27.1-8)

38 Bezalel built an altar of acacia
wood for offering sacrifices. It
was seven and a half feet square and
four and a half feet high 2 with each of
its four corners sticking up like the horn
of a bull, and it was completely covered
with bronze. 3 The equipment for the altar was also made of bronze—the pans
for the hot ashes, the shovels, the meat
forks, and the fire pans. 4 Midway up the
altar he built a ledge around it and covered the bottom half of the altar with a
decorative bronze grating. 5 Then he attached a bronze ring beneath the ledge
at the four corners to put the poles
through. 6 He covered two acacia wood
poles with bronze and 7 put them
through the rings for carrying the altar,
which was shaped like an open box.

The Large Bronze Bowl
(Exodus 30.18-21)

8 Bezalel made a large bowl and a
stand out of bronze from the mirrors of
the women who helped at the entrance
to the sacred tent.

The Courtyard around the Sacred Tent
(Exodus 27.9-19)

9-17 Around the sacred tent Bezalel
built a courtyard one hundred fifty feet
long on the south and north and seventy-five feet wide on the east and west.

[j] **37.6** *place of mercy*: See the note at 26.34. [k] **37.11,12** *a gold edging . . . wide*: Or "a gold edging around it three inches wide."

He used twenty bronze posts on bronze
stands for the south and north and ten
for the west. Then he hung a curtain of
fine linen on the posts along each of
these three sides by using silver hooks
and rods. He placed three bronze posts
on each side of the entrance at the east
and hung a curtain seven and a half
yards wide on each set of posts.

[18-19]For the entrance to the courtyard,
Bezalel made a curtain ten yards long,
which he hung on four bronze posts that
were set on bronze stands. This curtain
was the same height as the one for the
rest of the courtyard and was made of
fine linen embroidered and woven with
blue, purple, and red wool. He hung the
curtain on the four posts, using silver
hooks and rods. [20]The pegs for the tent
and for the curtain around the tent were
made of bronze.

The Sacred Tent

[21-23]Bezalel had worked closely with
Oholiab,[l] who was an expert at designing and engraving, and at embroidering
blue, purple, and red wool. The two of
them completed the work that the LORD
had commanded.

Moses made Aaron's son Ithamar responsible for keeping record of the metals used for the sacred tent. [24]According
to the official weights, the amount of
gold given was two thousand two hundred nine pounds, [25]and the silver that
was collected when the people were
counted[m] came to seven thousand five
hundred fifty pounds. [26]Everyone who
was counted paid the required amount,
and there was a total of 603,550 men
who were twenty years old or older.

[27]Seventy-five pounds of the silver
were used to make each of the one hundred stands for the sacred tent and the
curtain. [28]The remaining fifty pounds of
silver were used for the hooks and rods
and for covering the tops of the posts.

[29]Five thousand three hundred pounds
of bronze were given. [30]And it was used
to make the stands for the entrance to
the tent, the altar and its grating, the
equipment for the altar, [31]the stands for
the posts that surrounded the courtyard,
including those at the entrance to the
courtyard, and the pegs for the tent and
the courtyard.

Making the Priestly Clothes
(Exodus 28.1-14)

39 Beautiful priestly clothes were
made of blue, purple, and red
wool for Aaron to wear when he performed his duties in the holy place. This
was done exactly as the LORD had commanded Moses.

[2-3]The entire priestly vest was made of
fine linen, woven with blue, purple, and
red wool. Thin sheets of gold were hammered out and cut into threads that
were skillfully woven into the vest. [4-5]It
had two shoulder straps to support it
and a sash that fastened around the
waist. [6]Onyx[n] stones were placed in
gold settings, and each one was engraved with the name of one of Israel's
sons. [7]Then these were attached to the
shoulder straps of the vest, so the LORD
would never forget his people. Everything was done exactly as the LORD had
commanded Moses.

The Breastpiece
(Exodus 28.15-30)

[8]The breastpiece was made with the
same materials and designs as the
priestly vest. [9]It was nine inches square
and folded double [10]with four rows of
three precious stones: A carnelian, a
chrysolite, and an emerald were in the
first row; [11]a turquoise, a sapphire, and
a diamond were in the second row; [12]a
jacinth, an agate, and an amethyst were
in the third row; [13]and a beryl, an onyx,
and a jasper[o] were in the fourth row.
They were mounted in a delicate gold
setting, [14]and on each of them was engraved the name of one of the twelve
tribes of Israel.

[15-18]Two gold rings were attached to
the upper front corners of the breastpiece and fastened with two braided
gold chains to gold settings on the
shoulder straps. [19]Two other gold rings
were attached to the lower inside corners next to the vest, [20]and two more
near the bottom of the shoulder straps
right above the sash. [21]To keep the
breastpiece in place, a blue cord was
used to tie the two lower rings on the
breastpiece to those on the vest. These
things were done exactly as the LORD
had commanded Moses.

The Clothes for the Priests
(Exodus 28.31-43)

[22]The priestly robe was made of blue
wool [23]with an opening in the center for
the head. The material around the collar
was bound so as to keep it from raveling. [24-26]Along the hem of the robe were
woven pomegranates[p] of blue, purple,

[l] **38.21-23** *Bezalel . . . Oholiab*: Hebrew "Bezalel son of Uri and grandson of Hur of the Judah tribe had worked closely with Oholiab son of Ahisamach from the tribe of Dan."
[m] **38.25** *counted*: See 30.11-16; Numbers 1. [n] **39.6** *Onyx*: See the note at 25.7.
[o] **39.13** *jasper*: For the stones mentioned in verses 10-13, see the note at 28.20.
[p] **39.24-26** *pomegranates*: See the note at 28.33, 34.

and red wool with a bell of pure gold
between each of them. This robe was to
be worn by Aaron when he performed
his duties.
27-29 Everything that Aaron and his
sons wore was made of fine linen woven
with blue, purple, and red wool, including their robes and turbans, their fancy
caps and underwear, and even their
sashes that were embroidered with
needlework.
30 "Dedicated to the LORD" was engraved on a narrow strip of pure gold,
31 which was fastened to Aaron's turban.
These things were done exactly as the
LORD had commanded Moses.

The Work Is Completed

(Exodus 35.10-19)

32 So the people of Israel finished making everything the LORD had told Moses
to make. 33 Then they brought it all to
Moses: the sacred tent and its equipment, including the hooks, the framework and crossbars, and its posts and
stands; 34 the covering of tanned ram
skins and fine leather; the inside curtain; 35 the sacred chest with its carrying
poles and the place of mercy; 36 the table
with all that goes on it, including the sacred bread; 37 the lampstand of pure
gold, together with its equipment and
oil; 38 the gold-covered incense altar; the
ordination oil and the sweet-smelling incense; the curtain for the entrance to the
tent; 39 the bronze altar for sacrifices
with its bronze grating, its carrying
poles, and its equipment; the large
bronze bowl with its stand; 40 the curtain
with its posts and cords, and its pegs
and stands that go around the courtyard; everything needed for the sacred
tent; 41 and the finely woven priestly
clothes for Aaron and his sons.
42-43 When Moses saw that the people
had done everything exactly as the
LORD had commanded, he gave them his
blessing.

The LORD's Tent Is Set Up

40 The LORD said to Moses:
2 Set up my tent on the first
day of the year[q] 3 and put the chest
with the Ten Commandments behind the inside curtain[r] of the tent.
4 Bring in the table and set on it
those things that are made for it.
Also bring in the lampstand and attach the lamps to it. 5 Then place the
gold altar of incense in front of the
sacred chest and hang a curtain at
the entrance to the tent. 6 Set the altar for burning sacrifices in front of
the entrance to my tent. 7 Put the
large bronze bowl between the tent
and the altar and fill the bowl with
water. 8 Surround the tent and the altar with the wall of curtains and
hang the curtain that was made for
the entrance.
9 Use the sacred olive oil to dedicate the tent and everything in it to
me. 10 Do the same thing with the altar for offering sacrifices and its
equipment 11 and with the bowl and
its stand. 12 Bring Aaron and his sons
to the entrance of the tent and have
them wash themselves. 13 Dress
Aaron in the priestly clothes, then
use the sacred olive oil to ordain
him and dedicate him to me as my
priest. 14 Put the priestly robes on
Aaron's sons 15 and ordain them in
the same way, so they and their descendants will always be my priests.
16 Moses followed the LORD's instructions. 17 And on the first day of the first
month[s] of the second year, the sacred
tent was set up. 18 The posts, stands, and
framework were put in place, 19 then the
two layers of coverings were hung over
them. 20 The stones with the Ten Commandments written on them were
stored in the sacred chest, the place of
mercy[t] was put on top of it, and the carrying poles were attached. 21 The chest
was brought into the tent and set behind
the curtain in the most holy place. These
things were done exactly as the LORD
had commanded Moses.
22 The table for the sacred bread was
put along the north wall of the holy
place, 23 after which the bread was set on
the table. 24 The lampstand was put
along the south wall, 25 then the lamps
were attached to it there in the presence
of the LORD. 26 The gold incense altar
was set up in front of the curtain, 27 and
sweet-smelling incense was burned on
it. These things were done exactly as the
LORD had commanded Moses.
28 The curtain was hung at the entrance to the sacred tent. 29 Then the altar for offering sacrifices was put in
front of the tent, and animal sacrifices
and gifts of grain were offered there.
30 The large bronze bowl was placed between the altar and the entrance to the
tent. It was filled with water, 31 then
Moses and Aaron, together with Aaron's
sons, washed their hands and feet. 32 In
fact, they washed each time before entering the tent or offering sacrifices at
the altar. These things were done exactly as the LORD had commanded
Moses.

[q] **40.2** *first day of the year*: See the note at 12.2. [r] **40.3** *inside curtain*: Separating the holy place from the most holy place. [s] **40.17** *first month*: See the note at 12.2. [t] **40.20** *place of mercy*: See the note at 26.34.

33Finally, Moses had the curtain hung
around the courtyard.

The Glory of the LORD

34Suddenly the sacred tent was covered by a thick cloud and filled with the glory of the LORD. 35And so, Moses could not enter the tent. 36Whenever the cloud moved from the tent, the people would break camp and follow; 37then they would set up camp and stay there, until it moved again. 38No matter where the people traveled, the LORD was with them. Each day his cloud was over the tent, and each night a fire could be seen in the cloud.

LEVITICUS

ABOUT THIS BOOK

Leviticus tells how the Lord continued to give laws and instructions to Moses. The book's name is related to the word "Levite," a term referring to a person who belonged to the tribe of Levi. Levites were to be special servants of the Lord at the sacred tent, and the priests came from one of the Levite families. Much of the book deals with the responsibilities of the priests and other Levites, for example, sacrifices, gifts to the Lord, and religious festivals. But this book also contains laws about what animals could be used for food, what materials could be used for clothing, and how to care for the poor.

Most of the book is made up of laws, but it has a few stories telling what happened when the people or priests obeyed or disobeyed God's instructions. God was quick to punish those who rebelled, but he also made this promise to those who would obey him:

> *I will walk with you—I will be your God, and you will be my people. I am the LORD your God, and I rescued you from Egypt, so that you would never again be slaves. I have set you free; now walk with your heads held high.* (26.12, 13)

A QUICK LOOK AT THIS BOOK

---

1 1-3The LORD spoke to Moses from
the sacred tent and gave him instructions for the community of Israel to follow when they offered sacrifices.

Sacrifices To Please the LORD

The LORD said:

Sacrifices to please me[a] must be completely burned on the bronze altar.[b]
Bulls or rams or goats[c] are the animals to be used for these sacrifices. If the animal is a bull, it must not have anything wrong with it. Lead it to the entrance of the sacred tent, and I will let
you know if it is[d] acceptable to me. 4Lay
your hand on its head, and I will accept the animal as a sacrifice for taking away your sins.

[a]1.1-3 *Sacrifices to please me*: These sacrifices have traditionally been called "whole burnt offerings" because the whole animal was burned on the altar. A main purpose of such sacrifices was to please the LORD with the smell of the sacrifice, and so in the CEV they are often called "sacrifices to please the LORD." [b]1.1-3 *bronze altar*: This altar for offering sacrifices was in front of the entrance to the sacred tent; it was made of acacia wood covered with bronze. A smaller altar for offering incense was inside the tent; it was made of acacia wood covered with gold. [c]1.1-3 *goats*: Hebrew "male goats." [d]1.1-3 *if it is*: Or "if you are."

5After the bull is killed in my presence, some priests from Aaron's family
will offer its blood to me by splattering
it against the four sides of the altar.
6Skin the bull and cut it up, 7while the
priests pile wood on the altar fire to
make it start blazing. 8-9Wash the bull's
insides and hind legs, so the priests can
lay them on the altar with the head, the
fat, and the rest of the animal. A priest
will then send all of it up in smoke with
a smell that pleases me.
10If you sacrifice a ram or a goat, it
must not have anything wrong with it.
11Lead the animal to the north side of
the altar, where it is to be killed in my
presence. Then some of the priests will
splatter its blood against the four sides
of the altar.
12-13Cut up the animal and wash its insides and hind legs. A priest will put
these parts on the altar with the head,
the fat, and the rest of the animal. Then
he will send all of it up in smoke with a
smell that pleases me.
14If you offer a bird for this kind of
sacrifice, it must be a dove or a pigeon.
15A priest will take the bird to the
bronze altar, where he will wring its
neck and put its head on the fire. Then
he will drain out its blood on one side of
the altar, 16remove the bird's craw with
what is in it,[e] and throw them on the
ash heap at the east side of the altar.[f]
17Finally, he will take the bird by its
wings, tear it partially open,[g] and send
it up in smoke with a smell that pleases
me.

Sacrifices To Give Thanks to the LORD

The LORD said:

2 When you offer sacrifices to give
thanks to me,[h] you must use only
your finest flour. Put it in a dish, sprinkle olive oil and incense on the flour,
2and take it to the priests from Aaron's
family. One of them will scoop up the incense together with a handful of the
flour and oil. Then, to show that the
whole offering belongs to me, the priest
will lay this part on the bronze altar and
send it up in smoke with a smell that
pleases me. 3The rest of this sacrifice is
for the priests; it is very holy because it
was offered to me.
4If you bake bread in an oven for this
sacrifice, use only your finest flour, but
without any yeast. You may make the
flour into a loaf mixed with olive oil, or
you may make it into thin wafers and
brush them with oil.
5If you cook bread in a shallow pan
for this sacrifice, use only your finest
flour. Mix it with olive oil, but do not use
any yeast. 6Then break the bread into
small pieces and sprinkle them with oil.
7If you cook your bread in a pan with a
lid on it, you must also use the finest
flour mixed with oil.
8You may prepare sacrifices to give
thanks in any of these three ways. Bring
your sacrifice to a priest, and he will
take it to the bronze altar. 9Then, to
show that the whole offering belongs to
me, the priest will lay part of it on the
altar and send it up in smoke with a
smell that pleases me. 10The rest of this
sacrifice is for the priests; it is very holy
because it was offered to me.
11Yeast and honey must never be
burned on the altar, so don't ever mix either of these in a grain sacrifice. 12You
may offer either of them separately,[i]
when you present the first part of your
harvest to me, but they must never be
burned on the altar.
13Salt is offered when you make an
agreement with me, so sprinkle salt on
these sacrifices.
14Freshly cut grain, either roasted or
coarsely ground,[j] must be used when
you offer the first part of your grain harvest. 15You must mix in some olive oil
and put incense on top, because this is a
grain sacrifice. 16A priest will sprinkle
all of the incense and some of the grain
and oil on the altar and send them up in
smoke to show that the whole offering
belongs to me.

Sacrifices To Ask the LORD's Blessing

The LORD said:

3 When you offer sacrifices to ask my
blessing,[k] you may offer either a
bull or a cow, but there must be nothing
wrong with the animal. 2Lead it to the
entrance of the sacred tent, lay your
hand on its head, and have it killed
there. A priest from Aaron's family will
splatter its blood against the four sides
of the altar.
3Offer all of the fat on the animal's in-

[e]**1.16** *with what is in it*: One possible meaning for the difficult Hebrew text. [f]**1.16** *ash heap at the east side of the altar*: Ashes were piled here, then once a day they were taken to the ash heap outside the camp (see 4.11, 12; 6.10, 11). [g]**1.17** *tear it partially open*: Or "tear it open without pulling off the wings." [h]**2.1** *sacrifices to give thanks to me*: These sacrifices have traditionally been called "grain offerings." A main purpose of such sacrifices was to thank the LORD with a gift of grain, and so in the CEV they are sometimes called "sacrifices to give thanks to the LORD." [i]**2.12** *You . . . separately*: One possible meaning for the difficult Hebrew text. [j]**2.14** *either . . . ground*: Or "roasted and coarsely ground." [k]**3.1** *sacrifices to ask my blessing*: These sacrifices have traditionally been called "peace offerings" or "offerings of well-being." A main purpose was to ask for the LORD's blessing, and so in the CEV they are sometimes called "sacrifices to ask the LORD's blessing."

sides, 4as well as the lower part of the liver and the two kidneys with their fat. 5Some of the priests will lay these pieces on the altar and send them up in smoke with a smell that pleases me, together with the sacrifice that is offered to please me.[l]

6Instead of a bull or a cow, you may offer any sheep or goat that has nothing wrong with it. 7If you offer a sheep, you must present it to me at the entrance to the sacred tent. 8Lay your hand on its head and have it killed there. A priest will then splatter its blood against the four sides of the altar.

9Offer the fat on the tail, the tailbone, and the insides, 10as well as the lower part of the liver and the two kidneys with their fat. 11One of the priests will lay these pieces on the altar and send them up in smoke as a food offering for me.

12If you offer a goat, you must also present it to me 13at the entrance to the sacred tent. Lay your hand on its head and have it killed there. A priest will then splatter its blood against the four sides of the altar.

14Offer all of the fat on the animal's insides, 15as well as the lower part of the liver and the two kidneys with their fat. 16One of the priests will put these pieces on the altar and send them up in smoke as a food offering with a smell that pleases me.

All fat belongs to me. 17So you and your descendants must never eat any fat or any blood, not even in the privacy of your own homes.[m] This law will never change.

Sacrifices for Sin

(Leviticus 6.24-30)

4 The LORD told Moses 2to say to the community of Israel:

Offer a sacrifice to ask forgiveness when you sin by accidentally doing something I have told you not to do.

When the High Priest Sins

The LORD said:

3When the high priest sins, he makes everyone else guilty too. And so, he must sacrifice a young bull that has nothing wrong with it. 4The priest will lead the bull to the entrance of the sacred tent, lay his hand on its head, and kill it there. 5He will take a bowl of the blood inside the tent, 6dip a finger in the blood, and sprinkle some of it seven times toward the sacred chest behind the curtain. 7Then, in my presence, he will smear some of the blood on each of the four corners of the incense altar, before pouring out the rest at the foot of the bronze altar[n] near the entrance to the tent.

8-10The priest will remove the fat from the bull, just as he does when he sacrifices a bull to ask my blessing.[o] This includes the fat on the insides, as well as the lower part of the liver and the two kidneys with their fat. He will then send it all up in smoke.

11-12The skin and flesh of the bull, together with its legs, insides, and the food still in its stomach, are to be taken outside the camp and burned on a wood fire near the ash heap.[p]

When the Whole Nation Sins

The LORD said:

13When the nation of Israel disobeys me without meaning to, the whole nation is still guilty. 14Once you realize what has happened, you must sacrifice a young bull to ask my forgiveness. Lead the bull to the entrance of the sacred tent, 15where your tribal leaders will lay their hands on its head, before having it killed in my presence.

16The priest will take a bowl of the animal's blood inside the sacred tent, 17dip a finger in the blood, and sprinkle some of it seven times toward the sacred chest behind the curtain. 18Then, in my presence, he must smear some of the blood on each of the four corners of the incense altar, before pouring out the rest at the foot of the bronze altar[q] near the entrance to the tent. 19-21After this, the priest will remove the fat from the bull and send it up in smoke on the altar. Finally, he will burn its remains outside the camp, just as he did with the other bull. By this sacrifice the sin of the whole nation will be forgiven.

When a Tribal Leader Sins

The LORD God said:

22Any tribal leader who disobeys me without meaning to is still guilty. 23As soon as the leader realizes what has happened, he must sacrifice a goat[r] that has nothing wrong with it. 24This is a sacrifice for sin. So he will lay his hand on the animal's head, before having it killed in my presence at the north side of the bronze altar. 25The priest will dip a finger in the blood, smear some of it on each of the four corners of the altar, and pour out the rest at the foot of the altar. 26Then he must send all of the fat up in smoke, just as he does when a

---

[l] **3.5** *sacrifice . . . to please me*: See the note at 1.1-3. [m] **3.17** *not even . . . homes*: Or "no matter where you live." [n] **4.7** *incense altar . . . bronze altar*: See the note at 1.1-3. [o] **4.8-10** *to ask my blessing*: See the note at 3.1. [p] **4.11,12** *ash heap*: See the note at 1.16. [q] **4.18** *incense altar . . . bronze altar*: See the note at 1.1-3. [r] **4.23** *goat*: See the note at 1.1-3.

sacrifice is offered to ask my blessing.[s]
By this sacrifice the leader's sin will be
forgiven.

When Ordinary People Sin

The LORD *said:*
27 When any of you ordinary people
disobey me without meaning to, you are
still guilty. 28 As soon as you realize what
you have done, you must sacrifice a female goat that has nothing wrong with
it. 29 Lead the goat to the north side of
the bronze altar and lay your hand on
its head, before having it killed. 30 Then a
priest will dip a finger in the blood; he
will smear some of it on each of the four
corners of the altar and pour out the
rest at the foot of the altar. 31 After this,
the priest will remove all of the fat, just
as he does when an animal is sacrificed
to ask my blessing.[s] The priest will then
send the fat up in smoke with a smell
that pleases me. This animal is sacrificed so that I will forgive you ordinary
people when you sin.
32 If you offer a lamb instead of a goat
as a sacrifice for sin, it must be a female
that has nothing wrong with it. 33 Lead
the lamb to the altar and lay your hand
on its head, before having it killed.
34 The priest will dip a finger in the
blood, smear some of it on each of the
four corners of the altar, and pour out
the rest at the foot of the altar. 35 After
this, all of the fat must be removed, just
as when an animal is sacrificed to ask
my blessing. Then the priest will send it
up in smoke to me, together with a food
offering, and your sin will be forgiven.

The LORD *said:*
5 If you refuse to testify in court about
something you saw or know has
happened, you have sinned and can be
punished.
2 You are guilty and unfit to worship
me, if you accidentally touch the dead
body of any kind of unclean animal.
3 You are guilty if you find out that you
have accidentally touched any waste
that comes from a human body.
4 You are guilty the moment you realize that you have made a hasty promise
to do something good or bad.
5 As soon as you discover that you
have committed any of these sins, you
must confess what you have done.
6 Then you must bring a female sheep or
goat to me as the price for your sin. A
priest will sacrifice the animal, and you
will be forgiven.
7 If you are poor and cannot afford to
bring an animal, you may bring two
doves or two pigeons. One of these will
be a sacrifice to ask my forgiveness, and
the other will be a sacrifice to please
me.
8 Give both birds to the priest, who will
offer one as a sacrifice to ask my forgiveness. He will wring its neck without
tearing off its head, 9 splatter some of its
blood on one side of the bronze altar,
and drain out the rest at the foot of the
altar. 10 Then he will follow the proper
rules for offering the other bird as a sacrifice to please me.
You will be forgiven when the priest
offers these sacrifices as the price for
your sin.
11 If you are so poor that you cannot
afford doves or pigeons, you may bring
two pounds of your finest flour. This is a
sacrifice to ask my forgiveness, so don't
sprinkle olive oil or sweet-smelling incense on it. 12 Give the flour to a priest,
who will scoop up a handful and send it
up in smoke together with the other offerings. This is a reminder that all of the
flour belongs to me. 13 By offering this
sacrifice, the priest pays the price for
any of these sins you may have committed. The priest gets the rest of the flour,
just as he does with grain sacrifices.

Sacrifices To Make Things Right

(Leviticus 7.1-10)

14-15 The LORD told Moses what the
people must do to make things right
when they find out they have cheated
the LORD without meaning to:
If this happens, you must either sacrifice a ram that has nothing wrong with
it or else pay the price of a ram with the
official money used by the priests. 16 In
addition, you must pay what you owe
plus a fine of twenty percent. Then the
priest will offer the ram as a sacrifice to
make things right, and you will be forgiven.
17-19 If you break any of my commands
without meaning to, you are still guilty,
and you can be punished. When you realize what you have done, you must either bring to the priest a ram that has
nothing wrong with it or else pay him
for one. The priest will then offer it as a
sacrifice to make things right, and you
will be forgiven.

Other Sins That Need Sacrifices or Payments

(Numbers 5.5-10)

6 1-3 The LORD told Moses what the
people must do when they commit
other sins against the LORD:
You have sinned if you rob or cheat
someone, if you keep back money or
valuables left in your care, or if you find
something and claim not to have it.
4 When this happens, you must return

[s] **4.26** *sacrifice . . . blessing*: See the note at 3.1.

[s] **4.31** *sacrificed to ask my blessing*: See the note at 3.1.

what doesn't belong to you 5and pay the
owner a fine of twenty percent. 6-7In addition, you must either bring to the
priest a ram that has nothing wrong
with it or else pay him for one. The
priest will then offer it as a sacrifice to
make things right, and you will be forgiven for what you did wrong.

Daily Sacrifices

(Exodus 29.38-43; Numbers 28.1-8)

8-9The LORD told Moses to tell Aaron
and his sons how to offer the daily sacrifices that are sent up in smoke to
please the LORD:[t]

You must put the animal for the sacrifice on the altar in the evening and let it
stay there all night. But make sure the
fire keeps burning. 10The next morning
you will dress in your priestly clothes,
including your linen underwear. Then
clean away the ashes left by the sacrifices and pile them beside the altar.
11Change into your everyday clothes,
take the ashes outside the camp, and
pile them in the special place.[u]

12The fire must never go out, so put
wood on it each morning. After this, you
are to lay an animal on the altar next to
the fat that you sacrifice to ask my
blessing.[v] Then send it all up in smoke
to me.

13The altar fire must always be kept
burning—it must never go out.

Sacrifices To Give Thanks to the LORD

The LORD said:

14When someone offers a sacrifice to
give thanks to me,[w] the priests from
Aaron's family must bring it to the front
of the bronze altar, 15where one of them
will scoop up a handful of the flour and
oil, together with all the incense on it.
Then, to show that the whole offering
belongs to me, he will lay all of this on
the altar and send it up in smoke with a
smell that pleases me. 16-17The rest of it
is to be baked without yeast and eaten
by the priests in the sacred courtyard of
the sacred tent. This bread is very holy,
just like the sacrifices for sin or for
making things right, and I have given
this part to the priests from what is offered to me on the altar.

18Only the men in Aaron's family are
allowed to eat this bread, and they must
go through a ceremony to be made holy
before touching it.[x] This law will never
change.

When Priests Are Ordained

19The LORD spoke to Moses 20and told
him what sacrifices the priests must offer on the morning and evening of the
day they are ordained:

It is the same as the regular morning
and evening sacrifices—a pound of flour
21mixed with olive oil and cooked in a
shallow pan. The bread must then be
crumbled into small pieces[y] and sent up
in smoke with a smell that pleases me.
22-23Each of Aaron's descendants who is
ordained as a priest must perform this
ceremony and make sure that the bread
is completely burned on the altar. None
of it may be eaten!

Sacrifices for Sin

(Leviticus 4.1, 2)

24The LORD told Moses 25how the
priests from Aaron's family were to offer the sacrifice for sin:

This sacrifice is very sacred, and the
animal must be killed in my presence at
the north side of the bronze altar. 26The
priest who offers this sacrifice must eat
it in the sacred courtyard of the sacred
tent, 27and anyone or anything that
touches the meat will be holy.[z] If any of
the animal's blood is splattered on the
clothes of the priest, they must be
washed in a holy place. 28If the meat
was cooked in a clay pot, the pot must
be destroyed,[a] but if it was cooked in a
bronze pot, the pot must be scrubbed
and rinsed with water.

29This sacrifice is very holy, and only
the priests may have any part of it.
30None of the meat may be eaten from
the sacrifices for sin that require blood
to be brought into the sacred tent.[b]
These sacrifices must be completely
burned.

Sacrifices To Make Things Right

(Leviticus 5.14-19)

The LORD said:

7 The sacrifice to make things right is
very sacred. 2The animal must be
killed in the same place where the sacrifice to please me[c] is killed, and the animal's blood must be splattered against
the four sides of the bronze altar. 3Offer
all of the animal's fat, including the fat
on its tail and on its insides, 4as well as
the lower part of the liver and the two
kidneys with their fat. 5One of the
priests will lay these pieces on the altar

[t]**6.8,9** *to please the LORD*: See the note at 1.1-3. [u]**6.11** *ashes . . . in the special place*: See the note at 1.16. [v]**6.12** *sacrifice to ask my blessing*: See the note at 3.1. [w]**6.14** *a sacrifice to give thanks to me*: See the note at 2.1. [x]**6.18** *and they . . . touching it*: One possible meaning for the difficult Hebrew text. [y]**6.21** *crumbled . . . pieces*: One possible meaning for the difficult Hebrew text. [z]**6.27** *that touches . . . holy*: One possible meaning for the difficult Hebrew text. [a]**6.28** *clay pot . . . destroyed*: Juice from the meat cannot be completely cleaned from a clay pot. [b]**6.30** *that require blood . . . tent*: See 4.1-21. [c]**7.2** *sacrifice to please me*: See the note at 1.1-3.

and send them up in smoke to me. 6This
sacrifice for making things right is very
holy. Only the priests may eat it, and
they must eat it in a holy place.[d]
7The ceremony for this sacrifice and
the one for sin are just alike, and the
meat may be eaten only by the priest
who performs this ceremony of forgiveness.
8In fact, the priest who offers a sacrifice to please me[e] may keep the skin of
the animal, 9just as he may eat the bread
from a sacrifice to give thanks to me.[f]
10All other grain sacrifices—with or
without olive oil in them—are to be divided equally among the priests of
Aaron's family.

Sacrifices To Ask the LORD's Blessing

The LORD said:
11Here are the instructions for offering a sacrifice to ask my blessing:[g] 12If
you offer it to give thanks, you must
offer some bread together with it. Use
the finest flour to make three kinds of
bread without yeast—two in the form of
loaves mixed with olive oil and one in
the form of thin wafers brushed with oil.
13You must also make some bread with
yeast. 14Give me one loaf or wafer from
each of these four kinds of bread, after
which they will belong to the priest who
splattered the blood against the bronze
altar.
15When you offer an animal to ask a
blessing from me or to thank me, the
meat belongs to you, but it must be
eaten the same day. 16It is different with
the sacrifices you offer when you make
me a promise or voluntarily give me
something. The meat from those sacrifices may be kept and eaten the next
day, 17-18but any that is left must be destroyed. If you eat any after the second
day, your sacrifice will be useless and
unacceptable, and you will be both disgusting and guilty.
19Don't eat any of the meat that
touches something unclean. Instead,
burn it. The rest of the meat may be
eaten by anyone who is clean and acceptable to me. 20-21But don't eat any of
this meat if you have become unclean
by touching something unclean from a
human or an animal or from any other
creature. If you do, you will no longer
belong to the community of Israel.
22The LORD told Moses 23to say to the
people:
Don't eat the fat of cattle, sheep, or
goats. 24If one of your animals dies or is
killed by some wild animal, you may do
anything with its fat except eat it. 25If
you eat the fat of an animal that can be
used as a sacrifice to me, you will no
longer belong to the community of Israel. 26And no matter where you live,
you must not eat the blood of any bird
or animal, 27or you will no longer belong to the community of Israel.
28The LORD also told Moses 29-30to say
to the people of Israel:
If you want to offer a sacrifice to ask
my blessing, you must bring the part to
be burned and lay it on the bronze altar.
But you must first lift up[h] the choice
ribs with their fat to show that the offering is dedicated to me. 31A priest from
Aaron's family will then send the fat up
in smoke, but the ribs belong to the
priests. 32-33The upper joint of the right
hind leg is for the priest who offers the
blood and the fat of the animal. 34I have
decided that the people of Israel must
always give the choice ribs and the upper joint of the right hind leg to Aaron's
descendants 35who have been ordained
as priests to serve me. 36This law will
never change. I am the LORD!
37These are the ceremonies for sacrifices to please the LORD, to give him
thanks, and to ask his blessing or his
forgiveness, as well as the ceremonies
for those sacrifices that demand a payment and for the sacrifices that are offered when priests are ordained. 38While
Moses and the people of Israel were in
the desert at Mount Sinai, the LORD
commanded them to start offering these
sacrifices.

The Ceremony for Ordaining Priests
(Exodus 29.1-37)

8 The LORD said to Moses:
2Send for Aaron and his sons, as
well as their priestly clothes, the oil
for ordination, the bull for the sin offering, the two rams, and a basket of
bread made without yeast. 3Then
bring the whole community of Israel
together at the entrance to the sacred tent.
4Moses obeyed the LORD, and when
everyone had come together, 5he said,
"We are here to follow the LORD's instructions."
6After Moses told Aaron and his sons
to step forward, he had them wash
themselves. 7He put the priestly shirt
and robe on Aaron and wrapped the
sash around his waist. Then he put the
sacred vest on Aaron and fastened it
with the finely woven belt. 8Next, he put
on Aaron the sacred breastpiece that
was used in learning what the LORD
wanted his people to do. 9He placed the
turban on Aaron's head, and on the
front of the turban was the narrow strip

[d]**7.6** *holy place*: The courtyard of the sacred tent (see 6.16,17). [e]**7.8** *sacrifice to please me*: See the note at 1.1-3. [f]**7.9** *sacrifice to give thanks to me*: See the note at 2.1. [g]**7.11** *sacrifice to ask my blessing*: See the note at 3.1. [h]**7.29,30** *lift up*: Or "wave."

of thin gold as a sign of his dedication to the LORD.

10 Moses then dedicated the sacred tent and everything in it to the LORD by sprinkling them with some of the oil for ordination. 11 He sprinkled the bronze altar seven times, and he sprinkled its equipment, as well as the large bronze bowl and its base. 12 He also poured some of the oil on Aaron's head to dedicate him to the LORD. 13 At last, Moses dressed Aaron's sons in their shirts, then tied sashes around them and put special caps on them, just as the LORD had commanded.

14 Moses led out the bull that was to be sacrificed for sin, and Aaron and his sons laid their hands on its head. 15 After it was killed, Moses dipped a finger in the blood and smeared some of it on each of the four corners of the bronze altar, before pouring out the rest at the foot of the altar. This purified the altar and made it a fit place for offering the sacrifice for sin. 16 Moses then took the fat on the bull's insides, as well as the lower part of the liver and the two kidneys with their fat, and sent them up in smoke on the altar fire. 17 Finally, he took the skin and the flesh of the bull, together with the food still in its stomach, and burned them outside the camp, just as the LORD had commanded.

18 Moses led out the ram for the sacrifice to please the LORD.[i] After Aaron and his sons had laid their hands on its head, 19 Moses killed the ram and splattered its blood against the four sides of the altar. 20-21 Moses had the animal cut up, and he washed its insides and hind legs. Then he laid the head, the fat, and the rest of the ram on the altar and sent them up in smoke with a smell that pleased the LORD. All this was done just as the LORD had commanded.

22 Moses led out the ram for the ceremony of ordination. Aaron and his sons laid their hands on its head, 23 and it was killed. Moses smeared some of its blood on Aaron's right earlobe, some on his right thumb, and some on the big toe of his right foot. 24 Moses did the same thing for Aaron's sons, before splattering the rest of the blood against the four sides of the altar. 25 He took the animal's fat tail, the fat on its insides, and the lower part of the liver and the two kidneys with their fat, and the right hind leg. 26 Then he took from a basket some of each of the three kinds of bread[j] that had been made without yeast and had been dedicated to the LORD.

27 Moses placed the bread on top of the meat and gave it all to Aaron and his sons, who lifted it up[k] to show that it was dedicated to the LORD. 28 After this, Moses placed it on the fires of the altar and sent it up in smoke with a smell that pleased the LORD. This was part of the ordination ceremony. 29 Moses lifted up[k] the choice ribs of the ram to show that they were dedicated to the LORD. This was the part that the LORD had said Moses could have.

30 Finally, Moses sprinkled the priestly clothes of Aaron and his sons with some of the oil for ordination and with some of the blood from the altar. So Aaron and his sons, together with their priestly clothes, were dedicated to the LORD.

31 Moses said to Aaron and his sons:

The LORD told me that you must boil this meat at the entrance to the sacred tent and eat it there with the bread. 32 Burn what is left over 33 and stay near the entrance to the sacred tent until the ordination ceremony ends seven days from now. 34 We have obeyed the LORD in everything that has been done today, so that your sins may be forgiven.[l] 35 The LORD has told me that you must stay near the entrance to the tent for seven days and nights, or else you will die.

36 Aaron and his sons obeyed everything that the LORD had told Moses they must do.

The First Sacrifices Offered by Aaron and His Sons

9 Eight days later Moses called together Aaron, his sons, and Israel's leaders. 2 Then he said to Aaron:

Find a young bull and a ram that have nothing wrong with them. Offer the bull to the LORD as a sacrifice for sin and the ram as a sacrifice to please him.[m]

3 Tell the people of Israel that they must offer sacrifices as well. They must offer a goat[n] as a sacrifice for sin, and a bull and a ram as a sacrifice to please the LORD. The bull and the ram must be a year old and have nothing wrong with them. 4 Then the people must offer a bull and a ram as a sacrifice to ask the LORD's blessing[o] and also a grain sacrifice[p]

[i] **8.18** *sacrifice to please the LORD*: See the note at 1.1-3. [j] **8.26** *three kinds of bread*: Made from the finest wheat flour; olive oil was mixed into part of the dough, and some of it was made into thin wafers brushed with oil (see Exodus 29.2, 3). [k] **8.27** *lifted it up*: See the note at 7.29, 30. [k] **8.29** *lifted up*: See the note at 7.29, 30. [l] **8.34** *forgiven*: One possible meaning for the difficult Hebrew text of verse 34. [m] **9.2** *sacrifice to please him*: See the note at 1.1-3. [n] **9.3** *goat*: See the note at 1.1-3. [o] **9.4** *to ask the LORD's blessing*: See the note at 3.1. [p] **9.4** *grain sacrifice*: To give thanks to the LORD (see the note at 2.1).

mixed with oil. Do this, because the
LORD will appear to you today.
5After the animals and the grain had
been brought to the front of the sacred
tent, and the people were standing there
in the presence of the LORD, 6Moses
said:

The LORD has ordered you to do
this, so that he may appear to you in
all of his glory. 7Aaron, step up to
the altar and offer the sacrifice to
please the LORD, then offer the sacrifices for the forgiveness of your sins
and for the sins of the people, just as
the LORD has commanded.

8Aaron stepped up to the altar and
killed the bull that was to be the sacrifice for his sins. 9His sons brought him
the blood. He dipped a finger in it,
smeared some on the four corners of the
bronze altar, and poured out the rest at
its foot. 10But he sent up in smoke the
fat, the kidneys, and the lower part of
the liver, just as the LORD had commanded Moses. 11Then Aaron burned
the skin and the flesh outside the camp.
12After Aaron had killed the ram that
was sacrificed to please the LORD,
Aaron's sons brought him the blood,
and he splattered it against all four
sides of the altar. 13They brought him
each piece of the animal, including the
head, and he burned them all on the altar. 14He washed the insides and the
hind legs and also sent them up in
smoke.
15Next, Aaron sacrificed the goat for
the sins of the people, as he had done
with the sacrifice for his own sins.
16And so, he burned this sacrifice on the
altar in the proper way. 17He also presented the grain sacrifice and burned a
handful of the flour on the altar as part
of the morning sacrifice.
18At last, he killed the bull and the
ram as a sacrifice to ask the LORD's
blessing on the people. Aaron's sons
brought him the blood, and he splattered it against the four sides of the altar. 19His sons placed all the fat, as well
as the kidneys and the lower part of the
liver 20on top of the choice ribs. 21Then
Aaron burned the fat on the altar and
lifted up[q] the ribs and the right hind leg
to show that these were dedicated to the
LORD. This was done just as the LORD
had instructed Moses.
22Aaron held out his hand and gave
the people his blessing, before coming
down from the bronze altar where he
had offered the sacrifices. 23He and
Moses went into the sacred tent, and
when they came out, they gave the people their blessing. Then the LORD appeared to the people in all of his glory.
24The LORD sent fiery flames that
burned up everything on the altar, and
when everyone saw this, they shouted
and fell to their knees to worship the
LORD.

Nadab and Abihu

10 Nadab and Abihu were two of
Aaron's sons, but they disobeyed
the LORD by burning incense to him on a
fire pan, when they were not supposed
to.[r] 2Suddenly the LORD sent fiery
flames and burned them to death. 3Then
Moses told Aaron that this was exactly
what the LORD had meant when he said:

"I demand respect
from my priests,
and I will be praised
by everyone!"

Aaron was speechless.
4Moses sent for Mishael and Elzaphan, the two sons of Aaron's uncle
Uzziel. Then he told them, "Take these
two dead relatives of yours outside the
camp far from the entrance to the sacred tent." 5So they dragged the dead
men away by their clothes.
6Then Moses told Aaron and his other
two sons, Eleazar and Ithamar:

Don't show your sorrow by mess-
ing up your hair and tearing your
priestly clothes, or the LORD will get
angry. He will kill the three of you
and punish everyone else. It's all
right for your relatives, the people of
Israel, to mourn for those he destroyed by fire. 7But you are the
LORD's chosen priests, and you must
not leave the sacred tent, or you will
die.

Aaron and his two sons obeyed
Moses.
8The LORD said to Aaron:

9When you or your sons enter the
sacred tent, you must never drink
beer or wine. If you do, you will die
right there! This law will never
change. 10You must learn the difference between what is holy and what
isn't holy and between the clean and
the unclean. 11You must also teach
the people of Israel everything that I
commanded Moses to say to them.

12Moses told Aaron and his two sons,
Eleazar and Ithamar:

The grain sacrifice that was offered to give thanks to the LORD[s] is
very holy. So make bread without
yeast from the part that wasn't sent
up in smoke and eat it beside the altar. 13The LORD has said that this be-

[q]**9.21** *lifted up*: See the note at 7.29, 30. [r]**10.1** *when they . . . to*: One possible meaning for the difficult Hebrew text. [s]**10.12** *grain sacrifice . . . to give thanks to the LORD*: See the note at 2.1.

longs to you and your sons, and that
it must be eaten in a holy place.
14-15 But the choice ribs and the hind
leg that were lifted up[t] may be eaten
by your entire family, as long as you
do so in an acceptable place.[u] These
parts are yours from the sacrifices
that the people offer to ask the
LORD's blessing.[v] This is what the
LORD has commanded, and it will
never change.
16 When Moses asked around and
learned that the ram for the sin sacrifice
had already been burned on the altar, he
became angry with Eleazar and Ithamar
and said, 17 "Why didn't you eat the meat
from this sacrifice in an acceptable
place? It is very holy, and the LORD has
given you this sacrifice to remove Israel's sin and guilt. 18 Whenever an animal's blood isn't brought into the sacred
tent, I commanded you to eat its meat in
an acceptable place, but you burned it
instead."
19 Their father Aaron replied, "Today
two of my sons offered the sacrifice for
sin and the sacrifice to please the LORD,
and look what has happened to me!
Would the LORD have approved if I had
eaten the sacrifice for sin?"
20 Moses was satisfied with Aaron's reply.

Clean and Unclean Animals

(Deuteronomy 14.3-21)

11 The LORD told Moses and Aaron
2 to say to the community of Israel:
You may eat 3 any animal that has divided hoofs and chews the cud.[w] 4-8 But
you must not eat animals such as
camels, rock badgers, and rabbits that
chew the cud but don't have divided
hoofs. And you must not eat pigs—they
have divided hoofs, but don't chew the
cud. All of these animals are unclean,[x]
and you are forbidden even to touch
their dead bodies.
9-12 You may eat anything that lives in
water and has fins and scales. But it
would be disgusting for you to eat anything else that lives in water, and you
must not even touch their dead bodies.
13-19 Eagles, vultures, buzzards, crows,
ostriches, hawks, sea gulls, owls, pelicans, storks, herons, hoopoes,[y] and bats
are also disgusting, and you are forbidden to eat any of them.
20-23 The only winged insects you may
eat are locusts, grasshoppers, and crickets. All other winged insects that crawl
are too disgusting for you to eat.
24-28 Don't even touch the dead bodies
of animals that have divided hoofs but
don't chew the cud. And don't touch the
dead bodies of animals that have
paws. If you do, you must wash your
clothes, but you are still unclean until
evening.
29-30 Moles, rats, mice, and all kinds of
lizards are unclean. 31 Anyone who
touches their dead bodies or anything
touched by their dead bodies becomes
unclean until evening. 32 If something
made of wood, cloth, or leather touches
one of their dead bodies, it must be
washed, but it is still unclean until
evening. 33 If any of these animals is
found dead in a clay pot, the pot must
be broken to pieces, and everything in it
becomes unclean. 34 If you pour water
from this pot on any food, that food becomes unclean, and anything drinkable
in the pot becomes unclean.
35 If the dead body of one of these animals touches anything else, including
ovens and stoves, that thing becomes
unclean and must be destroyed. 36 A
spring or a cistern where one of these
dead animals is found is still clean, but
anyone who touches the animal becomes unclean. 37 If the dead body of
one of these animals is found lying on
seeds that have been set aside for planting, the seeds remain clean. 38 But seeds
that are soaking in water become unclean, if the dead animal is found in the
water.
39 If an animal that may be eaten happens to die, and you touch it, you become unclean until evening. 40 If you eat
any of its meat or carry its body away,
you must wash your clothes, but you are
still unclean until evening.
41-42 Don't eat any of those disgusting
little creatures that crawl or walk close
to the ground. 43 If you eat any of them,
you will become just as disgusting and
unclean as they are. 44 I am the LORD
your God, and you must dedicate yourselves to me and be holy, just as I am
holy. Don't become disgusting by eating
any of these unclean creatures. 45 I
brought you out of Egypt so that I could
be your God. Now you must become
holy, because I am holy!

[t] **10.14,15** *lifted up*: See the note at 7.29, 30. [u] **10.14,15** *acceptable place*: See 6.24-30. [v] **10.14,15** *to ask the LORD's blessing*: See the note at 3.1. [w] **11.3** *chews the cud*: Some animals that eat grass and leaves have more than one stomach and chew their food a second time after it has been partly digested in the first stomach. This partly digested food is called the "cud." [x] **11.4-8** *unclean*: In the Old Testament "clean" and "unclean" refer to whatever makes a person, animal, or object acceptable or unacceptable to God. For example, a person became unclean by eating certain foods, touching certain objects, and having certain kinds of diseases or bodily discharges. [y] **11.13-19** *Eagles . . . hoopoes*: Some of the birds in this list are difficult to identify.

46-47I have given these laws so that you
will know what animals, birds, and fish
are clean and may be eaten, and which
ones are unclean and may not be eaten.

What Women Must Do after Giving Birth

12 The LORD told Moses 2to say to
the community of Israel:
If a woman gives birth to a son, she is
unclean for seven days, just as she is
during her monthly period. 3Her son
must be circumcised on the eighth day,
4but her loss of blood keeps her from
being completely clean for another
thirty-three days. During this time she
must not touch anything holy or go to
the place of worship. 5Any woman who
gives birth to a daughter is unclean for
two weeks, just as she is during her period. And she won't be completely clean
for another sixty-six days.
6When the mother has completed her
time of cleansing, she must come to the
front of the sacred tent and bring to the
priest a year-old lamb as a sacrifice to
please me[z] and a dove or a pigeon as a
sacrifice for sin. 7After the priest offers
the sacrifices to me, the mother will become completely clean from her loss of
blood, whether her child is a boy or a
girl. 8If she cannot afford a lamb, she
can offer two doves or two pigeons, one
as a sacrifice to please me and the other
as a sacrifice for sin.

Skin Diseases

13 The LORD told Moses and Aaron
to say to the people:
2If sores or boils or a skin rash should
break out and start spreading on your
body, you must be brought to Aaron or
to one of the other priests. 3If the priest
discovers that the hair in the infected
area has turned white and that the infection seems more than skin deep, he
will say, "This is leprosy[a]—you are unclean."
4But if the infected area is white and
only skin deep, and if the hair in it
hasn't turned white, the priest will order
you to stay away from everyone else for
seven days. 5If the disease hasn't spread
by that time, he will order you to stay
away from everyone else for another
seven days. 6Then if the disease hasn't
gotten any worse or spread, the priest
will say, "You are clean. It was only a
sore. After you wash your clothes, you
may go home."
7However, if the disease comes back,
you must return to the priest. 8If it is discovered that the disease has started
spreading, he will say, "This is leprosy—
you are unclean."
9Any of you with a skin disease must
be brought to a priest. 10If he discovers
that the sore spot is white with pus and
that the hair around it has also turned
white, 11he will say, "This is leprosy. You
are unclean and must stay away from
everyone else." 12-13But if the disease has
run its course and only the scars remain, he will say, "You are clean." 14-15If
the sores come back and turn white
with pus, he will say, "This is leprosy—
you are unclean."
16-17However, if the sores heal and
only white spots remain, the priest will
say, "You are now clean."
18-19If you have a sore that either
swells or turns reddish-white after it has
healed, then you must show it to a
priest. 20If he discovers that the hair in
the infected area has turned white and
that the infection seems more than skin
deep, he will say, "This is leprosy—you
are unclean." 21But if the white area is
only on the surface of the skin and
hasn't gotten any worse, and if the hair
in it hasn't turned white, he will have
you stay away from everyone else for
seven days.
22If the sore begins spreading during
this time, the priest will say, "You are
unclean because you have a disease."
23But if it doesn't spread, and only a
scar remains, he will say, "You are now
clean."
24If you have a burn that gets infected
and turns red or reddish-white, 25a
priest must examine it. Then if he discovers that the hair in the infected area
has turned white and that the infection
seems more than skin deep, he will say,
"The burn has turned into leprosy, and
you are unclean." 26But if the priest
finds that the hair in the infected area
hasn't turned white and that the sore is
only skin deep and it is healing, he will
have you stay away from everyone else
for seven days. 27On the seventh day the
priest will examine you again, and if the
infection is spreading, he will say, "This
is leprosy—you are unclean." 28How-
ever, if the infection hasn't spread and
has begun to heal, and if only a scar remains, he will say, "Only a scar remains
from the burn, and you are clean."
29If you have a sore on your head or
chin, 30it must be examined by a priest.
If the infection seems more than skin
deep, and the hair in it has thinned out
and lost its color, he will say, "This is
leprosy—you are unclean." 31On the
other hand, if he discovers that the itchy
spot is only skin deep, but that the hair
still isn't healthy, he will order you to
stay away from everyone else for seven
days. 32By that time, if the itch hasn't
spread, if the hairs seem healthy, and if

[z] **12.6** *sacrifice to please me*: See the note at 1.1-3. [a] **13.3** *leprosy*: The word translated "leprosy" was used for many different kinds of skin diseases.

the itch is only skin deep, 33you must
shave off the hairs around the infection,
but not those on it. Then the priest will
tell you to stay away from everyone else
for another seven days. 34By that time, if
the itch hasn't spread and seems no
more than skin deep, he will say, "You
are clean; now you must wash your
clothes."

35-36Later, if the itch starts spreading,
even though the hair is still healthy, the
priest will say, "You are unclean." 37But
if he thinks you are completely well, he
will say, "You are clean."

38If white spots break out on your
skin, 39but the priest discovers that it is
only a rash, he will say, "You are clean."

40-41If you become bald on any part of
your head, you are still clean. 42-43But if
a priest discovers that a reddish-white
sore has broken out on the bald spot
and looks like leprosy, he will say,
44"This is leprosy—you are unclean."

45If you ever have leprosy, you must
tear your clothes, leave your hair un-
combed, cover the lower part of your
face, and go around shouting, "I'm unclean! I'm unclean!" 46As long as you
have the disease, you are unclean and
must live alone outside the camp.

47-50If a greenish or reddish spot[b] appears anywhere on any of your clothing
or on anything made of leather, you
must let the priest examine the clothing
or the leather. He will put it aside for
seven days, 51and if the mildew has
spread in that time, he will say, "This is
unclean 52because the mildew has
spread." Then he will burn the clothing
or the piece of leather.

53If the priest discovers that the
mildew hasn't spread, 54he will tell you
to wash the clothing or leather and put
it aside for another seven days, 55after
which he will examine it again. If the
spot hasn't spread, but is still greenish
or reddish, the clothing or leather is unclean and must be burned. 56But if the
spot has faded after being washed, he
will tear away the spot. 57Later, if the
spot reappears elsewhere on the clothing or the leather, you must burn it.
58Even if the spot completely disappears
after being washed, it must be washed
again before it is clean.

59These are the rules for deciding if
clothing is clean or unclean after a spot
appears on it.

The Ceremony for People Healed of Leprosy

14 The LORD told Moses to say to the
people:

2-3After you think you are healed of
leprosy,[c] you must ask for a priest to
come outside the camp and examine
you. And if you are well, 4he will have
someone bring out two live birds that
are acceptable for sacrifice, together
with a stick of cedar wood, a piece of
red yarn, and a branch from a hyssop
plant. 5The priest will have someone kill
one of the birds over a clay pot of spring
water. 6Then he will dip the other bird,
the cedar, the red yarn, and the hyssop
in the blood of the dead bird. 7Next, he
will sprinkle you seven times with the
blood and say, "You are now clean." Finally, he will release the bird and let it
fly away.

8After this you must wash your
clothes, shave your entire body, and
take a bath before you are completely
clean. You may move back into camp,
but you must not enter your tent for
seven days. 9Then you must once again
shave your head, face, and eyebrows, as
well as the hair on the rest of your body.
Finally, wash your clothes and take a
bath, and you will be completely clean.

10On the eighth day you must bring to
the priest two rams and a year-old female lamb that have nothing wrong
with them; also bring a half pint of olive
oil and six pounds of your finest flour
mixed with oil. 11Then the priest will
present you and your offerings to me at
the entrance to my sacred tent. 12There
he will offer one of the rams, together
with the pint of oil, as a sacrifice to
make things right.[d] He will also lift
them up[e] to show that they are dedicated to me. 13This sacrifice is very holy.
It belongs to the priest and must be
killed in the same place where animals
are killed as sacrifices for sins and as
sacrifices to please me.[f]

14The priest will smear some of the
blood from this sacrifice on your right
ear lobe, some on your right thumb, and
some on the big toe of your right foot.
15He will then pour some of the olive oil
into the palm of his left hand, 16dip a
finger of his right hand into the oil, and
sprinkle some of it seven times toward
the sacred tent. 17Next, he will smear
some of the oil on your right ear lobe,
some on your right thumb, and some on
the big toe of your right foot, 18-20and
pour the rest of the oil from his palm on
your head. Then he will offer the other
two animals—one as a sacrifice for sin
and the other as a sacrifice to please
me, together with a grain sacrifice. After
this you will be completely clean.

21If you are poor and cannot afford to

[b]**13.47-50** *spot*: The Hebrew word translated "spot" and "mildew" in verses 47-59 is the same one translated "leprosy" earlier in the chapter. [c]**14.2,3** *leprosy*: See the note at 13.3. [d]**14.12** *sacrifice to make things right*: See 7.1-10. [e]**14.12** *lift them up*: See the note at 7.29, 30. [f]**14.13** *sacrifices to please me*: See the note at 1.1-3.

offer this much, you may offer a ram as
a sacrifice to make things right, together
with a half pint of olive oil and two
pounds of flour mixed with oil as a
grain sacrifice. The priest will then lift
these up[g] to dedicate them to me. 22De-
pending on what you can afford, you
must also offer either two doves or two
pigeons, one as a sacrifice for sin and
the other as a sacrifice to please me.
23The priest will offer these to me in
front of the sacred tent on the eighth
day.

24-25The priest will kill this ram for the
sacrifice to make things right, and he
will lift it up[g] with the olive oil in dedication to me. Then he will smear some
of the blood on your right ear lobe,
some on your right thumb, and some on
the big toe of your right foot.

26The priest will pour some of the
olive oil into the palm of his left hand,
27then dip a finger of his right hand in
the oil and sprinkle some of it seven
times toward the sacred tent. 28He will
smear some of the oil on your right ear
lobe, some on your right thumb, and
some on the big toe of your right foot,
just as he did with the blood of the sacrifice to make things right. 29-31And he
will pour the rest of the oil from his
palm on your head.

Then, depending on what you can afford, he will offer either the doves or the
pigeons together with the grain sacrifice. One of the birds is the sacrifice for
sin, and the other is the sacrifice to
please me. After this you will be completely clean.

32These are the things you must do if
you have leprosy and cannot afford the
usual sacrifices to make you clean.

When Mildew Is in a House

33The LORD told Moses and Aaron to
say to the people:

34After I have given you the land of
Canaan as your permanent possession,
here is what you must do, if I ever put
mildew[h] on the walls of any of your
homes. 35First, you must say to a priest,
"I think mildew is on the wall of my
house."

36The priest will reply, "Empty the
house before I inspect it, or else everything in it will be unclean."

37If the priest discovers greenish or
reddish spots that go deeper than the
surface of the walls, 38he will have the
house closed for seven days. 39Then he
will return and check to see if the
mildew has spread. 40-41If so, he will
have someone scrape the plaster from
the walls, remove the filthy stones, then
haul everything off and dump it in an
unclean place outside the town. 42After-
wards the wall must be repaired with
new stones and fresh plaster.

43If the mildew appears a second time,
44the priest will come and say, "This
house is unclean. It's covered with
mildew that can't be removed." 45Then
he will have the house torn down and
every bit of wood, stone, and plaster
hauled off to an unclean place outside
the town. 46Meanwhile, if any of you entered the house while it was closed, you
will be unclean until evening. 47And if
you either slept or ate in the house, you
must wash your clothes.

48On the other hand, if the priest discovers that mildew hasn't reappeared
after the house was newly plastered, he
will say, "This house is clean—the
mildew has gone." 49Then, to show that
the house is now clean, he will get two
birds, a stick of cedar wood, a piece of
red yarn, and a branch from a hyssop
plant and bring them to the house. 50He
will kill one of the birds over a clay pot
of spring water 51-52and let its blood
drain into the pot. Then he will dip the
cedar, the hyssop, the yarn, and the
other bird into the mixture of blood and
water. Next, he will sprinkle the house
seven times with the mixture, then the
house will be completely clean. 53Fi-
nally, he will release the bird and let it
fly away, ending the ceremony for purifying the house.

54-57These are the things you must do
if you discover that you are unclean because of an itch or a sore, or that your
clothing or house is unclean because of
mildew.

Sexual Uncleanness

15 The LORD told Moses and Aaron
2to say to the community of Israel:

Any man with an infected penis is unclean, 3whether it is stopped up or keeps
dripping. 4Anything that he rests on or
sits on is also unclean, 5-7and if you
touch either these or him, you must
wash your clothes and take a bath, but
you still remain unclean until evening.

8If you are spit on by the man, you
must wash your clothes and take a bath,
but you still remain unclean until
evening. 9-10Any saddle or seat on which
the man sits is unclean. And if you
touch or carry either of these, you must
wash your clothes and take a bath, but
you still remain unclean until evening.
11If the man touches you without first
washing his hands, you must wash your
clothes and take a bath, but you still re-

[g] **14.21** *lift these up*: See the note at 7.29, 30. [g] **14.24,25** *lift it up*: See the note at 7.29, 30.
[h] **14.34** *mildew*: The Hebrew word translated "mildew" is the same one translated "leprosy" and "spot" in chapter 13.

main unclean until evening. 12Any clay
pot that he touches must be destroyed,
and any wooden bowl that he touches
must be washed.
13Seven days after the man gets well,
he will be considered clean, if he
washes his clothes and takes a bath in
spring water. 14On the eighth day he
must bring either two doves or two pigeons to the front of my sacred tent and
give them to a priest. 15The priest will
offer one of the birds as a sacrifice for
sin and the other as a sacrifice to please
me,[i] then I will consider the man completely clean.
16Any man who has a flow of semen
must take a bath, but he still remains
unclean until evening. 17If the semen
touches anything made of cloth or
leather, these must be washed, but they
still remain unclean until evening. 18Af-
ter having sex, both the man and the
woman must take a bath, but they still
remain unclean until evening.
19When a woman has her monthly period, she remains unclean for seven
days, and if you touch her, you must
take a bath, but you remain unclean until evening. 20-23Anything that she rests
on or sits on is also unclean, and if you
touch either of these, you must wash
your clothes and take a bath, but you
still remain unclean until evening. 24Any
man who has sex with her during this
time becomes unclean for seven days,
and anything he rests on is also unclean.
25Any woman who has a flow of blood
outside her regular monthly period is
unclean until it stops, just as she is during her monthly period. 26Anything that
she rests on or sits on during this time is
also unclean, just as it would be during
her period. 27If you touch either of these,
you must wash your clothes and take a
bath, but you still remain unclean until
evening.
28Seven days after the woman gets
well, she will be considered clean. 29On
the eighth day, she must bring either
two doves or two pigeons to the front of
my sacred tent and give them to a
priest. 30He will offer one of the birds as
a sacrifice for sin and the other as a sacrifice to please me; then I will consider
the woman completely clean.
31When any of you are unclean, you
must stay away from the rest of the
community of Israel. Otherwise, my sacred tent will become unclean, and the
whole nation will die.
32-33These are the things you men
must do if you become unclean because
of an infected penis or if you have a
flow of semen. And these are the things
you women must do when you become
unclean either because of your monthly
period or an unusual flow of blood. This
is also what you men must do if you
have sex with a woman who is unclean.

The Great Day of Forgiveness

16 1-2Two of Aaron's sons had already lost their lives for disobeying the LORD,[j] so the LORD told Moses to
say to Aaron:
I, the LORD, appear in a cloud over the
place of mercy on the sacred chest,
which is behind the inside curtain[k] of
the sacred tent. And I warn you not to
go there except at the proper time.
Otherwise, you will die!
3Before entering this most holy place,
you must offer a bull as a sacrifice for
your sins[l] and a ram as a sacrifice to
please me.[m] 4You will take a bath and
put on the sacred linen clothes, including the underwear, the robe, the sash,
and the turban. 5Then the community of
Israel will bring you a ram and two
goats, both of them males. The goats are
to be used as sacrifices for sin, and the
ram is to be used as a sacrifice to please
me.
6Aaron, you must offer the bull as a
sacrifice of forgiveness for your own
sins and for the sins of your family.
7Then you will lead the two goats into
my presence at the front of the sacred
tent, 8where I will show you[n] which goat
will be sacrificed to me and which one
will be sent into the desert to the demon
Azazel.[o] 9After you offer the first goat
as a sacrifice for sin, 10the other one
must be presented to me alive, before
you send it into the desert to take away
the sins of the people.
11You must offer the bull as a sacrifice
to ask forgiveness for your own sins
and for the sins of your family. 12Then
you will take a fire pan of live coals
from the bronze altar, together with two
handfuls of finely ground incense, into
the most holy place. 13There you will
present them to me by placing the incense on the coals, so that the place of
mercy will be covered with a cloud of
smoke. Do this, or you will die right
there! 14Next, use a finger to sprinkle
some of the blood on the place of mercy,
which is on the lid of the sacred chest;

[i] **15.15** *sacrifice to please me*: See the note at 1.1-3. [j] **16.1,2** *lost . . . disobeying the LORD*: See 10.1, 2. [k] **16.1,2** *inside curtain*: That separated the holy place from the most holy place. [l] **16.3** *for your sins*: See 4.3-12. [m] **16.3** *sacrifice to please me*: See the note at 1.1-3. [n] **16.8** *I will show you*: The Hebrew text has "you must cast lots to find out." Pieces of wood or stone (called "lots") were used to find out what God wanted his people to do. [o] **16.8** *Azazel*: It was believed that a demon named Azazel lived in the desert.

then sprinkle blood seven times in front
of the chest.
15Aaron, you must next sacrifice the
goat for the sins of the people, and you
must sprinkle its blood inside the most
holy place, just as you did with the
blood of the bull. 16By doing this, you
will take away the sins that make both
the most holy place and the people of Israel unclean. Do the same for the sacred
tent, which is here among the people.
17Only you are allowed in the sacred
tent from the time you enter until the
time you come out. 18After leaving the
tent, you will purify the bronze altar by
smearing each of its four corners with
some of the blood from the bull and
from the goat. 19Use a finger to sprinkle
the altar seven times with the blood, and
it will be completely clean from the sins
of the people.
20After you have purified the most
holy place, the sacred tent, and the
bronze altar, you must bring the live
goat to the front of the tent. 21There you
will lay your hands on its head, while
confessing every sin the people have
committed, and you will appoint someone to lead the goat into the desert, so
that it can take away their sins. 22Fi-
nally, this goat that carries the heavy
burden of Israel's sins must be released
deep in the desert.
23-24Aaron, after this you must go inside the sacred tent, take a bath, put on
your regular priestly clothes, and leave
there the clothes you put on before entering the most holy place. Then you
will come out and offer sacrifices to
please me and sacrifices for your sins
and for the sins of the people. 25The fat
from these sacrifices for sin must be
sent up in smoke on the bronze altar.
26The one who led the goat into the
desert and sent it off to the demon
Azazel must take a bath and wash his
clothes before coming back into camp.
27The remains of the bull and the goat
whose blood was taken into the most
holy place must be taken outside the
camp and burned. 28And whoever does
this must take a bath and change
clothes before coming back into camp.

The LORD told Moses to say to the people:

29On the tenth day of the seventh
month[p] of each year, you must go without eating to show sorrow for your sins,
and no one, including foreigners who
live among you, is allowed to work.
30This is the day on which the sacrifice
for the forgiveness of your sins will be
made in my presence, 31and from now
on, it must be celebrated each year. Go
without eating and make this a day of
complete rest just like the Sabbath.
32The high priest must offer the sacrifices for cleansing from sin, while wearing the sacred linen clothes. 33He will
offer these sacrifices for the most holy
place, the sacred tent, the bronze altar,
all the priests, and for the whole community. 34You must celebrate this day
each year—it is the Great Day of Forgiveness[q] for all the sins of the people
of Israel.
Moses did exactly as the LORD had
commanded.

Where To Offer Sacrifices

17 The LORD told Moses 2to tell
Aaron, his sons, and everyone
else in Israel:
3-4Whenever you kill any of your cattle, sheep, or goats as sacrifices to me,
you must do it at the entrance to the sacred tent. If you don't, you will be guilty
of pouring out blood, and you will no
longer belong to the community of Israel. 5And so, when you sacrifice an animal to ask my blessing,[r] it must not be
done out in a field, 6but in front of the
sacred tent. Then a priest can splatter
its blood against the bronze altar and
send its fat up in smoke with a smell
that pleases me. 7Don't ever turn from
me again and offer sacrifices to goat-
demons. This law will never change.
8Remember! No one in Israel, including foreigners, is to offer a sacrifice anywhere 9except at the entrance to the sacred tent. If you do, you will no longer
belong to my people.

Do Not Eat Blood

The LORD said:
10I will turn against any of my people
who eat blood. This also includes any
foreigners living among you. 11Life is in
the blood, and I have given you the
blood of animals to sacrifice in place of
your own. 12That's also why I have forbidden you to eat blood. 13Even if you
should hunt and kill a bird or an animal,
you must drain out the blood and cover
it with soil.
14The life of every living creature is in
its blood. That's why I have forbidden
you to eat blood and why I have warned
you that anyone who does will no
longer belong to my people.
15If you happen to find a dead animal
and eat it, you must take a bath and
wash your clothes, but you are still unclean until evening. 16If you don't take a
bath, you will suffer for what you did
wrong.

[p]16.29 *seventh month*: Tishri (also called Ethanim), the seventh month of the Hebrew calendar, from about mid-September to mid-October. [q]16.34 *Great Day of Forgiveness*: Traditionally known as the Day of Atonement. [r]17.5 *sacrifice . . . to ask my blessing*: See the note at 3.1.

Forbidden Sex

18 The LORD told Moses 2to tell the people of Israel:

I am the LORD your God! 3So don't follow the customs of Egypt where you used to live or those of Canaan where I am bringing you. 4I am the LORD your God, and you must obey my teachings. 5Obey them and you will live. I am the LORD.

6Don't have sex with any of your close relatives, 7especially your own mother. This would disgrace your father. 8And don't disgrace him by having sex with any of his other wives. 9Don't have sex with your sister or stepsister, whether you grew up together or not. 10Don't disgrace yourself by having sex with your granddaughter 11or half sister 12-13or a sister of your father or mother. 14Don't disgrace your uncle by having sex with his wife. 15Don't have sex with your daughter-in-law 16or sister-in-law. 17And don't have sex with the daughter or granddaughter of any woman that you have earlier had sex with. You may be having sex with a relative, and that would make you unclean. 18As long as your wife is alive, don't cause trouble for her by taking one of her sisters as a second wife.

19When a woman is having her monthly period, she is unclean, so don't have sex with her.

20Don't have sex with another man's wife—that would make you unclean.

21Don't sacrifice your children on the altar fires to the god Molech. I am the LORD your God, and that would disgrace me.

22It is disgusting for a man to have sex with another man.

23Anyone who has sex with an animal is unclean.

24Don't make yourselves unclean by any of these disgusting practices of those nations that I am forcing out of the land for you. They made themselves 25and the land so unclean, that I punished the land because of their sins, and I made it vomit them up. 26-27Now don't do these sickening things that make the land filthy. Instead, obey my laws and teachings. 28Then the land won't become sick of you and vomit you up, just as it did them. 29-30If any of you do these vulgar, disgusting things, you will be unclean and no longer belong to my people. I am the LORD your God, and I forbid you to follow their sickening way of life.

Moral and Religious Laws

19 The LORD told Moses 2to say to the community of Israel:

I am the LORD your God. I am holy, and you must be holy too! 3-4Respect your father and your mother, honor the Sabbath, and don't make idols or images. I am the LORD your God.

5When you offer a sacrifice to ask my blessing,[r] be sure to follow my instructions. 6You may eat the meat either on the day of the sacrifice or on the next day, but you must burn anything left until the third day. 7If you eat any of it on the third day, the sacrifice will be disgusting to me, and I will reject it. 8In fact, you will be punished for not respecting what I say is holy, and you will no longer belong to the community of Israel.

9When you harvest your grain, always leave some of it standing along the edges of your fields and don't pick up what falls on the ground. 10Don't strip your grapevines clean or gather the grapes that fall off the vines. Leave them for the poor and for those foreigners who live among you. I am the LORD your God.

11Do not steal or tell lies or cheat others.

12Do not misuse my name by making promises you don't intend to keep. I am the LORD your God.

13Do not steal anything or cheat anyone, and don't fail to pay your workers at the end of each day.[s]

14I am the LORD your God, and I command you not to make fun of the deaf or to cause a blind person to stumble.

15Be fair, no matter who is on trial—don't favor either the poor or the rich.

16Don't be a gossip, but never hesitate to speak up in court, especially if your testimony can save someone's life.[t]

17Don't hold grudges. On the other hand, it's wrong not to correct someone who needs correcting. 18Stop being angry and don't try to take revenge. I am the LORD, and I command you to love others as much as you love yourself.

19Breed your livestock animals only with animals of the same kind, and don't plant two kinds of seed in the same field or wear clothes made of different kinds of material.

20If a man has sex with a slave woman who is promised in marriage to someone else, he must pay a fine, but they are not to be put to death. After all, she was still a slave at the time.[u] 21-22The man must bring a ram to the entrance of

[r] **19.5** *to ask my blessing*: See the note at 3.1. [s] **19.13** *to pay . . . end of each day*: Day laborers needed their wages to buy food for their evening meal, which was the main meal of the day. [t] **19.16** *but never . . . someone's life*: One possible meaning for the difficult Hebrew text. [u] **19.20** *time*: One possible meaning for the difficult Hebrew text of verse 20.

the sacred tent and give it to a priest,
who will then offer it as a sacrifice to
me, so the man's sins will be forgiven.
23After you enter the land, you will
plant fruit trees, but you are not to eat
any of their fruit for the first three
years. 24In the fourth year the fruit must
be set apart, as an expression of thanks
25to me, the LORD God. Do this, and in
the fifth year, those trees will produce
an abundant harvest of fruit for you to
eat.
26Don't eat the blood of any animal.
Don't practice any kind of witchcraft.
27-28I forbid you to shave any part of
your head or beard or to cut and tattoo
yourself as a way of worshiping the
dead.
29Don't let your daughters serve as
temple prostitutes—this would bring
disgrace both to them and the land.
30I command you to respect the Sabbath and the place where I am worshiped.
31Don't make yourselves disgusting to
me by going to people who claim they
can talk to the dead.
32I command you to show respect for
older people and to obey me with fear
and trembling.
33Don't mistreat any foreigners who
live in your land. 34Instead, treat them
as well as you treat citizens and love
them as much as you love yourself. Remember, you were once foreigners in
the land of Egypt. I am the LORD your
God.
35-36Use honest scales and don't cheat
when you weigh or measure anything.
I am the LORD your God. I rescued you
from Egypt, 37and I command you to
obey my laws.

Penalties for Disobeying God's Laws

20 The LORD told Moses 2to say to
the community of Israel:
Death by stoning is the penalty for
any citizens or foreigners in the country
who sacrifice their children to the god
Molech. 3They have disgraced both the
place where I am worshiped and my
holy name, and so I will turn against
them and no longer let them belong to
my people. 4Some of you may let them
get away with human sacrifice, 5but not
me. If any of you worship Molech, I will
turn against you and your entire family,
and I will no longer let you belong to my
people.
6I will be your enemy if you go to
someone who claims to speak with the
dead, and I will destroy you from among
my people. 7Dedicate yourselves to me
and be holy because I am the LORD your
God. 8I have chosen you as my people,
and I expect you to obey my laws.
9If you curse your father or mother,
you will be put to death, and it will be
your own fault.
10If any of you men have sex with another man's wife, both you and the
woman will be put to death.
11Having sex with one of your father's
wives disgraces him. So both you and
the woman will be put to death, just as
you deserve. 12It isn't natural to have
sex with your daughter-in-law, and both
of you will be put to death, just as you
deserve. 13It's disgusting for men to
have sex with one another, and those
who do will be put to death, just as they
deserve. 14It isn't natural for a man to
marry both a mother and her daughter,
and so all three of them will be burned
to death. 15-16If any of you have sex
with an animal, both you and the
animal will be put to death, just as you
deserve.
17If you marry one of your sisters, you
will be punished, and the two of you will
be disgraced by being openly forced out
of the community. 18If you have sex with
a woman during her monthly period,
both you and the woman will be cut off
from the people of Israel. 19The sisters
of your father and mother are your own
relatives, and you will be punished for
having sex with any of them. 20If you
have sex with your uncle's wife, neither
you nor she will ever have any children.
21And if you marry your sister-in-law,
neither of you will ever have any children.[v]
22Obey my laws and teachings. Or else
the land I am giving you will become
sick of you and throw you out. 23The nations I am chasing out did these disgusting things, and I hated them for it, so
don't follow their example. 24I am the
LORD your God, and I have promised
you their land that is rich with milk and
honey. I have chosen you to be different
from other people. 25That's why you
must make a difference between animals and birds that I have said are clean
and unclean[w]—this will keep you from
becoming disgusting to me. 26I am the
LORD, the holy God. You have been chosen to be my people, and so you must be
holy too.
27If you claim to receive messages
from the dead, you will be put to death
by stoning, just as you deserve.

[v] **20.21** *And . . . children*: According to Deuteronomy 25.5, 6 a man was supposed to marry his brother's widow if his brother had died without having children. Otherwise, such marriages were forbidden (see also Matthew 22.23-33; Mark 12.18-27; Luke 20.27-40).

[w] **20.25** *clean and unclean*: See the note at 11.4-8.

Instructions for Priests

21 The LORD gave Moses these instructions for Aaron's sons, the
priests:
Touching a dead body will make you
unclean. So don't go near a dead relative, 2except your mother, father, son,
daughter, brother, 3or an unmarried sister, who has no husband to take care of
her. 4Don't make yourself unclean by at-
tending the funeral of someone related
to you by marriage.[x] 5Don't shave any
part of your head or trim your beard or
cut yourself to show that you are
mourning. 6I am the LORD your God, and
I have chosen you alone to offer sacrifices of food to me on the altar. That's
why you must keep yourselves holy.
7Don't marry a divorced woman or a
woman who has served as a temple
prostitute. You are holy, 8because I am
holy. And so, you must be treated with
proper respect, since you offer food sacrifices to me, the God of holiness.
9If any of you priests has a daughter
who disgraces you by serving as a temple prostitute, she must be burned to
death.
10If you are the high priest, you must
not mess up your hair or tear your
clothes in order to mourn for the dead.
11Don't make yourself unclean by going
near a dead body, not even that of your
own father or mother. 12If you leave the
sacred place to attend a funeral, both
you and the sacred place become unclean, because you are the high priest.
13If you are the high priest, you must
marry only a virgin 14from your own
tribe. Don't marry a divorced woman or
any other woman who has already had
sex, including a temple prostitute. 15In
this way, your descendants will be quali-
fied to serve me. Remember—I am the
LORD, and I have chosen you.
16The LORD told Moses 17-18to say to
Aaron:
No descendant of yours can ever
serve as my priest if he is blind or lame,
if his face is disfigured, if one leg is
shorter than the other, 19if either a foot
or a hand is crippled, 20if he is a hunch-
back or a dwarf, if an eye or his skin is
diseased, or if his testicles have been
damaged. 21These men may not serve as
my priests and burn sacrifices to me.
22They may eat the food offerings presented to me, 23but they may not enter
the sacred place or serve me at the altar.
Remember—I am the LORD, the one who
makes a priest holy.
24Moses told all of this to Aaron, his
sons, and the people of Israel.

The Offerings Are Holy

22 The LORD told Moses 2to say to
Aaron and his sons:
I am the LORD God, and I demand that
you honor my holy name by showing
proper respect for the offerings brought
to me by the people of Israel. 3If any of
you are unclean when you accept an offering for me, I will no longer let you
serve as a priest. 4None of you may take
part in the sacred meals while you have
a skin disease or an infected penis, or
after you have been near a dead body or
have had a flow of semen, 5or if you
have touched an unclean creature of
any sort, including an unclean person.
6-7Once you are unclean, you must take
a bath, but you still cannot eat any of
the sacred food until evening. 8I command you not to eat anything that is
killed by a wild animal or dies a natural
death. This would make you unclean.
9Obey me, or you will die on duty for
disgracing the place of worship. Remember—I am the LORD, the one who
makes a priest holy.
10Only you priests and your families
may eat the food offerings; these are too
sacred for any of your servants. 11How-
ever, any slave that you own, including
those born into your household, may eat
this food. 12If your daughter marries
someone who isn't a priest, she can no
longer have any of this food. 13But if she
returns to your home, either widowed or
divorced, and has no children, she may
join in the meal. Only members of a
priestly family can eat this food, 14and
anyone else who accidentally does so,
must pay for the food plus a fine of
twenty percent.
15I warn you not to treat lightly the offerings that are brought by the people of
Israel. 16Don't let them become guilty of
eating this sacred food. Remember—I
am the LORD, the one who makes these
offerings holy.

Acceptable Sacrifices

17The LORD told Moses 18to tell Aaron
and his sons and everyone else the rules
for offering sacrifices. He said:
The animals that are to be completely
burned on the altar 19-20must have nothing wrong with them, or else I won't accept them. Bulls or rams or goats[y] are
the animals to be used for these sacrifices.
21When you offer a sacrifice to ask my
blessing,[z] there must be nothing wrong
with the animal. This is true, whether
the sacrifice is part of a promise or
something you do voluntarily. 22Don't

[x] **21.4** *marriage*: One possible meaning for the difficult Hebrew text of verse 4.
[y] **22.19,20** *goats*: See the note at 1.1-3.
[z] **22.21** *sacrifice to ask my blessing*: See the note at 3.1.

offer an animal that is blind or injured or that has an infection or a skin disease. [23]If one of your cattle or lambs has a leg that is longer or shorter than the others, you may offer it voluntarily, but not as part of a promise. [24]As long as you live in this land, don't offer an animal with injured testicles. [25]And don't bring me animals you bought from a foreigner. I won't accept them, because they are no better than one that has something wrong with it.

[26]The LORD told Moses to say:

[27]Newborn cattle, sheep, or goats must remain with their mothers for seven days, but on the eighth day, you may send them up in smoke to me, and I will accept the offering. [28]Don't sacrifice a newborn animal and its mother on the same day.

[29]When you offer a sacrifice to give thanks[a] to me, you must do it in a way that is acceptable. [30]Eat all of the meat that same day and don't save any for the next day. I am the LORD your God!

[31]Obey my laws and teachings—I am the LORD. [32-33]I demand respect from the people of Israel, so don't disgrace my holy name. Remember—I am the one who chose you to be priests and rescued all of you from Egypt, so that I would be your LORD.

Religious Festivals

23 The LORD told Moses [2]to say to the community of Israel:

I have chosen certain times for you to come together and worship me.

[3]You have six days when you can do your work, but the seventh day of each week is holy because it belongs to me. No matter where you live, you must rest on the Sabbath and come together for worship. This law will never change.

Passover and the Festival of Thin Bread

(Numbers 28.16-25)

The LORD said:

[4-5]Passover is another time when you must come together to worship me, and it must be celebrated on the evening of the fourteenth day of the first month[b] of each year.

[6]The Festival of Thin Bread begins on the fifteenth day of that same month; it lasts seven days, and during this time you must honor me by eating bread made without yeast. [7]On the first day of this festival you must rest from your work and come together for worship. [8]Each day of this festival you must offer sacrifices. Then on the final day you must once again rest from your work and come together for worship.

Offering the First Part of the Harvest

[9]The LORD told Moses [10]to say to the community of Israel:

After you enter the land I am giving you, the first bundle of wheat from each crop must be given to me. So bring it to a priest [11]on the day after the Sabbath. He will lift it up[c] in dedication to me, and I will accept you. [12]You must also offer a sacrifice to please me.[d] So bring the priest a one-year-old lamb that has nothing wrong with it [13]and four pounds of your finest flour mixed with olive oil. Then he will place these on the bronze altar and send them up in smoke with a smell that pleases me. Together with these, you must bring a quart of wine as a drink offering. [14]I am your God, and I forbid you to eat any new grain or anything made from it until you have brought these offerings. This law will never change.

The Harvest Festival

(Numbers 28.26-31)

The LORD said:

[15]Seven weeks after you offer this bundle of grain, each family must bring another offering of new grain. [16]Do this exactly fifty days later, which is the day following the seventh Sabbath. [17]Bring two loaves of bread to be lifted up[e] in dedication to me. Each loaf is to be made with yeast and with four pounds of the finest flour from the first part of your harvest.

[18]At this same time, the entire community of Israel must bring seven lambs that are a year old, a young bull, and two rams. These animals must have nothing wrong with them, and they must be offered as a sacrifice to please me.[f] You must also offer the proper grain and wine sacrifices with each animal.[g] [19]Offer a goat[h] as a sacrifice for sin, and two rams a year old as a sacrifice to ask my blessing.[i] [20]The priest will lift up[j] the rams together with the bread in dedication to me. These offerings are holy and are my gift to the priest. [21]This is a day of celebration and worship, a time of rest from your work. You and your descendants must obey this law.

[22]When you harvest your grain, always leave some of it standing around

---

[a]**22.29** *sacrifice to give thanks*: See 7.12. [b]**23.4,5** *first month*: Abib (also called Nisan), the first month of the Hebrew calendar, from about mid-March to mid-April. [c]**23.11** *lift it up*: See the note at 7.29, 30. [d]**23.12** *sacrifice to please me*: See the note at 1.1-3. [e]**23.17** *lifted up*: See the note at 7.29, 30. [f]**23.18** *sacrifice to please me*: See the note at 1.1-3. [g]**23.18** *proper grain . . . animal*: See Numbers 15.1-16. [h]**23.19** *goat*: See the note at 1.1-3. [i]**23.19** *sacrifice to ask my blessing*: See the note at 3.1. [j]**23.20** *lift up*: See the note at 7.29, 30.

the edges of your fields and don't pick
up what falls on the ground. Leave it for
the poor and for those foreigners who
live among you. I am the LORD your
God!

The Festival of Trumpets

(Numbers 29.1-6)

23 The LORD told Moses 24-25 to say to
the people of Israel:
The first day of the seventh month[k]
must be a day of complete rest. Then at
the sound of the trumpets, you will
come together to worship and to offer
sacrifices on the altar.

The Great Day of Forgiveness

(Numbers 29.7-11)

26 The LORD God said to Moses:
27 The tenth day of the seventh month[l]
is the Great Day of Forgiveness.[m] It is a
solemn day of worship; everyone must
go without eating to show sorrow for
their sins, and sacrifices must be
burned. 28 No one is to work on that
day—it is the Great Day of Forgiveness,
when sacrifices will be offered to me, so
that I will forgive your sins. 29 I will destroy anyone who refuses to go without
eating. 30-31 None of my people are ever
to do any work on that day—not now or
in the future. And I will wipe out those
who do! 32 This is a time of complete rest
just like the Sabbath, and everyone
must go without eating from the
evening of the ninth to the evening of
the tenth.

The Festival of Shelters

(Numbers 29.12-40)

33 The LORD told Moses 34 to say to the
community of Israel:
Beginning on the fifteenth day of the
seventh month,[n] and continuing for
seven days, everyone must celebrate the
Festival of Shelters in honor of me. 35 No
one is to do any work on the first day of
the festival—it is a time when everyone
must come together for worship. 36 For
seven days, sacrifices must be offered
on the altar. The eighth day is also to be
a day of complete rest, as well as a time
of offering sacrifices on the altar and of
coming together for worship.
37 I have chosen these festivals as
times when my people must come together for worship and when animals,
grain, and wine are to be offered on the
proper days. 38 These festivals must be
celebrated in addition to the Sabbaths
and the times when you offer special
gifts or sacrifices to keep a promise or
as a voluntary offering.
39 Remember to begin the Festival of
Shelters on the fifteenth day of the seventh month after you have harvested
your crops. Celebrate this festival for
seven days in honor of me and don't do
any work on the first day or on the day
following the festival. 40 Pick the best
fruit from your trees[o] and cut leafy
branches to use during the time of this
joyous celebration in my honor. 41 I command you and all of your descendants
to celebrate this festival during the seventh month of each year. 42 For seven
days every Israelite must live in a shelter, 43 so future generations will know
that I made their ancestors live in shelters when I brought them out of Egypt. I
am the LORD your God.
44 This is how Moses instructed the
people of Israel to celebrate the LORD's
festivals.

Caring for the Lamps

(Exodus 27.20, 21)

24 The LORD told Moses 2 to say to
the community of Israel:
You must supply the purest olive oil
for the lamps in the sacred tent, so they
will keep burning. 3-4 Aaron will set up
the gold lampstand in the holy place of
the sacred tent. Then he will light the
seven lamps that must be kept burning
there in my presence, every night from
now on. This law will never change.

The Sacred Bread

The LORD said:
5 Use your finest flour to bake twelve
loaves of bread about four pounds each,
6 then take them into the sacred tent and
lay them on the gold table in two rows
of six loaves. 7 Alongside each row put
some pure incense that will be sent up
by fire in place of the bread as an offering to me. 8 Aaron must lay fresh loaves
on the table each Sabbath, and priests
in all generations must continue this
practice as part of Israel's agreement
with me. 9 This bread will always belong
to Aaron and his family; it is very holy
because it was offered to me, and it
must be eaten in a holy place.[p]

Punishment for Cursing the LORD

10-11 Shelomith, the daughter of Dibri
from the tribe of Dan, had married an
Egyptian, and they had a son. One day
their son got into a fight with an Israelite man in camp and cursed the
name of the LORD. So the young man
was dragged off to Moses, 12 who had
him guarded while everyone waited for
the LORD to tell them what to do.

[k] **23.24,25** *seventh month*: See the note at 16.29. [l] **23.27** *seventh month*: See the note at 16.29. [m] **23.27** *Great Day of Forgiveness*: See the note at 16.34. [n] **23.34** *seventh month*: See the note at 16.29. [o] **23.40** *best fruit from your trees*: One possible meaning for the difficult Hebrew text. [p] **24.9** *holy place*: The courtyard of the sacred tent (see 6.16, 17).

13Finally, the LORD said to Moses:
14This man has cursed me! Take
him outside the camp and have the
witnesses lay their hands on his
head. Then command the whole
community of Israel to stone him to
death. 15-16And warn the others that
everyone else who curses me will
die in the same way, whether they
are Israelites by birth or foreigners
living among you.
17Death is also the penalty for
murder, 18but the killing of an animal that belongs to someone else requires only that the animal be replaced. 19Personal injuries to others
must be dealt with in keeping with
the crime—20a broken bone for a
broken bone, an eye for an eye, or a
tooth for a tooth. 21It's possible to
pay the owner for an animal that
has been killed, but death is the
penalty for murder. 22I am the LORD
your God, and I demand equal justice both for you Israelites and for
those foreigners who live among
you.
23When Moses finished speaking, the
people did what the LORD had told
Moses, and they stoned to death the
man who had cursed the LORD.

The Seventh Year
(Deuteronomy 15.1-11)

25 When Moses was on Mount Sinai,
the LORD told him 2to say to the
community of Israel:
After you enter the land that I am
giving you, it must be allowed to rest
one year out of every seven. 3You
may raise grain and grapes for six
years, 4but the seventh year you
must let your fields and vineyards
rest in honor of me, your LORD. 5This
is to be a time of complete rest for
your fields and vineyards, so don't
harvest anything they produce.
6-7However, you and your slaves and
your hired workers, as well as any
domestic or wild animals, may eat
whatever grows on its own.

The Year of Celebration

The LORD said to his people:
8Once every forty-nine years 9on the
tenth day of the seventh month,[q] which
is also the Great Day of Forgiveness,[r]
trumpets are to be blown everywhere in
the land. 10This fiftieth year[s] is sacred—
it is a time of freedom and of celebration when everyone will receive back
their original property, and slaves will
return home to their families. 11This is a
year of complete celebration, so don't
plant any seed or harvest what your
fields or vineyards produce. 12In this
time of sacred celebration you may eat
only what grows on its own.
13During this year, all property must
go back to its original owner. 14-15So
when you buy or sell farmland, the price
is to be determined by the number of
crops it can produce before the next
Year of Celebration. Don't try to cheat.
16If it is a long time before the next Year
of Celebration, the price will be higher,
because what is really being sold are
the crops that the land can produce. 17I
am the LORD your God, so obey me and
don't cheat anyone.
18-19If you obey my laws and teachings, you will live safely in the land and
enjoy its abundant crops. 20Don't ever
worry about what you will eat during
the seventh year when you are forbidden to plant or harvest. 21I will see to it
that you harvest enough in the sixth
year to last for three years. 22In the
eighth year you will live on what you
harvested in the sixth year, but in the
ninth year you will eat what you plant
and harvest in the eighth year.
23No land may be permanently bought
or sold. It all belongs to me—it isn't
your land, and you only live there for a
little while.
24When property is being sold, the
original owner must be given the first
chance to buy it.
25If any of you Israelites become so
poor that you are forced to sell your
property, your closest relative must buy
it back, 26if that relative has the money.
Later, if you can afford to buy it, 27you
must pay enough to make up for what
the present owner will lose on it before
the next Year of Celebration, when the
property would become yours again.
28But if you don't have the money to pay
the present owner a fair price, you will
have to wait until the Year of Celebration, when the property will once again
become yours.
29If you sell a house in a walled city,
you have only one year in which to buy
it back. 30If you don't buy it back before
that year is up, it becomes the permanent property of the one who bought it,
and it will not be returned to you in the
Year of Celebration. 31But a house out in
a village may be bought back at any
time just like a field. And it must be returned to its original owner in the Year
of Celebration. 32If any Levites own
houses inside a walled city, they will always have the right to buy them back.
33And any houses that they do not buy
back will be returned to them in the
Year of Celebration, because these
homes are their permanent property

[q]**25.9** *seventh month*: See the note at 16.29. [r]**25.9** *Great Day of Forgiveness*: See the note at 16.34. [s]**25.10** *fiftieth year*: The year following seven periods of seven years.

among the people of Israel. 34No pastureland owned by the Levi tribe can
ever be sold; it is their permanent possession.

Help for the Poor

The LORD said:
35If any of your people become poor
and unable to support themselves, you
must help them, just as you are supposed to help foreigners who live
among you. 36-37Don't take advantage of
them by charging any kind of interest or
selling them food for profit. Instead,
honor me by letting them stay where
they now live. 38Remember—I am the
LORD your God! I rescued you from
Egypt and gave you the land of Canaan,
so that I would be your God.
39Suppose some of your people become so poor that they have to sell
themselves and become your slaves.
40Then you must treat them as servants,
rather than as slaves. And in the Year of
Celebration they are to be set free, 41so
they and their children may return
home to their families and property. 42I
brought them out of Egypt to be my servants, not to be sold as slaves. 43So obey
me, and don't be cruel to the poor.
44If you want slaves, buy them from
other nations 45or from the foreigners
who live in your own country, and make
them your property. 46You can own
them, and even leave them to your children when you die, but do not make
slaves of your own people or be cruel to
them.
47Even if some of you Israelites become so much in debt that you must sell
yourselves to foreigners in your country,
48you still have the right to be set free by
a relative, such as a brother 49or uncle
or cousin, or some other family member.
In fact, if you ever get enough money,
you may buy your own freedom 50by
paying your owner for the number of
years you would still be a slave before
the next Year of Celebration. 51-52The
longer the time until then, the more you
will have to pay. 53And even while you
are the slaves of foreigners in your own
country, your people must make sure
that you are not mistreated. 54If you cannot gain your freedom in any of these
ways, both you and your children will
still be set free in the Year of Celebration. 55People of Israel, I am the LORD
your God, and I brought you out of
Egypt to be my own servants.

Blessings for Obeying the LORD

The LORD said:
26 I am the LORD your God! So don't
make or worship any sort of idols
or images. 2Respect the Sabbath and
honor the place where I am worshiped,
because I am the LORD.
3Faithfully obey my laws, 4and I will
send rain to make your crops grow and
your trees produce fruit. 5Your harvest
of grain and grapes will be so abundant,
that you won't know what to do with it
all. You will eat and be satisfied, and you
will live in safety. 6I will bless your
country with peace, and you will rest
without fear. I will wipe out the dangerous animals and protect you from enemy attacks. 7You will chase and destroy your enemies, 8even if there are
only five of you and a hundred of them,
or only a hundred of you and ten thousand of them. 9I will treat you with such
kindness that your nation will grow
strong, and I will also keep my promises
to you. 10Your barns will overflow with
grain each year. 11I will live among you
and never again look on you with disgust. 12I will walk with you—I will be
your God, and you will be my people. 13I
am the LORD your God, and I rescued
you from Egypt, so that you would
never again be slaves. I have set you
free; now walk with your heads held
high.

Punishment for Disobeying the LORD

The LORD said:
14-15If you disobey me and my laws,
and if you break our agreement, 16I will
punish you terribly, and you will be ruined. You will be struck with incurable
diseases and with fever that leads to
blindness and depression. Your enemies
will eat the crops you plant, 17and I will
turn from you and let you be destroyed
by your attackers. You will even run at
the very rumor of attack. 18Then, if you
still refuse to obey me, I will punish you
seven times for each of your sins, 19until
your pride is completely crushed. I will
hold back the rain, so the sky above you
will be like iron, and the ground beneath your feet will be like copper. 20All
of your hard work will be for nothing—
and there will be no harvest of grain or
fruit.
21If you keep rebelling against me, I'll
punish you seven times worse, just as
your sins deserve! 22I'll send wild animals to attack you, and they will gobble
down your children and livestock. So
few of you will be left that your roads
will be deserted.
23If you remain my enemies after this,
24I'll remain your enemy and punish you
even worse. 25War will break out because you broke our agreement, and if
you escape to your walled cities, I'll
punish you with horrible diseases, and
you will be captured by your enemies.
26You will have such a shortage of
bread, that ten women will be able to
bake their bread in the same oven. Each
of you will get only a few crumbs, and
you will go hungry.

[27]Then if you don't stop rebelling, [28]I'll really get furious and punish you terribly for your sins! [29]In fact, you will be so desperate for food that you will eat your own children. [30]I'll destroy your shrines and tear down your incense altars, leaving your dead bodies piled on top of your idols. And you will be disgusting to me. [31]I'll wipe out your towns and your places of worship and will no longer be pleased with the smell of your sacrifices. [32]Your land will become so desolate that even your enemies who settle there will be shocked when they see it. [33]After I destroy your towns and ruin your land with war, I'll scatter you among the nations.

[34-35]While you are prisoners in foreign lands, your own land will enjoy years of rest and refreshment, as it should have done each seventh year when you lived there. [36-37]In the land of your enemies, you will tremble at the rustle of a leaf, as though it were a sword. And you will become so weak that you will stumble and fall over each other, even when no one is chasing you. [38]Many of you will die in foreign lands, [39]and others of you will waste away in sorrow as the result of your sins and the sins of your ancestors.

[40-41]Then suppose you realize that I turned against you and brought you to the land of your enemies because both you and your ancestors had stubbornly sinned against me. If you humbly confess what you have done and start living right, [42]I'll keep the promise I made to your ancestors Abraham, Isaac, and Jacob. I will bless your land [43]and let it rest during the time that you are in a foreign country, paying for your rebellion against me and my laws.

[44]No matter what you have done, I am still the LORD your God, and I will never completely reject you or become absolutely disgusted with you there in the land of your enemies. [45]While nations watched, I rescued your ancestors from Egypt so that I would be their God. Yes, I am your LORD, and I will never forget our agreement.

[46]Moses was on Mount Sinai when the LORD gave him these laws and teachings for the people of Israel.

Making Promises to the LORD

27 The LORD told Moses [2]to say to the community of Israel:

If you ever want to free someone who has been promised to me, [3-7]you may do so by paying the following amounts, weighed according to the official standards:

fifty pieces of silver for men
 ages twenty to sixty,
and thirty pieces for women;
twenty pieces of silver
 for young men
ages five to twenty,
and ten pieces
 for young women;
fifteen pieces of silver for men
ages sixty and above
 and ten pieces for women;
five pieces of silver for boys
ages one month to five years,
 and three pieces for girls.

[8]If you have promised to give someone to me and can't afford to pay the full amount for that person's release, you will be taken to a priest, and he will decide how much you can afford.

[9]If you promise to sacrifice an animal to me, it becomes holy, and there is no way you can set it free. [10]If you try to substitute any other animal, no matter how good, for the one you promised, they will both become holy and must be sacrificed. [11]Donkeys are unfit for sacrifice, so if you promise me a donkey,[t] you must bring it to the priest, [12]and let him determine its value. [13]But if you want to buy it back, you must pay an additional twenty percent.

[14]If you promise a house to me, a priest will set the price, whatever the condition of the house. [15]But if you decide to buy it back, you must pay an additional twenty percent.

[16]If you promise part of your family's land to me, its value must be determined by the bushels of seed needed to plant the land, and the rate will be ten pieces of silver for every bushel of seed. [17]If this promise is made in the Year of Celebration,[u] the land will be valued at the full price. [18]But any time after that, the price will be figured according to the number of years before the next Year of Celebration. [19]If you decide to buy back the land, you must pay the price plus an additional twenty percent, [20]but you cannot buy it back once someone else has bought it. [21]When the Year of Celebration comes, the land becomes holy because it belongs to me, and it will be given to the priests.

[22]If you promise me a field that you have bought, [23]its value will be decided by a priest, according to the number of years before the next Year of Celebration, and the money you pay will be mine. [24]However, on the next Year of Celebration, the land will go back to the

[t]**27.11** *Donkeys . . . donkey*: The Hebrew text has "If you promise me an unclean animal," which probably refers to a donkey (see Exodus 13.13; 34.20). [u]**27.17** *Year of Celebration*: See 25.8-34.

family of its original owner. 25 Every
price will be set by the official standards.

Various Offerings

The LORD said:
26 All first-born animals of your flocks
and herds are already mine, and so you
cannot promise any of them to me. 27 If
you promise me a donkey,[v] you may buy
it back by adding an additional twenty
percent to its value. If you don't buy
it back, it can be sold to someone else
for whatever a priest has said it is
worth.
28 Anything that you completely dedicate to me must be completely destroyed.[w] It cannot be bought back or
sold. Every person, animal, and piece of
property that you dedicate completely is
only for me. 29 In fact, any humans who
have been promised to me in this way
must be put to death.
30 Ten percent of everything you harvest is holy and belongs to me, whether
it grows in your fields or on your fruit
trees. 31 If you want to buy back this part
of your harvest, you may do so by paying what it is worth plus an additional
twenty percent.
32 When you count your flocks and
herds, one out of ten of every newborn
animal[x] is holy and belongs to me, 33 no
matter how good or bad it is. If you substitute one animal for another, both of
them become holy, and neither can be
bought back.
34 Moses was on Mount Sinai when the
LORD gave him these laws for the people
of Israel.

[v] **27.27** *donkey*: See the note at verse 11. [w] **27.28** *completely dedicate . . . completely destroyed*: In order to show that something belonged completely to the LORD and could not be used by anyone else, it was destroyed. This law most often applied to towns and people captured in war (see Joshua 6.16, 17). [x] **27.32** *one out of ten of every newborn animal*: Or "one out of every ten animals."

NUMBERS

ABOUT THIS BOOK

The book of Numbers continues the history of the people of Israel after they escaped from Egypt, and it tells what happened during the forty years when the Israelites lived in the desert on their journey from Mount Sinai to Canaan. This book is named "Numbers" because it begins with Moses counting the Israelites to find out the number of people in each of Israel's twelve tribes.

Numbers can be divided into three parts. In the first part (1.1—10.10) the Lord has Moses count the people, and then he gives Moses instructions for setting up Israel's camp and for assigning the Levites their duties. This part ends with everyone celebrating Passover and offering sacrifices to the Lord.

The second part (10.11—21.20) includes events that happened while the Israelites were on their way to Moab, a nation living east of the Jordan River. This was a very difficult journey through the desert, and the people often complained and even rebelled against Moses and against God. The Israelites refused to enter Canaan after hearing about the nations that lived there, and so the Lord punished the Israelites by making them remain in the desert for forty years. This part of Numbers ends with the people camped in Moab near Mount Pisgah.

The third part of the book (21.21—36.13) begins with the Israelites conquering the land just east of the Jordan River, from the border with Moab in the south to Lake Galilee in the north. Then the king of Moab hired the foreign prophet Balaam to curse the people of Israel. But the Lord told Balaam to bless the Israelites, and Balaam obeyed.

The Israelites prepared to cross the Jordan River and conquer the land of Canaan, although some of the people decided to settle east of the Jordan River. The Israelites were counted a second time, then the Lord appointed Joshua to be Israel's next leader and chose other leaders to help Joshua divide the land among the tribes. The book concludes with the Lord giving the Israelites more laws.

Numbers is about people who were rebellious and discouraged and who refused to believe that the Lord would take care of them. But the book also shows how the Lord protected them in war and gave them food and water in the barren desert. The Lord wanted the Israelites to realize that he did not want them to be destroyed; he wanted to bless them, just as Aaron prayed:

> *"I pray that the LORD*
> *will bless and protect you,*
> *and that he will show you mercy*
> *and kindness.*
> *May the LORD be good to you*
> *and give you peace."*
> *(6.24-26)*

A QUICK LOOK AT THIS BOOK

The People of Israel Are Counted (1.1—4.49)
Various Laws and the Dedication of the Levites (5.1—8.26)
Passover Is Celebrated and a Cloud Covers the Sacred Tent (9.1-23)
The People Begin Their Journey (10.1-36)
The People Complain (11.1-35)
Miriam and Aaron Are Jealous of Moses (12.1-16)
Twelve Men Are Sent into Canaan (13.1-33)

The People of Israel Are Counted

1 The people of Israel had left Egypt
and were living in the Sinai Desert.
Then on the first day of the second
month[a] of the second year, Moses was
in the sacred tent when the LORD said:

> 2-3 I want you and Aaron to find out
> how many people are in each of Israel's clans and families. And make
> a list of all the men twenty years and
> older who are able to fight in battle.
> 4-15 The following twelve family leaders, one from each tribe, will help
> you:
>
> Elizur son of Shedeur
> from Reuben,
> Shelumiel son of Zurishaddai
> from Simeon,
> Nahshon son of Amminadab
> from Judah,
> Nethanel son of Zuar
> from Issachar,
> Eliab son of Helon
> from Zebulun,
> Elishama son of Ammihud
> from Ephraim,
> Gamaliel son of Pedahzur
> from Manasseh,
> Abidan son of Gideoni
> from Benjamin,
> Ahiezer son of Ammishaddai
> from Dan,
> Pagiel son of Ochran
> from Asher,
> Eliasaph son of Deuel
> from Gad,
> and Ahira son of Enan
> from Naphtali.

16-17 Moses and Aaron, together with
these twelve tribal leaders, 18 called together the people that same day. They
were counted according to their clans
and families. Then Moses and the others
listed the names of the men twenty
years and older, 19 just as the LORD had
commanded. 20-46 The number of men
from each tribe who were at least
twenty years old and strong enough to
fight in Israel's army was as follows:

46,500 from Reuben,
the oldest son of Jacob,[b]
59,300 from Simeon,
45,650 from Gad,
74,600 from Judah,
54,400 from Issachar,
57,400 from Zebulun,
40,500 from Ephraim,
32,200 from Manasseh,
35,400 from Benjamin,
62,700 from Dan,
41,500 from Asher,
53,400 from Naphtali.

The total number of men registered
by Moses, Aaron, and the twelve leaders
was 603,550.
47 But those from the Levi tribe were
not included 48 because the LORD had
said to Moses:

> 49 When you count the Israelites,
> do not include those from the Levi
> tribe. 50-51 Instead, give them the job
> of caring for the sacred tent, its furnishings, and the objects used for
> worship. They will camp around the
> tent, and whenever you move, they
> will take it down, carry it to the new
> camp, and set it up again. Anyone
> else who tries to go near it must be
> put to death.
> 52 The rest of the Israelites will

[a] 1.1 *second month*: Ziv, the second month of the Hebrew calendar, from about mid-April to mid-May. [b] 1.20-46 *Jacob*: The Hebrew text has "Israel," Jacob's name after God renamed him.

camp in their own groups and under
their own banners. [53]But the Levites
will camp around the sacred tent to
make sure that no one goes near it
and makes me furious with the Israelites.
[54]The people of Israel did everything
the LORD had commanded.

Instructions for Setting Up Israel's Camp

2 The LORD told Moses and Aaron
[2]how the Israelites should arrange
their camp:
Each tribe must set up camp under its
own banner and under the flags of its
ancestral families. These camps will be
arranged around the sacred tent, but not
close to it.
[3-4]Judah and the tribes that march
with it must set up camp on the east
side of the sacred tent, under their own
banner. The 74,600 troops of the tribe of
Judah will be arranged by divisions and
led by Nahshon son of Amminadab.
[5-6]On one side of Judah will be the tribe
of Issachar, with Nethanel son of Zuar
as the leader of its 54,400 troops. [7-8]On
the other side will be the tribe of Zebulun, with Eliab son of Helon as the
leader of its 57,400 troops. [9]These
186,400 troops will march into battle
first.
[10-11]Reuben and the tribes that march
with it must set up camp on the south
side of the sacred tent, under their own
banner. The 46,500 troops of the tribe of
Reuben will be arranged by divisions
and led by Elizur son of Shedeur. [12-13]On
one side of Reuben will be the tribe of
Simeon, with Shelumiel son of Zurishaddai as the leader of its 59,300
troops. [14-15]On the other side will be the
tribe of Gad, with Eliasaph son of Deuel
as the leader of its 45,650 troops.
[16]These 151,450 troops will march into
battle second.
[17]Marching behind Reuben will be the
Levites, arranged in groups, just as they
are camped. They will carry the sacred
tent and their own banners.
[18-19]Ephraim and the tribes that march
with it must set up camp on the west
side of the sacred tent, under their own
banner. The 40,500 troops of the tribe of
Ephraim will be arranged by divisions
and led by Elishama son of Ammihud.
[20-21]On one side of Ephraim will be the
tribe of Manasseh, with Gamaliel son of
Pedahzur as the leader of its 32,200
troops. [22-23]On the other side will be the
tribe of Benjamin, with Abidan son of
Gideoni as the leader of its 35,400
troops. [24]These 108,100 troops will
march into battle third.
[25-26]Dan and the tribes that march
with it must set up camp on the north
side of the sacred tent, under their own
banner. The 62,700 troops of the tribe of
Dan will be arranged by divisions and
led by Ahiezer son of Ammishaddai.
[27-28]On one side of Dan will be the tribe
of Asher, with Pagiel son of Ochran as
the leader of its 41,500 troops. [29-30]On
the other side will be the tribe of Naphtali with Ahira son of Enan as the leader
of its 53,400 troops. [31]These 157,600
troops will march into battle last.
[32]So all the Israelites in the camp
were counted according to their ancestral families. The troops were arranged
by divisions and totaled 603,550. [33]The
only Israelites not included were the
Levites, just as the LORD had commanded Moses.
[34]Israel did everything the LORD had
told Moses. They arranged their camp
according to clans and families, with
each tribe under its own banner. And
that was the order by which they
marched into battle.

The Sons of Aaron

3 When the LORD talked with Moses
on Mount Sinai, [2]Aaron's four sons,
Nadab, Abihu, Eleazar, and Ithamar,
[3]were the ones to be ordained as priests.
[4]But the LORD killed Nadab and Abihu
in the Sinai Desert when they used fire
that was unacceptable[c] in their offering
to the LORD.[d] And because Nadab and
Abihu had no sons, only Eleazar and
Ithamar served as priests with their
father Aaron.

The Duties of the Levites

[5]The LORD said to Moses:
[6]Assign the Levi tribe to Aaron the
priest. They will be his assistants
[7]and will work at the sacred tent for
him and for all the Israelites. [8]The
Levites will serve the community by
being responsible for the furnishings of the tent. [9]They are assigned
to help Aaron and his sons, [10]who
have been appointed to be priests.
Anyone else who tries to perform
the duties of a priest must be put to
death.
[11-13]Moses, I have chosen these
Levites from all Israel, and they will
belong to me in a special way. When
I killed the first-born sons of the
Egyptians, I decided that the first-
born sons in every Israelite family
and the first-born males of their
flocks and herds would be mine.[e]
But now I accept these Levites in

[c]**3.4** *fire that was unacceptable*: One possible meaning for the difficult Hebrew text.
[d]**3.4** *the LORD killed Nadab and Abihu . . . to the LORD*: See Leviticus 10.1, 2. [e]**3.11-13** *When I killed . . . mine*: See Exodus 13.1, 2, 11-16.

place of the first-born sons of the Israelites.

The Levites Are Counted

14In the Sinai Desert the LORD said to Moses, 15"Now I want you to count the men and boys in the Levi tribe by families and by clans. Include every one at least a month old." 16So Moses obeyed and counted them.

17Levi's three sons, Gershon, Kohath, and Merari, had become the heads of their own clans. 18Gershon's sons were Libni and Shimei. 19Kohath's sons were Amram, Izhar, Hebron, and Uzziel. 20And Merari's sons were Mahli and Mushi. These were the sons and grandsons of Levi, and they had become the leaders of the Levite clans.

21The two Gershon clans were the Libnites and Shimeites, 22and they had seven thousand five hundred men and boys at least one month old. 23The Gershonites were to camp on the west side of the sacred tent, 24under the leadership of Eliasaph son of Lael. 25Their duties at the tent included taking care of the tent itself, along with its outer covering, the curtain for the entrance, 26the curtains hanging inside the courtyard around the tent, as well as the curtain and ropes for the entrance to the courtyard and its altar. The Gershonites were responsible for setting these things up and taking them down.

27The four Kohath clans were the Amramites, Izharites, Hebronites, and the Uzzielites, 28and they had eight thousand six hundred[f] men and boys at least one month old. 29The Kohathites were to camp on the south side of the sacred tent, 30under the leadership of Elizaphan son of Uzziel. 31Their duties at the tent included taking care of the sacred chest, the table for the sacred bread, the lampstand, the altars, the objects used for worship, and the curtain in front of the most holy place. The Kohathites were responsible for setting these things up and taking them down.

32Eleazar son of Aaron was the head of the Levite leaders, and he made sure that the work at the sacred tent was done.

33The two Merari clans were the Mahlites and the Mushites, 34and they had six thousand two hundred men and boys at least one month old. 35The Merarites were to camp on the north side of the sacred tent, under the leadership of Zuriel son of Abihail. 36-37Their duties included taking care of the tent frames and the pieces that held the tent up: the bars, the posts, the stands, and its other equipment. They were also in charge of the posts that supported the courtyard, as well as their stands, tent pegs, and ropes. The Merari clans were responsible for setting these things up and taking them down.

38Moses, Aaron, and his sons were to camp in front of the sacred tent, on the east side, and to make sure that the Israelites worshiped in the proper way. Anyone else who tried to do the work of Moses and Aaron was to be put to death.

39So Moses and Aaron obeyed the LORD and counted the Levites by their clans. The total number of Levites at least one month old was twenty-two thousand.

The Levites Are Accepted as Substitutes for the First-Born Sons

40The LORD said to Moses, "Make a list and count the first-born sons at least one month old in each of the Israelite families. 41They belong to me, but I will accept the Levites as substitutes for them, and I will accept the Levites' livestock as substitutes for the Israelites' first-born livestock."

42Moses obeyed the LORD and counted the first-born sons; 43there were 22,273 of them.

44Then the LORD said, 45"The Levites will belong to me and will take the place of the first-born sons; their livestock will take the place of the Israelites' first-born livestock. 46But since there are more first-born sons than Levites, the extra two hundred seventy-three men and boys must be bought back from me. 47For each one, you are to collect five pieces of silver, weighed according to the official standards. 48This money must then be given to Aaron and his sons."

49Moses collected the silver from the extra two hundred seventy-three first-born men and boys, 50and it amounted to one thousand three hundred sixty-five pieces of silver, weighed according to the official standards. 51Then he gave it to Aaron and his sons, just as the LORD had commanded.

The Duties of the Kohathite Clans

4 The LORD told Moses and Aaron:
2-3Find out how many men between the ages of thirty and fifty are in the four Levite clans of Kohath. Count only those who are able to work at the sacred tent.

4The Kohathites will be responsible for carrying the sacred objects used in worship at the sacred tent. 5When the Israelites are ready to move their camp, Aaron and his sons will enter the tent

[f] 3.28 *eight thousand six hundred*: Hebrew; some manuscripts of one ancient translation "eight thousand three hundred."

and take down the curtain that separates the sacred chest from the rest of the tent. They will cover the chest with this curtain, 6and then with a piece of fine leather, and cover it all with a solid blue cloth. After this they will put the carrying poles in place.

7Next, Aaron and his sons will use another blue cloth to cover the table for the sacred bread.[g] On the cloth they will place the dishes, the bowls for incense, the cups, the jugs for wine, as well as the bread itself. 8They are to cover all of this with a bright red cloth, and then with a piece of fine leather, before putting the carrying poles in place.

9With another blue cloth they will cover the lampstand, along with the lamps, the lamp snuffers, the fire pans, and the jars of oil for the lamps. 10All of this will then be covered with a piece of fine leather and placed on a carrying frame.

11The gold incense altar[h] is to be covered with a blue cloth, and then with a piece of fine leather, before its carrying poles are put in place.

12Next, Aaron and his sons will take blue cloth and wrap all the objects used in worship at the sacred tent. These will need to be covered with a piece of fine leather, then placed on a carrying frame.

13They are to remove the ashes from the bronze altar and cover it with a purple cloth. 14On that cloth will be placed the utensils used at the altar, including the fire pans, the meat forks, the shovels, and the sprinkling bowls. All of this will then be covered with a piece of fine leather, before the carrying poles are put in place.

15When the camp is ready to be moved, the Kohathites will be responsible for carrying the sacred objects and the furnishings of the sacred tent. But Aaron and his sons must have already covered those things so the Kohathites won't touch them and die.

16Eleazar son of Aaron the priest will be in charge of the oil for the lamps, the sweet-smelling incense, the grain for the sacrifices, and the olive oil used for dedications and ordinations. Eleazar is responsible for seeing that the sacred tent, its furnishings, and the sacred objects are taken care of.

17-20The Kohathites must not go near or even look at the sacred objects until Aaron and his sons have covered those objects. If they do, their entire clan will be wiped out. So make sure that Aaron and his sons go into the tent with them and tell them what to carry.

The Duties of the Gershonite Clans

21The LORD said to Moses:

22-23Find out how many men between the ages of thirty and fifty are in the two Levite clans of Gershon. Count only those who are able to work at the sacred tent.

24The Gershonites will be responsible 25for carrying the curtains of the sacred tent, its two outer coverings,[i] the curtain for the entrance to the tent, 26the curtains hanging around the courtyard of the tent, and the curtain and ropes for the entrance to the courtyard. The Gershonites are to do whatever needs to be done to take care of these things, 27and they will carry them wherever Aaron and his sons tell them to. 28These are the duties of the Gershonites at the sacred tent, and Ithamar son of Aaron will make sure they do their work.

The Duties of the Merarite Clans

29-30The LORD said:

Moses, find out how many men between thirty and fifty are in the two Levite clans of Merari, but count only those who are able to work at the sacred tent.

31The Merarites will be responsible for carrying the frames of the tent and its other pieces, including the bars, the posts, the stands, 32as well as the posts that support the courtyard, together with their stands, tent pegs, and ropes. The Merarites are to be told exactly what objects they are to carry, 33and Ithamar son of Aaron will make sure they do their work.

The Levites Are Counted Again

34-49Moses, Aaron, and the other Israelite leaders obeyed the LORD and counted the Levi tribe by families and clans, to find out how many men there were between the ages of thirty and fifty who could work at the sacred tent. There were two thousand seven hundred fifty Kohathites, two thousand six hundred thirty Gershonites, and three thousand two hundred Merarites, making a total of eight thousand five hundred eighty. Then they were all assigned their duties.

[g]**4.7** *sacred bread*: This bread was offered to the LORD and was a symbol of his presence in the sacred tent. It was put out on a special table and was replaced with fresh bread each Sabbath (Leviticus 24.5-9). [h]**4.11** *gold incense altar*: This altar for offering incense was inside the sacred tent; it was made of acacia wood covered with gold. A large altar for offering sacrifices was in front of the entrance to the tent; it was made of acacia wood covered with bronze (see verse 13). [i]**4.25** *two outer coverings*: See Exodus 26.14.

People Are Sent Outside the Camp

5 The LORD told Moses 2-3to say to the
people of Israel, "Put out of the
camp everyone who has leprosy[j] or a
bodily discharge or who has touched a
dead body. Now that I live among my
people, their camp must be kept clean."
4The Israelites obeyed the LORD's instructions.

The Penalty for Committing a Crime

(Leviticus 6.1-7)

5The LORD told Moses 6to say to the
community of Israel:
If any of you commit a crime against
someone, you have sinned against me.
7You must confess your guilt and pay
the victim in full for whatever damage
has been done, plus a fine of twenty percent. 8If the victim has no relative who
can accept this money, it belongs to me
and will be paid to the priest. In addition to that payment, you must take a
ram for the priest to sacrifice so your
sin will be forgiven.
9-10When you make a donation to the
sacred tent, that money belongs only to
the priest, and each priest will keep
what is given to him.

A Suspicious Husband

11The LORD told Moses 12-14to say to
the people of Israel:
Suppose a man becomes jealous and
suspects that his wife has been unfaithful, but he has no proof. 15He must take
his wife to the priest, together with two
pounds of ground barley as an offering
to find out if she is guilty. No olive oil or
incense is to be put on that offering.
16The priest is to have the woman
stand at my altar, 17where he will pour
sacred water into a clay jar and stir in
some dust from the floor of the sacred
tent. 18-22Next, he will remove her veil,
then hand her the barley offering, and
say, "If you have been faithful to your
husband, this water won't harm you. But
if you have been unfaithful, it will bring
down the LORD's curse—you will never
be able to give birth to a child, and
everyone will curse your name."
Then the woman will answer, "If I am
guilty, let it happen just as you say."
23The priest will write these curses on
special paper and wash them off into
the bitter water, 24so that when the
woman drinks this water, the curses will
enter her body. 25He will take the barley
offering from her and lift it up[k] in dedication to me, the LORD. Then he will
place it on my altar 26and burn part of it
as a sacrifice. After that, the woman
must drink the bitter water.
27If the woman has been unfaithful,
the water will immediately make her
unable to have children, and she will be
a curse among her people. 28But if she is
innocent, her body will not be harmed,
and she will still be able to have children.
29-30This is the ceremony that must
take place at my altar when a husband
suspects that his wife has been unfaithful. The priest must have the woman
stand in my presence and carefully follow these instructions. 31If the husband
is wrong, he will not be punished; but if
his wife is guilty, she will be punished.

Rules for Nazirites

6 The LORD told Moses 2to say to the
people of Israel:
If any of you want to dedicate yourself
to me by vowing to become a Nazirite,
3you must no longer drink any wine or
beer or use any kind of vinegar. Don't
drink grape juice or eat grapes or
raisins—4not even the seeds or skins.
5Even the hair of a Nazirite is sacred
to me, and as long as you are a Nazirite,
you must never cut your hair.
6During the time that you are a
Nazirite, you must never go close to a
dead body, 7-8not even that of your
father, mother, brother, or sister. That
would make you unclean. Your hair is
the sign that you are dedicated to me, so
remain holy.
9If someone suddenly dies near you,
your hair is no longer sacred, and you
must shave it seven days later during
the ceremony to make you clean. 10Then
on the next day, bring two doves or two
pigeons to the priest at the sacred tent.
11He will offer one of the birds as a sacrifice for sin and the other as a sacrifice
to please me.[l] You will then be forgiven
for being too near a dead body, and your
hair will again become sacred. 12But the
dead body made you unacceptable, so
you must make another vow to become
a Nazirite and be dedicated once more.
Finally, a year-old ram must be offered
as the sacrifice to make things right.
13When you have completed your
promised time of being a Nazirite, go to
the sacred tent 14and offer three animals
that have nothing wrong with them: a
year-old ram as a sacrifice to please me,
a year-old female lamb as a sacrifice for
sin, and a full-grown ram as a sacrifice

[j]**5.2,3** *leprosy*: The word translated "leprosy" was used for many different kinds of skin diseases. [k]**5.25** *lift it up*: Or "wave it." [l]**6.11** *sacrifice to please me*: This sacrifice has traditionally been called a "whole burnt offering," because the whole animal was burned on the altar. A main purpose of such a sacrifice was to please the LORD with the smell of the sacrifice, and so in the CEV it is often called "a sacrifice to please the LORD."

to ask my blessing.[m] 15Wine offerings
and grain sacrifices must also be
brought with these animals. Finally, you
are to bring a basket of bread made
with your finest flour and olive oil, but
without yeast. Also bring some thin
wafers brushed with oil.

16The priest will take these gifts to my
altar and offer them, so that I will be
pleased and will forgive you. 17Then he
will sacrifice the ram and offer the wine,
grain, and bread.

18After that, you will stand at the entrance to the sacred tent, shave your
head, and put the hair in the fire where
the priest has offered the sacrifice to
ask my blessing.

19Once the meat from the ram's shoulder has been boiled, the priest will take
it, along with one loaf of bread and one
wafer brushed with oil, and give them to
you. 20You will hand them back to the
priest, who will lift them up[n] in dedication to me. Then he can eat the meat
from the ram's shoulder, its choice ribs,
and its hind leg, because this is his
share of the sacrifice. After this, you will
no longer be a Nazirite and will be free
to drink wine.

21These are the requirements for
Nazirites. However, if you can afford to
offer more, you must do so.

The Blessing for the People

22The LORD told Moses, 23"When
Aaron and his sons bless the people of
Israel, they must say:

24 I pray that the LORD
will bless and protect you,
25 and that he will show you mercy
and kindness.
26 May the LORD be good to you
and give you peace."

27Then the LORD said, "If Aaron and
his sons ask me to bless the Israelites, I
will give them my blessing."

The Leaders Bring Gifts to the Sacred Tent

7 When Moses had finished setting up
the sacred tent, he dedicated it to
the LORD, together with its furnishings,
the altar, and its equipment. 2Then the
twelve tribal leaders of Israel, the same
men who had been in charge of counting the people,[o] came to the tent 3with
gifts for the LORD. They brought six
strong carts and twelve oxen—one ox
from each leader and a cart from every
two.

4The LORD said to Moses, 5"Accept
these gifts, so the Levites can use them
here at the sacred tent for carrying the
sacred things."

6Then Moses took the carts and oxen
and gave them to the Levites, 7-8who
were under the leadership of Ithamar
son of Aaron. Moses gave two carts and
four oxen to the Gershonites for their
work, and four carts and eight oxen to
the Merarites for their work. 9But Moses
did not give any to the Kohathites, because they were in charge of the sacred
objects that had to be carried on their
shoulders.

10On the day the altar was dedicated,
the twelve leaders brought offerings for
its dedication. 11The LORD said to Moses,
"Each day one leader is to give his offering for the dedication."

12-83So each leader brought the following gifts:

a silver bowl that weighed over three
pounds and a silver sprinkling bowl
weighing almost two pounds, both of
them filled with flour and olive oil as
grain sacrifices and weighed according
to the official standards;

a small gold dish filled with incense;

a young bull, a full-grown ram, and a
year-old ram as sacrifices to please the
LORD;[p]

a goat[q] as a sacrifice for sin;

and two bulls, five full-grown rams,
five goats, and five rams a year old as
sacrifices to ask the LORD's blessing.[r]

The tribal leaders brought their gifts
and offerings in the following order:

On the first day
Nahshon from Judah,
on the second day
Nethanel from Issachar,
on the third day
Eliab from Zebulun,
on the fourth day
Elizur from Reuben,
on the fifth day
Shelumiel from Simeon,
on the sixth day
Eliasaph from Gad,
on the seventh day
Elishama from Ephraim,
on the eighth day
Gamaliel from Manasseh,
on the ninth day
Abidan from Benjamin,
on the tenth day
Ahiezer from Dan,
on the eleventh day
Pagiel from Asher,

[m]**6.14** *sacrifice to ask my blessing*: This sacrifice has traditionally been called a "peace offering" or an "offering of well-being." A main purpose of such a sacrifice was to ask the LORD's blessing, and so in the CEV it is often called a "sacrifice to ask the LORD's blessing." [n]**6.20** *lift them up*: See the note at 5.25. [o]**7.2** *the same men . . . the people*: See 1.1-19. [p]**7.12-83** *sacrifices to please the LORD*: See the note at 6.11. [q]**7.12-83** *goat*: Hebrew "male goat." [r]**7.12-83** *sacrifices to ask the LORD's blessing*: See the note at 6.14.

on the twelfth day
Ahira from Naphtali.
84-88And so when the altar was dedicated to the LORD, these twelve leaders
brought the following gifts:
twelve silver bowls and twelve silver
sprinkling bowls, weighing a total of
about sixty pounds, according to the official standards;
twelve gold dishes filled with incense
and weighing about three pounds;
twelve bulls, twelve full-grown rams,
and twelve rams a year old as sacrifices
to please the LORD, along with the
proper grain sacrifices;
twelve goats as sacrifices for sin;
and twenty-four bulls, sixty full-
grown rams, sixty goats, and sixty rams
a year old as sacrifices to ask the LORD's
blessing.
89Whenever Moses needed to talk
with the LORD, he went into the sacred
tent, where he heard the LORD's voice
coming from between the two winged
creatures above the lid of the sacred
chest.

Aaron Puts the Gold Lamps in Place

8 The LORD said to Moses, 2"Tell
Aaron to put the seven lamps on the
lampstand so they shine toward the
front."
3Aaron obeyed and placed the lamps
as he was told. 4The lampstand was
made of hammered gold from its base to
the decorative flowers on top, exactly
like the pattern the LORD had described
to Moses.

Instructions for Ordaining the Levites

5The LORD said to Moses:
6The Levites must be acceptable to me
before they begin working at the sacred
tent. So separate them from the rest of
the Israelites 7and sprinkle them with
the water that washes away their sins.
Then have them shave their entire bodies and wash their clothes.
8They are to bring a bull and its
proper grain sacrifice of flour mixed
with olive oil. And they must bring a
second bull as a sacrifice for sin.
9Then you, Moses, will call together
all the people of Israel and have the
Levites go to my sacred tent, 10where
the people will place their hands on
them. 11Aaron will present the Levites to
me as a gift from the people, so that the
Levites will do my work.
12After this, the Levites are to place
their hands on the heads of the bulls.
Then one of the bulls will be sacrificed
for the forgiveness of sin, and the other
to make sure that I am pleased. 13The
Levites will stand at my altar in front of
Aaron and his sons, who will then dedicate the Levites to me.
14This ceremony will show that the
Levites are different from the other Israelites and belong to me in a special
way. 15After they have been made acceptable and have been dedicated, they
will be allowed to work at my sacred
tent. 16They are mine and will take the
place of the first-born Israelite sons.
17When I killed the oldest sons of the
Egyptians, I decided that the first-born
sons in each Israelite family would be
mine, as well as every first-born male
from their flocks and herds. 18But now I
have chosen these Levites as substitutes
for the first-born sons, 19and I have
given them as gifts to Aaron and his
sons to serve at the sacred tent. I will
hold them responsible for what happens
to anyone who gets too close to the sacred tent.[s]

The Levites Are Dedicated to the LORD

20Moses, Aaron, and the other Israelites made sure that the Levites did
everything the LORD had commanded.
21The Levites sprinkled themselves with
the water of forgiveness and washed
their clothes. Then Aaron brought them
to the altar and offered sacrifices to forgive their sins and make them acceptable to the LORD. 22After this, the Levites
worked at the sacred tent as assistants
to Aaron and his sons, just as the LORD
had commanded.
23The LORD also told Moses, 24-25"Levites who are between the ages of
twenty-five and fifty can work at my sacred tent. But once they turn fifty, they
must retire. 26They may help the other
Levites in their duties, but they must no
longer be responsible for any work
themselves. Remember this when you
assign their duties."

Regulations for Celebrating Passover

9 During the first month of Israel's
second year in the Sinai Desert,[t] the
LORD had told Moses 2to say to the people, "Celebrate Passover 3in the evening
of the fourteenth day of this month[u] and
do it by following all the regulations."
4-5Moses told the people what the LORD
had said, and they celebrated Passover
there in the desert in the evening of the
fourteenth day of the first month.

[s] **8.19** *I will hold . . . sacred tent*: One possible meaning for the difficult Hebrew text.
[t] **9.1** *first month . . . Sinai Desert*: The book of Numbers begins in the second month of the second year (see 1.1), so 9.1-5 refers to a Passover celebration that had already taken place.
[u] **9.3** *this month*: Abib (also called Nisan), the first month of the Hebrew calendar, from about mid-March to mid-April.

[6]Some people in Israel's camp had touched a dead body and had become unfit to worship the LORD, and they could not celebrate Passover. But they asked Moses and Aaron, [7]"Even though we have touched a dead body, why can't we celebrate Passover and offer sacrifices to the LORD at the same time as everyone else?"

[8]Moses said, "Wait here while I go into the sacred tent and find out what the LORD says about this."

[9]The LORD then told Moses [10]to say to the community of Israel:

> If any of you or your descendants touch a dead body and become unfit to worship me, or if you are away on a long journey, you may still celebrate Passover. [11]But it must be done in the second month,[v] in the evening of the fourteenth day. Eat the Passover lamb with thin bread and bitter herbs, [12]and don't leave any of it until morning or break any of the animal's bones. Be sure to follow these regulations.
>
> [13]But if any of you refuse to celebrate Passover when you are not away on a journey, you will no longer belong to my people. You will be punished because you did not offer sacrifices to me at the proper time.
>
> [14]Anyone, including foreigners who live among you, can celebrate Passover, if they follow all the regulations.

The Cloud over the Sacred Tent
(Exodus 40.34-38)

[15-16]As soon as the sacred tent was set up,[w] a thick cloud appeared and covered it. The cloud was there each day, and during the night, a fire could be seen in it. [17-19]The LORD used this cloud to tell the Israelites when to move their camp and where to set it up again. As long as the cloud covered the tent, the Israelites did not break camp. But when the cloud moved, they followed it, and wherever it stopped, they camped and stayed there, [20-22]whether it was only one night, a few days, a month, or even a year. As long as the cloud remained over the tent, the Israelites stayed where they were. But when the cloud moved, so did the Israelites. [23]They obeyed the LORD's commands and went wherever he directed Moses.

The Silver Trumpets

10 The LORD told Moses:

> [2]Have someone make two trumpets out of hammered silver. These will be used to call the people together and to give the signal for moving your camp. [3]If both trumpets are blown, everyone is to meet with you at the entrance to the sacred tent. [4]But if just one is blown, only the twelve tribal leaders need to come together.
>
> [5-6]Give a signal on a trumpet when it is time to break camp. The first blast will be the signal for the tribes camped on the east side, and the second blast will be the signal for those on the south. [7]But when you want everyone to come together, sound a different signal on the trumpet. [8]The priests of Aaron's family will be the ones to blow the trumpets, and this law will never change.
>
> [9]Whenever you go into battle against an enemy attacking your land, give a warning signal on the trumpets. Then I, the LORD, will hear it and rescue you. [10]During the celebration of the New Moon Festival and other religious festivals, sound the trumpets while you offer sacrifices. This will be a reminder that I am the LORD your God.

The Israelites Begin Their Journey

[11]On the twentieth day of the second month[x] of that same year, the cloud over the sacred tent moved on. [12]So the Israelites broke camp and left the Sinai Desert. And some time later, the cloud stopped in the Paran Desert.[y] [13]This was the first time the LORD had told Moses to command the people of Israel to move on.

[14]Judah and the tribes that camped alongside it marched out first, carrying their banner. Nahshon son of Amminadab was the leader of the Judah tribe, [15]Nethanel son of Zuar was the leader of the Issachar tribe, [16]and Eliab son of Helon was the leader of the Zebulun tribe.

[17]The sacred tent had been taken down, and the Gershonites and the Merarites carried it, marching behind the Judah camp.

[18]Reuben and the tribes that camped alongside it marched out second, carrying their banner. Elizur son of Shedeur was the leader of the Reuben tribe,

[v]**9.11** *second month*: See the note at 1.1. [w]**9.15,16** *As soon as the sacred tent was set up*: According to Exodus 40.17, this took place "on the first day of the first month of the second year" of the Israelites' stay in the desert. [x]**10.11** *second month*: See the note at 1.1. [y]**10.12** *the Paran Desert*: Probably a general name for the northernmost part of the Sinai Desert.

[19]Shelumiel son of Zurishaddai was the
leader of the Simeon tribe, [20]and Eliasaph son of Deuel was the leader of the
Gad tribe.
[21]Next were the Kohathites, carrying
the objects for the sacred tent, which
was to be set up before they arrived at
the new camp.
[22]Ephraim and the tribes that camped
alongside it marched next, carrying
their banner. Elishama son of Ammihud
was the leader of the Ephraim tribe,
[23]Gamaliel son of Pedahzur was the
leader of the Manasseh tribe, [24]and
Abidan son of Gideoni was the leader of
the Benjamin tribe.
[25]Dan and the tribes that camped
alongside it were to protect the Israelites against an attack from behind,
and so they marched last, carrying
their banner. Ahiezer son of Ammishaddai was the leader of the tribe of Dan,
[26]Pagiel son of Ochran was the leader
of the Asher tribe, [27]and Ahira son of
Enan was the leader of the Naphtali
tribe.
[28]This was the order in which the Israelites marched each time they moved
their camp.
[29]Hobab[z] the Midianite, the father-in-
law of Moses, was there. And Moses
said to him, "We're leaving for the place
the LORD has promised us. He has said
that all will go well for us. So come
along, and we will make sure that all
goes well for you."
[30]"No, I won't go," Hobab answered.
"I'm returning home to be with my own
people."
[31]"Please go with us!" Moses said.
"You can be our guide because you
know the places to camp in the desert.
[32]Besides that, if you go, we will give
you a share of the good things the LORD
gives us."
[33]The people of Israel began their
journey from Mount Sinai.[a] They traveled three days, and the Levites who
carried the sacred chest led the way, so
the LORD could show them where to
camp. [34]And the cloud always stayed
with them.
[35]Each day as the Israelites began
their journey, Moses would pray, "Our
LORD, defeat your enemies and make
them run!" [36]And when they stopped to
set up camp, he would pray, "Our LORD,
stay close to Israel's thousands and
thousands of people."

The Israelites Complain

11 One day the Israelites started
complaining about their troubles.
The LORD heard them and became so
angry that he destroyed the outer edges
of their camp with fire.
[2]When the people begged Moses to
help, he prayed, and the fire went out.
[3]They named the place "Burning,"[b] because in his anger the LORD had set
their camp on fire.

The People Grumble about Being Hungry

[4]One day some worthless foreigners
among the Israelites became greedy for
food, and even the Israelites themselves
began moaning, "We don't have any
meat! [5]In Egypt we could eat all the fish
we wanted, and there were cucumbers,
melons, onions, and garlic. [6]But we're
starving out here, and the only food we
have is this manna."
[7]The manna was like small whitish
seeds [8-9]and tasted like something
baked with sweet olive oil. It appeared
at night with the dew. In the morning
the people would collect the manna,
grind or crush it into flour, then boil it
and make it into thin wafers.
[10]The Israelites stood around their
tents complaining. Moses heard them
and was upset that they had made the
LORD angry. [11]He prayed:

I am your servant, LORD, so why
are you doing this to me? What have
I done to deserve this? You've made
me responsible for all these people,
[12]but they're not my children. You
told me to nurse them along and to
carry them to the land you promised
their ancestors. [13]They keep whining
for meat, but where can I get meat
for them? [14]This job is too much for
me. How can I take care of all these
people by myself? [15]If this is the way
you're going to treat me, just kill me
now and end my miserable life!

Seventy Leaders Are Chosen To Help Moses

[16]The LORD said to Moses:

Choose seventy of Israel's respected leaders and go with them to
the sacred tent. [17]While I am talking
with you there, I will give them some
of your authority, so they can share
responsibility for my people. You
will no longer have to care for them
by yourself.
[18]As for the Israelites, I have heard
them complaining about not having
meat and about being better off in
Egypt. So tell them to make themselves acceptable to me, because tomorrow they will have meat. [19-20]In
fact, they will have meat day after

[z]10.29 *Hobab*: Hebrew "Hobab son of Reuel." [a]10.33 *Mount Sinai*: Hebrew "the LORD's mountain." [b]11.3 *Burning*: Or "Taberah."

day for a whole month—not just a
few days, or even ten or twenty.
They turned against me and wanted
to return to Egypt. Now they will eat
meat until they get sick of it.
21Moses replied, "At least six hundred
thousand grown men are here with me.
How can you say there will be enough
meat to feed them and their families for
a whole month? 22Even if we butchered
all of our sheep and cattle, or caught
every fish in the sea, we wouldn't have
enough to feed them."
23The LORD answered, "I can do anything! Watch and you'll see my words
come true."
24Moses told the people what the LORD
had said. Then he chose seventy respected leaders and went with them to
the sacred tent. While the leaders stood
in a circle around the tent, Moses went
inside, 25and the LORD spoke with him.
Then the LORD took some authority[c]
from Moses and gave it to the seventy
leaders. And when the LORD's Spirit
took control of them, they started shouting like prophets. But they did it only
this one time.
26Eldad and Medad were two leaders
who had not gone to the tent. But when
the Spirit took control of them, they began shouting like prophets right there in
camp. 27A boy ran to Moses and told
him about Eldad and Medad.
28Joshua[d] was there helping Moses, as
he had done since he was young. And
he said to Moses, "Sir, you must stop
them!"
29But Moses replied, "Are you concerned what this might do to me? I wish
the LORD would give his Spirit to all his
people so everyone could be a prophet."
30Then Moses and the seventy leaders
went back to camp.

The LORD Sends Quails

31Some time later the LORD sent a
strong wind that blew quails in from the
sea until Israel's camp was completely
surrounded with birds, piled up about
three feet high for miles in every direction. 32The people picked up quails for
two days—each person filled at least
fifty bushels. Then they spread them out
to dry. 33But before the meat could be
eaten, the LORD became angry and sent
a disease through the camp.
34After they had buried the people
who had been so greedy for meat, they
called the place "Graves for the
Greedy."[e]
35Israel then broke camp and traveled
to Hazeroth.

Miriam and Aaron Are Jealous of Moses

12 1-3Although Moses was the most
humble person in all the world,
Miriam and Aaron started complaining,
"Moses had no right to marry that
woman from Ethiopia![f] Who does he
think he is? The LORD has spoken to us,
not just to him."
The LORD heard their complaint 4and
told Moses, Aaron, and Miriam to come
to the entrance of the sacred tent.
5There the LORD appeared in a cloud
and told Aaron and Miriam to come
closer. 6Then after commanding them to
listen carefully, he said:

"I, the LORD, speak to prophets
in visions and dreams.
7 But my servant Moses
is the leader of my people.
8 He sees me face to face,
and everything I say to him
is perfectly clear.
You have no right to criticize
my servant Moses."

9The LORD became angry at Aaron
and Miriam. And after the LORD left
10and the cloud disappeared from over
the sacred tent, Miriam's skin turned
white with leprosy.[g] When Aaron saw
what had happened to her, 11he said to
Moses, "Sir, please don't punish us for
doing such a foolish thing. 12Don't let
Miriam's flesh rot away like a child born
dead!"
13Moses prayed, "LORD God, please
heal her."
14But the LORD replied, "Miriam would
be disgraced for seven days if her father
had punished her by spitting in her face.
So make her stay outside the camp for
seven days, before coming back."
15The people of Israel did not move
their camp until Miriam returned seven
days later. 16Then they left Hazeroth and
set up camp in the Paran Desert.

Twelve Men Are Sent into Canaan

(Deuteronomy 1.19-33)

13 The LORD said to Moses, 2"Choose
a leader from each tribe and send
them into Canaan to explore the land I
am giving you."
3So Moses sent twelve tribal leaders
from Israel's camp in the Paran Desert
4-16with orders to explore the land of
Canaan. And here are their names:

Shammua son of Zaccur
from Reuben,
Shaphat son of Hori
from Simeon,

[c]**11.25** *some authority*: Or "some of the Spirit's power." [d]**11.28** *Joshua*: Hebrew "Joshua son of Nun." [e]**11.34** *Graves for the Greedy*: Or "Kibroth-Hattaavah." [f]**12.1-3** *Ethiopia*: The Hebrew text has "Cush," which was a region south of Egypt that included parts of the present countries of Ethiopia and Sudan. [g]**12.10** *leprosy*: See the note at 5.2, 3.

Caleb son of Jephunneh
from Judah,
Igal son of Joseph
from Issachar,
Joshua son of Nun
from Ephraim,[h]
Palti son of Raphu
from Benjamin,
Gaddiel son of Sodi
from Zebulun,
Gaddi son of Susi
from Manasseh,
Ammiel son of Gemalli
from Dan,
Sethur son of Michael
from Asher,
Nahbi son of Vophsi
from Naphtali,
and Geuel son of Machi
from Gad.

17 Before Moses sent them into Canaan, he said:
After you go through the Southern
Desert of Canaan, continue north
into the hill country 18 and find out
what those regions are like. Be sure
to remember how many people live
there, how strong they are, 19-20 and if
they live in open towns or walled
cities. See if the land is good for
growing crops and find out what
kinds of trees grow there. It's time
for grapes to ripen, so try to bring
back some of the fruit that grows
there.
21 The twelve men left to explore
Canaan from the Zin Desert in the south
all the way to the town of Rehob near
Lebo-Hamath in the north. 22 As they
went through the Southern Desert, they
came to the town of Hebron, which was
seven years older than the Egyptian
town of Zoan. In Hebron, they saw the
three Anakim[i] clans of Ahiman, Sheshai, and Talmai. 23-24 When they got to
Bunch Valley,[j] they cut off a branch with
such a huge bunch of grapes, that it
took two men to carry it on a pole.
That's why the place was called Bunch
Valley. Along with the grapes, they also
took back pomegranates[k] and figs.

The Men Report Back to the People

25 After exploring the land of Canaan
forty days, 26 the twelve men returned to
Kadesh in the Paran Desert and told
Moses, Aaron, and the people what they
had seen. They showed them the fruit
27 and said:
Look at this fruit! The land we explored is rich with milk and honey.
28 But the people who live there are
strong, and their cities are large and
walled. We even saw the three Anakim[l] clans. 29 Besides that, the Amalekites live in the Southern Desert;
the Hittites, Jebusites, and Amorites
are in the hill country; and the Canaanites[m] live along the Mediterranean Sea and the Jordan River.
30 Caleb calmed down the crowd and
said, "Let's go and take the land. I know
we can do it!"
31 But the other men replied, "Those
people are much too strong for us."
32 Then they started spreading rumors
and saying, "We won't be able to grow
anything in that soil. And the people are
like giants. 33 In fact, we saw the Nephilim who are the ancestors of the Anakim. They were so big that we felt as
small as grasshoppers."

The Israelites Rebel against Moses

14 After the Israelites heard the report from the twelve men who
had explored Canaan, the people cried
all night 2 and complained to Moses and
Aaron, "We wish we had died in Egypt
or somewhere out here in the desert! 3 Is
the LORD leading us into Canaan, just to
have us killed and our women and children captured? We'd be better off in
Egypt." 4 Then they said to one another,
"Let's choose our own leader and go
back."
5 Moses and Aaron bowed down to
pray in front of the crowd. 6 Joshua and
Caleb tore their clothes in sorrow 7 and
said:
We saw the land ourselves, and it's
very good. 8 If we obey the LORD, he
will surely give us that land rich
with milk and honey. 9 So don't rebel.
We have no reason to be afraid of
the people who live there. The LORD
is on our side, and they won't stand
a chance against us!
10 The crowd threatened to stone
Moses and Aaron to death. But just
then, the LORD appeared in a cloud at
the sacred tent.

Moses Prays for the People

11 The LORD said to Moses, "I have
done great things for these people, and
they still reject me by refusing to believe
in my power. 12 So they will no longer be
my people. I will destroy them, but I will
make you the ancestor of a nation even
stronger than theirs."

[h] 13.4-16 *Joshua . . . Ephraim*: Hebrew "Hoshea son of Nun from Ephraim; Moses renamed him Joshua." [i] 13.22 *Anakim*: Perhaps a group of very large people (see Deuteronomy 2.10, 11, 20, 21). [j] 13.23,24 *Bunch Valley*: Or "Eshcol Valley." [k] 13.23,24 *pomegranates*: A bright red fruit that looks like an apple. [l] 13.28 *Anakim*: See the note at verse 22. [m] 13.29 *Amalekites . . . Hittites . . . Jebusites . . . Amorites . . . Canaanites*: These people lived in Canaan before the Israelites.

13-16 Moses replied:
With your mighty power you rescued your people from Egypt, so
please don't destroy us here in the
desert. If you do, the Egyptians will
hear about it and tell the people of
Canaan. Those Canaanites already
know that we are your people, and
that we see you face to face. And
they have heard how you lead us
with a thick cloud during the day
and flaming fire at night. But if you
kill us, they will claim it was because you weren't powerful enough
to lead us into Canaan as you
promised.
17 Show us your great power, LORD.
You promised 18 that you love to
show mercy and kindness. And you
said that you are very patient, but
that you will punish everyone guilty
of doing wrong—not only them but
their children and grandchildren as
well.
19 You are merciful, and you treat
people better than they deserve. So
please forgive these people, just as
you have forgiven them ever since
they left Egypt.
20 Then the LORD said to Moses:
In answer to your prayer, I do forgive them. 21 But as surely as I live
and my power has no limit, 22-23 I
swear that not one of these Israelites
will enter the land I promised to give
their ancestors. These people have
seen my power in Egypt and in the
desert, but they will never see
Canaan. They have disobeyed and
tested me too many times.
24 But my servant Caleb isn't like
the others. So because he has faith
in me, I will allow him to cross into
Canaan, and his descendants will
settle there.
25 Now listen, Moses! The
Amalekites and the Canaanites live
in the valleys of Canaan.[n] And tomorrow morning, you'll need to turn
around and head back into the
desert toward the Red Sea.[o]

The Israelites Are Punished for Complaining

26 The LORD told Moses and Aaron
27-28 to give this message to the people of
Israel:
You sinful people have complained against me too many times!
Now I swear by my own life that I
will give you exactly what you
wanted.[p] 29 You will die right here in
the desert, and your dead bodies will
cover the ground. You have insulted
me, and none of you men who are
over twenty years old 30 will enter
the land that I solemnly promised to
give you as your own—only Caleb
and Joshua[q] will go in.
31 You were worried that your own
children would be captured. But I,
the LORD, will let them enter the
land you have rejected. 32 You will
die here in the desert! 33 Your children will wander around in this
desert forty years, suffering because
of your sins, until all of you are
dead. 34 I will cruelly punish you
every day for the next forty years—
one year for each day that the land
was explored. 35 You sinful people
who ganged up against me will die
here in the desert.
36 Ten of the men sent to explore the
land had brought back bad news and
had made the people complain against
the LORD. 37 So he sent a deadly disease
that killed those men, 38 but he let
Joshua and Caleb live.

The Israelites Fail To Enter Canaan

(Deuteronomy 1.41-45)

39 The people of Israel were very sad
after Moses gave them the LORD's message. 40 So they got up early the next
morning and got ready to head toward
the hill country of Canaan. They said,
"We were wrong to complain about the
LORD. Let's go into the land that he
promised us."
41 But Moses replied, "You're disobeying the LORD! Your plan won't work,
42-43 so don't even try it. The LORD refuses to help you, because you turned
your backs on him. The Amalekites and
the Canaanites are your enemies, and
they will attack and defeat you."
44 But the Israelites ignored Moses[r]
and marched toward the hill country,
even though the sacred chest and Moses
did not go with them. 45 The Amalekites
and the Canaanites came down from
the hill country, defeated the Israelites,
and chased them as far as the town of
Hormah.

Laws about Sacrifices

15 The LORD told Moses 2 to give the
Israelites the following laws
about offering sacrifices:
3 Bulls or rams or goats[s] are the animals that you may burn on the altar as

[n] **14.25** *The Amalekites and the Canaanites . . . valleys of Canaan*: That is, all possible ways into Canaan were blocked. [o] **14.25** *Red Sea*: Hebrew *yam suph*, here referring to the Gulf of Aqaba, since the term is extended to include the northeastern arm of the Red Sea (see also the note at Exodus 13.18). [p] **14.27,28** *wanted*: See verse 2. [q] **14.30** *Caleb and Joshua*: Hebrew "Caleb son of Jephunneh and Joshua son of Nun." [r] **14.44** *ignored Moses*: One possible meaning for the difficult Hebrew text. [s] **15.3** *goats*: See the note at 7.12-83.

sacrifices to please me.[t] You may also offer sacrifices voluntarily or because you made a promise, or because they are part of your regular religious ceremonies. The smell of the smoke from these sacrifices is pleasing to me.

4-5If you sacrifice a young ram or goat, you must also offer two pounds of your finest flour mixed with a quart of olive oil as a grain sacrifice. A quart of wine must also be poured on the altar.

6-7And if the animal is a full-grown ram, you must offer four pounds of flour mixed with one and a half quarts of olive oil. One and a half quarts of wine must also be poured on the altar. The smell of this smoke is pleasing to me.

8If a bull is offered as a sacrifice to please me or to ask my blessing,[u] 9you must offer six pounds of flour mixed with two quarts of olive oil. 10Two quarts of wine must also be poured on the altar. The smell of this smoke is pleasing to me.

11-13If you are a native Israelite, you must obey these rules each time you offer a bull, a ram, or a goat as a sacrifice. 14And the foreigners who live among you must also follow these rules. 15-16This law will never change. I am the LORD, and I consider all people the same, whether they are Israelites or foreigners living among you.

17-19When you eat food in the land that I am giving you, remember to set aside some of it as an offering to me. 20From the first batch of bread dough that you make after each new grain harvest, make a loaf of bread and offer it to me, just as you offer grain. 21All your descendants must follow this law and offer part of the first batch of bread dough.

22-23The LORD also told Moses to tell the people what must be done if they ever disobey his laws:

24If all of you disobey one of my laws without meaning to, you must offer a bull as a sacrifice to please me, together with a grain sacrifice, a wine offering, and a goat as a sacrifice for sin. 25Then the priest will pray and ask me to forgive you. And since you did not mean to do wrong, and you offered sacrifices, 26the sin of everyone—both Israelites and foreigners among you—will be forgiven.

27But if one of you does wrong without meaning to, you must sacrifice a year-old female goat as a sacrifice for sin. 28The priest will then ask me to forgive you, and your sin will be forgiven.

29The law will be the same for anyone who does wrong without meaning to, whether an Israelite or a foreigner living among you.

30-31But if one of you does wrong on purpose, whether Israelite or foreigner, you have sinned against me by disobeying my laws. You will be sent away and will no longer live among the people of Israel.

A Man Put to Death for Gathering Firewood on the Sabbath

32Once, while the Israelites were traveling through the desert, a man was caught gathering firewood on the Sabbath.[v] 33He was taken to Moses, Aaron, and the rest of the community. 34But no one knew what to do with him, so he was not allowed to leave.

35Then the LORD said to Moses, "Tell the people to take that man outside the camp and stone him to death!" 36So he was killed, just as the LORD had commanded Moses.

The Tassels on the People's Clothes

37The LORD told Moses 38to say to the people of Israel, "Sew tassels onto the bottom edge of your clothes and tie a purple string to each tassel. 39-40These will remind you that you must obey my laws and teachings. And when you do, you will be dedicated to me and won't follow your own sinful desires. 41I am the LORD your God who led you out of Egypt."

Korah, Dathan, and Abiram Lead a Rebellion

16 1-2Korah son of Izhar was a Levite from the Kohathite clan. One day he called together Dathan, Abiram, and On[w] from the Reuben tribe, and the four of them decided to rebel against Moses. So they asked two hundred fifty respected Israelite leaders for their support, and together they went to Moses 3and Aaron and said, "Why do you think you're so much better than anyone else? We're part of the LORD's holy people, and he's with all of us. What makes you think you're the only ones in charge?"

4When Moses heard this, he knelt down to pray.[x] 5Then he said to Korah and his followers:

> Tomorrow morning the LORD will show us the person he has chosen to be his priest, and that man will faithfully serve him.
>
> 6-7Korah, now here is what you and your followers must do: Get some fire pans, fill them with coals and incense, and place them near the sacred tent. And the man the

[t] **15.3** *sacrifices to please me*: See the note at 6.11. [u] **15.8** *to ask my blessing*: See the note at 6.14. [v] **15.32** *a man . . . Sabbath*: No work was to be done on the Sabbath (see Exodus 31.12-17). [w] **16.1,2** *Dathan, Abiram, and On*: Hebrew "Dathan and Abiram the sons of Eliab, and On son of Peleth." [x] **16.4** *he knelt down to pray*: Or "he fell to his knees in sorrow."

LORD chooses will be his priest.[y] Korah, this time you Levites have gone too far!

8-9You know that the God of Israel has chosen you Levites from all Israel to serve him by being in charge of the sacred tent and by helping the community to worship in the proper way. What more do you want? 10The LORD has given you a special responsibility, and now, Korah, you think you should also be his priest. 11You and your followers have rebelled against the LORD, not against Aaron.

12Then Moses sent for Dathan and Abiram, but they sent back this message: "We won't come! 13It's bad enough that you took us from our rich farmland in Egypt to let us die here in the desert. Now you also want to boss us around! 14You keep promising us rich farmlands with fertile fields and vineyards—but where are they? Stop trying to trick these people. No, we won't come to see you."

15Moses was very angry and said to the LORD, "Don't listen to these men! I haven't done anything wrong to them. I haven't taken as much as a donkey."

16Then he said to Korah, "Tomorrow you and your followers must go with Aaron to the LORD's sacred tent. 17Each of you take along your fire pan with incense in it and offer the incense to the LORD."

18The next day the men placed incense and coals in their fire pans and stood with Moses and Aaron at the entrance to the sacred tent. 19Meanwhile, Korah had convinced the rest of the Israelites to rebel against their two leaders.

When that happened, the LORD appeared in all his glory 20and said to Moses and Aaron, 21"Get away from the rest of the Israelites so I can kill them right now!"

22But the two men bowed down and prayed, "Our God, you gave these people life. Why would you punish everyone here when only one man has sinned?"

23The LORD answered Moses, 24"Tell the people to stay away from the tents of Korah, Dathan, and Abiram."

25Moses walked over to Dathan and Abiram, and the other leaders of Israel followed. 26Then Moses warned the people, "Get away from the tents of these sinful men! Don't touch anything that belongs to them or you'll be wiped out." 27So everyone moved away from those tents, except Korah, Dathan, Abiram, and their families.

28Moses said to the crowd, "The LORD has chosen me and told me to do these things—it wasn't my idea. And here's how you will know: 29If these men die a natural death, it means the LORD hasn't chosen me. 30But suppose the LORD does something that has never been done before. For example, what if a huge crack appears in the ground, and these men and their families fall into it and are buried alive, together with everything they own? Then you will know they have turned their backs on the LORD!"

31As soon as Moses said this, the ground under the men opened up 32-33and swallowed them alive, together with their families and everything they owned. Then the ground closed back up, and they were gone.

34The rest of the Israelites heard their screams, so they ran off, shouting, "We don't want that to happen to us!"

35Suddenly the LORD sent a fire that burned up the two hundred fifty men who had offered incense to him.

36Then the LORD said to Moses, 37"Tell Aaron's son Eleazar to take the fire pans from the smoldering fire and scatter the coals. The pans are now sacred, 38because they were used for offering incense to me. Have them hammered into a thin layer of bronze as a covering for the altar. Those men died because of their sin, and now their fire pans will become a warning for the rest of the community."

39Eleazar collected the pans and had them hammered into a thin layer of bronze as a covering for the altar, 40just as the LORD had told Moses. The pans were a warning to the Israelites that only Aaron's descendants would be allowed to offer incense to the LORD. Anyone else who tried would be punished like Korah and his followers.

The Israelites Rebel and Are Punished

41The next day the people of Israel again complained against Moses and Aaron, "The two of you killed some of the LORD's people!"

42As the people crowded around them, Moses and Aaron turned toward the sacred tent, and the LORD appeared in his glory in the cloud covering the tent. 43So Moses and Aaron walked to the front of the tent, 44where the LORD said to them, 45"Stand back! I am going to wipe out these Israelites once and for all."

They immediately bowed down and prayed. 46Then Moses told Aaron, "Grab your fire pan and fill it with hot coals from the altar. Put incense in it, then quickly take it to where the people are

[y]16.6,7 *Get some fire pans . . . his priest*: Only priests could offer incense at the sacred altar; anyone else who tried would be killed. In this case, the man who lived would be the one the LORD had chosen.

and offer it to the LORD, so they can be
forgiven. The LORD is very angry, and
people have already started dying!"
47-48 Aaron did exactly what he had
been told. He ran over to the crowd of
people and stood between the dead bodies and the people who were still alive.
He placed the incense on the pan, then
offered it to the LORD and asked him to
forgive the people's sin. The disease immediately stopped spreading, and no
one else died from it. 49 But fourteen
thousand seven hundred Israelites were
dead, not counting those who had died
with Korah and his followers.
50 Aaron walked back and stood with
Moses at the sacred tent.

Aaron's Walking Stick Blooms and Produces Almonds

17 The LORD told Moses:
2-3 Call together the twelve
tribes of Israel and tell the leader of
each tribe to write his name on the
walking stick he carries as a symbol
of his authority. Make sure Aaron's
name is written on the one from the
Levi tribe, then collect all the sticks.
4 Place these sticks in the tent right
in front of the sacred chest where I
appear to you. 5 I will then choose a
man to be my priest, and his stick
will sprout. After that happens, I
won't have to listen to any more
complaints about you.
6 Moses told the people what the LORD
had commanded, and they gave him the
walking sticks from the twelve tribal
leaders, including Aaron's from the Levi
tribe. 7 Moses took them and placed
them in the LORD's sacred tent.
8 The next day when Moses went into
the tent, flowers and almonds were already growing on Aaron's stick. 9 Moses
brought the twelve sticks out of the tent
and showed them to the people. Each of
the leaders found his own and took it.
10 But the LORD told Moses, "Put
Aaron's stick back! Let it stay near the
sacred chest as a warning to anyone
who might think about rebelling. If
these people don't stop their grumbling
about me, I will wipe them out." 11 Moses
did what he was told.
12 The Israelites cried out to Moses,
"We're done for 13 and doomed if we
even get near the sacred tent!"

The Duties of the Priests and Levites

18 The LORD said to Aaron:
You, your sons, and the other
Levites of the Kohath clan, are responsible for what happens at the sacred tent.[z]
And you and your sons will be responsible for what the priests do. 2 The Levites
are your relatives and are here to help
you in your service at the tent. 3 You
must see that they perform their duties.
But if they go near any of the sacred objects or the altar, all of you will die. 4 No
one else is allowed to take care of the
sacred tent or to do anything connected
with it. 5 Follow these instructions, so I
won't become angry and punish the Israelites ever again.
6 I alone chose the Levites from all the
other tribes to belong to me, and I have
given them to you as your helpers. 7 But
only you and your sons can serve as
priests at the altar and in the most holy
place. Your work as priests is a gift from
me, and anyone else who tries to do that
work must be put to death.

The Priests' Share of Offerings Given to the LORD

(Deuteronomy 18.1-8)

8-9 The LORD said to Aaron:
I have put you in charge of the sacred
gifts and sacrifices that the Israelites
bring to me. And from now on, you,
your sons, and your descendants will receive part of the sacrifices for sin, as
well as part of the grain sacrifices, and
the sacrifices to make things right. Your
share of these sacrifices will be the
parts not burned on the altar. 10 Since
these things are sacred, they must be
eaten near the sacred tent, but only men
are allowed to eat them.
11 You will also receive part of the special gifts and offerings that the Israelites
bring to me. Any member of your family
who is clean and acceptable for worship
can eat these things. 12 For example,
when the Israelites bring me the first
batches of oil, wine, and grain, you can
have the best parts of those gifts. 13 And
the first part of the crops from their
fields and vineyards also belongs to
you. The people will offer this to me,
then anyone in your family who is clean
may have some of it.
14 Everything in Israel that has been
completely dedicated to me[a] will now
belong to you.
15 The first-born son in every Israelite
family, as well as the first-born males of
their flocks and herds, belong to me. But
a first-born son and every first-born
donkey[b] must be bought back from me.
16 The price for a first-born son who is at

[z] 18.1 *are responsible . . . sacred tent*: Or "are to make sure that no one gets near the sacred tent." [a] 18.14 *that has been completely dedicated to me*: This translates a Hebrew word that describes property and things that were taken away from humans and given to God forever. Sometimes such things had to be completely destroyed (see Joshua 6.15-19).
[b] 18.15 *donkey*: The Hebrew text has "unclean animal," which probably refers to a donkey (see Exodus 13.13; 34.20).

least one month old will be five pieces
of silver, weighed according to the official standards. 17However, all first-born
cattle, sheep, and goats belong to me
and cannot be bought back. Splatter
their blood on the altar and send their
fat up in smoke, so I can smell it and be
pleased. 18You are allowed to eat the
meat of those animals, just as you can
eat the choice ribs and the right hind leg
of the special sacrifices.
19From now on, the sacred offerings
that the Israelites give to me will belong
to you, your sons, and your daughters.
This is my promise to you and your descendants, and it will never change.
20You will not receive any land in Israel as your own. I am the LORD, and I
will give you whatever you need.

What the Levites Receive

The LORD said to Aaron:
21Ten percent of the Israelites' crops
and one out of every ten of their newborn animals belong to me. But I am
giving all this to the Levites as their pay
for the work they do at the sacred tent.
22-23They are the only ones allowed to
work at the tent, and they must not let
anyone else come near it. Those who do
must be put to death, and the Levites
will also be punished. This law will
never change.
Since the Levites won't be given any
land in Israel as their own, 24they will be
given the crops and newborn animals
that the Israelites offer to me.

What the Levites Must Give

25The LORD told Moses 26to say to the
Levites:
When you receive from the people of
Israel ten percent of their crops and
newborn animals, you must offer a
tenth of that to me. 27Just as the Israelites give me part of their grain and
wine, you must set aside part of what
you receive 28as an offering to me. That
amount must then be given to Aaron,
29so the best of what you receive will be
mine.
30After you have dedicated the best
parts to me, you can eat the rest, just as
the Israelites eat part of their grain and
wine after offering them to me.[c] 31Your
share may be eaten anywhere by anyone in your family, because it is your
pay for working at the sacred tent. 32You
won't be punished for eating it, as long
as you have already offered the best
parts to me.
The gifts and sacrifices brought by the
people must remain sacred, and if you
eat any part of them before they are offered to me, you will be put to death.

The Ceremony To Wash Away Sin

19 1-2The LORD gave Moses and
Aaron the following law:
The people of Israel must bring Moses
a reddish-brown cow that has nothing
wrong with it and that has never been
used for plowing. 3Moses will give it to
Eleazar the priest, then it will be led
outside the camp and killed while
Eleazar watches. 4He will dip his finger
into the blood and sprinkle it seven
times in the direction of the sacred tent.
5Then the whole cow, including its skin,
meat, blood, and insides must be
burned. 6A priest[d] is to throw a stick of
cedar wood, a hyssop[e] branch, and a
piece of red yarn into the fire.
7After the ceremony, the priest is to
take a bath and wash his clothes. Only
then can he go back into the camp, but
he remains unclean and unfit for worship until evening. 8The man who
burned the cow must also wash his
clothes and take a bath, but he is also
unclean until evening.
9A man who isn't unclean must collect
the ashes of the burnt cow and store
them outside the camp in a clean place.
The people of Israel can mix these ashes
with the water used in the ceremony to
wash away sin. 10The man who collects
the ashes must wash his clothes, but
will remain unclean until evening. This
law must always be obeyed by the people of Israel and the foreigners living
among them.

What Must Be Done after Touching a Dead Body

The LORD said:
11If you touch a dead body, you will be
unclean for seven days. 12But if you
wash with the water mixed with the
cow's ashes on the third day and again
on the seventh day, you will be clean
and acceptable for worship. You must
wash yourself on those days; if you
don't, you will remain unclean. 13Sup-
pose you touch a dead body, but refuse
to be made clean by washing with the
water mixed with ashes. You will be
guilty of making my sacred tent unclean
and will no longer belong to the people
of Israel.
14If someone dies in a tent while you
are there, you will be unclean for seven
days. And anyone who later enters the
tent will also be unclean. 15Any open jar
in the tent is unclean.
16If you touch the body of someone

[c] **18.30** *just as the Israelites . . . to me*: One possible meaning for the difficult Hebrew text.
[d] **19.6** *A priest*: Or "Eleazar." [e] **19.6** *hyssop*: A plant with small clusters of blue flowers and sweet-smelling leaves.

who was killed or who died of old age,
or if you touch a human bone or a
grave, you will be unclean for seven
days.
17-18 Before you can be made clean,
someone who is clean must take some
of the ashes from the burnt cow and stir
them into a pot of spring water. That
same person must dip a hyssop branch
in the water and ashes, then sprinkle it
on the tent and everything in it, including everyone who was inside. If you
have touched a human bone, a grave, or
a dead body, you must be sprinkled with
that water. 19 If this is done on the third
day and on the seventh day, you will be
clean. Then after you take a bath and
wash your clothes, you can worship that
evening.
20 If you are unclean and refuse to be
made clean by washing with the water
mixed with ashes, you will be guilty of
making my sacred tent unclean, and you
will no longer belong to the people of Israel. 21 These laws will never change.
The man who sprinkled the water and
the ashes on you when you were unclean must also wash his clothes. And
whoever touches this water is unclean
until evening. 22 When you are unclean,
everything you touch becomes unclean,
and anyone who touches you will be unclean until evening.

Water from a Rock
(Exodus 17.1-7)

20 The people of Israel arrived at the
Zin Desert during the first month[f]
and set up camp near the town of
Kadesh. It was there that Miriam died
and was buried.
2 The Israelites had no water, so they
went to Moses and Aaron 3 and complained, "Moses, we'd be better off if we
had died along with the others in front
of the LORD's sacred tent.[g] 4 You brought
us into this desert, and now we and our
livestock are going to die! 5 Egypt was
better than this horrible place. At least
there we had grain and figs and
grapevines and pomegranates.[h] But
now we don't even have any water."
6 Moses and Aaron went to the entrance to the sacred tent, where they
bowed down. The LORD appeared to
them in all of his glory 7-8 and said,
"Moses, get your walking stick.[i] Then
you and Aaron call the people together
and command that rock to give you water. That's how you will provide water
for the people of Israel and their livestock."
9 Moses obeyed and took his stick
from the sacred tent. 10 After he and
Aaron had gathered the people around
the rock, he said, "Look, you rebellious
people, and you will see water flow from
this rock!" 11 He raised his stick in the
air and struck the rock two times. At
once, water gushed from the rock, and
the people and their livestock had water
to drink.
12 But the LORD said to Moses and
Aaron, "Because you refused to believe
in my power, these people did not respect me. And so, you will not be the
ones to lead them into the land I have
promised."
13 The Israelites had complained
against the LORD, and he had shown
them his holy power by giving them water to drink. So they named the place
Meribah, which means "Complaining."

Israel Isn't Allowed To Go through Edom

14 Moses sent messengers from Israel's
camp near Kadesh with this message
for the king of Edom:

> We are Israelites, your own rela-
> tives, and we're sure you have heard
> the terrible things that have hap-
> pened to us. 15 Our ancestors settled
> in Egypt and lived there a long time.
> But later the Egyptians were cruel to
> us, 16 and when we begged our LORD
> for help, he answered our prayer
> and brought us out of that land.
>
> Now we are camped at the border
> of your territory, near the town of
> Kadesh. 17 Please let us go through
> your country. We won't go near your
> fields and vineyards, and we won't
> drink any water from your wells. We
> will stay on the main road[j] until we
> leave your territory.

18 But the Edomite king answered,
"No, I won't let you go through our
country! And if you try, we will attack
you."
19 Moses sent back this message: "We
promise to stay on the main road, and if
any of us or our livestock drink your
water, we will pay for it. We just want to
pass through."
20 But the Edomite king insisted, "You
can't go through our land!"
Then Edom sent out its strongest
troops 21 to keep Israel from passing
through its territory. So the Israelites
had to go in another direction.

Aaron Dies

22 After the Israelites had left Kadesh
and had gone as far as Mount Hor 23 on

[f] **20.1** *first month*: See the note at 9.3. [g] **20.3** *if we had died . . . sacred tent*: See 16.41-49. [h] **20.5** *pomegranates*: See the note at 13.23, 24. [i] **20.7,8** *walking stick*: A symbol of his authority. [j] **20.17** *the main road*: The Hebrew text has "the King's Highway," which was an important trade route through what is today the country of Jordan. It connected the city of Damascus in Syria with the Gulf of Aqaba in southern Jordan.

the Edomite border, the LORD said,
24“Aaron, this is where you will die. You
and Moses disobeyed me at Meribah,
and so you will not enter the land I
promised the Israelites. 25Moses, go with
Aaron and his son Eleazar to the top of
the mountain. 26Then take Aaron's
priestly robe from him and place it on
Eleazar. Aaron will die there.”
27Moses obeyed, and everyone
watched as he and Aaron and Eleazar
walked to the top of Mount Hor. 28Moses
then took the priestly robe from Aaron
and placed it on Eleazar. Aaron died
there.

When Moses and Eleazar came down,
29the people knew that Aaron had died,
and they mourned his death for thirty
days.

Israel Defeats the Canaanites at Hormah

21 The Canaanite king of Arad lived
in the Southern Desert of Canaan, and when he heard that the Israelites were on their way to the village of
Atharim, he attacked and took some of
them hostage.
2The Israelites prayed, “Our LORD, if
you will help us defeat these Canaanites, we will completely destroy their
towns and everything in them, to show
that they belong to you.”[k]
3The LORD answered their prayer and
helped them wipe out the Canaanite
army and completely destroy their
towns. That's why one of the towns is
named Hormah, which means “Destroyed Place.”

Moses Makes a Bronze Snake

4The Israelites had to go around the
territory of Edom, so when they left
Mount Hor, they headed south toward
the Red Sea.[l] But along the way, the
people became so impatient 5that they
complained against God and said to
Moses, “Did you bring us out of Egypt,
just to let us die in the desert? There's
no water out here, and we can't stand
this awful food!”
6Then the LORD sent poisonous snakes
that bit and killed many of them.
7Some of the people went to Moses
and admitted, “It was wrong of us to insult you and the LORD. Now please ask
him to make these snakes go away.”

Moses prayed, 8and the LORD answered, “Make a snake out of bronze
and place it on top of a pole. Anyone
who gets bitten can look at the snake
and won't die.”
9Moses obeyed the LORD. And all of
those who looked at the bronze snake
lived, even though they had been bitten
by the poisonous snakes.

Israel's Journey to Moab

10As the Israelites continued their
journey to Canaan, they camped at
Oboth, 11then at Iye-Abarim in the
desert east of Moab, 12and then in the
Zered Gorge. 13After that, they crossed
the Arnon River gorge and camped in
the Moabite desert bordering Amorite
territory. The Arnon was the border between the Moabites and the Amorites.
14A song in *The Book of the LORD's Battles*[m] mentions the town of Waheb with
its creeks in the territory of Suphah. It
also mentions the Arnon River, 15with
its valleys that lie alongside the Moabite
border and extend to the town of Ar.
16From the Arnon, the Israelites went
to the well near the town of Beer, where
the LORD had said to Moses, “Call the
people together, and I will give them
water to drink.”
17That's also the same well the Israelites sang about in this song:

Let's celebrate!
  The well has given us water.
18 With their royal scepters,
our leaders pointed out
  where to dig the well.

The Israelites left the desert and
camped near the town of Mattanah,
19then at Nahaliel, and then at Bamoth.
20Finally, they reached Moabite territory, where they camped near Mount
Pisgah[n] in a valley overlooking the
desert north of the Dead Sea.

Israel Defeats King Sihon the Amorite

(Deuteronomy 2.26-37)

21The Israelites sent this message to
King Sihon of the Amorites:

22Please let us pass through your
territory. We promise to stay away
from your fields and vineyards, and
we won't drink any water from your
wells. As long as we're in your land,
we won't get off the main road.[o]

23But Sihon refused to let Israel travel
through his land. Instead, he called together his entire army and marched into
the desert to attack Israel near the town
of Jahaz. 24Israel defeated them and
took over the Amorite territory from the
Arnon River gorge in the south to the
Jabbok River gorge in the north. Beyond the Jabbok was the territory of the

[k]**21.2** *completely destroy . . . belong to you*: The complete destruction of a town and everything in it, including its people and animals, showed that the town belonged to the LORD and could no longer be used by humans. [l]**21.4** *Red Sea*: See the note at 14.25. [m]**21.14** *The Book of the LORD's Battles*: This may have been a collection of ancient war songs. [n]**21.20** *Mount Pisgah*: This probably refers to the highest peak in the Abarim Mountains in Moab. [o]**21.22** *the main road*: See the note at 20.17.

Ammonites, who were much stronger
than Israel.
25 The Israelites settled in the Amorite
towns, including the capital city of
Heshbon with its surrounding villages.
26 King Sihon had ruled from Heshbon,
after defeating the Moabites and taking
over their land north of the Arnon River
gorge. 27 That's why the Amorites had
written this poem about Heshbon:

Come and rebuild Heshbon,
  King Sihon's capital city!
28 His armies marched out
  like fiery flames,
burning down the town of Ar
and destroying[p] the hills
  along the Arnon River.
29 You Moabites are done for!
Your god Chemosh
  deserted your people;
they were captured, taken away
  by King Sihon the Amorite.
30 We completely defeated Moab.
The towns of Heshbon and Dibon,
  of Nophah and Medeba
  are ruined and gone.[q]

31 After the Israelites had settled in the
Amorite territory, 32 Moses sent some
men to explore the town of Jazer. Later,
the Israelites captured the villages surrounding it and forced out the Amorites
who lived there.

Israel Defeats King Og of Bashan
(Deuteronomy 3.1-11)

33 The Israelites headed toward the region of Bashan, where King Og ruled,
and he led his entire army to Edrei to
meet Israel in battle.
34 The LORD said to Moses, "Don't be
afraid of Og. I will help you defeat him
and his army, just as you did King Sihon
who ruled in Heshbon. Og's territory
will be yours."
35 So the Israelites wiped out Og, his
family, and his entire army—there were
no survivors. Then Israel took over the
land of Bashan.

22 Israel moved from there to the
hills of Moab, where they camped
across the Jordan River from the town
of Jericho.

King Balak of Moab Hires Balaam To Curse Israel

2-3 When King Balak[r] of Moab and his
people heard how many Israelites there
were and what they had done to the
Amorites, he and the Moabites were terrified and panicked. 4 They said to the
Midianite leaders, "That bunch of Israelites will wipe out everything in
sight, like a bull eating grass in a field."
So King Balak 5 sent a message to Balaam son of Beor who lived among his
relatives in the town of Pethor near the
Euphrates River. It said:

> I need your help. A huge group of
> people has come here from Egypt
> and settled near my territory. 6 They
> are too powerful for us to defeat, so
> would you come and place a curse
> on them? Maybe then we can run
> them off. I know that anyone you
> bless will be successful, but anyone
> you curse will fail.

7 The leaders of Moab and Midian left
and took along money to pay Balaam
for his work. When they got to his
house, they gave him Balak's message.
8 "Spend the night here," Balaam
replied, "and tomorrow I will tell you
the LORD's answer." So the officials
stayed at his house.
9 During the night, God asked Balaam,
"Who are these people at your house?"
10 "They are messengers from King
Balak of Moab," Balaam answered. "He
sent them 11 to ask me to go to Moab and
place a curse on the people who have
come there from Egypt. They have settled everywhere around him, and he
wants to run them off."
12 But God replied, "Don't go with Balak's messengers. I have blessed those
people who have come from Egypt, so
don't curse them."
13 The next morning, Balaam said to
Balak's officials, "Go on back home. The
LORD says I cannot go with you."
14 The officials left and told Balak that
Balaam refused to come.
15 Then Balak sent a larger group of
officials, who were even more important
than the first ones. 16 They went to Balaam and told him that Balak had said,
"Balaam, if you come to Moab, 17 I'll pay
you very well and do whatever you ask.
Just come and place a curse on these
people."
18 Balaam answered, "Even if Balak offered me a palace full of silver or gold, I
wouldn't do anything to disobey the
LORD my God. 19 You are welcome to
spend the night here, just as the others
did. I will find out if the LORD has something else to say about this."
20 That night, God said, "Balaam, I'll let
you go to Moab with Balak's messengers, but do only what I say."
21 So Balaam got up the next morning
and saddled his donkey, then left with
the Moabite officials.

Balaam and His Donkey Meet an Angel

22 Balaam was riding his donkey to
Moab, and two of his servants were with

[p]21.28 *destroying*: One ancient translation; Hebrew "the rulers of." [q]21.30 *gone*: One possible meaning for the difficult Hebrew text of verse 30. [r]22.2,3 *Balak*: Hebrew "Balak son of Zippor."

him. But God was angry that Balaam
had gone, so one of the LORD's angels
stood in the road to stop him. 23When
Balaam's donkey saw the angel standing there with a sword, it walked off the
road and into an open field. Balaam had
to beat the donkey to get it back on the
road.
24Then the angel stood between two
vineyards, in a narrow path with a stone
wall on each side. 25When the donkey
saw the angel, it walked so close to one
of the walls that Balaam's foot scraped
against the wall. Balaam beat the donkey again.
26The angel moved once more and
stood in a spot so narrow that there was
no room for the donkey to go around.
27So it just lay down. Balaam lost his
temper, then picked up a stick and
smacked the donkey.
28When that happened, the LORD told
the donkey to speak, and it asked Balaam, "What have I done to you that
made you beat me three times?"
29"You made me look stupid!" Balaam
answered. "If I had a sword, I'd kill you
here and now!"
30"But you're my owner," replied the
donkey, "and you've ridden me many
times. Have I ever done anything like
this before?"
"No," Balaam admitted.
31Just then, the LORD let Balaam see
the angel standing in the road, holding a
sword, and Balaam bowed down.
32The angel said, "You had no right to
treat your donkey like that! I was the
one who blocked your way, because I
don't think you should go to Moab.[s] 33If
your donkey had not seen me and
stopped those three times, I would have
killed you and let the donkey live."
34Balaam replied, "I was wrong. I
didn't know you were trying to stop me.
If you don't think I should go, I'll return
home right now."
35"It's all right for you to go," the
LORD's angel answered. "But you must
say only what I tell you." So Balaam
went on with Balak's officials.

King Balak Meets Balaam

36When Balak heard that Balaam was
coming, he went to meet him at the
town of Ir, which is on the northern border of Moab. 37Balak asked, "Why didn't
you come when I invited you the first
time? Did you think I wasn't going to
pay you?"
38"I'm here now," Balaam answered.
"But I will say only what God tells me to
say."
39They left and went to the town of
Kiriath-Huzoth, 40where Balak sacrificed cattle and sheep and gave some of
the meat to Balaam and the officials
who were with him.
41The next morning, Balak took Balaam to the town of Bamoth-Baal. From
there, Balaam could see some of the Israelites.[t]

Balaam's First Message

23 Balaam said to Balak, "Build
seven altars here, then bring
seven bulls and seven rams."
2After Balak had done this, they sacrificed a bull and a ram on each altar.
3Then Balaam said, "Wait here beside
your offerings, and I'll go somewhere to
be alone. Maybe the LORD will appear to
me. If he does, I will tell you everything
he says." And he left.
4When God appeared to him, Balaam
said, "I have built seven altars and have
sacrificed a bull and a ram on each
one."
5The LORD gave Balaam a message,
then sent him back to tell Balak. 6When
Balaam returned, he found Balak and
his officials standing beside the offerings.
7Balaam said:

"King Balak of Moab brought me
    from the hills of Syria
to curse Israel
    and announce its doom.
8 But I can't go against God!
He did not curse
    or condemn Israel.

*9 "From the mountain peaks,
I look down and see Israel,
    the obedient people of God.
10 They are living alone in peace.
And though they are many,
    they don't bother
    the other nations.

"I hope to obey God
for as long as I live
    and to die in such peace."

11Balak said, "What are you doing? I
asked you to come and place a curse on
my enemies. But you have blessed them
instead!"
12Balaam answered, "I can say only
what the LORD tells me."

Balaam's Second Message

13Balak said to Balaam, "Let's go
somewhere else. Maybe if you see a
smaller part of the Israelites, you will be
able to curse them for me." 14So he took

[s]22.32 *I don't think you should go to Moab*: One possible meaning for the difficult Hebrew text. [t]22.41 *Balaam could see some of the Israelites*: For a curse to work, the people or thing being cursed had to be seen.

Balaam to a field on top of Mount Pisgah where lookouts were stationed.[u]
Then he built seven altars there and sacrificed a bull and a ram on each one.
15"Wait here beside your offerings,"
Balaam said. "The LORD will appear to
me over there."
16The LORD appeared to Balaam and
gave him another message, then he told
him to go and tell Balak. 17Balaam went
back and saw him and his officials
standing beside the offerings.
Balak asked, "What did the LORD
say?"
18Balaam answered:

"Pay close attention
to my words—
19 God is no mere human!
He doesn't tell lies
or change his mind.
God always keeps his promises.

20 "My command from God
was to bless these people,
and there's nothing I can do
to change what he has done.
21 Israel's king is the LORD God.
He lives there with them
and intends them no harm.
22 With the strength of a wild ox,
God led Israel out of Egypt.
23 No magic charms can work
against them—
just look what God has done
for his people.
24 They are like angry lions
ready to attack;
and they won't rest
until their victim
is gobbled down."

25Balak shouted, "If you're not going
to curse Israel, then at least don't bless
them."
26"I've already told you," Balaam answered. "I will say only what the LORD
tells me."

Balaam's Third Message

27Balak said to Balaam, "Come on,
let's try another place. Maybe God will
let you curse Israel from there." 28So he
took Balaam to Mount Peor overlooking
the desert north of the Dead Sea.
29Balaam said, "Build seven altars
here, then bring me seven bulls and
seven rams."
30After Balak had done what Balaam
asked, he sacrificed a bull and a ram on
each altar.

24 Balaam was sure that the LORD
would tell him to bless Israel
again. So he did not use any magic to
find out what the LORD wanted him to
do, as he had the first two times. Instead, he looked out toward the desert
2and saw the tribes of Israel camped below. Just then, God's Spirit took control
of him, 3and Balaam said:

"I am the son of Beor,
and my words are true,[v]
so listen to my message!
4 It comes from the LORD,
the God All-Powerful.
I bowed down to him
and saw a vision of Israel.

5 "People of Israel,
your camp is lovely.
6 It's like a grove of palm trees[w]
or a garden beside a river.
You are like tall aloe trees
that the LORD has planted,
or like cedars
growing near water.
7 You and your descendants
will prosper like an orchard
beside a stream.
Your king will rule with power
and be a greater king
than Agag the Amalekite.[x]
8 With the strength of a wild ox,
God led you out of Egypt.
You will defeat your enemies,
shooting them with arrows[y]
and crushing their bones.
9 Like a lion you lie down,
resting after an attack.
Who would dare disturb you?

"Anyone who blesses you
will be blessed;
anyone who curses you
will be cursed."

10When Balak heard this, he was so
furious that he pounded his fist against
his hand and said, "I called you here to
place a curse on my enemies, and
you've blessed them three times.
11Leave now and go home! I told you I
would pay you well, but since the LORD
didn't let you do what I asked, you won't
be paid."
12Balaam answered, "I told your messengers 13that even if you offered me a
palace full of silver or gold, I would still
obey the LORD. And I explained that I
would say only what he told me. 14So
I'm going back home, but I'm leaving
you with a warning about what the Israelites will someday do to your nation."

[u]**23.14** *a field . . . where lookouts were stationed*: Or "Zophim Field on the top of Mount Pisgah." [v]**24.3** *my words are true*: One possible meaning for the difficult Hebrew text. [w]**24.6** *grove of palm trees*: Or "green valley." [x]**24.7** *Agag the Amalekite*: The Amalekites were long-time enemies of the Israelites (see Exodus 17.8-16), and Agag was one of their most powerful kings. [y]**24.8** *shooting them with arrows*: One possible meaning for the difficult Hebrew text.

Balaam's Fourth Message

15Balaam said:

"I am the son of Beor,
and my words are true,[z]
so listen to my message!
16 My knowledge comes
from God Most High,
the LORD All-Powerful.
I bowed down to him
and saw a vision of Israel.

17 "What I saw in my vision
hasn't happened yet.
But someday, a king of Israel
will appear like a star.
He will wipe out you Moabites[a]
and destroy[b] those tribes
who live in the desert.[c]
18 Israel will conquer Edom
and capture the land
of that enemy nation.
19 The king of Israel will rule
and destroy the survivors
of every town there.[d]

20 "And I saw this vision
about the Amalekites:[e]
Their nation is now great,
but it will someday
disappear forever.[f]

21 "And this is what I saw
about the Kenites:[g]
They think they're safe,
living among the rocks,
22 but they will be wiped out
when Assyria conquers them.[h]

23 "No one can survive
if God plans destruction.[i]
24 Ships will come from Cyprus,
bringing people who will invade
the lands of Assyria and Eber.
But finally, Cyprus itself
will be ruined."

25After Balaam finished, he started
home, and Balak also left.

The Israelites Worship Baal

25 While the Israelites were camped
at Acacia, some of the men had
sex with Moabite women. 2These
women then invited the men to ceremonies where sacrifices were offered to
their gods. The men ate the meat from
the sacrifices and worshiped the
Moabite gods.
3The LORD was angry with Israel because they had worshiped the god Baal
Peor. 4So he said to Moses, "Take the
Israelite leaders who are responsible for
this and have them killed in front of my
sacred tent where everyone can see.
Maybe then I will stop being angry with
the Israelites."
5Moses told Israel's officials,[j] "Each of
you must put to death any of your men
who worshiped Baal."
6Later, Moses and the people were at
the sacred tent, crying, when one of the
Israelite men brought a Midianite[k]
woman to meet his family. 7Phinehas,
the grandson of Aaron[l] the priest, saw
the couple and left the crowd. He found
a spear 8and followed the man into his
tent, where he ran the spear through the
man and into the woman's stomach. The
LORD immediately stopped punishing Israel with a deadly disease, 9but twenty-
four thousand Israelites had already
died.
10The LORD said to Moses, 11"In my
anger, I would have wiped out the Israelites if Phinehas had not been faithful to me. 12-13But instead of punishing
them, I forgave them. So because of the
loyalty that Phinehas showed, I
solemnly promise that he and his descendants will always be my priests."
14The Israelite man that was killed
was Zimri son of Salu, who was one of
the leaders of the Simeon tribe. 15And
the Midianite woman killed with him
was Cozbi, the daughter of a Midianite
clan leader named Zur.
16The LORD told Moses, 17-18"The Midianites are now enemies of Israel, so attack and defeat them! They tricked the
people of Israel into worshiping their
god at Peor, and they are responsible for
the death of Cozbi, the daughter of one
of their own leaders."

The Israelites Are Counted a Second Time

26 After the LORD had stopped the
deadly disease from killing the Is-

[z]24.15 *my words are true*: One possible meaning for the difficult Hebrew text. [a]24.17 *you Moabites*: Or "the territories of Moab." [b]24.17 *destroy*: The Standard Hebrew Text; the Samaritan Hebrew Text "the skulls of." [c]24.17 *those tribes . . . desert*: The Hebrew text has "the descendants of Sheth," which probably refers to the people who lived in the desert areas of Canaan before the Israelites. [d]24.19 *every town there*: Or "Ir in Moab." [e]24.20 *the Amalekites*: See the note at 24.7. [f]24.20 *but . . . forever*: One possible meaning for the difficult Hebrew text. [g]24.21 *the Kenites*: A group of people who lived in the desert south of Israel. [h]24.22 *them*: One possible meaning for the difficult Hebrew text of verse 22.
[i]24.23 *destruction*: One possible meaning for the difficult Hebrew text of verse 23.
[j]25.5 *officials*: These were special leaders who were probably responsible for an entire tribe or part of a tribe. [k]25.6 *Midianite*: Used here as a general term for various peoples who lived east of the Jordan River. Some of these people were probably ruled by the Moabite king (see Genesis 36.35). [l]25.7 *Phinehas . . . Aaron*: Hebrew "Phinehas, son of Eleazar and grandson of Aaron."

raelites, he said to Moses and Eleazar son of Aaron, 2“I want you to find out how many Israelites are in each family. And list every man twenty years and older who is able to serve in Israel’s army.”

3Israel was now camped in the hills of Moab across the Jordan River from the town of Jericho. Moses and Eleazar told them 4what the LORD had said about counting the men twenty years and older, just as Moses and their ancestors had done when they left Egypt.[m]

5-7There were 43,730 men from the tribe of Reuben, the oldest son of Jacob.[n] These men were from the clans of Hanoch, Pallu, Hezron, and Carmi. 8Pallu was the father of Eliab 9and the grandfather of Nemuel, Dathan, and Abiram. These are the same Dathan and Abiram who had been chosen by the people, but who followed Korah and rebelled against Moses, Aaron, and the LORD. 10That’s when the LORD made the earth open up and swallow Dathan, Abiram, and Korah. At the same time, fire destroyed two hundred fifty men as a warning to the other Israelites.[o] 11But the Korahite clan wasn’t destroyed.

12-14There were 22,200 men from the tribe of Simeon; they were from the clans of Nemuel, Jamin, Jachin, Zerah, and Shaul.

15-18There were 40,500 men from the tribe of Gad; they were from the clans of Zephon, Haggi, Shuni, Ozni, Eri, Arod, and Areli.

19-22There were 76,500 men from the tribe of Judah; they were from the clans of Shelah, Perez, Zerah, Hezron, and Hamul. Judah’s sons Er and Onan had died in Canaan.[p]

23-25There were 64,300 men from the tribe of Issachar; they were from the clans of Tola, Puvah, Jashub, and Shimron.

26-27There were 60,500 men from the tribe of Zebulun; they were from the clans of Sered, Elon, and Jahleel.

28-34There were 52,700 men from the tribe of Manasseh son of Joseph; they were from the clan of Machir, the clan of Gilead his son, and the clans of his six grandsons: Iezer, Helek, Asriel, Shechem, Shemida, and Hepher. Zelophehad son of Hepher had no sons, but he had five daughters: Mahlah, Noah, Hoglah, Milcah, and Tirzah.[q]

35-37There were 32,500 men from the tribe of Ephraim son of Joseph; they were from the clans of Shuthelah, Becher, Tahan, and Eran the son of Shuthelah.

38-41There were 45,600 men from the tribe of Benjamin; they were from the clans of Bela, Ashbel, Ahiram, Shephupham, Hupham, as well as from Ard and Naaman, the two sons of Bela.

42-43There were 64,400 men from the tribe of Dan; they were all from the clan of Shuham.

44-47There were 53,400 men from the tribe of Asher; they were from the clans of Imnah, Ishvi, and Beriah, and from the two clans of Heber and Malchiel, the sons of Beriah. Asher’s daughter was Serah.

48-50There were 45,400 men from the tribe of Naphtali; they were from the clans of Jahzeel, Guni, Jezer, and Shillem.

51The total number of Israelite men listed was 601,730.

52The LORD said to Moses, 53“Divide the land of Canaan among these tribes, according to the number of people in each one, 54so the larger tribes have more land than the smaller ones. 55-56I will show you[r] what land to give each tribe, and they will receive as much land as they need, according to the number of people in it.”

57The tribe of Levi included the clans of the Gershonites, Kohathites, Merarites, 58as well as the clans of Libni, Hebron, Mahli, Mushi, and Korah. Kohath the Levite was the father of Amram, 59the husband of Levi’s daughter Jochebed, who was born in Egypt. Amram and Jochebed’s three children were Aaron, Moses, and Miriam. 60Aaron was the father of Nadab, Abihu, Eleazar, and Ithamar. 61But Nadab and Abihu had died when they offered fire that was unacceptable to the LORD.[s]

62In the tribe of Levi there were 23,000 men and boys at least a month old. They were not listed with the other tribes, because they would not receive any land in Canaan.

63Moses and Eleazar counted the Israelites while they were camped in the hills of Moab across the Jordan River from Jericho. 64None of the people that Moses and Aaron had counted in the Sinai Desert were still alive, 65except Caleb son of Jephunneh and Joshua son of Nun. The LORD had said that everyone else would die there in the desert.[t]

[m]**26.4** *just as . . . Egypt*: One possible meaning for the difficult Hebrew text. [n]**26.5-7** *Jacob*: The Hebrew text has “Israel,” Jacob’s name after God renamed him. [o]**26.10** *Israelites*: See 16.1-35. [p]**26.19-22** *Judah’s sons . . . Canaan*: See Genesis 38.1-10. [q]**26.28-34** *Zelophehad . . . Tirzah*: See also 27.1-11; 36.1-12. [r]**26.55,56** *I will show you*: The Hebrew text has “Cast lots to find out.” Pieces of wood or stone (called “lots”) were used to find out what the LORD wanted his people to do. [s]**26.61** *Nadab and Abihu . . . the LORD*: See 3.1-4 and Leviticus 10.1, 2. [t]**26.64,65** *None of the people . . . the desert*: See 14.26-30.

The Daughters of Zelophehad Are Given Land

27 Zelophehad[u] was from the Manasseh tribe, and he had five
daughters, whose names were Mahlah,
Noah, Hoglah, Milcah, and Tirzah.
2One day his daughters went to the
sacred tent, where they met with Moses,
Eleazar, and some other leaders of Israel, as well as a large crowd of Israelites. The young women said:
3You know that our father died in
the desert. But it was for something
he did wrong, not for joining with
Korah in rebelling against the LORD.
Our father left no sons 4to carry
on his family name. But why should
his name die out for that reason?
Give us some land like the rest of his
relatives in our clan, so our father's
name can live on.
5Moses asked the LORD what should
be done, 6and the LORD answered:
7Zelophehad's daughters are right.
They should each be given part of
the land their father would have received.
8Tell the Israelites that when a
man dies without a son, his daughter
will inherit his land. 9If he has no
daughter, his brothers will inherit
the land. 10But if he has no brothers,
his father's brothers will inherit the
land. 11And if his father has no
brothers, the land must be given to
his nearest relative in the clan. This
is my law, and the Israelites must
obey it.

Joshua Is Appointed Israel's Leader
(Deuteronomy 31.1-8)

12The LORD said to Moses, "One day
you will go up into the Abarim Mountains, and from there you will see the
land I am giving the Israelites. 13After
you have seen it, you will die,[v] just like
your brother Aaron, 14because both of
you disobeyed me at Meribah near the
town of Kadesh in the Zin Desert. When
the Israelites insulted me there, you
didn't believe in my holy power."[w]
15Moses replied, 16"You are the LORD
God, and you know what is in everyone's heart. So I ask you to appoint a
leader for Israel. 17Your people need
someone to lead them into battle, or else
they will be like sheep wandering
around without a shepherd."
18The LORD answered, "Joshua son of
Nun can do the job. Place your hands on
him to show that he is the one to take
your place. 19Then go with him and have
him stand in front of Eleazar the priest
and the Israelites. Appoint Joshua as
their new leader 20and tell them they
must now obey him, just as they obey
you. 21But Joshua must depend on
Eleazar to find out from me[x] what I
want him to do as he leads Israel into
battle."
22Moses followed the LORD's instructions and took Joshua to Eleazar and
the people, 23then he placed his hands
on Joshua and appointed him Israel's
leader.

Regular Daily Sacrifices
(Exodus 29.38-43; Leviticus 6.8-13)

28 The LORD told Moses 2to say to
the people of Israel:
Offer sacrifices to me at the appointed
times of worship, so that I will smell the
smoke and be pleased.
3Each day offer two rams a year old
as sacrifices to please me.[y] The animals
must have nothing wrong with them;
4one will be sacrificed in the morning,
and the other in the evening. 5Along
with each of them, two pounds of your
finest flour mixed with a quart of olive
oil must be offered as a grain sacrifice.
6This sacrifice to please me was first offered on Mount Sinai. 7Finally, along
with each of these two sacrifices, a
quart of wine must be poured on the altar as a drink offering. 8The second ram
will be sacrificed that evening, along
with the other offerings, just like the
one sacrificed that morning. The smell
of the smoke from these sacrifices will
please me.

The Sacrifice on the Sabbath

The LORD said:
9-10On the Sabbath, in addition to the
regular daily sacrifices,[z] you must sacrifice two rams a year old to please me.[a]
These rams must have nothing wrong
with them, and they will be sacrificed
with a drink offering and four pounds of
your finest flour mixed with olive oil.

The Sacrifices on the First Day of the Month

The LORD said:
11On the first day of each month,
bring to the altar two bulls, one full-
grown ram, and seven rams a year old
that have nothing wrong with them.
Then offer these as sacrifices to please
me.[a] 12Six pounds of your finest flour

[u]**27.1** *Zelophehad*: Hebrew "Zelophehad son of Hepher son of Gilead son of Machir son of Manasseh son of Joseph." [v]**27.12,13** *One day . . . you will die*: The story of Moses' death is in Deuteronomy 34.1-8. [w]**27.14** *both of you . . . my holy power*: See 20.1-13.
[x]**27.21** *from me*: The Hebrew text has "by the urim," something used by the priests to get answers from the LORD. [y]**28.3** *sacrifices to please me*: See the note at 6.11.
[z]**28.9,10** *regular daily sacrifices*: See 28.1-8. [a]**28.9,10** *sacrifice . . . to please me*: See the note at 6.11. [a]**28.11** *sacrifices to please me*: See the note at 6.11.

mixed with olive oil must be offered with each bull as a grain sacrifice. Four pounds of flour mixed with oil must be offered with the ram, 13 and two pounds of flour mixed with oil must be offered with each of the young rams. The smell of the smoke from these sacrifices will please me.

14-15 Offer two quarts of wine as a drink offering with each bull, one and a half quarts with the ram, and one quart with each of the young rams.

Finally, you must offer a goat[b] as a sacrifice for sin.

These sacrifices are to be offered on the first day of each month, in addition to the regular daily sacrifices.[c]

The Sacrifices during Passover and the Festival of Thin Bread

(Leviticus 23.4-8)

The LORD said:

16 Celebrate Passover in honor of me on the fourteenth day of the first month[d] of each year. 17 The following day will begin the Festival of Thin Bread, which will last for a week. During this time you must honor me by eating bread made without yeast.

18 On the first day of this festival, you must rest from your work and come together for worship. 19 Bring to the altar two bulls, one full-grown ram, and seven rams a year old that have nothing wrong with them. And then offer these as sacrifices to please me.[e] 20 Six pounds of your finest flour mixed with olive oil must be offered with each bull as a grain sacrifice. Four pounds of flour mixed with oil must be offered with the ram, 21 and two pounds of flour mixed with oil must be offered with each of the young rams. 22 Also offer a goat[f] as a sacrifice for the sins of the people. 23-24 All of these are to be offered in addition to the regular daily sacrifices,[g] and the smoke from them will please me. 25 Then on the last day of the festival, you must once again rest from work and come together for worship.

The Sacrifices during the Harvest Festival

(Leviticus 23.15-22)

The LORD said:

26 On the first day of the Harvest Festival, you must rest from your work, come together for worship, and bring a sacrifice of new grain. 27 Offer two young bulls, one full-grown ram, and seven rams a year old as sacrifices to please me.[h] 28 Six pounds of your finest flour mixed with olive oil must be offered with each bull as a grain sacrifice. Four pounds of flour mixed with oil must be offered with the ram, 29 and two pounds of flour mixed with oil must be offered with each of the young rams. 30 Also offer a goat[i] as a sacrifice for sin. 31 The animals must have nothing wrong with them and are to be sacrificed along with the regular daily sacrifices.[j]

The Sacrifices at the Festival of Trumpets

(Leviticus 23.23-25)

The LORD said:

29 On the first day of the seventh month,[k] you must rest from your work and come together to celebrate at the sound of the trumpets. 2 Bring to the altar one bull, one full-grown ram, and seven rams a year old that have nothing wrong with them. And then offer these as sacrifices to please me.[l] 3 Six pounds of your finest flour mixed with olive oil must be offered with the bull as a grain sacrifice. Four pounds of flour mixed with oil must be offered with the ram, 4 and two pounds of flour mixed with oil must be offered with each of the young rams. 5 You must also offer a goat[m] as a sacrifice for sin. 6 These sacrifices will be made in addition to the regular daily sacrifices[n] and the sacrifices for the first day of the month.[o] The smoke from these sacrifices will please me.

The Sacrifices on the Great Day of Forgiveness

(Leviticus 23.26-32)

The LORD said:

7 The tenth day of the seventh month[p] is the Great Day of Forgiveness.[q] On that day you must rest from all work and come together for worship. Show sorrow for your sins by going without food, 8 and bring to the altar one young bull, one full-grown ram, and seven rams a year old that have nothing wrong with them. Then offer these as sacrifices to please me.[r] 9 Six pounds of your finest flour mixed with olive oil must be offered with the bull as a grain

[b] **28.14,15** *goat*: See the note at 7.12-83. [c] **28.14,15** *regular daily sacrifices*: See 28.1-8. [d] **28.16** *first month*: See the note at 9.3. [e] **28.19** *sacrifices to please me*: See the note at 6.11. [f] **28.22** *goat*: See the note at 7.12-83. [g] **28.23,24** *regular daily sacrifices*: See 28.1-8. [h] **28.27** *sacrifices to please me*: See the note at 6.11. [i] **28.30** *goat*: See the note at 7.12-83. [j] **28.31** *regular daily sacrifices*: See 28.1-8. [k] **29.1** *seventh month*: Tishri (also called Ethanim), the seventh month of the Hebrew calendar, from about mid-September to mid-October. [l] **29.2** *sacrifices to please me*: See the note at 6.11. [m] **29.5** *goat*: See the note at 7.12-83. [n] **29.6** *regular daily sacrifices*: See 28.1-8. [o] **29.6** *sacrifices . . . month*: See 28.11-15. [p] **29.7** *seventh month*: See the note at 29.1. [q] **29.7** *Great Day of Forgiveness*: Traditionally known as the Day of Atonement. [r] **29.8** *sacrifices to please me*: See the note at 6.11.

sacrifice. Four pounds of flour mixed
with oil must be offered with the ram,
10and two pounds of flour mixed with oil
must be offered with each of the young
rams. 11A goat[s] must also be sacrificed
for the sins of the people. You will offer
these sacrifices in addition to the sacrifice to ask forgiveness and the regular
daily sacrifices.[t]

The Sacrifices during the Festival of Shelters

(Leviticus 23.33-44)

The LORD said:
12Beginning on the fifteenth day of the
seventh month[u] and continuing for
seven days, everyone must celebrate the
Festival of Shelters in honor of me.
13On the first day, you must rest from
your work and come together for worship. Bring to the altar thirteen bulls,
two full-grown rams, and fourteen rams
a year old that have nothing wrong with
them. Then offer these as sacrifices to
please me.[v] 14Six pounds of your finest
flour mixed with olive oil must be offered with each bull as a grain sacrifice.
Four pounds of flour mixed with oil
must be offered with each of the rams,
15and two pounds of flour mixed with oil
must be offered with each of the young
rams. 16You must also offer a goat[w] as a
sacrifice for sin. These are to be offered
in addition to the regular daily sacrifices.[x]
17-34For the next six days of the festival, you will sacrifice one less bull than
the day before, so that on the seventh
day, seven bulls will be sacrificed. The
other sacrifices and offerings must remain the same for each of these days.
35On the eighth day, you must once
again rest from your work and come together for worship. 36Bring to the altar
one bull, one full-grown ram, and seven
rams a year old that have nothing
wrong with them. Then offer these as
sacrifices to please me. 37You must also
offer the proper grain sacrifices and
drink offerings of wine with each animal. 38And offer a goat[y] as the sacrifice
to ask forgiveness for the people. These
sacrifices are made in addition to the
regular daily sacrifices.[z]
39You must offer all these sacrifices to
me at the appointed times of worship,
together with any offerings that are voluntarily given or given because of a
promise.
40Moses told the people of Israel
everything the LORD had told him about
the sacrifices.

Making Promises to the LORD

30 The LORD told Moses to say to Israel's tribal leaders:
2When one of you men makes a
promise to the LORD,[a] you must keep
your word.
3Suppose a young woman who is still
living with her parents makes a promise
to the LORD. 4If her father hears about it
and says nothing, she must keep her
promise. 5But if he hears about it and
objects, then she no longer has to keep
her promise. The LORD will forgive her,
because her father did not agree with
the promise.
6-7Suppose a woman makes a promise
to the LORD and then gets married. If
her husband later hears about the
promise but says nothing, she must do
what she said, whether she meant it or
not. 8But if her husband hears about the
promise and objects, she no longer has
to keep it, and the LORD will forgive her.
9Widows and divorced women must
keep every promise they make to the
LORD.
10Suppose a married woman makes a
promise to the LORD. 11If her husband
hears about the promise and says nothing, she must do what she said. 12But if
he hears about the promise and does
object, she no longer has to keep it. The
LORD will forgive her, because her husband would not allow her to keep the
promise. 13Her husband has the final
say about any promises she makes to
the LORD. 14If her husband hears about a
promise and says nothing about it for a
whole day, she must do what she said—
since he did not object, the promise
must be kept. 15But if he waits until the
next day to stop her from keeping her
promise, he is the one who must be punished.
16These are the laws that the LORD
gave Moses about husbands and wives,
and about young daughters who still
live at home.

Israel's War against Midian

31 The LORD said to Moses, 2"Before
you die, make sure that the Midianites are punished for what they did to
Israel."[b]
3Then Moses told the people, "The
LORD wants to punish the Midianites.

[s]**29.11** *goat*: See the note at 7.12-83. [t]**29.11** *regular daily sacrifices*: See 28.1-8.
[u]**29.12** *seventh month*: See the note at 29.1. [v]**29.13** *sacrifices to please me*: See the note at 6.11. [w]**29.16** *goat*: See the note at 7.12-83. [x]**29.16** *regular daily sacrifices*: See 28.1-8.
[y]**29.38** *goat*: See the note at 7.12-83. [z]**29.38** *regular daily sacrifices*: See 28.1-8.
[a]**30.2** *a promise to the LORD*: Either the promise of a gift or the promise to do something.
[b]**31.2** *Midianites . . . to Israel*: See 25.1-18.

So have our men prepare for battle.
4 Each tribe will send a thousand men to
fight."
5 Twelve thousand men were picked
from the tribes of Israel, and after they
were prepared for battle, 6 Moses sent
them off to war. Phinehas the son of
Eleazar went with them and took along
some things from the sacred tent[c] and
the trumpets for sounding the battle signal.
7 The Israelites fought against the Midianites, just as the LORD had commanded Moses. They killed all the men,
8 including Balaam son of Beor and the
five Midianite kings, Evi, Rekem, Zur,
Hur, and Reba. 9 The Israelites captured
every woman and child, then led away
the Midianites' cattle and sheep, and
took everything else that belonged to
them. 10 They also burned down the Midianite towns and villages.
11 Israel's soldiers gathered together
everything they had taken from the
Midianites, including the captives and
the animals. 12-13 Then they returned to
their own camp in the hills of Moab
across the Jordan River from Jericho,
where Moses, Eleazar, and the other Israelite leaders met the troops outside
camp.
14 Moses became angry with the army
commanders 15 and said, "I can't believe
you let the women live! 16 They are the
ones who followed Balaam's advice and
invited our people to worship the god
Baal-Peor. That's why the LORD punished us by killing so many of our people. 17 You must put to death every boy
and all the women who have ever had
sex. 18 But do not kill the young women
who have never had sex. You may keep
them for yourselves."
19 Then Moses said to the soldiers, "If
you killed anyone or touched a dead
body, you are unclean and have to stay
outside the camp for seven days. On the
third and seventh days, you must go
through a ceremony to make yourselves
and your captives clean. 20 Then wash
your clothes and anything made from
animal skin, goat's hair, or wood."
21-23 Eleazar then explained, "If you
need to purify something that won't
burn, such as gold, silver, bronze, iron,
tin, or lead, you must first place it in a
hot fire. After you take it out, sprinkle it
with the water that purifies. Everything
else should only be sprinkled with the
water. Do all of this, just as the LORD
commanded Moses. 24 Wash your clothes
on the seventh day, and after that, you
will be clean and may return to the
camp."

Everything Taken from the Midianites Is Divided

25 The LORD told Moses:
26-27 Make a list of everything
taken from the Midianites, including
the captives and the animals. Then
divide them between the soldiers
and the rest of the people. Eleazar
the priest and the family leaders will
help you.
28-29 From the half that belongs to
the soldiers, set aside for the LORD
one out of every five hundred people
or animals and give these to Eleazar.
30 From the half that belongs to the
people, set aside one out of every
fifty and give these to the Levites in
charge of the sacred tent.
31 Moses and Eleazar followed the
LORD's instructions 32-35 and listed everything that had been taken from the Midianites. The list included 675,000 sheep
and goats, 72,000 cattle, 61,000 donkeys,
and 32,000 young women who had
never had sex.
36-47 Each half included 337,500 sheep
and goats, 36,000 cattle, 30,500 donkeys,
and 16,000 young women. From the half
that belonged to the soldiers, Moses
counted out 675 sheep and goats, 72 cattle, 61 donkeys, and 32 women and gave
them to Eleazar to be dedicated to the
LORD. Then from the half that belonged
to the people, Moses set aside one out of
every fifty animals and women, as the
LORD had said, and gave them to the
Levites.
48 The army commanders went to
Moses 49 and said, "Sir, we have counted
our troops, and not one soldier is missing. 50 So we want to give the LORD all
the gold jewelry we took from the Midianites. It's our gift to him for watching
over us and our troops."
51 Moses and Eleazar accepted the
jewelry from the commanders, 52 and its
total weight was over four hundred
pounds. 53 This did not include the things
that the soldiers had kept for themselves. 54 So Moses and Eleazar placed
the gold in the LORD's sacred tent to remind Israel of what had happened.[d]

Land East of the Jordan River Is Settled

(Deuteronomy 3.12-22)

32 The tribes of Reuben and Gad
owned a lot of cattle and sheep,
and they saw that the regions of Jazer
and Gilead had good pastureland. 2 So
they went to Moses, Eleazar, and the
other leaders of Israel and said, 3-4 "The
LORD has helped us capture the land
around the towns of Ataroth, Dibon,

[c] **31.6** *Phinehas . . . sacred tent*: Phinehas would serve as the priest during the battle, so he took along the things needed to ask God what he wanted done. [d] **31.54** *to remind . . . happened*: Or "so the LORD would continue to help Israel."

Jazer, Nimrah, Heshbon, Elealeh, Se-
bam, Nebo, and Beon. That's good
pastureland, and since we own cattle
and sheep, 5would you let us stay here
east of the Jordan River and have this
land as our own?"
6Moses answered:
You mean you'd stay here while
the rest of the Israelites go into battle? 7If you did that, it would discourage the others from crossing over
into the land the LORD promised
them. 8This is exactly what happened when I sent your ancestors
from Kadesh-Barnea to explore the
land. 9They went as far as Eshcol
Valley, then returned and told the
people that we should not enter it.
10The LORD became very angry.
11And he said that no one who was
twenty years or older when they left
Egypt would enter the land he had
promised to Abraham, Isaac, and Jacob. Not one of those people believed in the LORD's power, 12except
Caleb and Joshua.[e] They remained
faithful to the LORD, 13but he was so
angry with the others that he forced
them to wander around in the desert
forty years. By that time everyone
who had sinned against him had
died.
14Now you people of Reuben and
Gad are doing the same thing and
making the LORD even angrier. 15If
you reject the LORD, he will once
again abandon his people and leave
them here in the desert. And you
will be to blame!
16The men from Reuben and Gad replied:
Let us build places to keep our
sheep and goats, and towns for our
wives and children, 17where they
can stay and be safe. Then we'll prepare to fight and lead the other
tribes into battle. 18We will stay with
them until they have settled in their
own tribal lands. 19The land on this
side of the Jordan River will be ours,
so we won't expect to receive any on
the other side.
20Moses said:
You promised that you would be
ready to fight for the LORD. 21You
also agreed to cross the Jordan and
stay with the rest of the Israelites,
until the LORD forces our enemies
out of the land. If you do these
things, 22then after the LORD helps
Israel capture the land, you can return to your own land. You will no
longer have to stay with the others.
23But if you don't keep your promise,
you will sin against the LORD and be
punished.
24Go ahead and build towns for
your wives and children, and places
for your sheep and goats. Just be
sure to do what you have promised.
25The men from Reuben and Gad answered:
Sir, we will do just what you have
said. 26Our wives and children and
sheep and cattle will stay here in the
towns in Gilead. 27But those of us
who are prepared for battle will
cross the Jordan and fight for the
LORD.
28Then Moses said to Eleazar, Joshua,
and the family leaders, 29"Make sure
that the tribes of Gad and Reuben prepare for battle and cross the Jordan
River with you. If they do, then after the
land is in your control, give them the region of Gilead as their tribal land. 30But
if they break their promise, they will receive land on the other side of the Jordan, like the rest of the tribes."
31The tribes of Gad and Reuben replied, "We are your servants and will do
whatever the LORD has commanded.
32We will cross the Jordan River, ready
to fight for the LORD in Canaan. But the
land we will inherit as our own will be
on this side of the river."
33So Moses gave the tribes of Gad,
Reuben, and half of Manasseh[f] the territory and towns that King Sihon the
Amorite had ruled, as well as the territory and towns that King Og of Bashan
had ruled.[g]
34The tribe of Gad rebuilt the towns of
Dibon, Ataroth, Aroer, 35Atroth-
Shophan, Jazer, Jogbehah, 36Beth-
Nimrah, and Beth-Haran. They built
walls around them and also built places
to keep their sheep and goats.
37The tribe of Reuben rebuilt Heshbon, Elealeh, Kiriathaim, 38Sibmah, as
well as the towns that used to be known
as Nebo and Baal-Meon. They renamed
all those places.
39The clan of Machir from the tribe of
East Manasseh went to the region of
Gilead, captured its towns, and forced
out the Amorites. 40So Moses gave the
Machirites the region of Gilead, and
they settled there.
41Jair from the Manasseh tribe captured villages and renamed them "Villages of Jair."[h]
42Nobah captured the town of Kenath
with its villages and renamed it Nobah.

Israel's Journey from Egypt to Moab

33 As Israel traveled from Egypt under the command of Moses and

[e]**32.12** *Caleb and Joshua*: Hebrew "Caleb son of Jephunneh the Kenizzite and Joshua son of Nun." [f]**32.33** *half of Manasseh*: Or "East Manasseh." [g]**32.33** *ruled*: One possible meaning for the difficult Hebrew text of verse 33. [h]**32.41** *Villages of Jair*: Or "Havvoth-Jair."

Aaron, 2 Moses kept a list of the places
they camped, just as the LORD had instructed. Here is the record of their journey:
3-4 Israel left the Egyptian city of
Rameses on the fifteenth day of the first
month.[i] This was the day after the LORD
had punished Egypt's gods by killing
the first-born sons in every Egyptian
family. So while the Egyptians were
burying the bodies, they watched the Israelites proudly[j] leave their country.
5 After the Israelites left Rameses, they
camped at Succoth, 6 and from there,
they moved their camp to Etham on the
edge of the desert. 7 Then they turned
back toward Pi-Hahiroth, east of Baal-
Zephon, and camped near Migdol.
8 They left Pi-Hahiroth,[k] crossed the Red
Sea,[l] then walked three days into the
Etham Desert and camped at Marah.
9 Next, they camped at Elim, where there
were twelve springs of water and seventy palm trees. 10 They left Elim and
camped near the Red Sea,[m] 11 then
turned east and camped along the western edge of the Sinai Desert.[n] 12-14 From
there they went to Dophkah, Alush, and
Rephidim, where they had no water.[o]
15 They left Rephidim and finally
reached the Sinai Desert.
16-36 As Israel traveled from the Sinai
Desert to Kadesh in the Zin Desert, they
camped at Kibroth-Hattaavah, Hazeroth, Rithmah, Rimmon-Perez, Libnah,
Rissah, Kehelathah, Mount Shepher,
Haradah, Makheloth, Tahath, Terah,
Mithkah, Hashmonah, Moseroth, Bene-
Jaakan, Hor-Haggidgad, Jotbathah,
Abronah, Ezion-Geber, and finally
Kadesh. 37 When they left Kadesh, they
came to Mount Hor, on the border of
Edom.
38 That's where the LORD commanded
Aaron the priest to go to the top of the
mountain. Aaron died there on the first
day of the fifth month,[p] forty years after
the Israelites left Egypt. 39 He was one
hundred twenty-three years old at the
time.
40 It was then that the Canaanite king
of Arad, who lived in the Southern
Desert of Canaan, heard that Israel was
headed that way.
41-47 The Israelites left Mount Hor and
headed toward Moab. Along the way,
they camped at Zalmonah, Punon,
Oboth, Iye-Abarim in the territory of
Moab, Dibon-Gad, Almon-Diblathaim,
at a place near Mount Nebo in the
Abarim Mountains, 48 and finally in the
lowlands of Moab across the Jordan
River from Jericho. 49 Their camp
stretched from Beth-Jeshimoth to Acacia.

The LORD's Command To Conquer Canaan

50 While Israel was camped in the lowlands of Moab across the Jordan River
from Jericho, the LORD told Moses 51 to
give the people of Israel this message:
When you cross the Jordan River
and enter Canaan, 52 you must force
out the people living there. Destroy
their idols and tear down their altars. 53 Then settle in the land—I
have given it to you as your own.
54 I will show you[q] how to divide
the land among the tribes, according
to the number of clans in each one,
so that the larger tribes will have
more land than the smaller ones.
55 If you don't force out all the people there, they will be like pointed
sticks in your eyes and thorns in
your back. They will always be trouble for you, 56 and I will treat you as
cruelly as I planned on treating
them.

Israel's Borders

34 The LORD told Moses 2 to tell the
people of Israel that their land in
Canaan would have the following borders:
3 The southern border will be the
Zin Desert and the northwest part of
Edom. This border will begin at the
south end of the Dead Sea. 4 It will
go west from there, but will turn
southward to include Scorpion Pass,
the village of Zin, and the town of
Kadesh-Barnea. From there, the border will continue to Hazar-Addar
and on to Azmon. 5 It will run along
the Egyptian Gorge and end at the
Mediterranean Sea.
6 The western border will be the
Mediterranean Sea.
7 The northern border will begin at
the Mediterranean, then continue
eastward to Mount Hor.[r] 8 After that,
it will run to Lebo-Hamath and

[i] **33.3,4** *first month*: See the note at 9.3. [j] **33.3,4** *proudly*: Or "bravely." [k] **33.8** *Pi-Hahiroth*: Two ancient translations and the Samaritan Hebrew Text; the Standard Hebrew Text "a place near Hahiroth." [l] **33.8** *Red Sea*: Hebrew *hayyam* "the Sea," understood as *yam suph*, "Sea of Reeds" (see also the note at Exodus 13.18). [m] **33.10** *Red Sea*: Hebrew *yam suph*, here referring to the Gulf of Suez, since the term is extended to include the northwestern arm of the Red Sea (see also the note at Exodus 13.18). [n] **33.11** *the western edge of the Sinai Desert*: Hebrew "the Sin Desert." [o] **33.12-14** *Rephidim . . . no water*: See Exodus 17.1-7. [p] **33.38** *fifth month*: Ab, the fifth month of the Hebrew calendar, from about mid-July to mid-August. [q] **33.54** *I will show you*: See the note at 26.55, 56. [r] **34.7** *Mount Hor*: Not the same as in 33.37.

across to Zedad, which is the northern edge of your land. 9From Zedad,
the border will continue east to
Ziphron and end at Hazar-Enan.
10The eastern border will begin at
Hazar-Enan in the north, then run
south to Shepham, 11and on down to
Riblah on the east side of Ain. From
there, it will go south to the eastern
hills of Lake Galilee,[s] 12then follow
the Jordan River down to the north
end of the Dead Sea.
The land within those four borders will belong to you.
13Then Moses told the people, "You
will receive the land inside these borders. It will be yours, but the LORD has
commanded you to divide it among the
nine and a half tribes. 14The tribes of
Reuben, Gad, and East Manasseh have
already been given their land 15across
from Jericho, east of the Jordan River."

The Leaders Who Will Divide the Land

16The LORD said to Moses, 17"Eleazar
the priest and Joshua son of Nun will divide the land for the Israelites. 18One
leader from each tribe will help them,
19-28and here is the list of their names:

Caleb son of Jephunneh
from Judah,
Shemuel son of Ammihud
from Simeon,
Elidad son of Chislon
from Benjamin,
Bukki son of Jogli
from Dan,
Hanniel son of Ephod
from Manasseh,
Kemuel son of Shiphtan
from Ephraim,
Elizaphan son of Parnach
from Zebulun,
Paltiel son of Azzan
from Issachar,
Ahihud son of Shelomi
from Asher,
and Pedahel son of Ammihud
from Naphtali."

29These are the men the LORD commanded to help Eleazar and Joshua divide the land for the Israelites.

The Towns for the Levites

35 While the people of Israel were
still camped in the lowlands of
Moab across the Jordan River from Jericho, the LORD told Moses 2to say to
them:
When you receive your tribal lands,
you must give towns and pastures to the
Levi tribe. 3That way, the Levites will
have towns to live in and pastures for
their animals. 4-5The pasture around
each of these towns must be in the
shape of a square, with the town itself in
the center. The pasture is to measure
three thousand feet on each side, with
fifteen hundred feet of land outside each
of the town walls. This will be the
Levites' pastureland.
6Six of the towns you give them will
be Safe Towns where a person who has
accidentally killed someone can run for
protection. But you will also give the
Levites forty-two other towns, 7so they
will have a total of forty-eight towns
with their surrounding pastures.
8Since the towns for the Levites must
come from Israel's own tribal lands, the
larger tribes will give more towns than
the smaller ones.

The Safe Towns

(Deuteronomy 19.1–13; Joshua 20.1–9)

9The LORD then told Moses 10to tell the
people of Israel:
After you have crossed the Jordan
River and are settled in Canaan,
11choose Safe Towns, where a person
who has accidentally killed someone can
run for protection. 12If the victim's relatives think it was murder, they might try
to take revenge.[t] Anyone accused of
murder can run to one of these Safe
Towns for protection and not be killed
before a trial is held.
13There are to be six of these Safe
Towns, 14Three on each side of the
Jordan River. 15They will be places of
protection for anyone who lives in Israel
and accidentally kills someone.

Laws about Murder and Accidental Killing

The LORD said:
16-18Suppose you hit someone with a
piece of iron or a large stone or a dangerous wooden tool. If that person dies,
then you are a murderer and must be
put to death 19by one of the victim's relatives.[t] He will take revenge for his relative's death as soon as he finds you.
20-21Or suppose you get angry and kill
someone by pushing or hitting or by
throwing something. You are a murderer
and must be put to death by one of the
victim's relatives.
22-24But if you are not angry and accidentally kill someone in any of these
ways, the townspeople must hold a trial
and decide if you are guilty. 25If they decide that you are innocent, you will be

[s]34.11 *Lake Galilee*: The Hebrew text has "Lake Chinnereth," an earlier name for Lake Galilee.
[t]35.12 *the victim's relatives . . . revenge*: At this time in Israel's history, the clan would appoint the closest male relative to find and kill a person who had killed a member of their clan.
[t]35.19 *one of the victim's relatives*: At this time in Israel's history, the clan would appoint the closest male relative to find and kill a person who had killed a member of their clan.

protected from the victim's relative and
sent to stay in one of the Safe Towns until the high priest dies. 26But if you ever
leave the Safe Town 27and are killed by
the victim's relative, he cannot be punished for killing you. 28You must stay inside the town until the high priest dies;
only then can you go back home.
29The community of Israel must always obey these laws.
30Death is the penalty for murder. But
no one accused of murder can be put to
death unless there are at least two witnesses to the crime. 31You cannot give
someone money to escape the death
penalty; you must pay with your own
life! 32And if you have been proven innocent of murder and are living in a
Safe Town, you cannot pay to go back
home; you must stay there until the high
priest dies.
33-34I, the LORD, live among you people
of Israel, so your land must be kept
pure. But when a murder takes place,
blood pollutes the land, and it becomes
unclean. If that happens, the murderer
must be put to death, so the land will be
clean again. Keep murder out of Israel!

The Laws about Married Women and Land

36 One day the family leaders from
the Gilead clan of the Manasseh
tribe went to Moses and the other family leaders of Israel 2and said, "Sir, the
LORD has said that he will show[u] what
land each tribe will receive as their own.
And the LORD has commanded you to
give the daughters of our relative
Zelophehad the land that he would have
received. 3But if they marry men from
other tribes of Israel, the land they receive will become part of that tribe's inheritance and will no longer belong to
us. 4Even when land is returned to its
original owner in the Year of Celebration,[v] we will not get back Zelophehad's
land—it will belong to the tribe into
which his daughters married."
5So Moses told the people that the
LORD had said:

> These men from the Manasseh
> tribe are right. 6I will allow Zelophe-
> had's daughters to marry anyone, as
> long as those men belong to one of
> the clans of the Manasseh tribe.
> 7Tribal land must not be given to
> another tribe—it will remain the
> property of the tribe that received it.
> 8-9In the future, any daughter who
> inherits land must marry someone
> from her own tribe. Israel's tribal
> land is never to be passed from one
> tribe to another.

10-11Mahlah, Tirzah, Hoglah, Milcah,
and Noah the daughters of Zelophehad
obeyed the LORD and married their uncles' sons 12and remained part of the
Manasseh tribe. So their land stayed in
their father's clan.
13These are the laws that the LORD
gave to Moses and the Israelites while
they were camped in the lowlands of
Moab across the Jordan River from Jericho.

[u]**36.2** *that he will show*: See the note at 26.55, 56. [v]**36.4** *Year of Celebration*: This was a sacred year for Israel, traditionally called the "Year of Jubilee." During this year, all property had to go back to its original owner. But here, the property was not sold; it became part of the other tribe's land when the daughter who owned it married into that tribe. So the property could not be returned even during this year.

DEUTERONOMY

ABOUT THIS BOOK

It was almost time for the people of Israel to cross the Jordan River and conquer Canaan. But God refused to let Moses lead them into the land. Instead, Moses had been told that he was going to die on the eastern side of the Jordan. So Moses gave several farewell speeches to the people of Israel in which he repeated many of God's laws.

Because Moses was giving these laws to Israel for a second time, the book is now called "Deuteronomy," which comes from a Greek phrase meaning "second law."

Moses also reminded the Israelites about the past forty years. God had rescued them from Egypt and taken care of them in the desert, but they had not always been faithful or obedient to him.

Moses told the Israelites that if they kept their agreement to worship and obey the Lord, they would be a successful and powerful nation. But if they broke their agreement and worshiped idols, the Lord promised to put terrible curses on the people. They would be defeated by their enemies and lose their land and their lives.

Much later, when Jesus was asked which one of God's commands was the most important, he answered by quoting one of the commands from Deuteronomy:

> *Listen, Israel! The LORD our God is the only true God! So love the LORD your God with all your heart, soul, and strength.* (6.4, 5)

A QUICK LOOK AT THIS BOOK

The First Speech: Moses Reviews the Past (1.1—4.43)
The Second Speech: Moses Tells What the Lord Requires (4.44—29.1)
The Third Speech: Israel Must Keep Its Agreement with the Lord (29.2—30.20)
Joshua Is Appointed Leader of Israel (31.1-13)
Israel Will Reject the Lord (31.14-29)
The Song of Moses (31.30—32.47)
Moses Sees the Land and Blesses the Tribes of Israel (32.48—33.29)
The Death of Moses (34.1-12)

The Final Speeches of Moses

1 1-5 This book contains the speeches that Moses made while Israel was in the land of Moab, camped near the town of Suph in the desert east of the Jordan River. The town of Paran was in one direction from their camp, and the towns of Tophel, Laban, Hazeroth, and Dizahab[a] were in the opposite direction.

Earlier, Moses had defeated the Amorite King Sihon of Heshbon. Moses had also defeated King Og of Bashan, who used to live in Ashtaroth for part of the year and in Edrei for the rest of the year.

Although it takes only eleven days to walk from Mount Sinai[b] to Kadesh-Barnea by way of the Mount Seir Road, these speeches were not made until forty years after Israel left Egypt.[c]

[a]**1.1-5** *Suph . . . Paran . . . Tophel, Laban, Hazeroth, and Dizahab*: The exact location of these towns is not known. [b]**1.1-5** *Mount Sinai*: The Hebrew text has "Horeb," another name for Mount Sinai. [c]**1.1-5** *Egypt*: The Israelites would soon enter Canaan, but they would have entered the land of Canaan from Kadesh-Barnea forty years earlier if they had not rebelled against God (see verses 6-40).

THE FIRST SPEECH: MOSES REVIEWS THE PAST

The LORD's Command at Mount Sinai

The LORD had given Moses his laws
for the people of Israel. And on the first
day of the eleventh month,[d] Moses began explaining those laws by saying:
[6]People of Israel, when we were in our
camp at Mount Sinai,[e] the LORD our
God told us:
You have stayed here long enough.
[7]Leave this place and go into the
land that belongs to the Amorites
and their neighbors the Canaanites.
This land includes the Jordan River
valley, the hill country, the western
foothills, the Southern Desert, the
Mediterranean seacoast, the Lebanon Mountains, and all the territory
as far as the Euphrates River. [8]I give
you this land, just as I promised
your ancestors Abraham, Isaac, and
Jacob. Now you must go and take
the land.

Leaders Were Appointed
(Exodus 18.13-27)

Moses said:
[9]Right after the LORD commanded us
to leave Mount Sinai,[e] I told you:
Israel, being your leader is too big
a job for one person. [10]The LORD our
God has blessed us, and so now
there are as many of us as there are
stars in the sky. [11]God has even
promised to bless us a thousand
times more, and I pray that he will.
[12]But I cannot take care of all your
problems and settle all your arguments alone. [13]Each tribe must
choose some experienced men who
are known for their wisdom and understanding, and I will make those
men the official leaders of their
tribes.
[14]You answered, "That's a good idea!"
[15]Then I took these men, who were already wise and respected leaders, and I
appointed them as your official leaders.
Some of them became military officers
in charge of groups of a thousand, or a
hundred, or fifty, or ten, [16]and others became judges. I gave these judges the following instructions:
When you settle legal cases, your
decisions must be fair. It doesn't
matter if the case is between two Israelites, or between an Israelite and
a foreigner living in your community. [17]And it doesn't matter if one is
helpless and the other is powerful.
Don't be afraid of anyone! No matter who shows up in your court, God
will help you make a fair decision.
If any case is too hard for you,
bring the people to me, and I will
make the decision.
[18]After I gave these instructions to the
judges, I taught you the LORD's commands.

Men Were Sent To Explore the Hill Country
(Numbers 13.1-33)

Moses said to Israel:
[19]The LORD had commanded us to
leave Mount Sinai[e] and go to the hill
country that belonged to the Amorites,
so we started out into the huge desert.
You remember how frightening it was,
but soon we were at Kadesh-Barnea,
[20-21]and I told you, "We have reached the
hill country. It belongs to the Amorites
now, but the LORD our God is giving it to
us. He is the same God our ancestors
worshiped, and he has told us to go in
and take this land, so don't hesitate and
be afraid."
[22]Then all of you came to me and said,
"Before we go into the land, let's send
some men to explore it. When they
come back, they can tell us about the
towns we will find and what roads we
should take to get there."
[23]It seemed like a good idea, so I
chose twelve men, one from each tribe.
[24]They explored the hill country as far
as Bunch Valley[f] [25]and even brought
back some of the fruit. They said, "The
LORD our God is giving us good land."

Israel Refused To Obey the LORD
(Numbers 14.1-45)

Moses said to Israel:
[26]You did not want to go into the land,
and you refused to obey the LORD your
God. [27]You stayed in your tents and
grumbled, "The LORD must hate us—he
brought us out of Egypt, just so he could
hand us over to the Amorites and get rid
of us. [28]We are afraid, because the men
who explored the land told us that the
cities are large, with walls that reach to
the sky. The people who live there are
taller and stronger than we are,[g] and
some of them are Anakim.[h] We have
nowhere to go."
[29]Then I said, "Don't worry! [30]The

[d]**1.1-5** *eleventh month*: Shebat, the eleventh month of the Hebrew calendar, from about mid-January to mid-February. [e]**1.6** *Mount Sinai*: See the note at 1.1-5. [e]**1.9** *Mount Sinai*: See the note at 1.1-5. [e]**1.19** *Mount Sinai*: See the note at 1.1-5. [f]**1.24** *Bunch Valley*: Or "Eshcol Valley," famous for its large bunches of grapes. [g]**1.28** *The people . . . we are*: Most Hebrew manuscripts; a few Hebrew manuscripts and one ancient translation "the people who live there are stronger than we are, and there are more of them than there are of us."
[h]**1.28** *Anakim*: Perhaps a group of very tall people that lived in or near Palestine before the Israelites. See also 2.10, 11, 20, 21; Numbers 13.33.

LORD our God will lead the way. He will
fight on our side, just as he did when we
saw him do all those things to the Egyptians. 31And you know that the LORD has
taken care of us the whole time we've
been in the desert, just as you might
carry one of your children."
32But you still would not trust the
LORD, 33even though he had always been
with us in the desert. During the daytime, the LORD was in the cloud, leading
us in the right direction and showing us
where to camp. And at night, he was
there in the fire.[i]
34You had made the LORD angry, and
he said:

35You people of this generation are
evil, and I refuse to let you go into
the good land that I promised your
ancestors. 36Caleb son of Jephunneh
is the only one of your generation
that I will allow to go in. He obeyed
me completely, so I will give him
and his descendants the land he explored.

37The LORD was even angry with me
because of you people, and he said,
"Moses, I won't let you go into the land
either. 38Instead, I will let Joshua[j] your
assistant lead Israel to conquer the land.
So encourage him."
39Then the LORD spoke to you again:

People of Israel, you said that your
innocent young children would be
taken prisoner in the battle for the
land. But someday I will let them go
into the land, and with my help they
will conquer it and live there.
40Now, turn around and go back
into the desert by way of Red Sea[k]
Road.

41Then you told me, "We disobeyed
the LORD our God, but now we want to
obey him. We will go into the hill country and fight, just as he told us to do." So
you picked up your weapons, thinking it
would be easy to take over the hill country.
42But the LORD said, "Moses, warn
them not to go into the hill country. I
won't help them fight, and their enemies
will defeat them."
43I told you what the LORD had said,
but you paid no attention. You disobeyed
him and went into the hill country anyway. You thought you were so great!
44But when the Amorites in the hill
country attacked from their towns, you
ran from them as you would run from a
swarm of bees. The Amorites chased
your troops into Seir[l] as far as Hormah,
killing them as they went. 45Then you
came back to the place of worship at
Kadesh-Barnea and wept, but the LORD
would not listen to your prayers.

Israel Spent Years in the Desert

Moses said to Israel:
46After we had been in Kadesh for a
few months, we obeyed the LORD and
headed back into the desert by way of
2 Red Sea[m] Road. 1We spent many
years wandering around outside the
hill country of Seir,[n] 2until the LORD
said:

Moses, 3Israel has wandered in
these hills long enough. Turn and go
north. 4And give the people these orders: "Be very careful, because you
will soon go through the land that
belongs to your relatives, the descendants of Esau.[o] They are afraid
of you, 5but don't start a war with
them. I have given them the hill
country of Seir, so I won't give any
of it to you, not even enough to set a
foot on. 6And as you go through
their land, you will have to buy food
and water from them."

7The LORD has helped us and taken
care of us during the past forty years
that we have been in this huge desert.
We've had everything we needed, and
the LORD has blessed us and made us
successful in whatever we have done.
8We went past the territory that belonged to our relatives, the descendants
of Esau.[p] We followed Arabah Road that
starts in the south at Elath and Ezion-
Geber, then we turned onto the desert
road that leads to Moab.
9The LORD told me, "Don't try to start
a war with Moab. Leave them alone, because I gave the land of Ar[q] to them,[r]
and I will not let you have any of it."

Tribes That Lived near Canaan

10Before the LORD gave the Moabites
their land, a large and powerful tribe

[i]**1.33** *the cloud . . . the fire*: See Exodus 40.34-38; Numbers 9.15-23. [j]**1.38** *Joshua*: Hebrew "Joshua son of Nun." [k]**1.40** *Red Sea*: Hebrew *yam suph*, here referring to the Gulf of Aqaba, since the term is extended to include the northeastern arm of the Red Sea (see also the note at 11.4). [l]**1.44** *Seir*: An area of hills and mountains that was part of the territory of Edom. [m]**1.46** *Red Sea*: See the notes at 1.40; 11.4. [n]**2.1** *hill country of Seir*: See the note at 1.44. [o]**2.4** *your relatives, the descendants of Esau*: Esau was the brother of Jacob, the ancestor of the nation of Israel. Esau's descendants were also known as the nation of Edom. [p]**2.8** *We went past . . . Esau*: According to Numbers 20.14-21, the king of Edom did not let the Israelites go through his land. [q]**2.9** *Ar*: One of the main cities of Moab (see Numbers 21.28); sometimes it may have stood for the whole territory of Moab. [r]**2.9** *them*: The Hebrew text has "the descendants of Lot"; the nation of Moab descended from Moab, who was the son of Lot, the nephew of Abraham.

lived there. They were the Emim, and
they were as tall as the Anakim. 11The
Moabites called them Emim, though
others sometimes used the name
Rephaim[s] for both the Anakim and the
Emim.
12The Horites used to live in Seir, but
the Edomites[t] took over that region.
They killed many of the Horites and
forced the rest of them to leave, just as
Israel did to the people in the land that
the LORD gave them.

Israel Crossed the Zered Gorge

Moses said to Israel:
13When we came to the Zered Gorge
along the southern border of Moab, the
LORD told us to cross the gorge into
Moab, and we did. 14This was thirty-
eight years after we left Kadesh-Barnea,
and by that time all the men who had
been in the army at Kadesh-Barnea had
died, just as the LORD had said they
would. 15-16The LORD kept getting rid of[u]
them until finally none of them were
left.
17Then the LORD told me, 18"Moses,
now go past the town of Ar and cross
Moab's northern border 19into Ammon.
But don't start a war with the Ammonites. I gave them[v] their land, and I
won't give any of it to Israel."

More Nations That Lived near Canaan

20Before the Ammonites conquered
the land that the LORD had given them
some of the Rephaim used to live
there, although the Ammonites called
them Zamzummim. 21The Zamzummim
were a large and powerful tribe and
were as tall as the Anakim.[w] But the
LORD helped the Ammonites, and they
killed many of the Zamzummim and
forced the rest to leave. Then the Ammonites settled there. 22The LORD helped
them as he had helped the Edomites,[x]
who killed many of the Horites in Seir
and forced the rest to leave before settling there themselves.
23A group called the Avvim used to
live in villages as far south as Gaza, but
the Philistines[y] killed them and settled
on their land.

Israel Crossed the Arnon Gorge

Moses said:
24After we went through Ammon, the
LORD told us:
Israel, pack up your possessions,
take down your tents, and cross the
Arnon River gorge.[z] The territory of
the Amorite King Sihon of Heshbon
lies on the other side of the river, but
I now give you his land. So attack
and take it! 25Today I will start making all other nations afraid of you.
They will tremble with fear when
anyone mentions you, and they will
be terrified when you show up.

The Defeat of King Sihon of Heshbon

(Numbers 21.21-30)

Moses said to Israel:
26After we had crossed the Arnon and
had set up camp in the Kedemoth
Desert, I sent messengers to King Sihon
of Heshbon, telling him that his nation
and ours could be at peace. I said:
27Please let Israel go across your
country. We will walk straight
through, without turning off the
road. 28-29You can even sell us food
and water, and we will pay with silver. We need to reach the Jordan
River and cross it, because the LORD
our God is giving us the land on the
west side. The Edomites and Moabites[a] have already let us cross
their land. Please let us cross your
land as well.
30-31But Sihon refused to let us go
across his country, because the LORD
made him stubborn and eager to fight
us. The LORD told me, "I am going to
help you defeat Sihon and take his land,
so attack him!"
32We met Sihon and his army in battle
at Jahaz, 33and the LORD our God helped
us defeat them. We killed Sihon, his
sons, and everyone else in his army.
34Then we captured and destroyed every
town in Sihon's kingdom, killing everyone, 35but keeping the livestock and
everything else of value. 36The LORD
helped us capture every town from the
Arnon River gorge north to the boundary of Gilead, including the town of
Aroer on the edge of the gorge and the
town in the middle of the gorge.
37However, we stayed away from all

[s] **2.10,11** *Emim . . . Anakim . . . Rephaim*: These may refer to a group or groups of very tall people that lived in or near Palestine before the Israelites (see also Numbers 13.33).
[t] **2.12** *Edomites*: The Hebrew text has "the descendants of Esau," who became the nation of Edom. [u] **2.15,16** *getting rid of*: Or "sending diseases on." [v] **2.19** *them*: The Hebrew text has "descendants of Lot"; the nation of Ammon descended from Benammi, who was the son of Lot, the nephew of Abraham. [w] **2.21** *Anakim*: See the note at 2.10, 11. [x] **2.22** *Edomites*: See the note at 2.12. [y] **2.23** *Philistines*: The Hebrew text has "the Caphtorim from Caphtor," probably referring to the Philistines who originally came from Crete. [z] **2.24** *Arnon River gorge*: The northern boundary of Moab's territory and the southern boundary of Sihon's kingdom. [a] **2.28,29** *Edomites and Moabites*: Hebrew "descendants of Esau, who live in Seir and Moabites who live in Ar."

the Ammonite towns, both in the hill
country and near the Jabbok River, just
as the LORD had commanded.

The Defeat of King Og of Bashan

(Numbers 21.31-35)

Moses said to Israel:

3 When we turned onto the road that
leads to Bashan, King Og of Bashan
led out his whole army to fight us at
Edrei. 2 But the LORD told me, "Moses,
don't be afraid of King Og. I am going to
help you defeat him and his army and
take over his land. Destroy him and his
people, just as you did with the Amorite
King Sihon of Heshbon."

3-6 The LORD our God helped us destroy Og and his army and conquer his
entire kingdom of Bashan, including the
Argob region. His kingdom had lots of
villages and sixty towns with high walls
and gates that locked with bars. We
completely destroyed[b] them all, killing
everyone, 7 but keeping the livestock and
everything else of value.

8 Sihon and Og had ruled Amorite
kingdoms east of the Jordan River.
Their land stretched from the Arnon
River gorge in the south to Mount Hermon in the north, and we captured it all.
9 Mount Hermon is called Mount Sirion
by the people of Sidon, and it is called
Mount Senir by the Amorites. 10 We captured all the towns in the highlands, all
of Gilead, and all of Bashan as far as
Salecah and Edrei, two of the towns that
Og had ruled.

Og's Coffin

11 King Og was the last of the
Rephaim,[c] and his coffin[d] is in the town
of Rabbah in Ammon. It is made of hard
black rock[e] and is thirteen and a half
feet long and six feet wide.

The Land East of the Jordan River Is Divided

(Numbers 32.1-42)

Moses said to Israel:

12-17 I gave some of the land and towns
we captured to the tribes of Reuben and
Gad. Their share started at the Arnon
River gorge in the south, took in the
town of Aroer on the edge of the gorge,
and went far enough north to include
the southern half of the Gilead region.
The northern part of their land went as
far east as the upper Jabbok River
gorge, which formed their border with
the Ammonites.[f] I also gave them the
eastern side of the Jordan River valley,
from Lake Galilee[g] south to the Dead
Sea[h] below the slopes of Mount Pisgah.

I gave the northern half of Gilead and
all of the Bashan region to half the tribe
of Manasseh.[i] Bashan had belonged to
King Og, and the Argob region in
Bashan used to be called the Land of
the Rephaim. Jair from the Manasseh
tribe conquered the Argob region as far
west as the kingdoms of Geshur and
Maacah. The Israelites even started calling Bashan by the name "Villages of
Jair,"[j] and that is still its name. I gave
the northern half of Gilead to the
Machir clan.[k]

18-19 At that time I told the men of
Reuben, Gad, and East Manasseh:

> The LORD our God told me to give
> you this land with its towns, and
> that's what I have done. Now your
> wives and children can stay here
> with your large flocks of sheep and
> goats and your large herds of cattle.
> But all of you men that can serve in
> our army must cross the Jordan
> River and help the other tribes, be-
> cause they are your relatives. 20 The
> LORD will let them defeat the enemy
> nations on the west side of the Jor-
> dan and take their land. Afterwards,
> you can come back here to the land I
> gave you.

21-22 Then I told Joshua, "You saw how
the LORD our God helped us destroy
King Sihon and King Og. So don't be
afraid! Wherever you go, the LORD will
fight on your side and help you destroy
your enemies."

God Refused To Let Moses Enter Canaan

Moses said to Israel:

23 At that time I prayed and begged,
24 "Our LORD, it seems that you have just
begun to show me your great power. No
other god in the sky or on earth is able
to do the mighty things that you do.
25 The land west of the Jordan is such
good land. Please let me cross the Jordan and see the hills and the Lebanon
Mountains."

[b] **3.3-6** *completely destroyed*: The Hebrew word means that the town was given completely to the LORD, and since it could not be used for normal purposes any more, it had to be destroyed. Every person was killed and sometimes all the animals as well. [c] **3.11** *Rephaim*: See the note at 2.10, 11. [d] **3.11** *coffin*: Or "bed." [e] **3.11** *hard black rock*: The Hebrew text has "iron," which probably refers to basalt, a hard black rock. [f] **3.12-17** *The northern part . . . border with the Ammonites*: The Jabbok River flowed from south to north, then it turned west and formed the northern border of the land belonging to the Reuben and Gad tribes.
[g] **3.12-17** *Lake Galilee*: The Hebrew text has "Lake Chinnereth," an earlier name.
[h] **3.12-17** *the Dead Sea*: Hebrew "the Sea of the Arabah, the Salt Sea." [i] **3.12-17** *half the tribe of Manasseh*: Or "East Manasseh." [j] **3.12-17** *Villages of Jair*: Or "Havvoth-Jair."
[k] **3.12-17** *Machir clan*: One of the clans of the Manasseh tribe.

26 But the LORD was angry with me because of you people,[l] and he refused to
listen. "That's enough!" he said. "I don't
want to hear any more. 27 Climb to the
top of Mount Pisgah and look north,
south, east, and west. Take a good look,
but you are not going to cross the Jordan River. 28 Joshua will lead Israel
across the Jordan to take the land, so
help him be strong and brave and tell
him what he must do."
29 After this we stayed in the valley at
Beth-Peor.

Israel Must Obey God

Moses said:

4 Israel, listen to these laws and
teachings! If you obey them, you
will live, and you will go in and take the
land that the LORD is giving you. He is
the God your ancestors worshiped, 2 and
now he is your God. I am telling you
everything he has commanded, so don't
add anything or take anything away.
3 You saw how he killed everyone who
worshiped the god Baal-Peor.[m] 4 But all
of you that were faithful to the LORD
your God are still alive today.
5-8 No other nation has laws that are as
fair as the ones the Lord my God told
me to give you. If you faithfully obey
them when you enter the land, you will
show other nations how wise you are. In
fact, everyone that hears about your
laws will say, "That great nation certainly is wise!" And what makes us
greater than other nations? We have a
God who is close to us and answers our
prayers.
9 You must be very careful not to forget the things you have seen God do for
you. Keep reminding yourselves, and
tell your children and grandchildren as
well. 10 Do you remember the day you
stood in the LORD's presence at Mount
Sinai?[n] The LORD said, "Moses, bring
the people of Israel here. I want to
speak to them so they will obey me as
long as they live, and so they will teach
their children to obey me too."
11 Mount Sinai[n] was surrounded by
deep dark clouds, and fire went up to
the sky. You came to the foot of the
mountain, 12 and the LORD spoke to you
from the fire. You could hear him and
understand what he was saying, but you
couldn't see him. 13 The LORD said he
was making an agreement with you,
and he told you that your part of the
agreement is to obey the Ten Commandments. Then the LORD wrote these Commandments on two flat stones.
14 That's when the LORD commanded
me to give you the laws and teachings
you must obey in the land that you will
conquer west of the Jordan River.

Don't Worship Idols

Moses said to Israel:

15 When God spoke to you from the
fire, he was invisible. So be careful 16 not
to commit the sin of worshiping idols.
Don't make idols to be worshiped,
whether they are shaped like men,
women, 17 animals, birds, 18 reptiles, or
fish. 19 And when you see the sun or
moon or stars, don't be tempted to bow
down and worship them. The LORD put
them there for all the other nations to
worship. 20 But you are the LORD's people, because he led you through fiery trials and rescued you from Egypt.
21 The LORD was angry at me because
of what you said,[o] and he told me that
he would not let me cross the Jordan
River into the good land that he is giving you.[p] 22 So I must stay here and die
on this side of the Jordan, but you will
cross the river and take the land.
23 Always remember the agreement
that the LORD your God made with you,
and don't make an idol in any shape or
form. 24 The LORD will be angry if you
worship other gods, and he can be like a
fire destroying everything in its path.
25-26 Soon you will cross the Jordan
River and settle down in the land. Then
in the years to come, you will have children, and they will give you grandchildren. After many years, you might lose
your sense of right and wrong and make
idols, even though the LORD your God
hates them. So I am giving you fair
warning today, and I call the earth and
the sky as witnesses. If you ever make
idols, the LORD will be angry, and you
won't have long to live, because the
LORD will let you be wiped out. 27 Only a
few of you will survive, and the LORD
will force you to leave the land and will
scatter you among the nations. 28 There
you will have to worship gods made of
wood and stone, and these are nothing
but idols that can't see or hear or eat or
smell.
29-30 In all of your troubles, you may finally decide that you want to worship
only the LORD. And if you turn back to
him and obey him completely, he will
again be your God. 31 The LORD your
God will have mercy—he won't destroy
you or desert you. The LORD will remember his promise, and he will keep
the agreement he made with your ancestors.
32-34 When the LORD your God brought

[l] **3.26** *But the LORD . . . people*: See 1.37.
[m] **4.3** *Baal-Peor*: See Numbers 25.1-9.
[n] **4.10** *Mount Sinai*: See the note at 1.1-5.
[n] **4.11** *Mount Sinai*: See the note at 1.1-5.
[o] **4.21** *what you said*: Or "you people."
[p] **4.21** *The LORD was angry . . . giving you*: See 1.37; 3.26.

you out of Egypt, you saw how he
fought for you and showed his great
power by performing terrifying miracles. You became his people, and at
Mount Sinai you heard him talking to
you out of fiery flames. And yet you are
still alive! Has anything like this ever
happened since the time God created
humans? No matter where you go or
who you ask, you will get the same answer. No one has ever heard of another
god even trying to do such things as the
LORD your God has done for you.
35-36 The LORD wants you to know he is
the only true God, and he wants you to
obey him. That's why he let you see his
mighty miracles and his fierce fire on
earth, and why you heard his voice from
that fire and from the sky.
37 The LORD loved your ancestors and
decided that you would be his people.
So the LORD used his great power to
bring you out of Egypt. 38 Now you face
other nations more powerful than you
are, but the LORD has already started
forcing them out of their land and giving it to you.
39 So remember that the LORD is the
only true God, whether in the sky above
or on the earth below. 40 Today I am explaining his laws and teachings. And if
you always obey them, you and your descendants will live long and be successful in the land the LORD is giving you.

Safe Towns

41-43 Moses said, "People of Israel, you
must set aside the following three towns
east of the Jordan River as Safe Towns:
Bezer in the desert highlands belonging
to the Reuben tribe; Ramoth in Gilead,
belonging to the Gad tribe; and Golan in
Bashan, belonging to the Manasseh
tribe. If you kill a neighbor without
meaning to, and if you had not been angry with that person, you can run to one
of these towns and find safety."[q]

THE SECOND SPEECH: MOSES TELLS WHAT THE LORD DEMANDS

Israel at Beth-Peor

44-46 The Israelites had come from
Egypt and were camped east of the Jordan River near Beth-Peor, when Moses
gave these laws and teachings. The land
around their camp had once belonged to
King Sihon of Heshbon. But Moses and
the Israelites defeated him 47 and King
Og of Bashan, and took their lands.
These two Amorite kings had ruled the
territory east of the Jordan River 48 from
the town of Aroer on the edge of the
Arnon River gorge, north to Mount Hermon.[r] 49 Their land included the eastern
side of the Jordan River valley, as far
south as the Dead Sea[s] below the slopes
of Mount Pisgah.

The Ten Commandments

(Exodus 20.1-17)

5 Moses called together the people of
Israel and said:
Today I am telling you the laws and
teachings that you must follow, so listen
carefully. 2 The LORD our God made an
agreement with our nation at Mount
Sinai.[t] 3 That agreement wasn't only
with[u] our ancestors but with us, who
are here today. 4 The LORD himself spoke
to you out of the fire, 5 but you were
afraid of the fire and refused to go up
the mountain. So I spoke with the LORD
for you, then I told you that he had said:
6 I am the LORD your God, the one
who brought you out of Egypt where
you were slaves.
7 Do not worship any god except
me.
8 Do not make idols that look like
anything in the sky or on earth or in
the ocean under the earth. 9 Don't
bow down and worship idols. I am
the LORD your God, and I demand all
your love. If you reject me and worship idols, I will punish your families
for three or four generations. 10 But if
you love me and obey my laws, I will
be kind to your families for thousands of generations.
11 Do not misuse my name.[v] I am
the LORD your God, and I will punish
anyone who misuses my name.
12 Show respect for the Sabbath
Day—it belongs to me. 13 You have
six days when you can do your
work, 14 but the seventh day of the
week belongs to me, your God. No
one is to work on that day—not you,
your children, your oxen or donkeys
or any other animal, not even those
foreigners who live in your towns.
And don't make your slaves do any
work. 15 This special day of rest will
remind you that I reached out my
mighty arm and rescued you from
slavery in Egypt.
16 Respect your father and mother,

[q] **4.41-43** *find safety*: From the victim's clan, who might appoint one of their men to track down and put to death the killer (see also 19.1-13). [r] **4.48** *Hermon*: The Hebrew text also includes the name "Sion," probably another form of "Sirion," the name used by the Sidonians. [s] **4.49** *the Dead Sea*: Hebrew "the Sea of the Arabah." [t] **5.2** *Mount Sinai*: See the note at 1.1-5. [u] **5.3** *wasn't only with*: Hebrew "wasn't with." [v] **5.11** *misuse my name*: Probably includes breaking promises, telling lies after swearing to tell the truth, using the LORD's name as a curse word or a magic formula, and trying to control the LORD by using his name.

and you will live a long and successful life in the land I am giving you.
17 Do not murder.
18 Be faithful in marriage.
19 Do not steal.
20 Do not tell lies about others.
21 Do not want anything that belongs to someone else. Don't want
anyone's wife or husband, house,
land, slaves, oxen, donkeys, or anything else.
22 When we were gathered on the
mountain, the LORD spoke to us in a
loud voice from the dark fiery cloud.
The LORD gave us these commands, and
only these. Then he wrote them on two
flat stones and gave them to me.

The People Were Afraid

(Exodus 20.18-21)

Moses said to Israel:
23 When fire blazed from the mountain, and you heard the voice coming
from the darkness, your tribal leaders
came to me 24 and said:
Today the LORD our God has
shown us how powerful and glorious he is. He spoke to us from the
fire, and we learned that people can
live, even though God speaks to
them. 25 But we don't want to take a
chance on being killed by that terrible fire, and if we keep on hearing
the LORD's voice, we will die. 26 Has
anyone else ever heard the only true
God speaking from fire, as we have?
And even if they have, would they
live to tell about it? 27 Moses, go up
close and listen to the LORD. Then
come back and tell us, and we will
do everything he says.
28 The LORD heard you and said:
Moses, I heard what the people
said to you, and I approve. 29 I wish
they would always worship me with
fear and trembling and be this willing to obey me! Then they and their
children would always enjoy a successful life.
30 Now, tell them to return to their
tents, 31 but you come back here to
me. After I tell you my laws and
teachings, you will repeat them to
the people, so they can obey these
laws in the land I am giving them.

Moses said:
32 Israel, you must carefully obey the
LORD's commands. 33 Follow them, because they make a path that will lead to
a long successful life in the land the
LORD your God is giving you.

The Most Important Commandment

Moses said to Israel:
6 The LORD told me to give you these
laws and teachings,[w] so you can
obey them in the land he is giving you.
Soon you will cross the Jordan River
and take that land. 2 And if you and your
descendants want to live a long time,
you must always worship the LORD and
obey his laws. 3 Pay attention, Israel! Our
ancestors worshiped the LORD, and he
promised to give us this land that is rich
with milk and honey. Be careful to obey
him, and you will become a successful
and powerful nation.
4 Listen, Israel! The LORD our God is
the only true God![x] 5 So love the LORD
your God with all your heart, soul, and
strength. 6 Memorize his laws 7 and tell
them to your children over and over
again. Talk about them all the time,
whether you're at home or walking
along the road or going to bed at night,
or getting up in the morning. 8 Write
down copies and tie them to your wrists
and foreheads to help you obey them.
9 Write these laws on the door frames of
your homes and on your town gates.

Worship Only the LORD

Moses said to Israel:
10 The LORD promised your ancestors
Abraham, Isaac, and Jacob that he
would give you this land. Now he will
take you there and give you large
towns, with good buildings that you
didn't build, 11 and houses full of good
things that you didn't put there. The
LORD will give you wells[y] that you didn't
have to dig, and vineyards and olive orchards that you didn't have to plant. But
when you have eaten so much that you
can't eat any more, 12 don't forget it was
the LORD who set you free from slavery
and brought you out of Egypt. 13 Worship
and obey the LORD your God with fear
and trembling, and promise that you
will be loyal to him.
14 Don't have anything to do with gods
that are worshiped by the nations
around you. 15 If you worship other gods,
the LORD will be furious and wipe you
off the face of the earth. The LORD your
God is with you, 16 so don't try to make
him prove that he can help you, as you
did at Massah.[z] 17 Always obey the laws
that the LORD has given you 18-19 and live
in a way that pleases him. Then you will
be able to go in and take this good land
from your enemies, just as he promised
your ancestors.
20 Someday your children will ask,

[w] **6.1** *these laws and teachings*: Or "the following commandment with its laws and teachings" (see 6.4, 5). [x] **6.4** *The LORD . . . true God*: Or "Only the LORD is our God." [y] **6.11** *wells*: Cisterns cut into the rock to collect rainwater. [z] **6.16** *Massah*: See Exodus 17.1-7; Numbers 20.2-13.

"Why did the LORD give us these laws
and teachings?"
[21]Then you will answer:
We were slaves of the king of
Egypt, but the LORD used his great
power and set us free. [22]We saw him
perform miracles and make horrible
things happen to the king, his officials, and everyone else. [23]The LORD
rescued us from Egypt, so he could
bring us into this land, as he had
promised our ancestors. [24-25]That's
why the LORD our God demands that
we obey his laws and worship him
with fear and trembling. And if we
do, he will protect us and help us be
successful.

Force the Other Nations Out of the Land

(Exodus 34.11-16)

Moses said:

7 People of Israel, the LORD your God
will help you take the land of the
Hittites, the Girgashites, the Amorites,
the Canaanites, the Perizzites, the
Hivites, and the Jebusites. These seven
nations have more people and are
stronger than Israel, but when you attack them, [2]the LORD will force them out
of the land. Then you must destroy them
without mercy. Don't make any peace
treaties with them, [3]and don't let your
sons and daughters marry any of them.
[4]If you do, those people will lead your
descendants to worship other gods and
to turn their backs on the LORD. That
will make him very angry, and he will
quickly destroy Israel.
[5]So when you conquer these nations,
tear down the altars where they worship
their gods. Break up their sacred stones,
cut down the poles that they use in worshiping the goddess Asherah, and throw
their idols in the fire.

The LORD's Chosen People

Moses said:

[6]Israel, you are the chosen people of
the LORD your God. There are many nations on this earth, but he chose only Israel to be his very own. [7]You were the
weakest of all nations, [8]but the LORD
chose you because he loves you and because he had made a promise to your
ancestors. Then with his mighty arm, he
rescued you from the king of Egypt,
who had made you his slaves.
[9]You know that the LORD your God is
the only true God. So love him and obey
his commands, and he will faithfully
keep his agreement with you and your
descendants for a thousand generations.
[10]But if you turn against the LORD, he
will quickly destroy you. [11]So be sure to
obey his laws and teachings I am giving
you today.

The LORD Will Bless You if You Obey

(Deuteronomy 28.1-14; Leviticus 26.3-13)

Moses said to Israel:

[12]If you completely obey these laws,
the LORD your God will be loyal and
keep the agreement he made with you,
just as he promised our ancestors. [13]The
LORD will love you and bless you by giving you many children and plenty of
food, wine, and olive oil. Your herds of
cattle will have many calves, and your
flocks of sheep will have many lambs.
[14]God will bless you more than any
other nation—your families will grow
and your livestock increase. [15]You will
no longer suffer with the same horrible
diseases that you sometimes had in
Egypt. You will be healthy, but the LORD
will make your enemies suffer from
those diseases.

Destroy the Nations and Their Gods

Moses said to Israel:

[16]When the LORD helps you defeat
your enemies, you must destroy them
without pity! And don't get trapped into
worshiping their gods.
[17]You may be thinking, "How can we
destroy these nations? They are more
powerful than we are." [18]But stop worrying! Just remember what the LORD your
God did to Egypt and its king. [19]You saw
how the LORD used his tremendous
power to work great miracles and bring
you out of Egypt. And he will again
work miracles for you when you face
these enemies you fear so much. [20]Some
of them may try to survive by hiding
from you, but the LORD will make them
panic, and soon they will be dead.[a] [21]So
don't be frightened when you meet them
in battle. The LORD your God is great
and fearsome, and he will fight at your
side.
[22]As you attack these nations, the
LORD will force them out little by little.
He won't let you get rid of them all at
once—if he did, there wouldn't be
enough people living in the land to keep
down the number of wild animals.
[23-24]But when you attack your enemies,
the LORD will make them panic, and you
will easily destroy them. You will defeat
them one after another until they are
gone, and no one will remember they
ever lived.
[25]After you conquer a nation, burn
their idols. Don't get trapped into wanting the silver or gold on an idol. Even
the metal on an idol is disgusting to the
LORD, [26]so destroy it. If you bring it
home with you, both you and your

[a]**7.20** *make them . . . dead*: Or "send hornets to kill them."

house will be destroyed. Stay away from
those disgusting idols!

The LORD Takes Care of You

Moses said:

8 Israel, do you want to go into the
land the LORD promised your ancestors? Do you want to capture it, live
there, and become a powerful nation?
Then be sure to obey every command I
am giving you.
[2]Don't forget how the LORD your God
has led you through the desert for the
past forty years. He wanted to find out if
you were truly willing to obey him and
depend on him, [3]so he made you go
hungry. Then he gave you manna,[b] a
kind of food that you and your ancestors had never even heard about. The
LORD was teaching you that people need
more than food to live—they need every
word that the LORD has spoken.
[4]Over the past forty years, your clothing hasn't worn out, and your feet
haven't swollen. [5]So keep in mind that
the LORD has been correcting you, just
as parents correct their children. [6]Obey
the commands the LORD your God has
given you and worship him with fear
and trembling.
[7]The LORD your God is bringing you
into a good land with streams that flow
from springs in the valleys and hills.
[8-9]You can dig for copper in those hills,
and the stones are made of iron ore.
And you won't go hungry. Wheat and
barley fields are everywhere, and so are
vineyards and orchards full of fig,
pomegranate,[c] and olive trees, and there
is plenty of honey.

Don't Forget the LORD

Moses said to Israel:
[10]After you eat and are full, give
praise to the LORD your God for the
good land he gave you. [11]Make sure that
you never forget the LORD or disobey his
laws and teachings that I am giving you
today. If you always obey them, [12]you
will have plenty to eat, and you will
build good houses to live in. [13]You will
get more and more cattle, sheep, silver,
gold, and other possessions.
[14]But when all this happens, don't be
proud! Don't forget that you were once
slaves in Egypt and that it was the LORD
who set you free. [15]Remember how he
led you in that huge and frightening
desert where poisonous snakes and
scorpions live. There was no water, but
the LORD split open a rock, and water
poured out so you could drink. [16]He also
gave you manna,[d] a kind of food your
ancestors had never even heard about.
The LORD was testing you to make you
trust him, so that later on he could be
good to you.
[17]When you become successful, don't
say, "I'm rich, and I've earned it all myself." [18]Instead, remember that the LORD
your God gives you the strength to
make a living. That's how he keeps the
promise he made to your ancestors.
[19-20]But I'm warning you—if you forget the LORD your God and worship
other gods, the LORD will destroy you,
just as he destroyed the nations you
fought.

Why the LORD Will Help Israel

Moses said:

9 Israel, listen to me! You will soon
cross the Jordan River and go into
the land to force out the nations that
live there. They are more powerful than
you are, and the walls around their
cities reach to the sky. [2]Some of these
nations are descendants of the
Anakim.[e] You know how tall and strong
they are, and you've heard that no one
can defeat them in battle. [3]But the LORD
your God has promised to go ahead of
you, like a raging fire burning everything in its path. So when you attack
your enemies, it will be easy for you to
destroy them and take their land.
[4-6]After the LORD helps you wipe out
these nations and conquer their land,
don't think he did it because you are
such good people. You aren't good—you
are stubborn! No, the LORD is going to
help you, because the nations that live
there are evil, and because he wants to
keep the promise he made to your ancestors Abraham, Isaac, and Jacob.

When Israel Made an Idol

(Exodus 32)

Moses said to Israel:
[7]Don't ever forget how you kept rebelling and making the LORD angry the
whole time you were in the desert. You
rebelled from the day you left Egypt until the day you arrived here.
[8]At Mount Sinai[f] you made the LORD
so angry that he was going to destroy
you. [9-11]It happened during those forty
days and nights that I was on the mountain, without anything to eat or drink.
He had told me to come up there so he
could give me the agreement he made
with us. And this agreement was actually the same Ten Commandments[g] he

[b]**8.3** *manna*: See Exodus 16.1-36. [c]**8.8,9** *pomegranate*: A bright red fruit that looks like an apple. [d]**8.16** *manna*: See the note at 8.3. [e]**9.2** *Anakim*: See the note at 2.10, 11. [f]**9.8** *Mount Sinai*: See the note at 1.1-5. [g]**9.9-11** *Ten Commandments*: Hebrew "commandments."

had announced to you when he spoke
from the fire on the mountain. The LORD
had written them on two flat stones with
his own hand. But after giving me the
two stones, 12 he said:
Moses, hurry down the mountain
to those people you led out of Egypt.
They have already disobeyed me
and committed the terrible sin of
making an idol.
13 I've been watching the Israelites,
and I've seen how stubborn and rebellious they are. 14 So don't try to
stop me! I am going to wipe them
out, and no one on earth will remember they ever lived. Then I will
let your descendants become an
even bigger and more powerful nation than Israel.

Moses said:
15 Fire was raging on the mountaintop
as I went back down, carrying the two
stones with the commandments on
them. 16 I saw how quickly you had
sinned and disobeyed the LORD your
God. There you were, worshiping the
metal idol you had made in the shape of
a calf. 17 So I threw down the two stones
and smashed them before your very
eyes.
18-20 I bowed down at the place of worship and prayed to the LORD, without
eating or drinking for forty days and
nights. You had committed a terrible sin
by making that idol, and the LORD hated
what you had done. He was angry
enough to destroy all of you and Aaron
as well. So I prayed for you and Aaron
as I had done before, and this time the
LORD answered my prayers.[h]
21 It was a sin for you to make that
idol, so I threw it into the fire to melt it
down. Then I took the lump of gold,
ground it into powder, and threw the
powder into the stream flowing down
the mountain.
22 You also made the LORD angry when
you were staying at Taberah,[i] at Massah,[j] and at Kibroth-Hattaavah.[k] 23 Then
at Kadesh-Barnea the LORD said, "I am
giving you the land, so go ahead and
take it!" But since you didn't trust the
LORD, you rebelled and disobeyed his
command.[l] 24 In fact, you've rebelled
against the LORD for as long as he has[m]
known you.
25 After you had made the idol in the
shape of a calf, the LORD said he was going to destroy you. So I bowed down in
front of the sacred tent for forty days
and nights, 26 and I prayed:
Our LORD, please don't wipe out
your people. You used your great
power to rescue them from Egypt
and to make them your very own.
27 Israel's ancestors Abraham, Isaac,
and Jacob obeyed you faithfully.
Think about them, and not about Israel's stubbornness, evil, and sin. 28 If
you destroy your people, the Egyptians will say, "The LORD promised
to give Israel land, but he wasn't
powerful enough to keep his promise. In fact, he hated them so much
that he took them into the desert
and killed them." 29 But you, our
LORD, chose the people of Israel to
be your own, and with your mighty
power you rescued them from
Egypt.

The Second Set of Commandments
(Exodus 34.1-10)

Moses said to the people:
10 The LORD told me to chisel out
two flat stones, just like the ones
he had given me earlier. He also commanded me to make a wooden chest,
then come up the mountain and meet
with him. 2 He told me that he would
write the same words on the new stones
that he had written on the ones I broke,
and that I could put these stones in this
sacred chest.
3 So I made a chest out of acacia wood,
and I chiseled two flat stones like the
ones I broke. Then I carried the stones
up the mountain, 4 where the LORD wrote
the Ten Commandments on them, just
as he had done the first time. The commandments were exactly what he had
announced from the fire, when you were
gathered at the mountain.
After the LORD returned the stones to
me, 5 I took them down the mountainside
and put them in the chest, just as he had
commanded. And they are still there.

Aaron Died
(Numbers 20.22-29)

Moses said to Israel:
6 Later we set up camp at the wells belonging to the descendants of Jaakan.[n]
Then we moved on and camped at
Moserah, where Aaron died and was
buried, and his son Eleazar became the
priest. 7 Next, we camped at Gudgodah
and then at Jotbathah, where there are
flowing streams.

[h] **9.18-20** *as I had done before . . . prayers*: This may refer to Moses' praying for Israel before he came down from the mountain (see Exodus 32.11-14). [i] **9.22** *Taberah*: See Numbers 11.1-3.
[j] **9.22** *Massah*: See the note at 6.16. [k] **9.22** *Kibroth-Hattaavah*: See Numbers 11.31-34.
[l] **9.23** *Kadesh-Barnea . . . you rebelled and disobeyed his command*: See Numbers 13, 14.
[m] **9.24** *he has*: The Samaritan Hebrew Text and one ancient translation; the Standard Hebrew Text "I have." [n] **10.6** *the wells . . . Jaakan*: Or "Beeroth Bene-Jaakan."

The Levites Were Appointed To Carry the Chest

Moses said to Israel:
[8]After I put the two stones in the sacred chest,[o] the LORD chose the tribe of
Levi, not only to carry the chest, but
also to serve as his priests at the place
of worship and to bless the other tribes
in his name. And they still do these
things. [9]The LORD promised that he
would always provide for the tribe of
Levi, and that's why he won't give them
any land, when he divides it among the
other tribes.

The LORD Answered the Prayers of Moses

(Exodus 34.9, 10, 27-29)

Moses said to Israel:
[10]When I had taken the second set of
stones up the mountain, I spent forty
days and nights there, just as I had done
before. Once again, the LORD answered
my prayer and did not destroy you. [11]In-
stead, he told me, "Moses, get ready to
lead the people into the land that I
promised their ancestors."[p]

What the LORD Wants

Moses said:
[12]People of Israel, what does the LORD
your God want from you? The LORD
wants you to respect and follow him, to
love and serve him with all your heart
and soul, [13]and to obey his laws and
teachings that I am giving you today. Do
this, and all will go well for you.
[14]Everything belongs to the LORD your
God, not only the earth and everything
on it, but also the sky and the highest
heavens. [15]Yet the LORD loved your ancestors and wanted them to belong to
him. So he chose them and their descendants rather than any other nation, and
today you are still his people.
[16]Remember your agreement with the
LORD and stop being so stubborn. [17]The
LORD your God is more powerful than
all other gods and lords, and his tremendous power is to be feared. His decisions are always fair, and you cannot
bribe him to change his mind. [18]The
LORD defends the rights of orphans and
widows. He cares for foreigners and
gives them food and clothing. [19]And you
should also care for them, because you
were foreigners in Egypt.
[20]Respect the LORD your God, serve
only him, and make promises in his
name alone. [21]Offer your praises to him,
because you have seen him work such
terrifying miracles for you.
[22]When your ancestors went to live in
Egypt, there were only seventy of them.
But the LORD has blessed you, and now
there are more of you than there are
stars in the sky.

If You Are Loyal to the LORD, He Will Bless You

Moses said to Israel:
11 The LORD is your God, so you
must always love him and obey
his laws and teachings. [2]Remember, he
corrected you and not your children. You
are the ones who saw the LORD use his
great power [3]when he worked miracles
in Egypt, making terrible things happen
to the king and all his people. [4]And
when the Egyptian army chased you in
their chariots, you saw the LORD drown
them and their horses in the Red Sea.[q]
Egypt still suffers from that defeat!
[5]You saw what the LORD did for you
while you were in the desert, right up to
the time you arrived here. [6]And you saw
how the LORD made the ground open up
in the middle of our camp underneath
the tents of Dathan and Abiram,[r] who
were swallowed up along with their
families, their animals, and their tents.
[7]With your own eyes, you saw the
LORD's mighty power do all these
things.
[8]Soon you will cross the Jordan River,
and if you obey the laws and teachings
I'm giving you today, you will be strong
enough to conquer the land [9]that the
LORD promised your ancestors and their
descendants. It's rich with milk and
honey, and you will live there and enjoy
it for a long time. [10]It's better land than
you had in Egypt, where you had to
struggle just to water your crops.[s] [11]But
the hills and valleys in the promised
land are watered by rain from heaven,[t]
[12]because the LORD your God keeps his
eye on this land and takes care of it all
year long.
[13]The LORD your God commands you
to love him and to serve him with all

[o]**10.8** *After . . . chest*: Or "After Israel reached Jotbathah." [p]**10.11** *lead . . . ancestors*: The LORD would later tell Moses that he would not be allowed to enter the land (see 1.37; 3.23-28; Numbers 20.10-12). [q]**11.4** *Red Sea*: Hebrew *yam suph* "Sea of Reeds," one of the marshes or fresh water lakes near the eastern part of the Nile Delta. This identification is based on Exodus 13.7—14.9, which lists towns on the route of the Israelites before crossing the sea. In the Greek translation of the Scriptures made about 200 B.C., the "Sea of Reeds," was named "Red Sea." [r]**11.6** *Dathan and Abiram*: Hebrew "Dathan and Abiram, the sons of Eliab from the Reuben tribe." [s]**11.10** *where . . . crops*: One possible meaning for the difficult Hebrew text. [t]**11.10,11** *to water your crops . . . rain from heaven*: Egypt was flat and had very little rain. All water for crops had to come from the Nile River.

your heart and soul. If you obey him,
14-15 he will send rain at the right seasons,[u] so you will have more than
enough food, wine, and olive oil, and
there will be plenty of grass for your
cattle.
16 But watch out! You will be tempted
to turn your backs on the LORD. And if
you worship other gods, 17 the LORD will
become angry and keep the rain from
falling. Nothing will grow in your fields,
and you will die and disappear from the
good land that the LORD is giving you.
18 Memorize these laws and think
about them. Write down copies and tie
them to your wrists and your foreheads
to help you obey them. 19 Teach them to
your children. Talk about them all the
time—whether you're at home or walking along the road or going to bed at
night, or getting up in the morning.
20 Write them on the door frames of your
homes and on your town gates. 21 Then
you and your descendants will live a
long time in the land that the LORD
promised your ancestors. Your families
will live there as long as the sky is
above the earth.
22 Love the LORD your God and obey
all the laws and teachings that I'm giving you today. If you live the way the
LORD wants, 23 he will help you take the
land. And even though the nations there
are more powerful than you, the LORD
will force them to leave when you attack. 24 You will capture the land everywhere you go, from the Southern Desert
to the Lebanon Mountains, and from the
Euphrates River west to the Mediterranean Sea. 25 No one will be able to
stand up to you. The LORD will make
everyone terrified of you, just as he
promised.
26 You have a choice—do you want the
LORD to bless you, or do you want him
to put a curse on you? 27 Today I am giving you his laws, and if you obey him,
he will bless you. 28 But if you disobey
him and worship those gods that have
never done anything for you, the LORD
will put a curse on you.
29 After the LORD your God helps you
take the land, you must have a ceremony where you announce his blessings
from Mount Gerizim and his curses
from Mount Ebal. 30 You know that these
two mountains are west of the Jordan
River in land now controlled by the
Canaanites living in the Jordan River
valley. The mountains are west of the
road near the sacred trees of Moreh on
the other side of Gilgal.
31 Soon you will cross the Jordan River
to conquer the land that the LORD your
God is giving you. And when you have
settled there, 32 be careful to obey his
laws and teachings that I am giving you
today.

Only One Place To Worship the LORD

Moses said to Israel:

12 Now I'll tell you the laws and
teachings that you have to obey
as long as you live. Your ancestors worshiped the LORD, and he is giving you
this land. 2 But the nations that live there
worship other gods. So after you capture the land, you must completely destroy their places of worship—on mountains and hills or in the shade of large
trees. 3 Wherever these nations worship
their gods, you must tear down their altars, break their sacred stones, burn the
sacred poles[v] used in worshiping the
goddess Asherah, and smash their idols
to pieces. Destroy these places of worship so completely that no one will remember they were ever there. 4 Don't
worship the LORD your God in the way
those nations worship their gods.
5-19 Soon you will cross the Jordan,
and the LORD will help you conquer
your enemies and let you live in peace,
there in the land he has given you. But
after you are settled, life will be different. You must not offer sacrifices just
anywhere you want to. Instead, the
LORD will choose a place somewhere in
Israel where you must go to worship
him. All of your sacrifices and offerings
must be taken there, including sacrifices
to please the LORD[w] and any gift you
promise or voluntarily give him. That's
where you must also take one tenth of
your grain, wine, and olive oil,[x] as well
as the first-born of your cattle, sheep,
and goats.[y] You and your family and servants will eat your gifts and sacrifices[z]
and celebrate there at the place of worship, because the LORD your God has

[u] **11.14,15** *rain . . . seasons*: In Palestine, almost all the rain for the year comes during the months from October through April. [v] **12.3** *sacred poles*: Or "trees," used as symbols of Asherah, the goddess of fertility. [w] **12.5-19** *sacrifices to please the LORD*: These sacrifices have traditionally been called "whole burnt offerings" because the whole animal was burned on the altar. A main purpose of such sacrifices was to please the LORD with the smell of the sacrifice, and so in the CEV they are often called "sacrifices to please the LORD."
[x] **12.5-19** *one tenth of your grain, wine, and olive oil*: The Israelites had to give one tenth of their harvest of these products to the LORD each year (see 14.22-29; 26.12, 13; Leviticus 27.30-33). [y] **12.5-19** *the first-born of your cattle, sheep, and goats*: The Israelites had to sacrifice these to the LORD (see 15.19-22). [z] **12.5-19** *sacrifices*: Some sacrifices were completely burned on the altar; in other sacrifices, part of the animal was burned and part was given to the priests, but most of the meat was eaten by the worshipers as a sacred meal.

made you successful in everything you
have done. And since Levites will not
have any land of their own, you must
ask some of them to come along and
celebrate with you.

Sometimes you may want to kill an
animal for food and not as a sacrifice. If
the LORD has blessed you and given you
enough cows or sheep or goats, then
you can butcher one of them where you
live. You can eat it just like the meat
from a deer or gazelle that you kill
when you go hunting. And even those
people who are unclean and unfit for
worship can have some of the meat. But
you must not eat the blood of any animal—let the blood drain out on the
ground.

20-21 The LORD has promised that later
on he will give Israel more land, and
some of you may not be able to travel all
the way from your homes to the place of
worship each time you are hungry for
meat.[a] But the LORD will give you cattle,
sheep, and goats, and you can butcher
any of those animals at home and eat as
much as you want. 22 It is the same as
eating the meat from a deer or a gazelle
that you kill when you go hunting. And
in this way, anyone who is unclean and
unfit for worship can have some of the
meat.[b]

23-24 But don't eat the blood. It is the
life of the animal, so let it drain out on
the ground before you eat the meat.
25 Do you want the LORD to make you
successful? Do you want your children
to be successful even after you are
gone? Then do what pleases the LORD
and don't eat blood.

26-27 All sacrifices and offerings to the
LORD must be taken to the place where
he chooses to be worshiped. If you offer
a sacrifice to please the LORD, all of its
meat must be burned on the altar. You
can eat the meat from certain kinds of
sacrifices, but you must always pour out
the animal's blood on the altar.

28 If you obey these laws, you will be
doing what the LORD your God says is
right and good. Then he will help you
and your descendants be successful.

Worship the LORD in the Right Way

Moses said:

29 Israel, as you go into the land and
attack the nations that are there, the
LORD will get rid of them, and you can
have their land.

30 But that's when you must be especially careful not to ask, "How did those
nations worship their gods? Shouldn't
we worship the LORD in the same way?"
31 No, you should not! The LORD hates
the disgusting way those nations worship their gods, because they even burn
their sons and daughters as sacrifices.

32 Obey all the laws and teachings I am
giving you. Don't add any, and don't
take any away.

Don't Worship Other Gods

Moses said to Israel:

13 1-2 Someday a prophet[c] may come
along who is able to perform miracles or tell what will happen in the future. Then the prophet may say, "Let's
start worshiping some new gods—some
gods that we know nothing about." 3 If
the prophet says this, don't listen! The
LORD your God will be watching to find
out whether or not you love him with all
your heart and soul. 4 You must be completely faithful to the LORD. Worship and
obey only the LORD and do this with
fear and trembling, 5 because he rescued
you from slavery in Egypt.

If a prophet tells you to disobey the
LORD your God and to stop worshiping
him, then that prophet is evil and must
be put to death.

6-10 Someone else may say to you,
"Let's worship other gods." That person
may be your best friend, your brother or
sister, your son or daughter, or your
own dear wife or husband. But you must
not listen to people who say such things.
Instead, you must stone them to death.
You must be the first to throw the
stones, then others from the community
will finish the job. Don't show any pity.

The gods worshiped by other nations
have never done anything for you or
your ancestors. People who ask you to
worship other gods are trying to get you
to stop worshiping the LORD, who rescued you from slavery in Egypt. So put
to death anyone who asks you to worship another god. 11 And when the rest
of Israel hears about it, they will be
afraid, and no one else will ever do such
an evil thing again.

12 After the LORD your God gives you
towns to live in, you may hear a rumor
about one of the towns. 13 You may hear
that some worthless people have talked
everyone there into worshiping other
gods, even though these gods had never
done anything for them. 14 You must
carefully find out if the rumor is true.
Then if the people of that town have actually done such a disgusting thing in
your own country, 15 you must take your
swords and kill every one of them, and

[a] **12.20,21** *meat*: Usually eaten only on special occasions, such as during a sacred meal when sacrifices were offered to the LORD. [b] **12.22** *anyone . . . the meat*: Only those who were properly prepared for worship, or "clean," could eat a sacred meal, but anyone could eat this kind of meat. [c] **13.1,2** *a prophet*: Hebrew adds "or a dreamer of dreams," another name for a prophet.

their livestock too. [16-17]Gather all the possessions of the people who lived there, and pile them up in the marketplace, without keeping anything for yourself. Set the pile and the whole town on fire, and don't ever rebuild the town. The whole town will be a sacrifice to the LORD your God. Then he won't be angry anymore, and he will have mercy on you and make you successful, just as he promised your ancestors. [18]That's why you must do what the LORD your God says is right. I am giving you his laws and teachings today, and you must obey them.

Don't Mourn like Other Nations

Moses said:

14 People of Israel, you are the LORD's children, so when you mourn for the dead, you must not cut yourselves or shave your forehead.[d] [2]Out of all the nations on this earth, the LORD your God chose you to be his own. You belong to the LORD, so don't behave like those who worship other gods.

Animals That Can Be Eaten

(Leviticus 11.1-47)

[3]Don't eat any disgusting animals.

[4-5]You may eat the meat of cattle, sheep, and goats; wild sheep and goats; and gazelles, antelopes, and all kinds of deer. [6]It is all right to eat meat from any animals that have divided hoofs and also chew the cud.[e]

[7]But don't eat camels, rabbits, and rock badgers. These animals chew the cud but do not have divided hoofs. You must treat them as unclean. [8]And don't eat pork, since pigs have divided hoofs, but they do not chew their cud. Don't even touch a dead pig!

[9]You can eat any fish that has fins and scales. But there are other creatures that live in the water, [10]and if they do not have fins and scales, you must not eat them. Treat them as unclean.

[11]You can eat any clean bird. [12-18]But don't eat the meat of any of the following birds: eagles, vultures, falcons, kites, ravens, ostriches, owls, sea gulls, hawks, pelicans, ospreys, cormorants, storks, herons, and hoopoes.[f] You must not eat bats. [19]Swarming insects are unclean, so don't eat them. [20]However, you are allowed to eat certain kinds of winged insects.[g]

[21]You belong to the LORD your God, so if you happen to find a dead animal, don't eat its meat. You may give it to foreigners who live in your town or sell it to foreigners who are visiting your town.

Don't boil a young goat in its mother's milk.

Give the LORD Ten Percent of Your Harvest

Moses said:

[22]People of Israel, every year you must set aside ten percent of your grain harvest. [23]Also set aside ten percent of your wine and olive oil, and the first-born of every cow, sheep, and goat. Take these to the place where the LORD chooses to be worshiped, and eat them there. This will teach you to always respect the LORD your God.

[24]But suppose you can't carry that ten percent of your harvest to the place where the LORD chooses to be worshiped. If you live too far away, or if the LORD gives you a big harvest, [25]then sell this part and take the money there instead. [26]When you and your family arrive, spend the money on food for a big celebration. Buy cattle, sheep, goats, wine, beer, and if there are any other kinds of food that you want, buy those too. [27]And since people of the Levi tribe won't own any land for growing crops, remember to ask the Levites to celebrate with you.

[28]Every third year, instead of using the ten percent of your harvest for a big celebration, bring it into town and put it in a community storehouse. [29]The Levites have no land of their own, so you must give them food from the storehouse. You must also give food to the poor who live in your town, including orphans, widows, and foreigners. If they have enough to eat, then the LORD your God will be pleased and make you successful in everything you do.

Loans

(Leviticus 25.1-7)

Moses said:

15 [1-2]Every seven years you must announce, "The LORD says loans do not need to be paid back." Then if you have loaned money to another Israelite, you can no longer ask for payment.[h] [3]This law applies only to loans you have

[d]14.1 *when you mourn . . . forehead*: Or "you must not worship Baal, cutting yourselves and shaving your forehead." [e]14.6 *chew the cud*: Some animals that eat grass and leaves have more than one stomach, and they chew their food a second time, after it has been partly digested in the first stomach. This partly digested food is called "cud." [f]14.12-18 *eagles . . . hoopoes*: Some of the birds in this list are difficult to identify. [g]14.20 *certain kinds of winged insects*: These were locusts, crickets, and grasshoppers; see Leviticus 11.21, 22.
[h]15.1,2 *The LORD says . . . no longer ask for payment*: Or " 'The LORD says loans do not need to be paid back this year.' Then if you have loaned money to another Israelite, you cannot ask for payment until the next year."

made to other Israelites. Foreigners will
still have to pay back what you have
loaned them.
4-6No one in Israel should ever be
poor. The LORD your God is giving you
this land, and he has promised to make
you very successful, if you obey his laws
and teachings that I'm giving you today.
You will lend money to many nations,
but you won't have to borrow. You will
rule many nations, but they won't rule
you.
7After the LORD your God gives land
to each of you, there may be poor Israelites in the town where you live. If
there are, then don't be mean and selfish with your money. 8Instead, be kind
and lend them what they need. 9Be careful! Don't say to yourself, "Soon it will
be the seventh year, and then I won't be
able to get my money back." It would be
horrible for you to think that way and to
be so selfish that you refuse to help the
poor. They are your relatives, and if you
don't help them, they may ask the LORD
to decide whether you have done wrong.
And he will say that you are guilty.
10You should be happy to give the poor
what they need, because then the LORD
will make you successful in everything
you do.
11There will always be some Israelites
who are poor and needy. That's why I
am commanding you to be generous
with them.

Setting Slaves Free

(Exodus 21.1-11)

Moses said to Israel:
12If any of you buy Israelites as slaves,
you must set them free after six years.
13And don't just tell them they are free
to leave—14give them sheep and goats
and a good supply of grain and wine.
The more the LORD has given you, the
more you should give them. 15I am commanding you to obey the LORD as a reminder that you were slaves in Egypt
before he set you free. 16But one of your
slaves may say, "I love you and your
family, and I would be better off staying
with you, so please don't make me
leave." 17Take the slave to the door of
your house and push a sharp metal rod
through one earlobe and into the door.
Such slaves will belong to you for life,
whether they are men or women.
18Don't complain when you have to
set a slave free. After all, you got six
years of service at half the cost of hiring
someone to do the work.[i]

First-Born Animals

(Leviticus 27.26, 27; Numbers 18.15-18)

Moses said to Israel:
19If the first-born animal of a cow or
sheep or goat is a male, it must be given
to the LORD. Don't put first-born cattle
to work or cut wool from first-born
sheep. 20Instead, each year you must
take the first-born of these animals to
the place where the LORD your God
chooses to be worshiped. You and your
family will sacrifice them to the LORD
and then eat them as part of a sacred
meal.
21But if the animal is lame or blind or
has something else wrong with it, you
must not sacrifice it to the LORD your
God. 22You can butcher it where you
live, and eat it just like the meat of a
deer or gazelle that you kill while hunting. Even those people who are unclean
and unfit for worship can have some.
23But you must never eat the blood of an
animal—let it drain out on the ground.

Passover

(Exodus 12.1-20; Leviticus 23.4-8)

Moses said:
16 People of Israel, you must celebrate Passover in the month of
Abib,[j] because one night in that month
years ago, the LORD your God rescued
you from Egypt. 2The Passover sacrifice
must be a cow, a sheep, or a goat, and
you must offer it at the place where the
LORD chooses to be worshiped. 3-4Eat all
of the meat of the Passover sacrifice that
same night. But don't serve bread made
with yeast at the Passover meal. Serve
the same kind of thin bread that you ate
when you were slaves suffering in
Egypt[k] and when you had to leave
Egypt quickly. As long as you live, this
thin bread will remind you of the day
you left Egypt.
For seven days following Passover,[l]
don't make any bread with yeast. In
fact, there should be no yeast anywhere
in Israel.
5Don't offer the Passover sacrifice in
just any town where you happen to live.
6It must be offered at the place where
the LORD chooses to be worshiped. Kill
the sacrifice at sunset, the time of day

[i] **15.18** *six years . . . work*: Or "six years of service, and it cost you no more than if you had hired someone to do the work"; or "six years of service, for what you would have had to pay a worker for two years." [j] **16.1** *in the month of Abib*: Abib (also called Nisan), the first month of the Hebrew calendar, from about mid-March to mid-April. Passover was celebrated on the evening of the fourteenth of Abib (see Exodus 12.6; Leviticus 23.4, 5). [k] **16.3,4** *the same kind . . . in Egypt*: One possible meaning for the difficult Hebrew text. [l] **16.3,4** *seven days following Passover*: This period was called the Festival of Thin Bread (see also verse 16).

when you left Egypt.[m] [7]Then cook it and
eat it there at the place of worship, returning to your tents the next morning.
[8]Eat thin bread for the next six days.
Then on the seventh day, don't do any
work. Instead, come together and worship the LORD.

The Harvest Festival

(Exodus 34.22; Leviticus 23.15-21)

Moses said to Israel:
[9]Seven weeks after you start your
grain harvest, [10-11]go to the place where
the LORD chooses to be worshiped and
celebrate the Harvest Festival[n] in honor
of the LORD your God. Bring him an offering as large as you can afford, depending on how big a harvest he has
given you. Be sure to take along your
sons and daughters and all your servants. Also invite the poor, including
Levites, foreigners, orphans, and widows. [12]Remember that you used to be
slaves in Egypt, so obey these laws.

The Festival of Shelters

(Leviticus 23.33-43; Numbers 29.12-38)

Moses said to Israel:
[13-15]After you have finished the grain
harvest and the grape harvest,[o] take
your sons and daughters and all your
servants to the place where the LORD
chooses to be worshiped. Celebrate the
Festival of Shelters for seven days. Also
invite the poor, including Levites, foreigners, orphans, and widows.

The LORD will give you big harvests
and make you successful in everything
you do. You will be completely happy, so
celebrate this festival in honor of the
LORD your God.

Three Festivals at the Place of Worship

(Exodus 23.14-17)

Moses said:
[16]Each year there are three festivals
when all Israelite men must go to the
place where the LORD chooses to be
worshiped. These are the Festival of
Thin Bread, the Harvest Festival,[p] and
the Festival of Shelters. And don't forget
to take along a gift for the LORD. [17]The
bigger the harvest the LORD gives you,
the bigger your gift should be.

Treat Everyone with Justice

Moses said to Israel:
[18-19]After you are settled in the towns
that you will receive from the LORD your
God, the people in each town must appoint judges and other officers. Those of
you that become judges must be completely fair when you make legal decisions, even if someone important is involved. Don't take bribes to give unfair
decisions. Bribes keep people who are
wise from seeing the truth and turn honest people into liars.[q]
[20]People of Israel, if you want to enjoy
a long and successful life, make sure
that everyone is treated with justice in
the land the LORD is giving you.

Don't Set Up Sacred Poles or Stones

Moses said to Israel:
[21]When you build the altar for offering sacrifices to the LORD your God,
don't set up a sacred pole[r] for the worship of the goddess Asherah. [22]And
don't set up a sacred stone! The LORD
hates these things.

Sacrifices That Have Something Wrong with Them

Moses said to Israel:
17 If an ox or a sheep has something
wrong with it, don't offer it as a
sacrifice to the LORD your God—he will
be disgusted!

Put To Death People Who Worship Idols

Moses said to Israel:
[2-3]The LORD your God is giving you
towns to live in. But later, a man or a
woman in your town may start worshiping other gods, or even the sun, moon,
or stars.[s] I have warned you not to worship other gods, because whoever worships them is disobeying the LORD and
breaking the agreement he made with
you. [4]So when you hear that someone in
your town is committing this disgusting
sin, you must carefully find out if that
person really is guilty. [5-7]But you will
need two or three witnesses—one witness isn't enough to prove a person
guilty.

Get rid of those who are guilty of such
evil. Take them outside your town gates
and have everyone stone them to death.
But the witnesses must be the first to
throw stones.

Difficult Cases

Moses said to Israel:
[8-12]It may be difficult to find out the
truth in some legal cases in your town.
You may not be able to decide if some-

[m] **16.6** *sunset, the time of day when you left Egypt*: Or "sunset on the same date as when you left Egypt." [n] **16.10,11** *Harvest Festival*: Traditionally called the "Festival of Weeks," and known in New Testament times as "Pentecost." [o] **16.13-15** *After you . . . harvest*: Leviticus 23.34 gives the exact date as the fifteenth day of the seventh month of the Hebrew calendar, which would be early in October. [p] **16.16** *Harvest Festival*: See the note at 16.10, 11. [q] **16.18,19** *turn . . . liars*: Or "keep innocent people from getting justice." [r] **16.21** *sacred pole*: See the note at 12.3. [s] **17.2,3** *sun, moon, or stars*: Some people thought these were gods and worshiped them.

one was killed accidentally or murdered. Or you may not be able to tell
whether an injury or some property
damage was done by accident or on
purpose. If the case is too difficult, take
it to the court at the place where the
LORD your God chooses to be worshiped.
This court will be made up of one
judge and several priests[t] who serve at
the LORD's altar. They will explain the
law to you and give you their decision
about the case. Do exactly what they tell
you, or you will be put to death. [13]When
other Israelites hear about it, they will
be afraid and obey the decisions of the
court.

The King

Moses said:
[14]People of Israel, after you capture
the land the LORD your God is giving
you, and after you settle on it, you will
say, "We want a king, just like the nations around us."
[15]Go ahead and appoint a king, but
make sure that he is an Israelite and
that he is the one the LORD has chosen.
[16]The king should not have many
horses, especially those from Egypt. The
LORD has said never to go back there
again. [17]And the king must not have a
lot of wives—they might tempt him to
be unfaithful to the LORD.[u] Finally, the
king must not try to get huge amounts
of silver and gold.
[18]The official copy of God's laws[v] will
be kept by the priests of the Levi tribe.
So, as soon as anyone becomes king, he
must go to the priests and write out a
copy of these laws while they watch.
[19]Each day the king must read and obey
these laws, so that he will learn to worship the LORD with fear and trembling
[20]and not think that he's better than
everyone else.
If the king completely obeys the
LORD's commands, he and his descendants will rule Israel for many years.

Special Privileges for Priests and Levites

(Numbers 18.8-32)

Moses said to Israel:
18 The people of the Levi tribe, including the priests, will not receive any land. Instead, they will receive
part of the sacrifices that are offered to
the LORD, [2]because he has promised to
provide for them in this way.
[3]When you sacrifice a bull or sheep,
the priests will be given the shoulder,
the jaws, and the stomach.[w] [4]In addition, they will receive the first part of
your grain harvest and part of your first
batches of wine and olive oil.[x] You must
also give them the first wool that is cut
from your sheep each year. [5]Give these
gifts to the priests, because the LORD
has chosen them and their descendants
out of all the tribes of Israel to be his
special servants at the place of worship.
[6]Any Levite can leave his hometown,
and go to the place where the LORD
chooses to be worshiped, [7]and then be a
special servant of the LORD[y] there, just
like all the other Levites. [8]Some Levites
may have money from selling family
possessions, and others may not. But all
Levites serving at the place of worship
will receive the same amount of food
from the sacrifices and gifts brought by
the people.

Don't Do Disgusting Things

Moses said to Israel:
[9]Soon you will go into the land that
the LORD your God is giving you. The
nations that live there do things that are
disgusting to the LORD, and you must
not follow their example. [10-11]Don't sacrifice your son or daughter. And don't
try to use any kind of magic or witchcraft to tell fortunes[z] or to cast spells or
to talk with spirits of the dead.
[12]The LORD is disgusted with anyone
who does these things, and that's why
he will help you destroy the nations that
are in the land. [13]Never be guilty of doing any of these disgusting things!

A Prophet like Moses

Moses said to Israel:
[14]You will go in and take the land
from nations that practice magic and
witchcraft. But the LORD your God won't
allow you to do those things. [15]Instead,
he will choose one of your own people
to be a prophet just like me, and you
must do what that prophet says. [16]You
were asking for a prophet the day you

[t] **17.8-12** *several priests*: The Hebrew text has "the priests, the Levites"; priests belonged to the Levi tribe. [u] **17.17** *a lot of wives . . . unfaithful to the LORD*: A king would often marry the daughter of another king that he was making a treaty with. These foreign women would naturally want to worship their own gods, and would want their husband the king to do so as well. [v] **17.18** *God's laws*: Or "God's laws for the king." [w] **18.3** *stomach*: Certain portions of the stomach were considered a delicacy. [x] **18.4** *grain . . . olive oil*: An Israelite was supposed to offer the first part of the harvest as a gift to the LORD (see Leviticus 23.10, 11). [y] **18.7** *a special servant of the LORD*: Or "one of the LORD's priests." [z] **18.10,11** *tell fortunes*: Fortunetellers thought they could learn secrets or learn about the future by watching the flight of birds or looking at the livers of animals or in many other ways.

were gathered at Mount Sinai[a] and said
to the LORD, "Please don't let us hear
your voice or see this terrible fire
again—if we do, we will die!"
17 Then the LORD told me:
Moses, they have said the right
thing. 18 So when I want to speak to
them, I will choose one of them to be
a prophet like you. I will give my
message to that prophet, who will
tell the people exactly what I have
said. 19 Since the message comes
from me, anyone who doesn't obey
the message will have to answer to
me.
20 But if I haven't spoken, and a
prophet claims to have a message
from me, you must kill that prophet,
and you must also kill any prophet
who claims to have a message from
another god.

Moses said to Israel:
21 You may be asking yourselves,
"How can we tell if a prophet's message
really comes from the LORD?" 22 You will
know, because if the LORD says something will happen, it will happen. And if
it doesn't, you will know that the
prophet was falsely claiming to speak
for the LORD. Don't be afraid of any
prophet whose message doesn't come
from the LORD.

Safe Towns

(Numbers 35.9-28; Joshua 20.1-9)

Moses said to Israel:
19 Soon you will go into the land
and attack the nations. The LORD
your God will destroy them and give
you their lands, towns, and homes. Then
after you are settled, 2-4 you must choose
three of your towns to be Safe Towns.
Divide the land into three regions with
one Safe Town near the middle of each,
so that a Safe Town can be easily
reached from anywhere in your land.
Then, if one of you accidentally kills
someone, you can run to a Safe Town
and find protection from being put to
death. But you must not have been angry with the person you killed.
5 For example, suppose you and a
friend go into the forest to cut wood. You
are chopping down a tree with an ax,
when the ax head slips off the handle,
hits your friend, and kills him. You can
run to one of the Safe Towns and save
your life. 6 You don't deserve to die, since
you did not mean to harm your friend.
But he did get killed, and his relatives
might be very angry. They might even
choose one of the men from their family
to track you down and kill you. If it is
too far to one of the Safe Towns, the victim's relative might be able to catch you
and kill you. 7 That's why I said there
must be three Safe Towns.
8-9 Israel, the LORD your God has
promised that if you obey his laws and
teachings I'm giving you, and if you always love him, then he will give you the
land he promised your ancestors. When
that happens, you must name three
more Safe Towns in the new territory.
10 You will need them, so innocent people won't be killed on your land while
they are trying to reach a Safe Town
that is too far away. You will be guilty of
murder, if innocent people lose their
lives because you didn't name enough
Safe Towns in the land the LORD your
God will give you.
11 But what if you really do commit
murder? Suppose one of you hates a
neighbor. So you wait in a deserted
place, kill the neighbor, and run to a
Safe Town. 12 If that happens, the leaders
of your town must send messengers to
bring you back from the Safe Town.
They will hand you over to one of the
victim's relatives, who will put you to
death.
13 Israel, for the good of the whole
country, you must kill anyone who murders an innocent person. Never show
mercy to a murderer!

Property Lines

Moses said to Israel:
14 In the land the LORD is giving you,
there are already stones set up to mark
the property lines between fields. So
don't move those stones.

Witnesses Must Tell the Truth

Moses said to Israel:
15 Before you are convicted of a crime,
at least two witnesses must be able to
testify that you did it.
16 If you accuse someone of a crime,
but seem to be lying, 17-18 then both you
and the accused must be taken to the
court at the place where the LORD is
worshiped. There the priests and judges
will find out if you are lying or telling
the truth.
If you are lying and the accused is innocent, 19-21 then you will be punished
without mercy. You will receive the same
punishment the accused would have received if found guilty, whether it means
losing an eye, a tooth, a hand, a foot, or
even your life.
Israel, the crime of telling lies in court
must be punished. And when people
hear what happens to witnesses that lie,
everyone else who testifies in court will
tell the truth.

[a] **18.16** *Mount Sinai*: See the note at 1.1-5.

Laws for Going to War

Moses said to Israel:

20 If you have to go to war, you may find yourselves facing an enemy army that is bigger than yours and that has horses and chariots. But don't be afraid! The LORD your God rescued you from Egypt, and he will help you fight. 2Before you march into battle, a priest will go to the front of the army 3and say, "Soldiers of Israel, listen to me! Today when you go into battle, don't be afraid of the enemy, and when you see them, don't panic. 4The LORD your God will fight alongside you and help you win the battle."

5Then the tribal officials will say to the troops:

> If any of you have built a new house, but haven't yet moved in, you may go home. It isn't right for you to die in battle and for somebody else to live in your new house.
>
> 6If any of you have planted a vineyard but haven't had your first grape harvest, you may go home. It isn't right for you to die in battle and for somebody else to enjoy your grapes.
>
> 7If any of you are engaged to be married, you may go back home and get married. It isn't right for you to die in battle and for somebody else to marry the woman you are engaged to.
>
> 8Finally, if any of you are afraid, you may go home. We don't want you to discourage the other soldiers.

9When the officials are finished giving these orders, they will appoint officers to be in command of the army.

10-15Before you attack a town that is far from your land, offer peace to the people who live there. If they surrender and open their town gates, they will become your slaves. But if they reject your offer of peace and try to fight, surround their town and attack. Then, after the LORD helps you capture it, kill all the men. Take the women and children as slaves and keep the livestock and everything else of value.

16Whenever you capture towns in the land the LORD your God is giving you, be sure to kill all the people and animals. 17He has commanded you to completely wipe out the Hittites, the Amorites, the Canaanites, the Perizzites, the Hivites, and the Jebusites. 18If you allow them to live, they will persuade you to worship their disgusting gods, and you will be unfaithful to the LORD.

19When you are attacking a town, don't chop down its fruit trees, not even if you have had the town surrounded for a long time. Fruit trees aren't your enemies, and they produce food that you can eat, so don't cut them down. 20You may need wood to make ladders and towers to help you get over the walls and capture the town. But use only trees that you know are not fruit trees.

Unsolved Murder

Moses said to Israel:

21 Suppose the body of a murder victim is found in a field in the land the LORD your God is giving you, and no one knows who the murderer is. 2The judges and other leaders from the towns around there must find out what town is the closest to where the body was found. 3The leaders from that town will go to their cattle herds and choose a young cow that has never been put to work.[b] 4-5They and some of the priests will take this cow to a nearby valley where there is a stream, but no crops. Once they reach the valley, the leaders will break the cow's neck.

The priests must be there, because the LORD your God has chosen them to be his special servants at the place of worship. The LORD has chosen them to bless the people in his name and to be judges in all legal cases, whether property or injury is involved.

6The town leaders will wash their hands over the body of the dead cow 7and say, "We had no part in this murder, and we don't know who did it. 8-9But since an innocent person was murdered, we beg you, our LORD, to accept this sacrifice and forgive Israel. We are your people, and you rescued us. Please don't hold this crime against us."

If you obey the LORD and do these things, he will forgive Israel.

Marrying a Woman Taken Prisoner in War

Moses said to Israel:

10From time to time, you men will serve as soldiers and go off to war. The LORD your God will help you defeat your enemies, and you will take many prisoners. 11-13One of these prisoners may be a beautiful woman, and you may want to marry her. But first you must bring her into your home, and have her shave her head, cut her nails, get rid of her foreign clothes, and start wearing Israelite clothes. She will mourn a month for her father and mother, then you can marry her.

14Later on, if you are not happy with the woman, you can divorce her, and she can go free. But you have slept with her as your wife, so you cannot sell her as a slave or make her into your own slave.

[b]**21.3** *young cow . . . work*: Cows and oxen pulled plows and wagons.

Rights of a First-Born Son

Moses said to Israel:

15-17 Suppose a man has two wives and loves one more than the other. The first son of either wife is the man's first-born son, even if the boy's mother is the wife the man doesn't love. Later, when the man is near death and is dividing up his property, he must give a double share to his first-born son, simply because he was the first to be born.

A Son Who Rebels

Moses said to Israel:

18 A father and a mother may have a stubborn and rebellious son who refuses to obey them even after he has been punished. 19 If a son is like that, his parents must drag him to the town gate, where the leaders of the town hold their meetings. 20 The parents will tell the leaders, "This son of ours is stubborn and never obeys. He spends all his time drinking and partying."

21 The men of the town will stone that son to death, because they must get rid of the evil he brought into the community. Everyone in Israel will be afraid when they hear how he was punished.

The Body of a Criminal

Moses said to Israel:

22 If a criminal is put to death, and you hang the dead body on a tree, 23 you must not let it hang there overnight. Bury it the same day, because the dead body of a criminal will bring God's curse on the land. The LORD your God is giving this land to you, so don't make it unclean by leaving the bodies of executed criminals on display.

Helping Others

Moses said to Israel:

22 If you see a cow or sheep wandering around lost, take the animal back to its owner. 2 If the owner lives too far away, or if you don't know who the owner is, take the animal home with you and take care of it. The owner will come looking for the animal, and then you can give it back. 3 That's what you should do if you find anything that belongs to someone else. Do whatever you can to help, whether you find a cow or sheep or donkey or some clothing.

4 Oxen and donkeys that carry heavy loads can stumble and fall, and be unable to get up by themselves. So as you walk along the road, help anyone who is trying to get an ox or donkey back on its feet.

Don't Pretend To Be the Opposite Sex

Moses said to Israel:

5 Women must not pretend to be men, and men must not pretend to be women.[c] The LORD your God is disgusted with people who do that.

Don't Take a Mother Bird

Moses said to Israel:

6-7 As you walk along the road, you might see a bird's nest in a tree or on the ground. If the mother bird is in the nest with either her eggs or her baby birds, you are allowed to take the baby birds or the eggs, but not the mother bird. Let her go free, and the LORD will bless you with a long and successful life.

Put a Wall around Your Flat Roof

8 If you build a house, make sure to put a low wall around the edge of the flat roof.[d] Then if someone falls off the roof and is killed, it won't be your fault.

Laws against Mixing Different Things

Moses said to Israel:

9 If you plant a vineyard, don't plant any other fruit tree or crop in it. If you do plant something else there, you must bring to the place of worship everything you harvest from the vineyard.

10 Don't hitch an ox and a donkey to your plow at the same time.

11 When you weave cloth for clothing, you can use thread made of flax[e] or wool, but not both together. 12 And when you make a coat, sew a tassel on each of the four corners.

When a Husband Accuses His Wife

Moses said to Israel:

13 Suppose a man starts hating his wife soon after they are married. 14 He might tell ugly lies about her, and say, "I married this woman, but when we slept together, I found out she wasn't a virgin."

15 If this happens, the bride's father and mother must go to the town gate to show the town leaders the proof that the woman was a virgin. 16 Her father will say, "I let my daughter marry this man, but he started hating her 17 and accusing her of not being a virgin. But he is

[c] **22.5** *pretend to be men . . . pretend to be women*: Or "wear men's clothing . . . wear women's clothing." [d] **22.8** *flat roof*: Houses usually had flat roofs. In hot dry weather, it was cooler on the roof than in the house, and so roofs were used for sleeping and living quarters, and for entertaining guests. [e] **22.11** *flax*: The stalks of flax plants were harvested, soaked in water, and dried, then their fibers were separated and spun into thread, which was woven into linen cloth.

wrong, because here is proof that she
was a virgin!" Then the bride's parents
will show them the bed sheet from the
woman's wedding night.
18The town leaders will beat the man
with a whip 19because he accused his
bride of not being a virgin. He will have
to pay her father one hundred pieces of
silver and will never be allowed to divorce her.
20But if the man was right and there is
no proof that his bride was a virgin,
21the men of the town will take the
woman to the door of her father's house
and stone her to death.
This woman brought evil into your
community by sleeping with someone
before she got married, and you must
get rid of that evil by killing her.

Laws about Illegal Sex

Moses said:
22People of Israel, if a man is caught
having sex with someone else's wife,
you must put them both to death. That
way, you will get rid of the evil they
have done in Israel.
23-24If a man is caught in town having
sex with an engaged woman who isn't
screaming for help, they both must be
put to death. The man is guilty of having
sex with a married woman.[f] And the
woman is guilty because she didn't call
for help, even though she was inside a
town and people were nearby. Take
them both to the town gate and stone
them to death. You must get rid of the
evil they brought into your community.
25If an engaged woman is raped out in
the country, only the man will be put to
death. 26Do not punish the woman at all;
she has done nothing wrong, and certainly nothing deserving death. This
crime is like murder, 27because the
woman was alone out in the country
when the man attacked her. She
screamed, but there was no one to help
her.
28Suppose a woman isn't engaged to
be married, and a man talks her into
sleeping with him. If they are caught,
29they will be forced to get married. He
must give her father fifty pieces of silver
as a bride-price and[g] can never divorce
her.
30A man must not marry a woman
who was married to his father. This
would be a disgrace to his father.

Who Cannot Become One of the LORD's People

Moses said to Israel:
23 If a man's private parts have been
crushed or cut off,[h] he cannot
fully belong to the LORD's people.
2No one born outside of a legal marriage, or any of their descendants for
ten generations, can fully belong to the
LORD's people.
3No Ammonites or Moabites, or any of
their descendants for ten generations,
can become part of Israel, the LORD's
people. 4This is because when you came
out of Egypt, they refused to provide
you with food and water. And besides,
they hired Balaam[i] to put a curse on
you. 5But the LORD your God loves you,
so he refused to listen to Balaam and
turned Balaam's curse into a blessing.
6Don't even think of signing a peace
treaty with Moab or Ammon.
7But Edomites are your relatives, and
you lived as foreigners in the country of
Egypt. Now you must be kind to
Edomites and Egyptians 8and let their
great-grandchildren become part of Israel, the LORD's people.

Keep the Army Camp Acceptable

Moses said to Israel:
9When you men go off to fight your
enemies, make sure your camp is acceptable to the LORD.
10For example, if something happens
at night that makes a man unclean and
unfit for worship, he[j] must go outside
the camp and stay there 11until late afternoon. Then he must take a bath, and
at sunset he can go back into camp.
12Set up a place outside the camp to
be used as a toilet area. 13And make
sure that you have a small shovel in
your equipment. When you go out to the
toilet area, use the shovel to dig a hole.
Then, after you relieve yourself, bury
the waste in the hole. 14You must keep
your camp clean of filthy and disgusting
things. The LORD is always present in
your camp, ready to rescue you and give
you victory over your enemies. But if he
sees something disgusting in your camp,
he may turn around and leave.

Runaway Slaves from Other Countries

Moses said:
15When runaway slaves from other
countries come to Israel and ask for

[f]**22.23,24** *engaged woman . . . married woman*: An engaged woman was legally married, but had not yet slept with her husband or started living with him. [g]**22.28,29** *talks her into sleeping with him . . . bride-price and*: Or "forces her to have sex. 29Then if they are caught, he will have to marry her. He must give her father fifty pieces of silver as a bride-price and."
[h]**23.1** *a man's private parts have been crushed or cut off*: This was sometimes done to show devotion to pagan gods. [i]**23.4** *Balaam*: Hebrew "Balaam son of Beor from Pethor."
[j]**23.10** *if something . . . worship, he*: Or "if a man has a flow of semen at night, he is unclean and unfit for worship, and he."

protection, you must not hand them back to their owners. [16]Instead, you must let them choose which one of your towns they want to live in. Don't be cruel to runaway slaves.

Temple Prostitutes

Moses said:

[17]People of Israel, don't any of you ever be temple prostitutes.[k] [18]The LORD your God is disgusted with men and women who are prostitutes of any kind, and he will not accept a gift from them, even if it had been promised to him.

Interest on Loans

Moses said:

[19]When you lend money, food, or anything else to another Israelite, you are not allowed to charge interest. [20]You can charge a foreigner interest. But if you charge other Israelites interest, the LORD your God will not let you be successful in the land you are about to take.

Sacred Promises to the LORD

Moses said:

[21]People of Israel, if you make a sacred promise to give a gift to the LORD, then do it as soon as you can. If the LORD has to come looking for the gift you promised, you will be guilty of breaking that promise. [22]On the other hand, if you never make a sacred promise, you can't be guilty of breaking it. [23]You must keep whatever promises you make to the LORD. After all, you are the one who chose to make the promises.

Eating Someone Else's Produce

[24]If you go into a vineyard that belongs to someone else, you are allowed to eat as many grapes as you want while you are there. But don't take any with you when you leave. [25]In the same way, if you are in a grain field that belongs to someone else, you can pick heads of grain and eat the kernels. But don't cut down the stalks of grain and take them with you.

A Law about Divorce

Moses said to Israel:

24 Suppose a woman was divorced by her first husband because he found something disgraceful about her.[l] He wrote out divorce papers, gave them to her, and sent her away. [2]Later she married another man, [3]who then either divorced her in the same way or died. [4]Since she has slept with her second husband, she cannot marry her first husband again. Their marriage would pollute the land that the LORD your God is giving you, and he would be disgusted.

Newlyweds

Moses said to Israel:

[5]If a man and a woman have been married less than one year, he must not be sent off to war or sent away to do forced labor. He must be allowed to stay home for a year and be happy with his wife.

Loans

Moses said to Israel:

[6]When you lend money to people, you are allowed to keep something of theirs as a guarantee that they will pay back the loan. But don't take one or both of their millstones, or else they may starve. They need these stones for grinding grain into flour to make bread.

Kidnapping

Moses said to Israel:

[7]If you are guilty of kidnapping Israelites and forcing them into slavery, you will be put to death to remove this evil from the community.

Skin Diseases

Moses said to Israel:

[8]I have told the priests[m] what to do if any of you have leprosy,[n] so do exactly what they say. [9]And remember what the LORD your God did to Miriam[o] after you left Egypt.

Loans

Moses said to Israel:

[10]When you lend money to people, you are allowed to keep something of theirs as a guarantee that the money will be paid back. But you must not go into their house to get it. [11]Wait outside, and they will bring out the item you have agreed on.

[12]Suppose someone is so poor that a coat is the only thing that can be offered as a guarantee on a loan. Don't keep the coat overnight. [13]Instead, give it back before sunset, so the owner can keep warm and sleep and ask the LORD to bless you. Then the LORD your God will notice that you have done the right thing.

[k]23.17 *temple prostitutes*: Some Canaanites worshiped by going to their temples and having sex with prostitutes that represented their gods. [l]24.1 *something disgraceful about her*: One possible meaning for the difficult Hebrew text. [m]24.8 *the priests*: See the note at 17.8-12. [n]24.8 *leprosy*: The word "leprosy" was used for many different kinds of skin diseases. [o]24.9 *what the LORD your God did to Miriam*: See Numbers 12.1-16.

Poor People's Wages

Moses said:
14 If you hire poor people to work for
you, don't hold back their pay,[p] whether
they are Israelites or foreigners who live
in your town. 15 Pay them their wages at
the end of each day, because they live in
poverty and need the money to survive.
If you don't pay them on time, they will
complain about you to the LORD, and he
will punish you.

The Death Penalty

Moses said to Israel:
16 Parents must not be put to death for
crimes committed by their children, and
children must not be put to death for
crimes committed by their parents.
Don't put anyone to death for someone
else's crime.

Don't Mistreat the Powerless

Moses said to Israel:
17 Make sure that orphans and foreigners are treated fairly. And if you lend
money to a widow and want to keep
something of hers to guarantee that she
will pay you back, don't take any of her
clothes. 18 You were slaves in Egypt until
the LORD your God rescued you. That's
why I am giving you these laws.

Leave Some of Your Harvest for the Poor

Moses said to Israel:
19 If you forget to bring in a stack of
harvested grain, don't go back in the
field to get it. Leave it for the poor, including foreigners, orphans, and widows, and the LORD will make you successful in everything you do.
20 When you harvest your olives, don't
try to get them all for yourself, but leave
some for the poor. 21 And when you pick
your grapes, go over the vines only
once, then let the poor have what is left.
22 You lived in poverty as slaves in Egypt
until the LORD your God rescued you.
That's why I am giving you these laws.

Whipping as Punishment for a Crime

Moses said to Israel:
25 1-2 Suppose you and someone else
each accuse the other of doing
something wrong, and you go to court,
where the judges decide you are guilty.
If your punishment is to be beaten with
a whip,[q] one of the judges will order you
to lie down, and you will receive the
number of lashes you deserve. 3 Forty
lashes is the most that you can be given,
because more than that might make
other Israelites think you are worthless.

Don't Muzzle an Ox

Moses said to Israel:
4 Don't muzzle an ox while it is threshing grain.[r]

A Son for a Dead Brother

Moses said to Israel:
5-6 Suppose two brothers are living on
the same property, when one of them
dies without having a son to carry on
his name. If this happens, his widow
must not marry anyone outside the family. Instead, she must marry her late
husband's brother, and their first son
will be the legal son of the dead man.
7 But suppose the brother refuses to
marry the widow. She must go to a
meeting of the town leaders at the town
gate and say, "My husband died without
having a son to carry on his name. And
my husband's brother refuses to marry
me so I can have a son."
8 The leaders will call the living
brother to the town gate and try to persuade him to marry the widow. But if he
doesn't change his mind and marry her,
9 she must go over to him while the town
leaders watch. She will pull off one of
his sandals and spit in his face, while
saying, "That's what happens to a man
who won't help provide descendants for
his dead brother." 10 From then on, that
man's family will be known as "the family of the man whose sandal was pulled
off."

When Two Men Fight

Moses said to Israel:
11 If two men are fighting, and the wife
of one man tries to rescue her husband
by grabbing the other man's private
parts, 12 you must cut off her hand. Don't
have any mercy.

Be Honest in Business

Moses said to Israel:
13-14 Don't try to cheat people by having two sets of weights or measures, one
to get more when you are buying, and
the other to give less when you are selling. 15 If you weigh and measure things
honestly, the LORD your God will let you
enjoy a long life in the land he is giving
you. 16 But the LORD is disgusted with
anyone who cheats or is dishonest.

Wipe Out Amalek

Moses said:
17 People of Israel, do you remember
what the Amalekites did to you after
you came out of Egypt? 18 You were
tired, and they followed along behind,

[p] 24.14 *don't hold back their pay*: The Dead Sea Scrolls; the Standard Hebrew Text "treat them right." [q] 25.1,2 *whip*: Or "rod." [r] 25.4 *threshing grain*: Oxen were used at the threshing place to walk on heads of grain, or pull heavy slabs of wood over it, to separate the kernels from the husks.

attacking those who could not keep up
with the others. This showed that the
Amalekites have no respect for God.
19 The LORD your God will help you
capture the land, and he will give you
peace. But when that day comes,
you must wipe out Amalek so completely that no one will remember they
ever lived.

Give the LORD the First Part of Your Harvest

Moses said to Israel:

26 The LORD is giving you the land,
and soon you will conquer it, settle down, 2 and plant crops. And when
you begin harvesting each of your
crops, the very first things you pick
must be put in a basket. Take them to
the place where the LORD your God
chooses to be worshiped, 3 and tell the
priest, "Long ago the LORD our God
promised our ancestors that he would
give us this land. And today, I thank him
for keeping his promise and giving me a
share of the land."
4 The priest will take the basket and
set it in front of the LORD's altar. 5 Then,
standing there in front of the place of
worship, you must pray:

My ancestor was homeless,
an Aramean who went to live
in Egypt.
There were only a few
in his family then,
but they became great
and powerful,
a nation of many people.

6 The Egyptians were cruel
and had no pity on us.
They mistreated our people
and forced us into slavery.
7 We called out for help
to you, the LORD God
of our ancestors.
You heard our cries;
you knew we were in trouble
and abused.
8 Then you terrified the Egyptians
with your mighty miracles
and rescued us from Egypt.
9 You brought us here
and gave us this land
rich with milk and honey.
10 Now, LORD, I bring to you
the best of the crops
that you have given me.

After you say these things, place the
basket in front of the LORD's altar and
bow down to worship him.
11 Then you and your family must celebrate by eating a meal at the place of
worship to thank the LORD your God for
giving you such a good harvest. And remember to invite the Levites and the
foreigners who live in your town.

Ten Percent of the Harvest

Moses said to Israel:

12 Every year you are to give ten percent of your harvest to the LORD.[s] But
every third year,[t] this ten percent must
be given to the poor who live in your
town, including Levites, foreigners, orphans, and widows. That way, they will
have enough to eat. 13 Then you must
pray:

Our LORD and our God, you have
said that ten percent of my harvest
is sacred. I have obeyed your command and given this to the poor, including the Levites, foreigners, orphans, and widows.
14 I have not eaten any of this sacred food while I was in mourning;
in fact, I never touched it when I was
unclean.[u] And none of it has been
offered as a sacrifice to the spirits of
the dead. I have done everything exactly as you commanded.
15 Our LORD, look down from your
temple in heaven and bless your
people Israel. You promised our ancestors that you would give us this
land rich with milk and honey, and
you have kept your promise.

The LORD Is Your God, and You Are His People

Moses said to Israel:

16 Today the LORD your God has commanded you to obey these laws and
teachings with all your heart and soul.
17 In response, you have agreed that
the LORD will be your God, that you will
obey all his laws and teachings, and that
you will listen when he speaks to you.
18 Since you have agreed to obey the
LORD, he has agreed that you will be his
people and that you will belong to him,
just as he promised. 19 The LORD created
all nations, but he will make you more
famous than any of them, and you will
receive more praise and honor. You will
belong only to the LORD your God, just
as he promised.

Build an Altar on Mount Ebal

27 Moses stood together with the
leaders and told the people of Israel:
Obey all the laws and teachings that I
am giving you today. 2-4 Soon you will
enter the land that the LORD your God is

[s] **26.12** *Every year . . . LORD*: See 14.22-29. [t] **26.12** *every third year*: Probably the third and sixth years of the seven-year cycle described in 15.1-11 and Leviticus 25.1-7. [u] **26.14** *in mourning . . . unclean*: Touching a dead body made a person unclean and unfit to worship God. Ten percent of the harvest belonged to God, and was not to be touched by an unclean person.

giving to you. He is the God your ancestors worshiped, and he has promised
that this land is rich with milk and
honey.
After you cross the Jordan River, go to
Mount Ebal. Set up large slabs of stone,
then cover them with white plaster and
write on them a copy of these laws.
5 At this same place, build an altar for
offering sacrifices to the LORD your
God. But don't use stones that have
been cut with iron tools. 6 Look for
stones that can be used without being
cut. Then offer sacrifices to please the
LORD,[v] burning them completely on the
altar. 7 Next, offer sacrifices to ask the
LORD's blessing,[w] and serve the meat at
a sacred meal where you will celebrate
in honor of the LORD.
8 Don't forget to write out a copy of
these laws on the stone slabs that you
are going to set up. Make sure that the
writing is easy to read.

Curses on Those Who Disobey

9 Moses stood together with the
priests[x] and said, "Israel, be quiet and
listen to me! Today you have become the
people of the LORD your God.[y] 10 So you
must obey his laws and teachings that I
am giving you."
11 That same day, Moses gave them the
following instructions:
12-13 After you cross the Jordan River,
you will go to Mount Gerizim and
Mount Ebal.[z] The tribes of Simeon,
Levi, Judah, Issachar, Ephraim, Manasseh,[a] and Benjamin will go up on
Mount Gerizim, where they will bless
the people of Israel. The tribes of
Reuben, Gad, Asher, Zebulun, Dan, and
Naphtali will go up on Mount Ebal
where they will agree to the curses.
14-26 The people of the Levi tribe will
speak each curse in a loud voice, then
the rest of the people[b] will agree to that
curse by saying, "Amen!" Here are the
curses:

We ask the LORD to put a curse on anyone who makes an idol or worships idols, even secretly. The LORD is disgusted with idols.

We ask the LORD to put a curse on all who do not show respect for their father and mother.

We ask the LORD to put a curse on anyone who moves the rocks that mark property lines.

We ask the LORD to put a curse on anyone who tells blind people to go the wrong way.

We ask the LORD to put a curse on anyone who keeps the poor from getting justice, whether these poor are foreigners, widows, or orphans.

We ask the LORD to put a curse on any man who sleeps with his father's wife; that man has shown no respect for his father's marriage.

We ask the LORD to put a curse on anyone who has sex with an animal.

We ask the LORD to put a curse on any man who sleeps with his sister or his half sister or his mother-in-law.

We ask the LORD to put a curse on anyone who commits murder, even when there are no witnesses to the crime.

We ask the LORD to put a curse on anyone who accepts money to murder an innocent victim.

We ask the LORD to put a curse on anyone who refuses to obey his laws.

And so, to each of these curses, the people will answer, "Amen!"

The LORD Will Bless You if You Obey

Moses said to Israel:

28 1-2 Today I am giving you the laws
and teachings of the LORD your
God. Always obey them, and the LORD
will make Israel the most famous and
important nation on earth, and he will
bless you in many ways.
3 The LORD will make your businesses
and your farms successful.
4 You will have many children. You will
harvest large crops, and your herds of
cattle and flocks of sheep and goats will
produce many young.
5 You will have plenty of bread[c] to eat.
6 The LORD will make you successful in
your daily work.
7 The LORD will help you defeat your
enemies and make them scatter in all directions.
8 The LORD your God is giving you the
land, and he will make sure you are successful in everything you do. Your harvests will be so large that your storehouses will be full.
9 If you follow and obey the LORD, he
will make you his own special people,

[v]27.6 *sacrifices to please the LORD*: See the note at 12.5-19. [w]27.7 *sacrifices to ask the LORD's blessing*: These sacrifices have traditionally been called "peace offerings" or "offerings of well-being." A main purpose was to ask for the LORD's blessing, and so in the CEV they are sometimes called "sacrifices to ask the LORD's blessing." [x]27.9 *priests*: See the note at 17.8-12. [y]27.9 *Today you have become the people of the LORD your God*: As a result of the agreement that the LORD had made with them, recorded in 26.16-19. [z]27.12,13 *Mount Gerizim and Mount Ebal*: These mountains were separated by a valley. [a]27.12,13 *Ephraim, Manasseh*: The Hebrew text has "Joseph"; the descendants of Joseph formed the two tribes of Ephraim and Manasseh. [b]27.14-26 *the rest of the people*: Or "all the people who are standing on Mount Ebal." [c]28.5 *bread*: The main food of the Israelites.

just as he promised. [10]Then everyone on
earth will know that you belong to the
LORD, and they will be afraid of you.
[11]The LORD will give you a lot of children and make sure that your animals
give birth to many young. The LORD
promised your ancestors that this land
would be yours, and he will make it produce large crops for you.
[12]The LORD will open the storehouses
of the skies where he keeps the rain,
and he will send rain on your land at
just the right times. He will make you
successful in everything you do. You will
have plenty of money to lend to other
nations, but you won't need to borrow
any yourself.
[13]Obey the laws and teachings that
I'm giving you today, and the LORD your
God will make Israel a leader among
the nations, and not a follower. Israel
will be wealthy and powerful, not poor
and weak. [14]But you must not reject any
of his laws and teachings or worship
other gods.

The LORD Will Put Curses on You if You Disobey

(Leviticus 26.14-46)

Moses said:
[15]Israel, today I am giving you the
laws and teachings of the LORD your
God. And if you don't obey them all, he
will put many curses on you.
[16]Your businesses and farms will fail.
[17]You won't have enough bread[c] to
eat.
[18]You'll have only a few children, your
crops will be small, and your herds of
cattle and flocks of sheep and goats
won't produce many young.
[19]The LORD will make you fail in
everything you do.
[20]No matter what you try to accom-
plish, the LORD will confuse you, and
you will feel his anger. You won't last
long, and you may even meet with disaster, all because you rejected the LORD.
[21-23]The LORD will send terrible diseases to attack you, and you will never
be well again. You will suffer with burning fever and swelling and pain until
you die somewhere in the land that you
captured.
The LORD will make the sky overhead
seem like a bronze roof that keeps out
the rain, and the ground under your feet
will become as hard as iron. Your crops
will be scorched by the hot east wind or
ruined by mildew. [24]He will send dust
and sandstorms instead of rain, and you
will be wiped out.
[25]The LORD will let you be defeated by
your enemies, and you will scatter in all
directions. You will be a horrible sight
for the other nations to see, [26]and no
one will disturb the birds and wild animals while they eat your dead bodies.
[27]The LORD will make you suffer with
diseases that will cause oozing sores or
crusty itchy patches on your skin or
boils like the ones that are common in
Egypt. And there will be no cure for
you! [28]You will become insane and go
blind. The LORD will make you so confused, [29]that even in bright sunshine you
will have to feel your way around like a
blind person, who cannot tell day from
night. For the rest of your life, people
will beat and rob you, and no one will
be able to stop them.
[30]A man will be engaged to a woman,
but before they can get married, she will
be raped by enemy soldiers. Some of
you will build houses, but never get to
live in them. If you plant a vineyard, you
won't be around long enough to enjoy
the first harvest. [31]Your cattle will be
killed while you watch, but you won't
get to eat any of the meat. Your donkeys
and sheep will be stolen from you, and
no one will be around to force your enemies to give them back. [32]Your sons and
daughters will be dragged off to a foreign country, while you stand there
helpless. And even if you watch for
them until you go blind, you will never
see them again.
[33]You will work hard on your farms,
but everything you harvest will be eaten
by foreigners, who will mistreat you and
abuse you for the rest of your life.
[34]What you see will be so horrible that
you will go insane, [35]and the LORD will
punish you from head to toe with boils
that never heal.
[36]The LORD will let you and your king
be taken captive to a country that you
and your ancestors have never even
heard of, and there you will have to worship idols[d] made of wood and stone.
[37]People of nearby countries will shudder when they see your terrible troubles, but they will still make fun of you.
[38]You will plant a lot of seed, but
gather a small harvest, because locusts[e]
will eat your crops. [39]You will plant
vineyards and work hard at taking care
of them, but you won't gather any
grapes, much less get any wine, and the
vines themselves will be eaten by
worms. [40]Even if your olive trees grow
everywhere in your country, the olives
will fall off before they are ready, and
there won't be enough olive oil for
combing your hair.[f]

[c]28.17 *bread*: The main food of the Israelites. [d]28.36 *have to worship idols*: It was sometimes thought that only the gods of a country could be worshiped within the borders of that country. [e]28.38 *locusts*: A type of grasshopper that comes in swarms and causes great damage to plant life. [f]28.40 *olive oil . . . hair*: Olive oil was used for combing the hair.

41Even your infant sons and daughters will be taken as prisoners of war.
42Locusts[g] will eat your crops and
strip your trees of leaves and fruit.
43Foreigners in your towns will become wealthy and powerful, while you
become poor and powerless. 44You will
be so short of money that you will have
to borrow from those foreigners. They
will be the leaders in the community,
and you will be the followers.

More Curses for Disobedience

Moses said:
45Israel, if you don't obey the laws and
teachings that the LORD your God is giving you, he will send these curses to
chase, attack, and destroy you. 46Then
everyone will look at you and your descendants and realize that the LORD has
placed you under a curse.
47If the LORD makes you wealthy, but
you don't joyfully worship and honor
him, 48he will send enemies to attack
you and make you their slaves. Then
you will live in poverty with nothing to
eat, drink, or wear, and your owners will
work you to death.
49Foreigners who speak a strange language will be sent to attack you without
warning, just like an eagle swooping
down. 50They won't show any mercy,
and they will have no respect for old
people or pity for children. 51They will
take your cattle, sheep, goats, grain,
wine, and olive oil, then leave you to
starve.
52All over the land that the LORD your
God gave you, the enemy army will surround your towns. You may feel safe inside your town walls, but the enemy will
tear them down, 53while you wait in horror. Finally, you will get so hungry that
you will eat the sons and daughters that
the LORD gave you. 54-55Because of
hunger, a man who had been gentle and
kind will eat his own children and
refuse to share the meal with his
brother or wife or with his other children. 56-57A woman may have grown up
in such luxury that she never had to put
a foot on the ground. But times will be
so bad that she will secretly eat both her
newborn baby and the afterbirth, without sharing any with her husband or her
other children.

Disobedience Brings Destruction

Moses said to Israel:
58You must obey everything in *The
Book of God's Law*. Because if you don't
respect the LORD, 59he will punish you
and your descendants with incurable
diseases, 60like those you were so afraid
of in Egypt. 61Remember! If the LORD
decides to destroy your nation, he can
use any disease or disaster, not just the
ones written in *The Book of God's Law*.
62There are as many of you now as the
stars in the sky, but if you disobey the
LORD your God, only a few of you will
be left. 63The LORD is happy to make you
successful and to help your nation grow
while you conquer the land. But if you
disobey him, he will be just as happy to
pull you up by your roots.
64Those of you that survive will be
scattered to every nation on earth, and
you will have to worship stone and
wood idols[h] that never helped you or
your ancestors. 65You will be restless—
always longing for home, but never able
to return. 66You will live in constant fear
of death. 67Each morning you will wake
up to such terrible sights that you will
say, "I wish it were night!" But at night
you will be terrified and say, "I wish it
were day!"
68I told you never to go back to Egypt.
But now the LORD himself will load you
on ships and send you back. Then you
will even try to sell yourselves as slaves,
but no one will be interested.

The Agreement in Moab

29 So Moses finished telling the Israelites what they had to do in order to keep the agreement the LORD was
making with them in Moab, which was
in addition to the one the LORD had
made with them at Mount Sinai.[i]

THE THIRD SPEECH: ISRAEL MUST KEEP ITS AGREEMENT WITH THE LORD

The LORD Is Your God

2-3Moses called the nation of Israel together and told them:
When you were in Egypt, you saw the
LORD perform great miracles that
caused trouble for the king, his officials,
and everyone else in the country. 4-6He
has even told you, "For forty years I, the
LORD, led you through the desert, but
your clothes and your sandals didn't
wear out, and I gave you special food.[j] I
did these things so you would realize
that I am your God."
But the LORD must give you a change
of heart before you truly understand
what you have seen and heard.
7When we first camped here, King Sihon of Heshbon and King Og of Bashan
attacked, but we defeated them. 8Then
we captured their land and divided it

[g]**28.42** *Locusts*: See the note at 28.38. [h]**28.64** *have to worship . . . idols*: See the note at 28.36. [i]**29.1** *Mount Sinai*: See the note at 1.1-5. [j]**29.4-6** *I gave . . . food*: Hebrew "you didn't eat bread or drink any wine or beer."

among the tribes of Reuben, Gad, and
East Manasseh.

Keep the Agreement

Moses said:

9 Israel, the LORD has made an agreement with you, and if you keep your
part, you will be successful in everything you do. 10-12 Today everyone in our
nation is standing here in the LORD's
presence, including leaders and officials, parents and children, and even
those foreigners who cut wood and
carry water for us. We are at this place
of worship to promise that we will keep
our part of the agreement with the LORD
our God.

13-15 In this agreement, the LORD
promised that you would be his people
and that he would be your God. He first
made this promise to your ancestors
Abraham, Isaac, and Jacob, and today
the LORD is making this same promise
to you. But it isn't just for you; it is also
for your descendants.

16-17 When we lived in Egypt, you saw
the Egyptians worship disgusting idols
of wood, stone, silver, and gold. Then as
we traveled through other nations, you
saw those people worship other disgusting idols. 18 So make sure that everyone
in your tribe remains faithful to the
LORD and never starts worshiping gods
of other nations.

If even one of you worships idols, you
will be like the root of a plant that produces bitter, poisonous fruit. 19 You may
be an Israelite and know all about the
LORD's agreement with us, but he won't
bless you if you rebel against him. You
may think you can get away with it, but
you will cause the rest of Israel to be
punished along with you.[k] 20-21 The LORD
will be furious, and instead of forgiving
you, he will separate you from the other
tribes. Then he will destroy you, by piling on you all the curses in *The Book of
God's Law*, and you will be forgotten
forever.

22 The LORD will strike your country
with diseases and disasters. Your descendants and foreigners from distant
countries will see that your land 23 has
become a scorching desert of salt and
sulfur, where nothing is planted, nothing sprouts, and nothing grows. It will
be as lifeless as the land around the
cities of Sodom, Gomorrah, Admah, and
Zeboiim, after the LORD became angry
and destroyed them.[l]

24 People from other nations will ask,
"Why did the LORD destroy this country?
Why was he so furious?"

25 And they will be given this answer:

Our ancestors worshiped the
LORD, but after he brought them out
of Egypt and made an agreement
with them, they rejected the agreement 26 and decided to worship gods
that had never helped them. The
LORD had forbidden Israel to worship these gods, 27-28 and so he became furious and punished the land
with all the curses in *The Book of
God's Law*. Then he pulled up Israel
by the roots and tossed them into a
foreign country, where they still are
today.

29 The LORD our God hasn't explained
the present or the future, but he has
commanded us to obey the laws he gave
to us and our descendants.

The LORD Will Bring You Back

Moses said to Israel:

30 I have told you everything the
LORD your God will do for you,
and I've also told you the curses he will
put on you if you reject him. He will
scatter you in faraway countries, but
when you realize that he is punishing
you, 2 return to him with all your heart
and soul and start obeying the commands I have given to you today. 3-4 Then
he will stop punishing you and treat you
with kindness. He may have scattered
you to the farthest countries on earth,
but he will bring you back 5 to the land
that had belonged to your ancestors and
make you even more successful and
powerful than they ever were.

6 You and your descendants are stubborn, but the LORD will make you willing to obey him and love him with all
your heart and soul, and you will enjoy
a long life.

7 Then the LORD your God will remove
the curses from you and put them on
those enemies who hate and attack you.

8 You will again obey the laws and
teachings of the LORD, 9 and he will bless
you with many children, large herds and
flocks, and abundant crops. The LORD
will be happy to do good things for you,
just as he did for your ancestors. 10 But
you must decide once and for all to worship him with all your heart and soul
and to obey everything in *The Book of
God's Law*.

Choose Life, Not Death

Moses said to Israel:

11 You know God's laws, and it isn't
impossible to obey them. 12 His commands aren't in heaven, so you can't excuse yourselves by saying, "How can we
obey the LORD's commands? They are in
heaven, and no one can go up to get

[k] **29.19** *you will cause the rest of Israel to be punished along with you*: Hebrew "The mud will be swept away as well as the dust." [l] **29.23** *Sodom . . . destroyed them*: See Genesis 18.16-28.

them, then bring them down and explain them to us." [13]And you can't say,
"How can we obey the LORD's commands? They are across the sea, and
someone must go across, then bring
them back and explain them to us."
[14]No, these commands are nearby and
you know them by heart. All you have to
do is obey!
[15]Today I am giving you a choice. You
can choose life and success or death
and disaster. [16-18]I am commanding you
to be loyal to the LORD, to live the way
he has told you, and to obey his laws
and teachings. You are about to cross
the Jordan River and take the land that
he is giving you. If you obey him, you
will live and become successful and
powerful.
On the other hand, you might choose
to disobey the LORD and reject him. So
I'm warning you that if you bow down
and worship other gods, you won't have
long to live.
[19]Right now I call the sky and the
earth to be witnesses that I am offering
you this choice. Will you choose for the
LORD to make you prosperous and give
you a long life? Or will he put you under
a curse and kill you? Choose life! [20]Be
completely faithful to the LORD your
God, love him, and do whatever he tells
you. The LORD is the only one who can
give life, and he will let you live a long
time in the land that he promised to
your ancestors Abraham, Isaac, and Jacob.

FINAL SPEECHES AND THE DEATH OF MOSES

Joshua Is Appointed the Leader of Israel

31 Moses again spoke to the whole
nation of Israel:
[2]I am a hundred twenty years old, and
I am no longer able to be your leader.
And besides that, the LORD your God
has told me that he won't let me cross
the Jordan River. [3-5]But he has promised
that he and Joshua will lead you across
the Jordan to attack the nations that live
on the other side. The LORD will destroy
those nations just as he destroyed Sihon
and Og, those two Amorite kings. Just
remember—whenever you capture a
place, kill everyone who lives there.
[6]Be brave and strong! Don't be afraid
of the nations on the other side of the
Jordan. The LORD your God will always
be at your side, and he will never abandon you.
[7]Then Moses called Joshua up in front
of the crowd and said:
Joshua, be brave and strong as
you lead these people into their
land. The LORD made a promise long
ago to Israel's ancestors that this
land would someday belong to Israel. That time has now come, and
you must divide up the land among
the people. [8]The LORD will lead you
into the land. He will always be with
you and help you, so don't ever be
afraid of your enemies.

Read These Laws

[9]Moses wrote down all of these laws
and teachings and gave them to the
priests and the leaders of Israel. The
priests were from the Levi tribe, and
they carried the sacred chest that belonged to the LORD. [10-11]Moses told these
priests and leaders:
Each year the Israelites must
come together to celebrate the Festival of Shelters at the place where
the LORD chooses to be worshiped.
You must read these laws and teachings to the people at the festival
every seventh year, the year when
loans do not need to be repaid.[m]
[12-13]Everyone must come—men,
women, children, and even the foreigners who live in your towns. And
each new generation will listen and
learn to worship the LORD their God
with fear and trembling and to do
exactly what is said in God's Law.

Israel Will Reject the LORD

[14]The LORD told Moses, "You will soon
die, so bring Joshua to the sacred tent,
and I will appoint him the leader of Israel."
Moses and Joshua went to the sacred
tent, [15]and the LORD appeared in a thick
cloud right over the entrance to the tent.
[16]The LORD said:
Moses, you will soon die. But Israel is going into a land where other
gods are worshiped, and Israel will
reject me and start worshiping these
gods. The people will break the
agreement I made with them, [17]and I
will be so furious that I will abandon
them and ignore their prayers. I will
send disasters and suffering that
will nearly wipe them out. Finally,
they will realize that the disasters
happened because I abandoned
them. [18]They will pray to me, but I
will ignore them because they were
evil and started worshiping other
gods.
[19]Moses and Joshua, I am going to
give you the words to a new song.
Write them down and teach the
song to the Israelites. If they learn it,
they will know what I want them to
do, and so they will have no excuse
for not obeying me. [20]I am bringing

[m]31.10,11 *every seventh year . . . repaid*: See 15.1, 2 and the note there.

them into the land that I promised
their ancestors. It is a land rich with
milk and honey, and the Israelites
will have more than enough food to
eat. But they will get fat and turn
their backs on me and start worshiping other gods. The Israelites will reject me and break the agreement
that I made with them.
21When I punish the Israelites and
their descendants with suffering and
disasters, I will remind them that
they know the words to this song, so
they have no excuse for not obeying
me.
I will give them the land that I
promised, but I know the way they
are going to live later on.
22Moses wrote down the words to the
song[n] right away, and he taught it to the
Israelites.
23The LORD told Joshua, "Be brave and
strong! I will help you lead the people of
Israel into the land that I have promised
them."
24Moses wrote down all these laws
and teachings in a book, 25then he went
to the Levites who carried the sacred
chest and said:
26This is *The Book of God's Law*.
Keep it beside the sacred chest that
holds the agreement the LORD your
God made with Israel. This book is
proof that you know what the LORD
wants you to do. 27I know how stubborn and rebellious you and the rest
of the Israelites are. You have rebelled against the LORD while I have
been alive, and it will only get worse
after I am gone. 28So call together
the leaders and officials of the tribes
of Israel. I will bring this book and
read every word of it to you, and I
will call the sky and the earth as witnesses that all of you know what
you are supposed to do.
29I am going to die soon, and I
know that in the future you will stop
caring about what is right and what
is wrong, and so you will disobey
the LORD and stop living the way I
told you to live. The LORD will be angry, and terrible things will happen
to you.

The Song of Moses

30Moses called a meeting of all the
people of Israel, so he could teach them
the words to the song that the LORD had
given him. And here are the words:

32 Earth and Sky,
listen to what I say!
2 Israel, I will teach you.
My words will be like gentle rain
on tender young plants,
or like dew on the grass.

3 Join with me in praising
the wonderful name
of the LORD our God.
4 The LORD is a mighty rock,[o]
and he never does wrong.
God can always be trusted
to bring justice.
5 But you lie and cheat
and are unfaithful to him.
You have disgraced yourselves
and are no longer worthy
to be his children.[p]
6 Israel, the LORD is your Father,
the one who created you,
but you repaid him
by being foolish.
7 Think about past generations.
Ask your parents
or any of your elders.
They will tell you
8 that God Most High
gave land to every nation.
He assigned a guardian angel
to each of them,[q]
9 but the LORD himself
takes care of Israel.[r]

10 Israel, the LORD discovered you
in a barren desert
filled with howling winds.
God became your fortress,
protecting you as though
you were his own eyes.
11 The LORD was like an eagle
teaching its young to fly,
always ready to swoop down
and catch them on its back.
12 Israel, the LORD led you,
and without the aid
of a foreign god,
13 he helped you
capture the land.
Your fields were rich
with grain.
Olive trees grew
in your stony soil,
and honey was found
among the rocks.
14 Your flocks and herds
produced milk and yogurt,
and you got choice meat
from your sheep and goats
that grazed in Bashan.

[n]**31.22** *the words to the song*: See 32.1-43. [o]**32.4** *mighty rock*: The Hebrew text has "rock," which is sometimes used in poetry to compare the LORD to a mountain where his people can run for protection from their enemies. [p]**32.5** *and are unfaithful . . . children*: One possible meaning for the difficult Hebrew text. [q]**32.8** *He assigned . . . them*: The Dead Sea Scrolls and one ancient translation; the Standard Hebrew Text "So there were as many nations as Israel (that is, Jacob) had children." [r]**32.9** *Israel*: The Hebrew text has "Jacob," another name for Israel's ancestor.

Your wheat was the finest,
and you drank the best wine.

15 Israel,[s] you grew fat and rebelled
against God, your Creator;
you rejected the Mighty Rock,[t]
your only place of safety.
16 You made God jealous and angry
by worshiping disgusting idols
and foreign gods.
17 You offered sacrifices
to demons, those useless gods[u]
that never helped you,
new gods that your ancestors
never worshiped.
18 You turned away
from God, your Creator;
you forgot the Mighty Rock,[v]
the source of your life.
19 You were the LORD's children,
but you made him angry.
Then he rejected you 20 and said,
"You are unfaithful
and can't be trusted.
So I won't answer your prayers;
I'll just watch and see
what happens to you.
21 You worshiped worthless idols,
and made me jealous
and angry!
Now I will send a cruel[w]
and worthless nation
to make you jealous and angry.

22 "My people, I will breathe out fire
that sends you down
to the world of the dead.
It will scorch your farmlands
and burn deep down
under the mountains.
23 I'll send disaster after disaster
to strike you like arrows.
24 You'll be struck by starvation
and deadly diseases,
by the fangs of wild animals
and poisonous snakes.
25 Young and old alike
will be killed in the streets
and terrified at home.

26 "I wanted to scatter you,
so no one would remember
that you had ever lived.
27 But I dreaded the sound
of your enemies saying,
'We defeated Israel with no help
from the LORD.' "

28 People of Israel,
that's what the LORD
has said to you.
But you don't have good sense,
and you never listen
to advice.
29 If you did, you could see
where you are headed.
30 How could one enemy soldier
chase a thousand
of Israel's troops?
Or how could two of theirs
pursue ten thousand of ours?
It can only happen if the LORD
stops protecting Israel
and lets the enemy win.
31 Even our enemies know
that only our God
is a Mighty Rock.[x]

32 Our enemies are grapevines
rooted in the fields
of Sodom and Gomorrah.[y]
The grapes they produce
are full of bitter poison;
33 their wine is more deadly
than cobra venom.
34 But the LORD has written
a list of their sins
and locked it in his vault.
35 Soon our enemies will get
what they deserve[z]—
suddenly they will slip,
and total disaster
will quickly follow.

36 When only a few
of the LORD's people remain,
when their strength is gone,
and some of them are slaves,
the LORD will feel sorry for them
and give them justice.

37 But first the LORD will say,
"You ran for safety to other gods—
couldn't they help you?
38 You offered them wine
and your best sacrifices.
Can't those gods help you now
or give you protection?
39 Don't you understand?
I am the only God;
there are no others.
I am the one who takes life
and gives it again.
I punished you with suffering.

[s] **32.15** *Israel*: The Standard Hebrew Text has "Jeshurun," a rare name for Israel related to a word meaning "honest." The Samaritan Hebrew Text and one ancient translation also use "Jacob," another name for the ancestor of the nation of Israel. [t] **32.15** *Mighty Rock*: See the note at 32.4. [u] **32.16,17** *disgusting idols . . . foreign gods . . . demons . . . those useless gods*: Different ways of referring to gods of other nations. [v] **32.18** *Mighty Rock*: See the note at 32.4. [w] **32.21** *cruel*: One possible meaning for the difficult Hebrew text. [x] **32.31** *Mighty Rock*: See the note at 32.4. [y] **32.32** *Sodom and Gomorrah*: Two cities that the LORD destroyed because their people were so evil (see Genesis 18.16—19.28). [z] **32.35** *our enemies . . . deserve*: The Samaritan Hebrew Text and one ancient translation; the Standard Hebrew Text "I will pay them back."

But now I will heal you,
and nothing can stop me!

40 "I make this solemn promise:
Just as I live forever,
41 I will take revenge
on my hateful enemies.
I will sharpen my sword
and let it flash
like lightning.
42 My arrows will get drunk
on enemy blood;
my sword will taste the flesh
and the blood of the enemy.
It will kill prisoners,
and cut off the heads
of their leaders."[a]

43 Tell the heavens to celebrate
and all gods to bow down
to the LORD,[b]
because he will take revenge
on those hateful enemies
who killed his people.
He will forgive the sins of Israel
and purify their land.[c]

44-45Moses spoke the words of the
song so that all the Israelites could hear,
and Joshua[d] helped him. When Moses
had finished, 46he said, "Always remember this song I have taught you today.
And let it be a warning that you must
teach your children to obey everything
written in *The Book of God's Law*. 47The
Law isn't empty words. It can give you a
long life in the land that you are going
to take."

Moses Will See the Land

48Later that day the LORD said to
Moses:
49Go up into the Abarim Mountain
range here in Moab across the Jordan River valley from Jericho. And
when you reach the top of Mount
Nebo, you will be able to see the
land of Canaan, which I am giving
to Israel. 50Then you will die and be
buried on the mountaintop, just as
your brother Aaron died and was
buried on Mount Hor. 51Both of you
were unfaithful to me at Meribah
Spring near Kadesh in the Zin
Desert.[e] I am God, but there in front
of the Israelites, you did not treat me
with the honor and respect I deserve. 52So I will give the land to the
people of Israel, but you will only
get to see it from a distance.

Moses Blesses the Tribes of Israel

33 Moses was a prophet, and before
he died, he blessed the tribes of
Israel by saying:

2 The LORD came from Mount Sinai.
From Edom, he gave light
to his people,
and his glory was shining
from Mount Paran.
Thousands of his warriors
were with him, and fire
was at his right hand.[f]
3 The LORD loves the tribes
of Israel,[g]
and he protects his people.
They listen to his words
and worship at his feet.
*4 I called a meeting
of the tribes of Israel[h]
and gave you God's Law.
5 Then you and your leaders
made the LORD your king.

6 Tribe of Reuben, you will live,
even though your tribe
will always be small.[i]

7 The LORD will listen to you,
tribe of Judah, as you beg
to come safely home.
You fought your enemies alone;[j]
now the LORD will help you.

8 At Massah and Meribah Spring,[k]
the LORD tested you,
tribe of Levi.
You were faithful,[l]
and so the priesthood[m] belongs
to the Levi tribe.
9 Protecting Israel's agreement
with the LORD
was more important to you
than the life of your father
or mother,

[a]**32.42** *leaders*: Or "long-haired warriors," who let their hair grow to show that they had made sacred promises to their gods. [b]**32.43** *Tell . . . LORD*: The Dead Sea Scrolls and one ancient translation; the Standard Hebrew Text "Let the nations, his people, celebrate."
[c]**32.43** *because he will . . . land*: One possible meaning for the difficult Hebrew text.
[d]**32.44,45** *Joshua*: The Hebrew text has "Hoshea," another form of Joshua's name.
[e]**32.51** *Both of you were unfaithful . . . the Zin Desert*: See Numbers 20.1-13.
[f]**33.2** *Thousands . . . right hand*: One possible meaning for the difficult Hebrew text.
[g]**33.3** *the tribes of Israel*: Or "the nations." [h]**33.4** *Israel*: The Hebrew text also uses the name "Jeshurun," a rare name for "Israel." [i]**33.6** *even though . . . small*: One possible meaning for the difficult Hebrew text. [j]**33.7** *beg . . . alone*: One possible meaning for the difficult Hebrew text. [k]**33.8** *Massah and Meribah Spring*: See Exodus 17.1-7; Numbers 20.1-13. [l]**33.8** *the LORD tested you, tribe of Levi. You were faithful*: Or "the LORD tested me. I was faithful" or "the LORD tested Aaron and me. We were faithful." [m]**33.8** *priesthood*: The Hebrew text has "your thummim and your urim," objects that were used by priests to get answers from God.

or brothers or sisters,
or your own children.[n]

10 You teach God's laws to Israel,[o]
and at the place of worship
you offer sacrifices
and burn incense.
11 I pray that the LORD will bless
everything you do,
and make you strong enough
to crush your enemies.

12 The LORD Most High[p] loves you,
tribe of Benjamin.
He will live among your hills
and protect you.

13 Descendants of Joseph,
the LORD will bless you
with precious water
from deep wells
and with dew from the sky.
14 Month by month, your fruit
will ripen in the sunshine.
15 You will have a rich harvest
from the slopes
of the ancient hills.
16 The LORD who appeared
in the burning bush
wants to give you the best
the land can produce,
and it will be a princely crown
on Joseph's head.

17 The armies of Ephraim
and Manasseh
are majestic and fierce
like a bull or a wild ox.
They will run their spears
through faraway nations.

18 Be happy, Zebulun,
as your boats set sail;
be happy, Issachar,
in your tents.
19 The sea will make you wealthy,
and from the sandy beach
you will get treasure.[q]
So invite the other tribes[r]
to celebrate with you
and offer sacrifices to God.

20 Tribe of Gad,
the LORD will bless you
with more land.
So shout his praises!
Your tribe is like a lion
ripping up its victim.
21 Your leaders met together
and chose the best land
for your tribe,
but you obeyed the LORD
and helped the other tribes.[s]

22 Tribe of Dan,
you are like a lion cub,
startled by a snake.[t]

23 The LORD is pleased with you,
people of Naphtali.
He will bless you
and give you the land
to the west and the south.[u]

24 The LORD's greatest blessing
is for you, tribe of Asher.
You will be the favorite
of all the other tribes.
You will be rich with olive oil
25 and have strong town gates
with bronze and iron bolts.
Your people will be powerful
for as long as they live.

26 Israel,[v] no other god
is like ours—
the clouds are his chariot
as he rides across the skies
to come and help us.
27 The eternal God
is our hiding place;
he carries us in his arms.
When God tells you
to destroy your enemies,
he will make them run.
28 Israel, you will live in safety;
your enemies will be gone.[w]
The dew will fall from the sky,
and you will have plenty
of grain and wine.
29 The LORD has rescued you
and given you more blessings
than any other nation.
He protects you like a shield
and is your majestic sword.
Your enemies will bow in fear,
and you will trample
on their backs.

The Death of Moses

34 Sometime later, Moses left the lowlands of Moab. He went up

[n]**33.9** *Protecting Israel's agreement . . . your own children*: See Exodus 32.25-29. [o]**33.10** *Israel*: See the note at 32.9. [p]**33.12** *Most High*: One possible meaning for the difficult Hebrew text. [q]**33.19** *sandy beach . . . treasure*: Possibly a reference to glass made from sand; glass was rare and very valuable. [r]**33.19** *other tribes*: Or "nations." [s]**33.21** *tribes*: One possible meaning for the difficult Hebrew text of verse 21. The Gad tribe asked for some of the land east of the Jordan River, but promised that their warriors would cross the Jordan and help the other tribes take over the land west of the Jordan (see Numbers 32.1-33; Joshua 4.10-13). [t]**33.22** *startled by a snake*: Or "jumping out from the forest of Bashan." [u]**33.23** *land to the west and the south*: Or "land south as far as Lake Galilee." [v]**33.26** *Israel*: See the note at 33.4. [w]**33.28** *your enemies will be gone*: One possible meaning for the difficult Hebrew text.

Mount Pisgah to the peak of Mount
Nebo,[x] which is across the Jordan River
from Jericho. The LORD showed him all
the land as far north as Gilead and the
town of Dan. 2 He let Moses see the territories that would soon belong to the
tribes of Naphtali, Ephraim, Manasseh,
and Judah, as far west as the Mediterranean Sea. 3 The LORD also showed him
the land in the south, from the valley
near the town of Jericho, known as The
City of Palm Trees, down to the town of
Zoar.
4 The LORD said, "Moses, this is the
land I was talking about when I
solemnly promised Abraham, Isaac, and
Jacob that I would give land to their descendants. I have let you see it, but you
will not cross the Jordan and go in."
5 And so, Moses the LORD's servant
died there in Moab, just as the LORD had
said. 6 The LORD buried him in a valley
near the town of Beth-Peor, but even today no one knows exactly where.
7 Moses was a hundred twenty years old
when he died, yet his eyesight was still
good, and his body was strong.
8 The people of Israel stayed in the
lowlands of Moab, where they mourned
and grieved thirty days for Moses, as
was their custom.

Joshua Becomes the Leader of Israel

9 Before Moses died, he had placed his
hands on Joshua, and the LORD had
given Joshua wisdom. The Israelites
paid attention to what Joshua said and
obeyed the commands that the LORD
had given Moses.

Moses Was a Great Prophet

10 There has never again been a
prophet in Israel like Moses. The LORD
spoke face to face with him 11 and sent
him to perform powerful miracles in the
presence of the king of Egypt and his
entire nation. 12 No one else has ever had
the power to do such great things as
Moses did for everyone to see.

[x] **34.1** *Mount Pisgah . . . Mount Nebo*: Mount Nebo was probably one peak of the ridge known as Mount Pisgah.

JOSHUA

ABOUT THIS BOOK

The book of Joshua tells how Israel settled in Canaan, the land God promised to give them. The book gets its name from its main character, Joshua, who had become the leader of Israel following the death of Moses.

The book of Joshua has two parts. In the first part (1–12) the Lord helped Israel capture many of the cities and towns of Canaan. Sometimes this help involved miracles. For example, in the battle at Jericho the Lord made the city walls collapse (6.20). Later, in the battle at Gibeon the Lord made huge hailstones fall from the sky and crush the enemy soldiers. Then he made the sun stand still so the Israelites had a longer period of daylight to catch and kill as many of the enemy soldiers as possible before night came (10.1-15).

But the Lord refused to help Israel if the people broke their agreement to worship only him and to obey his commands. For example, in the battle at Ai, Israel was defeated because one person broke Israel's agreement with the Lord (7.1-12).

The second part of the book (13–24) describes how each tribe received its land. Israel had captured territory east of the Jordan River. This land had already been promised to the tribes of Reuben, Gad, and half of Manasseh, but they had to help the other tribes take over the rest of Canaan. The tribes of Judah, Ephraim, and West Manasseh took over their sections of the land fairly quickly. Then the rest of the land was explored and divided into sections, and the Lord showed Joshua which sections to assign to each of the remaining tribes. But since the Levites were the special servants of the Lord, they did not receive a large area of land like the other tribes. Instead, they were given towns scattered throughout the whole country.

At the end of the book, Joshua made two speeches emphasizing how good the Lord had been to the Israelites. Then Joshua gave them a challenge:

Worship the LORD, obey him, and always be faithful. *(24.14a)*

A QUICK LOOK AT THIS BOOK

Joshua Becomes the Leader of Israel (1.1-9)
Israel Crosses the Jordan River and Conquers Jericho (1.10—6.27)
Achan Disobeys the Lord (7.1-26)
The Battle at Ai (8.1-35)
The People of Gibeon Trick the Leaders of Israel (9.1-27)
Joshua Commands the Sun To Stand Still (10.1-15)
Israel Takes Over Much of the Land of Canaan (10.16—12.24)
Land that Israel Did Not Take Over (13.1-7)
Tribal Lands that Moses Had Assigned East of the Jordan (13.8-33)
Tribal Lands West of the Jordan (14.1—19.51)
Towns for Protecting People Accused of Murder (20.1-9)
Towns for the Levi Tribe (21.1-45)
The Eastern Tribes Return Home (22.1-34)
Joshua's Farewell Speeches and Death (23.1—24.33)

Joshua Becomes the Leader of Israel

1 Moses, the LORD's servant, was
dead. So the LORD spoke to Joshua
son of Nun, who had been the assistant
of Moses. The LORD said:
2 My servant Moses is dead. Now
you must lead Israel across the Jordan River into the land I'm giving to
all of you. 3 Wherever you go, I'll give
you that land, as I promised Moses.
4 It will reach from the Southern
Desert to the Lebanon Mountains in
the north, and to the northeast as far
as the great Euphrates River. It will
include the land of the Hittites,[a] and
the land from here at the Jordan
River to the Mediterranean Sea on
the west. 5 Joshua, I will always be
with you and help you as I helped
Moses, and no one will ever be able
to defeat you.
6-8 Long ago I promised the ancestors of Israel that I would give this
land to their descendants. So be
strong and brave! Be careful to do
everything my servant Moses taught
you. Never stop reading *The Book of
the Law*[b] he gave you. Day and
night you must think about what it
says. If you obey it completely, you
and Israel will be able to take this
land.
9 I've commanded you to be strong
and brave. Don't ever be afraid or
discouraged! I am the LORD your
God, and I will be there to help you
wherever you go.

The Eastern Tribes Promise To Help

10 Joshua ordered the tribal leaders
11 to go through the camp and tell everyone:
In a few days we will cross the
Jordan River to take the land that
the LORD our God is giving us. So fix
as much food as you'll need for the
march into the land.
12 Joshua told the men of the tribes of
Reuben, Gad, and East Manasseh:[c]
13-14 The LORD's servant Moses said
that the LORD our God has given you
land here on the east side of the Jordan River, where you could live in
peace. Your wives and children and
your animals can stay here in the
land Moses gave you. But all of you
that can serve in our army must pick
up your weapons and lead the men
of the other tribes across the Jordan
River. They are your relatives, so
you must help them 15 conquer the
land that the LORD is giving them.
The LORD will give peace to them as
he has given peace to you, and then
you can come back and settle here
in the land that Moses promised
you.
16 The men answered:
We'll cross the Jordan River and
help our relatives. We'll fight anywhere you send us. 17-18 If the LORD
our God will help you as he helped
Moses, and if you are strong and
brave, we will obey you as we
obeyed Moses. We'll even put to
death anyone who rebels against
you or refuses to obey you.

Rahab Helps the Israelite Spies

2 Joshua chose two men as spies and
sent them from their camp at Acacia
with these instructions: "Go across the
river and find out as much as you can
about the whole region, especially about
the town of Jericho."
The two spies left the Israelite camp
at Acacia and went to Jericho, where
they decided to spend the night at the
house of a prostitute[d] named Rahab.
2 But someone found out about them
and told the king of Jericho, "Some Israelite men came here tonight, and they
are spies." 3-7 So the king sent soldiers to
Rahab's house to arrest the spies.
Meanwhile, Rahab had taken the men
up to the flat roof of her house and had
hidden them under some piles of flax
plants[e] that she had put there to dry.
The soldiers came to her door and
demanded, "Let us have the men who
are staying at your house. They are
spies."
She answered, "Some men did come
to my house, but I didn't know where
they had come from. They left about
sunset, just before it was time to close
the town gate.[f] I don't know where they
were going, but if you hurry, maybe you
can catch them."
The guards at the town gate let the
soldiers leave Jericho, but they closed
the gate again as soon as the soldiers
went through. Then the soldiers headed
toward the Jordan River to look for the
spies at the place where people cross
the river.
8 Rahab went back up to her roof. The
spies were still awake, so she told them:
9 I know that the LORD has given
Israel this land. Everyone shakes

[a] **1.4** *the land . . . Hittites*: This refers to the northern part of Syria, which had been the southernmost part of the Hittite empire. [b] **1.6-8** *the Law*: Or "Teachings." [c] **1.12** *East Manasseh*: The half of Manasseh that settled east of the Jordan River. [d] **2.1** *prostitute*: Rahab was possibly an innkeeper. [e] **2.3-7** *flax plants*: The stalks of flax plants were harvested, soaked in water, and dried, then their fibers were separated and spun into thread, which was woven into linen cloth. [f] **2.3-7** *gate*: Many towns and cities had walls with heavy gates that were closed at night for protection.

with fear because of you. 10We heard
how the LORD dried up the Red Sea[g]
so you could leave Egypt. And we
heard how you destroyed Sihon and
Og, those two Amorite kings east of
the Jordan River. 11We know that the
LORD your God rules heaven and
earth, and we've lost our courage
and our will to fight.
12Please promise me in the LORD's
name that you will be as kind to my
family as I have been to you. Do
something to show 13that you won't
let your people kill my father and
mother and my brothers and sisters
and their families.
14"Rahab," the spies answered, "if you
keep quiet about what we're doing, we
promise to be kind to you when the
LORD gives us this land. We pray that the
LORD will kill us if we don't keep our
promise!"[h]
15Rahab's house was built into the
town wall,[i] and one of the windows in
her house faced outside the wall. She
gave the spies a rope, showed them the
window, and said, "Use this rope to let
yourselves down to the ground outside
the wall. 16Then hide in the hills. The
men who are looking for you won't be
able to find you there. They'll give up
and come back after a few days, and
you can be on your way."
17-20The spies said:
You made us promise to let you
and your family live. We will keep
our promise, but you can't tell anyone why we were here. You must tie
this red rope on your window when
we attack, and your father and
mother, your brothers, and everyone
else in your family must be here
with you. We'll take the blame if
anyone who stays in this house gets
hurt. But anyone who leaves your
house will be killed, and it won't be
our fault.
21"I'll do exactly what you said," Rahab promised. Then she sent them on
their way and tied the red rope to the
window.
22The spies hid in the hills for three
days while the king's soldiers looked for
them along the roads. As soon as the
soldiers gave up and returned to Jericho, 23the two spies went down into the
Jordan valley and crossed the river.
They reported to Joshua and told him
everything that had happened. 24"We're
sure the LORD has given us the whole
country," they said. "The people there
shake with fear every time they think
of us."

Israel Crosses the Jordan River

3 Early the next morning, Joshua and
the Israelites packed up and left
Acacia. They went to the Jordan River
and camped there that night. 2Two days
later[j] their leaders went through the
camp, 3-4shouting, "When you see some
of the priests[k] carrying the sacred
chest, you'll know it is time to cross
to the other side. You've never been
there before, and you won't know the
way, unless you follow the chest. But
don't get too close! Stay about half a
mile back."
5Joshua told the people, "Make yourselves acceptable[l] to worship the LORD,
because he is going to do some amazing
things for us."
6Then Joshua turned to the priests
and said, "Take the chest and cross the
Jordan River ahead of us." So the
priests picked up the chest by its carrying poles and went on ahead.
7The LORD told Joshua, "Beginning today I will show the people that you are
their leader, and they will know that I
am helping you as I helped Moses.
8Now, tell the priests who are carrying
the chest to go a little way into the river
and stand there."
9Joshua spoke to the people:
Come here and listen to what the
LORD our God said he will do! 10The
Canaanites, the Hittites, the Hivites,
the Perizzites, the Girgashites, the
Amorites, and the Jebusites control
the land on the other side of the
river. But the living God will be with
you and will force them out of the
land when you attack. And now,
God is going to prove that he's powerful enough to force them out.
11-13Just watch the sacred chest that
belongs to the LORD, the ruler of the
whole earth. As soon as the priests

[g]2.10 *Red Sea*: Hebrew *yam suph* "Sea of Reeds," one of the marshes or fresh water lakes near the eastern part of the Nile Delta. This identification is based on Exodus 13.17—14.9, which lists the towns on the route of the Israelites before crossing the sea. In the Greek translation of the Scriptures made about 200 B.C., the "Sea of Reeds" was named "Red Sea." [h]2.14 *We pray . . . promise*: Or "If you save our lives, we will save yours!" [i]2.15 *wall*: In ancient times, cities and larger towns had high walls around them to protect them against attack. Sometimes houses were built against the wall so that the city wall formed one wall of the house. This added strength to the city wall. [j]3.2 *Two days later*: The Hebrew text has "At the end of three days," two days after they had set up camp. [k]3.3,4 *the priests*: The Hebrew text has "the priests, the Levites"; priests belonged to the tribe of Levi. [l]3.5 *Make yourselves acceptable*: People had to do certain things to make themselves acceptable to worship the LORD (see Leviticus 7.20, 21; 15.2, 33; 22.4-8; Deuteronomy 23.10, 11).

carrying the chest step into the Jordan, the water will stop flowing and
pile up as if someone had built a
dam across the river.
The LORD has also said that each
of the twelve tribes should choose
one man to represent it.
14 The Israelites packed up and left
camp. The priests carrying the chest
walked in front, 15 until they came to the
Jordan River. The water in the river had
risen over its banks, as it often does
in springtime.[m] But as soon as the feet
of the priests touched the water, 16-17 the
river stopped flowing, and the water
started piling up at the town of Adam
near Zarethan. No water flowed toward
the Dead Sea, and the priests stood in
the middle of the dry riverbed near Jericho while everyone else crossed over.

The People Set Up a Monument

4 After Israel had crossed the Jordan,
the LORD said to Joshua:
2-3 Tell[n] one man from each of the
twelve tribes to pick up a large rock
from where the priests are standing.
Then have the men set up those
rocks as a monument at the place
where you camp tonight.
4 Joshua chose twelve men; he called
them together, 5 and told them:
Go to the middle of the riverbed
where the sacred chest is, and pick
up a large rock. Carry it on your
shoulder to our camp. There are
twelve of you, so there will be one
rock for each tribe. 6-7 Someday your
children will ask, "Why are these
rocks here?" Then you can tell them
how the water stopped flowing
when the chest was being carried
across the river. These rocks will always remind our people of what
happened here today.
8 The men followed the instructions
that the LORD had given Joshua. They
picked up twelve rocks, one for each
tribe, and carried them to the camp,
where they put them down.
9 Joshua had some other men set up a
monument next to the place where the
priests were standing. This monument
was also made of twelve large rocks,
and it is still there in the middle of the
river.

The People of Israel Set Up Camp at Gilgal

10-13 The army got ready for battle and
crossed the Jordan. They marched
quickly past the sacred chest[o] and into
the desert near Jericho. Forty thousand
soldiers from the tribes of Reuben, Gad,
and East Manasseh[p] led the way, as
Moses had ordered.[q]
The priests stayed right where they
were until the army had followed the orders that the LORD had given Moses and
Joshua. Then the army watched as the
priests carried the chest the rest of the
way across.
14-18 "Joshua," the LORD said, "have the
priests come up from the Jordan and
bring the chest with them." So Joshua
went over to the priests and told them
what the LORD had said. And as soon as
the priests carried the chest past the
highest place that the floodwaters of the
Jordan had reached, the river flooded its
banks again.
That's how the LORD showed the Israelites that Joshua was their leader.[r]
For the rest of Joshua's life, they respected him as they had respected
Moses.
19 It was the tenth day of the first
month[s] of the year when Israel crossed
the Jordan River. They set up camp at
Gilgal, which was east of the land controlled by Jericho. 20 The men who had
carried the twelve rocks from the Jordan brought them to Joshua, and they
made them into a monument. 21 Then
Joshua told the people:
Years from now your children will
ask you why these rocks are here.
22-23 Tell them, "The LORD our God
dried up the Jordan River so we
could walk across. He did the same
thing here for us that he did for our
people at the Red Sea,[t] 24 because he
wants everyone on earth to know
how powerful he is. And he wants us
to worship only him."

5 The Amorite kings west of the Jordan River and the Canaanite kings
along the Mediterranean Sea lost their
courage and their will to fight, when
they heard how the LORD had dried
up the Jordan River to let Israel go
across.

[m] **3.15** *springtime*: Or "harvest time"; the grain harvest was in late spring. [n] **4.1-3** *Joshua . . . Tell*: Or "Joshua, you and the other leaders must tell." [o] **4.10-13** *the sacred chest*: The Hebrew text has "the LORD." The army was marching past the sacred chest, which was a symbol of God's throne on earth (see 1 Samuel 4.4 and Exodus 25.10-22; 37.1-9).
[p] **4.10-13** *Forty thousand soldiers from the tribes of Reuben, Gad, and East Manasseh*: Or "There were forty thousand soldiers altogether, and those from the tribes of Reuben, Gad, and East Manasseh." [q] **4.10-13** *Moses . . . ordered*: See Numbers 32.16-32; Joshua 1.12-16.
[r] **4.14-18** *leader*: See 3.7. [s] **4.19** *first month*: Abib (also called Nisan), the first month of the Hebrew calendar, from about mid-March to mid-April. [t] **4.22,23** *Red Sea*: See the note at 2.10.

Israel Gets Ready To Celebrate Passover

2 While Israel was camped at Gilgal,
the LORD said, "Joshua, make some flint
knives[u] and circumcise the rest of the
Israelite men and boys."[v]
3 Joshua made the knives, then circumcised those men and boys at Haaraloth Hill.[w] 4-7 This had to be done, because none of Israel's baby boys had
been circumcised during the forty years
that Israel had wandered through the
desert after leaving Egypt.

And why had they wandered for forty
years? It was because right after they
left Egypt, the men in the army had disobeyed the LORD. And the LORD had
said, "None of you men will ever live to
see the land that I promised Israel. It is
a land rich with milk and honey, and
someday your children will live there,
but not before you die here in the
desert."
8 Everyone who had been circumcised
needed time to heal, and they stayed in
camp.
9 The LORD told Joshua, "It was a disgrace for my people to be slaves in
Egypt, but now I have taken away that
disgrace." So the Israelites named
the place Gilgal,[x] and it still has that
name.
10 Israel continued to camp at Gilgal in
the desert near Jericho, and on the fourteenth day of the same month,[y] they celebrated Passover.
11-12 The next day, God stopped sending the Israelites manna[z] to eat each
morning, and they started eating food
grown in the land of Canaan. They ate
roasted grain[a] and thin bread[b] made of
the barley they had gathered from
nearby fields.

Israel Captures Jericho

13 One day, Joshua was near Jericho
when he saw a man standing some distance in front of him. The man was
holding a sword, so Joshua walked up to
him and asked, "Are you on our side or
on our enemies' side?"
14 "Neither," he answered. "I am here
because I am the commander of the
LORD's army."

Joshua fell to his knees and bowed
down to the ground. "I am your servant," he said. "Tell me what to do."
15 "Take off your sandals," the commander answered. "This is a holy place."

So Joshua took off his sandals.

6 Meanwhile, the people of Jericho
had been locking the gates in their
town wall because they were afraid of
the Israelites. No one could go out or
come in.
2-3 The LORD said to Joshua:

> With my help, you and your army
> will defeat the king of Jericho and
> his army, and you will capture the
> town. Here is how to do it: March
> slowly around Jericho once a day
> for six days. 4 Take along the sacred
> chest and have seven priests walk in
> front of it, carrying trumpets.[c]
>
> But on the seventh day, march
> slowly around the town seven times
> while the priests blow their trum-
> pets. 5 Then the priests will blast on
> their trumpets, and everyone else
> will shout. The wall will fall down,
> and your soldiers can go straight in
> from every side.

6 Joshua called the priests together
and said, "Take the chest and have
seven priests carry trumpets and march
ahead of it."
7-10 Next, he gave the army their orders: "March slowly around Jericho. A
few of you will go ahead of the chest to
guard it, but most of you will follow it.
Don't shout the battle cry or yell or even
talk until the day I tell you to. Then let
out a shout!"

As soon as Joshua finished giving the
orders, the army started marching. One
group of soldiers led the way, with seven
priests marching behind them and
blowing trumpets. Then came the
priests carrying the chest, followed by
the rest of the soldiers. 11 They obeyed
Joshua's orders and carried the chest
once around the town before returning
to camp for the night.
12-14 Early the next morning, Joshua
and everyone else started marching
around Jericho in the same order as the
day before. One group of soldiers was in
front, followed by the seven priests with

[u] **5.2** *flint knives*: Flint is a stone that can be chipped until it forms a very sharp edge.
[v] **5.2** *circumcise . . . men and boys*: They could not celebrate Passover unless they were circumcised (see Exodus 12.43-49). [w] **5.3** *Haaraloth Hill*: Or "Foreskin Hill." [x] **5.9** *Gilgal*: In Hebrew "Gilgal" sounds like "take away." [y] **5.10** *the same month*: See the note at 4.19.
[z] **5.11,12** *manna*: The special food that God provided for the Israelites while they were in the desert for forty years. It was about the size of a small seed, and it appeared on the ground during the night, except on the Sabbath. It was gathered early in the morning, ground up, and then baked or boiled (see Exodus 16.13-35; Numbers 11.4-9). [a] **5.11,12** *roasted grain*: Roasted grain was made by cooking the grain in a dry pan or on a flat rock, or by holding a bunch of grain stalks over a fire. [b] **5.11,12** *thin bread*: Bread made without yeast. Israelites were not supposed to eat bread made with yeast for the week following Passover. That week is called the Festival of Thin Bread (see Exodus 12.14-20; 13.3-7). [c] **6.4** *trumpets*: These were hollowed-out ram's horns.

trumpets and the priests who carried
the chest. The rest of the army came
next. The seven priests blew their trumpets while everyone marched slowly
around Jericho and back to camp. They
did this once a day for six days.
15On the seventh day, the army got up
at daybreak. They marched slowly
around Jericho the same as they had
done for the past six days, except on
this day they went around seven times.
16Then the priests blew the trumpets,
and Joshua yelled:

Get ready to shout! The LORD will
let you capture this town. 17But you
must destroy it and everything in it,
to show that it now belongs to the
LORD.[d] The woman Rahab helped
the spies we sent,[e] so protect her
and the others who are inside her
house. But kill everyone else in the
town. 18-19The silver and gold and
everything made of bronze and iron
belong to the LORD and must be put
in his treasury. Be careful to follow
these instructions, because if you
see something you want and take it,
the LORD will destroy Israel. And it
will be all your fault.[f]

20The priests blew their trumpets
again, and the soldiers shouted as loud
as they could. The walls of Jericho fell
flat. Then the soldiers rushed up the hill,
went straight into the town, and captured it. 21-25They killed everyone, men
and women, young and old, everyone
except Rahab and the others in her
house. They even killed every cow,
sheep, and donkey.

Joshua said to the two men who had
been spies, "Rahab kept you safe when I
sent you to Jericho. We promised to protect her and her family, and we will
keep that promise. Now go into her
house and bring them out."

The two men went into Rahab's house
and brought her out, along with her
father and mother, her brothers, and her
other relatives. Rahab and her family
had to stay in a place just outside the Israelite army camp.[g] But later they were
allowed to live among the Israelites, and
her descendants still do.

The Israelites took the silver and gold
and the things made of bronze and iron
and put them with the rest of the treasure that was kept at the LORD's house.[h]
Finally, they set fire to Jericho and
everything in it.
26After Jericho was destroyed, Joshua
warned the people, "Someday a man
will rebuild Jericho, but the LORD will
put a curse on him, and the man's oldest
son will die when he starts to build the
town wall. And by the time he finishes
the wall and puts gates in it, all his children will be dead."[i]
27The LORD helped Joshua in everything he did, and Joshua was famous
everywhere in Canaan.

Achan Is Punished for Stealing from the LORD

7 The LORD had said that everything
in Jericho belonged to him.[j] But
Achan[k] from the Judah tribe took some
of the things from Jericho for himself.
And so the LORD was angry with the Israelites, because one of them had disobeyed him.[l]
2While Israel was still camped near
Jericho, Joshua sent some spies with
these instructions: "Go to the town of
Ai[m] and find out whatever you can
about the region around the town."

The spies left and went to Ai, which is
east of Bethel and near Beth-Aven. 3They
went back to Joshua and reported, "You
don't need to send the whole army to attack Ai—two or three thousand troops
will be enough. Why bother the whole
army for a town that small?"
4-5Joshua sent about three thousand
soldiers to attack Ai. But the men of Ai
fought back and chased the Israelite soldiers away from the town gate and
down the hill to the stone quarries.[n]
Thirty-six Israelite soldiers were killed,
and the Israelite army felt discouraged.
6Joshua and the leaders of Israel tore
their clothes and put dirt on their heads
to show their sorrow. They lay facedown
on the ground in front of the sacred
chest until sunset. 7Then Joshua said:

Our LORD, did you bring us across
the Jordan River just so the Amo-

[d]**6.17** *destroy . . . now belongs to the LORD*: Destroying a city and everything in it, including its people and animals, showed that it belonged to the LORD and could no longer be used by humans. [e]**6.17** *sent*: See 2.1, 21. [f]**6.18,19** *Be careful . . . fault*: One ancient translation; Hebrew "Don't keep any of it for yourself. If you do, the LORD will destroy both you and Israel."
[g]**6.21-25** *camp*: Rahab and her family were Canaanites and were considered unclean. If they stayed in the Israelite army camp, the Lord would not help the Israelite army in battle (see Deuteronomy 23.9-14). However, Rahab and her family later became part of Israel.
[h]**6.21-25** *the LORD's house*: A name for the place of worship, which at that time was the sacred tent. [i]**6.26** *by the time . . . dead*: Or "when he puts gates into the town wall, his youngest son will die." [j]**7.1** *belonged to him*: See the note at 6.17. [k]**7.1** *Achan*: The Hebrew text has "Achan, son of Carmi, grandson of Abdi, and great-grandson of Zerah." [l]**7.1** *the LORD was angry . . . disobeyed him*: Even though only one person had disobeyed, it meant that the LORD's instructions to the people of Israel had not been followed, and the whole nation was held responsible. [m]**7.2** *of Ai*: Or "called The Ruins." [n]**7.4,5** *stone quarries*: Or "Shebarim."

rites could destroy us? This wouldn't
have happened if we had agreed to
stay on the other side of the Jordan.
[8]I don't even know what to say to
you, since Israel's army has turned
and run from the enemy. [9]Everyone
will think you weren't strong
enough to protect your people. Now
the Canaanites and everyone else
who lives in the land will surround
us and wipe us out.
[10]The LORD answered:
Stop lying there on the ground!
Get up! [11]I said everything in Jericho
belonged to me and had to be destroyed. But the Israelites have kept
some of the things for themselves.
They stole from me and hid what
they took. Then they lied about it.
[12]What they stole was supposed to
be destroyed, and now Israel itself
must be destroyed. I cannot help you
anymore until you do exactly what I
have said. That's why Israel turns
and runs from its enemies instead of
standing up to them.
[13]Tell the people of Israel, "Tomorrow you will meet with the LORD
your God, so make yourselves acceptable to worship him. The LORD
says that you have taken things that
should have been destroyed. You
won't be able to stand up to your enemies until you get rid of those
things.
[14]"Tomorrow morning everyone
must gather near the place of worship. You will come forward tribe by
tribe, and the LORD will show which
tribe is guilty. Next, the clans in that
tribe must come forward, and the
LORD will show which clan is guilty.
The families in that clan must come,
and the LORD will point out the
guilty family. Finally, the men in that
family must come, [15]and the LORD
will show who stole what should
have been destroyed. That man must
be put to death, his body burned,
and his possessions thrown into the
fire. He has done a terrible thing by
breaking the sacred agreement that
the LORD made with Israel."
[16]Joshua got up early the next morning and brought each tribe to the place
of worship, where the LORD showed that
the Judah tribe was guilty. [17]Then
Joshua brought the clans of Judah to
the LORD, and the LORD showed that the
Zerah clan was guilty. One by one he
brought the leader of each family in the
Zerah clan to the LORD, and the LORD
showed that Zabdi's family was guilty.
[18]Finally, Joshua brought each man in
Zabdi's family to the LORD, and the
LORD showed that Achan was the guilty
one.
[19]"Achan," Joshua said, "the LORD God
of Israel has decided that you are guilty.
Is this true? Tell me what you did, and
don't try to hide anything."
[20]"It's true," Achan answered. "I
sinned and disobeyed the LORD God of
Israel. [21-22]While we were in Jericho, I
saw a beautiful Babylonian robe, two
hundred pieces of silver, and a gold bar
that weighed the same as fifty pieces of
gold. I wanted them for myself, so I took
them. I dug a hole under my tent and
hid the silver, the gold, and the robe."
Joshua had some people run to
Achan's tent, where they found the silver, the gold, and the robe. [23]They
brought them back and put them in
front of the sacred chest, so Joshua and
the rest of the Israelites could see them.
[24]Then everyone took Achan and the
things he had stolen to Trouble Valley.[o]
They also took along his sons and
daughters, his cattle, donkeys, and
sheep, his tent, and everything else that
belonged to him.
[25]Joshua said, "Achan, you caused us
a lot of trouble. Now the LORD is paying
you back with the same kind of trouble."
The people of Israel then stoned to
death Achan and his family. They made
a fire and burned the bodies, together
with what Achan had stolen, and all his
possessions. [26]They covered the remains
with a big pile of rocks, which is still
there. Then the LORD stopped being angry with Israel.
That's how the place came to be
called Trouble Valley.

Israel Destroys the Town of Ai

8 [1-2]The LORD told Joshua:
Don't be afraid, and don't be discouraged by what happened at the
town of Ai. Take the army and attack again. But first, have part of the
army set up an ambush on the other
side of the town. I will help you defeat the king of Ai and his army, and
you will capture the town and the
land around it. Destroy Ai and kill
its king as you did at Jericho. But
you may keep the livestock and
everything else you want.
[3-4]Joshua quickly got the army ready
to attack Ai. He chose thirty thousand of
his best soldiers and gave them these
orders:
Tonight, while it is dark, march to
Ai and take up a position behind the
town. Get as close to the town as
you can without being seen, but be
ready to attack.
[5-6]The rest of the army will come

[o] 7.24 *Trouble Valley*: Or "Achor Valley."

with me and attack near the gate.
When the people of Ai come out to
fight, we'll run away and let them
chase us. They will think we are running from them just like the first
time. But when we've let them chase
us far enough away, 7 you come out
of hiding. The LORD our God will
help you capture the town. 8 Then set
it on fire, as the LORD has told us to
do. Those are your orders, 9 now go!
The thirty thousand soldiers went to a
place on the west side of Ai, between Ai
and Bethel, where they could hide and
wait to attack.
That night, Joshua stayed in camp
with the rest of the army. 10 Early the
next morning he got his troops ready to
move out, and he and the other leaders
of Israel led them to Ai. 11 They set up
camp in full view of the town, across the
valley to the north. 12 Joshua had already
sent five thousand soldiers to the west
side of the town to hide and wait to attack. 13 Now all his troops were in place.
Part of the army was in the camp to the
north of Ai, and the others were hiding
to the west, ready to make a surprise attack. That night, Joshua went into the
valley.[p]
14-15 The king of Ai saw Joshua's army,
so the king and his troops hurried out
early the next morning to fight them.
Joshua and his army pretended to be
beaten, and they let the men of Ai chase
them toward the desert. The king and
his army were facing the Jordan valley
as Joshua had planned.
The king did not realize that some Israelite soldiers were hiding behind the
town. 16-17 So he called out every man in
Ai to go after Joshua's troops. They all
rushed out to chase the Israelite army,
and they left the town gates wide open.
Not one man was left in Ai or in Bethel.[q]
Joshua let the men of Ai chase him
and his army farther and farther away
from Ai. 18 Finally, the LORD told Joshua,
"Point your sword[r] at the town of Ai, because now I am going to help you defeat
it!"
As soon as Joshua pointed his sword
at the town, 19 the soldiers who had been
hiding got up and ran into the town.
They captured it and set it on fire.
20-21 When Joshua and his troops saw
smoke rising from the town, they knew
that the other part of their army had
captured it. So they turned and attacked.
The men of Ai looked back and saw
smoke rising from their town. But they
could not escape, because the soldiers
they had been chasing had suddenly
turned and started fighting. 22-24 Meanwhile, the other Israelite soldiers had
come from the town and attacked the
men of Ai from the rear. The Israelites
captured the king of Ai and brought him
to Joshua. They also chased the rest of
the men of Ai into the desert and killed
them.[s]
The Israelite army went back to Ai
and killed everyone there. 25-26 Joshua
kept his sword pointed at the town of Ai
until every last one of Ai's twelve thousand people was dead. 27 But the Israelites took the animals and the other
possessions of the people of Ai, because
this was what the LORD had told Joshua
to do.
28-29 Joshua made sure every building
in Ai was burned to the ground. He told
his men to kill the king of Ai and hang
his body on a tree. Then at sunset he
told the Israelites to take down the
body,[t] throw it in the gateway of the
town, and cover it with a big pile of
rocks. Those rocks are still there, and
the town itself has never been rebuilt.

Joshua Reads the Blessings and Curses

(Deuteronomy 27.1-26)

30-32 One day, Joshua led the people of
Israel to Mount Ebal, where he told
some of his men, "Build an altar for offering sacrifices to the LORD. And use
stones that have never been cut with
iron tools,[u] because that is what Moses
taught in *The Book of the Law*."[v]
Joshua offered sacrifices to please the
LORD[w] and to ask his blessing.[x] Then
with the Israelites still watching, he
copied parts of *The Book of the Law*[y] of
Moses onto stones.
33-35 Moses had said that everyone in
Israel was to go to the valley between
Mount Ebal and Mount Gerizim, where
they were to be blessed. So everyone
went there, including the foreigners, the

[p] **8.13** *valley*: This may refer either to the Jordan River valley or to the valley between the Israelite camp and Ai. [q] **8.16,17** *Ai or in Bethel*: Hebrew; one ancient translation "Ai." [r] **8.18** *sword*: Or "spear." [s] **8.22-24** *Joshua. They also chased . . . them*: Or "Joshua. The men of Ai had chased the Israelites into the desert, but the Israelites killed them there." [t] **8.28,29** *take down the body*: See Deuteronomy 21.22, 23. [u] **8.30-32** *use stones . . . iron tools*: See Exodus 20.25. [v] **8.30-32** *taught . . . Law*: Or "commanded . . . Teachings." [w] **8.30-32** *sacrifices to please the LORD*: These sacrifices have been traditionally called "whole burnt offerings" because the whole animal was burned on the altar. A main purpose of such sacrifices was to please the LORD with the smell of the sacrifice, and so in the CEV they are often called "sacrifices to please the LORD." [x] **8.30-32** *to ask his blessing*: These sacrifices have traditionally been called "peace offerings," or "offerings of well-being." A main purpose was to ask for the LORD's blessing, and so in the CEV they are often called "sacrifices to ask the LORD's blessing." [y] **8.30-32** *Law*: Or "Teachings."

leaders, officials, and judges. Half of the
people stood on one side of the valley,
and half on the other side, with the
priests from the Levi tribe standing in
the middle with the sacred chest. Then
in a loud voice, Joshua read the blessings and curses from *The Book of the*
Law[y] of Moses.[z]

The People of Gibeon Trick the Leaders of Israel

9 1-2 The kings west of the Jordan
River heard about Joshua's victories, and so they got together and decided to attack Joshua and Israel. These
kings were from the hill country and
from the foothills to the west, as well
as from the Mediterranean seacoast as
far north as the Lebanon Mountains.
Some of them were Hittites, others were
Amorites or Canaanites, and still
others were Perizzites, Hivites, or Jebusites.
3 The people of Gibeon had also heard
what Joshua had done to Jericho and
Ai. 4 So they decided that some of their
men should pretend to be messengers to
Israel from a faraway country.[a] The men
put worn-out bags on their donkeys and
found some old wineskins that had
cracked and had been sewn back together. 5 Their sandals were old and
patched, and their clothes were worn
out. They even took along some dry and
crumbly bread. 6 Then they went to the
Israelite camp at Gilgal, where they said
to Joshua and the men of Israel, "We
have come from a country that is far
from here. Please make a peace treaty
with us."
7-8 The Israelites replied, "But maybe
you really live near us. We can't make a
peace treaty with you if you live
nearby."[b]
The Gibeonites[c] said, "If you make a
peace treaty with us, we will be your
servants."
"Who are you?" Joshua asked. "Where
do you come from?"
They answered:
9 We are your servants, and we live
far from here. We came because the
LORD your God is so famous. We
heard what the LORD did in Egypt
10 and what he did to those two
Amorite kings on the other side of
the Jordan: King Og of Bashan, who
lived in Ashtaroth, and King Sihon
of Heshbon.
11 Our leaders and everyone who
lives in our country told us to meet
with you and tell you that all of us
are your servants. They said to ask
you to make a peace treaty with our
people. They told us to be sure and
take along enough food for our journey. 12 See this dry, crumbly bread of
ours? It was hot out of the oven
when we packed the food on the day
we left our homes. 13 These cracked
wineskins were new when we filled
them, and our clothes and sandals
are worn out because we have traveled so far.
14 The Israelites tried some of the
food,[d] but they did not ask the LORD if
he wanted them to make a treaty. 15 So
Joshua made a peace treaty with the
messengers and promised that Israel
would not kill their people. Israel's leaders swore that Israel would keep this
promise.
16-17 A couple of days later,[e] the Israelites found out that these people actually lived in the nearby towns of Gibeon, Chephirah, Beeroth, and Kiriath-
Jearim.[f] So the Israelites left the place
where they had camped and arrived at
the four towns two days later.[g] 18 But
they did not attack the towns, because
the Israelite leaders had sworn in the
name of the LORD that they would let
these people live.
The Israelites complained about their
leaders' decision not to attack, 19-21 but
the leaders reminded them, "We promised these people in the name of the
LORD God of Israel that we would let
them live, so we must not harm them. If
we break our promise, God will punish
us. We'll let them live, but we'll make
them cut wood and carry water for our
people."
22 Joshua told some of his soldiers, "I
want to meet with the Gibeonite leaders.
Bring them here."
When the Gibeonites came, Joshua
said, "You live close to us. Why did you
lie by claiming you lived far away?
23 Now you are under a curse, and your
people will have to send workers to cut

[y] **8.33-35** *Law*: Or "Teachings." [z] **8.33-35** *the blessings . . . Moses*: Or "all of *The Book of the Law of Moses*, including the blessings and the curses." [a] **9.4** *So . . . country*: One possible meaning for the difficult Hebrew text. [b] **9.7,8** *nearby*: See Deuteronomy 20.10-18. [c] **9.7,8** *Gibeonites*: Hebrew "Hivites." [d] **9.14** *tried . . . food*: Probably to see if it really was old or to show that they wanted peace. [e] **9.16,17** *A couple . . . later*: The Hebrew text has "At the end of three days," meaning two days after the day the treaty was made. [f] **9.16,17** *Gibeon, Chephirah, Beeroth, and Kiriath-Jearim*: These towns were twenty to thirty miles west of the Israelite camp at Gilgal. [g] **9.16,17** *A couple of days . . . later*: Or "A couple of days later, the Israelites moved their camp to the area near the towns of Gibeon, Chephirah, Beeroth, and Kiriath-Jearim. When they arrived, they realized that they had made a peace treaty with the people of these nearby towns!"

wood and carry water for the place of
worship."[h]
24The Gibeonites answered, "The
LORD your God told his servant Moses
that you were to kill everyone who lives
here and take their land for yourselves.
We were afraid you would kill us, and so
we tricked you into making a peace
treaty. But we agreed to be your servants, 25and you are strong enough to
do anything to us that you want. We just
ask you to do what seems right."
26Joshua did not let the Israelites kill
the Gibeonites, 27but he did tell the
Gibeonites that they would have to be
servants of the nation of Israel. They
would have to cut firewood and bring it
for the priests to use for burning sacrifices on the LORD's altar, wherever the
LORD decided the altar would be. The
Gibeonites would also have to carry water for the priests. And that is still the
work of the Gibeonites.

Joshua Commands the Sun To Stand Still

10 King Adonizedek of Jerusalem[i]
heard that Joshua had captured
and destroyed the town of Ai, and then
killed its king as he had done at Jericho.
He also learned that the Gibeonites had
signed a peace treaty with Israel. 2This
frightened Adonizedek and his people.
They knew that Gibeon was a large
town, as big as the towns that had
kings, and even bigger than the town of
Ai had been. And all of the men of
Gibeon were warriors. 3So Adonizedek
sent messages to the kings of four other
towns: King Hoham of Hebron, King Pi-
ram of Jarmuth, King Japhia of Lachish,
and King Debir of Eglon. The messages
said, 4"The Gibeonites have signed a
peace treaty with Joshua and the Israelites. Come and help me attack
Gibeon!"
5When these five Amorite kings called
their armies together and attacked
Gibeon, 6the Gibeonites sent a message
to the Israelite camp at Gilgal: "Joshua,
please come and rescue us! The Amorite
kings from the hill country have joined
together and are attacking us. We are
your servants, so don't let us down.
Please hurry!"
7Joshua and his army, including his
best warriors, left Gilgal. 8"Joshua," the
LORD said, "don't be afraid of the Amorites. They will run away when you attack, and I will help you defeat them."
9Joshua marched all night from Gilgal
to Gibeon and made a surprise attack
on the Amorite camp. 10The LORD made
the enemy panic, and the Israelites
started killing them right and left. They[j]
chased the Amorite troops up the road
to Beth-Horon and kept on killing them,
until they reached the towns of Azekah
and Makkedah.[k] 11And while these
troops were going down through Beth-
Horon Pass,[l] the LORD made huge hailstones fall on them all the way to
Azekah. More of the enemy soldiers
died from the hail than from the Israelite weapons.
12-13The LORD was helping the Israelites defeat the Amorites that day. So
about noon, Joshua prayed to the LORD
loud enough for the Israelites to hear:

"Our LORD, make the sun stop
  in the sky over Gibeon,
and the moon stand still
  over Aijalon Valley."[m]
So the sun and the moon
  stopped and stood still
until Israel defeated its enemies.

This poem can be found in *The Book of
Jashar*.[n] The sun stood still and didn't
go down for about a whole day. 14Never
before and never since has the LORD
done anything like that for someone
who prayed. The LORD was really fighting for Israel.
15After the battle, Joshua and the Israelites went back to their camp at Gilgal.

Joshua Kills the Five Enemy Kings

16While the enemy soldiers were running from the Israelites, the five enemy
kings ran away and hid in a cave near
Makkedah. 17Joshua's soldiers told him,
"The five kings have been found in a
cave near Makkedah."
18Joshua answered, "Roll some big
stones over the mouth of the cave and
leave a few soldiers to guard it. 19But
you and everyone else must keep after
the enemy troops, because they will be
safe if they reach their walled towns.
Don't let them get away! The LORD our
God is helping us get rid of them." 20So
Joshua and the Israelites almost wiped
out the enemy soldiers. Only a few
safely reached their walled towns.
21The Israelite army returned to their
camp at Makkedah, where Joshua was
waiting for them. No one around there
dared say anything bad about the Is-

[h] **9.23** *the place of worship*: The Hebrew text has "God's house," which at that time was the sacred tent. [i] **10.1** *Jerusalem*: Jerusalem was not an Israelite city at this time.
[j] **10.10** *They*: Or "The LORD." [k] **10.10** *Makkedah*: A total distance of about twenty-five miles.
[l] **10.11** *Beth-Horon Pass*: A two-mile long, steeply-sloping valley between the towns of Upper Beth-Horon and Lower Beth-Horon. [m] **10.12,13** *Aijalon Valley*: A valley southwest of Beth-Horon Pass. [n] **10.12,13** *Book of Jashar*: This book may have been a collection of ancient war songs.

raelites. [22]Joshua told his soldiers, "Now, move the rocks from the entrance to the cave and bring those five kings to me."

[23]The soldiers opened the entrance to the cave and brought out the kings of Jerusalem, Hebron, Jarmuth, Lachish, and Eglon. [24]After Joshua had called the army together, he forced the five kings to lie down on the ground. Then he called his officers forward and told them, "You fought these kings along with me, so put your feet on their necks." The officers did, [25]and Joshua continued, "Don't ever be afraid or discouraged. Be brave and strong. This is what the LORD will do to all your enemies."

[26]Joshua killed the five kings and told his men to hang each body on a tree. Then at sunset [27]he told some of his troops, "Take the bodies down and throw them into the cave where the kings were found. Cover the entrance to the cave with big rocks."

Joshua's troops obeyed his orders, and those rocks are still there.

Joshua Continues the Fighting

[28]Later that day, Joshua captured Makkedah and killed its king and everyone else in the town, just as he had done at Jericho.

[29]Joshua and his army left Makkedah and attacked the town of Libnah. [30]The LORD let them capture the town and its king, and they killed the king and everyone else, just as they had done at Jericho.

[31]Joshua then led his army to Lachish, and they set up camp around the town. They attacked, [32]and the next day the LORD let them capture the town. They killed everyone, as they had done at Libnah. [33]King Horam of Gezer arrived to help Lachish, but Joshua and his troops attacked and destroyed him and his army.

[34]From Lachish, Joshua took his troops to Eglon, where they set up camp surrounding the town. They attacked, [35]captured it that same day, then killed everyone, as they had done at Lachish.

[36]Joshua and his army left Eglon and attacked Hebron. [37]They captured the town and the nearby villages, then killed everyone, including the king. They destroyed Hebron in the same way they had destroyed Eglon.

[38]Joshua and the Israelite army turned and attacked Debir. [39]They captured the town, and its nearby villages. Then they destroyed Debir and killed its king, together with everyone else, just as they had done with Hebron and Libnah.

[40]Joshua captured towns everywhere in the land: In the central hill country and the foothills to the west, in the Southern Desert and the region that slopes down toward the Dead Sea. Whenever he captured a town, he would kill the king and everyone else, as the LORD God of Israel had commanded. [41]Joshua wiped out towns from Kadesh-Barnea to Gaza, everywhere in the region of Goshen,[o] and as far north as Gibeon. [42-43]The LORD fought on Israel's side, so Joshua and the Israelite army were able to capture these kings and take their land. They fought one battle after another, then they went back to their camp at Gilgal after capturing all that land.

Joshua Captures Towns in the North

11 King Jabin of Hazor heard about Joshua's victories, so he sent messages to many nearby kings and asked them to join him in fighting Israel. He sent these messages to King Jobab of Madon, the kings of Shimron and Achshaph, [2]the kings in the northern hill country and in the Jordan River valley south of Lake Galilee,[p] and the kings in the foothills and in Naphath-Dor to the west. [3]He sent messages to the Canaanite kings in the east and the west, to the Amorite, Hittite, Perizzite, and Jebusite kings in the hill country, and to the Hivite kings in the region of Mizpah, near the foot of Mount Hermon.[q]

[4-5]The kings and their armies went to Merom Pond,[r] where they set up camp, and got ready to fight Israel. It seemed as though there were more soldiers and horses and chariots than there are grains of sand on a beach.

[6]The LORD told Joshua:

Don't let them frighten you! I'll
help you defeat them, and by this
time tomorrow they will be dead.

When you attack, the first thing
you have to do is to cripple their
horses. Then after the battle is over,[s]
burn their chariots.

[7]Joshua and his army made a surprise attack against the enemy camp at Merom Pond[t] [8-9]and crippled the enemies'

[o]**10.41** *Goshen*: A region between the hill country of Judah and the desert further south. Not the same Goshen as in Genesis 47.4-6. [p]**11.2** *Lake Galilee*: The Hebrew text has "Lake Chinnereth," an earlier name. [q]**11.3** *Mizpah, near the foot of Mount Hermon*: Probably the same region as Mizpeh Valley in verses 8, 9, but different from the two other places named Mizpeh in 15.37-41; 18.25-28, and also different from the Mizpah mentioned in Genesis 31.49 and Judges 10.17. [r]**11.4,5** *Pond*: Or "Gorge." [s]**11.6** *When . . . over*: Or "After the battle is over, cripple their horses and burn their chariots." [t]**11.7** *Pond*: See the note at 11.4, 5.

horses.[u] Joshua followed the LORD's instructions, and the LORD helped Israel
defeat the enemy. The Israelite army
even chased enemy soldiers as far as
Misrephoth-Maim to the northwest,[v] the
city of Sidon to the north, and Mizpeh
Valley to the northeast.[w] None of the enemy soldiers escaped alive. The Israelites came back after the battle and
burned the enemy's chariots.
10 Up to this time, the king of Hazor
had controlled the kingdoms that had
joined together to attack Israel, so
Joshua led his army back and captured
Hazor. They killed its king 11 and everyone else, then they set the town on fire.
12-15 Joshua captured all the towns
where the enemy kings had ruled. These
towns were built on small hills,[x] and
Joshua did not set fire to any of these
towns, except Hazor. The Israelites kept
the animals and everything of value
from these towns, but they killed everyone who lived in them, including their
kings. That's what the LORD had told his
servant Moses to do, that's what Moses
had told Joshua to do, and that's exactly
what Joshua did.
16 Joshua and his army took control of
the northern and southern hill country,
the foothills to the west, the Southern
Desert, the whole region of Goshen,[y]
and the Jordan River valley. 17-18 They
took control of the land from Mount Halak near the country of Edom in the
south to Baal-Gad in Lebanon Valley at
the foot of Mount Hermon in the north.
Joshua and his army were at war with
the kings in this region for a long time,
but finally they captured and put to
death the last king.
19-20 The LORD had told Moses that he
wanted the towns in this region destroyed and their people killed without
mercy. That's why the LORD made the
people in the towns stubborn and determined to fight Israel. The only town that
signed a peace treaty with Israel was
the Hivite town of Gibeon. The Israelite
army captured the rest of the towns in
battle.
21 During this same time, Joshua and
his army killed the Anakim[z] from the
northern and southern hill country.
They also destroyed the towns where
the Anakim had lived, including Hebron, Debir, and Anab. 22 There were not
any Anakim left in the regions where
the Israelites lived, although there were
still some in Gaza, Gath, and Ashdod.[a]
23 That's how Joshua captured the
land, just as the LORD had commanded
Moses, and Joshua divided it up among
the tribes.
Finally, there was peace in the land.

The Kings Defeated by the Israelites

12 Before Moses died, he and the
people of Israel had defeated two
kings east of the Jordan River. These
kings had ruled the region from the
Arnon River gorge in the south to
Mount Hermon in the north, including
the eastern side of the Jordan River valley.
2 The first king that Moses and the Israelites defeated was an Amorite, King
Sihon of Heshbon.[b] The southern border of his kingdom ran down the middle
of the Arnon River gorge, taking in the
town of Aroer on the northern edge of
the gorge. The Jabbok River separated
Sihon's kingdom from the Ammonites
on the east. Then the Jabbok turned
west and became his northern border,
so his kingdom included the southern
half of the region of Gilead. 3 Sihon also
controlled the eastern side of the Jordan
River valley from Lake Galilee[c] south to
Beth-Jeshimoth and the Dead Sea. In
addition to these regions, he ruled the
town called Slopes of Mount Pisgah[d]
and the land south of there at the foot of
the hill.
4 Next, Moses and the Israelites defeated King Og of Bashan,[e] who lived in
the town of Ashtaroth part of each year
and in Edrei the rest of the year. Og was
one of the last of the Rephaim.[f] 5 His
kingdom stretched north to Mount
Hermon, east to the town of Salecah,
and included the land of Bashan as far
west as the borders of the kingdoms of
Geshur and Maacah. He also ruled the
northern half of Gilead.
6 Moses, the LORD's servant, had led
the people of Israel in defeating Sihon
and Og. Then Moses gave their land to

[u] **11.8,9** *and crippled the enemies' horses*: It is also possible that the Israelites crippled the enemies' horses after the battle at the same time they burned the enemies' chariots; see the note at 11.6. [v] **11.8,9** *Misrephoth-Maim . . . northwest*: Or "the town of Misrephoth to the northwest" or "the Misrephoth River." [w] **11.8,9** *northeast*: These three areas were twenty to thirty-five miles north of Merom. [x] **11.12-15** *small hills*: Towns were often built on top of the ruins of a previous town that had been destroyed. When this happened many times at one place, a hill was formed. [y] **11.16** *Goshen*: See the note at 10.41. [z] **11.21** *Anakim*: Perhaps a group of very large people that lived in Palestine before the Israelites (see Numbers 13.33 and Deuteronomy 2.10, 11, 20, 21). [a] **11.22** *Gaza, Gath, and Ashdod*: Towns in Philistia.
[b] **12.2** *King Sihon of Heshbon*: See Numbers 21.21-31. [c] **12.3** *Lake Galilee*: See the note at 11.2. [d] **12.3** *the town called Slopes of Mount Pisgah*: Or "the slopes of Mount Pisgah."
[e] **12.4** *King Og of Bashan*: See Numbers 21.33-35. [f] **12.4** *Rephaim*: Perhaps a group of very large people that lived in Palestine before the Israelites (see Deuteronomy 2.10, 11, 20, 21).

the tribes of Reuben, Gad, and East
Manasseh.
7–8Later, Joshua and the Israelites defeated many kings west of the Jordan
River, from Baal-Gad in Lebanon Valley
in the north to Mount Halak near the
country of Edom in the south. This region included the hill country and the
foothills, the Jordan River valley and its
western slopes, and the Southern
Desert. Joshua and the Israelites took
this land from the Hittites, the Amorites,
the Canaanites, the Perizzites, the
Hivites, and the Jebusites. Joshua di-
vided up the land among the tribes of Israel.
The Israelites defeated the kings of
the following towns west of the Jordan
River:
9-24Jericho, Ai near Bethel, Jeru-
salem, Hebron, Jarmuth, Lachish,
Eglon, Gezer, Debir, Geder, Hormah,
Arad, Libnah, Adullam, Makkedah,
Bethel, Tappuah, Hepher, Aphek,
Lasharon,[g] Madon, Hazor, Shimron-
Meron, Achshaph, Taanach,
Megiddo, Kedesh, Jokneam on
Mount Carmel, Dor in Naphath-Dor,
Goiim in Galilee,[h] and Tirzah.[i]
There were thirty-one of these kings in
all.

The Land Israel Had Not Yet Taken

13 Many years later, the LORD told
Joshua:
Now you are very old, but there is
still a lot of land that Israel has not
yet taken. 2-7First, there is the Canaanite territory that starts at the
Shihor River just east of Egypt and
goes north to Ekron. The southern
part of this region belongs to the
Avvites and the Geshurites,[j] and the
land around Gaza, Ashdod, Ashkelon, Gath, and Ekron belongs to
the five Philistine rulers.
The other Canaanite territory is in
the north. Its northern border starts
at the town of Arah, which belongs
to the Sidonians. From there, it goes
to Aphek,[k] then along the Amorite
border[l] to Hamath Pass.[m] The eastern border starts at Hamath Pass
and goes south to Baal-Gad at the
foot of Mount Hermon, and its
southern boundary runs west from
there to Misrephoth-Maim.[n] This
northern region includes the Lebanon Mountains and the land that
belongs to the Gebalites[o] and the
Sidonians who live in the hill country from the Lebanon Mountains to
Misrephoth-Maim.
With my help, Israel will capture
these Canaanite territories and force
out the people who live there. But
you must divide up the land from
the Jordan River to the Mediterranean Sea[p] among the nine tribes
and the half of Manasseh that don't
have any land yet. Then each tribe
will have its own land.

The Land East of the Jordan River

8Moses had already given land east of
the Jordan River to the tribes of
Reuben, Gad, and half of Manasseh.
9This region stretched north from the
town in the middle of the Arnon River
valley, and included the town of Aroer
on the northern edge of the valley. It
covered the flatlands of Medeba north
of Dibon, 10and took in the towns that
had belonged to Sihon, the Amorite
king of Heshbon. Some of these towns
were as far east as the Ammonite border.
11–12Geshur and Maacah were part of
this region, and so was the whole territory that King Og had ruled, that is,
Gilead, Mount Hermon, and all of
Bashan as far east as Salecah. Og had
lived in Ashtaroth part of each year, and
he had lived in Edrei the rest of the year.
Og had been one of the last of the
Rephaim,[q] but Moses had defeated
Sihon and Og and their people[r] and had
forced them to leave their land. 13How-
ever, the Israelites did not force the people of Geshur and Maacah to leave, and
they still live there among the Israelites.

Moses Did Not Give Land to the Levi Tribe

14Moses did not give any land to the
Levi tribe, because the LORD God of Israel had told them, "Instead of land, you
will receive the sacrifices offered at my
altar."

[g] **12.9-24** *Aphek, Lasharon*: Or "Aphek in the Sharon Plain." [h] **12.9-24** *Galilee*: One ancient translation; Hebrew "Gilgal." [i] **12.9-24** *Jericho . . . Tirzah*: There are some differences in this list between the Hebrew and several ancient translations. [j] **13.2-7** *Geshurites*: Not the same Geshur as in 12.5 and 13.11. One ancient translation has "Gezerites." Gezer was a town north of Ekron that the Israelites did not capture (see Judges 1.29). [k] **13.2-7** *Aphek*: Not the same Aphek as in 12.9-24. [l] **13.2-7** *Amorite border*: What had been the southern border of the old Amorite kingdom of Amurru. [m] **13.2-7** *Hamath Pass*: Or "Lebo-Hamath." [n] **13.2-7** *Misrephoth-Maim*: Or "Misrephoth" or "the Misrephoth River." [o] **13.2-7** *Gebalites*: Gebal was another name for Byblos. [p] **13.2-7** *from . . . Sea*: One ancient translation; the Hebrew text does not have these words. [q] **13.11,12** *Rephaim*: See the note at 12.4. [r] **13.11,12** *Sihon . . . people*: Or "the Rephaim."

Moses Gives Land to the Reuben Tribe

15 Moses gave land to each of the clans
in the Reuben tribe. 16 Their land started
in the south at the town in the middle of
the Arnon River valley, took in the town
of Aroer on the northern edge of the
valley, and went as far north as the flatlands around Medeba. 17-21 The Amorite
King Sihon had lived in Heshbon and
had ruled the towns in the flatlands.
Now Heshbon belonged to Reuben, and
so did the following towns in the flatlands: Dibon, Bamoth-Baal, Beth-Baal-
Meon, Jahaz, Kedemoth, Mephaath,
Kiriathaim, Sibmah, Zereth-Shahar on
the hill in the valley, Beth-Peor, Slopes
of Mount Pisgah, and Beth-Jeshimoth.
Moses defeated Sihon and killed him
and the Midianite chiefs who ruled
parts of his kingdom for him. Their
names were Evi, Rekem, Zur, Hur, and
Reba. 22 The Israelites also killed Balaam the son of Beor, who had been a
fortuneteller.
23 This region with its towns and villages was the land for the Reuben tribe,
and the Jordan River was its western
border.

Moses Gives Land to the Gad Tribe

24 Moses also gave land to each of the
clans in the Gad tribe. 25 It included the
town of Jazer, and in the Gilead region
their territory took in the land and
towns as far east as the town of Aroer[s]
just west of Rabbah.[t] This was about
half of the land that had once belonged
to the Ammonites. 26 The land given to
Gad stretched from Heshbon in the
south to Ramath-Mizpeh and Betonim
in the north, and even further north to
Mahanaim and Lidebor.[u] 27 Gad also received the eastern half of the Jordan
River valley, which had been ruled by
King Sihon of Heshbon. This territory
stretched as far north as Lake Galilee,[v]
and included the towns of Beth-Haram,
Beth-Nimrah, Succoth, and Zaphon.
28 These regions with their towns and
villages were given to the Gad tribe.

Moses Gives Land to Half of the Manasseh Tribe

29 Moses gave land east of the Jordan
River to half of the clans from the Manasseh tribe. 30-31 Their land started at
Mahanaim and took in the region that
King Og of Bashan had ruled, including
Ashtaroth and Edrei, the two towns
where he had lived. The villages where
the Jair clan settled were part of Manasseh's land, and so was the northern
half of the region of Gilead. The clans of
this half of Manasseh had sixty towns in
all.
The Manasseh tribe is sometimes
called the Machir tribe, after Manasseh's son Machir.
32 That was how Moses divided up the
Moab Plains to the east of Jericho on
the other side of the Jordan River, so
these two and a half tribes would have
land of their own. 33 But Moses did not
give any land to the Levi tribe, because
the LORD had promised that he would
always provide for them.

The Land West of the Jordan River

14 1-5 Nine and a half tribes still did
not have any land, although two
and a half tribes had already received
land east of the Jordan River. Moses had
divided that land among them, and he
had also said that the Levi tribe would
not receive a large region like the other
tribes. Instead, the people of Levi would
receive towns and the nearby pastures
for their sheep, goats, and cattle. And
since the descendants of Joseph had become the two tribes of Ephraim and
Manasseh, there were still nine and a
half tribes that needed land. The LORD
had told Moses that he would show
those tribes[w] how to divide up the land
of Canaan.
When the priest Eleazar, Joshua, and
the leaders of the families and tribes of
Israel met to divide up the land of
Canaan, the LORD showed them how to
do it.

Joshua Gives Hebron to Caleb

6 One day while the Israelites were still
camped at Gilgal, Caleb the son of Jephunneh went to talk with Joshua.
Caleb belonged to the Kenaz clan, and
many other people from the Judah tribe
went with Caleb. He told Joshua:
You know that back in Kadesh-
Barnea the LORD talked to his
prophet Moses about you and me. 7 I
was forty years old at the time
Moses sent me from Kadesh-Barnea
into Canaan as a spy. When I came
back and told him about the land,
everything I said was true. 8 The
other spies said things that made
our people afraid, but I completely
trusted the LORD God. 9 The same
day I came back, Moses told me,
"Since you were faithful to the LORD

[s] **13.25** *Aroer*: Not the same town as the Aroer in verse 16. [t] **13.25** *Rabbah*: The capital city of Ammon. [u] **13.26** *Lidebor*: This may be another name for Lodebar, a town a few miles east of the Jordan River and about ten miles south of Lake Galilee. [v] **13.27** *Lake Galilee*: See the note at 11.2. [w] **14.1-5** *he would show those tribes*: The Hebrew text has "those tribes must cast lots to find out." Pieces of wood or stone (called "lots") were used to find out what God wanted his people to do.

God, I promise that the places where
you went as a spy will belong to you
and your descendants forever."
10 Joshua, it was forty-five years
ago that the LORD told Moses to
make that promise, and now I am
eighty-five. Even though Israel has
moved from place to place in the
desert, the LORD has kept me alive
all this time as he said he would.
11 I'm just as strong today as I was
then, and I can still fight as well in
battle.
12 So I'm asking you for the hill
country that the LORD promised me
that day. You were there. You heard
the other spies talk about that part
of the hill country and the large,
walled towns where the Anakim[x]
live. But maybe the LORD will help
me take their land, just as he
promised.
13 Joshua prayed that God would help
Caleb, then he gave Hebron to Caleb and
his descendants. 14 And Hebron still belongs to Caleb's descendants, because
he was faithful to the LORD God of Israel.
15 Hebron used to be called Arba's
Town,[y] because Arba had been one of
the greatest[z] of the Anakim.
There was peace in the land.

Judah's Land

15 The clans of the Judah tribe were
given land that went south along
the border of Edom, and at its farthest
point south it even reached the Zin
Desert. 2 Judah's southern border started
at the south end of the Dead Sea. 3 As it
went west from there, it ran south of
Scorpion Pass[a] to Zin, and then came
up from the south to Kadesh-Barnea. It
continued past Hezron up to Addar,
turned toward Karka, 4 and ran along to
Azmon. After that, it followed the
Egyptian Gorge and ended at the Mediterranean Sea. This was also Israel's
southern border.
5 Judah's eastern border ran the full
length of the Dead Sea.
The northern border started at the
northern end of the Dead Sea.[b] 6 From
there it went west up to Beth-Hoglah,
continued north of Beth-Arabah, and
went up to the Monument of Bohan,[c]
who belonged to the Reuben tribe.
7 From there, it went to Trouble Valley[d]
and Debir,[e] then turned north and went
to Gilgal,[f] which is on the north side of
the valley across from Adummim Pass.
It continued on to Enshemesh, Enrogel,
8 and up through Hinnom Valley on the
land sloping south from Jerusalem. The
city of Jerusalem itself belonged to the
Jebusites.
Next, the border went up to the top of
the mountain on the west side of Hinnom Valley and at the north end of
Rephaim Valley. 9 At the top of the mountain it turned and went to Nephtoah
Spring and then to the ruins[g] on Mount
Ephron. From there, it went to Baalah,
which is now called Kiriath-Jearim.
10 From Baalah the northern border
curved west to Mount Seir and then ran
along the northern ridge of Mount
Jearim, where Chesalon is located. Then
it went down to Beth-Shemesh[h] and
over to Timnah. 11 It continued along to
the hillside north of Ekron, curved
around to Shikkeron, and then went to
Mount Baalah. After going to Jabneel,
the border finally ended at the Mediterranean Sea, 12 which was Judah's western border.
The clans of Judah lived within these
borders.

Caleb's Land

(Judges 1.12-15)

13 Joshua gave Caleb some land
among the people of Judah, as God had
told him to do. Caleb's share was Hebron, which at that time was known as
Arba's Town,[i] because Arba was the famous ancestor of the Anakim.[j]
14 Caleb attacked Hebron and forced
the three Anakim clans of[k] Sheshai,
Ahiman, and Talmai to leave. 15 Next,
Caleb started a war with the town of
Debir, which at that time was called
Kiriath-Sepher. 16 He told his men, "The
man who captures Kiriath-Sepher can
marry my daughter Achsah."
17 Caleb's nephew Othniel[l] captured
Kiriath-Sepher, and Caleb let him marry
Achsah. 18 Right after the wedding,
Achsah started telling Othniel that he[m]

[x] **14.12** *Anakim*: See the note at 11.21. [y] **14.15** *Arba's Town*: Or "Kiriath-Arba." [z] **14.15** *Arba's Town, because . . . greatest*: Hebrew; one ancient translation "Arba's Town. It was one of the main towns." [a] **15.3** *Scorpion Pass*: Or "Akrabbim Pass." [b] **15.5** *at . . . Dead Sea*: One possible meaning for the difficult Hebrew text. [c] **15.6** *Monument of Bohan*: Or "Bohan Rock," possibly a natural rock formation. [d] **15.7** *Trouble Valley*: Or "Achor Valley." [e] **15.7** *Debir*: Not the same town as in 10.38, 39. [f] **15.7** *Gilgal*: Not the same "Gilgal" as in 4.19. [g] **15.9** *ruins*: Hebrew; one ancient translation "towns." [h] **15.10** *Beth-Shemesh*: Probably the same town as the Ir-Shemesh of 19.41-46. Two other towns were also named Beth-Shemesh (see 19.17-23 and 19.35-39). [i] **15.13** *Arba's Town*: See the note at 14.15. [j] **15.13** *Anakim*: See the note at 11.21. [k] **15.14** *clans of*: Or "warriors." [l] **15.17** *Caleb's nephew Othniel*: Hebrew "Othniel the son of Caleb's brother Kenaz." [m] **15.18** *Achsah . . . Othniel . . . he*: Hebrew; one manuscript of one ancient translation and two ancient translations of the parallel in Judges 1.14 "Othniel . . . Achsah . . . she."

ought to ask her father for a field. She
went to see her father, and while she was
getting down from[n] her donkey, Caleb
asked her, "What's bothering you?"
19She answered, "I need your help.
The land you gave me is in the Southern
Desert, so I really need some spring-fed
ponds[o] for a water supply."
Caleb gave her a couple of small
ponds, named Higher Pond and Lower
Pond.[p]

Towns in Judah's Land

20The following is a list of the towns
in each region given to the Judah clans:
21-32The first region was located in the
Southern Desert along the border with
Edom, and it had the following twenty-
nine towns with their surrounding vil-
lages:
Kabzeel, Eder, Jagur, Kinah, Di-
monah, Aradah,[q] Kedesh, Hazor of
Ithnan,[r] Ziph, Telem, Bealoth, Hazor-
Hadattah, Kerioth-Hezron, which is
also called Hazor, Amam, Shema,
Moladah, Hazar-Gaddah, Heshmon,
Beth-Pelet, Hazar-Shual, Beersheba
and its surrounding villages,[s]
Baalah, Iim, Ezem, Eltolad, Chesil,
Hormah, Ziklag, Madmannah,
Sansannah, Lebaoth, Shilhim, and
Enrimmon.[t]
33-36The second region was located in
the northern part of the lower foothills,
and it had the following fourteen towns
with their surrounding villages:
Eshtaol, Zorah, Ashnah, Zanoah,
En-Gannim, Tappuah, Enam, Jarmuth, Adullam, Socoh, Azekah,
Shaaraim, Adithaim, Gederah, and
Gederothaim.
37-41The third region was located in
the southern part of the lower foothills,
and it had the following sixteen towns
with their surrounding villages:
Zenan, Hadashah, Migdalgad, Dilan,
Mizpeh, Joktheel, Lachish, Bozkath,
Eglon, Cabbon, Lahmas,[u] Chitlish,
Gederoth, Beth-Dagon, Naamah,
and Makkedah.
42-44The fourth region was located in
the central part of the lower foothills,
and it had the following nine towns with
their surrounding villages:
Libnah, Ether, Ashan, Iphtah, Ashnah, Nezib, Keilah, Achzib, and
Mareshah.
45-47The fifth region was located along
the Mediterranean seacoast, and it had
the following towns with their surrounding settlements and villages:
Ekron and the towns between there
and the coast, Ashdod and the larger
towns nearby, Gaza, the towns from
Gaza to the Egyptian Gorge, and the
towns along the coast of the
Mediterranean Sea.
48-51The sixth region was in the south-
western part of the hill country, and it
had the following eleven towns with
their surrounding villages:
Shamir, Jattir, Socoh, Dannah,
Kiriath-Sannah, which is now called
Debir, Anab, Eshtemoh,[v] Anim,
Goshen, Holon, and Giloh.
52-54The seventh region was located in
the south-central part of Judah's hill
country, and it had the following nine
towns with their surrounding villages:
Arab, Dumah,[w] Eshan, Janim, Beth-
Tappuah, Aphekah, Humtah,
Kiriath-Arba, which is now called
Hebron, and Zior.
55-57The eighth region was located in
the southeastern part of the hill country,
and it had the following ten towns with
their surrounding villages:
Maon, Carmel, Ziph, Juttah,
Jezreel,[x] Jokdeam,[y] Zanoah, Kain,
Gibeah,[z] and Timnah.
58-59The ninth region was located in
the central part of Judah's hill country,
and it had the following six towns with
their surrounding villages:
Halhul, Beth-Zur, Gedor, Maarath,
Beth-Anoth, and Eltekon.
The tenth region was located in the
north-central part of Judah's hill country, and it had the following eleven
towns with their surrounding villages:
Tekoa, Ephrath, which is also
called Bethlehem, Peor, Etam, Culon,
Tatam, Shoresh, Kerem, Gallim,
Bether, and Manahath.[a]
60The eleventh region was located in
the northern part of Judah's hill country, and it had the following two towns
with their surrounding villages:

[n] **15.18** *getting down from*: One possible meaning for the difficult Hebrew text.
[o] **15.19** *spring-fed ponds*: Or "wells." [p] **15.19** *small ponds . . . Pond . . . Pond*: Or "wells . . . Well . . . Well." [q] **15.21-32** *Aradah*: One possible meaning for the difficult Hebrew text. [r] **15.21-32** *Hazor of Ithnan*: One ancient translation; Hebrew "Hazor and Ithnan." [s] **15.21-32** *its . . . villages*: One ancient translation; Hebrew "Biziothiah."
[t] **15.21-32** *Enrimmon*: One ancient translation; Hebrew "Ain and Rimmon."
[u] **15.37-41** *Lahmas*: Most Hebrew manuscripts; many other Hebrew manuscripts and one manuscript of one ancient translation "Lahmam." [v] **15.48-51** *Eshtemoh*: Another spelling for the name Eshtemoa (see 21.9-19). [w] **15.52-54** *Dumah*: Most Hebrew manuscripts; some Hebrew manuscripts and one ancient translation "Rumah." [x] **15.55-57** *Jezreel*: Not the same Jezreel as in 19.17-23. [y] **15.55-57** *Jokdeam*: Hebrew; one ancient translation "Jorkeam." [z] **15.55-57** *Gibeah*: Not the same Gibeah as in 18.25-28. [a] **15.58,59** *The tenth region . . . Manahath*: One ancient translation; the Hebrew text does not have these words.

Rabbah, and Kiriath-Baal, which is
also called Kiriath-Jearim.
61-62The twelfth region was located in
the desert along the Dead Sea, and it
had the following six towns with their
surrounding villages:
Beth-Arabah, Middin, Secacah, Nib-
shan, Salt Town, and En-Gedi.

The Jebusites

63The Jebusites lived in Jerusalem,
and the people of the Judah tribe could
not capture the city and get rid of them.
That's why Jebusites still live in Jerusalem along with the people of Judah.[b]

Ephraim's Land

16 1-4Ephraim and Manasseh are the
two tribes descended from
Joseph, and the following is a description of the land they received. The
southern border of their land started at
the Jordan River east of the spring at
Jericho. From there it went west through
the desert up to the hill country around
Bethel. From Bethel it went to Luz and
then[c] to the border of the Archites in
Ataroth.[d] It continued west down to the
land that belonged to the Japhlet clan,
then went on to Lower Beth-Horon,
Gezer, and the Mediterranean Sea.
5The following is a description of the
land that was divided among the clans
of the Ephraim tribe. Their southern
border started at Ataroth-Addar and
went west to Upper Beth-Horon 6-8and
the Mediterranean Sea. Their northern
border started on the east at Janoah,
curved a little to the north, then came
back south to Michmethath and Tappuah, where it followed the Kanah
Gorge west to the Mediterranean Sea.
The eastern border started on the
north near Janoah and went between
Janoah on the southwest and Taanath-
Shiloh on the northeast. Then it went
south to Ataroth, Naarah, and on as far
as the edge of the land that belonged to
Jericho. At that point it turned east and
went to the Jordan River. The clans of
Ephraim received this region as their
tribal land. 9Ephraim also had some
towns and villages that were inside
Manasseh's tribal land.
10Ephraim could not force the
Canaanites out of Gezer, so there are
still some Canaanites who live there
among the Israelites. But now these
Canaanites have to work as slaves for
the Israelites.

Manasseh's Land West of the Jordan River

17 1-6Manasseh was Joseph's oldest
son, and Machir was Manasseh's
oldest son. Machir had a son named
Gilead, and some of his descendants
had already received the regions of
Gilead and Bashan because they were
good warriors. The other clans of the
Manasseh tribe descended from Gilead's sons Abiezer, Helek, Asriel,
Shechem, Hepher, and Shemida. The
following is a description of the land
they received.
Hepher's son Zelophehad did not
have any sons, but he did have five
daughters: Mahlah, Noah, Hoglah,
Milcah, and Tirzah. One day the clans
that were descendants of Zelophehad's
five daughters went to the priest
Eleazar, Joshua, and the leaders of Israel. The people of these clans said,
"The LORD told Moses to give us land
just as he gave land to our relatives."[e]
Joshua followed the LORD's instructions and gave land to these five clans,
as he had given land to the five clans
that had descended from Hepher's
brothers.[f] So Manasseh's land west of
the Jordan River was divided into ten
parts.
7The land of the Manasseh tribe went
from its northern border with the Asher
tribe south to Michmethath, which is to
the east of Shechem. The southern border started there, but curved even farther south to include the people who
lived around Tappuah Spring.[g] 8The
town of Tappuah was on Manasseh's
border with Ephraim. Although the land
around Tappuah belonged to Manasseh,
the town itself belonged to Ephraim.
9-10Then the border went west to the
Kanah Gorge and ran along the northern edge of the gorge to the Mediterranean Sea. The land south of the gorge
belonged to Ephraim. And even though
there were a few towns that belonged to
Ephraim north of the gorge, the land
north of the gorge belonged to Manasseh.

[b] **15.63** *Jebusites . . . Judah*: Israel captured Jerusalem in King David's time, but even then the Jebusites were not forced to leave. [c] **16.1-4** *it . . . then*: Or "which is also called Luz, it went." [d] **16.1-4** *Ataroth*: This is the same Ataroth as Ataroth-Addar in verse 5, but a different Ataroth from the one in verses 6-8. [e] **17.1-6** *The LORD told Moses . . . relatives*: See Numbers 27.1-11; 36.1-12. [f] **17.1-6** *the clans that were descendants of Zelophehad's five daughters . . . Hepher's brothers*: Or "Zelophehad's five daughters went to the priest Eleazar, Joshua, and the leaders of Israel. The five sisters said, 'The LORD told Moses to give us land just as he gave land to our relatives.' Joshua followed the LORD's instructions and gave land to these five sisters, as he had given land to Hepher's brothers." [g] **17.7** *to include . . . Tappuah Spring*: Hebrew; one ancient translation "to Jassiben-Tappuah" or "and turns toward Tappuah Spring."

The western border of Manasseh was
the Mediterranean Sea, and the tribe
shared a border with the Asher tribe on
the northwest and with the Issachar
tribe on the northeast.
11 Manasseh was supposed to have the
following towns with their surrounding
villages inside the borders of Issachar's
and Asher's tribal lands:

Beth-Shan, Ibleam, Endor, Taanach,
Megiddo, and Dor, which is also
called Naphath.[h]

12 But the people of Manasseh could not
capture these towns, so the Canaanites
kept on living in them. 13 When the
Israelites grew stronger, they made the
Canaanites in these towns work as their
slaves, though they never did force them
to leave.

Joseph's Descendants Ask for More Land

14 One day the Joseph tribes[i] came to
Joshua and asked, "Why didn't you give
us more land? The LORD has always
been kind to us, and we have too many
people for this small region."
15 Joshua replied, "If you have so many
people that you don't have enough room
in the hill country of Ephraim, then go
into the forest that belonged to the
Perizzites and the Rephaim.[j] Clear out
the trees and make more room for yourselves there."
16 "Even if we do that," they answered,
"there still won't be enough land for us
in the hill country. And we can't move
down into Jezreel Valley, because the
Canaanites who live in Beth-Shan and
in other parts of the valley have iron
chariots."
17 "Your tribes do have a lot of people,"
Joshua admitted. "I'll give you more
land. Your tribes are powerful, 18 so you
can have the rest of the hill country, but
it's a forest, and you'll have to cut down
the trees and clear the land. You can
also have Jezreel Valley. Even though
the Canaanites there are strong and
have iron chariots, you can force them
to leave the valley."

Joshua Gives Out the Rest of the Land

18 After Israel had captured the
land, they met at Shiloh and set
up the sacred tent.[k] 2 There were still
seven tribes without any land, 3-7 so
Joshua told the people:

The Judah tribe has already settled in its land in the south, and the
Joseph tribes[l] have settled in their
land in the north. The tribes of Gad,
Reuben, and East Manasseh already
have the land that the LORD's servant Moses gave them east of the
Jordan River. And the people of Levi
won't get a single large region of the
land like the other tribes. Instead,
they will serve the LORD as priests.

But the rest of you haven't done a
thing to take over any land. The
LORD God who was worshiped by
your ancestors has given you the
land, and now it's time to go ahead
and settle there.

Seven tribes still don't have any
land. Each of these tribes should
choose three men, and I'll send them
to explore the remaining land. They
will divide it into seven regions,
write a description of each region,
and bring these descriptions back to
me. I will find out[m] from the LORD
our God what region each tribe
should get.

8 Just before the men left camp, Joshua
repeated their orders: "Explore the land
and write a description of it. Then come
back to Shiloh, and I will find out from
the LORD how to divide the land."
9 The men left and went across the
land, dividing it into seven regions.
They wrote down a description of each
region, town by town, and returned to
Joshua at the camp at Shiloh. 10 Joshua
found out from the LORD how to divide
the land, and he told the tribes what the
LORD had decided.

Benjamin's Land

11 Benjamin was the first tribe chosen
to receive land. The region for its clans
lay between the Judah tribe on the
south and the Joseph tribes[n] on the
north. 12 Benjamin's northern border
started at the Jordan River and went up
the ridge north of Jericho, then on west
into the hill country as far as the Beth-
Aven Desert. 13-14 From there it went to
Luz, which is now called Bethel. The
border ran along the ridge south of Luz,
then went to Ataroth-Orech[o] and on as
far as the mountain south of Lower
Beth-Horon. At that point it turned
south and became the western border.
It went as far south as Kiriath-Baal, a
town in Judah now called Kiriath-
Jearim.
15 Benjamin's southern border started
at the edge of Kiriath-Jearim and went

[h] **17.11** *Dor . . . Naphath*: One possible meaning for the difficult Hebrew text. [i] **17.14** *Joseph tribes*: Ephraim and the half of Manasseh that lived west of the Jordan River. [j] **17.15** *Rephaim*: See the note at 12.4. [k] **18.1** *sacred tent*: Or "meeting tent." [l] **18.3-7** *Joseph tribes*: See the note at 17.14. [m] **18.3-7** *find out*: Hebrew "cast lots to find out" (see the note at 14.1-5). [n] **18.11** *Joseph tribes*: See the note at 17.14. [o] **18.13,14** *Ataroth-Orech*: One ancient translation; Hebrew "Ataroth-Addar."

east to the ruins[p] and on to Nephtoah
Spring. 16 From there it went to the bottom of the hill at the northern end of
Rephaim Valley. The other side of this
hill faces Hinnom Valley, which is on the
land that slopes south from Jerusalem.[q]
The border went down through Hinnom
Valley until it reached Enrogel.
17 At Enrogel the border curved north
and went to Enshemesh and on east to
Geliloth,[r] which is across the valley
from Adummim Pass. Then it went
down to the Monument of Bohan,[s] who
belonged to the Reuben tribe. 18 The border ran along the hillside north of Beth-
Arabah,[t] then down into the Jordan
River valley. 19 Inside the valley it went
south as far as the northern hillside of
Beth-Hoglah. The last section of the border went from there to the northern end
of the Dead Sea,[u] at the mouth of the
Jordan River. 20 The Jordan River itself
was Benjamin's eastern border.

These were the borders of Benjamin's tribal land, where the clans of Benjamin lived.

21-24 One region of Benjamin's tribal land had twelve towns with their surrounding villages. Those towns were Jericho, Beth-Hoglah, Emek-Keziz, Beth-Arabah, Zemaraim, Bethel, Avvim, Parah, Ophrah, Chephar-Ammoni, Ophni, and Geba.

25-28 In the other region there were the following fourteen towns with their surrounding villages: Gibeon, Ramah, Beeroth, Mizpeh, Chephirah, Mozah, Rekem, Irpeel, Taralah, Zelah, Haeleph, Gibeah, Kiriath-Jearim,[v] and Jerusalem, which is also called Jebusite Town.

These regions are the tribal lands of Benjamin.

Simeon's Land

19 Simeon was the second tribe chosen to receive land, and the region for its clans was inside Judah's
borders. 2-6 In one region of Simeon's tribal land there were the following thirteen towns with their surrounding villages:

Beersheba, Shema,[w] Moladah, Hazarshual, Balah, Ezem, Eltolad, Bethul, Hormah, Ziklag, Beth-Marcaboth, Hazar-Shual, Beth-Lebaoth, and Sharuhen.

7 In another region, Simeon had the following four towns with their surrounding villages:

Enrimmon,[x] Tachan,[y] Ether, and Ashan.

8 Simeon's land also included all the other towns and villages as far south as Baalath-Beer, which is also called Ramah of the South.

9 Simeon's tribal land was actually inside Judah's territory. Judah had received too much land for the number of people in its tribe, so part of Judah's land was given to Simeon.

Zebulun's Land

10-12 Zebulun was the third tribe chosen to receive land. The southern border for its clans started in the west at the edge of the gorge near Jokneam. It went east to the edge of the land that belongs to the town of Dabbesheth, and continued on to Maralah and Sarid. It took in the land that belongs to Chislothtabor, then ended at Daberath.

The eastern border went up to Japhia
13 and continued north to Gath-Hepher,
Ethkazin, and Rimmonah,[z] where it
curved[a] toward Neah 14 and became the
northern border. Then it curved south
around Hannathon and went as far west
as Iphtahel Valley.
15 Zebulun had twelve towns with their
surrounding villages. Some of these
were Kattath, Nahalal, Shimron, Jiralah,[b] and Bethlehem.[c]
16 This is the tribal land, and these are
the towns and villages of the Zebulun
clans.

Issachar's Land

17-23 Issachar was the fourth tribe chosen to receive land. The northern border for its clans went from Mount Tabor east to the Jordan River. Their land

[p] 18.15 *the ruins*: One possible meaning for the difficult Hebrew text. [q] 18.16 *Jerusalem*: Hebrew "the Jebusite town." [r] 18.17 *Geliloth*: Probably another name for Gilgal.
[s] 18.17 *Monument of Bohan*: See the note at 15.6. [t] 18.18 *hillside north of Beth-Arabah*: One ancient translation (see also the border description in 15.6); Hebrew "the northern hillside overlooking the Jordan River valley." [u] 18.19 *northern . . . Dead Sea*: One possible meaning for the difficult Hebrew text. [v] 18.25-28 *Kiriath-Jearim*: One ancient translation; Hebrew "Kiriath." [w] 19.2-6 *Shema*: One ancient translation and some manuscripts of another ancient translation (see also the list at 15.21-32); Hebrew and some manuscripts of one ancient translation "Sheba." The list in 1 Chronicles 4.28 does not have either "Shema" or "Sheba."
[x] 19.7 *Enrimmon*: Some Hebrew manuscripts and one ancient translation; most Hebrew manuscripts "Ain, Rimmon." [y] 19.7 *Tachan*: Some manuscripts of one ancient translation; the Hebrew text does not have this word. [z] 19.13 *Rimmonah*: Or "Rimmon."
[a] 19.13 *Rimmonah . . . curved*: One possible meaning for the difficult Hebrew text.
[b] 19.15 *Jiralah*: Some Hebrew manuscripts and two ancient translations; most Hebrew manuscripts "Idalah." [c] 19.15 *Bethlehem*: This town is different from the Bethlehem in 15.58, 59.

included the following sixteen towns with their surrounding villages:

Jezreel, Chesulloth, Shunem, Hapharaim, Shion, Anaharath, Debirath,[d] Kishion, Ebez, Remeth, En-Gannim, Enhaddah, Beth-Pazzez, Tabor,[e] Shahazumah and Beth-Shemesh.[f]

Asher's Land

24-26Asher was the fifth tribe chosen to receive land, and the region for its clans included the following towns:

Helkath, Hali, Beten, Achshaph, Allammelech, Amad, and Mishal.

Asher's southern border ran from the Mediterranean Sea southeast along the Shihor-Libnath River at the foot of Mount Carmel, 27then east to Beth-Dagon. On the southeast, Asher shared a border with Zebulun along the Iphtahel Valley. On the eastern side their border ran north to Beth-Emek, went east of Cabul, and then on to Neiel, 28Abdon,[g] Rehob, Hammon, Kanah, and as far north as the city of Sidon. 29-31Then it turned west to become the northern border and went to Ramah[h] and the fortress-city of Tyre.[i] Near Tyre it turned toward Hosah and ended at the Mediterranean Sea.

Asher had a total of twenty-two towns with their surrounding villages, including Mahalab,[j] Achzib, Acco,[k] Aphek, and Rehob.

Naphtali's Land

32-34Naphtali was the sixth tribe chosen to receive land. The southern border for its clans started in the west, where the tribal lands of Asher and Zebulun meet near Hukkok. From that point it ran east and southeast along the border with Zebulun as far as Aznoth-Tabor. From there the border went east to Heleph, Adami-Nekeb, Jabneel,[l] then to the town called Oak in Zaanannim,[m] and Lakkum. The southern border ended at the Jordan River, at the edge of the town named Jehudah.[n] Naphtali shared a border with Asher on the west.

35-39The Naphtali clans received this region as their tribal land, and it included nineteen towns with their surrounding villages. The following towns had walls around them:

Ziddim, Zer, Hammath, Rakkath, Chinnereth, Adamah, Ramah,[o] Hazor, Kedesh, Edrei,[p] Enhazor, Iron, Migdalel, Horem, Beth-Anath, and Beth-Shemesh.[q]

Dan's Land

40-46Dan was the seventh tribe chosen to receive land, and the region for its clans included the following towns:

Zorah, Eshtaol, Ir-Shemesh,[r] Shaalabbin, Aijalon, Ithlah, Elon, Timnah, Ekron, Eltekeh, Gibbethon, Baalath, Jehud, Azor,[s] Beneberak, Gath-Rimmon, Mejarkon, and Rakkon.

Dan's tribal land[t] went almost as far as Joppa. 47-48Its clans received this land and these towns with their surrounding villages.

Later, when enemies[u] forced them to leave their tribal land, they went to the town of Leshem. They attacked the town, captured it, and killed the people who lived there. Then they settled there themselves and renamed the town Dan after their ancestor.

Joshua's Land

49-51The Israelites were still gathered in Shiloh in front of the sacred tent,[v] when Eleazar the priest, Joshua, and the family leaders of Israel finished giving out the land to the tribes. The LORD had told the people to give Joshua whatever town he wanted. So Joshua chose Timnath-Serah in the hill country of Ephraim, and the people gave it to him. Joshua went to Timnath-Serah, rebuilt it, and lived there.

[d] **19.17-23** *Debirath*: One ancient translation; Hebrew "Rabbith." Debirath is probably the same place as Daberath in verse 12. [e] **19.17-23** *Mount Tabor . . . Tabor*: In Hebrew the name "Tabor" is used only once. It was probably intended as the name of a town located at the foot of Mount Tabor and which formed one point on the northern border of Issachar.
[f] **19.17-23** *Beth-Shemesh*: Not the same Beth-Shemesh as in 15.10 or 19.35-39.
[g] **19.28** *Abdon*: A few Hebrew manuscripts and one ancient translation; most Hebrew manuscripts "Ebron." [h] **19.29-31** *Ramah*: Not the same "Ramah" as in 18.25-28 or 19.35-39.
[i] **19.29-31** *fortress-city of Tyre*: Tyre was a walled city built on an island about half a mile from shore. [j] **19.29-31** *Mahalab*: One possible meaning for the difficult Hebrew text.
[k] **19.29-31** *Acco*: One ancient translation; Hebrew "Ummah." [l] **19.32-34** *Jabneel*: This town is not the same Jabneel as in 15.11. [m] **19.32-34** *the town . . . Zaanannim*: Or "the oak tree in the town of Zaanannim." [n] **19.32-34** *at . . . Jehudah*: One possible meaning for the difficult Hebrew text. [o] **19.35-39** *Ramah*: Not the same "Ramah" as in 18.25-28 or 19.29-31.
[p] **19.35-39** *Edrei*: Not the same Edrei as the town in Bashan east of the Jordan River where King Og had lived (see 12.4; 13.11, 12, 30, 31). [q] **19.35-39** *Beth-Shemesh*: Not the same Beth-Shemesh as in 15.10 or 19.17-23. [r] **19.40-46** *Ir-Shemesh*: Possibly the same town as the Beth-Shemesh of 15.10. [s] **19.40-46** *Azor*: Some manuscripts of one ancient translation; the Hebrew text does not have this word. [t] **19.40-46** *Gath-Rimmon, Mejarkon, and Rakkon. Dan's tribal land:* Or Gath-Rimmon, and Rakkon. Dan's tribal land included the Yarkon River and." [u] **19.47,48** *enemies*: Probably the Philistines. [v] **19.40-51** *sacred text*: Or "meeting tent."

The Safe Towns

(Numbers 35.9-15; Deuteronomy 19.1-13)

20 One day the LORD told Joshua:
2 When Moses was still alive, I
had him tell the Israelites about the
Safe Towns. Now you tell them that
it is time to set up these towns. 3-4 If a
person accidentally kills someone
and the victim's relatives say it was
murder, they might try to take revenge.[w] Anyone accused of murder
can run to one of the Safe Towns
and be safe from the victim's relatives. The one needing protection
will stand at the entrance to the
town gate and explain to the town
leaders what happened. Then the
leaders will bring that person in and
provide a place to live in their town.
5 One of the victim's relatives
might come to the town, looking for
revenge. But the town leaders must
not simply hand over the person accused of murder. After all, the accused and the victim had been
neighbors, not enemies. 6 The citizens of that Safe Town must come
together and hold a trial. They may
decide that the victim was killed accidentally and that the accused is
not guilty of murder.
Everyone found not guilty[x] must
still live in the Safe Town until the
high priest dies. Then they can go
back to their own towns and their
homes that they had to leave behind.
7 The Israelites decided that the following three towns west of the Jordan
River would be Safe Towns:
Kedesh in Galilee in Naphtali's hill
country, Shechem in Ephraim's hill
country, and Kiriath-Arba in Judah's
hill country. Kiriath-Arba is now
called Hebron.
8 The Israelites had already decided on
the following three towns east of the
Jordan River:
Bezer in the desert flatlands of
Reuben, Ramoth in Gilead, which
was a town that belonged to Gad,
and Golan in Bashan, which belonged to Manasseh.
9 These Safe Towns were set up, so
that if Israelites or even foreigners who
lived in Israel accidentally killed someone, they could run to one of these
towns. There they would be safe until a
trial could be held, even if one of the
victim's relatives came looking for revenge.

Levi's Towns

21 1-2 While the Israelites were still
camped at Shiloh in the land of
Canaan, the family leaders of the Levi
tribe went to speak to the priest Eleazar,
Joshua, and the family leaders of the
other Israelite tribes. The leaders of Levi
said, "The LORD told Moses that you
have to give us towns and provide pastures for our animals."[y]
3 Since the LORD had said this, the
leaders of the other Israelite tribes
agreed to give some of the towns and
pastures from their tribal lands to Levi.
4 The leaders asked the LORD to show
them[z] in what order the clans of Levi
would be given towns, and which towns
each clan would receive.
The Kohath clans were first. The descendants of Aaron, Israel's first priest,[a]
were given thirteen towns from the
tribes of Judah, Simeon, and Benjamin.
5 The other members of the Kohath clans
received ten towns from the tribes of
Ephraim, Dan, and West Manasseh.
6 The clans that were descendants of
Gershon were given thirteen towns
from the tribes of Issachar, Asher, Naphtali, and East Manasseh. 7 The clans that
were descendants of Merari[b] received
twelve towns from the tribes of Reuben,
Gad, and Zebulun.
8 The LORD had told Moses that he
would show the Israelites which towns
and pastures to give to the clans of Levi,
and he did.

Towns from Judah, Simeon, Benjamin

9-19 The descendants of Aaron from the
Kohath clans of Levi were priests, and
they were chosen to receive towns first.
They were given thirteen towns and the
pastureland around them. Nine of these
towns were from the tribes of Judah and
Simeon and four from Benjamin.
Hebron, Libnah, Jattir, Eshtemoa,
Holon, Debir, Ashan,[c] Juttah, and Beth-
Shemesh were from Judah and Simeon.
Hebron, located in the hill country of
Judah, was earlier called Arba's Town.[d]
It had been named after Arba, the

[w] **20.3,4** *revenge*: At this time in Israel's history, the clan could appoint a close male relative to find and kill a person who had killed a member of their clan. [x] **20.6** *not guilty*: If the person was found to be guilty of murder, the citizens of the Safe Town were to let the victim's relatives kill the murderer (see Deuteronomy 19.11-13). [y] **21.1,2** *The LORD told Moses . . . animals*: See Numbers 35.1-8. [z] **21.4** *asked the LORD to show them*: Hebrew "cast lots to find out." See the note at 14.1-5. [a] **21.4** *The descendants . . . priest*: Hebrew text; three ancient translations "The priests, the descendants of Aaron." The male descendants of Aaron would also be priests. [b] **21.4-7** *Kohath . . . Gershon . . . Merari*: Sons of Levi, the ancestor of the tribe of Levi. [c] **21.9-19** *Ashan*: One ancient translation and the parallel in 1 Chronicles 6.59; Hebrew "Ain." [d] **21.9-19** *Arba's Town*: See the note at 14.15.

ancestor of the Anakim.[e] Hebron's pasturelands went along with the town, but
its farmlands and the villages around it
had been given to Caleb.[f] Hebron was
also one of the Safe Towns for people
who had accidentally killed someone.
Gibeon, Geba, Anathoth, and Almon
were from Benjamin.

Towns from Ephraim, Dan, West Manasseh

20-26 The rest of the Kohath clans of the
Levi tribe received ten towns and the
pastureland around them. Four of these
towns were from the tribe of Ephraim,
four from Dan, and two from West Manasseh.
Shechem, Gezer, Kibzaim, and Beth-
Horon were from Ephraim. Shechem
was located in the hill country, and it
was also one of the Safe Towns for people who had accidentally killed someone.
Elteke, Gibbethon, Aijalon, and Gath-
Rimmon were from Dan.
Taanach and Jibleam[g] were from
West Manasseh.

Towns from East Manasseh, Issachar, Asher, Naphtali

27-33 The clans of Levi that were de-
scendants of Gershon received thirteen
towns and the pastureland around
them. Two of these towns were from the
tribe of East Manasseh, four from Is-
sachar, four from Asher, and three from
Naphtali.
Golan in Bashan and Beeshterah were
from East Manasseh.
Kishion, Daberath, Jarmuth, and En-
Gannim were from Issachar.
Mishal, Abdon, Helkath, and Rehob
were from Asher.
Kedesh in Galilee, Hammothdor, and
Kartan were from Naphtali. Golan in
Bashan and Kedesh in Galilee were also
Safe Towns for people who had acciden-
tally killed someone.

Towns from Zebulun, Reuben, Gad

34-40 The rest of the Levi clans were descendants of Merari, and they received
twelve towns with the pastureland
around them. Four towns were from the
tribe of Zebulun, four from Reuben, and
four from Gad.
Jokneam, Kartah, Rimmonah,[h] and
Nahalal were from Zebulun.
Bezer, Jazah, Kedemoth, and Mephaath were from Reuben. Bezer was
located in the desert flatlands east of the
Jordan River across from Jericho.[i]
Ramoth in Gilead, Mahanaim, Heshbon, and Jazer were from Gad.
Bezer and Ramoth in Gilead were
Safe Towns[j] for people who had accidentally killed someone.
41-42 The people of the Levi tribe had a
total of forty-eight towns within Israel,
and they had pastures around each one
of their towns.

Israel Settles in the Land

43 The LORD gave the Israelites the
land he had promised their ancestors,
and they captured it and settled in it.
44 There still were enemies around Israel, but the LORD kept his promise to let
his people live in peace. And whenever
the Israelites did have to go to war, no
enemy could defeat them. The LORD always helped Israel win. 45 The LORD
promised to do many good things for Israel, and he kept his promise every time.

The Two and a Half Tribes Return Home

22 Joshua had the men of the tribes
of Reuben, Gad, and East Manasseh come for a meeting, and he told
them:

2-3 You have obeyed every command of the LORD your God and of
his servant Moses. And you have
done everything I've told you to do.
It's taken a long time, but you have
stayed and helped your relatives.
4 The LORD promised to give peace to
your relatives, and that's what he
has done. Now it's time for you to go
back to your own homes in the land
that Moses gave you east of the Jordan River.
5 Moses taught you to love the
LORD your God, to be faithful to him,
and to worship and obey him with
your whole heart and with all your
strength. So be very careful to do
everything Moses commanded.
6-9 You've become rich from what
you've taken from your enemies. You
have big herds of cattle, lots of silver, gold, bronze, and iron, and
plenty of clothes. Take everything
home with you and share with the
people of your tribe.
I pray that God will be kind to
you. You are now free to go home.

The tribes of Reuben and Gad started
back to Gilead, their own land. Moses
had given the land of Bashan to the East
Manasseh tribe, so they started back
along with Reuben and Gad. God had
told Moses that these two and a half

[e]21.9-19 *Anakim*: See the note at 11.21. [f]21.9-19 *Caleb*: See 14.6-14 [g]21.20-26 *Jibleam*: One ancient translation and the parallel in 1 Chronicles 6.70; Hebrew "Gath-Rimmon." [h]21.34-40 *Rimmonah*: One possible meaning for the difficult Hebrew text. [i]21-34-40 *Bezer . . . Jericho*: One possible meaning for the difficult Hebrew text. [j]21.34-40 *Bezer and Ramoth in Gilead were Safe Towns*: One ancient translation; Hebrew "Ramoth in Gilead was a Safe Town."

tribes should conquer Gilead and Bashan, and they had done so.

Joshua had given land west of the Jordan River to the other half of the Manasseh tribe, so they stayed at Shiloh in the land of Canaan with the rest of the Israelites.

10-11The tribes of Reuben, Gad, and East Manasseh reached the western side of the Jordan River valley[k] and built a huge altar there beside the river.

When the rest of the Israelites heard what these tribes had done,[l] 12the Israelite men met at Shiloh to get ready to attack the two and a half tribes. 13But first they sent a priest, Phinehas the son of Eleazar, to talk with the two and a half tribes. 14Each of the tribes at Shiloh sent the leader of one of its families along with Phinehas.

15Phinehas and these leaders went to Gilead and met with the tribes of Reuben, Gad, and East Manasseh. They said:

16All of the LORD's people have gathered together and have sent us to find out why you are unfaithful to our God. You have turned your backs on the LORD by building that altar. Why are you rebelling against him? 17Wasn't our people's sin at Peor[m] terrible enough for you? The LORD punished us by sending a horrible sickness that killed many of us, and we still suffer because of that sin.[n] 18Now you are turning your backs on the LORD again.

If you don't stop rebelling against the LORD right now, he will be angry at the whole nation. 19If you don't think your land is a fit place to serve God, then move across the Jordan and live with us in the LORD's own land, where his sacred tent is located. But don't rebel against the LORD our God or against us by building another altar besides the LORD's own altar.[o] 20Don't you remember what happened when Achan was unfaithful[p] and took some of the things that belonged to God? This made God angry with the entire nation. Achan died because he sinned, but he also caused the death of many others.

21The tribes of Reuben, Gad, and East Manasseh answered:

22The LORD is the greatest God! We ask him to be our witness, because he knows whether or not we were rebellious or unfaithful when we built that altar. If we were unfaithful, then we pray that God won't rescue us today. Let us tell you why we built that altar, 23and we ask the LORD to punish us if we are lying. We didn't build it so we could turn our backs on the LORD. We didn't even build it so we could offer animal or grain sacrifices to please the LORD or ask his blessing.

24-25We built that altar because we were worried. Someday your descendants might tell our descendants, "The LORD made the Jordan River the boundary between us Israelites and you people of Reuben and Gad. The LORD is Israel's God, but you're not part of Israel, so you can't take part in worshiping the LORD."

Your descendants might say that and try to make our descendants stop worshiping and obeying the LORD. 26That's why we decided to build the altar. It isn't for offering sacrifices, not even sacrifices to please the LORD.[q] 27-29To build another altar for offering sacrifices would be the same as turning our backs on the LORD and rebelling against him. We could never do that! No, we built the altar to remind us and you and the generations to come that we will worship the LORD. And so we will keep bringing our sacrifices to the LORD's altar, there in front of his sacred tent. Now your descendants will never be able to say to our descendants, "You can't worship the LORD."

But if they do say this, our descendants can answer back, "Look at this altar our ancestors built! It's like the LORD's altar, but it isn't for offering sacrifices. It's here to remind us and you that we belong to the LORD, just as much as you do."

30-31Phinehas and the clan leaders were pleased when they heard the tribes of Reuben, Gad, and East Manasseh explain why they had built the altar. Then Phinehas told them, "Today we know that the LORD is helping us. You have not been unfaithful to him, and this means that the LORD will not be angry with us."

32Phinehas and the clan leaders left Gilead and went back to Canaan to tell

[k]**22.10,11** *western . . . valley*: Or "the town of Geliloth, which is in the land of Canaan near the Jordan River." [l]**22.10,11** *built a huge altar . . . tribes had done*: According to Deuteronomy 12.5-14, the LORD wanted the Israelites to have only one altar for offering sacrifices. To build another altar would be to disobey the LORD. [m]**22.17** *our people's sin at Peor*: See Numbers 25. [n]**22.17** *we still . . . sin*: Or "There are still people in Israel who want to worship other gods." [o]**22.19** *or against . . . altar*: Or "by building another altar besides the LORD's own altar. That would even make us into rebels along with you." [p]**22.20** *Achan was unfaithful*: See 7.1, 26. [q]**22.26** *sacrifices to please the LORD*: See the note at 8.30-32.

the Israelites about their meeting with
the Reuben and Gad tribes. 33The Israelites were happy and praised God.
There was no more talk about going to
war and wiping out the tribes of Reuben
and Gad.
34The people of Reuben and Gad
named the altar "A Reminder to Us All
That the LORD Is Our God."[r]

Joshua's Farewell Speech

23 The LORD let Israel live in peace
with its neighbors for a long time,
and Joshua lived to a ripe old age. 2One
day he called a meeting of the leaders of
the tribes of Israel, including the old
men, the judges, and the officials. Then
he told them:
I am now very old. 3You have seen
how the LORD your God fought for
you and helped you defeat the nations who lived in this land. 4-5There
are still some nations left, but the
LORD has promised you their land.
So when you attack them, he will
make them run away. I have already
divided their land among your
tribes, as I did with the land of the
nations I defeated between the Jordan River and the Mediterranean
Sea.
6Be sure that you carefully obey
everything written in *The Book of
the Law*[s] of Moses and do exactly
what it says.
7Don't have anything to do with
the nations that live around you.
Don't worship their gods or pray to
their idols or make promises in the
names of their gods. 8Be as faithful
to the LORD as you have always
been.
9When you attacked powerful nations, the LORD made them run
away, and no one has ever been able
to stand up to you. 10Any one of you
can defeat a thousand enemy soldiers, because the LORD God fights
for you, just as he promised. 11Be
sure to always love the LORD your
God. 12-13Don't ever turn your backs
on him by marrying people from the
nations that are left in the land.
Don't even make friends with them.
I tell you that if you are friendly with
those nations, the LORD won't chase
them away when you attack. Instead, they'll be like a trap for your
feet, a whip on your back, and
thorns in your eyes. And finally,
none of you will be left in this good
land that the LORD has given you.
14I will soon die, as everyone must.
But deep in your hearts you know
that the LORD has kept every promise he ever made to you. Not one of
them has been broken. 15-16Yes,
when the LORD makes a promise, he
does what he has promised. But
when he makes a threat, he will also
do what he has threatened. The
LORD is our God. He gave us this
wonderful land and made an agreement with us that we would worship
only him. But if you worship other
gods, it will make the LORD furious.
He will start getting rid of you, and
soon not one of you will be left in
this good land that he has given you.

We Will Worship and Obey the LORD

24 Joshua called the tribes of Israel
together for a meeting at Shechem. He had the leaders, including the
old men, the judges, and the officials,
come up and stand near the sacred
tent.[t] 2Then Joshua told everyone to listen to this message from the LORD, the
God of Israel:
Long ago your ancestors lived on
the other side of the Euphrates
River, and they worshiped other
gods. This continued until the time
of your ancestor Terah and his two
sons, Abraham and Nahor. 3But I
brought Abraham across the Euphrates River and led him through
the land of Canaan. I blessed him by
giving him Isaac, the first in a line of
many descendants. 4Then I gave
Isaac two sons, Jacob and Esau. I
had Esau live in the hill country of
Mount Seir, but your ancestor Jacob
and his children went to live in
Egypt.
5-6Later I sent Moses and his
brother Aaron to help your people,
and I made all those horrible things
happen to the Egyptians. I brought
your ancestors out of Egypt, but the
Egyptians got in their chariots and
on their horses and chased your ancestors, catching up with them at the
Red Sea.[u] 7Your people cried to me
for help, so I put a dark cloud between them and the Egyptians. Then
I opened up the sea and let your
people walk across on dry ground.
But when the Egyptians tried to follow, I commanded the sea to swal-

[r]**22.34** *named . . . God*: Or "gave a name to the altar. They explained, 'This altar is here to remind us all that the LORD is our God' "; most Hebrew manuscripts. A few Hebrew manuscripts and one ancient translation "named the altar 'Reminder.' They explained, 'This altar is here to remind us all that the LORD is our God.' " [s]**23.6** *Law*: See the note at 8.30-32.
[t]**24.1** *near . . . tent*: Or "in front of the sacred chest"; Hebrew "in the presence of God."
[u]**24.5,6** *Red Sea*: See the note at 2.10.

low them, and they drowned while
you watched.
You lived in the desert for a long
time, 8then I brought you into the
land east of the Jordan River. The
Amorites were living there, and they
fought you. But with my help, you
defeated them, wiped them out, and
took their land. 9King Balak decided
that his nation Moab would go to
war against you, so he asked Balaam[v] to come and put a curse on
you. 10But I wouldn't listen to Balaam, and I rescued you by making
him bless you instead of curse you.
11You crossed the Jordan River
and came to Jericho. The rulers of
Jericho fought you, and so did the
Amorites, the Perizzites, the Canaanites, the Hittites, the Girgashites,
the Hivites, and the Jebusites. I
helped you defeat them all. 12Your
enemies ran from you, but not because you had swords and bows and
arrows. I made your enemies panic
and run away, as I had done with the
two Amorite kings east of the
Jordan River.
13You didn't have to work for this
land—I gave it to you. Now you live
in towns you didn't build, and you
eat grapes and olives from vineyards
and trees you didn't plant.
14Then Joshua told the people:
Worship the LORD, obey him, and
always be faithful. Get rid of the
idols your ancestors worshiped
when they lived on the other side of
the Euphrates River and in Egypt.
15But if you don't want to worship
the LORD, then choose right now!
Will you worship the same idols
your ancestors did? Or since you're
living on land that once belonged to
the Amorites, maybe you'll worship
their gods. I won't. My family and I
are going to worship and obey the
LORD!
16The people answered:
We could never worship other
gods or stop worshiping the LORD.
17The LORD is our God. We were
slaves in Egypt as our ancestors had
been, but we saw the LORD work
miracles to set our people free and
to bring us out of Egypt. Even
though other nations were all
around us, the LORD protected us
wherever we went. 18And when we
fought the Amorites and the other
nations that lived in this land, the
LORD made them run away. Yes, we
will worship and obey the LORD, because the LORD is our God.
19Joshua said:
The LORD is fearsome; he is the
one true God, and I don't think you
are able to worship and obey him in
the ways he demands. You would
have to be completely faithful, and if
you sin or rebel, he won't let you get
away with it. 20If you turn your
backs on the LORD and worship the
gods of other nations, the LORD will
turn against you. He will make terrible things happen to you and wipe
you out, even though he had been
good to you before.
21But the people shouted, "We won't
worship any other gods. We will worship and obey only the LORD!"
22Joshua said, "You have heard yourselves say that you will worship and
obey the LORD. Isn't that true?"
"Yes, it's true," they answered.
23Joshua said, "But you still have
some idols, like those the other nations
worship. Get rid of your idols! You must
decide once and for all that you really
want to obey the LORD God of Israel."
24The people said, "The LORD is our
God, and we will worship and obey only
him."
25Joshua helped Israel make an agreement with the LORD that day at Shechem. Joshua made laws for Israel 26and
wrote them down in *The Book of the
Law*[w] *of God*. Then he set up a large
stone under the oak tree at the place of
worship in Shechem 27and told the people, "Look at this stone. It has heard
everything that the LORD has said to us.
Our God can call this stone as a witness
if we ever reject him."
28Joshua sent everyone back to their
homes.

Joshua, Joseph, and Eleazar Are Buried

29Not long afterwards, the LORD's servant Joshua died at the age of one hundred ten. 30The Israelites buried him in
his own land at Timnath-Serah, north of
Mount Gaash in the hill country of
Ephraim.
31As long as Joshua lived, Israel worshiped and obeyed the LORD. There
were other leaders old enough to remember everything that the LORD had
done for Israel. And for as long as these
men lived, Israel continued to worship
and obey the LORD.
32When the people of Israel left Egypt,
they brought the bones of Joseph along
with them. They took the bones to the
town of Shechem and buried them in
the field that Jacob had bought for one
hundred pieces of silver[x] from Hamor,
the founder of Shechem. The town and

[v] **24.9** *King Balak . . . Balaam*: The Hebrew text has "King Balak the son of Zippor . . . Balaam the son of Beor." [w] **24.26** *Law*: See the note at 8.30-32. [x] **24.32** *pieces of silver*: One possible meaning for the difficult Hebrew word.

the field both[y] became part of the land
belonging to the descendants of Joseph.
33 When Eleazar the priest[z] died, he
was buried in the hill country of
Ephraim on a hill that belonged to his
son Phinehas.

[y]24.32 *town . . . both*: One possible meaning for the difficult Hebrew text. [z]24.33 *Eleazar the priest*: Hebrew "Eleazar the son of Aaron."

JUDGES

ABOUT THIS BOOK

The book of Judges tells how the Israelites kept rejecting the Lord and worshiping idols. Each time they did this, the Lord punished them by letting other nations attack and defeat them. As a result, the Israelites turned back to the Lord and asked for his help, and he sent a special leader called a "judge," who helped them defeat their enemies. A time of peace followed, and the Israelites were faithful to the Lord for as long as the judge lived. But then they again rejected the Lord. All these things happened time after time.

Some judges may have led the entire nation, but usually a judge led a few tribes at the most. Israel at this time was a loosely-bound group of tribes, and the Israelites did not think of themselves as being a single, united country. They did not yet have a king, and so during this time "everyone did what they thought was right" (21.25). But the people had to learn that they were to worship only the Lord, and when they were unfaithful, the Lord punished them.

A QUICK LOOK AT THIS BOOK

The Tribes of Judah and Simeon Fight the Canaanites

1 After the death of Joshua, the Israelites asked the LORD, "Which of
our tribes should attack the Canaanites
first?"
2"Judah!" the LORD answered. "I'll
help them take the land."
3The people of Judah went to their relatives, the Simeon tribe, and said,
"Canaanites live in the land God gave
us. Help us fight them, and we will help
you."
Troops from Simeon came to help Judah. 4-5Together they attacked an army
of ten thousand Canaanites and Perizzites at Bezek, and the LORD helped
Judah defeat them. During the battle,
Judah's army found out where the king
of Bezek[a] was, and they attacked there.
6Bezek tried to escape, but soldiers from
Judah caught him. They cut off his
thumbs and big toes, 7and he said, "I've
cut off the thumbs and big toes of
seventy kings and made those
kings crawl around under my table for
scraps of food. Now God is paying me
back."

[a]1.4,5 *king of Bezek*: Or "Adoni-Bezek."

The army of Judah took the king of
Bezek along with them to Jerusalem,
where he died. 8 They attacked Jerusalem,[b] captured it, killed everyone
who lived there, and then burned it to
the ground.
9 Judah's army fought the Canaanites
who lived in the hill country, the Southern Desert, and the foothills to the west.
10 After that, they attacked the Canaanites who lived at Hebron, defeating the
three clans called[c] Sheshai, Ahiman,
and Talmai. At that time, Hebron was
called Kiriath-Arba.
11 From Hebron, Judah's army went to
attack Debir, which at that time was
called Kiriath-Sepher. 12 Caleb[d] told his
troops, "The man who captures Kiriath-
Sepher can marry my daughter
Achsah."
13 Caleb's nephew Othniel captured
Kiriath-Sepher, so Caleb let him marry
Achsah. Othniel was the son of Caleb's
younger brother Kenaz.[e] 14 Right after
the wedding, Achsah started telling Othniel that he[f] ought to ask her father for
a field. She went to see her father, and
while she was getting down from[g] her
donkey, Caleb asked, "What's bothering
you?"
15 She answered, "I need your help.
The land you gave me is in the Southern
Desert, so please give me some spring-
fed ponds for a water supply."
Caleb gave her a couple of small
ponds named Higher Pond and Lower
Pond.[h]
16 The people who belonged to the
Kenite clan were the descendants of the
father-in-law of Moses. They left
Jericho[i] with the people of Judah and
settled near Arad in the Southern
Desert of Judah not far from the
Amalekites.[j]
17 Judah's army helped Simeon's army
attack the Canaanites who lived at
Zephath. They completely destroyed[k]
the town and renamed it Hormah.[l]
18-19 The LORD helped the army of Judah capture Gaza, Ashkelon, Ekron, and
the land near those towns. They also
took the hill country. But the people
who lived in the valleys had iron chariots, so Judah was not able to make them
leave or to take their land.
20 The tribe of Judah gave the town of
Hebron to Caleb, as Moses had told
them to do. Caleb defeated the three
Anakim[m] clans[n] and took over the
town.

The Benjamin Tribe Does Not Capture Jerusalem

21 The Jebusites were living in
Jerusalem, and the Benjamin tribe did
not defeat them or capture the town.
That's why Jebusites still live in
Jerusalem along with the people of Ben-
jamin.

The Ephraim and Manasseh Tribes Capture Bethel

22-23 The Ephraim and Manasseh
tribes[o] were getting ready to attack
Bethel, which at that time was called
Luz. And the LORD helped them when
they sent spies to find out as much as
they could about Bethel. 24 While the
spies were watching the town, a man
came out, and they told him, "If you
show us how our army can get into the
town,[p] we will make sure that you
aren't harmed." 25 The man showed
them, and the two Israelite tribes attacked Bethel, killing everyone except
the man and his family. The two tribes
made the man and his family leave, 26 so
they went to the land of the Hittites,[q]
where he built a town. He named the
town Luz, and that is still its name.

[b] **1.8** *Jerusalem*: This probably refers to towns and villages belonging to Jerusalem but lying in Judah's territory south of the city wall. Jerusalem itself was just inside Benjamin's territory, but was not captured by Israel at this time (see verse 21; Joshua 15.5-9; 18.15-18). [c] **1.10** *clans called*: Or "warriors." [d] **1.12** *Caleb*: One of the leaders of Judah; see Joshua 14.6-14 and Numbers 13.6, 30; 14.6, 10, 20-24. For verses 12-15, see Joshua 15.13-19. [e] **1.13** *Othniel was the son of . . . Kenaz*: Or "Othniel and Caleb both belonged to the Kenaz clan, but Othniel was younger than Caleb." [f] **1.14** *Achsah . . . Othniel . . . he*: Hebrew; two ancient translations "Othniel . . . Achsah . . . she." [g] **1.14** *getting down from*: One possible meaning for the difficult Hebrew text. [h] **1.15** *spring-fed ponds . . . small ponds . . . Higher Pond and Lower Pond*: Or "wells . . . wells . . . Higher Well and Lower Well." [i] **1.16** *Jericho*: The Hebrew text has "Town of Palm Trees," another name for Jericho. [j] **1.16** *not far . . . Amalekites*: One possible meaning for the difficult Hebrew text. [k] **1.17** *completely destroyed*: The Hebrew word means that the town was given completely to the LORD, and since it could not be used for normal purposes any more, it had to be destroyed. [l] **1.17** *Hormah*: In Hebrew "Hormah" sounds like "completely destroyed." [m] **1.20** *Anakim*: Perhaps a group of very large people that lived in Palestine before the Israelites (see Numbers 13.33 and Deuteronomy 2.10, 11, 20, 21). [n] **1.20** *clans*: See the note at 1.10. [o] **1.22,23** *The Ephraim and Manasseh tribes*: The Hebrew text has "The Joseph family," which was divided into these two tribes named after Joseph's sons. [p] **1.24** *If you . . . town*: Sometimes there were small doors in the town wall that could be opened from the inside even when the main town gates were shut and locked. [q] **1.26** *land of the Hittites*: The Hittites had an empire centered in what is now Turkey. At one time their empire reached south into Syria, north of Israel.

Israel Does Not Get Rid of All the Canaanites

27-28 Canaanites lived in the towns of
Beth-Shan, Taanach, Dor, Ibleam,
Megiddo, and all the villages nearby.
The Canaanites were determined to stay,
and the Manasseh tribe never did get rid
of them. But later on, when the Israelites
grew more powerful, they made slaves
of the Canaanites.
29 The Ephraim tribe did not get rid of
the Canaanites who lived in Gezer, so
the Canaanites lived there with Israelites all around them.
30 The Zebulun tribe did not get rid of
the Canaanites who lived in Kitron and
Nahalol, and the Canaanites stayed
there with Israelites around them. But
the people of Zebulun did force the
Canaanites into slave labor.
31-32 The Asher tribe did not get rid of
the Canaanites who lived in Acco,
Sidon, Ahlab, Achzib, Helbah, Aphik,
and Rehob, and the Asher tribe lived
with Canaanites all around them.
33 The Naphtali tribe did not get rid of
the Canaanites who lived in Beth-
Shemesh and Beth-Anath, but they did
force the Canaanites into slave labor.
The Naphtali tribe lived with Canaanites around them.
34 The Amorites[r] were strong enough
to keep the tribe of Dan from settling in
the valleys, so Dan had to stay in the hill
country.
35 The Amorites on Mount Heres and
in Aijalon and Shaalbim were also determined to stay. Later on, as Ephraim
and Manasseh grew more powerful,
they forced those Amorites into slave labor.

The Amorite-Edomite Border

36 The old Amorite-Edomite border
used to go from Sela through Scorpion
Pass[s] into the hill country.[t]

The LORD's Angel Speaks to Israel

2 The LORD's angel went from Gilgal
to Bochim[u] and gave the Israelites
this message from the LORD:

I promised your ancestors that I
would give this land to their families, and I brought your people here
from Egypt. We made an agreement
that I promised never to break, 2 and
you promised not to make any peace
treaties with the other nations that
live in the land. Besides that, you
agreed to tear down the altars where
they sacrifice to their idols. But you
didn't keep your promise.
3 And so, I'll stop helping you defeat your enemies. Instead, they will
be there to trap[v] you into worshiping their idols.

4 The Israelites started crying loudly,
5 and they offered sacrifices to the LORD.
From then on, they called that place
"Crying."[w]

Israel Stops Worshiping the LORD

6-9 Joshua had been faithful to the
LORD. And after Joshua sent the Israelites to take the land they had been
promised, they remained faithful to the
LORD until Joshua died at the age of one
hundred ten. He was buried on his land
in Timnath-Heres, in the hill country of
Ephraim north of Mount Gaash. Even
though Joshua was gone, the Israelites
were faithful to the LORD during the lifetime of those men who had been leaders
with Joshua and who had seen the wonderful things the LORD had done for Israel.
10 After a while the people of Joshua's
generation died, and the next generation did not know the LORD or any of the
things he had done for Israel. 11-13 The
LORD had brought their ancestors out of
Egypt, and they had worshiped him. But
now the Israelites stopped worshiping
the LORD and worshiped the idols of
Baal and Astarte, as well as the idols of
other gods from nearby nations.
The LORD was so angry 14-15 at the Israelites that he let other nations raid Israel and steal their crops and other possessions. Enemies were everywhere, and
the LORD always let them defeat Israel
in battle. The LORD had warned Israel he
would do this, and now the Israelites
were miserable.

The LORD Chooses Leaders for Israel

16 From time to time, the LORD would
choose special leaders known as
judges.[x] These judges would lead the Israelites into battle and defeat the enemies that made raids on them. 17 In years
gone by, the Israelites had been faithful
to the LORD, but now they were quick to
be unfaithful and to refuse even to listen
to these judges. The Israelites would disobey the LORD, and instead of worshiping him, they would worship other gods.
18 When enemies made life miserable
for the Israelites, the LORD would feel

[r] **1.34** *Amorites*: Used in the general sense of nations that lived in Canaan before the Israelites.
[s] **1.36** *Scorpion Pass*: Or "Akrabbim Pass."
[t] **1.36** *country*: One possible meaning for the difficult Hebrew text of verse 36.
[u] **2.1** *Bochim*: In Hebrew "Bochim" means "crying" (see verse 5).
[v] **2.3** *trap*: One possible meaning for the difficult Hebrew text.
[w] **2.5** *Crying*: Or "Bochim."
[x] **2.16** *special leaders known as judges*: The Hebrew text has "judges." In addition to leading Israelites in battle, these special leaders also decided legal cases and sometimes performed religious duties.

sorry for them. He would choose a judge
and help that judge rescue Israel from
its enemies. The LORD would be kind to
Israel as long as that judge lived. 19But
afterwards, the Israelites would become
even more sinful than their ancestors
had been. The Israelites were stubborn—they simply would not stop worshiping other gods or following the
teachings of other religions.

The LORD Lets Enemies Test Israel

20The LORD was angry with Israel and
said:

> The Israelites have broken the
> agreement I made with their ances-
> tors. They won't obey me, 21so I'll
> stop helping them defeat their ene-
> mies. Israel still had a lot of enemies
> when Joshua died, 22and I'm going
> to let those enemies stay. I'll use
> them to test Israel, because then I
> can find out if Israel will worship
> and obey me as their ancestors did.

23That's why the LORD had not let
Joshua get rid of all those enemy nations right away.

3 1-2And the LORD had another reason
for letting these enemies stay. The
Israelites needed to learn how to fight in
war, just as their ancestors had done.
Each new generation would have to
learn by fighting 3the Philistines and
their five rulers, as well as the Canaanites, the Sidonians, and the Hivites that
lived in the Lebanon Mountains from
Mount Baal-Hermon to Hamath Pass.[y]

4Moses had told the Israelites what
the LORD had commanded them to do,
and now the LORD was using these nations to find out if Israel would obey.
5-6But they refused. And it was because
of the Canaanites, Hittites, Amorites,
Perizzites, Hivites, and Jebusites who
lived all around them. Some of the Israelites married the people of these nations, and that's how they started worshiping foreign gods.

Othniel

7The Israelites sinned against the
LORD by forgetting him and worshiping
idols of Baal and Astarte. 8This made
the LORD angry, so he let Israel be defeated by King Cushan Rishathaim of
northern Syria,[z] who ruled Israel eight
years and made everyone pay taxes.
9The Israelites begged the LORD for
help, and he chose Othniel to rescue
them. Othniel was the son of Caleb's
younger brother Kenaz.[a] 10The Spirit of
the LORD took control of Othniel, and he
led Israel in a war against Cushan
Rishathaim. The LORD gave Othniel victory, 11and Israel was at peace until Othniel died about forty years later.

Ehud

12Once more the Israelites started disobeying the LORD. So he let them be defeated by King Eglon of Moab, 13who
had joined forces with the Ammonites
and the Amalekites to attack Israel.
Eglon and his army captured Jericho.[b]
14Then he ruled Israel for eighteen years
and forced the Israelites to pay heavy
taxes.

15-16The Israelites begged the LORD for
help, and the LORD chose Ehud[c] from
the Benjamin tribe to rescue them. They
put Ehud in charge of taking the taxes
to King Eglon, but before Ehud went, he
made a double-edged dagger. Ehud was
left-handed, so he strapped the dagger
to his right thigh, where it would be hidden under his robes.

17-18Ehud and some other Israelites
took the taxes to Eglon, who was a very
fat man. As soon as they gave the taxes
to Eglon, Ehud said it was time to go
home.

19-20Ehud went with the other Israelites as far as the statues[d] at Gilgal.[e]
Then he turned back and went upstairs
to the cool room[f] where Eglon had his
throne. Ehud said, "Your Majesty, I need
to talk with you in private."

Eglon replied, "Don't say anything
yet!" His officials left the room, and
Eglon stood up as Ehud came closer.

"Yes," Ehud said, "I have a message
for you from God!" 21Ehud pulled out
the dagger with his left hand and
shoved it so far into Eglon's stomach
22-23that even the handle was buried in
his fat. Ehud left the dagger there. Then
after closing and locking the doors to
the room, he climbed through a window
onto the porch[g] 24and left.

When the king's officials came back
and saw that the doors were locked,
they said, "The king is probably inside
relieving himself." 25They stood there
waiting until they felt foolish, but Eglon

[y]**3.3** *Hamath Pass*: Or "Lebo-Hamath." [z]**3.8** *northern Syria*: The Hebrew text has "Aram-Naharaim," probably referring to the land around the city of Haran (see Genesis 24.10; 25.20; 28.2, 6; 31.18, 20; 33.18; 35.23-26; 46.8-15; 48.7). [a]**3.9** *Othniel was the son of . . . Kenaz*: See the note at 1.13. [b]**3.13** *Jericho*: See the note at 1.16. [c]**3.15,16** *Ehud*: Hebrew "Ehud the son of Gera." [d]**3.19,20** *statues*: Or "stone idols" or "stone monuments." [e]**3.19,20** *Gilgal*: About a mile and a half from Jericho, where Eglon probably was (see verse 13).
[f]**3.19,20** *upstairs . . . cool room*: Houses usually had flat roofs, and sometimes a room was built on one corner of the roof where it could best catch the breeze and be kept cooler than the rest of the house. [g]**3.22,23** *he climbed . . . porch*: One possible meaning for the difficult Hebrew text.

never opened the doors. Finally, they unlocked the doors and found King Eglon lying dead on the floor. 26But by that time, Ehud had already escaped past the statues.[h]

Ehud went to the town of Seirah 27-28in the hill country of Ephraim and started blowing a signal on a trumpet. The Israelites came together, and he shouted, "Follow me! The LORD will help us defeat the Moabites."

The Israelites followed Ehud down to the Jordan valley, and they captured the places where people cross the river on the way to Moab. They would not let anyone go across, 29and before the fighting was over, they killed about ten thousand Moabite warriors—not one escaped alive.

30Moab was so badly defeated that it was a long time before they were strong enough to attack Israel again. And Israel was at peace for eighty years.

Shamgar

31Shamgar the son of Anath was the next to rescue Israel. In one battle, he used a sharp wooden pole[i] to kill six hundred Philistines.

Deborah and Barak

4 After the death of Ehud, the Israelites again started disobeying the LORD. 2So the LORD let the Canaanite King Jabin of Hazor conquer Israel. Sisera, the commander of Jabin's army, lived in Harosheth-Ha-Goiim. 3Jabin's army had nine hundred iron chariots, and for twenty years he made life miserable for the Israelites, until finally they begged the LORD for help.

4Deborah the wife of Lappidoth was a prophet and a leader[j] of Israel during those days. 5She would sit under Deborah's Palm Tree between Ramah and Bethel in the hill country of Ephraim, where Israelites would come and ask her to settle their legal cases.

6One day, Barak the son of Abinoam was in Kedesh in Naphtali, and Deborah sent word for him to come and talk with her. When he arrived, she said:

> I have a message for you from the LORD God of Israel! You are to get together an army of ten thousand men from the Naphtali and Zebulun tribes and lead them to Mount Tabor. 7The LORD will trick Sisera into coming out to fight you at the Kishon River. Sisera will be leading King Jabin's army as usual, and they will have their chariots, but the LORD has promised to help you defeat them.

8"I'm not going unless you go!" Barak told her.

9"All right, I'll go!" she replied. "But I'm warning you that the LORD is going to let a woman defeat Sisera, and no one will honor you for winning the battle."

Deborah and Barak left for Kedesh, 10where Barak called together the troops from Zebulun and Naphtali. Ten thousand soldiers gathered there, and Barak led them out from Kedesh. Deborah went too.

11At this time, Heber of the Kenite clan was living near the village of Oak in Zaanannim,[k] not far from Kedesh. The Kenites were descendants of Hobab, the father-in-law of Moses, but Heber had moved and had set up his tents away from the rest of the clan.

12When Sisera learned that Barak had led an army to Mount Tabor, 13he called his troops together and got all nine hundred iron chariots ready. Then he led his army away from Harosheth-Ha-Goiim to the Kishon River.

14Deborah shouted, "Barak, it's time to attack Sisera! Because today the LORD is going to help you defeat him. In fact, the LORD has already gone on ahead to fight for you."

Barak led his ten thousand troops down from Mount Tabor. 15And during the battle, the LORD confused Sisera, his chariot drivers, and his whole army. Everyone was so afraid of Barak and his army, that even Sisera jumped down from his chariot and tried to escape. 16Barak's forces went after Sisera's chariots and army as far as Harosheth-Ha-Goiim.

Sisera's entire army was wiped out. 17Only Sisera escaped. He ran to Heber's camp, because Heber and his family had a peace treaty with the king of Hazor. Sisera went to the tent that belonged to Jael, Heber's wife. 18She came out to greet him and said, "Come in, sir! Please come on in. Don't be afraid."

After they had gone inside, Sisera lay down, and Jael covered him with a blanket. 19"Could I have a little water?" he asked. "I'm thirsty."

Jael opened a leather bottle and poured him some milk, then she covered him back up.

20"Stand at the entrance to the tent," Sisera told her. "If someone comes by and asks if anyone is inside, tell them 'No.' "

21Sisera was exhausted and soon fell fast asleep. Jael took a hammer and

[h]**3.26** *statues*: See the note at 3.19, 20. [i]**3.31** *sharp wooden pole*: The Hebrew text has "cattle-prod," a pole with a sharpened tip or metal point at one end. [j]**4.4** *leader*: See 2.16 and the note there. [k]**4.11** *the village . . . Zaanannim*: Or "the oak tree in the town of Zaanannim."

drove a tent-peg through his head into
the ground, and he died.
22 Meanwhile, Barak had been following Sisera, and Jael went out to meet
him. "The man you're looking for is inside," she said. "Come in and I'll show
him to you."

They went inside, and there was Sisera—dead and stretched out with a tent-peg through his skull.
23 That same day the Israelites defeated the Canaanite King Jabin, and
his army was no longer powerful
enough to attack the Israelites.
24 Jabin
grew weaker while the Israelites kept
growing stronger, and at last the Israelites destroyed him.

Deborah and Barak Sing for the LORD

5 After the battle was over that day,
Deborah and Barak sang this song:

2 We praise you, LORD!
Our soldiers volunteered,
ready to follow you.
3 Listen, kings and rulers,
while I sing for the LORD,
the God of Israel.

*4 Our LORD, God of Israel,
when you came from Seir,
where the Edomites live,
5 rain poured from the sky,
the earth trembled,
and mountains shook.

6 In the time of Shamgar
son of Anath,
and now again in Jael's time,
roads were too dangerous
for caravans.
Travelers had to take
the back roads,
7 and villagers couldn't work
in their fields.[l]
Then Deborah[m] took command,
protecting Israel as a mother
protects her children.

8 The Israelites worshiped
other gods,
and the gates of their towns
were then attacked.[n]
But they had no shields
or spears to fight with.
9 I praise you, LORD,
and I am grateful
for those leaders and soldiers
who volunteered.
10 Listen, everyone!
Whether you ride a donkey
with a padded saddle
or have to walk.
11 Even those who carry water[o]
to the animals will tell you,
"The LORD has won victories,
and so has Israel."

Then the LORD's people marched
down to the town gates
12 and said, "Deborah, let's go!
Let's sing as we march.
Barak, capture our enemies."

13 The LORD's people who were left
joined with their leaders
and fought at my side.[p]
14 Troops came from Ephraim,
where Amalekites once lived.
Others came from Benjamin;
officers and leaders came
from Machir and Zebulun.
15 The rulers of Issachar
came along with Deborah,
and Issachar followed Barak
into the valley.

But the tribe of Reuben
was no help at all![q]
16 Reuben, why did you stay
among your sheep pens?[r]
Was it to listen to shepherds
whistling for their sheep?
No one could figure out
why Reuben wouldn't come.[s]
17 The people of Gilead stayed
across the Jordan.
Why did the tribe of Dan
remain on their ships
and the tribe of Asher
stay along the coast
near the harbors?

18 But soldiers of Zebulun
and Naphtali
risked their lives
to attack the enemy.[t]
19 Canaanite kings fought us
at Taanach by the stream
near Megiddo[u]—
but they couldn't rob us
of our silver.[v]
20 From their pathways in the sky
the stars[w] fought Sisera,

[l] **5.7** *villagers . . . fields*: One possible meaning for the difficult Hebrew text. [m] **5.7** *Deborah*: Or "I, Deborah." [n] **5.8** *The Israelites . . . attacked*: One possible meaning for the difficult Hebrew text. [o] **5.11** *Even . . . water*: One possible meaning for the difficult Hebrew text. [p] **5.13** *side*: One possible meaning for the difficult Hebrew text of verse 13. [q] **5.15** *But . . . at all*: Or "But the people of Reuben couldn't make up their minds." [r] **5.16** *sheep pens*: Or "campfires." [s] **5.16** *No . . . come*: Or "The people of Reuben couldn't make up their minds." [t] **5.18** *to attack the enemy*: One possible meaning for the difficult Hebrew text. [u] **5.19** *stream near Megiddo*: Probably refers to one of the streams that flow into the Kishon River. [v] **5.19** *rob us of our silver*: The army that won a battle would take everything of value from the dead enemy soldiers. [w] **5.20** *stars*: In ancient times, the stars were sometimes regarded as supernatural beings.

21 and his soldiers were swept away
by the ancient Kishon River.

I will march on and be brave.

22 Sisera's horses galloped off,
their hoofs thundering
in retreat.

23 The LORD's angel said,
"Put a curse on Meroz Town!
Its people refused
to help the LORD fight
his powerful enemies."

24 But honor Jael,
the wife of Heber
from the Kenite clan.
Give more honor to her
than to any other woman
who lives in tents.
Yes, give more honor to her
than to any other woman.
25 Sisera asked for water,
but Jael gave him milk—
cream in a fancy cup.
26 She reached for a tent-peg
and held a hammer
in her right hand.
And with a blow to the head,
she crushed his skull.
27 Sisera sank to his knees
and fell dead at her feet.

28 Sisera's mother looked out
through her window.
"Why is he taking so long?"
she asked.
"Why haven't we heard
his chariots coming?"
29 She and her wisest women
gave the same answer:
30 "Sisera and his troops
are finding treasures
to bring back—
a woman, or maybe two,
for each man,
and beautiful dresses
for those women to wear."[x]

31 Our LORD, we pray
that all your enemies
will die like Sisera.
But let everyone who loves you
shine brightly like the sun
at dawn.

Midian Steals Everything from Israel

6 There was peace in Israel for about
forty years. 1 Then once again the Israelites started disobeying the LORD, so
he let the nation of Midian control Israel
for seven years. 2 The Midianites were so
cruel that many Israelites ran to the
mountains and hid in caves.
3 Every time the Israelites would plant
crops, the Midianites invaded Israel together with the Amalekites and other
eastern nations. 4-5 They rode in on their
camels, set up their tents, and then let
their livestock eat the crops as far as the
town of Gaza. The Midianites stole food,
sheep, cattle, and donkeys. Like a
swarm of locusts,[y] they could not be
counted, and they ruined the land wherever they went.
6-7 The Midianites took almost everything that belonged to the Israelites, and
the Israelites begged the LORD for help.
8-9 Then the LORD sent a prophet to them
with this message:

I am the LORD God of Israel, so listen to what I say. You were slaves in
Egypt, but I set you free and led you
out of Egypt into this land. And
when nations here made life miserable for you, I rescued you and
helped you get rid of them and take
their land. 10 I am your God, and I
told you not to worship Amorite
gods, even though you are living in
the land of the Amorites. But you refused to listen.

The LORD Chooses Gideon

11 One day an angel from the LORD
went to the town of Ophrah and sat
down under the big tree that belonged
to Joash, a member of the Abiezer clan.
Joash's son Gideon was nearby, threshing grain in a shallow pit, where he
could not be seen by the Midianites.
12 The angel appeared and spoke to
Gideon, "The LORD is helping you, and
you are a strong warrior."
13 Gideon answered, "Please don't take
this wrong, but if the LORD is helping us,
then why have all of these awful things
happened? We've heard how the LORD
performed miracles and rescued our ancestors from Egypt. But those things
happened long ago. Now the LORD has
abandoned us to the Midianites."
14 Then the LORD himself said,
"Gideon, you will be strong, because I
am giving you the power to rescue Israel from the Midianites."
15 Gideon replied, "But how can I rescue Israel? My clan is the weakest one
in Manasseh, and everyone else in my
family is more important than I am."
16 "Gideon," the LORD answered, "you
can rescue Israel because I am going to
help you! Defeating the Midianites will
be as easy as beating up one man."
17 Gideon said, "It's hard to believe
that I'm actually talking to the LORD.

[x] **5.30** *and beautiful . . . wear*: One possible meaning for the difficult Hebrew text.
[y] **6.4,5** *locusts*: Insects like grasshoppers that travel in swarms and cause great damage to crops.

Please do something so I'll know that
you really are the LORD. 18And wait here
until I bring you an offering."

"All right, I'll wait," the LORD answered.

19Gideon went home and killed a
young goat, then started boiling the
meat. Next, he opened a big sack of
flour and made it into thin bread.[z]
When the meat was done, he put it in a
basket and poured the broth into a clay
cooking pot. He took the meat, the
broth, and the bread and placed them
under the big tree.

20God's angel said, "Gideon, put the
meat and the bread on this rock, and
pour the broth over them." Gideon did
as he was told. 21The angel was holding
a walking stick, and he touched the
meat and the bread with the end of the
stick. Flames jumped from the rock and
burned up the meat and the bread.

When Gideon looked, the angel was
gone. 22Gideon realized that he had seen
one of the LORD's angels. "Oh!" he
moaned. "Now I'm going to die."[a]

23"Calm down!" the LORD told Gideon.
"There's nothing to be afraid of. You're
not going to die."

24Gideon built an altar for worshiping
the LORD and called it "The LORD Calms
Our Fears." It still stands there in
Ophrah, a town in the territory of the
Abiezer clan.

Gideon Tears Down Baal's Altar

25That night the LORD spoke to Gideon
again:

> Get your father's second-best bull, the one that's seven years old. Use it to pull down the altar where your father worships Baal and cut down the sacred pole[b] next to the altar.
> 26Then build an altar for worshiping
> me on the highest part of the hill where your town is built. Use layers of stones for my altar, not just a pile of rocks. Cut up the wood from the pole, make a fire, kill the bull, and burn it as a sacrifice to me.

27Gideon chose ten of his servants to
help him, and they did everything God
had said. But since Gideon was afraid of
his family and the other people in town,
he did it all at night.

28When the people of the town got up
the next morning, they saw that Baal's
altar had been knocked over, and the sacred pole next to it had been cut down.
Then they noticed the new altar covered
with the remains of the sacrificed bull.

29"Who could have done such a
thing?" they asked. And they kept on
asking, until finally someone told them,
"Gideon the son of Joash did it."

30The men of the town went to Joash
and said, "Your son Gideon knocked
over Baal's altar and cut down the sacred pole next to it. Hand him over, so
we can kill him!"

31The crowd pushed closer and closer,
but Joash replied, "Are you trying to
take revenge for Baal? Are you trying to
rescue Baal? If you are, you will be the
ones who are put to death, and it will
happen before another day dawns. If
Baal really is a god, let him take his
own revenge on someone who tears
down his altar."

32That same day, Joash changed
Gideon's name to Jerubbaal, explaining,
"He tore down Baal's altar, so let Baal
take revenge himself."[c]

Gideon Defeats the Midianites

33All the Midianites, Amalekites, and
other eastern nations got together and
crossed the Jordan River. Then they invaded the land of Israel and set up camp
in Jezreel Valley.

34The LORD's Spirit took control of
Gideon, and Gideon blew a signal on a
trumpet to tell the men in the Abiezer
clan to follow him. 35He also sent messengers to the tribes of Manasseh,
Asher, Zebulun, and Naphtali, telling
the men of these tribes to come and join
his army. Then they set out toward the
enemy camp.

36-37Gideon prayed to God, "I know
that you promised to help me rescue Israel, but I need proof. Tonight I'll put
some wool on the stone floor of that
threshing-place over there. If you really
will help me rescue Israel, then tomorrow morning let there be dew on the
wool, but let the stone floor be dry."

38And that's just what happened.
Early the next morning, Gideon got up
and checked the wool. He squeezed out
enough water to fill a bowl. 39But
Gideon prayed to God again. "Don't be
angry at me," Gideon said. "Let me try
this just one more time, so I'll really be
sure you'll help me. Only this time, let
the wool be dry and the stone floor be
wet with dew."

40That night, God made the stone floor
wet with dew, but he kept the wool dry.

7 Early the next morning, Gideon and
his army got up and moved their
camp to Fear Spring.[d] The Midianite

[z]6.19 *thin bread*: Bread made without yeast, since there was no time for the dough to rise.
[a]6.22 *Now I'm going to die*: The Hebrew text has "I have seen an angel of the LORD face to face." Some people believed that if they saw one of the LORD's angels, they would die (see 13.22). [b]6.25 *sacred pole*: Or "sacred tree," used as a symbol of Asherah, the Canaanite goddess of fertility. [c]6.32 *Jerubbaal . . . take revenge himself*: In Hebrew, "Jerubbaal" means "Let Baal take revenge." [d]7.1 *Fear Spring*: Or "Harod Spring."

camp was to the north, in the valley at
the foot of Moreh Hill.[e]
2 The LORD said, "Gideon, your army is
too big. I can't let you win with this
many soldiers. The Israelites would
think that they had won the battle all by
themselves and that I didn't have anything to do with it. 3 So call your troops
together and tell them that anyone who
is really afraid can leave Mount Gilead[f]
and go home."
Twenty-two thousand men returned
home, leaving Gideon with only ten
thousand soldiers.
4 "Gideon," the LORD said, "you still
have too many soldiers. Take them
down to the spring and I'll test them. I'll
tell you which ones can go along with
you and which ones must go back
home."
5 When Gideon led his army down to
the spring, the LORD told him, "Watch
how each man gets a drink of water.
Then divide them into two groups—
those who lap the water like a dog and
those who kneel down to drink."
6 Three hundred men scooped up water in their hands and lapped it, and the
rest knelt to get a drink. 7 The LORD said,
"Gideon, your army will be made up of
everyone who lapped the water from
their hands. Send the others home. I'm
going to rescue Israel by helping you
and your army of three hundred defeat
the Midianites."
8 Then Gideon gave these orders, "You
three hundred men stay here. The rest
of you may go home, but leave your
food and trumpets with us."
Gideon's army camp was on top of a
hill overlooking the Midianite camp in
the valley.
9 That night, the LORD said to Gideon.
"Get up! Attack the Midianite camp. I
am going to let you defeat them, 10 but if
you're still afraid, you and your servant
Purah should sneak down to their camp.
11 When you hear what the Midianites
are saying, you'll be brave enough to attack."
Gideon and Purah worked their way
to the edge of the enemy camp, where
soldiers were on guard duty. 12 The camp
was huge. The Midianites, Amalekites,
and other eastern nations covered the
valley like a swarm of locusts.[g] And it
would be easier to count the grains of
sand on a beach than to count their
camels. 13 Gideon overheard one enemy
guard telling another, "I had a dream
about a flat[h] loaf of barley bread that
came tumbling into our camp. It hit the
headquarters tent,[i] and the tent flipped
over and fell down."
14 The other soldier answered, "Your
dream must have been about Gideon,
the Israelite commander. It means God
will let him and his army defeat the
Midianite army and everyone else in our
camp."
15 As soon as Gideon heard about the
dream and what it meant, he bowed
down to praise God. Then he went back
to the Israelite camp and shouted, "Let's
go! The LORD is going to let us defeat
the Midianite army."
16 Gideon divided his little army into
three groups of one hundred men, and
he gave each soldier a trumpet and a
large clay jar with a burning torch inside. 17-18 Gideon said, "When we get to
the enemy camp, spread out and surround it. Then wait for me to blow a signal on my trumpet. As soon as you hear
it, blow your trumpets and shout, 'Fight
for the LORD! Fight for Gideon!' "
19 Gideon and his group reached the
edge of the enemy camp a few hours after dark, just after the new guards had
come on duty.[j] Gideon and his soldiers
blew their trumpets and smashed the
clay jars that were hiding the torches.
20 The rest of Gideon's soldiers blew the
trumpets they were holding in their
right hands. Then they smashed the jars
and held the burning torches in their
left hands. Everyone shouted, "Fight
with your swords for the LORD and for
Gideon!"
21 The enemy soldiers started yelling
and tried to run away. Gideon's troops
stayed in their positions surrounding
the camp 22 and blew their trumpets
again. As they did, the LORD made the
enemy soldiers pull out their swords
and start fighting each other.
The enemy army tried to escape from
the camp. They ran to Acacia Tree
Town, toward Zeredah,[k] and as far as
the edge of the land that belonged to the
town of Abel-Meholah near Tabbath.[l]
23 Gideon sent word for more Israelite

[e] **7.1** *Moreh Hill*: About 5 miles north of Fear Spring. [f] **7.3** *Mount Gilead*: Usually "Gilead" refers to an area east of the Jordan River, but in this verse it refers to a place near Jezreel Valley west of the Jordan. [g] **7.12** *locusts*: See the note at 6.4, 5. [h] **7.13** *flat*: Or "moldy." [i] **7.13** *the headquarters tent*: Or "a tent." [j] **7.19** *a few hours after dark, just . . . duty*: The Hebrew text has "at the beginning of the second watch, just . . . duty." The night was divided into three periods called "watches," each about four hours long, and different guards would come on duty at the beginning of each watch. The first watch began at sunset, so the beginning of the second watch would have been shortly after 10:00 P.M. [k] **7.22** *Zeredah*: Some Hebrew manuscripts; most Hebrew manuscripts "Zererah"; these may be different names for the town of Zarethan in the Jordan River valley. [l] **7.22** *Acacia Tree Town . . . Zeredah . . . Abel-Meholah near Tabbath*: These were places east of the Jordan River.

soldiers to come from the tribes of
Naphtali, Asher, and both halves of
Manasseh[m] to help fight the Midianites.
24He also sent messengers to tell all the
men who lived in the hill country of
Ephraim, "Come and help us fight the
Midianites! Put guards at every spring,
stream, and well, as far as Beth-Barah
before the Midianites can get to them.
And guard the Jordan River."

Troops from Ephraim did exactly
what Gideon had asked, 25and they even
helped chase the Midianites on the east
side of the Jordan River. These troops
captured Raven and Wolf,[n] the two Midianite leaders. They killed Raven at a
large rock that has come to be known as
Raven Rock, and they killed Wolf near a
wine-pit that has come to be called Wolf
Wine-Pit.[o]

The men of Ephraim brought the
heads of the two Midianite leaders to
8 Gideon. 1But the men were really
upset with Gideon and complained,
"When you went to war with Midian,
you didn't ask us to help! Why did you
treat us like that?"

2Gideon answered:

> Don't be upset! Even though you
> came later, you were able to do
> much more than I did. It's just like
> the grape harvest: The grapes your
> tribe doesn't even bother to pick are
> better than the best grapes my fam-
> ily can grow. 3Besides, God chose
> you to capture Raven and Wolf. I
> didn't do a thing compared to you.

By the time Gideon had finished talking, the men of Ephraim had calmed
down and were no longer angry at him.

Gideon Finishes Destroying the Midianite Army

4After Gideon and his three hundred
troops had chased the Midianites as far
as the Jordan River, they were exhausted. 5The town of Succoth was
nearby, so he went there and asked,
"Please give my troops some food. They
are worn out, but we have to keep chasing Zebah and Zalmunna, the two Midianite kings."

6The town leaders of Succoth answered, "Why should we feed your
army? We don't know if you really will
defeat Zebah and Zalmunna."

7"Just wait!" Gideon said. "After the
LORD helps me defeat them, I'm coming
back here. I'll make a whip out of thorns
and rip the flesh from your bones."

8After leaving Succoth, Gideon went
to Penuel and asked the leaders there
for some food. But he got the same answer as he had gotten at Succoth. 9"I'll
come back safe and sound," Gideon
said, "but when I do, I'm going to tear
down your tower!"[p]

10Zebah and Zalmunna were in
Karkor[q] with an army of fifteen thousand troops. They were all that was left
of the army of the eastern nations, because one hundred twenty thousand of
their warriors had been killed in the
battle.

11Gideon reached the enemy camp
by going east along Nomad[r] Road
past Nobah and Jogbehah. He made a
surprise attack, 12and the enemy panicked. Zebah and Zalmunna tried to escape, but Gideon chased and captured
them.

13After the battle, Gideon set out for
home. As he was going through Heres
Pass, 14he caught a young man who
lived in Succoth. Gideon asked him who
the town officials of Succoth were, and
the young man wrote down seventy-
seven names.

15Gideon went to the town officials
and said, "Here are Zebah and Zalmunna. Remember how you made fun
of me? You said, 'We don't know if you
really will defeat those two Midianite
kings. So why should we feed your
worn-out army?' "

16Gideon made a whip from thorn
plants and used it to beat the town officials. 17Afterwards he went to Penuel,
where he tore down the tower and killed
all the town officials[s] there.

18Then Gideon said, "Zebah and Zalmunna, tell me about the men you killed
at Tabor."

"They were a lot like you," the two
kings answered. "They were dignified,
almost like royalty."

19"They were my very own brothers!"
Gideon said. "I swear by the living LORD
that if you had let them live, I would let
you live."

20Gideon turned to Jether, his oldest
son. "Kill them!" Gideon said.

But Jether was young,[t] and he was
too afraid to even pull out his sword.

21"What's the matter, Gideon?" Zebah
and Zalmunna asked. "Do it yourself, if
you're not too much of a coward!"

Gideon jumped up and killed them
both. Then he took the fancy gold ornaments from the necks of their camels.

[m]**7.23** *both halves of Manasseh*: Half of Manasseh lived east of the Jordan River, and the other half lived on the west. [n]**7.25** *Raven and Wolf*: Or "Oreb and Zeeb." [o]**7.25** *Raven Rock . . . Wolf Wine-Pit*: Or "Oreb Rock . . . Zeeb Wine-Pit." [p]**8.9** *tower*: Towers were often part of a town wall. [q]**8.10** *Karkor*: A little over 100 miles east of the Dead Sea. [r]**8.11** *Nomad*: A person who lives in a tent and moves from place to place. [s]**8.17** *all . . . officials*: Or "every man in town." [t]**8.20** *young*: Gideon wanted to insult the kings by having a young boy kill them.

The Israelites Ask Gideon To Be Their King

22 After the battle with the Midianites,
the Israelites said, "Gideon, you rescued
us! Now we want you to be our king.
Then after your death, your son and
then your grandson will rule."
23 "No," Gideon replied, "I won't be
your king, and my son won't be king either. Only the LORD is your ruler. 24 But I
will ask you to do one thing: Give me all
the earrings you took from the enemy."
The enemy soldiers had been Ishmaelites,[u] and they wore gold earrings.
25 The Israelite soldiers replied, "Of
course we will give you the earrings."
Then they spread out a robe on the
ground and tossed the earrings on it.
26 The total weight of this gold was over
forty pounds. In addition, there was the
gold from the camels' ornaments and
from the beautiful jewelry worn by the
Midianite kings. Gideon also took their
purple robes.
27-29 Gideon returned to his home in
Ophrah and had the gold made into a
statue, which the Israelites soon started
worshiping. They became unfaithful to
God, and even Gideon and his family
were trapped into worshiping the
statue.[v]
The Midianites had been defeated so
badly that they were no longer strong
enough to attack Israel. And so Israel
was at peace for the remaining forty
years of Gideon's life.

Gideon Dies

30 Gideon had many wives and seventy
sons. 31 He even had a wife[w] who lived at
Shechem.[x] They had a son, and Gideon
named him Abimelech.
32 Gideon lived to be an old man. And
when he died, he was buried in the family tomb in his hometown of Ophrah,
which belonged to the Abiezer clan.
33 Soon after Gideon's death, the Israelites turned their backs on God
again. They set up idols of Baal and
worshiped Baal Berith[y] as their god.
34 The Israelites forgot that the LORD was
their God, and that he had rescued them
from the enemies who lived around
them. 35 Besides all that, the Israelites
were unkind to Gideon's family, even
though Gideon had done so much for Israel.

Abimelech Tries To Be King

9 Abimelech the son of Gideon[z] went
to Shechem. While there, he met
with his mother's relatives 2 and told
them to say to the leaders of Shechem,
"Do you think it would be good to have
all seventy of Gideon's sons ruling us?
Wouldn't you rather have just one man
be king? Abimelech would make a good
king, and he's related to us."
3 Abimelech's uncles talked it over
with the leaders of Shechem who
agreed, "Yes, it would be better for one
of our relatives to be king." 4 Then they
gave Abimelech seventy pieces[a] of silver from the temple of their god Baal
Berith.[b]
Abimelech used the silver to hire a
gang of rough soldiers who would do
anything for money. 5 Abimelech and his
soldiers went to his father's home in
Ophrah and brought out Gideon's other
sons to a large rock, where they murdered all seventy. Gideon's youngest son
Jotham hid from the soldiers, but he
was the only one who escaped.
6 The leaders of Shechem, including
the priests and the military officers,[c]
met at the tree next to the sacred rock[d]
in Shechem to crown Abimelech king.
7 Jotham heard what they were doing. So
he climbed to the top of Mount Gerizim
and shouted down to the people who
were there at the meeting:

Leaders of Shechem,
listen to me,
and maybe God
will listen to you.

8 Once the trees searched
for someone to be king;
they asked the olive tree,
"Will you be our king?"
9 But the olive tree replied,
"My oil brings honor
to people and gods.
I won't stop making oil,
just to have my branches wave
above the other trees."

[u] **8.24** *Ishmaelites*: According to Genesis 25.1, 2, 12, both Ishmaelites and Midianites were descendants of Abraham. It is possible that in this passage "Ishmaelites" has the meaning "nomadic traders," while "Midianites" (verses 22, 26-29) refers to their ethnic origin. [v] **8.27-29** *statue . . . statue*: Or "sacred priestly vest . . . vest." [w] **8.31** *wife*: This translates a Hebrew word for a woman who was legally bound to a man, but without the full privileges of a wife. [x] **8.31** *who lived at Shechem*: Sometimes marriages were arranged so that the wife lived with her parents, and the husband visited her from time to time. [y] **8.33** *Baal Berith*: Or "Baal of the Agreement" or "the Lord of the Agreement." [z] **9.1** *Gideon*: The Hebrew text has "Jerubbaal," another name for Gideon (see 6.32). [a] **9.4** *seventy pieces*: About 28 ounces. [b] **9.4** *Baal Berith*: See the note at 8.33. [c] **9.6** *including the priests and the military officers*: The Hebrew text has "and the Millo house," another name for the temple of Baal Berith. It probably also served as a military fortress. [d] **9.6** *tree . . . rock*: One ancient translation; Hebrew "propped-up sacred tree."

10 Then they asked the fig tree,
"Will you be our king?"
11 But the fig tree replied,
"I won't stop growing
my delicious fruit,
just to have my branches wave
above the other trees."

12 Next they asked the grape vine,
"Will you be our king?"
13 But the grape vine replied,
"My wine brings cheer
to people and gods.
I won't stop making wine,
just to have my branches wave
above the other trees."

14 Finally, they went
to the thornbush and asked,
"Will you be our king?"
15 The thornbush replied,
"If you really want me
to be your king,
then come into my shade
and I will protect you.
But if you're deceiving me,
I'll start a fire
that will spread out and destroy
the cedars of Lebanon."[e]

After Jotham had finished telling this story, he said:

16-18My father Gideon risked his life for you when he fought to rescue you from the Midianites. Did you reward Gideon by being kind to his family? No, you did not! You attacked his family and killed all seventy of his sons on that rock.

And was it right to make Abimelech your king? He's merely the son of my father's slave girl.[f] But just because he's your relative, you made him king of Shechem.

19So, you leaders of Shechem, if you treated Gideon and his family the way you should have, then I hope you and Abimelech will make each other very happy. 20But if it was wrong to treat Gideon and his family the way you did, then I pray that Abimelech will destroy you with fire, and I pray that you will do the same to him.

21Jotham ran off and went to live in the town of Beer, where he could be safe from his brother Abimelech.

Abimelech Destroys Shechem

22Abimelech had been a military commander of Israel for three years,
23-24when God decided to punish him and the leaders of Shechem for killing Gideon's seventy sons. So God turned the leaders of Shechem against Abimelech. 25Then they sent some men to hide on the hilltops and watch for Abimelech and his troops, while they sent others to rob everyone that went by on the road. But Abimelech found out what they were doing.

26One day, Gaal son of Ebed went to live in Shechem. His brothers moved there too, and soon the leaders of Shechem started trusting him.

27The time came for the grape harvest, and the people of Shechem went into their vineyards and picked the grapes. They put the grapes in their wine-pits and walked on them to squeeze out the juice in order to make wine. Then they went into the temple of their god and threw a big party. There was a lot of eating and drinking, and before long they were cursing Abimelech.

28Gaal said:

Hamor was the founder of Shechem, and one of his descendants should be our ruler. But Abimelech's father was Gideon, so Abimelech isn't really one of us. He shouldn't be our king, and we shouldn't have to obey him or Zebul, who rules Shechem for him. 29If I were the ruler of Shechem, I'd get rid of that Abimelech. I'd tell him, "Get yourself an even bigger army, and we will still defeat you."

30Zebul was angry when he found out what Gaal had said. 31And so he sent some messengers to Abimelech. But they had to pretend to be doing something else, or they would not have been allowed to leave Shechem.[g] Zebul told the messengers to say:

Gaal the son of Ebed has come to Shechem along with his brothers, and they have persuaded the people to let Gaal rule Shechem instead of you. 32This is what I think you should do. Lead your army here during the night and hide in the fields. 33Get up the next morning at sunrise and rush out of your hiding places to attack the town. Gaal and his followers will come out to fight you, but you will easily defeat them.

34So one night, Abimelech led his soldiers to Shechem. He divided them into four groups, and they all hid near the town.

35The next morning, Gaal went out and stood in the opening of the town gate. Abimelech and his soldiers left their hiding places, 36and Gaal saw them. Zebul was standing there with Gaal, and Gaal remarked, "Zebul, that

[e]9.15 *cedars of Lebanon*: The cedars that grew in the Lebanon mountains were some of the largest trees in that part of the world. [f]9.16-18 *son of . . . slave girl*: See 8.31. [g]9.31 *But . . . Shechem*: One possible meaning for the difficult Hebrew text.

looks like a crowd of people coming down from the mountaintops."

"No," Zebul answered, "it's just the shadows of the mountains. It only looks like people moving."

37"But Zebul, look over there," Gaal said. "There's a crowd coming down from the sacred mountain,[h] and another group is coming along the road from the tree where people talk with the spirits of the dead."

38Then Zebul replied, "What good is all of your bragging now? You were the one who said Abimelech shouldn't be the ruler of Shechem. Out there is the army that you made fun of. So go out and fight them!"

39Gaal and the leaders of Shechem went out and fought Abimelech. 40Soon the people of Shechem turned and ran back into the town. However, Abimelech and his troops were close behind and killed many of them along the way.

41Abimelech stayed at Arumah,[i] and Zebul forced Gaal and his brothers out of Shechem.

42The next morning, the people of Shechem were getting ready to work in their fields as usual, but someone told Abimelech about it. 43Abimelech divided his army into three groups and set up an ambush in the fields near Shechem. When the people came out of the town, he and his army rushed out from their hiding places and attacked. 44Abimelech and the troops with him ran to the town gate and took control of it, while two other groups attacked and killed the people who were in the fields. 45He and his troops fought in Shechem all day, until they had killed everyone in town. Then he and his men tore down the houses and buildings and scattered salt[j] everywhere.

46Earlier that day, the leaders of the temple of El Berith[k] at Shechem had heard about the attack. So they went into the temple fortress, 47but Abimelech found out where they were. 48He led his troops to Mount Zalmon, where he took an ax and chopped off a tree branch. He lifted the branch onto his shoulder and shouted, "Hurry! Cut off a branch just as I did."

49When they all had branches, they followed Abimelech back to Shechem. They piled the branches against the fortress and set them on fire, burning down the fortress and killing about one thousand men and women.

50After destroying Shechem, Abimelech went to Thebez. He surrounded the town and captured it. 51But there was a tall fortress in the middle of the town, and the town leaders and everyone else went inside. Then they barred the gates and went up to the flat roof.

52Abimelech and his army rushed to the fortress and tried to force their way inside. Abimelech himself was about to set the heavy wooden doors on fire, 53when a woman on the roof dropped a large rock[l] on his head and cracked his skull. 54The soldier who carried his weapons was nearby, and Abimelech told him, "Take out your sword and kill me. I don't want people to say that I was killed by a woman!"

So the soldier ran his sword through Abimelech. 55And when the Israelite soldiers saw that their leader was dead, they went back home.

56That's how God punished Abimelech for killing his brothers and bringing shame on his father's family. 57God also punished the people of Shechem for helping Abimelech.[m] Everything happened just as Jotham's curse said it would.

Tola

10 Tola was the next person to rescue Israel. He belonged to the Issachar tribe, but he lived in Shamir, a town in the hill country of Ephraim. His father was Puah, and his grandfather was Dodo. 2Tola was a leader[n] of Israel for twenty-three years, then he died and was buried in Shamir.

Jair

3The next leader[n] of Israel was Jair, who lived in Gilead. He was a leader for twenty-two years. 4He had thirty sons, and each son had his own mule[o] and was in charge of one town in Gilead. Those thirty towns are still called The Settlements of Jair.[p] 5When he died, he was buried in the town of Kamon.

Israel Is Unfaithful Again

6Before long, the Israelites began disobeying the LORD by worshiping Baal,

[h]9.37 *sacred mountain*: The Hebrew text has "the navel of the land," which probably refers to Mount Gerizim as a sacred mountain linking heaven and earth. [i]9.41 *Arumah*: About five miles from Shechem. [j]9.45 *scattered salt*: This may have been part of a ceremony to place a curse on the town. [k]9.46 *temple of El Berith*: The Hebrew text also calls all or part of this temple the "Fortress of Shechem." El Berith, "the God of the Agreement," was also known as Baal Berith, "the Lord of the Agreement" (see also 8.33; 9.4). [l]9.53 *large rock*: One that was used in the grinding of grain. [m]9.57 *helping Abimelech*: Hebrew "their evil" (see 9.3, 4). [n]10.2 *leader*: See 2.16 and the note there. [n]10.3 *leader*: See 2.16 and the note there. [o]10.4 *each son had his own mule*: A sign that the family was wealthy. [p]10.4 *The Settlements of Jair*: Or "Havvoth-Jair."

Astarte, and gods from Syria, Sidon,
Moab, Ammon, and Philistia.
7The LORD was angry at Israel and decided to let Philistia and Ammon conquer them. 8So the same year that Jair
died, Israel's army was crushed by these
two nations. For eighteen years, Ammon
was cruel to the Israelites who lived in
Gilead, the region east of the Jordan
River that had once belonged to the
Amorites. 9Then the Ammonites began
crossing the Jordan and attacking the
tribes of Judah, Benjamin, and Ephraim.
Life was miserable for the Israelites.
10They begged the LORD for help and
confessed, "We were unfaithful to you,
our LORD. We stopped worshiping you
and started worshiping idols of Baal."
11-12The LORD answered:

In the past when you came crying
to me for help, I rescued you. At one
time or another I've rescued you
from the Egyptians, the Amorites,
the Ammonites, the Philistines, the
Sidonians, the Amalekites, and the
Maonites.[q] 13-14But I'm not going to
rescue you any more! You've left me
and gone off to worship other gods.
If you're in such big trouble, go cry
to them for help!

15"We have been unfaithful," the Israelites admitted. "If we must be punished, do it yourself, but please rescue
us from the Ammonites."
16Then the Israelites got rid of the
idols of the foreign gods, and they began worshiping only the LORD. Finally,
there came a time when the LORD could
no longer stand to see them suffer.

The Ammonites Invade Gilead

17The rulers of Ammon called their
soldiers together and led them to
Gilead, where they set up camp.
The Israelites gathered at Mizpah[r]
and set up camp there. 18The leaders of
Gilead asked each other, "Who can lead
an attack on the Ammonites?" Then
they agreed, "If we can find someone
who can lead the attack, we'll make him
the ruler of Gilead."

Jephthah

11 1-5The leaders of the Gilead clan
decided to ask a brave warrior
named Jephthah son of Gilead to lead
the attack against the Ammonites.
Even though Jephthah belonged to
the Gilead clan, he had earlier been
forced to leave the region where they
had lived. Jephthah was the son of a
prostitute, but his half-brothers were the
sons of his father's wife.
One day his half-brothers told him,
"You don't really belong to our family,
so you can't have any of the family
property." Then they forced Jephthah to
leave home.
Jephthah went to the country of Tob,
where he was joined by a number of
men who would do anything for money.
So the leaders of Gilead went to Jephthah and said, 6"Please come back to
Gilead! If you lead our army, we will be
able to fight off the Ammonites."
7"Didn't you hate me?" Jephthah
replied. "Weren't you the ones who
forced me to leave my family? You're
coming to me now, just because you're
in trouble."
8"But we do want you to come back,"
the leaders said. "And if you lead us in
battle against the Ammonites, we will
make you the ruler of Gilead."
9"All right," Jephthah said. "If I go
back with you and the LORD lets me defeat the Ammonites, will you really
make me your ruler?"
10"You have our word," the leaders answered. "And the LORD is a witness to
what we have said."
11So Jephthah went back to Mizpah[r]
with the leaders of Gilead. The people of
Gilead gathered at the place of worship
and made Jephthah their ruler. Jephthah also made promises to them.
12After the ceremony, Jephthah sent
messengers to say to the king of Ammon, "Are you trying to start a war? You
have invaded my country, and I want to
know why!"
13The king of Ammon replied, "Tell
Jephthah that the land really belongs to
me, all the way from the Arnon River in
the south, to the Jabbok River in the
north, and west to the Jordan River.
When the Israelites came out of Egypt,
they stole it. Tell Jephthah to return it to
me, and there won't be any war."
14Jephthah sent the messengers back
to the king of Ammon, 15and they told
him that Jephthah had said:

Israel hasn't taken any territory
from Moab or Ammon. 16When the
Israelites came from Egypt, they
traveled in the desert to the Red
Sea[s] and then to Kadesh. 17They
sent messengers to the king of Edom
and said, "Please, let us go through
your country." But the king of Edom
refused. They also sent messengers
to the king of Moab, but he wouldn't

[q] **10.11,12** *Maonites*: Hebrew; one ancient translation "Midianites." [r] **10.17** *Mizpah*: In chapters 10–12, Mizpah is the name of a town in Gilead (see 11.29), not the same town as the Mizpah of chapters 20, 21. [r] **11.11** *Mizpah*: In chapters 10–12, Mizpah is the name of a town in Gilead (see 11.29), not the same town as the Mizpah of chapters 20, 21. [s] **11.16** *Red Sea*: Hebrew *yam suph*, here referring to the Gulf of Aqaba, since the term is extended to include the northeastern arm of the Red Sea (see also the note at Exodus 13.18).

let them cross his country either.
And so the Israelites stayed at
Kadesh.
18 A little later, the Israelites set out
into the desert, going east of Edom
and Moab, and camping on the eastern side of the Arnon River gorge.
The Arnon is the eastern border of
Moab, and since the Israelites didn't
cross it, they didn't even set foot in
Moab.
19 The Israelites sent messengers to
the Amorite King Sihon of Heshbon.
"Please," they said, "let our people
go through your country to get to
our own land."
20 Sihon didn't think the Israelites
could be trusted, so he called his
army together. They set up camp at
Jahaz, then they attacked the Israelite camp. 21 But the LORD God
helped Israel defeat Sihon and his
army. Israel took over all of the
Amorite land where Sihon's people
had lived, 22 from the Arnon River in
the south to the Jabbok River in the
north, and from the desert in the
east to the Jordan River in the west.
23 The messengers also told the king of
Ammon that Jephthah had said:
The LORD God of Israel helped his
nation get rid of the Amorites and
take their land. Now do you think
you're going to take over that same
territory? 24 If Chemosh your god[t]
takes over a country and gives it to
you, don't you have a right to it? And
if the LORD takes over a country and
gives it to us, the land is ours!
25 Are you better than Balak the
son of Zippor? He was the king of
Moab, but he didn't quarrel with Israel or start a war with us.
26 For three hundred years, Israelites have been living in Heshbon
and Aroer and the nearby villages,
and in the towns along the Arnon
River gorge. If the land really belonged to you Ammonites, you
wouldn't have waited until now to
try to get it back.
27 I haven't done anything to you,
but it's certainly wrong of you to
start a war. I pray that the LORD will
show whether Israel or Ammon is in
the right.
28 But the king of Ammon paid no attention to Jephthah's message.
29 Then the LORD's Spirit took control
of Jephthah, and Jephthah went
through Gilead and Manasseh, raising
an army. Finally, he arrived at Mizpah in
Gilead, where 30 he promised the LORD,
"If you will let me defeat the Ammonites
31 and come home safely, I will sacrifice
to you whoever comes out to meet me
first."
32 From Mizpah, Jephthah attacked the
Ammonites, and the LORD helped him
defeat them.
33 Jephthah and his army destroyed
the twenty towns between Aroer and
Minnith, and others as far as Abel-
Keramim. After that, the Ammonites
could not invade Israel any more.

Jephthah's Daughter

34 When Jephthah returned to his
home in Mizpah, the first one to meet
him was his daughter. She was playing
a tambourine and dancing to celebrate
his victory, and she was his only child.
35 "Oh!" Jephthah cried. Then he tore
his clothes in sorrow and said to his
daughter, "I made a sacred promise to
the LORD, and I must keep it. Your coming out to meet me has broken my
heart."
36 "Father," she said, "you made a sacred promise to the LORD, and he let you
defeat the Ammonites. Now, you must
do what you promised, even if it means I
must die. 37 But first, please let me spend
two months, wandering in the hill country with my friends. We will cry together, because I can never get married
and have children."
38 "Yes, you may have two months,"
Jephthah said.
She and some other girls left, and for
two months they wandered in the hill
country, crying because she could never
get married and have children. 39 Then
she went back to her father. He did what
he had promised, and she never got
married.
That's why 40 every year, Israelite girls
walk around for four days, weeping for[u]
Jephthah's daughter.

The Ephraim Tribe Fights Jephthah's Army

12 The men of the Ephraim tribe got
together an army and went across
the Jordan River to Zaphon to meet
with Jephthah. They said, "Why did you
go to war with the Ammonites without
asking us to help? Just for that, we're
going to burn down your house with
you inside!"
2 "But I did ask for your help," Jephthah answered. "That was back when
the people of Gilead and I were having
trouble with the Ammonites, and you
wouldn't do a thing to help us. 3 So when
we realized you weren't coming, we

[t] 11.24 *Chemosh your god*: Chemosh was actually the national god of Moab, not Ammon. The land that Ammon was trying to take over had belonged to the Moabites before belonging to the Amorites (see Numbers 21.26). So the Ammonites may have thought that Chemosh controlled it. [u] 11.40 *weeping for*: Or "remembering."

risked our lives and attacked the Ammonites. And the LORD let us defeat
them. There's no reason for you to come
here today to attack me."
4But the men from Ephraim said, "You
people of Gilead are nothing more than
refugees from Ephraim. You even live on
land that belongs to the tribes of
Ephraim and Manasseh."[v]
So Jephthah called together the army
of Gilead, then they attacked and defeated the army from Ephraim. 5The
army of Gilead also posted guards at all
the places where the soldiers from
Ephraim could cross the Jordan River to
return to their own land.
Whenever one of the men from
Ephraim would try to cross the river, the
guards would say, "Are you from
Ephraim?"
"No," the man would answer, "I'm not
from Ephraim."
6The guards would then tell them to
say "Shiboleth," because they knew that
people of Ephraim could say "Sibboleth," but not "Shiboleth."
If the man said "Sibboleth," the
guards would grab him and kill him
right there. Altogether, forty-two thousand men from Ephraim were killed in
the battle and at the Jordan.
7Jephthah was a leader[w] of Israel for
six years, before he died and was buried
in his hometown Mizpah[x] in Gilead.

Ibzan

8Ibzan, the next leader[y] of Israel,
came from Bethlehem. 9He had thirty
daughters and thirty sons, and he let
them all marry outside his clan.
Ibzan was a leader for seven years,
10before he died and was buried in Bethlehem.

Elon

11Elon from the Zebulun tribe was the
next leader[y] of Israel. He was a leader
for ten years, 12before he died and was
buried in Aijalon that belonged to the
Zebulun tribe.

Abdon

13-15Abdon the son of Hillel was the
next leader[y] of Israel. He had forty sons
and thirty grandsons, and each one of
them had his own donkey.[z] Abdon was
a leader for eight years, before he died
and was buried in his hometown of
Pirathon, which is located in the part of
the hill country of Ephraim where Amalekites used to live.

Samson Is Born

13 Once again the Israelites started
disobeying the LORD. So he let the
Philistines take control of Israel for
forty years.
2Manoah from the tribe of Dan lived
in the town of Zorah. His wife was not
able to have children, 3-5but one day an
angel from the LORD appeared to her
and said:

> You have never been able to have
> any children, but very soon you will
> be pregnant and have a son. He will
> belong to God[a] from the day he is
> born, so his hair must never be cut.
> And even before he is born, you
> must not drink any wine or beer or
> eat any food forbidden by God's
> laws.
>
> Your son will begin to set Israel
> free from the Philistines.

6She went to Manoah and said, "A
prophet who looked like an angel of
God came and talked to me. I was so
frightened, that I didn't even ask where
he was from. He didn't tell me his name,
7but he did say that I'm going to have a
baby boy. I'm not supposed to drink any
wine or beer or eat any food forbidden
by God's laws. Our son will belong to
God for as long as he lives."
8Then Manoah prayed, "Our LORD,
please send that prophet again and let
him tell us what to do for the son we are
going to have."
9God answered Manoah's prayer, and
the angel went back to Manoah's wife
while she was resting in the fields.
Manoah wasn't there at the time, 10so
she found him and said, "That same
man is here again! He's the one I saw
the other day."
11Manoah went with his wife and
asked the man, "Are you the one who
spoke to my wife?"
"Yes, I am," he answered.
12Manoah then asked, "When your
promise comes true, what rules must he
obey and what will be his work?"
13"Your wife must be careful to do
everything I told her," the LORD's angel
answered. 14"She must not eat or drink
anything made from grapes. She must
not drink wine or beer or eat anything
forbidden by God's laws. I told her exactly what to do."
15"Please," Manoah said, "stay here

[v] **12.4** *You people of Gilead . . . Ephraim and Manasseh*: One possible meaning for the difficult Hebrew text. [w] **12.7** *leader*: See 2.16 and the note there. [x] **12.7** *his hometown Mizpah*: One possible meaning for the difficult Hebrew text. [y] **12.8** *leader*: See 2.16 and the note there. [y] **12.11** *leader*: See 2.16 and the note there. [y] **12.13-15** *leader*: See 2.16 and the note there. [z] **12.13-15** *each . . . donkey*: A sign that the family was wealthy.
[a] **13.3-5** *belong to God*: The Hebrew text has "be a Nazirite of God." Nazirites were dedicated to God and had to follow special rules to stay that way (see Numbers 6.1, 21).

with us for just a little while, and we'll
fix a young goat for you to eat."
16Manoah didn't realize that he was really talking to one of the LORD's angels.
The angel answered, "I can stay for a
little while, although I won't eat any of
your food. But if you would like to offer
the goat as a sacrifice to the LORD, that
would be fine."
17Manoah said, "Tell us your name, so
we can honor you after our son is born."
18"No," the angel replied. "You don't
need to know my name. And if you did,
you couldn't understand it."
19So Manoah took a young goat over
to a large rock he had chosen for an altar, and he built a fire on the rock. Then
he killed the goat, and offered it with
some grain as a sacrifice to the LORD.
But then an amazing thing happened.
20The fire blazed up toward the sky, and
the LORD's angel went up toward heaven
in the fire. Manoah and his wife bowed
down low when they saw what happened.
21The angel was gone, but Manoah
and his wife realized that he was one of
the LORD's angels. 22Manoah said, "We
have seen an angel.[b] Now we're going
to die."[c]
23"The LORD isn't going to kill us,"
Manoah's wife responded. "The LORD
accepted our sacrifice and grain offering, and he let us see something amazing. Besides, he told us that we're going
to have a son."
24Later, Manoah's wife did give birth
to a son, and she named him Samson.
As the boy grew, the LORD blessed him.
25Then, while Samson was staying at
Dan's Camp[d] between the towns of Zorah and Eshtaol, the Spirit of the LORD
took control of him.

Samson Gets Married

14 One day, Samson went to Timnah,
where he saw a Philistine woman.
2When he got back home, he told his
parents, "I saw a Philistine woman in
Timnah, and I want to marry her. Get
her for me!"[e]
3His parents answered, "There are a
lot of women in our clan and even more
in the rest of Israel. Those Philistines
are pagans. Why would you want to
marry one of their women?"
"She looks good to me," Samson answered. "Get her for me!"
4At that time, the Philistines were in
control of Israel, and the LORD wanted
to stir up trouble for them. That's why
he made Samson desire that woman.
5As Samson and his parents reached
the vineyards near Timnah, a fierce
young lion suddenly roared and attacked Samson. 6But the LORD's Spirit
took control of Samson, and with his
bare hands he tore the lion apart, as
though it had been a young goat. His
parents didn't know what he had done,
and he didn't tell them.
7When they got to Timnah, Samson
talked to the woman, and he was sure
that she was the one for him.
8Later,[f] Samson returned to Timnah
for the wedding. And when he came
near the place where the lion had attacked, he left the road to see what was
left of the lion. He was surprised to see
that bees were living in the lion's skeleton, and that they had made some
honey. 9He scooped up the honey in his
hands and ate some of it as he walked
along. When he got back to his parents,
he gave them some of the honey, and
they ate it too. But he didn't tell them he
had found the honey in the skeleton of a
lion.[g]
10While Samson's father went to
make the final arrangements with the
bride and her family, Samson threw a
big party,[h] as grooms[i] usually did.
11When the Philistines saw what Samson was like, they told thirty of their
young men to stay with him at the party.
12Samson told the thirty young men,
"This party will last for seven days.
Let's make a bet: I'll tell you a riddle,
and if you can tell me the right answer
before the party is over, I'll give each
one of you a shirt and a full change of
clothing. 13But if you can't tell me the
answer, then each of you will have to
give me a shirt and a full change of
clothing."
"It's a bet!" the Philistines said. "Tell
us the riddle."
14Samson said:

Once so strong and mighty—
now so sweet and tasty!

Three days went by, and the Philistine
young men had not come up with the
right answer. 15Finally, on the seventh[j]
day of the party they went to Samson's
bride and said, "You had better trick

[b]13.22 *angel*: The Hebrew text has "god," which can be used of God or of other supernatural beings. [c]13.22 *We have seen an angel. Now we're going to die*: Some people believed that if they saw the LORD or one of the LORD's angels, they would die. [d]13.25 *Dan's Camp*: Or "Mahaneh-Dan." [e]14.2 *Get her for me*: At that time, parents arranged marriages for their children. [f]14.8 *Later*: Or "The following year." [g]14.9 *But he didn't tell them . . . skeleton of a lion*: To eat anything that had touched a skeleton was against God's laws (see Leviticus 11.27-40). [h]14.10 *party*: The Hebrew term means a party that involved a lot of drinking. [i]14.10 *grooms*: Or "warriors." [j]14.15 *Finally, on the seventh*: Hebrew; three ancient translations "on the fourth."

your husband into telling you the answer to his riddle. Have you invited us
here just to rob us? If you don't find out
the answer, we will burn you and your
family to death."
16Samson's bride went to him and
started crying in his arms. "You must really hate me," she sobbed. "If you loved
me at all, you would have told me the
answer to your riddle."
"But I haven't even told my parents
the answer!" Samson replied. "Why
should I tell you?"
17For the entire seven days of the
party, she had been whining and trying
to get the answer from him. But that
seventh day she put so much pressure
on Samson that he finally gave in and
told her the answer. She went straight to
the young men and told them.
18Before sunset that day, the men of
the town went to Samson with this answer:

A lion is the strongest—
    honey is the sweetest!

Samson replied,

This answer you have given me
doubtless came
    from my bride-to-be.

19Then the LORD's Spirit took control
of Samson. He went to Ashkelon,[k]
where he killed thirty men and took
their clothing. Samson then gave it to
the thirty young men at Timnah and
stormed back home to his own family.
20The father of the bride had Samson's wife marry one of the thirty young
men that had been at Samson's party.[l]
15 Later, during the wheat harvest,
Samson went to visit the young
woman he thought was still his wife.[m]
He brought along a young goat as a gift
and said to her father, "I want to go into
my wife's bedroom."
"You can't do that," he replied.
2"When you left the way you did, I
thought you were divorcing[n] her. So I
arranged for her to marry one of the
young men who were at your party. But
my younger daughter is even prettier,
and you can have her as your wife."
3"This time," Samson answered, "I
have a good reason for really hurting
some Philistines."

Samson Takes Revenge

4Samson went out and caught three
hundred foxes and tied them together in
pairs with oil-soaked rags around their
tails. 5Then Samson took the foxes into
the Philistine wheat fields that were
ready to be harvested. He set the rags
on fire and let the foxes go. The wheat
fields went up in flames, and so did the
stacks of wheat that had already been
cut. Even the Philistine vineyards and
olive orchards burned.
6Some of the Philistines started asking around, "Who could have done such
a thing?"
"It was Samson," someone told them.
"He married the daughter of that man in
Timnah, but then the man gave Samson's wife to one of the men at the wedding."
The Philistine leaders went to Timnah
and burned to death Samson's wife and
her father.[o]
7When Samson found out what they
had done, he went to them and said,
"You killed them! And I won't rest until I
get even with you." 8Then Samson
started hacking them to pieces with his
sword.[p]
Samson left Philistia and went to live
in the cave at Etam Rock. 9But it wasn't
long before the Philistines invaded Judah[q] and set up a huge army camp at
Jawbone.[r]
10The people of Judah asked, "Why
have you invaded our land?"
The Philistines answered, "We've
come to get Samson. We're going to do
the same things to him that he did to
our people."
11Three thousand men from Judah
went to the cave at Etam Rock and said
to Samson, "Don't you know that the
Philistines rule us, and they will punish
us for what you did?"
"I was only getting even with them,"
Samson replied. "They did the same
things to me first."
12"We came here to tie you up and
turn you over to them," said the men of
Judah.
"I won't put up a fight," Samson answered, "but you have to promise not to
hurt me yourselves."
13-14"We promise," the men said. "We
will only tie you up and turn you over to
the Philistines. We won't kill you." Then
they tied up his hands and arms with
two brand-new ropes and led him away
from Etam Rock.
When the Philistines saw that Samson
was being brought to their camp at Jaw-

[k]14.19 *Ashkelon*: Another Philistine town. [l]14.20 *one . . . at Samson's party*: One possible meaning for the difficult Hebrew text. [m]15.1 *Samson went to visit . . . his wife*: See the note at 8.31. [n]15.2 *divorcing*: It was often very easy for a husband to divorce his wife. [o]15.6 *and her father*: Most Hebrew manuscripts; many Hebrew manuscripts and two ancient translations "and her family." [p]15.8 *hacking . . . sword*: One possible meaning for the difficult Hebrew text. [q]15.9 *Judah*: Samson belonged to the Dan tribe, but his hideout in the cave at Etam Rock was in Judah, a few miles southwest of Bethlehem. [r]15.9 *Jawbone*: Or "Lehi" (see verse 17).

bone, they started shouting and ran toward him. But the LORD's Spirit took
control of Samson, and Samson broke
the ropes, as though they were pieces of
burnt cloth. 15 Samson glanced around
and spotted the jawbone of a donkey.
The jawbone had not yet dried out, so it
was still hard and heavy. Samson
grabbed it and started hitting
Philistines—he killed a thousand of
them! 16 After the fighting was over, he
made up this poem about what he had
done to the Philistines:

I used a donkey's jawbone
to kill a thousand men;
I beat them with this jawbone
over and over again.[s]

17 Samson tossed the jawbone on the
ground and decided to call the place
Jawbone Hill.[t] It is still called that today.
18 Samson was so thirsty that he
prayed, "Our LORD, you helped me win a
battle against a whole army. Please
don't let me die of thirst now. Those
heathen Philistines will carry off my
dead body."
19 Samson was tired and weary, but
God sent water gushing from a rock.[u]
Samson drank some and felt strong
again.
Samson named the place Caller
Spring,[v] because he had called out to
God for help. The spring is still there at
Jawbone.
20 Samson was a leader[w] of Israel for
twenty years, but the Philistines were
still the rulers of Israel.

Samson Carries Off the Gates of Gaza

16 One day while Samson was in
Gaza, he saw a prostitute and
went to her house to spend the night.
2 The people who lived in Gaza found
out he was there, and they decided
to kill him at sunrise. So they went
to the city gate and waited all night in
the guardrooms on each side of the
gate.[x]
3 But Samson got up in the middle of
the night and went to the town gate. He
pulled the gate doors and doorposts out
of the wall and put them on his shoulders. Then he carried them all the way
to the top of the hill that overlooks Hebron,[y] where he set the doors down, still
closed and locked.

Delilah Tricks Samson

4 Some time later, Samson fell in love
with a woman named Delilah, who lived
in Sorek Valley. 5 The Philistine rulers[z]
went to Delilah and said, "Trick Samson
into telling you what makes him so
strong and what can make him weak.
Then we can tie him up so he can't get
away. If you find out his secret, we will
each give you eleven hundred pieces of
silver."[a]
6 The next time Samson was at
Delilah's house, she asked, "Samson,
what makes you so strong? How can I
tie you up so you can't get away? Come
on, you can tell me."
7 Samson answered, "If someone ties
me up with seven new bowstrings that
have never been dried,[b] it will make me
just as weak as anyone else."
8-9 The Philistine rulers gave seven
new bowstrings to Delilah. They also
told some of their soldiers to go to
Delilah's house and hide in the room
where Samson and Delilah were. If the
bowstrings made Samson weak, they
would be able to capture him.
Delilah tied up Samson with the bowstrings and shouted, "Samson, the
Philistines are attacking!"
Samson snapped the bowstrings, as
though they were pieces of scorched
string. The Philistines had not found out
why Samson was so strong.
10 "You lied and made me look like a
fool," Delilah said. "Now tell me. How
can I really tie you up?"
11 Samson answered, "Use some new
ropes. If I'm tied up with ropes that have
never been used, I'll be just as weak as
anyone else."
12 Delilah got new ropes and again had
some Philistines hide in the room. Then
she tied up Samson's arms and shouted,
"Samson, the Philistines are attacking!"
Samson snapped the ropes as if they
were threads.
13 "You're still lying and making a fool
of me," Delilah said. "Tell me how I can
tie you up!"
"My hair is in seven braids," Samson
replied. "If you weave my braids into the
threads on a loom and nail the loom[c] to

[s] 15.16 *I beat . . . again*: One possible meaning for the difficult Hebrew text. [t] 15.17 *Jawbone Hill*: Or "Ramath-Lehi." [u] 15.19 *God sent . . . a rock*: One possible meaning for the difficult Hebrew text. [v] 15.19 *Caller Spring*: Or "Enhakkore." [w] 15.20 *leader*: See 2.16 and the note there. [x] 16.2 *guardrooms . . . gate*: The gate was often in a part of the town wall that was thicker and taller than the rest of the wall, and that had rooms where guards stayed when they were on duty. [y] 16.3 *Hebron*: About forty miles from Gaza. [z] 16.5 *Philistine rulers*: There were five rulers, each one controlling part of Philistia. [a] 16.5 *silver*: About 140 pounds of silver altogether. [b] 16.7 *new bowstrings . . . dried*: The string for a bow was often made from sinews or internal organs of animals. These strings were made while the animal tissues were still moist, and they became much stronger, once they were dry. [c] 16.13 *loom*: A large wooden frame on which cloth is woven.

a wall, then I will be as weak as anyone
else."
14 While Samson was asleep, Delilah
wove his braids into the threads on a
loom and nailed the loom to a wall.[d]
Then she shouted, "Samson, the
Philistines are attacking!"
Samson woke up and pulled the loom
free from its posts in the ground and
from the nails in the wall. Then he
pulled his hair free from the woven
cloth.
15 "Samson," Delilah said, "you claim
to love me, but you don't mean it! You've
made me look like a fool three times
now, and you still haven't told me why
you are so strong." 16 Delilah started
nagging and pestering him day after
day, until he couldn't stand it any
longer.
17 Finally, Samson told her the truth. "I
have belonged to God[e] ever since I was
born, so my hair has never been cut. If it
were ever cut off, my strength would
leave me, and I would be as weak as
anyone else."
18 Delilah realized that he was telling
the truth. So she sent someone to tell
the Philistine rulers, "Come to my house
one more time. Samson has finally told
me the truth."
The Philistine rulers went to Delilah's
house, and they brought along the silver
they had promised her. 19 Delilah had
lulled Samson to sleep with his head
resting in her lap. She signaled to one
of the Philistine men as she began cutting off Samson's seven braids. And by
the time she was finished, Samson's
strength was gone. Delilah tied him up
20 and shouted, "Samson, the Philistines
are attacking!"
Samson woke up and thought, "I'll
break loose and escape, just as I always
do." He did not realize that the LORD
had stopped helping him.
21 The Philistines grabbed Samson and
poked out his eyes. They took him to the
prison in Gaza and chained him up.
Then they put him to work, turning a
millstone to grind grain. 22 But they
didn't cut his hair any more, so it started
growing back.
23 The Philistine rulers threw a big
party and sacrificed a lot of animals to
their god Dagon. The rulers said:

Samson was our enemy,
but our god Dagon
    helped us capture him!

24-25 Everyone there was having a good
time, and they shouted, "Bring out Samson—he's still good for a few more
laughs!"
The rulers had Samson brought from
the prison, and when the people saw
him, this is how they praised their god:

Samson ruined our crops
    and killed our people.
He was our enemy,
but our god helped us
    capture him.

They made fun of Samson for a while,
then they told him to stand near the
columns that supported the roof. 26 A
young man was leading Samson by the
hand, and Samson said to him, "I need
to lean against something. Take me over
to the columns that hold up the roof."
27 The Philistine rulers were celebrating in a temple packed with people and
with three thousand[f] more on the flat
roof. They had all been watching Samson and making fun of him.[g]
28 Samson prayed, "Please remember
me, LORD God. The Philistines poked
out my eyes, but make me strong one
last time, so I can take revenge for at
least one of my eyes!"[h]
29 Samson was standing between the
two middle columns that held up the
roof. He felt around and found one column with his right hand, and the other
with his left hand. 30 Then he shouted,
"Let me die with the Philistines!" He
pushed against the columns as hard as
he could, and the temple collapsed with
the Philistine rulers and everyone else
still inside. Samson killed more
Philistines when he died than he had
killed during his entire life.
31 His brothers and the rest of his family went to Gaza and took his body back
home. They buried him in his father's
tomb,[i] which was located between Zorah and Eshtaol.
Samson was a leader[j] of Israel for
twenty years.

Micah Makes Idols and Hires a Priest

17 Micah[k] belonged to the Ephraim
tribe and lived in the hill country.
2 One day he told his mother, "Do you remember those eleven hundred pieces
of silver[l] that were stolen from you? I
was there when you put a curse on whoever stole them. Well, I'm the one who
did it."

[d] **16.13,14** *If you weave . . . to a wall*: Some manuscripts of one ancient translation; Hebrew "Weave my braids into the threads on a loom. She nailed the loom to a wall."
[e] **16.17** *belonged to God*: See the note at 13.3-5.
[f] **16.27** *three thousand*: Hebrew; some manuscripts of one ancient translation "seven hundred."
[g] **16.27** *They . . . him*: Samson may have been in a courtyard visible from the roof.
[h] **16.28** *one of my eyes*: Or "my eyes."
[i] **16.31** *buried him in his father's tomb*: Several family members were often buried in one tomb.
[j] **16.31** *leader*: See 2.16 and the note there.
[k] **17.1** *Micah*: The Hebrew also uses the longer form "Micaiah."
[l] **17.2** *eleven hundred . . . silver*: About 28 pounds.

His mother answered, "I pray that the
LORD will bless[m] you, my son."
3-4 Micah returned the silver to his
mother, and she said, "I give this silver
to the LORD, so my son can use it to
make an idol." Turning to her son, she
said, "Micah, now the silver belongs to
you."
But Micah handed it back to his
mother. She took two hundred pieces[n]
of the silver and gave them to a silver
worker, who made them into an idol.[o]
They kept the idol in Micah's house. 5 He
had a shrine for worshiping God there
at his home, and he had made some
idols and a sacred priestly vest. Micah
chose one of his own sons to be the
priest for his shrine.
6 This was before kings ruled Israel, so
all the Israelites did whatever they
thought was right.
7-8 One day a young Levite came to
Micah's house in the hill country of
Ephraim. He had been staying with one
of the clans of Judah in Bethlehem, but
he had left Bethlehem to find a new
place to live[p] where he could be a
priest.[q]
9 "Where are you from?" Micah asked.
"I am a Levite from Bethlehem in Judah," the man answered, "and I'm on my
way to find a new place to live."
10 Micah said, "Why don't you stay
here with me? You can be my priest and
tell me what God wants me to do. Every
year I'll give you ten pieces of silver and
one complete set of clothes, and I'll provide all your food."
The young man went for a walk,
11-12 then he agreed to stay with Micah
and be his priest. He lived in Micah's
house, and Micah treated him like one
of his own sons. 13 Micah said, "I have a
Levite as my own priest. Now I know
that the LORD will be kind to me."
18 These things happened before
kings ruled Israel.

The Tribe of Dan Takes Micah's Priest and Idols

About this time, the tribe of Dan was
looking for a place to live. The other
tribes had land, but the people of Dan
did not really have any to call their own.
2 The tribe chose five warriors to represent their clans and told them, "Go and
find some land where we can live."
The warriors left the area of Zorah
and Eshtaol and went into the hill country of Ephraim. One night they stayed at
Micah's house, 3 because they heard the
young Levite talking, and they knew
from his accent that he was from the
south. They asked him, "What are you
doing here? Who brought you here?"
4 The Levite replied, "Micah hired me
as his priest." Then he told them how
well Micah had treated him.
5 "Please talk to God for us," the men
said. "Ask God if we will be successful
in what we are trying to do."
6 "Don't worry," answered the priest.
"The LORD is pleased with what you are
doing."
7 The five men left and went to the
town of Laish, whose people were from
Sidon,[r] but Sidon was too far away to
protect them. Even though their town
had no walls, the people thought they
were safe from attack. So they had not
asked anyone else[s] for protection, which
meant that the tribe of Dan could easily
take over Laish.[t]
8 The five men went back to Zorah and
Eshtaol, where their relatives asked,
"Did you find any land?"
9-10 "Let's go!" the five men said. "We
saw some very good land with enough
room for all of us, and it has everything
we will ever need. What are you waiting
for? Let's attack and take it. You'll find
that the people think they're safe, but
God is giving the land to us."
11 Six hundred men from the tribe of
Dan strapped on their weapons and left
Zorah and Eshtaol with their families.[u]
12 One night they camped near Kiriath-
Jearim in the territory of Judah, and
that's why the place just west of Kiriath-
Jearim is still known as Dan's Camp.[v]
13 Then they went into the hill country of
Ephraim.
When they came close to Micah's
house, 14 the five men who had been
spies asked the other warriors, "Did you
know that someone in this village has
several idols and a sacred priestly vest?
What do you think we should do about
it?"
15-18 The six hundred warriors left the
road and went to the house on Micah's
property where the young Levite priest
lived. They stood at the gate and greeted
the priest. Meanwhile, the five men who
had been there before went into Micah's

[m] **17.2** *curse . . . bless*: A curse could not be taken back, but it could be made powerless by a blessing. [n] **17.3,4** *two hundred pieces*: About 5 pounds. [o] **17.3,4** *idol*: Probably carved from wood and covered with the silver. [p] **17.7,8** *place to live*: The people of the Levi tribe did not have a large area of land like the other tribes. [q] **17.7,8** *to find . . . priest*: Or "and was on his way to find a new place to live." [r] **18.7** *whose people . . . Sidon*: One possible meaning for the difficult Hebrew text. [s] **18.7** *anyone else*: Hebrew; one ancient translation has "the Arameans," who were a short distance to the north. [t] **18.7** *which . . . Laish*: One possible meaning for the difficult Hebrew text. [u] **18.11** *Eshtaol with their families*: Hebrew "Eshtaol" (see verse 21). [v] **18.12** *Dan's Camp*: See the note at 13.25.

house and took the sacred priestly vest
and the idols.
"Hey!" the priest shouted. "What do
you think you're doing?"
19"Quiet!" the men said. "Keep your
mouth shut and listen. Why don't you
come with us and be our priest, so you
can tell us what God wants us to do? You
could stay here and be a priest for one
man's family, but wouldn't you rather be
the priest for a clan or even a whole
tribe of Israel?"
20The priest really liked that idea. So
he took the vest and the idols and joined
the others 21from the tribe of Dan. Then
they turned and left, after putting their
children, their cattle, and the rest of
their other possessions in front.
22They had traveled for some time, before Micah asked his neighbors to help
him get his things back. He and his men
caught up with the people of Dan 23and
shouted for them to stop.
They turned to face him and asked,
"What's wrong? Why did you bring all
these men?"
24Micah answered, "You know what's
wrong. You stole the gods[w] I made, and
you took my priest. I don't have anything left."
25"We don't want to hear any more
about it," the people of Dan said. "And if
you make us angry, you'll only get yourself and your family killed." 26After saying this, they turned and left.
Micah realized there was no way he
could win a fight with them, and so he
went back home.

The Tribe of Dan Captures Laish

27-28The tribe of Dan took Micah's
priest and the things Micah had made,
and headed for Laish, which was located in a valley controlled by the town
of Beth-Rehob. Laish was defenseless,
because it had no walls and was too far
from Sidon for the Sidonians to help defend it. The leaders of Laish had not
even asked nearby towns to help them
in case of an attack.
The warriors from Dan made a surprise attack on Laish, killing everyone
and burning it down. Then they rebuilt
the town and settled there themselves.
29But they named it Dan, after one of Israel's[x] sons, who was the ancestor of
their tribe.
30-31Even though the place of worship[y]
was in Shiloh, the people of Dan set up
the idol Micah had made. They worshiped the idol, and the Levite was their
priest. His name was Jonathan, and he
was a descendant of Gershom the son of
Moses.[z] His descendants served as
priests for the tribe of Dan, until the
people of Israel were taken away as
prisoners by their enemies.

A Woman Is Murdered

19 Before kings ruled Israel, a
Levite[a] was living deep in the hill
country of the Ephraim tribe. He married[b] a woman from Bethlehem in Judah, 2but she was unfaithful and went
back to live with her family in Bethlehem.
Four months later 3her husband decided to try and talk her into coming
back. So he went to Bethlehem, taking
along a servant and two donkeys. He
talked with his wife, and she invited him
into her family's home. Her father was
glad to see him 4and did not want him to
leave. So the man stayed three days, eating and drinking with his father-in-law.
5When everyone got up on the fourth
day, the Levite started getting ready to
go home. But his father-in-law said,
"Don't leave until you have a bite to eat.
You'll need strength for your journey."
6The two men sat down together and
ate a big meal. "Come on," the man's
father-in-law said. "Stay tonight and
have a good time."
7The Levite tried to leave, but his
father-in-law insisted, and he spent one
more night. 8The fifth day, the man got
up early to leave, but his wife's father
said, "You need to keep up your
strength! Why don't you leave right after lunch?" So the two of them started
eating.
9Finally, the Levite got up from the
meal, so he and his wife and servant
could leave. "Look," his father-in-law
said, "it's already late afternoon, and if
you leave now, you won't get very far
before dark. Stay with us one more
night and enjoy yourself. Then you can
get up early tomorrow morning and
start home."
10But the Levite decided not to spend
the night there again. He had the sad-
dles put on his two donkeys, then he
and his wife and servant traveled as far
as Jebus, which is now called
Jerusalem. 11It was beginning to get
dark, and the man's servant said, "Let's
stop and spend the night in this town
where the Jebusites live."

[w] **18.24** *gods*: Or "god." [x] **18.29** *Israel's*: Israel was another name for Jacob, the father of the twelve ancestors of the tribes of Israel. [y] **18.30,31** *place of worship*: The Hebrew text has "house of God," which at this time was probably the sacred tent. [z] **18.30,31** *Moses*: Some manuscripts of two ancient translations; the Standard Hebrew Text has "Manasseh," but written in a special way that tells the reader "Moses" had been changed to "Manasseh."
[a] **19.1** *a Levite*: Someone from the Levi tribe, which had no tribal lands of its own.
[b] **19.1** *married*: See the note at 8.31.

12“No,” the Levite answered. “They aren’t Israelites, and I refuse to spend the night there. We’ll stop for the night at Gibeah, 13because we can make it to Gibeah or maybe even to Ramah[c] before dark.”

14They walked on and reached Gibeah in the territory of Benjamin just after sunset. 15They left the road and went into Gibeah. But the Levite couldn’t find a house where anyone would let them spend the night, and they sat down in the open area just inside the town gates.

16Soon an old man came in through the gates on his way home from working in the fields. Most of the people who lived in Gibeah belonged to the tribe of Benjamin, but this man was originally from the hill country of Ephraim. 17He noticed that the Levite was just in town to spend the night. “Where are you going?” the old man asked. “Where did you come from?”

18“We’ve come from Bethlehem in Judah,” the Levite answered. “We went there on a visit. Now we’re going to the place where the LORD is worshiped, and later we will return to our home in the hill country of Ephraim. But no one here will let us spend the night[d] in their home. 19We brought food for our donkeys and bread and wine for ourselves, so we don’t need anything except a place to sleep.”

20The old man said, “You are welcome to spend the night in my home and to be my guest, but don’t stay out here!”

21The old man brought them into his house and fed their donkeys. Then he and his guests washed their feet[e] and began eating and drinking. 22They were having a good time, when some worthless men of that town surrounded the house and started banging on the door and shouting, “A man came to your house tonight. Send him out, so we can have sex with him!”

23The old man went outside and said, “My friends, please don’t commit such a horrible crime against a man who is a guest in my house. 24Let me send out my daughter instead. She’s a virgin. And I’ll even send out the man’s wife.[f] You can rape them or do whatever else you want, but please don’t do such a horrible thing to this man.”

25The men refused to listen, so the Levite grabbed his wife and shoved her outside. The men raped her and abused her all night long. Finally, they let her go just before sunrise, 26and it was almost daybreak when she went back to the house where her husband[g] was staying. She collapsed at the door and lay there until sunrise.

27About that time, her husband woke up and got ready to leave. He opened the door and went outside, where he found his wife lying at the door with her hands on the doorstep. 28“Get up!” he said. “It’s time to leave.”

But his wife didn’t move.[h]

He lifted her body onto his donkey and left. 29When he got home, he took a butcher knife and cut her body into twelve pieces. Then he told some messengers, “Take one piece to each tribe of Israel 30and ask everyone if anything like this has ever happened since Israel left Egypt. Tell them to think about it, talk it over, and tell us what should be done.”

Everyone who saw a piece of the body said, “This is horrible! Nothing like this has ever happened since the day Israel left Egypt.”[i]

Israel Gets Ready for War

20 1-3The Israelites called a meeting of the nation. And since they were God’s people, the meeting was held at the place of worship in Mizpah. Men who could serve as soldiers came from everywhere in Israel—from Dan in the north, Beersheba in the south, and Gilead east of the Jordan River. Four hundred thousand of them came to Mizpah, and they each felt the same about what those men from the tribe of Benjamin had done.

News about the meeting at Mizpah reached the tribe of Benjamin.

As soon as the leaders of the tribes of Israel took their places, the Israelites said, “How could such a horrible thing happen?”

4The husband of the murdered woman answered:

My wife[j] and I went into the town
of Gibeah in Benjamin to spend the

[c]**19.13** *Gibeah . . . Ramah*: It was about three miles from Jerusalem to Gibeah, and another three miles to Ramah. [d]**19.18** *spend the night*: People usually considered it a duty to ask travelers to spend the night in their homes, since there were often no other places to stay. [e]**19.21** *washed their feet*: This was a custom, since people wore open sandals and their feet would be dirty after walking on the dirt roads or working in the fields. [f]**19.24** *wife*: See the note at 8.31. [g]**19.26** *husband*: Or “owner”; the Hebrew word may mean that she was his slave and had no legal rights. [h]**19.28** *move*: Hebrew; one ancient translation “move. She was dead.” [i]**19.29,30** *he told some messengers . . . since the day Israel left Egypt*: One ancient translation; Hebrew “he told some messengers, ‘Take one piece to each tribe of Israel.’ Everyone who saw a piece of the body said, ‘This is horrible! Nothing like this has ever happened since Israel left Egypt. Think of it! Let’s talk it over and decide what to do.’ ” [j]**20.4** *wife*: See the note at 8.31.

night. [5]Later that night, the men of
Gibeah surrounded the house. They
wanted to kill me, but instead they
raped and killed my wife. [6]It was a
terrible thing for Israelites to do! So
I cut up her body and sent pieces
everywhere in Israel.
[7]You are the people of Israel, and
you must decide today what to do
about the men of Gibeah.
[8]The whole army was in agreement,
and they said, "None of us will go home.
[9-10]We'll send one tenth of the men from
each tribe to get food for the army. And
we'll ask God[k] who should attack
Gibeah, because those men[l] deserve to
be punished for committing such a horrible crime in Israel."
[11]Everyone agreed that Gibeah had to
be punished.
[12]The tribes of Israel sent messengers
to every town and village in Benjamin.
And wherever the messengers went,
they said, "How could those worthless
men in Gibeah do such a disgusting
thing? [13]We can't allow such a terrible
crime to go unpunished in Israel! Hand
the men over to us, and we will put them
to death."
But the people of Benjamin refused to
listen to the other Israelites. [14]Men from
towns all over Benjamin's territory went
to Gibeah and got ready to fight Israel.
[15]The Benjamin tribe had twenty-six
thousand soldiers, not counting the
seven hundred who were Gibeah's best
warriors. [16]In this army there were
seven hundred left-handed experts who
could sling a rock[m] at a target the size
of a hair and hit it every time.
[17]The other Israelite tribes organized
their army and found they had four
hundred thousand experienced soldiers.
[18]So they went to the place of worship at
Bethel[n] and asked God, "Which tribe
should be the first to attack the people
of Benjamin?"
"Judah," the LORD answered.
[19]The next morning the Israelite army
moved its camp to a place near Gibeah.
[20]Then they left their camp and got into
position to attack the army of Benjamin.

The War Between Israel and Benjamin

[21]Benjamin's soldiers came out of
Gibeah and attacked, and when the day
was over, twenty-two thousand Israelite
soldiers lay dead on the ground.
[22-24]The people of Israel went to the
place of worship and cried until sunset.
Then they asked the LORD, "Should we
attack the people of Benjamin again,
even though they are our relatives?"
"Yes," the LORD replied, "attack them
again!"
The Israelite soldiers encouraged
each other to be brave and to fight hard.
Then the next day they went back to
Gibeah and took up the same positions
as they had before.
[25]That same day, Benjamin's soldiers
came out of Gibeah and attacked, leaving another eighteen thousand Israelite
soldiers dead on the battlefield.
[26-28]The people of Israel went to the
place of worship at Bethel,[n] where the
sacred chest was being kept. They sat
on the ground, crying and not eating for
the rest of the day. Then about sunset,
they offered sacrifices to please the
LORD and to ask his blessing.[o]
Phinehas[p] the priest then prayed, "Our
LORD, the people of Benjamin are our
relatives. Should we stop fighting or attack them again?"
"Attack!" the LORD answered. "Tomorrow I will let you defeat them."
[29]The Israelites surrounded Gibeah,
but stayed where they could not be
seen. [30]Then the next day, they took the
same positions as twice before, [31-41]but
this time they had a different plan. They
said, "When the men of Benjamin attack, we will run off and let them chase
us away from the town and into the
country roads."
The soldiers of Benjamin attacked the
Israelite army and started pushing it
back from the town. They killed about
thirty Israelites in the fields and along
the road between Gibeah and Bethel.
The men of Benjamin were thinking,
"We're mowing them down like we did
before."
The Israelites were running away, but
they headed for Baal-Tamar, where they
regrouped. They had set an ambush,
and they were sure it would work. Ten
thousand of Israel's best soldiers had
been hiding west of Gibeah,[q] and as
soon as the men of Benjamin chased the
Israelites into the countryside, these ten

[k]**20.9,10** *ask God*: The Hebrew text has "use lots to decide"; small pieces of wood or stone called "lots" were used to find out what God wanted his people to do. [l]**20.9,10** *those men*: One Hebrew manuscript and one ancient translation; The Standard Hebrew text "the men of Geba." [m]**20.16** *sling a rock*: By using a sling made from a leather strap. [n]**20.18** *place . . . Bethel*: The Hebrew text has "beth-el," which means "house of God." This could refer to the town of Bethel, to the place of worship at Mizpah, or to the sacred tent at Shiloh (see 18.30, 31).
[n]**20.26-28** *place . . . Bethel*: The Hebrew text has "beth-el," which means "house of God." This could refer to the town of Bethel, to the place of worship at Mizpah, or to the sacred tent at Shiloh (see 18.30, 31). [o]**20.26-28** *sacrifices . . . blessing*: See Leviticus 1–3.
[p]**20.26-28** *Phinehas*: Hebrew "Phinehas the son of Eleazar the son of Aaron."
[q]**20.31-41** *west of Gibeah*: three ancient translations; Hebrew "in a field at Geba."

thousand soldiers made a surprise attack on the town gates. They dashed in
and captured Gibeah, killing everyone
there. Then they set the town on fire, because the smoke would be the signal for
the other Israelite soldiers to turn and
attack the soldiers of Benjamin.
The fighting had been so heavy
around the soldiers of Benjamin, that
they did not know the trouble they were
in. But then they looked back and saw
clouds of smoke rising from the town.
They looked in front and saw the soldiers of Israel turning to attack. This
terrified them, because they realized
that something horrible was happening.
And it was horrible—over twenty-five
thousand[r] soldiers of Benjamin died
that day, and those who were left alive
knew that the LORD had given Israel the
victory.
42 The men of Benjamin headed down
the road toward the desert, trying to escape from the Israelites. But the Israelites stayed right behind them, keeping up their attack. Men even came out
of the nearby towns to help kill the men
of Benjamin, 43 who were having to fight
on all sides. The Israelite soldiers never
let up their attack.[s] They chased and
killed the warriors of Benjamin as far as
a place directly east of Gibeah,[t] 44 until
eighteen thousand of these warriors lay
dead.
45 Some other warriors of Benjamin
turned and ran down the road toward
Rimmon Rock in the desert. The Israelites killed five thousand of them on
the road, then chased the rest until they
had killed[u] two thousand more.
46 Twenty-five thousand soldiers of Benjamin died that day, all of them experienced warriors. 47 Only six hundred of
them finally made it into the desert to
Rimmon Rock, where they stayed for
four months.
48 The Israelites turned back and went
to every town in Benjamin's territory,
killing all the people and animals, and
setting the towns on fire.

Wives for the Men of Benjamin

21 When the Israelites had met at
Mizpah before the war with Benjamin,[v] they had made this sacred
promise: "None of us will ever let our
daughters marry any man from Benjamin."
2 After the war with Benjamin, the Israelites went to the place of worship at
Bethel and sat there until sunset. They
cried loudly and bitterly 3 and prayed,
"Our LORD, you are the God of Israel.
Why did you let this happen? Now one
of our tribes is almost gone."
4 Early the next morning, the Israelites
built an altar and offered sacrifices to
please the LORD and to ask his
blessing.[w] 5 Then they asked each other,
"Did any of the tribes of Israel fail to
come to the place of worship? We made
a sacred promise that anyone who
didn't come to the meeting at Mizpah
would be put to death."
6 The Israelites were sad about what
had happened to the Benjamin tribe,
and they said, "One of our tribes was almost wiped out. 7 Only a few men of
Benjamin weren't killed in the war. We
need to get wives for them, so the tribe
won't completely disappear. But how
can we do that, after promising in the
LORD's name that we wouldn't let them
marry any of our daughters?"
8-9 Again the Israelites asked, "Did any
of the tribes stay away from the meeting
at Mizpah?"
After asking around, they discovered
that no one had come from Jabesh in
Gilead. 10-11 So they sent twelve thousand warriors with these orders: "Attack
Jabesh in Gilead and kill everyone, except the women who have never been
married."
12 The warriors attacked Jabesh in
Gilead, and returned to their camp in
Canaan[x] with four hundred young
women.
13 The Israelites met and sent messengers to the men of Benjamin at Rimmon
Rock, telling them that the Israelites
were willing to make peace with them.
14 So the men of Benjamin came back
from Rimmon Rock, and the Israelites
let them marry the young women from
Jabesh. But there weren't enough
women.
15 The Israelites were very sad, because the LORD had almost wiped out
one of their tribes. 16 Then their national
leaders said:

> All the women of the Benjamin
> tribe were killed. How can we get
> wives for the men of Benjamin who
> are left? 17 If they don't have chil-
> dren, one of the Israelite tribes will
> die out. 18 But we can't let the men of
> Benjamin marry any of our daugh-
> ters. We made a sacred promise not
> to do that, and if we break our
> promise, we will be under our own
> curse.

[r] **20.31-41** *over twenty-five thousand*: Hebrew "twenty-five thousand one hundred."
[s] **20.42,43** *Men even came out . . . their attack*: One possible meaning for the difficult Hebrew text. [t] **20.43** *Gibeah*: Or "Geba." [u] **20.45** *until . . . killed*: Or "as far as Gidom, killing."
[v] **21.1** *the Israelites . . . Benjamin*: See 20.1-3. [w] **21.4** *sacrifices . . . blessing*: See the note at 20.26-28. [x] **21.12** *in Canaan*: Jabesh was in Gilead, across the Jordan River from the land of Canaan.

19 Then someone suggested, "What
about the LORD's Festival that takes
place each year in Shiloh? It's held
north of Bethel, south of Lebonah, and
just east of the road that goes from
Bethel to Shechem."
20 The leaders told the men of Benjamin who still did not have wives:

Go to Shiloh and hide in the vineyards near the festival. 21 Wait there
for the young women of Shiloh to
come out and perform their dances.
Then rush out and grab one of the
young women, then take her home
as your wife. 22 If the fathers or
brothers of these women complain
about this, we'll say, "Be kind
enough to let those men keep your
daughter. After all, we couldn't get
enough wives for all the men of Benjamin in the battle at Jabesh. And
because you didn't give them permission to marry your daughters,
you won't be under the curse we
earlier agreed on.[y]

23 The men of Benjamin went to Shiloh
and hid in the vineyards. The young
women soon started dancing, and each
man grabbed one of them and carried
her off. Then the men of Benjamin went
back to their own land and rebuilt
their towns and started living in them
again.
24 Afterwards, the rest of the Israelites
returned to their homes and families.

Israel Was Not Ruled by a King

25 In those days Israel wasn't ruled by
a king, and everyone did what they
thought was right.

[y] **21.22** *on*: One possible meaning for the difficult Hebrew text of verse 22.

RUTH

ABOUT THIS BOOK

The book of Ruth gives a glimpse into the life of an Israelite family during the period of the judges. This family later became very important to Israel, because one of Ruth's great-grandchildren was King David.

In addition to Ruth, the other main character in the book is Naomi, who lived in Bethlehem with her husband and two sons. But the crops failed, and the family moved to the country of Moab. Naomi's husband died, and her sons married Moabite women. Ruth was one of those women.

After Naomi's two sons died in Moab, she decided to return to Bethlehem. Naomi told her two daughters-in-law to stay in Moab and find new husbands. But Ruth refused to stay and instead went to Bethlehem with her. The rest of the book tells how Ruth married a rich relative named Boaz.

According to the law, Moabites were not allowed to become Israelites. But this book tells how Ruth became completely loyal and faithful to the Lord and was allowed to join the people of Israel. She told Naomi:

I will go where you go,
I will live where you live;
your people will be my people,
your God will be my God.
I will die where you die
and be buried beside you.
May the LORD punish me
if we are ever separated,
even by death!

(1.16b, 17)

A QUICK LOOK AT THIS BOOK

Ruth Is Loyal to Naomi (1)
Ruth Meets Boaz (2)
Naomi Makes Plans for Ruth (3)
Ruth and Boaz Get Married (4)

Ruth Is Loyal to Naomi

1 1-2Before Israel was ruled by kings,
Elimelech from the tribe of Ephrath
lived in the town of Bethlehem. His wife
was named Naomi, and their two sons
were Mahlon and Chilion. But when
their crops failed, they moved to the
country of Moab.[a] And while they were
there, 3Elimelech died, leaving Naomi
with only her two sons.
4Later, Naomi's sons married
Moabite women. One was named Orpah
and the other Ruth. About ten years
later, 5Mahlon and Chilion also died.
Now Naomi had no husband or sons.
6-7When Naomi heard that the LORD
had given his people a good harvest, she

[a] 1.1,2 *Moab*: The people of Moab worshiped idols and were usually enemies of the people of Israel.

and her two daughters-in-law got ready
to leave Moab and go to Judah. As they
were on their way there, 8Naomi said to
them, "Don't you want to go back home
to your own mothers? You were kind to
my husband and sons, and you have always been kind to me. I pray that the
LORD will be just as kind to you. 9May
he give each of you another husband
and a home of your own."
Naomi kissed them. They cried 10and
said, "We want to go with you and live
among your people."
11But she replied, "My daughters, why
don't you return home? What good will
it do you to go with me? Do you think I
could have more sons for you to
marry?[b] 12You must go back home, because I am too old to marry again. Even
if I got married tonight and later had
more sons, 13would you wait for them to
become old enough to marry? No, my
daughters! Life is harder for me than it
is for you, because the LORD has turned
against me."[c]
14They cried again. Orpah kissed her
mother-in-law good-by, but Ruth held on
to her. 15Naomi then said to Ruth,
"Look, your sister-in-law is going back
to her people and to her gods! Why
don't you go with her?"
16Ruth answered,

"Please don't tell me
to leave you
    and return home!
I will go where you go,
    I will live where you live;
your people will be my people,
    your God will be my God.
17 I will die where you die
    and be buried beside you.
May the LORD punish me
if we are ever separated,
    even by death!"[d]

18When Naomi saw that Ruth had
made up her mind to go with her, she
stopped urging her to go back.
19They reached Bethlehem, and the
whole town was excited to see them.
The women who lived there asked, "Can
this really be Naomi?"
20Then she told them, "Don't call me
Naomi any longer! Call me Mara,[e] because God has made my life bitter. 21I
had everything when I left, but the LORD
has brought me back with nothing. How
can you still call me Naomi, when God
has turned against me and made my life
so hard?"
22The barley harvest was just beginning when Naomi and Ruth, her
Moabite daughter-in-law, arrived in
Bethlehem.

Ruth Meets Boaz

2 1-3One day, Ruth said to Naomi, "Let
me see if I can find someone who
will let me pick up the grain left in the
fields by the harvest workers."[f]
Naomi answered, "Go ahead, my
daughter." So right away, Ruth went out
to pick up grain in a field owned by
Boaz. He was a relative of Naomi's husband Elimelech, as well as a rich and
important man.
4When Boaz left Bethlehem and went
out to his field, he said to the harvest
workers, "The LORD bless you!"
They replied, "And may the LORD
bless you!"
5Then Boaz asked the man in charge
of the harvest workers, "Who is that
young woman?"
6The man answered, "She is the one
who came back from Moab with Naomi.
7She asked if she could pick up grain
left by the harvest workers, and she has
been working all morning without a moment's rest."[g]
8Boaz went over to Ruth and said, "I
think it would be best for you not to
pick up grain in anyone else's field. Stay
here with the women 9and follow along
behind them, as they gather up what the
men have cut. I have warned the men
not to bother you, and whenever you are
thirsty, you can drink from the water
jars they have filled."
10Ruth bowed down to the ground and
said, "You know I come from another
country. Why are you so good to me?"
11Boaz answered, "I've heard how
you've helped your mother-in-law ever
since your husband died. You even left
your own father and mother to come
and live in a foreign land among people
you don't know. 12I pray that the LORD
God of Israel will reward you for what
you have done. And now that you have
come to him for protection, I pray that
he will bless you."
13Ruth replied, "Sir, it's good of you to
speak kindly to me and make me feel so
welcome. I'm not even one of your servants."

[b] **1.11** *for you to marry*: When a married man died and left no children, it was the custom for one of his brothers to marry his widow. Any children they had would then be thought of as those of the dead man, so that his family name would live on. [c] **1.13** *Life . . . me*: Or "I'm sorry that the LORD has turned against me and made life so hard for you." [d] **1.17** *even by death*: Or "by anything but death." [e] **1.20** *Mara*: In Hebrew "Naomi" means "pleasant," and "Mara" means "bitter." [f] **2.1-3** *grain left . . . workers*: It was the custom at harvest time to leave some grain in the field for the poor to pick up (see Leviticus 19.10; 23.22). [g] **2.7** *she has . . . rest*: One possible meaning for the difficult Hebrew text.

14At mealtime Boaz said to Ruth, "Come, eat with us. Have some bread and dip it in the sauce." Right away she sat down with the workers, and Boaz handed her some roasted grain. Ruth ate all she wanted and had some left over.

15When Ruth got up to start picking up grain, Boaz told his men, "Don't stop her, even if she picks up grain from where it is stacked. 16Be sure to pull out some stalks of grain from the bundles and leave them on the ground for her. And don't speak harshly to her!"

17Ruth worked in the field until evening. Then after she had pounded the grain off the stalks, she had a large basket full of grain. 18She took the grain to town and showed Naomi how much she had picked up. Ruth also gave her the food left over from her lunch.

19Naomi said, "Where did you work today? Whose field was it? God bless the man who treated you so well!" Then Ruth told her that she had worked in the field of a man named Boaz.

20"The LORD bless Boaz!" Naomi replied. "He[h] has shown that he is still loyal to the living and to the dead. Boaz is a close relative, one of those who is supposed to look after us."

21Ruth told her, "Boaz even said I could stay in the field with his workers until they had finished gathering all his grain."

22Naomi replied, "My daughter, it's good that you can pick up grain alongside the women who work in his field. Who knows what might happen to you in someone else's field!" 23And so, Ruth stayed close to the women, while picking up grain in his field.

Ruth worked in the fields until the barley and wheat were harvested. And all this time she lived with Naomi.

Naomi Makes Plans for Ruth

3 One day, Naomi said to Ruth:

It's time I found you a husband, who will give you a home and take care of you.

2You have been picking up grain alongside the women who work for Boaz, and you know he is a relative of ours. Tonight he will be threshing the grain. 3Now take a bath and put on some perfume, then dress in your best clothes. Go where he is working, but don't let him see you until he has finished eating and drinking. 4Watch where he goes to spend the night, then when he is asleep, lift the cover and lie down at his feet.[i] He will tell you what to do.

5Ruth answered, "I'll do whatever you say." 6She went out to the place where Boaz was working and did what Naomi had told her.

7After Boaz finished eating and drinking and was feeling happy, he went over and fell asleep near the pile of grain. Ruth slipped over quietly. She lifted the cover and lay down near his feet.

8In the middle of the night, Boaz suddenly woke up and was shocked to see a woman lying at his feet. 9"Who are you?" he asked.

"Sir, I am Ruth," she answered, "and you are the relative who is supposed to take care of me. So spread the edge of your cover over me."[j]

10Boaz replied:

The LORD bless you! This shows how truly loyal you are to your family. You could have looked for a younger man, either rich or poor, but you didn't. 11Don't worry, I'll do what you have asked. You are respected by everyone in town.

12It's true that I am one of the relatives who is supposed to take care of you, but there is someone who is an even closer relative. 13Stay here until morning, then I will find out if he is willing to look after you. If he isn't, I promise by the living God to do it myself. Now go back to sleep until morning.

14Ruth lay down again, but she got up before daylight, because Boaz did not want anyone to know she had been there. 15Then he told her to spread out her cape. And he filled it with a lot of grain and placed it on her shoulder.

When Ruth got back to town, 16Naomi asked her[k] what had happened, and Ruth told her everything. 17She also said, "Boaz gave me this grain, because he didn't want me to come back without something for you."

18Naomi replied, "Just be patient and don't worry about what will happen. He won't rest until everything is settled today!"

Ruth and Boaz Get Married

4 In the meanwhile, Boaz had gone to the meeting place at the town gate and was sitting there when the other close relative came by. So Boaz invited him to come over and sit down, and he did. 2Then Boaz got ten of the town leaders and also asked them to sit down. After they had sat down, 3he said to the man:

[h]**2.20** *He*: Or "The LORD." [i]**3.4** *lift the cover . . . feet*: To ask for protection and possibly for marriage. [j]**3.9** *So . . . me*: To show that he would protect and take care of her.
[k]**3.15,16** *When . . . her*: Some Hebrew manuscripts and two ancient translations; most Hebrew manuscripts "Boaz went back to town. [16]Naomi asked Ruth."

Naomi has come back from Moab
and is selling the land that belonged
to her husband Elimelech. 4 I am
telling you about this, since you are
his closest relative and have the
right to buy the property. If you
want it, you can buy it now. These
ten men and the others standing
here can be witnesses. But if you
don't want the property, let me
know, because I am next in line.
The man replied, "I will buy it!"
5 "If you do buy it from Naomi," Boaz
told him, "you must also marry Ruth.
Then if you have a son by her, the property will stay in the family of Ruth's first
husband."
6 The man answered, "If that's the
case, I don't want to buy it! That would
make problems with the property I already own.[l] You may buy it yourself, because I cannot."
7 To make a sale legal in those days,
one person would take off a sandal and
give it to the other. 8 So after the man
had agreed to let Boaz buy the property,
he took off one of his sandals and
handed it to Boaz.
9 Boaz told the town leaders and
everyone else:
All of you are witnesses that today
I have bought from Naomi the property that belonged to Elimelech and
his two sons, Chilion and Mahlon.
10 You are also witnesses that I have
agreed to marry Mahlon's widow
Ruth, the Moabite woman. This will
keep the property in his family's
name, and he will be remembered in
this town.
11 The town leaders and the others
standing there said:
We are witnesses to this. And we
pray that the LORD will give your
wife many children, just as he did
Leah and Rachel, the wives of
Jacob. May you be a rich man in
the tribe of Ephrath and an important man in Bethlehem. 12 May the
children you have by this young
woman make your family as famous
as the family of Perez,[m] the son of
Tamar and Judah.
13 Boaz married Ruth, and the LORD
blessed her with a son. 14 After his birth,
the women said to Naomi:
Praise the LORD! Today he has
given you a grandson to take care of
you. We pray that the boy will grow
up to be famous everywhere in Israel. 15 He will[n] make you happy and
take care of you in your old age, because he is the son of your daughter-
in-law. And she loves you more than
seven sons of your own would love
you.
16 Naomi loved the boy and took good
care of him. 17 The neighborhood women
named him Obed, but they called him
"Naomi's Boy."
When Obed grew up he had a son
named Jesse, who later became the
father of King David. 18-22 Here is a list of
the ancestors of David: Jesse, Obed,
Boaz, Salmon, Nahshon, Amminadab,
Ram, Hezron, and Perez.

[l] **4.6** *property . . . own*: This property would then have to be shared with Ruth and her children as well as with his own family. [m] **4.12** *Perez*: One of the sons of Judah; he was an ancestor of Boaz and of many others who lived in Bethlehem. [n] **4.14,15** *We pray that . . . famous . . .* 15 *He will*: Or "We pray that the LORD will be praised everywhere in Israel. 15 Your grandson will."

1 SAMUEL

ABOUT THIS BOOK

First Samuel is actually the first half of a single book that was divided into two parts, 1 and 2 Samuel, because together they were too long to fit on one scroll. The books are named for one of the main characters, who was a prophet and also the last judge to lead Israel.

The first part of 1 Samuel (1–7) tells about the life of Samuel and how he helped Israel's army fight against enemies that were making raids in Israel. But when he grew old, the people decided to ask the Lord for a king who could lead the army.

In the second part of this book (8.1–15.35) the Lord told Samuel to appoint Saul son of Kish to be the first king of Israel. Saul and his oldest son Jonathan won several battles against the Ammonites and Philistines, but Saul did not completely obey the Lord.

In the third part of the book (15.35—31.13), the Lord told Samuel to secretly appoint a young man named David to be the next king. The book tells how David soon became a national hero after he killed the giant Philistine warrior, Goliath from Gath. But as David continued to become more popular, Saul became suspicious of David. Saul tried to have him killed, even though David was married to Saul's daughter Michal and was best friends with Saul's son Jonathan. The rest of 1 Samuel tells how David escaped and became the leader of his own small army in the desert. Saul continued to hunt for David, and so David finally had to lead his followers to Philistia to be safe from Saul.

The book concludes with the death of Saul and his sons in a battle with the Philistine army. The Lord was keeping his promise to make David the king of Israel:

> *I've rejected Saul, and I refuse to let him be king any longer. Stop feeling sad about him. . . . go visit a man named Jesse, who lives in Bethlehem. I've chosen one of his sons to be my king.* (16.1)

A QUICK LOOK AT THIS BOOK

The Birth and Early Childhood of Samuel (1.1—2.10)
Samuel at the Sacred Tent (2.11—4.1)
The Sacred Chest Is Captured and Returned (4.1—7.2)
Samuel as the Leader of Israel (7.3-17)
Saul, the First King of Israel (8.1—11.15)
Samuel's Farewell Speech (12.1-25)
Saul Disobeys the Lord, and the Lord Rejects Him as King (13.1—15.35)
The Lord Chooses David To Be the Next King (15.35—16.13)
David Plays a Harp For Saul (16.14-23)
David Kills Goliath (17.1—18.5)
Saul Tries To Kill David (18.6-30)
Jonathan, Michal, Samuel, and Ahimelech Help David (19.1—21.9)
David Runs from Saul (21.10—22.5)
Saul Kills the Priests of the Lord (22.6-23)
David Refuses To Kill Saul (23.1—26.25)
David in Philistia (26.25—27.12)
Saul Talks with Samuel's Ghost (28.1-25)
David Rescues the Families of His Troops (29.1—30.31)
Saul and His Sons Die in Battle against the Philistines (31.1-13)

Hannah Asks the LORD for a Child

1 Elkanah lived in Ramah,[a] a town in
the hill country of Ephraim. His
great-great-grandfather was Zuph, so
Elkanah was a member of the Zuph
clan of the Ephraim tribe. Elkanah's father was Jeroham, his grandfather was
Elihu, and his great-grandfather was
Tohu.
2 Elkanah had two wives,[b] Hannah
and Peninnah. Although Peninnah had
children, Hannah did not have any.
3 Once a year Elkanah traveled from
his hometown to Shiloh, where he worshiped the LORD All-Powerful and offered sacrifices. Eli was the LORD's
priest there, and his two sons Hophni
and Phinehas served with him as
priests.[c]
4 Whenever Elkanah offered a sacrifice, he gave some of the meat[d] to Peninnah and some to each of her sons and
daughters. 5 But he gave Hannah even
more, because he loved Hannah very
much, even though the LORD had kept
her from having children of her own.
6 Peninnah liked to make Hannah feel
miserable about not having any children, 7 especially when the family went
to the house of the LORD[e] each year.
One day, Elkanah was there offering a
sacrifice, when Hannah began crying
and refused to eat. 8 So Elkanah asked,
"Hannah, why are you crying? Why
won't you eat? Why do you feel so bad?
Don't I mean more to you than ten
sons?"
9 When the sacrifice had been offered,
and they had eaten the meal, Hannah
got up and went to pray. Eli was sitting
in his chair near the door to the place of
worship. 10 Hannah was brokenhearted
and was crying as she prayed, 11 "LORD
All-Powerful, I am your servant, but I
am so miserable! Please let me have a
son. I will give him to you for as long as
he lives, and his hair will never be cut."[f]
12-13 Hannah prayed silently to the
LORD for a long time. But her lips were
moving, and Eli thought she was drunk.
14 "How long are you going to stay
drunk?" he asked. "Sober up!"
15-16 "Sir, please don't think I'm no
good!" Hannah answered. "I'm not
drunk, and I haven't been drinking. But
I do feel miserable and terribly upset.
I've been praying all this time, telling
the LORD about my problems."
17 Eli replied, "You may go home now
and stop worrying. I'm sure the God of
Israel will answer your prayer."
18 "Sir, thank you for being so kind to
me," Hannah said. Then she left, and after eating something, she felt much better.

Samuel Is Born

19 Elkanah and his family got up early
the next morning and worshiped the
LORD. Then they went back home to
Ramah. Later the LORD blessed Elkanah
and Hannah 20 with a son. She named
him Samuel because she had asked the
LORD for him.[g]

Hannah Gives Samuel to the LORD

21 The next time Elkanah and his family went to offer their yearly sacrifice,
he took along a gift that he had
promised to give to the LORD. 22 But Hannah stayed home, because she had told
Elkanah, "Samuel and I won't go until
he's old enough for me to stop nursing
him. Then I'll give him to the LORD, and
he can stay there at Shiloh for the rest
of his life."
23 "You know what's best," Elkanah
said. "Stay here until it's time to stop
nursing him. I'm sure the LORD will help
you do what you have promised."[h] Hannah did not go to Shiloh until she
stopped nursing Samuel.
24-25 When it was the time of year to go
to Shiloh again, Hannah and Elkanah[i]
took Samuel to the LORD's house. They
brought along a three-year-old bull,[j] a
twenty-pound sack of flour, and a clay
jar full of wine. Hannah and Elkanah offered the bull as a sacrifice, then
brought the little boy to Eli.
26 "Sir," Hannah said, "a few years ago
I stood here beside you and asked the
LORD 27 to give me a child. Here he is!
The LORD gave me just what I asked for.

[a] **1.1** *Ramah*: The Hebrew has "Ramathaim," a longer form of "Ramah" (see verse 19).
[b] **1.2** *two wives*: Having more than one wife was allowed in those times. [c] **1.3** *Eli . . . priests*: One ancient translation; Hebrew "Hophni and Phinehas, the two sons of Eli, served the LORD as priests." [d] **1.4** *meat*: For some sacrifices, like this one, only part of the meat was burned. Some was given to the priest, and the rest was eaten by the family and guests of the worshiper (see Leviticus 3.1-17; 7.11-18). [e] **1.7** *house of the LORD*: Another name for the place of worship at Shiloh, which still may have been the sacred tent at this time. [f] **1.11** *his hair . . . cut*: Never cutting the child's hair would be a sign that he would belong to the LORD (see Numbers 6.1, 21, especially verse 5). [g] **1.20** *him*: In Hebrew "Samuel" sounds something like "Someone from God" or "The name of God" or "His name is God." [h] **1.23** *the LORD . . . promised*: The Dead Sea Scrolls and two ancient translations; the Standard Hebrew Text "the LORD will do what he said." [i] **1.24,25** *When it was the time of year to go to Shiloh again, Hannah and Elkanah*: The Dead Sea Scrolls and one ancient translation; the Standard Hebrew Text "she." [j] **1.24,25** *a three-year-old bull*: The Dead Sea Scrolls and two ancient translations; the Standard Hebrew Text "three bulls."

[28]Now I am giving him to the LORD, and he will be the LORD's servant for as long as he lives."

Hannah Prays

2 Elkanah[k] worshiped the LORD there at Shiloh, and [1]Hannah prayed:

You make me strong
and happy, LORD.
You rescued me.
Now I can be glad
and laugh at my enemies.
[2] No other god[l] is like you.
We're safer with you
than on a high mountain.[m]
[3] I can tell those proud people,
"Stop your boasting!
Nothing is hidden from the LORD,
and he judges what we do."

[4] Our LORD, you break
the bows of warriors,
but you give strength
to everyone who stumbles.
[5] People who once
had plenty to eat
must now hire themselves out
for only a piece of bread.
But you give the hungry more
than enough to eat.
A woman did not have a child,
and you gave her seven,
but a woman who had many
was left with none.
[6] You take away life,
and you give life.
You send people down
to the world of the dead
and bring them back again.

[7] Our LORD, you are the one
who makes us rich or poor.
You put some in high positions
and bring disgrace on others.
[8] You lift the poor and homeless
out of the garbage dump
and give them places of honor
in royal palaces.

You set the world on foundations,
and they belong to you.
[9] You protect your loyal people,
but everyone who is evil
will die in darkness.

We cannot win a victory
by our own strength.
[10] Our LORD, those who attack you
will be broken in pieces
when you fight back
with thunder from heaven.
You will judge the whole earth
and give power and strength
to your chosen king.

Samuel Stays with Eli

[11]Elkanah and Hannah went back home to Ramah, but the boy Samuel stayed to help Eli serve the LORD.

Eli's Sons

[12-13]Eli's sons were priests, but they
were dishonest and refused to obey the
LORD. So, while people were boiling the
meat from their sacrifices, these priests
would send over a servant with a large,
three-pronged fork. [14]The servant would
stick the fork into the cooking pot, and
whatever meat came out on the fork
was taken back to the priests. That is
how these two priests treated every Israelite who came to offer sacrifices in
Shiloh. [15]Sometimes, when people were
offering sacrifices, the servant would
come over, even before the fat had been
cut off and sacrificed to the LORD.[n]

Then the servant would tell them, "The priest doesn't want his meat boiled! Give him some raw meat that he can roast!"

[16]Usually the people answered, "Take what you want. But first, let us sacrifice the fat to the LORD."

"No," the servant would reply. "If you don't give it to me now, I'll take it by force."

[17]Eli's sons did not show any respect for the sacrifices that the people offered. This was a terrible sin, and it made the LORD very angry.

Hannah Visits Samuel

[18]The boy Samuel served the LORD
and wore a special linen garment[o] [19]and
the clothes[p] his mother made for him.
She would bring new clothes every year, when she and her husband came to offer sacrifices at Shiloh.

[20]Eli would always bless Elkanah and his wife and say, "Samuel was born in answer to your prayers. Now you have given him to the LORD. I pray that the LORD will bless you with more children to take his place." After Eli had blessed them, Elkanah and Hannah would return home.

[k]**1.28** *Elkanah*: Or "They" or "Samuel." [l]**2.2** *god*: The Hebrew text has "holy one," a term for supernatural beings or gods. [m]**2.2** *mountain*: One possible meaning for the difficult Hebrew text of verse 2. [n]**2.15** *sacrificed to the LORD*: The fat belonged to the LORD and was supposed to be burned as a sacrifice before the rest of the animal was cooked and eaten (see Leviticus 3.3, 4, 9, 10, 14, 15). [o]**2.18** *a special linen garment*: Either a loin cloth or a jacket or a vest worn only by priests. [p]**2.19** *clothes*: The Hebrew word means a sleeveless coat or robe that was worn by priests. Samuel was a small child, but his mother made him clothes just like those worn by priests.

21The LORD was kind to Hannah, and she had three more sons and two daughters. But Samuel grew up at the LORD's house in Shiloh.

Eli Warns His Sons

22Eli was now very old, and he heard what his sons were doing to the people of Israel.[q] 23-24"Why are you doing these awful things?" he asked them. "I've been hearing nothing but complaints about you from all of the LORD's people. 25If you harm another person, God can help make things right between the two of you. But if you commit a crime against the LORD, no one can help you!"

But the LORD had already decided to kill them. So he kept them from listening to their father.

A Prophet Speaks to Eli

26Each day the LORD and his people liked Samuel more and more.

27One day a prophet came to Eli and gave him this message from the LORD:

When your ancestors were slaves of the king of Egypt, I came and showed them who I am. 28-29Out of all the tribes of Israel, I chose your family to be my priests. I wanted them to offer sacrifices and burn incense to me and to find out from me what I want my people to do. I commanded everyone to bring their sacrifices here where I live, and I allowed you and your family to keep those that were not offered to me on the altar.

But you honor your sons instead of me! You don't respect[r] the sacrifices and offerings that are brought to me, and you've all gotten fat from eating the best parts.

30I am the LORD, the God of Israel. I promised to always let your family serve me as priests, but now I tell you that I cannot do this any longer! I honor anyone who honors me, but I put a curse on anyone who hates me. 31The time will come when I will kill you and everyone else in your family. Not one of you will live to an old age.

32Your family[s] will have a lot of trouble. I will be kind to Israel,[t] but everyone in your family will die young. 33If I let anyone from your family be a priest, his[u] life will be full of sadness and sorrow. But most of the men in your family will die a violent death![v] 34To prove to you that I will do these things, your two sons, Hophni and Phinehas, will die on the same day.

35I have chosen someone else to be my priest, someone who will be faithful and obey me. I will always let his family serve as priests and help my chosen king. 36But if anyone is left from your family, he will come to my priest and beg for money or a little bread. He may even say to my priest, "Please let me be a priest, so I will at least have something to eat."

The LORD Speaks to Samuel

3 1-2Samuel served the LORD by helping Eli the priest, who was by that time almost blind. In those days, the LORD hardly ever spoke directly to people, and he did not appear to them in dreams very often. But one night, Eli was asleep in his room, 3and Samuel was sleeping on a mat near the sacred chest in the LORD's house. They had not been asleep very long[w] 4when the LORD called out Samuel's name.

"Here I am!" Samuel answered. 5Then he ran to Eli and said, "Here I am. What do you want?"

"I didn't call you," Eli answered. "Go back to bed."

Samuel went back.

6Again the LORD called out Samuel's name. Samuel got up and went to Eli. "Here I am," he said. "What do you want?"

Eli told him, "Son, I didn't call you. Go back to sleep."

7The LORD had not spoken to Samuel before, and Samuel did not recognize the voice. 8When the LORD called out his name for the third time, Samuel went to Eli again and said, "Here I am. What do you want?"

Eli finally realized that it was the LORD who was speaking to Samuel. 9So he said, "Go back and lie down! If someone speaks to you again, answer, 'I'm listening, LORD. What do you want me to do?' "

Once again Samuel went back and lay down.

10The LORD then stood beside Samuel

[q]**2.22** *Israel*: The Dead Sea Scrolls and one ancient translation; the Standard Hebrew Text adds "He heard that his sons were even sleeping with the women who worked at the entrance to the sacred tent." [r]**2.28,29** *don't respect*: The Standard Hebrew Text; the Dead Sea Scrolls and one ancient translation "are greedy for." [s]**2.32** *Your family*: Or "My house of worship." [t]**2.31,32** *Not one . . . to Israel*: The Standard Hebrew Text; the Dead Sea Scrolls and one ancient translation do not have these words. [u]**2.33** *his*: The Dead Sea Scrolls and one ancient translation; the Standard Hebrew Text "your." [v]**2.33** *die a violent death*: The Dead Sea Scrolls and one ancient translation; the Standard Hebrew Text "die." [w]**3.3** *They . . . long*: The Hebrew text has "The lamp was still burning." An olive oil lamp would go out after a few hours if the wick was not adjusted.

and called out as he had done before,
"Samuel! Samuel!"
"I'm listening," Samuel answered.
"What do you want me to do?"
11The LORD said:
Samuel, I am going to do something in Israel that will shock everyone who hears about it! 12I will punish Eli and his family, just as I
promised. 13He knew that his sons
refused to respect me,[x] and he let
them get away with it, even though I
said I would punish his family forever. 14I warned Eli that sacrifices or
offerings could never make things
right! His family has done too many
disgusting things.
15The next morning, Samuel got up
and opened the doors to the LORD's
house. He was afraid to tell Eli what
the LORD had said. 16But Eli told him,
"Samuel, my boy, come here!"
"Here I am," Samuel answered.
17Eli said, "What did God say to you?
Tell me everything. I pray that God will
punish you terribly if you don't tell me
every word he said!"
18Samuel told Eli everything. Then Eli
said, "He is the LORD, and he will do
what's right."

The LORD Helps Samuel

19As Samuel grew up, the LORD helped
him and made everything Samuel said
come true. 20From the town of Dan in
the north to the town of Beersheba in
the south, everyone in the country knew
that Samuel was truly the LORD's
prophet. 21The LORD often appeared to
Samuel at Shiloh and told him what
4 to say. 1Then Samuel would speak
to the whole nation of Israel.

The Philistines Capture the Sacred Chest

One day the Israelites went out to
fight the Philistines. They set up camp
near Ebenezer, and the Philistines
camped at Aphek. 2The Philistines made
a fierce attack. They defeated the Israelites and killed about four thousand
of them.
3The Israelite army returned to their
camp, and the leaders said, "Why did
the LORD let us lose to the Philistines today? Let's get the sacred chest where
the LORD's agreement with Israel is
kept. Then the LORD[y] will help us and
rescue us from our enemies."
4The army sent some soldiers to bring
back the sacred chest from Shiloh, because the LORD All-Powerful has his
throne on the winged creatures on top
of the chest.
As Eli's two sons, Hophni and Phinehas, 5brought the chest into camp, the
army cheered so loudly that the ground
shook. 6The Philistines heard the noise
and said, "What are those Hebrews
shouting about?"
When the Philistines learned that the
sacred chest had been brought into the
camp, 7they were scared to death and
said:
The gods have come into their
camp. Now we're in real trouble!
Nothing like this has ever happened
to us before. 8We're in big trouble!
Who can save us from these powerful gods? They're the same gods
who made all those horrible things
happen to the Egyptians in the
desert.
9Philistines, be brave and fight
hard! If you don't, those Hebrews
will rule us, just as we've been ruling them. Fight and don't be afraid.
10The Philistines did fight. They killed
thirty thousand Israelite soldiers, and all
the rest ran off to their homes. 11Hophni
and Phinehas were killed, and the sacred chest was captured.

Eli Dies

12That same day a soldier from the
tribe of Benjamin ran from the battle-
front to Shiloh. He had torn his clothes
and put dirt on his head to show his sorrow. 13He went into town and told the
news about the battle, and everyone
started crying.
Eli was afraid that something might
happen to the sacred chest. So he was
sitting on his chair beside the road, just
waiting. 14-15He was ninety-eight years
old and blind, but he could hear everyone crying, and he asked, "What's all
that noise?"
The soldier hurried over and told Eli,
16"I escaped from the fighting today and
ran here."
"Young man, what happened?" Eli
asked.
17"Israel ran away from the Philistines," the soldier answered. "Many
of our people were killed, including
your two sons, Hophni and Phinehas.
But worst of all, the sacred chest was
captured."
18Eli was still sitting on a chair beside
the wall of the town gate. And when the
man said that the Philistines had taken
the sacred chest, Eli fell backwards. He
was a very heavy old man, and the fall
broke his neck and killed him. He had
been a leader[z] of Israel for forty years.
19The wife of Phinehas was about to
give birth. And soon after she heard that
the sacred chest had been captured and
that her husband and his father had

[x]**3.13** *refused . . . me*: Or "were insulting everyone." [y]**4.3** *LORD*: Or "chest." [z]**4.18** *leader*: The Hebrew word means that Eli may have been an army commander, a judge, and a priest.

died, her baby came. The birth was very
hard, 20and she was dying. But the
women taking care of her said, "Don't
be afraid—it's a boy!"
She didn't pay any attention to them.
21-22Instead she kept thinking about losing her husband and her father-in-law.
So she said, "My son will be named Ichabod,[a] because the glory of Israel left
our country when the sacred chest was
captured."

God Causes Trouble for the Philistines

5 The Philistines took the sacred chest
from near Ebenezer to the town of
Ashdod. 2They brought it into the temple of their god Dagon and put it next to
the statue of Dagon, which they worshiped.
3When the people of Ashdod got up
early the next morning, they found the
statue lying facedown on the floor in
front of the sacred chest. They put the
statue back where it belonged. 4But
early the next morning, it had fallen
over again and was lying facedown on
the floor in front of the chest. The body
of the statue was still in one piece, but
its head and both hands had broken off
and were lying on the stone floor in the
doorway. 5This is the reason the priests
and everyone else step over that part of
the doorway when they enter the temple
of Dagon in Ashdod.
6The LORD caused a lot of trouble for
the people of Ashdod and their neighbors. He made sores break out all over
their bodies,[b] and everyone was in a
panic.[c] 7Finally, they said, "The God of
Israel did this. He is the one who caused
all this trouble for us and our god
Dagon. We've got to get rid of this chest."
8The people of Ashdod had all the
Philistine rulers come to Ashdod, and
they asked them, "What can we do with
the sacred chest that belongs to the God
of Israel?"
"Send it to Gath," the rulers answered.
But after they took it there, 9the LORD
made sores break out on everyone in
town. The people of Gath were frightened, 10so they sent the sacred chest to
Ekron. But before they could take it
through the town gates, the people of
Ekron started screaming, "They've
brought the sacred chest that belongs to
the God of Israel! It will kill us and our
families too!"

The Philistines Send Back the Sacred Chest

11The people of Ekron called for another meeting of the Philistine rulers
and told them, "Send this chest back
where it belongs. Then it won't kill us."
Everyone was in a panic, because God
was causing a lot of people to die, 12and
those who had survived were suffering
from the sores. They all cried to their
gods for help.

6 After the sacred chest had been in
Philistia for seven months,[d] 2the
Philistines called in their priests and
fortunetellers, and asked, "What should
we do with this sacred chest? Tell us
how to send it back where it belongs!"
3"Don't send it back without a gift,"
the priests and fortunetellers answered.
"Send along something to Israel's God
to make up for taking the chest in the
first place. Then you will be healed, and
you will find out why the LORD was
causing you so much trouble."
4"What should we send?" the Philistines asked.
The priests and fortunetellers answered:

There are five Philistine rulers,
and they all have the same disease
that you have. 5So make five gold
models of the sores and five gold
models of the rats that are wiping
out your crops. If you honor the God
of Israel with this gift, maybe he will
stop causing trouble for you and
your gods and your crops. 6Don't be
like the Egyptians and their king.
They were stubborn, but when Israel's God was finished with them,
they had to let Israel go.
7Get a new cart and two cows that
have young calves and that have
never pulled a cart. Hitch the cows
to the cart, but take the calves back
to their barn. 8Then put the chest on
the cart. Put the gold rats and sores
into a bag and put it on the cart next
to the chest. Then send it on its way.
9Watch to see if the chest goes on
up the road to the Israelite town of
Beth-Shemesh. If it goes back to its
own country, you will know that it
was the LORD who made us suffer so
badly. But if the chest doesn't go
back to its own country, then the
LORD had nothing to do with the disease that hit us—it was simply bad
luck.

10The Philistines followed their advice. They hitched up the two cows to
the cart, but they kept their calves in a
barn. 11Then they put the chest on the
cart, along with the bag that had the
gold rats and sores in it.
12The cows went straight up the road
toward Beth-Shemesh, mooing as they

[a]**4.21,22** *Ichabod*: Ichabod means "where is the glory?" or "there is no glory." [b]**5.6** *sores . . . bodies*: Or "He struck them with bubonic plague." [c]**5.6** *panic*: Two ancient translations add "Rats came from their ships, and people were dying right and left." [d]**6.1** *months*: One ancient translation adds "and rats were everywhere" or "and rats ate the crops."

went. The Philistine rulers followed
them until they got close to Beth-
Shemesh.
13 The people of Beth-Shemesh were
harvesting their wheat[e] in the valley.
When they looked up and saw the chest,
they were so happy that they stopped
working and started celebrating.
14-15 The cows left the road and pulled
the cart into a field that belonged to
Joshua from Beth-Shemesh, and they
stopped beside a huge rock. Some men
from the tribe of Levi were there. So
they took the chest off the cart and
placed it on the rock, and then they did
the same thing with the bag of gold rats
and sores. A few other people chopped
up the cart and made a fire. They killed
the cows and burned them as sacrifices
to the LORD. After that, they offered
more sacrifices.
16 When the five rulers of the Philistines saw what had happened, they went
back to Ekron that same day.
17 That is how the Philistines sent gifts
to the LORD to make up for taking the
sacred chest. They sent five gold sores,
one each for their towns of Ashdod,
Gaza, Ashkelon, Gath, and Ekron.
18 They also sent one gold rat for each
walled town and for every village that
the five Philistine rulers controlled. The
huge stone[f] where the Levites set the
chest is still there in Joshua's field as a
reminder of what happened.

The Sacred Chest Is Sent to Kiriath-Jearim

19 Some of the men of Beth-Shemesh
looked inside the sacred chest, and the
LORD God killed seventy[g] of them. This
made the people of Beth-Shemesh very
sad, 20 and they started saying, "No other
God is like the LORD! Who can go near
him and still live? We'll have to send the
chest away from here. But where can we
send it?"
21 They sent messengers to tell the
people of Kiriath-Jearim, "The Philistines have sent back the sacred chest.
Why don't you take it and keep it there
with you?"
7 The people of Kiriath-Jearim got the
chest and took it to Abinadab's
house, which was on a hill in their town.
They chose his son Eleazar to take care
of it, 2 and it stayed there for twenty
years.
During this time everyone in Israel
was very sad and begged the LORD for
help.[h]

The People of Israel Turn Back to the LORD

3 One day, Samuel told all the people
of Israel, "If you really want to turn
back to the LORD, then prove it. Get rid
of your foreign idols, including the ones
of the goddess Astarte. Turn to the LORD
with all your heart and worship only
him. Then he will rescue you from the
Philistines."
4 The people got rid of their idols of
Baal and Astarte and began worshiping
only the LORD.
5 Then Samuel said, "Tell everyone in
Israel to meet together at Mizpah, and I
will pray to the LORD for you."
6 The Israelites met together at Mizpah
with Samuel as their leader. They drew
water from the well and poured it out as
an offering to the LORD. On that same
day they went without eating to show
their sorrow, and they confessed they
had been unfaithful to the LORD.

The Philistines Attack Israel

7 When the Philistine rulers found out
about the meeting at Mizpah, they sent
an army there to attack the people of Israel.
The Israelites were afraid when they
heard that the Philistines were coming.
8 "Don't stop praying!" they told Samuel.
"Ask the LORD our God to rescue us."
9-10 Samuel begged the LORD to rescue
Israel, then he sacrificed a young lamb
to the LORD. Samuel had not even finished offering the sacrifice when the
Philistines started to attack. But the
LORD answered his prayer and made
thunder crash all around them. The
Philistines panicked and ran away.
11 The men of Israel left Mizpah and
went after them as far as the hillside below Beth-Car, killing every enemy soldier they caught.
12-13 The Philistines were so badly
beaten that it was quite a while before
they attacked Israel again. After the
battle, Samuel set up a monument between Mizpah and the rocky cliffs. He
named it "Help Monument"[i] to remind
Israel how much the LORD had helped
them.
For as long as Samuel lived, the LORD
helped Israel fight the Philistines. 14 The
Israelites were even able to recapture
their towns and territory between Ekron
and Gath.
Israel was also at peace with the
Amorites.[j]

[e] **6.13** *wheat*: The wheat harvest took place in May and June. [f] **6.18** *stone*: A few Hebrew manuscripts; most Hebrew manuscripts "meadow" or "stream." [g] **6.19** *seventy*: A few Hebrew manuscripts; most Hebrew manuscripts "seventy men, fifty thousand men." [h] **7.2** *Israel . . . help*: Or "Israel turned to the Lord and begged him for help." [i] **7.12,13** *Help Monument*: Or "Ebenezer." [j] **7.14** *Amorites*: In this verse, the non-Israelite peoples of Canaan.

Samuel Is a Leader in Israel

15 Samuel was a leader[k] in Israel all
his life. 16 Every year he would go
around to the towns of Bethel, Gilgal,
and Mizpah where he served as judge
for the people. 17 Then he would go back
to his home in Ramah and do the same
thing there. He also had an altar built
for the LORD at Ramah.

The People of Israel Want a King

8 1-2 Samuel had two sons. The older
one was Joel, and the younger one
was Abijah. When Samuel was getting
old, he let them be leaders[k] at Beersheba. 3 But they were not like their father. They were dishonest and accepted
bribes to give unfair decisions.
4 One day the nation's leaders came to
Samuel at Ramah 5 and said, "You are an
old man. You set a good example for
your sons, but they haven't followed it.
Now we want a king to be our leader,[k]
just like all the other nations. Choose
one for us!"
6 Samuel was upset to hear the leaders
say they wanted a king, so he prayed
about it. 7 The LORD answered:

> Samuel, do everything they want
> you to do. I am really the one they
> have rejected as their king. 8 Ever
> since the day I rescued my people
> from Egypt, they have turned from
> me to worship idols. Now they are
> turning away from you. 9 Do every-
> thing they ask, but warn them and
> tell them how a king will treat them.

10 Samuel told the people who were
asking for a king what the LORD had
said:

> 11 If you have a king, this is how he
> will treat you. He will force your
> sons to join his army. Some of them
> will ride in his chariots, some will
> serve in the cavalry, and others will
> run ahead of his own chariot.[l]
> 12 Some of them will be officers in
> charge of a thousand soldiers, and
> others will be in charge of fifty. Still
> others will have to farm the king's
> land and harvest his crops, or make
> weapons and parts for his chariots.
> 13 Your daughters will have to make
> perfume or do his cooking and bak-
> ing.
>
> 14 The king will take your best
> fields, as well as your vineyards, and
> olive orchards and give them to his
> own officials. 15 He will also take a
> tenth of your grain and grapes and
> give it to his officers and officials.
>
> 16 The king will take your slaves
> and your best young men and your
> donkeys and make them do his
> work. 17 He will also take a tenth of
> your sheep and goats. You will be-
> come the king's slaves, 18 and you
> will finally cry out for the LORD to
> save you from the king you wanted.
> But the LORD won't answer your
> prayers.

19-20 The people would not listen to
Samuel. "No!" they said. "We want to be
like other nations. We want a king to
rule us and lead us in battle."
21 Samuel listened to them and then
told the LORD exactly what they had
said. 22 "Do what they want," the LORD
answered. "Give them a king."
Samuel told the people to go back to
their homes.

Saul Meets Samuel

9 Kish was a wealthy man who belonged to the tribe of Benjamin. His
father was Abiel, his grandfather was
Zeror, his great-grandfather was Beco-
rath, and his great-great-grandfather
was Aphiah. 2 Kish had a son named
Saul, who was better looking and more
than a head taller than anyone else in
all Israel.
3 Kish owned some donkeys, but they
had run off. So he told Saul, "Take one
of the servants and go look for the donkeys."
4 Saul and the servant went through
the hill country of Ephraim and the territory of Shalishah, but they could not
find the donkeys. Then they went
through the territories of Shaalim and
Benjamin, but still there was no sign of
the donkeys. 5 Finally they came to the
territory where the clan of Zuph[m] lived.
"Let's go back home," Saul told his servant. "If we don't go back soon, my
father will stop worrying about the donkeys and start worrying about us!"
6 "Wait!" the servant answered.
"There's a man of God who lives in a
town near here. He's amazing! Everything he says comes true. Let's talk to
him. Maybe he can tell us where to look."
7 Saul said, "How can we talk to the
prophet when I don't have anything to
give him? We don't even have any bread
left in our sacks. What can we give him?"
8 "I have a small piece of silver," the
servant answered. "We can give him
that, and then he will tell us where to
look for the donkeys."
9-10 "Great!" Saul replied. "Let's go to
the man who can see visions!" He said
this because in those days God would
answer questions by giving visions to
prophets.

[k]7.15 *leader*: The Hebrew word could mean an army commander, a judge, and a religious leader. [k]8.1,2 *leaders*: See the note at 7.15. [k]8.5 *leader*: See the note at 7.15.
[l]8.11 *others . . . chariot*: These men were probably his bodyguards. [m]9.5 *Zuph*: Samuel's father Elkanah was from the Zuph clan.

Saul and his servant went to the town
where the prophet lived. 11As they were
going up the hill to the town, they met
some young women coming out to get
water,[n] and the two men said to them,
"We're looking for the man who can see
visions. Is he in town?"
12"Yes, he is," they replied. "He's in
town today because there's going to be
a sacrifice and a sacred meal at the
place of worship. In fact, he's just ahead
of you. Hurry 13and you should find him
right inside the town gate. He's on his
way out to the place of worship to eat
with the invited guests. They can't start
eating until he blesses the sacrifice. If
you go now, you should find him."
14They went to the town, and just as
they were going through the gate,
Samuel was coming out on his way to
the place of worship.
15The day before Saul came, the LORD
had told Samuel, 16"I've seen how my
people are suffering, and I've heard
their call for help. About this time tomorrow I'll send you a man from the
tribe of Benjamin, who will rescue my
people from the Philistines. I want you
to pour olive oil[o] on his head to show
that he will be their leader."
17Samuel looked at Saul, and the LORD
told Samuel, "This is the man I told you
about. He's the one who will rule Israel."
18Saul went over to Samuel in the
gateway and said, "A man who can see
visions lives here in town. Could you tell
me the way to his house?"
19"I am the one who sees visions!"
Samuel answered. "Go on up to the
place of worship. You will eat with me
today, and in the morning I'll answer
your questions. 20Don't worry about
your donkeys that ran off three days
ago. They've already been found. Everything of value in Israel now belongs to
you and your family."[p]
21"Why are you telling me this?" Saul
asked. "I'm from Benjamin, the smallest
tribe in Israel, and my clan is the least
important in the tribe."

Saul Eats with Samuel and Stays at His House

22Samuel took Saul and his servant
into the dining room at the place of worship. About thirty people were there for
the dinner, but Samuel gave Saul and
his servant the places of honor. 23-24Then
Samuel told the cook, "I gave you the
best piece of meat and told you to set it
aside. Bring it here now."
The cook brought the meat over and
set it down in front of Saul. "This is for
you," Samuel told him. "Go ahead and
eat it. I had this piece saved especially
for you, and I invited these guests to eat
with you."
After Saul and Samuel had finished
eating, 25they went down from the place
of worship and back into town. A bed
was set up for Saul on the flat roof[q] of
Samuel's house, 26and Saul slept there.
About sunrise the next morning,[r]
Samuel called up to Saul on the roof,
"Time to get up! I'll help you get started
on your way."
Saul got up. He and Samuel left together 27and had almost reached the
edge of town when Samuel stopped and
said, "Have your servant go on. Stay
here with me for a few minutes, and I'll
tell you what God has told me."

Samuel Tells Saul He Will Be King

10 After the servant had gone,
1Samuel took a small jar of olive
oil and poured it on Saul's head. Then
he kissed[s] Saul and told him:

> The LORD has chosen you to be the
> leader and ruler of his people.[t]
> 2When you leave me today, you'll
> meet two men near Rachel's tomb at
> Zelzah in the territory of Benjamin.
> They'll tell you, "The donkeys you've
> been looking for have been found.
> Your father has forgotten about
> them, and now he's worrying about
> you! He's wondering how he can
> find you."
> 3Go on from there until you reach
> the big oak tree at Tabor, where
> you'll meet three men on their way
> to worship God at Bethel. One of
> them will be leading three young
> goats, another will be carrying three
> round loaves of bread, and the last
> one will be carrying a clay jar of
> wine. 4After they greet you, they'll
> give you two loaves of bread.

[n]9.11 *water*: Towns were often built on a hill near a source of water, which would often be down in the valley outside of the town. It was usually the job of women to get water for their family. [o]9.16 *olive oil*: Olive oil was poured on the head of someone who was chosen to be a priest, a prophet, or a king. [p]9.20 *Everything . . . family*: Or "You and your family are what all Israel wants." [q]9.25 *roof*: Guests often slept on the flat roof of their host's house, where it was cool and breezy. [r]9.25,26 *was set . . . morning*: One ancient translation; Hebrew "Samuel spoke with Saul on the flat roof of his house. They got up early the next morning, around sunrise, and . . . " [s]10.1 *kissed*: Relatives or close friends often greeted one another with a kiss. But this may have been a ceremonial kiss after Samuel poured oil on Saul's head to show that he was to be the king. [t]10.1 *people*: One ancient translation adds "You will rule the Lord's people and save them from their enemies who are all around them. These things will prove that what I say is true."

5Next, go to Gibeah,[u] where the Philistines have an army camp. As you're going into the town, you'll meet a group of prophets coming down from the place of worship. They'll be going along prophesying while others are walking in front of them, playing small harps, small drums, and flutes.

6The Spirit of the LORD will suddenly take control of you.[v] You'll become a different person and start prophesying right along with them. 7After these things happen, do whatever you think is right! God will help you.

8Then you should go to Gilgal. I'll come a little later, so wait for me. It may even take a week for me to get there, but when I come, I'll offer sacrifices and offerings to the LORD. I'll also tell you what to do next.

Saul Goes Back Home

9As Saul turned around to leave Samuel, God made Saul feel like a different person. That same day, everything happened just as Samuel had said. 10When Saul arrived at Gibeah, a group of prophets met him. The Spirit of God suddenly took control of him,[w] and right there in the middle of the group he began prophesying.

11Some people who had known Saul for a long time saw that he was speaking and behaving like a prophet. They said to each other, "What's happened? How can Saul be a prophet?"

12"Why not?" one of them answered. "Saul has as much right to be a prophet as anyone else!"[x] That's why everyone started saying, "How can Saul be a prophet?"

13After Saul stopped prophesying, he went to the place of worship.

14Later, Saul's uncle asked him, "Where have you been?"

Saul answered, "Looking for the donkeys. We couldn't find them, so we went to talk with Samuel."

15"And what did he tell you?" Saul's uncle asked.

16Saul answered, "He told us the donkeys had been found." But Saul didn't mention that Samuel had chosen him to be king.

The LORD Shows Israel that Saul Will Be King

17Samuel sent messengers to tell the Israelites to come to Mizpah and meet with the LORD. 18When everyone had arrived, Samuel said:

The LORD God of Israel told me to remind you that he had rescued you from the Egyptians and from the other nations that abused you.

19God has rescued you from your troubles and hard times. But you have rejected your God and have asked for a king. Now each tribe and clan must come near the place of worship so the LORD can choose a king.

20Samuel brought each tribe, one after the other, to the altar, and the LORD chose the Benjamin tribe. 21Next, Samuel brought each clan of Benjamin there, and the LORD chose the Matri clan. Finally, Saul the son of Kish was chosen. But when they looked for him, he was nowhere to be found.

22The people prayed, "Our LORD, is Saul here?"

"Yes," the LORD answered, "he is hiding behind the baggage."

23The people ran and got Saul and brought him into the middle of the crowd. He was more than a head taller than anyone else. 24"Look closely at the man the LORD has chosen!" Samuel told the crowd. "There is no one like him!"

The crowd shouted, "Long live the king!"

25Samuel explained the rights and duties of a king and wrote them all in a book. He put the book in a temple building at one of the places where the LORD was worshiped. Then Samuel sent everyone home.

26God had encouraged some young men to become followers of Saul, and when he returned to his hometown of Gibeah, they went with him. 27But some worthless fools said, "How can someone like Saul rescue us from our enemies?" They did not want Saul to be their king, and so they didn't bring him any gifts. But Saul kept calm.

Saul Rescues the Town of Jabesh in Gilead

11 About this time,[y] King Nahash of Ammon came with his army and

[u]**10.5** *Gibeah*: The Hebrew text has "Gibeah of God," which may or may not have been the same Gibeah as Saul's hometown. [v]**10.6** *take . . . you*: Or "will take control of you in a powerful way." [w]**10.10** *suddenly . . . him*: Or "came over him in a powerful way." [x]**10.12** *Why not . . . anyone else*: Or "Sure he is! He's probably the leader of the prophets!" or "How can he be? Those prophets are nobodies!" [y]**10.27—11.1** *But Saul . . . time*: The Standard Hebrew Text; the Dead Sea Scrolls add "King Nahash of Ammon was making the people of Gad and Reuben miserable. He was poking out everyone's right eye, and no one in Israel could stop him. He had poked out the right eye of every Israelite man who lived east of the Jordan River. Only seven thousand men had escaped from the Ammonites, and they had gone into the town of Jabesh in Gilead. About a month later . . ."

surrounded the town of Jabesh in
Gilead. The people who lived there told
Nahash, "If you will sign a peace treaty
with us, you can be our ruler, and we
will pay taxes to you."
2Nahash answered, "Sure, I'll sign a
treaty! But not before I insult Israel by
poking out the right eye of every man
who lives in Jabesh."
3The town leaders said, "Give us
seven days so we can send messengers
everywhere in Israel to ask for help. If
no one comes here to save us, we will
surrender to you."
4Some of the messengers went to
Gibeah, Saul's hometown. They told
what was happening at Jabesh, and
everyone in Gibeah started crying. 5Just
then, Saul came in from the fields, walking behind his oxen.
"Why is everyone crying?" Saul
asked.
They told him what the men from
Jabesh had said. 6Then the Spirit of God
suddenly took control of Saul and made
him furious. 7Saul killed two of his
oxen, cut them up in pieces, and gave
the pieces to the[z] messengers. He told
them to show the pieces to everyone in
Israel and say, "Saul and Samuel are
getting an army together. Come and join
them. If you don't, this is what will happen to your oxen!"
The LORD made the people of Israel
terribly afraid. So all the men came together 8at Bezek. Saul had them organized and counted. There were three
hundred thousand from Israel and thirty
thousand[a] from Judah.
9Saul and his officers sent the messengers back to Jabesh with this
promise: "We will rescue you tomorrow
afternoon." The messengers went back
to the people at Jabesh and told them
that they were going to be rescued.
Everyone was encouraged! 10So they
told the Ammonites, "We will surrender
to you tomorrow, and then you can do
whatever you want to."
11The next day, Saul divided his army
into three groups and attacked before
daylight. They started killing Ammonites and kept it up until afternoon.
A few Ammonites managed to escape,
but they were scattered far from each
other.
12The Israelite soldiers went to
Samuel and demanded, "Where are the
men who said they didn't want Saul to
be king? Bring them to us, and we will
put them to death!"
13"No you won't!" Saul told them.
"The LORD rescued Israel today, and no
one will be put to death."

Saul Is Accepted as King

14"Come on!" Samuel said. "Let's go to
Gilgal and make an agreement that Saul
will continue to be our king."
15Everyone went to the place of worship at Gilgal, where they agreed that
Saul would be their king. Saul and the
people sacrificed animals to ask for the
LORD's blessing,[b] and they had a big celebration.

Samuel's Farewell Speech

12 Samuel told the Israelites:
I have given you a king, just
as you asked. 2You have seen how I
have led you ever since I was a
young man. I'm already old. My hair
is gray, and my own sons are grown.
Now you must see how well your
king will lead you.
3Let me ask this. Have I ever taken
anyone's ox or donkey or forced you
to give me anything? Have I ever
hurt anyone or taken a bribe to give
an unfair decision? Answer me so
the LORD and his chosen king can
hear you. And if I have done any of
these things, I will give it all back.
4"No," the Israelites answered. "You've
never cheated us in any way!"
5Samuel said, "The LORD and his chosen king are witnesses to what you have
said."
"That's true," they replied.
6Then Samuel told them:
The LORD brought your ancestors
out of Egypt and chose Moses and
Aaron to be your leaders. 7Now the
LORD will be your judge. So stand
here and listen, while I remind you
how often the LORD has saved you
and your ancestors from your enemies.
8After Jacob went to Egypt, your
ancestors cried out to the LORD for
help, and he sent Moses and Aaron.
They led your ancestors out of Egypt
and had them settle in this land. 9But
your ancestors forgot the LORD, so
he let them be defeated by the
Philistines, the king of Moab, and
Sisera, the commander of Hazor's
army.
10Again your ancestors cried out
to the LORD for help. They said, "We
have sinned! We stopped worshiping
you, our LORD, and started worshiping Baal and Astarte. But now, if you

[z] 11.7 *the*: Or "some other." [a] 11.8 *three hundred thousand . . . thirty thousand*: The Dead Sea Scrolls and some ancient translations have different numbers. [b] 11.15 *sacrificed . . . blessing*: This kind of sacrifice is described in Leviticus 3; 7.11-36; 19.5-8. People who offered these sacrifices were allowed to eat most of the meat, and they could invite others to share it with them.

rescue us from our enemies, we will
worship you."
11The LORD sent Gideon,[c] Bedan,
Jephthah, and Samuel to rescue you
from your enemies, and you didn't
have to worry about being attacked.
12Then you saw that King Nahash of
Ammon was going to attack you.
And even though the LORD your God
is your king, you told me, "This time
it's different. We want a king to rule
us!"
13You asked for a king, and you
chose one. Now he stands here
where all of you can see him. But it
was really the LORD who made him
your king. 14If you and your king
want to be followers of the LORD,
you must worship him[d] and do what
he says. Don't be stubborn! 15If
you're stubborn and refuse to obey
the LORD, he will turn against you
and your king.[e]
16Just stand here and watch the
LORD show his mighty power. 17Isn't
this the dry season?[f] I'm going to
ask the LORD to send a thunderstorm. When you see it, you will realize how wrong you were to ask for
a king.
18Samuel prayed, and that same day
the LORD sent a thunderstorm. Everyone
was afraid of the LORD and of Samuel.
19They told Samuel, "Please, pray to the
LORD your God for us! We don't want to
die. We have sinned many times in the
past, and we were very wrong to ask for
a king."
20Samuel answered:
Even though what you did was
wrong, you don't need to be afraid.
But you must always follow the
LORD and worship him with all your
heart. 21Don't worship idols! They
don't have any power, and they can't
help you or save you when you're in
trouble. 22But the LORD has chosen
you to be his own people. He will always take care of you so that everyone will know how great he is.
23I would be disobeying the LORD
if I stopped praying for you! I will always teach you how to live right.
24You also must obey the LORD—you
must worship him with all your
heart and remember the great things
he has done for you. 25But if you and
your king do evil, the LORD will wipe
you out.

Saul Disobeys the LORD

13 Saul was a young man[g] when he
became king, and he ruled Israel
for two years. 2Then[h] he chose three
thousand men from Israel to be full-time
soldiers and sent everyone else[i] home.
Two thousand of these troops stayed
with him in the hills around Michmash
and Bethel. The other thousand were
stationed with Jonathan[j] at Gibeah[k] in
the territory of Benjamin.
3Jonathan led an attack on the Philistine army camp at Geba.[l] The Philistine
camp was destroyed, but[m] the other
Philistines heard what had happened.
Then Saul told his messengers, "Go to
every village in the country. Give a signal with the trumpet, and when the people come together, tell them what has
happened."
4The messengers then said to the people of Israel, "Saul has destroyed the
Philistine army camp at Geba.[n] Now the
Philistines really hate Israel, so every
town and village must send men to join
Saul's army at Gilgal."
5The Philistines called their army together to fight Israel. They had three
thousand[o] chariots, six thousand cavalry, and as many foot soldiers as there
are grains of sand on the beach. They
went to Michmash and set up camp
there east of Beth-Aven.[p]
6The Israelite army realized that they
were outnumbered and were going to
lose the battle. Some of the Israelite
men hid in caves or in clumps of
bushes,[q] and some ran to places where
they could hide among large rocks. Others hid in tombs[r] or in deep dry pits.

[c]**12.11** *Gideon*: The Hebrew text has "Jerubbaal," another name for "Gideon." [d]**12.14** *If . . . him*: Or "If you and your king want things to go well for you, then you must worship the LORD." [e]**12.15** *and your king*: One ancient translation; Hebrew "and your ancestors" or "as he was against your ancestors." [f]**12.17** *the dry season*: The Hebrew text has "time for wheat harvest," which was usually in the spring, the beginning of the dry season. [g]**13.1** *a young man*: One possible meaning for the difficult Hebrew text; several manuscripts of one ancient translation have "thirty years old." [h]**13.1,2** *for . . . Then*: One possible meaning for the difficult Hebrew text. [i]**13.2** *everyone else*: People who were not full-time soldiers, but fought together with the army when the nation was in danger. [j]**13.2** *Jonathan*: Saul's son (see verse 16). [k]**13.2** *Michmash . . . Bethel . . . Gibeah*: These three towns form a triangle, with Bethel to the north. [l]**13.3** *Geba*: Geba was between Gibeah and Michmash. [m]**13.3** *led an attack . . . destroyed, but*: Or "killed the Philistine military governor who lived at Geba, and . . ." [n]**13.4** *destroyed . . . Geba*: Or "killed the Philistine military governor who lived at Geba." [o]**13.5** *three thousand*: Some ancient translations; Hebrew "thirty thousand." [p]**13.5** *Beth-Aven*: This Beth-Aven was probably located about a mile southwest of Michmash, between Michmash and Geba. [q]**13.6** *in . . . bushes*: Or "in cracks in the rocks." [r]**13.6** *tombs*: The Hebrew word may mean a room cut into solid rock and used as a burial place, or it may mean a cellar.

7Still others[s] went to Gad and Gilead on
the other side of the Jordan River.
Saul stayed at Gilgal. His soldiers
were shaking with fear, 8and they were
starting to run off and leave him. Saul
waited there seven days, just as Samuel
had ordered him to do,[t] but Samuel did
not come. 9Finally, Saul commanded,
"Bring me some animals, so we can offer sacrifices to please the LORD and ask
for his help."
Saul killed one of the animals, 10and
just as he was placing it on the altar,
Samuel arrived. Saul went out to welcome him.
11"What have you done?" Samuel
asked.
Saul answered, "My soldiers were
leaving in all directions, and you didn't
come when you were supposed to. The
Philistines were gathering at Michmash,
12and I was worried that they would attack me here at Gilgal. I hadn't offered a
sacrifice to ask for the LORD's help, so I
forced myself to offer a sacrifice on the
altar fire."
13"That was stupid!" Samuel said.
"You didn't obey the LORD your God. If
you had obeyed him, someone from
your family would always have been
king of Israel. 14But no, you disobeyed,
and so the LORD won't choose anyone
else from your family to be king. In fact,
he has already chosen the one he wants
to be the next leader of his people."
15Then Samuel left Gilgal.
Part of Saul's army had not deserted
him, and he led them to Gibeah in Benjamin to join his other troops. Then he
counted them[u] and found that he still
had six hundred men. 16Saul, Jonathan,
and their army set up camp at Geba in
Benjamin.

Jonathan Attacks the Philistines

The Philistine army was camped at
Michmash. 17Each day they sent out patrols to attack and rob villages and then
destroy them. One patrol would go
north along the road to Ophrah in the
region of Shual. 18Another patrol would
go west along the road to Beth-Horon. A
third patrol would go east toward the
desert on the road to the ridge that overlooks Zeboim Valley.
19The Philistines would not allow any
Israelites to learn how to make iron
tools. "If we allowed that," they said,
"those worthless Israelites would make
swords and spears."
20-21Whenever the Israelites wanted to
get an iron point put on a cattle prod,[v]
they had to go to the Philistines. Even if
they wanted to sharpen plow-blades,
picks, axes, sickles,[w] and pitchforks[x]
they still had to go to them. And the
Philistines charged high prices. 22So,
whenever the Israelite soldiers had to
go into battle, none of them had a sword
or a spear except Saul and his son
Jonathan. 23The Philistines moved their
14 camp to the pass at Michmash,
1-3and Saul was in Geba[y] with his
six hundred men. Saul's own tent was
set up under a fruit tree[z] by the threshing place[a] at the edge of town. Ahijah
was serving as priest, and one of his
jobs was to get answers from the LORD
for Saul. Ahijah's father was Ahitub,
and his father's brother was Ichabod.
Ahijah's grandfather was Phinehas, and
his great-grandfather Eli had been the
LORD's priest at Shiloh.
One day, Jonathan told the soldier
who carried his weapons that he wanted
to attack the Philistine camp on the
other side of the valley. So they slipped
out of the Israelite camp without anyone
knowing it. Jonathan didn't even tell his
father he was leaving.
4-5Jonathan decided to get to the
Philistine camp by going through the
pass that led between Shiny Cliff and
Michmash to the north and Thornbush
Cliff[b] and Geba to the south.
6Jonathan and the soldier who carried
his weapons talked as they went toward
the Philistine camp. "It's just the two of
us against all those godless men,"
Jonathan said. "But the LORD can help a
few soldiers win a battle just as easily
as he can help a whole army. Maybe the
LORD will help us win this battle."
7"Do whatever you want," the soldier
answered. "I'll be right there with you."
8"This is what we will do," Jonathan
said. "We will go across and let them see
us. 9If they agree to come down the hill
and fight where we are, then we won't
climb up to their camp. 10But we will go
if they tell us to come up the hill and

[s] **13.7** *Still others*: This translates a Hebrew word which may be used of wandering groups of people who sometimes became outlaws or hired soldiers (see also 14.21). [t] **13.8** *Samuel . . . to do*: See 10.8. [u] **13.15** *Then Samuel . . . counted them*: Two ancient translations; Hebrew "Then Samuel left Gilgal and went to Gibeah in Benjamin. Saul counted his army."
[v] **13.20,21** *cattle prod*: A pole used to poke cattle and make them move. [w] **13.20,21** *sickles*: One ancient translation; Hebrew "plow-blades." [x] **13.20,21** *pitchforks*: One possible meaning for the difficult Hebrew text. [y] **14.1-3** *Geba*: Or "Gibeah." In 13.16 and 14.5 the name "Geba" is used, while 14.2,16 have "Gibeah." In ancient Hebrew writing there is only one letter different between the two words. [z] **14.1-3** *fruit tree*: Hebrew "pomegranate tree." A pomegranate is a bright red fruit that looks like an apple. [a] **14.1-3** *threshing place*: Or "in Migron." [b] **14.4,5** *Shiny Cliff . . . Thornbush Cliff*: Or "Bozez Cliff . . . Seneh Cliff."

fight. That will mean the LORD is going
to help us win."
11-12 Jonathan and the soldier stood at
the bottom of the hill where the Philistines could see them. The Philistines
said, "Look! Those worthless Israelites
have crawled out of the holes where
they've been hiding." Then they yelled
down to Jonathan and the soldier,
"Come up here, and we will teach you a
thing or two!"
Jonathan turned to the soldier and
said, "Follow me! The LORD is going to
let us win."
13 Jonathan crawled up the hillside
with the soldier right behind him. When
they got to the top, Jonathan killed the
Philistines who attacked from the front,
and the soldier killed those who attacked from behind.[c] 14 Before they had
gone a hundred feet,[d] they had killed
about twenty Philistines.
15 The whole Philistine army panicked—those in camp, those on guard
duty, those in the fields, and those on
raiding patrols. All of them were afraid
and confused. Then God sent an earthquake, and the ground began to tremble.[e]

Israel Defeats the Philistines

16 Saul's lookouts at Geba[f] saw that
the Philistine army was running in
every direction, like melted wax. 17 Saul
told his officers, "Call the roll and find
out who left our camp." When they had
finished, they found out that Jonathan
and the soldier who carried his weapons
were missing.
18 At that time, Ahijah was serving as
priest for the army of Israel, and Saul
told him, "Come over here! Let's ask
God what we should do."[g] 19 Just as Saul
finished saying this, he could see that
the Philistine army camp was getting
more and more confused, and he said,
"Ahijah, never mind!"
20 Saul quickly called his army together, then led them to the Philistine
camp. By this time the Philistines were
so confused that they were killing each
other.
21 There were also some hired
soldiers[h] in the Philistine camp, who
now switched to Israel's side and fought
for Saul and Jonathan.
22 Many Israelites had been hiding in
the hill country of Ephraim. And when
they heard that the Philistines were running away, they came out of hiding and
joined in chasing the Philistines.
23-24 So the LORD helped Israel win the
battle that day.

Saul's Curse on Anyone Who Eats

Saul had earlier told his soldiers, "I
want to get even with those Philistines
by sunset. If any of you eat before then,
you will be under a curse!" So he made
them swear not to eat.
By the time the fighting moved past
Beth-Aven,[i] the Israelite troops were
weak from hunger. 25-26 The army and
the people who lived nearby had gone
into a forest, and they came to a place
where honey was dripping on the
ground.[j] But no one ate any of it, because they were afraid of being put under the curse.
27 Jonathan did not know about Saul's
warning to the soldiers. So he dipped
the end of his walking stick in the
honey and ate some with his fingers. He
felt stronger and more alert. 28 Then a
soldier told him, "Your father swore that
anyone who ate food today would be put
under a curse, and we agreed not to eat.
That's why we're so weak."
29 Jonathan said, "My father has
caused you a lot of trouble. Look at me!
I had only a little of this honey, but already I feel strong and alert. 30 I wish
you had eaten some of the food the
Philistines left behind. We would have
been able to kill a lot more of them."
31 By evening the Israelite army was
exhausted from killing Philistines all
the way from Michmash to Aijalon.[k]
32 They grabbed the food they had captured from the Philistines and started
eating. They even killed sheep and cows
and calves right on the ground and ate
the meat without draining the blood.[l]
33 Someone told Saul, "Look! The army
is disobeying the LORD by eating meat
before the blood drains out."
"You're right," Saul answered. "They
are being unfaithful to the LORD! Hurry!
Roll a big rock over here.[m] 34 Then tell

[c] **14.13** *Jonathan killed . . . from behind*: Or "Jonathan attacked the Philistines with his sword, and the soldier killed those who fell to the ground wounded." [d] **14.14** *a hundred feet*: One possible meaning for the difficult Hebrew text. [e] **14.15** *Then . . . tremble*: Or "Then the ground began to tremble, and everyone was in a terrible panic." Or "Then the ground began to tremble, and God made them all panic." [f] **14.16** *Geba*: See the note at 14.1-3. [g] **14.18** *At that time . . . should do*: One ancient translation; Hebrew "Saul told Ahijah, 'Bring the sacred chest,' because at that time it was with the army of Israel." [h] **14.21** *hired soldiers*: See the note at 13.7. [i] **14.23,24** *Beth-Aven*: See the note at 13.5. [j] **14.25,26** *The army . . . ground*: One possible meaning for the difficult Hebrew text. [k] **14.31** *Aijalon*: About 20 miles west of Michmash. [l] **14.32** *blood*: The Israelites were supposed to drain the blood from a butchered animal before the meat was cooked and eaten (see Genesis 9.4; Leviticus 17.11; Deuteronomy 12.23). [m] **14.33** *over here*: One ancient translation; Hebrew "today."

everyone in camp to bring their cattle
and lambs to me. They can kill the animals on this rock,[n] then eat the meat.
That way no one will disobey the LORD
by eating meat with blood still in it."
That night the soldiers brought their
cattle over to the big rock and killed
them there. 35It was the first altar Saul
had built for offering sacrifices to the
LORD.[o]

The Army Rescues Jonathan

36Saul said, "Let's attack the Philistines again while it's still dark. We can
fight them all night. Let's kill them and
take everything they own!"
The people answered, "We will do
whatever you want."
"Wait!" Ahijah the priest said. "Let's
ask God what we should do."
37Saul asked God, "Should I attack the
Philistines? Will you help us win?"
This time God did not answer. 38Saul
called his army officers together and
said, "We have to find out what sin has
kept God from answering. 39I swear by
the living LORD that whoever sinned
must die, even if it turns out to be my
own son Jonathan."
No one said a word.
40Saul told his army, "You stand on
that side of the priest, and Jonathan and
I will stand on the other side."
Everyone agreed.
41Then Saul prayed, "Our LORD, God
of Israel, why haven't you answered me
today? Please show us who sinned. Was
it my son Jonathan and I, or was it your
people Israel?"[p]
The answer came back that Jonathan
or Saul had sinned, not the army. 42Saul
told Ahijah, "Now ask the LORD to decide between Jonathan and me."
The answer came back that Jonathan
had sinned. 43"Jonathan," Saul exclaimed, "tell me what you did!"
"I dipped the end of my walking stick
in some honey and ate a little. Now you
say I have to die!"
44"Yes, Jonathan. I swear to God that
you must die."
45"No!" the soldiers shouted. "God
helped Jonathan win the battle for us.
We won't let you kill him. We swear to
the LORD that we won't let you kill him
or even lay a hand on him!" So the army
kept Saul from killing Jonathan.
46Saul stopped hunting down the
Philistines, and they went home.

Saul Fights His Enemies

47-48When Saul became king, the
Moabites, the Ammonites, the Edomites,
the kings of Zobah, the Philistines, and
the Amalekites had all been robbing the
Israelites. Saul fought back against
these enemies and stopped them from
robbing Israel. He was a brave commander and always won his battles.[q]

Saul's Family

49-51Saul's wife was Ahinoam, the
daughter of Ahimaaz. They had three
sons: Jonathan, Ishvi,[r] and Malchishua.
They also had two daughters: The older
one was Merab, and the younger one
was Michal.
Abner, Saul's cousin, was the commander of the army. Saul's father Kish
and Abner's father Ner were sons of
Abiel.

War with the Philistines

52Saul was at war with the Philistines
for as long as he lived. Whenever he
found a good warrior or a brave man,
Saul made him join his army.

Saul Disobeys the LORD

15 One day, Samuel told Saul:
The LORD had me choose you
to be king of his people, Israel. Now
listen to this message from the LORD:
2"When the Israelites were on their
way out of Egypt, the nation of
Amalek attacked them. I am the
LORD All-Powerful, and now I am going to make Amalek pay!
3"Go and attack the Amalekites!
Destroy them and all their possessions. Don't have any pity. Kill their
men, women, children, and even
their babies. Slaughter their cattle,
sheep, camels, and donkeys."
4Saul sent messengers who told every
town and village to send men to join the
army at Telaim. There were two hundred ten thousand troops in all, and ten
thousand of these were from Judah.
Saul organized them, 5then led them to
a valley near one of the towns in[s]
Amalek, where they got ready to make
a surprise attack. 6Some Kenites lived
nearby, and Saul told them, "Your people were kind to our nation when we left
Egypt, and I don't want you to get killed
when I wipe out the Amalekites. Leave
here and stay away from them."
The Kenites left, 7and Saul attacked
the Amalekites from Havilah[t] to Shur,

[n] **14.34** *kill . . . rock*: That is, up off the ground so the blood could drain out. [o] **14.35** *offering sacrifices to the LORD*: Even when animals were killed for food, it was often done as a sacrifice to the LORD. [p] **14.41** *why . . . Israel*: One ancient translation; Hebrew "give me an answer." [q] **14.47,48** *won his battles*: One ancient translation; Hebrew "hurt them." [r] **14.49-51** *Ishvi*: Also known as Eshbaal (see 1 Chronicles 8.33; 9.39) and Ishbosheth (see 2 Samuel 2.8-13; 3.8-15; 4.5-12). [s] **15.5** *one . . . in*: Or "the town of." [t] **15.7** *from Havilah*: Or "from the valley" (see 15.5).

which is just east of Egypt. [8]Every
Amalekite was killed except King Agag.
[9]Saul and his army let Agag live, and
they also spared the best sheep and cattle. They didn't want to destroy anything of value, so they only killed the
animals that were worthless or weak.[u]

The LORD Rejects Saul

[10]The LORD told Samuel, [11]"Saul has
stopped obeying me, and I'm sorry that I
made him king."
Samuel was angry, and he cried out in
prayer to the LORD all night. [12]Early the
next morning he went to talk with Saul.
Someone told him, "Saul went to
Carmel, where he had a monument built
so everyone would remember his victory. Then he left for Gilgal."
[13]Samuel finally caught up with Saul,[v]
and Saul told him, "I hope the LORD will
bless you! I have done what the LORD
told me."
[14]"Then why," Samuel asked, "do I
hear sheep and cattle?"
[15]"The army took them from the
Amalekites," Saul explained. "They kept
the best sheep and cattle, so they could
sacrifice them to the LORD your God.
But we destroyed everything else."
[16]"Stop!" Samuel said. "Let me tell
you what the LORD told me last night."
"All right," Saul answered.
[17]Samuel continued, "You may not
think you're very important, but the
LORD chose you to be king, and you are
in charge of the tribes of Israel. [18]When
the LORD sent you on this mission, he
told you to wipe out those worthless
Amalekites. [19]Why didn't you listen to
the LORD? Why did you keep the animals and make him angry?"
[20]"But I did listen to the LORD!" Saul
answered. "He sent me on a mission,
and I went. I captured King Agag and
destroyed his nation. [21]All the animals
were going to be destroyed[w] anyway.
That's why the army brought the best
sheep and cattle to Gilgal as sacrifices
to the LORD your God."
[22]"Tell me," Samuel said. "Does the
LORD really want sacrifices and offerings? No! He doesn't want your sacrifices. He wants you to obey him. [23]Re-
belling against God or disobeying him
because you are proud is just as bad as
worshiping idols or asking them for advice. You refused to do what God told
you, so God has decided that you can't
be king."
[24]"I have sinned," Saul admitted. "I
disobeyed both you and the LORD. I was
afraid of the army, and I listened to
them instead. [25]Please forgive me and
come back with me so I can worship the
LORD."
[26]"No!" Samuel replied, "You disobeyed the LORD, and I won't go back
with you. Now the LORD has said that
you can't be king of Israel any longer."
[27]As Samuel turned to go, Saul
grabbed the edge of Samuel's robe. It
tore! [28]Samuel said, "The LORD has torn
the kingdom of Israel away from you today, and he will give it to someone who
is better than you. [29]Besides, the
eternal[x] God of Israel isn't a human being. He doesn't tell lies or change his
mind."
[30]Saul said, "I did sin, but please
honor me in front of the leaders of the
army and the people of Israel. Come
back with me, so I can worship the LORD
your God."
[31]Samuel followed Saul back, and
Saul worshiped the LORD. [32]Then
Samuel shouted, "Bring me King Agag
of Amalek!"
Agag came in chains,[y] and he was
saying to himself, "Surely they won't
kill me now."[z]
[33]But Samuel said, "Agag, you have
snatched children from their mothers'
arms and killed them. Now your mother
will be without children." Then Samuel
chopped Agag to pieces at the place of
worship in Gilgal.
[34]Samuel went home to Ramah, and
Saul returned to his home in Gibeah.
[35]Even though Samuel felt sad about
Saul, Samuel never saw him again.

The LORD Chooses David To Be King

16 The LORD was sorry he had made
Saul the king of Israel. [1]One day
he said, "Samuel, I've rejected Saul, and
I refuse to let him be king any longer.
Stop feeling sad about him. Put some
olive oil[a] in a small container[b] and go
visit a man named Jesse, who lives in
Bethlehem. I've chosen one of his sons
to be my king."
[2]Samuel answered, "If I do that, Saul
will find out and have me killed."
"Take a calf with you," the LORD
replied. "Tell everyone that you've come

[u]**15.9** *animals . . . weak*: One possible meaning for the difficult Hebrew text. [v]**15.13** *Saul*: One ancient translation adds "Saul had sacrificed to the LORD the best animals they had taken from Amalek, when Samuel came up to him . . ." [w]**15.21** *animals . . . destroyed*: The Hebrew means things that were set aside for God. They could not be used for anything else, so they had to be destroyed. [x]**15.29** *eternal*: Or "glorious." [y]**15.32** *in chains*: One possible meaning for the difficult Hebrew text. [z]**15.32** *Surely . . . now*: Hebrew; one ancient translation "It would have been better to die in battle!" [a]**16.1** *olive oil*: See the note at 9.16. [b]**16.1** *small container*: Hebrew "horn"; animal horns were sometimes hollowed out and used as containers.

to offer it as a sacrifice to me, 3then invite Jesse to the sacrifice.[c] When I show
you which one of his sons I have chosen, pour the olive oil on his head."
4Samuel did what the LORD told him
and went to Bethlehem. The town leaders went to meet him, but they were terribly afraid and asked, "Is this a friendly
visit?"
5"Yes, it is!" Samuel answered. "I've
come to offer a sacrifice to the LORD.
Get yourselves ready[d] to take part in the
sacrifice and come with me." Samuel
also invited Jesse and his sons to come
to the sacrifice, and he got them ready
to take part.
6When Jesse and his sons arrived,
Samuel noticed Jesse's oldest son, Eliab.
"He has to be the one the LORD has chosen," Samuel said to himself.
7But the LORD told him, "Samuel, don't
think Eliab is the one just because he's
tall and handsome. He isn't the one I've
chosen. People judge others by what
they look like, but I judge people by
what is in their hearts."
8Jesse told his son Abinadab to go
over to Samuel, but Samuel said, "No,
the LORD hasn't chosen him."
9Next, Jesse sent his son Shammah to
him, and Samuel said, "The LORD hasn't
chosen him either."
10Jesse had all seven of his sons go
over to Samuel. Finally, Samuel said,
"Jesse, the LORD hasn't chosen any of
these young men. 11Do you have any
more sons?"

"Yes," Jesse answered. "My youngest
son David is out taking care of the
sheep."

"Send for him!" Samuel said. "We
won't start the ceremony until he gets
here."
12Jesse sent for David. He was a
healthy, good-looking boy with a
sparkle in his eyes. As soon as David
came, the LORD told Samuel, "He's the
one! Get up and pour the olive oil on his
head."[e]
13Samuel poured the oil on David's
head while his brothers watched. At that
moment, the Spirit of the LORD took
control of David and stayed with him
from then on.

Samuel returned home to Ramah.

David Plays the Harp for Saul

14The Spirit of the LORD had left Saul,
and an evil spirit from the LORD was terrifying him. 15"It's an evil spirit from
God that's frightening you," Saul's officials told him. 16"Your Majesty, let us go
and look for someone who is good at
playing the harp. He can play for you
whenever the evil spirit from God both-
ers you, and you'll feel better."
17"All right," Saul answered. "Find me
someone who is good at playing the
harp and bring him here."
18"A man named Jesse who lives in
Bethlehem has a son who can play the
harp," one official said. "He's a brave
warrior, he's good-looking, he can speak
well, and the LORD is with him."
19Saul sent a message to Jesse: "Tell
your son David to leave your sheep and
come here to me."
20Jesse loaded a donkey with bread
and a goatskin full of wine,[f] then he told
David to take the donkey and a young
goat to Saul. 21David went to Saul and
started working for him. Saul liked him
so much that he put David in charge of
carrying his weapons. 22Not long after
this, Saul sent another message to Jesse:
"I really like David. Please let him stay
with me."
23Whenever the evil spirit from God
bothered Saul, David would play his
harp. Saul would relax and feel better,
and the evil spirit would go away.

Goliath Challenges Israel's Army

17 The Philistines got ready for war
and brought their troops together
to attack the town of Socoh in Judah.
They set up camp at Ephes-Dammim,
between Socoh and Azekah.[g] 2-3King
Saul and the Israelite army set up camp
on a hill overlooking Elah Valley, and
they got ready to fight the Philistine
army that was on a hill on the other side
of the valley.
4The Philistine army had a hero
named Goliath who was from the town
of Gath and was over nine feet[h] tall.
5-6He wore a bronze helmet and had
bronze armor to protect his chest and
legs. The chest armor alone weighed
about one hundred twenty-five pounds.
He carried a bronze sword strapped on
his back, 7and his spear was so big that
the iron spearhead alone weighed more
than fifteen pounds. A soldier always
walked in front of Goliath to carry his
shield.
8Goliath went out and shouted to the
army of Israel:

[c]**16.3** *sacrifice*: A sacrifice often involved a dinner where the meat from the sacrificed animal would be served. [d]**16.5** *Get yourselves ready*: The people of Israel sometimes had to perform certain ceremonies to make themselves acceptable to God. [e]**16.12** *olive oil on his head*: See the note at 9.16. [f]**16.20** *wine*: Wine was sometimes kept in bottles made of goatskin sewn up with the fur on the outside. [g]**17.1** *Socoh and Azekah*: Socoh was controlled by the Israelites, while Azekah was in Philistine hands. [h]**17.4** *over nine feet*: The Standard Hebrew Text; the Dead Sea Scrolls and some manuscripts of one ancient translation have "almost seven feet."

Why are you lining up for battle?
I'm the best soldier in our army, and
all of you are in Saul's army. Choose
your best soldier to come out and
fight me! 9 If he can kill me, our people will be your slaves. But if I kill
him, your people will be our slaves.
10 Here and now I challenge Israel's
whole army! Choose someone to
fight me!
11 Saul and his men heard what Goliath said, but they were so frightened of
Goliath that they couldn't do a thing.

David Meets King Saul

12 David's father Jesse was an old
man, who belonged to the Ephrath
clan and lived in Bethlehem in Judah.
Jesse had eight sons: 13-14 the oldest was
Eliab, the next was Abinadab, and
Shammah was the third. The three of
them had gone off to fight in Saul's
army.
David was Jesse's youngest son. 15 He
took care of his father's sheep, and he
went back and forth between Bethlehem
and Saul's camp.
16 Goliath came out and gave his challenge every morning and every evening
for forty days.
17 One day, Jesse told David, "Hurry
and take this sack of roasted grain and
these ten loaves of bread to your brothers at the army camp. 18 And here are
ten large chunks of cheese to take to
their commanding officer. Find out how
your brothers are doing and bring back
something that shows that they're all
right. 19 They're with Saul's army, fighting the Philistines in Elah Valley."
20 David obeyed his father. He got up
early the next morning and left someone else in charge of the sheep; then he
loaded the supplies and started off. He
reached the army camp just as the soldiers were taking their places and
shouting the battle cry. 21 The army of Israel and the Philistine army stood there
facing each other.
22 David left his things with the man in
charge of supplies and ran up to the battle line to ask his brothers if they were
well. 23 While David was talking with
them, Goliath came out from the line of
Philistines and started boasting as
usual. David heard him.
24 When the Israelite soldiers saw Goliath, they were scared and ran off.
25 They said to each other, "Look how he
keeps coming out to insult us. The king
is offering a big reward to the man who
kills Goliath. That man will even get to
marry the king's daughter, and no one
in his family will ever have to pay taxes
again."
26 David asked some soldiers standing
nearby, "What will a man get for killing
this Philistine and stopping him from insulting our people? Who does that
worthless Philistine think he is? He's
making fun of the army of the living
God!"
27 The soldiers told David what the
king would give the man who killed Goliath.
28 David's oldest brother Eliab heard
him talking with the soldiers. Eliab was
angry at him and said, "What are you
doing here, anyway? Who's taking care
of that little flock of sheep out in the
desert? You spoiled brat! You came here
just to watch the fighting, didn't you?"
29 "Now what have I done?" David answered. "Can't I even ask a question?"
30 Then he turned and asked another soldier the same thing he had asked the
others, and he got the same answer.
31 Some soldiers overheard David talking, so they told Saul what David had
said. Saul sent for David, and David
came. 32 "Your Majesty," he said, "this
Philistine shouldn't turn us into cowards. I'll go out and fight him myself!"
33 "You don't have a chance against
him," Saul replied. "You're only a boy,
and he's been a soldier all his life."
34 But David told him:
Your Majesty, I take care of my
father's sheep. And when one of
them is dragged off by a lion or a
bear, 35 I go after it and beat the wild
animal until it lets the sheep go. If
the wild animal turns and attacks
me, I grab it by the throat and kill it.
36 Sir, I have killed lions and bears
that way, and I can kill this worthless Philistine. He shouldn't have
made fun of the army of the living
God! 37 The LORD has rescued me
from the claws of lions and bears,
and he will keep me safe from the
hands of this Philistine.
"All right," Saul answered, "go ahead
and fight him. And I hope the LORD will
help you."
38 Saul had his own military clothes
and armor put on David, and he gave
David a bronze helmet to wear. 39 David
strapped on a sword and tried to walk
around, but he was not used to wearing
those things.
"I can't move with all this stuff on,"
David said. "I'm just not used to it."
David took off the armor 40 and picked
up his shepherd's stick. He went out to a
stream and picked up five smooth rocks
and put them in his leather bag. Then
with his sling in his hand, he went
straight toward Goliath.

David Kills Goliath

41 Goliath came toward David, walking
behind the soldier who was carrying his
shield. 42 When Goliath saw that David
was just a healthy, good-looking boy, he
made fun of him. 43 "Do you think I'm a

dog?" Goliath asked. "Is that why you've
come after me with a stick?" He cursed
David in the name of the Philistine gods
44and shouted, "Come on! When I'm finished with you, I'll feed you to the birds
and wild animals!"
45David answered:

You've come out to fight me with a
sword and a spear and a dagger. But
I've come out to fight you in the
name of the LORD All-Powerful. He
is the God of Israel's army, and you
have insulted him too!

46Today the LORD will help me defeat you. I'll knock you down and
cut off your head, and I'll feed the
bodies of the other Philistine soldiers to the birds and wild animals.
Then the whole world will know that
Israel has a real God. 47Everybody
here will see that the LORD doesn't
need swords or spears to save his
people. The LORD always wins his
battles, and he will help us defeat
you.

48When Goliath started forward,
David ran toward him. 49He put a rock
in his sling and swung the sling around
by its straps. When he let go of one
strap, the rock flew out and hit Goliath
on the forehead. It cracked his skull,
and he fell facedown on the ground.
50David defeated Goliath with a sling
and a rock. He killed him without even
using a sword.
51David ran over and pulled out Goliath's sword. Then he used it to cut off
Goliath's head.

When the Philistines saw what had
happened to their hero, they started
running away. 52But the soldiers of Israel and Judah let out a battle cry and
went after them as far as Gath[i] and
Ekron. The bodies of the Philistines
were scattered all along the road from
Shaaraim to Gath and Ekron.
53When the Israelite army returned
from chasing the Philistines, they took
what they wanted from the enemy
camp. 54David took Goliath's head to
Jerusalem, but he kept Goliath's
weapons in his own tent.

David Becomes One of Saul's Officers

55After King Saul had watched David
go out to fight Goliath, Saul turned to
the commander of his army and said,
"Abner, who is that young man?"

"Your Majesty," Abner answered, "I
swear by your life that I don't know."
56"Then find out!" Saul told him.
57When David came back from fighting Goliath, he was still carrying Goliath's head.
Abner took David to Saul, 58and Saul
asked, "Who are you?"

"I am David the son of Jesse, a loyal
Israelite from Bethlehem."

18 David and Saul finished talking,
and soon David and Jonathan[j]
became best friends. Jonathan thought
as much of David as he did of himself.
2From that time on, Saul kept David in
his service and would not let David go
back to his own family.
3Jonathan liked David so much that
they promised to always be loyal
friends. 4Jonathan took off the robe that
he was wearing and gave it to David.
He also gave him his military clothes,[k]
his sword, his bow and arrows, and his
belt.
5David was a success in everything
that Saul sent him to do, and Saul made
him a high officer in his army. That
pleased everyone, including Saul's other
officers.

Saul Becomes David's Enemy

6David had killed Goliath, the battle
was over, and the Israelite army set out
for home. As the army went along,
women came out of each Israelite town
to welcome King Saul. They were
singing happy songs and dancing to the
music of tambourines and harps. 7They
sang:

Saul has killed
a thousand enemies;
David has killed
ten thousand enemies!

8This song made Saul very angry, and
he thought, "They are saying that David
has killed ten times more enemies than I
ever did. Next they will want to make
him king." 9Saul never again trusted
David.
10The next day the LORD let an evil
spirit take control of Saul, and he began
acting like a crazy man inside his
house. David came to play the harp for
Saul as usual, but this time Saul had a
spear in his hand. 11Saul thought, "I'll
pin David to the wall." He threw the
spear at David twice, but David dodged
and got away both times.
12Saul was afraid of David, because
the LORD was helping David and was no
longer helping him. 13Saul put David in
charge of a thousand soldiers and sent
him out to fight. 14The LORD helped
David, and he and his soldiers always
won their battles. 15This made Saul even
more afraid of David. 16But everyone
else in Judah and Israel was loyal to[l]
David, because he led the army in battle.

[i] 17.52 *Gath*: One ancient translation; Hebrew "a valley." (see chapter 14).
[k] 18.4 *military clothes*: Or "armor."
[j] 18.1 *Jonathan*: Saul's oldest son
[l] 18.16 *was loyal to*: Or "loved."

17One day, Saul told David, "If you'll be brave and fight the LORD's battles for me, I'll let you marry my oldest daughter Merab." But Saul was really thinking, "I don't want to kill David myself, so I'll let the Philistines do it for me."

18David answered, "How could I possibly marry your daughter? I'm not very important, and neither is my family."

19But when the time came for David to marry Saul's daughter Merab, Saul told her to marry Adriel from the town of Meholah.

20Saul had another daughter. Her name was Michal, and Saul found out that she was in love with David. This made Saul happy, 21and he thought, "I'll tell David he can marry Michal, but I'll set it up so that the Philistines will kill him." He told David, "I'm going to give you a second chance to marry one of my daughters."

22-23Saul ordered his officials to speak to David in private, so they went to David and said, "Look, the king likes you, and all of his officials are loyal to you. Why not ask the king if you can marry his daughter Michal?"

"I'm not rich[m] or famous enough to marry princess Michal!" David answered.

24The officials went back to Saul and told him exactly what David had said. 25Saul was hoping that the Philistines would kill David, and he told his officials to tell David, "The king doesn't want any silver or gold. He only wants to get even with his enemies. All you have to do is to bring back proof that you have killed a hundred Philistines!"[n] 26The officials told David, and David wanted to marry the princess.

King Saul had set a time limit, and before it ran out, 27David and his men left and killed two hundred Philistines. He brought back the proof and showed it to Saul, so he could marry Michal. Saul agreed to let David marry Michal. 28Saul knew that she loved David,[o] and he also realized that the LORD was helping David. 29But knowing those things made Saul even more afraid of David, and he was David's enemy for the rest of his life.

30The Philistine rulers kept coming to fight Israel, but whenever David fought them, he won. He was famous because he won more battles against the Philistines than any of Saul's other officers.

Saul Tries To Have David Killed

19 One day, Saul told his son Jonathan and his officers to kill David. But Jonathan liked David a lot, 2-3and he warned David, "My father is trying to have you killed, so be very careful. Hide in a field tomorrow morning, and I'll bring him there. Then I'll talk to him about you, and if I find out anything, I'll let you know."

4-5The next morning, Jonathan reminded Saul about the many good things David had done for him. Then he said, "Why do you want to kill David? He hasn't done anything to you. He has served in your army and has always done what's best for you. He even risked his life to kill Goliath. The LORD helped Israel win a great victory that day, and it made you happy."

6Saul agreed and promised, "I swear by the living LORD that I won't have David killed!"

7Jonathan called to David and told him what Saul had said. Then he brought David to Saul, and David served in Saul's army just as he had done before.

8The next time there was a war with the Philistines, David fought hard and forced them to retreat.

Michal Helps David Escape

9-10One night, David was in Saul's home, playing the harp for him. Saul was sitting there, holding a spear, when an evil spirit from the LORD took control of him. Saul tried to pin David to the wall with the spear, but David dodged, and it stuck in the wall. David ran out of the house and escaped.

11Saul sent guards to watch David's house all night and then to kill him in the morning.

Michal, David's wife, told him, "If you don't escape tonight, they'll kill you tomorrow!" 12She helped David go through a window and climb down to the ground.[p] As David ran off, 13Michal put a statue in his bed. She put goat hair on its head and dressed it in some of David's clothes.

14The next morning, Saul sent guards to arrest David. But Michal told them, "David is sick."

15Saul sent the guards back and told them, "Get David out of his bed and bring him to me, so I can have him killed."

[m] **18.22,23** *not rich*: It was the custom for a man to give the bride's father some silver or gold in order to marry his daughter, and it would take a large amount to marry the daughter of the king. [n] **18.25** *proof . . . Philistines*: Hebrew "one hundred Philistine foreskins." In ancient times soldiers would sometimes cut off body parts of their dead enemies to prove how many they had killed. [o] **18.28** *she . . . David*: Hebrew; one ancient translation "all Israel was loyal to David." [p] **19.12** *ground*: The house was probably built into the town wall, allowing David to come down outside the wall.

16When the guards went in, all they
found in the bed was the statue with the
goat hair on its head.
17"Why have you tricked me this
way?" Saul asked Michal. "You helped
my enemy get away!"
She answered, "He said he would kill
me if I didn't help him escape!"

Samuel Helps David Escape

18Meanwhile, David went to Samuel at
Ramah and told him what Saul had
done. Then Samuel and David went to
Prophets Village[q] and stayed there.
19Someone told Saul, "David is at
Prophets Village in Ramah."
20Saul sent a few soldiers to bring
David back. They went to Ramah and
found Samuel in charge of a group of
prophets who were all prophesying.
Then the Spirit of God took control of
the soldiers and they started prophesying too.
21When Saul heard what had happened, he sent another group of soldiers, but they prophesied the same way.
He sent a third group of soldiers, but the
same thing happened to them. 22Finally,
Saul left for Ramah himself. He went as
far as the deep pit[r] at the town of Secu,
and he asked, "Where are Samuel and
David?"
"At Prophets Village in Ramah," the
people answered.
23Saul left for Ramah. But as he
walked along, the Spirit of God took
control of him, and he started prophesying. Then, when he reached Prophets
Village, 24he stripped off his clothes and
prophesied in front of Samuel. He
dropped to the ground and lay there
naked all day and night. That's how the
saying started, "Is Saul now a prophet?"

Jonathan Helps David Escape

20 David escaped from Prophets Village. Then he ran to see Jonathan
and asked, "Why does your father Saul
want to kill me? What have I done
wrong?"
2"My father can't be trying to kill you!
He never does anything without telling
me about it. Why would he hide this
from me? It can't be true!"
3"Jonathan, I swear it's true! But your
father knows how much you like me,
and he didn't want to break your heart.
That's why he didn't tell you. I swear by
the living LORD and by your own life
that I'm only one step ahead of death."
4Then Jonathan said, "Tell me what to
do, and I'll do it."
5David answered:
Tomorrow is the New Moon Festival,[s] and I'm supposed to eat dinner
with your father. But instead, I'll
hide in a field until the evening of
the next day. 6If Saul wonders where
I am, tell him, "David asked me to let
him go to his hometown of Bethlehem, so he could take part in a sacrifice his family makes there every
year."
7If your father says it's all right,
then I'm safe. But if he gets angry,
you'll know he wants to harm me.
8Be kind to me. After all, it was your
idea to promise the LORD that we
would always be loyal friends. If I've
done anything wrong, kill me yourself, but don't hand me over to your
father.
9"Don't worry," Jonathan said. "If I
find out that my father wants to kill you,
I'll certainly let you know."
10"How will you do that?" David
asked.
11"Let's go out to this field, and I'll tell
you," Jonathan answered.
When they got there, 12Jonathan said:
I swear by the LORD God of Israel,
that two days from now I'll know
what my father is planning. Of
course I'll let you know if he's
friendly toward you. 13But if he
wants to harm you, I promise to tell
you and help you escape. And I ask
the LORD to punish me severely if I
don't keep my promise.
I pray that the LORD will bless you,
just as he used to bless my father.
14-15Someday the LORD will wipe out
all of your enemies. Then if I'm still
alive, please be as kind to me as the
LORD has been. But if I'm dead, be
kind to my family.
16Jonathan and David made an agreement that even David's descendants
would have to keep.[t] Then Jonathan
said, "I pray that the LORD will take revenge on your descendants if they break
our promise."[u]
17Jonathan thought as much of David
as he did of himself, so he asked David
to promise once more that he would be
a loyal friend. 18After this Jonathan
said:
Tomorrow is the New Moon Festival, and people will wonder where
you are, because your place will be
empty. 19By the day after tomorrow,

[q] **19.18** *Prophets Village*: Or "Naioth."
[r] **19.22** *pit*: A cistern, a large pit dug down into the rock and used for storing rainwater.
[s] **20.5** *New Moon Festival*: The first day of the month, when Israelites offered special sacrifices to the LORD and had special sacred meals.
[t] **20.16** *Jonathan . . . keep*: Or, continuing Jonathan's statement to David, "You and your descendants must not kill off my descendants."
[u] **20.16** *I pray . . . promise*: Or "I pray that the LORD take revenge on you if you break our promise!"

everyone will think you've been
gone a long time.[v] Then go to the
place where you hid before and stay
beside Going-Away Rock.[w] 20I'll
shoot three arrows at a target off to
the side of the rock, 21and send my
servant to find the arrows.

You'll know if it's safe to come out
by what I tell him. If it is safe, I
swear by the living LORD that I'll say,
"The arrows are on this side of you!
Pick them up!" 22But if it isn't safe,
I'll say to the boy, "The arrows are
farther away!" This will mean that
the LORD wants you to leave, and
you must go. 23But he will always
watch us to make sure that we keep
the promise we made to each other.
24So David hid there in the field.

During the New Moon Festival, Saul
sat down to eat 25by the wall, just as he
always did. Jonathan sat across from
him,[x] and Abner sat next to him. But
David's place was empty. 26Saul didn't
say anything that day, because he was
thinking, "Something must have happened to make David unfit to be at the
Festival.[y] Yes, something must have happened."

27The day after the New Moon Festival, when David's place was still empty,
Saul asked Jonathan, "Why hasn't that
son of Jesse come to eat with us? He
wasn't here yesterday, and he still isn't
here today!"

28-29Jonathan answered, "The reason
David hasn't come to eat with you is
that he begged me to let him go to Bethlehem. He said, 'Please let me go. My
family is offering a sacrifice, and my
brother told me I have to be there. Do
me this favor and let me slip away to see
my brothers.' "

30Saul was furious with Jonathan and
yelled, "You're no son of mine, you traitor! I know you've chosen to be loyal to
that son of Jesse. You should be
ashamed of yourself! And your own
mother should be ashamed that you
were ever born. 31You'll never be safe,
and your kingdom will be in danger as
long as that son of Jesse is alive. Turn
him over to me now! He deserves to
die!"

32"Why do you want to kill David?"
Jonathan asked. "What has he done?"

33Saul threw his spear at Jonathan
and tried to kill him. Then Jonathan was
sure that his father really did want to
kill David. 34Jonathan was angry that
his father had insulted David[z] so terribly. He got up, left the table, and didn't
eat anything all that day.

35In the morning, Jonathan went out
to the field to meet David. He took a servant boy along 36and told him, "When I
shoot the arrows, you run and find them
for me."

The boy started running, and Jonathan shot an arrow so that it would go
beyond him. 37When the boy got near
the place where the arrow had landed,
Jonathan shouted, "Isn't the arrow on
past you?" 38Jonathan shouted to him
again, "Hurry up! Don't stop!"

The boy picked up the arrows and
brought them back to Jonathan, 39but
he had no idea about what was going
on. Only Jonathan and David knew.
40Jonathan gave his weapons to the boy
and told him, "Take these back into
town."

41After the boy had gone, David got
up from beside the mound[a] and bowed
very low three times. Then he and
Jonathan kissed[b] each other and cried,
but David cried louder. 42Jonathan said,
"Take care of yourself. And remember,
we each have asked the LORD to watch
and make sure that we and our descendants keep our promise forever."

David left and Jonathan went back to
town.

Ahimelech Helps David

21 David went to see Ahimelech, a
priest who lived in the town of
Nob. Ahimelech was trembling with
fear as he came out to meet David.
"Why are you alone?" Ahimelech asked.
"Why isn't anyone else with you?"

2"I'm on a mission for King Saul,"
David answered. "He ordered me not to
tell anyone what the mission is all
about, so I had my soldiers stay somewhere else. 3Do you have any food you
can give me? Could you spare five
loaves of bread?"

4"The only bread I have is the sacred
bread," the priest told David. "You can
have it if your soldiers didn't sleep with
women last night."[c]

5"Of course we didn't sleep with
women," David answered. "I never let

[v]20.19 *By . . . time*: One possible meaning for the difficult Hebrew text. [w]20.19 *Going-Away Rock*: Or "Ezel Rock"; one ancient translation "that mound" (see 20.41). [x]20.25 *sat . . . him*: One ancient translation; Hebrew "stood up." [y]20.26 *unfit . . . Festival*: During the New Moon Festival a sacred meal was served that could only be eaten by people who were properly prepared. Some of the things that could make a person unfit are listed in Leviticus 7.20, 21; 15.2, 31; 22.4-8; Deuteronomy 23.10, 11. [z]20.34 *insulted David*: Or "insulted him" (that is, Jonathan). [a]20.41 *the mound*: One ancient translation; Hebrew "from the south side." [b]20.41 *kissed*: A common way of greeting or saying good-by in biblical times (see Mark 14.44). [c]21.4 *night*: Having sex was one of the things that would make someone temporarily unfit to take part in worship or a sacred meal (see Exodus 19.15; Leviticus 15.18).

my men do that when we're on a mission. They have to be acceptable to worship God even when we're on a regular
mission, and today we're on a special
mission."
6 The only bread the priest had was
the sacred bread that he had taken from
the place of worship after putting out
the fresh loaves. So he gave it to David.
7 It so happened that one of Saul's officers was there, worshiping the LORD
that day. His name was Doeg the
Edomite,[d] and he was the strongest of[e]
Saul's shepherds.
8 David asked Ahimelech, "Do you
have a spear or a sword? I had to leave
so quickly on this mission for the king
that I didn't bring along my sword or
any other weapons."
9 The priest answered, "The only
sword here is the one that belonged to
Goliath the Philistine. You were the one
who killed him in Elah Valley, and so
you can take his sword if you want to.
It's wrapped in a cloth behind the
statue."
"It's the best sword there is," David
said. "I'll take it!"

David Tries To Find Safety in Gath

10 David kept on running from Saul
that day until he came to Gath,[f] where
he met with King Achish. 11 The officers
of King Achish were also there, and
they asked Achish, "Isn't David a king
back in his own country? Don't the Israelites dance and sing,

'Saul has killed
    a thousand enemies;
David has killed
    ten thousand enemies'?"

12 David thought about what they were
saying, and it made him afraid of
Achish. 13 So right there in front of
everyone, he pretended to be insane. He
acted confused and scratched up the
doors of the town gate, while drooling in
his beard.
14 "Look at him!" Achish said to his officers. "You can see he's crazy. Why did
you bring him to me? 15 I have enough
crazy people without your bringing another one here. Keep him away from my
palace!"

People Join David

22 When David escaped from the
town of Gath, he went to Adullam
Cave. His brothers and the rest of his
family found out where he was, and
they followed him there. 2 A lot of other
people joined him too. Some were in
trouble, others were angry or in debt,
and David was soon the leader of four
hundred men.
3 David left Adullam Cave and went to
the town of Mizpeh in Moab, where he
talked with the king of Moab. "Please,"
David said, "let my father and mother
stay with you until I find out what God
will do with me." 4 So he brought his
parents to the king of Moab, and they
stayed with him while David was in hiding.
5 One day the prophet Gad told David,
"Don't stay here! Go back to Judah."
David then left and went to Hereth Forest.

Saul Kills the Priests of the LORD

6 Saul was sitting under a small tree
on top of the hill at Gibeah when he
heard that David and his men had been
seen. Saul was holding his spear, and
his officers were standing in front of
him. 7 He told them:
    Listen to me! You belong to the
    Benjamin tribe,[g] so if that son of
    Jesse ever becomes king, he won't
    give you fields or vineyards. He
    won't make you officers in charge of
    thousands or hundreds as I have
    done. 8 But you're all plotting against
    me! Not one of you told me that my
    own son Jonathan had made an
    agreement with him. Not one of you
    cared enough to tell me that
    Jonathan had helped one of my offi-
    cers[h] rebel. Now that son of Jesse is
    trying to ambush me.
9 Doeg the Edomite was standing with
the other officers and spoke up, "When I
was in the town of Nob, I saw that son
of Jesse. He was visiting the priest
Ahimelech the son of Ahitub. 10 Ahimelech talked to the LORD for him, then
gave him food and the sword that had
belonged to Goliath the Philistine."
11 Saul sent a message to Ahimelech
and his whole family of priests at Nob,
ordering them to come to him. When
they came, 12 Saul told them, "Listen to
me, you son of Ahitub."
"Certainly, Your Majesty," Ahimelech
answered.
13 Saul demanded, "Why did you plot
against me with that son of Jesse? You
helped him rebel against me by giving
him food and a sword, and by talking
with God for him. Now he's trying to
ambush me!"
14 "Your Majesty, none of your officers
is more loyal than David!" Ahimelech

[d] 21.7 *Edomite*: A person from the country of Edom, to the south of Israel. [e] 21.7 *the strongest of*: Or "in charge of." [f] 21.10 *Gath*: One of the five main Philistine towns.
[g] 22.7 *You . . . Benjamin tribe*: David was from the Judah tribe and would have given special privileges to the people of his own tribe rather than to those of Benjamin. [h] 22.7,8 *son of Jesse . . . officers*: That is, David. Saul avoids even saying David's name.

replied. "He's your son-in-law and the
captain of your bodyguard. Everyone in
your family respects him. 15This isn't the
first time I've talked with God for David,
and it's never made you angry before!
Please don't accuse me or my family
like this. I have no idea what's going
on!"
16"Ahimelech," Saul said, "you and
your whole family are going to die."
17Saul shouted to his bodyguards,
"These priests of the LORD helped
David! They knew he was running
away, but they didn't tell me. Kill them!"
But the king's officers would not attack the priests of the LORD.
18Saul turned to Doeg, who was from
Edom, and said, "Kill the priests!"
On that same day, Doeg killed eighty-
five priests. 19Then he attacked the town
of Nob, where the priests had lived, and
he killed everyone there—men, women,
children, and babies. He even killed
their cattle, donkeys, and sheep.

Only Abiathar Escapes from Nob

20Ahimelech's son Abiathar was the
only one who escaped. He ran to David
21and told him, "Saul has murdered the
priests at Nob!"
22David answered, "That day when I
saw Doeg, I knew he would tell Saul!
Your family died because of me. 23Stay
here. Isn't the same person trying to kill
both of us? Don't worry! You'll be safe
here with me."

David Rescues the Town of Keilah

23 One day some people told David,
"The Philistines keep attacking
the town of Keilah and stealing grain
from the threshing place."
2David asked the LORD, "Should I attack these Philistines?"
"Yes," the LORD answered. "Attack
them and rescue Keilah."
3But David's men said, "Look, even
here in Judah we're afraid of the
Philistines. We will be terrified if we try
to fight them at Keilah!"[i]
4David asked the LORD about it again.
"Leave right now," the LORD answered.
"I will give you victory over the
Philistines at Keilah."
5David and his men went there and
fiercely attacked the Philistines. They
killed many of them, then led away their
cattle, and rescued the people of Keilah.
6-8Meanwhile, Saul heard that David
was in Keilah. "God has let me catch
David," Saul said. "David is trapped inside a walled town where the gates can
be locked." Saul decided to go there and
surround the town, in order to trap
David and his men. He sent messengers
who told the towns and villages, "Send
men to serve in Saul's army!"
By this time, Abiathar had joined
David in Keilah and had brought along
everything he needed to get answers
from God.
9David heard about Saul's plan to
capture him, and he told Abiathar, "Let's
ask God what we should do."
10David prayed, "LORD God of Israel, I
was told that Saul is planning to come
here. What should I do? Suppose he
threatens to destroy the town because of
me. 11Would the leaders of Keilah turn
me over to Saul? Or is he really coming?
Please tell me, LORD."
"Yes, he will come," the LORD answered.
12David asked, "Would the leaders of
Keilah hand me and my soldiers over to
Saul?"
"Yes, they would," the LORD answered.
13David and his six hundred men got
out of there fast and started moving
from place to place. Saul heard that
David had left Keilah, and he decided
not to go after him.

Jonathan Says David Will Be King

14David stayed in hideouts in the hill
country of Ziph Desert. Saul kept
searching, but God never let Saul catch
him.
15One time, David was at Horesh in
Ziph Desert. He was afraid because[j]
Saul had come to the area to kill him.
16But Jonathan went to see David, and
God helped him encourage David.
17"Don't be afraid," Jonathan said. "My
father Saul will never get his hands on
you. In fact, you're going to be the next
king of Israel, and I'll be your highest
official. Even my father knows it's true."
18They both promised the LORD that
they would always be loyal to each
other. Then Jonathan went home, but
David stayed at Horesh.

David Escapes from Saul

19Some people from the town of Ziph
went to Saul at Gibeah and said, "Your
Majesty, David has a hideout not far
from us! It's near Horesh, somewhere
on Mount Hachilah south of Jeshimon.[k]
20If you come, we will help you catch
him."
21Saul told them:
You've done me a big favor, and I
pray that the LORD will bless you.
22Now please do just a little more for
me. Find out exactly where David is,
as well as where he goes, and who
has seen him there. I've been told

[i] 23.3 *Keilah*: Keilah was probably not controlled by Israelites at this time. [j] 23.15 *He . . . because*: Or "He saw that." [k] 23.19 *Jeshimon*: A place in the desert near the southern border of Judah.

that he's very tricky. 23 Find out
where all his hiding places are and
come back when you're sure. Then
I'll go with you. If he is still in the
area, or anywhere among the clans
of Judah, I'll find him.
24 The people from Ziph went back
ahead of Saul, and they found out that
David and his men were still south of
Jeshimon in the Maon Desert. 25 Saul
and his army set out to find David. But
David heard that Saul was coming, and
he went to a place called The Rock, one
of his hideouts in Maon Desert.
Saul found out where David was and
started closing in on him. 26 Saul was going around a hill on one side, and David
and his men were on the other side, trying to get away. Saul and his soldiers
were just about to capture David and
his men, 27 when a messenger came to
Saul and said, "Come quickly! The
Philistines are attacking Israel and taking everything."
28 Saul stopped going after David and
went back to fight the Philistines. That's
why the place is called "Escape Rock."
29 David left and went to live in the
hideouts at En-Gedi.

David Lets Saul Live

24 When Saul got back from fighting
off the Philistines, he heard that
David was in the desert around En-
Gedi. 2 Saul led three thousand of Israel's best soldiers out to look for David
and his men near Wild Goat Rocks at
En-Gedi. 3 There were some sheep pens
along the side of the road, and one of
them was built around the entrance to a
cave. Saul went into the cave to relieve
himself.
David and his men were hiding at the
back of the cave. 4 They whispered to
David, "The LORD told you he was going
to let you defeat your enemies and do
whatever you want with them. This
must be the day the LORD was talking
about."
David sneaked over and cut off a
small piece[l] of Saul's robe, but Saul
didn't notice a thing. 5 Afterwards, David
was sorry that he had even done that,
6–7 and he told his men, "Stop talking
foolishly. We're not going to attack Saul.
He's my king, and I pray that the LORD
will keep me from doing anything to
harm his chosen king."
Saul left the cave and started down
the road. 8 Soon, David also got up and
left the cave. "Your Majesty!" he shouted
from a distance.
Saul turned around to look. David
bowed down very low 9 and said:

Your Majesty, why do you listen to
people who say that I'm trying to
harm you? 10 You can see for yourself
that the LORD gave me the chance to
catch you in the cave today. Some of
my men wanted to kill you, but I
wouldn't let them do it. I told them,
"I will not harm the LORD's chosen
king!" 11 Your Majesty, look at what
I'm holding. You can see that it's a
piece of your robe. If I could cut off a
piece of your robe, I could have
killed you. But I let you live, and that
should prove I'm not trying to harm
you or to rebel. I haven't done anything to you, and yet you keep trying
to ambush and kill me.
12 I'll let the LORD decide which one
of us has done right. I pray that the
LORD will punish you for what
you're doing to me, but I won't do
anything to you. 13 An old proverb
says, "Only evil people do evil
things," and so I won't harm you.
14 Why should the king of Israel be
out chasing me, anyway? I'm as
worthless as a dead dog or a flea. 15 I
pray that the LORD will help me escape and show that I am in the right.
16 "David, my son—is that you?" Saul
asked. Then he started crying 17 and
said:

David, you're a better person than
I am. You treated me with kindness,
even though I've been cruel to you.
18 You've told me how you were kind
enough not to kill me when the LORD
gave you the chance. 19 If you really
were my enemy, you wouldn't have
let me leave here alive. I pray that
the LORD will give you a big reward
for what you did today.
20 I realize now that you will be the
next king, and a powerful king at
that. 21 Promise me with the LORD as
your witness, that you won't wipe
out my descendants. Let them live to
keep my family name alive.
22 So David promised, and Saul went
home. David and his men returned to
their hideout.

Samuel Dies

25 Samuel died, and people from all
over Israel gathered to mourn for
him when he was buried at his home[m]
in Ramah. Meanwhile, David moved his
camp to Paran Desert.[n]

Abigail Keeps David from Killing Innocent People

2-3 Nabal was a very rich man who
lived in Maon. He owned three thousand sheep and a thousand goats, which

[l] 24.4 *small piece*: Hebrew "corner" or "lower hem." [m] 25.1 *at his home*: Hebrew "in his house." Family tombs were sometimes underneath the house or in the courtyard of the home.
[n] 25.1 *Paran Desert*: Hebrew; some manuscripts of one ancient translation "Maon Desert."

he kept at Carmel.[o] His wife Abigail
was sensible and beautiful, but he was
from the Caleb clan[p] and was rough and
mean.
4 One day, Nabal was in Carmel, having his servants cut the wool from his
sheep. David was in the desert when he
heard about it. 5-6 So he sent ten men to
Carmel with this message for Nabal:
I hope that you and your family
are healthy and that all is going well
for you. 7 I've heard that you are cutting the wool from your sheep.
When your shepherds were with
us in Carmel, we didn't harm them,
and nothing was ever stolen from
them. 8 Ask your shepherds, and
they'll tell you the same thing.
My servants are your servants,
and you are like a father to me. This
is a day for celebrating,[q] so please
be kind and share some of your food
with us.
9 David's men went to Nabal and gave
him David's message, then they waited
for Nabal's answer.
10 This is what he said:
Who does this David think he is?
That son of Jesse is just one more
slave on the run from his master,
and there are too many of them
these days. 11 What makes you think
I would take my bread, my water,
and the meat that I've had cooked
for my own servants[r] and give it to
you? Besides, I'm not sure that
David sent you![s]
12 The men returned to their camp and
told David everything Nabal had said.
13 "Everybody get your swords!" David
ordered.
They all strapped on their swords.
Two hundred men stayed behind to
guard the camp, but the other four hundred followed David.
14-16 Meanwhile, one of Nabal's servants told Abigail:
David's men were often nearby
while we were taking care of the
sheep in the fields. They were very
good to us, they never hurt us, and
nothing was ever stolen from us
while they were nearby. With them
around day or night, we were as safe
as we would have been inside a
walled city.
David sent some messengers from
the desert to wish our master well,
but he shouted insults at them.
17 He's a bully who won't listen to
anyone.
Isn't there something you can do?
Please think of something! Or else
our master and his family and
everyone who works for him are all
doomed.
18 Abigail quickly got together two
hundred loaves of bread, two large clay
jars of wine, the meat from five sheep, a
large sack of roasted grain, a hundred
handfuls of raisins, and two hundred
handfuls of dried figs. She loaded all the
food on donkeys 19 and told her servants,
"Take this on ahead, and I'll catch up
with you." She didn't tell her husband
Nabal what she was doing.
20 Abigail was riding her donkey on
the path that led around the hillside,
when suddenly she met David and his
men heading straight at her.
21 David had just been saying, "I surely
wasted my time guarding Nabal's things
in the desert and keeping them from being stolen! I was good to him, and now
he pays me back with insults. 22 I swear
that by morning, there won't be a man
or boy left from his family or his servants' families. I pray that God will punish me[t] if I don't do it!"
23 Abigail quickly got off her donkey
and bowed down in front of David.
24 Then she said:
Sir, please let me explain! 25 Don't
pay any attention to that good-for-
nothing Nabal. His name means
"fool," and it really fits him!
I didn't see the men you sent,
26-27 but please take this gift of food
that I've brought and share it with
your followers. The LORD has kept
you from taking revenge and from
killing innocent people. But I hope
your enemies and anyone else who
wants to harm you will end up like
Nabal. I swear this by the living
LORD and by your life.
28 Please forgive me if I say a little
more. The LORD will always protect
you and your family, because you
fight for him. I pray that you won't
ever do anything evil as long as you
live. 29 The LORD your God will keep
you safe when your enemies try to
kill you. But he will snatch away
their lives quicker than you can
throw a rock from a sling.
30 The LORD has promised to do
many good things for you, even to
make you the ruler of Israel. The
LORD will keep his promises to you,
31 and now your conscience will be
clear, because you won't be guilty of

[o] **25.2,3** *Carmel*: About one mile north of Maon in the Southern Desert of Judah.
[p] **25.2,3** *from the Caleb clan*: Or "behaved like a dog." [q] **25.8** *celebrating*: Cutting the wool from the sheep was a time for celebrating as well as for working. [r] **25.11** *servants*: Hebrew "shearers," the servants who cut the wool from the sheep. [s] **25.11** *I'm not sure . . . sent you*: Or "I don't know where you come from." [t] **25.22** *me*: One ancient translation; Hebrew "my enemies."

taking revenge and killing innocent
people.
When the LORD does all those
good things for you, please remember me.
32David told her:
I praise the LORD God of Israel! He
must have sent you to meet me today. 33And you should also be
praised. Your good sense kept me
from taking revenge and killing innocent people. 34If you hadn't come
to meet me so quickly, every man
and boy in Nabal's family and in his
servants' families would have been
killed by morning. I swear by the living LORD God of Israel who protected you that this is the truth.
35David accepted the food Abigail had
brought. "Don't worry," he said. "You
can go home now. I'll do what you
asked."
36Abigail went back home and found
Nabal throwing a party fit for a king. He
was very drunk and feeling good, so she
didn't tell him anything that night. 37But
when he sobered up the next morning,
Abigail told him everything that had
happened. Nabal had a heart attack,
and he lay in bed as still as a stone.
38Ten days later, the LORD took his life.
39-40David heard that Nabal had died.
"I praise the LORD!" David said. "He has
judged Nabal guilty for insulting me.
The LORD kept me from doing anything
wrong, and he made sure that Nabal
hurt only himself with his own evil."

David and Abigail Are Married

Abigail was still at Carmel. So David
sent messengers to ask her if she would
marry him.
41She bowed down and said, "I would
willingly be David's slave and wash his
servants' feet."
42Abigail quickly got ready and went
back with David's messengers. She rode
on her donkey, while five of her servant
women walked alongside. She and
David were married as soon as she arrived.
43David had earlier married Ahinoam
from the town of Jezreel, so both she
and Abigail were now David's wives.[u]
44Meanwhile, Saul had arranged for
Michal[v] to marry Palti the son of Laish,
who came from the town of Gallim.

David Again Lets Saul Live

26 Once again,[w] some people from
Ziph went to Gibeah to talk with
Saul. "David has a hideout on Mount
Hachilah near Jeshimon out in the
desert," they told him.
2Saul took three thousand of Israel's
best soldiers and went to look for David
there in Ziph Desert. 3Saul set up camp
on Mount Hachilah, which is across the
road from Jeshimon. But David was hiding out in the desert.
When David heard that Saul was following him, 4he sent some spies to find
out if it was true. 5Then he sneaked up
to Saul's camp. He noticed that Saul and
his army commander Abner the son of
Ner were sleeping in the middle of the
camp, with soldiers sleeping all around
them. 6David asked Ahimelech the Hittite and Joab's brother Abishai,[x] "Which
one of you will go with me into Saul's
camp?"
"I will!" Abishai answered.
7That same night, David and Abishai
crept into the camp. Saul was sleeping,
and his spear was stuck in the ground
not far from his head. Abner and the
soldiers were sound asleep all around
him.
8Abishai whispered, "This time God
has let you get your hands on your enemy! I'll pin him to the ground with one
thrust of his own spear."
9"Don't kill him!" David whispered
back. "The LORD will punish anyone
who kills his chosen king. 10As surely as
the LORD lives, the LORD will kill Saul, or
Saul will die a natural death or be killed
in battle. 11But I pray that the LORD will
keep me from harming his chosen king.
Let's grab his spear and his water jar
and get out of here!"
12David took the spear and the water
jar, then left the camp. None of Saul's
soldiers knew what had happened or
even woke up—the LORD had made all
of them fall sound asleep. 13David and
Abishai crossed the valley and went to
the top of the next hill, where they were
at a safe distance. 14"Abner!" David
shouted toward Saul's army. "Can you
hear me?"
Abner shouted back. "Who dares disturb the king?"
15"Abner, what kind of a man are
you?" David replied. "Aren't you supposed to be the best soldier in Israel?
Then why didn't you protect your king?
Anyone who went into your camp could
have killed him tonight.[y] 16You're a
complete failure! I swear by the living
LORD that you and your men deserve to
die for not protecting the LORD's chosen
king. Look and see if you can find the

[u]25.43 *wives*: Having more than one wife was allowed in those times. [v]25.44 *Michal*: David's first wife (see 18.20—19.17). [w]26.1 *again*: See 23.19. [x]26.6 *Abishai*: Hebrew "Abishai the son of Zeruiah." Zeruiah was David's older sister, so Abishai and Joab were David's nephews (see 1 Chronicles 2.12-17; 2 Samuel 17.25 and the note there).
[y]26.15 *Anyone . . . tonight*: Or "Someone went into your camp to kill him tonight."

king's spear and the water jar that were
near his head."
17Saul could tell it was David's voice,
and he called out, "David, my son! Is
that you?"
"Yes it is, Your Majesty. 18Why are you
after me? Have I done something
wrong, or have I committed a crime?
19Please listen to what I have to say. If
the LORD has turned you against me,
maybe a sacrifice will make him change
his mind. But if some people have
turned you against me, I hope the LORD
will punish them! They have forced me
to leave the land that belongs to the
LORD and have told me to worship foreign gods.[z] 20Don't let me die in a land
far away from the LORD. I'm no more
important than a flea! Why should the
king of Israel hunt me down as if I were
a bird in the mountains?"
21"David, you had the chance to kill
me today. But you didn't. I was very
wrong about you. It was a terrible mistake for me to try to kill you. I've acted
like a fool, but I'll never try to harm you
again. You're like a son to me, so please
come back."
22"Your Majesty, here's your spear!
Have one of your soldiers come and get
it. 23The LORD put you in my power today, but you are his chosen king and I
wouldn't harm you. The LORD rewards
people who are faithful and live right.
24I saved your life today, and I pray that
the LORD will protect me and keep me
safe."
25"David, my son, I pray that the Lord
will bless you and make you successful!"

David in Philistia

27 Saul went back home. David also
left, 1but he thought to himself,
"One of these days, Saul is going to kill
me. The only way to escape from him is
to go to Philistia. Then I'll be outside of
Israel, and Saul will give up trying to
catch me."
2-3David and his six hundred men
went across the border to stay in Gath
with King Achish the son of Maoch. His
men brought their families with them.
David brought his wife Ahinoam whose
hometown was Jezreel, and he also
brought his wife Abigail who had been
married to Nabal from Carmel. 4When
Saul found out that David had run off to
Gath, he stopped trying to catch him.
5One day, David was talking with
Achish and said, "If you are happy with
me, then let me live in one of the towns
in the countryside. I'm not important
enough to live here with you in the royal
city."
6Achish gave David the town of Ziklag that same day, and Ziklag has belonged to the kings of Judah ever since.
7David was in Philistia for a year and
four months. 8The Geshurites, the
Girzites, and the Amalekites lived in the
area from Telam to Shur[a] and on as far
as Egypt, and David often attacked their
towns. 9Whenever David and his men
attacked a town, they took the sheep,
cattle, donkeys, camels, and the clothing, and killed everyone who lived
there.
After he returned from a raid, David
always went to see Achish, 10who would
ask, "Where did you attack today?"[b]
David would answer, "Oh, we attacked
some desert town that belonged to the
Judah tribe." Sometimes David would
say, "Oh, we attacked a town in the
desert where the Jerahmeel clan lives"
or "We attacked a town in the desert
where the Kenites[c] live." 11That's why
David killed everyone in the towns he
attacked. He thought, "If I let any of
them live, they might come to Gath and
tell what I've really been doing."
David made these raids all the time he
was in Philistia. 12But Achish trusted
David and thought, "David's people
must be furious with him. From now on
he will have to take orders from me."

Saul Talks with Samuel's Ghost

28 1-3Samuel had died some time
earlier,[d] and people from all over
Israel had attended his funeral in his
hometown of Ramah.
Meanwhile, Saul had been trying to
get rid of everyone who spoke with the
spirits of the dead.[e] But one day the
Philistines brought their soldiers together to attack Israel.
Achish told David, "Of course, you
know that you and your men must fight
as part of our Philistine army."
David answered, "That will give you a
chance to see for yourself just how well
we can fight!"
"In that case," Achish said, "you and
your men will always be my bodyguards."
4The Philistines went to Shunem and

[z]**26.19** *gods*: In ancient times it was often believed that gods (even the God of Israel) could only be properly worshiped in their own countries, and only a country's gods should be worshiped in that country. [a]**27.8** *lived . . . Shur*: One ancient translation; Hebrew "had lived for a long time in Shur." [b]**27.10** *Where . . . today*: A few Hebrew manuscripts, the Dead Sea Scrolls, and three ancient translations; most Hebrew manuscripts "Didn't you make a raid today?" [c]**27.10** *Jerahmeel . . . Kenites*: These were clans of the Judah tribe. [d]**28.1-3** *earlier*: See 25.1. [e]**28.1-3** *dead*: Many people believed that it was possible to talk to spirits of the dead, and that these spirits could tell the future.

set up camp. Saul called the army of Israel together, and they set up their camp
in Gilboa. 5 Saul took one look at the
Philistine army and started shaking
with fear. 6 So he asked the LORD what to
do. But the LORD would not answer, either in a dream or by a priest or a
prophet. 7 Then Saul told his officers,
"Find me a woman who can talk to the
spirits of the dead. I'll go to her and find
out what's going to happen."

His servants told him, "There's a
woman at Endor who can talk to spirits
of the dead."

8 That night, Saul put on different
clothing so nobody would recognize
him. Then he and two of his men went
to the woman, and asked, "Will you
bring up the ghost of someone for us?"

9 The woman said, "Why are you trying to trick me and get me killed? You
know King Saul has gotten rid of everyone who talks to the spirits of the dead!"

10 Saul replied, "I swear by the living
LORD that nothing will happen to you
because of this."

11 "Who do you want me to bring up?"
she asked.

"Bring up the ghost of Samuel," he answered.

12 When the woman saw Samuel, she
screamed. Then she turned to Saul and
said, "You've tricked me! You're the
king!"

13 "Don't be afraid," Saul replied. "Just
tell me what you see."

She answered, "I see a spirit rising up
out of the ground."

14 "What does it look like?"

"It looks like an old man wearing a
robe."

Saul knew it was Samuel, so he
bowed down low.

15 "Why are you bothering me by
bringing me up like this?" Samuel
asked.

"I'm terribly worried," Saul answered.
"The Philistines are about to attack me.
God has turned his back on me and
won't answer any more by prophets or
by dreams. What should I do?"

16 Samuel said:

If the LORD has turned away from
you and is now your enemy, don't
ask me what to do. 17 I've already
told you: The LORD has sworn to
take the kingdom from you and give
it to David. And that's just what he's
doing! 18 When the LORD was angry
with the Amalekites, he told you to
destroy them, but you didn't do it.
That's why the LORD is doing this to
you. 19 Tomorrow the LORD will let
the Philistines defeat Israel's army,
then you and your sons will join me
down here in the world of the dead.

20 At once, Saul collapsed and lay
stretched out on the floor, terrified at
what Samuel had said. He was weak because he had not eaten anything since
the day before.

21 The woman came over to Saul, and
when she saw that he was completely
terrified, she said, "Your Majesty, I listened to you and risked my life to do
what you asked. 22 Now please listen to
me. Let me get you a little something to
eat. It will give you strength for your
walk back to camp."

23 "No, I won't eat!"

But his officers and the woman kept
on urging Saul, until he finally agreed.
He got up off the floor and sat on the
bed. 24 Right away the woman killed a
calf that she had been fattening up. She
cooked part of the meat and baked
some thin bread.[f] 25 Then she served the
food to Saul and his officers, who ate
and left before daylight.

The Philistines Send David Back

29 The Philistines had brought their
whole army to Aphek,[g] while Israel's army was camping near Jezreel
Spring. 2-3 The Philistine rulers and their
troops were marching past the Philistine army commanders in groups of a
hundred and a thousand. When David
and his men marched by at the end with
Achish, the commanders said, "What
are these worthless Israelites doing
here?"

"They are David's men," Achish answered. "David used to be one of Saul's
officers, but he left Saul and joined my
army a long time ago. I've never had
even one complaint about him."

4 The Philistine army commanders
were angry and shouted:

Send David back to the town you
gave him. We won't have him going
into the battle with us. He could turn
and fight against us! Saul would
take David back as an officer if
David brought him the heads of our
soldiers. 5 The Israelites even dance
and sing,

"Saul has killed
a thousand enemies;
David has killed
ten thousand enemies!"

6 Achish called David over and said:

I swear by the living LORD that
you've been honest with me, and I
want you to fight by my side. I don't
think you've done anything wrong
from the day you joined me until

[f] **28.24** *thin bread*: Bread made without yeast, since there was no time for the bread to rise.
[g] **29.1** *Aphek*: The events of chapter 29 probably took place as the Philistine army was on its way to Shunem, which they reached in 28.4.

this very moment. But the other
Philistine rulers don't want you to
come along. 7Go on back home and
try not to upset them.
8"But what have I done?" David asked.
"Do you know of anything I've ever
done that would keep me from fighting
the enemies of my king?"[h]
9Achish said:

I believe that you're as good as an
angel of God, but our army commanders have decided that you can't
fight in this battle. 10You and your
troops will have to go back to the
town I gave you.[i] Get up and leave
tomorrow morning as soon as it's
light. I am pleased with you, so don't
let any of this bother you.[j]

11David and his men got up early in
the morning and headed back toward
Philistia, while the Philistines left for
Jezreel.

David Rescues His Soldiers' Families

30 It took David and his men three
days to reach Ziklag. But while
they had been away, the Amalekites had
been raiding in the desert around there.
They had attacked Ziklag, burned it to
the ground, 2and had taken away the
women and children. 3When David and
his men came to Ziklag, they saw the
burned-out ruins and learned that their
families had been taken captive. 4They
started crying and kept it up until they
were too weak to cry any more. 5David's
two wives, Ahinoam and Abigail, had
been taken captive with everyone else.
6David was desperate. His soldiers
were so upset over what had happened
to their sons and daughters that they
were thinking about stoning David to
death. But he felt the LORD God giving
him strength, 7and he said to the priest,
"Abiathar, let's ask God what to do."
Abiathar brought everything he
needed to get answers from God, and he
went over to David. 8Then David asked
the LORD, "Should I go after the people
who raided our town? Can I catch up
with them?"
"Go after them," the LORD answered.
"You will catch up with them, and you
will rescue your families."
9-10David led his six hundred men to
Besor Gorge, but two hundred of them
were too tired to go across. So they
stayed behind, while David and the
other four hundred men crossed the
gorge.
11Some of David's men found an
Egyptian out in a field and took him to
David. They gave the Egyptian some
bread, and he ate it. Then they gave him
a drink of water, 12some dried figs, and
two handfuls of raisins. This was the
first time in three days he had tasted
food or water. Now he felt much better.
13"Who is your master?" David asked.
"And where do you come from?"
"I'm from Egypt," the young man answered. "I'm the servant of an
Amalekite, but he left me here three
days ago because I was sick. 14We had
attacked some towns in the desert
where the Cherethites live, in the area
that belongs to Judah, and in the desert
where the Caleb clan lives. And we
burned down Ziklag."
15"Will you take me to those
Amalekites?" David asked.
"Yes, I will, if you promise with God
as a witness that you won't kill me or
hand me over to my master."
16He led David to the Amalekites.
They were eating and drinking everywhere, celebrating because of what they
had taken from Philistia and Judah.
17David attacked just before sunrise the
next day and fought until sunset.[k] Four
hundred Amalekites rode away on
camels, but they were the only ones who
escaped.
18David rescued his two wives and
everyone else the Amalekites had taken
from Ziklag. 19No one was missing—
young or old, sons or daughters. David
brought back everything that had been
stolen, 20including their livestock.
David also took the sheep and cattle
that the Amalekites had with them, but
he kept these separate from the others.
Everyone agreed that these would be
David's reward.
21On the way back, David went to the
two hundred men he had left at Besor
Gorge, because they had been too tired
to keep up with him. They came toward
David and the people who were with
him. When David was close enough, he
greeted the two hundred men and asked
how they were doing.
22Some of David's men were good-for-
nothings, and they said, "Those men
didn't go with us to the battle, so they
don't get any of the things we took back
from the Amalekites. Let them take
their wives and children and go!"
23But David said:

My friends, don't be so greedy
with what the LORD has given us!
The LORD protected us and gave us
victory over the people who attacked. 24Who would pay attention
to you, anyway? Soldiers who stay

[h]**29.8** *my king*: David may be referring to either Saul or Achish. [i]**29.10** *go . . . you*: One ancient translation; these words are not in the Hebrew text. [j]**29.10** *I am . . . bother you*: One ancient translation; these words are not in the Hebrew text. [k]**30.17** *just . . . sunset*: Or "at dusk, and fought until sunset on the next day."

behind to guard the camp get as
much as those who go into battle.

25 David made this a law for Israel, and it has been the same ever since.

26 David went back to Ziklag with everything they had taken from the Amalekites. He sent some of these things as gifts to his friends who were leaders of Judah, and he told them, "We took these things from the LORD's enemies. Please accept them as a gift."

27-31 This is a list of the towns where David sent gifts: Bethel,[l] Ramoth in the Southern Desert, Jattir, Aroer, Siphmoth, Eshtemoa, Racal, the towns belonging to the Jerahmeelites and the Kenites, Hormah, Bor-Ashan, Athach, and Hebron. He also sent gifts to the other towns where he and his men had traveled.

Saul and His Sons Die

31 Meanwhile, the Philistines were fighting Israel at Mount Gilboa. Israel's soldiers ran from the Philistines, and many of them were killed. 2 The Philistines closed in on Saul and his sons, and they killed his sons Jonathan, Abinadab, and Malchishua. 3 The fighting was fierce around Saul, and he was badly wounded by enemy arrows.

4 Saul told the soldier who carried his weapons, "Kill me with your sword! I don't want those worthless Philistines to torture me and make fun." But the soldier was afraid to kill him.

Saul then took out his own sword; he stuck the blade into his stomach, and fell on it. 5 When the soldier knew that Saul was dead, he killed himself in the same way.

6 Saul was dead, his three sons were dead, and the soldier who carried his weapons was dead. They and all his soldiers died on that same day. 7 The Israelites on the other side of Jezreel Valley[m] and the other side of the Jordan learned that Saul and his sons were dead. They saw that the Israelite army had run away. So they ran away too, and the Philistines moved into the towns the Israelites had left behind.

8 The day after the battle, when the Philistines returned to the battlefield to take the weapons of the dead Israelite soldiers, they found Saul and his three sons lying dead on Mount Gilboa. 9-10 The Philistines cut off Saul's head and pulled off his armor. Then they put his armor in the temple of the goddess Astarte, and they nailed his body to the city wall of Beth-Shan. They also sent messengers everywhere in Philistia to spread the good news in the temples of their idols and among their people.

11 The people who lived in Jabesh in Gilead heard what the Philistines had done to Saul's body. 12 So one night, some brave men from Jabesh went to Beth-Shan. They took down the bodies of Saul and his sons, then brought them back to Jabesh and burned them. 13 They buried the bones under a small tree in Jabesh, and for seven days, they went without eating to show their sorrow.

[l] **30.27-31** *Bethel*: Or "Bethuel" (see Joshua 19.4). [m] **31.7** *Jezreel Valley*: Hebrew "valley." Shunem (see 28.4) and Gilboa (see verse 1) were across the Jezreel Valley from each other.

2 SAMUEL

ABOUT THIS BOOK

Second Samuel is actually the second half of a single book that was divided into two parts, 1 and 2 Samuel, because together they were too long to fit on one scroll. Most of 2 Samuel is a history of the rule of King David.

After the death of King Saul, the people of the Judah tribe chose David to be their king. And for the next seven years David was at war with Saul's son, King Ishbosheth of Israel. Then David became king of the entire nation.

David captured Jerusalem from the Jebusites, made it his new capital, and brought the sacred chest there. He wanted to build a temple to honor the Lord and as a place to keep the sacred chest, but the Lord refused to let him do so. Instead, the Lord promised that David would be a powerful ruler and that one of his descendants would always be king.

David conquered the enemies of Israel and became the ruler of a small empire. But he also had an affair with Bathsheba, the wife of an army officer who was away at war. As a result, the Lord allowed David to have serious troubles later on, and many of those troubles came from within his own family. For example, one of David's sons, Amnon, raped David's daughter Tamar. Amnon was then killed by David's son Absalom, who later led a rebellion against David.

David wasn't perfect, but he was loyal to the Lord and worshiped only him. And for as long as Judah continued as a nation, the Lord kept the promise he made to David:

> *Now I promise that you and your descendants will be kings. I'll choose one of your sons to be king when you reach the end of your life and are buried in the tomb of your ancestors. I'll make him a strong ruler, and no one will be able to take his kingdom away from him. . . . I will be his father, and he will be my son.* (7.11-14)

A QUICK LOOK AT THIS BOOK

David Mourns for Saul (1.1-27)
David, King of Judah (2.1—4.12)
David, King of All Israel (5.1—6.23)
The Lord's Promise to David (7.1-29)
The Wars of King David (8.1—10.19)
David's Affair with Bathsheba (11.1—12.31)
Violence in David's Family: Tamar, Amnon, and Absalom (13.1—14.33)
Absalom Leads a Rebellion (15.1—20.22)
Other Events from David's Rule (20.22—21.22)
Two Poems by David (22.1—23.7)
David's Warriors (23.8-39)
David Counts the People of Israel, and Israel is Punished (24.1-25)

David Finds Out about Saul's Death

1 Saul was dead.
Meanwhile, David had defeated
the Amalekites and returned to Ziklag.
[2]Three days later, a soldier came from
Saul's army. His clothes were torn,
and dirt was on his head.[a] He went to

[a] **1.2** *His clothes . . . his head*: People tore their clothes and put dirt on their heads to show they were sad because someone had died.

David and knelt down in front of
him.
3 David asked, "Where did you come
from?"
The man answered, "From Israel's
army. I barely escaped with my life."
4 "Who won the battle?" David asked.
The man said, "Our army turned and
ran, but many were wounded and died.
Even King Saul and his son Jonathan
are dead."
5 David asked, "How do you know
Saul and Jonathan are dead?"
6 The young man replied:
I was on Mount Gilboa and saw
King Saul leaning on his spear. The
enemy's war chariots and cavalry
were closing in on him. 7 When he
turned around and saw me, he called
me over. I went and asked what he
wanted.
8 Saul asked me, "Who are you?"
"An Amalekite," I answered.
9 Then he said, "Kill me! I'm dying,
and I'm in terrible pain."[b]
10 So I killed him. I knew he was
too badly wounded to live much
longer. Then I took his crown and
his arm-band, and I brought them to
you, Your Majesty. Here they are.
11 Right away, David and his soldiers
tore their clothes in sorrow. 12 They cried
all day long and would not eat anything.
Everyone was sad because Saul, his son
Jonathan, and many of the LORD's people had been killed in the battle.
13 David asked the young man, "Where
is your home?"
The man replied, "My father is an
Amalekite, but we live in Israel."
14-16 David said to him, "Why weren't
you afraid to kill the LORD's chosen
king? And you even told what you did.
It's your own fault that you're going to
die!"
Then David told one of his soldiers,
"Come here and kill this man!"

David Sings in Memory of Saul

17 David sang a song in memory of
Saul and Jonathan, 18 and he ordered his
men to teach the song to everyone in Judah. He called it "The Song of the Bow,"
and it can be found in *The Book of
Jashar*.[c] This is the song:

19 Israel, your famous hero
lies dead on the hills,
and your mighty warriors
have fallen!
20 Don't tell it in Gath
or spread the news
on the streets of Ashkelon.
The godless Philistine women
will be happy
and jump for joy.
21 Don't let dew or rain fall
on the hills of Gilboa.
Don't let its fields
grow offerings for God.
There the warriors' shields
were smeared with mud,
and Saul's own shield
was left unpolished.[d]

22 The arrows of Jonathan struck,
and warriors died.
The sword of Saul cut
the enemy apart.

23 It was easy to love Saul
and Jonathan.
Together in life,
together in death,
they were faster than eagles
and stronger than lions.

24 Women of Israel, cry for Saul.
He brought you fine red cloth
and jewelry made of gold.
25 Our warriors have fallen
in the heat of battle,
and Jonathan lies dead
on the hills of Gilboa.

26 Jonathan, I miss you most!
I loved you
like a brother.
You were truly loyal to me,
more faithful than a wife
to her husband.[e]

27 Our warriors have fallen,
and their weapons[f]
are destroyed.

David Becomes King of Judah

2 Later, David asked the LORD,
"Should I go back to one of the
towns of Judah?"
The LORD answered, "Yes."
David asked, "Which town should I go
to?"
"Go to Hebron," the LORD replied.
2 David went to Hebron with his two
wives, Ahinoam and Abigail. Ahinoam
was from Jezreel, and Abigail was the
widow of Nabal from Carmel. 3 David
also had his men and their families
come and live in the villages near Hebron.
4 The people of Judah met with David
at Hebron and poured olive oil on his
head to show that he was their new

[b] 1.9 *in terrible pain*: Or "very weak." [c] 1.18 *The Book of Jashar*: This book may have been a collection of ancient war songs. [d] 1.21 *unpolished*: Some shields were made of leather and were polished with olive oil. [e] 1.26 *You . . . husband*: Or "You loved me more than a wife could possibly love her husband." [f] 1.27 *weapons*: This may refer to Saul and Jonathan.

king. Then they told David, "The people
from Jabesh in Gilead buried Saul."
5David sent messengers to tell them:

> The LORD bless you! You were kind
> enough to bury Saul your ruler, 6and
> I pray that the LORD will be kind and
> faithful to you. I will be your friend
> because of what you have done.
> 7Saul is dead, but the tribe of Judah
> has made me their king. So be
> strong and have courage.

Ishbosheth Becomes King of Israel

8Abner the son of Ner[g] had been the
general of Saul's army. He took Saul's
son Ishbosheth[h] across the Jordan River
to Mahanaim 9and made him king of Israel,[i] including the areas of Gilead,
Asher,[j] Jezreel, Ephraim, and Benjamin.
10Ishbosheth was forty years old at the
time, and he ruled for two years. But the
tribe of Judah made David their king,
11and he ruled from Hebron for seven
and a half years.

The War between David and Ishbosheth

12One day, Abner and the soldiers of
Ishbosheth[k] left Mahanaim and went to
Gibeon. 13Meanwhile, Joab the son of
Zeruiah[l] was leading David's soldiers,
and the two groups met at the pool in
Gibeon.[m] Abner and his men sat down
on one side of the pool, while Joab and
his men sat on the other side. 14Abner
yelled to Joab, "Let's have some of our
best soldiers get up and fight each
other!"

Joab agreed, 15and twelve of Ishbosheth's men from the tribe of Benjamin got up to fight twelve of David's
men. 16They grabbed each other by the
hair and stabbed each other in the side
with their daggers. They all died right
there! That's why the place in Gibeon is
called "Field of Daggers."[n] 17Then everyone started fighting. Both sides fought
very hard, but David's soldiers defeated
Abner and the soldiers of Israel.
18Zeruiah's three sons were there:
Joab, Abishai, and Asahel. Asahel could
run as fast as a deer in an open field,
19and he ran straight after Abner, without looking to the right or to the left.
20When Abner turned and saw him, he
said, "Is that you, Asahel?"

Asahel answered, "Yes it is."
21Abner said, "There are soldiers all
around. Stop chasing me and fight one
of them! Kill him and take his clothes
and weapons for yourself."

But Asahel refused to stop.
22Abner said, "If you don't turn back,
I'll have to kill you! Then I could never
face your brother Joab again."
23But Asahel would not turn back, so
Abner struck him in the stomach with
the back end of his spear. The spear
went all the way through and came out
of his back. Asahel fell down and died.
Everyone who saw Asahel lying dead
just stopped and stood still. 24But Joab
and Abishai went after Abner. Finally,
about sunset, they came to the hill of
Ammah, not far from Giah on the road
to Gibeon Desert. 25Abner brought the
men of Benjamin together in one group
on top of a hill, and they got ready to
fight.
26Abner shouted to Joab, "Aren't we
ever going to stop killing each other?
Don't you know that the longer we keep
on doing this, the worse it's going to be
when it's all over? When are you going
to order your men to stop chasing their
own relatives?"
27Joab shouted back, "I swear by the
living God, if you hadn't spoken, my
men would have chased their relatives
all night!" 28Joab took his trumpet and
blew the signal for his soldiers to stop
chasing the soldiers of Israel. Right
away, the fighting stopped.
29Abner and his troops marched
through the Jordan River valley all that
night. Then they crossed the river and
marched all morning[o] until they arrived
back at Mahanaim.
30As soon as Joab stopped chasing
Abner, he got David's troops together
and counted them. There were nineteen
missing besides Asahel. 31But David's
soldiers had killed 360 of Abner's men
from the tribe of Benjamin. 32Joab and
his troops carried Asahel's body to
Bethlehem and buried him in the family
burial place. Then they marched all

[g]**2.8** *son of Ner*: Abner was Saul's cousin (see 1 Samuel 14.50). [h]**2.8** *Ishbosheth*: One ancient translation has "Ishbaal" (see also 1 Chronicles 8.33). In Hebrew "baal" means "lord" and was used as the name of a Canaanite god. The people of Israel often changed "baal" to "bosheth" (which means "shame") in personal names. Ishbosheth was probably called Ishvi or Ishyo in 1 Samuel 14.49. [i]**2.9** *Israel*: Sometimes "Israel" means the northern tribes and does not include the tribes of Judah and Simeon. That is how it is used in this verse. [j]**2.9** *Asher*: The Hebrew text has "Ashur," which is the Hebrew name for the Assyrians. It may be another spelling for Asher (one of the tribes of Israel) or it may refer to Geshur (a small area between Gilead and Jezreel, east of Lake Galilee). [k]**2.12** *Ishbosheth*: See the note at 2.8. [l]**2.13** *the son of Zeruiah*: Zeruiah was David's older sister, so Joab was David's nephew (see 1 Chronicles 2.12-17 and the note at 2 Samuel 17.25). [m]**2.13** *pool in Gibeon*: This pool was located just inside the city wall and was used for storing water. It was in the shape of a circle and was 36 feet wide and 36 feet deep. [n]**2.16** *Field of Daggers*: Or "Field of Opponents" or "Battlefield." [o]**2.29** *all morning*: One possible meaning for the difficult Hebrew text.

night and reached Hebron before sunrise.

3 This battle was the beginning of a
long war between the followers of
Saul and the followers of David. Saul's
power grew weaker, but David's grew
stronger.

David's Sons Born in Hebron

(1 Chronicles 3.1-4)

2-5Several of David's sons were born
while he was living in Hebron. His oldest son was Amnon, whose mother was
Ahinoam from Jezreel. David's second
son was Chileab, whose mother was
Abigail, who had been married to Nabal
from Carmel. Absalom was the third.
His mother was Maacah, the daughter
of King Talmai of Geshur. The fourth
was Adonijah, whose mother was Haggith. The fifth was Shephatiah, whose
mother was Abital. The sixth was
Ithream, whose mother was Eglah, another one of David's wives.

Abner Decides To Help David

6As the war went on between the families of David and Saul, Abner was gaining more power than ever in Saul's family. 7He had even slept with a wife[p] of
Saul by the name of Rizpah the daughter of Aiah. But Saul's son Ishbosheth[q]
told Abner, "You shouldn't have slept
with one of my father's wives!"

8Abner was very angry at what Ishbosheth had said, and he told Ishbosheth:

> Am I some kind of worthless dog
> from Judah? I've always been loyal
> to your father's family and to his rel-
> atives and friends. I haven't turned
> you over to David. And yet you talk
> to me as if I've committed a crime
> with this woman.
>
> 9I ask God to punish me if I don't
> help David get what the LORD
> promised him! 10God said that he
> wouldn't let anyone in Saul's family
> ever be king again and that David
> would be king instead. He also said
> that David would rule both Israel
> and Judah, all the way from Dan in
> the north to Beersheba in the south.[r]

11Ishbosheth was so afraid of Abner
that he could not even answer.

12Abner sent some of his men to
David with this message: "You should
be the ruler of the whole nation.[s] If you
make an agreement with me, I will persuade everyone in Israel to make you
their king."

13David sent this message back:
"Good! I'll make an agreement with
you. But before I will even talk with you
about it, you must get Saul's daughter
Michal back for me."

14David sent a few of his officials to
Ishbosheth to give him this message:
"Give me back my wife Michal! I killed
a hundred Philistines so I could marry
her."[t]

15Ishbosheth sent some of his men to
take Michal away from her new husband, Paltiel the son of Laish. 16Paltiel
followed Michal and the men all the
way to Bahurim, crying as he walked.
But he went back home after Abner ordered him to leave.

17Abner talked with the leaders of the
tribes of Israel and told them, "You've
wanted to make David your king for a
long time now. 18So do it! After all,
God said he would use his servant
David to rescue his people Israel from
their enemies, especially from the
Philistines."

19Finally, Abner talked with the tribe
of Benjamin. Then he left for Hebron to
tell David everything that the tribe of
Benjamin and the rest of the people of
Israel wanted to do. 20Abner took
twenty soldiers with him, and when
they got to Hebron, David gave a big
feast for them.

21After the feast, Abner said, "Your
Majesty, let me leave now and bring Israel here to make an agreement with
you. You'll be king of the whole nation,
just as you've been wanting."

David told Abner he could leave, and
he left without causing any trouble.

Joab Kills Abner

22Soon after Abner had left Hebron,
Joab and some of David's soldiers came
back, bringing a lot of things they had
taken from an enemy village. 23Right after they arrived, someone told Joab,
"Abner visited the king, and the king let
him go. Abner even left without causing
any trouble."

24Joab went to David and said, "What
have you done? Abner came to you, and
you let him go. Now he's long gone!
25You know Abner—he came to trick
you. He wants to find out how strong
your army is and to know everything
you're doing."

26Joab left David, then he sent some
messengers to catch up with Abner.
They brought him back from the well at
Sirah,[u] but David did not know anything about it. 27When Abner returned
to Hebron, Joab pretended he wanted

[p]**3.7** *wife*: This translates a Hebrew word for a woman who was legally bound to a man, but without the full privileges of a wife. [q]**3.7** *Ishbosheth*: See the note at 2.8. [r]**3.10** *from . . . south*: Hebrew "from Dan to Beersheba." This was one way of describing all of the Israelite land, from north to south. [s]**3.12** *You . . . nation*: Or "I like you." [t]**3.14** *I killed . . . marry her*: See 1 Samuel 18.20-27. [u]**3.26** *well at Sirah*: Or "oasis of Sirah" or "cistern at Sirah."

to talk privately with him. So he took
Abner into one of the small rooms that
were part of the town gate and stabbed
him in the stomach. Joab killed him because Abner had killed Joab's brother
Asahel.

Abner's Funeral

28David heard how Joab had killed
Abner, and he said, "I swear to the LORD
that I am completely innocent of Abner's death! 29Joab and his family are
the guilty ones. I pray that Joab's family
will always be sick with sores and other
skin diseases. May they all be cowards,[v]
and may they die in war or starve to
death."
30Joab and his brother Abishai killed
Abner because he had killed their
brother Asahel in the battle at Gibeon.
31David told Joab and everyone with
him, "Show your sorrow by tearing your
clothes and wearing sackcloth![w] Walk
in front of Abner's body and cry!"
David walked behind the stretcher on
which Abner's body was being carried.
32Abner was buried in Hebron, while
David and everyone else stood at the
tomb and cried loudly. 33Then the king
sang a funeral song about Abner:

Abner, why should you
have died like an outlaw?[x]
34 No one tied your hands
or chained your feet,
yet you died as a victim
of murderers.

Everyone started crying again. 35Then
they brought some food to David and
told him he would feel better if he had
something to eat. It was still daytime,
and David said, "I swear to God that I'll
not take a bite of bread or anything else
until sunset!"
36Everyone noticed what David did,
and they liked it, just as they always
liked what he did. 37Now the people of
Judah and Israel were certain that
David had nothing to do with killing
Abner.
38David said to his officials, "Don't
you realize that today one of Israel's
great leaders has died? 39I am the chosen king, but Joab and Abishai have
more power than I do. So God will have
to pay them back[y] for the evil thing they
did."

Ishbosheth Is Killed

4 Ishbosheth[z] felt like giving up
after he heard that Abner had died
in Hebron. Everyone in Israel was terrified.
2Ishbosheth had put the two brothers
Baanah and Rechab in charge of the
soldiers who raided enemy villages.
Rimmon was their father, and they were
from the town of Beeroth, which belonged to the tribe of Benjamin. 3The
people who used to live in Beeroth had
run away to Gittaim, and they still live[a]
there.
4Saul's son Jonathan had a son
named Mephibosheth,[b] who had not
been able to walk since he was five
years old. It happened when someone
from Jezreel told his nurse that Saul
and Jonathan had died.[c] She hurried off
with the boy in her arms, but he fell and
injured his legs.
5One day about noon, Rechab and
Baanah went to Ishbosheth's house.
It was a hot day, and he was resting
6-7in his bedroom. The two brothers
went into the house, pretending to
get some flour. But once they were
inside, they stabbed Ishbosheth in
the stomach and killed him. Then
they cut off his head and took it with
them.
Rechab and Baanah walked through
the Jordan River valley all night long.
8Finally they turned west and went to
Hebron. They went in to see David and
told him, "Your Majesty, here is the head
of Ishbosheth, the son of your enemy
Saul who tried to kill you! The LORD has
let you get even with Saul and his family."
9David answered:
I swear that only the LORD rescues
me when I'm in trouble! 10When a
man came to Ziklag and told me
that Saul was dead, he thought he
deserved a reward for bringing good
news. But I grabbed him and killed
him.
11You evil men have done something much worse than he did.
You've killed an innocent man in his
own house and on his own bed. I'll
make you pay for that. I'll wipe you
from the face of the earth!
12Then David said to his troops, "Kill
these two brothers! Cut off their hands
and feet and hang their bodies by the
pool in Hebron. But bury Ishbosheth's

[v]3.29 *cowards*: One possible meaning for the difficult Hebrew text. [w]3.31 *sackcloth*: Sackcloth was a rough, dark-colored cloth made from goat or camel hair and was used to make grain sacks. People wore sackcloth or tore their clothes in times of trouble or sorrow. [x]3.33 *outlaw*: Or "fool." [y]3.39 *God . . . back*: Or "I pray that God will pay them back." [z]4.1 *Ishbosheth*: Hebrew "The Son of Saul." [a]4.3 *live*: The Hebrew word means that they did not have the full legal rights of citizens. [b]4.4 *Mephibosheth*: Some manuscripts of one ancient translation have "Mephibaal." In 1 Chronicles 8.34 and 9.40 he is called "Meribbaal." See the note on "baal" and "bosheth" at 2.8. [c]4.4 *Saul . . . died*: See 1 Samuel 31.1-6.

head in Abner's tomb near Hebron." And they did.

David Becomes King of Israel
(1 Chronicles 11.1-3)

5 Israel's leaders met with David at Hebron and said, "We are your relatives. [2]Even when Saul was king, you led our nation in battle. And the LORD promised that someday you would rule Israel and take care of us like a shepherd."

[3]During the meeting, David made an agreement with the leaders and asked the LORD to be their witness. Then the leaders poured olive oil on David's head to show that he was now the king of Israel.

[4]David was thirty years old when he became king, and he ruled for forty years. [5]He lived in Hebron for the first seven and a half years and ruled only Judah. Then he moved to Jerusalem, where he ruled both Israel and Judah for thirty-three years.

How David Captured Jerusalem
(1 Chronicles 11.4-9; 14.1-2)

[6]The Jebusites lived in Jerusalem, and David led his army there to attack them. The Jebusites did not think he could get in, so they told him, "You can't get in here! We could run you off, even if we couldn't see or walk!"

[7-9]David told his troops, "You will have to go up through the water tunnel to get those Jebusites. I hate people like them who can't walk or see."[d]

That's why there is still a rule that says, "Only people who can walk and see are allowed in the temple."[e]

David captured the fortress on Mount Zion, then he moved there and named it David's City. He had the city rebuilt, starting with the landfill to the east. [10]David became a great and strong ruler, because the LORD All-Powerful was on his side.

[11]King Hiram of Tyre sent some officials to David. Carpenters and stone workers came with them, and they brought cedar logs so they could build David a palace.

[12]David knew that the LORD had made him king of Israel and that he had made him a powerful ruler for the good of his people.

David's Sons Born in Jerusalem
(1 Chronicles 14.3-7)

[13]After David left Hebron and moved to Jerusalem, he married many women[f] from Jerusalem,[g] and he had a lot of children. [14]His sons who were born there were Shammua, Shobab, Nathan, Solomon, [15]Ibhar, Elishua, Nepheg, Japhia, [16]Elishama, Eliada,[h] and Eliphelet.

David Fights the Philistines
(1 Chronicles 14.8-17)

[17]The Philistines heard that David was now king of Israel, and they came into the hill country to try and capture him. But David found out and went into his fortress.[i] [18]So the Philistines camped in Rephaim Valley.[j]

[19]David asked the LORD, "Should I attack the Philistines? Will you let me win?"

The LORD told David, "Attack! I will let you win."

[20]David attacked the Philistines and defeated them. Then he said, "I watched the LORD break through my enemies like a mighty flood." So he named the place "The Lord Broke Through."[k] [21]David and his troops also carried away the idols that the Philistines had left behind.

[22]Some time later, the Philistines came back into the hill country and camped in Rephaim Valley. [23]David asked the LORD what he should do, and the LORD answered:

> Don't attack them from the front.
> Circle around behind and attack
> from among the balsam[l] trees.
> [24]Wait until you hear a sound like
> troops marching through the tops of
> the trees. Then attack quickly! That
> sound will mean I have marched out
> ahead of you to fight the Philistine
> army.

[25]David obeyed the LORD and defeated the Philistines. He even chased them all the way from Geba to the entrance to Gezer.

David Brings the Sacred Chest Back to Jerusalem
(1 Chronicles 13.1-14; 15.1—16.3,43)

6 David brought together thirty thousand of Israel's best soldiers and [2]led them to Baalah in Judah, which was

[d]**5.7-9** *You will . . . or see*: One possible meaning for the difficult Hebrew text. [e]**5.7-9** *temple*: Or "palace." [f]**5.13** *married many women*: Some of these women were second-class wives (see the note at 3.7). [g]**5.13** *from Jerusalem*: Or "in Jerusalem." [h]**5.16** *Eliada*: See 1 Chronicles 3.8. First Chronicles 14.7 has "Baalyada." [i]**5.17** *fortress*: Probably the fortress of Adullam, which was David's former hideout (see 1 Samuel 22.1, 4; 24.22). Or it could refer to the older walled city of Jerusalem, called the "fortress on Mount Zion" in verses 7-9. [j]**5.18** *Rephaim Valley*: A few miles southwest of Jerusalem. [k]**5.20** *The Lord Broke Through*: Or "Baal-Perazim." [l]**5.23** *balsam*: One possible meaning for the difficult Hebrew text.

also called Kiriath-Jearim. They were
going there[m] to get the sacred chest and
bring it back to Jerusalem. The throne
of the LORD All-Powerful is above the
winged creatures[n] on top of this chest,
and he is worshiped there.[o]
3They put the sacred chest on a new
ox cart and started bringing it down the
hill from Abinadab's house. Abinadab's
sons Uzzah and Ahio were guiding the
ox cart, 4with Ahio[p] walking in front of
it. 5Some of the people of Israel were
playing music on small harps and other
stringed instruments, and on tambourines, castanets, and cymbals. David
and the others were happy, and they
danced for the LORD with all their
might.
6But when they came to Nacon's
threshing-floor, the oxen stumbled, so
Uzzah reached out and took hold of the
sacred chest. 7The LORD God was very
angry at Uzzah for doing this, and he
killed Uzzah right there beside the
chest.
8David got angry at God for killing
Uzzah. He named that place "Bursting
Out Against Uzzah,"[q] and that's what
it's still called.
9David was afraid of the LORD and
thought, "Should I really take the sacred
chest to my city?" 10He decided not to
take it there. Instead, he turned off the
road and took it to the home of Obed
Edom, who was from Gath.[r]
11-12The chest stayed there for three
months, and the LORD greatly blessed
Obed Edom, his family, and everything
he owned. Then someone told King
David, "The LORD has done this because
the sacred chest is in Obed Edom's
house."
Right away, David went to Obed
Edom's house to get the chest and bring
it to David's City. Everyone was celebrating. 13The people carrying the chest
walked six steps, then David sacrificed
an ox and a choice cow. 14He was dancing for the LORD with all his might, but
he wore only a linen cloth.[s] 15He and
everyone else were celebrating by
shouting and blowing horns while the
chest was being carried along.
16Saul's daughter Michal looked out
her window and watched the chest being brought into David's City. But when
she saw David jumping and dancing for
the LORD, she was disgusted.
17They put the chest inside a tent that
David had set up for it. David worshiped
the LORD by sacrificing animals and
burning them on an altar,[t] 18then he
blessed the people in the name of the
LORD All-Powerful. 19He gave all the
men and women in the crowd a small
loaf of bread, some meat, and a handful
of raisins, and everyone went home.

Michal Talks to David

20David went home so he could ask
the LORD to bless his family. But Saul's
daughter Michal went out and started
yelling at him. "You were really great today!" she said. "You acted like a dirty
old man, dancing around half-naked in
front of your servants' slave-girls."
21David told her, "The LORD didn't
choose your father or anyone else in
your family to be the leader of his people. The LORD chose me, and I was celebrating in honor of him. 22I'll show you
just how great I can be! I'll even be disgusting to myself. But those slave-girls
you talked about will still honor me!"
23Michal never had any children.

The LORD's Message to David

(1 Chronicles 17.1-15)

7 King David moved into his new
palace, and the LORD let his kingdom be at peace. 2Then one day, as
David was talking with Nathan the
prophet, David said, "Look around! I
live in a palace made of cedar, but the
sacred chest has to stay in a tent."
3Nathan replied, "The LORD is with
you, so do what you want!"
4That night, the LORD told Nathan 5to
go to David and give him this message:
David, you are my servant, so listen to what I say. Why should you
build a temple for me? 6I didn't live
in a temple when I brought my people out of Egypt, and I don't live in
one now. A tent has always been my
home wherever I have gone with
them. 7I chose leaders and told them
to be like shepherds for my people
Israel. But did I ever say anything to
even one of them about building a
cedar temple for me?
8David, this is what I, the LORD

[m]**6.2** *to Baalah . . . there*: The Dead Sea Scrolls and 1 Chronicles 13.6; the Standard Hebrew Text "from Baalah in Judah. They had gone there." [n]**6.2** *winged creatures*: Two golden statues of winged creatures were on top of the sacred chest and were symbols of the LORD's throne on earth (see Exodus 25.18). [o]**6.2** *he is worshiped there*: Or "the chest belongs to him." [p]**6.3,4** *Ahio . . . Ahio*: Or "his brother . . . his brother." [q]**6.8** *Bursting . . . Uzzah*: Or "Perez-Uzzah." [r]**6.10** *Gath*: Or perhaps, "Gittaim." [s]**6.14** *only a linen cloth*: The Hebrew word is "ephod," which can mean either a piece of clothing like a skirt that went from the waist to the knee or a garment like a vest or a jacket that only the priests wore. [t]**6.17** *sacrificing . . . altar*: The Hebrew mentions two kinds of sacrifices. In one kind of sacrifice, the whole animal was burned on the altar. In the other kind, only part was burned, and the worshipers ate the rest, as in verse 19 (see Leviticus 1.2-17; 3.1-17).

All-Powerful, say to you. I brought
you in from the fields where you
took care of sheep, and I made you
the leader of my people. 9Wherever
you went, I helped you and destroyed your enemies right in front
of your eyes. I have made you one of
the most famous people in the
world.
10I have given my people Israel a
land of their own where they can
live in peace, and they won't have to
tremble with fear any more. Evil nations won't bother them, as they did
11when I let judges rule my people.
And I have kept your enemies from
attacking you.
Now I promise that you and your
descendants will be kings. 12I'll
choose one of your sons to be king
when you reach the end of your life
and are buried in the tomb of your
ancestors. I'll make him a strong
ruler, 13and no one will be able to
take his kingdom away from him.
He will be the one to build a temple
for me. 14I will be his father, and he
will be my son.
When he does wrong, I'll see that
he is corrected, just as children are
corrected by their parents. 15But I
will never put an end to my agreement with him, as I put an end to my
agreement with Saul, who was king
before you. 16I will make sure that
one of your descendants will always
be king.
17Nathan told David exactly what he
had heard in the vision.

David Gives Thanks to the LORD
(1 Chronicles 17.16-27)

18David went into the tent he had set
up for the sacred chest. Then he sat
there and prayed:
LORD All-Powerful, my family and
I don't deserve what you have already done for us, 19and yet you
have promised to do even more. Is
this the way you usually treat people?[u] 20I am your servant, and you
know my thoughts, so there is nothing more that I need to say. 21You
have done this wonderful thing, and
you have let me know about it, because you wanted to keep your
promise.
22LORD All-Powerful, you are
greater than all others. No one is
like you, and you alone are God.
Everything we have heard about you
is true. 23And there is no other nation on earth like Israel, the nation
you rescued from slavery in Egypt to
be your own. You became famous by
using great and wonderful miracles
to force other nations and their gods
out of your land, so your people
could live here.[v] 24You have chosen
Israel to be your people forever, and
you have become their God.
25And now, LORD God, please do
what you have promised me and my
descendants. 26Then you will be famous forever, and everyone will say,
"The LORD God All-Powerful rules
Israel, and David's descendants are
his chosen kings." 27After all, you really are Israel's God, the LORD All-
Powerful. You've told me that you
will let my descendants be kings.
That's why I have the courage to
pray to you like this, even though I
am only your servant.
28LORD All-Powerful, you are God.
You have promised me some very
good things, and you can be trusted
to do what you promise. 29Please
bless my descendants and let them
always be your chosen kings. You
have already promised, and I'm sure
that you will bless my family forever.

A List of David's Victories in War
(1 Chronicles 18.1-13)

8 Later, David attacked and badly defeated the Philistines. Israel was
now free from their control.[w]
2David also defeated the Moabites.
Then he made their soldiers lie down on
the ground, and he measured them off
with a rope. He would measure off two
lengths of the rope and have those men
killed, then he would measure off one
length and let those men live. The people of Moab had to accept David as their
ruler and pay taxes to him.
3David set out for the Euphrates River
to build a monument[x] there. On his
way,[y] he defeated the king of Zobah,
whose name was Hadadezer the son of
Rehob. 4In the battle, David captured
seventeen hundred cavalry[z] and twenty
thousand foot soldiers. He also captured
war chariots, but he destroyed all but
one hundred of them.[a] 5When troops

[u]**7.19** *Is this . . . people*: One possible meaning for the difficult Hebrew text. [v]**7.23** *You . . . here*: One possible meaning for the difficult Hebrew text. [w]**8.1** *Israel . . . control*: Or "David also took the town of Metheg-Ammah away from them." [x]**8.3** *monument*: Kings sometimes set up monuments in lands they had conquered. [y]**8.3** *David . . . way*: One possible meaning for the difficult Hebrew text. It may have been Hadadezer who was going to the Euphrates River. And he may have gone there either to build a monument or to put down a rebellion. [z]**8.4** *seventeen hundred cavalry*: Hebrew; one ancient translation and 1 Chronicles 18.4 "a thousand chariots and seven thousand cavalry." [a]**8.4** *He also captured . . . them*: Or "He crippled all but one hundred of the horses."

from the Aramean kingdom of Damascus came to help Hadadezer, David
killed twenty thousand of them. 6He left
some of his soldiers in Damascus, and
the Arameans had to accept David as
their ruler and pay taxes to him.

Everywhere David went, the LORD
helped him win battles.

7Hadadezer's officers had carried
their arrows in gold cases hung over
their shoulders, but David took these
cases[b] and brought them to Jerusalem.
8He also took a lot of bronze from the
cities of Betah and Berothai, which had
belonged to Hadadezer.

9-10King Toi of Hamath and King
Hadadezer had been enemies. So when
Toi heard that David had attacked and
defeated[c] Hadadezer's whole army, he
sent his son Joram to praise and congratulate David. Joram also brought him
gifts made of silver, gold, and bronze.
11David gave these to the LORD, just as
he had done with the silver and gold
that he had captured from 12Edom,[d]
Moab, Ammon, Philistia, and from King
Hadadezer of Zobah.

13David fought the Edomite[e] army in
Salt Valley and killed eighteen thousand
of their soldiers. When he returned,
he built a monument.[f] 14David left soldiers all through Edom, and the people
of Edom had to accept him as their
ruler.

Wherever David went, the LORD
helped him.

A List of David's Officials

(1 Chronicles 18.14-17)

15David ruled all Israel with fairness
and justice.

16Joab the son of Zeruiah was the
commander in chief of the army.

Jehoshaphat the son of Ahilud kept
the government records.

17Zadok the son of Ahitub, and Abiathar the son of Ahimelech,[g] were the
priests.

Seraiah was the secretary.

18Benaiah the son of Jehoiada was
the commander of[h] David's bodyguard.[i]

David's sons were priests.

David Is Kind to Mephibosheth

9 One day, David thought, "I wonder if
any of Saul's family are still alive. If
they are, I will be kind to them, because
I made a promise to Jonathan." 2David
called in Ziba, one of the servants of
Saul's family. David said, "So you are
Ziba."

"Yes, Your Majesty, I am."

3David asked, "Are any of Saul's family still alive? If there are, I want to be
kind to them."

Ziba answered, "One of Jonathan's
sons is still alive, but he can't walk."

4"Where is he?" David asked.

Ziba replied, "He lives in Lo-Debar
with Machir the son of Ammiel."

5-6David sent some servants to bring
Jonathan's son from Lo-Debar. His
name was Mephibosheth,[j] and he was
the grandson of Saul. He came to David
and knelt down.

David asked, "Are you Mephibosheth?"

"Yes, I am, Your Majesty."

7David said, "Don't be afraid. I'll be
kind to you because Jonathan was your
father. I'm going to give you back the
land that belonged to your grandfather
Saul. Besides that, you will always eat
with me at my table."

8Mephibosheth knelt down again and
said, "Why should you care about me?
I'm worth no more than a dead dog."

9David called in Ziba, Saul's chief servant, and told him, "Since Mephibosheth is Saul's grandson, I've given
him back everything that belonged to
your master Saul and his family. 10You
and your fifteen sons and twenty servants will work for Mephibosheth. You
will farm his land and bring in his
crops, so that Saul's family and
servants[k] will have food. But Mephibosheth will always eat with me at my
table."

11-13Ziba replied, "Your Majesty, I will
do exactly what you tell me to do." So
Ziba's family and servants worked for
Mephibosheth.

Mephibosheth was lame, but he lived
in Jerusalem and ate at David's[l] table,
just like one of David's own sons. And

[b]8.7 *Hadadezer's . . . cases*: Or "Hadadezer's soldiers carried gold shields, but David took these shields." [c]8.9,10 *defeated*: Or "killed." [d]8.12 *Edom*: Some Hebrew manuscripts and two ancient translations (see also 1 Chronicles 18.11); most Hebrew manuscripts "Aram." In Hebrew the words for "Edom" and "Aram" look almost alike. [e]8.13 *Edomite*: Some Hebrew manuscripts and two ancient translations (see also 1 Chronicles 18.12); most Hebrew manuscripts "Aramean." In Hebrew the words for "Edomite" and "Aramean" look almost alike. [f]8.13 *built a monument*: Or "was famous." [g]8.17 *Abiathar the son of Ahimelech*: One ancient translation and 1 Samuel 22.11-23; Hebrew "Ahimelech the son of Abiathar." [h]8.18 *was the commander of*: Not in the Hebrew text of this verse, but see 1 Chronicles 18.17. [i]8.18 *David's bodyguard*: The Hebrew text has "the Cherethites and the Pelethites," who were foreign soldiers hired by David to be his bodyguard. [j]9.5,6 *Mephibosheth*: Or "Mephibaal" (see the note at 4.4). [k]9.10 *Saul's family and servants*: Some manuscripts of one ancient translation; Hebrew "the son of your master." [l]9.11-13 *David's*: Hebrew "my."

he had a young son of his own, named
Mica.

Israel Fights Ammon
(1 Chronicles 19.1-19)

10 Some time later, King Nahash of
Ammon died, and his son Hanun
became king. 2David said, "Nahash was
kind to me, and I will be kind to his
son." So he sent some officials to the
country of Ammon to tell Hanun
how sorry he was that his father had
died.
3But Hanun's officials told him, "Do
you really believe David is honoring
your father by sending these people to
comfort you? He probably sent them to
spy on our city, so he can destroy it."
4Hanun arrested David's officials and
had their beards shaved off on one side
of their faces. He had their robes cut
off just below the waist, and then he
sent them away. 5They were terribly
ashamed.
When David found out what had happened to his officials, he sent a message
and told them, "Stay in Jericho until
your beards grow back. Then you can
come home."
6The Ammonites realized that they
had made David very angry, so they
hired more foreign soldiers. Twenty
thousand of them were foot soldiers
from the Aramean cities of Beth-Rehob
and Zobah, one thousand were from the
king of Maacah, and twelve thousand
were from the region of Tob. 7David
heard what they had done, and he sent
out Joab with all of his well-trained soldiers.
8The Ammonite troops came out and
got ready to fight in front of the gate to
their city. The Arameans from Zobah
and Rehob and the soldiers from Tob
and Maacah formed a separate group in
the nearby fields.
9Joab saw that he had to fight in front
and behind at the same time, and he
picked some of the best Israelite soldiers to fight the Arameans. 10He put his
brother Abishai in command of the rest
of the army and had them fight the
Ammonites. 11Joab told his brother, "If
the Arameans are too much for me to
handle, you can come and help me.
If the Ammonites are too strong for
you, I'll come and help you. 12Be brave
and fight hard to protect our people
and the cities of our God. I pray that
the LORD will do whatever pleases
him."
13Joab and his soldiers attacked the
Arameans, and the Arameans ran from
them. 14When the Ammonite soldiers
saw that the Arameans had run away,
they ran from Abishai's soldiers and
went back into their own city. Joab
stopped fighting the Ammonites and returned to Jerusalem.
15The Arameans realized they had lost
the battle, so they brought all their
troops together again. 16Hadadezer sent
messengers to call in the Arameans who
were on the other side of the Euphrates
River. Then Shobach, the commander of
Hadadezer's army, led them to the town
of Helam.
17David found out what the Arameans
were doing, and he brought Israel's
whole army together. They crossed the
Jordan River and went to Helam, where
the Arameans were ready to meet them.
18The Arameans attacked, but then they
ran from Israel. David killed seven hundred chariot drivers and forty thousand
cavalry.[m] He also killed Shobach, their
commander.
19When the kings who had been under
Hadadezer's rule saw that Israel had
beaten them, they made peace with Israel and accepted David as their ruler.
The Arameans were afraid to help Ammon any more.

David and Bathsheba
(1 Chronicles 20.1a)

11 It was now spring, the time when
kings go to war.[n] David sent out
the whole Israelite army under the command of Joab and his officers. They destroyed the Ammonite army and surrounded the capital city of Rabbah, but
David stayed in Jerusalem.
2-4Late one afternoon, David got up
from a nap and was walking around on
the flat roof of his palace. A beautiful
young woman was down below in her
courtyard, bathing as her religion required.[o] David happened to see her, and
he sent one of his servants to find out
who she was.
The servant came back and told
David, "Her name is Bathsheba. She is
the daughter of Eliam, and she is the
wife of Uriah the Hittite."
David sent some messengers to bring
her to his palace. She came to him, and
he slept with her. Then she returned
home. 5But later, when she found out
that she was going to have a baby, she
sent someone to David with this message: "I'm pregnant!"
6David sent a message to Joab: "Send
Uriah the Hittite to me."
Joab sent Uriah 7to David's palace,
and David asked him, "Is Joab well?

[m] **10.18** *cavalry*: The Hebrew manuscripts and ancient translations differ as to how many and what kind of soldiers were killed. [n] **11.1** *when . . . war*: Or "when the messengers had gone to Ammon" (see 10.2) or "the time when the kings had gone to war" (see 10.6-8). [o] **11.2-4** *as . . . required*: This bathing was often a requirement for worshiping God.

How is the army doing? And how about
the war?" 8Then David told Uriah, "Go
home and clean up."[p] Uriah left the
king's palace, and David had dinner
sent to Uriah's house. 9But Uriah didn't
go home. Instead, he slept outside the
entrance to the royal palace, where the
king's guards slept.
10Someone told David that Uriah had
not gone home. So the next morning
David asked him, "Why didn't you go
home? Haven't you been away for a
long time?"
11Uriah answered, "The sacred chest
and the armies of Israel and Judah are
camping out somewhere in the fields[q]
with our commander Joab and his officers and troops. Do you really think I
would go home to eat and drink and
sleep with my wife? I swear by your life
that I would not!"
12Then David said, "Stay here in
Jerusalem today, and I will send you
back tomorrow."
Uriah stayed in Jerusalem that day.
Then the next day, 13David invited him
for dinner. Uriah ate with David and
drank so much that he got drunk, but he
still did not go home. He went out and
slept on his mat near the palace guards.
14Early the next morning, David wrote a
letter and told Uriah to deliver it to
Joab. 15The letter said: "Put Uriah on the
front line where the fighting is the
worst. Then pull the troops back from
him, so that he will be wounded and
die."
16Joab had been carefully watching
the city of Rabbah, and he put Uriah in
a place where he knew there were some
of the enemy's best soldiers. 17When the
men of the city came out, they fought
and killed some of David's soldiers—
Uriah the Hittite was one of them.
18Joab sent a messenger to tell David
everything that was happening in the
war. 19He gave the messenger these orders:

> When you finish telling the king
> everything that has happened, 20he
> may get angry and ask, "Why did
> you go so near the city to fight?
> Didn't you know they would shoot
> arrows from the wall? 21Don't you
> know how Abimelech the son of
> Gideon[r] was killed at Thebez?
> Didn't a woman kill him by drop-
> ping a large rock from the top of the
> city wall? Why did you go so close to
> the city walls?"
> Then you tell him, "One of your
> soldiers who was killed was Uriah
> the Hittite."

22The messenger went to David and
reported everything Joab had told him.
23He added, "The enemy chased us from
the wall and out into the open fields. But
we pushed them back as far as the city
gate. 24Then they shot arrows at us from
the top of the wall. Some of your soldiers were killed, and one of them was
Uriah the Hittite."
25David replied, "Tell Joab to cheer up
and not to be upset about what happened. You never know who will be
killed in a war. Tell him to strengthen
his attack against the city and break
through its walls."[s]
26When Bathsheba heard that her husband was dead, she mourned for him.
27Then after the time for mourning was
over, David sent someone to bring her to
the palace. She became David's wife,
and they had a son.

The LORD's Message for David

The LORD was angry at what David
had done,
12 1and he sent Nathan the prophet
to tell this story to David:

> A rich man and a poor man lived
> in the same town. 2The rich man
> owned a lot of sheep and cattle, 3but
> the poor man had only one little
> lamb that he had bought and raised.
> The lamb became a pet for him and
> his children. He even let it eat from
> his plate and drink from his cup and
> sleep on his lap. The lamb was like
> one of his own children.
> 4One day someone came to visit
> the rich man, but the rich man didn't
> want to kill any of his own sheep or
> cattle and serve it to the visitor. So
> he stole the poor man's little lamb
> and served it instead.

5David was furious with the rich man
and said to Nathan, "I swear by the living LORD that the man who did this deserves to die! 6And because he didn't
have any pity on the poor man, he will
have to pay four times what the lamb
was worth."
7Then Nathan told David:

> You are that rich man! Now listen
> to what the LORD God of Israel says
> to you: "I chose you to be the king of
> Israel. I kept you safe from Saul
> 8and even gave you his house and
> his wives. I let you rule Israel and
> Judah, and if that had not been
> enough, I would have given you
> much more. 9Why did you disobey
> me and do such a horrible thing?
> You murdered Uriah the Hittite by

[p]**11.8** *and clean up*: Or "and sleep with your wife." [q]**11.11** *somewhere in the fields*: Or "at Succoth." [r]**11.21** *Gideon*: The Hebrew text has Jerubbesheth, which stands for "Jerubbaal," another name for Gideon. See Judges 6.32 and the note on "bosheth" at 2.8 ("besheth" means the same as "bosheth"). [s]**11.25** *break . . . walls*: Or "destroy it."

having the Ammonites kill him, so
you could take his wife.
10"Because you wouldn't obey me
and took Uriah's wife for yourself,
your family will never live in peace.
11Someone from your own family
will cause you a lot of trouble, and I
will take your wives and give them
to another man before your very
eyes. He will go to bed with them
while everyone looks on. 12What you
did was in secret, but I will do this in
the open for everyone in Israel to
see."
13-14David said, "I have disobeyed the
LORD."
"Yes, you have!" Nathan answered.
"You showed you didn't care what the
LORD wanted.[t] He has forgiven you, and
you won't die. But your newborn son
will." 15Then Nathan went back home.

David's Young Son Dies

The LORD made David's young son
very sick.
16So David went without eating to
show his sorrow, and he begged God to
make the boy well. David would not
sleep on his bed, but spent each night
lying on the floor. 17His officials stood
beside him and tried to talk him into
getting up. But he would not get up or
eat with them.
18After the child had been sick for
seven days, he died, but the officials
were afraid to tell David. They said to
each other, "Even when the boy was
alive, David wouldn't listen to us. How
can we tell him his son is dead? He
might do something terrible!"
19David noticed his servants whisper-
ing, and he knew the boy was dead.
"Did my son die?" he asked his servants.
"Yes, he did," they answered.
20David got up off the floor; he took a
bath, combed his hair, and dressed. He
went into the LORD's tent and worshiped, then he went back home. David
asked for something to eat, and when
his servants brought him some food, he
ate it.
21His officials said, "What are you doing? You went without eating and cried
for your son while he was alive! But
now that he's dead, you're up and eating."
22David answered:
While he was still alive, I went
without food and cried because
there was still hope. I said to myself,
"Who knows? Maybe the LORD will
have pity on me and let the child
live." 23But now that he's dead, why
should I go without eating? I can't
bring him back! Someday I will join
him in death, but he can't return to
me.

Solomon Is Born

24David comforted his wife Bathsheba
and slept with her. Later on, she gave
birth to another son and named him
Solomon. The LORD loved Solomon
25and sent Nathan the prophet to tell
David, "The LORD will call him Jedidiah."[u]

The End of the War with Ammon

(1 Chronicles 20.1b-3)

26Meanwhile, Joab had been in the
country of Ammon, attacking the city of
Rabbah. He captured the royal fortress
27and sent a messenger to tell David:
I have attacked Rabbah and captured the fortress guarding the city
water supply. 28Call the rest of the
army together. Then surround the
city, and capture it yourself. If you
don't, everyone will remember that I
captured the city.
29David called the rest of the army together and attacked Rabbah. He captured the city 30and took the crown from
the statue of their god Milcom.[v] The
crown was made of seventy-five pounds
of gold, and there was a valuable jewel
on it. David put the jewel on his own
crown.[w] He also carried off everything
else of value. 31David made the people
of Rabbah tear down the city walls[x]
with iron picks and axes, and then he
put them to work making bricks. He did
the same thing with all the other Ammonite cities.
David went back to Jerusalem, and
the people of Israel returned to their
homes.

Amnon Disgraces Tamar

13 David had a beautiful daughter
named Tamar, who was the sister
of Absalom. She was also the half sister
of Amnon,[y] who fell in love with her.
2But Tamar was a virgin, and Amnon
could not think of a way to be alone
with her. He was so upset about it that
he made himself sick.
3Amnon had a friend named Jonadab,
who was the son of David's brother
Shimeah. Jonadab always knew how to

[t] **12.13,14** *what . . . wanted*: One manuscript of one ancient translation; one Hebrew manuscript "what the LORD had said"; most Hebrew manuscripts "what the enemies of the Lord would think." [u] **12.25** *Jedidiah*: In Hebrew this name means "Loved by the LORD." [v] **12.30** *the statue of their god Milcom*: Or "their king." [w] **12.30** *David . . . crown*: Or "and David wore the crown." [x] **12.31** *tear . . . walls*: One possible meaning for the difficult Hebrew text. [y] **13.1** *Tamar . . . Absalom . . . Amnon*: David was their father, but Amnon had a different mother.

get what he wanted, 4and he said to Amnon, "What's the matter? You're the
king's son! You shouldn't have to go
around feeling sorry for yourself every
morning."
Amnon said, "I'm in love with Tamar,
my brother Absalom's sister."
5Jonadab told him, "Lie down on your
bed and pretend to be sick. When your
father comes to see you, ask him to send
Tamar, so you can watch her cook something for you. Then she can serve you
the food."
6So Amnon went to bed and pretended to be sick. When the king came
to see him, Amnon said, "Please, ask
Tamar to come over. She can make
some special bread[z] while I watch, and
then she can serve me the bread."
7David told Tamar, "Go over to Amnon's house and fix him some food."
8When she got there, he was lying in
bed. She mixed the dough, made the
loaves, and baked them while he
watched. 9Then she took the bread out
of the pan and put it on his plate, but he
refused to eat it.
Amnon said, "Send the servants out of
the house." After they had gone, 10he
said to Tamar, "Serve the food in my
bedroom."
Tamar picked up the bread that she
had made and brought it into Amnon's
bedroom. 11But as she was taking it over
to him, he grabbed her and said, "Come
to bed with me!"
12She answered, "No! Please don't
force me! This sort of thing isn't done in
Israel. It's too disgusting! 13Think of me.
I'll be disgraced forever! And think
of yourself. Everyone in Israel will
say you're nothing but trash! Just
ask the king, and he will let you marry
me."
14But Amnon would not listen to what
she said. He was stronger than she was,
so he overpowered her and raped her.
15Then Amnon hated her even more
than he had loved her before. So he told
her, "Get up and get out!"
16She said, "Don't send me away! That
would be worse than what you have already done."
But Amnon would not listen. 17He
called in his servant and said, "Throw
this woman out and lock the door!"
18The servant made her leave, and he
locked the door behind her.
The king's unmarried daughters used
to wear long robes with sleeves.[a]
19Tamar tore the robe she was wearing
and put ashes on her head. Then she
covered her face with her hands and
cried loudly as she walked away.

Absalom Kills Amnon

20Tamar's brother Absalom said to
her, "How could Amnon have done such
a terrible thing to you! But since he's
your brother, don't tell anyone what
happened. Just try not to think about it."
Tamar soon moved into Absalom's
house, but she was always sad and
lonely. 21When David heard what had
happened to Tamar, he was very angry.
But Amnon was his oldest son and also
his favorite, and David would not do
anything to make Amnon unhappy.[b]
22Absalom treated Amnon as though
nothing had happened, but he hated
Amnon for what he had done to his sister Tamar.
23Two years later, Absalom's servants
were cutting wool from his sheep in
Baal-Hazor near the town of Ephraim,
and Absalom invited all of the king's
sons to be there.[c] 24Then he went to
David and said, "My servants are cutting the wool from my sheep. Please
come and join us!"
25David answered, "No, my son, we
won't go. It would be too expensive for
you." Absalom tried to get him to
change his mind, but David did not
want to go. He only said that he hoped
they would have a good time.
26Absalom said, "If you won't go, at
least let my brother Amnon come with
us."
David asked, "Why should he go with
you?" 27But Absalom kept on insisting,
and finally David let Amnon and all his
other sons go with Absalom.
Absalom prepared a banquet fit for a
king.[d] 28But he told his servants, "Keep
an eye on Amnon. When he gets a little
drunk from the wine and is feeling
good, I'll give the signal. Then kill him!
I've commanded you to do it, so don't be
afraid. Be strong and brave."
29Absalom's servants killed Amnon,
just as Absalom had told them. The rest
of the king's sons quickly rode away on
their mules to escape from Absalom.
30While they were on their way to
Jerusalem, someone told David, "Absalom has killed all of your sons! Not even
one is left." 31David got up, and in his
sorrow he tore his clothes and lay down
on the ground. His servants remained
standing, but they tore their clothes
too.

[z] **13.6** *special bread*: Or "heart-shaped bread" or "dumplings." [a] **13.18** *long . . . sleeves*: One possible meaning for the difficult Hebrew text. [b] **13.21** *But Amnon . . . unhappy*: The Dead Sea Scrolls and one ancient translation; these words are not in the Standard Hebrew Text. [c] **13.23** *invited . . . there*: Cutting the wool from sheep was a time for celebrating as well as working. [d] **13.27** *Absalom prepared . . . king*: One ancient translation; these words are not in the Hebrew text.

32 Then David's nephew[e] Jonadab
said, "Your Majesty, not all of your sons
were killed! Only Amnon is dead. On
the day that Amnon raped Tamar, Absalom decided to kill him. 33 Don't worry
about the report that all your sons were
killed. Only Amnon is dead, 34 and Absalom has run away."

One of the guards noticed a lot of people coming along the hillside on the
road to Horonaim.[f] He went and told the
king, "I saw some men coming along
Horonaim Road."[g]

35 Jonadab said, "Your Majesty, look!
Here come your sons now, just as I told
you."

36 No sooner had he said it, than
David's sons came in. They were weeping out loud, and David and all his officials cried just as loudly. 37-38 David was
sad for a long time because Amnon was
dead.

David Lets Absalom Come Home

Absalom had run away to Geshur,
where he stayed for three years with
King Talmai[h] the son of Ammihud.
39 David still felt so sad over the loss of
Amnon that he wanted to take his army
there and capture Absalom.[i]

14 Joab knew that David couldn't
stop thinking about Absalom,
2-3 and he sent someone to bring in the
wise woman who lived in Tekoa. Joab
told her, "Put on funeral clothes and
don't use any makeup. Go to the king
and pretend you have spent a long time
mourning the death of a loved one."
Then he told her what to say.

4 The woman from Tekoa went to
David. She bowed very low and said,
"Your Majesty, please help me!"

5 David asked, "What's the matter?"

She replied:

> My husband is dead, and I'm a
> widow. 6 I had two sons, but they got
> into a fight out in a field where there
> was no one to pull them apart, and
> one of them killed the other. 7 Now
> all of my relatives have come to me
> and said, "Hand over your son!
> We're going to put him to death for
> killing his brother." But what they
> really want is to get rid of him, so
> they can take over our land.
>
> Please don't let them put out my
> only flame of hope! There won't be
> anyone left on this earth to carry on
> my husband's name.

8 "Go on home," David told her. "I'll
take care of this matter for you."

9 The woman said, "I hope your decision doesn't cause any problems for
you. But if it does, you can blame me."[j]

10 He said, "If anyone gives you any
trouble, bring them to me, and it won't
happen again!"

11 "Please," she replied, "swear by the
LORD your God that no one will be allowed to kill my son!"

He said, "I swear by the living LORD
that no one will touch even a hair on his
head!"

12 Then she asked, "Your Majesty, may
I say something?"

"Yes," he answered.

13 The woman said:

> Haven't you been hurting God's
> people? Your own son had to leave
> the country. And when you judged in
> my favor, it was the same as admit-
> ting that you should have let him
> come back. 14 We each must die and
> disappear like water poured out on
> the ground. But God doesn't take
> our lives.[k] Instead, he figures out
> ways of bringing us back when we
> run away.
>
> 15 Your Majesty, I came here to tell
> you about my problem, because I
> was afraid of what someone might
> do to me. I decided to come to you,
> because I thought you could help.
> 16 In fact, I knew that you would lis-
> ten and save my son and me from
> those who want to take the land that
> God gave us.[l]
>
> 17 I can rest easy now that you
> have given your decision. You know
> the difference between right and
> wrong just like an angel of God, and
> I pray that the LORD your God will
> be with you.

18 Then David said to the woman,
"Now I'm going to ask you a question,
and don't try to hide the truth!"

The woman replied, "Please go ahead,
Your Majesty."

19 David asked, "Did Joab put you up
to this?"

The woman answered, "Your Majesty,
I swear by your life that no one can hide
the truth from you. Yes, Joab did tell me
what to say, 20 but only to show you the
other side of this problem. You must be
as wise as the angel of God to know
everything that goes on in this country."

21 David turned to Joab and said, "It

[e] **13.32** *David's nephew*: The Hebrew text has "the son of David's brother Shimeah."
[f] **13.34** *the road to Horonaim*: Or "the road behind him" or "the road to the west."
[g] **13.34** *He . . . Road*: One ancient translation; these words are not in the Hebrew text.
[h] **13.37,38** *King Talmai*: Absalom's grandfather (see 3.3). [i] **13.39** *David . . . Absalom*: Or "David was comforted over the loss of Amnon, and he no longer wanted to take his army there to capture Absalom." [j] **14.9** *I hope . . . me*: Or "May I speak some more?" [k] **14.14** *take our lives*: Or "make any exceptions." [l] **14.16** *take . . . us*: Or "make sure we have no part in God's people."

seems that I have already given my decision. Go and bring Absalom back."
22Joab bowed very low and said,
"Your Majesty, I thank you for giving
your permission. It shows that you approve of me."
23Joab went to Geshur to get Absalom. But when they came back to
Jerusalem, 24David told Joab, "I don't
want to see my son Absalom. Tell him to
stay away from me." So Absalom went
to his own house without seeing his
father.

Absalom Was Handsome

25No one in all Israel was as handsome and well-built as Absalom. 26He
got his hair cut once a year, and when
the hair was weighed, it came to about
five pounds.
27Absalom had three sons. He also
had a daughter named Tamar, who grew
up to be very beautiful.

Absalom Finally Sees David

28Absalom lived in Jerusalem for two
years without seeing his father. 29He
wanted Joab to talk to David for him. So
one day he sent a message asking Joab
to come over, but Joab refused. Absalom
sent another message, but Joab still refused. 30Finally, Absalom told his servants, "Joab's barley field is right next
to mine. Go set it on fire!" And they did.
31Joab went to Absalom's house and
demanded, "Why did your servants set
my field on fire?"
32Absalom answered, "You didn't pay
any attention when I sent for you. I want
you to ask my father why he told me to
come back from Geshur. I was better off
there. I want to see my father now! If
I'm guilty, let him kill me."
33Joab went to David and told him
what Absalom had said. David sent for
Absalom, and Absalom came. He bowed
very low, and David leaned over and
kissed him.

Absalom Rebels against David

15 Some time later, Absalom got
himself a chariot with horses to
pull it, and he had fifty men run in front.
2He would get up early each morning
and wait by the side of the road that led
to the city gate.[m] Anyone who had a
complaint to bring to King David would
have to go that way, and Absalom would
ask each of them, "Where are you
from?"
If they said, "I'm from a tribe in the
north," 3Absalom would say, "You deserve to win your case. It's too bad the
king doesn't have anyone to hear complaints like yours. 4I wish someone
would make me the judge around here! I
would be fair to everyone."
5Whenever anyone would come to Absalom and start bowing down, he would
reach out and hug and kiss them.
6That's how he treated everyone from
Israel who brought a complaint to the
king. Soon everyone in Israel liked Absalom better than they liked David.
7Four years[n] later, Absalom said to
David, "Please, let me go to Hebron. I
have to keep a promise that I made to
the LORD, 8when I was living with the
Arameans in Geshur. I promised that if
the LORD would bring me back to live in
Jerusalem, I would worship him in Hebron."[o]
9David gave his permission, and Absalom went to Hebron. 10-12He took two
hundred men from Jerusalem with him,
but they had no idea what he was going
to do. Absalom offered sacrifices in Hebron and sent someone to Gilo to tell
David's advisor Ahithophel to come.
More and more people were joining
Absalom and supporting his plot. Meanwhile, Absalom had secretly sent some
messengers to the northern tribes of Israel. The messengers told everyone,
"When you hear the sound of the trumpets, you must shout, 'Absalom now
rules as king in Hebron!' "

David Has To Leave Jerusalem

13A messenger came and told David,
"Everyone in Israel is on Absalom's
side!"
14David's officials were in Jerusalem
with him, and he told them, "Let's get
out of here! We'll have to leave soon, or
none of us will escape from Absalom.
Hurry! If he moves fast, he could catch
us while we're still here. Then he will
kill us and everyone else in the city."
15The officials said, "Your Majesty,
we'll do whatever you say."
16-17David left behind ten of his wives[p]
to take care of the palace, but the rest of
his family and his officials and soldiers
went with him.
They stopped at the last house at the
edge of the city. 18Then David stood
there and watched while his regular
troops and his bodyguards[q] marched
past. The last group was the six hundred
soldiers who had followed him from
Gath.[r] Their commander was Ittai.
19David spoke to Ittai and said,
"You're a foreigner from the town of

[m] **15.2** *the city gate*: Or "the entrance to the king's palace." [n] **15.7** *Four years*: The Hebrew text has "forty years." [o] **15.8** *in Hebron*: Some manuscripts of one ancient translation; these words are not in the Hebrew text. [p] **15.16,17** *wives*: See the note at 3.7. [q] **15.18** *bodyguards*: See the note at 8.18. [r] **15.18** *the six . . . Gath*: These were Philistine soldiers who were loyal to David.

Gath. You don't have to leave with us.
Go back and join the new king! 20You
haven't been with me very long, so why
should you have to follow me, when I
don't even know where I'm going? Take
your soldiers and go back. I pray that
the Lord will be[s] kind and faithful to
you."
21Ittai answered, "Your Majesty, just
as surely as you and the LORD live, I will
go where you go, no matter if it costs me
my life."
22"Then come on!" David said.
So Ittai and all his men and their families walked on past David.

David Sends the Sacred Chest Back to Jerusalem

23The people of Jerusalem were crying and moaning as David and everyone with him passed by. He led them across Kidron Valley[t] and along the road toward the desert.
24Zadok and Abiathar the priests were there along with several men from the tribe of Levi who were carrying the sacred chest. They set the chest down, and left it there until David and his followers had gone out of the city.
25Then David said:

Zadok, take the sacred chest back
to Jerusalem. If the LORD is pleased
with me, he will bring me back and
let me see it and his tent again. 26But
if he says he isn't pleased with me,
then let him do what he knows is
best.
27Zadok, you are a good judge of
things,[u] so return to the city and
don't cause any trouble. Take your
son Ahimaaz with you. Abiathar and
his son Jonathan will also go back.
28I'll wait at the river crossing in the
desert until I hear from you.

29Zadok and Abiathar took the sacred
chest back into Jerusalem and stayed
there. 30David went on up the slope of
the Mount of Olives. He was barefoot and crying, and he covered his head to show his sorrow. Everyone with him was crying, and they covered their heads too.
31Someone told David, "Ahithophel is helping Absalom plot against you!"
David said, "Please, LORD, keep Ahithophel's plans from working!"

David Sends Hushai Back as a Spy

32When David reached the top of the Mount of Olives, he met Hushai the Archite[v] at a place of worship. Hushai's
robe was torn, and dust was on his
head.[w] 33David told him:

If you come with me, you might
slow us down.[x] 34Go back into the
city and tell Absalom, "Your Majesty, I am your servant. I will serve you now, just as I served your father in the past."
Hushai, if you do that, you can help me ruin Ahithophel's plans.
35Zadok and Abiathar the priests
will be there with you, and you can
tell them everything you hear in the
palace. 36Then have them send their
sons Ahimaaz and Jonathan to tell
me what you've heard.

37David's advisor Hushai slipped back into Jerusalem, just about the same time that Absalom was coming in.

Ziba Gives Food to David

16 David had started down the other side of the Mount of Olives, when he was met by Ziba, the chief servant of Mephibosheth.[y] Ziba had two donkeys that were carrying two hundred loaves of bread, a hundred handfuls of raisins, a hundred figs,[z] and some wine.
2"What's all this?" David asked.
Ziba said, "The donkeys are for your family to ride. The bread and fruit are for the people to eat, and the wine is for them to drink in the desert when they are tired out."
3"And where is Mephibosheth?" David asked.
Ziba answered, "He stayed in Jerusalem, because he thinks the people of Israel want him to rule the kingdom of his grandfather Saul."
4David then told him, "Everything that used to belong to Mephibosheth is now yours."
Ziba said, "Your Majesty, I am your humble servant, and I hope you will be pleased with me."

Shimei Curses David

5David was near the town of Bahurim
when a man came out and started cursing him. The man was Shimei the son of Gera, and he was one of Saul's distant
relatives. 6He threw stones at David, at
his soldiers, and at everyone else, including the bodyguards who walked on each side of David.
7Shimei was yelling at David, "Get out
of here, you murderer! You good-for-
nothing, 8the LORD is paying you back
for killing so many in Saul's family. You stole his kingdom, but now the LORD

[s]15.20 *I pray . . . be*: One ancient translation; these words are not in the Hebrew text. [t]15.23 *Kidron Valley*: This was considered the eastern boundary of Jerusalem. [u]15.27 *you . . . things*: Or "You are a prophet" or "You are not a prophet." [v]15.32 *Archite*: The Archites were part of the tribe of Benjamin (see Joshua 16.2). [w]15.32 *Hushai's . . . head*: See the note at 1.2. [x]15.33 *you might slow us down*: Hushai was probably very old. [y]16.1 *chief servant of Mephibosheth*: See 9.1-13. [z]16.1 *figs*: Or "pomegranates," a bright red fruit that looks like an apple.

has given it to your son Absalom. You're
a murderer, and that's why you're in
such big trouble!"
9Abishai said, "Your Majesty, this man
is as useless as a dead dog! He shouldn't
be allowed to curse you. Let me go over
and chop off his head."
10David replied, "What will I ever do
with you and your brother Joab? If
Shimei is cursing me because the LORD
has told him to, then who are you to tell
him to stop?"
11Then David said to Abishai and all
his soldiers:
My own son is trying to kill me!
Why shouldn't this man from the
tribe of Benjamin want me dead
even more? Let him curse all he
wants. Maybe the LORD did tell him
to curse me. 12But if the LORD hears
these curses and sees the trouble I'm
in, maybe he will have pity on me instead.
13David and the others went on down
the road. Shimei went along the hillside
by the road, cursing and throwing rocks
and dirt at them. 14When David and
those with him came to the Jordan
River, they were tired out. But after they
rested, they[a] felt much better.

Hushai Meets Absalom

15By this time, Absalom, Ahithophel,
and the others had reached Jerusalem.
16David's friend Hushai came to Absalom and said, "Long live the king! Long
live the king!"
17But Absalom asked Hushai, "Is this
how you show loyalty to your friend
David? Why didn't you go with him?"
18Hushai answered, "The LORD and
the people of Israel have chosen you to
be king. I can't leave. I have to stay and
serve the one they've chosen. 19Besides,
it seems right for me to serve you, just
as I served your father."

Ahithophel's Advice

20Absalom turned to Ahithophel and
said, "Give us your advice! What should
we do?"
21Ahithophel answered, "Some of
your father's wives[b] were left here to
take care of the palace. You should have
sex with them. Then everyone will find
out that you have publicly disgraced
your father. This will make you and
your followers even more powerful."
22Absalom had a tent set up on the
flat roof of the palace, and everyone
watched as he went into the tent with
his father's wives.
23Ahithophel gave such good advice in
those days that both Absalom and
David thought it came straight from
God.

17 Ahithophel said to Absalom:
Let me choose twelve thousand men and attack David tonight,
2while he is tired and discouraged.
He will panic, and everyone with
him will run away. I won't kill anyone except David, 3since he's the
one you want to get rid of. Then I'll
bring the whole nation back to you
like a bride coming home to her husband.[c] This way there won't be a
civil war.

Hushai Fools Absalom

4Absalom and all the leaders of the
tribes of Israel agreed that Ahithophel
had a good plan. 5Then Absalom said,
"Bring in Hushai the Archite. Let's hear
what he has to say."
6Hushai came in, and Absalom told
him what Ahithophel had planned. Then
Absalom said, "Should we do what he
says? And if we shouldn't, can you come
up with anything better?"
7Hushai said:
This time Ahithophel's advice isn't
so good. 8You know that your father
and his followers are real warriors.
Right now they are as fierce as a
mother bear whose cubs have just
been killed. Besides, your father has
a lot of experience in fighting wars,
and he won't be spending the night
with the others. 9He has probably already found a hiding place in a cave
or somewhere else.
As soon as anyone hears that
some of your soldiers have been
killed, everyone will think your
whole army has been destroyed.
10Then even those who are as brave
as a lion will lose their courage. All
Israel knows what a great warrior
your father is and what brave soldiers he has.
11My advice is to gather all the
fighting men of Israel from the town
of Dan in the north down to the
town of Beersheba in the south. You
will have more soldiers than there
are grains of sand on the seashore.
Absalom, you should lead them
yourself, 12and we will all go to fight
David wherever he is. We will fall on
him just as dew falls and covers the
ground. He and all his soldiers will
die! 13If they go into a walled town,
we will put ropes around that town
and drag it into the river. We won't

[a]16.14 *they*: Hebrew "he." [b]16.21 *wives*: See the note at 3.7. [c]17.3 *back to you . . . husband*: One ancient translation; Hebrew "back to you. The man you are chasing is like bringing back the whole nation."

leave even one small piece of a
stone.
14 Absalom and the others liked
Hushai's plan better than Ahithophel's
plan. This was because the LORD had decided to keep Ahithophel's plan from
working and to cause trouble for Absalom.

Jonathan and Ahimaaz Tell David the News

15 Right away, Hushai went to Zadok
and Abiathar. He told them what advice
Ahithophel had given to Absalom and
to the leaders of Israel. He also told
them about the advice he had given.
16 Then he said, "Hurry! Send someone
to warn David not to spend the night on
this side of the river. He must get across
the river, so he and the others won't be
wiped out!"
17 Jonathan and Ahimaaz[d] had been
waiting at Rogel Spring[e] because they
did not want to be seen in Jerusalem. A
servant girl went to the spring and gave
them the message for David. 18 But a
young man saw them and went to tell
Absalom. So Jonathan and Ahimaaz left
and hurried to the house of a man who
lived in Bahurim. Then they climbed
down into a well in the courtyard. 19 The
man's wife put the cover on the well and
poured grain on top of it, so the well
could not be seen.[f]
20 Absalom's soldiers came to the
woman and demanded, "Where are Ahimaaz and Jonathan?"
The woman answered, "They went
across the stream."
The soldiers went off to look for the
two men. But when they did not find the
men, they went back to Jerusalem.
21 After the soldiers had gone,
Jonathan and Ahimaaz climbed out of
the well. They went to David and said,
"Hurry! Get ready to cross the river!"
Then they told him about Ahithophel's
plan.
22 David and the others got ready and
started crossing the Jordan River. By
sunrise all of them were on the other
side.

Ahithophel Kills Himself

23 When Ahithophel saw that Absalom
and the leaders of Israel were not going
to follow his advice, he saddled his donkey and rode back to his home in Gilo.
He told his family and servants what to
do. Then he hanged himself, and they
buried him in his family's burial place.

Absalom Puts Amasa in Charge of the Army

24 David went to the town of Mahanaim, and Absalom crossed the Jordan River with the army of Israel. 25 Absalom put Amasa in Joab's place as
commander of the army. Amasa's father
was Ithra[g] from the family of Ishmael,[h]
and his mother was Abigal,[i] the daughter of Nahash and the sister of Joab's
mother Zeruiah. 26 The Israelites under
Absalom's command set up camp in the
region of Gilead.

Friends Bring Supplies to David

27 After David came to the town of Mahanaim, Shobi the son of Nahash came
from Rabbah in Ammon,[j] Machir the
son of Ammiel came from Lo-Debar,
and Barzillai the Gileadite came from
Rogelim.
28-29 Here is a list of what they brought:
sleeping mats, blankets, bowls, pottery
jars, wheat, barley, flour, roasted grain,
beans, lentils, honey, yogurt, sheep, and
cheese.
They brought the food for David and
the others because they knew that
everyone would be hungry, tired, and
thirsty from being out in the desert.

David Gets Ready for Battle

18 David divided his soldiers into
groups of a hundred and groups
of a thousand. Then he chose officers to
be in command of each group. 2 He sent
out one-third of his army under the
command of Joab, another third under
the command of Abishai the son of
Zeruiah, and the rest under the command of Ittai from Gath. He told the soldiers, "I'm going into battle with you."
3 But the soldiers said, "No, don't go
into battle with us! It won't matter to
our enemies if they make us all run
away, or even if they kill half of us. But
you are worth ten thousand of us. It
would be better for you to stay in town
and send help if we need it."
4-6 David said, "All right, if you think I
should."
Then in a voice loud enough for

[d] **17.17** *Jonathan and Ahimaaz*: See 15.27. [e] **17.17** *Rogel Spring*: South of Jerusalem in Kidron Valley. [f] **17.19** *The man's wife . . . seen*: Everyone would have thought that the woman was drying grain on a mat that she had spread on the ground. [g] **17.25** *Ithra*: Or "Jether." [h] **17.25** *the family of Ishmael*: Some manuscripts of one ancient translation; other manuscripts of the same translation "the town of Jezreel"; Hebrew "the people of Israel." [i] **17.25** *Amasa . . . Abigal*: Abigal and Zeruiah (Joab's mother) were full sisters, and David was evidently their half-brother with the same mother, but a different father. This made Amasa one of David's nephews (see 1 Chronicles 2.12-17). [j] **17.27** *Shobi . . . Ammon*: Shobi was probably the new king of the Ammonites that David had appointed after he captured Rabbah (see 2 Samuel 10.1-3; 12.26-31).

everyone to hear, he said, "Joab!
Abishai! Ittai! For my sake, be sure that
Absalom comes back unharmed."
David stood beside the town gate as
his army marched past in groups of a
hundred and in groups of a thousand.

Joab Kills Absalom

The war with Israel took place in
Ephraim Forest. 7-8Battles were being
fought all over the forest, and David's
soldiers were winning. Twenty thousand
soldiers were killed[k] that day, and more
of them died from the dangers of the
forest than from the fighting itself.
9Absalom was riding his mule under a
huge tree when his head[l] caught in the
branches. The mule ran off and left Absalom hanging in midair. Some of
David's soldiers happened by, 10and one
of them went and told Joab, "I saw Absalom hanging in a tree!"
11Joab said, "You saw Absalom? Why
didn't you kill him? I would have given
you ten pieces of silver and a special
belt."
12The man answered, "Even if you
paid me a thousand pieces of silver here
and now, I still wouldn't touch the king's
son. We all heard King David tell you
and Abishai and Ittai not to harm Absalom. 13He always finds out what's going
on. I would have been risking my life to
kill Absalom, because you would have
let me take the blame."
14Joab said, "I'm not going to waste
any more time on you!"
Absalom was still alive, so Joab took
three spears and stuck them through
Absalom's chest. 15Ten of Joab's bodyguards came over and finished him off.
16Then Joab blew a trumpet to signal his
troops to stop chasing Israel's soldiers.
17They threw Absalom's body into a
deep pit in the forest and put a big pile
of rocks over it.
Meanwhile, the people of Israel had
all run back to their own homes.
18When Absalom was alive, he had set
up a stone monument for himself in
King's Valley. He explained, "I don't
have any sons[m] to keep my name alive."
He called it Absalom's Monument, and
that is the name it still has today.[n]

Ahimaaz Wants To Tell David

19Ahimaaz the son of Zadok said,
"Joab, let me run and tell King David
that the LORD has rescued him from his
enemies."
20Joab answered, "You're not the one
to tell the king that his son is dead. You
can take him a message some other
time, but not today."
21Someone from Ethiopia[o] was standing there, and Joab told him, "Go and
tell the king what you have seen." The
man knelt down in front of Joab and
then got up and started running.
22Ahimaaz spoke to Joab again, "No
matter what happens, I still want to run.
And besides, the Ethiopian has already
left."
Joab said, "Why should you run? You
won't get a reward for the news you
have!"
23"I'll run no matter what!" Ahimaaz
insisted.
"All right then, run!" Joab said.
Ahimaaz took the road through the
Jordan Valley and outran the Ethiopian.
24Meanwhile, David was sitting between the inner and outer gates[p] in the
city wall. One of his soldiers was watching from the roof of the gate-tower. He
saw a man running toward the town
25and shouted down to tell David.
David answered, "If he's alone, he
must have some news."
The runner was getting closer, 26when
the soldier saw someone else running.
He shouted down to the gate, "Look!
There's another runner!"
David said, "He must have some news
too."
27The soldier on the roof shouted,
"The first one runs just like Ahimaaz the
son of Zadok."
This time David said, "He's a good
man. He must have some good news."
28Ahimaaz called out, "We won! We
won!" Then he bowed low to David and
said, "Your Majesty, praise the LORD
your God! He has given you victory over
your enemies."
29"Is my son Absalom all right?"
David asked.
Ahimaaz said, "When Joab sent your
personal servant and me, I saw a noisy
crowd. But I don't know what it was all
about."
30David told him, "Stand over there
and wait."
Ahimaaz went over and stood there.
31The Ethiopian came and said, "Your
Majesty, today I have good news! The

[k]18.7,8 *Twenty . . . killed*: This may refer to the total number or to the number of Absalom's soldiers who were killed. [l]18.9 *head*: Or "hair." [m]18.18 *I don't have any sons*: According to 14.27, Absalom had three sons. But they could have died young or been put to death for Absalom's murder of Amnon. [n]18.18 *today*: That is, at the time of writing. This monument is not the same as the structure now known as "Absalom's Tomb," which was built at least 600 years later. [o]18.21 *Ethiopia*: The Hebrew text has "Cush," which was a region south of Egypt that included parts of the present countries of Ethiopia and Sudan.
[p]18.24 *between . . . gates*: The city gate was often like a tower in the city wall, with one gate on the outside of the wall and another gate on the inside of the wall.

LORD has rescued you from all your enemies!"
32"Is my son Absalom all right?"
David asked.
The Ethiopian replied, "I wish that all
Your Majesty's enemies and everyone
who tries to harm you would end up like
him!"

David Cries for Absalom

33David started trembling. Then he
went up to the room above the city gate
to cry. As he went, he kept saying, "My
son Absalom! My son, my son Absalom!
I wish I could have died instead of you!
Absalom, my son, my son!"[q]

19 Someone told Joab, "The king is
crying because Absalom is dead."
2David's army found out he was crying because his son had died, and their
day of victory suddenly turned into a
day of sadness. 3The troops were sneaking into Mahanaim, just as if they had
run away from a battle and were
ashamed.
4David held his hands over his face
and kept on crying loudly, "My son, Absalom! Absalom, my son, my son!"
5Joab went to the house where David
was staying and told him:

> You've made your soldiers
> ashamed! Not only did they save
> your life, they saved your sons and
> daughters and wives as well. 6You're
> more loyal to your enemies than to
> your friends. What you've done to-
> day has shown your officers and sol-
> diers that they don't mean a thing to
> you. You would be happy if Absalom
> was still alive, even if the rest of us
> were dead.
> 7Now get up! Go out there and
> thank them for what they did. If you
> don't, I swear by the LORD that you
> won't even have one man left on
> your side tomorrow morning. You
> may have had a lot of troubles in the
> past, but this will be the worst thing
> that has ever happened to you!

8David got up and went to the town
gate and sat down. When the people
heard that he was sitting there, they
came to see him.

Israel and Judah Want David Back

After Israel's soldiers had all returned
home, 9-10everyone in Israel started arguing. They were saying to each other,
"King David rescued us from the
Philistines and from our other enemies.
But then we chose Absalom to be our
new leader, and David had to leave the
country to get away. Absalom died in
battle, so why hasn't something been
done to bring David back?"

11When David found out what they
were saying, he sent a message to
Zadok and Abiathar the priests. It said:

> Say to the leaders of Judah, "Why
> are you the last tribe to think about
> bringing King David back home?
> 12He is your brother, your own rela-
> tive! Why haven't you done anything
> to bring him back?"
> 13And tell Amasa, "You're my
> nephew, and with God as a witness, I
> swear I'll make you commander of
> my army instead of Joab."

14Soon the tribe of Judah again became followers of David, and they sent
him this message: "Come back, and
bring your soldiers with you."

David Starts Back for Jerusalem

15David started back and had gone as
far as the Jordan River when he met the
people of Judah. They had gathered at
Gilgal and had come to help him cross
the river.
16Shimei[r] the son of Gera was there
with them. He had hurried from
Bahurim to meet David. Shimei was
from the tribe of Benjamin, and 17a
thousand others from Benjamin had
come with him.
Ziba, the chief servant of Saul's family, also came to the Jordan River. He
and his fifteen sons and twenty servants
waded across[s] to meet David. 18Then
they brought David's family and servants back across the river, and they did
everything he wanted them to do.

Shimei Meets with David

Shimei crossed the Jordan River and
bowed down in front of David. 19He
said, "Your Majesty, I beg you not to
punish me! Please, forget what I did
when you were leaving Jerusalem. Don't
even think about it. 20I know I was
wrong. That's why I wanted to be the
first one from the northern tribes to
meet you."
21But Abishai shouted, "You should be
killed for cursing the LORD's chosen
king!"
22David said, "Abishai, what will I ever
do with you and your brother Joab? Is it
your job to tell me who has done
wrong? I've been made king of all Israel
today, and no one will be put to death!"
23Then David promised Shimei that he
would not be killed.

Mephibosheth Meets with David

24Mephibosheth, the grandson of Saul,
also came to meet David. He had missed
David so much that he had not taken a
bath or trimmed his beard or washed

[q]**18.33** *son*: In Hebrew, this verse is 19.1. [r]**19.16** *Shimei*: See 16.5-13. [s]**19.17** *waded across*: Or "rushed."

his clothes the whole time David was
gone.
25After they had gone back to
Jerusalem, Mephibosheth came to see
David, who asked him, "Why didn't you
go with me?"
26He answered, "Your Majesty, you
know I can't walk. I told my servant to
saddle a donkey for me[t] so I could go
with you. But my servant left without
me, and 27then he lied about me. You're
as wise as an angel of God, so do what
you think is right. 28After all, you could
have killed my whole family and me.
But instead, you let me eat at your own
table. Your Majesty, what more could I
ask?"
29David answered, "You've said
enough! I've decided to divide the property[u] between you and Ziba."
30Mephibosheth replied, "He can have
it all! I'm just glad you've come home
safely."

Barzillai Returns Home

31Barzillai came from Rogelim in
Gilead to meet David at the Jordan
River and go across with him. 32Barzillai
was eighty years old. He was very rich
and had sent food to David in Mahanaim.
33David said to him, "Cross the river
and go to Jerusalem with me. I will take
care of you."
34Barzillai answered:
Your Majesty, why should I go to
Jerusalem? I don't have much
longer to live. 35I'm already eighty
years old, and my body is almost
numb. I can't taste my food or hear
the sound of singing, and I would
be nothing but a burden. 36I'll cross
the river with you, but I'll only go a
little way on the other side. You
don't have to be so kind to me.
37Just let me return to my hometown, where I can someday be
buried near my father and mother.
My servant Chimham[v] can go with
you, and you can treat him as your
own.
38David said, "I'll take Chimham with
me, and whatever you ask me to do for
him, I'll do. And if there's anything else
you want, I'll also do that."
39David's soldiers went on across the
river, while he stayed behind to tell
Barzillai good-by and to wish him well.
Barzillai returned home, but 40Chimham
crossed the river with David.

Israel and Judah Argue

All of Judah's army and half of Israel's army were there to help David
cross the river. 41The soldiers from Israel came to him and said, "Why did our
relatives from Judah sneak you and
your family and your soldiers across the
Jordan?"
42The people of Judah answered,
"Why are you so angry? We are the
king's relatives. He didn't give us any
food, and we didn't take anything for
ourselves!"
43Those from Israel said, "King David
belongs to us ten times more than he belongs to you.[w] Why didn't you think we
were good enough to help you? After
all, we were the first ones to think of
bringing him back!"
The people of Judah spoke more
harshly than the people of Israel.

Sheba Rebels against David

20 A troublemaker from the tribe of
Benjamin was there. His name
was Sheba the son of Bichri, and he
blew a trumpet to get everyone's attention. Then he said, "People of Israel,
David the son of Jesse doesn't belong to
us! Let's go home."
2So they stopped following David and
went off with Sheba. But the people of
Judah stayed close to David all the way
from the Jordan to Jerusalem.

David's Ten Wives

3David had left ten of his wives in
Jerusalem to take care of his palace.
But when he came back, he had
them taken to another house, and he
placed soldiers there to guard them.
He gave them whatever they needed,
but he never slept with any of them
again.[x] They had to live there for the
rest of their lives as if they were widows.

The Army Goes after Sheba

4David said to Amasa, "Three days
from now I want you and all of Judah's
army to be here!"
5Amasa started bringing the army together, but it was taking him more than
three days. 6So David said to Abishai,
"Sheba will hurt us more than Absalom
ever did. Take my best soldiers and go
after him. We don't want him to take
over any walled cities and get away
from us."[y]

[t] **19.26** *I told . . . me*: Two ancient translations; Hebrew, "I said, 'I will saddle a donkey for myself.'" [u] **19.29** *the property*: The property that had belonged to Saul (see 9.7; 16.4). [v] **19.37** *My servant Chimham*: Or "My son Chimham." [w] **19.43** *King David . . . you*: In this verse "Israel" stands for the ten northern tribes and does not include the tribe of Judah in the south. [x] **20.3** *he . . . again*: Because of what Absalom had done (see 16.21, 22). [y] **20.6** *get . . . us*: One possible meaning for the difficult Hebrew text.

Joab Kills Amasa

7 Abishai left Jerusalem to try and capture Sheba. He took along Joab and his
soldiers, as well as David's bodyguard[z]
and best troops. 8 They had gone as far
as the big rock at Gibeon when Amasa
caught up with them. Joab had a dagger
strapped around his waist over his military uniform, but it fell out as he started
toward Amasa.
9 Joab said, "Amasa, my cousin, how
are you?" Then Joab took hold of
Amasa's beard with his right hand, so
that he could greet him with a kiss.
10 Amasa did not see the dagger in
Joab's other hand. Joab stuck it in
Amasa's stomach, and his insides
spilled out on the ground. Joab only
struck him once, but Amasa was dying.
Joab and his brother Abishai went off
to chase Sheba. 11 One of Joab's soldiers
stood by Amasa and shouted, "If any of
you like Joab, and if you are for David,
then follow Joab!"
12 Amasa was still rolling in his own
blood in the middle of the road. The soldier who had shouted noticed that
everyone who passed by would stop, so
he dragged Amasa off the road and covered him with a blanket. 13 After this, no
one else stopped. They all walked
straight past him on their way to help
Joab capture Sheba.

Sheba Hides Out in the Town of Abel

14 Sheba had gone through all of the
tribes of Israel when he came to the
town of Abel Beth-Maacah. All of his
best soldiers[a] met him there and followed him into the town.
15 Joab and his troops came and surrounded Abel, so that no one could go
in or come out. They made a dirt ramp
up to the town wall and then started to
use a battering ram to knock the wall
down.

A Wise Woman Saves the Town

16 A wise woman shouted from the top
of the wall,[b] "Listen to me! Listen to me!
I have to talk to Joab! Tell him to come
here!" 17 When he came, the woman
said, "Are you Joab?"
"Yes, I am," he answered.
She said, "Please, listen to what I have
to say."
"All right," he said. "I'll listen."
18 She said, "Long ago people used to
say, 'If you want good advice, go to the
town of Abel to get it.' The answers they
got here were all that was needed to settle any problem. 19 We are Israelites, and
we want peace! You can trust us. Why
are you trying to destroy a town that's
like a mother in Israel? Why do you
want to wipe out the LORD's people?"
20 Joab answered, "No, no! I'm not trying to wipe you out or destroy your
town! 21 That's not it at all. There's a
man in your town from the hill country
of Ephraim. His name is Sheba, and he
is the leader of a rebellion against King
David. Turn him over to me, and we will
leave your town alone."
The woman told Joab, "We will throw
his head over the wall."
22 She went to the people of the town
and talked them into doing it. They cut
off Sheba's head and threw it to Joab.
Joab blew a signal on his trumpet,
and the soldiers returned to their
homes. Joab went back to David in Jerusalem.

Another List of David's Officials[c]

23 Joab was the commander of Israel's
entire army.
Benaiah the son of Jehoiada was in
command of David's bodyguard.[d]
24 Adoram[e] was in charge of the slave-
labor force.
Jehoshaphat the son of Ahilud kept
government records.
25 Sheva was the secretary.
Zadok and Abiathar were the priests.
26 Ira from Jair was David's priest.

The Gibeonites Hang Saul's Descendants

21 While David was king, there were
three years in a row when the nation of Israel could not grow enough
food. So David asked the LORD for help,
and the LORD answered, "Saul and his
family are guilty of murder, because he
had the Gibeonites killed."
2 The Gibeonites were not Israelites;
they were descendants of the Amorites.
The people of Israel had promised not to
kill them,[f] but Saul had tried to kill
them because he wanted Israel and Judah to control all the land.
David had the Gibeonites come, and
he talked with them. 3 He said, "What
can I do to make up for what Saul did,
so that you'll ask the LORD to be kind to
his people again?"[g]

[z] 20.7 *bodyguard*: See the note at 8.18. [a] 20.14 *best soldiers*: One ancient translation; the difficult Hebrew text may mean either "Berites" or "Bichrites," Sheba's relatives. [b] 20.16 *the top of the wall*: Or "the town." [c] 20.23 *Another List of David's Officials*: See also the list in 8.16, 17. [d] 20.23 *David's bodyguard*: See the note at 8.18. [e] 20.24 *Adoram*: One ancient translation "Adoniram" (see 1 Kings 4.6; 5.14). [f] 21.2 *promised . . . them*: See Joshua 9.3-27. [g] 21.3 *ask . . . again*: Saul's guilt had become a curse on Israel that had resulted in famine. For the effects of this curse to be removed, the Gibeonites would have to ask the LORD to be kind to Israel.

4The Gibeonites answered, "Silver and
gold from Saul and his family are not
enough. On the other hand, we don't
have the right to put any Israelite to
death."
David said, "I'll do whatever you
ask."[h]
5They replied, "Saul tried to kill all
our people so that none of us would be
left in the land of Israel. 6Give us seven
of his descendants. We will hang[i] these
men near the place where the LORD is
worshiped in Gibeah, the hometown of
Saul, the LORD's chosen king."
"I'll give them to you," David said.
7David had made a promise to
Jonathan with the LORD as his witness,
so he spared Jonathan's son Mephibosheth, the grandson of Saul. 8But Saul
and Rizpah the daughter of Aiah had
two sons named Armoni and Mephibosheth. Saul's daughter Merab[j] had five
sons whose father was Adriel the son of
Barzillai from Meholah.[k] David took
Rizpah's two sons and Merab's five sons
and 9turned them over to the Gibeonites, who hanged[l] all seven of them
on the mountain near the place where
the LORD was worshiped. This happened
right at the beginning of the barley
harvest.[m]

Rizpah Takes Care of the Bodies

10Rizpah spread out some sackcloth[n]
on a nearby rock. She wouldn't let the
birds land on the bodies during the day,
and she kept the wild animals away at
night. She stayed there from the beginning of the harvest until it started to
rain.[o]

The Burial of Saul and His Descendants

11-12Earlier the Philistines had killed
Saul and Jonathan on Mount Gilboa and
had hung their bodies in the town
square at Beth-Shan. The people of
Jabesh in Gilead had secretly taken the
bodies away, but David found out what
Saul's wife[p] Rizpah had done, and he
went to the leaders of Jabesh to get the
bones of Saul and his son Jonathan.
13-14David had their bones taken to
the land of Benjamin and buried in a
side room in Saul's family burial place.
Then he gave orders for the bones of
the men who had been hanged[q]
to be buried there. It was done, and
God answered prayers to bless the
land.

The Descendants of the Rephaim

(1 Chronicles 20.4-8)

15One time David got very tired when
he and his soldiers were fighting the
Philistines. 16One of the Philistine
warriors was Ishbibenob, who was
a descendant of the Rephaim,[r] and
he tried to kill David. Ishbibenob was
armed with a new sword,[s] and his
bronze spearhead[t] alone weighed seven
and a half pounds. 17But Abishai[u]
came to the rescue and killed the
Philistine.
David's soldiers told him, "We can't
let you risk your life in battle anymore!
You give light to our nation, and we
want that flame to keep burning."
18There was another battle with the
Philistines at Gob, where Sibbecai from
Hushah killed a descendant of the
Rephaim named Saph.
19There was still another battle with
the Philistines at Gob. A soldier named
Elhanan killed Goliath[v] from Gath,
whose spear shaft was like a weaver's
beam.[w] Elhanan's father was Jari[x] from
Bethlehem.
20There was another war, this time in
Gath. One of the enemy soldiers was a
descendant of the Rephaim. He was as
big as a giant and had six fingers on
each hand and six toes on each foot.
21But when he made fun of Israel,
David's nephew Jonathan killed him.
Jonathan was the son of David's brother
Shimei.
22David and his soldiers killed these
four men who were descendants of the
Rephaim from Gath.

[h]**21.4** *I'll . . . ask*: Or "What are you asking me to do for you?" [i]**21.6** *hang*: One possible meaning for the difficult Hebrew text. [j]**21.8** *Merab*: Some Hebrew manuscripts and some manuscripts of one ancient translation. Most other manuscripts have "Michal," Saul's daughter who was one of David's wives, but she never had any children (see 2 Samuel 6.23). According to 1 Samuel 18.19, Merab was Saul's daughter, and she married Adriel from Meholah. [k]**21.8** *Meholah*: Also known as Abel-Meholah. [l]**21.9** *hanged*: One possible meaning for the difficult Hebrew text. [m]**21.9** *This . . . harvest*: This would have been late in April. [n]**21.10** *sackcloth*: See the note at 3.31. [o]**21.10** *started to rain*: This may have been the beginning of the rainy season in September or October. It usually didn't rain from May to September. Or, it may have been a sign that now there would be enough rain again. [p]**21.11,12** *wife*: See the note at 3.7. [q]**21.13,14** *hanged*: One possible meaning for the difficult Hebrew text. [r]**21.16** *the Rephaim*: This may refer to a group of people that lived in Palestine before the Israelites and who were famous for their large size. [s]**21.16** *new sword*: One possible meaning for the difficult Hebrew text. [t]**21.16** *spearhead*: Or "helmet." [u]**21.17** *Abishai*: David's nephew, the brother of Joab. [v]**21.19** *Goliath*: According to 1 Chronicles 20.5, Elhanan killed the brother of Goliath. [w]**21.19** *weaver's beam*: A large wooden rod used by a weaver when making cloth. [x]**21.19** *Jari*: Or "Jaare."

David Sings to the LORD

(Psalm 18.1-50)

22 David sang a song to the LORD after the LORD had rescued him from his enemies, especially Saul. These are the words to David's song:

2 Our LORD and our God,
you are my mighty rock,[y]
my fortress, my protector.
3 You are the rock
where I am safe.
You are my shield,
my powerful weapon,[z]
and my place of shelter.

You rescue me and keep me
from being hurt.
4 I praise you, our LORD!
I prayed to you,
and you rescued me
from my enemies.
5 Death, like ocean waves,
surrounded me,
and I was almost swallowed
by its flooding waters.

6 Ropes from the world
of the dead
had coiled around me,
and death had set a trap
in my path.
7 I was in terrible trouble
when I called out to you,
but from your temple
you heard me
and answered my prayer.
8 Earth shook and shivered!
The columns supporting the sky[a]
rocked back and forth.
You were angry
9 and breathed out smoke.
Scorching heat and fiery flames
spewed from your mouth.

10 You opened the heavens
like curtains,
and you came down
with storm clouds
under your feet.
11 You rode on the backs
of flying creatures.[b]
You appeared[c]
with the wind as wings.
12 Darkness was your tent!
Thunderclouds filled the sky,
hiding you from sight.
13 Fiery coals lit up the sky
in front of you.

14 LORD Most High, your voice
thundered from the heavens.
15 You scattered your enemies
with arrows of lightning.
16 You roared at the sea,
and its deepest channels
could be seen.
You snorted,
and the earth shook
to its foundations.

17 You reached down from heaven,
and you lifted me
from deep in the ocean.
18 You rescued me from enemies
who were hateful
and too powerful for me.
19 On the day disaster struck,
they came and attacked,
but you defended me.
20 When I was fenced in,
you freed and rescued me
because you love me.
21 You are good to me, LORD,
because I do right,
and you reward me
because I am innocent.
22 I do what you want
and never turn to do evil.
23 I keep your laws in mind
and never turn away
from your teachings.
24 I obey you completely
and guard against sin.
25 You have been good to me
because I do right;
you have rewarded me
for being innocent
by your standards.

26 You are always loyal
to your loyal people,
and you are faithful
to the faithful.
27 With all who are sincere
you are sincere,
but you treat the unfaithful
as their deeds deserve.
28 You rescue the humble,
but you look for ways
to put down the proud.

29 Our LORD and God,
you are my lamp.
You turn darkness to light.
30 You help me defeat armies
and capture cities.

31 Your way is perfect, LORD,
and your word is correct.
You are a shield for those
who run to you for help.
32 You alone are God!
Only you are a mighty rock.[d]

[y]22.2 *mighty rock*: The Hebrew text has "rock," which is sometimes used in poetry to compare the LORD to a mountain where his people can run for protection from their enemies.
[z]22.3 *powerful weapon*: The Hebrew has "the horn," which refers to the horn of a bull, one of the most powerful animals in ancient Palestine. [a]22.8 *columns . . . sky*: The sky was sometimes described as a dome that was held up by a foundation or pillars. [b]22.11 *flying creatures*: These were supernatural beings (see the note at 6.2). [c]22.11 *appeared*: Most Hebrew manuscripts; some Hebrew manuscripts "swooped down" (see Psalm 18.10).
[d]22.32 *mighty rock*: See the note at 22.2.

33 You are my strong fortress,
and you set me free.
34 You make my feet run as fast
as those of a deer,
and you help me stand
on the mountains.

35 You teach my hands to fight
and my arms to use
a bow of bronze.
36 You alone are my shield,
and by coming to help me,
you have made me famous.
37 You clear the way for me,
and now I won't stumble.

38 I kept chasing my enemies
until I caught them
and destroyed them.
39 I destroyed them!
I stuck my sword
through my enemies,
and they were crushed
under my feet.
40 You helped me win victories
and forced my attackers
to fall victim to me.

41 You made my enemies run,
and I killed them.
42 They cried out for help,
but no one saved them;
they called out to you,
but there was no answer.
43 I ground them to dust,
and I squashed them
like mud in the streets.

44 You rescued me
from my stubborn people
and made me the leader
of foreign nations,
who are now my slaves.
45 They obey and come crawling.
46 They have lost all courage
and from their fortresses
they come trembling.

47 You are the living LORD!
I will praise you!
You are a mighty rock.[d]
I will honor you
for keeping me safe.
48 You took revenge for me,
and you put nations
in my power.
49 You protected me
from violent enemies,
and you made me much greater
than all of them.

50 I will praise you, LORD,
and I will honor you
among the nations.
51 You give glorious victories
to your chosen king.
Your faithful love for David
and for his descendants
will never end.

David's Last Words

23 These are the last words
of David the son of Jesse.
The God of Jacob chose David
and made him a great king.
The Mighty God of Israel
loved him.[e]
When God told him to speak,
David said:
2 The Spirit of the LORD
has told me what to say.
3 Our Mighty Rock,[f]
the God of Jacob, told me,
"A ruler who obeys God
and does right
4 is like the sunrise
on a cloudless day,
or like rain that sparkles
on the grass."[g]

5 I have ruled this way,
and God will never break
his promise to me.
God's promise is complete
and unchanging;
he will always help me
and give me what I hope for.
6 But evil people are pulled up
like thornbushes.
They are not dug up by hand,
7 but with a sharp spear
and are burned on the spot.

The Three Warriors

(1 Chronicles 11.10-19)

8 These are the names of David's warriors:

Ishbosheth[h] the son of Hachmon[i] was the leader of the Three Warriors.[j] In one battle, he killed eight hundred men with his spear.[k]

9 The next one of the Three Warriors
was Eleazar the son of Dodo the Ahohite. One time when the Philistines were at war with Israel, he and David dared

[d]22.47 *mighty rock*: See the note at 22.2. [e]23.1 *The Mighty . . . him*: Or "He wrote Israel's favorite songs." [f]23.3 *Mighty Rock*: See the note at 22.2. [g]23.4 *sparkles . . . grass*: Or "makes the grass grow." [h]23.8 *Ishbosheth*: Hebrew "Josheb Bashebeth," which seems to be another spelling of Ishbosheth. See the note at 2.8, although this is a different Ishbosheth. [i]23.8 *the son of Hachmon*: Or "the Tahchemonite" (see 1 Chronicles 11.11). [j]23.8 *the Three Warriors*: The most honored group of warriors. They may have been part of the Thirty Warriors. "Three" and "thirty" are spelled almost the same in Hebrew, so there is some confusion in the manuscripts as to which group is being talked about in some places in the following lists. [k]23.8 *with . . . spear*: One possible meaning for the difficult Hebrew text (see 1 Chronicles 11.11).

the Philistines to fight them. Every one
of the Israelite soldiers turned and ran,
10except Eleazar. He killed Philistines
until his hand was cramped, and he
couldn't let go of his sword. When
Eleazar finished, all the Israelite troops
had to do was come back and take the
enemies' weapons and armor. The LORD
gave Israel a great victory that day.
11Next was Shammah the son of Agee
the Hararite. One time the Philistines
brought their army together to destroy a
crop of peas growing in a field near
Lehi. The rest of Israel's soldiers ran
away from the Philistines, 12but Shammah stood in the middle of the field and
killed the Philistines. The crops were
saved, and the LORD gave Israel a great
victory.
13One year at harvest time, the Three
Warriors[l] went to meet David at Adullam Cave.[m] The Philistine army had set
up camp in Rephaim Valley 14and had
taken over Bethlehem. David was in his
fortress, 15and he was very thirsty. He
said, "I wish I had a drink from the well
by the gate at Bethlehem."
16The Three Warriors[n] sneaked into
the Philistine camp and got some water
from the well near Bethlehem's gate.
But after they brought the water back to
David, he refused to drink it. Instead, he
poured it out as a sacrifice 17and said to
the LORD, "I can't drink this water! It's
like the blood of these men who risked
their lives to get it for me."
The Three Warriors did these brave
deeds.

The Thirty Warriors

(1 Chronicles 11.20-47)

18Joab's brother Abishai was the
leader of the Thirty Warriors,[o] and in
one battle he killed three hundred men
with his spear. He was as famous as the
Three Warriors 19and certainly just as
famous as the rest of the Thirty Warriors. He was the commander of the
Thirty Warriors, but he still did not become one of the Three Warriors.
20Benaiah the son of Jehoiada was a
brave man from Kabzeel who did some
amazing things. He killed two of Moab's
best fighters,[p] and on a snowy day he
went down into a pit and killed a lion.
21Another time, he killed an Egyptian,
as big as a giant.[q] The Egyptian was
armed with a spear, but Benaiah only
had a club. Benaiah grabbed the spear
from the Egyptian and killed him with
it. 22-23Benaiah did these things. He
never became one of the Three Warriors, but he was just as famous as they
were and certainly just as famous as the
rest of the Thirty Warriors. David made
him the leader of his bodyguard.
24-39Some of the Thirty Warriors were:

Asahel the brother of Joab
Elhanan the son of Dodo from Bethlehem
Shammah from Harod
Elika from Harod
Helez the Paltite
Ira the son of Ikkesh from Tekoa
Abiezer from Anathoth
Mebunnai[r] the Hushathite
Zalmon the Ahohite
Maharai from Netophah
Heleb the son of Baanah from Netophah
Ittai the son of Ribai from Gibeah of the tribe of Benjamin
Benaiah from Pirathon
Hiddai from the streams on Mount Gaash
Abialbon from Beth-Arabah
Azmaveth from Bahurim[s]
Eliahba from Shaalbon
Jashen[t]
Jonathan the son of Shammah the Hararite[u]
Ahiam the son of Sharar the Hararite
Eliphelet the son of Ahasbai from Maacah
Eliam the son of Ahithophel from Gilo
Hezro from Carmel
Paarai the Arbite
Igal the son of Nathan from Zobah
Bani the Gadite
Zelek from Ammon
Naharai from Beeroth, who carried the weapons of Joab the son of Zeruiah
Ira the Ithrite
Gareb the Ithrite
Uriah the Hittite
There were thirty-seven in all.

David Counts the People

(1 Chronicles 21.1-6)

24 The LORD was angry at Israel
again, and he made David think it

[l]**23.13** *the Three Warriors*: Or "three warriors." Hebrew "three of the thirty most important." [m]**23.13** *Adullam Cave*: This may have happened during the time that David was an outlaw (see 1 Samuel 22.1-6). [n]**23.16** *the Three Warriors*: Or "three warriors." [o]**23.18** *the Thirty Warriors*: The second most honored group of warriors. They may have also been officers in the army (see the note at 23.8). [p]**23.20** *Moab's best fighters*: Or "big lions in Moab;" one ancient translation "sons of Ariel from Moab." [q]**23.21** *Egyptian . . . giant*: First Chronicles 11.23; in this verse the Hebrew text has "good-looking Egyptian." [r]**23.24-39** *Mebunnai*: Or "Sibbecai" (see 1 Chronicles 11.26-47). [s]**23.24-39** *Bahurim*: Or "Barhum." [t]**23.24-39** *Jashen*: Hebrew "sons of Jashen." [u]**23.24-39** *Jonathan . . . Hararite*: Some manuscripts of one ancient translation (see 1 Chronicles 26-47). In the Hebrew text Jonathan and Shamah are separate members of the list.

would be a good idea to count the people in Israel and Judah. 2So David told
Joab and the army officers,[v] "Go to
every tribe in Israel, from the town of
Dan in the north all the way south to
Beersheba, and count everyone who can
serve in the army. I want to know how
many there are."
3Joab answered, "I hope the LORD
your God will give you a hundred times
more soldiers than you already have. I
hope you will live to see that day! But
why do you want to do a thing like
this?"
4But when David refused to change
his mind, Joab and the army officers
went out and started counting the people. 5They crossed the Jordan River and
began with[w] Aroer and the town in the
middle of the river valley. From there
they went toward Gad and on as far as
Jazer. 6They went to Gilead and to
Kadesh in Syria.[x] Then they went to
Dan, Ijon,[y] and on toward Sidon. 7They
came to the fortress of Tyre, then went
through every town of the Hivites and
the Canaanites. Finally, they went to
Beersheba in the Southern Desert of Judah. 8After they had gone through the
whole land, they went back to
Jerusalem. It had taken them nine
months and twenty days.
9Joab came and told David, "In Israel
there are eight hundred thousand who
can serve in the army, and in Judah
there are five hundred thousand."

The LORD Punishes David
(1 Chronicles 21.7-17)

10After David had everyone counted,
he felt guilty and told the LORD, "What I
did was stupid and terribly wrong.
LORD, please forgive me."
11Before David even got up the next
morning, the LORD had told David's
prophet Gad 12-13to take a message to
David. Gad went to David and told him:

> You must choose one of three
> ways for the LORD to punish you:
> Will there be seven[z] years when the
> land won't grow enough food for
> your people? Or will your enemies
> chase you and make you run from
> them for three months? Or will there
> be three days of horrible disease in
> your land? Think about it and de-
> cide, because I have to give your an-
> swer to God, who sent me.

14David was really frightened and
said, "It's a terrible choice to make! But
the LORD is kind, and I'd rather have
him punish us than for anyone else to
do it."
15-16So that morning, the LORD sent an
angel to spread a horrible disease everywhere in Israel, from Dan to Beersheba.
And before it was over, seventy thousand people had died.

When the angel was about to destroy
Jerusalem, the LORD felt sorry for all the
suffering he had caused and told the angel, "That's enough! Don't touch them."
This happened at the threshing place
that belonged to Araunah the Jebusite.
17David saw the angel killing everyone and told the LORD, "These people
are like sheep with me as their shepherd.[a] I have sinned terribly, but
they have done nothing wrong. Please,
punish me and my family instead of
them!"

David Buys Araunah's Threshing Place
(1 Chronicles 21.18—22.1)

18-19That same day the prophet Gad
came and told David, "Go to the threshing place that belongs to Araunah and
build an altar there for the LORD."

So David went.
20Araunah looked and saw David and
his soldiers coming up toward him. He
went over to David, bowed down low,
21and said, "Your Majesty! Why have
you come to see me?"

David answered, "I've come to buy
your threshing place. I have to build the
LORD an altar here, so this disease will
stop killing the people."
22Araunah said, "Take whatever you
want and offer your sacrifice. Here are
some oxen for the sacrifice. You can use
the threshing-boards[b] and the wooden
yokes for the fire. 23Take them—they're
yours! I hope the LORD your God will be
pleased with you."
24But David answered, "No! I have to
pay you what they're worth. I can't offer
the LORD my God a sacrifice that I got
for nothing." So David bought the
threshing place and the oxen for fifty
pieces of silver. 25Then he built an altar
for the LORD. He sacrificed animals and
burned them on the altar.

The LORD answered the prayers of the
people, and no one else died from the
terrible disease.

[v]**24.2** *Joab . . . officers*: Some manuscripts of one ancient translation (see 24.4); 1 Chronicles 21.2; Hebrew "Joab, the officer of the army." [w]**24.5** *began with*: Some manuscripts of one ancient translation; Hebrew "set up camp in." [x]**24.6** *Kadesh in Syria*: Or "the lower slopes of Mount Hermon." [y]**24.6** *Dan, Ijon*: Or "Danjaan," an unknown place. [z]**24.12,13** *seven*: Hebrew; some manuscripts of one ancient translation "three" (see 1 Chronicles 21.12). [a]**24.17** *as their shepherd*: The Dead Sea Scrolls, and some manuscripts of two ancient translations (see 1 Chronicles 21.17); these words are not in the Standard Hebrew Text of this verse. [b]**24.22** *threshing-boards*: Heavy boards with bits of rock or metal on the bottom. They were dragged across the grain to separate the husks from the kernels.

1 KINGS

ABOUT THIS BOOK

First Kings is the first half of a single book that was divided into two parts, 1 and 2 Kings, because together they were too long to fit on one scroll. These books continue the history of Israel.

The book of 1 Kings has three parts. The first part (1–2) tells about the last years of King David's life and how his son Solomon became the king of Israel. The second part (chapters 3–11) includes events from Solomon's rule and tells how famous and rich he was. Much of this second part tells how Solomon built and dedicated the temple in Jerusalem. The last part of the book (12–22) reports what happened after Solomon's death—the northern tribes rebelled against Rehoboam his son, and the nation of Israel was divided into two separate kingdoms: Judah in the south and Israel in the north. This part of 1 Kings includes stories about the kings of these two kingdoms. The book concludes with the rule of King Jehoshaphat of Judah and King Ahaziah of Israel.

Each king in the book is judged according to his faithfulness to the Lord. If the king was faithful and obeyed God's Law, he was praised as being good; but if he disobeyed and did wrong, he was condemned as being evil. All the kings of Israel were judged to be evil, because they rejected the Lord and worshiped idols. However, most of the kings of Judah were judged to be good, because they followed the example of their ancestor King David and worshiped the Lord.

First Kings also includes the familiar stories about Elijah the prophet, who opposed the evil King Ahab and Queen Jezebel of the northern kingdom. Elijah warned the people of Israel to obey the Lord and not to worship other gods. Elijah wanted to prove that the Lord was the one true God, and so he arranged a contest between the Lord and the pagan god Baal. Elijah and the prophets of Baal would offer a sacrifice to their own God, but the fire on the altars would not be lit. Elijah explained to the people:

> *"How much longer will you try to have things both ways? If the LORD is God, worship him! But if Baal is God, worship him! . . . The prophets of Baal will pray to their god, and I will pray to the LORD. The one who answers by starting the fire is God."*
>
> *(18.21, 24)*

A QUICK LOOK AT THIS BOOK

Solomon Becomes King (1.1-53)
David's Final Words and His Death (2.1-12)
Solomon Takes Control of the Kingdom (2.13-46)
Solomon's Wisdom and His Officials (3.1—4.34)
Building and Dedication of the Jerusalem Temple (5.1—8.66)
Other Events During Solomon's Rule (9.1—10.29)
Solomon's Unfaithfulness, Enemies, and Death (11.1-43)
The Northern Tribes of Israel Rebel against King Rehoboam (12.1-24)
King Jeroboam of Israel Makes Two Gold Statues of Calves (12.25-33)
Prophets Condemn Jeroboam (13.1—14.20)
Kings of Judah and Israel (14.21—16.34)
Elijah the Prophet (17.1—19.21)
King Ahab and Queen Jezebel (20.1—22.40)
King Jehoshaphat of Judah and King Ahaziah of Israel (22.41-53)

David in His Old Age

1 King David was now an old man,
and he always felt cold, even under
a lot of blankets. 2His officials said,
"Your Majesty, we will look for a young
woman to take care of you. She can lie
down beside you and keep you warm."
3-4They looked everywhere in Israel until they found a very beautiful young
woman named Abishag, who lived in
the town of Shunem.[a] They brought her
to David, and she took care of him. But
David did not have sex with her.

Adonijah Tries To Become King

5-6Adonijah was the son of David and
Haggith. He was Absalom's younger
brother[b] and was very handsome. One
day, Adonijah started bragging, "I'm going to make myself king!" So he got
some chariots and horses, and he hired
fifty men as bodyguards. David did not
want to hurt his feelings, so he never
asked Adonijah why he was doing these
things.
7Adonijah met with Joab the son of
Zeruiah and Abiathar the priest and
asked them if they would help him become king. Both of them agreed to help.
8But Zadok the priest, Benaiah the son
of Jehoiada, Nathan the prophet,
Shimei, Rei,[c] and David's bodyguards
all refused.
9Adonijah invited his brothers and
David's officials from Judah to go with
him to Crawling Rock[d] near Rogel
Spring, where he sacrificed some sheep,
cattle, and fat calves.[e] 10But he did not
invite Nathan, Benaiah, David's bodyguards, or his own brother Solomon.
11When Nathan heard what had happened, he asked Bathsheba, Solomon's
mother:

Have you heard that Adonijah the
son of Haggith has made himself
king? But David doesn't know a
thing about it. 12You and your son
Solomon will be killed, unless you
do what I tell you. 13Go say to David,
"You promised me that Solomon
would be the next king. So why is
Adonijah now king?"
14While you are still talking to
David, I'll come in and tell him that
everything you said is true.

15Meanwhile, David was in his bedroom where Abishag was taking care of
him because he was so old. Bathsheba
went in 16and bowed down.
"What can I do for you?" David asked.
17Bathsheba answered:

Your Majesty, you promised me in
the name of the LORD your God that
my son Solomon would be the next
king. 18But Adonijah has already
been made king, and you didn't
know anything about it. 19He sacrificed a lot of cattle, calves, and
sheep. And he invited Abiathar the
priest, Joab your army commander,
and all your sons to be there, except
Solomon, your loyal servant.
20Your Majesty, everyone in Israel
is waiting for you to announce who
will be the next king. 21If you don't,
they will say that Solomon and I
have rebelled. They will treat us like
criminals and kill us as soon as you
die.

22Just then, Nathan the prophet arrived. 23Someone told David that he
was there, and Nathan came in. He
bowed with his face to the ground 24and
said:

Your Majesty, did you say that
Adonijah would be king? 25Earlier
today, he sacrificed a lot of cattle,
calves, and sheep. He invited the
army commanders, Abiathar, and all
your sons to be there. Right now
they are eating and drinking and
shouting, "Long live King Adonijah!" 26But he didn't invite me or
Zadok the priest or Benaiah or
Solomon. 27Did you say they could
do this without telling the rest of us
who would be the next king?

Solomon Becomes King

28David said, "Tell Bathsheba to come
here." She came and stood in front of
him. 29-30Then he said, "The living LORD
God of Israel has kept me safe. And so
today, I will keep the promise I made to
you in his name: Solomon will be the
next king!"
31Bathsheba bowed with her face to
the ground and said, "Your Majesty, I
pray that you will live a long time!"
32Then David said, "Tell Zadok,
Nathan, and Benaiah to come here."
When they arrived, 33he told them:

Take along some of my officials
and have Solomon ride my own
mule to Gihon Spring. 34When you
get there, Zadok and Nathan will
make Solomon the new king of Israel. Then after the ceremony[f] is
over, have someone blow a trumpet
and tell everyone to shout, "Long
live King Solomon!" 35Bring him
back here, and he will take my place

[a]1.3,4 *Shunem*: A town in northern Israel, just north of Jezreel Valley. [b]1.5,6 *brother*: Since Absalom was dead, Adonijah was now David's oldest living son and would be next in line to be king. [c]1.8 *Shimei, Rei*: Or "Shimei his advisor." [d]1.9 *Crawling Rock*: Or "Zoheleth Rock." [e]1.9 *sacrificed . . . calves*: This was part of a ceremony where Adonijah was made the new king. [f]1.34 *the ceremony*: Part of this ceremony was pouring olive oil on Solomon's head to show that he was now king.

as king. He is the one I have chosen to rule Israel and Judah.

36 Benaiah answered, "We will do it, Your Majesty. I pray that the LORD your God will let it happen. 37 The LORD has always watched over you, and I pray that he will now watch over Solomon. May the LORD help Solomon to be an even greater king than you."

38 Zadok, Nathan, and Benaiah left and took along the two groups of David's special bodyguards.[g] Solomon rode on David's mule as they led him to Gihon Spring. 39 Zadok the priest brought some olive oil from the sacred tent and poured it on Solomon's head to show that he was now king. A trumpet was blown and everyone shouted, "Long live King Solomon!" 40 Then they played flutes and celebrated as they followed Solomon back to Jerusalem. They made so much noise that the ground shook.

41 Adonijah and his guests had almost finished eating when they heard the noise. Joab also heard the trumpet and asked, "What's all that noise about in the city?"

42 Just then, Jonathan son of Abiathar came running up. "Come in," Adonijah said. "An important man like you must have some good news."

43 Jonathan answered:

No, I don't! David has just announced that Solomon will be king.
44-45 Solomon rode David's own mule to Gihon Spring, and Zadok, Nathan, Benaiah, and David's special bodyguards[h] went with him. When they got there, Zadok and Nathan made Solomon king. Then everyone celebrated all the way back to Jerusalem. That's the noise you hear in the city. 46 Solomon is now king.

47 And listen to this! David's officials told him, "We pray that your God will help Solomon to be an even greater king!"

David was in his bed at the time, but he bowed 48 and prayed, "I praise you, LORD God of Israel. You have made my son Solomon king and have let me live to see it."

49 Adonijah's guests shook with fear when they heard this news, and they left as fast as they could. 50 Adonijah himself was afraid of what Solomon might do to him, so he ran to the sacred tent and grabbed hold of the corners of the altar for protection.[i]

51 Someone told Solomon, "Adonijah is afraid of you and is holding onto the corners of the altar. He wants you to promise that you won't kill him."

52 Solomon answered, "If Adonijah doesn't cause any trouble, I won't hurt him. But if he does, I'll have him killed." 53 Then he sent someone to the altar to get Adonijah.

After Adonijah came and bowed down, Solomon said, "Adonijah, go home."

David's Instructions to Solomon

2 Not long before David died, he told Solomon:

2 My son, I will soon die, as everyone must. But I want you to be strong and brave. 3 Do what the LORD your God commands and follow his teachings. Obey everything written in the Law of Moses. Then you will be a success, no matter what you do or where you go. 4 You and your descendants must always faithfully obey the LORD. If you do, he will keep the solemn promise he made to me that someone from our family will always be king of Israel.

5 Solomon, don't forget what Joab did to me by killing Abner son of Ner and Amasa son of Jether, the two commanders of Israel's army. He killed them as if they were his enemies in a war, but he did it when there was no war.[j] He is guilty, and now it's up to you to punish him 6 in the way you think best. Whatever you do, don't let him die peacefully in his old age.

7 The sons of Barzillai from Gilead helped me when I was running from your brother Absalom.[k] Be kind to them and let them eat at your table.

8 Be sure to do something about Shimei son of Gera from Bahurim in the territory of Benjamin. He cursed and insulted me the day I went to Mahanaim. But later, when he came to meet me at the Jordan River, I promised that I wouldn't kill him.[l] 9 Now you must punish him. He's an old man, but you're wise enough to know that you must have him killed.

David Dies

10-11 David was king of Israel forty years. He ruled seven years from Hebron and thirty-three years from

[g] **1.38** *the two . . . bodyguards*: The Hebrew text has "the Cherethites and the Pelethites," who were foreign soldiers hired by David to be part of his bodyguard. [h] **1.44,45** *David's special bodyguards*: See the note at 1.38. [i] **1.50** *the corners . . . for protection*: The four corners of some ancient altars looked like animal horns. Since the entire altar was sacred, anyone holding on to its corners was supposed to be safe from being killed. [j] **2.5** *war*: See 2 Samuel 3.22-27 and 20.7-10. [k] **2.7** *Absalom*: See 2 Samuel 17.27-29. [l] **2.8** *him*: See 2 Samuel 16.5-14 and 19.16-23.

Jerusalem. Then he died and was buried
in Jerusalem.[m] 12His son Solomon became king and took control of David's
kingdom.

Adonijah Is Killed

13One day, Adonijah went to see
Bathsheba, Solomon's mother, and she
asked, "Is this a friendly visit?"
"Yes. 14I just want to talk with you."
"All right," she told him, "go ahead."
15"You know that I was king for a little
while," Adonijah replied. "And everyone
in Israel accepted me as their ruler. But
the LORD wanted my brother to be king,
so now things have changed. 16Would
you do me a favor?"
"What do you want?" Bathsheba
asked.
17"Please ask Solomon to let me
marry Abishag. He won't say no to you."
18"All right," she said. "I'll ask him."
19When Bathsheba went to see
Solomon, he stood up to meet her, then
bowed low. He sat back down and had
another throne brought in, so his
mother could sit at his right side.[n]
20Bathsheba sat down and then asked,
"Would you do me a small favor?"
Solomon replied, "Mother, just tell me
what you want, and I will do it."
21"Allow your brother Adonijah to
marry Abishag," she answered.
22Solomon said:

What? Let my older brother marry
Abishag? You may as well ask me to
let him rule the kingdom! And why
don't you ask such favors for Abiathar and Joab?[o]
23I swear in the name of the LORD
that Adonijah will die because he
asked for this! If he doesn't, I pray
that God will severely punish me.
24The LORD made me king in my
father's place and promised that the
kings of Israel would come from my
family. Yes, I swear by the living
LORD that Adonijah will die today.

25"Benaiah," Solomon shouted, "go
kill Adonijah." So Adonijah died.

Abiathar Is Sent Back Home

26Solomon sent for Abiathar the priest
and said:

Abiathar, go back home to
Anathoth! You ought to be killed too,
but I won't do it now. When my
father David was king, you were in
charge of the sacred chest, and you
went through a lot of hard times
with my father. 27But I won't let you
be a priest of the LORD anymore.

And so the promise that the LORD had
made at Shiloh about the family of Eli
came true.[p]

Joab Is Killed

28Joab had not helped Absalom try to
become king, but he had helped Adonijah. So when Joab learned that Adonijah had been killed, he ran to the sacred
tent and grabbed hold of the corners of
the altar for protection.[q] 29When Solomon heard about this, he sent someone to ask Joab, "Why did you run to
the altar?"
Joab sent back his answer, "I was
afraid of you, and I ran to the LORD for
protection."[r]
Then Solomon shouted, "Benaiah, go
kill Joab!"
30Benaiah went to the sacred tent and
yelled, "Joab, the king orders you to
come out!"
"No!" Joab answered. "Kill me right
here."
Benaiah went back and told Solomon
what Joab had said.
31-32Solomon replied:

Do what Joab said. Kill him and
bury him! Then my family and I
won't be responsible for what he did
to Abner the commander of Israel's
army and to Amasa the commander
of Judah's army. He killed those innocent men without my father
knowing about it. Both of them were
better men than Joab. Now the LORD
will make him pay for those murders. 33Joab's family will always suffer because of what he did, but the
LORD will always bless David's family and his kingdom with peace.

34Benaiah went back and killed Joab.
His body was taken away and buried
near his home in the desert.
35Solomon put Benaiah in Joab's
place as army commander, and he put
Zadok in Abiathar's place as priest.

Shimei Is Killed

36Solomon sent for Shimei and said,
"Build a house here in Jerusalem and
live in it. But whatever you do, don't
leave the city! 37If you ever cross Kidron
Valley and leave Jerusalem, you will be
killed. And it will be your own fault."
38"That's fair, Your Majesty," Shimei
answered. "I'll do that." So Shimei lived
in Jerusalem from then on.
39About three years later, two of
Shimei's servants ran off to King Achish
in Gath. When Shimei found out where
they were, 40he saddled his donkey and

[m]**2.10,11** *Jerusalem*: Hebrew "the city of David." [n]**2.19** *at his right side*: The place of honor. [o]**2.22** *And why . . . Joab*: One possible meaning for the difficult Hebrew text. [p]**2.27** *the promise . . . came true*: See 1 Samuel 2.27-34. [q]**2.28** *the corners . . . for protection*: See the note at 1.50. [r]**2.29** *he sent someone . . . for protection*: One ancient translation; these words are not in the Hebrew text.

went after them. He found them and
brought them back to Jerusalem.
41 Someone told Solomon that Shimei
had gone to Gath and was back. 42 Solomon sent for him and said:

Shimei, you promised in the name
of the LORD that you would never
leave Jerusalem. I warned you that
you would die if you did. You agreed
that this was fair, didn't you? 43 You
have disobeyed me and have broken
the promise you made to the LORD.

44 I know you remember all the
cruel things you did to my father
David. Now the LORD is going to
punish you for what you did. 45 But
the LORD will bless me and make my
father's kingdom strong forever.

46 "Benaiah," Solomon shouted, "kill
Shimei." So Shimei died.

Solomon was now in complete control
of his kingdom.

The LORD Makes Solomon Wise

(2 Chronicles 1.1-13)

3 Solomon signed a treaty with the
king of Egypt and married his
daughter. She lived in the older part of
Jerusalem[s] until the palace, the LORD's
temple, and the wall around Jerusalem
were completed.
2 At that time, there was no temple for
worshiping the LORD, and everyone offered sacrifices at the local shrines.[t]
3 Solomon loved the LORD and followed
his father David's instructions, but Solomon also offered sacrifices and burned
incense at the shrines.
4 The most important shrine was in
Gibeon, and Solomon had offered more
than a thousand sacrifices on that altar.
5 One night while Solomon was in
Gibeon, the LORD God appeared to him
in a dream and said, "Solomon, ask for
anything you want, and I will give it to
you."
6 Solomon answered:

My father David, your servant,
was honest and did what you commanded. You were always loyal to
him, and you gave him a son who is
now king. 7 LORD God, I'm your servant, and you've made me king in
my father's place. But I'm very
young and know so little about being a leader. 8 And now I must rule
your chosen people, even though
there are too many of them to count.

9 Please make me wise and teach
me the difference between right and
wrong. Then I will know how to rule
your people. If you don't, there is no
way I could rule this great nation of
yours.

10-11 God said:

Solomon, I'm pleased that you
asked for this. You could have asked
to live a long time or to be rich. Or
you could have asked for your enemies to be destroyed. Instead, you
asked for wisdom to make right decisions. 12 So I'll make you wiser
than anyone who has ever lived or
ever will live.

13 I'll also give you what you didn't
ask for. You'll be rich and respected
as long as you live, and you'll be
greater than any other king. 14 If you
obey me and follow my commands,
as your father David did, I'll let you
live a long time.

15 Solomon woke up and realized that
God had spoken to him in the dream.
He went back to Jerusalem and stood
in front of the sacred chest, where he
offered sacrifices to please the Lord[u]
and sacrifices to ask his blessing.[v]
Then Solomon gave a feast for his officials.

Solomon Makes a Difficult Decision

16 One day two women[w] came to King
Solomon, 17 and one of them said:

Your Majesty, this woman and I
live in the same house. Not long ago
my baby was born at home, 18 and
three days later her baby was born.
Nobody else was there with us.

19 One night while we were all
asleep, she rolled over on her baby,
and he died. 20 Then while I was still
asleep, she got up and took my son
out of my bed. She put him in her
bed, then she put her dead baby next
to me.

21 In the morning when I got up to
feed my son, I saw that he was dead.
But when I looked at him in the
light, I knew he wasn't my son.

22 "No!" the other woman shouted. "He
was your son. My baby is alive!"

"The dead baby is yours," the first
woman yelled. "Mine is alive!"

They argued back and forth in front
of Solomon, 23 until finally he said, "Both
of you say this live baby is yours.
24 Someone bring me a sword."

A sword was brought, and Solomon
ordered, 25 "Cut the baby in half! That
way each of you can have part of him."
26 "Please don't kill my son," the
baby's mother screamed. "Your Majesty,
I love him very much, but give him to
her. Just don't kill him."

The other woman shouted, "Go ahead

[s] **3.1** *the older . . . Jerusalem*: Hebrew "the city of David." [t] **3.2** *local shrines*: The Hebrew text has "high places," which were local places to worship God or foreign gods.
[u] **3.15** *sacrifices to please the Lord*: See Leviticus 1.1-17. [v] **3.15** *sacrifices to ask his blessing*: See Leviticus 3.1-17. [w] **3.16** *women*: Hebrew "prostitutes."

and cut him in half. Then neither of us
will have the baby."
27 Solomon said, "Don't kill the baby."
Then he pointed to the first woman,
"She is his real mother. Give the baby to
her."
28 Everyone in Israel was amazed
when they heard how Solomon had
made his decision. They realized that
God had given him wisdom to judge
fairly.

Solomon's Officials

4 1-6 Here is a list of Solomon's highest
officials while he was king of Israel:

Azariah son of Zadok was the priest;
Elihoreph and Ahijah sons of Shisha
were the secretaries;
Jehoshaphat son of Ahilud kept the
government records;
Benaiah son of Jehoiada was the
army commander;
Zadok and Abiathar were priests;
Azariah son of Nathan was in charge
of the regional officers;
Zabud son of Nathan was a priest
and the king's advisor;
Ahishar was the prime minister;
Adoniram son of Abda was in charge
of the forced labor.

7 Solomon chose twelve regional officers, who took turns bringing food for
him and his household. Each officer
provided food from his region for one
month of the year. 8 These were the
twelve officers:
The son of Hur was in charge of the
hill country of Ephraim.
9 The son of Deker was in charge of
the towns of Makaz, Shaalbim, Beth
Shemesh, and Elon-Beth-Hanan.
10 The son of Hesed was in charge of
the towns of Arubboth and Socoh, and
the region of Hepher.
11 The son of Abinadab was in charge
of Naphath-Dor and was married to
Solomon's daughter Taphath.
12 Baana son of Ahilud was in charge
of the towns of Taanach and Megiddo.
He was also in charge of the whole region of Beth-Shan near the town of
Zarethan, south of Jezreel from Beth-
Shan to Abel-Meholah to the other side
of Jokmeam.
13 The son of Geber was in charge of
the town of Ramoth in Gilead and the
villages in Gilead belonging to the family of Jair, a descendant of Manasseh.
He was also in charge of the region of
Argob in Bashan, which had sixty
walled towns with bronze bars on their
gates.
14 Ahinadab son of Iddo was in charge
of the territory of Mahanaim.
15 Ahimaaz was in charge of the territory of Naphtali and was married to
Solomon's daughter Basemath.
16 Baana son of Hushai was in charge
of the territory of Asher and the town of
Bealoth.
17 Jehoshaphat son of Paruah was in
charge of the territory of Issachar.
18 Shimei son of Ela was in charge of
the territory of Benjamin.
19 Geber son of Uri was in charge of
Gilead, where King Sihon of the Amorites and King Og of Bashan had lived.
And one officer was in charge of the
territory of Judah.[x]

The Size of Solomon's Kingdom

20 There were so many people living in
Judah and Israel while Solomon was
king that they seemed like grains of
sand on a beach. Everyone had enough
to eat and drink, and they were happy.
21 Solomon ruled every kingdom between the Euphrates River and the land
of the Philistines down to Egypt. These
kingdoms paid him taxes as long as he
lived.
22 Every day, Solomon needed one
hundred fifty bushels of fine flour, three
hundred bushels of coarsely-ground
flour, 23 ten grain-fed cattle, twenty
pasture-fed cattle, one hundred sheep,
as well as deer, gazelles, and geese.
24 Solomon ruled the whole region
west of the Euphrates River, from Tiphsah to Gaza, and he was at peace with
all of the countries around him. 25 Everyone living in Israel, from the town of
Dan in the north to Beersheba in the
south, was safe as long as Solomon
lived. Each family sat undisturbed beneath its own grape vines and fig trees.
26 Solomon had forty thousand stalls
of chariot horses and twelve thousand
chariot soldiers.
27 Each of the twelve regional officers
brought food to Solomon and his household for one month of the year. They
provided everything he needed, 28 as
well as barley and straw for the horses.

Solomon's Wisdom

29 Solomon was brilliant. God had
blessed him with insight and understanding. 30-31 He was wiser than anyone
else in the world, including the wisest
people of the east and of Egypt. He was
even wiser than Ethan the Ezrahite, and
Mahol's three sons, Heman, Calcol, and
Darda. Solomon became famous in
every country around Judah and Israel.
32 Solomon wrote three thousand wise
sayings and composed more than one
thousand songs. 33 He could talk about
all kinds of plants, from large trees to

[x]**4.19** *of Judah*: One ancient translation; these words are not in the Hebrew text.

small bushes, and he taught about animals, birds, reptiles, and fish. 34Kings all
over the world heard about Solomon's
wisdom and sent people to listen to him
teach.

Solomon Asks Hiram To Help Build the Temple

(2 Chronicles 2.1-16)

5 King Hiram of Tyre[y] had always
been friends with Solomon's father
David. When Hiram learned that Solomon was king, he sent some of his officials to meet with Solomon.
2Solomon sent a message back to Hiram:
3Remember how my father David
wanted to build a temple where the
LORD his God could be worshiped?
But enemies kept attacking my
father's kingdom, and he never had
the chance. 4Now, thanks to the
LORD God, there is peace in my kingdom and no trouble or threat of war
anywhere.
5The LORD God promised my
father that when his son became
king, he would build a temple for
worshiping the LORD. So I've decided to do that.
6I'd like you to have your workers
cut down cedar trees in Lebanon for
me. I will pay them whatever you
say and will even have my workers
help them. We both know that your
workers are more experienced than
anyone else at cutting lumber.
7Hiram was so happy when he heard
Solomon's request that he said, "I am
grateful that the LORD gave David such
a wise son to be king of that great nation!" 8Then he sent back his answer:
I received your message and will
give you all the cedar and pine logs
you need. 9My workers will carry
them down from Lebanon to the
Mediterranean Sea. They will tie the
logs together and float them along
the coast to wherever you want
them. Then they will untie the logs,
and your workers can take them
from there.

To pay for the logs, you can provide the grain I need for my household.
10Hiram gave Solomon all the cedar
and pine logs he needed. 11In return,
Solomon gave Hiram about one hundred twenty-five thousand bushels of
wheat and about one thousand one hundred gallons of pure olive oil each year.
12The LORD kept his promise and
made Solomon wise. Hiram and Solomon signed a treaty and never went to
war against each other.

Solomon's Workers

13Solomon ordered thirty thousand
people from all over Israel to cut logs
for the temple, 14and he put Adoniram
in charge of these workers. Solomon divided them into three groups of ten
thousand. Each group worked one
month in Lebanon and had two months
off at home.
15He also had eighty thousand workers to cut stone in the hill country of Israel, seventy thousand workers to carry
the stones, 16and over three thousand
assistants to keep track of the work and
to supervise the workers. 17He ordered
the workers to cut and shape large
blocks of good stone for the foundation
of the temple.
18Solomon's and Hiram's men worked
with men from the city of Gebal,[z] and
together they got the stones and logs
ready for the temple.

The Outside of the Temple Is Completed

6 Solomon's workers started building
the temple during Ziv,[a] the second
month of the year. It had been four
years since Solomon became king of Israel, and four hundred eighty years
since the people of Israel left Egypt.
2The inside of the LORD's temple was
ninety feet long, thirty feet wide, and
forty-five feet high. 3A fifteen-foot porch
went all the way across the front of the
temple. 4The windows were narrow on
the outside but wide on the inside.
5-6Along the sides and back of the
temple, there were three levels of storage rooms. The rooms on the bottom
level were seven and a half feet wide,
the rooms on the middle level were nine
feet wide, and those on the top level
were ten and a half feet wide. There
were ledges on the outside of the temple
that supported the beams of the storage
rooms, so that nothing was built into the
temple walls.
7Solomon did not want the noise of
hammers and axes to be heard at the
place where the temple was being built.
So he had the workers shape the blocks
of stone at the quarry.
8The entrance to the bottom storage
rooms was on the south side of the
building, and stairs to the other rooms
were also there. 9The roof of the temple
was made out of beams and cedar
boards.

The workers finished building the outside of the temple. 10 Storage rooms

[y]5.1 *Tyre*: The most important city in Phoenicia. It was located on the coast of the Mediterranean Sea north of Israel, in what is today southern Lebanon. [z]5.18 *Gebal*: Later known as Byblos. [a]6.1 *Ziv*: The second month of the Hebrew calendar, from about mid-April to mid-May.

seven and a half feet high were all
around the temple, and they were attached to the temple by cedar beams.
11 The LORD told Solomon:

> 12-13 If you obey my commands and
> do what I say, I will keep the prom-
> ise I made to your father David. I
> will live among my people Israel in
> this temple you are building, and I
> will not desert them.

14 So Solomon's workers finished
building the temple.

The Inside of the Temple Is Furnished
(2 Chronicles 3.8-14)

15 The floor of the temple was made
out of pine, and the walls were lined
with cedar from floor to ceiling.[b]
16 The most holy place was in the back
of the temple, and it was thirty feet
square. Cedar boards standing from
floor to ceiling[c] separated it from the
rest of the temple. 17 The temple's main
room was sixty feet long, and it was in
front of the most holy place.
18 The inside walls were lined with
cedar to hide the stones, and the cedar
was decorated with carvings of gourds
and flowers.
19 The sacred chest was kept in the
most holy place. 20-22 This room was
thirty feet long, thirty feet wide, and
thirty feet high, and it was lined with
pure gold. There were also gold chains
across the front of the most holy place.
The inside of the temple, as well as the
cedar altar in the most holy place, was
covered with gold.
23 Solomon had two statues of winged
creatures[d] made from olive wood to put
in the most holy place. Each creature
was fifteen feet tall 24-26 and fifteen feet
across. They had two wings, and the
wings were seven and a half feet long.
27 Solomon put them next to each other
in the most holy place. Their wings were
spread out and reached across the
room. 28 The creatures were also covered
with gold.
29 The walls of the two rooms were
decorated with carvings of palm trees,
flowers, and winged creatures. 30 Even
the floor was covered with gold.
31-32 The two doors to the most holy
place were made out of olive wood and
were decorated with carvings of palm
trees, flowers, and winged creatures.
The doors and the carvings were covered with gold. The door frame came to
a point at the top.
33-34 The two doors to the main room of
the temple were made out of pine, and
each one had two sections[e] so they
could fold open. The door frame was
shaped like a rectangle and was made
out of olive wood. 35 The doors were covered with gold and were decorated with
carvings of palm trees, flowers, and
winged creatures.
36 The inner courtyard of the temple
had walls made out of three layers of
cut stones with one layer of cedar
beams.
37 Work began on the temple during
Ziv,[f] the second month of the year, four
years after Solomon became king of Israel. 38 Seven years later the workers finished building it during Bul,[g] the eighth
month of the year. It was built exactly as
it had been planned.

Solomon's Palace Is Built

7 Solomon's palace took thirteen
years to build.
2-3 Forest Hall was the largest room in
the palace. It was one hundred fifty feet
long, seventy-five feet wide, and forty-
five feet high, and was lined with cedar
from Lebanon. It had four rows of cedar
pillars, fifteen in a row, and they held up
forty-five cedar beams. The ceiling was
covered with cedar. 4 Three rows of windows on each side faced each other,
5 and there were three doors on each
side near the front of the hall.
6 Pillar Hall was seventy-five feet long
and forty-five feet wide. A covered
porch supported by pillars went all the
way across the front of the hall.
7 Solomon's throne was in Justice Hall,
where he judged cases. This hall was
completely lined with cedar.
8 The section of the palace where
Solomon lived was behind Justice Hall
and looked exactly like it. He had a similar place built for his wife, the daughter
of the king of Egypt.
9 From the foundation all the way to
the top, these buildings and the courtyard were made out of the best stones[h]
carefully cut to size, then smoothed on
every side with saws. 10 The foundation
stones were huge, good stones—some of
them fifteen feet long and others twelve
feet long. 11 The cedar beams and other
stones that had been cut to size were on
top of these foundation stones. 12 The
walls around the palace courtyard were
made out of three layers of cut stones
with one layer of cedar beams, just like

[b] **6.15** *from floor to ceiling*: One possible meaning for the difficult Hebrew text.
[c] **6.16** *standing . . . ceiling*: One possible meaning for the difficult Hebrew text.
[d] **6.23** *statues of winged creatures*: These were symbols of the LORD's throne on earth (see Exodus 25.18-22).
[e] **6.33,34** *two sections*: One possible meaning for the difficult Hebrew text.
[f] **6.37** *Ziv*: See the note at 6.1.
[g] **6.38** *Bul*: The eighth month of the Hebrew calendar, from about mid-October to mid-November.
[h] **7.9** *From . . . best stones*: One possible meaning for the difficult Hebrew text.

the front porch and the inner courtyard
of the temple.

Hiram Makes the Bronze Furnishings

(2 Chronicles 3.15-17; 4.1-10)

13-14 Hiram was a skilled bronze
worker from the city of Tyre.[i] His father
was now dead, but he also had been a
bronze worker from Tyre, and his
mother was from the tribe of Naphtali.
King Solomon asked Hiram to come
to Jerusalem and make the bronze
furnishings to use for worship in
the LORD's temple, and he agreed to do
it.
15 Hiram made two bronze columns
twenty-seven feet tall and about six feet
across. 16 For the top of each column, he
also made a bronze cap seven and a
half feet high. 17 The caps were decorated with seven rows of designs that
looked like chains,[j] 18 with two rows
of designs that looked like pomegranates.[k]
19 The caps for the columns of the
porch were six feet high and were
shaped like lilies.[l]
20 The chain designs on the caps were
right above the rounded tops of the two
columns, and there were two hundred
pomegranates in rows around each cap.
21 Hiram placed the two columns on
each side of the main door of the temple. The column on the south side was
called Jachin,[m] and the one on the north
was called Boaz.[n]
22 The lily-shaped caps were on top of
the columns.
This completed the work on the columns.
23 Hiram also made a large bowl called
the Sea. It was seven and a half feet
deep, about fifteen feet across, and
forty-five feet around. 24 Two rows of
bronze gourds were around the outer
edge of the bowl, ten gourds to every
eighteen inches. 25 The bowl itself sat on
top of twelve bronze bulls with three
bulls facing outward in each of four directions. 26 The sides of the bowl were
four inches thick, and its rim was like a
cup that curved outward like flower
petals. The bowl held about eleven thousand gallons.
27 Hiram made ten movable bronze
stands, each one four and a half feet
high, six feet long, and six feet wide.
28-29 The sides were made with panels attached to frames decorated with flower
designs. The panels themselves were
decorated with figures of lions, bulls,
and winged creatures. 30-31 Each stand
had four bronze wheels and axles and a
round frame twenty-seven inches
across, held up by four supports eighteen inches high. A small bowl rested in
the frame. The supports were decorated
with flower designs, and the frame with
carvings.
The side panels of the stands were
square, 32 and the wheels and axles
were underneath them. The wheels were
about twenty-seven inches high 33 and
looked like chariot wheels. The axles,
rims, spokes, and hubs were made out
of bronze.
34-35 Around the top of each stand was
a nine-inch strip, and there were four
braces[o] attached to the corners of each
stand. The panels and the supports
were attached to the stands, 36 and the
stands were decorated with flower designs and figures of lions, palm trees,
and winged creatures. 37 Hiram made the
ten bronze stands from the same mold,
so they were exactly the same size and
shape.
38 Hiram also made ten small bronze
bowls, one for each stand. The bowls
were six feet across and could hold
about two hundred thirty gallons.
39 He put five stands on the south side
of the temple, five stands on the north
side, and the large bowl at the southeast
corner of the temple.
40 Hiram made pans for hot ashes, and
also shovels and sprinkling bowls.

A List of Everything inside the Temple

(2 Chronicles 4.11—5.1)

This is a list of the bronze items that
Hiram made for the LORD's temple:
41 two columns; two bowl-shaped caps
for the tops of the columns; two chain
designs on the caps; 42 four hundred
pomegranates[p] for the chain designs;
43 ten movable stands; ten small bowls
for the stands; 44 a large bowl; twelve
bulls that held up the bowl; 45 pans for
hot ashes, and also shovels and sprinkling bowls.
Hiram made these bronze things for
Solomon 46 near the Jordan River between Succoth and Zarethan by pouring
melted bronze into clay molds.
47 There were so many bronze things
that Solomon never bothered to weigh
them, and no one ever knew how much
bronze was used.
48 Solomon gave orders to make the

[i] **7.13,14** *Hiram . . . city of Tyre*: This is not the same person as "King Hiram of Tyre" (see 5.1).
[j] **7.17** *seven rows . . . chains*: One possible meaning for the difficult Hebrew text.
[k] **7.18** *pomegranates*: One possible meaning for the difficult Hebrew text of verse 18. A pomegranate is a bright red fruit that looks like an apple. In ancient times, it was a symbol of life. [l] **7.19** *lilies*: One possible meaning for the difficult Hebrew text of verse 19.
[m] **7.21** *Jachin*: Or "He makes secure." [n] **7.21** *Boaz*: Or "He is strong." [o] **7.34,35** *braces*: Or "handles." [p] **7.42** *pomegranates*: See the note at 7.18.

following temple furnishings out of
gold: the altar; the table that held the sacred loaves of bread;[q] 49ten lampstands
that went in front of the most holy
place; flower designs; lamps and tongs;
50cups, lamp snuffers, and small sprinkling bowls; dishes for incense; fire
pans; and the hinges for the doors to the
most holy place and the main room of
the temple.
51After the LORD's temple was finished, Solomon put into its storage
rooms everything that his father David
had dedicated to the LORD, including the
gold and the silver.

Solomon Brings the Sacred Chest to the Temple

(2 Chronicles 5.2—6.2)

8 1-2The sacred chest had been kept
on Mount Zion, also known as the
city of David. But Solomon decided to
have the chest moved to the temple
while everyone was in Jerusalem, celebrating the Festival of Shelters during
Ethanim,[r] the seventh month of the
year.
Solomon called together the important leaders of Israel. 3-4Then the priests
and the Levites carried to the temple the
sacred chest, the sacred tent, and the
objects used for worship. 5Solomon and
a crowd of people walked in front of the
chest, and along the way they sacrificed
more sheep and cattle than could be
counted.
6The priests carried the chest into the
most holy place and put it under the
winged creatures, 7whose wings covered
the chest and the poles used for carrying it. 8The poles were so long that they
could be seen from right outside the
most holy place, but not from anywhere
else. And they stayed there from then
on.
9The only things kept in the chest
were the two flat stones Moses had put
there when the LORD made his agreement with the people of Israel at Mount
Sinai,[s] after bringing them out of Egypt.
10Suddenly a cloud filled the temple
as the priests were leaving the most
holy place. 11The LORD's glory was in
the cloud, and the light from it was so
bright that the priests could not stay inside to do their work. 12Then Solomon
prayed:

"Our LORD, you said that you
would live in a dark cloud.
13 Now I have built a glorious temple
where you can live forever."

Solomon Speaks to the People

(2 Chronicles 6.3-11)

14Solomon turned toward the people
standing there. Then he blessed them
15-16and said:
Praise the LORD God of Israel!
Long ago he brought his people out
of Egypt. He later kept his promise
to make my father David the king of
Israel. The LORD also said that he
had not chosen the city where his
temple would be built.
17So when David wanted to build a
temple for the LORD God of Israel,
18the LORD said, "It's good that you
want to build a temple where I can
be worshiped. 19But you're not the
one to do it. Your son will build a
temple to honor me."
20The LORD has done what he
promised. I am the king of Israel like
my father, and I've built a temple for
the LORD our God. 21I've also made a
place in the temple for the sacred
chest. And in that chest are the two
flat stones on which is written the
solemn agreement the LORD made
with our ancestors when he led
them out of Egypt.

Solomon Prays at the Temple

(2 Chronicles 6.12-42)

22Solomon stood facing the altar with
everyone standing behind him. Then he
lifted his arms toward heaven 23and
prayed:
LORD God of Israel, no other god
in heaven or on earth is like you!
You never forget the agreement
you made with your people, and you
are loyal to anyone who faithfully
obeys your teachings. 24My father
David was your servant, and today
you have kept every promise you
made to him.
25LORD God of Israel, you
promised my father that someone
from his family would always be
king of Israel, if they do their best to
obey you, just as he did. 26Please
keep this promise you made to your
servant David.
27There's not enough room in all
of heaven for you, LORD God. How
could you possibly live on earth in
this temple I have built? 28But I ask
you to answer my prayer. 29This is
the temple where you have chosen
to be worshiped. Please watch over
it day and night and listen when I
turn toward it and pray. 30 I am your
servant, and the people of Israel be-

[q]**7.48** *sacred loaves of bread*: This bread was offered to the LORD and was a symbol of the LORD's presence in the temple. It was put out on a special table, and was replaced with fresh bread each week (see Leviticus 24.5-9). [r]**8.1,2** *Ethanim*: The seventh month of the Hebrew calendar, from about mid-September to mid-October. [s]**8.9** *Sinai*: Hebrew "Horeb."

long to you. So whenever any of us
look toward this temple and pray,
answer from your home in heaven
and forgive our sins.
31 Suppose someone accuses a person of a crime, and the accused has
to stand in front of the altar in your
temple and say, "I swear I am innocent!" 32 Listen from heaven and decide who is right. Then punish the
guilty person and let the innocent
one go free.
33 Suppose your people Israel sin
against you, and then an enemy defeats them. If they come to this temple and beg for forgiveness, 34 listen
from your home in heaven. Forgive
them and bring them back to the
land you gave their ancestors.
35 Suppose your people sin against
you, and you punish them by holding back the rain. If they turn toward this temple and pray in your
name and stop sinning, 36 listen from
your home in heaven and forgive
them. The people of Israel are your
servants, so teach them to live right.
And please send rain on the land
you promised them forever.
37 Sometimes the crops may dry up
or rot or be eaten by locusts[t] or
grasshoppers, and your people will
be starving. Sometimes enemies
may surround their towns, or your
people will become sick with deadly
diseases. 38 Listen when anyone in Israel truly feels sorry and sincerely
prays with arms lifted toward your
temple. 39 You know what is in everyone's heart. So from your home in
heaven answer their prayers, according to the way they live and
what is in their hearts. 40 Then your
people will worship and obey you
for as long as they live in the land
you gave their ancestors.
41-42 Foreigners will hear about you
and your mighty power, and some of
them will come to live among your
people Israel. If any of them pray toward this temple, 43 listen from your
home in heaven and answer their
prayers. Then everyone on earth will
worship you, just like your people Israel, and they will know that I have
built this temple to honor you.
44 Our LORD, sometimes you will
order your people to attack their enemies. Then your people will turn toward this temple I have built for you
in your chosen city, and they will
pray to you. 45 Answer their prayers
from heaven and give them victory.
46 Everyone sins. But when your
people sin against you, suppose you
get angry enough to let their enemies drag them away to foreign
countries. 47-49 Later, they may feel
sorry for what they did and ask your
forgiveness. Answer them when they
pray toward this temple I have built
for you in your chosen city, here in
this land you gave their ancestors.
From your home in heaven, listen to
their sincere prayers and do what
they ask. 50 Forgive your people no
matter how much they have sinned
against you. Make the enemies who
defeated them be kind to them. 51 Remember, they are the people you
chose and rescued from Egypt that
was like a blazing fire to them.
52 I am your servant, and the people of Israel belong to you. So listen
when any of us pray and cry out for
your help. 53 When you brought our
ancestors out of Egypt, you told your
servant Moses to say to them, "From
all people on earth, the LORD God
has chosen you to be his very own."

Solomon Blesses the People

54 When Solomon finished his prayer
at the altar, he was kneeling with his
arms lifted toward heaven. He stood up,
55 turned toward the people, blessed
them, and said loudly:
56 Praise the LORD! He has kept his
promise and given us peace. Every
good thing he promised to his servant Moses has happened.
57 The LORD our God was with our
ancestors to help them, and I pray
that he will be with us and never
abandon us. 58 May the LORD help us
obey him and follow all the laws and
teachings he gave our ancestors.
59 I pray that the LORD our God will
remember my prayer day and night.
May he help everyone in Israel each
day, in whatever way we need it.
60 Then every nation will know that
the LORD is the only true God.
61 Obey the LORD our God and follow his commands with all your
heart, just as you are doing today.

Solomon Dedicates the Temple

(2 Chronicles 7.4-10)

62-63 Solomon and the people dedicated
the temple to the LORD by offering
twenty-two thousand cattle and one
hundred twenty thousand sheep as sacrifices to ask the LORD's blessing.[u] 64 On
that day, Solomon dedicated the courtyard in front of the temple and made it
acceptable for worship. He offered the
sacrifices there because the bronze altar
in front of the temple was too small.

[t] **8.37** *locusts*: A type of grasshopper that comes in swarms and causes great damage to plant life. [u] **8.62,63** *sacrifices to ask the LORD's blessing*: See Leviticus 3.1-17.

65 Solomon and the huge crowd celebrated the Festival of Shelters at the
temple for seven days.[v] There were people from as far away as the Egyptian
Gorge in the south and Lebo-Hamath in
the north. 66 Then on the eighth day, he
sent everyone home. They said good-by
and left, very happy, because of all
the good things the LORD had done
for his servant David and his people
Israel.

The LORD Appears to Solomon Again
(2 Chronicles 7.11-22)

9 The LORD's temple and Solomon's
palace were now finished, and
Solomon had built everything he
wanted. 2 Some time later the LORD appeared to him again in a dream, just as
he had done at Gibeon. 3 The LORD said:

> I heard your prayer and what you
> asked me to do. This temple you
> have built is where I will be wor-
> shiped forever. It belongs to me, and
> I will never stop watching over it.
> 4 You must obey me, as your father
> David did, and be honest and fair.
> Obey my laws and teachings, 5 and I
> will keep my promise to David that
> someone from your family will al-
> ways be king of Israel.
> 6 But if you or any of your descen-
> dants disobey my commands or start
> worshiping foreign gods, 7 I will no
> longer let my people Israel live in
> this land I gave them. I will desert
> this temple where I said I would be
> worshiped. Then people everywhere
> will think this nation is only a joke
> and will make fun of it. 8 This temple
> will become a pile of rocks![w] Every-
> one who walks by will be shocked,
> and they will ask, "Why did the
> LORD do such a terrible thing to his
> people and to this temple?" 9 Then
> they will answer, "We know why the
> LORD did this. The people of Israel
> rejected the LORD their God, who
> rescued their ancestors from Egypt,
> and they started worshiping other
> gods."

Other Things Solomon Did
(2 Chronicles 8.1-18)

10 It took twenty years for the LORD's
temple and Solomon's palace to be
built. 11 Later, Solomon gave King Hiram
of Tyre twenty towns in the region of
Galilee to repay him for the cedar, pine,
and gold he had given Solomon.
12 When Hiram went to see the towns,
he did not like them. 13 He said, "Solomon, my friend, are these the kind of
towns you want to give me?" So Hiram
called the region Cabul because he
thought it was worthless.[x] 14 He sent
Solomon only five tons of gold in return.
15 After Solomon's workers had finished the temple and the palace, he ordered them to fill in the land on the east
side of Jerusalem,[y] to build a wall
around the city, and to rebuild the towns
of Hazor, Megiddo, and Gezer.
16 Earlier, the king of Egypt had captured the town of Gezer; he burned it to
the ground and killed the Canaanite
people living there. Then he gave it to
his daughter as a wedding present when
she married Solomon. 17 So Solomon
had the town rebuilt.
Solomon had his workers rebuild
Lower Beth-Horon, 18 Baalath, and Tamar in the desert of Judah. 19 They also
built towns where he could keep his
supplies and his chariots and horses.
Solomon had them build whatever he
wanted in Jerusalem, Lebanon, and anywhere in his kingdom.
20-22 Solomon did not force the Israelites to do his work. They were his
soldiers, officials, leaders, commanders,
chariot captains, and chariot drivers.
But he did make slaves of the Amorites,
Hittites, Perizzites, Hivites, and Jebusites who were living in Israel. These
were the descendants of those foreigners the Israelites could not destroy, and
they remained Israel's slaves.
23 Solomon appointed five hundred
fifty officers to be in charge of his workers and to watch over his building projects.
24 Solomon's wife, the daughter of the
king of Egypt, moved from the older
part of Jerusalem[z] to her new palace.
Then Solomon had the land on the east
side of Jerusalem filled in.[a]
25 Three times a year, Solomon burned
incense and offered sacrifices to the
LORD on the altar he had built.
Solomon had now finished building
the LORD's temple.
26 He also had a lot of ships at Ezion-
Geber, a town in Edom near Eloth on
the Red Sea.[b] 27-28 King Hiram let some
of his experienced sailors go to the

---

[v] **8.65** *seven days*: One ancient translation; Hebrew "seven days and seven more days, fourteen days in all." [w] **9.8** *a pile of rocks*: Some ancient translations; Hebrew "high." [x] **9.13** *Cabul . . . worthless*: Cabul sounds like the Hebrew word for "worthless." [y] **9.15** *fill . . . Jerusalem*: The Hebrew text has "build the Millo," which probably refers to a landfill to strengthen and extend the hill where the city was built. [z] **9.24** *the older . . . Jerusalem*: See the note at 3.1. [a] **9.24** *the land . . . filled in*: See the note at 9.15. [b] **9.26** *Red Sea*: Hebrew *yam suph*, here referring to the Gulf of Aqaba, since the term is extended to include the northeastern arm of the Red Sea (see also the note at Exodus 13.11).

country of Ophir[c] with Solomon's own
sailors, and they brought back about
sixteen tons of gold for Solomon.

The Queen of Sheba Visits Solomon

(2 Chronicles 9.1-12)

10 The Queen of Sheba heard how
famous Solomon was, so she
went to Jerusalem to test him with difficult questions. 2 She took along several
of her officials, and she loaded her
camels with gifts of spices, jewels, and
gold. When she arrived, she and
Solomon talked about everything she
could think of. 3 He answered every
question, no matter how difficult it was.
4-5 The Queen was amazed at Solomon's wisdom. She was breathless
when she saw his palace, the food on
his table, his officials, his servants in
their uniforms, the people who served
his food, and the sacrifices he offered at
the LORD's temple. 6 She said:

Solomon, in my own country I had
heard about your wisdom and all
you've done. 7 But I didn't believe it
until I saw it with my own eyes! And
there's so much I didn't hear about.
You are wiser and richer than I was
told. 8 Your wives[d] and officials are
lucky to be here where they can listen to the wise things you say.

9 I praise the LORD your God. He is
pleased with you and has made you
king of Israel. The LORD loves Israel,
so he has given them a king who
will rule fairly and honestly.

10 The Queen of Sheba gave Solomon
almost five tons of gold, many jewels,
and more spices than anyone had ever
brought into Israel.
11-13 In return, Solomon gave her the
gifts he would have given any other
ruler, but he also gave her everything
else she wanted. Then she and her
officials went back to their own country.

Solomon's Wealth

(2 Chronicles 9.13-28)

King Hiram's ships brought gold, juniper wood, and jewels from the country
of Ophir. Solomon used the wood to
make steps[e] for the temple and palace,
and harps and other stringed instruments for the musicians. It was the best
juniper wood anyone in Israel had ever
seen.
14 Solomon received about twenty-five
tons of gold a year. 15 The merchants and
traders, as well as the kings of Arabia
and rulers from Israel, also gave him
gold.
16 Solomon made two hundred gold
shields and used about seven and a half
pounds of gold for each one. 17 He also
made three hundred smaller gold
shields, using almost four pounds for
each one, and he put the shields in his
palace in Forest Hall.
18 His throne was made of ivory and
covered with pure gold. 19-20 The back of
the throne was rounded at the top, and it
had armrests on each side. There was a
statue of a lion on both sides of the
throne, and there was a statue of a lion
at both ends of each of the six steps
leading up to the throne. No other
throne in the world was like Solomon's.
21 Since silver was almost worthless in
those days, everything was made of
gold, even the cups and dishes used in
Forest Hall.
22 Solomon had a lot of seagoing
ships.[f] Every three years he sent them
out with Hiram's ships to bring back
gold, silver, and ivory, as well as mon-
keys and peacocks.[g]
23 He was the richest and wisest king
in the world. 24 People from every nation
wanted to hear the wisdom God had
given him. 25 Year after year people
came and brought gifts of silver and
gold, as well as clothes, weapons,
spices, horses, or mules.
26 Solomon had one thousand four
hundred chariots and twelve thousand
horses that he kept in Jerusalem and
other towns.
27 While he was king, there was silver
everywhere in Jerusalem, and cedar was
as common as ordinary sycamore trees
in the foothills.
28-29 Solomon's merchants bought his
horses and chariots in the regions of
Musri and Kue.[h] They paid about fifteen
pounds of silver for a chariot and almost four pounds of silver for a horse.
They also sold horses and chariots to
the Hittite and Syrian kings.

Solomon Disobeys the LORD

11 1-2 The LORD did not want the Israelites to worship foreign gods,
so he had warned them not to marry
anyone who was not from Israel.
Solomon loved his wife, the daughter
of the king of Egypt. But he also loved
some women from Moab, Ammon, and
Edom, and others from Sidon and the
land of the Hittites. 3-4 Seven hundred of

[c] **9.27,28** *Ophir*: The location of this place is not known. [d] **10.8** *wives*: Two ancient translations; Hebrew "men." [e] **10.11-13** *steps*: Or "stools" or "railings." [f] **10.22** *seagoing ships*: The Hebrew text has "ships of Tarshish," which may have been a Phoenician city in Spain. "Ships of Tarshish" probably means large, seagoing ships. [g] **10.22** *peacocks*: Or "baboons." [h] **10.28,29** *Musri and Kue*: Hebrew "Egypt and Kue." Musri and Kue were regions located in what is today southeast Turkey.

his wives were daughters of kings, but
he also married three hundred other
women.[i]
As Solomon got older, some of his
wives led him to worship their gods. He
wasn't like his father David, who had
worshiped only the LORD God. 5Sol-
omon also worshiped Astarte the goddess of Sidon, and Milcom the disgusting god of Ammon. 6Solomon's father
had obeyed the LORD with all his heart,
but Solomon disobeyed and did what
the LORD hated.
7Solomon built shrines on a hill east
of Jerusalem to worship Chemosh the
disgusting god of Moab, and Molech the
disgusting god of Ammon. 8In fact, he
built a shrine for each of his foreign
wives, so all of them could burn incense
and offer sacrifices to their own gods.
9-10The LORD God of Israel had appeared to Solomon two times and
warned him not to worship foreign
gods. But Solomon disobeyed and did it
anyway. This made the LORD very angry,
11and he said to Solomon:

You did what you wanted and not
what I told you to do. Now I'm going
to take your kingdom from you and
give it to one of your officials. 12But
because David was your father, you
will remain king as long as you live.
I will wait until your son becomes
king, then I will take the kingdom
from him. 13When I do, I will still let
him rule one tribe, because I have
not forgotten that David was my servant and Jerusalem is my city.

Hadad Becomes an Enemy of Solomon

14Hadad was from the royal family of
Edom, and here is how the LORD made
him Solomon's enemy:
15-16Some time earlier, when David
conquered the nation of Edom,[j] Joab his
army commander went there to bury
those who had died in battle. Joab and
his soldiers stayed in Edom six months,
and during that time they killed every
man and boy who lived there.
17-19Hadad was a boy at the time, but
he escaped to Midian with some of his
father's officials. At Paran some other
men joined them, and they went to the
king of Egypt. The king liked Hadad
and gave him food, some land, and a
house, and even let him marry the sister
of Queen Tahpenes. 20Hadad and his
wife had a son named Genubath, and
the queen let the boy grow up in the
palace with her own children.
21When Hadad heard that David and
Joab were dead, he said to the king,
"Your Majesty, please let me go back to
my own country."
22"Why?" asked the king. "Do you
want something I haven't given you?"
"No, I just want to go home."

Rezon Becomes an Enemy of Solomon

23Here is how God made Rezon son of
Eliada an enemy of Solomon:
Rezon had run away from his master,
King Hadadezer of Zobah. 24-25He
formed his own small army and became
its leader after David had defeated Hadadezer's troops.[k] Then Rezon and his
army went to Damascus, where he became the ruler of Syria and an enemy of
Israel.
Both Hadad and Rezon were enemies
of Israel while Solomon was king, and
they caused him a lot of trouble.

The LORD Makes a Promise to Jeroboam

26Jeroboam was from the town of
Zeredah in Ephraim. His father Nebat
had died, but his mother Zeruah was
still alive. Jeroboam was one of
Solomon's officials, but even he rebelled
against Solomon. 27Here is how it happened:
While Solomon's workers were filling
in the land on the east side of Jerusalem[l]
and repairing the city walls, 28Solomon
noticed that Jeroboam was a hard
worker. So he put Jeroboam in charge
of the work force from Manasseh
and Ephraim.
29-30One day when Jeroboam was
leaving Jerusalem, he met Ahijah, a
prophet from Shiloh. No one else was
anywhere around. Suddenly, Ahijah
took off his new coat and ripped it into
twelve pieces. 31Then he said:

Jeroboam, take ten pieces of this
coat and listen to what the LORD
God of Israel says to you. "Jeroboam, I am the LORD God, and I am
about to take Solomon's kingdom
from him and give you ten tribes to
rule. 32But Solomon will still rule
one tribe,[m] since he is the son of
David my servant, and Jerusalem is
my chosen city.
33"Solomon and the Israelites are
not like their ancestor David. They
will not listen to me, obey me, or do
what is right. They have turned from
me to worship Astarte the goddess
of Sidon, Chemosh the god of Moab,
and Milcom the god of Ammon.

[i] **11.3,4** *other women*: This translates a Hebrew word for a woman who was legally bound to a man, but without the full privileges of a wife. [j] **11.15,16** *Edom*: See 2 Samuel 8.13, 14. [k] **11.24,25** *troops*: See 2 Samuel 8.3-6. [l] **11.27** *filling . . . Jerusalem*: See the note at 9.15. [m] **11.31,32** *ten tribes . . . one tribe*: By this time the tribe of Simeon had become part of the tribe of Judah. "One tribe" refers to Judah. Instead of "one tribe," one ancient translation has "two tribes."

34"Solomon is David's son, and
David was my chosen leader, who
did what I commanded. So I will let
Solomon be king until he dies.
35Then I will give you ten tribes to
rule, 36but Solomon's son will still
rule one tribe. This way, my servant
David will always have a descendant
ruling in Jerusalem, the city where I
have chosen to be worshiped.
37"You will be king of Israel and
will rule every nation you want. 38I'll
help you if you obey me. And if you
do what I say, as my servant David
did, I will always let someone from
your family rule in Israel, just as
someone from David's family will
always rule in Judah. The nation of
Israel will be yours.
39"I will punish the descendants of
David, but not forever."
40When Solomon learned what the
LORD had told Jeroboam, Solomon tried
to kill Jeroboam. But he escaped to King
Shishak of Egypt and stayed there until
Solomon died.

Solomon Dies
(2 Chronicles 9.29-31)

41Everything else Solomon did while
he was king is written in the book about
him and his wisdom. 42After he had
ruled forty years from Jerusalem, 43he
died and was buried there in the city of
his father David. His son Rehoboam
then became king.

Some of the People Rebel against Rehoboam
(2 Chronicles 10.1-19)

12 Rehoboam went to Shechem
where everyone was waiting to
crown him king.
2Jeroboam son of Nebat heard what
was happening, and he stayed in
Egypt,[n] where he had gone to hide from
Solomon. 3But the people from the
northern tribes of Israel sent for him.
Then together they went to Rehoboam
and said, 4"Your father Solomon forced
us to work very hard. But if you make
our work easier, we will serve you and
do whatever you ask."
5"Give me three days to think about
it," Rehoboam replied, "then come back
for my answer." So the people left.
6Rehoboam went to some leaders who
had been his father's senior officials,
and he asked them, "What should I tell
these people?"
7They answered, "If you want them to
serve and obey you, then you should do
what they ask today. Tell them you will
make their work easier."
8But Rehoboam refused their advice
and went to the younger men who had
grown up with him and were now his
officials. 9He asked, "What do you think
I should say to these people who asked
me to make their work easier?"
10His younger advisors said:
Here's what we think you should
say to them: "Compared to me, my
father was weak.[o] 11He made you
work hard, but I'll make you work
even harder. He punished you with
whips, but I'll use whips with pieces
of sharp metal!"
12Three days later, Jeroboam and the
others came back. 13Rehoboam ignored
the advice of the older advisors. 14He
spoke bluntly and told them exactly
what his own advisors had suggested:
"My father made you work hard, but I'll
make you work even harder. He punished you with whips, but I'll use whips
with pieces of sharp metal!"
15-19When the people realized that Rehoboam would not listen to them, they
shouted: "We don't have to be loyal to
David's family. We can do what we
want. Come on, people of Israel, let's go
home! Rehoboam can rule his own people."

Adoniram[p] was in charge of the
forced labor, and Rehoboam sent him to
talk to the people. But they stoned him
to death. Then Rehoboam ran to his
chariot and hurried back to Jerusalem.

So the people from the northern tribes
of Israel went home, leaving Rehoboam
to rule only the people from the towns
in Judah. Ever since that day, the people
of Israel have opposed David's family in
Judah. All of this happened just as the
LORD's prophet Ahijah had told Jeroboam.
20When the Israelites heard that Jeroboam was back, they called everyone
together. Then they sent for Jeroboam
and made him king of Israel. Only the
people from the tribe of Judah[q] remained loyal to David's family.

Shemaiah Warns Rehoboam
(2 Chronicles 11.1-4)

21After Rehoboam returned to
Jerusalem, he decided to attack Israel
and take control of the whole country.
So he called together one hundred
eighty thousand soldiers from the tribes
of Judah and Benjamin.

[n]12.2 *he stayed in Egypt*: Hebrew; two ancient translations "he returned from Egypt" (see also 2 Chronicles 10.2). [o]12.10 *Compared . . . weak*: Hebrew "My little finger is bigger than my father's waist." [p]12.15-19 *Adoniram*: Two ancient translations (see also 4.6 and 5.14); Hebrew "Adoram." [q]12.20 *Israelites . . . Israel . . . Judah*: From this time on, "Israel" usually refers to the northern kingdom, and "Israelites" refers to the people who lived there. The southern kingdom is called "Judah."

[22]Meanwhile, God told Shemaiah the
prophet [23]to give Rehoboam and everyone from Judah and Benjamin this
warning: [24]"Don't go to war against the
people from Israel—they are your relatives. Go home! I am the LORD, and I
made these things happen."
Rehoboam and his army obeyed the
LORD and went home.

Jeroboam Makes Religious Changes

[25]Jeroboam rebuilt Shechem in
Ephraim and made it a stronger town,
then he moved there. He also fortified
the town of Penuel.
[26-27]One day, Jeroboam started thinking, "Everyone in Israel still goes to the
temple in Jerusalem to offer sacrifices
to the LORD. What if they become loyal
to David's family again? They will kill
me and accept Rehoboam as their king."
[28]Jeroboam asked for advice and then
made two gold statues of calves. He
showed them to the people and said,
"Listen everyone! You won't have to go
to Jerusalem to worship anymore. Here
are your gods[r] who rescued you from
Egypt." [29-30]Then he put one of the gold
calves in the town of Bethel. He put the
other one in the town of Dan, and the
crowd walked out in front as the calf
was taken there.[s] What Jeroboam did
was a terrible sin.
[31]Jeroboam built small places of worship at the shrines[t] and appointed men
who were not from the tribe of Levi to
serve as priests. [32-33]He also decided to
start a new festival for the Israelites on
the fifteenth day of the eighth month,
just like the one in Judah.[u] On that day,
Jeroboam went to Bethel and offered
sacrifices on the altar to the gold calf he
had put there. Then he assigned the
priests their duties.

A Prophet Condemns the Altar at Bethel

13 [1-2]One day, Jeroboam was standing at the altar in Bethel, ready to
make an offering. Suddenly one of
God's prophets[v] arrived from Judah and
shouted:

> The LORD sent me with a message
> about this altar. A child named
> Josiah will be born into David's fam-
> ily. He will sacrifice on this altar the
> priests who make offerings here,
> and human bones will be burned
> on it.
> [3]You will know that the LORD has
> said these things when the altar
> splits in half, and the ashes on it fall
> to the ground.

[4]Jeroboam pointed at the prophet and
shouted, "Grab him!" But right away,
Jeroboam's hand became stiff, and he
could not move it. [5]The altar split in
half, and the ashes fell to the ground,
just as the prophet had warned.
[6]"Please pray to the LORD your God
and ask him to heal my hand," Jeroboam begged.
The prophet prayed, and Jeroboam's
hand was healed.
[7]"Come home with me and eat something," Jeroboam said. "I want to give
you a gift for what you have done."
[8]"No, I wouldn't go with you, even if
you offered me half of your kingdom. I
won't eat or drink here either. [9]The
LORD said I can't eat or drink anything
and that I can't go home the same way I
came." [10]Then he started home down a
different road.

An Old Prophet from Bethel

[11]At that time an old prophet lived in
Bethel, and one of his sons told him
what the prophet from Judah had said
and done.
[12]"Show me which way he went," the
old prophet said, and his sons pointed
out the road. [13]"Put a saddle on my donkey," he told them. After they did, he got
on the donkey [14]and rode off to look for
the prophet from Judah.
The old prophet found him sitting under an oak tree and asked, "Are you the
prophet from Judah?"
"Yes, I am."
[15]"Come home with me," the old
prophet said, "and have something to
eat."
[16]"I can't go back with you," the
prophet replied, "and I can't eat or drink
anything with you. [17]The LORD warned
me not to eat or drink or to go home the
same way I came."
[18]The old prophet said, "I'm a prophet
too. One of the LORD's angels told me to
take you to my house and give you
something to eat and drink."
The prophet from Judah did not know
that the old prophet was lying, [19]so he
went home with him and ate and drank.
[20]During the meal the LORD gave the
old prophet [21]a message for the prophet
from Judah:

> Listen to the LORD's message. You
> have disobeyed the LORD your God.
> [22]He told you not to eat or drink
> anything here, but you came home
> and ate with me. And so, when you
> die, your body won't be buried in
> your family tomb.

[r]12.28 *Here are your gods*: Or "Here is your God." One possible meaning for the difficult Hebrew text. [s]12.29,30 *the crowd . . . taken there*: [t]12.31 *shrines*: See the note at 3.2. [u]12.32,33 *the one in Judah*: This probably refers to the Festival of Shelters. [v]13.1,2 *one of God's prophets*: Hebrew "a man of God."

23After the meal the old prophet got a
donkey ready, 24and the prophet from
Judah left. Along the way, a lion attacked and killed him, and the donkey
and the lion stood there beside his dead
body.
25Some people walked by and saw the
body with the lion standing there. They
ran into Bethel, telling everyone what
they had seen.
26When the old prophet heard the
news, he said, "That must be the
prophet from Judah. The LORD warned
him, but he disobeyed. So the LORD sent
a lion to kill him."
27The old prophet told his sons to saddle his donkey, and when it was ready,
28he left. He found the body lying on the
road, with the donkey and lion standing
there. The lion had not eaten the body
or attacked the donkey. 29The old
prophet picked up the body, put it on his
own donkey, and took it back to Bethel,
so he could bury it and mourn for the
prophet from Judah.
30He buried the body in his own family tomb and cried for the prophet. 31He
said to his sons, "When I die, bury my
body next to this prophet. 32I'm sure
that everything he said about the altar
in Bethel and the shrines in Samaria
will happen."
33But Jeroboam kept on doing evil
things. He appointed men to be priests
at the local shrines, even if they were
not Levites. In fact, anyone who wanted
to be a priest could be one. 34This sinful
thing led to the downfall of his kingdom.

Jeroboam's Son Dies

14 About the same time, Abijah son
of Jeroboam got sick. 2-3Jeroboam
told his wife:

> Disguise yourself so no one will
> know you're my wife, then go to
> Shiloh, where the prophet Ahijah
> lives. Take him ten loaves of bread,
> some small cakes, and honey, and
> ask him what will happen to our
> son. He can tell you, because he's
> the one who told me I would become
> king.

4She got ready and left for Ahijah's
house in Shiloh.
Ahijah was now old and blind, 5but
the LORD told him, "Jeroboam's wife is
coming to ask about her son. I will tell
you what to say to her."
Jeroboam's wife came to Ahijah's
house, pretending to be someone else.
6But when Ahijah heard her walking up
to the door, he said:

> Come in! I know you're Jer-
> oboam's wife—why are you pretend-
> ing to be someone else? I have some
> bad news for you. 7Give your hus-
> band this message from the LORD
> God of Israel: "Jeroboam, you know
> that I, the LORD, chose you over any-
> one else to be the leader of my peo-
> ple Israel. 8I even took David's king-
> dom away from his family and gave
> it to you. But you are not like my
> servant David. He always obeyed me
> and did what was right.
> 9"You have made me very angry
> by rejecting me and making idols
> out of gold. Jeroboam, you have
> done more evil things than any king
> before you.
> 10"Because of this, I will destroy
> your family by killing every man
> and boy in it, whether slave or free. I
> will wipe out your family, just as fire
> burns up trash. 11Dogs will eat the
> bodies of your relatives who die in
> town, and vultures will eat the bod-
> ies of those who die in the country. I,
> the LORD, have spoken and will not
> change my mind!"
> 12That's the LORD's message to
> your husband. As for you, go back
> home, and right after you get there,
> your son will die. 13Everyone in Is-
> rael will mourn at his funeral. But he
> will be the last one from Jeroboam's
> family to receive a proper burial, be-
> cause he's the only one the LORD
> God of Israel is pleased with.
> 14The LORD will soon choose a
> new king of Israel, who will destroy
> Jeroboam's family. And I mean very
> soon.[w] 15The people of Israel have
> made the LORD angry by setting up
> sacred poles[x] for worshiping the
> goddess Asherah. So the LORD will
> punish them until they shake like
> grass in a stream. He will take them
> out of the land he gave to their an-
> cestors, then scatter them as far
> away as the Euphrates River. 16Jer-
> oboam sinned and caused the Is-
> raelites to sin. Now the LORD will
> desert Israel.

17Jeroboam's wife left and went back
home to the town of Tirzah. As soon as
she set foot in her house, her son died.
18Everyone in Israel came and mourned
at his funeral, just as the LORD's servant
Ahijah had said.

Jeroboam Dies

19Everything else Jeroboam did while
he was king, including the battles he
won, is written in *The History of the
Kings of Israel.* 20He was king of Israel
for twenty-two years, then he died, and
his son Nadab became king.

[w] **14.14** *And I mean very soon*: One possible meaning for the difficult Hebrew text.
[x] **14.15** *sacred poles*: Or "trees," used as symbols of Asherah, the goddess of fertility.

King Rehoboam of Judah
(2 Chronicles 11.5—12.16)

21Rehoboam son of Solomon was
forty-one years old when he became
king of Judah, and he ruled seventeen
years from Jerusalem, the city where
the LORD had chosen to be worshiped.
His mother Naamah was from Ammon.
22The people of Judah disobeyed the
LORD and made him even angrier than
their ancestors had. 23They also built
their own local shrines[y] and stone images of foreign gods, and they set up sacred poles[z] for worshiping the goddess
Asherah on every hill and in the shade
of large trees. 24Even worse, they allowed prostitutes[a] at the shrines, and
followed the disgusting customs of the
foreign nations that the LORD had forced
out of Canaan.
25After Rehoboam had been king
for four years, King Shishak of Egypt
attacked Jerusalem. 26He took everything of value from the temple and the
palace, including Solomon's gold
shields.
27Rehoboam had bronze shields made
to replace the gold ones, and he ordered
the guards at the city gates to keep them
safe. 28Whenever Rehoboam went to the
LORD's temple, the guards carried the
shields. But they always took them back
to the guardroom as soon as he was finished.
29Everything else Rehoboam did while
he was king is written in *The History of
the Kings of Judah*. 30He and Jeroboam
were constantly at war. 31Rehoboam's
mother Naamah was from Ammon, but
when Rehoboam died, he was buried
beside his ancestors in Jerusalem.[b] His
son Abijam then became king.

King Abijam of Judah
(2 Chronicles 13.1-22)

15 Abijam became king of Judah in
Jeroboam's eighteenth year as
king of Israel, 2and he ruled from
Jerusalem for three years. His mother
was Maacah the daughter of Abishalom.
3Abijam did not truly obey the LORD
his God as his ancestor David had done.
Instead, he was sinful just like his father
Rehoboam. 4-5David had always obeyed
the LORD's commands by doing right,
except in the case of Uriah.[c] And since
Abijam was David's great-grandson, the
LORD kept Jerusalem safe and let Abijam have a son who would be the next
king.
6-7The war that had broken out between Rehoboam and Jeroboam continued during the time that Abijam was
king.
Everything else Abijam did while he
was king is written in *The History of the
Kings of Judah*. 8Abijam died and was
buried in Jerusalem,[d] and his son Asa
became king.

King Asa of Judah
(2 Chronicles 15.16—16.6, 11-13)

9Asa became king of Judah in the
twentieth year of Jeroboam's rule in Israel, 10and he ruled forty-one years from
Jerusalem. His grandmother was
Maacah the daughter of Abishalom.
11Asa obeyed the LORD, as David had
done. 12He forced the prostitutes[e] at the
shrines to leave the country, and he got
rid of the idols his ancestors had made.
13His own grandmother Maacah had
made an idol of Asherah, and Asa took
it and burned it in Kidron Valley. Then
he removed Maacah from her position
as queen mother.[f]
14As long as Asa lived, he was completely faithful to the LORD, even though
he did not destroy the local shrines.
15He placed in the temple all the silver
and gold objects that he and his father
had dedicated to the LORD.
16Asa was always at war with King
Baasha of Israel. 17One time, Baasha invaded Judah and captured the town of
Ramah. He started making the town
stronger, so he could put troops there to
stop people from going in and out of Judah.
18When Asa heard about this, he took
the silver and gold from his palace and
from the LORD's temple. He gave it to
some of his officials and sent them to
Damascus with this message for
King Benhadad[g] of Syria: 19"Our
fathers signed a peace treaty. Why don't
we do the same thing? This silver
and gold is a present for you. So,
would you please break your treaty
with Baasha and force him to leave my
country?"
20Benhadad did what Asa asked and
sent the Syrian army into Israel. They
captured the towns of Ijon, Dan, and
Abel-Bethmaacah, and the territories of
Chinneroth and Naphtali. 21When

[y] **14.23** *local shrines*: See the note at 3.2. [z] **14.23** *sacred poles*: See the note at 14.15.
[a] **14.24** *prostitutes*: Men and women sometimes served at the local shrines as prostitutes in the worship of Canaanite gods, but the LORD had forbidden the people of Israel to worship in this way (see Deuteronomy 23.17, 18). [b] **14.31** *Jerusalem*: See the note at 2.10, 11.
[c] **15.4,5** *Uriah*: A Hittite who served in David's army; David had him killed so he could marry his wife Bathsheba (see 2 Samuel 11.1-27). [d] **15.8** *Jerusalem*: See the note at 2.10, 11.
[e] **15.12** *prostitutes*: See the note at 14.24. [f] **15.13** *queen mother*: Or "the mother of the king," an important position in biblical times (see 2.19). [g] **15.18** *Benhadad*: Hebrew "Benhadad son of Tabrimmon son of Hezion."

Baasha heard about it, he left Ramah
and went back to Tirzah.
22 Asa ordered everyone in Judah to
carry away the stones and wood Baasha
had used to strengthen the town of
Ramah. Then he used these same stones
and wood to fortify the town of Geba in
the territory of Benjamin and the town
of Mizpah.
23 Everything else Asa did while he
was king, including his victories and the
towns he rebuilt, is written in *The History of the Kings of Judah*. When he got
older, he had a foot disease.
24 Asa died
and was buried in the tomb of his ancestors in Jerusalem.[h] His son Jehoshaphat
then became king.

King Nadab of Israel

25 Nadab son of Jeroboam became
king of Israel in Asa's second year as
king of Judah, and he ruled two years.
26 Nadab disobeyed the LORD by following the evil example of his father, who
had caused the Israelites to sin.
27-28 Baasha son of Ahijah was from
the tribe of Issachar, and he made plans
to kill Nadab. When Nadab and his
army went to attack the town of Gibbethon in Philistia, Baasha killed Nadab
there. So in the third year of Asa's rule,
Baasha became king of Israel.
29 The LORD's prophet Ahijah had earlier said, "Not one man or boy in Jeroboam's family will be left alive." And,
as soon as Baasha became king, he
killed everyone in Jeroboam's family,
30 because Jeroboam had made the LORD
God of Israel angry by sinning and
causing the Israelites to sin.
31 Everything else Nadab did while he
was king is written in *The History of the
Kings of Israel*.
32 King Asa of Judah and King Baasha
of Israel were always at war.

King Baasha of Israel

33 Baasha son of Ahijah became king
of Israel in Asa's third year as king of
Judah, and he ruled twenty-four years
from Tirzah.
34 Baasha also disobeyed
the LORD by acting like Jeroboam, who
had caused the Israelites to sin.

16 The LORD sent Jehu son of Hanani to say to Baasha:

2 Nobody knew who you were until
I, the LORD, chose you[i] to be the
leader of my people Israel. And now
you're acting exactly like Jeroboam
by causing the Israelites to sin. What
you've done has made me so angry
3 that I will destroy you and your
family, just as I did the family of Jeroboam.
4 Dogs will eat the bodies of
your relatives who die in town, and
vultures will eat the bodies of those
who die in the country.

5-7 Baasha made the LORD very angry,
and that's why the LORD gave Jehu this
message for Baasha and his family.
Baasha constantly disobeyed the LORD
by following Jeroboam's sinful example—but even worse, he killed everyone
in Jeroboam's family!
Everything else Baasha did while he
was king, including his brave deeds, is
written in *The History of the Kings of
Israel*. Baasha died and was buried in
Tirzah, and his son Elah became king.

King Elah of Israel

8 Elah son of Baasha became king of
Israel after Asa had been king of Judah
for twenty-five years, and he ruled from
Tirzah for two years.
9 Zimri commanded half of Elah's
chariots, and he made plans to kill Elah.
One day, Elah was in Tirzah, getting
drunk at the home of Arza, his prime
minister,
10 when Zimri went there and
killed Elah. So Zimri became king in the
twenty-seventh year of Asa's rule in Judah.
11 As soon as Zimri became king, he
killed everyone in Baasha's family. Not
one man or boy in his family was left
alive—even his close friends were
killed.
12 Baasha's family was completely
wiped out, just as the LORD's prophet
Jehu had warned.
13 Baasha and Elah
sinned and caused the Israelites to sin,
and they made the LORD angry by worshiping idols.
14 Everything else Elah did while he
was king is written in *The History of the
Kings of Israel*.

King Zimri of Israel

15-16 Zimri became king of Israel in
Asa's twenty-seventh year as king of Judah, but he ruled only seven days from
Tirzah.
Israel's army was camped near Gibbethon in Philistia under the command
of Omri. The soldiers heard that Zimri
had killed Elah, and they made Omri
their king that same day.
17 At once,
Omri and his army marched to Tirzah
and attacked.
18 When Zimri saw that
the town was captured, he ran into the
strongest part of the palace and killed
himself by setting it on fire.
19 Zimri had
disobeyed the LORD by following the evil
example of Jeroboam, who had caused
the Israelites to sin.
20 Everything else Zimri did while he
was king, including his rebellion against
Elah, is written in *The History of the
Kings of Israel*.

[h] **15.24** *Jerusalem*: Hebrew "the city of David his ancestor." [i] **16.2** *Nobody . . . you*: Hebrew "I pulled you up out of the dust."

King Omri of Israel

21After Zimri died, some of the Israelites wanted Tibni son of Ginath to
be king, but others wanted Omri.
22Omri's followers were stronger than
Tibni's, so Tibni was killed, and Omri
became king of Israel 23in the thirty-first
year of Asa's rule in Judah.
Omri ruled Israel for twelve years.
The first six years he ruled from Tirzah,
24then he bought the hill of Samaria
from Shemer for about one hundred
fifty pounds of silver. He built a town
there and named it Samaria, after Shemer who had owned the hill.
25Omri did more evil things than any
king before him. 26He acted just like Jeroboam and made the LORD God of Israel
angry by causing the Israelites to sin
and to worship idols.
27Everything else Omri did while he
was king, including his brave deeds, is
written in *The History of the Kings of
Israel*. 28Omri died and was buried in
Samaria, and his son Ahab became
king.

King Ahab of Israel

29Ahab son of Omri became king of
Israel in the thirty-eighth year of Asa's
rule in Judah, and he ruled twenty-two
years from Samaria.
30Ahab did more things to disobey the
LORD than any king before him. 31He
acted just like Jeroboam. Even worse,
he married Jezebel the daughter of King
Ethbaal of Sidon[j] and started worshiping Baal. 32Ahab built an altar and temple for Baal in Samaria 33and set up a
sacred pole[k] for worshiping the goddess
Asherah. Ahab did more to make the
LORD God of Israel angry than any king
of Israel before him.
34While Ahab was king, a man from
Bethel named Hiel rebuilt the town of
Jericho. But while Hiel was laying the
foundation for the town wall, his oldest
son Abiram died. And while he was finishing the gates, his youngest son Segub
died. This happened just as the LORD
had told Joshua to say many years ago.[l]

Elijah Stops the Rain

17 Elijah was a prophet from Tishbe
in Gilead.[m] One day he went to
King Ahab and said, "I'm a servant of
the living LORD, the God of Israel. And I
swear in his name that it won't rain until I say so. There won't even be any dew
on the ground."
2Later, the LORD said to Elijah,
3"Leave and go across the Jordan River
so you can hide near Cherith Creek.
4You can drink water from the creek,
and eat the food I've told the ravens to
bring you."
5Elijah obeyed the LORD and went to
live near Cherith Creek. 6Ravens
brought him bread and meat twice a
day, and he drank water from the creek.
7But after a while, it dried up because
there was no rain.

Elijah Helps a Widow in Zarephath

8The LORD told Elijah, 9"Go to the
town of Zarephath in Sidon and live
there. I've told a widow in that town to
give you food."
10When Elijah came near the town
gate of Zarephath, he saw a widow
gathering sticks for a fire. "Would you
please bring me a cup of water?" he
asked. 11As she left to get it, he asked,
"Would you also please bring me a piece
of bread?"
12The widow answered, "In the name
of the living LORD your God, I swear
that I don't have any bread. All I have is
a handful of flour and a little olive oil.
I'm on my way home now with these
few sticks to cook what I have for my
son and me. After that, we will starve to
death."
13Elijah said, "Everything will be fine.
Do what you said. Go home and fix
something for you and your son. But
first, please make a small piece of bread
and bring it to me. 14The LORD God of Israel has promised that your jar of flour
won't run out and your bottle of oil
won't dry up before he sends rain for
the crops."
15The widow went home and did exactly what Elijah had told her. She and
Elijah and her family had enough food
for a long time. 16The LORD kept the
promise that his prophet Elijah had
made, and she did not run out of flour
or oil.

Elijah Brings a Boy Back to Life

17Several days later, the son of the
woman who owned the house[n] got sick,
and he kept getting worse, until finally
he died.
18The woman shouted at Elijah, "What
have I done to you? I thought you were
God's prophet. Did you come here to
cause the death of my son as a reminder
that I've sinned against God?"[o]

[j]**16.31** *Sidon*: One of the most important cities in Phoenicia. It was located on the coast of the Mediterranean Sea, north of Israel, in what is today southern Lebanon. [k]**16.33** *sacred pole*: See the note at 14.15. [l]**16.34** *a man from Bethel . . . ago*: See Joshua 6.26. [m]**17.1** *from Tishbe in Gilead*: Or "from the settlers in Gilead." [n]**17.17** *the woman who owned the house*: This may or may not be the same woman as the widow in verses 8-16. [o]**17.18** *Did you . . . God*: In ancient times people sometimes thought that if they sinned, something terrible would happen to them.

19"Bring me your son," Elijah said.
Then he took the boy from her arms and
carried him upstairs to the room where
he was staying. Elijah laid the boy on
his bed 20and prayed, "LORD God, why
did you do such a terrible thing to this
woman? She's letting me stay here, and
now you've let her son die." 21Elijah
stretched himself out over the boy three
times, while praying, "LORD God, bring
this boy back to life!"
22The LORD answered Elijah's prayer,
and the boy started breathing again.
23Elijah picked him up and carried him
downstairs. He gave the boy to his
mother and said, "Look, your son is
alive."
24"You are God's prophet!" the woman
replied. "Now I know that you really do
speak for the LORD."

Elijah Proves He Is the LORD's Prophet

18 1-2For three years no rain fell in
Samaria, and there was almost
nothing to eat anywhere. The LORD said
to Elijah, "Go and meet with King Ahab.
I will soon make it rain." So Elijah went
to see Ahab.
3-4At that time Obadiah was in charge
of Ahab's palace, but he faithfully worshiped the LORD. In fact, when Jezebel
was trying to kill the LORD's prophets,
Obadiah hid one hundred of them in
two caves and gave them food and water.
Ahab sent for Obadiah 5and said, "We
have to find something for our horses
and mules to eat. If we don't, we will
have to kill them. Let's look around
every creek and spring in the country
for some grass. 6You go one way, and I'll
go the other." Then they left in separate
directions.
7As Obadiah was walking along, he
met Elijah. Obadiah recognized him,
bowed down, and asked, "Elijah, is it really you?"
8"Yes. Go tell Ahab I'm here."
9Obadiah replied:
King Ahab would kill me if I told
him that. And I haven't even done
anything wrong. 10I swear to you in
the name of the living LORD your
God that the king has looked everywhere for you. He sent people to
look in every country, and when
they couldn't find you, he made the
leader of each country swear that
you were not in that country. 11Do
you really want me to tell him you're
here?
12What if the LORD's Spirit takes
you away as soon as I leave? When
Ahab comes to get you, he won't
find you. Then he will surely kill me.
I have worshiped the LORD since I
was a boy. 13I even hid one hundred
of the LORD's prophets in caves
when Jezebel was trying to kill
them. I also gave them food and water. 14Do you really want me to tell
Ahab you're here? He will kill me!
15Elijah said, "I'm a servant of the living LORD All-Powerful, and I swear in
his name that I will meet with Ahab today."
16Obadiah left and told Ahab where to
find Elijah.
Ahab went to meet Elijah, 17and when
he saw him, Ahab shouted, "There you
are, the biggest troublemaker in Israel!"
18Elijah answered:
You're the troublemaker—not me!
You and your family have disobeyed
the LORD's commands by worshiping
Baal.
19Call together everyone from Israel and have them meet me on
Mount Carmel. Be sure to bring
along the four hundred fifty prophets of Baal and the four hundred
prophets of Asherah who eat at Jezebel's table.
20Ahab got everyone together, then
they went to meet Elijah on Mount
Carmel. 21Elijah stood in front of them
and said, "How much longer will you try
to have things both ways? If the LORD is
God, worship him! But if Baal is God,
worship him!"
The people did not say a word.
22Then Elijah continued:
I am the LORD's only prophet, but
Baal has four hundred fifty
prophets.
23Bring us two bulls. Baal's
prophets can take one of them, kill
it, and cut it into pieces. Then they
can put the meat on the wood without lighting the fire. I will do the
same thing with the other bull, and I
won't light a fire under it either.
24The prophets of Baal will pray to
their god, and I will pray to the
LORD. The one who answers by starting the fire is God.
"That's a good idea," everyone agreed.
25Elijah said to Baal's prophets,
"There are more of you, so you go first.
Pick out a bull and get it ready, but don't
light the fire. Then pray to your god."
26They chose their bull, then they got
it ready and prayed to Baal all morning,
asking him to start the fire. They danced
around the altar and shouted, "Answer
us, Baal!" But there was no answer.
27At noon, Elijah began making fun of
them. "Pray louder!" he said. "Baal must
be a god. Maybe he's day-dreaming or
using the toilet or traveling somewhere.
Or maybe he's asleep, and you have to
wake him up."
28The prophets kept shouting louder
and louder, and they cut themselves
with swords and knives until they were
bleeding. This was the way they wor-

shiped, 29and they kept it up all afternoon. But there was no answer of any
kind.
30Elijah told everyone to gather
around him while he repaired the
LORD's altar. 31-32Then he used twelve
stones to build an altar in honor of the
LORD. Each stone stood for one of the
tribes of Israel, which was the name
the LORD had given to their ancestor Jacob. Elijah dug a ditch around the altar,
large enough to hold about thirteen
quarts. 33He placed the wood on the altar, then they cut the bull into pieces
and laid the meat on the wood.
He told the people, "Fill four large jars
with water and pour it over the meat
and the wood." After they did this, 34he
told them to do it two more times. They
did exactly as he said 35until finally, the
water ran down the altar and filled the
ditch.
36When it was time for the evening
sacrifice, Elijah prayed:

Our LORD, you are the God of
Abraham, Isaac, and Israel. Now,
prove that you are the God of this
nation,[p] and that I, your servant,
have done this at your command.
37Please answer me, so these people
will know that you are the LORD
God, and that you will turn their
hearts back to you.[q]

38The LORD immediately sent fire, and
it burned up the sacrifice, the wood, and
the stones. It scorched the ground
everywhere around the altar and dried
up every drop of water in the ditch.
39When the crowd saw what had happened, they all bowed down and
shouted, "The LORD is God! The LORD is
God!"
40Just then, Elijah said, "Grab the
prophets of Baal! Don't let any of them
get away."
So the people captured the prophets
and took them to Kishon River, where
Elijah killed every one of them.

It Starts To Rain

41Elijah told Ahab, "Get something to
eat and drink. I hear a heavy rain coming."
42Ahab left, but Elijah climbed back to
the top of Mount Carmel. Then he
stooped down with his face almost to
the ground 43and said to his servant,
"Look toward the sea."
The servant left. And when he came
back, he said, "I looked, but I didn't see
anything." Elijah told him to look seven
more times.
44After the seventh time the servant
replied, "I see a small cloud coming this
way. But it's no bigger than a fist."
Elijah told him, "Tell Ahab to get his
chariot ready and start home now.
Otherwise, the rain will stop him."
45-46A few minutes later, it got very
cloudy and windy, and rain started
pouring down. So Elijah wrapped his
coat around himself, and the LORD gave
him strength to run all the way to
Jezreel. Ahab followed him.

Elijah Runs Away from Ahab and Jezebel

19 Ahab told his wife Jezebel what
Elijah had done and that he had
killed the prophets. 2She sent a message
to Elijah: "You killed my prophets. Now
I'm going to kill you! I pray that the
gods will punish me even more severely
if I don't do it by this time tomorrow."
3Elijah was afraid when he got her
message, and he ran to the town of
Beersheba in Judah. He left his servant
there, 4then walked another whole day
into the desert. Finally, he came to a
large bush and sat down in its shade. He
begged the LORD, "I've had enough. Just
let me die! I'm no better off than my ancestors." 5Then he lay down in the shade
and fell asleep.
Suddenly an angel woke him up and
said, "Get up and eat." 6Elijah looked
around, and by his head was a jar of water and some baked bread. He sat up,
ate and drank, then lay down and went
back to sleep.
7Soon the LORD's angel woke him
again and said, "Get up and eat, or else
you'll get too tired to travel." 8So Elijah
sat up and ate and drank.
The food and water made him strong
enough to walk forty more days. At last,
he reached Mount Sinai,[r] the mountain
of God, 9and he spent the night there in
a cave.

The LORD Appears to Elijah

While Elijah was on Mount Sinai, the
LORD asked, "Elijah, why are you here?"
10He answered, "LORD God All-
Powerful, I've always done my best to
obey you. But your people have broken
their solemn promise to you. They have
torn down your altars and killed all
your prophets, except me. And now they
are even trying to kill me!"
11"Go out and stand on the mountain,"
the LORD replied. "I want you to see me
when I pass by."
All at once, a strong wind shook the
mountain and shattered the rocks. But
the LORD was not in the wind. Next,
there was an earthquake, but the LORD
was not in the earthquake. 12Then there

[p] **18.36** *this nation*: Hebrew "Israel." [q] **18.37** *will turn . . . to you*: One possible meaning for the difficult Hebrew text. [r] **19.8** *Sinai*: Hebrew "Horeb."

was a fire, but the LORD was not in the
fire.
Finally, there was a gentle breeze,[s]
13 and when Elijah heard it, he covered
his face with his coat. He went out and
stood at the entrance to the cave.
The LORD[t] asked, "Elijah, why are you
here?"
14 Elijah answered, "LORD God All-
Powerful, I've always done my best
to obey you. But your people have
broken their solemn promise to you.
They have torn down your altars and
killed all your prophets, except me.
And now they are even trying to kill
me!"
15 The LORD said:
Elijah, you can go back to the
desert near Damascus. And when
you get there, appoint[u] Hazael to be
king of Syria. 16 Then appoint Jehu
son of Nimshi to be king of Israel,
and Elisha son of Shaphat[v] to take
your place as my prophet.
17 Hazael will start killing the people who worship Baal. Jehu will kill
those who escape from Hazael, and
Elisha will kill those who escape
from Jehu.
18 But seven thousand Israelites
have refused to worship Baal, and
they will live.

Elisha Becomes Elijah's Assistant

19 Elijah left and found Elisha plowing
a field with a pair of oxen. There were
eleven other men in front of him, and
each one was also plowing with a pair
of oxen. Elijah went over and put his
own coat on Elisha.[w]
20 Elisha stopped plowing and ran after him. "Let me kiss my parents good-
by, then I'll go with you," he said.
"You can go," Elijah said. "But remember what I've done for you."
21 Elisha left and took his oxen with
him. He killed them and boiled them
over a fire he had made with the wood
from his plow. He gave the meat to the
people who were with him, and they ate
it. Then he left with Elijah and became
his assistant.

Syria Attacks Israel

20 King Benhadad of Syria[x] called
his army together. He was joined
by thirty-two other kings with their
horses and chariots, and together they
marched to Samaria and attacked. 2 Benhadad sent a messenger to tell King
Ahab of Israel, 3 "Ahab, give me your silver and gold, your wives,[y] and your
strongest sons!"
4 "Your Majesty," Ahab replied, "everything I have is yours, including me."
5 Later, Benhadad sent another messenger to say to Ahab, "I already told
you to give me your silver and gold,
your wives, and your children. 6 But tomorrow at this time, I will send my
officials into your city to search your
palace and the houses of your officials.
They will take everything else that you[z]
own."
7 Ahab called a meeting with the leaders of Israel and said, "Benhadad is
causing real trouble. He told me to give
him my wives and children, as well as
my silver and gold. And I agreed."
8 "Don't listen to him!" they answered.
"You don't have to do what he says."
9 So Ahab sent someone to tell Benhadad, "Your Majesty, I'll give you my
silver and gold, and even my wives and
children. But I won't let you have anything else."
When Benhadad got his answer, 10 he
replied, "I'll completely destroy Samaria! There won't even be enough of it
left for my soldiers to carry back in
their hands. If I don't do it, I pray that
the gods will punish me terribly."
11 Ahab then answered, "Benhadad,
don't brag before the fighting even begins. Wait and see if you live through it."
12 Meanwhile, Benhadad and the other
kings had been drinking in their tents.
But when Ahab's reply came, he ordered his soldiers to prepare to attack
Samaria, and they all got ready.
13 At that very moment, a prophet ran
up to Ahab and said, "You can see that
Benhadad's army is very strong. But the
LORD has promised to help you defeat
them today. Then you will know that the
LORD is in control."
14 "Who will fight the battle?" Ahab
asked.
The prophet answered, "The young
bodyguards who serve the district officials."
"But who will lead them into battle?"
Ahab asked.
"You will!" the prophet replied.
15 So Ahab called together the two
hundred thirty-two young soldiers and
the seven thousand troops in Israel's
army, and he got them ready to fight the
Syrians.

[s] **19.12** *a gentle breeze*: Or "a soft whisper" or "hardly a sound." [t] **19.13** *The LORD*: Hebrew "A voice." [u] **19.15** *appoint*: This would have included a ceremony in which olive oil would be poured on his head to show that he was now king. [v] **19.16** *Shaphat*: Hebrew "Shaphat from Abel-Meholah." [w] **19.19** *put . . . Elisha*: This was a sign that Elijah wanted Elisha to follow him and become a prophet. [x] **20.1** *King Benhadad of Syria*: This is probably not the same Benhadad mentioned in 15.18-21. [y] **20.3** *wives*: Having more than one wife was allowed in those times. [z] **20.6** *you*: Hebrew; three ancient translations "they."

Israel Defeats the Syrians

16-17At noon, King Ahab and his Israelite army marched out of Samaria,
with the young soldiers in front.

King Benhadad of Syria and the
thirty-two kings with him were drunk
when the scouts he had sent out ran up
to his tent, shouting, "We just now saw
soldiers marching out of Samaria!"

18"Take them alive!" Benhadad ordered. "I don't care if they have come
out to fight or to surrender."

19The young soldiers led Israel's
troops into battle, 20and each of them attacked and killed an enemy soldier. The
rest of the Syrian army turned and ran,
and the Israelites went after them. Benhadad and some others escaped on
horses, 21but Ahab and his soldiers followed them and captured[a] their horses
and chariots.

Ahab and Israel's army crushed the
Syrians.

22Later, the prophet[b] went back and
warned Ahab, "Benhadad will attack
you again next spring. Build up your
troops and make sure you have some
good plans."

Syria Attacks Israel Again

23Meanwhile, Benhadad's officials
went to him and explained:

> Israel's gods are mountain gods.
> We fought Israel's army in the hills,
> and that's why they defeated us. But
> if we fight them on flat land, there's
> no way we can lose.
>
> 24Here's what you should do. First,
> get rid of those thirty-two kings and
> put army commanders in their
> places. 25Then get more soldiers,
> horses, and chariots, so your army
> will be as strong as it was before.
> We'll fight Israel's army on flat land
> and wipe them out.

Benhadad agreed and did what they
suggested.

26In the spring, Benhadad got his
army together, and they marched to the
town of Aphek to attack Israel. 27The Israelites also prepared to fight. They
marched out to meet the Syrians, and
the two armies camped across from
each other. The Syrians covered the
whole area, but the Israelites looked like
two little flocks of goats.

28The prophet went to Ahab and said,
"The Syrians think the LORD is a god of
the hills and not of the valleys. So he
has promised to help you defeat their
powerful army. Then you will know that
the LORD is in control."

29For seven days the two armies
stayed in their camps, facing each other.
Then on the seventh day the fighting
broke out, and before sunset the Israelites had killed one hundred thousand Syrian troops. 30The rest of the
Syrian army ran back to Aphek, but the
town wall fell and crushed twenty-seven
thousand of them.

Benhadad also escaped to Aphek and
hid in the back room of a house. 31His
officials said, "Your Majesty, we've
heard that Israel's kings keep their
agreements. We will wrap sackcloth
around our waists, put ropes around our
heads, and ask Ahab to let you live."

32They dressed in sackcloth and put
ropes on their heads, then they went to
Ahab and said, "Your servant Benhadad
asks you to let him live."

"Is he still alive?" Ahab asked. "Benhadad is like a brother to me."

33Benhadad's officials were trying to
figure out what Ahab was thinking, and
when he said "brother," they quickly
replied, "You're right! You and Benhadad are like brothers."

"Go get him," Ahab said.

When Benhadad came out, Ahab had
him climb up into his chariot.

34Benhadad said, "I'll give back the
towns my father took from your father.
And you can have shops in Damascus,
just as my father had in Samaria."

Ahab replied, "If you do these things,
I'll let you go free." Then they signed a
peace treaty, and Ahab let Benhadad go.

A Prophet Condemns Ahab

35About this time the LORD commanded a prophet to say to a friend,
"Hit me!" But the friend refused, 36and
the prophet told him, "You disobeyed
the LORD, and as soon as you walk
away, a lion will kill you." The friend
left, and suddenly a lion killed him.

37The prophet found someone else
and said, "Hit me!" So this man beat
him up.

38The prophet left and put a bandage
over his face to disguise himself. Then
he went and stood beside the road, waiting for Ahab to pass by.

39When Ahab went by, the prophet
shouted, "Your Majesty, right in the heat
of battle, someone brought a prisoner to
me and told me to guard him. He said if
the prisoner got away, I would either be
killed or forced to pay seventy-five
pounds of silver. 40But I got busy doing
other things, and the prisoner escaped."

Ahab answered, "You will be punished just as you have said."

41The man quickly tore the bandage
off his face, and Ahab saw that he was
one of the prophets. 42The prophet said,
"The LORD told you to kill Benhadad,

[a]**20.21** *captured*: One ancient translation; Hebrew "attacked." [b]**20.22** *the prophet*: See verse 13.

but you let him go. Now you will die in
his place, and your people will die in
place of his people."
43 Ahab went back to Samaria, angry
and depressed.

Jezebel Has Naboth Killed

21 Naboth owned a vineyard in
Jezreel near King Ahab's palace.
2 One day, Ahab said, "Naboth, your
vineyard is near my palace. Give it to
me so I can turn it into a vegetable garden. I'll give you a better vineyard or
pay whatever you want for yours."
3 Naboth answered, "This vineyard has
always been in my family. I won't let
you have it."
4 So Ahab went home, angry and depressed because of what Naboth had
told him. He lay on his bed, just staring
at the wall and refusing to eat a thing.
5 Jezebel his wife came in and asked,
"What's wrong? Why won't you eat?"
6 "I asked Naboth to sell me his vineyard or to let me give him a better one,"
Ahab replied. "And he told me I couldn't
have it."
7 "Aren't you the king of Israel?" Jezebel asked. "Get out of bed and eat something! Don't worry, I'll get Naboth's
vineyard for you."
8-10 Jezebel wrote a letter to each of the
leaders of the town where Naboth lived.
In the letters she said:

> Call everyone together and tell
> them to go without eating[c] today.
> When they come together, give
> Naboth a seat at the front. Have two
> liars sit across from him and swear
> that Naboth has cursed God and the
> king. Then take Naboth outside and
> stone him to death!

She signed Ahab's name to the letters
and sealed them with his seal. Then she
sent them to the town leaders.
11 After receiving her letters, they did
exactly what she had asked. 12 They told
the people that it was a day to go without eating, and when they all came together, they seated Naboth at the front.
13 The two liars came in and sat across
from Naboth. Then they accused him of
cursing God and the king, so the people
dragged Naboth outside and stoned him
to death.
14 The leaders of Jezreel sent a message back to Jezebel that said, "Naboth
is dead."
15 As soon as Jezebel got their message, she told Ahab, "Now you can have
the vineyard Naboth refused to sell.
He's dead." 16 Ahab got up and went to
take over the vineyard.

Elijah Condemns Ahab

17 The LORD said to Elijah the prophet,
18 "King Ahab of Israel is in Naboth's
vineyard right now, taking it over. 19 Go
tell him that I say, 'Ahab, you murdered
Naboth and took his property. And so,
in the very spot where dogs licked up
Naboth's blood, they will lick up your
blood.' "
When Elijah found him, 20 Ahab said,
"So, my enemy, you found me at last."
Elijah answered:

> Yes, I did! Ahab, you have man-
> aged to do everything the LORD
> hates. 21 Now you will be punished.
> You and every man and boy in your
> family will die, whether slave or
> free. 22 Your whole family will be
> wiped out, just like the families of
> King Jeroboam and King Baasha.
> You've made the LORD very angry by
> sinning and causing the Israelites to
> sin.
> 23 And as for Jezebel, dogs will eat
> her body there in Jezreel. 24 Dogs
> will also eat the bodies of your rela-
> tives who die in town, and vultures
> will eat the bodies of those who die
> in the country.

25-29 When Ahab heard this, he tore his
clothes and wore sackcloth day and
night. He was depressed and refused to
eat.
Some time later, the LORD said, "Elijah, do you see how sorry Ahab is for
what he did? I won't punish his family
while he is still alive. I'll wait until his
son is king."
No one was more determined than
Ahab to disobey the LORD. And Jezebel
encouraged him. Worst of all, he had
worshiped idols, just as the Amorites[d]
had done before the LORD forced them
out of the land and gave it to Israel.

Micaiah Warns Ahab about Disaster

(2 Chronicles 18.2-27)

22 For the next three years there was
peace between Israel and Syria.
2 During the third year King Jehoshaphat of Judah went to visit King
Ahab of Israel.
3 Ahab asked his officials, "Why
haven't we tried to get Ramoth in Gilead
back from the Syrians? It belongs to us."
4 Then he asked Jehoshaphat, "Would
you go to Ramoth with me and attack
the Syrians?"
"Just tell me what to do," Jehoshaphat
answered. "My army and horses are at
your command. 5 But first, let's ask the
LORD."

[c] **21.8-10** *to go without eating*: People sometimes came together to worship and to go without eating to show that they were sorry for their sins. [d] **21.25-29** *Amorites*: A name sometimes used of the people who lived in Palestine before the Israelites.

6 Ahab sent for about four hundred
prophets and asked, "Should I attack
the Syrians at Ramoth?"
"Yes!" the prophets answered. "The
Lord will help you defeat them."
7 But Jehoshaphat said, "Just to make
sure, is there another of the LORD's
prophets we can ask?"
8 "We could ask Micaiah son of Imlah,"
Ahab said. "But I hate Micaiah. He always has bad news for me."
"Don't say that!" Jehoshaphat replied.
9 Then Ahab sent someone to bring Micaiah as soon as possible.
10 All this time, Ahab and Jehoshaphat
were dressed in their royal robes and
were seated on their thrones at the
threshing place near the gate of
Samaria. They were listening to the
prophets tell them what the LORD had
said.
11 Zedekiah son of Chenaanah was
one of the prophets. He had made some
horns out of iron and shouted, "Ahab,
the LORD says you will attack the Syrians like a bull with iron horns and wipe
them out!"
12 All the prophets agreed that Ahab
should attack the Syrians at Ramoth,
and they promised that the LORD would
help him defeat them.
13 Meanwhile, the messenger who
went to get Micaiah whispered, "Micaiah, all the prophets have good news for
Ahab. Now go and say the same thing."
14 "I'll say whatever the living LORD
tells me to say," Micaiah replied.
15 Then Micaiah went to Ahab, and
Ahab asked, "Micaiah, should I attack
the Syrians at Ramoth?"
"Yes!" Micaiah answered. "The LORD
will help you defeat them."
16 "Micaiah, I've told you over and over
to tell me the truth!" Ahab shouted.
"What does the LORD really say?"
17 He answered, "In a vision[e] I saw Israelite soldiers walking around in the
hills like sheep without a shepherd to
guide them. The LORD said, 'This army
has no leader. They should go home and
not fight.' "
18 Ahab turned to Jehoshaphat and
said, "I told you he would bring bad
news!"
19 Micaiah replied:

Listen to this! I also saw the LORD
seated on his throne with every
creature in heaven gathered around
him. 20 The LORD asked, "Who can
trick Ahab and make him go to
Ramoth where he will be killed?"
They talked about it for a while,
21 then finally a spirit came forward
and said to the LORD, "I can trick
Ahab."
"How?" the LORD asked.
22 "I'll make Ahab's prophets lie to
him."
"Good!" the LORD replied. "Now go
and do it."
23 This is exactly what has happened, Ahab. The LORD made all
your prophets lie to you, and he
knows you will soon be destroyed.

24 Zedekiah walked up to Micaiah and
slapped him on the face. Then he asked,
"Do you really think the LORD would
speak to you and not to me?"
25 Micaiah answered, "You'll find out
on the day you have to hide in the back
room of some house."
26 Ahab shouted, "Arrest Micaiah! Take
him to Prince Joash and Governor
Amon of Samaria. 27 Tell them to put
him in prison and to give him nothing
but bread and water until I come back
safely."
28 Micaiah said, "If you do come back,
I was wrong about what the LORD
wanted me to say." Then he told the
crowd, "Don't forget what I said!"

Ahab Dies at Ramoth

(2 Chronicles 18.28-34)

29 Ahab and Jehoshaphat led their
armies to Ramoth in Gilead. 30 Before
they went into battle, Ahab said, "Jehoshaphat, I'll disguise myself, but you
wear your royal robe." Then Ahab disguised himself and went into battle.
31 The king of Syria had ordered his
thirty-two chariot commanders to attack only Ahab. 32 So when they saw Jehoshaphat in his robe, they thought he
was Ahab and started to attack him. But
when Jehoshaphat shouted out to them,
33 they realized he wasn't Ahab, and they
left him alone.
34 However, during the fighting a soldier shot an arrow without even aiming,
and it hit Ahab where two pieces of his
armor joined. He shouted to his chariot
driver, "I've been hit! Get me out of
here!"
35 The fighting lasted all day, with
Ahab propped up in his chariot so he
could see the Syrian troops. He bled so
much that the bottom of the chariot was
covered with blood, and by evening he
was dead.
36 As the sun was going down, someone in Israel's army shouted to the others, "Retreat! Go back home!"
37 Ahab's body was taken to Samaria
and buried there. 38 Some workers
washed his chariot near a spring in
Samaria, and prostitutes washed themselves in his blood.[f] Dogs licked Ahab's
blood off the ground, just as the LORD
had warned.

[e] 22.17 *vision*: In ancient times, prophets often told about future events from what they had seen in visions or dreams. [f] 22.38 *prostitutes . . . blood*: Or "they cleaned his weapons."

39 Everything else Ahab did while he
was king, including the towns he
strengthened and the palace he built
and furnished with ivory, is written in
The History of the Kings of Israel.
40 Ahab died, and his son Ahaziah became king.

King Jehoshaphat of Judah

(2 Chronicles 20.31—21.1)

41 Jehoshaphat son of Asa became
king of Judah in Ahab's fourth year as
king of Israel. 42 Jehoshaphat was thirty-
five years old when he became king,
and he ruled from Jerusalem for twenty-
five years. His mother was Azubah
daughter of Shilhi.
43-46 Jehoshaphat obeyed the LORD, just
as his father Asa had done, and during
his rule he was at peace with the king of
Israel.
He got rid of the rest of the prostitutes[g] from the local shrines, but he
did not destroy the shrines, and they
were still used as places for offering
sacrifices.
Everything else Jehoshaphat did
while he was king, including his brave
deeds and military victories, is written
in *The History of the Kings of Judah*.
47 The country of Edom had no king at
the time, so a lower official ruled the
land.
48 Jehoshaphat had seagoing ships[h]
built to sail to Ophir for gold. But they
were wrecked at Ezion-Geber and never
sailed. 49 Ahaziah son of Ahab offered to
let his sailors go with Jehoshaphat's
sailors, but Jehoshaphat refused.
50 Jehoshaphat died and was buried
beside his ancestors in Jerusalem,[i] and
his son Jehoram became king.

King Ahaziah of Israel

51 Ahaziah son of Ahab became king
of Israel in the seventeenth year of Jehoshaphat's rule in Judah, and he ruled
two years from Samaria.
52 Ahaziah disobeyed the LORD, just as
his father, his mother, and Jeroboam
had done. They all led Israel to sin.
53 Ahaziah worshiped Baal and made the
LORD God of Israel very angry, just as
his father had done.

[g] **22.43-46** *prostitutes*: See the note at 14.24. [h] **22.48** *seagoing ships*: See the note at 10.22.
[i] **22.50** *Jerusalem*: Hebrew "the city of his ancestor David."

2 KINGS

ABOUT THIS BOOK

Second Kings is the second half of a single book that was divided into two parts, 1 and 2 Kings, because together they were too long to fit on one scroll. The book of 2 Kings continues the history of the two separate kingdoms of Judah and Israel.

The book of 2 Kings has two main parts. The first part (1–17) is the history of the two kingdoms until 722 B.C., when the northern kingdom was conquered by the Assyrians. Samaria, the capital city of Israel, was destroyed, and the people of that kingdom were taken as prisoners to Assyria. Only Judah, the southern kingdom, was left.

The second part of the book (18–25) is the history of Judah until 586 B.C., when it was conquered by King Nebuchadnezzar of Babylonia. Jerusalem, the capital city, was completely destroyed, and many of the people of Judah and Jerusalem were led away as prisoners to Babylonia. King Nebuchadnezzar then made Gedaliah ruler of those left in Judah. The book concludes with some hope for Judah's future: King Jehoiachin is released from prison in Babylon and is invited to eat with the Babylonian king every day.

According to the book of 2 Kings, Israel and Judah were destroyed because the people refused to be faithful to the Lord. He had sent prophets over and over to warn the people and their kings to stop worshiping other gods and to turn back to him. Finally, the people were punished. The two kingdoms were destroyed, and the people were forced to live in foreign nations, far from their own land. The fall of Jerusalem is one of the most important events in Israel's history. The book itself explains why this disaster took place:

> *The people of Judah and Jerusalem had made the LORD so angry that he finally turned his back on them. That's why these horrible things were happening.*
>
> *(24.20b)*

A QUICK LOOK AT THIS BOOK

Elijah the Prophet Condemns King Ahaziah of Israel (1.1-18)
Elisha the Prophet (2.1—8.15)
Kings of Judah and Israel (8.16—16.20)
King Hoshea of Israel and the Defeat of the Northern Kingdom (17.1-41)
King Hezekiah of Judah and the Assyrian Invasion (18.1—20.21)
Two Evil Kings of Judah: Manasseh and Amon (21.1-26)
The Rule of King Josiah and *The Book of God's Law* (22.1—23.30)
The Last Kings of Judah (23.31—24.20)
Jerusalem Is Destroyed and the People Are Taken to Babylonia (25.1-21)
Gedaliah Is Made Ruler and King Jehoiachin Is Released from Prison (25.22-30)

The LORD Condemns Ahaziah

1 1-2Soon after King Ahab of Israel
died, the country of Moab rebelled
against his son King Ahaziah.[a]
One day, Ahaziah fell through the
wooden slats around the porch on the
flat roof of his palace in Samaria, and
he was badly injured. So he sent some
messengers to the town of Ekron[b] with
orders to ask the god Baalzebub if he
would get well.
3About the same time, an angel from

[a]1.1,2 *the country . . . King Ahaziah*: The story of Moab's rebellion is in 3.4-27.
[b]1.1,2 *Ekron*: An important Philistine town about forty miles southwest of Samaria.

the LORD sent Elijah the prophet from
Tishbe to say to the king's messengers,
"Ahaziah has rejected Israel's own God
by sending you to ask Baalzebub about
his injury. 4 Tell him that because he has
done this, he's on his deathbed!" And
Elijah did what he was told.
5 When the messengers returned to
Ahaziah, he asked, "Why are you back
so soon?"
6 "A man met us along the road with a
message for you from the LORD," they
answered. "The LORD wants to know
why you sent us to ask Baalzebub about
your injury and why you don't believe
there's a God in Israel. The man also
told us that the LORD says you're going
to die."
7 "What did the man look like?"
Ahaziah asked.
8 "He was hairy[c] and had a leather belt
around his waist," they answered.
"It must be Elijah!" replied Ahaziah.
9 So at once he sent an army officer and
fifty soldiers to meet Elijah.
Elijah was sitting on top of a hill[d] at
the time. The officer went up to him and
said, "Man of God,[e] the king orders you
to come down and talk with him."
10 "If I am a man of God," Elijah answered, "God will send down fire on you
and your fifty soldiers." Fire immediately came down from heaven and
burned up the officer and his men.
11 Ahaziah sent another officer and
fifty more soldiers to Elijah. The officer
said, "Man of God, the king orders you
to come see him right now."
12 "If I am a man of God," Elijah answered, "fire will destroy you and your
fifty soldiers." And God sent down fire[f]
from heaven on the officer and his men.
13 Ahaziah sent a third army officer
and fifty more soldiers. This officer
went up to Elijah, then he got down on
his knees and begged, "Man of God,
please be kind to me and these fifty servants of yours. Let us live! 14 Fire has already wiped out the other officers and
their soldiers. Please don't let it happen
to me."
15 The angel from the LORD said to Elijah, "Go with him and don't be afraid."
So Elijah got up and went with the officer.
16 When Elijah arrived, he told Ahaziah, "The LORD wants to know why you
sent messengers to Ekron to ask Baalzebub about your injury. Don't you believe
there's a God in Israel? Ahaziah, because you did that, the LORD says you
will die."
17 Ahaziah died, just as the LORD had
said. But since Ahaziah had no sons, Joram[g] his brother[h] then became king.
This happened in the second year that
Jehoram son of Jehoshaphat was king
of Judah.[i] 18 Everything else Ahaziah did
while he was king is written in *The History of the Kings of Israel.*

The LORD Takes Elijah Away

2 Not long before the LORD took Elijah up into heaven in a strong wind,
Elijah and Elisha were leaving Gilgal.
2 Elijah said to Elisha, "The LORD wants
me to go to Bethel, but you must stay
here."
Elisha replied, "I swear by the living
LORD and by your own life that I will
stay with you no matter what!" And he
went with Elijah to Bethel.
3 A group of prophets who lived there
asked Elisha, "Do you know that today
the LORD is going to take away your
master?"
"Yes, I do," Elisha answered. "But
don't remind me of it."
4 Elijah then said, "Elisha, now the
LORD wants me to go to Jericho, but you
must stay here."
Elisha replied, "I swear by the living
LORD and by your own life, that I will
stay with you no matter what!" And he
went with Elijah to Jericho.
5 A group of prophets who lived there
asked Elisha, "Do you know that today
the LORD is going to take away your
master?"
"Yes, I do," Elisha answered. "But
don't remind me of it."
6 Elijah then said to Elisha, "Now the
LORD wants me to go to the Jordan
River, but you must stay here."
Elisha replied, "I swear by the living
LORD and by your own life that I will
never leave you!" So the two of them
walked on together.
7 Fifty prophets followed Elijah and
Elisha from Jericho, then stood at a distance and watched as the two men
walked toward the river. 8 When they got
there, Elijah took off his coat, then he
rolled it up and struck the water with it.
At once a path opened up through the
river, and the two of them walked across
on dry ground.
9 After they had reached the other

[c] **1.8** *hairy*: Or "wearing a furry coat." [d] **1.9** *a hill*: Probably Mount Carmel. [e] **1.9** *Man of God*: Another name for a prophet of the LORD. [f] **1.12** *God sent down fire*: Or "A mighty fire came down." [g] **1.17** *Joram*: The Hebrew text has "Jehoram," another spelling of the name. [h] **1.17** *his brother*: Some ancient translations (see also 3.1); these words are not in the Hebrew text. [i] **1.17** *This happened . . . Judah*: According to 3.1, this was also the eighteenth year of Jehoshaphat's rule in Judah. In biblical times, a father and son would sometimes rule as kings at the same time. This way, when the father died, the son would already have control of the kingdom (see also 8.16).

side, Elijah said, “Elisha, the LORD will
soon take me away. What can I do for
you before that happens?”
Elisha answered, “Please give me
twice as much of your power as you
give the other prophets, so I can be the
one who takes your place as their
leader.”
10“It won’t be easy,” Elijah answered.
“It can happen only if you see me as I
am being taken away.”
11Elijah and Elisha were walking
along and talking, when suddenly there
appeared between them a flaming chariot pulled by fiery horses. Right away, a
strong wind took Elijah up into heaven.
12Elisha saw this and shouted, “Israel’s
cavalry and chariots have taken my
master away!”[j] After Elijah had gone,
Elisha tore his clothes in sorrow.
13Elijah’s coat had fallen off, so Elisha
picked it up and walked back to the Jordan River. 14He struck the water with
the coat and wondered, “Will the LORD
perform miracles for me as he did for
Elijah?” As soon as Elisha did this, a dry
path opened up through the water, and
he walked across.
15When the prophets from Jericho
saw what happened, they said to each
other, “Elisha now has Elijah’s power.”
They walked over to him, bowed
down, 16and said, “There are fifty strong
men here with us. Please let them go
look for your master. Maybe the Spirit
of the LORD carried him off to some
mountain or valley.”
“No,” Elisha replied, “they won’t find
him.”
17They kept begging until he was embarrassed to say no. He finally agreed,
and the prophets sent the men out. They
looked three days for Elijah but never
found him. 18They returned to Jericho,
and Elisha said, “I told you that you
wouldn’t find him.”

Elisha Makes the Water Pure at Jericho

19One day the people of Jericho said,
“Elisha, you can see that our city is in a
good spot. But the water from our
spring is so bad that it even keeps our
crops from growing.”
20He replied, “Put some salt in a new
bowl and bring it to me.”
They brought him the bowl of salt,
21and he carried it to the spring. He
threw the salt into the water and said,
“The LORD has made this water pure
again. From now on you’ll be able to
grow crops, and no one will starve.”
22The water has been fine ever since,
just as Elisha said.

Some Boys Make Fun of Elisha

23Elisha left and headed toward
Bethel. Along the way some boys
started making fun of him by shouting,
“Go away, baldy! Get out of here!”
24Elisha turned around and stared at
the boys. Then he cursed them in the
name of the LORD. Right away two bears
ran out of the woods and ripped to
pieces forty-two of the boys.
25Elisha went up to Mount Carmel,
then returned to Samaria.

King Joram of Israel

3 Joram[k] son of Ahab became king of
Israel in Jehoshaphat’s eighteenth
year as king of Judah.[l] Joram ruled
twelve years from Samaria 2and disobeyed the LORD by doing wrong. He
tore down the stone image his father
had made to honor Baal, and so he
wasn’t as sinful as his parents. 3But he
kept doing the sinful things that Jeroboam son of Nebat had led Israel to
do.[m]

The Country of Moab Rebels against Israel

4For many years the country of Moab
had been controlled by Israel and was
forced to pay taxes to the kings of Israel. King Mesha of Moab raised sheep,
so he paid the king of Israel one hundred thousand lambs and the wool from
one hundred thousand rams. 5But soon
after the death of Ahab, Mesha rebelled
against Israel.
6One day, Joram left Samaria and
called together Israel’s army. 7He sent
this message to King Jehoshaphat of Judah, “The king of Moab has rebelled.
Will you go with me to attack him?”
“Yes, I will,” Jehoshaphat answered.
“I’m on your side, and my soldiers and
horses are at your command. 8But
which way should we go?”
“We will march through Edom
Desert,” Joram replied.
9So Joram, Jehoshaphat, and the king
of Edom led their troops out. But seven
days later, there was no drinking water
left for them or their animals. 10Joram
cried out, “This is terrible! The LORD
must have led us out here to be captured
by Moab’s army.”
11Jehoshaphat said, “Which of the
LORD’s prophets is with us? We can find

[j]**2.12** *Israel’s . . . away*: Or “Master, you were like cavalry and chariots for the people of Israel!”
[k]**3.1** *Joram*: See the note at 1.17. [l]**3.1** *Joram . . . Judah*: See 1.17 and 8.16 and the notes there. [m]**3.3** *the sinful things . . . to do*: When Jeroboam became king of Israel, he made two gold statues of calves and put them in the towns of Bethel and Dan, so the people of Israel could worship them (see 1 Kings 12.26-30).

out from him what the LORD wants us to
do."
One of Joram's officers answered,
"Elisha son of Shaphat is here. He was
one of Elijah's closest followers."
12 Jehoshaphat replied, "He can give us
the LORD's message."
The three kings went over to Elisha,
13 and he asked Joram, "Why did you
come to me? Go talk to the prophets of
the foreign gods your parents worshiped."[n]
"No," Joram answered. "It was the
LORD who led us out here, so that
Moab's army could capture us."
14 Elisha said to him, "I serve the LORD
All-Powerful, and as surely as he lives, I
swear I wouldn't even look at you if I
didn't respect King Jehoshaphat."
15 Then Elisha said, "Send for someone
who can play the harp."
The harpist began playing, and the
LORD gave Elisha this message for Joram:

> 16 The LORD says that this dry
> riverbed will be filled with water.[o]
> 17 You won't feel any wind or see any
> rain, but there will be plenty of wa-
> ter for you and your animals.
> 18 That simple thing isn't all the
> LORD is going to do. He will also
> help you defeat Moab's army. 19 You
> will capture all their walled cities
> and important towns. You will chop
> down every good tree and stop up
> every spring of water, then ruin their
> fertile fields by covering them with
> rocks.

20 The next morning, while the sacrifice was being offered, water suddenly
started flowing from the direction of
Edom, and it flooded the land.
21 Meanwhile, the people of Moab had
heard that the three kings were coming
to attack them. They had called together
all of their fighting men, from the
youngest to the oldest, and these troops
were now standing at their border,
ready for battle. 22 When they got up that
morning, the sun was shining across the
water, making it look red. The Moabite
troops took one look 23 and shouted,
"Look at that blood! The armies of those
kings must have fought and killed each
other. Come on, let's go take what's left
in their camp."
24 But when they arrived at Israel's
camp, the Israelite soldiers came out
and attacked them, until they turned
and ran away. Israel's army chased
them all the way back to Moab, and
even there they kept up the attack.[p]
25 The Israelites destroyed the Moabite
towns. They chopped down the good
trees and stopped up the springs of water, then covered the fertile fields with
rocks.
Finally, the only city left standing was
Kir-Hareseth, but soldiers armed with
slings surrounded and attacked it.
26 King Mesha of Moab saw that he was
about to be defeated. So he took along
seven hundred soldiers with swords and
tried to break through the front line
where the Edomite troops were posi-
tioned. But he failed. 27 He then grabbed
his oldest son who was to be the next
king and sacrificed him as an offering
on the city wall. The Israelite troops
were so horrified that[q] they left the city
and went back home.

Elisha Helps a Poor Widow

4 One day the widow of one of the
LORD's prophets said to Elisha, "You
know that before my husband died, he
was a follower of yours and a worshiper
of the LORD. But he owed a man some
money, and now that man is on his way
to take my two sons as his slaves."
2 "Maybe there's something I can do to
help," Elisha said. "What do you have in
your house?"
"Sir, I have nothing but a small bottle
of olive oil."
3 Elisha told her, "Ask your neighbors
for their empty jars. And after you've
borrowed as many as you can, 4 go home
and shut the door behind you and your
sons. Then begin filling the jars with oil
and set each one aside as you fill it."
5 The woman left.
Later, when she and her sons were
back inside their house, the two sons
brought her the jars, and she began filling them.
6 At last, she said to one of her sons,
"Bring me another jar."
"We don't have any more," he answered, and the oil stopped flowing
from the small bottle.
7 After she told Elisha what had happened, he said, "Sell the oil and use part
of the money to pay what you owe the
man. You and your sons can live on
what is left."

Elisha Brings a Rich Woman's Son Back to Life

8 Once, while Elisha was in the town of
Shunem,[r] he met a rich woman who invited him to her home for dinner. After
that, whenever he was in Shunem, he

[n] 3.13 *the prophets . . . worshiped*: These were prophets of the Canaanite god Baal and the goddess Asherah (see 1 Kings 16.30-33; 18.19). [o] 3.16 *that . . . water*: Or "to dig holes everywhere in this riverbed." [p] 3.24 *chased . . . attack*: One possible meaning for the difficult Hebrew text. [q] 3.27 *The Israelite . . . that*: One possible meaning for the difficult Hebrew text. [r] 4.8 *Shunem*: A town in Israel, about twenty-five miles north of Samaria.

would have a meal there with her and
her husband.
9Some time later the woman said to
her husband, "I'm sure the man who
comes here so often is a prophet of God.
10Why don't we build him a small room
on the flat roof of our house? We can put
a bed, a table and chair, and an oil lamp
in it. Then whenever he comes, he can
stay with us."
11The next time Elisha was in
Shunem, he stopped at their house and
went up to his room to rest. 12-13He said
to his servant Gehazi, "This woman has
been very helpful. Have her come up
here to the roof for a moment." She
came, and Elisha told Gehazi to say to
her, "You've gone to a lot of trouble for
us, and we want to help you. Is there
something we can request the king or
army commander to do?"[s]
The woman answered, "With my relatives nearby, I have everything I need."
14"Then what can we do for her?"
Elisha asked Gehazi.
Gehazi replied, "I do know that her
husband is old, and that she doesn't
have a son."
15"Ask her to come here again," Elisha
told his servant. He called for her, and
she came and stood in the doorway of
Elisha's room.
16Elisha said to her, "Next year at this
time, you'll be holding your own baby
son in your arms."
"You're a man of God," the woman
replied. "Please don't lie to me."
17But a few months later, the woman
got pregnant. She gave birth to a son,
just as Elisha had promised.
18One day while the boy was still
young, he was out in the fields with his
father, where the workers were harvesting the crops. 19Suddenly he shouted,
"My head hurts. It hurts a lot!"
"Carry him back to his mother," the
father said to his servant. 20The servant
picked up the boy and carried him to his
mother. The boy lay on her lap all morning, and by noon he was dead. 21She
carried him upstairs to Elisha's room
and laid him across the bed. Then she
walked out and shut the door behind
her.
22The woman called to her husband, "I
need to see the prophet. Let me use one
of the donkeys. Send a servant along
with me, and let me leave now, so I can
get back quickly."
23"Why do you need to see him today?" her husband asked. "It's not the
Sabbath or time for the New Moon Festival."
"That's all right," she answered. 24She
saddled the donkey and said to her servant, "Let's go. And don't slow down unless I tell you to." 25She left at once for
Mount Carmel to talk with Elisha.[t]
When Elisha saw her coming, he said,
"Gehazi, look! It's the woman from
Shunem. 26Run and meet her. And ask
her if everything is all right with her
and her family."
"Everything is fine," she answered Gehazi. 27But as soon as she got to the top
of the mountain, she went over and
grabbed Elisha by the feet.
Gehazi started toward her to push her
away, when Elisha said, "Leave her
alone! Don't you see how sad she is?
But the LORD hasn't told me why."
28The woman said, "Sir, I begged you
not to get my hopes up, and I didn't even
ask you for a son."
29"Gehazi, get ready and go to her
house," Elisha said. "Take along my
walking stick, and when you get there,
lay it on the boy's face. Don't stop to
talk to anyone, even if they try to talk to
you."
30But the boy's mother said to Elisha,
"I swear by the living LORD and by
your own life that I won't leave without
you." So Elisha got up and went with
them.
31Gehazi ran on ahead and laid Elisha's walking stick on the boy's face,
but the boy didn't move or make a
sound. Gehazi ran back to Elisha and
said, "The boy didn't wake up."
32Elisha arrived at the woman's house
and went straight to his room, where he
saw the boy's body on his bed. 33He
walked in, shut the door, and prayed to
the LORD. 34Then he got on the bed and
stretched out over the dead body, with
his mouth on the boy's mouth, his eyes
on his eyes, and his hand on his hands.
As he lay there, the boy's body became
warm. 35Elisha got up and walked back
and forth in the room, then he went
back and leaned over the boy's body.
The boy sneezed seven times and
opened his eyes.
36Elisha called out to Gehazi, "Have
the boy's mother come here." Gehazi
did, and when she was at the door, Elisha said, "You can take your son."
37She came in and bowed down at Elisha's feet. Then she picked up her son
and left.

Elisha Makes Some Stew Taste Better

38Later, Elisha went back to Gilgal,
where there was almost nothing to eat,
because the crops had failed.
One day while the prophets who lived
there were meeting with Elisha, he said

[s]**4.12,13** *request the king . . . do*: Elisha may have meant that he could ask these leaders to lower her taxes. [t]**4.25** *Elisha*: Mount Carmel is about twenty-five miles from Shunem.

to his servant, "Fix a big pot of stew for
these prophets."
39 One of them went out into the
woods to gather some herbs. He found a
wild vine and picked as much of its fruit
as he could carry, but he didn't know
that the fruit was very sour. When he
got back, he cut up the fruit and put it in
the stew.
40 The stew was served, and when the
prophets started eating it, they shouted,
"Elisha, this stew tastes terrible! We
can't eat it."
41 "Bring me some flour," Elisha said.
He sprinkled the flour in the stew and
said, "Now serve it to them." And the
stew tasted fine.

Elisha Feeds One Hundred People

42 A man from the town of Baal-
Shalishah[u] brought Elisha some freshly
cut grain and twenty loaves of bread
made from the first barley that was harvested. Elisha said, "Give it to the people
so they can eat."
43 "There's not enough here for a hundred people," his servant said.
"Just give it to them," Elisha replied.
"The LORD has promised there will be
more than enough."
44 So the servant served the bread and
grain to the people. They ate and still
had some left over, just as the LORD had
promised.

Elisha Heals Naaman

5 Naaman was the commander of the
Syrian army. The LORD had helped
him and his troops defeat their enemies,
so the king of Syria respected Naaman
very much. Naaman was a brave soldier,
but he had leprosy.[v]
2 One day while the Syrian troops
were raiding Israel, they captured a girl,
and she became a servant of Naaman's
wife. 3 Some time later the girl said, "If
your husband Naaman would go to the
prophet in Samaria, he would be cured
of his leprosy."
4 When Naaman told the king what the
girl had said, 5 the king replied, "Go
ahead! I will give you a letter to take to
the king of Israel."
Naaman left and took along seven
hundred fifty pounds of silver, one hundred fifty pounds of gold, and ten new
outfits. 6 He also carried the letter to the
king of Israel. It said, "I am sending my
servant Naaman to you. Would you cure
him of his leprosy?"
7 When the king of Israel read the letter, he tore his clothes in fear and
shouted, "That Syrian king believes I
can cure this man of leprosy! Does he
think I'm God with power over life and
death? He must be trying to pick a fight
with me."
8 As soon as Elisha the prophet[w] heard
what had happened, he sent the Israelite
king this message: "Why are you
so afraid? Send the man to me, so that
he will know there is a prophet in Israel."
9 Naaman left with his horses and
chariots and stopped at the door of Elisha's house. 10 Elisha sent someone outside to say to him, "Go wash seven times
in the Jordan River. Then you'll be completely cured."
11 But Naaman stormed off, grumbling,
"Why couldn't he come out and talk to
me? I thought for sure he would stand in
front of me and pray to the LORD his
God, then wave his hand over my skin
and cure me. 12 What about the Abana
River[x] or the Pharpar River? Those
rivers in Damascus are just as good as
any river in Israel. I could have washed
in them and been cured."
13 His servants went over to him and
said, "Sir, if the prophet had told you to
do something difficult, you would have
done it. So why don't you do what he
said? Go wash and be cured."
14 Naaman walked down to the Jordan;
he waded out into the water and
stooped down in it seven times, just as
Elisha had told him. Right away, he was
cured, and his skin became as smooth
as a child's.
15 Naaman and his officials went back
to Elisha. Naaman stood in front of him
and announced, "Now I know that the
God of Israel is the only God in the
whole world. Sir, would you please accept a gift from me?"
16 "I am a servant of the living LORD,"
Elisha answered, "and I swear that I will
not take anything from you."
Naaman kept begging, but Elisha kept
refusing. 17 Finally Naaman said, "If you
won't accept a gift, then please let me
take home as much soil as two mules
can pull in a wagon. Sir, from now on I
will offer sacrifices only to the LORD.[y]
18 But I pray that the LORD will forgive
me when I go into the temple of the god
Rimmon and bow down there with the
king of Syria."
19 "Go on home, and don't worry about
that," Elisha replied. Then Naaman
left.

[u] **4.42** *Baal-Shalishah*: The exact location of this town is not known, but it was probably somewhere near Shechem. [v] **5.1** *leprosy*: The word translated "leprosy" was used for many different kinds of skin diseases. [w] **5.8** *the prophet*: Hebrew "the man of God."
[x] **5.12** *Abana River*: Most Hebrew manuscripts; some Hebrew manuscripts and two ancient translations "Amana River." [y] **5.17** *let me take . . . the LORD*: It was believed that the LORD had to be worshiped in Israel or on soil taken from Israel.

Elisha Places a Curse on Gehazi

After Naaman had gone only a short
distance, 20Gehazi said to himself, "Elisha let that Syrian off too easy. He
should have taken Naaman's gift. I
swear by the living LORD that I will talk
to Naaman myself and get something
from him." 21So he hurried after Naaman.
When Naaman saw Gehazi running
after him, he got out of his chariot to
meet him. Naaman asked, "Is everything
all right?"
22"Yes," Gehazi answered. "But my
master has sent me to tell you about two
young prophets from the hills of
Ephraim. They came asking for help,
and now Elisha wants to know if you
would give them about seventy-five
pounds of silver and some new
clothes?"
23"Sure," Naaman replied. "But why
don't you take twice that amount of silver?" He convinced Gehazi to take it all,
then put the silver in two bags. He
handed the bags and the clothes to his
two servants, and they carried them for
Gehazi.
24When they reached the hill where
Gehazi lived, he took the bags from the
servants and placed them in his house,
then sent the men away. After they had
gone, 25Gehazi went in and stood in
front of Elisha, who asked, "Gehazi,
where have you been?"
"Nowhere, sir," Gehazi answered.
26Elisha asked, "Don't you know that
my spirit was there when Naaman got
out of his chariot to talk with you? Gehazi, you have no right to accept money
or clothes, olive orchards or vineyards,
sheep or cattle, or servants. 27Because of
what you've done, Naaman's leprosy[z]
will now be on you and your descendants forever!"
Suddenly, Gehazi's skin became white
with leprosy, and he left.

Elisha Makes an Ax Head Float

6 One day the prophets said to Elisha,
"The place where we meet with you
is too small. 2Why don't we build a new
meeting place near the Jordan River?
Each of us could get some wood, then
we could build it."
"That's a good idea," Elisha replied,
"get started."
3"Aren't you going with us?" one of
the prophets asked.
"Yes, I'll go," Elisha answered, 4and
he left with them.
They went to the Jordan River and began chopping down trees. 5While one of
the prophets was working, his ax head
fell off and dropped into the water.
"Oh!" he shouted. "Sir, I borrowed this
ax."
6"Where did it fall in?" Elisha asked.
The prophet pointed to the place, and
Elisha cut a stick and threw it into the
water at that spot. The ax head floated
to the top of the water.
7"Now get it," Elisha told him. And the
prophet reached in and grabbed it.

Elisha Stops an Invasion of the Syrian Army

8Time after time, when the king of
Syria was at war against the Israelites,
he met with his officers and announced,
"I've decided where we will set up
camp."
9Each time, Elisha[a] would send this
warning to the king of Israel: "Don't go
near there. That's where the Syrian
troops have set up camp."[b] 10So the king
would warn the Israelite troops in that
place to be on guard.
11The king of Syria was furious when
he found out what was happening. He
called in his officers and asked, "Which
one of you has been telling the king of
Israel our plans?"
12"None of us, Your Majesty," one of
them answered. "It's an Israelite named
Elisha. He's a prophet, so he can tell his
king everything—even what you say in
your own room."
13"Find out where he is!" the king ordered. "I'll send soldiers to bring him
here."
They learned that Elisha was in the
town of Dothan[c] and reported it to the
king. 14He ordered his best troops to go
there with horses and chariots. They
marched out during the night and surrounded the town.
15When Elisha's servant got up the
next morning, he saw that Syrian troops
had the town surrounded. "Sir, what are
we going to do?" he asked.
16"Don't be afraid," Elisha answered.
"There are more troops on our side than
on theirs." 17Then he prayed, "LORD,
please help him to see." And the LORD
let the servant see that the hill[d] was covered with fiery horses and flaming chariots all around Elisha.
18As the Syrian army came closer, Elisha prayed, "LORD, make those soldiers
blind!" And the LORD blinded them with
a bright light.
19Elisha told the enemy troops,
"You've taken the wrong road and are in
the wrong town. Follow me. I'll lead you
to the man you're looking for." Elisha

[z]**5.27** *leprosy*: See the note at 5.1. [a]**6.9** *Elisha*: Hebrew "the man of God." [b]**6.9** *have set up camp*: Or "are going." [c]**6.13** *Dothan*: About ten miles north of Samaria. [d]**6.17** *the hill*: The hill on which the town was built.

led them straight to the capital city of
Samaria.
20When all the soldiers were inside
the city, Elisha prayed, "LORD, now let
them see again." The LORD let them see
that they were standing in the middle of
Samaria.
21The king of Israel saw them and
asked Elisha, "Should I kill them, sir?"
22"No!" Elisha answered. "You didn't
capture these troops in battle, so you
have no right to kill them. Instead, give
them something to eat and drink and let
them return to their leader."
23The king ordered a huge meal to be
prepared for Syria's army, and when
they finished eating, he let them go.
For a while, the Syrian troops stopped
invading Israel's territory.

King Benhadad of Syria Attacks Samaria

24Some time later, King Benhadad of
Syria[e] called his entire army together,
then they marched to Samaria and attacked. 25They kept up the attack until
there was nothing to eat in the city. In
fact, a donkey's head cost about two
pounds of silver, and a small bowl of pigeon droppings[f] cost about two ounces
of silver.
26One day as the king of Israel[g] was
walking along the top of the city wall, a
woman shouted to him, "Please, Your
Majesty, help me!"
27"Let the LORD help you!" the king
said. "Do you think I have grain or wine
to give you?" 28Then he asked, "What's
the matter anyway?"
The woman answered, "Another
woman and I were so hungry that we
agreed to eat our sons. She said if we
ate my son one day, we could eat hers
the next day. 29So yesterday we cooked
my son and ate him. But today when I
went to her house to eat her son, she
had hidden him."
30The king tore off his clothes in sorrow, and since he was on top of the city
wall, the people saw that he was wearing sackcloth underneath. 31He said, "I
pray that God will punish me terribly, if
Elisha's head is still on his shoulders by
this time tomorrow." 32Then he sent a
messenger to Elisha.
Elisha was home at the time, and the
important leaders of Israel were meeting with him. Even before the king's
messenger arrived, Elisha told the leaders, "That murderer[h] is sending someone to cut off my head. When you see
him coming, shut the door and don't let
him in. I'm sure the king himself will be
right behind him."
33Before Elisha finished talking, the
messenger[i] came up and said, "The
LORD has made all these terrible things
happen to us. Why should I think he will
help us now?"

7 Elisha answered, "I have a message
for you. The LORD promises that tomorrow here in Samaria, you will be
able to buy a large sack of flour or two
large sacks of barley for almost nothing."
2The chief officer there with the king
replied, "I don't believe it! Even if the
LORD sent a rainstorm, it couldn't produce that much grain by tomorrow."
"You will see it happen, but you won't
eat any of the food," Elisha warned him.

The Syrian Army Stops Its Attack

3About the same time, four men with
leprosy[j] were just outside the gate of
Samaria. They said to each other, "Why
should we sit here, waiting to die?
4There's nothing to eat in the city, so we
would starve if we went inside. But if we
stay out here, we will die for sure. Let's
sneak over to the Syrian army camp
and surrender. They might kill us, but
they might not." 5-8That evening the
four men got up and left for the Syrian
camp.
As they walked toward the camp, the
Lord caused the Syrian troops to hear
what sounded like the roar of a huge
cavalry. The soldiers said to each other,
"Listen! The king of Israel must have
hired Hittite and Egyptian troops to attack us. Let's get out of here!" So they
ran out of their camp that night, leaving
their tents and horses and donkeys.
When the four men with leprosy
reached the edge of the Syrian camp, no
one was there. They walked into one of
the tents, where they ate and drank, before carrying off clothes, as well as silver and gold. They hid all this, then
walked into another tent; they took
what they wanted and hid it too.
9They said to each other, "This isn't
right. Today is a day to celebrate, and
we haven't told anyone else what has
happened. If we wait until morning, we
will be punished. Let's go to the king's
palace right now and tell the good
news."
10They went back to Samaria and
shouted up to the guards at the gate,

[e]**6.24** *King Benhadad of Syria*: This may or may not be the same Benhadad mentioned in 1 Kings 20.1. Several of the Syrian kings were named Benhadad. [f]**6.25** *pigeon droppings*: This may have been used for food or to burn for fuel. It also may have been a popular name for roasted beans or the shells of certain seeds. [g]**6.26** *the king of Israel*: Probably either Jehoahaz or Jehoash, but possibly even Joram. [h]**6.32** *That murderer*: Hebrew "That murderer's son." [i]**6.33** *messenger*: Or "king" (see 7.2, 18); the two Hebrew words are very similar. [j]**7.3** *leprosy*: See the note at 5.1.

"We've just come from the Syrian army
camp, and all the soldiers are gone! The
tents are empty, and the horses and
donkeys are still tied up. We didn't see
or hear anybody."
11The guards reported the news to the
king's palace. 12The king got out of bed
and said to his officers, "I know what
those Syrians are doing. They know
we're starving, so they're hiding in the
fields, hoping we will go out to look for
food. When we do, they can capture us
and take over our city."
13One of his officers replied, "We have
a few horses left—why don't we let
some men take five of them and go to
the Syrian camp and see what's happening? We're going to die anyway like
those who have already died."[k] 14They
found two chariots, and the king commanded the men to find out what had
happened to the Syrian troops.
15The men rode as far as the Jordan
River. All along the way they saw
clothes and equipment that the Syrians
had thrown away as they escaped. Then
they went back to the king and told him
what they had seen.
16At once the people went to the Syrian camp and carried off what was left.
They took so much that a large sack of
flour and two large sacks of barley sold
for almost nothing, just as the LORD had
promised.
17The king of Israel had put his chief
officer in charge of the gate, but he died
when the people trampled him as they
rushed out of the city. 18Earlier, when
the king was at Elisha's house, Elisha
had told him that flour or barley would
sell for almost nothing. 19But the officer
refused to believe that even the LORD
could do that. So Elisha warned him
that he would see it happen, but would
not eat any of the food. 20And that's exactly what happened—the officer was
trampled to death.

The Woman from Shunem Is Given Back Her Land

8 Elisha told the woman whose son he
had brought back to life,[l] "The LORD
has warned that there will be no food
here for seven years. Take your family
and go live somewhere else for a while."
2The woman did exactly what Elisha
had said and went to live in Philistine
territory.
She and her family lived there seven
years. 3Then she returned to Israel and
immediately begged the king to give
back her house and property.
4Meanwhile, the king was asking Gehazi the servant of Elisha about the
amazing things Elisha had been doing.
5While Gehazi was telling him that
Elisha had brought a dead boy back to
life, the woman and her son arrived.
"Here's the boy, Your Majesty," Gehazi
said. "And this is his mother."
6The king asked the woman to tell her
story, and she told him everything that
had happened. He then said to one of
his officials, "I want you to make sure
that this woman gets back everything
that belonged to her, including the
money her crops have made since the
day she left Israel."

Hazael Kills Benhadad

7Some time later Elisha went to the
capital city of Damascus to visit King
Benhadad of Syria, who was sick. And
when Benhadad was told he was there,
8he said to Hazael,[m] "Go meet with Elisha the man of God and have him ask
the LORD if I will get well. And take
along a gift for him."
9Hazael left with forty camel loads of
the best things made in Damascus as a
gift for Elisha. He found the prophet
and said, "Your servant, King Benhadad,
wants to know if he will get well."
10"Tell him he will," Elisha said to
Hazael. "But the LORD has already told
me that Benhadad will definitely die."
11Elisha stared at him until Hazael was
embarrassed, then Elisha began crying.[n]
12"Sir, why are you crying?" Hazael
asked.
Elisha answered, "Because I know the
terrible things you will do to the people
of Israel. You will burn down their
walled cities and slaughter their young
men. You will even crush the heads of
their babies and rip open their pregnant
women."
13"How could I ever do anything like
that?" Hazael replied. "I'm only a servant and don't have that kind of power."
"Hazael, the LORD has told me that
you will be the next king of Syria."
14Hazael went back to Benhadad and
told him, "Elisha said that you will get
well." 15But the very next day, Hazael
got a thick blanket; he soaked it in
water and held it over Benhadad's
face until he died. Hazael then became
king.

King Jehoram of Judah

(2 Chronicles 21.2-20)

16Jehoram son of Jehoshaphat became king of Judah in Joram's fifth year
as king of Israel, while Jehoshaphat was

[k]**7.13** *We're going . . . died*: One possible meaning for the difficult Hebrew text. [l]**8.1** *Elisha . . . life*: See 4.8-37. [m]**8.8** *Hazael*: Probably one of Benhadad's officials. [n]**8.11** *Elisha stared . . . crying*: Or "Hazael stared at him until Elisha was embarrassed and began to cry."

still king of Judah.[o] 17 Jehoram was
thirty-two years old when he became
king, and he ruled eight years from
Jerusalem.
18 Jehoram disobeyed the LORD by doing wrong. He married Ahab's daughter
and was as sinful as Ahab's family and
the kings of Israel. 19 But the LORD refused to destroy Judah, because he had
promised his servant David that someone from his family would always rule
in Judah.
20 While Jehoram was king, the people
of Edom rebelled and chose their own
king. 21 So Jehoram[p] and his cavalry
marched to Zair, where the Edomite
army surrounded him and his commanders. During the night he attacked the
Edomites, but he was defeated, and his
troops escaped to their homes.[q] 22 Judah
was never able to regain control of
Edom. Even the town of Libnah[r] rebelled at that time.
23 Everything else Jehoram did while
he was king is written in *The History of
the Kings of Judah*. 24 Jehoram died and
was buried beside his ancestors in
Jerusalem.[s] His son Ahaziah then became king.

King Ahaziah of Judah

(2 Chronicles 22.1-6)

25 Ahaziah son of Jehoram became
king of Judah in the twelfth year of Joram's rule in Israel. 26 Ahaziah was
twenty-two years old when he became
king, and he ruled from Jerusalem for
only one year. His mother was Athaliah,
a granddaughter of King Omri of Israel.
27 Since Ahaziah was related to Ahab's
family,[t] he acted just like them and disobeyed the LORD by doing wrong.
28 Ahaziah went with King Joram of
Israel to attack King Hazael and the
Syrian troops at Ramoth in Gilead. Joram was wounded in that battle, 29 so he
went to the town of Jezreel to recover.
Ahaziah went there to visit him.

Jehu Becomes King of Israel

9 One day, Elisha called for one of the
other prophets and said:
Take this bottle of olive oil and get
ready to go to the town of Ramoth in
Gilead. 2 When you get there, find
Jehu son of Jehoshaphat and grandson of Nimshi. Take him to a place
where the two of you can be alone,
3 then pour olive oil on his head to
show that he is the new king. Say to
him, "The LORD has chosen you to
be king of Israel." Then leave
quickly—don't wait around for anything!
4 The young prophet left for Ramoth.
5 When he arrived, the army officers
were meeting together. "Sir, I have a
message for you," he said.
"For which one of us?" Jehu asked.
"You, sir," the prophet answered. 6 So
Jehu got up and went inside.[u] The
prophet poured olive oil on Jehu's head
and told him:
The LORD God of Israel has this
message for you: "I am the LORD,
and I have chosen you to be king of
my people Israel. 7 I want you to
wipe out the family of Ahab, so
Jezebel will be punished for killing
the prophets and my other servants.
8 Every man and boy in Ahab's family must die, whether slave or free.
9 His whole family must be destroyed, just like the families of Jeroboam son of Nebat and Baasha son
of Ahijah. 10 As for Jezebel, her body
will be eaten by dogs in the town of
Jezreel. There won't be enough left
of her to bury."
Then the young prophet opened the
door and ran out.
11 Jehu went back to his officers, and
one of them asked, "What did that crazy
prophet want? Is everything all right?"
"You know him and how he talks,"
Jehu answered.
12 "No, we don't. What did he say?"
they asked.
"He had a message from the LORD,"
Jehu replied. "He said that the LORD has
chosen me to be the next king of Israel."
13 They quickly grabbed their coats
and spread them out on the steps where
Jehu was standing. Someone blew a
trumpet, and everyone shouted, "Jehu is
king!"

Jehu Kills Joram and Ahaziah

14-16 King Joram[v] of Israel had been
badly wounded in the battle at Ramoth,
trying to defend it against King Hazael
and the Syrian army. Joram was now recovering in Jezreel, and King Ahaziah
of Judah was there, visiting him.

[o] 8.16 *while Jehoshaphat . . . Judah*: In biblical times, a father and son would sometimes rule as kings at the same time. That way, when the father died, his son would already have control of the kingdom. [p] 8.21 *Jehoram*: The Hebrew text has "Joram," another spelling of the name.
[q] 8.21 *he attacked . . . homes*: One possible meaning for the difficult Hebrew text.
[r] 8.22 *Even the town of Libnah*: This was a town on the border between Philistia and Judah, which means that Jehoram was facing rebellion on two sides of his kingdom.
[s] 8.24 *Jerusalem*: Hebrew "the city of David." [t] 8.27 *Since . . . family*: Ahaziah's mother was Ahab's daughter (see verse 18). [u] 9.6 *went inside*: The officers were probably meeting outside in an open courtyard of some building. [v] 9.14-16 *Joram*: The Hebrew text has "Jehoram," another spelling of the name.

Meanwhile, Jehu was in Ramoth,
making plans to kill Joram. He said to
his officers, "If you want me to be king,
then don't let anyone leave this town.
They might go to Jezreel and tell Joram." Then Jehu got in his chariot and
rode to Jezreel.
17 When the guard in the watchtower
at Jezreel saw Jehu and his men riding
up, he shouted to the king, "I see a
bunch of men coming this way."
Joram ordered, "Send someone out to
ask them if this is a friendly visit."
18 One of the soldiers rode out and said
to Jehu, "King Joram wants to know if
this is a friendly visit."
"What's it to you?" Jehu asked. "Just
stay behind me with the rest of my
troops!"
About the same time the guard in the
watchtower said, "Your Majesty, the
rider got there, but he isn't coming
back."
19 So Joram sent out another rider,
who rode up to Jehu and said, "The king
wants to know if this is a friendly visit."
"What's it to you?" Jehu asked. "Just
get behind me with the rest of my
troops!"
20 The guard in the watchtower said,
"Your Majesty, the rider got there, but
he isn't coming back either. Wait a
minute! That one man is a reckless
chariot driver—it must be Jehu!"
21 Joram commanded, "Get my chariot
ready." Then he and Ahaziah got in their
chariots and rode out to meet Jehu.
They all met on the land that had belonged to Naboth.[w] 22 Joram asked,
"Jehu, is this a peaceful visit?"
"How can there be peace?" Jehu
asked. "Your mother Jezebel has caused
everyone to worship idols and practice
witchcraft."
23 "Ahaziah, let's get out of here!" Joram yelled. "It's a trap!" As Joram tried
to escape, 24 Jehu shot an arrow. It hit
Joram between his shoulders, then it
went through his heart and came out
his chest. He fell over dead in his chariot.
25-26 Jehu commanded his assistant
Bidkar, "Get Joram's body and throw it
in the field that Naboth once owned. Do
you remember when you and I used to
ride side by side behind Joram's father
Ahab? It was then that the LORD swore
to Ahab that he would be punished in
the same field where he had killed
Naboth and his sons. So throw Joram's
body there, just as the LORD said."
27 Ahaziah saw all of this happen and
tried to escape to the town of Beth-Hag-
gan, but Jehu caught up with him and
shouted, "Kill him too!" So his troops
shot Ahaziah with an arrow while he
was on the road to Gur near Ibleam. He
went as far as Megiddo, where he died.
28 Ahaziah's officers put his body in a
chariot and took it back to Jerusalem,
where they buried him beside his ancestors.
29 Ahaziah had become king of Judah
in the eleventh year of the rule of
Ahab's son Joram.

Jehu Kills Jezebel

30 Jehu headed toward Jezreel, and
when Jezebel heard he was coming, she
put on eye shadow and brushed her
hair. Then she stood at the window,
waiting for him to arrive. 31 As he
walked through the city gate, she
shouted down to him, "Why did you
come here, you murderer? To kill the
king? You're no better than Zimri!"[x]
32 He looked up toward the window
and asked, "Is anyone up there on my
side?" A few palace workers stuck their
heads out of a window, 33 and Jehu
shouted, "Throw her out the window!"
They threw her down, and her blood
splattered on the walls and on the
horses that trampled her body.[y]
34 Jehu left to get something to eat and
drink. Then he told some workers,
"Even though she was evil, she was a
king's daughter,[z] so make sure she has
a proper burial."
35 But when they went out to bury her
body, they found only her skull, her
hands, and her feet. 36 They reported this
to Jehu, and he said, "The LORD told Elijah the prophet that Jezebel's body
would be eaten by dogs right here in
Jezreel. 37 And he warned that her bones
would be spread all over the ground like
manure, so that no one could tell who it
was."

Jehu Kills All of Ahab's Descendants

10 Ahab still had seventy descendants living in Samaria. So Jehu
wrote a letter to each of the important
leaders and officials of the town,[a] and to
those who supported Ahab. In the letters he wrote:

2 Your town is strong, and you're
protected by chariots and an armed
cavalry. And I know that King
Ahab's descendants live there with
you. So as soon as you read this letter, 3 choose the best person for the

[w] **9.21** *the land . . . Naboth*: See 1 Kings 21. [x] **9.31** *Zimri*: An Israelite king who killed King Elah and his family so he could become king, but who ruled only seven days (see 1 Kings 16.8-20). [y] **9.33** *horses . . . her body*: Two ancient translations; Hebrew "horses. Then Jehu trampled her body." [z] **9.34** *she . . . daughter*: Her father was King Ethbaal of Sidon (see 1 Kings 16.31). [a] **10.1** *the town*: Two ancient translations; Hebrew "Jezreel."

job and make him the next king.
Then be prepared to defend Ahab's
family.
4The officials and leaders read the letters and were very frightened. They said
to each other, "Jehu has already killed
King Joram and King Ahaziah! We have
to do what he says." 5The prime minister, the mayor of the city, as well as the
other leaders and Ahab's supporters,
sent this answer to Jehu, "We are your
servants, Your Majesty, and we will do
whatever you tell us. But it's not our
place to choose someone to be king. You
do what you think is best."
6Jehu then wrote another letter which
said, "If you are on my side and will
obey me, then prove it. Bring me the
heads of the descendants of Ahab! And
be here in Jezreel by this time tomorrow."
The seventy descendants of King
Ahab were living with some of the most
important people of the city. 7And when
these people read Jehu's second letter,
they called together all seventy of
Ahab's descendants. They killed them,
put their heads in baskets, and sent
them to Jezreel.
8When Jehu was told what had happened, he said, "Put the heads in two
piles at the city gate, and leave them
there until morning."
9The next morning, Jehu went out and
stood where everyone could hear him,
and he said, "You people are not guilty
of anything. I'm the one who plotted
against Joram and had him killed. But
who killed all these men? 10Listen to me.
Everything the LORD's servant Elijah
promised about Ahab's family will come
true."[b]
11Then Jehu killed the rest of Ahab's
relatives living in Jezreel, as well as his
highest officials, his priests, and his
closest friends. No one in Ahab's family
was left alive in Jezreel.
12-13Jehu left for Samaria, and along
the way, he met some relatives of King
Ahaziah of Judah at a place where
shepherds meet.[c] He asked, "Who are
you?"
"We are relatives of Ahaziah," they
answered. "We're going to visit his family."
14"Take them alive!" Jehu said to his
officers. So they grabbed them and led
them to the well near the shepherds'
meeting place, where they killed all
forty-two of them.
15As Jehu went on, he saw Jehonadab
son of Rechab[d] coming to meet him.
Jehu greeted him, then said, "Jehonadab, I'm on your side. Are you on
mine?"
"Yes, I am."
"Then give me your hand," Jehu answered. He helped Jehonadab into his
chariot 16and said, "Come with me and
see how faithful I am to the LORD."
They rode together in Jehu's chariot
17to Samaria. Jehu killed everyone there
who belonged to Ahab's family, as well
as all his officials. Everyone in his family was now dead, just as the LORD had
promised Elijah.

Jehu Kills All the Worshipers of Baal

18Jehu called together the people in
Samaria and said:
> King Ahab sometimes worshiped
> Baal, but I will be completely faith-
> ful to Baal. 19I'm going to offer a
> huge sacrifice to him. So invite his
> prophets and priests, and be sure
> everyone who worships him is there.
> Anyone who doesn't come will be
> killed.

But this was a trick—Jehu was really
planning to kill the worshipers of Baal.
20He said, "Announce a day of worship
for Baal!" After the day had been announced, 21Jehu sent an invitation to
everyone in Israel. All the worshipers of
Baal came, and the temple was filled
from one end to the other. 22Jehu told
the official in charge of the sacred robes
to make sure that everyone had a robe
to wear.
23Jehu and Jehonadab went into the
temple, and Jehu said to the crowd,
"Look around and make sure that only
the worshipers of Baal are here. No one
who worships the LORD is allowed in."
24Then they began to offer sacrifices to
Baal.
Earlier, Jehu had ordered eighty soldiers to wait outside the temple. He had
warned them, "I will get all these worshipers here, and if any of you let even
one of them escape, you will be killed
instead!"
25As soon as Jehu finished offering
the sacrifice, he told the guards and soldiers, "Come in and kill them! Don't let
anyone escape." They slaughtered
everyone in the crowd and threw the
bodies outside. Then they went back
into the temple 26and carried out the image of Baal. They burned it 27and broke
it into pieces, then they completely destroyed Baal's temple. And since that
time, it's been nothing but a public toilet.[e]
28That's how Jehu stopped the worship of Baal in Israel. 29But he did not

[b]10.10 *Everything . . . come true*: See 1 Kings 21.17-24. [c]10.12,13 *at a place where shepherds meet*: Or "at Betheked of the Shepherds." [d]10.15 *Jehonadab son of Rechab*: Or "Jehonadab the chariot driver." [e]10.27 *public toilet*: Or "garbage dump."

stop the worship of the gold statues of
calves at Dan and Bethel that Jeroboam
had made for the people to worship.[f]
30Later the LORD said, "Jehu, you have
done right by destroying Ahab's entire
family, just as I had planned. So I will
make sure that the next four kings of Israel will come from your own family."
31But Jehu did not completely obey
the commands of the LORD God of Israel. Instead, he kept doing the sinful
things that Jeroboam had caused the Israelites to do.

Jehu Dies

32In those days the LORD began to re-
duce the size of Israel's territory. King
Hazael of Syria defeated the Israelites
and took control 33of the regions of
Gilead and Bashan east of the Jordan
River and north of the town of Aroer
near the Arnon River. This was the land
where the tribes of Gad, Reuben, and
Manasseh had once lived.
34Everything else Jehu did while he
was king, including his brave deeds, is
written in *The History of the Kings of
Israel*. 35Jehu died and was buried in
Samaria, and his son Jehoahaz became
king. 36Jehu had ruled Israel twenty-
eight years from Samaria.

Queen Athaliah of Judah
(2 Chronicles 22.10-12)

11 As soon as Athaliah heard that
her son King Ahaziah was dead,
she decided to kill any relative who
could possibly become king. She would
have done that, 2but Jehosheba rescued
Joash son of Ahaziah just as he was
about to be murdered. Jehosheba, who
was Jehoram's[g] daughter and Ahaziah's
half sister, hid her nephew Joash and
his personal servant in a bedroom in the
LORD's temple where he was safe from
Athaliah. 3Joash hid in the temple with
Jehosheba[h] for six years while Athaliah
ruled as queen of Judah.

Jehoiada Makes Joash King of Judah
(2 Chronicles 23.1-21)

4Joash son of Ahaziah had hidden in
the LORD's temple six years. Then in the
seventh year, Jehoiada the priest sent
for the commanders of the king's special bodyguards[i] and the commanders
of the palace guards. They met him at
the temple, and he asked them to make
a promise in the name of the LORD. Then
he brought out Joash 5and said to them:

Here's what I want you to do.
Three of your guard units will be on
duty on the Sabbath. I want one unit
to guard the palace. 6Another unit
will guard Sur Gate, and the third
unit will guard the palace gate and
relieve the palace guards.
7The other two guard units are
supposed to be off duty on the Sabbath. But I want both of them to stay
here at the temple and protect King
Joash. 8Make sure they follow him
wherever he goes, and have them
keep their swords ready to kill anyone who tries to get near him.

9The commanders followed Jehoiada's orders. Each one called together his guards—those coming on
duty and those going off duty. 10Je-
hoiada brought out the swords and
shields that had belonged to King David
and gave them to the commanders.
11Then they gave the weapons to their
guards, who took their positions around
the temple and the altar to protect Joash
on every side.
12Jehoiada brought Joash outside,
where he placed the crown on his head
and gave him a copy of instructions for
ruling the nation. Olive oil was poured
on his head to show that he was now
king, while the crowd clapped and
shouted, "Long live the king!"
13Queen Athaliah heard the crowd
and went to the temple. 14There she saw
Joash standing by one of the columns,
which was the usual place for the king.
The singers[j] and the trumpet players
were standing next to him, and the people were celebrating and blowing trumpets. Athaliah tore her clothes in anger
and shouted, "You betrayed me, you
traitors!"
15Right away, Jehoiada said to the
army commanders, "Kill her! But don't
do it anywhere near the LORD's temple.
Take her out in front of the troops and
kill anyone who is with her!" 16So the
commanders dragged her to the gate
where horses are led into the palace,
and they killed her there.
17Jehoiada the priest asked King
Joash and the people to promise that
they would be faithful to each other and
to the LORD. 18Then the crowd went to
the temple built to honor Baal and tore
it down. They smashed the altars and
idols and killed Mattan the priest of
Baal right in front of the altars.
After Jehoiada had placed guards
around the LORD's temple, 19he called

[f] **10.29** *gold statues . . . to worship*: See 1 Kings 12.26-30. [g] **11.2** *Jehoram's*: The Hebrew text has "Joram's," another spelling of the name. [h] **11.3** *Jehosheba*: Jehosheba was the wife of Jehoiada the priest (see 2 Chronicles 22.11), which is why she could hide Joash in one of the private bedrooms used only by the priests. [i] **11.4** *the king's special bodyguards*: The Hebrew text has "the Carites," who were probably foreign soldiers hired to serve as royal bodyguards. [j] **11.14** *singers*: Two ancient translations; Hebrew "commanders."

together all the commanders, the king's
special bodyguards,[k] the palace guards,
and the people. They led Joash from the
temple, through the Guards' Gate, and
into the palace. He took his place on the
throne and became king of Judah.
20Everyone celebrated because Athaliah
had been killed and Jerusalem was
peaceful again. 21Joash was only seven
years old when this happened.

King Joash of Judah

(2 Chronicles 24.1-16)

12 Joash[l] became king of Judah in
Jehu's seventh year as king of Israel, and he ruled forty years from
Jerusalem. His mother Zibiah was from
the town of Beersheba.

2Jehoiada the priest taught Joash
what was right, and so for the rest of his
life Joash obeyed the LORD. 3But even
Joash did not destroy the local shrines,[m]
and they were still used as places for offering sacrifices.

4One day, Joash said to the priests,
"Collect all the money that has been
given to the LORD's temple, whether
from taxes or gifts, 5and use it to repair
the temple. You priests can contribute
your own money too."[n]

6But the priests never started repairing the temple. So in the twenty-third
year of his rule, 7Joash called for Jehoiada and the other priests and said,
"Why aren't you using the money to repair the temple? Don't take any more
money for yourselves. It is only to be
used to pay for the repairs." 8The priests
agreed that they would not collect any
more money or be in charge of the temple repairs.

9Jehoiada found a wooden box; he cut
a hole in the top of it and set it on the
right side of the altar where people went
into the temple. Whenever someone
gave money to the temple, the priests
guarding the entrance would put it into
this box. 10When the box was full of
money, the king's secretary and the
chief priest would count the money and
put it in bags. 11Then they would give it
to the men supervising the repairs to the
temple. Some of the money was used to
pay the builders, the woodworkers, 12the
stonecutters, and the men who built the
walls. And some was used to buy wood
and stone and to pay any other costs for
repairing the temple.

13While the repairs were being made,
the money that was given to the temple
was not used to make silver bowls, lamp
snuffers, small sprinkling bowls, trumpets, or anything gold or silver for the
temple. 14It went only to pay for repairs.
15The men in charge were honest, so no
one had to keep track of the money.

16The fines that had to be paid along
with the sacrifices to make things right
and the sacrifices for sin did not go to
the temple. This money belonged only
to the priests.

17About the same time, King Hazael of
Syria attacked the town of Gath and
captured it. Next, he decided to attack
Jerusalem. 18So Joash collected everything he and his ancestors Jehoshaphat,
Jehoram, and Ahaziah had dedicated to
the LORD, as well as the gold in the storage rooms in the temple and palace. He
sent it all to Hazael as a gift, and when
Hazael received it, he ordered his troops
to leave Jerusalem.

19Everything else Joash did while he
was king is written in *The History of the
Kings of Judah*. 20-21At the end of his
rule, some of his officers rebelled
against him. Jozabad[o] son of Shimeath
and Jehozabad son of Shomer murdered him in a building where the land
was filled in on the east side of
Jerusalem,[p] near the road to Silla. Joash
was buried beside his ancestors in
Jerusalem,[q] and his son Amaziah became king.

King Jehoahaz of Israel

13 Jehoahaz son of Jehu became
king of Israel in the twenty-third
year of Joash's rule in Judah. Jehoahaz
ruled seventeen years from Samaria
2and disobeyed the LORD by doing
wrong. He never stopped following the
example of Jeroboam, who had caused
the Israelites to sin.

3The LORD was angry at the Israelites,
so he let King Hazael of Syria and his
son Benhadad rule over them for a long
time. 4Jehoahaz prayed to the LORD for
help, and the LORD saw how terribly
Hazael was treating the Israelites. He
answered Jehoahaz 5by sending Israel a
leader who rescued them from the Syrians,[r] and the Israelites lived in peace as
they had before. 6-7But Hazael had defeated Israel's army so badly that Jehoahaz had only ten chariots, fifty cavalry

[k]**11.19** *the king's special bodyguards*: See the note at verse 4. [l]**12.1** *Joash*: The Hebrew text has "Jehoash," another spelling of the name. [m]**12.3** *local shrines*: The Hebrew text has "high places," which were local places to worship God or foreign gods. [n]**12.5** *You priests . . . money too*: One possible meaning for the difficult Hebrew text. [o]**12.20,21** *Jozabad*: Some manuscripts of the Hebrew text; other manuscripts "Jozacar." [p]**12.20,21** *where . . . Jerusalem*: The Hebrew text has "on the Millo," which probably refers to a landfill to strengthen and extend the hill where the city was built. [q]**12.20,21** *Jerusalem*: See the note at 8.24. [r]**13.5** *by sending . . . the Syrians*: The name of this leader is not given, but it may refer to Elisha the prophet, King Jehoash of Israel, or his son King Jeroboam.

troops, and ten thousand regular soldiers left in his army.

The Israelites kept sinning and following the example of Jeroboam's family. They did not tear down the sacred poles[s] that had been set up in Samaria for the worship of the goddess Asherah.

[8]Everything else Jehoahaz did while he was king, including his brave deeds, is written in *The History of the Kings of Israel.* [9]Jehoahaz died and was buried in Samaria, and his son Jehoash became king.

King Jehoash of Israel

[10]Jehoash became king of Israel in the thirty-seventh year of Joash's rule in Judah, and he ruled sixteen years from Samaria. [11]He disobeyed the LORD by doing just like Jeroboam, who had caused the Israelites to sin.

[12]Everything else Jehoash did while he was king, including his war against King Amaziah of Judah, is written in *The History of the Kings of Israel.* [13]Jehoash died and was buried in Samaria beside the other Israelite kings. His son Jeroboam then became king.

Elisha the Prophet Dies

[14]Some time before the death of King Jehoash, Elisha the prophet was very sick and about to die. Jehoash went in and stood beside him, crying. He said, "Master, what will Israel's chariots and cavalry be able to do without you?"[t]

[15-16]"Grab a bow and some arrows," Elisha told him, "and hold them in your hand." Jehoash grabbed the bow and arrows and held them. Elisha placed his hand on the king's hand [17]and said, "Open the window facing east." When it was open, Elisha shouted, "Now shoot!" Jehoash shot an arrow and Elisha said, "That arrow is a sign that the LORD will help you completely defeat the Syrian army at Aphek."

[18]Elisha said, "Pick up the arrows and hit the ground with them." Jehoash grabbed the arrows and hit the ground three times, then stopped. [19]Elisha became angry at the king and exclaimed, "If you had struck it five or six times, you would completely wipe out the Syrians. Now you will defeat them only three times."

[20]Elisha died and was buried.

Every year in the spring, Moab's leaders sent raiding parties into Israel. [21]Once, while some Israelites were burying a man's body, they saw a group of Moabites. The Israelites quickly threw the body into Elisha's tomb and ran away. As soon as the man's body touched the bones of Elisha, the man came back to life and stood up.

Israel Defeats Syria

[22]Israel was under the power of King Hazael of Syria during the entire rule of Jehoahaz. [23]But the LORD was kind to the Israelites and showed them mercy because of his solemn agreement with their ancestors Abraham, Isaac, and Jacob. In fact, he has never turned his back on them or let them be completely destroyed.

[24]Hazael died, and his son Benhadad then became king of Syria. [25]King Jehoash of Israel attacked and defeated the Syrian army three times. He took back from Benhadad all the towns Hazael had captured in battle from his father Jehoahaz.

King Amaziah of Judah

(2 Chronicles 25.1-24)

14 Amaziah son of Joash became king of Judah in the second year of Jehoash's rule in Israel. [2]Amaziah was twenty-five years old when he became king, and he ruled twenty-nine years from Jerusalem, which was also the hometown of his mother Jehoaddin.

[3]Amaziah followed the example of his father Joash by obeying the LORD and doing right. But he was not as faithful as his ancestor David. [4]Amaziah did not destroy the local shrines, and they were still used as places for offering sacrifices.

[5]As soon as Amaziah had control of Israel, he arrested and killed the officers who had murdered his father. [6]But the children of those officers were not killed. The LORD had commanded in the Law of Moses that only the people who sinned were to be punished, not their parents or children.[u]

[7]While Amaziah was king, he killed ten thousand Edomite soldiers in Salt Valley. He captured the town of Sela and renamed it Joktheel, which is still its name.

[8]One day, Amaziah sent a message to King Jehoash of Israel: "Come out and face me in battle!"

[9]Jehoash sent back this reply:

> Once upon a time, a small thornbush in Lebanon announced that his son was going to marry the daughter of a large cedar tree. But a wild animal came along and trampled the small bush.
>
> [10]Amaziah, you think you're so powerful because you defeated Edom. Go ahead and celebrate—but stay at home. If you cause any trou-

[s] **13.6,7** *sacred poles*: Or "trees," used as symbols of Asherah, the goddess of fertility.
[t] **13.14** *Master . . . without you*: Or "Master, you were like chariots and cavalry for Israel!"
[u] **14.6** *The LORD had commanded . . . children*: See Deuteronomy 24.16.

ble, both you and your kingdom of
Judah will be destroyed.
11 But Amaziah refused to listen. So
Jehoash and his troops marched to the
town of Beth-Shemesh in Judah to attack Amaziah and his troops. 12 During
the battle, Judah's army was crushed.
Every soldier from Judah ran back
home, 13 and Jehoash captured Amaziah.
Jehoash then marched to Jerusalem
and broke down the city wall from
Ephraim Gate to Corner Gate, a section
about six hundred feet long. 14 He took
the gold and silver, as well as everything
of value from the LORD's temple and the
king's treasury. He took hostages, then
returned to Samaria.
15 Everything else Jehoash did while
he was king, including his brave deeds
and how he defeated King Amaziah of
Judah, is written in *The History of the
Kings of Israel.* 16 Jehoash died and was
buried in Samaria beside the other Israelite kings. His son Jeroboam then became king.
17 Fifteen years after Jehoash died,
18-20 some people in Jerusalem plotted
against Amaziah. He was able to escape
to the town of Lachish, but another
group of people caught him and killed
him there. His body was taken back to
Jerusalem on horseback and buried beside his ancestors.
Everything else Amaziah did while he
was king is written in *The History of the
Kings of Judah.* 21 After his death the
people of Judah made his son Azariah
king, even though he was only sixteen
at the time. 22 Azariah was the one who
later recaptured and rebuilt the town of
Elath.

King Jeroboam the Second of Israel

23 Jeroboam son of Jehoash became
king of Israel in the fifteenth year of
Amaziah's rule in Judah. Jeroboam
ruled forty-one years from Samaria.
24 He disobeyed the LORD by following
the evil example of Jeroboam son of
Nebat, who had caused the Israelites to
sin.
25 Jeroboam extended the boundaries
of Israel from Lebo-Hamath in the north
to the Dead Sea in the south, just as the
LORD had promised his servant Jonah
son of Amittai, who was a prophet from
Gath-Hepher. 26 The LORD helped Jeroboam do this because he had seen how
terribly the Israelites were suffering,
whether slave or free, and no one was
left to help them. 27 And since the LORD
had promised that he would not let Israel be completely destroyed, he helped
Jeroboam rescue them.
28 Everything else Jeroboam did while
he was king, including his brave deeds
and how he recaptured the towns of
Damascus and Hamath,[v] is written in
The History of the Kings of Israel. 29 Jeroboam died and was buried, and his son
Zechariah became king.

King Azariah of Judah

(2 Chronicles 26.1-23)

15 Azariah son of Amaziah became
king of Judah in Jeroboam's
twenty-seventh year as king of Israel.
2 He was only sixteen years old when he
became king, and he ruled fifty-two
years from Jerusalem, which was also
the hometown of his mother Jecoliah.
3 Azariah obeyed the LORD by doing
right, as his father Amaziah had done.
4 But Azariah did not destroy the local
shrines,[w] and they were still used as
places for offering sacrifices.
5 The LORD punished Azariah with leprosy[x] for the rest of his life. He wasn't
allowed to live in the royal palace, so his
son Jotham lived there and ruled in his
place.
6 Everything else Azariah did while he
was king is written in *The History of the
Kings of Judah.* 7 Azariah died and was
buried beside his ancestors in Jerusalem. His son Jotham then became king.

King Zechariah of Israel

8 Zechariah son of Jeroboam became
king of Israel in the thirty-eighth year of
Azariah's rule in Judah, but he ruled
only six months from Samaria. 9 Like his
ancestors, Zechariah disobeyed the
LORD by following the evil ways of Jeroboam son of Nebat, who had caused
the Israelites to sin.
10 Shallum son of Jabesh plotted
against Zechariah and killed him in
public.[y] Shallum then became king.
11-12 So the LORD had kept his promise to
Jehu that the next four kings of Israel
would come from his family.[z]
Everything else Zechariah did while
he was king is written in *The History of
the Kings of Israel.*

King Shallum of Israel

13 Shallum became king of Israel in the
thirty-ninth year of Azariah's[a] rule in
Judah. But only one month after Shallum became king, 14-16 Menahem son of
Gadi came to Samaria from Tirzah and
killed him. Menahem then became king.

[v] **14.28** *how he recaptured . . . Hamath*: One possible meaning for the difficult Hebrew text. [w] **15.4** *local shrines*: See the note at 12.3. [x] **15.5** *leprosy*: See the note at 5.1. [y] **15.10** *in public*: Hebrew; some manuscripts of one ancient translation "in Ibleam." [z] **15.11,12** *So the LORD . . . family*: See 10.28-31. [a] **15.13** *Azariah's*: The Hebrew text has "Uzziah's," another spelling of the name.

The town of Tiphsah would not surrender to him, so he destroyed it and all the
surrounding towns as far as Tirzah. He
killed everyone living in Tiphsah, and
with his sword he even ripped open
pregnant women.
Everything else Shallum did while he
was king, including his plot against
Zechariah, is written in *The History of
the Kings of Israel.*

King Menahem of Israel

17 Menahem became king of Israel in
Azariah's thirty-ninth year as king of
Judah, and he ruled Israel ten years
from Samaria. 18 He constantly disobeyed the LORD by following the example of Jeroboam son of Nebat, who had
caused the Israelites to sin.
19 During Menahem's rule, King
Tiglath Pileser[b] of Assyria invaded Israel. He agreed to help Menahem keep
control of his kingdom, if Menahem
would pay him over thirty tons of silver.
20 So Menahem ordered every rich person in Israel to give him at least one
pound of silver, and he gave it all to
Tiglath Pileser, who stopped his attack
and left Israel.
21 Everything else Menahem did while
he was king is written in *The History of
the Kings of Israel.* 22 Menahem died,
and his son Pekahiah became king.

King Pekahiah of Israel

23 Pekahiah became king of Israel in
the fiftieth year of Azariah's rule in Judah, and he ruled two years from
Samaria. 24 He disobeyed the LORD and
caused the Israelites to sin, just as Jeroboam son of Nebat had done.
25 Pekah son of Remaliah was
Pekahiah's chief officer, but he made
plans to kill the king. So he and fifty
men from Gilead broke into the
strongest part of the palace in Samaria
and murdered Pekahiah, together with
Argob and Arieh.[c] Pekah then became
king.
26 Everything else Pekahiah did while
he was king is written in *The History of
the Kings of Israel.*

King Pekah of Israel

27 Pekah son of Remaliah became king
of Israel in Azariah's fifty-second year
as king of Judah, and he ruled twenty
years from Samaria. 28 He disobeyed the
LORD and followed the evil example of
Jeroboam son of Nebat, who had caused
the Israelites to sin.
29 During Pekah's rule, King Tiglath
Pileser of Assyria marched into Israel.
He captured the territories of Gilead
and Galilee, including the towns of Ijon,
Abel-Bethmaacah, Janoah, Kedesh, and
Hazor, as well as the entire territory of
Naphtali. Then he took Israelites from
those regions to Assyria as prisoners.[d]
30 In the twentieth year of Jotham's
rule in Judah, Hoshea son of Elah plotted against Pekah and murdered him.
Hoshea then became king of Israel.
31 Everything else Pekah did while he
was king is written in *The History of the
Kings of Israel.* .

King Jotham of Judah

(2 Chronicles 27.1-9)

32 Jotham son of Azariah[e] became
king of Judah in the second year of
Pekah's rule in Israel. 33 Jotham was
twenty-five years old when he became
king, and he ruled sixteen years from
Jerusalem. His mother Jerusha was the
daughter of Zadok.
34 Jotham followed the example of his
father by obeying the LORD and doing
right. 35 It was Jotham who rebuilt the
Upper Gate that led into the court
around the LORD's temple. But the local
shrines were not destroyed, and they
were still used as places for offering
sacrifices.
36 Everything else Jotham did while he
was king is written in *The History of the
Kings of Judah.* 37 During his rule, the
LORD let King Rezin of Syria and King
Pekah of Israel start attacking Judah.
38 Jotham died and was buried beside his
ancestors in Jerusalem, and his son
Ahaz became king.

King Ahaz of Judah

(2 Chronicles 28.1-27)

16 Ahaz son of Jotham became king
of Judah in the seventeenth year
of Pekah's rule in Israel. 2 He was twenty
years old at the time, and he ruled from
Jerusalem for sixteen years.
Ahaz wasn't like his ancestor David.
Instead, he disobeyed the LORD 3 and
was even more sinful than the kings of
Israel. He sacrificed his own son, which
was a disgusting custom of the nations
that the LORD had forced out of Israel.
4 Ahaz offered sacrifices at the local
shrines, as well as on every hill and in
the shade of large trees.
5-6 While Ahaz was ruling Judah, the
king of Edom recaptured the town of
Elath from Judah and forced out the

[b] **15.19** *Tiglath Pileser*: The Hebrew text has "Pul," another name for Tiglath Pileser, who ruled Assyria from 745 to 727 B.C. [c] **15.25** *together with Argob and Arieh*: One possible meaning for the difficult Hebrew text. [d] **15.29** *prisoners*: The events in this verse probably took place around 733 B.C. [e] **15.32** *Azariah*: See the note at 15.13.

people of Judah. Edomites[f] then moved
into Elath, and they still live there.
About the same time, King Rezin of
Syria and King Pekah of Israel marched
to Jerusalem and attacked, but they
could not capture it.
7Ahaz sent a message to King Tiglath
Pileser of Assyria that said, "Your
Majesty, King Rezin and King Pekah are
attacking me, your loyal servant. Please
come and rescue me." 8Along with the
message, Ahaz sent silver and gold from
the LORD's temple and from the palace
treasury as a gift for the Assyrian king.
9As soon as Tiglath Pileser received
the message, he and his troops marched
to Syria. He captured the capital city of
Damascus, then he took the people living there to the town of Kir as prisoners
and killed King Rezin.[g]
10Later, Ahaz went to Damascus to
meet Tiglath Pileser. And while Ahaz
was there, he saw an altar and sent a
model of it back to Uriah the priest,
along with the plans for building one.
11Uriah followed the plans and built an
altar exactly like the one in Damascus,
finishing it just before Ahaz came back.
12When Ahaz returned, he went to see
the altar and to offer sacrifices on it. He
walked up to the altar 13and poured
wine over it. Then he offered sacrifices
to please the LORD, to give him thanks,
and to ask for his blessings.[h] 14After
that, he had the bronze altar moved
aside,[i] so his new altar would be right in
front of the LORD's temple. 15He told
Uriah the priest:

> From now on, the morning and
> evening sacrifices as well as all gifts
> of grain and wine are to be offered
> on this altar. The sacrifices for the
> people and for the king must also be
> offered here. Sprinkle the blood
> from all the sacrifices on it, but leave
> the bronze altar for me to use for
> prayer and finding out what God
> wants me to do.

16Uriah did everything Ahaz told him.
17Ahaz also had the side panels and
the small bowls taken off the movable
stands in the LORD's temple. He had the
large bronze bowl, called the Sea, removed from the bronze bulls on which it
rested and had it placed on a stand
made of stone. 18He took down the special tent that was used for worship on
the Sabbath[j] and closed up the private
entrance that the kings of Judah used
for going into the temple. He did all
these things to please Tiglath Pileser.
19Everything else Ahaz did while he
was king is written in *The History of the
Kings of Judah*. 20Ahaz died and was
buried beside his ancestors in Jerusalem,[k] and his son Hezekiah became
king.

King Hoshea of Israel

17 Hoshea son of Elah became king
of Israel in the twelfth year of
Ahaz's rule in Judah, and he ruled nine
years from Samaria. 2Hoshea disobeyed
the LORD and sinned, but not as much as
the earlier Israelite kings had done.
3During Hoshea's rule, King Shalmaneser of Assyria[l] invaded Israel; he
took control of the country and made
Hoshea pay taxes. 4But later, Hoshea refused to pay the taxes and asked King
So of Egypt to help him rebel. When
Shalmaneser found out, he arrested
Hoshea and put him in prison.

Samaria Is Destroyed and the Israelites Are Taken to Assyria

5Shalmaneser invaded Israel and attacked the city of Samaria for three
years, 6before capturing it in the ninth
year of Hoshea's rule. The Assyrian
king[m] took the Israelites away to Assyria as prisoners. He forced some of
them to live in the town of Halah, others
to live near the Habor River in the territory of Gozan, and still others to live in
towns where the Median people lived.
7All of this happened because the people of Israel had sinned against the
LORD their God, who had rescued them
from Egypt, where they had been slaves.
They worshiped foreign gods, 8followed
the customs of the nations that the LORD
had forced out of Israel, and were just
as sinful as the Israelite kings. 9Even
worse, the Israelites tried to hide their
sins from the LORD their God. They built
their own local shrines everywhere in
Israel—from small towns to large,
walled cities. 10They also built stone images of foreign gods and set up sacred

[f] **16.5,6** *the king of Edom . . . Edomites*: The Hebrew text has "King Rezin of Syria . . . Syrians"; in Hebrew, there is only one letter difference between "Edom" and "Aram," which is the usual Hebrew name for Syria in the Bible (see also 2 Chronicles 28.17). [g] **16.9** *King Rezin*: This probably took place around 734 B.C., before the events in 15.29. [h] **16.13** *offered . . . blessings*: In traditional translations, these sacrifices are usually called "whole burnt offerings," "grain offerings," and "peace offerings." These are described in Leviticus 1–3. [i] **16.14** *aside*: Hebrew "to the north." [j] **16.18** *the special tent . . . Sabbath*: One possible meaning for the difficult Hebrew text. [k] **16.20** *Jerusalem*: See the note at 8.24. [l] **17.3** *King Shalmaneser of Assyria*: The son of Tiglath Pileser, who ruled Assyria from 727 to 722 B.C. [m] **17.6** *The Assyrian king*: Probably Sargon, Shalmaneser's successor. Shalmaneser died after the city of Samaria was captured (722 B.C.) but before the people were taken away as prisoners (720 B.C.). Sargon ruled Assyria from 721 to 705 B.C.

poles[n] for the worship of Asherah on
every hill and under every shady tree.
11 They offered sacrifices at the shrines,[o]
just as the foreign nations had done before the LORD forced them out of Israel.
They did sinful things that made the
LORD very angry.
12 Even though the LORD had commanded the Israelites not to worship
idols,[p] they did it anyway. 13 So the LORD
made sure that every prophet warned
Israel and Judah with these words: "I,
the LORD, command you to stop doing
sinful things and start obeying my laws
and teachings! I gave them to your ancestors, and I told my servants the
prophets to repeat them to you."
14 But the Israelites would not listen;
they were as stubborn as their ancestors
who had refused to worship the LORD
their God. 15 They ignored the LORD's
warnings and commands, and they rejected the solemn agreement he had
made with their ancestors. They worshiped worthless idols and became
worthless themselves. The LORD had
told the Israelites not to do the things
that the foreign nations around them
were doing, but Israel became just like
them.
16 The people of Israel disobeyed all
the commands of the LORD their God.
They made two gold statues of calves
and set up a sacred pole for Asherah;
they also worshiped the stars and the
god Baal. 17 They used magic and witchcraft and even sacrificed their own children. The Israelites were determined to
do whatever the LORD hated. 18 The LORD
became so furious with the people of Israel that he allowed them to be carried
away as prisoners.
Only the people living in Judah were
left, 19 but they also disobeyed the LORD's
commands and acted like the Israelites.
20 So the LORD turned his back on everyone in Israel and Judah[q] and let them be
punished and defeated until no one was
left.
21 Earlier, when the LORD took the
northern tribes away from David's family,[r] the people living in northern Israel
chose Jeroboam son of Nebat as their
king. Jeroboam caused the Israelites to
sin and to stop worshiping the LORD.
22 The people kept on sinning like Jeroboam, 23 until the LORD got rid of them,
just as he had warned his servants the
prophets.
That's why the people of Israel were
taken away as prisoners to Assyria, and
that's where they remained.

Foreigners Are Resettled in Israel

24 The king of Assyria took people who
were living in the cities of Babylon,
Cuthah, Avva, Hamath, and Sepharvaim, and forced them to move to Israel.
They took over the towns where the Israelites had lived, including the capital
city of Samaria.
25 At first these people did not worship
the LORD, so he sent lions to attack
them, and the lions killed some of them.
26 A messenger told the king of Assyria,
"The people you moved to Israel don't
know how to worship the god of that
country. So he sent lions that have attacked and killed some of them."
27 The king replied, "Get one of the Israelite priests we brought here and send
him back to Israel. He can live there and
teach them about the god of that country." 28 One of the Israelite priests was
chosen to go back to Israel. He lived in
Bethel and taught the people how to
worship the LORD.
29 But in towns all over Israel, the different groups of people made statues of
their own gods, then they placed these
idols in local Israelite[s] shrines. 30 The
people from Babylonia made the god
Succoth-Benoth; those from Cuthah
made the god Nergal; those from
Hamath made Ashima; 31 those from
Avva made Nibhaz and Tartak; and the
people from Sepharvaim sacrificed their
children to their own gods Adrammelech and Anammelech. 32-33 They worshiped their own gods, just as they had
before they were taken away to Israel.
They also worshiped the LORD, but they
chose their own people to be priests at
the shrines. 34 Everyone followed their
old customs. None of them worshiped
only the LORD, and they refused to obey
the laws and commands that the LORD
had given to the descendants of Jacob,
the man he named Israel. 35 At the time
when the LORD had made his solemn
agreement with the people of Israel, he
told them:

Do not worship any other gods!
Do not bow down to them or offer
them a sacrifice. 36 Worship only me!
I am the one who rescued you from
Egypt with my mighty power. Bow
down to me and offer sacrifices.
37 Never worship any other god, always obey my laws and teachings,
38 and remember the solemn agreement between us.
I will say it again: Do not worship
any god 39 except me. I am the LORD

[n] **17.10** *sacred poles*: See the note at 13.6, 7. [o] **17.11** *shrines*: See the note at 12.3. [p] **17.12** *the LORD . . . idols*: See Exodus 20.4, 5. [q] **17.20** *Israel and Judah*: Or "Israel," that is, the northern kingdom only. [r] **17.21** *when the LORD . . . family*: See 1 Kings 11.29-39. [s] **17.29** *Israelite*: The Hebrew text has "Samaritan," which is a later word to describe the people who lived in northern Israel at this time.

your God, and I will rescue you from
all your enemies.
40But the people living in Israel ignored that command and kept on following their old customs. 41They did
worship the LORD, but they also worshiped their own idols. Their descendants did the same thing.

King Hezekiah of Judah

(2 Chronicles 29.1, 2; 31.1)

18 Hezekiah son of Ahaz became
king of Judah in the third year of
Hoshea's rule in Israel. 2Hezekiah was
twenty-five years old when he became
king, and he ruled twenty-nine years
from Jerusalem. His mother Abi was the
daughter of Zechariah.
3Hezekiah obeyed the LORD, just as
his ancestor David had done. 4He destroyed the local shrines, then tore
down the images of foreign gods and
cut down the sacred pole for worshiping
the goddess Asherah. He also smashed
the bronze snake Moses had made. The
people had named it Nehushtan[t] and
had been offering sacrifices to it.
5Hezekiah trusted the LORD God of Israel. No other king of Judah was like
Hezekiah, either before or after him.
6He was completely faithful to the LORD
and obeyed the laws the LORD had given
to Moses for the people. 7The LORD
helped Hezekiah, so he was successful
in everything he did. He even rebelled
against the king of Assyria, refusing to
be his servant. 8Hezekiah defeated the
Philistine towns as far away as Gaza—
from the smallest towns to the large,
walled cities.
9During the fourth year of Hezekiah's
rule, which was the seventh year of
Hoshea's rule in Israel, King Shalmaneser of Assyria led his troops to
Samaria, the capital city of Israel. They
attacked 10and captured it three years
later,[u] in the sixth year of Hezekiah's
rule and the ninth year of Hoshea's rule.
11The king of Assyria[v] took the Israelites away as prisoners; he forced
some of them to live in the town of Halah, others to live near the Habor River
in the territory of Gozan, and still others
to live in towns where the Median people lived. 12All of that happened because
the people of Israel had not obeyed the
LORD their God. They rejected the
solemn agreement he had made with
them, and they ignored everything
that the LORD's servant Moses had told
them.

King Sennacherib of Assyria Invades Judah

(2 Chronicles 32.1-19; Isaiah 36.1-22)

13In the fourteenth year of Hezekiah's
rule in Judah, King Sennacherib of Assyria invaded the country and captured
every walled city,[w] except Jerusalem.
14Hezekiah sent this message to Sennacherib, who was in the town of
Lachish: "I know I am guilty of rebellion. But I will pay you whatever you
want, if you stop your attack."
Sennacherib told Hezekiah to pay
about eleven tons of silver and almost a
ton of gold. 15So Hezekiah collected all
the silver from the LORD's temple and
the royal treasury. 16He even stripped
the gold that he had used to cover the
doors and doorposts[x] in the temple. He
gave it all to Sennacherib.
17The king of Assyria ordered his
three highest military officers to leave
Lachish and take a large army to
Jerusalem. When they arrived, the officers stood on the road near the cloth
makers' shops along the canal from the
upper pool. 18They called out to Hezekiah, and three of his highest officials
came out to meet them. One of them
was Hilkiah's son Eliakim, who was the
prime minister. The other two were
Shebna, assistant to the prime minister,
and Joah son of Asaph, keeper of the
government records.
19One of the Assyrian commanders
told them:
I have a message for Hezekiah
from the great king of Assyria. Ask
Hezekiah why he feels so sure of
himself. 20Does he think he can plan
and win a war with nothing but
words? Who is going to help him,
now that he has turned against the
king of Assyria? 21Is he depending
on Egypt and its king? That's the
same as leaning on a broken stick,
and it will go right through his hand.
22Is Hezekiah now depending on
the LORD your God? Didn't Hezekiah
tear down all except one of the
LORD's altars and places of worship?[y] Didn't he tell the people of

[t] **18.4** *the bronze snake . . . Nehushtan*: See Numbers 21.8, 9. "Nehushtan" is a nickname that sounds like the Hebrew words for "snake" and "bronze." [u] **18.10** *three years later*: When the Israelites measured time, part of a year could be counted as a whole year. [v] **18.11** *The king of Assyria*: Probably Sargon, Shalmaneser's successor (see the note at 17.6).
[w] **18.13** *King Sennacherib . . . walled city*: Sennacherib ruled Assyria 705-681 B.C., and this event probably took place in 701 B.C. [x] **18.16** *doorposts*: One possible meaning for the difficult Hebrew text. [y] **18.22** *worship*: Hezekiah actually had torn down the places where idols were worshiped, and he had told the people to worship the LORD at the one place of worship in Jerusalem. But the Assyrian leader was confused and thought these were also places where the LORD was supposed to be worshiped.

Jerusalem and Judah to worship at
that one place?
23The king of Assyria wants to
make a bet with you people. He will
give you two thousand horses, if you
have enough troops to ride them.
24How could you even defeat our
lowest ranking officer, when you
have to depend on Egypt for chariots and cavalry? 25Don't forget
that it was the LORD who sent me
here with orders to destroy your nation!
26Eliakim, Shebna, and Joah said, "Sir,
we don't want the people listening from
the city wall to understand what you are
saying. So please speak to us in Aramaic instead of Hebrew."
27The Assyrian army commander answered, "My king sent me to speak to
everyone, not just to you leaders. These
people will soon have to eat their own
body waste and drink their own urine!
And so will the three of you."
28Then, in a voice loud enough
for everyone to hear, he shouted in Hebrew:
Listen to what the great king of
Assyria says! 29Don't be fooled by
Hezekiah. He can't save you. 30Don't
trust him when he tells you that the
LORD will protect you from the king
of Assyria. 31Stop listening to
Hezekiah! Pay attention to my
king. Surrender to him. He will let
you keep your own vineyards,
fig trees, and cisterns 32for a while.
Then he will come and take you
away to a country just like yours,
where you can plant vineyards,
raise your own grain, and have
plenty of olive oil and honey.
Believe me, you won't starve
there.
Hezekiah claims the LORD will
save you. But don't be fooled by him.
33Were any other gods able to defend their land against the king of
Assyria? 34What happened to the
gods of Hamath and Arpad? What
about the gods of Sepharvaim,
Hena, and Ivvah? Were the gods of
Samaria able to protect their land
against the Assyrian forces? 35None
of these gods kept their people safe
from the king of Assyria. Do you
think the LORD your God can do any
better?
36-37Eliakim, Shebna, and Joah had
been warned by King Hezekiah not to
answer the Assyrian commander. So
they tore their clothes in sorrow and reported to Hezekiah everything the commander had said.

Hezekiah Asks Isaiah the Prophet for Advice

(Isaiah 37.1-13)

19 As soon as Hezekiah heard the
news, he tore off his clothes in
sorrow and put on sackcloth. Then he
went into the temple of the LORD. 2He
told Prime Minister Eliakim, Assistant
Prime Minister Shebna, and the senior
priests to dress in sackcloth and tell the
prophet Isaiah:
3These are difficult and disgraceful times. Our nation is like a woman
too weak to give birth, when it's
time for her baby to be born. 4Please
pray for those of us who are left
alive. The king of Assyria sent his
army commander to insult the living
God. Perhaps the LORD heard what
he said and will do something, if you
will pray.
5When these leaders went to Isaiah,
6he told them that the LORD had this
message for Hezekiah:
I am the LORD. Don't worry about
the insulting things that have been
said about me by these messengers
from the king of Assyria. 7I will upset him with rumors about what's
happening in his own country. He
will go back, and there I will make
him die a violent death.
8Meanwhile, the commander of the
Assyrian forces heard that his king had
left the town of Lachish and was now
attacking Libnah. So he went there.
9About this same time the king of
Assyria learned that King Tirhakah of
Ethiopia[z] was on his way to attack
him. Then the king of Assyria sent
some messengers with this note for
Hezekiah:
10Don't trust your God or be
fooled by his promise to defend
Jerusalem against me. 11You have
heard how we Assyrian kings have
completely wiped out other nations.
What makes you feel so safe? 12The
Assyrian kings before me destroyed
the towns of Gozan, Haran, Rezeph,
and everyone from Eden who lived
in Telassar. What good did their
gods do them? 13The kings of
Hamath, Arpad, Sepharvaim, Hena,
and Ivvah have all disappeared.

Hezekiah Prays

(Isaiah 37.14-20)

14After Hezekiah had read the note
from the king of Assyria, he took it to
the temple and spread it out for the
LORD to see. 15He prayed:
LORD God of Israel, your throne is

[z] **19.9** *Ethiopia*: The Hebrew text has "Cush," which was a region south of Egypt that included parts of the present countries of Ethiopia and Sudan.

above the winged creatures.[a] You
created the heavens and the earth,
and you alone rule the kingdoms of
this world. 16But just look how Sennacherib has insulted you, the living
God.
17It is true, our LORD, that Assyrian
kings have turned nations into
deserts. 18They destroyed the idols of
wood and stone that the people of
those nations had made and worshiped. 19But you are our LORD and
our God! We ask you to keep us safe
from the Assyrian king. Then everyone in every kingdom on earth will
know that you are the only God.

The LORD's Answer to Hezekiah

(Isaiah 37.21-35)

20Isaiah went to Hezekiah and told
him that the LORD God of Israel had
said:
Hezekiah, I heard your prayer
about King Sennacherib of Assyria.
21Now this is what I say to that king:

The people of Jerusalem
hate and make fun of you;
they laugh
behind your back.

22 Sennacherib, you cursed,
shouted, and sneered at me,
the holy God of Israel.
23 You let your officials
insult me, the Lord.
And here is what you
have said about yourself,
"I led my chariots
to the highest heights
of Lebanon's mountains.
I went deep into its forest,
cutting down the best cedar
and cypress trees.
24 I dried up every stream
in the land of Egypt,
and I drank water
from wells I had dug."

25 Sennacherib, now listen
to me, the Lord.
I planned all this long ago.
And you don't even realize
that I alone am the one
who decided that you
would do these things.
I let you make ruins
of fortified cities.
26 Their people became weak,
terribly confused.
They were like wild flowers
or tender young grass
growing on a flat roof,
scorched before it matures.[b]
27 I know all about you,
even how fiercely angry
you are with me.
28 I have seen your pride
and the tremendous hatred
you have for me.
Now I will put a hook
in your nose,
a bit in your mouth,[c]
then I will send you back
to where you came from.

29Hezekiah, I will tell you what's
going to happen. This year you will
eat crops that grow on their own,
and the next year you will eat whatever springs up where those crops
grew. But the third year you will
plant grain and vineyards, and you
will eat what you harvest. 30Those
who survive in Judah will be like a
vine that puts down deep roots
and bears fruit. 31I, the LORD All-
Powerful, will see to it that some
who live in Jerusalem will survive.
32I promise that the king of Assyria won't get into Jerusalem, or
shoot an arrow into the city, or even
surround it and prepare to attack.
33As surely as I am the LORD, he will
return by the way he came and will
never enter Jerusalem. 34I will protect it for myself and for my servant
David.

The Death of King Sennacherib

(Isaiah 37.36-38)

35That same night the LORD sent an
angel to the camp of the Assyrians, and
he killed one hundred eighty-five thousand of them. And so the next morning,
the camp was full of dead bodies. 36Af-
ter this King Sennacherib went back to
Assyria and lived in the city of Nineveh.
37One day he was worshiping in the
temple of his god Nisroch, when his
sons, Adrammelech and Sharezer, killed
him with their swords. They escaped to
the land of Ararat, and his son Esarhaddon became king.[d]

Hezekiah Gets Sick and Almost Dies

(2 Chronicles 32.24-26; Isaiah 38.1-8, 21, 22)

20 About this time, Hezekiah got
sick and was almost dead. Isaiah
the prophet went in and told him, "The
LORD says you won't ever get well. You

[a] **19.15** *winged creatures*: Two winged creatures made of gold were on the top of the sacred chest and were symbols of the LORD's throne on earth (see Exodus 25.18; 2 Samuel 6.2).
[b] **19.26** *tender young grass . . . matures*: Many of the houses had roofs made of packed earth. Grass would sometimes grow out of the roof, but would die quickly because of the sun and hot winds.
[c] **19.28** *I will put . . . your mouth*: This is how the Assyrians treated their prisoners, and now the LORD will treat Sennacherib the same way.
[d] **19.37** *Esarhaddon became king*: Ruled Assyria 681-669 B.C.

are going to die, so you had better start
doing what needs to be done."
2 Hezekiah turned toward the wall
and prayed, 3 "Don't forget that I have
been faithful to you, LORD. I have
obeyed you with all my heart, and I do
whatever you say is right." After this, he
cried hard.
4 Before Isaiah got to the middle court
of the palace, 5 the LORD sent him back
to Hezekiah with this message:

> Hezekiah, you are the ruler of my
> people, and I am the LORD God, who
> was worshiped by your ancestor
> David. I heard you pray, and I saw
> you cry. I will heal you, so that three
> days from now you will be able to
> worship in my temple. 6 I will let you
> live fifteen years more, while I pro-
> tect you and your city from the king
> of Assyria. I will defend this city as
> an honor to me and to my servant
> David.

7 Then Isaiah said to the king's servants, "Bring some mashed figs and
place them on the king's open sore. He
will then get well."
8 Hezekiah asked Isaiah, "Can you
prove that the LORD will heal me, so that
I can worship in his temple in three
days?"
9 Isaiah replied, "The LORD will prove
to you that he will keep his promise.
Will the shadow made by the setting sun
on the stairway go forward ten steps or
back ten steps?"[e]
10 "It's normal for the sun to go forward," Hezekiah answered. "But how
can it go back?"
11 Isaiah prayed, and the LORD made
the shadow go back ten steps on the
stairway built for King Ahaz.[f]

The LORD Is Still with Hezekiah

(Isaiah 39.1-8)

12 Merodach[g] Baladan, the son of Baladan, was now king of Babylonia.[h] And
when he learned that Hezekiah had
been sick, he sent messengers with letters and a gift for him. 13 Hezekiah welcomed[i] the messengers and showed
them all the silver, the gold, the spices,
and the fine oils that were in his storehouse. He even showed them where he
kept his weapons. Nothing in his palace
or in his entire kingdom was kept hidden from them.
14 Isaiah asked Hezekiah, "Where did
these men come from? What did they
want?"
"They came all the way from Babylonia," Hezekiah answered.
15 "What did you show them?" Isaiah
asked.
Hezekiah answered, "I showed them
everything in my kingdom."
16 Then Isaiah told Hezekiah:

> I have a message for you from the
> LORD. 17 One day everything you and
> your ancestors have stored up will
> be taken to Babylonia. The LORD has
> promised that nothing will be left.
> 18 Some of your own sons will be
> taken to Babylonia, where they will
> be disgraced and made to serve in
> the king's palace.

19 Hezekiah thought, "At least our nation will be at peace for a while." So he
told Isaiah, "The message you brought
me from the LORD is good."

Hezekiah Dies

(2 Chronicles 32.32, 33)

20 Everything else Hezekiah did while
he was king, including how he made the
upper pool and tunnel to bring water
into Jerusalem, is written in *The History
of the Kings of Judah.* 21 Hezekiah died,
and his son Manasseh became king.

King Manasseh of Judah

(2 Chronicles 33.1-20)

21 Manasseh was twelve years old
when he became king of Judah,
and he ruled fifty-five years from
Jerusalem. His mother was Hephzibah.
2 Manasseh disobeyed the LORD by following the disgusting customs of the nations that the LORD had forced out of Israel. 3 He rebuilt the local shrines that
his father Hezekiah had torn down. He
built altars for the god Baal and set up a
sacred pole for worshiping the goddess
Asherah, just as King Ahab of Israel had
done. And he faithfully worshiped the
stars in heaven.
4 In the temple, where only the LORD
was supposed to be worshiped, Manasseh built altars for pagan gods 5 and
for the stars. He placed these altars in
both courts of the temple, 6-7 and even
set up the pole for Asherah there. Manasseh practiced magic and witchcraft;
he asked fortunetellers for advice and
sacrificed his own son. He did many sinful things and made the LORD very angry.
Years ago the LORD had told David
and his son Solomon:

> Jerusalem is the place I prefer
> above all others in Israel. It belongs
> to me, and there I will be worshiped
> forever. 8 If my people will faithfully
> obey all the commands in the Law of

[e] **20.9** *Will . . . steps*: One possible meaning for the difficult Hebrew text. [f] **20.11** *the shadow . . . Ahaz*: One possible meaning for the difficult Hebrew text. [g] **20.12** *Merodach*: The Hebrew text has "Berodach," another spelling of the name. [h] **20.12** *Merodach Baladan . . . Babylonia*: Ruled Babylonia 722-710 and 704-703 B.C. [i] **20.13** *welcomed*: Or "listened to."

my servant Moses, I will never make
them leave the land I gave to their
ancestors.
9But the people of Judah disobeyed
the LORD. They listened to Manasseh
and did even more sinful things than the
nations the LORD had wiped out.
10One day the LORD said to some of
his prophets:
11King Manasseh has done more
disgusting things than the Amorites,[j] and he has led my people to
sin by forcing them to worship his
idols. 12Now I, the LORD God of Israel, will destroy both Jerusalem
and Judah! People will hear about it
but won't believe it. 13Jerusalem is
as sinful as Ahab and the people of
Samaria were. So I will wipe out
Jerusalem and be done with it, just
as someone wipes water off a plate
and turns it over to dry.
14I will even get rid of my people
who survive. They will be defeated
and robbed by their enemies. 15My
people have done what I hate and
have not stopped making me angry
since their ancestors left Egypt.
16Manasseh was guilty of causing the
people of Judah to sin and disobey the
LORD. He also refused to protect innocent people—he even let so many of
them be killed[k] that their blood filled
the streets of Jerusalem.
17Everything else Manasseh did while
he was king, including his terrible sins,
is written in *The History of the Kings of
Judah*. 18He died and was buried in Uzza
Garden near his palace, and his son
Amon became king.

King Amon of Judah
(2 Chronicles 33.21-25)

19Amon was twenty-two years old
when he became king of Judah, and he
ruled from Jerusalem for two years. His
mother Meshullemeth was the daughter
of Haruz from Jotbah. 20Amon disobeyed the LORD, just as his father Manasseh had done. 21Amon worshiped the
idols Manasseh had made and 22refused
to be faithful to the LORD, the God his
ancestors had worshiped.
23Some of Amon's officials plotted
against him and killed him in his
palace. 24-26He was buried in Uzza Garden. Soon after that, the people of Judah
killed the murderers of Amon, then they
made his son Josiah king.
Everything else Amon did while he
was king is written in *The History of the
Kings of Judah*.

King Josiah of Judah
(2 Chronicles 34.1, 2)

22 Josiah was eight years old when
he became king of Judah, and he
ruled thirty-one years from Jerusalem.
His mother Jedidah was the daughter of
Adaiah from Bozkath. 2Josiah always
obeyed the LORD, just as his ancestor
David had done.

Hilkiah Finds *The Book of God's Law*
(2 Chronicles 34.8-28)

3After Josiah had been king for eighteen years, he told Shaphan,[l] one of his
highest officials:
Go to the LORD's temple 4and ask
Hilkiah the high priest to collect
from the guards all the money that
the people have donated. 5Have
Hilkiah give it to the men supervising the repairs to the temple. They
can use some of the money to pay
6the workers, and with the rest of it
they can buy wood and stone for the
repair work. 7They are honest, so we
won't ask them to keep track of the
money.
8While Shaphan was at the temple,
Hilkiah handed him a book and said,
"Look what I found here in the temple—
The Book of God's Law."
Shaphan read it, 9then went back to
Josiah and reported, "Your officials collected the money in the temple and gave
it to the men supervising the repairs.
10But there's something else, Your
Majesty. The priest Hilkiah gave me this
book." Then Shaphan read it out loud.
11When Josiah heard what was in *The
Book of God's Law*, he tore his clothes
in sorrow. 12At once he called together
Hilkiah, Shaphan, Ahikam son of
Shaphan, Achbor son of Micaiah, and
his own servant Asaiah. He said, 13"The
LORD must be furious with me and
everyone else in Judah, because our ancestors did not obey the laws written in
this book. Go find out what the LORD
wants us to do."
14The five men left right away and
went to talk with Huldah the prophet.
Her husband was Shallum,[m] who was in
charge of the king's clothes. Huldah
lived in the northern part of Jerusalem,
and when they met in her home, 15she
said:
You were sent here by King
Josiah, and this is what the LORD
God of Israel says to him: 16"Josiah, I
am the LORD! And I will see to it that
this country and everyone living in it
will be destroyed. It will happen just

[j]21.11 *Amorites*: Here used in the general sense of nations that lived in Canaan before the Israelites. [k]21.16 *He also refused . . . killed*: Or "He killed so many innocent people." [l]22.3 *Shaphan*: Hebrew "Shaphan son of Azaliah son of Meshullam." [m]22.14 *Shallum*: Hebrew "Shallum son of Tikvah son of Harhas."

as this book says. 17 The people of Judah have rejected me. They have offered sacrifices to foreign gods and have worshiped their own idols. I cannot stand it any longer. I am furious.

18 "Josiah, listen to what I am going to do. 19 I noticed how sad you were when you read that this country and its people would be completely wiped out. You even tore your clothes in sorrow, and I heard you cry. 20 So I will let you die in peace, before I destroy this place."

The men left and took Huldah's answer back to Josiah.

Josiah Reads *The Book of God's Law*

(2 Chronicles 34.29-33)

23 King Josiah called together the older leaders of Judah and Jerusalem. 2 Then he went to the LORD's temple, together with the people of Judah and Jerusalem, the priests, and the prophets. Finally, when everybody was there, he read aloud *The Book of God's Law*[n] that had been found in the temple.

3 After Josiah had finished reading, he stood by one of the columns. He asked the people to promise in the LORD's name to faithfully obey the LORD and to follow his commands. The people agreed to do everything written in the book.

Josiah Follows the Teachings of God's Law

(2 Chronicles 34.3-7)

4 Josiah told Hilkiah the priest, the assistant priests, and the guards at the temple door to go into the temple and bring out the things used to worship Baal, Asherah, and the stars. Josiah had these things burned in Kidron Valley just outside Jerusalem, and he had the ashes carried away to the town of Bethel.

5 Josiah also got rid of the pagan priests at the local shrines in Judah and around Jerusalem. These were the men that the kings of Judah had appointed to offer sacrifices to Baal and to the sun, moon, and stars. 6 Josiah had the sacred pole[o] for Asherah brought out of the temple and taken to Kidron Valley, where it was burned. He then had its ashes ground into dust and scattered over the public cemetery there. 7 He had the buildings torn down where the male prostitutes[p] lived next to the temple, and where the women wove sacred robes[q] for the idol of Asherah.

8 In almost every town in Judah, priests had been offering sacrifices to the LORD at local shrines.[r] Josiah brought these priests to Jerusalem and had their shrines made unfit for worship—every shrine from Geba just north of Jerusalem to Beersheba in the south. He even tore down the shrine at Beersheba that was just to the left of Joshua Gate, which was named after the highest official of the city. 9 Those local priests could not serve at the LORD's altar in Jerusalem, but they were allowed to eat sacred bread,[s] just like the priests from Jerusalem.

10 Josiah sent some men to Hinnom Valley just outside Jerusalem with orders to make the altar there unfit for worship. That way, people could no longer use it for sacrificing their children to the god Molech. 11 He also got rid of the horses that the kings of Judah used in their ceremonies to worship the sun, and he destroyed the chariots along with them. The horses had been kept near the entrance to the LORD's temple, in a courtyard[t] close to where an official named Nathan-Melech lived.

12 Some of the kings of Judah, especially Manasseh, had built altars in the two courts of the temple and in the room that Ahaz had built on the palace roof. Josiah had these altars torn down and smashed to pieces, and he had the pieces thrown into Kidron Valley, just outside Jerusalem. 13 After that, he closed down the shrines that Solomon had built east of Jerusalem and south of Spoil Hill to honor Astarte the disgusting goddess of Sidon, Chemosh the disgusting god of Moab, and Milcom the disgusting god of Ammon.[u] 14 He tore down the stone images of foreign gods and cut down the sacred pole used in the worship of Asherah. Then he had the whole area covered with human bones.[v]

15 But Josiah was not finished yet. At

[n] **23.2** *The Book of God's Law*: The Hebrew text has "The Book of God's Agreement," which is the same as "The Book of God's Law" in 22.8, 11. In traditional translations this is called "The Book of the Covenant." [o] **23.6** *sacred pole*: See the note at 13.6, 7. [p] **23.7** *male prostitutes*: Young men or boys sometimes served as prostitutes in the worship of Canaanite gods, but the LORD had forbidden the people of Israel and Judah to worship in this way (see Deuteronomy 23.17, 18). [q] **23.7** *sacred robes*: Or "coverings." [r] **23.8** *local shrines*: See the note at 12.3. [s] **23.9** *sacred bread*: The Hebrew text has "thin bread," which may be either the pieces of thin bread made without yeast to be eaten during the Passover Festival (see verses 21-23) or the baked flour used in sacrifices to give thanks to the LORD (see Leviticus 2.4, 5). [t] **23.11** *in a courtyard*: One possible meaning for the difficult Hebrew text. [u] **23.13** *the shrines . . . Ammon*: See 1 Kings 11.5-7. [v] **23.14** *Then he . . . human bones*: This made the whole area unfit for the worship of any god.

Bethel he destroyed the shrine and the
altar that Jeroboam son of Nebat had
built and that had caused the Israelites
to sin. Josiah had the shrine and the
Asherah pole burned and ground into
dust. 16As he looked around, he saw
graves on the hillside. He had the bones
in them dug up and burned on the altar,
so that it could no longer be used. This
happened just as God's prophet had
said when Jeroboam was standing at
the altar, celebrating a festival.[w]

Then Josiah saw the grave of the
prophet who had said this would happen 17and he asked,[x] "Whose grave is
that?"

Some people who lived nearby answered, "It belongs to the prophet from
Judah who told what would happen to
this altar."

18Josiah replied, "Then leave it alone.
Don't dig up his bones." So they did not
disturb his bones or the bones of the old
prophet from Israel who had also been
buried there.[y]

19Some of the Israelite kings had
made the LORD angry by building pagan
shrines all over Israel. So Josiah sent
troops to destroy these shrines just as
he had done to the one in Bethel. 20He
killed the priests who served at them
and burned their bones on the altars.

After all that, Josiah went back to
Jerusalem.

Josiah and the People of Judah Celebrate Passover

(2 Chronicles 35.1-19)

21Josiah told the people of Judah, "Celebrate Passover in honor of the LORD
your God, just as it says in *The Book
of God's Law*."[z]

22This festival had not been celebrated
in this way since kings ruled Israel and
Judah. 23But in Josiah's eighteenth year
as king of Judah, everyone came to
Jerusalem to celebrate Passover.

The LORD Is Still Angry at the People of Judah

24Josiah got rid of every disgusting
person and thing in Judah and Jerusalem—including magicians, fortunetellers, and idols. He did his best to obey
every law written in the book that the
priest Hilkiah found in the LORD's temple. 25No other king before or after
Josiah tried as hard as he did to obey
the Law of Moses.

26But the LORD was still furious with
the people of Judah because Manasseh
had done so many things to make him
angry. 27The LORD said, "I will desert the
people of Judah, just as I deserted the
people of Israel. I will reject Jerusalem,
even though I chose it to be mine. And I
will abandon this temple built to honor
me."

Josiah Dies in Battle

(2 Chronicles 35.20—36.1)

28Everything else Josiah did while he
was king is written in *The History of the
Kings of Judah*. 29During Josiah's rule,
King Neco of Egypt led his army north
to the Euphrates River to help the king
of Assyria. Josiah led his troops north to
fight Neco, but when they met in battle
at Megiddo, Josiah was killed.[a] 30A few
of Josiah's servants put his body in a
chariot and took it back to Jerusalem,
where they buried it in his own tomb.
Then the people of Judah found his son
Jehoahaz and poured olive oil on his
head to show that he was their new
king.

King Jehoahaz of Judah

(2 Chronicles 36.2-4)

31Jehoahaz was twenty-three years
old when he became king of Judah, and
he ruled from Jerusalem only three
months. His mother Hamutal was the
daughter of Jeremiah from Libnah. 32Je-
hoahaz disobeyed the LORD, just as
some of his ancestors had done.

33King Neco of Egypt had Jehoahaz
arrested and put in prison at Riblah[b]
near Hamath. Then he forced the people
of Judah to pay him almost four tons of
silver and about seventy-five pounds of
gold as taxes. 34Neco appointed Josiah's
son Eliakim king of Judah, and changed
his name to Jehoiakim. He took Jehoahaz as a prisoner to Egypt, where he
died.

35Jehoiakim forced the people of Judah to pay higher taxes, so he could
give Neco the silver and gold he demanded.

King Jehoiakim of Judah

(2 Chronicles 36.5-8)

36Jehoiakim was twenty-five years old
when he was appointed king, and he
ruled eleven years from Jerusalem. His
mother Zebidah was the daughter of
Pedaiah from Rumah. 37Jehoiakim disobeyed the LORD by following the example of his ancestors.

[w]**23.16** *just . . . festival*: See 1 Kings 13.1, 2. [x]**23.16,17** *said when Jeroboam . . . asked*: One ancient translation; Hebrew "said. 17Then Josiah asked." [y]**23.18** *old prophet . . . there*: See 1 Kings 13.11-32. [z]**23.21** *The Book of God's Law*: See the note at verse 2. [a]**23.29** *killed*: At this time, King Neco of Egypt (609-595 B.C.) was fighting on the side of the Assyrians. He marched north to fight the Babylonian army and help Assyria keep control of its land. Since Josiah considered Assyria an enemy, he set out to stop Neco and the Egyptian troops.
[b]**23.33** *Riblah*: An important town in Syria on the Orontes River.

24 During Jehoiakim's rule, King Nebuchadnezzar of Babylonia[c] invaded and took control of Judah. Jehoiakim obeyed Nebuchadnezzar for three years, but then he rebelled.

2 At that time, the LORD started sending troops to rob and destroy towns in Judah. Some of these troops were from Babylonia, and others were from Syria, Moab, and Ammon. The LORD had sent his servants the prophets to warn Judah about this, 3 and now he was making it happen. The country of Judah was going to be wiped out, because Manasseh had sinned 4 and caused many innocent people to die. The LORD would not forgive this.

5 Everything else Jehoiakim did while he was king is written in *The History of the Kings of Judah*. 6 Jehoiakim died, and his son Jehoiachin became king.

7 King Nebuchadnezzar defeated King Neco of Egypt and took control of his land from the Egyptian Gorge all the way north to the Euphrates River. So Neco never invaded Judah again.[d]

King Jehoiachin of Judah Is Taken to Babylon

(2 Chronicles 36.9, 10)

8 Jehoiachin was eighteen years old when he became king of Judah, and he ruled only three months from Jerusalem. His mother Nehushta was the daughter of Elnathan from Jerusalem. 9 Jehoiachin disobeyed the LORD, just as his father Jehoiakim had done.

10 King Nebuchadnezzar of Babylonia sent troops to attack Jerusalem soon after Jehoiachin became king. 11 During the attack, Nebuchadnezzar himself arrived at the city. 12 Jehoiachin immediately surrendered, together with his mother and his servants, as well as his army officers and officials. Then Nebuchadnezzar had Jehoiachin arrested. These things took place in the eighth year of Nebuchadnezzar's rule in Babylonia.[e]

13 The LORD had warned[f] that someday the treasures would be taken from the royal palace and from the temple, including the gold objects that Solomon had made for the temple. And that's exactly what Nebuchadnezzar ordered his soldiers to do. 14 He also led away as prisoners the Jerusalem officials, the military leaders, and the skilled workers—ten thousand in all. Only the very poorest people were left in Judah.

15 Nebuchadnezzar took Jehoiachin to Babylon, along with his mother, his wives, his officials, and the most important leaders of Judah. 16 He also led away seven thousand soldiers, one thousand skilled workers, and anyone who would be useful in battle.

17 Then Nebuchadnezzar appointed Jehoiachin's uncle Mattaniah king of Judah and changed his name to Zedekiah.

King Zedekiah of Judah

(2 Chronicles 36.11-16; Jeremiah 52.1-3)

18 Zedekiah was twenty-one years old when he was appointed king of Judah, and he ruled from Jerusalem for eleven years. His mother Hamutal was the daughter of Jeremiah from Libnah. 19 Zedekiah disobeyed the LORD, just as Jehoiakim had done. 20 It was Zedekiah who finally rebelled against Nebuchadnezzar.

The people of Judah and Jerusalem had made the LORD so angry that he finally turned his back on them. That's why these horrible things were happening.

Jerusalem Is Captured and Destroyed

(2 Chronicles 36.17-21; Jeremiah 52.3-30)

25 In Zedekiah's ninth year as king, on the tenth day of the tenth month,[g] King Nebuchadnezzar of Babylonia led his entire army to attack Jerusalem. The troops set up camp outside the city and built ramps up to the city walls.

2-3 After a year and a half, all the food in Jerusalem was gone. Then on the ninth day of the fourth[h] month, 4 the Babylonian troops broke through the city wall.[i] That same night, Zedekiah and his soldiers tried to escape through the gate near the royal garden, even though they knew the enemy had the city surrounded. They headed toward the desert, 5 but the Babylonian troops caught up with them near Jericho. They arrested Zedekiah, but his soldiers scattered in every direction.

6 Zedekiah was taken to Riblah, where Nebuchadnezzar put him on trial and found him guilty. 7 Zedekiah's sons were killed right in front of him. His eyes were then poked out, and he was put in chains and dragged off to Babylon.

[c] **24.1** *King Nebuchadnezzar of Babylonia*: Ruled Babylonia 605-562 B.C. [d] **24.7** *again*: Nebuchadnezzar defeated the Egyptian army in 605 B.C. at the town of Carchemish. But a few years later, he was forced to retreat all the way back to Babylonia, which allowed Jehoiakim to rebel (see verse 1). [e] **24.12** *Babylonia*: These events took place in 597 B.C. [f] **24.13** *warned*: See 20.16-18. [g] **25.1** *tenth month*: Tebeth, the tenth month of the Hebrew calendar, from about mid-December to mid-January. [h] **25.2,3** *fourth*: This word is not in the Hebrew text here, but see the parallel in Jeremiah 52.5, 6. [i] **25.4** *wall*: Jerusalem was destroyed in 586 B.C.

8About a month later,[j] in Nebuchadnezzar's nineteenth year as king, Nebuzaradan, who was his official in charge
of the guards, arrived in Jerusalem.
9Nebuzaradan burned down the LORD's
temple, the king's palace, and every important building in the city, as well as all
the houses. 10Then he ordered the Babylonian soldiers to break down the
walls around Jerusalem. 11He led away
as prisoners the people left in the city,
including those who had become loyal
to Nebuchadnezzar. 12Only some of the
poorest people were left behind to work
the vineyards and the fields.
13The Babylonian soldiers took the
two bronze columns that stood in front
of the temple, the ten movable bronze
stands, and the large bronze bowl called
the Sea. They broke them into pieces so
they could take the bronze to Babylonia.
14They carried off the bronze things
used for worship at the temple, including the pans for hot ashes, and the shovels, snuffers, and also the dishes for incense, 15as well as the fire pans and the
sprinkling bowls. Nebuzaradan ordered
his soldiers to take everything made of
gold or silver.
16The pile of bronze from the
columns, the stands, and the large bowl
that Solomon had made for the temple
was too large to be weighed. 17Each column had been twenty-seven feet tall
with a bronze cap four and a half feet
high. These caps were decorated with
bronze designs—some of them like
chains and others like pomegranates.[k]
18Next, Nebuzaradan arrested Seraiah
the chief priest, Zephaniah his assistant,
and three temple officials. 19Then he arrested one of the army commanders, the
king's five personal advisors, and the officer in charge of gathering the troops
for battle. He also found sixty more soldiers who were still in Jerusalem. 20Neb-
uzaradan led them all to Riblah 21near
Hamath, where Nebuchadnezzar had
them killed.
The people of Judah no longer lived in
their own country.

Gedaliah Is Made Ruler of the People Left in Judah

(Jeremiah 40.7-9; 41.1-3)

22King Nebuchadnezzar appointed
Gedaliah son of Ahikam[l] to rule the few
people still living in Judah. 23When the
army officers and troops heard that
Gedaliah was their ruler, the officers
met with him at Mizpah. These men
were Ishmael son of Nethaniah, Johanan son of Kareah, Seraiah son of
Tanhumeth from Netophah, and Jaazaniah from Maacah.
24Gedaliah said to them, "Everything
will be fine, I promise. We don't need to
be afraid of the Babylonian rulers, if we
live here peacefully and do what Nebuchadnezzar says."
25Ishmael[m] was from the royal family.
And about two months after Gedaliah
began his rule,[n] Ishmael and ten other
men went to Mizpah. They killed
Gedaliah and his officials, including
those from Judah and those from Babylonia. 26After that, the army officers
and all the people in Mizpah, whether
important or not, were afraid of what
the Babylonians might do. So they left
Judah and went to Egypt.

Jehoiachin Is Set Free

(Jeremiah 52.31-34)

27Jehoiachin was a prisoner in Babylon for thirty-seven years. Then Evil-
Merodach became king of Babylonia,[o]
and in the first year of his rule, on the
twenty-seventh day of the twelfth
month,[p] he let Jehoiachin out of prison.
28Evil-Merodach was kind to Jehoiachin
and honored him more than any of the
other kings held prisoner there. 29Je-
hoiachin was even allowed to wear regular clothes, and he ate at the king's
table every day. 30As long as Jehoiachin
lived, he was paid a daily allowance to
buy whatever he needed.

[j]**25.8** *About a month later*: Hebrew "On the seventh day of the fifth month." [k]**25.17** *pomegranates*: A bright red fruit that looks like an apple. [l]**25.22** *Ahikam*: Hebrew "Ahikam son of Shaphan." [m]**25.25** *Ishmael*: Hebrew "Ishmael son of Nethaniah son of Elishama." [n]**25.25** *about two months . . . his rule*: Hebrew "in the seventh month." [o]**25.27** *Evil-Merodach . . . Babylonia*: The son of Nebuchadnezzar, who ruled Babylonia from 562 to 560 B.C. [p]**25.27** *twelfth month*: Adar, the twelfth month of the Hebrew calendar, from about mid-February to mid-March.

1 CHRONICLES

ABOUT THIS BOOK

First Chronicles is the first half of a single book that was divided into two parts, 1 and 2 Chronicles, because together they were too long to fit on one scroll. These two books retell the history of Israel from a slightly different viewpoint than that of Samuel and Kings, although many of the same stories are repeated.

King David is the most important person in the book of 1 Chronicles. He is the one who made Jerusalem the center for the worship of the Lord God, and who made sure the Lord was worshiped in the proper way. David is also honored as the founder of the temple, even though it was his son Solomon who actually built it.

Much of 1 Chronicles is made up of lists that trace the descendants of Adam to the time of King Saul (1–9). After reporting how Saul died (10), the rest of the book (11–29) focuses on King David, and these chapters can be divided into four parts. The first part (11–12) tells how David became king and made Jerusalem his capital city. This part also includes information about David's warriors and military officers. The second part (13–16) describes how David moved the sacred chest to its new home in Jerusalem. The third part (17–20) includes events during his rule, and the final part (21–29) describes his preparations for building the Lord's temple and his instructions to his son Solomon about the proper worship of the Lord.

In 1 Chronicles, David is used as an example of someone who faithfully worships and obeys the Lord. At the end of David's rule, he praises the Lord in front of everyone in Israel and says:

> *I praise you forever, LORD! You are the God our ancestor Jacob worshiped. Your power is great, and your glory is seen everywhere in heaven and on earth. You are king of the entire world, and you rule with strength and power.* *(29.10b-12a)*

A QUICK LOOK AT THIS BOOK

Descendants of Adam until the Time of King Saul (1.1—9.44)
The Death of Saul and His Sons (10.1-14)
David Becomes King of Israel and Captures Jerusalem (11.1-9)
David's Warriors (11.10—12.40)
The Sacred Chest Is Moved to Jerusalem (13.1—16.43)
Solomon Will Build the Lord's Temple (17.1-27)
David's Military Victories (18.1—20.8)
David's Preparations for Building the Temple (21.1—28.21)
The People Bring Gifts for Building the Temple (29.1-20)
Solomon Is Crowned King (29.21-25)
The Death of David (29.26-30)

The Descendants of Adam
(Genesis 5.1-32; 10.1-32; 11.10-32)

1 [1-4]Adam was the father of Seth, and
his descendants were Enosh, Kenan,
Mahalalel, Jared, Enoch, Methuselah,
Lamech, and Noah, who had three sons:
Shem, Ham, and Japheth.
[5]Japheth was the father of Gomer,
Magog, Madai, Javan, Tubal, Meshech,
and Tiras, and they were the ancestors
of the kingdoms named after them.

6Gomer was the ancestor of Ashkenaz,
Riphath,[a] and Togarmah. 7Javan was
the ancestor of Elishah, Tarshish, Kittim, and Dodanim.[b]
8Ham was the father of Ethiopia,[c]
Egypt, Put, and Canaan, and they were
the ancestors of the kingdoms named
after them. 9Ethiopia was the ancestor
of Seba, Havilah, Sabta, Raamah, and
Sabteca. Raamah was the ancestor of
Sheba and Dedan. 10Ethiopia was also
the father of Nimrod, the world's first
mighty warrior. 11Egypt was the ancestor of Ludim, Anamim, Lehabim, Naphtuhim, 12Pathrusim, Casluhim, and
Caphtorim, the ancestor of the Philistines.[d] 13Canaan's oldest son was Sidon; his other son was Heth. 14-16Ca-
naan was also the ancestor of the
Jebusites, the Amorites, the Girgashites,
the Hivites, and Arkites, the Sinites,
the Arvadites, the Zemarites, and the
Hamathites.
17Shem was the ancestor of Elam,
Asshur, Arpachshad, Lud, Aram, Uz,
Hul, Gether, and Meshech;[e] they were
the ancestors of the kingdoms named
after them. 18Arpachshad was Shelah's
father and Eber's grandfather. 19Eber
named his first son Peleg,[f] because in
his time the earth was divided into
tribal regions. Eber's second son was
Joktan, 20-23the ancestor of Almodad,
Sheleph, Hazarmaveth, Jerah, Hadoram,
Uzal, Diklah, Ebal, Abimael, Sheba,
Ophir, Havilah, and Jobab.
24-27Shem's descendants included
Arpachshad, Shelah, Eber, Peleg, Reu,
Serug, Nahor, Terah, and Abram, later
renamed Abraham.

Abraham's Family

(Genesis 25.1-4, 12-16)

28Abraham was the father of Isaac
and Ishmael.
29-31Ishmael had twelve sons, who
were born in the following order:
Nebaioth, Kedar, Adbeel, Mibsam,
Mishma, Dumah, Massa, Hadad, Tema,
Jetur, Naphish, and Kedemah.
32Abraham and his slave woman Keturah had six sons: Zimran, Jokshan,
Medan, Midian, Ishbak, and Shuah. Jokshan was the father of Sheba and
Dedan. 33Midian was the father of
Ephah, Epher, Hanoch, Abida, and Eldaah.

Esau's Family

(Genesis 36.1-14)

34Abraham's son Isaac was the father
of Esau and Jacob.[g] 35Esau was the
father of Eliphaz, Reuel, Jeush, Jalam,
and Korah. 36Eliphaz was the father of
Teman, Omar, Zephi, Gatam, Kenaz,
Timna, and Amalek. 37Reuel was the
father of Nahath, Zerah, Shammah, and
Mizzah.

The First Edomites and Their Kings

(Genesis 36.20-43)

38Seir was the father of Lotan, Shobal,
Zibeon, Anah, Dishon, Ezer, and Dishan. 39Lotan was the father of Hori and
Homam; Lotan's sister was Timna.
40Shobal was the father of Alvan,[h] Manahath, Ebal, Shephi, and Onam. Zibeon
was the father of Aiah and Anah.
41Anah was the father of Dishon and
the grandfather of Hemdan,[i] Eshban,
Ithran, and Cheran. 42Ezer was the
father of Bilhan, Zaavan, and Jaakan.[j]
Dishan[k] was the father of Uz and Aran.
43Before kings ruled in Israel, Bela
son of Beor ruled the country of Edom
from its capital of Dinhabah. 44After
Bela's death, Jobab son of Zerah from
Bozrah became king. 45After Jobab's
death, Husham from the land of Teman
became king. 46After Husham's death,
Hadad son of Bedad became king and
ruled from Avith. Earlier, Bedad had defeated the Midianites in the territory of
Moab. 47After Hadad's death, Samlah
from Masrekah became king; 48after
Samlah's death, Shaul from the town of
Rehoboth on the Euphrates River became king; 49and after Shaul's death,
Baal Hanan son of Achbor became king.
50After Baal Hanan's death, Hadad ruled
from Pai. His wife was Mehetabel, the
daughter of Matred and granddaughter
of Mezahab.
51The Edomite clans[l] were Timna,

[a]**1.6** *Riphath*: Most Hebrew manuscripts and two ancient translations (see also Genesis 10.2-5); some Hebrew manuscripts "Diphath." In Hebrew the letters "d" and "r" look almost exactly the same. [b]**1.7** *Dodanim*: Most Hebrew manuscripts and one ancient translation (see also Genesis 10.2-5); some Hebrew manuscripts "Rodanim." In Hebrew the letters "d" and "r" look almost exactly the same. [c]**1.8** *Ethiopia*: The Hebrew text has "Cush," which was a region south of Egypt that included parts of the present countries of Ethiopia and Sudan.
[d]**1.12** *Casluhim, and Caphtorim, the ancestor of the Philistines*: The Hebrew text has "Casluhim, the ancestor of the Philistines, and Caphtorim"; but see Jeremiah 47.4 and Amos 9.7. [e]**1.17** *Meshech*: Most Hebrew manuscripts; a few Hebrew manuscripts and some manuscripts of one ancient translation "Mash" (see also Genesis 10.21-31). [f]**1.19** *Peleg*: In Hebrew "Peleg" means "divided." [g]**1.34** *Jacob*: The Hebrew text has "Israel," which was Jacob's name after God renamed him. [h]**1.40** *Alvan*: Or "Alian." [i]**1.41** *Hemdan*: Most Hebrew manuscripts and some manuscripts of one ancient translation (see also Genesis 36.26); other Hebrew manuscripts "Hamran." [j]**1.42** *Jaakan*: Or "Akan" (see Genesis 36.27).
[k]**1.42** *Dishan*: The Hebrew text has "Dishon," another spelling of the name (see Genesis 36.28).
[l]**1.51** *The Edomite clans*: Or "The leaders of the Edomite clans."

Alvah,[m] Jetheth, [52]Oholibamah, Elah,
Pinon, [53]Kenaz, Teman, Mibzar, [54]Mag-
diel, and Iram.

The Descendants of Judah

2 [1-2]Jacob[n] was the father of twelve
sons: Reuben, Simeon, Levi, Judah,
Issachar, Zebulun, Dan, Joseph, Benjamin, Naphtali, Gad, and Asher.
[3]Judah and his Canaanite wife
Bathshua had three sons: Er, Onan, and
Shelah. But the LORD had Er put to
death, because he disobeyed and did
what the LORD hated. [4]Judah and his
daughter-in-law Tamar also had two
sons: Perez and Zerah.
[5]Perez was the father of Hezron and
Hamul. [6]Zerah was the father of Zimri,
Ethan, Heman, Calcol, and Darda.[o]
[7]Achan,[p] who was a descendant of
Zerah and the son of Carmi, caused
trouble for Israel, because he kept for
himself things that belonged only to the
LORD.[q] [8]Ethan's son was Azariah.

The Ancestors of King David

[9]Hezron was the father of Jerahmeel,
Ram, and Caleb.[r] [10]Ram was the father
of Amminadab and the grandfather of
Nahshon, a tribal leader of Judah. [11]Nah-
shon's descendants included Salma,
Boaz, [12]Obed, and Jesse. [13-15]Jesse had
seven sons, who were born in the following order: Eliab, Abinadab, Shimea,
Nethanel, Raddai, Ozem, and David.
[16]Jesse also had two daughters: Zeruiah
and Abigail. Zeruiah was the mother of
Abishai, Joab, and Asahel. [17]Abigail's
husband was Jether, who was a descendant of Ishmael, and their son was
Amasa.

The Descendants of Hezron

[18]Hezron's son Caleb married
Azubah, and their daughter was
Jerioth,[s] the mother of Jesher, Shobab,
and Ardon. [19]After the death of Azubah,
Caleb married Ephrath. Their son Hur
[20]was the father of Uri and the grandfather of Bezalel.
[21]When Hezron was sixty years old,
he married the daughter of Machir, who
settled the region of Gilead. Their son
Segub [22]was the father of Jair, who
ruled twenty-three villages in the region
of Gilead. [23]Some time later the nations
of Geshur and Aram captured sixty
towns in that region, including the villages that belonged to Jair, as well as
the town of Kenath and the nearby villages. Everyone from the region of
Gilead was a descendant of Machir.
[24]After the death of Hezron, Caleb
married Ephrath, his father's wife. Their
son was Ashhur,[t] who later settled the
town of Tekoa.

The Descendants of Jerahmeel

[25]Jerahmeel, Hezron's oldest son, was
the father of Ram, Bunah, Oren, Ozem,
and Ahijah. [26]Jerahmeel had a second
wife, Atarah, who gave birth to Onam.
[27]Ram was the father of Maaz, Jamin,
and Eker. [28]Onam was the father of
Shammai and Jada.
Shammai was the father of Nadab
and Abishur. [29]Abishur married Abihail,
and their two sons were Ahban and
Molid. [30]Nadab was the father of Seled
and Appaim. Seled had no children;
[31]Appaim's son was Ishi, the father of
Sheshan and the grandfather of Ahlai.
[32]Jada was the father of Jether and
Jonathan. Jether had no children, [33]but
Jonathan had two sons: Peleth and
Zaza.
[34-35]Sheshan had no sons, and so he
let one of his daughters marry Jarha, his
Egyptian slave. Their son was Attai,
[36]the father of Nathan and the grandfather of Zabad. [37-41]Zabad's descendants included Ephlal, Obed, Jehu,
Azariah, Helez, Eleasah, Sismai, Shallum, Jekamiah, and Elishama.

The Descendants of Caleb

[42]Caleb, Jerahmeel's brother, had the
following descendants: Mesha,[u] Ziph,
Mareshah,[v] Hebron, [43]and Hebron's
four sons, Korah, Tappuah, Rekem, and
Shema. [44]Shema was the father of Ra-
ham and the grandfather of Jorkeam.
Rekem was the father of Shammai, [45]the
grandfather of Maon, and the great-
grandfather of Bethzur.
[46]Ephah was one of Caleb's wives,[w]
and their sons were Haran, Moza, and
Gazez. Haran named his son after his
brother Gazez. [47]Ephah was the daughter of Jahdai, who was also the father of
Regem, Jotham, Geshan, Pelet, and
Shaaph.[x]
[48]Maacah was another of Caleb's

[m] **1.51** *Alvah*: Or "Aliah." [n] **2.1,2** *Jacob*: See the note at 1.34. [o] **2.6** *Darda*: Most Hebrew manuscripts and two ancient translations (see also 1 Kings 4.30, 31); some Hebrew manuscripts "Dara." [p] **2.7** *Achan*: The Hebrew text has "Achar," which means "trouble." [q] **2.7** *Achan . . . the LORD*: See Joshua 7.1-26. [r] **2.9** *Caleb*: The Hebrew text has "Chelubai," another form of the name. [s] **2.18** *married Azubah . . . Jerioth*: One possible meaning for the difficult Hebrew text. [t] **2.24** *After the death of Hezron . . . Ashhur*: Two ancient translations; Hebrew "After Hezron died in Caleb-Ephrathah, Abijah his wife gave birth to Ashhur." [u] **2.42** *Mesha*: Hebrew; one ancient translation "Mareshah." [v] **2.42** *following descendants . . . Mareshah*: One possible meaning for the difficult Hebrew text. [w] **2.46** *wives*: See the note at 3.9. [x] **2.47** *Shaaph*: One possible meaning for the difficult Hebrew text of verse 47.

wives,[y] and their sons were Sheber and Tirhanah. 49Later, they had two more sons: Shaaph the father of Madmannah, and Sheva the father of Machbenah and Gibea. Caleb's daughter was Achsah. 50-51All of these were Caleb's descendants.

Hur, the oldest son of Caleb and Ephrath, had three sons: Shobal, Salma, and Hareph, who settled the town of Beth-Gader. 52Shobal, who settled the town of Kiriath-Jearim, was the ancestor of Haroeh, half of the Menuhoth clan, 53and the clans that lived near Kiriath-Jearim; they were the Ithrites, the Puthites, the Shumathites, and the Mishraites. The Zorathites and the Eshtaolites were descendants of the Mishraites.

54Salma settled the town of Bethlehem and was the ancestor of the Netophathites, the people of Atroth-Bethjoab, half of the Manahathite clan, and the Zorites. 55Salma was also the ancestor of the clans in Jabez that kept the court and government records; they were the Tirathites, the Shimeathites, and the Sucathites. These clans were the descendants of Hammath the Kenite, who was also the ancestor of the Rechabites.

The Descendants of King David

3 1-4King David ruled from Hebron for seven years and six months, and during that time he had six sons, who were born in the following order: Amnon, Daniel, Absalom, Adonijah, Shephatiah, and Ithream. Ahinoam from Jezreel was the mother of Amnon; Abigail from Carmel was the mother of Daniel; Maacah daughter of King Talmai of Geshur was the mother of Absalom; Haggith was the mother of Adonijah; Abital was the mother of Shephatiah; and Eglah was the mother of Ithream.

David then ruled from Jerusalem for thirty-three years, 5and during that time, he had thirteen more sons. His wife Bathsheba[z] daughter of Ammiel gave birth to Shimea, Shobab, Nathan, and Solomon. 6-8David's other sons included Ibhar, Elishua,[a] Eliphelet, Nogah, Nepheg, Japhia, Elishama, Eliada, and Eliphelet. 9David's other wives[b] also gave birth to sons. Tamar was his daughter.

The Descendants of King Solomon

10-15Solomon's descendants included the following kings: Rehoboam, Abijah, Asa, Jehoshaphat, Jehoram,[c] Ahaziah, Joash, Amaziah, Azariah, Jotham, Ahaz, Hezekiah, Manasseh, Amon, and Josiah and his four sons, Johanan, Jehoiakim, Zedekiah, and Jehoahaz.[d] 16Jehoiakim was the father of Jehoiachin and Zedekiah.

17Jehoiachin, who was taken to Babylon as a prisoner, had seven sons: Shealtiel, 18Malchiram, Pedaiah, Shenazzar, Jekamiah, Hoshama, and Nedabiah. 19Pedaiah had two sons: Zerubbabel and Shimei. Zerubbabel was the father of Meshullam, Hananiah, and Shelomith their sister. 20He also had five other sons: Hashubah, Ohel, Berechiah, Hasadiah, and Jushabhesed. 21Hananiah's descendants were Pelatiah, Jeshaiah, Rephaiah, Arnan, Obadiah, and Shecaniah,[e] 22the father of Shemaiah and the grandfather of Hattush, Igal, Bariah, Neariah, and Shaphat. 23Neariah was the father of Elioenai, Hizkiah, and Azrikam. 24Elioenai was the father of Hodaviah, Eliashib, Pelaiah, Akkub, Johanan, Delaiah, and Anani.

The Descendants of Judah

4 Judah was the father of five sons: Perez, Hezron, Carmi, Hur, and Shobal. 2Shobal was the father of Reaiah, the grandfather of Jahath, and the great-grandfather of Ahumai and Lahad. These men all belonged to the Zorathite clan.

3-4Hur was the oldest son of Caleb and Ephrath. Some of his descendants settled the town of Bethlehem. Hur's other descendants included Etam, Penuel, and Ezer. Etam's sons[f] were Jezreel, Ishma, and Idbash, and his daughter was Hazzelelponi. Penuel settled the town of Gedor, and Ezer settled the town of Hushah.

5Ashhur, who settled the town of Tekoa, had two wives: Helah and Naarah. 6Ashhur and Naarah were the parents of Ahuzzam, Hepher, Temeni, and Haahashtari. 7Ashhur and Helah were the parents of Zereth, Izhar, and Ethnan.

8Koz, the father of Anub and Zobebah, was also the ancestor of the clans of Aharhel, the son of Harum.

[y]**2.48** *wives*: See the note at 3.9. [z]**3.5** *Bathsheba*: Two ancient translations (see also 2 Samuel 11); Hebrew "Bathshua." [a]**3.6-8** *Elishua*: Some Hebrew manuscripts and some manuscripts of one ancient translation (see also 2 Samuel 5.14, 15); most Hebrew manuscripts "Elishama." [b]**3.9** *other wives*: This translates a Hebrew word for women who were legally bound to a man, but without the full privileges of a wife. [c]**3.10-15** *Jehoram*: The Hebrew text has "Joram," another spelling of the name. [d]**3.10-15** *Jehoahaz*: The Hebrew text has "Shallum," probably another name for Jehoahaz (see also 2 Kings 23.30). [e]**3.21** *Shecaniah*: One possible meaning for the difficult Hebrew text of verse 21. [f]**4.3,4** *Etam's sons*: Some manuscripts of one ancient translation; Hebrew "Etam's ancestors."

9 Jabez was a man who got his name
because of the pain he caused his
mother during birth.[g] But he was still
the most respected son in his family.
10 One day he prayed to Israel's God,
"Please bless me and give me a lot of
land. Be with me so I will be safe from
harm."[h] And God did just what Jabez
had asked.

11 Chelub was the brother of Shuhah
and the father of Mehir. Later, Mehir
had a son, Eshton, 12 whose three sons
were Bethrapha, Paseah, and Tehinnah.
It was Tehinnah who settled the town of
Nahash.[i] These men and their families
lived in the town of Recah.

13 Kenaz was the father of Othniel and
Seraiah. Othniel had two sons: Hathath
and Meonothai,[j] 14 who was the father of
Ophrah. Seraiah was the father of Joab,
who settled a place called "Valley of
Crafts"[k] because the people who lived
there were experts in making things.

15 Caleb son of Jephunneh had three
sons: Iru, Elah, and Naam. Elah was the
father of Kenaz.

16 Jehallelel was the father of Ziph,
Ziphah, Tiria, and Asarel.

17-18 Ezrah was the father of Jether,
Mered, Epher, and Jalon. Mered was
married to Bithiah the daughter of the
king of Egypt. They had a daughter
named Miriam and two sons: Shammai
and Ishbah. It was Ishbah who settled
the town of Eshtemoa. Mered was also
married to a woman from the tribe of
Judah, and their sons were Jered, Heber,
and Jekuthiel. Jered settled the town of
Gedor; Heber settled the town of Soco;
and Jekuthiel settled the town of
Zanoah.

19 A man named Hodiah was married
to the sister of Naham. Hodiah's descendants included Keilah of the Gar-
mite clan and Eshtemoa of the Maaca-
thite clan.

20 Shimon was the father of Amnon,
Rinnah, Benhanan, and Tilon.

Ishi was the father of Zoheth and
Benzoheth.

21-22 Judah also had a son named Shelah, whose descendants included Jokim
and the people of the town of Cozeba,
as well as Er who settled the town of
Lecah and Laadah who settled the town
of Mareshah. The people who lived in
Beth-Ashbea were also descendants of
Shelah, and they were experts in weav-
ing cloth. Shelah was the ancestor of
Joash and Saraph, two men who married Moabite women and then settled
near Bethlehem[l]—but these family
records are very old. 23 The members of
these clans were the potters who lived
in the towns of Netaim and Gederah
and worked for the king.

The Descendants of Simeon

24 Simeon had five sons: Nemuel,
Jamin, Jarib, Zerah, and Shaul. 25 The
descendants of Shaul included his son
Shallum, his grandson Mibsam, and his
great-grandson Mishma. 26 The descendants of Mishma included his son Ham-
muel, his grandson Zaccur, and his
great-grandson Shimei. 27 Shimei had
sixteen sons and six daughters. But his
brothers did not have as many children,
so the Simeon tribe was smaller than
the Judah tribe.

28-31 Before David became king, the
people of the Simeon tribe lived in the
following towns: Beersheba, Moladah, Hazar-Shual, Bilhah, Ezem, To-
lad, Bethuel, Hormah, Ziklag, Beth-
Marcaboth, Hazarsusim, Bethbiri, and
Shaaraim. 32 They also lived in the five
villages of Etam, Ain, Rimmon, Tochen,
and Ashan, 33 as well as in the nearby
villages as far as the town of Baal.
These are the places where Simeon's
descendants had settled, according to
their own family records.

34-38 As their families and clans became larger, the people of Simeon had
the following leaders: Meshobab, Jam-
lech, Joshah son of Amaziah, Joel,
Jehu,[m] Elioenai, Jaakobah, Jeshohaiah,
Asaiah, Adiel, Jesimiel, Benaiah, and
Ziza.[n] 39 When the people needed more
pastureland for their flocks and herds,
they looked as far as the eastern side of
the valley where the town of Gerar[o] is
located, 40 and they found a lot of good
pastureland that was quiet and undisturbed. This had once belonged to the
Hamites, 41 but when Hezekiah was king
of Judah, the descendants of Simeon attacked and forced the Hamites and
Meunites off the land, then settled there.

42 Some time later, five hundred men
from the Simeon tribe went into Edom[p]
under the command of Pelatiah, Neariah, Rephaiah, and Uzziel the sons of

[g] **4.9** *Jabez . . . pain . . . birth*: In Hebrew "Jabez" sounds like "pain." [h] **4.10** *I . . . harm*: Or "keep me from harm, so I won't cause any pain." [i] **4.12** *who settled the town of Nahash*: Or "who was the father of Irnahash." [j] **4.13** *and Meonothai*: Two ancient translations; these words are not in the Hebrew text. [k] **4.14** *Valley of Crafts*: Hebrew "Geharashim."
[l] **4.21,22** *who married Moabite women and then settled near Bethlehem*: Or "who ruled in Moab and Jashubi-Lahem" or "who ruled in Moab but then returned to Lahem."
[m] **4.34-38** *Jehu*: Hebrew "Jehu son of Joshibiah son of Seraiah son of Asiel." [n] **4.34-38** *Ziza*: Hebrew "Ziza son of Shiphi son of Allon son of Jedaiah son of Shimri son of Shemaiah."
[o] **4.39** *Gerar*: One ancient translation; Hebrew "Gedor." [p] **4.42** *Edom*: The Hebrew text has "Mount Seir," a common name for the nation of Edom.

Ishi. 43They killed the last of the Amalekites and lived there from then on.

The Descendants of Reuben

5 Reuben was the oldest son of Jacob,[q] but he lost his rights as the first-born son[r] because he slept with one of his father's wives.[s] The honor of the first-born son was then given to Joseph, 2even though it was the Judah tribe that became the most powerful and produced a leader.

3Reuben had four sons: Hanoch, Pallu, Hezron, and Carmi.

4-6The descendants of Joel included Shemaiah, Gog, Shimei, Micah, Reaiah, Baal, and Beerah, a leader of the Reuben tribe. Later, King Tiglath Pileser of Assyria took Beerah away as prisoner.

7-8The family records also include Jeiel, who was a clan leader, Zechariah, and Bela son of Azaz and grandson of Shema of the Joel clan. They lived in the territory around the town of Aroer, as far north as Nebo and Baal-Meon, 9and as far east as the desert just west of the Euphrates River. They needed this much land because they owned too many cattle to keep them all in Gilead.

10When Saul was king, the Reuben tribe attacked and defeated the Hagrites, then took over their land east of Gilead.

The Descendants of Gad

11The tribe of Gad lived in the region of Bashan, north of the Reuben tribe. Gad's territory extended all the way to the town of Salecah. 12Some of the clan leaders were Joel, Shapham, Janai, and Shaphat. 13Their relatives included Michael, Meshullam, Sheba, Jorai, Jacan, Zia, and Eber.

14They were all descendants of Abihail, whose family line went back through Huri, Jaroah, Gilead, Michael, Jeshishai, Jahdo, and Buz. 15Ahi, the son of Abdiel and the grandson of Guni, was the leader of their clan.

16The people of Gad lived in the towns in the regions of Bashan and Gilead, as well as in the pastureland of Sharon. 17Their family records were written when Jotham was king of Judah and Jeroboam was king of Israel.

18The tribes of Reuben, Gad, and East Manasseh had 44,760 soldiers trained to fight in battle with shields, swords, bows, and arrows. 19They fought against the Hagrites and the tribes of Jetur, Naphish, and Nodab. 20Whenever these soldiers went to war against their enemies, they prayed to God and trusted him to help. That's why the tribes of Reuben, Gad, and East Manasseh defeated the Hagrites and their allies. 21These Israelite tribes captured fifty thousand camels, two hundred fifty thousand sheep, two thousand donkeys, and one hundred thousand people. 22Many of the Hagrites died in battle, because God was fighting this battle against them. The tribes of Reuben, Gad, and East Manasseh lived in that territory until they were taken as prisoners to Assyria.[t]

The Tribe of East Manasseh

23East Manasseh was a large tribe, so its people settled in the northern region of Bashan, as far north as Baal-Hermon,[u] Senir, and Mount Hermon. 24Epher, Ishi, Eliel, Azriel, Jeremiah, Hodaviah, and Jahdiel were their clan leaders; they were well-known leaders and brave soldiers.

The Tribes of Reuben, Gad, and East Manasseh Are Defeated

25The people of the tribes of Reuben, Gad, and East Manasseh were unfaithful to the God their ancestors had worshiped, and they started worshiping the gods of the nations that God had forced out of Canaan. 26So God sent King Tiglath Pileser[v] of Assyria to attack these Israelite tribes. The king led them away as prisoners to Assyria, and from then on, he forced them to live in Halah, Habor, Hara, and near the Gozan River.

The Descendants of Levi

6 Levi was the father of Gershon, Kohath, and Merari.

2Kohath was the father of Amram, Izhar, Hebron, and Uzziel. 3Amram was the father of Aaron, Moses, and Miriam.

Aaron had four sons: Nadab, Abihu, Eleazar, and Ithamar.

4-14Eleazar's descendants included Phinehas, Abishua, Bukki, Uzzi, Zerahiah, Meraioth, Amariah, Ahitub, Zadok, Ahimaaz, Azariah, Johanan, Azariah the priest who served in the temple built by King Solomon, Amariah, Ahitub, Zadok, Shallum, Hilkiah, Azariah, Seraiah, and Jehozadak. 15King Nebuchadnezzar of Babylonia took Jehozadak to Babylon as prisoner when the LORD let the people of Judah

[q]**5.1** *Jacob*: See the note at 1.34. [r]**5.1** *rights as the first-born son*: The first-born son inherited the largest amount of property, as well as the leadership of the family. [s]**5.1** *wives*: See Genesis 35.22; 49.3, 4. [t]**5.22** *they were taken as prisoners to Assyria*: See 2 Kings 15.29; 17.5-23. [u]**5.23** *Baal-Hermon*: The location of this place is unknown. [v]**5.26** *King Tiglath Pileser*: The Hebrew text also includes "King Pul," another name by which he was known.

and Jerusalem be dragged from their land.[w]

16 Levi's three sons had sons of their own. 17 Gershon was the father of Libni and Shimei. 18 Kohath was the father of Amram, Izhar, Hebron, and Uzziel. 19 Merari was the father of Mahli and Mushi. These descendants of Levi each became leaders of their own clans.

20-21 Gershon's descendants included Libni, Jahath, Zimmah, Joah, Iddo, Zerah, and Jeatherai.

22-24 Kohath's descendants included Amminadab, Korah, Assir, Elkanah, Ebiasaph, Assir, Tahath, Uriel, Uzziah, and Shaul.

25 Elkanah was the father of Amasai and Ahimoth. 26-27 Ahimoth's descendants included Elkanah, Zophai, Nahath, Eliab, Jeroham, and Elkanah.

28 Samuel was the father of Joel[x] and Abijah, born in that order.

29-30 Merari's descendants included Mahli, Libni, Shimei, Uzzah, Shimea, Haggiah, and Asaiah.

The Temple Musicians

31 After King David had the sacred chest moved to Jerusalem, he appointed musicians from the Levi tribe to be in charge of the music at the place of worship. 32 These musicians served at the sacred tent and later at the LORD's temple that King Solomon built.

33-38 Here is a list of these musicians and their family lines:

Heman from the Kohathite clan was the director. His ancestors went all the way back to Jacob and included Joel, Samuel, Elkanah, Jeroham, Eliel, Toah, Zuph, Elkanah, Mahath, Amasai, Elkanah, Joel, Azariah, Zephaniah, Tahath, Assir, Ebiasaph, Korah, Izhar, Kohath, Levi.

39-43 Asaph was Heman's relative and served as his assistant. Asaph's ancestors included Berechiah, Shimea, Michael, Baaseiah, Malchijah, Ethni, Zerah, Adaiah, Ethan, Zimmah, Shimei, Jahath, Gershon, and Levi.

44-47 Ethan was also Heman's relative and served as his assistant. Ethan belonged to the Merari clan, and his ancestors included Kishi, Abdi, Malluch, Hashabiah, Amaziah, Hilkiah, Amzi, Bani, Shemer, Mahli, Mushi, Merari, and Levi.

48 The rest of the Levites were appointed to work at the sacred tent.

The Descendants of Aaron

49 Only Aaron and his descendants were allowed to offer sacrifices and incense on the two altars at the sacred tent.[y] They were in charge of the most holy place and the ceremonies to forgive sins, just as God's servant Moses had commanded.

50-53 Aaron's descendants included his son Eleazar, Phinehas, Abishua, Bukki, Uzzi, Zerahiah, Meraioth, Amariah, Ahitub, Zadok, and Ahimaaz.

The Towns for the Levites

(Joshua 21.1-42)

54 Aaron's descendants belonged to the Levite clan of Kohath, and they were the first group chosen to receive towns to live in. 55 They received the town of Hebron in the territory of Judah and the pastureland around it. 56 But the farmland and villages around Hebron were given to Caleb son of Jephunneh. 57-59 So Aaron's descendants received the following Safe Towns[z] and the pastureland around them: Hebron, Libnah, Jattir, Eshtemoa, Hilen, Debir, Ashan, and Beth-Shemesh. 60 From the Benjamin tribe they were given the towns of Geba, Alemeth, and Anathoth and the pastureland around them. Thirteen towns were given to Aaron's descendants.

61 The rest of the Levite clan of Kohath received ten towns from West Manasseh.

62 The Levite clan of Gershon received thirteen towns from the tribes of Issachar, Asher, Naphtali, and East Manasseh in Bashan.

63 The Levite clan of Merari received twelve towns from the tribes of Reuben, Gad, and Zebulun.

64 So the people of Israel gave the Levites towns to live in and the pastureland around them. 65 All the towns were chosen with the LORD's help,[a] including those towns from the tribes of Judah, Simeon, and Benjamin.

66 Some of the families of the Kohath clan received their towns from the tribe of Ephraim. 67-69 These families received the following Safe Towns and the pastureland around them: Shechem in the hill country, Gezer, Jokmeam, Beth-Horon, Aijalon, and Gath-Rimmon.

[w] **6.15** *King Nebuchadnezzar . . . dragged from their land*: See 2 Kings 24.8-17; 25.1-21.
[x] **6.28** *Joel*: Two ancient translations (see also verse 33 and 1 Samuel 8.1, 2); this name is not in the Hebrew text. [y] **6.49** *the two altars at the sacred tent*: The Hebrew text mentions two different altars: A large altar for offering sacrifices, and a smaller altar for offering incense.
[z] **6.57-59** *Safe Towns*: These were special towns set aside where a person who had accidently killed someone could run for protection from the victim's relatives (see Numbers 35.9-15; Deuteronomy 19.1-13; Joshua 20.1-9). [a] **6.65** *with the LORD's help*: The Hebrew text has "by lot." Pieces of wood or stone (called "lots") were used to find out what God wanted his people to do.

[70]And from West Manasseh they received Aner and Bileam, together with
their pastureland.
[71]The Gershonite clan received two
towns from the tribe of East Manasseh:
Golan in Bashan and Ashtaroth, including the pastureland around them.
[72-73]The Gershonites also received four
towns from the tribe of Issachar:
Kedesh, Daberath, Ramoth, and Anem,
including the pastureland around them.
[74-75]The Gershonites received four
towns from the tribe of Asher: Mashal,
Abdon, Hukok, and Rehob, including
the pastureland around them. [76]Finally,
the Gershonites received three towns
from the tribe of Naphtali: Kedesh in
Galilee, Hammon, and Kiriathaim, including the pastureland around them.
[77]The rest of the Merari clan received
the towns of Rimmono and Tabor and
their pastureland from the tribe of
Zebulun. [78-79]They also received four
towns east of the Jordan River from the
tribe of Reuben: Bezer in the flatlands,
Jahzah, Kedemoth, and Mephaath,
including the pastures around them.
[80-81]And from the tribe of Gad the Merarites received the towns of Ramoth in
Gilead, Mahanaim, Heshbon, and Jazer,
including the pastureland around them.

The Descendants of Issachar

7 Issachar was the father of four sons:
Tola, Puah, Jashub, and Shimron.
[2]Tola was the father of Uzzi, Rephaiah, Jeriel, Jahmai, Ibsam, and Shemuel,
who were all brave soldiers and family
leaders in their clan. There were 22,600
people in Tola's family by the time
David became king.
[3]Uzzi was the father of Izrahiah and
the grandfather of Michael, Obadiah,
Joel, and Isshiah, who were also family
leaders. [4]Their families were so large
that they had 36,000 soldiers in their
clans. [5]In fact, according to family
records, the tribe of Issachar had a total
of 87,000 warriors.

The Descendants of Benjamin and Dan

[6]Benjamin was the father of three
sons: Bela, Becher, and Jediael.
[7]Bela was the father of Ezbon, Uzzi,
Uzziel, Jerimoth, and Iri. They were all
brave soldiers and family leaders in
their father's clan. The number of soldiers in their clan was 22,034.
[8]Becher was the father of Zemirah,
Joash, Eliezer, Elioenai, Omri, Jeremoth,
Abijah, Anathoth, and Alemeth. [9]The official family records listed 20,200 soldiers in the families of this clan, as well
as their family leaders.
[10]Jediael was the father of Bilhan and
the grandfather of Jeush, Benjamin,
Ehud, Chenaanah, Zethan, Tarshish,
and Ahishahar. [11]They were family leaders in their clan, which had 17,200 soldiers prepared to fight in battle. [12]Ir was
the father of Shuppim and Huppim, who
also belonged to this clan.
Dan[b] was the father of Hushim.

The Descendants of Naphtali

[13]Naphtali's mother was Bilhah,[c] and
he was the father of Jahziel, Guni, Jezer,
and Shallum.

The Descendants of Manasseh

[14]Manasseh and his Syrian wife[d] were
the parents of Asriel and Machir the
father of Gilead. [15]Machir found a wife
for Huppim and one for Shuppim.
Machir had a sister named Maacah.
Zelophehad was also a descendant of
Manasseh, and he had five daughters.[e]
[16]Machir and his wife Maacah were
the parents of Peresh and Sheresh.
Peresh was the father of Ulam and
Rekem. [17]Ulam was the father of Bedan.
These were all descendants of Gilead,
the son of Machir and the grandson of
Manasseh.
[18]Gilead's sister Hammolecheth was
the mother of Ishhod, Abiezer, and
Mahlah.
[19]Shemida, another descendant of
Manasseh, was the father of Ahian,
Shechem, Likhi, and Aniam.

The Descendants of Ephraim

[20]Ephraim was the father of Shuthelah and the ancestor of Bered, Tahath,
Eleadah, Tahath, [21]Zabad, and Shuthelah.
Ephraim had two other sons, Ezer and
Elead. But they were killed when they
tried to steal livestock from the people
who lived in the territory of Gath.
[22]Ephraim mourned for his sons a long
time, and his relatives came to comfort
him. [23]Some time later his wife gave
birth to another son, and Ephraim
named him Beriah, because he was born
during a time of misery.[f]
[24]Ephraim's daughter was Sheerah.
She built the towns of Lower Beth-
Horon, Upper Beth-Horon, and Uzzen-
Sheerah.
[25]Ephraim also had a son named
Rephah, and his descendants included
Resheph, Telah, Tahan, [26]Ladan, Ammihud, Elishama, [27]Nun, and Joshua.

[b]**7.12** *Dan*: The Hebrew text has "Aher," which can mean "someone else" (see Genesis 46.23-25). [c]**7.13** *Bilhah*: One of Jacob's wives and the mother of Dan and Naphtali (see Genesis 46.23-25). [d]**7.14** *wife*: See the note at 3.9. [e]**7.15** *Zelophehad . . . daughters*: One possible meaning for the difficult Hebrew text (see also Numbers 26.28-33). [f]**7.23** *Beriah . . . misery*: In Hebrew "Beriah" sounds like "in misery."

28 The descendants of Ephraim took over the territory as far south as Bethel, as far east as Naaran, and as far west as Gezer. Their territory included all the villages around these towns, as well as Shechem, Ayyah, and the nearby villages.

29 The descendants of Manasseh settled in the territory that included Beth-Shan, Taanach, Megiddo, Dor, and the nearby villages.

The descendants of Joseph[g] lived in these towns and villages.

The Descendants of Asher

30 Asher had four sons, Imnah, Ishvah, Ishvi, and Beriah, and one daughter, Serah.

31 Beriah was the father of Heber and Malchiel the father of Birzaith. 32 Heber was the father of three sons, Japhlet, Shomer, and Hotham, and one daughter, Shua. 33 Japhlet was the father of Pasach, Bimhal, and Ashvath. 34 Shomer was the father of Ahi, Rohgah, Hubbah, and Aram. 35 And Japhlet's brother Hotham[h] was the father of Zophah, Imna, Shelesh, and Amal. 36 Zophah was the father of Suah, Harnepher, Shual, Beri, Imrah, 37 Bezer, Hod, Shamma, Shilshah, Ithran, and Beera. 38 Jether was the father of Jephunneh, Pispa, and Ara.

39 Ulla was the father of Arah, Hanniel, and Rizia.

40 These were the descendants of Asher, and they were all respected family leaders and brave soldiers. The tribe of Asher had a total of 26,000 soldiers.

More Descendants of Benjamin

8 Benjamin had five sons, who were born in the following order: Bela, Ashbel, Aharah, 2 Nohah, and Rapha. 3 Bela was the father of Addar, Gera, Abihud, 4 Abishua, Naaman, Ahoah, 5 Gera, Shephuphan, and Huram.

6-7 Ehud was the father of Naaman, Ahijah, and Gera. They were clan leaders in the town of Geba, but were later forced to move to the town of Manahath, and Gera led the way. He had two sons: Uzza and Ahihud.

8-11 Shaharaim and his wife Hushim had two sons: Abitub and Elpaal. But Shaharaim later divorced her and his other wife, Baara. Then he moved to the country of Moab and married Hodesh, and they had seven sons: Jobab, Zibia, Mesha, Malcam, Jeuz, Sachia, and Mirmah. They were all family leaders in his clan. 12 Elpaal was the father of Eber, Misham, and Shemed, who settled the towns of Ono and Lod, as well as the nearby villages.

13 Beriah and Shema were family leaders in the clan that lived in the town of Aijalon and that forced out the people of Gath. 14-16 Beriah's descendants included Ahio, Shashak, Jeremoth, Zebadiah, Arad, Eder, Michael, Ishpah, and Joha. 17-18 Elpaal's descendants included Zebadiah, Meshullam, Hizki, Heber, Ishmerai, Izliah, and Jobab. 19-21 Shimei's descendants included Jakim, Zichri, Zabdi, Elienai, Zillethai, Eliel, Adaiah, Beraiah, and Shimrath. 22-25 Shashak's descendants included Ishpan, Eber, Eliel, Abdon, Zichri, Hanan, Hananiah, Elam, Anthothijah, Iphdeiah, and Penuel. 26-27 Jeroham's descendants included Shamsherai, Shehariah, Athaliah, Jaareshiah, Elijah, and Zichri. 28 These were the family leaders in their ancestor's clan, and they and their descendants lived in Jerusalem.

29 Jeiel[i] settled the town of Gibeon. He and his wife Maacah lived there 30 along with their sons, who were born in the following order: Abdon, Zur, Kish, Baal, Ner,[j] Nadab, 31 Gedor, Ahio, Zecher, 32 and Mikloth the father of Shimeah. Some of them went to live in Jerusalem near their relatives.

The Descendants of King Saul

33 Ner was the father of Kish and the grandfather of King Saul.

Saul had four sons: Jonathan, Malchishua, Abinadab, and Eshbaal.[k] 34 Jonathan was the father of Meribbaal,[l] the grandfather of Micah, 35 and the great-grandfather of Pithon, Melech, Tarea, and Ahaz. 36 Saul's other descendants were Jehoaddah, Alemeth, Azmaveth, Zimri, Moza, 37 Binea, Raphah, Eleasah, Azel, 38 as well as Azel's six sons: Azrikam, Bocheru, Ishmael, Sheariah, Obadiah, and Hanan. 39 Azel's brother Eshek was the father of Ulam, Jeush, and Eliphelet. 40 Ulam's sons were brave soldiers who were experts at using a bow and arrows. They had a total of one hundred fifty children and grandchildren.

All of these belonged to the tribe of Benjamin.

The People Who Returned from Babylonia and Settled in Jerusalem

9 Everyone in Israel was listed in the official family records that were included in the history of Israel's kings.

The people of Judah were taken to

[g] **7.29** *Joseph*: Hebrew "Joseph son of Israel." [h] **7.35** *Hotham*: The Hebrew text has "Helem," another spelling of the name. [i] **8.29** *Jeiel*: One ancient translation and 9.35; the Hebrew text does not have this name. [j] **8.30** *Ner*: One ancient translation and 9.36; the Hebrew text does not have this name. [k] **8.33** *Eshbaal*: Also called "Ishbosheth" (see 2 Samuel 2.8 and the note there). [l] **8.34** *Meribbaal*: Also called "Mephibosheth" (see 2 Samuel 4.4 and the note there).

Babylonia as prisoners because they
sinned against the LORD. 2And the first
people to return to their towns included
priests, Levites, temple workers, and
other Israelites. 3People from the tribes
of Judah, Benjamin, Ephraim, and Manasseh settled in Jerusalem.
4-6There were six hundred ninety people from the Judah tribe who settled in
Jerusalem. They were all descendants of
Judah's three sons: Perez, Shelah, and
Zerah. Their leaders were Uthai, Asaiah, and Jeuel. Uthai was the son of Ammihud and a descendant of Omri, Imri,
Bani, and Perez. Asaiah was a descendant of Shelah; Jeuel was a descendant
of Zerah.
7-9There were also nine hundred fifty-
six family leaders from the Benjamin
tribe who settled in Jerusalem. They included: Sallu son of Meshullam, grandson of Hodaviah, and great-grandson of
Hassenuah; Ibneiah son of Jeroham;
Elah son of Uzzi and grandson of
Michri; Meshullam son of Shephatiah,
grandson of Reuel, and great-grandson
of Ibnijah.

The Priests Who Settled in Jerusalem

10-12Here is a list of priests who settled
in Jerusalem: Jedaiah; Jehoiarib; Jachin;
Azariah, who was a temple official, and
whose ancestors included Hilkiah,
Meshullam, Zadok, Meraioth, and Ahitub; Adaiah son of Jeroham, whose ancestors included Pashhur and Malchijah; Maasai son of Adiel, whose
ancestors included Jahzerah, Meshullam, Meshillemith, and Immer.
13There was a total of 1,760 priests, all
of them family leaders in their clan and
trained in the work at the temple.

The Levites Who Settled in Jerusalem

14-16Here is a list of Levites who settled in Jerusalem: Shemaiah from the
Merari clan, whose ancestors included
Hasshub, Azrikam, and Hashabiah;
Bakbakkar; Heresh; Galal; Mattaniah
son of Mica, whose ancestors included
Zichri and Asaph; Obadiah son of Shemaiah, whose ancestors included Galal
and Jeduthun; Berechiah son of Asa and
grandson of Elkanah, who had lived in
the villages near the town of Netophah.

The Temple Guards Who Settled in Jerusalem

17Shallum, Akkub, Talmon, Ahiman,
and their relatives were the guards at
the temple gates. Shallum was the
leader of this clan, 18and for a long time
they had been the guards at the King's
Gate on the east side of the city. Before
that, their ancestors guarded the entrance to the Levite camp.
19Shallum son of Kore,[m] as well as the
other men in the Korahite clan, guarded
the entrance to the temple, just as their
ancestors had guarded the entrance to
the sacred tent. 20Phinehas son of
Eleazar had supervised their work because the LORD was with him.
21Zechariah son of Meshelemiah was
also one of the guards at the temple.
22There was a total of two hundred
twelve guards, all of them listed in the
family records in their towns. Their ancestors had been chosen by King David
and by Samuel the prophet to be responsible for this work, 23and now they
guarded the temple gates.
24There was one full-time guard appointed to each of the four sides of the
temple. 25Their assistants lived in the
villages outside the city, and every seven
days a group of them would come into
the city and take their turn at guard
duty. 26The four full-time guards were
Levites, and they supervised the other
guards and were responsible for the
rooms in the temple and the supplies
kept there. 27They guarded the temple
day and night and opened its doors
every morning.

The Duties of the Levites

28Some of the Levites were responsible for the equipment used in worship at
the temple, and they had to count everything before and after it was used.
29Others were responsible for the temple furnishings and its sacred objects, as
well as the flour, wine, olive oil, incense,
and spices. 30But only the priests could
mix the spices. 31Mattithiah, Shallum's
oldest son, was a member of the Levite
clan of Korah, and he was in charge of
baking the bread used for offerings.[n]
32The Levites from the Kohath clan were
in charge of baking the sacred loaves of
bread for each Sabbath.[o]
33The Levite family leaders who were
the musicians also lived at the temple.
They had no other responsibilities, because they were on duty day and night.
34All of these men were family leaders
in the Levi tribe and were listed that
way in their family records. They lived
in Jerusalem.

King Saul's Family

(1 Chronicles 8.29-38)

35Jeiel had settled the town of Gibeon,
where he and his wife Maacah lived.
36They had ten sons, who were born
in the following order: Abdon, Zur,
Kish, Baal, Ner, Nadab, 37Gedor, Ahio,

[m]**9.19** *Shallum son of Kore*: Hebrew "Shallum son of Kore, grandson of Ebiasaph, and great-grandson of Korah." [n]**9.31** *the bread used for offerings*: See Leviticus 2.4-7.
[o]**9.32** *the sacred loaves of bread for each Sabbath*: See Leviticus 24.5-9.

Zechariah, and Mikloth [38]the father of Shimeam. Some of them went to live in Jerusalem near their relatives.

[39]Ner was the father of Kish and the grandfather of King Saul.

Saul had four sons: Jonathan, Malchishua, Abinadab, and Eshbaal.[p] [40-41]Jonathan was the father of Meribbaal,[q] the grandfather of Micah, and the great-grandfather of Pithon, Melech, Tahrea, and Ahaz.[r] [42-44]The descendants of Ahaz included Jarah, Alemeth, Azmaveth, Zimri, Moza, Binea, Rephaiah, Eleasah, and Azel and his six sons: Azrikam, Bocheru, Ishmael, Sheariah, Obadiah, and Hanan.

King Saul and His Sons Die

(1 Samuel 31.1-13)

10 The Philistines fought against Israel in a battle at Mount Gilboa. Israel's soldiers ran from the Philistines, and many of them were killed. [2]The Philistines closed in on Saul and his sons and killed three of them: Jonathan, Abinadab, and Malchishua. [3]The fighting was fierce around Saul, and he was badly wounded by enemy arrows.

[4]Saul told the soldier who carried his weapons, "Kill me with your sword! I don't want those godless Philistines to torture and make fun of me."

But the soldier was afraid to kill him. Then Saul stuck himself in the stomach with his own sword and fell on the blade. [5]When the soldier realized that Saul was dead, he killed himself in the same way.

[6]Saul, three of his sons, and all his male relatives were dead. [7]The Israelites who lived in Jezreel Valley[s] learned that their army had run away and that Saul and his sons were dead. They ran away too, and the Philistines moved into the towns the Israelites left behind.

[8]The next day the Philistines came back to the battlefield to carry away the weapons of the dead Israelite soldiers. When they found the bodies of Saul and his sons on Mount Gilboa, [9]they took Saul's weapons, pulled off his armor, and cut off his head. Then they sent messengers everywhere in Philistia to spread the news among their people and to thank the idols of their gods. [10]They put Saul's armor in the temple of their gods and hung his head in the temple of their god Dagon.

[11]When the people who lived in Jabesh in Gilead heard what the Philistines had done to Saul, [12]some brave men went to get his body and the bodies of his three sons. The men brought the bodies back to Jabesh, where they buried them under an oak tree. Then for seven days, they went without eating to show their sorrow.

[13]Saul died because he was unfaithful and disobeyed the LORD. He even asked advice from a woman who talked to spirits of the dead, [14]instead of asking the LORD. So the LORD had Saul killed and gave his kingdom to David, the son of Jesse.

David Becomes King of Israel

(2 Samuel 5.1-3)

11 Israel's leaders met with David at Hebron and said, "We are your relatives, [2]and we know that you have led our army into battle, even when Saul was still our king. The LORD God has promised that you would rule our country and take care of us like a shepherd. [3]So we have come to crown you king of Israel."

David made an agreement with the leaders and asked the LORD to be their witness. Then the leaders poured olive oil on David's head to show that he was now king of Israel. This happened just as the LORD's prophet Samuel had said.

David Captures Jerusalem

(2 Samuel 5.6-10)

[4]Jerusalem was called Jebus at the time, and David led Israel's army to attack the town. [5]The Jebusites said, "You won't be able to get in here!" But David captured the fortress of Mount Zion, which is now called the City of David.

[6]David had told his troops, "The first soldier to kill a Jebusite will become my army commander." And since Joab son of Zeruiah attacked first, he became commander.

[7]Later, David moved to the fortress—that's why it's called the City of David. [8]He had the city rebuilt, starting at the landfill on the east side.[t] Meanwhile, Joab supervised the repairs to the rest of the city.

[9]David became a great and strong ruler, because the LORD All-Powerful was on his side.

The Three Warriors

(2 Samuel 23.8-17)

[10]The LORD had promised that David would become king, and so everyone in Israel gave David their support. Certain warriors also helped keep his kingdom strong.

[11]The first of these warriors was Ja-

[p] **9.39** *Eshbaal*: See the note at 8.33. [q] **9.40** *Meribbaal*: See the note at 8.34. [r] **9.41** *and Ahaz*: Most ancient translations and 8.35; the Hebrew text does not have this name.
[s] **10.7** *Jezreel Valley*: Hebrew "the valley." [t] **11.8** *the landfill on the east side*: The Hebrew text has "the Millo," which probably refers to a landfill to strengthen and extend the hill where the city was built.

shobeam the son of Hachmoni, the
leader of the Three Warriors.[u] In one
battle he killed three hundred men with
his spear.
12Another one of the Three Warriors
was Eleazar son of Dodo the Ahohite.
13During a battle against the Philistines
at Pas-Dammim, all the Israelite soldiers
ran away, 14except Eleazar, who stayed
with David. They took their positions in
a nearby barley field and defeated the
Philistines! The LORD gave Israel a great
victory that day.
15One time the Three Warriors[v] went
to meet David among the rocks at Adullam Cave. The Philistine army had set
up camp in Rephaim Valley 16and had
taken over Bethlehem. David was in a
fortress, 17and he said, "I'm very thirsty.
I wish I had a drink of water from the
well by the gate to Bethlehem."
18The Three Warriors sneaked
through the Philistine camp and got
some water from the well near Bethlehem's gate. They took it back to David,
but he refused to drink it. Instead, he
poured out the water as a sacrifice to
the LORD 19and said, "Drinking this water would be like drinking the blood of
these men who risked their lives to get it
for me."
The Three Warriors did these brave
deeds.

The Thirty Warriors
(2 Samuel 23.18-39)

20Joab's brother Abishai was the
leader of the Thirty Warriors,[w] and in
one battle he killed three hundred men
with his spear. He was just as famous as
the Three Warriors 21and was more famous than the rest of the Thirty Warriors. He was their commander, but he
never became one of the Three Warriors.[x]
22Benaiah the son of Jehoiada was a
brave man from Kabzeel who did some
amazing things. One time he killed two
of Moab's best fighters, and one snowy
day he went into a pit and killed a lion.
23Another time he killed an Egyptian
who was seven and a half feet tall and
was armed with a spear. Benaiah only
had a club, so he grabbed the spear
from the Egyptian and killed him with
it. 24Benaiah did things like that; he was
just as brave as the Three Warriors,
25even though he never became one of
them. And he was certainly as famous
as the rest of the Thirty Warriors. So
David made him the leader of his own
bodyguard.
26-47Here is a list of the other famous
warriors:
Asahel the brother of Joab; Elhanan
the son of Dodo from Bethlehem; Sham-
moth from Haror; Helez from Pelon; Ira
the son of Ikkesh from Tekoa; Abiezer
from Anathoth; Sibbecai the Hushathite;
Ilai[y] the Ahohite; Maharai from Netophah; Heled the son of Baanah from
Netophah; Ithai the son of Ribai from
Gibeah in Benjamin; Benaiah from Pirathon; Hurai[z] from near the streams on
Mount Gaash; Abiel from Arbah; Azmaveth from Baharum; Eliahba from
Shaalbon; Hashem[a] the Gizonite;
Jonathan the son of Shagee from Harar;
Ahiam the son of Sachar the Hararite;
Eliphal the son of Ur; Hepher from
Mecherah; Ahijah from Pelon; Hezro
from Carmel; Naarai the son of Ezbai;
Joel the brother of Nathan; Mibhar the
son of Hagri; Zelek from Ammon; Na-
harai from Beeroth who carried Joab's
weapons; Ira the Ithrite; Gareb the
Ithrite; Uriah the Hittite; Zabad the son
of Ahlai; Adina the son of Shiza, a
leader in the Reuben tribe, and thirty of
his soldiers; Hanan the son of Maacah;
Joshaphat from Mithan; Uzzia from
Ashterah; Shama and Jeiel the sons of
Hotham from Aroer; Jediael and Joha
the sons of Shimri from Tiz; Eliel from
Mahavah; Jeribai and Joshaviah the
sons of Elnaam; Ithmah from Moab;
Eliel, Obed, and Jaasiel from Mezobah.

David's Men at Ziklag

12 Some time earlier, David had
gone to live in the town of Ziklag
to escape from King Saul. While David
was there, several brave warriors joined
him to help fight his battles.[b]

Warriors from the Benjamin tribe
2Several of these warriors were from
King Saul's own tribe of Benjamin. They

[u] **11.11** *the Three Warriors*: One ancient translation and 2 Samuel 23.8; Hebrew "the Thirty Warriors." The "Three Warriors" was the most honored group of warriors and may have been part of the "Thirty Warriors." "Three" and "thirty" are spelled almost the same in Hebrew, so there is some confusion in the manuscripts as to which group is being talked about in some places in the following lists. [v] **11.15** *the Three Warriors*: Hebrew "three of the thirty most important warriors." [w] **11.20** *the Thirty Warriors*: One ancient translation; Hebrew "the Three Warriors." The "Thirty Warriors" was the second most honored group of warriors and may have also been officers in the army. [x] **11.20,21** *Warriors*: One possible meaning for the difficult Hebrew text of these verses. [y] **11.26-47** *Ilai*: Or "Zalmon" (see 2 Samuel 23.24-39). [z] **11.26-47** *Hurai*: Or "Hiddai" (see 2 Samuel 23.24-39). [a] **11.26-47** *Hashem*: One ancient translation; Hebrew "the sons of Hashem." [b] **12.1** *David had gone . . . battles*: Ziklag was the Philistine town that King Achish of Gath gave David in return for his loyalty (see 1 Samuel 27.6). This happened during the time that David was living as an outlaw, so the events in this chapter actually took place before chapter 11 when David became king of Israel.

were experts at using a bow and arrows,
and they could shoot an arrow or sling a
stone with either hand. 3-7Their leaders
were Ahiezer and Joash, the sons of
Shemaah from Gibeah. Here is a list of
those men from Benjamin: Jeziel and
Pelet the sons of Azmaveth; Beracah
and Jehu from Anathoth; Ishmaiah from
Gibeon, who was the leader of the
Thirty Warriors; Jeremiah, Jahaziel, Johanan, and Jozabad from Gederah;
Eluzai, Jerimoth, Bealiah, Shemariah,
and Shephatiah from Haruph; Elkanah,
Isshiah, Azarel, Joezer, and Jashobeam
from the Korah clan; Joelah and Zebadiah the sons of Jeroham from Gedor.

Warriors from the Gad tribe

8Men from the tribe of Gad also joined
David at his fortress in the desert and
served as his warriors. They were also
brave soldiers—fierce as lions and quick
as gazelles. They were always prepared
to fight with shields and spears.
9-13There were eleven of them, ranked
in the following order: Ezer the leader,
then Obadiah, Eliab, Mishmannah,
Jeremiah, Attai, Eliel, Johanan, Elzabad,
Jeremiah, and Machbannai.
14All these men were army officers;
some were high-ranking officers over a
thousand troops, and others were officers over a hundred troops. 15Earlier,
they had crossed the Jordan River when
it flooded, and they chased out the people who lived in the valleys on each side
of the river.

Warriors from the Benjamin and Judah tribes

16One time a group of men from the
tribes of Benjamin and Judah went to
the fortress where David was staying.
17David met them outside and said, "If
you are coming as friends to fight on my
side, then stay and join us. But if you try
to turn me over to my enemies, the God
our ancestors worshiped will punish
you, because I have done nothing
wrong."
18Amasai, who later became the
leader of the Thirty Warriors, was one of
these men who went to David. God's
Spirit took control of him, and he said,
"We will join you, David son of Jesse!
You and your followers will always be
successful, because God fights on your
side."

So David agreed to let them stay, and he even put them in charge of his soldiers who raided enemy villages.

Warriors from the Manasseh tribe

19Some of the warriors who joined
David were from the tribe of Manasseh.
They had earlier gone with David when
he agreed to fight on the side of the
Philistines against King Saul. But as
soon as the Philistine rulers realized
that David might turn against them and
rejoin Saul, they sent David away to
the town of Ziklag. 20That's when the
following men from Manasseh joined
him: Adnah, Jozabad, Jediael, Michael,
Jozabad, Elihu, and Zillethai. They had
all been commanders in Saul's army
21and brave soldiers, and so David made
them officers in his army. They fought
on his side when enemy troops attacked.
22Day after day, new men came to join
David, and soon he had a large, powerful army.

David's Men at Hebron

23-37The kingdom of Israel had been
taken away from Saul, and it now belonged to David. He was ruling from Hebron, and thousands of well-trained soldiers from each tribe went there to
crown David king of all Israel, just as
the LORD had promised. These soldiers,
who were always prepared for battle, included: 6,800 from Judah, who were
armed with shields and spears; 7,100
from Simeon; 4,600 from Levi, including
Jehoiada, who was a leader from
Aaron's descendants, and his 3,700 men,
as well as Zadok, who was a brave soldier, and 22 of his relatives, who were
also officers; 3,000 from Benjamin, because this was Saul's own tribe and
most of the men had remained loyal to
him; 20,800 from Ephraim, who were
not only brave, but also famous in their
clans; 18,000 from West Manasseh, who
had been chosen to help make David
king; 200 leaders from Issachar, along
with troops under their command—
these leaders knew the right time to
do what needed to be done; 50,000
from Zebulun, who were not only
loyal, but also trained to use any
weapon; 1,000 officers from Naphtali
and 37,000 soldiers armed with shields
and spears; 28,600 from Dan; 40,000
from Asher; and 120,000 from the tribes
of Reuben, Gad, and East Manasseh,
who were armed with all kinds of
weapons.
38All of these soldiers voluntarily
came to Hebron because they wanted
David to become king of Israel. In fact,
everyone in Israel wanted the same
thing. 39The soldiers stayed in Hebron
three days, eating and drinking what
their relatives had prepared for them.
40Other Israelites from as far away as
the territories of Issachar, Zebulun, and
Naphtali brought cattle and sheep to
slaughter for food. They also brought
donkeys, camels, mules, and oxen that
were loaded down with flour, dried figs,
wine, and olive oil.

Everyone in Israel was very happy.

David Moves the Sacred Chest to Jerusalem
(2 Samuel 6.1-12a)

13 Some time later, David talked
with his army commanders,
2-3and then announced to the people of
Israel:

> While Saul was king, the sacred chest was ignored. But now it's time to bring the chest to Jerusalem. We will invite everyone in Israel to come here, including the priests and the Levites in the towns surrounded by pastureland. But we will do these things only if you agree, and if the LORD our God wants us to.

4The people agreed this was the right
thing to do.
5David gathered everyone from the
Shihor River in Egypt to Lebo-Hamath
in the north. 6Then he led them to
Baalah in Judah, which was also called
Kiriath-Jearim. They went there to get
the sacred chest and bring it to
Jerusalem, because it belonged to the
LORD God, whose throne is above
the winged creatures[c] on the lid of the
chest.
7The sacred chest was still at Abinadab's house,[d] and when David and the
crowd arrived there, they brought the
chest outside and placed it on a new ox
cart. Abinadab's sons[e] Uzzah and Ahio
guided the cart, 8while David and the
crowd danced and sang praises to the
LORD with all their might. They played
music on small harps and other stringed
instruments, and on tambourines, cymbals, and trumpets.
9But when they came to Chidon's
threshing place, the oxen stumbled, and
Uzzah reached out and took hold of the
chest to stop it from falling. 10The LORD
God was very angry at Uzzah for doing
this, and he killed Uzzah right there beside the chest.
11David then got angry at God for
killing Uzzah. So he named that place
"Attack on Uzzah,"[f] and it's been called
that ever since.
12David was afraid what the LORD
might do to him, and he asked himself,
"Should I really be the one to take care
of the sacred chest?" 13So instead of taking it to Jerusalem, David decided to
take it to the home of Obed-Edom, who
lived in the town of Gath.
14The chest stayed there for three
months, and the LORD blessed Obed-
Edom, his family, and everything he
owned.

David's Palace in Jerusalem
(2 Samuel 5.11-16)

14 King Hiram of Tyre sent some officials to David. They brought
along carpenters and stone workers,
and enough cedar logs to build David a
palace. 2David now knew that the LORD
had made him a powerful king of Israel
for the good of his people.
3After David moved to Jerusalem, he
married more women and had more
sons and daughters. 4-7His children born
there were Shammua, Shobab, Nathan,
Solomon, Ibhar, Elishua, Elpelet, Nogah,
Nepheg, Japhia, Elishama, Beeliada,[g]
and Eliphelet.

David Defeats the Philistines
(2 Samuel 5.17-25)

8When the Philistines heard that
David had become king of Israel, they
came to capture him. But David heard
about their plan and marched out
to meet them in battle. 9The Philistines
had already camped in Rephaim
Valley and were raiding the nearby villages.
10David asked God, "Should I attack
the Philistines? Will you help me win?"
The LORD told David, "Yes, attack
them! I will give you victory."
11David and his army marched to
Baal-Perazim, where they attacked and
defeated the Philistines. He said, "I defeated my enemies because God broke
through them like a mighty flood." So
he named the place "The Lord Broke
Through."[h] 12Then David ordered his
troops to burn the idols that the
Philistines had left behind.
13Some time later, the Philistines came
back into the hill country and camped
in Rephaim Valley. 14David asked
God what he should do, and God
answered, "Don't attack them from
the front. Circle around behind
them where the balsam[i] trees are.
15Wait there until you hear the tree-
tops making the sound of marching
troops. That sound will mean I have
marched out ahead of you to fight the
Philistine army. So you must then attack
quickly!"
16David obeyed God and he defeated
the Philistines. He even chased them all
the way from Gibeon to the entrance to
Gezer.
17From then on, David became even
more famous, and the LORD made all the
nations afraid of him.

[c]**13.6** *winged creatures*: Two golden statues of winged creatures were on top of the sacred chest and were symbols of the LORD's throne on earth (see Exodus 25.18). [d]**13.7** *The sacred chest . . . Abinadab's house*: See 1 Samuel 6.19—7.2. [e]**13.7** *Abinadab's sons*: These words are not in the Hebrew text, but see 2 Samuel 6.3. [f]**13.11** *Attack on Uzzah*: Or "Perez-Uzzah." [g]**14.4-7** *Beeliada*: Or "Eliada" (see 3.6-8). [h]**14.11** *The Lord Broke Through*: Or "Baal-Perazim." [i]**14.14** *balsam*: One possible meaning for the difficult Hebrew text.

David Gets Ready To Bring the Sacred Chest to Jerusalem

15 David had several buildings built
in Jerusalem, and he had a tent
set up where the sacred chest would be
kept. 2He said, "Only Levites will be allowed to carry the chest, because the
LORD has chosen them to do that work
and to serve him forever."
3Next, David invited everyone to come
to Jerusalem and watch the sacred chest
being carried to the place he had set up
for it. 4He also sent for Aaron's descendants and for the Levites. The Levites
that came were: 5Uriel, the leader of the
Kohath clan, and one hundred twenty of
his relatives; 6Asaiah, the leader of the
Merari clan, and two hundred twenty of
his relatives; 7Joel, the leader of the Gershon clan, and one hundred thirty of his
relatives; 8Shemaiah, the leader of the
Elizaphan clan, and two hundred of his
relatives; 9Eliel, the leader of the Hebron clan, and eighty of his relatives;
and 10Amminadab, the leader of the
Uzziel clan, with one hundred twelve of
his relatives.
11David called together these six
Levites and the two priests, Zadok and
Abiathar. 12He said to them, "You are
the leaders of the clans in the Levi tribe.
You and your relatives must first go
through the ceremony to make yourselves clean and acceptable to the LORD.
Then you may carry the sacred chest
that belongs to the LORD God of Israel
and bring it to the place I have prepared
for it. 13The first time we tried to bring
the chest to Jerusalem, we didn't ask the
LORD what he wanted us to do. He was
angry at us, because you Levites weren't
there to carry the chest."
14The priests and the Levites made
themselves clean. They were now ready
to carry the sacred chest 15on poles that
rested on their shoulders, just as the
LORD had told Moses to do.
16David then told the leaders to
choose some Levites to sing and play
music on small harps, other stringed instruments, and cymbals. 17-21The men
chosen to play the cymbals were Heman
the son of Joel, his relative Asaph the
son of Berechiah, and Ethan the son of
Kushaiah from the Merari clan. Some of
their assistants played the smaller
harps: they were Zechariah, Aziel,
Shemiramoth, Jehiel, Unni, Eliab, Maaseiah, and Benaiah. Others played the
larger harps: they were Mattithiah,
Eliphelehu, Mikneiah, Azaziah, and two
of the temple guards, Obed-Edom and
Jeiel.
22Chenaniah was chosen to be the music director, because he was a skilled
musician.
23-24Four Levites were then appointed
to guard the sacred chest. They were
Berechiah, Elkanah, Obed-Edom, and
Jehiah.
Finally, David chose priests to walk in
front of the sacred chest and blow trumpets. They were Shebaniah, Joshaphat,
Nethanel, Amasai, Zechariah, Benaiah,
and Eliezer.

The Sacred Chest Is Brought to Jerusalem

(2 Samuel 6.12-22)

25David, the leaders of Israel, and the
army commanders were very happy as
they went to Obed-Edom's house to get
the sacred chest. 26God gave the Levites
the strength they needed to carry the
chest, and so they sacrificed seven bulls
and seven rams.
27David, the Levites, Chenaniah the
music director, and all the musicians
were wearing linen robes, and David
was also wearing a linen cloth.[j] 28While
the sacred chest was being carried into
Jerusalem, everyone was celebrating by
shouting and playing music on horns,
trumpets, cymbals, harps, and other
stringed instruments.
29Saul's daughter Michal[k] looked out
her window and watched the chest being brought into David's City. But when
she saw David jumping and dancing in
honor of the LORD, she was disgusted.
16 They put the sacred chest inside
the tent that David had set up for
it, then they offered sacrifices to please
the LORD[l] and sacrifices to ask his blessing.[m] 2After David had finished, he
blessed the people in the name of the
LORD 3and gave every person in the
crowd a small loaf of bread, some meat,
and a handful of raisins.
4David appointed some of the Levites
to serve at the sacred chest; they were
to play music and sing praises to the
LORD God of Israel. 5Asaph was their
leader, and Zechariah was his assistant.
Jeiel, Shemiramoth, Jehiel, Mattithiah,
Eliab, Benaiah, Obed-Edom, and an-

[j] **15.27** *a linen cloth*: The Hebrew word is "ephod," which can mean either a piece of clothing like a skirt that went from the waist to the knee or a garment like a vest or jacket that only the priests wore. [k] **15.29** *Michal*: One of David's wives. [l] **16.1** *sacrifices to please the LORD*: These sacrifices have traditionally been called "whole burnt offerings" because the whole animal was burned on the altar. A main purpose of such sacrifices was to please the LORD with the smell of the sacrifice, and so in the CEV they are often called "sacrifices to please the LORD." [m] **16.1** *sacrifices to ask his blessing*: These sacrifices have traditionally been called "peace offerings" or "offerings of well-being." A main purpose was to ask for the LORD's blessing, and so in the CEV they are sometimes called "sacrifices to ask the LORD's blessing."

other man named Jeiel were appointed
to play small harps and stringed instruments. Asaph himself played the cymbals, 6and the two priests Benaiah and
Jahaziel were to blow trumpets every
day in front of the sacred chest.

David's Song of Praise

(Psalms 105.1-15; 96.1-13; 106.1, 47, 48)

7That same day, David instructed
Asaph and his relatives for the first time
to sing these praises to the LORD:

8 Praise the LORD
and pray in his name!
Tell everyone
what he has done.
9 Sing praises to the LORD!
Tell about his miracles.
10 Celebrate and worship
his holy name
with all your heart.

11 Trust the LORD
and his mighty power.
Worship him always.
12 Remember his miracles
and all his wonders
and his fair decisions.
13 You belong to the family
of Israel, his servant;
you are his chosen ones,
the descendants of Jacob.

14 The LORD is our God,
bringing justice
everywhere on earth.
15 We must never forget
his agreement and his promises,
not in thousands of years.
*16 God made an eternal promise
17 to Abraham, Isaac, and Jacob
18 when he said, "I'll give you
the land of Canaan."

19 At the time there were
only a few of us,
and we were homeless.
20 We wandered from nation
to nation, from one country
to another.
21 God did not let anyone
mistreat our people.
Instead he protected us
by punishing rulers
22 and telling them,
"Don't touch my chosen leaders
or harm my prophets!"

23 Everyone on this earth,
sing praises to the LORD.
Day after day announce,
"The LORD has saved us!"
24 Tell every nation on earth,
"The LORD is wonderful
and does marvelous things!
25 The LORD is great and deserves
our greatest praise!
He is the only God
worthy of our worship.
26 Other nations worship idols,
but the LORD created
the heavens.
27 Give honor and praise
to the LORD,
whose power and beauty
fill his holy temple."

28 Tell everyone of every nation,
"Praise the glorious power
of the LORD.
29 He is wonderful! Praise him
and bring an offering
into his temple.
Worship the LORD,
majestic and holy.
30 Everyone on earth, now tremble!"

The world stands firm,
never to be shaken.
31 Tell the heavens and the earth
to be glad and celebrate!
And announce to the nations,
"The LORD is King!"
32 Command the ocean to roar
with all of its creatures
and the fields to rejoice
with all of their crops.
33 Then every tree in the forest
will sing joyful songs
to the LORD.
He is coming to judge
all people on earth.

34 Praise the LORD
because he is good to us,
and his love never fails.
35 Say to him, "Save us, LORD God!
Bring us back
from among the nations.
Let us celebrate and shout
in praise of your holy name.
36 LORD God of Israel,
you deserve to be praised
forever and ever."

After David finished, the people
shouted, "Amen! Praise the LORD!"

David Appoints Worship Leaders at Jerusalem and Gibeon

37David chose Asaph and the Levites
in his clan to be in charge of the daily
worship at the place where the sacred
chest was kept. 38Obed-Edom and sixty-
eight of his relatives were their assistants, and Hosah and Obed-Edom the
son of Jeduthun were the guards.
39David also chose Zadok the priest
and his relatives who were priests to
serve at the LORD's sacred tent at
Gibeon. 40They were to offer sacrifices
on the altar every morning and evening,
just as the LORD had commanded in the
Law he gave Israel. 41Heman and Jeduthun were their assistants, as well as the

other men who had been chosen to
praise the LORD for his never-ending
love. 42Heman and Jeduthun were also
responsible for blowing the trumpets,
and for playing the cymbals and other
instruments during worship at the tent.
The Levites in Jeduthun's clan were the
guards at Gibeon.
43After that, everyone went home, and
David went home to his family.

The LORD's Message to David

(2 Samuel 7.1-17)

17 Soon after David moved into his
new palace, he said to Nathan the
prophet, "Look around! I live in a palace
made of cedar, but the sacred chest is
kept in a tent."
2Nathan replied, "The LORD is with
you—do what you want."
3That night, the LORD told Nathan 4to
go to David and tell him:
David, you are my servant, so listen carefully: You are not the one to
build a temple for me. 5I didn't live
in a temple when I brought my people out of Egypt, and I don't live in
one now. A tent has always been my
home wherever I have gone with
them. 6I chose special leaders and
told them to be like shepherds for
my people Israel. But did I ever say
anything to even one of them about
building a cedar temple for me?
7David, this is what I, the LORD
All-Powerful, say to you. I brought
you in from the fields where you
took care of sheep, and I made you
the leader of my people. 8Wherever
you went, I helped you and destroyed your enemies right in front
of your eyes. I have made you one of
the most famous people in the
world.
9I have given my people Israel a
land of their own where they can
live in peace. They will no longer
have to tremble with fear—evil nations won't bother them, as they did
10when I let judges rule my people,
and I will keep your enemies from
attacking you.
Now I promise that like you, your
descendants will be kings. 11I'll
choose one of your sons to be king
when you reach the end of your life
and are buried beside your ancestors. I'll make him a strong ruler,
12and no one will be able to take his
kingdom away from him. He will be
the one to build a temple for me. 13I
will be like a father to him, and he
will be like a son to me. I will never
put an end to my agreement with
him, as I put an end to my agreement with Saul, who was king before you. 14I will make sure that your
son and his descendants will rule
my people and my kingdom forever.
15Nathan told David exactly what the
LORD had said.

David Gives Thanks to the LORD

(2 Samuel 7.18-29)

16David went into the tent he had set
up for the sacred chest. He sat there and
prayed:
LORD God, my family and I don't
deserve what you have already done
for us, 17and yet you have promised
to do even more for my descendants.
You are treating me as if I am a very
important person.[n] 18I am your servant, and you know my thoughts.
What else can I say, except that you
have honored me? 19It was your
choice to do these wonderful things
for me and to make these promises.
20No other god is like you, LORD—
you alone are God. Everything we
have heard about you is true. 21And
there is no other nation on earth like
Israel, the nation you rescued from
slavery in Egypt to be your own. You
became famous by using great and
wonderful miracles to force other
nations and their gods out of your
land, so that your people could live
here. 22You have chosen Israel to be
your people forever, and you have
become their God.
23LORD God, please do what you
promised me and my descendants.
24Then you will be famous forever,
and everyone will say, "The LORD
All-Powerful rules Israel and is their
God."
My kingdom will be strong, 25be-
cause you are my God, and you have
promised that my descendants will
be kings. That's why I have the
courage to pray to you like this, even
though I am only your servant.
26You are the LORD God, and you
have made this good promise to me.
27Now please bless my descendants
forever, and let them always be your
chosen kings. You have already
blessed my family, and I know you
will bless us forever.

A List of David's Victories in War

(2 Samuel 8.1-14)

18 Later, David attacked and defeated the Philistines. He captured their town of Gath and the nearby
villages.
2David also defeated the Moabites,
and so they had to accept him as their
ruler and pay taxes to him.
3While King Hadadezer of Zobah was
trying to gain control of the territory

[n] **17.17** *You are treating me . . . person*: One possible meaning for the difficult Hebrew text.

near the Euphrates River, David met
him in battle at Hamath and defeated
him. 4David captured one thousand
chariots, seven thousand chariot drivers, and twenty thousand soldiers. And
he crippled all but one hundred of the
horses.
5When troops from the Syrian kingdom of Damascus came to help Hadadezer, David killed twenty-two thousand of them. 6Then David stationed
some of his troops in Damascus, and the
people there had to accept David as
their ruler and pay taxes to him.
Everywhere David went, the LORD
helped him win battles.
7Hadadezer's officers had carried gold
shields, but David took these shields
and brought them back to Jerusalem.
8He also took a lot of bronze from the
cities of Tibhath and Cun, which had belonged to Hadadezer. Later, Solomon
used this bronze to make the large
bowl called the Sea, and to make the
pillars and other furnishings for the
temple.
9-10King Tou of Hamath and King
Hadadezer had been enemies. So
when Tou heard that David had defeated Hadadezer's whole army, he
sent his son Hadoram to congratulate
David on his victory. Hadoram also
brought him gifts made of gold, silver,
and bronze. 11David gave these gifts to
the LORD, just as he had done with the
silver and gold he had captured from
Edom, Moab, Ammon, Philistia, and
Amalek.
12Abishai the son of Zeruiah defeated
the Edomite army in Salt Valley and
killed eighteen thousand of their troops.
13Then he stationed troops in Edom, and
the people there had to accept David as
their ruler.
Everywhere David went, the LORD
gave him victory in war.

A List of David's Officials

(2 Samuel 8.15-18)

14David ruled all Israel with fairness
and justice.
15Joab the son of Zeruiah was the
commander in chief of the army.
Jehoshaphat the son of Ahilud kept
the government records.
16Zadok the son of Ahitub and Ahimelech the son of Abiathar were the
priests.
Shavsha was the secretary.
17Benaiah the son of Jehoiada was the
commander of David's bodyguard.[o]
David's sons were his highest-ranking
officials.

Israel Fights Ammon and Syria

(2 Samuel 10.1-19)

19 Some time later, King Nahash of
Ammon died, and his son Hanun
became king. 2David said, "Nahash was
kind to me, so I will be kind to his son."
He sent some officials to Ammon to tell
Hanun how sorry he was that his father
had died.
But when David's officials arrived at
Ammon, 3the Ammonite leaders said to
Hanun, "Do you really believe King
David is honoring your father by sending these men to comfort you? He probably sent them to spy on our country, so
he can come and destroy it."
4Hanun arrested David's officials and
had their beards shaved off and their
robes cut off just below the waist, and
then he sent them away. 5They were terribly ashamed.
When David found out what had happened to his officials, he sent a message
that told them, "Stay in Jericho until
your beards grow back. Then you can
come home."
6The Ammonites realized they had
made David furious. So they paid over
thirty tons of silver to hire chariot
troops from Mesopotamia and from the
Syrian kingdoms of Maacah and Zobah.
7Thirty-two thousand troops, as well as
the king of Maacah and his army, came
and camped near Medeba. The Ammonite troops also left their towns and
came to prepare for battle.
8David heard what was happening,
and he sent out Joab with his army. 9The
Ammonite troops marched to the entrance of the city[p] and prepared for battle, while the Syrian troops took their
positions in the open fields.
10Joab saw that the enemy troops
were lined up on both sides of him. So
he picked some of the best Israelite soldiers to fight the Syrians. 11Then he put
his brother Abishai in command of the
rest of the army and told them to fight
against the Ammonites. 12Joab told his
brother, "If the Syrians are too much for
me to handle, come and help me. And if
the Ammonites are too strong for you,
I'll come and help you. 13Be brave and
fight hard to protect our people and the
towns of our LORD God. I pray he will do
whatever pleases him."
14Joab and his soldiers attacked the
Syrians, and the Syrians ran from them.
15When the Ammonite troops saw that
the Syrians had run away, they ran from
Abishai's soldiers and went back into
their own city. Joab then returned to
Jerusalem.

[o] **18.17** *David's bodyguard*: The Hebrew text has "the Cherethites and the Pelethites," who were foreign soldiers hired by David to be his bodyguard. [p] **19.9** *the city*: Probably Rabbah, the capital city of Ammon.

16 As soon as the Syrians realized they
had been defeated, they sent for their
troops that were stationed on the other
side of the Euphrates River. Shophach,
the commander of Hadadezer's army,
led these troops to Ammon.
17 David found out what the Syrians
were doing, and he brought Israel's entire army together. They crossed the Jordan River, and he commanded them to
take their positions facing the Syrian
troops.
Soon after the fighting began, 18 the
Syrians ran from Israel. David killed
seven thousand chariot troops and forty
thousand regular soldiers. He also killed
Shophach, their commander.
19 When the kings who had been under
Hadadezer's rule saw that Israel had defeated them, they made peace with
David and accepted him as their new
ruler. The Syrians never helped the Ammonites again.

The End of the War with Ammon
(2 Samuel 11.1; 12.26-31)

20 The next spring, the time when
kings go to war, Joab marched
out in command of the Israelite army
and destroyed towns all over the country of Ammon. He attacked the capital
city of Rabbah and left it in ruins. But
David stayed in Jerusalem.
2 Later, David himself went to Rabbah,
where he took the crown from the
statue of their god Milcom.[q] The crown
was made of seventy-five pounds of
gold, and there was a valuable jewel on
it. David put the jewel on his crown,[r]
then carried off everything else of value.
3 He forced the people of Rabbah to
work with saws, iron picks, and axes.
He also did the same thing with the people in all the other Ammonite towns.
David then led Israel's army back to
Jerusalem.

The Descendants of the Rephaim
(2 Samuel 21.15-22)

4 Some time later, Israel fought a battle
against the Philistines at Gezer. During
this battle, Sibbecai from Hushah killed
Sippai, a descendant of the Rephaim,[s]
and the Philistines were defeated.
5 In another battle against the Philistines, Elhanan the son of Jair killed
Lahmi the brother of Goliath from Gath,
whose spear shaft was like a weaver's
beam.[t]
6 Another one of the Philistine soldiers
who was a descendant of the Rephaim
was as big as a giant and had six fingers on each hand and six toes on each
foot. During a battle at Gath, 7 he made
fun of Israel, so David's nephew
Jonathan[u] killed him.
8 David and his soldiers killed these
three men from Gath who were descendants of the Rephaim.

David Counts the People
(2 Samuel 24.1-9)

21 Satan decided to cause trouble
for Israel by making David think
it was a good idea to find out how many
people there were in Israel and Judah.
2 David told Joab and the army commanders, "Count everyone in Israel, from the
town of Beersheba in the south all the
way north to Dan. Then I will know how
many people can serve in my army."
3 Joab answered, "Your Majesty, even
if the LORD made your kingdom a hundred times larger, you would still rule
everyone in it. Why do you need to
know how many soldiers there are?
Don't you think that would make the
whole nation angry?"
4 But David would not change his
mind. And so Joab went everywhere in
Israel and Judah and counted the people. He returned to Jerusalem 5 and told
David that the total number of men who
could serve in the army was one million
one hundred thousand in Israel and four
hundred seventy thousand in Judah.
6 Joab refused to include anyone from
the tribes of Levi and Benjamin, because he still disagreed with David's orders.

God Punishes Israel
(2 Samuel 24.10-17)

7 David's order to count the people
made God angry, and he punished Israel. 8 David prayed, "I am your servant.
But what I did was stupid and terribly
wrong. Please forgive me."
9 The LORD said to Gad, one of David's
prophets, 10 "Tell David that I will punish
him in one of three ways. But he will
have to choose which one it will be."
11 Gad went to David and told him:
You must choose how the LORD
will punish you: 12 Will there be three
years when the land won't grow
enough food for its people? Or will
your enemies constantly defeat you
for three months? Or will the LORD
send a horrible disease to strike
your land for three days? Think
about it and decide, because I have

[q] **20.2** *the statue of their god Milcom*: Or "their king." [r] **20.2** *David put the jewel on his crown*: Or "David put the crown on his head." [s] **20.4** *the Rephaim*: This may refer to a group of people that lived in Palestine before the Israelites and who were famous for their large size. [t] **20.5** *weaver's beam*: When a weaver made cloth, one set of threads was tied onto a large wooden rod that was known as a weaver's beam. [u] **20.7** *David's nephew Jonathan*: Hebrew "Jonathan son of Shimea, David's brother."

to give your answer to God who sent me.

13David was miserable and said, "It's a terrible choice to make! But the LORD is kind, and I'd rather have him punish me than for anyone else to do it."

14So the LORD sent a horrible disease on Israel, and seventy thousand Israelites died. 15Then he sent an angel to destroy the city of Jerusalem. But just as the angel was about to do that, the LORD felt sorry for all the suffering he had caused the people, and he told the angel, "Stop! They have suffered enough." This happened at the threshing place that belonged to Araunah[v] the Jebusite.

16David saw the LORD's angel in the air, holding a sword over Jerusalem. He and the leaders of Israel, who were all wearing sackcloth,[w] bowed with their faces to the ground, 17and David prayed, "It's my fault! I sinned by ordering the people to be counted. They have done nothing wrong—they are innocent sheep. LORD God, please punish me and my family. Don't let the disease wipe out your people."

David Buys Araunah's Threshing Place

(2 Samuel 24.18-25)

18The LORD's angel told the prophet Gad to tell David that he must go to Araunah's threshing place and build an altar in honor of the LORD. 19David followed the LORD's instructions.

20Araunah and his four sons were threshing wheat at the time, and when they saw the angel, the four sons ran to hide. 21Just then, David arrived, and when Araunah saw him, he stopped his work and bowed down.

22David said, "Would you sell me your threshing place, so I can build an altar on it to the LORD? Then this disease will stop killing the people. I'm willing to pay whatever you say it's worth."

23Araunah answered, "Take it, Your Majesty, and do whatever you want with it. I'll even give you the oxen for the sacrifice and the wheat for the grain sacrifice. And you can use the threshing-boards[x] for the fire. It's all yours!"

24But David replied, "No! I want to pay you what they're worth. I can't just take something from you and then offer the LORD a sacrifice that cost me nothing."

25So David paid Araunah six hundred gold coins for his threshing place. 26David built an altar and offered sacrifices to please the LORD[y] and sacrifices to ask his blessing.[z] David prayed, and the LORD answered him by sending fire down on the altar. 27Then the LORD commanded the angel to put the sword away.[a]

28When David saw that the LORD had answered his prayer, he offered more sacrifices there at the threshing place, 29-30because he was afraid of the angel's sword and did not want to go all the way to Gibeon. That's where the sacred tent that Moses had made in the desert was kept, as well as the altar where sacrifices were offered to the LORD.

22 David said, "The temple of the LORD God must be built right here at this threshing place. And the altar for offering sacrifices will also be here."

David Prepares To Build the Temple

2David ordered the foreigners living in Israel to come to Jerusalem. Then he assigned some to cut blocks of stone for building the temple. 3He got a large supply of iron to make into nails and hinges for the doors, and he provided so much bronze that it could not be weighed. 4He also had cedar logs brought in from the cities of Sidon and Tyre.

5He said, "The temple for the LORD must be great, so that everyone in the world will know about it. But since my son Solomon is young and has no experience, I will make sure that everything is ready for the temple to be built."

That's why David did all these things before he died.

David Instructs Solomon To Build the Temple

6David sent for his son Solomon and told him to build a temple for the LORD God of Israel. 7He said:

> My son, I wanted to build a temple where the LORD my God would be worshiped. 8But some time ago, he told me, "David, you have killed too many people and have fought too many battles. That's why you are not the one to build my temple. 9But when your son becomes king, I will give him peace throughout his kingdom. His name will be Solomon, because during his rule I will keep Israel safe and peaceful.[b] 10Solomon will build my temple. He will be like a son to me, and I will be like a

[v]21.15 *Araunah*: The Hebrew text has "Ornan," another spelling of Araunah (see 2 Samuel 24.16). [w]21.16 *sackcloth*: A rough, dark-colored cloth made from goat or camel hair and used to make grain sacks. It was worn in times of trouble or sorrow. [x]21.23 *threshing-boards*: Heavy boards with bits of rock or metal on the bottom. They were dragged across the grain to separate the husks from the kernels. [y]21.26 *sacrifices to please the LORD*: See the note at 16.1. [z]21.26 *sacrifices to ask his blessing*: See the note at 16.1. [a]21.27 *the LORD commanded the angel to put the sword away*: See verse 16. [b]22.9 *Solomon . . . safe and peaceful*: In Hebrew "Solomon" sounds like "peace."

father to him. In fact, one of his descendants will always rule in Israel."
11 Solomon, my son, I now pray
that the LORD your God will be with
you and keep his promise to help
you build a temple for him. 12 May he
give you wisdom and knowledge, so
that you can rule Israel according to
his Law. 13 If you obey the laws and
teachings that the LORD gave Moses,
you will be successful. Be strong and
brave and don't get discouraged or
be afraid of anything.
14 I have all the supplies you'll
need to build the temple: You have
four thousand tons of gold and forty
thousand tons of silver. There's also
plenty of wood, stone, and more
bronze and iron than I could weigh.
Ask for anything else you need. 15 I
have also assigned men who will cut
and lay the stone. And there are carpenters and people who are experts
in working with 16 gold, silver,
bronze, and iron. You have plenty of
workers to do the job. Now get
started, and I pray that the LORD will
be with you in your work.
17 David then gave orders for the leaders of Israel to help Solomon. 18 David
said:
The LORD our God has helped me
defeat all the people who lived here
before us, and he has given you
peace from all your enemies. Now
this land belongs to the LORD and
his people. 19 Obey the LORD your
God with your heart and soul. Begin
work on the temple to honor him, so
that the sacred chest and the things
used for worship can be kept there.

David Assigns the Levites Their Duties

23 David was old when he chose his
son Solomon to be king of Israel.
2 Some time later, David called together
all of Israel's leaders, priests, and
Levites. 3 He then counted the Levite
men who were at least thirty years old,
and the total was thirty-eight thousand.
4 He said, "Twenty-four thousand of the
Levites will be in charge of the temple,
six thousand will be temple officials and
judges, 5 four thousand will be guards at
the temple, and four thousand will
praise the LORD by playing the musical
instruments I have given them."
6 David then divided the Levites into
three groups according to the clans of
Levi's sons, Gershon, Kohath, and Merari.
7 Gershon had two sons: Ladan and
Shimei. 8 Ladan was the father of Jehiel,
Zetham, and Joel. 9 They were all family
leaders among their father's descendants. Shimei was the father of Shelomoth, Haziel, and Haran. 10-11 Later,
Shimei had four more sons, in the following order: Jahath, Zina, Jeush, and
Beriah. But Jeush and Beriah didn't
have many children, so their descendants were counted as one family.
12 Kohath had four sons: Amram,
Izhar, Hebron, and Uzziel. 13 Amram was
the father of Aaron and Moses. Aaron
and his descendants were chosen to be
in charge of all the sacred things. They
served the LORD by offering sacrifices to
him and by blessing the people in his
name. 14-15 Moses, the man of God, was
the father of Gershom and Eliezer, and
their descendants were considered
Levites. 16 Gershom's oldest son was
Shebuel. 17 Rehabiah, who was Eliezer's
only son, had many children. 18 The second son born to Kohath was Izhar, and
his oldest son was Shelomith. 19 Hebron,
the third son of Kohath, was the father
of Jeriah, Amariah, Jahaziel, and
Jekameam. 20 Kohath's youngest son,
Uzziel, was the father of Micah and Isshiah.
21 Merari had two sons: Mahli and
Mushi. Mahli was the father of Eleazar
and Kish. 22 Eleazar had no sons, only
daughters, and they married their uncle's sons. 23 Mushi the second son of
Merari, was the father of Mahli, Eder,
and Jeremoth.
24 These were the clans and families of
the tribe of Levi. Those who were
twenty years and older were assigned to
work at the LORD's temple.
25 David said:
The LORD God of Israel has given
his people peace, and he will live in
Jerusalem forever. 26 And so, the
Levites won't need to move the sacred tent and the things used for
worship from place to place. 27 From
now on, all Levites at least twenty
years old 28 will serve the LORD by
helping Aaron's descendants do
their work at the temple, by keeping
the courtyards and rooms of the
temple clean, and by making sure
that everything used in worship
stays pure. 29 They will also be in
charge of the sacred loaves of bread,
the flour for the grain sacrifices, the
thin wafers, any offerings to be
baked, and the flour mixed with
olive oil. These Levites will weigh
and measure these offerings.
30 Every morning and evening, the
Levites are to give thanks to the
LORD and sing praises to him. 31 They
must also give thanks and sing
praises when sacrifices are offered
on each Sabbath, as well as during
New Moon Festivals and other religious feasts. There must always be
enough Levites on duty at the temple to do everything that needs to be
done. 32 They were once in charge of
taking care of the sacred tent; now

they are responsible for the temple
and for helping Aaron's descendants.

David Assigns the Priests Their Duties

24 Aaron's descendants were then
divided into work groups. Aaron
had four sons: Nadab, Abihu, Eleazar,
and Ithamar. [2]But Nadab and Abihu
died long before their father, without
having any sons. That's why Eleazar
and Ithamar served as priests.
[3]David divided Aaron's descendants
into groups, according to their assigned
work. Zadok, one of Eleazar's descendants, and Ahimelech, one of Ithamar's
descendants, helped David.
[4]Eleazar's descendants were divided
into sixteen groups, and Ithamar's were
divided into eight groups, because
Eleazar's family included more family
leaders. [5]However, both families included temple officials and priests, and
so to make sure the work was divided
fairly, David asked God what to do.[c]
[6]As each group was assigned their duties, Shemaiah the son of Nethanel the
Levite wrote down the name of the family leader in charge of that group. The
witnesses were David and his officials,
as well as Zadok the priest, Ahimelech
the son of Abiathar, and the family leaders from the clans of the priests and the
Levites.
[7-18]Each group of priests went by the
name of its family leader, and they were
assigned their duties in the following order: Jehoiarib, Jedaiah, Harim, Seorim,
Malchijah, Mijamin, Hakkoz, Abijah,
Jeshua, Shecaniah, Eliashib, Jakim,
Huppah, Jeshebeab, Bilgah, Immer,
Hezir, Happizzez, Pethahiah, Jehezkel,
Jachin, Gamul, Delaiah, Maaziah.
[19]These men were assigned their duties
at the temple, just as the LORD God of Israel had commanded their ancestor
Aaron.

The Rest of the Levites Are Assigned Their Duties

[20]Here is a list of the other descendants of Levi:

Amram was the ancestor of Shubael
and Jehdeiah.
[21]Rehabiah was the ancestor of
Isshiah, the oldest son in his family.
[22]Izhar was the father of Shelomoth
and the grandfather of Jahath.
[23]Hebron had four sons, in the
following order: Jeriah, Amariah,
Jahaziel, and Jekameam.
[24]Uzziel was the father of Micah and
the grandfather of Shamir.
[25]Isshiah, Micah's brother, was the
father of Zechariah.
[26]Merari was the father of Mahli,
Mushi, and Jaaziah.

[27]Jaaziah had three sons: Shoham,
Zaccur, and Ibri.[d] [28-29]Mahli was the
father of Eleazar and Kish. Eleazar had
no sons, but Kish was the father of Jerahmeel. [30]Mushi had three sons: Mahli,
Eder, and Jerimoth.
These were the descendants of Levi,
according to their clans. [31]Each one was
assigned his duties in the same way that
their relatives the priests had been assigned their duties. David, Zadok, Ahimelech, and the family leaders of the
priests and Levites were the witnesses.

David Assigns the Temple Musicians Their Duties

25 David and the temple officials
chose the descendants of Asaph,
Heman, and Jeduthun to be in charge of
music. They were to praise the LORD by
playing cymbals, harps and other
stringed instruments. Here is a list of
the musicians and their duties:
[2]Asaph's four sons, Zaccur, Joseph,
Nethaniah, and Asarelah, were under
the direction of their father and played
music whenever the king told them to.
[3]Jeduthun's six sons, Gedaliah, Zeri,
Jeshaiah, Shimei,[e] Hashabiah, and Mattithiah, were under the direction of their
father and played harps and sang
praises to the LORD.
[4]Heman had fourteen sons: Bukkiah,
Mattaniah, Uzziel, Shebuel, Jerimoth,
Hananiah, Hanani, Eliathah, Giddalti,
Romamtiezer, Joshbekashah, Mallothi,
Hothir, Mahazioth. [5]Heman was one of
the king's prophets, and God honored
Heman by giving him fourteen sons and
three daughters. [6]His sons were under
his direction and played cymbals, harps,
and other stringed instruments during
times of worship at the temple.
Asaph, Jeduthun, and Heman took
their orders directly from the king.
[7]There were two hundred eighty-eight
of these men, and all of them were
skilled musicians. [8]David assigned them
their duties by asking the LORD what he
wanted.[f] Everyone was responsible for
something, whether young or old,
teacher or student.
[9-31]The musicians were divided into
twenty-four groups of twelve, and each
group went by the name of their family

[c]**24.5** *asked God what to do*: The Hebrew text has "cast lots" (see the note at 6.65).
[d]**24.26,27** *Ibri*: One possible meaning for the difficult Hebrew text of verses 26, 27.
[e]**25.3** *Shimei*: One Hebrew manuscript and two ancient translations; other Hebrew manuscripts do not have this name. [f]**25.8** *asking the LORD what he wanted*: The Hebrew text has "casting lots" (see the note at 6.65).

leader. They were assigned their duties
in the following order: Joseph, Ged-
aliah, Zaccur, Zeri, Nethaniah, Bukkiah,
Asarelah, Jeshaiah, Mattaniah, Shimei,
Uzziel, Hashabiah, Shebuel, Mattithiah,
Jerimoth, Hananiah, Joshbekashah,
Hanani, Mallothi, Eliathah, Hothir, Gid-
dalti, Mahazioth, and Romamtiezer.

The Temple Guards Are Assigned Their Duties

26 The temple guards were also divided into groups according to
clans.
Meshelemiah son of Kore was from
the Korah clan and was a descendant of
Asaph. 2 He had seven sons, who were
born in the following order: Zechariah,
Jediael, Zebadiah, Jathniel, 3 Elam, Jehohanan, and Eliehoenai.
4-5 Obed-Edom had been blessed with
eight sons: Shemaiah, Jehozabad, Joah,
Sachar, Nethanel, Ammiel, Issachar, and
Peullethai.
6-7 Shemaiah was the father of Othni,
Rephael, Obed, Elzabad, Elihu, and
Semachiah. They were all respected
leaders in their clan. 8 There were sixty-
two descendants of Obed-Edom who
were strong enough to be guards at the
temple.
9 Eighteen descendants of Meshelemiah were chosen for this work.
10-11 Hosah, from the Merari clan, was
the father of Shimri, Hilkiah, Tebaliah,
and Zechariah. Hosah had made Shimri
the family leader, even though he was
not the oldest son. Thirteen men from
Hosah's family were chosen to be temple guards.
12 The guards were divided into
groups, according to their family leaders, and they were assigned duties at the
temple, just like the other Levites.
13 Each group, no matter how large or
small, was assigned a gate to guard, and
they let the LORD show them what he
wanted done.[g]
14 Shelemiah[h] was chosen to guard the
East Gate. Zechariah his son was a wise
man and was chosen to guard the North
Gate. 15 Obed-Edom was then chosen to
guard the South Gate, and his sons were
chosen to guard the storerooms. 16 Shuppim and Hosah were chosen to guard
the West Gate and the Shallecheth Gate
on the upper road.
The guards were assigned the following work schedule: 17 Each day six
guards were on duty on the east side of
the temple, four were on duty on the
north side, and four were on duty on the
south side. Two guards were stationed at
each of the two storerooms, 18 four were
stationed along the road leading to the
west courtyard,[i] and two guards stayed
in the court itself.
19 These were the guard duties assigned to the men from the clans of Korah and Merari.

Guards Are Assigned to the Treasury

20 The Levites who were relatives of
the Korahites and the Merarites were[j] in
charge of guarding the temple treasury
and the gifts that had been dedicated to
God.
21 Ladan was from the Gershon clan
and was the father of Jehieli. Many of
his other descendants were family leaders in the clan.[k] 22 Jehieli was the father
of Zetham and Joel, and they were responsible for guarding the treasury.
23 Other guards at the treasury were
from the Kohathite clans of Amram,
Izhar, Hebron, and Uzziel.
24 Shebuel was a descendant of Gershom the son of Moses. He was the chief
official in charge of the temple treasury.
25 The descendants of Gershom's brother
Eliezer included Rehabiah, Jeshaiah, Joram, Zichri, and Shelomoth.
26 Shelomoth and his relatives were in
charge of all the gifts that were dedicated to the LORD. These included the
gifts that King David had dedicated, as
well as those dedicated by the family
leaders, army officers, and army commanders. 27 And whenever valuable
things were captured in battle, these
men brought some of them to the temple. 28 Shelomoth and his relatives were
responsible for any gifts that had been
given to the temple, including those
from Samuel the prophet, King Saul the
son of Kish, Abner the son of Ner,[l] and
Joab the son of Zeruiah.

Other Officers Are Assigned Their Duties

29 Chenaniah from the Izhar clan and
his sons were government officials and
judges. They did not work at the temple.
30 Hashabiah from the Hebron clan
and one thousand seven hundred of his
skilled relatives were the officials in
charge of all religious and government
business in the Israelite territories west
of the Jordan River.
31-32 Jerijah was the leader of the Hebron clan. David assigned him and two
thousand seven hundred of his relatives,

[g]**26.13** *they let the LORD show them what he wanted done*: The Hebrew text has "they cast lots to find out what the LORD wanted done" (see the note at 6.65). [h]**26.14** *Shelemiah*: Another spelling for Meshelemiah. [i]**26.18** *courtyard*: One possible meaning for the difficult Hebrew text. [j]**26.20** *The Levites . . . were*: One ancient translation; Hebrew "Ahijah the Levite was." [k]**26.21** *Many of his other . . . clan*: One possible meaning for the difficult Hebrew text. [l]**26.28** *Abner the son of Ner*: Abner was King Saul's uncle (see 9.39).

who were all respected family leaders,
to be the officials in charge of all religious and government business in the
tribes of Reuben, Gad, and East Manasseh. David found out about these
men during the fortieth year of his rule,
when he had a list made of all the families in the Hebron clan. They were from
the town of Jazer in the territory of
Gilead.

David Assigns Army Commanders

27 Each month a group of twenty-
four thousand men served as soldiers in Israel's army. These men, which
included the family leaders, army commanders, and officials of the king, were
under the command of the following
men, arranged by the month of their
service:
[2]In the first month, Jashobeam the
son of Zabdiel, [3]a descendant of Perez;
[4]in the second month, Dodai the Ahohite, whose assistant was Mikloth;[m]
[5]in the third month, Benaiah the son
of Jehoiada the priest, [6]who was the
leader of the Thirty Warriors, and whose
son Ammizabad was also an army commander;[n]
[7]in the fourth month, Asahel the
brother of Joab, whose son Zebadiah
took over command after him;
[8]in the fifth month, Shamhuth from
the Izrah clan;
[9]in the sixth month, Ira the son of
Ikkesh from Tekoa;
[10]in the seventh month, Helez from
Pelon in the territory of Ephraim;
[11]in the eighth month, Sibbecai from
Hushah of the Zerah clan;
[12]in the ninth month, Abiezer from
Anathoth in the territory of Benjamin;
[13]in the tenth month, Maharai from
Netophah of the Zerah clan;
[14]in the eleventh month, Benaiah from
Pirathon in the territory of Ephraim;
[15]in the twelfth month, Heldai from
Netophah, who was a descendant of
Othniel.

David Assigns Tribal Leaders

[16-22]Here is a list of the leaders of each
tribe in Israel:
Eliezer son of Zichri was over
Reuben: Shephatiah son of Maacah was
over Simeon; Hashabiah son of Kemuel
was over the Levites, and Zadok the
priest was over the descendants of
Aaron; Elihu the brother of David was
over Judah; Omri son of Michael was
over Issachar; Ishmaiah son of Obadiah
was over Zebulun; Jerimoth son of
Azriel was over Naphtali; Hoshea son of
Azaziah was over Ephraim; Joel son of
Pedaiah was over West Manasseh; Iddo
son of Zechariah was over East Manasseh; Jaasiel son of Abner was over
Benjamin; Azarel son of Jeroham was
over Dan.
[23]When David decided to count the
people of Israel, he gave orders not to
count anyone under twenty years of
age, because the LORD had promised
long ago that Israel would have as many
people as there are stars in the sky.
[24]Joab the son of Zeruiah had begun to
count the people, but he stopped when
the LORD began punishing Israel. So the
total number was never included in
David's official records.

Officials in Charge of the King's Property

[25]Azmaveth the son of Adiel was in
charge of the king's personal storage
rooms. Jonathan the son of Uzziah was
in charge of the king's other storerooms
that were in the towns, the villages, and
the defense towers in Israel.
[26]Ezri the son of Chelub was in charge
of the workers who farmed the king's
land.
[27]Shimei from Ramah was in charge
of the vineyards, and Zabdi from Shepham was in charge of storing the wine.
[28]Baal Hanan from Geder was in
charge of the olive and sycamore trees
in the western foothills, and Joash was
in charge of storing the olive oil.
[29]Shitrai from Sharon was responsible
for the cattle that were kept in Sharon
Plain, and Shaphat son of Adlai was responsible for those kept in the valleys.
[30]Obil the Ishmaelite was in charge of
the camels, Jehdeiah from Meronoth
was in charge of the donkeys, and Jaziz
the Hagrite was in charge of the sheep
and goats.
[31]These were the men in charge of
David's royal property.

David's Personal Advisors

[32]David's uncle Jonathan was a wise
and intelligent advisor. He and Jehiel
the son of Hachmoni taught David's
sons.
[33]Ahithophel and Hushai the Archite
were two of David's advisors. [34]Je-
hoiada the son of Benaiah was the
king's advisor after Ahithophel, and
later, Abiathar was his advisor.
Joab was commander of Israel's army.

David Gives Solomon the Plans for the Temple

28 David called a meeting in
Jerusalem for all of Israel's leaders, including the tribal leaders, the government officials, the army commanders, the officials in charge of the royal

[m]27.4 *whose . . . Mikloth*: One possible meaning for the difficult Hebrew text. [n]27.6 *whose son Ammizabad . . . army commander*: One possible meaning for the difficult Hebrew text.

property and livestock, the palace officials, and the brave warriors.

2After everyone was there, David stood up and said:

Listen to me, my people. I wanted to build a place where the sacred chest would be kept, so we could go there and worship the LORD our God. I have prepared all the supplies for building a temple, 3but the LORD has refused to let me build it, because he said I have killed too many people in battle.

4The LORD God chose Judah to be the leading tribe in Israel. Then from Judah, he chose my father's family, and from that family, he chose me to be the king of Israel, and he promised that my descendants will also rule as kings. 5The LORD has blessed me with many sons, but he chose my son Solomon to be the next king of Israel. 6The LORD said to me, "Your son Solomon will build my temple, and it will honor me. Solomon will be like a son to me, and I will be like a father to him. 7If he continues to obey my laws and commands, his kingdom will never end."

8My friends, you are the LORD's people. And now, with God as your witness, I want you to promise that you will do your best to obey everything the LORD God has commanded us. Then this land will always belong to you and your descendants.

9Solomon, my son, worship God and obey him with all your heart and mind, just as I have done. He knows all your thoughts and your reasons for doing things, and so if you turn to him, he will hear your prayers. But if you ignore him, he will reject you forever. 10The LORD has chosen you to build a temple for worshiping him. Be confident and do the work you have been assigned.

11After David finished speaking, he gave Solomon the plans for building the main rooms of the temple, including the porch, the storerooms, the rooms upstairs and downstairs, as well as the most holy place. 12He gave Solomon his plans for the courtyards and the open areas around the temple, and for the rooms to store the temple treasures and gifts that had been dedicated to God.

13David also gave Solomon his plans for dividing the priests and the Levites into groups, as well as for the work that needed to be done at the temple and for taking care of the objects used for worship. 14He told Solomon how much gold and silver was to be used in making the sacred objects, 15including the lampstands and lamps, 16the gold table which held the sacred loaves of bread, the tables made of silver, 17the meat forks, the bowls and cups, 18the gold incense altar, and the gold statue of a chariot for the winged creatures which were on the lid of the sacred chest.

19David then said to Solomon:

The LORD showed me how his temple is to be built. 20But you must see that everything is done according to these plans. Be confident, and never be afraid of anything or get discouraged. The LORD my God will help you do everything needed to finish the temple, so it can be used for worshiping him. 21The priests and Levites have been assigned their duties, and all the skilled workers are prepared to do their work. The people and their leaders will do anything you tell them.

Gifts for Building the Temple

29 David told the crowd:

God chose my son Solomon to build the temple, but Solomon is young and has no experience. This is not just any building—this is the temple for the LORD God! 2That's why I have done my best to get everything Solomon will need to build it—gold, silver, bronze, iron, wood, onyx, turquoise, colored gems, all kinds of precious stones, and marble.

3Besides doing all that, I have promised to give part of my own gold and silver as a way of showing my love for God's temple. 4Almost one hundred twenty tons of my finest gold and over two hundred fifty tons of my silver will be used to decorate its walls 5and to make the gold and silver objects. Now, who else will show their dedication to the LORD by giving gifts for building his temple?

6After David finished speaking, the family leaders, the tribal leaders, the army commanders, and the government officials voluntarily gave gifts 7for the temple. These gifts included almost two hundred tons of gold, three hundred eighty tons of silver, almost seven hundred tons of bronze, and three thousand seven hundred fifty tons of iron. 8Everyone who owned precious stones also donated them to the temple treasury, where Jehiel from the Levite clan of Gershon guarded them.

9David and the people were very happy that so much had been given to the LORD, and they all celebrated.

David Praises the LORD

10Then, in front of everyone, David sang praises to the LORD:

I praise you forever, LORD! You are

the God our ancestor Jacob[o] worshiped. 11Your power is great, and
your glory is seen everywhere in
heaven and on earth. You are king of
the entire world, 12and you rule with
strength and power. You make people rich and powerful and famous.
13We thank you, our God, and praise
you.
14But why should we be happy
that we have given you these gifts?
They belong to you, and we have
only given back what is already
yours. 15We are only foreigners living here on earth for a while, just as
our ancestors were. And we will
soon be gone, like a shadow that
suddenly disappears.
16Our LORD God, we have brought
all these things for building a temple
to honor you. They belong to you,
and you gave them to us. 17But we
are happy, because everyone has
voluntarily given you these things.
You know what is in everyone's
heart, and you are pleased when
people are honest. 18Always make us
eager to give, and help us be faithful
to you, just as our ancestors Abraham, Isaac, and Jacob faithfully
worshiped you. 19And give Solomon
the desire to completely obey your
laws and teachings, and the desire to
build the temple for which I have
provided these gifts.
20David then said to the people, "Now
it's your turn to praise the LORD, the
God your ancestors worshiped!" So
everyone praised the LORD, and they
bowed down to honor him and David
their king.

Solomon Is Crowned King

21The next day, the Israelites slaughtered a thousand bulls, a thousand
rams, and a thousand lambs, and they
offered them as sacrifices to please the
LORD,[p] along with offerings of wine.
22The people were very happy, and they
ate and drank there at the LORD's altar.
That same day, Solomon was crowned
king. The people celebrated and poured
olive oil on Solomon's head to show
that he would be their next king. They
also poured oil on Zadok's head to show
that he was their priest.
23So Solomon became king after
David his father. Solomon was successful, and everyone in Israel obeyed him.
24Every official and every soldier, as
well as all of David's other sons, were
loyal to him. 25The LORD made Solomon
a great king, and the whole nation was
amazed at how famous he was. In fact,
no other king of Israel was as great as
Solomon.

David Dies

26David the son of Jesse was king of
Israel 27for forty years. He ruled from
Hebron for seven years and from
Jerusalem for thirty-three years. 28David
was rich and respected and lived to be
an old man. Then he died, and his son
Solomon became king.
29Everything David did while he was
king is included in the history written
by the prophets Samuel, Nathan, and
Gad. 30They wrote about his powerful
rule and about the things that happened
not only to him, but also to Israel and
the other nations.

[o]**29.10** *Jacob*: See the note at 1.34. [p]**29.21** *sacrifices to please the LORD*: See the note at 16.1.

2 CHRONICLES

ABOUT THIS BOOK

Second Chronicles continues the history of Israel that was begun in 1 Chronicles. This book repeats information and many stories that are in 1 and 2 Kings, but from a slightly different viewpoint.

The book of 2 Chronicles begins with the rule of King Solomon, then tells the history of the two separate kingdoms of Judah and Israel down to the fall of Jerusalem in 586 B.C.

King Solomon is honored as the ideal king of Israel. The first part of 2 Chronicles (1–9) includes events from his rule, especially the building and dedication of the temple in Jerusalem and the beginning of worship there.

The second part of the book (10–36) begins with the rebellion of the northern tribes of Israel and the division of the country into two separate kingdoms, Judah in the south and Israel in the north. This part of 2 Chronicles is the history of Judah down to the time of Jerusalem's fall and destruction. Unlike 2 Kings, the book of 2 Chronicles includes very little information about the northern kingdom. According to 2 Chronicles, the people of Israel were sinful and turned their backs on the Lord, and so their history did not deserve to be told.

Second Chronicles, like 1 Chronicles, is very concerned that the Lord be worshiped in the proper way. Hezekiah and Josiah are two of the most respected kings of Judah, because they were always faithful to the Lord and did many things to see that he was properly worshiped and that his Law was obeyed.

This book tells how Jerusalem was destroyed and the people of Judah were led away as prisoners to Babylonia. But the book concludes with hope for the Jews. King Cyrus of Persia lets them return to Judah, and he promises:

The LORD God will watch over any of his people who want to go back to Judah.

(36.23b)

A QUICK LOOK AT THIS BOOK

Solomon's Wisdom and Wealth (1.1-17)
Building and Dedication of the Jerusalem Temple (2.1—7.22)
Other Events During Solomon's Rule (8.1—9.28)
The Death of Solomon (9.29-31)
The Northern Tribes of Israel Rebel against King Rehoboam (10.1-19)
Kings of Judah (11.1—28.27)
King Hezekiah and the Assyrian Invasion (29.1—32.33)
King Manasseh and King Amon (33.1-25)
King Josiah and *The Book of God's Law* (34.1—35.27)
The Last Kings of Judah (36.1-16)
Jerusalem Is Destroyed and the People Are Taken to Babylonia (36.17-21)
King Cyrus of Persia Lets the Jews Return to Judah (36.22, 23)

The LORD Makes Solomon Wise

(1 Kings 3.1-15)

1 King Solomon, the son of David,
was now in complete control of his
kingdom, because the LORD God had
blessed him and made him a powerful
king.
2-5At that time, the sacred tent that
Moses the servant of the LORD had
made in the desert was still kept
at Gibeon, and in front of the tent was
the bronze altar that Bezalel[a] had
made.
One day, Solomon told the people of
Israel, the army commanders, the officials, and the family leaders, to go with
him to the place of worship at Gibeon,
even though his father King David
had already moved the sacred chest
from Kiriath-Jearim to the tent that
he had set up for it in Jerusalem.
Solomon and the others went to Gibeon
to worship the LORD, 6and there at the
bronze altar, Solomon offered a thousand animals as sacrifices to please the
LORD.[b]
7God appeared to Solomon that night
in a dream and said, "Solomon, ask for
anything you want, and I will give it to
you."
8Solomon answered:
LORD God, you were always loyal
to my father David, and now you
have made me king of Israel. 9I am
supposed to rule these people, but
there are as many of them as there
are specks of dust on the ground. So
keep the promise you made to my
father 10and make me wise. Give me
the knowledge I'll need to be the
king of this great nation of yours.
11God replied:
Solomon, you could have asked
me to make you rich or famous or to
let you live a long time. Or you could
have asked for your enemies to be
destroyed. Instead, you asked for
wisdom and knowledge to rule my
people. 12So I will make you wise
and intelligent. But I will also make
you richer and more famous than
any king before or after you.
13Solomon then left Gibeon and returned to Jerusalem, the capital city of
Israel.

Solomon's Wealth

(1 Kings 10.26-29)

14Solomon had a force of one thousand four hundred chariots and twelve
thousand horses that he kept in
Jerusalem and other towns.
15While Solomon was king of Israel,
there was silver and gold everywhere
in Jerusalem, and cedar was as common
as ordinary sycamore trees in the
foothills.
16-17Solomon's merchants bought his
horses and chariots in the regions
of Musri and Kue.[c] They paid about
fifteen pounds of silver for a chariot
and almost four pounds of silver for
a horse. They also sold horses and
chariots to the Hittite and Syrian
kings.

Solomon Asks Hiram To Help Build the Temple

(1 Kings 5.1-12)

2 Solomon decided to build a temple
where the LORD would be worshiped, and also to build a palace for
himself. 2He assigned seventy thousand
men to carry building supplies and
eighty thousand to cut stone from the
hills. And he chose three thousand six
hundred men to supervise these workers.
3Solomon sent the following message
to King Hiram of Tyre:
Years ago, when my father David
was building his palace, you supplied him with cedar logs. Now will
you send me supplies? 4I am building a temple where the LORD my
God will be worshiped. Sweet-
smelling incense will be burned
there, and sacred bread will be offered to him. Worshipers will offer
sacrifices to the LORD every morning
and evening, every Sabbath, and on
the first day of each month, as well
as during all our religious festivals.
These things will be done for all
time, just as the LORD has commanded.
5This will be a great temple, because our God is greater than all
other gods. 6No one can ever build a
temple large enough for God—even
the heavens are too small a place for
him to live in! All I can do is build a
place where we can offer sacrifices
to him.
7Send me a worker who can not
only carve, but who can work with
gold, silver, bronze, and iron, as well
as make brightly colored cloth. The
person you send will work here in
Judah and Jerusalem with the

[a] **1.2-5** *Bezalel*: Hebrew "Bezalel son of Uri son of Hur." [b] **1.6** *sacrifices to please the LORD*: These sacrifices have traditionally been called "whole burnt offerings," because the whole animal was burned on the altar. A main purpose of such sacrifices was to please the LORD with the smell of the sacrifice, and so in the CEV they are often called "sacrifices to please the LORD." [c] **1.16,17** *Musri and Kue*: Hebrew "Egypt and Kue." Musri and Kue were regions located in what is today southeast Turkey.

skilled workers that my father has
already hired.
8I know that you have workers
who are experts at cutting lumber in
Lebanon. So would you please send
me some cedar, pine, and juniper
logs? My workers will be there to
help them, 9because I'll need a lot of
lumber to build such a large and glorious temple. 10I will pay your wood-
cutters one hundred twenty-five
thousand bushels of wheat, the same
amount of barley, one hundred fifteen thousand gallons of wine, and
that same amount of olive oil.
11Hiram sent his answer back to
Solomon:
I know that the LORD must love his
people, because he has chosen you
to be their king. 12Praise the LORD
God of Israel who made heaven and
earth! He has given David a son who
isn't only wise and smart, but who
has the knowledge to build a temple
for the LORD and a palace for himself.
13I am sending Huram Abi to you.
He is very bright. 14His mother was
from the Israelite tribe of Dan, and
his father was from Tyre. Not only is
Huram an expert at working with
gold, silver, bronze, iron, stone, and
wood, but he can also make colored
cloth and fine linen. And he can
carve anything if you give him a pattern to follow. He can help your
workers and those hired by your
father King David.
15Go ahead and send the wheat,
barley, olive oil, and wine you
promised to pay my workers. 16I will
tell them to start cutting down trees
in Lebanon. They will cut as many
as you need, then tie them together
into rafts, and float them down
along the coast to Joppa. Your workers can take them to Jerusalem from
there.

Solomon's Work Force

17Solomon counted all the foreigners
who were living in Israel, just as his
father David had done when he was
king, and the total was 153,600. 18He assigned 70,000 of them to carry building
supplies and 80,000 of them to cut stone
from the hills. He chose 3,600 others to
supervise the workers and to make sure
the work was completed.

The Temple Is Built

(1 Kings 6.1-38)

3 1-2Solomon's workers began building the temple in Jerusalem on the
second day of the second month,[d] four
years after Solomon had become king
of Israel. It was built on Mount Moriah
where the LORD had appeared to David
at the threshing place that had belonged
to Araunah[e] from Jebus.
3The inside of the temple was ninety
feet long and thirty feet wide, according
to the older standards.[f] 4Across the
front of the temple was a porch thirty
feet wide and thirty feet[g] high. The inside walls of the porch were covered
with pure gold.
5Solomon had the inside walls of the
temple's main room paneled first with
pine and then with a layer of gold, and
he had them decorated with carvings of
palm trees and designs that looked like
chains. 6He used precious stones to decorate the temple, and he used gold im-
ported from Parvaim[h] 7to decorate the
ceiling beams, the doors, the door
frames, and the walls. Solomon also had
the workers carve designs of winged
creatures into the walls.
8The most holy place was thirty feet
square, and its walls were covered with
almost twenty-five tons of fine gold.
9More than a pound of gold was used to
cover the heads of the nails. The walls
of the small storage rooms were also
covered with gold.[i]
10Solomon had two statues of winged
creatures[j] made to put in the most holy
place, and he covered them with gold.
11-13Each creature had two wings and
was fifteen feet from the tip of one wing
to the tip of the other wing. Solomon set
them next to each other in the most holy
place, facing the doorway. Their wings
were spread out and reached all the way
across the thirty foot room.
14A curtain[k] was made of fine linen
woven with blue, purple, and red wool,
and embroidered with designs of
winged creatures.

The Two Columns

(1 Kings 7.15-22)

15Two columns were made for the entrance to the temple. Each one was fifty-

[d]**3.1,2** *second month*: Ziv, the second month of the Hebrew calendar, from about mid-April to mid-May. [e]**3.1,2** *Araunah*: The Hebrew text has "Ornan," another spelling of the name (see 2 Samuel 24.18-25; 1 Chronicles 21.18—22.1). [f]**3.3** *according to the older standards*: There were possibly two different standards of measurement during Israel's history. [g]**3.4** *thirty feet*: Some manuscripts of two ancient translations; Hebrew "one hundred eighty feet." [h]**3.6** *Parvaim*: An unknown place. [i]**3.9** *The walls . . . gold*: One possible meaning for the difficult Hebrew text. [j]**3.10** *statues of winged creatures*: These were symbols of the LORD's throne on earth (see Exodus 25.18-22). [k]**3.14** *A curtain*: To separate the most holy place from the main room of the temple.

two feet tall and had a cap on top that
was seven and a half feet high. 16The top
of each column was decorated with designs that looked like chains[l] and with a
hundred carvings of pomegranates.[m]
17Solomon had one of the columns
placed on the south side of the temple's
entrance; it was called Jachin.[n] The
other one was placed on the north side
of the entrance; it was called Boaz.[o]

The Furnishings for the Temple
(1 Kings 7.23-51)

4 Solomon had a bronze altar made
that was thirty feet square and fifteen feet high. 2He also gave orders to
make a large metal bowl called the Sea.
It was fifteen feet across, about seven
and a half feet deep, and forty-five feet
around. 3Its outer edge was decorated
with two rows of carvings of bulls, ten
bulls to every eighteen inches, all made
from the same piece of metal as the
bowl. 4The bowl itself sat on top of
twelve bronze bulls, with three bulls facing outward in each of four directions.
5The sides of the bowl were four inches
thick, and its rim was in the shape of a
cup that curved outward like flower
petals. The bowl held about fifteen thousand gallons.
6He also made ten small bowls and
put five on each side of the large bowl.
The small bowls were used to wash the
animals that were burned on the altar as
sacrifices, and the priests used the water
in the large bowl to wash their hands.
7Ten gold lampstands were also made
according to the plans. Solomon placed
these lampstands inside the temple, five
on each side of the main room. 8He also
made ten tables and placed them in the
main room, five on each side. And he
made a hundred small gold sprinkling
bowls.
9Solomon gave orders to build two
courtyards: a smaller one that only
priests could use and a larger one. The
doors to these courtyards were covered
with bronze. 10The large bowl called the
Sea was placed near the southeast corner of the temple.
11Huram made shovels, sprinkling
bowls, and pans for hot ashes. Here is a
list of the other furnishings he made for
God's temple: 12two columns, two bowl-
shaped caps for the tops of these
columns, two chain designs on the caps,
13four hundred pomegranates[p] for the
chain designs, 14the stands and the
small bowls, 15the large bowl and
the twelve bulls that held it up, 16pans
for hot ashes, as well as shovels and
meat forks.
Huram made all these things out of
polished bronze 17by pouring melted
bronze into the clay molds he had set up
near the Jordan River, between Succoth
and Zeredah.
18There were so many bronze furnishings that no one ever knew how much
bronze it took to make them.
19Solomon also gave orders to make
the following temple furnishings out of
gold: the altar, the tables that held the
sacred loaves of bread,[q] 20the lampstands and the lamps that burned in
front of the most holy place, 21flower designs, lamps and tongs, 22lamp snuffers,
small sprinkling bowls, ladles, fire pans,
and the doors to the most holy place
and the main room of the temple.
5 After the LORD's temple was finished, Solomon put in its storage
rooms everything that his father David
had dedicated to the LORD, including the
gold and silver, and the objects used in
worship.

Solomon Brings the Sacred Chest to the Temple
(1 Kings 8.1-13)

2-3The sacred chest had been kept on
Mount Zion, also known as the city of
David. But Solomon decided to have the
chest moved to the temple while everyone was in Jerusalem to celebrate the
Festival of Shelters during the seventh
month.[r]
Solomon called together all the important leaders of Israel. 4-5Then the
priests and the Levites picked up the sacred chest, the sacred tent, and the objects used for worship, and they carried
them to the temple. 6Solomon and a
crowd of people walked in front of the
chest, and along the way they sacrificed
more sheep and cattle than could be
counted.
7The priests carried the chest into the
most holy place and put it under the
winged creatures, 8whose wings covered
the chest and the poles used for carrying it. 9The poles were so long that they
could be seen from just outside the most
holy place, but not from anywhere else.
And they stayed there from then on.
10The only things kept in the chest

[l] **3.16** *designs that looked like chains*: One possible meaning for the difficult Hebrew text.
[m] **3.16** *pomegranates*: A pomegranate is a small red fruit that looks like an apple. In ancient times, it was a symbol of life.
[n] **3.17** *Jachin*: Or "He (God) makes secure."
[o] **3.17** *Boaz*: Or "He (God) is strong."
[p] **4.13** *pomegranates*: See the note at 3.16.
[q] **4.19** *sacred loaves of bread*: This bread was offered to the LORD and was a symbol of the LORD's presence in the temple. It was put out on special tables, and was replaced with fresh bread every week (see Leviticus 24.5-9).
[r] **5.2,3** *seventh month*: Tishri (also called Ethanim), the seventh month of the Hebrew calendar, from about mid-September to mid-October.

were the two flat stones Moses had put
there when the LORD made his agreement with the people of Israel at Mount
Sinai,[s] after bringing them out of Egypt.
11-13 The priests of every group had
gone through the ceremony to make
themselves clean and acceptable to the
LORD. The Levite musicians, including
Asaph, Heman, Jeduthun, and their sons
and relatives, were wearing robes of
fine linen. They were standing on the
east side of the altar, playing cymbals,
small harps, and other stringed instruments. One hundred twenty priests were
with these musicians, and they were
blowing trumpets.
They were praising the LORD by playing music and singing:

"The LORD is good,
and his love never ends."

Suddenly a cloud filled the temple as
the priests were leaving the holy place.
14 The LORD's glory was in that cloud,
and the light from it was so bright that
the priests could not stay inside to do
their work.

6 Solomon prayed:
"Our LORD, you said that you
would live in a dark cloud.
2 Now I've built a glorious temple
where you can live forever."

Solomon Speaks to the People

(1 Kings 8.14-21)

3 Solomon turned toward the people
standing there. Then he blessed them
4-6 and said:
Praise the LORD God of Israel! He
brought his people out of Egypt long
ago and later kept his promise to
make my father David the king of Israel. The LORD also promised him
that Jerusalem would be the city
where his temple will be built, and
now that promise has come true.
7 When my father wanted to build
a temple for the LORD God of Israel,
8 the LORD said, "It's good that you
want to build a temple where I can
be worshiped. 9 But you're not the
one to do it. Your son will build the
temple to honor me."
10 The LORD has done what he
promised. I am now the king of Israel, and I've built a temple for the
LORD our God. 11 I've also put the sacred chest in the temple. And in that
chest are the two flat stones on
which is written the solemn agreement the LORD made with our ancestors when he rescued them from
Egypt.

Solomon Prays at the Temple

(1 Kings 8.22-53)

12-13 Earlier, Solomon had a bronze
platform made that was about eight feet
square and five feet high, and he put it
in the center of the outer courtyard near
the altar. Solomon stood on the platform
facing the altar with everyone standing
behind him. Then he lifted his arms toward heaven; he knelt down 14 and
prayed:
LORD God of Israel, no other god
in heaven or on earth is like you!
You never forget the agreement
you made with your people, and you
are loyal to anyone who faithfully
obeys your teachings. 15 My father
David was your servant, and today
you have kept every promise you
made to him.
16 You promised that someone from
his family would always be king of
Israel, if they do their best to obey
you, just as he did. 17 Please keep this
promise you made to your servant
David. 18 There's not enough room in
all of heaven for you, LORD God.
How could you possibly live on
earth in this temple I have built?
19 But I ask you to answer my prayer.
20 This is the temple where you have
chosen to be worshiped. Please
watch over it day and night and listen when I turn toward it and pray.
21 I am your servant, and the people
of Israel belong to you, and so whenever any of us look toward this temple and pray, answer from your
home in heaven and forgive our
sins.
22 Suppose someone accuses a person of a crime, and the accused has
to stand in front of the altar in your
temple and say, "I swear I am innocent!" 23 Listen from heaven and decide who is right. Then punish the
guilty person and let the innocent
one go free.
24 Suppose your people Israel sin
against you, and then an enemy defeats them. If they come to this temple and beg for forgiveness, 25 listen
from your home in heaven. Forgive
them and bring them back to the
land you gave their ancestors.
26 Suppose your people sin against
you, and you punish them by holding back the rain. If they stop sinning and turn toward this temple to
pray in your name, 27 listen from
your home in heaven and forgive
them. The people of Israel are your
servants, so teach them to live right.
And send rain on the land you
promised them forever.

[s] **5.10** *Sinai*: Hebrew "Horeb."

28Sometimes the crops may dry up
or rot or be eaten by locusts[t] or
grasshoppers, and your people will
be starving. Sometimes enemies
may surround their towns, or your
people will become sick with deadly
diseases. 29Please listen when anyone in Israel truly feels sorry and
sincerely prays with arms lifted toward your temple. 30You know what
is in everyone's heart. So from your
home in heaven answer their
prayers, according to what they
do and what is in their hearts.
31Then your people will worship
you and obey you for as long as they
live in the land you gave their ancestors.
32Foreigners will hear about you
and your mighty power, and some of
them will come to live among your
people Israel. If any of them pray toward this temple, 33listen from your
home in heaven and answer their
prayers. Then everyone on earth will
worship you, just as your own people Israel do, and they will know
that I have built this temple in your
honor.
34Sometimes you will order your
people to attack their enemies. Then
your people will turn toward this
temple I have built for you in your
chosen city, and they will pray to
you. 35Answer their prayers from
heaven and give them victory.
36Everyone sins. But when your
people sin against you, suppose you
get angry enough to let their enemies drag them away to foreign
countries. 37-39Later, they may feel
sorry for what they did and ask your
forgiveness. Answer them when they
pray toward this temple I have built
for you in your chosen city, here in
this land you gave their ancestors.
From your home in heaven, listen to
their sincere prayers and forgive
your people who have sinned
against you.
40LORD God, hear us when we pray
in this temple. 41Come to your new
home, where we have already placed
the sacred chest, which is the symbol of your strength. I pray that
when the priests announce your
power to save people, those who are
faithful to you will celebrate what
you've done for them. 42Always remember the love you had for your
servant David,[u] so that you will not
reject your chosen kings.

Solomon Dedicates the Temple

(1 Kings 8.62-66)

7 As soon as Solomon finished praying, fire came down from heaven
and burned up the offerings. The LORD's
dazzling glory then filled the temple,
2and the priests could not go in.
3When the crowd of people saw the
fire and the LORD's glory, they knelt
down and worshiped the LORD. They
prayed:

"The LORD is good,
and his love never ends."

4-5Solomon and the people dedicated
the temple to the LORD by sacrificing
twenty-two thousand cattle and one
hundred twenty thousand sheep.
6Everybody stood up during the ceremony. The priests were in their assigned
places, blowing their trumpets. And the
Levites faced them, playing the musical
instruments that David had made for
them to use when they praised the LORD
for his never-ending love.
7On that same day, Solomon dedicated
the courtyard in front of the temple and
got it ready to be used for worship. The
bronze altar he had made was too small,
so he used the courtyard to offer sacrifices to please the LORD[v] and grain sacrifices, and also to send up in smoke the
fat from the other offerings.
8For seven days, Solomon and the
crowd celebrated the Festival of Shelters, and people came from as far away
as the Egyptian Gorge in the south and
Lebo-Hamath in the north. 9Then on the
next day, everyone came together for
worship. They had celebrated a total of
fourteen days, seven days for the dedication of the altar and seven more days
for the festival. 10Then on the twenty-
third day of the seventh month,[w]
Solomon sent everyone home. They left
very happy because of all the good
things the LORD had done for David and
Solomon, and for his people Israel.

The LORD Appears to Solomon Again

(1 Kings 9.1-9)

11The LORD's temple and Solomon's
palace were now finished. In fact, everything Solomon had planned to do was
completed.
12Some time later, the LORD appeared
to Solomon in a dream and said:
I heard your prayer, and I have
chosen this temple as the place
where sacrifices will be offered to
me.

[t]**6.28** *locusts*: A type of grasshopper that comes in swarms and causes great damage to crops.
[u]**6.42** *the love you had for your servant David*: Or "how loyal your servant David was to you."
[v]**7.7** *sacrifices to please the LORD*: See the note at 1.6. [w]**7.10** *seventh month*: See the note at 5.2, 3.

13 Suppose I hold back the rain or
send locusts[x] to eat the crops or
make my people suffer with deadly
diseases. 14 If my own people will
humbly pray and turn back to me
and stop sinning, then I will answer
them from heaven. I will forgive
them and make their land fertile
once again. 15 I will hear the prayers
made in this temple, 16 because it belongs to me, and this is where I will
be worshiped forever. I will never
stop watching over it.
17 Your father David obeyed me,
and now, Solomon, you must do the
same. Obey my laws and teachings,
18 and I will keep my solemn promise
to him that someone from your family will always be king of Israel.
19 But if you or any of the people of
Israel disobey my laws or start worshiping foreign gods, 20 I will pull
you out of this land I gave you. I will
desert this temple where I said I
would be worshiped, so that people
everywhere will think it is only a
joke and will make fun of it. 21 This
temple is now magnificent. But
when these things happen, everyone
who walks by it will be shocked and
will ask, "Why did the LORD do such
a terrible thing to his people and to
this temple?" 22 Then they will answer, "It was because the people of
Israel rejected the LORD their God,
who rescued their ancestors from
Egypt, and they started worshiping
other gods."

Other Things Solomon Did

(1 Kings 9.10-28)

8 It took twenty years for the LORD's
temple and Solomon's palace to be
built. 2 After that, Solomon had his
workers rebuild the towns that Hiram
had given him. Then Solomon sent Israelites to live in those towns.
3 Solomon attacked and captured the
town of Hamath-Zobah. 4 He had his
workers build the town of Tadmor in the
desert and some towns in Hamath
where he could keep his supplies. 5 He
strengthened Upper Beth-Horon and
Lower Beth-Horon by adding walls and
gates that could be locked. 6 He did the
same thing to the town of Baalath and
to the cities where he kept supplies,
chariots, and horses. Solomon had his
workers build whatever he wanted in
Jerusalem, Lebanon, and anywhere else
in his kingdom.
7-9 Solomon did not force the Israelites
to do his work. Instead, they were his
soldiers, officers, army commanders,
and cavalry troops. But he did make
slaves of the Hittites, Amorites, Perizzites, Hivites, and Jebusites who were
living in Israel. These were the descendants of those foreigners the Israelites
did not destroy, and they remained Israel's slaves.
10 Solomon appointed two hundred
fifty officers to be in charge of his workers.
11 Solomon's wife, the daughter of the
king of Egypt, moved from the part of
Jerusalem called David's City to her
new palace that Solomon had built. The
sacred chest had been kept in David's
City, which made his palace sacred, and
so Solomon's wife could no longer live
there.
12 Solomon offered sacrifices to the
LORD on the altar he had built in front of
the temple. 13 He followed the requirements that Moses had given for sacrifices offered on the Sabbath, on the first
day of each month, the Festival of Thin
Bread, the Harvest Festival, and the Festival of Shelters.
14 Solomon then assigned the priests
and the Levites their duties at the temple, and he followed the instructions
that his father David had given him.
Some of the Levites were to lead music
and help the priests in their duties, and
others were to guard the temple gates
15 and the storage rooms. The priests and
Levites followed these instructions exactly.
16 Everything Solomon had planned to
do was now finished—from the laying of
the temple's foundation to its completion.
17 Solomon went to Ezion-Geber and
Eloth, two Edomite towns on the
Red Sea.[y] 18 Hiram sent him ships and
some of his experienced sailors. They
went with Solomon's own sailors to the
country of Ophir[z] and brought back
about seventeen tons of gold for Solomon.

The Queen of Sheba Visits Solomon

(1 Kings 10.1-13)

9 The Queen of Sheba heard how famous Solomon was, so she went to
Jerusalem to test him with difficult
questions. She took along several of her
officials, and she loaded her camels
with gifts of spices, jewels, and gold.
When she arrived, she and Solomon
talked about everything she could think
of. 2 He answered every question, no
matter how difficult it was.
3-4 The Queen was amazed at Solomon's wisdom. She was breathless

[x] **7.13** *locusts*: See the note at 6.28. [y] **8.17** *Red Sea*: Hebrew *yam suph*, here referring to the Gulf of Aqaba, since the term is extended to include the northeastern arm of the Red Sea (see also the note at Exodus 13.18). [z] **8.18** *Ophir*: The location of this place is not known.

when she saw his palace,[a] the food on
his table, his officials, all his servants in
their uniforms, and the sacrifices he offered at the LORD's temple. 5She said:

> Solomon, in my own country I had
> heard about your wisdom and all
> you've done. 6But I didn't believe it
> until I saw it with my own eyes! And
> there's so much I didn't hear about.
> You are greater than I was told.
> 7Your people and officials are lucky
> to be here where they can listen to
> the wise things you say.
>
> 8I praise the LORD your God. He is
> pleased with you and has made you
> king of Israel. God loves the people
> of this country and will never desert
> them, so he has given them a king
> who will rule fairly and honestly.

9The Queen of Sheba gave Solomon
almost five tons of gold, a large amount
of jewels, and the best spices anyone
had ever seen.

10-12In return, Solomon gave her
everything she wanted—even more than
she had given him. Then she and her officials went back to their own country.

Solomon's Wealth
(1 Kings 10.14-29)

Hiram's and Solomon's sailors
brought gold, juniper wood, and jewels
from the country of Ophir. Solomon
used the wood to make steps[b] for the
temple and palace, and harps and other
stringed instruments for the musicians.
Nothing like these had ever been made
in Judah.

13Solomon received about twenty-five
tons of gold each year, 14not counting
what the merchants and traders brought
him. The kings of Arabia and the leaders of Israel also gave him gold and silver.

15Solomon made two hundred gold
shields that weighed about seven and a
half pounds each. 16He also made three
hundred smaller gold shields that
weighed almost four pounds, and he put
these shields in his palace in Forest Hall.

17His throne was made of ivory and
covered with pure gold. 18It had a gold
footstool attached to it and armrests on
each side. There was a statue of a lion
on each side of the throne, 19and there
were two lion statues on each of the six
steps leading up to the throne. No other
throne in the world was like Solomon's.

20Solomon's cups and dishes in Forest
Hall were made of pure gold, because
silver was almost worthless in those
days.

21Solomon had a lot of seagoing
ships.[c] Every three years he sent them
out with Hiram's ships to bring back
gold, silver, and ivory, as well as mon-
keys and peacocks.[d]

22Solomon was the richest and wisest
king in the world. 23-24Year after year,
other kings came to hear the wisdom
God had given him. And they brought
gifts of silver and gold, as well as
clothes, weapons, spices, horses, and
mules.

25Solomon had four thousand stalls
for his horses and chariots, and he
owned twelve thousand horses that he
kept in Jerusalem and other towns.

26He ruled all the nations from the Euphrates River in the north to the land of
Philistia in the south, as far as the border of Egypt.

27While Solomon was king, there was
silver everywhere in Jerusalem, and
cedar was as common as the sycamore
trees in the western foothills. 28Sol-
omon's horses were brought in from
other countries, including Musri.[e]

Solomon Dies
(1 Kings 11.41-43)

29Everything else Solomon did while
he was king is written in the records of
Nathan the prophet, Ahijah the prophet
from Shiloh, and Iddo the prophet who
wrote about Jeroboam son of Nebat.
30After Solomon had ruled forty years
from Jerusalem, 31he died and was
buried in the city of his father David.
His son Rehoboam then became king.

Some of the People Rebel against Rehoboam
(1 Kings 12.1-20)

10 Rehoboam went to Shechem
where everyone was waiting to
crown him king.

2Jeroboam son of Nebat heard what
was happening, and he returned from
Egypt, where he had gone to hide from
Solomon. 3The people from the northern
tribes of Israel sent for him. Then together they went to Rehoboam and said,
4"Your father Solomon forced us to
work very hard. But if you make our
work easier, we will serve you and do
whatever you ask."

5Rehoboam replied, "Come back in
three days for my answer." So the people left.

6Rehoboam went to some leaders who
had been his father's senior officials,
and he asked them, "What should I tell
these people?"

7They answered, "If you want them to

[a]**9.3,4** *his palace*: Or "the temple." [b]**9.10-12** *steps*: Or "stools" or "railings."
[c]**9.21** *seagoing ships*: The Hebrew text has "ships of Tarshish," which may have been a Phoenician city in Spain. "Ships of Tarshish" probably means large, seagoing ships.
[d]**9.21** *peacocks*: Or "baboons." [e]**9.28** *Musri*: See the note at 1.16, 17.

serve and obey you, then you should be
kind and promise to make their work
easier."
8But Rehoboam refused their advice
and went to the younger men who had
grown up with him and were now his
officials. 9He asked, "What do you think
I should say to these people who asked
me to make their work easier?"
10His younger advisors said:

> Here's what we think you should
> say to them: "Compared to me, my
> father was weak.[f] 11He made you
> work hard, but I'll make you work
> even harder. He punished you with
> whips, but I'll use whips with pieces
> of sharp metal!"

12Three days later, Jeroboam and the
others came back. 13Rehoboam ignored
the advice of the older advisors. He
spoke bluntly 14and told them exactly
what his own advisors had suggested.
He said: "My father made you work
hard, but I'll make you work even
harder. He punished you with whips, but
I'll use whips with pieces of sharp
metal!"
15-19When the people realized that Rehoboam would not listen to them, they
shouted: "We don't have to be loyal to
David's family. We can do what we
want. Come on, people of Israel, let's go
home! Rehoboam can rule his own people."

Adoniram[g] was in charge of the work
force, and Rehoboam sent him to talk to
the people. But they stoned him to
death. Then Rehoboam ran to his chariot and hurried back to Jerusalem.

Everyone from Israel's northern tribes
went home, leaving Rehoboam to rule
only the people from Judah. And since
that day, the people of Israel have been
opposed to David's descendants in Judah.[h] All of this happened just as Ahijah
the LORD's prophet from Shiloh had told
Jeroboam.

Shemaiah the Prophet Warns Rehoboam

(1 Kings 12.21-24)

11 After Rehoboam returned to
Jerusalem, he decided to attack
Israel and regain control of the whole
country. So he called together one hundred eighty thousand soldiers from the
tribes of Judah and Benjamin.
2Meanwhile, the LORD had told Shemaiah the prophet 3to tell Rehoboam
and everyone from Judah and Benjamin, 4"The LORD warns you not to go
to war against the people from the
northern tribes—they are your relatives.
Go home! The LORD is the one who
made these things happen."

Rehoboam and his army obeyed the
LORD's message and did not attack Jeroboam and his troops.

Rehoboam Fortifies Cities in Judah

5Rehoboam ruled from Jerusalem,
and he had several cities in Judah
turned into fortresses so he could use
them to defend his country. These cities
included 6Bethlehem, Etam, Tekoa,
7Beth-Zur, Soco, Adullam, 8Gath, Mareshah, Ziph, 9Adoraim, Lachish, Azekah,
10Zorah, Aijalon, and Hebron. After he
had fortified these cities in the territories of Judah and Benjamin, 11he assigned an army commander to each of
them and stocked them with supplies of
food, olive oil, and wine, 12as well as
with shields and spears. He used these
fortified cities to keep control of Judah
and Benjamin.

The Priests and the Levites Support Rehoboam

13The priests and Levites from the
northern tribes of Israel gave their support to King Rehoboam. 14And since
Jeroboam and the kings of Israel that
followed him would not allow any
Levites to serve as priests, most Levites
left their towns and pasturelands in Israel and moved to Jerusalem and other
towns in Judah. 15Jeroboam chose his
own priests to serve at the local shrines[i]
in Israel and at the places of worship
where he had set up statues of goat-
demons and of calves.
16But some of the people from Israel
wanted to worship the LORD God, just as
their ancestors had done. So they followed the priests and Levites to Jerusalem, where they could offer sacrifices to the LORD. 17For the next three
years, they lived in Judah and were
loyal to Rehoboam and his kingdom,
just as they had been loyal to David and
Solomon.

Rehoboam's Family

18Rehoboam married Mahalath,
whose father was Jerimoth son of
David, and whose mother was Abihail the daughter of Eliab and granddaughter of Jesse. 19Rehoboam and
Mahalath had three sons: Jeush, Shemariah, and Zaham. 20Then Rehoboam
married Maacah the daughter of Absalom. Their sons were Abijah, Attai, Ziza,
and Shelomith.
21Rehoboam had eighteen wives, but

[f] **10.10** *Compared . . . weak*: Hebrew "My little finger is bigger than my father's waist."
[g] **10.15-19** *Adoniram*: The Hebrew text has "Hadoram," another spelling of the name.
[h] **10.15-19** *the people of Israel have been opposed . . . Judah*: From this time on, "Israel" usually refers only to the northern kingdom. The southern kingdom is called "Judah."
[i] **11.15** *local shrines*: The Hebrew text has "high places," which were local places to worship foreign gods.

he also married sixty other women,[j] and he was the father of twenty-eight sons and sixty daughters. Rehoboam loved his wife Maacah the most, 22so he chose their oldest son Abijah to be the next king. 23Rehoboam was wise enough to put one of his sons in charge of each fortified city in his kingdom. He gave them all the supplies they needed and found wives for every one of them.

King Shishak of Egypt Invades Judah

(1 Kings 14.25-28)

12 Soon after Rehoboam had control of his kingdom, he and everyone in Judah stopped obeying the LORD. 2So in the fifth year of Rehoboam's rule, the LORD punished them for their unfaithfulness and allowed King Shishak of Egypt to invade Judah. 3Shishak attacked with his army of one thousand two hundred chariots and sixty thousand cavalry troops, as well as Egyptian soldiers from Libya, Sukkoth, and Ethiopia.[k] 4He captured every one of the fortified cities in Judah and then marched to Jerusalem.

5Rehoboam and the leaders of Judah had gone to Jerusalem to escape Shishak's invasion. And while they were there, Shemaiah the prophet told them, "The LORD says that because you have disobeyed him, he has now abandoned you. The LORD will not help you against Shishak!"

6Rehoboam and the leaders were sorry for what they had done and admitted, "The LORD is right. We have deserted him."

7When the LORD heard this, he told Shemaiah:

The people of Judah are truly
sorry for their sins, and so I won't let
Shishak completely destroy them.
But because I am still angry, 8he will
conquer and rule them.

Then my people will know what
it's like to serve a foreign king instead of serving me.

9Shishak attacked Jerusalem and took all the valuable things from the temple and from the palace, including Solomon's gold shields.

10Rehoboam had bronze shields made to replace the gold ones, and he ordered the guards at the city gates to keep them safe. 11Whenever Rehoboam went to the LORD's temple, the guards carried the shields. But they always took them back to the guardroom as soon as he had finished worshiping.

12Rehoboam turned back to the LORD, and so the LORD did not let Judah be completely destroyed, and Judah was prosperous again.

Rehoboam's Rule in Judah

(1 Kings 14.21, 29-31)

13Rehoboam was forty-one years old when he became king, and he ruled seventeen years from Jerusalem, the city where the LORD had chosen to be worshiped. His mother Naamah was from Ammon. Rehoboam was a powerful king, 14but he still did wrong and refused to obey the LORD.

15Everything else Rehoboam did while he was king, including a history of his family, is written in the records of the two prophets, Shemaiah and Iddo. During Rehoboam's rule, he and King Jeroboam of Israel were constantly at war. 16When Rehoboam died, he was buried beside his ancestors in Jerusalem, and his son Abijah became king.

King Abijah of Judah

(1 Kings 15.1-8)

13 Abijah[l] became king of Judah in Jeroboam's eighteenth year as king of Israel, 2and he ruled from Jerusalem for three years. His mother was Micaiah the daughter of Uriel from Gibeah.

Some time later, Abijah and King Jeroboam of Israel went to war against each other. 3Abijah's army had four hundred thousand troops, and Jeroboam met him in battle with eight hundred thousand troops.

4Abijah went to the top of Mount Zemaraim[m] in the hills of Ephraim and shouted:

Listen, Jeroboam and all you Israelites! 5The LORD God of Israel has made a solemn promise that every king of Israel will be from David's family. 6But Jeroboam, you were King Solomon's official, and you rebelled. 7Then right after Rehoboam became king, you and your bunch of worthless followers challenged Rehoboam, who was too young to know how to stop you.

8Now you and your powerful army think you can stand up to the kingdom that the LORD has given to David's descendants. The only gods you have are those gold statues of calves that Jeroboam made for you. 9You don't even have descendants of Aaron on your side, because you forced out the LORD's priests and Levites. In their place, you appoint

[j]11.21 *other women*: This translates a Hebrew word for women who were legally bound to a man, but without the full privileges of a wife. [k]12.3 *Ethiopia*: The Hebrew text has "Cush," which was a region south of Egypt that included parts of the present countries of Ethiopia and Sudan. [l]13.1 *Abijah*: In 1 Kings 15.1-8 his name is spelled "Abijam." [m]13.4 *Mount Zemaraim*: Probably located on the northern border of the territory of Benjamin.

ordinary people to be priests, just as
the foreign nations do. In fact, anyone who brings a bull and seven
rams to the altar can become a
priest of your so-called gods.
10But we have not turned our
backs on the LORD God! Aaron's own
descendants serve as our priests, and
the Levites are their assistants. 11Two
times every day they offer sacrifices
and burn incense to the LORD. They
set out the sacred loaves of bread on
a table that has been purified, and
they light the lamps in the gold
lampstand every day at sunset. We
follow the commands of the LORD
our God—you have rejected him!
12That's why God is on our side and
will lead us into battle when the
priests sound the signal on the trumpets. It's no use, Israelites. You might
as well give up. There's no way you
can defeat the LORD, the God your
ancestors worshiped.
13But while Abijah was talking, Jeroboam had sent some of his troops to
attack Judah's army from behind, while
the rest attacked from the front. 14Ju-
dah's army realized they were trapped,
and so they prayed to the LORD. The
priests blew the signal on the trumpet,
15and the troops let out a battle cry.
Then with Abijah leading them into battle, God defeated Jeroboam and Israel's
army. 16The Israelites ran away, and God
helped Judah's soldiers slaughter 17five
hundred thousand enemy troops. 18Ju-
dah's army won because they had
trusted the LORD God of their ancestors.
19Abijah kept up his attack on Jeroboam's army and captured the Israelite
towns of Bethel, Jeshanah, and Ephron,
as well as the villages around them.
20Jeroboam never regained his power
during the rest of Abijah's rule. The
LORD punished Jeroboam, and he died,
but Abijah became more powerful.
21Abijah had a total of fourteen wives,
twenty-two sons, and sixteen daughters.
22Everything Abijah said and did while
he was king is written in the records of
Iddo the prophet.

King Asa of Judah

14 Abijah died and was buried in
Jerusalem. Then his son Asa became king, and Judah had ten years of
peace.
2Asa obeyed the LORD his God and did
right. 3He destroyed the local shrines[n]
and the altars to foreign gods. He
smashed the stone images of gods and
cut down the sacred poles[o] used in worshiping the goddess Asherah. 4Then he
told everyone in Judah to worship the
LORD God, just as their ancestors had
done, and to obey his laws and teachings. 5He destroyed every local shrine
and incense altar in Judah.
6The LORD blessed Judah with peace
while Asa was king, and so during that
time, Asa fortified many of the towns.
7He said to the people, "Let's build walls
and defense towers for these towns, and
put in gates that can be locked with
bars. This land still belongs to us, because we have obeyed the LORD our
God. He has given us peace from all our
enemies." The people did everything
Asa had suggested.
8Asa had a large army of brave soldiers: Three hundred thousand of them
were from the tribe of Judah and were
armed with shields and spears; two hundred eighty thousand were from Benjamin and were armed with bows and
arrows.

Judah Defeats Ethiopia's Army

9Zerah from Ethiopia[p] led an army of
a million soldiers and three hundred
chariots to the town of Mareshah[q] in Judah. 10Asa met him there, and the two
armies prepared for battle in Zephathah
Valley.
11Asa prayed:

LORD God, only you can help a
powerless army defeat a stronger
one. So we depend on you to help
us. We will fight against this powerful army to honor your name, and
we know that you won't be defeated.
You are the LORD our God.

12The LORD helped Asa and his army
defeat the Ethiopians. The enemy soldiers ran away, 13but Asa and his troops
chased them as far as Gerar. It was a total defeat—the Ethiopians could not
even fight back![r]
The soldiers from Judah took everything that had belonged to the Ethiopians. 14The people who lived in the villages around Gerar learned what had
happened and were afraid of the LORD.
So Judah's army easily defeated them
and carried off everything of value that
they wanted from these towns. 15They
also attacked the camps where the shepherds lived and took a lot of sheep,
goats, and camels. Then they went back
to Jerusalem.

Asa Destroys the Idols in Judah

15 Some time later, God spoke to
Azariah son of Oded. 2At once,
Azariah went to Asa and said:

[n]**14.3** *local shrines*: See the note at 11.15. [o]**14.3** *sacred poles*: Or "trees," used as symbols of Asherah, the goddess of fertility. [p]**14.9** *Ethiopia*: See the note at 12.3. [q]**14.9** *Mareshah*: About twenty-five miles southwest of Jerusalem. [r]**14.13** *the Ethiopians could not even fight back*: Or "not one of the Ethiopians survived!"

Listen to me, King Asa and you
people of Judah and Benjamin. The
LORD will be with you and help you,
as long as you obey and worship
him. But if you disobey him, he will
desert you.
3For a long time, the people of Israel did not worship the true God or
listen to priests who could teach
them about God. They refused to
obey God's Law. 4But whenever
trouble came, Israel turned back to
the LORD their God and worshiped
him.
5There was so much confusion in
those days that it wasn't safe to go
anywhere in Israel. 6Nations were
destroying each other, and cities
were wiping out other cities, because God was causing trouble and
unrest everywhere.
7So you must be brave. Don't give
up! God will honor you for obeying
him.
8As soon as Asa heard what Azariah
the prophet said, he gave orders for all
the idols in Judah and Benjamin to be
destroyed, including those in the towns
he had captured in the territory of
Ephraim. He also repaired the LORD's altar that was in front of the temple porch.
9Asa called together the people from
Judah and Benjamin, as well as the people from the territories of Ephraim, West
Manasseh, and Simeon who were living
in Judah. Many of these people were
now loyal to Asa, because they had seen
that the LORD was with him.
10In the third month of the fifteenth
year of Asa's rule, they all met in
Jerusalem. 11That same day, they took
seven hundred bulls and seven thousand sheep and goats from what they
had brought back from Gerar and sacrificed them as offerings to the LORD.
12They made a solemn promise to faithfully worship the LORD God their ancestors had worshiped, 13and to put to
death anyone who refused to obey him.
14The crowd solemnly agreed to keep
their promise to the LORD, then they celebrated by shouting and blowing trumpets and horns. 15Everyone was happy
because they had made this solemn
promise, and in return, the LORD blessed
them with peace from all their enemies.
16Asa's grandmother Maacah had
made a disgusting idol of the goddess
Asherah, so he cut it down, crushed it,
and burned it in Kidron Valley. Then he
removed Maacah from her position as
queen mother.[s] 17As long as Asa lived,
he was faithful to the LORD, even though
he did not destroy the local shrines[t] in
Israel. 18He placed in the temple all the
silver and gold objects that he and his
father had dedicated to God.
19There was peace in Judah until the
thirty-fifth year of Asa's rule.

King Baasha of Israel Invades Judah

(1 Kings 15.16-22)

16 In the thirty-sixth year of Asa's
rule, King Baasha of Israel invaded Judah and captured the town of
Ramah. He started making the town
stronger, and he put troops there to stop
people from going in and out of Judah.
2When Asa heard about this, he took
the silver and gold from his palace and
from the LORD's temple. Then he sent it
to Damascus with this message for King
Benhadad of Syria: 3"I think we should
sign a peace treaty, just as our fathers
did. This silver and gold is a present for
you. Would you please break your treaty
with King Baasha of Israel and force
him to leave my country?"
4Benhadad did what Asa asked and
sent the Syrian army into Israel. They
captured the towns of Ijon, Dan, Abel-
Maim,[u] and all the towns in Naphtali
where supplies were kept. 5When
Baasha heard about it, he stopped his
work on the town of Ramah.
6Asa ordered everyone in Judah to
carry away the stones and wood Baasha
had used to fortify Ramah. Then he fortified the towns of Geba and Mizpah
with these same stones and wood.

Hanani the Prophet Condemns Asa

7Soon after that happened, Hanani the
prophet went to Asa and said:
You depended on the king of Syria
instead of depending on the LORD
your God. And so, you will never defeat the Syrian army. 8Remember
how powerful the Ethiopian[v] and
Libyan army was, with all their
chariots and cavalry troops! You
trusted the LORD to help you then,
and you defeated them. 9The LORD is
constantly watching everyone, and
he gives strength to those who faithfully obey him. But you have done a
foolish thing, and your kingdom will
never be at peace again.
10When Asa heard this, he was so angry that he put Hanani in prison. Asa
was also cruel to some of his people.[w]

Asa Dies

(1 Kings 15.23, 24)

11Everything Asa did while he was king
is written in *The History of the Kings*

[s] **15.16** *queen mother*: Or "the mother of the king," which was an important position in biblical times (see 1 Kings 2.19). [t] **15.17** *local shrines*: See the note at 11.15. [u] **16.4** *Abelmaim*: Also called "Abel-Bethmaacah" (see 1 Kings 15.20). [v] **16.8** *Ethiopian*: See the note at 12.3. [w] **16.10** *Asa was also cruel . . . people*: Or "Asa also started being cruel to some of his people."

of Judah and Israel. 12In the thirty-ninth
year of his rule, he got a very bad
foot disease, but he relied on doctors
and refused to ask the LORD for help.
13He died two years later.
14Earlier, Asa had his own tomb cut
out of a rock hill in Jerusalem. So he
was buried there, and the tomb was
filled with spices and sweet-smelling
oils. Then the people built a bonfire in
his honor.

King Jehoshaphat of Judah

17 Jehoshaphat son of Asa became
king and strengthened his defenses against Israel. 2He assigned
troops to the fortified cities in Judah, as
well as to other towns in Judah and to
those towns in Ephraim that his father
Asa had captured.
3-4When Jehoshaphat's father had
first become king of Judah, he was
faithful to the LORD and refused to worship the god Baal as the kings of Israel
did. Jehoshaphat followed his father's
example and obeyed and worshiped the
LORD. And so the LORD blessed Jehoshaphat 5and helped him keep firm
control of his kingdom. The people of
Judah brought gifts to Jehoshaphat, but
even after he became very rich and respected, 6he remained completely faithful to the LORD. He destroyed all the local shrines[x] in Judah, including the
places where the goddess Asherah was
worshiped.
7In the third year of Jehoshaphat's
rule, he chose five officials and gave
them orders to teach the LORD's Law in
every city and town in Judah. They were
Benhail, Obadiah, Zechariah, Nethanel,
and Micaiah. 8Their assistants were the
following nine Levites: Shemaiah,
Nethaniah, Zebadiah, Asahel, Shemiramoth, Jehonathan, Adonijah, Tobijah,
and Tob-Adonijah. Two priests, Elishama and Jehoram, also went along.
9They carried with them a copy of the
LORD's Law wherever they went and
taught the people from it.
10The nations around Judah were
afraid of the LORD's power, so none of
them attacked Jehoshaphat. 11Phi-
listines brought him silver and other
gifts to keep peace. Some of the Arab
people brought him seventy-seven hundred rams and the same number of
goats.
12As Jehoshaphat became more powerful, he built fortresses and cities
13where he stored supplies. He also kept
in Jerusalem some experienced soldiers
14from the Judah and Benjamin tribes.
These soldiers were grouped according
to their clans.
Adnah was the commander of the
troops from Judah, and he had three
hundred thousand soldiers under his
command. 15Jehohanan was second in
command, with two hundred eighty
thousand soldiers under him. 16Amasiah
son of Zichri, who had volunteered to
serve the LORD, was third in command,
with two hundred thousand soldiers under him.
17Eliada was a brave warrior who
commanded the troops from Benjamin.
He had two hundred thousand soldiers
under his command, all of them armed
with bows and shields. 18Jehozabad was
second in command, with one hundred
eighty thousand soldiers under him.
19These were the troops who protected
the king in Jerusalem, not counting
those he had assigned to the fortified
cities throughout the country.

Micaiah Warns King Ahab of Israel

(1 Kings 22.1-28)

18 Jehoshaphat was now very rich
and famous. He signed a treaty
with King Ahab of Israel by arranging
the marriage of his son and Ahab's
daughter.
2One day, Jehoshaphat went to visit
Ahab in his capital city of Samaria.
Ahab slaughtered sheep and cattle and
prepared a big feast to honor Jehoshaphat and the officials with him.
Ahab talked about attacking the city of
Ramoth in Gilead,[y] 3and finally asked,
"Jehoshaphat, would you go with me to
attack Ramoth?"
"Yes," Jehoshaphat answered. "My
army is at your command. 4But first let's
ask the LORD what to do."
5Ahab sent for four hundred prophets
and asked, "Should I attack the city of
Ramoth?"
"Yes!" the prophets answered. "God
will help you capture the city."
6But Jehoshaphat said, "Just to make
sure, is there another of the LORD's
prophets we can ask?"
7"We could ask Micaiah son of Imlah,"
Ahab said. "But I hate Micaiah. He always has bad news for me."
"Don't say that!" Jehoshaphat replied.
8Then Ahab sent someone to bring Micaiah as soon as possible.
9All this time, Ahab and Jehoshaphat
were dressed in their royal robes and
were seated on their thrones at the
threshing place near the gate of Samaria, listening to the prophets tell
them what the LORD had said.
10Zedekiah son of Chenaanah was
one of the prophets. He had made some
horns out of iron and shouted, "Ahab,
the LORD says you will attack the Syri-

[x] **17.6** *local shrines*: See the note at 11.15. [y] **18.2** *attacking the city of Ramoth in Gilead*: The Syrians had taken control of Ramoth (see 1 Kings 22.3, 4).

ans like a bull with iron horns and wipe
them out!"
11All the prophets agreed that Ahab
should attack the Syrians at Ramoth
and promised that the LORD would help
him defeat them.
12Meanwhile, the messenger who
went to get Micaiah whispered, "Micaiah, all the prophets have good news
for Ahab. Now go and say the same
thing."
13"I'll say whatever the living LORD my
God tells me to say," Micaiah replied.
14Then Micaiah went up to Ahab, who
asked, "Micaiah, should we attack
Ramoth?"
"Yes!" Micaiah answered. "The LORD
will help you capture the city."
15Ahab shouted, "Micaiah, I've told
you over and over to tell me the truth!
What does the LORD really say?"
16Micaiah answered, "In a vision[z] I
saw Israelite soldiers wandering
around, lost in the hills like sheep without a shepherd. The LORD said, 'These
troops have no leader. They should go
home and not fight.' "
17Ahab turned to Jehoshaphat and
said, "I told you he would bring me bad
news!"
18Micaiah replied:

I then saw the LORD seated on his
throne with every creature in heaven
gathered around him. 19The LORD
asked, "Who can trick Ahab and
make him go to Ramoth where he
will be killed?"
They talked about it for a while,
20then finally a spirit came forward
and said to the LORD, "I can trick
Ahab."
"How?" the LORD asked.
21"I'll make Ahab's prophets lie to
him."
"Good!" the LORD replied. "Now go
and do it. You will be successful."
22Ahab, this is exactly what has
happened. The LORD made all your
prophets lie to you, and he knows
you will soon be destroyed.

23Zedekiah walked over and slapped
Micaiah on the face. Then he asked, "Do
you really think the LORD would speak
to you and not to me?"
24Micaiah answered, "You'll find out
on the day you have to hide in the back
room of some house."
25Ahab shouted, "Arrest Micaiah! Take
him to Prince Joash and Governor
Amon of Samaria. 26Tell them to put
him in prison and to give him nothing
but bread and water until I come back
safely."
27Micaiah said, "If you do come back,
I was wrong about what the LORD
wanted me to say." Then he told the
crowd, "Don't forget what I said!"

Ahab Dies at Ramoth

(1 Kings 22.29-35)

28Ahab and Jehoshaphat led their
armies to Ramoth in Gilead. 29Before
they went into battle, Ahab said, "Jehoshaphat, I'll disguise myself, but you
wear your royal robe." Ahab disguised
himself and went into battle.
30The king of Syria had ordered his
chariot commanders to attack only
Ahab. 31So when they saw Jehoshaphat
in his robe, they thought he was Ahab
and started to attack him. But Jehoshaphat prayed, and the LORD made
the Syrian soldiers stop. 32And when
they realized he wasn't Ahab, they left
him alone.
33However, during the fighting a soldier shot an arrow without even aiming,
and it hit Ahab between two pieces of
his armor. He shouted to his chariot
driver, "I've been hit! Get me out of
here!"
34The fighting lasted all day, with
Ahab propped up in his chariot so he
could see the Syrian troops. He stayed
there until evening, and by sundown he
was dead.

19 Jehoshaphat returned safely to
his palace in Jerusalem. 2But the
prophet Jehu son of Hanani met him
and said:

By helping that wicked Ahab, you
have made friends with someone
who hates the LORD. Now the LORD
God is angry at you! 3But not everything about you is bad. You destroyed the sacred poles[a] used in
worshiping the goddess Asherah—
that shows you have tried to obey
the LORD.

Jehoshaphat Appoints Judges To Settle Cases

4Jehoshaphat lived in Jerusalem, but
he often traveled through his kingdom,
from Beersheba in the south to the edge
of the hill country of Ephraim in the
north. He talked with the people and
convinced them to turn back to the
LORD God and worship him, just as their
ancestors had done.
5He assigned judges to each of the
fortified cities in Judah 6and told them:

Be careful when you make your
decisions in court, because these are
the LORD's people, and he will know
what you decide. 7So do your work
in honor of him and know that he
won't allow you to be unfair to anyone or to take bribes.

[z]**18.16** *vision*: In ancient times, prophets often told about future events from what they had seen in visions or dreams. [a]**19.3** *sacred poles*: See the note at 14.3.

8Jehoshaphat also chose some Levites, some priests, and some of the family leaders, and he appointed them to
serve as judges in Jerusalem. 9He told
them:

Faithfully serve the LORD! 10The
people of Judah will bring you legal
cases that involve every type of
crime, including murder. You must
settle these cases and warn the people to stop sinning against the LORD,
so that he won't get angry and punish Judah. Remember, if you follow
these instructions, you won't be held
responsible for anything that happens.

11Amariah the high priest will
have the final say in any religious
case. And Zebadiah, the leader[b] of
the Judah tribe, will have the final
say in all other cases. The rest of the
Levites will serve as your assistants.
Be brave, and I pray that the LORD
will help you do right.

Moab and Ammon Are Defeated

20 Some time later, the armies of
Moab and Ammon, together with
the Meunites,[c] went to war against Jehoshaphat. 2Messengers told Jehoshaphat, "A large army from Edom[d]
east of the Dead Sea has invaded our
country. They have already reached En-
Gedi."[e]

3Jehoshaphat was afraid, so he asked
the LORD what to do. He then told the
people of Judah to go without eating to
show their sorrow. 4They immediately
left for Jerusalem to ask for the LORD's
help.

5After everyone from Judah and
Jerusalem had come together at the
LORD's temple, Jehoshaphat stood in
front of the new courtyard 6and prayed:

You, LORD, are the God our ancestors worshiped, and from heaven
you rule every nation in the world.
You are so powerful that no one can
defeat you. 7Our God, you forced out
the nations who lived in this land
before your people Israel came here,
and you gave it to the descendants
of your friend Abraham forever.
8Our ancestors lived in this land and
built a temple to honor you. 9They
believed that whenever this land is
struck by war or disease or famine,
your people can pray to you at the
temple, and you will hear their
prayer and save them.

10You can see that the armies of
Ammon, Moab, and Edom are attacking us! Those are the nations
you would not let our ancestors invade on their way from Egypt, so
these nations were not destroyed.
11Now they are coming to take back
the land you gave us. 12Aren't you
going to punish them? We won't
stand a chance when this army attacks. We don't know what to do—
we are begging for your help.

13While every man, woman, and child
of Judah was standing there at the temple, 14the LORD's Spirit suddenly spoke
to Jahaziel, a Levite from the Asaph
clan.[f] 15Then Jahaziel said:

Your Majesty and everyone from
Judah and Jerusalem, the LORD says
that you don't need to be afraid or
let this powerful army discourage
you. God will fight on your side!
16So here's what you must do. Tomorrow the enemy armies will
march through the desert around
the town of Jeruel. March down and
meet them at the town of Ziz as they
come up the valley. 17You won't even
have to fight. Just take your positions and watch the LORD rescue you
from your enemy. Don't be afraid.
Just do as you're told. And as you
march out tomorrow, the LORD will
be there with you.

18Jehoshaphat bowed low to the
ground and everyone worshiped the
LORD. 19Then some Levites from the Kohath and Korah clans stood up and
shouted praises to the LORD God of Israel.

20Early the next morning, as everyone
got ready to leave for the desert near
Tekoa, Jehoshaphat stood up and said,
"Listen my friends, if we trust the LORD
God and believe what these prophets
have told us, the LORD will help us, and
we will be successful." 21Then he explained his plan and appointed men to
march in front of the army and praise
the LORD for his holy power by singing:[g]

"Praise the LORD!
His love never ends."

22As soon as they began singing, the
LORD confused the enemy camp, 23so
that the Ammonite and Moabite troops

[b]**19.11** *Zebadiah, the leader*: Hebrew "Zebadiah son of Ishmael, who is the leader." [c]**20.1** *Meunites*: One ancient translation (see also 26.7); Hebrew "Ammonites." [d]**20.2** *Edom*: The Hebrew text has "Syria"; in Hebrew there is only one letter difference between "Edom" and "Aram," which is the usual Hebrew name for Syria in the Bible. [e]**20.2** *En-Gedi*: The Hebrew text has "Hazazon-Tamar, also known as En-Gedi," a city on the west shore of the Dead Sea, about twenty-five miles southeast of Jerusalem. [f]**20.14** *Jahaziel, a Levite from the Asaph clan*: Hebrew "Jahaziel son of Zechariah son of Benaiah son of Jeiel son of Mattaniah, who was a Levite from the Asaph clan." [g]**20.21** *to march in front . . . singing*: Or "to put on their sacred robes, lead the army into battle, and praise the LORD by singing."

attacked and completely destroyed those from Edom. Then they turned against each other and fought until the entire camp was wiped out!

24When Judah's army reached the tower that overlooked the desert, they saw that every soldier in the enemy's army was lying dead on the ground. 25So Jehoshaphat and his troops went into the camp to carry away everything of value. They found a large herd of livestock,[h] a lot of equipment, clothes,[i] and other valuable things. It took them three days to carry it all away, and there was still some left over.

26Then on the fourth day, everyone came together in Beracah Valley and sang praises to the LORD. That's why that place was called Praise Valley.[j]

27-28Jehoshaphat led the crowd back to Jerusalem. And as they marched, they played harps and blew trumpets. They were very happy because the LORD had given them victory over their enemies, so when they reached the city, they went straight to the temple.

29When the other nations heard how the LORD had fought against Judah's enemies, they were too afraid 30to invade Judah. The LORD let Jehoshaphat's kingdom be at peace.

Jehoshaphat Dies

(1 Kings 22.41-50)

31Jehoshaphat was thirty-five years old when he became king of Judah, and he ruled from Jerusalem for twenty-five years. His mother was Azubah daughter of Shilhi. 32Jehoshaphat obeyed the LORD, just as his father Asa had done, 33but he did not destroy the local shrines.[k] So the people still worshiped foreign gods, instead of faithfully serving the God their ancestors had worshiped.

34Everything else Jehoshaphat did while he was king is written in the records of Jehu son of Hanani that are included in *The History of the Kings of Israel.*

35While Jehoshaphat was king, he signed a peace treaty with Ahaziah the wicked king of Israel. 36They agreed to build several seagoing ships[l] at Ezion-Geber. 37But the prophet Eliezer[m] warned Jehoshaphat, "The LORD will destroy these ships because you have supported Ahaziah." The ships were wrecked and never sailed.

21 Jehoshaphat died and was buried beside his ancestors in Jerusalem, and his son Jehoram became king.

King Jehoram of Judah

(2 Kings 8.16-24)

2King Jehoshaphat had seven sons: Jehoram, Azariah, Jehiel, Zechariah, Azariah, Michael, and Shephatiah. 3Jehoshaphat gave each of them silver and gold, as well as other valuable gifts. He also put them in charge of the fortified cities in Judah, but he had chosen his oldest son Jehoram to succeed him as king.

4After Jehoram had taken control of Judah, he had his brothers killed, as well as some of the nation's leaders. 5He was thirty-two years old when he became king, and he ruled eight years from Jerusalem.

6Jehoram married Ahab's daughter and followed the sinful example of Ahab's family and the other kings of Israel. He disobeyed the LORD by doing wrong, 7but because the LORD had made a solemn promise to King David that someone from his family would always rule in Judah, he refused to wipe out David's descendants.

8While Jehoram was king, the people of Edom rebelled and chose their own king. 9Jehoram, his officers, and his cavalry marched to Edom, where the Edomite army surrounded them. He escaped during the night, 10but Judah was never able to regain control of Edom. Even the town of Libnah[n] rebelled at that time.

Those things happened because Jehoram had turned away from the LORD, the God his ancestors had worshiped. 11Jehoram even built local shrines[o] in the hills of Judah and let the people sin against the LORD by worshiping foreign gods.

12One day, Jehoram received a letter from Elijah the prophet that said:

> I have a message for you from the LORD God your ancestor David worshiped. He knows that you have not followed the example of Jehoshaphat your father or Asa your grandfather. 13Instead you have acted like those sinful kings of Israel and have encouraged the people of Judah to stop worshiping the LORD, just as Ahab and his descendants did. You even murdered your own

[h]**20.25** *a large herd of livestock*: One ancient translation; Hebrew "among the bodies a large herd of." [i]**20.25** *clothes*: One ancient translation; Hebrew "dead bodies." [j]**20.26** *Beracah Valley . . . sang praises . . . Praise Valley*: In Hebrew the name "Beracah" means "praise." [k]**20.33** *local shrines*: See the note at 11.15. [l]**20.36** *seagoing ships*: See the note at 9.21. [m]**20.37** *Eliezer*: Hebrew "Eliezer son of Dodavahu from Mareshah." [n]**21.10** *Even the town of Libnah*: This was a town on the border between Philistia and Judah, which means that Jehoram was facing rebellion on both sides of his kingdom. [o]**21.11** *local shrines*: See the note at 11.15.

brothers, who were better men than you.

14Because you have done these terrible things, the LORD will severely punish the people in your kingdom, including your own family, and he will destroy everything you own. 15You will be struck with a painful stomach disease and suffer until you die.

16The LORD later caused the Philistines and the Arabs who lived near the Ethiopians[p] to become angry at Jehoram. 17They invaded Judah and stole the royal property from the palace, and they led Jehoram's wives and sons away as prisoners. The only one left behind was Ahaziah,[q] his youngest son.

18After this happened, the LORD struck Jehoram with an incurable stomach disease. 19About two years later, Jehoram died in terrible pain. No bonfire was built to honor him, even though the people had done this for his ancestors.

20Jehoram was thirty-two years old when he became king, and he ruled eight years from Jerusalem. He died, and no one even felt sad. He was buried in Jerusalem, but not in the royal tombs.

King Ahaziah of Judah

(2 Kings 8.25-29; 9.21, 27, 28)

22 Earlier, when the Arabs led a raid against Judah, they killed all of Jehoram's sons, except Ahaziah, the youngest one. So the people of Jerusalem crowned him their king. 2He was twenty-two[r] years old at the time, and he ruled only one year from Jerusalem.

Ahaziah's mother was Athaliah, a granddaughter of King Omri of Israel, 3and she encouraged her son to sin against the LORD. He followed the evil example of King Ahab and his descendants. 4In fact, after his father's death, Ahaziah sinned against the LORD by appointing some of Ahab's relatives to be his advisors.

Their advice led to his downfall. 5He listened to them and went with King Joram of Israel to attack King Hazael and the Syrian troops at Ramoth in Gilead. Joram was wounded in that battle, 6and he went to the town of Jezreel to recover. And Ahaziah later went there to visit him. 7It was during that visit that God had Ahaziah put to death.

When Ahaziah arrived at Jezreel, he and Joram went to meet with Jehu grandson of Nimshi. The LORD had already told Jehu to kill every male in Ahab's family, 8and while Jehu was doing that, he saw some of Judah's leaders and Ahaziah's nephews who had come with Ahaziah. Jehu killed them on the spot, 9then gave orders to find Ahaziah. Jehu's officers found him hiding in Samaria. They brought Ahaziah to Jehu, who immediately put him to death. They buried Ahaziah only because they respected Jehoshaphat his grandfather, who had done his best to obey the LORD.

There was no one from Ahaziah's family left to become king of Judah.

Queen Athaliah of Judah

(2 Kings 11.1-3)

10As soon as Athaliah heard that her son King Ahaziah was dead, she decided to kill any relative who could possibly become king. She would have done just that, 11but Jehosheba[s] rescued Joash son of Ahaziah just as the others were about to be murdered. Jehosheba, who was Jehoram's daughter and Ahaziah's half sister, was married to Jehoiada the priest. So she was able to hide her nephew Joash and his personal servant in a bedroom in the LORD's temple where he was safe from Athaliah. 12Joash hid in the temple with them for six years while Athaliah ruled as queen of Judah.

Jehoiada Makes Joash King of Judah

(2 Kings 11.4-21)

23 After Ahaziah's son Joash had hidden in the temple for six years, Jehoiada the priest knew that something had to be done. So he made sure he had the support of several army officers. They were Azariah son of Jeroham, Ishmael son of Jehohanan, Azariah son of Obed, Maaseiah son of Adaiah, and Elishaphat son of Zichri. 2These five men went to the towns in Judah and called together the Levites and the clan leaders. They all came to Jerusalem 3and gathered at the temple, where they agreed to help Joash.

Jehoiada said to them:

Joash will be our next king, because long ago the LORD promised that one of David's descendants would always be king. 4Here is what we will do. Three groups of priests and Levites will be on guard duty on the Sabbath—one group will guard the gates of the temple, 5one will guard the palace, and the other will guard Foundation Gate. The rest of you will stand guard in the temple courtyards. 6Only the priests and Levites who are on duty will be able to enter the temple, because they

[p]21.16 *Ethiopians*: See the note at 12.3. [q]21.17 *Ahaziah*: The Hebrew text has "Jehoahaz," another spelling of the name. [r]22.2 *twenty-two*: One ancient translation (see also 2 Kings 8.26); Hebrew "forty-two." [s]22.11 *Jehosheba*: The Hebrew text has "Jehoshabeath," another spelling of the name.

will be the only ones who have gone
through the ceremony to make
themselves clean and acceptable.
The others must stay outside in the
courtyards, just as the LORD has
commanded. 7You Levites must protect King Joash. Don't let him out of
your sight! And keep your swords
ready to kill anyone who comes into
the temple.
8The Levites and the people of Judah
followed Jehoiada's orders. The guards
going off duty were not allowed to go
home, and so each commander had all
his guards available—those going off
duty as well as those coming on duty.
9Jehoiada went into the temple and
brought out the swords and shields that
had belonged to King David, and he
gave them to the commanders. 10They
gave the weapons to the guards, and Jehoiada then made sure that the guards
took their positions around the temple
and the altar to protect the king on
every side.
11Jehoiada and his sons brought
Joash outside, where they placed the
crown on his head and gave him a copy
of the instructions for ruling the nation.
Olive oil was poured on his head to
show that he was now king, and the
crowd cheered and shouted, "Long live
the king!"
12As soon as Queen Athaliah heard
the crowd cheering for Joash, she went
to the temple. 13There she saw Joash
standing by one of the columns near the
entrance, which was the usual place for
the king. The commanders and the
trumpet players were standing next to
him, and the musicians were playing instruments and leading the people as
they celebrated and blew trumpets.
Athaliah tore her clothes in anger and
shouted, "You betrayed me, you traitors!"
14Right away, Jehoiada said to the
army commanders, "Don't kill her near
the LORD's temple. Take her out in front
of the troops, and be sure to kill all of
her followers!" 15She tried to escape, but
the commanders caught and killed her
near the gate where horses are led into
the palace.
16Jehoiada asked King Joash and the
people to join with him in being faithful
to the LORD. They agreed, 17then rushed
to the temple of the god Baal and tore it
down. They smashed the altars and the
idols and killed Mattan the priest of
Baal in front of the altars.
18Jehoiada assigned the priests and
Levites their duties at the temple, just as
David had done. They were in charge of
offering sacrifices to the LORD according
to the Law of Moses, and they were responsible for leading the celebrations
with singing. 19Jehoiada ordered the
guards at the temple gates to keep out
anyone who was unclean.
20Finally, Jehoiada called together the
army commanders, the most important
citizens of Judah, and the government
officials. The crowd of people followed
them as they led Joash from the temple,
through the Upper Gate, and into the
palace, where he took his place as king
of Judah. 21Everyone celebrated because
Athaliah had been killed and Jerusalem
was peaceful again.

King Joash of Judah

(2 Kings 12.1-16)

24 Joash was only seven years old
when he became king of Judah,
and he ruled forty years from Jerusalem. His mother Zibiah was from the
town of Beersheba.
2While Jehoiada the priest was alive,
Joash obeyed the LORD by doing right.
3Jehoiada even chose two women for
Joash to marry so he could have a family.
4Some time later, Joash decided it was
time to repair the temple. 5He called together the priests and Levites and said,
"Go everywhere in Judah and collect the
annual tax from the people. I want this
done right away—we need that money
to repair the temple."
But the Levites were in no hurry to
follow the king's orders. 6So he sent for
Jehoiada the high priest and asked,
"Why didn't you send the Levites to collect the taxes? The LORD's servant
Moses and the people agreed long
ago that this tax would be collected
and used to pay for the upkeep of the
sacred tent. 7And now we need it to
repair the temple because the sons
of that evil woman Athaliah came in
and wrecked it. They even used some
of the sacred objects to worship the god
Baal."
8Joash gave orders for a wooden box
to be made and had it placed outside,
near the gate of the temple. 9He then
sent letters everywhere in Judah and
Jerusalem, asking everyone to bring
their taxes to the temple, just as Moses
had required their ancestors to do.
10The people and their leaders agreed,
and they brought their money to
Jerusalem and placed it in the box.
11Each day, after the Levites took the
box into the temple, the king's secretary
and the high priest's assistant would
dump out the money and count it. Then
the empty box would be taken back outside.
This happened day after day, and
soon a large amount of money was collected. 12Joash and Jehoiada turned the
money over to the men who were supervising the repairs to the temple. They
used the money to hire stonecutters,

carpenters, and experts in working with
iron and bronze.
13These workers went right to work
repairing the temple, and when they
were finished, it looked as good as new.
14They did not use all the tax money for
the repairs, so the rest of it was handed
over to Joash and Jehoiada, who then
used it to make dishes and other gold
and silver objects for the temple.
Sacrifices to please the LORD[t] were offered regularly in the temple for as long
as Jehoiada lived. 15He died at the ripe
old age of one hundred thirty years,
16and he was buried in the royal tombs
in Jerusalem, because he had done so
much good for the people of Israel, for
God, and for the temple.

Joash Turns Away from the LORD

17After the death of Jehoiada the
priest, the leaders of Judah went to
Joash and talked him into doing what
they wanted. 18Right away, the people of
Judah stopped worshiping in the temple
of the LORD God, and they started worshiping idols and the symbols of the
goddess Asherah. These sinful things
made the LORD God angry at the people
of Judah and Jerusalem, 19but he still
sent prophets who warned them to turn
back to him. The people refused to listen.
20God's Spirit spoke to Zechariah son
of Jehoiada the priest, and Zechariah
told everyone that God was saying:
"Why are you disobeying me and my
laws? This will only bring punishment!
You have deserted me, so now I will
desert you."
21-22King Joash forgot that Zechariah's father had always been a loyal
friend. So when the people of Judah
plotted to kill Zechariah, Joash joined
them and gave orders for them to stone
him to death in the courtyard of the
temple. As Zechariah was dying, he
said, "I pray that the LORD will see this
and punish all of you."

Joash Is Killed

23In the spring of the following year,
the Syrian army invaded Judah and
Jerusalem, killing all of the nation's
leaders. They collected everything of
value that belonged to the people and
took it back to their king in Damascus.
24The Syrian army was very small, but
the LORD let them defeat Judah's large
army, because he was punishing Joash
and the people of Judah for turning
away from him.
25-26Joash was severely wounded during the battle, and as soon as the Syrians left Judah, two of his officials,
Zabad and Jehozabad,[u] decided to revenge the death of Zechariah. They plotted and killed Joash while he was in
bed, recovering from his wounds. Joash
was buried in Jerusalem, but not in the
royal tombs. 27*The History of the Kings*
also tells more about the sons of Joash,
what the prophets said about him, and
how he repaired the temple. Amaziah
son of Joash became king after his
father's death.

King Amaziah of Judah

(2 Kings 14.1-6)

25 Amaziah was twenty-five years
old when he became king, and he
ruled twenty-nine years from Jerusalem,
the hometown of his mother Jehoaddin.[v]
2Even though Amaziah obeyed the
LORD by doing right, he refused to be
completely faithful. 3For example, as
soon as he had control of Judah, he arrested and killed the officers who had
murdered his father. 4But the children of
those officers were not killed; the LORD
had commanded in the Law of Moses
that only the people who sinned were to
be punished.[w]

Edom Is Defeated

(2 Kings 14.7)

5Amaziah sent a message to the tribes
of Judah and Benjamin and called together all the men who were twenty
years old and older. Three hundred
thousand men went to Jerusalem, all of
them ready for battle and able to fight
with spears and shields. Amaziah
grouped these soldiers according to
their clans and put them under the command of his army officers. 6Amaziah
also paid almost four tons of silver to
hire one hundred thousand soldiers
from Israel.
7One of God's prophets said, "Your
Majesty, don't let these Israelite soldiers
march into battle with you. The LORD
has refused to help anyone from the
northern kingdom of Israel, 8and so he
will let your enemies defeat you, even if
you fight hard. He is the one who brings
both victory and defeat."
9Amaziah replied, "What am I supposed to do about all the silver I paid
those troops?"
"The LORD will give you back even
more than you paid," the prophet answered.
10Amaziah ordered the troops from Is-

[t]**24.14** *Sacrifices to please the LORD*: See the note at 1.6. [u]**24.25,26** *Zabad and Jehozabad*: Hebrew "Zabad son of Shimeath from Ammon and Jehozabad son of Shimrith from Moab."
[v]**25.1** *Jehoaddin*: The Hebrew text has "Jehoaddan," another spelling of the name.
[w]**25.4** *the LORD had commanded . . . punished*: See Deuteronomy 24.16.

rael to go home, but when they left,
they were furious with the people of
Judah.
11After Amaziah got his courage back,
he led his troops to Salt Valley, where he
killed ten thousand Edomite soldiers in
battle. 12He captured ten thousand more
soldiers and dragged them to the top of
a high cliff. Then he pushed them over
the side, and they all were killed on the
rocks below.
13Meanwhile, the Israelite troops that
Amaziah had sent home, raided the
towns in Judah between Samaria and
Beth-Horon. They killed three thousand
people and carried off their possessions.
14After Amaziah had defeated the
Edomite army, he returned to Jerusalem. He took with him the idols of the
Edomite gods and set them up. Then he
bowed down and offered them sacrifices. 15This made the LORD very angry,
and he sent a prophet to ask Amaziah,
"Why would you worship these foreign
gods that couldn't even save their own
people from your attack?"
16But before the prophet finished
speaking, Amaziah interrupted and
said, "You're not one of my advisors!
Don't say another word, or I'll have you
killed."

The prophet stopped. But then he added, "First you sinned and now you've ignored my warning. It's clear that God has decided to punish you!"

Israel Defeats Judah
(2 Kings 14.8-14)

17King Amaziah of Judah talked with
his officials, then sent a message to
King Jehoash[x] of Israel: "Come out and
face me in battle!"
18Jehoash sent back a reply that said:

Once upon a time, a small thornbush in Lebanon arranged the marriage between his son and the
daughter of a large cedar tree. But a
wild animal came along and trampled the small bush.
19Amaziah, you think you're so
powerful because you defeated
Edom. But stay at home and do your
celebrating. If you cause any trouble, both you and your kingdom of
Judah will be destroyed.

20God made Amaziah stubborn because he was planning to punish him
for worshiping the Edomite gods.
Amaziah refused to listen to Jehoash's
warning, 21so Jehoash led his army to
the town of Beth-Shemesh in Judah to
attack Amaziah and his troops. 22Dur-
ing the battle, Judah's army was
crushed. Every soldier from Judah ran
back home, 23and Jehoash captured
Amaziah.

Jehoash took Amaziah with him when he went to attack Jerusalem. Jehoash broke down the city wall from Ephraim Gate to Corner Gate, a section about six hundred feet long.
24He carried away
the gold, the silver, and all the valuable
furnishings from God's temple where
the descendants of Obed-Edom stood
guard. He robbed the king's treasury,
took hostages, then returned to Samaria.

Amaziah Is Killed
(2 Kings 14.15-20)

25Amaziah lived fifteen years after Jehoash died. 26Everything else Amaziah
did while he was king is written in *The
History of the Kings of Judah and Israel.*
27As soon as Amaziah started disobeying the LORD, some people in
Jerusalem plotted against Amaziah. He
was able to escape to the town of
Lachish, but another group of people
caught him and killed him there. 28His
body was taken to Jerusalem on horseback and buried beside his ancestors.

King Uzziah of Judah
(2 Kings 14.21, 22; 15.1-7)

26 1-3After the death of King Amaziah, the people of Judah crowned
his son Uzziah[y] king, even though
he was only sixteen at the time.
Uzziah ruled fifty-two years from
Jerusalem, the hometown of his mother
Jecoliah. During his rule, he recaptured
and rebuilt the town of Elath.
4He obeyed the LORD by doing right,
as his father Amaziah had done.
5Zechariah was Uzziah's advisor and
taught him to obey God. And so, as long
as Zechariah was alive, Uzziah was
faithful to God, and God made him successful.
6While Uzziah was king, he started a
war against the Philistines. He smashed
the walls of the cities of Gath, Jabneh,
and Ashdod, then rebuilt towns around
Ashdod and in other parts of Philistia.
7God helped him defeat the Philistines,
the Arabs living in Gur-Baal, and the
Meunites. 8Even the Ammonites paid
taxes to Uzziah. He became very powerful, and people who lived as far away as
Egypt heard about him.
9In Jerusalem, Uzziah built fortified
towers at the Corner Gate, the Valley
Gate, and the place where the city wall

[x]**25.17** *King Jehoash*: The Hebrew text has "King Joash son of Jehoahaz son of Jehu"; Jehoash is another spelling for the name Joash. [y]**26.1-3** *Uzziah*: In the parallel passages in 2 Kings, he is called "Azariah" (see also 1 Chronicles 3.10-15). He is also called "Uzziah" in 2 Kings 15.13; Isaiah 1.1; Hosea 1.1; and Amos 1.1. One of these names was probably his birth name, while the other was his name after he became king.

turned inward.[z] 10He also built defense towers out in the desert.

He owned such a large herd of livestock in the western foothills and in the flatlands, that he had cisterns dug there to catch the rainwater. He loved farming, so he had crops and vineyards planted in the hill country wherever there was fertile soil, and he hired farmers to take care of them.

11Uzziah's army was always ready for battle. Jeiel and Maaseiah were the officers who kept track of the number of soldiers, and these two men were under the command of Hananiah, one of Uzziah's officials. 12-13There were 307,500 trained soldiers, all under the command of 2,600 clan leaders. These powerful troops protected the king against any enemy. 14Uzziah supplied his army with shields, spears, helmets, armor, bows, and stones used for slinging. 15Some of his skilled workers invented machines that could shoot arrows and sling large stones. Uzziah set these up in Jerusalem at his defense towers and at the corners of the city wall.

God helped Uzziah become more and more powerful, and he was famous all over the world.

Uzziah Becomes Too Proud

16Uzziah became proud of his power, and this led to his downfall.

One day, Uzziah disobeyed the LORD his God by going into the temple and burning incense as an offering to him.[a] 17Azariah the priest and eighty other brave priests followed Uzziah into the temple 18and said, "Your Majesty, this isn't right! You are not allowed to burn incense to the LORD. That must be done only by priests who are descendants of Aaron. You will have to leave! You have sinned against the LORD, and so he will no longer bless you."

19Uzziah, who was standing next to the incense altar at the time, was holding the incense burner, ready to offer incense to the LORD. He became very angry when he heard Azariah's warning, and leprosy[b] suddenly appeared on his forehead! 20Azariah and the other priests saw it and immediately told him to leave the temple. Uzziah realized that the LORD had punished him, so he hurried to get outside.

21Uzziah had leprosy the rest of his life. He was no longer allowed in the temple or in his own palace. That's why his son Jotham lived there and ruled in his place.

22Everything else Uzziah did while he was king is in the records written by the prophet Isaiah son of Amoz. 23Since Uzziah had leprosy, he could not be buried in the royal tombs. Instead, he was buried in a nearby cemetery that the kings owned. His son Jotham then became king.

King Jotham of Judah

(2 Kings 15.32-38)

27 Jotham was twenty-five years old when he became king of Judah, and he ruled from Jerusalem for sixteen years. Jerushah his mother was the daughter of Zadok.

2Jotham obeyed the LORD and did right. He followed the example of his father Uzziah, except he never burned incense in the temple as his father had done. But the people of Judah kept sinning against the LORD.

3Jotham rebuilt the Upper Gate of the temple and did a lot of work to repair the wall near Mount Ophel. 4He built towns in the mountains of Judah and built fortresses and defense towers in the forests.

5During his rule he attacked and defeated the Ammonites. Then every year for the next three years, he forced them to pay four tons of silver, sixty thousand bushels of wheat, and sixty thousand bushels of barley.

6Jotham remained faithful to the LORD his God and became a very powerful king.

7Everything else Jotham did while he was king, including the wars he fought, is written in *The History of the Kings of Israel and Judah*. 8After he had ruled Judah sixteen years, he died at the age of forty-one. 9He was buried in Jerusalem, and his son Ahaz became king.

King Ahaz of Judah

(2 Kings 16.1-4)

28 Ahaz was twenty years old when he became king of Judah, and he ruled from Jerusalem for sixteen years.

Ahaz was nothing like his ancestor David. Ahaz disobeyed the LORD 2and was as sinful as the kings of Israel. He made idols of the god Baal, 3and he offered sacrifices in Hinnom Valley. Worst of all, Ahaz sacrificed his own sons, which was a disgusting custom of the nations that the LORD had forced out of Israel. 4Ahaz offered sacrifices at the local shrines,[c] as well as on every hill and in the shade of large trees.

[z] **26.9** *the place where the city wall turned inward*: One possible meaning for the difficult Hebrew text. [a] **26.16** *going into the temple and burning incense as an offering to him*: This was to be done only by priests (see Exodus 30.1-10; Numbers 16.39, 40). [b] **26.19** *leprosy*: The word translated "leprosy" was used for many different kinds of skin diseases.
[c] **28.4** *local shrines*: See the note at 11.15.

Syria and Israel Attack Judah
(2 Kings 16.5, 6)

5-6Ahaz and the people of Judah
sinned and turned away from the LORD,
the God their ancestors had worshiped.
So the LORD punished them by letting
their enemies defeat them.
The king of Syria attacked Judah and
took many of its people to Damascus as
prisoners. King Pekah[d] of Israel later
defeated Judah and killed one hundred
twenty thousand of its bravest soldiers
in one day. 7During that battle, an Israelite soldier named Zichri killed three
men from Judah: Maaseiah the king's
son; Azrikam, the official in charge of
the palace; and Elkanah, the king's second in command. 8The Israelite troops
captured two hundred thousand women
and children and took them back to
their capital city of Samaria, along with
a large amount of their possessions.
They did these things even though the
people of Judah were their own relatives.

Oded the Prophet Condemns Israel

9Oded lived in Samaria and was one
of the LORD's prophets. He met Israel's
army on their way back from Judah and
said to them:

> The LORD God of your ancestors
> let you defeat Judah's army only be-
> cause he was angry with them. But
> you should not have been so cruel!
> 10If you make slaves of the people of
> Judah and Jerusalem, you will be as
> guilty as they are of sinning against
> the LORD.
> 11Send these prisoners back
> home—they are your own relatives.
> If you don't, the LORD will punish
> you in his anger.

12About the same time, four of Israel's
leaders arrived. They were Azariah son
of Johanan, Berechiah son of Meshillemoth, Jehizkiah son of Shallum, and
Amasa son of Hadlai. They agreed with
Oded that the Israelite troops were
wrong, 13and they said:

> If you bring these prisoners into
> Samaria, that will be one more thing
> we've done to sin against the LORD.
> And he is already angry enough at
> us.

14So in front of the leaders and the
crowd, the troops handed over their
prisoners and the property they had
taken from Judah. 15The four leaders
took some of the stolen clothes and gave
them to the prisoners who needed
something to wear. They later gave
them all a new change of clothes and
shoes, then fixed them something to eat
and drink, and cleaned their wounds
with olive oil. They gave donkeys to
those who were too weak to walk, and
led all of them back to Jericho, the city
known for its palm trees. The leaders
then returned to Samaria.

Ahaz Asks the King of Assyria for Help
(2 Kings 16.7-9)

16-18Some time later, the Edomites attacked the eastern part of Judah again
and carried away prisoners. And at the
same time, the Philistines raided towns
in the western foothills and in the
Southern Desert. They conquered the
towns of Beth-Shemesh, Aijalon,
Gederoth, Soco, Timnah, and Gimzo, including the villages around them. Then
some of the Philistines went to live in
these places.
Ahaz sent a message to King Tiglath
Pileser of Assyria and begged for help.
19But God was punishing Judah with
these disasters, because Ahaz had disobeyed him and refused to stop Judah
from sinning. 20So Tiglath Pileser came
to Judah, but instead of helping, he
made things worse. 21Ahaz gave him
gifts from the LORD's temple and the
king's palace, as well as from the homes
of Israel's other leaders. The Assyrian
king still refused to help Ahaz.

The Final Sin of Ahaz and His Death

22Even after all these terrible things
happened to Ahaz, he sinned against
the LORD even worse than before. 23He
said to himself, "The Syrian gods must
have helped their kings defeat me.
Maybe if I offer sacrifices to those gods,
they will help me." That was the sin that
finally led to the downfall of Ahaz, as
well as to the destruction of Judah.
24Ahaz collected all the furnishings of
the temple and smashed them to pieces.
Then he locked the doors to the temple
and set up altars to foreign gods on
every street corner in Jerusalem. 25In
every city and town in Judah he built local shrines[e] to worship foreign gods. All
of this made the LORD God of his ancestors very angry.
26Everything else Ahaz did while he
was king is written in *The History of the
Kings of Judah and Israel.* 27Ahaz died
and was buried in Jerusalem, but not in
the royal tombs. His son Hezekiah then
became king.

King Hezekiah of Judah
(2 Kings 18.1-3)

29 Hezekiah was twenty-five years
old when he became king of Judah, and he ruled twenty-nine years

[d]28.5,6 *Pekah*: Hebrew "Pekah son of Remaliah."

[e]28.25 *local shrines*: See the note at 11.15.

from Jerusalem. His mother was Abijah daughter of Zechariah. 2Hezekiah obeyed the LORD by doing right, just as his ancestor David had done.

The Temple Is Purified

3In the first month[f] of the first year of Hezekiah's rule, he unlocked the doors to the LORD's temple and had them repaired.[g] 4Then he called the priests and Levites to the east courtyard of the temple 5and said:

> It's time to purify the temple of the LORD God of our ancestors. You Levites must first go through the ceremony to make yourselves clean, then go into the temple and bring out everything that is unclean and unacceptable to the LORD. 6Some of our ancestors were unfaithful and disobeyed the LORD our God. Not only did they turn their backs on the LORD, but they also completely ignored his temple. 7They locked the doors, then let the lamps go out and stopped burning incense and offering sacrifices to him. 8The LORD became terribly angry at the people of Judah and Jerusalem, and everyone was shocked and horrified at what he did to punish them. Not only were 9our ancestors killed in battle, but our own children and wives were taken captive.
>
> 10So I have decided to renew our agreement with the LORD God of Israel. Maybe then he will stop being so angry at us. 11Let's not waste any time, my friends. You are the ones who were chosen to be the LORD's priests and to offer him sacrifices.

12-14When Hezekiah finished talking, the following Levite leaders went to work:

Mahath son of Amasai and Joel son of Azariah from the Kohath clan; Kish son of Abdi and Azariah son of Jehallelel from the Merari clan; Joah son of Zimmah and Eden son of Joah from the Gershon clan; Shimri and Jeuel from the Elizaphan clan; Zechariah and Mattaniah from the Asaph clan; Jehuel and Shimei from the Heman clan; Shemaiah and Uzziel from the Jeduthun clan.

15These leaders gathered together the rest of the Levites, and they all went through the ceremony to make themselves clean. Then they began to purify the temple according to the Law of the LORD, just as Hezekiah had commanded.

16The priests went into the temple and carried out everything that was unclean. They put these things in the courtyard, and from there, the Levites carried them outside the city to Kidron Valley.

17The priests and Levites began their work on the first day of the first month.[h] It took them one week to purify the courtyards of the temple and another week to purify the temple. So on the sixteenth day of that same month 18they went back to Hezekiah and said:

> Your Majesty, we have finished our work. The entire temple is now pure again, and so is the altar and its utensils, as well as the table for the sacred loaves of bread and its utensils. 19And we have brought back all the things that King Ahaz took from the temple during the time he was unfaithful to God. We purified them and put them back in front of the altar.

Worship in the Temple

20Right away, Hezekiah called together the officials of Jerusalem, and they went to the temple. 21They brought with them seven bulls, seven rams, seven lambs, and seven goats[i] as sacrifices to take away the sins of Hezekiah's family and of the people of Judah, as well as to purify the temple. Hezekiah told the priests, who were descendants of Aaron, to sacrifice these animals on the altar.

22The priests killed the bulls, the rams, and the lambs, then splattered the blood on the altar. 23They took the goats to Hezekiah and the worshipers, and they laid their hands on the animals. 24The priests then killed the goats and splattered the blood on the altar as a sacrifice to take away the sins of everyone in Israel, because Hezekiah had commanded that these sacrifices be made for all the people of Israel.

25Next, Hezekiah assigned the Levites to their places in the temple. He gave them cymbals, harps, and other stringed instruments, according to the instructions that the LORD had given King David and the two prophets, Gad and Nathan. 26The Levites were ready to play the instruments that had belonged to David; the priests were ready to blow the trumpets.

27As soon as Hezekiah gave the signal for the sacrifices to be burned on the altar, the musicians began singing praises to the LORD and playing their instruments, 28and everyone worshiped the LORD. This continued until the last animal was sacrificed.

[f]**29.3** *first month*: Abib (also called Nisan), the first month of the Hebrew calendar, from about mid-March to mid-April. [g]**29.3** *he unlocked the doors . . . repaired*: King Ahaz had locked the doors and stopped everyone from worshiping the LORD (see 28.24, 25). [h]**29.17** *first month*: See the note at 29.3. [i]**29.21** *goats*: Hebrew "male goats."

29After that, Hezekiah and the crowd
of worshipers knelt down and worshiped the LORD. 30Then Hezekiah and
his officials ordered the Levites to sing
the songs of praise that David and Asaph the prophet had written. And so
they bowed down and joyfully sang
praises to the LORD.
31Hezekiah said to the crowd, "Now
that you are once again acceptable to
the LORD, bring sacrifices and offerings
to give him thanks."
The people did this, and some of them
voluntarily brought animals to be offered as sacrifices. 32Seventy bulls, one
hundred rams, and two hundred lambs
were brought as sacrifices to please the
LORD;[j] 33six hundred bulls and three
thousand sheep were brought as sacrifices to ask the LORD's blessing.[k]
34There were not enough priests to skin
all these animals, because many of the
priests had not taken the time to go
through the ceremony to make themselves clean. However, since all the
Levites had made themselves clean,
they helped the priests until the last animal was skinned. 35Besides all the sacrifices that were burned on the altar, the
fat from the other animal sacrifices was
burned, and the offerings of wine were
poured over the altar.
So the temple was once again used for
worshiping the LORD. 36Hezekiah and
the people of Judah celebrated, because
God had helped them make this happen
so quickly.

Hezekiah Prepares To Celebrate Passover

30 1-4Passover wasn't celebrated in
the first month,[l] which was the
usual time, because many of the priests
were still unclean and unacceptable to
serve, and because not everyone in Judah had come to Jerusalem for the festival. So Hezekiah, his officials, and the
people agreed to celebrate Passover in
the second month.[m]
Hezekiah sent a message to everyone
in Israel and Judah, including those
in the territories of Ephraim and
West Manasseh, inviting them to the
temple in Jerusalem for the celebration
of Passover in honor of the LORD God
of Israel. 5Everyone from Beersheba
in the south to Dan in the north was
invited. This was the largest crowd of
people that had ever celebrated
Passover, according to the official
records.
6Hezekiah's messengers went everywhere in Israel and Judah with the following letter:

> People of Israel, now that you
> have survived the invasion of the As-
> syrian kings,[n] it's time for you to
> turn back to the LORD God our an-
> cestors Abraham, Isaac, and Jacob
> worshiped. If you do this, he will
> stop being angry. 7Don't follow the
> example of your ancestors and your
> Israelite relatives in the north. They
> were unfaithful to the LORD, and he
> punished them horribly. 8Don't be
> stubborn like your ancestors. Decide
> now to obey the LORD our God!
> Come to Jerusalem and worship him
> in the temple that will belong to him
> forever. Then he will stop being an-
> gry, 9and the enemies that have
> captured your families will show
> pity and send them back home.
> The LORD God is kind and mer-
> ciful, and if you turn back to him,
> he will no longer turn his back on
> you.

10The messengers went to every town
in Ephraim and West Manasseh as far
north as the territory of Zebulun, but
everyone laughed and insulted them.
11Only a few people from the tribes of
Asher, West Manasseh, and Zebulun
were humble and went to Jerusalem.
12God also made everyone in Judah eager to do what Hezekiah and his officials had commanded.

Passover Is Celebrated

13In the second month,[o] a large crowd
of people gathered in Jerusalem to celebrate the Festival of Thin Bread.[p] 14They
took all the foreign altars and incense
altars in Jerusalem and threw them into
Kidron Valley.
15-17Then, on the fourteenth day of
that same month, the Levites began
killing the lambs for Passover, because
many of the worshipers were unclean
and were not allowed to kill their own
lambs. Meanwhile, some of the priests
and Levites felt ashamed because they
had not gone through the ceremony to
make themselves clean. They immediately went through that ceremony and
went to the temple, where they offered

[j]**29.32** *sacrifices to please the LORD*: See the note at 1.6. [k]**29.33** *sacrifices to ask the LORD's blessing*: These sacrifices have traditionally been called "peace offerings" or "offerings of well-being." A main purpose was to ask for the LORD's blessing, and so in the CEV they are sometimes called "sacrifices to ask the LORD's blessing." [l]**30.1-4** *first month*: See the note at 29.3. [m]**30.1-4** *second month*: See the note at 3.1,2. [n]**30.6** *the invasion of the Assyrian kings*: See 2 Kings 17.1-22. [o]**30.13** *second month*: See the note at 3.1,2. [p]**30.13** *the Festival of Thin Bread*: The celebration of this Festival began one day after Passover. And so these two festivals were often referred to as one.

sacrifices to please the LORD.[q] Then the
priests and Levites took their positions,
according to the Law of Moses, the servant of God.

As the Levites killed the lambs, they
handed some of the blood to the priests,
who splattered it on the altar.

18-19Most of the people that came from
Ephraim, West Manasseh, Issachar, and
Zebulun had not made themselves
clean, but they ignored God's Law and
ate the Passover lambs anyway.
Hezekiah found out what they had done
and prayed, "LORD God, these people
are unclean according to the laws of
holiness. But they are worshiping you,
just as their ancestors did. So, please be
kind and forgive them." 20The LORD answered Hezekiah's prayer and did not
punish them.

21The worshipers in Jerusalem were
very happy and celebrated the Festival
for seven days. The Levites and priests
sang praises to the LORD every day and
played their instruments. 22Hezekiah
thanked the Levites for doing such a
good job, leading the celebration.

The worshipers celebrated for seven
days by offering sacrifices, by eating the
sacred meals, and by praising the LORD
God of their ancestors. 23Everyone was
so excited that they agreed to celebrate
seven more days.

24So Hezekiah gave the people one
thousand bulls and seven thousand
sheep to be offered as sacrifices and to
be used as food for the sacred meals.
His officials gave one thousand bulls
and ten thousand sheep, and many more
priests agreed to go through the ceremony to make themselves clean.
25Everyone was very happy, including
those from Judah and Israel, the priests
and Levites, and the foreigners living in
Judah and Israel. 26It was the biggest
celebration in Jerusalem since the days
of King Solomon, the son of David.
27The priests and Levites asked God to
bless the people, and from his home in
heaven, he did.

The People Destroy the Local Shrines

(2 Kings 18.4)

31 After the Festival, the people
went to every town in Judah and
smashed the stone images of foreign
gods and cut down the sacred poles[r] for
worshiping the goddess Asherah. They
destroyed all the local shrines[s] and foreign altars in Judah, as well as those in
the territories of Benjamin, Ephraim,
and West Manasseh. Then everyone
went home.

Offerings for the Priests and Levites

2Hezekiah divided the priests and
Levites into groups, according to their
duties. Then he assigned them the responsibilities of offering sacrifices to
please the LORD[t] and sacrifices to ask
his blessing.[u] He also appointed people
to serve at the temple and to sing
praises at the temple gates. 3Hezekiah
provided animals from his own herds
and flocks to use for the morning and
evening sacrifices, as well as for the sacrifices during the Sabbath celebrations,
the New Moon Festivals, and the other
religious feasts required by the Law of
the LORD.

4He told the people of Jerusalem to
bring the offerings that were to be given
to the priests and Levites, so that they
would have time to serve the LORD with
their work. 5As soon as the people heard
what the king wanted, they brought a
tenth of everything they owned, including their best grain, wine, olive oil,
honey, and other crops. 6The people
from the other towns of Judah brought a
tenth of their herds and flocks, as well
as a tenth of anything they had dedicated to the LORD. 7The people started
bringing their offerings to Jerusalem in
the third month,[v] and the last ones arrived four months later. 8When Hezekiah and his officials saw these offerings, they thanked the LORD and the
people.

9Hezekiah asked the priests and
Levites about the large amount of offerings. 10The high priest at the time was
Azariah, a descendant of Zadok, and he
replied, "Ever since the people have
been bringing us their offerings, we
have had more than enough food and
supplies. The LORD has certainly blessed
his people. Look at how much is left
over!"

11So the king gave orders for storerooms to be built in the temple, and
when they were completed, 12-13all the
extra offerings were taken there.
Hezekiah and Azariah then appointed
Conaniah the Levite to be in charge of
these storerooms. His brother Shimei
was his assistant, and the following
Levites worked with them: Jehiel,
Azaziah, Nahath, Asahel, Jerimoth, Jozabad, Eliel, Ismachiah, Mahath, and Benaiah. 14Kore son of Imnah was assigned to guard the East Gate, and he
was put in charge of receiving the offerings voluntarily given to God and of dividing them among the priests and
Levites. 15-16He had six assistants who
were responsible for seeing that all the

[q]**30.15-17** *sacrifices to please the LORD*: See the note at 1.6. [r]**31.1** *sacred poles*: See the note at 14.3. [s]**31.1** *local shrines*: See the note at 11.15. [t]**31.2** *sacrifices to please the LORD*: See the note at 1.6. [u]**31.2** *sacrifices to ask his blessing*: See the note at 29.33. [v]**31.7** *third month*: Sivan, the third month of the Hebrew calendar, from about mid-May to mid-June.

priests in the other towns of Judah also
got their share of these offerings. They
were Eden, Miniamin, Jeshua, Shemaiah, Amariah, and Shecaniah.
Every priest and every Levite over
thirty[w] years old who worked daily in
the temple received part of these offerings, according to their duties. 17The
priests were listed in the official records
by clans, and the Levites twenty years
old and older were listed by their duties.
18The official records also included their
wives and children, because they had
also been faithful in keeping themselves
clean and acceptable to serve the LORD.
19Hezekiah also appointed other men
to take food and supplies to the priests
and Levites whose homes were in the
pastureland around the towns of Judah.
But the priests had to be descendants of
Aaron, and the Levites had to be listed
in the official records.
20-21Everything Hezekiah did while he
was king of Judah, including what he
did for the temple in Jerusalem, was
right and good. He was a successful
king, because he obeyed the LORD God
with all his heart.

King Sennacherib of Assyria Invades Judah

(2 Kings 18.13-37; Isaiah 36.1-22)

32 After King Hezekiah had faithfully obeyed the LORD's instructions by doing these things, King Sennacherib of Assyria invaded Judah. He
attacked the fortified cities and thought
he would capture every one of them.
2As soon as Hezekiah learned that
Sennacherib was planning to attack
Jerusalem, 3-4he and his officials worked
out a plan to cut off the supply of water
outside the city, so that the Assyrians
would have no water when they came to
attack. The officials got together a large
work force that stopped up the springs
and streams near Jerusalem.
5Hezekiah also had workers repair
the broken sections of the city wall.
Then they built defense towers and an
outer wall to help protect the one already there. The landfill on the east side
of David's City was also strengthened.
He gave orders to make a large supply
of weapons and shields, 6and he appointed army commanders over the
troops. Then he gathered the troops together in the open area in front of the
city gate and said to them:

7Be brave and confident! There's
no reason to be afraid of King Sennacherib and his powerful army. We
are much more powerful, 8because
the LORD our God fights on our side.
The Assyrians must rely on human
power alone.

These words encouraged the army of
Judah.
9When Sennacherib and his troops
were camped at the town of Lachish, he
sent a message to Hezekiah and the
people in Jerusalem. It said:

10I am King Sennacherib of Assyria, and I have Jerusalem surrounded. Do you think you can survive my attack? 11Hezekiah your
king is telling you that the LORD
your God will save you from me. But
he is lying, and you'll die of hunger
and thirst. 12Didn't Hezekiah tear
down all except one of the LORD's altars and places of worship?[x] And
didn't he tell you people of
Jerusalem and Judah to worship at
that one place?
13You've heard what my ancestors
and I have done to other nations.
Were the gods of those nations able
to defend their land against us?
14None of those gods kept their people safe from the kings of Assyria.
Do you really think your God can do
any better? 15Don't be fooled by
Hezekiah! No god of any nation has
ever been able to stand up to Assyria. Believe me, your God cannot
keep you safe!

16The Assyrian officials said terrible
things about the LORD God and his servant Hezekiah. 17Sennacherib's letter
even made fun of the LORD. It said, "The
gods of other nations could not save
their people from Assyria's army, and
neither will the God that Hezekiah worships." 18The officials said all these
things in Hebrew, so that everyone listening from the city wall would understand and be terrified and surrender.
19The officials talked about the LORD God
as if he were nothing but an ordinary
god or an idol that someone had made.

The Death of King Sennacherib

(2 Kings 19.14-19, 35-37; Isaiah 37.14-20; 37.36-38)

20Hezekiah and the prophet Isaiah son
of Amoz asked the LORD for help, 21and
he sent an angel that killed every soldier and commander in the Assyrian
camp.
Sennacherib returned to Assyria,
completely disgraced. Then one day he

[w]**31.15,16** *thirty*: The Hebrew text has "three" instead of "thirty"; in Hebrew, these two words look almost exactly the same (see also Numbers 4.3; 1 Chronicles 23.3). [x]**32.12** *worship*: Hezekiah actually had torn down the places where idols were worshiped, and he had told the people to worship the LORD at the one place of worship in Jerusalem. But the Assyrian leader was confused and thought these were also places where the LORD was supposed to be worshiped.

went into the temple of his god where
some of his sons killed him.
22The LORD rescued Hezekiah and the
people of Jerusalem from Sennacherib
and also protected them from other enemies. 23People brought offerings to
Jerusalem for the LORD and expensive
gifts for Hezekiah, and from that day
on, every nation on earth respected
Hezekiah.

Hezekiah Gets Sick and Almost Dies
(2 Kings 20.1-11; Isaiah 38.1-8)

24About this same time, Hezekiah got
sick and was almost dead. He prayed,
and the LORD gave him a sign that he
would recover. 25But Hezekiah was so
proud that he refused to thank the LORD
for everything he had done for him.
This made the LORD angry, and he punished Hezekiah and the people of Judah
and Jerusalem. 26Hezekiah and the people later felt sorry and asked the LORD
to forgive them. So the LORD did not
punish them as long as Hezekiah was
king.

Hezekiah's Wealth
(2 Kings 20.12-19; Isaiah 39.1-8)

27Hezekiah was very rich, and everyone respected him. He built special
rooms to store the silver, the gold, the
precious stones and spices, the shields,
and the other valuable possessions.
28Storehouses were also built for his
supply of grain, wine, and olive oil;
barns were built for his cattle, and pens
were put up for his sheep. 29God made
Hezekiah extremely rich, so he bought
even more sheep, goats, and cattle. And
he built towns where he could keep all
these animals.
30It was Hezekiah who built a tunnel
that carried the water from Gihon
Spring into the city of Jerusalem. In
fact, everything he did was successful!
31Even when the leaders of Babylonia
sent messengers to ask Hezekiah about
the sign God had given him, God let
Hezekiah give his own answer to test
him and to see if he would remain faithful.

Hezekiah Dies
(2 Kings 20.20, 21)

32Everything else Hezekiah did while
he was king, including how faithful he
was to the LORD, is included in the
records kept by Isaiah the prophet.
These are written in *The History of the
Kings of Judah and Israel*. 33When
Hezekiah died, he was buried in the section of the royal tombs that was reserved for the most respected kings,[y]
and everyone in Judah and Jerusalem
honored him. His son Manasseh then
became king.

King Manasseh of Judah
(2 Kings 21.1-9, 17, 18)

33 Manasseh was twelve years old
when he became king of Judah,
and he ruled fifty-five years from
Jerusalem. 2Manasseh disobeyed the
LORD by following the disgusting customs of the nations that the LORD had
forced out of Israel. 3He rebuilt the local
shrines[z] that his father Hezekiah had
torn down. He built altars for the god
Baal and set up sacred poles[a] for worshiping the goddess Asherah. And he
faithfully worshiped the stars in the sky.
4In the temple, where only the LORD
was supposed to be worshiped, Manasseh built altars for pagan gods 5and
for the stars. He placed these altars in
both courtyards of the temple 6-7and
even set up a stone image of a foreign
god. Manasseh practiced magic and
witchcraft; he asked fortunetellers for
advice and sacrificed his own sons in
Hinnom Valley. He did many other sinful
things and made the LORD very angry.
Years ago, God had told David and
Solomon:

> Jerusalem is the place I prefer
> above all others in Israel. It belongs
> to me, and there in the temple I will
> be worshiped forever. 8If my people
> will faithfully obey all the laws and
> teaching I gave to my servant
> Moses, I will never again force them
> to leave the land I gave to their an-
> cestors.

9But the people of Judah and
Jerusalem listened to Manasseh and did
even more sinful things than the nations
the LORD had wiped out.
10The LORD tried to warn Manasseh
and the people about their sins, but they
ignored the warning. 11So he let Assyrian army commanders invade Judah
and capture Manasseh. They put a hook
in his nose and tied him up in chains,
and they took him to Babylon. 12While
Manasseh was held captive there, he
asked the LORD God to forgive him and
to help him. 13The LORD listened to Manasseh's prayer and saw how sorry he
was, and so he let him go back to
Jerusalem and rule as king. Manasseh
knew from then on that the LORD was
God.
14Later, Manasseh rebuilt the eastern
section of Jerusalem's outer wall and
made it taller. This section went
from Gihon Valley north to Fish Gate
and around the part of the city called

[y]**32.33** *in the section . . . reserved for the most respected kings*: One possible meaning for the difficult Hebrew text. [z]**33.3** *local shrines*: See the note at 11.15. [a]**33.3** *sacred poles*: See the note at 14.3.

Mount Ophel. He also assigned army officers to each of the fortified cities in Judah.[b]

15 Manasseh also removed the idols and the stone image of the foreign god from the temple, and he gathered the altars he had built near the temple and in other parts of Jerusalem. He threw all these things outside the city. 16 Then he repaired the LORD's altar and offered sacrifices to thank him and sacrifices to ask his blessing.[c] He gave orders that everyone in Judah must worship the LORD God of Israel. 17 The people obeyed Manasseh, but they worshiped the LORD at their own shrines.

18 Everything else Manasseh did while he was king, including his prayer to the LORD God and the warnings from his prophets, is written in *The History of the Kings of Israel.* 19 Hozai[d] wrote a lot about Manasseh, including his prayer and God's answer. But Hozai also recorded the evil things Manasseh did before turning back to God, as well as a list of places where Manasseh set up idols, and where he built local shrines and places to worship Asherah. 20 Manasseh died and was buried near the palace, and his son Amon became king.

King Amon of Judah

(2 Kings 21.19-26)

21 Amon was twenty-two years old when he became king of Judah, and he ruled from Jerusalem for two years. 22 Amon disobeyed the LORD, just as his father Manasseh had done, and he worshiped and offered sacrifices to the idols his father had made. 23 Manasseh had turned back to the LORD, but Amon refused to do that. Instead, he sinned even more than his father.

24 Some of Amon's officials plotted against him and killed him in his palace. 25 But the people of Judah killed the murderers of Amon and made his son Josiah king.

King Josiah of Judah

(2 Kings 22.1, 2)

34 Josiah was eight years old when he became king of Judah, and he ruled thirty-one years from Jerusalem. 2 He followed the example of his ancestor David and always obeyed the LORD.

Josiah Stops the Worship of Foreign Gods

(2 Kings 23.4-20)

3 When Josiah was only sixteen years old he began worshiping God, just as his ancestor David had done. Then, four years later, he decided to destroy the local shrines[e] in Judah and Jerusalem, as well as the sacred poles[f] for worshiping the goddess Asherah and the idols of foreign gods. 4 He watched as the altars for the worship of the god Baal were torn down, and as the nearby incense altars were smashed. The Asherah poles, the idols, and the stone images were also smashed, and the pieces were scattered over the graves of their worshipers. 5 Josiah then had the bones of the pagan priests burned on the altars.[g]

And so Josiah got rid of the worship of foreign gods in Judah and Jerusalem. 6 He did the same things in the towns and ruined villages[h] in the territories of West Manasseh, Ephraim, and Simeon, as far as the border of Naphtali. 7 Everywhere in the northern kingdom of Israel, Josiah tore down pagan altars and Asherah poles; he crushed idols to dust and smashed incense altars.

Then Josiah went back to Jerusalem.

Hilkiah Finds *The Book of God's Law*

(2 Kings 22.3-20)

8 In the eighteenth year of Josiah's rule in Judah, after he had gotten rid of all the sinful things from the land and from the LORD's temple, he sent three of his officials to repair the temple. They were Shaphan son of Azaliah, Governor Maaseiah of Jerusalem, and Joah son of Joahaz, who kept the government records.

9 These three men went to Hilkiah the high priest. They gave him the money that the Levite guards had collected from the people of West Manasseh, Ephraim, and the rest of Israel, as well as those living in Judah, Benjamin, and Jerusalem. 10 Then the money was turned over to the men who supervised the repairs to the temple. They used some of it to pay the workers, 11 and they gave the rest of it to the carpenters and builders, who used it to buy the stone and wood they needed to repair the other buildings that Judah's kings had not taken care of.

12 The workers were honest, and their

[b] **33.14** *fortified cities in Judah*: At this time, Judah was under the control of Assyria. The fortifications mentioned in this verse may have been done under orders from Assyrian officials, hoping to strengthen their southern border against the rising power of Egypt.
[c] **33.16** *sacrifices to ask his blessing*: See the note at 29.33. [d] **33.19** *Hozai*: Or "The prophets." [e] **34.3** *local shrines*: See the note at 11.15. [f] **34.3** *sacred poles*: See the note at 14.3. [g] **34.5** *the bones of the pagan priests burned on the altars*: This made the altars unclean, so that they could not be used in worshiping any god. [h] **34.6** *ruined villages*: One possible meaning for the difficult Hebrew text.

supervisors were Jahath and Obadiah from the Levite clan of Merari, and Zechariah and Meshullam from the Levite clan of Kohath. Other Levites, who were all skilled musicians, [13]were in charge of carrying supplies and supervising the workers. Other Levites were appointed to stand guard around the temple.

[14]While the money was being given to these supervisors, Hilkiah found the book that contained the laws that the LORD had given to Moses. [15]Hilkiah handed the book to Shaphan the official and said, "Look what I found here in the temple—*The Book of God's Law*."

[16]Shaphan took the book to Josiah and reported, "Your officials are doing everything you wanted. [17]They have collected the money from the temple and have given it to the men supervising the repairs. [18]But there's something else, Your Majesty. The priest Hilkiah gave me this book." Then Shaphan read it aloud.

[19]When Josiah heard what was in *The Book of God's Law*, he tore his clothes in sorrow. [20]At once he called together Hilkiah, Shaphan, Ahikam son of Shaphan, Abdon son of Micah,[i] and his own servant Asaiah. He said, [21]"The LORD must be furious with me and everyone else in Israel and Judah, because our ancestors did not obey the laws written in this book. Go find out what the LORD wants us to do."

[22]Hilkiah and the four other men left right away and went to talk with Huldah the prophet. Her husband was Shallum,[j] who was in charge of the king's clothes. Huldah lived in the northern part of Jerusalem, and when they met in her home, [23]she said:

> You were sent here by King Josiah, and this is what the LORD God of Israel says to him: [24]"Josiah, I am the LORD! And I intend to punish this country and everyone in it, just as this book says. [25]The people of Judah and Israel have rejected me. They have offered sacrifices to foreign gods and have worshiped their own idols. I can't stand it any longer. I am furious.
>
> [26-27]"Josiah, listen to what I am going to do. I noticed how sad you were when you heard that this country and its people would be completely wiped out. You even tore your clothes in sorrow, and I heard you cry. [28]So before I destroy this place, I will let you die in peace."

The men left and reported to Josiah what Huldah had said.

Josiah Reads *The Book of God's Law*
(2 Kings 23.1-3)

[29]King Josiah called together the leaders of Judah and Jerusalem. [30]Then he went to the LORD's temple, together with all the people of Judah and Jerusalem, the priests, and the Levites.

Finally, when everybody was there, he read aloud *The Book of God's Law*[k] that had been found in the temple.

[31]After Josiah had finished reading, he stood in the place reserved for the king. He promised in the LORD's name to faithfully obey the LORD and to follow his laws and teachings that were written in the book. [32]Then he asked the people of Jerusalem and Benjamin to make that same promise and to obey the God their ancestors had worshiped.

[33]Josiah destroyed all the idols in the territories of Israel, and he commanded everyone in Israel to worship only the LORD God. The people did not turn away from the LORD God of their ancestors for the rest of Josiah's rule as king.

Passover Is Celebrated
(2 Kings 23.21-23)

35 Josiah commanded that Passover be celebrated in Jerusalem to honor the LORD. So, on the fourteenth day of the first month,[l] the lambs were killed for the Passover celebration.

[2]On that day, Josiah made sure the priests knew what duties they were to do in the temple. [3]He called together the Levites who served the LORD and who taught the people his laws, and he said:

> No longer will you have to carry the sacred chest from place to place. It will stay in the temple built by King Solomon son of David, where you will serve the LORD and his people Israel. [4]Get ready to do the work that David and Solomon assigned to you, according to your clans. [5]Divide yourselves into groups, then arrange yourselves throughout the temple so that each family of worshipers will be able to get help from one of you.[m] [6]When the people bring you their Passover lamb, you must kill it and prepare it to be sacrificed to the LORD. Make sure the people celebrate according to the instructions that the LORD gave Moses, and don't do anything to make yourselves unclean and unacceptable.

[i] **34.20** *Abdon son of Micah*: Also called "Achbor son of Micaiah" (see 2 Kings 22.12). [j] **34.22** *Shallum*: Hebrew "Shallum son of Tokhath son of Hasrah." [k] **34.30** *The Book of God's Law*: The Hebrew text has "The Book of God's Agreement," which is the same as "The Book of God's Law" in verses 15 and 19. In traditional translations this is called "The Book of the Covenant." [l] **35.1** *first month*: See the note at 29.3. [m] **35.5** *each family of worshipers . . . you*: One possible meaning for the difficult Hebrew text.

7 Josiah donated thirty thousand sheep
and goats, and three thousand bulls
from his own flocks and herds for the
people to offer as sacrifices. 8 Josiah's officials also voluntarily gave some of
their animals to the people, the priests,
and the Levites as sacrifices. Hilkiah,
Zechariah, and Jehiel, who were the officials in charge of the temple, gave the
priests twenty-six hundred sheep and
lambs and three hundred bulls to sacrifice during the Passover celebration.
9 Conaniah, his two brothers Shemaiah
and Nethanel, as well as Hashabiah,
Jeiel, and Jozabad were leaders of the
Levites, and they gave the other Levites
five thousand sheep and goats, and five
hundred bulls to offer as sacrifices.

10 When everything was ready to celebrate Passover, the priests and the
Levites stood where Josiah had told
them. 11 Then the Levites killed and
skinned the Passover lambs, and they
handed some of the blood to the priests,
who splattered it on the altar. 12 The
Levites set aside the parts of the animal
that the worshipers needed for their
sacrifices to please the LORD,[n] just as
the Law of Moses required. They also
did the same thing with the bulls. 13 They
sacrificed the Passover animals on the
altar and boiled the meat for the other
offerings in pots, kettles, and pans. Then
they quickly handed the meat to the
people so they could eat it.

14 All day long, the priests were busy
offering sacrifices and burning the animals' fat on the altar. And when everyone had finished, the Levites prepared
Passover animals for themselves and for
the priests.

15 During the celebration some of the
Levites prepared Passover animals for
the musicians and the guards, so that
the Levite musicians would not have to
leave their places, which had been assigned to them according to the instructions of David, Asaph, Heman, and Jeduthun the king's prophet. Even the
guards at the temple gates did not have
to leave their posts.

16 So on that day, Passover was celebrated to honor the LORD, and sacrifices
were offered on the altar to him, just as
Josiah had commanded. 17 The worshipers then celebrated the Festival of
Thin Bread for the next seven days.

18 People from Jerusalem and from
towns all over Judah and Israel were
there. Passover had not been observed
like this since the days of Samuel the
prophet. In fact, this was the greatest
Passover celebration in Israel's history!

19 All these things happened in the eighteenth year of Josiah's rule in Judah.

Josiah Dies in Battle

(2 Kings 23.28-30)

20 Some time later, King Neco of Egypt
led his army to the city of Carchemish
on the Euphrates River. And Josiah led
his troops north to meet the Egyptians
in battle.[o]

21 Neco sent the following message to
Josiah:

> I'm not attacking you, king of Ju-
> dah! We're not even at war. But God
> has told me to quickly attack my en-
> emy. God is on my side, so if you try
> to stop me, he will punish you.

22 But Josiah ignored Neco's warning,
even though it came from God! Instead,
he disguised himself and marched into
battle against Neco in the valley near
Megiddo.

23 During the battle an Egyptian soldier shot Josiah with an arrow. Josiah
told his servants, "Get me out of here!
I've been hit." 24 They carried Josiah out
of his chariot, then put him in the other
chariot he had there and took him back
to Jerusalem, where he soon died. He
was buried beside his ancestors, and
everyone in Judah and Jerusalem
mourned his death.

25 Jeremiah the prophet wrote a funeral song in honor of Josiah. And since
then, anyone in Judah who mourns the
death of Josiah sings that song. It is included in the collection of funeral songs.

26 Everything else Josiah did while he
was king, including how he faithfully
obeyed the LORD, 27 is written in *The History of the Kings of Israel and Judah*.

King Jehoahaz of Judah

(2 Kings 23.30-35)

36 After the death of Josiah, the people of Judah crowned his son Jehoahaz their new king. 2 He was twenty-
three years old at the time, and he ruled
only three months from Jerusalem.
3 King Neco of Egypt captured Jehoahaz
and forced Judah to pay almost four
tons of silver and seventy-five pounds of
gold as taxes. 4 Then Neco appointed Jehoahaz's brother Eliakim king of Judah
and changed his name to Jehoiakim. He
led Jehoahaz away to Egypt as his prisoner.

King Jehoiakim of Judah

(2 Kings 23.36—24.7)

5 Jehoiakim was twenty-five years old
when he was appointed king, and he
ruled eleven years from Jerusalem.

[n]35.12 *sacrifices to please the LORD*: See the note at 1.6. [o]35.20 *battle*: At this time, King Neco of Egypt (609-595 B.C.) was fighting on the side of the Assyrians. He marched north to fight the Babylonian army and help Assyria keep control of its land. Since Josiah considered Assyria an enemy, he set out to stop Neco and the Egyptian troops.

Jehoiakim disobeyed the LORD his God
by doing evil.
6During Jehoiakim's rule, King Nebuchadnezzar of Babylonia invaded Judah. He arrested Jehoiakim and put him
in chains, and he sent him to the capital
city of Babylon. 7Nebuchadnezzar also
carried off many of the valuable things
in the LORD's temple, and he put them in
his palace in Babylon.
8Everything else Jehoiakim did while
he was king, including all the disgusting
and evil things, is written in *The History
of the Kings of Israel and Judah*. His son
Jehoiachin then became king.

King Jehoiachin of Judah
(2 Kings 24.8-17)

9Jehoiachin was eighteen[p] years old
when he became king of Judah, and he
ruled only three months and ten days
from Jerusalem. Jehoiachin also disobeyed the LORD by doing evil. 10In the
spring of the year, King Nebuchadnezzar of Babylonia had Jehoiachin arrested and taken to Babylon, along with
more of the valuable items in the temple. Then Nebuchadnezzar appointed
Zedekiah king of Judah.

King Zedekiah of Judah
(2 Kings 24.18-20; Jeremiah 52.1-3)

11Zedekiah was twenty-one years old
when he was appointed king of Judah,
and he ruled from Jerusalem for eleven
years. 12He disobeyed the LORD his God
and refused to change his ways, even after a warning from Jeremiah, the LORD's
prophet.
13King Nebuchadnezzar of Babylonia
had forced Zedekiah to promise in
God's name that he would be loyal.
Zedekiah was stubborn and refused to
turn back to the LORD God of Israel, so
he rebelled against Nebuchadnezzar.
14The people of Judah and even the
priests who were their leaders became
more unfaithful. They followed the disgusting example of the nations around
them and made the LORD's holy temple
unfit for worship. 15But the LORD God
felt sorry for his people, and instead of
destroying the temple, he sent prophets
who warned the people over and over
about their sins. 16But the people only
laughed and insulted these prophets.
They ignored what the LORD God was
trying to tell them, until he finally became so angry that nothing could stop
him from punishing Judah and
Jerusalem.

Jerusalem Is Destroyed
(2 Kings 25.1-21; Jeremiah 52.3-30)

17The LORD sent King Nebuchadnezzar of Babylonia to attack Jerusalem.
Nebuchadnezzar killed the young men
who were in the temple, and he showed
no mercy to anyone, whether man or
woman, young or old. God let him kill
everyone in the city. 18Nebuchadnezzar
carried off everything that was left in
the temple; he robbed the treasury and
the personal storerooms of the king and
his officials. He took everything back to
Babylon.
19Nebuchadnezzar's troops burned
down the temple and destroyed every
important building in the city. Then they
broke down the city wall. 20The survivors were taken to Babylonia as prisoners, where they were slaves of the
king and his sons, until Persia became a
powerful nation.
21Judah was an empty desert, and it
stayed that way for seventy years, to
make up for all the years it was not allowed to rest.[q] These things happened
just as Jeremiah the LORD's prophet had
said.[r]

Cyrus Lets the Jews Return Home
(Ezra 1.1-4)

22In the first year that Cyrus was king
of Persia,[s] the LORD had Cyrus send a
message to all parts of his kingdom.
This happened just as Jeremiah the
LORD's prophet had promised. 23The
message said:

> I am King Cyrus of Persia.
> The LORD God of heaven has made me the ruler of every nation on earth. He has also chosen me to build a temple for him in Jerusalem, which is in Judah. The LORD God will watch over any of his people who want to go back to Judah.

[p]**36.9** *eighteen*: Some manuscripts of one ancient translation (see also 2 Kings 24.8); Hebrew "eight." [q]**36.21** *rest*: According to Leviticus 25.1-7, the land was supposed to rest every seventh year. [r]**36.21** *Jeremiah . . . said*: Jeremiah 25.11, 12; 29.10. According to the Law, the people had to allow the land to rest one out of every seven years (see Leviticus 25.1-7).
[s]**36.22** *the first year that Cyrus was king of Persia*: Probably 538 B.C., when Cyrus captured Babylonia. He had actually ruled Persia since 549 B.C.

EZRA

ABOUT THIS BOOK

This book is named after the main character of its second part.

The book of 2 Chronicles ended with an official message that King Cyrus of Persia sent in 538 B.C., which allowed the Jews to return to their land and to rebuild the Lord's temple. The first part of the book of Ezra (1–6) begins with that same message and then tells how many of the Jews returned to Jerusalem and began work on the temple. But the people in nearby areas caused a lot of trouble for them, and so the work went slowly and even stopped for several years. But the temple was finally finished in 515 B.C.

The first part of the book also tells about problems at a later time, when the Jews had to stop rebuilding the city walls during the rule of Artaxerxes (4.6-23).

The second part of the book (7–10) begins with Ezra arriving in Jerusalem to teach God's laws to the people of Judah. Ezra was horrified to learn that the people of Israel were committing the same sins as other nations. Israel was in serious danger of being punished or even destroyed by the Lord. So Ezra prayed and confessed Israel's sins, and the people agreed to begin obeying God's laws. The book of Nehemiah reports other things that Ezra did.

God's people were no longer an independent nation, but Ezra realized that God was in control, no matter what empire ruled over them. And so Ezra said:

> *Praise the LORD God of our ancestors! He made sure that the king honored the LORD's temple in Jerusalem. God has told the king, his advisors, and his powerful officials to treat me with kindness. The LORD God has helped me, and I have been able to bring many Jewish leaders back to Jerusalem.* (7.27b, 28)

A QUICK LOOK AT THIS BOOK

The Jews Return Home from Exile (1.1—2.70)
The Altar Is Rebuilt, and Work on the Temple Begins (3.1—4.5)
Later Trouble Rebuilding Jerusalem (4.6-23)
The Temple Is Rebuilt (4.24—6.22)
Ezra Leads Many Jews back to Jerusalem (7.1—8.36)
Ezra Forces Men To Divorce Their Gentile Wives (9.1—10.44)

Cyrus Lets the Jews Return Home

1 Years ago the LORD sent Jeremiah
with a message about a promise[a] for
the people of Israel. Then in the first
year that Cyrus was king of Persia,[b] the
LORD kept his promise by having Cyrus
send this official message to all parts of
his kingdom:
2-3I am King Cyrus of Persia.
The LORD God of heaven, who is
also the God of Israel, has made me
the ruler of all nations on earth. And
he has chosen me to build a temple
for him in Jerusalem, which is in Judah. The LORD God will watch over
and encourage any of his people
who want to go back to Jerusalem
and help build the temple.
4Everyone else must provide what
is needed. They must give money,

[a]1.1 *a promise*: That the people of Israel would be set free from Babylonia after seventy years (see Jeremiah 25.11; 29.10). [b]1.1 *the first year that Cyrus was king of Persia*: Probably 539 B.C., when Cyrus captured Babylonia. He had actually ruled Persia since 549 B.C.

supplies, and animals, as well as
gifts for rebuilding God's temple.
5 Many people felt that the LORD God
wanted them to help rebuild his temple,
and they made plans to go to Jerusalem.
Among them were priests, Levites, and
leaders of the tribes of Judah and Benjamin. 6 The others helped by giving silver articles, gold, personal possessions,
cattle, and other valuable gifts, as well
as offerings for the temple.
7 King Cyrus gave back the things that
Nebuchadnezzar[c] had taken from the
LORD's temple in Jerusalem and had put
in the temple of his own gods. 8 Cyrus
placed Mithredath, his chief treasurer,
in charge of these things. Mithredath
counted them and gave a list to Sheshbazzar, the governor of Judah. 9-10 Included among them were: 30 large gold
dishes; 1,000 large silver dishes; 29
other dishes;[d] 30 gold bowls; 410 silver
bowls; and 1,000 other articles.
11 Altogether, there were 5,400 gold
and silver dishes, bowls, and other articles. Sheshbazzar took them with him
when he and the others returned to
Jerusalem from Babylonia.

A List of People Who Returned from Exile

(Nehemiah 7.4-73)

2 King Nebuchadnezzar[e] of Babylonia had captured many of the people
of Judah and had taken them as prisoners to Babylonia. Now they were on
their way back to Jerusalem and to their
own towns everywhere in Judah.
2-20 Zerubbabel, Joshua,[f] Nehemiah,
Seraiah, Reelaiah, Mordecai, Bilshan,
Mispar, Bigvai, Rehum, and Baanah
were in charge of the ones who were
coming back. And here is a list of how
many returned from each family group:
2,172 from the family of Parosh; 372
from the family of Shephatiah; 775 from
the family of Arah; 2,812 descendants of
Jeshua and Joab[g] from the family of Pahath Moab; 1,254 from the family of
Elam; 945 from the family of Zattu; 760
from the family of Zaccai; 642 from the
family of Bani; 623 from the family of
Bebai; 1,222 from the family of Azgad;
666 from the family of Adonikam; 2,056
from the family of Bigvai; 454 from the
family of Adin; 98 from the family of
Ater, also known as Hezekiah; 323 from
the family of Bezai; 112 from the family
of Jorah; 223 from the family of
Hashum; and 95 from the family of Gib-
bar.
21-35 Here is how many people returned
whose ancestors had come from the following towns: 123 from Bethlehem; 56
from Netophah; 128 from Anathoth; 42
from Azmaveth; 743 from Kiriatharim,
Chephirah, and Beeroth; 621 from
Ramah and Geba; 122 from Michmas;
223 from Bethel and Ai; 52 from Nebo;
156 from Magbish; 1,254 from the other
Elam; 320 from Harim; 725 from Lod,
Hadid, and Ono; 345 from Jericho; and
3,630 from Senaah.
36-39 Here is a list of how many returned from each family of priests: 973
descendants of Jeshua from the family
of Jedaiah; 1,052 from the family of Immer; 1,247 from the family of Pashhur;
and 1,017 from the family of Harim.
40-42 And here is a list of how many returned from the families of Levites: 74
descendants of Hodaviah from the families of Jeshua and Kadmiel; 128 descendants of Asaph from the temple
musicians; and 139 descendants of Shallum, Ater, Talmon, Akkub, Hatita, and
Shobai from the temple guards.
43-54 Here is a list of the families of
temple workers whose descendants returned: Ziha, Hasupha, Tabbaoth, Keros,
Siaha, Padon, Lebanah, Hagabah,
Akkub, Hagab, Shamlai, Hanan, Giddel,
Gahar, Reaiah, Rezin, Nekoda, Gazzam,
Uzza, Paseah, Besai, Asnah, Meunim,
Nephisim, Bakbuk, Hakupha, Harhur,
Bazluth, Mehida, Harsha, Barkos, Sisera, Temah, Neziah, and Hatipha.
55-57 Here is a list of Solomon's servants whose descendants returned:
Sotai, Hassophereth, Peruda, Jaalah,
Darkon, Giddel, Shephatiah, Hattil,
Pochereth Hazzebaim, and Ami.
58 A total of 392 descendants of temple
workers and of Solomon's servants returned.
59-60 There were 652 who returned
from the families of Delaiah, Tobiah,
and Nekoda, though they could not
prove that they were Israelites. They
had lived in the Babylonian towns of
Tel-Melah, Tel-Harsha, Cherub, Addan,
and Immer.
61-62 The families of Habaiah, Hakkoz,
and Barzillai could not prove that they
were priests. The ancestor of the family
of Barzillai had married the daughter of
Barzillai from Gilead and had taken his
wife's family name. But the records of

[c] **1.7** *Nebuchadnezzar*: Known as Nebuchadnezzar II, who ruled Babylonia from 605 to 562 B.C. In 586 B.C. he destroyed Jerusalem and took many of its people to Babylonia. [d] **1.9,10** *other dishes*: One possible meaning for the difficult Hebrew text. [e] **2.1** *Nebuchadnezzar*: See the note at 1.7. [f] **2.2-20** *Joshua*: Hebrew "Jeshua." In this translation the name "Joshua" is used of the descendant of Jozadak, the last chief priest before the exile; this same Joshua is often mentioned together with Zerubbabel (2.2-20; 3.2, 8, 9; 4.3; 5.2; 10.18, 19). In other places the name "Jeshua" is used (2.2-20, 36-39, 40-42; 8.33). [g] **2.2-20** *Jeshua and Joab*: Hebrew "Jeshua Joab."

these three families could not be found,
and none of them were allowed to serve
as priests. 63In fact, the governor[h] told
them, "You cannot eat the food offered
to God until we find out if you really are
priests."
64-67There were 42,360 who returned,
in addition to 7,337 servants and
200 musicians, both women and men.
They brought with them 736 horses,
245 mules, 435 camels, and 6,720 donkeys.
68When the people came to where the
LORD's temple had been in Jerusalem,
some of the family leaders gave gifts so
it could be rebuilt in the same place.
69They gave all they could, and it came
to a total of 1,030 pounds of gold, 5,740
pounds of silver, and 100 robes for the
priests.
70Everyone returned to the towns
from which their families had come, including the priests, the Levites, the musicians, the temple guards, and the
workers.[i]

The First Offering on the New Altar

3 During the seventh month[j] of the
year, the Israelites who had settled
in their towns went to Jerusalem. 2The
priest Joshua son of Jozadak, together
with the other priests, and Zerubbabel
son of Shealtiel and his relatives rebuilt
the altar of Israel's God. Then they were
able to offer sacrifices there by following the instructions God had given to
Moses. 3And they built the altar where it
had stood before,[k] even though they
were afraid of the people who were already living around there. Then every
morning and evening they burned sacrifices and offerings to the LORD.
4The people followed the rules for celebrating the Festival of Shelters and offered the proper sacrifices each day.
5They offered sacrifices to please the
LORD,[l] sacrifices at each New Moon Festival, and sacrifices at the rest of the
LORD's festivals. Every offering the people had brought was presented to the
LORD.
6Although work on the temple itself
had not yet begun, the people started offering sacrifices on the LORD's altar on
the first day of the seventh month of
that year.

The Rebuilding of the Temple Begins

7King Cyrus of Persia had said the Israelites could have cedar trees brought
from Lebanon to Joppa by sea. So they
sent grain, wine, and olive oil to the
cities of Tyre and Sidon as payment for
these trees, and they gave money to the
stoneworkers and carpenters.
8During the second month[m] of the
second year after the people had returned from Babylonia, they started rebuilding the LORD's temple. Zerubbabel
son of Shealtiel, Joshua son of Jozadak,
the priests, the Levites, and everyone
else who had returned started working.
Every Levite over twenty years of age
was put in charge of some part of the
work. 9The Levites in charge of the
whole project were Joshua and his sons
and relatives and Kadmiel and his sons
from the family of Hodaviah.[n] The family of Henadad worked along with them.
10When the builders had finished laying the foundation of the temple, the
priests put on their robes and blew
trumpets in honor of the LORD, while the
Levites from the family of Asaph
praised God with cymbals. All of them
followed the instructions given years
before by King David.[o] 11They praised
the LORD and gave thanks as they took
turns singing:

"The LORD is good!
His faithful love for Israel
will last forever."

Everyone started shouting and praising the LORD because work on the foundation of the temple had begun. 12Many
of the older priests and Levites and the
heads of families cried aloud because
they remembered seeing the first temple
years before. But others were so happy
that they celebrated with joyful shouts.
13Their shouting and crying were so
noisy that it all sounded alike and could
be heard a long way off.

Foreigners[p] Want To Help Rebuild the Temple

4 The enemies of the tribes of Judah
and Benjamin heard that the people
had come back to rebuild the temple of
the LORD God of Israel. 2So they went to
Zerubbabel and to the family leaders

[h]**2.63** *governor*: In Nehemiah 8.9; 10.1, this same title is used of Nehemiah, though it is doubtful if he is the one referred to here. [i]**2.70** *workers*: One possible meaning for the difficult Hebrew text of verse 70. [j]**3.1** *seventh month*: Tishri (also called Ethanim), the seventh month of the Hebrew calendar, from about mid-September to mid-October.
[k]**3.3** *where it had stood before*: One possible meaning for the difficult Hebrew text.
[l]**3.5** *sacrifices to please the LORD*: In traditional translations these sacrifices are usually called "whole burnt offerings" (see Leviticus 1.1-16). [m]**3.8** *second month*: Ziv, the second month of the Hebrew calendar, from about mid-April to mid-May. [n]**3.9** *Hodaviah*: Or "Yehudah" or "Hodiah." [o]**3.10** *King David*: Ruled from about 1010 to 970 B.C. [p]**4.1** *Foreigners*: People from foreign countries who had been captured by Assyrian and Babylonian kings and forced to settle in Palestine.

and said, "Let us help! Ever since King Esarhaddon of Assyria[q] brought us here, we have worshiped your God and offered sacrifices to him."

3 But Zerubbabel, Joshua, and the family leaders answered, "You cannot take part in building a temple for the LORD our God! We will build it ourselves, just as King Cyrus of Persia commanded us."

4 Then the neighboring people began to do everything possible to frighten the Jews[r] and to make them stop building. 5 During the time that Cyrus was king and even until Darius[s] became king, they kept bribing government officials to slow down the work.

Trouble Rebuilding Jerusalem[t]

6 In the first year that Xerxes was king,[u] the neighboring people brought written charges against the people of Judah and Jerusalem.

7 Later, Bishlam, Mithredath, Tabeel, and their advisors got together and wrote a letter to Artaxerxes when he was king of Persia.[v] It was written in Aramaic and had to be translated.[w]

8-10 A letter was also written to Artaxerxes about Jerusalem by Governor Rehum, Secretary Shimshai, and their advisors, including the judges, the governors, the officials, and the local leaders. They were joined in writing this letter by people from Erech and Babylonia, the Elamites from Susa,[x] and people from other foreign nations that the great and famous Ashurbanipal[y] had forced to settle in Samaria and other parts of Western Province.[z]

11 This letter said:

> Your Majesty King Artaxerxes, we are your servants from everywhere in Western Province, and we send you our greetings.
>
> 12 You should know that the Jews who left your country have moved back to Jerusalem and are now rebuilding that terrible city. In fact, they have almost finished rebuilding the walls and repairing the foundations. 13 You should also know that if the walls are completed and the city is rebuilt, the Jews won't pay any kind of taxes, and there will be less money in your treasury.
>
> 14 We are telling you this, because you have done so much for us, and we want everyone to respect you. 15 If you look up the official records of your ancestors, you will find that Jerusalem has constantly rebelled and has led others to rebel against kings and provinces. That's why the city was destroyed in the first place. 16 If Jerusalem is rebuilt and its walls completed, you will no longer have control over Western Province.

17 King Artaxerxes answered:

> Greetings to Governor Rehum, Secretary Shimshai, and to your advisors in Samaria and other parts of Western Province.
>
> 18 After your letter was translated and read to me, 19 I had the old records checked. It is true that for years Jerusalem has rebelled and caused trouble for other kings and nations. 20 And powerful kings have ruled Western Province from Jerusalem and have collected all kinds of taxes.
>
> 21 I want you to command the people to stop rebuilding the city until I give further notice. 22 Do this right now, so that no harm will come to the kingdom.

23 As soon as this letter was read, Governor Rehum, Secretary Shimshai, and their advisors went to Jerusalem and forced everyone to stop rebuilding the city.

Work on the Temple Starts Again

24 The Jews were forced to stop work on the temple and were not able to do any more building until the year after Darius became king of Persia.[a]

5 1 Then the LORD God of Israel told the prophets Haggai and Zechariah[b] to speak in his name to the people of Judah and Jerusalem. And they did. 2 So Zerubbabel the governor and Joshua the priest urged the people to

[q] **4.2** *King Esarhaddon of Assyria*: Ruled from 681 to 669 B.C. These people may have been brought to Palestine in 677 or 676 B.C., when Esarhaddon invaded Syria. [r] **4.4** *Jews*: This was the name given to those Israelites who settled in Judah after returning from Babylonia. [s] **4.5** *Cyrus . . . Darius*: Cyrus ruled 539-530 B.C. (see the note at 1.1); Darius I, known as Darius the Great, ruled 522-486 B.C. [t] **4.6** *Jerusalem*: Verses 6-23, which tell about the events of a later period, are placed here because they are also concerned with the problem of stopping or slowing down work on the temple. [u] **4.6** *first year that Xerxes was king*: Either the end of 486 or the beginning of 485 B.C. The Hebrew has the king's Persian name "Ahasuerus," but he is better known as "Xerxes," the Greek form of the name. [v] **4.7** *Artaxerxes . . . Persia*: Artaxerxes I (465-425 B.C.). [w] **4.7** *It was . . . translated*: One possible meaning for the difficult Hebrew text. Ezra 4.8—6.18 is written in Aramaic, instead of in Hebrew like most of the Old Testament. [x] **4.8-10** *the judges . . . Susa*: One possible translation for the names and titles. [y] **4.8-10** *Ashurbanipal*: King of Assyria 669-633 (or possibly 627) B.C. In Aramaic the king's name is "Osnapper," but he is better known as Ashurbanipal. [z] **4.8-10** *Western Province*: The land from the Euphrates River west to the Mediterranean Sea. [a] **4.24** *year after . . . king of Persia*: 520 B.C. [b] **5.1** *Zechariah*: Aramaic "Zechariah son of Iddo."

start working on the temple again,
and God's prophets encouraged them.
3Governor Tattenai of Western Province and his assistant Shethar Bozenai
got together with some of their officials.
Then they went to Jerusalem and said to
the people, "Who told you to rebuild this
temple? 4Give us the names of the workers!"
5But God was looking after the Jewish
leaders. So the governor and his group
decided not to make the people stop
working on the temple until they could
report to Darius and get his advice.
6Governor Tattenai, Shethar Bozenai,
and their advisors sent a report to Darius, 7which said:
King Darius, we wish you the best!
8We went to Judah, where the temple of the great God is being built
with huge stones and wooden beams
set in the walls. Everyone is working
hard, and the building is going up
fast.
9We asked those in charge to tell
us who gave them permission to rebuild the temple. 10We also asked for
the names of their leaders, so that
we could write them down for you.
11They claimed to be servants of
the God who rules heaven and earth.
And they said they were rebuilding
the temple that was built many years
ago by one of Israel's greatest
kings.[c]
12We were told that their people
had made God angry, and he let
them be captured by Nebuchadnezzar,[d] the Babylonian king[e] who took
them away as captives to Babylonia.
Nebuchadnezzar tore down their
temple, 13-15took its gold and silver
articles, and put them in the temple
of his own god in Babylon.
They also said that during the first
year Cyrus was king of Babylonia,[f]
he gave orders for God's temple to
be rebuilt in Jerusalem where it had
stood before. So Cyrus appointed
Sheshbazzar governor of Judah and
sent these gold and silver articles for
him to put in the temple. 16Shesh-
bazzar then went to Jerusalem and
laid the foundation for the temple,
and the work is still going on.
17Your Majesty, please have someone look up the old records in Babylonia and find out if King Cyrus really did give orders to rebuild God's
temple in Jerusalem. We will do
whatever you think we should.

King Cyrus' Order Is Rediscovered

6 King Darius ordered someone to go
through the old records kept in
Babylonia. 2Finally, a scroll[g] was found
in Ecbatana, the capital of Media Province, and it said:
This official record will show 3that
in the first year Cyrus was king, he
gave orders to rebuild God's temple
in Jerusalem, so that sacrifices and
offerings could be presented there.[h]
It is to be built ninety feet high and
ninety feet wide, 4with one[i] row of
wooden beams for each three rows
of large stones. The royal treasury
will pay for everything. 5Then return
to their proper places the gold and
silver things that Nebuchadnezzar
took from the temple and brought to
Babylonia.

King Darius Orders the Work To Continue

6King Darius sent this message:
Governor Tattenai of Western
Province and Shethar Bozenai, you
and your advisors must stay away
from the temple. 7Let the Jewish
governor and leaders rebuild it
where it stood before. And stop
slowing them down!
8Starting right now, I am ordering
you to help the leaders by paying
their expenses from the tax money
collected in Western Province. 9And
don't fail to let the priests in Jerusalem have whatever they need each
day so they can offer sacrifices to
the God of heaven. Give them young
bulls, rams, sheep, as well as wheat,
salt, wine, and olive oil. 10I want
them to be able to offer pleasing sacrifices to God and to pray for me
and my family.
11If any of you don't obey this order, a wooden beam will be taken
from your house and sharpened on
one end. Then it will be driven
through your body,[j] and your house
will be torn down and turned into a
garbage dump. 12I ask the God who
is worshiped in Jerusalem to destroy
any king or nation who tries either
to change what I have said or to tear
down his temple. I, Darius, give

[c]**5.11** *one of Israel's greatest kings*: Solomon (ruled from about 970 to 931 B.C.).
[d]**5.12** *Nebuchadnezzar*: See the note at 1.7. [e]**5.12** *the Babylonian king*: Aramaic "the Babylonian king from Chaldea," but Chaldea is another name for Babylonia.
[f]**5.13-15** *Cyrus was king of Babylonia*: King Cyrus of Persia became king of Babylonia when the Persians conquered the city of Babylon in 539 B.C. [g]**6.2** *scroll*: A roll of paper or special leather used for writing on. [h]**6.3** *so that . . . there*: One possible meaning for the difficult Aramaic text. [i]**6.4** *one*: One possible meaning for the difficult Aramaic text.
[j]**6.11** *driven through your body*: A well-known punishment in the ancient Near East.

these orders, and I expect them to be
followed carefully.

The Temple Is Dedicated

13 Governor Tattenai, Shethar Bozenai,
and their advisors carefully obeyed
King Darius. 14 With great success the
Jewish leaders continued working on
the temple, while Haggai and Zechariah
encouraged them by their preaching.
And so, the temple was completed at the
command of the God of Israel and by
the orders of kings Cyrus, Darius, and
Artaxerxes of Persia.[k] 15 On the third
day of the month of Adar[l] in the sixth
year of the rule of Darius,[m] the temple
was finished.
16 The people of Israel, the priests, the
Levites, and everyone else who had returned from exile were happy and celebrated as they dedicated God's temple.
17 One hundred bulls, two hundred rams,
and four hundred lambs were offered as
sacrifices at the dedication. Also twelve
goats were sacrificed as sin offerings for
the twelve tribes of Israel. 18 Then the
priests and Levites were assigned their
duties in God's temple in Jerusalem, according to the instructions Moses had
written.

The Passover

19 Everyone who had returned from
exile celebrated Passover on the fourteenth day of the first month.[n] 20 The
priests and Levites had gone through a
ceremony to make themselves acceptable to lead in worship. Then some of
them killed Passover lambs for those
who had returned, including the other
priests and themselves.
21 The sacrifices were eaten by the Israelites who had returned and by the
neighboring people who had given up
the sinful customs of other nations in
order to worship the LORD God of Israel.
22 For seven days they celebrated the
Festival of Thin Bread. Everyone was
happy because the LORD God of Israel
had made sure that the king of Assyria[o]
would be kind to them and help them
build the temple.

Ezra Comes to Jerusalem

7 1-6 Much later, when Artaxerxes[p] was
king of Persia, Ezra came to Jerusalem from Babylonia. Ezra was the son
of Seraiah and the grandson of Azariah.
His other ancestors were Hilkiah, Shallum, Zadok, Ahitub, Amariah, Azariah,
Meraioth, Zerahiah, Uzzi, Bukki,
Abishua, Phinehas, Eleazar, and Aaron,
the high priest.
Ezra was an expert in the Law that
the LORD God of Israel had given to
Moses, and the LORD made sure that the
king gave Ezra everything he asked for.
7 Other Jews, including priests, Levites, musicians, the temple guards, and
servants, came to Jerusalem with Ezra.
This happened during the seventh year
that Artaxerxes[q] was king.
8-9 God helped Ezra, and he arrived in
Jerusalem on the first day of the fifth
month[r] of that seventh year, after leaving Babylonia on the first day of the
first month.[s] 10 Ezra had spent his entire
life studying and obeying the Law of the
LORD and teaching it to others.

Artaxerxes Gives a Letter to Ezra

11 Ezra was a priest and an expert in
the laws and commands that the LORD
had given to Israel. One day King Artaxerxes gave Ezra a letter which said:
12 Greetings from the great King
Artaxerxes to Ezra the priest and
expert in the teachings of the God of
heaven.
13-14 Any of the people of Israel or
their priests or Levites in my kingdom may go with you to Jerusalem
if they want to. My seven advisors
and I agree that you may go to
Jerusalem and Judah to find out if[t]
the laws of your God are being
obeyed.
15 When you go, take the silver and
gold that I and my advisors are
freely giving to the God of Israel,
whose temple is in Jerusalem. 16 Take
the silver and gold that you collect
from everywhere in Babylonia. Also
take the gifts that your own people
and priests have so willingly contributed for the temple of your God
in Jerusalem.
17 Use the money carefully to buy
the best bulls, rams, lambs, grain,
and wine. Then sacrifice them on the
altar at God's temple in Jerusalem.
18 If any silver or gold is left, you and
your people may use it for whatever
pleases your God. 19 Give your God

[k] **6.14** *Artaxerxes of Persia*: See the note at 4.7. [l] **6.15** *Adar*: The twelfth month of the Hebrew calendar, from about mid-February to about mid-March. [m] **6.15** *sixth year . . . Darius*: 515 B.C. [n] **6.19** *the first month*: Nisan, the first month of the Hebrew calendar, from about mid-March to mid-April. [o] **6.22** *king of Assyria*: Meaning the king of Persia, because Assyria was now part of the Persian Empire. [p] **7.1-6** *Artaxerxes*: Either Artaxerxes I (ruled from 465 to 425 B.C.) or Artaxerxes II (ruled from 405-358 B.C.). [q] **7.7** *seventh year . . . Artaxerxes*: 458 B.C. if this is Artaxerxes I; 398 B.C., if this is Artaxerxes II (see the note at 7.1-6). [r] **7.8,9** *fifth month*: Ab, the fifth month of the Hebrew calendar, from about mid-July to mid-August. [s] **7.8,9** *first month*: See the note at 6.19. [t] **7.13,14** *find out if*: Or "make sure that."

the other articles that have been
contributed for use in his temple. 20If
you need to get anything else for the
temple, you may have the money
you need from the royal treasury.
21Ezra, you are a priest and an expert in the laws of the God of heaven,
and I order all treasurers in Western
Province to do their very best to help
you. 22They will be allowed to give as
much as 7,500 pounds of silver, 500
bushels of wheat, 550 gallons of
wine, 550 gallons of olive oil, and all
the salt you need.
23They must provide whatever the
God of heaven demands for his temple, so that he won't be angry with
me and with the kings who rule after me. 24We want you to know that
no priests, Levites, musicians,
guards, temple servants, or any
other temple workers will have to
pay any kind of taxes.
25Ezra, use the wisdom God has
given you and choose officials and
leaders to govern the people of Western Province. These leaders should
know God's laws and have them
taught to anyone who doesn't know
them. 26Everyone who fails to obey
God's Law or the king's law will be
punished without pity. They will either be executed or put in prison or
forced to leave their country, or have
all they own taken away.

Ezra Praises God

27Because King Artaxerxes was so
kind, Ezra said:
Praise the LORD God of our ancestors! He made sure that the king
honored the LORD's temple in
Jerusalem. 28God has told the king,
his advisors, and his powerful officials to treat me with kindness. The
LORD God has helped me, and I have
been able to bring many Jewish
leaders back to Jerusalem.

The Families Who Came Back with Ezra

8 Artaxerxes was king of Persia when
I[u] led the following chiefs of the
family groups from Babylonia to Jerusalem:

2-14Gershom of the Phinehas family;
Daniel of the Ithamar family;
Hattush son of Shecaniah of the
David family;
Zechariah and 150 other men of the
Parosh family, who had family
records;
Eliehoenai son of Zerahiah with 200
men of the Pahath Moab family;
Shecaniah son of Jahaziel with 300
men of the Zattu family;[v]
Ebed son of Jonathan with 50 men of
the Adin family;
Jeshaiah son of Athaliah with 70 men
of the Elam family;
Zebadiah son of Michael with 80 men
of the Shephatiah family;
Obadiah son of Jehiel with 218 men
of the Joab family;
Shelomith son of Josiphiah with 160
men of the Bani family;[w]
Zechariah son of Bebai with 28 men
of the Bebai family;
Johanan son of Hakkatan with 110
men of the Azgad family;
Eliphelet, Jeuel, and Shemaiah who
returned sometime later with 60
men of the Adonikam family;
Uthai and Zaccur with 70 men of the
Bigvai family.

Ezra Finds Levites for the Temple

15I[x] brought everyone together by the
river[y] that flows to the town of Ahava[z]
where we camped for three days. Not
one Levite could be found among the
people and priests. 16So I sent for the
leaders Eliezer, Ariel, Shemaiah, Elnathan, Jarib, Elnathan, Nathan, Zechariah, and Meshullam. I also sent for
Joiarib and Elnathan, who were very
wise. 17Then I sent them to Iddo, the
leader at Casiphia,[a] and I told them to
ask him and his temple workers to send
people to serve in God's temple.
18God was kind to us and had them
send a skillful man named Sherebiah,
who was a Levite from the family of
Mahli. Eighteen of his relatives came
with him. 19We were also sent Hashabiah and Jeshaiah from the family of
Merari along with twenty of their relatives. 20In addition, 220 others came to
help the Levites in the temple. The ancestors of these workers had been chosen years ago by King David[b] and his
officials, and they were all listed by
name.

Ezra Asks the People To Go without Eating and To Pray

21Beside the Ahava River,[c] I[d] asked
the people to go without eating[e] and to

[u]**8.1** *I*: Ezra. [v]**8.2-14** *of the Zattu family*: One ancient translation; these words are not in the Hebrew text, but see 2.2-20, where Zattu is mentioned. [w]**8.2-14** *of the Bani family*: One ancient translation; these words are not in the Hebrew text, but see 2.2-20. [x]**8.15** *I*: See the note at 8.1. [y]**8.15** *river*: Or "canal." [z]**8.15** *town of Ahava*: A town (or place) in Babylonia, but the exact location is unknown. [a]**8.17** *Casiphia*: The location is not known. [b]**8.20** *King David*: See the note at 3.10. [c]**8.21** *River*: See the note at 8.15. [d]**8.21** *I*: See the note at 8.1. [e]**8.21** *to go without eating*: The Jews often went without eating as a way of worshiping God. This is sometimes called "fasting."

pray. We humbled ourselves and asked
God to bring us and our children safely
to Jerusalem with all of our possessions.
22I was ashamed to ask the king to send
soldiers and cavalry to protect us
against enemies along the way. After all,
we had told the king that our God takes
care of everyone who truly worships
him, but that he gets very angry and
punishes anyone who refuses to obey.
23So we went without food and asked
God himself to protect us, and he answered our prayers.

The Gifts for the Temple

24I[f] chose twelve of the leading
priests—Sherebiah, Hashabiah and ten
of their relatives. 25-27Then I weighed the
gifts that had been given for God's temple, and I divided them among the
twelve priests I had chosen. There were
gifts of silver and gold, as well as the articles that the king, his advisors and officials, and the people of Israel had contributed. In all there were: 25 tons of
silver; 100 silver articles weighing 150
pounds; 7,500 pounds of gold; 20 gold
bowls weighing 270 ounces; and 2 polished bronze articles as valuable as
gold.
28I said to the priests:
You belong to the LORD, the God
of your ancestors, and these things
also belong to him. The silver and
gold were willingly given as gifts to
the LORD. 29Be sure to guard them
and keep them safe until you reach
Jerusalem. Then weigh them inside
God's temple in the presence of the
chief priests, the Levites, and the
heads of the Israelite families.
30The priests and Levites then took
charge of the gifts that had been
weighed, so they could take them to the
temple of our God in Jerusalem.

The Return to Jerusalem

31On the twelfth day of the first
month,[g] we left the Ahava River[h] and
started for Jerusalem. Our God watched
over us, and as we traveled along, he
kept our enemies from ambushing us.
32After arriving in Jerusalem, we
rested for three days. 33Then on the
fourth day we went to God's temple,
where the silver, the gold, and the other
things were weighed and given to the
priest Meremoth son of Uriah. With him
were Eleazar son of Phinehas and the
two Levites, Jozabad son of Jeshua and
Noadiah son of Binnui. 34Everything
was counted, weighed, and recorded.
35Those who had returned from exile
offered sacrifices on the altar to the God
of Israel. Twelve bulls were offered for
all Israel. Ninety-six rams and seventy-
seven[i] lambs were offered on the altar.
And twelve goats were sacrificed for the
sins of the people. 36Some of those who
had returned took the king's orders to
the governors and officials in Western
Province. Then the officials did what
they could for the people and for the
temple of God.

Ezra Condemns Mixed Marriages

9 Later the Jewish leaders came to
me[j] and said:
Many Israelites, including priests
and Levites, are living just like the
people around them. They are even
guilty of some of the horrible sins of
the Canaanites, the Hittites, the Perizzites, the Jebusites, the Ammonites, the Moabites, the Egyptians,
and the Amorites.
2Some Israelite men have married
foreign women and have let their
sons do the same thing. Our own officials and leaders were the first to
commit this disgusting sin, and now
God's holy people are mixed with
foreigners.
3This news made me so angry that I
ripped my clothes and tore hair from
my head and beard. Then I just sat in
shock 4until time for the evening sacrifice. Many of our people were greatly
concerned and gathered around me, because the God of Israel had warned us
to stay away from foreigners.

Ezra's Prayer

5At the time of the evening sacrifice,
I was still sitting there in sorrow with
my clothes all torn. So I got down on
my knees, then lifted my arms, 6and
prayed:
I am much too ashamed to face
you, LORD God. Our sins and our
guilt have swept over us like a flood
that reaches up to the heavens.
7Since the time of our ancestors, all
of us have sinned. That's why we,
our kings, and our priests have often
been defeated by other kings. They
have killed some of us and made
slaves of others; they have taken our
possessions and made us ashamed,
just as we are today.
8But for now, LORD God, you have
shown great kindness to us. You
made us truly happy by letting some
of us settle in this sacred place and
by helping us in our time of slavery.
9We are slaves, but you have never
turned your back on us. You love us,
and because of you, the kings of Persia have helped us. It's as though
you have given us new life! You let

[f]8.24 *I*: See the note at 8.1. [g]8.31 *first month*: See the note at 6.19. [h]8.31 *River*: See the note at 8.15. [i]8.35 *seventy-seven*: Or "seventy-two." [j]9.1 *me*: Ezra.

us rebuild your temple and live
safely in Judah and Jerusalem.
10 Our God, what can we say now?
Even after all this, we have disobeyed the commands 11 that were
given to us by your servants the
prophets. They said the land you are
giving us is full of sinful and wicked
people, who never stop doing disgusting things.[k] 12 And we were
warned not to let our daughters and
sons marry their sons and daughters.
Your prophets also told us never
to help those foreigners or even let
them live in peace. You wanted us to
become strong and to enjoy the
good things in the land, then someday to leave it to our children forever.
13 You punished us because of our
terrible sins. But you did not punish
us nearly as much as we deserve,
and you have brought some of us
back home. 14 Why should we disobey your commands again by letting our sons and daughters marry
these foreigners who do such disgusting things? That would make
you angry enough to destroy us all!
15 LORD God of Israel, you have been
more than fair by letting a few of us
survive. But once again, our sins
have made us ashamed to face you.

The Plan for Ending Mixed Marriages

10 While Ezra was down on his
knees in front of God's temple,
praying with tears in his eyes, and confessing the sins of the people of Israel, a
large number of men, women, and children gathered around him and cried bitterly.
2 Shecaniah son of Jehiel from the
family of Elam said:
Ezra, we have disobeyed God by
marrying these foreign women. But
there is still hope for the people of
Israel, 3 if we follow your advice and
the advice of others who truly respect the laws of God. We must
promise God that we will divorce
our foreign wives and send them
away, together with their children.
4 Ezra, it's up to you to do something! We will support whatever you
do. So be brave!
5 Ezra stood up and made the chief
priests, the Levites, and everyone else in
Israel swear that they would follow the
advice of Shecaniah. 6 Then Ezra left
God's temple and went to spend the
night in the living quarters of Jehohanan son of Eliashib. He felt sorry for
what the people had done, and he did
not eat or drink a thing.
7-8 The officials and leaders sent a
message to all who had returned from
Babylonia and were now living in
Jerusalem and Judah. It told them to
meet in Jerusalem within three days, or
else they would lose everything they
owned and would no longer be considered part of the people that had returned from Babylonia.
9 Three days later, on the twentieth day
of the ninth month,[l] everyone from Judah and Benjamin came to Jerusalem
and sat in the temple courtyard. It was a
serious meeting, and they sat there,
trembling in the rain.
10 Ezra the priest stood up and said:
You have broken God's Law by
marrying foreign women, and you
have made the whole nation guilty!
11 Now you must confess your sins to
the LORD God of your ancestors and
obey him. Divorce your foreign
wives and don't have anything to do
with the rest of the foreigners who
live around here.
12 Everyone in the crowd shouted:
You're right! We will do what you
say. 13 But there are so many of us,
and we can't just stay out here in
this downpour. A lot of us have
sinned by marrying foreign women,
and the matter can't be settled in
only a day or two.
14 Why can't our officials stay on in
Jerusalem and take care of this for
us? Let everyone who has sinned in
this way meet here at a certain time
with leaders and judges from their
own towns. If we take care of this
problem, God will surely stop being
so terribly angry with us.
15 Jonathan son of Asahel and
Jahzeiah son of Tikvah were the only
ones who objected, except for the two
Levites, Meshullam and Shabbethai.
16 Everyone else who had returned
from exile agreed with the plan. So Ezra
the priest chose men[m] who were heads
of the families, and he listed their
names. They started looking into the
matter on the first day of the tenth
month,[n] 17 and they did not finish until
the first day of the first month[o] of the
next year.

The Men Who Had Foreign Wives

18-19 Here is a list of the priests who
had agreed to divorce their foreign

[k] **9.11** *doing disgusting things*: Probably worshiping idols. [l] **10.9** *ninth month*: Chislev, the ninth month of the Hebrew calendar, from about mid-November to mid-December. [m] **10.16** *So . . . men*: One possible meaning for the difficult Hebrew text. [n] **10.16** *tenth month*: Tebeth, the tenth month of the Hebrew calendar, from about mid-December to mid-January. [o] **10.17** *first month*: See the note at 6.19.

wives and to sacrifice a ram as a sin offering:

Maaseiah, Eliezer, Jarib, and Gedaliah from the family of Joshua son of Jozadak and his brothers;
20Hanani and Zebadiah from the family of Immer;
21Maaseiah, Elijah, Shemaiah, Jehiel, and Uzziah from the family of Harim;
22Elioenai, Maaseiah, Ishmael, Nethanel, Jozabad, and Elasah from the family of Pashhur.

23Those Levites who had foreign wives were: Jozabad, Shimei, Kelaiah (also known as Kelita), Pethahiah, Judah, and Eliezer.

24Eliashib, the musician, had a foreign wife.

These temple guards had foreign wives:

Shallum, Telem, and Uri.

25Here is a list of the others from Israel who had foreign wives:

Ramiah, Izziah, Malchijah, Mijamin, Eleazar, Hashabiah,[p] and Benaiah from the family of Parosh;

26Mattaniah, Zechariah, Jehiel, Abdi, Jeremoth, and Elijah from the family of Elam;

27Elioenai, Eliashib, Mattaniah, Jeremoth, Zabad, and Aziza from the family of Zattu;

28Jehohanan, Hananiah, Zabbai, and Athlai from the family of Bebai;

29Meshullam, Malluch, Adaiah, Jashub, Sheal, and Jeremoth from the family of Bani;

30Adna, Chelal, Benaiah, Maaseiah, Mattaniah, Bezalel, Binnui, and Manasseh from the family of Pahath Moab;

31-32Eliezer, Isshijah, Malchijah, Shemaiah, Shimeon, Benjamin, Malluch, and Shemariah from the family of Harim;

33Mattenai, Mattattah, Zabad, Eliphelet, Jeremai, Manasseh, and Shimei from the family of Hashum;

34-37Maadai, Amram, Uel, Benaiah, Bedeiah, Cheluhi, Vaniah, Meremoth, Eliashib, Mattaniah, Mattenai, and Jaasu from the family of Bani;

38-42Shimei, Shelemiah, Nathan, Adaiah, Machnadebai, Shashai, Sharai, Azarel, Shelemiah, Shemariah, Shallum, Amariah, and Joseph from the family of Binnui;[q]

43Jeiel, Mattithiah, Zabad, Zebina, Jaddai, Joel, and Benaiah from the family of Nebo.

44These men divorced their foreign wives, then sent them and their children away.[r]

[p] **10.25** *Hashabiah*: One ancient translation; Hebrew "Malchijah." [q] **10.38-42** *from the family of Binnui*: One possible meaning for the difficult Hebrew text. [r] **10.44** *away*: One possible meaning for the difficult Hebrew text of verse 44.

NEHEMIAH

ABOUT THIS BOOK

Twelve years after the last events of the book of Ezra, a Jew named Nehemiah received bad news about Jerusalem: The walls of the city were still broken down, and the burned gates had never been replaced.

Nehemiah lived in the Persian city of Susa and was a personal servant to King Artaxerxes. So Nehemiah prayed and asked God to have Artaxerxes send him to Jerusalem to rebuild the city. Artaxerxes did send Nehemiah, and he even provided the materials for the repairs.

After Nehemiah had arrived in Jerusalem and the repair work had begun, the officials from neighboring areas insulted the Jews and accused them of wanting to rebel against Persia. These enemies even planned attacks against Jerusalem and tried to have Nehemiah killed. Finally, the walls and gates were finished and dedicated to God, and they became a sign that God had blessed his people.

But Nehemiah realized that God would continue to bless his people only if they obeyed him. As Nehemiah said in one of his prayers:

> *LORD God of heaven, you are great and fearsome. And you faithfully keep your promises to everyone who loves you and obeys your commands.* (1.5)

A QUICK LOOK AT THIS BOOK

- King Artaxerxes Sends Nehemiah to Jerusalem (1.1—2.10)
- Rebuilding the Walls of Jerusalem (2.11—4.22)
- Nehemiah's Concern for the Poor (5.1-19)
- The Wall Is Finished, in Spite of Enemy Plots (6.1—7.3)
- Exiles Who Returned (7.4-73)
- Ezra Reads God's Law to the People, and They Celebrate the Festival of Shelters (8.1-18)
- The People Confess Their Sins (9.1-37)
- The People Sign an Agreement To Obey the Lord (9.38—10.39)
- The People Who Settled in Jerusalem and Judah (11.1-36)
- Priests and Levites Who Returned from Exile (12.1-26)
- Nehemiah Dedicates the City Wall (12.27-47)
- Changes Nehemiah Made (13.1-31)

Nehemiah's Prayer

1 I am Nehemiah son of Hacaliah, and
in this book I tell what I have done.
During the month of Chislev[a] in the
twentieth year that Artaxerxes[b] ruled
Persia, I was in his fortress city of
Susa,[c] 2when my brother Hanani came
with some men from Judah. So I asked
them about the Jews who had escaped[d]
from being captives in Babylonia. I also
asked them about the city of Jerusalem.
3They told me, "Those captives who
have come back are having all kinds of

[a]1.1 *Chislev*: The ninth month of the Hebrew calendar, from about mid-November to mid-December. [b]1.1 *Artaxerxes*: Probably Artaxerxes I, who ruled Persia 465-425 B.C.
[c]1.1 *Susa*: Capital of Elam Province, the winter home of Persian kings. [d]1.2 *escaped*: Or "returned."

troubles. They are terribly disgraced,
Jerusalem's walls are broken down, and
its gates have been burned."
4When I heard this, I sat down and
cried. Then for several days, I mourned;
I went without eating to show my sorrow, and I prayed:

5LORD God of heaven, you are
great and fearsome. And you faithfully keep your promises to everyone who loves you and obeys your
commands. 6I am your servant, so
please have mercy on me and answer the prayer that I make day and
night for these people of Israel who
serve you. I, my family, and the rest
of your people have sinned 7by
choosing to disobey you and the
laws and teachings you gave to your
servant Moses.

8Please remember the promise
you made to Moses. You told him
that if we were unfaithful, you would
scatter us among foreign nations.
9But you also said that no matter
how far away we were, we could
turn to you and start obeying your
laws. Then you would bring us back
to the place where you have chosen
to be worshiped.

10Our LORD, I am praying for your
servants—those you rescued by your
great strength and mighty power.
11Please answer my prayer and the
prayer of your other servants who
gladly honor your name. When I
serve the king his wine today, make
him pleased with me and have him
do what I ask.

Nehemiah Goes to Jerusalem

2 During the month of Nisan[e] in the
twentieth year that Artaxerxes was
king, I served him his wine, as I had
done before. But this was the first time I
had ever looked depressed. 2So the king
said, "Why do you look so sad? You're
not sick. Something must be bothering
you."
Even though I was frightened, 3I answered, "Your Majesty, I hope you live
forever! I feel sad because the city
where my ancestors are buried is in ruins, and its gates have been burned
down."
4The king asked, "What do you want
me to do?"
I prayed to the God who rules from
heaven. 5Then I told the king, "Sir, if it's
all right with you, please send me back
to Judah, so that I can rebuild the city
where my ancestors are buried."
6The queen was sitting beside the
king when he asked me, "How long will
it take, and when will you be back?" The
king agreed to let me go, and I told him
when I would return.
7Then I asked, "Your Majesty, would
you be willing to give me letters to the
governors of the provinces west of the
Euphrates River, so that I can travel
safely to Judah? 8I will need timber to
rebuild the gates of the fortress near the
temple and more timber to construct the
city wall and to build a place for me to
live. And so, I would appreciate a letter
to Asaph, who is in charge of the royal
forest." God was good to me, and the
king did everything I asked.
9The king sent some army officers
and cavalry troops along with me, and
as I traveled through the Western
Provinces, I gave the letters to the governors. 10But when Sanballat from
Horon[f] and Tobiah the Ammonite official heard about what had happened,
they became very angry, because they
didn't want anyone to help the people of
Israel.

Nehemiah Inspects the Wall of Jerusalem

11Three days after arriving in Jerusalem, 12I got up during the night and
left my house. I took some men with me,
without telling anyone what I thought
God wanted me to do for the city. The
only animal I took was the donkey I
rode on. 13I went through Valley Gate on
the west, then south past Dragon
Spring, before coming to Garbage Gate.
As I rode along, I took a good look at
the crumbled walls of the city and the
gates that had been torn down and
burned. 14On the east side of the city, I
headed north to Fountain Gate and
King's Pool, but then the trail became
too narrow for my donkey. 15So I went
down to Kidron Valley and looked at the
wall from there. Then before daylight I
returned to the city through Valley Gate.
16None of the city officials knew what
I had in mind. And I had not even told
any of the Jews—not the priests, the
leaders, the officials, or any other Jews
who would be helping in the work. 17But
when I got back, I said to them,
"Jerusalem is truly in a mess! The gates
have been torn down and burned, and
everything is in ruins. We must rebuild
the city wall so that we can again take
pride in our city."
18Then I told them how kind God had
been and what the king had said.
Immediately, they replied, "Let's start
building now!" So they got everything
ready.
19When Sanballat, Tobiah, and Ge-

[e]**2.1** *Nisan*: Or Abib, the first month of the Hebrew calendar, from about mid-March to mid-April. [f]**2.10** *Horon*: Possibly meaning that Sanballat was the official in charge of Beth-Horon, an important town on the road from Jerusalem to Lydda and the Mediterranean Sea.

shem the Arab heard about our plans,
they started insulting us and saying,
"Just look at you! Do you plan to rebuild
the walls of the city and rebel against
the king?"
20 I answered, "We are servants of the
God who rules from heaven, and he
will make our work succeed. So we
will start rebuilding Jerusalem, but you
have no right to any of its property, because you have had no part in its history."

Rebuilding the Wall of Jerusalem

3 These are the people who helped rebuild the wall and gates of Jerusalem:

The high priest Eliashib and the
other priests rebuilt Sheep Gate and
hung its doors. Then they dedicated
Sheep Gate and the section of the
wall as far as Hundred Tower and
Hananel Tower.
2 The people of Jericho rebuilt the
next section of the wall, and Zaccur
son of Imri rebuilt the section after
that.
3 The family of Hassenaah built
Fish Gate. They put the beams in
place and hung the doors, then they
added metal bolts and wooden
beams as locks.
4 Meremoth, son of Uriah and
grandson of Hakkoz, completed the
next section of the wall.
Meshullam, son of Berechiah and
grandson of Meshezabel, rebuilt the
next section, and Zadok son of
Baana rebuilt the section beside
that.
5 The next section was to be repaired by the men of Tekoa, but their
town leaders refused to do the hard
work they were assigned.[g]
6 Joiada son of Paseah and Meshullam son of Besodeiah restored Ancient Gate. They put the beams in
place, hung the doors, and added
metal bolts and wooden beams as
locks. 7 Melatiah from Gibeon, Jadon
from Meronoth, and the men from
Gibeon and Mizpah rebuilt the next
section of the wall. This section
reached as far as the house of the
governor of West Euphrates
Province.[h]
8 Uzziel son of Harhaiah the goldsmith rebuilt the next section.
Hananiah the perfume maker rebuilt the section next after that, and
it went as far as Broad Wall.
9 Rephaiah son of Hur ruled half of
the Jerusalem District, and he rebuilt the next section of the wall.
10 The section after that was close
to the home of Jedaiah son of
Harumaph, and he rebuilt it.
Hattush son of Hashabneiah con-
structed the next section of the wall.
11 Malchijah son of Harim and
Hasshub son of Pahath Moab rebuilt
the section after that, and they also
built Oven Tower.
12 Shallum son of Hallohesh ruled
the other half of the Jerusalem District, and he rebuilt the next section
of the wall. Shallum's daughters also
worked with him.
13 Hanun and the people who lived
in the town of Zanoah rebuilt Valley
Gate. They hung the doors and
added metal bolts and wooden
beams as locks. They also rebuilt the
wall for fifteen hundred feet, all the
way to Garbage Gate.
14 Malchijah son of Rechab ruled
the district of Beth-Haccherem, and
he rebuilt Garbage Gate. He hung
the doors and added metal bolts and
wooden beams as locks.
15 Shallum[i] son of Colhozeh ruled
the district of Mizpah, and he rebuilt
Fountain Gate. He put a cover over
the gateway, then hung the doors
and added metal bolts and wooden
beams as locks. He also rebuilt the
wall at Shelah Pool. This section was
next to the king's garden and went
as far as the stairs leading down
from David's City.
16 Nehemiah son of Azbuk ruled
half of the district of Beth-Zur, and
he rebuilt the next section of the
wall. It went as far as the royal
cemetery,[j] the artificial pool, and the
army barracks.

Levites Who Worked on the Wall

17 The Levites who worked on the next
sections of the wall were Rehum son of
Bani; Hashabiah, who ruled half of the
district of Keilah and did this work for
his district; 18 Binnui[k] son of Henadad,
who ruled the other half of the district
of Keilah; 19 Ezer son of Jeshua, who
ruled Mizpah, rebuilt the section of the
wall that was in front of the armory and
reached to the corner of the wall;
20 Baruch son of Zabbai eagerly rebuilt
the section of the wall that went all the
way to the door of the house of Eliashib
the high priest; 21 Meremoth, son of

[g] **3.5** *refused . . . assigned*: One possible meaning for the difficult Hebrew text. [h] **3.7** *as far as . . . Province*: One possible meaning for the difficult Hebrew text. [i] **3.15** *Shallum*: A few Hebrew manuscripts and one ancient translation; most Hebrew manuscripts "Shallun"; one ancient translation "Solomon." [j] **3.16** *royal cemetery*: Hebrew "David's tombs."
[k] **3.18** *Binnui*: Two ancient translations; Hebrew "Bavvai."

Uriah and grandson of Hakkoz, built up
to the far end of Eliashib's house.

Priests Who Worked on the Wall

22 Here is a list of the priests who
worked on the wall:
Priests from the region around
Jerusalem rebuilt the next section of
the wall.
23 Benjamin and Hasshub rebuilt
the wall in front of their own houses.
Azariah, who was the son of Maaseiah and the grandson of Ananiah,
rebuilt the section in front of his
house.
24 Binnui son of Henadad rebuilt
the section of the wall from Azariah's house to the corner of the wall.
25 Palal son of Uzai rebuilt the next
section, which began at the corner
of the wall and the tower of the upper palace near the court of the
guard.
Pedaiah son of Parosh rebuilt the
next section of the wall. 26 He
stopped at a place near the Water
Gate on the east and the tower
guarding the temple. This was close
to a section in the city called Ophel,
where the temple workers lived.[l]

Other Builders Who Worked on the Wall

27 The men from Tekoa rebuilt the
next section of the wall, and it was
their second section.[m] It started at a
place across from the large tower
that guarded the Temple, and it went
all the way to the wall near Ophel.
28 Some priests rebuilt the next
section of the wall. They began
working north of Horse Gate, and
each one worked on a section in
front of his own house.
29 Zadok son of Immer rebuilt the
wall in front of his house.
Shemaiah son of Shecaniah, who
looked after the East Gate, rebuilt
the section after that.
30 Hananiah and Hanun[n] rebuilt
the next section, which was the second section[o] for them.
Meshullam son of Berechiah rebuilt the next section, which happened to be in front of his house.
31 Malchijah, a goldsmith, rebuilt
the next section, as far as the house
used by the temple workers and
merchants. This area was across
from Gathering Gate, near the room
on top of the wall at the northeast
corner.
32 The goldsmiths and merchants
rebuilt the last section of the wall,
which went from the corner room all
the way to Sheep Gate.

Nehemiah's Enemies

4 When Sanballat, the governor of
Samaria, heard that we were rebuilding the walls of Jerusalem, he became angry and started insulting our
people. 2 In front of his friends and the
Samaritan army he said, "What is this
feeble bunch of Jews trying to do? Are
they going to rebuild the wall and offer
sacrifices all in one day? Do they think
they can make something out of this
pile of scorched stones?"
3 Tobiah from Ammon was standing
beside Sanballat and said, "Look at the
wall they are building! Why, even a fox
could knock over this pile of stones."
4 But I prayed, "Our God, these people
hate us and have wished horrible things
for us. Please answer our prayers and
make their insults fall on them! Let
them be the ones to be dragged away as
prisoners of war. 5 Don't forgive the
mean and evil way they have insulted
the builders."
6 The people worked hard, and we
built the walls of Jerusalem halfway up
again. 7 But Sanballat, Tobiah, the Arabs,
the Ammonites, and the people from the
city of Ashdod saw the walls going up
and the holes being repaired. So they
became angry 8 and decided to stir up
trouble, and to fight against the people
of Jerusalem. 9 But we kept on praying
to our God, and we also stationed
guards day and night.
10 Meanwhile, the people of Judah
were singing a sorrowful song:

"So much rubble for us to haul!
Worn out and weary,
will we ever finish this wall?"

11 Our enemies were saying, "Before
those Jews know what has happened,
we will sneak up and kill them and put
an end to their work."
12 On at least ten different occasions,
the Jews living near our enemies
warned us against attacks from every
side,[p] 13 and so I sent people to guard the
wall at its lowest places and where there
were still holes in it. I placed them according to families, and they stood
guard with swords and spears and with
bows and arrows. 14 Then I looked things
over and told the leaders, the officials,
and the rest of the people, "Don't be
afraid of your enemies! The Lord is
great and fearsome. So think of him and
fight for your relatives and children,
your wives and homes!"

[l] **3.26** *This . . . lived*: One possible meaning for the difficult Hebrew text. [m] **3.27** *second section*: See verse 5. [n] **3.30** *Hananiah and Hanun*: Hebrew "Hananiah son of Shelemiah and Hanun, Zalaph's sixth son." [o] **3.30** *second section*: See verses 8, 13. [p] **4.12** *against . . . side*: One possible meaning for the difficult Hebrew text.

15 Our enemies found out that we
knew about their plot against us, but
God kept them from doing what they
had planned. So we went back to work
on the wall.
16 From then on, I let half of the young
men work while the other half stood
guard. They wore armor and had spears
and shields, as well as bows and arrows.
The leaders helped the workers 17 who
were rebuilding the wall. Everyone who
hauled building materials kept one hand
free to carry a weapon. 18 Even the workers who were rebuilding the wall
strapped on a sword. The worker who
was to blow the signal trumpet stayed
with me.
19 I told the people and their officials
and leaders, "Our work is so spread out,
that we are a long way from one another. 20 If you hear the sound of the
trumpet, come quickly and gather
around me. Our God will help us fight."
21 Every day from dawn to dark, half
of the workers rebuilt the walls, while
the rest stood guard with their spears.
22 I asked the men in charge and their
workers to stay inside Jerusalem and
stand guard at night. So they guarded
the city at night and worked during the
day. 23 I even slept in my work clothes at
night; my children, the workers, and the
guards slept in theirs as well. And we always kept our weapons close by.[q]

Nehemiah's Concern for the Poor

5 Some of the men and their wives
complained about the Jews in power
2 and said, "We have large families, and
it takes a lot of grain merely to keep
them alive."
3 Others said, "During the famine we
even had to mortgage our fields, vineyards, and homes to them in order to
buy grain."
4 Then others said, "We had to borrow
money from those in power to pay the
government tax on our fields and vineyards. 5 We are Jews just as they are, and
our children are as good as theirs. But
we still have to sell our children as
slaves, and some of our daughters have
already been raped. We are completely
helpless; our fields and vineyards have
even been taken from us."
6 When I heard their complaints and
their charges, I became very angry. 7 So I
thought it over and said to the leaders
and officials, "How can you charge your
own people interest?"
Then I called a public meeting and accused the leaders 8 by saying, "We have
tried to buy back all of our people who
were sold into exile. But here you are,
selling more of them for us to buy
back!" The officials and leaders did not
say a word, because they knew this was
true.
9 I continued, "What you have done is
wrong! We must honor our God by the
way we live, so the Gentiles can't find
fault with us. 10 My relatives, my friends,
and I are also lending money and grain,
but we must no longer demand payment
in return. 11 Now give back the fields,
vineyards, olive orchards, and houses
you have taken and also the interest you
have been paid."
12 The leaders answered, "We will do
whatever you say and return their property, without asking to be repaid."
So I made the leaders promise in front
of the priests to give back the property.
13 Then I emptied my pockets and said,
"If you don't keep your promise, that's
what God will do to you. He will empty
out everything you own, even taking
away your houses."
The people answered, "We will keep
our promise." Then they praised the
LORD and did as they had promised.

Nehemiah Is Generous

14 I was governor of Judah from the
twentieth year that Artaxerxes[r] was
king until the thirty-second year. And
during these entire twelve years, my relatives and I refused to accept the food
that I was allowed. 15 Each governor before me had been a burden to the people
by making them pay for his food and
wine and by demanding forty silver
coins a day. Even their officials had
been a burden to the people. But I respected God, and I didn't think it was
right to be so hard on them. 16 I spent all
my time getting the wall rebuilt and did
not buy any property. Everyone working
for me did the same thing. 17 I usually
fed a hundred fifty of our own Jewish
people and their leaders, as well as foreign visitors from surrounding lands.
18 Each day one ox, six of the best sheep,
and lots of chickens were prepared.
Then every ten days, a large supply of
wine was brought in. I knew what a
heavy burden this would have been for
the people, and so I did not ask for my
food allowance as governor.
19 I pray that God will bless me for
everything I have done for my people.

Plots against Nehemiah

6 Sanballat, Tobiah, Geshem, and our
other enemies learned that I had
completely rebuilt the wall. All I lacked
was hanging the doors in the gates.
2 Then Sanballat and Geshem sent a
message, asking me to meet with them
in one of the villages in Ono Valley. I

[q] 4.23 *And . . . by*: One possible meaning for the difficult Hebrew text. [r] 5.14 *Artaxerxes*: See the note at 1.1.

knew they were planning to harm me in some way. 3So I sent messengers to tell them, "My work is too important to stop now and go there. I can't afford to slow down the work just to visit with you." 4They invited me four times, but each time I refused to go.

5Finally, Sanballat sent an official to me with an unsealed letter, 6which said:

> A rumor is going around among the nations that you and the other Jews are rebuilding the wall and planning to rebel, because you want to be their king. And Geshem[s] says it's true! 7You even have prophets in Jerusalem, claiming you are now the king of Judah. You know the Persian king will hear about this, so let's get together and talk it over.

8I sent a message back to Sanballat, saying, "None of this is true! You are making it all up."

9Our enemies were trying to frighten us and to keep us from our work. But I asked God to give me strength.

10One day I went to visit Shemaiah.[t] He was looking very worried, and[u] he said, "Let's hurry to the holy place of the temple and hide there.[v] We will lock the temple doors, because your enemies are planning to kill you tonight."

11I answered, "Why should someone like me have to run and hide in the temple to save my life? I won't go!"

12Suddenly I realized that God had not given Shemaiah this message. But Tobiah and Sanballat had paid him to trick me 13and to frighten me into doing something wrong, because they wanted to ruin my good name.

14Then I asked God to punish Tobiah and Sanballat for what they had done. I prayed that God would punish the prophet Noadiah and the other prophets who, together with her, had tried to frighten me.

The Work Is Finished

15On the twenty-fifth day of the month Elul,[w] the wall was completely rebuilt. It had taken fifty-two days. 16When our enemies in the surrounding nations learned that the work was finished, they felt helpless, because they knew that our God had helped us rebuild the wall.

17All this time the Jewish leaders and Tobiah had been writing letters back and forth. 18Many people in Judah were loyal to Tobiah for two reasons: Shecaniah son of Arah was his father-in-law, and Tobiah's son Jehohanan had married the daughter of Meshullam son of Berechiah.[x] 19The people would always tell me about the good things Tobiah had done, and then they would tell Tobiah everything I had said. So Tobiah kept sending letters, trying to frighten me.

7 After the wall had been rebuilt and the gates hung, then the temple guards, the singers, and the other Levites were assigned their work. 2I put my brother Hanani in charge of Jerusalem, along with Hananiah, the commander of the fortress, because Hananiah could be trusted, and he respected God more than most people did. 3I said to them, "Don't let the gates to the city be opened until the sun has been up for a while. And make sure that they are closed and barred before the guards go off duty at sunset. Choose people from Jerusalem to stand guard at different places around the wall and others to stand guard near their own houses."

A List of Exiles Who Returned

(Ezra 2.1-70)

4Although Jerusalem covered a large area, not many people lived there, and no new houses had been built. 5-6So God gave me the idea to bring together the people, their leaders, and officials and to check the family records of those who had returned from captivity in Babylonia, after having been taken there by King Nebuchadnezzar.[y] About this same time, I found records of those who had been the first to return to Jerusalem from Babylon Province.[z] By reading these records, I learned that they settled in their own hometowns, 7and that they had come with Zerubbabel, Joshua, Nehemiah, Azariah, Raamiah, Nahamani, Mordecai, Bilshan, Mispereth, Bigvai, Nehum, and Baanah.

8-25Here is how many had returned from each family group: 2,172 from Parosh; 372 from Shephatiah; 652 from Arah; 2,818 from Pahath Moab, who were all descendants of Jeshua and Joab; 1,254 from Elam; 845 from Zattu; 760 from Zaccai; 648 from Binnui; 628 from Bebai; 2,322 from Azgad; 667 from

[s] **6.6** *Geshem*: Hebrew "Gashmu" (see verse 1 and 2.19). [t] **6.10** *Shemaiah*: Hebrew "Shemaiah son of Delaiah son of Mehetabel." [u] **6.10** *was . . . worried, and*: Or "wasn't supposed to leave his house, but." [v] **6.10** *holy place . . . hide there*: Only priests were allowed to enter the holy place; anyone else could be put to death. [w] **6.15** *Elul*: The sixth month of the Hebrew calendar, from about mid-August to mid-September. [x] **6.18** *Shecaniah . . . Berechiah*: Jews who had helped rebuild the Jerusalem wall (see 3.4, 29, 30).
[y] **7.5,6** *Nebuchadnezzar*: Known as Nebuchadnezzar II, who ruled Babylonia from 605 to 562 B.C. In 586 B.C. he destroyed Jerusalem and took many of its people to Babylonia.
[z] **7.5,6** *first to return . . . Province*: Probably 539 B.C., when Cyrus, the ruler of Persia, captured the city of Babylon.

Adonikam; 2,067 from Bigvai; 655 from
Adin; 98 from Ater, also known as
Hezekiah; 328 from Hashum; 324 from
Bezai; 112 from Hariph; and 95 from
Gibeon.
26-38 Here is how many people returned
whose ancestors had come from the following towns: 188 from Bethlehem and
Netophah; 128 from Anathoth; 42 from
Beth-Azmaveth; 743 from Kiriath-
Jearim, Chephirah, and Beeroth; 621
from Ramah and Geba; 122 from Michmas; 123 from Bethel and Ai; 52 from
Nebo;[a] 1,254 from Elam;[b] 320 from
Harim; 345 from Jericho; 721 from Lod,
Hadid, and Ono; and 3,930 from Senaah.
39-42 Here is how many returned from
each family of priests: 973 descendants
of Jeshua from Jedaiah; 1,052 from Immer; 1,247 from Pashhur; and 1,017
from Harim.
43-45 Here is how many returned from
the families of Levites: 74 descendants
of Hodevah from the families of Jeshua
and Kadmiel; 148 descendants of Asaph
from the temple musicians; and 138 descendants of Shallum, Ater, Talmon,
Akkub, Hatita, and Shobai from the
temple guards.
46-56 Here are the names of the families of temple workers whose descendants returned: Ziha, Hasupha, Tabbaoth, Keros, Sia, Padon, Lebana,
Hagaba, Shalmai, Hanan, Giddel, Gahar, Reaiah, Rezin, Nekoda, Gazzam,
Uzza, Paseah, Besai, Meunim, Nephush-
esim, Bakbuk, Hakupha, Harhur,
Bazlith, Mehida, Harsha, Barkos, Sisera,
Temah, Neziah, and Hatipha.
57-59 Here are the names of Solomon's
servants whose descendants returned:
Sotai, Sophereth, Perida, Jaala, Darkon,
Giddel, Shephatiah, Hattil, Pochereth
Hazzebaim, and Amon.
60 A total of 392 descendants of temple
workers and of Solomon's servants returned.
61-62 There were 642 who returned
from the families of Delaiah, Tobiah,
and Nekoda, though they could not
prove they were Israelites. They had
lived in the Babylonian towns of Tel-
Melah, Tel-Harsha, Cherub, Addon, and
Immer.
63-64 The families of Hobaiah, Hakkoz,
and Barzillai could not prove they were
priests. The ancestor of the family of
Barzillai had married the daughter of
Barzillai from Gilead and had taken his
wife's family name. But the records of
these three families could not be found,
and none of them were allowed to serve
as priests. 65 In fact, the governor told
them, "You cannot eat the food offered
to God until he lets us know if you really are priests."[c]
66-69 There were 42,360 who returned,
in addition to 7,337 servants, and 245
musicians. Altogether, they brought
with them 736 horses, 245 mules,[d] 435
camels, and 6,720 donkeys.
70-72 Many people gave gifts to help
pay for the materials to rebuild the temple. The governor himself gave 17
pounds of gold, 50 bowls to be used in
the temple, and 530 robes for the
priests. Family leaders gave 337 pounds
of gold and 3,215 pounds of silver. The
rest of the people gave 337 pounds of
gold, 2,923 pounds of silver, and 67
robes for the priests.
73 And so, by the seventh month,[e]
priests, Levites, temple guards, musicians, workers, and many of the ordinary people had settled in the towns of
Judah.

Ezra Reads God's Law to the People

8 1-2 On the first day of the seventh
month,[e] the people came together in
the open area in front of the Water Gate.
Then they asked Ezra, who was a
teacher of the Law of Moses, to read to
them from this Law that the LORD had
given his people. Ezra the priest came
with the Law and stood before the
crowd of men, women, and the children
who were old enough to understand.
3 From early morning till noon, he read
the Law of Moses to them, and they listened carefully. 4 Ezra stood on a high
wooden platform that had been built
for this occasion. Mattithiah, Shema,
Anaiah, Uriah, Hilkiah, and Maaseiah
were standing to his right, while Pedaiah, Mishael, Malchijah, Hashum, Hash
Baddanah, Zechariah, and Meshullam
were standing to his left.
5 Ezra was up on the high platform,
where he could be seen by everyone,
and when he opened the book, they all
stood up. 6 Ezra praised the great LORD
God, and the people shouted, "Amen!
Amen!" Then they bowed with their
faces to the ground and worshiped the
LORD.
7-8 After this, the Levites Jeshua, Bani,
Sherebiah, Jamin, Akkub, Shabbethai,

[a] **7.26-38** *Nebo*: Hebrew "the other Nebo." [b] **7.26-38** *Elam*: Hebrew "the other Elam."
[c] **7.65** *until . . . priests*: The Hebrew text has "until a priest comes with the urim and thummim," sacred objects which were used in some way to receive answers from God. [d] **7.66-69** *736 horses, 245 mules*: A few Hebrew manuscripts; this is not found in most Hebrew manuscripts of verse 68. [e] **7.73** *seventh month*: Tishri (also called Ethanim), the seventh month of the Hebrew calendar, from about mid-September to mid-October. [e] **8.1,2** *seventh month*: Tishri (also called Ethanim), the seventh month of the Hebrew calendar, from about mid-September to mid-October.

Hodiah, Maaseiah, Kelita, Azariah, Jozabad, Hanan, and Pelaiah went among
the people, explaining the meaning of
what Ezra had read.
9The people started crying when
God's Law was read to them. Then Nehemiah the governor, Ezra the priest
and teacher, and the Levites who had
been teaching the people all said, "This
is a special day for the LORD your God.
So don't be sad and don't cry!"
10Nehemiah told the people, "Enjoy
your good food and wine and share
some with those who didn't have anything to bring. Don't be sad! This is a
special day for the LORD, and he will
make you happy and strong."
11The Levites encouraged the people
by saying, "This is a sacred day, so don't
worry or mourn!" 12When the people returned to their homes, they celebrated
by eating and drinking and by sharing
their food with those in need, because
they had understood what had been
read to them.

Celebrating the Festival of Shelters

13On the second day of the seventh
month,[f] the leaders of all the family
groups came together with the priests
and the Levites, so Ezra could teach
them the Law 14that the LORD had given
to Moses. They learned from the Law
that the people of Israel were to live in
shelters when they celebrated the festival in the seventh month of the year.
15They also learned that they were to go
into the woods and gather branches of
leafy trees such as olives, myrtles, and
palms for making these shelters.
16So the people gathered branches
and made shelters on the flat roofs of
their houses, in their yards, in the courtyard of the temple, and in the open areas around the Water Gate and Ephraim
Gate. 17Everyone who had returned
from Babylonia built shelters. They
lived in them and joyfully celebrated the
Festival of Shelters for the first time
since the days of Joshua son of Nun.
18On each of the first seven days of the
festival, Ezra read to the people from
God's Law. Then on the eighth day,
everyone gathered for worship, just as
the Law had said they must.

The People Confess Their Sins

9 On the twenty-fourth day of the seventh month,[f] the people of Israel
went without eating, and they dressed in
sackcloth and threw dirt on their heads
to show their sorrow. 2They refused to
let foreigners join them, as they met to
confess their sins and the sins of their
ancestors. 3For three hours they stood
and listened to the Law of the LORD
their God, and then for the next three
hours they confessed their sins and worshiped the LORD.
4Jeshua, Bani, Kadmiel, Shebaniah,
Bunni, Sherebiah, Bani, and Chenani
stood on the special platform for the
Levites and prayed aloud to the LORD
their God. 5Then the Levites Jeshua,
Kadmiel, Bani, Hashabneiah, Sherebiah,
Hodiah, Shebaniah, and Pethahiah said:

"Stand and shout praises
to your LORD,
the eternal God![g]
Praise his wonderful name,
though he is greater
than words can express."

The People Pray

6 You alone are the LORD,
Creator of the heavens
and all the stars,
Creator of the earth
and those who live on it,
Creator of the ocean
and all its creatures.
You are the source of life,
praised by the stars
that fill the heavens.
7 You are the LORD our God,
the one who chose Abram—
you brought him from Ur
in Babylonia
and named him Abraham.
8 Because he was faithful,
you made an agreement
to give his descendants
the land of the Canaanites
and Hittites,
of the Amorites and Perizzites,
and of the Jebusites
and Girgashites.
Now you have kept your promise,
just as you always do.

9 When our ancestors
were in Egypt,
you saw their suffering;
when they were at the Red Sea,[h]
you heard their cry for help.
10 You knew that the King of Egypt
and his officials and his nation
had mistreated your people.
So you worked fearsome miracles
against the Egyptians
and earned a reputation
that still remains.

[f]**8.13** *seventh month*: Hebrew "same month." [f]**9.1** *seventh month*: Hebrew "same month."
[g]**9.5** *shout . . . God*: Or "shout eternal praises to the LORD your God." [h]**9.9** *Red Sea*: Hebrew *yam suph* "Sea of Reeds," one of the marshes of fresh water lakes near the eastern part of the Nile Delta. This identification is based on Exodus 13.17—14.9, which lists the towns on the route of the Israelites before crossing the sea. In the Greek translation of the Scriptures made about 200 B.C., the "Sea of Reeds" was named "Red Sea."

11 You divided the deep sea,
and your people walked through
on dry land.
But you tossed their enemies in,
and they sank down
like a heavy stone.
12 Each day you led your people
with a thick cloud,
and at night you showed the way
with a flaming fire.
13 At Sinai you came down
from heaven,
and you gave your people
good laws and teachings
that are fair and honest.
14 You commanded them to respect
your holy Sabbath,
and you instructed
your servant Moses
to teach them your laws.
15 When they were hungry,
you sent bread from heaven,
and when they were thirsty,
you let water flow
from a rock.
Then you commanded them
to capture the land
that you had solemnly promised.

*16 Our stubborn ancestors
refused to obey—
they forgot about the miracles
you had worked for them,
and they were determined
to return to Egypt
and become slaves again.
17 But, our God, you are merciful
and quick to forgive;
you are loving, kind,
and very patient.
So you never turned away
from them—
18 not even when they made
an idol shaped like a calf
and insulted you by claiming,
"This is the god who rescued us
from Egypt."

19 Because of your great mercy,
you never abandoned them
in the desert.
And you always guided them
with a cloud by day
and a fire at night.
20 Your gentle Spirit
instructed them,[i]
and you gave them manna[j] to eat
and water to drink.
21 You took good care of them,
and for forty years
they never lacked a thing.
Their shoes didn't wear out,
and their feet were never swollen.

22 You let them conquer kings
and take their land,
including King Sihon of Heshbon
and King Og of Bashan.[k]
23 You brought them into the land
that you had promised
their ancestors,
and you blessed their nation
with people that outnumbered
the stars in the sky.

24 Then their descendants
conquered the land.
You helped them defeat
the kings and nations
and treat their enemies
however they wished.
25 They captured strong cities
and rich farmland;
they took furnished houses,
as well as cisterns,[l]
vineyards, olive orchards,
and numerous fruit trees.
They ate till they were satisfied,
and they celebrated
your abundant blessings.

26 In spite of this, they rebelled
and disobeyed your laws.
They killed your prophets,
who warned them
to turn back to you,
and they cursed your name.
27 So you handed them over
to their enemies,
who treated them terribly.
But in their sufferings,
they begged you to help.
From heaven you listened
to their prayers
and because of your great mercy,
you sent leaders to rescue them.

28 But when they were at peace,
they would turn against you,
and you would hand them over
to their enemies.
Then they would beg for help,
and because you are merciful,
you rescued them
over and over again.
29 You warned them to turn back
and discover true life
by obeying your laws.
But they stubbornly refused
and continued to sin.
30 For years, you were patient,
and your Spirit[m] warned them
with messages spoken
by your prophets.
Still they refused to listen,
and you handed them over
to their enemies.

[i]**9.20** *Your gentle Spirit instructed them*: Or "You gently instructed them." [j]**9.20** *manna*: This was something like a thin wafer (see Exodus 16.1-36). [k]**9.22** *Bashan*: One possible meaning for the difficult Hebrew text of verse 22. [l]**9.25** *cisterns*: Pits dug into the ground to hold water. [m]**9.30** *your Spirit*: Or "you."

31 But you are merciful and kind,
and so you never forgot them
or let them be destroyed.

32 Our God, you are powerful,
fearsome, and faithful,
always true to your word.
So please keep in mind
the terrible sufferings
of our people, kings, leaders,
priests, and prophets,
from the time Assyria ruled
until this very day.
33 You have always been fair
when you punished us
for our sins.

34 Our kings, leaders, and priests
have never obeyed your commands
or heeded your warnings.
35 You blessed them with a kingdom
and with an abundance
of rich, fertile land,
but they refused to worship you
or turn from their evil.
36 Now we are slaves
in this fruitful land
you gave to our ancestors.
37 Its plentiful harvest is taken
by kings you placed over us
because of our sins.
Our suffering is unbearable,
because they do as they wish
to us and our livestock.

The People Make an Agreement

38 And so, a firm agreement was made
that had the official approval of the
10 leaders, the Levites, and priests.
1 As governor, I[n] signed the
agreement together with Zedekiah and
the following priests: 2-8 Seraiah,
Azariah, Jeremiah, Pashhur, Amariah,
Malchijah, Hattush, Shebaniah, Malluch, Harim, Meremoth, Obadiah,
Daniel, Ginnethon, Baruch, Meshullam,
Abijah, Mijamin, Maaziah, Bilgai, and
Shemaiah.
9 The Levites who signed were: Jeshua
son of Azaniah, Binnui from the clan
of Henadad, Kadmiel, 10 Shebaniah,
Hodiah, Kelita, Pelaiah, Hanan, 11 Mica,
Rehob, Hashabiah, 12 Zaccur, Sherebiah,
Shebaniah, 13 Hodiah, Bani, and Beninu.
14 The leaders who signed were:
Parosh, Pahath Moab, Elam, Zattu, Bani,
15 Bunni, Azgad, Bebai, 16 Adonijah, Big-
vai, Adin, 17 Ater, Hezekiah, Azzur, 18 Ho-
diah, Hashum, Bezai, 19 Hariph, Anathoth, Nebai, 20 Magpiash, Meshullam,
Hezir, 21 Meshezabel, Zadok, Jaddua,
22 Pelatiah, Hanan, Anaiah, 23 Hoshea,
Hananiah, Hasshub, 24 Hallohesh, Pilha,
Shobek, 25 Rehum, Hashabnah, Maaseiah, 26 Ahiah, Hanan, Anan, 27 Malluch,
Harim, and Baanah.

The Agreement

28-29 All of us, including priests,
Levites, temple guards, singers, temple workers and leaders, together
with our wives and children, have
separated ourselves from the foreigners in this land and now enter
into an agreement with a complete
understanding of what we are doing.
And so, we now place ourselves under the curse of the LORD our God, if
we fail to obey his laws and teachings that were given to us by his servant Moses.
30 We won't let our sons and
daughters marry foreigners.
31 We won't buy goods or grain on
the Sabbath or on any other sacred
day, not even from foreigners.
Every seven years we will let our
fields rest, and we will cancel all
debts.
32 Once a year we will each donate
a small amount of silver to the temple of our God. 33 This is to pay for
the sacred bread, as well as for the
daily sacrifices and special sacrifices
such as those offered on the Sabbath and during the New Moon Festival and the other festivals. It will
also pay for the sacrifices to forgive
our sins and for all expenses connected with the worship of God in
the temple.
34 We have decided that the families[o] of priests, Levites, and ordinary
people will supply firewood for the
temple each year, so that sacrifices
can be offered on the altar, just as
the LORD our God has commanded.
35 Each year we will bring to the
temple the first part of our harvest
of grain and fruit.
36 We will bring our first-born sons
and the first-born males of our herds
and flocks and offer them to the
priests who serve in the temple, because this is what is written in God's
Law.[p]
37 To the priests in the temple of
our God, we will bring the bread
dough from the first harvest, together with our best fruit, and an
offering of new wine and olive oil.
We will bring ten percent of our
grain harvest to those Levites who
are responsible for collecting it in
our towns. 38 A priest from the family
of Aaron must be there when we
give this to the Levites. Then the

[n] **10.1** *I*: Hebrew "Nehemiah son of Hacaliah." [o] **10.34** *that the families*: Or "which families."
[p] **10.36** *first-born sons . . . God's Law*: See Exodus 13.2, 12-15; 34.19, 20.

Levites will put one tenth of this
part in the temple storeroom,
39 which is also the place for the sacred objects used by the priests, the
temple guards, and the singers.
Levites and everyone else must
bring their gifts of grain, wine, and
olive oil to this room.
We will not neglect the temple of
our God.

People Who Settled in Jerusalem

11 The nation's leaders and their
families settled in Jerusalem. But
there was room for only one out of
every ten of the remaining families, and
so they asked God to show them[q] who
would live there. 2 Then everyone else
asked God to bless those who were willing to live in Jerusalem.
3 Some of the people of Israel, the
priests, the Levites, the temple workers,
and the descendants of Solomon's servants lived on their own property in the
towns of Judah. But the leaders of the
province lived in Jerusalem with their
families.

The Judah Tribe

4-6 From the Judah tribe, two leaders
settled in Jerusalem with their relatives.
One of them was Athaiah son of Uzziah.
His ancestors were Zechariah, Amariah,
Shephatiah, Mahalalel, and Perez, the
son of Judah. From the descendants of
Perez, four hundred sixty-eight of the
best men lived in Jerusalem.
The other leader from Judah was
Maaseiah the son of Baruch. His ances-
tors were Colhozeh, Hazaiah, Adaiah,
Joiarib, Zechariah, and Shelah, the son
of Judah.

The Benjamin Tribe

7-8 From the Benjamin tribe, three leaders settled in Jerusalem. The first was
Sallu son of Meshullam, and the others
were Gabbai and Sallai. Sallu's ancestors were Joed, Pedaiah, Kolaiah, Maaseiah, Ithiel, and Jeshaiah. Altogether,
there were nine hundred twenty-eight
men of the Benjamin tribe living in
Jerusalem. 9 Joel son of Zichri was their
leader, and Judah son of Hassenuah was
second in command.

Priests

10 Four priests settled in Jerusalem.
The first was Jedaiah; he was the son of
Joiarib and the uncle of Jachin.[r]
11 The second priest to settle there was
Seraiah son of Hilkiah. His ancestors
were Meshullam, Zadok, Meraioth, and
Ahitub, who had been a high priest.
12 Altogether, there were eight hundred
twenty-two from his clan who served in
the temple.
The third priest to settle there was
Adaiah son of Jeroham. His ancestors
were Pelaliah, Amzi, Zechariah, Pashhur, and Malchijah. 13 Altogether, there
were two hundred forty-two clan leaders among his relatives.
The fourth priest to settle there was
Amashsai son of Azarel. His ancestors
were Ahzai, Meshillemoth, and Immer.
14 Altogether, there were one hundred
twenty-eight brave warriors from their
clans, and their leader was Zabdiel son
of Haggedolim.

Levites

15 Several Levites settled in Jerusalem.
First, there was Shemaiah son of Hasshub. His ancestors were Azrikam,
Hashabiah, and Bunni.
16 Next, there were Shabbethai and
Jozabad, who were in charge of the
work outside the temple.
17 Then there was Mattaniah son of
Mica. His ancestors were Zabdi and Asaph. Mattaniah led the temple choir in
the prayer of praise. Bakbukiah, who
also settled in Jerusalem, was his assistant.
Finally, there was Abda son of Shammua; his grandfather was Galal, and his
great-grandfather was Jeduthun.
18 Altogether, two hundred eighty-four
Levites settled in the holy city.

Temple Guards and Others

19 One hundred seventy-two temple
guards settled in Jerusalem; their leaders were Akkub and Talmon.
20 The rest of the Israelites, including
priests and Levites, lived on their own
property in the other towns of Judah.
21 But the temple workers lived in the
section of Jerusalem known as Ophel,
and the two men in charge of them were
Ziha and Gishpa.
22 Uzzi son of Bani was the leader of the
Levites in Jerusalem. His grandfather
was Hashabiah, his great-grandfather
was Mattaniah, and his great-great-
grandfather was Mica. He belonged
to the Asaph clan that was in charge
of the music for the temple services,
23 though the daily choice of music and
musicians was decided by royal decree
of the Persian king.
24 The people of Israel were represented at the Persian court by Pethahiah
son of Meshezabel from the Zerah clan
of the Judah tribe.

[q] **11.1** *asked God to show them*: The Hebrew text has "cast lots." These were made of wood or stone and were thrown on the ground by a priest or official to find out how and when to do something. [r] **11.10** *son of Joiarib and the uncle of Jachin*: See 1 Chronicles 9.10; the Hebrew text has "son of Joiarib, Jachin."

The People in the Other Towns and Villages

[25]Some of the people of Judah lived in the following towns near their farms: Kiriath-Arba, Dibon, Jekabzeel, [26]Jeshua, Moladah, Beth-Pelet, [27]Hazar-Shual, Beersheba, [28]Ziklag, Meconah, [29]Enrimmon, Zorah, Jarmuth, [30]Zanoah, Adullam, Lachish, and Azekah. In fact, they settled the towns from Beersheba in the south to Hinnom Valley in the north.

[31]The people of Benjamin lived in the towns of Geba, Michmash, Aija, Bethel with its nearby villages, [32]Anathoth, Nob, Ananiah, [33]Hazor, Ramah, Gittaim, [34]Hadid, Zeboim, Neballat, [35]Lod, and Ono, as well as in Craft Valley. [36]Several groups of Levites from the territory of Judah were sent to live among the people of Benjamin.

A List of Priests and Levites

12 Many priests and Levites had returned from Babylonia with Zerubbabel[s] and Joshua as their leaders. Those priests were Seraiah, Jeremiah, Ezra, [2]Amariah, Malluch, Hattush, [3]Shecaniah, Rehum, Meremoth, [4]Iddo, Ginnethoi, Abijah, [5]Mijamin, Maadiah, Bilgah, [6]Shemaiah, Joiarib, Jedaiah, [7]Sallu, Amok, Hilkiah, and another Jedaiah. These were the leading priests and their assistants during the time of Joshua.[t]

[8]The Levites who returned were Jeshua, Binnui, Kadmiel, Sherebiah, Judah, and Mattaniah. They and their assistants were responsible for the songs of praise, [9]while Bakbukiah and Unno, together with their assistants, were responsible for the choral responses.

Descendants of Joshua the High Priest

[10]Joshua was the father of Joiakim, the grandfather of Eliashib, and the great-grandfather of Joiada. [11]Joiada was the father of Jonathan and the grandfather of Jaddua.

Leaders of the Priestly Clans

[12]When Joiakim was high priest, the following priests were leaders of their clans: Meraiah of the Seraiah clan, Hananiah of Jeremiah, [13]Meshullam of Ezra, Jehohanan of Amariah, [14]Jonathan of Malluchi, Joseph of Shebaniah, [15]Adna of Harim, Helkai of Meraioth, [16]Zechariah of Iddo, Meshullam of Ginnethon, [17]Zichri of Abijah,[u] Piltai of Moadiah, [18]Shammua of Bilgah, Jehonathan of Shemaiah, [19]Mattenai of Joiarib, Uzzi of Jedaiah, [20]Kallai of Sallai, Eber of Amok, [21]Hashabiah of Hilkiah, and Nethanel of Jedaiah.

The Priestly and Levite Families

[22]During the time of the high priests Eliashib, Joiada, Johanan, and Jaddua, and including the time that Darius was king of Persia, a record was kept of the heads of the Levite and priestly families. [23]However, no official record was kept of the heads of the Levite clans after the death of Johanan,[v] the grandson of Eliashib.

[24]Hashabiah, Sherebiah, Jeshua son of Kadmiel,[w] and their assistants organized two choirs of Levites to offer praises to God, just as King David, the man of God, had commanded.

[25]Mattaniah, Bakbukiah, Obadiah, Meshullam, Talmon, and Akkub were responsible for guarding the storerooms near the temple gates.

[26]All of these men lived during the time of Joiakim[x] and during the time that I was governor and Ezra, a teacher of the Law of Moses, was priest.

Nehemiah Dedicates the City Wall

[27]When the city wall was dedicated, Levites from everywhere in Judah were invited to join in the celebration with songs of praise and with the music of cymbals, small harps, and other stringed instruments. [28-29]The Levite singers lived in villages around Jerusalem, and so they came from there, as well as from the villages around Netophah, Beth-Gilgal, Geba, and Azmaveth. [30]The priests and Levites held special ceremonies to make themselves holy, and then they did the same for the rest of the people and for the gates and walls of the city.

[31]I brought the leaders of Judah to the top of the city wall and put them in charge of the two groups that were to march around on top of the wall, singing praises to God. One group marched to the right in the direction of Garbage Gate. [32]Hoshaiah and half of the leaders followed them. [33]Then came the priests Azariah, Ezra, Meshullam, [34]Judah, Benjamin, Shemaiah, and Jeremiah, [35]all of them blowing trumpets. Next, there was Zechariah of the Asaph clan[y] [36]and his relatives, Shemaiah, Azarel, Milalai, Gilalai, Maai, Nethanel,

[s]**12.1** *Zerubbabel*: Hebrew "Zerubbabel son of Shealtiel." [t]**12.7** *Joshua*: Joshua the high priest and friend of Zerubbabel (see verse 1 and Haggai 1.1; 2.2). [u]**12.17** *of Abijah*: The Hebrew text adds " . . . of Miniamin." [v]**12.23** *death of Johanan*: Probably between 408 and 405 B.C., when Darius II died. [w]**12.24** *son of Kadmiel*: Or possibly "Binnui, Kadmiel" (see 10.9; 12.8). [x]**12.26** *Joiakim*: Hebrew "Joiakim son of Joshua son of Jozadak." [y]**12.35** *Zechariah of the Asaph clan*: Hebrew "Zechariah son of Jonathan son of Shemaiah son of Mattaniah son of Micaiah son of Zaccur son of Asaph."

Judah, and Hanani. They played musical
instruments like those that had been
played by David, the man of God. And
they marched behind Ezra, the teacher
of the Law. 37 When they reached Fountain Gate, they climbed the steps to
David's City and went past his palace,
before stopping at the Water Gate near
the eastern wall of the city.
38 The second group of singers
marched along the wall in the opposite
direction, and I followed them, together
with the other half of the leaders of Judah. We went past Oven Tower, Broad
Wall, 39 Ephraim Gate, Old Gate, Fish
Gate, Hananel Tower, Hundred Tower,
and on to Sheep Gate. Finally, we
stopped at Gate of the Guard, 40 where
we stood in front of the temple with the
other group, praising God. In the group
with me were half of the leaders, 41 as
well as the priests Eliakim, Maaseiah,
Miniamin, Micaiah, Elioenai, Zechariah,
and Hananiah, who were blowing trumpets. 42 Maaseiah, Shemaiah, Eleazar,
Uzzi, Jehohanan, Malchijah, Elam, and
Ezer also stood there, as Jezrahiah led
the singers. 43 God had made the people
very happy, and so on that day they celebrated and offered many sacrifices.
The women and children joined in the
festivities, and joyful shouts could be
heard far from the city of Jerusalem.

Preparation for Worship

44 On that same day, some leaders
were appointed to be responsible for the
safekeeping of gifts for the temple and
to be in charge of receiving the first part
of the harvest and the ten percent of the
crops and livestock that was offered to
God. These same leaders also collected
the part of crops that the Law of Moses
taught was to be given to the Levites.

Everyone was pleased with the work
of the priests and Levites, 45 when they
performed the ceremonies to make people acceptable to worship God. And the
singers and the temple guards did their
jobs according to the instructions given
by David and his son Solomon. 46 In fact,
ever since the days of David and Asaph,
there had been song leaders and songs
of praise and worship. 47 During the time
that Zerubbabel and I were in charge,
everyone in Israel gave what they were
supposed to give for the daily needs of
the singers and temple guards from the
Levi tribe. Then the Levites would give
the priests their share from what they
had received.

Foreigners Are Sent Away

13 On that day when the Law of
Moses was read aloud to everyone, it was discovered that Ammonites
and Moabites were forbidden to belong
to the people of God. 2 This was because
they had refused to give food and water
to Israel and had hired Balaam[z] to call
down a curse on them. However, our
God turned the curse into a blessing.
3 Following the reading of the Law of
Moses, the people of Israel started sending away anyone who had any foreign
ancestors.

Nehemiah Makes Other Changes

4 The priest Eliashib was a relative of
Tobiah and had earlier been put in
charge of the temple storerooms. 5 So he
let Tobiah live in one of these rooms,
where all kinds of things had been
stored—the grain offerings, incense,
utensils for the temple, as well as the
tenth of the grain, wine, and olive oil
that had been given for the use of the
Levites, singers, and temple guards, and
the gifts for the priests.
6 This happened in the thirty-second
year that Artaxerxes[a] ruled Babylonia. I
was away from Jerusalem at the time,
because I was visiting him. Later I received permission from the king 7 to return to Jerusalem. Only then did I find
out that Eliashib had done this terrible
thing of letting Tobiah have a room in
the temple. 8 It upset me so much that I
threw out every bit of Tobiah's furni-
ture. 9 Then I ordered the room to be
cleaned and the temple utensils, the
grain offerings, and the incense to be
brought back into the room.
10 I also found out that the temple
singers and several other Levites had
returned to work on their farms, because they had not been given their
share of the harvest. 11 I called the
leaders together and angrily asked
them, "Why is the temple neglected?"
Then I told them to start doing their
jobs. 12 After this, everyone in Judah
brought a tenth of their grain, wine,
and olive oil to the temple storeroom.
13 Finally, I appointed three men
with good reputations to be in charge
of what was brought there and to
distribute it to the others. They were
Shelemiah the priest, Zadok the teacher
of the Law, and Pedaiah the Levite.
Their assistant was Hanan, the son
of Zaccur and the grandson of Mattaniah.
14 I pray that my God will remember
these good things that I have done for
his temple and for those who worship
there.

The Sabbath

15 I also noticed what the people of Judah were doing on the Sabbath. Not

[z] **13.2** *Balaam*: See Numbers 22.1-6. [a] **13.6** *Artaxerxes*: See the note at 1.1.

only were they trampling grapes to
make wine, but they were harvesting
their grain, grapes, figs, and other crops,
and then loading these on donkeys to
sell in Jerusalem. So I warned them not
to sell food on the Sabbath. 16People
who had moved to Jerusalem from the
city of Tyre were bringing in fish and
other things to sell there on the Sabbath. 17I got angry and said to the leaders of Judah, "This evil you are doing is
an insult to the Sabbath! 18Didn't God
punish us and this city because our ancestors did these very same things?
And here you are, about to make God
furious again by disgracing the Sabbath!"

19I ordered the gates of Jerusalem to
be closed on the eve of the Sabbath[b]
and not to be opened until after the Sabbath had ended. Then I put some of
my own men in charge of the gates
to make certain that nothing was
brought in on the Sabbath. 20Once or
twice some merchants spent the night
outside Jerualem with their goods.
21But I warned them, "If you do this
again, I'll have you arrested." From then
on, they did not come on the Sabbath.
22I ordered the Levites to make themselves holy and to guard the gates on
the Sabbath, so that it would be kept
holy.

God is truly merciful, and I pray that
he will treat me with kindness and bless
me for doing this.

Mixed Marriages

23I discovered that some Jewish men
had married women from Ashdod, Ammon, and Moab. 24About half of their
children could not speak Hebrew—they
spoke only the language of Ashdod or
some other foreign language. 25So in my
anger, I called down curses on those
men. I had them beaten and even pulled
out the hair of some of them. Then I
made them promise:

> In the name of God we solemnly
> promise not to let our sons and
> daughters marry foreigners. 26God
> dearly loved King Solomon of Israel
> and made him the greatest king on
> earth, but Solomon's foreign wives
> led him into sin. 27So we will obey
> you and not rebel against our God
> by marrying foreign women.

28Jehoiada, the son of the high priest
Eliashib, had a son who had married a
daughter of Sanballat from Horon,[c] and
I forced his son to leave.

29I pray that God will punish them for
breaking their priestly vows and disgracing the Levi tribe.

30Then I made sure that the people
were free from every foreign influence,
and I assigned duties for the priests and
Levites. 31I also arranged for the people
to bring firewood to the altar each day
and for them to bring the first part of
their harvest to the temple.

I pray that God will bless me for the
good I have done.

[b] **13.19** *eve of the Sabbath*: The Jewish day began at sunset. [c] **13.28** *Horon*: See the note at 2.10.

ESTHER

ABOUT THIS BOOK

The story of Esther takes place in the city of Susa, in the winter palace of the Persian king. After King Xerxes divorced his queen, he chose a young Jewish woman named Esther as his new queen. She was an orphan but had been adopted and cared for by her cousin, Mordecai, who was given a job as a palace official. Mordecai warned her not to tell anyone that she was a Jew, and she obeyed.

The king's highest official was a man named Haman. He hated the Jews, and he tricked the king into giving permission to have them all killed. The rest of the book tells how Esther risked her own life to save the lives of her people.

Afterward, Mordecai and Esther wrote a letter telling all Jews to celebrate the festival of Purim every year to remember how the nation was saved.

The Hebrew text of the book of Esther doesn't mention God, but the whole plot shows that God was protecting his people by making Esther queen, and as Mordecai put it:

It could be that you were made queen for a time like this! (4.14b)

A QUICK LOOK AT THIS BOOK

Esther Becomes Queen (1.1—2.23)
Haman Plans To Destroy the Jews (3.1-15)
Mordecai Asks for Esther's Help (4.1-17)
Mordecai Is Honored, Not Killed (5.1—6.14)
Haman Is Put To Death (7.1-10)
The Jews Defend Themselves and Kill Their Enemies (8.1—9.19)
The Festival of Purim (9.20-32)
The Greatness of Xerxes and Mordecai (10.1-3)

Queen Vashti Disobeys King Xerxes

1 1-2King Xerxes[a] of Persia lived in his
capital city of Susa[b] and ruled one
hundred twenty-seven provinces from
India to Ethiopia.[c] 3During the third
year of his rule, Xerxes gave a big dinner for all his officials and officers. The
governors and leaders of the provinces
were also invited, and even the commanders of the Persian and Median
armies came. 4For one hundred eighty
days he showed off his wealth and spent
a lot of money to impress his guests
with the greatness of his kingdom.
5King Xerxes soon gave another dinner and invited everyone in the city of
Susa, no matter who they were. The eating and drinking lasted seven days in
the beautiful palace gardens. 6The area
was decorated with blue and white cot-
ton curtains tied back with purple linen
cords that ran through silver rings fastened to marble columns. Couches of
gold and silver rested on pavement that
had all kinds of designs made from
costly bright-colored stones and marble
and mother-of-pearl.
7The guests drank from gold cups,
and each cup had a different design.

[a]**1.1,2** *Xerxes*: The Hebrew text has "Ahasuerus," who was better known as King Xerxes I (485-465 B.C.). [b]**1.1,2** *in his capital city of Susa*: Or "in his royal fortress in the city of Susa." Susa was a city east of Babylon and a winter home for Persian kings. [c]**1.1,2** *Ethiopia*: The Hebrew text has "Cush," which was a region south of Egypt that included parts of the present countries of Ethiopia and Sudan.

The king was generous 8and said to
them, "Drink all you want!" Then he
told his servants, "Keep their cups full."
9While the men were enjoying themselves, Queen Vashti gave the women a
big dinner inside the royal palace.
10By the seventh day, King Xerxes was
feeling happy because of so much wine.
And he asked his seven personal servants, Mehuman, Biztha, Harbona,
Bigtha, Abagtha, Zethar, and Carkas,
11to bring Queen Vashti to him. The king
wanted her to wear her crown and let
his people and his officials see how
beautiful she was. 12The king's servants
told Queen Vashti what he had said, but
she refused to go to him, and this made
him terribly angry.
13-14The king called in the seven highest officials of Persia and Media. They
were Carshena, Shethar, Admatha,
Tarshish, Meres, Marsena, and Memucan. These men were very wise and
understood all the laws and customs of
the country, and the king always asked
them what they thought about such
matters.
15The king said to them, "Queen Vashti
refused to come to me when I sent my
servants for her. What does the law say I
should do about that?"
16Then Memucan told the king and
the officials:

Your Majesty, Queen Vashti has
not only embarrassed you, but she
has insulted your officials and
everyone else in all the provinces.
17The women in the kingdom will
hear about this, and they will refuse
to respect their husbands. They will
say, "If Queen Vashti doesn't obey
her husband, why should we?" 18Be-
fore this day is over, the wives of the
officials of Persia and Media will
find out what Queen Vashti has
done, and they will refuse to obey
their husbands. They won't respect
their husbands, and their husbands
will be angry with them.
19Your Majesty, if you agree, you
should write for the Medes and Persians a law that can never be
changed. This law would keep
Queen Vashti from ever seeing you
again. Then you could let someone
who respects you be queen in her
place.
20When the women in your great
kingdom hear about this new law,
they will respect their husbands, no
matter if they are rich or poor.

21King Xerxes and his officials liked
what Memucan had said, 22and he sent
letters to all of his provinces. Each letter
was written in the language of the
province to which it was sent, and it
said that husbands should have complete control over their wives and children.

Esther Becomes Queen

2 After a while, King Xerxes got over
being angry. But he kept thinking
about what Vashti had done and the law
that he had written because of her.
2Then the king's personal servants said:

Your Majesty, a search must be
made to find you some beautiful
young women. 3You can select officers in every province to bring them
to the place where you keep your
wives in the capital city of Susa. Put
your servant Hegai in charge of
them since that is his job. He can see
to it that they are given the proper
beauty treatments. 4Then let the
young woman who pleases you most
take Vashti's place as queen.

King Xerxes liked these suggestions,
and he followed them.
5At this time a Jew named Mordecai
was living in Susa. His father was Jair,
and his grandfather Shimei was the son
of Kish from the tribe of Benjamin.
6Kish[d] was one of the people that Nebuchadnezzar had taken from Jerusalem,
when he took King Jeconiah of Judah to
Babylonia.
7Mordecai had a very beautiful cousin
named Esther, whose Hebrew name was
Hadassah. He had raised her as his own
daughter, after her father and mother
died. 8When the king ordered the search
for beautiful women, many were taken
to the king's palace in Susa, and Esther
was one of them.
Hegai was put in charge of all the
women, 9and from the first day, Esther
was his favorite. He began her beauty
treatments at once. He also gave her
plenty of food and seven special maids
from the king's palace, and they had the
best rooms.
10Mordecai had warned Esther not to
tell anyone that she was a Jew, and she
obeyed him. 11He was anxious to see
how Esther was getting along and to
learn what had happened to her. So
each day he would walk back and forth
in front of the court where the women
lived.
12The young women were given
beauty treatments for one whole year.
The first six months their skin was
rubbed with olive oil and myrrh, and the
last six months it was treated with per-
fumes and cosmetics. Then each of them
spent the night alone with King Xerxes.
13When a young woman went to the
king, she could wear whatever clothes
or jewelry she chose from the women's
living quarters. 14In the evening she

[d]2.6 *Kish*: Or "Mordecai." The Hebrew text has "He."

would go to the king, and the following
morning she would go to the place
where his wives stayed after being with
him. There a man named Shaashgaz
was in charge of the king's wives.[e] Only
the ones the king wanted and asked for
by name could go back to the king.
15-16 Xerxes had been king for seven
years when Esther's turn came to go to
him during Tebeth,[f] the tenth month of
the year. Everyone liked Esther. The
king's personal servant Hegai was in
charge of the women, and Esther
trusted Hegai and asked him what she
ought to take with her.[g]
17 Xerxes liked Esther more than he
did any of the other young women.
None of them pleased him as much as
she did, and right away he fell in love
with her and crowned her queen in
place of Vashti. 18 In honor of Esther he
gave a big dinner for his leaders and officials. Then he declared a holiday
everywhere in his kingdom and gave expensive gifts.

Mordecai Saves the King's Life

19 When the young women were
brought together again, Esther's cousin
Mordecai had become a palace official.
20 He had told Esther never to tell anyone that she was a Jew, and she obeyed
him, just as she had always done.
21 Bigthana and Teresh were the two
men who guarded King Xerxes' rooms,
but they got angry with the king and decided to kill him. 22 Mordecai found out
about their plans and asked Queen Esther to tell the king what he had found
out. 23 King Xerxes learned that Mordecai's report was true, and he had the
two men hanged. Then the king had all
of this written down in his record book
as he watched.

Haman Plans To Destroy the Jews

3 Later, King Xerxes promoted
Haman the son of Hammedatha to
the highest position in his kingdom.
Haman was a descendant of Agag,[h]
2 and the king had given orders for his
officials at the royal gate to honor
Haman by kneeling down to him. All of
them obeyed except Mordecai. 3 When
the other officials asked Mordecai why
he disobeyed the king's command, 4 he
said, "Because I am a Jew." They spoke
to him for several days about kneeling
down, but he still refused to obey. Finally, they reported this to Haman, to
find out if he would let Mordecai get
away with it.
5 Haman was furious to learn that
Mordecai refused to kneel down and
honor him. 6 And when he found out that
Mordecai was a Jew, he knew that
killing only Mordecai was not enough.
Every Jew in the whole kingdom had to
be killed.
7 It was now the twelfth year of the
rule of King Xerxes. During Nisan,[i] the
first month of the year, Haman said,
"Find out the best time for me to do
this."[j] The time chosen was Adar,[k] the
twelfth month.
8 Then Haman went to the king and
said:

> Your Majesty, there are some peo-
> ple who live all over your kingdom
> and won't have a thing to do with
> anyone else. They have customs that
> are different from everyone else's,
> and they refuse to obey your laws.
> We would be better off to get rid of
> them! 9 Why not give orders for all of
> them to be killed? I can promise that
> you will get tons of silver for your
> treasury.

10 The king handed his official ring to
Haman, who hated the Jews, and the
king told him, 11 "Do what you want with
those people! You can keep their
money."
12 On the thirteenth day of Nisan,
Haman called in the king's secretaries
and ordered them to write letters in
every language used in the kingdom.
The letters were written in the name of
the king and sealed by using the king's
own ring.[l] At once they were sent to the
king's highest officials, the governors of
each province, and the leaders of the
different nations in the kingdom of
Xerxes.
13 The letters were taken by messengers to every part of the kingdom, and
this is what was said in the letters:

> On the thirteenth day of Adar, the
> twelfth month, all Jewish men,
> women, and children are to be
> killed. And their property is to be
> taken.

[e] **2.14** *wives*: This translates a Hebrew word for women who were legally bound to a man, but without the full privileges of a wife. [f] **2.15,16** *Tebeth*: The tenth month of the Hebrew calendar, from about mid-December to mid-January. [g] **2.15,16** *her*: The Hebrew text adds, "Esther was the daughter of Abihail and was the cousin of Mordecai, who had adopted her after her parents died" (see verse 7). [h] **3.1** *Agag*: Agag was a king who had fought against the Jews long before the time of Esther (see 1 Samuel 15.1-33). [i] **3.7** *Nisan*: The first month of the Hebrew calendar, from about mid-March to mid-April. [j] **3.7** *Find out . . . do this*: The Hebrew text has "cast lots," which were pieces of wood or stone used to find out how and when to do something. For "lots" the Hebrew text uses the Babylonian word "purim." [k] **3.7** *Adar*: The twelfth month of the Hebrew calendar, from about mid-February to mid-March.
[l] **3.12** *king's own ring*: Melted wax was used to seal a letter, and while the wax was still soft, the king's ring was pressed in the wax to show that the letter was official.

14-15 King Xerxes gave orders for these
letters to be posted where they could be
seen by everyone all over the kingdom.
The king's command was obeyed, and
one of the letters was read aloud to the
people in the walled city of Susa. Then
the king and Haman sat down to drink
together, but no one in the city[m] could
figure out what was going on.

Mordecai Asks for Esther's Help

4 When Mordecai heard about the letter, he tore his clothes in sorrow and
put on sackcloth. Then he covered his
head with ashes and went through the
city, crying and weeping. 2 But he could
go only as far as the palace gate, because no one wearing sackcloth was allowed inside the palace. 3 In every
province where the king's orders were
read, the Jews cried and mourned, and
they went without eating.[n] Many of
them even put on sackcloth and sat in
ashes.
4 When Esther's servant girls and her
other servants told her what Mordecai
was doing, she became very upset and
sent Mordecai some clothes to wear in
place of the sackcloth. But he refused to
take them.
5 Esther had a servant named Hathach, who had been given to her by
the king. So she called him in and said,
"Find out what's wrong with Mordecai
and why he's acting this way."
6 Hathach went to Mordecai in the city
square in front of the palace gate, 7 and
Mordecai told him everything that had
happened. He also told him how much
money Haman had promised to add to
the king's treasury, if all the Jews were
killed.
8 Mordecai gave Hathach a copy of the
orders for the murder of the Jews and
told him that these had been read in
Susa. He said, "Show this to Esther and
explain what it means. Ask her to go to
the king and beg him to have pity on
her people, the Jews!"
9 Hathach went back to Esther and
told her what Mordecai had said. 10 She
answered, "Tell Mordecai 11 there is a
law about going in to see the king, and
all his officials and his people know
about this law. Anyone who goes in to
see the king without being invited by
him will be put to death. The only way
that anyone can be saved is for the king
to hold out the gold scepter to that person. And it's been thirty days since he
has asked for me."
12 When Mordecai was told what Esther had said, 13 he sent back this reply,
"Don't think that you will escape being
killed with the rest of the Jews, just because you live in the king's palace. 14 If
you don't speak up now, we will somehow get help, but you and your family
will be killed. It could be that you were
made queen for a time like this!"
15 Esther sent a message to Mordecai,
saying, 16 "Bring together all the Jews in
Susa and tell them to go without eating
for my sake! Don't eat or drink for three
days and nights. My servant girls and I
will do the same. Then I will go in to see
the king, even if it means I must die."
17 Mordecai did everything Esther told
him to do.

Esther Invites the King and Haman to a Dinner

5 Three days later, Esther dressed in
her royal robes and went to the inner court of the palace in front of the
throne. The king was sitting there, facing the open doorway. 2 He was happy to
see Esther, and he held out the gold
scepter to her.
When Esther came up and touched
the tip of the scepter, 3 the king said, "Esther, what brings you here? Just ask,
and I will give you as much as half of
my kingdom."
4 Esther answered, "Your Majesty,
please come with Haman to a dinner I
will prepare for you later today."
5 The king said to his servants, "Hurry
and get Haman, so we can accept Esther's invitation."
The king and Haman went to Esther's
dinner, 6 and while they were drinking
wine, the king asked her, "What can I do
for you? Just ask, and I will give you as
much as half of my kingdom."
7-8 Esther replied, "Your Majesty, if you
really care for me and are willing to do
what I want, please come again tomorrow with Haman to the dinner I will
prepare for you. At that time I will answer Your Majesty's question."

Haman Plans To Kill Mordecai

9 Haman was feeling great as he left.
But when he saw Mordecai at the palace
gate, he noticed that Mordecai did not
stand up or show him any respect. This
made Haman really angry, 10 but he did
not say a thing.
When Haman got home, he called together his friends and his wife Zeresh
11 and started bragging about his great
wealth and all his sons. He told them
the many ways that the king had honored him and how all the other officials
and leaders had to respect him. 12 Haman added, "That's not all! Besides the
king himself, I'm the only person Queen

[m] **3.14,15** *walled city . . . city*: Or "royal fortress . . . rest of the city." [n] **4.3** *went without eating*: The Israelites would sometimes go without eating (also called "fasting") in times of great sorrow or danger.

Esther invited for dinner. She has also
invited the king and me to dinner tomorrow. 13But none of this makes me
happy, as long as I see that Jew Mordecai sitting at the palace gate."
14Haman's wife and friends said to
him, "Have a tower built about seventy-
five feet high, and tomorrow morning
ask the king to hang Mordecai there.
Then later, you can have dinner with the
king and enjoy yourself."
This seemed like a good idea to
Haman, and he had the tower built.

The King Honors Mordecai

6 That night the king could not sleep,
and he had a servant read him the
records of what had happened since he
had been king. 2When the servant read
how Mordecai had kept Bigthana and
Teresh from killing the king, 3the king
asked, "What has been done to reward
Mordecai for this?"
"Nothing, Your Majesty!" the king's
servants replied.
4About this time, Haman came in to
ask the king to have Mordecai hanged
on the tower he had built. The king saw
him and asked, "Who is that man waiting in front of the throne room?"
5The king's servants answered, "Your
Majesty, it is Haman."
"Have him come in," the king commanded.
6When Haman entered the room, the
king asked him, "What should I do for a
man I want to honor?"
Haman was sure that he was the one
the king wanted to honor. 7So he
replied, "Your Majesty, if you wish to
honor a man, 8have someone bring him
one of your own robes and one of your
own horses with a fancy headdress.
9Have one of your highest officials place
your robe on this man and lead him
through the streets on your horse, while
someone shouts, 'This is how the king
honors a man!' "
10The king replied, "Hurry and do just
what you have said! Don't forget a
thing. Get the robe and the horse for
Mordecai the Jew, who is on duty at the
palace gate!"
11Haman got the king's robe and put it
on Mordecai. He led him through the
city on the horse and shouted as he
went, "This is how the king honors a
man!"
12Afterwards, Mordecai returned to
his duties at the palace gate, and Haman
hurried home, hiding his face in shame.
13Haman told his wife and friends what
had happened. Then his wife and his advisors said, "If Mordecai is a Jew, this is
just the beginning of your troubles! You
will end up a ruined man." 14They were
still talking, when the king's servants
came and quickly took Haman to the
dinner that Esther had prepared.

Haman Is Punished

7 The king and Haman were dining
with Esther 2and drinking wine during the second dinner, when the king
again said, "Esther, what can I do for
you? Just ask, and I will give you as
much as half of my kingdom!"
3Esther answered, "Your Majesty, if
you really care for me and are willing to
help, you can save me and my people.
That's what I really want, 4because a reward has been promised to anyone who
kills my people. Your Majesty, if we were
merely going to be sold as slaves, I
would not have bothered you."[o]
5"Who would dare to do such a
thing?" the king asked.
6Esther replied, "That evil Haman is
the one out to get us!"
Haman was terrified, as he looked at
the king and the queen.
7The king was so angry that he got up,
left his wine, and went out into the
palace garden.
Haman realized that the king had already decided what to do with him, and
he stayed and begged Esther to save his
life.
8Just as the king came back into the
room, Haman got down on his knees beside Esther, who was lying on the couch.
The king shouted, "Now you're even trying to rape my queen here in my own
palace!"
As soon as the king said this, his servants covered Haman's head. 9Then
Harbona, one of the king's personal servants, said, "Your Majesty, Haman built
a tower seventy-five feet high beside his
house, so he could hang Mordecai on it.
And Mordecai is the very one who
spoke up and saved your life."
"Hang Haman from his own tower!"
the king commanded. 10Right away,
Haman was hanged on the tower he had
built to hang Mordecai, and the king
calmed down.

A Happy Ending for the Jews

8 Before the end of the day, King
Xerxes gave Esther everything that
had belonged to Haman, the enemy of
the Jews. Esther told the king that
Mordecai was her cousin. So the king
made Mordecai one of his highest officials 2and gave him the royal ring that
Haman had worn. Then Esther put
Mordecai in charge of Haman's property.
3Once again Esther went to speak to
the king. This time she fell down at his
feet, crying and begging, "Please stop

[o]**7.4** *I would . . . bothered you*: One possible meaning for the difficult Hebrew text.

Haman's evil plan to have the Jews
killed!" 4King Xerxes held out the
golden scepter to Esther, 5and she got
up and said, "Your Majesty, I know that
you will do the right thing and that you
really love me. Please stop what Haman
has planned. He has already sent letters
demanding that the Jews in all your
provinces be killed, 6and I can't bear to
see my people and my own relatives destroyed."
7King Xerxes then said to Esther and
Mordecai, "I have already ordered
Haman to be hanged and his house
given to Esther, because of his evil plans
to kill the Jews. 8I now give you permission to make a law that will save the
lives of your people. You may use my
ring to seal the law, so that it can never
be changed."
9On the twenty-third day of Sivan,[p]
the third month, the king's secretaries
wrote the law. They obeyed Mordecai
and wrote to the Jews, the rulers, the
governors, and the officials of all one
hundred twenty-seven provinces from
India to Ethiopia.[q] The letters were written in every language used in the kingdom, including the Jewish language.
10They were written in the name of
King Xerxes and sealed with his ring.
Then they were taken by messengers
who rode the king's finest and fastest
horses.
11-13In these letters the king said:

> On the thirteenth day of Adar,[r] the
> twelfth month, the Jews in every city
> and province will be allowed to get
> together and defend themselves.
> They may destroy any army that at-
> tacks them, and they may kill all of
> their enemies, including women and
> children. They may also take every-
> thing that belongs to their enemies.

A copy of this law is to be posted in
every province and read by everyone.
14-15Then the king ordered his messengers to take their fastest horses and deliver the law as quickly as possible to
every province. When Mordecai left, he
was wearing clothes fit for a king. He
wore blue and white robes, a large gold
crown, and a cape made of fine linen
and purple cloth.
After the law was announced in Susa,
everyone shouted and cheered, 16and
the Jews were no longer afraid. In fact,
they were very happy and felt that they
had won a victory.
17In every province and city where the
law was sent, the Jews had parties and
celebrated. Many of the people in the
provinces accepted the Jewish religion,
because they were now afraid of the
Jews.

The Jews Destroy Their Enemies

9 The first law that the king had made
was to be followed on the thirteenth
day of Adar,[r] the twelfth month. This
was the very day that the enemies of
the Jews had hoped to do away with
them. But the Jews turned things
around, 2and in the cities of every
province they came together to attack
their enemies. Everyone was afraid of
the Jews, and no one could do anything
to oppose them.
3The leaders of the provinces, the
rulers, the governors, and the court officials were afraid of Mordecai and took
sides with the Jews. 4Everyone in the
provinces knew that the king had promoted him and had given him a lot of
power.
5The Jews took their swords and did
away with their enemies, without showing any mercy. 6-10They killed five hundred people in Susa,[s] but they did not
take anything that belonged to the ones
they killed. Haman had been one of the
worst enemies of the Jews, and ten of
his sons were among those who were
killed. Their names were Parshandatha,
Dalphon, Aspatha, Poratha, Adalia, Ari-
datha, Parmashta, Arisai, Aridai, and
Vaizatha.
11Later that day, someone told the
king how many people had been killed
in Susa.[s] 12Then he told Esther, "Five
hundred people, including Haman's ten
sons, have been killed in Susa alone. If
that many were killed here, what must
have happened in the provinces? Is
there anything else you want done? Just
tell me, and it will be done."
13Esther answered, "Your Majesty,
please let the Jews in Susa fight to defend themselves tomorrow, just as they
did today. And order the bodies of
Haman's ten sons to be hanged in public."
14King Xerxes did what Esther had re-
quested, and the bodies of Haman's
sons were hung in Susa. 15Then on the
fourteenth day of Adar the Jews of the
city got together and killed three hundred more people. But they still did not
take anything that belonged to their enemies.
16-17On the thirteenth day of Adar, the
Jews in the provinces had come together to defend themselves. They killed
seventy-five thousand of their enemies,
but the Jews did not take anything that
belonged to the ones they killed. Then

[p]**8.9** *Sivan*: The third month of the Hebrew calendar, from about mid-May to mid-June.
[q]**8.9** *Ethiopia*: See the note at 1.1, 2. [r]**8.11-13** *Adar*: See the note at 3.7. [r]**9.1** *Adar*: See the note at 3.7. [s]**9.6-10** *in Susa*: Or "in the royal fortress in Susa." [s]**9.11** *in Susa*: Or "in the royal fortress in Susa."

on the fourteenth day of the month the Jews celebrated with a feast.

[18]On the fifteenth day of the month the Jews in Susa held a holiday and celebrated, after killing their enemies on the thirteenth and the fourteenth. [19]This is why the Jews in the villages now celebrate on the fourteenth day of the month. It is a joyful holiday that they celebrate by feasting and sending gifts of food to each other.

The Festival of Purim

[20]Mordecai wrote down everything that had happened. Then he sent letters to the Jews everywhere in the provinces [21]and told them:

> Each year you must celebrate on both the fourteenth and the fifteenth of Adar, [22]the days when we Jews defeated our enemies. Remember this month as a time when our sorrow was turned to joy, and celebration took the place of crying. Celebrate by having parties and by giving to the poor and by sharing gifts of food with each other.

[23]They followed Mordecai's instructions and set aside these two days every year as a time of celebration.

The Reason for the Festival of Purim

[24]Haman was the son of Hammedatha and a descendant of Agag. He hated the Jews so much that he planned to destroy them, but he wanted to find out the best time to do it. So he cast lots.[t]

[25]Esther went to King Xerxes and asked him to save her people. Then the king gave written orders for Haman and his sons to be punished in the same terrible way that Haman had in mind for the Jews. So they were hanged. [26]Mordecai's letter had said that the Jews must celebrate for two days because of what had happened to them. This time of celebration is called Purim,[u] which is the Hebrew word for the lots that were cast. [27]Now every year the Jews set aside these two days for having parties and celebrating, just as they were told to do. [28]From now on, all Jewish families must remember to celebrate Purim on these two days each year.

[29]Queen Esther, daughter of Abihail, wanted to give full authority to Mordecai's letter about the Festival of Purim, and with his help she wrote a letter about the feast. [30]Copies of this letter were sent to Jews in the one hundred twenty-seven provinces of King Xerxes. In the letter they said:

> We pray that all of you will live in peace and safety.
>
> [31]You and your descendants must always remember to celebrate Purim at the time and in the way that we have said. You must also follow the instructions that we have given you about mourning and going without eating.[v]
>
> [32]These laws about Purim are written by the authority of Queen Esther.

The Greatness of Xerxes and Mordecai

10 King Xerxes made everyone in his kingdom pay taxes, even those in lands across the sea. [2]All the great and famous things that King Xerxes did are written in the record books of the kings of Media and Persia. These records also tell about the honors that the king gave to Mordecai. [3]Next to the king himself, Mordecai was the highest official in the kingdom. He was a popular leader of the Jews, because he helped them in many ways and would even speak to the king for them.

[t]**9.24** *cast lots*: See the note at 3.7. [u]**9.26** *Purim*: The Jewish festival of Purim got its name from "purim," which is the Babylonian name for the lots that Haman used. Purim is celebrated each year on the 14th and 15th of Adar, which is about the first of March. [v]**9.31** *going without eating*: See the note at 4.3.

JOB

ABOUT THIS BOOK

Job was a very rich man, and although he did not belong to the people of Israel, he worshiped the Lord and was a truly good person. But Satan talked to God and accused Job of serving God only because God was blessing him. God agreed to let Satan take away Job's wealth, his children, and finally, his health, to see whether Job would stay faithful to God. Job did remain faithful.

Then three of Job's friends came to comfort him. They believed that health and prosperity were signs of God's blessing. And because Job had lost both his health and his prosperity, the three friends insisted that God must be punishing Job for some sin. Job answered that he was innocent, and this meant that they were wrong. Job and the friends argued back and forth, with neither side really proving the other wrong, although at the end of the argument, the friends gave up.

Job was suffering deeply, and several times during the argument he asked God to appear and explain the reason for his suffering. Then, after the friends stopped speaking, Job decided that human beings cannot find the kind of wisdom that gives answers to the deep questions of life. Only God has that wisdom. Job ended his speeches by swearing that he was innocent of doing wrong.

At this point, a young bystander named Elihu began talking. He repeated some of what had already been said, but he also criticized both sides of the argument. Elihu finished with a poem praising God's care for nature.

God finally did appear to Job, but he did not explain Job's suffering. Instead, God showed that the many things he does cannot be understood by humans; humans cannot do what God does. God criticized Job for talking so much when he knew so little, but he also said that Job had remained his faithful servant. And so, at the very end, the book tells how God blessed Job and made him twice as wealthy as he had been before.

Job never did understand why he had suffered; he felt bitter, but he never rejected God or turned away from him. Job was convinced that someday, God would rescue him:

I know that my Savior lives,
and at the end
he will stand on this earth.
My flesh may be destroyed,
yet from this body
I will see God.
Yes, I will see him for myself,
and I long for that moment.
(19.25-27)

A QUICK LOOK AT THIS BOOK

Job Loses His Wealth, Family, and Health (1.10—2.13)
Job Curses the Day of His Birth (3.1-26)
The First Round of the Debate (4.1—14.22)
The Second Round of the Debate (15.1—21.34)
The Third Round of the Debate (22.1—26.14)
Job's Closing Statements (27.1—30.31)
Job Swears that He Is Innocent (31.1-40)
Elihu's Speeches (32.1—37.24)
God's First Speech (38.1—39.30)

God's Second Speech and Job's Responses (40.1—42.6)
The Lord Again Blesses Job with Health, Wealth, and Family (42.7-17)

Job and His Family

1 Many years ago, a man named Job lived in the land of Uz.[a] He was a truly good person, who respected God and refused to do evil.

2 Job had seven sons and three daughters. 3 He owned seven thousand sheep, three thousand camels, five hundred pair of oxen, five hundred donkeys, and a large number of servants. He was the richest person in the East.

4 Job's sons took turns having feasts in their homes, and they always invited their three sisters to join in the eating and drinking. 5 After each feast, Job would send for his children and perform a ceremony, as a way of asking God to forgive them of any wrongs they may have done. He would get up early the next morning and offer a sacrifice for each of them, just in case they had sinned or silently cursed God.

Angels, the LORD, and Satan

6 One day, when the angels[b] had gathered around the LORD, and Satan[c] was there with them, 7 the LORD asked, "Satan, where have you been?"

Satan replied, "I have been going all over the earth."

8 Then the LORD asked, "What do you think of my servant Job? No one on earth is like him—he is a truly good person, who respects me and refuses to do evil."

9 "Why shouldn't he respect you?" Satan remarked. 10 "You are like a wall protecting not only him, but his entire family and all his property. You make him successful in whatever he does, and his flocks and herds are everywhere. 11 Try taking away everything he owns, and he will curse you to your face."

12 The LORD replied, "All right, Satan, do what you want with anything that belongs to him, but don't harm Job."

Then Satan left.

Job Loses Everything

13 Job's sons and daughters were having a feast in the home of his oldest son, 14 when someone rushed up to Job and said, "While your servants were plowing with your oxen, and your donkeys were nearby eating grass, 15 a gang of Sabeans[d] attacked and stole the oxen and donkeys! Your other servants were killed, and I was the only one who escaped to tell you."

16 That servant was still speaking, when a second one came running up and saying, "God sent down a fire that killed your sheep and your servants. I am the only one who escaped to tell you."

17 Before that servant finished speaking, a third one raced up and said, "Three gangs of Chaldeans[e] attacked and stole your camels! All of your other servants were killed, and I am the only one who escaped to tell you."

18 That servant was still speaking, when a fourth one dashed up and said, "Your children were having a feast and drinking wine at the home of your oldest son, 19 when suddenly a windstorm from the desert blew the house down, crushing all of your children. I am the only one who escaped to tell you."

20 When Job heard this, he tore his clothes and shaved his head because of his great sorrow. He knelt on the ground, then worshiped God 21 and said:

"We bring nothing at birth;
we take nothing
 with us at death.
The LORD alone gives and takes.
Praise the name of the LORD!"

22 In spite of everything, Job did not sin or accuse God of doing wrong.

Job Loses His Health

2 When the angels[f] gathered around the LORD again, Satan[g] was there with them, 2 and the LORD asked, "Satan, where have you been?"

Satan replied, "I have been going all over the earth."

3 Then the LORD asked, "What do you think of my servant Job? No one on earth is like him—he is a truly good person, who respects me and refuses to do evil. And he hasn't changed, even though you persuaded me to destroy him for no reason."

[a] **1.1** *Uz*: The exact location of this place is unknown, though it was possibly somewhere in northwest Arabia. [b] **1.6** *angels*: See the note at 15.8. [c] **1.6** *Satan*: Hebrew "the accuser." [d] **1.15** *Sabeans*: Perhaps the people of Sheba in what is now southwest Arabia (see Isaiah 60.6). [e] **1.17** *Chaldeans*: People from the region of Babylonia, northeast of Palestine. [f] **2.1** *angels*: See the note at 15.8. [g] **2.1** *Satan*: See the note at 1.6.

4Satan answered, "There's no pain
like your own.[h] People will do anything
to stay alive. 5Try striking Job's own
body with pain, and he will curse you to
your face."
6"All right!" the LORD replied. "Make
Job suffer as much as you want, but just
don't kill him." 7Satan left and caused
painful sores to break out all over Job's
body—from head to toe.
8Then Job sat on the ash-heap to show
his sorrow. And while he was scraping
his sores with a broken piece of pottery,
9his wife asked, "Why do you still trust
God? Why don't you curse him and
die?"
10Job replied, "Don't talk like a fool! If
we accept blessings from God, we must
accept trouble as well." In all that happened, Job never once said anything
against God.

Job's Three Friends

11Eliphaz from Teman, Bildad from
Shuah, and Zophar from Naamah[i] were
three of Job's friends, and they heard
about his troubles. So they agreed to
visit Job and comfort him. 12When they
came near enough to see Job, they could
hardly recognize him. And in their great
sorrow, they tore their clothes, then
sprinkled dust on their heads and cried
bitterly. 13For seven days and nights,
they sat silently on the ground beside
him, because they realized what terrible
pain he was in.

Job's First Speech

Blot Out the Day of My Birth

3 Finally, Job cursed the day
of his birth
2 by saying to God:
3 Blot out the day of my birth
and the night when my parents
created a son.
4 Forget about that day,
cover it with darkness,
5 and send thick, gloomy shadows
to fill it with dread.
6 Erase that night from the calendar
and conceal it with darkness.
7 Don't let children be created
or joyful shouts be heard
ever again in that night.
8 Let those with magic powers[j]
place a curse on that day.
9 Darken its morning stars
and remove all hope of light,
10 because it let me be born
into a world of trouble.

Why Didn't I Die at Birth?

11 Why didn't I die at birth?
12 Why was I accepted[k]
and allowed to nurse
at my mother's breast?
13 Now I would be at peace
in the silent world below
14 with kings and their advisors
whose palaces lie in ruins,
15 and with rulers once rich
with silver and gold.
16 I wish I had been born dead
and then buried, never to see
the light of day.
17 In the world of the dead,
the wicked and the weary rest
without a worry.
*18 Everyone is there—
19 where captives and slaves
are free at last.

Why Does God Let Me Live?

20 Why does God let me live
when life is miserable
and so bitter?
21 I keep longing for death
more than I would seek
a valuable treasure.
22 Nothing could make me happier
than to be in the grave.
23 Why do I go on living
when God has me surrounded,
and I can't see the road?
24 Moaning and groaning
are my food and drink,
25 and my worst fears
have all come true.
26 I have no peace or rest—
only troubles and worries.

Eliphaz's First Speech

Please Be Patient and Listen

4 Eliphaz from Teman[l] said:
2 Please be patient and listen
to what I have to say.
*3 Remember how your words
4 have guided and encouraged
many in need.

[h]2.4 *There's no pain like your own*: The Hebrew text has "Skin for skin," which was probably a popular saying. [i]2.11 *Teman . . . Shuah . . . Naamah*: Teman was a place in northern Edom; Shuah may have been a town on the Euphrates River or else further south, near the towns of Dedan and Sheba; Naamah may have been located on the road between Beirut and Damascus, though its exact location is unknown. [j]3.8 *those with magic powers*: The Hebrew text has "those who can place a curse on the day and rouse up Leviathan," which was some kind of sea monster. God's victory over this monster sometimes stood for God's power over all creation and sometimes for his defeat of his enemies (see Isaiah 27.1). In Job 41.1, Leviathan is either a sea monster or a crocodile with almost supernatural powers. [k]3.12 *Why was I accepted*: The Hebrew text has "Why were there knees to receive me," which may refer either to Job's mother or to his father, who would have placed Job on his knees to show that he had accepted him as his child. [l]4.1 *Teman*: See the note at 2.11.

5 But now you feel discouraged
when struck by trouble.
6 You respect God and live right,
so don't lose hope!
7 No truly innocent person
has ever died young.
8 In my experience, only those
who plant seeds of evil
harvest trouble,
9 and then they are swept away
by the angry breath of God.
10 They may roar and growl
like powerful lions.
But when God breaks their teeth,
11 they starve, and their children
are scattered.

A Secret Was Told to Me

12 A secret was told to me
in a faint whisper—
13 I was overcome by sleep,
but disturbed by dreams;
14 I trembled with fear,
15 and my hair stood on end,
as a wind blew past my face.
16 It stopped and stood still.
Then a form appeared—
a shapeless form.
And from the silence,
I heard a voice say,
17 "No humans are innocent
in the eyes of God
their Creator.
18 He finds fault with his servants
and even with his angels.
19 Humans are formed from clay
and are fragile as moths,
so what chance do you have?
20 Born after daybreak,
you die before nightfall
and disappear forever.
21 Your tent pegs are pulled up,
and you leave this life,
having gained no wisdom."

Eliphaz Continues

Call Out for Help

5 Job, call out for help
and see if an angel comes!

2 Envy and jealousy
will kill a stupid fool.
3 I have seen fools take root.
But God sends a curse,
suddenly uprooting them
4 and leaving their children
helpless in court.
5 Then hungry and greedy people
gobble down their crops
and grab up their wealth.[m]
6 Our suffering isn't caused
by the failure of crops;
7 it's all part of life,
like sparks shooting skyward.

8 Job, if I were you,
I would ask God for help.
9 His miracles are marvelous,
more than we can count.
10 God sends showers on earth
and waters the fields.
11 He protects the sorrowful
and lifts up those
who have been disgraced.
*12 God swiftly traps the wicked
13 in their own evil schemes,
and their wisdom fails.
14 Darkness is their only companion,
hiding their path at noon.
15 God rescues the needy
from the words of the wicked
and the fist of the mighty.
16 The poor are filled with hope,
and injustice is silenced.

Consider Yourself Fortunate

17 Consider yourself fortunate
if God All-Powerful
chooses to correct you.
18 He may cause injury and pain,
but he will bandage and heal
your cuts and bruises.
19 God will protect you from harm,
no matter how often
trouble may strike.

20 In times of war and famine,
God will keep you safe.
21 You will be sheltered,
without fear of hurtful words
or any other weapon.
22 You will laugh at the threat
of destruction and famine.
And you won't be afraid
of wild animals—
23 they will no longer be fierce,
and your rocky fields
will become friendly.
24 Your home will be secure,
and your sheep will be safe.
25 You will have more descendants
than there are blades of grass
on the face of the earth.
26 You will live a long life,
and your body will be strong
until the day you die.
27 Our experience has proven
these things to be true,
so listen and learn.

Job's Reply to Eliphaz

It's Impossible

6 Job said:
2 It's impossible to weigh
my misery and grief!
3 They outweigh the sand
along the beach,
and that's why I have spoken
without thinking first.

[m] 5.5 *wealth*: One possible meaning for the difficult Hebrew text of verse 5.

4 The fearsome arrows
of God All-Powerful
have filled my soul
with their poison.
5 Do oxen and wild donkeys
cry out in distress
unless they are hungry?
6 What is food without salt?
What is more tasteless
than the white of an egg?[n]
7 That's how my food tastes,
and my appetite is gone.

*8 How I wish that God
would answer my prayer
9 and do away with me.
10 Then I would be comforted,
knowing that in all of my pain
I have never disobeyed God.
11 Why should I patiently hope
when my strength is gone?
12 I am not strong as stone
or bronze,
13 and I have finally reached
the end of my rope.

My Friends, I Am Desperate

14 My friends, I am desperate,
and you should help me,
even if I no longer respect
God All-Powerful.[o]
*15 But you are treacherous
16 as streams that swell
with melting snow,
17 then suddenly disappear
in the summer heat.
18 I am like a caravan,
lost in the desert
while searching for water.
19 Caravans from Tema and Sheba[p]
20 thought they would find water.
But they were disappointed,
21 just as I am with you.[q]
Only one look at my suffering,
and you run away scared.

What Have I Done Wrong?

22 Have I ever asked any of you
to give me a gift
23 or to purchase my freedom
from brutal enemies?
24 What have I done wrong?
Show me,
and I will keep quiet.
25 The truth is always painful,
but your arguments
prove nothing.
26 Here I am desperate,
and you consider my words
as worthless as wind.
27 Why, you would sell an orphan
or your own neighbor!
28 Look me straight in the eye;
I won't lie to you.
29 Stop accusing me falsely;
my reputation is at stake.
30 I know right from wrong,
and I am not telling lies.

Job Continues

Why Is Life So Hard?

7 Why is life so hard?
Why do we suffer?
2 We are slaves in search of shade;
we are laborers longing
for our wages.
3 God has made my days drag on
and my nights miserable.
4 I pray for night to end,
but it stretches out
while I toss and turn.
5 My parched skin is covered
with worms, dirt, and sores,
6 and my days are running out
quicker than the thread
of a fast-moving needle.

Don't Forget!

7 I beg you, God, don't forget!
My life is just a breath,
and trouble lies ahead.
8 I will vanish from sight,
and no one, including you,
will ever see me again.
9 I will disappear in the grave
or vanish from sight
like a passing cloud.
10 Never will I return home;
soon I will be forgotten.

11 And so, I cry out to you
in agony and distress.
12 Am I the sea or a sea monster?
Is that why you imprison me?[r]
13 I go to bed, hoping for rest,
14 but you torture me
with terrible dreams.
*15 I'd rather choke to death
than live in this body.
16 Leave me alone and let me die;
my life has no meaning.
17 What makes you so concerned
about us humans?
18 Why do you test us
from sunrise to sunset?
19 Won't you look away

[n]**6.6** *What is more tasteless . . . egg*: One possible meaning for the difficult Hebrew text. [o]**6.14** *and you should help me . . . God All-Powerful*: Or "and if you don't help me, you no longer respect God All-Powerful." [p]**6.19** *Tema and Sheba*: Tema was a region in northwest Arabia, and Sheba was probably a region in southwest Arabia. [q]**6.21** *just . . . you*: One possible meaning for the difficult Hebrew text. [r]**7.12** *sea monster . . . imprison me*: "Sea monster" translates the Hebrew word "Tannin," which was possibly a sea monster similar to Leviathan (3.8), Rahab (9.13), and Behemoth (40.15). According to 38.8-11, God makes the sea his prisoner by setting its boundaries.

just long enough
for me to swallow?
20 Why do you watch us so closely?
What's it to you, if I sin?
Why am I your target
and such a heavy burden?
21 Why do you refuse to forgive?
Soon you won't find me,
because I'll be dead.

Bildad's First Speech

How Long Will You Talk?

8 Bildad from Shuah[s] said:
2 How long will you talk
and keep saying nothing?
3 Does God All-Powerful
stand in the way of justice?
4 He made your children pay
for their sins.
5 So why don't you turn to him
6 and start living right?
Then he will decide
to rescue and restore you
to your place of honor.
7 Your future will be brighter
by far than your past.

Our Ancestors Were Wise

8 Our ancestors were wise,
so learn from them.
9 Our own time has been short,
like a fading shadow,
and we know very little.
10 But they will instruct you
with great understanding.

11 Papyrus reeds grow healthy
only in a swamp,
12 and if the water dries up,
they die sooner than grass.
13 Such is the hopeless future
of all who turn from God
14 and trust in something as frail
as a spider's web—
15 they take hold and fall
because it's so flimsy.
16 Sinful people are like plants
with spreading roots and plenty
of sun and water.
17 They wrap their roots tightly
around rocks.[t]
18 But once they are pulled up,
they have no more place;
19 their life slips away,[u]
and other plants grow there.

20 We know God doesn't reject
an innocent person
or help a sinner.
21 And so, he will make you happy
and give you something
to smile about.
22 But your evil enemies
will be put to shame
and disappear forever.

Job's Reply to Bildad

What You Say Is True

9 Job said:
2 What you say is true.
No human is innocent
in the sight of God.
3 Not once in a thousand times
could we win our case
if we took him to court.
4 God is wise and powerful—
who could possibly
oppose him and win?
5 When God becomes angry,
he can move mountains
before they even know it.
6 God can shake the earth loose
from its foundations
7 or command the sun and stars
to hold back their light.
8 God alone stretched out the sky,
stepped on the sea,[v]
9 and set the stars in place—
the Big Dipper and Orion,
the Pleiades and the stars
in the southern sky.
10 Of all the miracles God works,
we cannot understand a one.
11 God walks right past me,
without making a sound.
12 And if he grabs something,
who can stop him
or raise a question?

13 When God showed his anger,
the servants of the sea monster[w]
fell at his feet.
14 How, then, could I possibly
argue my case with God?

Though I Am Innocent

15 Even though I am innocent,
I can only beg for mercy.
16 And if God came into court
when I called him,
he would not hear my case.
17 He would strike me with a storm[x]
and increase my injuries
for no reason at all.
18 Before I could get my breath,
my miseries would multiply.
19 God is much stronger than I am,
and who would call me into court
to give me justice?

[s] **8.1** *Shuah*: See the note at 2.11. [t] **8.17** *rocks*: One possible meaning for the difficult Hebrew text of verse 17. [u] **8.19** *their . . . away*: One possible meaning for the difficult Hebrew text. [v] **9.8** *sea*: Or "sea monster" (see verse 13 and the note there). [w] **9.13** *the sea monster*: The Hebrew text has "Rahab," which was some kind of sea monster with supernatural powers (see the notes at 3.18 and 26.12). [x] **9.17** *strike . . . storm*: One possible meaning for the difficult Hebrew text.

20 Even if I were innocent,
God would prove me wrong.[y]
21 I am not guilty,
but I no longer care
what happens to me.
22 What difference does it make?
God destroys the innocent
along with the guilty.
23 When a good person dies
a sudden death,
God sits back and laughs.
24 And who else but God
blindfolds the judges,
then lets the wicked
take over the earth?

My Life Is Speeding By

25 My life is speeding by,
without a hope of happiness.
26 Each day passes swifter
than a sailing ship
or an eagle swooping down.
27 Sometimes I try to be cheerful
and to stop complaining,
28 but my sufferings frighten me,
because I know that God
still considers me guilty.
29 So what's the use of trying
to prove my innocence?
30 Even if I washed myself
with the strongest soap,
31 God would throw me into a pit
of stinking slime, leaving me
disgusting to my clothes.

32 God isn't a mere human like me.
I can't put him on trial.
33 Who could possibly judge
between the two of us?
34 Can someone snatch away
the stick God carries
to frighten me?
35 Then I could speak up
without fear of him,
but for now, I cannot speak.[z]

Job Complains to God

I Am Sick of Life!

10 I am sick of life!
And from my deep despair,
I complain to you, my God.
2 Don't just condemn me!
Point out my sin.
3 Why do you take such delight
in destroying those you created
and in smiling on sinners?
4 Do you look at things
the way we humans do?
5 Is your life as short as ours?
6 Is that why you are so quick
to find fault with me?
7 You know I am innocent,
but who can defend me
against you?
8 Will you now destroy
someone you created?
9 Remember that you molded me
like a piece of clay.
So don't turn me back
into dust once again.
10 As cheese is made from milk,
you created my body
from a tiny drop.
11 Then you tied my bones together
with muscles and covered them
with flesh and skin.
12 You, the source of my life,
showered me with kindness
and watched over me.

You Have Not Explained

13 You have not explained
all of your mysteries,
14 but you catch and punish me
each time I sin.
15 Guilty or innocent,
I am condemned and ashamed
because of my troubles.
16 No matter how hard I try,
you keep hunting me down
like a powerful lion.[a]
17 You never stop accusing me;
you become furious and attack
over and over again.

18 Why did you let me be born?
I would rather have died
before birth
19 and been carried to the grave
without ever breathing.
20 I have only a few days left.
Why don't you leave me alone?[b]
Let me find some relief,
*21 before I travel to the land
22 of darkness and despair,
the place of no return.

Zophar's First Speech

So Much Foolish Talk

11 Zophar from Naamah[c] said:
2 So much foolish talk
cannot go unanswered.
3 Your words have silenced others
and made them ashamed;
now it is only right for you
to be put to shame.
4 You claim to be innocent
and argue that your beliefs
are acceptable to God.
5 But I wish he would speak
6 and let you know that wisdom
has many different sides.
You would then discover

[y] **9.20** *God . . . wrong*: Or "my own words would prove me wrong." [z] **9.35** *but . . . speak*: One possible meaning for the difficult Hebrew text. [a] **10.16** *lion*: One possible meaning for the difficult Hebrew text of verse 16. [b] **10.20** *I have only . . . alone*: One possible meaning for the difficult Hebrew text. [c] **11.1** *Naamah*: See the note at 2.11.

that God has punished you
less than you deserve.

7 Can you understand the mysteries
surrounding God All-Powerful?
8 They are higher than the heavens
and deeper than the grave.
So what can you do
when you know so little,
9 and these mysteries outreach
the earth and the ocean?

10 If God puts you in prison
or drags you to court,
what can you do?
11 God has the wisdom to know
when someone is worthless
and sinful,
12 but it's easier to tame
a wild donkey
than to make a fool wise.[d]

Surrender Your Heart to God

13 Surrender your heart to God,
turn to him in prayer,
14 and give up your sins—
even those you do in secret.
15 Then you won't be ashamed;
you will be confident
and fearless.
16 Your troubles will go away
like water beneath a bridge,
17 and your darkest night
will be brighter than noon.
18 You will rest safe and secure,
filled with hope
and emptied of worry.
19 You will sleep without fear
and be greatly respected.
20 But those who are evil
will go blind and lose their way.
Their only escape is death!

Job's Reply to Zophar

You Think You Are So Great

12 *1Job said to his friends:
2You think you are so great,
with all the answers.
3 But I know as much as you do,
and so does everyone else.
4 I have always lived right,
and God answered my prayers;
now friends make fun of me.
5 It's easy to condemn
those who are suffering,
when you have no troubles.
6 Robbers and other godless people
live safely at home and say,
"God is in our hands!"[e]

If You Want To Learn

7 If you want to learn,
then go and ask
the wild animals and the birds,
8 the flowers and the fish.
9 Any of them can tell you
what the LORD has done.[f]
10 Every living creature
is in the hands of God.

11 We hear with our ears,
taste with our tongues,
12 and gain some wisdom from those
who have lived a long time.
13 But God is the real source
of wisdom and strength.
14 No one can rebuild
what he destroys, or release
those he has imprisoned.
15 God can hold back the rain
or send a flood,
16 just as he rules over liars
and those they lie to.

17 God destroys counselors,
turns judges into fools,
18 and makes slaves of kings.
19 God removes priests and others
who have great power—
20 he confuses wise,
experienced advisors,
21 puts mighty kings to shame,
and takes away their power.
22 God turns darkness to light;
23 he makes nations strong,
then shatters their strength.
24 God strikes their rulers senseless,
then leaves them to roam
through barren deserts,
25 lost in the dark, staggering
like someone drunk.

Job Continues

I Know and Understand

13 I know and understand
every bit of this.
2 None of you are smarter
than I am;
there's nothing you know
that I don't.
3 But I prefer to argue my case
with God All-Powerful—
4 you are merely useless doctors,
who treat me with lies.
5 The wisest thing you can do
is to keep quiet 6and listen
to my argument.
7 Are you telling lies for God
8 and not telling the whole truth
when you argue his case?
9 If he took you to court,
could you fool him,
just as you fool others?
10 If you were secretly unfair,
he would correct you,

[d]**11.12** *it's . . . wise*: One possible meaning for the difficult Hebrew text. [e]**12.6** *God is in our hands*: One possible meaning for the difficult Hebrew text. [f]**12.9** *Any . . . done*: One possible meaning for the difficult Hebrew text.

[11] and his glorious splendor
would make you terrified.
[12] Your wisdom and arguments
are as delicate as dust.

Be Quiet While I Speak

[13] Be quiet while I speak,
then say what you will.
[14] I will be responsible
for what happens to me.
[15] God may kill me, but still
I will trust him[g]
and offer my defense.
[16] This may be what saves me,
because no guilty person
would come to his court.
[17] Listen carefully to my words!
[18] I have prepared my case well,
and I am certain to win.
[19] If you can prove me guilty,
I will give up and die.

Job Prays

I Ask Only Two Things

[20] I ask only two things
of you, my God,
and I will no longer
hide from you—
[21] stop punishing
and terrifying me!

[22] Then speak, and I will reply;
or else let me speak,
and you reply.
[23] Please point out my sins,
so I will know them.
[24] Why have you turned your back
and count me your enemy?
[25] Do you really enjoy
frightening a fallen leaf?
[26] Why do you accuse me
of horrible crimes
and make me pay for sins
I did in my youth?
[27] You have tied my feet down
and keep me surrounded;
[28] I am rotting away like cloth
eaten by worms.

Job Continues his Prayer

Life Is Short and Sorrowful

14 Life is short and sorrowful
for every living soul.
[2] We are flowers that fade
and shadows that vanish.
[3] And so, I ask you, God,
why pick on me?
[4] There's no way a human
can be completely pure.
[5] Our time on earth is brief;
the number of our days
is already decided by you.
[6] Why don't you leave us alone
and let us find some happiness
while we toil and labor?

When a Tree Is Chopped Down

[7] When a tree is chopped down,
there is always the hope
that it will sprout again.
[8] Its roots and stump may rot,
[9] but at the touch of water,
fresh twigs shoot up.
[10] Humans are different—
we die, and that's the end.
[11] We are like streams and lakes
after the water has gone;
[12] we fall into the sleep of death,
never to rise again,
until the sky disappears.
[13] Please hide me, God,
deep in the ground—
and when you are angry no more,
remember to rescue me.

Will We Humans Live Again?

[14] Will we humans live again?
I would gladly suffer
and wait for my time.
[15] My Creator, you would want me;
you would call out,
and I would answer.
[16] You would take care of me,
but not count my sins—
[17] you would put them in a bag,
tie it tight,
and toss them away.
[18] But in the real world,
mountains tumble,
and rocks crumble;
[19] streams wear away stones
and wash away soil.
And you destroy our hopes!
[20] You change the way we look,
then send us away,
wiped out forever.
[21] We never live to know
if our children are praised
or disgraced.
[22] We feel no pain but our own,
and when we mourn,
it's only for ourselves.

Eliphaz's Second Speech

If You Had Any Sense

15 Eliphaz from Teman[h] said:
*[2]Job, if you had any sense,
[3] you would stop spreading
all of this hot air.
[4] Your words are enough
to make others turn from God
and lead them to doubt.
[5] And your sinful, scheming mind
is the source of all you say.
[6] I am not here as your judge;

[g]**13.15** *God . . . trust him*: Or "God will surely kill me; I have lost all hope." [h]**15.1** *Teman*: See the note at 2.11.

your own words are witnesses
against you.

7 Were you the first human?
Are you older than the hills?
8 Have you ever been present
when God's council[i] meets?
Do you alone have wisdom?
9 Do you know and understand
something we don't?
10 We have the benefit of wisdom
older than your father.
11 And you have been offered
comforting words from God.
Isn't this enough?

12 Your emotions are out of control,
making you look fierce;
13 that's why you attack God
with everything you say.
14 No human is pure and innocent,
15 and neither are angels—
not in the sight of God.
If God doesn't trust his angels,
16 what chance do humans have?
We are so terribly evil
that we thirst for sin.

Just Listen to What I Know

17 Just listen to what I know,
and you will learn
18 wisdom known by others
since ancient times.
19 Those who gained such insights
also gained the land,
and they were not influenced
by foreign teachings.
20 But suffering is in store
each day for those who sin.
21 Even in times of success,
they constantly hear
the threat of doom.
22 Darkness, despair, and death
are their destiny.
23 They scrounge around for food,
all the while dreading
the approaching darkness.
24 They are overcome with despair,
like a terrified king
about to go into battle.
25 This is because they rebelled
against God All-Powerful
26 and have attacked him
with their weapons.

27 They may be rich and fat,
28 but they will live in the ruins
of deserted towns.
29 Their property and wealth
will shrink and disappear.
30 They won't escape the darkness,
and the blazing breath of God
will set their future aflame.
*31 They have put their trust
in something worthless;
now they will become worthless
32 like a date palm tree
without a leaf.[j]
33 Or like vineyards or orchards
whose blossoms and unripe fruit
drop to the ground.
34 Yes, the godless and the greedy
will have nothing but flames
feasting on their homes,
35 because they are the parents
of trouble and vicious lies.

Job's Reply to Eliphaz

I Have Often Heard This

16 Job said:
2 I have often heard this,
and it offers no comfort.
3 So why don't you keep quiet?
What's bothering you?
4 If I were in your place,
it would be easy to criticize
or to give advice.
5 But I would offer hope
and comfort instead.

6 If I speak, or if I don't,
I hurt all the same.
My torment continues.
7 God has worn me down
and destroyed my family;
8 my shriveled up skin proves
that I am his prisoner.
9 God is my hateful enemy,
glaring at me and attacking
with his sharp teeth.
10 Everyone is against me;
they sneer and slap my face.
11 And God is the one
who handed me over
to this merciless mob.

Everything Was Going Well

12 Everything was going well,
until God grabbed my neck
and shook me to pieces.
God set me up as the target
13 for his arrows,
and without showing mercy,
he slashed my stomach open,
spilling out my insides.
14 God never stops attacking,
15 and so, in my sorrow
I dress in sackcloth[k]
and sit in the dust.
16 My face is red with tears,
and dark shadows
circle my eyes,
17 though I am not violent,
and my prayers are sincere.

[i] **15.8** *God's council*: The angels and others who gather to discuss matters with God (see 1.6; 2.1). [j] **15.32** *leaf*: One possible meaning for the difficult Hebrew text of verses 31, 32.
[k] **16.15** *sackcloth*: A rough, dark-colored cloth made from goat hair and used to make grain sacks. It was worn in times of trouble or sorrow.

18 If I should die,
I beg the earth not to cover
my cry for justice.
19 Even now, God in heaven
is both my witness
and my protector.
20 My friends have rejected me,
but God is the one I beg[l]
21 to show that I am right,
just as a friend should.
22 Because in only a few years,
I will be dead and gone.

Job Complains to God

My Hopes Have Died

17 My hopes have died,
my time is up,
and the grave is ready.
2 All I can see are angry crowds,
making fun of me.
3 If you, LORD, don't help,
who will pay the price
for my release?
4 My friends won't really listen,
all because of you,
and so you must be the one
to prove them wrong.
5 They have condemned me,
just to benefit themselves;
now blind their children.

6 You, God, are the reason
I am insulted and spit on.
7 I am almost blind with grief;
my body is a mere shadow.

8 People who are truly good
would feel so alarmed,
that they would become angry
at my worthless friends.
9 They would do the right thing
and because they did,
they would grow stronger.[m]
10 But none of my friends
show any sense.

11 My life is drawing to an end;
hope has disappeared.
12 But all my friends can do
is offer empty hopes.[n]
13 I could tell the world below
to prepare me a bed.
14 Then I could greet the grave
as my father
and say to the worms,
"Hello, mother and sisters!"

15 But what kind of hope is that?
16 Will it keep me company
in the world of the dead?

Bildad's Second Speech

How Long Will You Talk?

18 Bildad from Shuah[o] said:
2 How long will you talk?
Be sensible! Let us speak.
3 Or do you think that we
are dumb animals?
4 You cut yourself in anger.
Will that shake the earth
or even move the rocks?

*5 The lamps of sinful people
soon are snuffed out,
6 leaving their tents dark.
7 Their powerful legs become weak,
and they stumble on schemes
of their own doing.
*8 Before they know it,
9 they are trapped in a net,
10 hidden along the path.
11 Terror strikes and pursues
from every side.
12 Starving, they run,
only to meet disaster,
13 then afterwards to be eaten alive
by death itself.

14 Those sinners are dragged
from the safety of their tents
to die a gruesome death.
15 Then their tents and possessions
are burned to ashes,
16 and they are left like trees,
dried up from the roots.
17 They are gone and forgotten,
18 thrown far from the light
into a world of darkness,
19 without any children
to carry on their name.
20 Everyone, from east to west,
is overwhelmed with horror.
21 Such is the fate of sinners
and their families
who don't know God.

Job's Reply to Bildad

How Long Will You Torture Me?

19 Job said:
2 How long will you torture me
with your words?
3 Isn't ten times enough
for you to accuse me?
Aren't you ashamed?
4 Even if I have sinned,
you haven't been harmed.
5 You boast of your goodness,
claiming I am suffering
because I am guilty.
6 But God is the one at fault
for finding fault with me.

[l] **16.20** *My friends . . . beg*: Or "God is my friend, and he is the one I beg." [m] **17.9** *stronger*: One possible meaning for the difficult Hebrew text of verses 8, 9. [n] **17.12** *hopes*: One possible meaning for the difficult Hebrew text of verse 12. [o] **18.1** *Shuah*: See the note at 2.11.

7 Though I pray to be rescued
from this torment,
no whisper of justice
answers me.
8 God has me trapped
with a wall of darkness
9 and stripped of respect.
10 God rips me apart,
uproots my hopes,
11 and attacks with fierce anger,
as though I were his enemy.
12 His entire army advances,
then surrounds my tent.

I Am Forgotten

*13 God has turned relatives
and friends against me,
14 and I am forgotten.
15 My guests and my servants
consider me a stranger,
16 and when I call my servants,
they pay no attention.
17 My breath disgusts my wife;
everyone in my family
turns away.
18 Young children can't stand me,
and when I come near,
they make fun.
19 My best friends and loved ones
have turned from me.
20 I am skin and bones—
just barely alive.
21 My friends, I beg you for pity!
God has made me his target.
22 Hasn't he already done enough?
Why do you join the attack?

23 I wish that my words
could be written down
24 or chiseled into rock.
25 I know that my Savior[p] lives,
and at the end
he will stand on this earth.
26 My flesh may be destroyed,
yet from this body
I will see God.[q]
27 Yes, I will see him for myself,
and I long for that moment.

28 My friends, you think up ways
to blame and torment me, saying
I brought it on myself.
29 But watch out for the judgment,
when God will punish you!

Zophar's Second Speech

Your Words Are Disturbing

20 Zophar from Naamah[r] said:
2 Your words are disturbing;
now I must speak.
3 You have accused
and insulted me,
and reason requires a reply.
4 Since the time of creation,
everyone has known
5 that sinful people are happy
for only a while.
6 Though their pride and power
may reach to the sky,
7 they will disappear like dust,
and those who knew them
will wonder what happened.
8 They will be forgotten
like a dream
9 and vanish from the sight
of family and friends.
10 Their children will have to repay
what the parents took
from the poor.
11 Indeed, the wicked will die
and go to their graves
in the prime of life.

Sinners Love the Taste of Sin

12 Sinners love the taste of sin;
they relish every bite
13 and swallow it slowly.
14 But their food will turn sour
and poison their stomachs.
15 Then God will make them lose
the wealth they gobbled down.
16 They will die from the fangs
of poisonous snakes
17 and never enjoy rivers flowing
with milk and honey.
18 Their hard work will result
in nothing gained,
19 because they cheated the poor
and took their homes.

20 Greedy people want everything
and are never satisfied.[s]
21 But when nothing remains
for them to grab,
they will be nothing.
22 Once they have everything,
distress and despair
will strike them down,
23 and God will make them swallow
his blazing anger.[t]

24 While running from iron spears,
they will be killed
by arrows of bronze,
25 whose shining tips go straight
through their bodies.
They will be trapped by terror,
26 and what they treasure most
will be lost in the dark.
God will send flames
to destroy them in their tents
with all their property.
27 The heavens and the earth
will testify against them,
28 and all their possessions

[p] **19.25** *Savior*: Or "Defender." [q] **19.26** *God*: One possible meaning for the difficult Hebrew text of verses 25, 26. [r] **20.1** *Naamah*: See the note at 2.11. [s] **20.20** *are never satisfied*: One possible meaning for the difficult Hebrew text. [t] **20.23** *anger*: One possible meaning for the difficult Hebrew text of verse 23.

will be dragged off
when God becomes angry.
29 This is what God has decided
for those who are evil.

Job's Reply to Zophar

If You Want To Offer Comfort

21 Job said:
2 If you want to offer comfort,
then listen to me.
3 And when I have finished,
you can start your insults
all over again.
4 My complaint is against God;
that's why I am impatient.
5 Just looking at me is enough
to make you sick,
6 and the very thought of myself
fills me with disgust.

7 Why do evil people live so long
and gain such power?
8 Why are they allowed to see
their children grow up?[u]
9 They have no worries at home,
and God never punishes them.
10 Their cattle have lots of calves
without ever losing one;
11 their children play and dance
safely by themselves.
12 These people sing and celebrate
to the sound of tambourines,
small harps, and flutes,
13 and they are successful,
without a worry,
until the day they die.

Leave Us Alone!

14 Those who are evil say
to God All-Powerful,
"Leave us alone! Don't bother us
with your teachings.
15 What do we gain from praying
and worshiping you?
16 We succeeded all on our own."
And so, I keep away from them
and their evil schemes.

17 How often does God become angry
and send disaster and darkness
to punish sinners?
18 How often does he strike them
like a windstorm
that scatters straw?

19 You say, "God will punish
those sinners' children
in place of those sinners."
But I say, "Let him punish
those sinners themselves
until they really feel it.
20 Let God All-Powerful force them
to drink their own destruction
from the cup of his anger.
21 Because after they are dead,
they won't care what happens
to their children."

Who Can Tell God What To Do?

22 Who can tell God what to do?
He judges powerful rulers.
*23 Some of us die prosperous,
24 enjoying good health,
25 while others die in poverty,
having known only pain.
26 But we all end up dead,
beneath a blanket of worms.

27 My friends, I know that you
are plotting against me.
28 You ask, "Where is the home
of that important person
who does so much evil?"

29 Everyone, near and far, agrees
30 that those who do wrong
never suffer disaster,
when God becomes angry.
31 No one points out their sin
or punishes them.
32 Then at their funerals,
they are highly praised;
33 the earth welcomes them home,
while crowds mourn.

34 But empty, meaningless words
are the comfort you offer me.

Eliphaz's Third Speech

What Use Are We Humans to God?

22 Eliphaz from Teman[v] said:
2 What use are we humans
to God,
even the wisest of us?
3 If you were completely sinless,
that would still mean nothing
to God All-Powerful.
4 Is he correcting you
for worshiping him?
5 No! It's because
of your terrible sins.
6 To guarantee payment of a debt,
you have taken clothes
from the poor.
7 And you refused bread and water
to the hungry and thirsty,
8 although you were rich,
respected, and powerful.
9 You have turned away widows
and have broken the arms
of orphans.
10 That's why you were suddenly
trapped by terror,
11 blinded by darkness,
and drowned in a flood.

[u]**21.8** *up*: One possible meaning for the difficult Hebrew text of verse 8. [v]**22.1** *Teman*: See the note at 2.11.

God Lives in the Heavens

12 God lives in the heavens
above the highest stars,
where he sees everything.
13 Do you think the deep darkness
hides you from God?
14 Do thick clouds cover his eyes,
as he walks around heaven's dome
high above the earth?
15 Give up those ancient ideas
believed by sinners,
16 who were swept away
without warning.
17 They rejected God All-Powerful,
feeling he was helpless,
18 although he had been kind
to their families.
The beliefs of these sinners
are truly disgusting.
19 When God's people see
the godless swept away,
they celebrate, 20 saying,
"Our enemies are gone,
and fire has destroyed
their possessions."

Surrender to God All-Powerful

21 Surrender to God All-Powerful!
You will find peace
and prosperity.
22 Listen to his teachings
and take them to heart.
23 If you return to God
and turn from sin,
all will go well for you.
24 So get rid of your finest gold,
as though it were sand.
25 Let God All-Powerful
be your silver and gold,
26 and you will find happiness
by worshiping him.
27 God will answer your prayers,
and you will keep the promises
you made to him.
28 He will do whatever you ask,
and life will be bright.
29 When others are disgraced,
God will clear their names
in answer to your prayers.
30 Even those who are guilty
will be forgiven,
because you obey God.[w]

Job's Reply to Eliphaz

Today I Complain Bitterly

23 Job said:
2 Today I complain bitterly,
because God has been cruel
and made me suffer.
3 If I knew where to find God,
I would go there
4 and argue my case.
5 Then I would discover
what he wanted to say.
6 Would he overwhelm me
with his greatness?
No! He would listen
7 because I am innocent,
and he would say,
"I now set you free!"

8 I cannot find God anywhere—
in front or back of me,
9 to my left or my right.
God is always at work,
though I never see him.
10 But he knows what I am doing,
and when he tests me,
I will be pure as gold.
*11 I have never refused to follow
any of his commands,
12 and I have always treasured
his teachings.[x]
13 But he alone is God,
and who can oppose him?
God does as he pleases,
14 and he will do exactly
what he intends with me.
*15 Merely the thought
of God All-Powerful
16 makes me tremble with fear.
17 God has covered me
with darkness,
but I refuse to be silent.[y]

Job Continues

Why Doesn't God Set a Time?

24 Why doesn't God
set a time for court?
Why don't his people know
where he can be found?
2 Sinners remove boundary markers
and take care of sheep
they have stolen.
3 They cheat orphans and widows
by taking their donkeys
and oxen.
4 The poor are trampled
and forced to hide
5 in the desert,
where they and their children
must live like wild donkeys
and search for food.
6 If they want grain or grapes,[z]
they must go to the property
of these sinners.
7 They sleep naked in the cold,
because they have no cover,
8 and during a storm
their only shelters are caves
among the rocky cliffs.

[w]**22.30** *God*: One possible meaning for the difficult Hebrew text of verses 29, 30.
[x]**23.12** *treasured his teachings*: One possible meaning for the difficult Hebrew text.
[y]**23.17** *silent*: One possible meaning for the difficult Hebrew text of verse 17. [z]**24.6** *If they want grain or grapes*: Poor people were allowed to gather what was left in the fields and vineyards after the harvest.

[9] Children whose fathers have died
are taken from their mothers
as payment for a debt.
[10] Then they are forced to work
naked in the grain fields
because they have no clothes,
and they go hungry.
[11] They crush olives to make oil
and grapes to make wine—
but still they go thirsty.
[12] And along the city streets,
the wounded and dying cry out,
yet God does nothing.

Some Reject the Light

[13] Some rebel and refuse
to follow the light.
[14] Soon after sunset they murder
the poor and the needy,
and at night they steal.

[15] Others wait for the dark,
thinking they won't be seen
if they sleep with the wife
or husband of someone else.
[16] Robbers hide during the day,
then break in after dark
because they reject the light.
[17] They prefer night to day,
since the terrors of the night
are their friends.

Sinners Are Filthy Foam

[18] Those sinners are filthy foam
on the surface of the water.
And so, their fields and vineyards
will fall under a curse
and won't produce.
[19] Just as the heat of summer
swallows the snow,
the world of the dead
swallows those who sin.
[20] Forgotten here on earth,
and with their power broken,
they taste sweet to worms.

[21] Sinners take advantage of widows
and other helpless women.[a]
[22] But God's mighty strength
destroys those in power.
Even if they seem successful,
they are doomed to fail.
[23] God may let them feel secure,
but they are never
out of his sight.
[24] Great for a while; gone forever!
Sinners are mowed down
like weeds,
then they wither and die.
[25] If I haven't spoken the truth,
then prove me wrong.

Bildad's Third Speech

God Is the One To Fear

25 Bildad from Shuah[b] said:
[2] God is the one to fear,
because God is in control
and rules the heavens.
[3] Who can count his army of stars?
Isn't God the source of light?
[4] How can anyone be innocent
in the sight of God?
[5] To him, not even the light
of the moon and stars
can ever be pure.
[6] So how can we humans,
when we are merely worms?

Job's Reply to Bildad

You Have Really Been Helpful

26 Job said:
[2] You have really been helpful
to someone weak and weary.
[3] You have given great advice
and wonderful wisdom
to someone truly in need.
[4] How can anyone possibly speak
with such understanding?

[5] Remember the terrible trembling
of those in the world of the dead
below the mighty ocean.
[6] Nothing in that land
of death and destruction
is hidden from God,
[7] who hung the northern sky
and suspended the earth
on empty space.
[8] God stores water in clouds,
but they don't burst,
[9] and he wraps them around
the face of the moon.
[10] On the surface of the ocean,
God has drawn a boundary line
between light and darkness.
[11] And columns supporting the sky
tremble at his command.

[12] By his power and wisdom,
God conquered the force
of the mighty ocean.[c]
[13] The heavens became bright
when he breathed,
and the escaping sea monster[d]
died at the hands of God.
[14] These things are merely a whisper
of God's power at work.
How little we would understand
if this whisper
ever turned into thunder!

[a] **24.21** *women*: One possible meaning for the difficult Hebrew text of verse 21.
[b] **25.1** *Shuah*: See the note at 2.11. [c] **26.12** *the force of the mighty ocean*: The Hebrew text has "the ocean . . . Rahab." In this passage the sea monster Rahab stands for the fearsome power of the ocean (see the notes at 3.8 and 9.13). [d] **26.13** *sea monster*: The Hebrew text has "snake," which probably stands for some kind of fearsome sea monster, such as Leviathan (see Isaiah 27.1).

Job Continues

I Am Desperate

27 Job said:
2I am desperate because
God All-Powerful refuses
to do what is right.
As surely as God lives,
3 and while he gives me breath,
4 I will tell only the truth.
5 Until the day I die,
I will refuse to do wrong
by saying you are right,
6 because each day my conscience
agrees that I am innocent.

7 I pray that my enemies
will suffer no less
than the wicked.
8 Such people are hopeless,
and God All-Powerful
will cut them down,
9 without listening
when they beg for mercy.
10 And that is what God should do,
because they don't like him
or ever pray.
11 Now I will explain in detail
what God All-Powerful does.
12 All of you have seen these things
for yourselves.
So you have no excuse.

How God Treats the Wicked

13 Here is how God All-Powerful
treats those who are wicked
and brutal.
14 They may have many children,
but most of them will go hungry
or suffer a violent death.
15 Others will die of disease,
and their widows
won't be able to weep.
16 The wicked may collect riches
and clothes in abundance
as easily as clay.
17 But God's people will wear
clothes taken from them
and divide up their riches.
18 No homes built by the wicked
will outlast a cocoon
or a shack.
19 Those sinners may go to bed rich,
but they will wake up poor.[e]
20 Terror will strike at night
like a flood or a storm.
21 Then a scorching wind
will sweep them away
22 without showing mercy,
as they try to escape.
23 At last, the wind will celebrate
because they are gone.

Job Continues

Gold and Silver Are Mined

28 Gold and silver are mined,
then purified;
2 the same is done
with iron and copper.
3 Miners carry lanterns
deep into the darkness
to search for these metals.
4 They dig tunnels
in distant, unknown places,
where they dangle by ropes.
5 Far beneath the grain fields,
fires are built
to break loose those rocks
6 that have jewels or gold.[f]

7 Miners go to places unseen
by the eyes of hawks;
8 they walk on soil unknown
to the proudest lions.
9 With their own hands
they remove sharp rocks
and uproot mountains.
10 They dig through the rocks
in search of jewels
and precious metals.
11 They also uncover
the sources of[g] rivers
and discover secret places.

Where Is Wisdom Found?

12 But where is wisdom found?
13 No human knows the way.[h]
14 Nor can it be discovered
in the deepest sea.
*15 It is worth much more
than silver or pure gold
16 or precious stones.
17 Nothing is its equal—
not gold or costly glass.[i]
18 Wisdom is worth much more than
coral, jasper,[j] or rubies.
19 All the topaz[k] of Ethiopia[l]
and the finest gold
cannot compare with it.
20 Where then is wisdom?
21 It is hidden from human eyes
and even from birds.
22 Death and destruction
have merely heard rumors
about where it is found.
23 God is the only one who knows
the way to wisdom,
24 because he sees everything
beneath the heavens.

[e]**27.19** *poor*: Or "dead." [f]**28.6** *gold*: One possible meaning for the difficult Hebrew text of verses 5, 6. [g]**28.11** *uncover the sources of*: Two ancient translations; Hebrew "dam up." [h]**28.13** *the way*: Or "its worth." [i]**28.17** *costly glass*: In the ancient world, objects made of glass were costly. [j]**28.18** *jasper*: A valuable stone, usually green or clear. [k]**28.19** *topaz*: A valuable, yellow stone. [l]**28.19** *Ethiopia*: The Hebrew text has "Cush," which was a region south of Egypt that included parts of the present countries of Ethiopia and Sudan.

25 When God divided out
the wind and the water,
26 and when he decided the path
for rain and lightning,
27 he also determined the truth
and defined wisdom.
28 God told us, "Wisdom means
that you respect me, the Lord,
and turn from sin."

Job Continues

I Long for the Past

29 Job said:
2 I long for the past,
when God took care of me,
3 and the light from his lamp
showed me the way
through the dark.
4 I was in the prime of life,
God All-Powerful
was my closest friend,
5 and all of my children
were nearby.
6 My herds gave enough milk
to bathe my feet,
and from my olive harvest
flowed rivers of oil.
*7 When I sat down at the meeting
of the city council,
8 the young leaders stepped aside,
*9 while the older ones stood
10 and remained silent.

Everyone Was Pleased

11 Everyone was pleased
with what I said and did.
12 When poor people or orphans
cried out for help,
I came to their rescue.
13 And I was highly praised
for my generosity to widows
and others in poverty.
14 Kindness and justice
were my coat and hat;
15 I was good to the blind
and to the lame.
16 I was a father to the needy,
and I defended them in court,
even if they were strangers.
17 When criminals attacked,
I broke their teeth
and set their victims free.

18 I felt certain that I would live
a long and happy life,
then die in my own bed.
19 In those days I was strong
like a tree with deep roots
and with plenty of water,
20 or like an archer's new bow.
21 Everyone listened in silence
to my welcome advice,
22 and when I finished speaking,
nothing needed to be said.
23 My words were eagerly accepted
like the showers of spring,
24 and the smile on my face
renewed everyone's hopes.
25 My advice was followed
as though I were a king
leading my troops,
or someone comforting
those in sorrow.

Job Continues

Young People Now Insult Me

30 Young people now insult me,
although their fathers
would have been a disgrace
to my sheep dogs.
2 And those who insult me
are helpless themselves.
3 They must claw the desert sand
in the dark for something
to satisfy their hunger.[m]
4 They gather tasteless shrubs
for food and firewood,
5 and they are run out of towns,
as though they were thieves.
6 Their only homes are ditches
or holes between rocks,
7 where they bray like donkeys
gathering around shrubs.
8 And like senseless donkeys
they are chased away.

Those Worthless Nobodies

9 Those worthless nobodies
make up jokes and songs
to disgrace me.
10 They are hateful
and keep their distance,
even while spitting
in my direction.
11 God has destroyed me,
and so they don't care
what they do.[n]
12 Their attacks never stop,
though I am defenseless,
and my feet are trapped.[o]
13 Without any help,
they prevent my escape,
destroying me completely[p]
14 and leaving me crushed.
15 Terror has me surrounded;
my reputation and my riches
have vanished like a cloud.

I Am Sick at Heart

16 I am sick at heart!
Pain has taken its toll.
17 Night chews on my bones,
causing endless torment,

[m] **30.3** *hunger*: One possible meaning for the difficult Hebrew text of verse 3.
[n] **30.11** *God . . . do*: Or "They have destroyed me, and so they don't care what else they do."
[o] **30.12** *trapped*: One possible meaning for the difficult Hebrew text of verse 12.
[p] **30.13** *destroying . . . completely*: One possible meaning for the difficult Hebrew text.

18 and God has shrunk my skin,
choking me to death.
19 I have been thrown in the dirt
and now am dirt myself.
20 I beg God for help,
but there is no answer;
and when I stand up,
he simply stares.
21 God has turned brutal,
22 stirring up a windstorm
to toss me about.
23 Soon he will send me home
to the world of the dead,
where we all must go.

24 No one refuses help to others,
when disaster strikes.[q]
25 I mourned for the poor
and those who suffered.
26 But when I beg for relief
and light,
all I receive are disaster
and darkness.
27 My stomach is tied in knots;
pain is my daily companion.
28 Suffering has scorched my skin,
and in the city council
I stand and cry out,
29 making mournful sounds
like jackals[r] and owls.
30 My skin is so parched,
that it peels right off,
and my bones are burning.
31 My only songs are sorrow
and sadness.

Job Continues

I Promised Myself

31 I promised myself
never to stare with desire
at a young woman.
2 God All-Powerful punishes
men who do that.
3 In fact, God sends disaster
on all who sin,
4 and he keeps a close watch
on everything I do.

5 I am not dishonest or deceitful,
6 and I beg God to prove
my innocence.
7 If I have disobeyed him
or even wanted to,
8 then others can eat my harvest
and uproot my crops.
9 If I have desired someone's wife
and chased after her,
10 then let some stranger
steal my wife from me.
11 If I took someone's wife,
it would be a horrible crime,
12 sending me to destruction
and my crops to the flames.[s]

13 When my servants
complained against me,
I was fair to them.
14 Otherwise, what answer
would I give to God
when he judges me?
15 After all, God is the one
who gave life to each of us
before we were born.

I Have Never Cheated Anyone

16 I have never cheated widows
or others in need,
17 and I have always shared
my food with orphans.
18 Since the time I was young,
I have cared for orphans
and helped widows.[t]
19 I provided clothes for the poor,
20 and I was praised
for supplying woolen garments
to keep them warm.
21 If I have ever raised my arm
to threaten an orphan
when the power was mine,
22 I hope that arm will fall
from its socket.
23 I could not have been abusive;
I was terrified at the thought
that God might punish me.
24 I have never trusted
the power of wealth,
25 or taken pride in owning
many possessions.
*26 I have never openly or secretly
27 worshiped the sun or moon.
28 Such horrible sins
would have deserved
punishment from God.

29 I have never laughed
when my enemies
were struck by disaster.
30 Neither have I sinned
by asking God
to send down on them
the curse of death.
31 No one ever went hungry[u]
at my house,
32 and travelers
were always welcome.
33 Many have attempted to hide
their sins from others—
but I refused.
34 And the fear of public disgrace
never forced me to keep silent
about what I had done.

[q]**30.24** *strikes*: One possible meaning for the difficult Hebrew text of verse 24.
[r]**30.29** *jackals*: Desert animals related to wolves, but smaller. [s]**31.12** *flames*: One possible meaning for the difficult Hebrew text of verse 12. [t]**31.18** *widows*: One possible meaning for the difficult Hebrew text of verse 18. [u]**31.31** *ever went hungry*: Or "was ever sexually abused" (see Genesis 19.1-11; Judges 17.22-30). In ancient Israel, the lives of one's guests were sacred and had to be protected at any cost.

Why Doesn't God Listen?

35 Why doesn't God All-Powerful
listen and answer?
If God has something against me,
let him speak up
or put it in writing!
36 Then I would wear his charges
on my clothes and forehead.
37 And with my head held high,
I would tell him everything
I have ever done.

38 I have never mistreated
the land I farmed
and made it mourn.[v]
39 Nor have I cheated
my workers
and caused them pain.[w]
40 If I had, I would pray
for weeds instead of wheat
to grow in my fields.
After saying these things,
Job was silent.

Elihu Is Upset with Job's Friends

32 Finally, these three men stopped
arguing with Job, because he refused to admit that he was guilty.
2 Elihu from Buz[x] was there, and he
had become upset with Job for blaming
God instead of himself. 3 He was also angry with Job's three friends for not being able to prove that Job was wrong.
4 Elihu was younger than these three,
and he let them speak first. 5 But he became irritated when they could not answer Job, 6 and he said to them:

I am much younger than you,
so I have shown respect
by keeping silent.
7 I once believed age
was the source of wisdom;
8 now I truly realize
wisdom comes from God.
9 Age is no guarantee of wisdom
and understanding.
10 That's why I ask you
to listen to me.

I Eagerly Listened

*11 I eagerly listened
to each of your arguments,
12 but not one of you proved
Job to be wrong.
13 You shouldn't say,
"We know what's right!
Let God punish him."
14 Job hasn't spoken against me,
and so I won't answer him
with your arguments.

15 All of you are shocked;
you don't know what to say.
16 But am I to remain silent,
just because you
have stopped speaking?
17 No! I will give my opinion,
18 because I have so much to say,
that I can't keep quiet.
19 I am like a swollen wineskin,
and I will burst[y]
20 if I don't speak.
*21 I don't know how to be unfair
or to flatter anyone—
22 if I did, my Creator
would quickly destroy me!

Elihu Speaks

Job, Listen to Me!

33 Job, listen to me!
Pay close attention.
*2 Everything I will say
3 is true and sincere,
4 just as surely as the Spirit
of God All-Powerful[z]
gave me the breath of life.
5 Now line up your arguments
and prepare to face me.
6 We each were made from clay,
and God has no favorites,
7 so don't be afraid of me
or what I might do.

I Have Heard You Argue

8 I have heard you argue
9 that you are innocent,
guilty of nothing.
10 You claim that God
has made you his enemy,
11 that he has bound your feet
and blocked your path.
12 But, Job, you're wrong—
God is greater
than any human.
13 So why do you challenge God
to answer you?[a]
14 God speaks in different ways,
and we don't always
recognize his voice.
*15 Sometimes in the night,
he uses terrifying dreams
16 to give us warnings.
17 God does this to make us turn
from sin and pride

[v] **31.38** *mourn*: In biblical times there were strict regulations for proper use of the land, and land that was abused was said to "mourn" and become no longer productive. [w] **31.39** *pain*: One possible meaning for the difficult Hebrew text of verse 39. [x] **32.2** *Elihu from Buz*: The Hebrew text has "Elihu son of Barachel from Buz of the family of Ram." Buz may have been somewhere in the territory of Edom; in Jeremiah 25.23 it is mentioned along with Dedan and Tema (see 6.19). [y] **32.19** *swollen wineskin . . . burst*: While the juice from grapes was becoming wine, it would swell and stretch the skins in which it had been stored; sometimes the swelling would burst the wineskins. [z] **33.4** *the Spirit of God All-Powerful*: Or "God All-Powerful." [a] **33.13** *answer you*: One possible meaning for the difficult Hebrew text of verse 13.

18 and to protect us
from being swept away
to the world of the dead.

19 Sometimes we are punished
with a serious illness
and aching joints.
20 Merely the thought
of our favorite food
makes our stomachs sick,
21 and we become so skinny
that our bones stick out.
22 We feel death and the grave
taking us in their grip.

23 One of a thousand angels
then comes to our rescue
by saying we are innocent.
24 The angel shows kindness,
commanding death to release us,
because the price was paid.
25 Our health is restored,
we feel young again,
26 and we ask God to accept us.
Then we joyfully worship God,
and we are rewarded
because we are innocent.
27 When that happens,
we tell everyone,
"I sinned and did wrong,
but God forgave me
28 and rescued me from death!
Now I will see the light."

29 God gives each of us
chance after chance
30 to be saved from death
and brought into the light
that gives life.
31 So, Job, pay attention
and don't interrupt,
32 though I would gladly listen
to anything you say
that proves you are right.
33 Otherwise, listen in silence
to my wisdom.

Elihu Continues

You Men Think You Are Wise

34 Elihu said:
2 You men think you are wise,
but just listen to me!
3 Think about my words,
as you would taste food.
4 Then we can decide the case
and give a just verdict.
5 Job claims he is innocent
and God is guilty
of mistreating him.
6 Job also argues that God
considers him a liar
and that he is suffering severely
in spite of his innocence.
7 But to tell the truth,
Job is shameless!
8 He spends his time with sinners,
9 because he has said,
"It doesn't pay to please God."

If Any of You Are Smart

10 If any of you are smart,
you will listen and learn
that God All-Powerful
does what is right.
11 God always treats everyone
the way they deserve,
12 and he is never unfair.
13 From the very beginning,
God has been in control
of all the world.

14 If God took back the breath
that he breathed into us,
15 we humans would die
and return to the soil.
16 So be smart and listen!
17 The mighty God is the one
who brings about justice,
and you are condemning him.
18 Indeed, God is the one
who condemns unfair rulers.
19 And God created us all;
he has no favorites,
whether rich or poor.
20 Even powerful rulers die
in the darkness of night
when they least expect it,
just like the rest of us.

God Watches Everything We Do

21 God watches everything we do.
22 No evil person can hide
in the deepest darkness.
23 And so, God doesn't need
to set a time for judgment.
24 Without asking for advice,
God removes mighty leaders
and puts others in their place.
25 He knows what they are like,
and he wipes them out
in the middle of the night.
26 And while others look on,
he punishes them
because they were evil
27 and refused to obey him.
28 The persons they mistreated
had prayed for help,
until God answered
their prayers.
29 When God does nothing,
can any person or nation
find fault with him?
30 But still, he punishes rulers
who abuse their people.[b]

31 Job, you should tell God
that you are guilty
and promise to do better.
32 Then ask him to point out
what you did wrong,
so you won't do it again.

[b] **34.30** *people*: One possible meaning for the difficult Hebrew text of verses 29, 30.

33 Do you make the rules,
or does God?
You have to decide—
I can't do it for you;
now make up your mind.
34 Job, anyone with good sense
can easily see
35 that you are speaking nonsense
and lack good judgment.
36 So I pray for you to suffer
as much as possible
for talking like a sinner.
37 You have rebelled against God,
time after time,
and have even insulted us.

Elihu Continues

Are You Really Innocent?

35 Elihu said:
2 Job, are you really innocent
in the sight of God?[c]
3 Don't you honestly believe
it pays to obey him?
4 I will give the answers
to you and your friends.
*5 Look up to the heavens
6 and think!
Do your sins hurt God?
7 Is any good you may have done
at all helpful to him?
8 The evil or good you do
only affects other humans.

9 In times of trouble,
everyone begs the mighty God
to have mercy.
10 But after their Creator
helps them through hard times,
they forget about him,
11 though he makes us wiser
than animals or birds.
12 God won't listen to the prayers
of proud and evil people.
13 If God All-Powerful refuses
to answer their empty prayers,
14 he will surely deny
your impatient request
to face him in court.
15 Job, you were wrong to say
God doesn't punish sin.
16 Everything you have said
adds up to nonsense.

Elihu Continues

Be Patient a While Longer

36 Elihu said:
2 Be patient a while longer;
I have something else to say
in God's defense.
3 God always does right—
and this knowledge
comes straight from God.[d]
4 You can rest assured
that what I say is true.
5 Although God is mighty,
he cares about everyone
and makes fair decisions.

6 The wicked are cut down,
and those who are wronged
receive justice.
7 God watches over good people
and places them in positions
of power and honor forever.
8 But when people are prisoners
of suffering and pain,
*9 God points out their sin
and their pride,
10 then he warns them
to turn back to him.
11 And if they obey,
they will be successful
and happy from then on.
12 But if they foolishly refuse,
they will be rewarded
with a violent death.

Godless People Are Too Angry

13 Godless people are too angry
to ask God for help
when he punishes them.
14 So they die young
in shameful disgrace.
15 Hard times and trouble
are God's way
of getting our attention!
16 And at this very moment,
God deeply desires
to lead you from trouble
and to spread your table
with your favorite food.

17 Now that the judgment
for your sins
has fallen upon you,
18 don't let your anger
and the pain you endured
make you sneer at God.
19 Your reputation and riches
cannot protect you
from distress,
20 nor can you find safety
in the dark world below.[e]
21 Be on guard! Don't turn to evil
as a way of escape.
22 God's power is unlimited.
He needs no teachers
23 to guide or correct him.

Others Have Praised God

24 Others have praised God
for what he has done,
so join with them.

[c] **35.2** *are . . . God*: Or "is it right for you to accuse God?" [d] **36.3** *comes straight from God*: The Hebrew text has "comes from a distant place," which refers to the place where God lives; Elihu is claiming that he learned this from God. [e] **36.20** *below*: One possible meaning for the difficult Hebrew text of verses 18-20.

25 From down here on earth,
everyone has looked up and seen
26 how great God is—
God is more than we imagine;
no one can count the years
he has lived.
*27 God gathers moisture
into the clouds
28 and supplies us with rain.
29 Who can understand
how God scatters the clouds
and speaks from his home
in the thunderstorm?
30 And when God sends lightning,
it can be seen
at the bottom of the sea.
31 By producing such rainstorms,
God rules the world
and provides us with food.
32 Each flash of lightning
is one of his arrows
striking its target,
33 and the thunder tells
of his anger against sin.[f]

Elihu Continues

I Am Frightened

37 I am frightened
and tremble all over,
2 when I hear the roaring voice
of God in the thunder,
3 and when I see his lightning
flash across the sky.
4 God's majestic voice
thunders his commands,[g]
5 creating miracles too marvelous
for us to understand.
6 Snow and heavy rainstorms
7 make us stop and think
about God's power,
8 and they force animals
to seek shelter.
9 The windstorms of winter strike,
10 and the breath of God
freezes streams and rivers.
11 Rain clouds filled with lightning
appear at God's command,
12 traveling across the sky
13 to release their cargo—
sometimes as punishment for sin,
sometimes as kindness.

Consider Carefully

14 Job, consider carefully
the many wonders of God.
15 Can you explain why lightning
flashes at the orders
16 of God who knows all things?
Or how he hangs the clouds
in empty space?
17 You almost melt in the heat
of fierce desert winds
when the sky is like brass.
18 God can spread out the clouds
to get relief from the heat,
but can you?

19 Tell us what to say to God!
Our minds are in the dark,
and we don't know how
to argue our case.
20 Should I risk my life
by telling God
that I want to speak?
21 No one can stare at the sun
after a breeze has blown
the clouds from the sky.
22 Yet the glorious splendor
of God All-Powerful
is brighter by far.
23 God cannot be seen—
but his power is great,
and he is always fair.
24 And so we humans fear God,
because he shows no respect
for those who are proud
and think they know so much.

The LORD Speaks

From Out of a Storm

38 From out of a storm,
the LORD said to Job:
2 Why do you talk so much
when you know so little?
3 Now get ready to face me!
Can you answer
the questions I ask?
4 How did I lay the foundation
for the earth?
Were you there?
5 Doubtless you know who decided
its length and width.
6 What supports the foundation?
Who placed the cornerstone,
7 while morning stars sang,
and angels rejoiced?

8 When the ocean was born,
I set its boundaries
9 and wrapped it in blankets
of thickest fog.
10 Then I built a wall around it,
locked the gates, 11and said,
"Your powerful waves stop here!
They can go no farther."

Did You Ever Tell the Sun To Rise?

12 Did you ever tell the sun to rise?
And did it obey?
13 Did it take hold of the earth
and shake out the wicked
like dust from a rug?
14 Early dawn outlines the hills
like stitches on clothing
or sketches on clay.
15 But its light is too much
for those who are evil,
and their power is broken.

[f]**36.33** *sin*: One possible meaning for the difficult Hebrew text of verse 33.
[g]**37.4** *commands*: One possible meaning for the difficult Hebrew text of verse 4.

16 Job, have you ever walked
on the ocean floor?
17 Have you seen the gate
to the world of the dead?
18 And how large is the earth?
Tell me, if you know!

19 Where is the home of light,
and where does darkness live?
20 Can you lead them home?
21 I'm certain you must be able to,
since you were already born
when I created everything.

22 Have you been to the places
where I keep snow and hail,
23 until I use them to punish
and conquer nations?
24 From where does lightning leap,
or the east wind blow?
25 Who carves out a path
for thunderstorms?
Who sends torrents of rain
26 on empty deserts
where no one lives?
27 Rain that changes barren land
to meadows green with grass.
28 Who is the father of the dew
and of the rain?
29 Who gives birth to the sleet
and the frost
30 that fall in winter,
when streams and lakes
freeze solid as a rock?

Can You Arrange Stars?

31 Can you arrange stars in groups
such as Orion
and the Pleiades?
32 Do you control the stars
or set in place the Big Dipper
and the Little Dipper?
33 Do you know the laws
that govern the heavens,
and can you make them rule
the earth?
34 Can you order the clouds
to send a downpour,
35 or will lightning flash
at your command?
36 Did you teach birds to know
that rain or floods
are on their way?[h]
37 Can you count the clouds
or pour out their water
38 on the dry, lumpy soil?

39 When lions are hungry,
do you help them hunt?
40 Do you send an animal
into their den?
41 And when starving young ravens
cry out to me for food,
do you satisfy their hunger?

The LORD Continues

When Do Mountain Goats Give Birth?

39 When do mountain goats
and deer give birth?
Have you been there
when their young are born?
*2 How long are they pregnant
3 before they deliver?
4 Soon their young grow strong
and then leave
to be on their own.

5 Who set wild donkeys free?
6 I alone help them survive
in salty desert sand.
7 They stay far from crowded cities
and refuse to be tamed.
8 Instead, they roam the hills,
searching for pastureland.

9 Would a wild ox agree
to live in your barn
and labor for you?
10 Could you force him to plow
or to drag a heavy log
to smooth out the soil?
11 Can you depend on him
to use his great strength
and do your heavy work?
12 Can you trust him
to harvest your grain
or take it to your barn
from the threshing place?

An Ostrich Proudly Flaps Her Wings

13 An ostrich proudly
flaps her wings,
but not because
she loves her young.
14 She abandons her eggs
and lets the dusty ground
keep them warm.
15 And she doesn't seem to worry
that the feet of an animal
could crush them all.
16 She treats her eggs as though
they were not her own,
unconcerned that her work
might be for nothing.
17 I myself made her foolish
and without common sense.
18 But once she starts running,[i]
she laughs at a rider
on the fastest horse.

Did You Give Horses Their Strength?

19 Did you give horses their strength
and the flowing hair
along their necks?

[h]**38.36** *way*: One possible meaning for the difficult Hebrew text of verse 36. [i]**39.18** *starts running*: One possible meaning for the difficult Hebrew text.

[20] Did you make them able
to jump like grasshoppers
or to frighten people
with their snorting?

[21] Before horses are ridden
into battle,
they paw at the ground,
proud of their strength.
[22] Laughing at fear, they rush
toward the fighting,
[23] while the weapons of their riders
rattle and flash in the sun.
[24] Unable to stand still,
they gallop eagerly into battle
when trumpets blast.
[25] Stirred by the distant smells
and sounds of war, they snort
in reply to the trumpet.

[26] Did you teach hawks to fly south
for the winter?
*[27] Did you train eagles[j] to build
[28] their nests on rocky cliffs,
[29] where they can look down
to spot their next meal?
[30] Then their young gather to feast
wherever the victim lies.

The LORD Continues

I Am the LORD All-Powerful

40 *[1]I am the LORD All-Powerful,
[2]but you have argued
that I am wrong.
Now you must answer me.

[3] Job said to the LORD:
[4] Who am I to answer you?
[5] I did speak once or twice,
but never again.

[6] Then out of the storm
the LORD said to Job:
[7] Face me and answer
the questions I ask!
[8] Are you trying to prove
that you are innocent
by accusing me of injustice?
[9] Do you have a powerful arm
and a thundering voice
that compare with mine?
[10] If so, then surround yourself
with glory and majesty.
*[11] Show your furious anger!
Throw down and crush
[12] all who are proud and evil.
[13] Wrap them in grave clothes
and bury them together
in the dusty soil.
[14] Do this, and I will agree
that you have won
this argument.

I Created You

[15] I created both you
and the hippopotamus.[k]
It eats only grass like an ox,
[16] but look at the mighty muscles
in its body [17]and legs.
Its tail is like a cedar tree,
and its thighs are thick.
[18] The bones in its legs
are like bronze or iron.

[19] I made it more powerful
than any other creature,
yet I am stronger still.
[20] Undisturbed, it eats grass
while the other animals
play nearby.[l]
*[21] It rests in the shade of trees
along the riverbank
[22] or hides among reeds
in the swamp.
[23] It remains calm and unafraid
with the Jordan River rushing
and splashing in its face.
[24] There is no way to capture
a hippopotamus—
not even by hooking its nose
or blinding its eyes.

The LORD Continues

Can You Catch a Sea Monster?

41 Can you catch a sea monster[m]
by using a fishhook?
Can you tie its mouth shut
with a rope?
[2] Can it be led around
by a ring in its nose
or a hook in its jaw?
[3] Will it beg for mercy?
[4] Will it surrender
as a slave for life?
[5] Can it be tied by the leg
like a pet bird
for little girls?
[6] Is it ever chopped up
and its pieces bargained for
in the fish-market?
[7] Can it be killed
with harpoons or spears?
[8] Wrestle it just once—
that will be the end.
[9] Merely a glimpse of this monster
makes all courage melt.
[10] And if it is too fierce

[j]39.27 *eagles*: Or "vultures." [k]40.15 *the hippopotamus*: The Hebrew text has "Behemoth," which was sometimes understood to be a sea monster like Rahab (9.13; 26.12), Leviathan (3.8; 41.1), and Tannin (7.12). [l]40.20 *nearby*: One possible meaning for the difficult Hebrew text of verse 20. [m]41.1 *sea monster*: The Hebrew text has "Leviathan," which may refer to a sea monster or possibly to a crocodile in this verse (see the note at 3.8).

for anyone to attack,
who would dare oppose me?
11 I am in command of the world
and in debt to no one.

12 What powerful legs,
what a stout body
this monster possesses!
13 Who could strip off its armor
or bring it under control
with a harness?
14 Who would try to open its jaws,
full of fearsome teeth?
*15 Its back[n] is covered
with shield after shield,
16 firmly bound and closer together
17 than breath to breath.

When This Monster Sneezes

18 When this monster sneezes,
lightning flashes, and its eyes
glow like the dawn.
19 Sparks and fiery flames
explode from its mouth.
20 And smoke spews from its nose
like steam
from a boiling pot,
21 while its blazing breath
scorches everything in sight.

22 Its neck is so tremendous
that everyone trembles,
23 the weakest parts of its body
are harder than iron,
24 and its heart is stone.
25 When this noisy monster appears,
even the most powerful[o]
turn and run in fear.
26 No sword or spear can harm it,
27 and weapons of bronze or iron
are as useless as straw
or rotten wood.
28 Rocks thrown from a sling
cause it no more harm
than husks of grain.
This monster fears no arrows,
29 it simply smiles at spears,
and striking it with a stick
is like slapping it with straw.

30 As it crawls through the mud,
its sharp and spiny hide
tears the ground apart.
31 And when it swims down deep,
the sea starts churning
like boiling oil,
32 and it leaves behind a trail
of shining white foam.
33 No other creature on earth
is so fearless.
34 It is king of all proud creatures,
and it looks upon the others
as nothing.

Job's Reply to the LORD

No One Can Oppose You

42 Job said:
2 No one can oppose you,
because you have the power
to do what you want.
3 You asked why I talk so much
when I know so little.
I have talked about things
that are far beyond
my understanding.
4 You told me to listen
and answer your questions.[p]
5 I heard about you from others;
now I have seen you
with my own eyes.
6 That's why I hate myself
and sit here in dust and ashes
to show my sorrow.

The LORD Corrects Job's Friends

7 The LORD said to Eliphaz:
What my servant Job has said
about me is true, but I am angry at
you and your two friends for not
telling the truth. 8 So I want you to go
over to Job and offer seven bulls and
seven goats on an altar as a sacrifice
to please me.[q] After this, Job will
pray, and I will agree not to punish
you for your foolishness.
9 Eliphaz, Bildad, and Zophar obeyed
the LORD, and he answered Job's prayer.

A Happy Ending

10 After Job had prayed for his three
friends, the LORD made Job twice as rich
as he had been before. 11 Then Job gave
a feast for his brothers and sisters and
for his old friends. They expressed their
sorrow for the suffering the LORD had
brought on him, and they each gave Job
some silver and a gold ring.
12 The LORD now blessed Job more
than ever; he gave him fourteen thousand sheep, six thousand camels, a
thousand pair of oxen, and a thousand
donkeys.
13 In addition to seven sons, Job had
three daughters, 14 whose names were
Jemimah, Keziah, and Keren Happuch.
15 They were the most beautiful women
in that part of the world, and Job gave
them shares of his property, along with
their brothers.
16 Job lived for another one hundred
forty years—long enough to see his
great-grandchildren have children of
their own—17 and when he finally died,
he was very old.

[n] **41.15** *back*: Two ancient translations; Hebrew "pride." [o] **41.25** *most powerful*: Or "gods."
[p] **42.4** *questions*: One possible meaning for the difficult Hebrew text of verse 4.
[q] **42.8** *sacrifice to please me*: These sacrifices have traditionally been called "whole burnt offerings" because the whole animal was burned on the altar. A main purpose of such sacrifices was to please the LORD with the smell of the sacrifice, and so in the CEV they are often called "sacrifices to please the LORD."

PSALMS

ABOUT THIS BOOK

The book of Psalms is the longest book in the Bible. Psalms are poems that can either be sung as songs or spoken as prayers by individuals or groups. There are 150 psalms in this book, and many of them list King David as their author. They were collected over a long period of time and became a very important part of the worship of the people of Israel.

Some of the psalms tell the music leader what instruments should be used and what tunes should be followed. For example, look at Psalm 4 and Psalm 45.

Many of the Bible's main ideas are echoed in the Psalms: praise, thankfulness, faith, hope, sorrow for sin, God's loyalty and help. And at the heart of all the psalms there is a deep trust in God. The writers of the psalms always express their true feelings, whether they are praising God for his blessings or complaining in times of trouble.

In ancient Israel the psalms were used in several different ways: (1) to praise God, as in Psalm 105; (2) to express sorrow, as in Psalm 13; (3) to teach, as in Psalm 1; (4) to honor Israel's king and pray for fairness in his rule, as in Psalm 72; (5) to tell of God's power over all creation, as in Psalm 47; (6) to show love for Jerusalem, as in Psalm 122; and (7) to celebrate festivals, as in Psalm 126. Of course, many of the psalms could be used for more than one purpose.

Jesus used the psalms when he preached and taught, and they were often quoted by the writers of the New Testament. The earliest Christians also used the psalms in worship, teaching, and telling others the good news about what God has done through Jesus Christ. A verse from Psalm 118, for example, is directly referred to six times in the New Testament:

The stone that the builders
tossed aside
has now become
the most important stone.
(118.22)

A QUICK LOOK AT THIS BOOK

The book of Psalms is divided into five sections or "books." Most of the psalms in Books I and II were written by David, while many in Book III were written by either Asaph or the people of Korah. Psalms 120–134 are all "celebration psalms." The five sections of the book of Psalms are:

Book I (1–41)
Book II (42–72)
Book III (73–89)
Book IV (90–106)
Book V (107–150)

BOOK I

(Psalms 1–41)

Psalm 1

The Way to Happiness

1 God blesses those people
who refuse evil advice
and won't follow sinners
or join in sneering at God.
2 Instead, the Law of the LORD
makes them happy,
and they think about it
day and night.

3 They are like trees
growing beside a stream,

trees that produce
fruit in season
and always have leaves.
Those people succeed
in everything they do.

4 That isn't true of those
who are evil,
because they are like straw
blown by the wind.
5 Sinners won't have an excuse
on the day of judgment,
and they won't have a place
with the people of God.
6 The LORD protects everyone
who follows him,
but the wicked follow a road
that leads to ruin.

Psalm 2

The LORD's Chosen King

1 Why do the nations plot,[a]
and why do their people
make useless plans?[b]
2 The kings of this earth
have all joined together
to turn against the LORD
and his chosen one.
3 They say, "Let's cut the ropes
and set ourselves free!"

4 In heaven the LORD laughs
as he sits on his throne,
making fun of the nations.
5 The LORD becomes furious
and threatens them.
His anger terrifies them
as he says,
6 "I've put my king on Zion,
my sacred hill."

7 I will tell the promise
that the LORD made to me:
"You are my son, because today
I have become your father.
8 Ask me for the nations,
and every nation on earth
will belong to you.
9 You will smash them
with an iron rod
and shatter them
like dishes of clay."

10 Be smart, all you rulers,
and pay close attention.
11 Serve and honor the LORD;
be glad and tremble.
12 Show respect to his son
because if you don't,
the LORD might become furious
and suddenly destroy you.[c]
But he blesses and protects
everyone who runs to him.

Psalm 3

[Written by David when he was running from his son Absalom.]

An Early Morning Prayer

1 I have a lot of enemies, LORD.
Many fight against 2 me and say,
"God won't rescue you!"

3 But you are my shield,
and you give me victory
and great honor.
4 I pray to you, and you answer
from your sacred hill.

5 I sleep and wake up refreshed
because you, LORD,
protect me.
6 Ten thousand enemies attack
from every side,
but I am not afraid.

7 Come and save me, LORD God!
Break my enemies' jaws
and shatter their teeth,
8 because you protect
and bless your people.

Psalm 4

[A psalm by David for the music leader. Use stringed instruments.]

An Evening Prayer

1 You are my God and protector.
Please answer my prayer.
I was in terrible distress,
but you set me free.
Now have pity and listen
as I pray.

2 How long will you people
refuse to respect me?[d]
You love foolish things,
and you run after
what is worthless.[e]

3 The LORD has chosen
everyone who is faithful
to be his very own,[f]
and he answers my prayers.
4 But each of you
had better tremble
and turn from your sins.
Silently search your heart
as you lie in bed.
5 Offer the proper sacrifices
and trust the LORD.

[a] **2.1** *Why . . . plot?*: Or "Why are the nations restless?" [b] **2.1** *make useless plans*: Or "grumble uselessly." [c] **2.11,12** *Serve . . . you*: One possible meaning for the difficult Hebrew text of verses 11, 12. [d] **4.2** *me*: Or "my God." [e] **4.2** *foolish . . . worthless*: This may refer to idols and false gods. [f] **4.3** *has chosen . . . very own*: Some Hebrew manuscripts have "work miracles for his faithful people."

[6] There are some who ask,
"Who will be good to us?"
Let your kindness, LORD,
shine brightly on us.
[7] You brought me more happiness
than a rich harvest
of grain and grapes.
[8] I can lie down
and sleep soundly
because you, LORD,
will keep me safe.

Psalm 5

[*A psalm by David*
for the music leader. Use flutes.]

A Prayer for Help

[1] Listen, LORD, as I pray!
Pay attention when I groan.[g]
[2] You are my King and my God.
Answer my cry for help
because I pray to you.
[3] Each morning you listen
to my prayer,
as I bring my requests[h] to you
and wait for your reply.

[4] You are not the kind of God
who is pleased with evil.
Sinners can't stay with you.
[5] No one who boasts can stand
in your presence, LORD,
and you hate evil people.
[6] You destroy every liar,
and you despise violence
and deceit.

[7] Because of your great mercy,
I come to your house, LORD,
and I am filled with wonder
as I bow down to worship
at your holy temple.
[8] You do what is right,
and I ask you to guide me.
Make your teaching clear
because of my enemies.

[9] Nothing they say is true!
They just want to destroy.
Their words are deceitful
like a hidden pit,
and their tongues are good
only for telling lies.
[10] Punish them, God,
and let their own plans
bring their downfall.
Get rid of them!
They keep committing crimes
and turning against you.

[11] Let all who run to you
for protection
always sing joyful songs.
Provide shelter for those
who truly love you
and let them rejoice.
[12] Our LORD, you bless those
who live right,
and you shield them
with your kindness.

Psalm 6

[*A psalm by David for the music leader.*
Use stringed instruments.[i]]

A Prayer in Time of Trouble

[1] Don't punish me, LORD,
or even correct me
when you are angry!
[2] Have pity on me and heal
my feeble body.
My bones tremble with fear,
[3] and I am in deep distress.
How long will it be?

[4] Turn and come to my rescue.
Show your wonderful love
and save me, LORD.
[5] If I die, I cannot praise you
or even remember you.
[6] My groaning has worn me out.
At night my bed and pillow
are soaked with tears.
[7] Sorrow has made my eyes dim,
and my sight has failed
because of my enemies.

[8] You, LORD, heard my crying,
and those hateful people
had better leave me alone.
[9] You have answered my prayer
and my plea for mercy.
[10] My enemies will be ashamed
and terrified,
as they quickly run away
in complete disgrace.

Psalm 7

[*Written by David.*[j] *He sang this to the LORD because of Cush from the tribe of Benjamin.*]

The LORD Always Does Right

[1] You, LORD God,
are my protector.
Rescue me and keep me safe
from all who chase me.
[2] Or else they will rip me apart
like lions attacking a victim,
and no one will save me.

[3] I am innocent, LORD God!
[4] I have not betrayed a friend
or had pity on an enemy[k]
who attacks for no reason.

[g] **5.1** *when I groan*: Or "to my thoughts" or "to my words." [h] **5.3** *requests*: Or "sacrifices." [i] **Psalm 6** *instruments*: The Hebrew text adds "according to the sheminith," which may refer to a musical instrument with eight strings. [j] **Psalm 7** *Written by David*: The Hebrew text has "a shiggaion by David," which may refer to a psalm of mourning. [k] **7.4** *had pity on an enemy*: Or "failed to have pity on an enemy."

5 If I have done any of this,
then let my enemies
chase and capture me.
Let them stomp me to death
and leave me in the dirt.

6 Get angry, LORD God!
Do something!
Attack my furious enemies.
See that justice is done.
7 Make the nations come to you,
as you sit on your throne[l]
above them all.

8 Our LORD, judge the nations!
Judge me and show that I
am honest and innocent.
9 You know every heart and mind,
and you always do right.
Now make violent people stop,
but protect all of us
who obey you.

10 You, God, are my shield,
the protector of everyone
whose heart is right.
11 You see that justice is done,
and each day
you take revenge.
12 Whenever your enemies refuse
to change their ways,
you sharpen your sword
and string your bow.
13 Your deadly arrows are ready
with flaming tips.

14 An evil person is like a woman
about to give birth
to a hateful, deceitful,
and rebellious child.
15 Such people dig a deep hole,
then fall in it themselves.
16 The trouble they cause
comes back on them,
and their heads are crushed
by their own evil deeds.

17 I will praise you, LORD!
You always do right.
I will sing about you,
the LORD Most High.

Psalm 8

[*A psalm by David for the music leader.*[m]]

The Wonderful Name of the LORD

1 Our LORD and Ruler,
your name is wonderful
everywhere on earth!
You let your glory be seen[n]
in the heavens above.
2 With praises from children
and from tiny infants,
you have built a fortress.
It makes your enemies silent,
and all who turn against you
are left speechless.

3 I often think of the heavens
your hands have made,
and of the moon and stars
you put in place.
4 Then I ask, "Why do you care
about us humans?
Why are you concerned
for us weaklings?"
5 You made us a little lower
than you yourself,[o]
and you have crowned us
with glory and honor.

6 You let us rule everything
your hands have made.
And you put all of it
under our power—
7 the sheep and the cattle,
and every wild animal,
8 the birds in the sky,
the fish in the sea,
and all ocean creatures.

9 Our LORD and Ruler,
your name is wonderful
everywhere on earth!

Psalm 9

[*A psalm by David for the music leader. To the tune "The Death of the Son."*]

Sing Praises to the LORD

1 I will praise you, LORD,
with all my heart
and tell about the wonders
you have worked.
2 God Most High, I will rejoice;
I will celebrate and sing
because of you.

3 When my enemies face you,
they run away and stumble
and are destroyed.
4 You take your seat as judge,
and your fair decisions prove
that I was in the right.
5 You warn the nations
and destroy evil people;
you wipe out their names
forever and ever.
6 Our enemies are destroyed
completely for all time.
Their cities are torn down,
and they will never
be remembered again.

[l] **7.7** *sit . . . throne*: Or "return to your place." [m] **Psalm 8** *leader*: The Hebrew text adds "according to the gittith," which may refer to either a musical instrument or a tune.
[n] **8.1** *You . . . seen*: Or "I will worship your glory." [o] **8.5** *you yourself*: Or "the angels" or "the beings in heaven."

7 You rule forever, LORD,
and you are on your throne,
ready for judgment.
8 You judge the world fairly
and treat all nations
with justice.
9 The poor can run to you
because you are a fortress
in times of trouble.
10 Everyone who honors your name
can trust you,
because you are faithful
to all who depend on you.

11 You rule from Zion, LORD,
and we sing about you
to let the nations know
everything you have done.
12 You did not forget
to punish the guilty
or listen to the cries
of those in need.

13 Please have mercy, LORD!
My enemies mistreat me.
Keep me from the gates
that lead to death,
14 and I will sing about you
at the gate to Zion.
I will be happy there
because you rescued me.

15 Our LORD, the nations fell
into their own pits,
and their feet were caught
in their own traps.
16 You showed what you are like,
and you made certain
that justice is done,
but evil people are trapped
by their own evil deeds.
17 The wicked will go down
to the world of the dead
to be with those nations
that forgot about you.

18 The poor and the homeless
won't always be forgotten
and without hope.

19 Do something, LORD!
Don't let the nations win.
Make them stand trial
in your court of law.
20 Make the nations afraid
and let them all discover
just how weak they are.

Psalm 10

A Prayer for Help

1 Why are you far away, LORD?
Why do you hide yourself
when I am in trouble?
2 Proud and brutal people
hunt down the poor.
But let them get caught
by their own evil plans!

3 The wicked brag about
their deepest desires.
Those greedy people hate
and curse you, LORD.
4 The wicked are too proud
to turn to you
or even think about you.
5 They are always successful,
though they can't understand
your teachings,
and they keep sneering
at their enemies.

6 In their hearts they say,
"Nothing can hurt us!
We'll always be happy
and free from trouble."
7 They curse and tell lies,
and all they talk about
is how to be cruel
or how to do wrong.

8 They hide outside villages,
waiting to strike and murder
some innocent victim.
9 They are hungry lions
hiding in the bushes,
hoping to catch
some helpless passerby.
They trap the poor in nets
and drag them away.
10 They crouch down and wait
to grab a victim.
11 They say, "God can't see!
He's got on a blindfold."

12 Do something, LORD God,
and use your powerful arm
to help those in need.
13 The wicked don't respect you.
In their hearts they say,
"God won't punish us!"

14 But you see the trouble
and the distress,
and you will do something.
The poor can count on you,
and so can orphans.
15 Now break the arms
of all merciless people.
Punish them for doing wrong
and make them stop.

16 Our LORD, you will always rule,
but nations will vanish
from the earth.
17 You listen to the longings
of those who suffer.
You offer them hope,
and you pay attention
to their cries for help.
18 You defend orphans
and everyone else in need,
so that no one on earth
can terrify others again.

Psalm 11

[*A psalm by David for the music leader.*]

Trusting the LORD

1 The LORD is my fortress!
Don't say to me,
"Escape like a bird
to the mountains!"
2 You tell me, "Watch out!
Those evil people have put
their arrows on their bows,
and they are standing
in the shadows,
aiming at good people.
3 What can an honest person do
when everything crumbles?"

4 The LORD is sitting
in his sacred temple
on his throne in heaven.
He knows everything we do
because he sees us all.
5 The LORD tests honest people,
but despises those
who are cruel
and love violence.
6 He will send fiery coals[p]
and flaming sulfur
down on the wicked,
and they will drink nothing
but a scorching wind.

7 The LORD always does right
and wants justice done.
Everyone who does right
will see his face.

Psalm 12

[*A psalm by David for the music leader.*[q]]

A Prayer for Help

1 Please help me, LORD!
All who were faithful
and all who were loyal
have disappeared.
2 Everyone tells lies,
and no one is sincere.
3 Won't you chop off
all flattering tongues
that brag so loudly?
4 They say to themselves,
"We are great speakers.
No one else has a chance."

5 But you, LORD, tell them,
"I will do something!
The poor are mistreated
and helpless people moan.
I'll rescue all who suffer."

6 Our LORD, you are true
to your promises,
and your word is like silver
heated seven times
in a fiery furnace.[r]
7 You will protect us
and always keep us safe
from those people.
8 But all who are wicked
will keep on strutting,
while everyone praises
their shameless deeds.[s]

Psalm 13

[*A psalm by David for the music leader.*]

A Prayer for the LORD's Help

1 How much longer, LORD,
will you forget about me?
Will it be forever?
How long will you hide?
2 How long must I be confused
and miserable all day?
How long will my enemies
keep beating me down?

3 Please listen, LORD God,
and answer my prayers.
Make my eyes sparkle again,
or else I will fall
into the sleep of death.
4 My enemies will say,
"Now we've won!"
They will be greatly pleased
when I am defeated.

5 I trust your love,
and I feel like celebrating
because you rescued me.
6 You have been good to me, LORD,
and I will sing about you.

Psalm 14

[*A psalm by David for the music leader.*]

No One Can Ignore the LORD

1 Only a fool would say,
"There is no God!"
People like that are worthless;
they are heartless and cruel
and never do right.

2 From heaven the LORD
looks down to see
if anyone is wise enough
to search for him.
3 But all of them are corrupt;
no one does right.

4 Won't you evil people learn?
You refuse to pray,
and you gobble down
the LORD's people.

[p] **11.6** *fiery coals*: Or "trouble, fire." [q] **Psalm 12** *leader*: The Hebrew text adds "according to the sheminith," which may be a musical instrument with eight strings. [r] **12.6** *in a fiery furnace*: The Hebrew text has "in a furnace to the ground," which may describe part of a process for refining silver in Old Testament times. [s] **12.8** *while . . . deeds*: One possible meaning for the difficult Hebrew text.

5 But you will be frightened,
because God is on the side
of every good person.
6 You may spoil the plans
of the poor,
but the LORD protects them.

7 I long for someone from Zion
to come and save Israel!
Our LORD, when you bless
your people again,
Jacob's family will be glad,
and Israel will celebrate.

Psalm 15
[*A psalm by David.*]

Who May Worship the LORD?

1 Who may stay in God's temple
or live on the holy mountain
of the LORD?

2 Only those who obey God
and do as they should.
They speak the truth
3 and don't spread gossip;
they treat others fairly
and don't say cruel things.

4 They hate worthless people,
but show respect for all
who worship the LORD.
And they keep their promises,
no matter what the cost.
5 They lend their money
without charging interest,
and they don't take bribes
to hurt the innocent.

Those who do these things
will always stand firm.

Psalm 16
[*A special psalm by David.*]

The Best Choice

1 Protect me, LORD God!
I run to you for safety,
2 and I have said,
"Only you are my Lord!
Every good thing I have
is a gift from you."

3 Your people are wonderful,
and they make me happy,[t]
4 but worshipers of other gods
will have much sorrow.[u]
I refuse to offer sacrifices
of blood to those gods
or worship in their name.

5 You, LORD, are all I want!
You are my choice,
and you keep me safe.
6 You make my life pleasant,
and my future is bright.

7 I praise you, LORD,
for being my guide.
Even in the darkest night,
your teachings fill my mind.
8 I will always look to you,
as you stand beside me
and protect me from fear.
9 With all my heart,
I will celebrate,
and I can safely rest.

10 I am your chosen one.
You won't leave me in the grave
or let my body decay.
11 You have shown me
the path to life,
and you make me glad
by being near to me.
Sitting at your right side,[v]
I will always be joyful.

Psalm 17
[*A prayer by David.*]

The Prayer of an Innocent Person

1 I am innocent, LORD!
Won't you listen as I pray
and beg for help?
I am honest!
Please hear my prayer.
2 Only you can say
that I am innocent,
because only your eyes
can see the truth.

3 You know my heart,
and even during the night
you have tested me
and found me innocent.
I have made up my mind
never to tell a lie.
4 I don't do like others.
I obey your teachings
and am not cruel.
5 I have followed you,
without ever stumbling.

6 I pray to you, God,
because you will help me.
Listen and answer my prayer!
7 Show your wonderful love.
Your mighty arm protects those
who run to you for safety
from their enemies.
8 Protect me as you would
your very own eyes;
hide me in the shadow
of your wings.

[t] **16.3** *Your people . . . happy*: Or "I was happy worshiping gods I thought were powerful."
[u] **16.4** *but . . . sorrow*: One possible meaning for the difficult Hebrew text.
[v] **16.11** *right side*: The place of power and honor.

[9] Don't let my brutal enemies
attack from all sides
and kill me.
[10] They refuse to show mercy,
and they keep bragging.

[11] They have caught up with me!
My enemies are everywhere,
eagerly hoping to smear me
in the dirt.
[12] They are like hungry lions
hunting for food,
or like young lions
hiding in ambush.

[13] Do something, LORD!
Attack and defeat them.
Take your sword and save me
from those evil people.
[14] Use your powerful arm
and rescue me
from the hands of mere humans
whose world won't last.[w]

You provide food
for those you love.
Their children have plenty,
and their grandchildren
will have more than enough.

[15] I am innocent, LORD,
and I will see your face!
When I awake, all I want
is to see you as you are.

Psalm 18

[*For the music leader. A psalm by David, the LORD's servant. David sang this to the LORD after the LORD had rescued him from his enemies, but especially from Saul.*]

David's Song of Thanks

[1] I love you, LORD God,
and you make me strong.
[2] You are my mighty rock,[x]
my fortress, my protector,
the rock where I am safe,
my shield, my powerful weapon,[y]
and my place of shelter.

[3] I praise you, LORD!
I prayed, and you rescued me
from my enemies.
[4] Death had wrapped
its ropes around me,
and I was almost swallowed
by its flooding waters.

[5] Ropes from the world
of the dead
had coiled around me,
and death had set a trap
in my path.

[6] I was in terrible trouble
when I called out to you,
but from your temple
you heard me
and answered my prayer.
[7] The earth shook and shivered,
and the mountains trembled
down to their roots.
You were angry
[8] and breathed out smoke.
Scorching heat and fiery flames
spewed from your mouth.

[9] You opened the heavens
like curtains,
and you came down
with storm clouds
under your feet.
[10] You rode on the backs
of flying creatures
and swooped down
with the wind as wings.
[11] Darkness was your robe;
thunderclouds filled the sky,
hiding you from sight.
[12] Hailstones and fiery coals
lit up the sky
in front of you.

[13] LORD Most High, your voice
thundered from the heavens,
as hailstones and fiery coals
poured down like rain.
[14] You scattered your enemies
with arrows of lightning.
[15] You roared at the sea,
and its deepest channels
could be seen.
You snorted,
and the earth shook
to its foundations.

[16] You reached down from heaven,
and you lifted me
from deep in the ocean.
[17] You rescued me from enemies,
who were hateful
and too powerful for me.
[18] On the day disaster struck,
they came and attacked,
but you defended me.
[19] When I was fenced in,
you freed and rescued me
because you love me.

[20] You are good to me, LORD,
because I do right,
and you reward me
because I am innocent.
[21] I do what you want
and never turn to do evil.

[w] **17.14** *last*: One possible meaning for the difficult Hebrew text of verse 14. [x] **18.2** *mighty rock*: The Hebrew text has "rock," which is sometimes used in poetry to compare the Lord to a mountain where his people can run for protection from their enemies. [y] **18.2** *my powerful weapon*: The Hebrew text has "the horn," which refers to the horn of a bull, one of the most powerful animals in ancient Palestine.

22 I keep your laws in mind
and never look away
from your teachings.
23 I obey you completely
and guard against sin.
24 You have been good to me
because I do right;
you have rewarded me
for being innocent
by your standards.

25 You are always loyal
to your loyal people,
and you are faithful
to the faithful.
26 With all who are sincere,
you are sincere,
but you treat the unfaithful
as their deeds deserve.
27 You rescue the humble,
but you put down all
who are proud.

28 You, the LORD God,
keep my lamp burning
and turn darkness to light.
29 You help me defeat armies
and capture cities.

30 Your way is perfect, LORD,
and your word is correct.
You are a shield for those
who run to you for help.
31 You alone are God!
Only you are a mighty rock.[z]
32 You give me strength
and guide me right.
33 You make my feet run as fast
as those of a deer,
and you help me stand
on the mountains.

34 You teach my hands to fight
and my arms to use
a bow of bronze.
35 You alone are my shield.
Your right hand supports me,
and by coming to help me,
you have made me famous.
36 You clear the way for me,
and now I won't stumble.

37 I kept chasing my enemies,
until I caught them
and destroyed them.
38 I stuck my sword
through my enemies,
and they were crushed
under my feet.
39 You helped me win victories,
and you forced my attackers
to fall victim to me.

40 You made my enemies run,
and I killed them.
41 They cried out for help,
but no one saved them;
they called out to you,
but there was no answer.
42 I ground them to dust
blown by the wind,
and I poured them out
like mud in the streets.

43 You rescued me
from stubborn people,
and you made me the leader
of foreign nations,
who are now my slaves.
44 They obey and come crawling.
45 They have lost all courage,
and from their fortresses,
they come trembling.

46 You are the living LORD!
I will praise you.
You are a mighty rock.[z]
I will honor you
for keeping me safe.
47 You took revenge for me,
and you put nations
in my power.
48 You protected me
from violent enemies
and made me much greater
than all of them.

49 I will praise you, LORD,
and I will honor you
among the nations.
50 You give glorious victories
to your chosen king.
Your faithful love for David
and for his descendants
will never end.

Psalm 19

[*A psalm by David for the music leader.*]

The Wonders of God and the Goodness of His Law

1 The heavens keep telling
the wonders of God,
and the skies declare
what he has done.
2 Each day informs
the following day;
each night announces
to the next.
3 They don't speak a word,
and there is never
the sound of a voice.
4 Yet their message reaches
all the earth,
and it travels
around the world.

In the heavens a tent
is set up for the sun.
5 It rises like a bridegroom

[z] **18.31** *mighty rock*: See the note at 18.2.

[z] **18.46** *mighty rock*: See the note at 18.2.

and gets ready like a hero
eager to run a race.
6 It travels all the way
across the sky.
Nothing hides from its heat.

7 The Law of the LORD is perfect;
it gives us new life.
His teachings last forever,
and they give wisdom
to ordinary people.
8 The LORD's instruction is right;
it makes our hearts glad.
His commands shine brightly,
and they give us light.

9 Worshiping the LORD is sacred;
he will always be worshiped.
All of his decisions
are correct and fair.
10 They are worth more
than the finest gold
and are sweeter than honey
from a honeycomb.

11 By your teachings, Lord,
I am warned;
by obeying them,
I am greatly rewarded.
12 None of us know our faults.
Forgive me when I sin
without knowing it.
13 Don't let me do wrong
on purpose, Lord,
or let sin have control
over my life.
Then I will be innocent,
and not guilty
of some terrible fault.

14 Let my words and my thoughts
be pleasing to you, LORD,
because you are my mighty rock[z]
and my protector.

Psalm 20

[*A psalm by David for the music leader.*]

A Prayer for Victory

1 I pray that the LORD
will listen when you
are in trouble,
and that the God of Jacob
will keep you safe.
2 May the LORD send help
from his temple
and come to your rescue
from Mount Zion.
3 May he remember your gifts
and be pleased
with what you bring.

4 May God do what you want most
and let all go well for you.
5 Then you will win victories,
and we will celebrate,
while raising our banners
in the name of our God.
May the LORD answer
all of your prayers!

6 I am certain, LORD,
that you will help
your chosen king.
You will answer my prayers
from your holy place
in heaven,
and you will save me
with your mighty arm.

7 Some people trust the power
of chariots or horses,
but we trust you, LORD God.
8 Others will stumble and fall,
but we will be strong
and stand firm.

9 Give the king victory, LORD,
and answer our prayers.[a]

Psalm 21

[*A psalm by David for the music leader.*]

Thanking the LORD for Victory

1 Our LORD, your mighty power
makes the king glad,
and he celebrates victories
that you have given him.
2 You did what he wanted most
and never told him "No."
3 You truly blessed the king,
and you placed on him
a crown of finest gold.
4 He asked to live a long time,
and you promised him life
that never ends.

5 The king is highly honored.
You have let him win victories
that have made him famous.
6 You have given him blessings
that will last forever,
and you have made him glad
by being so near to him.
7 LORD Most High,
the king trusts you,
and your kindness
keeps him from defeat.

8 With your mighty arm, LORD,
you will strike down all
of your hateful enemies.
9 They will be destroyed by fire
once you are here,
and because of your anger,
flames will swallow them.
10 You will wipe their families
from the earth,
and they will disappear.

[z] **19.14** *mighty rock*: See the note at 18.2.

[a] **20.9** *victory . . . prayers*: Or "victory. He (God or the king) answers us."

11 All their plans to harm you
will come to nothing.
12 You will make them run away
by shooting your arrows
at their faces.

13 Show your strength, LORD,
so that we may sing
and praise your power.

Psalm 22

[A psalm by David for the music leader. To the tune "A Deer at Dawn."]

Suffering and Praise

1 My God, my God, why have you
deserted me?
Why are you so far away?
Won't you listen to my groans
and come to my rescue?
2 I cry out day and night,
but you don't answer,
and I can never rest.

3 Yet you are the holy God,
ruling from your throne
and praised by Israel.
4 Our ancestors trusted you,
and you rescued them.
5 When they cried out for help,
you saved them,
and you did not let them down
when they depended on you.

6 But I am merely a worm,
far less than human,
and I am hated and rejected
by people everywhere.
7 Everyone who sees me
makes fun and sneers.
They shake their heads,
8 and say, "Trust the LORD!
If you are his favorite,
let him protect you
and keep you safe."

9 You, LORD, brought me
safely through birth,
and you protected me
when I was a baby
at my mother's breast.
10 From the day I was born,
I have been in your care,
and from the time of my birth,
you have been my God.

11 Don't stay far off
when I am in trouble
with no one to help me.
12 Enemies are all around
like a herd of wild bulls.
Powerful bulls from Bashan[b]
are everywhere.
13 My enemies are like lions
roaring and attacking
with jaws open wide.

14 I have no more strength
than a few drops of water.
All my bones are out of joint;
my heart is like melted wax.
15 My strength has dried up
like a broken clay pot,
and my tongue sticks
to the roof of my mouth.
You, God, have left me
to die in the dirt.

16 Brutal enemies attack me
like a pack of dogs,
tearing at[c] my hands
and my feet.
17 I can count all my bones,
and my enemies just stare
and sneer at me.
18 They took my clothes
and gambled for them.

19 Don't stay far away, LORD!
My strength comes from you,
so hurry and help.
20 Rescue me from enemy swords
and save me from those dogs.
21 Don't let lions eat me.

You rescued me from the horns
of wild bulls,
22 and when your people meet,
I will praise you, LORD.

23 All who worship the LORD,
now praise him!
You belong to Jacob's family
and to the people of Israel,
so fear and honor the LORD!
24 The LORD doesn't hate
or despise the helpless
in all of their troubles.
When I cried out, he listened
and did not turn away.

25 When your people meet,
you will fill my heart
with your praises, LORD,
and everyone will see me
keep my promises to you.
26 The poor will eat and be full,
and all who worship you
will be thankful
and live in hope.

27 Everyone on this earth
will remember you, LORD.
People all over the world
will turn and worship you,
28 because you are in control,
the ruler of all nations.

[b]**22.12** *Bashan*: A land east of the Jordan River, where there were pastures suitable for raising fine cattle. [c]**22.16** *tearing at*: One possible meaning for the difficult Hebrew text.

29 All who are rich
and have more than enough
will bow down to you, Lord.
Even those who are dying
and almost in the grave
will come and bow down.
30 In the future, everyone
will worship and learn
about you, our Lord.
31 People not yet born
will be told,
"The Lord has saved us!"

Psalm 23
[*A psalm by David.*]

The Good Shepherd

1 You, LORD, are my shepherd.
I will never be in need.
2 You let me rest in fields
of green grass.
You lead me to streams
of peaceful water,
3 and you refresh my life.

You are true to your name,
and you lead me
along the right paths.
4 I may walk through valleys
as dark as death,
but I won't be afraid.
You are with me,
and your shepherd's rod[d]
makes me feel safe.

5 You treat me to a feast,
while my enemies watch.
You honor me as your guest,
and you fill my cup
until it overflows.

6 Your kindness and love
will always be with me
each day of my life,
and I will live forever
in your house, LORD.

Psalm 24
[*A psalm by David.*]

Who Can Enter the LORD's Temple?

1 The earth and everything on it
belong to the LORD.
The world and its people
belong to him.
2 The LORD placed it all
on the oceans and rivers.

3 Who may climb the LORD's hill[e]
or stand in his holy temple?
4 Only those who do right
for the right reasons,
and don't worship idols
or tell lies under oath.
5 The LORD God, who saves them,
will bless and reward them,
6 because they worship and serve
the God of Jacob.[f]
7 Open the ancient gates,
so that the glorious king
may come in.

8 Who is this glorious king?
He is our LORD, a strong
and mighty warrior.

9 Open the ancient gates,
so that the glorious king
may come in.

10 Who is this glorious king?
He is our LORD,
the All-Powerful!

Psalm 25
[*By David.*]

A Prayer for Guidance and Help

1 I offer you my heart, LORD God,
2 and I trust you.
Don't make me ashamed
or let enemies defeat me.
3 Don't disappoint any
of your worshipers,
but disappoint all
deceitful liars.
4 Show me your paths
and teach me to follow;
5 guide me by your truth
and instruct me.
You keep me safe,
and I always trust you.

6 Please, LORD, remember,
you have always
been patient and kind.
7 Forget each wrong I did
when I was young.
Show how truly kind you are
and remember me.
8 You are honest and merciful,
and you teach sinners
how to follow your path.

9 You lead humble people
to do what is right
and to stay on your path.
10 In everything you do,
you are kind and faithful
to everyone who keeps
our agreement with you.

11 Be true to your name, LORD,
by forgiving each one
of my terrible sins.

[d]**23.4** *shepherd's rod*: The Hebrew text mentions two objects carried by the shepherd: a club to defend against wild animals and a long pole to guide and control the sheep. [e]**24.3** *the LORD's hill*: The hill in Jerusalem where the temple was built. [f]**24.6** *worship . . . Jacob*: Two ancient translations; Hebrew "worship God and serve the descendants of Jacob."

12 You will show the right path
to all who worship you.
13 They will have plenty,
and then their children
will receive the land.

14 Our LORD, you are the friend
of your worshipers,
and you make an agreement
with all of us.
15 I always look to you,
because you rescue me
from every trap.
16 I am lonely and troubled.
Show that you care
and have pity on me.
17 My awful worries keep growing.
Rescue me from sadness.
18 See my troubles and misery
and forgive my sins.

19 Look at all my enemies!
See how much they hate me.
20 I come to you for shelter.
Protect me, keep me safe,
and don't disappoint me.
21 I obey you with all my heart,
and I trust you, knowing
that you will save me.

22 Our God, please save Israel
from all of its troubles.

Psalm 26
[By David.]

The Prayer of an Innocent Person

1 Show that I am right, LORD!
I stay true to myself,
and I have trusted you
without doubting.
2 Test my thoughts and find out
what I am like.
3 I never forget your kindness,
and I am always faithful
to you.[g]
4 I don't spend my time
with worthless liars
5 or go with evil crowds.

6 I wash my hands, LORD,
to show my innocence,
and I worship at your altar,
7 while gratefully singing
about your wonders.
8 I love the temple
where you live, and where
your glory shines.
9 Don't sweep me away,
as you do sinners.
Don't punish me with death
as you do those people
who are brutal
10 or full of meanness
or who bribe others.

11 I stay true to myself.
Be kind and rescue me.

12 Now I stand on solid ground!
And when your people meet,
I will praise you, LORD.

Psalm 27
[By David.]

A Prayer of Praise

1 You, LORD, are the light
that keeps me safe.
I am not afraid of anyone.
You protect me,
and I have no fears.
2 Brutal people may attack
and try to kill me,
but they will stumble.
Fierce enemies may attack,
but they will fall.
3 Armies may surround me,
but I won't be afraid;
war may break out,
but I will trust you.

4 I ask only one thing, LORD:
Let me live in your house
every day of my life
to see how wonderful you are
and to pray in your temple.

5 In times of trouble,
you will protect me.
You will hide me in your tent
and keep me safe
on top of a mighty rock.[h]
6 You will let me defeat
all of my enemies.
Then I will celebrate,
as I enter your tent
with animal sacrifices
and songs of praise.

7 Please listen when I pray!
Have pity. Answer my prayer.
8 My heart tells me to pray.
I am eager to see your face,
9 so don't hide from me.
I am your servant,
and you have helped me.
Don't turn from me in anger.
You alone keep me safe.
Don't reject or desert me.
10 Even if my father and mother
should desert me,
you will take care of me.

11 Teach me to follow, LORD,
and lead me on the right path
because of my enemies.
12 Don't let them do to me
what they want.
People tell lies about me
and make terrible threats,

[g] 26.3 *I am . . . to you*: Or "I trust your faithfulness."
[h] 27.5 *mighty rock*: See the note at18.2.

13 but I know I will live
to see how kind you are.

14 Trust the LORD!
Be brave and strong
and trust the LORD.

Psalm 28
[*By David.*]

A Prayer for Help

1 Only you, LORD,
are a mighty rock![h]
Don't refuse to help me
when I pray.
If you don't answer me,
I will soon be dead.
2 Please listen to my prayer
and my cry for help,
as I lift my hands
toward your holy temple.

3 Don't drag me away, LORD,
with those cruel people,
who speak kind words,
while planning trouble.
4 Treat them as they deserve!
Punish them for their sins.
5 They don't pay any attention
to your wonderful deeds.
Now you will destroy them
and leave them in ruin.

6 I praise you, LORD,
for answering my prayers.
7 You are my strong shield,
and I trust you completely.
You have helped me,
and I will celebrate
and thank you in song.

8 You give strength
to your people, LORD,
and you save and protect
your chosen ones.
9 Come save us and bless us.
Be our shepherd and always
carry us in your arms.

Psalm 29
[*A psalm by David.*]

The Voice of the LORD in a Storm

1 All of you angels[i] in heaven,
honor the glory and power
of the LORD!
2 Honor the wonderful name
of the LORD,
and worship the LORD
most holy and glorious.[j]

3 The voice of the LORD
echoes over the oceans.
The glorious LORD God
thunders above the roar
of the raging sea,
4 and his voice is mighty
and marvelous.
5 The voice of the LORD
destroys the cedar trees;
the LORD shatters cedars
on Mount Lebanon.
6 God makes Mount Lebanon
skip like a calf
and Mount Hermon
jump like a wild ox.

7 The voice of the LORD
makes lightning flash
8 and the desert tremble.
And because of the LORD,
the desert near Kadesh
shivers and shakes.

9 The voice of the LORD
makes deer give birth
before their time.[k]
Forests are stripped of leaves,
and the temple is filled
with shouts of praise.

10 The LORD rules on his throne,
king of the flood[l] forever.
11 Pray that our LORD
will make us strong
and give us peace.

Psalm 30
[*A psalm by David for the dedication of the temple.*]

A Prayer of Thanks

1 I will praise you, LORD!
You saved me from the grave
and kept my enemies
from celebrating my death.
2 I prayed to you, LORD God,
and you healed me,
3 saving me from death
and the grave.

4 Your faithful people, LORD,
will praise you with songs
and honor your holy name.
5 Your anger lasts a little while,
but your kindness lasts
for a lifetime.
At night we may cry,
but when morning comes
we will celebrate.

6 I was carefree and thought,
"I'll never be shaken!"

[h] **28.1** *mighty rock*: See the note at 18.2. [i] **29.1** *angels*: Or "supernatural beings" or "gods." [j] **29.2** *most . . . glorious*: Or "in his holy place" or "and wear your glorious clothes." [k] **29.9** *makes . . . time*: Or "twists the oak trees around." [l] **29.10** *king of the flood*: In ancient times the people of Israel believed that a mighty ocean surrounded all of creation, and that God could release the water to flood the earth.

[7] You, LORD, were my friend,
and you made me strong
as a mighty mountain.
But when you hid your face,
I was crushed.

[8] I prayed to you, LORD,
and in my prayer I said,
[9] "What good will it do you
if I am in the grave?
Once I have turned to dust,
how can I praise you
or tell how loyal you are?
[10] Have pity, LORD! Help!"

[11] You have turned my sorrow
into joyful dancing.
No longer am I sad
and wearing sackcloth.[m]
[12] I thank you from my heart,
and I will never stop
singing your praises,
my LORD and my God.

Psalm 31

[*A psalm by David for the music leader.*]

A Prayer for Protection

[1] I come to you, LORD,
for protection.
Don't let me be ashamed.
Do as you have promised
and rescue me.
[2] Listen to my prayer
and hurry to save me.
Be my mighty rock[n]
and the fortress
where I am safe.

[3] You, LORD God,
are my mighty rock
and my fortress.
Lead me and guide me,
so that your name
will be honored.
[4] Protect me from hidden traps
and keep me safe.
[5] You are faithful,
and I trust you
because you rescued me.

[6] I hate the worshipers
of worthless idols,
but I trust you, LORD.
[7] I celebrate and shout
because you are kind.
You saw all my suffering,
and you cared for me.
[8] You kept me from the hands
of my enemies,
and you set me free.

[9] Have pity, LORD!
I am hurting and almost blind.
My whole body aches.

[10] I have known only sorrow
all my life long, and I suffer
year after year.
I am weak from sin,
and my bones are limp.

[11] My enemies insult me.
Neighbors are even worse,
and I disgust my friends.
People meet me on the street,
and they turn and run.
[12] I am completely forgotten
like someone dead.
I am merely a broken dish.
[13] I hear the crowds whisper,
"Everyone is afraid!"
They are plotting and scheming
to murder me.

[14] But I trust you, LORD,
and I claim you as my God.
[15] My life is in your hands.
Save me from enemies
who hunt me down.
[16] Smile on me, your servant.
Have pity and rescue me.

[17] I pray only to you.
Don't disappoint me.
Disappoint my cruel enemies
until they lie silent
in their graves.
[18] Silence those proud liars!
Make them stop bragging
and insulting your people.

[19] You are wonderful,
and while everyone watches,
you store up blessings for all
who honor and trust you.
[20] You are their shelter
from harmful plots,
and you are their protection
from vicious gossip.

[21] I will praise you, LORD,
for showing great kindness
when I was like a city
under attack.
[22] I was terrified and thought,
"They've chased me
far away from you!"
But you answered my prayer
when I shouted for help.

[23] All who belong to the LORD,
show how you love him.
The LORD protects the faithful,
but he severely punishes
everyone who is proud.
[24] All who trust the LORD,
be cheerful and strong.

[m] **30.11** *sackcloth*: A rough, dark-colored cloth made from goat or camel hair and used to make grain sacks. It was worn in times of trouble or sorrow. [n] **31.2** *mighty rock*: See the note at 18.2.

Psalm 32

[*A special psalm by David.*]

The Joy of Forgiveness

1 Our God, you bless everyone
whose sins you forgive
and wipe away.
2 You bless them by saying,
"You told me your sins,
without trying to hide them,
and now I forgive you."

3 Before I confessed my sins,
my bones felt limp,
and I groaned all day long.
4 Night and day your hand
weighed heavily on me,
and my strength was gone
as in the summer heat.

5 So I confessed my sins
and told them all to you.
I said, "I'll tell the LORD
each one of my sins."
Then you forgave me
and took away my guilt.

6 We worship you, Lord,
and we should always pray
whenever we find out
that we have sinned.[o]
Then we won't be swept away
by a raging flood.
7 You are my hiding place!
You protect me from trouble,
and you put songs in my heart
because you have saved me.

8 You said to me,
"I will point out the road
that you should follow.
I will be your teacher
and watch over you.
9 Don't be stupid
like horses and mules
that must be led with ropes
to make them obey."

10 All kinds of troubles
will strike the wicked,
but your kindness shields those
who trust you, LORD.
11 And so your good people
should celebrate and shout.

Psalm 33

Sing Praises to the LORD

1 You are the LORD's people.
Obey him and celebrate!
He deserves your praise.
2 Praise the LORD with harps!
Use harps with ten strings
to make music for him.
3 Sing a new song. Shout!
Play beautiful music.
4 The LORD is truthful;
he can be trusted.
5 He loves justice and fairness,
and he is kind to everyone
everywhere on earth.

6 The LORD made the heavens
and everything in them
by his word.
7 He scooped up the ocean
and stored the water.
8 Everyone in this world
should worship and honor
the LORD!
9 As soon as he spoke
the world was created;
at his command,
the earth was formed.

10 The LORD destroys the plans
and spoils the schemes
of the nations.
11 But what the LORD has planned
will stand forever.
His thoughts never change.
12 The LORD blesses each nation
that worships only him.
He blesses his chosen ones.
13 The LORD looks at the world
14 from his throne in heaven,
and he watches us all.
15 The LORD gave us each a mind,
and nothing we do
can be hidden from him.

16 Mighty armies alone
cannot win wars for a king;
great strength by itself
cannot keep a soldier safe.
17 In war the strength of a horse
cannot be trusted
to take you to safety.
18 But the LORD watches over
all who honor him
and trust his kindness.
19 He protects them from death
and starvation.

20 We depend on you, LORD,
to help and protect us.
21 You make our hearts glad
because we trust you,
the only God.
22 Be kind and bless us!
We depend on you.

Psalm 34

[*Written by David when he pretended to be crazy in front of Abimelech, so that Abimelech would send him away, and David could leave.*]

Honor the LORD

1 I will always praise the LORD.
2 With all my heart,
I will praise the LORD.

[o] **32.6** *whenever . . . sinned*: Hebrew "at a time of finding only."

Let all who are helpless,
listen and be glad.
3 Honor the LORD with me!
Celebrate his great name.

4 I asked the LORD for help,
and he saved me
from all my fears.
5 Keep your eyes on the LORD!
You will shine like the sun
and never blush with shame.
6 I was a nobody, but I prayed,
and the LORD saved me
from all my troubles.

7 If you honor the LORD,
his angel will protect you.
8 Discover for yourself
that the LORD is kind.
Come to him for protection,
and you will be glad.

9 Honor the LORD!
You are his special people.
No one who honors the LORD
will ever be in need.
10 Young lions[p] may go hungry
or even starve,
but if you trust the LORD,
you will never miss out
on anything good.

11 Come, my children, listen
as I teach you
to respect the LORD.
12 Do you want to live
and enjoy a long life?
13 Then don't say cruel things
and don't tell lies.
14 Do good instead of evil
and try to live at peace.

15 If you obey the LORD,
he will watch over you
and answer your prayers.
16 But God despises evil people,
and he will wipe them all
from the earth,
till they are forgotten.
17 When his people pray for help,
he listens and rescues them
from their troubles.
18 The LORD is there to rescue
all who are discouraged
and have given up hope.

19 The LORD's people
may suffer a lot,
but he will always
bring them safely through.
20 Not one of their bones
will ever be broken.

21 Wicked people are killed
by their own evil deeds,
and if you hate God's people
you will be punished.
22 The LORD saves the lives
of his servants.
Run to him for protection,
and you won't be punished.

Psalm 35

[*A psalm by David.*]

A Prayer for Protection from Enemies

1 Fight my enemies, LORD!
Attack my attackers!
2 Shield me and help me.
3 Aim your spear at everyone
who hunts me down,
but promise to save me.

4 Let all who want to kill me
be disappointed
and disgraced.
Chase away and confuse
all who plan to harm me.
5 Send your angel after them
and let them be like straw
in the wind.
6 Make them run in the dark
on a slippery road,
as your angel chases them.
7 I did them no harm,
but they hid a net
to trap me,
and they dug a deep pit
to catch and kill me.
8 Surprise them with disaster!
Trap them in their own nets
and let them fall and rot
in the pits they have dug.

9 I will celebrate and be joyful
because you, LORD,
have saved me.
10 Every bone in my body
will shout:
"No one is like the LORD!"
You protect the helpless
from those in power;
you save the poor and needy
from those who hurt them.

11 Liars accuse me of crimes
I know nothing about.
12 They repay evil for good,
and I feel all alone.
13 When they were sick,
I wore sackcloth[q]
and went without food.[r]
I truly prayed for them,[s]
14 as I would for a friend
or a relative.

[p] **34.10** *Young lions*: In the Psalms wild animals often stand for God's enemies.
[q] **35.13** *sackcloth*: See the note at 30.11.
[r] **35.13** *went without food*: People sometimes went without food (called "fasting") to show sorrow.
[s] **35.13** *I . . . them*: Or "My prayer wasn't answered, but I prayed."

I was in sorrow and mourned,
as I would for my mother.

15 I have stumbled,
and worthless liars
I don't even know
surround me and sneer.
16 Worthless people make fun[t]
and never stop laughing.
17 But all you do is watch!
When will you do something?
Save me from the attack
of those vicious lions.
18 And when your people meet,
I will praise you
and thank you, Lord,
in front of them all.

19 Don't let my brutal enemies
be glad because of me.
They hate me for no reason.
Don't let them wink
behind my back.
20 They say hurtful things,
and they lie to people
who want to live in peace.
21 They are quick to accuse me.
They say, "You did it!
We saw you ourselves."

22 You see everything, LORD!
Please don't keep silent
or stay so far away.
23 Fight to defend me, Lord God,
24 and prove that I am right
by your standards.
Don't let them laugh at me
25 or say to each other,
"Now we've got what we want!
We'll gobble him down!"

26 Disappoint and confuse
all who are glad
to see me in trouble,
but disgrace and embarrass
my proud enemies who say to me,
"You are nothing!"

27 Let all who want me to win
be happy and joyful.
From now on let them say,
"The LORD is wonderful!
God is glad when all goes well
for his servant."
28 Then I will shout all day,
"Praise the LORD God!
He did what was right."

Psalm 36

[For the music leader by David, the LORD's servant.]

Human Sin and God's Goodness

1 Sinners don't respect God;
sin is all they think about.
2 They like themselves too much
to hate their own sins
or even to see them.
3 They tell deceitful lies,
and they don't have the sense
to live right.
4 Those people stay awake,
thinking up mischief,
and they follow the wrong road,
refusing to turn from sin.

5 Your love is faithful, LORD,
and even the clouds in the sky
can depend on you.
6 Your decisions are always fair.
They are firm like mountains,
deep like the sea,
and all people and animals
are under your care.

7 Your love is a treasure,
and everyone finds shelter
in the shadow of your wings.
8 You give your guests a feast
in your house,
and you serve a tasty drink
that flows like a river.
9 The life-giving fountain
belongs to you,
and your light gives light
to each of us.

10 Our LORD, keep showing love
to everyone who knows you,
and use your power to save all
whose thoughts please you.
11 Don't let those proud
and merciless people
kick me around
or chase me away.

12 Look at those wicked people!
They are knocked down,
never to get up again.

Psalm 37

[By David.]

Trust the LORD

1 Don't be annoyed by anyone
who does wrong,
and don't envy them.
2 They will soon disappear
like grass without rain.

3 Trust the LORD and live right!
The land will be yours,
and you will be safe.
4 Do what the LORD wants,
and he will give you
your heart's desire.

5 Let the LORD lead you
and trust him to help.
6 Then it will be as clear

[t]35.16 *Worthless . . . fun*: One possible meaning for the difficult Hebrew text.

as the noonday sun
that you were right.

7 Be patient and trust the LORD.
Don't let it bother you
when all goes well for those
who do sinful things.
8 Don't be angry or furious.
Anger can lead to sin.
9 All sinners will disappear,
but if you trust the LORD,
the land will be yours.

10 Sinners will soon disappear,
never to be found,
11 but the poor will take the land
and enjoy a big harvest.

12 Merciless people make plots
against good people
and snarl like animals,
13 but the Lord laughs and knows
their time is coming soon.
14 The wicked kill with swords
and shoot arrows to murder
the poor and the needy
and all who do right.
15 But they will be killed
by their own swords,
and their arrows
will be broken.

16 It is better to live right
and be poor
than to be sinful and rich.
17 The wicked will lose all
of their power,
but the LORD gives strength
to everyone who is good.

18 Those who obey the LORD
are daily in his care,
and what he has given them
will be theirs forever.
19 They won't be in trouble
when times are bad,
and they will have plenty
when food is scarce.

20 Wicked people are enemies
of the LORD
and will vanish like smoke
from a field on fire.

21 An evil person borrows
and never pays back;
a good person is generous
and never stops giving.
22 Everyone the LORD blesses
will receive the land;
everyone the LORD curses
will be destroyed.

23 If you do what the LORD wants,
he will make certain
each step you take is sure.
24 The LORD will hold your hand,
and if you stumble,
you still won't fall.

25 As long as I can remember,
good people have never
been left helpless,
and their children have never
gone begging for food.
26 They gladly give and lend,
and their children
turn out good.

27 If you stop sinning
and start doing right,
you will keep living
and be secure forever.
28 The LORD loves justice,
and he won't ever desert
his faithful people.
He always protects them,
but destroys the children
of the wicked.
29 God's people will own the land
and live here forever.

30 Words of wisdom come
when good people speak
for justice.
31 They remember God's teachings,
and they never take
a wrong step.

32 The wicked try to trap
and kill good people,
33 but the LORD is on their side,
and he will defend them
when they are on trial.

34 Trust the LORD and follow him.
He will give you the land,
and you will see
the wicked destroyed.

35 I have seen brutal people
abuse others and grow strong
like trees in rich soil.[u]
36 Suddenly they disappeared!
I looked, but they were gone
and no longer there.

37 Think of the bright future
waiting for all the families
of honest and innocent
and peace-loving people.
38 But not a trace will be left
of the wicked
or their families.

39 The LORD protects his people,
and they can come to him
in times of trouble.
40 The LORD helps them

[u]**37.35** *like . . . soil*: One possible meaning for the difficult Hebrew text.

and saves them from the wicked
because they run to him.

Psalm 38

[A psalm by David to be used when an offering is made.]

A Prayer in Times of Trouble

1 When you are angry, LORD,
please don't punish me
or even correct me.
2 You shot me with your arrows,
and you struck me
with your hand.

3 My body hurts all over
because of your anger.
Even my bones are in pain,
and my sins 4 are so heavy
that I am crushed.

5 Because of my foolishness,
I am covered with sores
that stink and spread.
6 My body is twisted and bent,
and I groan all day long.
7 Fever has my back in flames,
and I hurt all over.
8 I am worn out and weak,
moaning and in distress.

9 You, Lord, know every one
of my deepest desires,
and my noisy groans
are no secret to you.
10 My heart is beating fast.
I feel weak all over,
and my eyes are red.

11 Because of my sickness,
no friends or neighbors
will come near me.
12 All who want me dead
set traps to catch me,
and those who want
to harm and destroy me
plan and plot all day.

13 I am not able to hear
or speak a word;
14 I am completely deaf
and can't make a sound.

15 I trust you, LORD God,
and you will do something.
16 I said, "Don't let them laugh
or brag because I slip."

17 I am about to collapse
from constant pain.
18 I told you my sins,
and I am sorry for them.
19 Many deadly and powerful
enemies hate me,
20 and they repay evil for good
because I try to do right.

21 You are the LORD God!
Stay nearby
and don't desert me.
22 You are the one who saves me.
Please hurry and help.

Psalm 39

[A psalm by David for Jeduthun, the music leader.]

A Prayer for Forgiveness

1 I told myself, "I'll be careful
not to sin by what I say,
and I'll muzzle my mouth
when evil people are near."
2 I kept completely silent,
but it did no good,[v]
and I hurt even worse.

3 I felt a fire burning inside,
and the more I thought,
the more it burned,
until at last I said:
4 "Please, LORD,
show me my future.
Will I soon be gone?
5 You made my life short,
so brief that the time
means nothing to you.

"Human life is but a breath,
6 and it disappears
like a shadow.
Our struggles are senseless;
we store up more and more,
without ever knowing
who will get it all.

7 "What am I waiting for?
I depend on you, Lord!
8 Save me from my sins.
Don't let fools sneer at me.
9 You treated me like this,
and I kept silent,
not saying a word.

10 "Won't you stop punishing me?
You have worn me down.
11 You punish us severely
because of our sins.
Like a moth, you destroy
what we treasure most.
We are as frail as a breath.

12 "Listen, LORD, to my prayer!
My eyes are flooded with tears,
as I pray to you.
I am merely a stranger
visiting in your home
as my ancestors did.
13 Stop being angry with me

[v] **39.2** *but . . . good*: One possible meaning for the difficult Hebrew text.

and let me smile again
before I am dead and gone."

Psalm 40

[*A psalm by David for the music leader.*]

A Prayer for Help

1 I patiently waited, LORD,
for you to hear my prayer.
You listened 2and pulled me
from a lonely pit
full of mud and mire.
You let me stand on a rock
with my feet firm,
3 and you gave me a new song,
a song of praise to you.
Many will see this,
and they will honor and trust
you, the LORD God.

4 You bless all of those
who trust you, LORD,
and refuse to worship idols
or follow false gods.
5 You, LORD God, have done
many wonderful things,
and you have planned
marvelous things for us.
No one is like you!
I would never be able to tell
all you have done.

6 Sacrifices and offerings
are not what please you;
gifts and payment for sin
are not what you demand.
But you made me willing
to listen and obey.
7 And so, I said, "I am here
to do what is written
about me in the book,
where it says,
8 'I enjoy pleasing you.
Your Law is in my heart.' "

9 When your people worshiped,
you know I told them,
"Our LORD always helps!"
10 When all your people met,
I did not keep silent.
I said, "Our LORD is kind.
He is faithful and caring,
and he saves us."

11 You, LORD, never fail
to have pity on me;
your love and faithfulness
always keep me secure.

12 I have more troubles
than I can count.
My sins are all around me,
and I can't find my way.
My sins outnumber
the hairs on my head,
and I feel weak.
13 Please show that you care
and come to my rescue.
Hurry and help me!

14 Disappoint and confuse
all who want me dead;
turn away and disgrace
all who want to hurt me.
15 Embarrass and shame
all of those who say,
"Just look at you now!"
16 Our LORD, let your worshipers
rejoice and be glad.
They love you for saving them,
so let them always say,
"The LORD is wonderful!"

17 I am poor and needy,
but, LORD God,
you care about me,
and you come to my rescue.
Please hurry and help.

Psalm 41

[*A psalm by David for the music leader.*]

A Prayer in Time of Sickness

1 You, LORD God, bless everyone
who cares for the poor,
and you rescue those people
in times of trouble.
2 You protect them
and keep them alive.
You make them happy here
in this land,
and you don't hand them over
to their enemies.
3 You always heal them
and restore their strength
when they are sick.
4 I prayed, "Have pity, LORD!
Heal me, though I have sinned
against you."

5 My vicious enemies ask me,
"When will you die
and be forgotten?"
6 When visitors come,
all they ever bring
are worthless words,
and when they leave,
they spread gossip.

7 My enemies whisper about me.
They think the worst,
8 and they say,
"You have some fatal disease!
You'll never get well."
9 My most trusted friend
has turned against me,
though he ate at my table.

10 Have pity, LORD! Heal me,
so I can pay them back.
11 Then my enemies
won't defeat me,
and I will know
that you really care.

12 You have helped me
because I am innocent,
and you will always
be close to my side.

13 You, the LORD God of Israel,
will be praised forever!
Amen and amen.

BOOK II

(Psalms 42–72)

Psalm 42

[*A special psalm for the people of Korah and for the music leader.*]

Longing for God

1 As a deer gets thirsty
for streams of water,
I truly am thirsty
for you, my God.
2 In my heart, I am thirsty
for you, the living God.
When will I see your face?
3 Day and night my tears
are my only food,
as everyone keeps asking,
"Where is your God?"

4 Sorrow floods my heart,
when I remember
leading the worshipers
to your house.[w]
I can still hear them shout
their joyful praises.
5 Why am I discouraged?
Why am I restless?
I trust you!
And I will praise you again
because you help me,
6 and you are my God.

I am deeply discouraged
as I think about you
from where the Jordan begins
at Mount Hermon
and from Mount Mizar.[x]
7 Your vicious waves
have swept over me
like an angry ocean
or a roaring waterfall.

8 Every day, you are kind,
and at night
you give me a song
as my prayer to you,
the living LORD God.

9 You are my mighty rock.[y]
Why have you forgotten me?
Why must enemies mistreat me
and make me sad?

10 Even my bones are in pain,
while all day long
my enemies sneer and ask,
"Where is your God?"

11 Why am I discouraged?
Why am I restless?
I trust you!
And I will praise you again
because you help me,
and you are my God.

Psalm 43

A Prayer in Times of Trouble

1 Show that I am right, God!
Defend me against everyone
who doesn't know you;
rescue me from each
of those deceitful liars.
2 I run to you
for protection.
Why have you turned me away?
Why must enemies mistreat me
and make me sad?

3 Send your light and your truth
to guide me.
Let them lead me to your house
on your sacred mountain.
4 Then I will worship
at your altar because you
make me joyful.
You are my God,
and I will praise you.
Yes, I will praise you
as I play my harp.

5 Why am I discouraged?
Why am I restless?
I trust you!
And I will praise you again
because you help me,
and you are my God.

Psalm 44

[*A special psalm for the people of Korah and for the music leader.*]

A Prayer for Help

1 Our God, our ancestors told us
what wonders you worked
and we listened carefully.
2 You chased off the nations
by causing them trouble
with your powerful arm.
Then you let our ancestors
take over their land.
3 Their strength and weapons
were not what won the land
and gave them victory!
You loved them and fought
with your powerful arm
and your shining glory.

[w]**42.4** *leading . . . house*: One possible meaning for the difficult Hebrew text. [x]**42.6** *Mount Mizar*: The location is not known. [y]**42.9** *mighty rock*: See the note at 18.2.

[4] You are my God and King,
and you give victory[z]
to the people of Jacob.
[5] By your great power,
we knocked our enemies down
and stomped on them.
[6] I don't depend on my arrows
or my sword to save me.
[7] But you saved us
from our hateful enemies,
and you put them to shame.
[8] We boast about you, our God,
and we are always grateful.

[9] But now you have rejected us;
you don't lead us into battle,
and we look foolish.
[10] You made us retreat,
and our enemies have taken
everything we own.
[11] You let us be slaughtered
like sheep,
and you scattered us
among the nations.
[12] You sold your people
for little or nothing,
and you earned no profit.

[13] You made us look foolish
to our neighbors,
and people who live nearby
insult us and sneer.
[14] Foreigners joke about us
and shake their heads.
[15] I am embarrassed every day,
and I blush with shame.
[16] But others mock and sneer,
as they watch my enemies
take revenge on me.

[17] All of this has happened to us,
though we didn't forget you
or break our agreement.
[18] We always kept you in mind
and followed your teaching.
[19] But you crushed us,
and you covered us
with deepest darkness
where wild animals live.

[20] We did not forget you
or lift our hands in prayer
to foreign gods.
[21] You would have known it
because you discover
every secret thought.
[22] We face death all day for you.
We are like sheep on their way
to be slaughtered.

[23] Wake up! Do something, Lord!
Why are you sleeping?
Don't desert us forever.
[24] Why do you keep looking away?
Don't forget our sufferings
and all of our troubles.
[25] We are flat on the ground,
holding on to the dust.
[26] Do something! Help us!
Show how kind you are
and come to our rescue.

Psalm 45

[A special psalm for the people of Korah and for the music leader. To the tune "Lilies." A love song.]

For a Royal Wedding

[1] My thoughts are filled
with beautiful words
for the king,
and I will use my voice
as a writer would use
pen and ink.

[2] No one is as handsome as you!
Your words are always kind.
That is why God
will always bless you.
[3] Mighty king, glorious ruler,
strap on your sword
[4] and ride out in splendor!
Win victories for truth
and mercy and justice.
Do fearsome things
with your powerful arm.
[5] Send your sharp arrows
through enemy hearts
and make all nations fall
at your feet.

[6] You are God, and you will rule
forever as king.[a]
Your royal power
brings about justice.
[7] You love justice and hate evil.
And so, your God chose you
and made you happier
than any of your friends.
[8] The sweet aroma of the spices
myrrh, aloes, and cassia,
covers your royal robes.
You enjoy the music of harps
in palaces decorated
with ivory.
[9] Daughters of kings are here,
and your bride stands
at your right side,
wearing a wedding gown
trimmed with pure gold.[b]

[10] Bride of the king,
listen carefully to me.
Forget your own people
and your father's family.

[z]**44.4** *and . . . victory*: One ancient translation; Hebrew "please give victory." [a]**45.6** *You . . . king*: Or "God has made you king, and you will rule forever." [b]**45.9** *trimmed with pure gold*: Hebrew has "with gold from Ophir," which may have been in Africa or India. Gold from there was considered the very best.

11 The king is your husband,
so do what he desires.
12 All of the richest people
from the city of Tyre
will try to influence you
13 with precious treasures.

Your bride, my king,
has inward beauty,[c]
and her wedding gown is woven
with threads of gold.
14 Wearing the finest garments,
she is brought to you,
followed by her young friends,
the bridesmaids.
15 Everyone is excited,
as they follow you
to the royal palace.

16 Your sons and your grandsons
will also be kings
as your ancestors were.
You will make them the rulers
everywhere on earth.

17 I will make your name famous
from now on,
and you will be praised
forever and ever.

Psalm 46

[*A special song for the people of Korah and for the music leader.*]

God Is Our Mighty Fortress

1 God is our mighty fortress,
always ready to help
in times of trouble.
2 And so, we won't be afraid!
Let the earth tremble
and the mountains tumble
into the deepest sea.
3 Let the ocean roar and foam,
and its raging waves
shake the mountains.

4 A river and its streams
bring joy to the city,
which is the sacred home
of God Most High.
5 God is in that city,
and it won't be shaken.
He will help it at dawn.

6 Nations rage! Kingdoms fall!
But at the voice of God
the earth itself melts.
7 The LORD All-Powerful
is with us.
The God of Jacob
is our fortress.

8 Come! See the fearsome things
the LORD has done on earth.
9 God brings wars to an end
all over the world.
He breaks the arrows,
shatters the spears,
and burns the shields.[d]
10 Our God says, "Calm down,
and learn that I am God!
All nations on earth
will honor me."

11 The LORD All-Powerful
is with us.
The God of Jacob
is our fortress.

Psalm 47

[*A psalm for the people of Korah and for the music leader.*]

God Rules the Nations

1 All of you nations,
clap your hands and shout
joyful praises to God.
2 The LORD Most High is fearsome,
the ruler of all the earth.
3 God has put every nation
under our power,
4 and he chose for us the land
that was the pride of Jacob,
his favorite.

5 God goes up to his throne,
as people shout
and trumpets blast.
6 Sing praises to God our King,
7 the ruler of all the earth!
Praise God with songs.

8 God rules the nations
from his sacred throne.
9 Their leaders come together
and are now the people
of Abraham's God.
All rulers on earth
surrender their weapons,
and God is greatly praised!

Psalm 48

[*A song and a psalm for the people of Korah.*]

The City of God

1 The LORD God is wonderful!
He deserves all praise
in the city where he lives.
His holy mountain,
2 beautiful and majestic,
brings joy to all on earth.
Mount Zion, truly sacred,
is home for the Great King.
3 God is there to defend it
and has proved to be
its protector.

4 Kings joined forces
to attack the city,
5 but when they saw it,

[c] **45.13** *has inward beauty*: Or "is dressed in her room."

[d] **46.9** *shields*: Or "chariots."

they were terrified
and ran away.
6 They trembled all over
like women giving birth
7 or like seagoing ships[e]
wrecked by eastern winds.
8 We had heard about it,
and now we have seen it
in the city of our God,
the LORD All-Powerful.
This is the city that God
will let stand forever.

9 Our God, here in your temple
we think about your love.
10 You are famous and praised
everywhere on earth,
as you win victories
with your powerful arm.
11 Mount Zion will celebrate,
and all Judah will be glad,
because you bring justice.

12 Let's walk around Zion
and count its towers.
13 We will see its strong walls
and visit each fortress.
Then you can say
to future generations,
14 "Our God is like this forever
and will always[f] guide us."

Psalm 49

[A psalm for the people of Korah and for the music leader.]

Don't Depend on Wealth

1 Everyone on this earth,
now listen to what I say!
2 Listen, no matter who you are,
rich or poor.
3 I speak words of wisdom,
and my thoughts make sense.
4 I have in mind a mystery
that I will explain
while playing my harp.

5 Why should I be afraid
in times of trouble,
when I am surrounded
by vicious enemies?
6 They trust in their riches
and brag about
all of their wealth.
7 You cannot buy back your life
or pay off God!
8 It costs far too much
to buy back your life.
You can never pay God enough
9 to stay alive forever
and safe from death.

10 We see that wise people die,
and so do stupid fools.
Then their money is left
for someone else.
11 The grave[g] will be their home
forever and ever,
although they once had land
of their own.
12 Our human glory disappears,
and, like animals, we die.

13 Here is what happens to fools
and to those who trust
the words of fools:
14 They are like sheep
with death as their shepherd,
leading them to the grave.[h]
In the morning God's people
will walk all over them,
as their bodies lie rotting
in their home, the grave.
15 But God will rescue me
from the power of death.

16 Don't let it bother you
when others get rich
and live in luxury.
17 Soon they will die
and all of their wealth
will be left behind.

18 We humans are praised
when we do well,
and all of us are glad
to be alive.
19 But we each will go down
to our ancestors,
never again to see
the light of day.
20 Our human glory disappears,
and, like animals, we die.

Psalm 50

[A psalm by Asaph.]

What Pleases God

1 From east to west,
the powerful LORD God
has been calling together
everyone on earth.
2 God shines brightly from Zion,
the most beautiful city.

3 Our God approaches,
but not silently;
a flaming fire comes first,
and a storm surrounds him.
4 God comes to judge his people.
He shouts to the heavens
and to the earth,
5 "Call my followers together!
They offered me a sacrifice,
and we made an agreement."

[e] **48.7** *seagoing ships*: The Hebrew text has "ships of Tarshish," which probably means large, seagoing ships. [f] **48.14** *always*: One possible meaning for the difficult Hebrew text.
[g] **49.11** *The grave*: Some ancient translations; Hebrew "Their inward thoughts." [h] **49.14** *as their . . . grave*: One possible meaning for the difficult Hebrew text.

6 The heavens announce,
"God is the judge,
and he is always honest."

7 My people, I am God!
Israel, I am your God.
Listen to my charges
against you.
8 Although you offer sacrifices
and always bring gifts,
9 I won't accept your offerings
of bulls and goats.

10 Every animal in the forest
belongs to me,
and so do the cattle
on a thousand hills.
11 I know all the birds
in the mountains,
and every wild creature
is in my care.

12 If I were hungry,
I wouldn't tell you,
because I own the world
and everything in it.
13 I don't eat the meat of bulls
or drink the blood of goats.
14 I am God Most High!
The only sacrifice I want
is for you to be thankful
and to keep your word.
15 Pray to me in time of trouble.
I will rescue you,
and you will honor me.

16 But to the wicked I say:
"You don't have the right
to mention my laws or claim
to keep our agreement!
17 You refused correction
and rejected my commands.
18 You made friends
with every crook you met,
and you liked people who break
their wedding vows.
19 You talked only about violence
and told nothing but lies;
20 you sat around gossiping,
ruining the reputation
of your own relatives."

21 When you did all of this,
I didn't say a word,
and you thought,
"God is just like us!"
But now I will accuse you.
22 You have ignored me!
So pay close attention
or I will tear you apart,
and no one can help you.

23 The sacrifice that honors me
is a thankful heart.
Obey me,[i] and I, your God,
will show my power to save.

Psalm 51

[For the music leader. A psalm by David when the prophet Nathan came to him after David had been with Bathsheba.]

A Prayer for Forgiveness

1 You are kind, God!
Please have pity on me.
You are always merciful!
Please wipe away my sins.
2 Wash me clean from all
of my sin and guilt.
3 I know about my sins,
and I cannot forget
my terrible guilt.
4 You are really the one
I have sinned against;
I have disobeyed you
and have done wrong.
So it is right and fair for you
to correct and punish me.

5 I have sinned and done wrong
since the day I was born.
6 But you want complete honesty,
so teach me true wisdom.
7 Wash me with hyssop[j]
until I am clean
and whiter than snow.
8 Let me be happy and joyful!
You crushed my bones,
now let them celebrate.
9 Turn your eyes from my sin
and cover my guilt.
10 Create pure thoughts in me
and make me faithful again.
11 Don't chase me away from you
or take your Holy Spirit
away from me.

12 Make me as happy as you did
when you saved me;
make me want to obey!
13 I will teach sinners your Law,
and they will return to you.
14 Keep me from any deadly sin.
Only you can save me!
Then I will shout and sing
about your power to save.

15 Help me to speak,
and I will praise you, Lord.
16 Offerings and sacrifices
are not what you want.
17 The way to please you
is to feel sorrow
deep in our hearts.
This is the kind of sacrifice
you won't refuse.

[i]50.23 *Obey me*: One possible meaning for the difficult Hebrew text. **[j]51.7** *hyssop*: A small bush with bunches of small, white flowers. It was sometimes used as a symbol for making a person clean from sin.

18 Please be willing, Lord,
to help the city of Zion
and to rebuild its walls.
19 Then you will be pleased
with the proper sacrifices,
and we will offer bulls
on your altar once again.

Psalm 52

[A special psalm by David for the music leader. He wrote this when Doeg from Edom went to Saul and said, "David has gone to Ahimelech's house."]

God Is in Control

1 You people may be strong
and brag about your sins,
but God can be trusted
day after day.
2 You plan brutal crimes,
and your lying words cut
like a sharp razor.
3 You would rather do evil
than good, and tell lies
than speak the truth.
4 You love to say cruel things,
and your words are a trap.

5 God will destroy you forever!
He will grab you and drag you
from your homes.
You will be uprooted
and left to die.
6 When good people see
this fearsome sight,
they will laugh and say,
7 "Just look at them now!
Instead of trusting God,
they trusted their wealth
and their cruelty."

8 But I am like an olive tree
growing in God's house,
and I can count on his love
forever and ever.
9 I will always thank God
for what he has done;
I will praise his good name
when his people meet.

Psalm 53

[A special psalm by David for the music leader. To the tune "Mahalath."[k]]

No One Can Ignore God

1 Only a fool would say,
"There is no God!"
People like that are worthless!
They are heartless and cruel
and never do right.

2 From heaven God
looks down to see
if anyone is wise enough
to search for him.
3 But all of them
are crooked and corrupt.
Not one of them does right.

4 Won't you lawbreakers learn?
You refuse to pray,
and you gobble down
the people of God.
5 But you will be terrified
worse than ever before.
God will scatter the bones
of his enemies,
and you will be ashamed
when God rejects you.

6 I long for someone from Zion
to come and save Israel!
Our God, when you bless
your people again,
Jacob's family will be glad,
and Israel will celebrate.

Psalm 54

[For the music leader. Use with stringed instruments. A special psalm that David wrote when the people of Ziph went to Saul and said, "David is hiding here with us."]

Trusting God in Times of Trouble

1 Save me, God, by your power
and prove that I am right.
2 Listen to my prayer
and hear what I say.
3 Cruel strangers have attacked
and want me dead.
Not one of them cares
about you.

4 You will help me, Lord God,
and keep me from falling;
5 you will punish my enemies
for their evil deeds.
Be my faithful friend
and destroy them.

6 I will bring a gift
and offer a sacrifice
to you, LORD.
I will praise your name
because you are good.
7 You have rescued me
from all of my troubles,
and my own eyes have seen
my enemies fall.

Psalm 55

[A special psalm by David for the music leader. Use with stringed instruments.]

Betrayed by a Friend

1 Listen, God, to my prayer!
Don't reject my request.
2 Please listen and help me.

[k]**Psalm 53** *Mahalath*: Or "For flutes," one possible meaning for the difficult Hebrew text.

My thoughts are troubled,
and I keep groaning
3 because my loud enemies
shout and attack.
They treat me terribly
and hold angry grudges.
4 My heart is racing fast,
and I am afraid of dying.
5 I am trembling with fear,
completely terrified.

6 I wish I had wings
like a dove,
so I could fly far away
and be at peace.
7 I would go and live
in some distant desert.
8 I would quickly find shelter
from howling winds
and raging storms.

9 Confuse my enemies, Lord!
Upset their plans.
Cruelty and violence
are all I see in the city,
10 and they are like guards
on patrol day and night.
The city is full of trouble,
evil, 11 and corruption.
Troublemakers and liars
freely roam the streets.

12 My enemies are not the ones
who sneer and make fun.
I could put up with that
or even hide from them.
13 But it was my closest friend,
the one I trusted most.
14 We enjoyed being together,
and we went with others
to your house, our God.

15 All who hate me are controlled
by the power of evil.
Sentence them to death
and send them down alive
to the world of the dead.

16 I ask for your help, LORD God,
and you will keep me safe.
17 Morning, noon, and night
you hear my concerns
and my complaints.
18 I am attacked from all sides,
but you will rescue me
unharmed by the battle.
19 You have always ruled,
and you will hear me.
You will defeat my enemies
because they won't turn
and worship you.

20 My friend turned against me
and broke his promise.
21 His words were smoother
than butter, and softer
than olive oil.
But hatred filled his heart,
and he was ready to attack
with a sword.

22 Our LORD, we belong to you.
We tell you what worries us,
and you won't let us fall.
23 But what about those people
who are cruel and brutal?
You will throw them down
into the deepest pit
long before their time.
I trust you, LORD!

Psalm 56

[For the music leader. To the tune "A Silent Dove in the Distance."[l] A special psalm by David when the Philistines captured him in Gath.]

A Prayer of Trust in God

1 Have pity, God Most High!
My enemies chase me all day.
2 Many of them are pursuing
and attacking me,
3 but even when I am afraid,
I keep on trusting you.
4 I praise your promises!
I trust you and am not afraid.
No one can harm me.

5 Enemies spend the whole day
finding fault with me;
all they think about
is how to do me harm.
6 They attack from ambush,
watching my every step
and hoping to kill me.
7 They won't get away[m]
with these crimes, God,
because when you get angry,
you destroy people.

8 You have kept record
of my days of wandering.
You have stored my tears
in your bottle
and counted each of them.

9 When I pray, LORD God,
my enemies will retreat,
because I know for certain
that you are with me.
10 I praise your promises!
11 I trust you and am not afraid.
No one can harm me.

12 I will keep my promises
to you, my God,
and bring you gifts.
13 You protected me from death
and kept me from stumbling,

[l]**Psalm 56** *A Silent . . . Distance*: One possible meaning for the difficult Hebrew text.
[m]**56.7** *They . . . away*: One possible meaning for the difficult Hebrew text.

so that I would please you
and follow the light
that leads to life.

Psalm 57

[*For the music leader. To the tune "Don't Destroy."*[n] *A special psalm by David when he was in the cave while running from Saul.*]

Praise and Trust in Times of Trouble

1 God Most High, have pity on me!
Have mercy. I run to you
for safety.
In the shadow of your wings,
I seek protection
till danger dies down.
2 I pray to you, my protector.
3 You will send help from heaven
and save me,
but you will bring trouble
on my attackers.
You are faithful,
and you can be trusted.

4 I live among lions,
who gobble down people!
They have spears and arrows
instead of teeth,
and they have sharp swords
instead of tongues.

5 May you, my God, be honored
above the heavens;
may your glory be seen
everywhere on earth.

6 Enemies set traps for my feet
and struck me down.
They dug a pit in my path,
but fell in it themselves.
7 I am faithful to you,
and you can trust me.
I will sing and play music
for you, my God.
8 I feel wide awake!
I will wake up my harp
and wake up the sun.
9 I will praise you, Lord,
for everyone to hear,
and I will sing hymns to you
in every nation.
10 Your love reaches higher
than the heavens;
your loyalty extends
beyond the clouds.

11 May you, my God, be honored
above the heavens;
may your glory be seen
everywhere on earth.

Psalm 58

[*A special psalm by David for the music leader. To the tune "Don't Destroy."*[n]]

A Prayer When All Goes Wrong

1 Do you mighty people[o] talk
only to oppose justice?[p]
Don't you ever judge fairly?
2 You are always planning evil,
and you are brutal.
3 You have done wrong and lied
from the day you were born.
4 Your words spread poison
like the bite of a cobra
5 that refuses to listen
to the snake charmer.

6 My enemies are fierce
as lions, LORD God!
Shatter their teeth.
Snatch out their fangs.
7 Make them disappear
like leaking water,
and make their arrows miss.
8 Let them dry up like snails
or be like a child that dies
before seeing the sun.
9 Wipe them out quicker
than a pot can be heated
by setting thorns on fire.[q]

10 Good people will be glad
when they see the wicked
getting what they deserve,
and they will wash their feet
in their enemies' blood.
11 Everyone will say, "It's true!
Good people are rewarded.
God does rule the earth
with justice."

Psalm 59

[*For the music leader. To the tune "Don't Destroy."*[r] *A special psalm by David when Saul had David's house watched so that he could kill him.*]

A Prayer for Protection

1 Save me, God! Protect me
from enemy attacks!
2 Keep me safe from brutal people
who want to kill me.

3 Merciless enemies, LORD,
are hiding and plotting,
hoping to kill me.
I have not hurt them
in any way at all.
4 But they are ready to attack.
Do something! Help me!
Look at what's happening.

[n]**Psalm 57** *Don't Destroy*: One possible meaning for the difficult Hebrew text.
[n]**Psalm 58** *Don't Destroy*: One possible meaning for the difficult Hebrew text. [o]**58.1** *mighty people*: Or "mighty rulers" or "mighty gods." [p]**58.1** *Do . . . justice*: One possible meaning for the difficult Hebrew text. [q]**58.9** *Wipe . . . fire*: See the note at Psalm 57.
[r]**Psalm 59** *Don't Destroy*: See the note at Psalm 57.

5 Lord God All-Powerful,
you are the God of Israel.
Punish the other nations
and don't pity those terrible
and rebellious people.

6 My enemies return at evening,
growling like dogs
roaming the city.
7 They curse and their words
cut like swords,
as they say to themselves,
"No one can hear us!"

8 You, Lord, laugh at them
and sneer at the nations.
9 You are my mighty fortress,
and I depend on you.
10 You love me and will let me
see my enemies defeated.
11 Don't kill them,
or everyone may forget!
Just use your mighty power
to make them tremble
and fall.

You are a shield
for your people.
12 My enemies are liars!
So let them be trapped
by their boastful lies.
13 Get angry and destroy them.
Leave them in ruin.
Then all the nations will know
that you rule in Israel.

14 Those liars return at evening,
growling like dogs
roaming the city.
15 They search for scraps of food,
and they snarl
until they are stuffed.

16 But I will sing about
your strength, my God,
and I will celebrate
because of your love.
You are my fortress,
my place of protection
in times of trouble.
17 I will sing your praises!
You are my mighty fortress,
and you love me.

Psalm 60

[For the music leader. To the tune "Lily of the Promise." A special psalm by David for teaching. He wrote it during his wars with the Arameans of northern Syria,[s] when Joab came back and killed twelve thousand Edomites[t] in Salt Valley.]

You Can Depend on God

1 You, God, are angry with us!
We are rejected and crushed.
Make us strong again!
2 You made the earth shake
and split wide open;
now heal its wounds
and stop its trembling.
3 You brought hard times
on your people,
and you gave us wine
that made us stagger.

4 You gave a signal to those
who worship you,
so they could escape
from enemy arrows.[u]
5 Answer our prayers!
Use your powerful arm
and give us victory.
Then the people you love
will be safe.

6 Our God, you solemnly promised,
"I would gladly divide up
the city of Shechem
and give away Succoth Valley
piece by piece.
7 The lands of Gilead
and Manasseh are mine.
Ephraim is my war helmet,
and Judah is the symbol
of my royal power.
8 Moab is merely my washbasin.
Edom belongs to me,
and I shout in triumph
over the Philistines."

9 Our God, who will bring me
to the fortress,
or lead me to Edom?
10 Have you rejected us
and deserted our armies?
11 Help us defeat our enemies!
No one else can rescue us.
12 You will give us victory
and crush our enemies.

Psalm 61

[A psalm by David for the music leader. Use with stringed instruments.]

Under the Protection of God

1 Please listen, God,
and answer my prayer!
2 I feel hopeless,
and I cry out to you
from a faraway land.

Lead me to the mighty rock[v]
high above me.
3 You are a strong tower,
where I am safe
from my enemies.

[s]**Psalm 60** *wars . . . Syria*: See 2 Samuel 8.3-8; 10.16-18; 1 Chronicles 18.3-11; 19.6-19.
[t]**Psalm 60** *killed . . . Edomites*: See 2 Samuel 8.13; 1 Chronicles 18.12.
[u]**60.4** *so . . . arrows*: Some ancient translations and one possible meaning for the difficult Hebrew text.
[v]**61.2** *mighty rock*: See the note at 18.2.

4 Let me live with you forever
and find protection
under your wings, my God.
5 You heard my promises,
and you have blessed me,
just as you bless everyone
who worships you.

6 Let the king have a long
and healthy life.
7 May he always rule
with you, God, at his side;
may your love and loyalty
watch over him.

8 I will sing your praises
forever and will always
keep my promises.

Psalm 62

[*A psalm by David
for Jeduthun, the music leader.*]

God Is Powerful and Kind

1 Only God can save me,
and I calmly wait for[w] him.
2 God alone is the mighty rock[x]
that keeps me safe
and the fortress
where I am secure.

3 I feel like a shaky fence
or a sagging wall.
How long will all of you
attack and assault me?
4 You want to bring me down
from my place of honor.
You love to tell lies,
and when your words are kind,
hatred hides in your heart.
5 Only God gives inward peace,
and I depend on him.
6 God alone is the mighty rock
that keeps me safe,
and he is the fortress
where I feel secure.
7 God saves me and honors me.
He is that mighty rock
where I find safety.

8 Trust God, my friends,
and always tell him
each one of your concerns.
God is our place of safety.

9 We humans are only a breath;
none of us are truly great.
All of us together weigh less
than a puff of air.
10 Don't trust in violence
or depend on dishonesty
or rely on great wealth.

11 I heard God say two things:
"I am powerful,
12 and I am very kind."
The Lord rewards each of us
according to what we do.

Psalm 63

[*A psalm by David
when he was in the desert of Judah.*]

God's Love Means More than Life

1 You are my God. I worship you.
In my heart, I long for you,
as I would long for a stream
in a scorching desert.

2 I have seen your power
and your glory
in the place of worship.
3 Your love means more
than life to me,
and I praise you.
4 As long as I live,
I will pray to you.
5 I will sing joyful praises
and be filled with excitement
like a guest at a banquet.

6 I think about you
before I go to sleep,
and my thoughts turn to you
during the night.
7 You have helped me,
and I sing happy songs
in the shadow of your wings.
8 I stay close to you,
and your powerful arm
supports me.

9 All who want to kill me
will end up in the ground.
10 Swords will run them through,
and wild dogs will eat them.

11 Because of you, our God,
the king will celebrate
with your faithful followers,
but liars will be silent.

Psalm 64

[*A psalm by David for the music leader.*]

Celebrate because of the Lord

1 Listen to my concerns, God,
and protect me
from my terrible enemies.
2 Keep me safe from secret plots
of corrupt and evil gangs.
3 Their words cut like swords,
and their cruel remarks
sting like sharp arrows.
4 They fearlessly ambush
and shoot innocent people.

5 They are determined to do evil,
and they tell themselves,

[w] **62.1** *calmly wait for*: Or "am at peace with."

[x] **62.2** *mighty rock*: See the note at 18.2.

"Let's set traps!
No one can see us."[y]
6 They make evil plans and say,
"We'll commit a perfect crime.
No one knows our thoughts."[z]

7 But God will shoot his arrows
and quickly wound them.
8 They will be destroyed
by their own words,
and everyone who sees them
will tremble with fear.[a]
9 They will be afraid and say,
"Look at what God has done
and keep it all in mind."

10 May the LORD bless his people
with peace and happiness
and let them celebrate.

Psalm 65

[*A psalm by David and a song for the music leader.*]

God Answers Prayer

1 Our God, you deserve[b] praise
in Zion, where we keep
our promises to you.
2 Everyone will come to you
because you answer prayer.
3 Our terrible sins get us down,
but you forgive us.
4 You bless your chosen ones,
and you invite them
to live near you
in your temple.
We will enjoy your house,
the sacred temple.

5 Our God, you save us,
and your fearsome deeds answer
our prayers for justice!
You give hope to people
everywhere on earth,
even those across the sea.
6 You are strong,
and your mighty power
put the mountains in place.
7 You silence the roaring waves
and the noisy shouts
of the nations.
8 People far away marvel
at your fearsome deeds,
and all who live under the sun
celebrate and sing
because of you.

9 You take care of the earth
and send rain to help the soil
grow all kinds of crops.
Your rivers never run dry,
and you prepare the earth
to produce much grain.
10 You water all of its fields
and level the lumpy ground.
You send showers of rain
to soften the soil
and help the plants sprout.
11 Wherever your footsteps
touch the earth,
a rich harvest is gathered.
12 Desert pastures blossom,
and mountains celebrate.
13 Meadows are filled
with sheep and goats;
valleys overflow with grain
and echo with joyful songs.

Psalm 66

[*A song and a psalm for the music leader.*]

Shout Praises to God

1 Tell everyone on this earth
to shout praises to God!
2 Sing about his glorious name.
Honor him with praises.
3 Say to God, "Everything you do
is fearsome,
and your mighty power makes
your enemies come crawling.
4 You are worshiped by everyone!
We all sing praises to you."

5 Come and see the fearsome things
our God has done!
6 When God made the sea dry up,
our people walked across,
and because of him,
we celebrated there.
7 His mighty power rules forever,
and nothing the nations do
can be hidden from him.
So don't turn against God.

8 All of you people,
come praise our God!
Let his praises be heard.
9 God protects us from death
and keeps us steady.

10 Our God, you tested us,
just as silver is tested.
11 You trapped us in a net
and gave us heavy burdens.
12 You sent war chariots
to crush our skulls.
We traveled through fire
and through floods,
but you brought us
to a land of plenty.

13 I will bring sacrifices
into your house, my God,
and I will do what I promised
14 when I was in trouble.
15 I will sacrifice my best sheep

[y]**64.5** *us*: One ancient translation; Hebrew "them." [z]**64.6** *thoughts*: One possible meaning for the difficult Hebrew text of verse 6. [a]**64.8** *tremble with fear*: Or "turn and run." [b]**65.1** *deserve*: One possible meaning for the difficult Hebrew text.

and offer bulls and goats
on your altar.

16 All who worship God,
come here and listen;
I will tell you everything
God has done for me.
17 I prayed to the Lord,
and I praised him.
18 If my thoughts had been sinful,
he would have refused
to hear me.
19 But God did listen
and answered my prayer.
20 Let's praise God!
He listened when I prayed,
and he is always kind.

Psalm 67

[*A psalm and a song for the music leader. Use with stringed instruments.*]

Tell the Nations To Praise God

1 Our God, be kind and bless us!
Be pleased and smile.
2 Then everyone on earth
will learn to follow you,
and all nations will see
your power to save us.

3 Make everyone praise you
and shout your praises.
4 Let the nations celebrate
with joyful songs,
because you judge fairly
and guide all nations.
5 Make everyone praise you
and shout your praises.

6 Our God has blessed the earth
with a wonderful harvest!
7 Pray for his blessings
to continue
and for everyone on earth
to worship our God.

Psalm 68

[*A psalm and a song by David for the music leader.*]

God Will Win the Battle

1 Do something, God!
Scatter your hateful enemies.
Make them turn and run.
2 Scatter them like smoke!
When you come near,
make them melt
like wax in a fire.
3 But let your people be happy
and celebrate because of you.

4 Our God, you are the one
who rides on the clouds,
and we praise you.
Your name is the LORD,
and we celebrate
as we worship you.

5 Our God, from your sacred home
you take care of orphans
and protect widows.
6 You find families
for those who are lonely.
You set prisoners free
and let them prosper,[c]
but all who rebel will live
in a scorching desert.

7 You set your people free,
and you led them
through the desert.
8 God of Israel,
the earth trembled,
and rain poured down.
You alone are the God
who rules from Mount Sinai.
9 When your land was thirsty,
you sent showers
to refresh it.
10 Your people settled there,
and you were generous
to everyone in need.

11 You gave the command,
and a chorus of women told
what had happened:
12 "Kings and their armies
retreated and ran,
and everything they left
is now being divided.
13 And for those who stayed back
to guard the sheep,
there are metal doves
with silver-coated wings
and shiny gold feathers."

14 God All-Powerful, you scattered
the kings like snow falling
on Mount Zalmon.[d]

15 Our LORD and our God,
Bashan is a mighty mountain
covered with peaks.
16 Why is it jealous of Zion,
the mountain you chose
as your home forever?

17 When you, LORD God, appeared
to your people[e] at Sinai,
you came with thousands
of mighty chariots.
18 When you climbed
the high mountain,
you took prisoners with you
and were given gifts.
Your enemies didn't want you

[c]**68.6** *and let them prosper*: Or "and give them a song." [d]**68.14** *Mount Zalmon*: The location of this mountain is not known. [e]**68.17** *to your people*: Or "in all your holiness" or "in your holy place."

to live there,
but they gave you gifts.

19 We praise you, Lord God!
You treat us with kindness
day after day,
and you rescue us.
20 You always protect us
and save us from death.

21 Our Lord and our God,
your terrible enemies
are ready for war,[f]
but you will crush
their skulls.
22 You promised to bring them
from Bashan
and from the deepest sea.
23 Then we could stomp
on their blood,
and our dogs could chew
on their bones.

24 We have seen crowds marching
to your place of worship,
our God and King.
25 The singers come first,
and then the musicians,
surrounded by young women
playing tambourines.
26 They come shouting,
"People of Israel,
praise the LORD God!"
27 The small tribe of Benjamin
leads the way,
followed by the leaders
from Judah.
Then come the leaders
from Zebulun and Naphtali.

28 Our God, show your strength!
Show us once again.
29 Then kings will bring gifts
to your temple
in Jerusalem.[g]

30 Punish that animal
that lives in the swamp![h]
Punish that nation
whose leaders and people
are like wild bulls.
Make them come crawling
with gifts of silver.
Scatter those nations
that enjoy making war.[i]
31 Force the Egyptians to bring
gifts of bronze;
make the Ethiopians[j] hurry
to offer presents.[k]

32 Now sing praises to God!
Every kingdom on earth,
sing to the Lord!
33 Praise the one who rides
across the ancient skies;
listen as he speaks
with a mighty voice.

34 Tell about God's power!
He is honored in Israel,
and he rules the skies.
35 The God of Israel is fearsome
in his temple,
and he makes us strong.
Let's praise our God!

Psalm 69

[By David for the music leader. To the tune "Lilies."]

God Can Be Trusted

1 Save me, God!
I am about to drown.
2 I am sinking deep in the mud,
and my feet are slipping.
I am about to be swept under
by a mighty flood.
3 I am worn out from crying,
and my throat is dry.
I have waited for you
till my eyes are blurred.

4 There are more people
who hate me for no reason
than there are hairs
on my head.
Many terrible enemies
want to destroy me, God.
Am I supposed to give back
something I didn't steal?
5 You know my foolish sins.
Not one is hidden from you.

6 LORD God All-Powerful,
ruler of Israel,
don't let me embarrass anyone
who trusts and worships you.
7 It is for your sake alone
that I am insulted
and blush with shame.
8 I am like a stranger
to my relatives
and like a foreigner
to my own family.

9 My love for your house
burns in me like a fire,
and when others insulted you,
they insulted me as well.

[f] **68.21** *are ready for war*: The Hebrew text has "have long hair," which probably refers to the ancient custom of wearing long hair on special occasions, such as a "holy war."
[g] **68.28,29** *Our God . . . Jerusalem*: One possible meaning for the difficult Hebrew text of verses 28, 29. [h] **68.30** *animal . . . swamp*: Probably Egypt. [i] **68.30** *war*: One possible meaning for the difficult Hebrew text of verse 30. [j] **68.31** *the Ethiopians*: The Hebrew text has "the people of Cush," which was a region south of Egypt that included parts of the present countries of Ethiopia and Sudan. [k] **68.31** *presents*: One possible meaning for the difficult Hebrew text of verse 31.

10 I cried and went without food,[l]
but they still insulted me.
11 They sneered at me
for wearing sackcloth[m]
to show my sorrow.
12 Rulers and judges gossip
about me,
and drunkards make up songs
to mock me.

13 But I pray to you, LORD.
So when the time is right,
answer me and help me
with your wonderful love.
14 Don't let me sink in the mud,
but save me from my enemies
and from the deep water.
15 Don't let me be
swept away by a flood
or drowned in the ocean
or swallowed by death.

16 Answer me, LORD!
You are kind and good.
Pay attention to me!
You are truly merciful.
17 Don't turn away from me.
I am your servant,
and I am in trouble.
Please hurry and help!
18 Come and save me
from my enemies.

19 You know how I am insulted,
mocked, and disgraced;
you know every one
of my enemies.
20 I am crushed by insults,
and I feel sick.
I had hoped for mercy and pity,
but there was none.
21 Enemies poisoned my food,
and when I was thirsty,
they gave me vinegar.

22 Make their table a trap
for them and their friends.
23 Blind them with darkness
and make them tremble.
24 Show them how angry you are!
Be furious and catch them.
25 Destroy their camp
and don't let anyone live
in their tents.

26 They cause trouble for people
you have already punished;
their gossip hurts those
you have wounded.
27 Make them guiltier than ever
and don't forgive them.
28 Wipe their names from the book
of the living;
remove them from the list
of the innocent.
29 I am mistreated and in pain.
Protect me, God,
and keep me safe!

30 I will praise the LORD God
with a song
and a thankful heart.
31 This will please the LORD
better than offering an ox
or a full-grown bull.
32 When those in need see this,
they will be happy,
and the LORD's worshipers
will be encouraged.
33 The LORD will listen
when the homeless cry out,
and he will never forget
his people in prison.

34 Heaven and earth
will praise our God,
and so will the oceans
and everything in them.
35 God will rescue Jerusalem,
and he will rebuild
the towns of Judah.
His people will live there
on their own land,
36 and when the time comes,
their children will inherit
the land.
Then everyone who loves God
will also settle there.

Psalm 70

[By David for the music leader. To be used when an offering is made.]

God Is Wonderful

1 Save me, LORD God!
Hurry and help.
2 Disappoint and confuse
all who want to kill me.
Turn away and disgrace
all who want to hurt me.
3 Embarrass and shame those
who say, "We told you so!"

4 Let your worshipers celebrate
and be glad because of you.
They love your saving power,
so let them always say,
"God is wonderful!"
5 I am poor and needy,
but you, the LORD God,
care about me.

You are the one who saves me.
Please hurry and help!

Psalm 71

A Prayer for God's Protection

1 I run to you, LORD,
for protection.
Don't disappoint me.

[l]69.10 *went without food*: See the note at 35.13.

[m]69.11 *sackcloth*: See the note at 30.11.

2 You do what is right,
so come to my rescue.
Listen to my prayer
and keep me safe.
3 Be my mighty rock,[n] the place
where I can always run
for protection.
Save me by your command!
You are my mighty rock
and my fortress.

4 Come and save me, LORD God,
from vicious and cruel
and brutal enemies!
5 I depend on you,
and I have trusted you
since I was young.
6 I have relied on you[o]
from the day I was born.
You brought me safely
through birth,
and I always praise you.

7 Many people think of me
as something evil.
But you are my mighty protector,
8 and I praise and honor you
all day long.
9 Don't throw me aside
when I am old;
don't desert me
when my strength is gone.
10 My enemies are plotting
because they want me dead.
11 They say, "Now we'll catch you!
God has deserted you,
and no one can save you."
12 Come closer, God!
Please hurry and help.
13 Embarrass and destroy
all who want me dead;
disgrace and confuse
all who want to hurt me.
14 I will never give up hope
or stop praising you.
15 All day long I will tell
the wonderful things you do
to save your people.
But you have done much more
than I could possibly know.
16 I will praise you, LORD God,
for your mighty deeds
and your power to save.

17 You have taught me
since I was a child,
and I never stop telling about
your marvelous deeds.
18 Don't leave me when I am old
and my hair turns gray.
Let me tell future generations
about your mighty power.
19 Your deeds of kindness
are known in the heavens.
No one is like you!

20 You made me suffer a lot,
but you will bring me
back from this deep pit
and give me new life.
21 You will make me truly great
and take my sorrow away.

22 I will praise you, God,
the Holy One of Israel.
You are faithful.
I will play the harp
and sing your praises.
23 You have rescued me!
I will celebrate and shout,
singing praises to you
with all my heart.
24 All day long I will announce
your power to save.
I will tell how you disgraced
and disappointed those
who wanted to hurt me.

Psalm 72

[*By Solomon.*]

A Prayer for God To Guide and Help the King

1 Please help the king
to be honest and fair
just like you, our God.
2 Let him be honest and fair
with all your people,
especially the poor.
3 Let peace and justice rule
every mountain and hill.
4 Let the king defend the poor,
rescue the homeless, and crush
everyone who hurts them.
5 Let the king live[p] forever
like the sun and the moon.
6 Let him be as helpful as rain
that refreshes the meadows
and the ground.
7 Let the king be fair
with everyone,
and let there be peace
until the moon
falls from the sky.

8 Let his kingdom reach
from sea to sea,
from the Euphrates River
across all the earth.
9 Force the desert tribes
to accept his rule,
and make his enemies
crawl in the dirt.
10 Force the rulers of Tarshish[q]
and of the islands
to pay taxes to him.

[n] **71.3** *mighty rock*: See the note at 18.2. [o] **71.6** *I . . . you*: One possible meaning for the difficult Hebrew text. [p] **72.5** *Let the king live*: One ancient translation; Hebrew "Let them worship you." [q] **72.10** *Tarshish*: Possibly a city in Spain.

Make the kings of Sheba
and of Seba[r] bring gifts.
11 Make other rulers bow down
and all nations serve him.

12 Do this because the king
rescues the homeless
when they cry out,
and he helps everyone
who is poor and in need.
13 The king has pity
on the weak and the helpless
and protects those in need.
14 He cares when they hurt,
and he saves them from cruel
and violent deaths.

15 Long live the king!
Give him gold from Sheba.
Always pray for the king
and praise him each day.
16 Let cities overflow with food
and hills be covered with grain,
just like Mount Lebanon.
Let the people in the cities
prosper like wild flowers.
17 May the glory of the king
shine brightly forever
like the sun in the sky.
Let him make nations prosper
and learn to praise him.

18 LORD God of Israel,
we praise you.
Only you can work miracles.
19 We will always praise
your glorious name.
Let your glory be seen
everywhere on earth.
Amen and amen.

20 This ends the prayers
of David, the son of Jesse.

BOOK III
(Psalms 73–89)

Psalm 73
[*A psalm by Asaph.*]

God Is Good

1 God is truly good to Israel,[s]
especially to everyone
with a pure heart.
2 But I almost stumbled and fell,
3 because it made me jealous
to see proud and evil people
and to watch them prosper.
4 They never have to suffer,[t]
they stay healthy,
5 and they don't have troubles
like everyone else.
6 Their pride is like a necklace,
and they commit sin more often
than they dress themselves.
7 Their eyes poke out with fat,
and their minds are flooded
with foolish thoughts.
8 They sneer and say cruel things,
and because of their pride,
they make violent threats.
9 They dare to speak against God
and to order others around.

10 God will bring his people back,
and they will drink the water
he so freely gives.[u]

11 Only evil people would say,
"God Most High cannot
know everything!"
12 Yet all goes well for them,
and they live in peace.
13 What good did it do me
to keep my thoughts pure
and refuse to do wrong?
14 I am sick all day,
and I am punished
each morning.
15 If I had said evil things,
I would not have been loyal
to your people.

16 It was hard for me
to understand all this!
17 Then I went to your temple,
and there I understood
what will happen
to my enemies.
18 You will make them stumble,
never to get up again.
19 They will be terrified,
suddenly swept away
and no longer there.
20 They will disappear, Lord,
despised like a bad dream
the morning after.

21 Once I was bitter
and brokenhearted.
22 I was stupid and ignorant,
and I treated you
as a wild animal would.
23 But I never really left you,
and you hold my right hand.
24 Your advice has been my guide,
and later you will welcome me
in glory.[v]
25 In heaven I have only you,
and on this earth
you are all I want.
26 My body and mind may fail,
but you are my strength
and my choice forever.

[r] **72.10** *Sheba . . . Seba*: Sheba may have been a place in what is now southwest Arabia, and Seba may have been in southern Arabia. [s] **73.1** *to Israel*: Or "to those who do right." [t] **73.4** *They . . . suffer*: Or "They die a painless death." [u] **73.10** *gives*: One possible meaning for the difficult Hebrew text of verse 10. [v] **73.24** *in glory*: Or "with honor."

27 Powerful LORD God,
all who stay far from you
will be lost,
and you will destroy those
who are unfaithful.
28 It is good for me
to be near you.
I choose you as my protector,
and I will tell about
your wonderful deeds.

Psalm 74

[*A special psalm by Asaph.*]

A Prayer for the Nation in Times of Trouble

1 Our God, why have you
completely rejected us?
Why are you so angry
with the ones you care for?
2 Remember the people
you rescued long ago,
the tribe you chose
to be your very own.
Think of Mount Zion,
your home;
3 walk over to the temple
left in ruins forever
by those who hate us.

4 Your enemies roared like lions
in your holy temple,
and they have placed
their banners there.
5 It looks like a forest
chopped to pieces.[w]
6 They used axes and hatchets
to smash the carvings.
7 They burned down your temple
and badly disgraced it.
8 They said to themselves,
"We'll crush them!"
Then they burned every one
of your meeting places
all over the country.
9 There are no more miracles
and no more prophets.
Who knows how long
it will be like this?

10 Our God, how much longer
will our enemies sneer?
Won't they ever stop
insulting you?
11 Why don't you punish them?
Why are you holding back?

12 Our God and King,
you have ruled
since ancient times;
you have won victories
everywhere on this earth.
13 By your power you made a path
through the sea,
and you smashed the heads
of sea monsters.
14 You crushed the heads
of the monster Leviathan,[x]
then fed him to wild creatures
in the desert.
15 You opened the ground
for streams and springs
and dried up mighty rivers.
16 You rule the day and the night,
and you put the moon
and the sun in place.
17 You made summer and winter
and gave them to the earth.[y]

18 Remember your enemies, LORD!
They foolishly sneer
and won't respect you.
19 You treat us like pet doves,
but they mistreat us.
Don't keep forgetting us
and letting us be fed
to those wild animals.
20 Remember the agreement
you made with us.
Violent enemies are hiding
in every dark corner
of the earth.
21 Don't disappoint those in need
or make them turn from you,
but help the poor and homeless
to shout your praises.
22 Do something, God!
Defend yourself.
Remember how those fools
sneer at you all day long.
23 Don't forget the loud shouts
of your enemies.

Psalm 75

[*A psalm and a song by Asaph for the music leader. To the tune "Don't Destroy."*[z]]

Praise God for All He Has Done

1 Our God, we thank you
for being so near to us!
Everyone celebrates
your wonderful deeds.

2 You have set a time
to judge with fairness.
3 The earth trembles,
and its people shake;
you alone keep
its foundations firm.
4 You tell every bragger,
"Stop bragging!"
And to the wicked you say,
"Don't boast of your power!

[w] **74.5** *pieces*: One meaning for the difficult Hebrew text of verse 5. [x] **74.14** *Leviathan*: God's victory over this monster sometimes stands for his power over all creation and sometimes for his defeat of Egypt. [y] **74.17** *gave . . . earth*: Or "made boundaries for the earth." [z] **Psalm 75** *Don't Destroy*: See the note at Psalm 57.

5 Stop bragging! Quit telling me
how great you are."

6 Our LORD and our God,
victory doesn't come
from the east or the west
or from the desert.
7 You are the one who judges.
You can take away power
and give it to others.
8 You hold in your hand
a cup filled with wine,[a]
strong and foaming.
You will pour out some
for every sinful person
on this earth,
and they will have to drink
until it is gone.
9 But I will always tell about
you, the God of Jacob,
and I will sing your praise.

10 Our Lord, you will destroy
the power of evil people,
but you will give strength
to those who are good.

Psalm 76

[*A song and a psalm for the music leader. Use stringed instruments.*]

God Always Wins

1 You, our God,
are famous in Judah
and honored in Israel.
2 Your home is on Mount Zion
in the city of peace.
3 There you destroyed
fiery arrows, shields, swords,
and all the other weapons.

4 You are more glorious than
the eternal mountains.[b]
5 Brave warriors were robbed
of what they had taken,
and now they lie dead,
unable to lift an arm.
6 God of Jacob, when you roar,
enemy chariots and horses
drop dead in their tracks.

7 Our God, you are fearsome,
and no one can oppose you
when you are angry.
8 From heaven you announced
your decisions as judge!
And all who live on this earth
were terrified and silent
9 when you took over as judge,
ready to rescue
everyone in need.
10 Even the most angry people
will praise you
when you are furious.[c]

11 Everyone, make your promises
to the LORD your God
and do what you promise.
The LORD is fearsome,
and all of his servants
should bring him gifts.
12 God destroys the courage
of rulers and kings
and makes cowards of them.

Psalm 77

[*A psalm by Asaph for Jeduthun, the music leader.*]

In Times of Trouble God Is with His People

1 I pray to you, Lord God,
and I beg you to listen.
2 In days filled with trouble,
I search for you.
And at night I tirelessly
lift my hands in prayer,
refusing comfort.
3 When I think of you,
I feel restless and weak.

4 Because of you, Lord God,
I can't sleep.
I am restless
and can't even talk.
5 I think of times gone by,
of those years long ago.
6 Each night my mind
is flooded with questions:[d]
7 "Have you rejected me forever?
Won't you be kind again?
8 Is this the end of your love
and your promises?
9 Have you forgotten
how to have pity?
Do you refuse to show mercy
because of your anger?"
10 Then I said, "God Most High,
what hurts me most
is that you no longer help us
with your mighty arm."

11 Our LORD, I will remember
the things you have done,
your miracles of long ago.
12 I will think about each one
of your mighty deeds.
13 Everything you do is right,
and no other god
compares with you.
14 You alone work miracles,
and you have let nations
see your mighty power.
15 With your own arm you rescued

[a]**75.8** *a cup . . . wine*: In the Old Testament "a cup filled with wine" sometimes stands for God's anger. [b]**76.4** *the eternal mountains*: One ancient translation; Hebrew "the mountains of victims (of wild animals)." [c]**76.10** *furious*: One possible meaning for the difficult Hebrew text of verse 10. [d]**77.6** *my mind . . . questions*: One ancient translation; Hebrew "I remember my music."

your people, the descendants
of Jacob and Joseph.

16 The ocean looked at you, God,
and it trembled deep down
with fear.
17 Water flowed from the clouds.
Thunder was heard above
as your arrows of lightning
flashed about.
18 Your thunder roared
like chariot wheels.
The world was made bright
by lightning,
and all the earth trembled.

19 You walked through the water
of the mighty sea,
but your footprints
were never seen.
20 You guided your people
like a flock of sheep,
and you chose Moses and Aaron
to be their leaders.

Psalm 78

[*A special psalm by Asaph.*]

What God Has Done for His People

1 My friends, I beg you
to listen as I teach.
2 I will give instruction
and explain the mystery
of what happened long ago.
3 These are things we learned
from our ancestors,
4 and we will tell them
to the next generation.
We won't keep secret
the glorious deeds
and the mighty miracles
of the LORD.

5 God gave his Law
to Jacob's descendants,
the people of Israel.
And he told our ancestors
to teach their children,
6 so that each new generation
would know his Law
and tell it to the next.
7 Then they would trust God
and obey his teachings,
without forgetting anything
God had done.
8 They would be different
from their ancestors,
who were stubborn, rebellious,
and unfaithful to God.

9 The warriors from Ephraim
were armed with arrows,
but they ran away
when the battle began.
10 They broke their agreement
with God,
and they turned their backs
on his teaching.
11 They forgot all he had done,
even the mighty miracles
12 he did for their ancestors
near Zoan[e] in Egypt.

13 God made a path in the sea
and piled up the water
as he led them across.
14 He guided them during the day
with a cloud,
and each night he led them
with a flaming fire.
15 God made water flow
from rocks he split open
in the desert,
and his people drank freely,
as though from a lake.
16 He made streams gush out
like rivers from rocks.

17 But in the desert,
the people of God Most High
kept sinning and rebelling.
18 They stubbornly tested God
and demanded from him
what they wanted to eat.
19 They challenged God by saying,
"Can God provide food
out here in the desert?
20 It's true God struck the rock
and water gushed out
like a river,
but can he give his people
bread and meat?"

21 When the LORD heard this,
he was angry and furious
with Jacob's descendants,
the people of Israel.
22 They had refused to trust him,
and they had doubted
his saving power.

23 But God gave a command
to the clouds,
and he opened the doors
in the skies.
24 From heaven he sent grain
that they called manna.[f]
25 He gave them more than enough,
and each one of them ate
this special food.

26 God's mighty power
brought a strong wind
from the southeast,
27 and it brought birds
that covered the ground,
like sand on the beach.

[e] **78.12** *Zoan*: A city in the eastern part of the Nile Delta. [f] **78.24** *manna*: When the people of Israel were wandering through the desert, the Lord gave them a special kind of food to eat. It tasted like a wafer and was called "manna," which in Hebrew means, "What is this?"

28 Then God made the birds fall
in the camp of his people
near their tents.

29 God gave his people
all they wanted,
and each of them ate
until they were full.
30 But before they had swallowed
the last bite,
31 God became angry and killed
the strongest and best
from the families of Israel.

32 But the rest kept on sinning
and would not trust
God's miracles.
33 So he cut their lives short
and made them terrified.
34 After he killed some of them,
the others turned to him
with all their hearts.
35 They remembered God Most High,
the mighty rock[g]
that kept them safe.
36 But they tried to flatter God,
and they told him lies;
37 they were unfaithful
and broke their promises.

38 Yet God was kind.
He kept forgiving their sins
and didn't destroy them.
He often became angry,
but never lost his temper.
39 God remembered that they
were made of flesh
and were like a wind
that blows once
and then dies down.

40 While they were in the desert,
they often rebelled
and made God sad.
41 They kept testing him
and caused terrible pain
for the Holy One of Israel.
42 They forgot about his power
and how he had rescued them
from their enemies.
43 God showed them all kinds
of wonderful miracles
near Zoan[h] in Egypt.
44 He turned the rivers of Egypt
into blood,
and no one could drink
from the streams.
45 He sent swarms of flies
to pester the Egyptians,
and he sent frogs
to cause them trouble.

46 God let worms and grasshoppers
eat their crops.
47 He destroyed their grapevines
and their fig trees
with hail and floods.[i]
48 Then he killed their cattle
with hail
and their other animals
with lightning.

49 God was so angry and furious
that he went into a rage
and caused them great trouble
by sending swarms
of destroying angels.
50 God gave in to his anger
and slaughtered them
in a terrible way.
51 He killed the first-born son
of each Egyptian family.

52 Then God led his people
out of Egypt
and guided them in the desert
like a flock of sheep.
53 He led them safely along,
and they were not afraid,
but their enemies drowned
in the sea.

54 God brought his people
to the sacred mountain
that he had taken
by his own power.
55 He made nations run
from the tribes of Israel,
and he let the tribes
take over their land.

56 But the people tested
God Most High,
and they refused
to obey his laws.
57 They were as unfaithful
as their ancestors,
and they were as crooked
as a twisted arrow.
58 God demanded all their love,
but they made him angry
by worshiping idols.

59 So God became furious
and completely rejected
the people of Israel.
60 Then he deserted his home
at Shiloh, where he lived
here on earth.
61 He let enemies capture
the sacred chest[j]
and let them dishonor him.

62 God took out his anger
on his chosen ones
and let them be killed
by enemy swords.
63 Fire destroyed the young men,

[g]**78.35** *mighty rock*: See the note at 18.2. [h]**78.43** *Zoan*: See the note at 78.12.
[i]**78.47** *floods*: Or "frost." [j]**78.61** *sacred chest*: The Hebrew text has "his power," which refers to the sacred chest. In Psalm 132.8 it is called "powerful."

and the young women were left
with no one to marry.
64 Priests died violent deaths,
but their widows
were not allowed to mourn.

65 Finally the Lord woke up,
and he shouted
like a drunken soldier.
66 God scattered his enemies
and made them ashamed
forever.

67 Then the Lord decided
not to make his home
with Joseph's descendants
in Ephraim.[k]
68 Instead he chose the tribe
of Judah,
and he chose Mount Zion,
the place he loves.
69 There he built his temple
as lofty as the mountains
and as solid as the earth
that he had made
to last forever.

70 The Lord God chose David
to be his servant and took him
from tending sheep
71 and from caring for lambs.
Then God made him the leader
of Israel, his own nation.
72 David treated the people fairly
and guided them with wisdom.

Psalm 79
[*A psalm by Asaph.*]

Have Pity on Jerusalem

1 Our God, foreign nations
have taken your land,
disgraced your temple,
and left Jerusalem in ruins.
2 They have fed the bodies
of your servants
to flesh-eating birds;
your loyal people are food
for savage animals.
3 All Jerusalem is covered
with their blood,
and there is no one left
to bury them.
4 Every nation around us
sneers and makes fun.

5 Our LORD, will you keep on
being angry?
Will your angry feelings
keep flaming up like fire?
6 Get angry with those nations
that don't know you
and won't worship you!
7 They have gobbled down
Jacob's descendants
and left the land in ruins.

8 Don't make us pay for the sins
of our ancestors.
Have pity and come quickly!
We are completely helpless.
9 Our God, you keep us safe.
Now help us! Rescue us.
Forgive our sins
and bring honor to yourself.

10 Why should nations ask us,
"Where is your God?"
Let us and the other nations
see you take revenge
for your servants who died
a violent death.

11 Listen to the prisoners groan!
Let your mighty power save all
who are sentenced to die.
12 Each of those nations sneered
at you, our Lord.
Now let others sneer at them,
seven times as much.
13 Then we, your people,
will always thank you.
We are like sheep
with you as our shepherd,
and all generations
will hear us praise you.

Psalm 80
[*A psalm by Asaph for the music leader. To the tune "Lilies of the Agreement."*]

Help Our Nation

1 Shepherd of Israel, you lead
the descendants of Joseph,
and you sit on your throne
above the winged creatures.[l]
Listen to our prayer
and let your light shine
2 for the tribes of Ephraim,
Benjamin, and Manasseh.
Save us by your power.

3 Our God, make us strong again!
Smile on us and save us.

4 LORD God All-Powerful,
how much longer
will the prayers of your people
make you angry?
5 You gave us tears for food,
and you made us drink them
by the bowlful.

[k]**78.67** *with . . . Ephraim*: Ephraim was Joseph's youngest son. One of the twelve tribes was named after him, and sometimes the northern kingdom of Israel was also known as Ephraim. The town of Shiloh was in the territory of Ephraim, but the place where God was worshiped was moved from there to Zion (Jerusalem) in the territory of Judah. [l]**80.1** *winged creatures*: Two winged creatures made of gold were on the top of the sacred chest and were symbols of the Lords's throne on earth (see Exodus 25.18).

[6] Because of you,
our enemies who live nearby
laugh and joke about us.
[7] But if you smile on us,
we will be saved.

[8] We were like a grapevine
you brought out of Egypt.
You chased other nations away
and planted us here.
[9] Then you cleared the ground,
and we put our roots deep,
spreading over the land.
[10] Shade from this vine covered
the mountains.
Its branches climbed
the mighty cedars
[11] and stretched to the sea;
its new growth reached
to the river.[m]

[12] Our Lord, why have you
torn down the wall
from around the vineyard?
You let everyone who walks by
pick the grapes.
[13] Now the vine is gobbled down
by pigs from the forest
and other wild animals.

[14] God All-Powerful,
please do something!
Look down from heaven
and see what's happening
to this vine.
[15] With your own hands
you planted its roots,
and you raised it
as your very own.

[16] Enemies chopped the vine down
and set it on fire.
Now show your anger
and destroy them.
[17] But help the one who sits
at your right side,[n]
the one you raised
to be your own.
[18] Then we will never turn away.
Put new life into us,
and we will worship you.

[19] LORD God All-Powerful,
make us strong again!
Smile on us and save us.

Psalm 81

[*By Asaph for the music leader.*[o]]

God Makes Us Strong

[1] Be happy and shout to God
who makes us strong!
Shout praises to the God
of Jacob.
[2] Sing as you play tambourines
and the lovely sounding
stringed instruments.
[3] Sound the trumpets and start
the New Moon Festival.[p]
We must also celebrate
when the moon is full.
[4] This is the law in Israel,
and it was given to us
by the God of Jacob.
[5] The descendants of Joseph
were told to obey it,
when God led them out
from the land of Egypt.

In a language unknown to me,
I heard someone say:
[6] "I lifted the burden
from your shoulder
and took the heavy basket
from your hands.
[7] When you were in trouble,
I rescued you,
and from the thunderclouds,
I answered your prayers.
Later I tested you
at Meribah Spring.[q]

[8] "Listen, my people,
while I, the Lord,
correct you!
Israel, if you would only
pay attention to me!
[9] Don't worship foreign gods
or bow down to gods
you know nothing about.
[10] I am the LORD your God.
I rescued you from Egypt.
Just ask, and I will give you
whatever you need.

[11] "But, my people, Israel,
you refused to listen,
and you would have nothing
to do with me!
[12] So I let you be stubborn
and keep on following
your own advice.

[m]**80.11** *the sea . . . the river*: The Mediterranean Sea and the Euphrates River were part of the ideal boundaries for Israel. [n]**80.17** *right side*: See the note at 16.11. [o]**Psalm 81** *leader*: See the note at Psalm 8. [p]**81.3** *New Moon Festival*: Celebrated on the first day of each new moon, which was the beginning of the month. But this may refer to either the New Year celebration or the Harvest Festival. "The moon is full" suggests a festival in the middle of the month. [q]**81.7** *Meribah Spring*: When the people of Israel complained to Moses about the need for water, God commanded Moses to strike a rock with his walking stick, and water came out. The place was then named Massah ("test") and Meribah ("complaining").

13 "My people, Israel,
if only you would listen
and do as I say!
14 I, the LORD, would quickly
defeat your enemies
with my mighty power.
15 Everyone who hates me
would come crawling,
and that would be the end
of them.
16 But I would feed you
with the finest bread
and with the best honey[r]
until you were full."

Psalm 82

[*A psalm by Asaph.*]

Please Do Something, God!

1 When all of the other gods[s]
have come together,
the Lord God judges them
and says:
2 "How long will you
keep judging unfairly
and favoring evil people?
3 Be fair to the poor
and to orphans.
Defend the helpless
and everyone in need.
4 Rescue the weak and homeless
from the powerful hands
of heartless people.

5 "None of you know
or understand a thing.
You live in darkness,
while the foundations
of the earth tremble.[t]

6 "I, the Most High God, say
that all of you are gods[u]
and also my own children.
7 But you will die,
just like everyone else,
including powerful rulers."

8 Do something, God!
Judge the nations of the earth;
they belong to you.

Psalm 83

[*A song and a psalm by Asaph.*]

God Rules All the Earth

1 Our God, don't just sit there,
silently doing nothing!
2 Your hateful enemies
are turning against you
and rebelling.
3 They are sly, and they plot
against those you treasure.
4 They say, "Let's wipe out
the nation of Israel
and make sure that no one
remembers its name!"

5 All of them fully agree
in their plans against you,
and among them are
6 Edom and the Ishmaelites;
Moab and the Hagrites;
7 Gebal, Ammon, and Amalek;
Philistia and Phoenicia.[v]
8 Even Assyria has joined forces
with Moab and Ammon.[w]

9 Our Lord, punish all of them
as you punished Midian.
Destroy them, as you destroyed
Sisera and Jabin
at Kishon Creek 10 near Endor,
and let their bodies rot.
11 Treat their leaders as you did
Oreb and Zeeb,
Zebah and Zalmunna.
12 All of them said, "We'll take
God's valuable land!"

13 Our God, scatter them around
like dust in a whirlwind.
14 Just as flames destroy forests
on the mountains,
15 pursue and terrify them
with storms of your own.
16 Make them blush with shame,
until they turn and worship
you, our LORD.
17 Let them be forever ashamed
and confused.
Let them die in disgrace.
18 Make them realize that you
are the LORD Most High,
the only ruler of earth!

Psalm 84

[*For the music leader.*[x]
A psalm for the people of Korah.]

The Joy of Worship

1 LORD God All-Powerful,
your temple is so lovely!
2 Deep in my heart I long
for your temple,
and with all that I am
I sing joyful songs to you.

[r]**81.16** *the best honey*: The Hebrew text has "honey from rocks," referring to honey taken from beehives in holes or cracks in large rocks. [s]**82.1** *the other gods*: This probably refers to the gods of the nations that God defeated, but it could refer to God's servants (angels) in heaven or even to human rulers. [t]**82.5** *foundations . . . tremble*: In ancient times it was believed that the earth was flat and supported by columns. [u]**82.6** *all of you are gods*: See the note at 82.1. [v]**83.7** *Phoenicia*: The Hebrew text has "Tyre," the main city in Phoenicia. [w]**83.8** *Moab and Ammon*: The Hebrew text has "the descendants of Lot," whose older daughter was the mother of the Moabites and whose younger daughter was the mother of the Ammonites (see Genesis 19.30-38). [x]**Psalm 84** *leader*: See the note at Psalm 8.

[3] LORD God All-Powerful,
my King and my God,
sparrows find a home
near your altars;
swallows build nests there
to raise their young.

[4] You bless everyone
who lives in your house,
and they sing your praises.
[5] You bless all who depend
on you for their strength
and all who deeply desire
to visit your temple.
[6] When they reach Dry Valley,[y]
springs start flowing,
and the autumn rain fills it
with pools of water.[z]
[7] Your people grow stronger,
and you, the God of gods,
will be seen in Zion.

[8] LORD God All-Powerful,
the God of Jacob,
please answer my prayer!
[9] You are the shield
that protects your people,
and I am your chosen one.
Won't you smile on me?

[10] One day in your temple
is better than a thousand
anywhere else.
I would rather serve
in your house,
than live in the homes
of the wicked.

[11] Our LORD and our God,
you are like the sun
and also like a shield.
You treat us with kindness
and with honor,
never denying any good thing
to those who live right.

[12] LORD God All-Powerful,
you bless everyone
who trusts you.

Psalm 85

[A psalm by the people of Korah for the music leader.]

A Prayer for Peace

[1] Our LORD, you have blessed
your land
and made all go well
for Jacob's descendants.
[2] You have forgiven the sin
and taken away the guilt
of your people.
[3] Your fierce anger is no longer
aimed at us.
[4] Our LORD and our God,
you save us!
Please bring us back home
and don't be angry.
[5] Will you always be angry
with us and our families?
[6] Won't you give us fresh life
and let your people be glad
because of you?
[7] Show us your love
and save us!

[8] I will listen to you, LORD God,
because you promise peace
to those who are faithful
and no longer foolish.
[9] You are ready to rescue
everyone who worships you,
so that you will live with us
in all of your glory.

[10] Love and loyalty
will come together;
goodness and peace
will unite.
[11] Loyalty will sprout
from the ground;
justice will look down
from the sky above.

[12] Our LORD, you will bless us;
our land will produce
wonderful crops.
[13] Justice will march in front,
making a path
for you to follow.

Psalm 86

[A prayer by David.]

A Prayer for Help

[1] Please listen, LORD,
and answer my prayer!
I am poor and helpless.
[2] Protect me and save me
because you are my God.
I am your faithful servant,
and I trust you.
[3] Be kind to me!
I pray to you all day.
[4] Make my heart glad!
I serve you,
and my prayer is sincere.
[5] You willingly forgive,
and your love is always there
for those who pray to you.
[6] Please listen, LORD!
Answer my prayer for help.
[7] When I am in trouble, I pray,
knowing you will listen.

[8] No other gods are like you;
only you work miracles.
[9] You created each nation,

[y] **84.6** *Dry Valley*: Or "Balsam Tree Valley." The exact location is not known. [z] **84.6** *and . . . water*: One possible meaning for the difficult Hebrew text.

and they will all bow down
to worship and honor you.
10 You perform great wonders
because you alone are God.

11 Teach me to follow you,
and I will obey your truth.
Always keep me faithful.
12 With all my heart I thank you.
I praise you, LORD God.
13 Your love for me is so great
that you protected me
from death and the grave.

14 Proud and violent enemies,
who don't care about you,
have ganged up to attack
and kill me.
15 But you, the Lord God,
are kind and merciful.
You don't easily get angry,
and your love
can always be trusted.
16 I serve you, LORD,
and I am the child
of one of your servants.
Look on me with kindness.
Make me strong and save me.
17 Show that you approve of me!
Then my hateful enemies
will feel like fools,
because you have helped
and comforted me.

Psalm 87

[*A psalm and a song by the people of Korah.*]

The Glory of Mount Zion

1 Zion was built by the LORD
on the holy mountain,
2 and he loves that city
more than any other place
in all of Israel.
3 Zion, you are the city of God,
and wonderful things
are told about you.

4 Egypt,[a] Babylonia, Philistia,
Phoenicia,[b] and Ethiopia[c]
are some of those nations
that know you,
and their people all say,
"I was born in Zion."

5 God Most High will strengthen
the city of Zion.
Then everyone will say,
"We were born here too."
6 The LORD will make a list
of his people,
and all who were born here
will be included.
7 All who sing or dance will say,
"I too am from Zion."

Psalm 88

[*A song and a psalm by the people of Korah for the music leader. To the tune "Mahalath Leannoth."*[d] *A special psalm by Heman the Ezrahite.*]

A Prayer When You Can't Find the Way

1 You keep me safe, LORD God.
So when I pray at night,
2 please listen carefully
to each of my concerns.

3 I am deeply troubled
and close to death;
4 I am as good as dead
and completely helpless.
5 I am no better off
than those in the grave,
those you have forgotten
and no longer help.

6 You have put me in the deepest
and darkest grave;
7 your anger rolls over me
like ocean waves.
8 You have made my friends turn
in horror from me.
I am a prisoner
who cannot escape,
9 and I am almost blind
because of my sorrow.

Each day I lift my hands
in prayer to you, LORD.
10 Do you work miracles
for the dead?
Do they stand up
and praise you?
11 Are your love and loyalty
announced in the world
of the dead?
12 Do they know of your miracles
or your saving power
in the dark world below
where all is forgotten?

13 Each morning I pray
to you, LORD.
14 Why do you reject me?
Why do you turn from me?
15 Ever since I was a child,
I have been sick
and close to death.
You have terrified me
and made me helpless.[e]

16 Your anger is like a flood!
And I am shattered
by your furious attacks

[a]**87.4** *Egypt*: The Hebrew text has "Rahab," the name of a monster that stands for Egypt (see Isaiah 30.7). [b]**87.4** *Phoenicia*: See the note at 83.7. [c]**87.4** *Ethiopia*: See the note at 68.31.
[d]**Psalm 88** *To . . . Leannoth*: Or "For the flutes," one possible meaning for the difficult Hebrew text. [e]**88.15** *and made me helpless*: One possible meaning for the difficult Hebrew text.

17 that strike each day
and from every side.
18 My friends and neighbors
have turned against me
because of you,
and now darkness
is my only companion.

Psalm 89

[*A special psalm by Ethan the Ezrahite.*]

The LORD's Agreement with David

1 Our LORD, I will sing
of your love forever.
Everyone yet to be born
will hear me praise
your faithfulness.
2 I will tell them, "God's love
can always be trusted,
and his faithfulness lasts
as long as the heavens."

3 You said, "David, my servant,
is my chosen one,
and this is the agreement
I made with him:
4 David, one of your descendants
will always be king."

5 Our LORD, let the heavens
now praise your miracles,
and let all of your angels
praise your faithfulness.

6 None who live in the heavens
can compare with you.
7 You are the most fearsome
of all who live in heaven;
all the others fear
and greatly honor you.
8 You are LORD God All-Powerful!
No one is as loving
and faithful as you are.
9 You rule the roaring sea
and calm its waves.
10 You crushed the monster Rahab,[f]
and with your powerful arm
you scattered your enemies.
11 The heavens and the earth
belong to you.
And so does the world
with all its people
because you created them
12 and everything else.[g]

Mount Tabor and Mount Hermon
gladly praise you.
13 You are strong and mighty!
14 Your kingdom is ruled
by justice and fairness
with love and faithfulness
leading the way.

15 Our LORD, you bless those
who join in the festival
and walk in the brightness
of your presence.
16 We are happy all day
because of you,
and your saving power
brings honor to us.
17 Your own glorious power
makes us strong,
and because of your kindness,
our strength increases.
18 Our LORD and our King,
the Holy One of Israel,
you are truly our shield.

19 In a vision, you once said
to your faithful followers:
"I have helped a mighty hero.
I chose him from my people
and made him famous.
20 David, my servant, is the one
I chose to be king,
21 and I will always be there
to help and strengthen him.

22 "No enemy will outsmart David,
and he won't be defeated
by any hateful people.
23 I will strike down and crush
his troublesome enemies.
24 He will always be able
to depend on my love,
and I will make him strong
with my own power.
25 I will let him rule the lands
across the rivers and seas.
26 He will say to me,
'You are my Father
and my God,
as well as the mighty rock[h]
where I am safe.'

27 "I have chosen David
as my first-born son,
and he will be the ruler
of all kings on earth.
28 My love for him will last,
and my agreement with him
will never be broken.

29 "One of David's descendants
will always be king,
and his family will rule
until the sky disappears.
30 Suppose some of his children
should reject my Law
and refuse my instructions.
31 Or suppose they should disobey
all of my teachings.
32 Then I will correct

[f]**89.10** *Rahab*: Many people in the ancient world thought that the world was controlled by this sea monster that the Lord destroyed at the time of creation (see Isaiah 51.9). [g]**89.12** *and everything else*: The Hebrew text has "Zaphon and Yamin," which may either be the names of mountains or refer to the directions "north and south," with the meaning "everything from north to south." [h]**89.26** *mighty rock*: See the note at 18.2.

and punish them
because of their sins.
33 But I will always love David
and faithfully keep all
of my promises to him.

34 "I won't break my agreement
or go back on my word.
35 I have sworn once and for all
by my own holy name,
and I won't lie to David.
36 His family will always rule.
I will let his kingdom last
as long as the sun 37 and moon
appear in the sky."

38 You are now angry, God,
and you have turned your back
on your chosen king.
39 You broke off your agreement
with your servant, the king,
and you completely destroyed
his kingdom.
40 The walls of his city
have been broken through,
and every fortress
now lies in ruin.
41 All who pass by
take what they want,
and nations everywhere
joke about the king.

42 You made his enemies powerful
and let them celebrate.
43 But you forced him to retreat
because you did not fight
on his side.
44 You took his crown[i]
and threw his throne
in the dirt.
45 You made an old man of him
and put him to shame.

46 How much longer, LORD?
Will you hide forever?
How long will your anger
keep burning like fire?
47 Remember, life is short![j]
Why did you empty our lives
of all meaning?
48 No one can escape the power
of death and the grave.

49 Our Lord, where is the love
you have always shown
and that you promised
so faithfully to David?
50 Remember your servant, Lord!
People make jokes about me,
and I suffer many insults.
51 I am your chosen one,
but your enemies chase
and make fun of me.

52 Our LORD, we praise you
forever. Amen and amen.

BOOK IV

(Psalms 90–106)

Psalm 90

[A prayer by Moses, the man of God.]

God Is Eternal

1 Our Lord, in all generations
you have been our home.
2 You have always been God—
long before the birth
of the mountains,
even before you created
the earth and the world.

3 At your command we die
and turn back to dust,
4 but a thousand years
mean nothing to you!
They are merely a day gone by
or a few hours in the night.

5 You bring our lives to an end
just like a dream.
We are merely tender grass
6 that sprouts and grows
in the morning,
but dries up by evening.
7 Your furious anger frightens
and destroys us,
8 and you know all of our sins,
even those we do in secret.

9 Your anger is a burden
each day we live,
then life ends like a sigh.
10 We can expect seventy years,
or maybe eighty,
if we are healthy,
but even our best years
bring trouble and sorrow.
Suddenly our time is up,
and we disappear.
11 No one knows the full power
of your furious anger,
but it is as great as the fear
that we owe to you.
12 Teach us to use wisely
all the time we have.

13 Help us, LORD! Don't wait!
Pity your servants.
14 When morning comes,
let your love satisfy
all our needs.
Then we can celebrate
and be glad for what time
we have left.
15 Make us happy for as long
as you caused us trouble
and sorrow.

[i] **89.44** *You took . . . crown*: One possible meaning for the difficult Hebrew text.
[j] **89.47** *Remember . . . short*: One possible meaning for the difficult Hebrew text.

16 Do wonderful things for us,
your servants,
and show your mighty power
to our children.
17 Our Lord and our God,
treat us with kindness
and let all go well for us.
Please let all go well!

Psalm 91
The LORD Is My Fortress

1 Live under the protection
of God Most High
and stay in the shadow
of God All-Powerful.
2 Then you will say to the LORD,
"You are my fortress,
my place of safety;
you are my God,
and I trust you."

3 The Lord will keep you safe
from secret traps
and deadly diseases.
4 He will spread his wings
over you
and keep you secure.
His faithfulness is like
a shield or a city wall.[k]

5 You won't need to worry
about dangers at night
or arrows during the day.
6 And you won't fear diseases
that strike in the dark
or sudden disaster at noon.

7 You will not be harmed,
though thousands fall
all around you.
8 And with your own eyes
you will see the punishment
of the wicked.
9 The LORD Most High
is your fortress.
Run to him for safety,
10 and no terrible disasters
will strike you
or your home.

11 God will command his angels
to protect you
wherever you go.
12 They will carry you
in their arms,
and you won't hurt your feet
on the stones.
13 You will overpower
the strongest lions
and the most deadly snakes.

14 The Lord says, "If you love me
and truly know who I am,
I will rescue you
and keep you safe.
15 When you are in trouble,
call out to me.
I will answer and be there
to protect and honor you.
16 You will live a long life
and see my saving power."

Psalm 92
[A psalm and a song for the Sabbath.]

Sing Praises to the LORD

1 It is wonderful to be grateful
and to sing your praises,
LORD Most High!
2 It is wonderful each morning
to tell about your love
and at night to announce
how faithful you are.
3 I enjoy praising your name
to the music of harps,
4 because everything you do
makes me happy,
and I sing joyful songs.

5 You do great things, LORD.
Your thoughts are too deep
6 for an ignorant fool
to know or understand.
7 Though the wicked sprout
and spread like grass,
they will be pulled up
by their roots.
8 But you will rule
over all of us forever,
9 and your hateful enemies
will be scattered
and then destroyed.

10 You have given me
the strength of a wild ox,
and you have chosen me
to be your very own.
11 My eyes have seen,
and my ears have heard
the doom and destruction
of my terrible enemies.

12 Good people will prosper
like palm trees,
and they will grow strong
like the cedars of Lebanon.
13 They will take root
in your house, LORD God,
and they will do well.
14 They will be like trees
that stay healthy and fruitful,
even when they are old.
15 And they will say about you,
"The LORD always does right!
God is our mighty rock."[l]

[k] **91.4** *city wall*: One possible meaning for a difficult Hebrew word; it may possibly mean some kind of shield or weapon. [l] **92.15** *mighty rock*: See the note at 18.2.

Psalm 93

The LORD Is King

1 Our LORD, you are King!
Majesty and power
are your royal robes.
You put the world in place,
and it will never be moved.
2 You have always ruled,
and you are eternal.

3 The ocean is roaring, LORD!
The sea is pounding hard.
4 Its mighty waves are majestic,
but you are more majestic,
and you rule over all.
5 Your decisions are firm,
and your temple will always
be beautiful and holy.

Psalm 94

The LORD Punishes the Guilty

1 LORD God, you punish
the guilty.
Show what you are like
and punish them now.
2 You judge the earth.
Come and help us!
Pay back those proud people
for what they have done.
3 How long will the wicked
celebrate and be glad?

4 All of those cruel people
strut and boast,
5 and they crush and wound
your chosen nation, LORD.
6 They murder widows,
foreigners, and orphans.
7 Then they say,
"The LORD God of Jacob
doesn't see or know."

8 Can't you fools see?
Won't you ever learn?
9 God gave us ears and eyes!
Can't he hear and see?
10 God instructs the nations
and gives knowledge to us all.
Won't he also correct us?
11 The LORD knows how useless
our plans really are.

12 Our LORD, you bless everyone
that you instruct and teach
by using your Law.
13 You give them rest
from their troubles,
until a pit can be dug
for the wicked.
14 You won't turn your back
on your chosen nation.
15 Justice and fairness
will go hand in hand,
and all who do right
will follow along.

16 Who will stand up for me
against those cruel people?
17 If you had not helped me, LORD,
I would soon have gone
to the land of silence.[m]
18 When I felt my feet slipping,
you came with your love
and kept me steady.
19 And when I was burdened
with worries,
you comforted me
and made me feel secure.
20 But you are opposed
to dishonest lawmakers
21 who gang up to murder
innocent victims.

22 You, LORD God, are my fortress,
that mighty rock[n]
where I am safe.
23 You will pay back my enemies,
and you will wipe them out
for the evil they did.

Psalm 95

Worship and Obey the LORD

1 Sing joyful songs to the LORD!
Praise the mighty rock[n]
where we are safe.
2 Come to worship him
with thankful hearts
and songs of praise.

3 The LORD is the greatest God,
king over all other gods.
4 He holds the deepest part
of the earth in his hands,
and the mountain peaks
belong to him.
5 The ocean is the Lord's
because he made it,
and with his own hands
he formed the dry land.

6 Bow down and worship
the LORD our Creator!
7 The LORD is our God,
and we are his people,
the sheep he takes care of
in his own pasture.

Listen to God's voice today!
8 Don't be stubborn and rebel
as your ancestors did
at Meribah and Massah[o]
out in the desert.
9 For forty years

[m]**94.17** *land of silence*: The grave or the world of the dead. [n]**94.22** *mighty rock*: See the note at 18.2. [n]**95.1** *mighty rock*: See the note at 18.2. [o]**95.8** *Meribah and Massah*: See the note at 81.7.

they tested God and saw
the things he did.
10 Then God got tired of them
and said,
"You never show good sense,
and you don't understand
what I want you to do."
11 In his anger, God told them,
"You people will never enter
my place of rest."

Psalm 96

Sing a New Song to the LORD

1 Sing a new song to the LORD!
Everyone on this earth,
sing praises to the LORD,
2 sing and praise his name.

Day after day announce,
"The LORD has saved us!"
3 Tell every nation on earth,
"The LORD is wonderful
and does marvelous things!
4 The LORD is great and deserves
our greatest praise!
He is the only God
worthy of our worship.
5 Other nations worship idols,
but the LORD created
the heavens.
6 Give honor and praise
to the LORD,
whose power and beauty
fill his holy temple."

7 Tell everyone of every nation,
"Praise the glorious power
of the LORD.
8 He is wonderful! Praise him
and bring an offering
into his temple.
9 Everyone on earth, now tremble
and worship the LORD,
majestic and holy."

10 Announce to the nations,
"The LORD is King!
The world stands firm,
never to be shaken,
and he will judge its people
with fairness."

11 Tell the heavens and the earth
to be glad and celebrate!
Command the ocean to roar
with all of its creatures
12 and the fields to rejoice
with all of their crops.
Then every tree in the forest
will sing joyful songs
13 to the LORD.
He is coming to judge
all people on earth
with fairness and truth.

Psalm 97

The LORD Brings Justice

1 The LORD is King!
Tell the earth to celebrate
and all islands to shout.
2 Dark clouds surround him,
and his throne is supported
by justice and fairness.
3 Fire leaps from his throne,
destroying his enemies,
4 and his lightning is so bright
that the earth sees it
and trembles.
5 Mountains melt away like wax
in the presence of the LORD
of all the earth.

6 The heavens announce,
"The LORD brings justice!"
Everyone sees God's glory.
7 Those who brag about
the useless idols they worship
are terribly ashamed,
and all the false gods
bow down to the LORD.

8 When the people of Zion
and of the towns of Judah
hear that God brings justice,
they will celebrate.
9 The LORD rules the whole earth,
and he is more glorious
than all the false gods.

10 Love the LORD
and hate evil!
God protects his loyal people
and rescues them
from violence.
11 If you obey and do right,
a light will show you the way
and fill you with happiness.
12 You are the LORD's people!
So celebrate and praise
the only God.

Psalm 98

The LORD Works Miracles

1 Sing a new song to the LORD!
He has worked miracles,
and with his own powerful arm,
he has won the victory.
2 The LORD has shown the nations
that he has the power to save
and to bring justice.
3 God has been faithful
in his love for Israel,
and his saving power is seen
everywhere on earth.

4 Tell everyone on this earth
to sing happy songs
in praise of the LORD.
5 Make music for him on harps.
Play beautiful melodies!

6 Sound the trumpets and horns
and celebrate with joyful songs
for our LORD and King!

7 Command the ocean to roar
with all of its creatures,
and the earth to shout
with all of its people.
8 Order the rivers
to clap their hands,
and all of the hills
to sing together.
9 Let them worship the LORD!
He is coming to judge
everyone on the earth,
and he will be honest
and fair.

Psalm 99

Our LORD Is King

1 Our LORD, you are King!
You rule from your throne
above the winged creatures,[p]
as people tremble
and the earth shakes.
2 You are praised in Zion,
and you control all nations.
3 Only you are God!
And your power alone,
so great and fearsome,
is worthy of praise.
4 You are our mighty King,[q]
a lover of fairness,
who sees that justice is done
everywhere in Israel.
5 Our LORD and our God,
we praise you
and kneel down to worship you,
the God of holiness!

6 Moses and Aaron were two
of your priests.
Samuel was also one of those
who prayed in your name,
and you, our LORD,
answered their prayers.
7 You spoke to them
from a thick cloud,
and they obeyed your laws.

8 Our LORD and our God,
you answered their prayers
and forgave their sins,
but when they did wrong,
you punished them.
9 We praise you, LORD God,
and we worship you
at your sacred mountain.
Only you are God!

Psalm 100

[*A psalm of praise.*]

The LORD Is God

1 Shout praises to the LORD,
everyone on this earth.
2 Be joyful and sing
as you come in
to worship the LORD!

3 You know the LORD is God!
He created us,
and we belong to him;
we are his people,
the sheep in his pasture.

4 Be thankful and praise the LORD
as you enter his temple.
5 The LORD is good!
His love and faithfulness
will last forever.

Psalm 101

[*A psalm by David.*]

A King and His Promises

1 I will sing to you, LORD!
I will celebrate your kindness
and your justice.
2 Please help me learn
to do the right thing,
and I will be honest and fair
in my own kingdom.
3 I refuse to be corrupt
or to take part
in anything crooked,
4 and I won't be dishonest
or deceitful.

5 Anyone who spreads gossip
will be silenced,
and no one who is conceited
will be my friend.

6 I will find trustworthy people
to serve as my advisors,
and only an honest person
will serve as an official.

7 No one who cheats or lies
will have a position
in my royal court.
8 Each morning I will silence
any lawbreakers I find
in the countryside
or in the city of the LORD.

Psalm 102

[*A prayer for someone who hurts
and needs to ask the LORD for help.*]

A Prayer in Time of Trouble

1 I pray to you, LORD!
Please listen.

[p] **99.1** *winged creatures*: See the note at 80.1.

[q] **99.4** *You . . . King*: One possible meaning for the difficult Hebrew text.

2 Don't hide from me
in my time of trouble.
Pay attention to my prayer
and quickly give an answer.

3 My days disappear like smoke,
and my bones are burning
as though in a furnace.
4 I am wasting away like grass,
and my appetite is gone.
5 My groaning never stops,
and my bones can be seen
through my skin.
6 I am like a lonely owl
in the desert
7 or a restless sparrow
alone on a roof.

8 My enemies insult me all day,
and they use my name
for a curse word.
9 Instead of food,
I have ashes to eat
and tears to drink,
10 because you are furious
and have thrown me aside.
11 My life fades like a shadow
at the end of day
and withers like grass.

12 Our LORD, you are King forever
and will always be famous.
13 You will show pity to Zion
because the time has come.
14 We, your servants,
love each stone in the city,
and we are sad to see them
lying in the dirt.

15 Our LORD, the nations
will honor you,
and all kings on earth
will praise your glory.
16 You will rebuild
the city of Zion.
Your glory will be seen,
17 and the prayers of the homeless
will be answered.

18 Future generations must also
praise the LORD,
so write this for them:
19 "From his holy temple,
the LORD looked down
at the earth.
20 He listened to the groans
of prisoners,
and he rescued everyone
who was doomed to die."

21 All Jerusalem should praise
you, our LORD,
22 when people from every nation
meet to worship you.

23 I should still be strong,
but you, LORD, have made
an old person of me.
24 You will live forever!
Years mean nothing to you.
Don't cut my life in half!

25 In the beginning, LORD,
you laid the earth's foundation
and created the heavens.
26 They will all disappear
and wear out like clothes.
You change them,
as you would a coat,
but you last forever.
27 You are always the same.
Years cannot change you.
28 Every generation of those
who serve you
will live in your presence.

Psalm 103

[*By David.*]

The LORD's Wonderful Love

1 With all my heart
I praise the LORD,
and with all that I am
I praise his holy name!
2 With all my heart
I praise the LORD!
I will never forget
how kind he has been.

3 The LORD forgives our sins,
heals us when we are sick,
4 and protects us from death.
His kindness and love
are a crown on our heads.
5 Each day that we live,[r]
he provides for our needs
and gives us the strength
of a young eagle.

6 For all who are mistreated,
the LORD brings justice.
7 He taught his Law to Moses
and showed all Israel
what he could do.

8 The LORD is merciful!
He is kind and patient,
and his love never fails.
9 The LORD won't always be angry
and point out our sins;
10 he doesn't punish us
as our sins deserve.

11 How great is God's love for all
who worship him?
Greater than the distance
between heaven and earth!
12 How far has the LORD taken
our sins from us?

[r] **103.5** *Each . . . live*: One possible meaning for the difficult Hebrew text.

Farther than the distance
from east to west!

13 Just as parents are kind
to their children,
the LORD is kind
to all who worship him,
14 because he knows
we are made of dust.
15 We humans are like grass
or wild flowers
that quickly bloom.
16 But a scorching wind blows,
and they quickly wither
to be forever forgotten.

17 The LORD is always kind
to those who worship him,
and he keeps his promises
to their descendants
18 who faithfully obey him.

19 God has set up his kingdom
in heaven, and he rules
the whole creation.
20 All of you mighty angels,
who obey God's commands,
come and praise your LORD!
21 All of you thousands
who serve and obey God,
come and praise your LORD!
22 All of God's creation
and all that he rules,
come and praise your LORD!
With all my heart
I praise the LORD!

Psalm 104

The LORD Takes Care of His Creation

1 I praise you, LORD God,
with all my heart.
You are glorious and majestic,
dressed in royal robes
2 and surrounded by light.
You spread out the sky
like a tent,
3 and you built your home
over the mighty ocean.
The clouds are your chariot
with the wind as its wings.
4 The winds are your messengers,
and flames of fire
are your servants.

5 You built foundations
for the earth, and it
will never be shaken.
6 You covered the earth
with the ocean that rose
above the mountains.
7 Then your voice thundered!
And the water flowed
8 down the mountains
and through the valleys
to the place you prepared.
9 Now you have set boundaries,
so that the water will never
flood the earth again.

10 You provide streams of water
in the hills and valleys,
11 so that the donkeys
and other wild animals
can satisfy their thirst.
12 Birds build their nests nearby
and sing in the trees.
13 From your home above
you send rain on the hills
and water the earth.
14 You let the earth produce
grass for cattle,
plants for our food,
15 wine to cheer us up,
olive oil for our skin,
and grain for our health.

16 Our LORD, your trees
always have water,
and so do the cedars
you planted in Lebanon.
17 Birds nest in those trees,
and storks make their home
in the fir trees.
18 Wild goats find a home
in the tall mountains,
and small animals can hide
between the rocks.

19 You created the moon
to tell us the seasons.
The sun knows when to set,
20 and you made the darkness,
so the animals in the forest
could come out at night.
21 Lions roar as they hunt
for the food you provide.
22 But when morning comes,
they return to their dens,
23 then we go out to work
until the end of day.

24 Our LORD, by your wisdom
you made so many things;
the whole earth is covered
with your living creatures.
25 But what about the ocean
so big and wide?
It is alive with creatures,
large and small.
26 And there are the ships,
as well as Leviathan,[s]
the monster you created
to splash in the sea.

27 All of these depend on you
to provide them with food,
28 and you feed each one
with your own hand,
until they are full.
29 But when you turn away,
they are terrified;

[s] **104.26** *Leviathan*: See the note at 74.14.

when you end their life,
they die and rot.
30 You created all of them
by your Spirit,
and you give new life
to the earth.

31 Our LORD, we pray
that your glory
will last forever
and that you will be pleased
with what you have done.
32 You look at the earth,
and it trembles.
You touch the mountains,
and smoke goes up.
33 As long as I live,
I will sing and praise you,
the LORD God.
34 I hope my thoughts
will please you,
because you are the one
who makes me glad.

35 Destroy all wicked sinners
from the earth
once and for all.
With all my heart
I praise you, LORD!
I praise you!

Psalm 105

The LORD Can Be Trusted

1 Praise the LORD
and pray in his name!
Tell everyone
what he has done.
2 Sing praises to the LORD!
Tell about his miracles.
3 Celebrate and worship
his holy name
with all your heart.

4 Trust the LORD
and his mighty power.
5 Remember his miracles
and all his wonders
and his fair decisions.
6 You belong to the family
of Abraham, his servant;
you are his chosen ones,
the descendants of Jacob.

7 The LORD is our God,
bringing justice
everywhere on earth.
8 He will never forget
his agreement or his promises,
not in thousands of years.
*9 God made an eternal promise
10 to Abraham, Isaac, and Jacob,
11 when he said, "I'll give you
the land of Canaan."

12 At the time there were
only a few of us,
and we were homeless.
13 We wandered from nation
to nation, from one country
to another.
14 God did not let anyone
mistreat our people.
Instead he protected us
by punishing rulers
15 and telling them,
"Don't touch my chosen leaders
or harm my prophets!"

16 God kept crops from growing
until food was scarce
everywhere in the land.
17 But he had already sent Joseph,
sold as a slave into Egypt,
18 with chains of iron
around his legs and neck.

19 Joseph remained a slave
until his own words
had come true,
and the LORD had finished
testing him.
20 Then the king of Egypt
set Joseph free
21 and put him in charge
of everything he owned.
22 Joseph was in command
of the officials,
and he taught the leaders
how to use wisdom.

23 Jacob and his family
came and settled in Egypt
as foreigners.
24 They were the LORD's people,
so he let them grow stronger
than their enemies.
25 They served the LORD,
and he made the Egyptians plan
hateful things against them.
26 God sent his servant Moses.
He also chose and sent Aaron
27 to his people in Egypt,
and they worked miracles
and wonders there.
28 Moses and Aaron obeyed God,
and he sent darkness
to cover Egypt.
29 God turned their rivers
into streams of blood,
and the fish all died.
30 Frogs were everywhere,
even in the royal palace.
31 When God gave the command,
flies and gnats
swarmed all around.

32 In place of rain,
God sent hailstones
and flashes of lightning.
33 He destroyed their grapevines
and their fig trees,
and he made splinters
of all the other trees.

34 God gave the command,
and more grasshoppers came
than could be counted.
35 They ate every green plant
and all the crops that grew
in the land of Egypt.
36 Then God took the life
of every first-born son.

37 When God led Israel from Egypt,
they took silver and gold,
and no one was left behind.
38 The Egyptians were afraid
and gladly let them go.
39 God hid them under a cloud
and guided them by fire
during the night.

40 When they asked for food,
he sent more birds
than they could eat.
41 God even split open a rock,
and streams of water
gushed into the desert.
42 God never forgot
his sacred promise
to his servant Abraham.

43 When the Lord rescued
his chosen people from Egypt,
they celebrated with songs.
44 The Lord gave them the land
and everything else
the nations had worked for.
45 He did this so that his people
would obey all of his laws.
Shout praises to the LORD!

Psalm 106

A Nation Asks for Forgiveness

1 We will celebrate
and praise you, LORD!
You are good to us,
and your love never fails.
2 No one can praise you enough
for all of the mighty things
you have done.
3 You bless those people
who are honest and fair
in everything they do.

4 Remember me, LORD,
when you show kindness
by saving your people.
5 Let me prosper with the rest
of your chosen ones,
as they celebrate with pride
because they belong to you.

6 We and our ancestors
have sinned terribly.
7 When they were in Egypt,
they paid no attention
to your marvelous deeds
or your wonderful love.
And they turned against you
at the Red Sea.[t]

8 But you were true to your name,
and you rescued them to prove
how mighty you are.
9 You said to the Red Sea,[t]
"Dry up!"
Then you led your people across
on land as dry as a desert.
10 You saved all of them
11 and drowned every one
of their enemies.
12 Then your people trusted you
and sang your praises.

13 But they soon forgot
what you had done
and rejected your advice.
14 They became greedy for food
and tested you there
in the desert.
15 So you gave them
what they wanted,
but later you destroyed them
with a horrible disease.

16 Everyone in camp was jealous
of Moses and of Aaron,
your chosen priest.
17 Dathan and Abiram rebelled,
and the earth opened up
and swallowed them.
18 Then fire broke out
and destroyed all
of their followers.

19 At Horeb your people
made and worshiped the statue
20 of a bull, instead of you,
their glorious God.
21 You worked powerful miracles
to save them from Egypt,
but they forgot about you
22 and the fearsome things
you did at the Red Sea.[t]

[t] **106.7** *Red Sea*: Hebrew *yam suph* "Sea of Reeds," one of the marshes or fresh water lakes near the eastern part of the Nile Delta. This identification is based on Exodus 13.17—14.9, which lists the towns on the route of the Israelites before crossing the sea. In the Greek translation of the Scriptures made about 200 B.C., the "Sea of Reeds" was named "Red Sea."
[t] **106.9** *Red Sea*: Hebrew *yam suph* "Sea of Reeds," one of the marshes or fresh water lakes near the eastern part of the Nile Delta. This identification is based on Exodus 13.17—14.9, which lists the towns on the route of the Israelites before crossing the sea. In the Greek translation of the Scriptures made about 200 B.C., the "Sea of Reeds" was named "Red Sea."
[t] **106.22** *Red Sea*: Hebrew *yam suph* "Sea of Reeds," one of the marshes or fresh water lakes near the eastern part of the Nile Delta. This identification is based on Exodus 13.17—14.9, which lists the towns on the route of the Israelites before crossing the sea. In the Greek translation of the Scriptures made about 200 B.C., the "Sea of Reeds" was named "Red Sea."

23 You were angry and started
to destroy them,
but Moses, your chosen leader,
begged you not to do it.

24 They would not trust
you, LORD,
and they did not like
the promised land.
25 They would not obey you,
and they grumbled
in their tents.
26 So you threatened them
by saying, "I'll kill you
out here in the desert!
27 I'll scatter your children
everywhere in the world."

28 Your people became followers
of a god named Baal Peor,
and they ate sacrifices
offered to the dead.[u]
29 They did such terrible things
that you punished them
with a deadly disease.
30 But Phinehas[v] helped them,
and the sickness stopped.
31 Now he will always
be highly honored.

32 At Meribah Spring[w]
they turned against you
and made you furious.
33 Then Moses got into trouble
for speaking in anger.

34 Our LORD, they disobeyed you
by refusing to destroy
the nations.
35 Instead they were friendly
with those foreigners
and followed their customs.
36 Then they fell into the trap
of worshiping idols.
37 They sacrificed their sons
and their daughters to demons
38 and to the gods of Canaan.
Then they poured out the blood
of these innocent children
and made the land filthy.
39 By doing such gruesome things,
they also became filthy.

40 Finally, LORD, you were angry
and terribly disgusted
with your people.
41 So you put them in the power
of nations that hated them.
42 They were mistreated and abused
by their enemies,
43 but you saved them
time after time.
They were determined to rebel,
and their sins caused
their downfall.

44 You answered their prayers
when they were in trouble.
45 You kept your agreement
and were so merciful
46 that their enemies
had pity on them.

47 Save us, LORD God!
Bring us back
from among the nations.
Let us celebrate and shout
in praise of your holy name.

48 LORD God of Israel,
you deserve to be praised
forever and ever.
Let everyone say, "Amen!
Shout praises to the LORD!"

BOOK V

(Psalms 107–150)

Psalm 107

The LORD Is Good to His People

1 Shout praises to the LORD!
He is good to us,
and his love never fails.
2 Everyone the LORD has rescued
from trouble
should praise him,
3 everyone he has brought
from the east and the west,
the north and the south.[x]

4 Some of you were lost
in the scorching desert,
far from a town.
5 You were hungry and thirsty
and about to give up.
6 You were in serious trouble,
but you prayed to the LORD,
and he rescued you.
7 Right away he brought you
to a town.
8 You should praise the LORD
for his love
and for the wonderful things
he does for all of us.
9 To everyone who is thirsty,
he gives something to drink;
to everyone who is hungry,
he gives good things to eat.

10 Some of you were prisoners
suffering in deepest darkness
and bound by chains,
11 because you had rebelled

[u] **106.28** *the dead*: Or "lifeless idols." [v] **106.30** *Phinehas*: The grandson of Aaron, who put two people to death and kept the Lord from being angry with the rest of his people (see Numbers 25.1-13). [w] **106.32** *Meribah Spring*: See the note at 81.7. [x] **107.3** *south*: The Hebrew text has "sea," probably referring to the Mediterranean Sea.

against God Most High
and refused his advice.
12 You were worn out
from working like slaves,
and no one came to help.
13 You were in serious trouble,
but you prayed to the LORD,
and he rescued you.
14 He brought you out
of the deepest darkness
and broke your chains.

15 You should praise the LORD
for his love
and for the wonderful things
he does for all of us.
16 He breaks down bronze gates
and shatters iron locks.

17 Some of you had foolishly
committed a lot of sins
and were in terrible pain.
18 The very thought of food
was disgusting to you,
and you were almost dead.
19 You were in serious trouble,
but you prayed to the LORD,
and he rescued you.
20 By the power of his own word,
he healed you and saved you
from destruction.

21 You should praise the LORD
for his love
and for the wonderful things
he does for all of us.
22 You should celebrate
by offering sacrifices
and singing joyful songs
to tell what he has done.

23 Some of you made a living
by sailing the mighty sea,
24 and you saw the miracles
the LORD performed there.
25 At his command a storm arose,
and waves covered the sea.
26 You were tossed to the sky
and to the ocean depths,
until things looked so bad
that you lost your courage.
27 You staggered like drunkards
and gave up all hope.
28 You were in serious trouble,
but you prayed to the LORD,
and he rescued you.
29 He made the storm stop
and the sea be quiet.
30 You were happy because of this,
and he brought you to the port
where you wanted to go.

31 You should praise the LORD
for his love
and for the wonderful things
he does for all of us.
32 Honor the LORD
when you and your leaders
meet to worship.

33 If you start doing wrong,
the LORD will turn rivers
into deserts,
34 flowing streams
into scorched land,
and fruitful fields
into beds of salt.

35 But the LORD can also turn
deserts into lakes
and scorched land
into flowing streams.
36 If you are hungry,
you can settle there
and build a town.
37 You can plant fields
and vineyards that produce
a good harvest.
38 The LORD will bless you
with many children
and with herds of cattle.

39 Sometimes you may be crushed
by troubles and sorrows,
until only a few of you
are left to survive.
40 But the LORD will take revenge
on those who conquer you,
and he will make them wander
across desert sands.
41 When you are suffering
and in need,
he will come to your rescue,
and your families will grow
as fast as a herd of sheep.
42 You will see this because
you obey the LORD,
but everyone who is wicked
will be silenced.

43 Be wise! Remember this
and think about the kindness
of the LORD.

Psalm 108

[*A song and a psalm by David.*]

With God on Our Side

1 Our God, I am faithful to you
with all my heart,
and you can trust me.
I will sing
and play music for you
with all that I am.
2 I will start playing my harps
before the sun rises.
3 I will praise you, LORD,
for everyone to hear;
I will sing hymns to you
in every nation.
4 Your love reaches higher
than the heavens,
and your loyalty extends
beyond the clouds.

5 Our God, may you be honored
above the heavens;
may your glory be seen
everywhere on earth.
6 Answer my prayers
and use your powerful arm
to give us victory.
Then the people you love
will be safe.

7 Our God, from your holy place
you made this promise:
"I will gladly divide up
the city of Shechem
and give away Succoth Valley
piece by piece.
8 The lands of Gilead
and Manasseh are mine.
Ephraim is my war helmet,
and Judah is my symbol
of royal power.
9 Moab is merely my washbasin,
and Edom belongs to me.
I shout with victory
over the Philistines."

10 Our God, who will bring me
to the fortress
or lead me to Edom?
11 Have you rejected us?
You don't lead our armies.
12 Help us defeat our enemies!
No one else can rescue us.
13 You are the one
who gives us victory
and crushes our enemies.

Psalm 109

[*A psalm by David for the music leader.*]

A Prayer for the LORD's Help

1 I praise you, God!
Don't keep silent.
2 Destructive and deceitful lies
are told about me,
3 and hateful things are said
for no reason.
4 I had pity and prayed[y]
for my enemies,
but their words to me
were harsh and cruel.
5 For being friendly and kind,
they paid me back
with meanness and hatred.
6 My enemies said,
"Find some worthless fools
to accuse him of a crime.
7 Try him and find him guilty!
Consider his prayers a lie.
8 Cut his life short
and let someone else
have his job.
9 Make orphans of his children
and a widow of his wife;
10 make his children beg for food
and live in the slums.

11 "Let the people he owes
take everything he owns.
Give it all to strangers.
12 Don't let anyone be kind to him
or have pity on the children
he leaves behind.
13 Bring an end to his family,
and from now on let him be
a forgotten man.

14 "Don't let the LORD forgive
the sins of his parents
and his ancestors.
15 Don't let the LORD forget
the sins of his family,
or let anyone remember
his family ever lived.
16 He was so cruel to the poor,
homeless, and discouraged
that they died young.

17 "He cursed others.
Now place a curse on him!
He never wished others well.
Wish only trouble for him!
18 He cursed others more often
than he dressed himself.
Let his curses strike him deep,
just as water and olive oil
soak through to our bones.
19 Let his curses surround him,
just like the clothes
he wears each day."

20 Those are the cruel things
my enemies wish for me.
Let it all happen to them!
21 Be true to your name, LORD God!
Show your great kindness
and rescue me.

22 I am poor and helpless,
and I have lost all hope.
23 I am fading away
like an evening shadow;
I am tossed aside
like a crawling insect.
24 I have gone without eating,[z]
until my knees are weak,
and my body is bony.
25 When my enemies see me,
they say cruel things
and shake their heads.

26 Please help me, LORD God!
Come and save me
because of your love.
27 Let others know that you alone
have saved me.
28 I don't care if they curse me,
as long as you bless me.

[y]109.4 *and prayed*: One possible meaning for the difficult Hebrew text. [z]**109.24** *without eating*: See the note at 35.13.

You will make my enemies fail
when they attack,
and you will make me glad
to be your servant.
29 You will cover them with shame,
just as their bodies
are covered with clothes.

30 I will sing your praises
and thank you, LORD,
when your people meet.
31 You help everyone in need,
and you defend them
when they are on trial.

Psalm 110

[*A psalm by David.*]

The LORD Gives Victory

1 The LORD said to my Lord,
"Sit at my right side,[a]
until I make your enemies
into a footstool for you."

2 The LORD will let your power
reach out from Zion,
and you will rule
over your enemies.
3 Your glorious power
will be seen on the day
you begin to rule.
You will wear the sacred robes
and shine like the morning sun
in all of your strength.[b]
4 The LORD has made a promise
that will never be broken:
"You will be a priest forever,
just like Melchizedek."

5 My Lord is at your right side,
and when he gets angry
he will crush
the other kings.
6 He will judge the nations
and crack their skulls,
leaving piles of dead bodies
all over the earth.
7 He will drink from any stream
that he chooses, while winning
victory after victory.[c]

Psalm 111

Praise the LORD for All He Has Done

1 Shout praises to the LORD!
With all my heart
I will thank the LORD
when his people meet.
2 The LORD has done
many wonderful things!
Everyone who is pleased
with God's marvelous deeds
will keep them in mind.
3 Everything the LORD does
is glorious and majestic,
and his power to bring justice
will never end.

4 The LORD God is famous
for his wonderful deeds,
and he is kind and merciful.
5 He gives food to his worshipers
and always keeps his agreement
with them.
6 He has shown his mighty power
to his people
and has given them the lands
of other nations.

7 God is always honest and fair,
and his laws can be trusted.
8 They are true and right
and will stand forever.
9 God rescued his people,
and he will never break
his agreement with them.
He is fearsome and holy.

10 Respect and obey the LORD!
This is the first step
to wisdom and good sense.[d]
God will always be respected.

Psalm 112

God Blesses His Worshipers

1 Shout praises to the LORD!
The LORD blesses everyone
who worships him and gladly
obeys his teachings.
2 Their descendants will have
great power in the land,
because the LORD blesses
all who do right.
3 They will get rich and prosper
and will always be remembered
for their fairness.
4 They will be so kind
and merciful and good,
that they will be a light
in the dark for others
who do the right thing.

5 Life will go well for those
who freely lend
and are honest in business.
6 They won't ever be troubled,
and the kind things they do
will never be forgotten.
7 Bad news won't bother them;
they have decided
to trust the LORD.
8 They are dependable
and not afraid,
and they will live to see
their enemies defeated.

[a] **110.1** *right side*: See the note at 16.11. [b] **110.3** *You will . . . strength*: One possible meaning for the difficult Hebrew text. [c] **110.7** *while . . . victory*: Or "God will give him victory after victory." [d] **111.10** *This . . . sense*: Or "This is what wisdom and good sense are all about."

9 They will always be remembered
and greatly praised,
because they were kind
and freely gave to the poor.
10 When evil people see this,
they angrily bite their tongues
and disappear.
They will never get
what they really want.

Psalm 113

The LORD Helps People in Need

1 Shout praises to the LORD!
Everyone who serves him,
come and praise his name.

2 Let the name of the LORD
be praised now and forever.
3 From dawn until sunset
the name of the LORD
deserves to be praised.
4 The LORD is far above
all of the nations;
he is more glorious
than the heavens.

5 No one can compare
with the LORD our God.
His throne is high above,
6 and he looks down to see
the heavens and the earth.
7 God lifts the poor and needy
from dust and ashes,
8 and he lets them take part
in ruling his people.
9 When a wife has no children,
he blesses her with some,
and she is happy.
Shout praises to the LORD!

Psalm 114

The LORD Works Wonders

1 God brought his people
out of Egypt, that land
with a strange language.
2 He made Judah his holy place
and ruled over Israel.

3 When the sea looked at God,
it ran away,
and the Jordan River
flowed upstream.
4 The mountains and the hills
skipped around like goats.

5 Ask the sea why it ran away
or ask the Jordan
why it flowed upstream.
6 Ask the mountains and the hills
why they skipped like goats!

7 Earth, you will tremble,
when the Lord God of Jacob
comes near,
8 because he turns solid rock
into flowing streams
and pools of water.

Psalm 115

The LORD Deserves To Be Praised

1 We don't deserve praise!
The LORD alone deserves
all of the praise,
because of his love
and faithfulness.
2 Why should the nations ask,
"Where is your God?"

3 Our God is in the heavens,
doing as he chooses.
4 The idols of the nations
are made of silver and gold.
5 They have a mouth and eyes,
but they can't speak or see.
6 Their ears can't hear,
and their noses can't smell.
7 Their hands have no feeling,
their legs don't move,
and they can't make a sound.
8 Everyone who made the idols
and all who trust them
are just as helpless
as those useless gods.

9 People of Israel,
you must trust the LORD
to help and protect you.
10 Family of Aaron the priest,
you must trust the LORD
to help and protect you.
11 All of you worship the LORD,
so you must trust him
to help and protect you.

12 The LORD will not forget
to give us his blessing;
he will bless all of Israel
and the family of Aaron.
13 All who worship the LORD,
no matter who they are,
will receive his blessing.

14 I pray that the LORD
will let your family
and your descendants
always grow strong.
15 May the LORD who created
the heavens and the earth
give you his blessing.

16 The LORD has kept the heavens
for himself,
but he has given the earth
to us humans.
17 The dead are silent
and cannot praise the LORD,
18 but we will praise him
now and forevermore.
Shout praises to the LORD!

Psalm 116

When the LORD Saves You from Death

1 I love you, LORD!
You answered my prayers.
2 You paid attention to me,
and so I will pray to you
as long as I live.
3 Death attacked from all sides,
and I was captured
by its painful chains.
But when I was really hurting,
4 I prayed and said, "LORD,
please don't let me die!"

5 You are kind, LORD,
so good and merciful.
6 You protect ordinary people,
and when I was helpless,
you saved me
7 and treated me so kindly
that I don't need
to worry anymore.

8 You, LORD, have saved
my life from death,
my eyes from tears,
my feet from stumbling.
9 Now I will walk at your side
in this land of the living.
10 I was faithful to you
when I was suffering,
11 though in my confusion I said,
"I can't trust anyone!"

12 What must I give you, LORD,
for being so good to me?
13 I will pour out an offering
of wine to you,
and I will pray in your name
because you
have saved me.
14 I will keep my promise to you
when your people meet.
15 You are deeply concerned
when one of your loyal people
faces death.

16 I worship you, LORD,
just as my mother did,
and you have rescued me
from the chains of death.
17 I will offer you a sacrifice
to show how grateful I am,
and I will pray.
18 I will keep my promise to you
when your people
19 gather at your temple
in Jerusalem.
Shout praises to the LORD!

Psalm 117

Come Praise the LORD

1 All of you nations,
come praise the LORD!
Let everyone praise him.
2 His love for us is wonderful;
his faithfulness never ends.
Shout praises to the LORD!

Psalm 118

The LORD Is Always Merciful

1 Tell the LORD
how thankful you are,
because he is kind
and always merciful.

2 Let Israel shout,
"God is always merciful!"
3 Let the family of Aaron
the priest shout,
"God is always merciful!"
4 Let every true worshiper
of the LORD shout,
"God is always merciful!"

5 When I was really hurting,
I prayed to the LORD.
He answered my prayer,
and took my worries away.
6 The LORD is on my side,
and I am not afraid
of what others can do to me.
7 With the LORD on my side,
I will defeat all
of my hateful enemies.
8 It is better to trust the LORD
for protection
than to trust anyone else,
9 including strong leaders.
10 Nations surrounded me,
but I got rid of them
by the power of the LORD.
11 They attacked from all sides,
but I got rid of them
by the power of the LORD.
12 They swarmed around like bees,
but by the power of the LORD,
I got rid of them
and their fiery sting.
13 Their attacks were so fierce
that I nearly fell,
but the LORD helped me.
14 My power and my strength
come from the LORD,
and he has saved me.

15 From the tents of God's people
come shouts of victory:
"The LORD is powerful!
16 With his mighty arm
the LORD wins victories!
The LORD is powerful!"

17 And so my life is safe,
and I will live to tell
what the LORD has done.
18 He punished me terribly,
but he did not let death
lay its hands on me.
19 Open the gates of justice!
I will enter and tell the LORD
how thankful I am.

20 Here is the gate of the LORD!
Everyone who does right
may enter this gate.

21 I praise the LORD
for answering my prayers
and saving me.
22 The stone that the builders
tossed aside
has now become
the most important stone.

23 The LORD has done this,
and it is amazing to us.
24 This day belongs to the LORD!
Let's celebrate
and be glad today.
25 We'll ask the LORD to save us!
We'll sincerely ask the LORD
to let us win.

26 God bless the one who comes
in the name of the LORD!
We praise you from here
in the house of the LORD.

27 The LORD is our God,
and he has given us light!
Start the celebration!
March with palm branches
all the way to the altar.[e]

28 The LORD is my God!
I will praise him and tell him
how thankful I am.

29 Tell the LORD
how thankful you are,
because he is kind
and always merciful.

Psalm 119

In Praise of the Law of the LORD

1 Our LORD, you bless everyone
who lives right
and obeys your Law.
2 You bless all of those
who follow your commands
from deep in their hearts
3 and who never do wrong
or turn from you.
4 You have ordered us always
to obey your teachings;
5 I don't ever want to stray
from your laws.
6 Thinking about your commands
will keep me from doing
some foolish thing.
7 I will do right and praise you
by learning to respect
your perfect laws.
8 I will obey all of them!
Don't turn your back on me.

9 Young people can live
a clean life
by obeying your word.
10 I worship you
with all my heart.
Don't let me walk away
from your commands.
11 I treasure your word
above all else;
it keeps me from sinning
against you.
12 I praise you, LORD!
Teach me your laws.
13 With my own mouth,
I tell others the laws
that you have spoken.
14 Obeying your instructions
brings as much happiness
as being rich.
15 I will study your teachings
and follow your footsteps.
16 I will take pleasure
in your laws
and remember your words.

17 Treat me with kindness, LORD,
so that I may live
and do what you say.
18 Open my mind
and let me discover
the wonders of your Law.
19 I live here as a stranger.
Don't keep me from knowing
your commands.
20 What I want most of all
and at all times
is to honor your laws.
21 You punish those boastful,
worthless nobodies who turn
from your commands.
22 Don't let them sneer
and insult me
for following you.
23 I keep thinking about
your teachings, LORD,
even if rulers plot
against me.
24 Your laws are my greatest joy!
I follow their advice.

25 I am at the point of death.
Let your teachings
breathe new life into me.
26 When I told you my troubles,
you answered my prayers.
Now teach me your laws.
27 Help me to understand
your teachings,
and I will think about
your marvelous deeds.
28 I am overcome with sorrow.
Encourage me,
as you have promised to do.
29 Keep me from being deceitful,
and be kind enough
to teach me your Law.

[e] 118.27 *Start . . . altar*: One possible meaning for the difficult Hebrew text.

30 I am determined to be faithful
and to respect your laws.
31 I follow your rules, LORD.
Don't let me be ashamed.
32 I am eager to learn all
that you want me to do;
help me to understand
more and more.

33 Point out your rules to me,
and I won't disobey
even one of them.
34 Help me to understand your Law;
I promise to obey it
with all my heart.
35 Direct me by your commands!
I love to do what you say.
36 Make me want to obey you,
rather than to be rich.
37 Take away my foolish desires,
and let me find life
by walking with you.
38 I am your servant!
Do for me what you promised
to those who worship you.
39 Your wonderful teachings
protect me from the insults
that I hate so much.
40 I long for your teachings.
Be true to yourself
and let me live.

41 Show me your love
and save me, LORD,
as you have promised.
42 Then I will have an answer
for everyone who insults me
for trusting your word.
43 I rely on your laws!
Don't take away my chance
to speak your truth.
44 I will keep obeying your Law
forever and ever.
45 I have gained perfect freedom
by following your teachings,
46 and I trust them so much
that I tell them to kings.
47 I love your commands!
They bring me happiness.
48 I love and respect them
and will keep them in mind.

49 Don't forget your promise
to me, your servant.
I depend on it.
50 When I am hurting,
I find comfort in your promise
that leads to life.
51 Conceited people sneer at me,
but I obey your Law.
52 I find true comfort, LORD,
because your laws have stood
the test of time.
53 I get furious when evil people
turn against your Law.
54 No matter where I am,
your teachings
fill me with songs.

55 Even in the night
I think about you, LORD,
and I obey your Law.
56 You have blessed me
because I have always followed
your teachings.

57 You, LORD, are my choice,
and I will obey you.
58 With all my heart
I beg you to be kind to me,
just as you have promised.
59 I pay careful attention
as you lead me,
and I follow closely.
60 As soon as you command,
I do what you say.
61 Evil people may set a trap,
but I obey your Law.
62 Your laws are so fair
that I wake up and praise you
in the middle of the night.
63 I choose as my friends
everyone who worships you
and follows your teachings.
64 Our LORD, your love is seen
all over the world.
Teach me your laws.

65 I am your servant, LORD,
and you have kept your promise
to treat me with kindness.
66 Give me wisdom and good sense.
I trust your commands.
67 Once you corrected me
for not obeying you,
but now I obey.
68 You are kindhearted,
and you do good things,
so teach me your laws.
69 My reputation is being ruined
by conceited liars,
but with all my heart
I follow your teachings.
70 Those liars have no sense,
but I find happiness
in your Law.
71 When you corrected me,
it did me good
because it taught me
to study your laws.
72 I would rather obey you
than to have a thousand pieces
of silver and gold.

73 You created me
and put me together.
Make me wise enough to learn
what you have commanded.
74 Your worshipers will see me,
and they will be glad
that I trust your word.
75 Your decisions are correct,
and you were right
to punish me.
76 I serve you, LORD.
Comfort me with your love,
just as you have promised.

77 I love to obey your Law!
Have mercy and let me live.
78 Put down those proud people
who hurt me with their lies,
because I have chosen
to study your teachings.
79 Let your worshipers come to me,
so they will learn
to obey your rules.
80 Let me truly respect your laws,
so I won't be ashamed.

81 I long for you to rescue me!
Your word is my only hope.
82 I am worn out from waiting
for you to keep your word.
When will you have mercy?
83 My life is wasting away
like a dried-up wineskin,[f]
but I have not forgotten
your teachings.
84 I am your servant!
How long must I suffer?
When will you punish
those troublemakers?
85 Those proud people reject
your teachings,
and they dig pits
for me to fall in.
86 Your laws can be trusted!
Protect me from cruel liars.
87 They have almost killed me,
but I have been faithful
to your teachings.
88 Show that you love me
and let me live,
so that I may obey all
of your commands.

89 Our LORD, you are eternal!
Your word will last as long
as the heavens.[g]
90 You remain faithful
in every generation,
and the earth you created
will keep standing firm.
91 All things are your servants,
and the laws you made
are still in effect today.
92 If I had not found happiness
in obeying your Law,
I would have died in misery.
93 I won't ever forget
your teachings,
because you give me new life
by following them.
94 I belong to you,
and I have respected your laws,
so keep me safe.
95 Brutal enemies are waiting
to ambush and destroy me,
but I obey your rules.
96 Nothing is completely perfect,
except your teachings.

97 I deeply love your Law!
I think about it all day.
98 Your laws never leave my mind,
and they make me much wiser
than my enemies.
99 Thinking about your teachings
gives me better understanding
than my teachers,
100 and obeying your laws
makes me wiser than those
who have lived a long time.
101 I obey your word
instead of following a way
that leads to trouble.
102 You have been my teacher,
and I won't reject
your instructions.
103 Your teachings are sweeter
than honey.
104 They give me understanding
and make me hate all lies.

105 Your word is a lamp
that gives light
wherever I walk.
106 Your laws are fair,
and I have given my word
to respect them all.
107 I am in terrible pain!
Save me, LORD,
as you said you would.
108 Accept my offerings of praise
and teach me your laws.
109 I never forget your teachings,
although my life is always
in danger.
110 Some merciless people
are trying to trap me,
but I never turn my back
on your teachings.
111 They will always be
my most prized possession
and my source of joy.
112 I have made up my mind
to obey your laws forever,
no matter what.

113 I hate anyone
whose loyalty is divided,
but I love your Law.
114 You are my place of safety
and my shield.
Your word is my only hope.

115 All of you worthless people,
get away from me!
I am determined to obey
the commands of my God.

[f]**119.83** *a dried-up wineskin*: The Hebrew text has "a wineskin in the smoke." In ancient times bags were made from animal skins to hold wine, but when the bags dried up they cracked and could no longer be used. [g]**119.89** *Our . . . heavens*: Or "Our LORD, your word is eternal. It will last as long as the heavens."

116 Be true to your word, LORD.
Keep me alive and strong;
don't let me be ashamed
because of my hope.
117 Keep me safe and secure,
so that I will always
respect your laws.
118 You reject all deceitful liars
because they refuse
your teachings.
119 As far as you are concerned,
all evil people are[h] garbage,
and so I follow your rules.
120 I tremble all over
when I think of you
and the way you judge.

121 I did what was fair and right!
Don't hand me over to those
who want to mistreat me.
122 Take good care of me,
your servant,
and don't let me be harmed
by those conceited people.
123 My eyes are weary from waiting
to see you keep your promise
to come and save me.
124 Show your love for me,
your servant,
and teach me your laws.
125 I serve you,
so let me understand
your teachings.
126 Do something, LORD!
They have broken your Law.
127 Your laws mean more to me
than the finest gold.
128 I follow all of your commands,[i]
but I hate anyone
who leads me astray.

129 Your teachings are wonderful,
and I respect them all.
130 Understanding your word
brings light to the minds
of ordinary people.
131 I honestly want to know
everything you teach.
132 Think about me and be kind,
just as you are to everyone
who loves your name.
133 Keep your promise
and don't let me stumble
or let sin control my life.
134 Protect me from abuse,
so I can obey your laws.
135 Smile on me, your servant,
and teach me your laws.
136 When anyone disobeys you,
my eyes overflow with tears.

137 Our LORD, you always do right,
and your decisions are fair.
138 All of your teachings are true
and trustworthy.
139 It upsets me greatly
when my enemies neglect
your teachings.
140 Your word to me, your servant,
is like pure gold;
I treasure what you say.
141 Everyone calls me a nobody,
but I remember your laws.
142 You will always do right,
and your teachings are true.
143 I am in deep distress,
but I love your teachings.
144 Your rules are always fair.
Help me to understand them
and live.

145 I pray to you, LORD!
Please answer me.
I promise to obey your laws.
146 I beg you to save me,
so I can follow your rules.
147 Even before sunrise,
I pray for your help,
and I put my hope
in what you have said.
148 I lie awake at night,
thinking of your promises.
149 Show that you love me, LORD,
and answer my prayer.
Please do the right thing
and save my life.
150 People who disobey your Law
have made evil plans
and want to hurt me,
151 but you are with me,
and all of your commands
can be trusted.
152 From studying your laws,
I found out long ago
that you made them
to last forever.

153 I have not forgotten your Law!
Look at the trouble I am in,
and rescue me.
154 Be my defender and protector!
Keep your promise
and save my life.
155 Evil people won't obey you,
and so they have no hope
of being saved.
156 You are merciful, LORD!
Please do the right thing
and save my life.
157 I have a lot of brutal enemies,
but still I never turn
from your laws.
158 All of those unfaithful people
who refuse to obey you
are disgusting to me.
159 Remember how I love your laws,

[h] **119.119** *As far as . . . are*: A few Hebrew manuscripts and ancient translations. Most Hebrew manuscripts have "You get rid of evil people as if they were." [i] **119.128** *I . . . commands*: One possible meaning for the difficult Hebrew text.

and show your love for me
by keeping me safe.
160 All you say can be trusted;
your teachings are true
and will last forever.

161 Rulers are cruel to me
for no reason.
But with all my heart
I respect your words,
162 because they bring happiness
like treasures taken in war.
163 I can't stand liars,
but I love your Law.
164 I praise you seven times a day
because your laws are fair.
165 You give peace of mind
to all who love your Law.
Nothing can make them fall.
166 You are my only hope
for being saved, LORD,
and I do all you command.
167 I love and obey your laws
with all my heart.
168 You know everything I do.
You know I respect every law
you have given.

169 Please, LORD, hear my prayer
and give me the understanding
that comes from your word.
170 Listen to my concerns
and keep me safe,
just as you have promised.
171 If you will teach me your laws,
I will praise you 172and sing
about your promise,
because all of your teachings
are what they ought to be.
173 Be ready to protect me
because I have chosen
to obey your laws.
174 I am waiting for you
to save me, LORD.
Your Law makes me happy.
175 Keep me alive,
so I can praise you,
and let me find help
in your teachings.
176 I am your servant,
but I have wandered away
like a lost sheep.
Please come after me,
because I have not forgotten
your teachings.

Psalm 120

[*A song for worship.*]

A Prayer for the LORD's Help

1 When I am in trouble, I pray,
2 "Come and save me, LORD,
from deceitful liars!"
3 What punishment is fitting
for you deceitful liars?
4 Your reward should be
sharp and flaming arrows!

5 But I must live as a foreigner
among the people of Meshech
and in the tents of Kedar.[j]
6 I have spent too much time
living among people
who hate peace.
7 I am in favor of peace,
but when I speak of it,
all they want is war.

Psalm 121

[*A song for worship.*]

The LORD Will Protect His People

1 I look to the hills!
Where will I find help?
2 It will come from the LORD,
who created the heavens
and the earth.

3 The LORD is your protector,
and he won't go to sleep
or let you stumble.
4 The protector of Israel
doesn't doze
or ever get drowsy.

5 The LORD is your protector,
there at your right side
to shade you from the sun.
6 You won't be harmed
by the sun during the day
or by the moon[k] at night.

7 The LORD will protect you
and keep you safe
from all dangers.
8 The LORD will protect you
now and always
wherever you go.

Psalm 122

[*A song by David for worship.*]

A Song of Praise

1 It made me glad
to hear them say,
"Let's go to the house
of the LORD!"
2 Jerusalem, we are standing
inside your gates.

3 Jerusalem, what a strong
and beautiful city you are!
4 Every tribe of the LORD
obeys him and comes to you
to praise his name.

[j] **120.5** *Meshech . . . Kedar*: Meshech was a country near the Black Sea, and Kedar was a tribe of the Syrian desert. [k] **121.6** *harmed . . . sun . . . moon*: In ancient times people saw the harmful effects of the rays of the sun, and they thought that certain illnesses (especially mental disorders) were also caused by the rays of the moon.

5 David's royal throne is here
where justice rules.

6 Jerusalem, we pray
that you will have peace,
and that all will go well
for those who love you.
7 May there be peace
inside your city walls
and in your palaces.
8 Because of my friends
and my relatives,
I will pray for peace.
9 And because of the house
of the LORD our God,
I will work for your good.

Psalm 123
[*A song for worship.*]

A Prayer for Mercy

1 Our LORD and our God,
I turn my eyes to you,
on your throne in heaven.
2 Servants look to their master,
but we will look to you,
until you have mercy on us.

3 Please have mercy, LORD!
We have been insulted
more than we can stand,
4 and we can't take more abuse
from those proud,
conceited people.

Psalm 124
[*A song by David for worship.*]

Thanking the LORD for Victory

1 The LORD was on our side!
Let everyone in Israel say:
2 "The LORD was on our side!
Otherwise, the enemy attack
3 would have killed us all,
because it was furious.
4 We would have been swept away
in a violent flood
5 of high and roaring waves."

6 Let's praise the LORD!
He protected us from enemies
who were like wild animals,
7 and we escaped like birds
from a hunter's torn net.

8 The LORD made heaven and earth,
and he is the one
who sends us help.

Psalm 125
[*A song for worship.*]

The LORD's People Are Safe

1 Everyone who trusts the LORD
is like Mount Zion
that cannot be shaken
and will stand forever.
2 Just as Jerusalem is protected
by mountains on every side,
the LORD protects his people
by holding them in his arms
now and forever.
3 He won't let the wicked
rule his people
or lead them to do wrong.
4 Let's ask the LORD to be kind
to everyone who is good
and completely obeys him.

5 When the LORD punishes
the wicked,
he will punish everyone else
who lives a crooked life.
Pray for peace in Israel!

Psalm 126
[*A song for worship.*]

Celebrating the Harvest

1 It seemed like a dream
when the LORD brought us back
to the city of Zion.[l]
2 We celebrated with laughter
and joyful songs.
In foreign nations it was said,
"The LORD has worked miracles
for his people."
3 And so we celebrated
because the LORD had indeed
worked miracles for us.

4 Our LORD, we ask you to bless
our people again,
and let us be like streams
in the Southern Desert.
5 We cried as we went out
to plant our seeds.
Now let us celebrate
as we bring in the crops.
6 We cried on the way
to plant our seeds,
but we will celebrate and shout
as we bring in the crops.

Psalm 127
[*A song by Solomon for worship.*]

Only the LORD Can Bless a Home

1 Without the help of the LORD
it is useless to build a home
or to guard a city.
2 It is useless to get up early
and stay up late
in order to earn a living.
God takes care of his own,
even while they sleep.[m]

3 Children are a blessing
and a gift from the LORD.

[l] **126.1** *brought . . . Zion*: Or "made the city of Zion prosperous again." [m] **127.2** *God . . . sleep*: One possible meaning for the difficult Hebrew text.

4 Having a lot of children
to take care of you
in your old age
is like a warrior
with a lot of arrows.
5 The more you have,
the better off you will be,
because they will protect you
when your enemies attack
with arguments.

Psalm 128
[*A song for worship.*]

The LORD Rewards His Faithful People

1 The LORD will bless you
if you respect him
and obey his laws.
2 Your fields will produce,
and you will be happy
and all will go well.
3 Your wife will be as fruitful
as a grapevine,
and just as an olive tree
is rich with olives,
your home will be rich
with healthy children.
4 That is how the LORD will bless
everyone who respects him.

5 I pray that the LORD
will bless you from Zion
and let Jerusalem prosper
as long as you live.
6 May you live long enough
to see your grandchildren.
Let's pray for peace in Israel!

Psalm 129
[*A song for worship.*]

A Prayer for Protection

1 Since the time I was young,
enemies have often attacked!
Let everyone in Israel say:
2 "Since the time I was young,
enemies have often attacked!
But they have not defeated me,
3 though my back is like a field
that has just been plowed."

4 The LORD always does right,
and he has set me free
from the ropes
of those cruel people.
5 I pray that all who hate
the city of Zion
will be made ashamed
and forced to turn and run.
6 May they be like grass
on the flat roof of a house,
grass that dries up
as soon as it sprouts.
7 Don't let them be like wheat
gathered in bundles.
8 And don't let anyone
who passes by say to them,
"The LORD bless you!
I give you my blessing
in the name of the LORD."

Psalm 130
[*A song for worship.*]

Trusting the LORD in Times of Trouble

1 From a sea of troubles
I call out to you, LORD.
2 Won't you please listen
as I beg for mercy?

3 If you kept record of our sins,
no one could last long.
4 But you forgive us,
and so we will worship you.

5 With all my heart,
I am waiting, LORD, for you!
I trust your promises.
6 I wait for you more eagerly
than a soldier on guard duty
waits for the dawn.
Yes, I wait more eagerly
than a soldier on guard duty
waits for the dawn.

7 Israel, trust the LORD!
He is always merciful,
and he has the power
to save you.
8 Israel, the LORD will save you
from all of your sins.

Psalm 131
[*A song by David for worship.*]

Trust the LORD!

1 I am not conceited, LORD,
and I don't waste my time
on impossible schemes.
2 But I have learned to feel safe
and satisfied,
just like a young child
on its mother's lap.

3 People of Israel,
you must trust the LORD
now and forever.

Psalm 132
[*A song for worship.*]

The LORD Is Always with His People

1 Our LORD, don't forget David
and how he suffered.
2 Mighty God of Jacob,
remember how he promised:
3 "I won't go home
or crawl into bed
4 or close my eyelids,

5 until I find a home for you,
the mighty LORD God of Jacob."

6 When we were in Ephrath,
we heard that the sacred chest
was somewhere near Jaar.
7 Then we said, "Let's go
to the throne of the LORD
and worship at his feet."

8 Come to your new home, LORD,
you and the sacred chest
with all of its power.
9 Let victory be like robes
for the priests;
let your faithful people
celebrate and shout.
10 David is your chosen one,
so don't reject him.
11 You made a solemn promise
to David, when you said,
"I, the LORD, promise
that someone in your family
will always be king.
12 If they keep our agreement
and follow my teachings,
then someone in your family
will rule forever."

13 You have gladly chosen Zion
as your home, our LORD.
14 You said, "This is my home!
I will live here forever.
15 I will bless Zion with food,
and even the poor will eat
until they are full.
16 Victory will be like robes
for the priests,
and its faithful people
will celebrate and shout.
17 I will give mighty power
to the kingdom of David.
Each one of my chosen kings
will shine like a lamp
18 and wear a sparkling crown.
But I will disgrace
their enemies."

Psalm 133

[*A song for worship.*]

Living Together in Peace

1 It is truly wonderful
when relatives live together
in peace.
2 It is as beautiful as olive oil
poured on Aaron's head[n]
and running down his beard
and the collar of his robe.
3 It is like the dew
from Mount Hermon,
falling on Zion's mountains,
where the LORD has promised
to bless his people
with life forevermore.

Psalm 134

[*A song for worship.*]

Praising the LORD at Night

1 Everyone who serves the LORD,
come and offer praises.
Everyone who has gathered
in his temple tonight,
2 lift your hands in prayer
toward his holy place
and praise the LORD.

3 The LORD is the Creator
of heaven and earth,
and I pray that the LORD
will bless you from Zion.

Psalm 135

In Praise of the LORD's Kindness

1 Shout praises to the LORD!
You are his servants,
so praise his name.
2 All who serve in the temple
of the LORD our God,
3 come and shout praises.
Praise the name of the LORD!
He is kind and good.
4 He chose the family of Jacob
and the people of Israel
for his very own.

5 The LORD is much greater
than any other god.
6 He does as he chooses
in heaven and on earth
and deep in the sea.
7 The LORD makes the clouds rise
from far across the earth,
and he makes lightning
to go with the rain.
Then from his secret place
he sends out the wind.

8 The LORD killed the first-born
of people and animals
in the land of Egypt.
9 God used miracles and wonders
to fight the king of Egypt
and all of his officials.
10 He destroyed many nations
and killed powerful kings,
11 including King Sihon
of the Amorites
and King Og of Bashan.
He conquered every kingdom
in the land of Canaan
12 and gave their property
to his people Israel.

13 The name of the LORD
will be remembered forever,
and he will be famous
for all time to come.
14 The LORD will bring justice
and show mercy to all
who serve him.

[n] **133.2** *head*: Olive oil was poured on Aaron's head to show that God had chosen him to be the high priest.

15 Idols of silver and gold
are made and worshiped
in other nations.
16 They have a mouth and eyes,
but they can't speak or see.
17 They are completely deaf,
and they can't breathe.
18 Everyone who makes idols
and all who trust them
will end up as helpless
as their idols.

19 Everyone in Israel,
come praise the LORD!
All the family of Aaron
20 and all the tribe of Levi,[o]
come praise the LORD!
All of his worshipers,
come praise the LORD.
21 Praise the LORD from Zion!
He lives here in Jerusalem.
Shout praises to the LORD!

Psalm 136

God's Love Never Fails

1 Praise the LORD! He is good.
God's love never fails.
2 Praise the God of all gods.
God's love never fails.
3 Praise the Lord of lords.
God's love never fails.

4 Only God works great miracles.[p]
God's love never fails.
5 With wisdom he made the sky.
God's love never fails.
6 The Lord stretched the earth
over the ocean.
God's love never fails.
7 He made the bright lights
in the sky.
God's love never fails.
8 He lets the sun rule each day.
God's love never fails.
9 He lets the moon and the stars
rule each night.
God's love never fails.

10 God struck down the first-born
in every Egyptian family.
God's love never fails.
11 He rescued Israel from Egypt.
God's love never fails.
12 God used his great strength
and his powerful arm.
God's love never fails.
13 He split the Red Sea[q] apart.
God's love never fails.

14 The Lord brought Israel safely
through the sea.
God's love never fails.
15 He destroyed the Egyptian king
and his army there.
God's love never fails.
16 The Lord led his people
through the desert.
God's love never fails.

17 Our God defeated mighty kings.
God's love never fails.
18 And he killed famous kings.
God's love never fails.
19 One of them was Sihon,
king of the Amorites.
God's love never fails.
20 Another was King Og of Bashan.
God's love never fails.
21 God took away their land.
God's love never fails.
22 He gave their land to Israel,
the people who serve him.
God's love never fails.

23 God saw the trouble we were in.
God's love never fails.
24 He rescued us from our enemies.
God's love never fails.
25 He gives food to all who live.
God's love never fails.

26 Praise God in heaven!
God's love never fails.

Psalm 137

A Prayer for Revenge

1 Beside the rivers of Babylon
we thought about Jerusalem,
and we sat down and cried.
2 We hung our small harps
on the willow[r] trees.
3 Our enemies had brought us here
as their prisoners,
and now they wanted us to sing
and entertain them.
They insulted us and shouted,
"Sing about Zion!"

4 Here in a foreign land,
how can we sing
about the LORD?
5 Jerusalem, if I forget you,
let my right hand go limp.
6 Let my tongue stick
to the roof of my mouth,
if I don't think about you
above all else.

7 Our LORD, punish the Edomites!
Because the day Jerusalem fell,
they shouted,
"Completely destroy the city!
Tear down every building!"

[o] **135.19,20** *Aaron . . . Levi*: Aaron was from the tribe of Levi, and all priests were from his family. The temple helpers, singers, and musicians were also from the tribe of Levi.
[p] **136.4** *great miracles*: One Hebrew manuscript and one ancient translation have "miracles."
[q] **136.13** *Red Sea*: See the note at 106.7. [r] **137.2** *willow*: Or "poplar."

8 Babylon, you are doomed!
I pray the Lord's blessings
on anyone who punishes you
for what you did to us.
9 May the Lord bless everyone
who beats your children
against the rocks!

Psalm 138

[*By David.*]

Praise the LORD with All Your Heart

1 With all my heart
I praise you, LORD.
In the presence of angels[s]
I sing your praises.
2 I worship at your holy temple
and praise you for your love
and your faithfulness.
You were true to your word
and made yourself more famous
than ever before.[t]
3 When I asked for your help,
you answered my prayer
and gave me courage.[u]

4 All kings on this earth
have heard your promises, LORD,
and they will praise you.
5 You are so famous
that they will sing about
the things you have done.
6 Though you are above us all,
you care for humble people,
and you keep a close watch
on everyone who is proud.

7 I am surrounded by trouble,
but you protect me
against my angry enemies.
With your own powerful arm
you keep me safe.

8 You, LORD, will always
treat me with kindness.
Your love never fails.
You have made us what we are.
Don't give up on us now![v]

Psalm 139

[*A psalm by David for the music leader.*]

The LORD Is Always Near

1 You have looked deep
into my heart, LORD,
and you know all about me.
2 You know when I am resting
or when I am working,
and from heaven
you discover my thoughts.

3 You notice everything I do
and everywhere I go.
4 Before I even speak a word,
you know what I will say,
5 and with your powerful arm
you protect me
from every side.
6 I can't understand all of this!
Such wonderful knowledge
is far above me.

7 Where could I go to escape
from your Spirit
or from your sight?
8 If I were to climb up
to the highest heavens,
you would be there.
If I were to dig down
to the world of the dead
you would also be there.

9 Suppose I had wings
like the dawning day
and flew across the ocean.
10 Even then your powerful arm
would guide and protect me.
11 Or suppose I said, "I'll hide
in the dark until night comes
to cover me over."
12 But you see in the dark
because daylight and dark
are all the same to you.

13 You are the one
who put me together
inside my mother's body,
14 and I praise you because of
the wonderful way
you created me.
Everything you do is marvelous!
Of this I have no doubt.

15 Nothing about me
is hidden from you!
I was secretly woven together
deep in the earth below,
16 but with your own eyes you saw
my body being formed.
Even before I was born,
you had written in your book
everything I would do.

17 Your thoughts are far beyond
my understanding,
much more than I
could ever imagine.
18 I try to count your thoughts,
but they outnumber the grains
of sand on the beach.
And when I awake,
I will find you nearby.

19 How I wish that you would kill
all cruel and heartless people
and protect me from them!

[s] **138.1** *angels*: Or "gods" or "supernatural beings" who worship and serve God in heaven or "rulers" or "leaders." [t] **138.2** *You were . . . before*: One possible meaning for the difficult Hebrew text. [u] **138.3** *and gave me courage*: One possible meaning for the difficult Hebrew text. [v] **138.8** *You have . . . now*: Or "Please don't desert your people."

20 They are always rebelling
and speaking evil of you.[w]
21 You know I hate anyone
who hates you, LORD,
and refuses to obey.
22 They are my enemies too,
and I truly hate them.

23 Look deep into my heart, God,
and find out everything
I am thinking.
24 Don't let me follow evil ways,
but lead me in the way
that time has proven true.

Psalm 140

[A psalm by David for the music leader.]

A Prayer for the LORD's Help

1 Rescue me from cruel
and violent enemies, LORD!
2 They think up evil plans
and always cause trouble.
3 Their words bite deep
like the poisonous fangs
of a snake.

4 Protect me, LORD, from cruel
and brutal enemies,
who want to destroy me.
5 Those proud people have hidden
traps and nets
to catch me as I walk.

6 You, LORD, are my God!
Please listen to my prayer.
7 You have the power to save me,
and you keep me safe
in every battle.

8 Don't let the wicked succeed
in doing what they want,
or else they might never
stop planning evil.
9 They have me surrounded,
but make them the victims
of their own vicious lies.[x]
10 Dump flaming coals on them
and throw them into pits
where they can't climb out.
11 Chase those cruel liars away!
Let trouble hunt them down.

12 Our LORD, I know that you
defend the homeless
and see that the poor
are given justice.
13 Your people will praise you
and will live with you
because they do right.

Psalm 141

[A psalm by David.]

A Prayer for the LORD's Protection

1 I pray to you, LORD!
Please listen when I pray
and hurry to help me.
2 Think of my prayer
as sweet-smelling incense,
and think of my lifted hands
as an evening sacrifice.

3 Help me to guard my words
whenever I say something.
4 Don't let me want to do evil
or waste my time doing wrong
with wicked people.
Don't let me even taste
the good things they offer.

5 Let your faithful people
correct and punish me.
My prayers condemn the deeds
of those who do wrong,
so don't let me be friends
with any of them.
6 Everyone will admit
that I was right
when their rulers are thrown
down a rocky cliff,
7 and their bones lie scattered
like broken rocks
on top of a grave.[y]

8 You are my LORD and God,
and I look to you for safety.
Don't let me be harmed.
9 Protect me from the traps
of those violent people,
10 and make them fall
into their own traps
while you help me escape.

Psalm 142

[A special psalm and a prayer by David when he was in the cave.]

A Prayer for Help

1 I pray to you, LORD.
I beg for mercy.
2 I tell you all of my worries
and my troubles,
3 and whenever I feel low,
you are there to guide me.

A trap has been hidden
along my pathway.
4 Even if you look,
you won't see anyone
who cares enough
to walk beside me.
There is no place to hide,
and no one who really cares.

[w]139.20 *you*: One possible meaning for the difficult Hebrew text of verse 20. [x]140.8,9 *or else . . . lies*: One possible meaning for the difficult Hebrew text. [y]141.5-7 *Let . . . grave*: One possible meaning for the difficult Hebrew text of verses 5-7.

5 I pray to you, LORD!
You are my place of safety,
and you are my choice
in the land of the living.
Please answer my prayer.
I am completely helpless.

6 Help! They are chasing me,
and they are too strong.
7 Rescue me from this prison,
so I can praise your name.
And when your people notice
your wonderful kindness to me,
they will rush to my side.

Psalm 143

[*A psalm by David.*]

A Prayer in Time of Danger

1 Listen, LORD, as I pray!
You are faithful and honest
and will answer my prayer.
2 I am your servant.
Don't try me in your court,
because no one is innocent
by your standards.
3 My enemies are chasing me,
crushing me in the ground.
I am in total darkness,
like someone long dead.
4 I have given up all hope,
and I feel numb all over.

5 I remember to think about
the many things you did
in years gone by.
6 Then I lift my hands in prayer,
because my soul is a desert,
thirsty for water from you.

7 Please hurry, LORD,
and answer my prayer.
I feel hopeless.
Don't turn away
and leave me here to die.
8 Each morning let me learn
more about your love
because I trust you.
I come to you in prayer,
asking for your guidance.

9 Please rescue me
from my enemies, LORD!
I come to you for safety.[z]
10 You are my God. Show me
what you want me to do,
and let your gentle Spirit
lead me in the right path.

11 Be true to your name, LORD,
and keep my life safe.
Use your saving power
to protect me from trouble.
12 I am your servant.
Show how much you love me
by destroying my enemies.

Psalm 144

[*By David.*]

A Prayer for the Nation

1 I praise you, LORD!
You are my mighty rock,[a]
and you teach me
how to fight my battles.
2 You are my friend,
and you are my fortress
where I am safe.
You are my shield,
and you made me the ruler
of our people.[b]

3 Why do we humans mean anything
to you, our LORD?
Why do you care about us?
4 We disappear like a breath;
we last no longer
than a faint shadow.

5 Open the heavens like a curtain
and come down, LORD.
Touch the mountains
and make them send up smoke.
6 Use your lightning as arrows
to scatter my enemies
and make them run away.
7 Reach down from heaven
and set me free.
Save me from the mighty flood
8 of those lying foreigners
who can't tell the truth.

9 In praise of you, our God,
I will sing a new song,
while playing my harp.
10 By your power, kings win wars,
and your servant David is saved
from deadly swords.
11 Won't you keep me safe
from those lying foreigners
who can't tell the truth?

12 Let's pray that our young sons
will grow like strong plants
and that our daughters
will be as lovely as columns
in the corner of a palace.
13 May our barns be filled
with all kinds of crops.
May our fields be covered
with sheep by the thousands,
14 and every cow have calves.[c]
Don't let our city be captured
or any of us be taken away,
and don't let cries of sorrow
be heard in our streets.

[z] **143.9** *I . . . safety*: Or "You are my hiding place." [a] **144.1** *mighty rock*: See the note at 18.2.
[b] **144.2** *of our people*: Some Hebrew manuscripts and ancient translations have "of the nations."
[c] **144.14** *have calves*: Or "grow fat."

15 Our LORD and our God,
you give these blessings
to all who worship you.

Psalm 145

[*By David for praise.*]

The LORD Is Kind and Merciful

1 I will praise you,
my God and King,
and always honor your name.
2 I will praise you each day
and always honor your name.
3 You are wonderful, LORD,
and you deserve all praise,
because you are much greater
than anyone can understand.

4 Each generation will announce
to the next your wonderful
and powerful deeds.
5 I will keep thinking about
your marvelous glory
and your mighty miracles.[d]
6 Everyone will talk about
your fearsome deeds,
and I will tell all nations
how great you are.
7 They will celebrate and sing
about your matchless mercy
and your power to save.

8 You are merciful, LORD!
You are kind and patient
and always loving.
9 You are good to everyone,
and you take care
of all your creation.

10 All creation will thank you,
and your loyal people
will praise you.
11 They will tell about
your marvelous kingdom
and your power.
12 Then everyone will know about
the mighty things you do
and your glorious kingdom.
13 Your kingdom will never end,
and you will rule forever.

Our LORD, you keep your word
and do everything you say.[e]
14 When someone stumbles or falls,
you give a helping hand.
15 Everyone depends on you,
and when the time is right,
you provide them with food.
16 By your own hand you satisfy
the desires of all who live.

17 Our LORD, everything you do
is kind and thoughtful,
18 and you are near to everyone
whose prayers are sincere.
19 You satisfy the desires
of all your worshipers,
and you come to save them
when they ask for help.
20 You take care of everyone
who loves you,
but you destroy the wicked.

21 I will praise you, LORD,
and everyone will respect
your holy name forever.

Psalm 146

Shout Praises to the LORD

1 Shout praises to the LORD!
With all that I am,
I will shout his praises.
2 I will sing and praise
the LORD God
for as long as I live.

3 You can't depend on anyone,
not even a great leader.
4 Once they die and are buried,
that will be the end
of all their plans.

5 The LORD God of Jacob blesses
everyone who trusts him
and depends on him.
6 God made heaven and earth;
he created the sea
and everything else.
God always keeps his word.
7 He gives justice to the poor
and food to the hungry.

The LORD sets prisoners free
8 and heals blind eyes.
He gives a helping hand
to everyone who falls.
The LORD loves good people
9 and looks after strangers.
He defends the rights
of orphans and widows,
but destroys the wicked.

10 The LORD God of Zion
will rule forever!
Shout praises to the LORD!

Psalm 147

Sing and Praise the LORD

1 Shout praises to the LORD!
Our God is kind,
and it is right and good
to sing praises to him.
2 The LORD rebuilds Jerusalem

[d]**145.5** *and . . . miracles*: One Hebrew manuscript and two ancient translations have "as others tell about your mighty miracles." [e]**145.13** *Our . . . say*: These words are found in one Hebrew manuscript and two ancient translations.

and brings the people of Israel
back home again.
3 He renews our hopes
and heals our bodies.
4 He decided how many stars
there would be in the sky
and gave each one a name.
5 Our LORD is great and powerful!
He understands everything.
6 The LORD helps the poor,
but he smears the wicked
in the dirt.

7 Celebrate and sing!
Play your harps
for the LORD our God.
8 He fills the sky with clouds
and sends rain to the earth,
so that the hills
will be green with grass.
9 He provides food for cattle
and for the young ravens,
when they cry out.
10 The LORD doesn't care about
the strength of horses
or powerful armies.
11 The LORD is pleased only
with those who worship him
and trust his love.

12 Everyone in Jerusalem,
come and praise
the LORD your God!
13 He makes your city gates strong
and blesses your people
by giving them children.
14 God lets you live in peace,
and he gives you
the very best wheat.
15 As soon as God speaks,
the earth obeys.
16 He covers the ground with snow
like a blanket of wool,
and he scatters frost
like ashes on the ground.
17 God sends down hailstones
like chips of rocks.
Who can stand the cold?
18 At his command the ice melts,
the wind blows,
and streams begin to flow.

19 God gave his laws and teachings
to the descendants of Jacob,
the nation of Israel.
20 But he has not given his laws
to any other nation.
Shout praises to the LORD!

Psalm 148

Come Praise the LORD

1 Shout praises to the LORD!
Shout the LORD's praises
in the highest heavens.
2 All of you angels,
and all who serve him above,
come and offer praise.

3 Sun and moon,
and all of you bright stars,
come and offer praise.
4 Highest heavens, and the water
above the highest heavens,[f]
come and offer praise.

5 Let all things praise
the name of the LORD,
because they were created
at his command.
6 He made them to last forever,
and nothing can change
what he has done.[g]

7 All creatures on earth,
you obey his commands,
so come praise the LORD!

8 Sea monsters and the deep sea,
fire and hail, snow and frost,
and every stormy wind,
come praise the LORD!

9 All mountains and hills,
fruit trees and cedars,
10 every wild and tame animal,
all reptiles and birds,
come praise the LORD!
11 Every king and every ruler,
all nations on earth,
12 every man and every woman,
young people and old,
come praise the LORD!

13 All creation, come praise
the name of the LORD.
Praise his name alone.
The glory of God is greater
than heaven and earth.

14 Like a bull with mighty horns,
the LORD protects
his faithful nation Israel,
because they belong to him.
Shout praises to the LORD!

Psalm 149

A New Song of Praise

1 Shout praises to the LORD!
Sing him a new song of praise
when his loyal people meet.
2 People of Israel, rejoice
because of your Creator.
People of Zion, celebrate
because of your King.

[f] 148.4 *the water . . . heavens*: It was believed that the earth and the heavens were surrounded by water. [g] 148.6 *nothing . . . done*: Or "his laws will never change."

3 Praise his name by dancing
and playing music on harps
and tambourines.
4 The LORD is pleased
with his people,
and he gives victory
to those who are humble.
5 All of you faithful people,
praise our glorious Lord!
Celebrate and worship.
6 Praise God with songs
on your lips
and a sword in your hand.
7 Take revenge and punish
the nations.
8 Put chains of iron
on their kings and rulers.
9 Punish them as they deserve;
this is the privilege
of God's faithful people.
Shout praises to the LORD!

Psalm 150

The LORD Is Good to His People

1 Shout praises to the LORD!
Praise God in his temple.
Praise him in heaven,
his mighty fortress.
2 Praise our God!
His deeds are wonderful,
too marvelous to describe.
3 Praise God with trumpets
and all kinds of harps.
4 Praise him with tambourines
and dancing,
with stringed instruments
and woodwinds.
5 Praise God with cymbals,
with clashing cymbals.
6 Let every living creature
praise the LORD.
Shout praises to the LORD!

PROVERBS

ABOUT THIS BOOK

The book of Proverbs is a collection of sayings that were used in ancient Israel to teach God's people how to live right. For the most part, these sayings go back to Solomon, but others are traced back to Agur (30.1) and King Lemuel (31.1).

Like the psalms, all the proverbs are written in poetic form. A typical proverb takes the form of a short verse in which the first half states the theme and the second half echoes it. What makes the Bible's proverbs so popular is that they make such powerful statements with very few words. This makes them easy to memorize and apply to daily life.

One of the main teachings in Proverbs is that all wisdom is a gift from God. This wisdom supplies practical advice for everyday living, in the home, in society, in politics, at school and at work. The book of Proverbs also teaches the importance of fairness, humility, loyalty and concern for the poor and needy.

Because most proverbs are so brief, and make their point in one verse, many are often not connected to those around them. In some parts of the book, however, a common theme can be found. How not to be a fool is the theme of chapter 26.1-12, for example. In chapters 8-9, Wisdom is pictured as a woman who advises people to turn from their foolish ways and to live wisely.

A QUICK LOOK AT THIS BOOK

Introduction: How Proverbs Can Be Used (1.1-7)
Parental Advice on the Importance of Seeking Wisdom and Not Being Foolish (1.8—7.27)
In Praise of Wisdom (8.1-35)
Wisdom's Feast (9.1-18)
Solomon's Wise Sayings (10.1—24.34)
More of Solomon's Wise Sayings (25.1—29.27)
The Sayings of Agur (30.1-33)
What King Lemuel's Mother Taught Him (31.1-31)

How Proverbs Can Be Used

1 These are the proverbs
of King Solomon of Israel,
the son of David.
2 Proverbs will teach you
wisdom and self-control
and how to understand
sayings with deep meanings.
3 You will learn what is right
and honest and fair.
4 From these, an ordinary person
can learn to be smart,
and young people can gain
knowledge and good sense.

5 If you are already wise,
you will become even wiser.
And if you are smart,
you will learn to understand
6 proverbs and sayings,
as well as words of wisdom
and all kinds of riddles.
7 Respect and obey the LORD!
This is the beginning
of knowledge.[a]
Only a fool rejects wisdom
and good advice.

Warnings against Bad Friends

8 My child, obey the teachings
of your parents,
9 and wear their teachings
as you would a lovely hat
or a pretty necklace.

[a] **1.7** *the beginning of knowledge*: Or "what knowledge is all about."

10 Don't be tempted by sinners
or listen 11 when they say,
"Come on! Let's gang up
and kill somebody,
just for the fun of it!
12 They're well and healthy now,
but we'll finish them off
once and for all.
13 We'll take their valuables
and fill our homes
with stolen goods.
14 If you join our gang,
you'll get your share."

15 Don't follow anyone like that
or do what they do.
16 They are in a big hurry
to commit some crime,
perhaps even murder.
17 They are like a bird
that sees the bait,
but ignores the trap.[b]
18 They gang up to murder someone,
but they are the victims.
19 The wealth you get from crime
robs you of your life.

Wisdom Speaks

20 Wisdom[c] shouts in the streets
wherever crowds gather.
21 She shouts in the marketplaces
and near the city gates
as she says to the people,
22 "How much longer
will you enjoy
being stupid fools?
Won't you ever stop sneering
and laughing at knowledge?
23 Listen as I correct you
and tell you what I think.
24 You completely ignored me
and refused to listen;
25 you rejected my advice
and paid no attention
when I warned you.

26 "So when you are struck
by some terrible disaster,
27 or when trouble and distress
surround you like a whirlwind,
I will laugh and make fun.
28 You will ask for my help,
but I won't listen;
you will search,
but you won't find me.
29 No, you would not learn,
and you refused
to respect the LORD.
30 You rejected my advice
and paid no attention
when I warned you.

31 "Now you will eat the fruit
of what you have done,
until you are stuffed full
with your own schemes.
32 Sin and self-satisfaction
bring destruction and death
to stupid fools.
33 But if you listen to me,
you will be safe and secure
without fear of disaster."

Wisdom and Bad Friends

2 My child, you must follow
and treasure my teachings
and my instructions.
2 Keep in tune with wisdom
and think what it means
to have common sense.
3 Beg as loud as you can
for good common sense.
4 Search for wisdom
as you would search for silver
or hidden treasure.
5 Then you will understand
what it means to respect
and to know the LORD God.

6 All wisdom comes from the LORD,
and so do common sense
and understanding.
7 God gives helpful advice[d]
to everyone who obeys him
and protects all of those
who live as they should.
8 God sees that justice is done,
and he watches over everyone
who is faithful to him.
9 With wisdom you will learn
what is right
and honest and fair.

10 Wisdom will control your mind,
and you will be pleased
with knowledge.
11 Sound judgment and good sense
will watch over you.
12 Wisdom will protect you
from evil schemes
and from those liars
13 who turned from doing good
to live in the darkness.
14 Most of all they enjoy
being mean and deceitful.
15 They are dishonest themselves,
and all they do is crooked.

Wisdom and Sexual Purity

16 Wisdom will protect you
from the smooth talk
of a sinful woman,
17 who breaks her wedding vows
and leaves the man she married
when she was young.
18 The road to her house leads

[b] **1.17** *They are . . . trap*: Or "Be like a bird that won't go for the bait, if it sees the trap."
[c] **1.20** *Wisdom*: In the book of Proverbs the word "wisdom" is sometimes used as though wisdom were a supernatural being who was with God at the time of creation.
[d] **2.7** *helpful advice*: Or "wisdom."

down to the dark world
of the dead.
19 Visit her, and you will never
find the road to life again.

20 Follow the example
of good people
and live an honest life.
21 If you are honest and innocent,
you will keep your land;
22 if you do wrong
and can never be trusted,
you will be rooted out.

Trust God

3 My child, remember
my teachings and instructions
and obey them completely.
2 They will help you live
a long and prosperous life.
3 Let love and loyalty
always show like a necklace,
and write them in your mind.
4 God and people will like you
and consider you a success.

5 With all your heart
you must trust the LORD
and not your own judgment.
6 Always let him lead you,
and he will clear the road
for you to follow.
7 Don't ever think that you
are wise enough,
but respect the LORD
and stay away from evil.
8 This will make you healthy,
and you will feel strong.
9 Honor the LORD by giving him
your money and the first part
of all your crops.
10 Then you will have
more grain and grapes
than you will ever need.

11 My child, don't turn away
or become bitter
when the LORD corrects you.
12 The LORD corrects
everyone he loves,
just as parents correct
their favorite child.

The Value of Wisdom

13 God blesses everyone
who has wisdom
and common sense.
14 Wisdom is worth more
than silver;
it makes you much richer
than gold.
15 Wisdom is more valuable
than precious jewels;
nothing you want
compares with her.

16 In her right hand
Wisdom holds a long life,
and in her left hand
are wealth and honor.
17 Wisdom makes life pleasant
and leads us safely along.
18 Wisdom is a life-giving tree,
the source of happiness
for all who hold on to her.

19 By his wisdom and knowledge
the LORD created
heaven and earth.
20 By his understanding
he let the ocean break loose
and clouds release the rain.
21 My child, use common sense
and sound judgment!
Always keep them in mind.
22 They will help you to live
a long and beautiful life.
23 You will walk safely
and never stumble;
24 you will rest without a worry
and sleep soundly.
25 So don't be afraid
of sudden disasters
or storms that strike
those who are evil.
26 You can be sure that the LORD
will protect you from harm.

27 Do all you can for everyone
who deserves your help.
28 Don't tell your neighbor
to come back tomorrow,
if you can help today.
29 Don't try to be mean
to neighbors who trust you.
30 Don't argue just to be arguing,
when you haven't been hurt.
31 Don't be jealous
of cruel people
or follow their example.

32 The LORD doesn't like
anyone who is dishonest,
but he lets good people
be his friends.
33 He places a curse on the home
of everyone who is evil,
but he blesses the home
of every good person.
34 The LORD sneers at those
who sneer at him,
but he is kind to everyone
who is humble.
35 You will be praised
if you are wise,
but you will be disgraced
if you are a stubborn fool.

Advice to Young People

4 My child, listen closely
to my teachings
and learn common sense.
2 My advice is useful,
so don't turn away.
3 When I was still very young
and my mother's favorite child,

my father [4]said to me:
"If you follow my teachings
and keep them in mind,
you will live.
5 Be wise and learn good sense;
remember my teachings
and do what I say.

6 If you love Wisdom
and don't reject her,
she will watch over you.
7 The best thing about Wisdom
is Wisdom herself;
good sense is more important
than anything else.
8 If you value Wisdom
and hold tightly to her,
great honors will be yours.
9 It will be like wearing
a glorious crown
of beautiful flowers.

The Right Way and the Wrong Way

10 My child, if you listen
and obey my teachings,
you will live a long time.
11 I have shown you the way
that makes sense;
I have guided you
along the right path.
12 Your road won't be blocked,
and you won't stumble
when you run.
13 Hold firmly to my teaching
and never let go.
It will mean life for you.
14 Don't follow the bad example
of cruel and evil people.
15 Turn aside and keep going.
Stay away from them.
16 They can't sleep or rest
until they do wrong or harm
some innocent victim.
17 Their food and drink
are violence and cruelty.

18 The lifestyle of good people
is like sunlight at dawn
that keeps getting brighter
until broad daylight.
19 The lifestyle of the wicked
is like total darkness,
and they will never know
what makes them stumble.

20 My child, listen carefully
to everything I say.
21 Don't forget a single word,
but think about it all.
22 Knowing these teachings
will mean true life
and good health for you.
23 Carefully guard your thoughts
because they are the source
of true life.
24 Never tell lies or be deceitful
in what you say.
25 Keep looking straight ahead,
without turning aside.
26 Know where you are headed,
and you will stay
on solid ground.
27 Don't make a mistake by turning
to the right or the left.

Be Faithful to Your Wife

5 My son, if you listen closely
to my wisdom and good sense,
2 you will have sound judgment,
and you will always know
the right thing to say.
3 The words of an immoral woman
may be as sweet as honey
and as smooth as olive oil.
4 But all that you really get
from being with her
is bitter poison and pain.
5 If you follow her,
she will lead you down
to the world of the dead.
6 She has missed the path
that leads to life
and doesn't even know it.

7 My son, listen to me
and do everything I say.
8 Stay away from a bad woman!
Don't even go near the door
of her house.
9 You will lose your self-respect
and end up in debt
to some cruel person
for the rest of your life.
10 Strangers will get your money
and everything else
you have worked for.
11 When it's all over,
your body will waste away,
as you groan [12]and shout,
"I hated advice and correction!
13 I paid no attention
to my teachers,
14 and now I am disgraced
in front of everyone."

15 You should be faithful
to your wife,
just as you take water
from your own well.[e]
16 And don't be like a stream
from which just any woman
may take a drink.
17 Save yourself for your wife
and don't have sex
with other women.
18 Be happy with the wife
you married
when you were young.
19 She is beautiful and graceful,
just like a deer;
you should be attracted to her
and stay deeply in love.

[e]**5.15** *own well*: In biblical times water was scarce and wells were carefully guarded.

20 Don't go crazy over a woman
who is unfaithful
to her own husband!
21 The LORD sees everything,
and he watches us closely.
22 Sinners are trapped and caught
by their own evil deeds.
23 They get lost and die
because of their foolishness
and lack of self-control.

Don't Be Foolish

6 My child, suppose you agree
to pay the debt of someone,
who cannot repay a loan.
2 Then you are trapped
by your own words,
3 and you are now in the power
of someone else.
Here is what you should do:
Go and beg for permission
to call off the agreement.
4 Do this before you fall asleep
or even get sleepy.
5 Save yourself, just as a deer
or a bird tries to escape
from a hunter.

6 You lazy people can learn
by watching an anthill.
7 Ants don't have leaders,
8 but they store up food
during harvest season.
9 How long will you lie there
doing nothing at all?
When are you going to get up
and stop sleeping?
10 Sleep a little. Doze a little.
Fold your hands
and twiddle your thumbs.
11 Suddenly, everything is gone,
as though it had been taken
by an armed robber.

12 Worthless liars go around
13 winking and giving signals
to deceive others.
14 They are always thinking up
something cruel and evil,
and they stir up trouble.
15 But they will be struck
by sudden disaster
and left without a hope.

16 There are six or seven
kinds of people
the LORD doesn't like:
17 Those who are too proud
or tell lies or murder,
18 those who make evil plans
or are quick to do wrong,
19 those who tell lies in court
or stir up trouble
in a family.

20 Obey the teaching
of your parents—
21 always keep it in mind
and never forget it.
22 Their teaching will guide you
when you walk,
protect you when you sleep,
and talk to you
when you are awake.

23 The Law of the Lord is a lamp,
and its teachings
shine brightly.
Correction and self-control
will lead you through life.
24 They will protect you
from the flattering words
of someone else's wife.[f]
25 Don't let yourself be attracted
by the charm and lovely eyes
of someone like that.
26 A woman who sells her love
can be bought for as little
as the price of a meal.
But making love
to another man's wife
will cost you everything.
27 If you carry burning coals,
you burn your clothes;
28 if you step on hot coals,
you burn your feet.
29 And if you go to bed
with another man's wife,
you pay the price.

30 We don't put up with thieves,
not even[g] with one who steals
for something to eat.
31 And thieves who get caught
must pay back
seven times what was stolen
and lose everything.
32 But if you go to bed
with another man's wife,
you will destroy yourself
by your own stupidity.
33 You will be beaten
and forever disgraced,
34 because a jealous husband
can be furious and merciless
when he takes revenge.
35 He won't let you pay him off,
no matter what you offer.

The Foolishness of Unfaithfulness

7 My son, pay close attention
and don't forget
what I tell you to do.
2 Obey me, and you will live!
Let my instructions be
your greatest treasure.
3 Keep them at your fingertips
and write them
in your mind.
4 Let wisdom be your sister

[f] **6.24** *someone else's wife*: Or "an evil woman."

[g] **6.30** *not even*: Or "except."

and make common sense
your closest friend.
5 They will protect you
from the flattering words
of someone else's wife.

6 From the window of my house,
I once happened to see
7 some foolish young men.
8 It was late in the evening,
sometime after dark.
9 One of these young men
turned the corner
and was walking by the house
of an unfaithful wife.
10 She was dressed fancy
like a woman of the street
with only one thing in mind.
11 She was one of those women
who are loud and restless
and never stay at home,
12 who walk street after street,
waiting to trap a man.

13 She grabbed him and kissed him,
and with no sense of shame,
she said:
14 "I had to offer a sacrifice,
and there is enough meat
left over for a feast.
15 So I came looking for you,
and here you are!
16 The sheets on my bed
are bright-colored cloth
from Egypt.
17 And I have covered it
with perfume made of myrrh,
aloes, and cinnamon.

18 "Let's go there
and make love all night.
19 My husband is traveling,
and he's far away.
20 He took a lot of money along,
and he won't be back home
before the middle
of the month."

21 And so, she tricked him
with all of her sweet talk
and her flattery.
22 Right away he followed her
like an ox on the way
to be slaughtered,
or like a fool on the way
to be punished[h]
23 and killed with arrows.
He was no more than a bird
rushing into a trap,
without knowing
it would cost him his life.

24 My son, pay close attention
to what I have said.
25 Don't even think about
that kind of woman
or let yourself be misled
by someone like her.
26 Such a woman has caused
the downfall and destruction
of a lot of men.
27 Her house is a one-way street
leading straight down
to the world of the dead.

In Praise of Wisdom

8 With great understanding,
Wisdom[i] is calling out
2 as she stands at the crossroads
and on every hill.
3 She stands by the city gate
where everyone enters the city,
and she shouts:
4 "I am calling out
to each one of you!
5 Good sense and sound judgment
can be yours.
6 Listen, because what I say
is worthwhile and right.
7 I always speak the truth
and refuse to tell a lie.
8 Every word I speak is honest,
not one is misleading
or deceptive.

9 "If you have understanding,
you will see that my words
are just what you need.
10 Let instruction and knowledge
mean more to you than silver
or the finest gold.
11 Wisdom is worth much more
than precious jewels
or anything else you desire."

Wisdom Speaks

12 I am Wisdom[i]—Common Sense
is my closest friend;
I possess knowledge
and sound judgment.
13 If you respect the LORD,
you will hate evil.
I hate pride and conceit
and deceitful lies.
14 I am strong, and I offer
sensible advice
and sound judgment.
15 By my power kings govern,
and rulers make laws
that are fair.
16 Every honest leader rules
with help from me.

17 I love everyone who loves me,
and I will be found by all
who honestly search.
18 I can make you rich and famous,
important and successful.

[h]**7.22** *a fool . . . punished*: One possible meaning for the difficult Hebrew text. [i]**8.1** *Wisdom*: See the note at 1.20. [i]**8.12** *Wisdom*: See the note at 1.20.

19 What you receive from me
is more valuable
than even the finest gold
or the purest silver.
20 I always do what is right,
21 and I give great riches
to everyone who loves me.

22 From the beginning,
I was with the LORD.[j]
I was there before he began
23 to create the earth.
At the very first,
the LORD gave life to[k] me.
24 When I was born,
there were no oceans
or springs of water.
25 My birth was before
mountains were formed
or hills were put in place.
26 It happened long before God
had made the earth
or any of its fields
or even the dust.

27 I was there when the LORD
put the heavens in place
and stretched the sky
over the surface of the sea.
28 I was with him when he placed
the clouds in the sky
and created the springs
that fill the ocean.
29 I was there when he set
boundaries for the sea
to make it obey him,
and when he laid foundations
to support the earth.

30 I was right beside the LORD,
helping him plan and build.[l]
I made him happy each day,
and I was happy at his side.
31 I was pleased with his world
and pleased with its people.

32 Pay attention, my children!
Follow my advice,
and you will be happy.
33 Listen carefully
to my instructions,
and you will be wise.

34 Come to my home each day
and listen to me.
You will find happiness.
35 By finding me, you find life,
and the LORD will be pleased
with you.
36 But if you don't find me,
you hurt only yourself,
and if you hate me,
you are in love with death.

Wisdom Gives a Feast

9 Wisdom has built her house
with its seven columns.
2 She has prepared the meat
and set out the wine.
Her feast is ready.

3 She has sent her servant women
to announce her invitation
from the highest hills:
4 "Everyone who is ignorant
or foolish is invited!
5 All of you are welcome
to my meat and wine.
6 If you want to live,
give up your foolishness
and let understanding
guide your steps."

True Wisdom

7 Correct a worthless bragger,
and all you will get
are insults and injuries.
8 Any bragger you correct
will only hate you.
But if you correct someone
who has common sense,
you will be loved.
9 If you have good sense,
instruction will help you
to have even better sense.
And if you live right,
education will help you
to know even more.

10 Respect and obey the LORD!
This is the beginning
of wisdom.[m]
To have understanding,
you must know the Holy God.
11 I am Wisdom. If you follow me,
you will live a long time.
12 Good sense is good for you,
but if you brag,
you hurt yourself.

A Foolish Invitation

13 Stupidity[n] is reckless,
senseless, and foolish.
14 She sits in front of her house
and on the highest hills
in the town.
15 She shouts to everyone
who passes by,
16 "If you are stupid,
come on inside!"
And to every fool she says,
17 "Stolen water tastes best,
and the food you eat in secret
tastes best of all."
18 None who listen to Stupidity
understand that her guests
are as good as dead.

[j] **8.22** *From the beginning . . . with the LORD*: Or "In the very beginning, the LORD created me."
[k] **8.23** *gave life to*: Or "formed." [l] **8.30** *helping . . . build*: Or "like his own child."
[m] **9.10** *the beginning of wisdom*: Or "what wisdom is all about." [n] **9.13** *Stupidity*: Or "A foolish woman."

Solomon's Wise Sayings

10 Here are some proverbs
of Solomon:
Children with good sense
make their parents happy,
but foolish children
make them sad.
2 What you gain by doing evil
won't help you at all,
but being good[o]
can save you from death.

3 If you obey the LORD,
you won't go hungry;
if you are wicked,
God won't let you have
what you want.
4 Laziness leads to poverty;
hard work makes you rich.
5 At harvest season
it's smart to work hard,
but stupid to sleep.

6 Everyone praises good people,
but evil hides behind
the words of the wicked.
7 Good people are remembered
long after they are gone,
but the wicked
are soon forgotten.

8 If you have good sense,
you will listen and obey;
if all you do is talk,
you will destroy yourself.
9 You will be safe,
if you always do right,
but you will get caught,
if you are dishonest.
10 Deceit causes trouble,
and foolish talk
will bring you to ruin.[p]
11 The words of good people
are a source of life,
but evil hides behind
the words of the wicked.

12 Hatred stirs up trouble;
love overlooks the wrongs
that others do.
13 If you have good sense,
it will show when you speak.
But if you are stupid,
you will be beaten
with a stick.
14 If you have good sense,
you will learn all you can,
but foolish talk
will soon destroy you.

15 Great wealth can be a fortress,
but poverty
is no protection at all.

16 If you live right,
the reward is a good life;
if you are evil,
all you have is sin.

17 Accept correction,
and you will find life;
reject correction,
and you will miss the road.
18 You can hide your hatred
by telling lies,
but you are a fool
to spread lies.
19 You will say the wrong thing
if you talk too much—
so be sensible and watch
what you say.
20 The words of a good person
are like pure silver,
but the thoughts
of an evil person
are almost worthless.
21 Many are helped
by useful instruction,
but fools are killed
by their own stupidity.

22 When the LORD blesses you
with riches,
you have nothing to regret.[q]
23 Fools enjoy doing wrong,
but anyone with good sense
enjoys acting wisely.
24 What evil people dread most
will happen to them,
but good people will get
what they want most.
25 Those crooks will disappear
when a storm strikes,
but God will keep safe
all who obey him.
26 Having a lazy person on the job
is like a mouth full of vinegar
or smoke in your eyes.

27 If you respect the LORD,
you will live longer;
if you keep doing wrong,
your life will be cut short.
28 If you obey the Lord,
you will be happy,
but there is no future
for the wicked.
29 The LORD protects everyone
who lives right,
but he destroys anyone
who does wrong.
30 Good people will stand firm,
but the wicked
will lose their land.
31 Honest people speak sensibly,
but deceitful liars
will be silenced.

[o] **10.2** *good*: Or "generous." [p] **10.10** *and foolish . . . ruin*: One ancient translation "but you can help people by correcting them." [q] **10.22** *When . . . regret*: Or "No matter how hard you work, your riches really come from the Lord."

32 If you obey the Lord,
you will always know
the right thing to say.
But no one will trust you
if you tell lies.

Watch What You Say and Do

11 The LORD hates anyone
who cheats,
but he likes everyone
who is honest.
2 Too much pride
can put you to shame.
It's wiser to be humble.
3 If you do the right thing,
honesty will be your guide.
But if you are crooked,
you will be trapped
by your own dishonesty.

4 When God is angry,
money won't help you.
Obeying God is the only way
to be saved from death.
5 If you are truly good,
you will do right;
if you are wicked,
you will be destroyed
by your own sin.
6 Honesty can keep you safe,
but if you can't be trusted,
you trap yourself.
7 When the wicked die,
their hopes die with them.
8 Trouble goes right past
the LORD's people
and strikes the wicked.

9 Dishonest people use gossip
to destroy their neighbors;
good people are protected
by their own good sense.
10 When honest people prosper
and the wicked disappear,
the whole city celebrates.
11 When God blesses his people,
their city prospers,
but deceitful liars
can destroy a city.

12 It's stupid to say bad things
about your neighbors.
If you are sensible,
you will keep quiet.
13 A gossip tells everything,
but a true friend
will keep a secret.
14 A city without wise leaders
will end up in ruin;
a city with many wise leaders
will be kept safe.

15 It's a dangerous thing
to guarantee payment
for someone's debts.
Don't do it!
16 A gracious woman
will be respected,
but a man must work hard
to get rich.[r]
17 Kindness is rewarded—
but if you are cruel,
you hurt yourself.
18 Meanness gets you nowhere,
but goodness is rewarded.
19 Always do the right thing,
and you will live;
keep on doing wrong,
and you will die.

20 The LORD hates sneaky people,
but he likes everyone
who lives right.
21 You can be sure of this:
All crooks will be punished,
but God's people won't.
22 A beautiful woman
who acts foolishly
is like a gold ring
on the snout of a pig.
23 Good people want what is best,
but troublemakers
hope to stir up trouble.[s]

24 Sometimes you can become rich
by being generous
or poor by being greedy.
25 Generosity will be rewarded:
Give a cup of water,
and you will receive
a cup of water in return.
26 Charge too much for grain,
and you will be cursed;
sell it at a fair price,
and you will be praised.
27 Try hard to do right,
and you will win friends;
go looking for trouble,
and you will find it.
28 Trust in your wealth,
and you will be a failure,
but God's people will prosper
like healthy plants.

29 Fools who cause trouble
in the family
won't inherit a thing.
They will end up as slaves
of someone with good sense.
30 Live right, and you will eat
from the life-giving tree.
And if you act wisely,
others will follow.[t]
31 If good people are rewarded[u]
here on this earth,

[r]**11.16** *but . . . rich*: Or "a ruthless man will only get rich." [s]**11.23** *Good people . . . trouble*: Or "Good people do what is best, but troublemakers just stir up trouble." [t]**11.30** *act . . . follow*: Hebrew; one ancient translation "but violence leads to death." [u]**11.31** *rewarded*: Or "punished."

all who are cruel and mean
will surely be punished.

You Can't Hide behind Evil

12 To accept correction is wise,
to reject it is stupid.
2 The LORD likes everyone
who lives right,
but he punishes everyone
who makes evil plans.
3 Sin cannot offer security!
But if you live right,
you will be as secure
as a tree with deep roots.
4 A helpful wife is a jewel
for her husband,
but a shameless wife
will make his bones rot.

5 Good people have kind thoughts,
but you should never trust
the advice of someone evil.
6 Bad advice is a deadly trap,
but good advice
is like a shield.
7 Once the wicked are defeated,
they are gone forever,
but no one who obeys God
will ever be thrown down.
8 Good sense is worthy of praise,
but stupidity is a curse.
9 It's better to be ordinary
and have only one servant[v]
than to think you are somebody
and starve to death.
10 Good people are kind
to their animals,
but a mean person is cruel.

11 Hard working farmers have more
than enough food;
daydreamers are nothing more
than stupid fools.
12 An evil person tries to hide
behind evil;[w]
good people are like trees
with deep roots.
13 We trap ourselves
by telling lies,
but we stay out of trouble
by living right.
14 We are rewarded or punished
for what we say and do.
15 Fools think they know
what is best,
but a sensible person
listens to advice.

16 Losing your temper is foolish;
ignoring an insult is smart.
17 An honest person
tells the truth in court,
but a dishonest person
tells nothing but lies.
18 Sharp words cut like a sword,
but words of wisdom heal.
19 Truth will last forever;
lies are soon found out.
20 An evil mind is deceitful,
but gentle thoughts
bring happiness.
21 Good people never have trouble,
but troublemakers
have more than enough.
22 The LORD hates every liar,
but he is the friend of all
who can be trusted.
23 Be sensible and don't tell
everything you know—
only fools spread
foolishness everywhere.

24 Work hard, and you
will be a leader;
be lazy, and you
will end up a slave.
25 Worry is a heavy burden,
but a kind word
always brings cheer.
26 You are better off to do right,
than to lose your way
by doing wrong.[x]
27 Anyone too lazy to cook
will starve,
but a hard worker
is a valuable treasure.[y]
28 Follow the road to life,
and you won't be bothered
by death.

Wise Friends Make You Wise

13 Children with good sense
accept correction
from their parents,
but stubborn children
ignore it completely.
2 You will be well rewarded
for saying something kind,
but all some people think about
is how to be cruel and mean.
3 Keep what you know to yourself,
and you will be safe;
talk too much,
and you are done for.
4 No matter how much you want,
laziness won't help a bit,
but hard work will reward you
with more than enough.
5 A good person hates deceit,
but those who are evil
cause shame and disgrace.
6 Live right, and you are safe!
But sin will destroy you.

7 Some who have nothing
may pretend to be rich,

[v]12.9 *It's . . . servant*: Or "It is better just to have an ordinary job." [w]12.12 *An evil . . . evil*: Or "Evil people love what they get from being evil." [x]12.26 *wrong*: One possible meaning for the difficult Hebrew text of verse 26. [y]12.27 *but . . . treasure*: One possible meaning for the difficult Hebrew text.

and some who have everything
may pretend to be poor.
8 The rich may have
to pay a ransom,
but the poor don't have
that problem.
9 The lamp of a good person
keeps on shining;
the lamp of an evil person
soon goes out.
10 Too much pride causes trouble.
Be sensible and take advice.

11 Money wrongly gotten
will disappear bit by bit;
money earned little by little
will grow and grow.
12 Not getting what you want
can make you feel sick,
but a wish that comes true
is a life-giving tree.
13 If you reject God's teaching,
you will pay the price;
if you obey his commands,
you will be rewarded.

14 Sensible instruction
is a life-giving fountain
that helps you escape
all deadly traps.
15 Sound judgment is praised,
but people without good sense
are on the way to disaster.[z]
16 If you have good sense,
you will act sensibly,
but fools act like fools.
17 Whoever delivers your message
can make things better
or worse for you.

18 All who refuse correction
will be poor and disgraced;
all who accept correction
will be praised.
19 It's a good feeling
to get what you want,
but only a stupid fool
hates to turn from evil.
20 Wise friends make you wise,
but you hurt yourself
by going around with fools.
21 You are in for trouble
if you sin,
but you will be rewarded
if you live right.
22 If you obey God,
you will have something
to leave your grandchildren.
If you don't obey God,
those who live right
will get what you leave.

23 Even when the land of the poor
produces good crops,
they get cheated
out of what they grow.[a]
24 If you love your children,
you will correct them;
if you don't love them,
you won't correct them.
25 If you live right,
you will have plenty to eat;
if you don't live right,
you will go away empty.

Wisdom Makes Good Sense

14 A woman's family
is held together
by her wisdom,
but it can be destroyed
by her foolishness.
2 By living right, you show
that you respect the LORD;
by being deceitful, you show
that you despise him.
3 Proud fools are punished
for their stupid talk,
but sensible talk
can save your life.
4 Without the help of an ox
there can be no crop,
but with a strong ox
a big crop is possible.
5 An honest witness
tells the truth;
a dishonest witness
tells nothing but lies.

6 Make fun of wisdom,
and you will never find it.
But if you have understanding,
knowledge comes easily.
7 Stay away from fools,
or you won't learn a thing.
8 Wise people have enough sense
to find their way,
but stupid fools get lost.
9 Fools don't care
if they are wrong,[b]
but God is pleased
when people do right.

10 No one else can really know
how sad or happy you are.
11 The tent of a good person
stands longer than the house
of someone evil.
12 You may think you are
on the right road
and still end up dead.
13 Sorrow may hide
behind laughter,
and happiness may end
in sorrow.
14 You harvest what you plant,
whether good or bad.

15 Don't be stupid
and believe all you hear;

[z] **13.15** *people . . . disaster*: One possible meaning for the difficult Hebrew text.
[a] **13.23** *grow*: One possible meaning for the difficult Hebrew text of verse 23. [b] **14.9** *Fools . . . wrong*: One possible meaning for the difficult Hebrew text.

be smart and know
where you are headed.
16 Only a stupid fool
is never cautious—
so be extra careful
and stay out of trouble.
17 Fools have quick tempers,
and no one likes you
if you can't be trusted.
18 Stupidity leads to foolishness;
be smart and learn.

19 The wicked will come crawling
to those who obey God.
20 You have no friends
if you are poor,
but you have lots of friends
if you are rich.
21 It's wrong to hate others,
but God blesses everyone
who is kind to the poor.
22 It's a mistake
to make evil plans,
but you will have loyal friends
if you want to do right.
23 Hard work is worthwhile,
but empty talk
will make you poor.
24 Wisdom can make you rich,
but foolishness leads
to more foolishness.
25 An honest witness
can save your life,
but liars can't be trusted.

26 If you respect the LORD,
you and your children
have a strong fortress
27 and a life-giving fountain
that keeps you safe
from deadly traps.

28 Rulers of powerful nations
are held in honor;
rulers of weak nations
are nothing at all.
29 It's smart to be patient,
but it's stupid
to lose your temper.
30 It's healthy to be content,
but envy can eat you up.
31 If you mistreat the poor,
you insult your Creator;
if you are kind to them,
you show him respect.
32 In times of trouble
the wicked are destroyed,
but even at death
the innocent have faith.[c]

33 Wisdom is found in the minds
of people with good sense,
but fools don't know it.[d]
34 Doing right brings honor
to a nation,
but sin brings disgrace.
35 Kings reward servants
who act wisely,
but they punish those
who act foolishly.

The LORD Sees Everything

15 A kind answer
soothes angry feelings,
but harsh words
stir them up.
2 Words of wisdom
come from the wise,
but fools speak foolishness.

3 The LORD sees everything,
whether good or bad.
4 Kind words are good medicine,
but deceitful words
can really hurt.
5 Don't be a fool
and disobey your parents.
Be smart! Accept correction.
6 Good people become wealthy,
but those who are evil
will lose what they have.
7 Words of wisdom
make good sense;
the thoughts of a fool
make no sense at all.

8 The LORD is disgusted
by gifts from the wicked,
but it makes him happy
when his people pray.
9 The LORD is disgusted
with all who do wrong,
but he loves everyone
who does right.
10 If you turn from the right way,
you will be punished;
if you refuse correction,
you will die.

11 If the LORD can see everything
in the world of the dead,
he can see in our hearts.
12 Those who sneer at others
don't like to be corrected,
and they won't ask help
from someone with sense.
13 Happiness makes you smile;
sorrow can crush you.
14 Anyone with good sense
is eager to learn more,
but fools are hungry
for foolishness.

15 The poor have a hard life,
but being content is as good
as an endless feast.
16 It's better to obey the LORD
and have only a little,

[c] **14.32** *but even . . . faith*: One possible meaning for the difficult Hebrew text. Some ancient translations "but good people trust their innocence." [d] **14.33** *but . . . it*: One possible meaning for the difficult Hebrew text; some ancient translations "but not in the mind of a fool."

than to be very rich
and terribly confused.
17 A simple meal with love
is better than a feast
where there is hatred.

18 Losing your temper
causes a lot of trouble,
but staying calm
settles arguments.
19 Being lazy is like walking
in a thorn patch,
but everyone who does right
walks on a smooth road.
20 Children with good sense
make their parents happy,
but foolish children
are hateful to them.
21 Stupidity brings happiness
to senseless fools,
but everyone with good sense
follows the straight path.

22 Without good advice
everything goes wrong—
it takes careful planning
for things to go right.
23 Giving the right answer
at the right time
makes everyone happy.
24 All who are wise follow a road
that leads upward to life
and away from death.

25 The LORD destroys the homes
of those who are proud,
but he protects the property
of widows.
26 The LORD hates evil thoughts,
but kind words please him.
27 Being greedy causes trouble
for your family,
but you protect yourself
by refusing bribes.
28 Good people think
before they answer,
but the wicked speak evil
without ever thinking.

29 The LORD never even hears
the prayers of the wicked,
but he answers the prayers
of all who obey him.
30 A friendly smile
makes you happy,
and good news
makes you feel strong.
31 Healthy correction is good,
and if you accept it,
you will be wise.
32 You hurt only yourself
by rejecting instruction,
but it makes good sense
to accept it.
33 Showing respect to the LORD
will make you wise,
and being humble
will bring honor to you.

The LORD Has the Final Word

16 We humans make plans,
but the LORD
has the final word.
2 We may think we know
what is right,
but the LORD is the judge
of our motives.
3 Share your plans with the LORD,
and you will succeed.

4 The LORD has a reason
for everything he does,
and he lets evil people live
only to be punished.
5 The LORD doesn't like
anyone who is conceited—
you can be sure
they will be punished.
6 If we truly love God,
our sins will be forgiven;
if we show him respect,
we will keep away from sin.
7 When we please the LORD,
even our enemies
make friends with us.
8 It's better to be honest
and poor
than to be dishonest
and rich.

9 We make our own plans,
but the LORD decides
where we will go.
10 Rulers speak with authority
and are never wrong.
11 The LORD doesn't like it
when we cheat in business.
12 Justice makes rulers powerful.
They should hate evil
13 and like honesty and truth.
14 An angry ruler
can put you to death.
So be wise!
Don't make one angry.
15 When a ruler is happy
and pleased with you,
it's like refreshing rain,
and you will live.

16 It's much better to be wise
and sensible
than to be rich.
17 God's people avoid evil ways,
and they protect themselves
by watching where they go.
18 Too much pride
will destroy you.
19 You are better off
to be humble and poor
than to get rich
from what you take by force.
20 If you know what you're doing,[e]

[e] **16.20** *know what . . . doing*: Or "do what you're taught."

you will prosper.
God blesses everyone
who trusts him.
21 Good judgment proves
that you are wise,
and if you speak kindly,
you can teach others.
22 Good sense is a fountain
that gives life,
but fools are punished
by their foolishness.
23 You can persuade others
if you are wise
and speak sensibly.

24 Kind words are like honey—
they cheer you up
and make you feel strong.
25 Sometimes what seems right
is really a road to death.
26 The hungrier you are,
the harder you work.
27 Worthless people plan trouble.
Even their words burn
like a flaming fire.
28 Gossip is no good!
It causes hard feelings
and comes between friends.

29 Don't trust violent people.
They will mislead you
to do the wrong thing.
30 When someone winks
or grins behind your back,
trouble is on the way.
31 Gray hair is a glorious crown
worn by those
who have lived right.
32 Controlling your temper
is better than being a hero
who captures a city.
33 We make our own decisions,
but the LORD alone
determines what happens.

Our Thoughts Are Tested by the LORD

17 A dry crust of bread eaten
in peace and quiet
is better than a feast eaten
where everyone argues.
2 A hard-working slave
will be placed in charge
of a no-good child,
and that slave will be given
the same inheritance
that each child receives.
3 Silver and gold are tested
by flames of fire;
our thoughts are tested
by the LORD.
4 Troublemakers listen
to troublemakers,
and liars listen to liars.
5 By insulting the poor,
you insult your Creator.
You will be punished
if you make fun
of someone in trouble.

6 Grandparents are proud
of their grandchildren,
and children should be proud
of their parents.

7 It sounds strange for a fool
to talk sensibly,
but it's even worse
for a ruler to tell lies.
8 A bribe works miracles
like a magic charm
that brings good luck.
9 You will keep your friends
if you forgive them,
but you will lose your friends
if you keep talking about
what they did wrong.
10 A sensible person
accepts correction,
but you can't beat sense
into a fool.

11 Cruel people want to rebel,
and so vicious attackers
will be sent against them.
12 A bear robbed of her cubs
is far less dangerous
than a stubborn fool.
13 You will always have trouble
if you are mean to those
who are good to you.
14 The start of an argument
is like a water leak—
so stop it before
real trouble breaks out.
15 The LORD doesn't like those
who defend the guilty
or condemn the innocent.
16 Why should fools have money
for an education
when they refuse to learn?

17 A friend is always a friend,
and relatives are born
to share our troubles.
18 It's stupid to guarantee
someone else's loan.
19 The wicked and the proud
love trouble and keep begging
to be hurt.
20 Dishonesty does you no good,
and telling lies
will get you in trouble.
21 It's never pleasant
to be the parent of a fool
and have nothing but pain.
22 If you are cheerful,
you feel good;
if you are sad,
you hurt all over.

23 Crooks accept secret bribes
to keep justice
from being done.
24 Anyone with wisdom knows
what makes good sense,
but fools can never
make up their minds.

25 Foolish children bring sorrow
to their father
and pain to their mother.
26 It isn't fair
to punish the innocent
and those who do right.
27 It makes a lot of sense
to be a person of few words
and to stay calm.
28 Even fools seem smart
when they are quiet.

It's Wrong to Favor the Guilty

18 It's selfish and stupid
to think only of yourself
and to sneer at people
who have sense.[f]
2 Fools have no desire to learn;
they would much rather
give their own opinion.
3 Wrongdoing leads to shame
and disgrace.
4 Words of wisdom
are a stream that flows
from a deep fountain.
5 It's wrong to favor the guilty
and keep the innocent
from getting justice.

6 Foolish talk will get you
into a lot of trouble.
7 Saying foolish things
is like setting a trap
to destroy yourself.
8 There's nothing so delicious
as the taste of gossip!
It melts in your mouth.
9 Being lazy is no different
from being a troublemaker.

10 The LORD is a mighty tower
where his people can run
for safety—
11 the rich think their money
is a wall of protection.

12 Pride leads to destruction;
humility leads to honor.
13 It's stupid and embarrassing
to give an answer
before you listen.
14 Being cheerful helps
when we are sick,
but nothing helps
when we give up.
15 Everyone with good sense
wants to learn.
16 A gift will get you in
to see anyone.
17 You may think you have won
your case in court,
until your opponent speaks.
18 Drawing straws is one way
to settle a difficult case.
19 Making up with a friend
you have offended[g]
is harder than breaking
through a city wall.

20 Make your words good—
you will be glad you did.
21 Words can bring death or life!
Talk too much, and you will eat
everything you say.
22 A man's greatest treasure
is his wife—
she is a gift from the LORD.
23 The poor must beg for help,
but the rich can give
a harsh reply.
24 Some friends don't help,[h]
but a true friend is closer
than your own family.

It's Wise To Be Patient

19 It's better to be poor
and live right
than to be a stupid liar.
2 Willingness and stupidity
don't go well together.
If you are too eager,
you will miss the road.
3 We are ruined
by our own stupidity,
though we blame the LORD.

4 The rich have many friends;
the poor have none.
5 Dishonest witnesses and liars
won't escape punishment.
6 Everyone tries to be friends
of those who can help them.
7 If you are poor,
your own relatives reject you,
and your friends are worse.
When you really need them,
they are not there.[i]

8 Do yourself a favor
by having good sense—
you will be glad you did.
9 Dishonest witnesses and liars
will be destroyed.
10 It isn't right for a fool
to live in luxury
or for a slave to rule
in place of a king.
11 It's wise to be patient
and show what you are like
by forgiving others.
12 An angry king roars
like a lion,
but when a king is pleased,
it's like dew on the crops.

13 A foolish son brings disgrace
to his father.

[f]**18.1** *sense*: One possible meaning for the difficult Hebrew text of verse 1. [g]**18.19** *Making . . . offended*: One possible meaning for the difficult Hebrew text. [h]**18.24** *Some . . . help*: One possible meaning for the difficult Hebrew text. [i]**19.7** *When . . . there*: One possible meaning for the difficult Hebrew text.

A nagging wife goes on and on
like the drip, drip, drip
of the rain.
14 You may inherit all you own
from your parents,
but a sensible wife
is a gift from the LORD.
15 If you are lazy
and sleep your time away,
you will starve.

16 Obey the Lord's teachings
and you will live—
disobey and you will die.
17 Caring for the poor
is lending to the LORD,
and you will be well repaid.
18 Correct your children
before it's too late;
if you don't punish them,
you are destroying them.
19 People with bad tempers
are always in trouble,
and they need help
over and over again.[j]
20 Pay attention to advice
and accept correction,
so you can live sensibly.

21 We may make a lot of plans,
but the LORD will do
what he has decided.
22 What matters most is loyalty.
It's better to be poor
than to be a liar.
23 Showing respect to the LORD
brings true life—
if you do it, you can relax
without fear of danger.

24 Some people are too lazy
to lift a hand
to feed themselves.
25 Stupid fools learn good sense
by seeing others punished;
a sensible person learns
by being corrected.
26 Children who bring disgrace
rob their father
and chase their mother away.
27 If you stop learning,
you will forget
what you already know.
28 A lying witness makes fun
of the court system,
and criminals think crime
is really delicious.
29 Every stupid fool
is just waiting
to be punished.

Words of Wisdom Are Better than Gold

20 It isn't smart to get drunk!
Drinking makes a fool of you
and leads to fights.
2 An angry ruler
is like a roaring lion—
make either one angry,
and you are dead.
3 It makes you look good
when you avoid a fight—
only fools love to quarrel.
4 If you are too lazy to plow,
don't expect a harvest.
5 Someone's thoughts may be
as deep as the ocean,
but if you are smart,
you will discover them.

6 There are many who say,
"You can trust me!"
But can they be trusted?
7 Good people live right,
and God blesses the children
who follow their example.
8 When rulers decide cases,
they weigh the evidence.
9 Can any of us really say,
"My thoughts are pure,
and my sins are gone"?

10 Two things the LORD hates
are dishonest scales
and dishonest measures.
11 The good or bad
that children do
shows what they are like.
12 Hearing and seeing
are gifts from the LORD.
13 If you sleep all the time,
you will starve;
if you get up and work,
you will have enough food.
14 Everyone likes to brag
about getting a bargain.
15 Sensible words are better
than gold or jewels.

16 You deserve to lose your coat
if you loan it to someone
to guarantee payment
for the debt of a stranger.
17 The food you get by cheating
may taste delicious,
but it turns to gravel.
18 Be sure you have sound advice
before making plans
or starting a war.
19 Stay away from gossips—
they tell everything.
20 Children who curse their parents
will go to the land of darkness
long before their time.
21 Getting rich quick[k]
may turn out to be a curse.
22 Don't try to get even.
Trust the LORD,
and he will help you.

23 The LORD hates dishonest scales
and dishonest weights.

[j] **19.19** *and they . . . again*: One possible meaning for the difficult Hebrew text.
[k] **20.21** *quick*: Or "the wrong way."

So don't cheat!
24 How can we know
what will happen to us
when the LORD alone decides?
25 Don't fall into the trap
of making promises to God
before you think!
26 A wise ruler severely punishes
every criminal.
27 Our inner thoughts are a lamp
from the LORD,
and they search our hearts.
28 Rulers are protected
by God's mercy and loyalty,
but[l] they must be merciful
for their kingdoms to last.
29 Young people take pride
in their strength,
but the gray hairs of wisdom
are even more beautiful.
30 A severe beating can knock all
of the evil out of you!

The LORD Is In Charge

21 The LORD controls rulers,
just as he determines
the course of rivers.
2 We may think we are doing
the right thing,
but the LORD always knows
what is in our hearts.
3 Doing what is right and fair
pleases the LORD
more than an offering.
4 Evil people are proud
and arrogant,
but sin is the only crop
they produce.[m]
5 If you plan and work hard,
you will have plenty;
if you get in a hurry,
you will end up poor.

6 Cheating to get rich
is a foolish dream
and no less than suicide.[n]
7 You destroy yourself
by being cruel and violent
and refusing to live right.
8 All crooks are liars,
but anyone who is innocent
will do right.
9 It's better to stay outside
on the roof of your house
than to live inside
with a nagging wife.
10 Evil people want to do wrong,
even to their friends.
11 An ignorant fool learns
by seeing others punished;
a sensible person learns
by being instructed.
12 God is always fair!
He knows what the wicked do
and will punish them.
13 If you won't help the poor,
don't expect to be heard
when you cry out for help.
14 A secret bribe will save you
from someone's fierce anger.
15 When justice is done,
good citizens are glad
and crooks are terrified.
16 If you stop using good sense,
you will find yourself
in the grave.
17 Heavy drinkers and others
who live only for pleasure
will lose all they have.

18 God's people will escape,
but all who are wicked
will pay the price.
19 It's better out in the desert
than at home with a nagging,
complaining wife.
20 Be sensible and store up
precious treasures—
don't waste them
like a fool.
21 If you try to be kind and good,
you will be blessed with life
and goodness and honor.
22 One wise person can defeat
a city full of soldiers
and capture their fortress.
23 Watching what you say
can save you
a lot of trouble.
24 If you are proud and conceited,
everyone will say,
"You're a snob!"

25 If you want too much
and are too lazy to work,
it could be fatal.
26 But people who obey God
are always generous.

27 The Lord despises the offerings
of wicked people
with evil motives.
28 If you tell lies in court,
you are done for;
only a reliable witness
can do the job.
29 Wicked people bluff their way,
but God's people think
before they take a step.

30 No matter how much you know
or what plans you make,
you can't defeat the LORD.
31 Even if your army has horses
ready for battle,
the LORD will always win.

[l]20.28 *by God's mercy . . . but*: Or "by their mercy . . . and." [m]21.4 *but sin . . . produce*: Or "but sin is the only light they ever follow." [n]21.6 *and . . . suicide*: One possible meaning for the difficult Hebrew text.

The Value of a Good Reputation

22 A good reputation and respect
are worth much more
than silver and gold.
2 The rich and the poor
are all created
by the LORD.
3 When you see trouble coming,
don't be stupid
and walk right into it—
be smart and hide.

4 Respect and serve the LORD!
Your reward will be wealth,
a long life, and honor.
5 Crooks walk down a road
full of thorny traps.
Stay away from there!
6 Teach your children
right from wrong,
and when they are grown
they will still do right.
7 The poor are ruled by the rich,
and those who borrow
are slaves of moneylenders.
8 Troublemakers get in trouble,
and their terrible anger
will get them nowhere.

9 The LORD blesses everyone
who freely gives food
to the poor.
10 Arguments and fights
will come to an end,
if you chase away those
who insult others.
11 The king is the friend of all
who are sincere
and speak with kindness.

12 The LORD watches over everyone
who shows good sense,
but he frustrates the plans
of deceitful liars.
13 Don't be so lazy that you say,
"If I go to work,
a lion will eat me!"
14 The words of a bad woman
are like a deep pit;
if you make the LORD angry,
you will fall right in.
15 All children are foolish,
but firm correction
will make them change.
16 Cheat the poor to make profit
or give gifts to the rich—
either way you lose.

Thirty Wise Sayings

17 Here are some sayings
of people with wisdom,
so listen carefully
as I teach.
18 You will be glad
that you know these sayings
and can recite them.
19 I am teaching them today,
so that you
may trust the LORD.
20 I have written thirty sayings
filled with sound advice.
21 You can trust them completely
to give you the right words
for those in charge of you.

– 1 –

22 Don't take advantage
of the poor
or cheat them in court.
23 The LORD is their defender,
and what you do to them,
he will do to you.

– 2 –

24 Don't make friends with anyone
who has a bad temper.
25 You might turn out like them
and get caught in a trap.

– 3 –

26 Don't guarantee to pay
someone else's debt.
27 If you don't have the money,
you might lose your bed.

– 4 –

28 Don't move a boundary marker °
set up by your ancestors.

– 5 –

29 If you do your job well,
you will work for a ruler
and never be a slave.

– 6 –

23 When you are invited
to eat with a king,
use your best manners.
2 Don't go and stuff yourself!
That would be just the same
as cutting your throat.
3 Don't be greedy for all
of that fancy food!
It may not be so tasty.

– 7 –

4 Give up trying so hard
to get rich.
5 Your money flies away
before you know it,
just like an eagle
suddenly taking off.

– 8 –

6 Don't accept an invitation
to eat a selfish person's food,
no matter how good it is.
7 People like that take note

°22.28 *marker*: In ancient Israel boundary lines were sacred because all property was a gift from the Lord (see Deuteronomy 19.14).

of how much you eat.[p]
They say, "Take all you want!"
But they don't mean it.
8 Each bite will come back up,
and all your kind words
will be wasted.

– 9 –

9 Don't talk to fools—
they will just make fun.

– 10 –

10 Don't move a boundary marker [q]
or take the land
that belongs to orphans.
11 God All-Powerful is there
to defend them against you.

– 11 –

12 Listen to instruction
and do your best to learn.

– 12 –

13 Don't fail to correct
your children.
You won't kill them
by being firm,
14 and it may even
save their lives.

– 13 –

15 My children,
if you show good sense,
I will be happy,
16 and if you are truthful,
I will really be glad.

– 14 –

17 Don't be jealous of sinners,
but always honor the LORD.
18 Then you will truly have hope
for the future.

– 15 –

19 Listen to me, my children!
Be wise and have enough sense
to follow the right path.
20 Don't be a heavy drinker
or stuff yourself with food.
21 It will make you feel drowsy,
and you will end up poor
with only rags to wear.

– 16 –

22 Pay attention to your father,
and don't neglect your mother
when she grows old.
23 Invest in truth and wisdom,
discipline and good sense,
and don't part with them.
24 Make your father truly happy
by living right and showing
sound judgment.
25 Make your parents proud,
especially your mother.

– 17 –

26 My son, pay close attention,
and gladly follow
my example.
27 Bad women and unfaithful wives
are like a deep pit—
28 they are waiting to attack you
like a gang of robbers
with victim after victim.

– 18 –

29 Who is always in trouble?
Who argues and fights?
Who has cuts and bruises?
Whose eyes are red?
30 Everyone who stays up late,
having just one more drink.
31 Don't even look
at that colorful stuff
bubbling up in the glass!
It goes down so easily,
32 but later it bites
like a poisonous snake.
33 You will see weird things,
and your mind
will play tricks on you.
34 You will feel tossed about
like someone trying to sleep
on a ship in a storm.
35 You will be bruised all over,
without even remembering
how it all happened.
And you will lie awake asking,
"When will morning come,
so I can drink some more?"

– 19 –

24 Don't be jealous of crooks
or want to be their friends.
2 All they think about
and talk about
is violence and cruelty.

– 20 –

3 Use wisdom and understanding
to establish your home;
4 let good sense fill the rooms
with priceless treasures.

– 21 –

5 Wisdom brings strength,
and knowledge gives power.
6 Battles are won
by listening to advice
and making a lot of plans.

– 22 –

7 Wisdom is too much for fools!
Their advice is no good.

– 23 –

8 No one but troublemakers
think up trouble.
9 Everyone hates senseless fools
who think up ways to sin.

[p]**23.7** *People . . . eat*: One possible meaning for the difficult Hebrew text. [q]**23.10** *marker*: See the note at 22.28.

– 24 –

10 Don't give up and be helpless
in times of trouble.

– 25 –

11 Don't fail to rescue those
who are doomed to die.
12 Don't say, "I didn't know it!"
God can read your mind.
He watches each of us
and knows our thoughts.
And God will pay us back
for what we do.

– 26 –

13 Honey is good for you,
my children,
and it tastes sweet.
14 Wisdom is like honey
for your life—
if you find it,
your future is bright.

– 27 –

15 Don't be a cruel person
who attacks good people
and hurts their families.
16 Even if good people
fall seven times,
they will get back up.
But when trouble strikes
the wicked,
that's the end of them.

– 28 –

17 Don't be happy
to see your enemies trip
and fall down.
18 The LORD will find out
and be unhappy.
Then he will stop
being angry with them.

– 29 –

19 Don't let evil people
worry you
or make you jealous.
20 They will soon be gone
like the flame of a lamp
that burns out.

– 30 –

21 My children, you must respect
the LORD and the king,
and you must not make friends
with anyone who rebels
against either of them.
22 Who knows what sudden disaster
the LORD or a ruler
might bring?

More Sayings That Make Good Sense

23 Here are some more sayings
that make good sense:
When you judge,
you must be fair.
24 If you let the guilty
go free,
people of all nations
will hate and curse you.
25 But if you punish the guilty,
things will go well for you,
and you will prosper.
26 Giving an honest answer
is a sign
of true friendship.
27 Get your fields ready
and plant your crops
before starting a home.
28 Don't accuse anyone
who isn't guilty.
Don't ever tell a lie
29 or say to someone,
"I'll get even with you!"

30 I once walked by the field
and the vineyard
of a lazy fool.
31 Thorns and weeds
were everywhere,
and the stone wall
had fallen down.
32 When I saw this,
it taught me a lesson:
33 Sleep a little. Doze a little.
Fold your hands
and twiddle your thumbs.
34 Suddenly poverty hits you
and everything is gone!

More of Solomon's Wise Sayings

25 Here are more
of Solomon's proverbs.
They were copied by the officials
of King Hezekiah of Judah.
2 God is praised
for being mysterious;
rulers are praised
for explaining mysteries.
3 Who can fully understand
the thoughts of a ruler?
They reach beyond the sky
and go deep in the earth.

4 Silver must be purified
before it can be used
to make something of value.
5 Evil people must be removed
before anyone can rule
with justice.

6 Don't try to seem important
in the court of a ruler.
7 It's better for the ruler
to give you a high position
than for you to be embarrassed
in front of royal officials.
Be sure you are right
8 before you sue someone,
or you might lose your case
and be embarrassed.

9 When you and someone else
can't get along,

don't gossip about it.[r]
10 Others will find out,
and your reputation
will then be ruined.

11 The right word
at the right time
is like precious gold
set in silver.
12 Listening to good advice
is worth much more
than jewelry made of gold.
13 A messenger you can trust
is just as refreshing
as cool water in summer.
14 Broken promises
are worse than rain clouds
that don't bring rain.
15 Patience and gentle talk
can convince a ruler
and overcome any problem.

16 Eating too much honey
can make you sick.
17 Don't visit friends too often,
or they will get tired of it
and start hating you.
18 Telling lies about friends
is like attacking them
with clubs and swords
and sharp arrows.
19 A friend you can't trust
in times of trouble
is like having a toothache
or a sore foot.
20 Singing to someone
in deep sorrow
is like pouring vinegar
in an open cut.[s]

21 If your enemies are hungry,
give them something to eat.
And if they are thirsty,
give them something
to drink.
22 This will be the same
as piling burning coals
on their heads.
And the LORD
will reward you.
23 As surely as rain blows in
from the north,
anger is caused
by cruel words.
24 It's better to stay outside
on the roof of your house
than to live inside
with a nagging wife.

25 Good news from far away
refreshes like cold water
when you are thirsty.
26 When a good person gives in
to the wicked,
it's like dumping garbage
in a stream of clear water.
27 Don't eat too much honey
or always want praise.[t]
28 Losing self-control
leaves you as helpless
as a city without a wall.

Don't Be a Fool

26 Expecting snow in summer
and rain in the dry season
makes more sense
than honoring a fool.
2 A curse you don't deserve
will take wings and fly away
like a sparrow or a swallow.
3 Horses and donkeys
must be beaten and bridled—
and so must fools.
4 Don't make a fool of yourself
by answering a fool.
5 But if you answer any fools,
show how foolish they are,
so they won't feel smart.

6 Sending a message by a fool
is like chopping off your foot
and drinking poison.
7 A fool with words of wisdom
is like an athlete
with legs that can't move.[u]
8 Are you going to honor a fool?
Why not shoot a slingshot
with the rock tied tight?
9 A thornbush waved around
in the hand of a drunkard
is no worse than a proverb
in the mouth of a fool.

10 It's no smarter to shoot arrows
at every passerby
than it is to hire a bunch
of worthless nobodies.[v]
11 Dogs return to eat their vomit,
just as fools repeat
their foolishness.
12 There is more hope for a fool
than for someone who says,
"I'm really smart!"

13 Don't be lazy and keep saying,
"There's a lion outside!"
14 A door turns on its hinges,
but a lazy person
just turns over in bed.
15 Some of us are so lazy
that we won't lift a hand
to feed ourselves.
16 A lazy person says,

[r]**25.9** *When . . . it*: Or "Settle a problem privately between you and your neighbor and don't involve others." [s]**25.20** *cut*: One possible meaning for the difficult Hebrew text of verse 20. [t]**25.27** *or . . . praise*: One possible meaning for the difficult Hebrew text. [u]**26.7** *with . . . move*: One possible meaning for the difficult Hebrew text. [v]**26.10** *nobodies*: One possible meaning for the difficult Hebrew text of verse 10.

"I am smarter
than everyone else."

17 It's better to take hold
of a mad dog by the ears
than to take part
in someone else's argument.
18 It's no crazier to shoot
sharp and flaming arrows
19 than to cheat someone and say,
"I was only fooling!"

20 Where there is no fuel
a fire goes out;
where there is no gossip
arguments come to an end.
21 Troublemakers start trouble,
just as sparks and fuel
start a fire.
22 There is nothing so delicious
as the taste of gossip!
It melts in your mouth.

23 Hiding hateful thoughts
behind smooth[w] talk
is like coating a clay pot
with a cheap glaze.
24 The pleasant talk
of an enemy
hides more evil plans
25 than can be counted—
so don't believe a word!
26 Everyone will see through
those evil plans.
27 If you dig a pit,
you will fall in;
if you start a stone rolling,
it will roll back on you.
28 Watch out for anyone
who tells lies and flatters—
they are out to get you.

Don't Brag about Tomorrow

27 Don't brag about tomorrow!
Each day brings
its own surprises.
2 Don't brag about yourself—
let others praise you.
3 Stones and sand are heavy,
but trouble caused by a fool
is a much heavier load.
4 An angry person is dangerous,
but a jealous person
is even worse.

5 A truly good friend
will openly correct you.
6 You can trust a friend
who corrects you,
but kisses from an enemy
are nothing but lies.
7 If you have had enough to eat,
honey doesn't taste good,
but if you are really hungry,
you will eat anything.
8 When you are far from home,
you feel like a bird
without a nest.
9 The sweet smell of incense
can make you feel good,
but true friendship
is better still.[x]
10 Don't desert an old friend
of your family
or visit your relatives
when you are in trouble.
A friend nearby is better
than relatives far away.

11 My child, show good sense!
Then I will be happy
and able to answer anyone
who criticizes me.
12 Be cautious and hide
when you see danger—
don't be stupid and walk
right into trouble.
13 Don't loan money to a stranger
unless you are given something
to guarantee payment.
14 A loud greeting
early in the morning
is the same as a curse.
15 The steady dripping of rain
and the nagging of a wife
are one and the same.
16 It's easier to catch the wind
or hold olive oil in your hand
than to stop a nagging wife.

17 Just as iron sharpens iron,
friends sharpen the minds
of each other.
18 Take care of a tree,
and you will eat its fruit;
look after your master,
and you will be praised.
19 You see your face in a mirror
and your thoughts
in the minds of others.
20 Death and the grave
are never satisfied,
and neither are we.
21 Gold and silver are tested
in a red-hot furnace,
but we are tested by praise.
22 No matter how hard
you beat a fool,
you can't pound out
the foolishness.

23 You should take good care
of your sheep and goats,
24 because wealth and honor
don't last forever.
25 After the hay is cut
and the new growth appears
and the harvest is over,
26 you can sell lambs and goats
to buy clothes and land.

[w]**26.23** *smooth*: One ancient translation; Hebrew "hateful." [x]**27.9** *still*: One possible meaning for the difficult Hebrew text of verse 9.

27 From the milk of the goats,
you can make enough cheese
to feed your family
and all your servants.

The Law of God Makes Sense

28 Wicked people run away
when no one chases them,
but those who live right
are as brave as lions.
2 In time of civil war
there are many leaders,
but a sensible leader
restores law and order.[y]
3 When someone poor takes over
and mistreats the poor,
it's like a heavy rain
destroying the crops.

4 Lawbreakers praise criminals,
but law-abiding citizens
always oppose them.
5 Criminals don't know
what justice means,
but all who respect the LORD
understand it completely.
6 It's better to be poor
and live right,
than to be rich
and dishonest.

7 It makes good sense
to obey the Law of God,
but you disgrace your parents
if you make friends
with worthless nobodies.
8 If you make money by charging
high interest rates,
you will lose it all to someone
who cares for the poor.
9 God cannot stand the prayers
of anyone who disobeys
his Law.
10 By leading good people to sin,
you dig a pit for yourself,
but all who live right
will have a bright future.

11 The rich think highly
of themselves,
but anyone poor and sensible
sees right through them.
12 When an honest person wins,
it's time to celebrate;
when crooks are in control,
it's best to hide.
13 If you don't confess your sins,
you will be a failure.
But God will be merciful
if you confess your sins
and give them up.
14 The LORD blesses everyone
who is afraid to do evil,
but if you are cruel,
you will end up in trouble.

15 A ruler who mistreats the poor
is like a roaring lion
or a bear hunting for food.
16 A heartless leader is a fool,
but anyone who refuses
to get rich by cheating others
will live a long time.
17 Don't give help to murderers!
Make them stay on the run
for as long as they live.[z]

18 Honesty will keep you safe,
but everyone who is crooked
will suddenly fall.
19 Work hard, and you will have
a lot of food;
waste time, and you will have
a lot of trouble.

20 God blesses his loyal people,
but punishes all who want
to get rich quick.
21 It isn't right to be unfair,
but some people can be bribed
with only a piece of bread.
22 Don't be selfish
and eager to get rich—
you will end up worse off
than you can imagine.

23 Honest correction
is appreciated
more than flattery.
24 If you cheat your parents
and don't think it's wrong,
you are a common thief.
25 Selfish people cause trouble,
but you will live a full life
if you trust the LORD.
26 Only fools would trust
what they alone think,
but if you live by wisdom,
you will do all right.

27 Giving to the poor
will keep you from poverty,
but if you close your eyes
to their needs,
everyone will curse you.
28 When crooks are in control,
everyone tries to hide,
but when they lose power,
good people are everywhere.

Use Good Sense

29 If you keep being stubborn
after many warnings,
you will suddenly discover
you have gone too far.
2 When justice rules a nation,
everyone is glad;
when injustice rules,
everyone groans.
3 If you love wisdom
your parents will be glad,

[y]**28.2** *but . . . order*: One possible meaning for the difficult Hebrew text. [z]**28.17** *live*: One possible meaning for the difficult Hebrew text of verse 17.

but chasing after bad women
will cost you everything.
4 An honest ruler
makes the nation strong;
a ruler who takes bribes
will bring it to ruin.

5 Flattery is nothing less
than setting a trap.
6 Your sins will catch you,
but everyone who lives right
will sing and celebrate.
7 The wicked don't care
about the rights of the poor,
but good people do.
8 Sneering at others is a spark
that sets a city on fire;
using good sense can put out
the flames of anger.

9 Be wise and don't sue a fool.
You won't get satisfaction,
because all the fool will do
is sneer and shout.
10 A murderer hates everyone
who is honest
and lives right.[a]
11 Don't be a fool
and quickly lose your temper—
be sensible and patient.

12 A ruler who listens to lies
will have corrupt officials.
13 The poor and all who abuse them
must each depend on God
for light.
14 Kings who are fair to the poor
will rule forever.

15 Correct your children,
and they will be wise;
children out of control
disgrace their mothers.
16 Crime increases
when crooks are in power,
but law-abiding citizens
will see them fall.
17 If you correct your children,
they will bring you peace
and happiness.

18 Without guidance from God
law and order disappear,
but God blesses everyone
who obeys his Law.
19 Even when servants are smart,
it takes more than words
to make them obey.
20 There is more hope for a fool
than for someone who speaks
without thinking.
21 Slaves that you treat kindly
from their childhood
will cause you sorrow.[b]
22 A person with a quick temper
stirs up arguments
and commits a lot of sins.

23 Too much pride brings disgrace;
humility leads to honor.
24 If you take part in a crime
you are your worst enemy,
because even under oath
you can't tell the truth.
25 Don't fall into the trap
of being a coward—
trust the LORD,
and you will be safe.
26 Many try to make friends
with a ruler,
but justice comes
from the LORD.
27 Good people and criminals
can't stand each other.

The Sayings of Agur

30 These are the sayings
and the message
of Agur son of Jakeh.
Someone cries out to God,
"I am completely worn out!
How can I last?[c]
2 I am far too stupid
to be considered human.
3 I never was wise,
and I don't understand
what God is like."

4 Has anyone gone up to heaven
and come back down?
Has anyone grabbed hold
of the wind?
Has anyone wrapped up the sea
or marked out boundaries
for the earth?
If you know of any
who have done such things,
then tell me their names
and their children's names.

5 Everything God says is true—
and it's a shield for all
who come to him for safety.
6 Don't change what God has said!
He will correct you and show
that you are a liar.

7 There are two things, Lord,
I want you to do for me
before I die:
8 Make me absolutely honest
and don't let me be too poor
or too rich.
Give me just what I need.
9 If I have too much to eat,
I might forget about you;
if I don't have enough,

[a]**29.10** *and lives right*: Or "and those who live right are friends of honest people."
[b]**29.21** *will . . . sorrow*: One possible meaning for the difficult Hebrew text. [c]**30.1** *last*: One possible meaning for the difficult Hebrew text of verse 1.

I might steal
and disgrace your name.

10 Don't tell a slave owner
something bad about one
of the slaves.
That slave will curse you,
and you will be in trouble.

11 Some people curse their father
and even their mother;
12 others think they are perfect,
but they are stained by sin.
13 Some people are stuck-up
and act like snobs;
14 others are so greedy
that they gobble down
the poor and homeless.

15 Greed[d] has twins,
each named "Give me!"
There are three or four things
that are never satisfied:
16 The world of the dead
and a childless wife,
the thirsty earth
and a flaming fire.

17 Don't make fun of your father
or disobey your mother—
crows will peck out your eyes,
and buzzards will eat
the rest of you.

18 There are three or four things
I cannot understand:
19 How eagles fly so high
or snakes crawl on rocks,
how ships sail the ocean
or people fall in love.

20 An unfaithful wife says,
"Sleeping with another man
is as natural as eating."

21 There are three or four things
that make the earth tremble
and are unbearable:
22 A slave who becomes king,
a fool who eats too much,
23 a hateful woman
who finds a husband,
and a slave who takes the place
of the woman who owns her.

24 On this earth four things
are small but very wise:
25 Ants, who seem to be feeble,
but store up food
all summer long;
26 badgers, who seem to be weak,
but live among the rocks;
27 locusts, who have no king,
but march like an army;
28 lizards,[e] which can be caught
in your hand,
but sneak into palaces.

29 Three or four creatures
really strut around:
30 Those fearless lions
who rule the jungle,
31 those proud roosters,
those mountain goats,
and those rulers
who have no enemies.[f]

32 If you are foolishly bragging
or planning something evil,
then stop it now!
33 If you churn milk
you get butter;
if you pound on your nose,
you get blood—
and if you stay angry,
you get in trouble.

What King Lemuel's Mother Taught Him

31 These are the sayings
that King Lemuel of Massa
was taught by his mother.
2 My son Lemuel, you were born
in answer to my prayers,
so listen carefully.
3 Don't waste your life
chasing after women!
This has ruined many kings.

4 Kings and leaders
should not get drunk
or even want to drink.
5 Drinking makes you forget
your responsibilities,
and you mistreat the poor.
6 Beer and wine are only
for the dying or for those
who have lost all hope.
7 Let them drink and forget
how poor and miserable
they feel.
8 But you must defend
those who are helpless
and have no hope.
9 Be fair and give justice
to the poor and homeless.

In Praise of a Good Wife

10 A truly good wife
is the most precious treasure
a man can find!
11 Her husband depends on her,
and she never
lets him down.
12 She is good to him
every day of her life,
13 and with her own hands
she gladly makes clothes.

14 She is like a sailing ship
that brings food

[d]**30.15** *Greed*: Or "A leech." [e]**30.28** *lizards*: Or "spiders." [f]**30.31** *enemies*: One possible meaning for the difficult Hebrew text of verse 31.

from across the sea.
15 She gets up before daylight
to prepare food for her family
and for her servants.[g]
16 She knows how to buy land
and how to plant a vineyard,
17 and she always works hard.
18 She knows when to buy or sell,
and she stays busy
until late at night.
19 She spins her own cloth,
20 and she helps the poor
and the needy.
21 Her family has warm clothing,
and so she doesn't worry
when it snows.
22 She does her own sewing,
and everything she wears
is beautiful.

23 Her husband is a well-known
and respected leader
in the city.
24 She makes clothes to sell
to the shop owners.
25 She is strong and graceful,[h]
as well as cheerful
about the future.
26 Her words are sensible,
and her advice
is thoughtful.
27 She takes good care
of her family
and is never lazy.
28 Her children praise her,
and with great pride
her husband says,
29 "There are many good women,
but you are the best!"

30 Charm can be deceiving,
and beauty fades away,
but a woman
who honors the LORD
deserves to be praised.
31 Show her respect—
praise her in public
for what she has done.

[g]**31.15** *and . . . servants*: Or "and to tell her servants what to do." [h]**31.25** *She . . . graceful*: Or "The clothes she makes are attractive and of good quality."

ECCLESIASTES

ABOUT THIS BOOK

This book is a search for meaning in life. What can humans do to find satisfaction and happiness? What is worthwhile in life? The search begins with a gloomy outlook—life is boring and as senseless as chasing the wind.

Ecclesiastes looks at one area of life after another, to see whether meaning and purpose for living can be found. The book decides that humans cannot understand the meaning of life, and that life is too short and unfair. This may seem depressing, but Ecclesiastes also shows that some things in life are better than others. For example, it is better to be wise than to be foolish. And God does intend for people to enjoy his gifts of work, food, drink, friendship, and marriage. And most important of all:

Respect and obey God!
This is what life
is all about.
God will judge
everything we do,
even what is done in secret,
whether good or bad.
(12.13, 14)

A QUICK LOOK AT THIS BOOK

The Search for Meaning in Life (1.1—2.26)
Everything Has Its Time (3.1-8)
Life Isn't Always Fair, So Live Wisely (3.9—6.12)
No One Knows What the Future Will Bring (9.1—11.6)
Respect and Obey God (11.7—12.14)

Nothing Makes Sense

1 When the son of David was king in Jerusalem, he was known to be very wise,[a] and he said:

2 Nothing makes sense!
Everything is nonsense.
I have seen it all—
nothing makes sense!
3 What is there to show
for all of our hard work
here on this earth?
4 People come, and people go,
but still the world
never changes.
5 The sun comes up,
the sun goes down;
it hurries right back
to where it started from.
6 The wind blows south,
the wind blows north;
round and round it blows
over and over again.
7 All rivers empty into the sea,
but it never spills over;
one by one the rivers return
to their source.[b]

8 All of life is far more boring
than words could ever say.

[a]**1.1** *known to be very wise*: This stands for the Hebrew word often translated "preacher" or "teacher." The word may refer to someone who was a very wise leader or to someone who had become wise from collecting sayings about wisdom. [b]**1.7** *return to their source*: Or "flow into the sea."

Our eyes and our ears
are never satisfied
with what we see and hear.
9 Everything that happens
has happened before;
nothing is new,
nothing under the sun.
10 Someone might say,
"Here is something new!"
But it happened before,
long before we were born.
11 No one who lived in the past
is remembered anymore,
and everyone yet to be born
will be forgotten too.

It Is Senseless To Be Wise

12 I said these things when I lived in
Jerusalem as king of Israel. 13 With all
my wisdom I tried to understand everything that happens here on earth. And
God has made this so hard for us humans to do. 14 I have seen it all, and
everything is just as senseless as chasing the wind.[c]

15 If something is crooked,
it can't be made straight;
if something isn't there,
it can't be counted.

16 I said to myself, "You are by far the
wisest person who has ever lived in
Jerusalem. You are eager to learn, and
you have learned a lot." 17 Then I decided
to find out all I could about wisdom and
foolishness. Soon I realized that this too
was as senseless as chasing the wind.[c]

18 The more you know,
the more you hurt;
the more you understand,
the more you suffer.

It Is Senseless To Be Selfish

2 I said to myself, "Have fun and enjoy
yourself!" But this didn't make
sense. 2 Laughing and having fun is
crazy. What good does it do? 3 I wanted
to find out what was best for us during
the short time we have on this earth. So
I decided to make myself happy with
wine and find out what it means to be
foolish, without really being foolish myself.
4 I did some great things. I built houses
and planted vineyards. 5 I had flower
gardens and orchards full of fruit trees.
6 And I had pools where I could get water for the trees. 7 I owned slaves, and
their sons and daughters became my
slaves. I had more sheep and goats
than anyone who had ever lived in
Jerusalem. 8 Foreign rulers brought me
silver, gold, and precious treasures. Men
and women sang for me, and I had
many wives[d] who gave me great pleasure.
9 I was the most famous person who
had ever lived in Jerusalem, and I was
very wise. 10 I got whatever I wanted and
did whatever made me happy. But most
of all, I enjoyed my work. 11 Then I
thought about everything I had done, including the hard work, and it was simply chasing the wind.[e] Nothing on earth
is worth the trouble.

Wisdom Makes Sense

12 I asked myself, "What can the next
king do that I haven't done?" Then I decided to compare wisdom with foolishness and stupidity. 13 And I discovered
that wisdom is better than foolishness,
just as light is better than darkness.
14 Wisdom is like having two good eyes;
foolishness leaves you in the dark. But
wise or foolish, we all end up the same.
15 Finally, I said to myself, "Being wise
got me nowhere! The same thing will
happen to me that happens to fools.
Nothing makes sense. 16 Wise or foolish,
we all die and are soon forgotten."
17 This made me hate life. Everything we
do is painful; it's just as senseless as
chasing the wind.[e]
18 Suddenly I realized that others
would someday get everything I had
worked for so hard, then I started hating
it all. 19 Who knows if those people will
be sensible or stupid? Either way, they
will own everything I have earned by
hard work and wisdom. It doesn't make
sense.
20 I thought about all my hard work,
and I felt depressed. 21 When we use our
wisdom, knowledge, and skill to get
what we own, why do we have to leave
it to someone who didn't work for it?
This is senseless and wrong. 22 What do
we really gain from all of our hard
work? 23 Our bodies ache during the day,
and work is torture. Then at night our
thoughts are troubled. It just doesn't
make sense.
24 The best thing we can do is to enjoy
eating, drinking, and working.[f] I believe
these are God's gifts to us, 25 and no one
enjoys eating and living more than I do.
26 If we please God, he will make us
wise, understanding, and happy. But if
we sin, God will make us struggle for a
living, then he will give all we own to
someone who pleases him. This makes
no more sense than chasing the wind.[g]

[c] **1.14** *chasing the wind*: Or "eating the wind." [c] **1.17** *chasing the wind*: Or "eating the wind."
[d] **2.8** *many wives*: One possible meaning for the difficult Hebrew text. [e] **2.11** *chasing the wind*: See the note at 1.14. [e] **2.17** *chasing the wind*: See the note at 1.14. [f] **2.24** *The best . . . working*: One possible meaning for the difficult Hebrew text. [g] **2.26** *chasing the wind*: See the note at 1.14.

Everything Has Its Time

3 Everything on earth
has its own time
and its own season.
2 There is a time
for birth and death,
planting and reaping,
3 for killing and healing,
destroying and building,
4 for crying and laughing,
weeping and dancing,
5 for throwing stones
and gathering stones,
embracing and parting.
6 There is a time
for finding and losing,
keeping and giving,
7 for tearing and sewing,
listening and speaking.
8 There is also a time
for love and hate,
for war and peace.

What God Has Given Us To Do

9What do we gain by all of our hard
work? 10I have seen what difficult things
God demands of us. 11God makes everything happen at the right time. Yet none
of us can ever fully understand all he
has done, and he puts questions in our
minds about the past and the future. 12I
know the best thing we can do is to always enjoy life, 13because God's gift to
us is the happiness we get from our food
and drink and from the work we do.
14Everything God has done will last forever; nothing he does can ever be
changed. God has done all this, so that
we will worship him.

15 Everything that happens
has happened before,
and all that will be
has already been—
God does everything
over and over again.[h]

The Future Is Known Only to God

16Everywhere on earth I saw violence
and injustice instead of fairness and justice. 17So I told myself that God has set a
time and a place for everything. He will
judge everyone, both the wicked and the
good. 18I know that God is testing us to
show us that we are merely animals.
19Like animals we breathe and die, and
we are no better off than they are. It just
doesn't make sense. 20All living creatures go to the same place. We are made
from earth, and we return to the earth.
21Who really knows if our spirits go up
and the spirits of animals go down into
the earth? 22We were meant to enjoy our
work, and that's the best thing we can
do. We can never know the future.

4 I looked again and saw people being
mistreated everywhere on earth.
They were crying, but no one was there
to offer comfort, and those who mistreated them were powerful. 2I said to
myself, "The dead are better off than the
living. 3But those who have never been
born are better off than anyone else, because they have never seen the terrible
things that happen on this earth."
4Then I realized that we work and do
wonderful things just because we are
jealous of others. This makes no more
sense than chasing the wind.[i]

5 Fools will fold their hands
and starve to death.
6 Yet a very little food
eaten in peace
is better than twice as much
earned from overwork
and chasing the wind.[i]

7Once again I saw that nothing on
earth makes sense. 8For example, some
people don't have friends or family. But
they are never satisfied with what they
own, and they never stop working to get
more. They should ask themselves,
"Why am I always working to have
more? Who will get what I leave behind?" What a senseless and miserable
life!

It Is Better To Have a Friend

9You are better off to have a friend
than to be all alone, because then you
will get more enjoyment out of what
you earn. 10If you fall, your friend can
help you up. But if you fall without having a friend nearby, you are really in
trouble. 11If you sleep alone, you won't
have anyone to keep you warm on a
cold night. 12Someone might be able to
beat up one of you, but not both of
you. As the saying goes, "A rope made
from three strands of cord is hard to
break."
13You may be poor and young. But if
you are wise, you are better off than a
foolish old king who won't listen to advice. 14Even if you were not born into
the royal family and have been a prisoner and poor, you can still be king.
15I once saw everyone in the world follow a young leader who came to power
after the king was gone. 16His followers
could not even be counted. But years
from now, no one will praise him—this
makes no more sense than chasing the
wind.[i]

[h]**3.15** *God does . . . again*: One possible meaning for the difficult Hebrew text. [i]**4.4** *chasing the wind*: See the note at 1.14. [i]**4.6** *chasing the wind*: See the note at 1.14. [i]**4.16** *chasing the wind*: See the note at 1.14.

Be Careful How You Worship

5 Be careful what you do when you
enter the house of God. Some fools
go there to offer sacrifices, even though
they haven't sinned.[j] But it's best just to
listen when you go to worship. 2Don't
talk before you think or make promises
to God without thinking them through.
God is in heaven, and you are on earth,
so don't talk too much. 3If you keep
thinking about something, you will
dream about it. If you talk too much,
you will say the wrong thing.
4God doesn't like fools. So don't be
slow to keep your promises to God. 5It's
better not to make a promise at all than
to make one and not keep it. 6Don't let
your mouth get you in trouble! And
don't say to the worship leader,[k] "I
didn't mean what I said." God can destroy everything you have worked for,
so don't say something that makes God
angry.
7Respect and obey God! Daydreaming
leads to a lot of senseless talk.[l]
8Don't be surprised if the poor of your
country are abused, and injustice takes
the place of justice. After all, the lower
officials must do what the higher ones
order them to do. 9And since the king is
the highest official, he benefits most
from the taxes paid on the land.[m]
10If you love money and wealth, you
will never be satisfied with what you
have. This doesn't make sense either.
11The more you have, the more everyone
expects from you. Your money won't do
you any good—others will just spend it
for you. 12If you have to work hard for a
living, you can rest well at night, even if
you don't have much to eat. But if you
are rich, you can't even sleep.
13I have seen something terribly unfair. People get rich, but it does them no
good. 14Suddenly they lose everything in
a bad business deal, then have nothing
to leave for their children. 15They came
into this world naked, and when they
die, they will be just as naked. They
can't take anything with them, and they
won't have anything to show for all
their work. 16That's terribly unfair. They
leave the world just as they came into it.
They gained nothing from running after
the wind. 17Besides all this, they are always gloomy at mealtime, and they are
troubled, sick, and bitter.[n]
18What is the best thing to do in the
short life that God has given us? I think
we should enjoy eating, drinking, and
working hard. This is what God intends
for us to do. 19Suppose you are very rich
and able to enjoy everything you own.
Then go ahead and enjoy working
hard—this is God's gift to you. 20God
will keep you so happy that you won't
have time to worry about each day.

Don't Depend on Wealth

6 There is something else terribly unfair, and it troubles everyone on
earth. 2God may give you everything
you want—money, property, and wealth.
Then God doesn't let you enjoy it, and
someone you don't even know gets it
all. That's senseless and terribly unfair!
3You may live a long time and have a
hundred children. But a child born dead
is better off than you, unless you enjoy
life and have a decent burial. 4-5That
child will never live to see the sun or to
have a name, and it will go straight to
the world of darkness. But it will still
find more rest than you, 6even if you live
two thousand years and don't enjoy life.
As you know, we all end up in the same
place.
7We struggle just to have enough to
eat, but we are never satisfied. 8We may
be sensible, yet we are no better off than
a fool. And if we are poor, it still doesn't
do us any good to try to live right. 9It's
better to enjoy what we have than to always want something else, because that
makes no more sense than chasing the
wind.[o]
10Everything that happens was decided long ago. We humans know what
we are like, and we can't argue with
God, because he is[p] too strong for us.
11The more we talk, the less sense we
make, so what good does it do to talk?
12Life is short and meaningless, and it
fades away like a shadow. Who knows
what is best for us? Who knows what
will happen after we are gone?

The Best in Life

7 A good reputation
at the time of death
is better than loving care
at the time of birth.[q]
2 It's better to go to a funeral
than to attend a feast;
funerals remind us
that we all must die.
3 Choose sorrow over laughter
because a sad face
may hide a happy heart.
4 A sensible person mourns,
but fools always laugh.
5 Harsh correction is better

[j] **5.1** *even . . . sinned*: One possible meaning for the difficult Hebrew text. [k] **5.6** *worship leader*: Or "messenger." [l] **5.7** *Daydreaming . . . talk*: One possible meaning for the difficult Hebrew text. [m] **5.9** *land*: One possible meaning for the difficult Hebrew text of verse 9. [n] **5.17** *bitter*: One possible meaning for the difficult Hebrew text of verse 17. [o] **6.9** *chasing the wind*: See the note at 1.14. [p] **6.10** *with God, because he is*: Or "with anyone who is." [q] **7.1** *birth*: One possible meaning for the difficult Hebrew text of verse 1.

than the songs of a fool.
6 Foolish laughter is stupid.
It sounds like thorns
crackling in a fire.
7 Corruption[r] makes fools
of sensible people,
and bribes can ruin you.
8 Something completed is better
than something just begun;
patience is better
than too much pride.
9 Only fools get angry quickly
and hold a grudge.
10 It isn't wise to ask,
"Why is everything worse
than it used to be?"
11 Having wisdom is better
than an inheritance.
12 Wisdom will protect you
just like money;
knowledge with good sense
will lead you to life.
13 Think of what God has done!
If God makes something crooked,
can you make it straight?

14 When times are good,
you should be cheerful;
when times are bad,
think what it means.
God makes them both
to keep us from knowing
what will happen next.

Some of Life's Questions

15I have seen everything during this
senseless life of mine. I have seen good
citizens die for doing the right thing,
and I have seen criminals live to a ripe
old age. 16So don't destroy yourself by
being too good or acting too smart!
17Don't die before your time by being
too evil or acting like a fool. 18Keep to
the middle of the road. You can do this if
you truly respect God.
19Wisdom will make you stronger
than the ten most powerful leaders in
your city.
20No one in this world always does
right.
21Don't listen to everything that everyone says, or you might hear your servant cursing you. 22Haven't you cursed
many others?
23I told myself that I would be smart
and try to understand all of this, but it
was too much for me. 24The truth is beyond us. It's far too deep. 25So I decided
to learn everything I could and become
wise enough to discover what life is all
about. At the same time, I wanted to understand why it's stupid and senseless
to be an evil fool.
26Here is what I discovered: A bad
woman is worse than death. She is a
trap, reaching out with body and soul to
catch you. But if you obey God, you can
escape. If you don't obey, you are done
for. 27With all my wisdom I have tried to
find out how everything fits together,
28but so far I have not been able to. I do
know there is one good man in a thousand, but never have I found a good
woman. 29I did learn one thing: We were
completely honest when God created us,
but now we have twisted minds.

8 Who is smart enough
to explain everything?
Wisdom makes you cheerful
and gives you a smile.

Obey the King

2If you promised God that you would
be loyal to the king, I advise you to keep
that promise. 3Don't quickly oppose the
king or argue when he has already
made up his mind. 4The king's word is
law. No one can ask him, "Why are you
doing this?" 5If you obey the king, you
will stay out of trouble. So be smart and
learn what to do and when to do it. 6Life
is hard, but there is a time and a place
for everything, 7though no one can tell
the future. 8We cannot control the wind[s]
or determine the day of our death. There
is no escape in time of war, and no one
can hide behind evil. 9I noticed all this
and thought seriously about what goes
on in the world. Why does one person
have the power to hurt another?

Who Can Understand the Ways of God?

10I saw the wicked buried with honor,
but God's people had to leave the holy
city and were forgotten.[t] None of this
makes sense. 11When we see criminals
commit crime after crime without being
punished, it makes us want to start a life
of crime. 12They commit hundreds of
crimes and live to a ripe old age, in spite
of the saying:

Everyone who lives right
and respects God
will prosper,
13 but no one who sins
and rejects God
will prosper or live very long.

14There is something else that doesn't
make sense to me. Good citizens are
treated as criminals, while criminals are
honored as though they were good citizens. 15So I think we should get as much
out of life as we possibly can. There is
nothing better than to enjoy our food
and drink and to have a good time. Then
we can make it through this troublesome life that God has given us here on
earth.

[r]7.7 *Corruption*: Or "Oppression." [s]8.8 *control the wind*: Or "escape from death."
[t]8.10 *but . . . forgotten*: One possible meaning for the difficult Hebrew text.

16 Day and night I went without sleep,
trying to understand what goes on in
this world. 17 I saw everything God does,
and I realized that no one can really understand what happens. We may be very
wise, but no matter how much we try or
how much we claim to know, we cannot
understand it all.

One Day at a Time

9 I thought about these things. Then I
understood that God has power over
everyone, even those of us who are wise
and live right. Anything can happen to
any of us, and so we never know if life
will be good or bad.[u] 2 But exactly[v] the
same thing will finally happen to all of
us, whether we live right and respect
God or sin and don't respect God. Yes,
the same thing will happen if we offer
sacrifices to God or if we don't, if we
keep our promises or break them.

3 It's terribly unfair for the same thing
to happen to each of us. We are mean
and foolish while we live, and then we
die. 4 As long as we are alive, we still
have hope, just as a live dog is better off
than a dead lion. 5 We know that we will
die, but the dead don't know a thing.
Nothing good will happen to them—
they are gone and forgotten. 6 Their
loves, their hates, and their jealous feelings have all disappeared with them.
They will never again take part in anything that happens on this earth.

7 Be happy and enjoy eating and
drinking! God decided long ago that this
is what you should do. 8 Dress up, comb
your hair, and look your best. 9 Life is
short, and you love your wife, so enjoy
being with her. This is what you are supposed to do as you struggle through life
on this earth. 10 Work hard at whatever
you do. You will soon go to the world of
the dead, where no one works or thinks
or reasons or knows anything.

11 Here is something else I have
learned:

The fastest runners
 and the greatest heroes
don't always win races
 and battles.
Wisdom, intelligence, and skill
don't always make you healthy,
 rich, or popular.
We each have our share
 of bad luck.

12 None of us know when we might fall
victim to a sudden disaster and find ourselves like fish in a net or birds in a trap.

Better To Be Wise than Foolish

13 Once I saw what people really think
of wisdom. 14 It happened when a powerful ruler surrounded and attacked a
small city where only a few people
lived. The enemy army was getting
ready to break through the city walls.
15 But the city was saved by the wisdom
of a poor person who was soon forgotten. 16 So I decided that wisdom is better
than strength. Yet if you are poor, no one
pays any attention to you, no matter
how smart you are.

17 Words of wisdom spoken softly
 make much more sense
than the shouts of a ruler
 to a crowd of fools.
18 Wisdom is more powerful
 than weapons,
yet one mistake can destroy
 all the good you have done.

10 A few dead flies in perfume
 make all of it stink,
and a little foolishness
 outweighs a lot of wisdom.
2 Sensible thoughts lead you
 to do right;
foolish thoughts lead you
 to do wrong.
3 Fools show their stupidity
 by the way they live;
it's easy to see
 they have no sense.
4 Don't give up your job
 when your boss gets angry.
If you stay calm,
 you'll be forgiven.

5 Some things rulers do are terribly
unfair: 6 They honor fools, but dishonor
the rich; 7 they let slaves ride on horses,
but force slave owners to walk.

8 If you dig a pit,
 you might fall in;
if you break down a wall,
 a snake might bite you.[w]
9 You could even get hurt
by chiseling a stone
 or chopping a log.
10 If you don't sharpen your ax,
 it will be harder to use;
if you are smart,
 you'll know what to do.[x]
11 The power to charm a snake
does you no good
 if it bites you anyway.

12 If you talk sensibly,
 you will have friends;
if you talk foolishly,

[u] **9.1** *or bad*: Three ancient translations; the Hebrew text does not have these words. [v] **9.2** *exactly*: One possible meaning for the difficult Hebrew text. [w] **10.8** *a snake might bite you*: Walls of houses were often made of stones with mud to fill in the cracks between them. If some of the mud washed out, a snake could be living inside the wall. [x] **10.10** *do*: One possible meaning for the difficult Hebrew text of verse 10.

you will destroy yourself.
13 Fools begin with nonsense,
and their stupid chatter
ends with disaster.
14 They never tire of talking,
but none of us really know
what the future will bring.
15 Fools wear themselves out—
they don't know enough
to find their way home.[y]

16 A country is in for trouble
when its ruler is childish,
and its leaders
party all day long.
17 But a nation will prosper
when its ruler is mature,
and its leaders
don't party too much.
18 Some people are too lazy
to fix a leaky roof—
then the house falls in.
19 Eating and drinking
make you feel happy,
and bribes can buy
everything you need.
20 Don't even think
about cursing the king;
don't curse the rich,
not even in secret.
A little bird might hear
and tell everything.

It Pays To Work Hard

11 Be generous, and someday
you will be rewarded.[z]
2 Share what you have
with seven or eight others,
because you never know
when disaster may strike.
3 Rain clouds always bring rain;
trees always stay
wherever they fall.
4 If you worry about the weather
and don't plant seeds,
you won't harvest a crop.

5No one can explain how a baby
breathes before it is born.[a] So how can
anyone explain what God does? After
all, he created everything.
6Plant your seeds early in the morning and keep working in the field until
dark. Who knows? Your work might pay
off, and your seeds might produce.

Youth and Old Age

7Nothing on earth is more beautiful
than the morning sun. 8Even if you live
to a ripe old age, you should try to enjoy
each day, because darkness will come
and will last a long time. Nothing makes
sense.[b]
9Be cheerful and enjoy life while you
are young! Do what you want and find
pleasure in what you see. But don't forget that God will judge you for everything you do.
10Rid yourself of all worry and pain,
because the wonderful moments of
youth quickly disappear.

12 Keep your Creator in mind while
you are young! In years to come,
you will be burdened down with troubles and say, "I don't enjoy life anymore."

2 Someday the light of the sun
and the moon and the stars
will all seem dim to you.
Rain clouds will remain
over your head.
3 Your body will grow feeble,
your teeth will decay,
and your eyesight fail.
4 The noisy grinding of grain
will be shut out
by your deaf ears,
but even the song of a bird
will keep you awake.

5 You will be afraid
to climb up a hill
or walk down a road.
Your hair will turn as white
as almond blossoms.
You will feel lifeless
and drag along
like an old grasshopper.

We each go to our eternal home,
and the streets are filled
with those who mourn.
6 The silver cord snaps,
the golden bowl breaks;
the water pitcher is smashed,
and the pulley at the well
is shattered.
7 So our bodies return
to the earth,
and the life-giving breath[c]
returns to God.
8 Nothing makes sense.
I have seen it all—
nothing makes sense.

Respect and Obey God

9I was a wise teacher with much understanding, and I collected a number of
proverbs that I had carefully studied.
10Then I tried to explain these things in
the best and most accurate way.
11Words of wisdom are like the stick a

[y]**10.15** *home*: One possible meaning for the difficult Hebrew text of verse 15. [z]**11.1** *Be generous . . . rewarded*: Or "Don't be afraid to invest. Someday it will pay off." [a]**11.5** *how . . . born*: Or "what makes the wind blow or how a baby grows inside its mother." [b]**11.8** *Nothing makes sense*: Or "There's nothing to look forward to!" [c]**12.7** *life-giving breath*: Or "spirit."

farmer uses to make animals move.
These sayings come from God, our only
shepherd, and they are like nails that
fasten things together.[d] 12My child, I
warn you to stay away from any teachings except these.

There is no end to books,
and too much study
will wear you out.

13Everything you were taught can be
put into a few words:

Respect and obey God!
This is what life
is all about.
14 God will judge
everything we do,
even what is done in secret,
whether good or bad.

[d]12.11 *These sayings . . . together*: One possible meaning for the difficult Hebrew text.

SONG OF SONGS

ABOUT THIS BOOK

The title of this book means "the most beautiful of songs"; in some translations, it is called "The Song of Solomon" (see 1.1).

This book is a collection of songs, or poems, in which a woman and a man tell about their love for each other. Sometimes they speak to themselves, sometimes to each other or to friends, and in some of the poems they seem to be remembering earlier times in their relationship.

The poems have been interpreted in different ways. Some have thought that the man was King Solomon himself. Others read the book as a drama: The woman was taken to the court of Solomon, but she was still in love with a man back in her hometown, and finally the two are reunited. Some interpreters believe that the man and woman stand for God and his people or Christ and the Church.

But it is also possible to take the book as a collection of poems expressing the deep and powerful love that a woman and a man can have for each other. In fact, they may have been part of marriage celebrations in ancient Israel. As one of the poems says:

The passion of love
bursting into flame
is more powerful than death,
stronger than the grave.
Love cannot be drowned
by oceans or floods;
it cannot be bought,
no matter what is offered.
(8.6b, 7)

A QUICK LOOK AT THIS BOOK

Love Is Better than Wine (1.1-17)
Love Makes Everything Beautiful (2.1—3.5)
The Wedding (3.6—5.1)
Why Is the One You Love More Special than Others? (5.2—7.13)
If Only You and I . . . (8.1-14)

Love Is Better than Wine

1 This is Solomon's
most beautiful song.

She Speaks:
2 Kiss me tenderly!
Your love is better than wine,
3 and you smell so sweet.
All the young women adore you;
the very mention of your name
is like spreading perfume.
*4 Hurry, my king! Let's hurry.
5 Take me to your home.

The Young Women Speak:
We are happy for you!
And we praise your love
even more than wine.

She Speaks:
Young women of Jerusalem,
it is only right
that you should adore him.
My skin is dark and beautiful,
like a tent in the desert
or like Solomon's curtains.
6 Don't stare at me

just because the sun
has darkened my skin.
My brothers were angry with me;
they made me work in the vineyard,
and so I neglected
my complexion.

Don't let the other shepherds
think badly of me.[a]
7 I'm not one of those women
who shamelessly follow
after shepherds.[b]
My darling, I love you!
Where do you feed your sheep
and let them rest at noon?

He Speaks:
8 My dearest, if you don't know,
just follow the path
of the sheep.
Then feed your young goats
near the shepherds' tents.
9 You move as gracefully
as the pony that leads
the chariot of the king.
10 Earrings add to your beauty,
and you wear a necklace
of precious stones.
11 Let's make you some jewelry
of gold, woven with silver.

She Speaks:
12 My king, while you
were on your couch,
my love was a magic charm.[c]
13 My darling, you are perfume
between my breasts;
14 you are flower blossoms
from the gardens of En-Gedi.[d]

He Speaks:
15 My darling, you are lovely,
so very lovely—
your eyes are those of a dove.

She Speaks:
16 My love, you are handsome,
truly handsome—
the fresh green grass
will be our wedding bed
17 in the shade of cedar
and cypress trees.

Love Makes Everything Beautiful

She Speaks:
2 I am merely a rose[e]
from the land of Sharon,
a lily from the valley.

He Speaks:
2 My darling, when compared
with other young women,
you are a lily among thorns.

She Speaks:
3 And you, my love,
are an apple tree
among trees of the forest.
Your shade brought me pleasure;
your fruit was sweet.
4 You led me to your banquet room
and showered me with love.
5 Refresh and strengthen me
with raisins and apples.
I am hungry for love!
6 Put your left hand under my head
and embrace me
with your right arm.

7 Young women of Jerusalem,
promise me by the power
of deer and gazelles[f]
never to awaken love
before it is ready.

Winter Is Past

She Speaks:
8 I hear the voice
of the one I love,
as he comes leaping
over mountains and hills
9 like a deer or a gazelle.
Now he stands outside our wall,
looking through the window
10 and speaking to me.

He Speaks:
My darling, I love you!
Let's go away together.
11 Winter is past,
the rain has stopped;
12 flowers cover the earth,
it's time to sing.[g]
The cooing of doves
is heard in our land.
13 Fig trees are bearing fruit,
while blossoms on grapevines
fill the air with perfume.
My darling, I love you!
Let's go away together.
14 You are my dove
hiding among the rocks
on the side of a cliff.
Let me see how lovely you are!
Let me hear the sound
of your melodious voice.
15 Our vineyards are in blossom;

[a]**1.6** *Don't . . . me*: One possible meaning for the difficult Hebrew text. [b]**1.7** *I'm . . . shepherds*: One possible meaning for the difficult Hebrew text. [c]**1.12** *magic charm*: The Hebrew text has "spikenard" (or "nard"), a sweet-smelling ointment made from a plant that comes from India. The ointment was sometimes used as a love charm. [d]**1.14** *En-Gedi*: An oasis west of the Dead Sea. [e]**2.1** *rose*: The traditional translation. The exact variety of the flower is not known, though it may have been a crocus. [f]**2.7** *deer and gazelles*: Deer and gazelles were sacred animals in some religions of Old Testament times, and they were thought to have special powers. [g]**2.12** *sing*: Or "trim the vines."

we must catch the little foxes
that destroy the vineyards.[h]

She Speaks:
16 My darling, I am yours,
and you are mine,
as you feed your sheep
among the lilies.
17 Pretend to be a young deer
dancing on mountain slopes[i]
until daylight comes
and shadows fade away.

Beautiful Dreams

She Speaks:
3 While in bed at night,
I reached for the one I love
with heart and soul.
I looked for him,
but he wasn't there.
2 So I searched through the town
for the one I love.
I looked on every street,
but he wasn't there.
3 I even asked the guards
patrolling the town,
"Have you seen the one
I love so much?"
4 Right after that, I found him.
I held him and would not let go
until I had taken him
to the home of my mother.
5 Young women of Jerusalem,
promise me by the power
of deer and gazelles,[j]
never to awaken love
before it is ready.

The Groom and the Wedding Party

Their Friends Speak:
6 What do we see approaching
from the desert
like a cloud of smoke?
With it comes the sweet smell
of spices, including myrrh
and frankincense.
7 It is King Solomon
carried on a throne,
surrounded by sixty
of Israel's best soldiers.
8 Each of them wears a sword.
They are experts at fighting,
even in the dark.
9 The throne is made of trees
from Lebanon.
10 Its posts are silver,
the back is gold,
and the seat is covered
with purple cloth.
You women of Jerusalem
have taken great care
to furnish the inside.[k]
11 Now come and see the crown
given to Solomon by his mother
on his happy wedding day.

What a Beautiful Bride

He Speaks:
4 My darling, you are lovely,
so very lovely—
as you look through your veil,
your eyes are those of a dove.
Your hair tosses about
as gracefully as goats
coming down from Gilead.
2 Your teeth are whiter
than sheep freshly washed;
they match perfectly,
not one is missing.
3 Your lips are crimson cords,
your mouth is shapely;
behind your veil are hidden
beautiful rosy cheeks.[l]
4 Your neck is more graceful
than the tower of David,
decorated with thousands
of warriors' shields.

5 Your breasts are perfect;
they are twin deer
feeding among lilies.
6 I will hasten to those hills
sprinkled with sweet perfume
and stay there till sunrise.
7 My darling, you are lovely
in every way.
8 My bride, together
we will leave Lebanon!
We will say good-by
to the peaks of Mount Amana,
Senir, and Hermon,
where lions and leopards
live in the caves.
9 My bride, my very own,
you have stolen my heart!
With one glance from your eyes
and the glow of your necklace,
you have stolen my heart.
10 Your love is sweeter than wine;
the smell of your perfume
is more fragrant than spices.
11 Your lips are a honeycomb;
milk and honey
flow from your tongue.
Your dress has the aroma
of cedar trees from Lebanon.

12 My bride, my very own,
you are a garden, a fountain
closed off to all others.
13 Your arms[m] are vines,

[h] **2.15** *vineyards*: One possible meaning for the difficult Hebrew text of verse 15.
[i] **2.17** *mountain slopes*: One possible meaning for the difficult Hebrew text.
[j] **3.5** *deer and gazelles*: See the note at 2.7.
[k] **3.10** *inside*: One possible meaning for the difficult Hebrew text.
[l] **4.3** *beautiful rosy cheeks*: One possible meaning for the difficult Hebrew text.
[m] **4.13** *Your arms*: One possible meaning for the difficult Hebrew text.

covered with delicious fruits
and all sorts of spices—
henna, nard, 14 saffron,
calamus, cinnamon,
frankincense, myrrh, and aloes
— all the finest spices.
15 You are a spring in the garden,
a fountain of pure water,
and a refreshing stream
from Mount Lebanon.

She Speaks:
16 Let the north wind blow,
the south wind too!
Let them spread the aroma
of my garden,
so the one I love
may enter and taste
its delicious fruits.

He Speaks:
5 My bride, my very own,
I come to my garden
and enjoy its spices.
I eat my honeycomb and honey;
I drink my wine and milk.

Their Friends Speak:
Eat and drink until
you are drunk with love.

Another Dream

She Speaks:
2 I was asleep, but dreaming:
The one I love was at the door,
knocking and saying,
"My darling, my very own,
my flawless dove,
open the door for me!
My head is drenched
with evening dew."

3 But I had already undressed
and bathed my feet.
Should I dress again
and get my feet dirty?
4 Then my darling's hand
reached to open the latch,
and my heart stood still.
5 When I rose to open the door,
my hands and my fingers
dripped with perfume.

6 My heart stood still
while he spoke to me,
but when I opened the door,
my darling had disappeared.
I searched and shouted,
but I could not find him—
there was no answer.
7 Then I was found by the guards
patrolling the town
and guarding the wall.
They beat me up
and stripped off my robe.

8 Young women of Jerusalem,
if you find the one I love,
please say to him,
"She is weak with desire."

Their Friends Speak:
9 Most beautiful of women,
why is the one you love
more special than others?
Why do you ask us
to tell him how you feel?

She Speaks:
10 He is handsome and healthy,
the most outstanding
among ten thousand.
11 His head is purest gold;
his hair is wavy,
black as a raven.
12 His eyes are a pair of doves
bathing in a stream
flowing with milk.[n]
13 His face is a garden
of sweet-smelling spices;
his lips are lilies
dripping with perfume.

14 His arms are branches of gold
covered with jewels;
his body is ivory[o]
decorated with sapphires.
15 His legs are columns of marble
on feet of gold.
He stands there majestic
like Mount Lebanon
and its choice cedar trees.
16 His kisses are sweet.
I desire him so much!
Young women of Jerusalem,
he is my lover and friend.

Their Friends Speak:
6 Most beautiful of women,
tell us where he has gone.
Let us help you find him.

She Speaks:
2 My darling has gone down
to his garden of spices,
where he will feed his sheep
and gather lilies.
3 I am his, and he is mine,
as he feeds his sheep
among the lilies.

He Speaks:
4 My dearest, the cities of Tirzah
and Jerusalem
are not as lovely as you.
Your charms are more powerful
than all of the stars
in the heavens.[p]

[n]**5.12** *milk*: One possible meaning for the difficult Hebrew text of verse 12. [o]**5.14** *his . . . ivory*: One possible meaning for the difficult Hebrew text. [p]**6.4** *all . . . heavens*: Or "a mighty army ready for war."

5 Turn away your eyes—
they make me melt.
Your hair tosses about
as gracefully as goats
coming down from Gilead.
6 Your teeth are whiter
than sheep freshly washed;
they match perfectly,
not one is missing.
7 Behind your veil are hidden
beautiful rosy cheeks.[q]

8 What if I could have
sixty queens, eighty wives,
and thousands of others!
9 You would be my only choice,
my flawless dove,
the favorite child
of your mother.
The young women, the queens,
and all the others
tell how excited you are
as they sing your praises:
10 "You are as majestic
as the morning sky—
glorious as the moon—
blinding as the sun!
Your charms are more powerful
than all the stars above."[r]

She Speaks:
11 I went down to see if blossoms
were on the walnut trees,
grapevines, and fruit trees.
12 But in my imagination
I was suddenly riding
on a glorious chariot.[s]

Their Friends Speak:
13 Dance! Dance!
Beautiful woman from Shulam,
let us see you dance!

She Speaks:
Why do you want to see
this woman from Shulam
dancing with the others?[t]

The Wedding Dance

He Speaks:
7 You are a princess,
and your feet are graceful
in their sandals.
Your thighs are works of art,
each one a jewel;
2 your navel is a wine glass
filled to overflowing.
Your body is full and slender
like a bundle of wheat
bound together by lilies.
3 Your breasts are like twins
of a deer.
4 Your neck is like ivory,
and your eyes sparkle
like the pools of Heshbon
by the gate of Bath-Rabbim.
Your nose is beautiful
like Mount Lebanon
above the city of Damascus.
5 Your head is held high
like Mount Carmel;
your hair is so lovely
it holds a king prisoner.[u]

6 You are beautiful,
so very desirable!
7 You are tall and slender
like a palm tree,
and your breasts are full.
8 I will climb that tree
and cling to its branches.
I will discover that your breasts
are clusters of grapes,
and that your breath
is the aroma of apples.
9 Kissing you is more delicious
than drinking the finest wine.
How wonderful and tasty![v]

She Speaks:
10 My darling, I am yours,
and you desire me.
11 Let's stroll through the fields
and sleep in the villages.
12 At dawn let's slip out and see
if grapevines and fruit trees
are covered with blossoms.
When we are there,
I will give you my love.
13 Perfume from the magic flower[w]
fills the air, my darling.
Right at our doorstep
I have stored up for you
all kinds of tasty fruits.

If Only You and I . . .

She Speaks:
8 If you were my brother,
I could kiss you
whenever we happen to meet,
and no one would say
I did wrong.
2 I could take you to the home
of my mother,
who taught me all I know.[x]
I would give you delicious wine
and fruit juice as well.
3 Put your left hand under my head
and embrace me
with your right arm.

[q]**6.7** *cheeks*: One possible meaning for the difficult Hebrew text of verse 7. [r]**6.10** *all . . . above*: Or "a mighty army ready for war." [s]**6.12** *chariot*: One possible meaning for the difficult Hebrew text of verse 12. [t]**6.13** *dancing . . . others*: One possible meaning for the difficult Hebrew text. [u]**7.5** *it . . . prisoner*: One possible meaning for the difficult Hebrew text. [v]**7.9** *How . . . tasty*: One possible meaning for the difficult Hebrew text. [w]**7.13** *magic flower*: The Hebrew text has "mandrake," a plant that was thought to give sexual powers. [x]**8.2** *who . . . know*: One possible meaning for the difficult Hebrew text.

[4] Young women of Jerusalem,
promise me by the power
of deer and gazelles[y]
never to awaken love
before it is ready.

Their Friends Speak:
[5] Who is this young woman
coming in from the desert
and leaning on the shoulder
of the one she loves?

She Speaks:
I stirred up your passions
under the apple tree
where you were born.
[6] Always keep me in your heart
and wear this bracelet
to remember me by.
The passion of love
bursting into flame
is more powerful than death,
stronger than the grave.
[7] Love cannot be drowned
by oceans or floods;
it cannot be bought,
no matter what is offered.

Their Friends Speak:
[8] We have a little sister
whose breasts
are not yet formed.
If someone asks to marry her,
what should we do?
[9] She isn't a wall
that we can defend
behind a silver shield.
Neither is she a room
that we can protect
behind a wooden door.

She Speaks:
[10] I am a wall around a city,
my breasts are towers,
and just looking at me
brings him great pleasure.
[11] Solomon has a vineyard
at Baal-Hamon,
which he rents to others
for a thousand pieces
of silver each.
[12] My vineyard is mine alone!
Solomon can keep his silver
and the others can keep
their share of the profits.

He Speaks:
[13] You are in the garden
with friends all around.
Let me hear your voice!

She Speaks:
[14] Hurry to me, my darling!
Run faster than a deer
to mountains of spices.

[y]**8.4** *deer and gazelles*: See the note at 2.7.

ISAIAH

ABOUT THIS BOOK

Isaiah spoke for the Lord to the people of Judah during the reigns of four kings of Judah. Over this period of about forty years, the Assyrian empire was expanding. Nations joined together to fight Assyria, but Assyria finally conquered Israel and most other nearby countries. Thousands of people were led away as prisoners. And although the kingdom of Judah wasn't completely conquered, it had to pay heavy taxes.

The messages in this book can be divided into three parts. The first part (1–39) is especially concerned about the Lord's holiness and his power as king of the whole earth. As a holy king, the Lord was angry about evil in Judah. Government officials were corrupt; violence and injustice were everywhere. The Lord said he was going to have Assyria and Babylonia punish the people of Judah and other nations. But the Lord offered his people hope for the future, if they turned back to him and trusted him to protect their nation.

In the second part (40–55) the Lord spoke to people who had been punished (40.1, 2). They were discouraged, and he offered them hope. But the Lord wanted them to understand that idols have no power, and that he alone is the true God. If the people of Israel turned back to him, then he would rescue them from Babylonia and the other nations where they had been scattered. They would return to their own land, and he would bless them and make them prosperous. The Lord was able to make this tremendous promise to his people because he created and rules the entire earth.

In the third part (56–66) the Lord promises an especially bright future for those who are faithful to him. And in this section, people from all nations are included, not just the people of Judah. These promises are like windows that allow a glimpse into a future time when the Lord will create a new world full of joy and free from suffering:

I am creating new heavens
and a new earth;
everything of the past
will be forgotten.
Celebrate and be glad forever!
I am creating a Jerusalem,
full of happy people.
I will celebrate with Jerusalem
and all of its people;
there will be no more crying
or sorrow in that city.
(65.17-19)

A QUICK LOOK AT THIS BOOK

Introduction (1.1-31)
Messages about Judah and Israel (2.1—5.30)
Events from Isaiah's Ministry (6.1—9.7)
More Messages about Judah and Israel (9.8—12.6)
God Will Punish Other Nations (13.1—23.18)
Messages of Hope for the Lord's People Who Are Suffering (24.1—27.13)
The Lord Will Punish His Rebellious People (28.1—31.9)
The Lord Will Punish Edom and Bless Jerusalem (32.1—35.10)
Assyria, Babylonia, King Hezekiah, and Isaiah (36.1—39.8)
The Lord Will Rescue His People (40.1—48.22)
The Lord's Servant (49.1—53.12)

1 I am Isaiah, the son of Amoz.
And this is the message[a] that I was
given about Judah and Jerusalem when
Uzziah, Jotham, Ahaz, and Hezekiah
were the kings of Judah:[b]

A Guilty Nation

2 The LORD has said,
"Listen, heaven and earth!
The children I raised
have turned against me.
3 Oxen and donkeys know
who owns and feeds them,
but my people won't ever learn."

4 Israel, you are a sinful nation
loaded down with guilt.
You are wicked and corrupt
and have turned from the LORD,
the holy God of Israel.
5 Why be punished more?
Why not give up your sin?
Your head is badly bruised,
and you are weak all over.
6 From your head to your toes
there isn't a healthy spot.
Bruises, cuts, and open sores
go without care
or oil to ease the pain.

A Country in Ruins

7 Your country lies in ruins;
your towns are in ashes.
Foreigners and strangers
take and destroy your land
while you watch.
8 Enemies surround Jerusalem,
alone like a hut in a vineyard[c]
or in a cucumber field.
9 Zion would have disappeared
like Sodom and Gomorrah,[d]
if the LORD All-Powerful
had not let a few
of its people survive.

Justice, Not Sacrifices

10 You are no better
than the leaders and people
of Sodom and Gomorrah!
So listen to the LORD God:
11 "Your sacrifices
mean nothing to me.
I am sick of your offerings
of rams and choice cattle;
I don't like the blood
of bulls or lambs or goats.

12 "Who asked you to bring all this
when you come to worship me?
Stay out of my temple!
13 Your sacrifices are worthless,
and incense is disgusting.
I can't stand the evil you do
on your New Moon Festivals
or on your Sabbaths
and other times of worship.
14 I hate your New Moon Festivals
and all others as well.
They are a heavy burden
I am tired of carrying.

15 "No matter how much you pray,
I won't listen.
You are too violent.
16 Wash yourselves clean!
I am disgusted
with your filthy deeds.
Stop doing wrong
17 and learn to live right.
See that justice is done.
Defend widows and orphans
and help those in need."[e]

An Invitation from the LORD

18 I, the LORD, invite you
to come and talk it over.
Your sins are scarlet red,
but they will be whiter
than snow or wool.
19 If you willingly obey me,
the best crops in the land
will be yours.
20 But if you turn against me,
your enemies will kill you.
I, the LORD, have spoken.

[a]1.1 *message*: Or "vision." [b]1.1 *kings of Judah*: Uzziah (783-742 B.C.); Jotham (742-735 B.C.); Ahaz (735-715 B.C.); Hezekiah (715-687 B.C.). [c]1.8 *a hut in a vineyard*: When it was almost time for grapes to ripen, farmers would put up a temporary shelter or hut in the field or vineyard and stay there to keep thieves and wild animals away. [d]1.9 *Sodom and Gomorrah*: Two ancient cities of Palestine that God destroyed because the people were so wicked (see Genesis 19.1-29). [e]1.17 *and help those in need*: Or "and punish cruel people."

The LORD Condemns Jerusalem

21 Jerusalem, you are like
an unfaithful wife.
Once your judges were honest
and your people lived right;
now you are a city
full of murderers.
22 Your silver is fake,
and your wine
is watered down.
23 Your leaders have rejected me
to become friends of crooks;
your rulers are looking
for gifts and bribes.
Widows and orphans
never get a fair trial.

24 I am the LORD All-Powerful,
the mighty ruler of Israel,
and I make you a promise:
You are now my enemy,
and I will show my anger
by taking revenge on you.
25 I will punish you terribly
and burn away everything
that makes you unfit
to worship me.
26 Jerusalem, I will choose
judges and advisors
like those you had before.
Your new name will be
"Justice and Faithfulness."

The LORD Will Save Jerusalem

27 Jerusalem, you will be saved
by showing justice;[f]
Zion's people who turn to me
will be saved
by doing right.
28 But those rebellious sinners
who turn against me, the LORD,
will all disappear.

29 You will be made ashamed
of those groves of trees
where you worshiped idols.
30 You will be like a grove of trees
dying in a drought.
31 Your strongest leaders
will be like dry wood
set on fire by their idols.[g]
No one will be able to help,
as they all go up in flames.

Peace That Lasts Forever

2 This is the message[h] that I was
given about Judah and Jerusalem:

2 In the future, the mountain
with the LORD's temple
will be the highest of all.
It will reach above the hills;
every nation will rush to it.
3 Many people will come and say,
"Let's go to the mountain
of the LORD God of Jacob
and worship in his temple."

The LORD will teach us his Law
from Jerusalem,
and we will obey him.
4 He will settle arguments
between nations.
They will pound their swords
and their spears
into rakes and shovels;
they will never make war
or attack one another.
5 People of Israel, let's live
by the light of the LORD.

Following Sinful Customs

6 Our LORD, you have deserted
your people, Israel,
because they follow customs
of nations from the east.
They worship Philistine gods
and are close friends
of foreigners.[i]
7 They have endless treasures
of silver and gold;
they have countless horses
and war chariots.
8 Everywhere in the country
they worship the idols
they have made.
9 And so, all of them
will be ashamed and disgraced.
Don't help them!

A Day of Judgment

10 Every one of you,
go hide among the rocks
and in the ground,
because the LORD is fearsome,
marvelous, and glorious.
11 When the LORD comes,
everyone who is proud
will be made humble,
and the LORD alone
will be honored.
12 The LORD All-Powerful
has chosen a day
when those who are proud
and conceited
will be put down.

13 The tall and towering
cedars of Lebanon
will be destroyed.
So will the oak trees of Bashan,
14 all high mountains and hills,
15 every strong fortress,
16 all the seagoing ships,[j]
and every beautiful boat.

[f]**1.27** *by showing justice*: Or "by my saving power." [g]**1.31** *Your . . . idols*: Or "Your wealth will be like dry wood, set on fire by its owners." [h]**2.1** *message*: See the note at 1.1.
[i]**2.6** *because . . . foreigners*: One possible meaning for the difficult Hebrew text.
[j]**2.16** *seagoing ships*: The Hebrew text has "ships of Tarshish," which may have been a Phoenician city in Spain. "Ships of Tarshish" probably means large, seagoing ships.

17 When that day comes,
everyone who is proud
will be put down.
Only the LORD will be honored.
18 Idols will be gone for good.

19 You had better hide
in caves and holes—
the LORD will be fearsome,
marvelous, and glorious
when he comes to terrify
people on earth.

20 On that day everyone will throw
to the rats and bats
their idols of silver and gold
they made to worship.
21 The LORD will be fearsome,
marvelous, and glorious
when he comes to terrify
people on earth—
they will hide in caves
and in the hills.

22 Stop trusting the power
of humans.
They are all going to die,
so how can they help?

Judgment on Jerusalem and Judah

3 The mighty LORD All-Powerful
is going to take away
from Jerusalem and Judah
everything you need—
your bread and water,
*2 soldiers and heroes,
judges and prophets,
leaders and army officers,
3 officials and advisors,
fortunetellers and others
who tell the future.
4 He will let children and babies[k]
become your rulers.
5 You will each be cruel
to friends and neighbors.
Young people will insult
their elders;
no one will show respect
to those who deserve it.

6 Some of you will grab hold
of a relative and say,
"You still have a coat.
Be our leader and rule
this pile of ruins."
7 But the answer will be,
"I can't do you any good.
Don't make me your leader.
There's no food or clothing
left in my house."

8 Jerusalem and Judah,
you rebelled against
your glorious LORD—
your words and your actions,
made you stumble and fall.

9 The look on your faces shows
that you are sinful as Sodom,
and you don't try to hide it.
You are in for trouble,
and you have brought it all
on yourselves.

The Wrong Kind of Leaders

10 Tell those who obey God,
"You're very fortunate—
you will be rewarded
for what you have done."
11 Tell those who disobey,
"You're in big trouble—
what you did to others
will come back to you."
12 Though you are God's people,
you are ruled and abused
by women and children.
You are confused by leaders
who guide you
down the wrong path.

13 The LORD is ready to accuse
and judge all nations.
14 He will even judge
you rulers and leaders
of his own nation.
You destroyed his vineyard[l]
and filled your houses
by robbing the poor.
15 The LORD All-Powerful says,
"You have crushed my people
and rubbed in the dirt
the faces of the poor."

The Women of Jerusalem

16 The LORD says:
The women of Jerusalem
are proud and strut around,
winking shamelessly.
They wear anklets that jingle
and call attention
to the way they walk.
17 But I, the LORD, will cover
their heads with sores,
and I will uncover
their private parts.

18-23 When that day comes, I will take away from those women all the fine jewelry they wear on their ankles, heads, necks, ears, arms, noses, fingers, and on their clothes. I will remove their veils, their belts, their perfume, their magic charms, their royal robes, and all their fancy dresses, hats, and purses.

24 In place of perfume,
there will be a stink;
in place of belts,
there will be ropes;
in place of fancy hairdos,
they will have bald heads.
Instead of expensive clothes,
they will wear sackcloth;

[k] 3.4 *babies*: Or "worthless nobodies."

[l] 3.14 *his vineyard*: The nation Israel (see 5.1-7).

instead of beauty,
they will have ugly scars.
25 The fighting men of Jerusalem
will be killed in battle.
26 The city will mourn
and sit in the dirt,
emptied of its people.

4 When this happens, seven women will grab the same man, and each of them will say, "I'll buy my own food and clothes! Just marry me and take away my disgrace."[m]

The LORD Will Bless His People Who Survive

2The time is coming when the LORD will make his land fruitful and glorious again, and the people of Israel who survive will take great pride in what the land produces. 3Everyone who is left alive in Jerusalem will be called special, 4after the LORD sends a fiery judgment to clean the city and its people of their violent deeds.

5Then the LORD will cover the whole city and its meeting places with a thick cloud each day and with a flaming fire[n] each night. God's own glory will be like a huge tent that covers everything. 6It will provide shade from the heat of the sun and a place of shelter and protection from storms and rain.

A Song about a Vineyard

The LORD said:

5 I will sing a song
about my friend's vineyard
that was on the side
of a fertile hill.
2 My friend dug the ground,
removed the stones,
and planted the best vines.
He built a watchtower
and dug a pit in rocky ground
for pressing the grapes.
He hoped they would be sweet,
but bitter grapes
were all it produced.

3 Listen, people of Jerusalem
and of Judah!
You be the judge of me
and my vineyard.
4 What more could I have done
for my vineyard?
I hoped for sweet grapes,
but bitter grapes
were all that grew.

5 Now I will let you know
what I am going to do.
I will cut down the hedge
and tear down the wall.
My vineyard will be trampled
and left in ruins.
6 It will turn into a desert,
neither pruned nor hoed;
it will be covered
with thorns and briars.
I will command the clouds
not to send rain.

7 I am the LORD All-Powerful!
Israel is the vineyard,
and Judah is the garden
I tended with care.
I had hoped for honesty
and for justice,
but dishonesty
and cries for mercy
were all I found.

Isaiah Condemns Social Injustice

8You are in for trouble! You take over
house after house and field after field,
until there is no room left for anyone
else in all the land. 9But the LORD All-
Powerful has made this promise to me:

Those large and beautiful homes
will be left empty, with no one to
take care of them. 10Ten acres of
grapevines will produce only six
gallons of juice, and five bushels of
seed will produce merely a half-
bushel of grain.

11You are in for trouble! You get up
early to start drinking, and you keep it
up late into the night. 12At your drinking
parties you have the music of stringed
instruments, tambourines, and flutes.
But you never even think about all the
LORD has done, 13and so his people
know nothing about him. That's why
many of you will be dragged off to foreign lands. Your leaders will starve to
death, and everyone else will suffer
from thirst.

14The world of the dead has opened
its mouth wide and is eagerly waiting
for the leaders of Jerusalem and for its
noisy crowds, especially for those who
take pride in that city. 15Its citizens have
been put down, and its proud people
have been brought to shame. 16But the
holy LORD God All-Powerful is praised,
because he has shown who he is by
bringing justice. 17His people will be like
sheep grazing in their own pasture, and
they will take off what was left by others.[o]

18You are in for trouble! The lies you
tell are like ropes by which you drag
along sin and evil. 19And you say, "Let
the holy God of Israel hurry up and do
what he has promised, so we can see it
for ourselves." 20You are headed for

[m]4.1 *take away my disgrace*: If a woman did not have a husband or children, it was thought that God was punishing her. [n]4.5 *thick . . . fire*: This is how the LORD led the people of Israel during the forty years they were in the desert (see Exodus 13.20-22; 40.36-38).
[o]5.17 *and they . . . others*: One possible meaning for the difficult Hebrew text.

trouble! You say wrong is right, darkness is light, and bitter is sweet.
21 You think you are clever and smart.
22 And you are great at drinking and
mixing drinks. But you are in for trouble. 23 You accept bribes to let the guilty
go free, and you cheat the innocent out
of a fair trial.
24 You will go up in flames like straw
and hay! You have rejected the teaching
of the holy LORD God All-Powerful of Israel. Now your roots will rot, and your
blossoms will turn to dust.
25 You are the LORD's people, but you
made him terribly angry, and he struck
you with his mighty arm. Mountains
shook, and dead bodies covered the
streets like garbage. The LORD is still
angry, and he is ready to strike you
again.[p]

Foreign Nations Will Attack

26 The LORD has signaled for the foreign nations to come and attack you. He
has already whistled, and they are coming as fast as they can. 27 None of them
are tired. They don't sleep or get
drowsy, and they run without stumbling.
Their belts don't come loose; their sandal straps don't break. 28 Their arrows
are sharp, and their bows are ready. The
hoofs of their horses are hard as flint;
the wheels of their war chariots turn as
fast as a whirlwind.
29 They roar and growl like fierce
young lions as they grab their victims
and drag them off where no one can
rescue them. 30 On the day they attack,
they will roar like the ocean. And across
the land you will see nothing but darkness and trouble, because the light of
day will be covered by thick clouds.

A Vision of the LORD in the Temple

6 In the year that King Uzziah died,[q] I
had a vision of the LORD. He was on
his throne high above, and his robe
filled the temple. 2 Flaming creatures
with six wings each were flying over
him. They covered their faces with two
of their wings and their bodies with two
more. They used the other two wings for
flying, 3 as they shouted,

"Holy, holy, holy,
LORD All-Powerful!
The earth is filled
with your glory."

4 As they shouted, the doorposts of the
temple shook, and the temple was filled
with smoke. 5 Then I cried out, "I'm
doomed! Everything I say is sinful, and
so are the words of everyone around
me. Yet I have seen the King, the LORD
All-Powerful."
6 One of the flaming creatures flew
over to me with a burning coal that it
had taken from the altar with a pair of
metal tongs. 7 It touched my lips with the
hot coal and said, "This has touched
your lips. Your sins are forgiven, and
you are no longer guilty."
8 After this, I heard the LORD ask, "Is
there anyone I can send? Will someone
go for us?"
"I'll go," I answered. "Send me!"
9 Then the LORD told me to go and
speak this message to the people:

"You will listen and listen,
but never understand.
You will look and look,
but never see."

The LORD also said,

10 "Make these people stubborn!
Make them stop up
their ears,
cover their eyes,
and fail to understand.
Don't let them turn to me
and be healed."

11 Then I asked the LORD, "How long
will this last?"
The LORD answered:
Until their towns are destroyed
and their houses are deserted, until
their fields are empty, 12 and I have
sent them far away, leaving their
land in ruins. 13 If only a tenth of the
people are left, even they will be destroyed. But just as stumps remain
after trees have been cut down,[r]
some of my chosen ones will be left.

Isaiah Offers Hope to King Ahaz

7 Ahaz, the son of Jotham and the
grandson of Uzziah, was king of Judah when King Rezin of Syria and King
Pekah son of Remaliah of Israel went to
attack Jerusalem. But they were not
able to do what they had planned.[s]
2 When news reached the royal palace
that Syria had joined forces with Israel,
King Ahaz and everyone in Judah were
so terrified that they shook like trees in
a windstorm.
3 Then the LORD said to me:
Take your son Shearjashub[t] and
go see King Ahaz. You will find him
on the road near the cloth makers'
shops at the end of the canal that
brings water from the upper pool.
4 Tell Ahaz to stop worrying. There's

[p] **5.25** *is ready . . . again*: Or "hasn't given up on you yet." [q] **6.1** *the year that King Uzziah died*: Probably 742 B.C. [r] **6.13** *But just . . . down*: One possible meaning for the difficult Hebrew text. [s] **7.1** *went . . . had planned*: Or "attacked Jerusalem, but could not capture it." [t] **7.3** *Shearjashub*: In Hebrew "Shearjashub" means "a few will return."

no need for him to be afraid of King
Rezin and King Pekah. They are
very angry, but they are nothing
more than a dying fire. Ahaz doesn't
need to fear 5their evil threats 6to
invade and defeat Judah and Jerusalem and to let the son of Tabeel
be king in his place.
7I, the LORD, promise that this will
never happen. 8-9Damascus is just
the capital of Syria, and King Rezin
rules only in Damascus. Samaria is
just the capital of Israel, and King
Pekah rules only in Samaria. But in
less than sixty-five years, Israel will
be destroyed. And if Ahaz and his
officials don't trust me, they will be
defeated.

A Son Named Immanuel

10Once again the LORD God spoke to
King Ahaz. This time he said, 11"Ask me
for proof that my promise will come
true. Ask for something to happen deep
in the world of the dead or high in the
heavens above."
12"No, LORD," Ahaz answered. "I won't
test you!"
13Then I said:
Listen, every one of you in the
royal family of David. You have already tried my patience. Now you
are trying God's patience by refusing to ask for proof. 14But the LORD
will still give you proof. A virgin[u] is
pregnant; she will have a son and
will name him Immanuel.[v] 15-16Even
before the boy is old enough to
know how to choose between right
and wrong, he will eat yogurt and
honey,[w] and the countries of the two
kings you fear will be destroyed.
17But the LORD will make more trouble for your people and your kingdom than any of you have known
since Israel broke away from Judah.
He will even bring the king of Assyria to attack you.

The Threat of an Invasion

18When that time comes, the LORD
will whistle, and armies will come
from Egypt like flies and from Assyria like bees. 19They will settle
everywhere—in the deep valleys and
between the rocks, on every bush
and all over the pastureland.
20The Lord will pay the king of Assyria to bring a razor from across
the Euphrates River and shave your
head and every hair on your body,
including your beard.[x]
21No one will have more than one
young cow and two sheep, 22but
those who do will have enough milk
to make yogurt. In fact, everyone left
in the land will eat yogurt and
honey.[y]
23Vineyards that had a thousand
vines and were worth a thousand
pieces of silver will turn into thorn
patches. 24You will go there to hunt
with your bow and arrows, because
the whole country will be covered
with thornbushes. 25The hills where
you once planted crops will be over-
grown with thorns and thistles. You
will be afraid to go there, and your
cattle, sheep, and goats will be
turned loose on those hills.

A Warning and a Hope

8 The LORD said, "Isaiah, get something to write on. Then write in
big clear letters[z] the name, MAHER-
SHALAL-HASH-BAZ.[a] 2I will have Uriah
the priest and Zechariah son of Je-
berechiah serve as witnesses to this."
3Sometime later, my wife and I had a
son, and the LORD said, "Name him
Maher-Shalal-Hash-Baz. 4Because before he can say 'Mommy' or 'Daddy', the
king of Assyria will attack and take
everything of value from Damascus and
Samaria."
5The LORD spoke to me again and
said:
6These people have refused the
gentle waters of Shiloah[b] and have
gladly gone over to the side of King
Rezin and King Pekah. 7Now I will
send the king of Assyria against
them with his powerful army, which
will attack like the mighty Euphrates River overflowing its banks.
8Enemy soldiers will cover Judah
like a flood reaching up to your
neck.

[u]**7.14** *virgin*: Or "young woman." In this context the difficult Hebrew word did not imply a virgin birth. However, in the Greek translation made about 200 B.C. and used by the early Christians, the word *parthenos* had a double meaning. While the translator took it to mean "young woman," Matthew understood it to mean "virgin" and quoted the passage (Matthew 1.23) because it was the appropriate description of Mary, the mother of Jesus.

[v]**7.14** *Immanuel*: In Hebrew "Immanuel" means "God is with us." [w]**7.15,16** *yogurt and honey*: This may refer either to expensive foods eaten in a time of plenty or to a limited diet eaten in times of a food shortage. [x]**7.20** *shave . . . head . . . body . . . beard*: This would have been a terrible insult. [y]**7.22** *yogurt and honey*: See the note at 7.15, 16. [z]**8.1** *in big clear letters*: One possible meaning for the difficult Hebrew text. [a]**8.1** *MAHER-SHALAL-HASH-BAZ*: In Hebrew "Maher-Shalal-Hash-Baz" means "suddenly attacked, quickly taken."

[b]**8.6** *Shiloah*: The canal that brought water from Gihon Spring to Jerusalem.

But God is with us.[c]
He will spread his wings
and protect our land.[d]
9 All of you foreign nations,
go ahead and prepare for war,
but you will be crushed.
10 Get together and make plans,
but you will fail
because God is with us.

11The LORD took hold of me with his powerful hand and said:

I'm warning you! Don't act like
these people. 12Don't call something
a rebellious plot, just because they
do, and don't be afraid of something,
just because they are. 13I am the one
you should fear and respect. I am
the holy God, the LORD All-Powerful!
14-15Run to me for protection. I am a
rock that will make both Judah and
Israel stumble and break their
bones. I am a trap that will catch the
people of Jerusalem—they will be
captured and dragged away.

Isaiah and His Followers

16My message and my teachings are
to be sealed and given to my followers.
17Meanwhile, I patiently trust the LORD,
even though he is no longer pleased
with Israel. 18My children and I are
warning signs to Israel from the LORD
All-Powerful, who lives on Mount Zion.
19Someone may say to you, "Go to the
fortunetellers who make soft chirping
sounds or ask the spirits of the dead. After all, a nation ought to be able to ask
its own gods 20what it should do."

None of those who talk like that will
live to see the light of day! 21They will
go around in great pain and will become
so hungry that they will angrily curse
their king and their gods. And when
they try to find help in heaven 22and on
earth, they will find only trouble and
darkness, terrible trouble and deepest
darkness.

9 But those who have suffered will no longer be in pain.[e] The territories of Zebulun and Naphtali in Galilee were once hated. But this land of the Gentiles across the Jordan River and along the Mediterranean Sea will be greatly respected.

War Is Over

2 Those who walked in the dark
have seen a bright light.
And it shines upon everyone
who lives in the land
of darkest shadows.
3 Our LORD, you have made
your nation stronger.[f]
Because of you, its people
are glad and celebrate
like workers at harvest time
or like soldiers dividing up
what they have taken.

4 You have broken the power
of those who abused
and enslaved your people.
You have rescued them
just as you saved your people
from Midian.[g]
5 The boots of marching warriors
and the blood-stained uniforms
have been fed to flames
and eaten by fire.

A Child Has Been Born

6 A child has been born for us.
We have been given a son
who will be our ruler.
His names will be
Wonderful Advisor
and Mighty God,
Eternal Father
and Prince of Peace.
7 His power will never end;
peace will last forever.
He will rule David's kingdom
and make it grow strong.
He will always rule
with honesty and justice.
The LORD All-Powerful
will make certain
that all of this is done.

God Will Punish Israel

8The Lord had warned the people of
Israel, 9and all of them knew it, including everyone in the capital city of
Samaria. But they were proud and stubborn and said,

10 "Houses of brick and sycamore
have fallen to the ground,
but we will build houses
with stones and cedar."

11The LORD made their enemies[h] attack them. 12He sent the Arameans from
the east and the Philistines from the
west, and they swallowed up Israel. But
even this did not stop him from being
angry, so he kept on punishing them.[i]
13The people of Israel still did not turn
back to the LORD All-Powerful and worship him.

14In one day he cut off their head and
tail, their leaves and branches. 15Their
rulers and leaders were the head, and

[c]**8.8** *God is with us*: Here and in verse 10 this translates the Hebrew word "Immanuel" (see 7.14). [d]**8.8** *But . . . land*: One possible meaning for the difficult Hebrew text. [e]**9.1** *will . . . pain*: One possible meaning for the difficult Hebrew text. [f]**9.3** *stronger*: Or "happy" or "larger." [g]**9.4** *rescued . . . from Midian*: The time when Gideon defeated the people of Midian in Jezreel Valley (see Judges 6–8). [h]**9.11** *their enemies*: Hebrew "the enemies of Rezin." [i]**9.12** *so . . . them*: Or "but he hasn't given up on them yet."

the lying prophets were the tail. 16They
had led the nation down the wrong
path, and the people were confused.
17The Lord was angry with his people
and kept punishing them, because they
had turned against him.[j] They were evil
and spoke foolishly. That's why he did
not have pity on their young people or
on their widows and orphans.
18Evil had spread like a raging forest
fire sending thornbushes up in smoke.
19The LORD All-Powerful was angry and
used the people as fuel for a fire that
scorched the land. They turned against
each other 20like wild animals attacking
and eating everyone around them, even
their own relatives.[k] But still they were
not satisfied. 21The tribes of Ephraim
and Manasseh turned against each
other, then joined forces to attack Judah. But the LORD was still angry and
ready to punish the nation even more.
10 You people are in for trouble! You
have made cruel and unfair laws
2that let you cheat the poor and needy
and rob widows and orphans. 3But what
will you do when you are fiercely attacked and punished by foreigners?
Where will you run for help? Where will
you hide your valuables? 4How will you
escape being captured[l] or killed? The
Lord is still angry, and he isn't through
with you yet![m]

The Lord's Purpose and the King of Assyria

5The Lord says:
I am furious! And I will use the
king of Assyria[n] as a club 6to beat
down you godless people. I am angry with you, and I will send him to
attack you. He will take what he
wants and walk on you like mud in
the streets. 7He has even bigger
plans in mind, because he wants to
destroy many nations.
8The king of Assyria says:
My army commanders are kings!
9They have already captured[o] the
cities of Calno, Carchemish,
Hamath, Arpad, Samaria, and Damascus. 10-11The gods of Jerusalem
and Samaria are weaker than the
gods of those powerful nations. And
I will destroy Jerusalem, together
with its gods and idols, just as I did
Samaria.
12The Lord will do what he has
planned against Jerusalem and Mount
Zion. Then he will punish the proud and
boastful king of Assyria, 13who says:
I did these things by my own
power because I am smart and
clever. I attacked kings like a wild
bull, and I took the land and the
treasures of their nations. 14I have
conquered the whole world! And it
was easier than taking eggs from an
unguarded nest. No one even
flapped a wing or made a peep.
15King of Assyria, can an ax or a saw
overpower the one who uses it? Can a
wooden pole lift whoever holds it? 16The
mighty LORD All-Powerful will send a
terrible disease to strike down your
army, and you will burn with fever under your royal robes. 17The holy God,
who is the light of Israel, will turn into a
fire, and in one day you will go up in
flames, just like a thornbush. 18The Lord
will make your beautiful forests and fertile fields slowly rot. 19There will be so
few trees that even a young child can
count them.

Only a Few Will Come Back

20A time is coming when the survivors
from Israel and Judah will completely
depend on the holy LORD of Israel, instead of the nation[p] that defeated them.
21-22There were as many people as there
are grains of sand along the seashore,
but only a few will survive to come back
to Israel's mighty God. This is because
he has threatened to destroy their nation, just as they deserve. 23The LORD
All-Powerful has promised that everyone on this earth[q] will be punished.
24Now the LORD God All-Powerful
says to his people in Jerusalem:
The Assyrians will beat you with
sticks and abuse you, just as the
Egyptians did. But don't be afraid of
them. 25Soon I will stop being angry
with you, and I will punish them for
their crimes.[r] 26I will beat the Assyrians with a whip, as I did the people
of Midian near the rock at Oreb.
And I will show the same mighty
power that I used when I made a
path through the sea in Egypt.
27Then they will no longer rule your
nation. All will go well for you,[s] and
your burden will be lifted.

[j] **9.17** *and kept . . . against him*: Or "but even though they had turned against him, he still had not given up on them." [k] **9.20** *their own relatives*: One possible meaning for the difficult Hebrew text. [l] **10.4** *escape being captured*: One possible meaning for the difficult Hebrew text. [m] **10.4** *and he . . . yet*: Or "but he hasn't given up on you yet!" [n] **10.5** *king of Assyria*: Probably King Sennacherib who invaded Israel in 701 B.C. [o] **10.9** *already captured*: Calno (in northern Syria), Carchemish (on the Euphrates River), Hamath (on the Orontes River), Arpad (near Aleppo in northern Syria), Samaria, and Damascus had already been captured by Assyrian kings (738-717 B.C.). [p] **10.20** *nation*: That is, Assyria. [q] **10.23** *on this earth*: Or "in this land." [r] **10.25** *punish . . . crimes*: Or "completely destroy them." [s] **10.27** *All . . . you*: One possible meaning for the difficult Hebrew text.

[28]Enemy troops have reached the
town of Aiath.[t] They have gone through
Migron, and they stored their supplies
at Michmash, [29]before crossing the valley and spending the night at Geba.[u]
The people of Ramah are terrified;
everyone in Gibeah, the hometown of
Saul, has run away. [30]Loud crying can
be heard in the towns of Gallim,
Laishah, and sorrowful Anathoth. [31]No
one is left in Madmenah or Gebim. [32]To-
day the enemy will camp at Nob[v] and
shake a threatening fist at Mount Zion
in Jerusalem.

[33] But the LORD All-Powerful
will use his fearsome might
to bring down the tallest trees
and chop off every branch.
[34] With an ax, the glorious Lord
will destroy every tree
in the forests of Lebanon.[w]

Peace at Last

11 Like a branch that sprouts
from a stump,
someone from David's family[x]
will someday be king.
[2] The Spirit of the LORD
will be with him
to give him understanding,
wisdom, and insight.
He will be powerful,
and he will know
and honor the LORD.
[3] His greatest joy will be
to obey the LORD.

This king won't judge
by appearances
or listen to rumors.
[4] The poor and the needy
will be treated with fairness
and with justice.
His word will be law
everywhere in the land,
and criminals
will be put to death.
[5] Honesty and fairness
will be his royal robes.

[6] Leopards will lie down
with young goats,
and wolves will rest
with lambs.
Calves and lions
will eat together
and be cared for
by little children.
[7] Cows and bears will share
the same pasture;
their young will rest
side by side.
Lions and oxen
will both eat straw.

[8] Little children will play
near snake holes.
They will stick their hands
into dens of poisonous snakes
and never be hurt.

[9] Nothing harmful will take place
on the LORD's holy mountain.
Just as water fills the sea,
the land will be filled
with people who know
and honor the LORD.

God's People Will Come Back Home

[10]The time is coming when one of
David's descendants[y] will be the signal
for the people of all nations to come together. They will follow his advice, and
his own nation will become famous.
[11]When that day comes, the Lord will
again reach out his mighty arm and
bring home his people who have survived in Assyria, Egypt, Pathros, Ethiopia,[z] Elam, Shinar, Hamath, and the
land along the coast.[a] [12]He will give a
signal to the nations, and he will bring
together the refugees from Judah and
Israel, who have been scattered all over
the earth. [13]Israel will stop being jealous
of Judah, and Judah will no longer be
the enemy of Israel. [14]Instead, they will
get together and attack the Philistines in
the west. Then they will defeat the
Edomites, the Moabites, and the Ammonites in the east. They will rule those
people and take from them whatever
they want.
[15]The Lord will dry up the arm of the
Red Sea near Egypt,[b] and he will send a
scorching wind to divide the Euphrates
River into seven streams that anyone
can step across. [16]Then for his people
who survive, there will be a good road
from Assyria, just as there was a good
road for their ancestors when they left
Egypt.

A Song of Praise

12 At that time you will say,
"I thank you, LORD!
You were angry with me,

[t]**10.28** *Aiath*: Probably Ai (Joshua 7.2). [u]**10.29** *Geba*: Only six miles from Jerusalem. [v]**10.32** *Nob*: Perhaps within two miles of Jerusalem. [w]**10.34** *Lebanon*: One possible meaning for the difficult Hebrew text of verse 34. [x]**11.1** *David's family*: Hebrew "Jesse's family." Jesse was the father of King David. [y]**11.10** *David's descendants*: Hebrew "Jesse's descendants" (see the note at 11.1). [z]**11.11** *Ethiopia*: The Hebrew text has "Cush," which was a region south of Egypt that included parts of the present countries of Ethiopia and Sudan. [a]**11.11** *land along the coast*: Or "islands." [b]**11.15** *arm of the Red Sea near Egypt*: Gulf of Suez.

but you stopped being angry
and gave me comfort.
2 I trust you to save me,
LORD God,
and I won't be afraid.
My power and my strength[c]
come from you,
and you have saved me."

3 With great joy, you people
will get water
from the well of victory.
4 At that time you will say,
"Our LORD, we are thankful,
and we worship only you.
We will tell the nations
how glorious you are
and what you have done.
5 Because of your wonderful deeds
we will sing your praises
everywhere on earth."

6 Sing, people of Zion!
Celebrate the greatness
of the holy LORD of Israel.
God is here to help you.

Babylon Will Be Punished

13 This is the message[d] that I was
given about Babylon:
2 From high on a barren hill
give a signal, shout the orders,
and point the way
to enter the gates
of Babylon's proud rulers.
3 The LORD has commanded
his very best warriors
and his proud heroes
to show how angry he is.

4 Listen to the noisy crowds
on the mountains!
Kingdoms and nations
are joining forces.
The LORD All-Powerful
is bringing together
an army for battle.
5 From a distant land
the LORD is coming
fierce and furious—
he brings his weapons
to destroy the earth.

6 Cry and weep!
The day is coming
when the mighty LORD
will bring destruction.
*7 All people will be terrified.
Hands will grow limp;
courage will melt away.
8 Everyone will tremble with pain
like a woman giving birth;
they will stare at each other
with horror on their faces.

There Will Be No Mercy

9 I, the LORD,
will show no mercy or pity
when that time comes.
In my anger I will destroy
the earth and every sinner
who lives on it.
10 Light will disappear
from the stars in the sky;
the dawning sun will turn dark,
and the moon
will lose its glow.

11 I will punish this evil world
and its people
because of their sins.
I will crush the horrible pride
of those who are cruel.
12 Survivors will be harder to find
than the purest gold.
13 I, the LORD All-Powerful,
am terribly angry—
I will make the sky tremble
and the earth shake loose.

14 Everyone will run
to their homelands,
just as hunted deer run,
and sheep scatter
when they have no shepherd.
15 Those who are captured
will be killed by a sword.
16 They will see their children
beaten against rocks,
their homes robbed,
and their wives abused.

17 The Medes[e] can't be bought off
with silver or gold,
and I'm sending them
to attack Babylonia.
18 Their arrows will slaughter
the young men;
no pity will be shown
to babies and children.

The LORD Will Destroy Babylon

19 The city of Babylon
is glorious and powerful,
the pride of the nation.
But it will be like the cities
of Sodom and Gomorrah
after I, the Lord,
destroyed them.
20 No one will live in Babylon.
Even nomads won't camp nearby,
and shepherds won't let
their sheep rest there.
21 Only desert creatures,
hoot owls, and ostriches
will live in its ruins,
and goats[f] will leap about.

[c] **12.2** *strength*: Or "song." [d] **13.1** *message*: See the note at 1.1. [e] **13.17** *Medes*: People of a nation northeast of Babylonia, which became part of the Persian Empire. [f] **13.21** *goats*: Or "demons."

[22] Hyenas and wolves will howl
from Babylon's fortresses
and beautiful palaces.
Its time is almost up!

The LORD's People Will Come Home

14 The LORD will have mercy on Israel and will let them be his chosen people once again. He will bring them back to their own land, and foreigners will join them as part of Israel.
[2]Other nations will lead them home, and Israel will make slaves of them in the land that belongs to the Lord. Israel will rule over those who once governed and mistreated them.

Death to the King of Babylonia!

[3]The LORD will set you free from your sorrow, suffering, and slavery. [4]Then
you will make fun of the King of Babylonia by singing this song:

That cruel monster is done for!
He won't attack us again.[g]
[5] The LORD has crushed the power
of those evil kings,
[6] who were furious
and never stopped abusing
the people of other nations.

[7] Now all the world is at peace;
its people are celebrating
with joyful songs.
[8] King of Babylonia,
even the cypress trees
and the cedars of Lebanon
celebrate and say,
"Since you were put down,
no one comes along
to chop us down."

[9] The world of the dead
eagerly waits for you.
With great excitement,
the spirits of ancient rulers
hear about your coming.
[10] Each one of them will say,
"Now you are just as weak
as any of us!
[11] Your pride and your music
have ended here
in the world of the dead.
Worms are your blanket,
maggots are your bed."

[12] You, the bright morning star,
have fallen from the sky!
You brought down other nations;
now you are brought down.
[13] You said to yourself,
"I'll climb to heaven
and place my throne
above the highest stars.
I'll sit there with the gods
far away in the north.
[14] I'll be above the clouds,
just like God Most High."

[15] But now you are deep
in the world of the dead.
[16] Those who see you will stare
and wonder, "Is this the man
who made the world tremble
and shook up kingdoms?
[17] Did he capture every city
and make earth a desert?
Is he the one who refused
to let prisoners go home?"

[18] When kings die, they are buried
in glorious tombs.
[19] But you will be left unburied,
just another dead body
lying underfoot
like a broken branch.
You will be one of many
killed in battle and gone down
to the deep rocky pit.[h]
[20] You won't be buried with kings;
you ruined your country
and murdered your people.

You evil monster!
We hope that your family
will be forgotten forever.
[21] We will slaughter your sons
to make them pay for the crimes
of their ancestors.
They won't take over the world
or build cities
anywhere on this earth.

[22]The LORD All-Powerful has promised to attack Babylonia and destroy everyone there, so that none of them will ever be remembered again. [23]The LORD will sweep out the people, and the land will become a swamp for wild animals.

Assyria Will Be Punished

[24] The LORD All-Powerful
has made this promise:
Everything I have planned
will happen just as I said.
[25] I will wipe out every Assyrian
in my country,
and I will crush those
on my mountains.
I will free my people
from slavery
to the Assyrians.
[26] I have planned this
for the whole world,
and my mighty arm
controls every nation.
[27] I, the LORD All-Powerful,
have made these plans.
No one can stop me now!

[g]**14.4** *He . . . again*: One possible meaning for the difficult Hebrew text. [h]**14.19** *deep rocky pit*: The world of the dead.

The Philistines Will Be Punished

28 This message came from the LORD
in the year King Ahaz died:[i]
29 Philistines, don't be happy
just because the rod
that punished you
is broken.
That rod will become
a poisonous snake, and then
a flying fiery dragon.

30 The poor and needy will find
pastures for their sheep
and will live in safety.
But I will starve some of you,
and others will be killed.

31 Cry and weep in the gates
of your towns,
you Philistines!
Smoke blows in from the north,[j]
and every soldier is ready.
32 If a messenger comes
from a distant nation,
you must say:
"The LORD built Zion.
Even the poorest of his people
will find safety there."

Moab Will Be Punished

15 This is a message
about Moab:
The towns of Ar and Kir
were destroyed in a night.
Moab is left in ruins!
2 Everyone in Dibon has gone up
to the temple[k] and the shrines
to cry and weep.
All of Moab is crying.
Heads and beards are shaved[l]
because of what happened
at Nebo and Medeba.
3 In the towns and at home,
everyone wears sackcloth
and cries loud and long.
4 From Heshbon and Elealeh,
weeping is heard in Jahaz;
Moab's warriors scream
while trembling with fear.

Pity Moab

5 I pity Moab!
Its people are running to Zoar
and to Eglath-Shelishiyah.
They cry on their way up
to the town of Luhith;
on the road to Horonaim
they tell of disasters.
6 The streams of Nimrim
and the grasslands
have dried up.
Every plant is parched.

7 The people of Moab are leaving,
crossing over Willow Creek,
taking everything they own
and have worked for.
8 In the towns of Eglaim
and of Beerelim
and everywhere else in Moab
mournful cries are heard.
9 The streams near Dimon
are flowing with blood.
But the Lord will bring
even worse trouble to Dimon,[m]
because all in Moab who escape
will be attacked by lions.

More Troubles for Moab

16 Send lambs[n] as gifts
to the ruler of the land.
Send them across the desert
from Sela[o] to Mount Zion.
2 The women of Moab
crossing the Arnon River
are like a flock of birds
scattered from their nests.
3 Moab's messengers say
to the people of Judah,
"Be kind and help us!
Shade us from the heat
of the noon day sun.
Hide our refugees!
Don't turn them away.
4 Let our people live
in your country
and find safety here."

Moab, your cruel enemies
will disappear;
they will no longer attack
and destroy your land.
5 Then a kingdom of love
will be set up,
and someone from David's family
will rule with fairness.
He will do what is right
and quickly bring justice.

Moab's Pride Is Destroyed

6 We have heard of Moab's pride.
Its people strut and boast,
but without reason.
7 Tell everyone in Moab
to mourn for their nation.
Tell them to cry and weep
for those fancy raisins[p]
of Kir-Hareseth.

[i] **14.28** *King Ahaz died*: 715 B.C. [j] **14.31** *north*: The Assyrian and Babylonian attacks came from the north. [k] **15.2** *Everyone . . . temple*: One possible meaning for the difficult Hebrew text. [l] **15.2** *Heads . . . shaved*: As a sign of sorrow and mourning. [m] **15.9** *Dimon . . . Dimon*: The Standard Hebrew Text; the Dead Sea Scrolls and one ancient translation have *Dibon . . . Dibon.* [n] **16.1** *lambs*: The main product of Moab. [o] **16.1** *Sela*: A town in Edom. [p] **16.7** *fancy raisins*: The Hebrew text has "raisin-cakes," which could mean either the rich produce or the prosperous farmers.

[8] Vineyards near Heshbon
and Sibmah
have turned brown.
The rulers of nations
used to get drunk
on wine from those vineyards[q]
that spread to Jazer,
then across the desert
and beyond the sea.

[9] Now I mourn like Jazer
for the vineyards
of Sibmah.
I shed tears for Heshbon
and for Elealeh.
There will be no more
harvest celebrations
[10] or joyful and happy times,
while bringing in the crops.
Singing and shouting
are gone
from the vineyards.
There are no joyful shouts
where grapes were pressed.
God has silenced them all.

[11] Deep in my heart I hurt
for Moab and Kir-Heres.
[12] It's useless for Moab's people
to wear themselves out
by going to their altars
to worship and pray.

[13]The LORD has already said all of this
about Moab. [14]Now he says, "The contract of a hired worker is good for three
years, but Moab's glory and greatness
won't last any longer than that. Only a
few of its people will survive, and they
will be left helpless."

Damascus Will Be Punished

17 This is a message
about Damascus:
Damascus is doomed!
It will end up in ruins.
[2] The villages around Aroer[r]
will be deserted,
with only sheep living there
and no one to bother them.
[3] Israel[s] will lose its fortresses.
The kingdom of Damascus
will be destroyed;
its survivors will suffer
the same fate as Israel.
The LORD All-Powerful
has promised this.

Sin and Suffering

[4] When that time comes,
the glorious nation of Israel
will be brought down;
its prosperous people
will be skin and bones.
[5] Israel will be like wheat fields
in Rephaim Valley
picked clean of grain.
[6] It will be like an olive tree
beaten with a stick,
leaving two or three olives
or maybe four or five
on the highest
or most fruitful branches.
The LORD God of Israel
has promised this.

[7]At that time the people will turn and
trust their Creator, the holy God of Israel. [8]They have built altars and places
for burning incense to their goddess
Asherah, and they have set up sacred
poles[t] for her. But they will stop worshiping at these places.
[9]Israel captured powerful cities and
chased out the people who lived there.
But these cities will lie in ruins, covered
over with weeds and underbrush.[u]

[10] Israel, you have forgotten
the God who saves you,
the one who is the mighty rock[v]
where you find protection.
You plant the finest flowers
to honor a foreign god.
[11] The plants may sprout
and blossom
that very same morning,
but it will do you no good,
because you will suffer
endless agony.

God Defends His People

[12] The nations are a noisy,
thunderous sea.
[13] But even if they roar
like a fearsome flood,
God will give the command
to turn them back.
They will be like dust,
or like a tumbleweed
blowing across the hills
in a windstorm.
[14] In the evening
their attack is fierce,
but by morning
they are destroyed.
This is what happens to those
who raid and rob us.

[q] **16.8** *The rulers . . . vineyards*: Or "The rulers of nations have destroyed those vineyards."
[r] **17.2** *Aroer*: Either a city near Damascus with the same name as the Moabite city or the Moabite city itself, here used as an example of what will happen to Damascus. [s] **17.3** *Israel*: The Hebrew text has "Ephraim," another name for the northern kingdom. [t] **17.8** *sacred poles*: Or "trees," used as symbols of Asherah, the goddess of fertility. [u] **17.9** *covered . . . underbrush*: Hebrew; one ancient translation "like the cities of the Hivites and the Amorites."
[v] **17.10** *mighty rock*: The Hebrew text has "rock," which is sometimes used in poetry to compare the Lord to a mountain where his people can run for protection from their enemies.

Ethiopia Will Be Punished

18 Downstream from Ethiopia[w]
lies the country of Egypt,
swarming with insects.[x]
2 Egypt sends messengers
up the Nile River
on ships made of reeds.[y]
Send them fast to Ethiopia,
whose people are tall
and have smooth skin.
Their land is divided by rivers;
they are strong and brutal,
feared all over the world.[z]

3 Everyone on this earth,
listen with care!
A signal will be given
on the mountains,
and you will hear a trumpet.
4 The LORD said to me,
"I will calmly look down
from my home above—
as calmly as the sun at noon
or clouds in the heat
of harvest season."

5 Before the blossoms
can turn into grapes,
God will cut off the sprouts
and hack off the branches.
6 Ethiopians will be food
for mountain buzzards
during the summer
and for wild animals
during the winter.

7Those Ethiopians are tall and their
skin is smooth. They are feared all over
the world, because they are strong and
brutal. But at that time they will come
from their land divided by rivers, and
they will bring gifts to the LORD All-Powerful, who is worshiped on Mount Zion.

Egypt Will Be Punished

19 This is a message
about Egypt:
The LORD comes to Egypt,
riding swiftly on a cloud.
The people are weak from fear.
Their idols tremble
as he approaches and says,
2 "I will punish Egypt
with civil war—
neighbors, cities, and kingdoms
will fight each other.

3 "Egypt will be discouraged
when I confuse their plans.
They will try to get advice
from their idols,
from the spirits of the dead,
and from fortunetellers.
4 I will put the Egyptians
under the power of a cruel,
heartless king.
I, the LORD All-Powerful,
have promised this."

Trouble along the Nile

5 The Nile River will dry up
and become parched land.
6 Its streams will stink,
Egypt will have no water,
and the reeds and tall grass
will dry up.
7 Fields along the Nile
will be completely barren;
every plant will disappear.

8 Those who fish in the Nile
will be discouraged
and mourn.
9 None of the cloth makers[a]
will know what to do,
and they will turn pale.[b]
10 Weavers will be confused;
paid workers will cry and mourn.

Egypt's Helpless Leaders

11 The king's officials in Zoan[c]
are foolish themselves
and give stupid advice.
How can they say to him,
"We are very wise,
and our families go back
to kings of long ago?"
12 Where are those wise men now?
If they can, let them say
what the LORD All-Powerful
intends for Egypt.

13 The royal officials in Zoan
and in Memphis
are foolish and deceived.
The leaders in every state
have given bad advice
to the nation.
14 The LORD has confused Egypt;
its leaders have made it stagger
and vomit like a drunkard.
15 No one in Egypt can do a thing,
no matter who they are.

16When the LORD All-Powerful punishes Egypt with his mighty arm, the
Egyptians will become terribly weak
and will tremble with fear. 17They will
be so terrified of Judah that they will be
frightened by the very mention of its
name. This will happen because of what
the LORD All-Powerful is planning
against Egypt.

[w]18.1 *Ethiopia*: See the note at 11.11. [x]18.1 *insects*: Or "sailing ships." [y]18.2 *reeds*: Ancient Egypt was famous for the papyrus reeds that grew in the Nile Delta. [z]18.2 *world*: One possible meaning for the difficult Hebrew text of verse 2. [a]19.9 *cloth makers*: Cloth was made from several kinds of plants that grew in the fields along the Nile. [b]19.9 *turn pale*: One possible meaning for the difficult Hebrew text. [c]19.11 *Zoan*: The city of Tanis in the Nile delta.

The LORD Will Bless Egypt, Assyria, and Israel

18 The time is coming when Hebrew
will be spoken in five Egyptian cities,
and their people will become followers
of the LORD. One of these cities will be
called City of the Sun.[d]
19 In the heart of Egypt an altar will be
set up for the LORD; at its border a
shrine will be built to honor him.
20 These will remind the Egyptians that
the LORD All-Powerful is with them. And
when they are in trouble and ask for
help, he will send someone to rescue
them from their enemies. 21 The LORD
will show the Egyptians who he is, and
they will know and worship the LORD.
They will bring him sacrifices and offerings, and they will keep their promises
to him. 22 After the LORD has punished
Egypt, the people will turn to him. Then
he will answer their prayers, and the
Egyptians will be healed.
23 At that time a good road will run
from Egypt to Assyria. The Egyptians
and the Assyrians will travel back and
forth from Egypt to Assyria, and they
will worship together. 24 Israel will join
with these two countries. They will be a
blessing to everyone on earth, 25 then the
LORD All-Powerful will bless them by
saying,

"The Egyptians are my people.
I created the Assyrians
and chose the Israelites."

Isaiah Acts Out the Defeat of Egypt and Ethiopia

20 King Sargon of Assyria gave orders for his army commander to
capture the city of Ashdod.[e] 2 About this
same time the LORD had told me, "Isaiah, take off everything, including your
sandals!" I did this and went around
naked and barefoot 3 for three years.
Then the LORD said:
What Isaiah has done is a warning
to Egypt and Ethiopia.[f] 4 Everyone in
these two countries will be led away
naked and barefoot by the king of
Assyria. Young or old, they will be
taken prisoner, and Egypt will be
disgraced. 5 They will be confused
and frustrated, because they depended on Ethiopia and bragged
about Egypt. 6 When this happens,
the people who live along the coast[g]
will say, "Look what happened to
them! We ran to them for safety,
hoping they would protect us from
the king of Assyria. But now, there is
no escape for us."

The Fall of Babylonia[h]

21 This is a message about a desert
beside the sea:[i]

Enemies from a hostile nation
attack like a whirlwind
from the Southern Desert.
2 What a horrible vision
was shown to me—
a vision of betrayal
and destruction.
Tell Elam and Media[j]
to surround and attack
the Babylonians.
The LORD has sworn to end
the suffering they caused.

3 I'm in terrible pain
like a woman giving birth.
I'm shocked and hurt so much
that I can't hear or see.
4 My head spins; I'm horrified!
Early evening, my favorite time,
has become a nightmare.

5 In Babylon the high officials
were having a feast.
They were eating and drinking,
when someone shouted,
"Officers, take your places!
Grab your shields."

6 The LORD said to me,
"Send guards to find out
what's going on.
7 When they see cavalry troops
and columns of soldiers
on donkeys and camels,
tell them to be ready!"

8 Then a guard[k] said,
"I have stood day and night
on this watchtower, Lord.
9 Now I see column after column
of cavalry troops."

[d] **19.18** *City of the Sun*: Some manuscripts of the Standard Hebrew Text, the Dead Sea Scrolls, and one ancient translation; most manuscripts of the Standard Hebrew Text have "City of Destruction." This probably refers to Heliopolis which means "City of the Sun" (see Jeremiah 43.13). [e] **20.1** *Ashdod*: King Sargon II of Assyria captured this Philistine city in 711 B.C. [f] **20.3** *Ethiopia*: See the note at 11.11. [g] **20.6** *people . . . coast*: Probably the Philistines. [h] **21.1** *Babylonia*: King Cyrus and his army of Medes and Persians captured the city of Babylon in 539 B.C. [i] **21.1** *This . . . sea*: One possible meaning for the difficult Hebrew text. The prophet may be speaking of Babylonia as a desert, because of the terrible punishment God will bring on it. The southern part of Babylonia on the Persian Gulf was sometimes called "the land beside the sea." [j] **21.2** *Elam and Media*: People from the Iranian highlands; the capital of Elam was Susa, in the hill country east of Babylon. [k] **21.8** *guard*: The Dead Sea Scrolls and one ancient translation; the Standard Hebrew Text has "lion."

Right away someone shouted,
"Babylon has fallen!
Every idol in the city
lies broken on the ground."

10 Then I said, "My people,
you have suffered terribly,
but I have a message for you
from the LORD All-Powerful,
the God of Israel."

How Much Longer?

11 This is a message about Dumah:
From the country of Seir,[l]
someone shouts to me,
"Guard, how much longer
before daylight?"

12 From my guard post, I answered,
"Morning will soon be here,
but night will return.
If you want to know more,
come back later."

13 This is a message for Arabs
who live in the barren desert
in the region of Dedan:[m]
You must order your caravans
14 to bring water for those
who are thirsty.
You people of Tema[n]
must bring food
for the hungry refugees.
15 They are worn out and weary
from being chased by enemies
with swords and arrows.

16The Lord said to me:
A year from now the glory of the
people of Kedar[o] will all come to an
end, just as a worker's contract ends
after a year. 17Only a few of their
warriors will be left with bows and
arrows. This is a promise that I, the
LORD God of Israel, have made.

Trouble in Vision Valley

22 This is a message
about Vision Valley:[p]
Why are you celebrating
on the flat roofs[q]
of your houses?
2 Your city is filled
with noisy shouts.
Those who lie drunk
in your streets
were not killed in battle.
3 Your leaders ran away,
but they were captured
without a fight.
No matter how far they ran,
they were found and caught.[r]

4 Then I said, "Leave me alone!
Let me cry bitter tears.
My people have been destroyed,
so don't try to comfort me."

5 The LORD All-Powerful
had chosen a time
for noisy shouts and confusion
to fill Vision Valley,
and for everyone to beg
the mountains for help.[s]
6 The people of Elam and Kir[t]
attacked with chariots[u]
and carried shields.
7 Your most beautiful valleys
were covered with chariots;
your cities were surrounded
by cavalry troops.
8 Judah was left defenseless.

At that time you trusted in the
weapons you had stored in Forest
Palace.[v] 9You saw the holes in the outer
wall of Jerusalem, and you brought water from the lower pool.[w] 10You counted
the houses in Jerusalem and tore down
some of them, so you could get stones to
repair the city wall. 11Then you built a
large tank between the walls[x] to store
the water. But you refused to trust the
God who planned this long ago and
made it happen.

A Time To Weep

12 When all of this happened,
the LORD All-Powerful told you
to weep and mourn,
to shave your heads,
and wear sackcloth.
13 But instead, you celebrated

[l]21.11 *Dumah . . . Seir*: Dumah was an oasis in the Arabian desert. One ancient translation has "Edom," which may be what is meant. Seir is a mountainous region of Edom southwest of the Dead Sea. [m]21.13 *Dedan*: A region in northwest Arabia. [n]21.14 *Tema*: A region in north Arabia. [o]21.16 *Kedar*: A region in the Arabian desert. [p]22.1 *Vision Valley*: The exact location is not known. In Hebrew the name sounds something like "Hinnom Valley," where the people of Jerusalem sometimes offered human sacrifices to the gods of Canaan. [q]22.1 *flat roofs*: In Palestine the houses usually had a flat roof. Stairs on the outside led up to the roof, which was made of beams and boards covered with packed earth. [r]22.3 *No matter . . . caught*: One possible meaning for the difficult Hebrew text. [s]22.5 *and for . . . help*: One possible meaning for the difficult Hebrew text. [t]22.6 *Elam and Kir*: Regions in the Iranian highlands. [u]22.6 *chariots*: One possible meaning for the difficult Hebrew text. [v]22.8 *Forest Palace*: Built by Solomon (1 Kings 7.2) and used as a place for storing weapons. [w]22.9 *the lower pool*: Mentioned only here; probably in the southern part of the Central Valley (Tyropoean Valley) of Jerusalem. [x]22.11 *between the walls*: Some cities had two walls with a space between them. If the enemy broke through the outer wall, the city was still protected by the inner wall. The houses that were torn down to repair the outer wall were probably squatters' huts that had been built between the two walls.

by feasting on beef and lamb
and by drinking wine,
because you said,
"Let's eat and drink!
Tomorrow we may die."

14 The LORD All-Powerful
has spoken to me
this solemn promise:
"I won't forgive them for this,
not as long as they live."

Selfish Officials Are Doomed

15The LORD All-Powerful is sending you with this message for Shebna, the prime minister:

16Shebna, what gives you the right
to have a tomb carved out of rock in
this burial place of royalty? None of
your relatives are buried here. 17You
may be powerful, but the LORD is
about to snatch you up and throw
you away. 18He will roll you into a
ball and throw you into a wide open
country, where you will die and your
chariots will be destroyed. You're a
disgrace to those you serve.

19The LORD is going to take away
your job! 20-21He will give your official robes and your authority to his
servant Eliakim son of Hilkiah.

Eliakim will be like a father to the
people of Jerusalem and to the royal
family of Judah. 22The LORD will put
him in charge of the key that belongs to King David's family. No one
will be able to unlock what he locks,
and no one will be able to lock what
he unlocks. 23The LORD will make
him as firm in his position as a tent
peg hammered in the ground, and
Eliakim will bring honor to his family.

24His children and relatives will be
supported by him, like pans hanging
from a peg on the wall. 25That peg is
fastened firmly now, but someday it
will be shaken loose and fall down.
Then everything that was hanging
on it will be destroyed. This is what
the LORD All-Powerful has promised.

The City of Tyre Will Be Punished

23 This is a message
from distant islands
about the city of Tyre:[y]
Cry, you seagoing ships![z]
Tyre and its houses
lie in ruins.[a]
2 Mourn in silence,
you shop owners of Sidon,[b]
you people on the coast.
Your sailors crossed oceans,
making your city rich.
3 Your merchants sailed the seas,
making you wealthy by trading
with nation after nation.
They brought back grain
that grew along the Nile.[c]
4 Sidon, you are a mighty fortress
built along the sea.
But you will be disgraced
like a married woman
who never had children.[d]

5 When Egypt hears about Tyre,
it will tremble.
6 All of you along the coast
had better cry and sail
far across the ocean.[e]
7 Can this be the happy city
that has stood for centuries?
Its people have spread
to distant lands;
8 its merchants were kings
honored all over the world.
Who planned to destroy Tyre?
9 The LORD All-Powerful planned it
to bring shame and disgrace
to those who are honored
by everyone on earth.
10 People of Tyre,[f]
your harbor is destroyed!
You will have to become farmers
just like the Egyptians.[g]

Tyre Will Be Forgotten

11 The LORD's hand has reached
across the sea,
upsetting the nations.
He has given a command
to destroy fortresses
in the land of Canaan.
12 The LORD has said
to the people of Sidon,
"Your celebrating is over—
you are crushed.
Even if you escape to Cyprus,
you won't find peace."

13Look what the Assyrians have done
to Babylonia! They have attacked, destroying every palace in the land. Now
wild animals live among the ruins.[h]

[y]**23.1** *Tyre*: A fortress city built on an island in the Mediterranean Sea off the coast of what is now Lebanon. [z]**23.1** *seagoing ships*: See the note at 2.16. [a]**23.1** *Tyre . . . ruins*: One possible meaning for the difficult Hebrew text. [b]**23.2** *Sidon*: A coastal city just north of Tyre. [c]**23.3** *along the Nile*: The Hebrew text has "grain of Shihor, the harvest of the Nile," but Shihor is probably a name for a region near the lower part of the Nile. [d]**23.4** *children*: One possible meaning for the difficult Hebrew text. [e]**23.6** *far across the ocean*: The Hebrew text has "to Tarshish," probably meaning a long distance. [f]**23.10** *People of Tyre*: The Hebrew text has "the people of Tarshish," which stands for the colonies of Tyre. [g]**23.10** *Egyptians*: One possible meaning for the difficult Hebrew text of verse 10. [h]**23.13** *ruins*: One possible meaning for the difficult Hebrew text of verse 13.

14Not a fortress will be left standing, so tell all the seagoing ships[i] to mourn.
15The city of Tyre will be forgotten for seventy years, which is the lifetime of a king. Then Tyre will be like that evil woman in the song:

16 You're gone and forgotten,
you evil woman!
So strut through the town,
singing and playing
your favorite tune
to be remembered again.

17At the end of those seventy years,
the LORD will let Tyre get back into business. The city will be like a woman who sells her body to everyone of every nation on earth,
18but none of what is
earned will be kept in the city. That money will belong to the LORD, and it will be used to buy more than enough food and good clothes for those who worship the LORD.

The Earth Will Be Punished

24 The LORD is going to twist the earth out of shape and turn it into a desert. Everyone will be scattered,
2including ordinary people and priests, slaves and slave owners, buyers and sellers, lenders and borrowers, the rich and the poor.
3The earth will be stripped
bare and left that way. This is what the LORD has promised.

4 The earth wilts away;
its mighty leaders melt
to nothing.[j]
5 The earth is polluted
because its people
disobeyed the laws of God,
breaking their agreement
that was to last forever.

6 The earth is under a curse;
its people are dying out
because of their sins.
7 Grapevines have dried up;
wine is almost gone—
mournful sounds are heard
instead of joyful shouts.

8 No one plays tambourines
or stringed instruments;
all noisy celebrating
has come to an end.
9 They no longer sing
as they drink their wine,
and it tastes sour.

10 Towns are crushed and in chaos;
houses are locked tight.
11 Happy times have disappeared
from the earth,
and people shout in the streets,
"We're out of wine!"
12 Cities are destroyed;
their gates are torn down.
13 Nations will be stripped bare,
like olive trees or vineyards
after the harvest season.

Praise the God of Justice

14 People in the west shout;
they joyfully praise
the majesty of the LORD.
15 And so, everyone in the east
and those on the islands
should praise the LORD,
the God of Israel.
16 From all over the world
songs of praise are heard
for the God of justice.[k]
But I feel awful,
terribly miserable.
Can anyone be trusted?
So many are treacherous!

There's No Escape

17 Terror, traps, and pits
are waiting for everyone.
18 If you are terrified and run,
you will fall into a pit;
if you crawl out of the pit,
you will get caught in a trap.

The sky has split apart
like a window thrown open.
The foundations of the earth
have been shaken;
19 the earth is shattered,
ripped to pieces.
20 It staggers and shakes
like a drunkard
or a hut in a windstorm.
It is burdened down with sin;
the earth will fall,
never again to get up.

21 On that day the LORD
will punish the powers
in the heavens[l]
and the kings of the earth.
22 He will put them in a pit
and keep them prisoner.
Then later on,
he will punish them.
23 The moon and sun will both
be embarrassed and ashamed.
The LORD All-Powerful will rule
on Mount Zion in Jerusalem,
where he will show its rulers
his wonderful glory.

[i]23.14 *seagoing ships*: See the note at 2.16. [j]24.4 *its . . . to nothing*: One possible meaning for the difficult Hebrew text. [k]24.16 *God of justice*: Or "people who do right."
[l]24.21 *the powers in the heavens*: In ancient times the stars were thought of as powerful spiritual beings, and sometimes they stood for pagan gods.

A Prayer of Thanks to God

25 You, LORD, are my God!
I will praise you
for doing the wonderful things
you had planned and promised
since ancient times.
2 You have destroyed the fortress
of our enemies,
leaving their city in ruins.
Nothing in that foreign city
will ever be rebuilt.
3 Now strong and cruel nations
will fear and honor you.

4 You have been a place of safety
for the poor and needy
in times of trouble.
Brutal enemies pounded us
like a heavy rain
or the heat of the sun at noon,
but you were our shelter.
5 Those wild foreigners struck
like scorching desert heat.
But you were like a cloud,
protecting us from the sun.
You kept our enemies from singing
songs of victory.

The LORD Has Saved Us

6 On this mountain
the LORD All-Powerful
will prepare for all nations
a feast of the finest foods.
Choice wines and the best meats
will be served.
7 Here the LORD will strip away
the burial clothes
that cover the nations.
8 The LORD All-Powerful
will destroy the power of death
and wipe away all tears.
No longer will his people
be insulted everywhere.
The LORD has spoken!

9 At that time, people will say,
"The LORD has saved us!
Let's celebrate.
We waited and hoped—
now our God is here."
10 The powerful arm of the LORD
will protect this mountain.

The Moabites will be put down
and trampled on like straw
in a pit of manure.
11 They will struggle to get out,
but God will humiliate them
no matter how hard they try.[m]
12 The walls of their fortresses
will be knocked down
and scattered in the dirt.

A Song of Victory

26 The time is coming
when the people of Judah
will sing this song:
"Our city[n] is protected.
The LORD is our fortress,
and he gives us victory.
2 Open the city gates
for a law-abiding nation
that is faithful to God.
3 The LORD gives perfect peace
to those whose faith is firm.
4 So always trust the LORD
because he is forever
our mighty rock.[o]
5 God has put down our enemies
in their mountain city[p]
and rubbed it in the dirt.
6 Now the poor and abused
stomp all over that city."

The LORD Can Be Trusted

7 Our LORD, you always do right,
and you make the path smooth
for those who obey you.
8 You are the one we trust
to bring about justice;
above all else we want
your name to be honored.
9 Throughout the night,
my heart searches for you,
because your decisions
show everyone on this earth
how to live right.

10 Even when the wicked
are treated with mercy
in this land of justice,
they do wrong and are blind
to your glory, our LORD.
11 Your hand is raised and ready
to punish them,
but they don't see it.
Put them to shame!
Show how much you care for us
and throw them into the fire
intended for your enemies.

12 You will give us peace, LORD,
because everything we have done
was by your power.
13 Others have ruled over us
besides you, our LORD God,
but we obey only you.
14 Those enemies are now dead
and can never live again.
You have punished them—
they are destroyed,
completely forgotten.
15 Our nation has grown
because of you, our LORD.
We have more land than before,
and you are honored.

[m]**25.11** *no matter . . . try*: One possible meaning for the difficult Hebrew text. [n]**26.1** *city*: Probably Jerusalem. [o]**26.4** *mighty rock*: See the note at 17.10. [p]**26.5** *our enemies . . . city*: One possible meaning for the difficult Hebrew text.

The LORD Gives Life to the Dead

16 When you punished our people,
they turned and prayed
to you, our LORD.[q]
17 Because of what you did to us,
we suffered like a woman
about to give birth.
18 But instead of having a child,
our terrible pain
produced only wind.
We have won no victories,
and we have no descendants
to take over the earth.

19 Your people will rise to life!
Tell them to leave their graves
and celebrate with shouts.
You refresh the earth
like morning dew;
you give life to the dead.

20 Go inside and lock the doors,
my people.
Hide there for a little while,
until the LORD
is no longer angry.

The Earth and the Sea Will Be Punished

21 The LORD will come out
to punish everyone on earth
for their sins.
And when he does,
those who did violent crimes
will be known and punished.

27 On that day, Leviathan,[r]
the sea monster,
will squirm and try to escape,
but the LORD will kill him
with a cruel, sharp sword.

Protection and Forgiveness

The LORD said:
2 At that time you must sing
about a fruitful[s] vineyard.
3 I, the LORD, will protect it
and always keep it watered.
I will guard it day and night
to keep it from harm.
4 I am no longer angry.
But if it produces thorns,
I will go to war against it
and burn it to the ground.
5 Yet if the vineyard depends
on me for protection,
it will become my friend
and be at peace with me.

6 Someday Israel will take root
like a vine.
It will blossom and bear fruit
that covers the earth.

7 I, the LORD, didn't punish and kill
the people of Israel
as fiercely as I punished
and killed their enemies.
8 I carefully measured out
Israel's punishment[t]
and sent the scorching heat
to chase them far away.

9 There's only one way
that Israel's sin and guilt
can be completely forgiven:
They must crush the stones
of every pagan altar
and place of worship.

The LORD Will Bring His People Together

10 Fortress cities are left
like a desert
where no one lives.
Cattle walk through the ruins,
stripping the trees bare.
11 When broken branches
fall to the ground,
women pick them up
to feed the fire.
But these people are so stupid
that the God who created them
will show them no mercy.

12The time is coming when the LORD
will shake the land between the Euphrates River and the border of Egypt,
and one by one he will bring all of his
people together. 13A loud trumpet will
be heard. Then the people of Israel who
were dragged away to Assyria and
Egypt will return to worship the LORD
on his holy mountain in Jerusalem.

Samaria Will Be Punished

28 The city of Samaria
above a fertile valley
is in for trouble!
Its leaders are drunkards,
who stuff themselves
with food and wine.
But they will be like flowers
that dry up and wilt.
2 Only the Lord is strong
and powerful!
His mighty hand
will strike them down
with the force of a hailstorm
or a mighty whirlwind
or an overwhelming flood.

3 Every drunkard in Ephraim[u]
takes pride in Samaria,
but it will be crushed.

[q]**26.16** *LORD*: One possible meaning for the difficult Hebrew text of verse 16.
[r]**27.1** *Leviathan*: God's victory over this monster sometimes stands for God's power over all creation and sometimes for his defeat of his enemies, especially Egypt. [s]**27.2** *fruitful*: Some Hebrew manuscripts have "lovely." [t]**27.8** *I . . . punishment*: One possible meaning for the difficult Hebrew text. [u]**28.3** *Ephraim*: The northern kingdom of Israel; Samaria was its capital.

[4] Samaria above a fertile valley
will quickly lose its glory.
It will be gobbled down
like the first ripe fig
at harvest season.

[5] When this time comes,
the LORD All-Powerful
will be a glorious crown
for his people who survive.
[6] He will see that justice rules
and that his people are able
to defend their cities.

Corrupt Leaders Will Be Punished

[7] Priests and prophets stumble
because they are drunk.
Their minds are too confused
to receive God's messages
or give honest decisions.
[8] Their tables are covered,
completely covered,
with their stinking vomit.

[9] You drunken leaders
are like babies!
How can you possibly understand
or teach the LORD's message?
[10] You don't even listen—
all you hear is senseless sound
after senseless sound.[v]

[11] So, the Lord will speak
to his people
in strange sounds
and foreign languages.[w]
[12] He promised you
perfect peace and rest,
but you refused to listen.
[13] Now his message to you
will be senseless sound
after senseless sound.[x]
Then you will fall backwards,
injured and trapped.

False Security Is Fatal

[14] You rulers of Jerusalem
do nothing but sneer;
now you must listen
to what the LORD says.
[15] Do you think you have
an agreement with death
and the world of the dead?
Why do you trust in your lies
to keep you safe from danger
and the mighty flood?

[16] And so the LORD says,
"I'm laying a firm foundation
for the city of Zion.
It's a valuable cornerstone
proven to be trustworthy;
no one who trusts it
will ever be disappointed.
[17] Justice and fairness
will be the measuring lines
that help me build."

Hailstones and floods
will destroy and wash away
your shelter of lies.
[18] Your agreement with death
and the world of the dead
will be broken.
Then angry, roaring waves
will sweep over you.
[19] Morning, noon, and night
an overwhelming flood
will wash you away.
The terrible things that happen
will teach you this lesson:
[20] Your bed is too short,
your blanket too skimpy.[y]

[21] The LORD will fiercely attack
as he did at Mount Perazim[z]
and in Gibeon Valley.[a]
But this time the LORD
will do something surprising,
not what you expect.
[22] So you had better stop sneering
or you will be in worse shape
than ever before.
I heard the LORD All-Powerful
threaten the whole country
with destruction.

All Wisdom Comes from the LORD

[23] Pay close attention
to what I am saying.
[24] Farmers don't just plow
and break up the ground.
[25] When a field is ready,
they scatter the seeds
of dill and cumin;
they plant the seeds
of wheat and barley
in the proper places.
[26] They learn this from their God.

[27] After dill and cumin
have been harvested,
the stalks are pounded,
not run over with a wagon.
[28] Wheat and barley are pounded,
but not beaten to pulp;
they are run over with a wagon,
but not ground to dust.
[29] This wonderful knowledge comes
from the LORD All-Powerful,
who has such great wisdom.

[v]**28.10** *sound*: One possible meaning for the difficult Hebrew text of verses 9, 10. [w]**28.11** *in . . . foreign languages*: This probably refers to the language of the Assyrians. [x]**28.13** *Now . . . sound*: One possible meaning for the difficult Hebrew text. [y]**28.20** *Your bed . . . skimpy*: Isaiah quotes a popular saying to teach that the treaty made with Egypt (verse 18) cannot give the nation security from its enemies. [z]**28.21** *Mount Perazim*: This may refer to David's defeat of the Philistines at Baal Perazim (2 Samuel 5.17-21). [a]**28.21** *Gibeon Valley*: This refers to Joshua's victory at Gibeon (Joshua 10.1-11).

Jerusalem Will Suffer

The LORD *said:*

29 Jerusalem, city of David,
the place of my altar,[b]
you are in for trouble!
Celebrate your festivals
year after year.
2 I will still make you suffer,
and your people will cry
when I make an altar of you.[c]
3 I will surround you and prepare
to attack from all sides.[d]
4 From deep in the earth,
you will call out for help
with only a faint whisper.

5 Then your cruel enemies
will suddenly be swept away
like dust in a windstorm.
6 I, the LORD All-Powerful,
will come to your rescue
with a thundering earthquake
and a fiery whirlwind.

7 Every brutal nation
that attacks Jerusalem
and makes it suffer
will disappear like a dream
when night is over.
8 Those nations that attack
Mount Zion
will suffer from hunger
and thirst.
They will dream of food and drink
but wake up weary and hungry
and thirsty as ever.

Prophets Who Fool Themselves

9 Be shocked and stunned,
you prophets!
Refuse to see.
Get drunk and stagger,
but not from wine.
10 The LORD has made you drowsy;
he put you into a deep sleep
and covered your head.

11 Now his message is like a sealed letter to you. Some of you say, "We can't
read it, because it's sealed." 12 Others
say, "We can't read it, because we don't
know how to read."

13 The Lord has said:

"These people praise me
with their words,
but they never really
think about me.
They worship me by repeating
rules made up by humans.
14 So once again I will do things
that shock and amaze them,
and I will destroy the wisdom
of those who claim to know
and understand."

15 You are in for trouble,
if you try to hide your plans
from the LORD!
Or if you think what you do
in the dark can't be seen.
16 You have it all backwards.
A clay dish doesn't say
to the potter,
"You didn't make me.
You don't even know how."

Hope for the Future

17 Soon the forest of Lebanon
will become a field with crops,
thick as a forest.[e]
18 The deaf will be able to hear
whatever is read to them;
the blind will be freed
from a life of darkness.
19 The poor and the needy
will celebrate and shout
because of the LORD,
the holy God of Israel.

20 All who are cruel and arrogant
will be gone forever.
Those who live by crime
will disappear,
21 together with everyone
who tells lies in court
and keeps innocent people
from getting a fair trial.

22 The LORD who rescued Abraham
has this to say
about Jacob's descendants:
"They will no longer
be ashamed and disgraced.
23 When they see how great
I have made their nation,
they will praise and honor me,
the holy God of Israel.
24 Everyone who is confused
will understand,
and all who have complained
will obey my teaching."

Don't Expect Help from Egypt

30 This is the LORD's message
for his rebellious people:
"You follow your own plans
instead of mine;
you make treaties
without asking me,
and you keep on sinning.
2 You trust Egypt for protection.
So you refuse my advice

[b]29.1 *the place of my altar*: One possible meaning for "ariel, ariel" of the Hebrew text. In Hebrew "ariel" can mean "God's hero" or "God's lion" or "God's altar." [c]29.2 *when . . . you*: One possible meaning for the difficult Hebrew text. [d]29.3 *from all sides*: One possible meaning for the difficult Hebrew text. One ancient translation has "like David." [e]29.17 *with . . . forest*: Or "and Mount Carmel will be covered with forests."

and send messengers to Egypt
to beg their king for help.

3 You will be disappointed,
completely disgraced
for trusting Egypt.
4 The king's power reaches
from the city of Zoan
as far south as Hanes.[f]
5 But Egypt can't protect you,
and to trust that nation
is useless and foolish.

6 This is a message
about the animals
of the Southern Desert:
You people carry treasures
on donkeys and camels.
You travel to a feeble nation
through a troublesome desert
filled with lions
and flying fiery dragons.
7 Egypt can't help you!
That's why I call that nation
a helpless monster.[g]

Israel Refuses To Listen

8The LORD told me to write down his
message for his people, so that it would
be there forever. 9They have turned
against the LORD and can't be trusted.
They have refused his teaching 10and
have said to his messengers and
prophets:

Don't tell us what God has shown
you and don't preach the truth. Just
say what we want to hear, even if it's
false. 11Stop telling us what God has
said! We don't want to hear any
more about the holy God of Israel.

12 Now this is the answer
of the holy God of Israel:
"You rejected my message,
and you trust in violence
and lies.
13 This sin is like a crack
that makes a high wall
quickly crumble 14and shatter
like a crushed bowl.
There's not a piece left
big enough to carry hot coals
or to dip out water."

Trust the LORD

15 The holy LORD God of Israel
had told all of you,
"I will keep you safe
if you turn back to me
and calm down.
I will make you strong
if you quietly trust me."
Then you stubbornly 16said,
"No! We will safely escape
on speedy horses."

But those who chase you
will be even faster.
17 As few as five of them,
or even one, will be enough
to chase a thousand of you.
Finally, all that will be left
will be a few survivors
as lonely as a flag pole
on a barren hill.

The LORD Will Show Mercy

18 The LORD God is waiting
to show how kind he is
and to have pity on you.
The LORD always does right;
he blesses those who trust him.

19People of Jerusalem, you don't need
to cry anymore. The Lord is kind, and as
soon as he hears your cries for help, he
will come. 20The Lord has given you
trouble and sorrow as your food and
drink. But now you will again see the
Lord, your teacher, and he will guide
you. 21Whether you turn to the right or
to the left, you will hear a voice saying,
"This is the road! Now follow it." 22Then
you will treat your idols of silver and
gold like garbage; you will throw them
away like filthy rags.

23The Lord will send rain to water the
seeds you have planted—your fields will
produce more crops than you need, and
your cattle will graze in open pastures.
24Even the oxen and donkeys that plow
your fields will be fed the finest grain.[h]

25On that day people will be slaughtered and towers destroyed, but streams
of water will flow from high hills and
towering mountains. 26Then the LORD
will bandage his people's injuries and
heal the wounds he has caused. The
moon will shine as bright as the sun,
and the sun will shine seven times
brighter than usual. It will be like the
light of seven days all at once.

Assyria Will Be Punished

27 The LORD is coming
from far away
with his fiery anger
and thick clouds of smoke.[i]
His angry words flame up
like a destructive fire;
28 he breathes out a flood
that comes up to the neck.
He sifts the nations
and destroys them.

[f]**30.4** *Zoan . . . Hanes*: Or "Your messengers have reached the city of Zoan and gone as far as Hanes." Zoan was in northeast Egypt; Hanes was to the south. [g]**30.7** *a helpless monster*: One possible meaning for the difficult Hebrew text. [h]**30.24** *the finest grain*: The Hebrew text refers to grain with the husks removed. [i]**30.27** *with . . . smoke*: One possible meaning for the difficult Hebrew text.

Then he puts a bridle
in every foreigner's mouth
and leads them to doom.

29The LORD's people will sing as they do when they celebrate a religious festival[j] at night. The LORD is Israel's mighty rock,[k] and his people will be as happy as they are when they follow the sound of flutes to the mountain where he is worshiped.

30The LORD will get furious. His fearsome voice will be heard, his arm will be seen ready to strike, and his anger will be like a destructive fire, followed by thunderstorms and hailstones.
31When the Assyrians hear the LORD's voice and see him striking with his iron rod, they will be terrified. 32He will attack them in battle, and each time he strikes them, it will be to the music of tambourines and harps.

33Long ago the LORD got a place ready for burning the body of the dead king.[l] The place for the fire is deep and wide, the wood is piled high, and the LORD will start the fire by breathing out flaming sulfur.

Don't Trust the Power of Egypt

31 You are in for trouble
if you go to Egypt for help,
or if you depend on
an army of chariots
or a powerful cavalry.
Instead you should depend on
and trust the holy LORD God
of Israel.
2 The LORD isn't stupid!
He does what he promises,
and he can bring doom.
If you are cruel yourself,
or help those who are evil,
you will be destroyed.

3 The Egyptians are mere humans.
They aren't God.
Their horses are made of flesh;
they can't live forever.
When the LORD shows his power,
he will destroy the Egyptians
and all who depend on them.
Together they will fall.

4 The LORD All-Powerful
said to me,
"I will roar and attack
like a fearless lion
not frightened by the shouts
of shepherds trying to protect
their sheep.
That's how I will come down
and fight on Mount Zion.
5 I, the LORD All-Powerful,
will protect Jerusalem
like a mother bird circling
over her nest."

Come Back to the LORD

6 People of Israel, come back!
You have completely turned
from the LORD.
7 The time is coming
when you will throw away
your idols of silver and gold,
made by your sinful hands.

8 The Assyrians will be killed,
but not by the swords
of humans.
Their young men will try
to escape,
but they will be captured
and forced into slavery.
9 Their fortress[m] will fall
when terror strikes;
their army officers
will be frightened
and run from the battle.
This is what the LORD has said,
the LORD whose fiery furnace
is built on Mount Zion.

Justice Will Rule

32 A king and his leaders
will rule with justice.
2 They will be a place of safety
from stormy winds,
a stream in the desert,
and a rock that gives shade
from the heat of the sun.
3 Then everyone who has eyes
will open them and see,
and those who have ears
will pay attention.
4 All who are impatient
will take time to think;
everyone who stutters
will talk clearly.

5 Fools will no longer
be highly respected,
and crooks won't be given
positions of honor.
6 Fools talk foolishness.
They always make plans
to do sinful things,
to lie about the LORD,
to let the hungry starve,
and to keep water from those
who are thirsty.
7 Cruel people tell lies—
they do evil things,
and make cruel plans

[j]**30.29** *a religious festival*: Probably Passover. [k]**30.29** *mighty rock*: See the note at 17.10. [l]**30.33** *burning . . . king*: Or "sacrificing the king" or "sacrificing to Molech." Human sacrifices were sometimes offered to Molech, a god whose name sounds like the Hebrew word for "king" (see 2 Kings 23.10; Jeremiah 32.35). [m]**31.9** *fortress*: The Hebrew text has "rock," which may refer to the Assyrian god or king, or to their army.

to destroy the poor and needy,
even when they beg
for justice.
8 But helpful people
can always be trusted
to make helpful plans.

Punishment for the Women of Jerusalem

9 Listen to what I say,
you women who are carefree
and careless!
10 You may not have worries now,
but in about a year,
the grape harvest will fail,
and you will tremble.

11 Shake and shudder,
you women without a care!
Strip off your clothes—
put on sackcloth.
12 Slap your breasts in sorrow
because of what happened
to the fruitful fields
and vineyards,
13 and to the happy homes
in Jerusalem.
The land of my people
is covered with thorns.

14 The palace will be deserted,
the crowded city empty.
Fortresses and towers
will forever become
playgrounds for wild donkeys
and pastures for sheep.

God's Spirit Makes the Difference

15 When the Spirit is given to us
from heaven,
deserts will become orchards
thick as fertile forests.
16 Honesty and justice
will prosper there,
17 and justice will produce
lasting peace and security.

18 You, the LORD's people,
will live in peace,
calm and secure,
19 even if hailstones flatten
forests and cities.
20 You will have God's blessing,
as you plant your crops
beside streams,
while your donkeys and cattle
roam freely about.

Jerusalem Will Be Safe

33 You defeated my people.
Now you're in for trouble!
You've never been destroyed,
but you will be destroyed;
you've never been betrayed,
but you will be betrayed.
When you have finished
destroying and betraying,
you will be destroyed
and betrayed in return.

2 Please, LORD, be kind to us!
We depend on you.
Make us strong each morning,
and come to save us
when we are in trouble.
3 Nations scatter when you roar
and show your greatness.[n]
4 We attack our enemies
like swarms of locusts;[o]
we take everything
that belongs to them.[p]

5 You, LORD, are above all others,
and you live in the heavens.
You have brought justice
and fairness to Jerusalem;
6 you are the foundation
on which we stand today.
You always save us and give
true wisdom and knowledge.
Nothing means more to us[q]
than obeying you.

The LORD Will Do Something

7 Listen! Our bravest soldiers
are running through the streets,
screaming for help.[r]
Our messengers hoped for peace,
but came home crying.
8 No one travels anymore;
every road is empty.
Treaties are broken,
and no respect is shown
to any who keep promises.[s]
9 Fields are dry and barren;
Mount Lebanon wilts
with shame.
Sharon Valley is a desert;
the forests of Bashan and Carmel
have lost their leaves.

10 But the LORD says,
"Now I will do something
and be greatly praised.
11 Your deeds are straw
that will be set on fire
by your very own breath.
12 You will be burned to ashes
like thorns in a fire.
13 Everyone, both far and near,
come look at what I have done.
See my mighty power!"

[n] **33.3** *greatness*: One possible meaning for the difficult Hebrew text of verse 3.
[o] **33.4** *locusts*: Insects like grasshoppers that travel in swarms and cause great damage to crops.
[p] **33.4** *them*: One possible meaning for the difficult Hebrew text of verse 4. [q] **33.6** *Nothing . . . us*: One possible meaning for the difficult Hebrew text. [r] **33.7** *Listen . . . help*: Or "The LORD heard our shouts and will come to help us." [s] **33.8** *to any . . . promises*: The Dead Sea Scrolls; the Standard Hebrew Text "to those in the cities."

Punishment and Rewards

14 Those terrible sinners
on Mount Zion tremble
as they ask in fear,
"How can we possibly live
where a raging fire
never stops burning?"

15 But there will be rewards
for those who live right
and tell the truth,
for those who refuse
to take money by force
or accept bribes,
for all who hate murder
and violent crimes.
16 They will live in a fortress
high on a rocky cliff,
where they will have food
and plenty of water.

The LORD Is Our King

17 With your own eyes
you will see the glorious King;
you will see his kingdom
reaching far and wide.
18 Then you will ask yourself,
"Where are those officials
who terrified us and forced us
to pay such heavy taxes?"
19 You will never again have to see
the proud people who spoke
a strange and foreign language
you could not understand.

20 Look to Mount Zion
where we celebrate
our religious festivals.
You will see Jerusalem,
secure as a tent with pegs
that cannot be pulled up
and fastened with ropes
that can never be broken.
21 Our wonderful LORD
will be with us!
There will be deep rivers
and wide streams
safe from enemy ships.[t]

The LORD Is Our Judge

22 The LORD is our judge
and our ruler;
the LORD is our king
and will keep us safe.
23 But your nation[u] is a ship
with its rigging loose,
its mast shaky,
and its sail not spread.

Someday even you that are lame
will take everything you want
from your enemies.
24 The LORD will forgive your sins,
and none of you will say,
"I feel sick."

The Nations Will Be Judged

34 Everyone of every nation,
the entire earth,
and all of its creatures,
come here and listen!
2 The LORD is terribly angry
with the nations;
he has condemned them
to be slaughtered.
3 Their dead bodies will be left
to rot and stink;
their blood will flow
down the mountains.
4 Each star[v] will disappear—
the sky will roll up
like a scroll.[w]
Everything in the sky
will dry up and wilt
like leaves on a vine
or fruit on a tree.

Trouble for Edom

5 After the sword of the LORD
has done what it wants
to the skies above,[x]
it will come down on Edom,
the nation that the LORD
has doomed for destruction.

6 The sword of the LORD
is covered with blood
from lambs and goats,
together with fat
from kidneys of rams.
This is because the LORD
will slaughter many people
and make a sacrifice of them
in the city of Bozrah
and everywhere else
in Edom.
7 Edom's leaders are wild oxen.
They are powerful bulls,
but they will die
with the others.
Their country will be soaked
with their blood,
and its soil made fertile
with their fat.

8 The LORD has chosen
the year and the day,
when he will take revenge
and come to Zion's defense.
9 Edom's streams will turn into tar
and its soil into sulfur—
then the whole country
will go up in flames.

[t]**33.21** *safe . . . ships*: This probably means that Jerusalem will have a lot of water, without the danger of attacks from enemy ships. [u]**33.23** *your nation*: Possibly Judah or Assyria. [v]**34.4** *star*: Stars were worshiped as gods. [w]**34.4** *scroll*: A roll of paper or specially prepared leather used for writing on. [x]**34.5** *has done . . . above*: The Standard Hebrew Text; the Dead Sea Scrolls "appears in the skies above."

10 It will burn night and day
and never stop smoking.
Edom will be a desert,
generation after generation;
no one will ever travel
through that land.
11 Owls, hawks, and wild animals[y]
will make it their home.
God will leave it in ruins,
merely a pile of rocks.

The End of Edom

12 Edom will be called
"Kingdom of Nothing."
Its rulers will also be nothing.
13 Its palaces and fortresses
will be covered with thorns;
only wolves and ostriches
will make their home there.
14 Wildcats and hyenas
will hunt together,
demons will scream to demons,
and creatures of the night
will live among the ruins.
15 Owls will nest there
to raise their young
among its shadows,[z]
while families of buzzards
circle around.

16 In *The Book of the* LORD[a]
you can search and find
where it is written,
"The LORD brought together
all of his creatures
by the power of his Spirit.
Not one is missing."
17 The LORD has decided
where they each should live;
they will be there forever,
generation after generation.

God's Splendor Will Be Seen

35 Thirsty deserts will be glad;
barren lands will celebrate
and blossom with flowers.
2 Deserts will bloom everywhere
and sing joyful songs.
They will be as majestic
as Mount Lebanon,
as glorious as Mount Carmel
or Sharon Valley.
Everyone will see
the wonderful splendor
of the LORD our God.

God Changes Everything

*3 Here is a message for all
who are weak, trembling,
and worried:
4 "Cheer up! Don't be afraid.
Your God is coming
to punish your enemies.
God will take revenge on them
and rescue you."

5 The blind will see,
and the ears of the deaf
will be healed.
6 Those who were lame
will leap around like deer;
tongues once silent
will begin to shout.
Water will rush
through the desert.
7 Scorching sand
will turn into a lake,
and thirsty ground
will flow with fountains.
Grass will grow in wetlands,
where packs of wild dogs
once made their home.[b]

God's Sacred Highway

8 A good road will be there,
and it will be named
"God's Sacred Highway."
It will be for God's people;
no one unfit to worship God
will walk on that road.
And no fools can travel
on that highway.[c]
9 No lions or other wild animals
will come near that road;
only those the LORD has saved
will travel there.

10 The people the LORD has rescued
will come back singing
as they enter Zion.
Happiness will be a crown
they will always wear.
They will celebrate and shout
because all sorrows and worries
will be gone far away.

The Assyrians Surround Jerusalem

(2 Kings 18.13-27; 2 Chronicles 32.1-19)

36 Hezekiah had been king of Judah
for fourteen years when King
Sennacherib of Assyria invaded the
country and captured every walled city
2 except Jerusalem. The Assyrian king
ordered his army commander to leave
the city of Lachish and to take a large
army to Jerusalem.
The commander went there and stood
on the road near the cloth makers'
shops along the canal from the upper
pool. 3 Three of the king's highest officials came out of Jerusalem to meet

[y] 34.11 *Owls . . . animals*: One possible meaning for the difficult Hebrew text. [z] 34.15 *Owls . . . shadows*: One possible meaning for the difficult Hebrew text. [a] 34.16 *The Book of the* LORD: The book that Isaiah refers to is unknown. [b] 35.7 *where . . . home*: One possible meaning for the difficult Hebrew text. [c] 35.8 *And . . . highway*: Or "And not even a fool can miss that highway."

him. One of them was Hilkiah's son Eliakim, who was the prime minister. The
other two were Shebna, assistant to the
prime minister, and Joah son of Asaph,
keeper of the government records.
4The Assyrian commander told them:
I have a message for Hezekiah
from the great king of Assyria. Ask
Hezekiah why he feels so sure of
himself. 5Does he think he can plan
and win a war with nothing but
words? Who is going to help him,
now that he has turned against the
king of Assyria? 6Is he depending on
Egypt and its king? That's the same
as leaning on a broken stick, and it
will go right through his hand.
7Is Hezekiah now depending on
the LORD, your God? Didn't
Hezekiah tear down all except one
of the LORD's altars and places of
worship?[d] Didn't he tell the people
of Jerusalem and Judah to worship
at that one place?
8The king of Assyria wants to
make a bet with you people! He will
give you two thousand horses, if you
have enough troops to ride them.
9How could you even defeat our lowest ranking officer, when you have to
depend on Egypt for chariots and
cavalry? 10Don't forget that it was
the LORD who sent me here with orders to destroy your nation!
11Eliakim, Shebna, and Joah said, "Sir,
we don't want the people listening from
the city wall to understand what you are
saying. So please speak to us in Aramaic instead of Hebrew."
12The Assyrian army commander answered, "My king sent me to speak to
everyone, not just to you leaders. These
people will soon have to eat their own
body waste and drink their own urine!
And so will the three of you!"
13Then, in a voice loud enough for
everyone to hear, he shouted out in Hebrew:
Listen to what the great king of
Assyria says! 14Don't be fooled by
Hezekiah. He can't save you. 15Don't
trust him when he tells you that the
LORD will protect you from the king
of Assyria. 16Stop listening to
Hezekiah. Pay attention to my king.
Surrender to him. He will let you
keep your own vineyards, fig trees,
and cisterns 17for a while. Then he
will come and take you away to a
country just like yours, where you
can plant vineyards and raise your
own grain.
18Hezekiah claims the LORD will
save you. But don't be fooled by him.
Were any other gods able to defend
their land against the king of Assyria? 19What happened to the gods
of Hamath, Arpad, and Sepharvaim?
Were the gods of Samaria able to
protect their land against the Assyrian forces? 20None of these gods
kept their people safe from the king
of Assyria. Do you think the LORD,
your God, can do any better?
21-22Eliakim, Shebna, and Joah had
been warned by King Hezekiah not to
answer the Assyrian commander. So
they tore their clothes in sorrow and reported to Hezekiah everything the commander had said.

Hezekiah Asks Isaiah for Advice

(2 Kings 19.1-13)

37 As soon as Hezekiah heard the
news, he tore off his clothes in
sorrow and put on sackcloth. Then he
went into the temple of the LORD. 2He
told Prime Minister Eliakim, Assistant
Prime Minister Shebna, and the senior
priests to dress in sackcloth and tell me:
3Isaiah, these are difficult and disgraceful times. Our nation is like a
woman too weak to give birth, when
it's time for her baby to be born.
4Please pray for those of us who are
left alive. The king of Assyria sent
his army commander to insult the
living God. Perhaps the LORD heard
what he said and will do something,
if you will pray.
5When these leaders came to me, 6I
told them that the LORD had this message for Hezekiah:
I am the LORD. Don't worry about
the insulting things that have been
said about me by these messengers
from the king of Assyria. 7I will upset him with rumors about what's
happening in his own country. He
will go back, and there I will make
him die a violent death.
8Meanwhile the commander of the
Assyrian forces heard that his king had
left the town of Lachish and was now
attacking Libnah. So he went there.
9About this same time, the king of Assyria learned that King Tirhakah of
Ethiopia[e] was on his way to attack him.
Then the king of Assyria sent some
messengers with this note for Hezekiah:
10Don't trust your God or be
fooled by his promise to defend
Jerusalem against me. 11You have
heard how we Assyrian kings have

[d]**36.7** *worship*: Hezekiah actually had torn down the places where idols were worshiped, and he had told the people to worship the LORD at the one place of worship in Jerusalem. But the Assyrian leader was confused and thought these were also places where the LORD was supposed to be worshiped. [e]**37.9** *Ethiopia*: See the note at 11.11.

completely wiped out other nations.
What makes you feel so safe? 12The
Assyrian kings before me destroyed
the towns of Gozan, Haran, Rezeph,
and everyone from Eden who lived
in Telassar. What good did their
gods do them? 13The kings of
Hamath, Arpad, Sepharvaim, Hena,
and Ivvah have all disappeared.

Hezekiah Prays
(2 Kings 19.14-19)

14After Hezekiah had read the note
from the king of Assyria, he took it to
the temple and spread it out for the
LORD to see. 15Then he prayed:
16LORD God All-Powerful of Israel,
your throne is above the winged
creatures.[f] You created the heavens
and the earth, and you alone rule the
kingdoms of this world. 17Just look
and see how Sennacherib has insulted you, the living God.
18It is true, our LORD, that Assyrian
kings have turned nations into
deserts. 19They destroyed the idols of
wood and stone that the people of
those nations had made and worshiped. 20But you are our LORD and
our God! We ask you to keep us safe
from the Assyrian king. Then everyone in every kingdom on earth will
know that you are the only LORD.

Isaiah Gives the LORD's Answer to Hezekiah
(2 Kings 19.20-34)

21-22I went to Hezekiah and told him
that the LORD God of Israel had said:
Hezekiah, you prayed to me about
King Sennacherib of Assyria.[g] Now
this is what I say to that king:

The people of Jerusalem
hate and make fun of you;
they laugh behind your back.

23 Sennacherib, you cursed,
shouted, and sneered at me,
the holy God of Israel.
24 You let your officials
insult me, the Lord.
And here is what you
have said about yourself,
"I led my chariots
to the highest heights
of Lebanon's mountains.
I went deep into its forest,
cutting down the best cedar
and cypress trees.
25 I dried up every stream
in the land of Egypt,
and I drank water
from wells I had dug."

26 Sennacherib, now listen
to me, the LORD.
I planned all of this long ago.
And you don't even know
that I alone am the one
who decided that you
would do these things.
I let you make ruins
of fortified cities.
27 Their people became weak,
terribly confused.
They were like wild flowers
or like tender young grass
growing on a flat roof
or like a field of grain
before it matures.[h]

28 I know all about you,
even how fiercely angry
you are with me.
29 I have seen your pride
and the tremendous hatred
you have for me.
Now I will put a hook
in your nose,
a bit in your mouth,[i]
then I will send you back
to where you came from.

30Hezekiah, I will tell you what's
going to happen. This year you will
eat crops that grow on their own,
and the next year you will eat whatever springs up where those crops
grew. But the third year, you will
plant grain and vineyards, and you
will eat what you harvest. 31Those
who survive in Judah will be like a
vine that puts down deep roots and
bears fruit. 32I, the LORD All-Powerful, will see to it that some who live
in Jerusalem will survive.
33I promise that the king of Assyria won't get into Jerusalem, or
shoot an arrow into the city, or even
surround it and prepare to attack.
34As surely as I am the LORD, he will
return by the way he came and will
never enter Jerusalem. 35I will protect it for the sake of my own honor
and because of the promise I made
to my servant David.

[f]**37.16** *winged creatures*: Two winged creatures made of gold were on the top of the sacred chest and were symbols of the LORD's throne on earth (see Exodus 25.18; 2 Samuel 6.2).
[g]**37.21,22** *Hezekiah, you prayed . . . Assyria*: One possible meaning for the difficult Hebrew text. [h]**37.27** *tender young grass . . . matures*: The Standard Hebrew Text; the Dead Sea Scrolls and some Hebrew manuscripts "tender young grass, growing on a flat roof and scorched by the heat." Many of the houses had roofs made of packed earth. Grass would sometimes grow on the roof, but would die quickly because of the sun and hot winds.
[i]**37.29** *I will put . . . your mouth*: This is how the Assyrians treated their prisoners, and now the LORD will treat Sennacherib the same way.

The Death of King Sennacherib
(2 Kings 19.35-37)

36The LORD sent an angel to the camp
of the Assyrians, and he killed one hundred eighty-five thousand of them all in
one night. The next morning, the camp
was full of dead bodies. 37After this,
King Sennacherib went back to Assyria
and lived in the city of Nineveh. 38One
day he was worshiping in the temple of
his god Nisroch, when his sons, Adrammelech and Sharezer, killed him with
their swords. They escaped to the land
of Ararat, and his son Esarhaddon became king.[j]

Hezekiah Gets Sick and Almost Dies
(2 Kings 20.1-11; 2 Chronicles 32.24-26)

38 About this time, Hezekiah got sick and was almost dead. So I went in and told him, "The LORD says you won't ever get well. You are going to die, and so you had better start doing what needs to be done."

2Hezekiah turned toward the wall and
prayed, 3"Don't forget that I have been
faithful to you, LORD. I have obeyed you
with all my heart, and I do whatever you
say is right." After this, he cried hard.
4Then the LORD sent me 5with this
message for Hezekiah:

I am the LORD God, who was worshiped by your ancestor David. I
heard you pray, and I saw you cry. I
will let you live fifteen years more,
6while I protect you and your city
from the king of Assyria.

7Now I will prove to you that I will
keep my promise. 8Do you see the
shadow made by the setting sun on
the stairway built for King Ahaz? I
will make the shadow go back ten
steps.

Then the shadow went back ten steps.[k]

King Hezekiah's Song of Praise

9This is what Hezekiah wrote after he got well:

10 I thought I would die
during my best years
and stay as a prisoner forever
in the world of the dead.
11 I thought I would never again
see you, my LORD,
or any of the people
who live on this earth.
12 My life was taken from me
like the tent that a shepherd
pulls up and moves.
You cut me off like thread
from a weaver's loom;
you make a wreck of me
day and night.

13 Until morning came, I thought
you would crush my bones
just like a hungry lion;
both night and day
you make a wreck of me.[l]
14 I cry like a swallow;
I mourn like a dove.
My eyes are red
from looking to you, LORD.
I am terribly abused.
Please come and help me.[m]
15 There's nothing I can say
in answer to you,
since you are the one
who has done this to me.[n]
My life has turned sour;
I will limp until I die.

16 Your words and your deeds
bring life to everyone,
including me.[o]
Please make me healthy
and strong again.
17 It was for my own good
that I had such hard times.
But your love protected me
from doom in the deep pit,[p]
and you turned your eyes
away from my sins.

18 No one in the world of the dead
can thank you or praise you;
none of those in the deep pit
can hope for you to show them
how faithful you are.
19 Only the living can thank you,
as I am doing today.
Each generation tells the next
about your faithfulness.[q]

20 You, LORD, will save me,
and every day that we live
we will sing in your temple
to the music
of stringed instruments.

Isaiah's Advice to Hezekiah

21I had told King Hezekiah's servants
to put some mashed figs on the king's
open sore, and he would get well.
22Then Hezekiah asked for proof that he
would again worship in the LORD's temple.

[j]37.38 *Esarhaddon became king*: He ruled Assyria 681-669 B.C. [k]38.8 *steps*: One possible meaning for the difficult Hebrew text of verse 8. [l]38.13 *of me*: One possible meaning for the difficult Hebrew text of verse 13. [m]38.14 *help me*: One possible meaning for the difficult Hebrew text of verse 14. [n]38.15 *There's . . . me*: One possible meaning for the difficult Hebrew text. [o]38.16 *Your . . . me*: One possible meaning for the difficult Hebrew text. [p]38.17 *deep pit*: The world of the dead, as in verse 18. [q]38.19 *about your faithfulness*: One possible meaning for the difficult Hebrew text.

Isaiah Speaks the LORD's Message to Hezekiah

(2 Kings 20.12-19)

39 Merodach Baladan, the son of
Baladan, was now king of Babylonia. And when he learned that
Hezekiah was well, he sent messengers
with letters and a gift for him. 2 Hezekiah welcomed the messengers and
showed them all the silver, the gold, the
spices, and the fine oils that were in his
storehouse. He even showed them
where he kept his weapons. Nothing in
his palace or in his entire kingdom was
kept hidden from them.
3 I asked Hezekiah, "Where did these
men come from? What did they want?"
"They came all the way from Babylonia," Hezekiah answered.
4 "What did you show them?" I asked.
Hezekiah answered, "I showed them
everything in my kingdom."
5 Then I told Hezekiah:
I have a message for you from the
LORD All-Powerful. 6 One day everything you and your ancestors have
stored up will be taken to Babylonia.
The LORD has promised that nothing
will be left. 7 Some of your own sons
will be taken to Babylonia, where
they will be disgraced and made to
serve in the king's palace.
8 Hezekiah thought, "At least our nation will be at peace for a while." So he
told me, "The message you brought
from the LORD is good."

Encourage God's People

40 Our God has said:
"Encourage my people!
Give them comfort.
2 Speak kindly to Jerusalem
and announce:
Your slavery is past;
your punishment is over.
I, the LORD, made you pay
double for your sins."

3 Someone is shouting:
"Clear a path in the desert!
Make a straight road
for the LORD our God.
4 Fill in the valleys;
flatten every hill
and mountain.
Level the rough
and rugged ground.
5 Then the glory of the LORD
will appear for all to see.
The LORD has promised this!"

6 Someone told me to shout,
and I asked,
"What should I shout?"
We humans are merely grass,
and we last no longer
than wild flowers.
7 At the LORD's command,
flowers and grass disappear,
and so do we.
8 Flowers and grass fade away,
but what our God has said
will never change.

Your God Is Here!

9 There is good news
for the city of Zion.
Shout it as loud as you can[r]
from the highest mountain.
Don't be afraid to shout
to the towns of Judah,
"Your God is here!"
10 Look! The powerful LORD God
is coming to rule
with his mighty arm.
He brings with him
what he has taken in war,
and he rewards his people.
11 The LORD cares for his nation,
just as shepherds care
for their flocks.
He carries the lambs
in his arms,
while gently leading
the mother sheep.

Who Compares with God?

12 Did any of you measure
the ocean by yourself
or stretch out the sky
with your own hands?
Did you put the soil
of the earth in a bucket
or weigh the hills and mountains
on balance scales?

13 Has anyone told the LORD[s]
what he must do
or given him advice?
14 Did the LORD ask anyone
to teach him wisdom
and justice?
Who gave him knowledge
and understanding?
15 To the LORD, all nations
are merely a drop in a bucket
or dust on balance scales;
all of the islands
are but a handful of sand.
16 The cattle
on Lebanon's mountains
would not be enough to offer
as a sacrifice to God,
and the trees would not
be enough for the fire.
17 God thinks of the nations
as far less than nothing.

[r] **40.9** *There . . . can*: Or "City of Jerusalem, you have good news. Shout it as loud as you can."
[s] **40.13** *the LORD*: Or "the LORD's Spirit."

18 Who compares with God?
Is anything like him?
19 Is an idol at all like God?
It is made of bronze
with a thin layer of gold,
and decorated with silver.
20 Or special wood may be chosen[t]
because it doesn't rot—
then skilled hands
take care to make an idol
that won't fall on its face.

God Rules the Whole Earth

21 Don't you know?
Haven't you heard?
Isn't it clear that God
created the world?[u]
22 God is the one who rules
the whole earth,
and we that live here
are merely insects.
He spread out the heavens
like a curtain or an open tent.

23 God brings down rulers
and turns them into nothing.
24 They are like flowers
freshly sprung up
and starting to grow.
But when God blows on them,
they wilt and are carried off
like straw in a storm.

25 The holy God asks,
"Who compares with me?
Is anyone my equal?"

26 Look at the evening sky!
Who created the stars?
Who gave them each a name?
Who leads them like an army?
The LORD is so powerful
that none of the stars
are ever missing.

The LORD Gives Strength

27 You people of Israel, say,
"God pays no attention to us!
He doesn't care if we
are treated unjustly."

But how can you say that?
28 Don't you know?
Haven't you heard?
The LORD is the eternal God,
Creator of the earth.
He never gets weary or tired;
his wisdom cannot be measured.

29 The LORD gives strength
to those who are weary.
30 Even young people get tired,
then stumble and fall.
31 But those who trust the LORD
will find new strength.
They will be strong like eagles
soaring upward on wings;
they will walk and run
without getting tired.

The LORD Controls Human Events

41 Be silent and listen,
every island in the sea.
Have courage and come near,
every one of you nations.
Let's settle this matter!
2 Who appointed this ruler
from the east?[v]
Who puts nations and kings
in his power?[w]
His sword and his arrows
turn them to dust
blown by the wind.
3 He goes after them so quickly
that his feet
barely touch the ground—
he doesn't even get hurt.

4 Who makes these things happen?
Who controls human events?
I do! I am the LORD.
I was there at the beginning;
I will be there at the end.
5 Islands and foreign nations
saw what I did and trembled
as they came near.

What Can Idols Do?

6 Worshipers of idols
comfort each other,
saying, "Don't worry!"
7 Woodcarvers, goldsmiths,
and other workers[x]
encourage one another and say,
"We've done a great job!"
Then they nail the idol down,
so it won't fall over.

The LORD's Chosen Servant

8 Israel, you are my servant.
I chose you, the family
of my friend Abraham.
9 From far across the earth
I brought you here and said,
"You are my chosen servant.
I haven't forgotten you."

10 Don't be afraid. I am with you.
Don't tremble with fear.
I am your God.
I will make you strong,

[t]**40.20** *Or . . . chosen*: One possible meaning for the difficult Hebrew text. Two kinds of idols seem to be described: bronze idols covered with gold (verse 19) and wooden idols (verse 20). [u]**40.21** *Isn't . . . world*: Or "Hasn't it been clear since the time of creation?" [v]**41.2** *ruler from the east*: Probably Cyrus (see 44.28; 45.1; 48.14). [w]**41.2** *Who puts . . . power*: One possible meaning for the difficult Hebrew text. [x]**41.7** *and other workers*: One possible meaning for the difficult Hebrew text.

as I protect you with my arm
and give you victories.
11 Everyone who hates you
will be terribly disgraced;
those who attack
will vanish into thin air.
12 You will look around
for those brutal enemies,
but you won't find them
because they will be gone.

13 I am the LORD your God.
I am holding your hand,
so don't be afraid.
I am here to help you.

14 People of Israel, don't worry,
though others may say,
"Israel is only a worm!"
I am the holy God of Israel,
who saves and protects you.
15 I will let you be like a log
covered with sharp spikes.[y]
You will grind and crush
every mountain and hill[z]
until they turn to dust.
16 A strong wind will scatter them
in all directions.
Then you will celebrate
and praise me, your LORD,
the holy God of Israel.

The LORD Helps the Poor

17 When the poor and needy
are dying of thirst
and cannot find water,
I, the LORD God of Israel,
will come to their rescue.
I won't forget them.
18 I will make rivers flow
on mountain peaks.
I will send streams
to fill the valleys.
Dry and barren land
will flow with springs
and become a lake.
19 I will fill the desert
with all kinds of trees—
cedars, acacias, and myrtles;
olive and cypress trees;
fir trees and pines.
20 Everyone will see this
and know that I,
the holy LORD God of Israel,
created it all.

Idols Are Useless

21 I am the LORD,
the King of Israel!
Come argue your case with me.
Present your evidence.
22 Come near me, you idols.[a]
Tell us about the past,
and we will think about it.
Tell us about the future,
so we will know
what is going to happen.
23 Prove that you are gods
by making your predictions
come true.
Do something good or evil,
so we can be amazed
and terrified.[b]
24 You idols are nothing,
and you are powerless.[c]
To worship you
would be disgusting.

25 I, the LORD, appointed a ruler
in the north;
now he comes from the east
to honor my name.
He tramples[d] kings like mud,
as potters trample clay.[e]
26 Did any of you idols predict
what would happen?
Did any of you get it right?
None of you told about this
or even spoke a word.
27 I was the first to tell
the people of Jerusalem,
"Look, it's happening!"[f]
I was the one who announced
this good news to Zion.

28 None of these idols
are able to give advice
or answer questions.
29 They are nothing,[g]
and they can do nothing—
they are less
than a passing breeze.

The LORD's Servant

42 Here is my servant!
I have made him strong.
He is my chosen one;
I am pleased with him.
I have given him my Spirit,
and he will bring justice
to the nations.
2 He won't shout or yell
or call out in the streets.
3 He won't break off a bent reed
or put out a dying flame,
but he will make sure
that justice is done.

[y]**41.15** *I will let . . . sharp spikes*: In ancient times a heavy object was sometimes dragged over wheat or barley to separate the grain from the husk. This was called threshing.
[z]**41.15** *mountain and hill*: These stand for the power and pride of Israel's enemies.
[a]**41.22** *Come near . . . idols*: One possible meaning for the difficult Hebrew text.
[b]**41.23** *and terrified*: Or "when we see it."
[c]**41.24** *powerless*: One possible meaning for the difficult Hebrew text.
[d]**41.25** *tramples*: One possible meaning for the difficult Hebrew text.
[e]**41.25** *trample clay*: This was done to soften the clay and make it easier to shape.
[f]**41.27** *Look . . . happening*: One possible meaning for the difficult Hebrew text.
[g]**41.29** *nothing*: One possible meaning for the difficult Hebrew text.

4 He won't quit or give up
until he brings justice
everywhere on earth,
and people in foreign nations
long for his teaching.

5 I am the LORD God.
I created the heavens
like an open tent above.
I made the earth and everything
that grows on it.
I am the source of life
for all who live on this earth,
so listen to what I say.
6 I chose you to bring justice,
and I am here at your side.
I selected and sent you[h]
to bring light
and my promise of hope
to the nations.
7 You will give sight
to the blind;
you will set prisoners free
from dark dungeons.

8 My name is the LORD!
I won't let idols or humans
share my glory and praise.
9 Everything has happened
just as I said it would;
now I will announce
what will happen next.

Sing Praises to the LORD

10 Tell the whole world to sing
a new song to the LORD!
Tell those who sail the ocean
and those who live far away
to join in the praise.
11 Tell the tribes of the desert
and everyone in the mountains[i]
to celebrate and sing.
12 Let them announce
his praises everywhere.
13 The LORD is marching out
like an angry soldier,
shouting with all his might
while attacking his enemies.

The LORD Will Help His People

14 For a long time, I, the LORD,
have held my temper;
now I will scream and groan
like a woman giving birth.
15 I will destroy the mountains
and what grows on them;
I will dry up rivers and ponds.

16 I will lead the blind on roads
they have never known;
I will guide them on paths
they have never traveled.
Their road is dark and rough,
but I will give light
to keep them from stumbling.
This is my solemn promise.

17 Everyone who worships idols
as though they were gods
will be terribly ashamed.

God's People Won't Obey

18 You people are deaf and blind,
but the LORD commands you
to listen and to see.
19 No one is as blind or deaf
as his messenger,
his chosen servant,
20 who sees and hears so much,
but pays no attention.

21 The LORD always does right,
and so he wanted his Law
to be greatly praised.[j]
22 But his people were trapped
and imprisoned in holes
with no one to rescue them.
All they owned had been taken,
and no one was willing
to give it back.
23 Why won't his people
ever learn to listen?

24 Israel sinned and refused
to obey the LORD
or follow his instructions.
So the LORD let them be robbed
of everything they owned.
25 He was furious with them
and punished their nation
with the fires of war.
Still they paid no attention.
They didn't even care
when they were surrounded
and scorched by flames.

The LORD Has Rescued His People

43 Descendants of Jacob,
I, the LORD, created you
and formed your nation.
Israel, don't be afraid.
I have rescued you.
I have called you by name;
now you belong to me.
2 When you cross deep rivers,
I will be with you,
and you won't drown.
When you walk through fire,
you won't be burned
or scorched by the flames.

3 I am the LORD, your God,
the Holy One of Israel,
the God who saves you.

[h]**42.6** *I selected . . . you*: One possible meaning for the difficult Hebrew text. [i]**42.11** *desert . . . mountains*: The Hebrew text includes the place names of Kedar in the desert and Sela in the mountains. [j]**42.21** *greatly praised*: One possible meaning for the difficult Hebrew text of verse 21.

I gave up Egypt, Ethiopia,[k]
and the region of Seba[l]
in exchange for you.
4 To me, you are very dear,
and I love you.
That's why I gave up nations
and people to rescue you.

5 Don't be afraid! I am with you.
From both east and west
I will bring you together.
6 I will say to the north
and to the south,
"Free my sons and daughters!
Let them return
from distant lands.
7 They are my people—
I created each of them
to bring honor to me."

The LORD Alone Is God

The LORD said:
8 Bring my people together.
They have eyes and ears,
but they can't see or hear.
9 Tell everyone of every nation
to gather around.
None of them can honestly say,
"We told you so!"
If someone heard them say this,
then tell us about it now.

10 My people, you are my witnesses
and my chosen servant.
I want you to know me,
to trust me, and understand
that I alone am God.
I have always been God;
there can be no others.

11 I alone am the LORD;
only I can rescue you.
12 I promised to save you,
and I kept my promise.
You are my witnesses
that no other god did this.
I, the LORD, have spoken.
13 I am God now and forever.
No one can snatch you from me
or stand in my way.

The LORD Will Prepare the Way

14 I, the LORD, will rescue you!
I am Israel's holy God,
and this is my promise:
For your sake, I will send
an army against Babylon
to drag its people away,
crying as they go.[m]

15 I am the LORD, your holy God,
Israel's Creator and King.
16 I am the one who cut a path
through the mighty ocean.
17 I sent an army to chase you
with chariots and horses;
now they lie dead,
unable to move.
They are like an oil lamp
with the flame snuffed out.

Forget the Past

The LORD said:
18 Forget what happened long ago!
Don't think about the past.
19 I am creating something new.
There it is! Do you see it?
I have put roads in deserts,
streams[n] in thirsty lands.
20 Every wild animal honors me,
even jackals[o] and owls.
I provide water in deserts—
streams in thirsty lands
for my chosen people.
21 I made them my own nation,
so they would praise me.

22 I, the LORD, said to Israel:
You have become weary,
but not from worshiping me.
23 You have not honored me
by sacrificing sheep
or other animals.
And I have not burdened you
with demands for sacrifices
or sweet-smelling incense.

24 You have not brought
delicious spices for me
or given me the best part
of your sacrificed animals.
Instead, you burden me down
with your terrible sins.
25 But I wipe away your sins
because of who I am.
And so, I will forget
the wrongs you have done.

26 Meet me in court!
State your case and prove
that you are right.
27 Your earliest ancestor[p]
and all of your leaders[q]
rebelled against me.
28 That's why I don't allow
your priests to serve me;
I let Israel be destroyed
and your people disgraced.

The LORD's Promise to Israel

44 People of Israel,
I have chosen you
as my servant.
2 I am your Creator.

[k]43.3 *Ethiopia*: See the note at 11.11. [l]43.3 *Seba*: A region in southwest Arabia. Egypt, Ethiopia, and Seba probably stood for all that was known of Africa in biblical times. [m]43.14 *crying as they go*: Or "in their glorious ships." [n]43.19 *streams*: The Standard Hebrew Text; the Dead Sea Scrolls "paths." [o]43.20 *jackals*: Desert animals related to wolves, but smaller. [p]43.27 *earliest ancestor*: Jacob, also known as Israel. [q]43.27 *leaders*: Probably prophets, but perhaps also priests and kings.

You were in my care
even before you were born.
Israel, don't be terrified!
You are my chosen servant,
my very favorite.[r]

3 I will bless the thirsty land
by sending streams of water;
I will bless your descendants
by giving them my Spirit.
4 They will spring up like grass[s]
or like willow trees
near flowing streams.
5 They will worship me
and become my people.
They will write my name
on the back of their hands.[t]

6 I am the LORD All-Powerful,
the first and the last,
the one and only God.
Israel, I have rescued you!
I am your King.
7 Can anyone compare with me?
If so, let them speak up
and tell me now.
Let them say what has happened
since I made my nation
long ago,
and let them tell
what is going to happen.[u]
8 Don't tremble with fear!
Didn't I tell you long ago?
Didn't you hear me?
I alone am God—
no one else is a mighty rock.[v]

Idols Can't Do a Thing

The LORD said:
9 Those people who make idols
are nothing themselves,
and the idols they treasure
are just as worthless.
Worshipers of idols are blind,
stupid, and foolish.
10 Why make an idol or an image
that can't do a thing?
11 Everyone who makes idols
and all who worship them
are mere humans,
who will end up
sadly disappointed.
Let them face me in court
and be terrified.

Idols and Firewood

12 A metalworker shapes an idol
by using a hammer[w]
and heat from the fire.
In his powerful hand
he holds a hammer,
as he pounds the metal
into the proper shape.
But he gets hungry and thirsty
and loses his strength.

13 Some woodcarver measures
a piece of wood,
then draws an outline.
The idol is carefully carved
with each detail exact.
At last it looks like a person
and is placed in a temple.
14 Either cedar, cypress, oak,
or any tree from the forest
may be chosen.
Or even a pine tree planted
by the woodcarver
and watered by the rain.

15 Some of the wood is used
to make a fire for heating
or for cooking.
One piece is made into an idol,
then the woodcarver bows down
and worships it.
16 He enjoys the warm fire
and the meat that was roasted
over the burning coals.
17 Afterwards, he bows down
to worship the wooden idol.
"Protect me!" he says.
"You are my god."

18 Those who worship idols are stupid
and blind! 19 They don't have enough
sense to say to themselves, "I made a
fire with half of the wood and cooked
my bread and meat on it. Then I made
something worthless with the other half.
Why worship a block of wood?"
20 How can anyone be stupid enough
to trust something that can be burned to
ashes?[x] No one can save themselves
like that. Don't they realize that the
idols they hold in their hands are not really gods?

The LORD Won't Forget His People

21 People of Israel,
you are my servant,
so remember all of this.
Israel, I created you,
and you are my servant.
I won't forget you.[y]
22 Turn back to me!
I have rescued you
and swept away your sins
as though they were clouds.

[r] **44.2** *my very favorite*: Or "Jeshurun." [s] **44.4** *like grass*: One possible meaning for the difficult Hebrew text. [t] **44.5** *write . . . hands*: To show that they belong to the LORD and to Israel. [u] **44.7** *Let them say . . . happen*: One possible meaning for the difficult Hebrew text. [v] **44.8** *mighty rock*: See the note at 17.10. [w] **44.12** *by using a hammer*: One possible meaning for the difficult Hebrew text. [x] **44.20** *How . . . ashes*: One possible meaning for the difficult Hebrew text. [y] **44.21** *I won't forget you*: One possible meaning for the difficult Hebrew text.

Sing Praises to the LORD

23 Tell the heavens and the earth
to start singing!
Tell the mountains
and every tree in the forest
to join in the song!
The LORD has rescued his people;
now they will worship him.

The LORD Created Everything

24 Israel, I am your LORD.
I am your source of life,
and I have rescued you.
I created everything
from the sky above
to the earth below.

25 I make liars of false prophets
and fools of fortunetellers.
I take human wisdom
and turn it into nonsense.
26 I will make the message
of my prophets come true.
They are saying, "Jerusalem
will be filled with people,
and the LORD will rebuild
the towns of Judah."

27 I am the one who commands
the sea and its streams
to run dry.
28 I am also the one who says,
"Cyrus will lead my people
and obey my orders.
Jerusalem and the temple
will be rebuilt."

Cyrus Obeys the LORD's Commands

45 The LORD said to Cyrus,
his chosen one:
I have taken hold
of your right hand
to help you capture nations
and remove kings from power.
City gates will open for you;
not one will stay closed.
2 As I lead you,
I will level mountains[z]
and break the iron bars
on bronze gates of cities.

3 I will give you treasures
hidden in dark
and secret places.
Then you will know that I,
the LORD God of Israel,
have called you by name.
4 Cyrus, you don't even know me!
But I have called you by name
and highly honored you[a]
because of Israel,
my chosen servant.

5 Only I am the LORD!
There are no other gods.
I have made you strong,
though you don't know me.
6 Now everyone from east to west
will learn that I am the LORD.
No other gods are real.
7 I create light and darkness,
happiness and sorrow.
I, the LORD, do all of this.

8 Tell the heavens
to send down justice
like showers of rain.
Prepare the earth
for my saving power
to sprout and produce justice
that I, the LORD, create.[b]

The LORD's Mighty Power

The LORD said:
9 Israel, you have no right
to argue with your Creator.
You are merely a clay pot
shaped by a potter.
The clay doesn't ask,
"Why did you make me this way?
Where are the handles?"
10 Children don't have the right
to demand of their parents,
"What have you done
to make us what we are?"

11 I am the LORD, the Creator,
the holy God of Israel.
Do you dare question me
about my own nation
or about what I have done?
12 I created the world
and covered it with people;
I stretched out the sky
and filled it with stars.
13 I have done the right thing
by placing Cyrus in power,
and I will make the roads easy
for him to follow.
I am the LORD All-Powerful!
Cyrus will rebuild my city
and set my people free
without being paid a thing.
I, the LORD, have spoken.

The LORD Alone Can Save

14 My people, I, the LORD, promise
that the riches of Egypt
and the treasures of Ethiopia[c]
will belong to you.
You will force into slavery
those tall people of Seba.[d]

They will bow down and say,
"The only true God is with you;
there are no other gods."

[z]**45.2** *mountains*: The Dead Sea Scrolls and one ancient translation; the Standard Hebrew Text "rising waves." [a]**45.4** *But . . . you*: One possible meaning for the difficult Hebrew text.
[b]**45.8** *Prepare . . . create*: One possible meaning for the difficult Hebrew text.
[c]**45.14** *Ethiopia*: See the note at 11.11. [d]**45.14** *Seba*: See the note at 43.3.

15 People of Israel,
your God is a mystery,
though he alone can save.
16 Anyone who makes idols
will be confused
and terribly disgraced.
17 But Israel, I, the LORD,
will always keep you safe
and free from shame.

Everyone Is Invited

18 The LORD alone is God!
He created the heavens
and made a world
where people can live,
instead of creating
an empty desert.
The LORD alone is God;
there are no others.
19 The LORD did not speak
in a dark secret place
or command Jacob's descendants
to search for him in vain.

The LORD speaks the truth,
and this is what he says
20 to every survivor
from every nation:
"Gather around me!
Learn how senseless it is
to worship wooden idols
or pray to helpless gods.

21 "Why don't you get together
and meet me in court?
Didn't I tell you long ago
what would happen?
I am the only God!
There are no others.
I bring about justice,
and have the power to save.

22 "I invite the whole world
to turn to me and be saved.
I alone am God!
No others are real.
23 I have made a solemn promise,
one that won't be broken:
Everyone will bow down
and worship me.
24 They will admit that I alone
can bring about justice.
Everyone who is angry with me
will be terribly ashamed
and will turn to me.
25 I, the LORD, will give
victory and great honor
to the people of Israel."

Babylonia's Gods Are Helpless

The LORD said:

46 The gods Bel and Nebo[e]
are down on their knees,
as wooden images of them
are carried away
on weary animals.[f]
2 They are down on their knees
to rescue the heavy load,
but the images are still taken
to a foreign country.

3 You survivors in Israel,
listen to me, the LORD.
Since the day you were born,
I have carried you along.
4 I will still be the same
when you are old and gray,
and I will take care of you.
I created you. I will carry you
and always keep you safe.

5 Can anyone compare with me?
Is anyone my equal?
6 Some people hire a goldsmith
and give silver and gold
to be formed into an idol
for them to worship.
7 They carry the idol
on their shoulders,
then put it on a stand,
but it cannot move.

They call out to the idol
when they are in trouble,
but it doesn't answer,
and it cannot help.
8 Now keep this in mind,[g]
you sinful people.
And don't ever forget it.

The LORD Alone Is God

9 I alone am God!
There are no other gods;
no one is like me.
Think about what happened
many years ago.
10 From the very beginning,
I told what would happen
long before it took place.

I kept my word 11and brought
someone from a distant land
to do what I wanted.
He attacked from the east,
like a hawk swooping down.
Now I will keep my promise
and do what I planned.

12 You people are stubborn
and far from being safe,
so listen to me.
13 I will soon come to save you.
I am not far away
and will waste no time;
I take pride in Israel
and will save Jerusalem.

[e]**46.1** *Bel and Nebo*: Bel was another name for Marduk, the chief god of the Babylonians. Nebo was the son of Marduk and also an important god. [f]**46.1** *as . . . animals*: One possible meaning for the difficult Hebrew text. [g]**46.8** *Now . . . mind*: One possible meaning for the difficult Hebrew text.

Babylon Will Fall

The LORD *said:*

47 City of Babylon,
You are delicate
and untouched,
but that will change.
Surrender your royal power
and sit in the dirt.
2 Start grinding grain!
Take off your veil.
Strip off your fancy clothes
and cross over rivers.[h]
3 You will suffer the shame
of going naked,
because I will take revenge,
and no one can escape.[i]
4 I am the LORD All-Powerful,
the holy God of Israel.
I am their Savior.

5 Babylon, be silent!
Sit in the dark.
No longer will nations
accept you as their queen.
6 I was angry with my people.
So I let you take their land
and bring disgrace on them.
You showed them no mercy,
but were especially cruel
to those who were old.
7 You thought that you
would be queen forever.
You didn't care what you did;
it never entered your mind
that you might get caught.

8 You think that you alone
are all-powerful,
that you won't be a widow
or lose your children.
All you care about is pleasure,
but listen to what I say.
9 Your magic powers and charms
will suddenly fail,
then you will be a widow
and lose your children.

10 You hid behind evil
like a shield and said,
"No one can see me!"
You were fooled by your wisdom
and your knowledge;
you felt sure that you alone
were in full control.
11 But without warning,
disaster will strike—
and your magic charms
won't help at all.

12 Keep using your magic powers
and your charms
as you have always done.
Maybe—just maybe—
you will frighten somebody!
13 You have worn yourself out,
asking for advice
from those who study the stars
and tell the future
month after month.
Go ask them how to be saved
from what will happen.
14 People who trust the stars
are as helpless as straw
in a flaming fire.
No one can even keep warm,[j]
sitting by a fire
that feeds only on straw.
15 These are the fortunetellers
you have done business with
all of your life.
But they don't know
where they are going,
and they can't save you.

The LORD Corrects His People

48 People of Israel,
you come from Jacob's family
and the tribe[k] of Judah.
You claim to worship me,
the LORD God of Israel,
but you are lying.
2 You call Jerusalem your home
and say you depend on me,
the LORD All-Powerful,
the God of Israel.

3 Long ago I announced
what was going to be,
then without warning,
I made it happen.
4 I knew you were stubborn
and hardheaded.
5 And I told you these things,
so that when they happened
you would not say,
"The idols we worship did this."

6 You heard what I said,
and you have seen it happen.
Now admit that it's true!
I will show you secrets
you have never known.
7 Today I am doing something new,
something you cannot say
you have heard before.
8 You have never been willing
to listen to what I say;
from the moment of your birth,
I knew you would rebel.

The LORD Warns Israel

9 I, the LORD, am true to myself;
I will be praised for not punishing
and destroying you.

[h]**47.2** *Strip . . . rivers*: This may be a command to get ready for work that requires wading in the river, or it may be a warning that they are going to be taken away as slaves.
[i]**47.3** *escape*: Or "oppose me." [j]**47.14** *keep warm*: Or "cook food." [k]**48.1** *tribe*: Hebrew "waters."

10 I tested you in hard times
just as silver is refined
in a heated furnace.[l]
11 I did this because of who I am.
I refuse to be dishonored[m]
or share my praise
with any other god.

12 Israel, my chosen people,
listen to me.
I alone am the LORD,
the first and the last.
13 With my own hand
I created the earth
and stretched out the sky.
They obey my every command.

The LORD Speaks to the Nations

14 Gather around me, all of you!
Listen to what I say.
Did any of your idols
predict this would happen?
Did they say that my friend[n]
would do what I want done
to Babylonia?[o]
15 I was the one who chose him.
I have brought him this far,
and he will be successful.
16 Come closer and listen!
I have never kept secret
the things I have said,
and I was here
before time began.

It Is Best To Obey the LORD

By the power of his Spirit
the LORD God has sent me
17 with this message:
People of Israel,
I am the holy LORD God,
the one who rescues you.
For your own good,
I teach you, and I lead you
along the right path.
18 How I wish that you
had obeyed my commands!
Your success and good fortune
would then have overflowed
like a flooding river.
19 Your nation would be blessed
with more people
than there are grains of sand
along the seashore.
And I would never have let
your country be destroyed.

20 Now leave Babylon!
Celebrate as you go.
Be happy and shout
for everyone to hear,
"The LORD has rescued
his servant Israel!
21 He led us through the desert
and made water flow from a rock
to satisfy our thirst.
22 But the LORD has promised
that none who are evil
will live in peace."

The Work of the LORD's Servant

49 Everyone, listen,
even you foreign nations
across the sea.
The LORD chose me
and gave me a name
before I was born.
2 He made my words pierce
like a sharp sword
or a pointed arrow;
he kept me safely hidden
in the palm of his hand.
3 The LORD said to me,
"Israel, you are my servant;
and because of you
I will be highly honored."

4 I said to myself,
"I'm completely worn out;
my time has been wasted.
But I did it for the LORD God,
and he will reward me."

5 Even before I was born,
the LORD God chose me
to serve him and to lead back
the people of Israel.
So the LORD has honored me
and made me strong.

6 Now the LORD says to me,
"It isn't enough for you
to be merely my servant.
You must do more than lead back
survivors from the tribes
of Israel.
I have placed you here as a light
for other nations;
you must take my saving power
to everyone on earth."

The LORD Will Rescue His People

7 Israel, I am the holy LORD God,
the one who rescues you.
You are slaves of rulers
and of a nation
who despises you.[p]
Now this is what I promise:
Kings and rulers will honor you
by kneeling at your feet.
You can trust me! I am your LORD,
the holy God of Israel,
and you are my chosen ones.

[l] **48.10** *furnace*: One possible meaning for the difficult Hebrew text of verse 10. [m] **48.11** *I refuse to be dishonored*: One possible meaning for the difficult Hebrew text. [n] **48.14** *my friend*: Probably Cyrus (see 44.28; 45.1). [o] **48.14** *Babylonia*: One possible meaning for the difficult Hebrew text of verse 14. [p] **49.7** *You . . . you*: One possible meaning for the difficult Hebrew text.

The LORD Will Lead His People Home

8 This is what the LORD says:
I will answer your prayers
because I have set a time
when I will help
by coming to save you.
I have chosen you
to take my promise of hope
to other nations.[q]
You will rebuild the country
from its ruins,
then people will come
and settle there.
9 You will set prisoners free
from dark dungeons
to see the light of day.

On their way home,
they will find plenty to eat,
even on barren hills.
10 They won't go hungry
or get thirsty;
they won't be bothered
by the scorching sun
or hot desert winds.
I will be merciful
while leading them along
to streams of water.
11 I will level the mountains
and make roads.
12 Then my people will return
from distant lands
in the north and the west
and from the city of Syene.[r]

The LORD's Mercy

13 Tell the heavens and the earth
to celebrate and sing;
command every mountain
to join in the song.
The LORD's people have suffered,
but he has shown mercy
and given them comfort.

14 The people of Zion said,
"The LORD has turned away
and forgotten us."

15 The LORD answered,
"Could a mother forget a child
who nurses at her breast?
Could she fail to love an infant
who came from her own body?
Even if a mother could forget,
I will never forget you.
16 A picture of your city
is drawn on my hand.
You are always in my thoughts!

17 "Your city will be built faster
than it was destroyed[s]—
those who attacked it
will retreat and leave.
18 Look around! You will see
your people coming home.
As surely as I live,
I, the LORD, promise
that your city with its people
will be as lovely as a bride
wearing her jewelry."

Jerusalem's Bright Future

19 Jerusalem is now in ruins!
Nothing is left of the city.
But it will be rebuilt
and soon overcrowded;
its cruel enemies
will be gone far away.

20 Jerusalem is a woman
whose children were born
while she was in deep sorrow[t]
over the loss of her husband.
Now those children
will come and seek room
in the crowded city,
21 and Jerusalem will ask,
"Am I really their mother?
How could I have given birth
when I was still mourning
in a foreign land?
Who raised these children?
Where have they come from?"

22 The LORD God says:
"I will soon give a signal
for the nations
to return your sons
and your daughters
to the arms of Jerusalem.
23 The kings and queens
of those nations
where they were raised
will come and bow down.
They will take care of you
just like a slave
taking care of a child.
Then you will know
that I am the LORD.
You won't be disappointed
if you trust me."

The LORD Is on Our Side

24 Is it possible to rescue victims
from someone strong
and cruel?[u]
25 But the LORD has promised
to fight on our side
and to rescue our children
from those strong
and violent enemies.

[q]**49.8** *my . . . nations*: One possible meaning for the difficult Hebrew text. [r]**49.12** *Syene*: The Dead Sea Scrolls; the Standard Hebrew Text "Sinim." The reference may be to modern Aswan, a city in southern Egypt. [s]**49.17** *Your city . . . destroyed*: One possible meaning for the difficult Hebrew text. [t]**49.20** *whose children . . . sorrow*: These "children" are Jews who were born in foreign countries during the time that Jerusalem was in ruins. Jerusalem probably stands for all the cities in Judah that were destroyed by the Babylonians. [u]**49.24** *cruel*: The Dead Sea Scrolls and two ancient translations; the Standard Hebrew Text "good."

26 He will make those cruel people
dine on their own flesh
and get drunk from drinking
their own blood.
Then everyone will know
that the LORD is our Savior;
the powerful God of Israel
has rescued his people.

The LORD's Power To Punish

50 The LORD says, "Children,
I didn't divorce your mother
or sell you to pay debts;
I divorced her and sold you
because of your sins.
2 I came and called out,
but you didn't answer.
Have I lost my power
to rescue and save?
At my command oceans and rivers
turn into deserts;
fish rot and stink
for lack of water.
3 I make the sky turn dark
like the sackcloth
you wear at funerals."

God's Servant Must Suffer

4 The LORD God gives me
the right words
to encourage the weary.
Each morning he awakens me
eager to learn his teaching;
5 he made me willing to listen
and not rebel or run away.

6 I let them beat my back
and pull out my beard.
I didn't turn aside
when they insulted me
and spit in my face.
7 But the LORD God keeps me
from being disgraced.
So I refuse to give up,
because I know
God will never let me down.

8 My protector is nearby;
no one can stand here
to accuse me of wrong.
9 The LORD God will help me
and prove I am innocent.
My accusers will wear out
like moth-eaten clothes.

10 None of you respect the LORD
or obey his servant.
You walk in the dark
instead of the light;
you don't trust the name
of the LORD your God.[v]
11 Go ahead and walk in the light
of the fires you have set.[w]
But with his own hand,
the LORD will punish you
and make you suffer.

The LORD Will Bring Comfort

51 If you want to do right
and obey the LORD,
follow Abraham's example.
He was the rock from which
you were chipped.
2 God chose Abraham and Sarah
to be your ancestors.
The LORD blessed Abraham,
and from that one man
came many descendants.

3 Though Zion is in ruins,
the LORD will bring comfort,
and the city will be as lovely
as the garden of Eden
that he provided.
Then Zion will celebrate;
it will be thankful
and sing joyful songs.

The LORD's Victory Will Last

4 The LORD says:
You are my people and nation!
So pay attention to me.
My teaching will cause justice
to shine like a light
for every nation.
5 Those who live across the sea
are eagerly waiting
for me to rescue them.
I am strong and ready;
soon I will come to save
and to rule all nations.

6 Look closely at the sky!
Stare at the earth.
The sky will vanish like smoke;
the earth will wear out
like clothes.
Everyone on this earth
will die like flies.
But my victory will last;
my saving power never ends.

7 If you want to do right
and to obey my teaching
with all your heart,
then pay close attention.
Don't be discouraged
when others insult you
and say hurtful things.
8 They will be eaten away
like a moth-eaten coat.
But my victory will last;
my saving power
will never end.

A Prayer for the LORD's Help

9 Wake up! Do something, LORD.
Be strong and ready.

[v]**50.10** *God*: One possible meaning for the difficult Hebrew text of verse 10. [w]**50.11** *Go . . . set*: One possible meaning for the difficult Hebrew text.

Wake up! Do what you did
for our people long ago.
Didn't you chop up
Rahab[x] the monster?
10 Didn't you dry up the deep sea
and make a road for your people
to follow safely across?
11 Now those you have rescued
will return to Jerusalem,
singing on their way.
They will be crowned
with great happiness,
never again to be burdened
with sadness and sorrow.

The LORD Gives Hope

12 I am the LORD, the one
who encourages you.
Why are you afraid
of mere humans?
They dry up and die like grass.

13 I spread out the heavens
and laid foundations
for the earth.
But you have forgotten me,
your LORD and Creator.
All day long you were afraid
of those who were angry
and hoped to abuse you.
Where are they now?

14 Everyone crying out in pain
will be quickly set free;
they will be rescued
from the power of death
and never go hungry.
15 I will help them
because I am your God,
the LORD All-Powerful,
who makes the ocean roar.

16 I have told you what to say,
and I will keep you safe
in the palm of my hand.
I spread out the heavens
and laid foundations
for the earth.
Now I say, "Jerusalem,
your people are mine."

A Warning to Jerusalem

17 Jerusalem, wake up! Stand up!
You've drunk too much
from the cup filled
with the LORD's anger.
You have swallowed every drop,
and you can't walk straight.
18 Not one of your many children
is there to guide you
or to offer a helping hand.
19 You have been destroyed
by war and by famine;
I cannot comfort you.[y]

20 The LORD your God is angry,
and on every street corner
your children lie helpless,
like deer trapped in nets.

21 You are in trouble and drunk,
but not from wine.
So pay close attention
22 to the LORD your God,
who defends you and says,
"I have taken from your hands
the cup filled with my anger
that made you drunk.
You will never be forced
to drink it again.
23 Instead I will give it
to your brutal enemies,
who treated you like dirt
and walked all over you."

Jerusalem Can Celebrate

52 Jerusalem, wake up!
Stand up and be strong.
Holy city of Zion,
dress in your best clothes.
Those foreigners who ruined
your sacred city
won't bother you again.
2 Zion, rise from the dirt!
Free yourself from the rope
around your neck.

Suffering Will End

3 The LORD says:
My people, you were sold,
but not for money;
now you will be set free,
but not for a payment.
4 Long ago you went to Egypt
where you lived
as foreigners.
Then Assyria was cruel to you,
5 and now another nation[z]
has taken you prisoner
for no reason at all.
Your leaders groan with pain,[a]
and day after day
my own name is cursed.
6 My people, you will learn
who I am and who is speaking
because I am here.

A Message of Hope for Jerusalem

7 What a beautiful sight!
On the mountains a messenger
announces to Jerusalem,
"Good news! You're saved.
There will be peace.
Your God is now King."
8 Everyone on guard duty,
sing and celebrate!
Look! You can see the LORD
returning to Zion.

[x]**51.9** *Rahab*: This may refer to Egypt at the time of the exodus. [y]**51.19** *I . . . you*: One possible meaning for the difficult Hebrew text. [z]**52.5** *another nation*: Babylonia.
[a]**52.5** *groan with pain*: One possible meaning for the difficult Hebrew text.

9 Jerusalem, rise from the ruins!
Join in the singing.
The LORD has given comfort
to his people;
he comes to your rescue.
10 The LORD has shown all nations
his mighty strength;
now everyone will see
the saving power of our God.

A Command To Leave Babylon

11 Leave the city of Babylon!
Don't touch anything filthy.
Wash yourselves. Be ready
to carry back everything sacred
that belongs to the LORD.
12 You won't need to run.
No one is chasing you.
The LORD God of Israel
will lead and protect you
from enemy attacks.

The Suffering Servant

13 The LORD says:
My servant will succeed!
He will be given great praise
and the highest honors.
14 Many were horrified
at what happened to him.[b]
But everyone who saw him
was even more horrified
because he suffered until
he no longer looked human.[c]
15 My servant will make
nations worthy to worship me;[d]
kings will be silent
as they bow in wonder.[e]
They will see and think about
things they have never seen
or thought about before.

What God's Servant Did for Us

53 Has anyone believed us
or seen the mighty power
of the LORD in action?
2 Like a young plant or a root
that sprouts in dry ground,
the servant grew up
obeying the LORD.
He wasn't some handsome king.
Nothing about the way he looked
made him attractive to us.
3 He was hated and rejected;
his life was filled with sorrow
and terrible suffering.
No one wanted to look at him.
We despised him and said,
"He is a nobody!"

4 He suffered and endured
great pain for us,
but we thought his suffering
was punishment from God.
5 He was wounded and crushed
because of our sins;
by taking our punishment,
he made us completely well.
6 All of us were like sheep
that had wandered off.
We had each gone our own way,
but the LORD gave him
the punishment we deserved.

7 He was painfully abused,
but he did not complain.
He was silent like a lamb
being led to the butcher,
as quiet as a sheep
having its wool cut off.

8 He was condemned to death
without a fair trial.
Who could have imagined
what would happen to him?
His life was taken away
because of the sinful things
my people[f] had done.
9 He wasn't dishonest or violent,
but he was buried in a tomb
of cruel and rich people.[g]

10 The LORD decided his servant
would suffer as a sacrifice
to take away the sin
and guilt of others.
Now the servant will live
to see his own descendants.[h]
He did everything
the LORD had planned.

11 By suffering, the servant
will learn the true meaning
of obeying the LORD.
Although he is innocent,
he will take the punishment
for the sins of others,
so that many of them
will no longer be guilty.
12 The LORD will reward him
with honor and power
for sacrificing his life.
Others thought he was a sinner,
but he suffered for our sins
and asked God to forgive us.

A Promise of the LORD's Protection

54 Sing and shout,
even though you have never
had children!

[b]**52.14** *him*: One ancient translation; Hebrew "you." [c]**52.14** *human*: One possible meaning for the difficult Hebrew text of verse 14. [d]**52.15** *My . . . me*: Hebrew; one ancient translation "The nations will be amazed at him." [e]**52.15** *kings . . . wonder*: One possible meaning for the difficult Hebrew text. [f]**53.8** *my people*: Or "his people." [g]**53.9** *but he . . . people*: One possible meaning for the difficult Hebrew text. [h]**53.10** *The LORD . . . descendants*: One possible meaning for the difficult Hebrew text.

The LORD has promised that you
will have more children
than someone married
for a long time.
2 Make your tents larger!
Spread out the tent pegs;
fasten them firmly.
3 You and your descendants
will take over the land
of other nations.
You will settle in towns
that are now in ruins.

4 Don't be afraid or ashamed
and don't be discouraged.
You won't be disappointed.
Forget how sinful you were
when you were young;
stop feeling ashamed
for being left a widow.
5 The LORD All-Powerful,
the Holy God of Israel,
rules all the earth.
He is your Creator and husband,
and he will rescue you.

6 You were like a young wife,
brokenhearted and crying
because her husband
had divorced her.
But the LORD your God says,
"I am taking you back!
7 I rejected you for a while,
but with love and tenderness
I will embrace you again.
8 For a while, I turned away
in furious anger.
Now I will have mercy
and love you forever!
I, your protector and LORD,
make this promise."

The LORD Promises Lasting Peace

9 I once promised Noah that I
would never again destroy
the earth by a flood.
Now I have promised that I
will never again get angry
and punish you.
10 Every mountain and hill
may disappear.
But I will always be kind
and merciful to you;
I won't break my agreement
to give your nation peace.

The New Jerusalem

11 Jerusalem, you are sad
and discouraged,
tossed around in a storm.
But I, the LORD,
will rebuild your city
with precious stones;[i]
for your foundation
I will use blue sapphires.
12 Your fortresses[j]
will be built of rubies,
your gates of jewels,
and your walls of gems.
13 I will teach your children
and make them successful.

14 You will be built on fairness
with no fears of injustice;
every one of your worries
will be taken far from you.
15 I will never send anyone
to attack your city,
and you will make prisoners
of those who do attack.
16 Don't forget that I created
metalworkers who make weapons
over burning coals.
I also created armies
that can bring destruction.
17 Weapons made to attack you
won't be successful;
words spoken against you
won't hurt at all.

My servants, Jerusalem is yours!
I, the LORD, promise
to bless you with victory.

The LORD's Invitation

55 If you are thirsty,
come and drink water!
If you don't have any money,
come, eat what you want!
Drink wine and milk
without paying a cent.
2 Why waste your money
on what really isn't food?
Why work hard for something
that doesn't satisfy?
Listen carefully to me,
and you will enjoy
the very best foods.

3 Pay close attention!
Come to me and live.
I will promise you
the eternal love and loyalty
that I promised David.
4 I made him the leader and ruler
of the nations;
he was my witness to them.
5 You will call out to nations
you have never known.
And they have never known you,
but they will come running
because I am the LORD,
the holy God of Israel,
and I have honored you.

God's Words Are Powerful

6 Turn to the LORD!
He can still be found.
Call out to God! He is near.

[i]**54.11** *with precious stones*: One possible meaning for the difficult Hebrew text.
[j]**54.12** *fortresses*: One possible meaning for the difficult Hebrew text.

7 Give up your crooked ways
and your evil thoughts.
Return to the LORD our God.
He will be merciful
and forgive your sins.

8 The LORD says:
"My thoughts and my ways
are not like yours.
9 Just as the heavens
are higher than the earth,
my thoughts and my ways
are higher than yours.

10 "Rain and snow fall from the sky.
But they don't return
without watering the earth
that produces seeds to plant
and grain to eat.
11 That's how it is with my words.
They don't return to me
without doing everything
I send them to do."

God's People Will Celebrate

12 When you are set free,
you will celebrate
and travel home in peace.
Mountains and hills will sing
as you pass by,
and trees will clap.
13 Cypress and myrtle trees
will grow in fields
once covered by thorns.
And then those trees will stand
as a lasting witness
to the glory of the LORD.

All Nations Will Be Part of God's People

56 The LORD said:
Be honest and fair!
Soon I will come to save you;
my saving power will be seen
everywhere on earth.

2 I will bless everyone
who respects the Sabbath
and refuses to do wrong.

3 Foreigners who worship me
must not say,
"The LORD won't let us
be part of his people."
Men who are unable
to become fathers
must no longer say,
"We are dried-up trees."

4 To them, I, the LORD, say:
Respect the Sabbath,
obey me completely,
and keep our agreement.
5 Then I will set up monuments
in my temple with your names
written on them.
This will be much better
than having children,
because these monuments
will stand there forever.

6 Foreigners will follow me.
They will love me and worship
in my name;
they will respect the Sabbath
and keep our agreement.
7 I will bring them
to my holy mountain,
where they will celebrate
in my house of worship.
Their sacrifices and offerings
will always be welcome
on my altar.
Then my house will be known
as a house of worship
for all nations.
8 I, the LORD, promise
to bring together my people
who were taken away,
and let them join the others.

God Promises To Punish Israel's Leaders

9 Come from the forest,
you wild animals!
Attack and gobble down
your victims.
10 You leaders of Israel
should be watchdogs,
protecting my people.
But you can't see a thing,
and you never warn them.
Dozing and daydreaming
are all you ever do.
11 You stupid leaders are a pack
of hungry and greedy dogs
that never get enough.
You are shepherds
who mistreat your own sheep
for selfish gain.
12 You say to each other,
"Let's drink till we're drunk!
Tomorrow we'll do it again.
We'll really enjoy ourselves."

God's Faithful People Suffer

57 God's faithful people
are dragged off and killed,
and no one even cares.
Evil sweeps them away,
2 but in death they find peace
for obeying God.[k]

The LORD Condemns Idolatry

3 You people are unfaithful!
You go to fortunetellers,
and you worship idols.
Now pay close attention!
4 Who are you making fun of?
Who are you sneering at?

[k] **57.1,2** *Evil . . . God*: One possible meaning for the difficult Hebrew text.

Look how your sins
have made fools of you.

5 All you think about is sex
under those green trees
where idols are worshiped.
You sacrifice your children
on altars built in valleys
under rocky slopes.
6 You have chosen to worship
idols made of stone;[l]
you have given them offerings
of wine and grain.
Should I be pleased?

7 You have spread out your beds
on the tops of high mountains,
where you sacrifice to idols.
8 Even in your homes
you have placed pagan symbols
all around your huge beds.
Yes, you have rejected me,
sold yourselves to your lovers,
and gone to bed with them.[m]

9 You smear on olive oil
and all kinds of perfume
to worship the god Molech.[n]
You even seek advice
from spirits of the dead.
10 Though you tired yourself out
by running after idols,
you refused to stop.
Your desires were so strong
that they kept you going.

11 Did you forget about me
and become unfaithful
because you were more afraid
of someone else?
Have I been silent so long[o]
that you no longer fear me?
12 You think you're so good,
but I'll point out the truth.
13 Ask your idols to save you
when you are in trouble.
Be careful though—
it takes only a faint breath
to blow them over.
But if you come to me
for protection,
this land and my holy mountain
will always belong to you.

The LORD Helps the Helpless

14 The LORD says,
"Clear the road!
Get it ready for my people."

15 Our holy God lives forever
in the highest heavens,
and this is what he says:
Though I live high above
in the holy place,
I am here to help those
who are humble
and depend only on me.

16 My people, I won't stay angry
and keep on accusing you.
After all, I am your Creator.
I don't want you to give up
in complete despair.
17 Your greed made me furious.
That's why I punished you
and refused to be found,
while you kept returning
to your old sinful ways.

18 I know what you are like!
But I will heal you, lead you,
and give you comfort,
until those who are mourning
19 start singing my praises.[p]
No matter where you are,
I, the LORD, will heal you[q]
and give you peace.

20 The wicked are a restless sea
tossing up mud.
21 But I, the LORD, have promised
that none who are evil
will live in peace.

True Religion

58 Shout the message!
Don't hold back.
Say to my people Israel:
You've sinned! You've turned
against the LORD.
2 Day after day, you worship him
and seem eager to learn
his teachings.
You act like a nation
that wants to do right
by obeying his laws.
You ask him about justice,
and say you enjoy
worshiping the LORD.

3 You wonder why the LORD
pays no attention
when you go without eating
and act humble.
But on those same days
that you give up eating,
you think only of yourselves[r]
and abuse your workers.
4 You even get angry
and ready to fight.
No wonder God won't listen
to your prayers!

[l] **57.6** *You have . . . stone*: One possible meaning for the difficult Hebrew text. [m] **57.8** *them*: One possible meaning for the difficult Hebrew text of verse 8. [n] **57.9** *the god Molech*: Or "the king." In Hebrew "Molech" and "king" sound alike. [o] **57.11** *so long*: One possible meaning for the difficult Hebrew text. [p] **57.18,19** *until . . . praises*: One possible meaning for the difficult Hebrew text. [q] **57.19** *heal you*: One possible meaning for the difficult Hebrew text. [r] **58.3** *you think . . . yourselves*: One possible meaning for the difficult Hebrew text.

5 Do you think the LORD
wants you to give up eating
and to act as humble
as a bent-over bush?
Or to dress in sackcloth
and sit in ashes?
Is this really what he wants
on a day of worship?

6 I'll tell you
what it really means
to worship the LORD.
Remove the chains of prisoners
who are chained unjustly.
Free those who are abused!
7 Share your food with everyone
who is hungry;
share your home
with the poor and homeless.
Give clothes to those in need;
don't turn away your relatives.

8 Then your light will shine
like the dawning sun, and you
will quickly be healed.
Your honesty[s] will protect you
as you advance,
and the glory of the LORD
will defend you from behind.
9 When you beg the LORD for help,
he will answer, "Here I am!"

Don't mistreat others
or falsely accuse them
or say something cruel.
10 Give your food to the hungry
and care for the homeless.
Then your light will shine
in the dark;
your darkest hour will be
like the noonday sun.

11 The LORD will always guide you
and provide good things to eat
when you are in the desert.
He will make you healthy.
You will be like a garden
that has plenty of water
or like a stream
that never runs dry.
12 You will rebuild those houses
left in ruins for years;
you will be known
as a builder and repairer
of city walls and streets.

13 But first, you must start
respecting the Sabbath
as a joyful day of worship.
You must stop doing and saying
whatever you please
on this special day.
14 Then you will truly enjoy
knowing the LORD.
He will let you rule
from the highest mountains
and bless you with the land
of your ancestor Jacob.
The LORD has spoken!

Social Injustice Is Condemned

59 The LORD hasn't lost
his powerful strength;
he can still hear
and answer prayers.
2 Your sins are the roadblock
between you and your God.
That's why he doesn't answer
your prayers
or let you see his face.

3 Your talk is filled with lies
and plans for violence;
every finger on your hands
is covered with blood.
4 You falsely accuse others
and tell lies in court;
sin and trouble are the names
of your children.
5 You eat the deadly eggs
of poisonous snakes,
and more snakes crawl out
from the eggs left to hatch.
You weave spider webs,
6 but you can't make clothes
with those webs
or hide behind them.

You're sinful and brutal.
7 You hurry off to do wrong
or murder innocent victims.
All you think about is sin;
you leave ruin and destruction
wherever you go.
8 You don't know how
to live in peace
or to be fair with others.
The roads you make are crooked;
your followers cannot find peace.

The People Confess Their Sins

9 No one has come to defend us
or to bring about justice.
We hoped for a day of sunshine,
but all we found
was a dark, gloomy night.
10 We feel our way along,
as if we were blind;
we stumble at noon,
as if it were night.
We can see no better
than someone dead.[t]

11 We growl like bears
and mourn like doves.
We hope for justice and victory,
but they escape us.
12 How often have we sinned
and turned against you,
the LORD God?

[s]58.8 *honesty*: Or "honest leader."

[t]59.10 *We can . . . dead*: One possible meaning for the difficult Hebrew text.

Our sins condemn us!
We have done wrong.
13 We have rebelled and refused
to follow you.
Our hearts were deceitful,
and so we lied;
we planned to abuse others
and turn our backs on you.

14 Injustice is everywhere;
justice seems far away.
Truth is chased out of court;
honesty is shoved aside.
15 Everyone tells lies;
those who turn from crime
end up ruined.

The LORD Will Rescue His People

When the LORD noticed
that justice had disappeared,
he became very displeased.
16 It disgusted him even more
to learn that no one
would do a thing about it.
So with his own powerful arm,
he won victories for truth.
17 Justice was the LORD's armor;
saving power was his helmet;
anger and revenge
were his clothes.

18 Now the LORD will get furious
and do to his enemies,
both near and far,
what they did to his people.
19 He will attack like a flood
in a mighty windstorm.
Nations in the west and the east
will then honor and praise
his wonderful name.
20 The LORD has promised to rescue
the city of Zion
and Jacob's descendants
who turn from sin.

21 The LORD says: "My people,
I promise to give you my Spirit
and my message.
These will be my gifts to you
and your families forever.
I, the LORD, have spoken."

A New Day for Jerusalem

60 Jerusalem, stand up! Shine!
Your new day is dawning.
The glory of the LORD
shines brightly on you.
2 The earth and its people
are covered with darkness,
but the glory of the LORD
is shining upon you.
3 Nations and kings
will come to the light
of your dawning day.

Crowds Are Coming to Jerusalem

The LORD said:
4 Open your eyes! Look around!
Crowds are coming.
Your sons are on their way
from distant lands;
your daughters are being carried
like little children.
5 When you see this,
your faces will glow;
your hearts will pound
and swell with pride.[u]
Treasures from across the sea
and the wealth of nations
will be brought to you.
6 Your country will be covered
with caravans of young camels
from Midian and Ephah.[v]
The people of Sheba[w]
will bring gold and spices
in praise of me, the LORD.
7 Every sheep of Kedar
will come to you;
rams from Nebaioth[x]
will be yours as well.
I will accept them as offerings
and bring honor to my temple.

8 What is that sailing by
like clouds
or like doves flying home?
9 On those distant islands
your people are waiting
for me, the LORD.[y]
Seagoing ships[z] lead the way
to bring them home
with their silver and gold.
I, the holy LORD God of Israel,
do this to honor your people,
so they will honor me.

Jerusalem Will Be Rebuilt

The LORD said:
10 Jerusalem, your city walls
will be rebuilt by foreigners;
their rulers will become
your slaves.
I punished you in my anger;
now I will be kind
and treat you with mercy.

11 Your gates will be open
day and night
to let the rulers of nations
lead their people to you
with all their treasures.

[u]60.5 *swell with pride*: One possible meaning for the difficult Hebrew text. [v]60.6 *Midian . . . Ephah*: Midian was the ancestor of a nomadic tribe of the Arabian desert, east of the Gulf of Aqaba. Ephah was a clan within the tribe of Midian. [w]60.6 *Sheba*: Perhaps a place in what is now southwest Arabia. The Queen of Sheba brought gifts to Solomon (1 Kings 10.1-13). [x]60.7 *Kedar . . . Nebaioth*: Regions in northern Arabia. [y]60.9 *On . . . LORD*: One possible meaning for the difficult Hebrew text. [z]60.9 *Seagoing ships*: See the note at 2.16.

12 Any nation or kingdom
that refuses to serve you
will be wiped out.
13 Wood from Lebanon's best trees
will be brought to you—
the pines, the firs,
and the cypress trees.
It will be used in my temple
to make beautiful the place
where I rest my feet.

14 The descendants of enemies
who hated and mistreated you
will kneel at your feet.
They will say, "You are Zion,
the city of the LORD,
the holy God of Israel."

15 You were hated and deserted,
rejected by everyone.
But I will make you beautiful,
a city to be proud of
for all time to come.
16 You will drain the wealth
of kings and foreign nations.
You will know that I,
the mighty LORD God of Israel,
have saved and rescued you.

17 I will bring bronze and iron
in place of wood and stone;
in place of bronze and iron,
I will bring gold and silver.
I will appoint peace and justice
as your rulers and leaders.
18 Violence, destruction, and ruin
will never again be heard of
within your borders.
"Victory" will be the name
you give to your walls;
"Praise" will be the name
you give to your gates.

19 You won't need the light
of the sun or the moon.
I, the LORD your God,
will be your eternal light
and bring you honor.
20 Your sun will never set
or your moon go down.
I, the LORD, will be
your everlasting light,
and your days of sorrow
will come to an end.
21 Your people will live right
and always own the land;
they are the trees I planted
to bring praise to me.
22 Even the smallest family
will be a powerful nation.
I am the LORD,
and when the time comes,
I will quickly do all this.

The Good News of Victory

61 The Spirit of the LORD God
has taken control of me!
The LORD has chosen and sent me
to tell the oppressed
the good news,
to heal the brokenhearted,
and to announce freedom
for prisoners and captives.
2 This is the year
when the LORD God
will show kindness to us
and punish our enemies.

The LORD has sent me
to comfort those who mourn,
3 especially in Jerusalem.
He sent me to give them flowers
in place of their sorrow,
olive oil in place of tears,
and joyous praise
in place of broken hearts.
They will be called
"Trees of Justice,"
planted by the LORD
to honor his name.
4 Then they will rebuild cities
that have been in ruins
for many generations.

5 They will hire foreigners
to take care of their sheep
and their vineyards.
6 But they themselves will be
priests and servants
of the LORD our God.
The treasures of the nations
will belong to them,
and they will be famous.[a]
7 They were terribly insulted
and horribly mistreated;
now they will be greatly blessed
and joyful forever.

The LORD Loves Justice

8 I, the LORD, love justice!
But I hate robbery
and injustice.[b]
My people, I solemnly promise
to reward you
with an eternal agreement.
9 Your descendants will be known
in every nation.
All who see them will realize
that they have been blessed,
by me, the LORD.

Celebrate and Shout

10 I celebrate and shout
because of my LORD God.
His saving power and justice
are the very clothes I wear.
They are more beautiful

[a]**61.6** *and . . . famous*: One possible meaning for the difficult Hebrew text. [b]**61.8** *But . . . injustice*: One possible meaning for the difficult Hebrew text.

than the jewelry worn
by a bride or a groom.
11 The LORD will bring about
justice and praise
in every nation on earth,
like flowers blooming
in a garden.

Jerusalem Will Be Saved

62 Jerusalem, I will speak up
for your good.
I will never be silent
till you are safe and secure,
sparkling like a flame.
2 Your great victory will be seen
by every nation and king;
the LORD will even give you
a new name.
3 You will be a glorious crown,
a royal headband,
for the LORD your God.

4 Your name will no longer be
"Deserted and Childless,"
but "Happily Married."
You will please the LORD;
your country
will be his bride.
5 Your people will take the land,[c]
just as a young man
takes a bride.
The LORD will be pleased
because of you,
just as a husband is pleased
with his bride.

6 Jerusalem, on your walls
I have stationed guards,
whose duty it is
to speak out day and night,
without resting.
They must remind the LORD
7 and not let him rest
till he makes Jerusalem strong
and famous everywhere.

8 The LORD has given his word
and made this promise:
"Never again will I give
to your enemies
the grain and grapes
for which you struggled.
9 As surely as you harvest
your grain and grapes,
you will eat your bread
with thankful hearts,
and you will drink your wine
in my temple."

10 People of Jerusalem,
open your gates!
Repair the road to the city
and clear it of stones;
raise a banner to help
the nations find their way.
11 Here is what the LORD has said
for all the earth to hear:
"Soon I will come to save
the city of Zion,
and to reward you.
12 Then you will be called,
'The LORD's Own People,
The Ones He Rescued!'
Your city will be known
as a good place to live
and a city full of people."

The LORD's Victory over the Nations

63 Who is this coming
from Bozrah[d] in Edom
with clothes stained red?
Who is this hero marching
in his glorious uniform?

"It's me, the LORD!
I have won the battle,
and I can save you!"

2 What are those red spots?
Your clothes look stained
from stomping on grapes.[e]

3 "I alone stomped the grapes!
None of the nations helped.
I stomped nations in my anger
and stained my clothes
with their blood.
4 I did this because I wanted
to take revenge—
the time had come
to rescue my people.
5 No one was there to help me
or to give support;
my mighty arm won the battle,
strengthened by my anger.
6 In my fury I stomped on nations
and made them drunk;
their blood poured out
everywhere on earth."

The LORD's Goodness to His People

7 I will tell about the kind deeds
the LORD has done.
They deserve praise!
The LORD has shown mercy
to the people of Israel;
he has been kind and good.

8 The LORD rescued his people,
and said, "They are mine.
They won't betray me."
9 It troubled the LORD
to see them in trouble,
and his angel saved them.[f]
The LORD was truly merciful,
so he rescued his people.

[c] 62.5 *Your . . . land*: One possible meaning for the difficult Hebrew text. [d] 63.1 *Bozrah*: The main city of Edom. [e] 63.2 *stomping on grapes*: This is one way that grapes were crushed to make them into juice. [f] 63.9 *It . . . them*: One possible meaning for the difficult Hebrew text.

He took them in his arms
and carried them all those years.

10 Then the LORD's people
turned against him and made
his Holy Spirit sad.
So he became their enemy
and attacked them.
11 But his people remembered
what had happened
during the time of Moses.[g]
Didn't the LORD[h] bring them
and their leaders
safely through the sea?
Didn't he[i] give them
his Holy Spirit?
12 The glorious power of the LORD
marched beside Moses.
The LORD will be praised forever
for dividing the sea.
13 He led his people across
like horses running wild
without stumbling.
14 His Spirit gave them rest,
just as cattle find rest
when led into a valley.[j]
The name of the LORD was praised
for doing these things.

A Prayer for Mercy and Help

15 Please, LORD, look down
from your holy and glorious
home in the heavens
and see what's going on.
Have you lost interest?
Where is your power?
Show that you care about us[k]
and have mercy!
16 Our ancestors Abraham and Jacob
have both rejected us.
But you are still our Father;
you have been our protector
since ancient times.

17 Why did you make us turn away
from you, our LORD?
Why did you make us want
to disobey you?
Please change your mind!
We are your servants,
your very own people.
18 For a little while,
your temple belonged to us;[l]
and now our enemies
have torn it down.
19 We act as though you
had never ruled us
or called us your people.

64 Rip the heavens apart!
Come down, LORD;
make the mountains tremble.
2 Be a spark that starts a fire
causing water to boil.[m]
Then your enemies will know
who you are;
all nations will tremble
because you are nearby.

3 Your fearsome deeds
have completely amazed us;
even the mountains shake
when you come down.
4 You are the only God
ever seen or heard of
who works miracles
for his followers.

5 You help all who gladly obey
and do what you want,
but sin makes you angry.
Only by your help
can we ever be saved.[n]
6 We are unfit to worship you;
each of our good deeds
is merely a filthy rag.
We dry up like leaves;
our sins are storm winds
sweeping us away.
7 No one worships in your name
or remains faithful.
You have turned your back on us
and let our sins melt us away.[o]

8 You, LORD, are our Father.
We are nothing but clay,
but you are the potter
who molded us.
9 Don't be so furious
or keep our sins
in your thoughts forever!
Remember that all of us
are your people.
10 Every one of your towns
has turned into a desert,
especially Jerusalem.
11 Zion's glorious and holy temple
where our ancestors praised you
has been destroyed by fire.
Our beautiful buildings
are now a pile of ruins.
12 When you see these things,
how can you just sit there
and make us suffer more?

The LORD Will Punish the Guilty

65 I, the LORD, was ready
to answer even those
who were not asking
and to be found by those
who were not searching.
To a nation that refused
to worship me,[p]
I said, "Here I am!"

[g]63.11 *But* . . . *Moses*: One possible meaning for the difficult Hebrew text. [h]63.11 *the LORD*: Or "Moses." [i]63.11 *he*: Or "Moses." [j]63.14 *His* . . . *valley*: One possible meaning for the difficult Hebrew text. [k]63.15 *us*: Hebrew "me." [l]63.18 *For* . . . *us*: One possible meaning for the difficult Hebrew text. [m]64.2 *Be* . . . *boil*: One possible meaning for the difficult Hebrew text. [n]64.5 *saved*: One possible meaning for the difficult Hebrew text of verse 5. [o]64.7 *and let* . . . *away*: One possible meaning for the difficult Hebrew text. [p]65.1 *refused* . . . *me*: One possible meaning for the difficult Hebrew text.

2 All day long I have reached out
to stubborn and sinful people
going their own way.
3 They keep making me angry
by sneering at me,
while offering sacrifices
to idols in gardens
and burning incense
to them on bricks.
4 They spend their nights
hiding in burial caves;
they eat the meat of pigs,[q]
cooked in sauces
made of stuff unfit to eat.
5 And then they say to others,
"Don't come near us!
We're dedicated to God."
Such people are like smoke,
irritating my nose all day.
6 I have written this down;
I won't keep silent.
I'll pay them back
just as their sins deserve.
7 I, the LORD, will make them pay
for their sins and for those
of their ancestors—
they have disgraced me
by burning incense
on mountains.

8 Here is what the LORD says:
A cluster of grapes
that produces wine
is worth keeping!
So, because of my servants,
I won't destroy everyone.
9 I have chosen the people
of Israel and Judah,
and I will bless them
with many descendants.
They will settle here
in this land of mountains,
and it will be theirs.
10 My people will worship me.
Then the coastlands of Sharon
and the land as far
as Achor Valley[r]
will turn into pastureland
where cattle and sheep
will feed and rest.

11 What will I, the LORD, do
if any of you reject me
and my holy mountain?
What will happen to you
for offering food and wine
to the gods you call
"Good Luck" and "Fate"?
12 Your luck will end!
I will see to it that you
are slaughtered with swords.
You refused to answer
when I called out;
you paid no attention
to my instructions.
Instead, you did what I hated,
knowing it was wrong.

13 I, the LORD God, will give
food and drink to my servants,
and they will celebrate.
But all of you sinners
will go hungry and thirsty,
overcome with disgrace.
14 My servants will laugh and sing,
but you will be sad
and cry out in pain.
15 I, the LORD God, promise
to see that you are killed
and that my chosen servants use
your names as curse words.
But I will give new names[s]
to my servants.[t]
16 I am God! I can be trusted.
Your past troubles are gone;
I no longer think of them.
When you pray for someone
to receive a blessing,
or when you make a promise,
you must do it in my name.
I alone am the God
who can be trusted.

The LORD's New Creation

17 I am creating new heavens
and a new earth;
everything of the past
will be forgotten.
18 Celebrate and be glad forever!
I am creating a Jerusalem,
full of happy people.
19 I will celebrate with Jerusalem
and all of its people;
there will be no more crying
or sorrow in that city.

20 No child will die in infancy;
everyone will live
to a ripe old age.
Anyone a hundred years old
will be considered young,
and to die younger than that
will be considered a curse.

21 My people will live
in the houses they build;
they will enjoy grapes
from their own vineyards.
22 No one will take away
their homes or vineyards.
My chosen people will live
to be as old as trees,

[q]**65.4** *burial . . . pigs*: Coming in contact with the dead or eating the meat of pigs made a person unacceptable to God. [r]**65.10** *coastlands of Sharon . . . Achor Valley*: Sharon is the coastal plain on the west, and Achor Valley is in the east near Jericho. These two places stand for the whole country. [s]**65.15** *new names*: The giving of a new name suggests the beginning of a new life. [t]**65.15** *But I . . . servants*: One possible meaning for the difficult Hebrew text.

and they will enjoy
what they have earned.
23 Their work won't be wasted,
and their children won't die
of dreadful diseases.[u]
I will bless their children
and their grandchildren.
24 I will answer their prayers
before they finish praying.

25 Wolves and lambs
will graze together;
lions and oxen
will feed on straw.
Snakes will eat only dirt!
They won't bite or harm anyone
on my holy mountain.
I, the LORD, have spoken!

True Worship

66 The LORD said:
Heaven is my throne;
the earth is my footstool.
What kind of house
could you build for me?
In what place will I rest?
2 I have made everything;
that's how it all came to be.[v]
I, the LORD, have spoken.

The people I treasure most
are the humble—
they depend only on me
and tremble when I speak.

3 You sacrifice oxen to me,
and you commit murder;
you sacrifice lambs to me
and dogs to other gods;
you offer grain to me
and pigs' blood to idols;
you burn incense to me
and praise your idols.[w]
You have made your own choice
to do these disgusting things
that you enjoy so much.
4 You refused to answer
when I called out;
you paid no attention
to my instructions.
Instead, you did what I hated,
knowing it was wrong.
Now I will punish[x] you
in a way you dread the most.

The LORD Will Help Jerusalem

5 If you tremble
when the LORD speaks,
listen to what he says:
"Some of your own people hate
and reject you because of me.
They make fun and say,
'Let the LORD show his power!
Let us see him
make you truly happy.'[y]
But those who say these things
will be terribly ashamed."

6 Do you hear that noise
in the city and those shouts
coming from the temple?
It is the LORD shouting
as he punishes his enemies.

7 Have you ever heard of a woman
who gave birth to a child
before having labor pains?
8 Who ever heard of such a thing
or imagined it could happen?
Can a nation be born in a day
or come to life in a second?
Jerusalem is like a mother
who gave birth to her children
as soon as she was in labor.
9 The LORD is the one
who makes birth possible.
And he will see that Zion
has many more children.
The LORD has spoken.

10 If you love Jerusalem,
celebrate and shout!
If you were in sorrow
because of the city,
you can now be glad.
11 She will nurse and comfort you,
just like your own mother,
until you are satisfied.
You will fully enjoy
her wonderful glory.

12 The LORD has promised:
"I will flood Jerusalem
with the wealth of nations
and make the city prosper.
Zion will nurse you at her breast,
carry you in her arms,
and hold you in her lap.
13 I will comfort you there
like a mother
comforting her child."

14 When you see this happen,
you will celebrate;
your strength will return
faster than grass can sprout.
Then everyone will know
that the LORD is present
with his servants,

[u]**65.23** *their children . . . diseases*: One possible meaning for the difficult Hebrew text.
[v]**66.2** *that's . . . be*: One possible meaning for the difficult Hebrew text. [w]**66.3** *You sacrifice oxen . . . idols*: Or "Sacrificing oxen to me is the same as murder; sacrificing lambs to me is the same as sacrificing dogs to other gods; offering grain to me is the same as offering pigs' blood to idols; and burning incense to me is the same as praising idols." [x]**66.4** *punish*: One possible meaning for the difficult Hebrew text. [y]**66.5** *Some . . . happy*: One possible meaning for the difficult Hebrew text.

but he is angry
with his enemies.
15 The LORD will come down
like a whirlwind
with his flaming chariots.
He will be terribly furious
and punish his enemies
with fire.
16 The LORD's fiery sword
will bring justice
everywhere on this earth
and execute many people.

A Threat and a Promise

17Some of you get yourselves ready
and go to a garden to worship a foreign
goddess.[z] You eat the meat of pigs,
lizards, and mice. But I, the LORD, will
destroy you for this.
18I know everything you do and think!
The time has now come[a] to bring together the people of every language and
nation and to show them my glory 19by
proving what I can do.[b] I will send the
survivors to Tarshish, Pul,[c] Lud, Meshech,[d] Tubal, Javan,[e] and to the distant
islands. I will send them to announce
my wonderful glory to nations that have
never heard about me.
20They will bring your relatives from
the nations as an offering to me, the
LORD. They will come on horses, chariots, wagons, mules, and camels[f] to
Jerusalem, my holy mountain. It will be
like the people of Israel bringing the
right offering to my temple. 21I promise
that some of them will be priests and
others will be helpers in my temple. I,
the LORD, have spoken.
22I also promise that you will always
have descendants and will never be forgotten, just as the new heavens and the
new earth that I create will last forever.
23On the first day of each month and on
each Sabbath, everyone will worship
me. I, the LORD, have spoken.
24My people will go out and look at
the dead bodies of those who turned
against me. The worms there never die,
the fire never stops burning, and the
sight of those bodies will be disgusting
to everyone.

[z]**66.17** *Some . . . goddess*: One possible meaning for the difficult Hebrew text.
[a]**66.18** *I . . . come*: One possible meaning for the difficult Hebrew text. [b]**66.19** *by . . . do*: One possible meaning for the difficult Hebrew text. [c]**66.19** *Pul*: Hebrew; one ancient translation "Put," a country in Africa, but neither the location of Pul or Put is known for certain. [d]**66.19** *Meshech*: One ancient translation; Hebrew "those who use bows and arrows." [e]**66.19** *Tarshish . . . Javan*: Tarshish may have been a Phoenician city in Spain; Put (see note on Pul) and Lud were African people; Meshech and Tubal were regions south or southeast of the Black Sea; the Javan were people of Asia Minor and the Greek islands.
[f]**66.20** *camels*: One possible meaning for the difficult Hebrew text.

JEREMIAH

ABOUT THIS BOOK

The world of Jeremiah's time was full of wars as new empires conquered the old ones. The tiny kingdom of Judah was caught in the middle, and during Jeremiah's lifetime, Babylonia conquered Judah and ended its freedom as a nation.

Jeremiah began bringing the Lord's message to the people of Judah when he was young, possibly less than 20 years old. He continued until 586 B.C., when the Babylonians captured Jerusalem. Some of the people of Judah soon forced him to go with them to Egypt, where he continued to speak to them for the Lord.

Many of Jeremiah's messages include the date when they were originally spoken. But when his friend Baruch helped him put the messages into writing, they did not arrange the messages by these dates. Usually the messages are grouped together because they are about similar subjects.

Jeremiah acted out many of his messages, so that the people would know exactly what the Lord was saying (see 13.1-11; 19.1-11; 27.1—28.17; 32.1-44; 43.7-13).

Time after time, Jeremiah said God was going to punish Judah. But because he also said the people of Judah should surrender to the Babylonians, his enemies accused him of being a traitor. They had him thrown in prison and even tried to have him killed. Jeremiah complained to God about his problems, and these complaints are now known as his "Confessions" (see 11.18-23; 12.1-6; 15.10, 11, 15-21; 17.14-18; 18.19-23; 20.7-18.)

Jeremiah often reminded the people of Judah that they had broken their agreement to worship only the Lord. And so the Lord was going to punish them by letting the Babylonians take them away to Babylonia. But the Lord had also promised to bring his people back to their land someday, and at that time the Lord would make a new agreement with them:

"I will write my laws
on their hearts and minds.
I will be their God,
and they will be my people.

"No longer will they have to teach one another to obey me. I, the LORD, promise that all of them will obey me, ordinary people and rulers alike. I will forgive their sins and forget the evil things they have done." *(31.33b, 34)*

A QUICK LOOK AT THIS BOOK

God Chooses Jeremiah To Speak for Him (1)
God Will Punish the People of Judah and Jerusalem (2–26)
Jeremiah against the Lying Prophets (27–29)
God Will Someday Bring His People back to their Land (30–33)
Scenes from Jeremiah's Ministry (34–38)
The Fall of Jerusalem and Later Events in Judah (39–42)
Jeremiah in Egypt (43–44)
A Message for Baruch (45)
The Lord Speaks about the Nations (46–51)
Another Account of the Fall of Jerusalem (52)

1 My name is Jeremiah. I am a priest,
and my father Hilkiah and everyone
else in my family are from Anathoth in
the territory of the Benjamin tribe. This
book contains the things that the LORD
told me to say. 2The LORD first spoke to
me in the thirteenth year that Josiah[a]
was king of Judah, 3and he continued to
speak to me during the rule of Josiah's
son Jehoiakim.[b] The last time the LORD
spoke to me was in the fifth month[c] of
the eleventh year that Josiah's son
Zedekiah[d] was king. That was also
when the people of Jerusalem were
taken away as prisoners.

The LORD Chooses Jeremiah

4The LORD said:

5 "Jeremiah, I am your Creator,
and before you were born,
I chose you to speak for me
to the nations."

6I replied, "I'm not a good speaker,
LORD, and I'm too young."
7"Don't say you're too young," the
LORD answered. "If I tell you to go and
speak to someone, then go! And when I
tell you what to say, don't leave out a
word! 8I promise to be with you and
keep you safe, so don't be afraid."
9The LORD reached out his hand, then
he touched my mouth and said, "I am
giving you the words to say, 10and I am
sending you with authority to speak to
the nations for me. You will tell them of
doom and destruction, and of rising and
rebuilding again."
11The LORD showed me something in a
vision. Then he asked, "What do you
see, Jeremiah?"
I answered, "A branch of almonds that
ripen early."
12"That's right," the LORD replied, "and
I always rise early[e] to keep a promise."
13Then the LORD showed me something else and asked, "What do you see
now?"
I answered, "I see a pot of boiling water in the north, and it's about to spill
out toward us."
14The LORD said:

I will pour out destruction
all over the land.
15 Just watch while I send
for the kings of the north.
They will attack and capture
Jerusalem and other towns,
then set up their thrones
at the gates of Jerusalem.
16 I will punish my people,
because they are guilty
of turning from me
to worship idols.

17 Jeremiah, get ready!
Go and tell the people
what I command you to say.
Don't be frightened by them,
or I will make you terrified
while they watch.

18 My power will make you strong
like a fortress
or a column of iron
or a wall of bronze.
You will oppose all of Judah,
including its kings and leaders,
its priests and people.
19 They will fight back,
but they won't win.
I, the LORD, give my word—
I won't let them harm you.

Israel's Unfaithfulness

2 The LORD told me 2to go to Jerusalem and tell everyone that he had
said:

When you were my young bride,
you loved me and followed me
through the barren desert.
3 You belonged to me alone,
like the first part of the harvest,
and I severely punished
those who mistreated you.

4 Listen, people of Israel,[f]
5 and I, the LORD, will speak.
I was never unfair
to your ancestors,
but they left me
and became worthless
by following worthless idols.
6 Your ancestors refused
to ask for my help,
though I had rescued them
from Egypt
and led them through
a treacherous, barren desert,
where no one lives
or dares to travel.

7 I brought you here to my land,
where food is abundant,
but you made my land filthy
with your sins.
8 The priests who teach my laws
don't care to know me.
Your leaders rebel against me;

[a]**1.2** *Josiah*: Ruled 640-609 B.C. [b]**1.3** *Jehoiakim*: Ruled 609-598 B.C. [c]**1.3** *fifth month*: Ab, the fifth month of the Hebrew calendar, from about mid-July to mid-August. [d]**1.3** *Zedekiah*: Ruled 598-586 B.C. [e]**1.11,12** *almonds . . . rise early*: In Hebrew "almonds that ripen early" sounds like "always rise early." [f]**2.4** *Israel*: After the nation was divided, the northern kingdom was called "Israel," and the southern kingdom was called "Judah" (see 1 Kings 12.1-20). In 722 B.C. the Assyrians conquered the northern kingdom, and Judah was all that was left. And so in the book of Jeremiah the name "Israel" is most often used of the southern kingdom.

your prophets
give messages from Baal
and worship false gods.

The LORD Accuses His People

9 I will take you to court
and accuse you
and your descendants
*10 of a crime that no nation
has ever committed before.
Just ask anyone, anywhere,
from the eastern deserts
to the islands in the west.
11 You will find that no nation
has ever abandoned its gods
even though they were false.
I am the true and glorious God,
but you have rejected me
to worship idols.
12 Tell the heavens
to tremble with fear!
13 You, my people, have sinned
in two ways—
you have rejected me, the source
of life-giving water,
and you've tried to collect water
in cracked and leaking pits
dug in the ground.

14 People of Israel,
you weren't born slaves;
you were captured in war.
15 Enemies roared like lions
and destroyed your land;
towns lie burned and empty.
16 Soldiers from the Egyptian towns
of Memphis and Tahpanhes
have cracked your skulls.
17 It's all your own fault!
You stopped following me,
the LORD your God,
18 and you trusted the power
of Egypt and Assyria.[g]
19 Your own sins will punish you,
because it was a bitter mistake
for you to reject me
without fear of punishment.
I, the LORD All-Powerful,
have spoken.

20 Long ago you left me
and broke all ties between us,
refusing to be my servant.
Now you worship other gods
by having sex
on hilltops or in the shade
of large trees.[h]
21 You were a choice grapevine,
but now you produce nothing
but small, rotten grapes.

Israel Is Stained with Guilt

22The LORD said:

People of Israel,
you are stained with guilt,
and no soap or bleach
can wash it away.
23 You deny your sins
and say, "We aren't unclean.
We haven't worshiped Baal."[i]
But think about what you do
in Hinnom Valley.[j]
And you run back and forth
like young camels,
as you rush to worship one idol
after another.
24 You are a female donkey
sniffing the desert air,
wanting to mate
with just anyone.
You are an easy catch!
25 Your shoes are worn out,
and your throat is parched
from running here and there
to worship foreign gods.
"Stop!" I shouted,
but you replied, "No!
I love those gods too much."

26 You and your leaders
are more disgraceful
than thieves—
you and your kings,
your priests and prophets
27 worship stone idols
and sacred poles
as if they had created you
and had given you life.
You have rejected me,
but when you're in trouble,
you cry to me for help.
28 Go cry to the gods you made!
There should be enough of them
to save you,
because Judah has as many gods
as it has towns.

Israel Rebels against the LORD

29The LORD said to Israel:

You accuse me of not saving you,
but I say you have rebelled.
30 I tried punishing you,
but you refused
to come back to me,
and like fierce lions
you killed my prophets.

31 Now listen to what I say!
Did I abandon you in the desert
or surround you with darkness?

[g]**2.18** *trusted . . . Assyria*: Hebrew "went to Egypt and drank from the Shihor River, and you went to Assyria and drank from the Euphrates River." [h]**2.20** *having sex . . . trees*: In some Canaanite religions, worshipers had sex with temple prostitutes, who represented their gods; many of the Canaanite places of worship were on hilltops or under large trees. [i]**2.23** *Baal*: The Hebrew text has "the Baals," probably because the god Baal was believed to be present in different forms at different places of worship. [j]**2.23** *Hinnom Valley*: Hebrew "the valley" (see 7.31-32; 19.1-6).

You are my people,
yet you have told me,
"We'll do what we want,
and we refuse
to worship you!"
32 A bride could not forget
to wear her jewelry
to her wedding,
but you have forgotten me
day after day.
33 You are so clever
at finding lovers
that you could give lessons
to a prostitute.
34 You killed innocent people
for no reason at all.
And even though their blood
can be seen on your clothes,
35 you claim to be innocent,
and you want me to stop
being angry with you.
So I'll take you to court,
and we'll see who is right.

36 When Assyria let you down,
you ran to Egypt,
but you'll find no help there,
37 and you will leave
in great sadness.[k]
I won't let you find help
from those you trust.

Sin and Shame

3 The LORD said to the people of Israel:

If a divorced woman marries,
can her first husband
ever marry her again?
No, because this
would pollute the land.
But you have more gods
than a prostitute has lovers.
Why should I take you back?
2 Just try to find one hilltop
where you haven't gone
to worship other gods
by having sex.[l]
You sat beside the road
like a robber in ambush,
except you offered yourself
to every passerby.
Your sins of unfaithfulness
have polluted the land.
3 So I, the LORD, refused
to let the spring rains fall.
But just like a prostitute,
you still have no shame
for what you have done.
4 You call me your father
or your long-lost friend;
5 you beg me to stop being angry,
but you won't stop sinning.

The LORD Asks Israel To Come Back to Him

6When Josiah[m] was king, the LORD
said:
Jeremiah, the kingdom of Israel[n] was
like an unfaithful wife who became a
prostitute on the hilltops and in the
shade of large trees.[o] 7-8I knew that the
kingdom of Israel had been unfaithful
and committed many sins, yet I still
hoped she might come back to me. But
she didn't, so I divorced her and sent
her away.
Her sister, the kingdom of Judah, saw
what happened, but she wasn't worried
in the least, and I watched her become
unfaithful like her sister. 9The kingdom
of Judah wasn't sorry for being a prostitute, and she didn't care that she had
made both herself and the land unclean
by worshiping idols of stone and wood.
10And worst of all, the people of Judah
pretended to come back to me. 11Even
the people of Israel were honest enough
not to pretend.
12Jeremiah, shout toward the north:

Israel, I am your LORD—
come back to me!
You were unfaithful
and made me furious,
but I am merciful,
and so I will forgive you.
13 Just admit that you rebelled
and worshiped foreign gods
under large trees everywhere.
14 You are unfaithful children,
but you belong to me.
Come home!
I'll take one or two of you
from each town and clan
and bring you to Zion.
15 Then I'll appoint wise rulers
who will obey me,
and they will care for you
like shepherds.

16 You will increase in numbers,
and there will be no need
to remember the sacred chest
or to make a new one.[p]
17 The whole city of Jerusalem
will be my throne.[q]
All nations will come here
to worship me,
and they will no longer follow
their stubborn, evil hearts.
18 Then, in countries to the north,

[k]**2.37** *in great sadness*: Or "as prisoners." [l]**3.2** *hilltop . . . sex*: See the note at 2.20. [m]**3.6** *Josiah*: Ruled 640-609 B.C. [n]**3.6** *Israel*: The northern kingdom (see the note at 2.4). [o]**3.6** *prostitute . . . trees*: See the note at 2.20. [p]**3.16** *make a new one*: The sacred chest was probably destroyed or taken away by the Babylonians when they captured Jerusalem in 586 B.C. [q]**3.16,17** *sacred chest . . . throne*: The sacred chest was thought to be God's throne on earth.

you people of Judah and Israel
will be reunited,
and you will return to the land
I gave your ancestors.
19 I have always wanted
to treat you as my children
and give you the best land,
the most beautiful on earth.
I wanted you to call me "Father"
and not turn from me.
20 But instead, you are like a wife
who broke her wedding vows.
You have been unfaithful to me.
I, the LORD, have spoken.

The People Confess Their Sins

The LORD said:
21 Listen to the noise
on the hilltops!
It's the people of Israel,
weeping and begging me
to answer their prayers.
They forgot about me
and chose the wrong path.
22 I will tell them, "Come back,
and I will cure you
of your unfaithfulness."

They will answer,
"We will come back, because you
are the LORD our God.
23 On hilltops, we worshiped idols
and made loud noises,
but it was all for nothing—
only you can save us.
24 Since the days of our ancestors
when our nation was young,
that shameful god Baal[r] has taken
our crops and livestock,
our sons and daughters.
25 We have rebelled against you
just like our ancestors,
and we are ashamed of our sins."

How Israel Can Return to the LORD

4 The LORD said:
Israel, if you really want
to come back to me, get rid
of those disgusting idols.
2 Make promises only in my name,
and do what you promise!
Then all nations will praise me,
and I will bless them.
3 People of Jerusalem and Judah,
don't be so stubborn!
Your hearts have become hard,
like unplowed ground
where thornbushes grow.
4 With all your hearts,
keep the agreement
I made with you.
But if you are stubborn
and keep on sinning,
my anger will burn like a fire
that cannot be put out.

Disaster Is Coming

The Lord said:
*5 "Sound the trumpets, my people.
Warn the people of Judah,[s]
'Run for your lives!
6 Head for Jerusalem
or another walled town!'

"Jeremiah, tell them I'm sending
disaster from the north.
7 An army will come out,
like a lion from its den.
It will destroy nations
and leave your towns empty
and in ruins."

8 Then I said
to the people of Israel,
"Put on sackcloth![t]
Mourn and cry out,
'The LORD is still angry
with us.'"

9 The LORD said,

"When all this happens,
the king and his officials,
the prophets and the priests
will be shocked and terrified."

10 I said, "You are the LORD God. So
why have you fooled everyone, especially the people of Jerusalem? Why did
you promise peace, when a knife is at
our throats?"

The Coming Disaster

11-12 When disaster comes, the LORD
will tell you people of Jerusalem,

"I am sending a windstorm
from the desert—
not a welcome breeze.[u]
And it will sweep you away
as punishment for your sins.
13 Look! The enemy army
swoops down like an eagle;
their cavalry and chariots
race faster than storm clouds
blown by the wind."

Then you will answer,
"We are doomed!"

14 But Jerusalem, there is still time
for you to be saved.

[r] **3.24** *that shameful god Baal*: The Hebrew text has "The Shame," which was sometimes used as a way of making fun of the Canaanite god Baal. [s] **4.5** *Judah*: Hebrew "Judah and Jerusalem." [t] **4.8** *sackcloth*: A rough, dark-colored cloth made from goat or camel hair and used to make grain sacks. It was worn in times of trouble or sorrow. [u] **4.11,12** *a welcome breeze*: Hebrew "a wind to blow away the husks." Farmers used a special shovel to pitch grain and husks into the air. Wind would blow away the light husks, and the grain would fall back to the ground, where it could be gathered up.

Wash the evil from your hearts
and stop making sinful plans,
15 before a message of disaster
arrives from the hills of Ephraim
and the town of Dan.[v]

16-17 The LORD said,

"Tell the nations that my people
have rebelled against me.
And so an army will come
from far away
to surround Jerusalem
and the towns of Judah.
I, the LORD, have spoken.

18 "People of Judah,
your hearts will be in pain,
but it's your own fault
that you will be punished."

Jeremiah's Vision of the Coming Punishment

19 I can't stand the pain!
My heart pounds,
as I twist and turn in agony.
I hear the signal trumpet
and the battle cry of the enemy,
and I cannot be silent.
20 I see the enemy defeating us
time after time,
leaving everything in ruins.
Even my own home
is destroyed in a moment.
21 How long will I see enemy flags
and hear their trumpets?

22 I heard the LORD say,
"My people ignore me.
They are foolish children
who do not understand
that they will be punished.
All they know is how to sin."

23 After this, I looked around.
The earth was barren,
with no form of life.
The sun, moon, and stars
had disappeared.
24 The mountains were shaking;
25 no people could be seen,
and all the birds
had flown away.
26 Farmland had become a desert,
and towns were in ruins.
The LORD's fierce anger
had done all of this.

The Death of Jerusalem

27-28 The LORD said:

I have made my decision,
and I won't change my mind.
This land will be destroyed,
although not completely.
The sky will turn dark,
and the earth will mourn.

29 Enemy cavalry and archers
shout their battle cry.
People run for their lives
and try to find safety
among trees and rocks.
Every town is empty.

30 Jerusalem, your land
has been wiped out.
But you act like a prostitute
and try to win back your lovers,
who now hate you.
You can put on a red dress,
gold jewelry, and eye shadow,
but it's no use—
your lovers are out to kill you!

31 I heard groaning and crying.
Was it a woman giving birth
to her first child?
No, it was Jerusalem.
She was gasping for breath
and begging for help.
"I'm dying!" she said.
"They have murdered me."

Is Anyone Honest and Faithful?

The LORD said to me:
5 "Search Jerusalem
for honest people
who try to be faithful.
If you can find even one,
I'll forgive the whole city.
2 Everyone breaks promises
made in my name."

3 I answered, "I know
that you look for truth.
You punished your people
for their lies,
but in spite of the pain,
they became more stubborn
and refused to turn back
to you."
4 Then I thought to myself,
"These common people
act like fools,
and they have never learned
what the LORD their God
demands of them.
5 I'll go and talk to the leaders.
They know what God demands."
But even they had decided
not to obey the LORD.

6 The people have rebelled
and rejected the LORD
too many times.
So enemies will attack
like lions from the forest
or wolves from the desert.

[v] 4.15 *Ephraim . . . Dan*: The hills of Ephraim were to the north of Jerusalem, and Dan was even farther north. They would be reached by the invading army first.

Those enemies will watch
the towns of Judah,
and like leopards
they will tear to pieces
whoever goes outside.

Enemies Will Punish Judah

The LORD said:
7 People of Judah,
how can I forgive you?
I gave you everything,
but you abandoned me
and worshiped idols.
You men go to prostitutes
and are unfaithful
to your wives.
8 You are no better than animals,
and you always want sex
with someone else's wife.

9 Why shouldn't I punish
the people of Judah?
10 I will tell their enemies,
"Go through my vineyard.
Don't destroy the vines,
but cut off the branches,
because they are the people
who don't belong to me."

11 In every way, Judah and Israel
have been unfaithful to me.
*12 Their prophets lie and say,
"The LORD won't punish us.
We will have peace
and plenty of food."
13 They tell these lies in my name,
so now they will be killed in war
or starve to death.

14 I am the LORD God All-Powerful.
Jeremiah, I will tell you
exactly what to say.
Your words will be a fire;
Israel and Judah
will be the fuel.

15 People of Israel,
I have made my decision.
An army from a distant country
will attack you.
I've chosen an ancient nation,
and you won't understand
their language.
16 All of them are warriors,
and their arrows bring death.
17 This nation will eat your crops
and livestock;
they will leave no fruit
on your vines or trees.
And although you feel safe
behind thick walls,
your towns will be destroyed
and your children killed.

Israel Refused To Worship the LORD

18 The LORD said:
Jeremiah, the enemy army won't kill
everyone in Judah. 19 And the people
who survive will ask, "Why did the LORD
our God do such terrible things to us?"
Then tell them:

I am the LORD,
but you abandoned me
and worshiped other gods
in your own land.
Now you will be slaves
in a foreign country.
20 Tell these things to each other,
you people of Judah,
you descendants of Jacob.

21 You fools! Why don't you listen
when I speak?
Why can't you understand
22 that you should worship me
with fear and trembling?
I'm the one who made the shore
to hold back the ocean.
Waves may crash on the beach,
but they can come no farther.
23 You stubborn people have rebelled
and turned your backs on me.
24 You refuse to say,
"Let's worship the LORD!
He's the one who sends rain
in spring and autumn
and gives us a good harvest."
25 That's why I cannot bless you!

*26 A hunter traps birds
and puts them in a cage,
but some of you trap humans
and make them your slaves.
27 You are evil, and you lie and cheat
to make yourselves rich.
You are powerful
28 and prosperous,
but you refuse to help[w] the poor
get the justice they deserve.
29 You need to be punished,
and so I will take revenge.
30 Look at the terrible things
going on in this country.
I am shocked!
31 Prophets give their messages
in the name of a false god,[x]
my priests don't want
to serve me,[y]
and you—my own people—
like it this way!
But on the day of disaster,
where will you turn for help?

A Warning for the People of Jerusalem

The LORD said:
6 Run for your lives,
people of Benjamin.
Get out of Jerusalem.

[w] **5.28** *refuse to help*: One possible meaning for the difficult Hebrew text. [x] **5.31** *give . . . god*: Or "tell lies." [y] **5.31** *don't . . . me*: Or "don't care what I want."

Sound a trumpet in Tekoa
and light a signal fire
in Beth-Haccherem.
Soon you will be struck
by disaster from the north.
*2 Jerusalem is a lovely pasture,
but shepherds will surround it
and divide it up,
3 then let their flocks
eat all the grass.[z]
4 Kings will tell their troops,
"If we reach Jerusalem
in the morning,
we'll attack at noon.
But if we arrive later,
5 we'll attack after dark
and destroy its fortresses."

6 I am the LORD All-Powerful,
and I will command these armies
to chop down trees
and build a ramp up to the walls
of Jerusalem.

People of Jerusalem,
I must punish you
for your injustice.
7 Evil pours from your city
like water from a spring.
Sounds of violent crimes
echo within your walls;
victims are everywhere,
wounded and dying.

8 Listen to me,
you people of Jerusalem
and Judah.
I will abandon you,
and your land will become
an empty desert.
9 I will tell your enemies
to leave your nation bare
like a vine stripped of grapes.
I, the LORD All-Powerful,
have spoken.

Jeremiah's Anger

10 I have told the people
that you, LORD,
will punish them,
but they just laugh
and refuse to listen.
11 Your anger against Judah
flames up inside me,
and I can't hold it in
much longer.

The LORD's Anger Will Sweep Everyone Away

The LORD answered:
Don't hold back my anger!
Let it sweep away everyone—
the children at play
and all adults,
young and old alike.
12 I'll punish the people of Judah
and give to others
their houses and fields,
as well as their wives.
I, the LORD, have spoken.

13 Everyone is greedy and dishonest,
whether poor or rich.
Even the prophets and priests
cannot be trusted.
14 All they ever offer
to my deeply wounded people
are empty hopes for peace.
15 They should be ashamed
of their disgusting sins,
but they don't even blush.
And so, when I punish Judah,
they will end up on the ground,
dead like everyone else.
I, the LORD, have spoken.

The People of Judah Rejected God's Way of Life

16 The LORD said:

My people, when you stood
at the crossroads,
I told you, "Follow the road
your ancestors took,
and you will find peace."
But you refused.
17 I also sent prophets
to warn you of danger,
but when they sounded the alarm,
you paid no attention.
*18 So I tell all nations on earth,
"Watch what I will do!
19 My people ignored me
and rejected my laws.
They planned to do evil,
and now the evil they planned
will happen to them."

20 People of Judah,
you bring me incense from Sheba
and spices from distant lands.
You offer sacrifices of all kinds.
But why bother?
I hate these gifts of yours!
21 So I will put stumbling blocks
in your path,
and everyone will die,
including parents and children,
neighbors and friends.

An Army from the North

22 The LORD said,

"Look toward the north,
where a powerful nation
has prepared for war.
23 Its well-armed troops are cruel
and never show mercy.

[z] **6.2,3** *Jerusalem . . . grass*: One possible meaning for the difficult Hebrew text.

Their galloping horses sound
like ocean waves
pounding on the shore.
This army will attack you,
lovely Jerusalem."

[24]Then the people said,

"Just hearing about them
makes us tremble with fear,
and we twist and turn in pain
like a woman giving birth."

[25]The LORD said,

"Don't work in your fields
or walk along the roads.
It's too dangerous.
The enemy is well armed
26 and attacks without warning.
So mourn, my people, as though
your only child had died.
Wear clothes made of sackcloth[a]
and roll in the ash pile."

The LORD's People Must Be Tested

The LORD said:
27 Jeremiah, test my people
as though they were metal.
28 And you'll find they are hard
like bronze and iron.
They are stubborn rebels,
always spreading lies.
*29 Silver can be purified
in a fiery furnace,
30 but my people are too wicked
to be made pure,
and so I have rejected them.

Jeremiah Speaks in the Temple
(Jeremiah 26.1-6)

7 [1-3]The LORD told me to stand by the
gate of the temple[b] and to tell the
people who were going in that the LORD
All-Powerful, the God of Israel, had
said:
Pay attention, people of Judah!
Change your ways and start living right,
then I will let you keep on living in your
own country.[c] [4]Don't fool yourselves!
My temple is here in Jerusalem, but that
doesn't mean I will protect you. [5]I will
keep you safe only if you change your
ways. Be fair and honest with each
other. [6]Stop taking advantage of foreigners, orphans, and widows. Don't kill
innocent people. And stop worshiping
other gods. [7]Then I will let you enjoy a
long life in this land I gave your ancestors.
[8]But just look at what is happening!
You put your trust in worthless lies.
[9]You steal and murder; you lie in court
and are unfaithful in marriage. You worship idols and offer incense to Baal,
when these gods have never done anything for you. [10]And then you come into
my temple and worship me! Do you
think I will protect you so that you can
go on sinning? [11]You are thieves, and
you have made my temple your hideout.
But I've seen everything you have done.
[12]Go to Shiloh, where my sacred tent
once stood. Take a look at what I did
there. My people Israel sinned, and so I
destroyed Shiloh!
[13]While you have been sinning, I have
been trying to talk to you, but you
refuse to listen. [14]Don't think this temple will protect you. Long ago I told
your ancestors to build it and worship
me here, but now I have decided to tear
it down, just as I destroyed Shiloh.
[15]And as for you, people of Judah, I'm
going to send you away from my land,
just as I sent away the people of
Ephraim and the other northern tribes.

Punishment for Worshiping Other Gods

[16]Jeremiah, don't pray for these people! I, the LORD, would refuse to listen.
[17]Do you see what the people of Judah
are doing in their towns and in the
streets of Jerusalem? [18]Children gather
firewood, their fathers build fires, and
their mothers mix dough to bake bread
for the goddess they call the Queen of
Heaven.[d] They even offer wine sacrifices to other gods, just to insult me.
[19]But they are not only insulting me;
they are also insulting themselves by
doing these shameful things.
[20]And now, I, the LORD All-Powerful,
will flood Judah with my fiery anger until nothing is left—no people or animals,
no trees or crops.

It Is Useless To Offer Sacrifices

[21]The LORD told me to say to the people of Judah:
I am the LORD All-Powerful, the God
of Israel, but I won't accept sacrifices
from you. So don't even bother bringing
them to me. You might as well just cook
the meat for yourselves.
[22]At the time I brought your ancestors
out of Egypt, I didn't command them to
offer sacrifices to me. [23]Instead, I told
them, "If you listen to me and do what I
tell you, I will be your God, you will be
my people, and all will go well for you."
[24]But your ancestors refused to listen.
They were stubborn, and whenever I
wanted them to go one way, they always
went the other. [25]Ever since your ancestors left Egypt, I have been sending my
servants the prophets to speak for me.
[26]But you have ignored me and become
even more stubborn and sinful than
your ancestors ever were!

[a]**6.26** *sackcloth*: See the note at 4.8. [b]**7.1-3** *temple*: The Hebrew text has "house of the LORD," another name for the temple. [c]**7.1-3** *let you . . . own country*: Or "live here with you." [d]**7.18** *Queen of Heaven*: Probably another name for the goddess Astarte.

Slaughter Valley

The LORD *said:*
27 Jeremiah, no matter what you do,
the people won't listen. 28 So you must
say to them:
People of Judah, I am the LORD your
God, but you have refused to obey me,
and you didn't change when I punished
you. And now, you no longer even pretend to be faithful to me.

29 Shave your head bald
and throw away the hair.
Sing a funeral song
on top of a barren hill.
You people have made me angry,
and I have abandoned you.

30 You have disobeyed me by putting
your disgusting idols in my temple, and
now the temple itself is disgusting to
me. 31 At Topheth in Hinnom Valley you
have built altars where you kill your
children and burn them as sacrifices to
other gods. I would never think of
telling you to do this. 32 So watch out!
Someday that place will no longer be
called Topheth or Hinnom Valley. It will
be called Slaughter Valley, because you
will bury your dead there until you run
out of room, 33 and then bodies will lie
scattered on the ground. Birds and wild
animals will come and eat, and no one
will be around to scare them off. 34 When
I am finished with your land, there will
be deathly silence in the empty ruins of
Jerusalem and the towns of Judah—no
happy voices, no sounds of parties or
wedding celebrations.

8 Then the bones of the dead kings of
Judah and their officials will be dug
up, along with the bones of the priests,
the prophets, and everyone else in
Jerusalem 2 who loved and worshiped
the sun, moon, and stars. These bones
will be scattered and left lying on the
ground like trash, where the sun and
moon and stars can shine on them.
3 Some of you people of Judah will be
left alive, but I will force you to go to
foreign countries, and you will wish
you were dead. I, the LORD God All-
Powerful, have spoken.

The People Took the Wrong Road

4 The LORD said:

People of Jerusalem,
when you stumble and fall,
you get back up,
and if you take a wrong road,
you turn around and go back.[e]
5 So why do you refuse
to come back to me?
Why do you hold so tightly
to your false gods?

6 I listen carefully,
but none of you admit
that you've done wrong.
Without a second thought,
you run down the wrong road[f]
like cavalry troops
charging into battle.

7 Storks, doves, swallows,
and thrushes
all know when it's time
to fly away for the winter
and when to come back.
But you, my people,
don't know what I demand.
8 You say, "We are wise
because we have the teachings
and laws of the LORD."
But I say that your teachers
have turned my words
into lies!
9 Your wise men
have rejected what I say,
and so they have no wisdom.
Now they will be trapped
and put to shame;
they won't know what to do.
10 I'll give their wives and fields
to strangers.

Everyone is greedy and dishonest,
whether poor or rich.
Even the prophets and priests
cannot be trusted.
11 All they ever offer
to my deeply wounded people
are empty hopes for peace.
12 They should be ashamed
of their disgusting sins,
but they don't even blush.
And so, when I punish Judah,
they will end up on the ground,
dead like everyone else.
13 I will wipe them out.[g]
They are vines without grapes;
fig trees without figs or leaves.
They have not done a thing
that I told them![h]
I, the LORD, have spoken.

The People and Their Punishment

14 The people of Judah
say to each other,
"What are we waiting for?
Let's run to a town with walls
and die there.
We rebelled against the LORD,
and we were sentenced to die
by drinking poison.
15 We had hoped for peace

[e] 8.4 *if you take ... go back*: One possible meaning for the difficult Hebrew text. [f] 8.6 *you run down the wrong road*: One possible meaning for the difficult Hebrew text. [g] 8.13 *I will wipe them out*: One possible meaning for the difficult Hebrew text. [h] 8.13 *They have not ... them*: One possible meaning for the difficult Hebrew text.

and a time of healing,
but all we got was terror.
16 Our enemies have reached
the town of Dan in the north,
and the snorting of their horses
makes us tremble with fear.
The enemy will destroy Jerusalem
and our entire nation.
No one will survive."

17 "Watch out!" the LORD says.
"I'm sending poisonous snakes
to attack you,
and no one can stop them."

Jeremiah Mourns for His People

18 I'm burdened with sorrow
and feel like giving up.
19 In a foreign land
my people are crying.
Listen! You'll hear them say,
"Has the LORD deserted Zion?
Is he no longer its king?"

I hear the LORD reply,
"Why did you make me angry
by worshiping useless idols?"

20 The people complain,
"Spring and summer
have come and gone,
but still the LORD
hasn't rescued us."

21 My people are crushed,
and so is my heart.
I am horrified and mourn.
22 If medicine and doctors
may be found in Gilead,
why aren't my people healed?

9 I wish that my eyes
were fountains of tears,
so I could cry day and night
for my people
who were killed.
2 I wish I could go into the desert
and find a hiding place
from all who are treacherous
and unfaithful to God.

The LORD Answers Jeremiah

3The LORD replied:

Lies come from the mouths
of my people,
like arrows from a bow.
With each dishonest deed
their power increases,
and not one of them will admit
that I am God.

4 Jeremiah, all your friends
and relatives
tell lies about you,
so don't trust them.
5 They wear themselves out,
always looking for a new way
to cheat their friends.
6 Everyone takes advantage
of everyone else,
and no one will admit
that I am God.

7 And so I will purify
the hearts of my people
just as gold is purified
in a furnace.
I have no other choice.
8 They say they want peace,
but this lie is deadly,
like an arrow that strikes
when you least expect it.
9 Give me one good reason
not to punish them
as they deserve.
I, the LORD All-Powerful,
have spoken.

Jeremiah Weeps for His People

10 I weep for the pastureland
in the hill country.
It's so barren and scorched
that no one travels there.
No cattle can be found there,
and birds and wild animals
have all disappeared.

11 I heard the LORD reply,
"When I am finished,
Jerusalem and the towns of Judah
will be piles of ruins
where only jackals[i] live."

Why the Land Was Destroyed

12I said to the LORD, "None of us can
understand why the land has become
like an uncrossable desert. Won't you
explain why?"
13The LORD said:
I destroyed the land because the
people disobeyed me and rejected
my laws and teachings. 14They were
stubborn and worshiped Baal,[j] just
as their ancestors did. 15So I, the
LORD All-Powerful, the God of Israel,
promise them poison to eat and
drink.[k] 16I'll scatter them in foreign
countries that they and their ancestors have never even heard of. Finally, I will send enemy soldiers to
kill every last one of them.

The Women Who Are Paid To Weep

17 The LORD All-Powerful said,
"Send for the women

[i]**9.11** *jackals*: Desert animals related to wolves, but smaller. [j]**9.14** *Baal*: See the note at 2.23. [k]**9.15** *poison to eat and drink*: Or "bitter disappointment to eat, and tears to drink."

who are paid to weep
at funerals,[l]
especially the women
who can cry the loudest."

18 The people answered,
"Let them come quickly
and cry for us,
until our own eyes
are flooded with tears.
19 Now those of us on Zion cry,
'We are ruined!
We can't stand the shame.
Our homes have been destroyed,
and we must leave our land.'

20 "We ask you women
to pay attention
to what the LORD says.
We will teach you a funeral song
that you can teach
your daughters and friends:
21 'We were in our fortress,
but death sneaked in
through our windows.
It even struck down
children at play
and our strongest young men.'

22 "The LORD has told us
the ground will be covered
with dead bodies,
like stalks of ungathered grain
or like manure."

What the LORD Likes Best

23 The LORD says:

Don't brag about your wisdom
or strength or wealth.
24 If you feel you must brag,
then have enough sense
to brag about worshiping me,
the LORD.
What I like best
is showing kindness,
justice, and mercy
to everyone on earth.

25-26 Someday I will punish the nations
of Egypt, Edom, Ammon, and Moab, and
the tribes of the desert.[m] The men of
these nations are circumcised, but they
don't worship me. And it's the same
with you people of Judah. Your bodies
are circumcised, but your hearts are unchanged.

The LORD Talks about Idols

10 *1 The LORD said:

Listen to me,
you people of Israel.
2 Don't follow the customs
of those nations
who become frightened
when they see something strange
happen in the sky.
3 Their religion is worthless!
They chop down a tree,
carve the wood into an idol,
4 cover it with silver and gold,
and then nail it down
so it won't fall over.

5 An idol is no better
than a scarecrow.
It can't speak,
and it has to be carried,
because it can't walk.
Why worship an idol
that can't help or harm you?

Jeremiah Praises the LORD

6 Our LORD, great and powerful,
you alone are God.
7 You are King of the nations.
Everyone should worship you.
No human anywhere on earth
is wiser than you.
8 Idols are worthless,
and anyone who worships them
is a fool!
9 Idols are made by humans.
A carver shapes the wood.
A metalworker hammers out
a covering of gold from Uphaz
or of silver from Tarshish.
Then the idol is dressed
in blue and purple clothes.

10 You, LORD, are the only true
and living God.
You will rule for all time.
When you are angry
the earth shakes,
and nations are destroyed.

11 You told me to say
that idols did not create
the heavens and the earth,
and that you, the LORD,
will destroy every idol.

12 With your wisdom and power
you created the earth
and spread out the heavens.
13 The waters in the heavens roar
at your command.
You make clouds appear—
you send the winds
from your storehouse
and make lightning flash
in the rain.

14 People who make idols
are so stupid!
They will be disappointed,

[l]9.17 *women . . . weep at funerals*: Or "the women who weep for Baal"; the god Baal was believed to have died and come back to life, and some women would go to places of worship and weep over the death of Baal. [m]9.25,26 *the tribes of the desert*: One possible meaning for the difficult Hebrew text.

because their false gods
are not alive.
15 Idols are merely a joke,
and when the time is right,
they will be destroyed.

16 But you, Israel's God,
created all things,
and you chose Israel
to be your very own.
Your name is the LORD
All-Powerful.

Judah Will Be Thrown from Its Land

17 I said to the people of Judah,
"Gather your things;
you are surrounded.
18 The LORD said these troubles
will lead to your capture,
and he will throw you
from this land
like a rock from a sling."[n]

19 The people answered,
"We are wounded
and doomed to die.
Why did we say
we could stand the pain?
20 Our homes are destroyed;
our children are dead.
No one is left
to help us find shelter."

21 But I told them,
"Our leaders were stupid failures,
because they refused
to listen to the LORD.
And so we've been scattered
like sheep.

22 "Sounds of destruction
rumble from the north
like distant thunder.
Soon our towns will be ruins
where jackals[o] live."

Jeremiah Prays

23 I know, LORD, that we humans
are not in control
of our own lives.
24 Correct me, as I deserve,
but not in your anger,
or I will be dead.
25 Our enemies refuse
to admit that you are God
or to worship you.
They have wiped out our people
and left our nation
lying in ruins.
So get angry
and sweep them away!

Judah Has Broken the LORD's Agreement

11 1-3The LORD God told me to say
to the people of Judah and Jerusalem:
I, the LORD, am warning you that I
will put a curse on anyone who
doesn't keep the agreement I made
with Israel. So pay attention to what
it says. 4My commands haven't
changed since I brought your ancestors out of Egypt, a nation that
seemed like a blazing furnace where
iron ore is melted. I told your ancestors that if they obeyed my commands, I would be their God, and
they would be my people. 5Then I
did what I had promised and gave
them this wonderful land, where you
now live.
"Yes, LORD," I replied, "that's true."
6Then the LORD told me to say to
everyone on the streets of Jerusalem
and in the towns of Judah:
Pay attention to the commands in
my agreement with you. 7Ever since
I brought your ancestors out of
Egypt, I have been telling your people to obey me. But you and your ancestors 8have always been stubborn.
You have refused to listen, and instead you have done whatever your
sinful hearts have desired.
You have not kept the agreement
we made, so I will make you suffer
every curse that goes with it.
9The LORD said to me:
Jeremiah, the people of Judah and
Jerusalem are plotting against me.
10They have sinned in the same way
their ancestors did, by turning from
me and worshiping other gods. The
northern kingdom of Israel broke
the agreement I made with your ancestors, and now the southern kingdom of Judah[p] has done the same.
11Here is what I've decided to do. I
will bring suffering on the people of
Judah and Jerusalem, and no one
will escape. They will beg me to
help, but I won't listen to their
prayers. 12-13Then they will offer sacrifices to their other gods and ask
them for help. After all, the people of
Judah have more gods than towns,
and more altars for Baal than there
are streets in Jerusalem. But those
gods won't be able to rescue the
people of Judah from disaster.
14Jeremiah, don't pray for these
people or beg me to rescue them. If
you do, I won't listen, and I certainly
won't listen if they pray!
15Then the LORD told me to say to the
people of Judah:

You are my chosen people,
but you have no right
to be here in my temple,
doing such terrible things.

[n] **10.18** *like a rock from a sling*: One possible meaning for the difficult Hebrew text.
[o] **10.22** *jackals*: See the note at 9.11.
[p] **11.10** *Israel . . . Judah*: See the note at 2.4.

The sacrifices you offer me
won't protect you from disaster,
so stop celebrating.[q]
16 Once you were like an olive tree
covered with fruit.
But soon I will send a noisy mob
to break off your branches
and set you on fire.

17 I am the LORD All-Powerful. You people of Judah were like a tree that I had planted, but you have made me angry by offering sacrifices to Baal, just as the northern kingdom did. And now I'm going to pull you up by the roots.

The Plot To Kill Jeremiah

*18 Some people plotted to kill me.
And like a lamb
being led to the butcher,
I knew nothing
about their plans.
19 But then the LORD told me
that they had planned
to chop me down like a tree—
fruit and all—
so that no one would ever
remember me again.
20 I prayed, "LORD All-Powerful,
you always do what is right,
and you know every thought.
So I trust you to help me
and to take revenge."

21 Then the LORD said:
Jeremiah, some men from
Anathoth[r] say they will kill you, if
you keep on speaking for me. 22 But I
will punish them. Their young men
will die in battle, and their children
will starve to death. 23 And when I
am finished, no one from their families will be left alive.

Jeremiah Complains to the LORD

12 Whenever I complain
to you, LORD,
you are always fair.
But now I have questions
about your justice.
Why is life easy for sinners?
Why are they successful?
2 You plant them like trees;
you let them prosper
and produce fruit.
Yet even when they praise you,
they don't mean it.

3 But you know, LORD,
how faithful I've always been,
even in my thoughts.
So drag my enemies away
and butcher them like sheep!

4 How long will the ground be dry
and the pasturelands parched?
The birds and animals
are dead and gone.
And all of this happened because
the people are so sinful.
They even brag, "God can't see
the sins we commit."[s]

The LORD Answers Jeremiah

5 Jeremiah, if you get tired
in a race against people,
how can you possibly run
against horses?
If you fall in open fields,
what will happen in the forest
along the Jordan River?
6 Even your own family
has turned against you.
They act friendly,
but don't trust them.
They're out to get you,
and so is everyone else.

The LORD Is Furious with His People

7 I loved my people and chose them
as my very own.
But now I will reject them
and hand them over
to their enemies.
8 My people have turned against me
and roar at me like lions.
That's why I hate them.

9 My people are like a hawk
surrounded and attacked
by other hawks.[t]
Tell the wild animals
to come and eat their fill.
10 My beautiful land is ruined
like a field or a vineyard
trampled by shepherds
and stripped bare
by their flocks.
11 Every field I see lies barren,
and no one cares.

12 A destroying army
marches along desert roads
and attacks everywhere.
They are my deadly sword;
no one is safe from them.

13 My people, you planted wheat,
but because I was furious,
I let only weeds grow.
You wore yourselves out
for nothing!

The LORD Will Have Pity on Other Nations

14 The LORD said:
I gave this land to my people Israel,
but enemies around it have attacked

[q] **11.15** *celebrating*: One possible meaning for the difficult Hebrew text of verse 15.
[r] **11.21** *Anathoth*: Jeremiah's hometown (see 1.1).
[s] **12.4** *God can't see the sins we commit*: Or "Jeremiah won't live to see what happens to us."
[t] **12.9** *My people . . . other hawks*: Or "My land has become a hyena's den with vultures circling above."

and robbed it. So I will uproot them
from their own countries just as I will
uproot Judah from its land. 15But later, I
will have pity on these nations and
bring them back to their own lands.
16They once taught my people to worship Baal. But if they admit I am the
only true God, and if they let my people
teach them how to worship me, these
nations will also become my people.
17However, if they don't listen to me, I
will uproot them from their lands and
completely destroy them. I, the LORD,
have spoken.

Jeremiah's Linen Shorts

13 The LORD told me, "Go and buy a
pair of linen shorts. Wear them
for a while, but don't wash them." 2So I
bought a pair of shorts and put them on.
3Then the LORD said, 4"Take off the
shorts. Go to Parah[u] and hide the shorts
in a crack between some large rocks."
5And that's what I did.
6Some time later the LORD said, "Go
back and get the shorts." 7I went back
and dug the shorts out of their hiding
place, but the cloth had rotted, and the
shorts were ruined.
8Then the LORD said:
9Jeremiah, I will use Babylonia to[v]
destroy the pride of the people of Judah and Jerusalem. 10The people of
Judah are evil and stubborn. So instead of listening to me, they do
whatever they want and even worship other gods. When I am finished
with these people, they will be good
for nothing, just like this pair of
shorts. 11These shorts were tight
around your waist, and that's how
tightly I held onto the kingdoms of
Israel and Judah. I wanted them to
be my people. I wanted to make
them famous, so that other nations
would praise and honor me, but they
refused to obey me.

Wine Jars

The LORD said:
12Jeremiah, tell the people of Judah,
"The LORD God of Israel orders you to
fill your wine jars with wine."
They will answer, "Of course we fill
our wine jars with wine! Why are you
telling us something we already know?"
13Then say to them:
I am the LORD, and what I'm going
to do will make everyone in Judah
and Jerusalem appear to be full of
wine. And the worst ones will be the
kings of David's family and the
priests and the prophets. 14Then I
will smash them against each other
like jars. I will have no pity on the
young or the old, and they will all be
destroyed. I, the LORD, have spoken.

The People of Judah Will Be Taken Away

15 People of Judah,
don't be too proud to listen
to what the LORD has said.
16 You hope for light,
but God is sending darkness.
Evening shadows already deepen
in the hills.
So return to God
and confess your sins to him
before you trip and fall.
17 If you are too proud to listen,
I will weep alone.
Tears will stream from my eyes
when the LORD's people
are taken away as prisoners.

18 The LORD told me to tell you
that your king and his mother[w]
must surrender their thrones
and remove their crowns.[x]
19 The cities in the Southern Desert
are surrounded;
no one can get in or out.
Everyone in Judah
will be taken away.
20 Jerusalem, you were so proud
of ruling the people of Judah.
But where are they now?

Look north, and you will see
your enemies approaching.
21 You once trusted them to help,
but now I'll let them rule you.[y]
What do you say about that?
You will be in pain
like a woman giving birth.

22 Do you know why
your clothes were torn off
and you were abused?
It was because
of your terrible sins.
23 Can you ever change
and do what's right?
Can people change the color
of their skin,
or can a leopard
remove its spots?
If so, then maybe you can change
and learn to do right.

24 I will scatter you,
just as the desert wind
blows husks from grain
tossed in the air.

[u] **13.4** *Parah*: Or "the Euphrates River." Parah was a village about five and a half miles northeast of Jerusalem. [v] **13.9** *I will use Babylonia to*: Or "that's how I'm going to."
[w] **13.18** *mother*: The king's mother usually had an important position in the royal court.
[x] **13.18** *and remove their crowns*: One possible meaning for the difficult Hebrew text.
[y] **13.21** *You once . . . rule you*: One possible meaning for the difficult Hebrew text.

25 I won't change my mind.
I, the LORD, have spoken.

You rejected me
and worshiped false gods.
*26 You were married to me,
but you were unfaithful.
You even became a prostitute[z]
by worshiping disgusting gods
on hilltops and in fields.
27 So I'll rip off your clothes
and leave you naked and ashamed
for everyone to see.
You are doomed!
Will you ever be worthy
to worship me again?

The Land Dries Up

14 When there had been no rain for a long time, the LORD told me to say to the people:

2 Judah and Jerusalem weep
as the land dries up.
3 Rulers send their servants
to the storage pits for water.[a]
But there's none to be found;
they return in despair
with their jars still empty.

4 There has been no rain,
and farmers feel sick
as they watch cracks appear
in the dry ground.[b]

5 A deer gives birth in a field,
then abandons her newborn fawn
and leaves in search of grass.
6 Wild donkeys go blind
from starvation.
So they stand on barren hilltops
and sniff the air,[c]
hoping to smell green grass.

The LORD's People Pray

7 Our terrible sins may demand
that we be punished.
But if you rescue us, LORD,
everyone will see
how great you are.
8 You're our only hope;
you alone can save us now.
You help us one day,
but you're gone the next.
9 Did this disaster
take you by surprise?
Are you a warrior
with your hands tied?
You have chosen us,
and your temple is here.
Don't abandon us!

The LORD's Answer

10 My people,
you love to wander away;
you don't even try
to stay close to me.
So now I will reject you
and punish you for your sins.
I, the LORD, have spoken.

Lying Prophets

11The LORD said, "Jeremiah, don't ask
me to help these people. 12They may
even go without eating[d] and offer sacrifices to please me[e] and to give thanks.[f]
But when they cry out for my help, I
won't listen, and I won't accept their
sacrifices. Instead, I'll send war, starvation, and disease to wipe them out."
13I replied, "The other prophets keep
telling everyone that you won't send
starvation or war, and that you're going
to give us peace."
14The LORD answered:
They claim to speak for me, but
they're lying! I didn't even speak to
them, much less choose them to be
my prophets. Their messages come
from worthless dreams, useless fortunetelling, and their own imagina-
tions.
15Those lying prophets say there
will be peace and plenty of food. But
I say that those same prophets will
die from war and hunger. 16And
everyone who listens to them will be
killed, just as they deserve. Their
dead bodies will be thrown out into
the streets of Jerusalem, because
their families will also be dead, and
no one will be left to bury them.[g]
17Jeremiah, go and tell the people
how you feel about all this.
So I told them:

"Tears will flood my eyes
both day and night,

[z] 13.26 *prostitute*: See the note at 2.20. [a] 14.3 *storage pits for water*: Since water was scarce, pits were dug into solid rock for collecting and storing rainwater. These pits were called "cisterns." [b] 14.4 *cracks . . . ground*: One possible meaning for the difficult Hebrew text. [c] 14.6 *sniff the air*: The Hebrew text has "sniff the air, like jackals" (see the note at 9.11). [d] 14.12 *go without eating*: The people of Israel sometimes went without eating to show sorrow for their sins. [e] 14.12 *sacrifices to please me*: These sacrifices have traditionally been called "whole burnt offerings" because the whole animal was burned on the altar. A main purpose of such sacrifices was to please the LORD with the smell of the sacrifice, and so in the CEV they are sometimes called "sacrifices to please the LORD." [f] 14.12 *sacrifices . . . to give thanks*: These sacrifices have traditionally been called "grain offerings." A main purpose of such sacrifices was to thank the LORD with a gift of grain, and so in the CEV they are sometimes called "sacrifices to give thanks to the LORD." [g] 14.16 *dead bodies . . . bury them*: A proper burial was considered very important.

because my nation suffers
from a deadly wound.
18 In the fields I see the bodies
of those killed in battle.
And in the towns I see crowds
dying of hunger.
But the prophets and priests
go about their business,
without understanding
what has happened."[h]

Jeremiah Prays to the LORD

19 Have you rejected Judah, LORD?
Do you hate Jerusalem?
Why did you strike down Judah
with a fatal wound?
We had hoped for peace
and a time of healing,
but all we got was terror.
20 We and our ancestors are guilty
of rebelling against you.
21 If you save us, it will show
how great you are.
Don't let our enemies
disgrace your temple,
your beautiful throne.
Don't forget that you promised
to rescue us.
22 Idols can't send rain,
and showers don't fall
by themselves.
Only you control the rain,
so we put our trust in you,
the LORD our God.

The People of Judah Will Die

15 The LORD said to me:
Even if Moses and Samuel were
here, praying with you, I wouldn't
change my mind. So send the people of
Judah away. 2 And when they ask where
they are going, tell them that I, the
LORD, have said:

Some of you are going to die
of horrible diseases.
Others are going to die in war
or from starvation.
The rest will be led away
to a foreign country.
3 I will punish you
in four different ways:
You will be killed in war
and your bodies dragged off
by dogs,
your flesh will be eaten by birds,
and your bones will be chewed on
by wild animals.
4 This punishment will happen
because of the horrible things[i]
your King Manasseh[j] did.
And you will be disgusting
to all nations on earth.
5 People of Jerusalem,
who will feel sorry for you?
Will anyone bother
to ask if you are well?

6 My people, you abandoned me
and walked away.
I am tired of showing mercy;
that's why I'll destroy you
7 by scattering you like straw
blown by the wind.
I will punish you with sorrow
and death,
because you refuse
to change your ways.
8 There will be more widows
in Judah
than grains of sand on a beach.

A surprise attack at noon!
And the mothers in Jerusalem
mourn for their children.
9 A mother is in deep despair
and struggles for breath.
Her daylight has turned
to darkness—
she has suffered the loss
of her seven sons.

I will kill anyone who survives.
I, the LORD, have spoken.

Jeremiah Complains

10 I wish I had never been born!
I'm always in trouble
with everyone in Judah.
I never lend or borrow money,
but everyone curses me
just the same.

11 Then the LORD replied,
"I promise to protect you,
and when disaster comes,
even your enemies
will beg you for help."[k]

The Enemy Cannot Be Defeated

The LORD told me to say:
12 People of Judah,
just as you can't break iron
mixed with bronze,
you can't defeat the enemies
that will attack
from the north.
13 I will give them
everything you own,
because you have sinned
everywhere in your country.
14 My anger is a fire
that cannot be put out,[l]

[h] **14.18** *go about . . . has happened*: One possible meaning for the difficult Hebrew text. [i] **15.4** *the horrible things*: See 2 Kings 21.1-16. [j] **15.4** *Manasseh*: Hebrew "Manasseh son of Hezekiah"; he ruled 687-642 B.C. [k] **15.11** *help*: One possible meaning for the difficult Hebrew text of verse 11. [l] **15.14** *that cannot be put out*: Some Hebrew manuscripts; most Hebrew manuscripts "against you."

so I will make you slaves
of your enemies
in a foreign land.[m]

Jeremiah Complains Again

15 You can see how I suffer
insult after insult,
all because of you, LORD.
Don't be so patient
with my enemies;
take revenge on them
before they kill me.

16 When you spoke to me,
I was glad to obey,
because I belong to you,
the LORD All-Powerful.
17 I don't go to parties
and have a good time.
Instead, I keep to myself,
because you have filled me
with your anger.

18 I am badly injured
and in constant pain.
Are you going to disappoint me,
like a stream that goes dry
in the heat of summer?

The LORD Replies

19 Then the LORD told me:
Stop talking like a fool!
If you turn back to me
and speak my message,
I will let you be my prophet
once again.
I hope the people of Judah
will accept what you say.
But you can ignore their threats,
*20 because I am making you strong,
like a bronze wall.
They are evil and violent,
but when they attack,
21 I will be there to rescue you.
I, the LORD, have spoken.

Jeremiah Must Live His Message

16 The LORD said to me:
2Jeremiah, don't get married
and have children—Judah is no place to
raise a family. 3I'll tell you what's going
to happen to children and their parents
here. 4They will die of horrible diseases
and of war and starvation. No one will
give them a funeral or bury them, and
their bodies will be food for the birds
and wild animals. And what's left will
lie on the ground like manure.
5When someone dies, don't visit the
family or show any sorrow. I will no
longer love or bless or have any pity on
the people of Judah. 6Rich and poor
alike will die and be left unburied. No
one will mourn and show their sorrow
by cutting themselves or shaving their
heads.[n] 7No one will bring food and
wine to help comfort those who are
mourning the death of their father or
mother.
8Don't even set foot in a house where
there is eating and drinking and celebrating. 9Warn the people of Judah that
I, the LORD All-Powerful, will put an
end to all their parties and wedding celebrations. 10They will ask, "Why
has the LORD our God threatened us
with so many disasters? Have we done
something wrong or sinned against
him?"
11Then tell them I have said:
People of Judah, your ancestors
turned away from me; they rejected
my laws and teachings and started
worshiping other gods. 12And you
have done even worse! You are stubborn, and instead of obeying me,
you do whatever evil comes to your
mind. 13So I will throw you into a
land that you and your ancestors
know nothing about, a place where
you will have to worship other gods
both day and night. And I won't feel
the least bit sorry for you.
14A time will come when you will
again worship me. But you will no
longer call me the Living God who
rescued Israel from Egypt. 15Instead,
you will call me the Living God who
rescued you from that country in the
north and from the other countries
where I had forced you to go.
Someday I will bring you back to
this land that I gave your ancestors.
16But for now, I am sending enemies
who will catch you like fish and hunt
you down like wild animals in the
hills and the caves.
17I can see everything you are doing, even if you try to hide your sins
from me. 18I will punish you double
for your sins, because you have
made my own land disgusting. You
have filled it with lifeless idols that
remind me of dead bodies.

The LORD Gives Strength

I prayed to the LORD:
19 Our LORD, you are the one
who gives me strength
and protects me like a fortress
when I am in trouble.
People will come to you
from distant nations and say,
"Our ancestors worshiped
false and useless gods,

[m]**15.14** *I will make . . . land*: Many Hebrew manuscripts; most Hebrew manuscripts "I will make your enemies go through to a land you don't know about." [n]**16.6** *mourn and show their sorrow by cutting themselves or shaving their heads*: A custom in some Canaanite religions.

20 worthless idols
made by human hands."

21 Then the LORD replied,
"That's why I will teach them
about my power,
and they will know
that I am the true God."

The LORD Will Punish Judah

The LORD said:

17 People of Judah,
your sins cannot be erased.
They are written on your hearts
like words chiseled in stone
or carved on the corners
of your altars.[o]
*2 One generation after another
has set up pagan altars
and worshiped the goddess Asherah
everywhere in your country—
on hills and mountains,
and under large trees.
3 So I'll take everything you own,
including your altars,
and give it all
to your enemies.[p]
4 You will lose[q] the land
that I gave you,
and I will make you slaves
in a foreign country,
because you have made my anger
blaze up like a fire
that won't stop burning.

Trust the LORD

5 I, the LORD, have put a curse
on those who turn from me
and trust in human strength.
6 They will dry up like a bush
in salty desert soil,
where nothing can grow.

7 But I will bless those
who trust me.
8 They will be like trees
growing beside a stream—
trees with roots that reach
down to the water,
and with leaves
that are always green.
They bear fruit every year
and are never worried
by a lack of rain.

9 You people of Judah
are so deceitful
that you even fool yourselves,
and you can't change.
10 But I know your deeds
and your thoughts,
and I will make sure
you get what you deserve.
11 You cheated others,
but everything you gained
will fly away, like birds
hatched from stolen eggs.
Then you will discover
what fools you are.

Jeremiah Prays to the LORD

12 Our LORD, your temple
is a glorious throne
that has stood on a mountain
from the beginning.
13 You are a spring of water
giving Israel life and hope.
But if the people reject
what you have told me,
they will be swept away
like words written in dust.[r]

14 You, LORD, are the one I praise.
So heal me and rescue me!
Then I will be completely well
and perfectly safe.

15 The people of Judah say to me,
"Jeremiah, you claimed to tell us
what the LORD has said.
So why hasn't it come true?"

16 Our LORD, you chose me
to care for your people,
and that's what I have done.
You know everything I have said,
and I have never once
asked you to punish them.[s]
17 I trust you for protection
in times of trouble,
so don't frighten me.
18 Keep me from failure
and disgrace,
but make my enemies fail
and be disgraced.
Send destruction to make
their worst fears come true.

Resting on the Sabbath

19-20 The LORD said:
Jeremiah, stand at each city gate in
Jerusalem, including the one the king
uses, and speak to him and everyone
else. Tell them I have said:
I am the LORD, so pay attention.
21-24 If you value your lives, don't do
any work on the Sabbath. Don't
carry anything through the city
gates or through the door of your

[o] **17.1** *carved on the corners of your altars*: When sacrifices were offered to the LORD to ask him to forgive sins, some of the blood was smeared on the corners of the altar (see Leviticus 4.7, 18-20, 25, 26, 30, 31, 34, 35; 16.18). But now the LORD refuses to accept these sacrifices. [p] **17.3** *enemies*: One possible meaning for the difficult Hebrew text of verses 2, 3. [q] **17.4** *You will lose*: One possible meaning for the difficult Hebrew text. [r] **17.13** *reject . . . dust*: One possible meaning for the difficult Hebrew text. [s] **17.16** *you chose . . . punish them*: One possible meaning for the difficult Hebrew text.

house, or anywhere else. Keep the
Sabbath day sacred!
I gave this command to your ancestors, but they were stubborn and
refused to obey or to be corrected.
But if you obey, 25 then Judah and
Jerusalem will always be ruled by
kings from David's family. The king
and his officials will ride through
these gates on horses or in chariots,
and the people of Judah and
Jerusalem will be with them. There
will always be people living in
Jerusalem, 26 and others will come
here from the nearby villages, from
the towns of Judah and Benjamin,[t]
from the hill country and the
foothills to the west, and from the
Southern Desert. They will bring
sacrifices to please me and to give
me thanks,[u] as well as offerings of
grain and incense.
27 But if you keep on carrying
things through the city gates on the
Sabbath and keep treating it as any
other day, I will set fire to these
gates and burn down the whole city,
including the fortresses.

Jeremiah Goes to the Pottery Shop

18 The LORD told me, 2 "Go to the
pottery shop, and when you get
there, I will tell you what to say to the
people."
3 I went there and saw the potter making clay pots on his pottery wheel. 4 And
whenever the clay would not take the
shape he wanted, he would change his
mind and form it into some other shape.
5 Then the LORD told me to say:
6 People of Israel, I, the LORD, have
power over you, just as a potter has
power over clay. 7 If I threaten to uproot
and shatter an evil nation 8 and that nation turns from its evil, I will change my
mind.
9 If I promise to make a nation strong,
10 but its people start disobeying me and
doing evil, then I will change my mind
and not help them at all.
11 So listen to me, people of Judah and
Jerusalem! I have decided to strike you
with disaster, and I won't change my
mind unless you stop sinning and start
living right.
12 But I know you won't listen. You
might as well answer, "We don't care
what you say. We have made plans to
sin, and we are going to be stubborn
and do what we want!"
13 So I, the LORD, command you to ask
the nations, and find out if they have
ever heard of such a horrible sin as
what you have done.

14 The snow
on Lebanon's mountains
never melts away,
and the streams there
never run dry.[v]
15 But you, my people,
have turned from me
to burn incense
to worthless idols.
You have left the ancient road
to follow an unknown path
where you stumble over idols.

16 Your land will be ruined,
and every passerby
will look at it with horror
and make insulting remarks.
17 When your enemies attack,
I will scatter you like dust
blown by an eastern wind.
Then, on that day of disaster,
I will turn my back on you.

The Plot against Jeremiah

18 Some of the people said, "Let's get
rid of Jeremiah! We will always have
priests to teach us God's laws, as well as
wise people to give us advice, and
prophets to speak the LORD's messages.
So, instead of listening to Jeremiah any
longer, let's accuse him of a crime."

Jeremiah Prays about His Enemies

19 Please, LORD, answer my prayer.
Make my enemies stop
accusing me of evil.
20 I tried to help them,
but they are paying me back
by digging a pit to trap me.
I even begged you
not to punish them.
21 But now I am asking you
to let their children starve
or be killed in war.
Let women lose
their husbands and sons
to disease and violence.
22 These people have dug pits
and set traps for me, LORD.
Make them scream in fear
when you send enemy troops
to attack their homes.
23 You know they plan to kill me.
So get angry and punish them!
Don't ever forgive
their terrible crimes.

Jeremiah and the Clay Jar

19 The LORD said:
Jeremiah, go to the pottery shop
and buy a clay jar. Then take along

[t] **17.26** *Judah and Benjamin*: These two tribes made up the southern kingdom of Judah.
[u] **17.26** *sacrifices to please me and to give me thanks*: See the notes at 14.12. [v] **18.14** *dry*:
One possible meaning for the difficult Hebrew text of verse 14.

some of the city officials and leading
priests [2]and go to Hinnom Valley, just
outside Potsherd[w] Gate. Tell the people
that I have said:

[3]I am the LORD All-Powerful, the
God of Israel, and you kings of Judah and you people of Jerusalem
had better pay attention. I am going
to bring so much trouble on this valley that everyone who hears about it
will be shocked. [4-5]The people of Judah stopped worshiping me and
made this valley into a place of worship for Baal and other gods that
have never helped them or their ancestors or their kings. And they have
committed murder here, burning
their young, innocent children as
sacrifices to Baal. I have never even
thought of telling you to do that. [6]So
watch out! Someday this place will
no longer be called Topheth or Hinnom Valley. It will be called Slaughter Valley!

[7]You people of Judah and
Jerusalem may have big plans, but
here in this valley I'll ruin[x] those
plans. I'll let your enemies kill you,
and I'll tell the birds and wild animals to eat your dead bodies. [8]I will
turn Jerusalem into a pile of rubble,
and every passerby will be shocked
and horrified and will make insulting remarks. [9]And while your enemies are trying to break through
your city walls to kill you, the food
supply will run out. You will become
so hungry that you will eat the flesh
of your friends and even of your
own children.

[10]Jeremiah, as soon as you have said
this, smash the jar while the people are
watching. [11]Then tell them that I have
also said:

I am the LORD All-Powerful, and I
warn you that I will shatter Judah
and Jerusalem just like this jar that
is broken beyond repair. You will
bury your dead here in Topheth, but
so many of you will die that there
won't be enough room.

[12-13]I will make Jerusalem as unclean as Topheth, by filling the city
with your dead bodies. I will do this
because you and your kings have
gone up to the roofs of your houses
and burned incense to the stars in
the sky, as though they were gods.
And you have given sacrifices of
wine to foreign gods.

Jeremiah Speaks in the Temple Courtyard

[14]I went to Topheth, where I told the
people what the LORD had said. Then I
went to the temple courtyard and
shouted to the people, [15]"Listen, everyone! Some time ago, the LORD All-
Powerful, the God of Israel, warned you
that he would bring disaster on
Jerusalem and all nearby villages. But
you were stubborn and refused to listen.
Now the LORD is going to bring the disaster he promised."

Pashhur Arrests Jeremiah

20 Pashhur son of Immer was a
priest and the chief of temple security. He heard what I had said, [2]and so
he hit me.[y] Then he had me arrested
and put in chains[z] at the Benjamin Gate
in the LORD's temple.[a] [3]The next day,
when Pashhur let me go free, I told him
that the LORD had said:

No longer will I call you Pashhur.
Instead, I will call you Afraid-of-
Everything.[b] [4]You will be afraid, and
you will bring fear to your friends as
well. You will see enemies kill them
in battle. Then I will have the king of
Babylonia take everyone in Judah
prisoner, killing some and dragging
the rest away to Babylonia. [5]He will
clean out the royal treasury and take
everything else of value from
Jerusalem.

[6]Pashhur, you are guilty of telling
lies and claiming they were messages from me. That's why I will
have the Babylonians take you, your
family, and your friends as prisoners
to Babylonia, where you will all die
and be buried.

Jeremiah Complains to the LORD

7 You tricked me, LORD,
and I was really fooled.
You are stronger than I am,
and you have defeated me.
People never stop sneering
and insulting me.
8 You have let me announce
only destruction and death.
Your message has brought me
nothing but insults
and trouble.
9 Sometimes I tell myself
not to think about you, LORD,
or even mention your name.
But your message burns

[w]**19.2** *Potsherd*: A piece of broken pottery. [x]**19.7** *ruin*: In Hebrew "ruin" sounds like "jar" (see verse 1). [y]**20.2** *hit me*: Or "beat me up" or "had me beaten up." [z]**20.2** *in chains*: Or "in the stocks" (a wooden frame with holes for the hands, neck, or feet of a prisoner) or "in a prison cell." [a]**20.2** *the Benjamin Gate in the LORD's temple*: The Hebrew text has "the upper Benjamin Gate in the temple"; the lower Benjamin Gate may have been the city gate of that name. [b]**20.3** *Afraid-of-Everything*: Hebrew "Magor-Missabib."

in my heart and bones,
and I cannot keep silent.

10 I heard the crowds whisper,
"Everyone is afraid.
Now's our chance
to accuse Jeremiah!"
All of my so-called friends
are just waiting
for me to make a mistake.
They say, "Maybe Jeremiah
can be tricked.
Then we can overpower him
and get even at last."

11 But you, LORD,
are a mighty soldier,
standing at my side.
Those troublemakers
will fall down and fail—
terribly embarrassed,
forever ashamed.

12 LORD All-Powerful,
you test those who do right,
and you know every heart
and mind.
I have told you my complaints,
so let me watch you
take revenge on my enemies.
13 I sing praises to you, LORD.
You rescue the oppressed
from the wicked.

14 Put a curse on the day I was born!
Don't bless my mother.
15 Put a curse on the man
who told my father, "Good news!
You have a son."
16 May that man be like the towns
you destroyed without pity.
Let him hear shouts of alarm
in the morning
and battle cries at noon.
17 He deserves to die
for not killing me
before I was born.
Then my mother's body
would have been my grave.
18 Why did I have to be born?
Was it just to suffer
and die in shame?

The LORD Will Fight against Jerusalem

21 King Zedekiah[c] of Judah sent for
Pashhur son of Malchiah and for
a priest named Zephaniah son of Maaseiah. Then he told them, "Talk with Jeremiah for me."

So they came to me and said, 2"King
Nebuchadnezzar[d] of Babylonia has attacked Judah. Please ask the LORD to work miracles for our people, as he has done in the past, so that Nebuchadnezzar will leave us alone."

3-7I told them that the LORD God of Israel had told me to say to King Zedekiah:

The Babylonians have surrounded Jerusalem and want to kill you and your people. You are asking me to save you, but you have made me furious. So I will stretch out my mighty arm and fight against you myself. Your army is using spears and swords to fight the Babylonians, but I will make your own weapons turn and attack you. I will send a horrible disease to kill many of the people and animals in Jerusalem, and there will be nothing left to eat. Finally, I will let King Nebuchadnezzar and his army fight their way to the center of Jerusalem and capture everyone who is left alive, including you and your officials. But Nebuchadnezzar won't be kind or show any mercy—he will have you killed! I, the LORD, have spoken.

8Then I told them that the LORD had
said:

People of Jerusalem, I, the LORD, give you the choice of life or death.
9The Babylonian army has surrounded Jerusalem, so if you want to live, you must go out and surrender to them. But if you want to die because of hunger, disease, or war, then stay here in the city. 10I have
decided not to rescue Jerusalem. Instead, I am going to let the king of Babylonia burn it to the ground. I, the LORD, have spoken.

The LORD Warns the King of Judah

*11 Pay attention, you that belong
to the royal family.
12 Each new day, make sure
that justice is done,
and rescue those
who are being robbed.
Or else my anger will flame up
like a fire that never goes out.

13 Jerusalem,
from your mountaintop
you look out over the valleys[e]
and think you are safe.
But I, the LORD, am angry,
14 and I will punish you
as you deserve.
I'll set your palace[f] on fire,
and everything around you
will go up in smoke.

[c]21.1 *Zedekiah*: See the note at 1.3. [d]21.2 *Nebuchadnezzar*: Ruled 605-562 B.C.
[e]21.13 *Jerusalem . . . valleys*: One possible meaning for the difficult Hebrew text.
[f]21.14 *your palace*: The Hebrew text has "the forest"; the largest room in the king's palace was known as Forest Hall (see 1 Kings 7.2,3).

The LORD Will Punish the King of Judah

22 1-3The LORD sent me to the palace
of the king of Judah to speak to
the king, his officials, and everyone else
who was there. The LORD told me to say:

I am the LORD, so pay attention! You have been allowing people to cheat, rob, and take advantage of widows, orphans, and foreigners who live here. Innocent people have become victims of violence, and some of them have even been killed. But now I command you to do what is right and see that justice is done. Rescue everyone who has suffered from injustice.

4If you obey me, the kings from
David's family will continue to rule Judah from this palace. They and their officials will ride in and out on their
horses or in their chariots. 5But if you
ignore me, I promise in my own name
that this palace will lie in ruins. 6Listen
to what I think about it:

The palace of Judah's king
is as glorious as Gilead
or Lebanon's highest peaks.
But it will be as empty
as a ghost-town
when I'm through with it.
7 I'll send troops to tear it apart,
and its beautiful cedar beams
will be used for firewood.

8People from different nations will
pass by and ask, "Why did the LORD do
this to such a great city as Jerusalem?"
9Others will answer, "It's because the
people worshiped foreign gods and
broke the agreement that the LORD their
God had made with them."

King Jehoahaz

The LORD said:
10 King Josiah is dead,
so don't cry for him.[g]
Instead, cry for his son
King Jehoahaz,[h]
dragged off to another country,
never to return.

11-12Jehoahaz[i] became king of Judah after his father King Josiah died. But Jehoahaz was taken as a prisoner to a foreign country. Now I, the LORD, promise that he will die there without ever seeing his own land again.

King Jehoiakim

The LORD told me to say:
*13 King Jehoiakim,[j] you are doomed!
You built a palace
with large rooms upstairs.
14 You put in big windows
and used cedar paneling
and red paint.
But you were unfair
and forced the builders to work
without pay.

*15 More cedar in your palace
doesn't make you a better king
than your father Josiah.
He always did right—
he gave justice to the poor
and was honest.
16 That's what it means
to truly know me.
So he lived a comfortable life
and always had enough
to eat and drink.

17 But all you think about
is how to cheat
or abuse or murder
some innocent victim.
18 Jehoiakim, no one will cry
at your funeral.
They won't turn to each other
and ask,
"Why did our great king
have to die?"
19 You will be given a burial
fit for a donkey;
your body will be dragged
outside the city gates
and tossed in the dirt.
I, the LORD, have spoken.

King Jehoiachin and the People of Jerusalem

The LORD told me to say:
20 People of Jerusalem,
the nations[k] you trusted
have been crushed.
Go to Lebanon and weep;
cry in the land of Bashan
and in Moab.
21 When times were good,
I warned you.
But you ignored me,
just as you have done
since Israel was young.
22 Now you will be disgraced
because of your sins.
Your leaders will be swept away
by the wind,
and the nations you trusted
will be captured and dragged
to a foreign country.

[g]**22.10** *King Josiah . . . him*: The Hebrew text has "don't cry for the dead one," meaning King Josiah, who ruled 640-609 B.C. [h]**22.10** *his son, King Jehoahaz . . . country*: The Hebrew text has "the one who was dragged off to another country," meaning King Jehoahaz, who ruled for three months in 609 B.C. [i]**22.11,12** *Jehoahaz*: The Hebrew text has "Shallum," another name for Jehoahaz. [j]**22.13** *Jehoiakim*: See the note at 1.3. [k]**22.20** *nations*: Or "gods."

23 Those who live in the palace
paneled with cedar[l]
will groan with pain
like women giving birth.

24King Jehoiachin,[m] son of Jehoiakim,[n] even if you were the ring I
wear as the sign of my royal power, I
would still pull you from my finger. 25I
would hand you over to the enemy you
fear, to King Nebuchadnezzar[o] and his
army, who want to kill you. 26You and
your mother[p] were born in Judah, but I
will throw both of you into a foreign
country, where you will die, 27longing to
return home.

28 Jehoiachin, you are unwanted
like a broken clay pot.
So you and your children
will be thrown into a country
you know nothing about.

29 Land of Judah, I am the LORD.
Now listen to what I say!
30 Erase the names
of Jehoiachin's children
from the royal records.
He is a complete failure,
and so none of them
will ever be king.
I, the LORD, have spoken.

A Message of Hope

The LORD said:

23 You leaders of my people are like
shepherds that kill and scatter the
sheep. 2You were supposed to take care
of my people, but instead you chased
them away. So now I'll really take care
of you, and believe me, you will pay for
your crimes!

3I will bring the rest of my people
home from the lands where I have scattered them, and they will grow into a
mighty nation. 4I promise to choose
leaders who will care for them like real
shepherds. All of my people will be
there, and they will never again be
frightened.

5 Someday I will appoint
an honest king
from the family of David,
a king who will be wise
and rule with justice.
6 As long as he is king,
Israel will have peace,
and Judah will be safe.
The name of this king will be
"The LORD Gives Justice."

7A time will come when you will
again worship me. But you will no
longer call me the Living God who rescued Israel from Egypt. 8Instead, you
will call me the Living God who rescued
you from the land in the north and from
all the other countries where I had
forced you to go. And you will once
again live in your own land.

Jeremiah Thinks about Unfaithful Prophets

9 When I think of the prophets,
I am shocked, and I tremble[q]
like someone drunk,
because of the LORD
and his sacred words.
10 Those unfaithful prophets
misuse their power
all over the country.
So God turned the pasturelands
into scorching deserts.[r]

The LORD Will Punish Unfaithful Prophets

11The LORD told me to say:

You prophets and priests
think so little of me, the LORD,
that you even sin
in my own temple!
12 Now I will punish you
with disaster,
and you will slip and fall
in the darkness.
I, the LORD, have spoken.

13 The prophets in Samaria
were disgusting to me,
because they preached
in the name of Baal
and led my people astray.
14 And you prophets in Jerusalem
are even worse.
You're unfaithful in marriage[s]
and never tell the truth.[t]
You even lead others to sin
instead of helping them
turn back to me.
You and the people of Jerusalem
are evil like Sodom
and Gomorrah.[u]
15 You prophets in Jerusalem
have spread evil everywhere.
That's why I, the LORD, promise

[l]**22.23** *who live in the palace paneled with cedar*: The Hebrew text has "who live in Lebanon and who nest among the cedars," which probably means Forest Hall in the royal palace at Jerusalem, which was paneled with cedar and had cedar columns and a cedar ceiling, all from Lebanon (see 1 Kings 7.2, 3). [m]**22.24** *Jehoiachin*: The Hebrew text has "Coniah," another form of Jehoiachin's name; he ruled for three months in 598 B.C. [n]**22.24** *Jehoiakim*: See the note at 1.3. [o]**22.25** *Nebuchadnezzar*: See the note at 21.2. [p]**22.26** *mother*: See the note at 13.18. [q]**23.9** *tremble*: Or "become weak." [r]**23.10** *deserts*: One possible meaning for the difficult Hebrew text of verse 10. [s]**23.14** *in marriage*: Or "to me." [t]**23.14** *never tell the truth*: Or "worship other gods." [u]**23.14** *Sodom and Gomorrah*: Two cities that the LORD destroyed because their people were so evil (see Genesis 18.16—19.29).

to give you bitter poison
to eat and drink.

The LORD Gives a Warning

The LORD said:
16 Don't listen to the lies
of these false prophets,
you people of Judah!
The message they preach
is something they imagined;
it did not come from me,
the LORD All-Powerful.
17 These prophets go to people
who refuse to respect me
and who are stubborn
and do whatever they want.
The prophets tell them,
"The LORD has promised
everything will be fine."

18 But I, the LORD, tell you
that these prophets
have never attended a meeting
of my council in heaven[v]
or heard me speak.
19 They are evil! So in my anger
I will strike them
like a violent storm.
20 I won't calm down,
until I have finished
what I have decided to do.
Someday you will understand
exactly what I mean.
21 I did not send these prophets
or speak to them,
but they ran to find you
and to preach their message.
22 If they had been in a meeting
of my council in heaven,
they would have told
you people of Judah
to give up your sins
and come back to me.

23 I am everywhere—
both near and far,
24 in heaven and on earth.
There are no secret places
where you can hide from me.

25These unfaithful prophets claim that
I have given them a dream or a vision,
and then they tell lies in my name. 26But
everything they say comes from their
own twisted minds. How long can this
go on? 27They tell each other their
dreams and try to get my people to reject me, just as their ancestors left me
and worshiped Baal. 28Their dreams and
my truth are as different as straw and
wheat. But when prophets speak for me,
they must say only what I have told
them. 29My words are a powerful fire;
they are a hammer that shatters rocks.
30-32These unfaithful prophets claim I
give them their dreams, but it isn't true.
I didn't choose them to be my prophets,
and yet they babble on and on, speaking
in my name, while stealing words from
each other. And when my people hear
these liars, they are led astray instead of
being helped. So I warn you that I am
now the enemy of these prophets. I, the
LORD, have spoken.

News and Nuisance

The LORD said to me:
33Jeremiah, when a prophet or a priest
or anyone else comes to you and asks,
"Does the LORD have news for us?" tell
them, "You people are a nuisance[w] to
the LORD, and he[x] will get rid of you."
34If any of you say, "Here is news from
the LORD," I will punish you and your
families, even if you are a prophet or a
priest. 35Instead, you must ask your
friends and relatives, "What answer did
the LORD give?" or "What has the LORD
said?" 36It seems that you each have
your own news! So if you say, "Here is
news from the LORD," you are twisting
my words into a lie. Remember that I
am your God, the LORD All-Powerful.
37If you go to a prophet, it's all right to
ask, "What answer did the LORD give to
my question?" or "What has the LORD
said?" 38But if you disobey me and say,
"Here is news from the LORD," 39I will
pick you up[y] and throw you far away.
And I will abandon this city of
Jerusalem that I gave to your ancestors.
40You will never be free from your
shame and disgrace.

Jeremiah Has a Vision of Two Baskets of Figs

24 The LORD spoke to me in a vision
after King Nebuchadnezzar[z] of
Babylonia had come to Judah and taken
King Jehoiachin,[a] his officials, and all
the skilled workers back to Babylonia.
In this vision I saw two baskets of figs
in front of the LORD's temple. 2One basket was full of very good figs that
ripened early, and the other was full of
rotten figs that were not fit to eat.
3"Jeremiah," the LORD asked, "what do
you see?"

[v]**23.18** *a meeting of my council in heaven*: Sometimes, prophets had visions of the LORD meeting with his angels (see 1 Kings 22.19-23). [w]**23.33** *news . . . nuisance*: The Hebrew word for "news" in verses 33-38 is the same as "nuisance" and is related to "pick up" in verse 39. [x]**23.33** *You people are a nuisance to the LORD, and he*: Two ancient translations; Hebrew "Does the LORD have news for us? He." [y]**23.39** *pick you up*: A few Hebrew manuscripts and three ancient translations; most Hebrew manuscripts "forget you completely." [z]**24.1** *Nebuchadnezzar*: See the note at 21.2. [a]**24.1** *Jehoiachin*: The Hebrew text has "Jeconiah," another form of Jehoiachin's name; he ruled for three months in 598 B.C.

"Figs," I said. "Some are very good,
but the others are too rotten to eat."
4Then the LORD told me to say:
5People of Judah, the good figs
stand for those of you I sent away as
exiles to Babylonia, 6where I am
watching over them. Then someday I
will bring them back to this land. I
will plant them, instead of uprooting
them, and I will build them up,
rather than tearing them down. 7I
will give them a desire to know me
and to be my people. They will want
me to be their God, and they will
turn back to me with all their heart.
8The rotten figs stand for King
Zedekiah[b] of Judah, his officials,
and all the others who were not
taken away to Babylonia, whether
they stayed here in Judah or went to
live in Egypt. 9I will punish them
with a terrible disaster, and everyone on earth will tremble when they
hear about it. I will force the people
of Judah to go to foreign countries,
where they will be cursed and insulted. 10War and hunger and disease will strike them, until they finally disappear from the land that I
gave them and their ancestors.

Seventy Years of Exile

25 1-2In the fourth year that Jehoiakim was king of Judah,[c]
which was the first year that Nebuchadnezzar[d] was king of Babylonia, the
LORD told me to speak to the people of
Judah and Jerusalem. So I told them:
3For twenty-three years now, ever
since the thirteenth year that Josiah[e]
was king, I have been telling you what
the LORD has told me. But you have not
listened.
4The LORD has sent prophets to you
time after time, but you refused to listen. 5They told you that the LORD had
said:
Change your ways! If you stop doing evil, I will let you stay forever in
this land that I gave your ancestors.
6I don't want to harm you. So don't
make me angry by worshiping idols
and other gods.
7But you refused to listen to my
prophets. So I, the LORD, say that
you have made me angry by worshiping idols, and you are the ones
who were hurt by what you did. 8You
refused to listen to me, 9and now I
will let you be attacked by nations
from the north, and especially by my
servant, King Nebuchadnezzar of
Babylonia. You and other nearby nations will be destroyed and left in
ruins forever. Everyone who sees
what has happened will be shocked,
but they will still make fun of you.
10I will put an end to your parties
and wedding celebrations; no one
will grind grain or be here to light
the lamps at night. 11This country
will be as empty as a desert, because
I will make all of you the slaves of
the king of Babylonia for seventy
years.
12When that time is up, I will punish the king of Babylonia and his
people for everything they have
done wrong, and I will turn that
country into a wasteland forever.
13My servant Jeremiah has told you
what I said I will do to Babylonia
and to the other nations, and he
wrote it all down in this book. I will
do everything I threatened. 14I will
pay back the Babylonians for every
wrong they have done. Great kings
from many other nations will conquer the Babylonians and force
them to be slaves.

The Cup Full of God's Anger

15The LORD God of Israel showed me a
vision in which he said, "Jeremiah, here
is a cup filled with the wine of my anger.
Take it and make every nation drink
some. 16They will vomit and act crazy,
because of the war this cup of anger will
bring to them."
17I took the cup from the LORD's hand,
and I went to the kings of the nations
and made each of them drink some. 18I
started with Jerusalem and the towns of
Judah, and the king and his officials
were removed from power in disgrace.
Everyone still makes insulting jokes
about them and uses their names as
curse words. 19The second place I went
was Egypt, where everyone had to drink
from the cup, including the king and his
officials, the other government workers,
the rest of the Egyptians, 20and all the
foreigners who lived in the country.
Next I went to the king of Uz, and
then to the four kings of Philistia, who
ruled from Ashkelon, Gaza, Ekron, and
what was left of Ashdod.[f] 21Then I went
to the kings of Edom, Moab, Ammon,
22and to the kings of Tyre, Sidon, and
their colonies across the sea. 23-24After
this, I went to the kings of Dedan, Tema,
Buz, the tribes of the Arabian Desert,[g]
25Zimri, Elam, Media, 26and the countries in the north, both near and far.

[b]**24.8** *Zedekiah*: Ruled 598-586 B.C. [c]**25.1,2** *Jehoiakim . . . Judah*: See the note at 1.3. [d]**25.1,2** *Nebuchadnezzar*: See the note at 21.2. [e]**25.3** *Josiah*: Hebrew "Josiah son of Amon"; Josiah ruled 640-609 B.C. [f]**25.20** *what was left of Ashdod*: It was defeated by the king of Egypt after being surrounded for twenty-nine years. [g]**25.23,24** *the tribes of the Arabian Desert*: One possible meaning for the difficult Hebrew text.

I went to all the countries on earth,
one after another, and finally to Babylonia.[h]
27The LORD had said to tell each king,
"The LORD All-Powerful, the God of Israel, commands you to drink from this
cup that is full of the wine of his anger.
It will make you so drunk that you will
vomit. And when the LORD sends war
against the nations, you will be completely defeated."
28The LORD told me that if any of them
refused to drink from the cup, I must tell
them that he had said, "I, the LORD All-
Powerful, command you to drink.
29Starting with my own city of
Jerusalem, everyone on earth will suffer
from war. So there is no way I will let
you escape unharmed."
30The LORD told me to say:

From my sacred temple
I will roar like thunder,
while I trample my people
and everyone else
as though they were grapes.
31 My voice will be heard
everywhere on earth,
accusing nations of their crimes
and sentencing the guilty
to death.

Disaster Is Coming

32The LORD All-Powerful says:

You can see disaster spreading
from far across the earth,
from nation to nation
like a horrible storm.

33When it strikes, I will kill so many people that their bodies will cover the ground like manure. No one will be left to bury them or to mourn.

The Leaders of Judah Will Be Punished

34 The LORD's people are his flock,
and you leaders
were the shepherds.
But now it's your turn
to be butchered like sheep.
You'll shatter like fine pottery
dropped on the floor.[i]
So roll on the ground,
crying and mourning.
35 You have nowhere to run,
nowhere to hide.

*36 Listen to the cries
of the shepherds,
37 as the LORD's burning anger
turns[j] peaceful meadows
into barren deserts.
38 The LORD has abandoned
his people[k]
like a lion leaving its den.

Jeremiah's Message in the Temple

(Jeremiah 7.1-15)

26 Soon after Jehoiakim[l] became
king of Judah, the LORD said:
2Jeremiah, I have a message for everyone who comes from the towns of Judah
to worship in my temple. Go to the temple courtyard and speak every word that
I tell you. 3Maybe the people will listen
this time. And if they stop doing wrong,
I will change my mind and not punish
them for their sins. 4Tell them that I
have said:

You have refused to listen to me
and to obey my laws and teachings.
5Again and again I have sent my servants the prophets to preach to you,
but you ignored them as well. Now I
am warning you that if you don't
start obeying me right away, 6I will
destroy this temple, just as I destroyed the town of Shiloh.[m] Then
everyone on earth will use the name
"Jerusalem" as a curse word.

Jeremiah on Trial

7The prophets, the priests, and everyone else in the temple heard what I said,
8-9and as soon as I finished, they all
crowded around me and started shouting, "Why did you preach that the LORD
will destroy this temple, just as he destroyed Shiloh? Why did you say that
Jerusalem will be empty and lie in
ruins? You ought to be put to death for
saying such things in the LORD's name!"
Then they had me arrested.
10The royal officers heard what had
happened, and they came from the
palace to the new gate of the temple to
be the judges at my trial.[n] 11While they
listened, the priests and the prophets
said to the crowd, "All of you have heard
Jeremiah prophesy that Jerusalem will
be destroyed. He deserves the death
penalty."
12-13Then I told the judges and everyone else:

The LORD himself sent me to tell
you about the terrible things he will
do to you, to Jerusalem, and to the
temple. But if you change your ways
and start obeying the LORD, he will
change his mind.
14You must decide what to do with
me. Just do whatever you think is
right. 15But if you put me to death,

[h]**25.26** *Babylonia*: The Hebrew text has "Sheshach," a secret way of writing "Babylonia."
[i]**25.34** *You'll shatter . . . floor*: One possible meaning for the difficult Hebrew text.
[j]**25.37** *anger turns*: Or "anger and enemy armies turn." [k]**25.38** *The LORD has . . . people*: Or "And his people leave their homes." [l]**26.1** *Jehoiakim*: See the note at 1.3. [m]**26.6** *Shiloh*: The sacred tent had once stood at Shiloh. [n]**26.10** *new gate . . . trial*: Public trials were often held in an open area at a gate of a city, palace, or temple.

you and everyone else in Jerusalem
will be guilty of murdering an innocent man, because everything I
preached came from the LORD.
16 The judges and the other people told
the priests and prophets, "Since Jeremiah only told us what the LORD our
God had said, we don't think he deserves to die."
17 Then some of the leaders from other
towns stepped forward. They told the
crowd that 18 years ago when Hezekiah[o]
was king of Judah, a prophet named
Micah from the town of Moresheth had
said:

"I, the LORD All-Powerful, say
Jerusalem will be plowed under
and left in ruins.
Thorns will cover the mountain
where the temple
now stands."[p]

19 Then the leaders continued:
No one put Micah to death for saying that. Instead, King Hezekiah
prayed to the LORD with fear and
trembling and asked him to have
mercy. Then the LORD decided not to
destroy Jerusalem, even though he
had already said he would.
People of Judah, if Jeremiah is
killed, we will bring a terrible disaster on ourselves.
20-24 After these leaders finished
speaking, an important man named
Ahikam son of Shaphan spoke up for
me as well. And so, I wasn't handed over
to the crowd to be killed.

Uriah the Prophet

While Jehoiakim[q] was still king of Judah, a man named Uriah son of Shemaiah left his hometown of Kiriath-
Jearim and came to Jerusalem. Uriah
was one of the LORD's prophets, and he
was saying the same things about Judah
and Jerusalem that I had been saying.
And when Jehoiakim and his officials
and military officers heard what Uriah
said, they tried to arrest him, but he escaped to Egypt. So Jehoiakim sent Elnathan son of Achbor and some other
men after Uriah, and they brought him
back. Then Jehoiakim had Uriah killed
and his body dumped in a common burial pit.

Slaves of Nebuchadnezzar

27 1-2 Not long after Zedekiah became king of Judah,[r] the LORD
told me:
Jeremiah, make a wooden yoke[s] with
leather straps, and place it on your
neck. 3 Then send a message to the kings
of Edom, Moab, Ammon, Tyre, and
Sidon. Some officials from these countries are in Jerusalem, meeting with
Zedekiah. 4 So have them tell their kings
that I have said:
I am the All-Powerful LORD God of
Israel, 5 and with my power I created
the earth, its people, and all animals.
I decide who will rule the earth,
6-7 and I have chosen my servant
King Nebuchadnezzar[t] of Babylonia
to rule all nations, including yours. I
will even let him rule the wild animals. All nations will be slaves of
Nebuchadnezzar, his son, and his
grandson. Then many nations will
join together, and their kings will be
powerful enough to make slaves of
the Babylonians.
8 This yoke stands for the power of
King Nebuchadnezzar, and I will destroy any nation that refuses to obey
him. Nebuchadnezzar will attack,
and many will die in battle or from
hunger and disease. 9 You might have
people in your kingdom who claim
they can tell the future by magic or
by talking with the dead or by
dreams or messages from a god. But
don't pay attention if any of them
tell you not to obey Nebuchadnezzar. 10 If you listen to such lies, I will
have you dragged far from your
country and killed. 11 But if you and
your nation are willing to obey Nebuchadnezzar, I will let you stay in
your country, and your people will
continue to live and work on their
farms.
12 After I had spoken to the officials
from the nearby kingdoms, I went to
King Zedekiah and told him the same
thing. Then I said:
Zedekiah, if you and the people of
Judah want to stay alive, you must
obey Nebuchadnezzar and the
Babylonians. 13 But if you refuse,
then you and your people will die
from war, hunger, and disease, just
as the LORD has warned. 14 Your
prophets have told you that you
don't need to obey Nebuchadnezzar,
but don't listen to their lies. 15 Those
prophets claim to be speaking for
the LORD, but he didn't send them.
They are lying! If you do what they
say, he will have both you and them

[o] 26.18 *Hezekiah*: Ruled 716-687 B.C. [p] 26.18 *Jerusalem . . . stands*: See Micah 3.12.
[q] 26.20-24 *Jehoiakim*: See the note at 1.3. [r] 27.1,2 *Not long after Zedekiah became king of Judah*: A few manuscripts and one ancient translation; most Hebrew manuscripts "Not long after Jehoiakim became king of Judah"; most manuscripts of another ancient translation do not have these words. Jehoiakim ruled 609-598 B.C., and Zedekiah ruled 598-586 B.C.
[s] 27.1,2 *yoke*: A wooden collar that fits around the neck of an ox, so the ox can be made to pull a plow or a cart. [t] 27.6,7 *Nebuchadnezzar*: See the note at 21.2.

dragged off to another country and
killed. The LORD has spoken.
16 When I finished talking to the king, I
went to the priests and told them that
the LORD had said:
Don't listen to the prophets when
they say that very soon the Babylonians will return the things they
took from my temple. Those
prophets are lying! 17 If you choose
to obey the king of Babylonia, you
will live. But if you listen to those
prophets, this whole city will be
nothing but a pile of rubble.
18 If I really had spoken to those
prophets, they would know what I
am going to do. Then they would be
begging me not to let everything else
be taken from the temple and the
king's palace and the rest of
Jerusalem. 19-21 After all, when Nebuchadnezzar took King Jehoiachin[u]
to Babylonia as a prisoner, he didn't
take everything of value from
Jerusalem. He left the bronze pillars,
the huge bronze bowl called the Sea,
and the movable bronze stands in
the temple, and he left a lot of other
valuable things in the palace and in
the rest of Jerusalem.
But now I, the LORD All-Powerful,
the God of Israel, say that all these
things 22 will be taken to Babylonia,
where they will remain until I decide
to bring them back to Jerusalem. I,
the LORD, have spoken.

Jeremiah Accuses Hananiah of Being a False Prophet

28 Later that same year, in the fifth
month of the fourth year that
Zedekiah[v] was king,[w] the prophet
Hananiah son of Azzur from Gibeon
came up to me in the temple. And while
the priests and others in the temple
were listening, 2 he told me that the LORD
had said:
I am the LORD All-Powerful, the
God of Israel, and I will smash the
yoke[x] that Nebuchadnezzar[y] put on
the necks of the nations to make
them his slaves. 3 And within two
years, I will bring back to Jerusalem
everything that he took from my
temple and carried off to Babylonia.
4 King Jehoiachin[z] and the other
people who were taken from Judah
to Babylonia will be allowed to come
back here as well. All this will happen because I will smash the power
of the king of Babylonia!
5 The priests and the others were still
standing there, so I said:
6 Hananiah, I hope the LORD will
do exactly what you said. I hope he
does bring back everything the
Babylonians took from the temple,
and that our people who were taken
to Babylonia will be allowed to return home. 7 But let me remind you
and everyone else 8 that long before
we were born, prophets were saying
powerful kingdoms would be struck
by war, disaster, and disease. 9 Now
you are saying we will have peace.
We will just have to wait and see if
that is really what the LORD has
said.[a]
10 Hananiah grabbed the wooden yoke
from my neck and smashed it. 11 Then he
said, "The LORD says this is the way he
will smash the power Nebuchadnezzar
has over the nations, and it will happen
in less than two years."
I left the temple, 12 and a little while
later, the LORD told me 13-14 to go back
and say to Hananiah:
I am the LORD All-Powerful, the
God of Israel. You smashed a
wooden yoke, but I will replace it
with one made of iron. I will put iron
yokes on all the nations, and they
will have to do what King Nebuchadnezzar commands. I will even
let him rule the wild animals.
15-16 Hananiah, I have never sent
you to speak for me. And yet you
have talked my people into believing
your lies and rebelling against me.
So now I will send you—I'll send
you right off the face of the earth!
You will die before this year is over.
17 Two months later, Hananiah died.

Jeremiah's Letter to the People of Judah in Babylonia

29 1-2 I had been left in Jerusalem
when King Nebuchadnezzar[b]
took many of the people of Jerusalem
and Judah to Babylonia as prisoners, including King Jehoiachin,[c] his mother,
his officials, and the metal workers and
others in Jerusalem who were skilled in
making things. So I wrote a letter to the
prophets, the priests, the leaders, and
the rest of our people in Babylonia. 3 I
gave the letter to Elasah and
Gemariah,[d] two men that King

[u] **27.19-21** *Jehoiachin*: Hebrew "Jeconiah" (see the note at 24.1). [v] **28.1** *Zedekiah*: See the note at 1.3. [w] **28.1** *Later . . . king*: One possible meaning for the difficult Hebrew text. [x] **28.2** *yoke*: See the note at 27.1, 2. [y] **28.2** *Nebuchadnezzar*: See the note at 21.2. [z] **28.4** *Jehoiachin*: Hebrew "Jeconiah" (see the note at 24.1). [a] **28.9** *We will . . . said*: See Deuteronomy 18.21, 22. [b] **29.1,2** *Nebuchadnezzar*: See the note at 21.2. [c] **29.1,2** *Jehoiachin*: Hebrew "Jeconiah" (see the note at 24.1). [d] **29.3** *Elasah and Gemariah*: Hebrew "Elasah son of Shaphan and Gemariah son of Hilkiah."

Zedekiah[e] of Judah was sending to
Babylon to talk with Nebuchadnezzar.
In the letter, I wrote [4]that the LORD All-
Powerful, the God of Israel, had said:
I had you taken from Jerusalem to
Babylonia. Now I tell you [5]to settle
there and build houses. Plant gardens and eat what you grow in them.
[6]Get married and have children,
then help your sons find wives and
help your daughters find husbands,
so they can have children as well. I
want your numbers to grow, not to
get smaller.
[7]Pray for peace in Babylonia and
work hard to make it prosperous.
The more successful that nation is,
the better off you will be.
[8-9]Some of your people there in
Babylonia are fortunetellers, and
you have asked them to tell you
what will happen in the future. But
they will only lead you astray. And
don't let the prophets fool you, either. They speak in my name, but
they are liars. I have not spoken to
them.
[10]After Babylonia has been the
strongest nation for seventy years, I
will be kind and bring you back to
Jerusalem, just as I have promised.
[11]I will bless you with a future filled
with hope—a future of success, not
of suffering. [12]You will turn back to
me and ask for help, and I will answer your prayers. [13]You will worship me with all your heart, and I
will be with you [14]and accept your
worship. Then I will gather you from
all the nations where I scattered you,
and you will return to Jerusalem.
[15]You feel secure, because you
think I have sent prophets to speak
for me in Babylonia.
[16-19]But I have been sending
prophets to the people of Judah for a
long time, and the king from David's
family and the people who are left in
Jerusalem and Judah still don't obey
me. So I, the LORD All-Powerful, will
keep attacking them with war and
hunger and disease, until they are as
useless as rotten figs. I will force
them to leave the land, and all nations will be disgusted and shocked
at what happens to them. The nations will sneer and make fun of
them and use the names "Judah"
and "Jerusalem" as curse words.
And you have not obeyed me, even
though [20]I had you taken from
Jerusalem to Babylonia. But you had
better listen to me now. [21-23]You
think Ahab son of Kolaiah and
Zedekiah son of Maaseiah are
prophets because they claim to
speak for me. But they are lying! I
haven't told them anything. They are
also committing other horrible sins
in your community, such as sleeping
with the wives of their friends. So I
will hand them over to King Nebuchadnezzar, who will put them to
death while the rest of you watch.
And in the future, when you want to
put a curse on someone, you will
say, "I pray that the LORD will kill
you in the same way the king of
Babylonia burned Zedekiah and
Ahab to death!"

A Message for Shemaiah

[24-25]The LORD All-Powerful, the God of
Israel, told me what would happen to
Shemaiah,[f] who was one of our people
in Babylonia. After my letter reached
Babylonia, Shemaiah wrote letters to
the people of Jerusalem, including the
priest Zephaniah son of Maaseiah, and
the other priests. The letter to Zephaniah said:
[26]After the death of Jehoiada the
priest, the LORD chose you to be the
priest in charge of the temple security force. You know that anyone
who acts crazy and pretends to be a
prophet should be arrested and put
in chains[g] and iron collars. [27]Jere-
miah from the town of Anathoth is
pretending to be a prophet there in
Jerusalem, so why haven't you punished him? [28]He even wrote a letter
to the people here in Babylonia, saying we would be here a long time.
He told us to build homes and to
plant gardens and grow our own
food.
[29]When Zephaniah received Shemaiah's letter, he read it to me. [30]Then the
LORD told me what to write in a second
letter [31]to the people of Judah who had
been taken to Babylonia. In this letter, I
wrote that the LORD had said:
I, the LORD, have not chosen Shemaiah to be one of my prophets, and
he has misled you by telling lies in
my name. [32]He has even talked you
into disobeying me. So I will punish
Shemaiah. He and his descendants
won't live to see the good things I
will do for my people. I, the LORD,
have spoken.

The LORD Will Rescue Israel and Judah

30 [1-2]The LORD God of Israel said,
"Jeremiah, get a scroll[h] and write
down everything I have told you. [3]Some-
day I will let my people from both

[e]29.3 *Zedekiah*: See the note at 1.3. [f]29.24,25 *Shemaiah*: Hebrew "Shemaiah, who came from the town of Nehelam." [g]29.26 *in chains*: See the note at 20.2. [h]30.1,2 *scroll*: A roll of paper or special leather used for writing on.

Israel[i] and Judah return to the land I gave their ancestors."

4-5Then the LORD told me to say to Israel and Judah:

I, the LORD, hear screams
of terror,
and there is no peace.
6 Can men give birth?
Then why do I see them
looking so pale
and clutching their stomachs
like women in labor?
7 My people, soon you will suffer
worse than ever before,
but I will save you.

8 Now you are slaves
of other nations,
but I will break the chains
and smash the yokes[j]
that keep you in slavery.
9 Then you will be my servants,
and I will choose a king for you
from the family of David.

*10 Israel,[k] you belong to me,
so don't be afraid.
You deserved to be punished;
that's why I scattered you
in distant nations.
But I am with you,
and someday I will destroy
those nations.
11 Then I will bring you
and your descendants
back to your land,
where I will protect you
and give you peace.
Then your fears will be gone.
I, the LORD, have spoken.

The LORD Will Heal Israel and Judah

12The LORD said:

My people, you are wounded
and near death.
13 You are accused of a crime
with no one to defend you,
and you are covered with sores
that no medicine can cure.
*14 Your friends have forgotten you;
they don't care anymore.
Even I have acted like an enemy.
And because your sins
are horrible and countless,
I will be cruel
as I punish you.
15 So don't bother to cry out
for relief from your pain.

16 But if your enemies try to rob
or destroy you,
I will rob and destroy them,
and they will be led as captives
to foreign lands.
17 No one wants you as a friend
or cares what happens to you.
But I will heal your injuries,
and you will get well.

The LORD Will Rescue Israel and Judah

18The LORD said:

Israel, I will be kind to you
and let you come home.
Jerusalem now lies in ruins,
but you will rebuild it,
complete with a new palace.[l]
19 Other nations will respect
and honor you.
Your homes will be filled
with children,
and you will celebrate,
singing praises to me.

20 It will be just like old times.
Your nation will worship me,
and I will punish anyone
who abuses you.
21 One of your own people
will become your ruler.
And when I invite him
to come near me
at the place of worship,
he will do so.
No one would dare to come near
without being invited.
22 You will be my people,
and I will be your God.
I, the LORD, have spoken.

23 I am furious!
And like a violent storm
I will strike those
who do wrong.
24 I won't calm down
until I have finished
what I have decided to do.
Someday, you will understand
what I mean.

Israel Will Return to God

31 The LORD said:

Israel, I promise
that someday all your tribes
will again be my people,
and I will be your God.
2 In the desert I was kind
to those who escaped death.
I gave them peace,
and when the time is right,
I'll do the same for you.[m]
I, the LORD, have spoken.

[i]30.3 *Israel*: The northern kingdom. [j]30.8 *yokes*: See the note at 27.1, 2. [k]30.10 *Israel*: The people of the northern and southern kingdoms. [l]30.18 *Jerusalem . . . palace*: Or "Your towns lie in ruins, but you will rebuild them, and your homes will be where they were before." [m]31.2 *In the desert . . . same for you*: One possible meaning for the difficult Hebrew text.

The LORD Will Rebuild Israel

3 Some time ago, the LORD appeared to me[n] and told me to say:

Israel, I will always love you;
that's why I've been so patient
and kind.
4 You are precious to me,
and so I will rebuild
your nation.
Once again you will dance for joy
and play your tambourines.
5 You will plant vineyards
on the hills of Samaria
and enjoy the grapes.
6 Someday those who guard
the hill country of Ephraim
will shout, "Let's go to Zion
and worship the LORD our God."

Israel Will Return to Its Own Land

7 The LORD says:

Celebrate and sing for Israel,
the greatest of nations.
Offer praises and shout,
"Come and rescue
your people, LORD!
Save what's left of Israel."

8 I, the LORD, will bring
my people back from Babylonia[o]
and everywhere else on earth.
The blind and the lame
will be there.
Expectant mothers
and women about to give birth
will come and be part
of that great crowd.
9 They will weep and pray
as I bring them home.
I will lead them
to streams of water.
They will walk on a level[p] road
and not stumble.
I am a father to Israel,[q]
my favorite children.

10 Listen to me, you nations
nearby or across the sea.
I scattered the people of Israel,
but I will gather them again.
I will protect them like a shepherd
guarding a flock;
11 I will rescue them from enemies
who could overpower them.
12 My people will come
to Mount Zion
and celebrate;
their faces will glow
because of my blessings.
I'll give them grain, grapes,
and olive oil,
as well as sheep and cattle.
Israel will be prosperous
and grow like a garden
with plenty of water.
13 Young women and young men,
together with the elderly,
will celebrate and dance,
because I will comfort them
and turn their sorrow
into happiness.
14 I will bless my people
with more food
than they need,
and the priests will enjoy
the choice cuts of meat.
I, the LORD, have spoken.

The LORD Offers Hope

15 In Ramah[r] a voice is heard,
crying and weeping loudly.
Rachel mourns for her children[s]
and refuses to be comforted,
because they are dead.
*16 But I, the LORD, say
to dry your tears.
Someday your children
will come home
from the enemy's land.
Then all you have done for them
will be greatly rewarded.
17 So don't lose hope.
I, the LORD, have spoken.

18 The people of Israel[t] moan
and say to me,
"We were like wild bulls,
but you, LORD, broke us,
and we learned to obey.
You are our God—
please let us come home.
19 When we were young,
we strayed and sinned,
but then we realized
what we had done.
We are ashamed and disgraced
and want to return to you."

20 People of Israel,
you are my own dear children.
Don't I love you best of all?
Though I often make threats,
I want you to be near me,
so I will have mercy on you.
I, the LORD, have spoken.

[n] **31.3** *Some time . . . me*: Or "The LORD appeared to me from far away." [o] **31.8** *Babylonia*: The Hebrew text has "that country in the north," referring to Babylonia. [p] **31.9** *level*: Or "straight." [q] **31.9** *Israel*: The Hebrew text also has "Ephraim," the leading tribe of the northern kingdom of Israel, which sometimes stands for the whole northern kingdom. [r] **31.15** *In Ramah*: Or "In the hills." [s] **31.15** *Rachel . . . children*: Rachel was one of the wives of Jacob, the ancestor of the nation of Israel. She was the mother of Joseph and Benjamin. Joseph's two sons Ephraim and Manasseh were the ancestors of the leading tribes of the northern kingdom of Israel. [t] **31.18** *Israel*: Hebrew "Ephraim" (see the note at 31.9).

21 With rock piles and signposts,
mark the way home,
my dear people.
It is the same road
by which you left.
22 Will you ever decide
to be faithful?
I will make sure that someday
things will be different,
as different as a woman
protecting a man.[u]

The LORD Will Bring Judah Home

23The LORD All-Powerful, the God of Israel, said:

I promise to set the people of Judah free and to lead them back to their hometowns. And when I do, they will once again say,

"We pray that the LORD
will bless his home,
the sacred hill in Jerusalem
where his temple stands."

24The people will live in Jerusalem and in the towns of Judah. Some will be farmers, and others will be shepherds.
25Those who feel tired and worn out will
find new life and energy, 26and when
they sleep, they will wake up refreshed.[v]
27Someday, Israel and Judah will be
my field where my people and their livestock will grow. 28In the past, I took care
to uproot them, to tear them down, and
to destroy them. But when that day
comes, I will take care to plant them
and help them grow. 29No longer will
anyone go around saying,

"Sour grapes eaten by parents
leave a sour taste in the mouths
of their children."

30When that day comes, only those who eat sour grapes will get the sour taste, and only those who sin will be put to death.

The New Agreement with Israel and Judah

31The LORD said:

The time will surely come when I will
make a new agreement with the people
of Israel and Judah. 32It will be different
from the agreement I made with their
ancestors when I led them out of Egypt.
Although I was their God, they broke
that agreement.
33Here is the new agreement that I, the LORD, will make with the people of Israel:

"I will write my laws
on their hearts and minds.
I will be their God,
and they will be my people.

34"No longer will they have to teach one another to obey me. I, the LORD, promise that all of them will obey me, ordinary people and rulers alike. I will forgive their sins and forget the evil things they have done."

35 I am the LORD All-Powerful.
I command the sun
to give light each day,
the moon and stars
to shine at night,
and ocean waves to roar.
36 I will never forget
to give those commands,
and I will never let Israel
stop being a nation.
I, the LORD, have spoken.

37 Can you measure the heavens?
Can you explore
the depths of the earth?
That's how hard it would be
for me to reject Israel forever,
even though they have sinned.
I, the LORD, have spoken.

Jerusalem Will Be Rebuilt

38The LORD said:

Someday, Jerusalem will truly belong
to me. It will be rebuilt with a boundary
line running from Hananel Tower to
Corner Gate. 39From there, the boundary
will go in a straight line to Gareb Hill,
then turn toward Goah. 40Even that dis-
gusting Hinnom Valley[w] will be sacred to me, and so will the eastern slopes that go down from Horse Gate into Kidron Valley. Jerusalem will never again be destroyed.

Jeremiah Buys a Field

32 The LORD spoke to me in the tenth year that Zedekiah[x] was
king of Judah, which was the eighteenth
year that Nebuchadnezzar[y] was king of
Babylonia. 2At that time, the Babylonian
army had surrounded Jerusalem, and I
was in the prison at the courtyard of the
palace guards. 3Zedekiah had ordered
me to be held there because I told everyone that the LORD had said:

I am the LORD, and I am about to
let the king of Babylonia conquer
Jerusalem. 4King Zedekiah will be
captured and taken to King Neb-

[u]31.22 *I will make sure . . . a woman protecting a man*: One possible meaning for the difficult Hebrew text. [v]31.26 *and when they sleep . . . refreshed*: One possible meaning for the difficult Hebrew text. [w]31.40 *that disgusting Hinnom Valley*: The Hebrew text has "the whole valley of the dead bodies and of the fatty ashes," which probably refers to Hinnom Valley, just southwest of Jerusalem, where human sacrifices had been offered to foreign gods. [x]32.1 *Zedekiah*: See the note at 1.3. [y]32.1 *Nebuchadnezzar*: See the note at 21.2.

uchadnezzar, who will speak with
him face to face. 5Then Zedekiah
will be led away to Babylonia, where
he will stay until I am finished with
him. So, if you people of Judah fight
against the Babylonians, you will
lose. I, the LORD, have spoken.
6Later, when I was in prison, the LORD
said:
7Jeremiah, your cousin Hanamel,
the son of your uncle Shallum, will
visit you. He must sell his field near
the town of Anathoth, and because
you are his nearest relative, you
have the right and the responsibility
to buy it and keep it in the family.[z]
8Hanamel came, just as the LORD had
promised. And he said, "Please buy my
field near Anathoth in the territory of
the Benjamin tribe. You have the right to
buy it, and if you do, it will stay in our
family."
The LORD had told me to buy it 9from
Hanamel, and so I did. The price was
seventeen pieces of silver, and I weighed
out the full amount on a scale. 10-11I had
two copies of the bill of sale written out,
each containing all the details of our
agreement. Some witnesses and I signed
the official copy, which was folded and
tied, before being sealed shut with hot
wax.[a] Then I gave Hanamel the silver.
12And while he, the witnesses, and all
the other Jews sitting in the courtyard
were still watching, I gave both copies
to Baruch son of Neriah.[b]
13-14I told Baruch that the LORD had
said:
Take both copies of this bill of
sale, one sealed shut and the other
open, and put them in a clay jar so
they will last a long time. 15I am the
LORD All-Powerful, the God of Israel,
and I promise you that people will
once again buy and sell houses,
farms, and vineyards in this country.

Jeremiah Questions the LORD

16Then I prayed:
17LORD God, you stretched out your
mighty arm and made the sky and the
earth. You can do anything. 18You show
kindness for a thousand generations,[c]
but you also punish people for the sins
of their parents. You are the LORD All-
Powerful. 19With great wisdom you
make plans, and with your great power
you do all the mighty things you
planned. Nothing we do is hidden from
your eyes, and you reward or punish us
as we deserve.
20You are famous because you worked
miracles in Egypt, and you are still
working them in Israel and in the rest of
the world as well. 21You terrified the
Egyptians with your miracles, and you
reached out your mighty arm and rescued your people Israel from Egypt.
22Then you gave Israel this land rich
with milk and honey, just as you had
promised our ancestors.
23But when our ancestors took over
the land, they did not obey you. And
now you have punished Israel with disaster. 24Jerusalem is under attack, and
we suffer from hunger and disease. The
Babylonians have already built dirt
ramps up to the city walls, and you can
see that Jerusalem will be captured just
as you said.
25So why did you tell me to get some
witnesses and buy a field with my silver,
when Jerusalem is about to be captured
by the Babylonians?

The LORD Explains about the Field

26The LORD explained:
27Jeremiah, I am the LORD God. I rule
the world, and I can do anything!
28It is true that I am going to let King
Nebuchadnezzar[d] of Babylonia capture
Jerusalem. 29The Babylonian army is already attacking, and they will capture
the city and set it on fire. The people of
Jerusalem have made me angry by going up to the flat roofs of their houses
and burning incense to Baal and offering wine sacrifices to other gods. Now
these houses will be burned to the
ground!
30-33The kings and the officials, the
priests and the prophets, and everyone
else in Israel and Judah have turned
from me and made me angry by worshiping idols. Again and again I have
tried to teach my people to obey me, but
they refuse to be corrected.
I am going to get rid of Jerusalem, because its people have done nothing but
evil. 34They have set up disgusting idols
in my temple, and now it isn't a fit place
to worship me. 35And they led Judah
into sin by building places to worship
Baal in Hinnom Valley, where they also
sacrificed their sons and daughters to
the god Molech. I have never even
thought of telling them to commit such
disgusting sins.
36Jeremiah, what you said is true. The
people of Jerusalem are suffering from
hunger and disease, and so the king

[z]**32.7** *you have the right . . . in the family*: See Leviticus 25.25-32. [a]**32.10,11** *signed the official copy, which was folded and tied, before being sealed shut with hot wax*: The signing was actually done by pressing a carved clay stamp (called a "seal") into the hot wax, leaving the design in the wax. [b]**32.12** *Baruch son of Neriah*: Hebrew "Baruch son of Neriah and grandson of Mahseiah." [c]**32.18** *for a thousand generations*: Or "to thousands of people." [d]**32.28** *Nebuchadnezzar*: See the note at 21.2.

of Babylonia will be able to capture Jerusalem.

37 I am angry at the people of Jerusalem, and I will scatter them in foreign countries. But someday I will bring them back here and let them live in safety. 38 They will be my people, and I will be their God. 39-41 I will make their thoughts and desires pure. Then they will realize that, for their own good and the good of their children, they must worship only me. They will even be afraid to turn away from me. I will make an agreement with them that will never end, and I won't ever stop doing good things for them. With all my heart I promise that they will be planted in this land once again. 42 Even though I have brought disaster on the people, I will someday do all these good things for them.

43 Jeremiah, when you bought the field, you showed that fields will someday be bought and sold again. You say that this land has been conquered by the Babylonians and has become a desert, emptied of people and animals. 44 But someday, people will again spend their silver to buy fields everywhere—in the territory of Benjamin, the region around Jerusalem and the towns of Judah, and in the hill country, the foothills to the west, and the Southern Desert. Buyers and sellers and witnesses will sign and seal the bills of sale for the fields. It will happen, because I will give this land back to my people. I, the LORD, have spoken.

The LORD Promises To Give the Land Back to His People

33 1-2 I was still being held prisoner in the courtyard of the palace guards when the LORD told me:

I am the LORD, and I created the whole world.[e] 3 Ask me, and I will tell you things that you don't know and can't find out.

4-5 Many of the houses in Jerusalem and some of the buildings at the royal palace have been torn down to be used in repairing the walls to keep out the Babylonian attackers.[f] Now there are empty spaces where the buildings once stood. But I am furious, and these spaces will be filled with the bodies of the people I kill. The people of Jerusalem will cry out to me for help, but they are evil, and I will ignore their prayers.

6 Then someday, I will heal this place and my people as well, and let them enjoy unending peace.[g] 7 I will give this land to Israel and Judah once again, and I will make them as strong as they were before. 8 They sinned and rebelled against me, but I will forgive them and take away their guilt. 9 When that happens, all nations on earth will see the good things I have done for Jerusalem, and how I have given it complete peace. The nations will celebrate and praise and honor me, but they will also tremble with fear.

10 Jeremiah, you say that this land is a desert without people or animals, and for now, you are right. The towns of Judah and the streets of Jerusalem are deserted, and people and animals are nowhere to be seen. But someday you will hear 11 happy voices and the sounds of parties and wedding celebrations. And when people come to my temple to offer sacrifices to thank me, you will hear them say:

"We praise you,
    LORD All-Powerful!
You are good to us,
    and your love never fails."

The land will once again be productive. 12-13 Now it is empty, without people or animals. But when that time comes, shepherds will take care of their flocks in pastures near every town in the hill country, in the foothills to the west, in the Southern Desert, in the land of the Benjamin tribe, and around Jerusalem and the towns of Judah.

I, the LORD, have spoken.

The LORD's Wonderful Promise

14 The LORD said:

I made a wonderful promise to Israel and Judah,[h] and the days are coming when I will keep it.

15 I promise that the time will come
when I will appoint a king
    from the family of David,
a king who will be honest
    and rule with justice.
16 In those days,
    Judah will be safe;
Jerusalem will have peace
and will be named,
    "The LORD Gives Justice."

17 The king of Israel will be one of David's descendants, 18 and there will always be priests from the Levi tribe serving at my altar and offering sacrifices to please me and to give thanks.[i]

19 Then the LORD told me:

20 I, the LORD, have an agreement with

[e] **33.1,2** *the whole world*: One ancient translation; Hebrew "it." [f] **33.4,5** *have been torn down . . . Babylonian attackers*: One possible meaning for the difficult Hebrew text. [g] **33.6** *let them enjoy unending peace*: One possible meaning for the difficult Hebrew text. [h] **33.14** *Israel and Judah*: See the note at 2.4. [i] **33.18** *sacrifices to please me and to give thanks*: See the notes at 14.12.

day and night, so they always come at the right time. You can't break the agreement I made with them, 21 and you can't break the agreements I have made with David's family and with the priests from the Levi tribe who serve at my altar. A descendant of David will always rule as king of Israel, 22 and there will be more descendants of David and of the priests from the Levi tribe than stars in the sky or grains of sand on the beach.

23 The LORD also said:

24 You've heard foreigners insult my people by saying, "The LORD chose Israel and Judah, but now he has rejected them, and they are no longer a nation."

25 Jeremiah, I will never break my agreement with the day and the night or let the sky and the earth stop obeying my commands. 26 In the same way, I will never reject the descendants of Abraham, Isaac, and Jacob or break my promise that they will always have a descendant of David as their king. I will be kind to my people Israel, and they will be successful again.

Jeremiah Warns Zedekiah

34 King Nebuchadnezzar[i] had a large army made up of people from every kingdom in his empire. He and his army were attacking Jerusalem and all the nearby towns, when the LORD told me 2 to say to King Zedekiah:[k]

> I am the LORD, and I am going to let Nebuchadnezzar capture this city and burn it down. 3 You will be taken prisoner and brought to Nebuchadnezzar, and he will speak with you face to face. Then you will be led away to Babylonia.
>
> 4 Zedekiah, I promise that you won't die in battle. 5 You will die a peaceful death. People will mourn when you die, and they will light bonfires in your honor, just as they did for your ancestors, the kings who ruled before you.

6 I went to Zedekiah and told him what the LORD had said. 7 Meanwhile, the king of Babylonia was trying to break through the walls of Lachish, Azekah, and Jerusalem, the only three towns of Judah that had not been captured.

The People Break a Promise

8-10 King Zedekiah,[k] his officials, and everyone else in Jerusalem made an agreement to free all Hebrew[l] men and women who were slaves. No Jew would keep another as a slave. And so, all the Jewish slaves were given their freedom. 11 But those slave owners changed their minds and forced their former slaves back into slavery. 12 That's when the LORD told me to say to the people:

13 I am the LORD God of Israel, and I made an agreement with your ancestors when I brought them out of Egypt, where they had been slaves. 14 As part of this agreement, you must let a Hebrew slave go free after six years of service.

Your ancestors did not obey me, 15-16 but you decided to obey me and do the right thing by setting your Hebrew slaves completely free. You even went to my temple, and in my name you made an agreement to set them free. But you have abused my name, because you broke your agreement and forced your former slaves back into slavery.

17 You have disobeyed me by not giving your slaves their freedom. So I will give you freedom—the freedom to die in battle or from disease or hunger. I will make you disgusting to all other nations on earth.

18 You asked me to be a witness when you made the agreement to set your slaves free. And as part of the ceremony you cut a calf into two parts, then walked between the parts. But you people of Jerusalem have broken that agreement as well as my agreement with Israel. So I will do to you what you did to that calf. 19-20 I will let your enemies take all of you prisoner, including the leaders of Judah and Jerusalem, the royal officials, the priests, and everyone else who walked between the two parts of the calf. These enemies will kill you and leave your bodies lying on the ground as food for birds and wild animals.

21-22 These enemies are King Nebuchadnezzar[m] of Babylonia and his army. They have stopped attacking Jerusalem, but they want to kill King Zedekiah and his high officials. So I will command them to return and attack again. This time they will conquer the city and burn it down, and they will capture Zedekiah and his officials. I will also let them destroy the towns of Judah, so that no one can live there any longer.

Learn a Lesson from the Rechabites

35 When Jehoiakim[n] was king of Judah, the LORD told me, 2 "Go to the Rechabite clan and invite them to meet you in one of the side rooms[o] of the temple. When they arrive, offer them a drink of wine."

[i] 34.1 *Nebuchadnezzar*: See the note at 21.2. [k] 34.2 *Zedekiah*: See the note at 1.3. [k] 34.8-10 *Zedekiah*: See the note at 1.3. [l] 34.8-10 *Hebrew*: An earlier term for Israelite and Jewish. [m] 34.21,22 *Nebuchadnezzar*: See the note at 21.2. [n] 35.1 *Jehoiakim*: See the note at 1.3. [o] 35.2 *side rooms*: Probably a room with walls on three sides, and open to the courtyard on the fourth side.

3So I went to Jaazaniah,[p] the leader of
the clan, and I invited him and all the
men of his clan. 4I brought them into the
temple courtyard and took them upstairs to a room belonging to the
prophets who were followers of Hanan
son of Igdaliah. It was next to a room
belonging to some of the officials, and
that room was over the one belonging to
Maaseiah, a priest who was one of the
high officials in the temple.[q]
5I set out some large bowls full of
wine together with some cups, and then
I said to the Rechabites, "Have some
wine!"
6But they answered:
No! The ancestor of our clan, Jonadab son of Rechab,[r] made a rule
that we must obey. He said, "Don't
ever drink wine 7or build houses or
plant crops and vineyards. Instead,
you must always live in tents and
move from place to place. If you
obey this command, you will live a
long time."
8-10Our clan has always obeyed
Jonadab's command. To this very
day, we and our wives and sons and
daughters don't drink wine or build
houses or plant vineyards or crops.
And we have lived in tents, 11except
now we have to live inside Jerusalem because Nebuchadnezzar[s]
has taken over the countryside with
his army from Babylonia and Syria.
12-13Then the LORD told me to say to
the people of Judah and Jerusalem:
I, the LORD All-Powerful, the God
of Israel, want you to learn a lesson
14from the Rechabite clan. Their ancestor Jonadab told his descendants
never to drink wine, and to this very
day they have obeyed him. But I
have spoken to you over and over,
and you haven't obeyed me! 15You
refused to listen to my prophets,
who kept telling you, "Stop doing
evil and worshiping other gods!
Start obeying the LORD, and he will
let you live in this land he gave your
ancestors."
16The Rechabites have obeyed the
command of their ancestor Jonadab,
but you have not obeyed me, 17your
God. I am the LORD All-Powerful,
and I warned you about the terrible
things that would happen to you if
you did not listen to me. You have ignored me, so now disaster will strike
you. I, the LORD, have spoken.

The LORD Makes a Promise to the Rechabites

18Then the LORD told me to say to the
Rechabite clan:
I am the LORD All-Powerful, the God
of Israel. You have obeyed your ancestor
Jonadab, 19so I promise that your clan
will be my servants and will never die
out.

King Jehoiakim Burns Jeremiah's First Scroll

36 During the fourth year that Jehoiakim[t] son of Josiah[u] was king
of Judah, the LORD said to me, "Jeremiah, 2since the time Josiah was king, I
have been speaking to you about Israel,
Judah, and the other nations. Now, get a
scroll[v] and write down everything I
have told you, 3then read it to the people
of Judah. Maybe they will stop sinning
when they hear what terrible things I
plan for them. And if they turn to me, I
will forgive them."
4I sent for Baruch son of Neriah and
asked him to help me. I repeated everything the LORD had told me, and Baruch
wrote it all down on a scroll. 5Then I
said,
Baruch, the officials refuse to let
me go into the LORD's temple, 6so
you must go instead. Wait for the
next holy day when the people of Judah come to the temple to pray and
to go without eating.[w] Then take this
scroll to the temple and read it
aloud. 7The LORD is furious, and if
the people hear how he is going to
punish them, maybe they will ask to
be forgiven.
8-10In the ninth month[x] of the fifth
year that Jehoiakim was king, the leaders set a day when everyone who lived
in Jerusalem or who was visiting here
had to pray and go without eating. So
Baruch took the scroll to the upper
courtyard of the temple. He went over to
the side of the courtyard and stood in a
covered area near New Gate, where he
read the scroll aloud.
This covered area belonged to
Gemariah,[y] one of the king's highest officials. 11Gemariah's son Micaiah was

[p]**35.3** *Jaazaniah*: The Hebrew text has "Jaazaniah son of Jeremiah son of Habazziniah"; this is a different Jeremiah than the author of the book. [q]**35.4** *Maaseiah . . . temple*: Hebrew "Maaseiah son of Shallum, the keeper of the temple door." [r]**35.6** *Jonadab son of Rechab*: See 2 Kings 10.15-23. In the Hebrew of this chapter, "Jonadab" is sometimes spelled "Jehonadab." [s]**35.11** *Nebuchadnezzar*: See the note at 21.2. [t]**36.1** *Jehoiakim*: See the note at 1.3. [u]**36.1** *Josiah*: See the note at 3.6. [v]**36.2** *scroll*: See the note at 30.1, 2. [w]**36.6** *to go without eating*: As a way of asking for God's help. [x]**36.8-10** *ninth month*: Chislev, the ninth month of the Hebrew calendar, from about mid-November to mid-December. [y]**36.8-10** *Gemariah*: Hebrew "Gemariah son of Shaphan"; Gemariah's brother Ahikam had earlier protected Jeremiah (see 26.20-24).

there and heard Baruch read what
the LORD had said. 12 When Baruch finished reading, Micaiah went down to
the palace. His father Gemariah was in
the officials' room, meeting with the rest
of the king's officials, including Elishama, Delaiah, Elnathan, and
Zedekiah.[z] 13 Micaiah told them what he
had heard Baruch reading to the people.
14 Then the officials sent Jehudi and
Shelemiah[a] to tell Baruch, "Bring us
that scroll."

When Baruch arrived with the scroll,
15 the officials said, "Please sit down and
read it to us," which he did. 16 After they
heard what was written on the scroll,
they were worried and said to each
other, "The king needs to hear this!"
Turning to Baruch, they asked, 17 "Did
someone tell you what to write on this
scroll?"

18 "Yes, Jeremiah did," Baruch replied.
"I wrote down just what he told me."

19 The officials said, "You and Jeremiah must go into hiding, and don't tell
anyone where you are."

20-22 The officials put the scroll in
Elishama's room and went to see the
king, who was in one of the rooms
where he lived and worked during the
winter. It was the ninth month[b] of the
year, so there was a fire burning in the
fireplace,[c] and the king was sitting
nearby. After the officials told the king
about the scroll, he sent Jehudi to get it.
Then Jehudi started reading the scroll to
the king and his officials. 23-25 But every
time Jehudi finished reading three or
four columns, the king would tell him to
cut them off with his penknife and
throw them in the fire. Elnathan, Delaiah, and Gemariah begged the king
not to burn the scroll, but he ignored
them, and soon there was nothing left
of it.

The king and his servants listened to
what was written on the scroll, but they
were not afraid, and they did not tear
their clothes in sorrow.[d]

26 The king told his son Jerahmeel to
take Seraiah and Shelemiah[e] and to go
arrest Baruch and me.[f] But the LORD
kept them from finding us.

Jeremiah's Second Scroll

27 I had told Baruch what to write on
that first scroll,[g] but King Jehoiakim[h]
had burned it. So the LORD told me 28 to
get another scroll and write down
everything that had been on the first
one. 29 Then he told me to say to King Jehoiakim:

> Not only did you burn Jeremiah's
> scroll, you had the nerve to ask why
> he had written that the king of
> Babylonia would attack and ruin the
> land, killing all the people and even
> the animals. 30 So I, the LORD,
> promise that you will be killed and
> your body thrown out on the
> ground. The sun will beat down on it
> during the day, and the frost will set-
> tle on it at night. And none of your
> descendants will ever be king of Ju-
> dah. 31 You, your children, and your
> servants are evil, and I will punish
> all of you. I warned you and the peo-
> ple of Judah and Jerusalem that I
> would bring disaster, but none of
> you have listened. So now you are
> doomed!

32 After the LORD finished speaking to
me, I got another scroll and gave it to
Baruch. Then I told him what to write,
so this second scroll would contain even
more than was on the scroll Jehoiakim
had burned.

King Zedekiah Asks Jeremiah To Pray

37 King Nebuchadnezzar[i] of Babylo-
nia had removed Jehoiachin[j] son
of Jehoiakim[k] from being the king of
Judah and had made Josiah's[l] son
Zedekiah[m] king instead.[n] 2 But
Zedekiah, his officials, and everyone
else in Judah ignored everything the
LORD had told me.

3-5 Later, the Babylonian army attacked Jerusalem, but they left after
learning that the Egyptian army[o] was
headed in this direction.

One day, Zedekiah sent Jehucal and
the priest Zephaniah[p] to talk with me.
At that time, I was free to go wherever I
wanted, because I had not yet been put
in prison. Jehucal and Zephaniah said,

[z] **36.12** *Delaiah, Elnathan, and Zedekiah*: Hebrew "Delaiah son of Shemaiah, Elnathan son of Achbor, and Zedekiah son of Hananiah." [a] **36.14** *Jehudi and Shelemiah*: Hebrew "Jehudi son of Nethaniah and Shelemiah son of Cushi." [b] **36.20-22** *ninth month*: See the note at 36.8-10. [c] **36.20-22** *fireplace*: Probably a large metal or clay pot on a movable stand, with the fire burning inside. [d] **36.23-25** *they did not tear their clothes in sorrow*: Such actions would have shown that they were sorry for disobeying the LORD and were turning back to him. [e] **36.26** *Seraiah and Shelemiah*: Hebrew "Seraiah son of Azriel and Shelemiah son of Abdeel." [f] **36.26** *me*: Jeremiah. [g] **36.27** *scroll*: See the note at 30.1,2. [h] **36.27** *Jehoiakim*: See the note at 1.3. [i] **37.1** *Nebuchadnezzar*: See the note at 21.2. [j] **37.1** *Jehoiachin*: Hebrew "Coniah" (see the note at 22.24). [k] **37.1** *Jehoiakim*: See the note at 1.3. [l] **37.1** *Josiah's*: Josiah was the father of both Jehoiakim and Zedekiah. Josiah ruled 640-609 B.C. [m] **37.1** *Zedekiah*: See the note at 1.3. [n] **37.1** *King Nebuchadnezzar . . . instead*: See 2 Kings 24.10-17. [o] **37.3-5** *Egyptian army*: Led by King Apries, also known as Hophra. [p] **37.3-5** *Jehucal and the priest Zephaniah*: Hebrew "Jehucal son of Shelemiah, and the priest Zephaniah son of Maaseiah."

"Jeremiah, please pray to the LORD our
God for us."
6-7Then the LORD told me to send them
back to Zedekiah with this message:

> Zedekiah, you wanted Jeremiah to
> ask me, the LORD God of Israel, what
> is going to happen. So I will tell you.
> The king of Egypt and his army
> came to your rescue, but soon they
> will go back to Egypt. 8Then the
> Babylonians will return and attack
> Jerusalem, and this time they will
> capture the city and set it on fire.
> 9Don't fool yourselves into thinking
> that the Babylonians will leave as
> they did before. 10Even if you could
> defeat their entire army, their
> wounded survivors would still be
> able to leave their tents and set
> Jerusalem on fire.

Jeremiah Is Put in Prison

11The Babylonian army had left because the Egyptian army was on its way
to help us. 12So I decided to leave
Jerusalem and go to the territory of the
Benjamin tribe to claim my share of my
family's land. 13I was leaving Jerusalem
through Benjamin Gate, when I was
stopped by Irijah,[q] the officer in charge
of the soldiers at the gate. He said, "Jeremiah, you're under arrest for trying to
join the Babylonians."
14"I'm not trying to join them!" I answered. But Irijah wouldn't listen, and
he took me to the king's officials.
15-16They were angry and ordered the
soldiers to beat me. Then I was taken to
the house that belonged to Jonathan,
one of the king's officials. It had been
turned into a prison, and I was kept in a
basement room.
After I had spent a long time there,
17King Zedekiah secretly had me
brought to his palace, where he asked,
"Is there any message for us from the
LORD?"
"Yes, there is, Your Majesty," I replied.
"The LORD is going to let the king of
Babylonia capture you."
18Then I continued, "Your Majesty,
why have you put me in prison? Have I
committed a crime against you or
your officials or the nation? 19Have
you locked up the prophets who lied
to you and said that the king of Babylonia would never attack Jerusalem?
20Please, don't send me back to that
prison at Jonathan's house. If you do, I
will die."
21King Zedekiah had me taken to the
prison cells in the courtyard of the
palace guards. He told the soldiers to
give me a loaf of bread[r] from one of the
bakeries every day until the city ran out
of grain.

Jeremiah Is Held Prisoner in a Dry Well

38 One day, Shephatiah, Gedaliah,
Jehucal,[s] and Pashhur[t] heard me
tell the people of Judah 2-3that the LORD
had said, "If you stay here in Jerusalem,
you will die in battle or from disease or
hunger, and the Babylonian army will
capture the city anyway. But if you surrender to the Babylonians, they will let
you live."
4So the four of them went to the king
and said, "You should put Jeremiah to
death, because he is making the soldiers
and everyone else lose hope. He isn't
trying to help our people; he's trying to
harm them."
5Zedekiah replied, "Do what you want
with him. I can't stop you."
6Then they took me back to the courtyard of the palace guards and let me
down with ropes into the well that belonged to Malchiah, the king's son.
There was no water in the well, and I
sank down in the mud.
7-8Ebedmelech from Ethiopia[u] was
an official at the palace, and he
heard what they had done to me. So
he went to speak with King Zedekiah,
who was holding court at Benjamin
Gate. 9Ebedmelech said, "Your Majesty,
Jeremiah is a prophet, and those men
were wrong to throw him into a well.
And when Jerusalem runs out of food,
Jeremiah will starve to death down
there."
10Zedekiah answered, "Take thirty[v] of
my soldiers and pull Jeremiah out before he dies."
11Ebedmelech and the soldiers went to
the palace and got some rags from the
room under the treasury. He used ropes
to lower them into the well. 12Then he
said, "Put these rags under your arms so
the ropes won't hurt you." After I did,
13the men pulled me out. And from then
on, I was kept in the courtyard of the
palace guards.

[q] **37.13** *Irijah*: Hebrew "Irijah son of Shelemiah and grandson of Hananiah." [r] **37.21** *a loaf of bread*: Bread was the main food of the Israelites. During this time of emergency in Jerusalem, everyone probably received the same amount each day. [s] **38.1** *Jehucal*: The Hebrew text has "Jucal," another form of the name. [t] **38.1** *Shephatiah, Gedaliah, Jehucal, and Pashhur*: Hebrew "Shephatiah son of Mattan, Gedaliah son of Pashhur, Jucal son of Shelemiah, and Pashhur son of Malchiah." [u] **38.7,8** *Ethiopia*: The Hebrew text has "Cush," a region south of Egypt that included parts of the present countries of Ethiopia and Sudan. [v] **38.10** *thirty*: Most Hebrew manuscripts; one Hebrew manuscript "three."

King Zedekiah Questions Jeremiah

14King Zedekiah[w] had me brought to
his private entrance[x] to the temple, and
he said, "I'm going to ask you something, and I want to know the truth."
15"Why?" I replied. "You won't listen,
and you might even have me killed!"
16He said, "I swear in the name of the
living LORD our Creator that I won't
have you killed. No one else can hear
what we say, and I won't let anyone kill
you."
17Then I told him that the LORD had
said: "Zedekiah, I am the LORD God All-
Powerful, the God of Israel. I promise
that if you surrender to King Nebuchadnezzar's[y] officers, you and your family
won't be killed, and Jerusalem won't be
burned down. 18But if you don't surrender, I will let the Babylonian army capture Jerusalem and burn it down, and
you will be taken prisoner."
19Zedekiah answered, "I can't surrender to the Babylonians. I'm too afraid of
the Jews that have already joined them.
The Babylonians might hand me over to
those Jews, and they would torture me."
20I said, "If you will just obey the
LORD, the Babylonians won't hand you
over to those Jews. You will be allowed
to live, and all will go well for you. 21But
the LORD has shown me that if you
refuse to obey, 22then the women of your
palace will be taken prisoner by Nebuchadnezzar's officials. And those
women will say to you:

Friends you trusted led you astray.
  Now you're trapped in mud,
and those friends you trusted
  have all turned away.

23The Babylonian army will take your
wives and children captive, you will be
taken as a prisoner to the King of Babylonia, and Jerusalem will be burned
down."[z]
24Zedekiah said, "Jeremiah, if you tell
anyone what we have talked about, you
might lose your life. 25And I'm sure that
if my officials hear about our meeting,
they will ask you what we said to each
other. They might even threaten to kill
you if you don't tell them. 26So if they
question you, tell them you were begging me not to send you back to the
prison at Jonathan's house, because going back there would kill you."
27The officials did come and question
me about my meeting with the king, and
I told them exactly what he had ordered
me to say. They never spoke to me about
the meeting again, since no one had
heard us talking.
28I was held in the courtyard of the
palace guards until the day Jerusalem
was captured.

Jerusalem Is Captured by the Babylonians

(Jeremiah 52.4-16; 2 Kings 25.1-12)

39 1-3In the tenth month[a] of the ninth
year that Zedekiah[b] was king of
Judah, King Nebuchadnezzar[c] and the
Babylonian army began their attack on
Jerusalem. They kept the city surrounded for a year and a half. Then, on
the ninth day of the fourth month[d] of
the eleventh year that Zedekiah was
king, they broke through the city walls.
After Jerusalem was captured,[e] Nebuchadnezzar's highest officials,[f] including Nebo Sarsechim[g] and Nergal
Sharezer from Simmagir,[h] took their
places at Middle Gate to show they were
in control of the city.[i]
4When King Zedekiah and his troops
saw that Jerusalem had been captured,
they tried to escape from the city that
same night. They went to the king's garden, where they slipped through the
gate between the two city walls[j] and
headed toward the Jordan River valley.
5But the Babylonian troops caught up
with them near Jericho. They arrested
Zedekiah and took him to the town of
Riblah in the land of Hamath, where
Nebuchadnezzar put him on trial, then

[w]**38.14** *Zedekiah*: See the note at 1.3. [x]**38.14** *his private entrance*: One possible meaning for the difficult Hebrew text. [y]**38.17** *Nebuchadnezzar's*: See the note at 21.2. [z]**38.23** *Jerusalem will be burned down*: A few Hebrew manuscripts and three ancient translations; most Hebrew manuscripts "you will burn Jerusalem down"; one ancient translation "he will burn Jerusalem down." [a]**39.1-3** *the tenth month*: Tebeth, the tenth month of the Hebrew calendar, from about mid-December to mid-January. [b]**39.1-3** *Zedekiah*: See the note at 1.3. [c]**39.1-3** *Nebuchadnezzar*: See the note at 21.2. [d]**39.1-3** *fourth month*: Tammuz, the fourth month of the Hebrew calendar, from about mid-June to mid-July. [e]**39.1-3** *After Jerusalem was captured*: This phrase is from 38.28. [f]**39.1-3** *highest officials*: The Hebrew text gives Nergal Sharezer's title as "the Rabmag," and Nebo Sarsechim's title as "the Rabsaris," but the exact meaning of the titles and the duties of these offices are not known. [g]**39.1-3** *Nebo Sarsechim*: Probably another form of the name Nebushazban (see verse 13). [h]**39.1-3** *Nergal Sharezer from Simmagir*: One possible meaning for the difficult Hebrew text. Probably Nebuchadnezzar's son-in-law, who was king of Babylonia 560-556 B.C. It is also possible that the Hebrew text mentions a second official named Nergal Sharezer. [i]**39.1-3** *took their places . . . control of the city*: The rulers and leaders often sat in the broad open area at the gate of a city to take care of official business and hold trials. [j]**39.4** *the gate between the two city walls*: The construction of the city walls at this point is not known.

found him guilty 6and gave orders for
him to be punished. Zedekiah's sons
were killed there in front of him, and so
were the leaders of Judah's ruling families. 7His eyes were poked out, and he
was put in chains, so he could be
dragged off to Babylonia.
8Meanwhile, the Babylonian army had
burned the houses in Jerusalem, including[k] the royal palace, and they had broken down the city walls. 9Nebuzaradan,
the Babylonian officer in charge of the
guards, led away everyone from the city
as prisoners, even those who had deserted to Nebuchadnezzar. 10Only the
poorest people who owned no land were
left behind in Judah, and Nebuzaradan
gave them fields and vineyards.
11Nebuchadnezzar had given the following orders to Nebuzaradan: 12"Find
Jeremiah and keep him safe. Take good
care of him and do whatever he asks."
13Nebuzaradan, Nebushazban, Nergal
Sharezer, and the other officers of King
Nebuchadnezzar 14sent some of their
troops to bring me from the courtyard of
the royal palace guards. They put me in
the care of Gedaliah son of Ahikam[l] and
told him to take me to my home. And so
I was allowed to stay with the people
who remained in Judah.

The LORD Promises To Protect Ebedmelech

15While I was a prisoner in the courtyard of the palace guard, the LORD told
me to say 16to Ebedmelech from
Ethiopia:[m]
I am the LORD All-Powerful, the God
of Israel. I warned everyone that I would
bring disaster, not prosperity, to this
city. Now very soon I will do what I said,
and you will see it happen. 17-18But because you trusted me,[n] I will protect you
from the officials of Judah, and when
Judah is struck by disaster, I will rescue
you and keep you alive. I, the LORD,
have spoken.

Jeremiah Is Set Free

40 I was led away in chains along
with the people of Judah and
Jerusalem who were being taken to
Babylonia. Nebuzaradan was the officer
in charge of the guard, and while we
were stopped at Ramah, the LORD had
him set me free. 2Nebuzaradan said:
Jeremiah, the LORD your God
warned your people that he would
bring disaster on this land. 3But they
continued to rebel against him, and
now he has punished them just as he
threatened.
4Today I am taking the chains off
your wrists and setting you free! If
you want to, you can come with me
to Babylonia, and I will see that you
are taken care of. Or if you decide to
stay here, you can go wherever you
wish. 5King Nebuchadnezzar[o] has
chosen Gedaliah to rule Judah. You
can live near Gedaliah, and he will
provide for you, or you can live anywhere else you want.
Nebuzaradan gave me a supply of
food, then let me leave. 6I decided to
stay with the people of Judah, and I
went to live near Gedaliah in Mizpah.

The Harvest Is Brought In

7-8Ishmael the son of Nethaniah, together with Johanan and Jonathan, the
two sons of Kareah, had been officers in
Judah's army. And so had Seraiah the
son of Tanhumeth, the sons of Ephai the
Netophathite, and Jezaniah from
Maacah. They and their troops had been
stationed outside Jerusalem and had not
been captured. They heard that
Gedaliah had been chosen to rule Judah, and that the poorest men, women,
and children had not been taken away
to Babylonia. So they went to Mizpah
and met with their new ruler.
9Gedaliah told them, "There's no need
to be afraid of the Babylonians. Everything will be fine, if we live peacefully
and obey King Nebuchadnezzar.[o] 10I
will stay here at Mizpah and meet with
the Babylonian officials on each of their
visits. But you must go back to your
towns and bring in the harvest, then
store the wine, olive oil, and dried fruit."
11-12Earlier, when the Babylonians had
invaded Judah, many of the Jews escaped to Moab, Ammon, Edom, and several other countries. But these Jews
heard that the king of Babylonia had
appointed Gedaliah as ruler of Judah,
and that only a few people were left
there. So the Jews in these other countries came back to Judah and helped
with the grape and fruit harvest, which
was especially large that year.

Gedaliah Is Murdered

13One day, Johanan got together with
some of the other men who had been
army officers, and they came to Mizpah
and met with Gedaliah. 14They said,
"Gedaliah, we came to warn you that
King Baalis of Ammon hired Ishmael to
murder you!"
Gedaliah refused to believe them, 15so
Johanan went to Gedaliah privately and
said, "Let me kill Ishmael. No one will

[k]39.8 *the houses in Jerusalem, including*: Or "the temple and." [l]39.14 *son of Ahikam*: Hebrew "son of Ahikam and grandson of Shaphan." [m]39.16 *Ethiopia*: See the note at 38.7, 8. [n]39.17,18 *you trusted me*: See 38.7-13, where Ebedmelech helped Jeremiah. [o]40.5 *Nebuchadnezzar*: See the note at 21.2. [o]40.9 *Nebuchadnezzar*: See the note at 21.2.

find out who did it. There are only a few
people left in Judah, but they are depending on you. And if you are murdered, they will be scattered or killed."
16Gedaliah answered, "Don't kill Ishmael! What you've said about him can't
be true."

41 But in the seventh month,[p] Ishmael[q] came to Mizpah with ten of
his soldiers. He had been one of the
king's officials and was a member of the
royal family. Ishmael and his men were
invited to eat with Gedaliah. 2During the
meal, Ishmael and his soldiers killed
Gedaliah, the man chosen as ruler of Judah by the king of Babylonia. 3Then
they killed the Jews who were with
Gedaliah, and they also killed the Babylonian soldiers who were there.
4The next day, the murders had still
not been discovered, 5when eighty men
came down the road toward Mizpah
from the towns of Shechem, Shiloh, and
Samaria. They were on their way to the
temple to offer gifts of grain and incense to the LORD. They had shaved off
their beards, torn their clothes, and cut
themselves, because they were mourning.
6Ishmael went out the town gate to
meet them. He pretended to be weeping,
and he asked them to come into Mizpah
to meet with Gedaliah, the ruler of Judah. 7But after they were inside the
town, Ishmael had his soldiers kill them
and throw their bodies into a well. 8He
let ten of the men live, because they offered to give him supplies of wheat, barley, olive oil, and honey they had hidden
in a field. 9The well that he filled with
bodies had been dug by King Asa[r] of Judah to store rainwater, because he was
afraid that King Baasha[s] of Israel might
surround Mizpah and keep the people
from getting to their water supply.
10Nebuzaradan, King Nebuchadnez-
zar's[t] officer in charge of the guard, had
left King Zedekiah's[u] daughters and
many other people at Mizpah, and he
had put Gedaliah in charge of them. But
now Ishmael took them all prisoner and
led them toward Ammon, on the other
side of the Jordan River.
11Johanan and the other army officers
heard what Ishmael had done. 12So they
and their troops chased Ishmael and
caught up with him at the large pit at
Gibeon. 13When Ishmael's prisoners
saw Johanan and the officers, they were
happy 14and turned around and ran toward Johanan. 15But Ishmael and eight
of his men escaped and went to Ammon.

Johanan Decides To Take the People to Egypt

16Johanan and the officers had rescued the women, children, and royal officials that Ishmael had taken prisoner
after killing Gedaliah. Johanan led the
people from Gibeon 17-18toward Egypt.
They wanted to go there, because they
were afraid of what the Babylonians
would do when they found out that Ishmael had killed Gedaliah, the ruler appointed by King Nebuchadnezzar.[v]

The People Ask Jeremiah To Pray for Them

On the way to Egypt, we[w] stopped at
the town of Geruth Chimham near Beth-
42 lehem. 1Johanan, Jezaniah,[x] the
other army officers, and everyone
else in the group, came to me 2and said,
"Please pray to the LORD your God for
us. Judah used to have many people,
but as you can see, only a few of us are
left. 3Ask the LORD to tell us where he
wants us to go and what he wants us
to do."
4"All right," I answered, "I will pray to
the LORD your God, and I will tell you
everything he says."
5They answered, "The LORD himself
will be our witness that we promise to
do whatever he says, 6even if it isn't
what we want to do. We will obey the
LORD so that all will go well for us."
7Ten days later, the LORD gave me an
answer for 8Johanan, the officers, and
the other people. So I called them together 9and told them that the LORD God
of Israel had said:

> You asked Jeremiah to pray and
> find out what you should do. 10I am
> sorry that I had to punish you, and
> so I now tell you to stay here in Ju-
> dah, where I will plant you and build
> you up, instead of tearing you down
> and uprooting you. 11Don't be afraid
> of the King of Babylonia. I will pro-
> tect you from him, 12and I will even
> force him to have mercy on you and
> give back your farms.
> 13But you might keep on saying,
> "We won't stay here in Judah, and
> we won't obey the LORD our God.
> 14We are going to Egypt, where there

[p]41.1 *seventh month*: Tishri, also called Ethanim, the seventh month of the Hebrew calendar, from about mid-September to mid-October. [q]41.1 *Ishmael*: Hebrew "Ishmael son of Nethaniah and grandson of Elishama." [r]41.9 *Asa*: Ruled 911-870 B.C. [s]41.9 *Baasha*: Ruled 909-886 B.C. [t]41.10 *Nebuchadnezzar's*: See the note at 21.2. [u]41.10 *Zedekiah's*: See the note at 1.3. [v]41.17,18 *Nebuchadnezzar*: See the note at 21.2. [w]41.17,18 *we*: The group of people included Jeremiah, since he had been staying with Gedaliah near Mizpah (see 40.6). [x]42.1 *Jezaniah*: Hebrew "Jezaniah son of Hoshaiah"; one ancient translation "Azariah son of Hoshaiah" (see also 43.2 and the note there).

is plenty of food and no danger of
war."
15People of Judah, you survived
when the Babylonian army attacked.
Now you are planning to move to
Egypt, and if you do go, this is what
will happen. 16-17You are afraid of
war, starvation, and disease here in
Judah, but they will follow you to
Egypt and kill you there. None of
you will survive the disasters I will
send.
18I, the LORD, was angry with the
people of Jerusalem and punished
them. And if you go to Egypt, I will
be angry and punish you the same
way. You will never again see your
homeland. People will be horrified at
what I do to you, and they will use
the name of your city as a curse
word.

Jeremiah Gives a Warning

19I told the people:
You escaped the disaster that
struck Judah, but now the LORD
warns you to stay away from Egypt.
20You asked me to pray and find out
what the LORD our God wants you to
do, and you promised to obey him.
But that was a terrible mistake, 21be-
cause now that I have given you the
LORD's answer, you refuse to obey
him. 22And so, you will die in Egypt
from war, hunger, and disease.

The People Go to Egypt

43 I told the people everything the
LORD had told me. 2But Azariah,
Johanan[y] and some other arrogant men
said to me, "You're lying! The LORD
didn't tell you to say that we shouldn't
go to Egypt. 3Baruch son of Neriah must
have told you to say that. He wants the
Babylonians to capture us, so they can
take us away to Babylonia or even kill
us."
4Johanan, the other army officers, and
everyone else refused to stay in Judah in
spite of the LORD's command. 5So Johanan and the officers led us away toward Egypt. The group that left Judah
included those who had been scattered
in other countries and who had then
come back to live in Judah. 6Baruch and
I and others in the group had been staying with Gedaliah, because Nebuzaradan, the Babylonian officer in
charge of the guard, had ordered him to
take care of the king's daughters and
quite a few men, women, and children.
7The people disobeyed the LORD and
went to Egypt. The group had settled in
Tahpanhes, 8when the LORD told me:
9Jeremiah, carry some large
stones to the entrance of the government building in Tahpanhes. Bury
the stones underneath the brick
pavement[z] and be sure the Jews are
watching.
10Then tell them that I, the LORD
All-Powerful, the God of Israel, have
sent for my servant, Nebuchadnezzar[a] of Babylonia. I will bring him
here and have him set up his throne
and his royal tent over these stones
that I told you to bury. 11He will attack Egypt and kill many of its people; others will die of disease or be
dragged away as prisoners. 12-13I will
have him set Egypt's temples on fire,
and he will either burn or carry off
their idols. He will destroy the sacred monuments at the temple of the
sun-god.[b] Then Nebuchadnezzar
will pick the land clean, just like a
shepherd picking the lice off his
clothes. And he will return safely
home.

The LORD Will Destroy the People of Judah

44 The LORD told me to speak with
the Jews who were living in the
towns of Migdol, Tahpanhes, and Memphis in northern Egypt, and also to
those living in southern Egypt. He told
me to tell them:
2I am the LORD All-Powerful, the
God of Israel. You saw how I destroyed Jerusalem and the towns of
Judah. They lie empty and in ruins
today, 3because the people of Judah
made me angry by worshiping gods
that had never helped them or their
ancestors.
4Time after time I sent my servants the prophets to tell the people
of Judah how much I hated their disgusting sins. The prophets warned
them to stop sinning, 5but they refused to listen and would not stop
worshiping other gods. 6Finally, my
anger struck like a raging flood, and
today Jerusalem and the towns of
Judah are nothing but empty ruins.
7Why do you now insist on heading for another disaster? A disaster
that will destroy not only you, but
also your children and babies. 8You
have made me angry by worshiping
idols and burning incense to other
gods after you came here to Egypt.
You will die such a disgusting death,
that other nations will use the name

[y]**43.2** *Azariah, Johanan*: Hebrew "Azariah son of Hoshaiah, Johanan son of Kareah."
[z]**43.9** *underneath the brick pavement*: One possible meaning for the difficult Hebrew text.
[a]**43.10** *Nebuchadnezzar*: See the note at 21.2.
[b]**43.12,13** *at the temple of the sun-god*: Or "in the city of Heliopolis."

of Judah as a curse word. 9When
you were living in Jerusalem and Judah, you followed the example of
your ancestors in doing evil things,
just like your kings and queens.
10Even now, your pride keeps you
from respecting me and obeying the
laws and teachings I gave you and
your ancestors.
11I, the LORD All-Powerful, have
decided to wipe you out with disasters. 12There were only a few of you
left in Judah, and you decided to go
to Egypt. But you will die such horrible deaths in war or from starvation,
that people of other countries will
use the name of Judah as a curse
word. 13I punished Jerusalem with
war, hunger, and disease, and that's
how I will punish you. 14None of you
will survive. You may hope to return
to Judah someday, but only a very
few of you will escape death and be
able to go back.

The People Refuse To Worship the LORD

15A large number of Jews from both
northern and southern Egypt listened to
me as I told them what the LORD had
said. Most of the men in the crowd
knew that their wives often burned incense to other gods. So they and their
wives shouted:
16Jeremiah, what do we care if you
speak in the LORD's name? We
refuse to listen! 17We have promised
to worship the goddess Astarte, the
Queen of Heaven,[c] and that is exactly what we are going to do. We
will burn incense and offer sacrifices of wine to her, just as we, our
ancestors, our kings, and our leaders
did when we lived in Jerusalem and
the other towns of Judah. We had
plenty of food back then. We were
well off, and nothing bad ever happened to us. 18But since the time we
stopped burning incense and offering wine sacrifices to her, we have
been dying from war and hunger.
19Then the women said, "When we
lived in Judah, we worshiped the Queen
of Heaven and offered sacrifices of wine
and special loaves of bread shaped like
her. Our husbands knew what we were
doing, and they approved of it."
20Then I told the crowd:
21Don't you think the LORD knew
that you and your ancestors, your
leaders and kings, and the rest of
the people were burning incense to
other gods in Jerusalem and everywhere else in Judah? 22And when he
could no longer put up with your
disgusting sins, he placed a curse on
your land and turned it into a desert,
as it is today. 23This disaster happened because you worshiped other
gods and rebelled against the LORD
by refusing to obey him or follow his
laws and teachings.
24-25Then I told the men and their
wives, that the LORD All-Powerful, the
God of Israel, had said:
Here in Egypt you still keep your
promises to burn incense and offer
sacrifices of wine to the so-called
Queen of Heaven. 26Keep these
promises! But let me tell you what
will happen. As surely as I am the
LORD God, I swear that I will never
again accept any promises you
make in my name. 27Instead of
watching over you, I will watch for
chances to harm you. Some of you
will die in war, and others will starve
to death. 28Only a few will escape
and return to Judah. Then everyone
who went to live in Egypt will know
that when I say something will happen, it will—no matter what you say.
29And here is how you will know
that I will keep my threats to punish
you in Egypt. 30I will hand over King
Hophra of Egypt to those who want
to kill him,[d] just as I handed
Zedekiah[e] over to Nebuchadnezzar,[f]
who wanted to kill him.

The LORD Will Not Let Baruch Be Killed

45 In the fourth year that Jehoiakim[g] was king of Judah,
Baruch wrote down everything I had
told him.[h] 2Then later, the LORD God of
Israel told me to say to Baruch:
3You are moaning and blaming
me, the LORD, for your troubles and
sorrow, and for being so tired that
you can't even rest. 4But all over the
earth I am tearing down what I built
and pulling up what I planted. 5I am
bringing disaster everywhere, so
don't even think about making any
big plans for yourself. However, I
promise that wherever you go, I will
at least protect you from death. I, the
LORD, have spoken.

The LORD Speaks about the Nations

46 The LORD often told me what to
say about the different nations of
the world.

[c]**44.17** *the goddess Astarte, the Queen of Heaven*: The Hebrew text has "the queen of heaven," which probably refers to the goddess Astarte. [d]**44.30** *King Hophra . . . kill him*: Hophra, also known as Apries, ruled Egypt from 589 to 570 B.C., when he was killed by Ahmosis II, who then became king of Egypt and ruled until 526 B.C. [e]**44.30** *Zedekiah*: See the note at 1.3. [f]**44.30** *Nebuchadnezzar*: See the note at 21.2. [g]**45.1** *Jehoiakim*: See the note at 1.3. [h]**45.1** *Baruch wrote down everything I had told him*: See 36.1-32.

What the LORD Says about Egypt

2In the fourth year that Jehoiakim[i]
was king of Judah, King Nebuchadnezzar[j] of Babylonia defeated King Neco of
Egypt[k] in a battle at the city of Carchemish near the Euphrates River. And
here is what the LORD told me to say
about the Egyptian army:

3 It's time to go into battle!
So grab your shields,
4 saddle your horses,
and polish your spears.
Put on your helmets and armor,
then take your positions.

5 I can see the battle now—
you are defeated
and running away,
never once looking back.
Terror is all around.
6 You are strong and run fast,
but you can't escape.
You fall in battle
near the Euphrates River.

7 What nation is this,
that rises like the Nile River
overflowing its banks?
8 It is Egypt, rising with a roar
like a raging river
and saying,
"I'll flood the earth,
destroying cities, and killing
everyone in them."

9 Go ahead, Egypt.
Tell your chariots and cavalry
to attack and fight hard.
Order your troops to march out,
with Ethiopians[l] and Libyans
carrying shields,
and the Lydians[m] armed with bows
and arrows.

10 But the LORD All-Powerful
will win this battle
and take revenge
on his enemies.
His sword will eat them
and drink their blood
until it is full.
They will be killed in the north
near the Euphrates River,
as a sacrifice to the LORD.

11 Egypt, no medicine can heal you,
not even the soothing lotion
from Gilead.

12 All nations have heard you weep;
you are disgraced,
and they know it.
Your troops fall to the ground,
stumbling over each other.

A Warning for Egypt

13-14When King Nebuchadnezzar[n] of
Babylonia was on his way to attack
Egypt, the LORD sent me with a warning
for every Egyptian town, but especially
for Migdol, Memphis, and Tahpanhes.
He said to tell them:

Prepare to defend yourselves!
Everywhere in your nation,
people are dying in war.
15 I have struck down
your mighty god Apis[o]
and chased him away.[p]
16 Your soldiers stumble
over each other
and say, "Get up!
The enemy will kill us,
unless we can escape
to our own land."

17 Give the king of Egypt
this new name,
"Talks-Big-Does-Nothing."

18 Egypt, I am the true king,
the LORD All-Powerful,
and as surely as I live,
those enemies who attack
will tower over you
like Mount Tabor among the hills
or Mount Carmel by the sea.
19 You will be led away captive,
so pack a few things
to bring with you.
Your capital, Memphis,
will lie empty and in ruins.

20 An enemy from the north
will attack you, beautiful Egypt,
like a fly biting a cow.
21 The foreign soldiers you hired
will turn and run.
But they are doomed,
like well-fed calves
being led to the butcher.

*22 The enemy army will go forward
like a swarm of locusts.[q]
Your troops will feel helpless,
like a snake in a forest

[i]46.2 *Jehoiakim*: See the note at 1.3. [j]46.2 *King Nebuchadnezzar*: Ruled 605-562 B.C. At the time of the battle in 605 B.C., he was crown prince, but his father died a few months later, and he became king. [k]46.2 *King Neco of Egypt*: Neco II, ruled 609-594 B.C.
[l]46.9 *Ethiopians*: See the note at 38.7, 8. [m]46.9 *Lydians*: Probably hired soldiers from Lydia, an area in west-central Asia minor. [n]46.13,14 *Nebuchadnezzar*: See the note at 21.2.
[o]46.15 *Apis*: A sacred bull, kept in a temple at Memphis, Egypt, and worshiped as a god.
[p]46.15 *I have . . . him away*: One possible meaning for the difficult Hebrew text.
[q]46.22 *locusts*: A type of grasshopper that comes in swarms and causes great damage to plant life.

[23] when men with axes
start chopping down trees.
It can only hiss
and try to escape.
[24] Your people will be disgraced
and captured by the enemy
from the north.

[25]I am the LORD All-Powerful, the God
of Israel. Soon I will punish the god
Amon of Thebes[r] and the other Egyptian gods, the Egyptian kings, the people of Egypt, and everyone who trusts in
the Egyptian power. [26]I will hand them
over to King Nebuchadnezzar and his
army. But I also promise that Egypt will
someday have people living here again,
just as it had before. I, the LORD, have
spoken.

The LORD Will Bring Israel Home

The LORD said:
[27] Israel,[s] don't be afraid.
Someday I will bring you home
from foreign lands.
You and your descendants
will live in peace and safety,
with nothing to fear.
[28] So don't be afraid,
even though now
you deserve to be punished
and have been scattered
among other nations.
But when I destroy them,
I will protect you.
I, the LORD, have spoken.

What the LORD Says about the Philistines

47 Before the king of Egypt attacked
the town of Gaza,[t] the LORD told
me to say to the Philistines:

[2] I, the LORD, tell you
that your land will be flooded
with an army from the north.
It will destroy your towns
and sweep you away,
moaning and screaming.
[3] When you hear the thunder
of horses and chariots,
your courage will vanish,
and parents will abandon
their own children.

[4] You refugees from Crete,[u]
your time has now come,
and I will destroy you.
None of you will be left
to help the cities
of Tyre and Sidon.
[*5] The Anakim who survive[v]
in Gaza and Ashkelon
will mourn for you
by shaving their heads
and sitting in silence.
[6] You ask how long will I continue
to attack you with my sword,
then you tell me to put it away
and leave you alone.
[7] But how can my sword rest,
when I have commanded it
to attack Ashkelon
and the seacoast?

What the LORD Says about Moab

48 The LORD All-Powerful, the God
of Israel, told me to say to the nation of Moab:

The town of Nebo is doomed;
Kiriathaim will be captured
and disgraced,
and even its fortress
will be left in ruins.
[2] No one honors you, Moab.
In Heshbon, enemies make plans
to end your life.
My sword will leave only silence
in your town named "Quiet."[w]
[3] The people of Horonaim
will cry for help,
as their town is attacked
and destroyed.

[4] Moab will be shattered!
Your children will sob
[5] and cry on their way up
to the town of Luhith;
on the road to Horonaim
they will tell of disasters.

[6] Run for your lives!
Head into the desert
like a wild donkey.[x]
[7] You thought you could be saved
by your power and wealth,
but you will be captured
along with your god Chemosh,
his priests, and officials.
[8] Not one of your towns
will escape destruction.

I have told your enemies,
"Wipe out the valley
and the flatlands of Moab.

[r]**46.25** *the god Amon of Thebes*: Amon was the king of the Egyptian gods and was the special god of the Egyptian kings. [s]**46.27** *Israel*: See the note at 30.10, 11. [t]**47.1** *attacked the town of Gaza*: One of the major Philistine towns; nothing is known about this attack. [u]**47.4** *Crete*: Hebrew "Caphtor," another name for Crete, the original homeland of the ancestor of the Philistines. [v]**47.5** *Anakim who survive*: One ancient translation; Hebrew "people in the valley who survive." The Anakim may have been a group of very large people that lived in Palestine before the Israelites (see Numbers 13.33; Deuteronomy 2.10, 11, 20, 21; and Joshua 11.21, 22). [w]**48.2** *silence . . . Quiet*: In Hebrew the name of the town was "Madmen," which sounds like the word for "silence." [x]**48.6** *like a wild donkey*: One ancient translation; Hebrew "like (the town of) Aroer" (see verse 19).

9 Spread salt on the ground
to kill the crops.[y]
Leave its towns in ruins,
with no one living there.
10 I want you to kill the Moabites,
and if you let them escape,
I will put a curse on you."

11 Moab, you are like wine
left to settle undisturbed,
never poured from jar to jar.
And so, your nation continues
to prosper and improve.[z]
12 But now, I will send enemies
to pour out the wine
and smash the jars!
13 Then you will be ashamed,
because your god Chemosh
cannot save you,
just as Bethel[a] could not help
the Israelites.

14 You claim that your soldiers
are strong and brave.
15 But I am the LORD,
the all-powerful King,
and I promise that enemies
will overpower your towns.
Even your best warriors
will die in the battle.
16 It won't be long now—
disaster will hit Moab!

17 I will order the nearby nations
to mourn for you and say,
"Isn't it sad? Moab ruled others,
but now its glorious power
has been shattered."

18 People in the town of Dibon,[b]
you will be honored no more,
so have a seat in the dust.
Your walls will be torn down
when the enemies attack.

19 You people of Aroer,[c]
go wait beside the road,
and when refugees run by,
ask them, "What happened?"
20 They will answer,
"Moab has been defeated!
Weep with us in shame.
Tell everyone at the Arnon River
that Moab is destroyed."

*21 I will punish every town
that belongs to Moab,
but especially Holon,
Jahzah, Mephaath,
22 Dibon, Nebo,
Beth-Diblathaim, 23 Kiriathaim,
Beth-Gamul, Beth-Meon,
24 Kerioth, and Bozrah.[d]
25 My decision is final—
your army will be crushed,
and your power broken.

26 People of Moab, you claim
to be stronger than I am.
Now I will tell other nations
to make you drunk
and to laugh while you collapse
in your own vomit.
27 You made fun of my people
and treated them like criminals
caught in the act.
28 Now you must leave your towns
and live like doves
in the shelter of cliffs
and canyons.

29 I know about your pride,
and how you strut and boast.
30 But I also know bragging
will never save you.
31 So I will cry and mourn
for Moab
and its town of Kir-Heres.

32 People of Sibmah,
you were like a vineyard
heavy with grapes,
and with branches reaching
north to the town of Jazer
and west to the Dead Sea.[e]
But you have been destroyed,
and so I will weep for you,
as the people of Jazer weep
for the vineyards.

33 Harvest celebrations are gone
from the orchards and farms
of Moab.
There are no happy shouts
from people making wine.
34 Weeping from Heshbon
can be heard as far
as Elealeh and Jahaz;
cries from Zoar are heard
in Horonaim
and Eglath-Shelishiyah.
And Nimrim Creek has run dry.

35 I will get rid of anyone
who burns incense
to the gods of Moab
or offers sacrifices
at their shrines.
I, the LORD, have spoken.

[y]48.9 *Spread salt . . . crops*: One possible meaning for the difficult Hebrew text.
[z]48.11 *continues . . . improve*: Or "remains as evil as ever." [a]48.13 *Bethel*: It may refer to the Phoenician or Canaanite god of that name; or it may refer to the town where people of the northern kingdom worshiped at a local shrine (see 1 Kings 12.26-30). [b]48.18 *Dibon*: The capital city of Moab. [c]48.19 *Aroer*: A Moabite town located just north of the Arnon River. [d]48.24 *Bozrah*: Not the same Bozrah as in 49.13. [e]48.32 *reaching north . . . Dead Sea*: One possible meaning for the difficult Hebrew text.

36 In my heart I moan for Moab,
like a funeral song
played on a flute.
I mourn for the people
of the town of Kir-Herès,
because their wealth is gone.

*37 The people of Moab
mourn on the rooftops
and in the streets.
Men cut off their beards,
people shave their heads;
they make cuts on their hands
and wear sackcloth.[f]
38 And it's all because I, the LORD,
have shattered Moab like a jar
that no one wants.
39 Moab lies broken!
Listen to its people cry
as they turn away in shame.
Other nations are horrified
at what happened,
but still they laugh.

40 Moab, an enemy swoops down
like an eagle spreading its wings
over your land.
41 Your cities[g] and fortresses
will be captured,
and your warriors
gripped by fear.[h]
42 You are finished as a nation,
because you dared oppose me,
the LORD.
43 Terror, pits, and traps
are waiting for you.
44 If you are terrified and run,
you will fall into a pit;
and if you crawl out of the pit,
you'll get caught in a trap.
The time has come
for you to be punished.

45 Near the city of Heshbon,
where Sihon once ruled,
tired refugees stand in shadows
cast by the flames
of their burning city.
Soon, the towns on other hilltops,
where those warlike people live,
will also go up in smoke.

46 People of Moab, you worshiped
Chemosh, your god,
but now you are done for,
and your children are prisoners
in a foreign country.

47 Yet someday, I will bring
your people back home.
I, the LORD, have spoken.

What the LORD Says about Ammon

49 The LORD has this to say about the nation of Ammon:

The people of Israel
have plenty of children
to inherit their lands.
So why have you worshipers
of the god Milcom[i]
taken over towns and land
belonging to the Gad tribe?
2 Someday I will send an army
to attack you in Rabbah,
your capital city.
It will be left in ruins,
and the surrounding villages
will lie in ashes.
You took some of Israel's land,
but on that day
Israel will take yours!

3 Cry, people of Heshbon;[j]
your town will become
a pile of rubble.[k]
You will turn here and there,
but your path will be blocked.[l]

Put on sackcloth[m] and mourn,
you citizens of Rabbah,
because the idol you worship[n]
will be taken
to a foreign country,
along with its priests
and temple officials.
4 You rebellious Ammonites
trust your wealth and ask,
"Who could attack us?"
But I warn you not to boast
when your strength is fading.[o]
5 I, the LORD All-Powerful,
will send neighboring nations
to strike you with terror.
You will be scattered,
with no one to care
for your refugees.
6 Yet someday, I will bring
your people back home.
I, the LORD, have spoken.

What the LORD Says about Edom

7-8 The LORD All-Powerful says about Edom:

[f]**48.37** *sackcloth*: See the note at 4.8. [g]**48.41** *Your cities*: Or "Kerioth." [h]**48.41** *gripped by fear*: One possible meaning for the difficult Hebrew text. [i]**49.1** *Milcom*: The national god of Ammon, probably the same as the god Molech in 32.35. [j]**49.3** *Heshbon*: See also 48.45; since Heshbon was near the border of Moab and Ammon, it was probably ruled by the country that was stronger at the time. [k]**49.3** *your town will become a pile of rubble*: Or "because the town of Ai has been destroyed"; referring to an Ammonite town named Ai, not the town of that name near Bethel in the land of Israel. [l]**49.3** *You will turn . . . blocked*: One possible meaning for the difficult Hebrew text. [m]**49.3** *sackcloth*: See the note at 4.8. [n]**49.3** *the idol you worship*: Hebrew "Milcom" (see verse 1 and the note there). [o]**49.4** *when . . . fading*: One possible meaning for the difficult Hebrew text.

Wisdom and common sense
have vanished from Teman.[p]
I will send disaster to punish
you descendants of Esau,[q]
so anyone from Dedan[r]
had better turn around
and run back home.[s]
9 People who harvest grapes
leave some for the poor.
Thieves who break in at night
take only what they want.
10 But I will take everything
that belongs to you,
people of Edom,
and I will uncover every place
where you try to hide.
Then you will die,
and so will your children,
relatives, and neighbors.
11 But I can be trusted
to care for your orphans
and widows.

12Even those nations that don't deserve to be punished will have to drink
from the cup of my anger. So how
can you possibly hope to escape? 13I, the
LORD, swear in my own name that your
city of Bozrah[t] and all your towns will
suffer a horrible fate. They will lie in
ruins forever, and people will use the
name "Bozrah" as a curse word.

14 I have sent a messenger
to command the nations
to prepare for war
against you people of Edom.
15 Your nation will be small,
yet hated by other nations.
16 Pride tricks you into thinking
that other nations
look at you with fear.[u]
You live along the cliffs
and high in the mountains
like the eagles,
but I am the LORD,
and I will bring you down.
17 People passing by your country
will be shocked and horrified
to see a disaster
18 as bad as the destruction
of Sodom and Gomorrah
and towns nearby.
The towns of Edom will be empty.

19 I will attack you
like a lion from the forest,
attacking sheep in a meadow
along the Jordan.
In a moment the flock runs,
and the land is empty.
Who will I choose to attack you?
I will do it myself!
No one can force me to fight
or chase me away.
20 Listen to my plans for you,
people of Edom.[v]
Your children will be dragged off
and your country destroyed.
21 The sounds of your destruction
will reach the Red Sea[w]
and cause the earth to shake.
22 An enemy will swoop down
to attack you,
like an eagle spreading its wings
and circling over Bozrah.
Your warriors will be gripped
by fear.[x]

What the LORD Says about Damascus

23The LORD says about Damascus:

The towns of Hamath and Arpad[y]
have heard your bad news.
They have lost hope,
and worries roll over them
like ocean waves.[z]
24 You people of Damascus
have lost your courage,
and in panic you turn to run,
gripped by fear and pain.[a]

25 I once was pleased
with your famous city.
But now I warn you, "Escape
while you still can!"[b]
26 Soon, even your best soldiers
will lie dead in your streets.
I, the LORD All-Powerful,
have spoken.

[p]**49.7,8** *Teman*: The name of a town in Edom, sometimes used as the name of the northern half of the nation of Edom; here it probably stands for the whole nation. [q]**49.7,8** *Esau*: The ancestor of the nation of Edom. [r]**49.7,8** *Dedan*: The name of a town in northwest Arabia, also used of the northwest region of Arabia along the Red Sea. [s]**49.7,8** *anyone . . . home*: One possible meaning for the difficult Hebrew text. [t]**49.13** *Bozrah*: The main city and capital of Edom. [u]**49.16** *Pride . . . fear*: One possible meaning for the difficult Hebrew text. [v]**49.20** *Edom*: The Hebrew text also uses the name "Teman" (see the note at verses 7-8). [w]**49.21** *Red Sea*: Hebrew *yam suph*, here referring to the Gulf of Aqaba, since the term is extended to include the northeastern arm of the Red Sea (see also the note at Exodus 13.18). [x]**49.22** *will be gripped by fear*: One possible meaning for the difficult Hebrew text. [y]**49.23** *Hamath and Arpad*: Two towns in Syria that had been the capitals of small kingdoms allied with the more powerful kingdom whose capital was Damascus. [z]**49.23** *worries . . . waves*: One possible meaning for the difficult Hebrew text. [a]**49.24** *gripped by fear and pain*: One possible meaning for the difficult Hebrew text. [b]**49.25** *can*: One possible meaning for the difficult Hebrew text of verse 25.

27 I will set fire to your city walls
and burn down the fortresses
King Benhadad built.

Nebuchadnezzar and the People of the Desert

28Here is what the LORD says about the Kedar tribe and the desert villages[c] that were conquered by King Nebuchadnezzar[d] of Babylonia:

Listen, you people of Kedar
and the other tribes
of the eastern desert.
I have told Nebuchadnezzar
to attack and destroy you.
29 His fearsome army
will surround you,
taking your tents and possessions,
your sheep and camels.

30 Run and hide,
you people of the desert
who live in villages![e]
Nebuchadnezzar has big plans
for you.
31 You have no city walls
and no neighbors to help,
yet you think you're safe—
so I told him to attack.
32 Then your camels
and large herds
will be yours no longer.

People of the Arabian Desert,[f]
disaster will strike you
from every side,
and you will be scattered
everywhere on earth.
33 Only jackals[g] will live
where your villages[h] once stood.
I, the LORD, have spoken.

What the LORD Says about Elam

34-35Not long after Zedekiah[i] became
king of Judah, the LORD told me to say:

People of Elam,[j]
I, the LORD All-Powerful,
will kill the archers
who make your army strong.
36 Enemies will attack
from all directions,
and you will be led captive
to every nation on earth.
37 Their armies will crush
and kill you,
and you will face the disaster
that my anger brings.
38 Your king and his officials
will die, and I will rule
in their place.
I, the LORD, have spoken.

39 But I promise that someday
I will bring your people
back to their land.

Babylon Will Be Captured

50 *1The LORD told me to say:
Announce what will happen
and don't leave anything out.
2 Raise the signal flags;
shout so all nations can hear—
Babylon will be captured!

Marduk,[k] Babylon's god,
will be ashamed and terrified,
and his idols broken.
3 The attack on the Babylonians
will come from the north;
they and their animals will run,
leaving the land empty.

Israel and Judah Will Return to Their Land

4The LORD said:

People of Israel and Judah,
when these things happen
you will weep, and together
you will return to your land
and worship me,
the LORD your God.
5 You will ask the way to Zion
and then come and join with me
in making an agreement
you won't break or forget.

6 My people, you are lost sheep
abandoned by their shepherds
in the mountains.
You don't even remember
your resting place.
7 I am your true pastureland,
the one who gave hope
to your ancestors.
But you abandoned me,
so when your enemies found you,
they felt no guilt
as they gobbled you down.

8 Escape from Babylonia,
my people.
Get out of that country!
Don't wait for anyone else.
9 In the north I am bringing
great nations together.
They will attack Babylon
and capture it.

[c]**49.28** *desert villages*: The Hebrew text has "kingdoms of Hazor," which probably refers to several kingdoms of desert peoples who were not nomads, but who lived in small villages.
[d]**49.28** *Nebuchadnezzar*: See the note at 21.2.
[e]**49.30** *villages*: See the note at 49.28.
[f]**49.32** *People of the Arabian Desert*: One possible meaning for the difficult Hebrew text.
[g]**49.33** *jackals*: See the note at 9.11.
[h]**49.33** *villages*: See the note at 49.28.
[i]**49.34,35** *Zedekiah*: See the note at 1.3.
[j]**49.34,35** *Elam*: A nation east of Babylonia, attacked by Nebuchadnezzar about 596 B.C.
[k]**50.2** *Marduk*: The Hebrew text has "Bel" and "Marduk," two names for the same god.

The arrows they shoot
are like the best soldiers,[l]
always finding their target.
10 Babylonia will be conquered,
and its enemies will carry off
everything they want.

Babylon Will Be Disgraced

The LORD *said:*
11 People of Babylonia,
you were glad
to rob my people.
You had a good time,
making more noise
than horses
and jumping around
like calves threshing grain.[m]
12 The city of Babylon
was like a mother to you.
But it will be disgraced
and become nothing
but a barren desert.
13 My anger will destroy Babylon,
and no one will live there.
Everyone who passes by
will be shocked to see
what has happened.

14 Babylon has rebelled against me.
Archers, take your places.
Shoot all your arrows at Babylon.
15 Attack from every side!

Babylon surrenders!
The enemy tears down
its walls and towers.
I am taking my revenge
by doing to Babylon what it did
to other cities.
16 There is no one in Babylonia
to plant or harvest crops.
Even foreigners who lived there
have left for their homelands,
afraid of the enemy armies.

17 Israel is a flock of sheep
scattered by hungry lions.
The king of Assyria[n]
first gobbled Israel down.
Then Nebuchadnezzar,[o]
king of Babylonia,
crunched on Israel's bones.
18 I, the LORD All-Powerful,
the God of Israel,
punished the king of Assyria,
and I will also punish
the king of Babylonia.
19 But I will bring Israel
back to its own land.
The people will be like sheep
eating their fill
on Mount Carmel
and in Bashan,
in the hill country of Ephraim
and in Gilead.
20 I will rescue a few people
from Israel and Judah.
I will forgive them so completely
that their sin and guilt
will disappear,
never to be found.

The LORD's Commands to the Enemies of Babylonia

21 The LORD said:

I have told
the enemies of Babylonia,
"Attack the people of Merathaim
and Pekod.[p]
Kill them all!
Destroy their possessions!"

22 Sounds of war
and the noise of destruction
can be heard.
23 Babylonia was a hammer
pounding every country,
but now it lies broken.
What a shock to the nations
of the world!

24 Babylonia challenged me,
the LORD God All-Powerful,
but that nation doesn't know
it is caught in a trap
that I set.
25 I've brought out my weapons,
and with them I will put a curse
on Babylonia.

26 Come from far away,
you enemies of Babylon!
Pile up the grain
from its storehouses,
and destroy it completely,
along with everything else.
27 Kill the soldiers of Babylonia,
because the time has come
for them to be punished.

28 The Babylonian army
destroyed my temple,
but soon I will take revenge.

[l]**50.9** *the best soldiers*: Some Hebrew manuscripts and two ancient translations; most Hebrew manuscripts "soldiers that kill children." [m]**50.11** *threshing grain*: Hebrew; two ancient translations "in a pasture." [n]**50.17** *king of Assyria*: Either Shalmaneser V, who ruled 726-722 B.C., conquered most of the northern kingdom, and surrounded its capital city Samaria; or Sargon II, who ruled 721-705 B.C. and took thousands of prisoners back to Assyria. [o]**50.17** *Nebuchadnezzar*: See the note at 21.2. [p]**50.21** *Merathaim . . . Pekod*: Hebrew forms of two Babylonian names that refer to the land of Babylonia. Merathaim probably referred to lagoons near the mouth of the Tigris and Euphrates rivers or to the Persian Gulf, but in Hebrew it means "Twice as Rebellious." Pekod referred to a tribe of southeastern Babylonia, but in Hebrew it means "Punishment."

Then refugees from Babylon
will tell about it in Zion.

29 Attack Babylon, enemy archers;
set up camp around the city,
and don't let anyone escape.
It challenged me, the holy God,
so do to it
what it did to other cities.

Proud Babylon Will Fall

30 People of Babylon,
I, the LORD, promise
that even your best soldiers
will lie dead in the streets.

31 Babylon, you should be named,
"The Proud One."
But the time has come when I,
the LORD All-Powerful,
will punish you.
32 You are proud,
but you will stumble and fall,
and no one will help you up.
I will set your villages on fire,
and everything around you
will go up in flames.

33 You Babylonians were cruel
to Israel and Judah.
You took them captive, and now
you refuse to let them go.
34 But I, the LORD All-Powerful,
will rescue and protect them.
I will bring peace to their land
and trouble to yours.
35 I have declared war on you,
your officials, and advisors.
36 This war will prove
that your prophets
are liars and fools.
And it will frighten
your warriors.
37 Then your chariot horses
and the foreigners in your army
will refuse to go into battle,
and the enemy will carry away
everything you treasure.
38 Your rivers and canals
will dry up.

All of this will happen,
because your land
is full of idols,
and they have made fools
of you.
39 Never again will people live
in your land—
only desert animals, jackals,[q]
and unclean birds.
40 I destroyed Sodom and Gomorrah
and the nearby towns,
and I will destroy Babylon
just as completely.
No one will live there again.

Babylonia Is Invaded

The LORD said:
41 Far to the north,
a nation and its allies
have been awakened.
They are powerful
and ready for war.
42 Bows and arrows and swords
are in their hands.
The soldiers are cruel
and show no pity.
The hoofbeats of their horses
echo like ocean waves
crashing against the shore.
The army has lined up for battle
and is coming to attack you,
people of Babylonia!

43 Ever since your king heard
about this army,
he has been weak with fear;
he twists and turns in pain
like a woman giving birth.
44 Babylonia, I will attack you
like a lion from the forest,
attacking sheep in a meadow
along the Jordan.
In a moment the flock runs,
and the land is empty.
Who will I choose to attack you?
I will do it myself!
No one can force me to fight
or chase me away.
45 Listen to my plans for you,
people of Babylonia.
Your children will be dragged off,
and your country destroyed.
46 The sounds of your destruction
will be heard among the nations,
and the earth will shake.

Babylon Will Be Destroyed

51 I, the LORD, am sending
a wind[r] to destroy
the people of Babylonia[s]
and Babylon, its capital.
2 Foreign soldiers will come
from every direction,
and when the disaster is over,
Babylonia will be empty
and worthless.
3 I will tell these soldiers,
"Attack quickly,
before the Babylonians
can string their bows
or put on their armor.[t]
Kill their best soldiers
and destroy their army!"

[q]**50.39** *jackals*: See the note at 9.11. [r]**51.1** *wind*: Or "spirit." [s]**51.1** *Babylonia*: The Hebrew text has "Leb-Qamai," a secret way of writing "Babylonia." [t]**51.3** *I will tell . . . armor*: Or "Attack quickly! String your bows and put on your armor."

4 Their troops will fall wounded
in the streets of Babylon.

5 Everyone in Israel and Judah
is guilty.
But I, the LORD All-Powerful,
their holy God,
have not abandoned them.

6 Get out of Babylon!
Run for your lives!
If you stay, you will be killed
when I take revenge on the city
and punish it for its sins.

7 Babylon was my golden cup,
filled with the wine
of my anger.
The nations of the world
got drunk on this wine
and went insane.
8 But suddenly, Babylon will fall
and be destroyed.

I, the LORD, told the foreigners[u]
who lived there,
"Weep for the city!
Get medicine for its wounds;
maybe they will heal."

9 The foreigners answered,
"We have already tried
to treat Babylon's wounds,
but they would not heal.
Come on, let's all go home
to our own countries.
Nothing is left in Babylonia;
everything is destroyed."

10 The people of Israel said,
"Tell everyone in Zion!
The LORD has taken revenge
for what Babylon did to us."

The LORD Wants Babylon Destroyed

11 I, the LORD,
want Babylon destroyed,
because its army
destroyed my temple.
So, you kings of Media,[v]
sharpen your arrows
and pick up your shields.
12 Raise the signal flag
and attack the city walls.
Post more guards.
Have soldiers watch the city
and set up ambushes.
I have made plans
to destroy Babylon,
and nothing will stop me.

13 People of Babylon, you live
along the Euphrates River
and are surrounded by canals.
You are rich,
but now the time has come
for you to die.[w]
14 I, the LORD All-Powerful,
swear by my own life
that enemy soldiers
will fill your streets
like a swarm of locusts.[x]
They will shout
and celebrate their victory.

A Hymn of Praise
(Jeremiah 10.12-16)

15 God used his wisdom and power
to create the earth
and spread out the heavens.
16 The waters in the heavens roar
at his command.
He makes clouds appear;
he sends the wind
from his storehouse
and makes lightning flash
in the rain.

17 People who make idols
are stupid!
They will be disappointed,
because their false gods
cannot breathe.
18 Idols are merely a joke,
and when the time is right,
they will be destroyed.
19 But the LORD, Israel's God,
is all-powerful.
He created everything,
and he chose Israel
to be his very own.

God's Hammer

The LORD said:
20 Babylonia, you were my hammer;
I used you to pound nations
and break kingdoms,
21 to shatter cavalry and chariots,
22 as well as men and women,
young and old,
23 shepherds and their flocks,
farmers and their oxen,
and governors and leaders.

24 But now, my people will watch,
while I repay you
for what you did to Zion.

25 You destroyed the nations
and seem strong as a mountain,
but I am your enemy.
I might even grab you
and roll you off a cliff.
When I am finished,
you'll only be a pile
of scorched bricks.
26 Your stone blocks won't be reused

[u]**51.8** *the foreigners*: Or "my people." [v]**51.11** *kings of Media*: Probably kings of smaller kingdoms that were part of the Median empire (see also verse 27 and the note there). [w]**51.13** *for you to die*: One possible meaning for the difficult Hebrew text. [x]**51.14** *locusts*: See the note at 46.22, 23.

for cornerstones
or foundations,
and I promise that forever
you will be a desert.
I, the LORD, have spoken.

The Nations Will Attack Babylon

The LORD said:
27 Signal the nations
to get ready to attack.
Raise a flag and blow a trumpet.
Send for the armies of Ararat,
Minni, and Ashkenaz.[y]
Choose a commander;
let the cavalry attack
like a swarm of locusts.
28 Tell the kings and governors,
the leaders and the people
of the kingdoms of the Medes
to prepare for war!

29 The earth twists and turns
in torment,
because I have decided
to make Babylonia a desert
where no one can live,
and I won't change my mind.

30 The Babylonian soldiers
have lost their strength
and courage.[z]
They stay in their fortresses,
unable to fight,
while the enemy breaks through
the city gates,
then sets their homes on fire.
31 One messenger after another
announces to the king,
"Babylon has been captured!
32 The enemy now controls
the river crossings!
The marshes[a] are on fire!
Your army has panicked!"

33 I am the LORD All-Powerful,
the God of Israel,
and I make this promise—
"Soon Babylon will be leveled
and packed down
like a threshing place
at harvest time."[b]

Babylonia Will Pay!

34 The people of Jerusalem say,
"King Nebuchadnezzar[c]
made us panic.
That monster stuffed himself
with us and our treasures,
leaving us empty—
he gobbled down
what he wanted
and spit out the rest.
35 The people of Babylonia
harmed some of us[d]
and killed others.
Now, LORD, make them pay!"

The LORD Will Take Revenge on Babylon

36 My people, I am on your side,
and I will take revenge
on Babylon.
I will cut off its water supply,
and its stream[e] will dry up.
37 Babylon will be a pile of rubble
where only jackals[f] live.
People will laugh,
but they will be afraid
to walk among the ruins.
38 The Babylonians roar and growl
like young lions.
39 And since they are hungry,
I will give them a banquet.
They will celebrate, get drunk,
then fall asleep,
never to wake up!
40 I will lead them away to die,
like sheep, lambs, and goats
being led to the butcher.
41 All nations now praise Babylon,[g]
but when it is captured,
those same nations
will be horrified.
42 Babylon's enemies will rise
like ocean waves
and flood the city.
43 Horrible destruction will strike
the nearby towns.
The land will become
a barren desert,
where no one can live
or even travel.
44 I will punish Marduk,[h]
the god of Babylon,
and make him vomit up
everything he gobbled down.
Then nations will no longer
bring him gifts,
and Babylon's walls will crumble.

The LORD Offers Hope to His People

45 Get out of Babylon, my people,
and run for your lives,
before I strike the city
in my anger!

[y]**51.27** *Ararat, Minni, and Ashkenaz*: Kingdoms to the north of Babylonia that were part of the Median empire (see also verse 28). [z]**51.30** *have lost their strength and courage*: Hebrew "have lost their strength and have become like women." [a]**51.32** *marshes*: The tall grass in the marshes could have provided hiding places for people trying to escape from Babylon.
[b]**51.33** *leveled . . . harvest time*: A threshing place with a dirt surface had to be leveled and packed down before it could be used. [c]**51.34** *Nebuchadnezzar*: See the note at 21.2.
[d]**51.35** *harmed some of us*: One possible meaning for the difficult Hebrew text.
[e]**51.36** *stream*: Probably the Euphrates River. [f]**51.37** *jackals*: See the note at 9.11.
[g]**51.41** *Babylon*: The Hebrew text has "Sheshach," a secret way of writing the name "Babylon."
[h]**51.44** *Marduk*: Hebrew "Bel" (see the note at 50.2).

46 Don't be afraid or lose hope,
though year after year
there are rumors
of leaders fighting for control
in the city of Babylon.
47 The time will come
when I will punish
Babylon's false gods.
Everyone there will die,
and the whole nation
will be disgraced,
48 when an army attacks
from the north
and brings destruction.
Then the earth and the heavens
and everything in them
will celebrate.
49 Babylon must be overthrown,
because it slaughtered
the people of Israel
and of many other nations.

50 My people, you escaped death
when Jerusalem fell.
Now you live far from home,
but you should trust me
and think about Jerusalem.
Leave Babylon! Don't stay!

51 You feel ashamed and disgraced,
because foreigners have entered
my sacred temple.
52 Soon I will send a war
to punish Babylon's idols
and leave its wounded people
moaning everywhere.
53 Although Babylon's walls
reach to the sky,
the army I send
will destroy that city.
I, the LORD, have spoken.

Babylon Will Be Destroyed

The LORD said:
54 Listen to the cries for help
coming from Babylon.
Everywhere in the country
the sounds of destruction
can be heard.
55 The shouts of the enemy,
like crashing ocean waves,
will drown out Babylon's cries
as I level the city.

56 An enemy will attack
and destroy Babylon.
Its soldiers will be captured
and their weapons broken,
because I am a God
who takes revenge against nations
for what they do.
57 I, the LORD All-Powerful,
the true King, promise
that the officials and advisors,
the governors and leaders
and the soldiers of Babylon
will get drunk, fall asleep,
and never wake up.
58 The thick walls of that city
will be torn down,
and its huge gates burned.
Everything that nation
worked so hard to gain
will go up in smoke.

Jeremiah Gives Seraiah a Scroll

59During Zedekiah's[i] fourth year as
king of Judah, he went to Babylon. And
Baruch's brother Seraiah[j] went along as
the officer in charge of arranging for
places to stay overnight.[k]
60Before they left, I wrote on a scroll[l]
all the terrible things that would happen
to Babylon. 61I gave the scroll to Seraiah
and said:
When you get to Babylon, read
this scroll aloud, 62then pray, "Our
LORD, you promised to destroy this
place and make it into a desert
where no people or animals will
ever live."
63When you finish praying, tie the
scroll to a rock and throw it in the
Euphrates River. Then say, 64"This is
how Babylon will sink when the
LORD destroys it. Everyone in the
city will die, and it won't have the
strength to rise again."

The End of Jeremiah's Writing

Jeremiah's writing ends here.

Jerusalem Is Captured

(2 Kings 24.18—25.30; 2 Chronicles 36.11-21)

52 Zedekiah was twenty-one years old when he was appointed king of Judah,[m] and he ruled from Jerusalem for eleven years.[n] His mother Hamutal was the daughter of Jeremiah from the town of Libnah.[o]
2Zedekiah disobeyed
the LORD, just as Jehoiakim had done,
3and it was Zedekiah who finally rebelled against Nebuchadnezzar.[p]
The people of Judah and Jerusalem had made the LORD so angry that he finally turned his back on them. That's why horrible things were happening.

[i]51.59 *Zedekiah's*: See the note at 1.3. [j]51.59 *Baruch's brother Seraiah*: Hebrew "Seraiah son of Neriah and grandson of Mahseiah"; Baruch helped Jeremiah write down his messages (see 32.12; 36.4-10). [k]51.59 *arranging for places to stay overnight*: Hebrew and one ancient translation; two ancient translations, "the tax money." [l]51.60 *scroll*: See the note at 30.1, 2. [m]52.1 *appointed king of Judah*: By Nebuchadnezzar (see 37.1). [n]52.1 *he ruled . . . years*: Ruled 598-586 B.C. [o]52.1 *Jeremiah from the town of Libnah*: Not the same Jeremiah as the author of this book (see 1.1). [p]52.3 *Nebuchadnezzar*: See the note at 21.2.

4 In Zedekiah's ninth year as king, on the tenth day of the tenth month,[q] King Nebuchadnezzar of Babylonia led his entire army to attack Jerusalem. The troops set up camp outside the city and built ramps up to the city walls.

5-6 After a year and a half,[r] all the food in Jerusalem was gone. Then on the ninth day of the fourth month,[s] 7 the Babylonian troops broke through the city wall. That same night, Zedekiah and his soldiers tried to escape through the gate near the royal garden, even though they knew the enemy had the city surrounded. They headed toward the Jordan River valley, 8 but the Babylonian troops caught up with them near Jericho. The Babylonians arrested Zedekiah, but his soldiers scattered in every direction. 9 Zedekiah was taken to Riblah in the land of Hamath, where Nebuchadnezzar put him on trial and found him guilty. 10 Zedekiah's sons and the officials of Judah were killed while he watched, 11 then his eyes were poked out. He was put in chains, then dragged off to Babylon and kept in prison until he died.

12 Jerusalem was captured during Nebuchadnezzar's nineteenth year as king of Babylonia.

About a month later,[t] Nebuchadnezzar's officer in charge of the guards arrived in Jerusalem. His name was Nebuzaradan, 13 and he burned down the LORD's temple, the king's palace, and every important building in the city, as well as all the houses. 14 Then he ordered the Babylonian soldiers to break down the walls around Jerusalem. 15 He led away the people left in the city, including everyone who had become loyal to Nebuchadnezzar, the rest of the skilled workers,[u] and even some of the poor people of Judah. 16 Only the very poorest were left behind to work the vineyards and the fields.

17-20 Nebuzaradan ordered his soldiers to go to the temple and take everything made of gold or silver, including bowls, fire pans, sprinkling bowls, pans, lampstands, dishes for incense, and the cups for wine offerings. The Babylonian soldiers took all the bronze things used for worship at the temple, including the pans for hot ashes, and the shovels, lamp snuffers, sprinkling bowls, and dishes for incense. The soldiers also took everything else made of bronze, including the two columns that stood in front of the temple, the large bowl called the Sea, the twelve bulls that held it up, and the movable stands.[v] The soldiers broke these things into pieces so they could take them to Babylonia. There was so much bronze that it could not be weighed. 21 For example, the columns were about twenty-seven feet high and eighteen feet around. They were hollow, but the bronze was about three inches thick. 22 Each column had a bronze cap over seven feet high that was decorated with bronze designs. Some of these designs were like chains and others were like pomegranates.[w] 23 There were ninety-six pomegranates evenly spaced[x] around each column, and a total of one hundred pomegranates were located above the chains.

24 Next, Nebuzaradan arrested Seraiah the chief priest, Zephaniah his assistant, and three temple officials. 25 Then he arrested one of the army commanders, seven of King Zedekiah's personal advisors, and the officer in charge of gathering the troops for battle. He also found sixty more soldiers who were still in Jerusalem. 26-27 Nebuzaradan led them to Riblah in the land of Hamath, where Nebuchadnezzar had them killed.

The people of Judah no longer lived in their own country.

People of Judah Taken Prisoner

28-30 Here is a list of the number of the people of Judah that Nebuchadnezzar[y] took to Babylonia as prisoners:

In his seventh year as king, he took 3,023 people.
In his eighteenth year as king, he took 832 from Jerusalem.
In his twenty-third year as king, his officer Nebuzaradan took 745 people.

So, Nebuchadnezzar took a total of 4,600 people from Judah to Babylonia.

Jehoiachin Is Set Free
(2 Kings 25.27-30)

31 Jehoiachin was a prisoner in Babylon for thirty-seven years. Then Evil Merodach[z] became king of Babylonia,

[q] **52.4** *tenth month*: See the note at 39.1-3. [r] **52.5,6** *After a year and a half*: Jerusalem was captured in 586 B.C. [s] **52.5,6** *fourth month*: See the note at 39.1-3. [t] **52.12** *About a month later*: Hebrew "On the seventh day of the fifth month." [u] **52.15** *the rest of the skilled workers*: Nebuchadnezzar had taken away some of the skilled workers eleven years before (see 2 Kings 24.14-16). [v] **52.17-20** *the large bowl called the Sea, the twelve bulls that held it up, and the movable stands*: One ancient translation; Hebrew "the large bowl called the Sea, and the twelve bulls under the movable stands." [w] **52.22** *pomegranates*: A small red fruit that looks like an apple. [x] **52.23** *evenly spaced*: One possible meaning for the difficult Hebrew text. [y] **52.28-30** *Nebuchadnezzar*: See the note at 21.2. [z] **52.31** *Evil Merodach*: The son of Nebuchadnezzar who ruled Babylonia from 562-560 B.C.

and in the first year of his rule, on the
twenty-fifth day of the twelfth month,[a]
he let Jehoiachin out of prison. 32 Evil
Merodach was kind to Jehoiachin and
honored him more than any of the other
kings held prisoner there. 33 Jehoiachin
was allowed to wear regular clothes instead of a prison uniform, and he even
ate at the king's table every day. 34 As
long as Jehoiachin lived, he was paid a
daily allowance to buy whatever he
needed.

[a]**52.31** *twelfth month*: Adar, the twelfth month of the Hebrew calendar, from about mid-February to mid-March.

LAMENTATIONS

ABOUT THIS BOOK

This book is a collection of five poems expressing deep sorrow about the destruction of Jerusalem. The poems, sometimes called laments, are presented as being spoken by the city of Jerusalem and by the writer, who is called "the prophet" in the CEV.

The prophet realized that Jerusalem was being punished because its people had sinned, but the suffering seemed greater than what their sins deserved. Still, there was hope. Someday, God would be merciful again if the people would give up their sins and turn back to him.

Then I remember something
that fills me with hope.
The LORD's kindness never fails!
If he had not been merciful,
we would have been destroyed.
The LORD can always be trusted
to show mercy each morning.
Deep in my heart I say,
"The LORD is all I need;
I can depend on him!"
(3.21-24)

A QUICK LOOK AT THIS BOOK

Lonely Jerusalem

The Prophet Speaks:

1 Jerusalem, once so crowded,
lies deserted and lonely.
This city that was known
all over the world
is now like a widow.
This queen of the nations
has been made a slave.
2 Each night, bitter tears
flood her cheeks.
None of her former lovers
are there to offer comfort;
her friends[a] have betrayed her
and are now her enemies.

3 The people of Judah are slaves,
suffering in a foreign land,
with no rest from sorrow.
Their enemies captured them
and were terribly cruel.[b]
4 The roads to Zion mourn
because no one travels there
to celebrate the festivals.
The city gates are deserted;
priests are weeping.

[a]**1.2** *lovers . . . friends*: Israel's former allies. [b]**1.3** *Their . . . cruel*: One possible meaning for the difficult Hebrew text.

Young women are raped;[c]
Zion is in sorrow!
5 Enemies now rule the city
and live as they please.
The LORD has punished Jerusalem
because of her awful sins;
he has let her people
be dragged away.

6 Zion's glory has disappeared.
Her leaders are like deer
that cannot find pasture;
they are hunted down
till their strength is gone.
7 Her people recall the good life
that once was theirs;
now they suffer
and are scattered.
No one was there to protect them
from their enemies who sneered
when their city was taken.

8 Jerusalem's horrible sins
have made the city a joke.
Those who once admired her
now hate her instead—
she has been disgraced;
she groans and turns away.

9 Her sins had made her filthy,
but she wasn't worried
about what could happen.
And when Jerusalem fell,
it was so tragic.
No one gave her comfort
when she cried out,
"Help! I'm in trouble, LORD!
The enemy has won."

10 Zion's treasures were stolen.
Jerusalem saw foreigners
enter her place of worship,
though the LORD
had forbidden them
to belong to his people.[d]
11 Everyone in the city groans
while searching for food;
they trade their valuables
for barely enough scraps
to stay alive.

Jerusalem Speaks:
Jerusalem shouts to the LORD,
"Please look and see
how miserable I am!"
12 No passerby even cares.[e]
Why doesn't someone notice
my terrible sufferings?
You were fiercely angry, LORD,
and you punished me
worst of all.
13 From heaven you sent a fire
that burned in my bones;
you set a trap for my feet
and made me turn back.
All day long you leave me
in shock from constant pain.
14 You have tied my sins
around my neck,[f]
and they weigh so heavily
that my strength is gone.
You have put me in the power
of enemies too strong for me.

15 You, LORD, have turned back
my warriors and crushed
my young heroes.
Judah was a woman untouched,
but you let her be trampled
like grapes in a wine pit.
16 Because of this, I mourn,
and tears flood my eyes.
No one is here to comfort
or to encourage me;
we have lost the war—
my people are suffering.

The Prophet Speaks:
17 Zion reaches out her hands,
but no one offers comfort.
The LORD has turned
the neighboring nations
against Jacob's descendants.
Jerusalem is merely a filthy rag
to her neighbors.

Jerusalem Speaks:
18 The LORD was right,
but I refused to obey him.
Now I ask all of you to look
at my sufferings—
even my young people
have been dragged away.
19 I called out to my lovers,
but they betrayed me.
My priests and my leaders died
while searching the city
for scraps of food.

20 Won't you look and see
how upset I am, our LORD?
My stomach is in knots,
and my heart is broken
because I betrayed you.
In the streets and at home,
my people are slaughtered.

21 Everyone heard my groaning,
but no one offered comfort.
My enemies know of the trouble
that you have brought on me,
and it makes them glad.
Hurry and punish them,
as you have promised.
22 Don't let their evil deeds
escape your sight.
Punish them as much

[c] **1.4** *raped*: One possible meaning for the difficult Hebrew text. [d] **1.10** *to . . . people*: Or "to enter his temple." [e] **1.12** *No . . . cares*: One possible meaning for the difficult Hebrew text. [f] **1.14** *You . . . neck*: One possible meaning for the difficult Hebrew text.

as you have punished me
because of my sins.
I never stop groaning—
I've lost all hope!

The LORD Was Like an Enemy

The Prophet Speaks:

2 The Lord was angry!
So he disgraced[g] Zion
though it was Israel's pride
and his own place of rest.
In his anger he threw Zion down
from heaven to earth.
2 The LORD had no mercy!
He destroyed the homes
of Jacob's descendants.
In his anger he tore down
every walled city in Judah;
he toppled the nation
together with its leaders,
leaving them in shame.

3 The Lord was so furiously angry
that he wiped out
the whole army[h] of Israel
by not supporting them
when the enemy attacked.
He was like a raging fire
that swallowed up
the descendants of Jacob.
4 He attacked like an enemy
with a bow and arrows,
killing our loved ones.
He has burned to the ground
the homes on Mount Zion.[i]

5 The Lord was like an enemy!
He left Israel in ruins
with its palaces
and fortresses destroyed,
and with everyone in Judah
moaning and weeping.
6 He shattered his temple
like a hut in a garden;[j]
he completely wiped out
his meeting place,
and did away with festivals
and Sabbaths
in the city of Zion.
In his fierce anger he rejected
our king and priests.

7 The Lord abandoned his altar
and his temple;
he let Zion's enemies
capture her fortresses.
Noisy shouts were heard
from the temple,
as if it were a time
of celebration.

8 The LORD had decided
to tear down the walls of Zion
stone by stone.
So he started destroying
and did not stop
until walls and fortresses
mourned and trembled.
9 Zion's gates have fallen
facedown on the ground;
the bars that locked the gates
are smashed to pieces.
Her king and royal family
are prisoners
in foreign lands.
Her priests don't teach,
and her prophets don't have
a message from the LORD.

10 Zion's leaders are silent.
They just sit on the ground,
tossing dirt on their heads
and wearing sackcloth.
Her young women can do nothing
but stare at the ground.

11 My eyes are red from crying,
my stomach is in knots,
and I feel sick all over.
My people are being wiped out,
and children lie helpless
in the streets of the city.
12 A child begs its mother
for food and drink,
then blacks out
like a wounded soldier
lying in the street.
The child slowly dies
in its mother's arms.

13 Zion, how can I comfort you?
How great is your pain?[k]
Lovely city of Jerusalem,
how can I heal your wounds,
gaping as wide as the sea?
14 Your prophets deceived you
with false visions
and lying messages—
they should have warned you
to leave your sins
and be saved from disaster.
15 Those who pass by
shake their heads and sneer
as they make fun and shout,
"What a lovely city you were,
the happiest on earth,
but look at you now!"

16 Zion, your enemies curse you
and snarl like wild animals,
while shouting,
"This is the day

[g]**2.1** *disgraced*: One possible meaning for the difficult Hebrew text. [h]**2.3** *army*: The Hebrew text has "horn," which refers to the horn of a bull, one of the most powerful animals in ancient Palestine. [i]**2.4** *the homes on Mount Zion*: Or "the temple on Mount Zion." [j]**2.6** *He . . . garden*: Or "He shattered the temple walls, as if they were the walls of a garden."
[k]**2.13** *How great . . . pain*: Or "What are you really like?" or "What can I say about you?"

we've waited for!
At last, we've got you!"

17 The LORD has done everything
that he had planned
and threatened long ago.
He destroyed you without mercy
and let your enemies boast about
their powerful forces.[l]

18 Zion, deep in your heart
you cried out to the Lord.
Now let your tears overflow
your walls day and night.
Don't ever lose hope
or let your tears stop.
19 Get up and pray for help
all through the night.
Pour out your feelings
to the Lord,
as you would pour water
out of a jug.
Beg him to save your people,
who are starving to death
at every street crossing.

Jerusalem Speaks:
20 Think about it, LORD!
Have you ever been this cruel
to anyone before?
Is it right for mothers
to eat their children,
or for priests and prophets
to be killed in your temple?
21 My people, both young and old,
lie dead in the streets.
Because you were angry,
my young men and women
were brutally slaughtered.
22 When you were angry, LORD,
you invited my enemies
like guests for a party.
No one survived that day;
enemies killed my children,
my own little ones.

There Is Still Hope

The Prophet Speaks:
3 I have suffered much
because God was angry.
2 He chased me into a dark place,
where no light could enter.
3 I am the only one he punishes
over and over again,
without ever stopping.
4 God caused my skin and flesh
to waste away,
and he crushed my bones.
5 He attacked and surrounded me
with hardships and trouble;
6 he forced me to sit in the dark
like someone long dead.
7 God built a fence around me
that I cannot climb over,
and he chained me down.
8 Even when I shouted
and prayed for help,
he refused to listen.
9 God put big rocks in my way
and made me follow
a crooked path.
10 God was like a bear or a lion
waiting in ambush for me;
11 he dragged me from the road,
then tore me to shreds.[m]
12 God took careful aim
and shot his arrows
13 straight through my heart.

14 I am a joke to everyone—
no one ever stops
making fun of me.
15 God has turned my life sour.
16 He made me eat gravel
and rubbed me in the dirt.
17 I cannot find peace
or remember happiness.

18 I tell myself, "I am finished!
I can't count on the LORD
to do anything for me."
19 Just thinking of my troubles
and my lonely wandering
makes me miserable.
20 That's all I ever think about,
and I am depressed.[n]
21 Then I remember something
that fills me with hope.
22 The LORD's kindness never fails!
If he had not been merciful,
we would have been destroyed.[o]
23 The LORD can always be trusted
to show mercy each morning.
24 Deep in my heart I say,
"The LORD is all I need;
I can depend on him!"

25 The LORD is kind to everyone
who trusts and obeys him.
26 It is good to wait patiently
for the LORD to save us.
27 When we are young,
it is good to struggle hard
28 and to sit silently alone,
if this is what
the LORD intends.
29 Being rubbed in the dirt
can teach us a lesson;[p]
30 we can also learn from insults
and hard knocks.

31 The Lord won't always reject us!
32 He causes a lot of suffering,

[l] **2.17** *powerful forces*: The Hebrew text has "horn," which refers to the horn of a bull, one of the most powerful animals in ancient Palestine. [m] **3.11** *shreds*: One possible meaning for the difficult Hebrew text of verse 11. [n] **3.20** *I am depressed*: One possible meaning for the difficult Hebrew text. [o] **3.22** *destroyed*: One possible meaning for the difficult Hebrew text of verse 22. [p] **3.29** *lesson*: One possible meaning for the difficult Hebrew text of verse 29.

but he also has pity
because of his great love.
33 The Lord doesn't enjoy
sending grief or pain.

34 Don't trample prisoners
under your feet
35 or cheat anyone out of
what is rightfully theirs.
God Most High sees everything,
36 and he knows when you refuse
to give someone a fair trial.
37 No one can do anything
without the Lord's approval.
38 Good and bad each happen
at the command
of God Most High.
39 We're still alive!
We shouldn't complain
when we are being punished
for our sins.
40 Instead, we should think
about the way we are living,
and turn back to the LORD.

41 When we lift our hands
in prayer to God in heaven,
we should offer him our hearts
and say, 42"We've sinned!
We've rebelled against you,
and you haven't forgiven us!
43 Anger is written all over you,
as you pursue and slaughter us
without showing pity.
44 You are behind a wall of clouds
that blocks out our prayers.
45 You allowed nations
to treat us like garbage;
46 our enemies curse us.
47 We are terrified and trapped,
caught and crushed."

48 My people are destroyed!
Tears flood my eyes,
49 and they won't stop
50 until the LORD looks down
from heaven and helps.
51 I am horrified when I see
what enemies have done
to the young women of our city.

52 No one had reason to hate me,
but I was hunted down
like a bird.
53 Then they tried to kill me
by tossing me into a pit
and throwing stones at me.
54 Water covered my head—
I thought I was gone.

55 From the bottom of the pit,
I prayed to you, LORD.
56 I begged you to listen.
"Help!" I shouted. "Save me!"
You answered my prayer
57 and came when I was in need.
You told me, "Don't worry!"
58 You rescued me
and saved my life.
59 You saw them abuse me, LORD,
so make things right.
60 You know every plot
they have made against me.
61 Yes, you know their insults
and their evil plans.
62 All day long they attack
with words and whispers.
63 No matter what they are doing,
they keep on mocking me.

64 Pay them back for everything
they have done, LORD!
65 Put your curse on them
and make them suffer.[q]
66 Get angry and go after them
until not a trace is left
under the heavens.

The Punishment of Jerusalem

The Prophet Speaks:

4 The purest gold is ruined
and has lost its shine;
jewels from the temple
lie scattered in the streets.
2 These are Zion's people,
worth more than purest gold;
yet they are counted worthless
like dishes of clay.

3 Even jackals[r] nurse their young,
but my people are like ostriches
that abandon their own.
4 Babies are so thirsty
that their tongues are stuck
to the roof of the mouth.
Children go begging for food,
but no one gives them any.
5 All who ate expensive foods
lie starving in the streets;
those who grew up in luxury
now sit on trash heaps.

6 My nation was punished worse
than the people of Sodom,
whose city was destroyed
in a flash without the help
of human hands.[s]
7 The leaders of Jerusalem
were purer than snow
and whiter than milk;
their bodies were healthy
and glowed like jewels.[t]
8 Now they are blacker than tar,
and no one recognizes them;

[q]**3.65** *make them suffer*: One possible meaning for the difficult Hebrew text. [r]**4.3** *jackals*: Desert animals related to wolves, but smaller. [s]**4.6** *hands*: One possible meaning for the difficult Hebrew text of verse 6. [t]**4.7** *jewels*: One possible meaning for the difficult Hebrew text of verse 7.

their skin clings to their bones
and is drier than firewood.
9 Being killed with a sword
is better than slowly
starving to death.
10 Life in the city is so bad
that loving mothers have boiled
and eaten their own children.

11 The LORD was so fiercely angry
that he burned the city of Zion
to the ground.
12 Not a king on this earth
or the people of any nation
believed enemies could break
through her gates.

13 Jerusalem was punished because
her prophets and her priests
had sinned and caused the death
of innocent victims.
14 Yes, her prophets and priests
were covered with blood;
no one would come near them,
as they wandered
from street to street.
15 Instead, everyone shouted,
"Go away! Don't touch us!
You're filthy and unfit
to belong to God's people!"

So they had to leave
and become refugees.
But foreign nations told them,
"You can't stay here!"[u]
16 The LORD is the one
who sent them scattering,
and he has forgotten them.
No respect or kindness
will be shown
to the priests or leaders.
17 Our eyes became weary,
hopelessly looking
for help from a nation[v]
that could not save us.
18 Enemies hunted us down
on every public street.
Our time was up;
our doom was near.
19 They swooped down faster
than eagles from the sky.
They hunted for us in the hills
and set traps to catch us
out in the desert.
20 The LORD's chosen leader[w]
was our hope for survival!
We thought he would keep us safe
somewhere among the nations,
but even he was caught
in one of their traps.

21 You people of Edom
can celebrate now!
But your time will come
to suffer and stagger
around naked.
22 The people of Zion
have paid for their sins,
and the Lord will soon
let them return home.
But, people of Edom,
you will be punished,
and your sins exposed.

A Prayer for Mercy

The People of Jerusalem Pray:[x]

5 Our LORD, don't forget
how we have suffered
and been disgraced.
2 Foreigners and strangers
have taken our land
and our homes.
3 We are like children
whose mothers are widows.
4 The water we drink
and the wood we burn
cost far too much.
5 We are terribly mistreated;[y]
we are worn out
and can find no rest.
6 We had to surrender
to[z] Egypt and Assyria
because we were hungry.

7 Our ancestors sinned,
but they are dead,
and we are left to pay
for their sins.
8 Slaves are now our rulers,
and there is no one
to set us free.
9 We are in danger
from brutal desert tribes;
we must risk our lives
just to bring in our crops.[a]
10 Our skin is scorched
from fever and hunger.

11 On Zion and everywhere in Judah
our wives and daughters
are being raped.
12 Our rulers are strung up
by their arms,
and our nation's advisors
are treated shamefully.
13 Young men are forced
to do the work of slaves;
boys must carry
heavy loads of wood.
14 Our leaders are not allowed
to decide cases in court,

[u]4.15 *here*: One possible meaning for the difficult Hebrew text of verse 15. [v]4.17 *nation*: Egypt, a former ally of Judah. [w]4.20 *chosen leader*: Probably Zedekiah, the last king of Judah, taken away to Babylonia in 586 B.C. [x]5.1 *The People of Jerusalem Pray*: Or "The Prophet Prays." [y]5.5 *We . . . mistreated*: One possible meaning for the difficult Hebrew text. [z]5.6 *surrender to*: Or "make treaties with." [a]5.9 *crops*: One possible meaning for the difficult Hebrew text of verse 9.

and young people
no longer play music.

15 Our hearts are sad;
instead of dancing,
we mourn.
16 Zion's glory has disappeared!
And we are doomed
because of our sins.
17 We feel sick all over
and can't even see straight;
18 our city is in ruins,
overrun by wild dogs.

19 You will rule forever, LORD!
You are King for all time.
20 Why have you forgotten us
for so long?
21 Bring us back to you!
Give us a fresh start.
22 Or do you despise us so much
that you don't want us?

EZEKIEL

ABOUT THIS BOOK

Ezekiel was a priest and a prophet. He had been taken away as a prisoner to Babylonia, where he lived among the other exiles from Judah. The Lord chose Ezekiel to be his prophet and to preach his message, not only to the exiles in Babylonia, but also to the people still living in Jerusalem. Ezekiel's ministry probably began around 593 B.C., during the last years of the kingdom of Judah, and it ended sometime around 570 B.C., several years after the fall of Jerusalem (586 B.C.). Ezekiel preached before and after this horrible disaster, and so some of his messages threatened judgment and others offered hope.

The book of Ezekiel can be divided into five main parts. The first part (1–3) describes Ezekiel's vision of the Lord's glory and tells how the Lord appointed Ezekiel to be his prophet. The second part (4–24) includes several messages warning the people of Judah that they will soon be punished for turning away from the Lord. Ezekiel acted out many of these warnings. And the third part of the book (25–32) includes the Lord's judgments on nearby nations.

The fourth part of the book (33–39) is made up of Ezekiel's messages after he heard that Jerusalem had been captured. These are messages of hope. The Lord promises he will forgive his people and bring them back to Judah and Jerusalem. Finally, the fifth part of the book (40–48) is Ezekiel's vision of the new temple in Jerusalem, its regulations for proper worship, and how the restored land of Israel will be divided among the tribes.

When the Lord speaks to Ezekiel, he calls him "son of man." Although this expression shows that Ezekiel is a mere human, it also shows that he has been appointed to preach the Lord's message to the people of Judah and Jerusalem.

One of the most familiar passages in the book is Ezekiel's vision of the valley full of dried-out bones. Ezekiel watches the Lord's Spirit blow life into the dead bodies, and he sees them come back to life. The Lord then tells Ezekiel:

> *The people of Israel are like dead bones. They complain that they are dried up and that they have no hope for the future. So tell them, "I, the LORD God, promise to open your graves and set you free. I will bring you back to Israel . . . My Spirit will give you breath, and you will live again."* *(37.11, 12, 14a)*

A QUICK LOOK AT THIS BOOK

Ezekiel Sees the Lord's Glory and Is Chosen To Be His Prophet (1.1—3.27)
Ezekiel Acts Out the Coming Destruction of Judah and Jerusalem (4.1—5.17)
Disaster Is Near (6.1—7.27)
The Lord's Glory Leaves Sinful Jerusalem (8.1—11.25)
Messages of Doom for Judah and Jerusalem (12.1—24.27)
Judgment on Foreign Nations (25.1—32.32)
Ezekiel Must Warn the People To Turn from Their Sinful Ways (33.1-20)
The News of Jerusalem's Fall (33.21, 22)
The Lord Promises To Bring the People Home and To Restore Judah (34.1—37.28)
Gog Will Be Defeated and Israel Will Be Restored (38.1—39.29)
Ezekiel Sees the Future Temple in Jerusalem (40.1—46.24)
The Stream Flowing from the Temple (47.1-12)
The Borders of the Restored Land and Its Division Among the Tribes (47.13—48.35)

Ezekiel Sees the LORD's Glory

1 1-3 I am Ezekiel—a priest and the son
of Buzi.[a]
Five years after King Jehoiachin of
Judah had been led away as a prisoner
to Babylonia, I was living near the
Chebar River among those who had
been taken there with him. Then on the
fifth day of the fourth month[b] of the
thirtieth year,[c] the heavens suddenly
opened. The LORD placed his hand upon
me[d] and showed me some visions.
4 I saw a windstorm blowing in from
the north. Lightning flashed from a
huge cloud and lit up the whole sky
with a dazzling brightness. The fiery
center of the cloud was as shiny as polished metal, 5 and in that center I saw
what looked like four living creatures.
They were somewhat like humans, 6 except that each one had four faces and
four wings. 7 Their legs were straight,
but their feet looked like the hoofs of
calves and sparkled like bronze. 8 Under
each of their wings, these creatures had
a human hand. 9 The four creatures were
standing back to back with the tips of
their wings touching. They moved together in every direction, without turning their bodies.
10 Each creature had the face of a human in front, the face of a lion on the
right side, the face of a bull on the left,
and the face of an eagle in back. 11 Two
wings[e] of each creature were spread out
and touched the wings of the creatures
on either side. The other two wings of
each creature were folded against its
body.
12 Wherever the four living creatures
went, they moved together without turning their bodies, because each creature
faced straight ahead. 13 The creatures
were glowing like hot coals, and I saw
something like a flaming torch moving
back and forth among them. Lightning
flashed from the torch every time its
flame blazed up.[f] 14 The creatures themselves moved as quickly as sparks
jumping from a fire.[g]
15 I then noticed that on the ground beside each of the four living creatures
was a wheel,[h] 16 shining like chrysolite.[i]
Each wheel was exactly the same and
had a second wheel that cut through the
middle of it,[j] 17 so that they could move
in any direction without turning. 18 The
rims of the wheels were large and had
eyes all the way around them.[k] 19-21 The
creatures controlled when and where
the wheels moved—the wheels went
wherever the four creatures went and
stopped whenever they stopped. Even
when the creatures flew in the air, the
wheels were beside them.
22-23 Above the living creatures, I saw
something that was sparkling like ice,
and it reminded me of a dome. Each
creature had two of its wings stretched
out toward the creatures on either side,
with the other two wings folded against
its body. 24 Whenever the creatures flew,
their wings roared like an ocean or a
large army or even the voice of God All-
Powerful. And whenever the creatures
stopped, they folded their wings against
their bodies.
25 When the creatures stopped flap-
ping their wings, I heard a sound coming from above the dome. 26 I then saw
what looked like a throne made of sapphire,[l] and sitting on the throne was a
figure in the shape of a human. 27 From
the waist up, it was glowing like metal
in a hot furnace, and from the waist
down it looked like the flames of a fire.
The figure was surrounded by a bright
light, 28 as colorful as a rainbow that appears after a storm.
I realized I was seeing the brightness
of the LORD's glory! So I bowed with my
face to the ground, and just then I heard
a voice speaking to me.

The LORD Chooses Ezekiel

2 The LORD[m] said, "Ezekiel, son of
man,[n] I want you to stand up and
listen." 2 After he said this, his Spirit
took control of me and lifted me to my
feet. Then the LORD said:
3 Ezekiel, I am sending you to the
people of Israel. They are just like
their ancestors who rebelled against
me and refused to stop. 4 They are
stubborn and hardheaded. But I, the
LORD God, have chosen you to tell

[a] **1.1-3** *a priest and the son of Buzi*: Or "the son of Buzi the priest." [b] **1.1-3** *Five years . . . prisoner . . . fourth month*: Probably July of 593 B.C. [c] **1.1-3** *thirtieth year*: The event from which this date is figured is unknown. [d] **1.1-3** *The LORD placed his hand upon me*: This was a sign that the LORD had chosen Ezekiel to be his prophet. [e] **1.11** *Two wings*: One possible meaning for the difficult Hebrew text. [f] **1.13** *up*: One possible meaning for the difficult Hebrew text of verse 13. [g] **1.14** *as sparks jumping from a fire*: Or "as flashes of lightning."
[h] **1.15** *wheel*: One possible meaning for the difficult Hebrew text of verse 15.
[i] **1.16** *chrysolite*: A precious stone that has an olive green color. [j] **1.16** *a second wheel that cut through the middle of it*: Or "a smaller wheel inside it." [k] **1.18** *them*: One possible meaning for the difficult Hebrew text of verse 18. [l] **1.26** *sapphire*: A precious stone that has a blue color. [m] **2.1** *The LORD*: Hebrew "The voice." [n] **2.1** *Ezekiel, son of man*: The Hebrew text has "Son of man," which is often used in this book when the LORD speaks directly to Ezekiel. It means that Ezekiel is a mere human, yet he is the one the LORD has chosen to be his prophet who speaks for him to the people of Israel.

them what I say. 5Those rebels may
not even listen, but at least they will
know that a prophet has come to
them.
6Don't be afraid of them or of anything they say. You may think you're
in the middle of a thorn patch or a
bunch of scorpions. But be brave
7and preach my message to them,
whether they choose to listen or not.
8Ezekiel, don't rebel against me, as
they have done. Instead, listen to
everything I tell you.
And now, Ezekiel, open your
mouth and eat what I am going to
give you.
9Just then, I saw a hand stretched out
toward me. And in it was a scroll.[o] 10The
hand opened the scroll, and both sides
of it were filled with words of sadness,
mourning, and grief.
3 The LORD said, "Ezekiel, son of man,
after you eat this scroll, go speak to
the people of Israel."
2-3He handed me the scroll and said,
"Eat this and fill up on it." So I ate the
scroll, and it tasted sweet as honey.
4The LORD said:
Ezekiel, I am sending you to your
own people. 5-6They are Israelites,
not some strangers who speak a foreign language you can't understand.
If I were to send you to foreign nations, they would listen to you. 7But
the people of Israel will refuse to listen, because they have refused to listen to me. All of them are stubborn
and hardheaded, 8so I will make you
as stubborn as they are. 9You will be
so determined to speak my message
that nothing will stop you. I will
make you hard like a diamond, and
you'll have no reason to be afraid of
those arrogant rebels.
10Listen carefully to everything I
say and then think about it. 11Then
go to the people who were brought
here to Babylonia with you and tell
them you have a message from me,
the LORD God. Do this, whether they
listen to you or not.
12The Spirit[p] lifted me up, and as the
glory of the LORD started to leave,[q] I
heard a loud, thundering noise behind
me. 13It was the sound made by the
creatures' wings as they brushed
against each other, and by the rumble of
the wheels beside them. 14Then the
Spirit carried me away.
The LORD's power had taken complete
control of me, and I was both annoyed
and angry.
15When I was back with the others living at Abib Hill near the Chebar River, I
sat among them for seven days, shocked
at what had happened to me.

The LORD Appoints Ezekiel To Stand Watch

(Ezekiel 33.1-9)

16Seven days after I had seen the
brightness of the LORD's glory, the LORD
said:
17Ezekiel, son of man, I have appointed you to stand watch for the
people of Israel. So listen to what I
say, then warn them for me. 18When
I tell wicked people they will die because of their sins, you must warn
them to turn from their sinful ways
so they won't be punished. If you
refuse, you are responsible for their
death. 19However, if you do warn
them, and they keep on sinning, they
will die because of their sins, and
you will be innocent.
20Now suppose faithful people
start sinning, and I decide to put
stumbling blocks in their paths to
make them fall. They deserve to die
because of their sins. So if you
refuse to warn them, I will forget
about the times they were faithful,
and I will hold you responsible for
their death. 21But if you do warn
them, and they listen to you and stop
sinning, I will let them live. And you
will be innocent.

Ezekiel Cannot Talk

22The LORD took control of me and
said, "Stand up! Go into the valley, and I
will talk with you there."
23I immediately went to the valley,
where I saw the brightness of the LORD's
glory, just as I had seen near the Chebar
River, and I bowed with my face to the
ground. 24His Spirit took control of me
and lifted me to my feet. Then the LORD
said:
Go back and lock yourself in your
house! 25You will be tied up to keep
you inside, 26and I will make you unable to talk or to warn those who
have rebelled against me. 27But the
time will come, when I will tell you
what to say, and you will again be
able to speak my message.[r] Some of
them will listen; others will be stubborn and refuse to listen.

Ezekiel Acts Out an Attack on Jerusalem

The LORD said:

4 Ezekiel, son of man, find a brick
and sketch a picture of Jerusalem
on it. 2Then prepare to attack the brick
as if it were a real city. Build a dirt
mound and a ramp up to the top and

[o]**2.9** *scroll*: A roll of paper or special leather used for writing on. [p]**3.12** *The Spirit*: Or "A wind." [q]**3.12** *as the glory of the LORD started to leave*: One possible meaning for the difficult Hebrew text. [r]**3.27** *again . . . speak my message*: See 33.21, 22.

surround the brick with enemy camps. On every side put large wooden poles as though you were going to break down the gate to the city. [3]Set up an iron pan like a wall between you and the brick. All this will be a warning for the people of Israel.

[4-5]After that, lie down on your left side and stay there for three hundred ninety days as a sign of Israel's punishment[s]—one day for each year of its suffering. [6]Then turn over and lie on your right side forty more days. That will be a sign of Judah's punishment—one day for each year of its suffering.

[7]The brick stands for Jerusalem, so attack it! Stare at it and shout angry warnings. [8]I will tie you up, so you can't leave until your attack has ended.

[9]Get a large bowl. Then mix together wheat, barley, beans, lentils, and millet, and make some bread. This is what you will eat for the three hundred ninety days you are lying down. [10]Eat only a small loaf of bread each day [11]and drink only two large cups of water. [12]Use dried human waste to start a fire, then bake the bread on the coals where everyone can watch you. [13]When I scatter the people of Israel among the nations, they will also have to eat food that is unclean, just as you must do.[t]

[14]I said, "LORD God, please don't make me do that! Never in my life have I eaten food that would make me unacceptable to you. I've never eaten anything that died a natural death or was killed by a wild animal or that you said was unclean."

[15]The LORD replied, "Instead of human waste, I will let you bake your bread on a fire made from cow manure. [16]Ezekiel, the people of Jerusalem will starve. They will have so little food and water that they will be afraid and hopeless. [17]Everyone will be shocked at what is happening, and, because of their sins, they will die a slow death."

Jerusalem's Coming Destruction

The LORD said:

5 Ezekiel, son of man, get a sharp sword and use it to cut off your hair and beard. Weigh the hair and divide it into three equal piles. [2]After you attack the brick that stands for Jerusalem, burn one pile of your hair on the brick. Chop up the second pile and let the small pieces of hair fall around the brick. Throw the third pile into the wind, and I will strike it with my own sword.

[3]Keep a few of the hairs and wrap them in the hem of your clothes. [4]Then pull out a few of those hairs and throw them in the fire, so they will also burn. This fire will spread, destroying everyone in Israel.

[5]I am the LORD God, and I have made Jerusalem the most important place in the world, and all other nations admire it. [6]But the people of Jerusalem rebelled and refuse to obey me. They ignored my laws and have become even more sinful than the nations around them.

[7]So tell the people of Jerusalem:

I am the LORD God! You have refused to obey my laws and teachings, and instead you have obeyed the laws of the surrounding nations. You have become more rebellious than any of them! [8]Now all those nations will watch as I turn against you and punish you [9]for your sins. Your punishment will be more horrible than anything I've ever done or will ever do again. [10]Parents will be so desperate for food that they will eat their own children, and children will eat their parents. Those who survive this horror will be scattered in every direction.

[11]Your disgusting sins have made my temple unfit as a place to worship me. So I swear by my own life that I will turn my back on you and show you no pity. [12]A third of you will die here in Jerusalem from disease or starvation. Another third will be killed in war. And I will scatter the last third of you in every direction, then track you down and kill you.

[13]You will feel my fierce anger until I have finished taking revenge. Then you will know that I, the LORD, was furious because of your disobedience. [14]Every passerby will laugh at your destruction. Foreign nations [15]will insult you and make fun of you, but they will also be shocked and terrified at what I did in my anger. [16]I will destroy your crops until you starve to death, and disasters will strike you like arrows. [17]Starvation and wild animals will kill your children. I'll punish you with horrible diseases, and your enemies will

[s]4.4,5 *Israel's punishment*: Israel here refers to the northern kingdom that was destroyed in 722 B.C. [t]4.13 *have to eat food that is unclean, just as you must do*: The LORD had forbidden the people of Israel to mix certain things (see Deuteronomy 22.9-11), and so the people would not have been allowed to eat this bread under normal conditions. It is used here to show that when a city is under attack, people eat whatever food is left, even if the LORD had said it was unclean.

strike you down with their swords. I,
the LORD, have spoken.

Israel Is Doomed

6 The LORD God said:
2Ezekiel, son of man, face the hills
of Israel and tell them:
3Listen, you mountains and hills,
and every valley and gorge! I, the
LORD, am about to turn against you
and crush all the places where foreign gods are worshiped. 4Every altar will be smashed, and in front of
the idols I will put to death the people who worship them. 5Dead bodies
and bones will be lying around the
idols and the altars. 6Every town in
Israel will be destroyed to make sure
that each shrine, idol, and altar is
smashed—everything the Israelites
made will be a pile of ruins. 7All
over the country, your people will
die. And those who survive will
know that I, the LORD, did these
things. 8I will let some of the people
live through this punishment, but I
will scatter them among the nations,
9where they will be prisoners. And
when they think of me, they will realize that they disgraced me by rebelling and by worshiping idols.
They will hate themselves for the
evil things they did, 10and they will
know that I am the LORD and that
my warnings must be taken seriously.
11The LORD God then said:
Ezekiel, beat your fists together
and stomp your feet in despair!
Moan in sorrow, because the people
of Israel have done disgusting things
and now will be killed by enemy
troops, or they will die from starvation and disease. 12Those who live
far away will be struck with deadly
diseases. Those who live nearby will
be killed in war. And the ones who
are left will starve to death. I will let
loose my anger on them! 13These
people used to offer incense to idols
at altars built on hills and mountaintops and in the shade of large oak
trees. But when they see dead bodies
lying around those altars, they will
know that I am the LORD. 14I will
make their country a barren wasteland, from the Southern Desert to
the town of Diblah in the north.
Then they will know that I, the
LORD, have done these things.

Disaster Is Near

7 The LORD God said:
2Ezekiel, son of man, tell the
people of Israel that I am saying:
Israel will soon come to an end!
Your whole country is about to be
destroyed 3as punishment for your
disgusting sins. I, the LORD, am so
angry 4that I will show no pity. I will
punish you for the evil you've done,
and you will know that I am the
LORD.
5There's never been anything like
the coming disaster.[u] 6And when it
comes, your life will be over. 7You
people of Israel are doomed! Soon
there will be panic on the mountaintops instead of celebration.[v] 8I will
let loose my anger and punish you
for the evil things you've done. You'll
get what you deserve. 9Your sins are
so terrible, that you'll get no mercy
from me. Then you will know that I,
the LORD, have punished you.
10Disaster is near! Injustice and
arrogance are everywhere, 11and violent criminals run free. None of you
will survive the disaster, and everything you own and value will be
shattered.[w] 12The time is coming
when everyone will be ruined. Buying and selling will stop, 13and people who sell property will never get
it back, because all of you must be
punished for your sins. And I won't
change my mind![x]
14A signal has been blown on the
trumpet, and weapons are prepared
for battle. But no one goes to war,
because in my anger I will strike
down everyone in Israel.

Israel Is Surrounded

The LORD said to the people of Israel:
15War, disease, and starvation are
everywhere! People who live in the
countryside will be killed in battle, and
those who live in towns will die from
starvation or deadly diseases. 16Anyone
who survives will escape into the hills,
like doves who leave the valleys to find
safety.
All of you will moan[y] because of your
sins. 17Your hands will tremble, and
your knees will go limp. 18You will put
on sackcloth[z] to show your sorrow, but
terror will overpower you. Shame will
be written all over your faces, and you
will shave your heads in despair. 19Your
silver and gold will be thrown into the

[u] **7.5** *disaster*: One possible meaning for the difficult Hebrew text of verse 5.
[v] **7.7** *celebration*: One possible meaning for the difficult Hebrew text of verse 7.
[w] **7.11** *shattered*: One possible meaning for the difficult Hebrew text of verses 10, 11.
[x] **7.13** *mind*: One possible meaning for the difficult Hebrew text of verse 13. [y] **7.16** *will moan*: Hebrew; two ancient translations "will die." [z] **7.18** *sackcloth*: A rough, dark-colored cloth made from goat or camel hair and used to make grain sacks. It was worn in times of trouble or sorrow.

streets like garbage, because those are
the two things that led you into sin, and
now they cannot save you from my
anger. They are not even worth enough
to buy food. 20You took great pride in
using your beautiful jewelry to make
disgusting idols of foreign gods. So I
will make your jewelry worthless.
21Wicked foreigners will rob and disgrace you. 22They will break into my
temple[a] and leave it unfit as a place to
worship me, but I will look away and let
it happen.
23Your whole country is in confusion![b]
Murder and violence are everywhere in
Israel, 24so I will tell the most wicked
nations to come and take over your
homes. They will put an end to the pride
you have in your strong army, and they
will make your places of worship unfit
to use. 25You will be terrified and will
desperately look for peace—but there
will be no peace. 26One tragedy will follow another, and you'll hear only bad
news. People will beg prophets to give
them a message from me. Priests will
stop teaching my Law, and wise leaders
won't be able to give advice. 27Even
your king and his officials will lose hope
and cry in despair. Your hands will tremble with fear.

I will punish you for your sins and
treat you the same way you have treated
others. Then you will know that I am the
LORD.

Ezekiel Sees the Terrible Sins of Jerusalem

8 Six years after King Jehoiachin and
the rest of us had been led away as
prisoners to Babylonia, the leaders of
Judah were meeting with me in my
house. On the fifth day of the sixth
month,[c] the LORD God suddenly took
control of me, 2and I saw something in
the shape of a human.[d] This figure was
like fire from the waist down, and it
was bright as polished metal from the
waist up. 3It reached out what seemed
to be a hand and grabbed my hair. Then
in my vision the LORD's Spirit lifted
me into the sky and carried me to
Jerusalem.

The Spirit took me to the north gate of
the temple's inner courtyard, where
there was an idol that disgusted the
LORD and made him furious. 4Then I
saw the brightness of the glory of the
God of Israel, just as I had seen it near
the Chebar River.
5God said to me, "Ezekiel, son of man,
look north." And when I did, I saw that
disgusting idol by the altar near the
gate.
6God then said, "Do you see the terrible sins of the people of Israel? Their
sins are making my holy temple unfit as
a place to worship me. Yet you will see
even worse things than this."
7Next, I was taken to the entrance of
the courtyard, where I saw a hole in the
wall.
8God said, "Make this hole bigger."
And when I did, I realized it was a doorway. 9"Go in," God said, "and see what
horrible and evil things the people are
doing."
10Inside, I saw that the walls were covered with pictures of reptiles and disgusting, unclean animals,[e] as well as
with idols that the Israelites were worshiping. 11Seventy Israelite leaders were
standing there, including Jaazaniah son
of Shaphan. Each of these leaders was
holding an incense burner, and the
smell of incense filled the room.
12God said, "Ezekiel, do you see what
horrible things Israel's leaders are doing in secret? They have filled their
rooms with idols. And they say I can't
see them, because they think I have already deserted Israel. 13But I will show
you something even worse than this."
14He took me to the north gate of the
temple, where I saw women mourning
for the god Tammuz.[f] 15God asked me,
"Can you believe what these women are
doing? But now I want to show you
something worse."
16I was then led into the temple's inner courtyard, where I saw about
twenty-five men standing near the entrance, between the porch and the altar.
Their backs were to the LORD's temple,
and they were bowing down to the rising sun.
17God said, "Ezekiel, it's bad enough
that the people of Judah are doing these
disgusting things. But they have also
spread violence and injustice everywhere in Israel and have made me very
angry. They have disgraced and insulted
me in the worst possible way.[g] 18So in
my fierce anger, I will punish them without mercy and refuse to help them when
they cry out to me."

[a]7.22 *my temple*: The Hebrew text has "my treasure," which may refer to the temple, to Jerusalem, or to Israel itself. [b]7.23 *Your whole country is in confusion*: One ancient translation; Hebrew "Get chains ready to drag away the dead bodies of your people." [c]8.1 *Six years . . . sixth month*: Probably September of 592 B.C. [d]8.2 *a human*: One ancient translation; Hebrew "a fiery figure." [e]8.10 *disgusting, unclean animals*: See, for example, Leviticus 11.9-19. [f]8.14 *the god Tammuz*: A god of vegetation who was thought to die in the dry season. During the Hebrew month of Tammuz (from about mid-June to mid-July), women mourned the death of this god, hoping to bring him back to life. [g]8.17 *disgraced and insulted me . . . way*: One possible meaning for the difficult Hebrew text.

The LORD Gives the Command To Punish Jerusalem

9 After that, I heard the LORD shout,
"Come to Jerusalem, you men chosen to destroy the city. And bring your
weapons!"
2 I saw six men come through the
north gate of the temple, each one holding a deadly weapon. A seventh man
dressed in a linen robe was with them,
and he was carrying things to write
with. The men went into the temple and
stood by the bronze altar.
3 The brightness of God's glory then
left its place above the statues of the
winged creatures[h] inside the temple and
moved to the entrance. The LORD said to
the man in the linen robe, 4 "Walk
through the city of Jerusalem and mark
the forehead of anyone who is truly upset and sad about the disgusting things
that are being done here."
5-6 He turned to the other six men and
said, "Follow him and put to death
everyone who doesn't have a mark on
their forehead. Show no mercy or pity!
Kill men and women, parents and children. Begin here at my temple and be
sure not to harm those who are
marked."
The men immediately killed the leaders who were standing there.
7 Then the LORD said, "Pollute the temple by piling the dead bodies in the
courtyards. Now get busy!" They left
and started killing the people of
Jerusalem.
8 I was then alone, so I bowed down
and cried out to the LORD, "Why are you
doing this? Are you so angry at the people of Jerusalem that everyone must
die?"
9 The LORD answered, "The people of
Israel and Judah have done horrible
things. Their country is filled with murderers, and Jerusalem itself is filled with
violence. They think that I have deserted them, and that I can't see what
they are doing. 10 And so I will not have
pity on them or forgive them. They will
be punished for what they have done."
11 Just then, the man in the linen robe
returned and said, "I have done what
you commanded."

The LORD's Glory Leaves the Temple

10 I saw the dome that was above
the four winged creatures,[i] and
on it was the sapphire[j] throne.[k] 2 The
LORD said to the man in the linen robe,
"Walk among the four wheels beside the
creatures and pick up as many hot coals
as you can carry. Then scatter them over
the city of Jerusalem." I watched him as
he followed the LORD's instructions.
3 The winged creatures were standing
south of the temple when the man
walked among them. A cloud filled the
inner courtyard, 4 and the brightness of
the LORD's glory moved from above the
creatures and stopped at the entrance of
the temple. The entire temple was filled
with his glory, and the courtyard was
dazzling bright. 5 The sound of the creatures' wings was as loud as the voice of
God All-Powerful and could even be
heard in the outer courtyard.
6 The man in the robe was now standing beside a wheel. 7 One of the four
creatures reached its hand into the fire
among them and gave him some of the
hot coals. The man took the coals and
left.
8 I noticed again that each of the four
winged creatures had what looked like
human hands under their wings, 9 and I
saw the four wheels near the creatures.
These wheels were shining like chrysolite.[l] 10 Each wheel was exactly the same
and had a second wheel that cut
through the middle of it,[m] 11 so that they
could move in any direction without
turning. The wheels moved together
whenever the creatures moved. 12 I also
noticed that the wheels and the creatures' bodies, including their backs,
their hands, and their wings, were covered with eyes. 13 And I heard a voice
calling these "the wheels that spin."
14 Each of the winged creatures had
four faces: the face of a bull,[n] the face of
a human, the face of a lion, and the face
of an eagle. 15-17 These were the same
creatures I had seen near the Chebar
River. They controlled when and where
the wheels moved—the wheels went
wherever the creatures went and
stopped whenever they stopped. Even
when the creatures flew in the air, the
wheels stayed beside them.
18 Then I watched the brightness of the
LORD's glory move from the entrance of
the temple and stop above the winged
creatures. 19 They spread their wings
and flew into the air with the wheels at
their side. They stopped at the east gate
of the temple, and the LORD's glory was
above them.
20 I knew for sure that these were the
same creatures I had seen beneath the
LORD's glory near the Chebar River.
21-22 They had four wings with hands be-

[h] **9.3** *the statues of the winged creatures*: These were symbols of the LORD's throne on earth (see Exodus 25.18-22; 1 Kings 6.23-28). [i] **10.1** *winged creatures*: See the note at 9.3.
[j] **10.1** *sapphire*: See the note at 1.26. [k] **10.1** *dome . . . creatures . . . throne*: See 1.22-26.
[l] **10.9** *chrysolite*: See the note at 1.16. [m] **10.10** *a second wheel that cut through the middle of it*: See the note at 1.16. [n] **10.14** *a bull*: The Hebrew text has "a winged creature," but see 1.10.

neath them, and they had the same four
faces as those near the River. Each creature moved straight ahead without turning.

Ezekiel Condemns Jerusalem's Wicked Leaders

11 The LORD's Spirit[o] lifted me up
and took me to the east gate of
the temple, where I saw twenty-five
men, including the two leaders, Jaazaniah son of Azzur and Pelatiah son of
Benaiah. 2The LORD said, "Ezekiel, son
of man, these men are making evil plans
and giving dangerous advice to the people of Jerusalem. 3They say things like,
'Let's build more houses.[p] This city is
like a cooking pot over a fire, and we
are the meat, but at least the pot keeps
us from being burned in the fire.'[q] 4So,
Ezekiel, condemn them!"
5The LORD's Spirit took control of me
and told me to tell these leaders:
I, the LORD God, know what you
leaders are saying. 6You have murdered so many people that the city is
filled with dead bodies! 7This city is
indeed a cooking pot, but the bodies
of those you killed are the meat. And
so I will force you to leave
Jerusalem, 8and I'll send armies to
attack you, just as you fear. 9Then
you will be captured and punished
by foreign enemies.[r] 10You will be
killed in your own country, but not
before you realize that I, the LORD,
have done these things.
11You leaders claim to be meat in a
cooking pot, but you won't be protected by this city. No, you will die at
the border of Israel. 12You will realize that while you were following
the laws of nearby nations, you were
disobeying my laws and teachings.
And I am the LORD!
13Before I finished speaking, Pelatiah
dropped dead. I bowed down and cried
out, "Please, LORD God, don't kill everyone left in Israel."

A Promise of Hope

14The LORD replied:
15Ezekiel, son of man, the people living in Jerusalem claim that you and the
other Israelites who were taken to
Babylonia are too far away to worship
me. They also claim that the land of Israel now belongs only to them. 16But
here is what I want you to tell the Israelites in Babylonia:
It's true that I, the LORD God, have
forced you out of your own country
and made you live among foreign
nations. But for now, I will be with
you wherever you are, so that you
can worship me. 17And someday, I
will gather you from the nations
where you are scattered and let you
live in Israel again. 18When that happens, I want you to clear the land of
all disgusting idols. 19Then I will
take away your stubbornness and
make you eager to be completely
faithful to me. You will want to obey
me 20and all my laws and teachings.
You will be my people, and I will be
your God. 21But those who worship
idols will be punished and get what
they deserve. I, the LORD God, have
spoken.

The LORD's Glory Leaves Jerusalem

22After the LORD had finished speaking, the winged creatures spread their
wings and flew into the air, and the
wheels were beside them. The brightness of the LORD's glory above them
23left Jerusalem and stopped at a hill
east of the city.
24Then in my vision, the LORD's Spirit[s]
lifted me up and carried me back to the
other exiles in Babylonia. The vision
faded away, 25and I told them everything
the LORD had shown me.

Ezekiel Acts Out Israel's Captivity

12 The LORD said:
2Ezekiel, son of man, you are
living among rebellious people.
They have eyes, but refuse to see;
they have ears, but refuse to listen.
3So before it gets dark, here is what
I want you to do. Pack a few things
as though you were going to be
taken away as a prisoner. Then go
outside where everyone can see you
and walk around from place to
place. Maybe as they watch, they
will realize what rebels they are.
4After you have done this, return to
your house.
Later that evening leave your
house as if you were going into exile. 5Dig through the wall of your
house[t] and crawl out, carrying the
bag with you. Make sure everyone is
watching. 6Lift the bag to your
shoulders, and with your face covered, take it into the darkness, so
that you cannot see the land you are

[o] 11.1 *The LORD's Spirit*: Or "A wind." [p] 11.3 *Let's . . . houses*: One possible meaning for the difficult Hebrew text. [q] 11.3 *the pot keeps us from being burned in the fire*: These leaders were trying to convince the people of Jerusalem that they were secure, and that their future was bright. [r] 11.9 *foreign enemies*: That is, the Babylonians. [s] 11.24 *the LORD's Spirit*: See the note at 11.1. [t] 12.5 *Dig through the wall of your house*: The walls of most houses in Babylonia were made of mud bricks that had been dried in the sun. A hole could easily have been dug through these bricks.

leaving. All of this will be a warning for the people of Israel.

7I did everything the LORD had said. I packed a few things. Then as the sun was going down, and while everyone was watching, I dug a hole through one of the walls of my house. I pulled out my bag, then lifted it to my shoulders and left in the darkness.

8The next morning, the LORD 9reminded me that those rebellious people didn't even ask what I was doing. 10So he sent me back to tell them:

The LORD God has a message for the leader of Jerusalem and everyone living there!

11I have done these things to show them what will happen when they are taken away as prisoners.

12The leader of Jerusalem will lift his own bag to his shoulders at sunset and leave through a hole that the others have dug in the wall of his house. He will cover his face, so he can't see the land he is leaving. 13The LORD will spread out a net and trap him as he leaves Jerusalem. He will then be led away to the city of Babylon, but will never see that place,[u] even though he will die there. 14His own officials and troops will scatter in every direction, and the LORD will track them down and put them to death.

15The LORD will force the rest of the people in Jerusalem to live in foreign nations, where they will realize that he has done all these things. 16Some of them will survive the war, the starvation, and the deadly diseases. That way, they will be able to tell foreigners how disgusting their sins were, and that it was the LORD who punished them in this way.

A Sign of Fear

17The LORD said:

18Ezekiel, son of man, shake with fear when you eat, and tremble when you drink. 19Tell the people of Israel that I, the LORD, say that someday everyone in Jerusalem will shake when they eat and tremble when they drink. Their country will be destroyed and left empty, because they have been cruel and violent. 20Every town will lie in ruins, and the land will be a barren desert. Then they will know that I am the LORD.

The Words of the LORD Will Come True

21The LORD said:

22Ezekiel, son of man, you've heard people in Israel use the saying, "Time passes, and prophets are proved wrong." 23Now tell the people that I, the LORD, am going to prove that saying wrong. No one will ever be able to use it again in Israel, because very soon everything I have said will come true! 24The people will hear no more useless warnings and false messages. 25I will give them my message, and what I say will certainly happen. Warn those rebels that the time has come for them to be punished. I, the LORD, make this promise.

26-27Ezekiel, the people of Israel are also saying that your visions and messages are only about things in the future. 28So tell them that my words will soon come true, just as I have warned. I, the LORD, have spoken.

Lying Prophets

13 The LORD said:

2Ezekiel, son of man, condemn the prophets of Israel who say they speak in my name, but who preach messages that come from their own imagination. Tell them it's time to hear my message.

3I, the LORD God, say those lying prophets are doomed! They don't see visions—they make up their own messages! 4Israel's prophets are no better than jackals[v] that hunt for food among the ruins of a city. 5They don't warn the people about coming trouble or tell them how dangerous it is to sin against me. 6Those prophets lie by claiming they speak for me, but I have not even chosen them to be my prophets. And they still think their words will come true. 7They say they're preaching my messages, but they are full of lies—I did not speak to them!

8So I am going to punish those lying prophets for deceiving the people of Israel with false messages. 9I will turn against them and no longer let them belong to my people. They will not be allowed to call themselves Israelites or even to set foot in Israel. Then they will realize that I am the LORD God.

10Those prophets refuse to be honest. They tell my people there will be peace, even though there's no peace to be found. They are like workers who think they can fix a shaky wall by covering it with paint. 11But when I send rainstorms, hailstones, and strong winds, the wall will surely collapse. 12People will then ask the workers why the paint didn't hold it up.

13That wall is the city of Jerusalem. And I, the LORD God, am so angry that I will send strong winds, rainstorms, and hailstones to destroy it. 14The lying

[u] **12.13** *He will then be led away . . . that place*: According to 2 Kings 25.6, 7, King Zedekiah of Judah was blinded before he was taken to Babylon. [v] **13.4** *jackals*: Desert animals related to wolves, but smaller.

prophets have tried to cover up the evil
in Jerusalem, but I will tear down the
city, all the way to its foundations. And
when it collapses, those prophets will be
killed, and everyone will know that I
have done these things.
15 The city of Jerusalem and its lying
prophets will feel my fierce anger. Then
I will announce that the city has fallen
and that the lying prophets are dead,
16 because they promised my people
peace, when there was no peace. I, the
LORD God, have spoken.

Women Who Wear Magic Charms

The LORD said:
17 Ezekiel, son of man, now condemn
the women of Israel who preach messages that come from their own imagination. 18 Tell them they're doomed!
They wear magic charms on their wrists
and scarves on their heads, then trick
others into believing they can predict
the future.[w] They won't get away with
telling those lies. 19 They charge my people a few handfuls of barley and a couple pieces of bread, and then give messages that are insulting to me. They use
lies to sentence the innocent to death
and to help the guilty go free. And my
people believe them!
20 I hate the magic charms they use to
trick people into believing their lies. I
will rip those charms from their wrists
and set free the people they have
trapped like birds.[x] 21 I will tear the
scarves from their heads and rescue my
people from their power once and for
all. Then they will know that I am the
LORD God.
22 They do things I would never do.
They lie to good people and encourage
them to do wrong, and they convince
the wicked to keep sinning and ruin
their lives. 23 I will no longer let these
women give false messages and use
magic, and I will free my people from
their control. Then they will know that I,
the LORD, have done these things.

Ezekiel Encourages the People To Turn Back to the LORD

14 One day, some of Israel's leaders
came to me and asked for a message from the LORD. 2 While they were
there, the LORD said:
3 Ezekiel, son of man, these men have
started worshiping idols, though they
know it will cause them to sin even
more. So I refuse to give them a message!
4 Tell the people of Israel that if they
sin by worshiping idols and then go to a
prophet to find out what I say, I will give
them the answer their sins deserve.
5 When they hear my message, maybe
they will see that they need to turn back
to me and stop worshiping those idols.
6 Now, Ezekiel, tell everyone in Israel:
I am the LORD God. Stop worshiping your disgusting idols and come
back to me.
7 Suppose one of you Israelites or a
foreigner living in Israel rejects me
and starts worshiping idols. If you
then go to a prophet to find out what
I say, I will answer 8 by turning
against you. I will make you a warning to anyone who might think of
doing the same thing, and you will
no longer belong to my people. Then
you will know that I am the LORD
and that you have sinned against
me.
9 If a prophet gives a false message, I am the one who caused that
prophet to lie. But I will still reject
him and cut him off from my people,
10 and anyone who goes to that
prophet for a message will be punished in the same way. 11 I will do
this, so that you will come back to
me and stop destroying yourselves
with these disgusting sins. So turn
back to me! Then I will be your God,
and you will be my people. I, the
LORD God, make this promise.

Judgment on a Sinful Nation

12 The LORD God said:
13 Ezekiel, son of man, suppose an entire nation sins against me, and I punish
it by destroying the crops and letting its
people and livestock starve to death.
14 Even if Noah, Daniel,[y] and Job were
living in that nation, their faithfulness
would not save anyone but themselves.
15 Or suppose I punish a nation by
sending wild animals to eat people and
scare away every passerby, so that the
land becomes a barren desert. 16 As
surely as I live, I promise that even if
these three men lived in that nation,
their own children would not be spared.
The three men would live, but the land
would be an empty desert.
17 Or suppose I send an enemy to attack a sinful nation and kill its people
and livestock. 18 If these three men were
in that nation when I punished it, not
even their children would be spared.
Only the three men would live.
19 And suppose I am so angry that I
send a deadly disease to wipe out the
people and livestock of a sinful nation.
20 Again, even if Noah, Daniel, and Job
were living there, I, the LORD, promise
that the children of these faithful men

[w] 13.18 *They wear . . . the future*: One possible meaning for the difficult Hebrew text.
[x] 13.20 *like birds*: One possible meaning for the difficult Hebrew text. [y] 14.14 *Daniel*: Or "Danel," possibly a well-known hero or wise man.

would also die. Only the three of them
would be spared.
21 I am the LORD God, and I promise to
punish Jerusalem severely. I will send
war, starvation, wild animals, and
deadly disease to slaughter its people
and livestock. 22 And those who survive
will be taken from their country and led
here to Babylonia. Ezekiel, when you
see how sinful they are, you will know
why I did all these things to Jerusalem.
23 You will be convinced that I, the LORD
God, was right in doing what I did.

Jerusalem Is a Useless Vine

15 Some time later, the LORD said:
2 Ezekiel, son of man, what happens to the wood of a grapevine after
the grapes have been picked? It isn't
like other trees in the forest, 3 because
the wood of a grapevine can't be used to
make anything, not even a small peg to
hang things on. 4 It can only be used as
firewood. But after its ends are burnt
and its middle is charred, it can't be
used for anything. 5 The wood is useless
before it is burned, and afterwards, it is
completely worthless.
6 I, the LORD God, promise that just as
the wood of a grapevine is burned as
firewood, 7 I will punish the people of
Jerusalem with fire. Some of them have
escaped one destruction, but soon they
will be completely burned. And when
that happens, you, Ezekiel, will know
that I am the LORD. 8 I will make their
country an empty wasteland, because
they have not been loyal to me. I, the
LORD God, have spoken.

Jerusalem Is Unfaithful

16 The LORD said:
2 Ezekiel, son of man, remind
the people of Jerusalem of their disgusting sins 3and tell them that I, the Lord
God, am saying:
Jerusalem, you were born in the country where Canaanites lived. Your father
was an Amorite, and your mother was a
Hittite.[z] 4 When you were born, no one
cut you loose from your mother or
washed your body. No one rubbed your
skin with salt and olive oil,[a] and
wrapped you in warm blankets. 5 Not
one person loved you enough to do any
of these things, and no one even felt
sorry for you. You were despised,
thrown into a field, and forgotten.
6 I saw you lying there, rolling around
in your own blood, and I couldn't let you
die. 7 I took care of you, like someone
caring for a tender, young plant. You
grew up to be a beautiful young woman
with perfect breasts and long hair, but
you were still naked.
8 When I saw you again, you were old
enough to have sex. So I covered your
naked body with my own robe.[b] Then I
solemnly promised that you would belong to me and that I, the LORD God,
would take care of you.
9 I washed the blood off you and
rubbed your skin with olive oil. 10 I gave
you the finest clothes and the most expensive robes,[c] as well as sandals made
from the best leather. 11 I gave you
bracelets, a necklace, 12 a ring for your
nose, some earrings, and a beautiful
crown. 13 Your jewelry was gold and silver, and your clothes were made of only
the finest material and embroidered
linen. Your bread was baked from fine
flour, and you ate honey and olive oil.
You were as beautiful as a queen, 14 and
everyone on earth knew it. I, the LORD
God, had helped you become a lovely
young woman.
15 You learned that you were attractive
enough to have any man you wanted, so
you offered yourself to every passerby.[d]
16 You made shrines for yourself and
decorated them with some of your
clothes. That's where you took your visitors to have sex with them. These things
should never have happened![e] 17 You
made idols out of the gold and silver
jewelry I gave you, then you sinned by
worshiping those idols. 18 You dressed
them in the clothes you got from me,
and you offered them the olive oil and
incense I gave you. 19 I supplied you with
fine flour, olive oil, and honey, but you
sacrificed it all as offerings to please
those idols. I, the LORD God, watched
this happen.
20 But you did something even worse
than that—you sacrificed your own children to those idols! 21 You slaughtered
my children, so you could offer them as
sacrifices. 22 You were so busy sinning
and being a prostitute that you refused
to think about the days when you were
young and were rolling around naked in
your own blood.
23 Now I, the LORD God, say you are
doomed! Not only did you do these evil
things, 24 but you also built places on
every street corner 25 where you disgraced yourself by having sex with anyone who walked by. And you did that

[z] **16.3** *Amorite . . . Hittite*: People who lived in Canaan before the Israelites and who worshiped idols. [a] **16.4** *rubbed your skin with salt and olive oil*: People believed this toughened the skin of the babies. [b] **16.8** *I covered your naked body with my own robe*: To show that he would protect and take care of her. [c] **16.10** *most expensive robes*: One possible meaning for the difficult Hebrew text. [d] **16.15** *so you offered yourself to every passerby*: One possible meaning for the difficult Hebrew text. [e] **16.16** *These things should never have happened*: One possible meaning for the difficult Hebrew text.

more and more every day! [26]To make me angry, you even offered yourself to Egyptians, who were always ready to sleep with you.

[27]So I punished you by letting those greedy Philistine enemies take over some of your territory. But even they were offended by your disgusting behavior.

[28]You couldn't get enough sex, so you chased after Assyrians and slept with them. You still weren't satisfied, [29]so you went after Babylonians. But those merchants could not satisfy you either.

[30]I, the LORD God, say that you were so disgusting that you would have done anything to get what you wanted.[f] [31]You had sex on every street corner, and when you finished, you refused to accept money. That's worse than being a prostitute! [32]You are nothing but an unfaithful wife who would rather have sex with strangers than with your own husband. [33]Prostitutes accept money for having sex, but you bribe men from everywhere to have sex with you. [34]You're not like other prostitutes. Men don't ask you for sex—you offer to pay them!

Jerusalem Must Be Punished

The LORD said:

[35]Jerusalem, you prostitute, listen to me. [36]You chased after lovers, then took off your clothes and had sex. You even worshiped disgusting idols and sacrificed your own children as offerings to them. [37]So I, the LORD God, will gather every one of your lovers, those you liked and those you hated. They will stand around you, and I will rip off your clothes and let all of those lovers stare at your nakedness. [38]I will find you guilty of being an unfaithful wife and a murderer, and in my fierce anger I will sentence you to death! [39]Then I will hand you over to your lovers, who will tear down the places where you had sex. They will take your clothes and jewelry, leaving you naked and empty-handed.

[40]Your lovers and an angry mob will stone you to death; they will cut your dead body into pieces [41]and burn down your houses. Other women will watch these terrible things happen to you. I promise to stop you from being a prostitute and paying your lovers for sex.

[42]Only then will I calm down and stop being angry and jealous. [43]You made me furious by doing all these disgusting things and by forgetting how I took care of you when you were young. Then you made things worse by acting like a prostitute. You must be punished! I, the LORD God, have spoken.

Jerusalem's Two Sisters

The LORD said:

[44]People will use this saying about you, Jerusalem: "If the mother is bad, so is her daughter." [45]You are just like your mother, who hated her husband and her own children. You are also like your sisters, who hated their husbands and children. Your father was an Amorite, and your mother was a Hittite.[g] [46]Your older sister was Samaria, that city to your north with her nearby villages. Your younger sister was Sodom, that city to your south with her nearby villages. [47]You followed their way of life and their wicked customs, and soon you were more disgusting than they were.

[48]As surely as I am the living LORD God, the people of Sodom and its nearby villages were never as sinful as you. [49]They were arrogant and spoiled; they had everything they needed and still refused to help the poor and needy. [50]They thought they were better than everyone else, and they did things I hate. And so I destroyed them.

[51]You people of Jerusalem have sinned twice as much as the people of Samaria. In fact, your evil ways have made both Sodom and Samaria look innocent. [52]So their punishment will seem light compared to yours. You will be disgraced and put to shame because of your disgusting sins.

Jerusalem Will Be Ashamed

The LORD said to Jerusalem:

[53]Someday I will bless Sodom and Samaria and their nearby villages. I will also bless you, Jerusalem. [54]Then you will be ashamed of how you've acted, and Sodom and Samaria will be relieved that they weren't as sinful as you. [55]When that day comes, you and Sodom and Samaria will once again be well-off, and all nearby villages will be restored.

[56]Jerusalem, you were so arrogant that you sneered at Sodom. [57]But now everyone has learned how wicked you really are. The countries of Syria and Philistia, as well as your other neighbors, hate you and make insulting remarks. [58]You must pay for all the vulgar and disgusting things you have done. I, the LORD, have spoken.

The LORD Makes a Promise to Jerusalem

The LORD said:

[59]Jerusalem, you deserve to be punished, because you broke your promises and ignored our agreement. [60]But I

[f]**16.30** *wanted*: One possible meaning for the difficult Hebrew text of verse 30.
[g]**16.45** *Amorite . . . Hittite*: See the note at 16.3.

remember the agreement I made with you when you were young,[h] and so I will make you a promise that will last forever. 61 When you think about how you acted, you will be ashamed, especially when I return your sisters[i] to you as daughters, even though this was not part of our agreement.[j] 62 I will keep this solemn promise, and you will know that I am the LORD. 63 I will forgive you, but you will think about your sins and be too ashamed to say a word. I, the LORD God, have spoken.

A Story about Two Eagles and a Vine

17 The LORD said:

2 Ezekiel, son of man, tell the people of Israel the following story, 3 so they will understand what I am saying to them:

A large eagle with strong wings and beautiful feathers once flew to Lebanon. It broke the top branch off a cedar tree, 4 then carried it to a nation of merchants and left it in one of their cities. 5 The eagle also took seed from Israel and planted it in a fertile field with plenty of water, like a willow tree beside a stream.[k] 6 The seed sprouted and grew into a grapevine that spread over the ground. It had lots of leaves and strong, deep roots, and its branches grew upward toward the eagle.

7 There was another eagle with strong wings and thick feathers. The roots and branches of the grapevine soon turned toward this eagle, hoping it would bring water for the soil. 8 But the vine was already growing in fertile soil, where there was plenty of water to produce healthy leaves and large grapes.

9 Now tell me, Ezekiel, do you think this grapevine will live? Or will the first eagle pull it up by its roots and pluck off the grapes and let its new leaves die? The eagle could easily kill it without the help of a large and powerful army. 10 The grapevine is strong and healthy, but as soon as the scorching desert wind blows, it will quickly wither.

The LORD Explains the Story

11 The LORD said:

12 Ezekiel, ask the rebellious people of Israel if they know what this story means.

Tell them that the king of Babylonia came to Jerusalem, then he captured the king of Judah[l] and his officials, and took them back to Babylon as prisoners. 13 He chose someone from the family of Judah's king[m] and signed a treaty with him, then made him swear to be loyal. He also led away other important citizens, 14 so that the rest of the people of Judah would obey only him and never gain control of their own country again.

15 But this new king of Judah later rebelled against Babylonia and sent officials to Egypt to get horses and troops. Will this king be successful in breaking the treaty with Babylonia? Or will he be punished for what he's done?

16 As surely as I am the living LORD God, I swear that the king of Judah will die in Babylon, because he broke the treaty with the king of Babylonia, who appointed him king. 17 Even the king of Egypt and his powerful army will be useless to Judah when the Babylonians attack and build dirt ramps to invade the cities of Judah and kill its people. 18 The king of Judah broke his own promises and ignored the treaty with Babylonia. And so he will be punished!

19 He made a promise in my name and swore to honor the treaty. And now that he has broken that promise, my name is disgraced. He must pay for what he's done. 20 I will spread out a net to trap him. Then I will drag him to Babylon and see that he is punished for his unfaithfulness to me. 21 His best troops[n] will be killed in battle, and the survivors will be scattered in every direction. I, the LORD, have spoken.

*22 Someday, I, the LORD,
will cut a tender twig
from the top of a cedar tree,
then plant it on the peak
of Israel's tallest mountain,
where it will grow
strong branches
and produce large fruit.
23 All kinds of birds will find
shelter under the tree,
and they will rest in the shade
of its branches.
24 Every tree in the forest
will know that I, the LORD,
can bring down tall trees
and help short ones grow.
I dry up green trees
and make dry ones green.
I, the LORD, have spoken,
and I will keep my word.

[h] **16.60** *the agreement . . . when you were young*: See verse 8. [i] **16.61** *sisters*: Sodom and Samaria (see verses 44-52). [j] **16.61** *even though this was not part of our agreement*: One possible meaning for the difficult Hebrew text. [k] **17.5** *like a willow tree beside a stream*: One possible meaning for the difficult Hebrew text. [l] **17.12** *king of Judah*: Probably King Jehoiachin (see 2 Kings 24.10-12, 15, 16). [m] **17.13** *someone from the family of Judah's king*: Probably King Zedekiah (see 2 Kings 24.17). [n] **17.21** *best troops*: Two ancient translations; Hebrew "troops that ran away."

Those Who Sin Will Die

18 The LORD said:
2 Ezekiel, I hear the people of
Israel using the old saying,

"Sour grapes eaten by parents
leave a sour taste in the mouths
of their children."

3 Now tell them that I am the LORD
God, and as surely as I live, that saying
will no longer be used in Israel. 4 The
lives of all people belong to me—parents as well as children. Only those who
sin will be put to death.
5 Suppose there is a truly good man
who always does what is fair and right.
6 He refuses to eat meat sacrificed to foreign gods at local shrines or to worship
Israel's idols. He doesn't have sex with
someone else's wife or with a woman
having her monthly period. 7 He never
cheats or robs anyone and always returns anything taken as security for a
loan; he gives food and clothes to the
poor 8 and doesn't charge interest when
lending money. He refuses to do anything evil; he is fair to everyone 9 and
faithfully obeys my laws and teachings.
This man is good, and I promise he will
live.
10 But suppose this good man has an
evil son who is violent and commits sins
11 his father never did. He eats meat at
local shrines, has sex with someone
else's wife, 12 cheats the poor, and robs
people. He keeps what is given to him as
security for a loan. He worships idols,
does disgusting things, 13 and charges
high interest when lending money. An
evil man like that will certainly not live.
He is the one who has done these horrible sins, so it's his own fault that he will
be put to death.
14 But suppose this evil man has a son
who sees his father do these things and
refuses to act like him. 15 He doesn't eat
meat at local shrines or worship Israel's
idols, and he doesn't have sex with
someone else's wife. 16 He never cheats
or robs anyone and doesn't even demand security for a loan. He gives food
and clothes to the poor 17 and refuses to
do anything evil[o] or to charge interest.
And he obeys all my laws and teachings. Such a man will live. His own father sinned, but this good man will not
be put to death for the sins of his father.
18 It is his father who will die for cheating and robbing and doing evil.
19 You may wonder why a son isn't
punished for the sins of his father. It is
because the son does what is right and
obeys my laws. 20 Only those who sin
will be put to death. Children won't suffer for the sins of their parents, and parents won't suffer for the sins of their
children. Good people will be rewarded
for what they do, and evil people will be
punished for what they do.
21 Suppose wicked people stop sinning
and start obeying my laws and doing
right. They won't be put to death. 22 All
their sins will be forgiven, and they will
live because they did right. 23 I, the LORD
God, don't like to see wicked people die.
I enjoy seeing them turn from their sins
and live.
24 But when good people start sinning
and doing disgusting things, will they
live? No! All their good deeds will be
forgotten, and they will be put to death
because of their sins.
25 You people of Israel accuse me of
being unfair! But listen—I'm not unfair;
you are! 26 If good people start doing
evil, they must be put to death, because
they have sinned. 27 And if wicked people start doing right, they will save
themselves from punishment. 28 They
will think about what they've done and
stop sinning, and so they won't be put to
death. 29 But you still say that I am unfair. You are the ones who have done
wrong and are unfair!
30 I will judge each of you for what
you've done. So stop sinning, or else you
will certainly be punished. 31 Give up
your evil ways and start thinking pure
thoughts. And be faithful to me! Do you
really want to be put to death for your
sins? 32 I, the LORD God, don't want to
see that happen to anyone. So stop sinning and live!

A Funeral Song for Israel's Leaders

The LORD said:

19 Ezekiel, sing a funeral song for
two of Israel's leaders:[p]
2 Your mother was a brave lioness
who raised her cubs
among lions.
3 She taught one of them to hunt,
and he learned to eat people.
4 When the nations heard of him,
they trapped him in a pit,
then they used hooks
to drag him to Egypt.

5 His mother waited
for him to return.
But soon she lost all hope
and raised another cub,
who also became fierce.
6 He hunted with other lions
and learned to eat people.
7 He destroyed fortresses[q]
and ruined towns;

[o] 18.17 *evil*: One ancient translation; Hebrew "for the poor." [p] 19.1 *two of Israel's leaders*: Probably Jehoahaz (ruled three months in 609 B.C.) and Jehoiachin (ruled three months in 598 B.C.) or Zedekiah (598-586 B.C.). [q] 19.7 *He destroyed fortresses*: One possible meaning for the difficult Hebrew text.

his mighty roar
terrified everyone.
8 Nations plotted to kill him,
and people came from all over
to spread out a net
and catch him in a trap.
9 They put him in a cage
and took him to Babylonia.
The lion was locked away,
so that his mighty roar
would never again be heard
on Israel's hills.

10 Your mother was a vine[r]
growing near a stream.
There was plenty of water,
so she was filled with branches
and with lots of fruit.
11 Her strong branches
became symbols of authority,
and she was taller
than all other trees—
everyone could see how strong
and healthy she was.
12 But in anger, I pulled her up
by the roots
and threw her to the ground,
where the scorching desert wind
dried out her fruit.
Her strong branches wilted
and burned up.
13 Then she was planted
in a hot, dry desert,
14 where her stem caught fire,
and flames burned
her branches and fruit.
Not one strong branch is left;
she is stripped bare.

This funeral song must be sung with
sorrow.

Israel Keeps On Rebelling

20 Seven years after King Jehoiachin and the rest of us had
been led away as prisoners to Babylonia, some of Israel's leaders came to me
on the tenth day of the fifth month.[s]
They sat down and asked for a message
from the LORD. 2Just then, the LORD God
said:
3Ezekiel, son of man, these leaders
have come to find out what I want them
to do. As surely as I live, I will not give
them an answer of any kind.
4Are you willing to warn them,
Ezekiel? Then remind them of the disgusting sins of their ancestors.
5Tell them that long ago I, the LORD
God, chose Israel to be my own. I appeared to their ancestors in Egypt and
made a solemn promise that I would be
their God and the God of their descendants. 6I swore that I would rescue them
from Egypt and lead them to a land I
had already chosen. This land was rich
with milk and honey and was the most
splendid land of all. 7I told them to get
rid of their disgusting idols and not to
sin by worshiping the gods of Egypt. I
reminded them that I was the LORD their
God, 8but they still rebelled against me.
They refused to listen and kept on worshiping their idols and foreign gods.
In my anger, I decided to punish the
Israelites in Egypt. 9But that would have
made me look like a liar, because I had
already promised in front of everyone
that I would lead them out of Egypt.
10So I brought them out and led them
into the desert. 11I gave them my laws
and teachings, so they would know how
to live right. 12And I commanded them
to respect the Sabbath as a way of
showing that they were holy and belonged to me. 13But the Israelites rebelled against me in the desert. They refused to obey my laws and teachings,
and they treated the Sabbath like any
other day.
Then in my anger, I decided to destroy
the Israelites in the desert once and for
all. 14But that would have disgraced me,
because many other nations had seen
me bring the Israelites out of Egypt.
15Instead, I told them in the desert that I
would not lead them into the beautiful,
fertile land I had promised. 16I said this
because they had not only ignored my
laws and teachings, but had disgraced
my Sabbath and worshiped idols.
17Yet, I felt sorry for them and could
not let them die in the desert. 18So I
warned the children not to act like their
parents or follow their evil ways or worship their idols. 19I reminded them that I
was the LORD their God and that they
should obey my laws and teachings. 20I
told them to respect my Sabbath to
show that they were my people and that
I was the LORD their God. 21But the children also rebelled against me. They refused to obey my laws and teachings,
and they treated the Sabbath as any
other day.
I became angry and decided to punish
them in the desert. 22But I did not. That
would have disgraced me in front of the
nations that had seen me bring the Israelites out of Egypt. 23So I solemnly
swore that I would scatter the people of
Israel across the nations, 24because they
had disobeyed my laws and ignored my
teachings; they had disgraced my Sabbath and worshiped the idols their ancestors had made. 25I gave them laws
that bring punishment instead of life,
26and I let them offer me unacceptable
sacrifices, including their first-born
sons. I did this to horrify them and to let

[r] **19.10** *Your mother was a vine*: One possible meaning for the difficult Hebrew text.
[s] **20.1** *Seven years . . . fifth month*: Probably August of 591 B.C.

them know that I, the LORD, was punishing them.
[27]Ezekiel, tell the people of Israel that
their ancestors also rejected and insulted me [28]by offering sacrifices, incense, and wine to gods on every hill
and under every large tree. I was very
angry, because they did these things in
the land I had given them! [29]I asked
them where they went to worship those
gods, and they answered, "At the local
shrines."[t] And those places of worship
are still called shrines.
[30]Then ask the Israelites why they are
following the example of their wicked
ancestors [31]by worshiping idols and by
sacrificing their own children as offerings. They commit these sins and still
think they can ask me for a message. As
surely as I am the living LORD God, I
will give them no answer. [32]They may
think they can be like other nations and
get away with worshiping idols made of
wood and stone. But that will never happen!

The LORD Promises To Restore Israel

The LORD said to the people of Israel:
[33]As surely as I am the living LORD
God, I will rule over you with my powerful arm. You will feel my fierce anger
[34]and my power, when I gather you from
the places where you are scattered
[35]and lead you into a desert surrounded
by nations. I will meet you there face to
face. Then I will pass judgment on you
[36]and punish you, just as I punished
your ancestors in the desert near
Egypt.[u] [37]I will force each of you to obey
the regulations of our solemn agreement. [38]I will separate the sinful rebels
from the rest of you, and even though I
will bring them from the nations where
they live in exile, they won't be allowed
to return to Israel. Then you will know
that I am the LORD.
[39]Go ahead and worship your idols for
now, you Israelites, because soon I will
no longer let you dishonor me by offering gifts to them. You will have no
choice but to obey me![v] [40]When that day
comes, everyone in Israel will worship
me on Mount Zion, my holy mountain in
Jerusalem. I will once again call you my
own, and I will accept your sacred offerings and sacrifices. [41]When I bring you
home from the places where you are
now scattered, I will be pleased with
you, just as I am pleased with the smell
of the smoke from your sacrifices. Every
nation on earth will see that I am holy,
[42]and you will know that I, the LORD, am
the one who brought you back to Israel,
the land I promised your ancestors.
[43]Then you will remember your wicked
sins, and you will hate yourselves for
doing such horrible things. They have
made you unacceptable to me, [44]so you
deserve to be punished. But I will treat
you in a way that will bring honor to my
name, and you will know that I am the
LORD God.

Fire from the South

[45]The LORD said, [46]"Ezekiel, son of
man, turn toward the south and warn
the forests [47]that I, the LORD God, will
start a fire that will burn up every tree,
whether green or dry. Nothing will be
able to put out the blaze of that fire as it
spreads to the north and burns everything in its path. [48]Everyone will know
that I started it, and that it cannot be
stopped."
[49]But I complained, "LORD God, I don't
want to do that! People already say I
confuse them with my messages."

The LORD Will Punish Jerusalem

21 The LORD said:
[2]Ezekiel, son of man, condemn
the places in Jerusalem where people
worship. Warn everyone in Israel [3]that I
am about to punish them. I will pull
out my sword and have it ready to
kill everyone, whether good or evil.
[4]From south to north, people will die,
[5]knowing that my sword will never be
put away.
[6]Ezekiel, groan in sorrow and despair
so that everyone can hear you. [7]When
they ask why you are groaning, tell
them you have terrifying news that will
make them faint and tremble in fear and
lose all courage. These things will happen soon. I, the LORD God, make this
promise!

A Sword Is Ready To Attack Israel

[8]The LORD said:
[9-10]Ezekiel, son of man, tell the people
of Jerusalem:

I have sharpened my sword
to slaughter you;
it is shiny and will flash
like lightning!
Don't celebrate—
punishment is coming,
because everyone has ignored
my warnings.[w]
11 My sword has been polished;
it's sharp and ready to kill.

[t]**20.29** *where they went to worship those gods . . . local shrines*: In Hebrew "where they went" sounds like "local shrines." These were places to worship foreign gods. [u]**20.36** *the desert near Egypt*: The Sinai Desert. [v]**20.39** *me*: One possible meaning for the difficult Hebrew text of verse 39. [w]**21.9,10** *Don't celebrate . . . my warnings*: One possible meaning for the difficult Hebrew text.

12 Groan in sorrow, Ezekiel;
the sword is drawn against
my people and their leaders.
They will die!
So give up all hope.
13 I am testing my people,
and they can do nothing
to stop me.[x]
I, the LORD, have spoken.

14 Ezekiel, warn my people,
then celebrate my victory
by clapping your hands.
My vicious sword will attack
again and again,
killing my people
with every stroke.
15 They will lose all courage
and stumble with fear.
My slaughtering sword
is waiting at every gate,
flashing and ready to kill.[y]
16 It will slash right and left,
wherever the blade is pointed.
17 Then I will stop being angry,
and I will clap my hands
in victory.
I, the LORD, have spoken.

The King of Babylonia and His Sword

18 The LORD said:
19 Ezekiel, son of man, mark two roads
for the king of Babylonia to follow when
he comes with his sword. The roads will
begin at the same place, but be sure to
put up a signpost where the two roads
separate and go in different directions.
20 Clearly mark where the two roads
lead. One goes to Rabbah, the capital
of Ammon, and the other goes to
Jerusalem, the fortified capital of Judah.
21 When the Babylonian king stands at
that signpost, he will decide which way
to go by shaking his arrows, by asking
his idols, and by carefully looking at the
liver of a sacrificed animal.[z] 22 His right
hand will pull out the arrow marked
"Jerusalem." Then he will immediately
give the signal to shout the battle cry, to
build dirt ramps to the top of the city
walls, to break down its walls and gates
with large wooden poles, and to kill the
people. 23 Everyone in Jerusalem had
promised to be loyal to Babylonia, and
so none of them will believe that this
could happen to them. But Babylonia's
king will remind them of their sinful
ways and warn them of their coming
captivity.
24 Ezekiel, tell the people of Jerusalem
and their ruler that I, the LORD God, am
saying:

Everything you do is wicked and
shows how sinful you are. You are
guilty and will be taken away as
prisoners.
25 And now, you evil and wicked
ruler of Israel, your day of final punishment is almost here. 26 I, the LORD
God, command you to take off your
royal turban and your crown, because everything will be different.
Those who had no power will be put
in charge, and those who now rule
will become nobodies. 27 I will leave
Jerusalem in ruins when my chosen
one comes to punish this city.

Judgment against Ammon

28 The LORD God said:
Ezekiel, son of man, the Ammonites
have insulted Israel, so condemn them
and tell them I am saying:

A sword is drawn,
ready to slaughter;
it is polished and prepared
to kill as fast as lightning.

29 You wicked Ammonites see false visions and believe untrue messages. But
your day of punishment is coming soon,
and my sword will slaughter you!
30 Your days to punish others are over,
so put your swords away.[a] You will be
punished in the land of your birth. 31 My
furious anger will scorch you like fire,
and I will hand you over to cruel men
who are experts in killing. 32 You will be
burned and will die in your own land.
Then you will be forgotten forever. I, the
LORD, have spoken.

Jerusalem Is Condemned

22 Some time later, the LORD said:
2 Ezekiel, son of man, are you
ready to condemn Jerusalem? That city
is filled with murderers, so remind the
people of their sins 3 and tell them I am
saying:
Jerusalem, you have murdered many
of your own people and have worshiped
idols. You will soon be punished! 4 Those
crimes have made you guilty, and the
idols have made you unacceptable to
me. So your final punishment is near.
Other nations will laugh at you and
make insulting remarks, 5 and people far
and near will make fun of your misery.
6 Your own leaders use their power to
murder. 7 None of you honor your parents, and you cheat foreigners, orphans,
and widows. 8 You show no respect for
my sacred places and treat the Sabbath
just like any other day. 9 Some of your

[x] **21.13** *I am testing . . . me*: One possible meaning for the difficult Hebrew text. [y] **21.15** *My slaughtering sword . . . ready to kill*: One possible meaning for the difficult Hebrew text.
[z] **21.21** *shaking . . . animal*: These were ways the Babylonians found out what their gods wanted them to do. [a] **21.30** *Your days . . . put your swords away*: One possible meaning for the difficult Hebrew text.

own people tell lies, so that others will
be put to death. Some of you eat meat
sacrificed to idols at local shrines, and
others never stop doing vulgar things.
10Men have sex with their father's wife
or with women who are having their
monthly period 11or with someone else's
wife. Some men even sleep with their
own daughter-in-law or half sister.
12Others of you accept money to murder
someone. Your own people charge high
interest when making a loan to other Israelites, and they get rich by cheating.
Worst of all, you have forgotten me, the
LORD God.
13I will shake my fist in anger at your
violent crimes. 14When I'm finished with
you, your courage will disappear, and
you will be so weak that you won't be
able to lift your hands. I, the LORD, have
spoken and will not change my mind. 15I
will scatter you throughout every nation
on earth and put a stop to your sinful
ways. 16You[b] will be humiliated in the
eyes of other nations. Then you will
know that I, the LORD God, have done
these things.

Jerusalem Must Be Purified

17The LORD said:
18Ezekiel, son of man, I consider the
people of Israel as worthless as the leftover metal in a furnace after silver has
been purified. 19So I am going to bring
them together in Jerusalem. 20-21I will be
like a metalworker who collects that
metal from the furnace and melts it
down. I will collect the Israelites and
blow on them with my fiery anger. They
will melt inside the city of Jerusalem
22like silver in a furnace. Then they will
know that I, the LORD, have punished
them in my anger.

Everyone in Jerusalem Is Guilty

23The LORD said:
24Ezekiel, son of man, tell the people
of Israel that their country is full of sin,
and that I, the LORD, am furious! 25Their
leaders are like[c] roaring lions, tearing
apart their victims. They put people to
death, then steal everything of value.
Husbands are killed, and many women
are left as widows.
26The priests of Israel ignore my Law!
Not only do they refuse to respect any
of my sacred things, but they don't even
teach the difference between what is sacred and what is ordinary, or between
what is clean and what is unclean. They
treat my Sabbath like any other day,
and so my own people no longer honor
me.
27Israel's officials are like ferocious
wolves, ripping their victims apart. They
make a dishonest living by injuring and
killing people.
28And then the prophets in Israel
cover up these sins by giving false visions. I have never spoken to them, but
they lie and say they have a message
from me. 29The people themselves cheat
and rob; they abuse the poor and take
advantage of foreigners.
30I looked for someone to defend the
city and to protect it from my anger, as
well as to stop me from destroying it.
But I found no one. 31So in my fierce
anger, I will punish the Israelites for
what they have done, and they will
know that I am furious. I, the LORD, have
spoken.

Two Sinful Sisters

23 The LORD said:
2Ezekiel, son of man, listen to
this story about two sisters. 3While they
were young and living in Egypt, they became prostitutes. 4The older one was
named Oholah, which stands for
Samaria; the younger one was Oholibah, which stands for Jerusalem. [d] They
became my wives and gave birth to my
children.
5Even though Oholah was my wife,
she continued to be a prostitute and
chased after Assyrian lovers. 6She offered herself to soldiers in purple uniforms, to every handsome, high-ranking
officer, and to cavalry troops. 7She had
sex with all the important Assyrian officials and even worshiped their disgusting idols. 8Once she started doing these
things in Egypt, she never stopped. Men
slept with her, and she was always
ready for sex.
9So I gave Oholah to the Assyrian
lovers she wanted so badly. 10They
ripped off her clothes, then captured her
children and killed her. Women everywhere talked about what had happened
to Oholah.
11Oholibah saw all this, but she was
more sinful and wanted sex more than
her sister Oholah ever did. 12Oholibah
also chased after good-looking Assyrian
officers, uniformed soldiers, and cavalry
troops. 13Just like her sister, she did vulgar things.
14But Oholibah behaved worse than
her sister. Oholibah saw images of
Babylonian men carved into walls and
painted red. 15They had belts around

[b] **22.16** *You*: Hebrew; two ancient translations "Because of you, I." [c] **22.25** *Their leaders are like*: One ancient translation; Hebrew "Their prophets are like herds of." [d] **23.4** *Samaria . . . Jerusalem*: After the nation of Israel was divided, the northern kingdom was called "Israel," and the southern kingdom was called "Judah." Samaria was the capital of the northern kingdom, and Jerusalem was the capital of the southern kingdom.

their waists and large turbans on their
heads, and they reminded her of Babylonian cavalry officers. 16As soon as
she looked at them, she wanted to have
sex with them. And so, she sent messengers to bring them to her. 17Men from
Babylonia came and had sex with her so
many times that she got disgusted with
them. 18She let everyone see her naked
body and didn't care if they knew she
was a prostitute. That's why I turned my
back on her, just as I had done with her
older sister.

19Oholibah didn't stop there, but became even more immoral and acted as
she had back in Egypt. 20She eagerly
wanted to go to bed with Egyptian men,
who were famous for their sexual powers. 21And she longed for the days when
she was a young prostitute, when men
enjoyed having sex with her.

The Lord Will Punish Oholibah

22The Lord God said:

Oholibah,[e] though you no longer want
to be around your lovers, they will surround you like enemies, when I turn
them against you. 23I will gather all the
handsome young officials and the high-
ranking cavalry officers from Babylonia
and Assyria, as well as from the
Chaldean tribes of Pekod, Shoa, and
Koa. 24Their large armies will come
from the north[f] with chariots and wagons carrying weapons. They will wear
shields and helmets and will surround
you, and I will let them judge and sentence you according to their own laws.
25I am angry with you, so I will let them
be very cruel. They will cut off your
nose and ears; they will kill your children and put to death anyone in your
family who is still alive. 26Your clothes
and jewelry will be torn off. 27I will stop
your wickedness and the prostitution
you started back in Egypt. You will
never want to think about those days
again.

28I, the Lord God, am ready to hand
you over to those hateful enemies that
you find so disgusting. 29They will cruelly take away everything you have
worked for and strip you naked. Then
everyone will see you for the prostitute
you really are. Your own vulgar sins
30have led to this. You were the one determined to have sex with men from
other nations and to worship their
idols. 31You have turned out no better
than your older sister, and now you
must drink from the cup filled with my
anger.

32I, the Lord God, gave your sister a
large, deep cup filled with my anger.
And when you drink from that cup, you
will be mocked and insulted. 33You will
end up drunk and devastated, because
that cup is filled with horror and ruin.
34But you must drink every drop! Then
smash the cup to pieces and use them to
cut your breasts in sorrow. I, the Lord
God, have spoken.

35You have completely rejected me,
and so I promise that you will be punished for the disgusting things you did
as a prostitute.

The Two Sisters Are Condemned

36The Lord said:

Ezekiel, son of man, it's time for you
to tell Oholah and Oholibah[g] that they
are guilty. Remind them of their evil
ways! 37They have been unfaithful by
worshiping idols, and they have committed murder by sacrificing my own
children as offerings to idols. 38-39They
came into my temple that same day, and
that made it unfit as a place to worship
me. They have even stopped respecting
the Sabbath.

40They sent messengers to attract men
from far away. When those men arrived,
the two sisters took baths and put on
eye shadow and jewelry. 41They sat on a
fancy couch, and in front of them was a
table for the olive oil and incense that
had belonged to me. 42Their room was
always filled with a noisy crowd of
drunkards brought in from the desert.
These men gave the women bracelets
and beautiful crowns, 43and I noticed
that the men were eager to have sex
with these women, though they were exhausted from being prostitutes.[h] 44In
fact, the men had sex over and over
with Oholah and Oholibah, the two sinful sisters. 45But good men will someday
accuse those two of murder and of being unfaithful, because they are certainly guilty.

46So I, the Lord God, now say to these
sisters:

I will call together an angry mob
that will abuse and rob you. 47They
will stone you to death and cut you
to pieces; they will kill your children
and burn down your houses. 48I will
get rid of sinful prostitution in this
country, so that women everywhere
will be warned not to act as you
have. 49You will be punished for becoming prostitutes and for worshiping idols, and you will know that I
am the Lord God.

[e] **23.22** *Oholibah*: That is, Jerusalem (see verse 4). [f] **23.24** *from the north*: One ancient translation; Hebrew "with weapons." [g] **23.36** *Oholah and Oholibah*: That is, Samaria and Jerusalem (see verse 4). [h] **23.43** *prostitutes*: One possible meaning for the difficult Hebrew text of verse 43.

A Cooking Pot

24 Nine years after King Jehoiachin
and the rest of us had been led
away as prisoners to Babylonia, the
LORD spoke to me on the tenth day of
the tenth month.[i] He said:
2 Ezekiel, son of man, write down today's date, because the king of Babylonia has just begun attacking the city of
Jerusalem. 3 Then tell my rebellious people:

"Pour water in a cooking pot
and set it over a fire.
*4 Throw in the legs and shoulders
of your finest sheep
and put in the juicy bones.
5 "Pile wood[j] underneath the pot,
and let the meat and bones
boil until they are done."

6 These words mean that Jerusalem is
doomed! The city is filled with murderers and is like an old, rusty pot. The
meat is taken out piece by piece, and no
one cares what happens to it.[k] 7 The people of Jerusalem murdered innocent
people in the city and didn't even try to
cover up the blood that flowed out on
the hard ground. 8 But I have seen that
blood, and it cries out for me to take revenge.
9 I, the LORD God, will punish that city
of violence! I will make a huge pile of
firewood, 10 so bring more wood and
light it. Cook the meat and boil away the
broth[l] to let the bones scorch. 11 Then set
the empty pot over the hot coals until it
is red-hot. That will clean the pot and
burn off the rust. 12 I've tried everything
else. Now the rust must be burned
away.[m]
13 Jerusalem is so full of sin and evil
that I can't get it clean, even though I
have tried. It will stay filthy until I let
loose my fierce anger against it. 14 That
time will certainly come! And when it
does, I won't show the people of
Jerusalem any pity or change my mind.
They must be punished for the evil they
have done. I, the LORD God, have spoken.

Ezekiel's Wife Dies

15 The LORD said, 16 "Ezekiel, son of
man, I will suddenly take the life of the
person you love most. But I don't want
you to complain or cry. 17 Mourn in silence and don't show that you are grieving. Don't remove your turban or take
off your sandals; don't cover your face
to show your sorrow, or eat the food
that mourners eat."[n]
18 One morning, I was talking with the
people as usual, and by sunset my wife
was dead. The next day I did what the
LORD told me, 19 and when people saw
me, they asked, "Why aren't you mourning for your wife?"
20 I answered:
The LORD God says 21 he is ready
to destroy the temple in which you
take such pride and which makes
you feel so safe. Your children who
now live in Jerusalem will be killed.
22 Then you will do the same things I
have done. You will leave your face
uncovered and refuse to eat the food
that mourners usually eat. 23 You
won't take off your turbans and your
sandals.[o] You won't cry or mourn,
but all day long you will go around
groaning because of your sins.
24 I am a warning sign—everything
I have done, you will also do. And
then you will know the LORD God
has made these things happen.
25 The LORD said, "Ezekiel, I will soon
destroy the temple that makes everyone
feel proud and safe, and I will take away
their children as well. 26 On that same
day, someone will escape from the city
and come to tell you what has happened. 27 Then you will be able to speak
again,[p] and the two of you will talk. You
will be a warning sign to the people, and
they will know that I am the LORD."

Judgment on Ammon

25 The LORD God said:
2 Ezekiel, son of man, condemn
the people of Ammon 3 and tell them:
You celebrated when my temple
was destroyed, when Israel was defeated, and when my people were
taken away as prisoners. 4 Now I am
going to let you be conquered by
tribes from the eastern desert. They
will set up their camps in your land
and eat your fruit and drink your
milk. 5 Your capital city of Rabbah
will be nothing but pastureland for
camels, and the rest of the country
will be pastures for sheep. Then you
will know that I am the LORD God.

[i] **24.1** *Nine years . . . tenth month*: Probably January of 588 B.C. [j] **24.5** *Pile wood*: Or "Stack the bones." [k] **24.6** *and no one cares what happens to it*: One possible meaning for the difficult Hebrew text. [l] **24.10** *boil away the broth*: One ancient translation; Hebrew "mix the spices." [m] **24.12** *away*: One possible meaning for the difficult Hebrew text of verse 12.
[n] **24.17** *Don't remove your turban . . . take off your sandals . . . cover your face . . . eat the food that mourners eat*: The usual way people mourned was to remove anything worn on the head, to go barefoot, to cover their faces, and to eat special food to show they were grieving.
[o] **24.22,23** *You will leave your face uncovered . . . refuse to eat the food . . . won't take off your turbans and your sandals*: See the note at 24.17. [p] **24.27** *you will be able to speak again*: See 3.25-27; 33.21, 22.

6You hated Israel so much that you
clapped and shouted and celebrated.
7And so I will hand you over to enemies who will rob you. I will completely destroy you. There won't be
enough of your people left to be a
nation ever again, and you will
know that I, the LORD, have done
these things.

Judgment on Moab

8The LORD God said, "The people of
Moab[q] thought Judah was no different
from any other nation. 9So I will let
Moab's fortress towns along its border
be attacked, including Beth-Jeshimoth,
Baal-Meon, and Kiriathaim. 10The same
eastern desert tribes that invade Ammon will invade Moab, and just as Ammon will be forgotten forever, 11Moab
will be punished. Then the people there
will know that I am the LORD."

Judgment on Edom

12The LORD God then said, "The people of Edom are guilty of taking revenge
on Judah. 13So I will punish Edom by
killing all its people and livestock. It will
be an empty wasteland all the way from
Teman to Dedan. 14I will send my own
people to take revenge on the Edomites
by making them feel my fierce anger.
And when I punish them, they will
know that I am the LORD God."

Judgment on Philistia

15The LORD God said, "The cruel
Philistines have taken revenge on their
enemies over and over and have tried to
destroy them. 16Now it's my turn to treat
the Philistines as my enemies and to kill
everyone[r] living in their towns along the
seacoast. 17In my fierce anger, I will take
revenge on them. And when I punish
them, they will know that I am the
LORD."

Judgment on the City of Tyre

26 Eleven years[s] after King Jehoiachin and the rest of us had
been led away as prisoners to Babylonia, the LORD spoke to me on the first
day of the month. He said:
2Ezekiel, son of man, the people of the
city of Tyre[t] have celebrated Jerusalem's defeat by singing,

"Jerusalem has fallen!
It used to be powerful,
a center of trade.
Now the city is shattered,
and we will take its place."

3Because the people of Tyre have sung
that song, I have the following warning
for them: I am the LORD God, and I am
now your enemy! I will send nations to
attack you, like waves crashing against
the shore. 4They will tear down your
city walls and defense towers. I will
sweep away the ruins until all that's left
of you is a bare rock, 5where fishermen
can dry their nets along the coast. I
promise that you will be robbed 6and
that the people who live in your towns
along the coast will be killed. Then you
will know that I am the LORD.
7King Nebuchadnezzar of Babylonia
is the world's most powerful king, and I
will send him to attack you. He will
march from the north with a powerful
army, including horses and chariots and
cavalry troops. 8First, he will attack your
towns along the coast and kill the people who live there. Then he will build
dirt ramps up to the top of your city
walls and set up rows of shields around
you. 9He will command some of his
troops to use large wooden poles to beat
down your walls, while others use iron
rods to knock down your watchtowers.
10He will have so many horses that the
dust they stir up will seem like a thick
fog. And as his chariots and cavalry approach, even the walls will shake, especially when he proudly enters your ruined city. 11His troops will ride through
your streets, killing people left and
right, and your strong columns will
crumble to the ground. 12The troops will
steal your valuable possessions; they
will break down your walls, and crush
your expensive houses. Then the stones
and wood and all the remains will be
dumped into the sea. 13You will have no
reason to sing or play music on harps,
14because I will turn you into a bare
rock where fishermen can dry their
nets. And you will never rebuild your
city. I, the LORD God, make this promise.
15The people of the nations up and
down the coast will shudder when they
hear your screams and moans of death.
16The kings will step down from their
thrones, then take off their royal robes
and fancy clothes, and sit on the
ground, trembling. They will be so
shocked at the news of your defeat that
they will shake in fear 17and sing this
funeral song:

"The great city beside the sea
is destroyed![u]
Its people once ruled the coast
and terrified everyone there.

[q] **25.8** *Moab*: One ancient translation; Hebrew "Moab and Edom." [r] **25.16** *kill everyone*: The Hebrew text also has the name "Cherethites," which was a group of people that lived just southeast of Philistia, and was often identified with the Philistines. [s] **26.1** *Eleven years*: Probably late in 587 B.C. [t] **26.2** *Tyre*: One of the two major cities of Phoenicia; Sidon was the other. [u] **26.17** *The great city . . . is destroyed*: One possible meaning for the difficult Hebrew text.

18 But now Tyre is in ruins,
and the people on the coast
stare at it in horror
and tremble in fear."

19 I, the LORD God, will turn you into a
ghost-town. The ocean depths will rise
over you 20 and carry you down to the
world of the dead, where you will join
people of ancient times and towns ruined long ago. You will stay there and
never again be a city filled with people.[v]
21 You will die a horrible death! People
will come looking for your city, but it
will never be found. I, the LORD, have
spoken.

A Funeral Song for Tyre

27 The LORD said:
2 Ezekiel, son of man, sing a
funeral song for Tyre,[w] 3 the city that is
built along the sea and that trades with
nations along the coast. Tell the people
of Tyre that the following message is
from me:

Tyre, you brag about
your perfect beauty,
4 and your control of the sea.[x]

You are a ship
built to perfection.
5 Builders used cypress trees
from Mount Hermon
to make your planks
and a cedar tree from Lebanon
for your tall mast.
6 Oak trees from Bashan
were shaped into oars;
pine trees from Cyprus[y]
were cut for your deck,
which was then decorated
with strips of ivory.
7 The builders used fancy linen
from Egypt for your sails,
so everyone could see you.
Blue and purple cloth
from Cyprus was used
to shade your deck.
8 Men from Sidon and Arvad
did the rowing,
and your own skilled workers
were the captains.
9 Experienced men from Byblos
repaired any damages.
Sailors from all over
shopped at the stores
in your port.
10 Brave soldiers from Persia,
Lydia, and Libya
served in your navy,
protecting you with shields
and helmets,
and making you famous.
11 Your guards came from
Arvad and Cilicia,
and men from Gamad
stood watch in your towers.
With their weapons
hung on your walls,
your beauty was complete.

12 Merchants from southern Spain[z]
traded silver, iron, tin, and lead for your
products. 13 The people of Greece, Tubal,
and Meshech traded slaves and things
made of bronze, 14 and those from Beth-
Togarmah traded work horses, war
horses, and mules. 15 You also did business with people from Rhodes,[a] and
people from nations along the coast
gave you ivory and ebony[b] in exchange
for your goods. 16 Edom[c] traded emer-
alds, purple cloth, embroidery, fine
linen, coral, and rubies. 17 Judah and Israel gave you their finest wheat, fancy
figs,[d] honey, olive oil, and spices in exchange for your merchandise. 18 The
people of Damascus saw what you had
to offer and brought you wine from Hel-
bon and wool from Zahar. 19 Vedan and
Javan near Uzal[e] traded you iron and
spices. 20 The people of Dedan supplied
you with saddle blankets, 21 while people
from Arabia and the rulers of Kedar
traded lambs, sheep, and goats. 22 Merchants from Sheba and Raamah gave
you excellent spices, precious stones,
and gold in exchange for your products.
23 You also did business with merchants
from the cities of Haran, Canneh, Eden,
Sheba, Asshur, and Chilmad, 24 and they
gave you expensive clothing, purple and
embroidered cloth, brightly colored
rugs, and strong rope. 25 Large, seagoing
ships[f] carried your goods wherever they
needed to go.

You were like a ship
loaded with heavy cargo
26 and sailing across the sea,
but you were wrecked
by strong eastern winds.
27 Everything on board was lost—
your valuable cargo,

[v] **26.20** *You will stay there . . . with people*: One possible meaning for the difficult Hebrew text.
[w] **27.2** *Tyre*: See the note at 26.2.
[x] **27.4** *and your control of the sea*: One possible meaning for the difficult Hebrew text.
[y] **27.6** *pine trees from Cyprus*: One possible meaning for the difficult Hebrew text.
[z] **27.12** *southern Spain*: The Hebrew text has "Tarshish," which may have been a Phoenician city in southern Spain.
[a] **27.15** *Rhodes*: One ancient translation; Hebrew "Dedan."
[b] **27.15** *ebony*: A valuable black wood.
[c] **27.16** *Edom*: Some Hebrew manuscripts and one ancient translation; most Hebrew manuscripts "Syria."
[d] **27.17** *their finest wheat, fancy figs*: One possible meaning for the difficult Hebrew text.
[e] **27.19** *Vedan and Javan near Uzal*: One possible meaning for the difficult Hebrew text.
[f] **27.25** *Large, seagoing ships*: The Hebrew text has "Ships of Tarshish," which may have been a Phoenician city in Spain. "Ships of Tarshish" probably means large, seagoing ships.

your sailors and carpenters,
merchants and soldiers.
28 The shouts of your drowning crew
were heard on the shore.

29 Every ship is deserted;
rowers and sailors and captains
all stand on shore,
30 mourning for you.
They show their sorrow
by putting dust on their heads
and rolling in ashes;
31 they shave their heads
and dress in sackcloth[g]
as they cry in despair.
32 In their grief they sing
a funeral song for you:
"Tyre, you were greater
than all other cities.
But now you lie in silence
at the bottom of the sea.[h]

33 "Nations that received
your merchandise
were always pleased;
kings everywhere got rich
from your costly goods.
34 But now you are wrecked
in the deep sea,
with your cargo and crew
scattered everywhere.
35 People living along the coast
are shocked at the news.
Their rulers are horrified,
and terror is written
across their faces.
36 The merchants of the world
can't believe what happened.
Your death was gruesome,
and you are gone forever."

Judgment on the King of Tyre

28 The LORD God said:
2 Ezekiel, son of man, tell the
king of Tyre[i] that I am saying:
You are so arrogant that you think
you're a god and that the city of Tyre
is your throne. You may claim to be a
god, though you're nothing but a
mere human. 3 You think you're
wiser than Daniel[j] and know everything.[k]
4 Your wisdom has certainly made
you rich, because you have storehouses filled with gold and silver.
5 You're a clever businessman and
are extremely wealthy, but your
wealth has led to arrogance!
6 You compared yourself to a god,
so now I, the LORD God, 7 will make
you the victim of cruel enemies.
They will destroy all the possessions
you've worked so hard to get. 8 Your
enemies will brutally kill you, and
the sea will be your only grave.
9 When you face your enemies, will
you still claim to be a god? They will
attack, and you will suffer like any
other human. 10 Foreigners will kill
you, and you will die the death of
those who don't worship me. I, the
LORD, have spoken.

A Funeral Song for the King of Tyre

11 The LORD said:
12 Ezekiel, son of man, sing a funeral
song for the king of Tyre[l] and tell him I
am saying:
At one time, you were perfect,[m] intelligent, and good-looking. 13 You
lived in the garden of Eden and
wore jewelry made of brightly
colored gems and precious stones.
They were all set in gold[n] and were
ready for you on the day you were
born. 14 I appointed a winged creature to guard your home[o] on my
holy mountain, where you walked
among gems that dazzled like fire.
15 You were truly good from the
time of your birth, but later you
started doing wicked things. 16 You
traded with other nations and became more and more cruel and evil.
So I forced you to leave my mountain, and the creature that had been
your protector now chased you away
from the gems.
17 It was your good looks that
made you arrogant, and you were so
famous that you started acting like a
fool. That's why I threw you to the
ground and let other kings sneer at
you. 18 You have cheated so many
other merchants that your places of
worship are corrupt. So I set your
city on fire and burned it down. Now
everyone sees only ashes where
your city once stood, 19 and the people of other nations are shocked.
Your punishment was horrible, and
you are gone forever.

Judgment on Sidon and Peace for Israel

20 The LORD said:
21 Ezekiel, son of man, condemn the
city of Sidon[p] 22 and tell its people:
I, the LORD God, am your enemy!

[g] **27.31** *sackcloth*: See the note at 7.18. [h] **27.32** *Tyre, you were greater . . . the bottom of the sea*: One possible meaning for the difficult Hebrew text. [i] **28.2** *Tyre*: See the note at 26:2. [j] **28.3** *Daniel*: See the note at 14.14. [k] **28.3** *and know everything*: One possible meaning for the difficult Hebrew text. [l] **28.12** *Tyre*: See the note at 26.2. [m] **28.12** *you were perfect*: One possible meaning for the difficult Hebrew text. [n] **28.13** *They were all set in gold*: One possible meaning for the difficult Hebrew text. [o] **28.14** *I appointed a winged creature to guard your home*: One possible meaning for the difficult Hebrew text. [p] **28.21** *Sidon*: See the note at 26.2.

People will praise me when I punish
you, and they will see that I am holy.
23 I will send deadly diseases to wipe
you out, and I will send enemies to
invade and surround you. Your people will be killed, and you will know
that I am the LORD.
24 When that happens, the people
of Israel will no longer have cruel
neighbors that abuse them and
make them feel as though they are
in a field of thorns and briers. And
the Israelites will know that I, the
LORD God, have done these things.

A Blessing for Israel

25 The LORD God said:
Someday I will gather the people
of Israel from the nations where
they are now scattered, and every
nation will see that I am holy. The Israelites will once again live in the
land I gave to my servant Jacob.
26 They will be safe and will build
houses and plant vineyards. They
will no longer be in danger, because
I will punish their hateful neighbors.
Israel will know that I am the LORD
their God.

Judgment on the King of Egypt

29 Ten years after King Jehoiachin
and the rest of us had been led
away as prisoners to Babylonia, the
LORD spoke to me on the twelfth day of
the tenth month.[q] He said:
2 Ezekiel, son of man, condemn the
king of Egypt. Tell him and his people
3 that I am saying:
King of Egypt, you were like a giant crocodile lying in a river. You
acted as though you owned the Nile
and made it for yourself. But now I,
the LORD God, am your enemy! 4 I
will put a hook in your jaw and pull
you out of the water, and all the fish
in your river will stick to your scaly
body.[r] 5 I'll throw you and the fish
into the desert, and your body will
fall on the hard ground. You will be
left unburied,[s] and wild animals and
birds will eat your flesh. 6 Then
everyone in Egypt will know that I
am the LORD.
You and your nation refused to
help the people of Israel and were
nothing more than a broken stick.
7 When they reached out to you for
support, you broke in half, cutting
their arms and making them fall.[t]
8 So I, the LORD God, will send
troops to attack you, king of Egypt.
They will kill your people and livestock, 9 until your land is a barren
desert. Then you will know that I
have done these things.
You claimed that you made the
Nile River and control it. 10 Now I am
turning against you and your river.
Your nation will be nothing but an
empty wasteland all the way from
the town of Migdol in the north to
Aswan in the south, and as far as the
border of Ethiopia.[u] 11 No human or
animal will even dare travel through
Egypt, because no sign of life will be
found there for forty years. 12 It will
be the most barren place on earth.
Every city in Egypt will lie in ruins
during those forty years, and I will
scatter your people throughout the
nations of the world.
13 Then after those forty years have
passed, I will bring your people back
from the places where I scattered
them. 14 They will once again live in
their homeland in southern Egypt.
But they will be a weak kingdom
15 and won't ever be strong enough
to rule nations, as they did in the
past. 16 My own people Israel will
never again depend on your nation.
In fact, when the Israelites remember what happened to you Egyptians, they will realize how wrong
they were to turn to you for help.
Then the Israelites will know that I,
the LORD God, did these things.

King Nebuchadnezzar of Babylonia Will Conquer Egypt

17 Twenty-seven years after King Jehoiachin and the rest of us had been led
away as prisoners to Babylonia, the
LORD spoke to me on the first day of the
first month.[v] He said:
18 King Nebuchadnezzar of Babylonia has attacked the city of Tyre.
He forced his soldiers to carry so
many heavy loads that their heads
were rubbed bald, and their shoulders were red and sore. Nebuchadnezzar and his army still could not
capture the city. 19 So now I will hand
over the nation of Egypt to him. He
will take Egypt's valuable treasures
and give them to his own troops.

[q] **29.1** *Ten years . . . tenth month*: Probably January of 587 B.C. [r] **29.4** *all the fish in your river will stick to your scaly body*: All the king's officials will be removed from power and destroyed along with the king himself. [s] **29.5** *You will be left unburied*: A proper burial in a royal tomb was extremely important to Egyptian kings, because they often thought of themselves as gods. [t] **29.7** *making them fall*: One possible meaning for the difficult Hebrew text. [u] **29.10** *Ethiopia*: The Hebrew text has "Cush," which was a region south of Egypt that included parts of the present countries of Ethiopia and Sudan. [v] **29.17** *Twenty-seven . . . first month*: Probably March of 571 B.C.

20 Egypt will be his reward, because
he and his army have been following
my orders. I, the LORD God, have
spoken.
21 Ezekiel, when Egypt is defeated,
I will make the people of Israel
strong, and I will give you the power
to speak to them. Then they will
know that I, the LORD, have done
these things.

Egypt Will Be a Barren Desert

30 The LORD said:
2 Ezekiel, son of man, tell the
people of Egypt that I am saying:

Cry out in despair,
3 because you will soon
be punished!
That will be a time
of darkness and doom
for all nations.
4 Your own nation of Egypt
will be attacked,
and Ethiopia[w] will suffer.
You will be killed in battle,
and your land will be robbed
and left in ruins.

5 Soldiers hired from Ethiopia, Libya,
Lydia, Arabia, Kub, as well as from Israel,[x] will die in that battle. 6 All of your
allies will be killed, and your proud
strength will crumble. People will die
from Migdol in the north to Aswan in
the south. I, the LORD, have spoken.
7 Your nation of Egypt will be the most
deserted place on earth, and its cities
will lie in complete ruin. 8 I will set fire
to your land, and anyone who defended
your nation will die. Then you will know
that I am the LORD.
9 On the same day I destroy Egypt, I
will send messengers to the Ethiopians
to announce their coming destruction.
They think they are safe, but they will
be terrified.
10 Your Egyptian army is very strong,
but I will send King Nebuchadnezzar of
Babylonia to completely defeat that
army. 11 He and his cruel troops will invade and destroy your land and leave
your dead bodies piled everywhere.
12 I will dry up the Nile River, then sell
the land to evil buyers. I will send foreigners to turn your entire nation into a
barren desert. I, the LORD, have spoken.

Egypt's Proud Cities Will Lie in Ruins

The LORD said to the people of Egypt:
13 All the idols and images you Egyptians worship in the city of Memphis[y]
will be smashed. No one will be left to
rule your nation, and terror will fill the
land. 14 The city of Pathros will be left in
ruins, and Zoan will be burned to the
ground. Thebes,[z] your capital city, will
also be destroyed! 15 The fortress city of
Pelusium will feel my fierce anger, and
all the troops stationed at Thebes will be
slaughtered.
16 I will set fire to your nation of
Egypt! The city of Pelusium will be in
anguish. Thebes will fall, and the people
of Memphis will live in constant fear.[a]
17 The young soldiers in the cities of Heliopolis and Bubastis[b] will die in battle,
and the rest of the people will be taken
prisoner. 18 You were so proud of your
nation's power, but when I crush that
power and kill that pride, darkness will
fall over the city of Tahpanhes. A dark,
gloomy cloud will cover the land as you
are being led away into captivity.
19 When I'm through punishing Egypt,
you will know that I am the LORD.

Egypt's King Is Powerless

20 Eleven years after King Jehoiachin
and the rest of us had been led away as
prisoners to Babylonia, the LORD spoke
to me on the seventh day of the first
month.[c] He said:
21 Ezekiel, son of man, I, the LORD,
have defeated the king of Egypt! I broke
his arm, and no one has wrapped it or
put it in a sling, so that it could heal and
get strong enough to hold a sword. 22 So
tell him that I am now his worst enemy.
I will break both his arms—the good
one and the broken one! His sword will
drop from his hand forever, 23 and I will
scatter the Egyptians all over the world.
24-25 I will strengthen the power of
Babylonia's king and give him my
sword to use against Egypt. I will also
make the wounded king of Egypt powerless, and he will moan in pain and die
in front of the Babylonian king. Then
everyone on earth will know that I am
the LORD. 26 I will force the Egyptians to
live as prisoners in foreign nations, and
they will know that I, the LORD, have
punished them.

Egypt's King Will Be Chopped Down like a Cedar Tree

31 Eleven years after King Jehoiachin and the rest of us had
been led away as prisoners to Babylonia, the LORD spoke to me on the first
day of the third month.[d] He said:

[w] **30.4** *Ethiopia*: See the note at 29.10. [x] **30.5** *as well as from Israel*: One possible meaning for the difficult Hebrew text. [y] **30.13** *Memphis*: Hebrew "Noph." [z] **30.14** *Thebes*: Hebrew "No." [a] **30.16** *the people of Memphis . . . constant fear*: One possible meaning for the difficult Hebrew text. [b] **30.17** *Heliopolis and Bubastis*: Hebrew "On and Pi-Beseth." [c] **30.20** *Eleven years . . . first month*: Probably March of 587 B.C. [d] **31.1** *Eleven years . . . third month*: Probably May of 587 B.C.

2 Ezekiel, son of man, tell the king of
Egypt and his people that I am saying:

You are more powerful
than anyone on earth.
Now listen to this.
3 There was once a cedar tree
in Lebanon
with large, strong branches
reaching to the sky.[e]
4 This tree had plenty of water
to help it grow tall,
and nearby streams watered
the other trees
in the forest.
5 But this tree towered over
those other trees,
and its branches
grew long and thick.
6 Birds built nests
in its branches,
and animals were born
beneath it.
People from all nations
lived in the shade
of this strong tree.

7 It had beautiful,
long branches,
and its roots found water
deep in the soil.
8 None of the cedar trees
in my garden of Eden
were as beautiful
as this tree;
no tree of any kind
had such long branches.
9 I, the LORD, gave this tree
its beauty,
and I helped the branches
grow strong.
All other trees in Eden
wanted to be just like it.

10 King of Egypt, now listen to what I,
the LORD God, am saying about that
tree:
The tree grew so tall that it
reached the sky[f] and became very
proud and arrogant. 11 So I, the LORD
God, will reject the tree and hand it
over to a foreign ruler, who will punish it for its wickedness. 12 Cruel foreigners will chop it down and leave
it wherever it falls. Branches and
broken limbs will be scattered over
the mountains and in the valleys.
The people living in the shade of
those branches will go somewhere
else. 13 Birds will then nest on the
stump of the fallen tree, and wild animals will trample its branches.

14 Never again will any tree dare to
grow as tall as this tree, no matter
how much water it has. Every tree
must die, just as humans die and go
down to the world of the dead.
15 On the day this tree dies and
goes to the world below, I, the LORD
God, will command rivers and
streams to mourn its death. Every
underground spring of water and
every river will stop flowing.[g] The
mountains in Lebanon will be covered with darkness as a sign of their
sorrow, and all the trees in the forest
will wither. 16 This tree will crash to
the ground, and I will send it to the
world below. Then the nations of the
earth will tremble.
The trees from Eden and the
choice trees from Lebanon are now
in the world of the dead, and they
will be comforted when this tree
falls. 17 Those people who found protection in its shade will also be sent
to the world below, where they will
join the dead.[h]
18 King of Egypt, all these things
will happen to you and your people!
You were like this tree at one time—
taller and stronger than anyone on
earth. But now you will be chopped
down, just as every tree in the garden of Eden must die. You will be
sent down to the world of the dead,
where you will join the godless and
the other victims of violent death. I,
the LORD God, have spoken.

A Funeral Song for the King of Egypt

32 Twelve years after King Jehoiachin and the rest of us had
been led away as prisoners to Babylonia, the LORD spoke to me on the first
day of the twelfth month.[i] He said:
2 Ezekiel, son of man, condemn the
king of Egypt and tell him I am saying:

You act like a lion
roaming the earth;
but you are nothing more than
a crocodile in a river,
churning up muddy water
with your feet.

3 King of Egypt, listen to me. I, the
LORD God, will catch you in my net and
let a crowd of foreigners drag you to
shore. 4 I will throw you into an open
field, where birds and animals will come
to feed on your body. 5 I will spread your
rotting flesh[j] over the mountains and in
the valleys, 6 and your blood will flow

[e] 31.3 *sky*: One possible meaning for the difficult Hebrew text of verse 3. [f] 31.10 *the sky*: One ancient translation; Hebrew "over the thick branches." [g] 31.15 *rivers and streams . . . stop flowing*: One possible meaning for the difficult Hebrew text. [h] 31.17 *dead*: One possible meaning for the difficult Hebrew text of verse 17. [i] 32.1 *Twelve years . . . twelfth month*: Probably February of 585 B.C. [j] 32.5 *rotting flesh*: One possible meaning for the difficult Hebrew text.

throughout the land and fill up the
streams. 7I will cover the whole sky and
every star with thick clouds, so that the
sun and moon will stop shining. 8The
heavens will become black, leaving your
country in total darkness. I, the LORD,
have spoken.

9Foreign nations you have never
heard of will be shocked when I tell
them how I destroyed you.[k] 10They will
be horrified, and when I flash my sword
in victory on the day of your death, their
kings will tremble in the fear of what
could happen to them.

11The king of Babylonia is coming to
attack you, king of Egypt! 12Your soldiers will be killed by the cruelest army
in the world, and everything you take
pride in will be crushed. 13I will slaughter your cattle that graze by the river,[l]
and no people or livestock will be left to
muddy its water. 14The water will be
clear, and streams will be calm. I, the
LORD God, have spoken.

15Egypt will become a barren wasteland, and no living thing will ever survive there. Then you and your people
will know that I am the LORD.

16This is your warning, and it will be
used as a funeral song by foreign
women to mourn the death of your people. I, the LORD God, have spoken.

A Sad Ending for Egypt

17On the fifteenth day of that same
month,[m] the LORD said:

18Ezekiel, son of man, mourn for the
Egyptians and condemn them to the
world of the dead, where they will be
buried alongside the people of other
powerful nations.[n] 19Say to them:

You may be more beautiful
than the people
of other nations,
but you will also die
and join the godless
in the world below.

20You cannot escape! The enemy's
sword is ready to slaughter every one of
you.[o] 21Brave military leaders killed in
battle will gladly welcome you and your
allies into the world of the dead.

22-23The graves of soldiers from Assyria are there. They once terrified people, but they were killed in battle and
now lie deep in the world of the dead.[p]

24-25The graves of soldiers from Elam
are there. The very sight of those godless soldiers once terrified their enemies
and made them panic. But now they are
disgraced and ashamed as they lie in
the world of the dead, alongside others
who were killed in battle.

26The graves of soldiers from
Meshech and Tubal are there. These
godless soldiers who terrified people
were all killed in battle. 27They were not
given a proper burial like the heroes of
long ago,[q] who were buried with their
swords under their heads and with their
shields[r] over their bodies. These were
the heroes who made their enemies
panic.

28You Egyptians will be cruelly defeated, and you will be buried alongside
these other godless soldiers who died in
battle.

29The graves of kings and leaders
from Edom are there. They were powerful at one time. Now they are buried in
the world of the dead with other godless
soldiers killed in battle.

30The graves of the rulers of the
north[s] are there, as well as those of the
Sidonians. Their powerful armies once
terrified enemies. Now they lie buried in
the world of the dead, where they are
disgraced like other soldiers killed in
battle.

31The LORD God says:

When your king of Egypt sees all
of these graves, he and his soldiers
will be glad they are not the only
ones suffering. 32I sent him to terrify
people all over the earth. But he and
his army will be killed and buried
alongside other godless soldiers in
the world of the dead. I, the LORD
God, have spoken.

The LORD Appoints Ezekiel To Stand Watch

(Ezekiel 3.16-21)

33 The LORD said:
2Ezekiel, son of man, warn your
people by saying:

Someday, I, the LORD, may send an
enemy to invade a country. And suppose its people choose someone to
stand watch 3and to sound a warning signal when the enemy is seen
coming. 4-5If any of these people
hear the signal and ignore it, they
will be killed in battle. But it will be
their own fault, because they could
have escaped if they had paid attention.

[k]**32.9** *when I tell them how I destroyed you*: Hebrew; one ancient translation "when I scatter you like prisoners among them." [l]**32.13** *the river*: This possibly refers to the Nile River. [m]**32.17** *that same month*: See verse 1. [n]**32.18** *where they will be buried . . . powerful nations*: One possible meaning for the difficult Hebrew text. [o]**32.20** *The enemy's sword . . . you*: One possible meaning for the difficult Hebrew text. [p]**32.22,23** *deep in the world of the dead*: The place of greatest dishonor. [q]**32.27** *heroes of long ago*: One ancient translation; Hebrew "godless heroes." [r]**32.27** *shields*: One possible meaning for the difficult Hebrew text. [s]**32.30** *the rulers of the north*: Probably the Phoenicians.

6 But suppose the person watching
fails to sound the warning signal.
The enemy will attack and kill some
of the sinful people in that country,
and I, the LORD, will hold that person
responsible for their death.
7 Ezekiel, I have appointed you to
stand watch for the people of Israel. So
listen to what I say, then warn them for
me. 8 When I tell wicked people they will
die because of their sins, you must warn
them to turn from their sinful ways. But
if you refuse to warn them, you are responsible for their death. 9 If you do
warn them, and they keep sinning, they
will die because of their sins, and you
will be innocent.

The LORD Is Always Fair
(Ezekiel 18.21-30)

10 The LORD said:
Ezekiel, son of man, the people of Israel are complaining that the punishment for their sins is more than they
can stand. They have lost all hope for
survival, and they blame me. 11 Tell them
that as surely as I am the living LORD
God, I don't like to see wicked people
die. I enjoy seeing them turn from their
sins and live. So if the Israelites want to
live, they must stop sinning and turn
back to me.
12 Tell them that when good people
start sinning, all the good they did in the
past cannot save them from being punished. And remind them that when
wicked people stop sinning, their past
sins will be completely forgiven, and
they won't be punished.
13 Suppose I promise good people that
they will live, then later they start sinning and believe they will be saved by
the good they did in the past. These people will certainly be put to death because of their sins. Their good deeds
will be forgotten.
14 Suppose I warn wicked people that
they will die because of their sins, and
they stop sinning and start doing right.
15 For example, they need to return anything they have taken as security for a
loan and anything they have stolen.
Then if they stop doing evil and
start obeying my Law, they will live.
16 Their past sins will be forgiven, and
they will live because they have done
right.
17 Ezekiel, your people accuse me of
being unfair. But they are the ones who
are unfair. 18 If good people start doing
evil, they will be put to death, because
they have sinned. 19 And if wicked people stop sinning and start doing right,
they will save themselves from punishment. 20 But the Israelites still think I am
unfair. So warn them that they will be
punished for what they have done.

The News of Jerusalem's Fall

21 Twelve years after King Jehoiachin
and the rest of us had been led away as
prisoners to Babylonia, a refugee who
had escaped from Jerusalem came to
me on the fifth day of the tenth month.[t]
He told me that the city had fallen.
22 The evening before this man arrived
at my house, the LORD had taken control
of me. So when the man came to me the
next morning, I could once again speak.[u]

What Will Happen to Those Left in Israel?

23 Then the LORD said:
24 Ezekiel, son of man, the people living in the ruined cities of Israel are saying, "Abraham was just one man, and
the LORD gave him this whole land of Israel. There are many of us, and so this
land must be ours."
25 So, Ezekiel, tell them I am saying:
How can you think the land is still
yours? You eat meat with blood in it
and worship idols. You commit murder 26 and spread violence throughout the land. Everything you do is
wicked; you are even unfaithful in
marriage. And you claim the land is
yours!
27 As surely as I am the living LORD
God, you people in the ruined cities
will be killed in battle. Those of you
living in the countryside will be
eaten by wild animals, and those
hiding in caves and on rocky cliffs
will die from deadly diseases. 28 I will
make the whole country an empty
wasteland and crush the power in
which you take such pride. Even the
mountains will be bare, and no one
will try to cross them. 29 I will punish
you because of your sins, and I will
turn your nation into a barren
desert. Then you will know that I am
the LORD.

The People Listen, but Don't Change

The LORD said:
30 Ezekiel, son of man, the people with
you in Babylonia talk about you when
they meet by the city walls or in the
doorways of their houses. They say,
"Let's ask Ezekiel what the LORD has
said today." 31 So they all come and listen to you, but they refuse to do what
you tell them. They claim to be faithful,
but they are forever trying to cheat others out of their money. 32 They treat you
as though you were merely singing love
songs or playing music. They listen, but
don't do anything you say.

[t] 33.21 *Twelve years . . . tenth month*: Probably December of 586 B.C. [u] 33.22 *I could once again speak*: See 3.27.

33 Soon they will be punished, just as you warned, and they will know that a prophet has been among them.

Israel's Leaders Are Worthless Shepherds

34 The LORD God said:

2 Ezekiel, son of man, Israel's leaders are like shepherds taking care of my sheep, the people of Israel. But I want you to condemn these leaders and tell them:

I, the LORD God, say you shepherds of Israel are doomed! You take care of yourselves while ignoring my sheep. 3 You drink their milk and use their wool to make your clothes. Then you butcher the best ones for food. But you don't take care of the flock! 4 You have never protected the weak ones or healed the sick ones or bandaged those that get hurt. You let them wander off and never look for those that get lost. You are cruel and mean to my sheep. 5 They strayed in every direction, and because there was no shepherd to watch them, they were attacked and eaten by wild animals. 6 So my sheep were scattered across the earth. They roamed on hills and mountains, without anyone even bothering to look for them.

7-8 Now listen to what I, the living LORD God, am saying to you shepherds. My sheep have been attacked and eaten by wild animals, because you refused to watch them. You never went looking for the lost ones, and you fed yourselves without feeding my sheep. 9-10 So I, the LORD, will punish you! I will rescue my sheep from you and never let you be their shepherd again or butcher them for food. I, the LORD, have spoken.

The LORD Is the Good Shepherd

11 The LORD God then said:

I will look for my sheep and take care of them myself, 12 just as a shepherd looks for lost sheep. My sheep have been lost since that dark and miserable day when they were scattered throughout the nations.[v] But I will rescue them 13 and bring them back from the foreign nations where they now live. I will be their shepherd and will let them graze on Israel's mountains and in the valleys and fertile fields. 14 They will be safe as they feed on grassy meadows and green hills. 15 I promise to take care of them and keep them safe, 16 to look for those that are lost and bring back the ones that wander off, to bandage those that are hurt and protect the ones that are weak. I will also slaughter[w] those that are fat and strong, because I always do right.

Judgment on the Strong Sheep

17 The LORD God said to his sheep, the people of Israel:

I will carefully watch each one of you to decide which ones are the strong sheep and which ones are weak. 18 Some of you eat the greenest grass, then trample down what's left when you finish. Others drink clean water, then step in the water to make the rest of it muddy. 19 That means my other sheep have nothing fit to eat or drink.

20 So I, the LORD God, will separate you strong sheep from the weak. 21 You strong ones have used your powerful horns to chase off those that are weak, 22 but I will rescue them and no longer let them be mistreated. I will separate the good from the bad.

23 After that, I will give you a shepherd from the family of my servant King David. All of you, both strong and weak, will have the same shepherd, and he will take good care of you. 24 He will be your leader, and I will be your God. I, the LORD, have spoken.

A Bright Future for the LORD's Sheep

The LORD God said:

25 The people of Israel are my sheep, and I solemnly promise that they will live in peace. I will chase away every wild animal from the desert and the forest, so my sheep will not be afraid. 26 They will live around my holy mountain,[x] and I will bless them by sending more than enough rain 27 to make their trees produce fruit and their crops to grow. I will set them free from slavery and let them live safely in their own land. Then they will know that I am the LORD. 28 Foreign nations will never again rob them, and wild animals will no longer kill and eat them. They will have nothing to fear. 29 I will make their fields produce large amounts of crops, so they will never again go hungry or be laughed at by foreigners. 30 Then everyone will know that I protect my people Israel. I, the LORD, make this promise. 31 They are my sheep; I am their God, and I take care of them.

Edom Will Be a Wasteland

35 The LORD said:

2 Ezekiel, son of man, condemn the people of Edom[y] 3 and say to them:

[v] 34.12 *dark and miserable day . . . nations*: That is, the day the Babylonians defeated Jerusalem and led its people away as prisoners. [w] 34.16 *slaughter*: Hebrew; three ancient translations "take care of." [x] 34.26 *my holy mountain*: That is, Mount Zion in Jerusalem. [y] 35.2 *Edom*: The Hebrew text has "Mount Seir," another name for Edom.

I, the LORD God,
am now your enemy!
And I will turn your nation
into an empty wasteland,
4 leaving your towns in ruins.
Your land will be a desert,
and then you will know
that I am the LORD.

5 People of Edom, not only have you
been Israel's longtime enemy, you simply watched when disaster wiped out its
people as punishment for their sins.
6 And so, as surely as I am the living
LORD God, you are guilty of murder and
must be put to death. 7 I will destroy
your nation and kill anyone who travels through it. 8 Dead bodies will cover
your mountains and fill up your valleys,
9 and your land will lie in ruins forever. No one will live in your towns
ever again. You will know that I am the
LORD.

10 You thought the nations of Judah
and Israel belonged to you, and that you
could take over their territory. But I am
their God, 11 and as surely as I live, I will
punish you for treating my people with
anger and hatred. Then they will know
that I, the LORD, am punishing you!
12 And you will finally realize that I
heard you laugh at their destruction
and say their land was yours to take.
13 You even insulted me, but I heard it
all.

14 Everyone on earth will celebrate
when I destroy you, 15 just as you celebrated when Israel was destroyed. Your
nation of Edom will be nothing but a
wasteland. Then everyone will know
that I am the LORD.

A Message for Israel's Mountains

36 The LORD said:
Ezekiel, son of man, tell the
mountains of Israel 2 that I, the Lord
God, am saying:

Your enemies sneered and said that
you mountains belonged to them. 3 They
ruined and crushed you from every side,
and foreign nations captured and made
fun of you. 4 So all you mountains and
hills, streams and valleys, listen to what
I will do. Your towns may now lie in ruins, and nations may laugh and insult
you. 5 But in my fierce anger, I will turn
against those nations, and especially the
Edomites, because they laughed at you
the loudest and took over your pasturelands. 6 You have suffered long enough,
and, I, the LORD God, am very angry!
Nations have insulted you, 7 so I will
now insult and disgrace them. That is
my solemn promise.

8 Trees will grow on you mountains of
Israel and produce fruit for my people,
because they will soon come home. 9 I
will take care of you by plowing your
soil and planting crops on your fertile
slopes. 10 The people of Israel will return
and rebuild your ruined towns and live
in them. 11 Children will be born, and
animals will give birth to their young.
You will no longer be deserted as
you are now, but you will be covered
with people and treated better than
ever. Then you will know that I am the
LORD.

12 I will bring my people Israel home,
and they will live on you mountains, because you belong to them, and your fertile slopes will never again let them
starve. 13 It's true that you have been accused of not producing enough food and
of letting your people starve. 14-15 But
I, the LORD, promise that you won't
hear other nations laugh and sneer
at you ever again. From now on, you
will always produce plenty of food
for your people. I, the LORD God, have
spoken.

The LORD Will Be Honored

16 The LORD said:

17 Ezekiel, son of man, when the people of Israel were living in their own
country, they made the land unclean by
the way they behaved, just as a woman's
monthly period makes her unclean.
18 They committed murders and worshiped idols, which made the land even
worse. So in my anger, I punished my
people 19 and scattered them throughout
the nations, just as they deserved.
20 Wherever they went, my name was
disgraced, because foreigners insulted
my people by saying I had forced them
out of their own land.

21 I care what those foreigners think of
me, 22 so tell the Israelites that I am saying:

You have disgraced my holy name
among the nations where you now
live. So you don't deserve what I'm
going to do for you. I will lead you
home to bring honor to my name
23 and to show foreign nations that I
am holy. Then they will know that I
am the LORD God. I have spoken.

24 I will gather you from the foreign nations and bring you home. 25 I
will sprinkle you with clean water,
and you will be clean and acceptable
to me. I will wash away everything
that makes you unclean, and I will
remove your disgusting idols. 26 I will
take away your stubborn heart and
give you a new heart and a desire to
be faithful. You will have only pure
thoughts, 27 because I will put my
Spirit in you and make you eager to
obey my laws and teachings. 28 You
will once again live in the land I
gave your ancestors; you will be my
people, and I will be your God.

29 I will protect you from anything

that makes you unclean. Your fields
will overflow with grain, and no one
will starve. 30 Your trees will be filled
with fruit, and crops will grow in
your fields, so that you will never
again feel ashamed for not having
enough food. 31 You will remember
your evil ways and hate yourselves
for what you've done. 32 People of Israel, I'm not doing these things for
your sake. You sinned against me,
and you must suffer shame and disgrace for what you have done. I, the
LORD God, have spoken.
33 After I have made you clean, I
will let you rebuild your ruined
towns and let you live in them.
34 Your land will be plowed again,
and nobody will be able to see that it
was once barren. 35 Instead, they will
say that it looks as beautiful as the
garden of Eden. They won't see
towns lying in ruins, but they will
see your strong cities filled with people. 36 Then the nearby nations that
survive will know that I am the one
who rebuilt the ruined places and
replanted the barren fields. I, the
LORD, make this promise.
37 I will once again answer your
prayers, and I will let your nation
grow until you are like a large flock
of sheep. 38 The towns that now lie in
ruins will be filled with people, just
as Jerusalem was once filled with
sheep to be offered as sacrifices during a festival. Then you will know
that I am the LORD.

Dry Bones Live Again

37 Some time later, I felt the LORD's
power take control of me, and his
Spirit carried me to a valley full of
bones. 2 The LORD showed me all
around, and everywhere I looked I saw
bones that were dried out. 3 He said,
"Ezekiel, son of man, can these bones
come back to life?"
I replied, "LORD God, only you can answer that."
4 He then told me to say:
Dry bones, listen to what the LORD
is saying to you, 5 "I, the LORD God,
will put breath in you, and once
again you will live. 6 I will wrap you
with muscles and skin and breathe
life into you. Then you will know
that I am the LORD."
7 I did what the LORD said, but before I
finished speaking, I heard a rattling
noise. The bones were coming together!
8 I saw muscles and skin cover the
bones, but they had no life in them.
9 The LORD said:
Ezekiel, now say to the wind,[z]
"The LORD God commands you to
blow from every direction and to
breathe life into these dead bodies,
so they can live again."
10 As soon as I said this, the wind ble
among the bodies, and they came bac
to life! They all stood up, and there wer
enough to make a large army.
11 The LORD said:
Ezekiel, the people of Israel are
like dead bones. They complain that
they are dried up and that they have
no hope for the future. 12 So tell
them, "I, the LORD God, promise to
open your graves and set you free. I
will bring you back to Israel, 13 and
when that happens, you will realize
that I am the LORD. 14 My Spirit will
give you breath, and you will live
again. I will bring you home, and
you will know that I have kept my
promise. I, the LORD, have spoken."

Judah and Israel Together Again

15 The LORD said:
16 Ezekiel, son of man, get a stick an
write on it, "The kingdom of Judah
Then get another stick and write on i
"The kingdom of Israel."[a] 17 Hold thes
two sticks end to end, so they look lik
one stick. 18 And when your people as
you what this means, 19 tell them that
the LORD, will join together the stick
Israel and the stick of Judah. I will ho
them in my hand, and they will becom
one.
20 Hold these two sticks where the
can be seen by everyone 21 and then sa
I, the LORD God, will gather the
people of Israel and bring them
home from the foreign nations
where they now live. 22 I will make
them into one nation and let them
once again live in the land of Israel.
Only one king will rule them, and
they will never again be divided into
two nations. 23 They will no longer
worship idols and do things that
make them unacceptable to me. I
will wash away their sin and make
them clean, and I will protect them
from everything that makes them
unclean. They will be my people,
and I will be their God.
24-25 Their king will always come
from the family of my servant King
David and will care for them like a
shepherd. The people of Israel will
faithfully obey my laws. They and
their descendants will live in the
land I gave my servant Jacob, just as
their ancestors did. 26 I solemnly
promise to bless the people of Israel
with unending peace. I will protect
them and let them become a power-

[z] **37.9** *wind*: Or "breath." The Hebrew word may mean either. [a] **37.16** *Israel*: The Hebrew text has "Joseph, that is, Ephraim," the leading tribe in the northern kingdom.

ful nation. My temple will stand in
Israel for all time, 27and I will live
among my people and be their God.
28Every nation on earth will know
that my temple is in Israel and that I
have chosen the Israelites to be my
people.

Gog Invades Israel

38 The LORD said:
2Ezekiel, son of man, condemn
Gog, that wicked ruler of the kingdoms
of Meshech and Tubal in the land of Magog. Tell him:
3I, the LORD God, am your enemy,
4and I will make you powerless! I
will put a hook in your jaw and drag
away both you and your large army.
You command cavalry troops that
wear heavy armor and carry shields
and swords. 5Your army includes
soldiers from Persia, Ethiopia,[b] and
Libya, 6as well as from Gomer and
Beth-Togarmah in the north. Your
army is enormous!
7So keep your troops prepared to
fight, 8because in a few years, I will
command you to invade Israel, a
country that was ruined by war. It
was deserted for a long time, but its
people have returned from the foreign nations where they once lived.
The Israelites now live in peace in
the mountains of their own land.
9But you and your army will attack
them like a fierce thunderstorm and
surround them like a cloud.
10When that day comes, I know
that you will have an evil plan 11to
take advantage of Israel, that weak
and peaceful country where people
live safely inside towns that have no
walls or gates or locks. 12You will
rob the people in towns that were
once a pile of rubble. These people
lived as prisoners in foreign nations,
but they have returned to Israel, the
most important place in the world,
and they own livestock and property. 13The people of Sheba and
Dedan, along with merchants from
villages in[c] southern Spain,[d] will be
your allies. They will want some of
the silver and gold, as well as the
livestock and property that your
army takes from Israel.
14I, the LORD God, know that when
you see[e] my people Israel living in
peace, 15you will lead your powerful
cavalry from your kingdom in the
north. 16You will attack my people
like a storm-cloud that covers their
land. I will let you invade my country Israel, so that every nation on
earth will know that I, the LORD, am
holy.

Judgment on Gog

17The LORD said to Gog:
Long ago, I had my prophets warn the
people of Israel that someday I would
send an enemy to attack them. You, Gog,
are that enemy, and that day is coming.
18When you invade Israel, I will become
furious, 19and in my anger I will send a
terrible earthquake to shake Israel.
20Every living thing on earth will tremble in fear of me—every fish and bird,
every wild animal and reptile, and every
human. Mountains will crumble, cliffs
will fall, and cities will collapse. 21I, the
LORD, will make the mountains of Israel
turn against you.[f] Your troops will be so
terrified that they will attack each other.
22I will strike you with diseases and
punish you with death. You and your
army will be pounded with rainstorms,
hailstones, and burning sulfur. 23I will
do these things to show the world that
I, the LORD, am holy.

Gog Is Defeated

The LORD said:
39 Ezekiel, son of man, condemn
Gog and tell him:
You are the ruler of Meshech and
Tubal, but I, the LORD, am your enemy!
2I will turn you around and drag you
from the north until you reach the
mountains of Israel. 3I will knock the
bow out of your left hand and the arrows out of your right hand, 4and you
and your army will die on those mountains. Then birds and wild animals will
eat the flesh 5of your dead bodies left lying in open fields. I, the LORD, have spoken.
6I will set fire to the land of Magog
and to those nations along the seacoast
that think they are so secure, and they
will know that I am the LORD.
7My people Israel will know me, and
they will no longer disgrace my holy
name. Everyone on earth will know that
I am the holy LORD God of Israel. 8The
day is coming when these things will
happen, just as I have promised.
9When that day comes, the people in
the towns of Israel will collect the
weapons of their dead enemies. They
will use these shields, bows and arrows,
spears, and clubs as firewood, and there
will be enough to last for seven years.
10They will burn these weapons instead
of gathering sticks or chopping down
trees. That's how the Israelites will take

[b] **38.5** *Ethiopia*: See the note at 29.10. [c] **38.13** *from villages in*: One ancient translation; Hebrew "and soldiers from." [d] **38.13** *southern Spain*: See the note at 27.12. [e] **38.14** *when you see*: One possible meaning for the difficult Hebrew text. [f] **38.21** *I, the LORD . . . against you*: One possible meaning for the difficult Hebrew text.

revenge on those who robbed and
abused them. I, the LORD, have spoken.

The Burial of Gog

The LORD said:
11After Gog has been destroyed, I will
bury him and his army in Israel, in Travelers'[g] Valley, east of the Dead Sea. That
graveyard will be so large that it will
block the way of anyone who tries to
walk through the valley,[h] which will
then be known as "The Valley of Gog's
Army."[i] 12The Israelites will spend seven
months burying dead bodies and clean-
ing up their land. 13Everyone will help
with the burial, and they will be honored for this on the day the brightness
of my glory is seen. 14After those seven
months, the people will appoint a group
of men to look for any dead bodies left
unburied. This must be done for seven
months to make sure that the land is no
longer unclean. 15Whenever they find a
human bone, they will set up a marker
next to it. Then the gravediggers will
bury it in "The Valley of Gog's Army"
16near the town of "Gog's Army." After
that, the land will be pure again.
17Ezekiel, son of man, I am going to
hold a feast on Israel's mountains and
offer sacrifices there. So invite all the
birds and wild animals to come from
every direction and eat the meat of sacrifices and drink the blood. The birds
and animals 18will feast on the bodies of
warriors and foreign rulers that I will
sacrifice like sheep, goats, and bulls. 19I
want the birds and animals to eat until
they are full and drink until they are
drunk. 20They will come to my table and
stuff themselves with the flesh of horses
and warriors of every kind. I, the LORD
God, have spoken.

Israel Will Be Restored

The LORD said:
21When I punish the nations of the
earth, they will see the brightness of my
glory. 22The people of Israel will know
from then on that I am the LORD their
God. 23Foreign nations will realize that
the Israelites were forced to leave their
own land because they sinned against
me. I turned my back on my people and
let enemies attack and kill them. 24Their
lives were wicked and corrupt, and they
deserved to be punished.
25Now I will show mercy to the people
of Israel and bring them back from the
nations where they are living. They are
Jacob's descendants, so I will bless
them and show that I am holy. 26They
will live safely in their own land, but
will be ashamed when they remember
their evil ways and how they disgraced
me.[j] 27Foreign nations will watch as I
take the Israelites from enemy lands
and bring them back home, and those
nations will see that I am holy.
28My people will realize that I, the
LORD their God, sent them away as prisoners and now will bring them back to
their own land. 29Never again will I turn
my back on the people of Israel, and my
Spirit will live in them. I, the LORD, have
spoken.

Ezekiel Sees the Future Temple in Jerusalem

40 1-2Twenty-five years after King Jehoiachin and the rest of us had
been led away as prisoners to Babylonia, and fourteen years after the Babylonians had captured Jerusalem, the
LORD's power took control of me on the
tenth day of the first month.[k] The LORD
showed me some visions in which I was
carried to the top of a high mountain in
Jerusalem. I looked to the south and
saw what looked like a city full of buildings. 3In my vision the LORD took me
closer, and I saw a man who was
sparkling like polished bronze. He was
standing near one of the gates and
was holding a tape measure in one hand
and a measuring stick in the other. 4The
man said, "Ezekiel, son of man, pay
close attention to everything I'm going
to show you—that's why you've been
brought here. Listen carefully, because
you must tell the people of Israel what
you see."

The East Gate

5The first thing I saw was an outer
wall that completely surrounded the
temple area. The man took his measuring stick, which was ten feet long, and
measured the wall; it was ten feet high
and ten feet thick. 6-7Then he went to the
east gate, where he walked up steps that
led to a long passageway. On each side
of this passageway were three guardrooms, which were ten feet square, and
they were separated by walls over eight
feet thick. The man measured the distance between the opening of the gate
and the first guardroom, and it was ten
feet, the thickness of the outer wall.
At the far end of this passageway, I
saw an entrance room that faced the
courtyard of the temple itself. There was
also a distance of ten feet between the
last guardroom and the entrance room
8-9at the end of the passageway. The
man measured this room: It was thir-

[g] **39.11** *Travelers'*: Hebrew "Abarim." [h] **39.11** *That graveyard . . . the valley*: One possible meaning for the difficult Hebrew text. [i] **39.11** *Gog's Army*: Hebrew "Hamon-Gog." [j] **39.26** *me*: One possible meaning for the difficult Hebrew text of verse 26. [k] **40.1,2** *Twenty-five years . . . first month*: Probably March of 573 B.C.

teen feet from the doorway to the opposite wall, and the distance from the
doorway to the wall on either side was
three feet. 10 The three guardrooms on
each side of the passageway were the
same size, and the walls that separated
them were the same thickness.
11 Next, the man measured the width
of the passageway, and it was twenty-
two feet, but the two doors of the gate
were only sixteen feet wide.[l] 12 In front
of the guardrooms, which were ten feet
square, was a railing about twenty
inches high and twenty inches thick.
13 The man measured the distance from
the back wall[m] of one of these rooms to
the same spot in the room directly
across the passageway, and it was forty-
two feet. 14 He measured the entrance
room at the far end of the passageway,
and it was thirty-four feet wide.[n] 15 Finally, he measured the total length of
the passageway, from the outer wall to
the entrance room, and it was eighty-
five feet. 16 The three walls in the guardrooms had small windows in them, just
like the ones in the entrance room.[o] The
walls along the passageway were decorated with carvings of palm trees.

The Outer Courtyard

17 The man then led me through the
passageway and into the outer courtyard of the temple, where I saw thirty
rooms built around the outside of the
courtyard.[p] These side rooms were built
against the outer wall, and in front of
them was a sidewalk that circled the
courtyard. 18 This was known as the
lower sidewalk, and it was eighty-five
feet wide.
19 I saw the gates that led to the inner
courtyard of the temple and noticed that
they were higher than those leading to
the outer courtyard. The man measured
the distance between the outer and inner gates, and it was one hundred seventy feet.[q]

The North Gate

20 Next, the man measured the north
gate that led to the outer courtyard.
21 This gate also had three guardrooms
on each side of a passageway. The measurements of these rooms, the walls between them, and the entrance room at
the far end of the passageway were exactly the same as those of the east gate.
The north gate was also eighty-five feet
long and forty-two feet wide, 22 and the
windows, the entrance room, and the
carvings of palm trees were just like
those in the east gate. The entrance
room also faced the courtyard of the
temple and had seven steps leading up
to it. 23 Directly across the outer courtyard was a gate that led to the inner
courtyard, just as there was for the east
gate. The man measured the distance
between the outer and inner gate, and it
was one hundred seventy feet.

The South Gate

24 The man then took me to the south
gate. He measured the walls and the entrance room of this gate, and the measurements were exactly the same as
those of the other two gates. 25 There
were windows in the guardrooms of this
gate and in the entrance room, just like
the others, and this gate was also
eighty-five feet long and forty-two feet
wide. 26 Seven steps led up to the gate;
the entrance room was at the far end of
the passageway and faced the courtyard
of the temple. Carvings of palm trees
decorated the walls along the passageway. 27 And directly across the outer
courtyard was a gate on the south side
of the inner courtyard. The man measured the distance between the outer
and inner gate, and it was also one hundred seventy feet.

The Gates Leading to the Inner Courtyard

28 We then went into the inner courtyard, through the gate on the south side
of the temple. The man measured the
gate, and it was the same size as the
gates in the outer wall. 29-30 In fact,
everything along the passageway was
also the same size, including the guardrooms, the walls separating them, the
entrance room at the far end, and the
windows. This gate, like the others, was
eighty-five feet long and forty-two feet
wide. 31 The entrance room of this gate
faced the outer courtyard, and carvings
of palm trees decorated the walls of the
passageway. Eight steps led up to this
gate.
32 Next, we went through the east gate
to the inner courtyard. The man measured this gate, and it was the same size
as the others. 33 The guardrooms, the

[l] **40.11** *the width of the passageway . . . twenty-two feet . . . the two doors of the gate . . . sixteen feet wide*: The doors themselves probably were hung on stone sockets, which could explain the six-foot difference in width between the passageway and the doors.
[m] **40.13** *back wall*: One ancient translation; Hebrew "roof."
[n] **40.14** *wide*: One possible meaning for the difficult Hebrew text of verse 14.
[o] **40.16** *just like the ones in the entrance room*: One possible meaning for the difficult Hebrew text.
[p] **40.17** *thirty rooms built around the outside of the courtyard*: These were probably used by worshipers as places to meet and share sacrificial meals (see, for example, Jeremiah 35.2).
[q] **40.19** *feet*: The Hebrew text adds "the east and the north."

walls separating them, and its entrance
room had the same measurements as
the other gates. The guardrooms and
the entrance room had windows, and
the gate was eighty-five feet long
and forty-two feet wide. 34The entrance
room faced the outer courtyard, and the
walls in the passageway were decorated
with carvings of palm trees. Eight steps
also led up to this gate.
35Then the man took me to the north
gate. He measured it, and it was the
same size as the others, 36including the
guardrooms, the walls separating them,
and the entrance room. There were also
windows in this gate. It was eighty-five
feet long and forty-two feet wide, 37and
like the other inner gates, its entrance
room faced the outer courtyard, and its
walls were decorated with carvings of
palm trees. Eight steps also led up to
this gate.

The Rooms for Sacrificing Animals

38-39Inside the entrance room of the
north gate, I saw four tables, two on
each side of the room, where the animals to be sacrificed were killed. Just
outside[r] this room was a small building
used for washing the animals before
they were offered as sacrifices to please
the LORD[s] or sacrifices for sin[t] or sacrifices to make things right.[u] 40Four more
tables were in the outer courtyard, two
on each side of the steps leading into
the entrance room. 41So there was a total of eight tables, four inside and four
outside, where the animals were killed,
42-43and where the meat was placed until
it was sacrificed on the altar.[v]
Next to the tables in the entrance
room were four stone tables twenty
inches high and thirty inches square;
the equipment used for killing the animals was kept on top of these tables. All
around the walls of this room was a
three inch shelf.[w]

The Rooms Belonging to the Priests

44The man then took me to the inner
courtyard, where I saw two buildings,
one beside the inner gate on the north
and the other beside the inner gate on
the south.[x] 45He said, "The building beside the north gate belongs to the
priests who serve in the temple, 46and
the building beside the south gate belongs to those who serve at the altar. All
of them are descendants of Zadok and
are the only Levites allowed to serve as
the LORD's priests."

The Inner Courtyard and the Temple

47Now the man measured the inner
courtyard; it was one hundred seventy
feet square. I also saw an altar in front
of the temple.
48We walked to the porch of the temple, and the man measured the doorway
of the porch: It was twenty-four feet
long,[y] eight feet wide, and the distance
from the doorway to the wall on either
side was five feet. 49The porch itself was
thirty-four feet by twenty[z] feet, with
steps[a] leading up to it. There was a column on each side of these steps.

41 Next we went into the main room
of the temple. The man measured
the doorway of this room: It was ten feet
wide,[b] 2seventeen feet long, and the distance from the doorway to the wall on
either side was eight feet. The main
room itself was sixty-eight feet by
thirty-four feet.
3-4Then the man walked to the far end
of the temple's main room and said,
"Beyond this doorway is the most holy
place." He first measured the doorway:
It was three feet wide, ten feet long, and
the distance from the doorway to the
wall on either side was twelve feet. Then
he measured the most holy place, and it
was thirty-four feet square.

The Storage Rooms of the Temple

5The man measured the wall of the
temple, and it was ten feet thick. Storage rooms seven feet wide were built
against the outside of the wall. 6There
were three levels of rooms, with thirty
rooms on each level, and they rested on
ledges that were attached to the temple
walls, so that nothing was built into the
walls. 7The walls of the temple were
thicker at the bottom than at the top,
which meant that the storage rooms on
the top level were wider than those on
the bottom level.[c] Steps led from the

[r] **40.38,39** *Just outside*: Or "Inside." [s] **40.38,39** *sacrifices to please the LORD*: These sacrifices have traditionally been called "whole burnt offerings" because the whole animal was burned on the altar. A main purpose of such sacrifices was to please the LORD with the smell of the sacrifice, and so in the CEV they are often called "sacrifices to please the LORD."
[t] **40.38,39** *sacrifices for sin*: See Leviticus 4.1, 2; 6.24-30. [u] **40.38,39** *sacrifices to make things right*: See Leviticus 5.14-19; 7.1-10. [v] **40.42,43** *where the meat . . . altar*: One possible meaning for the difficult Hebrew text. [w] **40.42,43** *was a three inch shelf*: Or "were three inch pegs." [x] **40.44** *south*: One possible meaning for the difficult Hebrew text of verse 44.
[y] **40.48** *twenty-four feet long*: One ancient translation; these words are not in the Hebrew text of this verse. [z] **40.49** *twenty*: One ancient translation; Hebrew "eighteen." [a] **40.49** *steps*: Hebrew; one ancient translation "ten steps." [b] **41.1** *It was ten feet wide*: One possible meaning for the difficult Hebrew text. [c] **41.7** *which meant that . . . on the bottom level*: One possible meaning for the difficult Hebrew text.

bottom level, through the middle level,
and into the top level.
8The temple rested on a stone base
ten feet high, which also served as the
foundation for the storage rooms. 9The
outside walls of the storage rooms were
eight feet thick; there was nothing between these walls 10and the nearest
buildings thirty-four feet away. 11One
door led into the storage rooms on the
north side of the temple, and another
door led to those on the south side. The
stone base extended eight feet beyond
the outside wall of the storage rooms.

The West Building and the Measurements of the Temple

12I noticed another building: It faced
the west end of the temple and was one
hundred seventeen feet wide, one hundred fifty feet long, and had walls over
eight feet thick.
13The man measured the length of the
temple, and it was one hundred seventy
feet. He then measured from the back
wall of the temple, across the open
space behind the temple, to the back
wall of the west building; it was one
hundred seventy feet. 14The distance
across the front of the temple, including
the open space on either side, was also
one hundred seventy feet.
15Finally, the man measured the
length of the west building, including
the side rooms on each end, and it was
also one hundred seventy feet.

The Inside of the Temple

The inside walls of the temple's porch
and main room[d] 16were paneled with
wood all the way from the floor to the
windows, while the doorways, the small
windows, and the three side rooms were
trimmed in wood.[e] 17The paneling
stopped just above the doorway. These
walls were decorated[f] 18-20with carvings
of winged creatures and had a carving
of a palm tree between the creatures.
Each winged creature had two faces: A
human face looking at the palm tree on
one side, and a lion's face looking at the
palm tree on the other side. These designs were carved into the paneling all
the way around the two rooms.
21The doorframe to the temple's main
room was in the shape of a rectangle.

The Wooden Altar

In front of the doorway to the most
holy place was something that looked
like 22a wooden altar. It was five feet
high and four feet square,[g] and its corners, its base,[h] and its sides were made
of wood. The man said, "This is a reminder that the LORD is constantly
watching over his temple."

The Doors in the Temple

23Both the doorway to the main room
of the temple and the doorway to the
most holy place had two doors, 24and
each door had two sections that could
fold open. 25The doors to the main room
were decorated with carvings of winged
creatures and palm trees just like those
on the walls, and there was a wooden
covering over the porch just outside
these doors. 26The walls on each side of
this porch had small windows and were
also decorated with carvings of palm
trees.

The Sacred Rooms for the Priests

42 1-2After the man and I left the
temple and walked back to the
outer courtyard, he showed me a set of
rooms on the north side of the west
building.[i] This set of rooms was one
hundred seventy feet long and eighty-
five feet wide. 3On one side of them was
the thirty-four feet of open space that
ran alongside the temple,[j] and on the
other side was the sidewalk that circled
the outer courtyard.[k] The rooms were
arranged in three levels 4with doors that
opened toward the north, and in front of
them was a walkway seventeen feet
wide and one hundred seventy feet
long.[l] 5The rooms on the top level were
narrower than those on the middle level,
and the rooms on the middle level were
narrower than those on the bottom
level. 6The rooms on the bottom level
supported those on the two upper levels,
and so these rooms did not have
columns like other buildings in the
courtyard. 7-8To the north was a privacy
wall eighty-five feet long,[m] 9-10and at the
east end of this wall was the door leading from the courtyard to these rooms.
There was also a set of rooms on the
south[n] side of the west building. 11These
rooms were exactly like those on the

[d]**41.15** *The inside walls of the temple's porch and main room*: One possible meaning for the difficult Hebrew text. [e]**41.16** *were trimmed in wood*: One possible meaning for the difficult Hebrew text. [f]**41.17** *decorated*: One possible meaning for the difficult Hebrew text of verse 17. [g]**41.22** *four feet square*: One ancient translation; Hebrew "four feet wide." [h]**41.22** *base*: One ancient translation; Hebrew "length." [i]**42.1,2** *he showed me . . . the west building*: One possible meaning for the difficult Hebrew text. [j]**42.3** *the thirty-four feet of open space . . . the temple*: See 41.10. [k]**42.3** *the sidewalk that circled the outer courtyard*: See 40.17. [l]**42.4** *one hundred seventy feet long*: Two ancient translations; Hebrew "twenty inches long." [m]**42.7,8** *long*: One possible meaning for the difficult Hebrew text of verses 5-8. [n]**42.9,10** *south*: One ancient translation; Hebrew "east."

north side, and they also had a walkway in front of them. 12The door to these rooms was at the east end of the wall that stood in front of them.

13The man then said to me:

These rooms on the north and south sides of the temple are the sacred rooms where the LORD's priests will eat the most holy offerings. These offerings include the grain sacrifices, the sacrifices for sin, and the sacrifices to make things right. 14When the priests are ready to leave the temple, they must go through these rooms before they return to the outer courtyard. They must leave their sacred clothes in these rooms and put on regular clothes before going anywhere near other people.

The Size of the Temple Area

15After the man had finished measuring the buildings inside the temple area, he took me back through the east gate and measured the wall around this area. 16He used his measuring stick to measure the east side of this wall; it was eight hundred forty feet long. 17-19Then he measured the north side, the south side, and the west side of the wall, and they were each eight hundred forty feet long, 20and so the temple area was a perfect square. The wall around this area separated what was sacred from what was ordinary.

The LORD's Glory Returns to the Temple

43 The man took me back to the east gate of the temple, 2where I saw the brightness of the glory of Israel's God coming from the east. The sound I heard was as loud as ocean waves, and everything around was shining with the dazzling brightness of his glory. 3This vision was like the one I had seen when God came to destroy Jerusalem and like the one I had seen near the Chebar River.

I immediately bowed with my face to the ground, 4and the LORD's glory came through the east gate and into the temple.[o] 5The LORD's Spirit lifted me to my feet and carried me to the inner courtyard, where I saw that the LORD's glory had filled the temple.

6The man was standing beside me, and I heard the LORD[p] say from inside the temple:

7Ezekiel, son of man, this temple is my throne on earth. I will live here among the people of Israel forever. They and their kings will never again disgrace me by worshiping idols at local shrines or by setting up memorials to their dead kings.[q] 8Israel's kings built their palaces so close to my holy temple that only a wall separated them from me. Then these kings disgraced me with their evil ways, and in my fierce anger I destroyed them. 9But if the people and their kings stop worshiping other gods and tear down those memorials, I will live among them forever.

10The people of Israel must suffer shame for sinning against me, so tell them about my holy temple. Let them think about it, 11then if they are truly sorry, describe for them the design and shape of the temple, the gates, the measurements, and how the buildings are arranged. Explain the regulations about worshiping there, then write down these things, so they can study and obey them.

12The temple area on my holy mountain must be kept sacred! This is the most important law about the temple.

The Altar

13According to the official standards, the altar in the temple had the following measurements: Around the bottom of the altar was a gutter twenty inches wide and twenty inches deep, with a ten inch ledge on the outer rim. 14-17The altar rested on a base and had three sections, each one of them square. The bottom section was twenty-seven feet on each side and three feet high. The middle section was twenty-four feet on each side and seven feet high, and it had a ten inch rim around its outer edge. The top section, which was twenty feet on each side and seven feet high, was the place where sacrifices were burned, and the four corners of the top section looked like the horns of a bull. The steps leading up to the altar were on the east side.

The Dedication of the Altar

18The LORD God said:

Ezekiel, son of man, after the altar is built, it must be dedicated by offering sacrifices on it and by splattering it with blood. Here is what you must do: 19The priests of the Levi tribe from the family of Zadok the priest are the only ones who may serve in my temple—this is my law. So give them a young bull to slaughter as a sacrifice for sin. 20Take some of the animal's blood and smear it on the four corners of the altar, some on the corners of the middle section, and

[o]43.4 *the LORD's glory . . . temple*: This was the same gate the LORD's glory went through when it left Jerusalem (see 10.19 and 11.22, 23). [p]43.6 *the LORD*: Hebrew "a voice." [q]43.7 *by setting up memorials to their dead kings*: One possible meaning for the difficult Hebrew text.

some more on the rim around its edge. That will purify the altar and make it fit for offering sacrifices to me. 21Then take the body of the bull outside the temple area and burn it at the special place.

22The next day, a goat[r] that has nothing wrong with it must be offered as a sacrifice for sin. Purify the altar with its blood, just as you did with the blood of the bull. 23Then choose a young bull and a young ram that have nothing wrong with them, 24and bring them to my temple. The priests will sprinkle salt on them[s] and offer them as sacrifices to please me.[t]

25Each day for the next seven days, you must offer a goat and a bull and a ram as sacrifices for sin. These animals must have nothing wrong with them. 26The priests will purify the altar during those days, so that it will be acceptable to me and ready to use. 27From then on, the priests will use this altar to offer sacrifices to please me and sacrifices to ask my blessing.[u] Then I will be pleased with the people of Israel. I, the LORD God, have spoken.

The East Gate Must Remain Closed

44 The man took me back to the outer courtyard, near the east gate of the temple area. I saw that the doors to this gate were closed. 2The LORD said:

I, the LORD God of Israel, came through this gate, so it must remain closed forever! No one must ever use it. 3The ruler of Israel may come here to eat a sacrificial meal that has been offered to me, but he must use only the entrance room of this gate.

People Who Are Not Allowed in the Temple

4Then the man took me through the north gate to the front of the temple. I saw that the brightness of the LORD's glory had filled the temple, and I immediately bowed with my face to the ground.

5The LORD said:

Ezekiel, son of man, I am going to give you the laws for my temple. So pay attention and listen carefully to what kind of people are allowed to come in the temple, and what kind are not. 6Tell those rebellious people of Israel:

I, the LORD God, command you to stop your evil ways! 7My temple has been disgraced, because you have let godless, stubborn foreigners come here when sacrifices are being offered to me. You have sinned and have broken our solemn agreement. 8Instead of following the proper ways to worship me, you have put foreigners in charge of worship at my temple.

9And so I, the LORD God, say that no godless foreigner who disobeys me will be allowed in my temple. This includes any foreigner living in Israel.

The Levites Are Punished

The LORD said:

10Some of the Levites turned their backs on me and joined the other people of Israel in worshiping idols. So these Levites must be punished! 11They will still be allowed to serve me as temple workers by guarding the gates and by killing the animals to be sacrificed and by helping the worshipers. 12But because these Levites served the people of Israel when they worshiped idols, I, the LORD God, promise that the Levites will be punished. They did not stop the Israelites from sinning, 13and now I will no longer let the Levites serve as my priests or come near anything sacred to me. They must suffer shame and disgrace for their disgusting sins. 14They will be responsible for all the hard work that must be done in the temple.

Rules for Priests

The LORD said:

15The priests of the Levi tribe who are descendants of Zadok the priest were faithful to me, even when the rest of the Israelites turned away. And so, these priests will continue to serve as my priests and to offer the fat and the blood of sacrifices. 16They will come into my temple, where they will offer sacrifices at my altar and lead others in worship.

17When they come to the inner courtyard, they must wear their linen priestly clothes. My priests must never wear anything made of wool when they are on duty in this courtyard or in the temple. 18Even their turbans and underwear must be made of linen to keep my priests from sweating when they work. 19And before they leave to join the other people in the outer courtyard, they must take off their priestly clothes, then place them in the sacred rooms and put on their regular clothes.[v] That way, no one

[r]**43.22** *goat*: Hebrew "male goat." [s]**43.24** *The priests will sprinkle salt on them*: See Leviticus 2.13. [t]**43.24** *sacrifices to please me*: See the note at 40.38, 39.
[u]**43.27** *sacrifices to ask my blessing*: These sacrifices have traditionally been called "peace offerings" or "offerings of well-being." A main purpose was to ask for the LORD's blessing, and so in the CEV they are sometimes called "sacrifices to ask the LORD's blessing."
[v]**44.19** *take off their priestly clothes . . . put on their regular clothes*: See 42.14.

will touch their sacred clothes and be
harmed.[w]
20 Priests must never shave their heads
when they are mourning. But they must
keep their hair properly trimmed and
not let it grow too long. 21 They must not
drink wine before going to the inner
courtyard.
22 A priest must not marry a divorced
woman; he can marry only a virgin
from Israel or the widow of another
priest.
23 Priests must teach my people the
difference between what is sacred and
what is ordinary, and between what is
clean and what is unclean. 24 They will
make decisions in difficult legal cases,
according to my own laws. They must
also observe the religious festivals my
Law requires and must always respect
the Sabbath.
25 Touching a dead body will make a
person unclean. So a priest must not go
near a dead body, unless it is one of his
parents or children, or his brother or
unmarried sister. 26 If a priest touches a
dead body, he is unclean and must go
through a ceremony to make himself
clean. Then seven days later, 27 he must
go to the inner courtyard of the temple
and offer a sacrifice for sin. After that,
he may once again serve as my priest. I,
the LORD God, have spoken.
28 I myself will provide for my priests,
and so they won't receive any land of
their own. 29 Instead, they will receive
part of the grain sacrifices, as well as
part of the sacrifices for sin and sacrifices to make things right. They will also
be given everything in Israel that has
been completely dedicated to me.[x] 30 The
first part of every harvest will belong to
the priests. They will also receive part of
all special gifts and offerings the Israelites bring to me. And whenever any
of my people bake bread, they will give
their first loaf as an offering to the
priests, and I will bless the homes of the
people when they do this.
31 Priests must not eat any bird or animal that dies a natural death or that has
been killed by a wild animal.

The LORD's Sacred Land

The LORD said:
45 When the land of Israel is divided
among the twelve tribes, you
must set aside an area that will belong
to me. This sacred area will be eight
miles long and six[y] miles wide. 2 The
temple will be on a piece of land eight
hundred forty feet square, and the temple will be completely surrounded by an
open space eighty-four feet wide.
3-4 I will give half of my sacred land, a
section eight miles long and three miles
wide, to the priests who serve in the
temple. Their houses will be in this half,
as well as my temple, which is the most
sacred place of all.
5 I will give the other half of my land
to the Levites who work in my temple,
and the towns[z] where they will live will
be there.
6 Next to my sacred land will be an
area eight miles long and two miles
wide. This will belong to the people of
Israel and will include the city of
Jerusalem.

Land for Israel's Ruler

The LORD said:
7-8 The regions west and east of my sacred land and the city of Jerusalem will
belong to the ruler of Israel. He will be
given the region between the western
edge of my land and the Mediterranean
Sea, and between the eastern edge of
my land and the Jordan River. This will
mean that the length of his property will
be the same as the sections of land
given to the tribes.
This property will belong to every
ruler of Israel, so they will always be
fair to my people and will let them live
peacefully in the land given to their
tribes.

Israel's Rulers Must Be Honest

9 The LORD God said:
You leaders of Israel have robbed and
cheated my people long enough! I want
you to stop sinning and start doing what
is right and fair. You must never again
force my people off their own land. I,
the LORD, have spoken.
10 So from now on, you must use honest weights and measures. 11 The *ephah*
will be the standard dry measure, and
the *bath* will be the standard liquid
measure. Their size will be based on the
homer, which will equal ten *ephahs* or
ten *baths*.[a]
12 The standard unit of weight will be
the *shekel*.[b] One *shekel* will equal twen-

[w] **44.19** *no one will touch . . . and be harmed*: Ordinary people were forbidden to touch anything that was sacred. If they did, it was believed they would somehow be harmed. [x] **44.29** *that has been completely dedicated to me*: This translates a Hebrew word that describes property and things that were taken away from humans and given to God. In the early history of Israel, such things often had to be destroyed (see Joshua 6.15-19). [y] **45.1** *six*: One ancient translation; Hebrew "three." [z] **45.5** *the towns*: One ancient translation; Hebrew "the twenty rooms." [a] **45.11** *the homer . . . ten ephahs . . . ten baths*: A *homer* was either a dry or a liquid measure and equaled about five bushels or fifty-five gallons; an *ephah* would be about a half bushel, and a *bath* would be about five and a half gallons. [b] **45.12** *the shekel*: The *shekel* was about four-tenths of an ounce.

ty *gerahs*, and sixty *shekels* will equal one
mina.
13 Leaders of Israel, the people must
bring you one sixtieth of their grain harvests as offerings to me. 14 They will also
bring one percent of their olive oil.
These things will be measured according to the *bath*, and ten *baths* is the
same as one *homer* or one *cor*. 15 Finally,
they must bring one sheep out of every
two hundred from their flocks.
These offerings will be used as grain
sacrifices, as well as sacrifices to please
me[c] and those to ask my blessing.[d] I,
the LORD, will be pleased with these sacrifices and will forgive the sins of my
people.
16 The people of Israel will bring you
these offerings. 17 But during New Moon
Festivals, Sabbath celebrations, and
other religious feasts, you leaders
will be responsible for providing animals for the sacrifices, as well as the
grain and wine. All these will be used
for the sacrifices for sin, the grain sacrifices, the sacrifices to please me, and
those to ask my blessing. I will be
pleased and will forgive the sins of my
people.

The Festivals

(Exodus 12.1-20; Leviticus 23.33-43)

18 The LORD God said:
On the first day of the first month,[e] a
young bull that has nothing wrong with
it must be offered as a sacrifice to purify
the temple. 19 The priest will take some
blood from this sacrifice and smear it on
the doorposts of the temple, as well as
on the four corners of the altar and on
the doorposts of the gates that lead into
the inner courtyard.
20 The same ceremony must also be
done on the seventh day of the month,
so that anyone who sins accidentally or
without knowing it will be forgiven, and
so that my temple will remain holy.
21 Beginning on the fourteenth day of
the first month, and continuing for
seven days, everyone will celebrate
Passover and eat bread made without
yeast. 22 On the first day, the ruler will
bring a bull to offer as a sacrifice for his
sins and for the sins of the people.
23 Each day of the festival he is to bring
seven bulls and seven rams as sacrifices
to please me,[f] and he must bring a goat[g]
as a sacrifice for sin. These animals
must have nothing wrong with them.
24 He will also provide twenty pounds of
grain and four quarts of olive oil to be
offered with each bull and each ram.
25 The Festival of Shelters will begin
on the fifteenth day of the seventh
month[h] and will continue for seven
days. On each day of this festival, the
ruler will provide the same number of
animals that he did each day during
Passover, as well as the same amount of
grain and olive oil for the sacrifices.

Various Laws for the Ruler and the People

46 The LORD said:
The east gate of the inner courtyard must remain closed during the six
working days of each week. But on the
Sabbath and on the first day of the
month, this gate will be opened. 2 Israel's
ruler will go from the outer courtyard
into the entrance room of this gate and
stand in the doorway while the priest offers sacrifices to ask my blessing[i] and
sacrifices to please me.[j] The ruler will
bow with his face to the ground to show
that he has worshiped me. Then he will
leave, and the gate will remain open until evening.
3 Each Sabbath and on the first day of
each month, the people of Israel must
also come to the east gate and worship
me. 4 On the Sabbath, the ruler will bring
six lambs and one ram to be offered as
sacrifices to please me. There must be
nothing wrong with any of these animals. 5 With the ram, he is to offer
twenty pounds of grain, and with each
of the lambs, he can offer as much as he
wants. He must also offer four quarts of
olive oil with every twenty pounds of
grain.
6 The ruler is to bring six lambs, a bull,
and a ram to be offered as sacrifices at
the New Moon Festival. There must be
nothing wrong with any of these animals. 7 With the bull and the ram, he is
to offer twenty pounds of grain, and
with each of the lambs, he can offer as
much as he wants. He must also offer
four quarts of olive oil with every
twenty pounds of grain. 8 The ruler must
come through the entrance room of the
east gate and leave the same way.
9 When my people come to worship
me during any festival, they must always leave by the opposite gate from
which they came: Those who come in
the north gate must leave by the south
gate, and those who come in the south
gate must leave by the north gate.

[c] **45.15** *sacrifices to please me*: See the note at 40.38, 39. [d] **45.15** *sacrifices . . . to ask my blessing*: See the note at 43.27. [e] **45.18** *the first month*: Abib (also called Nisan), the first month of the Hebrew calendar, from about mid-March to mid-April. [f] **45.23** *sacrifices to please me*: See the note at 40.38,39. [g] **45.23** *goat*: See the note at 43.22. [h] **45.25** *seventh month*: Tishri (also called Ethanim), the seventh month of the Hebrew calendar, from about mid-September to mid-October. [i] **46.2** *sacrifices to ask my blessing*: See the note at 43.27. [j] **46.2** *sacrifices to please me*: See the note at 40.38, 39.

10Their ruler will come in at the same time they do and leave at the same time they leave.

11At all other festivals and celebrations, twenty pounds of grain will be offered with a bull, and twenty pounds will be offered with a ram. The worshipers can offer as much grain as they want with each lamb. Four quarts of olive oil must be offered with every twenty pounds of grain.

12If the ruler voluntarily offers a sacrifice to please me or to ask my blessing, the east gate of the inner courtyard will be opened for him. He will offer his sacrifices just as he does on each Sabbath; then he will leave, and the gate will be closed.

13Each morning a year-old lamb that has nothing wrong with it must be offered as a sacrifice to please me. 14Along with it, three pounds of fine flour mixed with a quart of olive oil must be offered as a grain sacrifice. This law will never change—15the lamb, the flour, and the olive oil will be offered to me every morning for all time.

Laws about the Ruler's Land

16The LORD God said:

If the ruler of Israel gives some of his land to one of his children, it will belong to the ruler's child as part of the family property. 17But if the ruler gives some of his land to one of his servants, the land will belong to the servant until the Year of Celebration, when it will be returned to the ruler.[k] Only the ruler's children can keep what is given to them.

18The ruler must never abuse my people by taking land from them. Any land he gives his children must already belong to him.

The Sacred Kitchens

19The man who was showing me the temple[l] then took me back to the inner courtyard. We walked to the south side of the courtyard and stopped at the door to the sacred rooms that belonged to the priests. He showed me more rooms at the western edge of the courtyard 20and said, "These are the kitchens where the priests must boil the meat to be offered as sacrifices to make things right[m] and as sacrifices for sin.[n] They will also bake the grain for sacrifices in these kitchens. That way, these sacred offerings won't have to be carried through the outer courtyard, where someone could accidentally touch them and be harmed."[o]

21We went back to the outer courtyard and walked past the four corners. 22At each corner I saw a smaller courtyard, sixty-eight feet long and fifty feet wide. 23Around the inside of these smaller courtyards was a low wall of stones, and against the wall were places to build fires.[p] 24The man said, "These are the kitchens where the temple workers will boil the meat that worshipers offer as sacrifices."

The Stream Flowing from the Temple

47 The man took me back to the temple, where I saw a stream flowing from under the entrance. It began in the south part of the temple, where it ran past the altar and continued east through the courtyard.

2We walked out of the temple area through the north gate and went around to the east gate. I saw the small stream of water flowing east from the south side of the gate.

3The man walked east, then took out his measuring stick and measured five hundred sixty yards downstream. He told me to wade through the stream there, and the water came up to my ankles. 4Then he measured another five hundred sixty yards downstream, and told me to wade through it there. The water came up to my knees. Another five hundred sixty yards downstream the water came up to my waist. 5Another five hundred sixty yards downstream, the stream had become a river that could be crossed only by swimming. 6The man said, "Ezekiel, son of man, pay attention to what you've seen."

We walked to the riverbank, 7where I saw dozens of trees on each side. 8The man said:

This water flows eastward to the Jordan River valley and empties into the Dead Sea, where it turns the salt water into fresh water. 9Wherever this water flows, there will be all kinds of animals and fish, because it will bring life and fresh water to the Dead Sea. 10From En-Gedi to Eneglaim, people will fish in the sea and dry their nets along the coast. There will be as many kinds of fish in the Dead Sea as there are in the Mediterranean Sea. 11But the marshes along the shore will remain salty, so that people can use the salt from them.

[k]**46.17** *the Year of Celebration . . . to the ruler*: This was a sacred year for Israel, traditionally called the "Year of Jubilee." During this year, all property had to go back to its original owner (see Leviticus 25.8-34). [l]**46.19** *The man . . . temple*: See 40.3. [m]**46.20** *sacrifices to make things right*: See the note at 40.38, 39. [n]**46.20** *sacrifices for sin*: See the note at 40.38, 39. [o]**46.20** *someone . . . touch them and be harmed*: See the note at 44.19. [p]**46.23** *fires*: One possible meaning for the difficult Hebrew text of verse 23.

[12]Fruit trees will grow all along
this river and produce fresh fruit
every month. The leaves will never
dry out, because they will always
have water from the stream that
flows from the temple, and they will
be used for healing people.

The Borders of the Land

[13-14]The LORD God said to the people
of Israel:
When the land is divided among the
twelve tribes of Israel, the Joseph tribe[q]
will receive two shares. Divide the land
equally, because I promised your ancestors that this land would someday belong to their descendants. These are the
borders of the land:
[15]The northern border will begin at
the Mediterranean Sea, then continue
eastward to Hethlon, to Lebo-Hamath,
then across to Zedad, [16]Berothah,[r] and
Sibraim, which is on the border between
the two kingdoms of Damascus and
Hamath. The border will end at Hazer-
Hatticon, which is on the border of Hauran. [17]So the northern border will run
between the Mediterranean Sea and
Hazar-Enon, which is on the border between Damascus and Hamath.[s]
[18]The eastern border will begin on the
border between the two kingdoms of
Hauran and Damascus. It will run south
along the Jordan River, which separates
the territories of Gilead and Israel, and
it will end at the Dead Sea near the
town of Tamar.[t]
[19]The southern border will begin at
Tamar, then run southwest to the
springs near Meribath-Kadesh. It will
continue along the Egyptian Gorge and
will end at the Mediterranean Sea.
[20]The western border will run north
along the Mediterranean Sea to a point
just west of Lebo-Hamath.
[21]That is the land to be divided among
the tribes of Israel. [22]It will belong to the
Israelites and to any foreigners living
among them whose children were born
in Israel. These foreigners must be
treated like any other Israelite citizen,
and they will receive [23]a share of the
land given to the tribe where they live. I,
the LORD God, have spoken.

The Division of Land among Tribes in the North

The LORD said:
48 [1-7]Each tribe will receive a section
of land that runs from the eastern
border of Israel west to the Mediterranean Sea. The northern border of Israel will run along the towns of Hethlon
and Lebo-Hamath, and will end at
Hazar-Enon, which is on the border between the kingdoms of Damascus and
Hamath. The tribes will receive their
share of land in the following order,
from north to south: Dan, Asher, Naphtali, Manasseh, Ephraim, Reuben, and
Judah.

The Special Section of Land

The LORD said:
[8]South of Judah's territory will be a
special section of land. Its length will be
eight miles, and its width will run from
the eastern border of Israel west to the
Mediterranean Sea. My temple will be
located in this section of land.
[9]An area in the center of this land will
belong to me. It will be eight miles long
and six[u] miles wide.
[10]I, the LORD, will give half of my sacred land to the priests. Their share will
be eight miles long and three miles
wide, and my temple will be right in the
middle. [11]Only priests who are descendants of Zadok will receive a share of
this sacred land, because they remained
faithful to me when the Levites and the
rest of the Israelites started sinning.
[12]The land belonging to the priests will
be the most sacred area and will lie
south of the area that belongs to the
Levites.
[13]I will give the other half of my sacred land to the Levites. Their share will
also be eight miles long and three miles
wide, [14]and they must never sell or trade
any of this land—it is the best land and
belongs to me.
[15]South of my sacred land will be a
section eight miles long and two miles
wide. It will not be sacred, but will belong to the people of Israel and will include the city of Jerusalem, together
with its houses and pastureland. [16]The
city will be a square: Each side will be a
mile and a half long, [17]and an open area
four hundred twenty feet wide will surround the city. [18]The land on the east
and west sides of the city limits will be
farmland for the people of Jerusalem;
both sections will be three miles long
and two miles wide. [19]People from the
city will farm the land, no matter which
tribe they belong to.
[20]And so the center of this special section of land will be for my sacred land,
as well as for the city and its property.

[q]**47.13,14** *the Joseph tribe*: That is, the two tribes of Manasseh and Ephraim, Joseph's sons.
[r]**47.15,16** *to Lebo-Hamath, then across to Zedad,* [16]Berothah: One ancient translation; Hebrew "to Lebo-Zedad, [16]then across to Hamath, Berothah." [s]**47.17** *which is on the border between Damascus and Hamath*: One possible meaning for the difficult Hebrew text.
[t]**47.18** *near the town of Tamar*: One possible meaning for the difficult Hebrew text.
[u]**48.9** *six*: The Hebrew text has "three" (but see 45.1 and the note there).

The land will be a square, eight miles on
each side.
[21]The regions east and west of this
square of land will belong to the ruler of
Israel. His property will run east to the
Jordan River and west to the Mediterranean Sea. In the very center of his
property will be my sacred land, as well
as the temple, [22]together with the share
belonging to the Levites and the city of
Jerusalem. The northern border of the
ruler's property will be the land that belongs to Judah, and the southern border
will be the land that belongs to Benjamin.

The Division of Land among Tribes in the South

The LORD God said:
[23-27]South of this special section will
be the land that belongs to the rest of Israel's tribes. Each tribe will receive a
section of land that runs from the eastern border of Israel west to the Mediterranean Sea. The tribes will receive their
share of land in the following order,
from north to south: Benjamin, Simeon,
Issachar, Zebulun, and Gad.
[28]Gad's southern border is also
the southern border of Israel. It will begin at the town of Tamar, then run
southwest to the springs near Meribath-
Kadesh. It will continue along the
Egyptian Gorge and end at the Mediterranean Sea.
[29]That's how the land of Israel will be
divided among the twelve tribes. I, the
LORD God, have spoken.

The Gates of Jerusalem

The LORD said:
[30-34]The city of Jerusalem will have
twelve gates, three on each of the four
sides of the city wall. These gates will be
named after the twelve tribes of Israel.
The gates of Reuben, Judah, and Levi
will be in the north; Joseph, Benjamin,
and Dan will be in the east; Simeon, Issachar, and Zebulun will be in the
south; Gad, Asher, and Naphtali will be
in the west. Each side of the city wall
will be a mile and a half long, [35]and so
the total length of the wall will be six
miles. The new name of the city will be
"The-LORD-Is-Here!"

DANIEL

ABOUT THIS BOOK

As a young man, Daniel had been taken prisoner by the Babylonian army when Jerusalem was captured. The first half of this book (1–6) tells how he and three of his friends from Judah became important officials in the government at Babylon. They remained completely faithful to the Lord, even when it meant risking their lives. This half of the book concludes with Daniel serving in the government of the Medo-Persian empire after it had conquered Babylonia.

In the second half of the book (7–12) Daniel reports several visions that he had and how the meanings of those visions were explained to him by angels.

This book shows that God is in control of human events. He guides empires into power, but later he lets them be conquered by other empires. God also cares for individuals who are faithful to him, and someday he will finally bring justice to the world and provide victory for his people. Here is how Daniel spoke about this future time of victory:

I saw what looked like
a son of man
coming with the clouds of heaven,
and he was presented
to the Eternal God.
He was crowned king
and given power and glory,
so that all people
of every nation and race
would serve him.
He will rule forever,
and his kingdom is eternal,
never to be destroyed.
(7.13, 14)

A QUICK LOOK AT THIS BOOK

Daniel and His Three Friends (1.1-21)
King Nebuchadnezzar's Dream (2.1-49)
God Rescues Shadrach, Meshach, and Abednego (3.1-30)
Nebuchadnezzar Loses His Kingdom for Seven Years (4.1-37)
King Belshazzar and the Writing on the Wall (5.1-31)
God Rescues Daniel from the Pit of Lions (6.1-28)
Daniel's Vision of Four Beasts (7.1-28)
Daniel's Vision of a Ram and a Goat (8.1-27)
Daniel Prays for His People (9.1-27)
Daniel Has a Vision beside the Tigris River (10.1—12.13)

Daniel and His Friends

1 In the third year that Jehoiakim was
king of Judah,[a] King Nebuchadnezzar of Babylonia attacked Jerusalem.
2The Lord let Nebuchadnezzar capture
Jehoiakim and take away some of the
things used in God's temple. And when
the king returned to Babylonia,[b] he put
these things in the temple of his own
god.
3One day the king ordered Ashpenaz,
his highest palace official, to choose
some young men from the royal family
of Judah and from other leading
Jewish families. 4The king said, "They
must be healthy, handsome, smart,
wise, educated, and fit to serve in
the royal palace. Teach them how
to speak and write our language 5and
give them the same food and wine that I
am served. Train them for three years,
and then they can become court officials."
6Four of the young Jews chosen were
Daniel, Hananiah, Mishael, and Azariah, all from the tribe of Judah. 7But the
king's chief official gave them Babylonian names: Daniel became Belteshazzar,
Hananiah became Shadrach, Mishael
became Meshach, and Azariah became
Abednego.
8Daniel made up his mind to eat and
drink only what God had approved
for his people to eat. And he asked
the king's chief official for permission
not to eat the food and wine served in
the royal palace. 9God had made the
official friendly and kind to Daniel.
10But the man still told him, "The
king has decided what you must eat
and drink. And I am afraid he will kill
me, if you eat something else and end
up looking worse than the other young
men."
11The king's official had put a guard
in charge of Daniel and his three
friends. So Daniel said to the guard,
12"For the next ten days, let us have only
vegetables and water at mealtime.
13When the ten days are up, compare
how we look with the other young men,
and decide what to do with us." 14The
guard agreed to do what Daniel had
asked.
15Ten days later, Daniel and his
friends looked healthier and better than
the young men who had been served
food from the royal palace. 16After this,
the guard let them eat vegetables instead of the rich food and wine.
17God made the four young men
smart and wise. They read a lot of
books and became well educated.
Daniel could also tell the meaning of
dreams and visions.
18At the end of the three-year period
set by King Nebuchadnezzar, his
chief palace official brought all
the young men to him. 19The king inter-
viewed them and discovered that
none of the others were as outstanding
as Daniel, Hananiah, Mishael, and
Azariah. So they were given positions
in the royal court. 20From then on,
whenever the king asked for advice,
he found their wisdom was ten times
better than that of any of his other
advisors and magicians. 21Daniel
served there until the first year of King
Cyrus.[c]

Nebuchadnezzar's Dream

2 During the second year that Nebuchadnezzar was king, he had such
horrible nightmares that he could not
sleep. 2So he called in his counselors,
advisors, magicians, and wise men, 3and
said, "I am disturbed by a dream that I
don't understand, and I want you to explain it."
4They answered in Aramaic,[d] "Your
Majesty, we hope you live forever! We
are your servants. Please tell us your
dream, and we will explain what it
means."
5But the king replied, "No! I have
made up my mind. If you don't tell me
both the dream and its meaning, you
will be chopped to pieces and your
houses will be torn down. 6However,
if you do tell me both the dream and
its meaning, you will be greatly rewarded and highly honored. Now tell
me the dream and explain what it
means."
7"Your Majesty," they said, "if you will
only tell us your dream, we will interpret it for you."
8The king replied, "You're just stalling
for time, 9because you know what's going to happen if you don't come up with
the answer. You've decided to make up a
bunch of lies, hoping I might change my
mind. Now tell me the dream, and that
will prove that you can interpret it."
10His advisors explained, "Your
Majesty, you are demanding the impossible! No king, not even the most famous and powerful, has ever ordered
his advisors, magicians, or wise men to
do such a thing. 11It can't be done, except by the gods, and they don't live
here on earth."
12-13This made the king so angry that
he gave orders for every wise man in

[a] **1.1** *Jehoiakim . . . king of Judah*: Ruled 609-598 B.C. [b] **1.2** *Babylonia*: The Hebrew text has "Shinar," another name for Babylonia. [c] **1.21** *first year of King Cyrus*: 539 B.C.
[d] **2.4** *Aramaic*: Chapter 2.4—7.28 is written in Aramaic, a language closely related to Hebrew.

Babylonia to be put to death, including Daniel and his three friends.

God Tells Nebuchadnezzar's Dream to Daniel

14Arioch was the king's official in charge of putting the wise men to death. He was on his way to have it done, when Daniel very wisely went to him 15and asked, "Why did the king give such cruel[e] orders?" After Arioch explained what had happened, 16Daniel rushed off and said to the king, "If you will just give me some time, I'll explain your dream."

17Daniel returned home and told his three friends. 18Then he said, "Pray that the God who rules from heaven will be merciful and explain this mystery, so that we and the others won't be put to death." 19In a vision one night, Daniel was shown the dream and its meaning. Then he praised the God who rules from heaven:

20 "Our God, your name
will be praised
forever and forever.
You are all-powerful,
and you know everything.
21 You control human events—
you give rulers their power
and take it away,
and you are the source
of wisdom and knowledge.

22 "You explain deep mysteries,
because even the dark
is light to you.
23 You are the God
who was worshiped
by my ancestors.
Now I thank you and praise you
for making me wise
and telling me the king's dream,
together with its meaning."

Daniel Interprets the Dream

24Daniel went back to Arioch, the official in charge of executing the wise men. Daniel said, "Don't kill those men! Take me to the king, and I will explain the meaning of his dream."

25Arioch rushed Daniel to the king and announced, "Your Majesty, I have found out that one of the men brought here from Judah can explain your dream."

26The king asked Daniel,[f] "Can you tell me my dream and what it means?"

27Daniel answered:

Your Majesty, not even the smartest person in all the world can
do what you are demanding. 28-29But
the God who rules from heaven can
explain mysteries. And while you
were sleeping, he showed you what
will happen in the future. 30However,
you must realize that these mysteries weren't explained to me because I am smarter than everyone else. Instead, it was done so that you would understand what you have seen.

31Your Majesty, what you saw
standing in front of you was a huge and terrifying statue, shining
brightly. 32Its head was made of
gold, its chest and arms were silver, and from its waist down to its knees,
it was bronze. 33From there to its ankles it was iron, and its feet were a mixture of iron and clay.

34As you watched, a stone was cut from a mountain—but not by human hands. The stone struck the feet, completely shattering the iron and
clay. 35Then the iron, the clay, the bronze, the silver, and the gold were crushed and blown away without a trace, like husks of wheat at threshing time. But the stone became a tremendous mountain that covered the entire earth.

36That was the dream, and now I'll
tell you what it means. 37Your
Majesty, you are the greatest of kings, and God has highly honored
you with power 38over all humans,
animals, and birds. You are the head
of gold. 39After you are gone, another kingdom will rule, but it won't be as strong. Then it will be followed by a kingdom of bronze that will
rule the whole world. 40Next, a kingdom of iron will come to power, crushing and shattering everything.[g]

41-42This fourth kingdom will be divided—it will be both strong and brittle, just as you saw that the feet and toes were a mixture of iron and
clay. 43This kingdom will be the result of a marriage between kingdoms, but it will crumble, just as iron and clay don't stick together.

44-45During the time of those kings, the God who rules from heaven will set up an eternal kingdom that will never fall. It will be like the stone that was cut from the mountain, but not by human hands—the stone that crushed the iron, bronze, clay, silver, and gold. Your Majesty, in your dream the great God has told you what is going to happen, and you can trust this interpretation.

[e]2.15 *cruel*: Or "urgent." [f]2.26 *Daniel*: Aramaic "Daniel whose name was Belteshazzar" (see 1.7). [g]2.40 *crushing . . . everything*: Three ancient translations; Aramaic adds "and like iron crushing."

Daniel Is Promoted

46 King Nebuchadnezzar bowed low to
the ground and worshiped Daniel. Then
he gave orders for incense to be burned
and a sacrifice of grain to be offered in
honor of Daniel. 47 The king said, "Now I
know that your God is above all other
gods and kings, because he gave you the
power to explain this mystery." 48 The
king then presented Daniel with a lot of
gifts; he promoted him to governor of
Babylon Province and put him in charge
of the other wise men. 49 At Daniel's request, the king appointed Shadrach, Meshach, and Abednego to high positions
in Babylon Province, and he let Daniel
stay on as a palace official.

King Nebuchadnezzar's Gold Statue

3 King Nebuchadnezzar ordered a
gold statue to be built ninety feet
high and nine feet wide. He had it set up
in Dura Valley near the city of Babylon,
2 and he commanded his governors, advisors, treasurers, judges, and his other
officials to come from everywhere in his
kingdom to the dedication of the statue.
3 So all of them came and stood in front
of it.
4 Then an official stood up and announced:

> People of every nation and race,
> now listen to the king's command!
> 5 Trumpets, flutes, harps, and all
> other kinds of musical instruments
> will soon start playing. When you
> hear the music, you must bow down
> and worship the statue that King
> Nebuchadnezzar has set up. 6 Any-
> one who refuses will at once be
> thrown into a flaming furnace.

7 As soon as the people heard the music, they bowed down and worshiped
the gold statue that the king had set up.
8 Some Babylonians used this as a
chance to accuse the Jews to King Nebuchadnezzar. 9 They said, "Your Majesty,
we hope you live forever! 10 You commanded everyone to bow down and
worship the gold statue when the music
played. 11 And you said that anyone who
did not bow down and worship it would
be thrown into a flaming furnace. 12 Sir,
you appointed three men to high positions in Babylon Province, but they have
disobeyed you. Those Jews, Shadrach,
Meshach, and Abednego, refuse to worship your gods and the statue you have
set up."
13 King Nebuchadnezzar was furious.
So he sent for the three young men and
said, 14 "I hear that you refuse to worship
my gods and the gold statue I have set
up. 15 Now I am going to give you one
more chance. If you bow down and worship the statue when you hear the music, everything will be all right. But if
you don't, you will at once be thrown
into a flaming furnace. No god can save
you from me."
16 The three men replied, "Your
Majesty, we don't need to defend ourselves. 17 The God we worship can save
us from you and your flaming furnace.
18 But even if he doesn't, we still won't
worship your gods and the gold statue
you have set up."
19 Nebuchadnezzar's face twisted with
anger at the three men. And he ordered
the furnace to be heated seven times
hotter than usual. 20 Next, he commanded some of his strongest soldiers
to tie up the men and throw them into
the flaming furnace. 21-23 The king
wanted it done at that very moment. So
the soldiers tied up Shadrach, Meshach,
and Abednego and threw them into the
flaming furnace with all of their clothes
still on, including their turbans. The fire
was so hot that flames leaped out and
killed the soldiers.
24 Suddenly the king jumped up and
shouted, "Weren't only three men tied
up and thrown into the fire?"
"Yes, Your Majesty," the people answered.
25 "But I see four men walking around
in the fire," the king replied. "None of
them is tied up or harmed, and the
fourth one looks like a god."[h]
26 Nebuchadnezzar went closer to the
flaming furnace and said to the three
young men, "You servants of the Most
High God, come out at once!"
They came out, 27 and the king's high
officials, governors, and advisors all
crowded around them. The men were
not burned, their hair wasn't scorched,
and their clothes didn't even smell like
smoke. 28 King Nebuchadnezzar said:

> Praise their God for sending an
> angel to rescue his servants! They
> trusted their God and refused to
> obey my commands. Yes, they chose
> to die rather than to worship or
> serve any god except their own.
> 29 And I won't allow people of any
> nation or race to say anything
> against their God. Anyone who does
> will be chopped up and their houses
> will be torn down, because no other
> god has such great power to save.

30 After this happened, the king appointed Shadrach, Meshach, and Abednego to even higher positions in Babylon Province.

King Nebuchadnezzar's Letter about His Second Dream

4 King Nebuchadnezzar sent the following letter to the people of all nations and races on the earth:

[h] **3.25** *a god*: Aramaic, "a son of the gods."

Greetings to all of you!
2 I am glad to tell about
the wonderful miracles
God Most High
has done for me.
3 His miracles are mighty
and marvelous.
He will rule forever,
and his kingdom
will never end.

4I was enjoying a time of peace and
prosperity, 5when suddenly I had some
horrifying dreams and visions. 6Then I
commanded every wise man in Babylonia to appear in my court, so they could
explain the meaning of my dream. 7After they arrived, I told them my dream,
but they were not able to say what it
meant. 8Finally, a young man named
Daniel came in, and I told him the
dream. The holy gods had given him
special powers, and I had renamed him
Belteshazzar after my own god.

9I said, "Belteshazzar, not only are
you the wisest of all advisors and counselors, but the holy gods have given you
special powers to solve the most difficult mysteries. So listen to what I
dreamed and tell me what it means:

10 In my sleep I saw
a very tall tree
in the center of the world.
11 It grew stronger and higher,
until it reached to heaven
and could be seen
from anywhere on earth.
12 It was covered with leaves
and heavy with fruit—
enough for all nations.
Wild animals enjoyed its shade,
birds nested in its branches,
and all creatures on earth
lived on its fruit.

13"While I was in bed, having this vision, a holy angel[i] came down from
heaven 14and shouted:

'Chop down the tree
and cut off its branches;
strip off its leaves
and scatter its fruit.
Make the animals leave its shade
and send the birds flying
from its branches.
15 But leave its stump and roots
in the ground,
surrounded by grass
and held by chains
of iron and bronze.

'Make sure that this ruler
lives like the animals
out in the open fields,
unprotected from the dew.
16 Give him the mind
of a wild animal
for seven long years.[j]
17 This punishment is given
at the command
of the holy angels.[k]
It will show to all who live
that God Most High
controls all kingdoms
and chooses for their rulers
persons of humble birth.'

18"Daniel,[l] that was the dream that
none of the wise men in my kingdom
were able to understand. But I am sure
that you will understand what it means,
because the holy gods have given you
some special powers."

19For a while, Daniel[l] was terribly
confused and worried by what he was
thinking. But I said, "Don't be bothered
either by the dream or by what it
means."

Daniel replied:

Your Majesty, I wish the dream
had been against your enemies.
20You saw a tree that grew so big
and strong that it reached up to
heaven and could be seen from anywhere on earth. 21Its leaves were
beautiful, and it produced enough
fruit for all living creatures; animals
lived in its shade, and birds nested
in its branches. 22Your Majesty, that
tree is you. Your glorious reputation
has reached heaven, and your kingdom covers the earth.

23Then you saw a holy angel[m]
come down from heaven and say,
"Chop down the tree and destroy it!
But leave its stump and roots in the
ground, fastened there by a chain of
iron and bronze. Let it stay for seven
years[n] out in the field with the wild
animals, unprotected from the dew."

24Your Majesty, God Most High
has sent you this message, and it
means 25that you will be forced to
live with the wild animals, far away
from humans. You will eat grass like
a wild animal and live outdoors for
seven years,[n] until you learn that
God Most High controls all earthly
kingdoms and chooses their rulers.
26But he gave orders not to disturb
the stump and roots. This is to show
that you will be king once again, after you learn that the God who rules
from heaven is in control. 27Your
Majesty, please be willing to do what
I say. Turn from your sins and start
living right; have mercy on those

[i]**4.13** *angel*: The Aramaic text has "watcher," which may be some special class of angel.
[j]**4.16** *long years*: Aramaic "times." [k]**4.17** *angels*: See the note at 4.13. [l]**4.18** *Daniel*: See the note at 2.26. [l]**4.19** *Daniel*: See the note at 2.26. [m]**4.23** *angel*: See the note at 4.13.
[n]**4.23** *years*: Aramaic "times." [n]**4.25** *years*: Aramaic "times."

who are mistreated. Then all will go
well with you for a long time.

The Rest of Nebuchadnezzar's Letter about His Second Dream

28-30 About twelve months later, I was
walking on the flat roof of my royal
palace and admiring the beautiful city
of Babylon, when these things started
happening to me. I was saying to myself, "Just look at this wonderful capital
city that I have built by my own power
and for my own glory!"
31 But before I could finish speaking, a
voice from heaven interrupted:

King Nebuchadnezzar, this kingdom is no longer yours. 32 You will be
forced to live with the wild animals,
away from people. For seven years[n]
you will eat grass, as though you
were an ox, until you learn that God
Most High is in control of all earthly
kingdoms and that he is the one who
chooses their rulers.

33 This was no sooner said than done—
I was forced to live like a wild animal; I
ate grass and was unprotected from the
dew. As time went by, my hair grew
longer than eagle feathers, and my fin-
gernails looked like the claws of a bird.
34 Finally, I prayed to God in heaven,
and my mind was healed. Then I said:

"I praise and honor
God Most High.
He lives forever,
and his kingdom
will never end.
35 To him the nations
are far less than nothing;
God controls the stars in the sky
and everyone on this earth.
When God does something,
we cannot change it
or even ask why."

36 At that time my mind was healed,
and once again I became the ruler of my
glorious kingdom. My advisors and officials returned to me, and I had greater
power than ever before. 37 That's why I
say:

"Praise and honor the King
who rules from heaven!
Everything he does
is honest and fair,
and he can shatter the power
of those who are proud."

King Belshazzar's Banquet

5 One evening, King Belshazzar gave
a great banquet for a thousand of
his highest officials, and he drank wine
with them. 2 He got drunk and ordered
his servants to bring in the gold and silver cups his father Nebuchadnezzar[o]
had taken from the temple in Jerusalem.
Belshazzar wanted the cups, so that he
and all his wives and officials could
drink from them.
3-4 When the gold cups were brought
in, everyone at the banquet drank from
them and praised their idols made of
gold, silver, bronze, iron, wood, and
stone.
5 Suddenly a human hand was seen
writing on the plaster wall of the palace.
The hand was just behind the lampstand, and the king could see it writing.
6 He was so frightened that his face
turned pale, his knees started shaking,
and his legs became weak.
7 The king called in his advisors, who
claimed they could talk with the spirits
of the dead and understand the meanings found in the stars. He told them,
"The man who can read this writing and
tell me what it means will become the
third most powerful man in my kingdom. He will wear robes of royal purple
and a gold chain around his neck."
8 All of King Belshazzar's highest officials came in, but not one of them could
read the writing or tell what it meant,
9 and they were completely puzzled.
Now the king was more afraid than ever
before, and his face turned white as a
ghost.
10 When the queen heard the king and
his officials talking, she came in and
said:

Your Majesty, I hope you live forever! Don't be afraid or look so pale.
11 In your kingdom there is a man
who has been given special powers
by the holy gods. When your father
Nebuchadnezzar was king, this man
was known to be as smart, intelligent, and wise as the gods themselves. Your father put him in charge
of all who claimed they could talk
with the spirits or understand the
meanings in the stars or tell about
the future. 12 He also changed the
man's name from Daniel to Belteshazzar. Not only is he wise and intelligent, but he can explain dreams
and riddles and solve difficult problems. Send for Daniel, and he will
tell you what the writing means.

13 When Daniel was brought in, the
king said:

So you are Daniel, one of the captives my father brought back from
Judah! 14 I was told that the gods
have given you special powers and
that you are intelligent and very
wise. 15 Neither my advisors nor the

[n] **4.32** *years*: Aramaic "times." [o] **5.2** *his father Nebuchadnezzar*: Belshazzar was actually the son of King Nabonidus, who was from another family. But in ancient times, it was possible to refer to a previous king as the "father" of the present king.

men who talk with the spirits of the dead could read this writing or tell me what it means. 16But I have been told that you understand everything and that you can solve difficult problems. Now then, if you can read this writing and tell me what it means, you will become the third most powerful man in my kingdom. You will wear royal purple robes and have a gold chain around your neck.

17Daniel answered:

Your Majesty, I will read the writing and tell you what it means. But you may keep your gifts or give them to someone else. 18Sir, the Most High God made your father a great and powerful man and brought him much honor and glory. 19God did such great things for him that people of all nations and races shook with fear.

Your father had the power of life or death over everyone, and he could honor or ruin anyone he chose. 20But when he became proud and stubborn, his glorious kingdom was taken from him. 21His mind became like that of an animal, and he was forced to stay away from people and live with wild donkeys. Your father ate grass like an ox, and he slept outside where his body was soaked with dew. He was forced to do this until he learned that the Most High God rules all kingdoms on earth and chooses their kings.

22King Belshazzar, you knew all of this, but you still refused to honor the Lord who rules from heaven. 23Instead, you turned against him and ordered the cups from his temple to be brought here, so that you and your wives and officials could drink wine from them. You praised idols made of silver, gold, bronze, iron, wood, and stone, even though they cannot see or hear or think. You refused to worship the God who gives you breath and controls everything you do. 24That's why he sent the hand to write this message on the wall.

25-28The words written there are *mene*, which means "numbered," *tekel*, which means "weighed," and *parsin*,[p] which means "divided." God has numbered the days of your kingdom and has brought it to an end. He has weighed you on his balance scales, and you fall short of what it takes to be king. So God has divided your kingdom between the Medes and the Persians.

29Belshazzar gave a command for Daniel to be made the third most powerful man in his kingdom and to be given a purple robe and a gold chain.

30That same night, the king was killed. 31Then Darius the Mede, who was sixty-two years old, took over his kingdom.

Daniel in a Pit of Lions

6 Darius divided his kingdom into a hundred and twenty states and placed a governor in charge of each one. 2In order to make sure that his government was run properly, Darius put three other officials in charge of the governors. One of these officials was Daniel. 3And he did his work so much better than the other governors and officials that the king decided to let him govern the whole kingdom.

4The other men tried to find something wrong with the way Daniel did his work for the king. But they could not accuse him of anything wrong, because he was honest and faithful and did everything he was supposed to do. 5Finally, they said to one another, "We will never be able to bring any charge against Daniel, unless it has to do with his religion."

6They all went to the king and said:

Your Majesty, we hope you live forever! 7All of your officials, leaders, advisors, and governors agree that you should make a law forbidding anyone to pray to any god or human except you for the next thirty days. Everyone who disobeys this law must be thrown into a pit of lions. 8Order this to be written and then sign it, so it cannot be changed, just as no written law of the Medes and Persians can be changed."

9So King Darius made the law and had it written down.

10Daniel heard about the law, but when he returned home, he went upstairs and prayed in front of the window that faced Jerusalem. In the same way that he had always done, he knelt down in prayer three times a day, giving thanks to God.

11The men who had spoken to the king watched Daniel and saw him praying to his God for help. 12They went back to the king and said, "Didn't you make a law that forbids anyone to pray to any god or human except you for the next thirty days? And doesn't the law say that everyone who disobeys it will be thrown into a pit of lions?"

"Yes, that's the law I made," the king agreed. "And just like all written laws of

[p]5.25-28 *mene . . . tekel . . . parsin*: In the Aramaic text of verse 25, the words "mene, tekel, parsin," are used, and in verses 26-28 the words "mene, tekel, peres" (the singular of "parsin") are used. "Parsin" means "divided," but "peres" can mean either "divided" or "Persia."

the Medes and Persians, it cannot be
changed."
13 The men then told the king, "That
Jew named Daniel, who was brought
here as a captive, refuses to obey you or
the law that you ordered to be written.
And he still prays to his god three times
a day." 14 The king was really upset to
hear about this, and for the rest of the
day he tried to think how he could save
Daniel.
15 At sunset the men returned and
said, "Your Majesty, remember that no
written law of the Medes and Persians
can be changed, not even by the king."
16 So Darius ordered Daniel to be
brought out and thrown into a pit of lions. But he said to Daniel, "You have
been faithful to your God, and I pray
that he will rescue you."
17 A stone was rolled over the pit, and
it was sealed. Then Darius and his officials stamped the seal to show that no
one should let Daniel out. 18 All night
long the king could not sleep. He did not
eat anything, and he would not let anyone come in to entertain him.
19 At daybreak the king got up and ran
to the pit. 20 He was anxious and
shouted, "Daniel, you were faithful and
served your God. Was he able to save
you from the lions?"
21 Daniel answered, "Your Majesty, I
hope you live forever! 22 My God knew
that I was innocent, and he sent an angel to keep the lions from eating me.
Your Majesty, I have never done anything to hurt you."
23 The king was relieved to hear
Daniel's voice, and he gave orders for
him to be taken out of the pit. Daniel's
faith in his God had kept him from being harmed. 24 And the king ordered
the men who had brought charges
against Daniel to be thrown into the
pit, together with their wives and children. But before they even reached
the bottom, the lions ripped them to
pieces.
25 King Darius then sent this message
to all people of every nation and race in
the world:

"Greetings to all of you!
26 I command everyone
in my kingdom
to worship and honor
the God of Daniel.
He is the living God,
the one who lives forever.
His power and his kingdom
will never end.
27 He rescues people
and sets them free
by working great miracles.
Daniel's God has rescued him
from the power of the lions."

28 All went well for Daniel while Darius was king, and even when Cyrus the
Persian ruled.[q]

Daniel's Vision of the Four Beasts

7 1-2 Daniel wrote:
In the first year of King Belshazzar[r] of Babylonia, I had some dreams
and visions while I was asleep one
night, and I wrote them down.
The four winds were stirring up the
mighty sea, 3 when suddenly four powerful beasts came out of the sea. Each
beast was different. 4 The first was like a
lion with the wings of an eagle. As I
watched, its wings were pulled off. Then
it was lifted to an upright position and
made to stand on two feet, just like a human, and it was given a human mind.
5 The second beast looked like a bear
standing on its hind legs.[s] It held three
ribs in its teeth, and it was told, "Attack!
Eat all the flesh you want."
6 The third beast was like a leopard—
except that it had four wings and four
heads. It was given authority to rule.
7 The fourth beast was stronger and
more terrifying than the others. Its huge
teeth were made of iron, and what it
didn't grind with its teeth, it smashed
with its feet. It was different from the
others, and it had horns on its head—
ten of them. 8 Just as I was thinking
about these horns, a smaller horn appeared, and three of the other horns
were pulled up by the roots to make
room for it. This horn had the eyes of a
human and a mouth that spoke with
great pride.

Judgment

Daniel wrote:
9 Thrones were set up
while I was watching,
and the Eternal God[t]
took his place.
His clothing and his hair
were white as snow.
His throne was a blazing fire
with fiery wheels,
10 and flames were dashing out
from all around him.
Countless thousands
were standing there
to serve him.
The time of judgment began,
and the books[u] were opened.

[q] **6.28** *Cyrus the Persian ruled*: 539-530 B.C. [r] **7.1,2** *first year of King Belshazzar*: 554 B.C.
[s] **7.5** *standing on its hind legs*: Or "higher on one side than the other" or "with a paw lifted up."
[t] **7.9** *Eternal God*: Aramaic "Ancient of Days." [u] **7.10** *books*: Containing the record of the good and evil that each person has done.

11I watched closely to see what would
happen to this smaller horn because of
the arrogant things it was saying. Then
before my very eyes, the fourth beast
was killed and its body destroyed by
fire. 12The other three beasts had their
authority taken from them, but they
were allowed to live a while longer.[v]
13As I continued to watch the vision that
night,

I saw what looked like
a son of man[w]
coming with the clouds of heaven,
and he was presented
to the Eternal God.[x]
14 He was crowned king
and given power and glory,
so that all people
of every nation and race
would serve him.
He will rule forever,
and his kingdom is eternal,
never to be destroyed.

The Meaning of Daniel's Vision

15Daniel wrote:
I was terrified by these visions, and I
didn't know what to think. 16So I asked
one of those standing there,[y] and he explained, 17"The four beasts are four
earthly kingdoms. 18But God Most High
will give his kingdom to his chosen
ones, and it will be theirs forever and
ever."
19I wanted to know more about the
fourth beast,[z] because it was so different and much more terrifying than the
others. What was the meaning of its iron
teeth and bronze claws and of its feet
that smashed what the teeth and claws
had not ground and crushed? 20I also
wanted to know more about all ten of
those horns on its head. I especially
wanted to know more about the one
that took the place of three of the others—the horn that had eyes and spoke
with arrogance and seemed greater
than the others. 21While I was looking,
this horn attacked God's chosen ones
and was winning the battle. 22Then God
Most High, the Eternal God,[a] came and
judged in favor of his chosen ones, because the time had arrived for them to
be given the kingdom.

23 Then I was told
by the one standing there:
"The fourth beast
will be a fourth kingdom
to appear on earth.
It will be different
from all the others—
it will trample the earth
and crush it to pieces.
24 All ten of those horns are kings
who will come from this kingdom,
and one more will follow.
This horn will be different
from the others,
and it will conquer
three other kings.

25 "This king will speak evil
of God Most High,
and he will be cruel
to God's chosen ones.
He will try to change God's Law
and the sacred seasons.
And he will be able to do this
for a time, two times,
and half a time.[b]
26 But he will finally be judged,
and his kingdom
completely destroyed.
27 "Then the greatest kingdom of all
will be given to the chosen ones
of God Most High.
His kingdom will be eternal,
and all others will serve
and obey him."

28That was what I saw and heard. I
turned pale with fear and kept it all to
myself.

Vision of a Ram and a Goat

8 Daniel wrote:
In the third year of King Belshazzar of Babylonia,[c] I had a second vision
2in which I was in Susa, the chief city of
Babylonia's Elam Province. I was beside
the Ulai River,[d] 3when I looked up and
saw a ram standing there with two
horns on its head—both of them were
long, but the second one was longer
than the first. 4The ram went charging
toward the west, the north, and the
south. No other animals were strong
enough to oppose him, and nothing
could save them from his power. So he
did as he pleased and became even
more powerful.
5I kept on watching and saw a goat
come from the west and charge across
the entire earth, without even touching
the ground. Between his eyes was a
powerful horn,[e] 6and with tremendous

[v]7.12 *a while longer*: Aramaic "for a time and a season." [w]7.13 *son of man*: Or "human." In Aramaic "son of man" may mean a human or even "oneself" ("I" or "me"). Jesus often used the phrase "the Son of Man" when referring to himself. [x]7.13 *Eternal God*: See the note at 7.9. [y]7.16 *one of those standing there*: Possibly an angel sent to interpret the visions or one of those thousands mentioned in verse 10. [z]7.19 *fourth beast*: See verses 7, 8. [a]7.22 *Eternal God*: See the note at 7.9. [b]7.25 *for . . . time*: Or "for a year, two years, and half a year." [c]8.1 *third year . . . Babylonia*: 552 B.C., two years after the first vision (see 7.1, 2). [d]8.2 *River*: Or "Gate." [e]8.5 *powerful horn*: Hebrew "horn of vision."

anger the goat started toward the ram
that I had seen beside the river.[f] 7The
goat was so fierce that its attack broke
both horns of the ram, leaving him powerless. Then the goat stomped on the
ram, and no one could do anything to
help. 8After this, the goat became even
more powerful. But at the peak of his
power, his mighty horn was broken, and
four other mighty horns took its place—
one pointing to the north and one to the
east, one to the south and one to the
west.
9A little horn came from one of these,
and its power reached to the south, the
east, and even to the holy land.[g] 10It became so strong that it attacked the stars
in the sky, which were heaven's army.[h]
Then it threw some of them down to the
earth and stomped on them. 11-12It humiliated heaven's army and dishonored
its leader[i] by keeping him from offering
the daily sacrifices. In fact, it was so terrible that it even disgraced the temple
and wiped out true worship. It also did
everything else it wanted to do.
13Then one of the holy angels asked
another, "When will the daily sacrifices
be offered again? What about this horrible rebellion? When will the temple and
heaven's army no longer be trampled in
the dust?"
14The other answered, "It will be two
thousand three hundred evenings and
mornings before the temple is dedicated
and in use again."

Gabriel Interprets the Vision

15Daniel wrote:
I was trying to figure out the meaning
of the vision, when someone suddenly
appeared there beside me. 16And from
beside the Ulai River,[j] a voice like that
of a human said, "Gabriel, help him understand the vision."
17Gabriel came over, and I fell to the
ground in fear. Then he said, "You are
merely a human, but you need to understand that this vision is about the end of
time."
18While he was speaking, I fell facedown in a deep sleep. But he lifted me to
my feet 19and said:
Listen, and I will tell you what will
happen at the end of time, when God
has chosen to show his anger. 20The
two horns of the ram are the kings
of Media and Persia, 21the goat is the
kingdom of Greece, and the powerful horn between his eyes is the first
of its kings. 22After this horn is broken, four other kingdoms will appear, but they won't be as strong.
23When these rulers have become
as evil as possible, their power will
end, and then a king who is dangerous and cannot be trusted will appear. 24He will gain strength, but not
on his own, and he will cause terrible destruction. He will wipe out
powerful leaders and God's people
as well. 25His deceitful lies will make
him so successful, that he will think
he is really great. Suddenly he will
kill many people, and he will even
attack God, the Supreme Ruler. But
God will crush him!
26This vision about the evenings
and mornings is true, but these
things won't happen for a long time,
so don't tell it to others.
27After this, I was so worn out and
weak that it was several days before I
could get out of bed and go about my
duties for the king. I was disturbed by
this vision that made no sense to me.

Daniel Prays for the People

9 1-2Daniel wrote:
Some years later, Darius the
Mede,[k] who was the son of Xerxes,[l] had
become king of Babylonia. And during
his first year as king, I found out from
studying the writings of the prophets
that the LORD had said to Jeremiah,
"Jerusalem will lie in ruins for seventy
years."[m] 3-4Then, to show my sorrow, I
went without eating and dressed in
sackcloth[n] and sat in ashes. I confessed
my sins and earnestly prayed to the
LORD my God:
Our Lord, you are a great and
fearsome God, and you faithfully
keep your agreement with those
who love and obey you. 5But we
have sinned terribly by rebelling
against you and rejecting your laws
and teachings. 6We have ignored the
message your servants the prophets
spoke to our kings, our leaders, our
ancestors, and everyone else.
7Everything you do is right, our
Lord. But still we suffer public disgrace because we have been unfaithful and have sinned against you.
This includes all of us, both far and
near—the people of Judah,
Jerusalem, and Israel, as well as

[f] **8.6** *river*: See the note at 8.2. [g] **8.9** *holy land*: Hebrew "the lovely land." [h] **8.10** *heaven's army*: In verses 10-13 the Hebrew word translated "heaven's army" may also mean "God's people." [i] **8.11,12** *leader*: Hebrew "prince." [j] **8.16** *River*: See the note at 8.2.
[k] **9.1,2** *Darius the Mede*: See 5.31. [l] **9.1,2** *Xerxes*: Hebrew "Ahasuerus." [m] **9.1,2** *seventy years*: See Jeremiah 25.11-13; 29.10. [n] **9.3,4** *sackcloth*: A rough, dark-colored cloth made from goat or camel hair and used to make grain sacks. It was worn in times of trouble or sorrow.

those you dragged away to foreign
lands, [8]and even our kings, our officials, and our ancestors. [9]LORD God,
you are merciful and forgiving, even
though we have rebelled against you
[10]and rejected your teachings that
came to us from your servants the
prophets.
[11]Everyone in Israel has stubbornly refused to obey your laws,
and so those curses written by your
servant Moses have fallen upon us.
[12]You warned us and our leaders
that Jerusalem would suffer the
worst disaster in human history, and
you did exactly as you had threatened. [13]We have not escaped any of
the terrible curses written by Moses,
and yet we have refused to beg you
for mercy and to remind ourselves
of how faithful you have always
been. [14]And when you finally punished us with this horrible disaster,
that was also the right thing to do,
because we deserved it so much.
[15]Our Lord God, with your own
mighty arm you rescued us from
Egypt and made yourself famous to
this very day, but we have sinned
terribly. [16]In the past, you treated us
with such kindness, that we now beg
you to stop being so terribly angry
with Jerusalem. After all, it is your
chosen city built on your holy mountain, even though it has suffered
public disgrace because of our sins
and those of our ancestors.
[17]I am your servant, Lord God, and
I beg you to answer my prayers and
bring honor to yourself by having
pity on your temple that lies in ruins. [18]Please show mercy to your
chosen city, not because we deserve
it, but because of your great kindness. [19]Forgive us! Hurry and do
something, not only for your city
and your chosen people, but to bring
honor to yourself.

The Seventy Weeks

Daniel wrote:

[20]I was still confessing my sins and
those of all Israel to the LORD my God,
and I was praying for the good of his
holy mountain,[o] [21]when Gabriel suddenly came flying in at the time of the
evening sacrifice. This was the same
Gabriel I had seen in my vision, [22]and
he explained:

Daniel, I am here to help you understand the vision. [23]God thinks
highly of you, and at the very moment you started praying, I was sent
to give you the answer. [24]God has
decided that for seventy weeks,[p]
your people and your holy city must
suffer as the price of their sins. Then
evil will disappear, and justice will
rule forever; the visions and words
of the prophets will come true, and a
most holy place will be dedicated.[q]
[25]You need to realize that from the
command to rebuild Jerusalem until
the coming of the Chosen Leader,[r] it
will be seven weeks and another
sixty-two weeks.[s] Streets will be
built in Jerusalem, and a trench will
be dug around the city for protection, but these will be difficult
times.[t] [26]At the end of the sixty-two
weeks,[u] the Chosen Leader[v] will be
killed and left with nothing.[w]

A foreign ruler and his army will
sweep down like a mighty flood,
leaving both the city and the temple
in ruins, and war and destruction
will continue until the end, just as
God has decided. [27]For one week[x]
this foreigner[y] will make a firm
agreement with many people, and
halfway through this week,[z] he will
end all sacrifices and offerings. Then
the "Horrible Thing" that causes destruction will be put there. And it
will stay there until the time God
has decided to destroy this one who
destroys.

Daniel's Vision beside the Tigris River

10 In the third year[a] of Cyrus the
king of Persia, a message came to
Daniel[b] from God, and it was explained
in a vision. The message was about a
horrible war, and it was true. [2]Daniel
wrote:

For three weeks I was in sorrow. [3]I ate
no fancy food or meat, I drank no wine,
and I put no olive oil on my face or

[o]9.20 *holy mountain*: Jerusalem (see verse 16) or the temple. [p]9.24 *seventy weeks*: Or "seventy times seven years." [q]9.24 *a most holy place will be dedicated*: Or "God's Holy One will appear." [r]9.25 *the Chosen Leader*: Or "a chosen leader." In Hebrew the word "chosen" means "to pour oil (on someone's head)." In Old Testament times it was the custom to pour oil on a person's head when that person was chosen to be a priest or a king. [s]9.25 *seven weeks and another sixty-two weeks*: Or "seven times seven years and another sixty-two times seven years." [t]9.25 *it will be seven . . . difficult times*: Or "it will be seven weeks. Then streets will be built in Jerusalem, and a trench will be dug around the city for protection. But Jerusalem will have difficult times for sixty-two weeks." [u]9.26 *sixty-two weeks*: Or "sixty-two times seven years." [v]9.26 *the Chosen Leader*: See the note at 9.25. [w]9.26 *left with nothing*: Or "no one will take his place." [x]9.27 *one week*: Or "seven years." [y]9.27 *this foreigner*: Or "the Chosen Leader." [z]9.27 *halfway through this week*: Or "for half of this week of seven years." [a]10.1 *third year*: 536 B.C. [b]10.1 *Daniel*: See the note at 2.26.

hair.[c] 4Then, on the twenty-fourth day of
the first month,[d] I was standing on the
banks of the great Tigris River, 5when I
looked up and saw someone dressed in
linen and wearing a solid gold belt.[e]
6His body was like a precious stone,[f] his
face like lightning, his eyes like flaming
fires, his arms and legs like polished
bronze, and his voice like the roar of a
crowd. 7Although the people who were
with me did not see the vision, they became so frightened that they scattered
and hid. 8Only I saw this great vision. I
became weak and pale, 9and at the
sound of his voice, I fell facedown in a
deep sleep.

10He raised me to my hands and knees
11and then said, "Daniel, your God
thinks highly of you, and he has sent
me. So stand up and pay close attention." I stood trembling, while the angel
said:

> 12Daniel, don't be afraid! God has
> listened to your prayers since the
> first day you humbly asked for un-
> derstanding, and he has sent me
> here. 13But the guardian angel[g] of
> Persia opposed me for twenty-one
> days. Then Michael, who is one of
> the strongest guardian angels,[h]
> came to rescue me from the kings of
> Persia.[i] 14Now I have come here to
> give you another vision about what
> will happen to your people in the fu-
> ture.

15While this angel was speaking to
me, I stared at the ground, speechless.
16Then he appeared in human form and
touched my lips. I said, "Sir, this vision
has brought me great pain and has
drained my strength. 17I am merely your
servant. How can I possibly speak with
someone so powerful, when I am almost
too weak to get my breath?"

18-19The angel touched me a second
time and said, "Don't be frightened! God
thinks highly of you, and he intends this
for your good, so be brave and strong."

At this, I regained my strength and
replied, "Please speak! You have already
made me feel much better."

20Then the angel said:

> Now do you understand why I
> have come? Soon I must leave to
> fight against the guardian angel of
> Persia. Then after I have defeated
> him, the guardian angel of Greece
> will attack me. 21I will tell you what
> is written in *The Book of Truth*. But
> first, you must realize that no one
> except Michael, the guardian angel
> of Israel, is on my side.

11 1You also need to know that I protected and helped Darius the
Mede[j] in his first year as king.

The Angel's Message to Daniel

Part One: The Four Kings and their Successors

2What I am going to tell you is certain
to happen. Four kings will rule Persia,
one after the other, but the fourth one
will become much richer than the others. In fact, his wealth will make him so
powerful that he will turn everyone
against the kingdom of Greece. 3Then a
mighty king will come to power and will
be able to do whatever he pleases. 4But
suddenly his kingdom will be crushed
and scattered to the four corners of the
earth, where four more kingdoms will
rise. But these won't be ruled by his descendants or be as powerful as his kingdom.

5The king of the south will grow powerful. Then one of his generals will rebel
and take over most of the kingdom.
6Years later the southern kingdom and
the northern kingdom will make a
treaty, and the daughter of the king of
the south will marry the king of the
north. But she will lose her power. Then
she, her husband, their child,[k] and the
servants who came with her will all be
killed.

After this, 7one of her relatives will
become the ruler of the southern kingdom. He will attack the army of the
northern kingdom and capture its
fortresses. 8Then he will carry their
idols to Egypt, together with their precious treasures of silver and gold, but it
will be a long time before he attacks the
northern kingdom again. Some years
later 9the king of the north will invade
the southern kingdom, but he will be
forced back to his own country.

10The sons of the king of the north
will gather a huge army that will sweep
down like a roaring flood, reaching all
the way to the fortress of the southern
kingdom. 11But this will make the king
of the south angry, and he will defeat
this large army from the north. 12The
king of the south will feel proud because of the many thousands he has
killed. But his victories won't last long,
13because the king of the north will

[c] **10.3** *olive oil . . . hair*: On special occasions, it was the custom to put olive oil on one's face and hair. [d] **10.4** *first month*: Nisan (also known as Abib), the first month of the Hebrew calendar, from about mid-March to mid-April. [e] **10.5** *solid gold belt*: Hebrew "belt of gold from Uphaz." [f] **10.6** *a precious stone*: The Hebrew text has "beryl," which is green or bluish-green. [g] **10.13** *guardian angel*: Hebrew "prince." [h] **10.13** *one of the strongest guardian angels*: Hebrew "chief prince." [i] **10.13** *came . . . Persia*: One possible meaning for the difficult Hebrew text. [j] **11.1** *Darius the Mede*: See 5.30. [k] **11.6** *their child*: One Hebrew manuscript and two ancient translations; most Hebrew manuscripts "her father."

gather a larger and more powerful army
than ever before. Then in a few years,
he will start invading other countries.
14 At this time many of your own people will try to make this vision come
true by rebelling against the king of the
south, but their rebellion will fail.
15 Then the army from the north will surround and capture a fortress in the
south, and not even the most experienced troops of the southern kingdom
will be able to make them retreat. 16 The
king who invaded from the north will do
as he pleases, and he will even capture
and destroy the holy land.[l] 17 In fact, he
will decide to invade the south with his
entire army. Then he will attempt to
make peace by giving the king of the
south a bride from the northern kingdom, but this won't be successful.
18 Afterwards, this proud king of the
north will invade and conquer many of
the nations along the coast, but a military leader will defeat him and make
him lose his pride. 19 He will retreat to
his fortresses in his own country, but on
the way he will be defeated and never
again be seen.
20 The next king of the north will try to
collect taxes for the glory of his kingdom. However, he will come to a sudden
end in some mysterious way, instead of
in battle or because of someone's anger.

Part Two: The Evil King from the North

21 The successor of this king of the
north will be a worthless nobody, who
doesn't come from a royal family. He
will suddenly appear and gain control
of the kingdom by treachery. 22 Then he
will destroy armies and remove God's
chosen high priest. 23 He will make a
treaty, but he will be deceitful and break
it, even though he has only a few followers. 24 Without warning, he will success-
fully invade a wealthy province, which
is something his ancestors never did.
Then he will divide among his followers
all of its treasures and property. But
none of this will last very long.
25 He will gather a large and powerful
army, and with great courage he will attack the king of the south. The king of
the south will meet him with a much
stronger army, but he will lose the battle, because he will be betrayed 26 by
members of the royal court. He will be
ruined, and most of his army will be
slaughtered.
27 The two kings will meet around a
table and tell evil lies to each other. But
their plans will fail, because God has already decided what will happen. 28 Then
the king of the north will return to his
country with great treasures. But on the
way, he will attack the religion of God's
people and do whatever else he pleases.
29 At the time God has decided, the
king of the north will invade the southern kingdom again, but this time, things
will be different. 30 Ships from the west
will come to attack him, and he will be
discouraged. Then he will start back to
his own country and take out his anger
on the religion of God's faithful people,
while showing kindness to those who
are unfaithful. 31 He will send troops to
pollute the temple and the fortress, and
he will stop the daily sacrifices. Then he
will set up that "Horrible Thing" that
causes destruction. 32 The king will use
deceit to win followers from those who
are unfaithful to God, but those who remain faithful will do everything possible
to oppose him.
33 Wise leaders will instruct many of
the people. But for a while, some of
these leaders will either be killed with
swords or burned alive, or else robbed
of their possessions and thrown into
prison. 34 They will receive only a little
help in their time of trouble, and many
of their followers will be treacherous.
35 Some of those who are wise will suffer, so that God will make them pure
and acceptable until the end, which will
still come at the time he has decided.
36 This king will do as he pleases. He
will proudly claim to be greater than
any god and will insult the only true
God. Indeed, he will be successful until
God is no longer angry with his people.
37 This king will reject the gods his ancestors worshiped and the god preferred by women.[m] In fact, he will put
himself above all gods 38 and worship
only the so-called god of fortresses, who
was unknown to his ancestors. And he
will honor it with gold, silver, precious
stones, and other costly gifts. 39 With the
help of this foreign god, he will capture
the strongest fortresses. Everyone who
worships this god will be put in a position of power and rewarded with wealth
and land.

Part Three: The Time of the End

40 At the time of the end, the king of
the south will attack the kingdom of the
north. But its king will rush out like a
storm with war chariots, cavalry, and
many ships. Indeed, his forces will flood
one country after another, 41 and when
they reach the holy land,[n] tens of thousands will be killed. But the countries of
Edom and Moab and the ruler of Ammon[o] will escape.
42 The king of the north will invade

[l] **11.16** *the holy land*: See the note at 8.9. [m] **11.37** *god preferred by women*: Perhaps Tammuz or Adonis, which were popular among the women of that time. [n] **11.41** *the holy land*: See the note at 8.9. [o] **11.41** *the ruler of Ammon*: Or "what is left of Ammon."

many countries, including Egypt, 43and
he will take its rich treasures of gold
and silver. He will also conquer Libya
and Ethiopia.[p] 44But he will be alarmed
by news from the east and the north,
and he will become furious and cause
great destruction. 45After this, he will set
up camp between the Mediterranean
Sea and Mount Zion. Then he will be
destroyed, and no one will be able to
save him.

Part Four: The Dead Will Rise to Life

12 Michael, the chief of the angels, is
the protector of your people, and
he will come at a time of terrible suffering, the worst in all of history. And your
people who have their names written in
The Book[q] will be protected. 2Many of
those who lie dead in the ground will
rise from death. Some of them will be
given eternal life, and others will receive nothing but eternal shame and
disgrace. 3Everyone who has been wise
will shine as bright as the sky above,
and everyone who has led others to
please God will shine like the stars.
4Daniel, I now command you to keep
the message of this book secret until the
end of time, even though many people
will go everywhere, searching for the
knowledge to be found in it.[r]

The End of Time

5Daniel wrote:
I looked around and saw two
other people—one on this side of the
river and one on the other side. 6The
angel who had spoken to me was
dressed in linen and was standing
upstream from them.[s] So one of the
two beside the river asked him,
"How long before these amazing
things happen?"
7The angel then raised both hands
toward heaven and said, "In the
name of the God who lives forever, I
solemnly promise that it will be a
time, two times, and half a time.[t]
Everything will be over, when the
suffering of God's holy people
comes to an end."
8I heard what the angel said, but I
didn't understand. So I asked, "Sir,
how will it all end?"
The angel in my vision then
replied:
9Daniel, go about your business,
because the meaning of this message will remain secret until the end
of time. 10Many people will have
their hearts and lives made pure and
clean, but those who are evil will
keep on being evil and never understand. Only the wise will understand. 11There will be one thousand
two hundred ninety days from the
time that the daily sacrifices are
stopped, until someone sets up the
"Horrible Thing" that causes destruction. 12God will bless everyone
who patiently waits until one thousand three hundred thirty-five days
have gone by.
13So, Daniel, be faithful until the
end! You will rest, and at the end of
time, you will rise from death to receive your reward.

[p]11.43 *Ethiopia*: The Hebrew text has "Cush," which was a region south of Egypt that included parts of the present countries of Ethiopia and Sudan. [q]12.1 *The Book*: Either the book with the names of God's people in it or the book with the record of the good and evil that people have done. [r]12.4 *even though . . . in it*: One possible meaning for the difficult Hebrew text. [s]12.6 *angel . . . upstream from them*: See 10.4-6. [t]12.7 *a time, two times, and half a time*: Or "a year, two years, and half a year," that is, about 1260 days.

HOSEA

ABOUT THIS BOOK

Hosea was a prophet in the northern kingdom during its final years as a nation. In the first three chapters of this book, Hosea's family life became a living picture of the message he preached to his country. The Lord told Hosea to marry a prostitute, as a way of showing how unfaithful Israel had been. Then the Lord told Hosea what to name his children, and these names were reminders that Israel was going to be punished. But Hosea was told to love his unfaithful wife, and his love was to be a picture of the Lord's continuing love for unfaithful Israel.

The rest of the book emphasizes the agreement that the Lord had made with Israel. This agreement demanded that Israel and the Lord be loyal and faithful to each other. The Lord had always lived up to the agreement, but the people had broken it time after time. They had trusted their own military strength and the power of foreign countries, rather than depending on the Lord to protect their nation. And the people had worshiped other gods and trusted them to provide good crops and large herds of livestock.

In this book the Lord put Israel and Judah on trial and charged them with breaking their agreement with him. They were guilty and would be punished.

But the Lord still loved his people in spite of everything they had done. And so he promised to forgive them and bless them again after they learned to be faithful to him:

Israel, you have rejected me,
but my anger is gone;
I will heal you and love you
without limit. (14.4)

A QUICK LOOK AT THIS BOOK

Hosea's Family Is a Picture of the Lord's Unfaithful People (1.1—3.5)
The Lord Accuses Israel, Judah, and Their Leaders (4.1—5.15)
The People Pretend To Turn to the Lord (6.1—7.10)
Israel Refused To Trust the Lord (7.11—8.14)
Israel Will Get the Punishment It Deserves (9.1-16)
Warnings for Israel (10.1-15)
God's Love for His People (11.1-11)
Israel and Judah Are Doomed (11.12—13.16)
Future Forgiveness and Blessings (14.1-9)

---

1 I am Hosea son of Beeri. When Uzziah, Jotham, Ahaz, and Hezekiah
were the kings of Judah, and when Jeroboam son of Jehoash[a] was king of
Israel,[b] the LORD spoke this message
to me.

[a]1.1 *Jehoash*: The Hebrew text has "Joash," another spelling of the name. [b]1.1 *kings of Judah . . . king of Israel*: Uzziah (781-740 B.C.), Jotham (740-736), Ahaz (736-716), Hezekiah (716-687), and Jeroboam II (783-743).

Hosea's Family

2 The LORD said, "Hosea, Israel has betrayed me like an unfaithful wife.[c]
Marry such a woman and have children
by her." 3 So I married Gomer the daughter of Diblaim, and we had a son.
4 Then the LORD said, "Hosea, name
your son Jezreel,[d] because I will soon
punish the descendants of King Jehu of
Israel for the murders he committed in
Jezreel Valley.[e] I will destroy his kingdom, 5 and in Jezreel Valley I will break
the power of Israel."
6 Later, Gomer had a daughter, and the
LORD said, "Name her Lo-Ruhamah,[f] because I will no longer have mercy and
forgive Israel. 7 But I am the LORD God
of Judah, and I will have mercy and save
Judah by my own power—not by wars
and arrows or swords and cavalry."
8 After Gomer had stopped nursing
Lo-Ruhamah, she had another son.
9 Then the LORD said, "Name him Lo-
Ammi,[g] because these people are not
mine, and I am not their God."

Hope for Israel

10 Someday it will be impossible to
count the people of Israel, because there
will be as many of them as there are
grains of sand along the seashore. They
are now called "Not My People," but in
the future they will be called "Children
of the Living God." 11 Israel and Judah
will unite and choose one leader. Then
they will take back their land, and this
will be a great day for Jezreel.[h]

2 1 So
let your brothers be called "My People" and your sisters be called "Shown
Mercy."[i]

The LORD Promises To Punish Israel

2 Accuse! Accuse your mother!
She is no longer my wife,
and now I, the LORD,
am not her husband.
Beg her to give up prostitution
and stop being unfaithful,[j]
3 or I will strip her naked
like the day she was born.
I will make her barren
like a desert,
and she will die of thirst.
4 You children are the result
of her unfaithfulness,
and I'll show you no pity.
5 Your mother was unfaithful.
She was disgraceful and said,
"I'll run after my lovers.
Everything comes from them—
my food and drink,
my linen and wool,
my olive oil and wine."

6 I, the LORD, will build
a fence of thorns
to block her path.
7 She will run after her lovers,
but not catch them;
she will search,
but not find them.
Then she will say, "I'll return
to my first husband.
Life was better then."
8 She didn't know that her grain,
wine, and olive oil
were gifts from me,
as were the gold and silver
she used in worshiping Baal.[k]

9 So I'll hold back the harvest
of grain and grapes.
I'll take back
my wool and my linen
that cover her body.
10 Then I'll strip her naked
in the sight of her lovers.[l]
No one can rescue her.

11 I'll stop Israel's celebrations—
no more New Moon Festivals,
Sabbaths, or other feasts.
12 She said, "My lovers gave me
vineyards and fig trees
as payment[m] for sex."

Now I, the LORD, will ruin
her vineyards and fig trees;
they will become clumps of weeds
eaten by wild animals.

[c] **1.2** *unfaithful wife*: In some Canaanite religions of Old Testament times, young women were expected to have sex with the worshipers of their god before marriage. Such women were called "temple prostitutes." Many of the Israelite women did this same thing, and Hosea is told to marry one of them to show that the nation has turned from the LORD to worship idols.
[d] **1.4** *Jezreel*: In Hebrew "Jezreel" means "God scatters (seed)." Here the name is used as a threat (meaning the LORD will punish Israel by scattering its people), while in verse 11 it is used as a promise (meaning the LORD will bless Israel by giving their nation many people, just as a big harvest comes when many seeds are scattered in a field).
[e] **1.4** *murders . . . Valley*: Jehu murdered the wife and relatives of King Ahab (see 2 Kings 9.15—10.14).
[f] **1.6** *Lo-Ruhamah*: In Hebrew "Lo-Ruhamah" means "No Mercy."
[g] **1.9** *Lo-Ammi*: In Hebrew "Lo-Ammi" means "Not My People."
[h] **1.11** *Jezreel*: See the note at verse 4.
[i] **2.1** *My People . . . Shown Mercy*: In Hebrew "My People" is "Ammi" and "Shown Mercy" is "Ruhamah" (see Lo-Ruhamah in 1.6 and Lo-Ammi in 1.9).
[j] **2.2** *prostitution . . . unfaithful*: See the note at 1.2.
[k] **2.8** *Baal*: A Canaanite god of fertility.
[l] **2.10** *I'll strip . . . lovers*: Or "I'll show her lovers how disgusting she is."
[m] **2.12** *fig trees . . . payment*: Hosea uses an unusual word for "fig tree," which is spelled something like the word for "payment."

13 I'll punish her for the days
she worshiped Baal
and burned incense to him.
I'll punish her for the times
she forgot about me
and wore jewelry and rings
to attract her lovers.
I, the LORD, have spoken!

The LORD Will Help Israel

14 Israel, I, the LORD,
will lure you into the desert
and speak gently to you.
15 I will return your vineyards,
and then Trouble Valley[n]
will become Hopeful Valley.
You will say "Yes" to me
as you did in your youth,
when leaving Egypt.

16I promise that from that day on, you
will call me your husband instead of
your master.[o] 17I will no longer even let
you mention the names of those pagan
gods that you called "Master." 18And I
will agree to let you live in peace—you
will no longer be attacked by wild animals and birds or by weapons of war. 19I
will accept you as my wife forever, and
instead of a bride price[p] I will give you
justice, fairness, love, kindness, 20and
faithfulness. Then you will truly know
who I am.
21I will command the sky to send rain
on the earth, 22and it will produce grain,
grapes, and olives in Jezreel Valley. 23I
will scatter the seeds and show mercy to
Lo-Ruhamah.[q] I will say to Lo-Ammi,[r]
"You are my people," and they will answer, "You are our God."

God's Love Offers Hope

3 Once again the LORD spoke to me.
And this time he said, "Hosea, fall in
love with an unfaithful woman[s] who has
a lover. Do this to show that I love the
people of Israel, even though they worship idols and enjoy the offering cakes
made with fruit."
2So I paid fifteen pieces of silver and
about ten bushels of grain for such a
woman. 3Then I said, "Now you are
mine! You will have to remain faithful to
me, though it will be a long time before
we sleep together."
4It will also be a long time before Israel has a king or before sacrifices are
offered at the temple or before there is
any way to get guidance from God. 5But
later, Israel will turn back to the LORD
their God and to David their king. At
that time they will come to the LORD
with fear and trembling, and he will be
good to them.

Israel Is Unfaithful

4 Israel, listen
as the LORD accuses
everyone in the land!
No one is faithful or loyal
or truly cares about God.
2 Cursing, dishonesty, murder,
robbery, unfaithfulness—
these happen all the time.
Violence is everywhere.
3 And so your land is a desert.
Every living creature is dying—
people and wild animals,
birds and fish.

The LORD Warns the Priests

4 Don't accuse just anyone!
Not everyone is at fault.
My case is against you,
the priests.[t]
5 You and the prophets
will stumble day and night;
I'll silence your mothers.
6 You priests have rejected me,
and my people are destroyed
by refusing to obey.
Now I'll reject you and forget
your children, because you
have forgotten my Law.

7 By adding more of you priests,
you multiply the number
of people who sin.
Now I'll change your pride
into shame.
8 You encourage others to sin,
so you can stuff yourselves
on their sin offerings.

9 That's why I will punish
the people for their deeds,
just as I will punish
you priests.
10 Their food won't satisfy,
and having sex at pagan shrines
won't produce children.
My people have rebelled

[n]**2.15** *Trouble Valley*: Or "Achor Valley." The exact location of the valley is unknown, but in Hebrew "Achor" sounds like "Achan," who brought trouble on Israel by disobeying the Lord (see Joshua 7.24-26). [o]**2.16** *husband . . . master*: In Hebrew the word "master" is the same as the name of the god Baal. But the LORD promises that his people will have a deep personal relationship with him (like a devoted wife and husband) rather than merely a legal tie (like a wife and her "master"). [p]**2.19** *bride price*: It was the custom for the husband to pay his wife's parents a bride price. Instead of money, the LORD will give much better benefits to Israel. [q]**2.23** *Lo-Ruhamah*: See the note at 1.6. [r]**2.23** *Lo-Ammi*: See the note at 1.9. [s]**3.1** *unfaithful woman*: This may refer to Gomer, the woman Hosea married (see 1.3), or it may refer to another woman. [t]**4.4** *priests*: One possible meaning for the difficult Hebrew text of verse 4. Hosea may have had in mind only one priest, possibly the chief priest.

11 and have been unfaithful
to me, their LORD.

God Condemns Israel's Idolatry

My people, you are foolish
because of too much pleasure
and too much wine.
12 You expect wooden idols
and other objects of wood
to give you advice.
Lusting for sex at pagan shrines
has made you unfaithful
to me, your God.
13 You offer sacrifices
on mountaintops and hills,
under oak trees, and wherever
good shade is found.

Your own daughters
and daughters-in-law
sell themselves for sex.
14 But I won't punish them.
You men are to blame,
because you go to prostitutes
and offer sacrifices with them
at pagan shrines.
Your own foolishness
will lead to your ruin.
15 Israel, you are unfaithful,
but don't lead Judah to sin.
Stop worshiping at Gilgal
or at sinful Bethel.[u]
And quit making promises
in my name— the name
of the living LORD.
16 You are nothing more
than a stubborn cow—
so stubborn that I, the LORD,
cannot feed you like lambs
in an open pasture.

17 You people of Israel[v]
are charmed by[w] idols.
Leave them alone!
18 You get drunk, then sleep
with prostitutes;
you would rather be vulgar
than lead a decent life.[x]
19 And so you will be swept away
in a whirlwind
for sacrificing to idols.

Israel and Judah Will Be Judged

The LORD said:
5 Listen, you priests!
Pay attention, Israel![y]
Listen, you members
of the royal family.
Justice was your duty.
But[z] at Mizpah and Mount Tabor
you trapped the people.
2 At the place of worship
you were a treacherous pit,[a]
and I will punish you.

3 Israel, I know all about you,
and because of your unfaithfulness,
I find you unacceptable.
4 Your evil deeds are the reason
you won't return to me,
your LORD God.
And your constant craving for sex
keeps you from knowing me.

5 Israel, your pride
testifies to your guilt;
it makes you stumble,
and Judah stumbles too.
6 You offer sheep and cattle
as sacrifices to me,
but I have turned away
and refuse to be found.
7 You have been unfaithful
to me, your LORD;
you have had children
by prostitutes.[b]
So at the New Moon Festival,
you and your crops
will be destroyed.[c]

The LORD Warns Israel and Judah

8 Give a warning on the trumpet!
Let it be heard in Gibeah,
Ramah, and sinful Bethel.[d]
Benjamin, watch out![e]
9 I, the LORD, will punish
and wipe out Israel.
This is my solemn promise
to every tribe of Israel.
10 Judah's leaders are like crooks
who move boundary markers;
that's why I will flood them
with my anger.

11 Israel was brutally crushed.
They got what they deserved
for worshiping useless idols.[f]
12 Now I, the LORD,
will fill Israel with maggots
and make Judah rot.
13 When Israel and Judah saw
their sickness and wounds,

[u]**4.15** *sinful Bethel*: The Hebrew text has "Beth-Aven," which means "house of sin" or "house of nothing," referring to "Bethel," which means "house of God." [v]**4.17** *Israel*: The Hebrew text has "Ephraim," the leading tribe of the northern kingdom of Israel, which sometimes stands for the whole kingdom. [w]**4.17** *charmed by*: Or "joined to." [x]**4.18** *life*: One possible meaning for the difficult Hebrew text of verse 18. [y]**5.1** *Israel*: Probably meaning the tribal leaders of Israel. [z]**5.1** *Justice . . . duty. But*: Or "You are doomed, because." [a]**5.2** *At . . . pit*: One possible meaning for the difficult Hebrew text. [b]**5.7** *prostitutes*: See 4.14, and the note at 1.2. [c]**5.7** *So . . . destroyed*: One possible meaning for the difficult Hebrew text. [d]**5.8** *sinful Bethel*: See the note at 4.15. Gibeah is three miles north of Jerusalem, Ramah is five miles north, and Bethel is eleven miles north. The attack comes from the south, and all the land of Benjamin (belonging to Israel) is in danger. [e]**5.8** *watch out*: Or "lead the way." [f]**5.11** *for . . . idols*: One possible meaning for the difficult Hebrew text.

Israel asked help from Assyria
and its mighty king.[g]

But the king cannot cure them
or heal their wounds.
14 So I'll become a fierce lion
attacking Israel and Judah.
I'll snatch and carry off
what I want,
and no one can stop me.
15 Then I'll return to my temple
until they confess their guilt
and worship me,
until they are desperate
and beg for my help.

The LORD's People Speak

6 Let's return to the LORD.
He has torn us to shreds,
but he will bandage our wounds
and make us well.
2 In two or three days
he will heal us
and restore our strength
that we may live with him.
3 Let's do our best
to know the LORD.
His coming is as certain
as the morning sun;
he will refresh us like rain
renewing the earth
in the springtime.

The LORD Speaks to Israel and Judah

4 People of Israel and Judah,
what can I do with you?
Your love for me disappears
more quickly than mist
or dew at sunrise.
5 That's why I slaughtered you
with the words
of my prophets.
That's why my judgments blazed
like the dawning sun.[h]
6 I'd rather for you to be faithful
and to know me
than to offer sacrifices.

7 At a place named Adam,
you[i] betrayed me
by breaking our agreement.
8 Everyone in Gilead is evil;
your hands are stained
with the blood of victims.[j]
9 You priests are like a gang
of robbers in ambush.[k]
On the road to Shechem[l]
you murder and commit
other horrible crimes.
10 I have seen a terrible thing
in Israel—
you are unfaithful
and unfit to worship me.
11 People of Judah,
your time is coming too.

The LORD Wants To Help Israel

I, the LORD, would like to make
my nation prosper again
7 1 and to heal its wounds.
But then I see the crimes
in Israel[m] and Samaria.
Everyone is deceitful;
robbers roam the streets.
2 No one realizes
that I have seen their sins
surround them like a flood.

3 The king and his officials
take great pleasure
in their sin and deceit.
4 Everyone burns with desire—
they are like coals in an oven,
ready to burst into flames.
5 On the day their king
was crowned,
his officials got him drunk,
and he joined
in their foolishness.[n]

6 Their anger is a fire
that smolders all night,
then flares up at dawn.
7 They are flames
destroying their leaders.
And their kings are powerless;
none of them trust me.

8 The people of Israel[o]
have mixed with foreigners;
they are a thin piece of bread
scorched on one side.
9 They don't seem to realize
how weak and feeble they are;
their hair has turned gray,
while foreigners rule.
10 I am the LORD, their God,
but in all of their troubles
their pride keeps them
from returning to me.

No Help from Foreign Nations

The LORD said:
11 Israel[o] is a senseless bird,
fluttering back and forth
between Egypt and Assyria.
12 But I will catch them in a net
as hunters trap birds;

[g]**5.13** *and . . . king*: One possible meaning for the difficult Hebrew text. [h]**6.5** *That's why my . . . sun*: One possible meaning for the difficult Hebrew text. [i]**6.7** *At . . . you*: Or "Like Adam, you" or "Each one of you." [j]**6.8** *your hands . . . victims*: This may refer to child sacrifice. [k]**6.9** *You . . . ambush*: One possible meaning for the difficult Hebrew text. [l]**6.9** *Shechem*: This was one of the towns where people could run for safety, if they had accidentally killed someone (see Joshua 20.1-9). [m]**7.1** *Israel*: See the note at 4.17. Samaria was the capital city of Israel. [n]**7.5** *foolishness*: One possible meaning for the difficult Hebrew text of verse 5. [o]**7.8** *Israel*: Hebrew "Ephraim" (see the note at 4.17). [o]**7.11** *Israel*: Hebrew "Ephraim" (see the note at 4.17).

I threatened to punish them,
and indeed I will.[p]
13 Trouble and destruction
will be their reward
for rejecting me.
I would have rescued them,
but they told me lies.

14 They don't really pray to me;
they just howl in their beds.
They have rejected me for Baal
and slashed themselves,[q]
in the hope that Baal
will bless their crops.
15 I taught them what they know,
and I made them strong.
Now they plot against me
16 and refuse to obey.[r]
They are more useless
than a crooked arrow.
Their leaders will die in war
for saying foolish things.
Egyptians will laugh at them.

Israel Rejects the LORD

The LORD said:

8 Sound a warning!
Israel, you broke our agreement
and ignored my teaching.
Now an eagle is swooping down
to attack my land.
2 Israel, you say, "We claim you,
the LORD, as our God."
3 But your enemies
will chase you for rejecting
our good agreement.[s]

4 You chose kings and leaders
without consulting me;
you made silver and gold idols
that led to your downfall.
5 City of Samaria, I'm angry
because of your idol
in the shape of a calf.
When will you ever
be innocent again?
6 Someone from Israel built
that idol for you,
but only I am God.
And so it will be smashed
to pieces.[t]

7 If you scatter wind
instead of wheat,
you will harvest a whirlwind
and have no wheat.
Even if you harvest grain,
enemies will steal it all.

8 Israel, you are ruined,
and now the nations
consider you worthless.
9 You are like a wild donkey
that goes its own way.
You've run off to Assyria
and hired them as allies.
10 You can bargain with nations,
but I'll catch you anyway.
Soon you will suffer abuse
by kings and rulers.

11 Israel, you have built
many altars where you offer
sacrifices for sin.
But these altars have become
places for sin.
12 My instructions for sacrifices
were written in detail,
but you ignored them.
13 You sacrifice your best animals
and eat the sacrificial meals,[u]
but I, the LORD,
refuse your offerings.
I will remember your sins
and punish you.
Then you will return to Egypt.[v]

14 Israel, I created you,
but you forgot me.
You and Judah built palaces
and many strong cities.[w]
Now I will send fire to destroy
your towns and fortresses.

Israel Will Be Punished

9 Israel, don't celebrate
or make noisy shouts[x]
like other nations.
You have been unfaithful
to your God.
Wherever grain is threshed,
you behave like prostitutes
because you enjoy
the money you receive.[y]

[p]7.12 *I threatened . . . will*: One possible meaning for the difficult Hebrew text. [q]7.14 *slashed themselves*: One ancient translation and some Hebrew manuscripts; other Hebrew manuscripts "gather together." Slashing themselves was one way of worshiping Baal (see 1 Kings 18.28). [r]7.16 *and . . . obey*: One possible meaning for the difficult Hebrew text. [s]8.3 *our good agreement*: Or "me, the Good One" (referring to God). [t]8.6 *smashed to pieces*: Or "destroyed by fire." [u]8.13 *sacrifice . . . sacrificial meals*: One possible meaning for the difficult Hebrew text. Two kinds of sacrifices are referred to: Those in which the whole animal is burned on the altar ("whole burnt offerings" in traditional translations) and those in which part is eaten by the worshipers ("fellowship offerings" in traditional translations). [v]8.13 *return to Egypt*: Either as slaves or to find help against Assyria. [w]8.14 *built palaces . . . cities*: They did this because they no longer trusted the LORD to protect them. "Palaces" may also mean "temples." [x]9.1 *or . . . shouts*: One possible meaning for the difficult Hebrew text. [y]9.1 *Wherever . . . receive*: Grain was threshed on hills or other places where the wind could blow away the husks. People also met at these places to worship Baal, the god they thought had given them the grain harvest.

2 But you will run short
of grain and wine,
3 and you will have to leave
the land of the LORD.
Some of you will go to Egypt;
others will go to Assyria
and eat unclean food.

4 You won't be able to offer
sacrifices of wine
to the LORD.
None of your sacrifices
will please him—
they will be unclean
like food offered to the dead.
Your food will only be used
to satisfy your hunger;
none of it will be brought
to the LORD's temple.
5 You will no longer be able
to celebrate the festival
of the LORD.[z]
6 Even if you escape alive,
you will end up in Egypt
and be buried in Memphis.[a]
Your silver treasures
will be lost among weeds;[b]
thorns will sprout in your tents.

7 Israel, the time has come.
You will get what you deserve,
and you will know it.
"Prophets are fools," you say.
"And God's messengers
are crazy."
Your terrible guilt
has filled you with hatred.

8 Israel, the LORD sent me
to look after you.[c]
But you trap his prophets
and flood his temple
with your hatred.
9 You are brutal and corrupt,
as were the men of Gibeah.[d]
But God remembers your sin,
and you will be punished.

Sin's Terrible Results

10 Israel, when I, the LORD,
found you long ago
it was like finding
grapes in a barren desert
or tender young figs.
Then you worshiped Baal Peor,
that disgusting idol,
and you became as disgusting
as the idol you loved.

11 And so, Israel, your glory
will fly away like birds—
your women will no longer
be able to give birth.
12 Even if you do have children,
I will take them all
and leave you to mourn.
I will turn away,
and you will sink down
in deep trouble.
13 Israel, when I first met you,
I thought of you as palm trees
growing in fertile ground.[e]
Now you lead your people out,
only to be slaughtered.

Hosea's Advice

14 Our LORD, do just one thing
for your people—
make their women unable
to have children
or to nurse their babies.

The LORD's Judgment on Israel

15 Israel, I first began
to hate you because
you did evil at Gilgal.[f]
Now I will chase you
out of my house.
No longer will I love you;
your leaders betrayed me.
16 Israel, you are a vine
with dried-up roots
and fruitless branches.
Even if you had more children
and loved them dearly,
I would slaughter them all.

Hosea Warns Israel

17 Israel, you disobeyed my God.
Now he will force you to roam
from nation to nation.

10 You were a healthy vine
covered with grapes.
But the more grapes you grew,
the more altars you built;
the better off you became,
the better shrines you set up
for pagan gods.
2 You are deceitful and disloyal.
So you will pay
for your sins,
because the LORD will destroy
your altars and images.

3 "We don't have a king,"
you will say.
"We don't fear the LORD.
And what good are kings?"
4 Israel, you break treaties
and don't keep promises;

[z]9.5 *festival of the LORD*: Probably the Festival of Shelters. [a]9.6 *Memphis*: An Egyptian city with a famous cemetery. [b]9.6 *Your silver . . . weeds*: One possible meaning for the difficult Hebrew text. [c]9.8 *Israel . . . you*: One possible meaning for the difficult Hebrew text. [d]9.9 *the men of Gibeah*: They raped and murdered a woman (see Judges 19). [e]9.13 *Israel, when . . . ground*: One possible meaning for the difficult Hebrew text. [f]9.15 *Gilgal*: See 4.15.

you turn justice
into poisonous weeds
where healthy plants should grow.[g]

5 All who live in Samaria tremble
with concern for the idols[h]
at sinful Bethel.[i]
The idol there was the pride
of the priests,
but it has been put to shame;
now everyone will cry.
6 It will be taken to Assyria
and given to the great king.
Then Israel will be disgraced
for worshiping that idol.

7 Like a twig in a stream,
the king of Samaria
will be swept away.
8 The altars at sinful Bethel
will be destroyed
for causing Israel to sin;
they will be grown over
with thorns and thistles.
Then everyone will beg
the mountains and hills
to cover and protect them.

The LORD Promises To Punish Israel

9 Israel, you have never
stopped sinning[j]
since that time at Gibeah.[k]
That's why you
will be attacked at Gibeah.[l]
10 Your sins have doubled,
and you are rebellious.
Now I have decided
to send nations to attack
and put you in chains.

11 Once you were obedient
like a calf
that loved to thresh grain.
But I will put a harness
on your powerful neck;
you and Judah must plow
and cultivate the ground.
12 Plow your fields,
scatter seeds of justice,
and harvest faithfulness.
Worship me, the LORD,
and I will send my saving power
down like rain.
13 You have planted evil,
harvested injustice, and eaten
the fruit of your lies.
You trusted your own strength
and your powerful forces.
14 So war will break out,
and your fortresses
will be destroyed.
Your enemies will do to you
what Shalman[m] did to the people
of Beth-Arbel—
mothers and their children
will be beaten to death
against rocks.
15 Bethel, this will be your fate
because of your evil.
Israel, at dawn your king
will be killed.

God's Love for His People

11 When Israel was a child,
I loved him, and I called
my son out of Egypt.
2 But as the saying goes,
"The more they were called,
the more they rebelled."[n]
They never stopped offering
incense and sacrifices
to the idols of Baal.

3 I took Israel by the arm
and taught them to walk.
But they would not admit
that I was the one
who had healed them.
4 I led them with kindness
and with love,
not with ropes.
I held them close to me;[o]
I bent down to feed them.

5 But they trusted Egypt
instead of returning to me;
now Assyria will rule them.
6 War will visit their cities,
and their plans will fail.[p]
7 My people are determined
to reject me for a god
they think is stronger,
but he can't help.[q]

8 Israel, I can't let you go.
I can't give you up.
How could I possibly destroy you
as I did the towns of Admah
and Zeboiim?[r]
I just can't do it.
My feelings for you
are much too strong.

[g] **10.4** *you turn . . . grow*: One possible meaning for the difficult Hebrew text. [h] **10.5** *idols*: The Hebrew text has "calves," referring to the idols made in the shape of calves. [i] **10.5** *sinful Bethel*: See the note at 4.15. [j] **10.9** *never stopped sinning*: One possible meaning for the difficult Hebrew text. [k] **10.9** *Gibeah*: See the note at 9.9. [l] **10.9** *That's why . . . Gibeah*: One possible meaning for the difficult Hebrew text. [m] **10.14** *Shalman*: Perhaps a Moabite king, also known as Salamanu. [n] **11.2** *But . . . rebelled*: One possible meaning for the difficult Hebrew text. [o] **11.4** *I held . . . to me*: One possible meaning for the difficult Hebrew text. [p] **11.6** *fail*: One possible meaning for the difficult Hebrew text of verse 6. [q] **11.7** *help*: One possible meaning for the difficult Hebrew text of verse 7. [r] **11.8** *Admah and Zeboiim*: When the LORD destroyed Sodom and Gomorrah, he also destroyed these two towns (see Deuteronomy 29.23).

9 Israel, I won't lose my temper
and destroy you again.
I am the Holy God—
not merely some human,
and I won't stay angry.

10 I, the LORD, will roar like a lion,
and my children will return,
trembling from the west.
11 They will come back,
fluttering like birds from Egypt
or like doves from Assyria.
Then I will bring them
back to their homes.
I, the LORD, have spoken!

Israel and Judah Compared

12 Israel is deceitful to me,
their loyal and holy God;
they surround me with lies,
and Judah worships
other gods.[s]

12 All day long Israel chases
wind from the desert;
deceit and violence
are found everywhere.
Treaties are made with Assyria;
olive oil is taken to Egypt.

Israel and Judah Condemned

2 The LORD also brings charges
against the people of Judah,
the descendants of Jacob.
He will punish them
for what they have done.
3 Even before Jacob was born,
he cheated his brother,[t]
and when he grew up,
he fought against God.[u]

4 At Bethel, Jacob wrestled
with an angel and won;
then with tears in his eyes,
he asked for a blessing,
and God spoke to us[v] there.
5 God's name is the LORD,
the LORD God All-Powerful.
6 So return to your God.
Patiently trust him,
and show love and justice.

7 Israel, you enjoy cheating
and taking advantage
of others.
8 You say to yourself, "I'm rich!
I earned it all on my own,
without committing a sin."[w]

The LORD Is Still the God of Israel

9 Israel, I, the LORD,
am still your God,
just as I have been
since the time
you were in Egypt.
Now I will force you
to live in tents once again,
as you did in the desert.[x]
10 I spoke to the prophets—
often I spoke in visions.
And so, I will send my prophets
with messages of doom.
11 Gilead is terribly sinful
and will end up ruined.
Bulls are sacrificed in Gilgal
on altars made of stones,
but those stones will be scattered
in every field.
12 Jacob[y] escaped to Syria[z]
where he tended sheep
to earn himself a wife.
13 I sent the prophet Moses
to lead Israel from Egypt
and to keep them safe.
14 Israel, I will make you pay
for your terrible sins
and for insulting me.

Israel Is Doomed

The LORD said:

13 When your leaders[a] spoke,
everyone in Israel trembled
and showed great respect.
But you sinned by worshiping Baal,
and you were destroyed.
2 Now you continue to sin
by designing and making
idols of silver
in the shape of calves.
You are told to sacrifice
to these idols[b]—
yes, even to kiss them.

[s] **11.12** *and Judah worships other gods*: Or "but Judah remains faithful." [t] **12.3** *Jacob . . . cheated . . . brother*: In Hebrew "Jacob" sounds like "cheat" and also like "heel." Jacob grabbed his twin brother Esau by the heel at the time of their birth (see Genesis 25.26). Later he cheated him out of his rights and blessings as the first-born son (see Genesis 25.29-34; 27.1-40). [u] **12.3** *fought against God*: See Genesis 32.22-32. [v] **12.4** *us*: Hebrew; two ancient translations "him." [w] **12.8** *without . . . sin*: One possible meaning for the difficult Hebrew text. [x] **12.9** *as . . . desert*: One possible meaning for the difficult Hebrew text. This probably refers to the forty years of wandering through the desert after leaving Egypt, though it could refer to the "tents" (or "shelters") in which the Israelites lived during the Festival of Shelters (see 9.5, 6). [y] **12.12** *Jacob*: His name was later changed to Israel (see Genesis 32.28), and he became the ancestor of the nation by that name. [z] **12.12** *Syria*: The Hebrew text has "Aram," probably referring to northern Syria in the region of Haran. [a] **13.1** *your leaders*: The Hebrew text has "Ephraim," here meaning Mount Ephraim, where the royal palace of Samaria (capital of the northern kingdom of Israel) was located. [b] **13.2** *You are told . . . idols*: One possible meaning for the difficult Hebrew text.

3 And so, all of you will vanish
like the mist or the dew
of early morning,
or husks of grain in the wind
or smoke from a chimney.

4 I, the LORD, have been your God
since the time
you were in Egypt.
I am the only God you know,
the only one who can save.
5 I took care of you
in a thirsty desert.[c]
6 I fed you till you were satisfied,
then you became proud
and forgot about me.
7 Now I will attack like a lion,
ambush you like a leopard,
8 and rip you apart like a bear
robbed of her cubs.
I will gnaw on your bones,
as though I were a lion
or some other wild animal.
9 Israel, you are done for.
Don't expect help from me.[d]
10 You wanted a king and rulers.
Where is your king now?
What cities have rulers?
11 In my anger, I gave you a king;
in my fury, I took him away.

Israel's Terrible Fate

The LORD said:
12 Israel, your terrible sins
are written down
and stored away.
13 You are like a senseless child
who refuses to be born
at the proper time.
14 Should I, the LORD, rescue you
from death and the grave?
No! I call death and the grave
to strike you like a plague.
I refuse to show mercy.

15 No matter how much you prosper
more than the other tribes,[e]
I, the LORD, will wipe you out,
just as a scorching desert wind
dries up streams of water.
I will take away
your precious treasures.
16 Samaria[f] will be punished
for turning against me.
It will be destroyed in war—
children will be beaten
against rocks,
and pregnant women
will be ripped open.

Turn Back to the LORD

14 Israel, return! Come back
to the LORD, your God.
Sin has made you fall.
2 Return to the LORD and say,
"Please forgive our sins.
Accept our good sacrifices
of praise instead of bulls.[g]
3 Assyria can't save us,
and chariots can't help.
So we will no longer worship
the idols we have made.
Our LORD, you show mercy
to orphans."

The LORD Promises To Forgive

4 Israel, you have rejected me,
but my anger is gone;
I will heal you and love you
without limit.
5 I will be like the dew—
then you will blossom like lilies
and have roots like a tree.[h]
6 Your branches will spread
with the beauty
of an olive tree
and with the aroma
of Lebanon Forest.
7 You will rest in my shade,
and your grain will grow.
You will blossom
like a vineyard
and be famous as the wine
from Lebanon.

8 Israel, give up your idols!
I will answer your prayers
and take care of you.[i]
I am that glorious tree,
the source of your fruit.[j]

9 If you are wise, you will know
and understand what I mean.
I am the LORD, and I lead you
along the right path.
If you obey me,
we will walk together,
but if you are wicked,
you will stumble.

[c] **13.5** *thirsty desert*: The forty years that Israel wandered through the desert, after leaving Egypt. [d] **13.9** *Don't . . . me*: Or "You are against me, the one who helps you."
[e] **13.15** *more . . . tribes*: One possible meaning for the difficult Hebrew text. [f] **13.16** *Samaria*: The capital of the northern kingdom of Israel. [g] **14.2** *Accept . . . bulls*: One possible meaning for the difficult Hebrew text. [h] **14.5** *like a tree*: The Hebrew text has "like Lebanon," probably referring to the famous cedar trees on Mount Lebanon. [i] **14.8** *Israel . . . you*: One possible meaning for the difficult Hebrew text. [j] **14.8** *I am . . . fruit*: This is the only place in the Old Testament where the LORD is compared to a tree. Hosea reminds the people that it is the LORD who is the source of life, rather than the Canaanite gods and goddesses that are worshiped under trees at the local shrines.

JOEL

ABOUT THIS BOOK

Joel was a prophet who had watched swarm after swarm of locusts cover the land of Israel and wipe out the crops. He described these locusts as though they were an enemy army destroying everything in sight, and he said that the Lord had sent the locusts as punishment for the sins of Israel. Joel also used the locusts as a way of talking about a real army that was going to attack Israel. But the Lord promised that if the people would turn back to him, he would forgive them and bless them once again.

The locusts caused horrible destruction, but it was only a small taste of what will happen on the judgment day of the Lord. At that time the Lord will put all nations on trial for what they have done to his people, and those who are guilty will be punished.

Crowds fill Decision Valley.
The judgment day of the LORD
will soon be here—
no light from the sun or moon,
and stars no longer shine.
From the heart of Jerusalem
the LORD roars like a lion,
shaking the earth and sky.
But the LORD is a fortress,
a place of safety
for his people Israel.
(3.14-16)

A QUICK LOOK AT THIS BOOK

Locusts and an Enemy Army (1.1—2.17)
The Lord Will Bless His People (2.18-32)
The Lord Will Punish the Nations (3.1-21)

---

1 I am Joel the son of Pethuel.
And this is the message
the LORD gave to me.

Locusts Cover the Land

2 Listen, you leaders
and everyone else
in the land.
Has anything like this
ever happened before?
3 Tell our children!
Let it be told
to our grandchildren
and their children too.
4 Swarm after swarm of locusts[a]
has attacked our crops,
eating everything in sight.
5 Sober up, you drunkards!
Cry long and loud;
your wine supply is gone.
6 A powerful nation[b]
with countless troops
has invaded our land.
They have the teeth and jaws
of powerful lions.
7 Our grapevines and fig trees
are stripped bare;
only naked branches remain.

[a] 1.4 *Swarm . . . locusts*: The Hebrew text lists either four kinds of locusts or locusts in four stages of their development. Locusts are a type of grasshopper that comes in swarms and causes great damage to plant life. [b] 1.6 *A powerful nation*: The swarms of locusts.

8 Grieve like a young woman
mourning for the man
she was to marry.
9 Offerings of grain and wine
are no longer brought
to the LORD's temple.
His servants, the priests,
are deep in sorrow.
10 Barren fields mourn;
grain, grapes, and olives
are scorched and shriveled.

11 Mourn for our farms
and our vineyards!
There's no wheat or barley
growing in our fields.
12 Grapevines have dried up
and so has every tree—
figs and pomegranates,[c]
date palms and apples.
All happiness has faded away.

Return to God

13 Mourn, you priests who serve
at the altar of my God.
Spend your days and nights
wearing sackcloth.[d]
Offerings of grain and wine
are no longer brought
to the LORD's temple.

14 Tell the leaders and people
to come together
at the temple.
Order them to go without eating[e]
and to pray sincerely.
15 We are in for trouble!
Soon the LORD All-Powerful
will bring disaster.
16 Our food is already gone;
there's no more celebrating
at the temple of our God.

17 Seeds dry up in the ground;[f]
no harvest is possible.
Our barns are in bad shape,
with no grain
to store in them.
18 Our cattle wander aimlessly,
moaning for lack of pasture,
and sheep are suffering.[g]
19 I cry out to you, LORD.
Grasslands and forests are eaten
by the scorching heat.
20 Wild animals have no water
because of you;
rivers and streams are dry,
and pastures are parched.

Locusts and an Enemy Army

2 Sound the trumpet on Zion,
the LORD's sacred hill.
Warn everyone to tremble!
The judgment day of the LORD
is coming soon.
2 It will be dark and gloomy
with storm clouds overhead.
Troops will cover the mountains
like thunderclouds.
No army this powerful
has ever been gathered before
or will ever be again.
3 Fiery flames surround them;
no one escapes.
Before they invaded,
the land was like Eden;
now only a desert remains.

4 They look like horses
and charge like cavalry.
5 They roar over mountains
like noisy chariots,
or a mighty army
ready for battle.
They are a forest fire
that feasts on straw.
6 The very sight of them
is frightening.[h]
7 They climb over walls
like warriors;
they march in columns
and never turn aside.
8 They charge straight ahead,
without pushing each other;
even arrows and spears
cannot make them retreat.
9 They swarm over city walls
and enter our homes;
they crawl in through windows,
just like thieves.

10 They make the earth tremble
and the heavens shake;
the sun and moon turn dark,
and stars stop shining.
11 The LORD God leads this army
of countless troops,
and they obey his commands.
The day of his judgment
is so terrible
that no one can stand it.

The LORD's Invitation

12 The LORD said:

It isn't too late.
You can still return to me
with all your heart.
Start crying and mourning!
Go without eating.
13 Don't rip your clothes
to show your sorrow.
Instead, turn back to me
with broken hearts.

[c] 1.12 *pomegranates*: A bright red fruit that looks like an apple. [d] 1.13 *sackcloth*: A rough, dark-colored cloth made from goat or camel hair and used to make grain sacks. It was worn i[n] times of trouble or sorrow. [e] 1.14 *go without eating*: As a way of showing sorrow for their sins. [f] 1.17 *Seeds . . . ground*: One possible meaning for the difficult Hebrew text. [g] 1.18 *sheep are suffering*: One possible meaning for the difficult Hebrew text. [h] 2.6 *The very . . . frightening*: One possible meaning for the difficult Hebrew text.

I am merciful, kind, and caring.
I don't easily lose my temper,
and I don't like to punish.

14 I am the LORD your God.
Perhaps I will change my mind
and treat you with mercy.
Then you will be blessed
with enough grain and wine
for offering sacrifices to me.

15 Sound the trumpet on Zion!
Call the people together.
Show your sorrow
by going without food.
16 Make sure that everyone
is fit to worship me.[i]
Bring adults, children, babies,
and even bring newlyweds
from their festivities.

17 Tell my servants, the priests,
to cry inside the temple
and to offer this prayer
near the altar:[j]
"Save your people, LORD God!
Don't let foreign nations
make jokes about us.
Don't let them laugh and ask,
'Where is your God?' "

The LORD Will Bless the Land

18 The LORD was deeply concerned
about his land
and had pity on his people.
19 In answer to their prayers
he said,
"I will give you enough grain,
wine, and olive oil
to satisfy your needs.
No longer will I let you
be insulted by the nations.
20 An army attacked from the north,
but I will chase it
into a scorching desert.
There it will rot and stink
from the Dead Sea
to the Mediterranean."

The LORD works wonders
21 and does great things.
So tell the soil to celebrate
22 and wild animals
to stop being afraid.
Grasslands are green again;
fruit trees and fig trees
are loaded with fruit.
Grapevines are covered
with grapes.

23 People of Zion,[k]
celebrate in honor
of the LORD your God!
He is generous and has sent
the autumn and spring rains
in the proper seasons.[l]
24 Grain will cover
your threshing places;
jars will overflow
with wine and olive oil.

The LORD Will Rescue His People

25 I, the LORD your God,
will make up for the losses
caused by those swarms
and swarms of locusts[m]
I sent to attack you.
26 My people, you will eat
until you are satisfied.
Then you will praise me
for the wonderful things
I have done.
Never again will you
be put to shame.

27 Israel, you will know
that I stand at your side.
I am the LORD your God—
there are no other gods.
Never again will you
be put to shame.

The LORD Will Work Wonders

The LORD said:
28 Later, I will give my Spirit
to everyone.
Your sons and daughters
will prophesy.
Your old men
will have dreams,
and your young men
will see visions.
29 In those days I will even give
my Spirit to my servants,
both men and women.

30 I will work wonders
in the sky above
and on the earth below.
There will be blood and fire
and clouds of smoke.
31 The sun will turn dark,
and the moon
will be as red as blood
before that great
and terrible day
when I appear.

32 Then the LORD will save everyone who faithfully worships him. He has promised there will be survivors on Mount Zion and in Jerusalem, and among them will be his chosen ones.

The LORD Will Judge the Nations

3 At that time I, the LORD, will make Judah and Jerusalem prosperous

[i]2.16 *fit to worship me*: This required going through certain kinds of ceremonies.
[j]2.17 *inside . . . altar*: The Hebrew text has "between the porch and the altar," which is the place where the priests usually prayed for the people. [k]2.23 *Zion*: Jerusalem. [l]2.23 *in . . . seasons*: Or "as he used to do." [m]2.25 *swarms . . . locusts*: See the note at 1.4.

again. [2]Then in Judgment Valley[n] I will
bring together the nations that scattered
my people Israel everywhere in the
world, and I will bring charges against
those nations. They divided up my land
[3]and gambled to see who would get my
people; they sold boys and girls to pay
for prostitutes and wine.
[4]You people of Tyre and Sidon[o] and
you Philistines, why are you doing this?
Are you trying to get even with me? I'll
strike back before you know what's
happened. [5]You've taken my prized possessions, including my silver and gold,
and carried them off to your temples.[p]
[6]You have dragged the people of Judah
and Jerusalem from their land and sold
them to the Greeks.
[7]But I'll make the people of Judah determined to come home, and what happened to them will happen to you. [8]I'll
hand over your sons and daughters to
the people of Judah, and they will sell
them to the Sabeans,[q] who live far
away. I, the LORD, have spoken!

Judgment in Judgment Valley

[9]Say to the nations:

"Get ready for war!
Be eager to fight.
Line up for battle
and prepare to attack.
10 Make swords out of plows
and spears out of garden tools.
Strengthen every weakling."

11 Hurry, all you nations!
Come quickly.
Ask the LORD to bring
his warriors along.[r]
12 You must come now
to Judgment Valley,[s]
where the LORD will judge
the surrounding nations.
13 They are a field of ripe crops.
Bring in the harvest!
They are grapes piled high.
Start trampling them now![t]
If our enemy's sins were wine,
every jar would overflow.
14 Crowds fill Decision Valley.
The judgment day of the LORD
will soon be here—
15 no light from the sun or moon,
and stars no longer shine.
16 From the heart of Jerusalem
the LORD roars like a lion,
shaking the earth and sky.
But the LORD is a fortress,
a place of safety
for his people Israel.

God Will Bless His People

17 I am the LORD your God.
And you will know I live on Zion,
my sacred hill,
because Jerusalem will be sacred,
untouched by foreign troops.
18 On that day, fruitful vineyards
will cover the mountains.
And your cattle and goats
that graze on the hills
will produce a lot of milk.
Streams in Judah
will never run dry;
a stream from my house
will flow in Acacia Valley.[u]

19 Egypt and Edom were cruel
and brutal to Judah,
without a reason.
Now their countries will become
a barren desert,
20 but Judah and Jerusalem
will always have people.
21 I, the LORD, live on Mount Zion.
I will punish the guilty
and defend the innocent.[v]

[n]3.2 *Judgment Valley*: The Hebrew text has "Jehoshaphat Valley," which means "Valley of the LORD's Judgment." This valley is mentioned here and in verse 12, but nowhere else in the Bible.
[o]3.4 *Tyre and Sidon*: Two Phoenician coastal cities.
[p]3.5 *temples*: Or "palaces."
[q]3.8 *Sabeans*: The people of Seba, a region in southwest Arabia.
[r]3.11 *Ask . . . along*: One possible meaning for the difficult Hebrew text.
[s]3.12 *Judgment Valley*: See the note at 3.2.
[t]3.13 *grapes . . . now*: People trampled grapes with their bare feet to squeeze out the juice.
[u]3.18 *Acacia Valley*: In the plains of Moab, northeast of the Dead Sea.
[v]3.21 *I will . . . innocent*: One possible meaning for the difficult Hebrew text.

AMOS

ABOUT THIS BOOK

Amos wasn't a professional prophet and had never been trained to be a prophet (7.14). But when the Lord gave him messages for the people in the northern kingdom, Amos left his hometown of Tekoa in Judah and went to preach in the town of Bethel in Israel, probably at the famous place of worship.

In this book, Amos first condemns many of the nearby nations, and then he condemns the people of Israel, especially the rich who lived in luxury. They had great power and used it to rob the poor and to make slaves of them. And even though most of the people were worshiping other gods besides the Lord, they still expected the Lord to protect them. But Amos warned the people that they would be punished, and he said:

Choose good instead of evil!
See that justice is done.
Maybe I, the LORD God All-Powerful,
will be kind to what's left
of your people. *(5.15)*

A QUICK LOOK AT THIS BOOK

Crimes of the Nations Will Be Punished (1.1—3.2)
Israel and Samaria Will Be Destroyed (3.3—6.14)
Five Visions of Israel's Punishment (7.1—9.10)
Israel's Bright Future (9.11-15)

---

1 I am Amos. And I raised sheep
near the town of Tekoa[a] when
Uzziah was king of Judah and Jeroboam[b] son of Jehoash[c] was king of
Israel.

Two years before the earthquake,[d] the
LORD gave me several messages[e] about
Israel, 2and I said:

When the LORD roars
from Jerusalem,
pasturelands and Mount Carmel
dry up and turn brown.

Judgment on Syria

3The LORD said:

I will punish Syria[f]
for countless crimes,
and I won't change my mind.
They dragged logs with spikes[g]
over the people of Gilead.
4 Now I will burn down the palaces
and fortresses of King Hazael
and of King Benhadad.[h]
5 I will break through
the gates of Damascus.

[a]1.1 *Tekoa*: In the hill country of Judah about five miles south of Bethlehem. [b]1.1 *Uzziah . . . Jeroboam*: Uzziah was king of Judah 781-740 B.C., and Jeroboam II was king of Israel 783-743 B.C. [c]1.1 *Jehoash*: The Hebrew text has "Joash," another spelling of the name. [d]1.1 *Two years . . . earthquake*: Possibly the earthquake of 760 B.C., which seems to have been especially violent. [e]1.1 *messages*: Or "visions." [f]1.3 *Syria*: The Hebrew text has "Damascus," the leading city of Syria. [g]1.3 *logs with spikes*: These were dragged over grain to thresh it. [h]1.4 *Hazael . . . Benhadad*: Two Syrian kings.

I will destroy the people[i]
of Wicked Valley[j]
and the ruler of Beth-Eden.[k]
Then the Syrians will be dragged
as prisoners to Kir.[l]
I, the LORD, have spoken!

Judgment on Philistia

6 The LORD said:

I will punish Philistia[m]
for countless crimes,
and I won't change my mind.
They dragged off my people[n]
from town after town
to sell them as slaves
to the Edomites.

7 That's why I will burn down
the walls and fortresses
of the city of Gaza.
8 I will destroy the king[o] of Ashdod
and the ruler of Ashkelon.
I will strike down Ekron,[p]
and that will be the end
of the Philistines.
I, the LORD, have spoken!

Judgment on Phoenicia

9 The LORD said:

I will punish Phoenicia[q]
for countless crimes,
and I won't change my mind.
They broke their treaty
and dragged off my people[r]
from town after town
to sell them as slaves
to the Edomites.
10 That's why I will send flames
to burn down the city of Tyre
along with its fortresses.

Judgment on Edom

11 The LORD said:

I will punish Edom
for countless crimes,
and I won't change my mind.
They killed their own relatives[s]
and were so terribly furious
that they showed no mercy.
12 Now I will send fire to wipe out
the fortresses of Teman
and Bozrah.[t]

Judgment on Ammon

13 The LORD said:

I will punish Ammon
for countless crimes,
and I won't change my mind.
In Gilead they ripped open
pregnant women,
just to take the land.

14 Now I will send fire to destroy
the walls and fortresses
of Rabbah.[u]
Enemies will shout and attack
like a whirlwind.
15 Ammon's king and leaders
will be dragged away.
I, the LORD, have spoken!

Judgment on Moab

2 The LORD said:
I will punish Moab
for countless crimes,
and I won't change my mind.
They made lime from the bones[v]
of the king of Edom.
2 Now I will send fire to destroy
the fortresses of Kerioth.[w]
Battle shouts and trumpet blasts
will be heard as I destroy Moab
3 with its king and leaders.
I, the LORD, have spoken!

Judgment on Judah

4 The LORD said:

I will punish Judah
for countless crimes,
and I won't change my mind.
They have rejected my teachings
and refused to obey me.
They were led astray
by the same false gods
their ancestors worshiped.
5 Now I will send fire on Judah
and destroy the fortresses
of Jerusalem.

[i] **1.5** *people*: Or "king." [j] **1.5** *Wicked Valley*: The Hebrew text has "Aven Valley," probably the fertile valley between the Lebanon and the anti-Lebanon mountains. [k] **1.5** *I will . . . Beth-Eden*: Or "I will destroy the people of Wicked Valley and the king who rules from Beth-Eden." Beth-Eden was a city-state on the banks of the Euphrates River. [l] **1.5** *Kir*: The exact location of this country is not known; in 9.7 Amos refers to Kir as the original home of the Syrians, and so the verse probably means that the Syrians will lose everything they have gained as a people. [m] **1.6** *Philistia*: The Hebrew text has "Gaza," one of the main Philistine cities. [n] **1.6** *my people*: The people of Israel. [o] **1.8** *king*: Or "people." [p] **1.8** *Ashdod . . . Ashkelon . . . Ekron*: Philistine cities. [q] **1.9** *Phoenicia*: The Hebrew text has "Tyre," which was one of the two Phoenician cities; the other was Sidon, which is not mentioned by Amos. [r] **1.9** *my people*: See the note at 1.6. [s] **1.11** *their own relatives*: The Edomites were descendants of Esau, the brother of Jacob, the ancestor of the Israelites. [t] **1.12** *Teman and Bozrah*: These stand for all of Edom; Teman may have been a city or a district. Bozrah, the chief city of northern Edom, was thirty miles southeast of the Dead Sea. [u] **1.14** *Rabbah*: The capital city of Ammon. [v] **2.1** *They . . . bones*: They dug up the bodies of kings and made lime out of them to use as whitewash on their houses and walls. [w] **2.2** *Kerioth*: A leading city of Moab and a center for the worship of Chemosh, the chief god of Moab.

Judgment on Israel

6 The LORD said:

I will punish Israel
for countless crimes,
and I won't change my mind.
They sell honest people for money,
and the needy are sold
for the price of sandals.
7 They smear the poor in the dirt
and push aside
those who are helpless.

My holy name is dishonored,
because fathers and sons sleep
with the same young women.
8 They lie down beside altars
on clothes taken
as security for loans.
And they drink wine in my temple,
wine bought with the money
they received from fines.

9 Israel, the Amorites[x] were there
when you entered Canaan.
They were tall as cedars
and strong as oaks.
But I wiped them out—
I destroyed their branches
and their roots.
10 I had rescued you from Egypt,
and for forty years I had led you
through the desert.
Then I gave you the land
of the Amorites.

11 I chose some of you
to be prophets
and others to be Nazirites.[y]
People of Israel,
you know this is true.
I, the LORD, have spoken!
12 But you commanded the prophets
not to speak their message,
and you pressured the Nazirites
into drinking wine.

13 And so I will crush you,
just as a wagon full of grain
crushes the ground.[z]
14 No matter how fast you run,
you won't escape.
No matter how strong you are,
you will lose your strength
and your life.
15 Even if you are an expert
with a bow and arrow,
you will retreat.
And you won't get away alive,
not even if you run fast
or ride a horse.
16 You may be brave and strong,
but you will run away,
stripped naked.
I, the LORD, have spoken!

3 People of Israel,
I rescued you from Egypt.
Now listen to my judgment
against you.
2 Of all nations on earth,
you are the only one
I have chosen.
That's why I will punish you
because of your sins.

The Work of a Prophet

3 Can two people walk together
without agreeing to meet?
4 Does a lion roar in the forest
unless it has caught
a victim?
Does it growl in its den
unless it is eating?
5 How can anyone catch a bird
without using a net?
Does a trap spring shut
unless something is caught?

6 Isn't the whole city frightened
when the trumpet
signals an attack?
Isn't it the LORD who brings
disaster on a city?
7 Whatever the LORD God
plans to do,
he tells his servants,
the prophets.
8 Everyone is terrified
when a lion roars—
and ordinary people
become prophets
when the LORD God speaks.

Samaria Is Doomed

9 Here is a message
for the leaders
of Philistia[a] and Egypt—
tell everyone to come together
on the hills of Samaria.
Let them see the injustice
and the lawlessness
in that city.
10 The LORD has said
that they don't even know how
to do right.
They have become rich
from violence and robbery.
11 And so the LORD God has sworn
that they will be surrounded.
Enemies will break through
their defenses
and steal their treasures.

[x] **2.9** *Amorites*: This word is used for all the people who lived in Canaan at the time Israel took over the land. [y] **2.11** *Nazirites*: People who promised the LORD that they would never drink wine or cut their hair or come in contact with a dead body. [z] **2.13** *ground*: One possible meaning for the difficult Hebrew text of verse 13. [a] **3.9** *Philistia*: The Hebrew text has "Ashdod," one of the leading cities of Philistia.

12 The LORD has promised
that only a few from Samaria
will escape with their lives
and with some broken pieces
of their beds and couches.[b]
It will be like when a shepherd
rescues two leg bones
and part of a sheep's ear
from the jaws of a lion.[c]

The Altars at Bethel

13 The LORD God All-Powerful
told me to speak this message
against Jacob's descendants:
14 When I, the LORD, punish Israel
for their sins,
I will destroy the altars
at Bethel.
Even the corners of the altar[d]
will be left in the dirt.
15 I will tear down winter homes
and summer homes.
Houses decorated with ivory
and all other mansions
will be gone forever.
I, the LORD, have spoken!

The Women of Samaria

The LORD said:
4 You women of Samaria
are fat cows![e]
You mistreat and abuse
the poor and needy,
then you say to your husbands,
"Bring us more drinks!"
2 I, the LORD God, have sworn
by my own name
that your time is coming.
Not one of you will be left—
you will be taken away
by sharp hooks.[f]
3 You will be dragged through holes
in your city walls,
and you will be thrown
toward Harmon.[g]
I, the LORD, have spoken!

Israel Refuses To Obey

The LORD said:
4 Come to Bethel and Gilgal.[h]
Sin all you want!
Offer sacrifices the next morning
and bring a tenth of your crops
on the third day.[i]
5 Bring offerings to show me
how thankful you are.
Gladly bring more offerings
than I have demanded.
You really love to do this.
I, the LORD God, have spoken!

How the LORD Warned Israel

6 I, the LORD, took away the food
from every town and village,
but still you rejected me.
7 Three months before harvest,
I kept back the rain.
Sometimes I would let it fall
on one town or field
but not on another,
and pastures dried up.
8 People from two or three towns
would go to a town
that still had water,
but it wasn't enough.
Even then you rejected me.
I, the LORD, have spoken!

9 I dried up your grain fields;
your gardens and vineyards
turned brown.
Locusts[j] ate your fig trees
and olive orchards,
but even then you rejected me.
I, the LORD, have spoken!

10 I did terrible things to you,
just as I did to Egypt—
I killed your young men in war;
I let your horses be stolen,
and I made your camp stink
with dead bodies.
Even then you rejected me.
I, the LORD, have spoken!

11 I destroyed many of you,
just as I did the cities
of Sodom and Gomorrah.
You were a burning stick
I rescued from the fire.
Even then you rejected me.
I, the LORD, have spoken!

12 Now, Israel, I myself
will deal with you.
Get ready to face your God!

[b]**3.12** *some . . . couches*: One possible meaning for the difficult Hebrew text. [c]**3.12** *lion*: When a wild animal attacked and killed a sheep, the shepherd had to rescue part of the sheep and take it to the owner as proof that it had been killed by an animal. Otherwise, the shepherd had to pay the owner the cost of the sheep. [d]**3.14** *altar*: Altars were places of worship but also places of protection. People whose lives were in danger could grab hold of the corners of an altar, and no one was allowed to kill them. [e]**4.1** *fat cows*: The Hebrew text has "cows of Bashan," a fertile plain famous for its rich pastures and well-fed cattle. [f]**4.2** *taken . . . hooks*: One possible meaning for the difficult Hebrew text. [g]**4.3** *Harmon*: Hebrew; some manuscripts of one ancient translation "Mount Hermon," a mountain in the north of Palestine, on the way to Assyria. [h]**4.4** *Bethel and Gilgal*: These were two of the most important centers of worship in northern Israel. Amos mentions these together again in 5.5. [i]**4.4** *Offer . . . day*: Or "Offer sacrifices each morning and bring a tenth of your crops every three days." In verses 4, 5 God is condemning the people for meaningless acts of worship. [j]**4.9** *Locusts*: A type of grasshopper that comes in swarms and causes great damage to plant life.

13 I created the mountains
and the wind.
I let humans know
what I am thinking.[k]
I bring darkness at dawn
and step over hills.
I am the LORD God All-Powerful!

Turn Back to the LORD

5 Listen, nation of Israel,
to my mournful message:
2 You, dearest Israel, have fallen,
never to rise again—
you lie deserted in your own land,
with no one to help you up.

3 The LORD God has warned,
"From every ten soldiers
only one will be left;
from a thousand troops,
only a hundred will survive."

4 The LORD keeps saying,
"Israel, turn back to me
and you will live!
5 Don't go to Gilgal or Bethel
or even to Beersheba.[l]
Gilgal will be dragged away,
and Bethel will end up
as nothing."[m]

6 Turn back to the LORD,
you descendants of Joseph,[n]
and you will live.
If you don't, the LORD
will attack like fire.
Bethel will burn to the ground,
and no one can save it.
7 You people are doomed!
You twist the truth
and stomp on justice.

8 But the LORD created the stars
and put them in place.[o]
He turns darkness to dawn
and daylight to darkness;
he scoops up the ocean
and empties it on the earth.
9 God destroys mighty soldiers
and strong fortresses.

Choose Good Instead of Evil!

The LORD said:
10 You people hate judges
and honest witnesses;
11 you abuse the poor and demand
heavy taxes from them.
You have built expensive homes,
but you won't enjoy them;
you have planted vineyards,
but you will get no wine.
12 I am the LORD, and I know
your terrible sins.
You cheat honest people
and take bribes;
you rob the poor of justice.
13 Times are so evil
that anyone with good sense
will keep quiet.

14 If you really want to live,
you must stop doing wrong
and start doing right.
I, the LORD God All-Powerful,
will then be on your side,
just as you claim I am.
15 Choose good instead of evil!
See that justice is done.
Maybe I, the LORD All-Powerful,
will be kind to what's left
of your people.[p]

Judgment Is Coming

16 This is what the LORD has sworn:

Noisy crying will be heard
in every town and street.
Even farmers will be told
to mourn for the dead,
together with those
who are paid to mourn.[q]
17 Your vineyards will be filled
with crying and weeping,[r]
because I will punish you.
I, the LORD, have spoken!

When the LORD Judges

18 You look forward to the day
when the LORD comes to judge.
But you are in for trouble!
It won't be a time of sunshine;
all will be darkness.
19 You will run from a lion,
only to meet a bear.
You will escape to your house,
rest your hand on the wall,
and be bitten by a snake.
20 The day when the LORD judges
will be dark, very dark,
without a ray of light.

[k] 4.13 *I let . . . thinking*: Or "No one's secret thoughts are hidden from me." [l] 5.5 *Gilgal . . . Bethel . . . Beersheba*: These were ancient places of worship, but the LORD had warned his people to stay away from them. [m] 5.5 *Gilgal . . . nothing*: In Hebrew "Gilgal" and "dragged away" sound something alike. Bethel (meaning "house of God") is sometimes called "house of nothing" or "house of sin" by the prophets (see Hosea 4.15; 5.8; 10.5-8). [n] 5.6 *descendants of Joseph*: Another name for the people of the northern kingdom of Israel. [o] 5.8 *the stars . . . place*: The Hebrew text mentions two groups of stars, Pleiades and Orion. Since the LORD is the Creator of the stars, he controls the seasons that are signaled by the different positions of the stars. Moreover, the stars are created objects and should not be worshiped. [p] 5.15 *your people*: Hebrew "Joseph's descendants" (see the note at verse 6). [q] 5.16 *paid to mourn*: In ancient times some people were paid to mourn and make loud cries at funerals. [r] 5.17 *Your vineyards . . . weeping*: Instead of happy celebrations that were often held in vineyards after the harvest.

What the LORD Demands

21 I, the LORD, hate and despise
your religious celebrations
and your times of worship.
22 I won't accept your offerings
or animal sacrifices—
not even your very best.
23 No more of your noisy songs!
I won't listen
when you play your harps.
24 But let justice and fairness
flow like a river
that never runs dry.

25 Israel, for forty years
you wandered in the desert,
without bringing offerings
or sacrifices to me.
26 Now you will have to carry
the two idols you made—
Sakkuth, the one you call king,
and Kaiwan, the one you built
in the shape of a star.[s]
27 I will force you to march
as captives beyond Damascus.
I, the LORD God All-Powerful,
have spoken![t]

Israel Will Be Punished

6 Do you rulers in Jerusalem
and in the city of Samaria
feel safe and at ease?
Everyone bows down to you,
and you think you are better
than any other nation.
But you are in for trouble!
2 Look what happened
to the cities of Calneh,
powerful Hamath,
and Gath[u] in Philistia.
Are you greater than any
of those kingdoms?
3 You are cruel, and you forget
the coming day of judgment.

4 You rich people lounge around
on beds with ivory posts,
while dining on the meat
of your lambs and calves.
5 You sing foolish songs
to the music of harps,
and you make up new tunes,
just as David used to do.
6 You drink all the wine you want
and wear expensive perfume,
but you don't care about
the ruin of your nation.[v]
7 So you will be the first
to be dragged off as captives;
your good times will end.

8 The LORD God All-Powerful
has sworn by his own name:
"You descendants of Jacob
make me angry by your pride,
and I hate your fortresses.
And so I will surrender your city
and possessions
to your enemies."

9 If only ten of you survive
by hiding in a house
you will still die.
10 As you carry out a corpse
to prepare it for burial,[w]
your relative in the house
will ask, "Are there others?"
You will answer, "No!"
Then your relative will reply,
"Be quiet! Don't dare mention
the name of the LORD."[x]
11 At the LORD's command,
houses great and small
will be smashed to pieces.

12 Horses can't gallop on rocks;
oceans[y] can't be plowed.
But you have turned justice
and fairness
into bitter poison.
13 You celebrate the defeat
of Lo-Debar and Karnaim,[z]
and you boast by saying,
"We did it on our own."

14 But the LORD God All-Powerful
will send a nation to attack
you people of Israel.
They will capture Lebo-Hamath
in the north,
Arabah Creek[a] in the south,
and everything in between.

[s]**5.26** *star*: One possible meaning for the difficult Hebrew text of verse 26. [t]**5.27** *I, the LORD . . . spoken*: Israel did not offer sacrifices and gifts to the LORD during the time they wandered through the desert. But now they have made idols to carry during their ceremonies. So the LORD warns that he will make them "march" away as captives beyond Damascus, where Israel had extended its borders by victories in war (see 2 Kings 14.28). [u]**6.2** *Calneh . . . Hamath . . . Gath*: City-states captured by the Assyrians: Calneh in 738 B.C., Hamath in 720, and Gath in 711. [v]**6.6** *your nation*: Hebrew "Joseph's descendants" (see the note at 5.6). [w]**6.10** *prepare . . . burial*: Or "burn it" or "burn incense for it." [x]**6.10** *the name of the LORD*: Two relatives seem to be carrying out corpses for burial. One of them warns the other to be careful not even to say "Thank the LORD!" for fear that the mention of his name may cause something worse to happen. [y]**6.12** *oceans*: Or "rocks." [z]**6.13** *Lo-Debar and Karnaim*: Two cities east of the Jordan River that were captured by Jeroboam II (see 2 Kings 14.25). In Hebrew "Lo-Debar" can mean "nothing," and "Karnaim" means "two horns (of a bull)." Horns were symbols of strength, and so the people are bragging about their military power (defeat of "two horns"), which Amos says is "nothing" (Lo-Debar). [a]**6.14** *Lebo-Hamath . . . Arabah Creek*: The northern and southern boundaries of the northern kingdom.

A Vision of Locusts

7 The LORD God showed me that he is
going to send locusts[b] to attack your
crops. It will happen after the king has
already been given his share of the
grain and before the rest of the grain
has been harvested.[c] 2In my vision the
locusts ate every crop in the land, and I
said to the LORD, "Forgive me for asking, but how can the nation survive? It's
so weak."
3Then the LORD felt sorry and answered, "I won't let it be destroyed."

A Vision of Fire

4The LORD showed me that he is
going to send a ball of fire to burn up
everything on earth, including the
ocean. 5Then I said, "Won't you please
stop? How can our weak nation survive?"
6Again the LORD felt sorry and answered, "I won't let it be destroyed."

A Vision of a Measuring Line

7The LORD showed me a vision of himself standing beside a wall and holding
a string with a weight tied to the end of
it. The string and weight had been used
to measure the straightness of the wall.
8Then he asked, "Amos, what do you
see?"
"A measuring line," I answered.
The LORD said, "I'm using this measuring line to show that my people Israel don't measure up, and I won't forgive them any more. 9Their sacred
places will be destroyed, and I will send
war against the nation of King Jeroboam."[d]

Amos and Amaziah

10Amaziah the priest at Bethel sent
this message to King Jeroboam of Israel, "Amos is plotting against you in the
very heart of Israel. Our nation cannot
put up with his message for very long.
11Here is what he is saying:

'Jeroboam will be put to death,
and the people will be taken
to a foreign country.' "

12Then Amaziah told me, "Amos, take
your visions and get out! Go back to Judah and earn your living there as a
prophet. 13Don't do any more preaching
at Bethel. The king worships here at our
national temple."
14I answered:

I'm not a prophet! And I wasn't
trained to be a prophet. I am a shepherd, and I take care of fig trees.
15But the LORD told me to leave my
herds and preach to the people of Israel. 16And here you are, telling me
not to preach! 17Now, listen to what
the LORD says about you:

Your wife will become
a prostitute in the city,
your sons and daughters
will be killed in war,
and your land will be divided
among others.
You will die in a country
of foreigners,
and the people of Israel
will be dragged
from their homeland.

A Basket of Fruit

8 The LORD God showed me a basket
of ripe fruit 2and asked, "Amos,
what do you see?"
"A basket of ripe fruit," I replied.
Then he said,

"This is the end[e]
for my people Israel.
I won't forgive them again.
3 Instead of singing
in the temple,
they will cry and weep.
Dead bodies will be everywhere.
So keep silent!
I, the LORD, have spoken!"

Israel Is Doomed

The LORD said:
4 You people crush those in need
and wipe out the poor.
5 You say to yourselves,
"How much longer before the end
of the New Moon Festival?
When will the Sabbath[f] be over?
Our wheat is ready,
and we want to sell it now.
We can't wait to cheat
and charge high prices
for the grain we sell.
We will use dishonest scales
6 and mix dust in the grain.
Those who are needy and poor
don't have any money.
We will make them our slaves
for the price
of a pair of sandals."

7 I, the LORD, won't forget
any of this,

[b]7.1 *locusts*: See the note at 4.9. [c]7.1 *harvested*: This would have been an especially bad time for a locust attack. The non-grain crops such as vegetables and onions were just beginning to sprout, and the grain crops were almost ready to be harvested.
[d]7.9 *Jeroboam*: Jeroboam II, who ruled Israel 783-743 B.C. [e]8.2 *end*: In Hebrew "ripe fruit" and "end" sound alike. [f]8.5 *New Moon Festival . . . Sabbath*: Selling grain at these times was forbidden by the Law of Moses.

though you take great pride
in your ancestor Jacob.[g]
8 Your country will tremble,
and you will mourn.
It will be like the Nile River
that rises and overflows,
then sinks back down.

9 On that day, I, the LORD God,
will make the sun
go down at noon,
and I will turn daylight
into darkness.
10 Your festivals and joyful singing
will turn into sorrow.
You will wear sackcloth[h]
and shave your heads,
as you would at the death
of your only son.
It will be a horrible day.

11 I, the LORD, also promise you
a terrible shortage,
but not of food and water.
You will hunger and thirst
to hear my message.
12 You will search everywhere—
from north to south,
from east to west.
You will go all over the earth,
seeking a message
from me, the LORD.
But you won't find one.

13 Your beautiful young women
and your young men
will faint from thirst.
14 You made promises
in the name of Ashimah,
the goddess of Samaria.
And you made vows in my name
at the shrines
of Dan and Beersheba.[i]
But you will fall
and never get up.

Judgment on Israel

9 I saw a vision of the LORD
standing by the temple altar,[j]
and he said,
"Shake the columns
until the tops fall loose,
and the doorposts crumble.
Then make the pieces fall
on the people below.
I will take a sword and kill
anyone who escapes.
2 "If they dig deep into the earth
or climb to the sky,
I'll reach out and get them.
3 If they escape to the peaks
of Mount Carmel,
I'll search and find them.
And if they hide from me
at the bottom of the ocean,
I'll command a sea monster
to bite them.
4 I'll send a sword to kill them,
wherever their enemies
drag them off as captives.
I'm determined to hurt them,
not to help them."

His Name Is the LORD

5 When the LORD God All-Powerful
touches the earth, it melts,
and its people mourn.
God makes the earth rise
and then fall,
just like the Nile River.
6 He built his palace in the heavens
and let its foundations
rest on the earth.[k]
He scoops up the ocean
and empties it on the earth.
His name is the LORD.

The LORD Is God

7 Israel, I am the LORD God,
and the Ethiopians[l]
are no less important to me
than you are.
I brought you out of Egypt,
but I also brought
the Philistines from Crete[m]
and the Arameans from Kir.[n]
8 My eyes have seen
what a sinful nation you are,
and I'll wipe you out.
But I will leave a few
of Jacob's descendants.
I, the LORD, have spoken!

9 At my command, all of you
will be sifted like grain.
Israelites who remain faithful
will be scattered
among the nations.
And the others will be trapped
like trash in a sifter.
10 Some of you are evil,
and you deny
that you will ever get caught.
But you will be killed.

[g] **8.7** *though . . . Jacob*: Or "though I am the God that Jacob proudly worshiped."
[h] **8.10** *sackcloth*: A rough, dark-colored cloth made from goat or camel hair and used to make grain sacks. It was worn in times of trouble or sorrow.
[i] **8.14** *You made . . . Beersheba*: Or "You made promises to the goddess Ashimah at Samaria, and you made vows in the names of other gods at the shrines of Dan and Beersheba."
[j] **9.1** *the temple altar*: The one at Bethel.
[k] **9.6** *He built . . . earth*: One possible meaning for the difficult Hebrew text.
[l] **9.7** *Ethiopians*: The Hebrew text has "people of Cush," which was a region south of Egypt that included parts of the present countries of Ethiopia and Sudan.
[m] **9.7** *Crete*: Hebrew "Caphtor."
[n] **9.7** *Philistines . . . Arameans from Kir*: The Philistines were Israel's enemies to the west, and the Arameans were enemies to the northeast. For Kir, see the note at 1.5.

The LORD's Promise to Israel

11 In the future, I will rebuild
David's fallen kingdom.
I will build it from its ruins
and set it up again,
just as it used to be.
12 Then you will capture Edom
and the other nations
that are mine.
I, the LORD, have spoken,
and my words will come true.

13 You will have such a harvest
that you won't be able
to bring in all of your wheat
before plowing time.
You will have grapes left over
from season to season;
your fruitful vineyards
will cover the mountains.

14 I'll make Israel prosper again.
You will rebuild your towns
and live in them.
You will drink wine
from your own vineyards
and eat the fruit you grow.
15 I'll plant your roots deep
in the land I have given you,
and you won't ever
be uprooted again.
I, the LORD God, have spoken!

OBADIAH

ABOUT THIS BOOK

Obadiah was a prophet, but nothing else is known about him. His name, meaning "worshiper of the Lord," was fairly common in ancient Israel.

Obadiah wrote about the nation of Edom, which was south of the Dead Sea. The Edomites had been cruel to the Lord's people Israel, and so the Lord was going to punish them and give their land to Israel.

The book of Obadiah is so short that it wasn't divided into chapters.

A QUICK LOOK AT THIS BOOK

Edom's Pride and Punishment (1-9)
Edom's Cruelty (10-14)
Victory for Israel (15-21)

Edom's Pride and Punishment

The LORD God gave Obadiah
a message[a] about Edom,
and this is what we heard:
"I, the LORD, have sent
a messenger
with orders for the nations
to attack Edom."

2 The LORD said to Edom:
I will make you the weakest
and most despised nation.
3 You live in a mountain fortress,[b]
because your pride
makes you feel safe from attack,
but you are mistaken.
4 I will still bring you down,
even if you fly higher
than an eagle
or nest among the stars.
I, the LORD, have spoken!

5 If thieves break in at night,
they steal
only what they want.
And people who harvest grapes
always leave some unpicked.
But, Edom, you are doomed!
6 Everything you treasure most
will be taken from you.
7 Your allies can't be trusted.
They will force you out
of your own country.
Your best friends
will trick and trap you,
even before you know it.

8 Edom, when this happens,
I, the LORD, will destroy
all your marvelous wisdom.
9 Warriors from the city of Teman[c]
will be terrified,
and you descendants of Esau[d]
will be wiped out.

The LORD Condemns Edom's Cruelty

10 You were cruel to your relatives,
the descendants of Jacob.[e]
Now you will be destroyed,
disgraced forever.
11 You stood there and watched
as foreigners entered Jerusalem
and took what they wanted.
In fact, you were no better
than those foreigners.

12 Why did you celebrate
when such a dreadful disaster
struck your relatives?
Why were you so pleased

[a] **1** *message*: Or "vision." [b] **3** *mountain fortress*: The Hebrew text has "rocky cliff," which sounds like "Sela," the capital of Edom, a fortress city built on a mountain. [c] **9** *Teman*: A famous city in Edom. [d] **9** *descendants of Esau*: The people of Edom were descendants of Esau, the brother of Jacob (Israel). [e] **10** *descendants of Jacob*: Jacob and Esau were brothers (see the note on Esau at verse 9).

when everyone in Judah
was suffering?
13 They are my people,
and you were cruel to them.
You went through their towns,
sneering and stealing
whatever was left.
14 In their time of torment,
you ambushed refugees
and handed them over
to their attackers.

The LORD Will Judge the Nations

15 The day is coming
when I, the LORD,
will judge the nations.
And, Edom, you will pay in full
for what you have done.

16 I forced the people of Judah[f]
to drink the wine of my anger
on my sacred mountain.
Soon the neighboring nations
must drink their fill—
then vanish without a trace.

Victory for Israel

17 The LORD's people who escape
will go to Mount Zion,
and it will be holy.
Then Jacob's descendants
will capture the land of those
who took their land.
18 Israel[g] will be a fire,
and Edom will be straw
going up in flames.
The LORD has spoken!

19 The people of Israel
who live in the Southern Desert
will take the land of Edom.
Those who live in the hills
will capture Philistia,
Ephraim, and Samaria.
And the tribe of Benjamin
will conquer Gilead.

20 Those who return from captivity
will control Phoenicia
as far as Zarephath.[h]
Captives from Jerusalem
who were taken to Sepharad[i]
will capture the towns
of the Southern Desert.
21 Those the LORD has saved
will live on Mount Zion
and rule over Edom.[j]
Then the kingdom will belong
to the LORD.

[f]**16** *I forced . . . Judah*: Or "I will force the people of Edom." [g]**18** *Israel*: Hebrew "The descendants of Jacob and of Joseph." [h]**20** *Those who return . . . Zarephath*: One possible meaning for the difficult Hebrew text. [i]**20** *Sepharad*: Possibly the city of Sardis, the capital of Lydia, a country north and west of Media. This would refer to those captives from Judah who had been taken beyond the kingdom of Babylonia. [j]**21** *Those the LORD . . . Edom*: Or "Leaders on (from) Mount Zion will save the people and rule over Edom."

JONAH

ABOUT THIS BOOK

The book of Jonah is different from the other prophetic books, because it gives only one sentence of what the prophet Jonah preached. Instead, this book tells how Jonah disobeyed the Lord and refused to warn Nineveh that it was going to be destroyed. Jonah even wanted the city to be destroyed, because it was the capital city of Assyria, a hated enemy of Israel. But the Lord corrected Jonah; then Jonah went to Nineveh and preached the Lord's message.

When many people think about the book of Jonah, they think only of Jonah being swallowed by a huge fish. However, the message of this book is that the Lord wants to have mercy on everyone; as Jonah says to him:

> *You are a kind and merciful God, and you are very patient. You always show love, and you don't like to punish anyone, not even foreigners.* *(4.2b)*

A QUICK LOOK AT THIS BOOK

Jonah Runs from the Lord (1)
Jonah Prays to the Lord (2)
Jonah Goes to Nineveh, and Its People Believe God's Message (3)
Jonah Is Angry Because the Lord Showed Mercy (4)

Jonah Runs from the LORD

1 One day the LORD told Jonah, the
son of Amittai, 2to go to the great
city of Nineveh[a] and say to the people,
"The LORD has seen your terrible sins.
You are doomed!"
3Instead, Jonah ran from the LORD. He
went to the seaport of Joppa and bought
a ticket on a ship that was going to
Spain. Then he got on the ship and
sailed away to escape.
4But the LORD made a strong wind
blow, and such a bad storm came up
that the ship was about to be broken to
pieces. 5The sailors were frightened, and
they all started praying to their gods.
They even threw the ship's cargo overboard to make the ship lighter.
All this time, Jonah was down below
deck, sound asleep. 6The ship's captain
went to him and said, "How can you
sleep at a time like this? Get up and
pray to your God! Maybe he will have
pity on us and keep us from drowning."
7Finally, the sailors got together and
said, "Let's ask our gods to show us[b]
who caused all this trouble." It turned
out to be Jonah.
8They started asking him, "Are you
the one who brought all this trouble on
us? What business are you in? Where do
you come from? What is your country?
Who are your people?"
9Jonah answered, "I'm a Hebrew, and
I worship the LORD God of heaven, who
made the sea and the dry land."
10When the sailors heard this, they
were frightened, because Jonah had already told them he was running from
the LORD. Then they said, "Do you know
what you have done?"
11The storm kept getting worse, until

[a]**1.2** *Nineveh*: Capital city of Assyria, a hated enemy of Israel. [b]**1.7** *ask . . . show us*: The Hebrew text has "cast lots," which were pieces of wood or stone used to find out how and when to do something. In this case, the lots would show who was the guilty person.

finally the sailors asked him, "What
should we do with you to make the sea
calm down?"
12 Jonah told them, "Throw me into the
sea, and it will calm down. I'm the cause
of this terrible storm."
13 The sailors tried their best to row to
the shore. But they could not do it, and
the storm kept getting worse every
minute. 14 So they prayed to the LORD,
"Please don't let us drown for taking
this man's life. Don't hold us guilty for
killing an innocent man. All of this happened because you wanted it to." 15 Then
they threw Jonah overboard, and the
sea calmed down. 16 The sailors were so
terrified that they offered a sacrifice to
the LORD and made all kinds of promises.
17 The LORD sent a big fish to swallow
Jonah, and Jonah was inside the fish for
three days and three nights.

Jonah's Prayer

2 From inside the fish, Jonah prayed
to the LORD his God:

2 When I was in trouble, LORD,
I prayed to you,
and you listened to me.
From deep in the world
of the dead,
I begged for your help,
and you answered my prayer.

3 You threw me down
to the bottom of the sea.
The water was churning
all around;
I was completely covered
by your mighty waves.
4 I thought I was swept away
from your sight,
never again to see
your holy temple.

5 I was almost drowned
by the swirling waters
that surrounded me.
Seaweed had wrapped
around my head.
6 I had sunk down below
the underwater mountains;
I knew that forever,
I would be a prisoner there.

But, you, LORD God,
rescued me from that pit.
7 When my life was slipping away,
I remembered you—
and in your holy temple
you heard my prayer.

8 All who worship worthless idols
turn from the God
who offers them mercy.
9 But with shouts of praise,
I will offer a sacrifice
to you, my LORD.
I will keep my promise,
because you are the one
with power to save.

10 The LORD commanded the fish to
vomit up Jonah on the shore. And it did.

Jonah Goes to Nineveh

3 Once again the LORD told Jonah 2 to
go to that great city of Nineveh and
preach his message of doom.
3 Jonah obeyed the LORD and went to
Nineveh. The city was so big that it took
three days just to walk through it. 4 After
walking for a day, Jonah warned the
people, "Forty days from now, Nineveh
will be destroyed!"
5 They believed God's message and set
a time when they would go without eating to show their sorrow. Then everyone
in the city, no matter who they were,
dressed in sackcloth.
6 When the king of Nineveh heard
what was happening, he also dressed in
sackcloth; he left the royal palace and
sat in dust.[c] 7-9 Then he and his officials
sent out an order for everyone in the
city to obey. It said:

None of you or your animals may
eat or drink a thing. Each of you
must wear sackcloth, and you must
even put sackcloth on your animals.
You must also pray to the LORD
God with all your heart and stop being sinful and cruel. Maybe God will
change his mind and have mercy on
us, so we won't be destroyed.

10 When God saw that the people had
stopped doing evil things, he had pity
and did not destroy them as he had
planned.

Jonah Gets Angry at the LORD

4 Jonah was really upset and angry.
2 So he prayed:

Our LORD, I knew from the very
beginning that you wouldn't destroy
Nineveh. That's why I left my own
country and headed for Spain. You
are a kind and merciful God, and
you are very patient. You always
show love, and you don't like to punish anyone, not even foreigners.
3 Now let me die! I'd be better off
dead.

4 The LORD replied, "What right do you
have to be angry?"

[c] **3.5,6** *dressed in sackcloth . . . sat in dust*: Sackcloth was a rough, dark-colored cloth made from goat or camel hair and used to make grain sacks. Sometimes people wore sackcloth and sat in dust to show how sorry they were for their sins.

5Jonah then left through the east gate
of the city and made a shelter to protect
himself from the sun. He sat under the
shelter, waiting to see what would happen to Nineveh.
6The LORD made a vine grow up to
shade Jonah's head and protect him
from the sun. Jonah was very happy to
have the vine, 7but early the next morning the LORD sent a worm to chew on
the vine, and the vine dried up. 8During
the day the LORD sent a scorching wind,
and the sun beat down on Jonah's head,
making him feel faint. Jonah was ready
to die, and he shouted, "I wish I were
dead!"
9But the LORD asked, "Jonah, do you
have the right to be angry about the
vine?"

"Yes, I do," he answered, "and I'm angry enough to die."
10But the LORD said:

You are concerned about a vine
that you did not plant or take care
of, a vine that grew up in one night
and died the next. 11In that city of
Nineveh there are more than a hundred twenty thousand people who
cannot tell right from wrong, and
many cattle are also there. Don't you
think I should be concerned about
that big city?

MICAH

ABOUT THIS BOOK

The messages in this book were especially for Samaria, the capital of Israel, and for Jerusalem, the capital of Judah. Instead of leading their nations to worship and obey the Lord, the officials and people of these capital cities had led their nations to worship other gods and to cheat and rob the poor. And so the Lord was going to punish Israel and Judah.

But the Lord had also promised that in the future the people of Israel and Judah would return to him. Then he and his chosen king would take care of the people, just as shepherds take care of sheep, and there would be peace everywhere:

He will settle arguments
between distant
and powerful nations.
They will pound their swords
and their spears
into rakes and shovels;
they will never again make war
or attack one another.
Everyone will find rest
beneath their own fig trees
or grape vines,
and they will live in peace.
(4.3, 4)

A QUICK LOOK AT THIS BOOK

The Lord Will Punish His People (1.1—2.11)
A Promise of Hope (2.12, 13)
The Lord Will Punish Evil Rulers and Lying Prophets (3.1-12)
A New Temple in a New Israel (4.1—5.15)
Israel Is Declared Guilty (6.1—7.7)
The Nation Turns to God (7.8-20)

---

1 I am Micah from Moresheth.[a] And
this is the message about Samaria
and Jerusalem[b] that the LORD gave to
me when Jotham, Ahaz, and Hezekiah[c]
were the kings of Judah.

Judgment on Samaria

2 Listen, all of you!
Earth and everything on it,
pay close attention.
The LORD God accuses you
from his holy temple.[d]
3 And he will come down
to crush underfoot
every pagan altar.
4 Mountains will melt
beneath his feet
like wax beside a fire.
Valleys will vanish like water
rushing down a ravine.

[a]**1.1** *Moresheth*: A town in southern Judah not far from Gath. In verse 14 it is called Moresheth-Gath. [b]**1.1** *Samaria and Jerusalem*: Samaria was the capital of the northern kingdom (Israel), and Jerusalem was the capital of the southern kingdom (Judah).
[c]**1.1** *Jotham, Ahaz, and Hezekiah*: Jotham, the son of Uzziah, ruled Judah 740–736 B.C.; Ahaz, the son of Jotham, ruled 736–716 B.C.; Hezekiah, the son of Ahaz, ruled 716–687 B.C.
[d]**1.2** *holy temple*: Possibly the one in heaven, though it may be the Jerusalem temple.

5 This will happen because of
the terrible sins of Israel,
the descendants of Jacob.
Samaria has led Israel to sin,
and pagan altars at Jerusalem
have made Judah sin.

6 So the LORD will leave Samaria
in ruins—
merely an empty field
where vineyards are planted.
He will scatter its stones
and destroy its foundations.
7 Samaria's idols will be smashed,
and the wages
of temple prostitutes[e]
will be destroyed by fire.
Silver and gold from those idols
will then be used by foreigners
as payment for prostitutes.

Judah Is Doomed

8 Because of this tragedy,[f]
I go barefoot and naked.
My crying and weeping
sound like howling wolves
or ostriches.
9 The nation is fatally wounded.
Judah is doomed.
Jerusalem will fall.

10 Don't tell it in Gath!
Don't even cry.
Instead, roll in the dust
at Beth-Leaphrah.[g]
11 Depart naked and ashamed,
you people of Shaphir.[h]
The town of Bethezel[i] mourns
because no one from Zaanan[j]
went out to help.[k]
12 Everyone in Maroth[l]
hoped for the best,
but the LORD sent disaster
down on Jerusalem.

13 Get the war chariots ready,
you people of Lachish.[m]
You led Jerusalem into sin,
just as Israel did.[n]
14 Now you will have to give
a going-away gift[o]
to Moresheth.[p]
Israel's kings will discover
that they cannot trust
the town of Achzib.[q]

15 People of Mareshah,[r]
the LORD will send someone
to capture your town.
Then Israel's glorious king
will be forced to hide
in Adullam Cave.[s]
16 Judah, shave your head
as bald as a buzzard
and start mourning.
Your precious children[t]
will be dragged off
to a foreign country.

Punishment for Those Who Abuse Their Power

2 Doomed! You're doomed!
At night you lie in bed,
making evil plans.
And when morning comes,
you do what you've planned
because you have the power.
2 You grab any field or house
that you want;
you cheat families
out of homes and land.

3 But here is what the LORD says:
"I am planning trouble for you.

[e] **1.7** *wages of temple prostitutes*: At pagan temples, people had sex with prostitutes as a way of worshiping the idols, and the money earned in this way was used to support the pagan religion. [f] **1.8** *this tragedy*: Either the destruction of Samaria (verses 6,7) or the coming destruction of Judah and Jerusalem. [g] **1.10** *Gath . . . Beth-Leaphrah*: Gath was a Philistine city; Beth-Leaphrah is unknown, but in Hebrew it sounds like "House of Dust." [h] **1.11** *Shaphir*: Mentioned only here in the Old Testament; in Hebrew "Shaphir" means "beautiful." [i] **1.11** *Bethezel*: Mentioned only here in the Old Testament; in Hebrew "Bethezel" means "house next door." [j] **1.11** *Zaanan*: Mentioned only here in the Old Testament; in Hebrew "Zaanan" means "one who goes out." [k] **1.11** *The town . . . help*: Or "No one from Zaanan refused to desert their town, and Bethezel mourns because it is left undefended." [l] **1.12** *Maroth*: Mentioned only here in the Old Testament; in Hebrew "Maroth" means "bitter." [m] **1.13** *Lachish*: The chief city of southwest Judah, about thirty miles from Jerusalem. [n] **1.13** *led . . . sin . . . did*: Or "You led Jerusalem and Israel into sin." In Hebrew "Lachish" sounds like "a team of horses (that pulls a war chariot)." And the sin may be that Lachish led the nation to trust the power of war chariots instead of the LORD. But the sin could be idolatry or some false teachings that were brought in from Egypt by way of Lachish. [o] **1.14** *going-away gift*: The gift (dowry) that a bride's father gave her when she left the home of her parents to live with the family of her husband. In Hebrew the word for "bride" or "fiancee" sounds like "Moresheth." [p] **1.14** *Moresheth*: Hebrew "Moresheth-Gath"; the home of Micah (see verse 1). [q] **1.14** *Achzib*: Meaning "lie" or "deception" was near Adullam Cave (verse 15), where David hid from King Saul (see 1 Samuel 22.1, 2). Micah probably means that the people of Israel (including their king) will have to run for their lives, but will find that all hope for escape is merely a "lie" (see verse 15). [r] **1.15** *Mareshah*: Sounds something like the Hebrew word for "conqueror" and was only a few miles northeast of Lachish. [s] **1.15** *Adullam Cave*: See the note at 1.14. [t] **1.16** *precious children*: The towns mentioned in verses 10-15.

Your necks will be caught
in a noose,
and you will be disgraced
in this time of disaster."

4 When that happens,
this sorrowful song
will be sung about you:
"Ruined! Completely ruined!
The LORD has taken our land
and given it to traitors."[u]
5 And so you will never again
own property
among the LORD's people.

6 "Enough of your preaching!"
That's what you tell me.
"We won't be disgraced,
so stop preaching!"

7 Descendants of Jacob,
is it right for you to claim
that the LORD did what he did
because he was angry?
Doesn't he always bless
those who do right?
8 My people, you have even stolen
clothes right off the backs
of your unsuspecting soldiers
returning home from battle.
9 You take over lovely homes
that belong to the women
of my nation.
Then you cheat their children
out of the inheritance
that comes from the LORD.[v]

10 Get out of here, you crooks!
You'll find no rest here.
You're not fit to belong
to the LORD's people,
and you will be destroyed.[w]
11 The only prophet you want
is a liar who will say,
"Drink and get drunk!"

A Promise of Hope

12 I, the LORD, promise
to bring together
the people of Israel
who have survived.
I will gather them,
just as a shepherd
brings sheep together,
and there will be many.
13 I will break down the gate
and lead them out—
then I will be their king.

Evil Rulers and Lying Prophets

3 Listen to me,
you rulers of Israel!
You know right from wrong,
2 but you prefer to do evil
instead of what is right.
You skin my people alive.
You strip off their flesh,
3 break their bones,
cook it all in a pot,
and gulp it down.

4 Someday you will beg the LORD
to help you,
but he will turn away
because of your sins.

5 You lying prophets promise
security for anyone
who gives you food,
but disaster for anyone
who refuses to feed you.
Here is what the LORD says
to you prophets:
6 "You will live in the dark,
far from the sight of the sun,
with no message from me.
7 You prophets and fortunetellers
will all be disgraced,
with no message from me."

8 But the LORD has filled me
with power and his Spirit.
I have been given the courage
to speak about justice
and to tell you people of Israel
that you have sinned.
9 So listen to my message,
you rulers of Israel!
You hate justice
and twist the truth.
10 You make cruelty and murder
a way of life in Jerusalem.
11 You leaders accept bribes
for dishonest decisions.
You priests and prophets
teach and preach,
but only for money.

Then you say,
"The LORD is on our side.
No harm will come to us."
12 And so, because of you,
Jerusalem will be plowed under
and left in ruins.
Thorns will cover the mountain
where the temple now stands.

Peace and Prosperity

4 In the future, the mountain
with the LORD's temple
will be the highest of all.
It will reach above the hills,
and every nation
will rush to it.
2 People of many nations
will come and say,

[u] 2.4 *The LORD . . . traitors*: One possible meaning for the difficult Hebrew text.
[v] 2.9 *inheritance . . . LORD*: The Hebrew text has "my glory," which refers to the inheritance of land that the LORD had promised his people.
[w] 2.10 *destroyed*: One possible meaning for the difficult Hebrew text.

"Let's go up to the mountain
of the LORD God of Jacob
and worship in his temple."

The LORD will teach us his Law
from Jerusalem,
and we will obey him.
3 He will settle arguments
between distant
and powerful nations.
They will pound their swords
and their spears
into rakes and shovels;
they will never again make war
or attack one another.
4 Everyone will find rest
beneath their own fig trees
or grape vines,
and they will live in peace.
This is a solemn promise
of the LORD All-Powerful.

5 Others may follow their gods,
but we will always follow
the LORD our God.

The LORD Will Lead His People Home

6 The LORD said:
At that time
I will gather my people—
the lame and the outcasts,
and all into whose lives
I have brought sorrow.
7 Then the lame and the outcasts
will belong to my people
and become a strong nation.
I, the LORD, will rule them
from Mount Zion forever.
8 Mount Zion in Jerusalem,
guardian of my people,
you will rule again.

9 Jerusalem, why are you crying?
Don't you have a king?
Have your advisors gone?
Are you suffering
like a woman in childbirth?
10 Keep on groaning with pain,
you people of Jerusalem!
If you escape from your city
to the countryside,
you will still be taken
as prisoners to Babylonia.
But later I will rescue you
from your enemies.

11 Zion, because of your sins
you are surrounded
by many nations who say,
"We can hardly wait
to see you disgraced."[x]
12 But they don't know
that I, the LORD,
have gathered them here
to grind them like grain.
13 Smash them to pieces, Zion!
I'll let you be like a bull
with iron horns
and bronze hoofs.
Crush those nations
and bring their wealth to me,
the LORD of the earth.

A Promised Ruler

5 Jerusalem, enemy troops
have surrounded you;[y]
they have struck Israel's ruler
in the face with a stick.

2 Bethlehem Ephrath,
you are one of the smallest towns
in the nation of Judah.
But the LORD will choose
one of your people
to rule the nation—
someone whose family
goes back to ancient times.[z]
3 The LORD will abandon Israel
only until this ruler is born,
and the rest of his family
returns to Israel.
4 Like a shepherd
taking care of his sheep,
this ruler will lead
and care for his people
by the power and glorious name
of the LORD his God.
His people will live securely,
and the whole earth will know
his true greatness,
5 because he will bring peace.

Assyria Will Be Defeated

Let Assyria attack our country
and our palaces.
We will counterattack,
led by a number of rulers
6 whose strong army will defeat
the nation of Assyria.[a]
Yes, our leaders will rescue us,
if those Assyrians
dare to invade our land.

The Survivors Will Be Safe

7 A few of Jacob's descendants
survived and are scattered
among the nations.
But the LORD will let them
cover the earth like dew and rain
that refreshes the soil.
8 At present they are scattered,
but later they will attack,
as though they were fierce lions
pouncing on sheep.

[x]**4.11** *We . . . disgraced*: Or "We'll pull up your skirt and expose your nakedness!"
[y]**5.1** *Jerusalem . . . you*: Or "Jerusalem, you are slashing yourself in sorrow, because of the enemy troops." [z]**5.2** *family . . . times*: Or "kingdom is eternal." [a]**5.6** *the nation of Assyria*: The Hebrew text uses both "land of Assyria" and "land of Nimrod," which was a poetic name for Assyria.

Their enemies will be torn
to shreds,
with no one to save them;
9 they will be helpless,
completely destroyed.

Idols Will Be Destroyed in Israel

10 The LORD said:
At that time I will wipe out
your cavalry and chariots,
11 as well as your cities
and your fortresses.
12 I will stop you
from telling fortunes
and practicing witchcraft.
13 You will no longer worship
the idols or stone images
you have made—
I will destroy them,
14 together with the sacred poles[b]
and even your towns.
15 I will become furious
and take revenge on the nations
that refuse to obey me.

The LORD's Challenge to His People

6 The LORD said to his people:
Come and present your case
to the hills and mountains.
2 Israel, I am bringing charges
against you—
I call upon the mountains
and the earth's firm foundation
to be my witnesses.

3 My people, have I wronged you
in any way at all?
Please tell me.
4 I rescued you from Egypt,
where you were slaves.
I sent Moses, Aaron, and Miriam
to be your leaders.
5 Don't forget the evil plans
of King Balak of Moab
or what Balaam son of Beor[c]
said to him.
Remember how I, the LORD,
saved you many times
on your way from Acacia
to Gilgal.[d]

True Obedience

6 What offering should I bring
when I bow down to worship
the LORD God Most High?
Should I try to please him[e]
by sacrificing
calves a year old?
7 Will thousands of sheep
or rivers of olive oil
make God satisfied with me?
Should I sacrifice to the LORD
my first-born child as payment
for my terrible sins?
8 The LORD God has told us
what is right
and what he demands:
"See that justice is done,
let mercy be your first concern,
and humbly obey your God."

Cheating and Violence

9 I am the LORD,
and it makes sense to respect
my power to punish.
So listen to my message
for the city of Jerusalem:[f]
10 You store up stolen treasures
and use dishonest scales.[g]
11 But I, the LORD, will punish you
for cheating with weights
and with measures.
12 You rich people are violent,
and everyone tells lies.

13 Because of your sins,
I will wound you and leave you
ruined and defenseless.
14 You will eat,
but still be hungry;
you will store up goods,
but lose everything—
I, the LORD, will let it all
be captured in war.
15 You won't harvest what you plant
or use the oil
from your olive trees
or drink the wine
from grapes you grow.

16 Jerusalem, this will happen
because you followed
the sinful example
of kings Omri and Ahab.[h]
Now I will destroy you
and your property.
Then the people of every nation
will make fun and insult you.

Israel Is Corrupt

7 I feel so empty inside—
like someone starving
for grapes or figs,

[b]**5.14** *sacred poles*: Used in the worship of Asherah, the fertility goddess. [c]**6.5** *Balak . . . Beor*: See Numbers 22–24. [d]**6.5** *Acacia to Gilgal*: Acacia was where the Israelites camped after the experience with Balaam (see Numbers 25.1; Joshua 2.1; 3.1); Gilgal was where they camped while waiting to attack Jericho (see Joshua 4.19—5.12). [e]**6.6** *try to please him*: This refers to what are traditionally called "burnt sacrifices," which were offered as a way of pleasing the LORD. [f]**6.9** *Jerusalem*: One possible meaning for the difficult Hebrew text of verse 9. [g]**6.10** *scales*: One possible meaning for the difficult Hebrew text of verse 10. [h]**6.16** *Omri and Ahab*: King Ahab was the son of Omri and the husband of the evil Jezebel. Almost two centuries before Micah, the prophet Elijah had spoken against the idolatry and the other sinful practices that Ahab had encouraged in Israel (see 1 Kings 16.21-34; 18.1-18; 21.1-26).

after the vines and trees
have all been picked clean.
2 No one is loyal to God;
no one does right.
Everyone is brutal
and eager to deceive
everyone else.
3 People cooperate to commit crime.
Judges and leaders demand bribes,
and rulers cheat in court.[i]
4 The most honest of them
is worse than a thorn patch.

Your doom has come!
Lookouts sound the warning,
and everyone panics.
5 Don't trust anyone,
not even your best friend,
and be careful what you say
to the one you love.

6 Sons refuse to respect
their own fathers,
daughters rebel against
their own mothers,
and daughters-in-law despise
their mothers-in-law.
Your family is now your enemy.
7 But I trust the LORD God
to save me,
and I will wait for him
to answer my prayer.

The Nation Turns to God

8 My enemies, don't be glad
because of my troubles!
I may have fallen,
but I will get up;
I may be sitting in the dark,
but the LORD is my light.
9 I have sinned against the LORD.
And so I must endure his anger,
until he comes to my defense.
But I know that I will see him
making things right for me
and leading me to the light.

10 You, my enemies, said,
"The LORD God is helpless."
Now each of you
will be disgraced
and put to shame.
I will see you trampled
like mud in the street.

A Bright Future

11 Towns of Judah, the day is coming
when your walls will be rebuilt,
and your boundaries enlarged.
12 People will flock to you
from Assyria and Egypt,
from Babylonia[j]
and everywhere else.
13 Those nations will suffer disaster
because of what they did.

Micah's Prayer and the LORD's Answer

14 Lead your people, LORD!
Come and be our shepherd.
Grasslands surround us,
but we live in a forest.
So lead us to Bashan and Gilead,[k]
and let us find pasture
as we did long ago.

15 I, the LORD, will work miracles
just as I did when I led you
out of Egypt.
16 Nations will see this
and be ashamed because
of their helpless armies.
They will be in shock,
unable to speak or hear,
17 because of their fear of me,
your LORD and God.
Then they will come trembling,
crawling out of their fortresses
like insects or snakes,
lapping up the dust.

No One Is Like God

The people said:
18 Our God, no one is like you.
We are all that is left
of your chosen people,
and you freely forgive
our sin and guilt.
You don't stay angry forever;
you're glad to have pity
19 and pleased to be merciful.
You will trample on our sins
and throw them in the sea.
20 You will keep your word
and be faithful to Jacob
and to Abraham,
as you promised our ancestors
many years ago.

[i]**7.3** *court*: One possible meaning for the difficult Hebrew text of verse 3. [j]**7.12** *Babylonia*: The Hebrew text has "the river," meaning the Euphrates River, which stood for Babylonia. [k]**7.14** *Bashan and Gilead*: Two regions east of the Jordan River, known for their fertile pasturelands.

NAHUM

ABOUT THIS BOOK

In this book, the prophet Nahum said the Lord was going to bring justice and punish Assyria, because it had been so cruel to other nations. Many Old Testament books also talk about the Lord's mercy when they discuss the Lord's justice. But in this book the Lord is merciful and good only to those who turn to him (1.7). Nahum also hinted that one way God has mercy on his people is to punish enemies like Assyria and give his people freedom from their power (1.13-15). And the Lord can do this because he rules the earth:

The LORD God demands loyalty.
In his anger, he takes revenge
on his enemies.
The LORD is powerful,
yet patient;
he makes sure that the guilty
are always punished.
He can be seen in storms
and in whirlwinds;
clouds are the dust from his feet.
(1.2, 3)

A QUICK LOOK AT THIS BOOK

---

1 I am Nahum from Elkosh.[a] And this
is the message[b] that I wrote down
about Nineveh.[c]

The Fierce Anger of the LORD

2 The LORD God demands loyalty.
In his anger, he takes revenge
on his enemies.
3 The LORD is powerful,
yet patient;
he makes sure that the guilty
are always punished.
He can be seen in storms
and in whirlwinds;
clouds are the dust from his feet.

4 At the LORD's command,
oceans and rivers dry up.
Bashan, Mount Carmel,
and Lebanon[d] wither,
and their flowers fade.
5 At the sight of the LORD,
mountains and hills
tremble and melt;
the earth and its people
shudder and shake.
6 Who can stand the heat
of his furious anger?
It flashes out like fire
and shatters stones.

The Power of Assyria Will Be Broken

7 The LORD is good.
He protects those who trust him
in times of trouble.
8 But like a roaring flood,

[a]**1.1** *Elkosh*: The location of Elkosh is not known. [b]**1.1** *message*: Or "vision." [c]**1.1** *Nineveh*: The capital of Assyria, the hated enemy of Israel. [d]**1.4** *Bashan, Mount Carmel, and Lebanon*: Three regions noted for their trees and flowers.

the LORD chases his enemies
into dark places
and destroys them.
9 So don't plot against the LORD!
He wipes out his enemies,
and they never revive.
10 They are like drunkards
overcome by wine,
or like dry thornbushes
burning in a fire.[e]
11 Assyria, one of your rulers
has made evil plans
against the LORD.

12 But the LORD says, "Assyria,
no matter how strong you are,
you are doomed!
My people Judah,
I have troubled you before,
but I won't do it again.
13 I'll snap your chains
and set you free
from the Assyrians."

14 Assyria, this is what else
the LORD says to you:
"Your name will be forgotten.
I will destroy every idol
in your temple,
and I will send you to the grave,
because you are worthless."

15 Look toward the mountains,
people of Judah!
Here comes a messenger
with good news of peace.
Celebrate your festivals.
Keep your promises to God.
Your evil enemies are destroyed
and will never again
invade your country.

Nineveh Will Fall

2 Nineveh, someone is coming
to attack and scatter you.
Guard your fortresses!
Watch the road! Be brave!
Prepare for battle!
2 Judah and Israel are like trees
with branches broken
by their enemies.
But the LORD is going to restore
their power and glory.

*3 Nineveh, on this day of attack,
your enemies' shields are red;
their uniforms are crimson.
4 Their horses[f] prance,
and their armored[g] chariots
dart around like lightning
or flaming torches.
5 An officer gives a command.
But his soldiers stumble,
as they hasten to build
a shelter to protect themselves
against rocks thrown down
from the city wall.

6 The river gates[h] fly open,
and panic floods the palace.
7 Nineveh is disgraced.
The queen is dragged off.
Her servant women mourn;
they sound like doves,
and they beat their breasts
in sorrow.[i]
8 Nineveh is like a pond
with leaking water.
Shouts of "Stop! Don't go!"
can be heard everywhere.
But everyone is leaving.

9 Enemy soldiers shout,
"The city is full of treasure
and all kinds of wealth.
Steal her silver! Grab her gold!"

10 Nineveh is doomed! Destroyed!
Her people tremble with fear;
their faces turn pale.[j]
11 What happened to this city?
They were safer there
than powerful lions in a den,
with no one to disturb them.
12 These are the same lions
that ferociously attacked
their victims,
then dragged away the flesh
to feed their young.

13 The LORD All-Powerful,
is against you, Nineveh.
God will burn your chariots
and send an army to kill
those young lions of yours.
You will never again
make victims of others
or send messengers to threaten
everyone on this earth.

Punishment for Nineveh

The LORD said:
3 Doom to the crime capital!
Nineveh, city of murder
and treachery,
2 here is your fate—
cracking whips,
churning wheels;
galloping horses,
roaring chariots;
3 cavalry attacking,
swords and spears flashing;
soldiers stumbling
over piles of dead bodies.

[e]**1.10** *fire*: One possible meaning for the difficult Hebrew text of verse 10. [f]**2.4** *horses*: Two ancient translations; Hebrew "spears." [g]**2.4** *armored*: One possible meaning for the difficult Hebrew text. [h]**2.6** *river gates*: Nineveh was protected by a moat filled with water from the nearby Tigris River. [i]**2.7** *sorrow*: One possible meaning for the difficult Hebrew text of verse 7. [j]**2.10** *faces turn pale*: Or "ashes cover their faces."

4 You were nothing more
than a prostitute
using your magical charms
and witchcraft
to attract and trap nations.

5 But I, the LORD All-Powerful,
am now your enemy.
I will pull up your skirt
and let nations and kingdoms
stare at your nakedness.
6 I will cover you with garbage,
treat you like trash,
and rub you in the dirt.
7 Everyone who sees you
will turn away and shout,
"Nineveh is done for!
Is anyone willing to mourn
or to give her comfort?"

Nineveh's Fate Is Sealed

8 Nineveh, do you feel safer
than the city of Thebes?[k]
The Nile River
was its wall of defense.[l]
9 Thebes trusted the mighty power
of Ethiopia[m] and Egypt;
the nations of Put[n] and Libya
were her allies.
10 But she was captured and taken
to a foreign country.
Her children were murdered
at every street corner.
The members of her royal family
were auctioned off,
and her high officials
were bound in chains.

11 Nineveh, now it's your turn!
You will get drunk and try to hide
from your enemy.
12 Your fortresses are fig trees
with ripe figs.
Merely shake the trees,
and fruit will fall
into every open mouth.
13 Your army is weak.
Fire has destroyed the crossbars
on your city gates;
now they stand wide open
to your enemy.

14 Your city is under attack.
Haul in extra water!
Strengthen your defenses!
Start making bricks!
Stir the mortar!
15 You will still go up in flames
and be cut down by swords
that will wipe you out like wheat
attacked by grasshoppers.
So, go ahead and increase
like a swarm of locusts![o]

16 More merchants are in your city
than there are stars
in the sky—
but they are like locusts
that eat everything,
then fly away.
17 Your guards and your officials
are swarms of locusts.
On a chilly day
they settle on a fence,
but when the sun comes out,
they take off
to who-knows-where.

18 King of Assyria,
your officials and leaders
sleep the eternal sleep,
while your people are scattered
in the mountains.
Yes, your people are sheep
without a shepherd.
19 You're fatally wounded.
There's no hope for you.
But everyone claps
when they hear this news,
because your constant cruelty
has caused them pain.

[k]**3.8** *Thebes*: In 663 B.C., the Assyrian King Ashurbanipal captured this Egyptian city, which seems to have been built with protection similar to that of Nineveh. [l]**3.8** *was its . . . defense*: One possible meaning for the difficult Hebrew text. [m]**3.9** *Ethiopia*: The Hebrew text has "Cush," which was a region south of Egypt that included parts of the present countries of Ethiopia and Sudan. [n]**3.9** *Put*: A region in Africa, possibly part of the present country of Libya. [o]**3.15** *locusts*: A type of grasshopper that comes in swarms and causes great damage to plant life.

HABAKKUK

ABOUT THIS BOOK

The first two chapters of this book report a conversation between Habakkuk and the Lord. Habakkuk complained that Judah was full of injustice and crime. The Lord answered that he was going to have the Babylonians punish the people of Judah. But then Habakkuk complained that this would be unfair, because the Babylonians were even worse sinners than the people of Judah! The Lord answered that Babylonia would be punished later.

The last chapter of the book is a prayer in which Habakkuk praises the Lord's power and glory.

A QUICK LOOK AT THIS BOOK

Habakkuk Complains, and the Lord Answers (1–2)
Habakkuk Gives Praise to the Lord (3)

---

1 I am Habakkuk the prophet. And this is the message[a] that the LORD gave me.

Habakkuk Complains to the LORD

2 Our LORD, how long must I beg
for your help
before you listen?
How long before you save us
from all this violence?
3 Why do you make me watch
such terrible injustice?
Why do you allow violence,
lawlessness, crime, and cruelty
to spread everywhere?
4 Laws cannot be enforced;
justice is always the loser;
criminals crowd out honest people
and twist the laws around.

The LORD Answers Habakkuk

5 Look and be amazed
at what's happening
among the nations!
Even if you were told,
you would never believe
what's taking place now.
6 I am sending the Babylonians.
They are fierce and cruel—
marching across the land,
conquering cities and towns.

7 How fearsome and frightening.
Their only laws and rules
are the ones they make up.
8 Their cavalry troops are faster
than leopards,
more ferocious than wolves
hunting at sunset,
and swifter than hungry eagles
suddenly swooping down.

9 They are eager to destroy,[b]
and they gather captives
like handfuls of sand.
10 They make fun of rulers
and laugh at fortresses,
while building dirt mounds
so they can capture cities.[c]
11 Then suddenly they disappear
like a gust of wind—
those sinful people who worship
their own strength.

Habakkuk Complains Again

12 Holy LORD God, mighty rock,[d]
you are eternal,
and we[e] are safe from death.

[a]**1.1** *message*: Or "vision." [b]**1.9** *eager to destroy*: One possible meaning for the difficult Hebrew text. [c]**1.10** *dirt mounds . . . cities*: Attacking armies often build dirt mounds against city walls to make it easier for them to climb the wall and capture the city.
[d]**1.12** *mighty rock*: The Hebrew text has "rock," which is sometimes used in poetry to compare the LORD to a mountain where his people can run for protection from their enemies.
[e]**1.12** *we*: Hebrew; one ancient Jewish tradition "you."

You are using those Babylonians
to judge and punish others.[f]
13 But you can't stand sin or wrong.
So don't sit by in silence
while they gobble down people
who are better than they are.

14 The people you put on this earth
are like fish or reptiles
without a leader.
15 Then an enemy comes along
and takes them captive
with hooks and nets.
It makes him so happy
16 that he offers sacrifices
to his fishing nets,
because they make him rich
and provide choice foods.
17 Will he keep hauling in his nets
and destroying nations
without showing mercy?

The LORD Answers Habakkuk Again

2 While standing guard
on the watchtower,
I waited for the LORD's answer,
before explaining the reason
for my complaint.[g]
2 Then the LORD told me:
"I will give you my message
in the form of a vision.
Write it clearly enough
to be read at a glance.
3 At the time I have decided,
my words will come true.
You can trust what I say
about the future.
It may take a long time,
but keep on waiting—
it will happen!

4 "I, the LORD, refuse to accept
anyone who is proud.
Only those who live by faith
are acceptable to me."[h]

Trouble for Evil People

5 Wine[i] is treacherous,
and arrogant people
are never satisfied.
They are no less greedy
than death itself—
they open their mouths as wide
as the world of the dead
and swallow everyone.

6 But they will be mocked
with these words:
You're doomed!
You stored up stolen goods
and cheated others
of what belonged to them.
7 But without warning,
those you owe
will demand payment.
Then you will become
a frightened victim.
8 You robbed cities and nations
everywhere on earth
and murdered their people.
Now those who survived
will be as cruel to you.

9 You're doomed!
You made your family rich
at the expense of others.
You even said to yourself,
"I'm above the law."
10 But you will bring shame
on your family
and ruin to yourself
for what you did to others.
11 The very stones and wood
in your home
will testify against you.

12 You're doomed! You built a city
on crime and violence.
13 But the LORD All-Powerful
sends up in flames
what nations and people
work so hard to gain.

14 Just as water fills the sea,
the land will be filled
with people who know
and honor the LORD.

15 You're doomed!
You get your friends drunk,
just to see them naked.
16 Now you will be disgraced
instead of praised.
The LORD will make you drunk,
and when others see you naked,
you will lose their respect.
17 You destroyed trees and animals
on Mount Lebanon;
you were ruthless to towns
and people everywhere.
Now you will be terrorized.

Idolatry Is Foolish

18 What is an idol worth?
It's merely a false god.
Why trust a speechless image
made from wood or metal
by human hands?
19 What can you learn from idols
covered with silver or gold?
They can't even breathe.
Pity anyone who says to an idol
of wood or stone,
"Get up and do something!"

[f]**1.12** *You . . . others*: Or "You will judge and punish those Babylonians." [g]**2.1** *I . . . complaint*: One possible meaning for the difficult Hebrew text. [h]**2.4** *Only . . . me*: Or "But those who are acceptable to me will live because of their faithfulness." [i]**2.5** *Wine*: The Standard Hebrew Text; the Dead Sea Scrolls "Wealth."

20 Let all the world be silent—
the LORD is present
in his holy temple.

Habakkuk's Prayer

3 This is my prayer:[j]
2 I know your reputation, LORD,
and I am amazed
at what you have done.
Please turn from your anger
and be merciful;
do for us what you did
for our ancestors.

3 You are the same Holy God
who came from Teman
and Paran[k] to help us.
The brightness of your glory
covered the heavens,
and your praises were heard
everywhere on earth.
4 Your glory shone like the sun,
and light flashed from your hands,
hiding your mighty power.
5 Dreadful diseases and plagues
marched in front
and followed behind.
6 When you stopped,
the earth shook;
when you stared,
nations trembled;
when you walked
along your ancient paths,
eternal mountains and hills
crumbled and collapsed.
7 The tents of desert tribes
in Cushan and Midian[l]
were ripped apart.

8 Our LORD, were you angry
with the monsters
of the deep?[m]
You attacked in your chariot
and wiped them out.
9 Your arrows were ready
and obeyed your commands.[n]

You split the earth apart
with rivers and streams;
10 mountains trembled
at the sight of you;
rain poured from the clouds;
ocean waves roared and rose.
11 The sun and moon stood still,
while your arrows and spears
flashed like lightning.

12 In your furious anger,
you trampled on nations
13 to rescue your people
and save your chosen one.[o]
You crushed a nation's ruler
and stripped his evil kingdom
of its power.[p]
14 His troops had come like a storm,
hoping to scatter us
and glad to gobble us down.
To them we were refugees
in hiding—
but you smashed their heads
with their own weapons.[q]
15 Then your chariots churned
the waters of the sea.

Habakkuk's Response to God's Message

16 When I heard this message,[r]
I felt weak from fear,
and my lips quivered.
My bones seemed to melt,
and I stumbled around.
But I will patiently wait.
Someday those vicious enemies
will be struck by disaster.[s]

Trust in a Time of Trouble

17 Fig trees may no longer bloom,
or vineyards produce grapes;
olive trees may be fruitless,
and harvest time a failure;
sheep pens may be empty,
and cattle stalls vacant—
18 but I will still celebrate
because the LORD God
saves me.
19 The LORD gives me strength.
He makes my feet as sure
as those of a deer,
and he helps me stand
on the mountains.[t]

To the music director:
Use stringed instruments.

[j] **3.1** *prayer*: The Hebrew text adds "according to the shigionoth," which may mean a prayer of request or a prayer to be accompanied by a special musical instrument. [k] **3.3** *Teman . . . Paran*: Teman is a district in Edom, but the name is sometimes used of the whole country of Edom; Paran is the hill country along the western border of the Gulf of Aqaba. In Judges 5.4, the LORD is said to have marched from Edom to help his people; in Deuteronomy 33.2, Paran is mentioned in connection with the LORD's appearance at Sinai. [l] **3.7** *Cushan and Midian*: Tribes of the Arabian desert who were enemies of Israel. [m] **3.8** *monsters of the deep*: The Hebrew text has "rivers and oceans," which may stand for the powerful monsters that were thought to have lived there before the LORD defeated them. [n] **3.9** *obeyed your commands*: One possible meaning for the difficult Hebrew text. [o] **3.13** *chosen one*: Or "chosen ones." [p] **3.13** *You crushed . . . power*: One possible meaning for the difficult Hebrew text. [q] **3.14** *but you . . . weapons*: One possible meaning for the difficult Hebrew text. [r] **3.16** *heard this message*: Or "saw this vision." [s] **3.16** *I will . . . disaster*: One possible meaning for the difficult Hebrew text. [t] **3.19** *stand on the mountains*: One possible meaning for the difficult Hebrew text.

ZEPHANIAH

ABOUT THIS BOOK

The people of Judah had thought that at a certain time in the future, the Lord was going to make them powerful and would wipe out their enemies. This future time of justice, victory, and celebration was called "the day of the Lord." But Zephaniah told the people that when the day of the Lord did come, the Lord would punish everyone who had not obeyed him. And this included Judah, as well as other nations. The only way that Judah could avoid being swept away by the Lord's anger was to obey the Lord and worship only him:

If you humbly obey the LORD,
then come and worship him.
If you do right and are humble,
perhaps you will be safe
on that day when the LORD
turns loose his anger.

(2.3)

A QUICK LOOK AT THIS BOOK

Judah and Jerusalem Will Be Punished on the Day of the Lord (1.1-18)
Turn to the Lord (2.1-3)
The Nations Will Be Punished (2.4-15)
Judah and Other Nations Will Turn to the Lord (3.1-20)

---

1 I am Zephaniah, the son of Cushi,
the grandson of Gedaliah, the great-
grandson of Amariah, and the great-
great-grandson of Hezekiah.[a]
When Josiah son of Amon was king of
Judah,[b] the LORD gave me this message.

Judgment on Judah

2 I, the LORD, now promise
to destroy everything
on this earth—
3 people and animals,
birds and fish.
Everyone who is evil
will crash to the ground,[c]
and I will wipe out
the entire human race.
4 I will reach out to punish
Judah and Jerusalem—
nothing will remain
of the god Baal;[d]
nothing will be remembered
of his pagan priests.
5 Not a trace will be found
of those who worship stars
from their rooftops,
or bow down to the god Milcom,[e]
while claiming loyalty
to me, the LORD.
6 Nothing will remain of anyone
who has turned away
and rejected me.

7 Be silent! I am the LORD God,
and the time is near.
I am preparing
to sacrifice my people
and to invite my guests.
8 On that day I will punish
national leaders
and sons of the king,
along with all who follow
foreign customs.[f]

[a] **1.1** *Hezekiah*: Ruled 716-687 B.C. [b] **1.1** *Josiah . . . king of Judah*: Ruled 640-609 B.C. [c] **1.3** *Everyone . . . ground*: One possible meaning for the difficult Hebrew text. [d] **1.4** *Baal*: A Caananite fertility god. [e] **1.5** *Milcom*: An Ammonite fertility god. [f] **1.8** *follow foreign customs*: Hebrew "wear foreign clothes."

[9] I will punish worshipers
of pagan gods[g]
and cruel palace officials
who abuse their power.

[10] I, the LORD, promise
that on that day
noisy crying will be heard
from Fish Gate, New Town,
and Upper Hills.
[11] Everyone in Lower Hollow[h]
will mourn loudly,
because merchants
and money changers
will be wiped out.
[12] I'll search Jerusalem with lamps
and punish those people
who sit there unworried
while thinking,
"The LORD won't do anything,
good or bad."
[13] Their possessions will be taken,
their homes left in ruins.
They won't get to live
in the houses they build,
or drink wine from the grapes
in their own vineyards.

A Terrible Day

[14] The great day of the LORD
is coming soon, very soon.
On that terrible day,
fearsome shouts of warriors
will be heard everywhere.
[15] It will be a time of anger—
of trouble and torment,
of disaster and destruction,
of darkness and despair,
of storm clouds and shadows,
[16] of trumpet calls
and battle cries
against fortified cities
and mighty fortresses.

[17] The LORD warns everyone
who has sinned against him,
"I'll strike you blind!
Then your blood and your insides
will gush out like vomit.
[18] Not even your silver or gold
can save you on that day
when I, the LORD, am angry.
My anger will flare up
like a furious fire
scorching the earth
and everyone on it."

Turn to the LORD

2 You disgraceful nation,
gather around,
[2] before it's too late.
The LORD has set a time
when his fierce anger
will strike like a storm
and sweep you away.
[3] If you humbly obey the LORD,
then come and worship him.
If you do right and are humble,
perhaps you will be safe
on that day when the LORD
turns loose his anger.

Judgment on Philistia

[4] Gaza and Ashkelon
will be deserted
and left in ruins.
Ashdod will be emptied
in broad daylight,
and Ekron[i] uprooted.
[5] To you people of Philistia[j]
who live along the coast,
the LORD has this to say:
"I am now your enemy,
and I'll wipe you out!"

[6] Your seacoast will be changed
into pastureland
and sheep pens.[k]
[7] The LORD God hasn't forgotten
those survivors in Judah,
and he will help them—
his people will take your land
to use for pasture.
And when evening comes,
they will rest
in houses at Ashkelon.[l]

Judgment on Moab and Ammon

[*8] The LORD All-Powerful,
the God of Israel, said:
I've heard Moab and Ammon
insult my people
and threaten their nation.[m]
[9] And so, I swear by my very life
that Moab and Ammon will end up
like Sodom and Gomorrah—
covered with thornbushes
and salt pits forever.
Then my people who survive
will take their land.
[10] This is how Moab and Ammon
will at last be repaid
for their pride—

[g]**1.9** *worshipers . . . gods*: The Hebrew text has "all who jump over the threshold," which was a Philistine religious practice (see 1 Samuel 5.5). [h]**1.10,11** *Fish Gate, New Town, and Upper Hills . . . Lower Hollow*: Names for different sections of Jerusalem: Fish Gate was probably the main gate on the north side of the city; New Town was a newer section; Upper Hills may have been a suburb north of the city; Lower Hollow was probably on the southern edge of town. [i]**2.4** *Gaza . . . Ekron*: Gaza, Ashkelon, Ashdod, Ekron, and Gath (not mentioned because it was already destroyed) were the five major Philistine towns. [j]**2.5** *people of Philistia*: The Hebrew text also mentions "Canaan" and "Cherethites," which are other ways of referring to the Philistines. [k]**2.6** *pens*: One possible meaning for the difficult Hebrew text of verse 6. [l]**2.7** *Ashkelon*: A Philistine town; see the note at 2.4. [m]**2.8** *threaten their nation*: Or "boast about their own nation."

and for sneering at the nation
that belongs to me,
the LORD All-Powerful.
11 I will fiercely attack.
Then every god on this earth
will shrink to nothing,
and everyone of every nation
will bow down to me,
right where they are.

Judgment on Ethiopia

12 People of Ethiopia,[n]
the sword of the LORD
will slaughter you!

Judgment on Assyria

13 The LORD will reach to the north
to crush Assyria
and overthrow Nineveh.[o]
14 Herds of wild animals
will live in its rubble;
all kinds of desert owls
will perch on its stones
and hoot in the windows.
Noisy ravens will be heard
inside its buildings,
stripped bare of cedar.[p]
15 This is the glorious city
that felt secure and said,
"I am the only one!"
Now it's merely ruins,
a home for wild animals.
Every passerby simply sneers
and makes vulgar signs.

Sinful Jerusalem

3 Too bad for that disgusting,
corrupt, and lawless city!
2 Forever rebellious
and rejecting correction,
Jerusalem refuses to trust
or obey the LORD God.
3 Its officials are roaring lions,
its judges are wolves;
in the evening they attack,
by morning nothing is left.
4 Jerusalem's prophets are proud
and not to be trusted.
The priests have disgraced
the place of worship
and abused God's Law.
5 All who do evil are shameless,
but the LORD does right
and is always fair.
With the dawn of each day,
God brings about justice.

6 The LORD wiped out nations
and left fortresses
crumbling in the dirt.
Their streets and towns
were reduced to ruins
and emptied of people.
7 God felt certain that Jerusalem
would learn to respect
and obey him.
Then he would hold back
from punishing the city
and not wipe it out.
But everyone there was eager
to start sinning again.

Nations Will Turn to the LORD

8 The LORD said:
Just wait for the day
when I accuse you nations.
I have decided on a day,
when I will bring together
every nation and kingdom
and punish them all
in my fiery anger.
I will become furious
and destroy the earth.

9 I will purify each language
and make those languages
acceptable for praising me.[q]
Then, with hearts united,
everyone will serve
only me, the LORD.
10 From across the rivers
of Ethiopia,[r]
my scattered people,
my true worshipers,
will bring offerings to me.

11 When that time comes,
you won't rebel against me
and be put to shame.
I'll do away with those
who are proud and arrogant.
Never will any of them
strut around
on my holy mountain.
12 But I, the LORD, won't destroy
any of your people
who are truly humble
and turn to me for safety.
13 The people of Israel who survive
will live right
and refuse to tell lies.
They will eat and rest
with nothing to fear.

A Song of Celebration

14 Everyone in Jerusalem and Judah,
celebrate and shout
with all your heart!
15 Zion, your punishment is over.

[n]**2.12** *Ethiopia*: The Hebrew text has "Cush," which was a region south of Egypt that included parts of the present countries of Ethiopia and Sudan. [o]**2.13** *Nineveh*: The capital of Assyria; Nineveh was protected by a moat filled with water from the nearby Tigris River. [p]**2.14** *stripped . . . cedar*: One possible meaning for the difficult Hebrew text. [q]**3.9** *I will . . . praising me*: Or "I will change the hearts of all people and make them fit for praising me." [r]**3.10** *Ethiopia*: See the note at 2.12.

The LORD has forced your enemies
to turn and retreat.
Your LORD is King of Israel
and stands at your side;
you don't have to worry
about any more troubles.

16 Jerusalem, the time is coming,
when it will be said to you:
"Don't be discouraged
or grow weak from fear!
17 The LORD your God
wins victory after victory
and is always with you.
He celebrates and sings
because of you,
and he will refresh your life
with his love."[s]

The LORD's Promise to His People

18 The LORD has promised:
Your sorrow has ended,
and you can celebrate.[t]
19 I will punish those
who mistreat you.
I will bring together the lame
and the outcasts,
then they will be praised,
instead of despised,
in every country on earth.
20 I will lead you home,
and with your own eyes
you will see me bless you
with all you once owned.
Then you will be famous
everywhere on this earth.
I, the LORD, have spoken!

[s]**3.17** *refresh . . . love*: Two ancient translations; Hebrew "silently show you his love."
[t]**3.18** *celebrate*: One possible meaning for the difficult Hebrew text of verse 18.

HAGGAI

ABOUT THIS BOOK

By 520 B.C., many of the Jews had returned to Judah from the exile in Babylonia. The leaders were fairly well off, but most of the people were struggling just to survive. The Lord told Haggai that the reason the people had to struggle was because the temple still had not been rebuilt. Their lack of respect for the Lord's temple showed that they did not respect the Lord himself, and so he refused to bless them.

The people began work on the temple, and then the Lord promised to bless them and make them prosperous.

A QUICK LOOK AT THIS BOOK

Rebuild the Temple

1 On the first day of the sixth month
of the second year that Darius was
king of Persia,[a] the LORD told Haggai
the prophet to speak his message to the
governor of Judah and to the high
priest.
So Haggai told Governor Zerubbabel
and High Priest Joshua[b] 2-5that the LORD
All-Powerful had said to them and to the
people:
You say this isn't the right time to
build a temple for me. But is it right
for you to live in expensive houses,[c]
while my temple is a pile of ruins?
Just look at what's happening. 6You
harvest less than you plant, you
never have enough to eat or drink,
your clothes don't keep you warm,
and your wages are stored in bags
full of holes.
7Think about what I have said!
8But first, go to the hills and get
wood for my temple, so I can take
pride in it and be worshiped there.
9You expected much, but received
only a little. And when you brought
it home, I made that little disappear.
Why have I done this? It's because
you hurry off to build your own
houses, while my temple is still in
ruins. 10That's also why the dew
doesn't fall and your harvest fails.
11And so, at my command everything will become barren—your
farmland and pastures, your vineyards and olive trees, your animals
and you yourselves. All your hard
work will be for nothing.
12Zerubbabel and Joshua, together
with the others who had returned from
exile in Babylonia, obeyed the LORD's
message spoken by his prophet Haggai,
and they started showing proper respect
for the LORD. 13 Haggai then told them
that the LORD had promised to be with
them. 14So the LORD God All-Powerful
made everyone eager to work on his
temple, especially Zerubbabel and
Joshua. 15And the work began on the
twenty-fourth day of that same month.

The Glorious New Temple

2 1-2On the twenty-first day of the next
month,[d] the LORD told Haggai the

[a]1.1 *sixth month . . . king of Persia*: Elul, the sixth month of the Hebrew calendar, from about mid-August to mid-September; the second year of the rule of Darius was 520 B.C.
[b]1.1 *Governor . . . Joshua*: Hebrew "Governor Zerubbabel son of Shealtiel and High Priest Joshua son of Jehozadak."
[c]1.2-5 *expensive houses*: Either houses with paneled interiors or with roofs; the temple was not yet completely rebuilt at this time.
[d]2.1,2 *the next month*: Tishri (also called Ethnim), the seventh month of the Hebrew calendar, from about mid-September to mid-October (see the note at 1.1).

prophet to speak this message to Governor Zerubbabel, High Priest Joshua, and
everyone else:
3Does anyone remember how glorious this temple used to be? Now it
looks like nothing. 4But cheer up!
Because I, the LORD All-Powerful,
will be here to help you with the
work, 5just as I promised your ancestors when I brought them out of
Egypt. Don't worry. My Spirit is[e]
right here with you.
6Soon I will again shake the heavens and the earth, the sea and the
dry land. 7I will shake the nations,
and their treasures[f] will be brought
here. Then the brightness of my
glory will fill this temple. 8All silver
and gold belong to me, 9and I promise that this new temple will be more
glorious than the first one. I will also
bless this city[g] with peace.

The Past and the Future

10On the twenty-fourth day of the ninth
month,[h] the LORD God All-Powerful
told the prophet Haggai 11to ask the
priests for their opinion on the following matter:
12Suppose meat ready to be sacrificed to God is being carried in the
folds of someone's clothing, and the
clothing rubs against some bread or
stew or wine or olive oil or any other
food. Would those foods that were
touched then become acceptable for
sacrifice?
"Of course not," the priests answered.
13Then Haggai said, "Suppose someone has touched a dead body and is
considered unacceptable to worship
God. If that person touches these foods,
would they become unclean?"
"Of course they would," the priests answered.
14So the LORD told Haggai to say:
That's how it is with this entire nation. Everything you do and every
sacrifice you offer is unacceptable to
me. 15But from now on, things will
get better. Before you started laying
the foundation for the temple, 16you
recalled what life was like in the
past.[i] When you wanted twenty
bushels of wheat, there were only
ten, and when you wanted fifty jars
of wine, there were only twenty. 17I
made all of your hard work useless
by sending mildew, mold, and hail—
but you still did not return to me,
your LORD.
18Today you have completed the
foundation for my temple, so listen
to what your future will be like. 19Al-
though you have not yet harvested
any grain, grapes, figs, pomegranates,[j] or olives, I will richly bless you
in the days ahead.

God's Promise to Zerubbabel

20That same day the LORD spoke to
Haggai again and said:
21Tell Governor Zerubbabel of Judah that I am going to shake the
heavens and the earth 22and wipe
out kings and their kingdoms. I will
overturn war chariots, and then cavalry troops will start slaughtering
each other. 23But tell my servant
Zerubbabel that I, the LORD All-
Powerful, have chosen him, and he
will rule in my name.[k]

[e]2.5 *My Spirit is*: Or "I am." [f]2.7 *their treasures*: Hebrew "what they most desire." [g]2.9 *city*: Or "temple." [h]2.10 *ninth month*: Chislev, the ninth month of the Hebrew calendar, from about mid-November to mid-December. [i]2.16 *you recalled . . . past*: One possible meaning for the difficult Hebrew text. [j]2.19 *pomegranates*: A bright red fruit that looks like an apple. [k]2.23 *rule in my name*: The Hebrew text has "be my signet ring," which signified authority.

ZECHARIAH

ABOUT THIS BOOK

The people of Jerusalem had problems. They had begun to rebuild the temple, but the new temple could never be as great as the original one. There was no king from David's family, and Judah was only a small part of the Medo-Persian empire.

In the first part of this book (1–8) Zechariah tells how the Lord gave him eight meaningful visions to help the people overcome these problems. Someday, the Lord's chosen king would again rule in Jerusalem, and all the nations would turn to the Lord and become his people. But for now, the Lord had chosen Zerubbabel to be the governor and Joshua to be the high priest, and they were to be in charge of the Lord's people.

In the second part of this book (9–11) the Lord promised he would punish many of the nearby nations and also the leaders of Judah who had been unfaithful.

In the third part (12–14) the Lord gave Zechariah messages about a time even farther in the future, when Jerusalem and Judah will be attacked by all nations. Many of the people of Judah will be killed, but the Lord himself will appear and rescue his people. They will turn back to him, and he will forgive them. Then mountains around Jerusalem will be flattened, but Jerusalem will remain on the mountain towering high above the land around it. Life-giving streams will flow from Jerusalem, and all people on earth will worship the Lord.

The Lord promised that someday he would again choose a king for his people. In the New Testament both Matthew and John quote part of this verse from the book of Zechariah, to show that God had chosen Jesus to be that king:

Everyone in Jerusalem,
celebrate and shout!
Your king has won a victory,
and he is coming to you.
He is humble
and rides on a donkey;
he comes on the colt
of a donkey. (9.9)

A QUICK LOOK AT THIS BOOK

Turn to the LORD

1 I am the prophet Zechariah, the son
of Berechiah and the grandson of
Iddo.
In the eighth month of the second
year that Darius was king of Persia,[a] the
LORD told me to say:
2-3 Israel, I, the LORD All-Powerful,
was very angry with your ancestors.
But if you people will return to me, I
will turn and help you. 4 Don't be
stubborn like your ancestors. They
were warned by the earlier prophets[b] to give up their evil and turn
back to me, but they paid no attention.
5 Where are your ancestors now?
Not even prophets live forever. 6 But
my warnings and my words spoken
by the prophets caught up with your
ancestors. So they turned back to
me and said, "LORD All-Powerful,
you have punished us for our sins,
just as you had planned."

First Vision: Horses and Riders

7-8 On the twenty-fourth day of
Shebat,[c] which was the eleventh month
of that same year,[d] the LORD spoke to
me in a vision during the night: In a valley among myrtle trees,[e] I saw someone
on a red horse, with riders on red,
brown, and white horses behind him.
9 An angel was there to explain things to
me, and I asked, "Sir, who are these riders?"
"I'll tell you," the angel answered.
10 Right away, the man standing
among the myrtle trees said, "These are
the ones the LORD has sent to find out
what's happening on earth."
11 Then the riders spoke to the LORD's
angel, who was standing among the
myrtle trees, and they said, "We have
gone everywhere and have discovered
that the whole world is at peace."
12 At this, the angel said, "LORD All-
Powerful, for seventy years you have
been angry with Jerusalem and the
towns of Judah. When are you ever going to have mercy on them?"
13 The LORD's answer was kind and
comforting. 14 So the angel told me to
announce:
I, the LORD All-Powerful, am very
protective of Jerusalem. 15 For a
while I was angry at the nations, but
now I am furious, because they have
made things worse for Jerusalem
and are not the least bit concerned.
16 And so, I will have pity on Jerusalem. The city will be completely
rebuilt, and my temple will stand
again. 17 I also promise that my
towns will prosper—Jerusalem will
once again be my chosen city, and I
will comfort the people of Zion.

Second Vision: Animal Horns

18 Next, I saw four animal horns.[f]
19-21 The angel who was sent to explain
was there, and so I asked, "What do
these mean?"
His answer was, "These horns are the
nations that scattered the people of Judah, Israel, and Jerusalem, and took
away their freedom."
Then the LORD showed me four black-
smiths, and I asked, "What are they going to do?"
He replied, "They are going to terrify
and crush those horns."

Third Vision: A Measuring Line

2 This time I saw someone holding a
measuring line, 2 and I asked,
"Where are you going?"
"To measure Jerusalem," was the answer. "To find out how wide and long
it is."
3 The angel who had spoken to me was
leaving, when another angel came up to
him 4 and said, "Hurry! Tell that man
with the measuring line that Jerusalem
won't have any boundaries. It will be
too full of people and animals even to
have a wall. 5 The LORD himself has
promised to be a protective wall of fire
surrounding Jerusalem, and he will be
its shining glory in the heart of the city."

A Call to Action

6 The LORD says to his people, "Run!
Escape from the land in the north,
where I scattered you to the four winds.
7 Leave Babylonia and hurry back to
Zion."
8 Then the glorious LORD All-Powerful
ordered me to say to the nations that
had raided and robbed Zion:
Zion is as precious to the LORD as
are his eyes. Whatever you do to
Zion, you do to him. 9 And so, he will
put you in the power of your slaves,

---

[a] **1.1** *eighth month . . . second year . . . king of Persia*: Bul, the eighth month of the Hebrew calendar, from about mid-October to mid-November; the second year of the rule of Darius was 520 B.C. [b] **1.4** *the earlier prophets*: Those who preached before the fall of Jerusalem in either 587 or 586 B.C. [c] **1.7,8** *Shebat*: The eleventh month of the Hebrew calendar, from about mid-January to mid-February. [d] **1.7,8** *that same year*: See verse 1 and the note there. [e] **1.7,8** *myrtle trees*: Evergreen shrubs, which in ancient times were symbols of fertility and renewal. [f] **1.18** *animal horns*: Horns, especially those of a bull, were symbols of power in ancient times. The number "four" would signal completeness, one representing each of the four directions.

and they will raid and rob you. Then
you will know that I am a prophet of
the LORD All-Powerful.
10 City of Zion, sing and celebrate!
The LORD has promised to come and
live with you. 11 When he does, many
nations will turn to him and become
his people. At that time you will
know that I am a prophet of the
LORD All-Powerful. 12 Then Judah
will be his part of the holy land, and
Jerusalem will again be his chosen
city.

13 Everyone, be silent!
The LORD is present
and moving about
in his holy place.

Fourth Vision: Joshua and Satan

3 I was given another vision. This
time Joshua the high priest was
standing in front of the LORD's angel.
And there was Satan, standing at
Joshua's right side, ready to accuse him.
2 But the LORD said, "Satan, you are
wrong. Jerusalem is my chosen city, and
this man was rescued like a stick from a
flaming fire."
3 Joshua's clothes were filthy. 4 So the
angel told some of the people to remove
Joshua's filthy clothes. Then he said to
Joshua, "This means you are forgiven.
Now I will dress you in priestly clothes."
5 I spoke up and said, "Also put a clean
priestly turban on his head." Then they
dressed him in priestly clothes and put
the turban on him, while the LORD's angel stood there watching.
6 After this, the angel encouraged
Joshua by telling him that the LORD All-
Powerful had promised:
7 If you truly obey me, I will put
you in charge of my temple, including the courtyard around it, and you
will be allowed to speak at any time
with the angels standing beside me.[g]
8 Listen carefully, High Priest Joshua
and all of you other priests. You are
a sign of things to come, because I
am going to bring back my servant,
the Chosen King.[h]
9 Joshua, I have placed in front of
you a stone with seven sides. I will
engrave something on that stone,
and in a single day I will forgive this
guilty country. 10 Then each of you
will live at peace and entertain your
friends in your own vineyard and
under your own fig trees.

Fifth Vision: A Lampstand and Olive Trees

4 The angel who explained the visions
woke me from what seemed like
sleep. 2 Then he asked, "What do you
see?"
"A solid gold lampstand with an oil
container above it," I answered. "On the
stand are seven lamps, each with seven
flames. 3 One olive tree is on the right
side and another on the left of the oil container. 4 But, sir, what do these mean?"
5 Then he asked, "Don't you know?"
"No sir," I replied.
6 So the angel explained that it was the
following message of the LORD to Zerubbabel:[i]
I am the LORD All-Powerful. So
don't depend on your own power or
strength, but on my Spirit. 7 Zerubbabel, that mountain in front of you
will be leveled to the ground. Then
you will bring out the temple's most
important stone and shout, "God has
been very kind."[j]
8 The LORD spoke to me again and
said:
9 Zerubbabel laid the foundation
for the temple, and he will complete
it. Then everyone will know that
you were sent by me, the LORD All-
Powerful. 10 Those who have made
fun of this day of small beginnings
will celebrate when they see Zerubbabel holding this important stone.[k]
Those seven lamps represent my
eyes—the eyes of the LORD—and
they see everything on this earth.
11 Then I asked the angel, "What about
the olive trees on each side of the lampstand? What do they represent? 12 And
what is the meaning of the two
branches from which golden olive oil[l]
flows through the two gold pipes?"
13 "Don't you know?" he asked.
"No sir, I don't," was my answer.
14 Then he told me, "These branches
are the two chosen leaders[m] who stand
beside the Lord of all the earth."

Sixth Vision: A Flying Scroll

5 When I looked the next time, I saw a
flying scroll,[n] 2 and the angel asked,
"What do you see?"

[g] **3.7** *with the angels . . . me*: Or "with me." The angels are members of God's Council, who stand beside the throne of God in heaven and are allowed to speak with him and for him. [h] **3.8** *Chosen King*: The Hebrew text has "Sprout" or "Branch," a term used of royalty (see Isaiah 11.1). [i] **4.6** *Zerubbabel*: Governor of Judah (see Haggai 1.1). [j] **4.7** *God . . . kind*: Or "What a beautiful stone." [k] **4.10** *important stone*: Or "measuring line (with a stone attached to the end)." [l] **4.12** *golden olive oil*: The Hebrew text has "gold," which possibly refers to the color of the olive oil as it flows through the gold pipe. [m] **4.14** *chosen leaders*: The Hebrew text has "people of oil." In ancient times prophets, priests, and kings had olive oil poured over their heads to show that they had been chosen (see 1 Samuel 10.1; 16.13). [n] **5.1** *scroll*: A roll of paper or special leather used for writing on.

"A flying scroll," I answered. "About
thirty feet long and fifteen feet wide."
3Then he told me:
This scroll puts a curse on everyone in the land who steals or tells
lies. The writing on one side tells
about the destruction of those who
steal, while the writing on the other
side tells about the destruction of
those who lie.
4The LORD All-Powerful has said,
"I am sending this scroll into the
house of everyone who is a robber
or tells lies in my name, and it will
remain there until every piece of
wood and stone in that house crumbles."

Seventh Vision: A Woman in a Basket

5Now the angel who was there to explain the visions came over and said,
"Look up and tell me what you see coming."
6"I don't know what it is," was my reply.
"It's a big basket," he said. "And it
shows what everyone in the land has in
mind."[o]
7The lead cover of the basket was
opened, and in the basket was a woman.
8"This woman represents evil," the angel
explained. Then he threw her back into
the basket and slammed the heavy
cover down tight.
9Right after this I saw two women
coming through the sky like storks with
wings outstretched in the wind. Suddenly they lifted the basket into the air,
10and I asked the angel, "Where are they
taking the basket?"
11"To Babylonia,"[p] he answered,
"where they will build a house for the
basket and set it down inside."

Eighth Vision: Four Chariots

6 Finally, I looked up and saw four
chariots coming from between two
bronze mountains. 2The first chariot
was pulled by red horses, and the second by black horses; 3the third chariot
was pulled by white horses, and the
fourth by spotted gray horses.
4"Sir," I asked the angel. "What do
these stand for?"
5Then he explained, "These are the
four winds[q] of heaven, and now they
are going out, after presenting themselves to the Lord of all the earth. 6The
chariot with black horses goes toward
the north, the chariot with white horses
goes toward the west,[r] and the one with
spotted horses goes toward the south."
7The horses came out eager to patrol
the earth, and the angel told them,
"Start patrolling the earth."
When they had gone on their way, 8he
shouted to me, "Those that have gone to
the country in the north will do what the
LORD's Spirit[s] wants them to do there."

The Chosen Leader

9The LORD said to me:
10-11Heldai, Tobijah, and Jedaiah
have returned from Babylonia. Collect enough silver and gold from
them to make a crown.[t] Then go
with them to the house of Josiah son
of Zephaniah and put the crown on
the head of the high priest Joshua
son of Jehozadak.[u] 12-13Tell him that
I, the LORD All-Powerful, say, "Someone will reach out from here like a
branch and build a temple for me. I
will name him 'Branch,' and he will
rule with royal honors. A priest will
stand beside his throne,[v] and the
two of them will be good friends.
14This crown will be kept in my temple as a reminder and will be taken
care of by Heldai,[w] Tobijah, Jedaiah,
and Josiah."[x]
15When people from distant lands
come and help build the temple of the
LORD All-Powerful, you will know that
the LORD is the one who sent me. And
this will happen, if you truly obey the
LORD your God.

A Question about Going without Eating

7 On the fourth day of Chislev, the
ninth month of the fourth year that
Darius was king of Persia,[y] the LORD
again spoke to me. 2-3It happened after
the people of Bethel had sent Sharezer
with Regem-Melech and his men to ask
the priests in the LORD's temple and the
prophets to pray for them. So they
prayed, "Should we mourn and go with-

[o] 5.6 *what . . . mind*: Hebrew; one ancient translation "the sin of everyone in the land."
[p] 5.11 *Babylonia*: The Hebrew text has "Shinar," an ancient name for Babylonia.
[q] 6.5 *winds*: Or "spirits." The Hebrew word may mean either. [r] 6.6 *goes toward the west*: Or "follows behind." [s] 6.8 *LORD's Spirit*: Or "LORD." [t] 6.10,11 *a crown*: Two ancient translations; Hebrew "some crowns." [u] 6.10,11 *Heldai . . . Jehozadak*: Or "Go to the house of Josiah son of Zephaniah, where you will find Heldai, Tobijah, and Jedaiah, who have returned from Babylonia. Collect enough silver and gold from them to make a crown. Then put it on the head of the high priest Joshua son of Jehozadak." [v] 6.12,13 *stand beside his throne*: Or "sit on a throne." [w] 6.14 *Heldai*: One ancient translation; Hebrew "Helem." [x] 6.14 *Josiah*: One ancient translation; Hebrew "Hen." [y] 7.1 *Chislev . . . fourth year . . . king of Persia*: Chislev, the ninth month of the Hebrew calendar, from about mid-November to mid-December; the fourth year of the rule of Darius was 518 B.C.

out eating during the fifth month,[z] as
we have done for many years?"
4-5It was then that the LORD All-
Powerful told me to say to everyone in
the country, including the priests:
For seventy years you have gone
without eating during the fifth and
seventh months of the year. But did
you really do it for me? 6And when
you eat and drink, isn't it for your
own enjoyment? 7My message today
is the same one I commanded the
earlier prophets[a] to speak to Jerusalem and its villages when they
were prosperous, and when all of Judah, including the Southern Desert
and the hill country, was filled with
people.
8-9So once again, I, the LORD All-
Powerful, tell you, "See that justice is
done and be kind and merciful to
one another! 10Don't mistreat widows or orphans or foreigners or anyone who is poor, and stop making
plans to hurt each other."
11-12But everyone who heard those
prophets, stubbornly refused to
obey. Instead, they turned their
backs on everything my Spirit[b] had
commanded the earlier prophets to
preach. So I, the LORD, became angry 13and said, "You people paid no
attention when I called out to you,
and now I'll pay no attention when
you call out to me."
14That's why I came with a whirlwind and scattered them among foreign nations, leaving their lovely
country empty of people and in
ruins.

The LORD's Promises to Zion

8 The LORD All-Powerful said to me:
2I love Zion so much that her enemies make me angry. 3I will return
to Jerusalem and live there on
Mount Zion. Then Jerusalem will be
known as my faithful city, and Zion
will be known as my holy mountain.
4Very old people with walking
sticks will once again sit around in
Jerusalem, 5while boys and girls
play in the streets. 6This may seem
impossible for my people who are
left, but it isn't impossible for me,
the LORD All-Powerful. 7I will save
those who were taken to lands in the
east and the west, 8and I will bring
them to live in Jerusalem. They will
be my people, and I will be their
God, faithful to bring about justice.
9I am the LORD All-Powerful! So
don't give up. Think about the message my prophets spoke when the
foundation of my temple was laid.
10Before that time, neither people
nor animals were rewarded for their
work, and no one was safe anywhere, because I had turned them
against each other.
11My people, only a few of you are
left, and I promise not to punish you
as I did before. 12Instead, I will make
sure that your crops are planted in
peace and your vineyards are fruitful, that your fields are fertile and
the dew falls from the sky. 13People
of Judah and Israel, you have been a
curse to the nations, but I will save
you and make you a blessing to
them. So don't be afraid or lose
courage.
14When your ancestors made me
angry, I decided to punish you with
disasters, and I didn't hold back.
15Now you no longer need to be
afraid. I have decided to treat Jerusalem and Judah with kindness.
16But you must be truthful with each
other, and in court you must give
fair decisions that lead to peace.
17Don't ever plan evil things against
others or tell lies under oath. I, the
LORD, hate such things.

A Time of Celebration

18The LORD All-Powerful told me to
say:
19People of Judah, I, the LORD, demand that whenever you go without
food as a way of worshiping me, it
should become a time of celebration.
No matter if it's the fourth month,
the fifth month, the seventh month,
or the tenth month, you should have
a joyful festival. So love truth and
live at peace.
20I tell you that people will come
here from cities everywhere. 21Those
of one town will go to another and
say, "We're going to ask the LORD
All-Powerful to treat us with kindness. Come and join us."
22Many people from strong nations will come to Jerusalem to worship me and to ask me to treat them
with kindness. 23When this happens,
ten people from nations with different languages will grab a Jew by his
clothes and say, "Let us go with you.
We've heard that God is on your
side." I, the LORD All-Powerful, have
spoken!

Israel's Enemies Will Be Punished

9 This is a message
from the LORD:
His eyes are on everyone,

[z]7.2,3 *fifth month*: Ab, the fifth month of the Hebrew calendar, from about mid-July to mid-August. The temple was destroyed by the Babylonians in the year 587 or 586 B.C. [a]7.7 *the earlier prophets*: See the note at 1.4. [b]7.11,12 *my Spirit*: Or "I."

especially the tribes
of Israel.[c]
So he pronounces judgment
against the cities
of Hadrach and Damascus.[d]
2 Judgment will also fall
on the nearby city
of Hamath,
as well as on Tyre and Sidon,[e]
whose people are clever.
3 Tyre has built a fortress
and piled up silver and gold,
as though they were dust
or mud from the streets.
4 Now the Lord will punish Tyre
with poverty;
he will sink its ships
and send it up in flames.

5 Both Ashkelon and Gaza
will tremble with fear;
Ekron will lose all hope.
Gaza's king will be killed,
and Ashkelon emptied
of its people.
6 A mob of half-breeds
will settle in Ashdod,[f]
and the Lord himself
will rob Philistia of pride.

7 No longer will the Philistines
eat meat with blood in it
or any unclean food.[g]
They will become part
of the people of our God
from the tribe of Judah.
And God will accept
the people of Ekron,
as he did the Jebusites.[h]

8 God says, "I will stand guard
to protect my temple from those
who come to attack.
I know what's happening,
and no one will mistreat
my people ever again."

The LORD Tells about the Coming King

9 Everyone in Jerusalem,
celebrate and shout!
Your king has won a victory,
and he is coming to you.
He is humble
and rides on a donkey;
he comes on the colt
of a donkey.
10 I, the LORD, will take away
war chariots and horses
from Israel[i] and Jerusalem.
Bows that were made for battle
will be broken.
I will bring peace to nations,
and your king will rule
from sea to sea.
His kingdom will reach
from the Euphrates River
across the earth.

The LORD Promises To Rescue Captives

11 When I made a sacred agreement
with you, my people,
we sealed it with blood.[j]
Now some of you are captives
in waterless pits,
but I will come to your rescue
12 and offer you hope.
Return to your fortress,
because today I will reward you
with twice what you had.
13 I will use Judah as my bow
and Israel[k] as my arrow.
I will take the people of Zion
as my sword
and attack the Greeks.

The LORD Will Protect His People

14 Like a cloud, the LORD God
will appear over his people,
and his arrows will flash
like lightning.
God will sound his trumpet
and attack in a whirlwind
from the south.
15 The LORD All-Powerful
will protect his people,
and they will trample down
the sharpshooters
and their slingshots.
They will drink and get rowdy;
they will be as full as a bowl
at the time of sacrifice.

16 The LORD God will save them
on that day,
because they are his people,
and they will shine on his land
like jewels in a crown.
17 How lovely they will be.
Young people will grow there
like grain in a field
or grapes in a vineyard.

[c]**9.1** *His . . . Israel*: One possible meaning for the difficult Hebrew text. [d]**9.1** *Hadrach and Damascus*: Hadrach was north of both Damascus (the main city of Syria) and Hamath (verse 2). [e]**9.2** *Tyre and Sidon*: Phoenician cities. [f]**9.5,6** *Ashkelon and Gaza . . . Ekron . . . Ashdod*: Philistine cities. [g]**9.7** *eat . . . food*: The Philistines will become part of Judah and no longer eat meat with blood in it (see Genesis 9.4) or any other forbidden foods (see Leviticus 11.1-23; Deuteronomy 14.3-21). [h]**9.7** *Jebusites*: The original people of Canaan, who lived in Jerusalem before it was captured by David (see 2 Samuel 5.6-10) and were later accepted as part of Israel. [i]**9.10** *Israel*: The Hebrew text has "Ephraim," the leading tribe of the northern kingdom of Israel, which sometimes stands for the whole kingdom. [j]**9.11** *an agreement . . . blood*: The agreement at Mount Sinai (see Exodus 24.7, 8). [k]**9.13** *Israel*: Hebrew "Ephraim" (see the note at 9.10).

A Bright Future for Judah and Israel

10 I, the LORD, am the one
who sends storm clouds
and showers of rain
to make fields produce.
So when the crops need rain,
you should pray to me.

2 You can't believe idols
and fortunetellers,
or depend on the hope
you receive from witchcraft
and interpreters of dreams.
But you have tried all of these,
and now you are like sheep
without a shepherd.

3 I, the LORD All-Powerful,
am fiercely angry
with you leaders,
and I will punish you.
I care for my people,
the nation of Judah,
and I will change
this flock of sheep
into charging war horses.

4 From this flock will come leaders
who will be strong
like cornerstones and tent pegs
and weapons of war.
5 They will join in the fighting,
and together they will trample
their enemies like mud.
They will fight,
because I, the LORD,
will be on their side.
And they will crush
the enemy cavalry.

6 I will strengthen
the kingdoms of Judah
and Israel.[l]
And I will show mercy
because I am the LORD,
their God.
I will answer their prayers
and bring them home.
Then it will seem as though
I had never rejected them.
7 Israel[m] will be like
a tribe of warriors
celebrating with wine.
When their children see this,
they will also be happy
because of me, the LORD.

8 I will give a signal
for them to come together
because I have rescued them.
And there will be as many
as ever before.
9 Although I scattered my people
in distant countries,
they won't forget me.
Once their children are raised,[n]
they will return—
10 I will bring them home
from Egypt and Assyria,
then let them settle
as far as Gilead and Lebanon,
until the land overflows
with them.
11 My people will go through
an ocean of troubles,
but I will overcome the waves
and dry up the deepest part
of the Nile.
Assyria's great pride
will be put down,
and the power of Egypt
will disappear.
12 I'll strengthen my people
because of who I am,
and they will follow me.
I, the LORD, have spoken!

Trouble for Israel's Enemies

11 Lebanon, open your gates!
Let the fire come in
to destroy your cedar trees.
2 Cry, you cyprus trees!
The glorious cedars have fallen
and are rotting.
Cry, you oak trees of Bashan!
The dense forest
has been chopped down.
3 Listen! Shepherds are crying.
Their glorious pastures
have been ruined.
Listen! Lions are roaring.
The forests of the Jordan Valley
are no more to be found.

Worthless Shepherds

4The LORD my God said to me:
Tend those sheep doomed for
slaughter! 5The people who buy and
butcher them go unpunished, while
everyone who sells them says,
"Praise the LORD! I'm rich." Not even
their shepherds have pity on them.
6Tend those sheep because I, the
LORD, will no longer have pity on the
people of this earth. I'll turn neighbor against neighbor and make
them slaves of a king. They will
bring disaster on the earth, and I'll
do nothing to rescue any of them.
7So I became a shepherd of those
sheep doomed to be slaughtered by the
sheep dealers.[o] And I gave names to the
two sticks I used for tending the sheep:
One of them was named "Mercy" and

[l] **10.6** *Israel*: The Hebrew text has "family of Joseph," the ancestor of Ephraim and Manasseh, the leading tribes of the northern kingdom (Israel). [m] **10.7** *Israel*: Hebrew "Ephraim" (see the note at 9.10). [n] **10.9** *Once . . . raised*: One possible meaning for the difficult Hebrew text.
[o] **11.7** *by the sheep dealers*: One ancient translation; Hebrew "especially the weak ones."

the other "Unity." [8]In less than a month,
I became impatient with three shepherds who didn't like me, and I got rid
of them. [9]Then I said, "I refuse to be
your shepherd. Let the sheep that are
going to die, go on and die, and those
that are going to be destroyed, go on
and be destroyed. Then let the others
eat one another alive."

[10]On that same day, I broke the stick
named "Mercy" to show that the LORD
had canceled his agreement with all
people. [11]The sheep dealers who saw me
knew right away that this was a message from the LORD. [12-13]I told them,
"Pay me my wages, if you think you
should; otherwise, forget it." So they
handed me my wages, a measly thirty
pieces of silver.

Then the LORD said, "Throw the
money into the treasury."[p] So I threw
the money into the treasury at the
LORD's temple. [14]Then I broke the stick
named "Unity" and canceled the ties between Judah and Israel.

[15]Next, the LORD said to me, "Act like
a shepherd again—this time a worthless
shepherd. [16]Once more I am going to let
a worthless nobody rule the land—one
who won't care for the strays or search
for the young or heal the sick or feed
the healthy. He will just dine on the fat-
test sheep, leaving nothing but a few
bones."

17 You worthless shepherd,
deserting the sheep!
I hope a sword
will cripple your arm
and blind your right eye.

Victory for Jerusalem

12 This is a message from the LORD
about Israel:
I am the LORD! I stretched out the
heavens; I put the earth on its foundations and gave breath to humans.
[2]I have decided that Jerusalem will
become a bowl of wine that makes
the neighboring nations drunk. And
when Jerusalem is attacked, Judah
will also be attacked.[q] [3]But I will
turn Jerusalem into a heavy stone
that crushes anyone who tries to
lift it.

When all nations on earth surround Jerusalem, [4]I will make every
horse panic and every rider confused. But at the same time, I will
watch over Judah. [5]Then every clan
in Judah will realize that I, the LORD
All-Powerful, am their God, and that
I am the source of their strength.

[6]At that time I will let the clans of
Judah be like a ball of fire in a wood
pile or a fiery torch in a hay stack.
Then Judah will send the surrounding nations up in smoke. And once
again the city of Jerusalem will be
filled with people.

[7]But I will first give victory to Judah, so the kingdom of David and
the city of Jerusalem in all of their
glory won't be thought of more
highly than Judah itself. [8]I, the LORD
God, will protect Jerusalem. Even
the weakest person there will be as
strong as David, and David's kingdom will rule as though my very
own angel were its leader. [9]I am determined to wipe out every nation
that attacks Jerusalem.

Mourning for the One Pierced with a Spear

[10]I, the LORD, will make the descendants of David and the people of Jerusalem feel deep sorrow and pray when
they see the one they pierced with a
spear. They will mourn and weep for
him, as parents weep over the death of
their only child or their first-born. [11]On
that day the people of Jerusalem will
mourn as much as everyone did for
Hadad Rimmon[r] on the flatlands near
Megiddo. [12]Everyone of each family in
the land will mourn, and the men will
mourn separately from the women. This
includes those from the family of David,
and the families of Nathan, [13]Levi,
Shimei,[s] [14]and all other families as well.

Getting Rid of Idols and False Prophets

13 In the future there will be a fountain, where David's descendants
and the people of Jerusalem can wash
away their sin and guilt.
[2]The LORD All-Powerful says:
When that time comes, I will get
rid of every idol in the country, and
they will be forgotten forever. I will
also do away with their prophets
and those evil spirits that control
them. [3]If any such prophets ever appear again, their own parents must
warn them that they will die for
telling lies in my name—the name of
the LORD. If those prophets don't
stop speaking, their parents must
then kill them with a sword.

[4]Those prophets will be ashamed
of their so-called visions, and they
won't deceive anyone by dressing
like a true prophet. [5]Instead, they

[p]**11.12,13** *Throw . . . treasury*: Hebrew "Throw the money to the potter." [q]**12.2** *Judah . . . attacked*: One possible meaning for the difficult Hebrew text. [r]**12.11** *Hadad Rimmon*: Not mentioned elsewhere in the Old Testament. [s]**12.13** *Shimei*: A descendant of Gershon son of Levi (see Numbers 3.18).

will say, "I'm no prophet. I've been a farmer all my life."[t]

6 And if any of them are asked why they are wounded,[u] they will answer, "It happened at the house of some friends."

A Wounded Shepherd and Scattered Sheep

7 The LORD All-Powerful said:

My sword, wake up! Attack
    my shepherd and friend.
Strike down the shepherd!
Scatter the little sheep,
    and I will destroy them.
8 Nowhere in the land
will more than a third of them
    be left alive.
9 Then I will purify them
    and put them to the test,
just as gold and silver
    are purified and tested.
They will pray in my name,
    and I will answer them.
I will say, "You are my people,"
and they will reply,
    "You, LORD, are our God!"

War and Victory

14 The LORD will have his day. And when it comes, everything that was ever taken from Jerusalem will be returned and divided among its people.
2 But first, he will bring many nations to attack Jerusalem—homes will be robbed, women raped, and half of the population dragged off, though the others will be allowed to remain.

3 The LORD will attack those nations like a warrior fighting in battle. 4 He will take his stand on the Mount of Olives east of Jerusalem, and the mountain will split in half, forming a wide valley that runs from east to west. 5 Then you people will escape from the LORD's mountain, through this valley, which reaches to Azal.[v] You will run in all directions, just as everyone did when the earthquake struck[w] in the time of King Uzziah of Judah. Afterwards, the LORD my God will appear with his holy angels.

6 It will be a bright day that won't turn cloudy.[x] 7 And the LORD has decided when it will happen—this time of unending day.

8 In both summer and winter, life-giving streams will flow from Jerusalem, half of them to the Dead Sea in the east and half to the Mediterranean Sea in the west. 9 Then there will be only one LORD who rules as King and whose name is worshiped everywhere on earth.

10-11 From Geba down to Rimmon[y] south of Jerusalem, the entire country will be turned into flatlands, with Jerusalem still towering above. Then the city will be full of people, from Benjamin Gate, Old Gate Place, and Hananel Tower in the northeast part of the city over to Corner Gate in the northwest and down to King's Wine Press in the south. Jerusalem will always be secure and will never again be destroyed.

12 Here is what the LORD will do to those who attack Jerusalem: While they are standing there, he will make their flesh rot and their eyes fall from their sockets and their tongues drop out.
13 The LORD will make them go into a frenzy and start attacking each other,
14-15 until even the people of Judah turn against those in Jerusalem.[z] This same terrible disaster will also strike every animal nearby, including horses, mules, camels, and donkeys. Finally, everything of value in the surrounding nations will be collected and brought to Jerusalem—gold, silver, and piles of clothing.

16 Afterwards, the survivors from those nations that attacked Jerusalem will go there each year to worship the King, the LORD All-Powerful, and to celebrate the Festival of Shelters. 17 No rain will fall on the land of anyone in any country who refuses to go to Jerusalem to worship the King, the LORD All-Powerful. 18-19 This horrible disaster will strike the Egyptians and everyone else who refuses to go there for the celebration.

20-21 At that time the words "Dedicated to the LORD" will be engraved on the bells worn by horses. In fact, every ordinary cooking pot in Jerusalem will be just as sacred to the LORD All-Powerful as the bowls used at the altar. Any one of them will be acceptable for boiling the meat of sacrificed animals, and there will no longer be a need to sell special pots and bowls.[a]

[t] **13.5** *I've . . . my life*: One possible meaning for the difficult Hebrew text. [u] **13.6** *wounded*: Probably from slashing themselves in the worship of a false god (see 1 Kings 18.28).
[v] **14.5** *to Azal*: One possible meaning for the difficult Hebrew text. The location of Azal is unknown. [w] **14.5** *earthquake struck*: See Amos 1.1. [x] **14.6** *a bright . . . cloudy*: One possible meaning for the difficult Hebrew text. [y] **14.10** *From Geba down to Rimmon*: Approximately the northern and southern borders of Judah before the exile (see 2 Kings 23.8); Geba is about ten miles north of Jerusalem, and Rimmon is about ten miles north of Beersheba. [z] **14.13-15** *each other . . . Jerusalem*: Or "each other. 14-15 But the people of Judah will fight on the side of Jerusalem." [a] **14.20,21** *special pots and bowls*: Since all pots and bowls will be considered acceptable for use in the temple, there will be no more need for merchants to sell special ones to those people who come to offer sacrifices.

MALACHI

ABOUT THIS BOOK

The book of Malachi comes from a time after many people of Judah had returned from Babylonia, but just before Ezra and Nehemiah returned. The temple had been rebuilt, and the priests were again offering the people's sacrifices to the Lord. But times were hard, and the people had lost most of their hope for a bright new future in Judah. The people and the priests were no longer showing the proper respect for the Lord or for his temple. They were also making wrong sacrifices and disobeying the laws of God. They were mistreating the poor and powerless, and men were divorcing their wives.

Malachi challenged the people and especially the priests to be faithful to the agreement the Lord had made with Israel. They were to honor the Lord by offering the right kind of sacrifices and by giving ten percent of their harvest to him. Then the Lord would bless them.

A QUICK LOOK AT THIS BOOK

The Lord's Love for Israel (1.1-5)
Against the Priests (1.6—2.9)
Broken Agreements (2.10-17)
The Lord Will Come (3.1-4)
Don't Cheat God (3.5-15)
The Lord Will Reward Faithful People and Punish Those Who Are Evil (3.16—4.6)

---

1 I am Malachi. And this is the message that the LORD gave me for Israel.

The LORD's Love for Israel

[2]Israel, I, the LORD, have loved you.
And yet you ask in what way have
I loved you. Don't forget that Esau
was the brother of your ancestor Jacob,
but I chose Jacob [3]instead of Esau.
And I turned Esau's hill country into a
barren desert where jackals[a] roam.
[4]Esau's descendants may say, "Although
our nation Edom is in ruins, we will rebuild."

But I, the LORD All-Powerful, promise
to tear down whatever they build. Then
everyone will know that I will never
stop being angry with them as long as
they are so sinful.

[5]Israel, when you see this, you will
shout, "The LORD's great reputation
reaches beyond our borders."

Judgment against Priests

[6]I, the LORD All-Powerful, have something to say to you priests. Children respect their fathers, and servants respect
their masters. I am your father and your
master, so why don't you respect me?
You priests have insulted me, and now
you ask, "How did we insult you?"

[7]You embarrass me by offering worthless food on my altar. Then you ask,
"How have we embarrassed you?" You
have done it by saying, "What's so great
about the LORD's altar?"

[8]But isn't it wrong to offer animals
that are blind, crippled, or sick? Just try
giving those animals to your governor.
That certainly wouldn't please him or
make him want to help you. [9]I am the
LORD God All-Powerful, and you had
better try to please me. You have sinned.
Now see if I will have mercy on any of
you.

[10]I wish someone would lock the
doors of my temple, so you would stop

[a]1.3 *jackals*: Desert animals related to wolves, but smaller.

wasting time building fires on my altar. I
am not pleased with you priests, and I
refuse to accept any more of your offerings. 11From dawn until dusk my name
is praised by every nation on this earth,
as they burn incense and offer the
proper sacrifices to me. 12But even you
priests insult me by saying, "There's
nothing special about the LORD's altar,
and these sacrifices are worthless."
13You get so disgusted that you even
make vulgar signs at me.[b] And for an
offering, you bring stolen[c] animals or
those that are crippled or sick. Should I
accept these? 14Instead of offering the
acceptable animals you have promised,
you bring me those that are unhealthy. I
will punish you for this, because I am
the great King, the LORD All-Powerful,
and I am worshiped by nations everywhere.

True and False Priests

2 I, the LORD All-Powerful, have something else to say to you priests. 2You
had better take seriously the need to
honor my name. Otherwise, when you
give a blessing, I will turn it into a curse.
In fact, I have already done this, because you haven't taken to heart your
duties as priests. 3I will punish your descendants and rub your faces in the manure from your animal sacrifices, and
then be done with you.[d]
4I am telling you this, so I can continue to keep my agreement with your
ancestor Levi. 5I blessed him with a full
life, as I had promised, and he kept his
part of the agreement by honoring me
and respecting my name. 6He taught the
truth and never told lies, and he led a lot
of people to turn from sin, because he
obeyed me and lived right.
7You priests should be eager to spread
knowledge, and everyone should come
to you for instruction, because you
speak for me, the LORD All-Powerful.
8But you have turned your backs on me.
Your teachings have led others to do
sinful things, and you have broken the
agreement I made with your ancestor
Levi. 9So I caused everyone to hate and
despise you, because you disobeyed me
and failed to treat all people alike.

A Broken Agreement

10Don't you know that we all have
God as our Father? Didn't the one God
create each of us? Then why do you
cheat each other by breaking the agreement God made with your ancestors?
11You people in Judah and Jerusalem
have been unfaithful to the LORD. You
have disgraced the temple that he loves,
and you have committed the disgusting
sin of worshiping other gods.[e] 12I pray
that the LORD will no longer let those
who are guilty belong to his people,
even if they eagerly decide to offer the
LORD a gift.[f]
13And what else are you doing? You
cry noisily and flood the LORD's altar
with your tears, because he isn't pleased
with your offerings and refuses to accept them. 14And why isn't God pleased?
It's because he knows that each of you
men has been unfaithful to the wife you
married when you were young. You
promised that she would be your partner, but now you have broken that
promise. 15Didn't God create you to become like one person with your wife?[g]
And why did he do this? It was so you
would have children, and then lead
them to become God's people. Don't
ever be unfaithful to your wife. 16The
LORD God All-Powerful of Israel hates
anyone who is cruel enough to divorce
his wife. So take care never to be unfaithful!
17You have worn out the LORD with
your words. And yet, you ask, "How did
we do that?"
You did it by saying, "The LORD is
pleased with evil and doesn't care about
justice."

The Promised Messenger

3 I, the LORD All-Powerful,
will send my messenger
to prepare the way for me.
Then suddenly the Lord
you are looking for
will appear in his temple.
The messenger you desire
is coming with my promise,
and he is on his way.

A Day of Change

2On the day the Lord comes, he will
be like a furnace that purifies silver or
like strong soap in a washbasin. No one
will be able to stand up to him. 3The
LORD will purify the descendants of
Levi,[h] as though they were gold or silver. Then they will bring the proper offerings to the LORD, 4and the offerings
of the people of Judah and Jerusalem
will please him, just as they did in the
past.

Don't Cheat God

5The LORD All-Powerful said:
I'm now on my way to judge you.

[b]**1.13** *me*: Or "the altar." [c]**1.13** *stolen*: Or "injured." [d]**2.3** *and then be done with you*: One possible meaning for the difficult Hebrew text. [e]**2.11** *worshiping other gods*: Or "marrying the worshipers of other gods." [f]**2.12** *even if . . . gift*: One possible meaning for the difficult Hebrew text. [g]**2.15** *Didn't . . . wife*: One possible meaning for the difficult Hebrew text. [h]**3.3** *descendants of Levi*: The priests.

And I will quickly condemn all who
practice witchcraft or cheat in marriage or tell lies in court or rob
workers of their pay or mistreat widows and orphans or steal the property of foreigners or refuse to respect me.
6Descendants of Jacob, I am the
LORD All-Powerful, and I never
change. That's why you haven't been
wiped out, 7even though you have ignored and disobeyed my laws ever
since the time of your ancestors. But
if you return to me, I will return to
you.

And yet you ask, "How can we return?"

8You people are robbing me, your
God. And, here you are, asking,
"How are we robbing you?"

You are robbing me of the offerings and of the ten percent that belongs to me.[i] 9That's why your
whole nation is under a curse. 10I am
the LORD All-Powerful, and I challenge you to put me to the test. Bring
the entire ten percent into the storehouse, so there will be food in my
house. Then I will open the windows
of heaven and flood you with blessing after blessing.[j] 11I will also stop
locusts[k] from destroying your crops
and keeping your vineyards from
producing. 12Everyone of every nation will talk about how I have
blessed you and about your wonderful land. I, the LORD All-Powerful,
have spoken!

13You have said horrible things
about me, and yet you ask, "What
have we said?"

14Here is what you have said: "It's
foolish to serve the LORD God All-
Powerful. What do we get for obeying him and from going around
looking sad? 15See how happy those
arrogant people are. Everyone who
does wrong is successful, and when
they put God to the test, they always
get away with it."

Faithfulness Is Rewarded

16All those who truly respected the
LORD and honored his name started dis-
cussing these things, and when God saw
what was happening, he had their
names[l] written as a reminder in his
book.
17Then the LORD All-Powerful said:

You people are precious to me,
and when I come to bring justice, I
will protect you, just as parents protect an obedient child. 18Then everyone will once again see the difference between those who obey me by
doing right and those who reject me
by doing wrong.

The Day of Judgment

The LORD said:

4 The day of judgment is certain to
come. And it will be like a red-hot
furnace with flames that burn up proud
and sinful people, as though they were
straw. Not a branch or a root will be left.
I, the LORD All-Powerful, have spoken!
2But for you that honor my name, victory will shine like the sun with healing
in its rays, and you will jump around
like calves at play. 3When I come to
bring justice, you will trample those
who are evil, as though they were
ashes under your feet. I, the LORD All-
Powerful, have spoken!

4Don't ever forget the laws and teachings I gave my servant Moses on Mount
Sinai.[m]

5I, the LORD, promise to send the
prophet Elijah before that great and terrible day comes. 6He will lead children
and parents to love each other more, so
that when I come, I won't bring doom to
the land.

[i]3.8 *the ten percent . . . to me*: The people of Israel were supposed to give a tenth of their harvests and of their flocks and herds to the LORD (see Leviticus 27.30-33; Deuteronomy 14.22-29). [j]3.10 *open the windows . . . blessing*: This may refer to rain, since there seems to have been a terrible drought at this time. [k]3.11 *locusts*: A kind of grasshopper that comes in swarms and causes great damage to plant life. [l]3.16 *names*: Or "deeds." [m]4.4 *Sinai*: Hebrew "Horeb."

The
HOLY
BIBLE

The New Testament

Contemporary English Version

About the New Testament

The New Testament is a collection of 27 books and letters written in Greek. They are arranged in four groups:

(1) Gospels and Acts. This group contains the four Gospels, which are Matthew, Mark, Luke, and John. The term "gospel" means "good news," and these four Gospels tell the good news about Jesus Christ. The group also contains the book of Acts, which tells how the good news spread in the years after Jesus died and was raised from death.

(2) Letters of Paul. This group is made up of Romans, 1 and 2 Corinthians, Galatians, Ephesians, Philippians, Colossians, 1 and 2 Thessalonians, 1 and 2 Timothy, Titus, and Philemon. These letters have traditionally been called "epistles," and each one is named for the group or person that it was written to.

(3) Other Letters. This group contains letters written by people other than Paul. It contains Hebrews, James, 1 and 2 Peter, 1, 2, and 3 John, and Jude. The Letter to the Hebrews doesn't give its author's name, but each of the other letters is named for the person who wrote it.

(4) Revelation. This book is quite different from the other New Testament books, because it is a book of visions and prophecies.

MATTHEW

ABOUT THIS BOOK

The Sermon on the Mount (5.1—7.28), the Lord's Prayer (6.9-13), and the Golden Rule (7.12: "Treat others as you want them to treat you") are all in this book. It is perhaps the best known and the most quoted of all the books that have ever been written about Jesus. That is one reason why Matthew was placed first among the four books about Jesus called Gospels.

One of the most important ideas found here is that God expects his people to obey him, and this is what is meant by the Greek word that appears in many translations as *righteousness.* It is used seven times by Matthew, but only once by Luke, and not at all by Mark. So it is an important clue to much of what Matthew wants his readers to understand about the teaching of Jesus.

Jesus first uses this word at his own baptism, when he tells John the Baptist, "We must do all that God wants us to do" (3.15). Then, during his Sermon on the Mount, he speaks five more times of what God's people must do to obey him (5.6, 10, 20; 6.1, 33). And finally, he reminds the chief priests and leaders of the people, "John the Baptist showed you how to do right" (21.32).

Matthew wanted to provide for the people of his time a record of Jesus' message and ministry. It is clear that the Old Testament Scriptures were very important to these people. And Matthew never fails to show when these texts point to the coming of Jesus as the Messiah sent from God. Matthew wrote this book to make sure Christians knew that their faith in Jesus as the Messiah was well anchored in the Old Testament Scriptures, and to help them grow in faith.

Matthew ends his story with the words of Jesus to his followers, which tell what they are to do after he leaves them:

> *I have been given all authority in heaven and on earth! Go to the people of all nations and make them my disciples. Baptize them in the name of the Father, the Son, and the Holy Spirit, and teach them to do everything I have told you. I will be with you always, even until the end of the world.* *(28.18b-20)*

A QUICK LOOK AT THIS BOOK

The Ancestors and Birth of Jesus (1.1—2.23)
The Message of John the Baptist (3.1-12)
The Baptism and Temptation of Jesus (3.13—4.11)
Jesus in Galilee (4.12—18.35)
Jesus Goes from Galilee to Jerusalem (19.1—20.34)
Jesus' Last Week: His Trial and Death (21.1—27.66)
Jesus Is Alive (28.1-20)

The Ancestors of Jesus
(Luke 3.23-38)

1 Jesus Christ came from the family
of King David and also from the
family of Abraham. And this is a list of
his ancestors. 2-6a From Abraham to King
David, his ancestors were:

Abraham, Isaac, Jacob, Judah and his brothers (Judah's sons were Perez and Zerah, and their mother was Tamar), Hezron;

Ram, Amminadab, Nahshon, Salmon, Boaz (his mother was Rahab), Obed (his mother was Ruth), Jesse, and King David.

6b-11 From David to the time of the exile in Babylonia, the ancestors of Jesus
were:
David, Solomon (his mother had been
Uriah's wife), Rehoboam, Abijah, Asa,
Jehoshaphat, Jehoram;
Uzziah, Jotham, Ahaz, Hezekiah, Manasseh, Amon, Josiah, and Jehoiachin
and his brothers.
12-16 From the exile to the birth of Jesus, his ancestors were:
Jehoiachin, Shealtiel, Zerubbabel,
Abiud, Eliakim, Azor, Zadok, Achim;
Eliud, Eleazar, Matthan, Jacob, and
Joseph, the husband of Mary, the
mother of Jesus, who is called the Messiah.
17 There were fourteen generations
from Abraham to David. There were
also fourteen from David to the exile in
Babylonia and fourteen more to the
birth of the Messiah.

The Birth of Jesus

(Luke 2.1-7)

18 This is how Jesus Christ was born. A
young woman named Mary was engaged to Joseph from King David's family. But before they were married, she
learned that she was going to have a
baby by God's Holy Spirit. 19 Joseph was
a good man[a] and did not want to embarrass Mary in front of everyone. So he
decided to quietly call off the wedding.
20 While Joseph was thinking about
this, an angel from the Lord came to
him in a dream. The angel said, "Joseph,
the baby that Mary will have is from the
Holy Spirit. Go ahead and marry her.
21 Then after her baby is born, name him
Jesus,[b] because he will save his people
from their sins."
22 So the Lord's promise came true,
just as the prophet had said, 23 "A virgin
will have a baby boy, and he will be
called Immanuel," which means "God is
with us."
24 After Joseph woke up, he and Mary
were soon married, just as the Lord's
angel had told him to do. 25 But they did
not sleep together before her baby was
born. Then Joseph named him Jesus.

The Wise Men

2 When Jesus was born in the village
of Bethlehem in Judea, Herod was
king. During this time some wise men[c]
from the east came to Jerusalem 2 and
said, "Where is the child born to be king
of the Jews? We saw his star in the east[d]
and have come to worship him."
3 When King Herod heard about this,
he was worried, and so was everyone
else in Jerusalem. 4 Herod brought together the chief priests and the teachers
of the Law of Moses and asked them,
"Where will the Messiah be born?"
5 They told him, "He will be born in
Bethlehem, just as the prophet wrote,

6 'Bethlehem in the land
    of Judea,
you are very important
    among the towns of Judea.
From your town
    will come a leader,
who will be like a shepherd
    for my people Israel.' "

7 Herod secretly called in the wise men
and asked them when they had first
seen the star. 8 He told them, "Go to
Bethlehem and search carefully for the
child. As soon as you find him, let me
know. I want to go and worship him
too."
9 The wise men listened to what the
king said and then left. And the star
they had seen in the east went on ahead
of them until it stopped over the place
where the child was. 10 They were
thrilled and excited to see the star.
11 When the men went into the house
and saw the child with Mary, his
mother, they knelt down and worshiped
him. They took out their gifts of gold,
frankincense, and myrrh[e] and gave
them to him. 12 Later they were warned
in a dream not to return to Herod, and
they went back home by another road.

The Escape to Egypt

13 After the wise men had gone, an angel from the Lord appeared to Joseph in
a dream and said, "Get up! Hurry and
take the child and his mother to Egypt!
Stay there until I tell you to return, because Herod is looking for the child and
wants to kill him."
14 That night, Joseph got up and took
his wife and the child to Egypt, 15 where
they stayed until Herod died. So the
Lord's promise came true, just as the
prophet had said, "I called my son out of
Egypt."

The Killing of the Children

16 When Herod found out that the wise
men from the east had tricked him, he
was very angry. He gave orders for his
men to kill all the boys who lived in or
near Bethlehem and were two years old

[a] **1.19** *good man*: Or "kind man," or "man who always did the right thing." [b] **1.21** *name him Jesus*: In Hebrew the name "Jesus" means "the Lord saves." [c] **2.1** *wise men*: People famous for studying the stars. [d] **2.2** *his star in the east*: Or "his star rise." [e] **2.11** *frankincense, and myrrh*: Frankincense was a valuable powder that was burned to make a sweet smell. Myrrh was a valuable sweet-smelling powder often used in perfume.

and younger. This was based on what he
had learned from the wise men.
17So the Lord's promise came true,
just as the prophet Jeremiah had said,

18 "In Ramah a voice was heard
crying and weeping loudly.
Rachel was mourning
for her children,
and she refused
to be comforted,
because they were dead."

The Return from Egypt

19After King Herod died, an angel
from the Lord appeared in a dream to
Joseph while he was still in Egypt. 20The
angel said, "Get up and take the child
and his mother back to Israel. The people who wanted to kill him are now
dead."
21Joseph got up and left with them for
Israel. 22But when he heard that Herod's
son Archelaus was now ruler of Judea,
he was afraid to go there. Then in a
dream he was told to go to Galilee,
23and they went to live there in the town
of Nazareth. So the Lord's promise
came true, just as the prophet had said,
"He will be called a Nazarene."[f]

The Preaching of John the Baptist

(Mark 1.1-8; Luke 3.1-18; John 1.19-28)

3 Years later, John the Baptist started
preaching in the desert of Judea.
2He said, "Turn back to God! The kingdom of heaven[g] will soon be here."[h]
3John was the one the prophet Isaiah
was talking about, when he said,

"In the desert someone
is shouting,
'Get the road ready
for the Lord!
Make a straight path
for him.' "

4John wore clothes made of camel's
hair. He had a leather strap around his
waist and ate grasshoppers and wild
honey.
5From Jerusalem and all Judea and
from the Jordan River Valley crowds of
people went to John. 6They told how
sorry they were for their sins, and he
baptized them in the river.
7Many Pharisees and Sadducees also
came to be baptized. But John said to
them:

You bunch of snakes! Who warned
you to run from the coming judgment? 8Do something to show that
you have really given up your sins.
9And don't start telling yourselves
that you belong to Abraham's family. I tell you that God can turn these
stones into children for Abraham.
10An ax is ready to cut the trees
down at their roots. Any tree that
doesn't produce good fruit will be
chopped down and thrown into a
fire.
11I baptize you with water so that
you will give up your sins.[i] But
someone more powerful is going to
come, and I am not good enough
even to carry his sandals.[j] He will
baptize you with the Holy Spirit and
with fire. 12His threshing fork is in
his hand, and he is ready to separate
the wheat from the husks.[k] He will
store the wheat in a barn and burn
the husks in a fire that never goes
out.

The Baptism of Jesus

(Mark 1.9-11; Luke 3.21, 22)

13Jesus left Galilee and went to the
Jordan River to be baptized by John.
14But John kept objecting and said, "I
ought to be baptized by you. Why have
you come to me?"
15Jesus answered, "For now this is
how it should be, because we must do
all that God wants us to do." Then John
agreed.
16So Jesus was baptized. And as soon
as he came out of the water, the sky
opened, and he saw the Spirit of God
coming down on him like a dove. 17Then
a voice from heaven said, "This is my
own dear Son, and I am pleased with
him."

Jesus and the Devil

(Mark 1.12, 13; Luke 4.1-13)

4 The Holy Spirit led Jesus into the
desert, so that the devil could test
him. 2After Jesus had gone without eating[l] for forty days and nights, he was
very hungry. 3Then the devil came to
him and said, "If you are God's Son, tell
these stones to turn into bread."

[f]**2.23** *He will be called a Nazarene*: The prophet who said this is not known. [g]**3.2** *kingdom of heaven*: In the Gospel of Matthew "kingdom of heaven" is used with the same meaning as "God's kingdom" in Mark and Luke. [h]**3.2** *will soon be here*: Or "is already here."
[i]**3.11** *so that you will give up your sins*: Or "because you have given up your sins."
[j]**3.11** *carry his sandals*: This was one of the duties of a slave. [k]**3.12** *His threshing fork is in his hand, and he is ready to separate the wheat from the husks*: After Jewish farmers had trampled out the grain, they used a large fork to pitch the grain and the husks into the air. Wind would blow away the light husks, and the grain would fall back to the ground, where it could be gathered up. [l]**4.2** *without eating*: The Jewish people sometimes went without eating (also called "fasting") to show their love for God or to show sorrow for their sins.

4 Jesus answered, "The Scriptures say:

'No one can live only on food.
People need every word
that God has spoken.' "

5 Next, the devil took Jesus to the holy
city and had him stand on the highest
part of the temple. 6 The devil said, "If
you are God's Son, jump off. The Scriptures say:

'God will give his angels
orders about you.
They will catch you
in their arms,
and you won't hurt
your feet on the stones.' "

7 Jesus answered, "The Scriptures also
say, 'Don't try to test the Lord your
God!' "
8 Finally, the devil took Jesus up on a
very high mountain and showed him all
the kingdoms on earth and their power.
9 The devil said to him, "I will give all
this to you, if you will bow down and
worship me."
10 Jesus answered, "Go away Satan!
The Scriptures say:

'Worship the Lord your God
and serve only him.' "

11 Then the devil left Jesus, and angels
came to help him.

Jesus Begins His Work

(Mark 1.14, 15; Luke 4.14, 15)

12 When Jesus heard that John had
been put in prison, he went to Galilee.
13 But instead of staying in Nazareth, Jesus moved to Capernaum. This town
was beside Lake Galilee in the territory
of Zebulun and Naphtali.[m] 14 So God's
promise came true, just as the prophet
Isaiah had said,

15 "Listen, lands of Zebulun
and Naphtali,
lands along the road
to the sea and east
of the Jordan!
Listen Galilee,
land of the Gentiles!
16 Although your people
live in darkness,
they will see
a bright light.
Although they live
in the shadow of death,
a light will shine
on them."

17 Then Jesus started preaching, "Turn
back to God! The kingdom of heaven
will soon be here."[n]

Jesus Chooses Four Fishermen

(Mark 1.16-20; Luke 5.1-11)

18 While Jesus was walking along the
shore of Lake Galilee, he saw two brothers. One was Simon, also known as Peter, and the other was Andrew. They
were fishermen, and they were casting
their net into the lake. 19 Jesus said to
them, "Come with me! I will teach you
how to bring in people instead of fish."
20 Right then the two brothers dropped
their nets and went with him.
21 Jesus walked on until he saw James
and John, the sons of Zebedee. They
were in a boat with their father, mending their nets. Jesus asked them to come
with him too. 22 Right away they left the
boat and their father and went with Jesus.

Jesus Teaches, Preaches, and Heals

(Luke 6.17-19)

23 Jesus went all over Galilee, teaching
in the Jewish meeting places and
preaching the good news about God's
kingdom. He also healed every kind of
disease and sickness. 24 News about him
spread all over Syria, and people with
every kind of sickness or disease were
brought to him. Some of them had a lot
of demons in them, others were thought
to be crazy,[o] and still others could not
walk. But Jesus healed them all.
25 Large crowds followed Jesus from
Galilee and the region around the ten
cities known as Decapolis.[p] They also
came from Jerusalem, Judea, and from
across the Jordan River.

The Sermon on the Mount

5 When Jesus saw the crowds, he
went up on the side of a mountain
and sat down.[q]

Blessings

(Luke 6.20-23)

Jesus' disciples gathered around him,
2 and he taught them:

3 God blesses those people
who depend only on him.
They belong to the kingdom
of heaven![r]

[m] **4.13** *Zebulun and Naphtali*: In Old Testament times these tribes were in northern Palestine, and in New Testament times many Gentiles lived where these tribes had once been.
[n] **4.17** *The kingdom of heaven will soon be here*: See the two notes at 3.2.
[o] **4.24** *thought to be crazy*: In ancient times people with epilepsy were thought to be crazy.
[p] **4.25** *the ten cities known as Decapolis*: A group of ten cities east of Samaria and Galilee, where the people followed the Greek way of life.
[q] **5.1** *sat down*: Teachers in the ancient world, including Jewish teachers, usually sat down when they taught.
[r] **5.3** *They belong to the kingdom of heaven*: Or "The kingdom of heaven belongs to them."

4 God blesses those people
who grieve.
They will find comfort!
5 God blesses those people
who are humble.
The earth will belong
to them!
6 God blesses those people
who want to obey him[s]
more than to eat or drink.
They will be given
what they want!
7 God blesses those people
who are merciful.
They will be treated
with mercy!
8 God blesses those people
whose hearts are pure.
They will see him!
9 God blesses those people
who make peace.
They will be called
his children!
10 God blesses those people
who are treated badly
for doing right.
They belong to the kingdom
of heaven.[t]

11God will bless you when people
insult you, mistreat you, and tell all
kinds of evil lies about you because
of me. 12Be happy and excited! You
will have a great reward in heaven.
People did these same things to the
prophets who lived long ago.

Salt and Light

(Mark 9.50; Luke 14.34, 35)

13You are like salt for everyone on
earth. But if salt no longer tastes like
salt, how can it make food salty? All
it is good for is to be thrown out and
walked on.
14You are like light for the whole
world. A city built on top of a hill
cannot be hidden, 15and no one
would light a lamp and put it under
a clay pot. A lamp is placed on a
lampstand, where it can give light to
everyone in the house. 16Make your
light shine, so that others will see
the good that you do and will praise
your Father in heaven.

The Law of Moses

17Don't suppose that I came to do
away with the Law and the
Prophets.[u] I did not come to do away
with them, but to give them their full
meaning. 18Heaven and earth may
disappear. But I promise you that
not even a period or comma will
ever disappear from the Law. Everything written in it must happen.
19If you reject even the least important command in the Law and
teach others to do the same, you will
be the least important person in the
kingdom of heaven. But if you obey
and teach others its commands, you
will have an important place in the
kingdom. 20You must obey God's
commands better than the Pharisees
and the teachers of the Law obey
them. If you don't, I promise you
that you will never get into the kingdom of heaven.

Anger

21You know that our ancestors
were told, "Do not murder" and "A
murderer must be brought to trial."
22But I promise you that if you are
angry with someone,[v] you will have
to stand trial. If you call someone a
fool, you will be taken to court. And
if you say that someone is worthless,
you will be in danger of the fires of
hell.
23So if you are about to place your
gift on the altar and remember that
someone is angry with you, 24leave
your gift there in front of the altar.
Make peace with that person, then
come back and offer your gift to
God.
25Before you are dragged into
court, make friends with the person
who has accused you of doing
wrong. If you don't, you will be
handed over to the judge and then to
the officer who will put you in jail.
26I promise you that you will not get
out until you have paid the last cent
you owe.

Marriage

27You know the commandment
which says, "Be faithful in marriage." 28But I tell you that if you
look at another woman and want
her, you are already unfaithful in
your thoughts. 29If your right eye
causes you to sin, poke it out and
throw it away. It is better to lose one
part of your body, than for your
whole body to end up in hell. 30If
your right hand causes you to sin,
chop it off and throw it away! It is
better to lose one part of your body,
than for your whole body to be
thrown into hell.

[s] **5.6** *who want to obey him*: Or "who want to do right" or "who want everyone to be treated right." [t] **5.10** *They belong to the kingdom of heaven*: See the note at 5.3. [u] **5.17** *the Law and the Prophets*: The Jewish Scriptures, that is, the Old Testament. [v] **5.22** *someone*: In verses 22-24 the Greek text has "brother," which may refer to people in general or to other followers.

Divorce

(Matthew 19.9; Mark 10.11, 12; Luke 16.18)

31 You have been taught that a man
who divorces his wife must write out
divorce papers for her.[w] 32 But I tell
you not to divorce your wife unless
she has committed some terrible
sexual sin.[x] If you divorce her, you
will cause her to be unfaithful, just
as any man who marries her is
guilty of taking another man's wife.

Promises

33 You know that our ancestors
were told, "Don't use the Lord's
name to make a promise unless you
are going to keep it." 34 But I tell you
not to swear by anything when you
make a promise! Heaven is God's
throne, so don't swear by heaven.
35 The earth is God's footstool, so
don't swear by the earth. Jerusalem
is the city of the great king, so don't
swear by it. 36 Don't swear by your
own head. You cannot make one hair
white or black. 37 When you make a
promise, say only "Yes" or "No."
Anything else comes from the devil.

Revenge

(Luke 6.29, 30)

38 You know that you have been
taught, "An eye for an eye and a
tooth for a tooth." 39 But I tell you not
to try to get even with a person who
has done something to you. When
someone slaps your right cheek,[y]
turn and let that person slap your
other cheek. 40 If someone sues you
for your shirt, give up your coat as
well. 41 If a soldier forces you to
carry his pack one mile, carry it two
miles.[z] 42 When people ask you for
something, give it to them. When
they want to borrow money, lend it
to them.

Love

(Luke 6.27, 28, 32-36)

43 You have heard people say,
"Love your neighbors and hate your
enemies." 44 But I tell you to love
your enemies and pray for anyone
who mistreats you. 45 Then you will
be acting like your Father in heaven.
He makes the sun rise on both good
and bad people. And he sends rain
for the ones who do right and for the
ones who do wrong. 46 If you love
only those people who love you, will
God reward you for that? Even tax
collectors[a] love their friends. 47 If you
greet only your friends, what's so
great about that? Don't even unbelievers do that? 48 But you must always act like your Father in heaven.

Giving

6 When you do good deeds, don't try
to show off. If you do, you won't get
a reward from your Father in heaven.
2 When you give to the poor, don't
blow a loud horn. That's what show-
offs do in the meeting places and on
the street corners, because they are
always looking for praise. I can assure you that they already have their
reward.
3 When you give to the poor, don't
let anyone know about it.[b] 4 Then
your gift will be given in secret. Your
Father knows what is done in secret,
and he will reward you.

Prayer

(Luke 11.2-4)

5 When you pray, don't be like
those show-offs who love to stand
up and pray in the meeting places
and on the street corners. They do
this just to look good. I can assure
you that they already have their
reward.
6 When you pray, go into a room
alone and close the door. Pray to
your Father in private. He knows
what is done in private, and he will
reward you.
7 When you pray, don't talk on and
on as people do who don't know
God. They think God likes to hear
long prayers. 8 Don't be like them.
Your Father knows what you need
before you ask.
9 You should pray like this:

Our Father in heaven,
help us to honor
your name.
10 Come and set up
your kingdom,
so that everyone on earth
will obey you,

[w] **5.31** *write out divorce papers for her*: Jewish men could divorce their wives, but the women could not divorce their husbands. The purpose of writing these papers was to make it harder for a man to divorce his wife. Before this law was made, all a man had to do was to send his wife away and say that she was no longer his wife. [x] **5.32** *some terrible sexual sin*: This probably refers to the laws about the wrong kinds of marriages that are forbidden in Leviticus 18.6-18 or to some serious sexual sin. [y] **5.39** *right cheek*: A slap on the right cheek was a bad insult. [z] **5.41** *two miles*: A Roman soldier had the right to force a person to carry his pack as far as one mile. [a] **5.46** *tax collectors*: These were usually Jewish people who paid the Romans for the right to collect taxes. They were hated by other Jews who thought of them as traitors to their country and to their religion. [b] **6.3** *don't let anyone know about it*: The Greek text has, "Don't let your left hand know what your right hand is doing."

as you are obeyed
in heaven.
11 Give us our food for today.[c]
12 Forgive us for doing wrong,
as we forgive others.
13 Keep us from being tempted
and protect us from evil.[d]

14 If you forgive others for the
wrongs they do to you, your Father
in heaven will forgive you. 15 But if
you don't forgive others, your Father
will not forgive your sins.

Worshiping God by Going without Eating

16 When you go without eating,[e]
don't try to look gloomy as those
show-offs do when they go without
eating. I can assure you that they already have their reward. 17 Instead,
comb your hair and wash your face.
18 Then others won't know that you
are going without eating. But your
Father sees what is done in private,
and he will reward you.

Treasures in Heaven

(Luke 12.33, 34)

19 Don't store up treasures on
earth! Moths and rust can destroy
them, and thieves can break in and
steal them. 20 Instead, store up your
treasures in heaven, where moths
and rust cannot destroy them, and
thieves cannot break in and steal
them. 21 Your heart will always be
where your treasure is.

Light

(Luke 11.34-36)

22 Your eyes are like a window for
your body. When they are good, you
have all the light you need. 23 But
when your eyes are bad, everything
is dark. If the light inside you is
dark, you surely are in the dark.

Money

(Luke 16.13)

24 You cannot be the slave of two
masters! You will like one more than
the other or be more loyal to one
than the other. You cannot serve
both God and money.

Worry

(Luke 12.22-31)

25 I tell you not to worry about your
life. Don't worry about having something to eat, drink, or wear. Isn't life
more than food or clothing? 26 Look
at the birds in the sky! They don't
plant or harvest. They don't even
store grain in barns. Yet your Father
in heaven takes care of them. Aren't
you worth more than birds?
27 Can worry make you live
longer?[f] 28 Why worry about clothes?
Look how the wild flowers grow.
They don't work hard to make their
clothes. 29 But I tell you that Solomon
with all his wealth[g] wasn't as well
clothed as one of them. 30 God gives
such beauty to everything that grows
in the fields, even though it is here
today and thrown into a fire tomorrow. He will surely do even more for
you! Why do you have such little faith?
31 Don't worry and ask yourselves,
"Will we have anything to eat? Will
we have anything to drink? Will we
have any clothes to wear?" 32 Only
people who don't know God are always worrying about such things.
Your Father in heaven knows that
you need all of these. 33 But more
than anything else, put God's work
first and do what he wants. Then the
other things will be yours as well.
34 Don't worry about tomorrow. It
will take care of itself. You have
enough to worry about today.

Judging Others

(Luke 6.37, 38, 41, 42)

7 Don't condemn others, and God
won't condemn you. 2 God will be as
hard on you as you are on others! He
will treat you exactly as you treat
them.
3 You can see the speck in your
friend's eye, but you don't notice the
log in your own eye. 4 How can you
say, "My friend, let me take the
speck out of your eye," when you
don't see the log in your own eye?
5 You're nothing but show-offs! First,
take the log out of your own eye.
Then you can see how to take the
speck out of your friend's eye.
6 Don't give to dogs what belongs
to God. They will only turn and attack you. Don't throw pearls down
in front of pigs. They will trample all
over them.

Ask, Search, Knock

(Luke 11.9-13)

7 Ask, and you will receive. Search,
and you will find. Knock, and the
door will be opened for you. 8 Everyone who asks will receive. Everyone
who searches will find. And the door

[c] **6.11** *our food for today*: Or "the food that we need" or "our food for the coming day."
[d] **6.13** *evil*: Or "the evil one," that is, the devil. Some manuscripts add, "The kingdom, the power, and the glory are yours forever. Amen." [e] **6.16** *without eating*: See the note at 4.2.
[f] **6.27** *live longer*: Or "grow taller." [g] **6.29** *Solomon with all his wealth*: The Jewish people thought that Solomon was the richest person who had ever lived.

will be opened for everyone who
knocks. 9Would any of you give your
hungry child a stone, if the child
asked for some bread? 10Would you
give your child a snake if the child
asked for a fish? 11As bad as you
are, you still know how to give good
gifts to your children. But your heavenly Father is even more ready to
give good things to people who ask.
12Treat others as you want them to
treat you. This is what the Law and
the Prophets[h] are all about.

The Narrow Gate
(Luke 13.24)

13Go in through the narrow gate.
The gate to destruction is wide, and
the road that leads there is easy to
follow. A lot of people go through
that gate. 14But the gate to life is
very narrow. The road that leads
there is so hard to follow that only a
few people find it.

A Tree and Its Fruit
(Luke 6.43-45)

15Watch out for false prophets!
They dress up like sheep, but inside
they are wolves who have come to
attack you. 16You can tell what they
are by what they do. No one picks
grapes or figs from thornbushes. 17A
good tree produces good fruit, and a
bad tree produces bad fruit. 18A
good tree cannot produce bad fruit,
and a bad tree cannot produce good
fruit. 19Every tree that produces bad
fruit will be chopped down and
burned. 20You can tell who the false
prophets are by their deeds.

A Warning
(Luke 13.26, 27)

21Not everyone who calls me their
Lord will get into the kingdom of
heaven. Only the ones who obey my
Father in heaven will get in. 22On the
day of judgment many will call me
their Lord. They will say, "We
preached in your name, and in your
name we forced out demons and
worked many miracles." 23But I will
tell them, "I will have nothing to do
with you! Get out of my sight, you
evil people!"

Two Builders
(Luke 6.47-49)

24Anyone who hears and obeys
these teachings of mine is like a
wise person who built a house on
solid rock. 25Rain poured down,
rivers flooded, and winds beat
against that house. But it did not
fall, because it was built on solid
rock.
26Anyone who hears my teachings
and doesn't obey them is like a foolish person who built a house on
sand. 27The rain poured down, the
rivers flooded, and the winds blew
and beat against that house. Finally,
it fell with a crash.
28When Jesus finished speaking, the
crowds were surprised at his teaching.
29He taught them like someone with authority, and not like their teachers of the
Law of Moses.

Jesus Heals a Man
(Mark 1.40-45; Luke 5.12-16)

8 As Jesus came down the mountain,
he was followed by large crowds.
2Suddenly a man with leprosy[i] came
and knelt in front of Jesus. He said,
"Lord, you have the power to make me
well, if only you wanted to."
3Jesus put his hand on the man and
said, "I want to! Now you are well." At
once the man's leprosy disappeared.
4Jesus told him, "Don't tell anyone
about this, but go and show the priest
that you are well. Then take a gift to the
temple just as Moses commanded, and
everyone will know that you have been
healed."[j]

Jesus Heals an Army Officer's Servant
(Luke 7.1-10; John 4.43-54)

5When Jesus was going into the town
of Capernaum, an army officer came up
to him and said, 6"Lord, my servant is at
home in such terrible pain that he can't
even move."
7"I will go and heal him," Jesus replied.
8But the officer said, "Lord, I'm not
good enough for you to come into my
house. Just give the order, and my servant will get well. 9I have officers who
give orders to me, and I have soldiers
who take orders from me. I can say to
one of them, 'Go!' and he goes. I can say
to another, 'Come!' and he comes. I can
say to my servant, 'Do this!' and he will
do it."
10When Jesus heard this, he was so
surprised that he turned and said to the
crowd following him, "I tell you that in
all of Israel I've never found anyone

[h]7.12 *the Law and the Prophets*: See the note at 5.17. [i]8.2 *leprosy*: In biblical times the word "leprosy" was used for many different kinds of skin diseases. [j]8.4 *everyone will know that you have been healed*: People with leprosy had to be examined by a priest and told that they were well (that is "clean") before they could once again live a normal life in the Jewish community. The gift that Moses commanded was the sacrifice of some lambs together with flour mixed with olive oil.

with this much faith! 11Many people will
come from everywhere to enjoy the
feast in the kingdom of heaven with
Abraham, Isaac, and Jacob. 12But the
ones who should have been in the kingdom will be thrown out into the dark.
They will cry and grit their teeth in
pain."
13Then Jesus said to the officer, "You
may go home now. Your faith has made
it happen."
Right then his servant was healed.

Jesus Heals Many People
(Mark 1.29-34; Luke 4.38-41)

14Jesus went to the home of Peter,
where he found that Peter's mother-in-
law was sick in bed with fever. 15He
took her by the hand, and the fever left
her. Then she got up and served Jesus a
meal.
16That evening many people with
demons in them were brought to Jesus.
And with only a word he forced out the
evil spirits and healed everyone who
was sick. 17So God's promise came true,
just as the prophet Isaiah had said,

"He healed our diseases
and made us well."

Some Who Wanted To Go with Jesus
(Luke 9.57-62)

18When Jesus saw the crowd,[k] he
went across Lake Galilee. 19A teacher of
the Law of Moses came up to him and
said, "Teacher, I'll go anywhere with
you!"
20Jesus replied, "Foxes have dens, and
birds have nests. But the Son of Man
doesn't have a place to call his own."
21Another disciple said to Jesus,
"Lord, let me wait till I bury my father."
22Jesus answered, "Come with me,
and let the dead bury their dead."[l]

A Storm
(Mark 4.35-41; Luke 8.22-25)

23After Jesus left in a boat with his
disciples, 24a terrible storm suddenly
struck the lake, and waves started
splashing into their boat.
Jesus was sound asleep, 25so the disciples went over to him and woke him up.
They said, "Lord, save us! We're going to
drown!"
26But Jesus replied, "Why are you so
afraid? You surely don't have much
faith." Then he got up and ordered the
wind and the waves to calm down. And
everything was calm.
27The men in the boat were amazed
and said, "Who is this? Even the wind
and the waves obey him."

Two Men with Demons in Them
(Mark 5.1-20; Luke 8.26-39)

28After Jesus had crossed the lake, he
came to shore near the town of Gadara[m]
and started down the road. Two men
with demons in them came to him from
the tombs.[n] They were so fierce that no
one could travel that way. 29Suddenly
they shouted, "Jesus, Son of God, what
do you want with us? Have you come to
punish us before our time?"
30Not far from there a large herd of
pigs was feeding. 31So the demons
begged Jesus, "If you force us out,
please send us into those pigs!" 32Jesus
told them to go, and they went out of the
men and into the pigs. All at once the
pigs rushed down the steep bank into
the lake and drowned.
33The people taking care of the pigs
ran to the town and told everything, especially what had happened to the two
men. 34Everyone in town came out to
meet Jesus. When they saw him, they
begged him to leave their part of the
country.

Jesus Heals a Crippled Man
(Mark 2.1-12; Luke 5.17-26)

9 Jesus got into a boat and crossed
back over to the town where he
lived.[o] 2Some people soon brought to
him a crippled man lying on a mat.
When Jesus saw how much faith they
had, he said to the crippled man, "My
friend, don't worry! Your sins are forgiven."
3Some teachers of the Law of Moses
said to themselves, "Jesus must think he
is God!"
4But Jesus knew what was in their
minds, and he said, "Why are you thinking such evil things? 5Is it easier for me
to tell this crippled man that his sins are
forgiven or to tell him to get up and
walk? 6But I will show you that the Son
of Man has the right to forgive sins here
on earth." So Jesus said to the man, "Get
up! Pick up your mat and go on home."
7The man got up and went home. 8When
the crowds saw this, they were afraid[p]
and praised God for giving such authority to people.

[k]**8.18** *saw the crowd*: Some manuscripts have "large crowd." Others have "large crowds."
[l]**8.22** *let the dead bury their dead*: For the Jewish people a proper burial of their dead was a very important duty. But Jesus teaches that following him is even more important.
[m]**8.28** *Gadara*: Some manuscripts have "Gergesa." Others have "Gerasa." [n]**8.28** *tombs*: It was thought that demons and evil spirits lived in tombs and in caves that were used for burying the dead. [o]**9.1** *where he lived*: Capernaum (see 4.13). [p]**9.8** *afraid*: Some manuscripts have "amazed."

Jesus Chooses Matthew

(Mark 2.13-17; Luke 5.27-32)

9As Jesus was leaving, he saw a tax
collector[q] named Matthew sitting at the
place for paying taxes. Jesus said to
him, "Come with me." Matthew got up
and went with him.
10Later, Jesus and his disciples were
having dinner at Matthew's house.[r]
Many tax collectors and other sinners
were also there. 11Some Pharisees asked
Jesus' disciples, "Why does your teacher
eat with tax collectors and other sinners?"
12Jesus heard them and answered,
"Healthy people don't need a doctor, but
sick people do. 13Go and learn what the
Scriptures mean when they say, 'Instead
of offering sacrifices to me, I want you
to be merciful to others.' I didn't come to
invite good people to be my followers. I
came to invite sinners."

People Ask about Going without Eating

(Mark 2.18-22; Luke 5.33-39)

14One day some followers of John the
Baptist came and asked Jesus, "Why do
we and the Pharisees often go without
eating,[s] while your disciples never do?"
15Jesus answered:

The friends of a bridegroom don't
go without eating while he is still
with them. But the time will come
when he will be taken from them.
Then they will go without eating.
16No one uses a new piece of cloth
to patch old clothes. The patch
would shrink and tear a bigger hole.
17No one pours new wine into old
wineskins. The wine would swell
and burst the old skins.[t] Then the
wine would be lost, and the skins
would be ruined. New wine must be
put into new wineskins. Both the
skins and the wine will then be safe.

A Dying Girl and a Sick Woman

(Mark 5.21-43; Luke 8.40-56)

18While Jesus was still speaking, an
official came and knelt in front of him.
The man said, "My daughter has just
now died! Please come and place your
hand on her. Then she will live again."
19Jesus and his disciples got up and
went with the man.
20A woman who had been bleeding
for twelve years came up behind Jesus
and barely touched his clothes. 21She
had said to herself, "If I can just touch
his clothes, I will get well."
22Jesus turned. He saw the woman
and said, "Don't worry! You are now
well because of your faith." At that moment she was healed.
23When Jesus went into the home of
the official and saw the musicians and
the crowd of mourners,[u] 24he said, "Get
out of here! The little girl isn't dead. She
is just asleep." Everyone started laughing at Jesus. 25But after the crowd had
been sent out of the house, Jesus went
to the girl's bedside. He took her by the
hand and helped her up.
26News about this spread all over that
part of the country.

Jesus Heals Two Blind Men

27As Jesus was walking along, two
blind men began following him and
shouting, "Son of David,[v] have pity on
us!"
28After Jesus had gone indoors, the
two blind men came up to him. He
asked them, "Do you believe I can make
you well?"
"Yes, Lord," they answered.
29Jesus touched their eyes and said,
"Because of your faith, you will be
healed." 30They were able to see, and Jesus strictly warned them not to tell anyone about him. 31But they left and talked
about him to everyone in that part of the
country.

Jesus Heals a Man Who Could Not Talk

32As Jesus and his disciples were on
their way, some people brought to him a
man who could not talk because a demon was in him. 33After Jesus had
forced the demon out, the man started
talking. The crowds were so amazed
that they began saying, "Nothing like
this has ever happened in Israel!"
34But the Pharisees said, "The leader
of the demons gives him the power to
force out demons."

Jesus Has Pity on People

35Jesus went to every town and village. He taught in their meeting places
and preached the good news about
God's kingdom. Jesus also healed every
kind of disease and sickness. 36When he
saw the crowds, he felt sorry for them.
They were confused and helpless, like
sheep without a shepherd. 37He said to
his disciples, "A large crop is in the
fields, but there are only a few workers.

[q]**9.9** *tax collector*: See the note at 5.46. [r]**9.10** *Matthew's house*: Or "Jesus' house." [s]**9.14** *without eating*: See the note at 4.2. [t]**9.17** *swell and burst the old skins*: While the juice from grapes was becoming wine, it would swell and stretch the skins in which it had been stored. If the skins were old and stiff, they would burst. [u]**9.23** *the crowd of mourners*: The Jewish people often hired mourners for funerals. [v]**9.27** *Son of David*: The Jewish people expected the Messiah to be from the family of King David, and for this reason the Messiah was often called the "Son of David."

38 Ask the Lord in charge of the harvest
to send out workers to bring it in."

Jesus Chooses His Twelve Apostles
(Mark 3.13-19; Luke 6.12-16)

10 Jesus called together his twelve
disciples. He gave them the power
to force out evil spirits and to heal every
kind of disease and sickness. 2 The first
of the twelve apostles was Simon, better
known as Peter. His brother Andrew
was an apostle, and so were James and
John, the two sons of Zebedee. 3 Philip,
Bartholomew, Thomas, Matthew the tax
collector,[w] James the son of Alphaeus,
and Thaddaeus were also apostles. 4 The
others were Simon, known as the Eager
One,[x] and Judas Iscariot,[y] who later betrayed Jesus.

Instructions for the Twelve Apostles
(Mark 6.7-13; Luke 9.1-6)

5 Jesus sent out the twelve apostles
with these instructions:
Stay away from the Gentiles and
don't go to any Samaritan town. 6 Go
only to the people of Israel, because
they are like a flock of lost sheep.
7 As you go, announce that the kingdom of heaven will soon be here.[z]
8 Heal the sick, raise the dead to life,
heal people who have leprosy,[a] and
force out demons. You received without paying, now give without being
paid. 9 Don't take along any gold, silver, or copper coins. 10 And don't
carry[b] a traveling bag or an extra
shirt or sandals or a walking stick.
Workers deserve their food. 11 So
when you go to a town or a village,
find someone worthy enough to
have you as their guest and stay
with them until you leave. 12 When
you go to a home, give it your blessing of peace. 13 If the home is deserving, let your blessing remain with
them. But if the home isn't deserving, take back your blessing of
peace. 14 If someone won't welcome
you or listen to your message, leave
their home or town. And shake the
dust from your feet at them.[c] 15 I
promise you that the day of judgment will be easier for the towns of
Sodom and Gomorrah[d] than for that
town.

Warning about Trouble
(Mark 13.9-13; Luke 21.12-17)

16 I am sending you like lambs into
a pack of wolves. So be as wise as
snakes and as innocent as doves.
17 Watch out for people who will take
you to court and have you beaten in
their meeting places. 18 Because of
me, you will be dragged before
rulers and kings to tell them and the
Gentiles about your faith. 19 But
when someone arrests you, don't
worry about what you will say or
how you will say it. At that time you
will be given the words to say. 20 But
you will not really be the one speaking. The Spirit from your Father will
tell you what to say.
21 Brothers and sisters will betray
one another and have each other put
to death. Parents will betray their
own children, and children will turn
against their parents and have them
killed. 22 Everyone will hate you because of me. But if you remain faithful until the end, you will be saved.
23 When people mistreat you in one
town, hurry to another one. I
promise you that before you have
gone to all the towns of Israel, the
Son of Man will come.
24 Disciples are not better than
their teacher, and slaves are not better than their master. 25 It is enough
for disciples to be like their teacher
and for slaves to be like their master. If people call the head of the
family Satan, what will they say
about the rest of the family?

The One To Fear
(Luke 12.2-7)

26 Don't be afraid of anyone!
Everything that is hidden will be
found out, and every secret will be
known. 27 Whatever I say to you in
the dark, you must tell in the light.
And you must announce from the
housetops whatever I have whispered to you. 28 Don't be afraid of
people. They can kill you, but they
cannot harm your soul. Instead, you
should fear God who can destroy
both your body and your soul in
hell. 29 Aren't two sparrows sold for
only a penny? But your Father

[w] **10.3** *tax collector*: See the note at 5.46. [x] **10.4** *Eager One*: The Greek text has "Zealot," a name later given to the members of a Jewish group that resisted and fought against the Romans. [y] **10.4** *Iscariot*: This may mean "a man from Kerioth" (a place in Judea). But more probably it means "a man who was a liar" or "a man who was a betrayer." [z] **10.7** *will soon be here*: Or "is already here." [a] **10.8** *leprosy*: See the note at 8.2. [b] **10.9,10** *Don't take along . . . don't carry*: Or "Don't accept . . . don't accept." [c] **10.14** *shake the dust from your feet at them*: This was a way of showing rejection (see Acts 13.51). [d] **10.15** *Sodom and Gomorrah*: During the time of Abraham the Lord destroyed these towns because the people there were so evil.

knows when any one of them falls to
the ground. 30 Even the hairs on your
head are counted. 31 So don't be
afraid! You are worth much more
than many sparrows.

Telling Others about Christ
(Luke 12.8, 9)

32 If you tell others that you belong
to me, I will tell my Father in heaven
that you are my followers. 33 But if
you reject me, I will tell my Father in
heaven that you don't belong to me.

Not Peace, but Trouble
(Luke 12.51-53; 14.26, 27)

34 Don't think that I came to bring
peace to the earth! I came to bring
trouble, not peace. 35 I came to turn
sons against their fathers, daughters against their mothers, and
daughters-in-law against their
mothers-in-law. 36 Your worst enemies will be in your own family.

37 If you love your father or mother
or even your sons and daughters
more than me, you are not fit to be
my disciples. 38 And unless you are
willing to take up your cross and
come with me, you are not fit to be
my disciples. 39 If you try to save
your life, you will lose it. But if you
give it up for me, you will surely
find it.

Rewards
(Mark 9.41)

40 Anyone who welcomes you welcomes me. And anyone who welcomes me also welcomes the one
who sent me. 41 Anyone who welcomes a prophet, just because that
person is a prophet, will be given the
same reward as a prophet. Anyone
who welcomes a good person, just
because that person is good, will be
given the same reward as a good
person. 42 And anyone who gives one
of my most humble followers a cup
of cool water, just because that person is my follower, will surely be rewarded.

John the Baptist
(Luke 7.18-35)

11 After Jesus had finished instruct-
ing his twelve disciples, he left
and began teaching and preaching in
the towns.[e]

2 John was in prison when he heard
what Christ was doing. So John sent
some of his followers 3 to ask Jesus, "Are
you the one we should be looking for?
Or must we wait for someone else?"

4 Jesus answered, "Go and tell John
what you have heard and seen. 5 The
blind are now able to see, and the lame
can walk. People with leprosy[f] are being
healed, and the deaf can hear. The dead
are raised to life, and the poor are hearing the good news. 6 God will bless
everyone who doesn't reject me because
of what I do."

7 As John's followers were going away,
Jesus spoke to the crowds about John:

What sort of person did you go out
into the desert to see? Was he like
tall grass blown about by the wind?
8 What kind of man did you go out to
see? Was he someone dressed in fine
clothes? People who dress like that
live in the king's palace. 9 What did
you really go out to see? Was he a
prophet? He certainly was. I tell you
that he was more than a prophet.
10 In the Scriptures God says about
him, "I am sending my messenger
ahead of you to get things ready for
you." 11 I tell you that no one ever
born on this earth is greater than
John the Baptist. But whoever is
least in the kingdom of heaven is
greater than John.

12 From the time of John the Baptist until now, violent people have
been trying to take over the kingdom of heaven by force. 13 All the
Books of the Prophets and the Law
of Moses[g] told what was going to
happen up to the time of John. 14 And
if you believe them, John is Elijah,
the prophet you are waiting for. 15 If
you have ears, pay attention!

16 You people are like children sitting in the market and shouting to
each other,

17 "We played the flute,
but you would not dance!
We sang a funeral song,
but you would not mourn!"

18 John the Baptist did not go around
eating and drinking, and you said,
"That man has a demon in him!"
19 But the Son of Man goes around
eating and drinking, and you say,
"That man eats and drinks too
much! He is even a friend of tax collectors[h] and sinners." Yet Wisdom is
shown to be right by what it does.

The Unbelieving Towns
(Luke 10.13-15)

20 In the towns where Jesus had
worked most of his miracles, the people

[e] **11.1** *the towns*: The Greek text has "their towns," which may refer to the towns of Galilee or to the towns where Jesus' disciples had lived. [f] **11.5** *leprosy*: See the note at 8.2.
[g] **11.13** *the Books of the Prophets and the Law of Moses*: The Jewish Scriptures, that is, the Old Testament. [h] **11.19** *tax collectors*: See the note at 5.46.

refused to turn to God. So Jesus was upset with them and said:

21 You people of Chorazin are in for trouble! You people of Bethsaida are in for trouble too! If the miracles that took place in your towns had happened in Tyre and Sidon, the people there would have turned to God long ago. They would have dressed in sackcloth and put ashes on their heads.[i] 22 I tell you that on the day of judgment the people of Tyre and Sidon will get off easier than you will.

23 People of Capernaum, do you think you will be honored in heaven? You will go down to hell! If the miracles that took place in your town had happened in Sodom, that town would still be standing. 24 So I tell you that on the day of judgment the people of Sodom will get off easier than you.

Come to Me and Rest

(Luke 10.21, 22)

25 At that moment Jesus said:

My Father, Lord of heaven and earth, I am grateful that you hid all this from wise and educated people and showed it to ordinary people.
26 Yes, Father, that is what pleased you.

27 My Father has given me everything, and he is the only one who knows the Son. The only one who truly knows the Father is the Son. But the Son wants to tell others about the Father, so that they can know him too.

28 If you are tired from carrying heavy burdens, come to me and I will give you rest. 29 Take the yoke[j] I give you. Put it on your shoulders and learn from me. I am gentle and humble, and you will find rest. 30 This yoke is easy to bear, and this burden is light.

A Question about the Sabbath

(Mark 2.23-28; Luke 6.1-5)

12 One Sabbath, Jesus and his disciples were walking through some wheat fields.[k] His disciples were hungry and began picking and eating grains of wheat. 2 Some Pharisees noticed this and said to Jesus, "Why are your disciples picking grain on the Sabbath? They are not supposed to do that!"

3 Jesus answered:

You surely must have read what David did when he and his followers were hungry. 4 He went into the house of God, and then they ate the sacred loaves of bread that only priests are supposed to eat. 5 Haven't you read in the Law of Moses that the priests are allowed to work in the temple on the Sabbath? But no one says that they are guilty of breaking the law of the Sabbath. 6 I tell you that there is something here greater than the temple. 7 Don't you know what the Scriptures mean when they say, "Instead of offering sacrifices to me, I want you to be merciful to others?" If you knew what this means, you would not condemn these innocent disciples of mine. 8 So the Son of Man is Lord over the Sabbath.

A Man with a Crippled Hand

(Mark 3.1-6; Luke 6.6-11)

9 Jesus left and went into one of the Jewish meeting places, 10 where there was a man whose hand was crippled. Some Pharisees wanted to accuse Jesus of doing something wrong, and they asked him, "Is it right to heal someone on the Sabbath?"

11 Jesus answered, "If you had a sheep that fell into a ditch on the Sabbath, wouldn't you lift it out? 12 People are worth much more than sheep, and so it is right to do good on the Sabbath." 13 Then Jesus told the man, "Hold out your hand." The man did, and it became as healthy as the other one.

14 The Pharisees left and started making plans to kill Jesus.

God's Chosen Servant

15 When Jesus found out what was happening, he left there and large crowds followed him. He healed all of their sick, 16 but warned them not to tell anyone about him. 17 So God's promise came true, just as Isaiah the prophet had said,

18 "Here is my chosen servant!
I love him,
and he pleases me.
I will give him my Spirit,
and he will bring justice
to the nations.
19 He won't shout or yell
or call out in the streets.
20 He won't break off a bent reed
or put out a dying flame,
but he will make sure
that justice is done.

[i] **11.21** *sackcloth . . . ashes on their heads*: This was one way that people showed how sorry they were for their sins. [j] **11.29** *yoke*: Yokes were put on the necks of animals, so that they could pull a plow or wagon. A yoke was a symbol of obedience and hard work.
[k] **12.1** *walking through some wheat fields*: It was the custom to let hungry travelers pick grains of wheat.

21 All nations will place
their hope in him."

Jesus and the Ruler of the Demons
(Mark 3.20-30; Luke 11.14-23; 12.10)

22Some people brought to Jesus a man
who was blind and could not talk because he had a demon in him. Jesus
healed the man, and then he was able to
talk and see. 23The crowds were so
amazed that they asked, "Could Jesus
be the Son of David?"[l]
24When the Pharisees heard this, they
said, "He forces out demons by the
power of Beelzebul, the ruler of the
demons!"
25Jesus knew what they were thinking, and he said to them:
Any kingdom where people fight
each other will end up ruined. And a
town or family that fights will soon
destroy itself. 26So if Satan fights
against himself, how can his kingdom last? 27If I use the power of
Beelzebul to force out demons,
whose power do your own followers
use to force them out? Your followers
are the ones who will judge you.
28But when I force out demons by
the power of God's Spirit, it proves
that God's kingdom has already
come to you. 29How can anyone
break into a strong man's house and
steal his things, unless he first ties
up the strong man? Then he can
take everything.
30If you are not on my side, you
are against me. If you don't gather
in the harvest with me, you scatter
it. 31-32I tell you that any sinful thing
you do or say can be forgiven. Even
if you speak against the Son of Man,
you can be forgiven. But if you
speak against the Holy Spirit, you
can never be forgiven, either in this
life or in the life to come.

A Tree and Its Fruit
(Luke 6.43-45)

33A good tree produces only good
fruit, and a bad tree produces bad
fruit. You can tell what a tree is like
by the fruit it produces. 34You are a
bunch of evil snakes, so how can
you say anything good? Your words
show what is in your hearts. 35Good
people bring good things out of their
hearts, but evil people bring evil
things out of their hearts. 36I
promise you that on the day of judgment, everyone will have to account
for every careless word they have
spoken. 37On that day they will be
told that they are either innocent or
guilty because of the things they
have said.

A Sign from Heaven
(Mark 8.11, 12; Luke 11.29-32)

38Some Pharisees and teachers of the
Law of Moses said, "Teacher, we want
you to show us a sign from heaven."
39But Jesus replied:
You want a sign because you are
evil and won't believe! But the only
sign you will get is the sign of the
prophet Jonah. 40He was in the
stomach of a big fish for three days
and nights, just as the Son of Man
will be deep in the earth for three
days and nights. 41On the day of
judgment the people of Nineveh[m]
will stand there with you and condemn you. They turned to God when
Jonah preached, and yet here is
something far greater than Jonah.
42The Queen of the South[n] will also
stand there with you and condemn
you. She traveled a long way to hear
Solomon's wisdom, and yet here is
something much greater than
Solomon.

Return of an Evil Spirit
(Luke 11.24-26)

43When an evil spirit leaves a person, it travels through the desert,
looking for a place to rest. But when
the demon doesn't find a place, 44it
says, "I will go back to the home I
left." When it gets there and finds
the place empty, clean, and fixed up,
45it goes off and finds seven other
evil spirits even worse than itself.
They all come and make their home
there, and the person ends up in
worse shape than before. That's how
it will be with you evil people of today.

Jesus' Mother and Brothers
(Mark 3.31-35; Luke 8.19-21)

46While Jesus was still speaking to the
crowds, his mother and brothers came
and stood outside because they wanted
to talk with him. 47Someone told Jesus,
"Your mother and brothers are standing
outside and want to talk with you."[o]
48Jesus answered, "Who is my mother
and who are my brothers?" 49Then he
pointed to his disciples and said, "These
are my mother and my brothers! 50Any-

[l] **12.23** *Could Jesus be the Son of David*: Or "Does Jesus think he is the Son of David?" See the note at 9.27. [m] **12.41** *Nineveh*: During the time of Jonah this city was the capital of the Assyrian Empire, which was Israel's worst enemy. But Jonah was sent there to preach, so that the people would turn to the Lord and be saved. [n] **12.42** *Queen of the South*: Sheba, probably a country in southern Arabia. [o] **12.47** *with you*: Some manuscripts do not have verse 47.

one who obeys my Father in heaven is
my brother or sister or mother."

A Story about a Farmer

(Mark 4.1-9; Luke 8.4-8)

13 That same day Jesus left the
house and went out beside Lake
Galilee, where he sat down to teach.[p]
2Such large crowds gathered around
him that he had to sit in a boat, while
the people stood on the shore. 3Then he
taught them many things by using stories. He said:
A farmer went out to scatter seed
in a field. 4While the farmer was
scattering the seed, some of it fell
along the road and was eaten by
birds. 5Other seeds fell on thin,
rocky ground and quickly started
growing because the soil wasn't very
deep. 6But when the sun came up,
the plants were scorched and dried
up, because they did not have
enough roots. 7Some other seeds fell
where thornbushes grew up and
choked the plants. 8But a few seeds
did fall on good ground where the
plants produced a hundred or sixty
or thirty times as much as was scattered. 9If you have ears, pay attention!

Why Jesus Used Stories

(Mark 4.10-12; Luke 8.9, 10)

10Jesus' disciples came to him and
asked, "Why do you use nothing but stories when you speak to the people?"
11Jesus answered:
I have explained the secrets about
the kingdom of heaven to you, but
not to others. 12Everyone who has
something will be given more. But
people who don't have anything will
lose even what little they have. 13I
use stories when I speak to them because when they look, they cannot
see, and when they listen, they cannot hear or understand. 14So God's
promise came true, just as the
prophet Isaiah had said,

"These people will listen
and listen,
but never understand.
They will look and look,
but never see.
15 All of them have
stubborn minds!
Their ears are stopped up,
and their eyes are covered.
They cannot see or hear
or understand.
If they could,
they would turn to me,
and I would heal them."

16But God has blessed you, because your eyes can see and your
ears can hear! 17Many prophets and
good people were eager to see what
you see and to hear what you hear.
But I tell you that they did not see or
hear.

Jesus Explains the Story about the Farmer

(Mark 4.13-20; Luke 8.11-15)

18Now listen to the meaning of the
story about the farmer:
19The seeds that fell along the
road are the people who hear the
message about the kingdom, but
don't understand it. Then the evil
one comes and snatches the message from their hearts. 20The seeds
that fell on rocky ground are the
people who gladly hear the message
and accept it right away. 21But they
don't have deep roots, and they don't
last very long. As soon as life gets
hard or the message gets them in
trouble, they give up.
22The seeds that fell among the
thornbushes are also people who
hear the message. But they start
worrying about the needs of this life
and are fooled by the desire to get
rich. So the message gets choked
out, and they never produce anything. 23The seeds that fell on good
ground are the people who hear and
understand the message. They produce as much as a hundred or sixty
or thirty times what was planted.

Weeds among the Wheat

24Jesus then told them this story:
The kingdom of heaven is like
what happened when a farmer scattered good seed in a field. 25But
while everyone was sleeping, an enemy came and scattered weed seeds
in the field and then left.
26When the plants came up and
began to ripen, the farmer's servants
could see the weeds. 27The servants
came and asked, "Sir, didn't you
scatter good seed in your field?
Where did these weeds come from?"
28"An enemy did this," he replied.
His servants then asked, "Do you
want us to go out and pull up the
weeds?"
29"No!" he answered. "You might
also pull up the wheat. 30Leave the
weeds alone until harvest time. Then
I'll tell my workers to gather the
weeds and tie them up and burn
them. But I'll have them store the
wheat in my barn."

[p] **13.1** *sat down to teach*: Teachers in the ancient world, including Jewish teachers, usually sat down when they taught.

Stories about a Mustard Seed and Yeast

(Mark 4.30-32; Luke 13.18-21)

31 Jesus told them another story:
The kingdom of heaven is like
what happens when a farmer plants
a mustard seed in a field. 32 Although
it is the smallest of all seeds, it
grows larger than any garden plant
and becomes a tree. Birds even come
and nest on its branches.
33 Jesus also said:
The kingdom of heaven is like
what happens when a woman mixes
a little yeast into three big batches
of flour. Finally, all the dough rises.

The Reason for Teaching with Stories

(Mark 4.33, 34)

34 Jesus used stories when he spoke to
the people. In fact, he did not tell them
anything without using stories. 35 So
God's promise came true, just as the
prophet[q] had said,

"I will use stories
to speak my message
and to explain things
that have been hidden
since the creation
of the world."

Jesus Explains the Story about the Weeds

36 After Jesus left the crowd and went
inside,[r] his disciples came to him and
said, "Explain to us the story about the
weeds in the wheat field."
37 Jesus answered:
The one who scattered the good
seed is the Son of Man. 38 The field is
the world, and the good seeds are
the people who belong to the kingdom. The weed seeds are those who
belong to the evil one, 39 and the one
who scattered them is the devil. The
harvest is the end of time, and angels are the ones who bring in the
harvest.
40 Weeds are gathered and burned.
That's how it will be at the end of
time. 41 The Son of Man will send out
his angels, and they will gather from
his kingdom everyone who does
wrong or causes others to sin.
42 Then he will throw them into a
flaming furnace, where people will
cry and grit their teeth in pain. 43 But
everyone who has done right will
shine like the sun in their Father's
kingdom. If you have ears, pay attention!

A Hidden Treasure

44 The kingdom of heaven is like
what happens when someone finds
treasure hidden in a field and buries
it again. A person like that is happy
and goes and sells everything in order to buy that field.

A Valuable Pearl

45 The kingdom of heaven is like
what happens when a shop owner is
looking for fine pearls. 46 After finding a very valuable one, the owner
goes and sells everything in order to
buy that pearl.

A Fish Net

47 The kingdom of heaven is like
what happens when a net is thrown
into a lake and catches all kinds of
fish. 48 When the net is full, it is
dragged to the shore, and the fishermen sit down to separate the fish.
They keep the good ones, but throw
the bad ones away. 49 That's how it
will be at the end of time. Angels
will come and separate the evil people from the ones who have done
right. 50 Then those evil people will
be thrown into a flaming furnace,
where they will cry and grit their
teeth in pain.

New and Old Treasures

51 Jesus asked his disciples if they understood all these things. They said,
"Yes, we do."
52 So he told them, "Every student of
the Scriptures who becomes a disciple
in the kingdom of heaven is like someone who brings out new and old treasures from the storeroom."

The People of Nazareth Turn against Jesus

(Mark 6.1-6; Luke 4.16-30)

53 When Jesus had finished telling
these stories, he left 54 and went to his
hometown. He taught in their meeting
place, and the people were so amazed
that they asked, "Where does he get all
this wisdom and the power to work
these miracles? 55 Isn't he the son of the
carpenter? Isn't Mary his mother, and
aren't James, Joseph, Simon, and Judas
his brothers? 56 Don't his sisters still live
here in our town? How can he do all
this?" 57 So the people were very unhappy because of what he was doing.
But Jesus said, "Prophets are honored
by everyone, except the people of their
hometown and their own family." 58 And
because the people did not have any
faith, Jesus did not work many miracles
there.

[q] **13.35** *the prophet*: Some manuscripts have "the prophet Isaiah." [r] **13.36** *went inside*: Or "went home."

The Death of John the Baptist
(Mark 6.14-29; Luke 9.7-9)

14 About this time Herod the ruler[s]
heard the news about Jesus 2and
told his officials, "This is John the Baptist! He has come back from death, and
that's why he has the power to work
these miracles."
3-4Herod had earlier arrested John
and had him chained and put in prison.
He did this because John had told him,
"It isn't right for you to take Herodias,
the wife of your brother Philip." 5Herod
wanted to kill John. But the people
thought John was a prophet, and Herod
was afraid of what they might do.
6When Herod's birthday came, the
daughter of Herodias danced for the
guests. She pleased Herod 7so much
that he swore to give her whatever she
wanted. 8But the girl's mother told her
to say, "Here on a platter I want the
head of John the Baptist!"
9The king was sorry for what he had
said. But he did not want to break the
promise he had made in front of his
guests. So he ordered a guard 10to go to
the prison and cut off John's head. 11It
was taken on a platter to the girl, and
she gave it to her mother. 12John's followers took his body and buried it. Then
they told Jesus what had happened.

Jesus Feeds Five Thousand
(Mark 6.30-44; Luke 9.10-17; John 6.1-14)

13After Jesus heard about John, he
crossed Lake Galilee[t] to go to some
place where he could be alone. But the
crowds found out and followed him on
foot from the towns. 14When Jesus got
out of the boat, he saw the large crowd.
He felt sorry for them and healed everyone who was sick.
15That evening the disciples came to
Jesus and said, "This place is like a
desert, and it is already late. Let the
crowds leave, so they can go to the villages and buy some food."
16Jesus replied, "They don't have to
leave. Why don't you give them something to eat?"
17But they said, "We have only five
small loaves of bread[u] and two fish."
18Jesus asked his disciples to bring the
food to him, 19and he told the crowd to
sit down on the grass. Jesus took the
five loaves and the two fish. He looked
up toward heaven and blessed the food.
Then he broke the bread and handed it
to his disciples, and they gave it to the
people.
20After everyone had eaten all they
wanted, Jesus' disciples picked up
twelve large baskets of leftovers.
21There were about five thousand men
who ate, not counting the women and
children.

Jesus Walks on the Water
(Mark 6.45-52; John 6.15-21)

22Right away, Jesus made his disciples
get into a boat and start back across the
lake.[v] But he stayed until he had sent
the crowds away. 23Then he went up on
a mountain where he could be alone
and pray. Later that evening, he was still
there.
24By this time the boat was a long way
from the shore. It was going against the
wind and was being tossed around by
the waves. 25A little while before morning, Jesus came walking on the water
toward his disciples. 26When they saw
him, they thought he was a ghost. They
were terrified and started screaming.
27At once, Jesus said to them, "Don't
worry! I am Jesus. Don't be afraid."
28Peter replied, "Lord, if it is really
you, tell me to come to you on the water."
29"Come on!" Jesus said. Peter then
got out of the boat and started walking
on the water toward him.
30But when Peter saw how strong the
wind was, he was afraid and started
sinking. "Save me, Lord!" he shouted.
31Right away, Jesus reached out his
hand. He helped Peter up and said, "You
surely don't have much faith. Why do
you doubt?"
32When Jesus and Peter got into the
boat, the wind died down. 33The men in
the boat worshiped Jesus and said, "You
really are the Son of God!"

Jesus Heals Sick People in Gennesaret
(Mark 6.53-56)

34Jesus and his disciples crossed the
lake and came to shore near the town of
Gennesaret. 35The people found out that
he was there, and they sent word to
everyone who lived in that part of the
country. So they brought all the sick
people to Jesus. 36They begged him just
to let them touch his clothes, and everyone who did was healed.

The Teaching of the Ancestors
(Mark 7.1-13)

15 About this time some Pharisees
and teachers of the Law of Moses
came from Jerusalem. They asked Jesus, 2"Why don't your disciples obey
what our ancestors taught us to do?

[s]14.1 *Herod the ruler*: Herod Antipas, the son of Herod the Great (see 2.1). [t]14.13 *crossed Lake Galilee*: To the east side. [u]14.17 *small loaves of bread*: These would have been flat and round or in the shape of a bun. [v]14.22 *back across the lake*: To the west side.

They don't even wash their hands[w] before they eat."
3 Jesus answered:
Why do you disobey God and follow your own teaching? 4 Didn't God
command you to respect your father
and mother? Didn't he tell you to put
to death all who curse their parents?
5 But you let people get by without
helping their parents when they
should. You let them say that what
they have has been offered to God.[x]
6 Is this any way to show respect to
your parents? You ignore God's commands in order to follow your own
teaching. 7 And you are nothing but
show-offs! Isaiah the prophet was
right when he wrote that God had
said,

8 "All of you praise me
with your words,
but you never really
think about me.
9 It is useless for you
to worship me,
when you teach rules
made up by humans."

What Really Makes People Unclean
(Mark 7.14-23)

10 Jesus called the crowd together and
said, "Pay attention and try to understand what I mean. 11 The food that you
put into your mouth doesn't make you
unclean and unfit to worship God. The
bad words that come out of your mouth
are what make you unclean."
12 Then his disciples came over to him
and asked, "Do you know that you insulted the Pharisees by what you said?"
13 Jesus answered, "Every plant that
my Father in heaven did not plant will
be pulled up by the roots. 14 Stay away
from those Pharisees! They are like
blind people leading other blind people,
and all of them will fall into a ditch."
15 Peter replied, "What did you mean
when you talked about the things that
make people unclean?"
16 Jesus then said:
Don't any of you know what I am
talking about by now? 17 Don't you
know that the food you put into your
mouth goes into your stomach and
then out of your body? 18 But the
words that come out of your mouth
come from your heart. And they are
what make you unfit to worship
God. 19 Out of your heart come evil
thoughts, murder, unfaithfulness in
marriage, vulgar deeds, stealing,
telling lies, and insulting others.
20 These are what make you unclean.
Eating without washing your hands
will not make you unfit to worship
God.

A Woman's Faith
(Mark 7.24-30)

21 Jesus left and went to the territory
near the cities of Tyre and Sidon. 22 Suddenly a Canaanite woman[y] from there
came out shouting, "Lord and Son of
David,[z] have pity on me! My daughter is
full of demons." 23 Jesus did not say a
word. But the woman kept following
along and shouting, so his disciples
came up and asked him to send her
away.
24 Jesus said, "I was sent only to the
people of Israel! They are like a flock of
lost sheep."
25 The woman came closer. Then she
knelt down and begged, "Please help
me, Lord!"
26 Jesus replied, "It isn't right to take
food away from children and feed it to
dogs."[a]
27 "Lord, that's true," the woman said,
"but even dogs get the crumbs that fall
from their owner's table."
28 Jesus answered, "Dear woman, you
really do have a lot of faith, and you will
be given what you want." At that moment her daughter was healed.

Jesus Heals Many People

29 From there, Jesus went along Lake
Galilee. Then he climbed a hill and sat
down. 30 Large crowds came and
brought many people who were crippled
or blind or lame or unable to talk. They
placed them, and many others, in front
of Jesus, and he healed them all.
31 Everyone was amazed at what they
saw and heard. People who had never
spoken could now speak. The lame were
healed, the crippled could walk, and the
blind were able to see. Everyone was
praising the God of Israel.

Jesus Feeds Four Thousand
(Mark 8.1-10)

32 Jesus called his disciples together
and told them, "I feel sorry for these
people. They have been with me for
three days, and they don't have anything to eat. I don't want to send them
away hungry. They might faint on their
way home."

[w] **15.2** *wash their hands*: The Jewish people had strict laws about washing their hands before eating, especially if they had been out in public. [x] **15.5** *has been offered to God*: According to Jewish custom, when people said something was offered to God, it belonged to him and could not be used for anyone else, not even for their own parents. [y] **15.22** *Canaanite woman*: This woman was not Jewish. [z] **15.22** *Son of David*: See the note at 9.27.
[a] **15.26** *feed it to dogs*: The Jewish people sometimes referred to Gentiles as dogs.

33His disciples said, "This place is like
a desert. Where can we find enough
food to feed such a crowd?"
34Jesus asked them how much food
they had. They replied, "Seven small
loaves of bread[b] and a few little fish."
35After Jesus had told the people to sit
down, 36he took the seven loaves of
bread and the fish and gave thanks. He
then broke them and handed them to
his disciples, who passed them around
to the crowds.
37Everyone ate all they wanted, and
the leftovers filled seven large baskets.
38There were four thousand men who
ate, not counting the women and children.
39After Jesus had sent the crowds
away, he got into a boat and sailed
across the lake. He came to shore near
the town of Magadan.[c]

A Demand for a Sign from Heaven

(Mark 8.11-13; Luke 12.54-56)

16 The Pharisees and Sadducees
came to Jesus and tried to test
him by asking for a sign from heaven.
2He told them:

If the sky is red in the evening,
you say the weather will be good.
3But if the sky is red and gloomy in
the morning, you say it is going to
rain. You can tell what the weather
will be like by looking at the sky. But
you don't understand what is happening now.[d] 4You want a sign because you are evil and won't believe!
But the only sign you will be given is
what happened to Jonah.[e]

Then Jesus left.

The Yeast of the Pharisees and Sadducees

(Mark 8.14-21)

5The disciples had forgotten to bring
any bread when they crossed the lake.[f]
6Jesus then warned them, "Watch out!
Guard against the yeast of the Pharisees
and Sadducees."
7The disciples talked this over and
said to each other, "He must be saying
this because we didn't bring along any
bread."
8Jesus knew what they were thinking
and said:

You surely don't have much faith!
Why are you talking about not having any bread? 9Don't you understand? Have you forgotten about the
five thousand people and all those
baskets of leftovers from just five
loaves of bread? 10And what about
the four thousand people and all
those baskets of leftovers from only
seven loaves of bread? 11Don't you
know by now that I am not talking
to you about bread? Watch out for
the yeast of the Pharisees and Sadducees!

12Finally, the disciples understood that
Jesus wasn't talking about the yeast
used to make bread, but about the
teaching of the Pharisees and Sadducees.

Who Is Jesus?

(Mark 8.27-30; Luke 9.18-21)

13When Jesus and his disciples were
near the town of Caesarea Philippi, he
asked them, "What do people say about
the Son of Man?"
14The disciples answered, "Some people say you are John the Baptist or
maybe Elijah[g] or Jeremiah or some
other prophet."
15Then Jesus asked them, "But who do
you say I am?"
16Simon Peter spoke up, "You are the
Messiah, the Son of the living God."
17Jesus told him:

Simon, son of Jonah, you are
blessed! You didn't discover this on
your own. It was shown to you by
my Father in heaven. 18So I will call
you Peter, which means "a rock." On
this rock I will build my church, and
death itself will not have any power
over it. 19I will give you the keys to
the kingdom of heaven, and God in
heaven will allow whatever you allow on earth. But he will not allow
anything that you don't allow.

20Jesus told his disciples not to tell
anyone that he was the Messiah.

Jesus Speaks about His Suffering and Death

(Mark 8.31—9.1; Luke 9.22-27)

21From then on, Jesus began telling
his disciples what would happen to him.
He said, "I must go to Jerusalem. There
the nation's leaders, the chief priests,
and the teachers of the Law of Moses
will make me suffer terribly. I will be
killed, but three days later I will rise to
life."
22Peter took Jesus aside and told him
to stop talking like that. He said, "God
would never let this happen to you,
Lord!"
23Jesus turned to Peter and said, "Satan, get away from me! You're in my way

[b]**15.34** *small loaves of bread*: See the note at 14.17. [c]**15.39** *Magadan*: The location is unknown. [d]**16.2, 3** *If the sky is red . . . what is happening now*: The words of Jesus in verses 2 and 3 are not in some manuscripts. [e]**16.4** *what happened to Jonah*: Jonah was in the stomach of a big fish for three days and nights (see 12.40). [f]**16.5** *crossed the lake*: To the east side. [g]**16.14** *Elijah*: Many of the Jewish people expected the prophet Elijah to come and prepare the way for the Messiah.

because you think like everyone else
and not like God."
24Then Jesus said to his disciples:
If any of you want to be my followers, you must forget about yourself. You must take up your cross and follow me. 25If you want to save your life,[h] you will destroy it. But if you give up your life for me, you will find it. 26What will you gain, if you own the whole world but destroy yourself? What would you give to get back your soul?
27The Son of Man will soon come in the glory of his Father and with his angels to reward all people for what they have done. 28I promise you that some of those standing here will not die before they see the Son of Man coming with his kingdom.

The True Glory of Jesus
(Mark 9.2-13; Luke 9.28-36)

17 Six days later Jesus took Peter
and the brothers James and John
with him. They went up on a very high
mountain where they could be alone.
2There in front of the disciples, Jesus
was completely changed. His face was
shining like the sun, and his clothes became white as light.
3All at once Moses and Elijah were
there talking with Jesus. 4So Peter said
to him, "Lord, it is good for us to be
here! Let us make three shelters, one for
you, one for Moses, and one for Elijah."
5While Peter was still speaking, the
shadow of a bright cloud passed over
them. From the cloud a voice said, "This
is my own dear Son, and I am pleased
with him. Listen to what he says!"
6When the disciples heard the voice,
they were so afraid that they fell flat on
the ground. 7But Jesus came over and
touched them. He said, "Get up and
don't be afraid!" 8When they opened
their eyes, they saw only Jesus.
9On their way down from the mountain, Jesus warned his disciples not to
tell anyone what they had seen until after the Son of Man had been raised
from death.
10The disciples asked Jesus, "Don't the
teachers of the Law of Moses say that
Elijah must come before the Messiah
does?"
11Jesus told them, "Elijah certainly
will come and get everything ready. 12In
fact, he has already come. But the people did not recognize him and treated
him just as they wanted to. They will
soon make the Son of Man suffer in the
same way." 13Then the disciples understood that Jesus was talking to them
about John the Baptist.

Jesus Heals a Boy
(Mark 9.14-29; Luke 9.37-43a)

14Jesus and his disciples returned to
the crowd. A man knelt in front of him
15and said, "Lord, have pity on my son!
He has a bad case of epilepsy and often
falls into a fire or into water. 16I brought
him to your disciples, but none of them
could heal him."
17Jesus said, "You people are too stubborn to have any faith! How much
longer must I be with you? Why do I
have to put up with you? Bring the boy
here." 18Then Jesus spoke sternly to the
demon. It went out of the boy, and right
then he was healed.
19Later the disciples went to Jesus in
private and asked him, "Why couldn't
we force out the demon?"
20-21Jesus replied:
It is because you don't have enough faith! But I can promise you this. If you had faith no larger than a mustard seed, you could tell this mountain to move from here to there. And it would. Everything would be possible for you.[i]

Jesus Again Speaks about His Death
(Mark 9.30-32; Luke 9.43b-45)

22While Jesus and his disciples were
going from place to place in Galilee, he
told them, "The Son of Man will be
handed over to people 23who will kill
him. But three days later he will rise to
life." All of this made the disciples very
sad.

Paying the Temple Tax

24When Jesus and the others arrived
in Capernaum, the collectors for the
temple tax came to Peter and asked,
"Does your teacher pay the temple tax?"
25"Yes, he does," Peter answered.
After they had returned home, Jesus
went up to Peter and asked him, "Simon, what do you think? Do the kings
of this earth collect taxes and fees from
their own people or from foreigners?"[j]
26Peter answered, "From foreigners."
Jesus replied, "Then their own
people[k] don't have to pay. 27But we
don't want to cause trouble. So go cast a
line into the lake and pull out the first
fish you hook. Open its mouth, and you
will find a coin. Use it to pay your taxes
and mine."

[h] **16.25** *life*: In verses 25 and 26 the same Greek word is translated "life," "yourself," and "soul." [i] **17.20,21** *for you*: Some manuscripts add, "But the only way to force out that kind of demon is by praying and going without eating." [j] **17.25** *from their own people or from foreigners*: Or "from their children or from others." [k] **17.26** *From foreigners . . . their own people*: Or "From other people . . . their children."

Who Is the Greatest?
(Mark 9.33-37; Luke 9.46-48)

18 About this time the disciples came to Jesus and asked him who would be the greatest in the kingdom of heaven. 2 Jesus called a child over and had the child stand near him. 3 Then he said:

I promise you this. If you don't change and become like a child, you will never get into the kingdom of heaven. 4 But if you are as humble as this child, you are the greatest in the kingdom of heaven. 5 And when you welcome one of these children because of me, you welcome me.

Temptations To Sin
(Mark 9.42-48; Luke 17.1, 2)

6 It will be terrible for people who cause even one of my little followers to sin. Those people would be better off thrown into the deepest part of the ocean with a heavy stone tied around their necks! 7 The world is in for trouble because of the way it causes people to sin. There will always be something to cause people to sin, but anyone who does this will be in for trouble.

8 If your hand or foot causes you to sin, chop it off and throw it away! You would be better off to go into life crippled or lame than to have two hands or two feet and be thrown into the fire that never goes out. 9 If your eye causes you to sin, poke it out and get rid of it. You would be better off to go into life with only one eye than to have two eyes and be thrown into the fires of hell.

The Lost Sheep
(Luke 15.3-7)

10-11 Don't be cruel to any of these little ones! I promise you that their angels are always with my Father in heaven.[l] 12 Let me ask you this. What would you do if you had a hundred sheep and one of them wandered off? Wouldn't you leave the ninety-nine on the hillside and go look for the one that had wandered away? 13 I am sure that finding it would make you happier than having the ninety-nine that never wandered off. 14 That's how it is with your Father in heaven. He doesn't want any of these little ones to be lost.

When Someone Sins
(Luke 17.3)

15 If one of my followers[m] sins against you, go and point out what was wrong. But do it in private, just between the two of you. If that person listens, you have won back a follower. 16 But if that one refuses to listen, take along one or two others. The Scriptures teach that every complaint must be proven true by two or more witnesses. 17 If the follower refuses to listen to them, report the matter to the church. Anyone who refuses to listen to the church must be treated like an unbeliever or a tax collector.[n]

Allowing and Not Allowing

18 I promise you that God in heaven will allow whatever you allow on earth, but he will not allow anything you don't allow. 19 I promise that when any two of you on earth agree about something you are praying for, my Father in heaven will do it for you. 20 Whenever two or three of you come together in my name,[o] I am there with you.

An Official Who Refused To Forgive

21 Peter came up to the Lord and asked, "How many times should I forgive someone[p] who does something wrong to me? Is seven times enough?" 22 Jesus answered:

Not just seven times, but seventy-seven times![q] 23 This story will show you what the kingdom of heaven is like:

One day a king decided to call in his officials and ask them to give an account of what they owed him. 24 As he was doing this, one official was brought in who owed him fifty million silver coins. 25 But he didn't have any money to pay what he owed. The king ordered him to be sold, along with his wife and children and all he owned, in order to pay the debt.

26 The official got down on his knees and began begging, "Have pity on me, and I will pay you every cent I owe!" 27 The king felt sorry for him and let him go free. He even told the official that he did not have to pay back the money.

28 As the official was leaving, he happened to meet another official,

[l] 18.10,11 *in heaven*: Some manuscripts add, "The Son of Man came to save people who are lost." [m] 18.15 *followers*: The Greek text has "brother," which is used here and elsewhere in this chapter to refer to a follower of Christ. [n] 18.17 *tax collector*: See the note at 5.46. [o] 18.20 *in my name*: Or "as my followers." [p] 18.21 *someone*: Or "a follower." See the note at 18.15. [q] 18.22 *seventy-seven times*: Or "seventy times seven." The large number means that one follower should never stop forgiving another.

who owed him a hundred silver
coins. So he grabbed the man by the
throat. He started choking him and
said, "Pay me what you owe!"
29The man got down on his knees
and began begging, "Have pity on
me, and I will pay you back." 30But
the first official refused to have pity.
Instead, he went and had the other
official put in jail until he could pay
what he owed.
31When some other officials found
out what had happened, they felt
sorry for the man who had been put
in jail. Then they told the king what
had happened. 32The king called the
first official back in and said,
"You're an evil man! When you
begged for mercy, I said you did not
have to pay back a cent. 33Don't you
think you should show pity to someone else, as I did to you?" 34The king
was so angry that he ordered the official to be tortured until he could
pay back everything he owed. 35That
is how my Father in heaven will
treat you, if you don't forgive each of
my followers with all your heart.

Teaching about Divorce

(Mark 10.1-12)

19 When Jesus finished teaching, he
left Galilee and went to the part
of Judea that is east of the Jordan River.
2Large crowds followed him, and he
healed their sick people.
3Some Pharisees wanted to test Jesus.
They came up to him and asked, "Is it
right for a man to divorce his wife for
just any reason?"
4Jesus answered, "Don't you know
that in the beginning the Creator made
a man and a woman? 5That's why a man
leaves his father and mother and gets
married. He becomes like one person
with his wife. 6Then they are no longer
two people, but one. And no one should
separate a couple that God has joined
together."
7The Pharisees asked Jesus, "Why did
Moses say that a man could write out divorce papers and send his wife away?"
8Jesus replied, "You are so heartless!
That's why Moses allowed you to divorce your wife. But from the beginning
God did not intend it to be that way. 9I
say that if your wife has not committed
some terrible sexual sin,[r] you must not
divorce her to marry someone else. If
you do, you are unfaithful."
10The disciples said, "If that's how it is
between a man and a woman, it's better
not to get married."
11Jesus told them, "Only those people
who have been given the gift of staying single can accept this teaching.
12Some people are unable to marry because of birth defects or because of
what someone has done to their bodies.
Others stay single for the sake of the
kingdom of heaven. Anyone who
can accept this teaching should do so."

Jesus Blesses Little Children

(Mark 10.13-16; Luke 18.15-17)

13Some people brought their children
to Jesus, so that he could place his
hands on them and pray for them. His
disciples told the people to stop bothering him. 14But Jesus said, "Let the children come to me, and don't try to stop
them! People who are like these children belong to God's kingdom."[s] 15After
Jesus had placed his hands on the children, he left.

A Rich Young Man

(Mark 10.17-31; Luke 18.18-30)

16A man came to Jesus and asked,
"Teacher, what good thing must I do to
have eternal life?"
17Jesus said to him, "Why do you ask
me about what is good? Only God is
good. If you want to have eternal life,
you must obey his commandments."
18"Which ones?" the man asked.
Jesus answered, "Do not murder. Be
faithful in marriage. Do not steal. Do
not tell lies about others. 19Respect your
father and mother. And love others as
much as you love yourself." 20The young
man said, "I have obeyed all of these.
What else must I do?"
21Jesus replied, "If you want to be perfect, go sell everything you own! Give
the money to the poor, and you will
have riches in heaven. Then come and
be my follower." 22When the young man
heard this, he was sad, because he was
very rich.
23Jesus said to his disciples, "It's terribly hard for rich people to get into the
kingdom of heaven! 24In fact, it's easier
for a camel to go through the eye of a
needle than for a rich person to get into
God's kingdom."
25When the disciples heard this, they
were greatly surprised and asked, "How
can anyone ever be saved?"
26Jesus looked straight at them and
said, "There are some things that people
cannot do, but God can do anything."
27Peter replied, "Remember, we have
left everything to be your followers!
What will we get?"
28Jesus answered:
Yes, all of you have become my

[r] **19.9** *some terrible sexual sin*: See the note at 5.32. [s] **19.14** *People who are like these children belong to God's kingdom*: Or "God's kingdom belongs to people who are like these children."

followers. And so in the future
world, when the Son of Man sits on
his glorious throne, I promise that
you will sit on twelve thrones to
judge the twelve tribes of Israel.
29All who have given up home or
brothers and sisters or father and
mother or children or land for me
will be given a hundred times as
much. They will also have eternal
life. 30But many who are now first
will be last, and many who are last
will be first.

Workers in a Vineyard

20 As Jesus was telling what the
kingdom of heaven would be like,
he said:

Early one morning a man went
out to hire some workers for his
vineyard. 2After he had agreed to
pay them the usual amount for a
day's work, he sent them off to his
vineyard.
3About nine that morning, the
man saw some other people standing in the market with nothing to do.
4He said he would pay them what
was fair, if they would work in his
vineyard. 5So they went.

At noon and again about three in
the afternoon he returned to the
market. And each time he made the
same agreement with others who
were loafing around with nothing
to do.
6Finally, about five in the afternoon the man went back and found
some others standing there. He
asked them, "Why have you been
standing here all day long doing
nothing?"
7"Because no one has hired us,"
they answered. Then he told them to
go work in his vineyard.
8That evening the owner of the
vineyard told the man in charge of
the workers to call them in and give
them their money. He also told the
man to begin with the ones who
were hired last. 9When the workers
arrived, the ones who had been
hired at five in the afternoon were
given a full day's pay.
10The workers who had been hired
first thought they would be given
more than the others. But when they
were given the same, 11they began
complaining to the owner of the
vineyard. 12They said, "The ones
who were hired last worked for only
one hour. But you paid them the
same that you did us. And we
worked in the hot sun all day long!"
13The owner answered one of
them, "Friend, I didn't cheat you. I
paid you exactly what we agreed on.
14Take your money now and go!
What business is it of yours if I want
to pay them the same that I paid
you? 15Don't I have the right to do
what I want with my own money?
Why should you be jealous, if I want
to be generous?"
16Jesus then said, "So it is. Everyone
who is now first will be last, and everyone who is last will be first."

Jesus Again Tells about His Death

(Mark 10.32-34; Luke 18.31-34)

17As Jesus was on his way to
Jerusalem, he took his twelve disciples
aside and told them in private:
18We are now on our way to
Jerusalem, where the Son of Man
will be handed over to the chief
priests and the teachers of the Law
of Moses. They will sentence him to
death, 19and then they will hand him
over to foreigners[t] who will make
fun of him. They will beat him and
nail him to a cross. But on the third
day he will rise from death.

A Mother's Request

(Mark 10.35-45)

20The mother of James and John[u]
came to Jesus with her two sons. She
knelt down and started begging him to
do something for her. 21Jesus asked her
what she wanted, and she said, "When
you come into your kingdom, please let
one of my sons sit at your right side and
the other at your left."[v]
22Jesus answered, "Not one of you
knows what you are asking. Are you
able to drink from the cup[w] that I must
soon drink from?"
James and John said, "Yes, we are!"
23Jesus replied, "You certainly will
drink from my cup! But it isn't for me to
say who will sit at my right side and at
my left. That is for my Father to say."
24When the ten other disciples heard
this, they were angry with the two
brothers. 25But Jesus called the disciples
together and said:

You know that foreign rulers like
to order their people around. And
their great leaders have full power
over everyone they rule. 26But don't
act like them. If you want to be
great, you must be the servant of all
the others. 27And if you want to be

[t]**20.19** *foreigners*: The Romans, who ruled Judea at this time. [u]**20.20** *mother of James and John*: The Greek text has "mother of the sons of Zebedee" (see 26.37). [v]**20.21** *right side . . . left*: The most powerful people in a kingdom sat at the right and left side of the king.
[w]**20.22** *drink from the cup*: In the Scriptures a cup is sometimes used as a symbol of suffering. To "drink from the cup" is to suffer.

first, you must be the slave of the
rest. 28The Son of Man did not come
to be a slave master, but a slave who
will give his life to rescue[x] many
people.

Jesus Heals Two Blind Men
(Mark 10.46-52; Luke 18.35-43)

29Jesus was followed by a large crowd
as he and his disciples were leaving
Jericho. 30Two blind men were sitting
beside the road. And when they heard
that Jesus was coming their way, they
shouted, "Lord and Son of David,[y] have
pity on us!"
31The crowd told them to be quiet, but
they shouted even louder, "Lord and
Son of David, have pity on us!"
32When Jesus heard them, he stopped
and asked, "What do you want me to do
for you?"
33They answered, "Lord, we want to
see!"
34Jesus felt sorry for them and
touched their eyes. Right away they
could see, and they became his followers.

Jesus Enters Jerusalem
(Mark 11.1-11; Luke 19.28-38; John 12.12-19)

21 When Jesus and his disciples
came near Jerusalem, he went to
Bethphage on the Mount of Olives and
sent two of them on ahead. 2He told
them, "Go into the next village, where
you will at once find a donkey and her
colt. Untie the two donkeys and bring
them to me. 3If anyone asks why you are
doing that, just say, 'The Lord[z] needs
them.' Right away he will let you have
the donkeys."
4So God's promise came true, just as
the prophet had said,

5 "Announce to the people
of Jerusalem:
'Your king is coming to you!
He is humble
and rides on a donkey.
He comes on the colt
of a donkey.' "

6The disciples left and did what Jesus
had told them to do. 7They brought the
donkey and its colt and laid some
clothes on their backs. Then Jesus got
on.
8Many people spread clothes in the
road, while others put down branches[a]
which they had cut from trees. 9Some
people walked ahead of Jesus and others followed behind. They were all
shouting,

"Hooray[b] for the Son of David![c]
God bless the one who comes
in the name of the Lord.
Hooray for God
in heaven above!"

10When Jesus came to Jerusalem,
everyone in the city was excited and
asked, "Who can this be?"
11The crowd answered, "This is Jesus,
the prophet from Nazareth in Galilee."

Jesus in the Temple
(Mark 11.15-19; Luke 19.45-48; John 2.13-22)

12Jesus went into the temple and
chased out everyone who was selling or
buying. He turned over the tables of the
moneychangers and the benches of the
ones who were selling doves. 13He told
them, "The Scriptures say, 'My house
should be called a place of worship.' But
you have turned it into a place where
robbers hide."
14Blind and lame people came to Jesus in the temple, and he healed them.
15But the chief priests and the teachers
of the Law of Moses were angry when
they saw his miracles and heard the
children shouting praises to the Son of
David.[c] 16The men said to Jesus, "Don't
you hear what those children are saying?"
"Yes, I do!" Jesus answered. "Don't
you know that the Scriptures say, 'Children and infants will sing praises'?"
17Then Jesus left the city and went out
to the village of Bethany, where he
spent the night.

Jesus Puts a Curse on a Fig Tree
(Mark 11.12-14, 20-24)

18When Jesus got up the next morning, he was hungry. He started out for
the city, 19and along the way he saw a
fig tree. But when he came to it, he
found only leaves and no figs. So he
told the tree, "You will never again grow
any fruit!" Right then the fig tree dried
up.
20The disciples were shocked when
they saw how quickly the tree had dried
up. 21But Jesus said to them, "If you
have faith and don't doubt, I promise
that you can do what I did to this tree.
And you will be able to do even more.
You can tell this mountain to get up and
jump into the sea, and it will. 22If you

[x]20.28 *rescue*: The Greek word often, though not always, means the payment of a price to free a slave or a prisoner. [y]20.30 *Son of David*: See the note at 9.27. [z]21.3 *The Lord*: Or "The master of the donkeys." [a]21.8 *spread clothes . . . put down branches*: This was one way that the Jewish people welcomed a famous person. [b]21.9 *Horray*: This translates a word that can mean "please save us." But it is most often used as a shout of praise to God. [c]21.9,15 *Son of David*: See the note at 9.27.

have faith when you pray, you will be
given whatever you ask for."

A Question about Jesus' Authority

(Mark 11.27-33; Luke 20.1-8)

23 Jesus had gone into the temple and
was teaching when the chief priests and
the leaders of the people came up to
him. They asked, "What right do you
have to do these things? Who gave you
this authority?"
24 Jesus answered, "I have just one
question to ask you. If you answer it, I
will tell you where I got the right to do
these things. 25 Who gave John the right
to baptize? Was it God in heaven or
merely some human being?"
They thought it over and said to each
other, "We can't say that God gave John
this right. Jesus will ask us why we
didn't believe John. 26 On the other hand,
these people think that John was a
prophet, and we are afraid of what they
might do to us. That's why we can't say
that it was merely some human who
gave John the right to baptize." 27 So
they told Jesus, "We don't know."
Jesus said, "Then I won't tell you who
gave me the right to do what I do."

A Story about Two Sons

28 Jesus said:
I will tell you a story about a man
who had two sons. Then you can tell
me what you think. The father went
to the older son and said, "Go work
in the vineyard today!" 29 His son
told him that he would not do it, but
later he changed his mind and went.
30 The man then told his younger son
to go work in the vineyard. The boy
said he would, but he didn't go.
31 Which one of the sons obeyed his
father?
"The older one," the chief priests and
leaders answered.
Then Jesus told them:
You can be sure that tax collectors[d]
and prostitutes will get into the kingdom of God before you ever will!
32 When John the Baptist showed you
how to do right, you would not believe him. But these evil people did
believe. And even when you saw
what they did, you still would not
change your minds and believe.

Renters of a Vineyard

(Mark 12.1-12; Luke 20.9-19)

33 Jesus told the chief priests and leaders to listen to this story:
A land owner once planted a vineyard. He built a wall around it and
dug a pit to crush the grapes in. He
also built a lookout tower. Then he
rented out his vineyard and left the
country.
34 When it was harvest time, the
owner sent some servants to get his
share of the grapes. 35 But the renters
grabbed those servants. They beat
up one, killed one, and stoned one of
them to death. 36 He then sent more
servants than he did the first time.
But the renters treated them in the
same way.
37 Finally, the owner sent his own
son to the renters, because he
thought they would respect him.
38 But when they saw the man's son,
they said, "Someday he will own the
vineyard. Let's kill him! Then we
can have it all for ourselves." 39 So
they grabbed him, threw him out of
the vineyard, and killed him.
40 Jesus asked, "When the owner of
that vineyard comes, what do you suppose he will do to those renters?"
41 The chief priests and leaders answered, "He will kill them in some horrible way. Then he will rent out his vineyard to people who will give him his
share of grapes at harvest time."
42 Jesus replied, "You surely know that
the Scriptures say,

'The stone that the builders
tossed aside
is now the most important
stone of all.
This is something
the Lord has done,
and it is amazing to us.'

43 I tell you that God's kingdom will be
taken from you and given to people who
will do what he demands. 44 Anyone who
stumbles over this stone will be
crushed, and anyone it falls on will be
smashed to pieces."[e]
45 When the chief priests and the Pharisees heard these stories, they knew that
Jesus was talking about them. 46 So they
looked for a way to arrest Jesus. But
they were afraid to, because the people
thought he was a prophet.

The Great Banquet

(Luke 14.15-24)

22 Once again Jesus used stories to
teach the people:
2 The kingdom of heaven is like
what happened when a king gave a
wedding banquet for his son. 3 The
king sent some servants to tell the
invited guests to come to the banquet, but the guests refused. 4 He
sent other servants to say to the

[d]21.31 *tax collectors*: See the note at 5.46.

[e]21.44 *pieces*: Verse 44 is not in some
manuscripts.

guests, "The banquet is ready! My
cattle and prize calves have all been
prepared. Everything is ready. Come
to the banquet!"
5But the guests did not pay any attention. Some of them left for their
farms, and some went to their places
of business. 6Others grabbed the servants, then beat them up and killed
them.
7This made the king so furious
that he sent an army to kill those
murderers and burn down their city.
8Then he said to the servants, "It is
time for the wedding banquet, and
the invited guests don't deserve to
come. 9Go out to the street corners
and tell everyone you meet to come
to the banquet." 10They went out on
the streets and brought in everyone
they could find, good and bad alike.
And the banquet room was filled
with guests.
11When the king went in to meet
the guests, he found that one of
them wasn't wearing the right kind
of clothes for the wedding. 12The
king asked, "Friend, why didn't you
wear proper clothes for the wedding?" But the guest had no excuse.
13So the king gave orders for that
person to be tied hand and foot
and to be thrown outside into the
dark. That's where people will cry
and grit their teeth in pain. 14Many
are invited, but only a few are chosen.

Paying Taxes

(Mark 12.13-17; Luke 20.20-26)

15The Pharisees got together and
planned how they could trick Jesus into
saying something wrong. 16They sent
some of their followers and some of
Herod's followers[f] to say to him,
"Teacher, we know that you are honest.
You teach the truth about what God
wants people to do. And you treat everyone with the same respect, no matter
who they are. 17Tell us what you think!
Should we pay taxes to the Emperor or
not?"
18Jesus knew their evil thoughts and
said, "Why are you trying to test me?
You show-offs! 19Let me see one of the
coins used for paying taxes." They
brought him a silver coin, 20and he
asked, "Whose picture and name are on
it?"
21"The Emperor's," they answered.
Then Jesus told them, "Give the Emperor what belongs to him and give God
what belongs to God." 22His answer surprised them so much that they walked
away.

Life in the Future World

(Mark 12.18-27; Luke 20.27-40)

23The Sadducees did not believe that
people would rise to life after death. So
that same day some of the Sadducees
came to Jesus and said:
24Teacher, Moses wrote that if a
married man dies and has no children, his brother should marry the
widow. Their first son would then be
thought of as the son of the dead
brother.
25Once there were seven brothers
who lived here. The first one married, but died without having any
children. So his wife was left to his
brother. 26The same thing happened
to the second and third brothers and
finally to all seven of them. 27At last
the woman died. 28When God raises
people from death, whose wife will
this woman be? She had been married to all seven brothers.
29Jesus answered:
You are completely wrong! You
don't know what the Scriptures
teach. And you don't know anything
about the power of God. 30When
God raises people to life, they won't
marry. They will be like the angels
in heaven. 31And as for people being
raised to life, God was speaking to
you when he said, 32"I am the God
worshiped by Abraham, Isaac, and
Jacob."[g] He isn't the God of the
dead, but of the living.
33The crowds were surprised to hear
what Jesus was teaching.

The Most Important Commandment

(Mark 12.28-34; Luke 10.25-28)

34After Jesus had made the Sadducees
look foolish, the Pharisees heard about
it and got together. 35One of them was
an expert in the Jewish Law. So he tried
to test Jesus by asking, 36"Teacher, what
is the most important commandment in
the Law?"
37Jesus answered:
Love the Lord your God with all
your heart, soul, and mind. 38This is
the first and most important commandment. 39The second most important commandment is like this
one. And it is, "Love others as much
as you love yourself." 40All the Law
of Moses and the Books of the

[f]**22.16** *Herod's followers*: People who were political followers of the family of Herod the Great (see 2.1) and his son Herod Antipas (see 14.1), and who wanted Herod to be king in Jerusalem.
[g]**22.32** *I am the God worshiped by Abraham, Isaac, and Jacob*: Jesus argues that if God is worshiped by these three, they must still be alive, because he is the God of the living.

Prophets[h] are based on these two
commandments.

About David's Son
(Mark 12.35-37; Luke 20.41-44)

41While the Pharisees were still there,
Jesus asked them, 42"What do you think
about the Messiah? Whose family will
he come from?"
They answered, "He will be a son of
King David."[i]
43Jesus replied, "How then could the
Spirit lead David to call the Messiah
his Lord? David said,

44 'The Lord said to my Lord:
Sit at my right side[j]
until I make your enemies
into a footstool for you.'

45If David called the Messiah his Lord,
how can the Messiah be a son of King
David?" 46No one was able to give Jesus
an answer, and from that day on, no one
dared ask him any more questions.

Jesus Condemns the Pharisees and the Teachers of the Law of Moses
(Mark 12.38-40; Luke 11.37-52; 20.45-47)

23 Jesus said to the crowds and to
his disciples:
2The Pharisees and the teachers of
the Law are experts in the Law of
Moses. 3So obey everything they
teach you, but don't do as they do.
After all, they say one thing and do
something else.
4They pile heavy burdens on people's shoulders and won't lift a finger to help. 5Everything they do is
just to show off in front of others.
They even make a big show of wearing Scripture verses on their foreheads and arms, and they wear big
tassels[k] for everyone to see. 6They
love the best seats at banquets and
the front seats in the meeting places.
7And when they are in the market,
they like to have people greet them
as their teachers.
8But none of you should be called
a teacher. You have only one teacher,
and all of you are like brothers and
sisters. 9Don't call anyone on earth
your father. All of you have the same
Father in heaven. 10None of you
should be called the leader. The
Messiah is your only leader. 11Who-
ever is the greatest should be the
servant of the others. 12If you put
yourself above others, you will be
put down. But if you humble yourself, you will be honored.
13-14You Pharisees and teachers of
the Law of Moses are in for trouble!
You're nothing but show-offs. You
lock people out of the kingdom of
heaven. You won't go in yourselves,
and you keep others from going in.[l]
15You Pharisees and teachers of
the Law of Moses are in for trouble!
You're nothing but show-offs. You
travel over land and sea to win one
follower. And when you have done
so, you make that person twice as fit
for hell as you are.
16You are in for trouble! You are
supposed to lead others, but you are
blind. You teach that it doesn't matter if a person swears by the temple.
But you say that it does matter if
someone swears by the gold in the
temple. 17You blind fools! Which is
greater, the gold or the temple that
makes the gold sacred?
18You also teach that it doesn't
matter if a person swears by the altar. But you say that it does matter if
someone swears by the gift on the
altar. 19Are you blind? Which is
more important, the gift or the altar
that makes the gift sacred? 20Anyone
who swears by the altar also swears
by everything on it. 21And anyone
who swears by the temple also
swears by God, who lives there. 22To
swear by heaven is the same as
swearing by God's throne and by the
one who sits on that throne.
23You Pharisees and teachers are
show-offs, and you're in for trouble!
You give God a tenth of the spices
from your garden, such as mint, dill,
and cumin. Yet you neglect the more
important matters of the Law, such
as justice, mercy, and faithfulness.
These are the important things you
should have done, though you
should not have left the others undone either. 24You blind leaders! You
strain out a small fly but swallow a
camel.
25You Pharisees and teachers are
show-offs, and you're in for trouble!

[h]**22.40** *the Law of Moses and the Books of the Prophets*: The Jewish Scriptures, that is, the Old Testament. [i]**22.42** *son of King David*: See the note at 9.27. [j]**22.44** *right side*: The place of power and honor. [k]**23.5** *wearing Scripture verses on their foreheads and arms . . . tassels*: As a sign of their love for the Lord and his teachings, the Jewish people had started wearing Scripture verses in small leather boxes. But the Pharisees tried to show off by making the boxes bigger than necessary. The Jewish people were also taught to wear tassels on the four corners of their robes to show their love for God. [l]**23.13,14** *from going in*: Some manuscripts add, "You Pharisees and teachers are in for trouble! And you're nothing but show-offs! You cheat widows out of their homes and then pray long prayers just to show off. So you will be punished most of all."

You wash the outside of your cups
and dishes, while inside there is
nothing but greed and selfishness.
26 You blind Pharisee! First clean the
inside of a cup, and then the outside
will also be clean.
27 You Pharisees and teachers are
in for trouble! You're nothing but
show-offs. You're like tombs that
have been whitewashed.[m] On the
outside they are beautiful, but inside
they are full of bones and filth.
28 That's what you are like. Outside
you look good, but inside you are
evil and only pretend to be good.
29 You Pharisees and teachers are
nothing but show-offs, and you're in
for trouble! You build monuments
for the prophets and decorate the
tombs of good people. 30 And you
claim that you would not have taken
part with your ancestors in killing
the prophets. 31 But you prove that
you really are the relatives of the
ones who killed the prophets. 32 So
keep on doing everything they did.
33 You are nothing but snakes and
the children of snakes! How can you
escape going to hell?
34 I will send prophets and wise
people and experts in the Law of
Moses to you. But you will kill them
or nail them to a cross or beat them
in your meeting places or chase
them from town to town. 35 That's
why you will be held guilty for the
murder of every good person, beginning with the good man Abel. This
also includes Barachiah's son
Zechariah,[n] the man you murdered
between the temple and the altar. 36 I
can promise that you people living
today will be punished for all these
things!

Jesus Loves Jerusalem

(Luke 13.34, 35)

37 Jerusalem, Jerusalem! Your people have killed the prophets and
have stoned the messengers who
were sent to you. I have often
wanted to gather your people, as a
hen gathers her chicks under her
wings. But you wouldn't let me.
38 And now your temple will be deserted. 39 You won't see me again until you say,

"Blessed is the one who comes
in the name of the Lord."

The Temple Will Be Destroyed

(Mark 13.1, 2; Luke 21.5, 6)

24 After Jesus left the temple, his
disciples came over and said,
"Look at all these buildings!"
2 Jesus replied, "Do you see these
buildings? They will certainly be torn
down! Not one stone will be left in
place."

Warning about Trouble

(Mark 13.3-13; Luke 21.7-19)

3 Later, as Jesus was sitting on the
Mount of Olives, his disciples came to
him in private and asked, "When will
this happen? What will be the sign of
your coming and of the end of the
world?"
4 Jesus answered:
Don't let anyone fool you. 5 Many
will come and claim to be me. They
will say that they are the Messiah,
and they will fool many people.
6 You will soon hear about wars
and threats of wars, but don't be
afraid. These things will have to
happen first, but that isn't the end.
7 Nations and kingdoms will go to
war against each other. People will
starve to death, and in some places
there will be earthquakes. 8 But this
is just the beginning of troubles.
9 You will be arrested, punished,
and even killed. Because of me, you
will be hated by people of all nations. 10 Many will give up and will
betray and hate each other. 11 Many
false prophets will come and fool a
lot of people. 12 Evil will spread and
cause many people to stop loving
others. 13 But if you keep on being
faithful right to the end, you will be
saved. 14 When the good news about
the kingdom has been preached all
over the world and told to all nations, the end will come.

The Horrible Thing

(Mark 13.14-23; Luke 21.20-24)

15 Someday you will see that "Horrible Thing" in the holy place, just as
the prophet Daniel said. Everyone
who reads this must try to understand! 16 If you are living in Judea at
that time, run to the mountains. 17 If
you are on the roof[o] of your house,
don't go inside to get anything. 18 If
you are out in the field, don't go
back for your coat. 19 It will be a ter-

[m] **23.27** *whitewashed*: Tombs were whitewashed to keep anyone from accidentally touching them. A person who touched a dead body or a tomb was considered unclean and could not worship with the rest of the Jewish people. [n] **23.35** *Zechariah*: Genesis is the first book in the Jewish Scriptures, and it tells that Abel was the first person to be murdered. Second Chronicles is the last book in the Jewish Scriptures, and the last murder that it tells about is that of Zechariah. [o] **24.17** *roof*: In Palestine the houses usually had a flat roof. Stairs on the outside led up to the roof, which was made of beams and boards covered with packed earth.

rible time for women who are expecting babies or nursing young
children. 20 And pray that you won't
have to escape in winter or on a
Sabbath.[p] 21 This will be the worst
time of suffering since the beginning
of the world, and nothing this terrible will ever happen again. 22 If God
doesn't make the time shorter, no
one will be left alive. But because of
God's chosen ones, he will make the
time shorter.
23 Someone may say, "Here is the
Messiah!" or "There he is!" But don't
believe it. 24 False messiahs and false
prophets will come and work great
miracles and signs. They will even
try to fool God's chosen ones. 25 But I
have warned you ahead of time. 26 If
you are told that the Messiah is out
in the desert, don't go there! And if
you are told that he is in some secret
place, don't believe it! 27 The coming
of the Son of Man will be like lightning that can be seen from east to
west. 28 Where there is a corpse,
there will always be buzzards.[q]

When the Son of Man Appears

(Mark 13.24-27; Luke 21.25-28)

29 Right after those days of suffering,

"The sun will become dark,
and the moon
will no longer shine.
The stars will fall,
and the powers in the sky[r]
will be shaken."

30 Then a sign will appear in the
sky. And there will be the Son of
Man.[s] All nations on earth will weep
when they see the Son of Man coming on the clouds of heaven with
power and great glory. 31 At the
sound of a loud trumpet, he will
send his angels to bring his chosen
ones together from all over the
earth.

A Lesson from a Fig Tree

(Mark 13.28-31; Luke 21.29-33)

32 Learn a lesson from a fig tree.
When its branches sprout and start
putting out leaves, you know that
summer is near. 33 So when you see
all these things happening, you will
know that the time has almost
come.[t] 34 I can promise you that
some of the people of this generation will still be alive when all this
happens. 35 The sky and the earth
won't last forever, but my words
will.

No One Knows the Day or Time

(Mark 13.32-37; Luke 17.26-30, 34-36)

36 No one knows the day or hour.
The angels in heaven don't know,
and the Son himself doesn't know.[u]
Only the Father knows. 37 When the
Son of Man appears, things will be
just as they were when Noah lived.
38 People were eating, drinking, and
getting married right up to the day
that the flood came and Noah went
into the big boat. 39 They didn't know
anything was happening until the
flood came and swept them all away.
That is how it will be when the Son
of Man appears.
40 Two men will be in the same
field, but only one will be taken. The
other will be left. 41 Two women will
be together grinding grain, but only
one will be taken. The other will be
left. 42 So be on your guard! You don't
know when your Lord will come.
43 Homeowners never know when a
thief is coming, and they are always
on guard to keep one from breaking
in. 44 Always be ready! You don't
know when the Son of Man will
come.

Faithful and Unfaithful Servants

(Luke 12.35-48)

45 Who are faithful and wise servants? Who are the ones the master
will put in charge of giving the other
servants their food supplies at the
proper time? 46 Servants are fortunate if their master comes and finds
them doing their job. 47 You may be
sure that a servant who is always
faithful will be put in charge of
everything the master owns. 48 But
suppose one of the servants thinks
that the master won't return until
late. 49 Suppose that evil servant

[p]**24.20** *in winter or on a Sabbath*: In Palestine the winters are cold and rainy and make travel difficult. The Jewish people were not allowed to travel much more than half a mile on the Sabbath. For these reasons it was hard for them to escape from their enemies in the winter or on a Sabbath. [q]**24.28** *Where there is a corpse, there will always be buzzards*: This saying may mean that when anything important happens, people soon know about it. Or the saying may mean that whenever something bad happens, curious people gather around and stare. But the word translated "buzzard" also means "eagle" and may refer to the Roman army, which had an eagle as its symbol. [r]**24.29** *the powers in the sky*: In ancient times people thought that the stars were spiritual powers. [s]**24.30** *And there will be the Son of Man*: Or "And it will be the Son of Man." [t]**24.33** *the time has almost come*: Or "he (that is, the Son of Man) will soon be here." [u]**24.36** *and the Son himself doesn't know*: These words are not in some manuscripts.

starts beating the other servants and
eats and drinks with people who are
drunk. 50If that happens, the master
will surely come on a day and at a
time when the servant least expects
him. 51That servant will then be punished and thrown out with the ones
who only pretended to serve their
master. There they will cry and grit
their teeth in pain.

A Story about Ten Girls

25 The kingdom of heaven is like
what happened one night when
ten girls took their oil lamps and
went to a wedding to meet the
groom.[v] 2Five of the girls were foolish and five were wise. 3The foolish
ones took their lamps, but no extra
oil. 4The ones who were wise took
along extra oil for their lamps.
5The groom was late arriving, and
the girls became drowsy and fell
asleep. 6Then in the middle of the
night someone shouted, "Here's the
groom! Come to meet him!"
7When the girls got up and started
getting their lamps ready, 8the foolish ones said to the others, "Let us
have some of your oil! Our lamps
are going out."
9The girls who were wise answered, "There's not enough oil for
all of us! Go and buy some for yourselves."
10While the foolish girls were on
their way to get some oil, the groom
arrived. The girls who were ready
went into the wedding, and the
doors were closed. 11Later the other
girls returned and shouted, "Sir, sir!
Open the door for us!"
12But the groom replied, "I don't
even know you!"
13So, my disciples, always be
ready! You don't know the day or the
time when all this will happen.

A Story about Three Servants

(Luke 19.11-27)

14The kingdom is also like what
happened when a man went away
and put his three servants in charge
of all he owned. 15The man knew
what each servant could do. So he
handed five thousand coins to the
first servant, two thousand to the
second, and one thousand to the
third. Then he left the country.
16As soon as the man had gone,
the servant with the five thousand
coins used them to earn five thousand more. 17The servant who had
two thousand coins did the same
with his money and earned two
thousand more. 18But the servant
with one thousand coins dug a hole
and hid his master's money in the
ground.
19Some time later the master of
those servants returned. He called
them in and asked what they had
done with his money. 20The servant
who had been given five thousand
coins brought them in with the five
thousand that he had earned. He
said, "Sir, you gave me five thousand
coins, and I have earned five thousand more."
21"Wonderful!" his master replied.
"You are a good and faithful servant.
I left you in charge of only a little,
but now I will put you in charge of
much more. Come and share in my
happiness!"
22Next, the servant who had been
given two thousand coins came in
and said, "Sir, you gave me two
thousand coins, and I have earned
two thousand more."
23"Wonderful!" his master replied.
"You are a good and faithful servant.
I left you in charge of only a little,
but now I will put you in charge of
much more. Come and share in my
happiness!"
24The servant who had been given
one thousand coins then came in
and said, "Sir, I know that you are
hard to get along with. You harvest
what you don't plant and gather
crops where you haven't scattered
seed. 25I was frightened and went
out and hid your money in the
ground. Here is every single
coin!"
26The master of the servant told
him, "You are lazy and good-for-
nothing! You know that I harvest
what I don't plant and gather crops
where I haven't scattered seed. 27You
could have at least put my money in
the bank, so that I could have earned
interest on it."
28Then the master said, "Now your
money will be taken away and given
to the servant with ten thousand
coins! 29Everyone who has something will be given more, and they
will have more than enough. But
everything will be taken from those
who don't have anything. 30You are a
worthless servant, and you will be
thrown out into the dark where people will cry and grit their teeth in
pain."

[v]25.1 *to meet the groom*: Some manuscripts add "and the bride." It was the custom for the groom to go to the home of the bride's parents to get his bride. Young girls and other guests would then go with them to the home of the groom's parents, where the wedding feast would take place.

The Final Judgment

31When the Son of Man comes in
his glory with all of his angels, he
will sit on his royal throne. 32The
people of all nations will be brought
before him, and he will separate
them, as shepherds separate their
sheep from their goats.
33He will place the sheep on his
right and the goats on his left.
34Then the king will say to those on
his right, "My father has blessed
you! Come and receive the kingdom
that was prepared for you before the
world was created. 35When I was
hungry, you gave me something to
eat, and when I was thirsty, you gave
me something to drink. When I was
a stranger, you welcomed me, 36and
when I was naked, you gave me
clothes to wear. When I was sick,
you took care of me, and when I was
in jail, you visited me."
37Then the ones who pleased the
Lord will ask, "When did we give you
something to eat or drink? 38When
did we welcome you as a stranger or
give you clothes to wear 39or visit
you while you were sick or in jail?"
40The king will answer, "Whenever
you did it for any of my people, no
matter how unimportant they
seemed, you did it for me."
41Then the king will say to those
on his left, "Get away from me! You
are under God's curse. Go into the
everlasting fire prepared for the
devil and his angels! 42I was hungry,
but you did not give me anything to
eat, and I was thirsty, but you did not
give me anything to drink. 43I was a
stranger, but you did not welcome
me, and I was naked, but you did not
give me any clothes to wear. I was
sick and in jail, but you did not take
care of me."
44Then the people will ask, "Lord,
when did we fail to help you when
you were hungry or thirsty or a
stranger or naked or sick or in jail?"
45The king will say to them,
"Whenever you failed to help any of
my people, no matter how unimportant they seemed, you failed to do it
for me."
46Then Jesus said, "Those people will
be punished forever. But the ones who
pleased God will have eternal life."

The Plot To Kill Jesus

(Mark 14.1, 2; Luke 22.1, 2; John 11.45-53)

26 When Jesus had finished teaching, he told his disciples, 2"You
know that two days from now will be
Passover. That is when the Son of Man
will be handed over to his enemies and
nailed to a cross."
3At that time the chief priests and the
nation's leaders were meeting at the
home of Caiaphas the high priest. 4They
planned how they could sneak around
and have Jesus arrested and put to
death. 5But they said, "We must not do it
during Passover, because the people will
riot."

At Bethany

(Mark 14.3-9; John 12.1-8)

6Jesus was in the town of Bethany,
eating at the home of Simon, who had
leprosy.[w] 7A woman came in with a bottle of expensive perfume and poured it
on Jesus' head. 8But when his disciples
saw this, they became angry and complained, "Why such a waste? 9We could
have sold this perfume for a lot of
money and given it to the poor."
10Jesus knew what they were thinking, and he said:
Why are you bothering this
woman? She has done a beautiful
thing for me. 11You will always have
the poor with you, but you won't always have me. 12She has poured perfume on my body to prepare it for
burial.[x] 13You may be sure that
wherever the good news is told all
over the world, people will remember what she has done. And they
will tell others.

Judas and the Chief Priests

(Mark 14.10, 11; Luke 22.3-6)

14Judas Iscariot[y] was one of the
twelve disciples. He went to the chief
priests 15and asked, "How much will you
give me if I help you arrest Jesus?" They
paid Judas thirty silver coins, 16and
from then on he started looking for a
good chance to betray Jesus.

Jesus Eats the Passover Meal with His Disciples

(Mark 14.12-21; Luke 22.7-13; John 13.21-30)

17On the first day of the Festival of
Thin Bread, Jesus' disciples came to him
and asked, "Where do you want us to
prepare the Passover meal?"
18Jesus told them to go to a certain
man in the city and tell him, "Our
teacher says, 'My time has come! I want
to eat the Passover meal with my disciples in your home.' " 19They did as Jesus
told them and prepared the meal.
20-21When Jesus was eating with his
twelve disciples that evening, he said,
"One of you will surely hand me over to
my enemies."

[w]**26.6** *leprosy*: See the note at 8.2. [x]**26.12** *poured perfume on my body to prepare it for burial*: The Jewish people taught that giving someone a proper burial was even more important than helping the poor. [y]**26.14** *Iscariot*: See the note at 10.4.

22 The disciples were very sad, and
each one said to Jesus, "Lord, you can't
mean me!"
23 He answered, "One of you men who
has eaten with me from this dish will
betray me. 24 The Son of Man will die, as
the Scriptures say. But it's going to be
terrible for the one who betrays me!
That man would be better off if he had
never been born."
25 Judas said, "Teacher, you surely
don't mean me!"
"That's what you say!" Jesus replied.
But later, Judas did betray him.

The Lord's Supper

(Mark 14.22-26; Luke 22.14-23; 1 Corinthians 11.23-25)

26 During the meal Jesus took some
bread in his hands. He blessed the bread
and broke it. Then he gave it to his disciples and said, "Take this and eat it. This
is my body."
27 Jesus picked up a cup of wine and
gave thanks to God. He then gave it to
his disciples and said, "Take this and
drink it. 28 This is my blood, and with it
God makes his agreement with you. It
will be poured out, so that many people
will have their sins forgiven. 29 From
now on I am not going to drink any
wine, until I drink new wine with you in
my Father's kingdom." 30 Then they sang
a hymn and went out to the Mount of
Olives.

Peter's Promise

(Mark 14.27-31; Luke 22.31-34; John 13.36-38)

31 Jesus said to his disciples, "During
this very night, all of you will reject me,
as the Scriptures say,

'I will strike down
the shepherd,
and the sheep
will be scattered.'

32 But after I am raised to life, I will go to
Galilee ahead of you."
33 Peter spoke up, "Even if all the others reject you, I never will!"
34 Jesus replied, "I promise you that
before a rooster crows tonight, you will
say three times that you don't know
me." 35 But Peter said, "Even if I have to
die with you, I will never say I don't
know you."
All the others said the same thing.

Jesus Prays

(Mark 14.32-42; Luke 22.39-46)

36 Jesus went with his disciples to a
place called Gethsemane. When they got
there, he told them, "Sit here while I go
over there and pray."
37 Jesus took along Peter and the two
brothers, James and John.[z] He was very
sad and troubled, 38 and he said to them,
"I am so sad that I feel as if I am dying.
Stay here and keep awake with me."
39 Jesus walked on a little way. Then
he knelt with his face to the ground and
prayed, "My Father, if it is possible,
don't make me suffer by having me
drink from this cup.[a] But do what you
want, and not what I want."
40 He came back and found his disciples sleeping. So he said to Peter, "Can't
any of you stay awake with me for just
one hour? 41 Stay awake and pray that
you won't be tested. You want to do what
is right, but you are weak."
42 Again Jesus went to pray and said,
"My Father, if there is no other way, and
I must suffer, I will still do what you
want."
43 Jesus came back and found them
sleeping again. They simply could not
keep their eyes open. 44 He left them and
prayed the same prayer once more.
45 Finally, Jesus returned to his disciples and said, "Are you still sleeping and
resting?[b] The time has come for the Son
of Man to be handed over to sinners.
46 Get up! Let's go. The one who will betray me is already here."

Jesus Is Arrested

(Mark 14.43-50; Luke 22.47-53; John 18.3-12)

47 Jesus was still speaking, when Judas
the betrayer came up. He was one of the
twelve disciples, and a large mob armed
with swords and clubs was with him.
They had been sent by the chief priests
and the nation's leaders. 48 Judas had
told them ahead of time, "Arrest the
man I greet with a kiss."[c]
49 Judas walked right up to Jesus and
said, "Hello, teacher." Then Judas kissed
him.
50 Jesus replied, "My friend, why are
you here?"[d]
The men grabbed Jesus and arrested
him. 51 One of Jesus' followers pulled out
a sword. He struck the servant of the
high priest and cut off his ear.
52 But Jesus told him, "Put your sword
away. Anyone who lives by fighting will
die by fighting. 53 Don't you know that I
could ask my Father, and right away he
would send me more than twelve armies
of angels? 54 But then, how could the
words of the Scriptures come true,
which say that this must happen?"

[z] **26.37** *the two brothers, James and John*: The Greek text has "the two sons of Zebedee" (see 27.56). [a] **26.39** *having me drink from this cup*: In the Scriptures "to drink from a cup" sometimes means to suffer (see the note at 20.22). [b] **26.45** *Are you still sleeping and resting?*: Or "You may as well keep on sleeping and resting." [c] **26.48** *the man I greet with a kiss*: It was the custom for people to greet each other with a kiss on the cheek. [d] **26.50** *why are you here?*: Or "do what you came for."

55Jesus said to the mob, "Why do you
come with swords and clubs to arrest
me like a criminal? Day after day I sat
and taught in the temple, and you didn't
arrest me. 56But all this happened, so that
what the prophets wrote would come true."
All of Jesus' disciples left him and ran
away.

Jesus Is Questioned by the Council

(Mark 14.53-65; Luke 22.54, 55, 63-71; John 18.13, 14, 19-24)

57After Jesus had been arrested, he
was led off to the house of Caiaphas the
high priest. The nation's leaders and the
teachers of the Law of Moses were
meeting there. 58But Peter followed
along at a distance and came to the
courtyard of the high priest's palace. He
went in and sat down with the guards to
see what was going to happen.
59The chief priests and the whole
council wanted to put Jesus to death. So
they tried to find some people who
would tell lies about him in court.[e] 60But
they could not find any, even though
many did come and tell lies. At last, two
men came forward 61and said, "This
man claimed that he would tear down
God's temple and build it again in three
days."
62The high priest stood up and asked
Jesus, "Why don't you say something in
your own defense? Don't you hear the
charges they are making against you?"
63But Jesus did not answer. So the high
priest said, "With the living God looking
on, you must tell the truth. Tell us, are
you the Messiah, the Son of God?"[f]
64"That is what you say!" Jesus answered. "But I tell all of you,

'Soon you will see
the Son of Man
sitting at the right side[g]
of God All-Powerful
and coming on the clouds
of heaven.' "

65The high priest then tore his robe and
said, "This man claims to be God! We
don't need any more witnesses! You have
heard what he said. 66What do you think?"
They answered, "He is guilty and deserves to die!" 67Then they spit in his
face and hit him with their fists. Others
slapped him 68and said, "You think you
are the Messiah! So tell us who hit you!"

Peter Says He Doesn't Know Jesus

(Mark 14.66-72; Luke 22.56-62; John 18.15-18, 25-27)

69While Peter was sitting out in the
courtyard, a servant girl came up to him
and said, "You were with Jesus from
Galilee."
70But in front of everyone Peter said,
"That isn't so! I don't know what you
are talking about!"
71When Peter had gone out to the
gate, another servant girl saw him and
said to some people there, "This man
was with Jesus from Nazareth."
72Again Peter denied it, and this time
he swore, "I don't even know that man!"
73A little while later some people
standing there walked over to Peter and
said, "We know that you are one of
them. We can tell it because you talk
like someone from Galilee."
74Peter began to curse and swear, "I
don't know that man!"
Right then a rooster crowed, 75and Peter remembered that Jesus had said,
"Before a rooster crows, you will say
three times that you don't know me."
Then Peter went out and cried hard.

Jesus Is Taken to Pilate

(Mark 15.1; Luke 23.1, 2; John 18.28-32)

27 Early the next morning all the
chief priests and the nation's
leaders met and decided that Jesus
should be put to death. 2They tied him
up and led him away to Pilate the governor.

The Death of Judas

(Acts 1.18, 19)

3Judas had betrayed Jesus, but when
he learned that Jesus had been sentenced to death, he was sorry for what
he had done. He returned the thirty silver coins to the chief priests and leaders
4and said, "I have sinned by betraying a
man who has never done anything
wrong."
"So what? That's your problem," they
replied. 5Judas threw the money into the
temple and then went out and hanged
himself.
6The chief priests picked up the
money and said, "This money was paid
to have a man killed. We can't put it in
the temple treasury." 7Then they had a
meeting and decided to buy a field that
belonged to someone who made clay
pots. They wanted to use it as a graveyard for foreigners. 8That's why people
still call that place "Field of Blood." 9So
the words of the prophet Jeremiah came
true,

"They took
the thirty silver coins,
the price of a person
among the people of Israel.

[e]**26.59** *some people who would tell lies about him in court*: The Law of Moses taught that two witnesses were necessary before a person could be put to death (see verse 60). [f]**26.63** *Son of God*: One of the titles used for the kings of Israel. [g]**26.64** *right side*: See the note at 22.44.

10 They paid it
for a potter's field,[h]
as the Lord
had commanded me."

Pilate Questions Jesus

(Mark 15.2-5; Luke 23.3-5; John 18.33-38)

11 Jesus was brought before Pilate the
governor, who asked him, "Are you the
king of the Jews?"
"Those are your words!" Jesus answered. 12 And when the chief priests
and leaders brought their charges
against him, he did not say a thing.
13 Pilate asked him, "Don't you hear
what crimes they say you have done?"
14 But Jesus did not say anything, and
the governor was greatly amazed.

The Death Sentence

(Mark 15.6-15; Luke 23.13-26; John 18.39—19.16)

15 During Passover the governor always freed a prisoner chosen by the
people. 16 At that time a well-known
terrorist named Jesus Barabbas[i] was in
jail. 17 So when the crowd came together,
Pilate asked them, "Which prisoner do
you want me to set free? Do you want
Jesus Barabbas or Jesus who is called
the Messiah?" 18 Pilate knew that the
leaders had brought Jesus to him because they were jealous.
19 While Pilate was judging the case,
his wife sent him a message. It said,
"Don't have anything to do with that innocent man. I have had nightmares because of him."
20 But the chief priests and the leaders
convinced the crowds to ask for Barabbas to be set free and for Jesus to be
killed. 21 Pilate asked the crowd again,
"Which of these two men do you want
me to set free?"
"Barabbas!" they replied.
22 Pilate asked them, "What am I to do
with Jesus, who is called the Messiah?"
They all yelled, "Nail him to a cross!"
23 Pilate answered, "But what crime
has he done?"
"Nail him to a cross!" they yelled even
louder.
24 Pilate saw that there was nothing he
could do and that the people were starting to riot. So he took some water and
washed his hands[j] in front of them and
said, "I won't have anything to do with
killing this man. You are the ones doing
it!"
25 Everyone answered, "We and our
own families will take the blame for his
death!"
26 Pilate set Barabbas free. Then he ordered his soldiers to beat Jesus with a
whip and nail him to a cross.

Soldiers Make Fun of Jesus

(Mark 15.16-21; John 19.2, 3)

27 The governor's soldiers led Jesus
into the fortress[k] and brought together
the rest of the troops. 28 They stripped
off Jesus' clothes and put a scarlet robe[l]
on him. 29 They made a crown out of
thorn branches and placed it on his
head, and they put a stick in his right
hand. The soldiers knelt down and pretended to worship him. They made fun
of him and shouted, "Hey, you king of
the Jews!" 30 Then they spit on him. They
took the stick from him and beat him on
the head with it.

Jesus Is Nailed to a Cross

(Mark 15.22-32; Luke 23.27-43; John 19.17-27)

31 When the soldiers had finished making fun of Jesus, they took off the robe.
They put his own clothes back on him
and led him off to be nailed to a cross.
32 On the way they met a man from
Cyrene named Simon, and they forced
him to carry Jesus' cross.
33 They came to a place named Golgotha, which means "Place of a Skull."[m]
34 There they gave Jesus some wine
mixed with a drug to ease the pain. But
when Jesus tasted what it was, he refused to drink it.
35 The soldiers nailed Jesus to a cross
and gambled to see who would get his
clothes. 36 Then they sat down to guard
him. 37 Above his head they put a sign
that told why he was nailed there. It
read, "This is Jesus, the King of the
Jews." 38 The soldiers also nailed two
criminals on crosses, one to the right of
Jesus and the other to his left.
39 People who passed by said terrible
things about Jesus. They shook their
heads and 40 shouted, "So you're the one
who claimed you could tear down the
temple and build it again in three days!
If you are God's Son, save yourself and
come down from the cross!"
41 The chief priests, the leaders, and
the teachers of the Law of Moses also

[h]**27.10** *a potter's field*: Perhaps a field owned by someone who made clay pots. But it may have been a field where potters came to get clay or to make pots or to throw away their broken pieces of pottery. [i]**27.16** *Jesus Barabbas*: Here and in verse 17 many manuscripts have "Barabbas." [j]**27.24** *washed his hands*: To show that he was innocent. [k]**27.27** *fortress*: The place where the Roman governor stayed. It was probably at Herod's palace west of Jerusalem, though it may have been Fortress Antonia north of the temple, where the Roman troops were stationed. [l]**27.28** *scarlet robe*: This was probably a Roman soldier's robe. [m]**27.33** *Place of a Skull*: The place was probably given this name because it was near a large rock in the shape of a human skull.

made fun of Jesus. They said, 42“He
saved others, but he can’t save himself.
If he is the king of Israel, he should
come down from the cross! Then we will
believe him. 43He trusted God, so let
God save him, if he wants to. He even
said he was God’s Son.” 44The two criminals also said cruel things to Jesus.

The Death of Jesus

(Mark 15.33-41; Luke 23.44-49; John 19.28-30)

45At noon the sky turned dark and
stayed that way until three o’clock.
46Then about that time Jesus shouted,
“Eli, Eli, lema sabachthani?”[n] which
means, “My God, my God, why have you
deserted me?”

47Some of the people standing there
heard Jesus and said, “He’s calling for
Elijah.”[o] 48One of them at once ran and
grabbed a sponge. He soaked it in wine,
then put it on a stick and held it up to
Jesus.

49Others said, “Wait! Let’s see if Elijah
will come[p] and save him.” 50Once again
Jesus shouted, and then he died.

51At once the curtain in the temple[q]
was torn in two from top to bottom. The
earth shook, and rocks split apart.
52Graves opened, and many of God’s
people were raised to life. 53Then after
Jesus had risen to life, they came out
of their graves and went into the holy
city, where they were seen by many
people.

54The officer and the soldiers guarding Jesus felt the earthquake and saw
everything else that happened. They
were frightened and said, “This man
really was God’s Son!”

55Many women had come with Jesus
from Galilee to be of help to him, and
they were there, looking on at a distance. 56Mary Magdalene, Mary the
mother of James and Joseph, and the
mother of James and John[r] were some
of these women.

Jesus Is Buried

(Mark 15.42-47; Luke 23.50-56; John 19.38-42)

57That evening a rich disciple named
Joseph from the town of Arimathea
58went and asked for Jesus’ body. Pilate
gave orders for it to be given to
Joseph, 59who took the body and
wrapped it in a clean linen cloth. 60Then
Joseph put the body in his own tomb
that had been cut into solid rock[s] and
had never been used. He rolled a big
stone against the entrance to the tomb
and went away.

61All this time Mary Magdalene and
the other Mary were sitting across from
the tomb.

62On the next day, which was a Sabbath, the chief priests and the Pharisees
went together to Pilate. 63They said, “Sir,
we remember what that liar said while
he was still alive. He claimed that in
three days he would come back from
death. 64So please order the tomb to be
carefully guarded for three days. If you
don’t, his disciples may come and steal
his body. They will tell the people that
he has been raised to life, and this last
lie will be worse than the first one.”[t]

65Pilate said to them, “All right, take
some of your soldiers and guard the
tomb as well as you know how.” 66So
they sealed it tight and placed soldiers
there to guard it.

Jesus Is Alive

(Mark 16.1-8; Luke 24.1-12; John 20.1-10)

28 The Sabbath was over, and it was
almost daybreak on Sunday
when Mary Magdalene and the other
Mary went to see the tomb. 2Suddenly a
strong earthquake struck, and the
Lord’s angel came down from heaven.
He rolled away the stone and sat on it.
3The angel looked as bright as lightning,
and his clothes were white as snow.
4The guards shook from fear and fell
down, as though they were dead.

5The angel said to the women, “Don’t
be afraid! I know you are looking for Jesus, who was nailed to a cross. 6He isn’t
here! God has raised him to life, just as
Jesus said he would. Come, see the
place where his body was lying. 7Now
hurry! Tell his disciples that he has been
raised to life and is on his way to
Galilee. Go there, and you will see him.
That is what I came to tell you.”

8The women were frightened and
yet very happy, as they hurried from
the tomb and ran to tell his disciples.
9Suddenly Jesus met them and greeted
them. They went near him, held on to
his feet, and worshiped him. 10Then
Jesus said, “Don’t be afraid! Tell my

[n] **27.46** *Eli . . . sabachthani*: These words are in Hebrew. [o] 27.47 Elijah: In Aramaic the name “Elijah” sounds like “Eli,” which means “my God.” [p] **27.49** *Elijah will come*: See the note at 16.14. [q] **27.51** *curtain in the temple*: There were two curtains in the temple. One was at the entrance, and the other separated the holy place from the most holy place that the Jewish people thought of as God’s home on earth. The second curtain is probably the one that is meant. [r] **27.56** *of James and John*: The Greek text has “of Zebedee’s sons” (see 26.37). [s] **27.60** *tomb . . . solid rock*: Some of the Jewish people buried their dead in rooms carved into solid rock. A heavy stone was rolled against the entrance. [t] **27.64** *the first one*: Probably the belief that Jesus is the Messiah.

followers to go to Galilee. They will see
me there."

Report of the Guard

11While the women were on their way,
some soldiers who had been guarding
the tomb went into the city. They told
the chief priests everything that had
happened. 12So the chief priests met
with the leaders and decided to bribe
the soldiers with a lot of money. 13They
said to the soldiers, "Tell everyone that
Jesus' disciples came during the night
and stole his body while you were
asleep. 14If the governor[u] hears about
this, we will talk to him. You won't have
anything to worry about." 15The soldiers
took the money and did what they were
told. The people of Judea still tell each
other this story.

What Jesus' Followers Must Do

(Mark 16.14-18; Luke 24.36-49;
John 20.19-23; Acts 1.6-8)

16Jesus' eleven disciples went to a
mountain in Galilee, where Jesus had
told them to meet him. 17They saw him
and worshiped him, but some of them
doubted.

18Jesus came to them and said:

I have been given all authority in
heaven and on earth! 19Go to the
people of all nations and make them
my disciples. Baptize them in the
name of the Father, the Son, and the
Holy Spirit, 20and teach them to do
everything I have told you. I will be
with you always, even until the end
of the world.

[u]**28.14** *governor*: Pontius Pilate.

MARK

ABOUT THIS BOOK

This is the shortest of the four New Testament books that tell about the life and teachings of Jesus, but it is also the most action-packed. From the very beginning of his ministry, Jesus worked mighty wonders. After choosing four followers (1.16-20), he immediately performed many miracles of healing. Among those healed were a man with an evil spirit in him (1.21-28), Simon's mother-in-law (1.30, 31), crowds of sick people (1.32-34), and a man with leprosy (1.40-45). Over and over Mark tells how Jesus healed people, but always in such a way as to show that he did these miracles by the power of God.

The religious leaders refused to accept Jesus. This led to conflicts (2.2—3.6) that finally made them start looking for a way to kill him (11.18). But the demons saw the power of Jesus, and they knew that he was the Son of God, although Jesus would not let them tell anyone.

This book is full of miracles that amazed the crowds and Jesus' followers. But, according to Mark, the most powerful miracle of Jesus is his suffering and death. The first person to understand this miracle was the Roman soldier who saw Jesus die on the cross and said, "This man really was the Son of God!" (15.39).

This Gospel is widely thought to be the first one written. The many explanations of Aramaic words and Jewish customs in Mark suggest that Mark wrote to Gentile or non-Jewish Christians. He wants to tell about Jesus and to encourage readers to believe in the power of Jesus to rescue them from sickness, demons, and death. He also wants to remind them that the new life of faith is not an easy life, and that they must follow Jesus by serving others and being ready to suffer as he did.

The first followers of Jesus to discover the empty tomb were three women, and the angel told them:

> *Don't be alarmed! You are looking for Jesus from Nazareth, who was nailed to a cross. God has raised him to life, and he isn't here.* *(16.6)*

A QUICK LOOK AT THIS BOOK

The Message of John the Baptist (1.1-8)
The Baptism and Temptation of Jesus (1.9-13)
Jesus in Galilee (1.14—9.50)
Jesus Goes from Galilee to Jerusalem (10.1-52)
Jesus' Last Week: His Trial and Death (11.1—15.47)
Jesus Is Alive (16.1-8)
Jesus Appears to His Followers (16.9-20)

The Preaching of John the Baptist
(Matthew 3.1-12; Luke 3.1-18; John 1.19-28)

1 This is the good news about Jesus
Christ, the Son of God.[a]
2 It began
just as God had said in the book written
by Isaiah the prophet,

"I am sending my messenger
to get the way ready
for you.
3 In the desert
someone is shouting,
'Get the road ready
for the Lord!

[a]**1.1** *the Son of God*: These words are not in some manuscripts.

Make a straight path
for him.' "

4So John the Baptist showed up in the
desert and told everyone, "Turn back to
God and be baptized! Then your sins
will be forgiven."
5From all Judea and Jerusalem
crowds of people went to John. They
told how sorry they were for their sins,
and he baptized them in the Jordan
River.
6John wore clothes made of camel's
hair. He had a leather strap around his
waist and ate grasshoppers and wild
honey.
7John also told the people, "Someone
more powerful is going to come. And I
am not good enough even to stoop down
and untie his sandals.[b] 8I baptize you
with water, but he will baptize you with
the Holy Spirit!"

The Baptism of Jesus

(Matthew 3.13-17; Luke 3.21, 22)

9About that time Jesus came from
Nazareth in Galilee, and John baptized
him in the Jordan River. 10As soon as Jesus came out of the water, he saw the
sky open and the Holy Spirit coming
down to him like a dove. 11A voice from
heaven said, "You are my own dear Son,
and I am pleased with you."

Jesus and Satan

(Matthew 4.1-11; Luke 4.1-13)

12Right away God's Spirit made Jesus
go into the desert. 13He stayed there for
forty days while Satan tested him. Jesus
was with the wild animals, but angels
took care of him.

Jesus Begins His Work

(Matthew 4.12-17; Luke 4.14, 15)

14After John was arrested, Jesus went
to Galilee and told the good news that
comes from God.[c] 15He said, "The time
has come! God's kingdom will soon be
here.[d] Turn back to God and believe the
good news!"

Jesus Chooses Four Fishermen

(Matthew 4.18-22; Luke 5.1-11)

16As Jesus was walking along the
shore of Lake Galilee, he saw Simon
and his brother Andrew. They were fishermen and were casting their nets into
the lake. 17Jesus said to them, "Come
with me! I will teach you how to bring
in people instead of fish." 18Right then
the two brothers dropped their nets and
went with him.
19Jesus walked on and soon saw
James and John, the sons of Zebedee.
They were in a boat, mending their nets.
20At once Jesus asked them to come
with him. They left their father in the
boat with the hired workers and went
with him.

A Man with an Evil Spirit

(Luke 4.31-37)

21Jesus and his disciples went to the
town of Capernaum. Then on the next
Sabbath he went into the Jewish meeting place and started teaching. 22Every-
one was amazed at his teaching. He
taught with authority, and not like the
teachers of the Law of Moses. 23Sud-
denly a man with an evil spirit[e] in him
entered the meeting place and yelled,
24"Jesus from Nazareth, what do you
want with us? Have you come to destroy
us? I know who you are! You are God's
Holy One."
25Jesus told the evil spirit, "Be quiet
and come out of the man!" 26The spirit
shook him. Then it gave a loud shout
and left.
27Everyone was completely surprised
and kept saying to each other, "What is
this? It must be some new kind of powerful teaching! Even the evil spirits obey
him." 28News about Jesus quickly
spread all over Galilee.

Jesus Heals Many People

(Matthew 8.14-17; Luke 4.38-41)

29As soon as Jesus left the meeting
place with James and John, they went
home with Simon and Andrew. 30When
they got there, Jesus was told that Simon's mother-in-law was sick in bed
with fever. 31Jesus went to her. He took
hold of her hand and helped her up. The
fever left her, and she served them a
meal.
32That evening after sunset,[f] all who
were sick or had demons in them were
brought to Jesus. 33In fact, the whole
town gathered around the door of the
house. 34Jesus healed all kinds of terrible diseases and forced out a lot of
demons. But the demons knew who he
was, and he did not let them speak.
35Very early the next morning, Jesus
got up and went to a place where he
could be alone and pray. 36Simon and
the others started looking for him.
37And when they found him, they said,
"Everyone is looking for you!"
38Jesus replied, "We must go to the
nearby towns, so that I can tell the good
news to those people. This is why I have

[b]**1.7** *untie his sandals*: This was the duty of a slave. [c]**1.14** *that comes from God*: Or "that is about God." [d]**1.15** *will soon be here*: Or "is already here." [e]**1.23** *evil spirit*: A Jewish person who had an evil spirit was considered "unclean" and was not allowed to eat or worship with other Jewish people. [f]**1.32** *after sunset*: The Sabbath was over, and a new day began at sunset.

come." [39]Then Jesus went to Jewish
meeting places everywhere in Galilee,
where he preached and forced out
demons.

Jesus Heals a Man

(Matthew 8.1-4; Luke 5.12-16)

[40]A man with leprosy[g] came to Jesus
and knelt down.[h] He begged, "You have
the power to make me well, if only you
wanted to."
[41]Jesus felt sorry for[i] the man. So he
put his hand on him and said, "I want
to! Now you are well." [42]At once the
man's leprosy disappeared, and he was
well.
[43]After Jesus strictly warned the man,
he sent him on his way. [44]He said,
"Don't tell anyone about this. Just go
and show the priest that you are well.
Then take a gift to the temple as Moses
commanded, and everyone will know
that you have been healed."[j]
[45]The man talked about it so much
and told so many people, that Jesus
could no longer go openly into a town.
He had to stay away from the towns, but
people still came to him from everywhere.

Jesus Heals a Crippled Man

(Matthew 9.1-8; Luke 5.17-26)

2 Jesus went back to Capernaum, and
a few days later people heard that
he was at home.[k] [2]Then so many of
them came to the house that there
wasn't even standing room left in front
of the door.
Jesus was still teaching [3]when four
people came up, carrying a crippled
man on a mat. [4]But because of the
crowd, they could not get him to Jesus.
So they made a hole in the roof[l] above
him and let the man down in front of
everyone.
[5]When Jesus saw how much faith they
had, he said to the crippled man, "My
friend, your sins are forgiven."
[6]Some of the teachers of the Law of
Moses were sitting there. They started
wondering, [7]"Why would he say such a
thing? He must think he is God! Only
God can forgive sins."
[8]Right away, Jesus knew what they
were thinking, and he said, "Why are
you thinking such things? [9]Is it easier
for me to tell this crippled man that his
sins are forgiven or to tell him to get up
and pick up his mat and go on home? [10]I
will show you that the Son of Man has
the right to forgive sins here on earth."
So Jesus said to the man, [11]"Get up!
Pick up your mat and go on home."
[12]The man got right up. He picked up
his mat and went out while everyone
watched in amazement. They praised
God and said, "We have never seen anything like this!"

Jesus Chooses Levi

(Matthew 9.9-13; Luke 5.27-32)

[13]Once again, Jesus went to the shore
of Lake Galilee. A large crowd gathered
around him, and he taught them. [14]As
he walked along, he saw Levi, the son of
Alphaeus. Levi was sitting at the place
for paying taxes, and Jesus said to him,
"Come with me!" So he got up and went
with Jesus.
[15]Later, Jesus and his disciples were
having dinner at Levi's house.[m] Many
tax collectors[n] and other sinners had
become followers of Jesus, and they
were also guests at the dinner.
[16]Some of the teachers of the Law of
Moses were Pharisees, and they saw
that Jesus was eating with sinners and
tax collectors. So they asked his disciples, "Why does he eat with tax collectors and sinners?"
[17]Jesus heard them and answered,
"Healthy people don't need a doctor, but
sick people do. I didn't come to invite
good people to be my followers. I came
to invite sinners."

People Ask about Going without Eating

(Matthew 9.14-17; Luke 5.33-39)

[18]The followers of John the Baptist
and the Pharisees often went without
eating.[o] Some people came and asked
Jesus, "Why do the followers of John
and those of the Pharisees often go
without eating, while your disciples
never do?"
[19]Jesus answered:

[g]**1.40** *leprosy*: In biblical times the word "leprosy" was used for many different kinds of skin diseases. [h]**1.40** *and knelt down*: These words are not in some manuscripts. [i]**1.41** *felt sorry for*: Some manuscripts have "was angry with." [j]**1.44** *everyone will know that you have been healed*: People with leprosy had to be examined by a priest and told that they were well (that is, "clean") before they could once again live a normal life in the Jewish community. The gift that Moses commanded was the sacrifice of some lambs together with flour mixed with olive oil. [k]**2.1** *at home*: Or "in the house" (perhaps Simon Peter's home). [l]**2.4** *roof*: In Palestine the houses usually had a flat roof. Stairs on the outside led up to the roof that was made of beams and boards covered with packed earth. [m]**2.15** *Levi's house*: Or "Jesus' house." [n]**2.15** *tax collectors*: These were usually Jewish people who paid the Romans for the right to collect taxes. They were hated by other Jews who thought of them as traitors to their country and to their religion. [o]**2.18** *without eating*: The Jewish people sometimes went without eating (also called "fasting") to show their love for God or to show sorrow for their sins.

The friends of a bridegroom don't
go without eating while he is still
with them. 20But the time will come
when he will be taken from them.
Then they will go without eating.
21No one patches old clothes by
sewing on a piece of new cloth. The
new piece would shrink and tear a
bigger hole.
22No one pours new wine into old
wineskins. The wine would swell
and burst the old skins.[p] Then the
wine would be lost, and the skins
would be ruined. New wine must be
put into new wineskins.

A Question about the Sabbath

(Matthew 12.1-8; Luke 6.1-5)

23One Sabbath Jesus and his disciples
were walking through some wheat
fields. His disciples were picking grains
of wheat as they went along.[q] 24Some
Pharisees asked Jesus, "Why are your
disciples picking grain on the Sabbath?
They are not supposed to do that!"
25Jesus answered, "Haven't you read
what David did when he and his followers were hungry and in need? 26It was
during the time of Abiathar the high
priest. David went into the house of God
and ate the sacred loaves of bread that
only priests are allowed to eat. He also
gave some to his followers."
27Jesus finished by saying, "People
were not made for the good of the Sabbath. The Sabbath was made for the
good of people. 28So the Son of Man is
Lord over the Sabbath."

A Man with a Crippled Hand

(Matthew 12.9-14; Luke 6.6-11)

3 The next time that Jesus went into
the meeting place, a man with a
crippled hand was there. 2The Pharisees[r] wanted to accuse Jesus of doing
something wrong, and they kept watching to see if Jesus would heal him on the
Sabbath.
3Jesus told the man to stand up where
everyone could see him. 4Then he asked,
"On the Sabbath should we do good
deeds or evil deeds? Should we save
someone's life or destroy it?" But no one
said a word.
5Jesus was angry as he looked around
at the people. Yet he felt sorry for them
because they were so stubborn. Then he
told the man, "Stretch out your hand."
He did, and his bad hand was healed.
6The Pharisees left. And right away
they started making plans with Herod's
followers[s] to kill Jesus.

Large Crowds Come to Jesus

7Jesus led his disciples down to the
shore of the lake. Large crowds followed him from Galilee, Judea, 8and
Jerusalem. People came from Idumea,
as well as other places east of the Jordan River. They also came from the region around the cities of Tyre and
Sidon. All of these crowds came because they had heard what Jesus was
doing. 9He even had to tell his disciples
to get a boat ready to keep him from being crushed by the crowds.
10After Jesus had healed many people,
the other sick people begged him to let
them touch him. 11And whenever any
evil spirits saw Jesus, they would fall to
the ground and shout, "You are the Son
of God!" 12But Jesus warned the spirits
not to tell who he was.

Jesus Chooses His Twelve Apostles

(Matthew 10.1-4; Luke 6.12-16)

13Jesus decided to ask some of his disciples to go up on a mountain with him,
and they went. 14Then he chose twelve
of them to be his apostles,[t] so that they
could be with him. He also wanted to
send them out to preach 15and to force
out demons. 16Simon was one of the
twelve, and Jesus named him Peter.
17There were also James and John, the
two sons of Zebedee. Jesus called them
Boanerges, which means "Thunderbolts." 18Andrew, Philip, Bartholomew,
Matthew, Thomas, James son of Alphaeus, and Thaddaeus were also apostles. The others were Simon, known as
the Eager One,[u] 19and Judas Iscariot,[v]
who later betrayed Jesus.

Jesus and the Ruler of Demons

(Matthew 12.22-32; Luke 11.14-23; 12.10)

20Jesus went back home,[w] and once
again such a large crowd gathered that

[p]**2.22** *swell and burst the old skins*: While the juice from grapes was becoming wine, it would swell and stretch the skins in which it had been stored. If the skins were old and stiff, they would burst. [q]**2.23** *went along*: It was the custom to let hungry travelers pick grains of wheat. [r]**3.2** *Pharisees*: The Greek text has "they" (but see verse 6). [s]**3.6** *Herod's followers*: People who were political followers of the family of Herod the Great and his son Herod Antipas. [t]**3.14** *to be his apostles*: These words are not in some manuscripts. [u]**3.18.** *Eager One*: The Greek text has "Zealot," a name later given to the members of a Jewish group that resisted and fought against the Romans. [v]**3.19** *Iscariot*: This may mean "a man from Kerioth" (a place in Judea). But more probably it means "a man who was a liar" or "a man who was a betrayer." [w]**3.20** *went back home*: Or "entered a house" (perhaps the home of Simon Peter).

there was no chance even to eat. 21 When
Jesus' family heard what he was doing,
they thought he was crazy and went to
get him under control.
22 Some teachers of the Law of Moses
came from Jerusalem and said, "This
man is under the power of Beelzebul,
the ruler of demons! He is even forcing
out demons with the help of Beelzebul."
23 Jesus told the people to gather
around him. Then he spoke to them in
riddles and said:

How can Satan force himself out?
24 A nation whose people fight each
other won't last very long. 25 And a
family that fights won't last long either. 26 So if Satan fights against
himself, that will be the end of him.
27 How can anyone break into the
house of a strong man and steal his
things, unless he first ties up the
strong man? Then he can take
everything.
28 I promise you that any of the sinful things you say or do can be forgiven, no matter how terrible those
things are. 29 But if you speak against
the Holy Spirit, you can never be
forgiven. That sin will be held
against you forever.

30 Jesus said this because the people
were saying that he had an evil spirit in
him.

Jesus' Mother and Brothers

(Matthew 12.46-50; Luke 8.19-21)

31 Jesus' mother and brothers came
and stood outside. Then they sent someone with a message for him to come out
to them. 32 The crowd that was sitting
around Jesus told him, "Your mother
and your brothers and sisters[x] are outside and want to see you."
33 Jesus asked, "Who is my mother and
who are my brothers?" 34 Then he looked
at the people sitting around him and
said, "Here are my mother and my
brothers. 35 Anyone who obeys God is
my brother or sister or mother."

A Story about a Farmer

(Matthew 13.1-9; Luke 8.4-8)

4 The next time Jesus taught beside
Lake Galilee, a big crowd gathered.
It was so large that he had to sit in a
boat out on the lake, while the people
stood on the shore. 2 He used stories to
teach them many things, and this is part
of what he taught:

3 Now listen! A farmer went out to
scatter seed in a field. 4 While the
farmer was scattering the seed,
some of it fell along the road and
was eaten by birds. 5 Other seeds fell
on thin, rocky ground and quickly
started growing because the soil
wasn't very deep. 6 But when the sun
came up, the plants were scorched
and dried up, because they did not
have enough roots. 7 Some other
seeds fell where thornbushes grew
up and choked out the plants. So
they did not produce any grain. 8 But
a few seeds did fall on good ground
where the plants grew and produced
thirty or sixty or even a hundred
times as much as was scattered.

9 Then Jesus said, "If you have ears,
pay attention."

Why Jesus Used Stories

(Matthew 13.10-17; Luke 8.9, 10)

10 When Jesus was alone with the
twelve apostles and some others, they
asked him about these stories. 11 He answered:

I have explained the secret about
God's kingdom to you, but for others
I can use only stories. 12 The reason
is,

"These people will look
and look, but never see.
They will listen and listen,
but never understand.
If they did,
they would turn to God,
and he would forgive them."

Jesus Explains the Story about the Farmer

(Matthew 13.18-23; Luke 8.11-15)

13 Jesus told them:

If you don't understand this story,
you won't understand any others.
14 What the farmer is spreading is really the message about the kingdom.
15 The seeds that fell along the road
are the people who hear the message. But Satan soon comes and
snatches it away from them. 16 The
seeds that fell on rocky ground are
the people who gladly hear the message and accept it right away. 17 But
they don't have any roots, and they
don't last very long. As soon as life
gets hard or the message gets them
in trouble, they give up.
18 The seeds that fell among the
thornbushes are also people who
hear the message. 19 But they start
worrying about the needs of this life.
They are fooled by the desire to get
rich and to have all kinds of other
things. So the message gets choked
out, and they never produce anything. 20 The seeds that fell on good
ground are the people who hear and
welcome the message. They produce
thirty or sixty or even a hundred
times as much as was planted.

[x] 3.32 *and sisters*: These words are not in some manuscripts.

Light
(Luke 8.16-18)

21 Jesus also said:
You don't light a lamp and put it
under a clay pot or under a bed.
Don't you put a lamp on a lampstand? 22 There is nothing hidden
that will not be made public. There
is no secret that will not be well
known. 23 If you have ears, pay attention!
24 Listen carefully to what you
hear! The way you treat others will
be the way you will be treated—and
even worse. 25 Everyone who has
something will be given more. But
people who don't have anything will
lose what little they have.

Another Story about Seeds

26 Again Jesus said:
God's kingdom is like what happens when a farmer scatters seed in
a field. 27 The farmer sleeps at night
and is up and around during the day.
Yet the seeds keep sprouting and
growing, and he doesn't understand
how. 28 It is the ground that makes
the seeds sprout and grow into
plants that produce grain. 29 Then
when harvest season comes and the
grain is ripe, the farmer cuts it with
a sickle.[y]

A Mustard Seed
(Matthew 13.31, 32; Luke 13.18, 19)

30 Finally, Jesus said:
What is God's kingdom like? What
story can I use to explain it? 31 It is
like what happens when a mustard
seed is planted in the ground. It is
the smallest seed in all the world.
32 But once it is planted, it grows
larger than any garden plant. It even
puts out branches that are big
enough for birds to nest in its shade.

The Reason for Teaching with Stories
(Matthew 13.34, 35)

33 Jesus used many other stories when
he spoke to the people, and he taught
them as much as they could understand.
34 He did not tell them anything without
using stories. But when he was alone
with his disciples, he explained everything to them.

A Storm
(Matthew 8.23-27; Luke 8.22-25)

35 That evening, Jesus said to his disciples, "Let's cross to the east side." 36 So
they left the crowd, and his disciples
started across the lake with him in the
boat. Some other boats followed along.
37 Suddenly a windstorm struck the lake.
Waves started splashing into the boat,
and it was about to sink.
38 Jesus was in the back of the boat
with his head on a pillow, and he was
asleep. His disciples woke him and said,
"Teacher, don't you care that we're
about to drown?"
39 Jesus got up and ordered the wind
and the waves to be quiet. The wind
stopped, and everything was calm.
40 Jesus asked his disciples, "Why
were you afraid? Don't you have any
faith?"
41 Now they were more afraid than
ever and said to each other, "Who is
this? Even the wind and the waves obey
him!"

A Man with Evil Spirits
(Matthew 8.28-34; Luke 8.26-39)

5 Jesus and his disciples crossed Lake
Galilee and came to shore near the
town of Gerasa.[z] 2 When he was getting
out of the boat, a man with an evil spirit
quickly ran to him 3 from the graveyard[a]
where he had been living. No one was
able to tie the man up anymore, not
even with a chain. 4 He had often been
put in chains and leg irons, but he broke
the chains and smashed the leg irons.
No one could control him. 5 Night and
day he was in the graveyard or on the
hills, yelling and cutting himself with
stones.
6 When the man saw Jesus in the distance, he ran up to him and knelt down.
7 He shouted, "Jesus, Son of God in
heaven, what do you want with me?
Promise me in God's name that you
won't torture me!" 8 The man said this
because Jesus had already told the evil
spirit to come out of him.
9 Jesus asked, "What is your name?"
The man answered, "My name is Lots,
because I have 'lots' of evil spirits." 10 He
then begged Jesus not to send them
away.
11 Over on the hillside a large herd of
pigs was feeding. 12 So the evil spirits
begged Jesus, "Send us into those pigs!
Let us go into them." 13 Jesus let them
go, and they went out of the man and
into the pigs. The whole herd of about
two thousand pigs rushed down the
steep bank into the lake and drowned.
14 The men taking care of the pigs ran
to the town and the farms to spread the
news. Then the people came out to see
what had happened. 15 When they came
to Jesus, they saw the man who had
once been full of demons. He was sitting
there with his clothes on and in his right
mind, and they were terrified.

[y] **4.29** *sickle*: A knife with a long curved blade, used to cut grain and other crops.
[z] **5.1** *Gerasa*: Some manuscripts have "Gadara," and others have "Gergesa." [a] **5.3** *graveyard*: It was thought that demons and evil spirits lived in graveyards.

16 Everyone who had seen what had happened told about the man and the pigs. 17 Then the people started begging Jesus to leave their part of the country.

18 When Jesus was getting into the boat, the man begged to go with him. 19 But Jesus would not let him. Instead, he said, "Go home to your family and tell them how much the Lord has done for you and how good he has been to you."

20 The man went away into the region near the ten cities known as Decapolis[b] and began telling everyone how much Jesus had done for him. Everyone who heard what had happened was amazed.

A Dying Girl and a Sick Woman

(Matthew 9.18-26; Luke 8.40-56)

21 Once again Jesus got into the boat and crossed Lake Galilee.[c] Then as he stood on the shore, a large crowd gathered around him. 22 The person in charge of the Jewish meeting place was also there. His name was Jairus, and when he saw Jesus, he went over to him. He knelt at Jesus' feet 23 and started begging him for help. He said, "My daughter is about to die! Please come and touch her, so she will get well and live." 24 Jesus went with Jairus. Many people followed along and kept crowding around.

25 In the crowd was a woman who had been bleeding for twelve years. 26 She had gone to many doctors, and they had not done anything except cause her a lot of pain. She had paid them all the money she had. But instead of getting better, she only got worse.

27 The woman had heard about Jesus, so she came up behind him in the crowd and barely touched his clothes. 28 She had said to herself, "If I can just touch his clothes, I will get well." 29 As soon as she touched them, her bleeding stopped, and she knew she was well.

30 At that moment Jesus felt power go out from him. He turned to the crowd and asked, "Who touched my clothes?"

31 His disciples said to him, "Look at all these people crowding around you! How can you ask who touched you?" 32 But Jesus turned to see who had touched him.

33 The woman knew what had happened to her. She came shaking with fear and knelt down in front of Jesus. Then she told him the whole story.

34 Jesus said to the woman, "You are now well because of your faith. May God give you peace! You are healed, and you will no longer be in pain."

35 While Jesus was still speaking, some men came from Jairus' home and said, "Your daughter has died! Why bother the teacher anymore?"

36 Jesus heard[d] what they said, and he said to Jairus, "Don't worry. Just have faith!"

37 Jesus did not let anyone go with him except Peter and the two brothers, James and John. 38 They went home with Jairus and saw the people crying and making a lot of noise.[e] 39 Then Jesus went inside and said to them, "Why are you crying and carrying on like this? The child isn't dead. She is just asleep." 40 But the people laughed at him.

After Jesus had sent them all out of the house, he took the girl's father and mother and his three disciples and went to where she was. 41-42 He took the twelve-year-old girl by the hand and said, "Talitha, koum!"[f] which means, "Little girl, get up!" The girl got right up and started walking around.

Everyone was greatly surprised. 43 But Jesus ordered them not to tell anyone what had happened. Then he said, "Give her something to eat."

The People of Nazareth Turn against Jesus

(Matthew 13.53-58; Luke 4.16-30)

6 Jesus left and returned to his hometown[g] with his disciples. 2 The next Sabbath he taught in the Jewish meeting place. Many of the people who heard him were amazed and asked, "How can he do all this? Where did he get such wisdom and the power to work these miracles? 3 Isn't he the carpenter,[h] the son of Mary? Aren't James, Joseph, Judas, and Simon his brothers? Don't his sisters still live here in our town?" The people were very unhappy because of what he was doing.

4 But Jesus said, "Prophets are honored by everyone, except the people of their hometown and their relatives and their own family." 5 Jesus could not work any miracles there, except to heal a few sick people by placing his hands on them. 6 He was surprised that the people did not have any faith.

Instructions for the Twelve Apostles

(Matthew 10.5-15; Luke 9.1-6)

Jesus taught in all the neighboring villages. 7 Then he called together his

[b] **5.20** *the ten cities known as Decapolis*: A group of ten cities east of Samaria and Galilee, where the people followed the Greek way of life. [c] **5.21** *crossed Lake Galilee*: To the west side. [d] **5.36** *heard*: Or "ignored." [e] **5.38** *crying and making a lot of noise*: The Jewish people often hired mourners for funerals. [f] **5.41,42** *Talitha, koum*: These words are in Aramaic, a language spoken in Palestine during the time of Jesus. [g] **6.1** *hometown*: Nazareth. [h] **6.3** *carpenter*: The Greek word may also mean someone who builds or works with stone or brick.

twelve apostles and sent them out two
by two with power over evil spirits. 8He
told them, "You may take along a walking stick. But don't carry food or a traveling bag or any money. 9It's all right to
wear sandals, but don't take along a
change of clothes. 10When you are welcomed into a home, stay there until you
leave that town. 11If any place won't
welcome you or listen to your message,
leave and shake the dust from your feet[i]
as a warning to them."
12The apostles left and started telling
everyone to turn to God. 13They forced
out many demons and healed a lot of
sick people by putting olive oil[j] on them.

The Death of John the Baptist

(Matthew 14.1-12; Luke 9.7-9)

14Jesus became so well-known that
Herod the ruler[k] heard about him. Some
people thought he was John the Baptist,
who had come back to life with the
power to work miracles. 15Others
thought he was Elijah[l] or some other
prophet who had lived long ago. 16But
when Herod heard about Jesus, he said,
"This must be John! I had his head cut
off, and now he has come back to life."
17-18Herod had earlier married Herodias, the wife of his brother Philip. But
John had told him, "It isn't right for you
to take your brother's wife!" So, in order
to please Herodias, Herod arrested John
and put him in prison.
19Herodias had a grudge against John
and wanted to kill him. But she could
not do it 20because Herod was afraid of
John and protected him. He knew that
John was a good and holy man. Even
though Herod was confused by what
John said,[m] he was glad to listen to him.
And he often did.
21Finally, Herodias got her chance
when Herod gave a great birthday celebration for himself and invited his officials, his army officers, and the leaders
of Galilee. 22The daughter of Herodias[n]
came in and danced for Herod and his
guests. She pleased them so much that
Herod said, "Ask for anything, and it's
yours! 23I swear that I will give you as
much as half of my kingdom, if you
want it."
24The girl left and asked her mother,
"What do you think I should ask for?"
Her mother answered, "The head of
John the Baptist!"
25The girl hurried back and told
Herod, "Right now on a platter I want
the head of John the Baptist!"
26The king was very sorry for what he
had said. But he did not want to break
the promise he had made in front of his
guests. 27At once he ordered a guard to
cut off John's head there in prison.
28The guard put the head on a platter
and took it to the girl. Then she gave it
to her mother.
29When John's followers learned that
he had been killed, they took his body
and put it in a tomb.

Jesus Feeds Five Thousand

*(Matthew 14.13-21; Luke 9.10-17;
John 6.1-14)*

30After the apostles returned to
Jesus,[o] they told him everything they
had done and taught. 31But so many
people were coming and going that Jesus and the apostles did not even have a
chance to eat. Then Jesus said, "Let's go
to a place[p] where we can be alone and
get some rest." 32They left in a boat for a
place where they could be alone. 33But
many people saw them leave and figured out where they were going. So people from every town ran on ahead and
got there first.
34When Jesus got out of the boat, he
saw the large crowd that was like sheep
without a shepherd. He felt sorry for the
people and started teaching them many
things.
35That evening the disciples came to
Jesus and said, "This place is like a
desert, and it is already late. 36Let the
crowds leave, so they can go to the
farms and villages near here and buy
something to eat."
37Jesus replied, "You give them something to eat."
But they asked him, "Don't you know
that it would take almost a year's
wages[q] to buy all of these people something to eat?"
38Then Jesus said, "How much bread
do you have? Go and see!"
They found out and answered, "We
have five small loaves of bread[r] and two
fish." 39Jesus told his disciples to have
the people sit down on the green grass.

[i] **6.11** *shake the dust from your feet*: This was a way of showing rejection. [j] **6.13** *olive oil*:
The Jewish people used olive oil as a way of healing people. Sometimes olive oil is a symbol
for healing by means of a miracle (see James 5.14). [k] **6.14** *Herod the ruler*: Herod Antipas,
the son of Herod the Great. [l] **6.15** *Elijah*: Many of the Jewish people expected the prophet
Elijah to come and prepare the way for the Messiah. [m] **6.20** *was confused by what John
said*: Some manuscripts have "did many things because of what John said." [n] **6.22** *Herodias*:
Some manuscripts have "Herod." [o] **6.30** *the apostles returned to Jesus*: From the mission on
which he had sent them (see 6.7, 12, 13). [p] **6.31** *a place*: This was probably northeast of
Lake Galilee (see verse 45). [q] **6.37** *almost a year's wages*: The Greek text has "two hundred
silver coins." Each coin was the average day's wage for a worker. [r] **6.38** *small loaves of
bread*: These would have been flat and round or in the shape of a bun.

40 They sat down in groups of a hundred
and groups of fifty.
41 Jesus took the five loaves and the
two fish. He looked up toward heaven
and blessed the food. Then he broke the
bread and handed it to his disciples to
give to the people. He also divided the
two fish, so that everyone could have
some.
42 After everyone had eaten all they
wanted, 43 Jesus' disciples picked up
twelve large baskets of leftover bread
and fish.
44 There were five thousand men who
ate the food.

Jesus Walks on the Water
(Matthew 14.22-33; John 6.15-21)

45 Right away, Jesus made his disciples
get into the boat and start back across
to Bethsaida. But he stayed until he had
sent the crowds away. 46 Then he told
them good-by and went up on the side
of a mountain to pray.
47 Later that evening he was still there
by himself, and the boat was somewhere
in the middle of the lake. 48 He could see
that the disciples were struggling hard,
because they were rowing against the
wind. Not long before morning, Jesus
came toward them. He was walking on
the water and was about to pass the
boat.
49 When the disciples saw Jesus walking on the water, they thought he was a
ghost, and they started screaming. 50 All
of them saw him and were terrified. But
at that same time he said, "Don't worry!
I am Jesus. Don't be afraid." 51 He then
got into the boat with them, and the
wind died down. The disciples were
completely confused. 52 Their minds
were closed, and they could not understand the true meaning of the loaves of
bread.

Jesus Heals Sick People in Gennesaret
(Matthew 14.34-36)

53 Jesus and his disciples crossed the
lake and brought the boat to shore near
the town of Gennesaret. 54 As soon as
they got out of the boat, the people recognized Jesus. 55 So they ran all over
that part of the country to bring their
sick people to him on mats. They
brought them each time they heard
where he was. 56 In every village or farm
or marketplace where Jesus went, the
people brought their sick to him. They
begged him to let them just touch his
clothes, and everyone who did was
healed.

The Teaching of the Ancestors
(Matthew 15.1-9)

7 Some Pharisees and several teachers of the Law of Moses from
Jerusalem came and gathered around
Jesus. 2 They noticed that some of his
disciples ate without first washing their
hands.[s]
3 The Pharisees and many other Jewish
people obey the teachings of their ancestors. They always wash their hands in
the proper way[t] before eating. 4 None of
them will eat anything they buy in the
market until it is washed. They also follow a lot of other teachings, such as
washing cups, pitchers, and bowls.[u]
5 The Pharisees and teachers asked
Jesus, "Why don't your disciples obey
what our ancestors taught us to do?
Why do they eat without washing their
hands?"
6 Jesus replied:
You are nothing but show-offs!
The prophet Isaiah was right when
he wrote that God had said,

"All of you praise me
with your words,
but you never really
think about me.
7 It is useless for you
to worship me,
when you teach rules
made up by humans."

8 You disobey God's commands in
order to obey what humans have
taught. 9 You are good at rejecting
God's commands so that you can
follow your own teachings! 10 Didn't
Moses command you to respect your
father and mother? Didn't he tell
you to put to death all who curse
their parents? 11 But you let people
get by without helping their parents
when they should. You let them say
that what they own has been offered
to God.[v] 12 You won't let those people
help their parents. 13 And you ignore
God's commands in order to follow
your own teaching. You do a lot of
other things that are just as bad.

What Really Makes People Unclean
(Matthew 15.10-20)

14 Jesus called the crowd together
again and said, "Pay attention and try to
understand what I mean. 15-16 The food
that you put into your mouth doesn't

[s] **7.2** *without first washing their hands*: The Jewish people had strict laws about washing their hands before eating, especially if they had been out in public. [t] **7.3** *in the proper way*: The Greek text has "with the fist," but the exact meaning is not clear. It could mean "to the wrist" or "to the elbow." [u] **7.4** *bowls*: Some manuscripts add "and sleeping mats." [v] **7.11** *has been offered to God*: According to Jewish custom, when anything was offered to God, it could not be used for anyone else, not even for a person's parents.

make you unclean and unfit to worship
God. The bad words that come out of
your mouth are what make you unclean."[w]
17After Jesus and his disciples had left
the crowd and had gone into the house,
they asked him what these sayings
meant. 18He answered, "Don't you know
what I am talking about by now? You
surely know that the food you put into
your mouth cannot make you unclean.
19It doesn't go into your heart, but into
your stomach, and then out of your
body." By saying this, Jesus meant that
all foods were fit to eat.
20Then Jesus said:

What comes from your heart is
what makes you unclean. 21Out of
your heart come evil thoughts, vulgar deeds, stealing, murder, 22un-
faithfulness in marriage, greed,
meanness, deceit, indecency, envy,
insults, pride, and foolishness. 23All
of these come from your heart, and
they are what make you unfit to
worship God.

A Woman's Faith
(Matthew 15.21-28)

24Jesus left and went to the region
near the city of Tyre, where he stayed in
someone's home. He did not want people to know he was there, but they
found out anyway. 25A woman whose
daughter had an evil spirit in her heard
where Jesus was. And right away she
came and knelt down at his feet. 26The
woman was Greek and had been born in
the part of Syria known as Phoenicia.
She begged Jesus to force the demon
out of her daughter. 27But Jesus said,
"The children must first be fed! It isn't
right to take away their food and feed it
to dogs."[x]
28The woman replied, "Lord, even
dogs eat the crumbs that children drop
from the table."
29Jesus answered, "That's true! You
may go now. The demon has left your
daughter." 30When the woman got back
home, she found her child lying on the
bed. The demon had gone.

Jesus Heals a Man Who Was Deaf and Could Hardly Talk

31Jesus left the region around Tyre
and went by way of Sidon toward Lake
Galilee. He went through the land near
the ten cities known as Decapolis.[y]
32Some people brought to him a man
who was deaf and could hardly talk.
They begged Jesus just to touch him.
33After Jesus had taken him aside
from the crowd, he stuck his fingers in
the man's ears. Then he spit and put it
on the man's tongue. 34Jesus looked up
toward heaven, and with a groan he
said, "Effatha!"[z] which means "Open
up!" 35At once the man could hear, and
he had no more trouble talking clearly.
36Jesus told the people not to say anything about what he had done. But the
more he told them, the more they talked
about it. 37They were completely
amazed and said, "Everything he does is
good! He even heals people who cannot
hear or talk."

Jesus Feeds Four Thousand
(Matthew 15.32-39)

8 One day another large crowd gathered around Jesus. They had not
brought along anything to eat. So Jesus
called his disciples together and said, 2"I
feel sorry for these people. They have
been with me for three days, and they
don't have anything to eat. 3Some of
them live a long way from here. If I send
them away hungry, they might faint on
their way home."
4The disciples said, "This place is like
a desert. Where can we find enough
food to feed such a crowd?"
5Jesus asked them how much food
they had. They replied, "Seven small
loaves of bread."[a]
6After Jesus told the crowd to sit
down, he took the seven loaves and
blessed them. He then broke the loaves
and handed them to his disciples, who
passed them out to the crowd. 7They
also had a few little fish, and after Jesus
had blessed these, he told the disciples
to pass them around.
8-9The crowd of about four thousand
people ate all they wanted, and the leftovers filled seven large baskets.
As soon as Jesus had sent the people
away, 10he got into the boat with the disciples and crossed to the territory near
Dalmanutha.[b]

A Sign from Heaven
(Matthew 16.1-4)

11The Pharisees came out and started
an argument with Jesus. They wanted to
test him by asking for a sign from
heaven. 12Jesus groaned and said, "Why
are you always looking for a sign? I can
promise you that you will not be given
one!" 13Then he left them. He again got
into a boat and crossed over to the other
side of the lake.

[w]**7.15,16** *unclean*: Some manuscripts add, "If you have ears, pay attention." [x]**7.27** *feed it to dogs*: The Jewish people often referred to Gentiles as dogs. [y]**7.31** *the ten cities known as Decapolis*: See the note at 5.20. [z]**7.34** *Effatha*: This word is in Aramaic, a language spoken in Palestine during the time of Jesus. [a]**8.5** *small loaves of bread*: See the note at 6.38. [b]**8.10** *Dalmanutha*: The place is unknown.

The Yeast of the Pharisees and of Herod
(Matthew 16.5-12)

14 The disciples had forgotten to bring
any bread, and they had only one loaf
with them in the boat. 15 Jesus warned
them, "Watch out! Guard against the
yeast of the Pharisees and of Herod."[c]
16 The disciples talked this over and
said to each other, "He must be saying
this because we don't have any bread."
17 Jesus knew what they were thinking
and asked, "Why are you talking about
not having any bread? Don't you understand? Are your minds still closed?
18 Are your eyes blind and your ears
deaf? Don't you remember 19 how many
baskets of leftovers you picked up when
I fed those five thousand people with
only five small loaves of bread?"
"Yes," the disciples answered. "There
were twelve baskets."
20 Jesus then asked, "And how many
baskets of leftovers did you pick up
when I broke seven small loaves of
bread for those four thousand people?"
"Seven," they answered.
21 "Don't you know what I am talking
about by now?" Jesus asked.

Jesus Heals a Blind Man at Bethsaida

22 As Jesus and his disciples were going into Bethsaida, some people brought
a blind man to him and begged him to
touch the man. 23 Jesus took him by the
hand and led him out of the village,
where he spit into the man's eyes. He
placed his hands on the blind man and
asked him if he could see anything.
24 The man looked up and said, "I see
people, but they look like trees walking
around."
25 Once again Jesus placed his hands
on the man's eyes, and this time the
man stared. His eyes were healed, and
he saw everything clearly. 26 Jesus said
to him, "You may return home now, but
don't go into the village."

Who Is Jesus?
(Matthew 16.13-20; Luke 9.18-21)

27 Jesus and his disciples went to the
villages near the town of Caesarea
Philippi. As they were walking along, he
asked them, "What do people say about
me?"
28 The disciples answered, "Some say
you are John the Baptist or maybe Elijah.[d] Others say you are one of the
prophets."
29 Then Jesus asked them, "But who do
you say I am?"
"You are the Messiah!" Peter replied.
30 Jesus warned the disciples not to tell
anyone about him.

Jesus Speaks about His Suffering and Death
(Matthew 16.21-28; Luke 9.22-27)

31 Jesus began telling his disciples
what would happen to him. He said,
"The nation's leaders, the chief priests,
and the teachers of the Law of Moses
will make the Son of Man suffer terribly. He will be rejected and killed, but
three days later he will rise to life."
32 Then Jesus explained clearly what he
meant.
Peter took Jesus aside and told him to
stop talking like that. 33 But when Jesus
turned and saw the disciples, he corrected Peter. He said to him, "Satan, get
away from me! You are thinking like
everyone else and not like God."
34 Jesus then told the crowd and the
disciples to come closer, and he said:

> If any of you want to be my fol-
> lowers, you must forget about your-
> self. You must take up your cross and
> follow me. 35 If you want to save your
> life,[e] you will destroy it. But if you
> give up your life for me and for the
> good news, you will save it. 36 What
> will you gain, if you own the whole
> world but destroy yourself? 37 What
> could you give to get back your
> soul?
> 38 Don't be ashamed of me and my
> message among these unfaithful and
> sinful people! If you are, the Son of
> Man will be ashamed of you when
> he comes in the glory of his Father
> with the holy angels.

> 9 I can assure you that some of the
> people standing here will not die
> before they see God's kingdom
> come with power.

The True Glory of Jesus
(Matthew 17.1-13; Luke 9.28-36)

2 Six days later Jesus took Peter,
James, and John with him. They went
up on a high mountain, where they
could be alone. There in front of the disciples, Jesus was completely changed.
3 And his clothes became much whiter
than any bleach on earth could make
them. 4 Then Moses and Elijah were
there talking with Jesus.
5 Peter said to Jesus, "Teacher, it is
good for us to be here! Let us make
three shelters, one for you, one for
Moses, and one for Elijah." 6 But Peter
and the others were terribly frightened,
and he did not know what he was talking about.
7 The shadow of a cloud passed over
and covered them. From the cloud a
voice said, "This is my Son, and I love
him. Listen to what he says!" 8 At once

[c] 8.15 *Herod*: Herod Antipas, the son of Herod the Great. [d] 8.28 *Elijah*: See the note at 6.15.
[e] 8.35 *life*: In verses 35-37 the same Greek word is translated "life," "yourself," and "soul."

the disciples looked around, but they saw only Jesus.

9 As Jesus and his disciples were coming down the mountain, he told them not to say a word about what they had seen, until the Son of Man had been raised from death. 10 So they kept it to themselves. But they wondered what he meant by the words "raised from death."

11 The disciples asked Jesus, "Don't the teachers of the Law of Moses say that Elijah must come before the Messiah does?"

12 Jesus answered:

Elijah certainly will come[f] to get
everything ready. But don't the
Scriptures also say that the Son of
Man must suffer terribly and be rejected? 13 I can assure you that Elijah
has already come. And people
treated him just as they wanted to,
as the Scriptures say they would.

Jesus Heals a Boy

(Matthew 17.14-20; Luke 9.37-43a)

14 When Jesus and his three disciples came back down, they saw a large crowd around the other disciples. The teachers of the Law of Moses were arguing with them.

15 The crowd was really surprised to see Jesus, and everyone hurried over to greet him.

16 Jesus asked, "What are you arguing about?"

17 Someone from the crowd answered, "Teacher, I brought my son to you. A demon keeps him from talking. 18 Whenever the demon attacks my son, it throws him to the ground and makes him foam at the mouth and grit his teeth in pain. Then he becomes stiff. I asked your disciples to force out the demon, but they couldn't do it."

19 Jesus said, "You people don't have any faith! How much longer must I be with you? Why do I have to put up with you? Bring the boy to me."

20 They brought the boy, and as soon as the demon saw Jesus, it made the boy shake all over. He fell down and began rolling on the ground and foaming at the mouth.

21 Jesus asked the boy's father, "How long has he been like this?"

The man answered, "Ever since he was a child. 22 The demon has often tried to kill him by throwing him into a fire or into water. Please have pity and help us if you can!"

23 Jesus replied, "Why do you say 'if you can'? Anything is possible for someone who has faith!"

24 Right away the boy's father shouted, "I do have faith! Please help me to have even more."

25 When Jesus saw that a crowd was gathering fast, he spoke sternly to the evil spirit that had kept the boy from speaking or hearing. He said, "I order you to come out of the boy! Don't ever bother him again."

26 The spirit screamed and made the boy shake all over. Then it went out of him. The boy looked dead, and almost everyone said he was. 27 But Jesus took hold of his hand and helped him stand up.

28 After Jesus and the disciples had gone back home and were alone, they asked him, "Why couldn't we force out that demon?"

29 Jesus answered, "Only prayer can force out that kind of demon."

Jesus Again Speaks about His Death

(Matthew 17.22, 23; Luke 9.43b-45)

30 Jesus left with his disciples and started through Galilee. He did not want anyone to know about it, 31 because he was teaching the disciples that the Son of Man would be handed over to people who would kill him. But three days later he would rise to life. 32 The disciples did not understand what Jesus meant, and they were afraid to ask.

Who Is the Greatest?

(Matthew 18.1-5; Luke 9.46-48)

33 Jesus and his disciples went to his home in Capernaum. After they were inside the house, Jesus asked them, "What were you arguing about along the way?" 34 They had been arguing about which one of them was the greatest, and so they did not answer.

35 After Jesus sat down and told the twelve disciples to gather around him, he said, "If you want the place of honor, you must become a slave and serve others!"

36 Then Jesus had a child stand near him. He put his arm around the child and said, 37 "When you welcome even a child because of me, you welcome me. And when you welcome me, you welcome the one who sent me."

For or against Jesus

(Luke 9.49, 50)

38 John said, "Teacher, we saw a man using your name to force demons out of people. But he wasn't one of us, and we told him to stop."

39 Jesus said to his disciples:

Don't stop him! No one who
works miracles in my name will
soon turn and say something bad
about me. 40 Anyone who isn't
against us is for us. 41 And anyone
who gives you a cup of water in my

[f] **9.12** *Elijah certainly will come*: See the note at 6.15.

name, just because you belong to
me, will surely be rewarded.

Temptations To Sin

(Matthew 18.6-9; Luke 17.1, 2)

42 It will be terrible for people who
cause even one of my little followers
to sin. Those people would be better
off thrown into the ocean with a
heavy stone tied around their necks.
43-44 So if your hand causes you to
sin, cut it off! You would be better off
to go into life crippled than to have
two hands and be thrown into the
fires of hell that never go out.[g] 45-46 If
your foot causes you to sin, chop it
off. You would be better off to go into
life lame than to have two feet and
be thrown into hell.[h] 47 If your eye
causes you to sin, get rid of it. You
would be better off to go into God's
kingdom with only one eye than to
have two eyes and be thrown into
hell. 48 The worms there never die,
and the fire never stops burning.
49 Everyone must be salted with
fire.[i]
50 Salt is good. But if it no longer
tastes like salt, how can it be made
salty again? Have salt among you
and live at peace with each other.[j]

Teaching about Divorce

(Matthew 19.1-12; Luke 16.18)

10 After Jesus left, he went to Judea
and then on to the other side of
the Jordan River. Once again large
crowds came to him, and as usual, he
taught them.
2 Some Pharisees wanted to test Jesus.
So they came up to him and asked if it
was right for a man to divorce his wife.
3 Jesus asked them, "What does the Law
of Moses say about that?"
4 They answered, "Moses allows a man
to write out divorce papers and send his
wife away."
5 Jesus replied, "Moses gave you this
law because you are so heartless. 6 But
in the beginning God made a man and a
woman. 7 That's why a man leaves his
father and mother and gets married. 8 He
becomes like one person with his wife.
Then they are no longer two people, but
one. 9 And no one should separate a couple that God has joined together."
10 When Jesus and his disciples were
back in the house, they asked him about
what he had said. 11 He told them, "A
man who divorces his wife and marries
someone else is unfaithful to his wife.
12 A woman who divorces her husband[k]
and marries again is also unfaithful."

Jesus Blesses Little Children

(Matthew 19.13-15; Luke 18.15-17)

13 Some people brought their children
to Jesus so that he could bless them by
placing his hands on them. But his disciples told the people to stop bothering
him.
14 When Jesus saw this, he became angry and said, "Let the children come to
me! Don't try to stop them. People who
are like these little children belong to
the kingdom of God.[l] 15 I promise you
that you cannot get into God's kingdom,
unless you accept it the way a child
does." 16 Then Jesus took the children in
his arms and blessed them by placing
his hands on them.

A Rich Man

(Matthew 19.16-30; Luke 18.18-30)

17 As Jesus was walking down a road,
a man ran up to him. He knelt down,
and asked, "Good teacher, what can I do
to have eternal life?"
18 Jesus replied, "Why do you call me
good? Only God is good. 19 You know the
commandments. 'Do not murder. Be
faithful in marriage. Do not steal. Do
not tell lies about others. Do not cheat.
Respect your father and mother.' "
20 The man answered, "Teacher, I have
obeyed all these commandments since I
was a young man."
21 Jesus looked closely at the man. He
liked him and said, "There's one thing
you still need to do. Go sell everything
you own. Give the money to the poor,
and you will have riches in heaven.
Then come with me."
22 When the man heard Jesus say this,
he went away gloomy and sad because
he was very rich.
23 Jesus looked around and said to his
disciples, "It's hard for rich people to get
into God's kingdom!" 24 The disciples
were shocked to hear this. So Jesus told
them again, "It's terribly hard[m] to get

[g] **9.43,44** *never go out*: Some manuscripts add, "The worms there never die, and the fire never stops burning." [h] **9.45,46** *thrown into hell*: Some manuscripts add, "The worms there never die, and the fire never stops burning." [i] **9.49** *salted with fire*: Some manuscripts add "and every sacrifice will be seasoned with salt." The verse may mean that Christ's followers must suffer because of their faith. [j] **9.50** *Have salt among you and live at peace with each other*: This may mean that when Christ's followers have to suffer because of their faith, they must still try to live at peace with each other. [k] **10.12** *A woman who divorces her husband*: Roman law let a woman divorce her husband, but Jewish law did not let a woman do this. [l] **10.14** *People who are like these little children belong to the kingdom of God*: Or "The kingdom of God belongs to people who are like these little children." [m] **10.24** *hard*: Some manuscripts add "for people who trust in their wealth." Others add "for the rich."

into God's kingdom! 25 In fact, it's easier
for a camel to go through the eye of a
needle than for a rich person to get into
God's kingdom."
26 Jesus' disciples were even more
amazed. They asked each other, "How
can anyone ever be saved?"
27 Jesus looked at them and said,
"There are some things that people cannot do, but God can do anything."
28 Peter replied, "Remember, we left
everything to be your followers!"
29 Jesus told him:

> You can be sure that anyone who
> gives up home or brothers or sisters
> or mother or father or children or
> land for me and for the good news
> 30 will be rewarded. In this world
> they will be given a hundred times
> as many houses and brothers and
> sisters and mothers and children
> and pieces of land, though they will
> also be mistreated. And in the world
> to come, they will have eternal life.
> 31 But many who are now first will be
> last, and many who are now last will
> be first.

Jesus Again Tells about His Death
(Matthew 20.17-19; Luke 18.31-34)

32 The disciples were confused as Jesus led them toward Jerusalem, and his
other followers were afraid. Once again,
Jesus took the twelve disciples aside
and told them what was going to happen to him. He said:

> 33 We are now on our way to
> Jerusalem where the Son of Man
> will be handed over to the chief
> priests and the teachers of the Law
> of Moses. They will sentence him to
> death and hand him over to foreign-
> ers,[n] 34 who will make fun of him and
> spit on him. They will beat him and
> kill him. But three days later he will
> rise to life.

The Request of James and John
(Matthew 20.20-28)

35 James and John, the sons of
Zebedee, came up to Jesus and asked,
"Teacher, will you do us a favor?"
36 Jesus asked them what they wanted,
37 and they answered, "When you come
into your glory, please let one of us sit at
your right side and the other at your
left."[o]
38 Jesus told them, "You don't really
know what you're asking! Are you able
to drink from the cup[p] that I must soon
drink from or be baptized as I must be
baptized?"[q]
39 "Yes, we are!" James and John answered.
Then Jesus replied, "You certainly will
drink from the cup from which I must
drink. And you will be baptized just as I
must! 40 But it isn't for me to say who
will sit at my right side and at my left.
That is for God to decide."
41 When the ten other disciples heard
this, they were angry with James and
John. 42 But Jesus called the disciples together and said:

> You know that those foreigners
> who call themselves kings like to or-
> der their people around. And their
> great leaders have full power over
> the people they rule. 43 But don't act
> like them. If you want to be great,
> you must be the servant of all the
> others. 44 And if you want to be first,
> you must be everyone's slave. 45 The
> Son of Man did not come to be a
> slave master, but a slave who will
> give his life to rescue[r] many people.

Jesus Heals Blind Bartimaeus
(Matthew 20.29-34; Luke 18.35-43)

46 Jesus and his disciples went to Jericho. And as they were leaving, they
were followed by a large crowd. A blind
beggar by the name of Bartimaeus son
of Timaeus was sitting beside the road.
47 When he heard that it was Jesus from
Nazareth, he shouted, "Jesus, Son of
David,[s] have pity on me!" 48 Many people told the man to stop, but he shouted
even louder, "Son of David, have pity on
me!"
49 Jesus stopped and said, "Call him
over!"
They called out to the blind man and
said, "Don't be afraid! Come on! He
is calling for you." 50 The man threw off
his coat as he jumped up and ran to
Jesus.
51 Jesus asked, "What do you want me
to do for you?"
The blind man answered, "Master,[t] I
want to see!"
52 Jesus told him, "You may go. Your
eyes are healed because of your faith."
Right away the man could see, and he
went down the road with Jesus.

[n] **10.33** *foreigners*: The Romans who ruled Judea at this time. [o] **10.37** *right side . . . left*: The most powerful people in a kingdom sat at the right and left side of the king. [p] **10.38** *drink from the cup*: In the Scriptures a "cup" is sometimes used as a symbol of suffering. To "drink from the cup" would be to suffer. [q] **10.38** *as I must be baptized*: Baptism is used with the same meaning that "cup" has in this verse. [r] **10.45** *rescue*: The Greek word often, though not always, means the payment of a price to free a slave or a prisoner. [s] **10.47** *Son of David*: The Jewish people expected the Messiah to be from the family of King David, and for this reason the Messiah was often called the "Son of David." [t] **10.51** *Master*: A Hebrew word that may also mean "Teacher."

Jesus Enters Jerusalem
(Matthew 21.1-11; Luke 19.28-40;
John 12.12-19)

11 Jesus and his disciples reached
Bethphage and Bethany near the
Mount of Olives. When they were getting close to Jerusalem, Jesus sent two
of them on ahead. 2He told them, "Go
into the next village. As soon as you enter it, you will find a young donkey that
has never been ridden. Untie the donkey
and bring it here. 3If anyone asks why
you are doing that, say, 'The Lord[u]
needs it and will soon bring it back.' "
4The disciples left and found the donkey tied near a door that faced the
street. While they were untying it, 5some
of the people standing there asked,
"Why are you untying the donkey?"
6They told them what Jesus had said,
and the people let them take it.
7The disciples led the donkey to Jesus.
They put some of their clothes on its
back, and Jesus got on. 8Many people
spread clothes on the road, while others
went to cut branches from the fields.[v]
9In front of Jesus and behind him,
people went along shouting,

"Hooray![w]
God bless the one who comes
in the name of the Lord!
10 God bless the coming kingdom
of our ancestor David.
Hooray for God
in heaven above!"

11After Jesus had gone to Jerusalem,
he went into the temple and looked
around at everything. But since it was
already late in the day, he went back to
Bethany with the twelve disciples.

Jesus Puts a Curse on a Fig Tree
(Matthew 21.18, 19)

12When Jesus and his disciples left
Bethany the next morning, he was hungry. 13From a distance Jesus saw a fig
tree covered with leaves, and he went to
see if there were any figs on the tree.
But there were not any, because it
wasn't the season for figs. 14So Jesus
said to the tree, "Never again will anyone eat fruit from this tree!" The disciples heard him say this.

Jesus in the Temple
(Matthew 21.12-17; Luke 19.45-48;
John 2.13-22)

15After Jesus and his disciples
reached Jerusalem, he went into the
temple and began chasing out everyone
who was selling and buying. He turned
over the tables of the moneychangers
and the benches of those who were selling doves. 16Jesus would not let anyone
carry things through the temple. 17Then
he taught the people and said, "The
Scriptures say, 'My house should be
called a place of worship for all nations.'
But you have made it a place where robbers hide!"
18The chief priests and the teachers of
the Law of Moses heard what Jesus
said, and they started looking for a way
to kill him. They were afraid of him,
because the crowds were completely
amazed at his teaching.
19That evening, Jesus and the disciples went outside the city.

A Lesson from the Fig Tree
(Matthew 21.20-22)

20As the disciples walked past the fig
tree the next morning, they noticed that
it was completely dried up, roots and
all. 21Peter remembered what Jesus
had said to the tree. Then Peter said,
"Teacher, look! The tree you put a curse
on has dried up."
22Jesus told his disciples:
Have faith in God! 23If you have
faith in God and don't doubt, you
can tell this mountain to get up and
jump into the sea, and it will.
24Everything you ask for in prayer
will be yours, if you only have faith.
25-26Whenever you stand up to
pray, you must forgive what others
have done to you. Then your Father
in heaven will forgive your sins.[x]

A Question about Jesus' Authority
(Matthew 21.23-27; Luke 20.1-8)

27Jesus and his disciples returned to
Jerusalem. And as he was walking
through the temple, the chief priests, the
nation's leaders, and the teachers of the
Law of Moses came over to him. 28They
asked, "What right do you have to do
these things? Who gave you this authority?"
29Jesus answered, "I have just one
question to ask you. If you answer it, I
will tell you where I got the right to do
these things. 30Who gave John the right
to baptize? Was it God in heaven or
merely some human being?"
31They thought it over and said to
each other, "We can't say that God gave
John this right. Jesus will ask us why we
didn't believe John. 32On the other hand,
these people think that John was a
prophet. So we can't say that it was

[u]11.3 *The Lord*: Or "The master of the donkey." [v]11.8 *spread . . . branches from the fields*: This was one way that the Jewish people welcomed a famous person. [w]11.9 *Hooray*: This translates a word that can mean "please save us." But it is most often used as a shout of praise to God. [x]11.25,26 *your sins*: Some manuscripts add, "But if you do not forgive others, God will not forgive you."

merely some human who gave John the
right to baptize."
They were afraid of the crowd 33and
told Jesus, "We don't know."
Jesus replied, "Then I won't tell you
who gave me the right to do what I do."

Renters of a Vineyard

(Matthew 21.33-46; Luke 20.9-19)

12 Jesus then told them this story:
A farmer once planted a vineyard. He built a wall around it and
dug a pit to crush the grapes in. He
also built a lookout tower. Then he
rented out his vineyard and left the
country.
2When it was harvest time, he sent
a servant to get his share of the
grapes. 3The renters grabbed the
servant. They beat him up and sent
him away without a thing.
4The owner sent another servant,
but the renters beat him on the head
and insulted him terribly. 5Then the
man sent another servant, and they
killed him. He kept sending servant
after servant. They beat some of
them and killed others.
6The owner had a son he loved
very much. Finally, he sent his son to
the renters because he thought they
would respect him. 7But they said to
themselves, "Someday he will own
this vineyard. Let's kill him! That
way we can have it all for ourselves." 8So they grabbed the
owner's son and killed him. Then
they threw his body out of the vineyard.
9Jesus asked, "What do you think the
owner of the vineyard will do? He will
come and kill those renters and let
someone else have his vineyard. 10You
surely know that the Scriptures say,

'The stone that the builders
tossed aside
is now the most important
stone of all.
11 This is something
the Lord has done,
and it is amazing to us.' "

12The leaders knew that Jesus was really talking about them, and they
wanted to arrest him. But because they
were afraid of the crowd, they let him
alone and left.

Paying Taxes

(Matthew 22.15-22; Luke 20.20-26)

13The Pharisees got together with
Herod's followers.[y] Then they sent some
men to trick Jesus into saying something wrong. 14They went to him and
said, "Teacher, we know that you are
honest. You treat everyone with the
same respect, no matter who they are.
And you teach the truth about what God
wants people to do. Tell us, should we
pay taxes to the Emperor or not?"
15Jesus knew what they were up to,
and he said, "Why are you trying to test
me? Show me a coin!"
16They brought him a silver coin, and
he asked, "Whose picture and name are
on it?"
"The Emperor's," they answered.
17Then Jesus told them, "Give the Emperor what belongs to him and give God
what belongs to God." The men were
amazed at Jesus.

Life in the Future World

(Matthew 22.23-33; Luke 20.27-40)

18The Sadducees did not believe that
people would rise to life after death. So
some of them came to Jesus and said:
19Teacher, Moses wrote that if a
married man dies and has no children, his brother should marry the
widow. Their first son would then be
thought of as the son of the dead
brother. 20There were once seven
brothers. The first one married, but
died without having any children.
21The second brother married his
brother's widow, and he also died
without having children. The same
thing happened to the third brother,
22and finally to all seven brothers. At
last the woman died. 23When God
raises people from death, whose
wife will this woman be? After all,
she had been married to all seven
brothers.
24Jesus answered:
You are completely wrong! You
don't know what the Scriptures
teach. And you don't know anything
about the power of God. 25When
God raises people to life, they won't
marry. They will be like the angels
in heaven. 26You surely know about
people being raised to life. You know
that in the story about Moses and
the burning bush, God said, "I am
the God worshiped by Abraham,
Isaac, and Jacob."[z] 27He isn't the
God of the dead, but of the living.
You Sadducees are all wrong.

The Most Important Commandment

(Matthew 22.34-40; Luke 10.25-28)

28One of the teachers of the Law of
Moses came up while Jesus and the Sadducees were arguing. When he heard

[y]**12.13** *Herod's followers*: People who were political followers of the family of Herod the Great and his son Herod Antipas. [z]**12.26** *"I am the God worshiped by Abraham, Isaac, and Jacob"*: Jesus argues that if God is worshiped by these three, they must still be alive, because he is the God of the living.

Jesus give a good answer, he asked
him, "What is the most important commandment?"
29 Jesus answered, "The most important one says: 'People of Israel, you have
only one Lord and God. 30 You must love
him with all your heart, soul, mind, and
strength.' 31 The second most important
commandment says: 'Love others as
much as you love yourself.' No other
commandment is more important than
these."
32 The man replied, "Teacher, you are
certainly right to say there is only one
God. 33 It is also true that we must love
God with all our heart, mind, and
strength, and that we must love others
as much as we love ourselves. These
commandments are more important
than all the sacrifices and offerings that
we could possibly make."
34 When Jesus saw that the man had
given a sensible answer, he told him,
"You are not far from God's kingdom."
After this, no one dared ask Jesus any
more questions.

About David's Son
(Matthew 22.41-46; Luke 20.41-44)

35 As Jesus was teaching in the temple,
he said, "How can the teachers of the
Law of Moses say that the Messiah will
come from the family of King David?
36 The Holy Spirit led David to say,

'The Lord said to my Lord:
Sit at my right side[a]
until I make your enemies
into a footstool for you.'

37 If David called the Messiah his Lord,
how can the Messiah be his son?"[b]
The large crowd enjoyed listening to
Jesus teach.

Jesus Condemns the Pharisees and the Teachers of the Law of Moses
(Matthew 23.1-36; Luke 20.45-47)

38 As Jesus was teaching, he said:
Guard against the teachers of the
Law of Moses! They love to walk
around in long robes and be greeted
in the market. 39 They like the front
seats in the meeting places and the
best seats at banquets. 40 But they
cheat widows out of their homes and
pray long prayers just to show off.
They will be punished most of all.

A Widow's Offering
(Luke 21.1-4)

41 Jesus was sitting in the temple near
the offering box and watching people
put in their gifts. He noticed that many
rich people were giving a lot of money.
42 Finally, a poor widow came up and put
in two coins that were worth only a few
pennies. 43 Jesus told his disciples to
gather around him. Then he said:
I tell you that this poor widow has
put in more than all the others.
44 Everyone else gave what they
didn't need. But she is very poor and
gave everything she had. Now she
doesn't have a cent to live on.

The Temple Will Be Destroyed
(Matthew 24.1, 2; Luke 21.5, 6)

13 As Jesus was leaving the temple,
one of his disciples said to him,
"Teacher, look at these beautiful stones
and wonderful buildings!"
2 Jesus replied, "Do you see these huge
buildings? They will certainly be torn
down! Not one stone will be left in
place."

Warning about Trouble
(Matthew 24.3-14; Luke 21.7-19)

3 Later, as Jesus was sitting on the
Mount of Olives across from the temple,
Peter, James, John, and Andrew came to
him in private. 4 They asked, "When will
these things happen? What will be the
sign that they are about to take place?"
5 Jesus answered:
Watch out and don't let anyone
fool you! 6 Many will come and claim
to be me. They will use my name
and fool many people.
7 When you hear about wars and
threats of wars, don't be afraid.
These things will have to happen
first, but that isn't the end. 8 Nations
and kingdoms will go to war against
each other. There will be earthquakes in many places, and people
will starve to death. But this is just
the beginning of troubles.
9 Be on your guard! You will be
taken to courts and beaten with
whips in their meeting places. And
because of me, you will have to
stand before rulers and kings to tell
about your faith. 10 But before the
end comes, the good news must be
preached to all nations.
11 When you are arrested, don't
worry about what you will say. You
will be given the right words when
the time comes. But you will not really be the ones speaking. Your
words will come from the Holy
Spirit.
12 Brothers and sisters will betray
each other and have each other put
to death. Parents will betray their
own children, and children will turn
against their parents and have them
killed. 13 Everyone will hate you
because of me. But if you keep on

[a] **12.36** *right side*: The place of power and honor.

[b] **12.37** *David . . . his son*: See the note at 10.47.

being faithful right to the end, you will be saved.

The Horrible Thing

(Matthew 24.15-21; Luke 21.20-24)

14 Someday you will see that "Horrible Thing" where it should not be.[c] Everyone who reads this must try to understand! If you are living in Judea at that time, run to the mountains. 15 If you are on the roof[d] of your house, don't go inside to get anything. 16 If you are out in the field, don't go back for your coat. 17 It will be an awful time for women who are expecting babies or nursing young children. 18 Pray that it won't happen in winter.[e] 19 This will be the worst time of suffering since God created the world, and nothing this terrible will ever happen again. 20 If the Lord doesn't make the time shorter, no one will be left alive. But because of his chosen and special ones, he will make the time shorter.

21 If someone should say, "Here is the Messiah!" or "There he is!" don't believe it. 22 False messiahs and false prophets will come and work miracles and signs. They will even try to fool God's chosen ones. 23 But be on your guard! That's why I am telling you these things now.

When the Son of Man Appears

(Matthew 24.29-31; Luke 21.25-28)

24 In those days, right after that time of suffering,

"The sun will become dark,
and the moon
will no longer shine.
25 The stars will fall,
and the powers in the sky[f]
will be shaken."

26 Then the Son of Man will be seen coming in the clouds with great power and glory. 27 He will send his angels to gather his chosen ones from all over the earth.

A Lesson from a Fig Tree

(Matthew 24.32-35; Luke 21.29-33)

28 Learn a lesson from a fig tree. When its branches sprout and start putting out leaves, you know summer is near. 29 So when you see all these things happening, you will know that the time has almost come.[g] 30 You can be sure that some of the people of this generation will still be alive when all this happens. 31 The sky and the earth will not last forever, but my words will.

No One Knows the Day or Time

(Matthew 24.36-44)

32 No one knows the day or the time. The angels in heaven don't know, and the Son himself doesn't know. Only the Father knows. 33 So watch out and be ready! You don't know when the time will come. 34 It is like what happens when a man goes away for a while and places his servants in charge of everything. He tells each of them what to do, and he orders the guard to keep alert. 35 So be alert! You don't know when the master of the house will come back. It could be in the evening or at midnight or before dawn or in the morning. 36 But if he comes suddenly, don't let him find you asleep. 37 I tell everyone just what I have told you. Be alert!

A Plot To Kill Jesus

(Matthew 26.1-5; Luke 22.1, 2; John 11.45-53)

14 It was now two days before Passover and the Festival of Thin Bread. The chief priests and the teachers of the Law of Moses were planning how they could sneak around and have Jesus arrested and put to death. 2 They were saying, "We must not do it during the festival, because the people will riot."

At Bethany

(Matthew 26.6-13; John 12.1-8)

3 Jesus was eating in Bethany at the home of Simon, who once had leprosy,[h] when a woman came in with a very expensive bottle of sweet-smelling perfume.[i] After breaking it open, she poured the perfume on Jesus' head. 4 This made some of the guests angry, and they complained, "Why such a waste? 5 We could have sold this perfume for more than three hundred silver coins and given the money to the poor!" So they started saying cruel things to the woman.

6 But Jesus said:

Leave her alone! Why are you bothering her? She has done a beautiful thing for me. 7 You will always have the poor with you. And whenever you want to, you can give to

[c] **13.14** *where it should not be*: Probably the holy place in the temple. [d] **13.15** *roof*: See the note at 2.4. [e] **13.18** *in winter*: In Palestine the winters are cold and rainy and make travel difficult. [f] **13.25** *the powers in the sky*: In ancient times people thought that the stars were spiritual powers. [g] **13.29** *the time has almost come*: Or "he (that is, the Son of Man) will soon be here." [h] **14.3** *leprosy*: In biblical times the word "leprosy" was used for many different skin diseases. [i] **14.3** *sweet-smelling perfume*: The Greek text has "perfume made of pure spikenard," a plant used to make perfume.

them. But you won't always have me
here with you. 8She has done all she
could by pouring perfume on my
body to prepare it for burial. 9You
may be sure that wherever the good
news is told all over the world, people will remember what she has
done. And they will tell others.

Judas and the Chief Priests

(Matthew 26.14-16; Luke 22.3-6)

10Judas Iscariot[j] was one of the twelve
disciples. He went to the chief priests
and offered to help them arrest Jesus.
11They were glad to hear this, and they
promised to pay him. So Judas started
looking for a good chance to betray Jesus.

Jesus Eats with His Disciples

(Matthew 26.17-25; Luke 22.7-14, 21-23; John 13.21-30)

12It was the first day of the Festival of
Thin Bread, and the Passover lambs
were being killed. Jesus' disciples asked
him, "Where do you want us to prepare
the Passover meal?"
13Jesus said to two of the disciples,
"Go into the city, where you will meet a
man carrying a jar of water.[k] Follow
him, 14and when he goes into a house,
say to the owner, 'Our teacher wants to
know if you have a room where he can
eat the Passover meal with his disciples.'
15The owner will take you upstairs and
show you a large room furnished and
ready for you to use. Prepare the meal
there."
16The two disciples went into the city
and found everything just as Jesus had
told them. So they prepared the
Passover meal.
17-18While Jesus and the twelve disciples were eating together that evening,
he said, "The one who will betray me is
now eating with me."
19This made the disciples sad, and one
after another they said to Jesus, "You
surely don't mean me!"
20He answered, "It is one of you
twelve men who is eating from this dish
with me. 21The Son of Man will die, just
as the Scriptures say. But it is going to
be terrible for the one who betrays me.
That man would be better off if he had
never been born."

The Lord's Supper

(Matthew 26.26-30; Luke 22.14-23; 1 Corinthians 11.23-25)

22During the meal Jesus took some
bread in his hands. He blessed the bread
and broke it. Then he gave it to his disciples and said, "Take this. It is my body."
23Jesus picked up a cup of wine and
gave thanks to God. He gave it to his disciples, and they all drank some. 24Then
he said, "This is my blood, which is
poured out for many people, and with it
God makes his agreement. 25From now
on I will not drink any wine, until I drink
new wine in God's kingdom." 26Then they
sang a hymn and went out to the Mount
of Olives.

Peter's Promise

(Matthew 26.31-35; Luke 22.31-34; John 13.36-38)

27Jesus said to his disciples, "All of
you will reject me, as the Scriptures say,

'I will strike down
the shepherd,
and the sheep
will be scattered.'

28But after I am raised to life, I will go
ahead of you to Galilee."
29Peter spoke up, "Even if all the others reject you, I never will!"
30Jesus replied, "This very night before a rooster crows twice, you will say
three times that you don't know me."
31But Peter was so sure of himself that
he said, "Even if I have to die with you, I
will never say that I don't know you!"
All the others said the same thing.

Jesus Prays

(Matthew 26.36-46; Luke 22.39-46)

32Jesus went with his disciples to a
place called Gethsemane, and he told
them, "Sit here while I pray."
33Jesus took along Peter, James, and
John. He was sad and troubled and
34told them, "I am so sad that I feel as if
I am dying. Stay here and keep awake
with me."
35-36Jesus walked on a little way. Then
he knelt down on the ground and
prayed, "Father,[l] if it is possible, don't let
this happen to me! Father, you can do
anything. Don't make me suffer by having me drink from this cup.[m] But do
what you want, and not what I want."
37When Jesus came back and found
the disciples sleeping, he said to Simon
Peter, "Are you asleep? Can't you stay
awake for just one hour? 38Stay awake
and pray that you won't be tested. You
want to do what is right, but you are
weak."
39Jesus went back and prayed the
same prayer. 40But when he returned to
the disciples, he found them sleeping
again. They simply could not keep their

[j] **14.10** *Iscariot*: See the note at 3.19. [k] **14.13** *a man carrying a jar of water*: A male slave carrying water could mean that the family was rich. [l] **14.35,36** *Father*: The Greek text has "Abba," which is an Aramaic word meaning "father." [m] **14.35,36** *by having me drink from this cup*: See the note at 10.38.

eyes open, and they did not know what
to say.
41When Jesus returned to the disciples
the third time, he said, "Are you still
sleeping and resting?[n] Enough of that!
The time has come for the Son of Man
to be handed over to sinners. 42Get up!
Let's go. The one who will betray me is
already here."

Jesus Is Arrested

(Matthew 26.47-56; Luke 22.47-53; John 18.3-12)

43Jesus was still speaking, when Judas
the betrayer came up. He was one of the
twelve disciples, and a mob of men
armed with swords and clubs were with
him. They had been sent by the chief
priests, the nation's leaders, and the
teachers of the Law of Moses. 44Judas
had told them ahead of time, "Arrest the
man I greet with a kiss.[o] Tie him up
tight and lead him away."
45Judas walked right up to Jesus and
said, "Teacher!" Then Judas kissed him,
46and the men grabbed Jesus and arrested him.
47Someone standing there pulled out a
sword. He struck the servant of the high
priest and cut off his ear.
48Jesus said to the mob, "Why do you
come with swords and clubs to arrest
me like a criminal? 49Day after day I
was with you and taught in the temple,
and you didn't arrest me. But what the
Scriptures say must come true."
50All of Jesus' disciples ran off and
left him. 51One of them was a young
man who was wearing only a linen
cloth. And when the men grabbed him,
52he left the cloth behind and ran away
naked.

Jesus Is Questioned by the Council

(Matthew 26.57-68; Luke 22.54, 55, 63-71; John 18.13, 14, 19-24)

53Jesus was led off to the high priest.
Then the chief priests, the nation's leaders, and the teachers of the Law of
Moses all met together. 54Peter had followed at a distance. And when he
reached the courtyard of the high
priest's house, he sat down with the
guards to warm himself beside a fire.
55The chief priests and the whole
council tried to find someone to accuse
Jesus of a crime, so they could put him
to death. But they could not find anyone
to accuse him. 56Many people did tell
lies against Jesus, but they did not agree
on what they said. 57Finally, some men
stood up and lied about him. They said,
58"We heard him say he would tear
down this temple that we built. He also
claimed that in three days he would
build another one without any help."
59But even then they did not agree on
what they said.
60The high priest stood up in the council and asked Jesus, "Why don't you say
something in your own defense? Don't
you hear the charges they are making
against you?" 61But Jesus kept quiet and
did not say a word. The high priest
asked him another question, "Are you
the Messiah, the Son of the glorious
God?"[p]
62"Yes, I am!" Jesus answered.

"Soon you will see
the Son of Man
sitting at the right side[q]
of God All-Powerful,
and coming with the clouds
of heaven."

63At once the high priest ripped his
robe apart and shouted, "Why do we
need more witnesses? 64You heard him
claim to be God! What is your decision?" They all agreed that he should be
put to death.
65Some of the people started spitting
on Jesus. They blindfolded him, hit him
with their fists, and said, "Tell us who
hit you!" Then the guards took charge of
Jesus and beat him.

Peter Says He Doesn't Know Jesus

(Matthew 26.69-75; Luke 22.56-62; John 18.15-18, 25-27)

66While Peter was still in the courtyard, a servant girl of the high priest
came up 67and saw Peter warming himself by the fire. She stared at him and
said, "You were with Jesus from Nazareth!"
68Peter replied, "That isn't true! I don't
know what you're talking about. I don't
have any idea what you mean." He went
out to the gate, and a rooster crowed.[r]
69The servant girl saw Peter again and
said to the people standing there, "This
man is one of them!"
70"No, I'm not!" Peter replied.
A little while later some of the people
said to Peter, "You certainly are one of
them. You're a Galilean!"
71This time Peter began to curse and
swear, "I don't even know the man
you're talking about!"
72Right away the rooster crowed a
second time. Then Peter remembered
that Jesus had told him, "Before a
rooster crows twice, you will say three

[n]**14.41** *Are you still sleeping and resting?*: Or "You may as well keep on sleeping and resting."
[o]**14.44** *greet with a kiss*: It was the custom for people to greet each other with a kiss on the cheek. [p]**14.61** *Son of the glorious God*: "Son of God" was one of the titles used for the kings of Israel. [q]**14.62** *right side*: See the note at 12.36. [r]**14.68** *a rooster crowed*: These words are not in some manuscripts.

times that you don't know me." So Peter started crying.

Pilate Questions Jesus

(Matthew 27.1, 2, 11-14; Luke 23.1-5; John 18.28-38)

15 Early the next morning the chief priests, the nation's leaders, and the teachers of the Law of Moses met together with the whole Jewish council. They tied up Jesus and led him off to Pilate.

2 He asked Jesus, "Are you the king of the Jews?"

"Those are your words," Jesus answered.

3 The chief priests brought many charges against Jesus. 4 Then Pilate questioned him again, "Don't you have anything to say? Don't you hear what crimes they say you have done?" 5 But Jesus did not answer, and Pilate was amazed.

The Death Sentence

(Matthew 27.15-26; Luke 23.13-25; John 18.39—19.16)

6 During Passover, Pilate always freed one prisoner chosen by the people. 7 And at that time there was a prisoner named Barabbas. He and some others had been arrested for murder during a riot. 8 The crowd now came and asked Pilate to set a prisoner free, just as he usually did.

9 Pilate asked them, "Do you want me to free the king of the Jews?" 10 Pilate knew that the chief priests had brought Jesus to him because they were jealous.

11 But the chief priests told the crowd to ask Pilate to free Barabbas.

12 Then Pilate asked the crowd, "What do you want me to do with this man you say is[s] the king of the Jews?"

13 They yelled, "Nail him to a cross!"

14 Pilate asked, "But what crime has he done?"

"Nail him to a cross!" they yelled even louder.

15 Pilate wanted to please the crowd. So he set Barabbas free. Then he ordered his soldiers to beat Jesus with a whip and nail him to a cross.

Soldiers Make Fun of Jesus

(Matthew 27.27-30; John 19.2, 3)

16 The soldiers led Jesus inside the courtyard of the fortress[t] and called together the rest of the troops. 17 They put a purple robe[u] on him, and on his head they placed a crown that they had made out of thorn branches. 18 They made fun of Jesus and shouted, "Hey, you king of the Jews!" 19 Then they beat him on the head with a stick. They spit on him and knelt down and pretended to worship him.

20 When the soldiers had finished making fun of Jesus, they took off the purple robe. They put his own clothes back on him and led him off to be nailed to a cross. 21 Simon from Cyrene happened to be coming in from a farm, and they forced him to carry Jesus' cross. Simon was the father of Alexander and Rufus.

Jesus Is Nailed to a Cross

(Matthew 27.31-44; Luke 23.27-43; John 19.17-27)

22 The soldiers took Jesus to Golgotha, which means "Place of a Skull."[v] 23 There they gave him some wine mixed with a drug to ease the pain, but he refused to drink it.

24 They nailed Jesus to a cross and gambled to see who would get his clothes. 25 It was about nine o'clock in the morning when they nailed him to the cross. 26 On it was a sign that told why he was nailed there. It read, "This is the King of the Jews." 27-28 The soldiers also nailed two criminals on crosses, one to the right of Jesus and the other to his left.[w]

29 People who passed by said terrible things about Jesus. They shook their heads and shouted, "Ha! So you're the one who claimed you could tear down the temple and build it again in three days. 30 Save yourself and come down from the cross!"

31 The chief priests and the teachers of the Law of Moses also made fun of Jesus. They said to each other, "He saved others, but he can't save himself. 32 If he is the Messiah, the king of Israel, let him come down from the cross! Then we will see and believe." The two criminals also said cruel things to Jesus.

The Death of Jesus

(Matthew 27.45-56; Luke 23.44-49; John 19.28-30)

33 About noon the sky turned dark and stayed that way until around three o'clock. 34 Then about that time Jesus shouted, "Eloi, Eloi, lema sabachthani?"[x] which means, "My God, my God, why have you deserted me?"

[s] **15.12** *this man you say is*: These words are not in some manuscripts. [t] **15.16** *fortress*: The place where the Roman governor stayed. It was probably at Herod's palace west of Jerusalem, though it may have been Fortress Antonia, north of the temple, where the Roman troops were stationed. [u] **15.17** *purple robe*: This was probably a Roman soldier's robe. [v] **15.22** *Place of a Skull*: The place was probably given this name because it was near a large rock in the shape of a human skull. [w] **15.27-28** *left*: Some manuscripts add, "So the Scriptures came true which say, 'He was accused of being a criminal.'" [x] **15.34** *Eloi . . . sabachthani*: These words are in Aramaic, a language spoken in Palestine during the time of Jesus.

35 Some of the people standing there heard Jesus and said, "He is calling for Elijah."[y] 36 One of them ran and grabbed a sponge. After he had soaked it in wine, he put it on a stick and held it up to Jesus. He said, "Let's wait and see if Elijah will come[z] and take him down!" 37 Jesus shouted and then died.

38 At once the curtain in the temple[a] tore in two from top to bottom.

39 A Roman army officer was standing in front of Jesus. When the officer saw how Jesus died, he said, "This man really was the Son of God!"

40-41 Some women were looking on from a distance. They had come with Jesus to Jerusalem. But even before this they had been his followers and had helped him while he was in Galilee. Mary Magdalene and Mary the mother of the younger James and of Joseph were two of these women. Salome was also one of them.

Jesus Is Buried

(Matthew 27.57-61; Luke 23.50-56; John 19.38-42)

42 It was now the evening before the Sabbath, and the Jewish people were getting ready for that sacred day. 43 A man named Joseph from Arimathea was brave enough to ask Pilate for the body of Jesus. Joseph was a highly respected member of the Jewish council, and he was also waiting for God's kingdom to come.

44 Pilate was surprised to hear that Jesus was already dead, and he called in the army officer to find out if Jesus had been dead very long. 45 After the officer told him, Pilate let Joseph have Jesus' body.

46 Joseph bought a linen cloth and took the body down from the cross. He had it wrapped in the cloth, and he put it in a tomb that had been cut into solid rock. Then he rolled a big stone against the entrance to the tomb.

47 Mary Magdalene and Mary the mother of Joseph were watching and saw where the body was placed.

Jesus Is Alive

(Matthew 28.1-8; Luke 24.1-12; John 20.1-10)

16 After the Sabbath, Mary Magdalene, Salome, and Mary the mother of James bought some spices to put on Jesus' body. 2 Very early on Sunday morning, just as the sun was coming up, they went to the tomb. 3 On their way, they were asking one another, "Who will roll the stone away from the entrance for us?" 4 But when they looked, they saw that the stone had already been rolled away. And it was a huge stone!

5 The women went into the tomb, and on the right side they saw a young man in a white robe sitting there. They were alarmed.

6 The man said, "Don't be alarmed! You are looking for Jesus from Nazareth, who was nailed to a cross. God has raised him to life, and he isn't here. You can see the place where they put his body. 7 Now go and tell his disciples, and especially Peter, that he will go ahead of you to Galilee. You will see him there, just as he told you."

8 When the women ran from the tomb, they were confused and shaking all over. They were too afraid to tell anyone what had happened.

ONE OLD ENDING TO MARK'S GOSPEL[b]

Jesus Appears to Mary Magdalene

(Matthew 28.9, 10; John 20.11-18)

9 Very early on the first day of the week, after Jesus had risen to life, he appeared to Mary Magdalene. Earlier he had forced seven demons out of her. 10 She left and told his friends, who were crying and mourning. 11 Even though they heard that Jesus was alive and that Mary had seen him, they would not believe it.

Jesus Appears to Two Disciples

(Luke 24.13-35)

12 Later, Jesus appeared in another form to two disciples, as they were on their way out of the city. 13 But when these disciples told what had happened, the others would not believe.

What Jesus' Followers Must Do

(Matthew 28.16-20; Luke 24.36-49; John 20.19-23; Acts 1.6-8)

14 Afterwards, Jesus appeared to his eleven disciples as they were eating. He scolded them because they were too stubborn to believe the ones who had seen him after he had been raised to life. 15 Then he told them:

Go and preach the good news to everyone in the world. 16 Anyone who believes me and is baptized will be saved. But anyone who refuses to believe me will be condemned.

17 Everyone who believes me will be

[y] **15.35** *Elijah*: The name "Elijah" sounds something like "Eloi," which means "my God."
[z] **15.36** *see if Elijah will come*: See the note at 6.15. [a] **15.38** *curtain in the temple*: There were two curtains in the temple. One was at the entrance, and the other separated the holy place from the most holy place that the Jewish people thought of as God's home on earth. The second curtain is probably the one which is meant. [b] **16.9** *One Old Ending to Mark's Gospel*: Verses 9-20 are not in some manuscripts.

able to do wonderful things. By using my name they will force out
demons, and they will speak new
languages. 18They will handle
snakes and will drink poison and
not be hurt. They will also heal sick
people by placing their hands on
them.

Jesus Returns to Heaven

(Luke 24.50-53; Acts 1.9-11)

19After the Lord Jesus had said these
things to the disciples, he was taken
back up to heaven where he sat down at
the right side[c] of God. 20Then the disciples left and preached everywhere. The
Lord was with them, and the miracles
they worked proved that their message
was true.

ANOTHER OLD ENDING TO MARK'S GOSPEL[d]

9-10The women quickly told Peter and his friends what had happened. Later, Jesus sent the disciples to the east and to the west with his sacred and everlasting message of how people can be saved forever.

[c] **16.19** *right side*: See the note at 12.36.

[d] **16.9,10** *Another Old Ending to Mark's Gospel*: Some manuscripts and early translations have both this shorter ending and the longer one (verses 9-20).

LUKE

ABOUT THIS BOOK

God's love is for everyone! Jesus came into the world to be the Savior of all people! These are two of the main thoughts in this book. Several of the best known stories that Jesus used for teaching about God's love are found only in Luke's Gospel: The Good Samaritan (10.25-37), A Lost Sheep (15.1-7), and A Lost Son (15.11-32). Only Luke tells how Jesus visited in the home of a hated tax collector (19.1-10) and promised life in paradise to a dying criminal (23.39-43).

Luke mentions God's Spirit more than any of the other New Testament writers. For example, the power of the Spirit was with John the Baptist from the time he was born (1.15). And the angel promised Mary, "The Holy Spirit will come down to you . . . So your child will be called the holy Son of God" (1.35). Jesus followed the Spirit (4.1, 14, 18; 10.21) and taught that the Spirit is God's greatest gift (11.13).

Luke shows how important prayer was to Jesus. Jesus prayed often: after being baptized (3.21), before choosing the disciples (6.12), before asking his disciples who they thought he was (9.18), and before giving up his life on the cross (23.34, 46). From Luke we learn of three stories that Jesus told to teach about prayer (11.5-9; 18.1-8, 9-14).

An important part of Luke's story is the way in which he shows the concern of Jesus for the poor: the good news is preached to them (4.18; 7.22), they receive God's blessings (6.20), they are invited to the great feast (14.13, 21), the poor man Lazarus is taken to heaven by angels (16.20, 22), and Jesus commands his disciples to sell what they have and give the money to the poor (12.33).

To make sure that readers would understand that Jesus was raised physically from death, Luke reports that the risen Jesus ate a piece of fish (24.42, 43). There could be no mistake about the risen Jesus: he was not a ghost. His being raised from death was real and not someone's imagination. Luke also wrote another book—the Acts of the Apostles—to show what happened to Jesus' followers after he was raised from death and taken up to heaven. No other Gospel has a second volume that continues the story.

Luke closes this first book that he wrote by telling that Jesus returned to heaven. But right before Jesus leaves, he tells his disciples:

> *The Scriptures say that the Messiah must suffer, then three days later he will rise from death. They also say that all people of every nation must be told in my name to turn to God, in order to be forgiven. So beginning in Jerusalem, you must tell everything that has happened.*
> *(24.46-48)*

A QUICK LOOK AT THIS BOOK

Why Luke Wrote this Book (1.1-4)
The Births of John the Baptist and Jesus (1.5—2.52)
The Message of John the Baptist (3.1-20)
The Baptism and Temptation of Jesus (3.21—4.13)
Jesus' Ministry in Galilee (4.14—9.50)
Jesus Goes from Galilee to Jerusalem (9.51—19.27)
Jesus' Last Week: His Trial and Death (19.28—23.56)
Jesus Is Alive (24.1-12)
Jesus Appears. He Is Taken to Heaven (24.13-53)

1 Many people have tried to tell the
story of what God has done among
us. 2They wrote what we had been told
by the ones who were there in the beginning and saw what happened. 3So
I made a careful study[a] of everything
and then decided to write and tell you
exactly what took place. Honorable
Theophilus, 4I have done this to let you
know the truth about what you have
heard.

An Angel Tells about the Birth of John

5When Herod was king of Judea, there
was a priest by the name of Zechariah
from the priestly group of Abijah. His
wife Elizabeth was from the family of
Aaron.[b] 6Both of them were good people and pleased the Lord God by obeying all that he had commanded. 7But
they did not have children. Elizabeth
could not have any, and both Zechariah
and Elizabeth were already old.

8One day Zechariah's group of priests
were on duty, and he was serving God
as a priest. 9According to the custom of
the priests, he had been chosen to go
into the Lord's temple that day and to
burn incense,[c] 10while the people stood
outside praying.

11All at once an angel from the Lord
appeared to Zechariah at the right side
of the altar. 12Zechariah was confused
and afraid when he saw the angel. 13But
the angel told him:

> Don't be afraid, Zechariah! God
> has heard your prayers. Your wife
> Elizabeth will have a son, and you
> must name him John. 14His birth will
> make you very happy, and many
> people will be glad. 15Your son will
> be a great servant of the Lord. He
> must never drink wine or beer, and
> the power of the Holy Spirit will be
> with him from the time he is born.
>
> 16John will lead many people in Is-
> rael to turn back to the Lord their
> God. 17He will go ahead of the Lord
> with the same power and spirit that
> Elijah[d] had. And because of John,
> parents will be more thoughtful of
> their children. And people who now
> disobey God will begin to think as
> they ought to. That is how John will
> get people ready for the Lord.

18Zechariah said to the angel, "How
will I know this is going to happen? My
wife and I are both very old."

19The angel answered, "I am Gabriel,
God's servant, and I was sent to tell you
this good news. 20You have not believed
what I have said. So you will not be able
to say a thing until all this happens. But
everything will take place when it is
supposed to."

21The crowd was waiting for Zechariah and kept wondering why he was
staying so long in the temple. 22When
he did come out, he could not speak,
and they knew he had seen a vision.
He motioned to them with his hands,
but did not say a thing.

23When Zechariah's time of service in
the temple was over, he went home.
24Soon after that, his wife was expecting
a baby, and for five months she did not
leave the house. She said to herself,
25"What the Lord has done for me will
keep people from looking down on
me."[e]

An Angel Tells about the Birth of Jesus

26One month later God sent the angel
Gabriel to the town of Nazareth in
Galilee 27with a message for a virgin
named Mary. She was engaged to
Joseph from the family of King David.
28The angel greeted Mary and said, "You
are truly blessed! The Lord is with you."

29Mary was confused by the angel's
words and wondered what they meant.
30Then the angel told Mary, "Don't be
afraid! God is pleased with you, 31and
you will have a son. His name will be Jesus. 32He will be great and will be called
the Son of God Most High. The Lord
God will make him king, as his ancestor
David was. 33He will rule the people of
Israel forever, and his kingdom will
never end."

34Mary asked the angel, "How can this
happen? I am not married!"

35The angel answered, "The Holy
Spirit will come down to you, and God's
power will come over you. So your child
will be called the holy Son of God.
36Your relative Elizabeth is also going to
have a son, even though she is old. No
one thought she could ever have a baby,
but in three months she will have a son.
37Nothing is impossible for God!"

38Mary said, "I am the Lord's servant!
Let it happen as you have said." And the
angel left her.

Mary Visits Elizabeth

39A short time later Mary hurried to a
town in the hill country of Judea. 40She
went into Zechariah's home, where she
greeted Elizabeth. 41When Elizabeth
heard Mary's greeting, her baby moved
within her.

The Holy Spirit came upon Elizabeth.
42Then in a loud voice she said to Mary:

[a]1.3 *a careful study*: Or "a study from the beginning." [b]1.5 *Aaron*: The brother of Moses and the first priest. [c]1.9 *burn incense*: This was done twice a day, once in the morning and again in the late afternoon. [d]1.17 *Elijah*: The prophet Elijah was known for his power to work miracles. [e]1.25 *keep people from looking down on me*: When a married woman could not have children, it was thought that the Lord was punishing her.

God has blessed you more than
any other woman! He has also
blessed the child you will have.
43Why should the mother of my Lord
come to me? 44As soon as I heard
your greeting, my baby became
happy and moved within me. 45The
Lord has blessed you because you
believed that he will keep his
promise.

Mary's Song of Praise

46Mary said:

With all my heart
I praise the Lord,
47 and I am glad
because of God my Savior.
48 He cares for me,
his humble servant.
From now on,
all people will say
God has blessed me.
49 God All-Powerful has done
great things for me,
and his name is holy.
50 He always shows mercy
to everyone
who worships him.
51 The Lord has used
his powerful arm
to scatter those
who are proud.
52 He drags strong rulers
from their thrones
and puts humble people
in places of power.
53 God gives the hungry
good things to eat,
and sends the rich away
with nothing.
54 He helps his servant Israel
and is always merciful
to his people.
55 The Lord made this promise
to our ancestors,
to Abraham and his family
forever!

56Mary stayed with Elizabeth about
three months. Then she went back
home.

The Birth of John the Baptist

57When Elizabeth's son was born,
58her neighbors and relatives heard how
kind the Lord had been to her, and they
too were glad.
59Eight days later they did for the child
what the Law of Moses commands.[f]
They were going to name him Zechariah, after his father. 60But Elizabeth
said, "No! His name is John."
61The people argued, "No one in your
family has ever been named John." 62So
they motioned to Zechariah to find out
what he wanted to name his son.
63Zechariah asked for a writing tablet.
Then he wrote, "His name is John."
Everyone was amazed. 64Right away,
Zechariah started speaking and praising God.
65All the neighbors were frightened
because of what had happened, and
everywhere in the hill country people
kept talking about these things. 66Every-
one who heard about this wondered
what this child would grow up to be.
They knew that the Lord was with him.

Zechariah Praises the Lord

67The Holy Spirit came upon Zechariah, and he began to speak:

68 Praise the Lord,
the God of Israel!
He has come
to save his people.
69 Our God has given us
a mighty Savior[g]
from the family
of David his servant.
70 Long ago the Lord promised
by the words
of his holy prophets
71 to save us from our enemies
and from everyone
who hates us.
72 God said he would be kind
to our people and keep
his sacred promise.
73 He told our ancestor Abraham
74 that he would rescue us
from our enemies.
Then we could serve him
without fear,
75 by being holy and good
as long as we live.

76 You, my son, will be called
a prophet of God
in heaven above.
You will go ahead of the Lord
to get everything ready
for him.
77 You will tell his people
that they can be saved
when their sins
are forgiven.
78 God's love and kindness
will shine upon us
like the sun that rises
in the sky.[h]
79 On us who live
in the dark shadow
of death

[f]**1.59** *what the Law of Moses commands*: This refers to circumcision. It is the cutting off of skin from the private part of Jewish boys eight days after birth to show that they belong to the Lord. [g]**1.69** *a mighty Savior*: The Greek text has "a horn of salvation." In the Scriptures animal horns are often a symbol of great strength. [h]**1.78** *like the sun that rises in the sky*: Or "like the Messiah coming from heaven."

this light will shine
to guide us
into a life of peace.

80 As John grew up, God's Spirit gave him great power. John lived in the desert until the time he was sent to the people of Israel.

The Birth of Jesus

(Matthew 1.18-25)

2 About that time Emperor Augustus gave orders for the names of all the people to be listed in record books.[i] 2 These first records were made when Quirinius was governor of Syria.[j]

3 Everyone had to go to their own hometown to be listed. 4 So Joseph had to leave Nazareth in Galilee and go to Bethlehem in Judea. Long ago Bethlehem had been King David's hometown, and Joseph went there because he was from David's family.

5 Mary was engaged to Joseph and traveled with him to Bethlehem. She was soon going to have a baby, 6 and while they were there, 7 she gave birth to her first-born[k] son. She dressed him in baby clothes[l] and laid him on a bed of hay, because there was no room for them in the inn.

The Shepherds

8 That night in the fields near Bethlehem some shepherds were guarding their sheep. 9 All at once an angel came down to them from the Lord, and the brightness of the Lord's glory flashed around them. The shepherds were frightened. 10 But the angel said, "Don't be afraid! I have good news for you, which will make everyone happy. 11 This very day in King David's hometown a Savior was born for you. He is Christ the Lord. 12 You will know who he is, because you will find him dressed in baby clothes and lying on a bed of hay."

13 Suddenly many other angels came down from heaven and joined in praising God. They said:

14 "Praise God in heaven!
Peace on earth to everyone
who pleases God."

15 After the angels had left and gone back to heaven, the shepherds said to each other, "Let's go to Bethlehem and see what the Lord has told us about."

16 They hurried off and found Mary and Joseph, and they saw the baby lying on a bed of hay.

17 When the shepherds saw Jesus, they told his parents what the angel had said about him. 18 Everyone listened and was surprised. 19 But Mary kept thinking about all this and wondering what it meant.

20 As the shepherds returned to their sheep, they were praising God and saying wonderful things about him. Everything they had seen and heard was just as the angel had said.

21 Eight days later Jesus' parents did for him what the Law of Moses commands.[m] And they named him Jesus, just as the angel had told Mary when he promised she would have a baby.

Simeon Praises the Lord

22 The time came for Mary and Joseph to do what the Law of Moses says a mother is supposed to do after her baby is born.[n]

They took Jesus to the temple in Jerusalem and presented him to the Lord, 23 just as the Law of the Lord says, "Each first-born[o] baby boy belongs to the Lord." 24 The Law of the Lord also says that parents have to offer a sacrifice, giving at least a pair of doves or two young pigeons. So that is what Mary and Joseph did.

25 At this time a man named Simeon was living in Jerusalem. Simeon was a good man. He loved God and was waiting for God to save the people of Israel. God's Spirit came to him 26 and told him that he would not die until he had seen Christ the Lord.

27 When Mary and Joseph brought Jesus to the temple to do what the Law of Moses says should be done for a new baby, the Spirit told Simeon to go into the temple. 28 Simeon took the baby Jesus in his arms and praised God,

29 "Lord, I am your servant,
and now I can die in peace,
because you have kept
your promise to me.
30 With my own eyes I have seen
what you have done
to save your people,
31 and foreign nations
will also see this.

[i] **2.1** *names . . . listed in record books*: This was done so that everyone could be made to pay taxes to the Emperor. [j] **2.2** *Quirinius was governor of Syria*: It is known that Quirinius made a record of the people in A.D. 6 or 7. But the exact date of the record taking that Luke mentions is not known. [k] **2.7** *first-born*: The Jewish people said that the first-born son in each of their families belonged to the Lord. [l] **2.7** *dressed him in baby clothes*: The Greek text has "wrapped him in wide strips of cloth," which was how young babies were dressed. [m] **2.21** *what the Law of Moses commands*: See the note at 1.59. [n] **2.22** *after her baby is born*: After a Jewish mother gave birth to a son, she was considered "unclean" and had to stay home until he was circumcised (see the note at 1.59). Then she had to stay home for another 33 days, before offering a sacrifice to the Lord. [o] **2.23** *first-born*: See the note at 2.7.

32 Your mighty power is a light
for all nations,
and it will bring honor
to your people Israel."

33 Jesus' parents were surprised at
what Simeon had said. 34 Then he
blessed them and told Mary, "This child
of yours will cause many people in Israel to fall and others to stand. The child
will be like a warning sign. Many people
will reject him, 35 and you, Mary, will suffer as though you had been stabbed by a
dagger. But all this will show what people are really thinking."

Anna Speaks about the Child Jesus

36 The prophet Anna was also there in
the temple. She was the daughter of
Phanuel from the tribe of Asher, and she
was very old. In her youth she had been
married for seven years, but her husband died. 37 And now she was eighty-
four years old.[p] Night and day she
served God in the temple by praying
and often going without eating.[q]
38 At that time Anna came in and
praised God. She spoke about the child
Jesus to everyone who hoped for
Jerusalem to be set free.

The Return to Nazareth

39 After Joseph and Mary had done
everything that the Law of the Lord
commands, they returned home to
Nazareth in Galilee. 40 The child Jesus
grew. He became strong and wise, and
God blessed him.

The Boy Jesus in the Temple

41 Every year Jesus' parents went to
Jerusalem for Passover. 42 And when Jesus was twelve years old, they all went
there as usual for the celebration. 43 After Passover his parents left, but they
did not know that Jesus had stayed on
in the city. 44 They thought he was traveling with some other people, and they
went a whole day before they started
looking for him. 45 When they could not
find him with their relatives and friends,
they went back to Jerusalem and started
looking for him there.
46 Three days later they found Jesus
sitting in the temple, listening to the
teachers and asking them questions.
47 Everyone who heard him was surprised at how much he knew and at the
answers he gave.
48 When his parents found him, they
were amazed. His mother said, "Son,
why have you done this to us? Your
father and I have been very worried,
and we have been searching for you!"
49 Jesus answered, "Why did you have
to look for me? Didn't you know that I
would be in my Father's house?"[r] 50 But
they did not understand what he meant.
51 Jesus went back to Nazareth with
his parents and obeyed them. His
mother kept on thinking about all that
had happened.
52 Jesus became wise, and he grew
strong. God was pleased with him and
so were the people.

The Preaching of John the Baptist

(Matthew 3.1-12; Mark 1.1-8; John 1.19-28)

3 For fifteen years[s] Emperor Tiberius
had ruled that part of the world.
Pontius Pilate was governor of Judea,
and Herod[t] was the ruler of Galilee.
Herod's brother, Philip, was the ruler in
the countries of Iturea and Trachonitis,
and Lysanias was the ruler of Abilene.
2 Annas and Caiaphas were the Jewish
high priests.[u]
At that time God spoke to Zechariah's
son John, who was living in the desert.
3 So John went along the Jordan Valley,
telling the people, "Turn back to God
and be baptized! Then your sins will be
forgiven." 4 Isaiah the prophet wrote
about John when he said,

"In the desert
someone is shouting,
'Get the road ready
for the Lord!
Make a straight path
for him.
5 Fill up every valley
and level every mountain
and hill.
Straighten the crooked paths
and smooth out
the rough roads.
6 Then everyone will see
the saving power of God.' "

7 Crowds of people came out to be
baptized, but John said to them, "You
bunch of snakes! Who warned you to
run from the coming judgment? 8 Do
something to show that you really have
given up your sins. Don't start saying
that you belong to Abraham's family.
God can turn these stones into children
for Abraham.[v] 9 An ax is ready to cut the

[p]**2.37** *And now she was eighty-four years old*: Or "And now she had been a widow for eighty-four years." [q]**2.37** *without eating*: The Jewish people sometimes went without eating (also called "fasting") to show their love for God or to show sorrow for their sins. [r]**2.49** *in my Father's house*: Or "doing my Father's work." [s]**3.1** *For fifteen years*: This was either A.D. 28 or 29, and Jesus was about thirty years old (see 3.23). [t]**3.1** *Herod*: Herod Antipas, the son of Herod the Great. [u]**3.2** *Annas and Caiaphas . . . high priests*: Annas was high priest from A.D. 6 until 15. His son-in-law Caiaphas was high priest from A.D. 18 until 37. [v]**3.8** *children for Abraham*: The Jewish people thought they were God's chosen people because of God's promises to their ancestor Abraham.

trees down at their roots. Any tree that
doesn't produce good fruit will be cut
down and thrown into a fire."
10The crowds asked John, "What
should we do?"
11John told them, "If you have two
coats, give one to someone who doesn't
have any. If you have food, share it with
someone else."
12When tax collectors[w] came to be
baptized, they asked John, "Teacher,
what should we do?"
13John told them, "Don't make people
pay more than they owe."
14Some soldiers asked him, "And what
about us? What do we have to do?"
John told them, "Don't force people to
pay money to make you leave them
alone. Be satisfied with your pay."
15Everyone became excited and wondered, "Could John be the Messiah?"
16John said, "I am just baptizing with
water. But someone more powerful is
going to come, and I am not good
enough even to untie his sandals.[x] He
will baptize you with the Holy Spirit
and with fire. 17His threshing fork[y] is in
his hand, and he is ready to separate the
wheat from the husks. He will store the
wheat in his barn and burn the husks
with a fire that never goes out."
18In many different ways John
preached the good news to the people.
19But to Herod the ruler, he said, "It was
wrong for you to take Herodias, your
brother's wife." John also said that
Herod had done many other bad things.
20Finally, Herod put John in jail, and this
was the worst thing he had done.

The Baptism of Jesus

(Matthew 3.13-17; Mark 1.9-11)

21While everyone else was being baptized, Jesus himself was baptized. Then
as he prayed, the sky opened up, 22and
the Holy Spirit came down upon him in
the form of a dove. A voice from heaven
said, "You are my own dear Son, and I
am pleased with you."

The Ancestors of Jesus

(Matthew 1.1-17)

23When Jesus began to preach, he was
about thirty years old. Everyone thought
he was the son of Joseph. But his family
went back through Heli, 24Matthat, Levi,
Melchi, Jannai, Joseph, 25Mattathias,
Amos, Nahum, Esli, Naggai, 26Maath,
Mattathias, Semein, Josech, Joda;
27Joanan, Rhesa, Zerubbabel, Shealtiel, Neri, 28Melchi, Addi, Cosam, El-
madam, Er, 29Joshua, Eliezer, Jorim,
Matthat, Levi;
30Simeon, Judah, Joseph, Jonam, Eliakim, 31Melea, Menna, Mattatha, Nathan, David, 32Jesse, Obed, Boaz, Salmon, Nahshon;
33Amminadab, Admin, Arni, Hezron,
Perez, Judah, 34Jacob, Isaac, Abraham,
Terah, Nahor, 35Serug, Reu, Peleg, Eber,
Shelah;
36Cainan, Arphaxad, Shem, Noah,
Lamech, 37Methuselah, Enoch, Jared,
Mahalaleel, Kenan, 38Enosh, and Seth.
The family of Jesus went all the way
back to Adam and then to God.

Jesus and the Devil

(Matthew 4.1-11; Mark 1.12, 13)

4 When Jesus returned from the Jordan River, the power of the Holy
Spirit was with him, and the Spirit led
him into the desert. 2For forty days Jesus was tested by the devil, and during
that time he went without eating.[z] When
it was all over, he was hungry.
3The devil said to Jesus, "If you are
God's Son, tell this stone to turn into
bread."
4Jesus answered, "The Scriptures say,
'No one can live only on food.' "
5Then the devil led Jesus up to a high
place and quickly showed him all the
nations on earth. 6The devil said, "I will
give all this power and glory to you. It
has been given to me, and I can give it
to anyone I want to. 7Just worship me,
and you can have it all."
8Jesus answered, "The Scriptures say:

'Worship the Lord your God
and serve only him!' "

9Finally, the devil took Jesus to
Jerusalem and had him stand on top of
the temple. The devil said, "If you are
God's Son, jump off. 10-11The Scriptures
say:

'God will tell his angels
to take care of you.
They will catch you
in their arms,
and you will not hurt
your feet on the stones.' "

12Jesus answered, "The Scriptures
also say, 'Don't try to test the Lord your
God!' "
13After the devil had finished testing
Jesus in every way possible, he left him
for a while.

[w] **3.12** *tax collectors*: These were usually Jewish people who paid the Romans for the right to collect taxes. They were hated by other Jews who thought of them as traitors to their country and to their religion. [x] **3.16** *untie his sandals*: This was the duty of a slave.
[y] **3.17** *threshing fork*: After Jewish farmers had trampled out the grain, they used a large fork to pitch the grain and the husks into the air. Wind would blow away the light husks, and the grain would fall back to the ground, where it could be gathered up. [z] **4.2** *went without eating*: See the note at 2.37.

Jesus Begins His Work
(Matthew 4.12-17; Mark 1.14, 15)

14 Jesus returned to Galilee with the
power of the Spirit. News about him
spread everywhere. 15 He taught in the
Jewish meeting places, and everyone
praised him.

The People of Nazareth Turn against Jesus
(Matthew 13.53-58; Mark 6.1-6)

16 Jesus went back to Nazareth, where
he had been brought up, and as usual he
went to the meeting place on the Sabbath. When he stood up to read from the
Scriptures, 17 he was given the book of
Isaiah the prophet. He opened it and
read,

18 "The Lord's Spirit
has come to me,
because he has chosen me
to tell the good news
to the poor.
The Lord has sent me
to announce freedom
for prisoners,
to give sight to the blind,
to free everyone
who suffers,
19 and to say, 'This is the year
the Lord has chosen.' "

20 Jesus closed the book, then handed
it back to the man in charge and sat
down. Everyone in the meeting place
looked straight at Jesus.
21 Then Jesus said to them, "What you
have just heard me read has come true
today."
22 All the people started talking about
Jesus and were amazed at the wonderful things he said. They kept on asking,
"Isn't he Joseph's son?"
23 Jesus answered:
You will certainly want to tell me
this saying, "Doctor, first make yourself well." You will tell me to do the
same things here in my own hometown that you heard I did in Capernaum. 24 But you can be sure that no
prophets are liked by the people of
their own hometown.
25 Once during the time of Elijah
there was no rain for three and a
half years, and people everywhere
were starving. There were many
widows in Israel, 26 but Elijah was
sent only to a widow in the town of
Zarephath near the city of Sidon.
27 During the time of the prophet Elisha, many men in Israel had leprosy.[a] But no one was healed, except
Naaman who lived in Syria.
28 When the people in the meeting
place heard Jesus say this, they became
so angry 29 that they got up and threw
him out of town. They dragged him to
the edge of the cliff on which the town
was built, because they wanted to throw
him down from there. 30 But Jesus
slipped through the crowd and got
away.

A Man with an Evil Spirit
(Mark 1.21-28)

31 Jesus went to the town of Capernaum in Galilee and taught the people
on the Sabbath. 32 His teaching amazed
them because he spoke with power.
33 There in the Jewish meeting place was
a man with an evil spirit. He yelled out,
34 "Hey, Jesus of Nazareth, what do you
want with us? Are you here to get rid of
us? I know who you are! You are God's
Holy One."
35 Jesus ordered the evil spirit to be
quiet and come out. The demon threw
the man to the ground in front of everyone and left without harming him.
36 They all were amazed and kept saying to each other, "What kind of teaching is this? He has power to order evil
spirits out of people!" 37 News about Jesus spread all over that part of the country.

Jesus Heals Many People
(Matthew 8.14-17; Mark 1.29-34)

38 Jesus left the meeting place and
went to Simon's home. When Jesus got
there, he was told that Simon's mother-
in-law was sick with a high fever. 39 So
Jesus went over to her and ordered the
fever to go away. Right then she was
able to get up and serve them a meal.
40 After the sun had set, people with all
kinds of diseases were brought to Jesus.
He put his hands on each one of them
and healed them. 41 Demons went out of
many people and shouted, "You are the
Son of God!" But Jesus ordered the
demons not to speak because they knew
he was the Messiah.
42 The next morning Jesus went out to
a place where he could be alone, and
crowds came looking for him. When
they found him, they tried to stop him
from leaving. 43 But Jesus said, "People
in other towns must hear the good news
about God's kingdom. That's why I was
sent." 44 So he kept on preaching in the
Jewish meeting places in Judea.[b]

Jesus Chooses His First Disciples
(Matthew 4.18-22; Mark 1.16-20)

5 Jesus was standing on the shore of
Lake Gennesaret,[c] teaching the people as they crowded around him to hear

[a] **4.27** *leprosy*: In biblical times the word "leprosy" was used for many different kinds of skin diseases. [b] **4.44** *Judea*: Some manuscripts have "Galilee." [c] **5.1** *Lake Gennesaret*: Another name for Lake Galilee.

God's message. 2Near the shore he saw
two boats left there by some fishermen
who had gone to wash their nets. 3Jesus
got into the boat that belonged to Simon
and asked him to row it out a little way
from the shore. Then Jesus sat down[d] in
the boat to teach the crowd.
4When Jesus had finished speaking,
he told Simon, "Row the boat out into
the deep water and let your nets down
to catch some fish."
5"Master," Simon answered, "we have
worked hard all night long and have not
caught a thing. But if you tell me to, I
will let the nets down." 6They did it and
caught so many fish that their nets began ripping apart. 7Then they signaled
for their partners in the other boat
to come and help them. The men
came, and together they filled the two
boats so full that they both began to
sink.
8When Simon Peter saw this happen,
he knelt down in front of Jesus and said,
"Lord, don't come near me! I am a sinner." 9Peter and everyone with him were
completely surprised at all the fish they
had caught. 10His partners James and
John, the sons of Zebedee, were surprised too.
Jesus told Simon, "Don't be afraid!
From now on you will bring in people
instead of fish." 11The men pulled their
boats up on the shore. Then they left
everything and went with Jesus.

Jesus Heals a Man

(Matthew 8.1-4; Mark 1.40-45)

12Jesus came to a town where there
was a man who had leprosy.[e] When the
man saw Jesus, he knelt down to the
ground in front of Jesus and begged,
"Lord, you have the power to make me
well, if only you wanted to."
13Jesus put his hand on him and said,
"I want to! Now you are well." At once
the man's leprosy disappeared. 14Jesus
told him, "Don't tell anyone about this,
but go and show yourself to the priest.
Offer a gift to the priest, just as Moses
commanded, and everyone will know
that you have been healed."[f]
15News about Jesus kept spreading.
Large crowds came to listen to him
teach and to be healed of their diseases.
16But Jesus would often go to some
place where he could be alone and pray.

Jesus Heals a Crippled Man

(Matthew 9.1-8; Mark 2.1-12)

17One day some Pharisees and experts
in the Law of Moses sat listening to Jesus teach. They had come from every
village in Galilee and Judea and from
Jerusalem.
God had given Jesus the power to
heal the sick, 18and some people came
carrying a crippled man on a mat. They
tried to take him inside the house and
put him in front of Jesus. 19But because
of the crowd, they could not get him to
Jesus. So they went up on the roof,[g]
where they removed some tiles and
let the mat down in the middle of the
room.
20When Jesus saw how much faith
they had, he said to the crippled man,
"My friend, your sins are forgiven."
21The Pharisees and the experts began arguing, "Jesus must think he is
God! Only God can forgive sins."
22Jesus knew what they were thinking, and he said, "Why are you thinking
that? 23Is it easier for me to tell this crippled man that his sins are forgiven or to
tell him to get up and walk? 24But now
you will see that the Son of Man has the
right to forgive sins here on earth." Jesus then said to the man, "Get up! Pick
up your mat and walk home."
25At once the man stood up in front of
everyone. He picked up his mat and
went home, giving thanks to God.
26Everyone was amazed and praised
God. What they saw surprised them, and
they said, "We have seen a great miracle
today!"

Jesus Chooses Levi

(Matthew 9.9-13; Mark 2.13-17)

27Later, Jesus went out and saw a tax
collector[h] named Levi sitting at the
place for paying taxes. Jesus said to
him, "Come with me." 28Levi left everything and went with Jesus.
29In his home Levi gave a big dinner
for Jesus. Many tax collectors and other
guests were also there.
30The Pharisees and some of their
teachers of the Law of Moses grumbled
to Jesus' disciples, "Why do you eat and
drink with those tax collectors and
other sinners?"
31Jesus answered, "Healthy people
don't need a doctor, but sick people do.

[d]**5.3** *sat down*: Teachers in the ancient world, including Jewish teachers, usually sat down when they taught. [e]**5.12** *leprosy*: See the note at 4.27. [f]**5.14** *everyone will know that you have been healed*: People with leprosy had to be examined by a priest and told that they were well (that is, "clean") before they could once again live a normal life in the Jewish community. The gift that Moses commanded was the sacrifice of some lambs together with flour mixed with olive oil. [g]**5.19** *roof*: In Palestine the houses usually had a flat roof. Stairs on the outside led up to the roof, which was made of beams and boards covered with packed earth. Luke says that the roof was made of (clay) tiles, which were also used for making roofs in New Testament times. [h]**5.27** *tax collector*: See the note at 3.12.

32I didn't come to invite good people to
turn to God. I came to invite sinners."

People Ask about Going without Eating

(Matthew 9.14-17; Mark 2.18-22)

33Some people said to Jesus, "John's
followers often pray and go without eating,[i] and so do the followers of the
Pharisees. But your disciples never go
without eating or drinking."
34Jesus told them, "The friends of a
bridegroom don't go without eating
while he is still with them. 35But the
time will come when he will be taken
from them. Then they will go without
eating."
36Jesus then told them these sayings:
No one uses a new piece of cloth
to patch old clothes. The patch
would shrink and make the hole
even bigger.
37No one pours new wine into old
wineskins. The new wine would
swell and burst the old skins.[j] Then
the wine would be lost, and the skins
would be ruined. 38New wine must
be put only into new wineskins.
39No one wants new wine after
drinking old wine. They say, "The
old wine is better."

A Question about the Sabbath

(Matthew 12.1-8; Mark 2.23-28)

6 One Sabbath when Jesus and his
disciples were walking through
some wheat fields,[k] the disciples picked
some wheat. They rubbed the husks off
with their hands and started eating the
grain.
2Some Pharisees said, "Why are you
picking grain on the Sabbath? You're
not supposed to do that!"
3Jesus answered, "You surely have
read what David did when he and his
followers were hungry. 4He went into
the house of God and took the sacred
loaves of bread that only priests were
supposed to eat. He not only ate some
himself, but even gave some to his followers."
5Jesus finished by saying, "The Son of
Man is Lord over the Sabbath."

A Man with a Crippled Hand

(Matthew 12.9-14; Mark 3.1-6)

6On another Sabbath[l] Jesus was
teaching in a Jewish meeting place, and
a man with a crippled right hand was
there. 7Some Pharisees and teachers of
the Law of Moses kept watching Jesus
to see if he would heal the man. They
did this because they wanted to accuse
Jesus of doing something wrong.
8Jesus knew what they were thinking.
So he told the man to stand up where
everyone could see him. And the man
stood up. 9Then Jesus asked, "On the
Sabbath should we do good deeds or
evil deeds? Should we save someone's
life or destroy it?"
10After he had looked around at
everyone, he told the man, "Stretch out
your hand." He did, and his bad hand
became completely well.
11The teachers and the Pharisees were
furious and started saying to each other,
"What can we do about Jesus?"

Jesus Chooses His Twelve Apostles

(Matthew 10.1-4; Mark 3.13-19)

12About that time Jesus went off to a
mountain to pray, and he spent the
whole night there. 13The next morning
he called his disciples together and
chose twelve of them to be his apostles.
14One was Simon, and Jesus named him
Peter. Another was Andrew, Peter's
brother. There were also James,
John, Philip, Bartholomew, 15Matthew,
Thomas, and James the son of Alphaeus. The rest of the apostles were Simon, known as the Eager One,[m] 16Jude,
who was the son of James, and Judas Iscariot,[n] who later betrayed Jesus.

Jesus Teaches, Preaches, and Heals

(Matthew 4.23-25)

17Jesus and his apostles went down
from the mountain and came to some
flat, level ground. Many other disciples
were there to meet him. Large crowds of
people from all over Judea, Jerusalem,
and the coastal cities of Tyre and Sidon
were there too. 18These people had come
to listen to Jesus and to be healed of
their diseases. All who were troubled by
evil spirits were also healed. 19Everyone
was trying to touch Jesus, because
power was going out from him and
healing them all.

Blessings and Troubles

(Matthew 5.1-12)

20Jesus looked at his disciples and
said:

[i]**5.33** *without eating*: See the note at 2.37. [j]**5.37** *swell and burst the old skins*: While the juice from grapes was becoming wine, it would swell and stretch the skins in which it had been stored. If the skins were old and stiff, they would burst. [k]**6.1** *walking through some wheat fields*: It was the custom to let hungry travelers pick grains of wheat. [l]**6.6** *On another Sabbath*: Some manuscripts have a reading which may mean "the Sabbath after the next." [m]**6.15** *known as the Eager One*: The word "eager" translates the Greek word "zealot," which was a name later given to the members of a Jewish group that resisted and fought against the Romans. [n]**6.16** *Iscariot*: This may mean "a man from Kerioth" (a place in Judea). But more probably it means "a man who was a liar" or "a man who was a betrayer."

God will bless you people
who are poor.
His kingdom belongs to you!
21 God will bless
you hungry people.
You will have plenty
to eat!
God will bless you people
who are crying.
You will laugh!

22 God will bless you when others
hate you and won't have anything to
do with you. God will bless you
when people insult you and say
cruel things about you, all because
you are a follower of the Son of
Man. 23 Long ago your own people
did these same things to the
prophets. So when this happens to
you, be happy and jump for joy! You
will have a great reward in heaven.

24 But you rich people
are in for trouble.
You have already had
an easy life!
25 You well-fed people
are in for trouble.
You will go hungry!
You people
who are laughing now
are in for trouble.
You are going to cry
and weep!

26 You are in for trouble when
everyone says good things about
you. That is what your own people
said about those prophets who told
lies.

Love for Enemies

(Matthew 5.38-48; 7.12a)

27 This is what I say to all who will
listen to me:
Love your enemies, and be good to
everyone who hates you. 28 Ask God
to bless anyone who curses you, and
pray for everyone who is cruel to
you. 29 If someone slaps you on one
cheek, don't stop that person from
slapping you on the other cheek. If
someone wants to take your coat,
don't try to keep back your shirt.
30 Give to everyone who asks and
don't ask people to return what they
have taken from you. 31 Treat others
just as you want to be treated.
32 If you love only someone who
loves you, will God praise you for
that? Even sinners love people who
love them. 33 If you are kind only to
someone who is kind to you, will
God be pleased with you for that?
Even sinners are kind to people who
are kind to them. 34 If you lend
money only to someone you think
will pay you back, will God be
pleased with you for that? Even sinners lend to sinners because they
think they will get it all back.
35 But love your enemies and be
good to them. Lend without expecting to be paid back.[o] Then you will
get a great reward, and you will be
the true children of God in heaven.
He is good even to people who are
unthankful and cruel. 36 Have pity on
others, just as your Father has pity
on you.

Judging Others

(Matthew 7.1-5)

37 Jesus said:
Don't judge others, and God won't
judge you. Don't be hard on others,
and God won't be hard on you. Forgive others, and God will forgive
you. 38 If you give to others, you will
be given a full amount in return. It
will be packed down, shaken together, and spilling over into your
lap. The way you treat others is the
way you will be treated.
39 Jesus also used some sayings as he
spoke to the people. He said:
Can one blind person lead another
blind person? Won't they both fall
into a ditch? 40 Are students better
than their teacher? But when they
are fully trained, they will be like
their teacher.
41 You can see the speck in your
friend's eye. But you don't notice the
log in your own eye. 42 How can you
say, "My friend, let me take the
speck out of your eye," when you
don't see the log in your own eye?
You show-offs! First, get the log out
of your own eye. Then you can see
how to take the speck out of your
friend's eye.

A Tree and Its Fruit

(Matthew 7.17-20; 12.34b, 35)

43 A good tree cannot produce bad
fruit, and a bad tree cannot produce
good fruit. 44 You can tell what a tree
is like by the fruit it produces. You
cannot pick figs or grapes from
thornbushes. 45 Good people do good
things because of the good in their
hearts. Bad people do bad things because of the evil in their hearts. Your
words show what is in your heart.

Two Builders

(Matthew 7.24-27)

46 Why do you keep on saying that
I am your Lord, when you refuse to

[o] 6.35 *without expecting to be paid back*: Some manuscripts have "without giving up on anyone."

do what I say? 47Anyone who comes
and listens to me and obeys me 48is
like someone who dug down deep
and built a house on solid rock.
When the flood came and the river
rushed against the house, it was
built so well that it didn't even
shake. 49But anyone who hears what
I say and doesn't obey me is like
someone whose house wasn't built
on solid rock. As soon as the river
rushed against that house, it was
smashed to pieces!

Jesus Heals an Army Officer's Servant
(Matthew 8.5-13; John 4.43-54)

7 After Jesus had finished teaching
the people, he went to Capernaum.
2In that town an army officer's servant
was sick and about to die. The officer
liked this servant very much. 3And
when he heard about Jesus, he sent
some Jewish leaders to ask him to come
and heal the servant.

4The leaders went to Jesus and
begged him to do something. They said,
"This man deserves your help! 5He loves
our nation and even built us a meeting
place." 6So Jesus went with them.

When Jesus wasn't far from the
house, the officer sent some friends to
tell him, "Lord, don't go to any trouble
for me! I am not good enough for you to
come into my house. 7And I am certainly not worthy to come to you. Just
say the word, and my servant will get
well. 8I have officers who give orders to
me, and I have soldiers who take orders
from me. I can say to one of them, 'Go!'
and he goes. I can say to another,
'Come!' and he comes. I can say to my
servant, 'Do this!' and he will do it."

9When Jesus heard this, he was so
surprised that he turned and said to the
crowd following him, "In all of Israel
I've never found anyone with this much
faith!"

10The officer's friends returned and
found the servant well.

A Widow's Son

11Soon Jesus and his disciples were
on their way to the town of Nain, and a
big crowd was going along with them.
12As they came near the gate of the
town, they saw people carrying out the
body of a widow's only son. Many people from the town were walking along
with her.

13When the Lord saw the woman, he
felt sorry for her and said, "Don't cry!"

14Jesus went over and touched the
stretcher on which the people were carrying the dead boy. They stopped, and
Jesus said, "Young man, get up!" 15The
boy sat up and began to speak. Jesus
then gave him back to his mother.

16Everyone was frightened and
praised God. They said, "A great
prophet is here with us! God has come
to his people."

17News about Jesus spread all over
Judea and everywhere else in that part
of the country.

John the Baptist
(Matthew 11.1-19)

18-19John's followers told John everything that was being said about Jesus.
So he sent two of them to ask the Lord,
"Are you the one we should be looking
for? Or must we wait for someone else?"

20When these messengers came to Jesus, they said, "John the Baptist sent us
to ask, 'Are you the one we should be
looking for? Or are we supposed to wait
for someone else?' "

21At that time Jesus was healing many
people who were sick or in pain or were
troubled by evil spirits, and he was giving sight to a lot of blind people. 22Jesus
said to the messengers sent by John,
"Go and tell John what you have seen
and heard. Blind people are now able to
see, and the lame can walk. People who
have leprosy[p] are being healed, and the
deaf can now hear. The dead are raised
to life, and the poor are hearing the
good news. 23God will bless everyone
who doesn't reject me because of what I
do."

24After John's messengers had gone,
Jesus began speaking to the crowds
about John:

What kind of person did you go
out to the desert to see? Was he like
tall grass blown about by the wind?
25What kind of man did you really
go out to see? Was he someone
dressed in fine clothes? People who
wear expensive clothes and live in
luxury are in the king's palace.
26What then did you go out to see?
Was he a prophet? He certainly was!
I tell you that he was more than a
prophet. 27In the Scriptures, God
calls John his messenger and says,
"I am sending my messenger ahead
of you to get things ready for you."
28No one ever born on this earth is
greater than John. But whoever is
least important in God's kingdom is
greater than John.

29Everyone had been listening to
John. Even the tax collectors[q] had
obeyed God and had done what was
right by letting John baptize them. 30But
the Pharisees and the experts in the
Law of Moses refused to obey God and
be baptized by John.

31Jesus went on to say:

[p] **7.22** *leprosy*: See the note at 4.27. [q] **7.29** *tax collectors*: See the note at 3.12.

What are you people like? What
kind of people are you? 32 You are
like children sitting in the market
and shouting to each other,

“We played the flute,
but you would not dance!
We sang a funeral song,
but you would not cry!”

33 John the Baptist did not go around
eating and drinking, and you said,
“John has a demon in him!” 34 But
because the Son of Man goes around
eating and drinking, you say, “Jesus
eats and drinks too much! He is
even a friend of tax collectors and
sinners.” 35 Yet Wisdom is shown to
be right by what its followers do.

Simon the Pharisee

36 A Pharisee invited Jesus to have dinner with him. So Jesus went to the Pharisee's home and got ready to eat.[r]
37 When a sinful woman in that town
found out that Jesus was there, she
bought an expensive bottle of perfume.
38 Then she came and stood behind Jesus. She cried and started washing his
feet with her tears and drying them with
her hair. The woman kissed his feet and
poured the perfume on them.
39 The Pharisee who had invited Jesus
saw this and said to himself, “If this man
really were a prophet, he would know
what kind of woman is touching him!
He would know that she is a sinner.”
40 Jesus said to the Pharisee, “Simon, I
have something to say to you.”
“Teacher, what is it?” Simon replied.
41 Jesus told him, “Two people were in
debt to a moneylender. One of them
owed him five hundred silver coins, and
the other owed him fifty. 42 Since neither
of them could pay him back, the moneylender said that they didn't have to pay
him anything. Which one of them will
like him more?”
43 Simon answered, “I suppose it
would be the one who had owed more
and didn't have to pay it back.”
“You are right,” Jesus said.
44 He turned toward the woman and
said to Simon, “Have you noticed this
woman? When I came into your home,
you didn't give me any water so I could
wash my feet. But she has washed my
feet with her tears and dried them with
her hair. 45 You didn't greet me with a
kiss, but from the time I came in, she
has not stopped kissing my feet. 46 You
didn't even pour olive oil on my head,[s]
but she has poured expensive perfume
on my feet. 47 So I tell you that all her
sins are forgiven, and that is why she
has shown great love. But anyone who
has been forgiven for only a little will
show only a little love.”
48 Then Jesus said to the woman, “Your
sins are forgiven.”
49 Some other guests started saying to
one another, “Who is this who dares to
forgive sins?”
50 But Jesus told the woman, “Because
of your faith, you are now saved.[t] May
God give you peace!”

Women Who Helped Jesus

8 Soon after this, Jesus was going
through towns and villages, telling
the good news about God's kingdom.
His twelve apostles were with him, 2 and
so were some women who had been
healed of evil spirits and all sorts of diseases. One of the women was Mary
Magdalene,[u] who once had seven
demons in her. 3 Joanna, Susanna, and
many others had also used what they
owned to help Jesus[v] and his disciples.
Joanna's husband Chuza was one of
Herod's officials.[w]

A Story about a Farmer

(Matthew 13.1-9; Mark 4.1-9)

4 When a large crowd from several
towns had gathered around Jesus, he
told them this story:
5 A farmer went out to scatter seed
in a field. While the farmer was doing it, some of the seeds fell along
the road and were stepped on or
eaten by birds. 6 Other seeds fell on
rocky ground and started growing.
But the plants did not have enough
water and soon dried up. 7 Some
other seeds fell where thornbushes
grew up and choked the plants. 8 The
rest of the seeds fell on good ground
where they grew and produced a
hundred times as many seeds.

[r] **7.36** *got ready to eat*: On special occasions the Jewish people often followed the Greek and Roman custom of lying down on their left side and leaning on their left elbow, while eating with their right hand. This is how the woman could come up behind Jesus and wash his feet (see verse 38). [s] **7.44-46** *washed my feet . . . greet me with a kiss . . . pour olive oil on my head*: Guests in a home were usually offered water so they could wash their feet, because most people either went barefoot or wore sandals and would come in the house with very dusty feet. Guests were also greeted with a kiss on the cheek, and special ones often had sweet-smelling olive oil poured on their head. [t] **7.50** *saved*: Or “healed.” The Greek word may have either meaning. [u] **8.2** *Magdalene*: Meaning “from Magdala,” a small town on the western shore of Lake Galilee. There is no hint that she is the sinful woman in 7.36-50. [v] **8.3** *used what they owned to help Jesus*: Women often helped Jewish teachers by giving them money. [w] **8.3** *Herod's officials*: Herod Antipas, the son of Herod the Great.

When Jesus had finished speaking, he said, "If you have ears, pay attention!"

Why Jesus Used Stories
(Matthew 13.10-17; Mark 4.10-12)

[9]Jesus' disciples asked him what the story meant. [10]So he answered:

I have explained the secrets about
God's kingdom to you, but for others
I can only use stories. These people
look, but they don't see, and they
hear, but they don't understand.

Jesus Explains the Story about a Farmer
(Matthew 13.18-23; Mark 4.13-20)

[11]This is what the story means:
The seed is God's message, [12]and the
seeds that fell along the road are the
people who hear the message. But
the devil comes and snatches the
message out of their hearts, so that
they will not believe and be saved.
[13]The seeds that fell on rocky
ground are the people who gladly
hear the message and accept it. But
they don't have deep roots, and they
believe only for a little while. As
soon as life gets hard, they give up.
[14]The seeds that fell among the
thornbushes are also people who
hear the message. But they are so
eager for riches and pleasures that
they never produce anything.
[15]Those seeds that fell on good
ground are the people who listen to
the message and keep it in good and
honest hearts. They last and produce
a harvest.

Light
(Mark 4.21-25)

[16]No one lights a lamp and puts it
under a bowl or under a bed. A lamp
is always put on a lampstand, so that
people who come into a house will
see the light. [17]There is nothing hidden that will not be found. There is
no secret that will not be well
known. [18]Pay attention to how you
listen! Everyone who has something
will be given more, but people who
have nothing will lose what little
they think they have.

Jesus' Mother and Brothers
(Matthew 12.46-50; Mark 3.31-35)

[19]Jesus' mother and brothers went to see him, but because of the crowd they could not get near him. [20]Someone told Jesus, "Your mother and brothers are standing outside and want to see you."

[21]Jesus answered, "My mother and my brothers are those people who hear and obey God's message."

A Storm
(Matthew 8.23-27; Mark 4.35-41)

[22]One day, Jesus and his disciples got into a boat, and he said, "Let's cross the lake."[x] They started out, [23]and while they were sailing across, he went to sleep.

Suddenly a windstorm struck the lake, and the boat started sinking. They were in danger. [24]So they went to Jesus and woke him up, "Master, Master! We are about to drown!"

Jesus got up and ordered the wind and waves to stop. They obeyed, and everything was calm. [25]Then Jesus asked the disciples, "Don't you have any faith?"

But they were frightened and amazed. They said to each other, "Who is this? He can give orders to the wind and the waves, and they obey him!"

A Man with Demons in Him
(Matthew 8.28-34; Mark 5.1-20)

[26]Jesus and his disciples sailed across Lake Galilee and came to shore near the town of Gerasa.[y] [27]As Jesus was getting out of the boat, he was met by a man from that town. The man had demons in him. He had gone naked for a long time and no longer lived in a house, but in the graveyard.[z]

[28]The man saw Jesus and screamed. He knelt down in front of him and shouted, "Jesus, Son of God in heaven, what do you want with me? I beg you not to torture me!" [29]He said this because Jesus had already told the evil spirit to go out of him.

The man had often been attacked by the demon. And even though he had been bound with chains and leg irons and kept under guard, he smashed whatever bound him. Then the demon would force him out into lonely places.

[30]Jesus asked the man, "What is your name?"

He answered, "My name is Lots." He said this because there were 'lots' of demons in him. [31]They begged Jesus not to send them to the deep pit,[a] where they would be punished.

[32]A large herd of pigs was feeding there on the hillside. So the demons begged Jesus to let them go into the pigs, and Jesus let them go. [33]Then the demons left the man and went into the pigs. The whole herd rushed down the steep bank into the lake and drowned.

[x]**8.22** *cross the lake*: To the eastern shore of Lake Galilee, where most of the people were not Jewish. [y]**8.26** *Gerasa*: Some manuscripts have "Gergesa." [z]**8.27** *graveyard*: It was thought that demons and evil spirits lived in graveyards. [a]**8.31** *deep pit*: The place where evil spirits are kept and punished.

34When the men taking care of the
pigs saw this, they ran to spread the
news in the town and on the farms.
35The people went out to see what had
happened, and when they came to Jesus, they also found the man. The
demons had gone out of him, and he
was sitting there at the feet of Jesus. He
had clothes on and was in his right
mind. But the people were terrified.
36Then all who had seen the man
healed told about it. 37Everyone from
around Gerasa[b] begged Jesus to leave,
because they were so frightened.
When Jesus got into the boat to start
back, 38the man who had been healed
begged to go with him. But Jesus sent
him off and said, 39"Go back home and
tell everyone how much God has done
for you." The man then went all over
town, telling everything that Jesus had
done for him.

A Dying Girl and a Sick Woman

(Matthew 9.18-26; Mark 5.21-43)

40Everyone had been waiting for Jesus, and when he came back, a crowd
was there to welcome him. 41Just then
the man in charge of the Jewish meeting
place came and knelt down in front of
Jesus. His name was Jairus, and he
begged Jesus to come to his home 42be-
cause his twelve-year-old child was dying. She was his only daughter.
While Jesus was on his way, people
were crowding all around him. 43In the
crowd was a woman who had been
bleeding for twelve years. She had spent
everything she had on doctors,[c] but
none of them could make her well.
44As soon as she came up behind Jesus and barely touched his clothes, her
bleeding stopped.
45"Who touched me?" Jesus asked.
While everyone was denying it, Peter
said, "Master, people are crowding all
around and pushing you from every
side."[d]
46But Jesus answered, "Someone
touched me, because I felt power going
out from me." 47The woman knew that
she could not hide, so she came trembling and knelt down in front of Jesus.
She told everyone why she had touched
him and that she had been healed right
away.
48Jesus said to the woman, "You are
now well because of your faith. May
God give you peace!"
49While Jesus was speaking, someone
came from Jairus' home and said, "Your
daughter has died! Why bother the
teacher anymore?"
50When Jesus heard this, he told Jairus, "Don't worry! Have faith, and your
daughter will get well."
51Jesus went into the house, but he did
not let anyone else go with him, except
Peter, John, James, and the girl's father
and mother. 52Everyone was crying and
weeping for the girl. But Jesus said,
"The child isn't dead. She is just asleep."
53The people laughed at him because
they knew she was dead.
54Jesus took hold of the girl's hand
and said, "Child, get up!" 55She came
back to life and got right up. Jesus told
them to give her something to eat. 56Her
parents were surprised, but Jesus ordered them not to tell anyone what had
happened.

Instructions for the Twelve Apostles

(Matthew 10.5-15; Mark 6.7-13)

9 Jesus called together his twelve
apostles and gave them complete
power over all demons and diseases.
2Then he sent them to tell about God's
kingdom and to heal the sick. 3He told
them, "Don't take anything with you!
Don't take a walking stick or a traveling
bag or food or money or even a change
of clothes. 4When you are welcomed
into a home, stay there until you leave
that town. 5If people won't welcome
you, leave the town and shake the dust
from your feet[e] as a warning to them."
6The apostles left and went from village to village, telling the good news
and healing people everywhere.

Herod Is Worried

(Matthew 14.1-12; Mark 6.14-29)

7Herod[f] the ruler heard about all that
was happening, and he was worried.
Some people were saying that John the
Baptist had come back to life. 8Others
were saying that Elijah had come[g] or
that one of the prophets from long ago
had come back to life. 9But Herod said,
"I had John's head cut off! Who is this I
hear so much about?" Herod was eager
to meet Jesus.

Jesus Feeds Five Thousand

(Matthew 14.13-21; Mark 6.30-44; John 6.1-14)

10The apostles came back and told Jesus everything they had done. He then
took them with him to the village of
Bethsaida, where they could be alone.
11But a lot of people found out about

[b]**8.37** *Gerasa*: See the note at 8.26. [c]**8.43** *She had spent everything she had on doctors*: Some manuscripts do not have these words. [d]**8.45** *from every side*: Some manuscripts add "and you ask, 'Who touched me?' " [e]**9.5** *shake the dust from your feet*: This was a way of showing rejection. [f]**9.7** *Herod*: Herod Antipas, the son of Herod the Great. [g]**9.8** *Elijah had come*: Many of the Jewish people expected the prophet Elijah to come and prepare the way for the Messiah.

this and followed him. Jesus welcomed
them. He spoke to them about God's
kingdom and healed everyone who was
sick.
12 Late in the afternoon the twelve
apostles came to Jesus and said, "Send
the crowd to the villages and farms
around here. They need to find a place
to stay and something to eat. There is
nothing in this place. It is like a desert!"
13 Jesus answered, "You give them
something to eat."
But they replied, "We have only five
small loaves of bread[h] and two fish. If
we are going to feed all these people, we
will have to go and buy food." 14 There
were about five thousand men in the
crowd.
Jesus said to his disciples, "Have the
people sit in groups of fifty." 15 They did
this, and all the people sat down. 16 Jesus
took the five loaves and the two fish. He
looked up toward heaven and blessed
the food. Then he broke the bread and
fish and handed them to his disciples to
give to the people.
17 Everyone ate all they wanted. What
was left over filled twelve baskets.

Who Is Jesus?

(Matthew 16.13-19; Mark 8.27-29)

18 When Jesus was alone praying, his
disciples came to him, and he asked
them, "What do people say about me?"
19 They answered, "Some say that you
are John the Baptist or Elijah[i] or a
prophet from long ago who has come
back to life."
20 Jesus then asked them, "But who do
you say I am?"
Peter answered, "You are the Messiah
sent from God."
21 Jesus strictly warned his disciples
not to tell anyone about this.

Jesus Speaks about His Suffering and Death

(Matthew 16.20-28; Mark 8.30—9.1)

22 Jesus told his disciples, "The nation's leaders, the chief priests, and the
teachers of the Law of Moses will make
the Son of Man suffer terribly. They will
reject him and kill him, but three days
later he will rise to life."
23 Then Jesus said to all the people:

> If any of you want to be my fol-
> lowers, you must forget about your-
> self. You must take up your cross
> each day and follow me. 24 If you
> want to save your life,[j] you will de-
> stroy it. But if you give up your life
> for me, you will save it. 25 What will
> you gain, if you own the whole
> world but destroy yourself or waste
> your life? 26 If you are ashamed of
> me and my message, the Son of Man
> will be ashamed of you when he
> comes in his glory and in the glory
> of his Father and the holy angels.
> 27 You can be sure that some of the
> people standing here will not die be-
> fore they see God's kingdom.

The True Glory of Jesus

(Matthew 17.1-8; Mark 9.2-8)

28 About eight days later Jesus took
Peter, John, and James with him and
went up on a mountain to pray. 29 While
he was praying, his face changed, and
his clothes became shining white. 30 Suddenly Moses and Elijah were there
speaking with him. 31 They appeared in
heavenly glory and talked about all that
Jesus' death[k] in Jerusalem would mean.
32 Peter and the other two disciples
had been sound asleep. All at once they
woke up and saw how glorious Jesus
was. They also saw the two men who
were with him.
33 Moses and Elijah were about to
leave, when Peter said to Jesus, "Master,
it is good for us to be here! Let us make
three shelters, one for you, one for
Moses, and one for Elijah." But Peter did
not know what he was talking about.
34 While Peter was still speaking, a
shadow from a cloud passed over them,
and they were frightened as the cloud
covered them. 35 From the cloud a voice
spoke, "This is my chosen Son. Listen to
what he says!"
36 After the voice had spoken, Peter,
John, and James saw only Jesus. For
some time they kept quiet and did not
say anything about what they had seen.

Jesus Heals a Boy

(Matthew 17.14-18; Mark 9.14-27)

37 The next day Jesus and his three
disciples came down from the mountain
and were met by a large crowd. 38 Just
then someone in the crowd shouted,
"Teacher, please do something for my
son! He is my only child! 39 A demon often attacks him and makes him scream.
It shakes him until he foams at the
mouth, and it won't leave him until it
has completely worn the boy out. 40 I
begged your disciples to force out the
demon, but they couldn't do it."
41 Jesus said to them, "You people are
stubborn and don't have any faith! How
much longer must I be with you? Why
do I have to put up with you?"
Then Jesus said to the man, "Bring
your son to me." 42 While the boy was

[h] **9.13** *small loaves of bread*: These would have been flat and round or in the shape of a bun.
[i] **9.19** *Elijah*: See the note at 9.8. [j] **9.24** *life*: In verses 24, 25 a Greek word which often means "soul" is translated "life" and "yourself." [k] **9.31** *Jesus' death*: In Greek this is "his departure," which probably includes his rising to life and his return to heaven.

being brought, the demon attacked him
and made him shake all over. Jesus ordered the demon to stop. Then he
healed the boy and gave him back to his
father. 43Everyone was amazed at God's
great power.

Jesus Again Speaks about His Death
(Matthew 17.22, 23; Mark 9.30-32)

While everyone was still amazed at
what Jesus was doing, he said to his disciples, 44"Pay close attention to what I
am telling you! The Son of Man will be
handed over to his enemies." 45But the
disciples did not know what he meant.
The meaning was hidden from them.
They could not understand it, and they
were afraid to ask.

Who Is the Greatest?
(Matthew 18.1-5; Mark 9.33-37)

46Jesus' disciples were arguing about
which one of them was the greatest.
47Jesus knew what they were thinking,
and he had a child stand there beside
him. 48Then he said to his disciples,
"When you welcome even a child because of me, you welcome me. And
when you welcome me, you welcome
the one who sent me. Whichever one of
you is the most humble is the greatest."

For or against Jesus
(Mark 9.38-40)

49John said, "Master, we saw a man
using your name to force demons out of
people. But we told him to stop, because
he isn't one of us."
50"Don't stop him!" Jesus said. "Anyone who isn't against you is for you."

A Samaritan Village Refuses To Receive Jesus

51Not long before it was time for Jesus
to be taken up to heaven, he made up
his mind to go to Jerusalem. 52He sent
some messengers on ahead to a Samaritan village to get things ready for him.
53But he was on his way to Jerusalem,
so the people there refused to welcome
him. 54When the disciples James and
John saw what was happening, they
asked, "Lord, do you want us to call
down fire from heaven to destroy these
people?"[l]
55But Jesus turned and corrected them
for what they had said.[m] 56Then they all
went on to another village.

Three People Who Wanted To Be Followers
(Matthew 8.19-22)

57Along the way someone said to Jesus, "I'll go anywhere with you!"
58Jesus said, "Foxes have dens, and
birds have nests, but the Son of Man
doesn't have a place to call his own."
59Jesus told someone else to come
with him. But the man said, "Lord, let
me wait until I bury my father."[n]
60Jesus answered, "Let the dead take
care of the dead, while you go and tell
about God's kingdom."
61Then someone said to Jesus, "I want
to go with you, Lord, but first let me go
back and take care of things at home."
62Jesus answered, "Anyone who starts
plowing and keeps looking back isn't
worth a thing to God's kingdom!"

The Work of the Seventy-Two Followers

10 Later the Lord chose seventy-
two[o] other followers and sent
them out two by two to every town and
village where he was about to go. 2He
said to them:

A large crop is in the fields, but
there are only a few workers. Ask
the Lord in charge of the harvest to
send out workers to bring it in. 3Now
go, but remember, I am sending you
like lambs into a pack of wolves.
4Don't take along a moneybag or a
traveling bag or sandals. And don't
waste time greeting people on the
road.[p] 5As soon as you enter a
home, say, "God bless this home
with peace." 6If the people living
there are peace-loving, your prayer
for peace will bless them. But if they
are not peace-loving, your prayer
will return to you. 7Stay with the
same family, eating and drinking
whatever they give you, because
workers are worth what they earn.
Don't move around from house to
house.
8If the people of a town welcome
you, eat whatever they offer. 9Heal
their sick and say, "God's kingdom
will soon be here!"[q]
10But if the people of a town refuse
to welcome you, go out into the

[l]**9.54** *to destroy these people*: Some manuscripts add "as Elijah did." [m]**9.55** *what they had said*: Some manuscripts add, "and said, 'Don't you know what spirit you belong to? The Son of Man did not come to destroy people's lives, but to save them.'" [n]**9.59** *bury my father*: The Jewish people taught that giving someone a proper burial was even more important than helping the poor. [o]**10.1** *seventy-two*: Some manuscripts have "seventy." According to Jewish tradition, there were seventy nations on earth. But the ancient Greek translation of the Old Testament has "seventy-two" in place of "seventy." Jesus probably chose this number of followers to show that his message was for everyone in the world.
[p]**10.4** *waste time greeting people on the road*: In those days a polite greeting could take a long time. [q]**10.9** *will soon be here*: Or "is already here."

street and say, [11]"We are shaking the dust from our feet[r] as a warning to you. And you can be sure that God's kingdom will soon be here!"[s] [12]I tell you that on the day of judgment the people of Sodom will get off easier than the people of that town!

The Unbelieving Towns
(Matthew 11.20-24)

[13]You people of Chorazin are in for trouble! You people of Bethsaida are also in for trouble! If the miracles that took place in your towns had happened in Tyre and Sidon, the people there would have turned to God long ago. They would have dressed in sackcloth and put ashes on their heads.[t] [14]On the day of judgment the people of Tyre and Sidon will get off easier than you will. [15]People of Capernaum, do you think you will be honored in heaven? Well, you will go down to hell!

[16]My followers, whoever listens to you is listening to me. Anyone who says "No" to you is saying "No" to me. And anyone who says "No" to me is really saying "No" to the one who sent me.

The Return of the Seventy-Two

[17]When the seventy-two[u] followers returned, they were excited and said, "Lord, even the demons obeyed when we spoke in your name!"

[18]Jesus told them:

I saw Satan fall from heaven like a flash of lightning. [19]I have given you the power to trample on snakes and scorpions and to defeat the power of your enemy Satan. Nothing can harm you. [20]But don't be happy because evil spirits obey you. Be happy that your names are written in heaven!

Jesus Thanks His Father
(Matthew 11.25-27; 13.16, 17)

[21]At that same time, Jesus felt the joy that comes from the Holy Spirit,[v] and he said:

My Father, Lord of heaven and earth, I am grateful that you hid all this from wise and educated people and showed it to ordinary people. Yes, Father, that is what pleased you.

[22]My Father has given me everything, and he is the only one who knows the Son. The only one who really knows the Father is the Son. But the Son wants to tell others about the Father, so that they can know him too.

[23]Jesus then turned to his disciples and said to them in private, "You are really blessed to see what you see! [24]Many prophets and kings were eager to see what you see and to hear what you hear. But I tell you that they did not see or hear."

The Good Samaritan

[25]An expert in the Law of Moses stood up and asked Jesus a question to see what he would say. "Teacher," he asked, "what must I do to have eternal life?"

[26]Jesus answered, "What is written in the Scriptures? How do you understand them?"

[27]The man replied, "The Scriptures say, 'Love the Lord your God with all your heart, soul, strength, and mind.' They also say, 'Love your neighbors as much as you love yourself.' "

[28]Jesus said, "You have given the right answer. If you do this, you will have eternal life."

[29]But the man wanted to show that he knew what he was talking about. So he asked Jesus, "Who are my neighbors?"

[30]Jesus replied:

As a man was going down from Jerusalem to Jericho, robbers attacked him and grabbed everything he had. They beat him up and ran off, leaving him half dead.

[31]A priest happened to be going down the same road. But when he saw the man, he walked by on the other side. [32]Later a temple helper[w] came to the same place. But when he saw the man who had been beaten up, he also went by on the other side.

[33]A man from Samaria then came traveling along that road. When he saw the man, he felt sorry for him [34]and went over to him. He treated his wounds with olive oil and wine[x] and bandaged them. Then he put him on his own donkey and took him to an inn, where he took care of him. [35]The next morning he gave the innkeeper two silver coins and said, "Please take care of the man. If you spend more than this on him, I will pay you when I return."

[36]Then Jesus asked, "Which one of

[r]**10.11** *shaking the dust from our feet*: This was a way of showing rejection. [s]**10.11** *will soon be here*: Or "is already here." [t]**10.13** *dressed in sackcloth . . . ashes on their heads*: This was one way that people showed how sorry they were for their sins. [u]**10.17** *seventy-two*: See the note at 10.1. [v]**10.21** *the Holy Spirit*: Some manuscripts have "his spirit." [w]**10.32** *temple helper*: A man from the tribe of Levi, whose job it was to work around the temple. [x]**10.34** *olive oil and wine*: In New Testament times these were used as medicine. Sometimes olive oil is a symbol for healing by means of a miracle (see James 5.14).

these three people was a real neighbor
to the man who was beaten up by robbers?"
37 The teacher answered, "The one
who showed pity."
Jesus said, "Go and do the same!"

Martha and Mary

38 The Lord and his disciples were
traveling along and came to a village.
When they got there, a woman named
Martha welcomed him into her home.
39 She had a sister named Mary, who sat
down in front of the Lord and was listening to what he said. 40 Martha was
worried about all that had to be done.
Finally, she went to Jesus and said,
"Lord, doesn't it bother you that my
sister has left me to do all the work
by myself? Tell her to come and help
me!"
41 The Lord answered, "Martha,
Martha! You are worried and upset
about so many things, 42 but only one
thing is necessary. Mary has chosen
what is best, and it will not be taken
away from her."

Prayer

(Matthew 6.9-13; 7.7-11)

11 When Jesus had finished praying,
one of his disciples said to him,
"Lord, teach us to pray, just as John
taught his followers to pray."
2 So Jesus told them, "Pray in this way:

'Father, help us
to honor your name.
Come and set up
your kingdom.
3 Give us each day
the food we need.[y]
4 Forgive our sins,
as we forgive everyone
who has done wrong to us.
And keep us
from being tempted.' "

5 Then Jesus went on to say:
Suppose one of you goes to a
friend in the middle of the night and
says, "Let me borrow three loaves
of bread. 6 A friend of mine has
dropped in, and I don't have a thing
for him to eat." 7 And suppose your
friend answers, "Don't bother me!
The door is bolted, and my children
and I are in bed. I cannot get up to
give you something."
8 He may not get up and give you
the bread, just because you are his
friend. But he will get up and give
you as much as you need, simply because you are not ashamed to keep
on asking.
9 So I tell you to ask and you will
receive, search and you will find,
knock and the door will be opened
for you. 10 Everyone who asks will
receive, everyone who searches will
find, and the door will be opened for
everyone who knocks. 11 Which one
of you fathers would give your hungry child a snake if the child asked
for a fish? 12 Which one of you would
give your child a scorpion if the
child asked for an egg? 13 As bad as
you are, you still know how to give
good gifts to your children. But your
heavenly Father is even more ready
to give the Holy Spirit to anyone
who asks.

Jesus and the Ruler of Demons

(Matthew 12.22-30; Mark 3.20-27)

14 Jesus forced a demon out of a man
who could not talk. And after the demon
had gone out, the man started speaking,
and the crowds were amazed. 15 But
some people said, "He forces out demons by the power of Beelzebul, the
ruler of the demons!"
16 Others wanted to put Jesus to the
test. So they asked him to show them a
sign from God. 17 Jesus knew what they
were thinking, and he said:
A kingdom where people fight
each other will end up in ruin. And a
family that fights will break up. 18 If
Satan fights against himself, how
can his kingdom last? Yet you say
that I force out demons by the power
of Beelzebul. 19 If I use his power to
force out demons, whose power do
your own followers use to force
them out? They are the ones who
will judge you. 20 But if I use God's
power to force out demons, it proves
that God's kingdom has already
come to you.
21 When a strong man arms himself and guards his home, everything
he owns is safe. 22 But if a stronger
man comes and defeats him, he will
carry off the weapons in which the
strong man trusted. Then he will
divide with others what he has
taken. 23 If you are not on my side,
you are against me. If you don't
gather in the crop with me, you
scatter it.

Return of an Evil Spirit

(Matthew 12.43-45)

24 When an evil spirit leaves a person, it travels through the desert,
looking for a place to rest. But when
it doesn't find a place, it says, "I will
go back to the home I left." 25 When
it gets there and finds the place

[y] **11.3** *the food we need*: Or "food for today" or "food for the coming day."

clean and fixed up, 26 it goes off and
finds seven other evil spirits even
worse than itself. They all come and
make their home there, and that person ends up in worse shape than before.

Being Really Blessed

27 While Jesus was still talking, a
woman in the crowd spoke up, "The
woman who gave birth to you and
nursed you is blessed!"
28 Jesus replied, "That's true, but the
people who are really blessed are the
ones who hear and obey God's message!"[z]

A Sign from God
(Matthew 12.38-42; Mark 8.12)

29 As crowds were gathering around
Jesus, he said:
You people of today are evil! You
keep looking for a sign from God.
But what happened to Jonah[a] is the
only sign you will be given. 30 Just as
Jonah was a sign to the people of
Nineveh, the Son of Man will be a
sign to the people of today. 31 When
the judgment comes, the Queen of
the South[b] will stand there with you
and condemn you. She traveled a
long way to hear Solomon's wisdom,
and yet here is something far
greater than Solomon. 32 The people
of Nineveh will also stand there with
you and condemn you. They turned
to God when Jonah preached, and
yet here is something far greater
than Jonah.

Light
(Matthew 5.15; 6.22, 23)

33 No one lights a lamp and then
hides it or puts it under a clay pot. A
lamp is put on a lampstand, so that
everyone who comes into the house
can see the light. 34 Your eyes are the
lamp for your body. When your eyes
are good, you have all the light you
need. But when your eyes are bad,
everything is dark. 35 So be sure
that your light isn't darkness. 36 If
you have light, and nothing is dark,
then light will be everywhere, as
when a lamp shines brightly on
you.

Jesus Condemns the Pharisees and Teachers of the Law of Moses
(Matthew 23.1-36; Mark 12.38-40; Luke 20.45-47)

37 When Jesus finished speaking, a
Pharisee invited him home for a meal.
Jesus went and sat down to eat.[c] 38 The
Pharisee was surprised that he did not
wash his hands[d] before eating. 39 So the
Lord said to him:
You Pharisees clean the outside of
cups and dishes, but on the inside
you are greedy and evil. 40 You fools!
Didn't God make both the outside
and the inside?[e] 41 If you would only
give what you have to the poor,
everything you do would please
God.
42 You Pharisees are in for trouble!
You give God a tenth of the spices
from your gardens, such as mint and
rue. But you cheat people, and you
don't love God. You should be fair
and kind to others and still give a
tenth to God.
43 You Pharisees are in for trouble!
You love the front seats in the meeting places, and you like to be
greeted with honor in the market.
44 But you are in for trouble! You are
like unmarked graves[f] that people
walk on without even knowing it.
45 A teacher of the Law of Moses spoke
up, "Teacher, you said cruel things
about us."
46 Jesus replied:
You teachers are also in for trouble! You load people down with
heavy burdens, but you won't lift a
finger to help them carry the loads.
47 Yes, you are really in for trouble.
You build monuments to honor the
prophets your own people murdered
long ago. 48 You must think that was
the right thing for your people to do,
or else you would not have built
monuments for the prophets they
murdered.
49 Because of your evil deeds, the
Wisdom of God said, "I will send
prophets and apostles to you. But
you will murder some and mistreat
others." 50 You people living today
will be punished for all the prophets
who have been murdered since the
beginning of the world. 51 This includes every prophet from the time

[z] **11.28** *"That's true, but the people who are really blessed . . . message"*: Or " 'That's not true, the people who are blessed . . . message.' " [a] **11.29** *what happened to Jonah*: Jonah was in the stomach of a big fish for three days and nights (see Matthew 12.40). [b] **11.31** *Queen of the South*: Sheba, probably a country in southern Arabia. [c] **11.37** *sat down to eat*: See the note at 7.36. [d] **11.38** *did not wash his hands*: The Jewish people had strict laws about washing their hands before eating, especially if they had been out in public. [e] **11.40** *Didn't God make both the outside and the inside?*: Or "Doesn't the person who washes the outside always wash the inside too?" [f] **11.44** *unmarked graves*: Tombs were whitewashed to keep anyone from accidentally touching them. A person who touched a dead body or a tomb was considered unclean and could not worship with other Jewish people.

of Abel to the time of Zechariah,[g]
who was murdered between the altar and the temple. You people will
certainly be punished for all of this.
52You teachers of the Law of
Moses are really in for trouble! You
carry the keys to the door of knowledge about God. But you never go
in, and you keep others from going
in.
53Jesus was about to leave, but the
teachers and the Pharisees wanted to
get even with him. They tried to make
him say what he thought about other
things, 54so that they could catch him
saying something wrong.

Warnings

12 As thousands of people crowded
around Jesus and were stepping
on each other, he told his disciples:
Be sure to guard against the dishonest teaching[h] of the Pharisees! It
is their way of fooling people.
2Everything that is hidden will be
found out, and every secret will be
known. 3Whatever you say in the
dark will be heard when it is day.
Whatever you whisper in a closed
room will be shouted from the
housetops.

The One To Fear
(Matthew 10.28-31)

4My friends, don't be afraid of
people. They can kill you, but after
that, there is nothing else they can
do. 5God is the one you must fear.
Not only can he take your life, but
he can throw you into hell. God is
certainly the one you should fear!
6Five sparrows are sold for just
two pennies, but God doesn't forget
a one of them. 7Even the hairs on
your head are counted. So don't be
afraid! You are worth much more
than many sparrows.

Telling Others about Christ
(Matthew 10.32, 33; 12.32; 10.19, 20)

8If you tell others that you belong
to me, the Son of Man will tell God's
angels that you are my followers.
9But if you reject me, you will be rejected in front of them. 10If you
speak against the Son of Man, you
can be forgiven, but if you speak
against the Holy Spirit, you cannot
be forgiven.
11When you are brought to trial in
the Jewish meeting places or before
rulers or officials, don't worry about
how you will defend yourselves or
what you will say. 12At that time the
Holy Spirit will tell you what to say.

A Rich Fool

13A man in a crowd said to Jesus,
"Teacher, tell my brother to give me my
share of what our father left us when he
died."
14Jesus answered, "Who gave me the
right to settle arguments between you
and your brother?"
15Then he said to the crowd, "Don't be
greedy! Owning a lot of things won't
make your life safe."
16So Jesus told them this story:
A rich man's farm produced a big
crop, 17and he said to himself, "What
can I do? I don't have a place large
enough to store everything."
18Later, he said, "Now I know what
I'll do. I'll tear down my barns and
build bigger ones, where I can store
all my grain and other goods. 19Then
I'll say to myself, 'You have stored
up enough good things to last for
years to come. Live it up! Eat, drink,
and enjoy yourself.' "
20But God said to him, "You fool!
Tonight you will die. Then who will
get what you have stored up?"
21"This is what happens to people who
store up everything for themselves, but
are poor in the sight of God."

Worry
(Matthew 6.25-34)

22Jesus said to his disciples:
I tell you not to worry about your
life! Don't worry about having something to eat or wear. 23Life is more
than food or clothing. 24Look at the
crows! They don't plant or harvest,
and they don't have storehouses or
barns. But God takes care of them.
You are much more important than
any birds. 25Can worry make you
live longer?[i] 26If you don't have
power over small things, why worry
about everything else?
27Look how the wild flowers grow!
They don't work hard to make their
clothes. But I tell you that Solomon
with all his wealth[j] wasn't as well
clothed as one of these flowers.
28God gives such beauty to everything that grows in the fields, even
though it is here today and thrown

[g] **11.51** *from the time of Abel . . . Zechariah*: Genesis is the first book in the Jewish Scriptures, and it tells that Abel was the first person to be murdered. Second Chronicles is the last book in the Jewish Scriptures, and the last murder that it tells about is that of Zechariah.
[h] **12.1** *dishonest teaching*: The Greek text has "yeast," which is used here of a teaching that is not true (see Matthew 16.6, 12). [i] **12.25** *live longer*: Or "grow taller." [j] **12.27** *Solomon with all his wealth*: The Jewish people thought that Solomon was the richest person who had ever lived.

into a fire tomorrow. Won't he do
even more for you? You have such
little faith!
29Don't keep worrying about having something to eat or drink. 30Only
people who don't know God are always worrying about such things.
Your Father knows what you need.
31But put God's work first, and these
things will be yours as well.

Treasures in Heaven
(Matthew 6.19-21)

32My little group of disciples, don't
be afraid! Your Father wants to give
you the kingdom. 33Sell what you
have and give the money to the poor.
Make yourselves moneybags that
never wear out. Make sure your
treasure is safe in heaven, where
thieves cannot steal it and moths
cannot destroy it. 34Your heart will
always be where your treasure is.

Faithful and Unfaithful Servants
(Matthew 24.45-51)

35Be ready and keep your lamps
burning 36just like those servants
who wait up for their master to return from a wedding feast. As soon
as he comes and knocks, they open
the door for him. 37Servants are fortunate if their master finds them
awake and ready when he comes! I
promise you that he will get ready
and have his servants sit down so he
can serve them. 38Those servants are
really fortunate if their master finds
them ready, even though he comes
late at night or early in the morning.
39You would surely not let a thief
break into your home, if you knew
when the thief was coming. 40So always be ready! You don't know
when the Son of Man will come.
41Peter asked Jesus, "Did you say this
just for us or for everyone?"
42The Lord answered:
Who are faithful and wise servants? Who are the ones the master
will put in charge of giving the other
servants their food supplies at the
proper time? 43Servants are fortunate if their master comes and finds
them doing their job. 44A servant
who is always faithful will surely be
put in charge of everything the master owns.
45But suppose one of the servants
thinks that the master won't return
until late. Suppose that servant
starts beating all the other servants
and eats and drinks and gets drunk.
46If that happens, the master will
come on a day and at a time when
the servant least expects him. That
servant will then be punished and
thrown out with the servants who
cannot be trusted.
47If servants are not ready or willing to do what their master wants
them to do, they will be beaten hard.
48But servants who don't know what
their master wants them to do will
not be beaten so hard for doing
wrong. If God has been generous
with you, he will expect you to serve
him well. But if he has been more
than generous, he will expect you to
serve him even better.

Not Peace, but Trouble
(Matthew 10.34-36)

49I came to set fire to the earth,
and I wish it were already on fire! 50I
am going to be put to a hard test.
And I will have to suffer a lot of pain
until it is over. 51Do you think that I
came to bring peace to earth? No indeed! I came to make people choose
sides. 52A family of five will be divided, with two of them against the
other three. 53Fathers and sons will
turn against one another, and
mothers and daughters will do
the same. Mothers-in-law and
daughters-in-law will also turn
against each other.

Knowing What To Do
(Matthew 16.2, 3; 5.25, 26)

54Jesus said to all the people:
As soon as you see a cloud coming
up in the west, you say, "It's going to
rain," and it does. 55When the south
wind blows, you say, "It's going to
get hot," and it does. 56Are you trying to fool someone? You can predict
the weather by looking at the earth
and sky, but you don't really know
what's going on right now. 57Why
don't you understand the right thing
to do? 58When someone accuses you
of something, try to settle things before you are taken to court. If you
don't, you will be dragged before the
judge. Then the judge will hand you
over to the jailer, and you will be
locked up. 59You won't get out until
you have paid the last cent you owe.

Turn Back to God

13 About this same time Jesus was
told that Pilate had given orders
for some people from Galilee to be
killed while they were offering sacrifices. 2Jesus replied:
Do you think that these people
were worse sinners than everyone
else in Galilee just because of what
happened to them? 3Not at all! But
you can be sure that if you don't
turn back to God, every one of you
will also be killed. 4What about
those eighteen people who died

when the tower in Siloam fell on
them? Do you think they were worse
than everyone else in Jerusalem?
5 Not at all! But you can be sure that
if you don't turn back to God, every
one of you will also die.

A Story about a Fig Tree

6 Jesus then told them this story:
A man had a fig tree growing in
his vineyard. One day he went out to
pick some figs, but he didn't find
any. 7 So he said to the gardener, "For
three years I have come looking for
figs on this tree, and I haven't found
any yet. Chop it down! Why should
it take up space?"
8 The gardener answered, "Master,
leave it for another year. I'll dig
around it and put some manure on it
to make it grow. 9 Maybe it will have
figs on it next year. If it doesn't, you
can have it cut down."

Healing a Woman on the Sabbath

10 One Sabbath, Jesus was teaching in
a Jewish meeting place, 11 and a woman
was there who had been crippled by an
evil spirit for eighteen years. She was
completely bent over and could not
straighten up. 12 When Jesus saw the
woman, he called her over and said,
"You are now well." 13 He placed his
hands on her, and right away she stood
up straight and praised God.
14 The man in charge of the meeting
place was angry because Jesus had
healed someone on the Sabbath. So he
said to the people, "Each week has six
days when we can work. Come and be
healed on one of those days, but not on
the Sabbath."
15 The Lord replied, "Are you trying to
fool someone? Won't any one of you untie your ox or donkey and lead it out to
drink on a Sabbath? 16 This woman belongs to the family of Abraham, but Satan has kept her bound for eighteen
years. Isn't it right to set her free on the
Sabbath?" 17 Jesus' words made his enemies ashamed. But everyone else in the
crowd was happy about the wonderful
things he was doing.

A Mustard Seed and Yeast

(Matthew 13.31-33; Mark 4.30-32)

18 Jesus said, "What is God's kingdom
like? What can I compare it with? 19 It is
like what happens when someone
plants a mustard seed in a garden. The
seed grows as big as a tree, and birds
nest in its branches."
20 Then Jesus said, "What can I compare God's kingdom with? 21 It is like
what happens when a woman mixes
yeast into three batches of flour. Finally,
all the dough rises."

The Narrow Door

(Matthew 7.13, 14, 21-23)

22 As Jesus was on his way to Jerusalem, he taught the people in the towns
and villages. 23 Someone asked him,
"Lord, are only a few people going to be
saved?"
Jesus answered:
24 Do all you can to go in by the
narrow door! A lot of people will try
to get in, but will not be able to.
25 Once the owner of the house gets
up and locks the door, you will be
left standing outside. You will knock
on the door and say, "Sir, open the
door for us!"
But the owner will answer, "I don't
know a thing about you!"
26 Then you will start saying, "We
dined with you, and you taught in
our streets."
27 But he will say, "I really don't
know who you are! Get away from
me, you evil people!"
28 Then when you have been
thrown outside, you will weep and
grit your teeth because you will see
Abraham, Isaac, Jacob, and all the
prophets in God's kingdom. 29 People
will come from all directions and sit
down to feast in God's kingdom.
30 There the ones who are now least
important will be the most important, and those who are now most
important will be least important.

Jesus and Herod

31 At that time some Pharisees came to
Jesus and said, "You had better get
away from here! Herod[k] wants to kill
you."
32 Jesus said to them:
Go tell that fox, "I am going to
force out demons and heal people
today and tomorrow, and three days
later I'll be through." 33 But I am going on my way today and tomorrow
and the next day. After all,
Jerusalem is the place where
prophets are killed.

Jesus Loves Jerusalem

(Matthew 23.37-39)

34 Jerusalem, Jerusalem! Your people have killed the prophets and
have stoned the messengers who
were sent to you. I have often
wanted to gather your people, as a
hen gathers her chicks under her
wings. But you wouldn't let me.
35 Now your temple will be deserted.

[k] 13.31 *Herod*: Herod Antipas, the son of Herod the Great.

You won't see me again until the
time when you say,

"Blessed is the one who comes
in the name of the Lord."

Jesus Heals a Sick Man

14 One Sabbath, Jesus was having
dinner in the home of an important Pharisee, and everyone was carefully watching Jesus. 2 All of a sudden a
man with swollen legs stood up in front
of him. 3 Jesus turned and asked the
Pharisees and the teachers of the Law
of Moses, "Is it right to heal on the Sabbath?" 4 But they did not say a word.
Jesus took hold of the man. Then he
healed him and sent him away. 5 Afterwards, Jesus asked the people, "If your
son or ox falls into a well, wouldn't you
pull him out right away, even on the
Sabbath?" 6 There was nothing they
could say.

How To Be a Guest

7 Jesus saw how the guests had tried to
take the best seats. So he told them:
8 When you are invited to a wedding feast, don't sit in the best place.
Someone more important may have
been invited. 9 Then the one who invited you will come and say, "Give
your place to this other guest!" You
will be embarrassed and will have to
sit in the worst place.
10 When you are invited to be a
guest, go and sit in the worst place.
Then the one who invited you may
come and say, "My friend, take a
better seat!" You will then be honored in front of all the other guests.
11 If you put yourself above others,
you will be put down. But if you
humble yourself, you will be honored.
12 Then Jesus said to the man who had
invited him:
When you give a dinner or a banquet, don't invite your friends and
family and relatives and rich neighbors. If you do, they will invite you
in return, and you will be paid back.
13 When you give a feast, invite the
poor, the crippled, the lame, and the
blind. 14 They cannot pay you back.
But God will bless you and reward
you when his people rise from
death.

The Great Banquet
(Matthew 22.1-10)

15 After Jesus had finished speaking,
one of the guests said, "The greatest
blessing of all is to be at the banquet in
God's kingdom!"
16 Jesus told him:
A man once gave a great banquet
and invited a lot of guests. 17 When
the banquet was ready, he sent a servant to tell the guests, "Everything is
ready! Please come."
18 One guest after another started
making excuses. The first one said,
"I bought some land, and I've got to
look it over. Please excuse me."
19 Another guest said, "I bought
five teams of oxen, and I need to try
them out. Please excuse me."
20 Still another guest said, "I have
just gotten married, and I can't be
there."
21 The servant told his master what
happened, and the master became
so angry that he said, "Go as fast as
you can to every street and alley in
town! Bring in everyone who is poor
or crippled or blind or lame."
22 When the servant returned, he
said, "Master, I've done what you
told me, and there is still plenty of
room for more people."
23 His master then told him, "Go
out along the back roads and fence
rows and make people come in, so
that my house will be full. 24 Not one
of the guests I first invited will get
even a bite of my food!"

Being a Disciple
(Matthew 10.37, 38)

25 Large crowds were walking along
with Jesus, when he turned and said:
26 You cannot be my disciple, unless you love me more than you love
your father and mother, your wife
and children, and your brothers and
sisters. You cannot come with me unless you love me more than you love
your own life.
27 You cannot be my disciple unless
you carry your own cross and come
with me.
28 Suppose one of you wants to
build a tower. What is the first thing
you will do? Won't you sit down and
figure out how much it will cost and
if you have enough money to pay for
it? 29 Otherwise, you will start building the tower, but not be able to finish. Then everyone who sees what is
happening will laugh at you. 30 They
will say, "You started building, but
could not finish the job."
31 What will a king do if he has
only ten thousand soldiers to defend
himself against a king who is about
to attack him with twenty thousand
soldiers? Before he goes out to battle, won't he first sit down and decide if he can win? 32 If he thinks he
won't be able to defend himself, he
will send messengers and ask for
peace while the other king is still a
long way off. 33 So then, you cannot
be my disciple unless you give away
everything you own.

Salt and Light
(Matthew 5.13; Mark 9.50)

34Salt is good, but if it no longer
tastes like salt, how can it be made
to taste salty again? 35It is no longer
good for the soil or even for the manure pile. People simply throw it out.
If you have ears, pay attention!

One Sheep
(Matthew 18.12-14)

15 Tax collectors[l] and sinners were
all crowding around to listen to
Jesus. 2So the Pharisees and the teachers of the Law of Moses started grumbling, "This man is friendly with sinners. He even eats with them."
3Then Jesus told them this story:
4If any of you has a hundred
sheep, and one of them gets lost,
what will you do? Won't you leave
the ninety-nine in the field and go
look for the lost sheep until you find
it? 5And when you find it, you will be
so glad that you will put it on your
shoulder 6and carry it home. Then
you will call in your friends and
neighbors and say, "Let's celebrate!
I've found my lost sheep."
7Jesus said, "In the same way there is
more happiness in heaven because of
one sinner who turns to God than over
ninety-nine good people who don't need
to."

One Coin

8Jesus told the people another story:
What will a woman do if she has
ten silver coins and loses one of
them? Won't she light a lamp, sweep
the floor, and look carefully until she
finds it? 9Then she will call in her
friends and neighbors and say,
"Let's celebrate! I've found the coin I
lost."
10Jesus said, "In the same way God's
angels are happy when even one person
turns to him."

Two Sons

11Jesus also told them another story:
Once a man had two sons. 12The
younger son said to his father, "Give
me my share of the property." So the
father divided his property between
his two sons.
13Not long after that, the younger
son packed up everything he owned
and left for a foreign country, where
he wasted all his money in wild living. 14He had spent everything,
when a bad famine spread through
that whole land. Soon he had nothing to eat.
15He went to work for a man in
that country, and the man sent him
out to take care of his pigs.[m] 16He
would have been glad to eat what
the pigs were eating,[n] but no one
gave him a thing.
17Finally, he came to his senses
and said, "My father's workers have
plenty to eat, and here I am, starving
to death! 18I will go to my father and
say to him, 'Father, I have sinned
against God in heaven and against
you. 19I am no longer good enough
to be called your son. Treat me like
one of your workers.' "
20The younger son got up and
started back to his father. But when
he was still a long way off, his father
saw him and felt sorry for him. He
ran to his son and hugged and
kissed him.
21The son said, "Father, I have
sinned against God in heaven and
against you. I am no longer good
enough to be called your son."
22But his father said to the servants, "Hurry and bring the best
clothes and put them on him. Give
him a ring for his finger and
sandals[o] for his feet. 23Get the best
calf and prepare it, so we can eat
and celebrate. 24This son of mine
was dead, but has now come back to
life. He was lost and has now been
found." And they began to celebrate.
25The older son had been out in
the field. But when he came near the
house, he heard the music and dancing. 26So he called one of the servants over and asked, "What's going
on here?"
27The servant answered, "Your
brother has come home safe and
sound, and your father ordered us to
kill the best calf." 28The older
brother got so angry that he would
not even go into the house.
His father came out and begged
him to go in. 29But he said to his
father, "For years I have worked for
you like a slave and have always
obeyed you. But you have never
even given me a little goat, so that I
could give a dinner for my friends.
30This other son of yours wasted

[l] **15.1** *Tax collectors*: See the note at 3.12. [m] **15.15** *pigs*: The Jewish religion taught that pigs were not fit to eat or even to touch. A Jewish man would have felt terribly insulted if he had to feed pigs, much less eat with them. [n] **15.16** *what the pigs were eating*: The Greek text has "(bean) pods," which came from a tree in Palestine. These were used to feed animals. Poor people sometimes ate them too. [o] **15.22** *ring . . . sandals*: These show that the young man's father fully accepted him as his son. A ring was a sign of high position in the family. Sandals showed that he was a son instead of a slave, since slaves did not usually wear sandals.

your money on prostitutes. And now
that he has come home, you ordered
the best calf to be killed for a feast."
31 His father replied, "My son, you
are always with me, and everything I
have is yours. 32 But we should be
glad and celebrate! Your brother was
dead, but he is now alive. He was
lost and has now been found."

A Dishonest Manager

16 Jesus said to his disciples:
A rich man once had a man-
ager to take care of his business. But
he was told that his manager was
wasting money. 2 So the rich man
called him in and said, "What is this
I hear about you? Tell me what you
have done! You are no longer going
to work for me."
3 The manager said to himself,
"What shall I do now that my master
is going to fire me? I can't dig
ditches, and I'm ashamed to beg. 4 I
know what I'll do, so that people will
welcome me into their homes after
I've lost my job."
5 Then one by one he called in the
people who were in debt to his master. He asked the first one, "How
much do you owe my master?"
6 "A hundred barrels of olive oil,"
the man answered.
So the manager said, "Take your
bill and sit down and quickly write
'fifty'."
7 The manager asked someone else
who was in debt to his master, "How
much do you owe?"
"A thousand bushels[p] of wheat,"
the man replied.
The manager said, "Take your bill
and write 'eight hundred'."
8 The master praised his dishonest
manager for looking out for himself
so well. That's how it is! The people
of this world look out for themselves
better than the people who belong to
the light.
9 My disciples, I tell you to use
wicked wealth to make friends for
yourselves. Then when it is gone,
you will be welcomed into an eternal
home. 10 Anyone who can be trusted
in little matters can also be trusted
in important matters. But anyone
who is dishonest in little matters will
be dishonest in important matters.
11 If you cannot be trusted with this
wicked wealth, who will trust you
with true wealth? 12 And if you cannot be trusted with what belongs to
someone else, who will give you
something that will be your own?
13 You cannot be the slave of two
masters. You will like one more than
the other or be more loyal to one
than to the other. You cannot serve
God and money.

Some Sayings of Jesus

(Matthew 11.12, 13; 5.31, 32; Mark 10.11, 12)

14 The Pharisees really loved money.
So when they heard what Jesus said,
they made fun of him. 15 But Jesus told
them:
You are always making yourselves
look good, but God sees what is in
your heart. The things that most
people think are important are
worthless as far as God is concerned.
16 Until the time of John the Baptist, people had to obey the Law of
Moses and the Books of the
Prophets.[q] But since God's kingdom
has been preached, everyone is trying hard to get in. 17 Heaven and
earth will disappear before the
smallest letter of the Law does.
18 It is a terrible sin[r] for a man to
divorce his wife and marry another
woman. It is also a terrible sin for a
man to marry a divorced woman.

Lazarus and the Rich Man

19 There was once a rich man who
wore expensive clothes and every
day ate the best food. 20 But a poor
beggar named Lazarus was brought
to the gate of the rich man's house.
21 He was happy just to eat the scraps
that fell from the rich man's table.
His body was covered with sores,
and dogs kept coming up to lick
them. 22 The poor man died, and angels took him to the place of honor
next to Abraham.[s]
The rich man also died and was
buried. 23 He went to hell[t] and was
suffering terribly. When he looked
up and saw Abraham far off and
Lazarus at his side, 24 he said to
Abraham, "Have pity on me! Send
Lazarus to dip his finger in water
and touch my tongue. I'm suffering
terribly in this fire."
25 Abraham answered, "My friend,

[p] **16.7** *A thousand bushels*: The Greek text has "A hundred measures," and each measure is about ten or twelve bushels. [q] **16.16** *the Law of Moses and the Books of the Prophets*: The Jewish Scriptures, that is, the Old Testament. [r] **16.18** *a terrible sin*: The Greek text uses a word that means the sin of being unfaithful in marriage. [s] **16.22** *the place of honor next to Abraham*: The Jewish people thought that heaven would be a banquet that God would give for them. Abraham would be the most important person there, and the guest of honor would sit next to him. [t] **16.23** *hell*: The Greek text has "hades," which the Jewish people often thought of as the place where the dead wait for the final judgment.

remember that while you lived, you
had everything good, and Lazarus
had everything bad. Now he is
happy, and you are in pain. 26 And
besides, there is a deep ditch between us, and no one from either
side can cross over."
27 But the rich man said, "Abraham, then please send Lazarus to
my father's home. 28 Let him warn
my five brothers, so they won't come
to this horrible place."
29 Abraham answered, "Your
brothers can read what Moses and
the prophets[u] wrote. They should
pay attention to that."
30 Then the rich man said, "No,
that's not enough! If only someone
from the dead would go to them,
they would listen and turn to God."
31 So Abraham said, "If they won't
pay attention to Moses and the
prophets, they won't listen even to
someone who comes back from the
dead."

Faith and Service

(Matthew 18.6, 7, 21, 22; Mark 9.42)

17 Jesus said to his disciples:
There will always be something that causes people to sin. But
anyone who causes them to sin is in
for trouble. A person who causes
even one of my little followers to sin
2 would be better off thrown into the
ocean with a heavy stone tied
around their neck. 3 So be careful
what you do.
Correct any followers[v] of mine
who sin, and forgive the ones who
say they are sorry. 4 Even if one of
them mistreats you seven times in
one day and says, "I am sorry," you
should still forgive that person.
5 The apostles said to the Lord, "Make
our faith stronger!"
6 Jesus replied:
If you had faith no bigger than a
tiny mustard seed, you could tell this
mulberry tree to pull itself up, roots
and all, and to plant itself in the
ocean. And it would!
7 If your servant comes in from
plowing or from taking care of the
sheep, would you say, "Welcome!
Come on in and have something to
eat"? 8 No, you wouldn't say that. You
would say, "Fix me something to eat.
Get ready to serve me, so I can have
my meal. Then later on you can eat
and drink." 9 Servants don't deserve
special thanks for doing what they
are supposed to do. 10 And that's how
it should be with you. When you've
done all you should, then say, "We
are merely servants, and we have
simply done our duty."

Ten Men with Leprosy

11 On his way to Jerusalem, Jesus went
along the border between Samaria and
Galilee. 12 As he was going into a village,
ten men with leprosy[w] came toward
him. They stood at a distance 13 and
shouted, "Jesus, Master, have pity on
us!"
14 Jesus looked at them and said, "Go
show yourselves to the priests."[x]
On their way they were healed.
15 When one of them discovered that he
was healed, he came back, shouting
praises to God. 16 He bowed down at the
feet of Jesus and thanked him. The man
was from the country of Samaria.
17 Jesus asked, "Weren't ten men
healed? Where are the other nine?
18 Why was this foreigner the only one
who came back to thank God?" 19 Then
Jesus told the man, "You may get up and
go. Your faith has made you well."

God's Kingdom

(Matthew 24.23-28, 37-41)

20 Some Pharisees asked Jesus when
God's kingdom would come. He answered, "God's kingdom isn't something
you can see. 21 There is no use saying,
'Look! Here it is' or 'Look! There it is.'
God's kingdom is here with you."[y]
22 Jesus said to his disciples:
The time will come when you will
long to see one of the days of the
Son of Man, but you will not.
23 When people say to you, "Look
there," or "Look here," don't go looking for him. 24 The day of the Son of
Man will be like lightning flashing
across the sky. 25 But first he must
suffer terribly and be rejected by the
people of today. 26 When the Son of
Man comes, things will be just as
they were when Noah lived. 27 People
were eating, drinking, and getting
married right up to the day when
Noah went into the big boat. Then
the flood came and drowned everyone on earth.
28 When Lot[z] lived, people were
also eating and drinking. They were
buying, selling, planting, and

[u] **16.29** *Moses and the prophets*: The Jewish Scriptures, that is, the Old Testament.
[v] **17.3** *followers*: The Greek text has "brothers," which is often used in the New Testament for followers of Jesus. [w] **17.12** *leprosy*: See the note at 4.27. [x] **17.14** *show yourselves to the priests*: See the note at 5.14. [y] **17.21** *here with you*: Or "in your hearts." [z] **17.27,28** *Noah . . . Lot*: When God destroyed the earth by a flood, he saved Noah and his family. And when God destroyed the cities of Sodom and Gomorrah and the evil people who lived there, he rescued Lot and his family (see Genesis 19.1-29).

building. 29But on the very day Lot
left Sodom, fiery flames poured
down from the sky and killed everyone. 30The same will happen on the
day when the Son of Man appears.
31At that time no one on a rooftop[a]
should go down into the house to get
anything. No one in a field should go
back to the house for anything. 32Re-
member what happened to Lot's
wife.[b]
33People who try to save their lives
will lose them, and those who lose
their lives will save them. 34On that
night two people will be sleeping in
the same bed, but only one will be
taken. The other will be left. 35-36Two
women will be together grinding
wheat, but only one will be taken.
The other will be left.[c]
37Then Jesus' disciples spoke up, "But
where will this happen, Lord?"
Jesus said, "Where there is a corpse,
there will always be buzzards."[d]

A Widow and a Judge

18 Jesus told his disciples a story
about how they should keep on
praying and never give up:
2In a town there was once a judge
who didn't fear God or care about
people. 3In that same town there was
a widow who kept going to the judge
and saying, "Make sure that I get
fair treatment in court."
4For a while the judge refused to
do anything. Finally, he said to himself, "Even though I don't fear God
or care about people, 5I will help this
widow because she keeps on bothering me. If I don't help her, she will
wear me out."
6The Lord said:
Think about what that crooked
judge said. 7Won't God protect his
chosen ones who pray to him day
and night? Won't he be concerned
for them? 8He will surely hurry and
help them. But when the Son of Man
comes, will he find on this earth
anyone with faith?

A Pharisee and a Tax Collector

9Jesus told a story to some people
who thought they were better than others and who looked down on everyone
else:
10Two men went into the temple to
pray.[e] One was a Pharisee and the
other a tax collector.[f] 11The Pharisee
stood over by himself and prayed,[g]
"God, I thank you that I am not
greedy, dishonest, and unfaithful in
marriage like other people. And I am
really glad that I am not like that tax
collector over there. 12I go without
eating[h] for two days a week, and I
give you one tenth of all I earn."
13The tax collector stood off at a
distance and did not think he was
good enough even to look up toward
heaven. He was so sorry for what he
had done that he pounded his chest
and prayed, "God, have pity on me! I
am such a sinner."
14Then Jesus said, "When the two men
went home, it was the tax collector and
not the Pharisee who was pleasing to
God. If you put yourself above others,
you will be put down. But if you humble
yourself, you will be honored."

Jesus Blesses Little Children

(Matthew 19.13-15; Mark 10.13-16)

15Some people brought their little children for Jesus to bless. But when his
disciples saw them doing this, they told
the people to stop bothering him. 16So
Jesus called the children over to him
and said, "Let the children come to me!
Don't try to stop them. People who are
like these children belong to God's kingdom.[i] 17You will never get into God's
kingdom unless you enter it like a
child!"

A Rich and Important Man

(Matthew 19.16-30; Mark 10.17-31)

18An important man asked Jesus,
"Good Teacher, what must I do to have
eternal life?"
19Jesus said, "Why do you call me
good? Only God is good. 20You know the
commandments: 'Be faithful in marriage. Do not murder. Do not steal. Do
not tell lies about others. Respect your
father and mother.' "
21He told Jesus, "I have obeyed all
these commandments since I was a
young man."

[a]**17.31** *rooftop*: See the note at 5.19. [b]**17.32** *what happened to Lot's wife*: She turned into a block of salt when she disobeyed God (see Genesis 19.26). [c]**17.35,36** *will be left*: Some manuscripts add, "Two men will be in the same field, but only one will be taken. The other will be left." [d]**17.37** *Where there is a corpse, there will always be buzzards*: This saying may mean that when anything important happens, people soon know about it. Or the saying may mean that whenever something bad happens, curious people gather around and stare. But the word translated "buzzard" also means "eagle" and may refer to the Roman army, which had an eagle as its symbol. [e]**18.10** *into the temple to pray*: Jewish people usually prayed there early in the morning and late in the afternoon. [f]**18.10** *tax collector*: See the note at 3.12. [g]**18.11** *stood over by himself and prayed*: Some manuscripts have "stood up and prayed to himself." [h]**18.12** *without eating*: See the note at 2.37. [i]**18.16** *People who are like these children belong to God's kingdom*: Or "God's kingdom belongs to people who are like these children."

22When Jesus heard this, he said,
"There is one thing you still need to do.
Go and sell everything you own! Give
the money to the poor, and you will
have riches in heaven. Then come and
be my follower." 23When the man heard
this, he was sad, because he was very
rich.
24Jesus saw how sad the man was. So
he said, "It's terribly hard for rich people to get into God's kingdom! 25In fact,
it's easier for a camel to go through the
eye of a needle than for a rich person to
get into God's kingdom."
26When the crowd heard this, they
asked, "How can anyone ever be
saved?"
27Jesus replied, "There are some
things that people cannot do, but God
can do anything."
28Peter said, "Remember, we left
everything to be your followers!"
29Jesus answered, "You can be sure
that anyone who gives up home or wife
or brothers or family or children because of God's kingdom 30will be given
much more in this life. And in the future
world they will have eternal life."

Jesus Again Tells about His Death

(Matthew 20.17-19; Mark 10.32-34)

31Jesus took the twelve apostles aside
and said:
We are now on our way to
Jerusalem. Everything that the
prophets wrote about the Son of
Man will happen there. 32He will be
handed over to foreigners,[j] who will
make fun of him, mistreat him, and
spit on him. 33They will beat him
and kill him, but three days later he
will rise to life.
34The apostles did not understand
what Jesus was talking about. They
could not understand, because the
meaning of what he said was hidden
from them.

Jesus Heals a Blind Beggar

(Matthew 20.29-34; Mark 10.46-52)

35When Jesus was coming close to
Jericho, a blind man sat begging beside
the road. 36The man heard the crowd
walking by and asked what was happening. 37Some people told him that Jesus from Nazareth was passing by. 38So
the blind man shouted, "Jesus, Son of
David,[k] have pity on me!" 39The people
who were going along with Jesus told
the man to be quiet. But he shouted
even louder, "Son of David, have pity on
me!"
40Jesus stopped and told some people
to bring the blind man over to him.
When the blind man was getting near,
Jesus asked, 41"What do you want me to
do for you?"
"Lord, I want to see!" he answered.
42Jesus replied, "Look and you will
see! Your eyes are healed because of
your faith." 43Right away the man could
see, and he went with Jesus and started
thanking God. When the crowds saw
what happened, they praised God.

Zacchaeus

19 Jesus was going through Jericho,
2where a man named Zacchaeus
lived. He was in charge of collecting
taxes[l] and was very rich. 3-4Jesus was
heading his way, and Zacchaeus wanted
to see what he was like. But Zacchaeus
was a short man and could not see over
the crowd. So he ran ahead and climbed
up into a sycamore tree.
5When Jesus got there, he looked up
and said, "Zacchaeus, hurry down! I
want to stay with you today." 6Zac-
chaeus hurried down and gladly welcomed Jesus.
7Everyone who saw this started grumbling, "This man Zacchaeus is a sinner!
And Jesus is going home to eat with
him."
8Later that day Zacchaeus stood up
and said to the Lord, "I will give half of
my property to the poor. And I will now
pay back four times as much[m] to everyone I have ever cheated."
9Jesus said to Zacchaeus, "Today you
and your family have been saved,[n] because you are a true son of Abraham.[o]
10The Son of Man came to look for and
to save people who are lost."

A Story about Ten Servants

(Matthew 25.14-30)

11The crowd was still listening to Jesus as he was getting close to Jerusalem. Many of them thought that God's
kingdom would soon appear, 12and
Jesus told them this story:
A prince once went to a foreign
country to be crowned king and
then to return. 13But before leaving,
he called in ten servants and gave

[j] **18.32** *foreigners*: The Romans, who ruled Judea at this time. [k] **18.38** *Son of David*: The Jewish people expected the Messiah to be from the family of King David, and for this reason the Messiah was often called the "Son of David." [l] **19.2** *in charge of collecting taxes*: See the note at 3.12. [m] **19.8** *pay back four times as much*: Both Jewish and Roman law said that a person must pay back four times the amount that was taken. [n] **19.9** *saved*: Zacchaeus was Jewish, but it is only now that he is rescued from sin and placed under God's care. [o] **19.9** *son of Abraham*: As used in this verse, the words mean that Zacchaeus is truly one of God's special people.

each of them some money. He told
them, "Use this to earn more money
until I get back."
14 But the people of his country
hated him, and they sent messengers
to the foreign country to say, "We
don't want this man to be our king."
15 After the prince had been made
king, he returned and called in his
servants. He asked them how much
they had earned with the money
they had been given.
16 The first servant came and said,
"Sir, with the money you gave me I
have earned ten times as much."
17 "That's fine, my good servant!"
the king said. "Since you have
shown that you can be trusted with
a small amount, you will be given
ten cities to rule."
18 The second one came and said,
"Sir, with the money you gave me, I
have earned five times as much."
19 The king said, "You will be given
five cities."
20 Another servant came and said,
"Sir, here is your money. I kept it
safe in a handkerchief.
21 You are a
hard man, and I was afraid of you.
You take what isn't yours, and you
harvest crops you didn't plant."
22 "You worthless servant!" the
king told him. "You have condemned
yourself by what you have just said.
You knew that I am a hard man, taking what isn't mine and harvesting
what I've not planted.
23 Why didn't
you put my money in the bank? On
my return, I could have had the
money together with interest."
24 Then he said to some other servants standing there, "Take the
money away from him and give it to
the servant who earned ten times as
much."
25 But they said, "Sir, he already
has ten times as much!"
26 The king replied, "Those who
have something will be given more.
But everything will be taken away
from those who don't have anything.
27 Now bring me the enemies who
didn't want me to be their king. Kill
them while I watch!"

Jesus Enters Jerusalem

(Matthew 21.1-11; Mark 11.1-11; John 12.12-19)

28 When Jesus had finished saying all
this, he went on toward Jerusalem.
29 As
he was getting near Bethphage and
Bethany on the Mount of Olives, he sent
two of his disciples on ahead.
30 He told
them, "Go into the next village, where
you will find a young donkey that has
never been ridden. Untie the donkey
and bring it here.
31 If anyone asks why
you are doing that, just say, 'The Lord[p]
needs it.' "
32 They went off and found everything
just as Jesus had said.
33 While they were
untying the donkey, its owners asked,
"Why are you doing that?"
34 They answered, "The Lord[p] needs
it."
35 Then they led the donkey to Jesus.
They put some of their clothes on its
back and helped Jesus get on.
36 And as
he rode along, the people spread clothes
on the road[q] in front of him.
37 When Je-
sus was starting down the Mount of
Olives, his large crowd of disciples were
happy and praised God because of all
the miracles they had seen.
38 They
shouted,

"Blessed is the king who comes
in the name of the Lord!
Peace in heaven
and glory to God."

39 Some Pharisees in the crowd said to
Jesus, "Teacher, make your disciples
stop shouting!"
40 But Jesus answered, "If they keep
quiet, these stones will start shouting."
41 When Jesus came closer and could
see Jerusalem, he cried
42 and said:
It is too bad that today your people don't know what will bring them
peace! Now it is hidden from them.
43 Jerusalem, the time will come
when your enemies will build walls
around you to attack you. Armies
will surround you and close in on
you from every side.
44 They will
level you to the ground and kill your
people. Not one stone in your buildings will be left on top of another.
This will happen because you did
not see that God had come to save
you.[r]

Jesus in the Temple

(Matthew 21.12-17; Mark 11.15-19; John 2.13-22)

45 When Jesus entered the temple, he
started chasing out the people who were
selling things.
46 He told them, "The
Scriptures say, 'My house should be a
place of worship.' But you have made it
a place where robbers hide!"
47 Each day, Jesus kept on teaching in
the temple. So the chief priests, the
teachers of the Law of Moses, and some

[p] **19.31,34** *The Lord*: Or "The master of the donkey." [q] **19.36** *spread clothes on the road*: This was one way that Jewish people welcomed a famous person. [r] **19.44** *that God had come to save you*: The Jewish people looked for the time when God would come and rescue them from their enemies. But when Jesus came, many of them refused to obey him.

other important people tried to have
him killed. [48]But they could not find a
way to do it, because everyone else was
eager to listen to him.

A Question about Jesus' Authority
(Matthew 21.23-27; Mark 11.27-33)

20 One day, Jesus was teaching in
the temple and telling the good
news. So the chief priests, the teachers,
and the nation's leaders [2]asked him,
"What right do you have to do these
things? Who gave you this authority?"
[3]Jesus replied, "I want to ask you a
question. [4]Who gave John the right to
baptize? Was it God in heaven or merely
some human being?"
[5]They talked this over and said to
each other, "We can't say that God gave
John this right. Jesus will ask us why we
didn't believe John. [6]And we can't say
that it was merely some human who
gave John the right to baptize. The
crowd will stone us to death, because
they think John was a prophet."
[7]So they told Jesus, "We don't know
who gave John the right to baptize."
[8]Jesus replied, "Then I won't tell you
who gave me the right to do what I do."

Renters of a Vineyard
(Matthew 21.33-46; Mark 12.1-12)

[9]Jesus told the people this story:

A man once planted a vineyard
and rented it out. Then he left the
country for a long time. [10]When it
was time to harvest the crop, he sent
a servant to ask the renters for his
share of the grapes. But they beat up
the servant and sent him away without anything. [11]So the owner sent
another servant. The renters also
beat him up. They insulted him terribly and sent him away without a
thing. [12]The owner sent a third servant. He was also beaten terribly
and thrown out of the vineyard.
[13]The owner then said to himself,
"What am I going to do? I know
what. I'll send my son, the one I love
so much. They will surely respect
him!"
[14]When the renters saw the
owner's son, they said to one another, "Someday he will own the
vineyard. Let's kill him! Then we
can have it all for ourselves." [15]So
they threw him out of the vineyard
and killed him.

Jesus asked, "What do you think the
owner of the vineyard will do? [16]I'll tell
you what. He will come and kill those
renters and let someone else have his
vineyard."

When the people heard this, they said,
"This must never happen!"
[17]But Jesus looked straight at them
and said, "Then what do the Scriptures
mean when they say, 'The stone that the
builders tossed aside is now the most
important stone of all'? [18]Anyone who
stumbles over this stone will get hurt,
and anyone it falls on will be smashed
to pieces."
[19]The chief priests and the teachers of
the Law of Moses knew that Jesus was
talking about them when he was telling
this story. They wanted to arrest him
right then, but they were afraid of the
people.

Paying Taxes
(Matthew 22.15-22; Mark 12.13-17)

[20]Jesus' enemies kept watching him
closely, because they wanted to hand
him over to the Roman governor. So
they sent some men who pretended to
be good. But they were really spies
trying to catch Jesus saying something wrong. [21]The spies said to him,
"Teacher, we know that you teach the
truth about what God wants people to
do. And you treat everyone with the
same respect, no matter who they are.
[22]Tell us, should we pay taxes to the Emperor or not?"
[23]Jesus knew that they were trying to
trick him. So he told them, [24]"Show me
a coin." Then he asked, "Whose picture
and name are on it?"

"The Emperor's," they answered.
[25]Then he told them, "Give the Emperor what belongs to him and give God
what belongs to God." [26]Jesus' enemies
could not catch him saying anything
wrong there in front of the people. They
were amazed at his answer and kept
quiet.

Life in the Future World
(Matthew 22.23-33; Mark 12.18-27)

[27]The Sadducees did not believe that
people would rise to life after death.
So some of them came to Jesus [28]and
said:

Teacher, Moses wrote that if a
married man dies and has no children, his brother should marry the
widow. Their first son would then be
thought of as the son of the dead
brother.
[29]There were once seven brothers.
The first one married, but died without having any children. [30]The second one married his brother's
widow, and he also died without
having any children. [31]The same
thing happened to the third one. Finally, all seven brothers married that
woman and died without having any
children. [32]At last the woman died.
[33]When God raises people from
death, whose wife will this woman
be? All seven brothers had married
her.

34 Jesus answered:
The people in this world get married. 35 But in the future world no one
who is worthy to rise from death will
either marry 36 or die. They will be
like the angels and will be God's
children, because they have been
raised to life.
37 In the story about the burning
bush, Moses clearly shows that people will live again. He said, "The
Lord is the God worshiped by Abraham, Isaac, and Jacob."[s] 38 So the
Lord isn't the God of the dead, but of
the living. This means that everyone
is alive as far as God is concerned.
39 Some of the teachers of the Law of
Moses said, "Teacher, you have given a
good answer!" 40 From then on, no one
dared to ask Jesus any questions.

About David's Son
(Matthew 22.41-46; Mark 12.35-37)

41 Jesus asked, "Why do people say
that the Messiah will be the son of King
David?[t] 42 In the book of Psalms, David
himself says,

'The Lord said to my Lord,
Sit at my right side[u]
43 until I make your enemies
into a footstool for you.'

44 David spoke of the Messiah as his
Lord, so how can the Messiah be his
son?"

Jesus and the Teachers of the Law of Moses
(Matthew 23.1-36; Mark 12.38-40; Luke 11.37-54)

45 While everyone was listening to Jesus, he said to his disciples:
46 Guard against the teachers of
the Law of Moses! They love to walk
around in long robes, and they like
to be greeted in the market. They
want the front seats in the meeting
places and the best seats at banquets. 47 But they cheat widows out
of their homes and then pray long
prayers just to show off. These
teachers will be punished most of all.

A Widow's Offering
(Mark 12.41-44)

21 Jesus looked up and saw some
rich people tossing their gifts into
the offering box. 2 He also saw a poor
widow putting in two pennies. 3 And he
said, "I tell you that this poor woman
has put in more than all the others.
4 Everyone else gave what they didn't
need. But she is very poor and gave
everything she had."

The Temple Will Be Destroyed
(Matthew 24.1, 2; Mark 13.1, 2)

5 Some people were talking about the
beautiful stones used to build the temple
and about the gifts that had been placed
in it. Jesus said, 6 "Do you see these
stones? The time is coming when not
one of them will be left in place. They
will all be knocked down."

Warning about Trouble
(Matthew 24.3-14; Mark 13.3-13)

7 Some people asked, "Teacher, when
will all this happen? How can we know
when these things are about to take
place?"
8 Jesus replied:
Don't be fooled by those who will
come and claim to be me. They will
say, "I am Christ!" and "Now is the
time!" But don't follow them. 9 When
you hear about wars and riots, don't
be afraid. These things will have to
happen first, but that isn't the end.
10 Nations will go to war against
one another, and kingdoms will attack each other. 11 There will be great
earthquakes, and in many places
people will starve to death and suffer terrible diseases. All sorts of
frightening things will be seen in the
sky.
12 Before all this happens, you will
be arrested and punished. You will
be tried in your meeting places and
put in jail. Because of me you will be
placed on trial before kings and governors. 13 But this will be your
chance to tell about your faith.
14 Don't worry about what you will
say to defend yourselves. 15 I will
give you the wisdom to know what
to say. None of your enemies will be
able to oppose you or to say that you
are wrong. 16 You will be betrayed by
your own parents, brothers, family,
and friends. Some of you will even
be killed. 17 Because of me, you will
be hated by everyone. 18 But don't
worry![v] 19 You will be saved by being
faithful to me.

Jerusalem Will Be Destroyed
(Matthew 24.15-21; Mark 13.14-19)

20 When you see Jerusalem surrounded by soldiers, you will know
that it will soon be destroyed. 21 If
you are living in Judea at that time,
run to the mountains. If you are in

[s] **20.37** *"The Lord is the God worshiped by Abraham, Isaac, and Jacob"*: Jesus argues that if God is worshiped by these three, they must be alive, because he is the God of the living. [t] **20.41** *the son of King David*: See the note at 18.38. [u] **20.42** *right side*: The place of power and honor. [v] **21.18** *But don't worry*: The Greek text has "Not a hair of your head will be lost," which means, "There's no need to worry."

the city, leave it. And if you are out
in the country, don't go back into the
city. [22]This time of punishment is
what is written about in the Scriptures. [23]It will be an awful time for
women who are expecting babies or
nursing young children! Everywhere
in the land people will suffer horribly and be punished. [24]Some of them
will be killed by swords. Others will
be carried off to foreign countries.
Jerusalem will be overrun by foreign
nations until their time comes to an
end.

When the Son of Man Appears

(Matthew 24.29-31; Mark 13.24-27)

[25]Strange things will happen to
the sun, moon, and stars. The nations on earth will be afraid of the
roaring sea and tides, and they
won't know what to do. [26]People will
be so frightened that they will faint
because of what is happening to the
world. Every power in the sky will
be shaken.[w] [27]Then the Son of Man
will be seen, coming in a cloud with
great power and glory. [28]When all of
this starts happening, stand up
straight and be brave. You will soon
be set free.

A Lesson from a Fig Tree

(Matthew 24.32-35; Mark 13.28-31)

[29]Then Jesus told them a story:
When you see a fig tree or any
other tree [30]putting out leaves, you
know that summer will soon come.
[31]So, when you see these things happening, you know that God's kingdom will soon be here. [32]You can be
sure that some of the people of this
generation will still be alive when all
of this takes place. [33]The sky and the
earth won't last forever, but my
words will.

A Warning

[34]Don't spend all of your time
thinking about eating or drinking or
worrying about life. If you do, the final day will suddenly catch you
[35]like a trap. That day will surprise
everyone on earth. [36]Watch out and
keep praying that you can escape all
that is going to happen and that the
Son of Man will be pleased with
you.
[37]Jesus taught in the temple each day,
and he spent each night on the Mount of
Olives. [38]Everyone got up early and
came to the temple to hear him teach.

A Plot To Kill Jesus

*(Matthew 26.1-5, 14, 16; Mark 14.1, 2, 10, 11;
John 11.45-53)*

22 The Festival of Thin Bread, also
called Passover, was near. [2]The
chief priests and the teachers of the
Law of Moses were looking for a way to
get rid of Jesus, because they were
afraid of what the people might do.
[3]Then Satan entered the heart of Judas
Iscariot,[x] who was one of the twelve
apostles.
[4]Judas went to talk with the chief
priests and the officers of the temple police about how he could help them arrest Jesus. [5]They were very pleased and
offered to pay Judas some money. [6]He
agreed and started looking for a good
chance to betray Jesus when the crowds
were not around.

Jesus Eats with His Disciples

*(Matthew 26.17-25; Mark 14.12-21;
John 13.21-30)*

[7]The day had come for the Festival of
Thin Bread, and it was time to kill the
Passover lambs. [8]So Jesus said to Peter
and John, "Go and prepare the Passover
meal for us to eat."
[9]But they asked, "Where do you want
us to prepare it?"
[10]Jesus told them, "As you go into the
city, you will meet a man carrying a jar
of water.[y] Follow him into the house
[11]and say to the owner, 'Our teacher
wants to know where he can eat the
Passover meal with his disciples.' [12]The
owner will take you upstairs and show
you a large room ready for you to use.
Prepare the meal there."
[13]Peter and John left. They found
everything just as Jesus had told them,
and they prepared the Passover meal.

The Lord's Supper

*(Matthew 26.26-30; Mark 14.22-26;
1 Corinthians 11.23-25)*

[14]When the time came for Jesus and
the apostles to eat, [15]he said to them, "I
have very much wanted to eat this
Passover meal with you before I suffer.
[16]I tell you that I will not eat another
Passover meal until it is finally eaten in
God's kingdom."
[17]Jesus took a cup of wine in his
hands and gave thanks to God. Then he
told the apostles, "Take this wine and
share it with each other. [18]I tell you that
I will not drink any more wine until
God's kingdom comes."
[19]Jesus took some bread in his hands
and gave thanks for it. He broke the

[w]**21.26** *Every power in the sky will be shaken*: In ancient times people thought that the stars were spiritual powers. [x]**22.3** *Iscariot*: See the note at 6.16. [y]**22.10** *a man carrying a jar of water*: A male slave carrying water would probably mean that the family was rich.

bread and handed it to his apostles.
Then he said, "This is my body, which is
given for you. Eat this as a way of remembering me!"
20After the meal he took another cup
of wine in his hands. Then he said, "This
is my blood. It is poured out for you, and
with it God makes his new agreement.
21The one who will betray me is here at
the table with me! 22The Son of Man
will die in the way that has been decided for him, but it will be terrible for
the one who betrays him!"
23Then the apostles started arguing
about who would ever do such a thing.

An Argument about Greatness

24The apostles got into an argument
about which one of them was the greatest. 25So Jesus told them:

Foreign kings order their people
around, and powerful rulers call
themselves everyone's friends.[z]
26But don't be like them. The most
important one of you should be like
the least important, and your leader
should be like a servant. 27Who do
people think is the greatest, a person
who is served or one who serves?
Isn't it the one who is served? But I
have been with you as a servant.

28You have stayed with me in all
my troubles. 29So I will give you the
right to rule as kings, just as my
Father has given me the right to rule
as a king. 30You will eat and drink
with me in my kingdom, and you
will each sit on a throne to judge the
twelve tribes of Israel.

Jesus' Disciples Will Be Tested
(Matthew 26.31-35; Mark 14.27-31; John 13.36-38)

31Jesus said, "Simon, listen to me! Satan has demanded the right to test each
one of you, as a farmer does when he
separates wheat from the husks.[a] 32But
Simon, I have prayed that your faith will
be strong. And when you have come
back to me, help the others."
33Peter said, "Lord, I am ready to go
with you to jail and even to die with
you."
34Jesus replied, "Peter, I tell you that
before a rooster crows tomorrow morning, you will say three times that you
don't know me."

Moneybags, Traveling Bags, and Swords

35Jesus asked his disciples, "When I
sent you out without a moneybag or a
traveling bag or sandals, did you need
anything?"
"No!" they answered.
36Jesus told them, "But now, if you
have a moneybag, take it with you. Also
take a traveling bag, and if you don't
have a sword,[b] sell some of your clothes
and buy one. 37Do this because the
Scriptures say, 'He was considered a
criminal.' This was written about me,
and it will soon come true."
38The disciples said, "Lord, here are
two swords!"
"Enough of that!" Jesus replied.

Jesus Prays
(Matthew 26.36-46; Mark 14.32-42)

39Jesus went out to the Mount of
Olives, as he often did, and his disciples
went with him. 40When they got there,
he told them, "Pray that you won't be
tested."
41Jesus walked on a little way before
he knelt down and prayed, 42"Father, if
you will, please don't make me suffer by
having me drink from this cup.[c] But do
what you want, and not what I want."
43Then an angel from heaven came to
help him. 44Jesus was in great pain and
prayed so sincerely that his sweat fell to
the ground like drops of blood.[d]
45Jesus got up from praying and went
over to his disciples. They were asleep
and worn out from being so sad. 46He
said to them, "Why are you asleep?
Wake up and pray that you won't be
tested."

Jesus Is Arrested
(Matthew 26.47-56; Mark 14.43-50; John 18.3-11)

47While Jesus was still speaking, a
crowd came up. It was led by Judas, one
of the twelve apostles. He went over to
Jesus and greeted him with a kiss.[e]
48Jesus asked Judas, "Are you betraying the Son of Man with a kiss?"
49When Jesus' disciples saw what was
about to happen, they asked, "Lord,
should we attack them with a sword?"
50One of the disciples even struck at the
high priest's servant with his sword and
cut off the servant's right ear.
51"Enough of that!" Jesus said. Then

[z]**22.25** *everyone's friends*: This translates a Greek word that rulers sometimes used as a title for themselves or for special friends. [a]**22.31** *separates wheat from the husks*: See the note at 3.17. [b]**22.36** *moneybag . . . traveling bag . . . sword*: These were things that someone would take on a dangerous journey. Jesus was telling his disciples to be ready for anything that might happen. They seem to have understood what he meant (see 22.49-51). [c]**22.42** *having me drink from this cup*: In the Scriptures "to drink from a cup" sometimes means to suffer.
[d]**22.43, 44** *Then an angel . . . like drops of blood*: Verses 43, 44 are not in some manuscripts.
[e]**22.47** *greeted him with a kiss*: It was the custom for people to greet each other with a kiss on the cheek.

he touched the servant's ear and healed
it.
52 Jesus spoke to the chief priests, the
temple police, and the leaders who had
come to arrest him. He said, "Why do
you come out with swords and clubs
and treat me like a criminal? 53 I was
with you every day in the temple, and
you didn't arrest me. But this is your
time, and darkness[f] is in control."

Peter Says He Doesn't Know Jesus

(Matthew 26.57, 58, 67-75; Mark 14.53, 54, 66-72; John 18.12-18, 25-27)

54 Jesus was arrested and led away to
the house of the high priest, while Peter
followed at a distance. 55 Some people
built a fire in the middle of the courtyard and were sitting around it. Peter
sat there with them, 56 and a servant girl
saw him. Then after she had looked at
him carefully, she said, "This man was
with Jesus!"
57 Peter said, "Woman, I don't even
know that man!"
58 A little later someone else saw Peter
and said, "You are one of them!"
"No, I'm not!" Peter replied.
59 About an hour later another man insisted, "This man must have been with
Jesus. They both come from Galilee."
60 Peter replied, "I don't know what
you are talking about!" Right then,
while Peter was still speaking, a rooster
crowed.
61 The Lord turned and looked at Peter.
And Peter remembered that the Lord
had said, "Before a rooster crows tomorrow morning, you will say three times
that you don't know me." 62 Then Peter
went out and cried hard.
63 The men who were guarding Jesus
made fun of him and beat him. 64 They
put a blindfold on him and said, "Tell us
who struck you!" 65 They kept on insulting Jesus in many other ways.

Jesus Is Questioned by the Council

(Matthew 26.59-66; Mark 14.55-64; John 18.19-24)

66 At daybreak the nation's leaders, the
chief priests, and the teachers of the
Law of Moses got together and brought
Jesus before their council. 67 They said,
"Tell us! Are you the Messiah?"
Jesus replied, "If I said so, you
wouldn't believe me. 68 And if I asked
you a question, you wouldn't answer.
69 But from now on, the Son of Man
will be seated at the right side of God
All-Powerful."
70 Then they asked, "Are you the Son
of God?"[g]
Jesus answered, "You say I am!"[h]
71 They replied, "Why do we need
more witnesses? He said it himself!"

Pilate Questions Jesus

(Matthew 27.1, 2, 11-14; Mark 15.1-5; John 18.28-38)

23 Everyone in the council got up
and led Jesus off to Pilate. 2 They
started accusing him and said, "We
caught this man trying to get our people
to riot and to stop paying taxes to the
Emperor. He also claims that he is the
Messiah, our king."
3 Pilate asked Jesus, "Are you the king
of the Jews?"
"Those are your words," Jesus answered.
4 Pilate told the chief priests and the
crowd, "I don't find him guilty of anything."
5 But they all kept on saying, "He has
been teaching and causing trouble all
over Judea. He started in Galilee and
has now come all the way here."

Jesus Is Brought before Herod

6 When Pilate heard this, he asked, "Is
this man from Galilee?" 7 After Pilate
learned that Jesus came from the
region ruled by Herod,[i] he sent him to
Herod, who was in Jerusalem at that
time.
8 For a long time Herod had wanted to
see Jesus and was very happy because
he finally had this chance. He had heard
many things about Jesus and hoped to
see him work a miracle.
9 Herod asked him a lot of questions,
but Jesus did not answer. 10 Then the
chief priests and the teachers of the
Law of Moses stood up and accused him
of all kinds of bad things.
11 Herod and his soldiers made fun
of Jesus and insulted him. They put a
fine robe on him and sent him back to
Pilate. 12 That same day Herod and Pilate
became friends, even though they had
been enemies before this.

The Death Sentence

(Matthew 27.15-26; Mark 15.6-15; John 18.39—19.16)

13 Pilate called together the chief
priests, the leaders, and the people. 14 He
told them, "You brought Jesus to me
and said he was a troublemaker. But I
have questioned him here in front of
you, and I have not found him guilty of
anything that you say he has done.
15 Herod didn't find him guilty either and
sent him back. This man doesn't deserve to be put to death! 16-17 I will just

[f] **22.53** *darkness*: Darkness stands for the power of the devil. [g] **22.70** *Son of God*: This was one of the titles used for the kings of Israel. [h] **22.70** *You say I am*: Or "That's what you say." [i] **23.7** *Herod*: Herod Antipas, the son of Herod the Great.

have him beaten with a whip and set
free."[j]
18But the whole crowd shouted, "Kill
Jesus! Give us Barabbas!" 19Now Barabbas was in jail because he had started a
riot in the city and had murdered someone.
20Pilate wanted to set Jesus free, so he
spoke again to the crowds. 21But they
kept shouting, "Nail him to a cross! Nail
him to a cross!"
22Pilate spoke to them a third time,
"But what crime has he done? I have
not found him guilty of anything for
which he should be put to death. I will
have him beaten with a whip and set
free."
23The people kept on shouting as loud
as they could for Jesus to be put to
death. 24Finally, Pilate gave in. 25He
freed the man who was in jail for rioting
and murder, because he was the one the
crowd wanted to be set free. Then Pilate
handed Jesus over for them to do what
they wanted with him.

Jesus Is Nailed to a Cross

(Matthew 27.31-44; Mark 15.21-32; John 19.17-27)

26As Jesus was being led away, some
soldiers grabbed hold of a man from
Cyrene named Simon. He was coming
in from the fields, but they put the cross
on him and made him carry it behind
Jesus.
27A large crowd was following Jesus,
and in the crowd a lot of women were
crying and weeping for him. 28Jesus
turned to the women and said:
Women of Jerusalem, don't cry for
me! Cry for yourselves and for your
children. 29Someday people will say,
"Women who never had children are
really fortunate!" 30At that time
everyone will say to the mountains,
"Fall on us!" They will say to the
hills, "Hide us!" 31If this can happen
when the wood is green, what do
you think will happen when it is
dry?[k]
32Two criminals were led out to be put
to death with Jesus. 33When the soldiers
came to the place called "The Skull,"[l]
they nailed Jesus to a cross. They also
nailed the two criminals to crosses, one
on each side of Jesus.
34-35Jesus said, "Father, forgive these
people! They don't know what they're
doing."[m]
While the crowd stood there watching
Jesus, the soldiers gambled for his
clothes. The leaders insulted him by
saying, "He saved others. Now he
should save himself, if he really is God's
chosen Messiah!"
36The soldiers made fun of Jesus and
brought him some wine. 37They said, "If
you are the king of the Jews, save yourself!"
38Above him was a sign that said,
"This is the King of the Jews."
39One of the criminals hanging there
also insulted Jesus by saying, "Aren't
you the Messiah? Save yourself and
save us!"
40But the other criminal told the first
one off, "Don't you fear God? Aren't you
getting the same punishment as this
man? 41We got what was coming to us,
but he didn't do anything wrong."
42Then he said to Jesus, "Remember me
when you come into power!"
43Jesus replied, "I promise that today
you will be with me in paradise."[n]

The Death of Jesus

(Matthew 27.45-56; Mark 15.33-41; John 19.28-30)

44Around noon the sky turned dark
and stayed that way until the middle of
the afternoon. 45The sun stopped shining, and the curtain in the temple[o] split
down the middle. 46Jesus shouted,
"Father, I put myself in your hands!"
Then he died.
47When the Roman officer saw what
had happened, he praised God and said,
"Jesus must really have been a good
man!"
48A crowd had gathered to see the
terrible sight. Then after they had seen
it, they felt brokenhearted and went
home. 49All of Jesus' close friends and
the women who had come with him
from Galilee stood at a distance and
watched.

[j] **23.16,17** *set free*: Some manuscripts add, "Pilate said this, because at every Passover he was supposed to set one prisoner free for the Jewish people." [k] **23.31** *If this can happen when the wood is green, what do you think will happen when it is dry?*: This saying probably means, "If this can happen to an innocent person, what do you think will happen to one who is guilty?" [l] **23.33** *"The Skull"*: The place was probably given this name because it was near a large rock in the shape of a human skull. [m] **23.34,35** *Jesus said, "Father, forgive these people! They don't know what they're doing."*: These words are not in some manuscripts. [n] **23.43** *paradise*: In the Greek translation of the Old Testament, this word is used for the Garden of Eden. In New Testament times it was sometimes used for the place where God's people are happy and at rest, as they wait for the final judgment. [o] **23.45** *curtain in the temple*: There were two curtains in the temple. One was at the entrance, and the other separated the holy place from the most holy place that the Jewish people thought of as God's home on earth. The second curtain is probably the one which is meant.

Jesus Is Buried

(Matthew 27.57-61; Mark 15.42-47; John 19.38-42)

[50-51]There was a man named Joseph, who was from Arimathea in Judea. Joseph was a good and honest man, and he was eager for God's kingdom to come. He was also a member of the council, but he did not agree with what they had decided.

[52]Joseph went to Pilate and asked for Jesus' body. [53]He took the body down from the cross and wrapped it in fine cloth. Then he put it in a tomb that had been cut out of solid rock and had never been used. [54]It was Friday, and the Sabbath was about to begin.[p]

[55]The women who had come with Jesus from Galilee followed Joseph and watched how Jesus' body was placed in the tomb. [56]Then they went to prepare some sweet-smelling spices for his burial. But on the Sabbath they rested, as the Law of Moses commands.

Jesus Is Alive

(Matthew 28.1-10; Mark 16.1-8; John 20.1-10)

24 Very early on Sunday morning the women went to the tomb, carrying the spices that they had prepared. [2]When they found the stone rolled away from the entrance, [3]they went in. But they did not find the body of the Lord[q] Jesus, [4]and they did not know what to think.

Suddenly two men in shining white clothes stood beside them. [5]The women were afraid and bowed to the ground. But the men said, "Why are you looking in the place of the dead for someone who is alive? [6]Jesus isn't here! He has been raised from death. Remember that while he was still in Galilee, he told you, [7]'The Son of Man will be handed over to sinners who will nail him to a cross. But three days later he will rise to life.' " [8]Then they remembered what Jesus had said.

[9-10]Mary Magdalene, Joanna, Mary the mother of James, and some other women were the ones who had gone to the tomb. When they returned, they told the eleven apostles and the others what had happened. [11]The apostles thought it was all nonsense, and they would not believe.

[12]But Peter ran to the tomb. And when he stooped down and looked in, he saw only the burial clothes. Then he returned, wondering what had happened.[r]

Jesus Appears to Two Disciples

(Mark 16.12, 13)

[13]That same day two of Jesus' disciples were going to the village of Emmaus, which was about seven miles from Jerusalem. [14]As they were talking and thinking about what had happened, [15]Jesus came near and started walking along beside them. [16]But they did not know who he was.

[17]Jesus asked them, "What were you talking about as you walked along?"

The two of them stood there looking sad and gloomy. [18]Then the one named Cleopas asked Jesus, "Are you the only person from Jerusalem who didn't know what was happening there these last few days?"

[19]"What do you mean?" Jesus asked.

They answered:

Those things that happened to Jesus from Nazareth. By what he did and said he showed that he was a powerful prophet, who pleased God and all the people. [20]Then the chief priests and our leaders had him arrested and sentenced to die on a cross. [21]We had hoped that he would be the one to set Israel free! But it has already been three days since all this happened.

[22]Some women in our group surprised us. They had gone to the tomb early in the morning, [23]but did not find the body of Jesus. They came back, saying that they had seen a vision of angels who told them that he is alive. [24]Some men from our group went to the tomb and found it just as the women had said. But they didn't see Jesus either.

[25]Then Jesus asked the two disciples, "Why can't you understand? How can you be so slow to believe all that the prophets said? [26]Didn't you know that the Messiah would have to suffer before he was given his glory?" [27]Jesus then explained everything written about himself in the Scriptures, beginning with the Law of Moses and the Books of the Prophets.[s]

[28]When the two of them came near the village where they were going, Jesus seemed to be going farther. [29]They begged him, "Stay with us! It's already late, and the sun is going down." So Jesus went into the house to stay with them.

[30]After Jesus sat down to eat, he took some bread. He blessed it and broke it. Then he gave it to them. [31]At once they knew who he was, but he disappeared.

[p]**23.54** *the Sabbath was about to begin*: The Sabbath begins at sunset on Friday. [q]**24.3** *the Lord*: These words are not in some manuscripts. [r]**24.12** *what had happened*: Verse 12 is not in some manuscripts. [s]**24.27** *the Law of Moses and the Books of the Prophets*: See the note at 16.16.

32They said to each other, "When he
talked with us along the road and explained the Scriptures to us, didn't it
warm our hearts?" 33So they got right
up and returned to Jerusalem.
The two disciples found the eleven
apostles and the others gathered together. 34And they learned from the
group that the Lord was really alive
and had appeared to Peter. 35Then the
disciples from Emmaus told what happened on the road and how they knew
he was the Lord when he broke the
bread.

What Jesus' Followers Must Do

(Matthew 28.16-20; Mark 16.14-18; John 20.19-23; Acts 1.6-8)

36While Jesus' disciples were talking
about what had happened, Jesus appeared and greeted them. 37They were
frightened and terrified because they
thought they were seeing a ghost.
38But Jesus said, "Why are you so
frightened? Why do you doubt? 39Look
at my hands and my feet and see who I
am! Touch me and find out for yourselves. Ghosts don't have flesh and
bones as you see I have."
40After Jesus said this, he showed
them his hands and his feet. 41The disciples were so glad and amazed that they
could not believe it. Jesus then asked
them, "Do you have something to eat?"
42They gave him a piece of baked fish.
43He took it and ate it as they watched.
44Jesus said to them, "While I was still
with you, I told you that everything written about me in the Law of Moses, the
Books of the Prophets, and in the
Psalms[t] had to happen."
45Then he helped them understand the
Scriptures. 46He told them:

> The Scriptures say that the Mes-
> siah must suffer, then three days
> later he will rise from death. 47They
> also say that all people of every na-
> tion must be told in my name to turn
> to God, in order to be forgiven. So
> beginning in Jerusalem, 48you must
> tell everything that has happened.
> 49I will send you the one my Father
> has promised,[u] but you must stay in
> the city until you are given power
> from heaven.

Jesus Returns to Heaven

(Mark 16.19, 20; Acts 1.9-11)

50Jesus led his disciples out to Bethany, where he raised his hands and
blessed them. 51As he was doing this, he
left and was taken up to heaven.[v] 52Af-
ter his disciples had worshiped him,[w]
they returned to Jerusalem and were
very happy. 53They spent their time in
the temple, praising God.

[t]**24.44** *Psalms*: The Jewish Scriptures were made up of three parts: (1) the Law of Moses, (2) the Books of the Prophets, (3) and the Writings, which included the Psalms. Sometimes the Scriptures were just called the Law or the Law (of Moses) and the Books of the Prophets.
[u]**24.49** *the one my Father has promised*: Jesus means the Holy Spirit.
[v]**24.51** *and was taken up to heaven*: These words are not in some manuscripts.
[w]**24.52** *After his disciples had worshiped him*: These words are not in some manuscripts.

JOHN

ABOUT THIS BOOK

Who is Jesus Christ? John answers this question in the first chapter of his Gospel. Using the words of an early Christian hymn, he calls Jesus the "Word" by which God created everything and by which he gave life to everyone (1.3, 4). He shows how John the Baptist announced Jesus' coming, "Here is the Lamb of God who takes away the sin of the world" (1.29). When Philip met Jesus he knew Jesus was "the one that Moses and the Prophets wrote about" (1.45). And, in the words of Nathanael, Jesus is "the Son of God and the King of Israel" (1.49).

In John's Gospel we learn a lot about who Jesus is by observing what he said and did when he was with other people. These include a Samaritan woman who received Jesus' offer of life-giving water, a woman who had been caught in sin, his friend Lazarus who was brought back to life by Jesus, and his follower Thomas who doubted that Jesus was raised from death. Jesus also refers to himself as "I am", a phrase which translates the most holy name for God in the Hebrew Scriptures. He uses this name for himself when he makes his claim to be the life-giving bread, the light of the world, the good shepherd, and the true vine.

Jesus performs seven miracles that are more than miracles. Each of them is a "sign" that tells us something about Jesus as the Son of God. For example, by healing a lame man (5.1-8), Jesus shows that he is just like his Father, who never stops working (5.17). This sign also teaches that the Son does only what he sees his Father doing (5.19), and that like the Father "the Son gives life to anyone he wants to" (5.21).

The way John tells the story of Jesus is quite different from the other three Gospels. Here, Jesus has long conversations with people about who he is and what God sent him to do. In these conversations he teaches many important things—for example, that he is the way, the truth and the life.

Why did John write? John himself tells us, "So that you will put your faith in Jesus as the Messiah and the Son of God" (20.31). How is this possible? Jesus answers that question in his words to Nicodemus:

> *God loved the people of this world so much that he gave his only Son, so that everyone who has faith in him will have eternal life and never really die.* (3.16)

A QUICK LOOK AT THIS BOOK

A Hymn in Praise of the Word (1.1-18)
The Message of John the Baptist (1.19-34)
Jesus Chooses His First Disciples (1.35-51)
Jesus' Seven Special Miracles (2.1—12.50)
Jesus' Last Week: His Trial and Death (13.1—19.42)
Jesus Is Alive (20.1-10)
Jesus Appears to His Disciples (20.11—21.25)

The Word of Life

1 In the beginning was the one
who is called the Word.
The Word was with God
and was truly God.
2 From the very beginning
the Word was with God.

3 And with this Word,
God created all things.
Nothing was made
without the Word.
Everything that was created
4 received its life from him,
and his life gave light
to everyone.
5 The light keeps shining
in the dark,
and darkness has never
put it out.[a]
6 God sent a man named John,
7 who came to tell
about the light
and to lead all people
to have faith.
8 John wasn't that light.
He came only to tell
about the light.

9 The true light that shines
on everyone
was coming into the world.
10 The Word was in the world,
but no one knew him,
though God had made the world
with his Word.
11 He came into his own world,
but his own nation
did not welcome him.
12 Yet some people accepted him
and put their faith in him.
So he gave them the right
to be the children of God.
13 They were not God's children
by nature or because
of any human desires.
God himself was the one
who made them his children.

14 The Word became
a human being
and lived here with us.
We saw his true glory,
the glory of the only Son
of the Father.
From him all the kindness
and all the truth of God
have come down to us.

15John spoke about him and shouted,
"This is the one I told you would come!
He is greater than I am, because he was
alive before I was born."
16Because of all that the Son is, we
have been given one blessing after another.[b] 17The Law was given by Moses,
but Jesus Christ brought us undeserved
kindness and truth. 18No one has ever
seen God. The only Son, who is truly
God and is closest to the Father, has
shown us what God is like.

John the Baptist Tells about Jesus

(Matthew 3.1-12; Mark 1.1-8; Luke 3.15-17)

19-20The Jewish leaders in Jerusalem
sent priests and temple helpers to ask
John who he was. He told them plainly,
"I am not the Messiah." 21Then when
they asked him if he were Elijah, he
said, "No, I am not!" And when they
asked if he were the Prophet,[c], he also
said "No!"
22Finally, they said, "Who are you
then? We have to give an answer to the
ones who sent us. Tell us who you are!"
23John answered in the words of the
prophet Isaiah, "I am only someone
shouting in the desert, 'Get the road
ready for the Lord!' "
24Some Pharisees had also been sent
to John. 25They asked him, "Why are
you baptizing people, if you are not the
Messiah or Elijah or the Prophet?"
26John told them, "I use water to baptize people. But here with you is someone you don't know. 27Even though I
came first, I am not good enough to untie his sandals." 28John said this as he
was baptizing east of the Jordan River
in Bethany.[d]

The Lamb of God

29The next day, John saw Jesus coming toward him and said:
Here is the Lamb of God who
takes away the sin of the world! 30He
is the one I told you about when I
said, "Someone else will come. He is
greater than I am, because he was
alive before I was born." 31I didn't
know who he was. But I came to
baptize you with water, so that
everyone in Israel would see him.
32I was there and saw the Spirit
come down on him like a dove from
heaven. And the Spirit stayed on
him. 33Before this I didn't know who
he was. But the one who sent me to
baptize with water had told me,
"You will see the Spirit come down
and stay on someone. Then you will

[a]**1.5** *put it out*: Or "understood it." [b]**1.16** *one blessing after another*: Or "one blessing in place of another." [c]**1.21** *the Prophet*: Many of the Jewish people expected God to send them a prophet who would be like Moses, but with even greater power (see Deuteronomy 18.15, 18). [d]**1.28** *Bethany*: An unknown village east of the Jordan with the same name as the village near Jerusalem.

know that he is the one who will
baptize with the Holy Spirit." 34 I saw
this happen, and I tell you that he is
the Son of God.

The First Disciples of Jesus

35 The next day, John was there again,
and two of his followers were with him.
36 When he saw Jesus walking by, he
said, "Here is the Lamb of God!"
37 John's two followers heard him, and
they went with Jesus.
38 When Jesus turned and saw them,
he asked, "What do you want?"
They answered, "Rabbi, where do you
live?" The Hebrew word "Rabbi" means
"Teacher."
39 Jesus replied, "Come and see!" It
was already about four o'clock in the afternoon when they went with him and
saw where he lived. So they stayed on
for the rest of the day.
40 One of the two men who had heard
John and had gone with Jesus was Andrew, the brother of Simon Peter. 41 The
first thing Andrew did was to find his
brother and tell him, "We have found
the Messiah!" The Hebrew word "Messiah" means the same as the Greek
word "Christ."
42 Andrew brought his brother to Jesus. And when Jesus saw him, he said,
"Simon son of John, you will be called
Cephas." This name can be translated as
"Peter."[e]

Jesus Chooses Philip and Nathanael

43-44 The next day Jesus decided to go
to Galilee. There he met Philip, who was
from Bethsaida, the hometown of Andrew and Peter. Jesus said to Philip,
"Come with me."
45 Philip then found Nathanael and
said, "We have found the one that
Moses and the Prophets[f] wrote about.
He is Jesus, the son of Joseph from
Nazareth."
46 Nathanael asked, "Can anything
good come from Nazareth?"
Philip answered, "Come and see."
47 When Jesus saw Nathanael coming
toward him, he said, "Here is a true descendant of our ancestor Israel. And he
isn't deceitful."[g]
48 "How do you know me?" Nathanael
asked.
Jesus answered, "Before Philip called
you, I saw you under the fig tree."
49 Nathanael said, "Rabbi, you are the
Son of God and the King of Israel!"
50 Jesus answered, "Did you believe me
just because I said that I saw you under
the fig tree? You will see something even
greater. 51 I tell you for certain that you
will see heaven open and God's angels
going up and coming down on the Son
of Man."[h]

Jesus at a Wedding in Cana

2 Three days later Mary, the mother of
Jesus, was at a wedding feast in the
village of Cana in Galilee. 2 Jesus and his
disciples had also been invited and were
there.
3 When the wine was all gone, Mary
said to Jesus, "They don't have any
more wine."
4 Jesus replied, "Mother, my time
hasn't yet come![i] You must not tell me
what to do."
5 Mary then said to the servants, "Do
whatever Jesus tells you to do."
6 At the feast there were six stone water jars that were used by the people for
washing themselves in the way that
their religion said they must. Each jar
held about twenty or thirty gallons. 7 Jesus told the servants to fill them to the
top with water. Then after the jars had
been filled, 8 he said, "Now take some
water and give it to the man in charge of
the feast."
The servants did as Jesus told them,
9 and the man in charge drank some of
the water that had now turned into
wine. He did not know where the wine
had come from, but the servants did. He
called the bridegroom over 10 and said,
"The best wine is always served first.
Then after the guests have had plenty,
the other wine is served. But you have
kept the best until last!"
11 This was Jesus' first miracle,[j] and he
did it in the village of Cana in Galilee.
There Jesus showed his glory, and his
disciples put their faith in him. 12 After
this, he went with his mother, his
brothers, and his disciples to the town
of Capernaum, where they stayed for a
few days.

[e] **1.42** *Peter*: The Aramaic name "Cephas" and the Greek name "Peter" each mean "rock."
[f] **1.45** *Moses and the Prophets*: The Jewish Scriptures, that is, the Old Testament.
[g] **1.47** *Israel . . . isn't deceitful*: Israel (meaning "a man who wrestled with God" or "a prince of God") was the name that the Lord gave to Jacob (meaning "cheater" or "deceiver"), the famous ancestor of the Jewish people. [h] **1.51** *going up and coming down on the Son of Man*: When Jacob (see the note at verse 47) was running from his brother Esau, he had a dream in which he saw angels going up and down on a ladder from earth to heaven (see Genesis 32.22-32).
[i] **2.4** *my time hasn't yet come!*: The time when the true glory of Jesus would be seen, and he would be recognized as God's Son (see 12.23). [j] **2.11,18,23** *miracle*: The Greek text has "sign." In the Gospel of John the word "sign" is used for the miracle itself and as a way of pointing to Jesus as the Son of God.

Jesus in the Temple
(Matthew 21.12, 13; Mark 11.15-17;
Luke 19.45, 46)

13 Not long before the Jewish festival
of Passover, Jesus went to Jerusalem.
14 There he found people selling cattle,
sheep, and doves in the temple. He also
saw moneychangers sitting at their tables. 15 So he took some rope and made
a whip. Then he chased everyone out of
the temple, together with their sheep
and cattle. He turned over the tables of
the moneychangers and scattered their
coins.
16 Jesus said to the people who had
been selling doves, "Get those doves out
of here! Don't make my Father's house a
marketplace."
17 The disciples then remembered that
the Scriptures say, "My love for your
house burns in me like a fire."
18 The Jewish leaders asked Jesus,
"What miracle[j] will you work to show
us why you have done this?"
19 "Destroy this temple," Jesus answered, "and in three days I will build it
again!"
20 The leaders replied, "It took forty-
six years to build this temple. What
makes you think you can rebuild it in
three days?"
21 But Jesus was talking about his
body as a temple. 22 And when he was
raised from death, his disciples remembered what he had told them. Then they
believed the Scriptures and the words of
Jesus.

Jesus Knows What People Are Like

23 In Jerusalem during Passover many
people put their faith in Jesus, because
they saw him work miracles.[j] 24 But Jesus knew what was in their hearts, and
he would not let them have power over
him. 25 No one had to tell him what people were like. He already knew.

Jesus and Nicodemus

3 There was a man named Nicodemus
who was a Pharisee and a Jewish
leader. 2 One night he went to Jesus and
said, "Sir, we know that God has sent
you to teach us. You could not work
these miracles, unless God were with
you."
3 Jesus replied, "I tell you for certain
that you must be born from above[k] before you can see God's kingdom!"
4 Nicodemus asked, "How can a grown
man ever be born a second time?"
5 Jesus answered:

I tell you for certain that before
you can get into God's kingdom, you
must be born not only by water, but
by the Spirit. 6 Humans give life to
their children. Yet only God's Spirit
can change you into a child of God.
7 Don't be surprised when I say that
you must be born from above. 8 Only
God's Spirit gives new life. The
Spirit is like the wind that blows
wherever it wants to. You can hear
the wind, but you don't know where
it comes from or where it is going.
9 "How can this be?" Nicodemus asked.
10 Jesus replied:

How can you be a teacher of Israel
and not know these things? 11 I tell
you for certain that we know what
we are talking about because we
have seen it ourselves. But none of
you will accept what we say. 12 If you
don't believe when I talk to you
about things on earth, how can you
possibly believe if I talk to you about
things in heaven?
13 No one has gone up to heaven
except the Son of Man, who came
down from there. 14 And the Son of
Man must be lifted up, just as that
metal snake was lifted up by Moses
in the desert.[l] 15 Then everyone who
has faith in the Son of Man will have
eternal life.
16 God loved the people of this
world so much that he gave his only
Son, so that everyone who has faith
in him will have eternal life and
never really die. 17 God did not send
his Son into the world to condemn
its people. He sent him to save them!
18 No one who has faith in God's Son
will be condemned. But everyone
who doesn't have faith in him has already been condemned for not having faith in God's only Son.
19 The light has come into the
world, and people who do evil things
are judged guilty because they love
the dark more than the light. 20 People who do evil hate the light and
won't come to the light, because it
clearly shows what they have done.
21 But everyone who lives by the
truth will come to the light, because
they want others to know that God
is really the one doing what they do.

Jesus and John the Baptist

22 Later, Jesus and his disciples went
to Judea, where he stayed with them for
a while and was baptizing people.
23-24 John had not yet been put in jail.

[j] **2.11,18,23** *miracle*: The Greek text has "sign." In the Gospel of John the word "sign" is used for the miracle itself and as a way of pointing to Jesus as the Son of God. [k] **3.3** *from above*: Or "in a new way." The same Greek word is used in verses 7, 31. [l] **3.14** *just as that metal snake was lifted up by Moses in the desert*: When the Lord punished the people of Israel by sending snakes to bite them, he told Moses to hold a metal snake up on a pole. Everyone who looked at the snake was cured of the snake bites (see Numbers 21.4-9).

He was at Aenon near Salim, where
there was a lot of water, and people
were coming there for John to baptize
them.
25 John's followers got into an argument with a Jewish man[m] about a ceremony of washing.[n] 26 They went to John
and said, "Rabbi, you spoke about a
man when you were with him east of
the Jordan. He is now baptizing people,
and everyone is going to him."
27 John replied:
No one can do anything unless
God in heaven allows it. 28 You surely
remember how I told you that I am
not the Messiah. I am only the one
sent ahead of him.
29 At a wedding the groom is the
one who gets married. The best man
is glad just to be there and to hear
the groom's voice. That's why I am
so glad. 30 Jesus must become more
important, while I become less important.

The One Who Comes from Heaven

31 God's Son comes from heaven
and is above all others. Everyone
who comes from the earth belongs
to the earth and speaks about
earthly things. The one who comes
from heaven is above all others. 32 He
speaks about what he has seen and
heard, and yet no one believes him.
33 But everyone who does believe
him has shown that God is truthful.
34 The Son was sent to speak God's
message, and he has been given the
full power of God's Spirit.
35 The Father loves the Son and has
given him everything. 36 Everyone
who has faith in the Son has eternal
life. But no one who rejects him will
ever share in that life, and God will
be angry with them forever.

4 Jesus knew that the Pharisees had
heard that he was winning and baptizing more followers than John was.
2 But Jesus' disciples were really the
ones doing the baptizing, and not Jesus
himself.

Jesus and the Samaritan Woman

3 Jesus left Judea and started for
Galilee again. 4 This time he had to go
through Samaria, 5 and on his way he
came to the town of Sychar. It was near
the field that Jacob had long ago given
to his son Joseph. 6-8 The well that Jacob
had dug was still there, and Jesus sat
down beside it because he was tired
from traveling. It was noon, and after
Jesus' disciples had gone into town to
buy some food, a Samaritan woman
came to draw water from the well.
Jesus asked her, "Would you please
give me a drink of water?"
9 "You are a Jew," she replied, "and I
am a Samaritan woman. How can you
ask me for a drink of water when Jews
and Samaritans won't have anything to
do with each other?"[o]
10 Jesus answered, "You don't know
what God wants to give you, and you
don't know who is asking you for a
drink. If you did, you would ask me for
the water that gives life."
11 "Sir," the woman said, "you don't
even have a bucket, and the well is deep.
Where are you going to get this life-
giving water? 12 Our ancestor Jacob dug
this well for us, and his family and animals got water from it. Are you greater
than Jacob?"
13 Jesus answered, "Everyone who
drinks this water will get thirsty again.
14 But no one who drinks the water I give
will ever be thirsty again. The water I
give is like a flowing fountain that gives
eternal life."
15 The woman replied, "Sir, please give
me a drink of that water! Then I won't
get thirsty and have to come to this well
again."
16 Jesus told her, "Go and bring your
husband."
17-18 The woman answered, "I don't
have a husband."
"That's right," Jesus replied, "you're
telling the truth. You don't have a husband. You have already been married
five times, and the man you are now living with isn't your husband."
19 The woman said, "Sir, I can see that
you are a prophet. 20 My ancestors worshiped on this mountain,[p] but you Jews
say Jerusalem is the only place to worship."
21 Jesus said to her:
Believe me, the time is coming
when you won't worship the Father
either on this mountain or in Jerusalem. 22 You Samaritans don't
really know the one you worship.
But we Jews do know the God we
worship, and by using us, God will
save the world. 23 But a time is coming, and it is already here! Even now
the true worshipers are being led by
the Spirit to worship the Father

[m] **3.25** *a Jewish man*: Some manuscripts have "some Jewish men." [n] **3.25** *about a ceremony of washing*: The Jewish people had many rules about washing themselves and their dishes, in order to make themselves fit to worship God. [o] **4.9** *won't have anything to do with each other*: Or "won't use the same cups." The Samaritans lived in the land between Judea and Galilee. They worshiped God differently from the Jews and did not get along with them. [p] **4.20** *this mountain*: Mount Gerizim, near the city of Shechem.

according to the truth. These are the
ones the Father is seeking to worship him. 24 God is Spirit, and those
who worship God must be led by the
Spirit to worship him according to
the truth.
25 The woman said, "I know that the
Messiah will come. He is the one we call
Christ. When he comes, he will explain
everything to us."
26 "I am that one," Jesus told her, "and I
am speaking to you now."
27 The disciples returned about this
time and were surprised to find Jesus
talking with a woman. But none of them
asked him what he wanted or why he
was talking with her.
28 The woman left her water jar and
ran back into town. She said to the people, 29 "Come and see a man who told me
everything I have ever done! Could he
be the Messiah?" 30 Everyone in town
went out to see Jesus.
31 While this was happening, Jesus'
disciples were saying to him, "Teacher,
please eat something."
32 But Jesus told them, "I have food
that you don't know anything about."
33 His disciples started asking each
other, "Has someone brought him something to eat?"
34 Jesus said:
My food is to do what God wants!
He is the one who sent me, and I
must finish the work that he gave
me to do. 35 You may say that there
are still four months until harvest
time. But I tell you to look, and you
will see that the fields are ripe and
ready to harvest.
36 Even now the harvest workers
are receiving their reward by gathering a harvest that brings eternal life.
Then everyone who planted the seed
and everyone who harvests the crop
will celebrate together. 37 So the saying proves true, "Some plant the
seed, and others harvest the crop."
38 I am sending you to harvest crops
in fields where others have done all
the hard work.
39 A lot of Samaritans in that town put
their faith in Jesus because the woman
had said, "This man told me everything I
have ever done." 40 They came and asked
him to stay in their town, and he stayed
on for two days.
41 Many more Samaritans put their
faith in Jesus because of what they
heard him say. 42 They told the woman,
"We no longer have faith in Jesus just
because of what you told us. We have
heard him ourselves, and we are certain
that he is the Savior of the world!"

Jesus Heals an Official's Son

(Matthew 8.5-13; Luke 7.1-10)

43-44 Jesus had said, "Prophets are honored everywhere, except in their own
country." Then two days later he left
45 and went to Galilee. The people there
welcomed him, because they had gone
to the festival in Jerusalem and had
seen everything he had done.
46 While Jesus was in Galilee, he returned to the village of Cana, where he
had turned the water into wine. There
was an official in Capernaum whose son
was sick. 47 And when the man heard
that Jesus had come from Judea, he
went and begged him to keep his son
from dying.
48 Jesus told the official, "You won't
have faith unless you see miracles and
wonders!"
49 The man replied, "Lord, please come
before my son dies!"
50 Jesus then said, "Your son will live.
Go on home to him." The man believed
Jesus and started back home.
51 Some of the official's servants met
him along the road and told him, "Your
son is better!" 52 He asked them when
the boy got better, and they answered,
"The fever left him yesterday at one
o'clock."
53 The boy's father realized that at one
o'clock the day before, Jesus had told
him, "Your son will live!" So the man
and everyone in his family put their
faith in Jesus.
54 This was the second miracle[q] that
Jesus worked after he left Judea and
went to Galilee.

Jesus Heals a Sick Man

5 Later, Jesus went to Jerusalem for
another Jewish festival.[r] 2 In the city
near the sheep gate was a pool with five
porches, and its name in Hebrew was
Bethzatha.[s]
3-4 Many sick, blind, lame, and crippled
people were lying close to the pool.[t]
5 Beside the pool was a man who had
been sick for thirty-eight years. 6 When
Jesus saw the man and realized that he
had been crippled for a long time, he
asked him, "Do you want to be healed?"
7 The man answered, "Lord, I don't
have anyone to put me in the pool when
the water is stirred up. I try to get in, but
someone else always gets there first."
8 Jesus told him, "Pick up your mat

[q] **4.54** *miracle*: See the note at 2.11. [r] **5.1** *another Jewish festival*: Either the Festival of Shelters or Passover. [s] **5.2** *Bethzatha*: Some manuscripts have "Bethesda" and others have "Bethsaida." [t] **5.3,4** *pool*: Some manuscripts add, "They were waiting for the water to be stirred, because an angel from the Lord would sometimes come down and stir it. The first person to get into the pool after that would be healed."

and walk!" 9Right then the man was healed. He picked up his mat and started walking around. The day on which this happened was a Sabbath.

10When the Jewish leaders saw the man carrying his mat, they said to him, "This is the Sabbath! No one is allowed to carry a mat on the Sabbath."

11But he replied, "The man who healed me told me to pick up my mat and walk."

12They asked him, "Who is this man that told you to pick up your mat and walk?" 13But he did not know who Jesus was, and Jesus had left because of the crowd.

14Later, Jesus met the man in the temple and told him, "You are now well. But don't sin anymore or something worse might happen to you." 15The man left and told the leaders that Jesus was the one who had healed him. 16They started making a lot of trouble for Jesus because he did things like this on the Sabbath.

17But Jesus said, "My Father has never stopped working, and that is why I keep on working." 18Now the leaders wanted to kill Jesus for two reasons. First, he had broken the law of the Sabbath. But even worse, he had said that God was his Father, which made him equal with God.

The Son's Authority

19Jesus told the people:

I tell you for certain that the Son cannot do anything on his own. He can do only what he sees the Father doing, and he does exactly what he sees the Father do. 20The Father loves the Son and has shown him everything he does. The Father will show him even greater things, and you will be amazed. 21Just as the Father raises the dead and gives life, so the Son gives life to anyone he wants to.

22The Father doesn't judge anyone, but he has made his Son the judge of everyone. 23The Father wants all people to honor the Son as much as they honor him. When anyone refuses to honor the Son, that is the same as refusing to honor the Father who sent him. 24I tell you for certain that everyone who hears my message and has faith in the one who sent me has eternal life and will never be condemned. They have already gone from death to life.

25I tell you for certain that the time will come, and it is already here, when all of the dead will hear the voice of the Son of God. And those who listen to it will live! 26The Father has the power to give life, and he has given that same power to the Son. 27And he has given his Son the right to judge everyone, because he is the Son of Man.

28Don't be surprised! The time will come when all of the dead will hear the voice of the Son of Man, 29and they will come out of their graves. Everyone who has done good things will rise to life, but everyone who has done evil things will rise and be condemned.

30I cannot do anything on my own. The Father sent me, and he is the one who told me how to judge. I judge with fairness, because I obey him, and I don't just try to please myself.

Witnesses to Jesus

31If I speak for myself, there is no way to prove I am telling the truth. 32But there is someone else who speaks for me, and I know what he says is true. 33You sent messengers to John, and he told them the truth. 34I don't depend on what people say about me, but I tell you these things so that you may be saved. 35John was a lamp that gave a lot of light, and you were glad to enjoy his light for a while.

36But something more important than John speaks for me. I mean the things that the Father has given me to do! All of these speak for me and prove that the Father sent me.

37The Father who sent me also speaks for me, but you have never heard his voice or seen him face to face. 38You have not believed his message, because you refused to have faith in the one he sent.

39You search the Scriptures, because you think you will find eternal life in them. The Scriptures tell about me, 40but you refuse to come to me for eternal life.

41I don't care about human praise, 42but I do know that none of you love God. 43I have come with my Father's authority, and you have not welcomed me. But you will welcome people who come on their own. 44How could you possibly believe? You like to have your friends praise you, and you don't care about praise that the only God can give!

45Don't think that I will be the one to accuse you to the Father. You have put your hope in Moses, yet he is the very one who will accuse you. 46Moses wrote about me, and if you had believed Moses, you would have believed me. 47But if you don't believe what Moses wrote, how can you believe what I say?

Feeding Five Thousand
*(Matthew 14.13-21; Mark 6.30-44;
Luke 9.10-17)*

6 Jesus crossed Lake Galilee, which
was also known as Lake Tiberias. 2A
large crowd had seen him work miracles to heal the sick, and those people
went with him. 3-4It was almost time for
the Jewish festival of Passover, and Jesus went up on a mountain with his disciples and sat down.[u]
5When Jesus saw the large crowd
coming toward him, he asked Philip,
"Where will we get enough food to feed
all these people?" 6He said this to test
Philip, since he already knew what he
was going to do.
7Philip answered, "Don't you know
that it would take almost a year's
wages[v] just to buy only a little bread for
each of these people?"
8Andrew, the brother of Simon Peter,
was one of the disciples. He spoke up
and said, 9"There is a boy here who has
five small loaves[w] of barley bread and
two fish. But what good is that with all
these people?"
10The ground was covered with grass,
and Jesus told his disciples to have
everyone sit down. About five thousand
men were in the crowd. 11Jesus took the
bread in his hands and gave thanks to
God. Then he passed the bread to the
people, and he did the same with the
fish, until everyone had plenty to eat.
12The people ate all they wanted, and
Jesus told his disciples to gather up the
leftovers, so that nothing would be
wasted. 13The disciples gathered them
up and filled twelve large baskets with
what was left over from the five barley
loaves.
14After the people had seen Jesus
work this miracle,[x] they began saying,
"This must be the Prophet[y] who is to
come into the world!" 15Jesus realized
that they would try to force him to be
their king. So he went up on a mountain, where he could be alone.

Jesus Walks on the Water
(Matthew 14.22-27; Mark 6.45-52)

16That evening, Jesus' disciples went
down to the lake. 17They got into a boat
and started across for Capernaum.
Later that evening Jesus had still not
come to them, 18and a strong wind was
making the water rough.
19When the disciples had rowed for
three or four miles, they saw Jesus
walking on the water. He kept coming
closer to the boat, and they were terrified. 20But he said, "I am Jesus![z] Don't
be afraid!" 21The disciples wanted to
take him into the boat, but suddenly the
boat reached the shore where they were
headed.

The Bread That Gives Life

22The people who had stayed on the
east side of the lake knew that only one
boat had been there. They also knew
that Jesus had not left in it with his disciples. But the next day 23some boats
from Tiberias sailed near the place
where the crowd had eaten the bread
for which the Lord had given thanks.
24They saw that Jesus and his disciples
had left. Then they got into the boats
and went to Capernaum to look for Jesus. 25They found him on the west side
of the lake and asked, "Rabbi, when did
you get here?"
26Jesus answered, "I tell you for certain that you are not looking for me because you saw the miracles,[a] but because you ate all the food you wanted.
27Don't work for food that spoils. Work
for food that gives eternal life. The Son
of Man will give you this food, because
God the Father has given him the right
to do so."
28"What exactly does God want us to
do?" the people asked.
29Jesus answered, "God wants you to
have faith in the one he sent."
30They replied, "What miracle will you
work, so that we can have faith in you?
What will you do? 31For example, when
our ancestors were in the desert, they
were given manna[b] to eat. It happened
just as the Scriptures say, 'God gave
them bread from heaven to eat.' "
32Jesus then told them, "I tell you for
certain that Moses wasn't the one who
gave you bread from heaven. My Father
is the one who gives you the true bread
from heaven. 33And the bread that God
gives is the one who came down from
heaven to give life to the world."
34The people said, "Lord, give us this
bread and don't ever stop!"
35Jesus replied:

> I am the bread that gives life! No
> one who comes to me will ever be
> hungry. No one who has faith in me

[u]**6.3,4** *sat down*: Possibly to teach. Teachers in the ancient world, including Jewish teachers, usually sat down to teach. [v]**6.7** *almost a year's wages*: The Greek text has "two hundred silver coins." Each coin was worth the average day's wages for a worker. [w]**6.9** *small loaves*: These would have been flat and round or in the shape of a bun. [x]**6.14** *miracle*: See the note at 2.11. [y]**6.14** *the Prophet*: See the note at 1.21. [z]**6.20** *I am Jesus*: The Greek text has "I am" (see the note at 8.24). [a]**6.26** *miracles*: The Greek text has "signs" here and "sign" in verse 30 (see the note at 2.11). [b]**6.31** *manna*: When the people of Israel were wandering through the desert, the Lord gave them a special kind of food to eat. It tasted like a wafer and was called "manna," which in Hebrew means, "What is this?"

will ever be thirsty. 36 I have told you
already that you have seen me and
still do not have faith in me. 37 Everything and everyone that the Father
has given me will come to me, and I
won't turn any of them away.
38 I didn't come from heaven to do
what I want! I came to do what the
Father wants me to do. He sent me,
39 and he wants to make certain that
none of the ones he has given me
will be lost. Instead, he wants me to
raise them to life on the last day.[c]
40 My Father wants everyone who
sees the Son to have faith in him and
to have eternal life. Then I will raise
them to life on the last day.
41 The people started grumbling because Jesus had said he was the bread
that had come down from heaven.
42 They were asking each other, "Isn't he
Jesus, the son of Joseph? Don't we
know his father and mother? How can
he say that he has come down from
heaven?"
43 Jesus told them:
Stop grumbling! 44 No one can
come to me, unless the Father who
sent me makes them want to come.
But if they do come, I will raise them
to life on the last day. 45 One of the
prophets wrote, "God will teach all
of them." And so everyone who listens to the Father and learns from
him will come to me.
46 The only one who has seen the
Father is the one who has come from
him. No one else has ever seen the
Father. 47 I tell you for certain that
everyone who has faith in me has
eternal life.
48 I am the bread that gives life!
49 Your ancestors ate manna[d] in the
desert, and later they died. 50 But the
bread from heaven has come down,
so that no one who eats it will ever
die. 51 I am that bread from heaven!
Everyone who eats it will live forever. My flesh is the life-giving
bread that I give to the people of this
world.
52 They started arguing with each
other and asked, "How can he give us
his flesh to eat?"
53 Jesus answered:
I tell you for certain that you won't
live unless you eat the flesh and
drink the blood of the Son of Man.
54 But if you do eat my flesh and
drink my blood, you will have eternal life, and I will raise you to life on
the last day. 55 My flesh is the true
food, and my blood is the true drink.
56 If you eat my flesh and drink my
blood, you are one with me, and I
am one with you.
57 The living Father sent me, and I
have life because of him. Now everyone who eats my flesh will live because of me. 58 The bread that comes
down from heaven isn't like what
your ancestors ate. They died, but
whoever eats this bread will live forever.
59 Jesus was teaching in a Jewish place
of worship in Capernaum when he said
these things.

The Words of Eternal Life

60 Many of Jesus' disciples heard him
and said, "This is too hard for anyone to
understand."
61 Jesus knew that his disciples were
grumbling. So he asked, "Does this
bother you? 62 What if you should see
the Son of Man go up to heaven where
he came from? 63 The Spirit is the one
who gives life! Human strength can do
nothing. The words that I have spoken
to you are from that life-giving Spirit.
64 But some of you refuse to have faith in
me." Jesus said this, because from the
beginning he knew who would have
faith in him. He also knew which one
would betray him.
65 Then Jesus said, "You cannot come
to me, unless the Father makes you
want to come. That is why I have told
these things to all of you."
66 Because of what Jesus said, many of
his disciples turned their backs on him
and stopped following him. 67 Jesus then
asked his twelve disciples if they were
going to leave him. 68 Simon Peter answered, "Lord, there is no one else that
we can go to! Your words give eternal
life. 69 We have faith in you, and we are
sure that you are God's Holy One."
70 Jesus told his disciples, "I chose all
twelve of you, but one of you is a demon!" 71 Jesus was talking about Judas,
the son of Simon Iscariot.[e] He would
later betray Jesus, even though he was
one of the twelve disciples.

Jesus' Brothers Don't Have Faith in Him

7 Jesus decided to leave Judea and to
start going through Galilee because
the Jewish leaders wanted to kill him.
2 It was almost time for the Festival of
Shelters, 3 and Jesus' brothers said to
him, "Why don't you go to Judea? Then
your disciples can see what you are doing. 4 No one does anything in secret, if
they want others to know about them.
So let the world know what you are

[c] **6.39** *the last day*: When God will judge all people. [d] **6.49** *manna*: See the note at 6.31.
[e] **6.71** *Iscariot*: This may mean "a man from Kerioth" (a place in Judea). But more probably it means "a man who was a liar" or "a man who was a betrayer."

doing!" 5 Even Jesus' own brothers had
not yet become his followers.
6 Jesus answered, "My time hasn't yet
come,[f] but your time is always here.
7 The people of this world cannot hate
you. They hate me, because I tell them
that they do evil things. 8 Go on to the
festival. My time hasn't yet come, and I
am not going." 9 Jesus said this and
stayed on in Galilee.

Jesus at the Festival of Shelters

10 After Jesus' brothers had gone to
the festival, he went secretly, without
telling anyone.
11 During the festival the Jewish leaders looked for Jesus and asked,
"Where is he?" 12 The crowds even got
into an argument about him. Some
were saying, "Jesus is a good man,"
while others were saying, "He is lying
to everyone." 13 But the people were
afraid of their leaders, and none of
them talked in public about him.
14 When the festival was about half
over, Jesus went into the temple and
started teaching. 15 The leaders were surprised and said, "How does this man
know so much? He has never been
taught!"
16 Jesus replied:
I am not teaching something that I
thought up. What I teach comes from
the one who sent me. 17 If you really
want to obey God, you will know if
what I teach comes from God or
from me. 18 If I wanted to bring
honor to myself, I would speak for
myself. But I want to honor the one
who sent me. That is why I tell the
truth and not a lie. 19 Didn't Moses
give you the Law? Yet none of you
obey it! So why do you want to kill
me?
20 The crowd replied, "You're crazy!
What makes you think someone wants
to kill you?"
21 Jesus answered:
I worked one miracle,[g] and it
amazed you. 22 Moses commanded
you to circumcise your sons. But it
wasn't really Moses who gave you
this command. It was your ancestors, and even on the Sabbath you
circumcise your sons 23 in order to
obey the Law of Moses. Why are you
angry with me for making someone
completely well on the Sabbath?
24 Don't judge by appearances. Judge
by what is right.
25 Some of the people from Jerusalem
were saying, "Isn't this the man they
want to kill? 26 Yet here he is, speaking
for everyone to hear. And no one is arguing with him. Do you suppose the authorities know that he is the Messiah?
27 But how could that be? No one knows
where the Messiah will come from, but
we know where this man comes from."
28 As Jesus was teaching in the temple,
he shouted, "Do you really think you
know me and where I came from? I
didn't come on my own! The one who
sent me is truthful, and you don't know
him. 29 But I know the one who sent me,
because I came from him."
30 Some of the people wanted to arrest
Jesus right then. But no one even laid a
hand on him, because his time had not
yet come.[h] 31 A lot of people in the crowd
put their faith in him and said, "When
the Messiah comes, he surely won't perform more miracles[i] than this man has
done!"

Officers Sent To Arrest Jesus

32 When the Pharisees heard the
crowd arguing about Jesus, they got together with the chief priests and sent
some temple police to arrest him. 33 But
Jesus told them, "I will be with you a little while longer, and then I will return to
the one who sent me. 34 You will look for
me, but you won't find me. You cannot
go where I am going."
35 The Jewish leaders asked each
other, "Where can he go to keep us
from finding him? Is he going to some
foreign country where our people live?
Is he going there to teach the Greeks?[j]
36 What did he mean by saying that we
will look for him, but won't find him?
Why can't we go where he is going?"

Streams of Life-Giving Water

37 On the last and most important day
of the festival, Jesus stood up and
shouted, "If you are thirsty, come to me
and drink! 38 Have faith in me, and you
will have life-giving water flowing from
deep inside you, just as the Scriptures
say." 39 Jesus was talking about the Holy
Spirit, who would be given to everyone
that had faith in him. The Spirit had not
yet been given to anyone, since Jesus
had not yet been given his full glory.[k]

The People Take Sides

40 When the crowd heard Jesus say
this, some of them said, "He must be the
Prophet!"[l] 41 Others said, "He is the Messiah!" Others even said, "Can the Mes-

[f] **7.6** *My time hasn't yet come*: See the note at 2.4. [g] **7.21** *one miracle*: The healing of the lame man (5.1-18; see also the note at 2.11). [h] **7.30** *his time had not yet come*: See the note at 2.4. [i] **7.31** *miracles*: See the note at 2.11. [j] **7.35** *Greeks*: Perhaps Gentiles or Jews who followed Greek customs. [k] **7.39** *had not yet been given his full glory*: In the Gospel of John, Jesus is given his full glory both when he is nailed to the cross and when he is raised from death to sit beside his Father in heaven. [l] **7.40** *the Prophet*: See the note at 1.21.

siah come from Galilee? 42The Scriptures say that the Messiah will come
from the family of King David. Doesn't
this mean that he will be born in
David's hometown of Bethlehem?"
43The people started taking sides
against each other because of Jesus.
44Some of them wanted to arrest him,
but no one laid a hand on him.

The Leaders Refuse To Have Faith in Jesus

45When the temple police returned to
the chief priests and Pharisees, they
were asked, "Why didn't you bring Jesus here?"
46They answered, "No one has ever
spoken like that man!"
47The Pharisees said to them, "Have
you also been fooled? 48Not one of the
chief priests or the Pharisees has faith
in him. 49And these people who don't
know the Law are under God's curse
anyway."
50Nicodemus was there at the time. He
was a member of the council, and was
the same one who had earlier come to
see Jesus.[m] He said, 51"Our Law doesn't
let us condemn people before we hear
what they have to say. We cannot judge
them before we know what they have
done."
52Then they said, "Nicodemus, you
must be from Galilee! Read the Scriptures, and you will find that no prophet
is to come from Galilee."

A Woman Caught in Sin

8 53Everyone else went home, 1but
Jesus walked out to the Mount of
Olives. 2Then early the next morning he
went to the temple. The people came to
him, and he sat down[n] and started
teaching them.
3The Pharisees and the teachers of the
Law of Moses brought in a woman who
had been caught in bed with a man who
wasn't her husband. They made her
stand in the middle of the crowd. 4Then
they said, "Teacher, this woman was
caught sleeping with a man who isn't
her husband. 5The Law of Moses
teaches that a woman like this should
be stoned to death! What do you say?"
6They asked Jesus this question, because they wanted to test him and bring
some charge against him. But Jesus simply bent over and started writing on the
ground with his finger.
7They kept on asking Jesus about the
woman. Finally, he stood up and said, "If
any of you have never sinned, then go
ahead and throw the first stone at her!"
8Once again he bent over and began
writing on the ground. 9The people left
one by one, beginning with the oldest.
Finally, Jesus and the woman were there
alone.
10Jesus stood up and asked her,
"Where is everyone? Isn't there anyone
left to accuse you?"
11"No sir," the woman answered.
Then Jesus told her, "I am not going to
accuse you either. You may go now, but
don't sin anymore."[o]

Jesus Is the Light for the World

12Once again Jesus spoke to the people. This time he said, "I am the light for
the world! Follow me, and you won't be
walking in the dark. You will have the
light that gives life."
13The Pharisees objected, "You are the
only one speaking for yourself, and
what you say isn't true!"
14Jesus replied:

Even if I do speak for myself, what
I say is true! I know where I came
from and where I am going. But you
don't know where I am from or
where I am going. 15You judge in the
same way that everyone else does,
but I don't judge anyone. 16If I did
judge, I would judge fairly, because I
would not be doing it alone. The
Father who sent me is here with me.
17Your Law requires two witnesses
to prove that something is true. 18I
am one of my witnesses, and the
Father who sent me is the other one.

19"Where is your Father?" they asked.
"You don't know me or my Father!"
Jesus answered. "If you knew me, you
would know my Father."
20Jesus said this while he was still
teaching in the place where the temple
treasures were stored. But no one arrested him, because his time had not yet
come.[p]

You Cannot Go Where I Am Going

21Jesus also told them, "I am going
away, and you will look for me. But you
cannot go where I am going, and you
will die with your sins unforgiven."
22The Jewish leaders asked, "Does he
intend to kill himself? Is that what he
means by saying we cannot go where
he is going?"
23Jesus answered, "You are from below, but I am from above. You belong
to this world, but I don't. 24That is why
I said you will die with your sins unforgiven. If you don't have faith in me for

[m]**7.50** *who had earlier come to see Jesus*: See 3.1-21. [n]**8.2** *sat down*: See the note at 6.3, 4.
[o]**8.11** *don't sin anymore*: Verses 1-11 are not in some manuscripts. In other manuscripts these verses are placed after 7.36 or after 21.25 or after Luke 21.38, with some differences in the text.
[p]**8.20** *his time had not yet come*: See the note at 2.4.

who I am,[q] you will die, and your sins will not be forgiven."

25"Who are you?" they asked Jesus.

Jesus answered, "I am exactly who I told you at the beginning. 26There is a lot more I could say to condemn you. But the one who sent me is truthful, and I tell the people of this world only what I have heard from him."

27No one understood that Jesus was talking to them about the Father.

28Jesus went on to say, "When you have lifted up the Son of Man,[r] you will know who I am. You will also know that I don't do anything on my own. I say only what my Father taught me. 29The one who sent me is with me. I always do what pleases him, and he will never leave me."

30After Jesus said this, many of the people put their faith in him.

The Truth Will Set You Free

31Jesus told the people who had faith in him, "If you keep on obeying what I have said, you truly are my disciples. 32You will know the truth, and the truth will set you free."

33They answered, "We are Abraham's children! We have never been anyone's slaves. How can you say we will be set free?"

34Jesus replied:

> I tell you for certain that anyone who sins is a slave of sin! 35And slaves don't stay in the family forever, though the Son will always remain in the family. 36If the Son gives you freedom, you are free! 37I know that you are from Abraham's family. Yet you want to kill me, because my message isn't really in your hearts. 38I am telling you what my Father has shown me, just as you are doing what your father has taught you.

Your Father Is the Devil

39The people said to Jesus, "Abraham is our father!"

Jesus replied, "If you were Abraham's children, you would do what Abraham did. 40Instead, you want to kill me for telling you the truth that God gave me. Abraham never did anything like that. 41But you are doing exactly what your father does."

"Don't accuse us of having someone else as our father!" they said. "We just have one father, and he is God."

42Jesus answered:

> If God were your Father, you would love me, because I came from God and only from him. He sent me. I did not come on my own. 43Why can't you understand what I am talking about? Can't you stand to hear what I am saying? 44Your father is the devil, and you do exactly what he wants. He has always been a murderer and a liar. There is nothing truthful about him. He speaks on his own, and everything he says is a lie. Not only is he a liar himself, but he is also the father of all lies.
>
> 45Everything I have told you is true, and you still refuse to have faith in me. 46Can any of you accuse me of sin? If you cannot, why won't you have faith in me? After all, I am telling you the truth. 47Anyone who belongs to God will listen to his message. But you refuse to listen, because you don't belong to God.

Jesus and Abraham

48The people told Jesus, "We were right to say that you are a Samaritan[s] and that you have a demon in you!"

49Jesus answered, "I don't have a demon in me. I honor my Father, and you refuse to honor me. 50I don't want honor for myself. But there is one who wants me to be honored, and he is also the one who judges. 51I tell you for certain that if you obey my words, you will never die."

52Then the people said, "Now we are sure that you have a demon. Abraham is dead, and so are the prophets. How can you say that no one who obeys your words will ever die? 53Are you greater than our father Abraham? He died, and so did the prophets. Who do you think you are?"

54Jesus replied, "If I honored myself, it would mean nothing. My Father is the one who honors me. You claim that he is your God, 55even though you don't really know him. If I said I didn't know him, I would be a liar, just like all of you. But I know him, and I do what he says. 56Your father Abraham was really glad to see me."

57"You are not even fifty years old!" they said. "How could you have seen Abraham?"

58Jesus answered, "I tell you for certain that even before Abraham was, I was, and I am."[t] 59The people picked up stones to kill Jesus, but he hid and left the temple.

Jesus Heals a Man Born Blind

9 As Jesus walked along, he saw a man who had been blind since birth. 2Jesus' disciples asked, "Teacher, why

[q]8.24 *I am*: For the Jewish people the most holy name of God is "Yahweh," which may be translated "I am." In the Gospel of John "I am" is sometimes used by Jesus to show that he is that one. [r]8.28 *lifted up the Son of Man*: See the note at 7.39. [s]8.48 *Samaritan*: See 4.9 and the note there. [t]8.58 *I am*: See the note at 8.24.

was this man born blind? Was it because
he or his parents sinned?"
3"No, it wasn't!" Jesus answered. "But
because of his blindness, you will see
God work a miracle for him. 4As long as
it is day, we must do what the one who
sent me wants me to do. When night
comes, no one can work. 5While I am in
the world, I am the light for the world."
6After Jesus said this, he spit on the
ground. He made some mud and
smeared it on the man's eyes. 7Then he
said, "Go and wash off the mud in
Siloam Pool." The man went and
washed in Siloam, which means "One
Who Is Sent." When he had washed off
the mud, he could see.
8The man's neighbors and the people
who had seen him begging wondered if
he really could be the same man. 9Some
of them said he was the same beggar,
while others said he only looked like
him. But he told them, "I am that man."
10"Then how can you see?" they
asked.
11He answered, "Someone named Jesus made some mud and smeared it on
my eyes. He told me to go and wash it
off in Siloam Pool. When I did, I could
see."
12"Where is he now?" they asked.
"I don't know," he answered.

The Pharisees Try To Find Out What Happened

13-14The day when Jesus made the
mud and healed the man was a Sabbath.
So the people took the man to the Pharisees. 15They asked him how he was
able to see, and he answered, "Jesus
made some mud and smeared it on my
eyes. Then after I washed it off, I could
see."
16Some of the Pharisees said, "This
man Jesus doesn't come from God. If he
did, he would not break the law of the
Sabbath."
Others asked, "How could someone
who is a sinner work such a miracle?"[u]
Since the Pharisees could not agree
among themselves, 17they asked the
man, "What do you say about this one
who healed your eyes?"
"He is a prophet!" the man told them.
18But the Jewish leaders would not believe that the man had once been blind.
They sent for his parents 19and asked
them, "Is this the son that you said was
born blind? How can he now see?"
20The man's parents answered, "We
are certain that he is our son, and we
know that he was born blind. 21But
we don't know how he got his sight or
who gave it to him. Ask him! He is old
enough to speak for himself."
22-23The man's parents said this because they were afraid of the Jewish
leaders. The leaders had already agreed
that no one was to have anything to do
with anyone who said Jesus was the
Messiah.
24The leaders called the man back and
said, "Swear by God to tell the truth! We
know that Jesus is a sinner."
25The man replied, "I don't know if he
is a sinner or not. All I know is that I
used to be blind, but now I can see!"
26"What did he do to you?" the Jewish
leaders asked. "How did he heal your
eyes?"
27The man answered, "I have already
told you once, and you refused to listen.
Why do you want me to tell you again?
Do you also want to become his disciples?"
28The leaders insulted the man and
said, "You are his follower! We are followers of Moses. 29We are sure that God
spoke to Moses, but we don't even know
where Jesus comes from."
30"How strange!" the man replied. "He
healed my eyes, and yet you don't know
where he comes from. 31We know that
God listens only to people who love and
obey him. God doesn't listen to sinners.
32And this is the first time in history that
anyone has ever given sight to someone
born blind. 33Jesus could not do anything unless he came from God."
34The leaders told the man, "You have
been a sinner since the day you were
born! Do you think you can teach us
anything?" Then they said, "You can
never come back into any of our meeting places!"
35When Jesus heard what had happened, he went and found the man.
Then Jesus asked, "Do you have faith in
the Son of Man?"
36He replied, "Sir, if you will tell me
who he is, I will put my faith in him."
37"You have already seen him," Jesus
answered, "and right now he is talking
with you."
38The man said, "Lord, I put my faith
in you!" Then he worshiped Jesus.
39Jesus told him, "I came to judge the
people of this world. I am here to give
sight to the blind and to make blind
everyone who can see."
40When the Pharisees heard Jesus say
this, they asked, "Are we blind?"
41Jesus answered, "If you were blind,
you would not be guilty. But now that
you claim to see, you will keep on being
guilty."

A Story about Sheep

10 Jesus said:
I tell you for certain that only
thieves and robbers climb over the
fence instead of going in through the
gate to the sheep pen. 2-3But the
gatekeeper opens the gate for the

[u]9.16 *miracle*: See the note at 2.11.

shepherd, and he goes in through it. The sheep know their shepherd's voice. He calls each of them by name and leads them out.

[4]When he has led out all of his sheep, he walks in front of them, and they follow, because they know his voice. [5]The sheep will not follow strangers. They don't recognize a stranger's voice, and they run away.

[6]Jesus told the people this story. But they did not understand what he was talking about.

Jesus Is the Good Shepherd

[7]Jesus said:

I tell you for certain that I am the gate for the sheep. [8]Everyone who came before me was a thief or a robber, and the sheep did not listen to any of them. [9]I am the gate. All who come in through me will be saved. Through me they will come and go and find pasture.

[10]A thief comes only to rob, kill, and destroy. I came so that everyone would have life, and have it in its fullest. [11]I am the good shepherd, and the good shepherd gives up his life for his sheep. [12]Hired workers are not like the shepherd. They don't own the sheep, and when they see a wolf coming, they run off and leave the sheep. Then the wolf attacks and scatters the flock. [13]Hired workers run away because they don't care about the sheep.

[14]I am the good shepherd. I know my sheep, and they know me. [15]Just as the Father knows me, I know the Father, and I give up my life for my sheep. [16]I have other sheep that are not in this sheep pen. I must bring them together too, when they hear my voice. Then there will be one flock of sheep and one shepherd.

[17]The Father loves me, because I give up my life, so that I may receive it back again. [18]No one takes my life from me. I give it up willingly! I have the power to give it up and the power to receive it back again, just as my Father commanded me to do.

[19]The people took sides because of what Jesus had told them. [20]Many of them said, "He has a demon in him! He is crazy! Why listen to him?"

[21]But others said, "How could anyone with a demon in him say these things? No one like that could give sight to a blind person!"

Jesus Is Rejected

[22]That winter, Jesus was in Jerusalem for the Temple Festival. [23]One day he was walking in that part of the temple known as Solomon's Porch,[v] [24]and the people gathered all around him. They said, "How long are you going to keep us guessing? If you are the Messiah, tell us plainly!"

[25]Jesus answered:

I have told you, and you refused to believe me. The things I do by my Father's authority show who I am. [26]But since you are not my sheep, you don't believe me. [27]My sheep know my voice, and I know them. They follow me, [28]and I give them eternal life, so that they will never be lost. No one can snatch them out of my hand. [29]My Father gave them to me, and he is greater than all others.[w] No one can snatch them from his hands, [30]and I am one with the Father.

[31]Once again the people picked up stones in order to kill Jesus. [32]But he said, "I have shown you many good things that my Father sent me to do. Which one are you going to stone me for?"

[33]They answered, "We are not stoning you because of any good thing you did. We are stoning you because you did a terrible thing. You are just a man, and here you are claiming to be God!"

[34]Jesus replied:

In your Scriptures doesn't God say, "You are gods"? [35]You can't argue with the Scriptures, and God spoke to those people and called them gods. [36]So why do you accuse me of a terrible sin for saying that I am the Son of God? After all, it is the Father who prepared me for this work. He is also the one who sent me into the world. [37]If I don't do as my Father does, you should not believe me. [38]But if I do what my Father does, you should believe because of that, even if you don't have faith in me. Then you will know for certain that the Father is one with me, and I am one with the Father.

[39]Again they wanted to arrest Jesus. But he escaped [40]and crossed the Jordan to the place where John had earlier been baptizing. While Jesus was there, [41]many people came to him. They were saying, "John didn't work any miracles, but everything he said about Jesus is true." [42]A lot of those people also put their faith in Jesus.

The Death of Lazarus

11 [1-2]A man by the name of Lazarus was sick in the village of Bethany. He had two sisters, Mary and Martha. This was the same Mary who later

[v]10.23 *Solomon's Porch*: A public place with tall columns along the east side of the temple.
[w]10.29 *he is greater than all others*: Some manuscripts have "they are greater than all others."

poured perfume on the Lord's head and
wiped his feet with her hair. 3The sisters
sent a message to the Lord and told him
that his good friend Lazarus was sick.
4When Jesus heard this, he said, "His
sickness won't end in death. It will bring
glory to God and his Son."
5Jesus loved Martha and her sister
and brother. 6But he stayed where he
was for two more days. 7Then he said to
his disciples, "Now we will go back to
Judea."
8"Teacher," they said, "the people
there want to stone you to death! Why
do you want to go back?"
9Jesus answered, "Aren't there twelve
hours in each day? If you walk during
the day, you will have light from the
sun, and you won't stumble. 10But if you
walk during the night, you will stumble,
because you don't have any light."
11Then he told them, "Our friend Lazarus is asleep, and I am going there to
wake him up."
12They replied, "Lord, if he is asleep,
he will get better." 13Jesus really meant
that Lazarus was dead, but they thought
he was talking only about sleep.
14Then Jesus told them plainly,
"Lazarus is dead! 15I am glad that I
wasn't there, because now you will have
a chance to put your faith in me. Let's
go to him."
16Thomas, whose nickname was
"Twin," said to the other disciples,
"Come on. Let's go, so we can die with
him."

Jesus Brings Lazarus to Life

17When Jesus got to Bethany, he
found that Lazarus had already been in
the tomb four days. 18Bethany was only
about two miles from Jerusalem, 19and
many people had come from the city to
comfort Martha and Mary because their
brother had died.
20When Martha heard that Jesus had
arrived, she went out to meet him, but
Mary stayed in the house. 21Martha said
to Jesus, "Lord, if you had been here, my
brother would not have died. 22Yet even
now I know that God will do anything
you ask."
23Jesus told her, "Your brother will
live again!"
24Martha answered, "I know that he
will be raised to life on the last day,[x]
when all the dead are raised."
25Jesus then said, "I am the one who
raises the dead to life! Everyone who
has faith in me will live, even if they die.
26And everyone who lives because of
faith in me will never really die. Do you
believe this?"
27"Yes, Lord!" she replied. "I believe
that you are Christ, the Son of God. You
are the one we hoped would come into
the world."
28After Martha said this, she went and
privately said to her sister Mary, "The
Teacher is here, and he wants to see
you." 29As soon as Mary heard this, she
got up and went out to Jesus. 30He was
still outside the village where Martha
had gone to meet him. 31Many people
had come to comfort Mary, and when
they saw her quickly leave the house,
they thought she was going out to the
tomb to cry. So they followed her.
32Mary went to where Jesus was. Then
as soon as she saw him, she knelt at his
feet and said, "Lord, if you had been
here, my brother would not have died."
33When Jesus saw that Mary and the
people with her were crying, he was terribly upset 34and asked, "Where have
you put his body?"
They replied, "Lord, come and you
will see."
35Jesus started crying, 36and the people said, "See how much he loved
Lazarus."
37Some of them said, "He gives sight
to the blind. Why couldn't he have kept
Lazarus from dying?"
38Jesus was still terribly upset. So he
went to the tomb, which was a cave with
a stone rolled against the entrance.
39Then he told the people to roll the
stone away. But Martha said, "Lord, you
know that Lazarus has been dead four
days, and there will be a bad smell."
40Jesus replied, "Didn't I tell you that
if you had faith, you would see the glory
of God?"
41After the stone had been rolled
aside, Jesus looked up toward heaven
and prayed, "Father, I thank you for answering my prayer. 42I know that you always answer my prayers. But I said this,
so that the people here would believe
that you sent me."
43When Jesus had finished praying, he
shouted, "Lazarus, come out!" 44The
man who had been dead came out. His
hands and feet were wrapped with
strips of burial cloth, and a cloth covered his face.
Jesus then told the people, "Untie him
and let him go."

The Plot To Kill Jesus

(Matthew 26.1-5; Mark 14.1, 2; Luke 22.1, 2)

45Many of the people who had come
to visit Mary saw the things that Jesus
did, and they put their faith in him.
46Others went to the Pharisees and told
what Jesus had done. 47Then the chief
priests and the Pharisees called the
council together and said, "What should
we do? This man is working a lot of miracles.[y] 48If we don't stop him now,

[x] **11.24** *the last day*: When God will judge all people.

[y] **11.47** *miracles*: See the note at 2.11.

everyone will put their faith in him.
Then the Romans will come and destroy
our temple and our nation."[z]
49One of the council members was Caiaphas, who was also high priest that
year. He spoke up and said, "You people
don't have any sense at all! 50Don't you
know it is better for one person to die
for the people than for the whole nation
to be destroyed?" 51Caiaphas did not say
this on his own. As high priest that year,
he was prophesying that Jesus would
die for the nation. 52Yet Jesus would
not die just for the Jewish nation. He
would die to bring together all of God's
scattered people. 53From that day on, the
council started making plans to put Jesus to death.
54Because of this plot against him, Jesus stopped going around in public. He
went to the town of Ephraim, which was
near the desert, and he stayed there
with his disciples.
55It was almost time for Passover.
Many of the Jewish people who lived
out in the country had come to Jerusalem to get themselves ready[a] for the
festival. 56They looked around for Jesus.
Then when they were in the temple,
they asked each other, "You don't think
he will come here for Passover, do you?"
57The chief priests and the Pharisees
told the people to let them know if any
of them saw Jesus. That is how they
hoped to arrest him.

At Bethany

(Matthew 26.6-13; Mark 14.3-9)

12 Six days before Passover Jesus
went back to Bethany, where he
had raised Lazarus from death. 2A meal
had been prepared for Jesus. Martha
was doing the serving, and Lazarus
himself was there.
3Mary took a very expensive bottle of
perfume[b] and poured it on Jesus' feet.
She wiped them with her hair, and the
sweet smell of the perfume filled the
house.
4A disciple named Judas Iscariot[c] was
there. He was the one who was going to
betray Jesus, and he asked, 5"Why
wasn't this perfume sold for three hundred silver coins and the money given to
the poor?" 6Judas did not really care
about the poor. He asked this because
he carried the moneybag and sometimes would steal from it.
7Jesus replied, "Leave her alone! She
has kept this perfume for the day of my
burial. 8You will always have the poor
with you, but you won't always have
me."

A Plot To Kill Lazarus

9A lot of people came when they
heard that Jesus was there. They also
wanted to see Lazarus, because Jesus
had raised him from death. 10So the
chief priests made plans to kill Lazarus.
11He was the reason that many of the
Jewish people were turning from them
and putting their faith in Jesus.

Jesus Enters Jerusalem

*(Matthew 21.1-11; Mark 11.1-11;
Luke 19.28-40)*

12The next day a large crowd was in
Jerusalem for Passover. When they
heard that Jesus was coming for the festival, 13they took palm branches and
went out to greet him.[d] They shouted,

"Hooray![e]
God bless the one who comes
in the name of the Lord!
God bless the King
of Israel!"

14Jesus found a donkey and rode on it,
just as the Scriptures say,

15 "People of Jerusalem,
don't be afraid!
Your King is now coming,
and he is riding
on a donkey."

16At first, Jesus' disciples did not
understand. But after he had been given
his glory,[f] they remembered all this.
Everything had happened exactly as the
Scriptures said it would.
17-18A crowd had come to meet Jesus
because they had seen him call Lazarus
out of the tomb. They kept talking about
him and this miracle.[g] 19But the Pharisees said to each other, "There is nothing that can be done! Everyone in the
world is following Jesus."

Some Greeks Want To Meet Jesus

20Some Greeks[h] had gone to Jerusalem to worship during Passover.

[z] **11.48** *destroy our temple and our nation*: The Jewish leaders were afraid that Jesus would lead his followers to rebel against Rome and that the Roman army would then destroy their nation. [a] **11.55** *get themselves ready*: The Jewish people had to do certain things to prepare themselves to worship God. [b] **12.3** *very expensive bottle of perfume*: The Greek text has "expensive perfume made of pure spikenard," a plant used to make perfume. [c] **12.4** *Iscariot*: See the note at 6.71. [d] **12.13** *took palm branches and went out to greet him*: This was one way that the Jewish people welcomed a famous person. [e] **12.13** *Hooray*: This translates a word that can mean "please save us." But it is most often used as a shout of praise to God. [f] **12.16** *had been given his glory*: See the note at 7.39. [g] **12.17,18** *miracle*: See the note at 2.11. [h] **12.20** *Greeks*: Perhaps Gentiles who worshiped with the Jews. See the note at 7.35.

21 Philip from Bethsaida in Galilee was
there too. So they went to him and said,
"Sir, we would like to meet Jesus."
22 Philip told Andrew. Then the two of
them went to Jesus and told him.

The Son of Man Must Be Lifted Up

23 Jesus said:
The time has come for the Son of
Man to be given his glory.[i] 24 I tell
you for certain that a grain of wheat
that falls on the ground will never be
more than one grain unless it dies.
But if it dies, it will produce lots of
wheat. 25 If you love your life, you
will lose it. If you give it up in this
world, you will be given eternal life.
26 If you serve me, you must go with
me. My servants will be with me
wherever I am. If you serve me, my
Father will honor you.
27 Now I am deeply troubled, and I
don't know what to say. But I must
not ask my Father to keep me from
this time of suffering. In fact, I came
into the world to suffer. 28 So Father,
bring glory to yourself.
A voice from heaven then said, "I have
already brought glory to myself, and I
will do it again!" 29 When the crowd
heard the voice, some of them thought it
was thunder. Others thought an angel
had spoken to Jesus.
30 Then Jesus told the crowd, "That
voice spoke to help you, not me. 31 This
world's people are now being judged,
and the ruler of this world[j] is already
being thrown out! 32 If I am lifted up
above the earth, I will make everyone
want to come to me." 33 Jesus was talking about the way he would be put to
death.
34 The crowd said to Jesus, "The Scriptures teach that the Messiah will live
forever. How can you say that the Son of
Man must be lifted up? Who is this Son
of Man?"
35 Jesus answered, "The light will be
with you for only a little longer. Walk in
the light while you can. Then you won't
be caught walking blindly in the dark.
36 Have faith in the light while it is with
you, and you will be children of the
light."

The People Refuse To Have Faith in Jesus

After Jesus had said these things, he
left and went into hiding. 37 He had
worked a lot of miracles[k] among the
people, but they were still not willing to
have faith in him. 38 This happened so
that what the prophet Isaiah had said
would come true,

"Lord, who has believed
our message?
And who has seen
your mighty strength?"

39 The people could not have faith in Jesus, because Isaiah had also said,

40 "The Lord has blinded
the eyes of the people,
and he has made
the people stubborn.
He did this so that they
could not see
or understand,
and so that they
would not turn to the Lord
and be healed."

41 Isaiah said this, because he saw the
glory of Jesus and spoke about him.[l]
42 Even then, many of the leaders put
their faith in Jesus, but they did not tell
anyone about it. The Pharisees had already given orders for the people not to
have anything to do with anyone who
had faith in Jesus. 43 And besides, the
leaders liked praise from others more
than they liked praise from God.

Jesus Came To Save the World

44 In a loud voice Jesus said:
Everyone who has faith in me also
has faith in the one who sent me.
45 And everyone who has seen me
has seen the one who sent me. 46 I
am the light that has come into the
world. No one who has faith in me
will stay in the dark.
47 I am not the one who will judge
those who refuse to obey my teachings. I came to save the people of
this world, not to be their judge.
48 But everyone who rejects me and
my teachings will be judged on the
last day[m] by what I have said. 49 I
don't speak on my own. I say only
what the Father who sent me has
told me to say. 50 I know that his
commands will bring eternal life.
That is why I tell you exactly what
the Father has told me.

Jesus Washes the Feet of His Disciples

13 It was before Passover, and Jesus
knew that the time had come for
him to leave this world and to return to
the Father. He had always loved his followers in this world, and he loved them
to the very end.

[i] **12.23** *be given his glory*: See the note at 7.39. [j] **12.31** *world*: In the Gospel of John "world" sometimes refers to the people who live in this world and to the evil forces that control their lives. [k] **12.37** *miracles*: See the note at 2.11. [l] **12.41** *he saw the glory of Jesus and spoke about him*: Or "he saw the glory of God and spoke about Jesus." [m] **12.48** *the last day*: See the note at 6.39.

2Even before the evening meal
started, the devil had made Judas, the
son of Simon Iscariot,[n] decide to betray
Jesus.
3Jesus knew that he had come from
God and would go back to God. He also
knew that the Father had given him
complete power. 4So during the meal Jesus got up, removed his outer garment,
and wrapped a towel around his waist.
5He put some water into a large bowl.
Then he began washing his disciples'
feet and drying them with the towel he
was wearing.
6But when he came to Simon Peter,
that disciple asked, "Lord, are you going
to wash my feet?"
7Jesus answered, "You don't really
know what I am doing, but later you will
understand."
8"You will never wash my feet!" Peter
replied.
"If I don't wash you," Jesus told him,
"you don't really belong to me."
9Peter said, "Lord, don't wash just my
feet. Wash my hands and my head."
10Jesus answered, "People who have
bathed and are clean all over need to
wash just their feet. And you, my disciples, are clean, except for one of you."
11Jesus knew who would betray him.
That is why he said, "except for one of
you."
12After Jesus had washed his disciples' feet and had put his outer garment
back on, he sat down again.[o] Then he
said:

Do you understand what I have
done? 13You call me your teacher
and Lord, and you should, because
that is who I am. 14And if your Lord
and teacher has washed your feet,
you should do the same for each
other. 15I have set the example, and
you should do for each other exactly
what I have done for you. 16I tell you
for certain that servants are not
greater than their master, and messengers are not greater than the one
who sent them. 17You know these
things, and God will bless you, if you
do them.

18I am not talking about all of you.
I know the ones I have chosen. But
what the Scriptures say must come
true. And they say, "The man who
ate with me has turned against me!"
19I am telling you this before it all
happens. Then when it does happen,
you will believe who I am.[p] 20I tell
you for certain that anyone who
welcomes my messengers also welcomes me, and anyone who welcomes me welcomes the one who
sent me.

Jesus Tells What Will Happen to Him

(Matthew 26.20-25; Mark 14.17-21; Luke 22.21-23)

21After Jesus had said these things, he
was deeply troubled and told his disciples, "I tell you for certain that one of
you will betray me." 22They were confused about what he meant. And they
just stared at each other.
23Jesus' favorite disciple was sitting
next to him at the meal, 24and Simon
motioned for that disciple to find out
which one Jesus meant. 25So the disciple
leaned toward Jesus and asked, "Lord,
which one of us are you talking about?"
26Jesus answered, "I will dip this piece
of bread in the sauce and give it to the
one I was talking about."
Then Jesus dipped the bread and gave
it to Judas, the son of Simon Iscariot.[q]
27Right then Satan took control of Judas.
Jesus said, "Judas, go quickly and do
what you have to do." 28No one at the
meal understood what Jesus meant.
29But because Judas was in charge of
the money, some of them thought that
Jesus had told him to buy something
they needed for the festival. Others
thought that Jesus had told him to give
some money to the poor. 30Judas took
the piece of bread and went out.
It was already night.

The New Command

31After Judas had gone, Jesus said:

Now the Son of Man will be given
glory, and he will bring glory to God.
32Then, after God is given glory because of him, God will bring glory to
him, and God will do it very soon.

33My children, I will be with you
for a little while longer. Then you
will look for me, but you won't find
me. I tell you just as I told the people, "You cannot go where I am going." 34But I am giving you a new
command. You must love each other,
just as I have loved you. 35If you love
each other, everyone will know that
you are my disciples.

Peter's Promise

(Matthew 26.31-35; Mark 14.27-31; Luke 22.31-34)

36Simon Peter asked, "Lord, where are
you going?"
Jesus answered, "You can't go with
me now, but later on you will."

[n]**13.2** *Iscariot*: See the note at 6.71. [o]**13.12** *sat down again*: On special occasions the Jewish people followed the Greek and Roman custom of lying down on their left side and leaning on their left elbow, while eating with their right hand. [p]**13.19** *I am*: See the note at 8.24. [q]**13.26** *Iscariot*: See the note at 6.71.

37Peter asked, "Lord, why can't I go
with you now? I would die for you!"
38"Would you really die for me?" Jesus
asked. "I tell you for certain that before
a rooster crows, you will say three times
that you don't even know me."

Jesus Is the Way to the Father

14 Jesus said to his disciples, "Don't
be worried! Have faith in God
and have faith in me.[r] 2There are many
rooms in my Father's house. I wouldn't
tell you this, unless it was true. I am going there to prepare a place for each of
you. 3After I have done this, I will come
back and take you with me. Then we
will be together. 4You know the way to
where I am going."
5Thomas said, "Lord, we don't even
know where you are going! How can we
know the way?"
6"I am the way, the truth, and the life!"
Jesus answered. "Without me, no one
can go to the Father. 7If you had known
me, you would have known the Father.
But from now on, you do know him, and
you have seen him."
8Philip said, "Lord, show us the
Father. That is all we need."
9Jesus replied:
Philip, I have been with you for a
long time. Don't you know who I
am? If you have seen me, you have
seen the Father. How can you ask
me to show you the Father? 10Don't
you believe that I am one with the
Father and that the Father is one
with me? What I say isn't said on my
own. The Father who lives in me
does these things.
11Have faith in me when I say that
the Father is one with me and that I
am one with the Father. Or else have
faith in me simply because of the
things I do. 12I tell you for certain
that if you have faith in me, you will
do the same things that I am doing.
You will do even greater things, now
that I am going back to the Father.
13Ask me, and I will do whatever you
ask. This way the Son will bring
honor to the Father. 14I will do whatever you ask me to do.

The Holy Spirit Is Promised

15Jesus said to his disciples:
If you love me, you will do as I
command. 16Then I will ask the Father to send you the Holy Spirit who
will help[s] you and always be with
you. 17The Spirit will show you what
is true. The people of this world cannot accept the Spirit, because they
don't see or know him. But you
know the Spirit, who is with you and
will keep on living in you.
18I won't leave you like orphans. I
will come back to you. 19In a little
while the people of this world won't
be able to see me, but you will see
me. And because I live, you will live.
20Then you will know that I am one
with the Father. You will know that
you are one with me, and I am one
with you. 21If you love me, you will
do what I have said, and my Father
will love you. I will also love you and
show you what I am like.
22The other Judas, not Judas Iscariot,[t]
then spoke up and asked, "Lord, what
do you mean by saying that you will
show us what you are like, but you will
not show the people of this world?"
23Jesus replied:
If anyone loves me, they will obey
me. Then my Father will love them,
and we will come to them and live in
them. 24But anyone who doesn't love
me, won't obey me. What they have
heard me say doesn't really come
from me, but from the Father who
sent me.
25I have told you these things
while I am still with you. 26But the
Holy Spirit will come and help[u] you,
because the Father will send the
Spirit to take my place. The Spirit
will teach you everything and will
remind you of what I said while I
was with you.
27I give you peace, the kind of
peace that only I can give. It isn't
like the peace that this world can
give. So don't be worried or afraid.
28You have already heard me say
that I am going and that I will also
come back to you. If you really love
me, you should be glad that I am going back to the Father, because he is
greater than I am.
29I am telling you this before I
leave, so that when it does happen,
you will have faith in me. 30I cannot
speak with you much longer, because the ruler of this world is coming. But he has no power over me. 31I
obey my Father, so that everyone in
the world might know that I love
him.
It is time for us to go now.

Jesus Is the True Vine

15 Jesus said to his disciples:
I am the true vine, and my
Father is the gardener. 2He cuts
away every branch of mine that

[r] **14.1** *Have faith in God and have faith in me*: Or "You have faith in God, so have faith in me."
[s] **14.16** *help*: The Greek word may mean "comfort," "encourage," or "defend."
[t] **14.22** *Iscariot*: See the note at 6.71. [u] **14.26** *help*: See the note at 14.16.

doesn't produce fruit. But he trims
clean every branch that does
produce fruit, so that it will produce
even more fruit. 3You are already
clean because of what I have said to
you.
4Stay joined to me, and I will stay
joined to you. Just as a branch cannot produce fruit unless it stays
joined to the vine, you cannot produce fruit unless you stay joined to
me. 5I am the vine, and you are the
branches. If you stay joined to me,
and I stay joined to you, then you
will produce lots of fruit. But you
cannot do anything without me. 6If
you don't stay joined to me, you will
be thrown away. You will be like dry
branches that are gathered up and
burned in a fire.
7Stay joined to me and let my
teachings become part of you. Then
you can pray for whatever you want,
and your prayer will be answered.
8When you become fruitful disciples
of mine, my Father will be honored.
9I have loved you, just as my Father
has loved me. So remain faithful to
my love for you. 10If you obey me, I
will keep loving you, just as my
Father keeps loving me, because I
have obeyed him.
11I have told you this to make you
as completely happy as I am. 12Now
I tell you to love each other, as I
have loved you. 13The greatest way
to show love for friends is to die for
them. 14And you are my friends, if
you obey me. 15Servants don't know
what their master is doing, and so I
don't speak to you as my servants. I
speak to you as my friends, and I
have told you everything that my
Father has told me.
16You did not choose me. I chose
you and sent you out to produce
fruit, the kind of fruit that will last.
Then my Father will give you whatever you ask for in my name.[v] 17So I
command you to love each other.

The World's Hatred

18If the people of this world[w] hate
you, just remember that they hated
me first. 19If you belonged to the
world, its people would love you. But
you don't belong to the world. I have
chosen you to leave the world behind, and that is why its people hate
you. 20Remember how I told you that
servants are not greater than their
master. So if people mistreat me,
they will mistreat you. If they do
what I say, they will do what you say.
21People will do to you exactly
what they did to me. They will do it
because you belong to me, and they
don't know the one who sent me. 22If
I had not come and spoken to them,
they would not be guilty of sin. But
now they have no excuse for their
sin.
23Everyone who hates me also
hates my Father. 24I have done
things that no one else has ever
done. If they had not seen me do
these things, they would not be
guilty. But they did see me do these
things, and they still hate me and my
Father too. 25That is why the Scriptures are true when they say, "People
hated me for no reason."
26I will send you the Spirit who
comes from the Father and shows
what is true. The Spirit will help[x]
you and will tell you about me.
27Then you will also tell others about
me, because you have been with me
from the beginning.

16 I am telling you this to keep you
from being afraid. 2You will be
chased out of the Jewish meeting
places. And the time will come when
people will kill you and think they
are doing God a favor. 3They will do
these things because they don't
know either the Father or me. 4I am
saying this to you now, so that when
the time comes, you will remember
what I have said.

The Work of the Holy Spirit

I was with you at the first, and so I
didn't tell you these things. 5But now
I am going back to the Father who
sent me, and none of you asks me
where I am going. 6You are very sad
from hearing all of this. 7But I tell
you that I am going to do what is
best for you. That is why I am going
away. The Holy Spirit cannot come
to help[x] you until I leave. But after I
am gone, I will send the Spirit to
you.
8The Spirit will come and show
the people of this world the truth
about sin and God's justice and the
judgment. 9The Spirit will show
them that they are wrong about sin,
because they didn't have faith in me.
10They are wrong about God's justice, because I am going to the
Father, and you won't see me again.
11And they are wrong about the
judgment, because God has already
judged the ruler of this world.
12I have much more to say to you,

[v]15.16 *in my name*: Or "because you are my followers." [w]15.18 *world*: See the note at 12.31. [x]15.26; 16.7 *help*: See the note at 14.16.

but right now it would be more than
you could understand. 13 The Spirit
shows what is true and will come
and guide you into the full truth. The
Spirit doesn't speak on his own. He
will tell you only what he has heard
from me, and he will let you know
what is going to happen. 14 The Spirit
will bring glory to me by taking my
message and telling it to you.
15 Everything that the Father has is
mine. That is why I have said that
the Spirit takes my message and
tells it to you.

Sorrow Will Turn into Joy

16 Jesus told his disciples, "For a little
while you won't see me, but after a
while you will see me."
17 They said to each other, "What does
Jesus mean by saying that for a little
while we won't see him, but after a
while we will see him? What does he
mean by saying that he is going to the
Father? 18 What is this 'little while' that
he is talking about? We don't know what
he means."
19 Jesus knew that they had some
questions, so he said:
You are wondering what I meant
when I said that for a little while you
won't see me, but after a while you
will see me. 20 I tell you for certain
that you will cry and be sad, but the
world will be happy. You will be sad,
but later you will be happy.
21 When a woman is about to give
birth, she is in great pain. But after it
is all over, she forgets the pain and
is happy, because she has brought a
child into the world. 22 You are now
very sad. But later I will see you, and
you will be so happy that no one will
be able to change the way you feel.
23 When that time comes, you won't
have to ask me about anything. I tell
you for certain that the Father will
give you whatever you ask for in my
name. 24 You have not asked for anything in this way before, but now
you must ask in my name.[y] Then it
will be given to you, so that you will
be completely happy.
25 I have used examples to explain
to you what I have been talking
about. But the time will come when I
will speak to you plainly about the
Father and will no longer use examples like these. 26 You will ask the
Father in my name,[z] and I won't
have to ask him for you. 27 God the
Father loves you because you love
me, and you believe that I have come
from him. 28 I came from the Father
into the world, but I am leaving the
world and returning to the Father.
29 The disciples said, "Now you are
speaking plainly to us! You are not using
examples. 30 At last we know that you
understand everything, and we don't
have any more questions. Now we believe that you truly have come from
God."
31 Jesus replied:
Do you really believe me? 32 The
time will come and is already here
when all of you will be scattered.
Each of you will go back home and
leave me by myself. But the Father
will be with me, and I won't be
alone. 33 I have told you this, so that
you might have peace in your hearts
because of me. While you are in the
world, you will have to suffer. But
cheer up! I have defeated the world.[a]

Jesus Prays

17 After Jesus had finished speaking
to his disciples, he looked up toward heaven and prayed:
Father, the time has come for you
to bring glory to your Son, in order
that he may bring glory to you. 2 And
you gave him power over all people,
so that he would give eternal life to
everyone you give him. 3 Eternal life
is to know you, the only true God,
and to know Jesus Christ, the one
you sent. 4 I have brought glory to
you here on earth by doing everything you gave me to do. 5 Now,
Father, give me back the glory that I
had with you before the world was
created.
6 You have given me some followers from this world, and I have
shown them what you are like. They
were yours, but you gave them to
me, and they have obeyed you.
7 They know that you gave me everything I have. 8 I told my followers
what you told me, and they accepted
it. They know that I came from you,
and they believe that you are the one
who sent me. 9 I am praying for
them, but not for those who belong
to this world.[a] My followers belong
to you, and I am praying for them.
10 All that I have is yours, and all that
you have is mine, and they will bring
glory to me.
11 Holy Father, I am no longer in
the world. I am coming to you, but
my followers are still in the world.

[y] **16.23,24** *in my name . . . in my name*: Or "as my disciples . . . as my disciples." [z] **16.26** *in my name*: Or "because you are my followers." [a] **16.33; 17.9** *world*: See the note at 12.31.

So keep them safe by the power of
the name that you have given me.
Then they will be one with each
other, just as you and I are one.
12While I was with them, I kept them
safe by the power you have given
me. I guarded them, and not one of
them was lost, except the one who
had to be lost. This happened so that
what the Scriptures say would come
true.
13I am on my way to you. But I say
these things while I am still in the
world, so that my followers will have
the same complete joy that I do. 14I
have told them your message. But
the people of this world hate them,
because they don't belong to this
world, just as I don't.
15Father, I don't ask you to take
my followers out of the world, but
keep them safe from the evil one.
16They don't belong to this world,
and neither do I. 17Your word is the
truth. So let this truth make them
completely yours. 18I am sending
them into the world, just as you sent
me. 19I have given myself completely
for their sake, so that they may belong completely to the truth.
20I am not praying just for these
followers. I am also praying for
everyone else who will have faith
because of what my followers will
say about me. 21I want all of them to
be one with each other, just as I am
one with you and you are one with
me. I also want them to be one with
us. Then the people of this world
will believe that you sent me.
22I have honored my followers in
the same way that you honored me,
in order that they may be one with
each other, just as we are one. 23I am
one with them, and you are one with
me, so that they may become completely one. Then this world's people
will know that you sent me. They
will know that you love my followers as much as you love me.
24Father, I want everyone you have
given me to be with me, wherever I
am. Then they will see the glory that
you have given me, because you
loved me before the world was created. 25Good Father, the people of
this world don't know you. But I
know you, and my followers know
that you sent me. 26I told them what
you are like, and I will tell them
even more. Then the love that you
have for me will become part of
them, and I will be one with them.

Jesus Is Betrayed and Arrested

(Matthew 26.47-56; Mark 14.43-50; Luke 22.47-53)

18 When Jesus had finished praying,
he and his disciples crossed the
Kidron Valley and went into a garden.[b]
2Jesus had often met there with his disciples, and Judas knew where the place
was.
3-5Judas had promised to betray Jesus.
So he went to the garden with some Roman soldiers and temple police, who
had been sent by the chief priests and
the Pharisees. They carried torches,
lanterns, and weapons. Jesus already
knew everything that was going to happen, but he asked, "Who are you looking
for?"
They answered, "We are looking for
Jesus from Nazareth!"
Jesus told them, "I am Jesus!"[c] 6At
once they all backed away and fell to
the ground.
7Jesus again asked, "Who are you
looking for?"
"We are looking for Jesus from
Nazareth," they answered.
8This time Jesus replied, "I have already told you that I am Jesus. If I am
the one you are looking for, let these
others go. 9Then everything will happen, just as I said, 'I did not lose anyone you gave me.' "
10Simon Peter had brought along a
sword. He now pulled it out and struck
at the servant of the high priest. The servant's name was Malchus, and Peter cut
off his right ear. 11Jesus told Peter, "Put
your sword away. I must drink from the
cup[d] that the Father has given me."

Jesus Is Brought to Annas

(Matthew 26.57, 58; Mark 14.53, 54; Luke 22.54)

12The Roman officer and his men, together with the temple police, arrested
Jesus and tied him up. 13They took him
first to Annas, who was the father-in-
law of Caiaphas, the high priest that
year. 14This was the same Caiaphas who
had told the Jewish leaders, "It is better
if one person dies for the people."

Peter Says He Doesn't Know Jesus

(Matthew 26.69, 70; Mark 14.66-68; Luke 22.55-57)

15Simon Peter and another disciple
followed Jesus. That disciple knew the
high priest, and he followed Jesus into
the courtyard of the high priest's house.
16Peter stayed outside near the gate. But
the other disciple came back out and

[b] **18.1** *garden*: The Greek word is usually translated "garden," but probably referred to an olive orchard. [c] **18.3-5** *I am Jesus*: The Greek text has "I am" (see the note at 8.24).
[d] **18.11** *drink from the cup*: In the Scriptures a cup is sometimes used as a symbol of suffering. To "drink from the cup" is to suffer.

spoke to the girl at the gate. She let Peter go in, 17but asked him, "Aren't you
one of that man's followers?"
"No, I am not!" Peter answered.
18It was cold, and the servants and
temple police had made a charcoal fire.
They were warming themselves around
it, when Peter went over and stood near
the fire to warm himself.

Jesus Is Questioned by the High Priest

(Matthew 26.59-66; Mark 14.55-64;
Luke 22.66-71)

19The high priest questioned Jesus
about his followers and his teaching.
20But Jesus told him, "I have spoken
freely in front of everyone. And I have
always taught in our meeting places and
in the temple, where all of our people
come together. I have not said anything
in secret. 21Why are you questioning
me? Why don't you ask the people who
heard me? They know what I have said."
22As soon as Jesus said this, one of the
temple police hit him and said, "That's
no way to talk to the high priest!"
23Jesus answered, "If I have done
something wrong, say so. But if not, why
did you hit me?" 24Jesus was still tied
up, and Annas sent him to Caiaphas the
high priest.

Peter Again Denies that He Knows Jesus

(Matthew 26.71-75; Mark 14.69-72;
Luke 22.58-62)

25While Simon Peter was standing
there warming himself, someone asked
him, "Aren't you one of Jesus' followers?"
Again Peter denied it and said, "No, I
am not!"
26One of the high priest's servants
was there. He was a relative of the servant whose ear Peter had cut off, and he
asked, "Didn't I see you in the garden
with that man?"
27Once more Peter denied it, and right
then a rooster crowed.

Jesus Is Tried by Pilate

(Matthew 27.1, 2, 11-14; Mark 15.1-5;
Luke 23.1-5)

28It was early in the morning when Jesus was taken from Caiaphas to the
building where the Roman governor
stayed. But the crowd waited outside.
Any of them who had gone inside would
have become unclean and would not be
allowed to eat the Passover meal.[e]
29Pilate came out and asked, "What
charges are you bringing against this
man?"
30They answered, "He is a criminal!
That's why we brought him to you."
31Pilate told them, "Take him and
judge him by your own laws."
The crowd replied, "We are not allowed to put anyone to death." 32And so
what Jesus said about his death[f] would
soon come true.
33Pilate then went back inside. He
called Jesus over and asked, "Are you
the king of the Jews?"
34Jesus answered, "Are you asking
this on your own or did someone tell
you about me?"
35"You know I'm not a Jew!" Pilate
said. "Your own people and the chief
priests brought you to me. What have
you done?"
36Jesus answered, "My kingdom
doesn't belong to this world. If it did, my
followers would have fought to keep me
from being handed over to the Jewish
leaders. No, my kingdom doesn't belong
to this world."
37"So you are a king," Pilate replied.
"You are saying that I am a king," Jesus told him. "I was born into this world
to tell about the truth. And everyone
who belongs to the truth knows my
voice."
38Pilate asked Jesus, "What is truth?"

Jesus Is Sentenced to Death

(Matthew 27.15-31; Mark 15.6-20;
Luke 23.13-25)

Pilate went back out and said, "I don't
find this man guilty of anything! 39And
since I usually set a prisoner free for
you at Passover, would you like for me
to set free the king of the Jews?"
40They shouted, "No, not him! We
want Barabbas." Now Barabbas was a
terrorist.[g]

19 Pilate gave orders for Jesus to be
beaten with a whip. 2The soldiers
made a crown out of thorn branches
and put it on Jesus. Then they put a purple robe on him. 3They came up to him
and said, "Hey, you king of the Jews!"
They also hit him with their fists.
4Once again Pilate went out. This time
he said, "I will have Jesus brought out to
you again. Then you can see for yourselves that I have not found him guilty."
5Jesus came out, wearing the crown of
thorns and the purple robe. Pilate said,
"Here is the man!"[h]

[e] **18.28** *would have become unclean and would not be allowed to eat the Passover meal*: Jewish people who came in close contact with foreigners right before Passover were not allowed to eat the Passover meal. [f] **18.32** *about his death*: Jesus had said that he would die by being "lifted up," which meant that he would die on a cross. The Romans killed criminals by nailing them on a cross, but they did not let the Jews kill anyone in this way. [g] **18.40** *terrorist*: Someone who stirred up trouble against the Romans in the hope of gaining freedom for the Jewish people. [h] **19.5** *"Here is the man!"*: Or "Look at the man!"

6 When the chief priests and the temple police saw him, they yelled, "Nail him to a cross! Nail him to a cross!"

Pilate told them, "You take him and nail him to a cross! I don't find him guilty of anything."

7 The crowd replied, "He claimed to be the Son of God! Our Jewish Law says that he must be put to death."

8 When Pilate heard this, he was terrified. 9 He went back inside and asked Jesus, "Where are you from?" But Jesus did not answer.

10 "Why won't you answer my question?" Pilate asked. "Don't you know that I have the power to let you go free or to nail you to a cross?"

11 Jesus replied, "If God had not given you the power, you couldn't do anything at all to me. But the one who handed me over to you did something even worse."

12 Then Pilate wanted to set Jesus free. But the crowd again yelled, "If you set this man free, you are no friend of the Emperor! Anyone who claims to be a king is an enemy of the Emperor."

13 When Pilate heard this, he brought Jesus out. Then he sat down on the judge's bench at the place known as "The Stone Pavement." In Aramaic this pavement is called "Gabbatha." 14 It was about noon on the day before Passover, and Pilate said to the crowd, "Look at your king!"

15 "Kill him! Kill him!" they yelled. "Nail him to a cross!"

"So you want me to nail your king to a cross?" Pilate asked.

The chief priests replied, "The Emperor is our king!" 16 Then Pilate handed Jesus over to be nailed to a cross.

Jesus Is Nailed to a Cross

(Matthew 27.32-44; Mark 15.21-32; Luke 23.26-43)

Jesus was taken away, 17 and he carried his cross to a place known as "The Skull."[i] In Aramaic this place is called "Golgotha." 18 There Jesus was nailed to the cross, and on each side of him a man was also nailed to a cross.

19 Pilate ordered the charge against Jesus to be written on a board and put above the cross. It read, "Jesus of Nazareth, King of the Jews." 20 The words were written in Hebrew, Latin, and Greek.

The place where Jesus was taken wasn't far from the city, and many of the people read the charge against him. 21 So the chief priests went to Pilate and said, "Why did you write that he is King of the Jews? You should have written, 'He claimed to be King of the Jews.' "

22 But Pilate told them, "What is written will not be changed!"

23 After the soldiers had nailed Jesus to the cross, they divided up his clothes into four parts, one for each of them. But his outer garment was made from a single piece of cloth, and it did not have any seams. 24 The soldiers said to each other, "Let's not rip it apart. We will gamble to see who gets it." This happened so that the Scriptures would come true, which say,

"They divided up my clothes
and gambled
for my garments."

The soldiers then did what they had decided.

25 Jesus' mother stood beside his cross with her sister and Mary the wife of Clopas. Mary Magdalene was standing there too.[j] 26 When Jesus saw his mother and his favorite disciple with her, he said to his mother, "This man is now your son." 27 Then he said to the disciple, "She is now your mother." From then on, that disciple took her into his own home.

The Death of Jesus

(Matthew 27.45-56; Mark 15.33-41; Luke 23.44-49)

28 Jesus knew that he had now finished his work. And in order to make the Scriptures come true, he said, "I am thirsty!" 29 A jar of cheap wine was there. Someone then soaked a sponge with the wine and held it up to Jesus' mouth on the stem of a hyssop plant. 30 After Jesus drank the wine, he said, "Everything is done!" He bowed his head and died.

A Spear Is Stuck in Jesus' Side

31 The next day would be both a Sabbath and the Passover. It was a special day for the Jewish people,[k] and they did not want the bodies to stay on the crosses during that day. So they asked

[i] **19.17** *The Skull*: The place was probably given this name because it was near a large rock in the shape of a human skull. [j] **19.25** *Jesus' mother stood beside his cross with her sister and Mary the wife of Clopas. Mary Magdalene was standing there too*: The Greek text may also be understood to include only three women ("Jesus' mother stood beside the cross with her sister, Mary the mother of Clopas. Mary Magdalene was standing there too.") or merely two women ("Jesus' mother was standing there with her sister Mary of Clopas, that is, Mary Magdalene."). "Of Clopas" may mean "daughter of" or "mother of." [k] **19.31** *a special day for the Jewish people*: Passover could be any day of the week. But according to the Gospel of John, Passover was on a Sabbath in the year that Jesus was nailed to a cross.

Pilate to break the men's legs[l] and take
their bodies down. 32The soldiers first
broke the legs of the other two men who
were nailed there. 33But when they came
to Jesus, they saw that he was already
dead, and they did not break his legs.
34One of the soldiers stuck his spear
into Jesus' side, and blood and water
came out. 35We know this is true, because it was told by someone who saw it
happen. Now you can have faith too.
36All this happened so that the Scriptures would come true, which say, "No
bone of his body will be broken" 37and,
"They will see the one in whose side
they stuck a spear."

Jesus Is Buried

(Matthew 27.57-61; Mark 15.42-47; Luke 23.50-56)

38Joseph from Arimathea was one of
Jesus' disciples. He had kept it secret
though, because he was afraid of the
Jewish leaders. But now he asked Pilate
to let him have Jesus' body. Pilate gave
him permission, and Joseph took it
down from the cross.
39Nicodemus also came with about
seventy-five pounds of spices made
from myrrh and aloes. This was the
same Nicodemus who had visited Jesus
one night.[m] 40The two men wrapped the
body in a linen cloth, together with the
spices, which was how the Jewish people buried their dead. 41In the place
where Jesus had been nailed to a cross,
there was a garden with a tomb that had
never been used. 42The tomb was
nearby, and since it was the time to prepare for the Sabbath, they were in a
hurry to put Jesus' body there.

Jesus Is Alive

(Matthew 28.1-10; Mark 16.1-8; Luke 24.1-12)

20 On Sunday morning while it was
still dark, Mary Magdalene went
to the tomb and saw that the stone had
been rolled away from the entrance.
2She ran to Simon Peter and to Jesus'
favorite disciple and said, "They have
taken the Lord from the tomb! We don't
know where they have put him."
3Peter and the other disciple started
for the tomb. 4They ran side by side, until the other disciple ran faster than Peter and got there first. 5He bent over and
saw the strips of linen cloth lying inside
the tomb, but he did not go in.
6When Simon Peter got there, he went
into the tomb and saw the strips of
cloth. 7He also saw the piece of cloth
that had been used to cover Jesus' face.
It was rolled up and in a place by itself.
8The disciple who got there first then
went into the tomb, and when he saw it,
he believed. 9At that time Peter and the
other disciple did not know that the
Scriptures said Jesus would rise to life.
10So the two of them went back to the
other disciples.

Jesus Appears to Mary Magdalene

(Mark 16.9-11)

11Mary Magdalene stood crying outside the tomb. She was still weeping,
when she stooped down 12and saw two
angels inside. They were dressed in
white and were sitting where Jesus'
body had been. One was at the head and
the other was at the foot. 13The angels
asked Mary, "Why are you crying?"
She answered, "They have taken away
my Lord's body! I don't know where
they have put him."
14As soon as Mary said this, she
turned around and saw Jesus standing
there. But she did not know who he was.
15Jesus asked her, "Why are you crying?
Who are you looking for?"
She thought he was the gardener and
said, "Sir, if you have taken his body
away, please tell me, so I can go and get
him."
16Then Jesus said to her, "Mary!"
She turned and said to him, "Rabboni." The Aramaic word "Rabboni"
means "Teacher."
17Jesus told her, "Don't hold on to me!
I have not yet gone to the Father. But tell
my disciples that I am going to the one
who is my Father and my God, as well
as your Father and your God." 18Mary
Magdalene then went and told the disciples that she had seen the Lord. She
also told them what he had said to her.

Jesus Appears to His Disciples

(Matthew 28.16-20; Mark 16.14-18; Luke 24.36-49)

19The disciples were afraid of the Jewish leaders, and on the evening of that
same Sunday they locked themselves in
a room. Suddenly, Jesus appeared in the
middle of the group. He greeted them
20and showed them his hands and his
side. When the disciples saw the Lord,
they became very happy.
21After Jesus had greeted them again,
he said, "I am sending you, just as the
Father has sent me." 22Then he breathed
on them and said, "Receive the Holy
Spirit. 23If you forgive anyone's sins,
they will be forgiven. But if you don't
forgive their sins, they will not be forgiven."

[l] **19.31** *break the men's legs*: This was the way that the Romans sometimes speeded up the death of a person who had been nailed to a cross. [m] **19.39** *Nicodemus who had visited Jesus one night*: See 3.1-21.

Jesus and Thomas

24 Although Thomas the Twin was one
of the twelve disciples, he wasn't with
the others when Jesus appeared to
them. 25 So they told him, "We have seen
the Lord!"

But Thomas said, "First, I must see the
nail scars in his hands and touch them
with my finger. I must put my hand
where the spear went into his side. I
won't believe unless I do this!"

26 A week later the disciples were together again. This time, Thomas was
with them. Jesus came in while the
doors were still locked and stood in the
middle of the group. He greeted his disciples 27 and said to Thomas, "Put your
finger here and look at my hands! Put
your hand into my side. Stop doubting
and have faith!"

28 Thomas replied, "You are my Lord
and my God!"

29 Jesus said, "Thomas, do you have
faith because you have seen me? The
people who have faith in me without
seeing me are the ones who are really
blessed!"

Why John Wrote His Book

30 Jesus worked many other miracles[n]
for his disciples, and not all of them are
written in this book. 31 But these are
written so that you will put your faith in
Jesus as the Messiah and the Son of
God. If you have faith in[o] him, you will
have true life.

Jesus Appears to Seven Disciples

21 Jesus later appeared to his disciples along the shore of Lake
Tiberias. 2 Simon Peter, Thomas the
Twin, Nathanael from Cana in Galilee,
and the brothers James and John,[p] were
there, together with two other disciples.
3 Simon Peter said, "I'm going fishing!"

The others said, "We will go with
you." They went out in their boat. But
they didn't catch a thing that night.

4 Early the next morning Jesus stood
on the shore, but the disciples did not
realize who he was. 5 Jesus shouted,
"Friends, have you caught anything?"

"No!" they answered.

6 So he told them, "Let your net down
on the right side of your boat, and you
will catch some fish."

They did, and the net was so full of
fish that they could not drag it up into
the boat.

7 Jesus' favorite disciple told Peter,
"It's the Lord!" When Simon heard that
it was the Lord, he put on the clothes
that he had taken off while he was
working. Then he jumped into the water. 8 The boat was only about a hundred
yards from shore. So the other disciples
stayed in the boat and dragged in the
net full of fish.

9 When the disciples got out of the
boat, they saw some bread and a charcoal fire with fish on it. 10 Jesus told his
disciples, "Bring some of the fish you
just caught." 11 Simon Peter got back into
the boat and dragged the net to shore.
In it were one hundred fifty-three large
fish, but still the net did not rip.

12 Jesus said, "Come and eat!" But
none of the disciples dared ask who he
was. They knew he was the Lord. 13 Jesus took the bread in his hands and
gave some of it to his disciples. He did
the same with the fish. 14 This was the
third time that Jesus appeared to his
disciples after he was raised from death.

Jesus and Peter

15 When Jesus and his disciples had
finished eating, he asked, "Simon son of
John, do you love me more than the others do?"[q]

Simon Peter answered, "Yes, Lord,
you know I do!"

"Then feed my lambs," Jesus said.

16 Jesus asked a second time, "Simon
son of John, do you love me?"

Peter answered, "Yes, Lord, you know
I love you!"

"Then take care of my sheep," Jesus
told him.

17 Jesus asked a third time, "Simon son
of John, do you love me?"

Peter was hurt because Jesus had
asked him three times if he loved him.
So he told Jesus, "Lord, you know
everything. You know I love you."

Jesus replied, "Feed my sheep. 18 I tell
you for certain that when you were a
young man, you dressed yourself and
went wherever you wanted to go. But
when you are old, you will hold out your
hands. Then others will wrap your belt
around you and lead you where you
don't want to go."

19 Jesus said this to tell how Peter
would die and bring honor to God. Then
he said to Peter, "Follow me!"

Jesus and His Favorite Disciple

20 Peter turned and saw Jesus' favorite
disciple following them. He was the
same one who had sat next to Jesus at
the meal and had asked, "Lord, who is
going to betray you?" 21 When Peter saw
that disciple, he asked Jesus, "Lord,
what about him?"

[n] **20.30** *miracles*: See the note at 2.11. [o] **20.31** *put your faith in . . . have faith in*: Some manuscripts have "keep on having faith in . . . keep on having faith in." [p] **21.2** *the brothers James and John*: Greek "the two sons of Zebedee." [q] **21.15** *more than the others do?*: Or "more than you love these things?"

22Jesus answered, "What is it to you, if
I want him to live until I return? You
must follow me." 23So the rumor spread
among the other disciples that this disciple would not die. But Jesus did not say he would not die. He simply said, "What is it to you, if I want him to live until I return?"

24This disciple is the one who told all of this. He wrote it, and we know he is telling the truth.

25Jesus did many other things. If they were all written in books, I don't suppose there would be room enough in the whole world for all the books.

ACTS

ABOUT THIS BOOK

This is the second book written by Luke. His first one is commonly known as the Gospel of Luke. In it he told "all that Jesus did and taught from the very first until he was taken up to heaven" (1.1, 2). In this book Luke continues the story by describing some of the struggles the disciples faced as they tried to obey the command of Jesus: "You will tell everyone about me in Jerusalem, in all Judea, in Samaria, and everywhere in the world" (1.8).

So many different countries are mentioned in Acts that the book may seem to have been written only to tell about the spread of the Christian message. But that is only part of the story. After Jesus was taken up to heaven, one of the big problems for his followers was deciding who could belong to God's people. And since Jesus and his first followers were Jews, it was only natural for many of them to think that his message was only for Jews. But in Acts, the Spirit is always present to show that Jesus came to save both Jews and Gentiles, and that God wants followers from every nation and race to be part of his people.

The first conflict between Christians and Jews took place when some of the Jewish religious leaders rejected the message about Jesus (4.1-31; 7.1-59). But the most serious problems for the early church happened because the disciples at first failed to understand that anyone could become a follower of Jesus without first becoming a Jew. This began to change when Philip dared to take the message to the Samaritans (8.7-25), and when Peter went to the home of Cornelius, a captain in the Roman army (10.1-48).

Finally, Peter reported to the church in Jerusalem (11.1-18) and a meeting was held there (15.3-35) to discuss the question of who could become followers of Christ. Before the meeting was over, everyone agreed that the Spirit of God was leading them to reach out to Gentiles as well as Jews with the good news of Jesus.

The one who did the most for the spread of the faith was a man named Paul, and much of the book tells about his preaching among the Gentiles. Finally, he took the message to Rome, the world's most important city at that time (28.16-31). One of Luke's main reasons for writing was to show that nothing could keep the Christian message from spreading everywhere:

> *For two years Paul stayed in a rented house and welcomed everyone who came to see him. He bravely preached about God's kingdom and taught about the Lord Jesus Christ, and no one tried to stop him.* *(28.30, 31)*

A QUICK LOOK AT THIS BOOK

Telling the Good News in Jerusalem (1.1—8.3)
The Good News in Judea and Samaria (8.4—12.25)
Paul's First Journey to Tell the Good News (13.1—14.28)
An Important Decision in Jerusalem (15.1-35)
Paul's Second Journey to Tell the Good News (15.36—18.22)
Paul's Third Journey to Tell the Good News (18.23—21.16)
Paul's Arrest in Jerusalem (21.17—23.22)
Paul Is Taken to Caesarea (23.23—26.32)
Paul Is Taken to Rome (27.1—28.31)

1

Theophilus, I first wrote to you[a]
about all that Jesus did and taught
from the very first 2until he was taken
up to heaven. But before he was taken
up, he gave orders to the apostles he
had chosen with the help of the Holy
Spirit.
3For forty days after Jesus had suffered and died, he proved in many ways
that he had been raised from death. He
appeared to his apostles and spoke to
them about God's kingdom. 4While he
was still with them, he said:

> Don't leave Jerusalem yet. Wait
> here for the Father to give you the
> Holy Spirit, just as I told you he has
> promised to do. 5John baptized with
> water, but in a few days you will be
> baptized with the Holy Spirit.

Jesus Is Taken to Heaven

6While the apostles were still with
Jesus, they asked him, "Lord, are you
now going to give Israel its own king
again?"[b]
7Jesus said to them, "You don't need
to know the time of those events that
only the Father controls. 8But the Holy
Spirit will come upon you and give
you power. Then you will tell everyone
about me in Jerusalem, in all Judea, in
Samaria, and everywhere in the world."
9After Jesus had said this and while
they were watching, he was taken up
into a cloud. They could not see him,
10but as he went up, they kept looking
up into the sky.
Suddenly two men dressed in white
clothes were standing there beside
them. 11They said, "Why are you men
from Galilee standing here and looking
up into the sky? Jesus has been taken to
heaven. But he will come back in the
same way that you have seen him go."

Someone To Take the Place of Judas

12-13The Mount of Olives was about
half a mile from Jerusalem. The apostles who had gone there were Peter,
John, James, Andrew, Philip, Thomas,
Bartholomew, Matthew, James the son
of Alphaeus, Simon, known as the Eager One,[c] and Judas the son of James.
After the apostles returned to the city,
they went upstairs to the room where
they had been staying.
14The apostles often met together and
prayed with a single purpose in mind.[d]
The women and Mary the mother of Jesus would meet with them, and so would
his brothers. 15One day there were
about one hundred twenty of the Lord's
followers meeting together, and Peter
stood up to speak to them. 16-17He said:

> My friends, long ago by the power
> of the Holy Spirit, David said some-
> thing about Judas, and what he said
> has now happened. Judas was one
> of us and had worked with us, but he
> brought the mob to arrest Jesus.
> 18Then Judas bought some land with
> the money he was given for doing
> that evil thing. He fell headfirst into
> the field. His body burst open, and
> all his insides came out. 19When the
> people of Jerusalem found out about
> this, they called the place Akeldama,
> which in the local language means
> "Field of Blood."
> 20In the book of Psalms it says,
>
> "Leave his house empty,
> and don't let anyone
> live there."
>
> It also says,
>
> "Let someone else
> have his job."
>
> 21-22So we need someone else to
> help us tell others that Jesus has
> been raised from death. He must
> also be one of the men who was
> with us from the very beginning. He
> must have been with us from the
> time the Lord Jesus was baptized by
> John until the day he was taken to
> heaven.

23Two men were suggested: One of
them was Joseph Barsabbas, known as
Justus, and the other was Matthias.
24Then they all prayed, "Lord, you know
what everyone is like! Show us the one
you have chosen 25to be an apostle and
to serve in place of Judas, who got what
he deserved." 26They drew names, and
Matthias was chosen to join the group
of the eleven apostles.

The Coming of the Holy Spirit

2

On the day of Pentecost[e] all the
Lord's followers were together in
one place. 2Suddenly there was a noise
from heaven like the sound of a mighty
wind! It filled the house where they
were meeting. 3Then they saw what
looked like fiery tongues moving in all
directions, and a tongue came and settled on each person there. 4The Holy

[a]**1.1** *I first wrote to you*: The Gospel of Luke. [b]**1.6** *are you now going to give Israel its own king again?*: Or "Are you now going to rule Israel as its king?" [c]**1.12,13** *known as the Eager One*: The Greek text has "Zealot," a name later given to the members of a Jewish group that resisted and fought against the Romans. [d]**1.14** *met together and prayed with a single purpose in mind*: Or "met together in a special place for prayer." [e]**2.1** *Pentecost*: A Jewish festival that came fifty days after Passover and celebrated the wheat harvest. Jews later celebrated Pentecost as the time when they were given the Law of Moses.

Spirit took control of everyone, and they
began speaking whatever languages the
Spirit let them speak.
5 Many religious Jews from every
country in the world were living in
Jerusalem. 6 And when they heard this
noise, a crowd gathered. But they were
surprised, because they were hearing
everything in their own languages.
7 They were excited and amazed, and
said:

Don't all these who are speaking
come from Galilee? 8 Then why do
we hear them speaking our very
own languages? 9 Some of us are
from Parthia, Media, and Elam. Others are from Mesopotamia, Judea,
Cappadocia, Pontus, Asia, 10 Phrygia,
Pamphylia, Egypt, parts of Libya
near Cyrene, Rome, 11 Crete, and
Arabia. Some of us were born Jews,
and others of us have chosen to be
Jews. Yet we all hear them using our
own languages to tell the wonderful
things God has done.

12 Everyone was excited and confused.
Some of them even kept asking each
other, "What does all this mean?"
13 Others made fun of the Lord's followers and said, "They are drunk."

Peter Speaks to the Crowd

14 Peter stood with the eleven apostles
and spoke in a loud and clear voice to
the crowd:

Friends and everyone else living in
Jerusalem, listen carefully to what I
have to say! 15 You are wrong to
think that these people are drunk.
After all, it is only nine o'clock in
the morning. 16 But this is what God
had the prophet Joel say,

17 "When the last days come,
I will give my Spirit
to everyone.
Your sons and daughters
will prophesy.
Your young men
will see visions,
and your old men
will have dreams.
18 In those days I will give
my Spirit to my servants,
both men and women,
and they will prophesy.

19 I will work miracles
in the sky above
and wonders
on the earth below.
There will be blood and fire
and clouds of smoke.
20 The sun will turn dark,
and the moon
will be as red as blood
before the great
and wonderful day
of the Lord appears.
21 Then the Lord
will save everyone
who asks for his help."

22 Now, listen to what I have to say
about Jesus from Nazareth. God
proved that he sent Jesus to you by
having him work miracles, wonders,
and signs. All of you know this.
23 God had already planned and decided that Jesus would be handed
over to you. So you took him and
had evil men put him to death on a
cross. 24 But God set him free from
death and raised him to life. Death
could not hold him in its power.
25 What David said are really the
words of Jesus,

"I always see the Lord
near me,
and I will not be afraid
with him at my right side.
26 Because of this,
my heart will be glad,
my words will be joyful,
and I will live in hope.
27 The Lord won't leave me
in the grave.
I am his holy one,
and he won't let
my body decay.
28 He has shown me
the path to life,
and he makes me glad
by being near me."

29 My friends, it is right for me to
speak to you about our ancestor
David. He died and was buried, and
his tomb is still here. 30 But David
was a prophet, and he knew that
God had made a promise he would
not break. He had told David that
someone from his own family would
someday be king.
31 David knew this would happen,
and so he told us that Christ would
be raised to life. He said that God
would not leave him in the grave or
let his body decay. 32 All of us can tell
you that God has raised Jesus to life!
33 Jesus was taken up to sit at the
right side[f] of God, and he was given
the Holy Spirit, just as the Father
had promised. Jesus is also the one
who has given the Spirit to us, and
that is what you are now seeing and
hearing.
34 David didn't go up to heaven. So
he wasn't talking about himself
when he said, "The Lord told my
Lord to sit at his right side, 35 until he
made my Lord's enemies into a foot-

[f] **2.33** *right side*: The place of honor and power.

stool for him." 36 Everyone in Israel
should then know for certain that
God has made Jesus both Lord and
Christ, even though you put him to
death on a cross.
37 When the people heard this, they
were very upset. They asked Peter and
the other apostles, "Friends, what shall
we do?"
38 Peter said, "Turn back to God! Be
baptized in the name of Jesus Christ, so
that your sins will be forgiven. Then you
will be given the Holy Spirit. 39 This
promise is for you and your children.
It is for everyone our Lord God will
choose, no matter where they live."
40 Peter told them many other things
as well. Then he said, "I beg you to save
yourselves from what will happen to all
these evil people." 41 On that day about
three thousand believed his message
and were baptized. 42 They spent their
time learning from the apostles, and
they were like family to each other.
They also broke bread[g] and prayed together.

Life among the Lord's Followers

43 Everyone was amazed by the many
miracles and wonders that the apostles
worked. 44 All the Lord's followers often
met together, and they shared everything they had. 45 They would sell their
property and possessions and give the
money to whoever needed it. 46 Day after
day they met together in the temple.
They broke bread[g] together in different
homes and shared their food happily
and freely, 47 while praising God. Everyone liked them, and each day the Lord
added to their group others who were
being saved.

Peter and John Heal a Lame Man

3 The time of prayer[h] was about three
o'clock in the afternoon, and Peter
and John were going into the temple. 2 A
man who had been born lame was being
carried to the temple door. Each day he
was placed beside this door, known as
the Beautiful Gate. He sat there and
begged from the people who were going
in.
3 The man saw Peter and John entering the temple, and he asked them for
money. 4 But they looked straight at him
and said, "Look up at us!"
5 The man stared at them and thought
he was going to get something. 6 But Peter said, "I don't have any silver or gold!
But I will give you what I do have. In the
name of Jesus Christ from Nazareth, get
up and start walking." 7 Peter then took
him by the right hand and helped him
up.
At once the man's feet and ankles became strong, 8 and he jumped up and
started walking. He went with Peter and
John into the temple, walking and jumping and praising God. 9 Everyone saw
him walking around and praising God.
10 They knew that he was the beggar
who had been lying beside the Beautiful
Gate, and they were completely surprised. They could not imagine what
had happened to the man.

Peter Speaks in the Temple

11 While the man kept holding on to
Peter and John, the whole crowd ran to
them in amazement at the place known
as Solomon's Porch.[i] 12 Peter saw that a
crowd had gathered, and he said:
Friends, why are you surprised at
what has happened? Why are you
staring at us? Do you think we have
some power of our own? Do you
think we were able to make this
man walk because we are so religious? 13 The God that Abraham,
Isaac, Jacob, and our other ancestors worshiped has brought honor to
his Servant[j] Jesus. He is the one you
betrayed. You turned against him
when he was being tried by Pilate,
even though Pilate wanted to set
him free.
14 You rejected Jesus, who was
holy and good. You asked for a murderer to be set free, 15 and you killed
the one who leads people to life. But
God raised him from death, and all
of us can tell you what he has done.
16 You see this man, and you know
him. He put his faith in the name of
Jesus and was made strong. Faith in
Jesus made this man completely
well while everyone was watching.
17 My friends, I am sure that you
and your leaders didn't know what
you were doing. 18 But God had his
prophets tell that his Messiah would
suffer, and now he has kept that
promise. 19 So turn to God! Give up
your sins, and you will be forgiven.
20 Then that time will come when the
Lord will give you fresh strength. He
will send you Jesus, his chosen Messiah. 21 But Jesus must stay in heaven
until God makes all things new, just
as his holy prophets promised long
ago.
22 Moses said, "The Lord your God
will choose one of your own people

[g] **2.42,46** *broke bread*: They ate together and celebrated the Lord's Supper. [h] **3.1** *The time of prayer*: Many of the Jewish people prayed in their homes at regular times each day (see Daniel 6.11), and on special occasions they prayed in the temple. [i] **3.11** *Solomon's Porch*: A public place with tall columns along the east side of the temple. [j] **3.13** *Servant*: Or "Son."

to be a prophet, just as he chose me.
Listen to everything he tells you.
23 No one who disobeys that prophet
will be one of God's people any
longer."
24 Samuel and all the other
prophets who came later also spoke
about what is now happening. 25 You
are really the ones God told his
prophets to speak to. And you were
given the promise that God made to
your ancestors. He said to Abraham,
"All nations on earth will be blessed
because of someone from your family." 26 God sent his chosen Son[k] to
you first, because God wanted to
bless you and make each one of you
turn away from your sins.

Peter and John Are Brought in Front of the Council

4 The apostles were still talking to the
people, when some priests, the captain of the temple guard, and some Sadducees arrived. 2 These men were angry
because the apostles were teaching the
people that the dead would be raised
from death, just as Jesus had been
raised from death. 3 It was already late in
the afternoon, and they arrested Peter
and John and put them in jail for the
night. 4 But a lot of people who had
heard the message believed it. So by
now there were about five thousand followers of the Lord.
5 The next morning the leaders, the elders, and the teachers of the Law of
Moses met in Jerusalem. 6 The high
priest Annas was there, as well as Caiaphas, John, Alexander, and other
members of the high priest's family.
7 They brought in Peter and John and
made them stand in the middle while
they questioned them. They asked, "By
what power and in whose name have
you done this?"
8 Peter was filled with the Holy Spirit
and told the nation's leaders and the elders:
9 You are questioning us today
about a kind deed in which a crippled man was healed. 10 But there is
something we must tell you and
everyone else in Israel. This man is
standing here completely well because of the power of Jesus Christ
from Nazareth. You put Jesus to
death on a cross, but God raised him
to life. 11 He is the stone that you
builders thought was worthless, and
now he is the most important stone
of all. 12 Only Jesus has the power to
save! His name is the only one in all
the world that can save anyone.

13 The officials were amazed to see
how brave Peter and John were, and
they knew that these two apostles were
only ordinary men and not well educated. The officials were certain that
these men had been with Jesus. 14 But
they could not deny what had happened. The man who had been healed
was standing there with the apostles.
15 The officials commanded them to
leave the council room. Then the officials said to each other, 16 "What can we
do with these men? Everyone in
Jerusalem knows about this miracle,
and we cannot say it didn't happen.
17 But to keep this thing from spreading,
we will warn them never again to speak
to anyone about the name of Jesus."
18 So they called the two apostles back in
and told them that they must never, for
any reason, teach anything about the
name of Jesus.
19 Peter and John answered, "Do you
think God wants us to obey you or to
obey him? 20 We cannot keep quiet about
what we have seen and heard."
21-22 The officials could not find any
reason to punish Peter and John. So
they threatened them and let them go.
The man who was healed by this miracle was more than forty years old, and
everyone was praising God for what had
happened.

Peter and Others Pray for Courage

23 As soon as Peter and John had been
set free, they went back and told the
others everything that the chief priests
and the leaders had said to them.
24 When the rest of the Lord's followers
heard this, they prayed together and
said:
Master, you created heaven and
earth, the sea, and everything in
them. 25 And by the Holy Spirit you
spoke to our ancestor David. He was
your servant, and you told him to
say:

"Why are all the Gentiles
so furious?
Why do people
make foolish plans?
26 The kings of earth
prepare for war,
and the rulers
join together
against the Lord
and his Messiah."

27 Here in Jerusalem, Herod[l] and
Pontius Pilate got together with the
Gentiles and the people of Israel.
Then they turned against your holy
Servant[m] Jesus, your chosen Mes-

[k] **3.26** *Son*: Or "Servant." [l] **4.27** *Herod*: Herod Antipas, the son of Herod the Great.
[m] **4.27,30** *Servant*: See the note at 3.13.

siah. 28They did what you in your
power and wisdom had already decided would happen.
29Lord, listen to their threats! We
are your servants. So make us brave
enough to speak your message.
30Show your mighty power, as we
heal people and work miracles and
wonders in the name of your holy
Servant[m] Jesus.
31After they had prayed, the meeting
place shook. They were all filled with
the Holy Spirit and bravely spoke God's
message.

Sharing Possessions

32The group of followers all felt the
same way about everything. None of
them claimed that their possessions
were their own, and they shared everything they had with each other. 33In a
powerful way the apostles told everyone
that the Lord Jesus was now alive. God
greatly blessed his followers,[n] 34and no
one went in need of anything. Everyone
who owned land or houses would sell
them and bring the money 35to the apostles. Then they would give the money to
anyone who needed it.
36-37Joseph was one of the followers
who had sold a piece of property and
brought the money to the apostles. He
was a Levite from Cyprus, and the apostles called him Barnabas, which means
"one who encourages others."

Peter Condemns Ananias and Sapphira

5 Ananias and his wife Sapphira also
sold a piece of property. 2But they
agreed to cheat and keep some of the
money for themselves.
So when Ananias took the rest of the
money to the apostles, 3Peter said, "Why
has Satan made you keep back some of
the money from the sale of the property? Why have you lied to the Holy
Spirit? 4The property was yours before
you sold it, and even after you sold it,
the money was still yours. What made
you do such a thing? You didn't lie to
people. You lied to God!"
5As soon as Ananias heard this, he
dropped dead, and everyone who heard
about it was frightened. 6Some young
men came in and wrapped up his body.
Then they took it out and buried it.
7Three hours later Sapphira came in,
but she did not know what had happened to her husband. 8Peter asked her,
"Tell me, did you sell the property for
this amount?"
"Yes," she answered, "that's the
amount."
9Then Peter said, "Why did the two of
you agree to test the Lord's Spirit?
The men who buried Ananias are by
the door, and they will carry you out!"
10At once she fell at Peter's feet and
died.
When the young men came back in,
they found Sapphira lying there dead.
So they carried her out and buried her
beside her husband. 11The church members were afraid, and so was everyone
else who heard what had happened.

Peter's Unusual Power

12The apostles worked many miracles
and wonders among the people. All of
the Lord's followers often met in the
part of the temple known as Solomon's
Porch.[o] 13No one outside their group
dared join them, even though everyone
liked them very much.
14Many men and women started having faith in the Lord. 15Then sick people
were brought out to the road and placed
on cots and mats. It was hoped that Peter would walk by, and his shadow
would fall on them and heal them. 16A
lot of people living in the towns near
Jerusalem brought those who were sick
or troubled by evil spirits, and they were
all healed.

Trouble for the Apostles

17The high priest and all the other
Sadducees who were with him became
jealous. 18They arrested the apostles and
put them in the city jail. 19But that night
an angel from the Lord opened the
doors of the jail and led the apostles
out. The angel said, 20"Go to the temple
and tell the people everything about this
new life." 21So they went into the temple
before sunrise and started teaching.
The high priest and his men called together their council, which included all
of Israel's leaders. Then they ordered
the apostles to be brought to them from
the jail. 22The temple police who were
sent to the jail did not find the apostles.
They returned and said, 23"We found the
jail locked tight and the guards standing
at the doors. But when we opened the
doors and went in, we didn't find anyone there." 24The captain of the temple
police and the chief priests listened to
their report, but they did not know what
to think about it.
25Just then someone came in and said,
"Right now those men you put in jail are
in the temple, teaching the people!"
26The captain went with some of the
temple police and brought the apostles
back. But they did not use force. They
were afraid that the people might start
throwing stones at them.

[m]**4.27,30** *Servant*: See the note at 3.13. [n]**4.33** *God greatly blessed his followers*: Or "Everyone highly respected his followers." [o]**5.12** *Solomon's Porch*: See the note at 3.11.

27When the apostles were brought before the council, the high priest said to
them, 28"We told you plainly not to teach
in the name of Jesus. But look what you
have done! You have been teaching all
over Jerusalem, and you are trying to
blame us for his death."
29Peter and the apostles replied:
We don't obey people. We obey
God. 30You killed Jesus by nailing
him to a cross. But the God our ancestors worshiped raised him to life
31and made him our Leader and
Savior. Then God gave him a place
at his right side,[p] so that the people
of Israel would turn back to him and
be forgiven. 32We are here to tell you
about all this, and so is the Holy
Spirit, who is God's gift to everyone
who obeys God.
33When the council members heard
this, they became so angry that they
wanted to kill the apostles. 34But one of
the members was the Pharisee Gamaliel, a highly respected teacher. He ordered the apostles to be taken out of the
room for a little while. 35Then he said to
the council:
People of Israel, be careful what
you do with these men. 36Not long
ago Theudas claimed to be someone
important, and about four hundred
men joined him. But he was killed.
All his followers were scattered,
and that was the end of that.
37Later, when the people of our nation were being counted, Judas from
Galilee showed up. A lot of people
followed him, but he was killed, and
all his followers were scattered.
38So I advise you to stay away
from these men. Leave them alone.
If what they are planning is something of their own doing, it will fail.
39But if God is behind it, you cannot
stop it anyway, unless you want to
fight against God.
The council members agreed with
what he said, 40and they called the apostles back in. They had them beaten with
a whip and warned them not to speak in
the name of Jesus. Then they let them
go.
41The apostles left the council and
were happy, because God had considered them worthy to suffer for the sake
of Jesus. 42Every day they spent time in
the temple and in one home after another. They never stopped teaching and
telling the good news that Jesus is the
Messiah.

Seven Leaders for the Church

6 A lot of people were now becoming
followers of the Lord. But some of
the ones who spoke Greek started complaining about the ones who spoke Aramaic. They complained that the Greek-
speaking widows were not given their
share when the food supplies were
handed out each day.
2The twelve apostles called the whole
group of followers together and said,
"We should not give up preaching God's
message in order to serve at tables.[q]
3My friends, choose seven men who are
respected and wise and filled with God's
Spirit. We will put them in charge of
these things. 4We can spend our time
praying and serving God by preaching."
5This suggestion pleased everyone,
and they began by choosing Stephen.
He had great faith and was filled with
the Holy Spirit. Then they chose Philip,
Prochorus, Nicanor, Timon, Parmenas,
and also Nicolaus, who worshiped with
the Jewish people[r] in Antioch. 6These
men were brought to the apostles. Then
the apostles prayed and placed their
hands on the men to show that they had
been chosen to do this work. 7God's
message spread, and many more people
in Jerusalem became followers. Even a
large number of priests put their faith in
the Lord.

Stephen Is Arrested

8God gave Stephen the power to work
great miracles and wonders among the
people. 9But some Jews from Cyrene
and Alexandria were members of a
group who called themselves "Free
Men."[s] They started arguing with
Stephen. Some others from Cilicia and
Asia also argued with him. 10But they
were no match for Stephen, who spoke
with the great wisdom that the Spirit
gave him. 11So they talked some men
into saying, "We heard Stephen say terrible things against Moses and God!"
12They turned the people and their
leaders and the teachers of the Law of
Moses against Stephen. Then they all
grabbed Stephen and dragged him in
front of the council.
13Some men agreed to tell lies about
Stephen, and they said, "This man keeps
on saying terrible things about this holy
temple and the Law of Moses. 14We have
heard him claim that Jesus from
Nazareth will destroy this place and
change the customs that Moses gave
us." 15Then all the council members

[p]**5.31** *right side*: See the note at 2.33. [q]**6.2** *to serve at tables*: This may mean either that they were in charge of handing out food to the widows or that they were in charge of the money, since the Greek word "table" may also mean "bank." [r]**6.5** *worshiped with the Jewish people*: This translates the Greek word "proselyte" that means a Gentile who had accepted the Jewish religion. [s]**6.9** *Free Men*: A group of Jewish men who had once been slaves, but had been freed.

stared at Stephen. They saw that his
face looked like the face of an angel.

Stephen's Speech

7 The high priest asked Stephen, "Are
they telling the truth about you?"
2Stephen answered:
Friends, listen to me. Our glorious
God appeared to our ancestor Abraham while he was still in
Mesopotamia, before he had moved
to Haran. 3God told him, "Leave
your country and your relatives and
go to a land that I will show you."
4Then Abraham left the land of the
Chaldeans and settled in Haran.
After his father died, Abraham
came and settled in this land where
you now live. 5God didn't give him
any part of it, not even a square foot.
But God did promise to give it to
him and his family forever, even
though Abraham didn't have any
children. 6God said that Abraham's
descendants would live for a while in
a foreign land. There they would be
slaves and would be mistreated four
hundred years. 7But he also said, "I
will punish the nation that makes
them slaves. Then later they will
come and worship me in this place."
8God said to Abraham, "Every son
in each family must be circumcised
to show that you have kept your
agreement with me." So when Isaac
was eight days old, Abraham circumcised him. Later, Isaac circumcised his son Jacob, and Jacob circumcised his twelve sons. 9 These
men were our ancestors.
Joseph was also one of our famous ancestors. His brothers were
jealous of him and sold him as a
slave to be taken to Egypt. But God
was with him 10and rescued him
from all his troubles. God made him
so wise that the Egyptian king
Pharaoh[x] thought highly of him.
The king even made Joseph governor over Egypt and put him in
charge of everything he owned.
11Everywhere in Egypt and Canaan
the grain crops failed. There was terrible suffering, and our ancestors
could not find enough to eat. 12But
when Jacob heard that there was
grain in Egypt, he sent our ancestors
there for the first time. 13It was on
their second trip that Joseph told his
brothers who he was, and Pharaoh
learned about Joseph's family.
14Joseph sent for his father and
his relatives. In all, there were seventy-five of them. 15His father went
to Egypt and died there, just as
our ancestors did. 15Later their bodies were taken back to Shechem and
placed in the tomb that Abraham
had bought from the sons of Hamor.
17Finally, the time came for God to
do what he had promised Abraham.
By then the number of our people in
Egypt had greatly increased. 18An-
other king was ruling Egypt, and he
didn't know anything about Joseph.
19He tricked our ancestors and was
cruel to them. He even made them
leave their babies outside, so they
would die.
20During this time Moses was
born. He was a very beautiful child,
and for three months his parents
took care of him in their home.
21Then when they were forced to
leave him outside, the king's daughter found him and raised him as her
own son. 22Moses was given the best
education in Egypt. He was a strong
man and a powerful speaker.
23When Moses was forty years old,
he wanted to help the Israelites because they were his own people.
24One day he saw an Egyptian mistreating one of them. So he rescued
the man and killed the Egyptian.
25Moses thought the rest of his people would realize that God was going to use him to set them free. But
they didn't understand.
26The next day Moses saw two of
his own people fighting, and he tried
to make them stop. He said, "Men,
you are both Israelites. Why are you
so cruel to each other?"
27But the man who had started the
fight pushed Moses aside and asked,
"Who made you our ruler and
judge? 28Are you going to kill me,
just as you killed that Egyptian yesterday?" 29When Moses heard this,
he ran away to live in the country of
Midian. His two sons were born there.
30Forty years later, an angel appeared to Moses from a burning
bush in the desert near Mount Sinai.
31Moses was surprised by what he
saw. He went closer to get a better
look, and the Lord said, 32"I am the
God who was worshiped by your ancestors, Abraham, Isaac, and Jacob."
Moses started shaking all over and
didn't dare to look at the bush.
33The Lord said to him, "Take off
your sandals. The place where you
are standing is holy. 34With my own
eyes I have seen the suffering of my
people in Egypt. I have heard their
groans and have come down to rescue them. Now I am sending you
back to Egypt."
35This was the same Moses that
the people rejected by saying, "Who

[x]7.10 *Pharaoh*: A Hebrew word sometimes used for the title of the King of Egypt.

made you our leader and judge?"
God's angel had spoken to Moses
from the bush. And God had even
sent the angel to help Moses rescue
the people and be their leader.
36 In Egypt and at the Red Sea[t] and
in the desert, Moses rescued the people by working miracles and wonders for forty years. 37 Moses is the
one who told the people of Israel,
"God will choose one of your people
to be a prophet, just as he chose me."
38 Moses brought our people together
in the desert, and the angel spoke to
him on Mount Sinai. There he was
given these life-giving words to pass
on to us. 39 But our ancestors refused
to obey Moses. They rejected him
and wanted to go back to Egypt.
40 The people said to Aaron, "Make
some gods to lead us! Moses led us
out of Egypt, but we don't know
what's happened to him now."
41 Then they made an idol in the
shape of a calf. They offered sacrifices to the idol and were pleased
with what they had done.
42 God turned his back on his people and left them. Then they worshiped the stars in the sky, just as it
says in the Book of the Prophets,
"People of Israel, you didn't offer
sacrifices and offerings to me during
those forty years in the desert. 43 Instead, you carried the tent where the
god Molech is worshiped, and you
took along the star of your god
Rephan. You made those idols and
worshiped them. So now I will have
you carried off beyond Babylonia."
44 The tent where our ancestors
worshiped God was with them in the
desert. This was the same tent that
God had commanded Moses to
make. And it was made like the
model that Moses had seen. 45 Later
it was given to our ancestors, and
they took it with them when they
went with Joshua. They carried the
tent along as they took over the land
from those people that God had
chased out for them. Our ancestors
used this tent until the time of King
David. 46 He pleased God and asked
him if he could build a house of worship for the people[u] of Israel. 47 And
it was finally King Solomon who
built a house for God.[v]
48 But the Most High God doesn't
live in houses made by humans. It is
just as the prophet said, when he
spoke for the Lord,

49 "Heaven is my throne,
and the earth
is my footstool.
What kind of house
will you build for me?
In what place will I rest?
50 I have made everything."

51 You stubborn and hardheaded
people! You are always fighting
against the Holy Spirit, just as your
ancestors did. 52 Is there one prophet
that your ancestors didn't mistreat?
They killed the prophets who told
about the coming of the One Who
Obeys God.[w] And now you have
turned against him and killed him.
53 Angels gave you God's Law, but
you still don't obey it.

Stephen Is Stoned to Death

54 When the council members heard
Stephen's speech, they were angry and
furious. 55 But Stephen was filled with
the Holy Spirit. He looked toward
heaven, where he saw our glorious God
and Jesus standing at his right side.[x]
56 Then Stephen said, "I see heaven open
and the Son of Man standing at the
right side of God!"
57 The council members shouted and
covered their ears. At once they all attacked Stephen 58 and dragged him out
of the city. Then they started throwing
stones at him. The men who had
brought charges against him put their
coats at the feet of a young man named
Saul.[y]
59 As Stephen was being stoned to
death, he called out, "Lord Jesus, please
welcome me!" 60 He knelt down and
shouted, "Lord, don't blame them for
what they have done." Then he died.
8 1-2 Saul approved the stoning of
Stephen. Some faithful followers of
the Lord buried Stephen and mourned
very much for him.

Saul Makes Trouble for the Church

At that time the church in Jerusalem
suffered terribly. All of the Lord's followers, except the apostles, were scattered everywhere in Judea and Samaria.
3 Saul started making a lot of trouble for
the church. He went from house to

[t] **7.36** *Red Sea*: This name comes from the Bible of the early Christians, a translation made into Greek about 200 B.C. It refers to the body of water that the Israelites crossed and was one of the marshes or fresh water lakes near the eastern part of the Nile Delta, where they lived and where the towns of Exodus 13.17—14.9 were located. [u] **7.46** *the people*: Some manuscripts have "God." [v] **7.47** *God*: Or "the people." [w] **7.52** *One Who Obeys God*: That is, Jesus. [x] **7.55** *standing at his right side*: The "right side" is the place of honor and power. "Standing" may mean that Jesus is welcoming Stephen (see verse 59). [y] **7.58** *Saul*: Better known as Paul, who became a famous follower of Jesus.

house, arresting men and women and
putting them in jail.

The Good News Is Preached in Samaria

4 The Lord's followers who had been
scattered went from place to place,
telling the good news. 5 Philip went to
the city of Samaria and told the people
about Christ. 6 They crowded around
Philip because they were eager to hear
what he was saying and to see him work
miracles. 7 Many people with evil spirits
were healed, and the spirits went out of
them with a shout. A lot of crippled and
lame people were also healed. 8 Everyone in that city was very glad because
of what was happening.

9 For some time a man named Simon
had lived in the city of Samaria and had
amazed the people. He practiced witchcraft and claimed to be somebody great.
10 Everyone, rich and poor, crowded
around him. They said, "This man is the
power of God called 'The Great Power.' "

11 For a long time, Simon had used
witchcraft to amaze the people, and
they kept crowding around him. 12 But
when they believed what Philip was saying about God's kingdom and about the
name of Jesus Christ, they were all baptized. 13 Even Simon believed and was
baptized. He stayed close to Philip, because he marveled at all the miracles
and wonders.

14 The apostles in Jerusalem heard that
some people in Samaria had accepted
God's message, and they sent Peter and
John. 15 When the two apostles arrived,
they prayed that the people would be
given the Holy Spirit. 16 Before this, the
Holy Spirit had not been given to anyone in Samaria, though some of them
had been baptized in the name of the
Lord Jesus. 17 Peter and John then
placed their hands on everyone who had
faith in the Lord, and they were given
the Holy Spirit.

18 Simon noticed that the Spirit was
given only when the apostles placed
their hands on the people. So he
brought money 19 and said to Peter and
John, "Let me have this power too! Then
anyone I place my hands on will also be
given the Holy Spirit."

20 Peter said to him, "You and your
money will both end up in hell if you
think you can buy God's gift! 21 You
don't have any part in this, and God
sees that your heart isn't right. 22 Get rid
of these evil thoughts and ask God to
forgive you. 23 I can see that you are jealous and bound by your evil ways."

24 Simon said, "Please pray to the
Lord, so that what you said won't happen to me."

25 After Peter and John had preached
about the Lord, they returned to
Jerusalem. On their way they told the
good news in many villages of Samaria.

Philip and an Ethiopian Official

26 The Lord's angel said to Philip, "Go
south[z] along the desert road that leads
from Jerusalem to Gaza."[a] 27 So Philip
left.

An important Ethiopian official happened to be going along that road in his
chariot. He was the chief treasurer for
Candace, the Queen of Ethiopia. The official had gone to Jerusalem to worship
28 and was now on his way home. He
was sitting in his chariot, reading the
book of the prophet Isaiah.

29 The Spirit told Philip to catch up
with the chariot. 30 Philip ran up close
and heard the man reading aloud from
the book of Isaiah. Philip asked him,
"Do you understand what you are reading?"

31 The official answered, "How can I
understand unless someone helps me?"
He then invited Philip to come up and
sit beside him.

32 The man was reading the passage
that said,

"He was led like a sheep
    on its way to be killed.
He was silent as a lamb
whose wool
    is being cut off,
and he did not say
    a word.
33 He was treated like a nobody
and did not receive
    a fair trial.
How can he have children,
if his life
    is snatched away?"

34 The official said to Philip, "Tell me,
was the prophet talking about himself
or about someone else?" 35 So Philip began at this place in the Scriptures and
explained the good news about Jesus.

36-37 As they were going along the
road, they came to a place where there
was some water. The official said,
"Look! Here is some water. Why can't I
be baptized?"[b] 38 He ordered the chariot
to stop. Then they both went down into
the water, and Philip baptized him.

39 After they had come out of the water, the Lord's Spirit took Philip away.
The official never saw him again, but he
was very happy as he went on his way.
40 Philip later appeared in Azotus. He

[z] **8.26** *Go south*: Or "About noon go." [a] **8.26** *the desert road that leads from Jerusalem to Gaza*: Or "the road that leads from Jerusalem to Gaza in the desert." [b] **8.36,37** *Why can't I be baptized*: Some manuscripts add, "Philip replied, 'You can, if you believe with all your heart.' "The official answered, 'I believe that Jesus Christ is the Son of God.' "

went from town to town, all the way to
Caesarea, telling people about Jesus.

Saul Becomes a Follower of the Lord

(Acts 22.6-16; 26.12-18)

9 Saul kept on threatening to kill the
Lord's followers. He even went to
the high priest [2]and asked for letters to
the Jewish leaders in Damascus. He did
this because he wanted to arrest and take
to Jerusalem any man or woman who
had accepted the Lord's Way.[c] [3]When
Saul had almost reached Damascus, a
bright light from heaven suddenly flashed
around him. [4]He fell to the ground and
heard a voice that said, "Saul! Saul! Why
are you so cruel to me?"
[5]"Who are you?" Saul asked.
"I am Jesus," the Lord answered. "I
am the one you are so cruel to. [6]Now get
up and go into the city, where you will
be told what to do."
[7]The men with Saul stood there
speechless. They had heard the voice,
but they had not seen anyone. [8]Saul got
up from the ground, and when he
opened his eyes, he could not see a
thing. Someone then led him by the
hand to Damascus, [9]and for three days
he was blind and did not eat or drink.
[10]A follower named Ananias lived in
Damascus, and the Lord spoke to him in
a vision. Ananias answered, "Lord, here
I am."
[11]The Lord said to him, "Get up and
go to the house of Judas on Straight
Street. When you get there, you will find
a man named Saul from the city of Tarsus. Saul is praying, [12]and he has seen a
vision. He saw a man named Ananias
coming to him and putting his hands on
him, so that he could see again."
[13]Ananias replied, "Lord, a lot of people have told me about the terrible
things this man has done to your followers in Jerusalem. [14]Now the chief priests
have given him the power to come here
and arrest anyone who worships in your
name."
[15]The Lord said to Ananias, "Go! I
have chosen him to tell foreigners,
kings, and the people of Israel about
me. [16]I will show him how much he
must suffer for worshiping in my name."
[17]Ananias left and went into the house
where Saul was staying. Ananias placed
his hands on him and said, "Saul, the
Lord Jesus has sent me. He is the same
one who appeared to you along the
road. He wants you to be able to see and
to be filled with the Holy Spirit."
[18]Suddenly something like fish scales
fell from Saul's eyes, and he could see.
He got up and was baptized. [19]Then he
ate and felt much better.

Saul Preaches in Damascus

For several days Saul stayed with the
Lord's followers in Damascus. [20]Soon
he went to the Jewish meeting places
and started telling people that Jesus is
the Son of God. [21]Everyone who heard
Saul was amazed and said, "Isn't this
the man who caused so much trouble
for those people in Jerusalem who worship in the name of Jesus? Didn't he
come here to arrest them and take them
to the chief priests?"
[22]Saul preached with such power that
he completely confused the Jewish people in Damascus, as he tried to show
them that Jesus is the Messiah.
[23]Later some of them made plans to
kill Saul, [24]but he found out about it. He
learned that they were guarding the
gates of the city day and night in order
to kill him. [25]Then one night his followers let him down over the city wall in a
large basket.

Saul in Jerusalem

[26]When Saul arrived in Jerusalem, he
tried to join the followers. But they were
all afraid of him, because they did not
believe he was a true follower. [27]Then
Barnabas helped him by taking him to
the apostles. He explained how Saul
had seen the Lord and how the Lord
had spoken to him. Barnabas also said
that when Saul was in Damascus, he
had spoken bravely in the name of Jesus.
[28]Saul moved about freely with the
followers in Jerusalem and told everyone about the Lord. [29]He was always arguing with the Jews who spoke Greek,
and so they tried to kill him. [30]But the
followers found out about this and took
Saul to Caesarea. From there they sent
him to the city of Tarsus.
[31]The church in Judea, Galilee, and
Samaria now had a time of peace and
kept on worshiping the Lord. The
church became stronger, as the Holy
Spirit encouraged it and helped it grow.

Peter Heals Aeneas

[32]While Peter was traveling from
place to place, he visited the Lord's followers who lived in the town of Lydda.
[33]There he met a man named Aeneas,
who for eight years had been sick in bed
and could not move. [34]Peter said to Aeneas, "Jesus Christ has healed you! Get
up and make up your bed."[d] Right away
he stood up.
[35]Many people in the towns of Lydda
and Sharon saw Aeneas and became
followers of the Lord.

[c]**9.2** *accepted the Lord's Way*: In the book of Acts, this means to become a follower of the Lord Jesus. [d]**9.34** *and make up your bed*: Or "and fix something to eat."

Peter Brings Dorcas Back to Life

36 In Joppa there was a follower
named Tabitha. Her Greek name was
Dorcas, which means "deer." She was
always doing good things for people
and had given much to the poor. 37 But
she got sick and died, and her body was
washed and placed in an upstairs room.
38 Joppa wasn't far from Lydda, and the
followers heard that Peter was there.
They sent two men to say to him,
"Please come with us as quickly as you
can!" 39 Right away, Peter went with
them.

The men took Peter upstairs into the
room. Many widows were there crying.
They showed him the coats and clothes
that Dorcas had made while she was
still alive.

40 After Peter had sent everyone out of
the room, he knelt down and prayed.
Then he turned to the body of Dorcas
and said, "Tabitha, get up!" The woman
opened her eyes, and when she saw Peter, she sat up. 41 He took her by the
hand and helped her to her feet.

Peter called in the widows and the
other followers and showed them that
Dorcas had been raised from death.
42 Everyone in Joppa heard what had
happened, and many of them put their
faith in the Lord. 43 Peter stayed on for a
while in Joppa in the house of a man
named Simon, who made leather.

Peter and Cornelius

10 In Caesarea there was a man
named Cornelius, who was the
captain of a group of soldiers called
"The Italian Unit." 2 Cornelius was a very
religious man. He worshiped God, and
so did everyone else who lived in his
house. He had given a lot of money to
the poor and was always praying to
God.

3 One afternoon at about three
o'clock,[e] Cornelius had a vision. He saw
an angel from God coming to him and
calling him by name. 4 Cornelius was
surprised and stared at the angel. Then
he asked, "What is this all about?"

The angel answered, "God has heard
your prayers and knows about your
gifts to the poor. 5 Now send some men
to Joppa for a man named Simon Peter.
6 He is visiting with Simon the leather
maker, who lives in a house near the
sea." 7 After saying this, the angel left.

Cornelius called in two of his servants
and one of his soldiers who worshiped
God. 8 He explained everything to them
and sent them off to Joppa.

9 The next day about noon these men
were coming near Joppa. Peter went up
on the roof[f] of the house to pray 10 and
became very hungry. While the food was
being prepared, he fell sound asleep and
had a vision. 11 He saw heaven open, and
something came down like a huge sheet
held up by its four corners. 12 In it were
all kinds of animals, snakes, and birds.
13 A voice said to him, "Peter, get up! Kill
these and eat them."

14 But Peter said, "Lord, I can't do that!
I've never eaten anything that is unclean and not fit to eat."[g]

15 The voice spoke to him again,
"When God says that something can be
used for food, don't say it isn't fit to eat."

16 This happened three times before
the sheet was suddenly taken back to
heaven.

17 Peter was still wondering what all of
this meant, when the men sent by Cornelius came and stood at the gate. They
had found their way to Simon's house
18 and were asking if Simon Peter was
staying there.

19 While Peter was still thinking about
the vision, the Holy Spirit said to him,
"Three[h] men are here looking for you.
20 Hurry down and go with them. Don't
worry, I sent them."

21 Peter went down and said to the
men, "I am the one you are looking for.
Why have you come?"

22 They answered, "Captain Cornelius
sent us. He is a good man who worships
God and is liked by the Jewish people.
One of God's holy angels told Cornelius
to send for you, so he could hear what
you have to say." 23 Peter invited them to
spend the night.

The next morning, Peter and some of
the Lord's followers in Joppa left with
the men who had come from Cornelius.
24 The next day they arrived in Caesarea
where Cornelius was waiting for them.
He had also invited his relatives and
close friends.

25 When Peter arrived, Cornelius
greeted him. Then he knelt at Peter's
feet and started worshiping him. 26 But
Peter took hold of him and said, "Stand
up! I am nothing more than a human."

27 As Peter entered the house, he was
still talking with Cornelius. Many people were there, 28 and Peter said to them,
"You know that we Jews are not allowed
to have anything to do with other people. But God has shown me that he
doesn't think anyone is unclean or unfit.
29 I agreed to come here, but I want to
know why you sent for me."

[e] **10.3** *at about three o'clock*: Probably while he was praying (see 3.1 and the note there).
[f] **10.9** *roof*: In Palestine the houses usually had a flat roof. Stairs on the outside led up to the roof, which was made of beams and boards covered with packed earth. [g] **10.14** *unclean and not fit to eat*: The Law of Moses taught that some foods were not fit to eat. [h] **10.19** *Three*: One manuscript has "two;" some manuscripts have "some."

30Cornelius answered:
Four days ago at about three
o'clock in the afternoon I was praying at home. Suddenly a man in
bright clothes stood in front of me.
31He said, "Cornelius, God has heard
your prayers, and he knows about
your gifts to the poor. 32Now send to
Joppa for Simon Peter. He is visiting
in the home of Simon the leather
maker, who lives near the sea."
33I sent for you right away, and
you have been good enough to
come. All of us are here in the presence of the Lord God, so that we can
hear what he has to say.
34Peter then said:
Now I am certain that God treats
all people alike. 35God is pleased
with everyone who worships him
and does right, no matter what nation they come from. 36This is the
same message that God gave to the
people of Israel, when he sent Jesus
Christ, the Lord of all, to offer peace
to them.
37You surely know what
happened[i] everywhere in Judea. It
all began in Galilee after John had
told everyone to be baptized. 38God
gave the Holy Spirit and power to
Jesus from Nazareth. He was with
Jesus, as he went around doing good
and healing everyone who was under the power of the devil. 39We all
saw what Jesus did both in Israel
and in the city of Jerusalem.
Jesus was put to death on a cross.
40But three days later, God raised
him to life and let him be seen. 41Not
everyone saw him. He was seen only
by us, who ate and drank with him
after he was raised from death. We
were the ones God chose to tell others about him.
42God told us to announce clearly
to the people that Jesus is the one he
has chosen to judge the living and
the dead. 43Every one of the
prophets has said that all who have
faith in Jesus will have their sins forgiven in his name.
44While Peter was still speaking, the
Holy Spirit took control of everyone
who was listening. 45Some Jewish followers of the Lord had come with Peter,
and they were surprised that the Holy
Spirit had been given to Gentiles.
46Now they were hearing Gentiles
speaking unknown languages and
praising God.
Peter said, 47"These Gentiles have
been given the Holy Spirit, just as we
have! I am certain that no one would
dare stop us from baptizing them." 48Pe-
ter ordered them to be baptized in the
name of Jesus Christ, and they asked
him to stay on for a few days.

Peter Reports to the Church in Jerusalem

11 The apostles and the followers in
Judea heard that Gentiles had accepted God's message. 2So when Peter
came to Jerusalem, some of the Jewish
followers started arguing with him.
They wanted Gentile followers to be circumcised, and 3they said, "You stayed in
the homes of Gentiles, and you even ate
with them!"
4Then Peter told them exactly what
had happened:
5I was in the town of Joppa and
was praying when I fell sound
asleep and had a vision. I saw
heaven open, and something like a
huge sheet held by its four corners
came down to me. 6When I looked in
it, I saw animals, wild beasts,
snakes, and birds. 7I heard a voice
saying to me, "Peter, get up! Kill
these and eat them."
8But I said, "Lord, I can't do that!
I've never taken a bite of anything
that is unclean and not fit to eat."[j]
9The voice from heaven spoke to
me again, "When God says that
something can be used for food,
don't say it isn't fit to eat." 10This
happened three times before it was
all taken back into heaven.
11Suddenly three men from Caesarea stood in front of the house
where I was staying. 12The Holy
Spirit told me to go with them and
not to worry. Then six of the Lord's
followers went with me to the home
of a man 13who told us that an angel
had appeared to him. The angel had
ordered him to send to Joppa for
someone named Simon Peter. 14Then
Peter would tell him how he and
everyone in his house could be
saved.
15After I started speaking, the
Holy Spirit was given to them, just
as the Spirit had been given to us at
the beginning. 16I remembered that
the Lord had said, "John baptized
with water, but you will be baptized
with the Holy Spirit." 17God gave
those Gentiles the same gift that he
gave us when we put our faith in the
Lord Jesus Christ. So how could I
have gone against God?
18When they heard Peter say this, they
stopped arguing and started praising
God. They said, "God has now let Gentiles turn to him, and he has given life to
them!"

[i] **10.37** *what happened*: Or "the message that went." the note at 10.14.

[j] **11.8** *unclean and not fit to eat*: See

The Church in Antioch

19Some of the Lord's followers had
been scattered because of the terrible
trouble that started when Stephen was
killed. They went as far as Phoenicia,
Cyprus, and Antioch, but they told the
message only to the Jews.
20Some of the followers from Cyprus
and Cyrene went to Antioch and started
telling Gentiles[k] the good news about
the Lord Jesus. 21The Lord's power was
with them, and many people turned to
the Lord and put their faith in him.
22News of what was happening reached
the church in Jerusalem. Then they sent
Barnabas to Antioch.
23When Barnabas got there and
saw what God had been kind enough
to do for them, he was very glad. So
he begged them to remain faithful to
the Lord with all their hearts. 24Barn-
abas was a good man of great faith,
and he was filled with the Holy
Spirit. Many more people turned to the
Lord.
25Barnabas went to Tarsus to look for
Saul. 26He found Saul and brought him
to Antioch, where they met with the
church for a whole year and taught
many of its people. There in Antioch the
Lord's followers were first called Christians.
27During this time some prophets
from Jerusalem came to Antioch. 28One
of them was Agabus. Then with the help
of the Spirit, he told that there would be
a terrible famine everywhere in the
world. And it happened when Claudius
was Emperor.[l] 29The followers in Antioch decided to send whatever help
they could to the followers in Judea.
30So they had Barnabas and Saul take
their gifts to the church leaders in
Jerusalem.

Herod Causes Trouble for the Church

12 At that time King Herod[m] caused
terrible suffering for some members of the church. 2He ordered soldiers
to cut off the head of James, the brother
of John. 3When Herod saw that this
pleased the Jewish people, he had Peter
arrested during the Festival of Thin
Bread. 4He put Peter in jail and ordered
four squads of soldiers to guard him.
Herod planned to put him on trial in
public after the festival.
5While Peter was being kept in jail,
the church never stopped praying to
God for him.

Peter Is Rescued

6The night before Peter was to be put
on trial, he was asleep and bound by
two chains. A soldier was guarding him
on each side, and two other soldiers
were guarding the entrance to the jail.
7Suddenly an angel from the Lord appeared, and light flashed around in the
cell. The angel poked Peter in the side
and woke him up. Then he said, "Quick!
Get up!"
The chains fell off his hands, 8and the
angel said, "Get dressed and put on your
sandals." Peter did what he was told.
Then the angel said, "Now put on your
coat and follow me." 9Peter left with the
angel, but he thought everything was
only a dream. 10They went past the two
groups of soldiers, and when they came
to the iron gate to the city, it opened by
itself. They went out and were going
along the street, when all at once the angel disappeared.
11Peter now realized what had happened, and he said, "I am certain that
the Lord sent his angel to rescue me
from Herod and from everything the
Jewish leaders planned to do to me."
12Then Peter went to the house of Mary
the mother of John whose other name
was Mark. Many of the Lord's followers
had come together there and were praying.
13Peter knocked on the gate, and a
servant named Rhoda came to answer.
14When she heard Peter's voice, she was
too excited to open the gate. She ran
back into the house and said that Peter
was standing there.
15"You are crazy!" everyone told her.
But she kept saying that it was Peter.
Then they said, "It must be his angel."[n]
16But Peter kept on knocking, until finally they opened the gate. They saw
him and were completely amazed.
17Peter motioned for them to keep
quiet. Then he told how the Lord had
led him out of jail. He also said, "Tell
James[o] and the others what has happened." After that, he left and went
somewhere else.
18The next morning the soldiers who
had been on guard were terribly worried and wondered what had happened
to Peter. 19Herod ordered his own soldiers to search for him, but they could
not find him. Then he questioned the
guards and had them put to death. After
this, Herod left Judea to stay in Caesarea for a while.

[k] **11.20** *Gentiles*: This translates a Greek word that may mean "people who speak Greek" or "people who live as Greeks do." Here the word seems to mean "people who are not Jews." Some manuscripts have "Greeks," which also seems to mean "people who are not Jews."
[l] **11.28** *when Claudius was Emperor*: A.D. 41-54.
[m] **12.1** *Herod*: Herod Agrippa I, the grandson of Herod the Great.
[n] **12.15** *his angel*: Probably meaning "his guardian angel."
[o] **12.17** *James*: The brother of the Lord.

Herod Dies

[20]Herod and the people of Tyre and Sidon were very angry with each other. But their country got its food supply from the region that he ruled. So a group of them went to see Blastus, who was one of Herod's high officials. They convinced Blastus that they wanted to make peace between their cities and Herod, [21]and a day was set for them to meet with him.

Herod came dressed in his royal robes. He sat down on his throne and made a speech. [22]The people shouted, "You speak more like a god than a man!" [23]At once an angel from the Lord struck him down because he took the honor that belonged to God. Later, Herod was eaten by worms and died.

[24]God's message kept spreading. [25]And after Barnabas and Saul had done the work they were sent to do, they went back to Jerusalem[p] with John, whose other name was Mark.

Barnabas and Saul Are Chosen and Sent

13 The church at Antioch had several prophets and teachers. They were Barnabas, Simeon, also called Niger, Lucius from Cyrene, Manaen, who was Herod's[q] close friend, and Saul. [2]While they were worshiping the Lord and going without eating,[r] the Holy Spirit told them, "Appoint Barnabas and Saul to do the work for which I have chosen them." [3]Everyone prayed and went without eating for a while longer. Next, they placed their hands on Barnabas and Saul to show that they had been appointed to do this work. Then everyone sent them on their way.

Barnabas and Saul in Cyprus

[4]After Barnabas and Saul had been sent by the Holy Spirit, they went to Seleucia. From there they sailed to the island of Cyprus. [5]They arrived at Salamis and began to preach God's message in the Jewish meeting places. They also had John[s] as a helper.

[6]Barnabas and Saul went all the way to the city of Paphos on the other end of the island, where they met a Jewish man named Bar-Jesus. He practiced witchcraft and was a false prophet. [7]He also worked for Sergius Paulus, who was very smart and was the governor of the island. Sergius Paulus wanted to hear God's message, and he sent for Barnabas and Saul. [8]But Bar-Jesus, whose other name was Elymas, was against them. He even tried to keep the governor from having faith in the Lord.

[9]Then Saul, better known as Paul, was filled with the Holy Spirit. He looked straight at Elymas [10]and said, "You son of the devil! You are a liar, a crook, and an enemy of everything that is right. When will you stop speaking against the true ways of the Lord? [11]The Lord is going to punish you by making you completely blind for a while."

Suddenly the man's eyes were covered by a dark mist, and he went around trying to get someone to lead him by the hand. [12]When the governor saw what had happened, he was amazed at this teaching about the Lord. So he put his faith in the Lord.

Paul and Barnabas in Antioch of Pisidia

[13]Paul and the others left Paphos and sailed to Perga in Pamphylia. But John[s] left them and went back to Jerusalem. [14]The rest of them went on from Perga to Antioch in Pisidia. Then on the Sabbath they went to the Jewish meeting place and sat down.

[15]After the reading of the Law and the Prophets,[t] the leaders sent someone over to tell Paul and Barnabas, "Friends, if you have anything to say that will help the people, please say it."

[16]Paul got up. He motioned with his hand and said:

> People of Israel, and everyone else who worships God, listen! [17]The God of Israel chose our ancestors, and he let our people prosper while they were living in Egypt. Then with his mighty power he led them out, [18]and for about forty years he took care of[u] them in the desert. [19]He destroyed seven nations in the land of Canaan and gave their land to our people. [20]All this happened in about 450 years.
>
> Then God gave our people judges until the time of the prophet Samuel, [21]but the people demanded a king. So for forty years God gave them King Saul, the son of Kish from the tribe of Benjamin. [22]Later, God removed Saul and let David rule in his place. God said about him, "David the son of Jesse is the kind of person who pleases me most! He does everything I want him to do."
>
> [23]God promised that someone

[p]**12.25** *went back to Jerusalem*: Some manuscripts have "left Jerusalem," and others have "went to Antioch." [q]**13.1** *Herod's*: Herod Antipas, the son of Herod the Great. [r]**13.2** *going without eating*: The Jews often went without eating as a way of showing how much they loved God. This is also called "fasting." [s]**13.5,13** *John*: Whose other name was Mark (see 12.12, 25). [t]**13.15** *the Law and the Prophets*: The Jewish Scriptures, that is, the Old Testament. [u]**13.18** *took care of*: Some manuscripts have "put up with."

from David's family would come to
save the people of Israel, and that
one is Jesus. 24But before Jesus
came, John was telling everyone in
Israel to turn back to God and be
baptized. 25Then, when John's work
was almost done, he said, "Who do
you people think I am? Do you think
I am the Promised One? He will
come later, and I am not good
enough to untie his sandals."
26Now listen, you descendants of
Abraham! Pay attention, all of you
Gentiles who are here to worship
God! Listen to this message about
how to be saved, because it is for
everyone. 27The people of Jerusalem
and their leaders didn't realize who
Jesus was. And they didn't understand the words of the prophets that
they read each Sabbath. So they
condemned Jesus just as the
prophets had said.
28-29They did exactly what the
Scriptures said they would. Even
though they couldn't find any reason
to put Jesus to death, they still asked
Pilate to have him killed.
After Jesus had been put to death,
he was taken down from the cross[v]
and placed in a tomb. 30But God
raised him from death! 31Then for
many days Jesus appeared to his followers who had gone with him from
Galilee to Jerusalem. Now they are
telling our people about him.
32God made a promise to our ancestors. And we are here to tell you
the good news 33that he has kept
this promise to us. It is just as the
second Psalm says about Jesus,

"You are my son because today
I have become your Father."

34God raised Jesus from death and
will never let his body decay. It is
just as God said,

"I will make to you
the same holy promise
that I made to David."

35And in another psalm it says, "God
will never let the body of his Holy
One decay."
36When David was alive, he
obeyed God. Then after he died, he
was buried in the family grave, and
his body decayed. 37But God raised
Jesus from death, and his body did
not decay.
38My friends, the message is that
Jesus can forgive your sins! The
Law of Moses could not set you free
from all your sins. 39But everyone
who has faith in Jesus is set free.
40Make sure that what the prophets
have said doesn't happen to you.
They said,

41 "Look, you people
who make fun of God!
Be amazed
and disappear.
I will do something today
that you won't believe,
even if someone
tells you about it!"

42As Paul and Barnabas were leaving
the meeting, the people begged them to
say more about these same things on
the next Sabbath. 43After the service,
many Jews and a lot of Gentiles who
worshiped God went with them. Paul
and Barnabas begged them all to remain faithful to God, who had been so
kind to them.
44The next Sabbath almost everyone
in town came to hear the message about
the Lord.[w] 45When the Jewish people
saw the crowds, they were very jealous.
They insulted Paul and spoke against
everything he said.
46But Paul and Barnabas bravely said:
We had to tell God's message to
you before we told it to anyone else.
But you rejected the message! This
proves that you don't deserve eternal life. Now we are going to the
Gentiles. 47The Lord has given us
this command,

"I have placed you here
as a light
for the Gentiles.
You are to take
the saving power of God
to people everywhere on earth."

48This message made the Gentiles
glad, and they praised what they had
heard about the Lord.[w] Everyone who
had been chosen for eternal life then
put their faith in the Lord.
49The message about the Lord spread
all over that region. 50But the Jewish
leaders went to some of the important
men in the town and to some respected
women who were religious. They turned
them against Paul and Barnabas and
started making trouble for them. They
even chased them out of that part of the
country.
51Paul and Barnabas shook the dust
from that place off their feet[x] and went
on to the city of Iconium.
52But the Lord's followers in Antioch

[v]13.28,29 *cross*: This translates a Greek word that means "wood," "pole," or "tree."
[w]13.44,48 *the Lord*: Some manuscripts have "God." [x]13.51 *shook the dust from that place off their feet*: This was a way of showing rejection.

were very happy and were filled with
the Holy Spirit.

Paul and Barnabas in Iconium

14 Paul and Barnabas spoke in the
Jewish meeting place in Iconium,
just as they had done at Antioch, and
many Jews and Gentiles[y] put their faith
in the Lord. [2]But the Jews who did not
have faith in him made the other Gentiles angry and turned them against the
Lord's followers.
[3]Paul and Barnabas stayed there for a
while, having faith in the Lord and
bravely speaking his message. The Lord
gave them the power to work miracles
and wonders, and he showed that their
message about his great kindness was
true.
[4]The people of Iconium did not know
what to think. Some of them believed
the Jewish group, and others believed
the apostles. [5]Finally, some Gentiles and
Jews, together with their leaders, decided to make trouble for Paul and
Barnabas and to stone them to death.
[6-7]But when the two apostles found
out what was happening, they escaped
to the region of Lycaonia. They
preached the good news there in the
towns of Lystra and Derbe and in the
nearby countryside.

Paul and Barnabas in Lystra

[8]In Lystra there was a man who had
been born with crippled feet and had
never been able to walk. [9]The man was
listening to Paul speak, when Paul saw
that he had faith in Jesus and could be
healed. So he looked straight at the man
[10]and shouted, "Stand up!" The man
jumped up and started walking around.
[11]When the crowd saw what Paul had
done, they yelled out in the language of
Lycaonia, "The gods have turned into
humans and have come down to us!"
[12]The people then gave Barnabas the
name Zeus, and they gave Paul the
name Hermes,[z] because he did the talking.
[13]The temple of Zeus was near the entrance to the city. Its priest and the
crowds wanted to offer a sacrifice to
Barnabas and Paul. So the priest
brought some bulls and flowers to the
city gates. [14]When the two apostles
found out about this, they tore their
clothes in horror and ran to the crowd,
shouting:

> [15]Why are you doing this? We are
> humans just like you. Please give up
> all this foolishness. Turn to the living
> God, who made the sky, the earth,
> the sea, and everything in them. [16]In
> times past, God let each nation go its
> own way. [17]But he showed that he
> was there by the good things he did.
> God sends rain from heaven and
> makes your crops grow. He gives
> food to you and makes your hearts
> glad.

[18]Even after Paul and Barnabas had
said all this, they could hardly keep the
people from offering a sacrifice to them.
[19]Some Jewish leaders from Antioch
and Iconium came and turned the
crowds against Paul. They hit him with
stones and dragged him out of the city,
thinking he was dead. [20]But when the
Lord's followers gathered around Paul,
he stood up and went back into the city.
The next day he and Barnabas went to
Derbe.

Paul and Barnabas Return to Antioch in Syria

[21]Paul and Barnabas preached the
good news in Derbe and won some people to the Lord. Then they went back to
Lystra, Iconium, and Antioch in Pisidia.
[22]They encouraged the followers and
begged them to remain faithful. They
told them, "We have to suffer a lot before we can get into God's kingdom."
[23]Paul and Barnabas chose some leaders
for each of the churches. Then they
went without eating[a] and prayed that
the Lord would take good care of these
leaders.
[24]Paul and Barnabas went on through
Pisidia to Pamphylia, [25]where they
preached in the town of Perga. Then
they went down to Attalia [26]and sailed
to Antioch in Syria. It was there that
they had been placed in God's care for
the work they had now completed.[b]
[27]After arriving in Antioch, they
called the church together. They told the
people what God had helped them do
and how he had made it possible for
the Gentiles to believe. [28]Then they
stayed there with the followers for a
long time.

15 Some people came from Judea
and started teaching the Lord's
followers that they could not be saved,
unless they were circumcised as Moses
had taught. [2]This caused trouble, and
Paul and Barnabas argued with them
about this teaching. So it was decided to
send Paul and Barnabas and a few others to Jerusalem to discuss this problem
with the apostles and the church leaders.

[y]**14.1** *Gentiles*: The Greek text has "Greeks," which probably means people who were not Jews. But it may mean Gentiles who worshiped with the Jews. [z]**14.12** *Hermes*: The Greeks thought of Hermes as the messenger of the other gods, especially of Zeus, their chief god. [a]**14.23** *went without eating*: See the note at 13.2. [b]**14.26** *the work they had now completed*: See 13.1-3.

The Church Leaders Meet in Jerusalem

3 The men who were sent by the
church went through Phoenicia and
Samaria, telling how the Gentiles had
turned to God. This news made the
Lord's followers very happy. 4 When the
men arrived in Jerusalem, they were
welcomed by the church, including the
apostles and the leaders. They told them
everything God had helped them do.
5 But some Pharisees had become followers of the Lord. They stood up and
said, "Gentiles who have faith in the
Lord must be circumcised and told to
obey the Law of Moses."

6 The apostles and church leaders met
to discuss this problem about Gentiles.
7 They had talked it over for a long time,
when Peter got up and said:

My friends, you know that God decided long ago to let me be the one
from your group to preach the good
news to the Gentiles. God did this so
that they would hear and obey him.
8 He knows what is in everyone's
heart. And he showed that he had
chosen the Gentiles, when he gave
them the Holy Spirit, just as he had
given his Spirit to us. 9 God treated
them in the same way that he
treated us. They put their faith in
him, and he made their hearts pure.

10 Now why are you trying to make
God angry by placing a heavy burden on these followers? This burden
was too heavy for us or our ancestors. 11 But our Lord Jesus was kind
to us, and we are saved by faith in
him, just as the Gentiles are.

12 Everyone kept quiet and listened as
Barnabas and Paul told how God had
given them the power to work a lot of
miracles and wonders for the Gentiles.
13 After they had finished speaking,
James[c] said:

My friends, listen to me! 14 Simon
Peter[d] has told how God first came
to the Gentiles and made some of
them his own people. 15 This agrees
with what the prophets wrote,

16 "I, the Lord, will return
and rebuild
David's fallen house.
I will build it from its ruins
and set it up again.
17 Then other nations
will turn to me
and be my chosen ones.
I, the Lord, say this.
18 I promised it long ago."

19 And so, my friends, I don't think
we should place burdens on the
Gentiles who are turning to God.
20 We should simply write and tell
them not to eat anything that has
been offered to idols. They should be
told not to eat the meat of any animal that has been strangled or that
still has blood in it. They must also
not commit any terrible sexual sins.[e]

21 We must remember that the Law
of Moses has been preached in city after city for many years, and every
Sabbath it is read when we Jews meet.

A Letter to Gentiles Who Had Faith in the Lord

22 The apostles, the leaders, and all the
church members decided to send some
men to Antioch along with Paul and
Barnabas. They chose Silas and Judas
Barsabbas,[f] who were two leaders of the
Lord's followers. 23 They wrote a letter
that said:

We apostles and leaders send
friendly greetings to all of you Gentiles who are followers of the Lord
in Antioch, Syria, and Cilicia.

24 We have heard that some people
from here have terribly upset you by
what they said. But we did not send
them! 25 So we met together and decided to choose some men and to
send them to you along with our
good friends Barnabas and Paul.
26 These men have risked their lives
for our Lord Jesus Christ. 27 We are
also sending Judas and Silas, who
will tell you in person the same
things that we are writing.

28 The Holy Spirit has shown us
that we should not place any extra
burden on you. 29 But you should not
eat anything offered to idols. You
should not eat any meat that still has
the blood in it or any meat of any
animal that has been strangled. You
must also not commit any terrible
sexual sins. If you follow these instructions, you will do well.

We send our best wishes.

30 The four men left Jerusalem and
went to Antioch. Then they called the
church members together and gave
them the letter. 31 When the letter was
read, everyone was pleased and greatly
encouraged. 32 Judas and Silas were
prophets, and they spoke a long time,
encouraging and helping the Lord's followers.

33 The men from Jerusalem stayed on

[c] **15.13** *James*: The Lord's brother. [d] **15.14** *Simon Peter*: The Greek text has "Simeon," which is another form of the name "Simon." The apostle Peter is meant. [e] **15.20** *not commit any terrible sexual sins*: This probably refers to the laws about the wrong kind of marriages that are forbidden in Leviticus 18.6-18 or to some serious sexual sin. [f] **15.22** *Judas Barsabbas*: He may have been a brother of Joseph Barsabbas (see 1.23), but the name "Barsabbas" was often used by the Jewish people.

in Antioch for a while. And when they
left to return to the ones who had sent
them, the followers wished them well.
34-35 But Paul and Barnabas stayed on in
Antioch, where they and many others
taught and preached about the Lord.[g]

Paul and Barnabas Go Their Separate Ways

36 Sometime later Paul said to Barnabas, "Let's go back and visit the
Lord's followers in the cities where we
preached his message. Then we will
know how they are doing." 37 Barnabas
wanted to take along John, whose other
name was Mark. 38 But Paul did not want
to, because Mark had left them in Pamphylia and had stopped working with
them.
39 Paul and Barnabas argued, then
each of them went his own way. Barnabas took Mark and sailed to Cyprus,
40 but Paul took Silas and left after the
followers had placed them in God's
care. 41 They traveled through Syria and
Cilicia, encouraging the churches.

Timothy Works with Paul and Silas

16 Paul and Silas went back to
Derbe and Lystra, where there
was a follower named Timothy. His
mother was also a follower. She was
Jewish, and his father was Greek. 2 The
Lord's followers in Lystra and Iconium
said good things about Timothy, 3 and
Paul wanted him to go with them. But
Paul first had him circumcised, because
all the Jewish people around there knew
that Timothy's father was Greek.[h]
4 As Paul and the others went from
city to city, they told the followers what
the apostles and leaders in Jerusalem
had decided, and they urged them to follow these instructions. 5 The churches
became stronger in their faith, and each
day more people put their faith in the
Lord.

Paul's Vision in Troas

6 Paul and his friends went through
Phrygia and Galatia, but the Holy Spirit
would not let them preach in Asia. 7 After they arrived in Mysia, they tried to
go into Bithynia, but the Spirit of Jesus
would not let them. 8 So they went on
through[i] Mysia until they came to Troas.
9 During the night, Paul had a vision of
someone from Macedonia who was
standing there and begging him, "Come
over to Macedonia and help us!" 10 After
Paul had seen the vision, we began
looking for a way to go to Macedonia.
We were sure that God had called us to
preach the good news there.

Lydia Becomes a Follower of the Lord

11 We sailed straight from Troas to
Samothrace, and the next day we arrived in Neapolis. 12 From there we went
to Philippi, which is a Roman colony in
the first district of Macedonia.[j]
We spent several days in Philippi.
13 Then on the Sabbath we went outside
the city gate to a place by the river,
where we thought there would be a Jewish meeting place for prayer. We sat
down and talked with the women who
came. 14 One of them was Lydia, who
was from the city of Thyatira and sold
expensive purple cloth. She was a worshiper of the Lord God, and he made
her willing to accept what Paul was saying. 15 Then after she and her family
were baptized, she kept on begging us,
"If you think I really do have faith in the
Lord, come stay in my home." Finally,
we accepted her invitation.

Paul and Silas Are Put in Jail

16 One day on our way to the place of
prayer, we were met by a slave girl. She
had a spirit in her that gave her the
power to tell the future. By doing this
she made a lot of money for her owners.
17 The girl followed Paul and the rest of
us and kept yelling, "These men are servants of the Most High God! They are
telling you how to be saved."
18 This went on for several days. Finally, Paul got so upset that he turned
and said to the spirit, "In the name of Jesus Christ, I order you to leave this girl
alone!" At once the evil spirit left her.
19 When the girl's owners realized that
they had lost all chances for making
more money, they grabbed Paul and
Silas and dragged them into court.
20 They told the officials, "These Jews
are upsetting our city! 21 They are telling
us to do things we Romans are not allowed to do."
22 The crowd joined in the attack on
Paul and Silas. Then the officials tore
the clothes off the two men and ordered
them to be beaten with a whip. 23 After
they had been badly beaten, they were
put in jail, and the jailer was told to
guard them carefully. 24 The jailer did as
he was told. He put them deep inside the
jail and chained their feet to heavy
blocks of wood.
25 About midnight Paul and Silas were
praying and singing praises to God,
while the other prisoners listened.

[g] **15.34,35** Verse 34, which says that Silas decided to stay on in Antioch, is not in some manuscripts. [h] **16.3** *had him circumcised . . . Timothy's father was Greek*: Timothy would not have been acceptable to the Jews unless he had been circumcised, and Greeks did not circumcise their sons. [i] **16.8** *went on through*: Or "passed by." [j] **16.12** *in the first district of Macedonia*: Some manuscripts have "and the leading city of Macedonia."

26 Suddenly a strong earthquake shook the jail to its foundations. The doors opened, and the chains fell from all the prisoners.

27 When the jailer woke up and saw that the doors were open, he thought that the prisoners had escaped. He pulled out his sword and was about to kill himself. 28 But Paul shouted, "Don't harm yourself! No one has escaped."

29 The jailer asked for a torch and went into the jail. He was shaking all over as he knelt down in front of Paul and Silas. 30 After he had led them out of the jail, he asked, "What must I do to be saved?"

31 They replied, "Have faith in the Lord Jesus and you will be saved! This is also true for everyone who lives in your home."

32 Then Paul and Silas told him and everyone else in his house about the Lord. 33 While it was still night, the jailer took them to a place where he could wash their cuts and bruises. Then he and everyone in his home were baptized. 34 They were very glad that they had put their faith in God. After this, the jailer took Paul and Silas to his home and gave them something to eat.

35 The next morning the officials sent some police with orders for the jailer to let Paul and Silas go. 36 The jailer told Paul, "The officials have ordered me to set you free. Now you can leave in peace."

37 But Paul told the police, "We are Roman citizens,[k] and the Roman officials had us beaten in public without giving us a trial. They threw us into jail. Now do they think they can secretly send us away? No, they cannot! They will have to come here themselves and let us out."

38 When the police told the officials that Paul and Silas were Roman citizens, the officials were afraid. 39 So they came and apologized. They led them out of the jail and asked them to please leave town. 40 But Paul and Silas went straight to the home of Lydia, where they saw the Lord's followers and encouraged them. Then they left.

Trouble in Thessalonica

17 After Paul and his friends had traveled through Amphipolis and Apollonia, they went on to Thessalonica. A Jewish meeting place was in that city. 2 So as usual, Paul went there to worship, and on three Sabbaths he spoke to the people. He used the Scriptures 3 to show them that the Messiah had to suffer, but that he would rise from death. Paul also told them that Jesus is the Messiah he was preaching about. 4 Some of them believed what Paul had said, and they became followers with Paul and Silas. Some Gentiles[l] and many important women also believed the message.

5 The Jewish leaders were jealous and got some worthless bums who hung around the marketplace to start a riot in the city. They wanted to drag Paul and Silas out to the mob, and so they went straight to Jason's home. 6 But when they did not find them there, they dragged out Jason and some of the Lord's followers. They took them to the city authorities and shouted, "Paul and Silas have been upsetting things everywhere. Now they have come here, 7 and Jason has welcomed them into his home. All of them break the laws of the Roman Emperor by claiming that someone named Jesus is king."

8 The officials and the people were upset when they heard this. 9 So they made Jason and the other followers pay bail before letting them go.

People in Berea Welcome the Message

10 That same night the Lord's followers sent Paul and Silas on to Berea, and after they arrived, they went to the Jewish meeting place. 11 The people in Berea were much nicer than those in Thessalonica, and they gladly accepted the message. Day after day they studied the Scriptures to see if these things were true. 12 Many of them put their faith in the Lord, including some important Greek women and several men.

13 When the Jewish leaders in Thessalonica heard that Paul had been preaching God's message in Berea, they went there and caused trouble by turning the crowds against Paul.

14 Right away the followers sent Paul down to the coast, but Silas and Timothy stayed in Berea. 15 Some men went with Paul as far as Athens, and then returned with instructions for Silas and Timothy to join him as soon as possible.

Paul in Athens

16 While Paul was waiting in Athens, he was upset to see all the idols in the city. 17 He went to the Jewish meeting place to speak to the Jews and to anyone who worshiped with them. Day after day he also spoke to everyone he met in the market. 18 Some of them were Epicureans[m] and some were

[k] **16.37** *Roman citizens*: Only a small number of the people living in the Roman Empire were citizens, and they had special rights and privileges. [l] **17.4** *Gentiles*: See the note at 14.1.
[m] **17.18** *Epicureans*: People who followed the teaching of a man named Epicurus, who taught that happiness should be the main goal in life.

Stoics,[n] and they started arguing with him.

People were asking, "What is this know-it-all trying to say?"

Some even said, "Paul must be preaching about foreign gods! That's what he means when he talks about Jesus and about people rising from death."[o]

19They brought Paul before a council called the Areopagus, and said, "Tell us what your new teaching is all about. 20We have heard you say some strange things, and we want to know what you mean."

21More than anything else the people of Athens and the foreigners living there loved to hear and to talk about anything new. 22So Paul stood up in front of the council and said:

> People of Athens, I see that you are very religious. 23As I was going through your city and looking at the things you worship, I found an altar with the words, "To an Unknown God." You worship this God, but you don't really know him. So I want to tell you about him. 24This God made the world and everything in it. He is Lord of heaven and earth, and he doesn't live in temples built by human hands. 25He doesn't need help from anyone. He gives life, breath, and everything else to all people. 26From one person God made all nations who live on earth, and he decided when and where every nation would be.
>
> 27God has done all this, so that we will look for him and reach out and find him. He isn't far from any of us, 28and he gives us the power to live, to move, and to be who we are. "We are his children," just as some of your poets have said.
>
> 29Since we are God's children, we must not think that he is like an idol made out of gold or silver or stone. He isn't like anything that humans have thought up and made. 30In the past, God forgave all this because people did not know what they were doing. But now he says that everyone everywhere must turn to him. 31He has set a day when he will judge the world's people with fairness. And he has chosen the man Jesus to do the judging for him. God has given proof of this to all of us by raising Jesus from death.

32As soon as the people heard Paul say that a man had been raised from death, some of them started laughing. Others said, "We will hear you talk about this some other time." 33When Paul left the council meeting, 34some of the men put their faith in the Lord and went with Paul. One of them was a council member named Dionysius. A woman named Damaris and several others also put their faith in the Lord.

Paul in Corinth

18 Paul left Athens and went to Corinth, 2where he met Aquila, a Jewish man from Pontus. Not long before this, Aquila had come from Italy with his wife Priscilla, because Emperor Claudius had ordered the Jewish people to leave Rome.[p] Paul went to see Aquila and Priscilla 3and found out that they were tent makers. Paul was a tent maker too. So he stayed with them, and they worked together.

4Every Sabbath, Paul went to the Jewish meeting place. He spoke to Jews and Gentiles[q] and tried to win them over. 5But after Silas and Timothy came from Macedonia, he spent all his time preaching to the Jews about Jesus the Messiah. 6Finally, they turned against him and insulted him. So he shook the dust from his clothes[r] and told them, "Whatever happens to you will be your own fault! I am not to blame. From now on I am going to preach to the Gentiles."

7Paul then moved into the house of a man named Titius Justus, who worshiped God and lived next door to the Jewish meeting place. 8Crispus was the leader of the meeting place. He and everyone in his family put their faith in the Lord. Many others in Corinth also heard the message, and all the people who had faith in the Lord were baptized.

9One night, Paul had a vision, and in it the Lord said, "Don't be afraid to keep on preaching. Don't stop! 10I am with you, and you won't be harmed. Many people in this city belong to me." 11Paul stayed on in Corinth for a year and a half, teaching God's message to the people.

12While Gallio was governor of Achaia, some of the Jewish leaders got together and grabbed Paul. They brought him into court 13and said, "This man is trying to make our people worship God in a way that is against our Law!"

14Even before Paul could speak, Gallio said, "If you were charging this man

[n] **17.18** *Stoics*: Followers of a man named Zeno, who taught that people should learn self-control and be guided by their consciences. [o] **17.18** *people rising from death*: Or "a goddess named 'Rising from Death.'" [p] **18.2** *Emperor Claudius had ordered all the Jewish people to leave Rome*: Probably A.D. 49, though it may have been A.D. 41. [q] **18.4** *Gentiles*: Here the word is "Greeks." But see the note at 14.1. [r] **18.6** *shook the dust from his clothes*: This means the same as shaking dust from the feet (see the note at 13.51).

with a crime or some other wrong, I
would have to listen to you. 15But since
this concerns only words, names, and
your own law, you will have to take care
of it. I refuse to judge such matters."
16Then he sent them out of the court.
17The crowd grabbed Sosthenes, the
Jewish leader, and beat him up in front
of the court. But none of this mattered
to Gallio.

Paul Returns to Antioch in Syria

18After Paul had stayed for a while
with the Lord's followers in Corinth, he
told them good-by and sailed on to
Syria with Aquila and Priscilla. But before he left, he had his head shaved[s] at
Cenchreae because he had made a
promise to God.
19The three of them arrived in Ephesus, where Paul left Priscilla and
Aquila. He then went into the Jewish
meeting place to talk with the people
there. 20They asked him to stay longer,
but he refused. 21He told them good-by
and said, "If God lets me, I will come
back."
22Paul sailed to Caesarea, where he
greeted the church. Then he went on to
Antioch. 23After staying there for a
while, he left and visited several places
in Galatia and Phrygia. He helped the
followers there to become stronger in
their faith.

Apollos in Ephesus

24A Jewish man named Apollos came
to Ephesus. Apollos had been born in
the city of Alexandria. He was a very
good speaker and knew a lot about the
Scriptures. 25He also knew much about
the Lord's Way,[t] and he spoke about it
with great excitement. What he taught
about Jesus was right, but all he knew
was John's message about baptism.
26Apollos started speaking bravely in
the Jewish meeting place. But when
Priscilla and Aquila heard him, they
took him to their home and helped him
understand God's Way even better.
27Apollos decided to travel through
Achaia. So the Lord's followers wrote
letters, encouraging the followers there
to welcome him. After Apollos arrived
in Achaia, he was a great help to everyone who had put their faith in the Lord
Jesus because of God's kindness. 28He
got into fierce arguments with the Jewish people, and in public he used the
Scriptures to prove that Jesus is the
Messiah.

Paul in Ephesus

19 While Apollos was in Corinth,
Paul traveled across the hill country to Ephesus, where he met some of
the Lord's followers. 2He asked them,
"When you put your faith in Jesus, were
you given the Holy Spirit?"
"No!" they answered. "We have never
even heard of the Holy Spirit."
3"Then why were you baptized?" Paul
asked.
They answered, "Because of what
John taught."[u]
4Paul replied, "John baptized people
so that they would turn to God. But he
also told them that someone else was
coming, and that they should put their
faith in him. Jesus is the one that John
was talking about." 5After the people
heard Paul say this, they were baptized
in the name of the Lord Jesus. 6Then
Paul placed his hands on them. The
Holy Spirit was given to them, and they
spoke unknown languages and prophesied. 7There were about twelve men in
this group.
8For three months Paul went to the
Jewish meeting place and talked
bravely with the people about God's
kingdom. He tried to win them over,
9but some of them were stubborn and
refused to believe. In front of everyone
they said terrible things about God's
Way. Paul left and took the followers
with him to the lecture hall of Tyrannus.
He spoke there every day 10for two
years, until every Jew and Gentile[v] in
Asia had heard the Lord's message.

The Sons of Sceva

11God gave Paul the power to work
great miracles. 12People even took hand-
kerchiefs and aprons that had touched
Paul's body, and they carried them to
everyone who was sick. All of the sick
people were healed, and the evil spirits
went out.
13Some Jewish men started going
around trying to force out evil spirits by
using the name of the Lord Jesus. They
said to the spirits, "Come out in the
name of that same Jesus that Paul
preaches about!"
14Seven sons of a Jewish high priest
named Sceva were doing this, 15when an
evil spirit said to them, "I know Jesus! And
I have heard about Paul. But who are
you?" 16Then the man with the evil spirit
jumped on them and beat them up. They
ran out of the house, naked and bruised.

[s] **18.18** *he had his head shaved*: Paul had promised to be a "Nazirite" for a while. This meant that for the time of the promise, he could not cut his hair or drink wine. When the time was over, he would have to cut his hair and offer a sacrifice to God. [t] **18.25** *the Lord's Way*: See the note at 9.2. [u] **19.3** *Then why were you baptized? . . . Because of what John taught*: Or "In whose name were you baptized? . . . We were baptized in John's name."
[v] **19.10,17** *Gentile(s)*: The text has "Greek(s)" (see the note at 14.1).

[17]When the Jews and Gentiles[v] in Ephesus heard about this, they were so frightened that they praised the name of the Lord Jesus. [18]Many who were followers now started telling everyone about the evil things they had been doing. [19]Some who had been practicing witchcraft even brought their books and burned them in public. These books were worth about fifty thousand silver coins. [20]So the Lord's message spread and became even more powerful.

The Riot in Ephesus

[21]After all of this had happened, Paul decided[w] to visit Macedonia and Achaia on his way to Jerusalem. Paul had said, "From there I will go on to Rome." [22]So he sent his two helpers, Timothy and Erastus, to Macedonia. But he stayed on in Asia for a while.

[23]At that time there was serious trouble because of the Lord's Way.[x] [24]A silversmith named Demetrius had a business that made silver models of the temple of the goddess Artemis. Those who worked for him earned a lot of money. [25]Demetrius brought together everyone who was in the same business and said:

> Friends, you know that we make a good living at this. [26]But you have surely seen and heard how this man Paul is upsetting a lot of people, not only in Ephesus, but almost everywhere in Asia. He claims that the gods we humans make are not really gods at all. [27]Everyone will start saying terrible things about our business. They will stop respecting the temple of the goddess Artemis, who is worshiped in Asia and all over the world. Our great goddess will be forgotten!

[28]When the workers heard this, they got angry and started shouting, "Great is Artemis, the goddess of the Ephesians!" [29]Soon the whole city was in a riot, and some men grabbed Gaius and Aristarchus, who had come from Macedonia with Paul. Then everyone in the crowd rushed to the place where the town meetings were held.

[30]Paul wanted to go out and speak to the people, but the Lord's followers would not let him. [31]A few of the local officials were friendly to Paul, and they sent someone to warn him not to go.

[32]Some of the people in the meeting were shouting one thing, and others were shouting something else. Everyone was completely confused, and most of them did not even know why they were there.

[33]Several of the Jewish leaders pushed a man named Alexander to the front of the crowd and started telling him what to say. He motioned with his hand and tried to explain what was going on. [34]But when the crowd saw that he was Jewish, they all shouted for two hours, "Great is Artemis, the goddess of the Ephesians!"

[35]Finally, a town official made the crowd be quiet. Then he said:

> People of Ephesus, who in the world doesn't know that our city is the center for worshiping the great goddess Artemis? Who doesn't know that her image which fell from heaven is right here? [36]No one can deny this, and so you should calm down and not do anything foolish. [37]You have brought men in here who have not robbed temples or spoken against our goddess.
>
> [38]If Demetrius and his workers have a case against these men, we have courts and judges. Let them take their complaints there. [39]But if you want to do more than that, the matter will have to be brought before the city council. [40]We could easily be accused of starting a riot today. There is no excuse for it! We cannot even give a reason for this uproar.

[41]After saying this, he told the people to leave.

Paul Goes through Macedonia and Greece

20 When the riot was over, Paul sent for the followers and encouraged them. He then told them good-by and left for Macedonia. [2]As he traveled from place to place, he encouraged the followers with many messages. Finally, he went to Greece[y] [3]and stayed there for three months.

Paul was about to sail to Syria. But some of the Jewish leaders plotted against him, so he decided to return by way of Macedonia. [4]With him were Sopater, son of Pyrrhus from Berea, and Aristarchus and Secundus from Thessalonica. Gaius from Derbe was also with him, and so were Timothy and the two Asians, Tychicus and Trophimus. [5]They went on ahead to Troas and waited for us there. [6]After the Festival of Thin Bread, we sailed from Philippi. Five days later we met them in Troas and stayed there for a week.

[v]**19.10,17** *Gentile(s)*: The text has "Greek(s)" (see the note at 14.1). [w]**19.21** *Paul decided*: Or "Paul was led by the Holy Spirit." [x]**19.23** *the Lord's Way*: See the note at 9.2.
[y]**20.2** *Greece*: Probably Corinth.

Paul's Last Visit to Troas

7 On the first day of the week[z] we met
to break bread together.[a] Paul spoke to
the people until midnight because he
was leaving the next morning. 8 In the
upstairs room where we were meeting,
there were a lot of lamps. 9 A young man
by the name of Eutychus was sitting on
a window sill. While Paul was speaking,
the young man got very sleepy. Finally,
he went to sleep and fell three floors all
the way down to the ground. When they
picked him up, he was dead.
10 Paul went down and bent over Eutychus. He took him in his arms and said,
"Don't worry! He's alive." 11 After Paul
had gone back upstairs, he broke bread,
and ate with us. He then spoke until
dawn and left. 12 Then the followers took
the young man home alive and were
very happy.

The Voyage from Troas to Miletus

13 Paul decided to travel by land to Assos. The rest of us went on ahead by
ship, and we were to take him aboard
there. 14 When he met us in Assos, he
came aboard, and we sailed on to Mity-
lene. 15 The next day we came to a place
near Chios, and the following day we
reached Samos. The day after that we
sailed to Miletus. 16 Paul had decided to
sail on past Ephesus, because he did not
want to spend too much time in Asia. He
was in a hurry and wanted to be in
Jerusalem in time for Pentecost.[b]

Paul Says Good-By to the Church Leaders of Ephesus

17 From Miletus, Paul sent a message
for the church leaders at Ephesus to
come and meet with him. 18 When they
got there, he said:
You know everything I did during
the time I was with you when I first
came to Asia. 19 Some of the Jews
plotted against me and caused me a
lot of sorrow and trouble. But I
served the Lord and was humble.
20 When I preached in public or
taught in your homes, I didn't hold
back from telling anything that
would help you. 21 I told Jews and
Gentiles to turn to God and have
faith in our Lord Jesus.
22 I don't know what will happen to
me in Jerusalem, but I must obey
God's Spirit and go there. 23 In every
city I visit, I am told by the Holy
Spirit that I will be put in jail and
will be in trouble in Jerusalem. 24 But
I don't care what happens to me, as
long as I finish the work that the
Lord Jesus gave me to do. And that
work is to tell the good news about
God's great kindness.
25 I have gone from place to place,
preaching to you about God's kingdom, but now I know that none of
you will ever see me again. 26 I tell
you today that I am no longer responsible for any of you! 27 I have
told you everything God wants you
to know. 28 Look after yourselves and
everyone the Holy Spirit has placed
in your care. Be like shepherds to
God's church. It is the flock that he
bought with the blood of his own
Son.[c]
29 I know that after I am gone, others will come like fierce wolves to
attack you. 30 Some of your own people will tell lies to win over the
Lord's followers. 31 Be on your
guard! Remember how day and
night for three years I kept warning
you with tears in my eyes.
32 I now place you in God's care.
Remember the message about his
great kindness! This message can
help you and give you what belongs
to you as God's people. 33 I have
never wanted anyone's money or
clothes. 34 You know how I have
worked with my own hands to make
a living for myself and my friends.
35 By everything I did, I showed how
you should work to help everyone
who is weak. Remember that our
Lord Jesus said, "More blessings
come from giving than from receiving."
36 After Paul had finished speaking, he
knelt down with all of them and prayed.
37 Everyone cried and hugged and kissed
him. 38 They were especially sad because
Paul had told them, "You will never see
me again."
Then they went with him to the ship.

Paul Goes to Jerusalem

21 After saying good-by, we sailed
straight to Cos. The next day we
reached Rhodes and from there sailed
on to Patara. 2 We found a ship going to
Phoenicia, so we got on board and
sailed off.
3 We came within sight of Cyprus and
then sailed south of it on to the port of
Tyre in Syria, where the ship was going
to unload its cargo. 4 We looked up the
Lord's followers and stayed with them
for a week. The Holy Spirit had told
them to warn Paul not to go on to
Jerusalem. 5 But when the week was

[z] **20.7** *On the first day of the week*: Since the Jewish day began at sunset, the meeting would have begun in the evening. [a] **20.7** *break bread together*: See the note at 2.46. [b] **20.16** *in time for Pentecost*: The Jewish people liked to be in Jerusalem for this festival (see the note at 2.1). [c] **20.28** *the blood of his own Son*: Or "his own blood."

over, we started on our way again. All
the men, together with their wives and
children, walked with us from the town
to the seashore. We knelt on the beach
and prayed. [6]Then after saying good-by
to each other, we got into the ship, and
they went back home.
[7]We sailed from Tyre to Ptolemais,
where we greeted the followers and
stayed with them for a day. [8]The next
day we went to Caesarea and stayed
with Philip, the preacher. He was one of
the seven men who helped the apostles,
[9]and he had four unmarried[d] daughters
who prophesied.
[10]We had been in Caesarea for several
days, when the prophet Agabus came to
us from Judea. [11]He took Paul's belt, and
with it he tied up his own hands and
feet. Then he told us, "The Holy Spirit
says that some of the Jewish leaders in
Jerusalem will tie up the man who owns
this belt. They will also hand him over
to the Gentiles." [12]After Agabus said
this, we and the followers living there
begged Paul not to go to Jerusalem.
[13]But Paul answered, "Why are you
crying and breaking my heart? I am not
only willing to be put in jail for the Lord
Jesus. I am even willing to die for him in
Jerusalem!"
[14]Since we could not get Paul to
change his mind, we gave up and
prayed, "Lord, please make us willing to
do what you want."
[15]Then we got ready to go to
Jerusalem. [16]Some of the followers from
Caesarea went with us and took us to
stay in the home of Mnason. He was
from Cyprus and had been a follower
from the beginning.

Paul Visits James

[17]When we arrived in Jerusalem, the
Lord's followers gladly welcomed us.
[18]Paul went with us to see James[e] the
next day, and all the church leaders
were present. [19]Paul greeted them and
told how God had used him to help the
Gentiles. [20]Everyone who heard this
praised God and said to Paul:

> My friend, you can see how many
> tens of thousands of the Jewish peo-
> ple have become followers! And all
> of them are eager to obey the Law
> of Moses. [21]But they have been told
> that you are teaching those who live
> among the Gentiles to disobey this
> Law. They claim that you are telling
> them not to circumcise their sons or
> to follow Jewish customs.
> [22]What should we do now that our
> people have heard that you are
> here? [23]Please do what we ask, be-
> cause four of our men have made
> special promises to God. [24]Join with
> them and prepare yourself for the
> ceremony that goes with the
> promises. Pay the cost for their
> heads to be shaved. Then everyone
> will learn that the reports about you
> are not true. They will know that
> you do obey the Law of Moses.
> [25]Some while ago we told the Gen-
> tile followers what we think they
> should do. We instructed them not to
> eat anything offered to idols. They
> were told not to eat any meat with
> blood still in it or the meat of an ani-
> mal that has been strangled. They
> were also told not to commit any ter-
> rible sexual sins.[f]

[26]The next day Paul took the four men
with him and got himself ready at the
same time they did. Then he went into
the temple and told when the final ceremony would take place and when an offering would be made for each of them.

Paul Is Arrested

[27]When the period of seven days for
the ceremony was almost over, some of
the Jewish people from Asia saw Paul in
the temple. They got a large crowd together and started attacking him. [28]They
were shouting, "Friends, help us! This
man goes around everywhere, saying
bad things about our nation and about
the Law of Moses and about this temple.
He has even brought shame to this holy
temple by bringing in Gentiles." [29]Some
of them thought that Paul had brought
Trophimus from Ephesus into the temple, because they had seen them together in the city.
[30]The whole city was in an uproar,
and the people turned into a mob. They
grabbed Paul and dragged him out of
the temple. Then suddenly the doors
were shut. [31]The people were about to
kill Paul when the Roman army commander heard that all Jerusalem was
starting to riot. [32]So he quickly took
some soldiers and officers and ran to
where the crowd had gathered.
As soon as the mob saw the commander and soldiers, they stopped beating
Paul. [33]The army commander went over
and arrested him and had him bound
with two chains. Then he tried to find
out who Paul was and what he had
done. [34]Part of the crowd shouted one
thing, and part of them shouted something else. But they were making so
much noise that the commander could
not find out a thing. Then he ordered
Paul to be taken into the fortress. [35]As
they reached the steps, the crowd became so wild that the soldiers had to lift
Paul up and carry him. [36]The crowd fol-

[d]**21.9** *unmarried*: Or "virgin." [e]**21.18** *James*: The Lord's brother. [f]**21.25** *not to commit any terrible sexual sins*: See the note at 15.20.

lowed and kept shouting, "Kill him! Kill him!"

Paul Speaks to the Crowd

37 When Paul was about to be taken into the fortress, he asked the commander, "Can I say something to you?"

"How do you know Greek?" the commander asked. 38 "Aren't you that Egyptian who started a riot not long ago and led four thousand terrorists into the desert?"

39 "No!" Paul replied. "I am a Jew from Tarsus, an important city in Cilicia. Please let me speak to the crowd."

40 The commander told him he could speak, so Paul stood on the steps and motioned to the people. When they were quiet, he spoke to them in Aramaic:

22 "My friends and leaders of our nation, listen as I explain what happened!" 2 When the crowd heard Paul speak to them in Aramaic, they became even quieter. Then Paul said:

3 I am a Jew, born and raised in the city of Tarsus in Cilicia. I was a student of Gamaliel and was taught to follow every single law of our ancestors. In fact, I was just as eager to obey God as any of you are today.

4 I made trouble for everyone who followed the Lord's Way,[g] and I even had some of them killed. I had others arrested and put in jail. I didn't care if they were men or women. 5 The high priest and all the council members can tell you that this is true. They even gave me letters to the Jewish leaders in Damascus, so that I could arrest people there and bring them to Jerusalem to be punished.

6 One day about noon I was getting close to Damascus, when a bright light from heaven suddenly flashed around me. 7 I fell to the ground and heard a voice asking, "Saul, Saul, why are you so cruel to me?"

8 "Who are you?" I answered.

The Lord replied, "I am Jesus from Nazareth! I am the one you are so cruel to." 9 The men who were traveling with me saw the light, but did not hear the voice.

10 I asked, "Lord, what do you want me to do?"

Then he told me, "Get up and go to Damascus. When you get there, you will be told what to do." 11 The light had been so bright that I couldn't see. And the other men had to lead me by the hand to Damascus.

12 In that city there was a man named Ananias, who faithfully obeyed the Law of Moses and was well liked by all the Jewish people living there. 13 He came to me and said, "Saul, my friend, you can now see again!"

At once I could see. 14 Then Ananias told me, "The God that our ancestors worshiped has chosen you to know what he wants done. He has chosen you to see the One Who Obeys God[h] and to hear his voice. 15 You must tell everyone what you have seen and heard. 16 What are you waiting for? Get up! Be baptized, and wash away your sins by praying to the Lord."

17 After this I returned to Jerusalem and went to the temple to pray. There I had a vision 18 of the Lord who said to me, "Hurry and leave Jerusalem! The people won't listen to what you say about me."

19 I replied, "Lord, they know that in many of our meeting places I arrested and beat people who had faith in you. 20 Stephen was killed because he spoke for you, and I stood there and cheered them on. I even guarded the clothes of the men who murdered him."

21 But the Lord told me to go, and he promised to send me far away to the Gentiles.

22 The crowd listened until Paul said this. Then they started shouting, "Get rid of this man! He doesn't deserve to live." 23 They kept shouting. They waved their clothes around and threw dust into the air.

Paul and the Roman Army Commander

24 The Roman commander ordered Paul to be taken into the fortress and beaten with a whip. He did this to find out why the people were screaming at Paul.

25 While the soldiers were tying Paul up to be beaten, he asked the officer standing there, "Is it legal to beat a Roman citizen before he has been tried in court?"

26 When the officer heard this, he went to the commander and said, "What are you doing? This man is a Roman citizen!"

27 The commander went to Paul and asked, "Tell me, are you a Roman citizen?"

"Yes," Paul answered.

28 The commander then said, "I paid a lot of money to become a Roman citizen."[i]

But Paul replied, "I was born a Roman citizen."

29 The men who were about to beat and question Paul quickly backed off.

[g] 22.4 *followed the Lord's Way*: See the note at 9.2. [h] 22.14 *One Who Obeys God*: See the note at 7.52. [i] 22.28 *Roman citizen*: See the note at 16.37.

And the commander himself was frightened when he realized that he had put a Roman citizen in chains.

Paul Is Tried by the Council

[30]The next day the commander wanted to know the real reason why the Jewish leaders had brought charges against Paul. So he had Paul's chains removed, and he ordered the chief priests and the whole council to meet. Then he had Paul led in and made him stand in front of them.

23 Paul looked straight at the council members and said, "My friends, to this day I have served God with a clear conscience!"

[2]Then Ananias the high priest ordered the men standing beside Paul to hit him on the mouth. [3]Paul turned to the high priest and said, "You whitewashed wall![j] God will hit you. You sit there to judge me by the Law of Moses. But at the same time you order men to break the Law by hitting me."

[4]The men standing beside Paul asked, "Don't you know you are insulting God's high priest?"

[5]Paul replied, "Oh! I didn't know he was the high priest. The Scriptures do tell us not to speak evil about a leader of our people."

[6]When Paul saw that some of the council members were Sadducees and others were Pharisees, he shouted, "My friends, I am a Pharisee and the son of a Pharisee. I am on trial simply because I believe that the dead will be raised to life."

[7]As soon as Paul said this, the Pharisees and the Sadducees got into a big argument, and the council members started taking sides. [8]The Sadducees do not believe in angels or spirits or that the dead will rise to life. But the Pharisees believe in all of these, [9]and so there was a lot of shouting. Some of the teachers of the Law of Moses were Pharisees. Finally, they became angry and said, "We don't find anything wrong with this man. Maybe a spirit or an angel really did speak to him."

[10]The argument became fierce, and the commander was afraid that Paul would be pulled apart. So he ordered the soldiers to go in and rescue Paul. Then they took him back into the fortress.

[11]That night the Lord stood beside Paul and said, "Don't worry! Just as you have told others about me in Jerusalem, you must also tell about me in Rome."

A Plot To Kill Paul

[12-13]The next morning more than forty Jewish men got together and vowed that they would not eat or drink anything until they had killed Paul. [14]Then some of them went to the chief priests and the nation's leaders and said, "We have promised God that we would not eat a thing until we have killed Paul. [15]You and everyone in the council must go to the commander and pretend that you want to find out more about the charges against Paul. Ask for him to be brought before your court. Meanwhile, we will be waiting to kill him before he gets there."

[16]When Paul's nephew heard about the plot, he went to the fortress and told Paul about it. [17]So Paul said to one of the army officers, "Take this young man to the commander. He has something to tell him."

[18]The officer took him to the commander and said, "The prisoner named Paul asked me to bring this young man to you, because he has something to tell you."

[19]The commander took the young man aside and asked him in private, "What do you want to tell me?"

[20]He answered, "Some men are planning to ask you to bring Paul down to the Jewish council tomorrow. They will claim that they want to find out more about him. [21]But please don't do what they say. More than forty men are going to attack Paul. They have made a vow not to eat or drink anything until they have killed him. Even now they are waiting to hear what you decide."

[22]The commander sent the young man away after saying to him, "Don't let anyone know that you told me this."

Paul Is Sent to Felix the Governor

[23]The commander called in two of his officers and told them, "By nine o'clock tonight have two hundred soldiers ready to go to Caesarea. Take along seventy men on horseback and two hundred foot soldiers with spears. [24]Get a horse ready for Paul and make sure that he gets safely through to Felix the governor."

[25]The commander wrote a letter that said:

> [26]Greetings from Claudius Lysias to the Honorable Governor Felix:
>
> [27]Some Jews grabbed this man and were about to kill him. But when I found out that he was a Roman citizen, I took some soldiers and rescued him.
>
> [28]I wanted to find out what they had against him. So I brought him before their council [29]and learned that the charges concern only their religious laws. This man isn't guilty of anything for which he should die or even be put in jail.

[j]23.3 *whitewashed wall*: Someone who pretends to be good, but really isn't.

30 As soon as I learned that there
was a plot against him, I sent him to
you and told their leaders to bring
charges against him in your court.
31 The soldiers obeyed the commander's orders, and that same night they
took Paul to the city of Antipatris. 32 The
next day the foot soldiers returned to
the fortress and let the soldiers on
horseback take him the rest of the way.
33 When they came to Caesarea, they
gave the letter to the governor and
handed Paul over to him.
34 The governor read the letter. Then
he asked Paul and found out that he was
from Cilicia. 35 The governor said, "I will
listen to your case as soon as the people
come to bring their charges against
you." After saying this, he gave orders
for Paul to be kept as a prisoner in
Herod's palace.[k]

Paul Is Accused in the Court of Felix

24 Five days later Ananias the high
priest, together with some of their
leaders and a lawyer named Tertullus,
went to the governor to present their
case against Paul. 2 So Paul was called in,
and Tertullus stated the case against him:[l]
Honorable Felix, you have brought
our people a long period of peace,
and because of your concern our nation is much better off. 3 All of us are
always grateful for what you have
done. 4 I don't want to bother you,
but please be patient with us and listen to me for just a few minutes.
5 This man has been found to be a
real pest and troublemaker for Jews
all over the world. He is also a
leader of a group called Nazarenes.
6-8 When he tried to disgrace the
temple, we arrested him.[m] If you
question him, you will find out for
yourself that our charges are true.
9 The Jewish crowd spoke up and
agreed with what Tertullus had said.

Paul Defends Himself

10 The governor motioned for Paul to
speak, and he began:
I know that you have judged the
people of our nation for many years,
and I am glad to defend myself in
your court.
11 It was no more than twelve days
ago that I went to worship in
Jerusalem. You can find this out easily enough. 12 Never once did the
Jews find me arguing with anyone in
the temple. I didn't cause trouble in
the Jewish meeting places or in the
city itself. 13 There is no way that
they can prove these charges that
they are now bringing against me.
14 I admit that their leaders think
that the Lord's Way[n] which I follow
is based on wrong beliefs. But I still
worship the same God that my ancestors worshiped. And I believe
everything written in the Law of
Moses and in the Prophets.[o] 15 I am
just as sure as these people are that
God will raise from death everyone
who is good or evil. 16 And because I
am sure, I try my best to have a clear
conscience in whatever I do for God
or for people.
17 After being away for several
years, I returned here to bring gifts
for the poor people of my nation and
to offer sacrifices. 18 This is what I
was doing when I was found going
through a ceremony in the temple. I
wasn't with a crowd, and there was
no uproar.
19 Some Jews from Asia were there
at that time, and if they have anything to say against me, they should
be here now. 20 Or ask the ones who
are here. They can tell you that they
didn't find me guilty of anything
when I was tried by their own council. 21 The only charge they can bring
against me is what I shouted out in
court, when I said, "I am on trial today because I believe that the dead
will be raised to life!"
22 Felix knew a lot about the Lord's
Way.[p] But he brought the trial to an end
and said, "I will make my decision after
Lysias the commander arrives." 23 He
then ordered the army officer to keep
Paul under guard, but not to lock him up
or to stop his friends from helping him.

Paul Is Kept under Guard

24 Several days later Felix and his wife
Drusilla, who was Jewish, went to the
place where Paul was kept under guard.
They sent for Paul and listened while he
spoke to them about having faith in
Christ Jesus. 25 But Felix was frightened
when Paul started talking to them about
doing right, about self-control, and
about the coming judgment. So he said
to Paul, "That's enough for now. You
may go. But when I have time I will send

[k] **23.35** *Herod's palace*: The palace built by Herod the Great and used by the Roman governors of Palestine. [l] **24.2** *Paul was called in, and Tertullus stated the case against him*: Or "Tertullus was called in and stated the case against Paul." [m] **24.6-8** *we arrested him*: Some manuscripts add, "We wanted to judge him by our own laws. But Lysias the commander took him away from us by force. Then Lysias ordered us to bring our charges against this man in your court." [n] **24.14** *the Lord's Way*: See the note at 9.2. [o] **24.14** *Law of Moses . . . the Prophets*: The Jewish Scriptures, that is, the Old Testament. [p] **24.22** *the Lord's Way*: See the note at 9.2.

for you.” [26]After this, Felix often sent
for Paul and talked with him, because
he hoped that Paul would offer him a
bribe.
[27]Two years later Porcius Festus became governor in place of Felix. But
since Felix wanted to do the Jewish
leaders a favor, he kept Paul in jail.

Paul Asks To Be Tried by the Roman Emperor

25 Three days after Festus had become governor, he went from
Caesarea to Jerusalem. [2]There the chief
priests and some Jewish leaders told
him about their charges against Paul.
They also asked Festus [3]if he would be
willing to bring Paul to Jerusalem. They
begged him to do this because they
were planning to attack and kill Paul on
the way. [4]But Festus told them, “Paul
will be kept in Caesarea, and I am soon
going there myself. [5]If he has done anything wrong, let your leaders go with
me and bring charges against him
there.”
[6]Festus stayed in Jerusalem for eight
or ten more days before going to Caesarea. Then the next day he took his
place as judge and had Paul brought
into court. [7]As soon as Paul came in, the
Jewish leaders from Jerusalem
crowded around him and said he was
guilty of many serious crimes. But they
could not prove anything. [8]Then Paul
spoke in his own defense, “I have not
broken the Law of my people. And I
have not done anything against either
the temple or the Emperor.”
[9]Festus wanted to please the leaders.
So he asked Paul, “Are you willing to go
to Jerusalem and be tried by me on
these charges?”
[10]Paul replied, “I am on trial in the
Emperor’s court, and that’s where I
should be tried. You know very well that
I have not done anything to harm the
Jewish nation. [11]If I had done something
deserving death, I would not ask to escape the death penalty. But I am not
guilty of any of these crimes, and no one
has the right to hand me over to these
people. I now ask to be tried by the Emperor himself.”
[12]After Festus had talked this over
with members of his council, he told
Paul, “You have asked to be tried by the
Emperor, and to the Emperor you will
go!”

Paul Speaks to Agrippa and Bernice

[13]A few days later King Agrippa and
Bernice came to Caesarea to visit Festus. [14]They had been there for several
days, when Festus told the king about
the charges against Paul. He said:
Felix left a man here in jail, [15]and
when I went to Jerusalem, the chief
priests and the Jewish leaders came
and asked me to find him guilty. [16]I
told them that it isn’t the Roman
custom to hand a man over to people who are bringing charges
against him. He must first have the
chance to meet them face to face
and to defend himself against their
charges.
[17]So when they came here with
me, I wasted no time. On the very
next day I took my place on the
judge’s bench and ordered him to be
brought in. [18]But when the men
stood up to make their charges
against him, they did not accuse him
of any of the crimes that I thought
they would. [19]Instead, they argued
with him about some of their beliefs
and about a dead man named Jesus,
who Paul said was alive.
[20]Since I did not know how to find
out the truth about all this, I asked
Paul if he would be willing to go to
Jerusalem and be put on trial there.
[21]But Paul asked to be kept in jail
until the Emperor could decide his
case. So I ordered him to be kept
here until I could send him to the
Emperor.
[22]Then Agrippa said to Festus, “I
would also like to hear what this man
has to say.”
Festus answered, “You can hear him
tomorrow.”
[23]The next day Agrippa and Bernice
made a big show as they came into the
meeting room. High ranking army officers and leading citizens of the town
were also there. Festus then ordered
Paul to be brought in [24]and said:
King Agrippa and other guests,
look at this man! Every Jew from
Jerusalem and Caesarea has come
to me, demanding for him to be put
to death. [25]I have not found him
guilty of any crime deserving death.
But because he has asked to be
judged by the Emperor, I have decided to send him to Rome.
[26]I have to write some facts about
this man to the Emperor. So I have
brought him before all of you, but
especially before you, King Agrippa.
After we have talked about his case,
I will then have something to write.
[27]It makes no sense to send a prisoner to the Emperor without stating
the charges against him.

Paul’s Defense before Agrippa

26 Agrippa told Paul, “You may now
speak for yourself.”
Paul stretched out his hand and said:
[2]King Agrippa, I am glad for this
chance to defend myself before you
today on all these charges that my
own people have brought against

me. 3You know a lot about our religious customs and the beliefs that
divide us. So I ask you to listen patiently to me.
4-5All the Jews have known me
since I was a child. They know what
kind of life I have lived in my own
country and in Jerusalem. And if
they were willing, they could tell you
that I was a Pharisee, a member of a
group that is stricter than any other.
6Now I am on trial because I believe
the promise God made to our people
long ago.
7Day and night our twelve tribes
have earnestly served God, waiting
for his promised blessings. King
Agrippa, because of this hope, the
Jewish leaders have brought
charges against me. 8Why should
any of you doubt that God raises
the dead to life?
9I once thought that I should do
everything I could to oppose Jesus
from Nazareth. 10I did this first in
Jerusalem, and with the authority of
the chief priests I put many of God's
people in jail. I even voted for them
to be killed. 11I often had them punished in our meeting places, and I
tried to make them give up their
faith. In fact, I was so angry with
them, that I went looking for them in
foreign cities.
12King Agrippa, one day I was on
my way to Damascus with the authority and permission of the chief
priests. 13About noon I saw a light
brighter than the sun. It flashed
from heaven on me and on everyone
traveling with me. 14We all fell to the
ground. Then I heard a voice say to
me in Aramaic, "Saul, Saul, why are
you so cruel to me? It's foolish to
fight against me!"
15"Who are you?" I asked.
Then the Lord answered, "I am
Jesus! I am the one you are so cruel
to. 16Now stand up. I have appeared
to you, because I have chosen you
to be my servant. You are to tell others what you have learned about
me and what I will show you
later."
17The Lord also said, "I will protect you from the Jews and from the
Gentiles that I am sending you to. 18I
want you to open their eyes, so that
they will turn from darkness to light
and from the power of Satan to God.
Then their sins will be forgiven, and
by faith in me they will become part
of God's holy people."
19King Agrippa, I obeyed this vision from heaven. 20First I preached
to the people in Damascus, and then
I went to Jerusalem and all over
Judea. Finally, I went to the Gentiles
and said, "Stop sinning and turn to
God! Then prove what you have
done by the way you live."
21That is why some men grabbed
me in the temple and tried to kill
me. 22But all this time God has
helped me, and I have preached both
to the rich and to the poor. I have
told them only what the prophets
and Moses said would happen. 23I
told them how the Messiah would
suffer and be the first to be raised
from death, so that he could bring
light to his own people and to the
Gentiles.
24Before Paul finished defending himself, Festus shouted, "Paul, you're crazy!
Too much learning has driven you out of
your mind."
25But Paul replied, "Honorable Festus,
I am not crazy. What I am saying is true,
and it makes sense. 26None of these
things happened off in a corner somewhere. I am sure that King Agrippa
knows what I am talking about. That's
why I can speak so plainly to him."
27Then Paul said to Agrippa, "Do you
believe what the prophets said? I know
you do."
28Agrippa asked Paul, "In such a short
time do you think you can talk me into
being a Christian?"
29Paul answered, "Whether it takes
a short time or a long time, I wish you
and everyone else who hears me today
would become just like me! Except, of
course, for these chains."
30Then King Agrippa, Governor Festus, Bernice, and everyone who was
with them got up. 31But before they left,
they said, "This man isn't guilty of anything. He doesn't deserve to die or to be
put in jail."
32Agrippa told Festus, "Paul could
have been set free, if he had not asked
to be tried by the Roman Emperor."

Paul Is Taken to Rome

27 When it was time for us to sail to
Rome, Captain Julius from the
Emperor's special troops was put in
charge of Paul and the other prisoners.
2We went aboard a ship from Adramyt-
tium that was about to sail to some
ports along the coast of Asia. Aristarchus from Thessalonica in Macedonia
sailed on the ship with us.
3The next day we came to shore at
Sidon. Captain Julius was very kind to
Paul. He even let him visit his friends, so
they could give him whatever he
needed. 4When we left Sidon, the winds
were blowing against us, and we sailed
close to the island of Cyprus to be
safe from the wind. 5Then we sailed
south of Cilicia and Pamphylia until we
came to the port of Myra in Lycia.
6There the army captain found a ship

from Alexandria that was going to Italy.
So he ordered us to board that ship.
7We sailed along slowly for several
days and had a hard time reaching
Cnidus. The wind would not let us go
any farther in that direction, so we
sailed past Cape Salmone, where the island of Crete would protect us from the
wind. 8We went slowly along the coast
and finally reached a place called Fair
Havens, not far from the town of Lasea.
9By now we had already lost a lot of
time, and sailing was no longer safe. In
fact, even the Great Day of Forgiveness[q]
was past. 10Then Paul spoke to the crew
of the ship, "Men, listen to me! If we sail
now, our ship and its cargo will be badly
damaged, and many lives will be lost."
11But Julius listened to the captain of
the ship and its owner, rather than to
Paul.
12The harbor at Fair Havens wasn't a
good place to spend the winter. Because
of this, almost everyone agreed that we
should at least try to sail along the coast
of Crete as far as Phoenix. It had a harbor that opened toward the southwest
and northwest,[r] and we could spend the
winter there.

The Storm at Sea

13When a gentle wind from the south
started blowing, the men thought it
was a good time to do what they had
planned. So they pulled up the anchor,
and we sailed along the coast of Crete.
14But soon a strong wind called "The
Northeaster" blew against us from the
island. 15The wind struck the ship, and
we could not sail against it. So we let
the wind carry the ship.
16We went along the island of Cauda
on the side that was protected from the
wind. We had a hard time holding the
lifeboat in place, 17but finally we got it
where it belonged. Then the sailors
wrapped ropes around the ship to hold
it together. They lowered the sail and let
the ship drift along, because they were
afraid it might hit the sandbanks in the
gulf of Syrtis.
18The storm was so fierce that the
next day they threw some of the ship's
cargo overboard. 19Then on the third
day, with their bare hands they threw
overboard some of the ship's gear. 20For
several days we could not see either the
sun or the stars. A strong wind kept
blowing, and we finally gave up all hope
of being saved.
21Since none of us had eaten anything
for a long time, Paul stood up and told
the men:

You should have listened to me! If
you had stayed on in Crete, you
would not have had this damage and
loss. 22But now I beg you to cheer
up, because you will be safe. Only
the ship will be lost.
23I belong to God, and I worship
him. Last night he sent an angel 24to
tell me, "Paul, don't be afraid! You
will stand trial before the Emperor.
And because of you, God will save
the lives of everyone on the ship."
25Cheer up! I am sure that God will
do exactly what he promised. 26But
we will first be shipwrecked on
some island.

27For fourteen days and nights we had
been blown around over the Mediterranean Sea. But about midnight the
sailors realized that we were getting
near land. 28They measured and found
that the water was about one hundred
twenty feet deep. A little later they measured again and found it was only about
ninety feet. 29The sailors were afraid
that we might hit some rocks, and they
let down four anchors from the back of
the ship. Then they prayed for daylight.
30The sailors wanted to escape from
the ship. So they lowered the lifeboat
into the water, pretending that they
were letting down an anchor from the
front of the ship. 31But Paul said to Captain Julius and the soldiers, "If the
sailors don't stay on the ship, you won't
have any chance to save your lives."
32The soldiers then cut the ropes that
held the lifeboat and let it fall into the
sea.
33Just before daylight Paul begged the
people to eat something. He told them,
"For fourteen days you have been so
worried that you haven't eaten a thing.
34I beg you to eat something. Your lives
depend on it. Do this and not one of you
will be hurt."
35After Paul had said this, he took a
piece of bread and gave thanks to God.
Then in front of everyone, he broke the
bread and ate some. 36They all felt encouraged, and each of them ate something. 37There were 276 people on the
ship, 38and after everyone had eaten,
they threw the cargo of wheat into the
sea to make the ship lighter.

The Shipwreck

39Morning came, and the ship's crew
saw a coast that they did not recognize.
But they did see a cove with a beach. So
they decided to try to run the ship
aground on the beach. 40They cut the
anchors loose and let them sink into the

[q]27.9 *Great Day of Forgiveness*: This Jewish festival took place near the end of September. The sailing season was dangerous after the middle of September, and it was stopped completely between the middle of November and the middle of March. [r]27.12 *southwest and northwest*: Or "northeast and southeast."

sea. At the same time they untied the
ropes that were holding the rudders.
Next, they raised the sail at the front of
the ship and let the wind carry the ship
toward the beach. 41But it ran aground
on a sandbank. The front of the ship
stuck firmly in the sand, and the rear
was being smashed by the force of the
waves.
42The soldiers decided to kill the prisoners to keep them from swimming
away and escaping. 43But Captain Julius
wanted to save Paul's life, and he did
not let the soldiers do what they had
planned. Instead, he ordered everyone
who could swim to dive into the water
and head for shore. 44Then he told the
others to hold on to planks of wood or
parts of the ship. At last, everyone safely
reached shore.

On the Island of Malta

28 When we came ashore, we
learned that the island was called
Malta. 2The local people were very
friendly, and they welcomed us by building a fire, because it was rainy and
cold.
3After Paul had gathered some wood
and had put it on the fire, the heat
caused a snake to crawl out, and it bit
him on the hand. 4When the local people saw the snake hanging from Paul's
hand, they said to each other, "This man
must be a murderer! He didn't drown in
the sea, but the goddess of justice will
kill him anyway."
5Paul shook the snake off into the fire
and wasn't harmed. 6The people kept
thinking that Paul would either swell up
or suddenly drop dead. They watched
him for a long time, and when nothing
happened to him, they changed their
minds and said, "This man is a god."
7The governor of the island was
named Publius, and he owned some of
the land around there. Publius was very
friendly and welcomed us into his home
for three days. 8His father was in bed,
sick with fever and stomach trouble,
and Paul went to visit him. Paul healed
the man by praying and placing his
hands on him.
9After this happened, everyone on the
island brought their sick people to Paul,
and they were all healed. 10The people
were very respectful to us, and when
we sailed, they gave us everything we
needed.

From Malta to Rome

11Three months later we sailed in a
ship that had been docked at Malta for
the winter. The ship was from Alexandria in Egypt and was known as "The
Twin Gods."[s] 12We arrived in Syracuse
and stayed for three days. 13From there
we sailed to Rhegium. The next day a
south wind began to blow, and two days
later we arrived in Puteoli. 14There we
found some of the Lord's followers, who
begged us to stay with them. A week
later we left for the city of Rome.
15Some of the followers in Rome
heard about us and came to meet us at
the Market of Appius and at the Three
Inns. When Paul saw them, he thanked
God and was encouraged.

Paul in Rome

16We arrived in Rome, and Paul was
allowed to live in a house by himself
with a soldier to guard him.
17Three days after we got there, Paul
called together some of the Jewish leaders and said:

> My friends, I have never done any-
> thing to hurt our people, and I have
> never gone against the customs of
> our ancestors. But in Jerusalem I
> was handed over as a prisoner to the
> Romans. 18They looked into the
> charges against me and wanted to
> release me. They found that I had
> not done anything deserving death.
> 19The Jewish leaders disagreed, so I
> asked to be tried by the Emperor.
>
> But I don't have anything to say
> against my own nation. 20I am
> bound by these chains because of
> what we people of Israel hope for.
> That's why I have called you here to
> talk about this hope of ours.

21The leaders replied, "No one from
Judea has written us a letter about you.
And not one of them has come here to
report on you or to say anything against
you. 22But we would like to hear what
you have to say. We understand that
people everywhere are against this new
group."
23They agreed on a time to meet with
Paul, and many of them came to his
house. From early morning until late in
the afternoon, Paul talked to them about
God's kingdom. He used the Law of
Moses and the Books of the Prophets[t] to
try to win them over to Jesus.
24Some of the leaders agreed with
what Paul said, but others did not.
25Since they could not agree among
themselves, they started leaving. But
Paul said, "The Holy Spirit said the right
thing when he sent Isaiah the prophet
26to tell our ancestors,

> 'Go to these people
> and tell them:

[s]**28.11** *known as "The Twin Gods"*: Or "carried on its bow a wooden carving of the Twin Gods." These gods were Castor and Pollux, two of the favorite gods among sailors. [t]**28.23** *Law of Moses and the Books of the Prophets*: The Jewish Bible, that is, the Old Testament.

You will listen and listen,
but never understand.
You will look and look,
but never see.
27 All of you
have stubborn hearts.
Your ears are stopped up,
and your eyes are covered.
You cannot see or hear
or understand.
If you could,
you would turn to me,
and I would heal you.' "

28-29 Paul said, "You may be sure that God wants to save the Gentiles! And they will listen."[u]
30 For two years Paul stayed in a rented house and welcomed everyone who came to see him. 31 He bravely preached about God's kingdom and taught about the Lord Jesus Christ, and no one tried to stop him.

[u]28.28,29 *And they will listen*: Some manuscripts add, "After Paul said this, the people left, but they got into a fierce argument among themselves."

ROMANS

ABOUT THIS BOOK

Paul wrote this letter to introduce himself and his message to the church at Rome. He had never been to this important city, although he knew the names of many Christians there and hoped to visit them soon (15.22—16.21). Paul tells them that he is an apostle, chosen to preach the good news (1.1). And the message he proclaims "is God's powerful way of saving all people who have faith, whether they are Jews or Gentiles" (1.16).

Paul reminds his readers, "All of us have sinned and fallen short of God's glory" (3.23). But how can we be made acceptable to God? This is the main question that Paul answers in this letter. He begins by showing how everyone has failed to do what God requires. The Jews have not obeyed the Law of Moses, and the Gentiles have refused even to think about God, although God has spoken to them in many different ways (1.18—3.20).

> *Now we see how God does make us acceptable to him. . . . He accepts people only because they have faith in Jesus Christ . . . God treats us much better than we deserve, and because of Christ Jesus, he freely accepts us and sets us free from our sins.*
> *(3.21a-24)*

> *God gave Jesus to die for our sins, and he raised him to life, so that we would be made acceptable to God.*
> *(4.25)*

A QUICK LOOK AT THIS LETTER

Paul and His Message of Good News (1.1-17)
Everyone Is Guilty (1.18—3.20)
God's Way of Accepting People (3.21—4.25)
A New Life for God's People (5.1—8.39)
What about the People of Israel? (9.1—11.36)
How to Live the New Life of Love (12.1—15.13)
Paul's Plans and Personal Greetings (15.14—16.27)

---

1 From Paul, a servant of Christ
Jesus.
God chose me to be an apostle, and he
appointed me to preach the good news
2that he promised long ago by what his
prophets said in the holy Scriptures. 3-4This
good news is about his Son, our Lord Jesus Christ! As a human, he was from the
family of David. But the Holy Spirit[a]
proved that Jesus is the powerful Son of
God,[b] because he was raised from death.
5Jesus was kind to me and chose me
to be an apostle,[c] so that people of all
nations would obey and have faith. 6You
are some of those people chosen by
Jesus Christ.
7This letter is to all of you in Rome.
God loves you and has chosen you to be
his very own people.
I pray that God our Father and our
Lord Jesus Christ will be kind to you
and will bless you with peace!

[a]1.4 *the Holy Spirit*: Or "his own spirit of holiness." [b]1.4 *proved that Jesus is the powerful Son of God*: Or "proved in a powerful way that Jesus is the Son of God." [c]1.5 *Jesus was kind to me and chose me to be an apostle*: Or "Jesus was kind to us and chose us to be his apostles."

A Prayer of Thanks

[8]First, I thank God in the name of Jesus Christ for all of you. I do this because people everywhere in the world are talking about your faith. [9]God has seen how I never stop praying for you, while I serve him with all my heart and tell the good news about his Son.

[10]In all my prayers, I ask God to make it possible for me to visit you. [11]I want to see you and share with you the same blessings that God's Spirit has given me. Then you will grow stronger in your faith. [12]What I am saying is that we can encourage each other by the faith that is ours.

[13]My friends, I want you to know that I have often planned to come for a visit. But something has always kept me from doing it. I want to win followers to Christ in Rome, as I have done in many other places. [14-15]It doesn't matter if people are civilized and educated, or if they are uncivilized and uneducated. I must tell the good news to everyone. That's why I am eager to visit all of you in Rome.

The Power of the Good News

[16]I am proud of the good news! It is God's powerful way of saving all people who have faith, whether they are Jews or Gentiles. [17]The good news tells how God accepts everyone who has faith, but only those who have faith.[d] It is just as the Scriptures say, "The people God accepts because of their faith will live."[e]

Everyone Is Guilty

[18]From heaven God shows how angry he is with all the wicked and evil things that sinful people do to crush the truth. [19]They know everything that can be known about God, because God has shown it all to them. [20]God's eternal power and character cannot be seen. But from the beginning of creation, God has shown what these are like by all he has made. That's why those people don't have any excuse. [21]They know about God, but they don't honor him or even thank him. Their thoughts are useless, and their stupid minds are in the dark. [22]They claim to be wise, but they are fools. [23]They don't worship the glorious and eternal God. Instead, they worship idols that are made to look like humans who cannot live forever, and like birds, animals, and reptiles.

[24]So God let these people go their own way. They did what they wanted to do, and their filthy thoughts made them do shameful things with their bodies. [25]They gave up the truth about God for a lie, and they worshiped God's creation instead of God, who will be praised forever. Amen.

[26]God let them follow their own evil desires. Women no longer wanted to have sex in a natural way, and they did things with each other that were not natural. [27]Men behaved in the same way. They stopped wanting to have sex with women and had strong desires for sex with other men. They did shameful things with each other, and what has happened to them is punishment for their foolish deeds.

[28]Since these people refused even to think about God, he let their useless minds rule over them. That's why they do all sorts of indecent things. [29]They are evil, wicked, and greedy, as well as mean in every possible way. They want what others have, and they murder, argue, cheat, and are hard to get along with. They gossip, [30]say cruel things about others, and hate God. They are proud, conceited, and boastful, always thinking up new ways to do evil.

These people don't respect their parents. [31]They are stupid, unreliable, and don't have any love or pity for others. [32]They know God has said that anyone who acts this way deserves to die. But they keep on doing evil things, and they even encourage others to do them.

God's Judgment Is Fair

2 Some of you accuse others of doing wrong. But there is no excuse for what you do. When you judge others, you condemn yourselves, because you are guilty of doing the very same things. [2]We know that God is right to judge everyone who behaves in this way. [3]Do you really think God won't punish you, when you behave exactly like the people you accuse? [4]You surely don't think much of God's wonderful goodness or of his patience and willingness to put up with you. Don't you know that the reason God is good to you is because he wants you to turn to him?

[5]But you are stubborn and refuse to turn to God. So you are making things even worse for yourselves on that day when he will show how angry he is and will judge the world with fairness. [6]God will reward each of us for what we have done. [7]He will give eternal life to everyone who has patiently done what is good in the hope of receiving glory, honor, and life that lasts forever. [8]But he will show how angry and furious he can be with every selfish person who rejects the truth and wants to do evil. [9]All who

[d] **1.17** *but only those who have faith*: Or "and faith is all that matters." [e] **1.17** *The people God accepts because of their faith will live*: Or "The people God accepts will live because of their faith."

are wicked will be punished with trouble and suffering. It doesn't matter if
they are Jews or Gentiles. [10]But all who
do right will be rewarded with glory,
honor, and peace, whether they are
Jews or Gentiles. [11]God doesn't have
any favorites!
[12]Those people who don't know about
God's Law will still be punished for
what they do wrong. And the Law will
be used to judge everyone who knows
what it says. [13]God accepts those who
obey his Law, but not those who simply
hear it.
[14]Some people naturally obey the
Law's commands, even though they
don't have the Law. [15]This proves that
the conscience is like a law written in
the human heart. And it will show
whether we are forgiven or condemned, [16]when God appoints Jesus
Christ to judge everyone's secret
thoughts, just as my message says.

The Jews and the Law

[17]Some of you call yourselves Jews.
You trust in the Law and take pride in
God. [18]By reading the Scriptures you
learn how God wants you to behave,
and you discover what is right. [19]You are
sure that you are a guide for the blind
and a light for all who are in the dark.
[20]And since there is knowledge and
truth in God's Law, you think you can
instruct fools and teach young people.
[21]But how can you teach others when
you refuse to learn? You preach that it is
wrong to steal. But do you steal? [22]You
say people should be faithful in marriage. But are you faithful? You hate
idols, yet you rob their temples. [23]You
take pride in the Law, but you disobey
the Law and bring shame to God. [24]It is
just as the Scriptures tell us, "You have
made foreigners say insulting things
about God."
[25]Being circumcised is worthwhile, if
you obey the Law. But if you don't obey
the Law, you are no better off than people who are not circumcised. [26]In fact, if
they obey the Law, they are as good as
anyone who is circumcised. [27]So everyone who obeys the Law, but has never
been circumcised, will condemn you.
Even though you are circumcised and
have the Law, you still don't obey its
teachings.
[28]Just because you live like a Jew and
are circumcised doesn't make you a real
Jew. [29]To be a real Jew you must obey
the Law. True circumcision is something
that happens deep in your heart, not
something done to your body. And besides, you should want praise from God
and not from humans.

3 What good is it to be a Jew? What
good is it to be circumcised? [2]It is
good in a lot of ways! First of all, God's
messages were spoken to the Jews. [3]It is
true that some of them did not believe
the message. But does this mean that
God cannot be trusted, just because they
did not have faith? [4]No, indeed! God
tells the truth, even if everyone else is a
liar. The Scriptures say about God,

"Your words
will be proven true,
and in court
you will win your case."

[5]If our evil deeds show how right God
is, then what can we say? Is it wrong for
God to become angry and punish us?
What a foolish thing to ask. [6]But the answer is, "No." Otherwise, how could God
judge the world? [7]Since your lies bring
great honor to God by showing how
truthful he is, you may ask why God still
says you are a sinner. [8]You might as
well say, "Let's do something evil, so
that something good will come of it!"
Some people even claim that we are
saying this. But God is fair and will
judge them as well.

No One Is Good

[9]What does all this mean? Does it
mean that we Jews are better off[f] than
the Gentiles? No, it doesn't! Jews, as
well as Gentiles, are ruled by sin, just as
I have said. [10]The Scriptures tell us,

"No one is acceptable to God!
11 Not one of them understands
or even searches for God.
12 They have all turned away
and are worthless.
There isn't one person
who does right.
13 Their words are like
an open pit,
and their tongues are good
only for telling lies.
Each word is as deadly
as the fangs of a snake,
14 and they say nothing
but bitter curses.
15 These people quickly
become violent.
16 Wherever they go,
they leave ruin
and destruction.
17 They don't know how
to live in peace.
18 They don't even fear God."

[19]We know that everything in the Law
was written for those who are under its
power. The Law says these things to
stop anyone from making excuses and
to let God show that the whole world is

[f]3.9 *better off*: Or "worse off."

guilty. [20]God doesn't accept people simply because they obey the Law. No, indeed! All the Law does is to point out our sin.

God's Way of Accepting People

[21]Now we see how God does make us acceptable to him. The Law and the Prophets[g] tell how we become acceptable, and it isn't by obeying the Law of Moses. [22]God treats everyone alike. He accepts people only because they have faith in Jesus Christ. [23]All of us have sinned and fallen short of God's glory. [24]But God treats us much better than we deserve,[h] and because of Christ Jesus, he freely accepts us and sets us free from our sins. [25-26]God sent Christ to be our sacrifice. Christ offered his life's blood, so that by faith in him we could come to God. And God did this to show that in the past he was right to be patient and forgive sinners. This also shows that God is right when he accepts people who have faith in Jesus.

[27]What is left for us to brag about? Not a thing! Is it because we obeyed some law? No! It is because of faith. [28]We see that people are acceptable to God because they have faith, and not because they obey the Law. [29]Does God belong only to the Jews? Isn't he also the God of the Gentiles? Yes, he is! [30]There is only one God, and he accepts Gentiles as well as Jews, simply because of their faith. [31]Do we destroy the Law by our faith? Not at all! We make it even more powerful.

The Example of Abraham

4 Well then, what can we say about our ancestor Abraham? [2]If he became acceptable to God because of what he did, then he would have something to brag about. But he would never be able to brag about it to God. [3]The Scriptures say, "God accepted Abraham because Abraham had faith in him."

[4]Money paid to workers isn't a gift. It is something they earn by working. [5]But you cannot make God accept you because of something you do. God accepts sinners only because they have faith in him. [6]In the Scriptures David talks about the blessings that come to people who are acceptable to God, even though they don't do anything to deserve these blessings. David says,

[7] "God blesses people
whose sins are forgiven
and whose evil deeds
are forgotten.
[8] The Lord blesses people
whose sins are erased
from his book."

[9]Are these blessings meant for circumcised people or for those who are not circumcised? Well, the Scriptures say that God accepted Abraham because Abraham had faith in him. [10]But when did this happen? Was it before or after Abraham was circumcised? Of course, it was before.

[11]Abraham let himself be circumcised to show that he had been accepted because of his faith even before he was circumcised. This makes Abraham the father of all who are acceptable to God because of their faith, even though they are not circumcised. [12]This also makes Abraham the father of everyone who is circumcised and has faith in God, as Abraham did before he was circumcised.

The Promise Is for All Who Have Faith

[13]God promised Abraham and his descendants that he would give them the world. This promise wasn't made because Abraham had obeyed a law, but because his faith in God made him acceptable. [14]If Abraham and his descendants were given this promise because they had obeyed a law, then faith would mean nothing, and the promise would be worthless.

[15]God becomes angry when his Law is broken. But where there isn't a law, it cannot be broken. [16]Everything depends on having faith in God, so that God's promise is assured by his great kindness. This promise isn't only for Abraham's descendants who have the Law. It is for all who are Abraham's descendants because they have faith, just as he did. Abraham is the ancestor of us all. [17]The Scriptures say that Abraham would become the ancestor of many nations. This promise was made to Abraham because he had faith in God, who raises the dead to life and creates new things.

[18]God promised Abraham a lot of descendants. And when it all seemed hopeless, Abraham still had faith in God and became the ancestor of many nations. [19]Abraham's faith never became weak, not even when he was nearly a hundred years old. He knew that he was almost dead and that his wife Sarah could not have children. [20]But Abraham never doubted or questioned God's promise. His faith made him strong, and he gave all the credit to God.

[g]**3.21** *The Law and the Prophets*: The Jewish Scriptures, that is, the Old Testament.
[h]**3.24** *treats us much better than we deserve*: The Greek word *charis*, traditionally rendered "grace," is translated here and other places in the CEV to express the overwhelming kindness of God.

21 Abraham was certain that God
could do what he had promised. 22 So
God accepted him, 23 just as we read in
the Scriptures. But these words were not
written only for Abraham. 24 They were
written for us, since we will also be accepted because of our faith in God, who
raised our Lord Jesus to life. 25 God gave
Jesus to die for our sins, and he raised
him to life, so that we would be made
acceptable to God.

What It Means To Be Acceptable to God

5 By faith we have been made acceptable to God. And now, because of
our Lord Jesus Christ, we live at peace[i]
with God. 2 Christ has also introduced
us[j] to God's undeserved kindness on
which we take our stand. So we are
happy, as we look forward to sharing in
the glory of God. 3 But that's not all! We
gladly suffer,[k] because we know that
suffering helps us to endure. 4 And en-
durance builds character, which gives us
a hope 5 that will never disappoint us. All
of this happens because God has given
us the Holy Spirit, who fills our hearts
with his love.
6 Christ died for us at a time when we
were helpless and sinful. 7 No one is really willing to die for an honest person,
though someone might be willing to
die for a truly good person. 8 But God
showed how much he loved us by having Christ die for us, even though we
were sinful.
9 But there is more! Now that God has
accepted us because Christ sacrificed
his life's blood, we will also be kept safe
from God's anger. 10 Even when we were
God's enemies, he made peace with us,
because his Son died for us. Yet something even greater than friendship is
ours. Now that we are at peace with
God, we will be saved by his Son's life.
11 And in addition to everything else, we
are happy because God sent our Lord
Jesus Christ to make peace with us.

Adam and Christ

12 Adam sinned, and that sin brought
death into the world. Now everyone has
sinned, and so everyone must die. 13 Sin
was in the world before the Law came.
But no record of sin was kept, because
there was no Law. 14 Yet death still had
power over all who lived from the time
of Adam to the time of Moses. This happened, though not everyone disobeyed a
direct command from God, as Adam
did.
In some ways Adam is like Christ who
came later. 15 But the gift that God was
kind enough to give was very different
from Adam's sin. That one sin brought
death to many others. Yet in an even
greater way, Jesus Christ alone brought
God's gift of kindness to many people.
16 There is a lot of difference between
Adam's sin and God's gift. That one sin
led to punishment. But God's gift made
it possible for us to be acceptable to
him, even though we have sinned many
times. 17 Death ruled like a king because
Adam had sinned. But that cannot compare with what Jesus Christ has done.
God has been so kind to us, and he has
accepted us because of Jesus. And so we
will live and rule like kings.
18 Everyone was going to be punished
because Adam sinned. But because of
the good thing that Christ has done,
God accepts us and gives us the gift of
life. 19 Adam disobeyed God and caused
many others to be sinners. But Jesus
obeyed him and will make many people
acceptable to God.
20 The Law came, so that the full
power of sin could be seen. Yet where
sin was powerful, God's kindness was
even more powerful. 21 Sin ruled by
means of death. But God's kindness
now rules, and God has accepted us because of Jesus Christ our Lord. This
means that we will have eternal life.

Dead to Sin but Alive because of Christ

6 What should we say? Should we
keep on sinning, so that God's wonderful kindness will show up even better? 2 No, we should not! If we are dead
to sin, how can we go on sinning?
3 Don't you know that all who share in
Christ Jesus by being baptized also
share in his death? 4 When we were baptized, we died and were buried with
Christ. We were baptized, so that we
would live a new life, as Christ was raised
to life by the glory of God the Father.
5 If we shared in Jesus' death by being
baptized, we will be raised to life with
him. 6 We know that the persons we used
to be were nailed to the cross with Jesus. This was done, so that our sinful
bodies would no longer be the slaves of
sin. 7 We know that sin doesn't have
power over dead people.
8 As surely as we died with Christ, we
believe we will also live with him. 9 We
know that death no longer has any
power over Christ. He died and was
raised to life, never again to die. 10 When
Christ died, he died for sin once and for
all. But now he is alive, and he lives only
for God. 11 In the same way, you must
think of yourselves as dead to the power
of sin. But Christ Jesus has given life to
you, and you live for God.
12 Don't let sin rule your body. After
all, your body is bound to die, so don't

[i] 5.1 *we live at peace*: Some manuscripts have "let us live at peace." [j] 5.2 *introduced us*: Some manuscripts add "by faith." [k] 5.3 *We gladly suffer*: Or "Let us gladly suffer."

obey its desires 13or let any part of it become a slave of evil. Give yourselves to God, as people who have been raised from death to life. Make every part of your body a slave that pleases God. 14Don't let sin keep ruling your lives. You are ruled by God's kindness and not by the Law.

Slaves Who Do What Pleases God

15What does all this mean? Does it mean we are free to sin, because we are ruled by God's wonderful kindness and not by the Law? Certainly not! 16Don't you know that you are slaves of anyone you obey? You can be slaves of sin and die, or you can be obedient slaves of God and be acceptable to him. 17You used to be slaves of sin. But I thank God that with all your heart you obeyed the teaching you received from me. 18Now you are set free from sin and are slaves who please God.

19I am using these everyday examples, because in some ways you are still weak. You used to let the different parts of your body be slaves of your evil thoughts. But now you must make every part of your body serve God, so that you will belong completely to him.

20When you were slaves of sin, you didn't have to please God. 21But what good did you receive from the things you did? All you have to show for them is your shame, and they lead to death. 22Now you have been set free from sin, and you are God's slaves. This will make you holy and will lead you to eternal life. 23Sin pays off with death. But God's gift is eternal life given by Jesus Christ our Lord.

An Example from Marriage

7 My friends, you surely understand enough about law to know that laws only have power over people who are alive. 2For example, the Law says that a man's wife must remain his wife as long as he lives. But once her husband is dead, she is free 3to marry someone else. However, if she goes off with another man while her husband is still alive, she is said to be unfaithful.

4That is how it is with you, my friends. You are now part of the body of Christ and are dead to the power of the Law. You are free to belong to Christ, who was raised to life so that we could serve God. 5When we thought only of ourselves, the Law made us have sinful desires. It made every part of our bodies into slaves who are doomed to die. 6But the Law no longer rules over us. We are like dead people, and it cannot have any power over us. Now we can serve God in a new way by obeying his Spirit, and not in the old way by obeying the written Law.

The Battle with Sin

7Does this mean that the Law is sinful? Certainly not! But if it had not been for the Law, I would not have known what sin is really like. For example, I would not have known what it means to want something that belongs to someone else, unless the Law had told me not to do that. 8It was sin that used this command as a way of making me have all kinds of desires. But without the Law, sin is dead.

9Before I knew about the Law, I was alive. But as soon as I heard that command, sin came to life, 10and I died. The very command that was supposed to bring life to me, instead brought death. 11Sin used this command to trick me, and because of it I died. 12Still, the Law and its commands are holy and correct and good.

13Am I saying that something good caused my death? Certainly not! It was sin that killed me by using something good. Now we can see how terrible and evil sin really is. 14We know that the Law is spiritual. But I am merely a human, and I have been sold as a slave to sin. 15In fact, I don't understand why I act the way I do. I don't do what I know is right. I do the things I hate. 16Although I don't do what I know is right, I agree that the Law is good. 17So I am not the one doing these evil things. The sin that lives in me is what does them.

18I know that my selfish desires won't let me do anything that is good. Even when I want to do right, I cannot. 19Instead of doing what I know is right, I do wrong. 20And so, if I don't do what I know is right, I am no longer the one doing these evil things. The sin that lives in me is what does them.

21The Law has shown me that something in me keeps me from doing what I know is right. 22With my whole heart I agree with the Law of God. 23But in every part of me I discover something fighting against my mind, and it makes me a prisoner of sin that controls everything I do. 24What a miserable person I am. Who will rescue me from this body that is doomed to die? 25Thank God! Jesus Christ will rescue me.

So with my mind I serve the Law of God, although my selfish desires make me serve the law of sin.

Living by the Power of God's Spirit

8 If you belong to Christ Jesus, you won't be punished. 2The Holy Spirit will give you life that comes from Christ Jesus and will set you[l] free from sin and

[l]8.2 *you*: Some manuscripts have "me."

death. 3The Law of Moses cannot do this, because our selfish desires make the Law weak. But God set you free when he sent his own Son to be like us sinners and to be a sacrifice for our sin. God used Christ's body to condemn sin. 4He did this, so that we would do what the Law commands by obeying the Spirit instead of our own desires.

5People who are ruled by their desires think only of themselves. Everyone who is ruled by the Holy Spirit thinks about spiritual things. 6If our minds are ruled by our desires, we will die. But if our minds are ruled by the Spirit, we will have life and peace. 7Our desires fight against God, because they do not and cannot obey God's laws. 8If we follow our desires, we cannot please God.

9You are no longer ruled by your desires, but by God's Spirit, who lives in you. People who don't have the Spirit of Christ in them don't belong to him. 10But Christ lives in you. So you are alive because God has accepted you, even though your bodies must die because of your sins. 11Yet God raised Jesus to life! God's Spirit now lives in you, and he will raise you to life by his Spirit.

12My dear friends, we must not live to satisfy our desires. 13If you do, you will die. But you will live, if by the help of God's Spirit you say "No" to your desires. 14Only those people who are led by God's Spirit are his children. 15God's Spirit doesn't make us slaves who are afraid of him. Instead, we become his children and call him our Father.[m] 16God's Spirit makes us sure that we are his children. 17His Spirit lets us know that together with Christ we will be given what God has promised. We will also share in the glory of Christ, because we have suffered with him.

A Wonderful Future for God's People

18I am sure that what we are suffering now cannot compare with the glory that will be shown to us. 19In fact, all creation is eagerly waiting for God to show who his children are. 20Meanwhile, creation is confused, but not because it wants to be confused. God made it this way in the hope 21that creation would be set free from decay and would share in the glorious freedom of his children. 22We know that all creation is still groaning and is in pain, like a woman about to give birth.

23The Spirit makes us sure about what we will be in the future. But now we groan silently, while we wait for God to show that we are his children.[n] This means that our bodies will also be set free. 24And this hope is what saves us. But if we already have what we hope for, there is no need to keep on hoping. 25However, we hope for something we have not yet seen, and we patiently wait for it.

26In certain ways we are weak, but the Spirit is here to help us. For example, when we don't know what to pray for, the Spirit prays for us in ways that cannot be put into words. 27All of our thoughts are known to God. He can understand what is in the mind of the Spirit, as the Spirit prays for God's people. 28We know that God is always at work for the good of everyone who loves him.[o] They are the ones God has chosen for his purpose, 29and he has always known who his chosen ones would be. He had decided to let them become like his own Son, so that his Son would be the first of many children. 30God then accepted the people he had already decided to choose, and he has shared his glory with them.

God's Love

31What can we say about all this? If God is on our side, can anyone be against us? 32God did not keep back his own Son, but he gave him for us. If God did this, won't he freely give us everything else? 33If God says his chosen ones are acceptable to him, can anyone bring charges against them? 34Or can anyone condemn them? No indeed! Christ died and was raised to life, and now he is at God's right side,[p] speaking to him for us. 35Can anything separate us from the love of Christ? Can trouble, suffering, and hard times, or hunger and nakedness, or danger and death? 36It is exactly as the Scriptures say,

"For you we face death
all day long.
We are like sheep
on their way
to be butchered."

37In everything we have won more than a victory because of Christ who loves us. 38I am sure that nothing can separate us from God's love—not life or death, not angels or spirits, not the present or the future, 39and not powers above or powers below. Nothing in all creation

[m]**8.15** *our Father*: The Greek text uses the Aramaic word "Abba" (meaning "father"), which shows the close relation between the children and their father. [n]**8.23** *to show that we are his children*: These words are not in some manuscripts. The translation of the remainder of the verse would then read, "while we wait for God to set our bodies free." [o]**8.28** *God is always at work for the good of everyone who loves him*: Or "All things work for the good of everyone who loves God" or "God's Spirit always works for the good of everyone who loves God." [p]**8.34** *right side*: The place of power and honor.

can separate us from God's love for us
in Christ Jesus our Lord!

God's Choice of Israel

9 I am a follower of Christ, and the
Holy Spirit is a witness to my conscience. So I tell the truth and I am not
lying when I say 2my heart is broken
and I am in great sorrow. 3I would
gladly be placed under God's curse and
be separated from Christ for the good of
my own people. 4They are the descendants of Israel, and they are also God's
chosen people. God showed them his
glory. He made agreements with them
and gave them his Law. The temple is
theirs and so are the promises that God
made to them. 5They have those famous
ancestors, who were also the ancestors
of Jesus Christ. I pray that God, who
rules over all, will be praised forever![q]
Amen.

6It cannot be said that God broke his
promise. After all, not all of the people
of Israel are the true people of God. 7-8In
fact, when God made the promise to
Abraham, he meant only Abraham's descendants by his son Isaac. God was
talking only about Isaac when he
promised 9Sarah, "At this time next year
I will return, and you will already have a
son."

10Don't forget what happened to the
twin sons of Isaac and Rebekah. 11-12Even
before they were born or had done anything good or bad, the Lord told
Rebekah that her older son would serve
the younger one. The Lord said this to
show that he makes his own choices
and that it wasn't because of anything
either of them had done. 13That's why
the Scriptures say that the Lord liked
Jacob more than Esau.

14Are we saying that God is unfair?
Certainly not! 15The Lord told Moses
that he has pity and mercy on anyone
he wants to. 16Everything then depends
on God's mercy and not on what people
want or do. 17In the Scriptures the Lord
says to the king of Egypt, "I let you become king, so that I could show you my
power and be praised by all people on
earth." 18Everything depends on what
God decides to do, and he can either
have pity on people or make them stubborn.

God's Anger and Mercy

19Someone may ask, "How can God
blame us, if he makes us behave in the
way he wants us to?" 20But, my friend, I
ask, "Who do you think you are to question God? Does the clay have the right
to ask the potter why he shaped it the
way he did? 21Doesn't a potter have the
right to make a fancy bowl and a plain
bowl out of the same lump of clay?"

22God wanted to show his anger and
reveal his power against everyone who
deserved to be destroyed. But instead,
he patiently put up with them. 23He did
this by showing how glorious he is
when he has pity on the people he has
chosen to share in his glory. 24Whether
Jews or Gentiles, we are those chosen
ones, 25just as the Lord says in the book
of Hosea,

"Although they are not
my people,
 I will make them my people.
I will treat with love
those nations
 that have never been loved.

26 "Once they were told,
 'You are not my people.'
But in that very place
they will be called
 children of the living God."

27And this is what the prophet Isaiah
said about the people of Israel,

"The people of Israel
 are as many
as the grains of sand
 along the beach.
But only a few who are left
 will be saved.
28 The Lord will be quick
 and sure to do on earth
what he has warned
 he will do."

29Isaiah also said,

"If the Lord All-Powerful
had not spared some
 of our descendants,
we would have been destroyed
like the cities of Sodom
 and Gomorrah."[r]

Israel and the Good News

30What does all of this mean? It
means that the Gentiles were not trying
to be acceptable to God, but they found
that he would accept them if they had
faith. 31-32It also means that the people
of Israel were not acceptable to God.
And why not? It was because they were
trying[s] to be acceptable by obeying the
Law instead of by having faith in God.
The people of Israel fell over the stone
that makes people stumble, 33just as
God says in the Scriptures,

[q]**9.5** *Christ. I pray that God, who rules over all, will be praised forever*: Or "Christ, who rules over all. I pray that God will be praised forever" or "Christ. And I pray that Christ, who is God and rules over all, will be praised forever." [r]**9.29** *Sodom and Gomorrah*: During the time of Abraham the Lord destroyed these two cities because their people were so sinful.
[s]**9.31** *because they were trying*: Or "while they were trying" or "even though they were trying."

“Look! I am placing in Zion
a stone to make people
stumble and fall.
But those who have faith
in that one will never
be disappointed.”

10 Dear friends, my greatest wish
and my prayer to God is for the
people of Israel to be saved. 2I know
they love God, but they don’t understand 3what makes people acceptable to
him. So they refuse to trust God, and
they try to be acceptable by obeying the
Law. 4But Christ makes the Law no
longer necessary[t] for those who become
acceptable to God by faith.

Anyone Can Be Saved

5Moses said that a person could become acceptable to God by obeying the
Law. He did this when he wrote, “If you
want to live, you must do all that the
Law commands.”
6But people whose faith makes them
acceptable to God will never ask, “Who
will go up to heaven to bring Christ
down?” 7Neither will they ask, “Who
will go down into the world of the dead
to raise him to life?”
8All who are acceptable because of
their faith simply say, “The message is
as near as your mouth or your heart.”
And this is the same message we preach
about faith. 9So you will be saved, if you
honestly say, “Jesus is Lord,” and if you
believe with all your heart that God
raised him from death. 10God will accept
you and save you, if you truly believe
this and tell it to others.
11The Scriptures say that no one who
has faith will be disappointed, 12no matter if that person is a Jew or a Gentile.
There is only one Lord, and he is generous to everyone who asks for his help.
13All who call out to the Lord will be
saved.
14How can people have faith in the
Lord and ask him to save them, if they
have never heard about him? And how
can they hear, unless someone tells
them? 15And how can anyone tell them
without being sent by the Lord? The
Scriptures say it is a beautiful sight to
see even the feet of someone coming to
preach the good news. 16Yet not everyone has believed the message. For example, the prophet Isaiah asked, “Lord,
has anyone believed what we said?”
17No one can have faith without hearing the message about Christ. 18But am I
saying that the people of Israel did not
hear? No, I am not! The Scriptures say,

“The message was told
everywhere on earth.
It was announced
all over the world.”

19Did the people of Israel understand or
not? Moses answered this question
when he told that the Lord had said,

“I will make Israel jealous
of people
who are a nation
of nobodies.
I will make them angry
at people
who don’t understand
a thing.”

20Isaiah was fearless enough to tell that
the Lord had said,

“I was found by people
who were not looking
for me.
I appeared to the ones
who were not asking
about me.”

21And Isaiah said about the people of Israel,

“All day long the Lord
has reached out
to people who are stubborn
and refuse to obey.”

God Has Not Rejected His People

11 Am I saying that God has turned
his back on his people? Certainly
not! I am one of the people of Israel, and
I myself am a descendant of Abraham
from the tribe of Benjamin. 2God did not
turn his back on his chosen people.
Don’t you remember reading in the
Scriptures how Elijah complained to
God about the people of Israel? 3He
said, “Lord, they killed your prophets
and destroyed your altars. I am the only
one left, and now they want to kill me.”
4But the Lord told Elijah, “I still have
seven thousand followers who have not
worshiped Baal.” 5It is the same way
now. God was kind to the people of Israel, and so a few of them are still his
followers. 6This happened because of
God’s undeserved kindness and not because of anything they have done. It
could not have happened except for
God’s kindness.
7This means that only a chosen few of
the people of Israel found what all of
them were searching for. And the rest of
them were stubborn, 8just as the Scriptures say,

“God made them so stupid
that their eyes are blind,
and their ears
are still deaf.”

9Then David said,

[t] **10.4** *But Christ makes the Law no longer necessary*: Or “But Christ gives the full meaning to the Law.”

"Turn their meals
into bait for a trap,
so that they will stumble
and be given
what they deserve.
10 Blindfold their eyes!
Don't let them see.
Bend their backs
beneath a burden
that will never be lifted."

Gentiles Will Be Saved

11 Do I mean that the people of Israel
fell, never to get up again? Certainly
not! Their failure made it possible for
the Gentiles to be saved, and this will
make the people of Israel jealous. 12 But
if the rest of the world's people were
helped so much by Israel's sin and loss,
they will be helped even more by their
full return.
13 I am now speaking to you Gentiles,
and as long as I am an apostle to you, I
will take pride in my work. 14 I hope in
this way to make some of my own people jealous enough to be saved. 15 When
Israel rejected God,[u] the rest of the people in the world were able to turn to
him. So when God makes friends with
Israel, it will be like bringing the dead
back to life. 16 If part of a batch of dough
is made holy by being offered to God,
then all of the dough is holy. If the roots
of a tree are holy, the rest of the tree is
holy too.
17 You Gentiles are like branches of a
wild olive tree that were made to be part
of a cultivated olive tree. You have taken
the place of some branches that were
cut away from it. And because of this,
you enjoy the blessings that come from
being part of that cultivated tree. 18 But
don't think you are better than the
branches that were cut away. Just remember that you are not supporting the
roots of that tree. Its roots are supporting you.
19 Maybe you think those branches
were cut away, so that you could be put
in their place. 20 That's true enough. But
they were cut away because they did not
have faith, and you are where you are
because you do have faith. So don't be
proud, but be afraid. 21 If God cut away
those natural branches, couldn't he do
the same to you?
22 Now you see both how kind and
how hard God can be. He was hard on
those who fell, but he was kind to you.
And he will keep on being kind to you,
if you keep on trusting in his kindness.
Otherwise, you will be cut away too.
23 If those other branches will start
having faith, they will be made a part of
that tree again. God has the power to
put them back. 24 After all, it wasn't natural for branches to be cut from a wild
olive tree and to be made part of a cultivated olive tree. So it is much more
likely that God will join the natural
branches back to the cultivated olive
tree.

The People of Israel Will Be Brought Back

25 My friends, I don't want you Gentiles to be too proud of yourselves. So I
will explain the mystery of what has
happened to the people of Israel. Some
of them have become stubborn, and
they will stay like that until the complete number of you Gentiles has come
in. 26 In this way all of Israel will be
saved, as the Scriptures say,

"From Zion someone will come
to rescue us.
Then Jacob's descendants
will stop being evil.
27 This is what the Lord
has promised to do
when he forgives their sins."

28 The people of Israel are treated as
God's enemies, so that the good news
can come to you Gentiles. But they are
still the chosen ones, and God loves
them because of their famous ancestors.
29 God doesn't take back the gifts he has
given or forget about the people he has
chosen.
30 At one time you Gentiles rejected
God. But now Israel has rejected God,
and you have been shown mercy. 31 And
because of the mercy shown to you, they
will also be shown mercy. 32 All people
have disobeyed God, and that's why he
treats them as prisoners. But he does
this, so that he can have mercy on all of
them.
33 Who can measure the wealth and
wisdom and knowledge of God? Who
can understand his decisions or explain
what he does?

34 "Has anyone known
the thoughts of the Lord
or given him advice?
35 Has anyone loaned
something to the Lord
that must be repaid?"

36 Everything comes from the Lord. All
things were made because of him and
will return to him. Praise the Lord forever! Amen.

Christ Brings New Life

12 Dear friends, God is good. So I
beg you to offer your bodies to
him as a living sacrifice, pure and pleasing. That's the most sensible way to
serve God. 2 Don't be like the people of
this world, but let God change the way

[u] 11.15 *When Israel rejected God*: Or "When Israel was rejected."

you think. Then you will know how to
do everything that is good and pleasing
to him.
[3]I realize how kind God has been to
me, and so I tell each of you not to think
you are better than you really are. Use
good sense and measure yourself by the
amount of faith that God has given you.
[4]A body is made up of many parts, and
each of them has its own use. [5]That's
how it is with us. There are many of us,
but we each are part of the body of
Christ, as well as part of one another.
[6]God has also given each of us different gifts to use. If we can prophesy, we
should do it according to the amount of
faith we have. [7]If we can serve others,
we should serve. If we can teach, we
should teach. [8]If we can encourage others, we should encourage them. If we
can give, we should be generous. If we
are leaders, we should do our best. If
we are good to others, we should do it
cheerfully.

Rules for Christian Living

[9]Be sincere in your love for others.
Hate everything that is evil and hold
tight to everything that is good. [10]Love
each other as brothers and sisters and
honor others more than you do yourself.
[11]Never give up. Eagerly follow the Holy
Spirit and serve the Lord. [12]Let your
hope make you glad. Be patient in time
of trouble and never stop praying.
[13]Take care of God's needy people and
welcome strangers into your home.
[14]Ask God to bless everyone who mistreats you. Ask him to bless them and
not to curse them. [15]When others are
happy, be happy with them, and when
they are sad, be sad. [16]Be friendly with
everyone. Don't be proud and feel that
you are smarter than others. Make
friends with ordinary people.[v] [17]Don't
mistreat someone who has mistreated
you. But try to earn the respect of others, [18]and do your best to live at peace
with everyone.
[19]Dear friends, don't try to get even.
Let God take revenge. In the Scriptures
the Lord says,

> "I am the one to take revenge
> and pay them back."

[20]The Scriptures also say,

> "If your enemies are hungry,
> give them something to eat.
> And if they are thirsty,
> give them something
> to drink.
> This will be the same
> as piling burning coals
> on their heads."

[21]Don't let evil defeat you, but defeat
evil with good.

Obey Rulers

13 Obey the rulers who have authority over you. Only God can give
authority to anyone, and he puts these
rulers in their places of power. [2]People
who oppose the authorities are oppos-
ing what God has done, and they will be
punished. [3]Rulers are a threat to evil
people, not to good people. There is no
need to be afraid of the authorities. Just
do right, and they will praise you for it.
[4]After all, they are God's servants, and it
is their duty to help you.
If you do something wrong, you ought
to be afraid, because these rulers have
the right to punish you. They are God's
servants who punish criminals to show
how angry God is. [5]But you should obey
the rulers because you know it is the
right thing to do, and not just because of
God's anger.
[6]You must also pay your taxes. The
authorities are God's servants, and it is
their duty to take care of these matters.
[7]Pay all that you owe, whether it is taxes
and fees or respect and honor.

Love

[8]Let love be your only debt! If you
love others, you have done all that the
Law demands. [9]In the Law there are
many commands, such as, "Be faithful
in marriage. Do not murder. Do not
steal. Do not want what belongs to others." But all of these are summed up in
the command that says, "Love others as
much as you love yourself." [10]No one
who loves others will harm them. So
love is all that the Law demands.

The Day When Christ Returns

[11]You know what sort of times we live
in, and so you should live properly. It is
time to wake up. You know that the day
when we will be saved is nearer now
than when we first put our faith in the
Lord. [12]Night is almost over, and day
will soon appear. We must stop behaving as people do in the dark and be
ready to live in the light. [13]So behave
properly, as people do in the day. Don't
go to wild parties or get drunk or be
vulgar or indecent. Don't quarrel or be
jealous. [14]Let the Lord Jesus Christ
be as near to you as the clothes you
wear. Then you won't try to satisfy your
selfish desires.

Don't Criticize Others

14 Welcome all the Lord's followers,
even those whose faith is weak.
Don't criticize them for having beliefs

[v]12.16 *Make friends with ordinary people*: Or "Do ordinary jobs."

that are different from yours. [2]Some
think it is all right to eat anything, while
those whose faith is weak will eat only
vegetables. [3]But you should not criticize
others for eating or for not eating. After
all, God welcomes everyone. [4]What
right do you have to criticize someone
else's servants? Only their Lord can decide if they are doing right, and the Lord
will make sure that they do right.
[5]Some of the Lord's followers think
one day is more important than another.
Others think all days are the same. But
each of you should make up your own
mind. [6]Any followers who count one
day more important than another day
do it to honor their Lord. And any followers who eat meat give thanks to
God, just like the ones who don't eat
meat.
[7]Whether we live or die, it must be for
God, rather than for ourselves.
[8]Whether we live or die, it must be for
the Lord. Alive or dead, we still belong
to the Lord. [9]This is because Christ died
and rose to life, so that he would be the
Lord of the dead and of the living.
[10]Why do you criticize other followers
of the Lord? Why do you look down on
them? The day is coming when God will
judge all of us. [11]In the Scriptures God
says,

"I swear by my very life
that everyone will kneel down
and praise my name!"

[12]And so, each of us must give an account to God for what we do.

Don't Cause Problems for Others

[13]We must stop judging others. We
must also make up our minds not to upset anyone's faith. [14]The Lord Jesus has
made it clear to me that God considers
all foods fit to eat. But if you think some
foods are unfit to eat, then for you they
are not fit.
[15]If you are hurting others by the
foods you eat, you are not guided by
love. Don't let your appetite destroy
someone Christ died for. [16]Don't let your
right to eat bring shame to Christ.
[17]God's kingdom isn't about eating and
drinking. It is about pleasing God, about
living in peace, and about true happiness. All this comes from the Holy
Spirit. [18]If you serve Christ in this way,
you will please God and be respected by
people. [19]We should try[w] to live at peace
and help each other have a strong faith.
[20]Don't let your appetite destroy what
God has done. All foods are fit to eat,
but it is wrong to cause problems for
others by what you eat. [21]It is best not to
eat meat or drink wine or do anything
else that causes problems for other followers of the Lord. [22]What you believe
about these things should be kept between you and God. You are fortunate, if
your actions don't make you have
doubts. [23]But if you do have doubts
about what you eat, you are going
against your beliefs. And you know that
is wrong, because anything you do
against your beliefs is sin.

Please Others and Not Yourself

15 If our faith is strong, we should
be patient with the Lord's followers whose faith is weak. We should try
to please them instead of ourselves. [2]We
should think of their good and try to
help them by doing what pleases them.
[3]Even Christ did not try to please himself. But as the Scriptures say, "The people who insulted you also insulted me."
[4]And the Scriptures were written to
teach and encourage us by giving us
hope. [5]God is the one who makes us patient and cheerful. I pray that he will
help you live at peace with each other,
as you follow Christ. [6]Then all of you together will praise God, the Father of our
Lord Jesus Christ.

The Good News Is for Jews and Gentiles

[7]Honor God by accepting each other,
as Christ has accepted you. [8]I tell you
that Christ came as a servant of the
Jews to show that God has kept the
promises he made to their famous ancestors. Christ also came, [9]so that the
Gentiles would praise God for being
kind to them. It is just as the Scriptures
say,

"I will tell the nations
about you,
and I will sing praises
to your name."

[10]The Scriptures also say to the Gentiles, "Come and celebrate with God's
people."
[11]Again the Scriptures say,

"Praise the Lord,
all you Gentiles.
All you nations, come
and worship him."

[12]Isaiah says,

"Someone from David's family
will come to power.
He will rule the nations,
and they will put their hope
in him."

[13]I pray that God, who gives hope, will
bless you with complete happiness and
peace because of your faith. And may
the power of the Holy Spirit fill you with
hope.

[w]**14.19** *We should try*: Some manuscripts have "We try."

Paul's Work as a Missionary

[14]My friends, I am sure that you are very good and that you have all the knowledge you need to teach each other. [15]But I have spoken to you plainly and have tried to remind you of some things. God was so kind to me! [16]He chose me to be a servant of Christ Jesus for the Gentiles and to do the work of a priest in the service of his good news. God did this so that the Holy Spirit could make the Gentiles into a holy offering, pleasing to him.

[17]Because of Christ Jesus, I can take pride in my service for God. [18]In fact, all I will talk about is how Christ let me speak and work, so that the Gentiles would obey him. [19]Indeed, I will tell how Christ worked miracles and wonders by the power of the Holy Spirit. I have preached the good news about him all the way from Jerusalem to Illyricum. [20]But I have always tried to preach where people have never heard about Christ. I am like a builder who doesn't build on anyone else's foundation. [21]It is just as the Scriptures say,

"All who haven't been told
about him
will see him,
and those who haven't heard
about him
will understand."

Paul's Plan To Visit Rome

[22]My work has always kept me from coming to see you. [23]Now there is nothing left for me to do in this part of the world, and for years I have wanted to visit you. [24]So I plan to stop off on my way to Spain. Then after a short, but refreshing, visit with you, I hope you will quickly send me on.

[25-26]I am now on my way to Jerusalem to deliver the money that the Lord's followers in Macedonia and Achaia collected for God's needy people. [27]This is something they really wanted to do. But sharing their money with the Jews was also like paying back a debt, because the Jews had already shared their spiritual blessings with the Gentiles. [28]After I have safely delivered this money, I will visit you and then go on to Spain. [29]And when I do arrive in Rome, I know it will be with the full blessings of Christ.

[30]My friends, by the power of the Lord Jesus Christ and by the love that comes from the Holy Spirit, I beg you to pray sincerely with me and for me. [31]Pray that God will protect me from the unbelievers in Judea, and that his people in Jerusalem will be pleased with what I am doing. [32]Ask God to let me come to you and have a pleasant and refreshing visit. [33]I pray that God, who gives peace, will be with all of you. Amen.

Personal Greetings

16 I have good things to say about Phoebe, who is a leader in the church at Cenchreae. [2]Welcome her in a way that is proper for someone who has faith in the Lord and is one of God's own people. Help her in any way you can. After all, she has proved to be a respected leader for many others, including me.

[3]Give my greetings to Priscilla and Aquila. They have not only served Christ Jesus together with me, [4]but they have even risked their lives for me. I am grateful for them and so are all the Gentile churches. [5]Greet the church that meets in their home.

Greet my dear friend Epaenetus, who was the first person in Asia to have faith in Christ.

[6]Greet Mary, who has worked so hard for you.

[7]Greet my relatives[x] Andronicus and Junias,[y] who were in jail with me. They are highly respected by the apostles and were followers of Christ before I was.

[8]Greet Ampliatus, my dear friend whose faith is in the Lord.

[9]Greet Urbanus, who serves Christ along with us.

Greet my dear friend Stachys.

[10]Greet Apelles, a faithful servant of Christ.

Greet Aristobulus and his family.

[11]Greet Herodion, who is a relative[z] of mine.

Greet Narcissus and the others in his family, who have faith in the Lord.

[12]Greet Tryphaena and Tryphosa, who work hard for the Lord.

Greet my dear friend Persis. She also works hard for the Lord.

[13]Greet Rufus, that special servant of the Lord, and greet his mother, who has been like a mother to me.

[14]Greet Asyncritus, Phlegon, Hermes, Patrobas, and Hermas, as well as our friends who are with them.

[15]Greet Philologus, Julia, Nereus and his sister, and Olympas, and all of God's people who are with them.

[16]Be sure to give each other a warm greeting.

All of Christ's churches greet you.

[17]My friends, I beg you to watch out for anyone who causes trouble and divides the church by refusing to do what all of you were taught. Stay away from them! [18]They want to serve themselves and not Christ the Lord. Their flattery and fancy talk fool people who don't know any better. [19]I am glad that

[x]**16.7** *relatives*: Or "Jewish friends." [y]**16.7** *Junias*: Or Junia. Some manuscripts have Julia.
[z]**16.11, 21** *relative(s)*: See the note at verse 7.

everyone knows how well you obey
the Lord. But still, I want you to understand what is good and not have
anything to do with evil. 20Then God,
who gives peace, will soon crush Satan
under your feet. I pray that our Lord
Jesus will be kind to you.
21Timothy, who works with me, sends
his greetings, and so do my relatives,[z]
Lucius, Jason, and Sosipater.
22I, Tertius, also send my greetings. I
am a follower of the Lord, and I wrote
this letter.[a]
23-24Gaius welcomes me and the
whole church into his home, and he
sends his greetings.
Erastus, the city treasurer, and our
dear friend Quartus send their greetings too.[b]

Paul's Closing Prayer

25Praise God! He can make you
strong by means of my good news,
which is the message about[c] Jesus
Christ. For ages and ages this message
was kept secret, 26but now at last it has
been told. The eternal God commanded
his prophets to write about the good
news, so that all nations would obey
and have faith. 27And now, because of
Jesus Christ, we can praise the only
wise God forever! Amen.[d]

[z]**16.11,21** *relative(s)*: See the note at verse 7. [a]**16.22** *I wrote this letter*: Paul probably dictated this letter to Tertius. [b]**16.23,24** *send their greetings too*: Some manuscripts add, "I pray that our Lord Jesus Christ will always be kind to you. Amen." [c]**16.25** *about*: Or "from." [d]**16.27** *Amen*: Some manuscripts have verses 25-27 after 14.23. Others have the verses here and after 14.23, and one manuscript has them after 15.33.

1 CORINTHIANS

ABOUT THIS LETTER

Although this letter is called the First Letter to the Corinthians, it is not really the first one that Paul wrote to this church. We know this because he mentions in this letter that he had written one before (5.9). The Christians in Corinth had also written to him (7.1), and part of First Corinthians contains Paul's answers to questions they had asked.

Corinth is a large port city in southern Greece. Paul began his work there in a Jewish meeting place, but he had to move next door to the home of a Gentile who had become a follower of Jesus (Acts 18.1-17). Most of the followers in Corinth were poor people (1 Corinthians 1.26-29), though some of them were wealthy (1 Corinthians 11.18-21), and one was even the city treasurer (Romans 16.23). While he was in Corinth, Paul worked as a tentmaker to earn a living (Acts 18.3; 1 Corinthians 4.12; 9.1-18).

Paul was especially concerned about the way the Corinthian Christians were always arguing and dividing themselves into groups (1.10—4.21) and about the way they treated one another (5.1—6.20). These are two of Paul's main concerns as he writes this letter. But he also wants to answer the questions they asked him about marriage (7.1-40) and food offered to idols (8.1-13). Paul encourages them to worship God the right way (10.1—14.40) and to be firm in their belief that God has given them victory over death (15.1-58).

Love, Paul tells them, is even more important than faith or hope. All of the problems in the church could be solved, if all the members would love one another, as Christians should:

Love is kind and patient,
never jealous, boastful,
proud, or rude.
Love rejoices in the truth,
but not in evil.
Love is always supportive,
loyal, hopeful,
and trusting.
Love never fails!
(13.4, 5a, 6-8a)

A QUICK LOOK AT THIS LETTER

Paul's Greeting and Prayer (1.1-9)
A Call for Unity (1.10—4.21)
Problems in Relationships (5.1—7.40)
Honoring God Instead of Idols (8.1—11.1)
Guidance for Worship and Church Life (11.2—14.40)
Christ's Victory Over Death (15.1-58)
An Offering for the Poor (16.1-4)
Paul's Travel Plans (16.5-12)
Personal Concerns and Greetings (16.13-24)

1 From Paul, chosen by God to be an
apostle of Christ Jesus, and from
Sosthenes, who is also a follower.
2To God's church in Corinth. Christ
Jesus chose you to be his very own people, and you worship in his name, as we
and all others do who call him Lord.
3My prayer is that God our Father and
the Lord Jesus Christ will be kind to you
and will bless you with peace!
4I never stop thanking my God for being kind enough to give you Christ Jesus, 5who helps you speak and understand so well. 6Now you are certain that
everything we told you about our Lord
Christ Jesus is true. 7You are not missing out on any blessings, as you wait for
him to return. 8And until the day Christ
does return, he will keep you completely
innocent. 9God can be trusted, and he
chose you to be partners with his Son,
our Lord Jesus Christ.

Taking Sides

10My dear friends, as a follower of our
Lord Jesus Christ, I beg you to get along
with each other. Don't take sides. Always try to agree in what you think.
11Several people from Chloe's family[a]
have already reported to me that you
keep arguing with each other. 12They
have said that some of you claim to follow me, while others claim to follow
Apollos or Peter[b] or Christ.
13Has Christ been divided up? Was I
nailed to a cross for you? Were you baptized in my name? 14I thank God[c] that I
didn't baptize any of you except Crispus
and Gaius. 15Not one of you can say that
you were baptized in my name. 16I did
baptize the family[d] of Stephanas, but I
don't remember if I baptized anyone
else. 17Christ did not send me to baptize.
He sent me to tell the good news without using big words that would make
the cross of Christ lose its power.

Christ Is God's Power and Wisdom

18The message about the cross doesn't
make any sense to lost people. But for
those of us who are being saved, it is
God's power at work. 19As God says in
the Scriptures,

"I will destroy the wisdom
of all who claim
 to be wise.
I will confuse those
who think they know
 so much."

20What happened to those wise people? What happened to those experts in
the Scriptures? What happened to the
ones who think they have all the answers? Didn't God show that the wisdom of this world is foolish? 21God was
wise and decided not to let the people of
this world use their wisdom to learn
about him.
Instead, God chose to save only those
who believe the foolish message we
preach. 22Jews ask for miracles, and
Greeks want something that sounds
wise. 23But we preach that Christ was
nailed to a cross. Most Jews have problems with this, and most Gentiles think
it is foolish. 24Our message is God's
power and wisdom for the Jews and the
Greeks that he has chosen. 25Even when
God is foolish, he is wiser than everyone
else, and even when God is weak, he is
stronger than everyone else.
26My dear friends, remember what
you were when God chose you. The people of this world didn't think that many
of you were wise. Only a few of you
were in places of power, and not many
of you came from important families.
27But God chose the foolish things of
this world to put the wise to shame. He
chose the weak things of this world to
put the powerful to shame.
28What the world thinks is worthless,
useless, and nothing at all is what God
has used to destroy what the world considers important. 29God did all this to
keep anyone from bragging to him.
30You are God's children. He sent Christ
Jesus to save us and to make us wise,
acceptable, and holy. 31So if you want to
brag, do what the Scriptures say and
brag about the Lord.

Telling about Christ and the Cross

2 Friends, when I came and told you
the mystery[e] that God had shared
with us, I didn't use big words or try to
sound wise. 2In fact, while I was with
you, I made up my mind to speak only
about Jesus Christ, who had been nailed
to a cross.
3At first, I was weak and trembling
with fear. 4When I talked with you or
preached, I didn't try to prove anything
by sounding wise. I simply let God's
Spirit show his power. 5That way you
would have faith because of God's
power and not because of human wisdom.
6We do use wisdom when speaking to
people who are mature in their faith.
But it isn't the wisdom of this world or
of its rulers, who will soon disappear.
7We speak of God's hidden and mysteri-

[a]**1.11** *family*: Family members and possibly slaves and others who may have lived in the house.
[b]**1.12** *Peter*: The Greek text has "Cephas," which is an Aramaic name meaning "rock." Peter is the Greek name with the same meaning. [c]**1.14** *I thank God*: Some manuscripts have "I thank my God." [d]**1.16** *family*: See the note at 1.11. [e]**2.1** *mystery*: Some manuscripts have "testimony."

ous wisdom that God decided to use for our glory long before the world began. 8The rulers of this world didn't know anything about this wisdom. If they had known about it, they would not have nailed the glorious Lord to a cross. 9But it is just as the Scriptures say,

> "What God has planned
> for people who love him
> is more than eyes have seen
> or ears have heard.
> It has never even
> entered our minds!"

10God's Spirit has shown you everything. His Spirit finds out everything, even what is deep in the mind of God. 11You are the only one who knows what is in your own mind, and God's Spirit is the only one who knows what is in God's mind. 12But God has given us his Spirit. That's why we don't think the same way that the people of this world think. That's also why we can recognize the blessings that God has given us.

13Every word we speak was taught to us by God's Spirit, not by human wisdom. And this same Spirit helps us teach spiritual things to spiritual people.[f] 14That's why only someone who has God's Spirit can understand spiritual blessings. Anyone who doesn't have God's Spirit thinks these blessings are foolish. 15People who are guided by the Spirit can make all kinds of judgments, but they cannot be judged by others. 16The Scriptures ask,

> "Has anyone ever known
> the thoughts of the Lord
> or given him advice?"

But we understand what Christ is thinking.[g]

Working Together for God

3 My friends, you are acting like the people of this world. That's why I could not speak to you as spiritual people. You are like babies as far as your faith in Christ is concerned. 2So I had to treat you like babies and feed you milk. You could not take solid food, and you still cannot, 3because you are not yet spiritual. You are jealous and argue with each other. This proves that you are not spiritual and that you are acting like the people of this world.

4Some of you say that you follow me, and others claim to follow Apollos. Isn't that how ordinary people behave? 5Apollos and I are merely servants who helped you to have faith. It was the Lord who made it all happen. 6I planted the seeds, Apollos watered them, but God made them sprout and grow. 7What matters isn't those who planted or watered, but God who made the plants grow. 8The one who plants is just as important as the one who waters. And each one will be paid for what they do. 9Apollos and I work together for God, and you are God's garden and God's building.

Only One Foundation

10God was kind and let me become an expert builder. I laid a foundation on which others have built. But we must each be careful how we build, 11because Christ is the only foundation. 12-13Whatever we build on that foundation will be tested by fire on the day of judgment. Then everyone will find out if we have used gold, silver, and precious stones, or wood, hay, and straw. 14We will be rewarded if our building is left standing. 15But if it is destroyed by the fire, we will lose everything. Yet we ourselves will be saved, like someone escaping from flames.

16All of you surely know that you are God's temple and that his Spirit lives in you. 17Together you are God's holy temple, and God will destroy anyone who destroys his temple.

18Don't fool yourselves! If any of you think you are wise in the things of this world, you will have to become foolish before you can be truly wise. 19This is because God considers the wisdom of this world to be foolish. It is just as the Scriptures say, "God catches the wise when they try to outsmart him." 20The Scriptures also say, "The Lord knows that the plans made by wise people are useless." 21-22So stop bragging about what anyone has done. Paul and Apollos and Peter[h] all belong to you. In fact, everything is yours, including the world, life, death, the present, and the future. Everything belongs to you, 23and you belong to Christ, and Christ belongs to God.

The Work of the Apostles

4 Think of us as servants of Christ who have been given the work of explaining God's mysterious ways. 2And since our first duty is to be faithful to the one we work for, 3it doesn't matter to me if I am judged by you or even by a court of law. In fact, I don't judge myself. 4I don't know of anything against me, but that doesn't prove that I am right. The Lord is my judge. 5So don't judge anyone until the Lord returns. He will show what is hidden in the dark and what is in everyone's heart. Then

[f]**2.13** *teach spiritual things to spiritual people*: Or "compare spiritual things with spiritual things." [g]**2.16** *we understand what Christ is thinking*: Or "we think as Christ does."
[h]**3.21,22** *Peter*: See the note at 1.12.

God will be the one who praises each of us.

6 Friends, I have used Apollos and myself as examples to teach you the meaning of the saying, "Follow the rules." I want you to stop saying that one of us is better than the other. 7 What is so special about you? What do you have that you were not given? And if it was given to you, how can you brag? 8 Are you already satisfied? Are you now rich? Have you become kings while we are still nobodies? I wish you were kings. Then we could have a share in your kingdom.

9 It seems to me that God has put us apostles in the worst possible place. We are like prisoners on their way to death. Angels and the people of this world just laugh at us. 10 Because of Christ we are thought of as fools, but Christ has made you wise. We are weak and hated, but you are powerful and respected. 11 Even today we go hungry and thirsty and don't have anything to wear except rags. We are mistreated and don't have a place to live. 12 We work hard with our own hands, and when people abuse us, we wish them well. When we suffer, we are patient. 13 When someone curses us, we answer with kind words. Until now we are thought of as nothing more than the trash and garbage of this world.

14 I am not writing to embarrass you. I want to help you, just as parents help their own dear children. 15 Ten thousand people may teach you about Christ, but I am your only father. You became my children when I told you about Christ Jesus, 16 and I want you to be like me. 17 That's why I sent Timothy to you. I love him like a son, and he is a faithful servant of the Lord. Timothy will tell you what I do to follow Christ and how it agrees with what I always teach about Christ in every church.

18 Some of you think I am not coming for a visit, and so you are bragging. 19 But if the Lord lets me come, I will soon be there. Then I will find out if the ones who are doing all this bragging really have any power. 20 God's kingdom isn't just a lot of words. It is power. 21 What do you want me to do when I arrive? Do you want me to be hard on you or to be kind and gentle?

Immoral Followers

5 I have heard terrible things about some of you. In fact, you are behaving worse than the Gentiles. A man is even sleeping with his own stepmother.[i] 2 You are proud, when you ought to feel bad enough to chase away anyone who acts like that.

3-4 I am with you only in my thoughts. But in the name of our Lord Jesus I have already judged this man, as though I were with you in person. So when you meet together and the power of the Lord Jesus is with you, I will be there too. 5 You must then hand that man over to Satan. His body will be destroyed, but his spirit will be saved when the Lord Jesus returns.

6 Stop being proud! Don't you know how a little yeast can spread through the whole batch of dough? 7 Get rid of the old yeast! Then you will be like fresh bread made without yeast, and that is what you are. Our Passover lamb is Christ, who has already been sacrificed. 8 So don't celebrate the festival by being evil and sinful, which is like serving bread made with yeast. Be pure and truthful and celebrate by using bread made without yeast.

9 In my other letter[j] I told you not to have anything to do with immoral people. 10 But I wasn't talking about the people of this world. You would have to leave this world to get away from everyone who is immoral or greedy or who cheats or worships idols. 11 I was talking about your own people who are immoral or greedy or worship idols or curse others or get drunk or cheat. Don't even eat with them! 12 Why should I judge outsiders? Aren't we supposed to judge only church members? 13 God judges everyone else. The Scriptures say, "Chase away any of your own people who are evil."

Taking Each Other to Court

6 When one of you has a complaint against another, do you take your complaint to a court of sinners? Or do you take it to God's people? 2 Don't you know that God's people will judge the world? And if you are going to judge the world, can't you settle small problems? 3 Don't you know that we will judge angels? And if that is so, we can surely judge everyday matters. 4 Why do you take everyday complaints to judges who are not respected by the church? 5 I say this to your shame. Aren't any of you wise enough to act as a judge between one follower and another? 6 Why should one of you take another to be tried by unbelievers?

7 When one of you takes another to court, all of you lose. It would be better to let yourselves be cheated and robbed. 8 But instead, you cheat and rob other followers.

9 Don't you know that evil people won't have a share in the blessings of

[i] **5.1** *is even sleeping with his own stepmother*: Or "has even married his own stepmother."
[j] **5.9** *other letter*: An unknown letter that Paul wrote to the Christians at Corinth before he wrote this one.

God's kingdom? Don't fool yourselves!
No one who is immoral or worships
idols or is unfaithful in marriage or is a
pervert or behaves like a homosexual
10will share in God's kingdom. Neither
will any thief or greedy person or
drunkard or anyone who curses and
cheats others. 11Some of you used to be
like that. But now the name of our Lord
Jesus Christ and the power of God's
Spirit have washed you and made you
holy and acceptable to God.

Honor God with Your Body

12Some of you say, "We can do anything we want to." But I tell you that not
everything is good for us. So I refuse to
let anything have power over me. 13You
also say, "Food is meant for our bodies,
and our bodies are meant for food." But
I tell you that God will destroy them
both. We are not supposed to do indecent things with our bodies. We are to
use them for the Lord who is in charge
of our bodies. 14God will raise us from
death by the same power that he used
when he raised our Lord to life.

15Don't you know that your bodies are
part of the body of Christ? Is it right for
me to join part of the body of Christ to a
prostitute? No, it isn't! 16Don't you know
that a man who does that becomes part
of her body? The Scriptures say, "The
two of them will be like one person."
17But anyone who is joined to the Lord
is one in spirit with him.

18Don't be immoral in matters of sex.
That is a sin against your own body in a
way that no other sin is. 19You surely
know that your body is a temple where
the Holy Spirit lives. The Spirit is in you
and is a gift from God. You are no longer
your own. 20God paid a great price for
you. So use your body to honor God.

Questions about Marriage

7 Now I will answer the questions that
you asked in your letter. You asked,
"Is it best for people not to marry?"[k]
2Well, having your own husband or wife
should keep you from doing something
immoral. 3Husbands and wives should
be fair with each other about having
sex. 4A wife belongs to her husband instead of to herself, and a husband belongs to his wife instead of to himself.
5So don't refuse sex to each other, unless you agree not to have sex for a little
while, in order to spend time in prayer.
Then Satan won't be able to tempt you
because of your lack of self-control. 6In
my opinion that is what should be done,
though I don't know of anything the
Lord said about this matter. 7I wish that
all of you were like me, but God has
given different gifts to each of us.

8Here is my advice for people who
have never been married and for widows. You should stay single, just as I am.
9But if you don't have enough self-
control, then go ahead and get married.
After all, it is better to marry than to
burn with desire.[l]

10I instruct married couples to stay together, and this is exactly what the Lord
himself taught. A wife who leaves her
husband 11should either stay single or
go back to her husband. And a husband
should not leave his wife.

12I don't know of anything else the
Lord said about marriage. All I can do is
to give you my own advice. If your wife
isn't a follower of the Lord, but is willing to stay with you, don't divorce her.
13If your husband isn't a follower, but is
willing to stay with you, don't divorce
him. 14Your husband or wife who isn't a
follower is made holy by having you as
a mate. This also makes your children
holy and keeps them from being unclean in God's sight.

15If your husband or wife isn't a follower of the Lord and decides to divorce
you, then you should agree to it. You are
no longer bound to that person. After
all, God chose you and wants you to live
at peace. 16And besides, how do you
know if you will be able to save your
husband or wife who isn't a follower?

Obeying the Lord at All Times

17In every church I tell the people to
stay as they were when the Lord Jesus
chose them and God called them to be
his own. Now I say the same thing to
you. 18If you are already circumcised,
don't try to change it. If you are not circumcised, don't get circumcised. 19Being
circumcised or uncircumcised isn't really what matters. The important thing
is to obey God's commands. 20So don't
try to change what you were when God
chose you. 21Are you a slave? Don't let
that bother you. But if you can win your
freedom, you should. 22When the Lord
chooses slaves, they become his free
people. And when he chooses free people, they become slaves of Christ. 23God
paid a great price for you. So don't become slaves of anyone else. 24Stay what
you were when God chose you.

Unmarried People

25I don't know of anything that the
Lord said about people who have never
been married.[m] But I will tell you what I
think. And you can trust me, because
the Lord has treated me with kindness.

[k]**7.1** *people not to marry*: Or "married couples not to have sex." [l]**7.9** *with desire*: Or "in the flames of hell." [m]**7.25** *people who have never been married*: Or "virgins."

26 We are now going through hard times, and I think it is best for you to stay as you are. 27 If you are married, stay married. If you are not married, don't try to get married. 28 It isn't wrong to marry, even if you have never been married before. But those who marry will have a lot of trouble, and I want to protect you from that.

29 My friends, what I mean is that the Lord will soon come,[n] and it won't matter if you are married or not. 30 It will be all the same if you are crying or laughing, or if you are buying or are completely broke. 31 It won't make any difference how much good you are getting from this world or how much you like it. This world as we know it is now passing away.

32 I want all of you to be free from worry. An unmarried man worries about how to please the Lord. 33 But a married man has more worries. He must worry about the things of this world, because he wants to please his wife. 34 So he is pulled in two directions. Unmarried women and women who have never been married[o] worry only about pleasing the Lord, and they keep their bodies and minds pure. But a married woman worries about the things of this world, because she wants to please her husband. 35 What I am saying is for your own good—it isn't to limit your freedom. I want to help you to live right and to love the Lord above all else.

36 But suppose you are engaged to someone old enough to be married, and you want her so much that all you can think about is getting married. Then go ahead and marry.[p] There is nothing wrong with that. 37 But it is better to have self-control and to make up your mind not to marry. 38 It is perfectly all right to marry, but it is better not to get married at all.

39 A wife should stay married to her husband until he dies. Then she is free to marry again, but only to a man who is a follower of the Lord. 40 However, I think I am obeying God's Spirit when I say she would be happier to stay single.

Food Offered to Idols

8 In your letter you asked me about food offered to idols. All of us know something about this subject. But knowledge makes us proud of ourselves, while love makes us helpful to others. 2 In fact, people who think they know so much don't know anything at all. 3 But God has no doubts about who loves him.

4 Even though food is offered to idols, we know that none of the idols in this world are alive. After all, there is only one God. 5 Many things in heaven and on earth are called gods and lords, but none of them really are gods or lords. 6 We have only one God, and he is the Father. He created everything, and we live for him. Jesus Christ is our only Lord. Everything was made by him, and by him life was given to us.

7 Not everyone knows these things. In fact, many people have grown up with the belief that idols have life in them. So when they eat meat offered to idols, they are bothered by a weak conscience. 8 But food doesn't bring us any closer to God. We are no worse off if we don't eat, and we are no better off if we do.

9 Don't cause problems for someone with a weak conscience, just because you have the right to eat anything. 10 You know all this, and so it doesn't bother you to eat in the temple of an idol. But suppose a person with a weak conscience sees you and decides to eat food that has been offered to idols. 11 Then what you know has destroyed someone Christ died for. 12 When you sin by hurting a follower with a weak conscience, you sin against Christ. 13 So if I hurt one of the Lord's followers by what I eat, I will never eat meat as long as I live.

The Rights of an Apostle

9 I am free. I am an apostle. I have seen the Lord Jesus and have led you to have faith in him. 2 Others may think that I am not an apostle, but you are proof that I am an apostle to you.

3 When people question me, I tell them 4 that Barnabas and I have the right to our food and drink. 5 We each have the right to marry one of the Lord's followers and to take her along with us, just as the other apostles and the Lord's brothers and Peter[q] do. 6 Are we the only ones who have to support ourselves by working at another job? 7 Do soldiers pay their own salaries? Don't people who raise grapes eat some of what they grow? Don't shepherds get milk from their own goats?

8-9 I am not saying this on my own authority. The Law of Moses tells us not to muzzle an ox when it is grinding grain. But was God concerned only about an

[n] 7.29 *the Lord will soon come*: Or "there's not much time left" or "the time for decision comes quickly." [o] 7.34 *women who have never been married*: Or "virgins." [p] 7.36 *But suppose you are engaged . . . go ahead and marry*: Verses 36-38 may also be translated: 36 "If you feel that you are not treating your grown daughter right by keeping her from getting married, then let her marry. You won't be doing anything wrong. 37 But it is better to have self-control and make up your mind not to let your daughter get married. 38 It is all right for you to let her marry. But it is better if you don't let her marry at all." [q] 9.5 *Peter*: See the note at 1.12.

ox? 10No, he wasn't! He was talking
about us. This was written in the Scriptures so that all who plow and all who
grind the grain will look forward to
sharing in the harvest.
11When we told the message to you, it
was like planting spiritual seed. So we
have the right to accept material things
as our harvest from you. 12If others have
the right to do this, we have an even
greater right. But we haven't used this
right of ours. We are willing to put up
with anything to keep from causing
trouble for the message about Christ.
13Don't you know that people who
work in the temple make their living
from what is brought to the temple?
Don't you know that a person who
serves at the altar is given part of what
is offered? 14In the same way, the Lord
wants everyone who preaches the good
news to make a living from preaching
this message.
15But I have never used these privileges of mine, and I am not writing this
because I want to start now. I would
rather die than have someone rob me of
the right to take pride in this. 16I don't
have any reason to brag about preaching the good news. Preaching is something God told me to do, and if I don't
do it, I am doomed. 17If I preach because
I want to, I will be paid. But even if I
don't want to, it is still something God
has sent me to do. 18What pay am I
given? It is the chance to preach the
good news free of charge and not to use
the privileges that are mine because I
am a preacher.
19I am not anyone's slave. But I have
become a slave to everyone, so that I
can win as many people as possible.
20When I am with the Jews, I live like a
Jew to win Jews. They are ruled by the
Law of Moses, and I am not. But I live
by the Law to win them. 21And when I
am with people who are not ruled by the
Law, I forget about the Law to win
them. Of course, I never really forget
about the law of God. In fact, I am ruled
by the law of Christ. 22When I am with
people whose faith is weak, I live as
they do to win them. I do everything I
can to win everyone I possibly can. 23I
do all this for the good news, because
I want to share in its blessings.

A Race and a Fight

24You know that many runners enter a
race, and only one of them wins the
prize. So run to win! 25Athletes work
hard to win a crown that cannot last,
but we do it for a crown that will last
forever. 26I don't run without a goal. And
I don't box by beating my fists in the air.
27I keep my body under control and
make it my slave, so I won't lose out after telling the good news to others.

Don't Worship Idols

10 Friends, I want to remind you that
all of our ancestors walked under
the cloud and went through the sea.
2This was like being baptized and becoming followers of Moses. 3All of them
also ate the same spiritual food 4and
drank the same spiritual drink, which
flowed from the spiritual rock that followed them. That rock was Christ. 5But
most of them did not please God. So
they died, and their bodies were scattered all over the desert.
6What happened to them is a warning
to keep us from wanting to do the same
evil things. 7They worshiped idols, just
as the Scriptures say, "The people sat
down to eat and drink. Then they got up
to dance around." So don't worship
idols. 8Some of those people did shameful things, and in a single day about
twenty-three thousand of them died.
Don't do shameful things as they did.
9And don't try to test Christ,[r] as some of
them did and were later bitten by poisonous snakes. 10Don't even grumble, as
some of them did and were killed by the
destroying angel. 11These things happened to them as a warning to us. All
this was written in the Scriptures to
teach us who live in these last days.
12Even if you think you can stand up
to temptation, be careful not to fall.
13You are tempted in the same way that
everyone else is tempted. But God can
be trusted not to let you be tempted too
much, and he will show you how to escape from your temptations.
14My friends, you must keep away
from idols. 15I am speaking to you as
people who have enough sense to know
what I am talking about. 16When we
drink from the cup that we ask God to
bless, isn't that sharing in the blood of
Christ? When we eat the bread that we
break, isn't that sharing in the body of
Christ? 17By sharing in the same loaf
of bread, we become one body, even
though there are many of us.
18Aren't the people of Israel sharing in
the worship when they gather around
the altar and eat the sacrifices offered
there? 19Am I saying that either the
idols or the food sacrificed to them is
anything at all? 20No, I am not! That
food is really sacrificed to demons and
not to God. I don't want you to have
anything to do with demons. 21You cannot drink from the cup of demons and
still drink from the Lord's cup. You cannot eat at the table of demons and still
eat at the Lord's table. 22We would make

[r]**10.9** *Christ*: Some manuscripts have "the Lord."

the Lord jealous if we did that. And we are not stronger than the Lord.

Always Honor God

23Some of you say, "We can do whatever we want to!" But I tell you that not everything may be good or helpful. 24We should think about others and not about ourselves. 25However, when you buy meat in the market, go ahead and eat it. Keep your conscience clear by not asking where the meat came from. 26The Scriptures say, "The earth and everything in it belong to the Lord."

27If an unbeliever invites you to dinner, and you want to go, then go. Eat whatever you are served. Don't cause a problem for someone's conscience by asking where the food came from. 28-29But if you are told that it has been sacrificed to idols, don't cause a problem by eating it. I don't mean a problem for yourself, but for the one who told you. Why should my freedom be limited by someone else's conscience? 30If I give thanks for what I eat, why should anyone accuse me of doing wrong?

31When you eat or drink or do anything else, always do it to honor God. 32Don't cause problems for Jews or Greeks or anyone else who belongs to God's church. 33I always try to please others instead of myself, in the hope that many of them will be saved.

11 1You must follow my example, as I follow the example of Christ.

Rules for Worship

2I am proud of you, because you always remember me and obey the teachings I gave you. 3Now I want you to know that Christ is the head over all men, and a man is the head over a woman. But God is the head over Christ. 4This means that any man who prays or prophesies with something on his head brings shame to his head.

5But any woman who prays or prophesies without something on her head brings shame to her head. In fact, she may as well shave her head.[s] 6A woman should wear something on her head. It is a disgrace for a woman to shave her head or cut her hair. But if she refuses to wear something on her head, let her cut off her hair.

7Men were created to be like God and to bring honor to God. This means that a man should not wear anything on his head. Women were created to bring honor to men. 8It was the woman who was made from a man, and not the man who was made from a woman. 9He wasn't created for her. She was created for him. 10And so, because of this, and also because of the angels, a woman ought to wear something on her head, as a sign of her authority.[t]

11As far as the Lord is concerned, men and women need each other. 12It is true that the first woman came from a man, but all other men have been given birth by women. Yet God is the one who created everything. 13Ask yourselves if it is proper for a woman to pray without something on her head. 14Isn't it unnatural and disgraceful for men to have long hair? 15But long hair is a beautiful way for a woman to cover her head. 16This is how things are done in all of God's churches,[u] and that's why none of you should argue about what I have said.

Rules for the Lord's Supper

17Your worship services do you more harm than good. I am certainly not going to praise you for this. 18I am told that you can't get along with each other when you worship, and I am sure that some of what I have heard is true. 19You are bound to argue with each other, but it is easy to see which of you have God's approval.

20When you meet together, you don't really celebrate the Lord's Supper. 21You even start eating before everyone gets to the meeting, and some of you go hungry, while others get drunk. 22Don't you have homes where you can eat and drink? Do you hate God's church? Do you want to embarrass people who don't have anything? What can I say to you? I certainly cannot praise you.

The Lord's Supper

(Matthew 26.26-29; Mark 14.22-25; Luke 22.14-20)

23I have already told you what the Lord Jesus did on the night he was betrayed. And it came from the Lord himself.

He took some bread in his hands.
24Then after he had given thanks, he
broke it and said, "This is my body,
which is given for you. Eat this and
remember me."
25After the meal, Jesus took a cup
of wine in his hands and said, "This
is my blood, and with it God makes
his new agreement with you. Drink
this and remember me."

26The Lord meant that when you eat this bread and drink from this cup, you tell about his death until he comes.

---

[s] **11.5** *she may as well shave her head*: A woman's hair was a mark of beauty, and it was shameful for a woman to cut her hair short or to shave her head, so that she looked like a man.
[t] **11.10** *as a sign of her authority*: Or "as a sign that she is under someone's authority."
[u] **11.16** *This is how things are done in all of God's churches*: Or "There is no set rule for this in any of God's churches."

27 But if you eat the bread and drink
the wine in a way that isn't worthy of
the Lord, you sin against his body and
blood. 28 That's why you must examine
the way you eat and drink. 29 If you fail
to understand that you are the body of
the Lord, you will condemn yourselves
by the way you eat and drink. 30 That's
why many of you are sick and weak and
why a lot of others have died. 31 If we
carefully judge ourselves, we won't be
punished. 32 But when the Lord judges
and punishes us, he does it to keep us
from being condemned with the rest of
the world.

33 My dear friends, you should wait until everyone gets there before you start
eating. 34 If you really are hungry, you
can eat at home. Then you won't condemn yourselves when you meet together.

After I arrive, I will instruct you about
the other matters.

Spiritual Gifts

12 My friends, you asked me about
spiritual gifts. 2 I want you to remember that before you became followers of the Lord, you were led in all the
wrong ways by idols that cannot even
talk. 3 Now I want you to know that if
you are led by God's Spirit, you will say
that Jesus is Lord, and you will never
curse Jesus.

4 There are different kinds of spiritual
gifts, but they all come from the same
Spirit. 5 There are different ways to serve
the same Lord, 6 and we can each do different things. Yet the same God works in
all of us and helps us in everything we
do.

7 The Spirit has given each of us a special way of serving others. 8 Some of us
can speak with wisdom, while others
can speak with knowledge, but these
gifts come from the same Spirit. 9 To others the Spirit has given great faith or the
power to heal the sick 10 or the power to
work mighty miracles. Some of us are
prophets, and some of us recognize
when God's Spirit is present.[v] Others
can speak different kinds of languages,
and still others can tell what these languages mean. 11 But it is the Spirit who
does all this and decides which gifts to
give to each of us.

One Body with Many Parts

12 The body of Christ has many different parts, just as any other body does.
13 Some of us are Jews, and others are
Gentiles. Some of us are slaves, and others are free. But God's Spirit baptized
each of us and made us part of the body
of Christ. Now we each drink from that
same Spirit.[w]

14 Our bodies don't have just one part.
They have many parts. 15 Suppose a foot
says, "I'm not a hand, and so I'm not
part of the body." Wouldn't the foot still
belong to the body? 16 Or suppose an ear
says, "I'm not an eye, and so I'm not
part of the body." Wouldn't the ear still
belong to the body? 17 If our bodies
were only an eye, we couldn't hear a
thing. And if they were only an ear, we
couldn't smell a thing. 18 But God has put
all parts of our body together in the way
that he decided is best.

19 A body isn't really a body, unless
there is more than one part. 20 It takes
many parts to make a single body.
21 That's why the eyes cannot say they
don't need the hands. That's also why
the head cannot say it doesn't need the
feet. 22 In fact, we cannot get along without the parts of the body that seem to be
the weakest. 23 We take special care to
dress up some parts of our bodies. We
are modest about our personal parts,
24 but we don't have to be modest about
other parts.

God put our bodies together in such a
way that even the parts that seem the
least important are valuable. 25 He did
this to make all parts of the body work
together smoothly, with each part caring about the others. 26 If one part of our
body hurts, we hurt all over. If one part
of our body is honored, the whole body
will be happy.

27 Together you are the body of Christ.
Each one of you is part of his body.
28 First, God chose some people to be
apostles and prophets and teachers for
the church. But he also chose some to
work miracles or heal the sick or help
others or be leaders or speak different
kinds of languages. 29 Not everyone is an
apostle. Not everyone is a prophet. Not
everyone is a teacher. Not everyone can
work miracles. 30 Not everyone can heal
the sick. Not everyone can speak different kinds of languages. Not everyone
can tell what these languages mean. 31 I
want you to desire the best gifts.[x] So I
will show you a much better way.

Love

13 What if I could speak
all languages of humans
and of angels?

[v] 12.10 *and some of us . . . present*: Or "and some of us recognize the difference between God's Spirit and other spirits." [w] 12.13 *Some of us are Jews . . . that same Spirit*: Verse 13 may also be translated, "God's Spirit is inside each of us, and all around us as well. So it doesn't matter that some of us are Jews and others are Gentiles and that some are slaves and others are free. Together we are one body." [x] 12.31 *I want you to desire the best gifts*: Or "You desire the best gifts."

If I did not love others,
I would be nothing more
than a noisy gong
or a clanging cymbal.
2 What if I could prophesy
and understand all secrets
and all knowledge?
And what if I had faith
that moved mountains?
I would be nothing,
unless I loved others.
3 What if I gave away all
that I owned
and let myself
be burned alive?[y]
I would gain nothing,
unless I loved others.
4 Love is kind and patient,
never jealous, boastful,
proud, or 5rude.
Love isn't selfish
or quick tempered.
It doesn't keep a record
of wrongs that others do.
6 Love rejoices in the truth,
but not in evil.
7 Love is always supportive,
loyal, hopeful,
and trusting.
8 Love never fails!

Everyone who prophesies
will stop,
and unknown languages
will no longer
be spoken.
All that we know
will be forgotten.
9 We don't know everything,
and our prophecies
are not complete.
10 But what is perfect
will someday appear,
and what isn't perfect
will then disappear.

11 When we were children,
we thought and reasoned
as children do.
But when we grew up,
we quit our childish ways.
12 Now all we can see of God
is like a cloudy picture
in a mirror.
Later we will see him
face to face.
We don't know everything,
but then we will,
just as God completely
understands us.
13 For now there are faith,
hope, and love.
But of these three,
the greatest is love.

Speaking Unknown Languages and Prophesying

14 Love should be your guide. Be eager to have the gifts that come
from the Holy Spirit, especially the gift
of prophecy. 2If you speak languages
that others don't know, God will understand what you are saying, though no
one else will know what you mean.
You will be talking about mysteries
that only the Spirit understands. 3But
when you prophesy, you will be understood, and others will be helped. They
will be encouraged and made to feel
better.
4By speaking languages that others
don't know, you help only yourself. But
by prophesying you help everyone in
the church. 5I am glad for you to speak
unknown languages, although I had
rather for you to prophesy. In fact,
prophesying does much more good than
speaking unknown languages, unless
someone can help the church by explaining what you mean.
6My friends, what good would it do, if
I came and spoke unknown languages
to you and didn't explain what I meant?
How would I help you, unless I told you
what God had shown me or gave you
some knowledge or prophecy or teaching? 7If all musical instruments sounded
alike, how would you know the difference between a flute and a harp? 8If a
bugle call isn't clear, how would you
know to get ready for battle?
9That's how it is when you speak unknown languages. If no one can understand what you are talking about, you
will only be talking to the wind. 10There
are many different languages in this
world, and all of them make sense. 11But
if I don't understand the language that
someone is using, we will be like foreigners to each other. 12If you really
want spiritual gifts, choose the ones that
will be most helpful to the church.
13When we speak languages that others don't know, we should pray for the
power to explain what we mean. 14For
example, if I use an unknown language
in my prayers, my spirit prays but my
mind is useless. 15Then what should I
do? There are times when I should pray
with my spirit, and times when I should
pray with my mind. Sometimes I should
sing with my spirit, and at other times I
should sing with my mind.
16Suppose some strangers are in your
worship service, when you are praising
God with your spirit. If they don't understand you, how will they know to
say, "Amen"? 17You may be worshiping
God in a wonderful way, but no one else
will be helped. 18I thank God that I

[y] **13.3** *and let myself be burned alive*: Some manuscripts have "so that I could brag."

speak unknown languages more than
any of you. 19But words that make sense
can help the church. That's why in
church I had rather speak five words
that make sense than to speak ten thousand words in a language that others
don't know.
20My friends, stop thinking like children. Think like mature people and be
as innocent as tiny babies. 21In the
Scriptures the Lord says,

"I will use strangers
who speak unknown languages
to talk to my people.
They will speak to them
in foreign languages,
but still my people
won't listen to me."

22Languages that others don't know
may mean something to unbelievers, but
not to the Lord's followers. Prophecy, on
the other hand, is for followers, not for
unbelievers. 23Suppose everyone in your
worship service started speaking unknown languages, and some outsiders
or some unbelievers come in. Won't they
think you are crazy? 24But suppose all
of you are prophesying when those unbelievers and outsiders come in. They
will realize that they are sinners, and
they will want to change their ways because of what you are saying. 25They
will tell what is hidden in their hearts.
Then they will kneel down and say to
God, "We are certain that you are with
these people."

Worship Must Be Orderly

26My friends, when you meet to worship, you must do everything for the
good of everyone there. That's how it
should be when someone sings or
teaches or tells what God has said or
speaks an unknown language or explains what the language means. 27No
more than two or three of you should
speak unknown languages during the
meeting. You must take turns, and someone should always be there to explain
what you mean. 28If no one can explain,
you must keep silent in church and
speak only to yourself and to God.
29Two or three persons may prophesy,
and everyone else must listen carefully.
30If someone sitting there receives a
message from God, the speaker must
stop and let the other person speak.
31Let only one person speak at a time,
then all of you will learn something and
be encouraged. 32A prophet should be
willing to stop and let someone else
speak. 33God wants everything to be
done peacefully and in order.
When God's people meet in church,
34the women must not be allowed to
speak. They must keep quiet and listen,
as the Law of Moses teaches. 35If there
is something they want to know, they
can ask their husbands when they get
home. It is disgraceful for women to
speak in church. 36God's message did
not start with you people, and you are
not the only ones it has reached.
37If you think of yourself as a prophet
or a spiritual person, you will know that
I am writing only what the Lord has
commanded. 38So don't pay attention to
anyone who ignores what I am writing.
39My friends, be eager to prophesy and
don't stop anyone from speaking languages that others don't know. 40But do
everything properly and in order.

Christ Was Raised to Life

15 My friends, I want you to remember the message that I preached
and that you believed and trusted. 2You
will be saved by this message, if you
hold firmly to it. But if you don't, your
faith was all for nothing.
3I told you the most important part of
the message exactly as it was told to
me. That part is:

Christ died for our sins,
as the Scriptures say.
4 He was buried,
and three days later
he was raised to life,
as the Scriptures say.
5 Christ appeared to Peter,[z]
then to the twelve.
6 After this, he appeared
to more than five hundred
other followers.
Most of them are still alive,
but some have died.
7 He also appeared to James,
and then to all
of the apostles.

8Finally, he appeared to me, even
though I am like someone who was
born at the wrong time.[a]
9I am the least important of all the
apostles. In fact, I caused so much trouble for God's church that I don't even
deserve to be called an apostle. 10But
God was kind! He made me what I am,
and his wonderful kindness wasn't
wasted. I worked much harder than any
of the other apostles, although it was really God's kindness at work and not me.
11But it doesn't matter if I preached or if
they preached. All of you believed the
message just the same.

God's People Will Be Raised to Life

12If we preach that Christ was raised
from death, how can some of you say

[z]**15.5** *Peter*: See the note at 1.12. [a]**15.8** *who was born at the wrong time*: The meaning of these words in Greek is not clear.

that the dead will not be raised to life?
13If they won't be raised to life, Christ
himself wasn't raised to life. 14And if
Christ wasn't raised to life, our message
is worthless, and so is your faith. 15If the
dead won't be raised to life, we have
told lies about God by saying that he
raised Christ to life, when he really did
not.

16So if the dead won't be raised to life,
Christ wasn't raised to life. 17Unless
Christ was raised to life, your faith is
useless, and you are still living in your
sins. 18And those people who died after
putting their faith in him are completely
lost. 19If our hope in Christ is good only
for this life, we are worse off than anyone else.

20But Christ has been raised to life!
And he makes us certain that others will
also be raised to life. 21Just as we will
die because of Adam, we will be raised
to life because of Christ. 22Adam
brought death to all of us, and Christ
will bring life to all of us. 23But we must
each wait our turn. Christ was the first
to be raised to life, and his people will
be raised to life when he returns. 24Then
after Christ has destroyed all powers
and forces, the end will come, and he
will give the kingdom to God the Father.

25Christ will rule until he puts all his
enemies under his power, 26and the last
enemy he destroys will be death.
27When the Scriptures say that he will
put everything under his power, they
don't include God. It was God who put
everything under the power of Christ.
28After everything is under the power of
God's Son, he will put himself under the
power of God, who put everything under his Son's power. Then God will
mean everything to everyone.

29If the dead are not going to be raised
to life, what will people do who are being baptized for them? Why are they being baptized for those dead people?
30And why do we always risk our lives
31and face death every day? The pride
that I have in you because of Christ Jesus our Lord is what makes me say this.
32What do you think I gained by fighting
wild animals in Ephesus? If the dead are
not raised to life,

"Let's eat and drink.
Tomorrow we die."

33Don't fool yourselves. Bad friends will
destroy you. 34Be sensible and stop sinning. You should be embarrassed that
some people still don't know about God.

What Our Bodies Will Be Like

35Some of you have asked, "How will
the dead be raised to life? What kind of
bodies will they have?" 36Don't be foolish. A seed must die before it can sprout
from the ground. 37Wheat seeds and all
other seeds look different from the
sprouts that come up. 38This is because
God gives everything the kind of body
he wants it to have. 39People, animals,
birds, and fish are each made of flesh,
but none of them are alike. 40Everything
in the heavens has a body, and so does
everything on earth. But each one is
very different from all the others. 41The
sun isn't like the moon, the moon isn't
like the stars, and each star is different.

42That's how it will be when our bodies are raised to life. These bodies will
die, but the bodies that are raised will
live forever. 43These ugly and weak bodies will become beautiful and strong.
44As surely as there are physical bodies,
there are spiritual bodies. And our physical bodies will be changed into spiritual
bodies.

45The first man was named Adam, and
the Scriptures tell us that he was a living person. But Jesus, who may be
called the last Adam, is a life-giving
spirit. 46We see that the one with a spiritual body did not come first. He came
after the one who had a physical body.
47The first man was made from the dust
of the earth, but the second man came
from heaven. 48Everyone on earth has a
body like the body of the one who was
made from the dust of the earth. And
everyone in heaven has a body like the
body of the one who came from heaven.
49Just as we are like the one who was
made out of earth, we will be like the
one who came from heaven.

50My friends, I want you to know that
our bodies of flesh and blood will decay.
This means that they cannot share in
God's kingdom, which lasts forever. 51I
will explain a mystery to you. Not every
one of us will die, but we will all be
changed. 52It will happen suddenly,
quicker than the blink of an eye. At the
sound of the last trumpet the dead will
be raised. We will all be changed, so that
we will never die again. 53Our dead and
decaying bodies will be changed into
bodies that won't die or decay. 54The
bodies we now have are weak and can
die. But they will be changed into bodies
that are eternal. Then the Scriptures will
come true,

"Death has lost the battle!
55 Where is its victory?
Where is its sting?"

56Sin is what gives death its sting, and
the Law is the power behind sin. 57But
thank God for letting our Lord Jesus
Christ give us the victory!

58My dear friends, stand firm and
don't be shaken. Always keep busy
working for the Lord. You know that
everything you do for him is worthwhile.

A Collection for God's People

16 When you collect money for
God's people, I want you to do exactly what I told the churches in Galatia
to do. 2That is, each Sunday each of you
must put aside part of what you have
earned. If you do this, you won't have to
take up a collection when I come.
3Choose some followers to take the
money to Jerusalem. I will send them on
with the money and with letters which
show that you approve of them. 4If you
think I should go along, they can go
with me.

Paul's Travel Plans

5After I have gone through Macedonia, I hope to see you 6and visit with you
for a while. I may even stay all winter,
so that you can help me on my way to
wherever I will be going next. 7If the
Lord lets me, I would rather come later
for a longer visit than to stop off now
for only a short visit. 8I will stay in Ephesus until Pentecost, 9because there is a
wonderful opportunity for me to do
some work here. But there are also
many people who are against me.
10When Timothy arrives, give him a
friendly welcome. He is doing the Lord's
work, just as I am. 11Don't let anyone
mistreat him. I am looking for him to return to me together with the other followers. So when he leaves, send him off
with your blessings.
12I have tried hard to get our friend
Apollos to visit you with the other followers. He doesn't want to come just
now, but he will come when he can.

Personal Concerns and Greetings

13Keep alert. Be firm in your faith.
Stay brave and strong. 14Show love in
everything you do.
15You know that Stephanas and his
family were the first in Achaia to have
faith in the Lord. They have done all
they can for God's people. My friends, I
ask you 16to obey leaders like them and
to do the same for all others who work
hard with you.
17I was glad to see Stephanas and For-
tunatus and Achaicus. Having them
here was like having you. 18They made
me feel much better, just as they made
you feel better. You should appreciate
people like them.
19Greetings from the churches in Asia.
Aquila and Priscilla, together with the
church that meets in their house, send
greetings in the name of the Lord.
20All of the Lord's followers send their
greetings.
Give each other a warm greeting.
21I am signing this letter myself:
PAUL.
22I pray that God will put a curse on
everyone who doesn't love the Lord.
And may the Lord come soon.
23I pray that the Lord Jesus will be
kind to you.
24I love everyone who belongs to
Christ Jesus.

2 CORINTHIANS

ABOUT THIS LETTER

In the beginning of this letter Paul answers the concerns of the Christians in Corinth who accused him of not living up to his promise to visit them. Paul had changed his mind for a good reason. He had stayed away from Corinth so that he would not seem to be too hard and demanding (1.23). He also wanted to see if they would follow his instructions about forgiving and comforting people who had sinned (2.5-11).

Paul reminds the Corinthians that God is generous and wants them to be just as generous in their giving to help God's people in Jerusalem and Judea (8.1—9.15).

Paul is a servant of God's new agreement (3.1-17). He is faithful in trying to bring people to God, even if it means terrible suffering for himself (4.1—6.13; 10.1—12.10). And what has God done to make it possible for us to come to him?

> *God has done it all! He sent Christ to make peace between himself and us, and he has given us the work of making peace between himself and others.*
>
> *What we mean is that God was in Christ, offering peace and forgiveness to the people of this world. And he has given us the work of sharing his message about peace.*
>
> *(5.18, 19)*

A QUICK LOOK AT THIS LETTER

Paul Gives Thanks to God (1.1-11)
The Work of an Apostle for God's People (1.12—2.17)
Guided by the Love of Christ (3.1—7.16)
Gifts for the Poor (8.1—9.15)
Paul Is a True Apostle (10.1—13.10)
Final Greetings (13.11-13)

---

1 From Paul, chosen by God to be an
apostle of Jesus Christ, and from
Timothy, who is also a follower.
To God's church in Corinth and to all
of God's people in Achaia.
2I pray that God our Father and the
Lord Jesus Christ will be kind to you
and will bless you with peace!

Paul Gives Thanks

3Praise God, the Father of our Lord Jesus Christ! The Father is a merciful God,
who always gives us comfort. 4He comforts us when we are in trouble, so that
we can share that same comfort with
others in trouble. 5We share in the terrible sufferings of Christ, but also in the
wonderful comfort he gives. 6We suffer
in the hope that you will be comforted
and saved. And because we are comforted, you will also be comforted, as
you patiently endure suffering like ours.
7You never disappoint us. You suffered
as much as we did, and we know that
you will be comforted as we were.
8My friends, I want you to know what
a hard time we had in Asia. Our sufferings were so horrible and so unbearable
that death seemed certain. 9In fact, we
felt sure that we were going to die. But
this made us stop trusting in ourselves
and start trusting God, who raises the
dead to life. 10God saved us from the
threat of death,[a] and we are sure that he
will do it again and again. 11Please help
us by praying for us. Then many people
will give thanks for the blessings we receive in answer to all these prayers.

[a]**1.10** *the threat of death*: Some manuscripts have "many threats of death."

Paul's Change of Plans

12We can be proud of our clear conscience. We have always lived honestly
and sincerely, especially when we were
with you. And we were guided by God's
wonderful kindness instead of by the
wisdom of this world. 13I am not writing
anything you cannot read and understand. I hope you will understand it
completely, 14just as you already partly
understand us. Then when our Lord Jesus returns, you can be as proud of us as
we are of you.
15I was so sure of your pride in us that
I had planned to visit you first of all. In
this way you would have the blessing of
two visits from me. 16Once on my way to
Macedonia and again on my return
from there. Then you could send me on
to Judea. 17Do you think I couldn't make
up my mind about what to do? Or do I
seem like someone who says "Yes" or
"No" simply to please others? 18God can
be trusted, and so can I, when I say that
our answer to you has always been
"Yes" and never "No." 19This is because
Jesus Christ the Son of God is always
"Yes" and never "No." And he is the one
that Silas,[b] Timothy, and I told you
about.
20Christ says "Yes" to all of God's
promises. That's why we have Christ to
say "Amen"[c] for us to the glory of God.
21And so God makes it possible for you
and us to stand firmly together with
Christ. God is also the one who chose us
22and put his Spirit in our hearts to
show that we belong only to him.
23God is my witness that I stayed
away from Corinth, just to keep from
being hard on you. 24We are not bosses
who tell you what to believe. We are
working with you to make you glad, because your faith is strong.

2 I have decided not to make my next
visit with you so painful. 2If I make
you feel bad, who would be left to cheer
me up, except the people I had made to
feel bad? 3The reason I want to be
happy is to make you happy. I wrote as I
did because I didn't want to visit you
and be made to feel bad, when you
should make me feel happy. 4At the time
I wrote, I was suffering terribly. My eyes
were full of tears, and my heart was broken. But I didn't want to make you feel
bad. I only wanted to let you know how
much I cared for you.

Forgiveness

5I don't want to be hard on you. But if
one of you has made someone feel bad,
I am not really the one who has been
made to feel bad. Some of you are the
ones. 6Most of you have already pointed
out the wrong that person did, and that
is punishment enough for what was done.
7When people sin, you should forgive
and comfort them, so they won't give up
in despair. 8You should make them sure
of your love for them.
9I also wrote because I wanted to test
you and find out if you would follow my
instructions. 10I will forgive anyone you
forgive. Yes, for your sake and with
Christ as my witness, I have forgiven
whatever needed to be forgiven. 11I have
done this to keep Satan from getting the
better of us. We all know what goes on
in his mind.
12When I went to Troas to preach the
good news about Christ, I found that the
Lord had already prepared the way.
13But I was worried when I didn't find
my friend Titus there. So I left the other
followers and went on to Macedonia.
14I am grateful that God always makes
it possible for Christ to lead us to victory. God also helps us spread the
knowledge about Christ everywhere,
and this knowledge is like the smell of
perfume. 15-16In fact, God thinks of us as
a perfume that brings Christ to everyone. For people who are being saved,
this perfume has a sweet smell and
leads them to a better life. But for people who are lost, it has a bad smell and
leads them to a horrible death.
No one really has what it takes to do
this work. 17A lot of people try to get
rich from preaching God's message. But
we are God's sincere messengers, and
by the power of Christ we speak our
message with God as our witness.

God's New Agreement

3 Are we once again bragging about
ourselves? Do we need letters to you
or from you to tell others about us?
Some people do need letters that tell
about them. 2But you are our letter, and
you are in our[d] hearts for everyone to
read and understand. 3You are like a letter written by Christ and delivered by
us. But you are not written with pen and
ink or on tablets made of stone. You are
written in our hearts by the Spirit of the
living God.
4We are sure about all this. Christ
makes us sure in the very presence of
God. 5We don't have the right to claim
that we have done anything on our own.
God gives us what it takes to do all that
we do. 6He makes us worthy to be the
servants of his new agreement that
comes from the Holy Spirit and not
from a written Law. After all, the Law
brings death, but the Spirit brings life.

[b]1.19 *Silas*: The Greek text has "Silvanus," which is another form of the name Silas.
[c]1.20 *Amen*: The word "amen" is used here with the meaning of "yes." [d]3.2 *our*: Some manuscripts have "your."

7The Law of Moses brought only the
promise of death, even though it was
carved on stones and given in a wonderful way. Still the Law made Moses' face
shine so brightly that the people of Israel could not look at it, even though it
was a fading glory. 8So won't the agreement that the Spirit brings to us be even
more wonderful? 9If something that
brings the death sentence is glorious,
won't something that makes us acceptable to God be even more glorious? 10In
fact, the new agreement is so wonderful
that the Law is no longer glorious at all.
11The Law was given with a glory that
faded away. But the glory of the new
agreement is much greater, because it
will never fade away.
12This wonderful hope makes us feel
like speaking freely. 13We are not like
Moses. His face was shining, but he covered it to keep the people of Israel from
seeing the brightness fade away. 14The
people were stubborn, and something
still keeps them from seeing the truth
when the Law is read. Only Christ can
take away the covering that keeps them
from seeing.
15When the Law of Moses is read,
they have their minds covered over
16with a covering that is removed only
for those who turn to the Lord. 17The
Lord and the Spirit are one and the
same, and the Lord's Spirit sets us free.
18So our faces are not covered. They
show the bright glory of the Lord, as the
Lord's Spirit makes us more and more
like our glorious Lord.

Treasure in Clay Jars

4 God has been kind enough to trust
us with this work. That's why we
never give up. 2We don't do shameful
things that must be kept secret. And we
don't try to fool anyone or twist God's
message around. God is our witness that
we speak only the truth, so others will
be sure that we can be trusted. 3If there
is anything hidden about our message,
it is hidden only to someone who is
lost.
4The god who rules this world has
blinded the minds of unbelievers. They
cannot see the light, which is the good
news about our glorious Christ, who
shows what God is like. 5We are not
preaching about ourselves. Our message
is that Jesus Christ is Lord. He also sent
us to be your servants. 6The Scriptures
say, "God commanded light to shine in
the dark." Now God is shining in our
hearts to let you know that his glory is
seen in Jesus Christ.
7We are like clay jars in which this
treasure is stored. The real power comes
from God and not from us. 8We often
suffer, but we are never crushed. Even
when we don't know what to do, we
never give up. 9In times of trouble, God
is with us, and when we are knocked
down, we get up again. 10-11We face
death every day because of Jesus. Our
bodies show what his death was like, so
that his life can also be seen in us.
12This means that death is working in
us, but life is working in you.
13In the Scriptures it says, "I spoke because I had faith." We have that same
kind of faith. So we speak 14because we
know that God raised the Lord Jesus to
life. And just as God raised Jesus, he
will also raise us to life. Then he will
bring us into his presence together with
you. 15All of this has been done for you,
so that more and more people will know
how kind God is and will praise and
honor him.

Faith in the Lord

16We never give up. Our bodies are
gradually dying, but we ourselves are
being made stronger each day. 17These
little troubles are getting us ready for an
eternal glory that will make all our troubles seem like nothing. 18Things that are
seen don't last forever, but things that
are not seen are eternal. That's why we
keep our minds on the things that cannot be seen.
5 Our bodies are like tents that we live
in here on earth. But when these
tents are destroyed, we know that God
will give each of us a place to live. These
homes will not be buildings that someone has made, but they are in heaven
and will last forever. 2While we are here
on earth, we sigh because we want to
live in that heavenly home. 3We want to
put it on like clothes and not be naked.
4These tents we now live in are like a
heavy burden, and we groan. But we
don't do this just because we want to
leave these bodies that will die. It is because we want to change them for bodies that will never die. 5God is the one
who makes all of this possible. He has
given us his Spirit to make us certain
that he will do it. 6So always be cheerful!
As long as we are in these bodies, we
are away from the Lord. 7But we live by
faith, not by what we see. 8We should be
cheerful, because we would rather leave
these bodies and be at home with the
Lord. 9But whether we are at home with
the Lord or away from him, we still try
our best to please him. 10After all, Christ
will judge each of us for the good or the
bad that we do while living in these
bodies.

Bringing People to God

11We know what it means to respect
the Lord, and we encourage everyone to
turn to him. God himself knows what

we are like, and I hope you also know what kind of people we are. 12We are not trying once more to brag about ourselves. But we want you to be proud of us, when you are with those who are not sincere and brag about what others think of them.

13If we seem out of our minds, it is between God and us. But if we are in our right minds, it is for your good. 14We are ruled by Christ's love for us. We are certain that if one person died for everyone else, then all of us have died. 15And Christ did die for all of us. He died so we would no longer live for ourselves, but for the one who died and was raised to life for us.

16We are careful not to judge people by what they seem to be, though we once judged Christ in that way. 17Anyone who belongs to Christ is a new person. The past is forgotten, and everything is new. 18God has done it all! He sent Christ to make peace between himself and us, and he has given us the work of making peace between himself and others.

19What we mean is that God was in Christ, offering peace and forgiveness to the people of this world. And he has given us the work of sharing his message about peace. 20We were sent to speak for Christ, and God is begging you to listen to our message. We speak for Christ and sincerely ask you to make peace with God. 21Christ never sinned! But God treated him as a sinner, so that Christ could make us acceptable to God.

6 We work together with God, and we beg you to make good use of God's kindness to you. 2In the Scriptures God says,

"When the time came,
I listened to you,
and when you needed help,
I came to save you."

That time has come. This is the day for you to be saved.

3We don't want anyone to find fault with our work, and so we try hard not to cause problems. 4But in everything and in every way we show that we truly are God's servants. We have always been patient, though we have had a lot of trouble, suffering, and hard times. 5We have been beaten, put in jail, and hurt in riots. We have worked hard and have gone without sleep or food. 6But we have kept ourselves pure and have been understanding, patient, and kind. The Holy Spirit has been with us, and our love has been real. 7We have spoken the truth, and God's power has worked in us. In all our struggles we have said and done only what is right.

8Whether we were honored or dishonored or praised or cursed, we always told the truth about ourselves. But some people said we did not. 9We are unknown to others, but well known to you. We seem to be dying, and yet we are still alive. We have been punished, but never killed, 10and we are always happy, even in times of suffering. Although we are poor, we have made many people rich. And though we own nothing, everything is ours.

11Friends in Corinth, we are telling the truth when we say that there is room in our hearts for you. 12We are not holding back on our love for you, but you are holding back on your love for us. 13I speak to you as I would speak to my own children. Please make room in your hearts for us.

The Temple of the Living God

14Stay away from people who are not followers of the Lord! Can someone who is good get along with someone who is evil? Are light and darkness the same? 15Is Christ a friend of Satan?[e] Can people who follow the Lord have anything in common with those who don't? 16Do idols belong in the temple of God? We are the temple of the living God, as God himself says,

"I will live with these people
and walk among them.
I will be their God,
and they will be
my people."

17The Lord also says,

"Leave them and stay away!
Don't touch anything
that isn't clean.
Then I will welcome you
18 and be your Father.
You will be my sons
and my daughters,
as surely as I am God,
the All-Powerful."

7 My friends, God has made us these promises. So we should stay away from everything that keeps our bodies and spirits from being clean. We should honor God and try to be completely like him.

The Church Makes Paul Happy

2Make a place for us in your hearts! We haven't mistreated or hurt anyone. We haven't cheated anyone. 3I am not saying this to be hard on you. But, as I have said before, you will always be in our thoughts, whether we live or die.

[e]6.15 *Satan*: The Greek text has "Beliar," which is another form of the Hebrew word "Belial," meaning "wicked" or "useless." The Jewish people sometimes used this as a name for Satan.

4 I trust you completely.[f] I am always
proud of you, and I am greatly encouraged. In all my trouble I am still very
happy.
5 After we came to Macedonia, we
didn't have any chance to rest. We were
faced with all kinds of problems. We
were troubled by enemies and troubled
by fears. 6 But God cheers up people in
need, and that is what he did when he
sent Titus to us. 7 Of course, we were
glad to see Titus, but what really made
us glad is the way you cheered him up.
He told how sorry you were and how
concerned you were about me. And this
made me even happier.
8 I don't feel bad anymore, even
though my letter[g] hurt your feelings. I
did feel bad at first, but I don't now. I
know that the letter hurt you for a
while. 9 Now I am happy, but not because
I hurt your feelings. It is because God
used your hurt feelings to make you
turn back to him, and none of you were
harmed by us. 10 When God makes you
feel sorry enough to turn to him and be
saved, you don't have anything to feel
bad about. But when this world makes
you feel sorry, it can cause your death.
11 Just look what God has done by
making you feel sorry! You sincerely
want to prove that you are innocent. You
are angry. You are shocked. You are eager to see that justice is done. You have
proved that you were completely right
in this matter. 12 When I wrote you, it
wasn't to accuse the one who was
wrong or to take up for the one who
was hurt. I wrote, so that God would
show you how much you do care for us.
13 And we were greatly encouraged.
Although we were encouraged, we felt
even better when we saw how happy Titus was, because you had shown that he
had nothing to worry about. 14 We had
told him how much we thought of you,
and you did not disappoint us. Just as
we have always told you the truth, so
everything we told him about you has
also proved to be true. 15 Titus loves all
of you very much, especially when he
remembers how you obeyed him and
how you trembled with fear when you
welcomed him. 16 It makes me really
glad to know that I can depend on you.

Generous Giving

8 My friends, we want you to know
that the churches in Macedonia[h]
have shown others how kind God is.
2 Although they were going through
hard times and were very poor, they
were glad to give generously. 3 They
gave as much as they could afford and
even more, simply because they wanted
to. 4 They even asked and begged us to
let them have the joy of giving their
money for God's people. 5 And they did
more than we had hoped. They gave
themselves first to the Lord and then to
us, just as God wanted them to do.
6 Titus was the one who got you
started doing this good thing, so we
begged him to have you finish what you
had begun. 7 You do everything better
than anyone else. You have stronger
faith. You speak better and know more.
You are eager to give, and you love us
better.[i] Now you must give more generously than anyone else.
8 I am not ordering you to do this. I am
simply testing how real your love is by
comparing it with the concern that others have shown. 9 You know that our
Lord Jesus Christ was kind enough to
give up all his riches and become poor,
so that you could become rich.
10 A year ago you were the first ones to
give, and you gave because you wanted
to. So listen to my advice. 11 I think
you should finish what you started.
If you give according to what you have,
you will prove that you are as eager to
give as you were to think about giving.
12 It doesn't matter how much you have.
What matters is how much you are willing to give from what you have.
13 I am not trying to make life easier
for others by making life harder for you.
But it is only fair 14 for you to share with
them when you have so much, and they
have so little. Later, when they have
more than enough, and you are in need,
they can share with you. Then everyone
will have a fair share, 15 just as the Scriptures say,

"Those who gathered
too much
had nothing left.
Those who gathered
only a little
had all they needed."

Titus and His Friends

16 I am grateful that God made Titus
care as much about you as we do.
17 When we begged Titus to visit you, he
said he would. He wanted to because he
cared so much for you. 18 With Titus we
are also sending one of the Lord's followers who is well known in every
church for spreading the good news.
19 The churches chose this follower to

[f] **7.4** *I trust you completely*: Or "I have always spoken the truth to you" or "I can speak freely to you." [g] **7.8** *my letter*: There is no copy of this letter that Paul wrote to the church at Corinth. [h] **8.1** *churches in Macedonia*: The churches that Paul had started in Philippi and Thessalonica. The church in Berea is probably also meant. [i] **8.7** *you love us better*: Some manuscripts have "we love you better."

travel with us while we carry this gift
that will bring praise to the Lord and
show how much we hope to help. [20]We
don't want anyone to find fault with the
way we handle your generous gift. [21]But
we want to do what pleases the Lord
and what people think is right.
[22]We are also sending someone else
with Titus and the other follower. We approve of this man. In fact, he has already shown us many times that he
wants to help. And now he wants to help
even more than ever, because he trusts
you so much. [23]Titus is my partner, who
works with me to serve you. The other
two followers are sent by the churches,
and they bring honor to Christ. [24]Treat
them in such a way that the churches
will see your love and will know why we
bragged about you.

The Money for God's People

9 I don't need to write you about the
money you plan to give for God's
people. [2]I know how eager you are to
give. And I have proudly told the Lord's
followers in Macedonia that you people
in Achaia have been ready for a whole
year. Now your desire to give has made
them want to give. [3]That's why I am
sending Titus and the two others to
you. I want you to be ready, just as I
promised. This will prove that we were
not wrong to brag about you.
[4]Some followers from Macedonia may
come with me, and I want them to find
that you have the money ready. If you
don't, I would be embarrassed for trusting you to do this. But you would be embarrassed even more. [5]So I have decided
to ask Titus and the others to spend
some time with you before I arrive. This
way they can arrange to collect the
money you have promised. Then you
will have the chance to give because
you want to, and not because you feel
forced to.
[6]Remember this saying,

"A few seeds make
a small harvest,
but a lot of seeds make
a big harvest."

[7]Each of you must make up your own
mind about how much to give. But don't
feel sorry that you must give and don't
feel that you are forced to give. God
loves people who love to give. [8]God can
bless you with everything you need, and
you will always have more than enough
to do all kinds of good things for others.
[9]The Scriptures say,

"God freely gives his gifts
to the poor,
and always does right."

[10]God gives seed to farmers and provides everyone with food. He will increase what you have, so that you can
give even more to those in need. [11]You
will be blessed in every way, and you
will be able to keep on being generous.
Then many people will thank God when
we deliver your gift.
[12]What you are doing is much more
than a service that supplies God's people with what they need. It is something
that will make many others thank God.
[13]The way in which you have proved
yourselves by this service will bring
honor and praise to God. You believed
the message about Christ, and you
obeyed it by sharing generously with
God's people and with everyone else.
[14]Now they are praying for you and
want to see you, because God used you
to bless them so very much. [15]Thank
God for his gift that is too wonderful for
words!

Paul Defends His Work for Christ

10 Do you think I am a coward when
I am with you and brave when I
am far away? Well, I ask you to listen,
because Christ himself was humble and
gentle. [2]Some people have said that we
act like the people of this world. So
when I arrive, I expect I will have to be
firm and forceful in what I say to them.
Please don't make me treat you that
way. [3]We live in this world, but we don't
act like its people [4]or fight our battles
with the weapons of this world. Instead,
we use God's power that can destroy
fortresses. We destroy arguments [5]and
every bit of pride that keeps anyone
from knowing God. We capture people's
thoughts and make them obey Christ.
[6]And when you completely obey him,
we will punish anyone who refuses to
obey.
[7]You judge by appearances.[j] If any of
you think you are the only ones who belong to Christ, then think again. We belong to Christ as much as you do.
[8]Maybe I brag a little too much about
the authority that the Lord gave me to
help you and not to hurt you. Yet I am
not embarrassed to brag. [9]And I am not
trying to scare you with my letters.
[10]Some of you are saying, "Paul's letters
are harsh and powerful. But in person,
he is a weakling and has nothing worth
saying." [11]Those people had better understand that when I am with you, I will
do exactly what I say in my letters.
[12]We won't dare compare ourselves
with those who think so much of themselves. But they are foolish to compare
themselves with themselves. [13]We won't
brag about something we don't have a
right to brag about. We will only brag

[j]**10.7** *You judge by appearances*: Or "Take a close look at yourselves."

about the work that God has sent us to
do, and you are part of that work. [14]We
are not bragging more than we should.
After all, we did bring the message
about Christ to you.

[15]We don't brag about what others
have done, as if we had done those
things ourselves. But I hope that as you
become stronger in your faith, we will
be able to reach many more of the people around you.[k] That has always been
our goal. [16]Then we will be able to
preach the good news in other lands
where we cannot take credit for work
someone else has already done. [17]The
Scriptures say, "If you want to brag,
then brag about the Lord." [18]You may
brag about yourself, but the only approval that counts is the Lord's approval.

Paul and the False Apostles

11 Please put up with a little of my
foolishness. [2]I am as concerned
about you as God is. You were like a virgin bride I had chosen only for Christ.
[3]But now I fear that you will be tricked,
just as Eve was tricked by that lying
snake. I am afraid that you might stop
thinking about Christ in an honest and
sincere way. [4]We told you about Jesus,
and you received the Holy Spirit and accepted our message. But you let some
people tell you about another Jesus.
Now you are ready to receive another
spirit and accept a different message. [5]I
think I am as good as any of those super
apostles. [6]I may not speak as well as
they do, but I know as much. And this
has already been made perfectly clear
to you.

[7]Was it wrong for me to lower myself
and honor you by preaching God's message free of charge? [8]I robbed other
churches by taking money from them to
serve you. [9]Even when I was in need, I
still didn't bother you. In fact, some of
the Lord's followers from Macedonia
brought me what I needed. I have not
been a burden to you in the past, and I
will never be a burden. [10]As surely as I
speak the truth about Christ, no one in
Achaia can stop me from bragging
about this. [11]And it isn't because I don't
love you. God himself knows how much
I do love you.

[12]I plan to go on doing just what I
have always done. Then those people
won't be able to brag about doing the
same things we are doing. [13]Anyway,
they are no more than false apostles
and dishonest workers. They only pretend to be apostles of Christ. [14]And it is
no wonder. Even Satan tries to make
himself look like an angel of light. [15]So
why does it seem strange for Satan's
servants to pretend to do what is right?
Someday they will get exactly what they
deserve.

Paul's Sufferings for Christ

[16]I don't want any of you to think that
I am a fool. But if you do, then let me be
a fool and brag a little. [17]When I do all
this bragging, I do it as a fool and not
for the Lord. [18]Yet if others want to brag
about what they have done, so will I.
[19]And since you are so smart, you will
gladly put up with a fool. [20]In fact, you
let people make slaves of you and cheat
you and steal from you. Why, you even
let them strut around and slap you
in the face. [21]I am ashamed to say that
we are too weak to behave in such a
way.

If they can brag, so can I, but it is a
foolish thing to do. [22]Are they Hebrews?
So am I. Are they Jews? So am I. Are
they from the family of Abraham? Well,
so am I. [23]Are they servants of Christ? I
am a fool to talk this way, but I serve
him better than they do. I have worked
harder and have been put in jail more
times. I have been beaten with whips
more and have been in danger of death
more often.

[24]Five times the Jews gave me thirty-
nine lashes with a whip. [25]Three times
the Romans beat me with a big stick,
and once my enemies stoned me. I have
been shipwrecked three times, and I
even had to spend a night and a day in
the sea. [26]During my many travels, I
have been in danger from rivers, robbers, my own people, and foreigners.
My life has been in danger in cities, in
deserts, at sea, and with people who
only pretended to be the Lord's followers.

[27]I have worked and struggled and
spent many sleepless nights. I have gone
hungry and thirsty and often had nothing to eat. I have been cold from not
having enough clothes to keep me
warm. [28]Besides everything else, each
day I am burdened down, worrying
about all the churches. [29]When others
are weak, I am weak too. When others
are tricked into sin, I get angry.[l]

[30]If I have to brag, I will brag about
how weak I am. [31]God, the Father of our
Lord Jesus, knows I am not lying. And
God is to be praised forever! [32]The governor of Damascus at the time of King
Aretas had the city gates guarded, so
that he could capture me. [33]But I escaped by being let down in a basket
through a window in the city wall.

[k] **10.15** *we will be able to reach many more of the people around you*: Or "you will praise us even more because of our work among you." [l] **11.29** *When others are tricked into sin, I get angry*: Or "When others stumble into sin, I hurt for them."

Visions from the Lord

12 I have to brag. There is nothing to
be gained by it, but I must brag
about the visions and other things that
the Lord has shown me. 2 I know about
one of Christ's followers who was taken
up into the third heaven fourteen years
ago. I don't know if the man was still in
his body when it happened, but God certainly knows.
3 As I said, only God really knows if
this man was in his body at the time.
4 But he was taken up into paradise,[m]
where he heard things that are too wonderful to tell. 5 I will brag about that
man, but not about myself, except to say
how weak I am.
6 Yet even if I did brag, I would not be
foolish. I would simply be speaking the
truth. But I will try not to say too much.
That way, none of you will think more
highly of me than you should because of
what you have seen me do and say. 7 Of
course, I am now referring to the wonderful things I saw. One of Satan's angels was sent to make me suffer terribly,
so that I would not feel too proud.[n]
8 Three times I begged the Lord to
make this suffering go away. 9 But he
replied, "My kindness is all you need.
My power is strongest when you are
weak." So if Christ keeps giving me his
power, I will gladly brag about how
weak I am. 10 Yes, I am glad to be weak
or insulted or mistreated or to have
troubles and sufferings, if it is for
Christ. Because when I am weak, I am
strong.

Paul's Concern for the Lord's Followers at Corinth

11 I have been making a fool of myself.
But you forced me to do it, when you
should have been speaking up for me. I
may be nothing at all, but I am as good
as those super apostles. 12 When I was
with you, I was patient and worked all
the powerful miracles and signs and
wonders of a true apostle. 13 You missed
out on only one blessing that the other
churches received. That is, you didn't
have to support me. Forgive me for doing you wrong.
14 I am planning to visit you for the
third time. But I still won't make a burden of myself. What I really want is you,
and not what you have. Children are not
supposed to save up for their parents,
but parents are supposed to take care of
their children. 15 So I will gladly give all
that I have and all that I am. Will you
love me less for loving you too much?
16 You agree that I wasn't a burden to
you. Maybe that's because I was trying
to catch you off guard and trick you.
17 Were you cheated by any of those I
sent to you? 18 I urged Titus to visit you,
and I sent another follower with him.
But Titus didn't cheat you, and we felt
and behaved the same way he did.
19 Have you been thinking all along
that we have been defending ourselves
to you? Actually, we have been speaking
to God as followers of Christ. But, my
friends, we did it all for your good.
20 I am afraid that when I come, we
won't be pleased with each other. I fear
that some of you may be arguing or jealous or angry or selfish or gossiping or
insulting each other. I even fear that you
may be proud and acting like a mob. 21 I
am afraid God will make me ashamed
when I visit you again. I will feel like
crying because many of you have never
given up your old sins. You are still doing things that are immoral, indecent,
and shameful.

Final Warnings and Greetings

13 I am on my way to visit you for
the third time. And as the Scriptures say, "Any charges must be proved
true by at least two or three witnesses."
2 During my second visit I warned you
that I would punish you and anyone else
who doesn't stop sinning. I am far away
from you now, but I give you the same
warning. 3 This should prove to you that
I am speaking for Christ. When he corrects you, he won't be weak. He will be
powerful! 4 Although he was weak when
he was nailed to the cross, he now lives
by the power of God. We are weak, just
as Christ was. But you will see that we
will live by the power of God, just as
Christ does.
5 Test yourselves and find out if you really are true to your faith. If you pass
the test, you will discover that Christ is
living in you. But if Christ isn't living in
you, you have failed. 6 I hope you will
discover that we have not failed. 7 We
pray that you will stop doing evil things.
We don't pray like this to make ourselves look good, but to get you to do
right, even if we are failures.
8 All we can do is to follow the truth
and not fight against it. 9 Even though
we are weak, we are glad that you are
strong, and we pray that you will do
even better. 10 I am writing these things
to you before I arrive. This way I won't
have to be hard on you when I use the
authority that the Lord has given me. I

[m] **12.4** *paradise*: In the Greek translation of the Old Testament, this word is used for the Garden of Eden. In New Testament times it was sometimes used for the place where God's people are happy and at rest, as they wait for the final judgment.

[n] **12.7** *Of course . . . too proud*: Or "Because of the wonderful things that I saw, one of Satan's angels was sent to make me suffer terribly, so that I would not feel too proud."

was given this authority, so that I could
help you and not destroy you.
11Good-by, my friends. Do better and
pay attention to what I have said. Try to
get along and live peacefully with each
other.
Now I pray that God, who gives love
and peace, will be with you. 12Give each
other a warm greeting. All of God's people send their greetings.
13I pray that the Lord Jesus Christ will
bless you and be kind to you! May God
bless you with his love, and may the
Holy Spirit join all your hearts together.

GALATIANS

ABOUT THIS LETTER

From the very beginning of this letter to the churches in the region of Galatia (in central Asia Minor), Paul makes two things clear to his readers: he is a true apostle, and his message is the only true message (1.1-10). These statements were very important, because some people claimed that Paul was a false apostle with a false message.

Paul was indeed a true apostle, and his mission to the Gentiles was given to him by the Lord and approved by the apostles in Jerusalem (1.18—2.10). Paul had even corrected the apostle Peter, when he had stopped eating with Gentile followers who were not obeying the Law of Moses (2.1-18).

Faith is the only way to be saved. Paul insists that this was true already for Abraham, who had received God's promise by faith. And Paul leaves no doubt about what his own faith means to him:

> *I have been nailed to the cross with Christ. I have died, but Christ lives in me. And I now live by faith in the Son of God, who loved me and gave his life for me.*
>
> *(2.19b, 20)*

A QUICK LOOK AT THIS LETTER

A True Apostle and the True Message (1.1-10)
God Chose Paul To Be an Apostle (1.11-24)
Paul Defends His Message (2.1-21)
Faith Is the Only Way To Be Saved (3.1—4.31)
Guided by the Spirit and Love (5.1—6.10)
Final Warnings (6.11-18)

---

1 [1-2]From the apostle Paul and from
all the Lord's followers with me.
I was chosen to be an apostle by Jesus
Christ and by God the Father, who
raised him from death. No mere human
chose or appointed me to this work.
To the churches in Galatia.
[3]I pray that God the Father and our
Lord Jesus Christ will be kind to you
and will bless you with peace! [4]Christ
obeyed God our Father and gave himself
as a sacrifice for our sins to rescue us
from this evil world. [5]God will be given
glory forever and ever. Amen.

The Only True Message

[6]I am shocked that you have so
quickly turned from God, who chose
you because of his wonderful kindness.[a]
You have believed another message,
[7]when there is really only one true message.
But some people are causing you
trouble and want to make you turn
away from the good news about Christ.
[8]I pray that God will punish anyone who
preaches anything different from our
message to you! It doesn't matter if that
person is one of us or an angel from
heaven. [9]I have said it before, and I will
say it again. I hope God will punish anyone
who preaches anything different
from what you have already believed.
[10]I am not trying to please people. I
want to please God. Do you think I am
trying to please people? If I were doing
that, I would not be a servant of Christ.

How Paul Became an Apostle

[11]My friends, I want you to know that
no one made up the message I preach.
[12]It wasn't given or taught to me by
some mere human. My message came

[a]1.6 *his wonderful kindness*: Some manuscripts have "the wonderful kindness of Christ."

directly from Jesus Christ when he appeared to me.
13You know how I used to live as a
Jew. I was cruel to God's church and
even tried to destroy it. 14I was a much
better Jew than anyone else my own
age, and I obeyed every law that our ancestors had given us. 15But even before I
was born, God had chosen me. He was
kind and had decided 16to show me his
Son, so that I would announce his message to the Gentiles. I didn't talk this
over with anyone. 17I didn't say a word,
not even to the men in Jerusalem who
were apostles before I was. Instead, I
went at once to Arabia, and afterwards I
returned to Damascus.
18Three years later I went to visit Peter[b] in Jerusalem and stayed with him
for fifteen days. 19The only other apostle
I saw was James, the Lord's brother.
20And in the presence of God I swear I
am telling the truth.
21Later, I went to the regions of Syria
and Cilicia. 22But no one who belonged
to Christ's churches in Judea had ever
seen me in person. 23They had only
heard that the one who had been cruel
to them was now preaching the message
that he had once tried to destroy. 24And
because of me, they praised God.
2 Fourteen years later I went to
Jerusalem with Barnabas. I also
took along Titus. 2But I went there because God had told me to go, and I explained the good news that I had been
preaching to the Gentiles. Then I met
privately with the ones who seemed to
be the most important leaders. I wanted
to make sure that my work in the past
and my future work would not be for
nothing.
3Titus went to Jerusalem with me. He
was a Greek, but still he wasn't forced
to be circumcised. 4We went there because of those who pretended to be followers and had sneaked in among us as
spies. They had come to take away the
freedom that Christ Jesus had given us,
and they were trying to make us their
slaves. 5But we wanted you to have the
true message. That's why we didn't give
in to them, not even for a second.
6Some of them were supposed to be
important leaders, but I didn't care who
they were. God doesn't have any favorites! None of these so-called special
leaders added anything to my message. 7They realized that God had sent
me with the good news for Gentiles,
and that he had sent Peter with the
same message for Jews. 8God, who
had sent Peter on a mission to the Jews,
was now using me to preach to the Gentiles.
9James, Peter,[b] and John realized that
God had given me the message about
his undeserved kindness. And these
men are supposed to be the backbone of
the church. They even gave Barnabas
and me a friendly handshake. This was
to show that we would work with Gentiles and that they would work with
Jews. 10They only asked us to remember
the poor, and that was something I had
always been eager to do.

Paul Corrects Peter at Antioch

11When Peter came to Antioch, I told
him face to face that he was wrong. 12He
used to eat with Gentile followers of the
Lord, until James sent some Jewish followers. Peter was afraid of the Jews and
soon stopped eating with Gentiles. 13He
and the other Jews hid their true feelings
so well that even Barnabas was fooled.
14But when I saw that they were not really obeying the truth that is in the good
news, I corrected Peter in front of everyone and said:

Peter, you are a Jew, but you live
like a Gentile. So how can you force
Gentiles to live like Jews?
15We are Jews by birth and are not
sinners like Gentiles. 16But we know
that God accepts only those who
have faith in Jesus Christ. No one
can please God by simply obeying
the Law. So we put our faith in
Christ Jesus, and God accepted us
because of our faith.
17When we Jews started looking
for a way to please God, we discovered that we are sinners too. Does
this mean that Christ is the one who
makes us sinners? No, it doesn't!
18But if I tear down something and
then build it again, I prove that I was
wrong at first. 19It was the Law itself
that killed me and freed me from
its power, so that I could live for
God.
I have been nailed to the cross
with Christ. 20I have died, but Christ
lives in me. And I now live by faith
in the Son of God, who loved me and
gave his life for me. 21I don't turn my
back on God's undeserved kindness.
If we can be acceptable to God by
obeying the Law, it was useless for
Christ to die.

Faith Is the Only Way

3 You stupid Galatians! I told you exactly how Jesus Christ was nailed to
a cross. Has someone now put an evil
spell on you? 2I want to know only one
thing. How were you given God's Spirit?
Was it by obeying the Law of Moses or
by hearing about Christ and having

[b]1.18;2.9 *Peter*: The Greek text has "Cephas," which is an Aramaic name meaning "rock."
Peter is the Greek name with the same meaning.

faith in him? [3]How can you be so stupid? Do you think that by yourself you can complete what God's Spirit started in you? [4]Have you gone through all of this for nothing? Is it all really for nothing? [5]God gives you his Spirit and works miracles in you. But does he do this because you obey the Law of Moses or because you have heard about Christ and have faith in him?

[6]The Scriptures say that God accepted Abraham because Abraham had faith. [7]And so, you should understand that everyone who has faith is a child of Abraham.[c] [8]Long ago the Scriptures said that God would accept the Gentiles because of their faith. That's why God told Abraham the good news that all nations would be blessed because of him. [9]This means that everyone who has faith will share in the blessings that were given to Abraham because of his faith.

[10]Anyone who tries to please God by obeying the Law is under a curse. The Scriptures say, "Everyone who doesn't obey everything in the Law is under a curse." [11]No one can please God by obeying the Law. The Scriptures also say, "The people God accepts because of their faith will live."[d]

[12]The Law isn't based on faith. It promises life only to people who obey its commands. [13]But Christ rescued us from the Law's curse, when he became a curse in our place. This is because the Scriptures say that anyone who is nailed to a tree is under a curse. [14]And because of what Jesus Christ has done, the blessing that was promised to Abraham was taken to the Gentiles. This happened so that by faith we would be given the promised Holy Spirit.

The Law and the Promise

[15]My friends, I will use an everyday example to explain what I mean. Once someone agrees to something, no one else can change or cancel the agreement.[e] [16]That is how it is with the promises God made to Abraham and his descendant.[f] The promises were not made to many descendants, but only to one, and that one is Christ. [17]What I am saying is that the Law cannot change or cancel God's promise that was made 430 years before the Law was given. [18]If we have to obey the Law in order to receive God's blessings, those blessings don't really come to us because of God's promise. But God was kind to Abraham and made him a promise.

[19]What is the use of the Law? It was given later to show that we sin. But it was only supposed to last until the coming of that descendant[g] who was given the promise. In fact, angels gave the Law to Moses, and he gave it to the people. [20]There is only one God, and the Law did not come directly from him.

Slaves and Children

[21]Does the Law disagree with God's promises? No, it doesn't! If any law could give life to us, we could become acceptable to God by obeying that law. [22]But the Scriptures say that sin controls everyone, so that God's promises will be for anyone who has faith in Jesus Christ.

[23]The Law controlled us and kept us under its power until the time came when we would have faith. [24]In fact, the Law was our teacher. It was supposed to teach us until we had faith and were acceptable to God. [25]But once a person has learned to have faith, there is no more need to have the Law as a teacher.

[26]All of you are God's children because of your faith in Christ Jesus. [27]And when you were baptized, it was as though you had put on Christ in the same way you put on new clothes. [28]Faith in Christ Jesus is what makes each of you equal with each other, whether you are a Jew or a Greek, a slave or a free person, a man or a woman. [29]So if you belong to Christ, you are now part of Abraham's family,[h] and you will be given what God has promised.

4 [1]Children who are under age are no better off than slaves, even though everything their parents own will someday be theirs. [2]This is because children are placed in the care of guardians and teachers until the time their parents have set. [3]That is how it was with us. We were like children ruled by the powers of this world.

[4]But when the time was right, God sent his Son, and a woman gave birth to him. His Son obeyed the Law, [5]so he could set us free from the Law, and we could become God's children. [6]Now that we are his children, God has sent the Spirit of his Son into our hearts. And his

[c]**3.7** *a child of Abraham*: God chose Abraham, and so it was believed that anyone who was a child of Abraham was also a child of God (see the note at 3.29). [d]**3.11** *The people God accepts because of their faith will live*: Or "The people God accepts will live because of their faith." [e]**3.15** *Once someone . . . cancel the agreement*: Or "Once a person makes out a will, no one can change or cancel it." [f]**3.16** *descendant*: The Greek text has "seed," which may mean one or many descendants. In this verse Paul says it means Christ. [g]**3.19** *that descendant*: Jesus. [h]**3.29** *you are now part of Abraham's family*: Paul tells the Galatians that faith in Jesus Christ is what makes someone a true child of Abraham and of God (see the note at 3.7).

Spirit tells us that God is our Father. [7]You are no longer slaves. You are God's children, and you will be given what he has promised.

Paul's Concern for the Galatians

[8]Before you knew God, you were slaves of gods that are not real. [9]But now you know God, or better still, God knows you. How can you turn back and become the slaves of those weak and pitiful powers?[i] [10]You even celebrate certain days, months, seasons, and years. [11]I am afraid I have wasted my time working with you.

[12]My friends, I beg you to be like me, just as I once tried to be like you. Did you mistreat me [13]when I first preached to you? No you didn't, even though you knew I had come there because I was sick. [14]My illness must have caused you some trouble, but you didn't hate me or turn me away because of it. You welcomed me as though I were one of God's angels or even Christ Jesus himself. [15]Where is that good feeling now? I am sure that if it had been possible, you would have taken out your own eyes and given them to me. [16]Am I now your enemy, just because I told you the truth?

[17]Those people may be paying you a lot of attention, but it isn't for your good. They only want to keep you away from me, so you will pay them a lot of attention. [18]It is always good to give your attention to something worthwhile, even when I am not with you. [19]My children, I am in terrible pain until Christ may be seen living in you. [20]I wish I were with you now. Then I would not have to talk this way. You really have me puzzled.

Hagar and Sarah

[21]Some of you would like to be under the rule of the Law of Moses. But do you know what the Law says? [22]In the Scriptures we learn that Abraham had two sons. The mother of one of them was a slave, while the mother of the other one had always been free. [23]The son of the slave woman was born in the usual way. But the son of the free woman was born because of God's promise.

[24]All of this has another meaning as well. Each of the two women stands for one of the agreements God made with his people. Hagar, the slave woman, stands for the agreement that was made at Mount Sinai. Everyone born into her family is a slave. [25]Hagar also stands for Mount Sinai in Arabia[j] and for the present city of Jerusalem. She[k] and her children are slaves.

[26]But our mother is the city of Jerusalem in heaven above, and she isn't a slave. [27]The Scriptures say about her,

"You have never had children,
 but now you can be glad.
You have never given birth,
 but now you can shout.
Once you had no children,
 but now you will have
more children than a woman
who has been married
 for a long time."

[28]My friends, you were born because of this promise, just as Isaac was. [29]But the child who was born in the natural way made trouble for the child who was born because of the Spirit. The same thing is happening today. [30]The Scriptures say, "Get rid of the slave woman and her son! He won't be given anything. The son of the free woman will receive everything." [31]My friends, we are children of the free woman and not of the slave.

Christ Gives Freedom

5 Christ has set us free! This means we are really free. Now hold on to your freedom and don't ever become slaves of the Law again.

[2]I, Paul, promise you that Christ won't do you any good if you get circumcised. [3]If you do, you must obey the whole Law. [4]And if you try to please God by obeying the Law, you have cut yourself off from Christ and his wonderful kindness. [5]But the Spirit makes us sure that God will accept us because of our faith in Christ. [6]If you are a follower of Christ Jesus, it makes no difference whether you are circumcised or not. All that matters is your faith that makes you love others.

[7]You were doing so well until someone made you turn from the truth. [8]And that person was certainly not sent by the one who chose you. [9]A little yeast can change a whole batch of dough, [10]but you belong to the Lord. That makes me certain that you will do what I say, instead of what someone else tells you to do. Whoever is causing trouble for you will be punished.

[11]My friends, if I still preach that people need to be circumcised, why am I in so much trouble? The message about the cross would no longer be a problem, if I told people to be circumcised. [12]I wish that everyone who is upsetting you

[i]**4.9** *powers*: Spirits were thought to control human lives and were believed to be connected with the movements of the stars. [j]**4.25** *Hagar also stands for Mount Sinai in Arabia*: Some manuscripts have "Sinai is a mountain in Arabia." This sentence would then be translated: "Sinai is a mountain in Arabia, and Hagar stands for the present city of Jerusalem."
[k]**4.25** *She*: "Hagar" or "Jerusalem."

would not only get circumcised, but
would cut off much more!
13 My friends, you were chosen to be
free. So don't use your freedom as an
excuse to do anything you want. Use it
as an opportunity to serve each other
with love. 14 All that the Law says can be
summed up in the command to love others as much as you love yourself. 15 But
if you keep attacking each other like
wild animals, you had better watch out
or you will destroy yourselves.

God's Spirit and Our Own Desires

16 If you are guided by the Spirit, you
won't obey your selfish desires. 17 The
Spirit and your desires are enemies of
each other. They are always fighting
each other and keeping you from doing
what you feel you should. 18 But if you
obey the Spirit, the Law of Moses has
no control over you.
19 People's desires make them give in
to immoral ways, filthy thoughts, and
shameful deeds. 20 They worship idols,
practice witchcraft, hate others, and are
hard to get along with. People become
jealous, angry, and selfish. They not
only argue and cause trouble, but they
are 21 envious. They get drunk, carry on
at wild parties, and do other evil things
as well. I told you before, and I am
telling you again: No one who does
these things will share in the blessings
of God's kingdom.
22 God's Spirit makes us loving, happy,
peaceful, patient, kind, good, faithful,
23 gentle, and self-controlled. There is no
law against behaving in any of these
ways. 24 And because we belong to
Christ Jesus, we have killed our selfish
feelings and desires. 25 God's Spirit has
given us life, and so we should follow
the Spirit. 26 But don't be conceited or
make others jealous by claiming to be
better than they are.

Help Each Other

6 My friends, you are spiritual. So if
someone is trapped in sin, you
should gently lead that person back to
the right path. But watch out, and don't
be tempted yourself. 2 You obey the law
of Christ when you offer each other a
helping hand.
3 If you think you are better than others, when you really aren't, you are
wrong. 4 Do your own work well, and
then you will have something to be
proud of. But don't compare yourself
with others. 5 We each must carry our
own load.
6 Share every good thing you have
with anyone who teaches you what God
has said.
7 You cannot fool God, so don't make a
fool of yourself! You will harvest what
you plant. 8 If you follow your selfish desires, you will harvest destruction, but if
you follow the Spirit, you will harvest
eternal life. 9 Don't get tired of helping
others. You will be rewarded when the
time is right, if you don't give up. 10 We
should help people whenever we can,
especially if they are followers of the
Lord.

Final Warnings

11 You can see what big letters I make
when I write with my own hand.
12 Those people who are telling you to
get circumcised are only trying to show
how important they are. And they don't
want to get into trouble for preaching
about the cross of Christ. 13 They are circumcised, but they don't obey the Law
of Moses. All they want is to brag about
having you circumcised. 14 But I will
never brag about anything except the
cross of our Lord Jesus Christ. Because
of his cross, the world is dead as far as I
am concerned, and I am dead as far as
the world is concerned.
15 It doesn't matter if you are circumcised or not. All that matters is that you
are a new person.
16 If you follow this rule, you will belong to God's true people. God will treat
you with undeserved kindness and will
bless you with peace.
17 On my own body are scars that
prove I belong to Christ Jesus. So I don't
want anyone to bother me anymore.
18 My friends, I pray that the Lord Jesus Christ will be kind to you! Amen.

EPHESIANS

ABOUT THIS LETTER

"Praise the God and Father of our Lord Jesus Christ for the spiritual blessings that Christ has brought us from heaven!" (1.3). Paul begins his letter to the Christians in Ephesus with a powerful reminder of the main theme of his message. Christ died on the cross to set us free (1.7, 8). But God raised Christ from death, and he now sits at God's right side in heaven, where he rules over this world. And he will rule over the future world as well (1.20, 21).

Christ brought Jews and Gentiles together by "breaking down the wall of hatred" that separated them (2.14) and he united them all as part of that holy temple where God's Spirit lives (2.22). This was according to God's eternal plan (3.11).

There is only one Lord, one Spirit of God, and one God, who is the Father of all people (4.4, 5). This means that Christians must let the Spirit keep their hearts united, so they can live at peace with each other (4.3). The idea of all Christians being one with Christ is so central to this letter that it occurs twenty times. There is one faith and one baptism by which believers become one body.

Ephesus was a port city on the western shore of Asia Minor (modern-day Turkey). In Paul's time this was the fourth largest city in the Roman Empire. It was also an ancient center of nature religion where the goddess Artemis was widely worshiped (Acts 19).

Paul lets the Ephesians know that much is expected of people who are called to a new life (4.17—5.20). Followers of the Lord are God's dear children, and they must do as God does (5.1). They used to live in the dark, but they must now live in the light and make their light shine (5.8, 9).

Paul then teaches husbands and wives, children and parents, and slaves and masters how to live as Christians (5.21—6.9).

Paul never forgets how kind God is:

God was merciful! We were dead because of our sins, but God loved us so much that he made us alive with Christ, and God's wonderful kindness is what saves you. *(2.4, 5)*

You were saved by faith in God, who treats us much better than we deserve. This is God's gift to you, and not anything you have done on your own. *(2.8)*

A QUICK LOOK AT THIS LETTER

Greetings (1.1, 2)
Christ Brings Spiritual Blessings (1.3—3.21)
A New Life in Unity with Christ (4.1—6.20)
Final Greetings (6.21-24)

---

1 From Paul, chosen by God to be an
apostle of Christ Jesus.
To God's people who live in Ephesus
and[a] are faithful followers of Christ Jesus.
2 I pray that God our Father and our
Lord Jesus Christ will be kind to you
and will bless you with peace!

Christ Brings Spiritual Blessings

3 Praise the God and Father of our
Lord Jesus Christ for the spiritual bless-

[a] **1.1** *live in Ephesus and*: Some manuscripts do not have these words.

ings that Christ has brought us from
heaven! [4]Before the world was created,
God had Christ choose us to live with
him and to be his holy and innocent and
loving people. [5]God was kind[b] and decided that Christ would choose us to be
God's own adopted children. [6]God was
very kind to us because of the Son he
dearly loves, and so we should praise
God.

[7-8]Christ sacrificed his life's blood to
set us free, which means that our sins
are now forgiven. Christ did this because God was so kind to us. God has
great wisdom and understanding, [9]and
by what Christ has done, God has
shown us his own mysterious ways.
[10]Then when the time is right, God will
do all that he has planned, and Christ
will bring together everything in heaven
and on earth.

[11]God always does what he plans, and
that's why he appointed Christ to choose
us. [12]He did this so that we Jews would
bring honor to him and be the first ones
to have hope because of him. [13]Christ
also brought you the truth, which is the
good news about how you can be saved.
You put your faith in Christ and were
given the promised Holy Spirit to show
that you belong to God. [14]The Spirit also
makes us sure that we will be given
what God has stored up for his people.
Then we will be set free, and God will
be honored and praised.

Paul's Prayer

[15]I have heard about your faith in the
Lord Jesus and your love for all of
God's people. [16]So I never stop being
grateful for you, as I mention you in my
prayers. [17]I ask the glorious Father and
God of our Lord Jesus Christ to give you
his Spirit. The Spirit will make you wise
and let you understand what it means to
know God. [18]My prayer is that light will
flood your hearts and that you will understand the hope that was given to you
when God chose you. Then you will discover the glorious blessings that will be
yours together with all of God's people.

[19]I want you to know about the great
and mighty power that God has for us
followers. It is the same wonderful
power he used [20]when he raised Christ
from death and let him sit at his right
side[c] in heaven. [21]There Christ rules
over all forces, authorities, powers, and
rulers. He rules over all beings in this
world and will rule in the future world
as well. [22]God has put all things under
the power of Christ, and for the good of
the church he has made him the head of
everything. [23]The church is Christ's
body and is filled with Christ who completely fills everything.[d]

From Death to Life

2 In the past you were dead because
you sinned and fought against God.
[2]You followed the ways of this world
and obeyed the devil. He rules the
world, and his spirit has power over
everyone who doesn't obey God. [3]Once
we were also ruled by the selfish desires
of our bodies and minds. We had made
God angry, and we were going to be
punished like everyone else.

[4-5]But God was merciful! We were
dead because of our sins, but God loved
us so much that he made us alive with
Christ, and God's wonderful kindness is
what saves you. [6]God raised us from
death to life with Christ Jesus, and he
has given us a place beside Christ in
heaven. [7]God did this so that in the future world he could show how truly
good and kind he is to us because of
what Christ Jesus has done. [8]You were
saved by faith in God, who treats us
much better than we deserve.[e] This is
God's gift to you, and not anything you
have done on your own. [9]It isn't something you have earned, so there is nothing you can brag about. [10]God planned
for us to do good things and to live as
he has always wanted us to live. That's
why he sent Christ to make us what we
are.

United by Christ

[11]Don't forget that you are Gentiles. In
fact, you used to be called "uncircumcised" by those who take pride in being
circumcised. [12]At that time you did not
know about Christ. You were foreigners
to the people of Israel, and you had no
part in the promises that God had made
to them. You were living in this world
without hope and without God, [13]and
you were far from God. But Christ offered his life's blood as a sacrifice and
brought you near God.

[14]Christ has made peace between
Jews and Gentiles, and he has united us
by breaking down the wall of hatred
that separated us. Christ gave his own
body [15]to destroy the Law of Moses with
all its rules and commands. He even
brought Jews and Gentiles together as
though we were only one person, when
he united us in peace. [16]On the cross

[b]**1.4,5** *holy and innocent and loving people. [5]God was kind*: Or "holy and innocent people. God was loving [5]and kind." [c]**1.20** *right side*: The place of power and honor. [d]**1.23** *and is filled with Christ who completely fills everything*: Or "which completely fills Christ and fully completes his work." [e]**2.8** *treats us much better than we deserve*: The Greek word *charis*, traditionally rendered "grace," is translated here and other places in the CEV to express the overwhelming kindness of God.

Christ did away with our hatred for
each other. He also made peace[f] between us and God by uniting Jews and
Gentiles in one body. 17 Christ came and
preached peace to you Gentiles, who
were far from God, and peace to us
Jews, who were near God. 18 And because of Christ, all of us can come to the
Father by the same Spirit.
19 You Gentiles are no longer strangers
and foreigners. You are citizens with
everyone else who belongs to the family
of God. 20 You are like a building with
the apostles and prophets as the foundation and with Christ as the most important stone. 21 Christ is the one who holds
the building together and makes it grow
into a holy temple for the Lord. 22 And
you are part of that building Christ has
built as a place for God's own Spirit to
live.

Paul's Mission to the Gentiles

3 Christ Jesus made me his prisoner,
so that I could help you Gentiles.
2 You have surely heard about God's
kindness in choosing me to help you. 3 In
fact, this letter tells you a little about
how God has shown me his mysterious
ways. 4 As you read the letter, you will
also find out how well I really do understand the mystery about Christ. 5 No one
knew about this mystery until God's
Spirit told it to his holy apostles and
prophets. 6 And the mystery is this: Because of Christ Jesus, the good news
has given the Gentiles a share in the
promises that God gave to the Jews.
God has also let the Gentiles be part of
the same body.
7 God treated me with kindness. His
power worked in me, and it became my
job to spread the good news. 8 I am the
least important of all God's people. But
God was kind and chose me to tell the
Gentiles that because of Christ there are
blessings that cannot be measured.
9 God, who created everything, wanted
me to help everyone understand the
mysterious plan that had always been
hidden in his mind. 10 Then God would
use the church to show the powers and
authorities in the spiritual world that
he has many different kinds of wisdom.
11 God did this according to his eternal
plan. And he was able to do what he had
planned because of all that Christ Jesus
our Lord had done. 12 Christ now gives
us courage and confidence, so that we
can come to God by faith. 13 That's why
you should not be discouraged when I
suffer for you. After all, it will bring
honor to you.

Christ's Love for Us

14 I kneel in prayer to the Father. 15 All
beings in heaven and on earth receive
their life from him.[g] 16 God is wonderful
and glorious. I pray that his Spirit will
make you become strong followers
17 and that Christ will live in your hearts
because of your faith. Stand firm and be
deeply rooted in his love. 18 I pray that
you and all of God's people will understand what is called wide or long or
high or deep.[h] 19 I want you to know all
about Christ's love, although it is too
wonderful to be measured. Then your
lives will be filled with all that God is.
20-21 I pray that Christ Jesus and the
church will forever bring praise to God.
His power at work in us can do far more
than we dare ask or imagine. Amen.

Unity with Christ

4 As a prisoner of the Lord, I beg you
to live in a way that is worthy of the
people God has chosen to be his own.
2 Always be humble and gentle. Patiently
put up with each other and love each
other. 3 Try your best to let God's Spirit
keep your hearts united. Do this by living at peace. 4 All of you are part of the
same body. There is only one Spirit of
God, just as you were given one hope
when you were chosen to be God's people. 5 We have only one Lord, one faith,
and one baptism. 6 There is one God who
is the Father of all people. Not only is
God above all others, but he works by
using all of us, and he lives in all of us.
7 Christ has generously divided out his
gifts to us. 8 As the Scriptures say,

"When he went up
  to the highest place,
he led away many prisoners
  and gave gifts to people."

9 When it says, "he went up," it means
that Christ had been deep in the earth.
10 This also means that the one who
went deep into the earth is the same one
who went into the highest heaven, so
that he would fill the whole universe.
11 Christ chose some of us to be apostles, prophets, missionaries, pastors, and
teachers, 12 so that his people would
learn to serve and his body would grow
strong. 13 This will continue until we are
united by our faith and by our understanding of the Son of God. Then we
will be mature, just as Christ is, and we
will be completely like him.[i]

[f] **2.16** *He also made peace*: Or "The cross also made peace." [g] **3.15** *receive their life from him*: Or "know who they really are because of him." [h] **3.18** *what is called wide or long or high or deep*: This may refer to the heavenly Jerusalem or to God's love or wisdom or to the meaning of the cross. [i] **4.13** *and we will be completely like him*: Or "and he is completely perfect."

14We must stop acting like children.
We must not let deceitful people trick us
by their false teachings, which are like
winds that toss us around from place to
place. 15Love should always make us tell
the truth. Then we will grow in every
way and be more like Christ, the head
16of the body. Christ holds it together
and makes all of its parts work perfectly, as it grows and becomes strong
because of love.

The Old Life and the New Life

17As a follower of the Lord, I order
you to stop living like stupid, godless
people. 18Their minds are in the dark,
and they are stubborn and ignorant and
have missed out on the life that comes
from God. They no longer have any feelings about what is right, 19and they are
so greedy that they do all kinds of indecent things.

20-21But that isn't what you were
taught about Jesus Christ. He is the
truth, and you heard about him and
learned about him. 22You were told that
your foolish desires will destroy you
and that you must give up your old way
of life with all its bad habits. 23Let the
Spirit change your way of thinking
24and make you into a new person. You
were created to be like God, and so you
must please him and be truly holy.

Rules for the New Life

25We are part of the same body. Stop
lying and start telling each other the
truth. 26Don't get so angry that you sin.
Don't go to bed angry 27and don't give
the devil a chance.

28If you are a thief, quit stealing. Be
honest and work hard, so you will have
something to give to people in need.

29Stop all your dirty talk. Say the right
thing at the right time and help others
by what you say.

30Don't make God's Spirit sad. The
Spirit makes you sure that someday you
will be free from your sins.

31Stop being bitter and angry and
mad at others. Don't yell at one another
or curse each other or ever be rude. 32In-
stead, be kind and merciful, and forgive
others, just as God forgave you because
of Christ.

5 Do as God does. After all, you are
his dear children. 2Let love be your
guide. Christ loved us[j] and offered his
life for us as a sacrifice that pleases
God.

3You are God's people, so don't let it
be said that any of you are immoral or
indecent or greedy. 4Don't use dirty or
foolish or filthy words. Instead, say how
thankful you are. 5Being greedy, indecent, or immoral is just another way of
worshiping idols. You can be sure that
people who behave in this way will
never be part of the kingdom that belongs to Christ and to God.

Living as People of Light

6Don't let anyone trick you with foolish talk. God punishes everyone who
disobeys him and says[k] foolish things.
7So don't have anything to do with anyone like that.

8You used to be like people living in
the dark, but now you are people of the
light because you belong to the Lord. So
act like people of the light 9and make
your light shine. Be good and honest
and truthful, 10as you try to please the
Lord. 11Don't take part in doing those
worthless things that are done in the
dark. Instead, show how wrong they
are. 12It is disgusting even to talk about
what is done in the dark. 13But the light
will show what these things are really
like. 14Light shows up everything,[l] just
as the Scriptures say,

"Wake up from your sleep
and rise from death.
Then Christ will shine on you."

15Act like people with good sense and
not like fools. 16These are evil times, so
make every minute count. 17Don't be
stupid. Instead, find out what the Lord
wants you to do. 18Don't destroy yourself by getting drunk, but let the Spirit
fill your life. 19When you meet together,
sing psalms, hymns, and spiritual songs,
as you praise the Lord with all your
heart. 20Always use the name of our
Lord Jesus Christ to thank God the
Father for everything.

Wives and Husbands

21Honor Christ and put others first.
22A wife should put her husband first, as
she does the Lord. 23A husband is the
head of his wife, as Christ is the head
and the Savior of the church, which is
his own body. 24Wives should always
put their husbands first, as the church
puts Christ first.

25A husband should love his wife as
much as Christ loved the church and
gave his life for it. 26He made the church
holy by the power of his word, and he
made it pure by washing it with water.
27Christ did this, so that he would have a
glorious and holy church, without faults
or spots or wrinkles or any other flaws.

28In the same way, a husband should
love his wife as much as he loves himself. A husband who loves his wife
shows that he loves himself. 29None of
us hate our own bodies. We provide for

[j]**5.2** *us*: Some manuscripts have "you." [k]**5.6** *says*: Or "does." [l]**5.14** *Light shows up everything*: Or "Everything that is seen in the light becomes light itself."

them and take good care of them, just as
Christ does for the church, 30because we
are each part of his body. 31As the Scriptures say, "A man leaves his father and
mother to get married, and he becomes
like one person with his wife." 32This is
a great mystery, but I understand it to
mean Christ and his church. 33So each
husband should love his wife as much
as he loves himself, and each wife
should respect her husband.

Children and Parents

6 Children, you belong to the Lord,
and you do the right thing when you
obey your parents. The first commandment with a promise says, 2"Obey your
father and your mother, 3and you will
have a long and happy life."
4Parents, don't be hard on your children. Raise them properly. Teach them
and instruct them about the Lord.

Slaves and Masters

5Slaves, you must obey your earthly
masters. Show them great respect and
be as loyal to them as you are to Christ.
6Try to please them at all times, and not
just when you think they are watching.
You are slaves of Christ, so with your
whole heart you must do what God
wants you to do. 7Gladly serve your
masters, as though they were the Lord
himself, and not simply people. 8You
know that you will be rewarded for any
good things you do, whether you are
slaves or free.
9Slave owners, you must treat your
slaves with this same respect. Don't
threaten them. They have the same Master in heaven that you do, and he doesn't
have any favorites.

The Fight against Evil

10Finally, let the mighty strength of
the Lord make you strong. 11Put on all
the armor that God gives, so you can defend yourself against the devil's tricks.
12We are not fighting against humans.
We are fighting against forces and authorities and against rulers of darkness
and powers in the spiritual world. 13So
put on all the armor that God gives.
Then when that evil day[m] comes, you
will be able to defend yourself. And
when the battle is over, you will still be
standing firm.
14Be ready! Let the truth be like a belt
around your waist, and let God's justice
protect you like armor. 15Your desire to
tell the good news about peace should
be like shoes on your feet. 16Let your
faith be like a shield, and you will be
able to stop all the flaming arrows of
the evil one. 17Let God's saving power
be like a helmet, and for a sword use
God's message that comes from the
Spirit.
18Never stop praying, especially for
others. Always pray by the power of the
Spirit. Stay alert and keep praying for
God's people. 19Pray that I will be given
the message to speak and that I may
fearlessly explain the mystery about the
good news. 20I was sent to do this work,
and that's the reason I am in jail. So
pray that I will be brave and will speak
as I should.

Final Greetings

21-22I want you to know how I am getting along and what I am doing. That's
why I am sending Tychicus to you. He is
a dear friend, as well as a faithful servant of the Lord. He will tell you how I
am doing, and he will cheer you up.
23I pray that God the Father and the
Lord Jesus Christ will give peace, love,
and faith to every follower! 24May God
be kind to everyone who keeps on loving our Lord Jesus Christ.

[m]**6.13** *that evil day*: Either the present (see 5.16) or "the day of death" or "the day of judgment."

PHILIPPIANS

ABOUT THIS LETTER

Paul wrote this letter from jail (1.7) to thank the Lord's followers at Philippi for helping him with their gifts and prayers (1.5; 4.10-19). He hopes to be set free, so that he can continue preaching the good news (3.17-19). But he knows that he might be put to death (1.21; 2.17; 3.10).

The city of Philippi is in the part of northern Greece known as Macedonia. It was at Philippi that Paul had entered Europe for the first time, and there he preached the good news and began a church (Acts 16). He now warns the Christians at Philippi that they may have to suffer, just as Christ suffered and Paul is now suffering. If this happens, the Philippians should count it a blessing that comes from having faith in Christ (1.28-30).

There were problems in the church at Philippi, because some of the members claimed that people must obey the law of Moses, or they could not be saved. But Paul has no patience with such members and warns the church, "Watch out for those people who behave like dogs!" (3.2-11). This letter is also filled with joy. Even in jail, Paul is happy because he has discovered how to make the best of a bad situation and because he remembers all the kindness shown to him by the people in the church at Philippi.

Paul reminds them that God's people are to live in harmony (2.2; 4.2, 3) and to think the same way that Christ Jesus did:

Christ was truly God.
But he did not try to remain
equal with God.
He gave up everything
and became a slave,
when he became
like one of us. (2.6, 7)

A QUICK LOOK AT THIS LETTER

Greetings and a Prayer (1.1-11)
What Life Means to Paul (1.12-30)
Christ's Example of True Humility (2.1-18)
News about Paul's Friends (2.19-30)
Being Acceptable to God (3.1—4.9)
Paul Thanks the Philippians (4.10-20)
Final Greetings (4.21-23)

---

1 From Paul and Timothy, servants of
Christ Jesus.
To all of God's people who belong to
Christ Jesus at Philippi and to all of
your church officials and officers.[a]
2I pray that God our Father and the
Lord Jesus Christ will be kind to you
and will bless you with peace!

Paul's Prayer for the Church in Philippi

3Every time I think of you, I thank my
God. 4And whenever I mention you in
my prayers, it makes me happy. 5This is
because you have taken part with me in
spreading the good news from the first
day you heard about it. 6God is the one

[a]**1.1** *church officials and officers*: Or "bishops and deacons."

who began this good work in you, and I
am certain that he won't stop before it is
complete on the day that Christ Jesus
returns.
7 You have a special place in my heart.
So it is only natural for me to feel the
way I do. All of you have helped in the
work that God has given me, as I defend
the good news and tell about it here in
jail. 8 God himself knows how much I
want to see you. He knows that I care
for you in the same way that Christ Jesus does.
9 I pray that your love will keep on
growing and that you will fully know
and understand 10 how to make the right
choices. Then you will still be pure and
innocent when Christ returns. And until
that day, 11 Jesus Christ will keep you
busy doing good deeds that bring glory
and praise to God.

What Life Means to Paul

12 My dear friends, I want you to know
that what has happened to me has
helped to spread the good news. 13 The
Roman guards and all the others know
that I am here in jail because I serve
Christ. 14 Now most of the Lord's followers have become brave and are fearlessly telling the message.[b]
15 Some are preaching about Christ
because they are jealous and envious of
us. Others are preaching because they
want to help. 16 They love Christ and
know that I am here to defend the good
news about him. 17 But the ones who are
jealous of us are not sincere. They just
want to cause trouble for me while I am
in jail. 18 But that doesn't matter. All that
matters is that people are telling about
Christ, whether they are sincere or not.
That is what makes me glad.
I will keep on being glad, 19 because I
know that your prayers and the help
that comes from the Spirit of Christ Jesus will keep me safe. 20 I honestly expect and hope that I will never do anything to be ashamed of. Whether I live
or die, I always want to be as brave as I
am now and bring honor to Christ.
21 If I live, it will be for Christ, and if I
die, I will gain even more. 22 I don't know
what to choose. I could keep on living
and doing something useful. 23 It is a
hard choice to make. I want to die and
be with Christ, because that would be
much better. 24-25 But I know that all of
you still need me. That's why I am sure I
will stay on to help you grow and be
happy in your faith. 26 Then, when I visit
you again, you will have good reason to
take great pride in Christ Jesus because
of me.[c]
27 Above all else, you must live in a
way that brings honor to the good news
about Christ. Then, whether I visit you
or not, I will hear that all of you think
alike. I will know that you are working
together and that you are struggling
side by side to get others to believe the
good news.
28 Be brave when you face your enemies. Your courage will show them that
they are going to be destroyed, and it
will show you that you will be saved.
God will make all of this happen, 29 and
he has blessed you. Not only do you
have faith in Christ, but you suffer for
him. 30 You saw me suffer, and you still
hear about my troubles. Now you must
suffer in the same way.

True Humility

2 Christ encourages you, and his love
comforts you. God's Spirit unites
you, and you are concerned for others.
2 Now make me completely happy! Live
in harmony by showing love for each
other. Be united in what you think, as if
you were only one person. 3 Don't be
jealous or proud, but be humble and
consider others more important than
yourselves. 4 Care about them as much
as you care about yourselves 5 and think
the same way that Christ Jesus
thought:[d]

6 Christ was truly God.
But he did not try to remain[e]
equal with God.
7 Instead he gave up everything[f]
and became a slave,
when he became
like one of us.

8 Christ was humble.
He obeyed God and even died
on a cross.
9 Then God gave Christ
the highest place
and honored his name
above all others.

10 So at the name of Jesus
everyone will bow down,
those in heaven, on earth,
and under the earth.
11 And to the glory
of God the Father
everyone will openly agree,
"Jesus Christ is Lord!"

Lights in the World

12 My dear friends, you always obeyed
when I was with you. Now that I am

[b] **1.14** *the message*: Some manuscripts have "the Lord's message," and others have "God's message." [c] **1.26** *take great pride in Christ Jesus because of me*: Or "take great pride in me because of Christ Jesus." [d] **2.5** *think the same way that Christ Jesus thought*: Or "think the way you should because you belong to Christ Jesus." [e] **2.6** *remain*: Or "become." [f] **2.7** *He gave up everything*: Greek, "He emptied himself."

away, you should obey even more. So
work with fear and trembling to discover what it really means to be saved.
[13]God is working in you to make you
willing and able to obey him.
[14]Do everything without grumbling or
arguing. [15]Then you will be the pure and
innocent children of God. You live
among people who are crooked and
evil, but you must not do anything that
they can say is wrong. Try to shine as
lights among the people of this world,
[16]as you hold firmly to[g] the message
that gives life. Then on the day when
Christ returns, I can take pride in you. I
can also know that my work and efforts
were not useless.
[17]Your faith in the Lord and your service are like a sacrifice offered to him.
And my own blood may have to be
poured out with the sacrifice.[h] If this
happens, I will be glad and rejoice with
you. [18]In the same way, you should be
glad and rejoice with me.

Timothy and Epaphroditus

[19]I want to be encouraged by news
about you. So I hope the Lord Jesus will
soon let me send Timothy to you. [20]I
don't have anyone else who cares about
you as much as he does. [21]The others
think only about what interests them
and not about what concerns Christ Jesus. [22]But you know what kind of person Timothy is. He has worked with me
like a son in spreading the good news.
[23]I hope to send him to you, as soon as I
find out what is going to happen to me.
[24]And I feel sure that the Lord will also
let me come soon.
[25]I think I ought to send my dear
friend Epaphroditus back to you. He is a
follower and a worker and a soldier of
the Lord, just as I am. You sent him to
look after me, [26]but now he is eager to
see you. He is worried, because you
heard he was sick. [27]In fact, he was very
sick and almost died. But God was kind
to him, and also to me, and he kept me
from being burdened down with sorrow.
[28]Now I am more eager than ever to
send Epaphroditus back again. You will
be glad to see him, and I won't have to
worry any longer. [29]Be sure to give him
a cheerful welcome, just as people who
serve the Lord deserve. [30]He almost died
working for Christ, and he risked his
own life to do for me what you could not.

Being Acceptable to God

3 Finally, my dear friends, be glad that
you belong to the Lord. It doesn't
bother me to write the same things to
you that I have written before. In fact, it
is for your own good.
[2]Watch out for those people who behave like dogs! They are evil and want
to do more than just circumcise you.
[3]But we are the ones who are truly circumcised, because we worship by the
power of God's Spirit[i] and take pride in
Christ Jesus. We don't brag about what
we have done, [4]although I could. Others
may brag about themselves, but I have
more reason to brag than anyone else. [5]I
was circumcised when I was eight days
old,[j] and I am from the nation of Israel
and the tribe of Benjamin. I am a true
Hebrew. As a Pharisee, I strictly obeyed
the Law of Moses. [6]And I was so eager
that I even made trouble for the church.
I did everything the Law demands in order to please God.
[7]But Christ has shown me that what I
once thought was valuable is worthless.
[8]Nothing is as wonderful as knowing
Christ Jesus my Lord. I have given up
everything else and count it all as
garbage. All I want is Christ [9]and to
know that I belong to him. I could not
make myself acceptable to God by obeying the Law of Moses. God accepted me
simply because of my faith in Christ.
[10]All I want is to know Christ and the
power that raised him to life. I want to
suffer and die as he did, [11]so that somehow I also may be raised to life.

Running toward the Goal

[12]I have not yet reached my goal, and
I am not perfect. But Christ has taken
hold of me. So I keep on running and
struggling to take hold of the prize.
[13]My friends, I don't feel that I have already arrived. But I forget what is behind, and I struggle for what is ahead.
[14]I run toward the goal, so that I can win
the prize of being called to heaven. This
is the prize that God offers because of
what Christ Jesus has done. [15]All of us
who are mature should think in this
same way. And if any of you think differently, God will make it clear to you.
[16]But we must keep going in the direction that we are now headed.
[17]My friends, I want you to follow my
example and learn from others who
closely follow the example we set for
you. [18]I often warned you that many
people are living as enemies of the cross
of Christ. And now with tears in my
eyes, I warn you again [19]that they are
headed for hell! They worship their
stomachs and brag about the disgusting
things they do. All they can think about
are the things of this world.

[g]**2.16** *hold firmly to*: Or "offer them." [h]**2.17** *my own blood may have to be poured out with the sacrifice*: Offerings of water or wine were sometimes poured out when animals were sacrificed on the altar. [i]**3.3** *by the power of God's Spirit*: Some manuscripts have "sincerely." [j]**3.5** *when I was eight days old*: Jewish boys are circumcised eight days after birth.

20 But we are citizens of heaven and are eagerly waiting for our Savior to come from there. Our Lord Jesus Christ 21 has power over everything, and he will make these poor bodies of ours like his own glorious body.

4 Dear friends, I love you and long to see you. Please keep on being faithful to the Lord. You are my pride and joy.

Paul Encourages the Lord's Followers

2 Euodia and Syntyche, you belong to the Lord, so I beg you to stop arguing with each other. 3 And, my true partner,[k] I ask you to help them. These women have worked together with me and with Clement and with the others in spreading the good news. Their names are now written in the book of life.[l]

4 Always be glad because of the Lord! I will say it again: Be glad. 5 Always be gentle with others. The Lord will soon be here. 6 Don't worry about anything, but pray about everything. With thankful hearts offer up your prayers and requests to God. 7 Then, because you belong to Christ Jesus, God will bless you with peace that no one can completely understand. And this peace will control the way you think and feel.

8 Finally, my friends, keep your minds on whatever is true, pure, right, holy, friendly, and proper. Don't ever stop thinking about what is truly worthwhile and worthy of praise. 9 You know the teachings I gave you, and you know what you heard me say and saw me do. So follow my example. And God, who gives peace, will be with you.

Paul Gives Thanks for the Gifts He Was Given

10 The Lord has made me very grateful that at last you have thought about me once again. Actually, you were thinking about me all along, but you didn't have any chance to show it. 11 I am not complaining about having too little. I have learned to be satisfied with[m] whatever I have. 12 I know what it is to be poor or to have plenty, and I have lived under all kinds of conditions. I know what it means to be full or to be hungry, to have too much or too little. 13 Christ gives me the strength to face anything.

14 It was good of you to help me when I was having such a hard time. 15 My friends at Philippi, you remember what it was like when I started preaching the good news in Macedonia.[n] After I left there, you were the only church that became my partner by giving blessings and by receiving them in return. 16 Even when I was in Thessalonica, you helped me more than once. 17 I am not trying to get something from you, but I want you to receive the blessings that come from giving.

18 I have been paid back everything, and with interest. I am completely satisfied with the gifts that you had Epaphroditus bring me. They are like a sweet-smelling offering or like the right kind of sacrifice that pleases God. 19 I pray that God will take care of all your needs with the wonderful blessings that come from Christ Jesus! 20 May God our Father be praised forever and ever. Amen.

Final Greetings

21 Give my greetings to all who are God's people because of Christ Jesus.

The Lord's followers here with me send you their greetings.

22 All of God's people send their greetings, especially those in the service of the Emperor.

23 I pray that our Lord Jesus Christ will be kind to you and will bless your life!

---

[k] **4.3** *partner*: Or "Syzygus," a person's name. [l] **4.3** *the book of life*: A book in which the names of God's people are written. [m] **4.11** *be satisfied with*: Or "get by on." [n] **4.15** *when I started preaching the good news in Macedonia*: Paul is talking about his first visit to Philippi (see Acts 16.12-40).

COLOSSIANS

ABOUT THIS LETTER

Colossae was an important city in western Asia Minor, about 100 miles east of the port city of Ephesus. Paul had never been to Colossae, but he was pleased to learn that the Christians there were strong in their faith (1.3-7; 2.6, 7). They had heard the good news from a man named Epaphras who had lived there (1.7; 4.12, 13), but was in jail with Paul (Philemon 23) at the time that Paul wrote this letter (1.14; 4.3, 10, 18).

Many of the church members in Colossae were Gentiles (1.27), and some of them were influenced by strange religious ideas and practices (2.16-23). They thought that to obey God fully they must give up certain physical desires and worship angels and other spiritual powers. But Paul wanted them to know that Christ was with God in heaven, ruling over all powers in the universe (3.1). And so, their worship should be directed to Christ.

Paul quotes a beautiful hymn that explains who Christ is:

Christ is exactly like God,
who cannot be seen.
He is the first-born Son,
superior to all creation.

God himself was pleased
to live fully in his Son.
And God was pleased
for him to make peace
by sacrificing his blood
on the cross.
(1.15, 19, 20a)

A QUICK LOOK AT THIS LETTER

Greetings (1.1, 2)
A Prayer of Thanks (1.3-8)
The Person and Work of Christ (1.9—2.19)
New Life with Christ (2.20—4.6)
Final Greetings (4.7-18)

---

1 From Paul, chosen by God to be an
apostle of Christ Jesus, and from
Timothy, who is also a follower.
2To God's people who live in Colossae
and are faithful followers of Christ.
I pray that God our Father will be
kind to you and will bless you with
peace!

A Prayer of Thanks

3Each time we pray for you, we thank
God, the Father of our Lord Jesus
Christ. 4We have heard of your faith in
Christ and of your love for all of God's
people, 5because what you hope for is
kept safe for you in heaven. You first
heard about this hope when you believed the true message, which is the
good news.
6The good news is spreading all over
the world with great success. It has
spread in that same way among you,
ever since the first day you learned the
truth about God's wonderful kindness
7from our good friend Epaphras. He
works together with us for Christ and is

a faithful worker for you.[a] 8He is also
the one who told us about the love that
God's Spirit has given you.

The Person and Work of Christ

9We have not stopped praying for you
since the first day we heard about you.
In fact, we always pray that God will
show you everything he wants you to do
and that you may have all the wisdom
and understanding that his Spirit gives.
10Then you will live a life that honors
the Lord, and you will always please
him by doing good deeds. You will come
to know God even better. 11His glorious
power will make you patient and strong
enough to endure anything, and you will
be truly happy.
12I pray that you will be grateful to
God for letting you[a] have part in what
he has promised his people in the kingdom of light. 13God rescued us from the
dark power of Satan and brought us
into the kingdom of his dear Son, 14who
forgives our sins and sets us free.

15 Christ is exactly like God,
who cannot be seen.
He is the first-born Son,
superior to all creation.
16 Everything was created by him,
everything in heaven
and on earth,
everything seen and unseen,
including all forces
and powers,
and all rulers
and authorities.
All things were created
by God's Son,
and everything was made
for him.

17 God's Son was before all else,
and by him everything
is held together.
18 He is the head of his body,
which is the church.
He is the very beginning,
the first to be raised
from death,
so that he would be
above all others.

19 God himself was pleased
to live fully in his Son.
20 And God was pleased
for him to make peace
by sacrificing his blood
on the cross,
so that all beings in heaven
and on earth
would be brought back to God.

21You used to be far from God. Your
thoughts made you his enemies, and
you did evil things. 22But his Son became a human and died. So God made
peace with you, and now he lets you
stand in his presence as people who are
holy and faultless and innocent. 23But
you must stay deeply rooted and firm in
your faith. You must not give up the
hope you received when you heard the
good news. It was preached to everyone
on earth, and I myself have become a
servant of this message.

Paul's Service to the Church

24I am glad that I can suffer for you. I
am pleased also that in my own body I
can continue[b] the suffering of Christ for
his body, the church. 25God's plan was
to make me a servant of his church and
to send me to preach his complete message to you. 26For ages and ages this
message was kept secret from everyone,
but now it has been explained to God's
people. 27God did this because he
wanted you Gentiles to understand his
wonderful and glorious mystery. And
the mystery is that Christ lives in you,
and he is your hope of sharing in God's
glory.
28We announce the message about
Christ, and we use all our wisdom to
warn and teach everyone, so that all of
Christ's followers will grow and become mature. 29That's why I work so
hard and use the mighty power he gives
me.

2 I want you to know what a struggle I
am going through for you, for God's
people at Laodicea, and for all of those
followers who have never met me. 2I do
it to encourage them. Then as their
hearts are joined together in love, they
will be wonderfully blessed with complete understanding. And they will truly
know Christ. Not only is he the key to
God's mystery, 3but all wisdom and
knowledge are hidden away in him. 4I
tell you these things to keep you from
being fooled by fancy talk. 5Even
though I am not with you, I keep thinking about you. I am glad to know that
you are living as you should and that
your faith in Christ is strong.

Christ Brings Real Life

6You have accepted Christ Jesus as
your Lord. Now keep on following him.
7Plant your roots in Christ and let him
be the foundation for your life. Be
strong in your faith, just as you were
taught. And be grateful.
8Don't let anyone fool you by using
senseless arguments. These arguments
may sound wise, but they are only human teachings. They come from the

[a]**1.7,12** *you*: Some manuscripts have "us." [b]**1.24** *continue*: Or "complete."

powers of this world[c] and not from Christ.

[9]God lives fully in Christ. [10]And you are fully grown because you belong to Christ, who is over every power and authority. [11]Christ has also taken away your selfish desires, just as circumcision removes flesh from the body. [12]And when you were baptized, it was the same as being buried with Christ. Then you were raised to life because you had faith in the power of God, who raised Christ from death. [13]You were dead, because you were sinful and were not God's people. But God let Christ make you[d] alive, when he forgave all our sins.

[14]God wiped out the charges that were against us for disobeying the Law of Moses. He took them away and nailed them to the cross. [15]There Christ defeated all powers and forces. He let the whole world see them being led away as prisoners when he celebrated his victory.

[16]Don't let anyone tell you what you must eat or drink. Don't let them say that you must celebrate the New Moon festival, the Sabbath, or any other festival. [17]These things are only a shadow of what was to come. But Christ is real!

[18]Don't be cheated by people who make a show of acting humble and who worship angels.[e] They brag about seeing visions. But it is all nonsense, because their minds are filled with selfish desires. [19]They are no longer part of Christ, who is the head of the whole body. Christ gives the body its strength, and he uses its joints and muscles to hold it together, as it grows by the power of God.

Christ Brings New Life

[20]You died with Christ. Now the forces of the universe[f] don't have any power over you. Why do you live as if you had to obey such rules as, [21]"Don't handle this. Don't taste that. Don't touch this."? [22]After these things are used, they are no longer good for anything. So why be bothered with the rules that humans have made up? [23]Obeying these rules may seem to be the smart thing to do. They appear to make you love God more and to be very humble and to have control over your body. But they don't really have any power over our desires.

3 You have been raised to life with Christ. Now set your heart on what is in heaven, where Christ rules at God's right side.[g] [2]Think about what is up there, not about what is here on earth. [3]You died, which means that your life is hidden with Christ, who sits beside God. [4]Christ gives meaning to your[h] life, and when he appears, you will also appear with him in glory.

[5]Don't be controlled by your body. Kill every desire for the wrong kind of sex. Don't be immoral or indecent or have evil thoughts. Don't be greedy, which is the same as worshiping idols. [6]God is angry with people who disobey him by doing[i] these things. [7]And that is exactly what you did, when you lived among people who behaved in this way. [8]But now you must stop doing such things. You must quit being angry, hateful, and evil. You must no longer say insulting or cruel things about others. [9]And stop lying to each other. You have given up your old way of life with its habits.

[10]Each of you is now a new person. You are becoming more and more like your Creator, and you will understand him better. [11]It doesn't matter if you are a Greek or a Jew, or if you are circumcised or not. You may even be a barbarian or a Scythian,[j] and you may be a slave or a free person. Yet Christ is all that matters, and he lives in all of us.

[12]God loves you and has chosen you as his own special people. So be gentle, kind, humble, meek, and patient. [13]Put up with each other, and forgive anyone who does you wrong, just as Christ has forgiven you. [14]Love is more important than anything else. It is what ties everything completely together.

[15]Each one of you is part of the body of Christ, and you were chosen to live together in peace. So let the peace that comes from Christ control your thoughts. And be grateful. [16]Let the message about Christ completely fill your lives, while you use all your wisdom to teach and instruct each other. With thankful hearts, sing psalms, hymns, and spiritual songs to God. [17]Whatever you say or do should be done in the name of the Lord Jesus, as you give thanks to God the Father because of him.

Some Rules for Christian Living

[18]A wife must put her husband first. This is her duty as a follower of the Lord.

[c]**2.8** *powers of this world*: Spirits and unseen forces were thought to control human lives and were believed to be connected with the movements of the stars. [d]**2.13** *you*: See the note at 1.7. [e]**2.18** *worship angels*: Or "worship with angels (in visions of heaven)." [f]**2.20** *forces of the universe*: See the note at 2.8. [g]**3.1** *right side*: The place of power and honor. [h]**3.4** *your*: Some manuscripts have "our." [i]**3.6** *people who disobey him by doing*: Some manuscripts do not have these words. [j]**3.11** *a barbarian or a Scythian*: Barbarians were people who could not speak Greek and would be in the lower class of society. Scythians were people who were known for their cruelty.

[19]A husband must love his wife and not abuse her.

[20]Children must always obey their parents. This pleases the Lord.

[21]Parents, don't be hard on your children. If you are, they might give up.

[22]Slaves, you must always obey your earthly masters. Try to please them at all times, and not just when you think they are watching. Honor the Lord and serve your masters with your whole heart. [23]Do your work willingly, as though you were serving the Lord himself, and not just your earthly master. [24]In fact, the Lord Christ is the one you are really serving, and you know that he will reward you. [25]But Christ has no favorites! He will punish evil people, just as they deserve.

4 Slave owners, be fair and honest with your slaves. Don't forget that you have a Master in heaven.

[2]Never give up praying. And when you pray, keep alert and be thankful. [3]Be sure to pray that God will make a way for us to spread his message and explain the mystery about Christ, even though I am in jail for doing this. [4]Please pray that I will make the message as clear as possible.

[5]When you are with unbelievers, always make good use of the time. [6]Be pleasant and hold their interest when you speak the message. Choose your words carefully and be ready to give answers to anyone who asks questions.

Final Greetings

[7]Tychicus is the dear friend, who faithfully works and serves the Lord with us, and he will give you the news about me. [8]I am sending him to cheer you up by telling you how we are getting along. [9]Onesimus, that dear and faithful follower from your own group, is coming with him. The two of them will tell you everything that has happened here.

[10]Aristarchus is in jail with me. He sends greetings to you, and so does Mark, the cousin of Barnabas. You have already been told to welcome Mark, if he visits you. [11]Jesus, who is known as Justus, sends his greetings. These three men are the only Jewish followers who have worked with me for the kingdom of God. They have given me much comfort.

[12]Your own Epaphras, who serves Christ Jesus, sends his greetings. He always prays hard that you may fully know what the Lord wants you to do and that you may do it completely. [13]I have seen how much trouble he has gone through for you and for the followers in Laodicea and Hierapolis.

[14]Our dear doctor Luke sends you his greetings, and so does Demas.

[15]Give my greetings to the followers at Laodicea, especially to Nympha and the church that meets in her home.

[16]After this letter has been read to your people, be sure to have it read in the church at Laodicea. And you should read the letter that I have sent to them.[k]

[17]Remind Archippus to do the work that the Lord has given him to do.

[18]I am signing this letter myself: PAUL.

Don't forget that I am in jail.

I pray that God will be kind to you.

[k]**4.16** *the letter that I have sent to them*: This is the only mention of the letter to the church at Laodicea.

1 THESSALONIANS

ABOUT THIS LETTER

Paul started the church in Thessalonica (2.13, 14), while working hard to support himself (2.9). In this important city of northern Greece, many of the followers had worshiped idols before becoming Christians (1.9). But they were faithful to the Lord, and because of them the Lord's message had spread everywhere in that region (1.8). This letter may have been the first one that Paul wrote, and maybe even the first of all the New Testament writings.

Some people in Thessalonica began to oppose Paul, and he had to escape to Athens. But he sent his young friend Timothy to find out how the Christians were doing (3.1-5). When Timothy returned, he gave Paul good reports of their faith and love (3.6-10).

The church itself had problems. Some of its members had quit working, since they thought that the Lord would soon return (4.11, 12). Others were worried because relatives and friends had already died before Christ's return. So Paul tried to explain to them more clearly what would happen when the Lord returns (4.13-15), and then told them how they should live in the meanwhile (5.1-11).

Paul's final instructions are well worth remembering:

Always be joyful and never stop praying. Whatever happens, keep thanking God because of Jesus Christ. This is what God wants you to do. *(5.16-18)*

A QUICK LOOK AT THIS LETTER

Greetings (1.1-3)
The Thessalonians' Faith and Example (1.4—3.13)
A Life That Pleases God (4.1-12)
What to Expect When the Lord Returns (4.13—5.11)
Final Instructions and Greetings (5.12-28)

---

1 From Paul, Silas,[a] and Timothy.
To the church in Thessalonica, the
people of God the Father and of the
Lord Jesus Christ.
I pray that God will be kind to you
and will bless you with peace!
2We thank God for you and always
mention you in our prayers. Each time
we pray, 3we tell God our Father about
your faith and loving work and about
your firm hope in our Lord Jesus Christ.

The Thessalonians' Faith and Example

4My dear friends, God loves you, and
we know he has chosen you to be his
people. 5When we told you the good
news, it was with the power and assurance that come from the Holy Spirit,
and not simply with words. You knew
what kind of people we were and how
we helped you. 6So, when you accepted
the message, you followed our example
and the example of the Lord. You suffered, but the Holy Spirit made you
glad.
7You became an example for all the
Lord's followers in Macedonia and
Achaia. 8And because of you, the Lord's
message has spread everywhere in
those regions. Now the news of your
faith in God is known all over the world,
and we don't have to say a thing about
it. 9Everyone is talking about how you
welcomed us and how you turned away
from idols to serve the true and living
God. 10They also tell how you are waiting for his Son Jesus to come from
heaven. God raised him from death, and

[a]1.1 *Silas*: The Greek text has "Silvanus," another form of the name Silas.

on the day of judgment Jesus will save
us from God's anger.

Paul's Work in Thessalonica

2 My friends, you know that our time
with you wasn't wasted. [2]As you remember, we had been mistreated and
insulted at Philippi. But God gave us the
courage to tell you the good news about
him, even though many people caused
us trouble. [3]We didn't have any hidden
motives when we won you over, and we
didn't try to fool or trick anyone. [4]God
was pleased to trust us with his message. We didn't speak to please people,
but to please God who knows our motives.
[5]You also know that we didn't try to
flatter anyone. God himself knows that
what we did wasn't a cover-up for greed.
[6]We were not trying to get you or anyone else to praise us. [7]But as apostles,
we could have demanded help from you.
After all, Christ is the one who sent us.
We chose to be like children or like a
mother[b] nursing her baby. [8]We cared so
much for you, and you became so dear
to us, that we were willing to give our
lives for you when we gave you God's
message.
[9]My dear friends, you surely haven't
forgotten our hard work and hardships.
You remember how night and day we
struggled to make a living, so that we
could tell you God's message without
being a burden to anyone. [10]Both you
and God are witnesses that we were
pure and honest and innocent in our
dealings with you followers of the Lord.
[11]You also know we did everything for
you that parents would do for their own
children. [12]We begged, encouraged, and
urged each of you to live in a way that
would honor God. He is the one who
chose you to share in his own kingdom
and glory.
[13]We always thank God that you believed the message we preached. It
came from him, and it isn't something
made up by humans. You accepted it as
God's message, and now he is working
in you. [14]My friends, you did just like
God's churches in Judea and like the
other followers of Christ Jesus there.
And so, you were mistreated by your
own people, in the same way they were
mistreated by their people.
[15]Those Jews killed the Lord Jesus
and the prophets, and they even
chased us away. God doesn't like what
they do and neither does anyone else.
[16]They keep us from speaking his message to the Gentiles and from leading
them to be saved. The Jews have always gone too far with their sins. Now
God has finally become angry and will
punish them.

Paul Wants To Visit the Church Again

[17]My friends, we were kept from coming to you for a while, but we never
stopped thinking about you. We were
eager to see you and tried our best to
visit you in person. [18]We really wanted
to come. I myself tried several times, but
Satan always stopped us. [19]After all,
when the Lord Jesus appears, who else
but you will give us hope and joy and be
like a glorious crown for us? [20]You
alone are our glory and joy!

3 Finally, we couldn't stand it any
longer. We decided to stay in Athens
by ourselves [2]and send our friend Timothy to you. He works with us as God's
servant and preaches the good news
about Christ. We wanted him to make
you strong in your faith and to encourage you. [3]We didn't want any of you to
be discouraged by all these troubles. You
knew we would have to suffer, [4]because
when we were with you, we told you
this would happen. And we did suffer, as
you well know. [5]At last, when I could
not wait any longer, I sent Timothy to
find out about your faith. I hoped that
Satan had not tempted you and made all
our work useless.
[6]Timothy has come back from his visit
with you and has told us about your
faith and love. He also said that you always have happy memories of us and
that you want to see us as much as we
want to see you.
[7]My friends, even though we have a
lot of trouble and suffering, your faith
makes us feel better about you. [8]Your
strong faith in the Lord is like a breath
of new life. [9]How can we possibly thank
God enough for all the happiness you
have brought us? [10]Day and night we
sincerely pray that we will see you
again and help you to have an even
stronger faith.
[11]We pray that God our Father and
our Lord Jesus will let us visit you.
[12]May the Lord make your love for each
other and for everyone else grow by
leaps and bounds. That's how our love
for you has grown. [13]And when our
Lord comes with all of his people, I pray
that he will make your hearts pure and
innocent in the sight of God the Father.

A Life That Pleases God

4 Finally, my dear friends, since you
belong to the Lord Jesus, we beg
and urge you to live as we taught you.
Then you will please God. You are already living that way, but try even
harder. [2]Remember the instructions we

[b]**2.7** *like children or like a mother*: Some manuscripts have "as gentle as a mother."

gave you as followers of the Lord Jesus.
3God wants you to be holy, so don't be
immoral in matters of sex. 4Respect and
honor your wife.[c] 5Don't be a slave of
your desires or live like people who
don't know God. 6You must not cheat
any of the Lord's followers in matters of
sex.[d] Remember, we warned you that he
punishes everyone who does such
things. 7God didn't choose you to be
filthy, but to be pure. 8So if you don't
obey these rules, you are not really disobeying us. You are disobeying God,
who gives you his Holy Spirit.
9We don't have to write you about the
need to love each other. God has taught
you to do this, 10and you already have
shown your love for all of his people in
Macedonia. But, my dear friends, we ask
you to do even more. 11Try your best to
live quietly, to mind your own business,
and to work hard, just as we taught you
to do. 12Then you will be respected by
people who are not followers of the
Lord, and you won't have to depend on
anyone.

The Lord's Coming

13My friends, we want you to understand how it will be for those followers
who have already died. Then you won't
grieve over them and be like people who
don't have any hope. 14We believe that
Jesus died and was raised to life. We
also believe that when God brings Jesus
back again, he will bring with him all
who had faith in Jesus before they died.
15Our Lord Jesus told us that when he
comes, we won't go up to meet him
ahead of his followers who have already
died.
16With a loud command and with the
shout of the chief angel and a blast of
God's trumpet, the Lord will return from
heaven. Then those who had faith in
Christ before they died will be raised to
life. 17Next, all of us who are still alive
will be taken up into the clouds together
with them to meet the Lord in the sky.
From that time on we will all be with the
Lord forever. 18Encourage each other
with these words.

5 I don't need to write you about the
time or date when all this will happen. 2You surely know that the Lord's
return[e] will be as a thief coming at
night. 3People will think they are safe
and secure. But destruction will suddenly strike them like the pains of a
woman about to give birth. And they
won't escape.
4My dear friends, you don't live in
darkness, and so that day won't surprise
you like a thief. 5You belong to the light
and live in the day. We don't live in the
night or belong to the dark. 6Others may
sleep, but we should stay awake and be
alert. 7People sleep during the night, and
some even get drunk. 8But we belong to
the day. So we must stay sober and let
our faith and love be like a suit of armor. Our firm hope that we will be
saved is our helmet.
9God doesn't intend to punish us, but
wants us to be saved by our Lord Jesus
Christ. 10Christ died for us, so that we
could live with him, whether we are
alive or dead when he comes. 11That's
why you must encourage and help each
other, just as you are already doing.

Final Instructions and Greetings

12My friends, we ask you to be
thoughtful of your leaders who work
hard and tell you how to live for the
Lord. 13Show them great respect and
love because of their work. Try to get
along with each other. 14My friends, we
beg you to warn anyone who isn't living
right. Encourage anyone who feels left
out, help all who are weak, and be patient with everyone. 15Don't be hateful
to people, just because they are hateful
to you. Rather, be good to each other
and to everyone else.
16Always be joyful 17and never stop
praying. 18Whatever happens, keep
thanking God because of Jesus Christ.
This is what God wants you to do.
19Don't turn away God's Spirit 20or ignore prophecies. 21Put everything to the
test. Accept what is good 22and don't
have anything to do with evil.
23I pray that God, who gives peace,
will make you completely holy. And
may your spirit, soul, and body be kept
healthy and faultless until our Lord Jesus Christ returns. 24The one who chose
you can be trusted, and he will do this.
25Friends, please pray for us.
26Give the Lord's followers a warm
greeting.
27In the name of the Lord I beg you to
read this letter to all his followers.
28I pray that our Lord Jesus Christ
will be kind to you!

[c] **4.4** *your wife*: Or "your body." [d] **4.6** *in matters of sex*: Or "in business." [e] **5.2** *the Lord's return*: The Greek text has "the day of the Lord."

2 THESSALONIANS

ABOUT THIS LETTER

In this letter to the believers in Thessalonica, Paul begins by thanking God that their faith and love keep growing all the time (1.3). They were going through a lot of troubles, but Paul insists that this is God's way of testing their faith, not a way of punishing them (1.4, 5).

Someone in Thessalonica claimed to have a letter from Paul, saying that the Lord had already returned (2.2). But Paul warns the church not to be fooled! The Lord will not return until after the "wicked one" has appeared (2.3).

Paul also warns against laziness (3.6-10), and he tells the church to guard against any followers who refuse to obey what he has written in this letter.

The letter closes with a prayer:

> *I pray that the Lord, who gives peace, will always bless you with peace. May the Lord be with all of you.* (3.16)

A QUICK LOOK AT THIS LETTER

Greetings (1.1, 2)
The Lord's Return Will Bring Justice (1.3-12)
The Lord Has Not Returned Yet (2.1-12)
Be Faithful (2.13-17)
Pray and Work (3.1-15)
A Final Prayer (3.16-18)

---

1 From Paul, Silas,[a] and Timothy.
To the church in Thessalonica, the
people of God our Father and of the
Lord Jesus Christ.
2I pray that God our Father and the
Lord Jesus Christ will be kind to you
and will bless you with peace!

When Christ Returns

3My dear friends, we always have
good reason to thank God for you, because your faith in God and your love
for each other keep growing all the
time. 4That's why we brag about you
to all of God's churches. We tell them
how patient you are and how you keep
on having faith, even though you are going through a lot of trouble and suffering.
5All of this shows that God judges
fairly and that he is making you fit to
share in his kingdom for which you are
suffering. 6It is only right for God to
punish everyone who is causing you
trouble, 7but he will give you relief from
your troubles. He will do the same for
us, when the Lord Jesus comes from
heaven with his powerful angels 8and
with a flaming fire.
Our Lord Jesus will punish anyone
who doesn't know God and won't obey
his message. 9Their punishment will be
eternal destruction, and they will be
kept far from the presence of our Lord
and his glorious strength. 10This will
happen on that day when the Lord returns to be praised and honored by all
who have faith in him and belong to
him. This includes you, because you believed what we said.
11God chose you, and we keep praying
that God will make you worthy of being
his people. We pray for God's power to
help you do all the good things that you
hope to do and that your faith makes
you want to do. 12Then, because God
and our Lord Jesus Christ are so kind,
you will bring honor to the name of our

[a]1.1 *Silas*: The Greek text has "Silvanus," which is another form of the name Silas.

Lord Jesus, and he will bring honor to you.

The Lord's Return

2 When our Lord Jesus returns, we will be gathered up to meet him. So I ask you, my friends, 2not to be easily upset or disturbed by people who claim that the Lord[b] has already come. They may say that they heard this directly from the Holy Spirit, or from someone else, or even that they read it in one of our letters. 3But don't be fooled! People will rebel against God. Then before the Lord returns, the wicked[c] one who is doomed to be destroyed will appear. 4He will brag and oppose everything that is holy or sacred. He will even sit in God's temple and claim to be God. 5Don't you remember that I told you this while I was still with you?

6You already know what is holding this wicked one back until it is time for him to come. 7His mysterious power is already at work, but someone is holding him back. And the wicked one won't appear until that someone is out of the way. 8Then he will appear, but the Lord Jesus will kill him simply by breathing on him. He will be completely destroyed by the Lord's glorious return.

9When the wicked one appears, Satan will pretend to work all kinds of miracles, wonders, and signs. 10Lost people will be fooled by his evil deeds. They could be saved, but they will refuse to love the truth and accept it. 11So God will make sure that they are fooled into believing a lie. 12All of them will be punished, because they would rather do evil than believe the truth.

Be Faithful

13My friends, the Lord loves you, and it is only natural for us to thank God for you. God chose you to be the first ones to be saved.[d] His Spirit made you holy, and you put your faith in the truth. 14God used our preaching as his way of inviting you to share in the glory of our Lord Jesus Christ. 15My friends, that's why you must remain faithful and follow closely what we taught you in person and by our letters.

16God our Father loves us. He is kind and has given us eternal comfort and a wonderful hope. We pray that our Lord Jesus Christ and God our Father 17will encourage you and help you always to do and say the right thing.

Pray for Us

3 Finally, our friends, please pray for us. This will help the message about the Lord to spread quickly, and others will respect it, just as you do. 2Pray that we may be kept safe from worthless and evil people. After all, not everyone has faith. 3But the Lord can be trusted to make you strong and protect you from harm. 4He has made us sure that you are obeying what we taught you and that you will keep on obeying. 5I pray that the Lord will guide you to be as loving as God and as patient as Christ.

Warnings against Laziness

6My dear friends, in the name of[e] the Lord Jesus, I beg you not to have anything to do with any of your people who loaf around and refuse to obey the instructions we gave you. 7You surely know that you should follow our example. We didn't waste our time loafing, 8and we didn't accept food from anyone without paying for it. We didn't want to be a burden to any of you, so night and day we worked as hard as we could.

9We had the right not to work, but we wanted to set an example for you. 10We also gave you the rule that if you don't work, you don't eat. 11Now we learn that some of you just loaf around and won't do any work, except the work of a busybody. 12So, for the sake of our Lord Jesus Christ, we ask and beg these people to settle down and start working for a living. 13Dear friends, you must never become tired of doing right.

14Be on your guard against any followers who refuse to obey what we have written in this letter. Put them to shame by not having anything to do with them. 15Don't consider them your enemies, but speak kindly to them as you would to any other follower.

Final Prayer

16I pray that the Lord, who gives peace, will always bless you with peace. May the Lord be with all of you.

17I always sign my letters as I am now doing: PAUL.

18I pray that our Lord Jesus Christ will be kind to all of you.

[b]**2.2** *Lord*: The Greek text has "day of the Lord." [c]**2.3** *wicked*: Some manuscripts have "sinful." [d]**2.13** *God chose you to be the first ones to be saved*: Some manuscripts have "From the beginning God chose you to be saved." [e]**3.6** *in the name of*: Or "as a follower of."

1 TIMOTHY

ABOUT THIS LETTER

Timothy traveled and worked with Paul (Romans 16.21; 1 Corinthians 16.10; Philippians 2.19), and because of their shared faith, Timothy was like a son to Paul (1.2). Timothy became one of Paul's most faithful co-workers, and Paul mentions Timothy in five of his letters.

Although this letter is addressed to Timothy personally, it actually addresses many of the concerns Paul had with the life of the entire church. Guidelines are given for choosing church officials (3.1-7), officers (3.8-13), and leaders (5.17-20).

Christians are to pray for everyone and to remember:

There is only one God,
and Christ Jesus
is the only one
who can bring us
to God. (2.5)

A QUICK LOOK AT THIS LETTER

Greetings (1.1, 2)
Instructions for Church Life (1.3—3.13)
The Mystery of Our Religion (3.14—4.5)
Paul's Advice to Timothy (4.6—6.21)

---

1 From Paul.
God our Savior and Christ Jesus
commanded me to be an apostle of
Christ Jesus, who gives us hope.
2Timothy, because of our faith, you are
like a son to me. I pray that God our Father and our Lord Jesus Christ will be
kind and merciful to you. May they
bless you with peace!

Warning against False Teaching

3When I was leaving for Macedonia, I
asked you to stay on in Ephesus and
warn certain people there to stop
spreading their false teachings. 4You
needed to warn them to stop wasting
their time on senseless stories and endless lists of ancestors. Such things only
cause arguments. They don't help anyone to do God's work that can only be
done by faith.
5You must teach people to have genuine love, as well as a good conscience
and true faith. 6There are some who
have given up these for nothing but
empty talk. 7They want to be teachers of
the Law of Moses. But they don't know
what they are talking about, even
though they think they do.
8We know that the Law is good, if it is
used in the right way. 9We also understand that it wasn't given to control people who please God, but to control lawbreakers, criminals, godless people, and
sinners. It is for wicked and evil people,
and for murderers, who would even kill
their own parents. 10The Law was written for people who are sexual perverts
or who live as homosexuals or are kid-
nappers or liars or won't tell the truth in
court. It is for anything else that opposes the correct teaching 11of the good
news that the glorious and wonderful
God has given me.

Being Thankful for God's Kindness

12I thank Christ Jesus our Lord. He
has given me the strength for my work
because he knew that he could trust me.
13I used to say terrible and insulting

things about him, and I was cruel. But he had mercy on me because I didn't know what I was doing, and I had not yet put my faith in him. 14Christ Jesus our Lord was very kind to me. He has greatly blessed my life with faith and love just like his own.

15"Christ Jesus came into the world to save sinners." This saying is true, and it can be trusted. I was the worst sinner of all! 16But since I was worse than anyone else, God had mercy on me and let me be an example of the endless patience of Christ Jesus. He did this so that others would put their faith in Christ and have eternal life. 17I pray that honor and glory will always be given to the only God, who lives forever and is the invisible and eternal King! Amen.

18Timothy, my son, the instructions I am giving you are based on what some prophets[a] once said about you. If you follow these instructions, you will fight like a good soldier. 19You will be faithful and have a clear conscience. Some people have made a mess of their faith because they didn't listen to their consciences. 20Two of them are Hymenaeus and Alexander. I have given these men over to the power of Satan, so they will learn not to oppose God.

How To Pray

2 First of all, I ask you to pray for everyone. Ask God to help and bless them all, and tell God how thankful you are for each of them. 2Pray for kings and others in power, so that we may live quiet and peaceful lives as we worship and honor God. 3This kind of prayer is good, and it pleases God our Savior. 4God wants everyone to be saved and to know the whole truth, which is,

5 There is only one God,
and Christ Jesus
is the only one
who can bring us
to God.
Jesus was truly human,
and he gave himself
to rescue all of us.
6 God showed us this
at the right time.

7This is why God chose me to be a preacher and an apostle of the good news. I am telling the truth. I am not lying. God sent me to teach the Gentiles about faith and truth.

8I want everyone everywhere to lift innocent hands toward heaven and pray, without being angry or arguing with each other.

9I would like for women to wear modest and sensible clothes. They should not have fancy hairdos, or wear expensive clothes, or put on jewelry made of gold or pearls. 10Women who claim to love God should do helpful things for others, 11and they should learn by being quiet and paying attention. 12They should be silent and not be allowed to teach or to tell men what to do. 13After all, Adam was created before Eve, 14and the man Adam wasn't the one who was fooled. It was the woman Eve who was completely fooled and sinned. 15But women will be saved by having children,[b] if they stay faithful, loving, holy, and modest.

Church Officials

3 It is true that[c] anyone who desires to be a church official[d] wants to be something worthwhile. 2That's why officials must have a good reputation and be faithful in marriage.[e] They must be self-controlled, sensible, well-behaved, friendly to strangers, and able to teach. 3They must not be heavy drinkers or troublemakers. Instead, they must be kind and gentle and not love money.

4Church officials must be in control of their own families, and they must see that their children are obedient and always respectful. 5If they don't know how to control their own families, how can they look after God's people?

6They must not be new followers of the Lord. If they are, they might become proud and be doomed along with the devil. 7Finally, they must be well-respected by people who are not followers. Then they won't be trapped and disgraced by the devil.

Church Officers

8Church officers[f] should be serious. They must not be liars, heavy drinkers, or greedy for money. 9And they must have a clear conscience and hold firmly to what God has shown us about our faith. 10They must first prove themselves. Then if no one has anything against them, they can serve as officers.

11Women[g] must also be serious. They must not gossip or be heavy drinkers,

[a]**1.18** *prophets*: Probably the Christian prophets referred to in 4.14. [b]**2.15** *saved by having children*: Or "brought safely through childbirth" or "saved by the birth of a child" (that is, by the birth of Jesus) or "saved by being good mothers." [c]**3.1** *It is true that*: These words may be taken with 2.15. If so, that verse would be translated: "It is true that women will be saved . . . holy, and modest." And 3.1 would be translated, "Anyone who desires . . . something worthwhile." [d]**3.1** *church official*: Or "bishop." [e]**3.2** *be faithful in marriage*: Or "be the husband of only one wife" or "have never been divorced." [f]**3.8** *Church officers*: Or "Deacons." [g]**3.11** *Women*: Either church officers or the wives of church officers.

and they must be faithful in everything
they do.
12Church officers must be faithful in
marriage.[h] They must be in full control
of their children and everyone else in
their home. 13Those who serve well as
officers will earn a good reputation and
will be highly respected for their faith in
Christ Jesus.

The Mystery of Our Religion

14I hope to visit you soon. But I am
writing these instructions, 15so that if I
am delayed, you will know how everyone who belongs to God's family ought
to behave. After all, the church of the
living God is the strong foundation of
truth.
16Here is the great mystery of our religion:

Christ[i] came as a human.
The Spirit proved
  that he pleased God,
and he was seen by angels.

Christ was preached
  to the nations.
People in this world
  put their faith in him,
and he was taken up to glory.

People Will Turn from Their Faith

4 God's Spirit clearly says that in the
last days many people will turn
from their faith. They will be fooled by
evil spirits and by teachings that come
from demons. 2They will also be fooled
by the false claims of liars whose consciences have lost all feeling. These liars
3will forbid people to marry or to eat
certain foods. But God created these
foods to be eaten with thankful hearts
by his followers who know the truth.
4Everything God created is good. And if
you give thanks, you may eat anything.
5What God has said and your prayer
will make it fit to eat.

Paul's Advice to Timothy

6If you teach these things to other followers, you will be a good servant of
Christ Jesus. You will show that you
have grown up on the teachings about
our faith and on the good instructions
you have obeyed. 7Don't have anything
to do with worthless, senseless stories.
Work hard to be truly religious. 8-9As the
saying goes,

"Exercise is good
  for your body,
but religion helps you
  in every way.
It promises life
  now and forever."

These words are worthwhile and should
not be forgotten. 10We have put our hope
in the living God, who is the Savior of
everyone, but especially of those who
have faith. That's why we work and
struggle so hard.[j]
11Teach these things and tell everyone
to do what you say. 12Don't let anyone
make fun of you, just because you are
young. Set an example for other followers by what you say and do, as well as
by your love, faith, and purity.
13Until I arrive, be sure to keep on
reading the Scriptures in worship, and
don't stop preaching and teaching.
14Use the gift you were given when the
prophets spoke and the group of church
leaders[k] blessed you by placing their
hands on you. 15Remember these things
and think about them, so everyone can
see how well you are doing. 16Be careful
about the way you live and about what
you teach. Keep on doing this, and you
will save not only yourself, but the people who hear you.

How To Act toward Others

5 Don't correct an older man. Encourage him, as you would your own father. Treat younger men as you would
your own brother, 2and treat older
women as you would your own mother.
Show the same respect to younger
women that you would to your sister.
3Take care of any widow who is really
in need. 4But if a widow has children or
grandchildren, they should learn to
serve God by taking care of her, as she
once took care of them. This is what
God wants them to do. 5A widow who is
really in need is one who doesn't have
any relatives. She has faith in God, and
she keeps praying to him night and day,
asking for his help.
6A widow who thinks only about having a good time is already dead, even
though she is still alive.
7Tell all of this to everyone, so they
will do the right thing. 8People who
don't take care of their relatives, and especially their own families, have given
up their faith. They are worse than
someone who doesn't have faith in the
Lord.
9For a widow to be put on the list of
widows, she must be at least sixty years
old, and she must have been faithful in

[h]**3.12** *be faithful in marriage*: See the note at 3.2. [i]**3.16** *Christ*: The Greek text has "he," probably meaning "Christ." Some manuscripts have "God." [j]**4.10** *struggle so hard*: Some manuscripts have "are treated so badly." [k]**4.14** *group of church leaders*: Or "group of elders" or "group of presbyters" or "group of priests." This translates one Greek word, and it is related to the one used in 5.17, 19.

marriage.[l] 10She must also be well-
known for doing all sorts of good
things, such as raising children, giving
food to strangers, welcoming God's people into her home,[m] helping people in
need, and always making herself useful.
11Don't put young widows on the list.
They may later have a strong desire to
get married. Then they will turn away
from Christ 12and become guilty of
breaking their promise to him. 13Be-
sides, they will become lazy and get into
the habit of going from house to house.
Next, they will start gossiping and become busybodies, talking about things
that are none of their business.
14I would prefer that young widows
get married, have children, and look after their families. Then the enemy won't
have any reason to say insulting things
about us. 15Look what's already happened to some of the young widows!
They have turned away to follow Satan.
16If a woman who is a follower has
any widows in her family, she[n] should
help them. This will keep the church
from having that burden, and then the
church can help widows who are really
in need.

Church Leaders

17Church leaders[o] who do their job
well deserve to be paid[p] twice as much,
especially if they work hard at preaching and teaching. 18It is just as the Scriptures say, "Don't muzzle an ox when
you are using it to grind grain." You also
know the saying, "Workers are worth
their pay."
19Don't listen to any charge against a
church leader, unless at least two or
three people bring the same charges.
20But if any of the leaders should keep
on sinning, they must be corrected in
front of the whole group, as a warning
to everyone else.
21In the presence of God and Christ
Jesus and their chosen angels, I order
you to follow my instructions! Be fair
with everyone, and don't have any favorites.
22Don't be too quick to accept people
into the service of the Lord[q] by placing
your hands on them.
Don't sin because others do, but stay
close to God.
23Stop drinking only water. Take a little wine to help your stomach trouble
and the other illnesses you always have.
24Some people get caught in their sins
right away, even before the time of judgment. But other people's sins don't show
up until later. 25It is the same with good
deeds. Some are easily seen, but none of
them can be hidden.

6 If you are a slave, you should respect and honor your owner. This
will keep people from saying bad things
about God and about our teaching. 2If
any of you slaves have owners who are
followers, you should show them respect. After all, they are also followers
of Christ, and he loves them. So you
should serve and help them the best you
can.

False Teaching and True Wealth

These are the things you must teach
and tell the people to do. 3Anyone who
teaches something different disagrees
with the correct and godly teaching of
our Lord Jesus Christ. 4Those people
who disagree are proud of themselves,
but they don't really know a thing. Their
minds are sick, and they like to argue
over words. They cause jealousy, disagreements, unkind words, evil suspi-
cions, 5and nasty quarrels. They have
wicked minds and have missed out on
the truth.
These people think religion is supposed to make you rich. 6And religion
does make your life rich, by making you
content with what you have. 7We didn't
bring anything into this world, and we
won't[r] take anything with us when we
leave. 8So we should be satisfied just to
have food and clothes. 9People who
want to be rich fall into all sorts of
temptations and traps. They are caught
by foolish and harmful desires that drag
them down and destroy them. 10The love
of money causes all kinds of trouble.
Some people want money so much that
they have given up their faith and
caused themselves a lot of pain.

Fighting a Good Fight for the Faith

11Timothy, you belong to God, so keep
away from all these evil things. Try your
best to please God and to be like him.
Be faithful, loving, dependable, and gentle. 12Fight a good fight for the faith and
claim eternal life. God offered it to you
when you clearly told about your faith,

[l]**5.9** *been faithful in marriage*: Or "been the wife of only one husband" or "never been divorced." [m]**5.10** *welcoming God's people into her home*: The Greek text has "washing the feet of God's people." In New Testament times most people either went barefoot or wore sandals, and a host would often wash the feet of special guests. [n]**5.16** *woman . . . she*: Some manuscripts have "man or woman . . . that person." [o]**5.17** *leaders*: Or "elders" or "presbyters" or "priests." [p]**5.17** *paid*: Or "honored" or "respected." [q]**5.22** *to accept people into the service of the Lord*: Or "to forgive people." [r]**6.7** *we won't*: Some manuscripts have "we surely won't."

while so many people listened. [13]Now I
ask you to make a promise. Make it in
the presence of God, who gives life to
all, and in the presence of Jesus Christ,
who openly told Pontius Pilate about his
faith. [14]Promise to obey completely and
fully all that you have been told until
our Lord Jesus Christ returns.

15 The glorious God
is the only Ruler,
the King of kings
and Lord of lords.
At the time that God
has already decided,
he will send Jesus Christ
back again.

16 Only God lives forever!
And he lives in light
that no one can come near.
No human has ever seen God
or ever can see him.
God will be honored,
and his power
will last forever. Amen.

[17]Warn the rich people of this world
not to be proud or to trust in wealth that
is easily lost. Tell them to have faith in
God, who is rich and blesses us with
everything we need to enjoy life. [18]In-
struct them to do as many good deeds
as they can and to help everyone. Remind the rich to be generous and share
what they have. [19]This will lay a solid
foundation for the future, so that they
will know what true life is like.

[20]Timothy, guard what God has placed
in your care! Don't pay any attention to
that godless and stupid talk that sounds
smart but really isn't. [21]Some people
have even lost their faith by believing
this talk.

I pray that the Lord will be kind to all
of you!

2 TIMOTHY

ABOUT THIS LETTER

In his second letter to Timothy, Paul is more personal than in his first one. Timothy is like a "dear child" to Paul, and Paul always mentions him in his prayers (1.2, 3) because he wants Timothy to be a "good soldier" of Christ Jesus and to learn to endure suffering (2.1, 3). Paul mentions Timothy's mother and grandmother by name in this letter and reminds Timothy how he had placed his hands on him as a special sign that the Spirit was guiding his work.

Some who claimed to be followers of the Lord had already been trapped by the devil, and Paul warns Timothy to run from those temptations that often catch young people (2.20-26; 3.1-9). He tells Timothy to keep preaching God's message, even if it is not the popular thing to do (4.2). He should also beware of false teachers.

Paul knows that he will soon die for his faith, but he will be rewarded for his faithfulness (4.6-8), and he reminds Timothy of the true message:

If we died with Christ,
we will live with him.
If we don't give up,
we will rule with him.
(2.11, 12a)

A QUICK LOOK AT THIS LETTER

Greetings and Prayer for Timothy (1.1, 2)
Do Not Be Ashamed of the Lord (1.3-18)
How To Be a Good Soldier of Christ (2.1-26)
What People Will Be Like in the Last Days (3.1-9)
Keep Being Faithful (3.10—4.8)
Personal Instructions and Final Greetings (4.9-22)

---

1 From Paul, an apostle of Christ Jesus.
God himself chose me to be an apostle, and he gave me the promised life
that Jesus Christ makes possible.
2Timothy, you are like a dear child to
me. I pray that God our Father and our
Lord Christ Jesus will be kind and merciful to you and will bless you with
peace!

Do Not Be Ashamed of the Lord

3Night and day I mention you in my
prayers. I am always grateful for you, as
I pray to the God my ancestors and I
have served with a clear conscience. 4I
remember how you cried, and I want to
see you, because that will make me truly
happy. 5I also remember the genuine
faith of your mother Eunice. Your grandmother Lois had the same sort of faith,
and I am sure that you have it as well.
6So I ask you to make full use of the gift
that God gave you when I placed my
hands on you.[a] Use it well. 7God's
Spirit[b] doesn't make cowards out of us.
The Spirit gives us power, love, and self-control.
8Don't be ashamed to speak for our
Lord. And don't be ashamed of me, just
because I am in jail for serving him. Use
the power that comes from God and join

[a]1.6 *when I placed my hands on you*: Church leaders placed their hands on people who were being appointed to preach or teach (see 1 Timothy 4.14). [b]1.7 *God's Spirit*: Or "God."

with me in suffering for telling the good
news.

9 God saved us and chose us
to be his holy people.
We did nothing
to deserve this,
but God planned it
because he is so kind.
Even before time began
God planned for Christ Jesus
to show kindness to us.

10 Now Christ Jesus has come
to show us the kindness
of God.
Christ our Savior defeated death
and brought us
the good news.
It shines like a light
and offers life
that never ends.

11 My work is to be a preacher, an
apostle, and a teacher.[c] 12 That's why I
am suffering now. But I am not
ashamed! I know the one I have faith in,
and I am sure that he can guard until
the last day what he has trusted me
with.[d] 13 Now follow the example of the
correct teaching I gave you, and let the
faith and love of Christ Jesus be your
model. 14 You have been trusted with a
wonderful treasure. Guard it with the
help of the Holy Spirit, who lives within
you.

15 You know that everyone in Asia has
turned against me, especially Phygelus
and Hermogenes.

16 I pray that the Lord will be kind to
the family of Onesiphorus. He often
cheered me up and wasn't ashamed of
me when I was put in jail. 17 Then after
he arrived in Rome, he searched everywhere until he found me. 18 I pray that
the Lord Jesus will ask God to show
mercy to Onesiphorus on the day of
judgment. You know how much he
helped me in Ephesus.

A Good Soldier of Christ Jesus

2 Timothy, my child, Christ Jesus is
kind, and you must let him make
you strong. 2 You have often heard me
teach. Now I want you to tell these same
things to followers who can be trusted
to tell others.

3 As a good soldier of Christ Jesus you
must endure your share of suffering.
4 Soldiers on duty don't work at outside
jobs. They try only to please their commanding officer. 5 No one wins an ath-
letic contest without obeying the rules.
6 And farmers who work hard are the
first to eat what grows in their field. 7 If
you keep in mind what I have told you,
the Lord will help you understand completely.

8 Keep your mind on Jesus Christ! He
was from the family of David and was
raised from death, just as my good news
says. 9 And because of this message, I
am locked up in jail and treated like a
criminal. But God's good news isn't
locked in jail, 10 and so I am willing to
put up with anything. Then God's special people will be saved. They will be
given eternal glory because they belong
to Christ Jesus. 11 Here is a true message:

"If we died with Christ,
we will live with him.
12 If we don't give up,
we will rule with him.
If we deny
that we know him,
he will deny
that he knows us.
13 If we are not faithful,
he will still be faithful.
Christ cannot deny
who he is."

An Approved Worker

14 Don't let anyone forget these things.
And with God[e] as your witness, you
must warn them not to argue about
words. These arguments don't help anyone. In fact, they ruin everyone who listens to them. 15 Do your best to win
God's approval as a worker who doesn't
need to be ashamed and who teaches
only the true message.

16 Keep away from worthless and useless talk. It only leads people farther
away from God. 17 That sort of talk is
like a sore that won't heal. And Hymenaeus and Philetus have been talking
this way 18 by teaching that the dead
have already been raised to life. This is
far from the truth, and it is destroying
the faith of some people.

19 But the foundation that God has laid
is solid. On it is written, "The Lord
knows who his people are. So everyone
who worships the Lord must turn away
from evil."

20 In a large house some dishes are
made of gold or silver, while others are
made of wood or clay. Some of these
are special, and others are not. 21 That's
also how it is with people. The ones who
stop doing evil and make themselves
pure will become special. Their lives
will be holy and pleasing to their Master, and they will be able to do all kinds
of good deeds.

22 Run from temptations that capture

[c] **1.11** *teacher*: Some manuscripts add "of the Gentiles." [d] **1.12** *what he has trusted me with*: Or "what I have trusted him with." [e] **2.14** *God*: Some manuscripts have "the Lord," and others have "Christ."

young people. Always do the right thing. Be faithful, loving, and easy to get along with. Worship with people whose hearts are pure. 23 Stay away from stupid and senseless arguments. These only lead to trouble, 24 and God's servants must not be troublemakers. They must be kind to everyone, and they must be good teachers and very patient.

25 Be humble when you correct people who oppose you. Maybe God will lead them to turn to him and learn the truth. 26 They have been trapped by the devil, and he makes them obey him, but God may help them escape.

What People Will Be Like in the Last Days

3 You can be certain that in the last days there will be some very hard times. 2 People will love only themselves and money. They will be proud, stuck-up, rude, and disobedient to their parents. They will also be ungrateful, godless, 3 heartless, and hateful. Their words will be cruel, and they will have no self-control or pity. These people will hate everything that is good. 4 They will be sneaky, reckless, and puffed up with pride. Instead of loving God, they will love pleasure. 5 Even though they will make a show of being religious, their religion won't be real. Don't have anything to do with such people.

6 Some men fool whole families, just to get power over those women who are slaves of sin and are controlled by all sorts of desires. 7 These women always want to learn something new, but they never can discover the truth. 8 Just as Jannes and Jambres[f] opposed Moses, these people are enemies of the truth. Their minds are sick, and their faith isn't real. 9 But they won't get very far with their foolishness. Soon everyone will know the truth about them, just as Jannes and Jambres were found out.

Paul's Last Instructions to Timothy

10 Timothy, you know what I teach and how I live. You know what I want to do and what I believe. You have seen how patient and loving I am, and how in the past I put up with 11 trouble and suffering in the cities of Antioch, Iconium, and Lystra. Yet the Lord rescued me from all those terrible troubles. 12 Anyone who belongs to Christ Jesus and wants to live right will have trouble from others. 13 But evil people who pretend to be what they are not will become worse than ever, as they fool others and are fooled themselves.

14 Keep on being faithful to what you were taught and to what you believed. After all, you know who taught you these things. 15 Since childhood, you have known the Holy Scriptures that are able to make you wise enough to have faith in Christ Jesus and be saved. 16 Everything in the Scriptures is God's Word. All of it is useful for teaching and helping people and for correcting them and showing them how to live. 17 The Scriptures train God's servants to do all kinds of good deeds.

4 When Christ Jesus comes as king, he will be the judge of everyone, whether they are living or dead. So with God and Christ as witnesses, I command you 2 to preach God's message. Do it willingly, even if it isn't the popular thing to do. You must correct people and point out their sins. But also cheer them up, and when you instruct them, always be patient. 3 The time is coming when people won't listen to good teaching. Instead, they will look for teachers who will please them by telling them only what they are itching to hear. 4 They will turn from the truth and eagerly listen to senseless stories. 5 But you must stay calm and be willing to suffer. You must work hard to tell the good news and to do your job well.

6 Now the time has come for me to die. My life is like a drink offering[g] being poured out on the altar. 7 I have fought well. I have finished the race, and I have been faithful. 8 So a crown will be given to me for pleasing the Lord. He judges fairly, and on the day of judgment he will give a crown to me and to everyone else who wants him to appear with power.

Personal Instructions

9 Come to see me as soon as you can. 10 Demas loves the things of this world so much that he left me and went to Thessalonica. Crescens has gone to Galatia, and Titus has gone to Dalmatia. 11 Only Luke has stayed with me.

Mark can be very helpful to me, so please find him and bring him with you. 12 I sent Tychicus to Ephesus.

13 When you come, bring the coat I left at Troas with Carpus. Don't forget to bring the scrolls, especially the ones made of leather.[h]

14 Alexander, the metalworker, has hurt me in many ways. But the Lord will

[f] **3.8** *Jannes and Jambres*: These names are not found in the Old Testament. But many believe these were the names of the two Egyptian magicians who opposed Moses when he wanted to lead the people of Israel out of Egypt (see Exodus 7.11, 22). [g] **4.6** *drink offering*: Water or wine was sometimes poured out as an offering when an animal sacrifice was made.
[h] **4.13** *the ones made of leather*: A scroll was a kind of rolled up book, and it could be made out of paper (called "papyrus") or leather (that is, animal skin) or even copper.

pay him back for what he has done.
15Alexander opposes what we preach.
You had better watch out for him.

16When I was first put on trial, no one
helped me. In fact, everyone deserted
me. I hope it won't be held against them.
17But the Lord stood beside me. He gave
me the strength to tell his full message,
so that all Gentiles would hear it. And I
was kept safe from hungry lions. 18The
Lord will always keep me from being
harmed by evil, and he will bring me
safely into his heavenly kingdom. Praise
him forever and ever! Amen.

Final Greetings

19Give my greetings to Priscilla and
Aquila and to the family of Onesiphorus.

20Erastus stayed at Corinth.

Trophimus was sick when I left him at Miletus.

21Do your best to come before winter.

Eubulus, Pudens, Linus, and Claudia send you their greetings, and so do the rest of the Lord's followers.

22I pray that the Lord will bless your life and will be kind to you.

TITUS

ABOUT THIS LETTER

Paul mentions Titus several times in his letters as someone who worked with him in Asia Minor and Greece (2 Corinthians 2.13; 7.6, 13; 8.6, 16, 23; 12.18; Galatians 2.3). He is told by Paul to appoint church leaders and officials in Crete.

Paul instructs Titus to make sure that church leaders and officials have good reputations (1.5-9) and that all of the Lord's followers keep themselves pure and avoid arguments (1.10—2.9).

Paul includes special instructions for the different groups within the church in Crete. He reminds Titus that a new way of life is possible because of what God has done by sending Jesus Christ: God has saved them, washed them by the power of the Holy Spirit, and given them a fresh start and the hope of eternal life.

Paul also tells how we are saved:

God our Savior showed us
how good and kind he is.
He saved us because
of his mercy,
and not because
of any good things
that we have done.
(3.4, 5)

A QUICK LOOK AT THIS LETTER

Greetings and a Prayer for Titus (1.1-4)
Instructions for Church Officials (1.5-16)
Instructions for Church People (2.1—3.11)
Personal Advice and Final Greetings (3.12-15)

---

1 From Paul, a servant of God and an
apostle of Jesus Christ.
I encourage God's own people to have
more faith and to understand the truth
about religion. 2Then they will have the
hope of eternal life that God promised
long ago. And God never tells a lie! 3So,
at the proper time, God our Savior gave
this message and told me to announce
what he had said.
4Titus, because of our faith, you are
like a son to me. I pray that God our Father
and Christ Jesus our Savior will be
kind to you and will bless you with
peace!

What Titus Was To Do in Crete

5I left you in Crete to do what had
been left undone and to appoint
leaders[a] for the churches in each town.
As I told you, 6they must have a good
reputation and be faithful in marriage.[b]
Their children must be followers of the
Lord and not have a reputation for being
wild and disobedient.
7Church officials[c] are in charge of

[a]1.5 *leaders*: Or "elders" or "presbyters" or "priests." [b]1.6 *be faithful in marriage*: Or "be the husband of only one wife" or "have never been divorced." [c]1.7 *Church officials*: Or "Bishops."

God's work, and so they must also have a good reputation. They must not be bossy, quick-tempered, heavy drinkers, bullies, or dishonest in business. 8Instead, they must be friendly to strangers and enjoy doing good things. They must also be sensible, fair, pure, and self-controlled. 9They must stick to the true message they were taught, so that their good teaching can help others and correct everyone who opposes it.

10There are many who don't respect authority, and they fool others by talking nonsense. This is especially true of some Jewish followers. 11But you must make them be quiet. They are after money, and they upset whole families by teaching what they should not. 12It is like one of their own prophets once said,

> "The people of Crete
> always tell lies.
> They are greedy and lazy
> like wild animals."

13That surely is a true saying. And you should be hard on such people, so you can help them grow stronger in their faith. 14Don't pay any attention to any of those senseless Jewish stories and human commands. These are made up by people who won't obey the truth.

15Everything is pure for someone whose heart is pure. But nothing is pure for an unbeliever with a dirty mind. That person's mind and conscience are destroyed. 16Such people claim to know God, but their actions prove that they really don't. They are disgusting. They won't obey God, and they are too worthless to do anything good.

Instructions for Different Groups of People

2 Titus, you must teach only what is correct. 2Tell the older men to have self-control and to be serious and sensible. Their faith, love, and patience must never fail.

3Tell the older women to behave as those who love the Lord should. They must not gossip about others or be slaves of wine. They must teach what is proper, 4so the younger women will be loving wives and mothers. 5Each of the younger women must be sensible and kind, as well as a good homemaker, who puts her own husband first. Then no one can say insulting things about God's message.

6Tell the young men to have self-control in everything.

7Always set a good example for others. Be sincere and serious when you teach. 8Use clean language that no one can criticize. Do this, and your enemies will be too ashamed to say anything against you.

9Tell slaves always to please their owners by obeying them in everything. Slaves must not talk back to their owners 10or steal from them. They must be completely honest and trustworthy. Then everyone will show great respect for what is taught about God our Savior.

God's Kindness and the New Life

11God has shown us how kind he is by coming to save all people. 12He taught us to give up our wicked ways and our worldly desires and to live decent and honest lives in this world. 13We are filled with hope, as we wait for the glorious return of our great God and Savior Jesus Christ.[d] 14He gave himself to rescue us from everything that is evil and to make our hearts pure. He wanted us to be his own people and to be eager to do right.

15Teach these things, as you use your full authority to encourage and correct people. Make sure you earn everyone's respect.

Doing Helpful Things

3 Remind your people to obey the rulers and authorities and not to be rebellious. They must always be ready to do something helpful 2and not say cruel things or argue. They should be gentle and kind to everyone. 3We used to be stupid, disobedient, and foolish, as well as slaves of all sorts of desires and pleasures. We were evil and jealous. Everyone hated us, and we hated everyone.

> 4 God our Savior showed us
> how good and kind he is.
> 5 He saved us because
> of his mercy,
> and not because
> of any good things
> that we have done.
>
> God washed us by the power
> of the Holy Spirit.
> He gave us new birth
> and a fresh beginning.
> 6 God sent Jesus Christ
> our Savior
> to give us his Spirit.
>
> 7 Jesus treated us much better
> than we deserve.

[d]**2.13** *the glorious return of our great God and Savior Jesus Christ*: Or "the glorious return of our great God and our Savior Jesus Christ" or "the return of Jesus Christ, who is the glory of our great God and Savior."

He made us acceptable to God
and gave us the hope
of eternal life.

8This message is certainly true.
These teachings are useful and helpful
for everyone. I want you to insist that the
people follow them, so that all who have
faith in God will be sure to do good
deeds. 9But don't have anything to do
with stupid arguments about ancestors.
And stay away from disagreements and
quarrels about the Law of Moses. Such
arguments are useless and senseless.
10Warn troublemakers once or twice.
Then don't have anything else to do
with them. 11You know that their minds
are twisted, and their own sins show
how guilty they are.

Personal Instructions and Greetings

12I plan to send Artemas or Tychicus
to you. After he arrives, please try your
best to meet me at Nicopolis. I have decided to spend the winter there.
13When Zenas the lawyer and Apollos
get ready to leave, help them as much as
you can, so they won't have need of anything.
14Our people should learn to spend
their time doing something useful and
worthwhile.
15Greetings to you from everyone
here. Greet all of our friends who share
in our faith.
I pray that the Lord will be kind to all
of you!

PHILEMON

ABOUT THIS LETTER

Philemon was a wealthy man who owned slaves and who used his large house for church meetings (2). He probably lived in Colossae, since Paul's letter to the Colossians mentions Onesimus, a slave of Philemon, and Archippus (Colossians 4.9, 17).

Paul is writing from jail on behalf of Onesimus, a runaway slave owned by Philemon. Onesimus had become a follower of the Lord and a valuable friend to Paul, and Paul is writing to encourage Philemon to accept Onesimus also as a friend and follower of the Lord.

This letter is an excellent example of the art of letter-writing in the Roman world, and it is the most personal of all Paul's letters. The way the letter is written suggests that Paul and Philemon were close friends.

A QUICK LOOK AT THIS LETTER

Greetings to Philemon (1-3)
Paul Speaks to Philemon about Onesimus (4-22)
Final Greetings and a Prayer (23-25)

1From Paul, who is in jail for serving
Christ Jesus, and from Timothy, who is
like a brother because of our faith.
Philemon, you work with us and are
very dear to us. This letter is to you 2and
to the church that meets in your home.
It is also to our dear friend Apphia and
to Archippus, who serves the Lord as we
do.
3I pray that God our Father and our
Lord Jesus Christ will be kind to you
and will bless you with peace!

Philemon's Love and Faith

4Philemon, each time I mention you in
my prayers, I thank God. 5I hear about
your faith in our Lord Jesus and about
your love for all of God's people. 6As
you share your faith with others, I pray
that they may come to know all the
blessings Christ has given us. 7My
friend, your love has made me happy
and has greatly encouraged me. It has
also cheered the hearts of God's people.

Paul Speaks to Philemon about Onesimus

8Christ gives me the courage to tell
you what to do. 9But I would rather ask
you to do it simply because of love. Yes,
as someone[a] in jail for Christ, 10I beg
you to help Onesimus![b] He is like a son
to me because I led him to Christ here in
jail. 11Before this, he was useless to you,
but now he is useful both to you and to
me.
12Sending Onesimus back to you
makes me very sad. 13I would like to
keep him here with me, where he could
take your place in helping me while I
am here in prison for preaching the
good news. 14But I won't do anything
unless you agree to it first. I want your
act of kindness to come from your
heart, and not be something you feel
forced to do.
15Perhaps Onesimus was taken from
you for a little while so that you could
have him back for good, 16but not as a
slave. Onesimus is much more than a
slave. To me he is a dear friend, but to
you he is even more, both as a person
and as a follower of the Lord.
17If you consider me a friend because
of Christ, then welcome Onesimus as
you would welcome me. 18If he has
cheated you or owes you anything,
charge it to my account. 19With my own

[a]**9** *someone*: Greek "a messenger" or "an old man." [b]**10** *Onesimus*: In Greek this name means "useful."

hand I write: I, PAUL, WILL PAY YOU
BACK. But don't forget that you owe me
your life. 20 My dear friend and follower
of Christ our Lord, please cheer me up
by doing this for me.
21 I am sure you will do all I have
asked, and even more. 22 Please get a
room ready for me. I hope your prayers will be answered, and I can visit you.
23 Epaphras is also here in jail for being a follower of Christ Jesus. He sends
his greetings, 24 and so do Mark,
Aristarchus, Demas, and Luke, who
work together with me.
25 I pray that the Lord Jesus Christ will
be kind to you!

HEBREWS

ABOUT THIS LETTER

Many religious people in the first century after Jesus' birth, both Jews and Gentiles, had questions about the religion of the early Christians. They were looking for evidence that this new faith was genuine. Jews had the miracle of crossing the Red Sea and the agreement made with God at Mount Sinai to support their faith. But what miracles did Christians have? Jews had beautiful worship ceremonies and a high priest who offered sacrifices in the temple so that the people would be forgiven. But what did Christians have? How could this new Christian faith, centered in Jesus, offer forgiveness of sins and friendship with God?

The letter to the Hebrews was written to answer exactly these kinds of questions. In it the author tells the readers how important Jesus really is. He is greater than any of God's angels (1.5-14), greater than any prophet, and greater even than Moses and Joshua (2.1—4.14). Jesus is the perfect high priest because he never sinned, and by offering his own life he has made the perfect sacrifice for sin once for all time (9.23—10.18). By his death and return from death he has opened the way for all people to come to God (4.14—5.10; 7.1—8.13).

This letter has much to say about the importance of faith. The writer points out that what Jesus offers comes only by faith. And this faith makes his followers sure of what they hope for and gives them proof of things that cannot be seen. The writer praises God's faithful people of the past (11.1-40) and encourages those who follow Jesus now to keep their eyes on him as they run the race (12.1-3).

What does it mean to have a high priest like Jesus?

> *Jesus understands every weakness of ours, because he was tempted in every way that we are. But he did not sin! So whenever we are in need, we should come bravely before the throne of our merciful God. There we will be treated with undeserved kindness, and we will find help.* *(4.15, 16)*

A QUICK LOOK AT THIS LETTER

The Greatness of God's Son (1.1-4)
Jesus Is Greater than Angels (1.5—2.18)
Jesus Is Greater than Moses and Joshua (3.1—4.13)
Jesus Is the Great High Priest (4.14—7.28)
Jesus Brings a Better Agreement (8.1—9.22)
Jesus' Sacrifice Is Once and for All (9.23—10.31)
Some of God's People Who Had Great Faith (11.1-40)
Follow the Example of Jesus (12.1—13.19)
Final Prayers and Greetings (13.20-25)

---

1 Long ago in many ways and at
many times God's prophets spoke
his message to our ancestors. 2But now
at last, God sent his Son to bring his
message to us. God created the universe
by his Son, and everything will someday
belong to the Son. 3God's Son has all
the brightness of God's own glory and is
like him in every way. By his own
mighty word, he holds the universe together.

After the Son had washed away our

sins, he sat down at the right side[a] of the glorious God in heaven. 4He had become much greater than the angels, and the name he was given is far greater than any of theirs.

God's Son Is Greater than Angels

5 God has never said
to any of the angels,
"You are my Son, because today
I have become your Father!"
Neither has God said
to any of them,
"I will be his Father,
and he will be my Son!"

6When God brings his first-born Son[b] into the world, he commands all of his angels to worship him.
7And when God speaks about the angels, he says,

"I change my angels into wind
and my servants
into flaming fire."

8But God says about his Son,

"You are God,
and you will rule
as King forever!
Your[c] royal power
brings about justice.
9 You loved justice
and hated evil,
and so I, your God,
have chosen you.
I appointed you
and made you happier
than any of your friends."

10The Scriptures also say,

"In the beginning, Lord,
you were the one
who laid the foundation
of the earth
and created the heavens.
11 They will all disappear
and wear out like clothes,
but you will last forever.
12 You will roll them up
like a robe
and change them
like a garment.
But you are always the same,
and you will live forever."

13 God never said to any
of the angels,
"Sit at my right side
until I make your enemies
into a footstool for you!"

14Angels are merely spirits sent to serve people who are going to be saved.

This Great Way of Being Saved

2 We must give our full attention to what we were told, so that we won't drift away. 2The message spoken by angels proved to be true, and all who disobeyed or rejected it were punished as they deserved. 3So if we refuse this great way of being saved, how can we hope to escape? The Lord himself was the first to tell about it, and people who heard the message proved to us that it was true. 4God himself showed that his message was true by working all kinds of powerful miracles and wonders. He also gave his Holy Spirit to anyone he chose to.

The One Who Leads Us To Be Saved

5We know that God did not put the future world under the power of angels.
6Somewhere in the Scriptures someone says to God,

"What makes you care
about us humans?
Why are you concerned
for weaklings such as we?
7 You made us lower
than the angels
for a while.
Yet you have crowned us
with glory and honor.[d]
8 And you have put everything
under our power!"

God has put everything under our power and has not left anything out of our power. But we still don't see it all under our power. 9What we do see is Jesus, who for a little while was made lower than the angels. Because of God's wonderful kindness, Jesus died for everyone. And now that Jesus has suffered and died, he is crowned with glory and honor!
10Everything belongs to God, and all things were created by his power. So God did the right thing when he made Jesus perfect by suffering, as Jesus led many of God's children to be saved and to share in his glory. 11Jesus and the people he makes holy all belong to the same family. That is why he isn't ashamed to call them his brothers and sisters. 12He even said to God,

"I will tell them your name
and sing your praises
when they come together
to worship."

13He also said,

"I will trust God."

Then he said,

[a]**1.3** *right side*: The place of honor and power. [b]**1.6** *first-born Son*: The first son born into a family had certain privileges that the other children did not have. In 12.23 "first-born" refers to God's special people. [c]**1.8** *Your*: Some manuscripts have "His." [d]**2.7** *and honor*: Some manuscripts add "and you have placed us in charge of all you created."

"Here I am with the children
God has given me."

14 We are people of flesh and blood.
That is why Jesus became one of us. He
died to destroy the devil, who had
power over death. 15 But he also died to
rescue all of us who live each day in
fear of dying. 16 Jesus clearly did not
come to help angels, but he did come to
help Abraham's descendants. 17 He had
to be one of us, so that he could serve
God as our merciful and faithful high
priest and sacrifice himself for the forgiveness of our sins. 18 And now that Jesus has suffered and was tempted, he
can help anyone else who is tempted.

Jesus Is Greater than Moses

3 My friends, God has chosen you to
be his holy people. So think about
Jesus, the one we call our apostle and
high priest! 2 Jesus was faithful to God,
who appointed him, just as Moses was
faithful in serving all of[e] God's people.
3 But Jesus deserves more honor than
Moses, just as the builder of a house deserves more honor than the house. 4 Of
course, every house is built by someone,
and God is really the one who built
everything.
5 Moses was a faithful servant and told
God's people what would be said in the
future. 6 But Christ is the Son in charge
of God's people. And we are those people, if we keep on being brave and don't
lose hope.

A Rest for God's People

7 It is just as the Holy Spirit says,

"If you hear God's voice today,
8 don't be stubborn!
Don't rebel like those people
who were tested
in the desert.
*9 For forty years your ancestors
tested God and saw
the things he did.

10 "Then God got tired of them
and said,
'You people never
show good sense,
and you don't understand
what I want you to do.'
11 God became angry
and told the people,
'You will never enter
my place of rest!' "

12 My friends, watch out! Don't let evil
thoughts or doubts make any of you
turn from the living God. 13 You must encourage one another each day. And you
must keep on while there is still a time
that can be called "today." If you don't,
then sin may fool some of you and make
you stubborn. 14 We were sure about
Christ when we first became his people.
So let's hold tightly to our faith until the
end. 15 The Scriptures say,

"If you hear his voice today,
don't be stubborn
like those who rebelled."

16 Who were those people that heard
God's voice and rebelled? Weren't they
the same ones that came out of Egypt
with Moses? 17 Who were the people that
made God angry for forty years?
Weren't they the ones that sinned and
died in the desert? 18 And who did God
say would never enter his place of rest?
Weren't they the ones that disobeyed
him? 19 We see that those people did not
enter the place of rest because they did
not have faith.

4 The promise to enter the place of
rest is still good, and we must take
care that none of you miss out. 2 We have
heard the message, just as they did. But
they failed to believe what they heard,
and the message did not do them any
good. 3 Only people who have faith will
enter the place of rest. It is just as the
Scriptures say,

"God became angry
and told the people,
'You will never enter
my place of rest!' "

God said this, even though everything
has been ready from the time of creation. 4 In fact, somewhere the Scriptures say that by the seventh day, God
had finished his work, and so he rested.
5 We also read that he later said, "You
people will never enter my place of
rest!" 6 This means that the promise to
enter is still good, because those who
first heard about it disobeyed and did
not enter. 7 Much later God told David to
make the promise again, just as I have
already said,

"If you hear his voice today,
don't be stubborn!"

8 If Joshua had really given the people
rest, there would not be any need for
God to talk about another day of rest.
9 But God has promised us a Sabbath
when we will rest, even though it has
not yet come. 10 On that day God's people will rest from their work, just as God
rested from his work.
11 We should do our best to enter that
place of rest, so that none of us will disobey and miss going there, as they did.
12 What God has said isn't only alive and
active! It is sharper than any double-
edged sword. His word can cut through
our spirits and souls and through our
joints and marrow, until it discovers the

[e] 3.2 *all of*: Some manuscripts do not have these words.

desires and thoughts of our hearts.
[13]Nothing is hidden from God! He sees
through everything, and we will have to
tell him the truth.

Jesus Is the Great High Priest

[14]We have a great high priest, who has
gone into heaven, and he is Jesus the
Son of God. That is why we must hold
on to what we have said about him. [15]Je-
sus understands every weakness of
ours, because he was tempted in every
way that we are. But he did not sin! [16]So
whenever we are in need, we should
come bravely before the throne of our
merciful God. There we will be treated
with undeserved kindness, and we will
find help.

5 Every high priest is appointed to
help others by offering gifts and
sacrifices to God because of their sins.
[2]A high priest has weaknesses of his
own, and he feels sorry for foolish and
sinful people. [3]That is why he must offer
sacrifices for his own sins and for the
sins of others. [4]But no one can have the
honor of being a high priest simply by
wanting to be one. Only God can choose
a priest, and God is the one who chose
Aaron.

[5]That is how it was with Christ. He became a high priest, but not just because
he wanted the honor of being one. It
was God who told him,

> "You are my Son, because today
> I have become your Father!"

[6]In another place, God says,

> "You are a priest forever
> just like Melchizedek."[f]

[7]God had the power to save Jesus
from death. And while Jesus was on
earth, he begged God with loud crying
and tears to save him. He truly worshiped God, and God listened to his
prayers. [8]Jesus is God's own Son, but
still he had to suffer before he could
learn what it really means to obey God.
[9]Suffering made Jesus perfect, and now
he can save forever all who obey him.
[10]This is because God chose him to be a
high priest like Melchizedek.

Warning against Turning Away

[11]Much more could be said about this
subject. But it is hard to explain, and all
of you are slow to understand. [12]By now
you should have been teachers, but once
again you need to be taught the simplest
things about what God has said. You
need milk instead of solid food. [13]People
who live on milk are like babies who
don't really know what is right. [14]Solid
food is for mature people who have
been trained to know right from wrong.

6 We must try to become mature and
start thinking about more than just
the basic things we were taught about
Christ. We shouldn't need to keep talking about why we ought to turn from
deeds that bring death and why we
ought to have faith in God. [2]And we
shouldn't need to keep teaching about
baptisms[g] or about the laying on of
hands[h] or about people being raised
from death and the future judgment.
[3]Let's grow up, if God is willing.

[4-6]But what about people who turn
away after they have already seen the
light and have received the gift from
heaven and have shared in the Holy
Spirit? What about those who turn away
after they have received the good message of God and the powers of the future world? There is no way to bring
them back. What they are doing is the
same as nailing the Son of God to a
cross and insulting him in public!

[7]A field is useful to farmers, if there is
enough rain to make good crops grow.
In fact, God will bless that field. [8]But
land that produces only thornbushes is
worthless. It is likely to fall under God's
curse, and in the end it will be set on
fire.

[9]My friends, we are talking this way.
But we are sure that you are doing those
really good things that people do when
they are being saved. [10]God is always
fair. He will remember how you helped
his people in the past and how you are
still helping them. You belong to God,
and he won't forget the love you have
shown his people. [11]We wish that each
of you would always be eager to show
how strong and lasting your hope really
is. [12]Then you would never be lazy. You
would be following the example of
those who had faith and were patient
until God kept his promise to them.

God's Promise Is Sure

[13]No one is greater than God. So he
made a promise in his own name when
he said to Abraham, [14]"I, the Lord, will
bless you with many descendants!"
[15]Then after Abraham had been very patient, he was given what God had
promised. [16]When anyone wants to settle an argument, they make a vow by using the name of someone or something
greater than themselves. [17]So when God
wanted to prove for certain that his

[f]**5.6** *Melchizedek*: When Melchizedek is mentioned in the Old Testament, he is described as a priest who lived before Aaron. Nothing is said about his ancestors or his death (see 7.3 and Genesis 14.17-20). [g]**6.2** *baptisms*: Or "ceremonies of washing." [h]**6.2** *laying on of hands*: This was a ceremony in which church leaders and others put their hands on people to show that those people were chosen to do some special kind of work.

promise to his people could not be broken, he made a vow. 18God cannot tell lies! And so his promises and vows are two things that can never be changed.

We have run to God for safety. Now his promises should greatly encourage us to take hold of the hope that is right in front of us. 19This hope is like a firm and steady anchor for our souls. In fact, hope reaches behind the curtain[i] and into the most holy place. 20Jesus has gone there ahead of us, and he is our high priest forever, just like Melchizedek.[j]

The Priestly Family of Melchizedek

7 Melchizedek was both king of Salem and priest of God Most High. He was the one who went out and gave Abraham his blessing, when Abraham returned from killing the kings. 2Then Abraham gave him a tenth of everything he had.

The meaning of the name Melchizedek is "King of Justice." But since Salem means "peace," he is also "King of Peace." 3We are not told that he had a father or mother or ancestors or beginning or end. He is like the Son of God and will be a priest forever.[k]

4Notice how great Melchizedek is! Our famous ancestor Abraham gave him a tenth of what he had taken from his enemies. 5The Law teaches that even Abraham's descendants must give a tenth of what they possess. And they are to give this to their own relatives, who are the descendants of Levi and are priests. 6Although Melchizedek wasn't a descendant of Levi, Abraham gave him a tenth of what he had. Then Melchizedek blessed Abraham, who had been given God's promise. 7Everyone agrees that a person who gives a blessing is greater than the one who receives the blessing.

8Priests are given a tenth of what people earn. But all priests die, except Melchizedek, and the Scriptures teach that he is alive. 9Levi's descendants are now the ones who receive a tenth from people. We could even say that when Abraham gave Melchizedek a tenth, Levi also gave him a tenth. 10This is because Levi was born later into the family of Abraham, who gave a tenth to Melchizedek.

11Even though the Law of Moses says that the priests must be descendants of Levi, those priests cannot make anyone perfect. So there needs to be a priest like Melchizedek, rather than one from the priestly family of Aaron.[l] 12And when the rules for selecting a priest are changed, the Law must also be changed.

13The person we are talking about is our Lord, who came from a tribe that had never had anyone to serve as a priest at the altar. 14Everyone knows he came from the tribe of Judah, and Moses never said that priests would come from that tribe.

15All of this becomes clearer, when someone who is like Melchizedek is appointed to be a priest. 16That person wasn't appointed because of his ancestors, but because his life can never end. 17The Scriptures say about him,

> "You are a priest forever,
> just like Melchizedek."

18In this way a weak and useless command was put aside, 19because the Law cannot make anything perfect. At the same time, we are given a much better hope, and it can bring us close to God.

20-21God himself made a promise when this priest was appointed. But he did not make a promise like this when the other priests were appointed. The promise he made is,

> "I, the Lord, promise that you
> will be a priest forever!
> And I will never
> change my mind!"

22This means that Jesus guarantees us a better agreement with God. 23There have been a lot of other priests, and all of them have died. 24But Jesus will never die, and so he will be a priest forever! 25He is forever able to save[m] the people he leads to God, because he always lives to speak to God for them.

26Jesus is the high priest we need. He is holy and innocent and faultless, and not at all like us sinners. Jesus is honored above all beings in heaven, 27and he is better than any other high priest. Jesus doesn't need to offer sacrifices each day for his own sins and then for the sins of the people. He offered a sacrifice once for all, when he gave himself. 28The Law appoints priests who have weaknesses. But God's promise, which came later than the Law, appoints his Son. And he is the perfect high priest forever.

A Better Promise

8 What I mean is that we have a high priest who sits at the right side[n] of God's great throne in heaven. 2He also

[i]**6.19** *behind the curtain*: In the tent that was used for worship, a curtain separated the "holy place" from the "most holy place," which only the high priest could enter. [j]**6.20** *Melchizedek*: See the note at 5.6. [k]**7.3** *will be a priest forever*: See the note at 5.6. [l]**7.11** *descendants of Levi . . . from the priestly family of Aaron*: Levi was the ancestor of the tribe from which priests and their helpers (called "Levites") were chosen. Aaron was the first high priest. [m]**7.25** *forever able to save*: Or "able to save forever." [n]**8.1** *right side*: See the note at 1.3.

serves as the priest in the most holy
place[o] inside the real tent there in
heaven. This tent of worship was set up
by the Lord, not by humans.
3Since all priests must offer gifts and
sacrifices, Christ also needed to have
something to offer. 4If he were here on
earth, he would not be a priest at all, because here the Law appoints other
priests to offer sacrifices. 5But the tent
where they serve is just a copy and a
shadow of the real one in heaven. Before Moses made the tent, he was told,
"Be sure to make it exactly like the pattern you were shown on the mountain!"
6Now Christ has been appointed to
serve as a priest in a much better way,
and he has given us much assurance of
a better agreement.
7If the first agreement with God had
been all right, there would not have
been any need for another one. 8But the
Lord found fault with it and said,

"I tell you the time will come,
when I will make
    a new agreement
with the people of Israel
    and the people of Judah.
9 It won't be like the agreement
that I made
    with their ancestors,
when I took them by the hand
    and led them out of Egypt.
They broke their agreement
    with me,
and I stopped caring
    about them!

10 "But now I tell the people
of Israel
    this is my new agreement:
'The time will come
    when I, the Lord,
will write my laws
    on their minds and hearts.
I will be their God,
and they will be
    my people.
11 Not one of them
will have to teach another
    to know me, their Lord.'

"All of them will know me,
    no matter who they are.
12 I will treat them with kindness,
even though they are wicked.
    I will forget their sins."

13When the Lord talks about a new
agreement, he means that the first one
is out of date. And anything that is old
and useless will soon disappear.

The Tent in Heaven

9 The first promise that was made included rules for worship and a tent
for worship here on earth. 2The first
part of the tent was called the holy
place, and a lampstand, a table, and the
sacred loaves of bread were kept there.
3Behind the curtain was the most holy
place. 4The gold altar that was used for
burning incense was in this holy place.
The gold-covered sacred chest was also
there, and inside it were three things.
First, there was a gold jar filled with
manna.[p] Then there was Aaron's walking stick that sprouted.[q] Finally, there
were the flat stones with the Ten Commandments written on them. 5On top of
the chest were the glorious creatures
with wings[r] opened out above the place
of mercy.[s]
Now isn't the time to go into detail
about these things. 6But this is how
everything was when the priests went
each day into the first part of the tent to
do their duties. 7However, only the high
priest could go into the second part of
the tent, and he went in only once a
year. Each time he carried blood to offer
for his sins and for any sins that the
people had committed without meaning
to.
8All of this is the Holy Spirit's way of
saying that no one could enter the most
holy place while the tent was still the
place of worship. 9This also has a meaning for today. It shows that we cannot
make our consciences clear by offering
gifts and sacrifices. 10These rules are
merely about such things as eating and
drinking and ceremonies for washing
ourselves. And rules about physical
things will last only until the time
comes to change them for something
better.
11Christ came as the high priest of the
good things that are now here.[t] He also
went into a much better tent that wasn't
made by humans and that doesn't belong to this world. 12Then Christ went
once for all into the most holy place and
freed us from sin forever. He did this by
offering his own blood instead of the
blood of goats and bulls.

[o]**8.2** *most holy place*: See the note at 6.19. [p]**9.4** *manna*: When the people of Israel were wandering through the desert, the Lord provided them with food that could be made into thin wafers. This food was called manna, which in Hebrew means "What is it?" [q]**9.4** *Aaron's walking stick that sprouted*: According to Numbers 17.1-11, Aaron's walking stick sprouted and produced almonds to show that the Lord was pleased with him and Moses.
[r]**9.5** *glorious creatures with wings*: Two of these creatures (called "cherubim" in Hebrew and Greek) with outspread wings were on top of the sacred chest and were symbols of God's throne. [s]**9.5** *place of mercy*: The lid of the sacred chest, which was thought to be God's throne on earth. [t]**9.11** *that are now here*: Some manuscripts have "that were coming."

13According to the Law of Moses, those people who become unclean are not fit to worship God. Yet they will be considered clean, if they are sprinkled with the blood of goats and bulls and with the ashes of a sacrificed calf. 14But Christ was sinless, and he offered himself as an eternal and spiritual sacrifice to God. That's why his blood is much more powerful and makes our[u] consciences clear. Now we can serve the living God and no longer do things that lead to death.

15Christ died to rescue those who had sinned and broken the old agreement. Now he brings his chosen ones a new agreement with its guarantee of God's eternal blessings! 16In fact, making an agreement of this kind is like writing a will. This is because the one who makes the will must die before it is of any use. 17In other words, a will doesn't go into effect as long as the one who made it is still alive.

18Blood was also used[v] to put the first agreement into effect. 19Moses told the people all that the Law said they must do. Then he used red wool and a hyssop plant to sprinkle the people and the book of the Law with the blood of bulls and goats[w] and with water. 20He told the people, "With this blood God makes his agreement with you." 21Moses also sprinkled blood on the tent and on everything else that was used in worship. 22The Law says that almost everything must be sprinkled with blood, and no sins can be forgiven unless blood is offered.

Christ's Great Sacrifice

23These things are only copies of what is in heaven, and so they had to be made holy by these ceremonies. But the real things in heaven must be made holy by something better. 24This is why Christ did not go into a tent that had been made by humans and was only a copy of the real one. Instead, he went into heaven and is now there with God to help us.

25Christ did not have to offer himself many times. He wasn't like a high priest who goes into the most holy place each year to offer the blood of an animal. 26If he had offered himself every year, he would have suffered many times since the creation of the world. But instead, near the end of time he offered himself once and for all, so that he could be a sacrifice that does away with sin.

27We die only once, and then we are judged. 28So Christ died only once to take away the sins of many people. But when he comes again, it will not be to take away sin. He will come to save everyone who is waiting for him.

10 The Law of Moses is like a shadow of the good things to come. This shadow isn't the good things themselves, because it cannot free people from sin by the sacrifices that are offered year after year. 2If there were worshipers who already have their sins washed away and their consciences made clear, there would not be any need to go on offering sacrifices. 3-4But the blood of bulls and goats cannot take away sins. It only reminds people of their sins from one year to the next.

5When Christ came into the world, he said to God,

"Sacrifices and offerings
are not what you want,
but you have given me
my body.
6 No, you are not pleased
with animal sacrifices
and offerings for sin."

7Then Christ said,

"And so, my God,
I have come to do
what you want,
as the Scriptures say."

8The Law teaches that offerings and sacrifices must be made because of sin. But why did Christ mention these things and say that God did not want them? 9Well, it was to do away with offerings and sacrifices and to replace them. That is what he meant by saying to God, "I have come to do what you want." 10So we are made holy because Christ obeyed God and offered himself once for all.

11The priests do their work each day, and they keep on offering sacrifices that can never take away sins. 12But Christ offered himself as a sacrifice that is good forever. Now he is sitting at God's right side,[x] 13and he will stay there until his enemies are put under his power. 14By his one sacrifice he has forever set free from sin the people he brings to God.

15The Holy Spirit also speaks of this by telling us that the Lord said,

16 "When the time comes,
I will make an agreement
with them.
I will write my laws
on their minds and hearts.
17 Then I will forget
about their sins
and no longer remember
their evil deeds."

[u]**9.14** *our*: Some manuscripts have "your," and others have "their." [v]**9.18** *Blood was also used*: Or "There also had to be a death." [w]**9.19** *blood of bulls and goats*: Some manuscripts do not have "and goats." [x]**10.12** *right side*: See the note at 1.3.

18When sins are forgiven, there is no
more need to offer sacrifices.

Encouragement and Warning

19My friends, the blood of Jesus gives
us courage to enter the most holy place
20by a new way that leads to life! And
this way takes us through the curtain
that is Christ himself.
21We have a great high priest who is
in charge of God's house. 22So let's
come near God with pure hearts and a
confidence that comes from having
faith. Let's keep our hearts pure, our
consciences free from evil, and our bodies washed with clean water. 23We must
hold tightly to the hope that we say is
ours. After all, we can trust the one who
made the agreement with us. 24We
should keep on encouraging each other
to be thoughtful and to do helpful
things. 25Some people have gotten out of
the habit of meeting for worship, but we
must not do that. We should keep on encouraging each other, especially since
you know that the day of the Lord's
coming is getting closer.
26No sacrifices can be made for people
who decide to sin after they find out
about the truth. 27They are God's enemies, and all they can look forward to is
a terrible judgment and a furious fire. 28If
two or more witnesses accused someone
of breaking the Law of Moses, that person could be put to death. 29But it is
much worse to dishonor God's Son and
to disgrace the blood of the promise that
made us holy. And it is just as bad to insult the Holy Spirit, who shows us mercy.
30We know that God has said he will
punish and take revenge. We also know
that the Scriptures say the Lord will
judge his people. 31It is a terrible thing to
fall into the hands of the living God!
32Don't forget all the hard times you
went through when you first received
the light. 33Sometimes you were abused
and mistreated in public, and at other
times you shared in the sufferings of
others. 34You were kind to people in jail.
And you gladly let your possessions be
taken away, because you knew you had
something better, something that would
last forever.
35Keep on being brave! It will bring
you great rewards. 36Learn to be patient,
so that you will please God and be given
what he has promised. 37As the Scriptures say,

"God is coming soon!
It won't be very long.
38 The people God accepts
will live because
of their faith.[y]
But he isn't pleased
with anyone
who turns back."

39We are not like those people who turn
back and get destroyed. We will keep on
having faith until we are saved.

The Great Faith of God's People

11 Faith makes us sure of what we
hope for and gives us proof of
what we cannot see. 2It was their faith
that made our ancestors pleasing to
God.
3Because of our faith, we know that
the world was made at God's command.
We also know that what can be seen
was made out of what cannot be seen.
4Because Abel had faith, he offered
God a better sacrifice than Cain did.
God was pleased with him and his gift,
and even though Abel is now dead, his
faith still speaks for him.
5Enoch had faith and did not die. He
pleased God, and God took him up to
heaven. That's why his body was never
found. 6But without faith no one can
please God. We must believe that God is
real and that he rewards everyone who
searches for him.
7Because Noah had faith, he was
warned about something that had not
yet happened. He obeyed and built a
boat that saved him and his family. In
this way the people of the world were
judged, and Noah was given the blessings that come to everyone who pleases
God.
8Abraham had faith and obeyed God.
He was told to go to the land that God
had said would be his, and he left for a
country he had never seen. 9Because
Abraham had faith, he lived as a
stranger in the promised land. He lived
there in a tent, and so did Isaac and Jacob, who were later given the same
promise. 10Abraham did this, because he
was waiting for the eternal city that God
had planned and built.
11Even when Sarah was too old to
have children, she had faith that God
would do what he had promised, and
she had a son. 12Her husband Abraham
was almost dead, but he became the ancestor of many people. In fact, there are
as many of them as there are stars in
the sky or grains of sand along the
beach.
13Every one of those people died. But
they still had faith, even though they
had not received what they had been
promised. They were glad just to see
these things from far away, and they
agreed that they were only strangers
and foreigners on this earth. 14When

[y]**10.38** *The people God accepts will live because of their faith*: Or "The people God accepts because of their faith will live."

people talk this way, it is clear that they are looking for a place to call their own. 15 If they had been talking about the land where they had once lived, they could have gone back at any time. 16 But they were looking forward to a better home in heaven. That's why God wasn't ashamed for them to call him their God. He even built a city for them.

17-18 Abraham had been promised that Isaac, his only son,[z] would continue his family. But when Abraham was tested, he had faith and was willing to sacrifice Isaac, 19 because he was sure that God could raise people to life. This was just like getting Isaac back from death.

20 Isaac had faith, and he promised blessings to Jacob and Esau. 21 Later, when Jacob was about to die, he leaned on his walking stick and worshiped. Then because of his faith he blessed each of Joseph's sons. 22 And right before Joseph died, he had faith that God would lead the people of Israel out of Egypt. So he told them to take his bones with them.

23 Because Moses' parents had faith, they kept him hidden until he was three months old. They saw that he was a beautiful child, and they were not afraid to disobey the king's orders.[a] 24 Then after Moses grew up, his faith made him refuse to be called the king's grandson. 25 He chose to be mistreated with God's people instead of having the good time that sin could bring for a little while. 26 Moses knew that the treasures of Egypt were not as wonderful as what he would receive from suffering for the Messiah,[b] and he looked forward to his reward.

27 Because of his faith, Moses left Egypt. Moses had seen the invisible God and wasn't afraid of the king's anger. 28 His faith also made him celebrate Passover. He sprinkled the blood of animals on the doorposts, so that the firstborn sons of the people of Israel would not be killed by the destroying angel.

29 Because of their faith, the people walked through the Red Sea[c] on dry land. But when the Egyptians tried to do it, they were drowned.

30 God's people had faith, and when they had walked around the city of Jericho for seven days, its walls fell down.

31 Rahab had been a prostitute, but she had faith and welcomed the spies. So she wasn't killed with the people who disobeyed.

32 What else can I say? There isn't enough time to tell about Gideon, Barak, Samson, Jephthah, David, Samuel, and the prophets. 33 Their faith helped them conquer kingdoms, and because they did right, God made promises to them. They closed the jaws of lions 34 and put out raging fires and escaped from the swords of their enemies. Although they were weak, they were given the strength and power to chase foreign armies away.

35 Some women received their loved ones back from death. Many of these people were tortured, but they refused to be released. They were sure that they would get a better reward when the dead are raised to life. 36 Others were made fun of and beaten with whips, and some were chained in jail. 37 Still others were stoned to death or sawed in two[d] or killed with swords. Some had nothing but sheep skins or goat skins to wear. They were poor, mistreated, and tortured. 38 The world did not deserve these good people, who had to wander in deserts and on mountains and had to live in caves and holes in the ground.

39 All of them pleased God because of their faith! But still they died without being given what had been promised. 40 This was because God had something better in store for us. And he did not want them to reach the goal of their faith without us.

A Large Crowd of Witnesses

12 Such a large crowd of witnesses is all around us! So we must get rid of everything that slows us down, especially the sin that just won't let go. And we must be determined to run the race that is ahead of us. 2 We must keep our eyes on Jesus, who leads us and makes our faith complete. He endured the shame of being nailed to a cross, because he knew that later on he would be glad he did. Now he is seated at the right side[e] of God's throne! 3 So keep your mind on Jesus, who put up with many insults from sinners. Then you won't get discouraged and give up.

4 None of you have yet been hurt[f] in your battle against sin. 5 But you have

[z] **11.17,18** *his only son*: Although Abraham had a son by a slave woman, his son Isaac was considered his only son, because he was born as a result of God's promise to Abraham.
[a] **11.23** *the king's orders*: The king of Egypt ordered all Israelite baby boys to be left outside of their homes, so they would die or be killed.
[b] **11.26** *the Messiah*: Or "Christ."
[c] **11.29** *Red Sea*: This name comes from the Bible of the early Christians, a translation made into Greek about 200 B.C. It refers to the body of water that the Israelites crossed and was one of the marshes or fresh water lakes near the eastern part of the Nile Delta, where they lived and where the towns of Exodus 13.17—14.9 were located.
[d] **11.37** *sawed in two*: Some manuscripts have "tested" or "tempted."
[e] **12.2** *right side*: See the note at 1.3.
[f] **12.4** *hurt*: Or "killed."

forgotten that the Scriptures say to God's children,

> "When the Lord punishes you,
> don't make light of it,
> and when he corrects you,
> don't be discouraged.
> 6 The Lord corrects the people
> he loves
> and disciplines those
> he calls his own."

7 Be patient when you are being corrected! This is how God treats his children. Don't all parents correct their children? 8 God corrects all of his children, and if he doesn't correct you, then you don't really belong to him. 9 Our earthly fathers correct us, and we still respect them. Isn't it even better to be given true life by letting our spiritual Father correct us?

10 Our human fathers correct us for a short time, and they do it as they think best. But God corrects us for our own good, because he wants us to be holy, as he is. 11 It is never fun to be corrected. In fact, at the time it is always painful. But if we learn to obey by being corrected, we will do right and live at peace.

12 Now stand up straight! Stop your knees from shaking 13 and walk a straight path. Then lame people will be healed, instead of getting worse.

Warning against Turning from God

14 Try to live at peace with everyone! Live a clean life. If you don't, you will never see the Lord. 15 Make sure that no one misses out on God's wonderful kindness. Don't let anyone become bitter and cause trouble for the rest of you. 16 Watch out for immoral and ungodly people like Esau, who sold his future blessing[g] for only one meal. 17 You know how he later wanted it back. But there was nothing he could do to change things, even though he begged his father and cried.

18 You have not come to a place like Mount Sinai[h] that can be seen and touched. There is no flaming fire or dark cloud or storm 19 or trumpet sound. The people of Israel heard a voice speak. But they begged it to stop, 20 because they could not obey its commands. They were even told to kill any animal that touched the mountain. 21 The sight was so frightening that Moses said he shook with fear.

22 You have now come to Mount Zion and to the heavenly Jerusalem. This is the city of the living God, where thousands and thousands of angels have come to celebrate. 23 Here you will find all of God's dearest children,[i] whose names are written in heaven. And you will find God himself, who judges everyone. Here also are the spirits of those good people who have been made perfect. 24 And Jesus is here! He is the one who makes God's new agreement with us, and his sprinkled blood says much better things than the blood of Abel.[j]

25 Make sure that you obey the one who speaks to you. The people did not escape, when they refused to obey the one who spoke to them at Mount Sinai. Do you think you can possibly escape, if you refuse to obey the one who speaks to you from heaven? 26 When God spoke the first time, his voice shook only the earth. This time he has promised to shake the earth once again, and heaven too.

27 The words "once again" mean that these created things will someday be shaken and removed. Then what cannot be shaken will last. 28 We should be grateful that we were given a kingdom that cannot be shaken. And in this kingdom we please God by worshiping him and by showing him great honor and respect. 29 Our God is like a destructive fire!

Service That Pleases God

13 Keep being concerned about each other as the Lord's followers should.

2 Be sure to welcome strangers into your home. By doing this, some people have welcomed angels as guests, without even knowing it.

3 Remember the Lord's people who are in jail and be concerned for them. Don't forget those who are suffering, but imagine that you are there with them.

4 Have respect for marriage. Always be faithful to your partner, because God will punish anyone who is immoral or unfaithful in marriage.

5 Don't fall in love with money. Be satisfied with what you have. The Lord has promised that he will not leave us or desert us. 6 That should make you feel like saying,

> "The Lord helps me!
> Why should I be afraid
> of what people
> can do to me?"

7 Don't forget about your leaders who taught you God's message. Remember

[g] **12.16** *sold his future blessing*: As the first-born son, Esau had certain privileges that were known as a "birthright." [h] **12.18** *a place like Mount Sinai*: The Greek text has "a place," but the writer is referring to the time that the Lord spoke to the people of Israel from Mount Sinai (see Exodus 19.16-25). [i] **12.23** *all of God's dearest children*: The Greek text has "the gathering of the first-born children" (see the note at 1.6). [j] **12.24** *blood of Abel*: Cain and Abel were the two sons of Adam and Eve. Cain murdered Abel (see Genesis 4.1-16).

what kind of lives they lived and try to
have faith like theirs.
[8]Jesus Christ never changes! He is the
same yesterday, today, and forever.
[9]Don't be fooled by any kind of strange
teachings. It is better to receive strength
from God's undeserved kindness than to
depend on certain foods. After all, these
foods don't really help the people who
eat them. [10]But we have an altar where
even the priests who serve in the place
of worship have no right to eat.
[11]After the high priest offers the blood
of animals as a sin offering, the bodies
of those animals are burned outside the
camp. [12]Jesus himself suffered outside
the city gate, so that his blood would
make people holy. [13]That's why we
should go outside the camp to Jesus and
share in his disgrace. [14]On this earth we
don't have a city that lasts forever, but
we are waiting for such a city.
[15]Our sacrifice is to keep offering
praise to God in the name of Jesus.
[16]But don't forget to help others and to
share your possessions with them. This
too is like offering a sacrifice that
pleases God.
[17]Obey your leaders and do what they
say. They are watching over you, and
they must answer to God. So don't make
them sad as they do their work. Make
them happy. Otherwise, they won't be
able to help you at all.
[18]Pray for us. Our consciences are
clear, and we always try to live right. [19]I
especially want you to pray that I can
visit you again soon.

Final Prayers and Greetings

[20]God gives peace, and he raised our
Lord Jesus Christ from death. Now Jesus is like a Great Shepherd whose
blood was used to make God's eternal
agreement with his flock.[k] [21]I pray that
God will make you ready to obey him
and that you will always be eager to do
right. May Jesus help you do what
pleases God. To Jesus Christ be glory
forever and ever! Amen.
[22]My friends, I have written only a
short letter to encourage you, and I beg
you to pay close attention to what I have
said.
[23]By now you surely must know that
our friend Timothy is out of jail. If he
gets here in time, I will bring him with
me when I come to visit you.
[24]Please give my greetings to your
leaders and to the rest of the Lord's people.
His followers from Italy send you
their greetings.
[25]I pray that God will be kind to all of
you![l]

[k] **13.20** *whose blood was used to make God's eternal agreement with his flock*: See 9.18-22.
[l] **13.25** *to all of you!*: Some manuscripts add "Amen."

JAMES

ABOUT THIS LETTER

This is a good example of a general letter, because it is addressed to Christians scattered throughout the Roman Empire. Though written as a letter, it is more like a short book of instructions for daily living.

For James faith means action! In fact, the entire book is a series of examples that show faith in action in wise and practical ways.

His advice was clear and to the point: If you are poor, don't despair! Don't give up when your faith is being tested. Don't get angry quickly. Don't favor the rich over the poor. Do good things for others. Control your tongue and desires. Surrender to God and rely on his wisdom. Resist the devil. Don't brag about what you are going to do. If you are rich, use your money to help the poor. Be patient and kind, and pray for those who need God's help.

A QUICK LOOK AT THIS LETTER

Greetings (1.1)
A Life of Faith and Wisdom (1.2-18)
Hearing and Obeying God's Message (1.19-27)
Don't Favor the Rich and Powerful (2.1-13)
Faith and Works (2.14-26)
Wisdom and Words (3.1-18)
Warning against Friendship with the World (4.1—5.6)
Patience, Kindness, and Prayer (5.7-20)

---

1 From James, a servant of God and of
our Lord Jesus Christ.
Greetings to the twelve tribes scattered all over the world.[a]

Faith and Wisdom

2 My friends, be glad, even if you have
a lot of trouble. 3 You know that you
learn to endure by having your faith
tested. 4 But you must learn to endure
everything, so that you will be completely mature and not lacking in anything.

5 If any of you need wisdom, you
should ask God, and it will be given to
you. God is generous and won't correct
you for asking. 6 But when you ask for
something, you must have faith and not
doubt. Anyone who doubts is like an
ocean wave tossed around in a storm.
7-8 If you are that kind of person, you
can't make up your mind, and you
surely can't be trusted. So don't expect
the Lord to give you anything at all.

Poor People and Rich People

9 Any of God's people who are poor
should be glad that he thinks so highly
of them. 10 But any who are rich should
be glad when God makes them humble.
Rich people will disappear like wild
flowers 11 scorched by the burning heat
of the sun. The flowers lose their blossoms, and their beauty is destroyed.
That is how the rich will disappear, as
they go about their business.

Trials and Temptations

12 God will bless you, if you don't give
up when your faith is being tested. He
will reward you with a glorious life,[b]
just as he rewards everyone who loves
him.

13 Don't blame God when you are

[a] **1.1** *twelve tribes scattered all over the world*: James is saying that the Lord's followers are like the tribes of Israel that were scattered everywhere by their enemies.

[b] **1.12** *a glorious life*: The Greek text has "the crown of life." In ancient times an athlete who had won a contest was rewarded with a crown of flowers as a sign of victory.

tempted! God cannot be tempted by evil,
and he doesn't use evil to tempt others.
14We are tempted by our own desires
that drag us off and trap us. 15Our desires make us sin, and when sin is finished with us, it leaves us dead.
16Don't be fooled, my dear friends.
17Every good and perfect gift comes
down from the Father who created all
the lights in the heavens. He is always
the same and never makes dark shadows by changing. 18He wanted us to be
his own special people,[c] and so he sent
the true message to give us new birth.

Hearing and Obeying

19My dear friends, you should be
quick to listen and slow to speak or to
get angry. 20If you are angry, you cannot
do any of the good things that God
wants done. 21You must stop doing anything immoral or evil. Instead be humble and accept the message that is
planted in you to save you.
22Obey God's message! Don't fool
yourselves by just listening to it. 23If you
hear the message and don't obey it, you
are like people who stare at themselves
in a mirror 24and forget what they look
like as soon as they leave. 25But you
must never stop looking at the perfect
law that sets you free. God will bless
you in everything you do, if you listen
and obey, and don't just hear and forget.
26If you think you are being religious,
but can't control your tongue, you are
fooling yourself, and everything you do
is useless. 27Religion that pleases God
the Father must be pure and spotless.
You must help needy orphans and widows and not let this world make you
evil.

Warning against Having Favorites

2 My friends, if you have faith in our
glorious Lord Jesus Christ, you
won't treat some people better than others. 2Suppose a rich person wearing
fancy clothes and a gold ring comes to
one of your meetings. And suppose a
poor person dressed in worn-out clothes
also comes. 3You must not give the best
seat to the one in fancy clothes and tell
the one who is poor to stand at the side
or sit on the floor. 4That is the same as
saying that some people are better than
others, and you would be acting like a
crooked judge.
5My dear friends, pay attention. God
has given a lot of faith to the poor people in this world. He has also promised
them a share in his kingdom that he will
give to everyone who loves him. 6You
mistreat the poor. But isn't it the rich
who boss you around and drag you off
to court? 7Aren't they the ones who
make fun of your Lord?
8You will do all right, if you obey the
most important law[d] in the Scriptures. It
is the law that commands us to love others as much as we love ourselves. 9But if
you treat some people better than others, you have done wrong, and the
Scriptures teach that you have sinned.
10If you obey every law except one,
you are still guilty of breaking them all.
11The same God who told us to be faithful in marriage also told us not to murder. So even if you are faithful in marriage, but murder someone, you still
have broken God's Law.
12Speak and act like people who will
be judged by the law that sets us free.
13Do this, because on the day of judgment there will be no pity for those who
have not had pity on others. But even in
judgment, God is merciful![e]

Faith and Works

14My friends, what good is it to say
you have faith, when you don't do anything to show that you really do have
faith? Can that kind of faith save
you? 15If you know someone who
doesn't have any clothes or food, 16you
shouldn't just say, "I hope all goes well
for you. I hope you will be warm and
have plenty to eat." What good is it to
say this, unless you do something to
help? 17Faith that doesn't lead us to do
good deeds is all alone and dead!
18Suppose someone disagrees and
says, "It is possible to have faith without
doing kind deeds."
I would answer, "Prove that you have
faith without doing kind deeds, and I
will prove that I have faith by doing
them." 19You surely believe there is only
one God. That's fine. Even demons believe this, and it makes them shake with
fear.
20Does some stupid person want proof
that faith without deeds is useless?
21Well, our ancestor Abraham pleased
God by putting his son Isaac on the altar to sacrifice him. 22Now you see how
Abraham's faith and deeds worked together. He proved that his faith was real
by what he did. 23This is what the Scriptures mean by saying, "Abraham had
faith in God, and God was pleased with
him." That's how Abraham became
God's friend.
24You can now see that we please God

[c]**1.18** *his own special people*: The Greek text has "the first of his creatures." The Law of Moses taught that the first-born of all animals and the first part of the harvest were special and belonged to the Lord. [d]**2.8** *most important law*: The Greek text has "royal law," meaning the one given by the king (that is, God). [e]**2.13** *But even in judgment, God is merciful!*: Or "So be merciful, and you will be shown mercy on the day of judgment."

by what we do and not only by what we
believe. 25For example, Rahab had been
a prostitute. But she pleased God when
she welcomed the spies and sent them
home by another way.
26Anyone who doesn't breathe is
dead, and faith that doesn't do anything
is just as dead!

The Tongue

3 My friends, we should not all try to
become teachers. In fact, teachers
will be judged more strictly than others.
2All of us do many wrong things. But if
you can control your tongue, you are
mature and able to control your whole
body.
3By putting a bit into the mouth of a
horse, we can turn the horse in different
directions. 4It takes strong winds to
move a large sailing ship, but the captain uses only a small rudder to make it
go in any direction. 5Our tongues are
small too, and yet they brag about big
things.
It takes only a spark to start a forest
fire! 6The tongue is like a spark. It is an
evil power that dirties the rest of the
body and sets a person's entire life on
fire with flames that come from hell itself. 7All kinds of animals, birds, reptiles, and sea creatures can be tamed
and have been tamed. 8But our tongues
get out of control. They are restless and
evil, and always spreading deadly poison.
9-10My dear friends, with our tongues
we speak both praises and curses. We
praise our Lord and Father, and we
curse people who were created to be
like God, and this isn't right. 11Can
clean water and dirty water both flow
from the same spring? 12Can a fig tree
produce olives or a grapevine produce
figs? Does fresh water come from a well
full of salt water?

Wisdom from Above

13Are any of you wise or sensible?
Then show it by living right and by being humble and wise in everything you
do. 14But if your heart is full of bitter
jealousy and selfishness, don't brag or
lie to cover up the truth. 15That kind of
wisdom doesn't come from above. It is
earthly and selfish and comes from the
devil himself. 16Whenever people are
jealous or selfish, they cause trouble
and do all sorts of cruel things. 17But the
wisdom that comes from above leads us
to be pure, friendly, gentle, sensible,
kind, helpful, genuine, and sincere.
18When peacemakers plant seeds of
peace, they will harvest justice.

Friendship with the World

4 Why do you fight and argue with
each other? Isn't it because you are
full of selfish desires that fight to control your body? 2You want something
you don't have, and you will do anything to get it. You will even kill! But you
still cannot get what you want, and you
won't get it by fighting and arguing. You
should pray for it. 3Yet even when you
do pray, your prayers are not answered,
because you pray just for selfish reasons.
4You people aren't faithful to God!
Don't you know that if you love the
world, you are God's enemies? And if
you decide to be a friend of the world,
you make yourself an enemy of God.
5Do you doubt the Scriptures that say,
"God truly cares about the Spirit he has
put in us"?[f] 6In fact, God treats us with
even greater kindness, just as the Scriptures say,

"God opposes everyone
who is proud,
but he is kind to everyone
who is humble."

7Surrender to God! Resist the devil,
and he will run from you. 8Come near to
God, and he will come near to you. Clean
up your lives, you sinners. Purify your
hearts, you people who can't make up
your mind. 9Be sad and sorry and weep.
Stop laughing and start crying. Be gloomy
instead of glad. 10Be humble in the
Lord's presence, and he will honor you.

Saying Cruel Things about Others

11My friends, don't say cruel things
about others! If you do, or if you condemn others, you are condemning God's
Law. And if you condemn the Law, you
put yourself above the Law and refuse
to obey either it 12or God who gave it.
God is our judge, and he can save or destroy us. What right do you have to condemn anyone?

Warning against Bragging

13You should know better than to say,
"Today or tomorrow we will go to the
city. We will do business there for a year
and make a lot of money!" 14What do
you know about tomorrow? How can
you be so sure about your life? It is
nothing more than mist that appears for
only a little while before it disappears.
15You should say, "If the Lord lets us
live, we will do these things." 16Yet you
are stupid enough to brag, and it is
wrong to be so proud. 17If you don't do
what you know is right, you have
sinned.

[f]**4.5** *God truly cares about the Spirit he has put in us*: One possible meaning for the difficult Greek text; other translations are possible, such as, "the Spirit that God put in us truly cares."

Warning to the Rich

5 You rich people should cry and
weep! Terrible things are going to
happen to you. [2]Your treasures have already rotted, and moths have eaten your
clothes. [3]Your money has rusted, and
the rust will be evidence against you, as
it burns your body like fire. Yet you keep
on storing up wealth in these last days.
[4]You refused to pay the people who
worked in your fields, and now their un-
paid wages are shouting out against
you. The Lord All-Powerful has surely
heard the cries of the workers who harvested your crops.
[5]While here on earth, you have
thought only of filling your own stomachs and having a good time. But now
you are like fat cattle on their way to be
butchered. [6]You have condemned and
murdered innocent people, who couldn't
even fight back.

Be Patient and Kind

[7]My friends, be patient until the Lord
returns. Think of farmers who wait patiently for the spring and summer rains
to make their valuable crops grow. [8]Be
patient like those farmers and don't give
up. The Lord will soon be here! [9]Don't
grumble about each other or you will be
judged, and the judge is right outside
the door.
[10]My friends, follow the example of
the prophets who spoke for the Lord.
They were patient, even when they had
to suffer. [11]In fact, we praise the ones
who endured the most. You remember
how patient Job was and how the Lord
finally helped him. The Lord did this because he is so merciful and kind.
[12]My friends, above all else, don't take
an oath. You must not swear by heaven
or by earth or by anything else. "Yes" or
"No" is all you need to say. If you say
anything more, you will be condemned.
[13]If you are having trouble, you should
pray. And if you are feeling good, you
should sing praises. [14]If you are sick,
ask the church leaders[g] to come and
pray for you. Ask them to put olive oil[h]
on you in the name of the Lord. [15]If you
have faith when you pray for sick people, they will get well. The Lord will
heal them, and if they have sinned, he
will forgive them.
[16]If you have sinned, you should tell
each other what you have done. Then
you can pray for one another and be
healed. The prayer of an innocent person is powerful, and it can help a lot.
[17]Elijah was just as human as we are,
and for three and a half years his
prayers kept the rain from falling. [18]But
when he did pray for rain, it fell from
the skies and made the crops grow.
[19]My friends, if any followers have
wandered away from the truth, you
should try to lead them back. [20]If you
turn sinners from the wrong way, you
will save them from death, and many of
their sins will be forgiven.

[g]**5.14** *church leaders*: Or "elders" or "presbyters" or "priests." [h]**5.14** *olive oil*: The Jewish people used olive oil for healing.

1 PETER

ABOUT THIS LETTER

In this letter Peter has much to say about suffering. He shows how it can be a way of serving the Lord, of sharing the faith, and of being tested. The letter was written to Christians scattered all over the northern part of Asia Minor. In this part of the Roman Empire many Christians had already suffered unfair treatment from people who did not believe in Jesus. And they could expect to suffer even more.

Peter was quick to offer encouragement. His letter reminds the readers that some of the Lord's followers may have to go through times of hard testing. But this should make them glad, Peter declares, because it will strengthen their faith and bring them honor on the day when Jesus Christ returns (1.6, 7).

Peter reminds them that Christ suffered here on earth, and when his followers suffer for doing right they are sharing his sufferings (2.18-25; 4.12-17). In fact, Christians should expect to suffer for their faith (3.8—4.19).

But because of who God is and because of what God has done by raising Jesus Christ from death, Christians can have hope in the future. Just as Christ suffered before he received honor from God, so will Christians be tested by suffering before they receive honor when the Lord returns. Peter uses poetic language to remind his readers of what Christ has done:

Christ died once for our sins.
An innocent person died
   for those who are guilty.
Christ did this
   to bring you to God,
when his body
   was put to death
and his spirit
   was made alive.   (3.18)

A QUICK LOOK AT THIS LETTER

Greetings and Prayer (1.1, 2)
A Real Reason for Hope (1.3-12)
Living as God's Holy People (1.13—2.17)
The Example of Christ's Suffering (2.18-25)
Being a Christian and Suffering (3.1—4.19)
Advice for Church Leaders (5.1-11)
Final Greetings (5.12-14)

---

1 From Peter, an apostle of Jesus Christ.
To God's people who are scattered
like foreigners in Pontus, Galatia, Cappadocia, Asia, and Bithynia.
2 God the Father decided to choose you
as his people, and his Spirit has made
you holy. You have obeyed Jesus Christ
and are sprinkled with his blood.[a]

[a] **1.2** *sprinkled with his blood*: According to Exodus 24.3-8 the people of Israel were sprinkled with the blood of cows to show they would keep their agreement with God. Peter says that it is the blood of Jesus that seals the agreement between God and his people (see Hebrews 9.18-21).

I pray that God will be kind to you
and will keep on giving you peace!

A Real Reason for Hope

3 Praise God, the Father of our Lord Jesus Christ. God is so good, and by raising Jesus from death, he has given us
new life and a hope that lives on. 4 God
has something stored up for you in
heaven, where it will never decay or be
ruined or disappear.
5 You have faith in God, whose power
will protect you until the last day.[b] Then
he will save you, just as he has always
planned to do. 6 On that day you will be
glad, even if you have to go through
many hard trials for a while. 7 Your faith
will be like gold that has been tested in
a fire. And these trials will prove that
your faith is worth much more than
gold that can be destroyed. They will
show that you will be given praise and
honor and glory when Jesus Christ returns.
8 You have never seen Jesus, and you
don't see him now. But still you love him
and have faith in him, and no words can
tell how glad and happy 9 you are to be
saved. That's why you have faith.
10 Some prophets told how kind God
would be to you, and they searched hard
to find out more about the way you
would be saved. 11 The Spirit of Christ
was in them and was telling them how
Christ would suffer and would then be
given great honor. So they searched to
find out exactly who Christ would be
and when this would happen. 12 But they
were told that they were serving you
and not themselves. They preached to
you by the power of the Holy Spirit,
who was sent from heaven. And their
message was only for you, even though
angels would like to know more about
it.

Chosen To Live a Holy Life

13 Be alert and think straight. Put all
your hope in how kind God will be to
you when Jesus Christ appears. 14 Behave like obedient children. Don't let
your lives be controlled by your desires,
as they used to be. 15 Always live as
God's holy people should, because God
is the one who chose you, and he is holy.
16 That's why the Scriptures say, "I am
the holy God, and you must be holy
too."
17 You say that God is your Father, but
God doesn't have favorites! He judges
all people by what they do. So you must
honor God while you live as strangers
here on earth. 18 You were rescued[c] from
the useless way of life that you learned
from your ancestors. But you know that
you were not rescued by such things as
silver or gold that don't last forever.
19 You were rescued by the precious
blood of Christ, that spotless and innocent lamb. 20 Christ was chosen even before the world was created, but because
of you, he did not come until these last
days. 21 And when he did come, it was to
lead you to have faith in God, who
raised him from death and honored him
in a glorious way. That's why you have
put your faith and hope in God.
22 You obeyed the truth,[d] and your
souls were made pure. Now you sincerely love each other. But you must
keep on loving with all your heart. 23 Do
this because God has given you new
birth by his message that lives on forever. 24 The Scriptures say,

"Humans wither like grass,
and their glory fades
  like wild flowers.
Grass dries up,
and flowers fall
  to the ground.
25 But what the Lord has said
  will stand forever."

Our good news to you is what the
Lord has said.

A Living Stone and a Holy Nation

2 Stop being hateful! Quit trying to
fool people, and start being sincere.
Don't be jealous or say cruel things
about others. 2 Be like newborn babies
who are thirsty for the pure spiritual
milk that will help you grow and be
saved. 3 You have already found out how
good the Lord really is.
4 Come to Jesus Christ. He is the living
stone that people have rejected, but
which God has chosen and highly honored. 5 And now you are living stones
that are being used to build a spiritual
house. You are also a group of holy
priests, and with the help of Jesus
Christ you will offer sacrifices that
please God. 6 It is just as God says in the
Scriptures,

"Look! I am placing in Zion
a choice and precious
  cornerstone.
No one who has faith
in that one
  will be disappointed."

7 You are followers of the Lord, and
that stone is precious to you. But it isn't
precious to those who refuse to follow

[b] **1.5** *the last day*: When God will judge all people. [c] **1.18** *rescued*: The Greek word often, though not always, means payment of a price to free a slave or prisoner. [d] **1.22** *You obeyed the truth*: Some manuscripts add "by the power of the Spirit."

him. They are the builders who tossed
aside the stone that turned out to be the
most important one of all. 8They disobeyed the message and stumbled and
fell over that stone, because they were
doomed.
9But you are God's chosen and special
people. You are a group of royal priests
and a holy nation. God has brought you
out of darkness into his marvelous light.
Now you must tell all the wonderful
things that he has done. The Scriptures
say,

10 "Once you were nobody.
Now you are God's people.
At one time no one
had pity on you.
Now God has treated you
with kindness.

Live as God's Servants Should

11Dear friends, you are foreigners and
strangers on this earth. So I beg you not
to surrender to those desires that fight
against you. 12Always let others see you
behaving properly, even though they
may still accuse you of doing wrong.
Then on the day of judgment, they will
honor God by telling the good things
they saw you do.
13The Lord wants you to obey all human authorities, especially the Emperor,
who rules over everyone. 14You must
also obey governors, because they are
sent by the Emperor to punish criminals
and to praise good citizens. 15God wants
you to silence stupid and ignorant people by doing right. 16You are free, but
still you are God's servants, and you
must not use your freedom as an excuse
for doing wrong. 17Respect everyone
and show special love for God's people.
Honor God and respect the Emperor.

The Example of Christ's Suffering

18Servants, you must obey your masters and always show respect to them.
Do this, not only to those who are kind
and thoughtful, but also to those who
are cruel. 19God will bless you, even if
others treat you unfairly for being loyal
to him. 20You don't gain anything by being punished for some wrong you have
done. But God will bless you, if you have
to suffer for doing something good.
21After all, God chose you to suffer as
you follow in the footsteps of Christ,
who set an example by suffering for
you.

22 Christ did not sin
or ever tell a lie.
23 Although he was abused,
he never tried to get even.
And when he suffered,
he made no threats.
Instead, he had faith in God,
who judges fairly.
24 Christ carried the burden
of our sins.
He was nailed to the cross,
so that we would stop sinning
and start living right.
By his cuts and bruises
you are healed.
25 You had wandered away
like sheep.
Now you have returned
to the one
who is your shepherd
and protector.

Wives and Husbands

3 If you are a wife, you must put your
husband first. Even if he opposes
our message, you will win him over by
what you do. No one else will have to
say anything to him, 2because he will
see how you honor God and live a pure
life. 3Don't depend on things like fancy
hairdos or gold jewelry or expensive
clothes to make you look beautiful. 4Be
beautiful in your heart by being gentle
and quiet. This kind of beauty will last,
and God considers it very special.
5Long ago those women who worshiped God and put their hope in him
made themselves beautiful by putting
their husbands first. 6For example,
Sarah obeyed Abraham and called him
her master. You are her true children, if
you do right and don't let anything
frighten you.
7If you are a husband, you should be
thoughtful of your wife. Treat her with
honor, because she isn't as strong as
you are, and she shares with you in the
gift of life. Then nothing will stand in
the way of your prayers.

Suffering for Doing Right

8Finally, all of you should agree and
have concern and love for each other.
You should also be kind and humble.
9Don't be hateful and insult people just
because they are hateful and insult you.
Instead, treat everyone with kindness.
You are God's chosen ones, and he will
bless you. The Scriptures say,

10 "Do you really love life?
Do you want to be happy?
Then stop saying cruel things
and quit telling lies.
11 Give up your evil ways
and do right,
as you find and follow
the road that leads
to peace.
12 The Lord watches over
everyone who obeys him,
and he listens
to their prayers.
But he opposes everyone
who does evil."

13 Can anyone really harm you for being eager to do good deeds? 14 Even if
you have to suffer for doing good
things, God will bless you. So stop being
afraid and don't worry about what people might do. 15 Honor Christ and let him
be the Lord of your life.

Always be ready to give an answer
when someone asks you about your
hope. 16 Give a kind and respectful answer and keep your conscience clear.
This way you will make people ashamed
for saying bad things about your good
conduct as a follower of Christ. 17 You
are better off to obey God and suffer for
doing right than to suffer for doing
wrong.

18 Christ died once for our sins.
An innocent person died
for those who are guilty.
Christ did this
to bring you to God,
when his body
was put to death
and his spirit
was made alive.

19 Christ then preached to the spirits
that were being kept in prison. 20 They
had disobeyed God while Noah was
building the boat, but God had been patient with them. Eight people went into
that boat and were brought safely
through the flood.

21 Those flood waters were like baptism that now saves you. But baptism is
more than just washing your body. It
means turning to God with a clear conscience, because Jesus Christ was raised
from death. 22 Christ is now in heaven,
where he sits at the right side[e] of God.
All angels, authorities, and powers are
under his control.

Being Faithful to God

4 Christ suffered here on earth. Now
you must be ready to suffer as he
did, because suffering shows that you
have stopped sinning. 2 It means you
have turned from your own desires and
want to obey God for the rest of your
life. 3 You have already lived long
enough like people who don't know
God. You were immoral and followed
your evil desires. You went around
drinking and partying and carrying on.
In fact, you even worshiped disgusting
idols. 4 Now your former friends wonder
why you have stopped running around
with them, and they curse you for it.
5 But they will have to answer to God,
who judges the living and the dead.
6 The good news has even been preached
to the dead,[f] so that after they have
been judged for what they have done in
this life, their spirits will live with God.

7 Everything will soon come to an end.
So be serious and be sensible enough to
pray.

8 Most important of all, you must sincerely love each other, because love
wipes away many sins.

9 Welcome people into your home and
don't grumble about it.

10 Each of you has been blessed with
one of God's many wonderful gifts to be
used in the service of others. So use
your gift well. 11 If you have the gift of
speaking, preach God's message. If you
have the gift of helping others, do it
with the strength that God supplies.
Everything should be done in a way that
will bring honor to God because of Jesus Christ, who is glorious and powerful
forever. Amen.

Suffering for Being a Christian

12 Dear friends, don't be surprised or
shocked that you are going through
testing that is like walking through fire.
13 Be glad for the chance to suffer as
Christ suffered. It will prepare you for
even greater happiness when he makes
his glorious return.

14 Count it a blessing when you suffer
for being a Christian. This shows that
God's glorious Spirit is with you. 15 But
you deserve to suffer if you are a murderer, a thief, a crook, or a busybody.
16 Don't be ashamed to suffer for being a
Christian. Praise God that you belong to
him. 17 God has already begun judging
his own people. And if his judgment begins with us, imagine how terrible it will
be for those who refuse to obey his message. The Scriptures say,

18 "If good people barely escape,
what will happen to sinners
and to others
who don't respect God?"

19 If you suffer for obeying God, you
must have complete faith in your faithful Creator and keep on doing right.

Helping Christian Leaders

5 Church leaders,[g] I am writing to encourage you. I too am a leader, as
well as a witness to Christ's suffering,
and I will share in his glory when it is
shown to us.

2 Just as shepherds watch over their
sheep, you must watch over everyone
God has placed in your care. Do it willingly in order to please God, and not
simply because you think you must. Let
it be something you want to do, instead
of something you do merely to make

[e] **3.22** *right side*: The place of honor and power. [f] **4.6** *the dead*: Either people who died after becoming followers of Christ or the people of Noah's day (see 3.19). [g] **5.1** *Church leaders*: Or "Elders" or "Presbyters" or "Priests."

money. [3]Don't be bossy to those people
who are in your care, but set an example for them. [4]Then when Christ the
Chief Shepherd returns, you will be
given a crown that will never lose its
glory.
[5]All of you young people should obey
your elders. In fact, everyone should be
humble toward everyone else. The
Scriptures say,

"God opposes proud people,
but he helps everyone
who is humble."

[6]Be humble in the presence of God's
mighty power, and he will honor you
when the time comes. [7]God cares for
you, so turn all your worries over to
him.
[8]Be on your guard and stay awake.
Your enemy, the devil, is like a roaring
lion, sneaking around to find someone
to attack. [9]But you must resist the devil
and stay strong in your faith. You know
that all over the world the Lord's followers are suffering just as you are. [10]But
God shows undeserved kindness to everyone. That's why he appointed
Christ Jesus to choose you to share in
his eternal glory. You will suffer for a
while, but God will make you complete, steady, strong, and firm. [11]God
will be in control forever! Amen.

Final Greetings

[12]Silvanus helped me write this short
letter, and I consider him a faithful follower of the Lord. I wanted to encourage you and tell you how kind God really is, so that you will keep on having
faith in him.
[13]Greetings from the Lord's followers
in Babylon.[h] They are God's chosen
ones.

Mark, who is like a son to me, sends
his greetings too.
[14]Give each other a warm greeting. I
pray that God will give peace to everyone who belongs to Christ.[i]

[h]**5.13** *Babylon*: This may be a secret name for the city of Rome. [i]**5.14** Christ: Some manuscripts add "Amen."

2 PETER

ABOUT THIS LETTER

The writer of this letter wants the readers to know that Christians must live in a way that pleases God (1.3) and hold firmly to the truth they were given (1.12).

He warns them that false prophets and teachers had entered the Christian community and were trying to lead the Lord's followers away from the truth. But they will be punished for their evil deeds (2.1-22). When false teachers are at work, Christians must stick to their faith and be examples for others of right living. They must have understanding, self-control and patience, and they should show love for God and all people.

The readers must never forget that the Lord's return is certain, no matter what others may say (3.1-18):

> *Don't forget that for the Lord one day is the same as a thousand years, and a thousand years is the same as one day. The Lord isn't slow about keeping his promises, as some people think he is. In fact, God is patient, because he wants everyone to turn from sin and no one to be lost.*
> *(3.8, 9)*

A QUICK LOOK AT THIS LETTER

Greetings and Prayer (1.1, 2)
How the Lord's Followers Should Live (1.3-15)
The Glory of Christ (1.16-21)
False Prophets and Teachers (2.1-22)
The Lord's Return Is Certain (3.1-18)

---

1 From Simon Peter, a servant and an
apostle of Jesus Christ.
To everyone who shares with us in the
privilege of believing that our God and
Savior Jesus Christ will do what is just
and fair.[a]
2 I pray that God will be kind to you
and will let you live in perfect peace!
May you keep learning more and more
about God and our Lord Jesus.

Living as the Lord's Followers

3 We have everything we need to live a
life that pleases God. It was all given to
us by God's own power, when we
learned that he had invited us to share
in his wonderful goodness. 4 God made
great and marvelous promises, so that
his nature would become part of us.
Then we could escape our evil desires
and the corrupt influences of this world.
5 Do your best to improve your faith.
You can do this by adding goodness, understanding, 6 self-control, patience, devotion to God, 7 concern for others, and
love. 8 If you keep growing in this way, it
will show that what you know about our
Lord Jesus Christ has made your lives
useful and meaningful. 9 But if you don't
grow, you are like someone who is near-
sighted or blind, and you have forgotten
that your past sins are forgiven.
10 My friends, you must do all you can
to show that God has really chosen and
selected you. If you keep on doing this,
you won't stumble and fall. 11 Then our
Lord and Savior Jesus Christ will give
you a glorious welcome into his kingdom that will last forever.
12 You are holding firmly to the truth

[a] 1.1 *To everyone who . . . just and fair*: Or "To everyone whose faith in the justice and fairness of our God and Savior Jesus Christ is as precious as our own faith."

that you were given. But I am still going
to remind you of these things. 13 In fact, I
think I should keep on reminding you
until I leave this body. 14 And our Lord
Jesus Christ has already told me that I
will soon leave it behind. 15 That is why I
am doing my best to make sure that
each of you remembers all of this after I
am gone.

The Message about the Glory of Christ

16 When we told you about the power
and the return of our Lord Jesus Christ,
we were not telling clever stories that
someone had made up. But with our
own eyes we saw his true greatness.
17 God, our great and wonderful Father,
truly honored him by saying, "This is
my own dear Son, and I am pleased
with him." 18 We were there with Jesus
on the holy mountain and heard this
voice speak from heaven.

19 All of this makes us even more certain that what the prophets said is true.
So you should pay close attention to
their message, as you would to a lamp
shining in some dark place. You must
keep on paying attention until daylight
comes and the morning star rises in
your hearts. 20 But you need to realize
that no one alone can understand any of
the prophecies in the Scriptures. 21 The
prophets did not think these things up
on their own, but they were guided by
the Spirit of God.

False Prophets and Teachers

2 Sometimes false prophets spoke to
the people of Israel. False teachers
will also sneak in and speak harmful
lies to you. But these teachers don't really belong to the Master who paid a
great price for them, and they will
quickly destroy themselves. 2 Many people will follow their evil ways and cause
others to tell lies about the true way.
3 They will be greedy and cheat you with
smooth talk. But long ago God decided
to punish them, and God doesn't sleep.

4 God did not have pity on the angels
that sinned. He had them tied up and
thrown into the dark pits of hell until
the time of judgment. 5 And during
Noah's time, God did not have pity on
the ungodly people of the world. He destroyed them with a flood, though he did
save eight people, including Noah, who
preached the truth.

6 God punished the cities of Sodom
and Gomorrah[b] by burning them to
ashes, and this is a warning to anyone
else who wants to sin.

7-8 Lot lived right and was greatly troubled by the terrible way those wicked
people were living. He was a good man,
and day after day he suffered because of
the evil things he saw and heard. So the
Lord rescued him. 9 This shows that the
Lord knows how to rescue godly people
from their sufferings and to punish evil
people while they wait for the day of
judgment.

10 The Lord is especially hard on people who disobey him and don't think of
anything except their own filthy desires.
They are reckless and proud and are not
afraid of cursing the glorious beings in
heaven. 11 Although angels are more
powerful than these evil beings,[c] even
the angels don't dare to accuse them to
the Lord.

12 These people are no better than
senseless animals that live by their feelings and are born to be caught and
killed. They speak evil of things they
don't know anything about. But their
own corrupt deeds will destroy them.
13 They have done evil, and they will be
rewarded with evil.

They think it is fun to have wild parties during the day. They are immoral,
and the meals they eat with you are
spoiled by the shameful and selfish way
they carry on.[d] 14 All they think about is
having sex with someone else's husband or wife. There is no end to their
wicked deeds. They trick people who
are easily fooled, and their minds are
filled with greedy thoughts. But they are
headed for trouble!

15 They have left the true road and
have gone down the wrong path by following the example of the prophet Balaam. He was the son of Beor and loved
what he got from being a crook. 16 But a
donkey corrected him for this evil deed.
It spoke to him with a human voice and
made him stop his foolishness.

17 These people are like dried up water
holes and clouds blown by a windstorm.
The darkest part of hell is waiting for
them. 18 They brag out loud about their
stupid nonsense. And by being vulgar
and crude, they trap people who have
barely escaped from living the wrong
kind of life. 19 They promise freedom to
everyone. But they are merely slaves of
filthy living, because people are slaves
of whatever controls them.

20 When they learned about our Lord
and Savior Jesus Christ, they escaped
from the filthy things of this world. But
they are again caught up and controlled
by these filthy things, and now they are

[b] **2.6** *Sodom and Gomorrah*: During the time of Abraham the Lord destroyed these cities because the people there were so evil (see Genesis 19.24). [c] **2.11** *evil beings*: Or "evil teachers." [d] **2.13** *and the meals they eat with you are spoiled by the shameful and selfish way they carry on*: Some manuscripts have "and the meals they eat with you are spoiled by the shameful way they carry on during your feasts of Christian love."

in worse shape than they were at first.
21 They would have been better off if
they had never known about the right
way. Even after they knew what was
right, they turned their backs on the
holy commandments that they were
given. 22 What happened to them is just
like the true saying,

"A dog will come back
to lick up its own vomit.
A pig that has been washed
will roll in the mud."

The Lord Will Return

3 My dear friends, this is the second
letter I have written to encourage
you to do some honest thinking. I don't
want you to forget 2 what God's prophets
said would happen. You must never forget what the holy prophets taught in the
past. And you must remember what the
apostles told you our Lord and Savior
has commanded us to do.
3 But first you must realize that in the
last days some people won't think about
anything except their own selfish desires. They will make fun of you 4 and
say, "Didn't your Lord promise to come
back? Yet the first leaders have already
died, and the world hasn't changed a
bit."
5 They will say this because they want
to forget that long ago the heavens and
the earth were made at God's command.
The earth came out of water and was
made from water. 6 Later it was destroyed by the waters of a mighty flood.
7 But God has commanded the present
heavens and earth to remain until the
day of judgment. Then they will be set
on fire, and ungodly people will be destroyed.
8 Dear friends, don't forget that for the
Lord one day is the same as a thousand
years, and a thousand years is the same
as one day. 9 The Lord isn't slow about
keeping his promises, as some people
think he is. In fact, God is patient, because he wants everyone to turn from
sin and no one to be lost.
10 The day of the Lord's return will
surprise us like a thief. The heavens will
disappear with a loud noise, and the
heat will melt the whole universe.[e] Then
the earth and everything on it will be
seen for what they are.[f]
11 Everything will be destroyed. So you
should serve and honor God by the way
you live. 12 You should look forward to
the day when God judges everyone, and
you should try to make it come soon.[g]
On that day the heavens will be destroyed by fire, and everything else will
melt in the heat. 13 But God has
promised us a new heaven and a new
earth, where justice will rule. We are really looking forward to that!
14 My friends, while you are waiting,
you should make certain that the Lord
finds you pure, spotless, and living at
peace. 15 Don't forget that the Lord is patient because he wants people to be
saved. This is also what our dear friend
Paul said when he wrote you with the
wisdom that God had given him. 16 Paul
talks about these same things in all his
letters, but part of what he says is hard
to understand. Some ignorant and un-
steady people even destroy themselves
by twisting what he said. They do the
same thing with other Scriptures too.
17 My dear friends, you have been
warned ahead of time! So don't let the
errors of evil people lead you down the
wrong path and make you lose your balance. 18 Let the wonderful kindness and
the understanding that come from our
Lord and Savior Jesus Christ help you
to keep on growing. Praise Jesus now
and forever! Amen.[h]

[e] **3.10** *the whole universe*: Probably the sun, moon, and stars, or the elements that everything in the universe is made of. [f] **3.10** *will be seen for what they are*: Some manuscripts have "will go up in flames." [g] **3.12** *and you should try to make it come soon*: Or "and you should eagerly desire for that day to come." [h] **3.18** *Amen*: Some manuscripts do not have "Amen."

1 JOHN

ABOUT THIS LETTER

John wants Christian believers to know that when we tell God about our sins, God will forgive us and take them away (1.9).

The true test of faith is love for each other (3.11-24). Because God is love, his people must be like him (4.1-21). For a complete victory over sin, we must not only love others, but we must believe that Jesus, the Son of God, is truly Christ, and that his death for us was real (5.1-12).

Remember:

The Word that gives life
was from the beginning,
and this is the one
our message is about.
(1.1a)

A QUICK LOOK AT THIS LETTER

The Word that Gives Life (1.1-4)
God Is Light and Christ Is Our Example (1.5—2.6)
The New Commandment (2.7-17)
The Enemies of Christ and God's Children (2.18—3.10)
God's Love and Our Love (3.11—4.21)
Victory Over the World (5.1-21)

---

1 The Word that gives life
was from the beginning,
and this is the one
our message is about.

Our ears have heard,
our own eyes have seen,
and our hands touched
this Word.

2The one who gives life appeared! We
saw it happen, and we are witnesses to
what we have seen. Now we are telling
you about this eternal life that was with
the Father and appeared to us. 3We are
telling you what we have seen and
heard, so that you may share in this life
with us. And we share in it with the Father and with his Son Jesus Christ. 4We
are writing to tell you these things, because this makes us[a] truly happy.

God Is Light

5Jesus told us that God is light and
doesn't have any darkness in him. Now
we are telling you.
6If we say that we share in life with
God and keep on living in the dark, we
are lying and are not living by the truth.
7But if we live in the light, as God does,
we share in life with each other. And the
blood of his Son Jesus washes all our
sins away. 8If we say that we have not
sinned, we are fooling ourselves, and
the truth isn't in our hearts. 9But if we
confess our sins to God, he can always
be trusted to forgive us and take our
sins away.

[a]1.4 *us:* Some manuscripts have "you."

10 If we say that we have not sinned,
we make God a liar, and his message
isn't in our hearts.[b]

Christ Helps Us

2 My children, I am writing this so
that you won't sin. But if you do sin,
Jesus Christ always does the right thing,
and he will speak to the Father for us.
2 Christ is the sacrifice that takes away
our sins and the sins of all the world's
people.
3 When we obey God, we are sure that
we know him. 4 But if we claim to know
him and don't obey him, we are lying
and the truth isn't in our hearts. 5 We
truly love God only when we obey him
as we should, and then we know that we
belong to him. 6 If we say we are his, we
must follow the example of Christ.

The New Commandment

7 My dear friends, I am not writing to
give you a new commandment. It is the
same one that you were first given, and
it is the message you heard. 8 But it really is a new commandment, and you
know its true meaning, just as Christ
does. You can see the darkness fading
away and the true light already shining.
9 If we claim to be in the light and hate
someone, we are still in the dark. 10 But
if we love others, we are in the light, and
we don't cause problems for them.[c] 11 If
we hate others, we are living and walking in the dark. We don't know where
we are going, because we can't see in
the dark.

12 Children, I am writing you,
because your sins
have been forgiven
in the name of Christ.
13 Parents, I am writing you,
because you have known
the one who was there
from the beginning.
Young people, I am writing you,
because you have defeated
the evil one.
14 Children, I am writing you,
because you have known
the Father.
Parents, I am writing you,
because you have known
the one who was there
from the beginning.
Young people, I am writing you,
because you are strong.
God's message is firm
in your hearts,
and you have defeated
the evil one.

15 Don't love the world or anything
that belongs to the world. If you love the
world, you cannot love the Father. 16 Our
foolish pride comes from this world, and
so do our selfish desires and our desire
to have everything we see. None of this
comes from the Father. 17 The world and
the desires it causes are disappearing.
But if we obey God, we will live forever.

The Enemy of Christ

18 Children, this is the last hour. You
heard that the enemy of Christ would
appear at this time, and many of
Christ's enemies have already appeared.
So we know that the last hour is here.
19 These people came from our own
group, yet they were not part of us. If
they had been part of us, they would
have stayed with us. But they left, which
proves that they did not belong to our
group.
20 Christ, the Holy One,[d] has blessed[e]
you, and now all of you understand.[f] 21 I
did not need to write you about the
truth, since you already know it. You
also know that liars do not belong to the
truth. 22 And a liar is anyone who says
that Jesus isn't truly Christ. Anyone
who says this is an enemy of Christ and
rejects both the Father and the Son. 23 If
we reject the Son, we reject the Father.
But if we say that we accept the Son, we
have the Father. 24 Keep thinking about
the message you first heard, and you
will always be one in your heart with
the Son and with the Father. 25 The Son[g]
has promised us[h] eternal life.
26 I am writing to warn you about
those people who are misleading you.
27 But Christ has blessed you with the
Holy Spirit.[i] Now the Spirit stays in you,
and you don't need any teachers. The

[b]**1.10** *and his message isn't in our hearts*: Or "because we have not accepted his message." [c]**2.10** *and we don't cause problems for them*: Or "and we can see anything that might make us fall." [d]**2.20** *Christ, the Holy One*: The Greek text has "the Holy One" which may refer either to Christ or to God the Father. [e]**2.20** *blessed*: This translates a word which means "to pour olive oil on (someone's head)." In Old Testament times it was the custom to pour olive oil on a person's head when that person was chosen to be a priest or a king. Here the meaning is not clear. It may refer to the ceremony of pouring olive oil on the followers of the Lord right before they were baptized or it may refer to the gift of the Holy Spirit which they were given at baptism (see verse 27). [f]**2.20** *now all of you understand*: Some manuscripts have "you understand all things." [g]**2.25** *The Son*: The Greek text has "he" and may refer to God the Father. [h]**2.25** *us*: Some manuscripts have "you." [i]**2.27** *Christ has blessed you with the Holy Spirit*: The Greek text has "You received a pouring on of olive oil from him" (see verse 20). The "pouring on of olive oil" is here taken to refer to the gift of the Holy Spirit, and "he" may refer either to Christ or to the Father.

Spirit is truthful and teaches you everything. So stay one in your heart with
Christ, just as the Spirit has taught you
to do.

Children of God

28Children, stay one in your hearts
with Christ. Then when he returns, we
will have confidence and won't have to
hide in shame. 29You know that Christ
always does right and that everyone
who does right is a child of God.

3 Think how much the Father loves
us. He loves us so much that he lets
us be called his children, as we truly
are. But since the people of this world
did not know who Christ[j] is, they don't
know who we are. 2My dear friends, we
are already God's children, though what
we will be hasn't yet been seen. But we
do know that when Christ returns, we
will be like him, because we will see
him as he truly is. 3This hope makes us
keep ourselves holy, just as Christ[k] is
holy.
4Everyone who sins breaks God's law,
because sin is the same as breaking
God's law. 5You know that Christ came
to take away sins. He isn't sinful, 6and
people who stay one in their hearts with
him won't keep on sinning. If they do
keep on sinning, they don't know
Christ, and they have never seen him.
7Children, don't be fooled. Anyone
who does right is good, just like Christ
himself. 8Anyone who keeps on sinning
belongs to the devil. He has sinned from
the beginning, but the Son of God came
to destroy all that he has done. 9God's
children cannot keep on being sinful.
His life-giving power[l] lives in them and
makes them his children, so that they
cannot keep on sinning. 10You can tell
God's children from the devil's children,
because those who belong to the devil
refuse to do right or to love each other.

Love Each Other

11From the beginning you were told
that we must love each other. 12Don't be
like Cain, who belonged to the devil and
murdered his own brother. Why did he
murder him? He did it because his
brother was good, and he was evil. 13My
friends, don't be surprised if the people
of this world hate you. 14Our love for
each other proves that we have gone
from death to life. But if you don't love
each other, you are still under the power
of death.
15If you hate each other, you are murderers, and we know that murderers do
not have eternal life. 16We know what
love is because Jesus gave his life for us.
That's why we must give our lives for
each other. 17If we have all we need and
see one of our own people in need, we
must have pity on that person, or else
we cannot say we love God. 18Children,
you show love for others by truly helping them, and not merely by talking
about it.
19When we love others, we know that
we belong to the truth, and we feel at
ease in the presence of God. 20But even
if we don't feel at ease, God is greater
than our feelings, and he knows everything. 21Dear friends, if we feel at ease
in the presence of God, we will have the
courage to come near him. 22He will
give us whatever we ask, because we
obey him and do what pleases him.
23God wants us to have faith in his Son
Jesus Christ and to love each other. This
is also what Jesus taught us to do. 24If
we obey God's commandments, we will
stay one in our hearts with him, and he
will stay one with us. The Spirit that he
has given us is proof that we are one
with him.

God Is Love

4 Dear friends, don't believe everyone
who claims to have the Spirit of
God. Test them all to find out if they really do come from God. Many false
prophets have already gone out into the
world, 2and you can know which ones
come from God. His Spirit says that Jesus Christ had a truly human body. 3But
when someone doesn't say this about
Jesus, you know that person has a spirit
that doesn't come from God and is the
enemy of Christ. You knew that this enemy was coming into the world and
now is already here.
4Children, you belong to God, and you
have defeated these enemies. God's
Spirit[m] is in you and is more powerful
than the one that is in the world. 5These
enemies belong to this world, and the
world listens to them, because they
speak its language. 6We belong to God,
and everyone who knows God will listen to us. But the people who don't
know God won't listen to us. That is
how we can tell the Spirit that speaks
the truth from the one that tells lies.
7My dear friends, we must love each
other. Love comes from God, and when
we love each other, it shows that we
have been given new life. We are now
God's children, and we know him. 8God
is love, and anyone who doesn't love
others has never known him. 9God
showed his love for us when he sent his
only Son into the world to give us life.
10Real love isn't our love for God, but

[j]**3.1** *Christ*: The Greek text has "he" and may refer to God. [k]**3.3** *Christ*: The Greek text has "that one" and may refer to God. [l]**3.9** *His life-giving power*: The Greek text has "his seed." [m]**4.4** *God's Spirit*: The Greek text has "he" and may refer to the Spirit or to God or to Jesus.

his love for us. God sent his Son to be the sacrifice by which our sins are forgiven. 11Dear friends, since God loved us this much, we must love each other.

12No one has ever seen God. But if we love each other, God lives in us, and his love is truly in our hearts.

13God has given us his Spirit. That is how we know that we are one with him, just as he is one with us. 14God sent his Son to be the Savior of the world. We saw his Son and are now telling others about him. 15God stays one with everyone who openly says that Jesus is the Son of God. That's how we stay one with God 16and are sure that God loves us.

God is love. If we keep on loving others, we will stay one in our hearts with God, and he will stay one with us. 17If we truly love others and live as Christ did in this world, we won't be worried about the day of judgment. 18A real love for others will chase those worries away. The thought of being punished is what makes us afraid. It shows that we have not really learned to love.

19We love because God loved us first. 20But if we say we love God and don't love each other, we are liars. We cannot see God. So how can we love God, if we don't love the people we can see? 21The commandment that God has given us is: "Love God and love each other!"

Victory over the World

5 If we believe that Jesus is truly Christ, we are God's children. Everyone who loves the Father will also love his children. 2If we love and obey God, we know that we will love his children. 3We show our love for God by obeying his commandments, and they are not hard to follow.

4Every child of God can defeat the world, and our faith is what gives us this victory. 5No one can defeat the world without having faith in Jesus as the Son of God.

Who Jesus Is

6Water and blood came out from the side of Jesus Christ. It wasn't just water, but water and blood.[n] The Spirit tells about this, because the Spirit is truthful. 7In fact, there are three who tell about it. 8They are the Spirit, the water, and the blood, and they all agree.

9We believe what people tell us. But we can trust what God says even more, and God is the one who has spoken about his Son. 10If we have faith in God's Son, we have believed what God has said. But if we don't believe what God has said about his Son, it is the same as calling God a liar. 11God has also said that he gave us eternal life and that this life comes to us from his Son. 12And so, if we have God's Son, we have this life. But if we don't have the Son, we don't have this life.

Knowing about Eternal Life

13All of you have faith in the Son of God, and I have written to let you know that you have eternal life. 14We are certain that God will hear our prayers when we ask for what pleases him. 15And if we know that God listens when we pray, we are sure that our prayers have already been answered.

16Suppose you see one of our people commit a sin that isn't a deadly sin. You can pray, and that person will be given eternal life. But the sin must not be one that is deadly. 17Everything that is wrong is sin, but not all sins are deadly.

18We are sure that God's children do not keep on sinning. God's own Son protects them, and the devil cannot harm them.

19We are certain that we come from God and that the rest of the world is under the power of the devil.

20We know that Jesus Christ the Son of God has come and has shown us the true God. And because of Jesus, we now belong to the true God who gives eternal life.

21Children, you must stay away from idols.

[n]**5.6** *Water and blood came out from the side of Jesus Christ. It wasn't just water, but water and blood*: See John 19.34. It is also possible to translate, "Jesus Christ came by the water of baptism and by the blood of his death! He was not only baptized, but he bled and died." The purpose of the verse is to tell that Jesus was truly human and that he really died.

2 JOHN

ABOUT THIS LETTER

John writes again about the importance of love in a Christian's life. He points out that truth and love must go together. We must also believe that Christ was truly human, and we must love each other.

A QUICK LOOK AT THIS LETTER

Greetings and Prayer (1-3)
Truth and Love (4-11)
Final Greetings (12, 13)

---

1 From the church leader.[a]
To a very special woman and her children.[b] I truly love all of you, and so does
everyone else who knows the truth. 2 We
love you because the truth is now in our
hearts, and it will be there forever.
3 I pray that God the Father and Jesus
Christ his Son will be kind and merciful
to us! May they give us peace and truth
and love.

Truth and Love

4 I was very glad to learn that some of
your children are obeying the truth, as
the Father told us to do. 5 Dear friend, I
am not writing to tell you and your children to do something you have not done
before. I am writing to tell you to love
each other, which is the first thing you
were told to do. 6 Love means that we do
what God tells us. And from the beginning, he told you to love him.
7 Many liars have gone out into the
world. These deceitful liars are saying
that Jesus Christ did not have a truly
human body. But they are liars and the
enemies of Christ. 8 So be sure not to
lose what we[c] have worked for. If you
do, you won't be given your full reward.
9 Don't keep changing what you were
taught about Christ, or else God will no
longer be with you. But if you hold
firmly to what you were taught, both the
Father and the Son will be with you. 10 If
people won't agree to this teaching,
don't welcome them into your home or
even greet them. 11 Greeting them is the
same as taking part in their evil deeds.

Final Greetings

12 I have much more to tell you, but I
don't want to write it with pen and ink. I
want to come and talk to you in person,
because that will make us[d] really happy.
13 Greetings from the children of your
very special sister.[e]

[a] 1 *church leader*: Or "elder" or "presbyter" or "priest." [b] 1 *very special woman and her children*: A group of the Lord's followers who met together for worship. "The children of your . . . sister" (see verse 13) is another group of followers. "Very special" (here and verse 13) probably means "chosen (by the Lord)." [c] 8 *we*: Some manuscripts have "you." [d] 12 *us*: Some manuscripts have "you." [e] 13 *sister*: See the note at verse 1.

3 JOHN

ABOUT THIS LETTER

In this letter the writer reminds Christian readers that they should help support those who go to other parts of the world to tell others about the Lord. The letter is written to an important church member named Gaius, who had been very helpful to Christians who traveled around and preached the good news.

A QUICK LOOK AT THIS LETTER

Greetings to Gaius (1-4)
The Importance of Working Together (5-12)
Final Greetings (13-15)

1From the church leader.[a]
To my dear friend Gaius.
I love you because we follow the
truth, 2dear friend, and I pray that all
goes well for you. I hope that you are as
strong in body, as I know you are in
spirit. 3It makes me very happy when
the Lord's followers come by and speak
openly of how you obey the truth.
4Nothing brings me greater happiness
than to hear that my children[b] are obeying the truth.

Working Together

5Dear friend, you have always been
faithful in helping other followers of the
Lord, even the ones you didn't know before. 6They have told the church about
your love. They say you were good
enough to welcome them and to send
them on their mission in a way that
God's servants deserve. 7When they left
to tell others about the Lord, they decided not to accept help from anyone
who wasn't a follower. 8We must support people like them, so that we can
take part in what they are doing to
spread the truth.
9I wrote to the church. But Diotrephes
likes to be the number-one leader, and
he won't pay any attention to us. 10So if
I come, I will remind him of how he has
been attacking us with gossip. Not only
has he been doing this, but he refuses to
welcome any of the Lord's followers
who come by. And when other church
members want to welcome them, he
puts them out of the church.
11Dear friend, don't copy the evil
deeds of others! Follow the example of
people who do kind deeds. They are
God's children, but those who are always doing evil have never seen God.
12Everyone speaks well of Demetrius,
and so does the true message that he
teaches. I also speak well of him, and
you know what I say is true.

Final Greetings

13I have much more to say to you, but
I don't want to write it with pen and ink.
14I hope to see you soon, and then we
can talk in person.
15I pray that God will bless you with
peace!
Your friends send their greetings.
Please give a personal greeting to each
of our friends.

[a]**1** *church leader*: Or "elder" or "presbyter" or "priest." [b]**4** *children*: Probably persons that the leader had led to be followers of the Lord.

JUDE

ABOUT THIS LETTER

Jude has much to say about false teachers. They are evil! God will punish them, and Christians should not follow their teaching or imitate the way they live.

Jude ends with a beautiful prayer-like blessing:

> *Offer praise to God our Savior because of our Lord Jesus Christ! Only God can keep you from falling and make you pure and joyful in his glorious presence. Before time began and now and forevermore, God is worthy of glory, honor, power, and authority. Amen.* (24, 25)

A QUICK LOOK AT THIS LETTER

1From Jude, a servant of Jesus Christ
and the brother of James.
To all who are chosen and loved by God the Father and are kept safe by Jesus Christ.
2I pray that God will greatly bless you
with kindness, peace, and love!

False Teachers

3My dear friends, I really wanted to
write you about God's saving power at
work in our lives. But instead, I must
write and ask you to defend the faith
that God has once for all given to his
people. 4Some godless people have
sneaked in among us and are saying,
"God treats us much better than we deserve, and so it is all right to be immoral." They even deny that we must
obey Jesus Christ as our only Master
and Lord. But long ago the Scriptures
warned that these godless people were
doomed.
5Don't forget what happened to those
people that the Lord rescued from
Egypt. Some of them did not have faith,
and he later destroyed them. 6You also
know about the angels[a] who didn't do
their work and left their proper places.
God chained them with everlasting
chains and is now keeping them in dark
pits until the great day of judgment. 7We
should also be warned by what happened to the cities of Sodom and Gomorrah[b] and the nearby towns. Their
people became immoral and did all
sorts of sexual sins. Then God made an
example of them and punished them
with eternal fire.
8The people I am talking about are behaving just like those dreamers who destroyed their own bodies. They reject all
authority and insult angels. 9Even
Michael, the chief angel, didn't dare to
insult the devil, when the two of them
were arguing about the body of Moses.[c]
All Michael said was, "The Lord will
punish you!"
10But these people insult powers they
don't know anything about. They
are like senseless animals that end up

---

[a]6 *angels*: This may refer to the angels who liked the women on earth so much that they came down and married them (see Genesis 6.2). [b]7 *Sodom and Gomorrah*: During the time of Abraham the Lord destroyed these cities because the people there were so evil. [c]9 *Michael . . . the body of Moses*: This refers to what was said in an ancient Jewish book about Moses.

getting destroyed, because they live
only by their feelings. 11Now they are in
for real trouble. They have followed
Cain's example[d] and have made the
same mistake that Balaam[e] did by caring only for money. They have also rebelled against God, just as Korah did.[f]
Because of all this, they will be destroyed.
12These people are filthy minded, and
by their shameful and selfish actions
they spoil the meals you eat together.
They are like clouds blown along by the
wind, but never bringing any rain. They
are like leafless trees, uprooted and
dead, and unable to produce fruit.
13Their shameful deeds show up like
foam on wild ocean waves. They are
like wandering stars forever doomed to
the darkest pits of hell.
14Enoch was the seventh person after
Adam, and he was talking about these
people when he said:

> Look! The Lord is coming with
> thousands and thousands of holy
> angels 15to judge everyone. He will
> punish all those ungodly people for
> all the evil things they have done.
> The Lord will surely punish those
> ungodly sinners for every evil thing
> they have ever said about him.

16These people grumble and complain
and live by their own selfish desires.
They brag about themselves and flatter
others to get what they want.

More Warnings

17My dear friends, remember the
warning you were given by the apostles
of our Lord Jesus Christ. 18They told
you that near the end of time, selfish
and godless people would start making
fun of God. 19And now these people are
already making you turn against each
other. They think only about this life,
and they don't have God's Spirit.
20Dear friends, keep building on the
foundation of your most holy faith, as
the Holy Spirit helps you to pray. 21And
keep in step with God's love, as you wait
for our Lord Jesus Christ to show how
kind he is by giving you eternal life.
22Be helpful to[g] all who may have
doubts. 23Rescue any who need to be
saved, as you would rescue someone
from a fire. Then with fear in your own
hearts, have mercy on everyone who
needs it. But hate even the clothes of
those who have been made dirty by
their filthy deeds.

Final Prayer

24-25Offer praise to God our Savior because of our Lord Jesus Christ! Only
God can keep you from falling and
make you pure and joyful in his glorious
presence. Before time began and now
and forevermore, God is worthy of
glory, honor, power, and authority.
Amen.

[d]11 *Cain's example*: Cain murdered his brother Abel. [e]11 *Balaam*: According to the biblical account, Balaam refused to curse the people of Israel for profit (see Numbers 22.18; 24.13), though he led them to be unfaithful to the Lord (see Numbers 25.1-3; 31.16). But by New Testament times, some Jewish teachers taught that Balaam was greedy and did accept money to curse them. [f]11 *just as Korah did*: Together with Dathan and Abiram, Korah led a rebellion against Moses and Aaron (see Numbers 16.1-35; 26.9, 10). [g]22 *Be helpful to*: Some manuscripts have "Correct."

REVELATION

ABOUT THIS BOOK

This book tells what John had seen in a vision about God's message and about what Jesus Christ had said and done (1.2). The message has three main parts: (1) There are evil forces at work in the world, and Christians may have to suffer and die; (2) Jesus is Lord, and he will conquer all people and powers who oppose God; and (3) God has wonderful rewards in store for his faithful people, who remain faithful to him, especially for those who lose their lives in his service.

This was a powerful message of hope for those early Christians who had to suffer or die for their faith. In this book they learned that, in spite of the cruel power of the Roman Empire, the Lamb of God would win the final victory. And this gave them the courage to be faithful.

Because this book is so full of visions that use ideas and word pictures from the Old Testament, it was like a book with secret messages for the early Christians. The book could be passed around and be understood by Christians, but an official of the Roman Empire would not be able to understand it. For example, when the fall of Babylon is described (chapter 18), the early Christians knew that this pointed to the fall of the Roman Empire. This knowledge gave them hope.

At the beginning of this book there are seven letters to seven churches. These letters show what different groups of the Lord's followers will do in times of persecution (2.1—3.22).

The author uses many powerful images to describe God's power and judgment. The vision of God's throne (4.1-11) and of the scroll and the Lamb (5.1-14) show that God and Christ are in control of all human and supernatural events. Opening seven seals (6.1—8.5), blowing the seven trumpets (8.6—11.19), and emptying the seven bowls (16.1-21) are among the visions that show God's fierce judgment on the world.

After the suffering has ended, God's faithful people will receive the greatest blessing of all:

> *God's home is now with his people. He will live with them, and they will be his own. Yes, God will make his home among his people. He will wipe all tears from their eyes, and there will be no more death, suffering, crying, or pain. These things of the past are gone forever.*
> *(21.3b, 4)*

A QUICK LOOK AT THIS BOOK

A Prophecy from John (1.1-8)
A Vision of the Living Lord (1.9-20)
Letters to the Seven Churches (2.1—3.22)
A Vision of Worship in Heaven (4.1-11)
A Scroll with Seven Seals (5.1—6.17)
Worship in Front of God's Throne (7.1-17)
Seven Trumpets (8.1—11.19)
A Dragon and Two Beasts (12.1—13.18)
Visions of God's Judgment and Protection (14.1—15.8)
Seven Bowls of God's Anger (16.1-21)
God's Enemies Are Defeated (17.1—20.10)
The Final Judgment (20.11-15)
A New Heaven and a New Earth (21.1-8)
New Jerusalem (21.9—22.5)
Christ Will Soon Return (22.6-21)

1 This is what God showed to Jesus
Christ, so that he could tell his servants what must happen soon. Christ
then sent his angel with the message to
his servant John. 2And John told everything that he had seen about God's message and about what Jesus Christ had
said and done.
3God will bless everyone who reads
this prophecy to others,[a] and he will
bless everyone who hears and obeys it.
The time is almost here.
4From John to the seven churches in
Asia.[b]

I pray that you
will be blessed
with kindness and peace
from God, who is and was
and is coming.
May you receive
kindness and peace
from the seven spirits
before the throne of God.
5 May kindness and peace
be yours
from Jesus Christ,
the faithful witness.

Jesus was the first
to conquer death,
and he is the ruler
of all earthly kings.
Christ loves us,
and by his blood
he set us free
from our sins.
6 He lets us rule as kings
and serve God his Father
as priests.
To him be glory and power
forever and ever! Amen.
7 Look! He is coming
with the clouds.
Everyone will see him,
even the ones who stuck
a sword through him.
All people on earth
will weep because of him.
Yes, it will happen! Amen.

8The Lord God says, "I am Alpha and
Omega,[c] the one who is and was and is
coming. I am God All-Powerful!"

A Vision of the Risen Lord

9I am John, a follower together with
all of you. We suffer because Jesus is
our king, but he gives us the strength to
endure. I was sent to Patmos Island,[d]
because I had preached God's message
and had told about Jesus. 10On the
Lord's day the Spirit took control of me,
and behind me I heard a loud voice that
sounded like a trumpet. 11The voice
said, "Write in a book what you see.
Then send it to the seven churches in
Ephesus, Smyrna, Pergamum, Thyatira,
Sardis, Philadelphia, and Laodicea."[e]
12When I turned to see who was
speaking to me, I saw seven gold lampstands. 13There with the lampstands was
someone who seemed to be the Son of
Man.[f] He was wearing a robe that
reached down to his feet, and a gold
cloth was wrapped around his chest.
14His head and his hair were white as
wool or snow, and his eyes looked like
flames of fire. 15His feet were glowing
like bronze being heated in a furnace,
and his voice sounded like the roar of a
waterfall. 16He held seven stars in his
right hand, and a sharp double-edged
sword was coming from his mouth. His
face was shining as bright as the sun at
noon.
17When I saw him, I fell at his feet like
a dead person. But he put his right hand
on me and said:
Don't be afraid! I am the first, the
last, 18and the living one. I died, but
now I am alive forevermore, and I
have the keys to death and the world
of the dead.[g] 19Write what you have
seen and what is and what will happen after these things. 20I will explain the mystery of the seven stars
that you saw at my right side and
the seven gold lampstands. The
seven stars are the angels[h] of the
seven churches, and the lampstands
are the seven churches.

The Letter to Ephesus

2 This is what you must write to the
angel of the church in Ephesus:
I am the one who holds the seven
stars in my right hand, and I walk
among the seven gold lampstands.
Listen to what I say.
2I know everything you have done,
including your hard work and how
you have endured. I know you won't
put up with anyone who is evil.
When some people pretended to be
apostles, you tested them and found
out that they were liars. 3You have

[a]**1.3** *who reads this prophecy to others*: A public reading, in a worship service. [b]**1.4** Asia: The section 1.4—3.22 is in the form of a letter. Asia was in the eastern part of the Roman Empire and is present day Turkey. [c]**1.8** *Alpha and Omega*: The first and last letters of the Greek alphabet, which sometimes mean "first" and "last." [d]**1.9** *Patmos Island*: A small island where prisoners were sometimes kept by the Romans. [e]**1.11** *Ephesus . . . Laodicea*: Ephesus was in the center with the six other cities forming a half-circle around it. [f]**1.13** *Son of Man*: That is, Jesus. [g]**1.18** *keys to death and the world of the dead*: That is, power over death and the world of the dead. [h]**1.20** *angels*: Perhaps guardian angels that represent the churches, or they may be church leaders or messengers sent to the churches.

endured and gone through hard
times because of me, and you have
not given up.
4But I do have something against
you! And it is this: You don't have as
much love as you used to. 5Think
about where you have fallen from,
and then turn back and do as you
did at first. If you don't turn back, I
will come and take away your lampstand. 6But there is one thing you
are doing right. You hate what the
Nicolaitans[i] are doing, and so do I.
7If you have ears, listen to what
the Spirit says to the churches. I will
let everyone who wins the victory
eat from the life-giving tree in God's
wonderful garden.

The Letter to Smyrna

8This is what you must write to the
angel of the church in Smyrna:
I am the first and the last. I died,
but now I am alive! Listen to what I
say.
9I know how much you suffer
and how poor you are, but you are
rich. I also know the cruel things
being said about you by people who
claim to be Jews. But they are not
really Jews. They are a group that
belongs to Satan.
10Don't worry about what you will
suffer. The devil will throw some of
you into jail, and you will be tested
and made to suffer for ten days. But
if you are faithful until you die, I will
reward you with a glorious life.[j]
11If you have ears, listen to what
the Spirit says to the churches. Whoever wins the victory will not be hurt
by the second death.[k]

The Letter to Pergamum

12This is what you must write to the
angel of the church in Pergamum:
I am the one who has the sharp
double-edged sword! Listen to what
I say.
13I know that you live where Satan
has his throne.[l] But you have kept
true to my name. Right there where
Satan lives, my faithful witness Antipas[m] was taken from you and put
to death. Even then you did not give
up your faith in me.
14I do have a few things against
you. Some of you are following the
teaching of Balaam.[n] Long ago he
told Balak to teach the people of Israel to eat food that had been offered to idols and to be immoral.
15Now some of you are following the
teaching of the Nicolaitans.[o] 16Turn
back! If you don't, I will come
quickly and fight against these people. And my words will cut like a
sword.
17If you have ears, listen to what
the Spirit says to the churches. To
everyone who wins the victory, I will
give some of the hidden food.[p] I will
also give each one a white stone[q]
with a new name[r] written on it. No
one will know that name except the
one who is given the stone.

The Letter to Thyatira

18This is what you must write to the
angel of the church in Thyatira:
I am the Son of God! My eyes are
like flames of fire, and my feet are
like bronze. Listen to what I say.
19I know everything about you, including your love, your faith, your
service, and how you have endured.
I know that you are doing more now
than you have ever done before.
20But I still have something against
you because of that woman Jezebel.[s]
She calls herself a prophet, and you
let her teach and mislead my servants to do immoral things and to
eat food offered to idols. 21I gave her

[i]**2.6** *Nicolaitans*: Nothing else is known about these people, though it is possible that they claimed to be followers of Nicolaus from Antioch (see Acts 6.5). [j]**2.10** *a glorious life*: The Greek text has "a crown of life." In ancient times an athlete who had won a contest was rewarded with a crown of flowers as a sign of victory. [k]**2.11** *second death*: The first death is physical death, and the "second death" is eternal death. [l]**2.13** *where Satan has his throne*: The meaning is uncertain, but it may refer to the city as a center of pagan worship or of Emperor worship. [m]**2.13** *Antipas*: Nothing else is known about this man, who is mentioned only here in the New Testament. [n]**2.14** *Balaam*: According to Numbers 22–24, Balaam refused to disobey the Lord. But in other books of the Old Testament, he is spoken of as evil (see Deuteronomy 23.4, 5; Joshua 13.22; 24.9, 10; Nehemiah 13.2). [o]**2.15** *Nicolaitans*: See the note at 2.6. [p]**2.17** *hidden food*: When the people of Israel were going through the desert, the Lord provided a special food for them. Some of this was placed in a jar and stored in the sacred chest (see Exodus 16). According to later Jewish teaching, the prophet Jeremiah rescued the sacred chest when the temple was destroyed by the Babylonians. He hid the chest in a cave, where it would stay until God came to save his people. [q]**2.17** *white stone*: The meaning of this is uncertain, though it may be the same as a ticket that lets a person into God's banquet where the "hidden food" is eaten. Or it may be a symbol of victory. [r]**2.17** *a new name*: Either the name of Christ or God or the name of the follower who is given the stone. [s]**2.20** *Jezebel*: Nothing else is known about her. This may have been her real name or a name that was given to her because she was like Queen Jezebel, who opposed the Lord (see 1 Kings 19.1, 2; 21.1-26).

a chance to turn from her sins, but
she did not want to stop doing these
immoral things.
22 I am going to strike down
Jezebel. Everyone who does these
immoral things with her will also be
punished, if they don't stop. 23 I will
even kill her followers.[t] Then all
the churches will see that I know
everyone's thoughts and feelings. I
will treat each of you as you deserve.
24 Some of you in Thyatira don't
follow Jezebel's teaching. You don't
know anything about what her followers call the "deep secrets of Satan." So I won't burden you down
with any other commands. 25 But until I come, you must hold firmly to
the teaching you have.
26 I will give power over the nations to everyone who wins the victory and keeps on obeying me until
the end. 27-28 I will give each of them
the same power that my Father has
given me. They will rule the nations
with an iron rod and smash those
nations to pieces like clay pots. I will
also give them the morning star.[u]
29 If you have ears, listen to what
the Spirit says to the churches.

The Letter to Sardis

3 This is what you must write to the
angel of the church in Sardis:
I have the seven spirits of God and
the seven stars. Listen to what I
say.
I know what you are doing. Everyone may think you are alive, but you
are dead. 2 Wake up! You have only a
little strength left, and it is almost
gone. So try to become stronger. I
have found that you are not completely obeying God. 3 Remember the
teaching that you were given and
that you heard. Hold firmly to it and
turn from your sins. If you don't
wake up, I will come when you least
expect it, just as a thief does.
4 A few of you in Sardis have not
dirtied your clothes with sin. You
will walk with me in white clothes,
because you are worthy. 5 Everyone
who wins the victory will wear white
clothes. Their names will not be
erased from the book of life,[v] and I
will tell my Father and his angels
that they are my followers.
6 If you have ears, listen to what
the Spirit says to the churches.

The Letter to Philadelphia

7 This is what you must write to the
angel of the church in Philadelphia:
I am the one who is holy and true,
and I have the keys that belonged to
David.[w] When I open a door, no one
can close it. And when I close a
door, no one can open it. Listen to
what I say.
8 I know everything you have
done. And I have placed before you
an open door that no one can close.
You were not very strong, but you
obeyed my message and did not
deny that you are my followers.[x]
9 Now you will see what I will do
with those people who belong to
Satan's group. They claim to be
Jews, but they are liars. I will make
them come and kneel down at your
feet. Then they will know that I
love you.
10 You obeyed my message and endured. So I will protect you from the
time of testing that everyone in all
the world must go through. 11 I am
coming soon. So hold firmly to what
you have, and no one will take away
the crown that you will be given as
your reward.
12 Everyone who wins the victory
will be made into a pillar in the temple of my God, and they will stay
there forever. I will write on each of
them the name of my God and the
name of his city. It is the new
Jerusalem that my God will send
down from heaven. I will also write
on them my own new name.
13 If you have ears, listen to what
the Spirit says to the churches.

The Letter to Laodicea

14 This is what you must write to the
angel of the church in Laodicea:
I am the one called Amen![y] I am
the faithful and true witness and the
source[z] of God's creation. Listen to
what I say.
15 I know everything you have
done, and you are not cold or hot. I
wish you were either one or the
other. 16 But since you are lukewarm
and neither cold nor hot, I will spit
you out of my mouth. 17 You claim to
be rich and successful and to have
everything you need. But you don't
know how bad off you are. You are
pitiful, poor, blind, and naked.
18 Buy your gold from me. It has

[t] **2.23** *her followers*: Or "her children." [u] **2.27,28** *the morning star*: Probably thought of as the star that signals the end of night and the beginning of day. In 22.16 Christ is called the "morning star." [v] **3.5** *book of life*: The book in which the names of God's people are written.
[w] **3.7** *the keys that belonged to David*: The keys stand for authority over David's kingdom.
[x] **3.8** *did not deny that you are my followers*: Or "did not say evil things about me."
[y] **3.14** *Amen*: Meaning "Trustworthy." [z] **3.14** *source*: Or "beginning."

been refined in a fire, and it will
make you rich. Buy white clothes
from me. Wear them and you can
cover up your shameful nakedness.
Buy medicine for your eyes, so that
you will be able to see.
19 I correct and punish everyone I
love. So make up your minds to turn
away from your sins. 20 Listen! I am
standing and knocking at your door.
If you hear my voice and open the
door, I will come in and we will eat
together. 21 Everyone who wins the
victory will sit with me on my
throne, just as I won the victory and
sat with my Father on his throne.
22 If you have ears, listen to what
the Spirit says to the churches.

Worship in Heaven

4 After this, I looked and saw a door
that opened into heaven. Then the
voice that had spoken to me at first and
that sounded like a trumpet said, "Come
up here! I will show you what must happen next." 2 Right then the Spirit took
control of me, and there in heaven I saw
a throne and someone sitting on it. 3 The
one who was sitting there sparkled like
precious stones of jasper[a] and carnelian.[b] A rainbow that looked like an
emerald[c] surrounded the throne.
4 Twenty-four other thrones were in a
circle around that throne. And on each
of these thrones there was an elder
dressed in white clothes and wearing a
gold crown. 5 Flashes of lightning and
roars of thunder came out from the
throne in the center of the circle. Seven
torches, which are the seven spirits of
God, were burning in front of the
throne. 6 Also in front of the throne was
something that looked like a glass sea,
clear as crystal.
Around the throne in the center were
four living creatures covered front and
back with eyes. 7 The first creature was
like a lion, the second one was like a
bull, the third one had the face of a human, and the fourth was like a flying eagle. 8 Each of the four living creatures
had six wings, and their bodies were
covered with eyes. Day and night they
never stopped singing,

"Holy, holy, holy is the Lord,
  the all-powerful God,
who was and is
  and is coming!"

9 The living creatures kept praising,
honoring, and thanking the one who sits
on the throne and who lives forever and
ever. 10 At the same time the twenty-four
elders knelt down before the one sitting
on the throne. And as they worshiped
the one who lives forever, they placed
their crowns in front of the throne and
said,

11 "Our Lord and God,
  you are worthy
to receive glory,
  honor, and power.
You created all things,
and by your decision they are
  and were created."

The Scroll and the Lamb

5 In the right hand of the one sitting
on the throne I saw a scroll[d] that
had writing on the inside and on the
outside. And it was sealed in seven
places. 2 I saw a mighty angel ask with a
loud voice, "Who is worthy to open the
scroll and break its seals?" 3 No one in
heaven or on earth or under the earth
was able to open the scroll or see inside
it.
4 I cried hard because no one was
found worthy to open the scroll or see
inside it. 5 Then one of the elders said to
me, "Stop crying and look! The one who
is called both the 'Lion from the Tribe of
Judah'[e] and 'King David's Great Descendant'[f] has won the victory. He will
open the book and its seven seals."
6 Then I looked and saw a Lamb standing in the center of the throne that was
surrounded by the four living creatures
and the elders. The Lamb looked as if it
had once been killed. It had seven horns
and seven eyes, which are the seven
spirits[g] of God, sent out to all the earth.
7 The Lamb went over and took the
scroll from the right hand of the one
who sat on the throne. 8 After he had
taken it, the four living creatures and
the twenty-four elders knelt down before him. Each of them had a harp and a
gold bowl full of incense,[h] which are the
prayers of God's people. 9 Then they
sang a new song,

"You are worthy
  to receive the scroll
and open its seals,
  because you were killed.
And with your own blood
  you bought for God

[a]**4.3** *jasper*: Usually green or clear. [b]**4.3** *carnelian*: Usually deep-red or reddish-white.
[c]**4.3** *emerald*: A precious stone, usually green. [d]**5.1** *scroll*: A roll of paper or special leather used for writing on. Sometimes a scroll would be sealed on the outside with one or more pieces of wax. [e]**5.5** *'Lion from the Tribe of Judah'*: In Genesis 49.9 the tribe of Judah is called a young lion, and King David was from Judah. [f]**5.5** *'King David's Great Descendant'*: The Greek text has "the root of David" which is a title for the Messiah based on Isaiah 11.1, 10.
[g]**5.6** *the seven spirits*: Some manuscripts have "the spirits." [h]**5.8** *incense*: A material that produces a sweet smell when burned. Sometimes it is a symbol for the prayers of God's people.

people from every tribe,
language, nation, and race.
10 You let them become kings
and serve God as priests,
and they will rule on earth."

11 As I looked, I heard the voices of a
lot of angels around the throne and the
voices of the living creatures and of the
elders. There were millions and millions
of them, 12 and they were saying in a
loud voice,

"The Lamb who was killed
is worthy to receive power,
riches, wisdom, strength,
honor, glory, and praise."

13 Then I heard all beings in heaven
and on the earth and under the earth
and in the sea offer praise. Together, all
of them were saying,

"Praise, honor, glory,
and strength
forever and ever
to the one who sits
on the throne
and to the Lamb!"

14 The four living creatures said
"Amen," while the elders knelt down
and worshiped.

Opening the Seven Seals

6 At the same time that I saw the
Lamb open the first of the seven
seals, I heard one of the four living creatures shout with a voice like thunder. It
said, "Come out!" 2 Then I saw a white
horse. Its rider carried a bow and was
given a crown. He had already won
some victories, and he went out to win
more.
3 When the Lamb opened the second
seal, I heard the second living creature
say, "Come out!" 4 Then another horse
came out. It was fiery red. And its rider
was given the power to take away all
peace from the earth, so that people
would slaughter one another. He was
also given a big sword.
5 When the Lamb opened the third
seal, I heard the third living creature
say, "Come out!" Then I saw a black
horse, and its rider had a balance scale
in one hand. 6 I heard what sounded like
a voice from somewhere among the four
living creatures. It said, "A quart of
wheat will cost you a whole day's
wages! Three quarts of barley will cost
you a day's wages too. But don't ruin
the olive oil or the wine."
7 When the Lamb opened the fourth
seal, I heard the voice of the fourth living creature say, "Come out!" 8 Then I
saw a pale green horse. Its rider was
named Death, and Death's Kingdom followed behind. They were given power
over one fourth of the earth, and they
could kill its people with swords,
famines, diseases, and wild animals.
9 When the Lamb opened the fifth seal,
I saw under the altar the souls of everyone who had been killed for speaking
God's message and telling about their
faith. 10 They shouted, "Master, you are
holy and faithful! How long will it be
before you judge and punish the people
of this earth who killed us?"
11 Then each of those who had been
killed was given a white robe and told
to rest for a little while. They had to
wait until the complete number of the
Lord's other servants and followers
would be killed.
12 When I saw the Lamb open the sixth
seal, I looked and saw a great earthquake. The sun turned as dark as sackcloth,[i] and the moon became as red as
blood. 13 The stars in the sky fell to
earth, just like figs shaken loose by a
windstorm. 14 Then the sky was rolled up
like a scroll,[j] and all mountains and islands were moved from their places.
15 The kings of the earth, its famous
people, and its military leaders hid in
caves or behind rocks on the mountains.
They hid there together with the rich
and the powerful and with all the slaves
and free people. 16 Then they shouted to
the mountains and the rocks, "Fall on
us! Hide us from the one who sits on the
throne and from the anger of the Lamb.
17 That terrible day has come! God and
the Lamb will show their anger, and
who can face it?"

The 144,000 Are Marked for God

7 1-2 After this I saw four angels. Each
one was standing on one of the
earth's four corners. The angels held
back the four winds, so that no wind
would blow on the earth or on the sea or
on any tree. These angels had also been
given the power to harm the earth and
the sea. Then I saw another angel come
up from where the sun rises in the east,
and he was ready to put the mark of the
living God on people. He shouted to the
four angels, 3 "Don't harm the earth or
the sea or any tree! Wait until I have
marked the foreheads of the servants of
our God."
4 Then I heard how many people had
been marked on the forehead. There
were one hundred forty-four thousand,
and they came from every tribe of Israel:

5 12,000 from Judah,
12,000 from Reuben,

[i] **6.12** *sackcloth*: A rough, dark-colored cloth made from goat or camel hair and used to make grain sacks. It was worn in times of trouble or sorrow. [j] **6.14** *scroll*: See the note at 5.1.

12,000 from Gad,
6 12,000 from Asher,
12,000 from Naphtali,
12,000 from Manasseh,
7 12,000 from Simeon,
12,000 from Levi,
12,000 from Issachar,
8 12,000 from Zebulun,
12,000 from Joseph, and
12,000 from Benjamin.

People from Every Nation

9 After this, I saw a large crowd with
more people than could be counted.
They were from every race, tribe, nation, and language, and they stood before the throne and before the Lamb.
They wore white robes and held palm
branches in their hands, 10 as they
shouted,

"Our God, who sits
upon the throne,
has the power
to save his people,
and so does the Lamb."

11 The angels who stood around the
throne knelt in front of it with their
faces to the ground. The elders and the
four living creatures knelt there with
them. Then they all worshiped God
12 and said,

"Amen! Praise, glory, wisdom,
thanks, honor, power,
and strength belong to our God
forever and ever! Amen!"

13 One of the elders asked me, "Do you
know who these people are that are
dressed in white robes? Do you know
where they come from?"
14 "Sir," I answered, "you must know."
Then he told me:

"These are the ones
who have gone through
the great suffering.
They have washed their robes
in the blood of the Lamb
and have made them white.
15 And so they stand
before the throne of God
and worship him in his temple
day and night.
The one who sits on the throne
will spread his tent
over them.
16 They will never hunger
or thirst again,
and they won't be troubled
by the sun
or any scorching heat.

17 The Lamb in the center
of the throne
will be their shepherd.
He will lead them to streams
of life-giving water,
and God will wipe all tears
from their eyes."

The Seventh Seal Is Opened

8 When the Lamb opened the seventh
seal, there was silence in heaven for
about half an hour. 2 I noticed that the
seven angels who stood before God
were each given a trumpet.
3 Another angel, who had a gold container for incense,[k] came and stood at
the altar. This one was given a lot of incense to offer with the prayers of God's
people on the gold altar in front of the
throne. 4 Then the smoke of the incense,
together with the prayers of God's people, went up to God from the hand of the
angel.
5 After this, the angel filled the incense
container with fire from the altar and
threw it on the earth. Thunder roared,
lightning flashed, and the earth shook.

The Trumpets

6 The seven angels now got ready to
blow their trumpets.
7 When the first angel blew his trumpet, hail and fire mixed with blood were
thrown down on the earth. A third of the
earth, a third of the trees, and a third of
all green plants were burned.
8 When the second angel blew his
trumpet, something like a great fiery
mountain was thrown into the sea. A
third of the sea turned to blood, 9 a third
of the living creatures in the sea died,
and a third of the ships were destroyed.
10 When the third angel blew his trumpet, a great star fell from heaven. It was
burning like a torch, and it fell on a
third of the rivers and on a third of the
springs of water. 11 The name of the star
was Bitter, and a third of the water
turned bitter. Many people died because
the water was so bitter.
12 When the fourth angel blew his
trumpet, a third of the sun, a third of the
moon, and a third of the stars were
struck. They each lost a third of their
light. So during a third of the day there
was no light, and a third of the night
was also without light.
13 Then I looked and saw a lone eagle
flying across the sky. It was shouting,
"Trouble, trouble, trouble to everyone
who lives on earth! The other three angels are now going to blow their trumpets."

9 When the fifth angel blew his trumpet, I saw a star[l] fall from the sky to
earth. It was given the key to the tunnel
that leads down to the deep pit. 2 As it
opened the tunnel, smoke poured out

[k] 8.3 *incense*: See the note at 5.8.

[l] 9.1 *star*: In the ancient world, stars were often thought of as living beings, such as angels.

like the smoke of a great furnace. The sun and the air turned dark because of the smoke. 3Locusts[m] came out of the smoke and covered the earth. They were given the same power that scorpions have.

4The locusts were told not to harm the grass on the earth or any plant or any tree. They were to punish only those people who did not have God's mark on their foreheads. 5The locusts were allowed to make them suffer for five months, but not to kill them. The suffering they caused was like the sting of a scorpion. 6In those days people will want to die, but they will not be able to. They will hope for death, but it will escape from them.

7These locusts looked like horses ready for battle. On their heads they wore something like gold crowns, and they had human faces. 8Their hair was like a woman's long hair, and their teeth were like those of a lion. 9On their chests they wore armor made of iron. Their wings roared like an army of horse-drawn chariots rushing into battle. 10Their tails were like a scorpion's tail with a stinger that had the power to hurt someone for five months. 11Their king was the angel in charge of the deep pit. In Hebrew his name was Abaddon, and in Greek it was Apollyon.[n]

12The first horrible thing has now happened! But wait. Two more horrible things will happen soon.

13Then the sixth angel blew his trumpet. I heard a voice speak from the four corners of the gold altar that stands in the presence of God. 14The voice spoke to this angel and said, "Release the four angels who are tied up beside the great Euphrates River." 15The four angels had been prepared for this very hour and day and month and year. Now they were set free to kill a third of all people.

16By listening, I could tell there were more than two hundred million of these war horses. 17In my vision their riders wore fiery-red, dark-blue, and yellow armor on their chests. The heads of the horses looked like lions, with fire and smoke and sulfur coming out of their mouths. 18One-third of all people were killed by the three terrible troubles caused by the fire, the smoke, and the sulfur. 19The horses had powerful mouths, and their tails were like poisonous snakes that bite and hurt.

20The people who lived through these terrible troubles did not turn away from the idols they had made, and they did not stop worshiping demons. They kept on worshiping idols that were made of gold, silver, bronze, stone, and wood. Not one of these idols could see, hear, or walk. 21No one stopped murdering or practicing witchcraft or being immoral or stealing.

The Angel and the Little Scroll

10 I saw another powerful angel come down from heaven. This one was covered with a cloud, and a rainbow was over his head. His face was like the sun, his legs were like columns of fire, 2and with his hand he held a little scroll[o] that had been unrolled. He stood there with his right foot on the sea and his left foot on the land. 3Then he shouted with a voice that sounded like a growling lion. Thunder roared seven times.

4After the thunder stopped, I was about to write what it had said. But a voice from heaven shouted, "Keep it secret! Don't write these things."

5The angel I had seen standing on the sea and the land then held his right hand up toward heaven. 6He made a promise in the name of God who lives forever and who created heaven, earth, the sea, and every living creature. The angel said, "You won't have to wait any longer. 7God told his secret plans to his servants the prophets, and it will all happen by the time the seventh angel sounds his trumpet."

8Once again the voice from heaven spoke to me. It said, "Go and take the open scroll from the hand of the angel standing on the sea and the land."

9When I went over to ask the angel for the little scroll, the angel said, "Take the scroll and eat it! Your stomach will turn sour, but the taste in your mouth will be as sweet as honey." 10I took the little scroll from the hand of the angel and ate it. The taste was as sweet as honey, but my stomach turned sour.

11Then some voices said, "Keep on telling what will happen to the people of many nations, races, and languages, and also to kings."

The Two Witnesses

11 An angel gave me a measuring stick and said:

Measure around God's temple. Be
sure to include the altar and everyone worshiping there. 2But don't
measure the courtyard outside the
temple building. Leave it out. It has
been given to those people who
don't know God, and they will trample all over the holy city for forty-
two months. 3My two witnesses will

[m]9.3 *Locusts*: A type of grasshopper that comes in swarms and causes great damage to crops.
[n]9.11 *Abaddon . . . Apollyon*: The Hebrew word "Abaddon" and the Greek word "Apollyon" each mean "destruction." [o]10.2 *scroll*: See the note at 5.1.

wear sackcloth,[p] while I let them
preach for one thousand two hundred sixty days.
4These two witnesses are the two
olive trees and the two lampstands that
stand in the presence of the Lord who
rules the earth. 5Any enemy who tries to
harm them will be destroyed by the fire
that comes out of their mouths. 6They
have the power to lock up the sky and to
keep rain from falling while they are
prophesying. And whenever they want
to, they can turn water to blood and
cause all kinds of terrible troubles on
earth.
7After the two witnesses have finished
preaching God's message, the beast that
lives in the deep pit will come up and
fight against them. It will win the battle
and kill them. 8Their bodies will be left
lying in the streets of the same great
city where their Lord was nailed to a
cross. And that city is spiritually like the
city of Sodom or the country of Egypt.
9For three and a half days the people
of every nation, tribe, language, and
race will stare at the bodies of these two
witnesses and refuse to let them be
buried. 10Everyone on earth will celebrate and be happy. They will give gifts
to each other, because of what happened to the two prophets who caused
them so much trouble. 11But three and a
half days later, God will breathe life into
their bodies. They will stand up, and
everyone who sees them will be terrified.
12The witnesses then heard a loud
voice from heaven, saying, "Come up
here." And while their enemies were
watching, they were taken up to heaven
in a cloud. 13At that same moment there
was a terrible earthquake that destroyed
a tenth of the city. Seven thousand people were killed, and the rest were frightened and praised the God who rules in
heaven.
14The second horrible thing has now
happened! But the third one will be here
soon.

The Seventh Trumpet

15At the sound of the seventh trumpet,
loud voices were heard in heaven. They
said,

"Now the kingdom
 of this world
belongs to our Lord
 and to his Chosen One!
And he will rule
 forever and ever!"

16Then the twenty-four elders, who
were seated on thrones in God's presence, knelt down and worshiped him.
17They said,

"Lord God All-Powerful,
you are and you were,
 and we thank you.
You used your great power
 and started ruling.
18 When the nations got angry,
 you became angry too!
Now the time has come
for the dead
 to be judged.
It is time for you to reward
 your servants the prophets
and all of your people
who honor your name,
 no matter who they are.
It is time to destroy everyone
who has destroyed
 the earth."

19The door to God's temple in heaven
was then opened, and the sacred chest[q]
could be seen inside the temple. I saw
lightning and heard roars of thunder.
The earth trembled and huge hailstones
fell to the ground.

The Woman and the Dragon

12 Something important appeared in
the sky. It was a woman whose
clothes were the sun. The moon was under her feet, and a crown made of
twelve stars was on her head. 2She was
about to give birth, and she was crying
because of the great pain.
3Something else appeared in the sky.
It was a huge red dragon with seven
heads and ten horns, and a crown on
each of its seven heads. 4With its tail, it
dragged a third of the stars from the sky
and threw them down to the earth. Then
the dragon turned toward the woman,
because it wanted to eat her child as
soon as it was born.
5The woman gave birth to a son, who
would rule all nations with an iron rod.
The boy was snatched away. He was
taken to God and placed on his throne.
6The woman ran into the desert to a
place that God had prepared for her.
There she would be taken care of for
one thousand two hundred sixty days.

Michael Fights the Dragon

7A war broke out in heaven. Michael
and his angels were fighting against the
dragon and its angels. 8But the dragon
lost the battle. It and its angels were
forced out of their places in heaven 9and
were thrown down to the earth. Yes, that
old snake and his angels were thrown
out of heaven! That snake, who fools
everyone on earth, is known as the devil

[p]**11.3** *sackcloth*: See the note at 6.12. [q]**11.19** *sacred chest*: In Old Testament times the sacred chest was kept in the tent used for worship. It was the symbol of God's presence with his people and also of his agreement with them.

and Satan. 10Then I heard a voice from
heaven shout,

"Our God has shown
his saving power,
and his kingdom has come!
God's own Chosen One
has shown his authority.
Satan accused our people
in the presence of God
day and night.
Now he has been thrown out!

11 Our people defeated Satan
because of the blood[r]
of the Lamb
and the message of God.
They were willing
to give up their lives.

12 The heavens should rejoice,
together with everyone
who lives there.
But pity the earth
and the sea,
because the devil
was thrown down
to the earth.
He knows his time is short,
and he is very angry."

13When the dragon realized that it
had been thrown down to the earth, it
tried to make trouble for the woman
who had given birth to a son. 14But the
woman was given two wings like those
of a huge eagle, so that she could fly
into the desert. There she would escape
from the snake and be taken care of for
a time, two times, and half a time.
15The snake then spewed out water
like a river to sweep the woman away.
16But the earth helped her and swallowed the water that had come from the
dragon's mouth. 17This made the dragon
terribly angry with the woman. So it
started a war against the rest of her
children. They are the people who obey
God and are faithful to what Jesus did
and taught. 18The dragon[s] stood on the
beach beside the sea.

The Two Beasts

13 I looked and saw a beast coming
up from the sea. This one had ten
horns and seven heads, and a crown
was on each of its ten horns. On each of
its heads were names that were an insult to God. 2The beast that I saw had
the body of a leopard, the feet of a bear,
and the mouth of a lion. The dragon
handed over its own power and throne
and great authority to this beast. 3One
of its heads seemed to have been fatally
wounded, but now it was well. Everyone
on earth marveled at this beast, 4and
they worshiped the dragon who had
given its authority to the beast. They
also worshiped the beast and said, "No
one is like this beast! No one can fight
against it."
5The beast was allowed to brag and
claim to be God, and for forty-two
months it was allowed to rule. 6The
beast cursed God, and it cursed the
name of God. It even cursed the place
where God lives, as well as everyone
who lives in heaven with God. 7It was
allowed to fight against God's people
and defeat them. It was also given authority over the people of every tribe,
nation, language, and race. 8The beast
was worshiped by everyone whose
name wasn't written before the time of
creation in the book of the Lamb who
was killed.[t]

9 If you have ears,
then listen!
10 If you are doomed
to be captured,
you will be captured.
If you are doomed
to be killed by a sword,
you will be killed
by a sword.

This means that God's people must
learn to endure and be faithful!
11I now saw another beast. This one
came out of the ground. It had two
horns like a lamb, but spoke like a
dragon. 12It worked for the beast whose
fatal wound had been healed. And it
used all its authority to force the earth
and its people to worship that beast. 13It
worked mighty miracles, and while people watched, it even made fire come
down from the sky.
14This second beast fooled people on
earth by working miracles for the first
one. Then it talked them into making an
idol in the form of the beast that did not
die after being wounded by a sword. 15It
was allowed to put breath into the idol,
so that it could speak. Everyone who refused to worship the idol of the beast
was put to death. 16All people were
forced to put a mark on their right hand
or forehead. Whether they were powerful or weak, rich or poor, free people or
slaves, 17they all had to have this mark,
or else they could not buy or sell anything. This mark stood for the name of
the beast and for the number of its
name.
18You need wisdom to understand the
number of the beast! But if you are
smart enough, you can figure this out.

[r]12.11 *blood*: Or "death." [s]12.18 *The dragon*: The text has "he," and some manuscripts have "I." [t]13.8 *wasn't written . . . was killed*: Or "not written in the book of the Lamb who was killed before the time of creation."

Its number is six hundred sixty-six, and
it stands for a person.

The Lamb and His 144,000 Followers

14 I looked and saw the Lamb standing on Mount Zion![u] With him
were a hundred forty-four thousand,
who had his name and his Father's
name written on their foreheads. 2Then
I heard a sound from heaven that was
like a roaring flood or loud thunder or
even like the music of harps. 3And a
new song was being sung in front of
God's throne and in front of the four living creatures and the elders. No one
could learn that song, except the one
hundred forty-four thousand who had
been rescued from the earth. 4All of
these are pure virgins, and they follow
the Lamb wherever he leads. They have
been rescued to be presented to God
and the Lamb as the most precious people[v] on earth. 5They never tell lies, and
they are innocent.

The Messages of the Three Angels

6I saw another angel. This one was
flying across the sky and had the eternal good news to announce to the people of every race, tribe, language, and
nation on earth. 7The angel shouted,
"Worship and honor God! The time has
come for him to judge everyone. Kneel
down before the one who created
heaven and earth, the oceans, and every
stream."

8A second angel followed and said,
"The great city of Babylon has fallen!
This is the city that made all nations
drunk and immoral. Now God is angry,
and Babylon has fallen."

9Finally, a third angel came and
shouted:

Here is what will happen if you
worship the beast and the idol and
have the mark of the beast on your
hand or forehead. 10You will have to
drink the wine that God gives to
everyone who makes him angry. You
will feel his mighty anger, and you
will be tortured with fire and burning sulfur, while the holy angels
and the Lamb look on.

11If you worship the beast and the
idol and accept the mark of its
name, you will be tortured day and
night. The smoke from your torture
will go up forever and ever, and you
will never be able to rest.

12God's people must learn to endure.
They must also obey his commands and
have faith in Jesus.

13Then I heard a voice from heaven
say, "Put this in writing. From now on,
the Lord will bless everyone who has
faith in him when they die."

The Spirit answered, "Yes, they will
rest from their hard work, and they will
be rewarded for what they have done."

The Earth Is Harvested

14I looked and saw a bright cloud, and
someone who seemed to be the Son of
Man[w] was sitting on the cloud. He wore
a gold crown on his head and held a
sharp sickle[x] in his hand. 15An angel
came out of the temple and shouted,
"Start cutting with your sickle! Harvest
season is here, and all crops on earth
are ripe." 16The one on the cloud swung
his sickle and harvested the crops.

17Another angel with a sharp sickle
then came out of the temple in heaven.
18After this, an angel with power over
fire came from the altar and shouted to
the angel who had the sickle. He said,
"All grapes on earth are ripe! Harvest
them with your sharp sickle." 19The angel swung his sickle on earth and cut off
its grapes. He threw them into a pit[y]
where they were trampled on as a sign
of God's anger. 20The pit was outside the
city, and when the grapes were mashed,
blood flowed out. The blood turned into
a river that was about two hundred
miles long and almost deep enough to
cover a horse.

The Last of the Terrible Troubles

15 After this, I looked at the sky and
saw something else that was
strange and important. Seven angels
were bringing the last seven terrible
troubles. When these are ended, God
will no longer be angry.

2Then I saw something that looked
like a glass sea mixed with fire, and
people were standing on it. They were
the ones who had defeated the beast
and the idol and the number that tells
the name of the beast. God had given
them harps, 3and they were singing the
song that his servant Moses and the
Lamb had sung. They were singing,

"Lord God All-Powerful,
you have done great
and marvelous things.
You are the ruler
of all nations,

[u]**14.1** *Mount Zion*: Another name for Jerusalem. [v]**14.4** *the most precious people*: The Greek text has "the first people." The Law of Moses taught that the first-born of all animals and the first part of the harvest were special and belonged to the Lord. [w]**14.14** *Son of Man*: See the note at 1.13. [x]**14.14** *sickle*: A knife with a long curved blade, used to cut grain and other crops. [y]**14.19** *pit*: It was the custom to put grapes in a pit (called a wine press) and stomp on them to make juice that would later turn to wine.

and you do what is
right and fair.
4 Lord, who doesn't honor
and praise your name?
You alone are holy,
and all nations will come
and worship you,
because you have shown
that you judge
with fairness."

5 After this, I noticed something else in
heaven. The sacred tent used for a temple was open. 6 And the seven angels
who were bringing the terrible troubles
were coming out of it. They were
dressed in robes of pure white linen and
wore belts made of pure gold. 7 One of
the four living creatures gave each of
the seven angels a bowl made of gold.
These bowls were filled with the anger
of God who lives forever and ever. 8 The
temple quickly filled with smoke from
the glory and power of God. No one
could enter it until the seven angels had
finished pouring out the seven last troubles.

The Bowls of God's Anger

16 From the temple I heard a voice
shout to the seven angels, "Go
and empty the seven bowls of God's
anger on the earth."
2 The first angel emptied his bowl on
the earth. At once ugly and painful
sores broke out on everyone who had
the mark of the beast and worshiped the
idol.
3 The second angel emptied his bowl
on the sea. Right away the sea turned
into blood like that of a dead person,
and every living thing in the sea died.
4 The third angel emptied his bowl into
the rivers and streams. At once they
turned to blood. 5 Then I heard the angel,
who has power over water, say,

"You have always been,
and you always will be
the holy God.
You had the right
to judge in this way.
6 They poured out the blood[z]
of your people
and your prophets.
So you gave them blood
to drink, as they deserve!"
7 After this, I heard
the altar shout,
"Yes, Lord God All-Powerful,
your judgments are honest
and fair."

8 The fourth angel emptied his bowl on
the sun, and it began to scorch people
like fire. 9 Everyone was scorched by its
great heat, and all of them cursed the
name of God who had power over these
terrible troubles. But no one turned to
God and praised him.
10 The fifth angel emptied his bowl on
the throne of the beast. At once darkness covered its kingdom, and its people
began biting their tongues in pain.
11 And because of their painful sores,
they cursed the God who rules in
heaven. But still they did not stop doing
evil things.
12 The sixth angel emptied his bowl on
the great Euphrates River, and it completely dried up to make a road for the
kings from the east. 13 An evil spirit that
looked like a frog came out of the
mouth of the dragon. One also came out
of the mouth of the beast, and another
out of the mouth of the false prophet.
14 These evil spirits had the power to
work miracles. They went to every king
on earth, to bring them together for a
war against God All-Powerful. But that
will be the day of God's great victory.
15 Remember that Christ says, "When I
come, it will surprise you like a thief!
But God will bless you, if you are awake
and ready. Then you won't have to walk
around naked and be ashamed."
16 Those armies came together in a
place that in Hebrew is called Armagedon.[a]
17 As soon as the seventh angel emptied his bowl in the air, a loud voice
from the throne in the temple shouted,
"It's done!" 18 There were flashes of
lightning, roars of thunder, and the
worst earthquake in all history. 19 The
great city of Babylon split into three
parts, and the cities of other nations fell.
So God made Babylon drink from the
wine cup that was filled with his anger.
20 Every island ran away, and the mountains disappeared. 21 Hailstones, weighing about a hundred pounds each, fell
from the sky on people. Finally, the people cursed God, because the hail was so
terrible.

The Prostitute and the Beast

17 One of the seven angels who had
emptied the bowls came over and
said to me, "Come on! I will show you
how God will punish that shameless
prostitute who sits on many oceans.
2 Every king on earth has slept with her,
and her shameless ways are like wine
that has made everyone on earth
drunk."
3 With the help of the Spirit, the angel
took me into the desert, where I saw a
woman sitting on a red beast. The beast

[z]**16.6** *They poured out the blood*: A way of saying, "They murdered." [a]**16.16** *Armagedon*: The Hebrew form of the name would be "Har Megiddo," meaning "Hill of Megiddo," where many battles were fought in ancient times (see Judges 5.19; 2 Kings 23.29, 30).

was covered with names that were an
insult to God, and it had seven heads
and ten horns. 4The woman was dressed
in purple and scarlet robes, and she
wore jewelry made of gold, precious
stones, and pearls. In her hand she held
a gold cup filled with the filthy and
nasty things she had done. 5On her
forehead a mysterious name was written:

I AM THE GREAT CITY OF
BABYLON, THE MOTHER
OF EVERY IMMORAL AND FILTHY
THING ON EARTH.

6I could tell that the woman was drunk
on the blood of God's people who had
given their lives for Jesus. This surprising sight amazed me, 7and the angel
said:

Why are you so amazed? I will explain the mystery about this woman and about the beast she is sitting on, with its seven heads and ten horns.
8The beast you saw is one that used
to be and no longer is. It will come back from the deep pit, but only to be destroyed. Everyone on earth whose names were not written in the book of life[b] before the time of creation will be amazed. They will see this beast that used to be and no longer is, but will be once more.

9Anyone with wisdom can figure this out. The seven heads that the woman is sitting on stand for seven hills. These heads are also seven
kings. 10Five of the kings are dead.
One is ruling now, and the other one has not yet come. But when he does, he will rule for only a little while.

11You also saw a beast that used to be and no longer is. That beast is one of the seven kings who will return as the eighth king, but only to be destroyed.

12The ten horns that you saw are ten more kings, who have not yet come into power, and they will rule with the beast for only a short time.
13They all think alike and will give their power and authority to the
beast. 14These kings will go to war against the Lamb. But he will defeat them, because he is Lord over all lords and King over all kings. His followers are chosen and special and faithful.

15The oceans that you saw the prostitute sitting on are crowds of people from all races and languages.
16The ten horns and the beast will start hating the shameless woman. They will strip off her clothes and leave her naked. Then they will eat her flesh and throw the rest of her
body into a fire. 17God is the one
who made these kings all think alike and decide to give their power to the beast. And they will do this until what God has said comes true.

18The woman you saw is the great city that rules over all kings on earth.

The Fall of Babylon

18 I saw another angel come from heaven. This one had great power, and the earth was bright because
of his glory. 2The angel shouted,

"Fallen! Powerful Babylon
has fallen
and is now the home
of demons.
It is the den
of every filthy spirit
and of all unclean birds,
and every dirty
and hated animal.
3 Babylon's evil and immoral wine
has made all nations drunk.
Every king on earth
has slept with her,
and every merchant on earth
is rich because of
her evil desires."

4 Then I heard another voice
from heaven shout,
"My people, you must escape
from Babylon.
Don't take part in her sins
and share her punishment.
5 Her sins are piled
as high as heaven.
God has remembered the evil
she has done.
6 Treat her as she
has treated others.
Make her pay double
for what she has done.
Make her drink twice as much
of what she mixed
for others.
7 That woman honored herself
with a life of luxury.
Reward her now
with suffering and pain.

"Deep in her heart
Babylon said,
'I am the queen!
Never will I be a widow
or know what it means
to be sad.'
8 And so, in a single day
she will suffer the pain
of sorrow, hunger, and death.
Fire will destroy
her dead body,

[b] 17.8 *book of life*: See the note at 3.5.

because her judge
is the powerful Lord God."

9Every king on earth who slept with
her and shared in her luxury will
mourn. They will weep, when they see
the smoke from that fire. 10Her sufferings will frighten them, and they will
stand at a distance and say,

"Pity that great
and powerful city!
Pity Babylon!
In a single hour
her judgment has come."

11Every merchant on earth will
mourn, because there is no one to buy
their goods. 12There won't be anyone to
buy their gold, silver, jewels, pearls, fine
linen, purple cloth, silk, scarlet cloth,
sweet-smelling wood, fancy carvings of
ivory and wood, as well as things made
of bronze, iron, or marble. 13No one will
buy their cinnamon, spices, incense,
myrrh, frankincense,[c] wine, olive oil,
fine flour, wheat, cattle, sheep, horses,
chariots, slaves, and other humans.

14 Babylon, the things
your heart desired
have all escaped
from you.
Every luxury
and all your glory
will be lost forever.
You will never
get them back.

15The merchants had become rich because of her. But when they saw her sufferings, they were terrified. They stood
at a distance, crying and mourning.
16Then they shouted,

"Pity the great city
of Babylon!
She dressed in fine linen
and wore purple
and scarlet cloth.
She had jewelry
made of gold
and precious stones
and pearls.
17 Yet in a single hour
her riches disappeared."

Every ship captain and passenger and
sailor stood at a distance, together with
everyone who does business by traveling on the sea. 18When they saw the
smoke from her fire, they shouted, "This
was the greatest city ever!"
19They cried loudly, and in their sorrow they threw dust on their heads, as
they said,

"Pity the great city
of Babylon!
Everyone who sailed the seas
became rich
from her treasures.
But in a single hour
the city was destroyed.
20 The heavens should be happy
with God's people
and apostles and prophets.
God has punished her
for them."

21A powerful angel then picked up a
huge stone and threw it into the sea.
The angel said,

"This is how the great city
of Babylon
will be thrown down,
never to rise again.
22 The music of harps and singers
and of flutes and trumpets
will no longer be heard.
No workers will ever
set up shop in that city,
and the sound
of grinding grain
will be silenced forever.
23 Lamps will no longer shine
anywhere in Babylon,
and couples will never again
say wedding vows there.
Her merchants ruled
the earth,
and by her witchcraft
she fooled all nations.
24 On the streets of Babylon
is found the blood
of God's people
and of his prophets,
and everyone else."

19 After this, I heard what sounded
like a lot of voices in heaven, and
they were shouting,

"Praise the Lord!
To our God belongs
the glorious power to save,
2 because his judgments
are honest and fair.
That filthy prostitute
ruined the earth
with shameful deeds.
But God has judged her
and made her pay
the price for murdering
his servants."

3Then the crowd shouted,

"Praise the Lord!
Smoke will never stop rising
from her burning body."

4After this, the twenty-four elders and
the four living creatures all knelt before
the throne of God and worshiped him.
They said, "Amen! Praise the Lord!"

[c] **18.13** *myrrh, frankincense*: Myrrh was a valuable sweet-smelling powder often used in perfume. Frankincense was a valuable powder that was burned to make a sweet smell.

The Marriage Supper of the Lamb

5From the throne a voice said,

"If you worship
and fear our God,
give praise to him,
no matter who you are."

6Then I heard what seemed to be a
large crowd that sounded like a roaring
flood and loud thunder all mixed together. They were saying,

"Praise the Lord!
Our Lord God All-Powerful
now rules as king.
7 So we will be glad and happy
and give him praise.
The wedding day of the Lamb
is here,
and his bride is ready.
8 She will be given
a wedding dress
made of pure
and shining linen.
This linen stands for
the good things
God's people have done."

9Then the angel told me, "Put this in
writing. God will bless everyone who is
invited to the wedding feast of the
Lamb." The angel also said, "These
things that God has said are true."
10I knelt at the feet of the angel and
began to worship him. But the angel
said, "Don't do that! I am a servant, just
like you and everyone else who tells
about Jesus. Don't worship anyone but
God. Everyone who tells about Jesus
does it by the power of the Spirit."

The Rider on the White Horse

11I looked and saw that heaven was
open, and a white horse was there. Its
rider was called Faithful and True, and
he is always fair when he judges or goes
to war. 12He had eyes like flames of fire,
and he was wearing a lot of crowns. His
name was written on him, but he was
the only one who knew what the name
meant.
13The rider wore a robe that was covered with[d] blood, and he was known as
"The Word of God." 14He was followed
by armies from heaven that rode on
horses and were dressed in pure white
linen. 15From his mouth a sharp sword
went out to attack the nations. He will
rule them with an iron rod and will
show the fierce anger of God All-
Powerful by trampling the grapes in the
pit where wine is made. 16On the part of
the robe that covered his thigh was written, "KING OF KINGS AND LORD OF
LORDS."
17I then saw an angel standing on the
sun, and he shouted to all the birds flying in the sky, "Come and join in God's
great feast! 18You can eat the flesh of
kings, rulers, leaders, horses, riders, free
people, slaves, important people, and
everyone else."
19I also saw the beast and all kings of
the earth come together. They fought
against the rider on the white horse and
against his army. 20But the beast was
captured and so was the false prophet.
This is the same prophet who had
worked miracles for the beast, so that
he could fool everyone who had the
mark of the beast and worshiped the
idol. The beast and the false prophet
were thrown alive into a lake of burning sulfur. 21But the rest of their army
was killed by the sword that came
from the mouth of the rider on the
horse. Then birds stuffed themselves
on the dead bodies.

The Thousand Years

20 I saw an angel come down from
heaven, carrying the key to the
deep pit and a big chain. 2He chained
the dragon for a thousand years. It is
that old snake, who is also known as the
devil and Satan. 3Then the angel threw
the dragon into the pit. He locked and
sealed it, so that a thousand years would
go by before the dragon could fool the
nations again. But after that, it would
have to be set free for a little while.
4I saw thrones, and sitting on those
thrones were the ones who had been
given the right to judge. I also saw the
souls of the people who had their heads
cut off because they had told about Jesus and preached God's message. They
were the same ones who had not worshiped the beast or the idol, and they
had refused to let its mark be put on
their hands or foreheads. They will
come to life and rule with Christ for a
thousand years.
5-6These people are the first to be
raised to life, and they are especially
blessed and holy. The second death[e] has
no power over them. They will be
priests for God and Christ and will rule
with them for a thousand years.
No other dead people were raised to
life until a thousand years later.

Satan Is Defeated

7At the end of the thousand years, Satan will be set free. 8He will fool the
countries of Gog and Magog, which are
at the far ends of the earth, and their
people will follow him into battle. They
will have as many followers as there are

[d]**19.13** *covered with*: Some manuscripts have "sprinkled with." [e]**20.5,6** *second death*: See the note at 2.11.

grains of sand along the beach, 9 and
they will march all the way across the
earth. They will surround the camp of
God's people and the city that his people
love. But fire will come down from
heaven and destroy the whole army.
10 Then the devil who fooled them will be
thrown into the lake of fire and burning
sulfur. He will be there with the beast
and the false prophet, and they will be in
pain day and night forever and ever.

The Judgment at the Great White Throne

11 I saw a great white throne with
someone sitting on it. Earth and heaven
tried to run away, but there was no
place for them to go. 12 I also saw all the
dead people standing in front of that
throne. Every one of them was there, no
matter who they had once been. Several
books were opened, and then the book
of life[f] was opened. The dead were
judged by what those books said they
had done.
13 The sea gave up the dead people
who were in it, and death and its kingdom also gave up their dead. Then
everyone was judged by what they had
done. 14 Afterwards, death and its kingdom were thrown into the lake of fire.
This is the second death.[g] 15 Anyone
whose name wasn't written in the book
of life was thrown into the lake of fire.

The New Heaven and the New Earth

21 I saw a new heaven and a new
earth. The first heaven and the
first earth had disappeared, and so had
the sea. 2 Then I saw New Jerusalem,
that holy city, coming down from God in
heaven. It was like a bride dressed in
her wedding gown and ready to meet
her husband.
3 I heard a loud voice shout from the
throne:

> God's home is now with his peo-
> ple. He will live with them, and they
> will be his own. Yes, God will make
> his home among his people. 4 He will
> wipe all tears from their eyes, and
> there will be no more death, suffer-
> ing, crying, or pain. These things of
> the past are gone forever.

5 Then the one sitting on the throne
said:

> I am making everything new.
> Write down what I have said. My
> words are true and can be trusted.
> 6 Everything is finished! I am Alpha
> and Omega,[h] the beginning and the
> end. I will freely give water from the
> life-giving fountain to everyone who
> is thirsty. 7 All who win the victory
> will be given these blessings. I will
> be their God, and they will be my
> people.
> 8 But I will tell you what will hap-
> pen to cowards and to everyone who
> is unfaithful or dirty-minded or who
> murders or is sexually immoral or
> uses witchcraft or worships idols or
> tells lies. They will be thrown into
> that lake of fire and burning sul-
> fur. This is the second death.[i]

The New Jerusalem

9 I saw one of the seven angels who
had the bowls filled with the seven last
terrible troubles. The angel came to me
and said, "Come on! I will show you the
one who will be the bride and wife of
the Lamb." 10 Then with the help of the
Spirit, he took me to the top of a very
high mountain. There he showed me the
holy city of Jerusalem coming down
from God in heaven.
11 The glory of God made the city
bright. It was dazzling and crystal clear
like a precious jasper stone. 12 The city
had a high and thick wall with twelve
gates, and each one of them was
guarded by an angel. On each of the
gates was written the name of one of the
twelve tribes of Israel. 13 Three of these
gates were on the east, three were on
the north, three more were on the south,
and the other three were on the west.
14 The city was built on twelve foundation stones. On each of the stones was
written the name of one of the Lamb's
twelve apostles.
15 The angel who spoke to me had a
gold measuring stick to measure the
city and its gates and its walls. 16 The
city was shaped like a cube, because it
was just as high as it was wide. When
the angel measured the city, it was
about fifteen hundred miles high and
fifteen hundred miles wide. 17 Then the
angel measured the wall, and by our
measurements it was about two hundred sixteen feet high.
18 The wall was built of jasper, and the
city was made of pure gold, clear as
crystal. 19 Each of the twelve foundations
was a precious stone. The first was
jasper,[j] the second was sapphire, the
third was agate, the fourth was emerald,
20 the fifth was onyx, the sixth was carnelian, the seventh was chrysolite, the

[f] **20.12** *book of life*: See the note at 3.5. [g] **20.14** *second death*: See the note at 2.11.
[h] **21.6** *Alpha and Omega*: See the note at 1.8. [i] **21.8** *second death*: See the note at 2.11.
[j] **21.19** *jasper*: The precious and semi-precious stones mentioned in verses 19, 20 are of different colors. *Jasper* is usually green or clear; *sapphire* is blue; *agate* has circles of brown and white; *emerald* is green; *onyx* has different bands of color; *carnelian* is deep-red or reddish-white; *chrysolite* is olive-green; *beryl* is green or bluish-green; *topaz* is yellow; *chrysoprase* is apple-green; *jacinth* is reddish-orange; and *amethyst* is deep purple.

eighth was beryl, the ninth was topaz, the tenth was chrysoprase, the eleventh was jacinth, and the twelfth was amethyst. [21]Each of the twelve gates was a solid pearl. The streets of the city were made of pure gold, clear as crystal.

[22]I did not see a temple there. The Lord God All-Powerful and the Lamb were its temple. [23]And the city did not need the sun or the moon. The glory of God was shining on it, and the Lamb was its light.

[24]Nations will walk by the light of that city, and kings will bring their riches there. [25]Its gates are always open during the day, and night never comes. [26]The glorious treasures of nations will be brought into the city. [27]But nothing unworthy will be allowed to enter. No one who is dirty-minded or who tells lies will be there. Only those whose names are written in the Lamb's book of life[k] will be in the city.

22 The angel showed me a river that was crystal clear, and its waters gave life. The river came from the throne where God and the Lamb were seated. [2]Then it flowed down the middle of the city's main street. On each side of the river are trees[l] that grow a different kind of fruit each month of the year. The fruit gives life, and the leaves are used as medicine to heal the nations.

[3]God's curse will no longer be on the people of that city. He and the Lamb will be seated there on their thrones, and its people will worship God [4]and will see him face to face. God's name will be written on the foreheads of the people. [5]Never again will night appear, and no one who lives there will ever need a lamp or the sun. The Lord God will be their light, and they will rule forever.

The Coming of Christ

[6]Then I was told:

These words are true and can be trusted. The Lord God controls the spirits of his prophets, and he is the one who sent his angel to show his servants what must happen right away. [7]Remember, I am coming soon! God will bless everyone who pays attention to the message of this book.

[8]My name is John, and I am the one who heard and saw these things. Then after I had heard and seen all this, I knelt down and began to worship at the feet of the angel who had shown it to me.

[9]But the angel said,

Don't do that! I am a servant, just like you. I am the same as a follower or a prophet or anyone else who obeys what is written in this book. God is the one you should worship.

[10]Don't keep the prophecies in this book a secret. These things will happen soon.

[11]Evil people will keep on being evil, and everyone who is dirty-minded will still be dirty-minded. But good people will keep on doing right, and God's people will always be holy.

[12]Then I was told:

I am coming soon! And when I come, I will reward everyone for what they have done. [13]I am Alpha and Omega,[m] the first and the last, the beginning and the end.

[14]God will bless all who have washed their robes. They will each have the right to eat fruit from the tree that gives life, and they can enter the gates of the city. [15]But outside the city will be dogs, witches, immoral people, murderers, idol worshipers, and everyone who loves to tell lies and do wrong.

[16]I am Jesus! And I am the one who sent my angel to tell all of you these things for the churches. I am David's Great Descendant,[n] and I am also the bright morning star.[o]

[17]The Spirit and the bride say, "Come!"

Everyone who hears this[p] should say, "Come!"

If you are thirsty, come! If you want life-giving water, come and take it. It's free!

[18]Here is my warning for everyone who hears the prophecies in this book:

If you add anything to them, God will make you suffer all the terrible troubles written in this book. [19]If you take anything away from these prophecies, God will not let you have part in the life-giving tree and in the holy city described in this book.

[20]The one who has spoken these things says, "I am coming soon!"

So, Lord Jesus, please come soon!

[21]I pray that the Lord Jesus will be kind to all of you.

[k]**21.27** *book of life*: See the note at 3.5. [l]**22.2** *trees*: The Greek has "tree," which is used in a collective sense of trees on both sides of the heavenly river. [m]**22.13** *Alpha and Omega*: See the note at 1.8. [n]**22.16** *David's Great Descendant*: See the note at 5.5. [o]**22.16** *the bright morning star*: Probably thought of as the brightest star (see 2.27, 28). [p]**22.17** *who hears this*: The reading of the book of Revelation in a service of worship.

The
HOLY
BIBLE

Mini-Dictionary
Chronology of Bible
Maps

A Mini Dictionary for the Bible

This dictionary is divided into 21 sections. The indexes below list all of the sections, and all of the entries in alphabetical order, so that you can find what you are looking for more easily.

Section Index

Alphabetical Index

1. A Few Basics

CEV The *Contemporary English Version* of the Bible.

Old Testament This first part of the Bible is made up of the 39 books from Genesis through Malachi. They were written mostly in Hebrew, with a few passages in Aramaic.

New Testament This second part of the Bible is made up of the 27 books from Matthew through Revelation. They were written in Greek.

Chapter and Verse Numbers These numbers were not part of the original books, but were added hundreds of years later as a way to refer to specific parts of the books of Scripture. For example, Genesis 1.3 means "the book of Genesis, chapter 1, verse 3." Genesis 2.4, 5 means "the book of Genesis, chapter 2, verses 4 through 5." And Genesis 1–2 means, "the book of Genesis, chapters 1 through 2." A few books are so short that they were not divided into chapters, and so these books only have verse numbers. In the text of the CEV, sometimes verse numbers have been combined, for example, 3-4. One reason verse numbers might be combined is that contemporary English says things in a different order than ancient Greek and Hebrew, and so two or more verses are sometimes blended together in the CEV translation. And in lists, the verse numbers are sometimes combined into a single heading to avoid confusion. But all the meaning from the original Greek and Hebrew has been carefully included in the CEV text.

2. Scriptures, Manuscripts

Ancient Translations The Old Testament was translated into Greek over the period 250–150 B.C. Later, the whole Bible was translated into Latin, Syriac, and some other languages. These ancient translations can sometimes show what the Hebrew or Greek text said at the time they were translated, and so the CEV notes will sometimes refer to them.

Commandments God's rules for his people to live by. The most famous are the Ten Commandments (see Exodus 20.1-17; Deuteronomy 5.6-21).

Dead Sea Scrolls Manuscripts found near the Dead Sea from 1947–1954. They date from about 250 B.C. to A.D. 68. These manuscripts include at least some parts of nearly all Old Testament books.

God's Law God's rules for his people to live by. They are found in the Old Testament, especially in the first five books.

Law and the Prophets A term used in New Testament times to refer to the sacred writings of the Jews. The Law and the Prophets were two of the three sections of the Old Testament, but the expression sometimes refers to the entire Old Testament.

Law of Moses and **Law of the Lord** Usually refers to the first five books of the Old Testament, but sometimes to the entire Old Testament.

Manuscript In ancient times, all books were copied by hand. A copy made this way is called "a manuscript."

Proverb A wise saying that is short and easy to remember.

Psalm A Hebrew poem. Psalms were often written in such a way that they could be prayed or sung by an individual or a group. Some of the psalms thank and praise God, while others ask God to take away sins or to give protection, comfort, vengeance, or mercy.

Samaritan Hebrew Text The Hebrew text of Genesis through Deuteronomy used and preserved by the Samaritans (see also "Samaria"). This text uses forms of letters and many spellings that are different from the Standard Hebrew Text. It has traditionally been called "the Samaritan Pentateuch."

Scriptures Although this term now refers to the whole Bible, in the New Testament it refers to the Old Testament.

Standard Hebrew Text The Hebrew text that is found in most Hebrew manuscripts of the Old Testament. Almost all of these manuscripts were copied after A.D. 900 (but see also "Dead Sea Scrolls").

Wisdom Often refers to the common sense and practical skill needed to solve everyday problems, but sometimes involves trying to find answers to the hard questions about the meaning of life.

3. Languages

Aramaic A language closely related to Hebrew. In New Testament times Aramaic was spoken by many Jews including Jesus. Ezra 4.8—6.18; 7.12-26; and Daniel 2.4b—7.28 were written in Aramaic.

Greek The language used throughout the Mediterranean world in New Testament times, and the language in which the New Testament was written.

Hebrew The language used by most of the people of Israel until the Exile. But after the people returned, more and more people spoke Aramaic instead. Most of the Old Testament was written in Hebrew.

4. People

Aaron The brother of Moses. Only he and his descendants were to serve as priests and offer sacrifices for the people of Israel (see Exodus 4.14-16; 28.1; Numbers 16.1—18.7).

Abel The second son of Adam and Eve and the younger brother of Cain. Abel was killed by Cain after God accepted Abel's offering and refused to accept Cain's (see Genesis 4.1-11).

Abraham The first of the three great ancestors of the people of Israel. Abraham was the husband of Sarah and the father of Isaac. At first Abraham's name was Abram, meaning "Great Father." Then, when Abram was ninety-nine years old, God changed Abram's name to Abraham, which means "Father of a Crowd." Abraham trusted God, and so God promised that Abraham and his wife Sarah would have a son and more descendants than could be counted. God also promised that Abraham would be a blessing to everyone on earth (see Genesis 12.1-7; 17.1—18.15).

Abram See "Abraham."

Adam The first man and the husband of Eve (see Genesis 1.26—3.21).

Agrippa (1) Herod Agrippa was king of Judea A.D. 41–44 and mistreated Christians (see Acts 12.1-5). (2) Agrippa II was the son of Herod Agrippa and ruled parts of Palestine from A.D. 53 to A.D. 93 or later. He and his sister Bernice listened to Paul defend himself (see Acts 25.13-26, 32).

Antipas (1) Herod Antipas, son of Herod the Great (see "Herod"). (2) An otherwise unknown Christian at Pergamum, who was killed because he was a follower of Christ (see Revelation 2.13).

Augustus A title meaning "honored," which was given to Octavian by the Romans when he began ruling the Roman world in 27 B.C. He was the Roman Emperor when Jesus was born.

Cain The first son of Adam and Eve; Cain killed his brother Abel after God accepted Abel's offering and refused to accept Cain's (see Genesis 4.1-17).

David King of Israel from about 1010–970 B.C. David was the most famous king Israel ever had, and many of the people of Israel hoped that one of his descendants would always be their king (see 1 Samuel 16-30; 2 Samuel; 1 Kings 12).

Esau The older son of Isaac and Rebekah, and the brother of Jacob. Esau was also known as Edom and as the ancestor of the Edomites (see Genesis 25.20-34; 26.34-46; 32.1—33.16).

Eve The first woman and the wife of Adam (see Genesis 1.26—3.21).

Felix The Roman governor of Palestine A.D. 52–60, who listened to Paul speak and kept him in jail (see Acts 23.24—24.27).

Festus The Roman governor after Felix, who sent Paul to stand trial in Rome (see Acts 24.27—26.32).

Hagar A slave of Sarah, the wife of Abraham. When Sarah could not have any children, she followed the ancient custom of letting her husband have a child by Hagar, her slave. The boy's name was Ishmael (see Genesis 16; 21.8-21).

Herod (1) Herod the Great was the king of all Palestine 37–4 B.C., and so he was king at the time Jesus was born (see the note at "A.D."). (2) Herod Antipas was the son of Herod the Great and was the ruler of Galilee 4 B.C.–A.D. 39. (3) Herod Agrippa I, the grandson of Herod the Great, ruled Palestine A.D. 41–44.

Isaac The second of the three great ancestors of the people of Israel. He was the son of Abraham and Sarah, and he was the father of Esau and Jacob.

Ishmael The son of Abraham and Hagar.

Israel See "Jacob."

Jacob The third great ancestor of the people of Israel. Jacob was the son of Isaac and Rebekah, and his name was changed to Israel when he struggled with God at Peniel near the Jabbok River (see Genesis 32.22-32).

Joseph A son of Jacob and Rachel. Joseph was sold as a slave by his brothers, but later he became governor of Egypt (see Genesis 37.12-36; 41.1-57).

Lot A nephew of Abraham and the ancestor of the Moabites and Ammonites (see Genesis 11.27; 13.1-13; 18.16—19.38).

Noah When God destroyed the world by a flood, Noah and his family were kept safe in a big boat that God had told him to build (see Genesis 6–8).

Rebekah The wife of Isaac, and the mother of Jacob and Esau (see Genesis 24.1-67; 25.19-28).

Sarah The wife of Abraham and the mother of Isaac. At first her name was Sarai, but when she was old, God promised her that she would have a son, and he changed her name to Sarah. Both names mean "princess" (see 11.29-30; 17.15-19; 18.9-15; 21.1-7).

Solomon A son of King David and Bathsheba. After David's death, Solomon ruled Israel about 970–931 B.C. Solomon built the temple in Jerusalem and was widely known for his wisdom. The Hebrew text indicates that he wrote many of the proverbs and two of the psalms.

5. Prophets

Anna A woman prophet who stayed in the temple night and day. Soon after Jesus was born, Mary and Joseph took him to the temple and presented him to the Lord, and Anna talked about the child Jesus to everyone who hoped for Jerusalem to be set free (see Luke 2.36-38).

Balaam A foreign prophet. Balaam was hired by the king of Moab to put a curse on Israel, but instead Balaam blessed Israel (see Numbers 22–24).

Deborah A prophet and judge who helped lead Israel to defeat King Jabin of Hazor (see Judges 4–5).

Elijah A prophet who spoke for God in the early ninth century B.C. and who opposed the evil King Ahab and Queen Jezebel of the northern kingdom. Many Jews in later centuries thought Elijah would return to get everything ready for the day of judgment or for the coming of the Messiah (see 1 Kings 17–21; 2 Kings 1–2; Malachi 4.1-6; Matthew 17.10, 11; Mark 9.11, 12).

Elisha A prophet who assisted Elijah and later took his place. Elisha spoke for God in the late ninth century B.C., and was the prophet who healed Naaman (see 1 Kings 19.19-21; 2 Kings 2–9; 13.14-21).

Huldah A prophet who spoke for God during the late seventh century B.C. After *The Book of God's Law* was found in the temple, King Josiah asked her what the Lord wanted him to do (see 2 Kings 22.14-20).

Micaiah The prophet who told King Ahab that he would die in battle against the Syrian army (see 1 Kings 22.5-38).

Moses The prophet who led the people of Israel when God rescued them from slavery in Egypt. Moses also received laws from God and gave them to Israel (see Exodus 2–12; 19–24; Numbers 12.68).

Prophesy To speak as a prophet (see "Prophet").

Prophet Someone who speaks God's message, which at times included telling what would happen in the future. Sometimes when the Spirit of God took control of prophets, they lost some or all control over their speech and actions or were not aware of what was happening around them.

6. Twelve Tribes of Israel

The Bible speaks of all the people in a tribe as having descended from one of the twelve sons of Jacob. The tribes of Ephraim and Manasseh were a little different, because the people in those tribes descended from the two sons of Joseph, who was one of Jacob's sons. That would make a total of thirteen tribes, but the Bible always counts only twelve. In some passages Ephraim and Manasseh are counted as one tribe, and in other passages the Levi tribe is left out, probably because they were designated for priestly service to all the tribes, and as such, were scattered throughout the land belonging to the other tribes. People from other nations were sometimes allowed to become Israelites (see Exodus 12.38; Deuteronomy 23.1-8; and the book of Ruth), and these people would then belong to one of the tribes.

Asher Occupied land along the Mediterranean coast from Mount Carmel to the border with the city of Tyre.

Benjamin Occupied land between Bethel and Jerusalem. When the northern tribes of Israel broke away following the death of Solomon, only the tribes of Benjamin and Judah were left to form the southern kingdom.

Dan First occupied land west of Judah, Benjamin, and Ephraim. But after the Philistines took control of this area, part of the tribe then moved to the northernmost area of Israel.

Ephraim One of the largest tribes. Ephraim occupied the land north of Benjamin and south of West Manasseh.

Gad Occupied land east of the Jordan River from the northern end of the Dead Sea north to the Jabbok River.

Issachar Occupied land southwest of Lake Galilee.

Judah Occupied the hill country west of the Dead Sea. When the ten northern tribes of Israel broke away following the death of Solomon, only the tribes of Judah and Benjamin were left to form the southern kingdom, and it was also called "Judah."

Levi The men of this tribe were to be the special servants of the Lord at the sacred tent and later at the temple, and so the people of this tribe were not given tribal land. Instead, they were given towns scattered throughout the other twelve tribes (see also "Levite").

Manasseh Occupied two areas of land: (1) East Manasseh lived east of the Jordan River and north of the Jabbok River in the areas of Bashan and northern Gilead. (2) West Manasseh lived west of the Jordan River and to the north of Ephraim.

Naphtali Occupied land north and west of Lake Galilee.

Reuben Occupied land east of the Dead Sea, from the Arnon River in the south to the northern end of the Dead Sea.

Simeon Occupied land southwest of Judah, and was later practically absorbed into Judah.

Zebulun Occupied land north of Manasseh from the eastern end of Mount Carmel to Mount Tabor.

7. Christ's Twelve Apostles

Apostle A person chosen and sent by Christ to take his message to others. Lists of the names of Christ's twelve apostles can be found in Matthew 10.2-4; Mark 3.16-19; Luke 6.14-16; Acts 1.12, 13. Later, others such as Paul and James the brother of Jesus also became known as apostles.

Simon also known as Peter or Cephas

Andrew Simon Peter's brother

James the son of Zebedee

John the son of Zebedee (James and John were also known as "Thunderbolts")

Philip from Bethsaida, the hometown of Simon and Andrew

Bartholomew mentioned in all New Testament lists of the apostles, but nowhere else

Thomas also known as "The Twin"

Matthew also known as Levi

James the son of Alphaeus

Thaddeus also known as Judas or Jude the son of James

Simon also known as "the Eager One"

Judas Iscariot who betrayed Jesus

Matthias who was chosen to replace Judas Iscariot

8. Cities, Nations, and Groups of People

Amalekites A nomadic nation living mostly in the area south and east of the Dead Sea. They were enemies of Israel.

Ammon A nation that lived east of Israel. According to Genesis 19.30-38, the people of Ammon descended from Lot, a nephew of Abraham.

Amorites Usually a name for all the non-Israelite nations who lived in Canaan, but in some passages it may refer to one nation scattered in several areas of Canaan.

Anakim Perhaps a group of very large people who lived in Palestine before the Israelites (see Numbers 13.33 and Deuteronomy 2.10, 11, 20, 21).

Asia A Roman province in what is today the nation of Turkey.

Assyria An empire of Old Testament times, whose capital city Nineveh was located in what is today northern Iraq. In 722 B.C. Assyria conquered the kingdom of Israel and took many Israelites as captives. The Assyrians then forced people from other parts of its empire to settle on Israel's land (see 2 Kings 18.9-12).

Avvites A nation that lived along the Mediterranean seacoast before the Philistines came and took their land. The Avvites who survived lived south of the Philistines.

Babylonia A large empire of Old Testament times, whose capital city Babylon was located in south-central Mesopotamia. The Babylonians defeated the southern kingdom of Judah in 586 B.C. and forced many of its people to live in Babylonia (see 2 Kings 25.1-12).

Canaanites The nations who lived in Canaan before the Israelites. Many Canaanites continued to live there even after the Israelites came.

Cush The Hebrew form for Ethiopia (see "Ethiopia" below).

Disciples Those who were followers of Jesus and learned from him. The term often refers to his twelve apostles.

Edomites A nation living in Edom or Seir, an area south and southeast of the Dead Sea. According to Genesis 36.1-43, the Edomites descended from Esau, Jacob's brother.

Empire A number of kingdoms ruled by one strong military power.

Epicureans People who followed the teachings of a man named Epicurus, who taught that happiness should be the main goal in life.

Ethiopia A region south of Egypt that included parts of the present countries of Ethiopia and Sudan.

Exiles Israelites who were taken away as prisoners to Babylonia (see also "Exile").

Gentiles Those people who are not Jews.

Girgashites One of the nations that lived in Canaan before the Israelites.

Hebrew An older term for "Israelite" or "Jewish."

Hittites A nation whose capital city was located in what is now Turkey. The Hittites had an empire that at times controlled some kingdoms in Canaan before 1200 B.C., and many Hittites remained in Canaan even after the Israelites came.

Hivites A nation that lived in Canaan before the Israelites, probably related to the Horites.

Horites A nation that lived in Canaan before the Israelites. The Horites were also known as "Hurrians."

Israel (1) The nation made up of the twelve tribes descended from Jacob (see Section 6, "Twelve Tribes of Israel"). (2) The northern kingdom, after the northern tribes broke away following the death of Solomon (see 1 Kings 12.1-20).

Jebusites A group of Canaanite people who lived at Jebus, also known as Jerusalem (see 2 Samuel 5.6-10).

Jews A name first used in referring to someone belonging to the tribe of Judah. Later, the term came to be used of any Israelite.

Kadesh A town in the desert of Paran southwest of the Dead Sea, near the southern border of Israel and the western border of Edom. Israel camped at Kadesh while the twelve tribal leaders explored Canaan (see Numbers 13–14).

Levites Those Israelites who belonged to the tribe of Levi. God chose the men of one Levite family, the descendants of Aaron, to be Israel's priests. The other men from this tribe helped with the work in the sacred tent and later in the temple (see Numbers 3.5-10).

Medes A nation that lived in what is today northwest Iran. Their kingdom, called "Media," later became one of the most important provinces of the Persian Empire, and Persian laws were referred to as the laws of the Medes and Persians (see Esther 1.19; Daniel 6.8, 12, 15).

Midianites A nomadic nation who lived mainly in the desert along the eastern shore of the Gulf of Aqaba.

Moab A nation that lived east of the Dead Sea. According to Genesis 19.30-38, the people of Moab descended from Lot, the nephew of Abraham.

Nazarenes A name that was sometimes used for the followers of Jesus, who came from the small town of Nazareth (see Acts 24.5).

Perizzites A nation that lived in the central hill country of Canaan, before the Israelites.

Persia A large empire of Old Testament times, whose capital was located in what is now southern Iran. It is sometimes called "the Medo-Persian Empire," because of the importance of the province of Media.

Pharisees A group of Jews who thought they could best serve God by strictly obeying the laws of the Old Testament as well as their own rules, traditions, and teachings.

Philistines The land along the Mediterranean coast controlled by the Philistine people was called "Philistia." There were five main cities, each with its own ruler: Ashdod, Ashkelon, Ekron, Gath, and Gaza. The Philistines were often at war with Israel.

Phoenicia The territory along the Mediterranean Sea controlled by the cities of Tyre, Sidon, Arvad, and Byblos. The coast of modern Lebanon covers about the same area.

Rapha Perhaps a group of very large people who lived in Palestine before the Israelites (see Deuteronomy 2.11, 20).

Roman Empire Controlled the area around the Mediterranean Sea in New Testament times. Its capital was Rome.

Sadducees A small and powerful group of Jews in New Testament times. They were closely connected with the high priests and accepted only the first five books of the Old Testament as their Bible. They also did not believe in life after death.

Samaria (1) The capital city of the northern kingdom of Israel beginning with the rule of King Omri (ruled 885–874 B.C.). (2) In New Testament times, a district between Judea and Galilee, named for the city of Samaria. The people of this district, called "Samaritans," worshiped God differently from the Jews, and these two groups refused to have anything to do with one another.

Sidon See "Phoenicia."

Stoics Followers of a man named Zeno, who taught that people should learn self-control and be guided by their consciences.

Tyre See "Phoenicia."

9. Places

Bashan The flat highlands and wooded hills of southern Syria. Bashan was just north of the region of Gilead and was known for its fat cattle and fine grain.

Canaan The area now covered by Israel plus Gaza, the West Bank of Jordan, Lebanon, and southern Syria (see Numbers 34.1-12). Many passages use the term to refer only to the area south of Lebanon.

Gethsemane A garden or olive orchard on the Mount of Olives (see "Mount of Olives").

Gilead A region east of the Jordan River. Moab lay to the south of Gilead, and Bashan was to the north.

Hinnom Valley A valley west and south of Jerusalem, where human sacrifice was sometimes made in Old Testament times (see "Molech").

Mount of Olives A mountain just east of Jerusalem, across Kidron Valley from the temple. Gethsemane, a place where Jesus and his disciples often went to pray, was on this mountain, and so were the villages of Bethany, Bethphage, and Bahurim (see Matthew 26.36; Mark 14.32; Luke 22.39; John 18.1, 2).

Palestine The area now covered by Israel, Gaza, and Jordan.

Peniel A place near the Jabbok River where Jacob wrestled with God. Then God changed Jacob's name to Israel (see Genesis 32.22-32).

Zion Another name for Jerusalem. Zion can also refer to the hill in Jerusalem where the temple was built.

10. Objects

Chariot A two-wheeled cart that was open at the back and that was pulled by horses.

Cistern A hole or pit used for storing rainwater. Cisterns were sometimes dug in the ground and lined with stones and plaster, and at other times they were cut into the rock. The CEV sometimes translates "cistern" as "well."

Cross A device used by the Romans to put people to death. It was made of two pieces of lumber crossed in a **"T,"** **"†,"** or **"X"** shape.

Piece of Silver In the Old Testament, this usually refers to an amount of silver weighing about 0.4 oz. Coins were not invented until late Old Testament times, so when silver or gold was used to buy things, it was weighed. In traditional translations this amount is called "a shekel." Silver and gold were worth more in biblical times than they are today.

Sackcloth A rough, dark-colored cloth made from goat or camel hair. Sackcloth was usually used to make grain sacks, but clothing made from it was worn in times of trouble or sorrow.

Scroll A roll of paper or special thin leather used for writing on.

Scepter A decorated rod, often made of gold, that a king held in his hand as a symbol of royal power.

Sling A weapon used to throw rocks a little smaller than a tennis ball. A sling was made of a piece of leather that wrapped almost around the rock and had a leather strap at each end. The person would hold the ends of the straps and swing the sling around and around. When the person let go of one strap, the rock would fly out of the sling.

Tomb A burial place, often made by cutting a small room out of the rock.

11. Festivals and Holy Days

Many of these festivals are still celebrated by Jewish people.

Festival of Shelters A festival in the early fall celebrating the period of forty years when the people of Israel walked through the desert and lived in small shelters. This happy celebration began on the fifteenth day of Tishri, and for the next seven days, the people lived in small shelters made of tree branches. The name of this festival in Hebrew is "Sukkoth."

Festival of Thin Bread A seven-day festival right after Passover. During this festival the Israelites ate a thin, flat bread made without yeast to remind themselves how God freed the people of Israel from slavery in Egypt and made them into a nation. The name of this festival in Hebrew is "Mazzoth."

Festival of Trumpets See "New Moon Festival."

Great Day of Forgiveness The tenth day of Tishri in the early fall. On this one day of the year, the high priest was allowed to go into the most holy part of the temple and sprinkle some of the blood of a sacrificed bull on the sacred chest. This was done so that the people's sins would be forgiven. In English this holy day has traditionally been called "the Day of Atonement," and its name in Hebrew is "Yom Kippur."

Harvest Festival See "Pentecost."

New Moon Festival A religious festival held on the day of the new moon, the day when only a thin edge of the moon can be seen. This day was always the first day of the month for the Hebrew calendar. The New Moon Festival was a time for rest from work, and a time for worship, sacrifices, celebration, and eating. The New Moon Festival in the month of Tishri in the early fall was also called "the Festival of Trumpets," and it involved even more sacrifices.

Passover A festival held on the fourteenth day of Abib in the early spring. At Passover the Israelites celebrated the time God rescued them from slavery in Egypt. The name of this festival in Hebrew is "Pesach."

Pentecost A Jewish festival held in mid-spring, fifty days after Passover. At this festival Israelites celebrated the wheat harvest. Pentecost was also known as "the Harvest Festival" and has traditionally been called "the Feast of Weeks"; in Hebrew, its name is "Shavuoth."

Festival of Purim A Jewish festival on the fourteenth and fifteenth of Adar, near the end of winter, when the Jews celebrated how they were saved from Haman, the evil prime minister of Persia who wanted to have them killed (see Esther 9.20-32).

Sabbath The seventh day of the week, from sunset on Friday to sunset on Saturday. Israelites worshiped on the Sabbath and rested from their work.

Temple Festival In 165 B.C. the Jewish people recaptured the temple in Jerusalem from their enemies and made it fit for worship again. They celebrated this event each year by an eight-day festival that began on the twenty-fifth day of the month of Chislev in the late fall. This festival is traditionally called "the Festival of Dedication," or in Hebrew, "Hanukkah."

12. Sacrifice, Temple, Worship

Altar A raised structure where sacrifices and offerings were presented to God or to pagan gods. Altars could be made of rocks, packed earth, metal, or pottery.

Amen A Hebrew word used after a prayer or a blessing and meaning that what had been said was right and true.

Fire Pan A metal pan used for burning incense or carrying hot coals from the altar.

God's Tent See "Sacred Tent."

High Priest See "Priest."

Holy Place The main room of the sacred tent and of the temple. This room contained the sacred bread, the golden incense altar, and the golden lampstand. A curtain or wall separated the holy place from the most holy place. A priest would go into the holy place once each morning and evening to burn incense on the golden altar (see also "Most Holy Place").

Incense A material that makes a sweet smell when burned. It was used in the worship of God.

Local Shrine See "Place of Worship."

Most Holy Place The inner room of the sacred tent and of the temple. In the sacred tent this room contained only the sacred chest; in Solomon's temple, the most holy place also held statues of winged creatures. Only the high priest could enter the most holy place, and even he could enter it only once a year on the Great Day of Forgiveness. The most holy place has traditionally been called "the holy of holies."

Offerings See "Sacrifices."

Place of Worship A place to worship God or pagan gods. These places were often on a hill outside of a town and have traditionally been called "high places." In the CEV they are sometimes called "local shrines."

Priest A man who led the worship in the sacred tent or in the temple and who offered sacrifices. Some of the more important priests were called "chief priests," and the most important priest was called the "high priest."

Sacred Chest The chest or box that contained the two flat stones with the Ten Commandments written on them. The chest was covered with gold, and two golden statues of winged creatures were on the lid of the chest. These winged creatures and the chest represented God's throne on earth. Two wooden poles, one on each side, were put through rings at the corners of the chest, so that the

Levites could carry the chest without touching it. The chest was kept in the most holy place (see Exodus 25.10-22).

Sacred Tent The tent where the people of Israel worshiped God before the temple was built. It has traditionally been called "the tabernacle" (see Exodus 26).

Sacrifices These gifts to God included certain animals, grains, fruits, and sweet-smelling spices. Israelites offered sacrifices to give thanks to God, to ask for his forgiveness and his blessing, and to make a payment for a wrong. Some sacrifices were completely burned on the altar. In the case of other sacrifices, a portion was given to the Lord and burned on the altar, then the rest was eaten by the priests or the worshipers who had offered the sacrifice.

Sacrifices To Ask the LORD's Blessing Traditionally called "peace offerings" or "offerings of well-being." A main purpose was to ask for the LORD's blessing, and so in the CEV they are sometimes called "sacrifices to ask the LORD's blessing" (see Leviticus 3).

Sacrifices To Give Thanks to the LORD Traditionally called "grain offerings." A main purpose of such sacrifices was to thank the LORD with a gift of grain, and so in the CEV they are sometimes called "sacrifices to give thanks to the LORD" (see Leviticus 2).

Sacrifices To Make Things Right Traditionally called "guilt offerings." A main purpose was to make things right when a person had cheated someone or the LORD. These sacrifices were also made when a person had broken certain religious rules (see Leviticus 5.14—6.7).

Sacrifices To Please the LORD Traditionally called "whole burnt offerings" because the whole animal was burned on the altar. While these sacrifices did involve forgiveness for sin, a main purpose was to please the LORD with the smell of the smoke from the sacrifice, and so in the CEV they are often called "sacrifices to please the LORD" (see Leviticus 1).

Snuffer A small tool used for putting out the flame of an oil lamp, or for trimming off the charred part of the wick.

Temple A building used as a place of worship. The god that was worshiped in a particular temple was believed to be present there in a special way. The LORD's temple was in Jerusalem.

13. Customs

Ashes People put ashes, dust, or dirt on their heads, or they rolled in ash piles or dust or dirt, as a way of showing sorrow.

Circumcise To cut off the foreskin from the male organ. This was done for Israelite boys eight days after they were born. God commanded that all newborn Israelite boys be circumcised to show that they belonged to his people (see Genesis 17.9-14).

Clean and Unclean (1) In Old Testament times, a person who was acceptable to worship God was called "clean." A person who had certain kinds of diseases, who had touched a dead body, or who had broken certain laws became "unclean," and was unacceptable to worship God. If a person was unclean because of disease, the disease would have to be cured before the person could be clean again. And becoming clean involved performing certain ceremonies that sometimes included sacrifices. (2) Animals that were acceptable as food were called "clean." Those that were not acceptable were called "unclean" (see Leviticus 11.1-47; Deuteronomy 14.3-21). (3) Many things including tools, dishes, houses, and land could also become unclean and unusable, especially if they were touched by something unclean. Some unclean objects had to be destroyed, but others could be made clean by being washed or placed in a fire for a short time.

Going without Eating This was a way of showing sorrow, or of asking for God's help. It is also called "fasting."

Tearing Clothes A way of showing sorrow or anger, or of asking for God's help.

14. God, Jesus, Angels

Angel A supernatural being who tells God's messages to people or protects those who belong to God.

Christ A Greek word meaning "the Chosen One" and used to translate the Hebrew word "Messiah." In New Testament times, many of the Jews believed that God was going to send the Messiah to set them free from the power of their enemies. The term "Christ" is used in the New Testament both as a title and as a name for Jesus.

Eternal Life Life that is the gift of God and that never ends.

Glory Something seen, heard, or felt that shows a person or thing is important, wonderful, or powerful. When God appeared to people, his glory was often seen as a bright light or as fire and smoke. Jesus' glory was seen when he performed miracles, when he was lifted up on the cross, and when he was raised from death.

God's Kingdom God's rule over people, both in this life and in the next.

Holy One A name for the Savior that God had promised to send (see "Savior").

Kingdom of Heaven See "God's kingdom."

LORD In the Old Testament the word "LORD" in capital letters stands for the Hebrew consonants *YHWH*, the personal name of God. Ancient Hebrew did not have vowel letters, and so anyone reading Hebrew would have to know what vowels to put with the consonants. It is not known for certain what vowel sounds were originally used with the consonants *YHWH*. The word "Lord" represents the Hebrew term *Adonai*, the usual word for "lord." By late Old Testament times, Jews considered God's personal name too holy to be pronounced. So they said *Adonai*, "Lord," whenever they read *YHWH*. When the Jewish scribes first translated the Hebrew Scriptures into ancient Greek, they translated the personal name of God as *Kurios*, "Lord." Since that time, most translations, including the *Contemporary English Version*, have followed their example and have avoided using the personal name of God.

Messiah See "Christ."

Promised One A title for the Savior that God promised to send (see "Savior").

Save To rescue people from the power of their enemies or from the power of evil, and to give them new life and place them under God's care (see also "Savior").

Savior The one that God has chosen to rescue or save his people (see also "Save").

Sin Turning away from God and disobeying the teachings or commandments of God.

Son of Man A title often used by Jesus to refer to himself. This title is also found in the Hebrew text of Daniel 7.13 and Psalm 8.4, and God uses it numerous times in the book of Ezekiel to refer to Ezekiel.

Way In the book of Acts the Christian life is sometimes called "the Way" or "the Way of the Lord" or "God's Way."

Winged Creature These supernatural beings represented the presence of God and supported his throne in Ezekiel 1.4-25; 10.1-22. Statues of winged creatures were on top of the sacred chest, and larger ones were in the most holy place in the temple built by Solomon. Wood carvings of winged creatures decorated the inside walls and doors of the temple, and figures of winged creatures were woven into the curtain separating the holy place from the most holy place in the sacred tent. The traditional term for winged creature is "cherub" (or "cherubim" for more than one).

15. Foreign Gods, Fortunetellers, Evil Spirits

Astarte A Canaanite goddess. Those who worshiped her believed that she gave them fertile land and many children, and that she helped their animals give birth to lots of young.

Baal A Canaanite god. The Canaanites believed that Baal was the most powerful of all the gods.

Dagon The chief god of the Philistines.

Demons and **Evil Spirits** Supernatural beings that do harmful things to people and sometimes cause them to do bad things. In the New Testament they are sometimes called "unclean spirits," because people under their power were thought to be unclean and unfit to worship God.

Devil The chief of the demons and evil spirits, also known as "Satan."

Evil Spirits See "Demons."

Fortuneteller Fortunetellers thought they could learn secrets or learn about the future by doing such things as watching the flight of birds, looking at the livers of animals, and rolling dice.

Hermes The Greek god of skillful speaking and the messenger of the other Greek gods.

Molech or **Milcom** The national god of the Ammonites. Some Israelites offered human sacrifices to Molech in Hinnom Valley near Jerusalem.

Satan See "Devil."

Zeus The chief god of the Greeks.

16. Plants, Animals, and Farming

Acacia A flowering tree that produces a hard, durable wood. The sacred chest, the altars, and certain other wooden objects in the sacred tent were made of acacia wood.

Aloes A sweet-smelling spice that was mixed with myrrh and used as a perfume.

Barley A grain that was used to make bread.

Cedar A tall tree once common in the Lebanon mountains and used for many of the royal building projects in Jerusalem.

Cumin A plant with small seeds used for seasoning food.

Flax The stalks of flax plants were harvested, soaked in water, and dried. Then their fibers were separated and spun into thread, which was woven to make linen cloth.

Hyssop A bush with clusters of small branches. In religious ceremonies, hyssop was sometimes dipped in a liquid and then used to sprinkle people or objects.

Jackal A wild desert animal related to wolves, but smaller.

Leviathan A legendary sea monster representing revolt and evil, also known from Canaanite writings.

Locust A type of grasshopper that comes in huge swarms and causes great damage to plant life.

Mint A garden plant used for seasoning and medicine.

Mustard A large plant with very small seeds, which were ground up and used as a spice.

Myrrh A valuable sweet-smelling powder used in perfume.

Pomegranate A reddish fruit with a hard rind. Figures of pomegranates were used as decorations on the high priest's robe and in the temple.

Reed Several kinds of tall plants related to the grass family can be called "reeds." Some varieties are hollow, and some grow in shallow water. The stems were strong and could be up to 18 feet long and 3 inches across at the base.

Rue A garden plant used for seasoning and medicine.

Threshing The process of separating grain from its husks. Grain was spread out at a "threshing place," a flat area of stone or packed earth. People or animals walked on the grain or dragged heavy boards across it to remove the husks. Then the grain and husks were tossed into the air with a special shovel called a "threshing fork." The wind would blow the light husks away, but the heavy grain would fall back to the surface of the threshing place.

Wine-pit A hollow place cut into the rock where the juice was squeezed from grapes to make wine.

Yoke A strong, heavy, wooden collar that fit around the neck of an ox, so that the ox could pull a plow or a cart.

17. Society and Its Leaders

Citizen A person who is given special rights and privileges by a nation or state. In return, a citizen was expected to be loyal to that nation or state.

Council (1) A group of leaders who meet and make decisions for their people. (2) The Old Testament refers to God's council as a group of angels who meet and talk with God in heaven.

Elders Men whose age and wisdom made them respected leaders.

Emperor The person who ruled an empire.

Generation One way of describing a group of people who live during the same period of time. In the Bible the time of one generation is often understood to be about forty years.

Judges Leaders chosen by the Lord for the people of Israel after the time of Joshua and before the time of the kings.

Tax Collectors See "Taxes."

Taxes Special fees collected by rulers. Taxes are usually part of the value of crops, property, or income. Taxes were collected at markets, city gates, ports, and border crossings. In New Testament times, Jews were hired by the Roman government to collect taxes from other Jews, and these tax collectors were hated by their own people.

18. Families, Relatives

Ancestor Someone born earlier in a family line, especially several generations earlier.

Clan A group of families who were related to each other and who often lived close to each other. A group of clans made up a tribe.

Descendant Someone born one or more generations later in a family line.

Tribe A large group of people descended from a common ancestor (see also "Clan" and Section 6, "Twelve Tribes of Israel").

19. Events

Exile The time in Israel's history (597–539 B.C.) when the Babylonians took away many of the people of Jerusalem and Judah as prisoners of war and made them live in Babylonia. The northern tribes had been taken away by Assyria in 722 B.C.

Exodus The people of Israel leaving Egypt, led by Moses and Aaron. This event is celebrated each year as Passover.

20. Dates

B.C. Before Christ. Used to date events that happened before Christ's birth. "B.C." is used after the number of the year.

A.D. *Anno Domini,* Latin for "In the year of the Lord." Used to date events that happened after Christ's birth. "A.D." is often used before the number of the year.[a]

931 B.C. The nation of Israel split into two parts, Israel, the northern kingdom, and Judah, the southern kingdom.

722 B.C. Samaria, the capital of the northern kingdom, was captured by the Assyrian army.

586 B.C. Jerusalem, the capital of the southern kingdom, was captured by the Babylonian army.

538 B.C. Cyrus of Persia allowed the Jews to return to Judah.

333 B.C. Alexander the Great took control of Palestine.

323 B.C. Palestine was taken over by the Ptolemy, who was one of Alexander's generals and who became the ruler of Egypt after Alexander's death.

198 B.C. Palestine was taken over by the Seleucids, the descendants of one of Alexander's generals. They had been the rulers of Syria since Alexander's death.

166 B.C. The Jews revolted, led by Judas Maccabeus and his brothers.

63 B.C. Rome took control of Palestine.

37 B.C. Herod the Great was appointed king of the Jews by the Roman government.

6 B.C. Jesus was born. (See the note following "A.D." above.)

A.D. 30 (Or possibly A.D. 33) Jesus died and was raised to life.

21. The Hebrew Calendar

Nisan or ***Abib*** first month, about mid-March to mid-April.

Iyyar or ***Ziv*** second month about mid-April to mid-May.

Sivan third month, about mid-May to mid-June.

Tammuz fourth month, about mid-June to mid-July.

Ab fifth month, about mid-July to mid-August.

Elul sixth month, about mid-August to mid-September.

Tishri or ***Ethanim*** seventh month, about mid-September to mid-October.

Marchesvan or ***Bul*** eighth month, about mid-October to mid-November.

[a]**Note:** The numbering system now in use was developed about A.D. 525. The plan was that the year of Christ's birth would be A.D. 1, and then the years would be numbered before and after. But an error was made in assigning A.D. 1, and by the time the error was discovered, the numbering system could not be changed. And so, the correct year of Christ's birth according to the numbering system is probably about 6 B.C.

Chislev ninth month, about mid-November to mid-December.

Tebeth tenth month, about mid-December to mid-January.

Shebat eleventh month, about mid-January to mid-February.

Adar twelfth month, about mid-February to mid-March.

CHRONOLOGY OF THE BIBLE

DATE Time scales represent varied number of years

B.C. = Before Christ
c. = circa (around)*

PREHISTORY

THE BEGINNINGS: EVENTS IN PREHISTORY

Creation

Adam and Eve in the Garden

Cain and Abel

Noah and the Flood

The Tower of Babel

2000 B.C.

THE ANCESTORS OF THE ISRAELITES

Abraham comes to Palestine. *c.* 1900

Isaac is born to Abraham.

Jacob is born to Isaac.

1800 B.C.

Jacob has twelve sons, who become the ancestors of the twelve tribes of Israel. The most prominent of these sons is Joseph, who becomes advisor to the King of Egypt.

THE ISRAELITES IN EGYPT

The descendants of Jacob are enslaved in Egypt. *c.* 1700 — *c.* 1290

1600 B.C.

Moses leads the Israelites out of Egypt *c.* 1290

1250 B.C.

The Israelites wander in the wilderness. During this time Moses receives the Law on Mount Sinai. *c.* 1290 — *c.*1250

THE CONQUEST AND SETTLEMENT OF CANAAN

Joshua leads the first stage of the invasion of Canaan. *c.* 1250

Israel remains a loose confederation of tribes, and leadership is exercised by heroic figures known as the Judges.

THE UNITED ISRAELITE KINGDOM

Reign of Saul *c.* 1030 — *c.* 1010

1000 B.C.

Reign of David *c.* 1010 — *c.* 970

Reign of Solomon *c.* 970 — *c.* 931

*A circa date is only an approximation. Generally speaking, the earlier the time, the less precise is the dating. From the time of the death of Solomon in 931 B.C. to the Edict of Cyrus in 538 B.C., the dates given are fairly accurate, but even in this epoch a possible error of a year or two must be allowed for.

CHRONOLOGY OF THE BIBLE

THE TWO ISRAELITE KINGDOMS

DATE	JUDAH (Southern Kingdom)		ISRAEL (Northern Kingdom)
	Kings		*Kings*
950 B.C.	Rehoboam 931-913		Jeroboam 931-910
	Abijah 913-911		Nadab 910-909
900 B.C.	Asa 911-870		Baasha 909-886
		Prophets	Elah 886-885
			Zimri 7 days in 885
	Jehoshaphat 870-848	Elijah	Omri 885-874
			Ahab 874-853
850 B.C.	Jehoram 848-841		Ahaziah 853-852
	Ahaziah 841		Joram 852-841
	Queen Athaliah 841-835	Elisha	Jehu 841-814
	Joash 835-796		Jehoahaz 814-798
800 B.C.	Amaziah 796-781		Jehoash 798-783
	Uzziah 781-740		
		Jonah	Jeroboam II 783-743
		Amos	
750 B.C.	Jotham 740-736		Zechariah 6 mo. in 743
		Hosea	Shallum 1 mo. in 743
	Ahaz 736-716		Menahem 743-738
		Micah	Pekahiah 738-737
		Isaiah	Pekah 737-732
	Hezekiah 716-687		Hosea 732-723
			Fall of Samaria 722

THE LAST YEARS OF THE KINGDOM OF JUDAH

DATE	Kings		Prophets
700 B.C.	Manasseh 687-642		
650 B.C.	Amon 642-640		
	Josiah 640-609		Zephaniah
	Joahaz 3 mo. in 609		Nahum
600 B.C.	Jehoiakim 609-598	Jeremiah	Habakkuk?
	Jehoiachin 3 mo. in 598		
	Zedekiah 598-587		Ezekiel

Fall of Jerusalem July 587 or 586

CHRONOLOGY OF THE BIBLE

DATE	
550 B.C.	**THE EXILE AND THE RESTORATION**
	The Judeans taken into exile in Babylonia after the fall of Jerusalem
	Persian rule begins. 539 — *Prophets*: Haggai, Zechariah, Obadiah, Daniel, Malachi, Joel?
	Edict of Cyprus allows Jews to return. 538
	Foundations of New Temple laid. 520
	Restoration of the walls of Jerusalem 445-443
400 B.C.	**THE TIME BETWEEN THE TESTAMENTS**
	Alexander the Great establishes Greek rule in Palestine. 333
	Palestine is ruled by the Ptolemies, descendants of one of Alexander's generals, who had been given the position of ruler over Egypt. 323 to 198
200 B.C.	Palestine is ruled by the Seleucids, descendants of one of Alexander's generals, who had acquired the rule of Syria. 198 to 166
	Jewish revolt under Judas Maccabeus reestablishes Jewish independence. Palestine is ruled by Judas' family and descendants, the Hasmoneans. 166 to 63
	The Roman general Pompey takes Jerusalem 63 B.C. Palestine is ruled by puppet kings appointed by Rome. One of these is Herod the Great, who rules from 37 B.C. to 4 B.C.
	THE TIME OF THE NEW TESTAMENT
	Birth of Jesus*
A.D. 1	Ministry of John the Baptist; baptism of Jesus and beginning of his public ministry
	Death and resurrection of Jesus
A.D. 30	Conversion of Paul (Saul of Tarsus) *c.* A.D. 37
	Ministry of Paul *c.* A.D. 41 to A.D. 65
	Final imprisonment of Paul *c.* A.D. 65

*The present era was calculated to begin with the birth of Jesus Christ, that is in A.D. 1 (A.D. standing for *Anno Domini* 'in the year of the Lord'). However, the original calculation was later found to be wrong by a few years, so that the birth of Christ took place perhaps about 6 B.C.

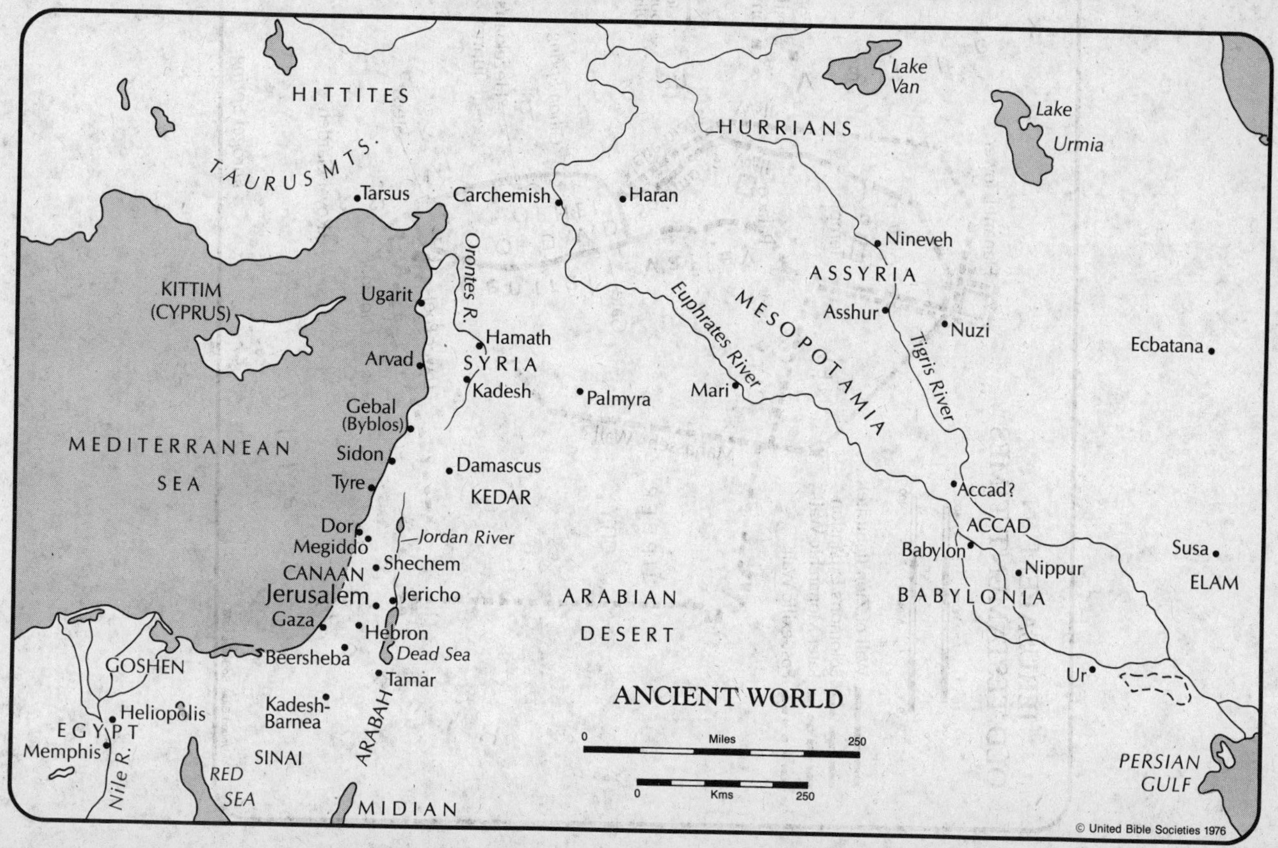
ANCIENT WORLD
HITTITES
TAURUS MTS.
Tarsus
Carchemish
Haran
HURRIANS
Lake Van
Lake Urmia
Nineveh
ASSYRIA
Asshur
Nuzi
Ecbatana
MESOPOTAMIA
Euphrates River
Tigris River
Mari
Palmyra
KITTIM (CYPRUS)
Ugarit
Orontes R.
Hamath
Arvad
SYRIA
Kadesh
Gebal (Byblos)
MEDITERRANEAN SEA
Sidon
Damascus
Tyre
KEDAR
Dor
Megiddo
Jordan River
Shechem
CANAAN
Jerusalem
Jericho
Gaza
Hebron
Dead Sea
Beersheba
Tamar
ARABIAN DESERT
Accad?
ACCAD
Babylon
Nippur
BABYLONIA
Susa
ELAM
Ur
PERSIAN GULF
GOSHEN
Heliopolis
EGYPT
Memphis
Nile R.
Kadesh-Barnea
SINAI
RED SEA
ARABAH
MIDIAN
0 Miles 250
0 Kms 250

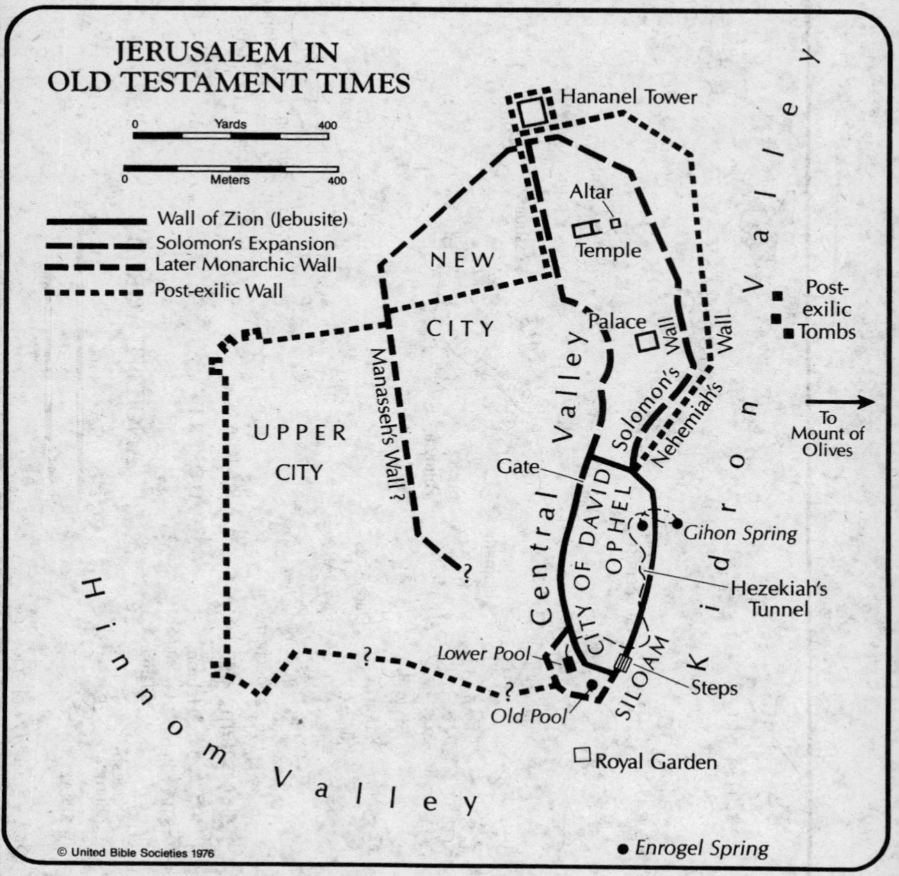

JERUSALEM IN OLD TESTAMENT TIMES
0 Yards 400
0 Meters 400
Wall of Zion (Jebusite)
Solomon's Expansion
Later Monarchic Wall
Post-exilic Wall
Hananel Tower
Altar
Temple
NEW CITY
Palace
Solomon's Wall
Nehemiah's Wall
Manasseh's Wall ?
UPPER CITY
Central Valley
Gate
CITY OF DAVID
OPHEL
Gihon Spring
Hezekiah's Tunnel
Kidron Valley
Post-exilic Tombs
To Mount of Olives
Lower Pool
Old Pool
SILOAM
Steps
Royal Garden
Hinnom Valley
Enrogel Spring
© United Bible Societies 1976

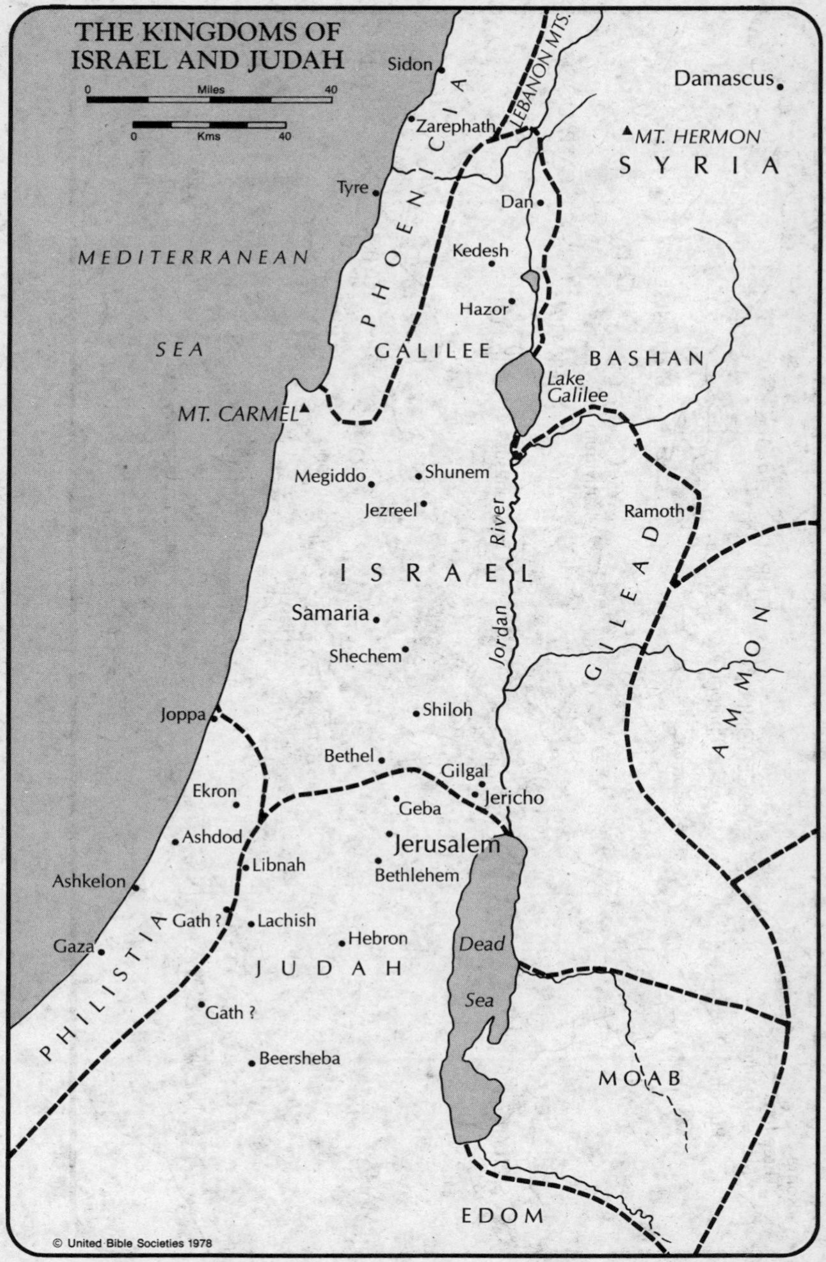
THE KINGDOMS OF ISRAEL AND JUDAH
0 Miles 40
0 Kms 40
Sidon
Zarephath
Tyre
PHOENICIA
LEBANON MTS.
Damascus
MT. HERMON
SYRIA
Dan
Kedesh
Hazor
MEDITERRANEAN
SEA
GALILEE
BASHAN
Lake Galilee
MT. CARMEL
Megiddo
Shunem
Jezreel
Ramoth
Jordan River
ISRAEL
GILEAD
Samaria
Shechem
AMMON
Joppa
Shiloh
Bethel
Gilgal
Ekron
Jericho
Geba
Ashdod
Jerusalem
Libnah
Bethlehem
Ashkelon
Gath ?
Lachish
Hebron
Gaza
Dead Sea
JUDAH
PHILISTIA
Gath ?
Beersheba
MOAB
EDOM
© United Bible Societies 1978

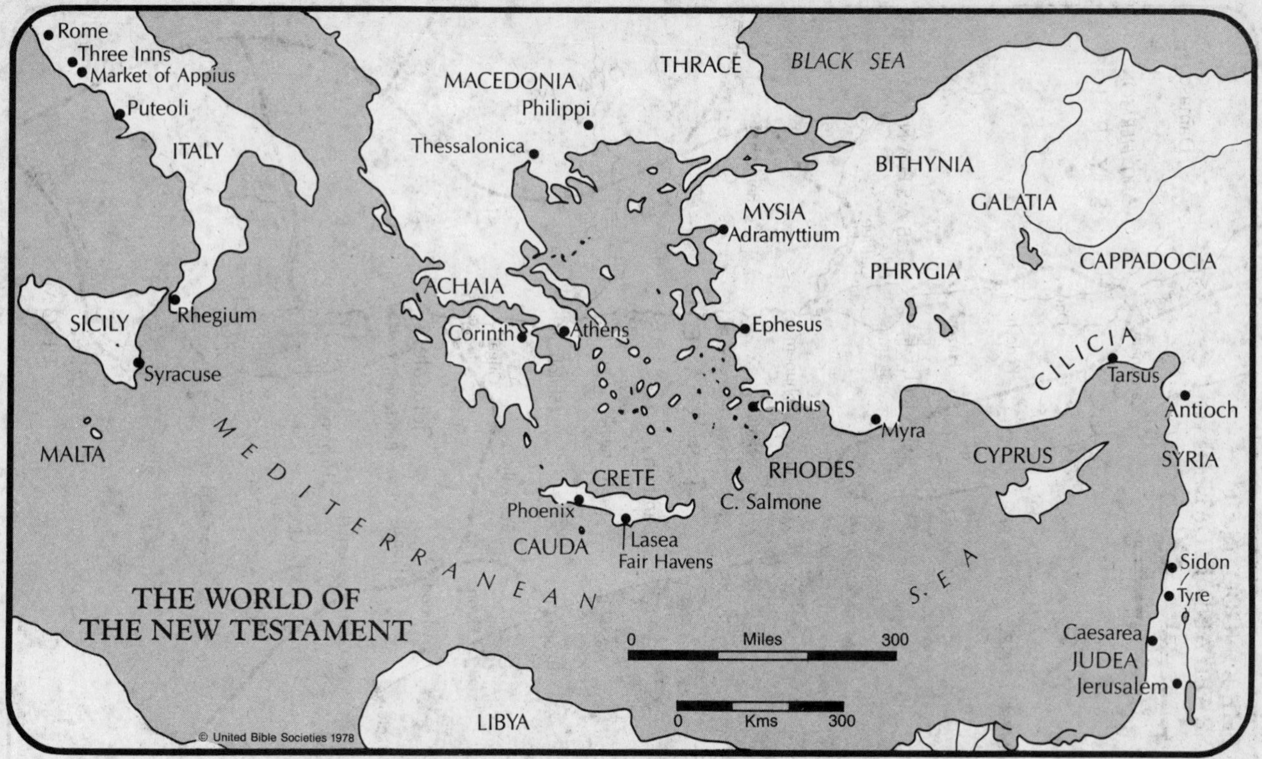

THE WORLD OF THE NEW TESTAMENT